Encyclopedia *of*
BRITISH
COLUMBIA

Encyclopedia *of*
BRITISH COLUMBIA

Editor
Daniel Francis

H A R B O U R   P U B L I S H I N G

Harbour Publishing Ltd
P.O. Box 219, Madeira Park, BC Canada V0N 2H0

Cover design and artwork by Martin Nichols

Cover photographs: Front cover, background (top to bottom): Clouds trapped behind a shoulder of Bute Mt (John Baldwin photo); mix of old-growth and regenerated forests after logging, Kamloops region (courtesy Working Forest Project). Right foreground (top to bottom): Carving of thunderbird at Discovery Harbour Centre, Campbell River, carved by Bill, Junior and Greg Henderson (courtesy Weiwaikum Band and Northwest Group); provincial legislative buildings in Victoria, designed by Francis Rattenbury and opened in 1898 (Roy Luckow photo); Paul Kariya, star hockey player with the Anaheim Mighty Ducks (Jeff Vinnick photo/Vancouver Canucks); cowboy in the Nicola Valley (Rick Blacklaws photo); Pauline Johnson, dressed for one of her stage performances, c 1904 (BC Archives A-09684); sockeye salmon spawning in the Horsefly River (Roy Luckow photo). Foreground (clockwise from top): James Douglas, first governor of the colony of BC (BC Archives HP-2652); Terry Fox during his Marathon of Hope, 1980 (Gail Harvey photo/Terry Fox Foundation); Sarah McLachlan, singer (Nettwerk Productions); hay bales in the Chilcotin (Rick Blacklaws photo); Green Island, BC's northernmost lighthouse (Chris Jaksa photo); grizzly bear at Knight Inlet on the Mid-Coast (Ian McAllister photo); blasting of Ripple Rock, 5 Apr 1958 (R.E. Olsen photo/MCR 12148); Science World BC, Vancouver; thunderbird headdress by Richard Hunt (Bob Matheson photo). Back cover (clockwise from top left): Silken Laumann displaying the bronze medal she won for rowing in the 1992 Olympics in Barcelona; cruise ship at Canada Place in Vancouver (Roy Luckow photo); Mt Robson (Jane Siska photo/Image Makers); Joe Gosnell, Nisga'a chief (Gary Fiegehen photo); Fort Steele (Duncan McDougall photo/Image Makers); (left) heli-logging at Khartoum Lake near Powell River, in a Canadian Air Crane S-64, 1996 (Keith Thirkell photo); (right) the ferry *Queen of the North* steaming through the Inside Passage (courtesy BC Ferry Corp); Pat John, Robert Clothier and Bruno Gerussi in the *Beachcombers* television series, 1981 (Roy Luckow photo); 1958 photograph of the seiner *BCP No 45*, a rendering of which appeared on the Canadian $5 bill (VMM); back country skiing in the Rogers Pass area (Jacy Schindel photo). Bottom right corner (clockwise from top left): South Chesterman Beach, serigraph by Roy Henry Vickers; T.C. Brayshaw illustration of a dogwood flower; Gulf of Georgia Cannery Historic Site at Steveston (Rick Blacklaws photo); restored buildings at Fort St James (Rick Blacklaws photo). Bottom left corner (clockwise from top): the Univ of Northern BC campus (courtesy UNBC); the Fraser River, looking east from New Westminster, with a view of working vessels and the Port Mann Bridge (Rick Blacklaws photo); the BC flag (Roy Luckow photo); sport fishers with a chinook salmon caught in the Cape Beale area (Martin Nichols photo); (left) Joy Kogawa, writer; (right) Cottonwood House after being restored (Rick Blacklaws photo); giant Douglas fir near Port Renfrew (Rick Blacklaws photo); David Suzuki, environmental activist; killer whale breaching (Chris Hopkins photo/Image Makers). Spine: killer whales in Johnstone Strait (Les Bazso photo/Vancouver Province).

Photographs on preliminary pages: half-title: BC Place from False Creek (Brian Gauvin photo); title pages: (l) snake fence in the Cariboo (Rick Blacklaws photo), (r) pounding surf at Wickaninnish Beach (courtesy Ucluelet Chamber of Commerce); contents page: driving the last spike of the CPR, Craigellachie (BC Archives E-02200); acknowledgements: *Echo Bay, Gilford Island*, a 1963 oil painting by E.J. Hughes; feller buncher at work (courtesy Western Forest Products); annual powwow in Kamloops, 1999 (Keith Thirkell photo); provincial legislative buildings at night (Roy Luckow photo); dancing at the Vancouver Folk Music Festival, 1998 (Peter Battistoni/Vancouver Sun); red-tailed hawk (R. Wayne Campbell photo); high school girls' field hockey, Comox, 1996 (Don MacKinnon/Vancouver Province}; map of BC (Roger Handling).

Printed in Hong Kong by Colorcraft

Every attempt has been made to identify and credit sources for photographs.
The publisher would appreciate receiving information as to any inaccuracies in the credits for subsequent editions.

Second Printing , 2000

Canadian Cataloguing in Publication Data

Main entry under title:
The encyclopedia of British Columbia

    Includes bibliographical references and index.

    ISBN 1-55017-200-X

    1. British Columbia—Encyclopedias. I. Francis, Daniel.
FC3804.E52 2000   971.1'003   C00-910782-7
F1087.E52 2000

For its timely and enthusiastic support of the overall *Encyclopedia of BC* project,
Harbour Publishing gratefully acknowledges

The Insurance Corporation of BC

"The Encyclopedia of BC is a wonderful source of knowledge where people of all
ages may learn more about our province and the contributions of British
Columbians, past and present. The Insurance Corporation of BC is proud to be a
contributor to this valuable information resource."

—Thom Thompson, Chief Executive Officer

Harbour Publishing gratefully acknowledges a major donation from

THE POWER IS YOURS

BChydro

BC Hydro and Power Authority

whose strong support of both the print and interactive editions of the
Encyclopedia of BC exemplifies great community spirit and bears witness to BC
Hydro's continuing efforts to enrich the communities it serves.

"The Encyclopedia is the result of a tremendous collaborative effort and a vital
living record of the accomplishments and achievements of the people of our
province. BC Hydro and its predecessor companies have been here since 1860
when the first gas lights were turned on in Victoria. We are proud of our history
and we are proud to sponsor this important work."

—Michael Costello,
President and Chief Executive Officer

Harbour Publishing wishes to acknowledge the following organizations for making major contributions to the *Encyclopedia of British Columbia* and the *Interactive Encyclopedia of British Columbia*:

The Telus BC New Media and Broadcast Fund

Canadian Broadcasting Corporation

Province of British Columbia
Ministry of Education: Curriculum Branch

Telefilm Canada

Canada
MULTIMEDIA FUND

Funded by the Department of Canadian Heritage
Administered by Telefilm Canada

Harbour Publishing wishes to recognize the following, some for organizational support they provided to the *Encyclopedia of British Columbia,* some for financial contributions and some for their long-term support of Harbour's publishing program:

THE UNIVERSITY OF BRITISH COLUMBIA LIBRARY
SPECIAL COLLECTIONS & UNIVERSITY ARCHIVES DIVISION

———————

THE CANADIAN CENTRE FOR STUDIES IN PUBLISHING
AT SIMON FRASER UNIVERSITY

———————

THE LEON AND THEA KOERNER FOUNDATION

———————

PACIFIC PRESS LTD

———————

THE GOVERNMENT OF CANADA
BOOK PUBLISHING INDUSTRY DEVELOPMENT PROGRAM

THE CANADA COUNCIL

THE BC ARTS COUNCIL

BEAUTIFUL BC PUBLISHING

Contents

Foreword

by Howard White

Most people, on hearing of the *Encyclopedia of British Columbia*, have had one of two reactions. The first—and, I would like to think, most common—is "At last. What a wonderful idea." The second is less definite and usually begins with the question "What will be in it?" Initially this struck me as odd, since by definition an encyclopedia has everything in it. It is, after all, made from two Greek words meaning "to encircle knowledge." But the waters have been much muddied by such usages as the "Encyclopedia of Hockey," or the "Encyclopedia of Hunting and Gathering," which contrive to reduce that most inclusive of concepts to something highly exclusive. We are not entirely innocent on that score, since our encyclopedia excludes everything that is unconnected with BC. But within the realm of Canada's westernmost province our intention has been to encircle all subjects: everything from BC soup to BC nuts.

The next most common question is "Oh. Do we need that?" We do, on several counts. First, the *EBC* provides practical information you can't conveniently get elsewhere, and will rival the phone book as a useful reference for anybody in BC or dealing with BC. But we have an ulterior motive that goes beyond practicality, and you will be able to tell what it is just by flipping through a few hundred pages. Even after having laboured for ten years to bring all these scattered bits of data together, we find ourselves awed by what it mounts up to now that it is collected and bound. You simply can't leaf through it without being struck by what a remarkable place BC is: how vast, how various, how unique. It is for this reason as much as any other—to show that not only does British Columbia occupy one of the world's most remarkable landscapes, but also it is the site of equally remarkable human doings—that we have compiled this massive work.

Some may consider the point sufficiently obvious as to make the effort unnecessary, and we wish that were so. But it is our experience here at Harbour Publishing, even after having published some 350 books on BC, that our own story is actually losing ground in the forefront of the public mind, especially among young people. As communications become more and more globalized, there is less and less place for local knowledge. Our hope is that by placing the essentials of the BC story in this concise, accessible form and by making it available not just in one handy volume but also in electronic media (www.knowbc.com), we will provide basic BC knowledge with the kind of state-of-the-art vehicle it needs to keep pace on the information highway.

To be the first to do anything is both a privilege and a peril. It is a privilege to be first to arrive at the place of asking "Who are BC's most important writers/athletes/high-tech corporations?" but it is also a terrible responsibility to have to carve the first path through so much new territory, knowing how closely one's choices will be scrutinized by those who follow. It is a challenge that backed me off for years, drawn though I was to the idea of an encyclopedia. The project would have remained in the daydream state had it not been for Daniel Francis. Dan, in addition to writing twelve books, worked on the first and second editions of the Hurtig *Canadian Encyclopedia* and the Hurtig *Junior Encyclopedia of Canada*, and served as editorial director of the encyclopedic *Horizon Canada* illustrated history project. Dan had learned many things from this experience, but the chief thing was not to be intimidated by that word "encyclopedia." He agreed to come aboard as editorial director of the EBC in 1990, and before we knew it he had either written or assigned 2,000 entries and the book was halfway to completion. It was only then that I fully began to understand that our dream was headed for reality. Now that it has completed that journey, I have no hesitation in saying the one person most responsible is Daniel Francis, without whose great experience, enormous productivity and weakness for unlikely causes the *EBC* would never have come to be.

Several others deserve mention for contributions far beyond the call of duty. First Mary Schendlinger, managing editor, whose dedication to editorial quality is such that I began to understand it as more of a religion than a discipline. On the same plane is Peter Robson, production manager, whose dedication to assembling and deploying the galaxy of illustrations, charts, graphs and other manifold moving parts at times approached the obsessive, and was still not a bit less than the task demanded. Craig Riggs had the double duty of leading the marketing team and also directing the interactive effort, and handled both with competence and aplomb.

In a groundbreaking project such as this, it was especially valuable to have the support of some highly respected professionals in the scholarly and archival fields to assure us that what we envisioned was do-able and worth doing. Jean

Barman, BC historian supreme, author of *The West Beyond the West* and co-editor of *BC Studies* in addition to serving as history advisor of the *EBC*, gave the project her formidable backing from inception to completion. The same can be said of Rowland Lorimer, Director of the Canadian Centre for Studies in Publishing at Simon Fraser University, and the matchless George Brandak, who with his colleague Brenda Peterson marshalled the invaluable resources of the University of BC Library Special Collections Division behind the project. The Hon Andrew Petter, then BC Minister of Advanced Education, and the Hon Ian Waddell, BC Minister of Small Business, Culture and Tourism, both took personal interest in the project and gave crucial assistance. Our subject advisors, Jean Barman, Richard Cannings, Ken Drushka, Mark Leier, Ken MacLeod, Charles Menzies, Jock Munro, Jay Powell, Peter Robson, June Ryder, Andrew Scott, Martin Segger and Silas White, each a leading authority in his/her field, graced the project with their presence and made contributions far beyond anything we had a right to expect. I want also to extend my thanks to James Marsh, editor of *The Canadian Encyclopedia*, and Michael Francis, both of whom were unstinting with their advice.

The *EBC* would not be what it is if not for a large group of enthusiastic professionals who came forward and generously offered special skills and resources, from the photographers Rick Blacklaws, Roy Luckow and Philip Stone to Reimut Lieder of Image Makers, to naturalist extraordinaire R. Wayne Campbell to military history specialist Ken MacLeod to art scholar Martin Segger to labour historian Mark Leier to pop music aficionado Mike Harling to sports experts Fred Hume, Jim Kearney, Archie McDonald and Clancy Loranger. These and dozens like them gave freely of their time, asking no reward except to have a hand in giving their province an encyclopedia worthy of its name. In addition hundreds of interested citizens from all over BC rallied round the project from the earliest stages, offering rare knowledge, writing up local histories, offering family photos, researching obscure topics, vetting endless materials. Their faith buoyed us on bad days.

Even with the best efforts of all its supporters, the long task of research and writing could not have been completed without external financial assistance, and that was provided first and foremost by BC Hydro & Power Authority and the Insurance Corporation of BC, whose chairmen, Brian Smith and Robert Williams, are both men of letters as well as action and became early and committed advocates of the *EBC*. Another key corporate sponsor was CBC Vancouver Television, under the direction of Rae Hull, whose film and video archives are a national treasure. The interactive edition of the EBC would not have been possible without the support of the Telus BC New Media and Broadcast Fund and the Telefilm Canada Multimedia Fund. The BC Ministry of Education: Curriculum Branch provided special funding for placing the encyclopedia in BC schools.

Howard White
Publisher

Did we miss something? Contact us!

The *Encyclopedia of BC* is an ongoing collaborative project between Harbour Publishing and the people of BC. We have taken great pains to be as careful and judicious as possible in our coverage, but it is inevitable in a project such as this that some things will have slipped through the cracks and some mistakes will have been made. It is our intention to continue updating and expanding the encyclopedia in its interactive edition, which will be reiussed periodically on CD-ROM and will be available by subscription on the Internet at **www.knowbc.com**. We want your input. Please accept this invitation to take part in this great ongoing project by contacting us with your comments, suggestions, corrections and additions at **ebc@harbourpublishing.com** or by post at

Box 219, Madeira Park, BC, Canada V0N 2H0.

Preface

When Howard White and I embarked on the *Encyclopedia of British Columbia*, we imagined a convenient reference work containing basic information about the province and geared to general readers. Our modest intention was to put an entire library between the covers of a single book: a work that included all aspects of life in the province, from prehistory to the present. The arts, sciences, First Nations cultures, sports, prominent people and places, history, geography, religions and industries—all are important and, we felt, deserved to be covered in a comprehensive encyclopedia about the place. It seemed like a straightforward enough job. After all, I'd grown up here. Surely I knew most of what there was to know already. In my naïveté, I expected to be finished in a couple of years.

As things turned out, a decade has passed since Howard and I began. During that time I discovered just how diverse, and fascinating, a place British Columbia is. I read hundreds of books about the province, and still did not exhaust the subject. I consulted scores of experts on every conceivable aspect of life in BC, from abalone to Nanaimo bars to rum-runners right on through the alphabet to the acclaimed bassoonist George Zukerman. At the same time I made several excursions up the coast and into the Interior—by car, airplane, ferry and sailboat—visiting smaller communities and exploring the different regions that make up the provincial mosaic. On Vancouver Island I stayed overnight in the former home of the famed nature writer Roderick Haig-Brown, the only historic site I know of that doubles as a bed and breakfast. Outside of Bella Coola my battered old Honda laboured up the infamous Big Hill, still unpaved and as terrifying as on the day it opened to traffic in 1953, to reach the stunningly beautiful Chilcotin plateau. At Hudson's Hope I plunged underground into the bowels of the W.A.C. Bennett Dam to view the giant turbines that generate close to 30 percent of the province's hydroelectricy. I saw whales in the Inside Passage, hoodoos at Farwell Canyon, the largest tree crusher in the world at Mackenzie, the open Pacific breaking onto the stone beach at Yuquot, the world's tallest totem pole at Alert Bay, the site of the Last Spike at Craigellachie, a historic salmon cannery at Port Edward, the goats on the roof at Coombs. And each time I returned home feeling I had hardly scratched the surface, there was so much still to see.

The story of British Columbia might fill forty volumes. We only had room for one. It was obvious that decisions had to be made. To help us decide what subjects should be included, we assembled a team of knowledgeable advisors, experts with long experience in their fields, who helped us to identify the most important BC people, places and events. With that outline we went about gathering more details, with the objective of providing useful information without becoming too technical or arcane. We were also concerned to make the *EBC* an encyclopedia for all British Columbians, wherever they happen to live. Too often British Columbia is considered to be synonymous with its southwest corner. We wanted to be sure to include the other three-quarters of the province, and to this end we consulted people in all the different regions to make sure that the *EBC* did justice to their areas. Many subjects are not specific to BC. Butterflies, for example, occur almost everywhere, as do whales and forest fires. However, BC does have its own species of butterflies, its own populations of whales and its own pattern of forest fires. In every *EBC* article, it is that local aspect of the subject that is emphasized; so that, for instance, the biographical article on the explorer Alexander Mackenzie concentrates on his expedition west of the Rocky Mountains, and the article on filmmaking is about the industry as it has evolved in "Hollywood North." There are other encyclopedias about the world, and about Canada; the *EBC* is the only one that takes British Columbia as its focus.

The *EBC* contains much that a reader will expect to find in a general knowledge encyclopedia. There are articles on every premier and lieutenant governor, every significant animal species and every populated place, and articles on writers, visual and performing artists, major businesses and industries, ethnic and religious groups and so on. But there are also many articles on topics that are unique to BC and reflect the singular, sometimes quirky, character of the province: Ogopogo and sasquatch, Chinook jargon, float houses, rain forests, A-frame logging, Baby Duck, argillite, Lotus Land, the Flying Seven and many others like them. Most of the articles were written by the staff of the *EBC*. Many others were written by experts in the field. Every article was then reviewed by a knowledgeable expert to ensure that subjects were treated fairly and comprehensively and that the information in the *EBC* is as reliable and objective as we can possibly make it. Contributors were allowed to express opinions—their own or someone else's— but they were asked to balance their articles by presenting opposing points of view. The *EBC* is a source of information, not a forum for pleading causes.

I want to express my special thanks to Howard White, without whom the *EBC* would never have been published because I am quite sure that I never would have found another publisher with enough faith in the idea to give it a try. Howard's urgent belief that the story of BC must be told and preserved inspires the *Encyclopedia of BC*, just as it does all the books produced by Harbour Publishing. I am grateful to have had the opportunity to work with him and with the dedicated people in his company.

Daniel Francis, Editor

Using the Encyclopedia

We have endeavoured to make the EBC as simple to use as possible. All entries are arranged alphabetically, with subject heads in **BOLDFACE**. Entries are alphabetized word by word rather than letter by letter. For simplicity and readability, "B.C.," "BC" and "British Columbia" are all written as "BC" and alphabetized as such, not as though they were spelled out as "British Columbia." (The one exception is the entry for the actual name of the province, BRITISH COLUMBIA.) Biographical subjects are alphabetized by the last name, followed by given names and, sometimes, the name that the individual was commonly called (eg, **PATTISON, James Allen "Jimmy"**). The maiden names of women, when included, are enclosed in parentheses. The exact places and dates of birth and death are given when they are known. Names that begin with Mc or Mac are presented as though they begin with Mac. Numbers are listed as if they were spelled out; for example, 100 Mile House is listed as if it were "One Hundred Mile House." The spelling of physical features and populated places follows the provincial gazetteer. Many entries end with one or more suggested readings. These are references to easily accessible books that readers may consult to further their study of a subject; they are not meant to be bibliographies of sources consulted for the entries. There is also a Further Reading section on British Columbia at the end of the encyclopedia. The name of the author of an entry appears at the end of the entry. Two members of our editorial team—Andrew Scott and Silas White—were particularly prolific; they are listed as *AS* and *SW*. When no author is listed it means that the entry was written by the editor, or in a few cases by more than one contributor.

A great deal of thought and discussion went into our presentation of the names of First Nations groups. Over the past twenty years many, if not most, of these groups have changed their names, understandably preferring to be known by designations they have chosen themselves rather than the names that were so long applied to them by Euro-Canadians. So, for instance, the Nootka have become the Nuu-chah-nulth, the Kutenai have become the Ktunaxa, and so on. We have decided to respect the evident wishes of First Nations people by using these contemporary names. At the same time we recognize that many readers will be familiar with the former nomenclature, so we have included these older names in parentheses where it seemed appropriate. First Nations nomenclature is an area in flux; if our choices have failed to keep up with common usage within the First Nations communities themselves, our intention is certainly not to insult anyone. For a list of current names of First Nations groups, along with former names by which the groups have been known, consult the chart on page 239.

To utilize space most efficiently, we have placed much information in chart form. As well, a system of cross-references has been employed. Words that appear in SMALL CAPITALS indicate a subject that has its own entry in the encyclopedia. This system allows us to provide a great deal of information without repeating much of it. It also allows readers some flexibility to explore a subject as deeply or as superficially as they desire. If you do not find an entry for the subject in which you are interested, consult the index at the back of the book. It locates topics that appear in the EBC but do not have entries of their own and lets you know where they can be found. Abbreviations have been kept to a minimum but some have been employed to save space. A list of them appears. Entries on communities usually include population figures. Unless another date is noted, our source is the 1996 national census. Sometimes we use the 1991 census because for a few smaller communities that is the latest official count. In a few other cases—for example, the size of the different religious communities in the province—the 1991 census also provides the latest reliable figure.

The EBC includes five long feature entries on the history of the province, its economy, its natural history, its physical geography and its First Nations, each written by an expert in the field. These essays are intended to introduce readers to a subject and may be used as jumping-off points for further discovery. There are also many longer feature entries that serve as introductions to their subjects. For example, a reader interested in knowing about BC writers should consult the entry on LITERATURE, which traces the evolution of writing in the province and includes the names of most of the major writers who have their own entries in the encyclopedia. Similarly for the film industry, the visual arts, architecture, the mining industry, forestry and so on. We hope that every entry in the EBC is a door that opens into an expanding world of knowledge about our province.

Staff

Published by Harbour Publishing Co Ltd

Publisher: Howard White
Editor: Daniel Francis

Managing Editor: Mary Schendlinger

Production Manager: Peter A. Robson

Marketing Manager: Craig Riggs

Designers: Roger Handling, Martin Nichols

Editorial

Contributing Editors: Andrew Scott, Silas White

Copy-editing: Helena Bryan, Wendy Fitzgibbons, Helen Godolphin, Susan Mayse,
Irene Niechoda, Maggie Paquet, Patricia Wolfe

Proofreading: Wendy Fitzgibbons, Helen Godolphin, Eda Kadar, Betty Keller, Irene Niechoda, Patricia Wolfe

Indexing: Betty Keller, Ann Macklem, Andrew Scott, Silas White

Production

Assembly: Martin Nichols/Lionheart Graphics, Roger Handling/Terra Firma Digital Arts

Graphics Editor: Peter A. Robson

Image Processing: Mary White

Maps: Roger Handling, Kim LaFave, Martin Nichols

Charts and Tables: Martin Nichols

Illustrations: Nola Johnston, Kim LaFave

Photo Research: Heidi Brown

Photo and Media Research: Mike Steele

Marketing

Marketing and Publicity: Marisa Alps, Bethan Hull, Patrick White

Warehousing and Shipping: Maureen Cochrane

Administration

Dani Lacusta, Regina Kasa, Karen Esplen

Acknowledgements

The *Encyclopedia of BC* would not have been completed without the help of many people who contributed their expert knowledge about the province. Some of these people contributed ideas for entries; others actually wrote entries; others helped to locate information or illustrations; others read over entries to make sure the information was accurate. A few contributors played a larger role in the project, as consultants and readers who made themselves constantly available as advisors and wrote the larger overview essays that are a unique feature of the *EBC*. All of these contributors are listed below.

Advisory Board

Jean Barman, Ed.D. Editor of BC Studies, Professor of Educational Studies, UBC.

Barry Broadfoot, C.M. LL.D. Author.

Senator Pat Carney, LL.D. Adjunct Professor of Community and Regional Planning, UBC.

Celia Duthie, LL.D. Bookseller.

Arthur Erickson, C.C. LL.D D.Litt., D.Eng. Architect.

Rowland M. Lorimer, Ph.D. Director of the Centre for Canadian Studies and Professor of Communication, SFU.

Peter C. Newman, C.C. LL.D. D.Litt. Author.

Jay Powell, Ph.D. Assistant Professor Emeritus of Anthropology, UBC.

Subject Consultants

History: **Jean Barman**, Ed.D.

Natural History: **Richard Cannings**, M.Sc. Biologist & Author.

Forest Industry: **Ken Drushka**, Author.

First Nations: **Charles Menzies**, Ph.D. Assistant Professor of Anthropology, UBC and **Jay Powell**, Ph.D.

Economy: **John M. Munro**, D.B.A. Professor of Economics, SFU.

Fisheries: **Peter A. Robson**, Journalist.

Geography: **June Ryder**, Ph.D. Adjunct Professor of Geography, UBC.

Places: **Andrew Scott**, M.A. Author.

Sports: **Silas White**, B.A. Author.

Military: **Ken MacLeod**, M.Ed. Educator & Historian.

Labour: **Mark Leier**, Ph.D. Associate Professor of History, SFU.

Visual Arts: **Martin Segger**, M.Phil. Director and Curator, Malwood Gallery, Adjunct Professor of Canadian Art & Architecture, Univ of Victoria.

Advisors and Contributors

Arts, Architecture and Culture: Barbara Clausen, David Conn, Karen Duffek, Ed Gould, Mike Harling, Jim Hoffman, Edith Iglauer, Peggy Imredy, Patrick Lane, David Lee, Sharon McGowan, David Mattison, Ted Mills, Stephen Osborne, Ann Pollock, Red Robinson, Norbert Ruebsaat, Sheryl Salloum, Karen Schendlinger, Minna Schendlinger, Bill Schermbrucker, Doris Shadbolt, Sid Tafler, Peggy Thompson, Alan Twigg, Michael Walsh, Frances Wasserlein, Robert D. Watt, Tony Westbridge, Hildegarde Westerkamp, Tom Woods, Max Wyman, Norman Young.

Business, Industry and Labour: Barry Ackerman, Robert Allington, Craig Aspinall, George Barber, David Barr, BC Ministry of Fisheries, BC Salmon Farmers' Association, Emil Bjarnason, Constance Brissenden, Parzival Copes, Peter Corley-Smith, Gordon Curry, Jan DeGrass, Michel Drouin, Derek Fairbridge, Fisheries and Oceans Canada, Terry Glavin, Bud Graham, Neil Gray, Lewis Green, Ian F. Greenwood, Alan Haig-Brown, Herschel Hardin, Jay Hartling, S.C. Heal, International Pacific Halibut Commission, Vickie Jensen, Nancy Knickerbocker, Athol Laing, David Lane, Deb Logan, Brian Ludwig, Francis Mansbridge, Ken Mather, Carmen Matthews, Geoff Meggs, Rob Morris, Don Pepper, Mike Poole, David Rahn, Jack Schofield, Will and Heidi Soltau, David Spalding, Duncan Stacey, John Stuart, Carol Swann, Terry Tarita, Blair Trousdale, Robert Turner, Bruce Turris, Daniel Ware, Jane Watt, Tom Wayman, John Willow, Ed Zyblut, Shane McCune.

First Nations: Howard Adams, Roy Carlson, Karen Duffek, Ken Favrholdt, Stephen Hume, Peter Macnair, Kerry Mason, Ralph Maud, Martine Reid, Alex Rose.

Government, Politics and History: John Atkin, Jamie Boyd, Brian Burtch, Veronica Delorme, Patrick Dunae, Ron Dutton, Clayton Evans, Russ Francis, Lyn Gough, Jacqueline Gresko, Bob Griffin, Peter Hebb, Irene Howard, Robin Inglis, Hugh Johnston, Keith Keller, Yvonne Klan, John

MacDonald, Robert McDonald, Edward McDonnell, Evelyn Peters McLellan, Gary Mitchell, Stephen Owen, John Plant, Bill Quackenbush, Toby Rainy, Patricia Roy, Charmaine Saulnier, David Schreck, Sandy Shreve, Freeman Tovell, Anna Tremere, Bruce Watson.

Peoples and Communities: Edward L. Affleck, Doreen Armitage, Graeme Balcom, Stewart Beaveridge, Lynn Blake, Peter Botham, Roger G. Burrows, Ken Campbell, John Cherrington, Michael Clague, Tracy Cooper, Roy Crowe, Ray Culos, Bill Dale, Kathleen Dalzell, Esther Darlington, Chuck Davis, Ruth Derksen Siemens, Phinder Dulai, Fran Duncan, Gail Edwards, Bob Ellenton, Ken Ellison, Shannon Emmerson, Derek Fairbridge, Marvin Fennessy, Diana French, David Goa, David Gregory, Tom Henry, Margaret Horsfield, Helen Inglis, Peter Jacobi, Sarjeet Singh Jagpal, Charlie Kadota, Diane Kadota, Leslie Kemp, David C.Y. Lai, Martin Lynch, Jack McIntosh, Dianne Mackay, Jill Mandrake, Ralph Maud, Susan Mayse, Jim Miller, Naomi Miller, Faith Moosang, John Morton, Jeremy Mouat, Bet Oliver, Stephen R. Pacholuk, Rosemarie Parent, Ajmer Rode, Andrew Scott, Wendy Scott, Cyril Shelford, Karen Southern, Jon Swainger, Don Tarassof, Jeanette Taylor, Leona Taylor, Adam Waldie, Tom Wayman, Ron Welwood, Paula Wild, Jim Wong-Chu.

Science and the Natural World: Peter Caverhill, Dennis Chalmers, T.C. Brayshaw, John Clague, Derek Fairbridge, John Ford, Howard Freeland, Chris Gainor, Kim Goldberg, Crispin S. Guppy, Rick Harbo, W.G. Hastings, Michael W. Hawkes, Rick Hudson, Andy Lamb, Colin Levings, Rolf Ludvigsen, Andy MacKinnon, Ron McLeod, Dan Moore, Jim Morison, Maggie Paquet, Guy Robertson, Marvin Roseanu, Hans Roemer, Klaus Schallie, Duane Sept, Bill Shaw, Claire Sowerbutt, Carol Swann, John Trelawny, Daniel Ware, Jim Woodey.

Sports: Alpine Canada, Peter Andrews, George Angelomatis, Don Arnold, Lorne Atkinson, John Baldwin, Basketball BC, BC Golf House, BC Lions, BC Sports Hall of Fame, Rudy Bianco, Alan Blair, Gordie Bowles, Chad Brealey, Harold Bridge, Judy Broom, Dave Brown, Roger M. Brunt, Canadian Lacrosse Hall of Fame, Sandy Chevallier, Doug Clement, Jeff Cross, Steve Daniel, Mark Dawson, Cleve Dheensaw, Alan Douglas, Bruce Fairley, Bert Fergus, Martha Fournier, Patrick Francis, Jimmy Gallagher, Joe Hailey, Mike Harling, Tom Hawthorn, Dan Hawthorne, Shirley Hewitt, Shirley Hills, Horse Council of BC, Graham Houston, Fred Hume, Norm Jewison, Tom Johnson, Mike Jones, Jim Kearney, Jack Kelso, Lyle Knight, John Kootnekoff, Kit Krieger, Jack Kyle, Geoff LaCasse, Bob Lenarduzzi, Clancy Loranger, John McBride, Archie McDonald, Neil McEvoy, Kevin McLane, Joan McMaster, Bill McNulty, Harold Mann, Ian Michaud, Jim Miller, Buzz Moore, Linda Moore, Margaret O'Reilly, John O'Shea, Tommy Paonessa, Marina Percy, Brian Pound, Fraser Pullen, Raiden, Nancy Greene Raine, Mike Riste, Jim Robson, Barbara Schrodt, Chic Scott, Flynn Sedden, Don Serl, Wendy Sewell, Paddy Sherman, Ken and Kathy Shields, Stan Shillington, Stanley F. Smith, Sport BC, Stan Stewardson, Annis Stukus, Roger Sumner, Derek A. Swain, Rikk Taylor, UBC Sports Hall of Fame, Vancouver Canucks, Vancouver 86ers, Vancouver Grizzlies, Ken Winslade, John Wirtanen.

As well, many individuals, museums and archives helped to collect and secure permissions for the hundreds of photographs, illustrations, sound and video clips that are such an important feature of the *EBC* in both book and interactive editions. They are Kelly Nolin at BC Archives; Liz Shorten at the BC Film Commission; Alice To at BC Film; Wayne Cousins and BC Hydro; Sherry Elchuk and the BC Museum of Mining; Kim Blake at Bruce Allen Talent; Eva Campbell; R. Wayne Campbell; Colin Preston and Janet Howey at CBC Vancouver; Kea Barker, Carol Vanelli and Alice Nellestijn at Cominco; Sue Kerr and Communication Design; Lisa Hayden at the David Suzuki Foundation; Alix Dunham; Derek Fairbridge; Sarah Goodman at Forest Alliance of BC; Miranda Holmes at Greenpeace; Connie Baxter, Chris Bogan and Lynne Waller at the Gulf of Georgia Cannery National Historic Site; Pam Kaatz and Bill Ahrens of Howe Sound Pulp and Paper; Jeff Edwards at Lakeside Studios; the staff at the Museum of Anthropology; Alexandria Stuart and Christina Dunkley at Nettwerk Productions; the Outdoor Recreation Council of BC; Kate Bird at Pacific Press; Malcolm Earle at Rainmaker Digital Productions; Gerry Truscott and Dan Savard at the Royal BC Museum; George Brandak at the UBC Library, Special Collections; the staff at the Vancouver Public Library; Hildegarde Westerkamp of the World Soundscape Project; Jennifer Jackiw and Tony Westbridge of Westbridge Fine Art; Sue Fox, Paul George and Joe Foy at the Western Canada Wilderness Committee; Western Forest Products and Diane Gudlaugsson; Whistler's Director of Communications Connie Rabold.

The work of many BC photographers is featured throughout the *Encyclopedia of BC*; credits appear in photo captions. Photographers and agencies who were particularly generous in providing photographs for the *EBC* include Rick Blacklaws, R. Wayne Campbell, Reimut Lieder of Image Makers, Roy Luckow, Eliza Massey, Malcolm Parry, Barry Peterson and Blaise Enright-Peterson, Hans Roemer and Alan Twigg.

Special thanks to Robert Dubberley, Michael Francis, Larry Kuehn, Ken Norton, Marg Penney, Doug Plant, Nora D. Randall, Sandra Smith, Harvey Thommasen, Patrick C. Trelawny, Drew Ann Wake.

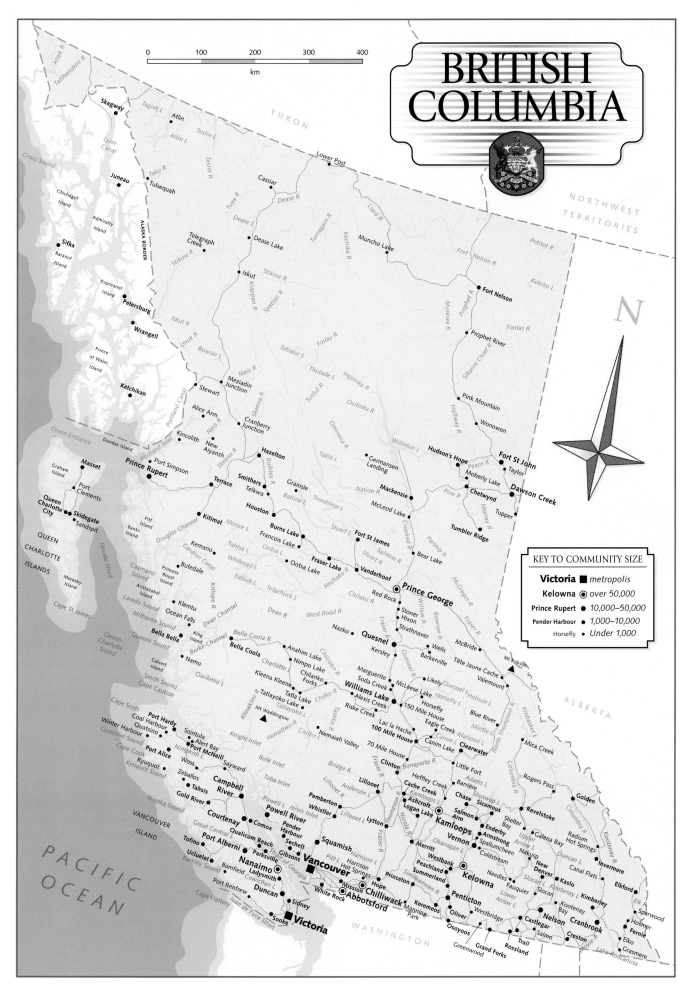

BRITISH COLUMBIA

0   100   200   300   400
km

KEY TO COMMUNITY SIZE

Victoria	■	*metropolis*
Kelowna	◉	*over 50,000*
Prince Rupert	●	*10,000–50,000*
Pender Harbour	●	*1,000–10,000*
Horsefly	•	*Under 1,000*

Abbreviations

AB Alberta
AK Alaska
AL Alabama
Apr April
AR Arkansas
Assoc Association
Aug August
AZ Arizona
b born
BC British Columbia
BCSHF BC Sports Hall of Fame
c circa
CA California
Capt Captain
CBC Canadian Broadcasting Corporation
CCF Co-operative Commonwealth Federation
CF Canadian Forces
CFL Canadian Football League
cm centimetre(s)
CMHC Canada Mortgage & Housing Corporation
CNR Canadian National Railway
CO Colorado
Co Company
Corp Corporation
CPR Canadian Pacific Railway
Crk Creek
CT Connecticut
CVA City of Vancouver Archives
d died
DC District of Columbia
DE Delaware
Dec December
E East
el elevation
est established
FABC Forest Alliance BC
Feb February
FL Florida
GA Georgia
gov gen governor general
GSC Geological Survey of Canada
GVRD Greater Vancouver Regional District
ha hectare(s)
HBC Hudson's Bay Company
HI Hawaii
Hwy Highway
IA Iowa
ID Idaho
IL Illinois
IN Indiana

Inc Incorporated
Jan January
km kilometre(s)
km/h kilometres per hour
KS Kansas
KY Kentucky
LA Louisiana
Lk Lake
LPGA Ladies' Professional Golf Association
lt gov lieutenant governor
Ltd Limited
m metre(s)
MA Massachusetts
Mar March
MB Manitoba
MCR Museum at Campbell River
MD Maryland
ME Maine
MI Michigan
MLA Member of the Legislative Assembly
MMBC Maritime Museum of BC
MN Minnesota
MO Missouri
MOA Museum of Anthropology
MP Member of Parliament
MS Mississippi
MT Montana
Mt Mount; Mountain
MVP Most Valuable Player
N North
NAC National Archives of Canada
NB New Brunswick
NBA National Basketball Association
NC North Carolina
NCAA National Collegiate Athletic Association
ND North Dakota
NDP New Democratic Party
NE Nebraska
NF Newfoundland
NFL National Football League
NH New Hampshire
NHL National Hockey League
NJ New Jersey
NM New Mexico
Nov November
NS Nova Scotia
NT Nunavut
NV Nevada
NWT Northwest Territories
NY New York
Oct October

OH Ohio
OK Oklahoma
ON Ontario
OR Oregon
PA Pennsylvania
PEI Prince Edward Island
PGA Professional Golfers' Association
PNE Pacific National Exhibition
pop population
QC Quebec
R River
RBCM Royal BC Museum
RI Rhode Island
Rwy Railway
S South
SC South Carolina
SD South Dakota
Sept September
SFU Simon Fraser University
SK Saskatchewan
sq square
St Saint
St Street
Ste Sainte
TN Tennessee
TX Texas
UBC University of British Columbia
UN United Nations
UNBC University of Northern British Columbia
UNESCO United Nations Educational, Scientific, and Cultural Organization
Univ University
UT Utah
VA Virginia
VMM Vancouver Maritime Museum
VPL Vancouver Public Library
VSO Vancouver Symphony Orchestra
VT Vermont
W West
WA Washington
WCWC Western Canada Wilderness Committee
WHL Western Hockey League
WI Wisconsin
WV West Virginia
WWI World War I
WWII World War II
WY Wyoming
YT Yukon

The annual Abbotsford International Airshow.
Brian Gauvin photo

Abbotsford International Airshow, North America's largest. The AIRPORT, which opened in 1944, is the weather alternate for the VANCOUVER INTERNATIONAL AIRPORT and supports a flight-training facility and a growing number of aerospace industries. The city's large MENNONITE population maintains a museum at CLEARBROOK and the Mennonite Educational Institute.

Population: 105,403
Rank in BC: 5th
Population increase since 1981: 93%
Date of incorporation: village 22 Feb 1924; district 17 Nov 1972; city 1 Jan 1995
Land area: 358.71 km²
Location: Fraser Valley Regional District
Economic base: agriculture, manufacturing, retail services

ABBOTT, Henry Braithwaite, engineer, CPR executive (b 14 June 1829, Abbottsford, QC; d 13 Sept 1915, Vancouver). Trained as an engineer at McGill Univ, he became a senior manager for the CPR during construction of the transcontinental railway. He was present at the Last Spike ceremony at CRAIGELLACHIE and was general superintendent of the CPR in BC from 1886 to 1897. Later he was president of the Vancouver & Lulu Island Rwy, the "Sockeye Ltd" that the CPR ran to STEVESTON in 1902-5. Abbott let the contract for clearing the VANCOUVER townsite in 1886 and his senior position with the CPR made him the leading business figure in the city during its first decade. He was a founding organizer of the Vancouver Club and first president of the Vancouver Lawn Tennis Club. He was a younger brother of John Abbott, prime minister of Canada from 1891 to 1892. ABBOTSFORD is named after H.B. Abbott.

ABERDEEN was the site of a SALMON CANNERY located on the north shore of the SKEENA R, 25 km southeast of PRINCE RUPERT. Established by the Windsor Canning Co in 1878, it was the second cannery built on the North Coast and served also as a trading centre for the region's MINERS. Aberdeen was rebuilt in 1895 after a serious fire. It burned again in 1902 and was abandoned. AS

ABALONE is a marine creature belonging to the class Gastropoda of the phylum Mollusca (*see* MOLLUSC). Abalone may be found intertidally in BC, but generally inhabit subtidal waters along rocky coasts to depths of 10 m, where they fasten to submerged rocks with a muscular "foot." Abalones are herbivores. Like most molluscs, the abalone has a radula, or rasplike "tongue," with which it scrapes algae and other plant material from rocks. Of the more than 70 species on earth, only one—the world's northernmost species—occurs in BC: the northern (pinto) abalone (*Haliotis kamtschatkana*). It grows to about 15 cm and has a thin, iridescent shell that is mottled green and red-brown on the outside and pearly white inside. The shell is perforated

Northern abalone, the only abalone species that occurs in BC. Duane Sept photo

by 3–6 holes along one side that allow water to exit the mantle cavity and take with it the wastes from the excretory organs and digestive tract. FIRST NATIONS people harvested abalone to eat the meat and to use the shells for ornamentation. Abalone was harvested commercially beginning in the early 1900s, particularly in the QUEEN CHARLOTTE ISLANDS. Commercial divers took substantial quantities in the 1970s and

1980s, until the threat of a population collapse resulted in a complete ban on harvesting in 1990. Surveys showed no evidence of populations rebuilding by the late 1990s and poaching remained a serious threat to recovery of this species. Abalone are cultured successfully in California; in BC, experiments with the culture of northern abalone in SAANICH INLET proved unsuccessful, but abalone culture in BC was still at the proposal stage in 1999.

ABBOTSFORD lies in the central FRASER VALLEY 75 km east of VANCOUVER. A townsite, originally spelled Abbottsford, was laid out beside the CPR track in 1889, the name referring to Henry ABBOTT, superintendent of the railway's Pacific Division. LOGGING and SAWMILLING were important from 1890 to 1930. The Abbotsford Lumber Co, owned by the TRETHEWEY family, built a sawmill on Mill Lk in 1909 and logged extensively until it closed in 1931. The BC ELECTRIC RWY linked the community to Vancouver in 1910. Abbotsford amalgamated with SUMAS PRAIRIE in 1972 and absorbed the district municipality of MATSQUI in 1995; its proximity to Vancouver resulted in rapid population growth during the 1990s. AGRICULTURE has always been important, principally DAIRY products, eggs and poultry, vegetables and BERRIES. Known as the Raspberry Capital of Canada, the area supplies 90% of all the raspberries consumed in the country. In the 1990s agriculture began to decline in importance as the local economy diversified into light manufacturing, mainly of building materials, furniture, metal fabrications and food products. The Univ College of the Fraser Valley opened in 1983, and since 1962 the community has become known for the annual

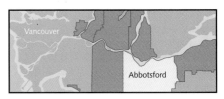

ABORIGINAL DEMOGRAPHY is a highly speculative subject, especially for the period before the arrival of the first European explorers when population figures are not available and can only be surmised. Estimates for the pre-contact aboriginal population of BC have reflected this uncertainty, ranging from a low of about 75,000 to a high of about 400,000. Most of the population was on the coast, where aboriginals achieved the highest density of any place in Canada. At contact, nearly half the aboriginal people in the country lived in BC. This population began to decrease dramatically at contact, due largely to the introduction of diseases against which the people had no immunity. Measles, whooping cough, INFLUENZA, tuberculosis, scarlet fever and SMALLPOX were particularly devastating. On the eve of CONFEDERATION (1871), the population had fallen below 26,000. Two groups—the PENTLATCH on VANCOUVER ISLAND and the TSETSAUT of the northern Interior—disappeared entirely. During the 1880s the non-aboriginal population of the province exceeded the aboriginal population for the first time. The aboriginal population continued to fall through the 1920s, principally because of high infant mortality rates, and reached a low of about 20,000. Since that time the population has grown; by 1996 it exceeded 139,000, 70% of whom were living off-RESERVE and 27% of whom lived in Greater VANCOUVER or Greater VICTORIA. BC aboriginals account for about 17% of the total Canadian FIRST NATIONS population. The following figures are from official government censuses and may under-represent the size of BC's aboriginal population. The numbers refer to so-called status Indians who meet the requirements of the *Indian Act*.

ABORIGINAL DEMOGRAPHY 1881–1996

YEAR	ABORIGINAL POP.	% of BC POPULATION
1881	25,661	51.9%
1891	27,305	27.8%
1901	28,949	16.2%
1911	20,174	5.1%
1921	22,377	4.3%
1931	24,599	3.5%
1941	24,882	3.0%
1951	28,504	2.4%
1961	38,814	2.4%
1971	52,430	2.4%
1981	73,670	2.7%
1991	118,731	3.6%
1996	139,655	3.8%

ABORIGINAL RIGHTS are rights of title, occupation and use of land and resources that existed prior to the arrival of European colonial powers and that in Canada are the subject of treaty agreements between federal and provincial governments and aboriginal groups. Colonial powers unsuccessfully wrestled with the issue of aboriginal rights for 400 years and any systematic codification of these rights has eluded almost every government. Since colonial times, aboriginal groups in BC have had a consistent view of what their pre-existing rights and titles are, and from whence those rights derive; they have sent many formal delegations to federal and provincial authorities to articulate their grievances over alienation from their lands and diminished access to their resources. In addition to the rights inherent in their traditional forms of governance and law, aboriginal groups point to the Royal Proclamation of 1763, in which the British Crown explicitly recognized the existence and continuation of aboriginal title in British N America and implicitly acknowledged the existence and continuity of aboriginal self-government. In BC, however, colonial authorities generally conducted themselves as though aboriginal rights did not exist or had been extinguished with the advent of colonial and later provincial governments (*see* COLONIAL GOVERNMENT). With the exception of a handful of treaties signed by James DOUGLAS on VANCOUVER ISLAND (*see* DOUGLAS TREATIES), and an extension of TREATY NO 8 in northeastern BC during the GOLD RUSH to the Klondike in 1899, most FIRST NATIONS in the province remained without treaties. In 1982 the Canadian Constitution recognized and affirmed "existing" aboriginal and treaty rights and a series of court rulings (notably the CALDER CASE, *Guerin*, SPARROW DECISION and DELGAMUUKW CASE) have defined the nature and extent of these rights. In 1990 the government of BC joined the federal government to negotiate a treaty with the NISGA'A people (*see* NISGA'A TREATY). And in 1993, following a BC Court of Appeal ruling in *Delgamuukw* that the GITKSAN and WET'SUWET'EN peoples have "unextinguished, non-exclusive aboriginal rights, other than right of ownership" to much of their traditional territories, the province established the BC TREATY COMMISSION to oversee 3-way negotiations between each First Nation and representatives from the federal and provincial governments.
Reading: Paul Tennant, *Aboriginal Peoples and Politics: The Indian Land Question in British Columbia, 1849–1989*, 1990.   *Stephen Hume*

ACKERY, Ivor Frederick Wilson "Ivan," theatre manager (b 30 Oct 1899, Bristol, England; d 29 Oct 1989, Vancouver). He immigrated to VANCOUVER in 1914 to join his widowed mother. During WWI he enlisted in the Canadian army and saw action in France. His long career in show business began in 1921 in Calgary, where he had gone looking for work and where he took a job as a theatre usher. He returned in 1923 to Vancouver, and Famous Players made him a manager of one of their movie theatres. He proved such a successful promoter that he became manager of the showcase ORPHEUM THEATRE in 1935. He remained there until his retirement at the end of 1969, earning a reputation as Vancouver's Mr Show Business (a.k.a. "Little Orpheum Ackery"). He was famous for his promotional stunts: once he had someone dress up in a gorilla costume and chase his secretary around the roof of the theatre to advertise "King Kong." Few Hollywood celebrities came to town without putting in an appearance at the Orpheum.

ACORN, Milton, poet (b 30 Mar 1923, Charlottetown; d 20 Aug 1986, Charlottetown). He was a carpenter by trade, a communist and Canadian nationalist by choice, who made poetry his profession, living hand-to-mouth, shunning academia and styling himself a "people's poet." Afflicted with a variety of physical and mental ailments, he lived a troubled life but in the end was recognized as one of the outstanding poets of his generation. He began publishing poetry in 1953 when living in Montreal, then moved to Toronto where in 1962 he married the poet Gwendolyn MacEwen. When his marriage

Milton Acorn, who inspired the People's Poet Award, c 1965. Courtesy Mary Hooper

broke up he moved in 1963 to VANCOUVER where for 5 years he was a familiar figure in literary-political circles. He was part of the small group that founded the GEORGIA STRAIGHT newspaper in 1967. He returned east in 1968 and published a book of poems, *I've Tasted My Blood*, the following year. When it was denied a GOV GEN'S LITERARY AWARD in favour of MacEwen's *The Shadow-Maker* and George BOWERING's *Rocky Mountain Foot* and *The Gangs of Kosmos*, a group of writers gathered at Grossman's Tavern in Toronto to present Acorn with the first ever People's Poet Award, which later became a regular event carried out in his memory. Acorn finally did win a Gov Gen's Award in 1975 for *The Island Means Minago*. Other books include *More Poems for People* (1972) and *Dig Up My Heart: Selected Poems 1952–83* (1983).

ACTIVE PASS, connecting GEORGIA STRAIT and the inner waters of the GULF ISLANDS between MAYNE and GALIANO ISLANDS, is the route followed by BC FERRIES travelling between TSAWWASSEN and Swartz Bay. It is named for the US survey ship that first navigated the pass in 1855. It is an excellent viewing area for many types of seabirds and large marine mammals that congregate to feed on the fish and plankton churned up by the current.

ADAMS, Alfred, Haida activist (b 1867, Masset; d 1945). One of the founders of the NATIVE BROTHERHOOD OF BC in 1931, he served as president of the organization until his death. He came from a long line of HAIDA chiefs and was a commercial fisher and an ANGLICAN lay minister. As a recruiter of labour for the canneries, he advocated employment and welfare for his people.

ADAMS, Bryan Guy, musician (b 5 Nov 1959, Kingston, ON). His father was in the military and Bryan was raised in a series of overseas NATO bases. His parents separated and he settled in VANCOUVER with his mother in 1974. As a 16-year-old he made his first recording with the short-lived Vancouver group Sweeney Todd. When the group dissolved he pursued a songwriting career with a partner, Jim VALLANCE. His first single appeared in 1979, his first album in 1980; in 1983 his third album, *Cuts Like a Knife*, established him as an international success. Subsequent albums—including *Into the Fire* (1987), *Waking Up the Neighbours* (1991), *18 'Til I Die* (1996) and *On a Day Like Today* (1998), his tenth—have sold millions of copies worldwide. His single "(Everything I Do) I Do It For You" from *Waking up the Neighbours* won a Grammy Award and made the *Guinness Book of World Records* as the longest-running number one single on the British pop charts (16 weeks). One of Canada's leading international rock music stars, he has won several Juno Awards and is a member of the ORDER OF BC (1990) and the Order of Canada (1990).

ADAMS LAKE, 145 km^2, lies north of SHUSWAP LK and northeast of KAMLOOPS. The region was an important territory of the SECWEPEMC (Shuswap) people. Prospectors arrived in the 1890s and several mines opened, 3 of them lasting until the 1930s. The area supplied timber from 1911 to 1925 for a sawmill at CHASE. The sternwheeler *Helen* was built on the 65-km-long lake to tow logs to the lower ADAMS R, where they were flushed downstream. A supply depot and wharf at the lake's south end became the nucleus of a settlement, also called Adams Lake. In 1945 Art Holding built a mill there that subsequently was purchased by INTERNATIONAL FOREST PRODUCTS. Cottages and several resorts line the lakeshore; FISHING and houseboating are popular. *See also* LOGGING; MINING; SAWMILLING. *AS*

ADAMS RIVER, northeast of KAMLOOPS, is divided into 2 units by ADAMS LK (145 km^2). The lower section (11 km) connects the lake to the west end of SHUSWAP LK. It is famous as the site of one of the largest sockeye SALMON runs on the continent. Every 4 years close to 2 million fish return to the river to spawn and die, attracting visitors from around the world. The turbulent river, which flows through Roderick HAIG-BROWN Provincial Park (9.88 km^2), is also popular with whitewater enthusiasts. Salmon runs on the upper section were destroyed early in the century but have begun to rebuild. The provincial government named it a HERITAGE RIVER in 1996. It is named for a 19th-century chief of the Sexqeltqin nation, a division of the SECWEPEMC (Shuswap), who live at Adams Lk and have fished the river for hundreds of years. *See also* RIVERS.

ADASKIN, Harry, musician (b 6 Oct 1901, Riga, Latvia; d 7 Apr 1994, Vancouver). The eldest member of a prominent musical family (his brother Murray is a composer and John was a radio producer), he came to Canada as an infant and grew up in Toronto, where he began playing violin at age 7. In 1924 he became one of the founding members of the acclaimed Hart

Harry Adaskin and his wife Frances.
Eliza Massey photo

House String Quartet, formed under the patronage of Vincent Massey. After leaving the quartet in 1938 he became a freelance musician and radio BROADCASTER. In 1946 he arrived in VANCOUVER to establish the music department at UBC, where he remained on the faculty until 1973. He and his wife Frances, a pianist, were well known for their passionate efforts to share their love of music with the public. Adaskin wrote two volumes of memoirs, *A Fiddler's World* (1977) and *A Fiddler's Choice* (1982).

ADBUSTERS is a MAGAZINE published in VANCOUVER since 1989 by the non-profit Media Foundation, a group of social activists promoting the decommercialization of everyday life. The magazine, billed as a "Journal of the Mental Environment," features parodies of advertisements and articles about advertising, media, ENVIRONMENTALISM and the corporate economy. Under its founding editor and chief adbuster, Kalle Lasn, a former market researcher and filmmaker, *Adbusters* was named Canadian magazine of the year in 1999. The foundation also sponsors a variety of anti-consumerism activities, including Buy Nothing Day, TV Turnoff Week, and the production of "uncommercials" through its own ad agency, Powershift.

AERO, 25 km south of SANDSPIT on Cumshewa Inlet, was the only site in the QUEEN CHARLOTTE ISLANDS where RAILWAY LOGGING took place. A.P. ALLISON established the MORESBY ISLAND camp in 1936 and it soon became a major supplier of Sitka SPRUCE. A crown corporation named Aero Timber took over the camp in WWII as spruce was vital for building airplanes. After the war the operation was sold at a low price to the POWELL RIVER CO. The railway ran until 1955. By 1967 the camp was abandoned. *AS*

AGAR, Carl Clare, aviator (b 28 Nov 1901, Lion's Head, ON; d 27 Jan 1968, Victoria). He grew up in Edmonton and became a farmer

Bryan Adams in performance. Inset: Danny Clinch photo; photos courtesy Bruce Allen Talent

L to r: Carl Agar, his business partner Alf Stringer and Igor Sikorsky, designer of the Sikorsky helicopter, 1954.
United Technologies/Sikorsky Aircraft

south of the city, and he obtained a pilot's licence. When WWII began he joined the RCAF as an instructor in the British Commonwealth Air Training Plan. Following his discharge in 1945 he co-founded Okanagan Air Services, a commercial flying business based in KELOWNA and PENTICTON. In 1947 he bought his first helicopter, using it to crop-dust orchards. As the business expanded into aerial supply for remote camps and construction sites, he pioneered techniques for flying in mountainous terrain and soon became an authority on this type of flying. By 1952, when the company became Okanagan Helicopters Ltd (*see* CANADIAN HELICOPTERS LTD), it was one of the largest commercial helicopter operators in the world. He was awarded the McKee Trophy for his contribution to Canadian AVIATION and is a member of Canada's Aviation Hall of Fame.

AGASSIZ is a rural community south of HARRISON HOT SPRINGS at the head of the FRASER VALLEY 35 km west of HOPE. The original settler was Louis Agassiz, postmaster of Hope, who pre-empted farmland at the site in 1862. He named the spot Ferney Coombe; the CPR changed the name to Agassiz in the 1880s. A Dominion Experimental Farm was established here in 1888.

AGRICULTURAL LAND RESERVE (ALR) was created in 1973 by the NDP government of Dave BARRETT to arrest shrinkage of the province's agricultural land base. With the best arable land comprising only .5% of BC's total area, it was a cause of great concern that through the 1960s and early 1970s more than 4,000 ha of farmland was being lost annually to other forms of development, primarily residential. Concern focussed on the lower FRASER VALLEY, where urban sprawl was rapidly consuming the province's most productive truck and DAIRY farms. The Land Commission Act, championed by RICHMOND MLA Harold Steves and introduced by Agriculture Minister Dave STUPICH, froze development on all agricultural land and established an Agricultural Land Commission to administer the legislation, create an inventory of agricultural lands and consider appeals. The ALR embraced 4 different land classifications from grazing land to the most fertile multi-crop land, and eventually involved about 47,000 km², representing about 5% of the province. Although the legislation initially provoked fierce opposi-

tion from landowners whose property values were reduced, it was copied in other jurisdictions across N America and in time became the proudest legacy of the Barrett government. Barrett's SOCIAL CREDIT PARTY successors weakened the legislation by introducing an appeal process that placed political "provincial interest" criteria above agricultural values and excluded many smaller properties, but the government was criticized so strongly when it allowed residential development on a large Richmond acreage known as the Terra Nova lands, that further large-scale removals were curtailed. The NDP government of Glen CLARK faced such a storm of criticism when it used the provincial interest exemption to allow a recreational complex on a KAMLOOPS property known as the Six Mile Ranch in 1998 that the provincial interest loophole was removed. In Apr 2000 the ALR was merged with the forest land commission to create the BC Land Reserve Commission. *See also* AGRICULTURE; FOREST POLICY. *Howard White*

AGRICULTURE is the third-largest resource industry in BC after the forest industry and mining, despite the fact that only 3% of the land area is suitable for farming—the smallest percentage of arable land of any province except Newfoundland. Since 1973 most of this land has been protected from non-agricultural use by the AGRICULTURAL LAND RESERVE. More than a quarter of BC's farms are concentrated in the lower FRASER VALLEY, the centre of DAIRY FARMING and BERRY, vegetable, poultry, pig and MUSHROOM production. The valley has the longest frost-free growing season in Canada. Cattle raising is centred around KAMLOOPS and in the CARIBOO and CHILCOTIN (*see* CATTLE INDUSTRY). TREE FRUITS are concentrated in the THOMPSON R and OKANAGAN VALLEYS, where another 25% of the farms are located. The PEACE R area accounts for

86% of BC's grain production. Other significant agricultural areas are southern VANCOUVER ISLAND and parts of the KOOTENAY.

The first crops were grown at NOOTKA SOUND in 1790 by the Spanish garrison posted there. Later the HBC began raising crops at some of its trading posts and established the first agricultural settlers on land near VICTORIA in the 1850s. From these modest beginnings, agriculture has grown into an industry accounting for 33,000 direct jobs and many more in processing and manufacturing. In 1998 there were 21,835 farms in BC. Of these, 97% were family-owned. During the 1990s the number of family farms actually grew; BC was the only province where this occurred. In 1998 farm cash receipts totalled $1.8 billion. The agricultural industry produces 200 different commodities, both livestock and plant products, annually accounting for $1.7 billion worth of international exports and $1.1 billion worth of exports to the rest of Canada. The marketing of several commodities is supervised by provincial marketing boards. There are 11 such boards or commissions in BC, regulating sales of vegetables, turkeys, tree fruits, mushrooms, milk, hogs, grapes, eggs, CRANBERRIES, chickens and broiler hatching eggs. Individual commodity boards are themselves regulated by the BC Marketing Board.

Among the most important livestock products, after cattle and dairying, are:

Poultry and Eggs. There are about 300 commercial chicken producers in BC, producing 100 million kg of chickens a year with a farm gate value of $179 million. Another 2.3 million laying chickens are kept by about 140 commercial egg producers to produce 53 million dozen eggs annually, worth $73 million at the gate. There is also a smaller market for turkeys, about 2 million of which are raised annually, mainly in the Fraser Valley.

Harvesting wheat, Peace R area, 1989.
Roy Luckow photo

AGRICULTURE IN BC: Farms with annual revenues over $2,500

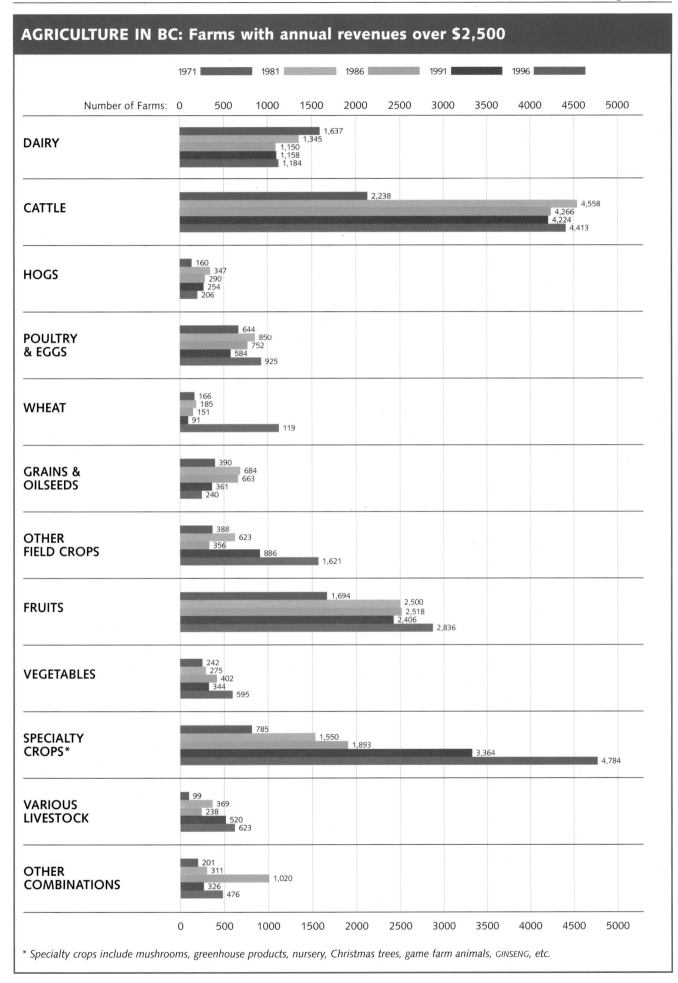

Legend: 1971 · 1981 · 1986 · 1991 · 1996

Number of Farms: 0 — 500 — 1000 — 1500 — 2000 — 2500 — 3000 — 3500 — 4000 — 4500 — 5000

DAIRY
- 1,637
- 1,345
- 1,150
- 1,158
- 1,184

CATTLE
- 2,238
- 4,558
- 4,266
- 4,224
- 4,413

HOGS
- 160
- 347
- 290
- 254
- 206

POULTRY & EGGS
- 644
- 850
- 752
- 584
- 925

WHEAT
- 166
- 185
- 151
- 91
- 119

GRAINS & OILSEEDS
- 390
- 684
- 663
- 361
- 240

OTHER FIELD CROPS
- 388
- 623
- 356
- 886
- 1,621

FRUITS
- 1,694
- 2,500
- 2,518
- 2,406
- 2,836

VEGETABLES
- 242
- 275
- 402
- 344
- 595

SPECIALTY CROPS*
- 785
- 1,550
- 1,893
- 3,364
- 4,784

VARIOUS LIVESTOCK
- 99
- 369
- 238
- 520
- 623

OTHER COMBINATIONS
- 201
- 311
- 1,020
- 326
- 476

0 — 500 — 1000 — 1500 — 2000 — 2500 — 3000 — 3500 — 4000 — 4500 — 5000

Specialty crops include mushrooms, greenhouse products, nursery, Christmas trees, game farm animals, GINSENG, etc.

Early grain farmers at Spillimacheen, c 1900.
UBC BC816

Hogs. There are 175 BC producers, once again mainly in the Fraser Valley, producing 300,000 animals a year for slaughter. In 1998 pigs had a farm gate value of $37 million. Local producers account for 25–30% of all the pork eaten in BC.

Sheep. There are about 75,000 sheep in BC, raised both for their wool (about 85 tonnes a year) and meat.

Goats. A small number of goats (9,000 –10,000) are raised for their milk (used to drink and make cheese), meat and wool.

Exotic livestock. This category includes llamas, which provide wool; emus and ostriches, raised at this point only to provide breeding stock; and reindeer, raised at a very few locations in the Peace R for meat.

Important plant crops include mushrooms, cranberries and other berries, tree fruits and vegetables. Another significant sector is floriculture, the production of cut flowers and potted and bedding plants in both greenhouses and fields. This industry includes close to 400 producers, 90% of whom are located in the lower Fraser

SELECTED BC AGRICULTURAL STATISTICS 1971–96

	1971	1981	1986	1991	1996
Number of farms	18,400	20,012	19,063	19,225	21,835
Total farm area (000 ha)	2,357	2,179	2,411	2,392	2,529
Average farm size (ha)	128	109	126	124	116
Total area owned (000 ha)	1,545	1,537	1,457	1,500	1,562
Total area rented (000 ha)	812	642	954	892	967
Total area in crops (000 ha)	442	568	571	557	566
Area in wheat (000 ha)	44	43	40	44	40
Area in oats (000 ha)	53	50	47	30	34
Area in barley (000 ha)	79	94	74	43	45
Area in fodder (000 ha)	217	305	303	327	348
Area in potatoes (ha)	3,676	3,510	3,182	3,369	3,642
Area in vegetables (ha)	7,250	7,867	7,568	8,275	7,117
Total area irrigated (000 ha)	89	100	118	95	115
Number of tractors	21,953	28,761	31,768	33,527	36,361
Number of combines	1,673	1,870	1,795	1,752	1,526
Number of farm trucks	17,243	23,097	25,346	26,773	28,789
Greenhouse area (000 m²)	476	1,008	1,306	1,787	2,834
Mushroom area (000 m²)	67	—	199	210	244
Cattle (000s)	573	790	690	752	814
Hogs (000s)	79	255	217	224	174
Sheep (000s)	53	67	57	74	72
Poultry (000s)	7,861	9,976	9,230	11,285	13,759
Turkeys (000s)	805	712	649	801	851
Horses (000s)	32	39	42	40	49
Goats (000s)	2	—	8	9	13
Rabbits (000s)	35	—	30	32	21
Mink (000s)	246	—	247	190	249

BC AGRICULTURAL REVENUES 1911-98 ($ million)

1911	17.4
1931	36.4
1951	69.0
1971	209.6
1981	800.0
1986	1,104.0
1991	1,324.0
1996	1,596.0
1998	1,812.0

Valley within a 2-hour drive of Vancouver. A related industry is the growing of nursery crops, including trees, shrubs and other plants. BC is the second-largest producer of nursery stock in Canada, producing 25% of national sales. In 1998 floriculture and nursery crops taken together accounted for $270 million in revenue for producers, making it the third most valuable agricultural sector after dairy farming and poultry production.

Harvesting strawberries near Chilliwack. Roy Luckow photo

AH-CHEE-WUN was a legendary Coast Salish chief, leader of the Lemalchi people who lived on KUPER ISLAND opposite CHEMAINUS in the mid-19th century (*see* SALISHAN FIRST NATIONS). A fearsome warrior believed by some to have supernatural powers, he opposed the entry of non-aboriginals into his territory. In Apr 1863, 3 white people were murdered in the GULF ISLANDS. Ah-Chee-Wun's people were blamed and Gov James DOUGLAS dispatched a gunboat to bring them in. At Kuper Island people said the suspects were not there, but the gunboat fired on the village anyway, destroying it and dispersing the inhabitants. A small flotilla of boats pursued the fugitives to MONTAGUE HARBOUR on GALIANO ISLAND, where Ah-Chee-Wun and his followers eventually surrendered. The chief and 2 other men were convicted of the murders and hanged. The incident marked the end of the Lemalchi as a distinct tribe.

AHOUSAT, pop 900, is a waterfront reserve on FLORES ISLAND in CLAYOQUOT SOUND on the west coast of VANCOUVER ISLAND, accessible only by boat or float plane. It was originally a village site of the Otsosaht people (NUU-CHAH-NULTH); it was conquered and absorbed early in the 19th century by the Ahousaht (also Nuu-chah-nulth) from nearby VARGAS ISLAND. From 1918 to the 1930s it was headquarters for the Gordon GIBSON family LOGGING operations. Also known as Marktosis, Ahousat offers services to cruising boats and there is a sulphur springs nearby. Many Ahousaht people live away from the island in order to find employment. Commercial FISHING is the major occupation locally.

AIDS (Acquired Immune Deficiency Syndrome) is a disease resulting from infection by a virus known as HIV, human immunodeficiency virus. The virus attacks the human immune system, leaving the victim vulnerable to infectious diseases and some types of cancer. Several years may elapse between infection with HIV and the onset of AIDS, and in some cases the virus never develops into full-blown disease. The virus is transmitted through sexual contact with an infected person, intravenous drug use, artificial insemination and the use of tainted blood or blood products. As well, an infected pregnant woman may spread the virus to her fetus. The first Canadian case of AIDS was reported in 1979, though it was not related to HIV until 1983. Initially the disease was thought to be confined to homosexual men, since the vast majority of early cases belonged to that group, but it soon appeared among women and the heterosexual population generally. By 1997, about 15,000 cases of AIDS had been reported in Canada and about 40,000 people were living with HIV. Death rates from the disease peaked in 1993, then began to decline markedly with advances in medical treatment and public education programs. However, the number of people in Canada infected with HIV continued to climb, reaching about 5,000 new cases a year, mainly as a result of intravenous drug use.

BC has been hard hit by the AIDS outbreak, especially but not exclusively VANCOUVER's Downtown Eastside area, where by 1997 the disease had reached epidemic proportions among injection-drug users. It is estimated that as many as 50% of these people are infected with HIV, having acquired it mainly by sharing needles. To combat the disease a needle exchange program was established in 1989, and in 1992 the BC CENTRE FOR EXCELLENCE IN HIV/AIDS was founded to distribute medication and train health-care workers. Nevertheless, by 1997 new cases of HIV infection were appearing at a rate of 2 per day and the situation was declared a medical emergency. There was also concern that HIV was spreading rapidly to the province's aboriginal community: a 1998 report revealed that 16% of people newly infected with HIV in BC were aboriginals, even though they comprised only about 4% of the population.

AINSWORTH HOT SPRINGS, pop 89, is on the west side of KOOTENAY LK 20 km south of KASLO. It was the first townsite in the Kootenay Lk–SLOCAN area, established in 1883 by John C. Ainsworth, a wealthy Portland steamboat operator, and registered in the name of his son George. High-grade SILVER prospects were discovered at the site so that in 1888 the Ainsworth syndicate commissioned Gustavus WRIGHT to develop both the townsite and several of its own claims. By 1891 it was the leading shipping camp on the lake, but in that year significant silver discoveries in the Slocan promoted the development of Kaslo as the major distribution point. Activity at the Ainsworth MINING camp settled into a modest pace of production that carried on in fits and starts until about 1960. During the 1930s John Burns, a retired building contractor, bought up much of the townsite and developed the natural chalybeate HOT SPRINGS as a resort. In 1999 the Ainsworth Hot Springs resort remained the major industry in what had become a bedroom suburb of NELSON and Kaslo.

AINSWORTH LUMBER CO is a diversified wood products company founded by the Ainsworth family in 1950. Based in VANCOUVER, it has 1,100 employees producing strand board and solid-wood products at operations in 100 MILE HOUSE, CLINTON, LILLOOET, SAVONA, ABBOTSFORD and Grande Prairie, AB. The company reported 1999 revenues of $433.4 million. *See also* FOREST PRODUCTS.

Ainsworth brothers en route to the Cariboo with their portable sawmill, 1952. Ainsworth collection/courtesy Ken Drushka

AIRPORTS in BC, as in the rest of Canada, have recently been transferred from the responsibility of Transport Canada to new airport authorities regulated by local government. There are more than 150 land- and water-based airports and heliports in the province. VANCOUVER INTERNATIONAL AIRPORT is the largest airport and the only one situated on major international routes and welcoming international airlines; it handles more than 87% of passengers travelling on scheduled services through BC. VICTORIA's is the second busiest airport in BC, with 4% of travellers; passenger traffic at the Victoria airport reached 1.2 million in 1998. There are another 15 airports with regularly scheduled local and regional service and connections to Vancouver International for longer flights. Of these, the busiest are at KELOWNA and PRINCE GEORGE.

Vancouver's first airport, Lulu Island, 1929.
Leonard Frank/Jewish Historical Society

BC AIRPORTS

100 Mile House	Hope (YHE)	Prince Rupert (YPR)
108 Mile Ranch (ZMH)	Houston (ZHO)	Princeton
Abbotsford (YXX)	Hudson's Hope (YNH)	Qualicum Beach
Alert Bay (YAL)	Kamloops (YKA)	Quesnel (YQZ)
Anahim Lake (YAA)	Kaslo	Revelstoke (YRV)
Atlin	Kelowna (YLW)	Salmon Arm (YSN)
Bella Bella (ZEL)	Langley (YNJ)	Sandspit (YZP)
Bella Coola (QBC)	Likely	Sechelt (YHS)
Blue River	Lillooet	Smithers (YYD)
Boundary Bay (YBB)	Mackenzie (YZY)	Sparwood
Burns Lake (YPZ)	Massett (ZMT)	Squamish (YSE)
Cache Creek	McBride	Stewart (ZST)
Campbell River (YBL)	Merritt (YMB)	Telegraph Creek (YTX)
Castlegar (YCG)	Midway	Terrace (YXT)
Chetwynd (YCQ)	Nakusp	Texada Island (YGB)
Chilliwack (YCW)	Nanaimo (YCD)	Tofino (YAZ)
Courtenay (YCA)	Nelson (ZNL)	Trail
Cranbrook (YXC)	Oliver	Tsey Keh (Prince George)
Creston (YCZ)	Osoyoos	Tumbler Ridge (TUX)
Dawson Creek (YDQ)	Pemberton	Valemount
Fairmont Hot Springs	Penticton (YYF)	Vancouver (YVR)
Fort Nelson (YYE)	Pitt Meadows (YPK)	Vanderhoof
Fort St James (YJM)	Port Alberni (YPB)	Vernon (YVE)
Fort St John (YXJ)	Port Hardy (YZT)	Victoria (YYJ)
Fraser Lake	Port McNeill (YMP)	Williams Lake (YWL)
Golden	Powell River (YPW)	
Grand Forks (ZGF)	Prince George (YXS)	

AIYANSH; *see* GITLAKDAMIKS.

AKAMINA PASS, in the southeast corner of BC, connects the Akamina–Kishinena Provincial PARK (109.22 km²) across the ROCKY MTS with Waterton Lakes National Park in Alberta. Isolated and unpopulated, it is the most easterly point in the province. The area is home to one of the densest populations of grizzly BEAR in N America. The name derives from a KTUNAXA (Kutenai) word meaning "mountain pass." In 1995 the United Nations declared the area encompassed by the BC park, Waterton Park and Montana's Glacier National Park to be a WORLD HERITAGE SITE.

ALAMO was a MINING camp (now abandoned), established in 1894 east of NEW DENVER between KOOTENAY and SLOCAN lakes, an area rich in SILVER-lead ore. Named after the nearby Alamo Mine, the camp had a population of more than 200 and a post office, hotel and general store. It was a stop on the Nakusp & Slocan Rwy, part of the CPR system. The camp was shut down in about 1904, although mining in the area continued into the late 1930s. *AS*

ALASKA BOUNDARY DISPUTE involved the border between BC and the Alaska Panhandle, the narrow strip of mainland and islands extending south from AK to latitude 54°40'.

The US purchased Alaska from Russia in 1867, claiming that the border of the Panhandle area passed inland around the heads of the major fjords. This interpretation was not tested for several years until the discovery of GOLD in the Klondike in 1896 brought the matter to a head. Most of the traffic to and from the goldfields flowed through Lynn Canal; to get a share of the lucrative Klondike trade, Canada asserted its claim to the head of the canal. In 1903 the dispute went to an international tribunal of 3 Americans, 2 Canadians and a British jurist, Lord Alverstone. A decision came down on 20 Oct 1903; Alverstone had endorsed the American claim, touching off a wave of indig-

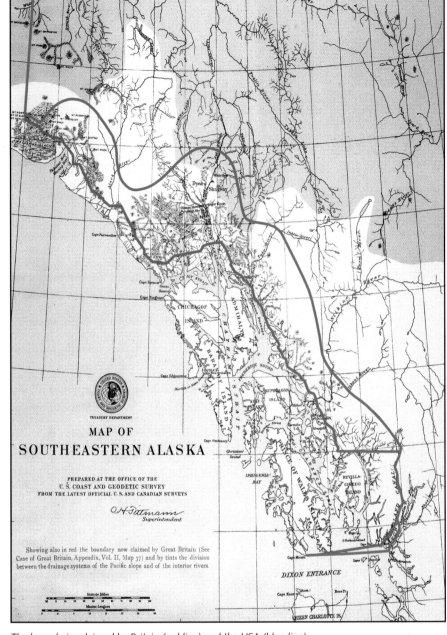

The boundaries claimed by Britain (red line) and the USA (blue line), 1903. Public Records Office, Surrey, UK/Historical Atlas of BC

ALASKA HIGHWAY

To Fairbanks, AK

Teslin

Watson Lake

Liard River

Muncho Lake

97

Fort Nelson

Prophet River

Sikanni Chief

Fort St. John

Taylor

Dawson Creek

nant protest by Canadians. Feelings eventually cooled but the dispute highlighted Canada's desire to have more control over its own foreign affairs.

ALASKA HIGHWAY winds across 2,451 km of mountain wilderness from DAWSON CREEK, BC, to Fairbanks, AK: 1,009 km are actually in BC. The original road was built hurriedly in the summer of 1942 by the American military. In the wake of the attack on Pearl Harbor, the Americans feared a Japanese invasion of the Northwest via the Aleutian Islands and wanted a secure land route into Alaska. The road, built and paid for by the Americans, opened to military through-traffic on Nov 20. Immediately the US Public Roads Administration began upgrading the route to civilian standards. At its peak the project employed 14,000 people. Reconstruction was completed by the end of 1943 and the US continued to maintain the highway until Apr 1946, when Canada paid $120 million and took formal possession of the 1,954-km portion of the highway up to the Alaska border. The following year the road opened to regular traffic and it has been an important transportation corridor linking northern BC, the Yukon and Alaska to the south. *See also* ROADS AND HIGHWAYS.

ALASKA PINE CO LTD began just before WWII with the arrival in VANCOUVER of 3 brothers with extensive experience in the European timber business. Otto, Leon and Walter KOERNER had fled the Nazi invasion of Czechoslovakia and sought to re-establish themselves in BC. They purchased a small box plant at Marpole called Universal Box Co and found a way to use western HEMLOCK, a prolific species with little export value because of its tendency to warp and stain during shipment. Once they had figured out how to cure hemlock lumber, the Koerners began to market it under the name "Alaska pine." In 1942 they purchased Jones Lake Logging Co to obtain a timber supply. The following year they bought Pioneer Timber Co at PORT MCNEILL and set up a subsidiary, Northern Timber Co, to acquire timber land in the same area.

After the war, the brothers joined with an Australian company to found Western Forest Industries, which purchased Lake Logging Co at COWICHAN LK, as well as the assets of the Canadian Puget Sound Lumber & Timber Co at JORDAN RIVER. In 1951 Alaska Pine joined Abitibi Power & Paper Co to form Alaska Pine & Cellulose Ltd, which purchased pulp mills at PORT ALICE on VANCOUVER ISLAND and WOODFIBRE on HOWE SOUND. In 1954 Rayonier Inc of New York purchased 80% of the company. The remaining shares were purchased in 1959 and the name changed to Rayonier Canada Ltd. In 1980 Rayonier was sold to 3 BC forest companies and its name changed to Western Forest Products which, in turn, was taken over by DOMAN INDUSTRIES in the early 1990s.

Ken Drushka

ALBAS was a tiny LOGGING community, site of a water-driven SAWMILL in the WWI era, on the east shore of SEYMOUR ARM of SHUSWAP LK, 60 km north of SALMON ARM. It was named after Al Bass, an early trapper in the area, and is now part of Shuswap Lake Provincial MARINE PARK.

AS

ALBATROSS is a pelagic seabird notable for its long, narrow wings, broad wingspan and graceful soaring flight. Like other members of the order Procellariiformes, the albatross comes to land only to reproduce. Most types are confined to the S Pacific but one, the black-footed albatross (*Phoebastria nigripes*), frequents the outer

The black-footed albatross, Queen Charlotte Sound. Peter A. Robson photo

coast of BC from Apr to Sept. This species has a wingspan over 2 metres. It is dusky black in colour, breeds in Hawaii and off Japan and, as a surface feeder, tends to follow boats picking up scraps. The Laysan albatross (*P. immutabilis*), notable for its white head and front, is a rare visitor to the coast, and the large short-tailed albatross (*P. albatros*) is even rarer.

ALBERNI, Pedro de, army officer (b 30 Jan 1747, Tortosa, Spain; d 11 Mar 1802, Monterey, CA). He arrived in New Spain with the Company of Catalonian Volunteers and became commanding officer in 1783. In 1789 Spain decided to establish a post in NOOTKA SOUND; Alberni led 76 soldiers accompanying Francisco ELIZA to Friendly Cove, arriving in April 1790. They fortified the harbour but the hard work, poor diet and wet climate weakened the corps. Alberni continued to develop the settlement, however, by digging wells, operating a bakery and planting gardens. He promoted good relations with the local NUU-CHAH-NULTH (Nootka) nations; his skill and leadership won the praise of both MALASPINA and BODEGA Y QUADRA. He left Nootka in July 1792 and later commanded the California presidios. PORT ALBERNI and ALBERNI INLET are named after him, though no evidence suggests that he visited that area. *See also* SPANISH EXPLORATION. *Robin Inglis*

ALBERNI INLET is a narrow FJORD formerly known as the Alberni Canal, extending 40 km inland from BARKLEY SOUND on the west coast of VANCOUVER ISLAND. It is the longest inlet on the

Island. The SOMASS R drains into the head of the inlet where the city of PORT ALBERNI is located. Named for Pedro de ALBERNI, captain of Spanish forces at NOOTKA SOUND in 1791, it has been occupied by groups of NUU-CHAH-NULTH (Nootka) since before contact with Europeans. The inlet has been a major LOGGING and SAWMILLING centre since ANDERSON'S MILL was established at Alberni in 1860. Important logging camps were at CHINA CRK, NAHMINT BAY, Franklin R and Coleman Crk. Several rivers draining into the inlet support rich SALMON runs, and FISHING, both sport and commercial, has been important. The inlet accommodates deep-sea vessels loading wood products at Port Alberni and is under the jurisdiction of the Port Alberni Harbour Commission. MV *LADY ROSE* services camps between Port Alberni and BAMFIELD and UCLUELET.
Reading: Jan Peterson, *Journeys: Down the Alberni Canal to Barkley Sound*, 1999.

ALBERT CANYON, a station on the CPR 35 km east of REVELSTOKE, became a service centre in the late 1890s for MINERS working on the north fork of the Illecillewaet R. It was named after Albert L. Rogers, who helped his uncle, the survey engineer A.B. ROGERS, find a route for the CPR through the SELKIRK MTS. Today, apart from a trading post, campground and mineral pool, it is a ghost town. AS

ALBERT HEAD is a rocky promontory along the south coast of VANCOUVER ISLAND west of VICTORIA. It was named for Prince Albert, husband of Queen Victoria. Manuel QUIMPER landed here in 1790 and claimed the island for Spain. The headland was the site of a quarantine station from 1883 to 1893, which was later transferred to WILLIAM HEAD. During WWII it was heavily fortified to guard the entrance to ESQUIMALT.

ALBION is a rural community on the north shore of the FRASER R east of HANEY. The name refers to the ancient Greek and Roman name for Britain, and reflects the background of the pioneer settlers. The earliest, Samuel Robertson, planted an orchard (*see* TREE FRUITS) in 1858. A car ferry links MAPLE RIDGE on the north side of the river with LANGLEY on the south.

ALBION IRON WORKS, one of the major industrial enterprises in late 19th-century BC, was at one time the largest iron works north of San Francisco, employing 230 workers and occupying a 1.5-ha site. Founded in VICTORIA in 1872 by Capt Joseph Spratt, and owned at one time by the prominent industrialists Robert DUNSMUIR and R.P. RITHET, it manufactured machinery, boilers, steam engines, water pipes and cast-iron storefronts and stoves. In the early years of the 20th century the company failed to adjust to changing markets, however; after a prolonged labour dispute and a disastrous fire in 1907, the company became mainly a stove manufacturer. It was sold in 1928 and the name was changed.

ALBREDA, 65 km north of BLUE RIVER on the Yellowhead Hwy (*see* ROADS AND HWYS) and a station on the CNR, was located on the Albreda R, named by Viscount Milton, an early traveller in BC, for his aunt, Lady Albreda Lyveden. A camp of Japanese internees was established here during WWII to help construct the highway (*see* JAPANESE, RELOCATION OF). Today all that remains is a pioneer cemetery with a view of Albreda Glacier. AS

ALCALA-GALIANO, Dionisio, naval officer (b 8 Oct 1760, Cabra, Spain; d 21 Oct 1805, Battle of Trafalgar). An officer in the Spanish navy and an experienced hydrographer, he explored BC waters in summer 1792. He joined the MALASPINA expedition in 1789 but stayed in New Spain (Mexico) in 1791 when Malaspina visited NOOTKA SOUND. On his return to Acapulco, Malaspina saw the new Spanish charts of JUAN DE FUCA STRAIT and GEORGIA STRAIT and assigned Alcalá-Galiano to continue the search for the Northwest Passage. Commanding the *Sutil*, one of 2 ships, he charted the INSIDE PASSAGE and sailed around VANCOUVER ISLAND to Nootka. During this trip, on 27 June, he made a historic rendezvous with Capt George VANCOUVER off Point Grey. An account of the voyage was published in 1802. Having died commanding *Bahama* at Trafalgar, Alcalá-Galiano was memorialized in the Spanish navy's pantheon of illustrious mariners in San Fernando, Cádiz. *See also* SPANISH EXPLORATION. *Robin Inglis*

ALCAN ALUMINUM CO is a Montreal-based multinational corporation, the world's second largest producer of aluminum and aluminum products. It originated in 1901 as the Northern Aluminum Co, the Canadian subsidiary of the Aluminum Company of America (Alcoa). In the 1920s Alcoa spun off its international operations to focus on the US domestic market. The

Alcan smelter at Kitimat. Ian Smith/Vancouver Sun

Transporting molten aluminum at Kitimat smelter. Jack Cornelis/Alcan

Aluminum Company of Canada was created to manage these international assets; in 1928 it became an independent Canadian company. The name "Alcan" was adopted in 1966. Along with operations and sales offices in more than 30 countries, Alcan has aluminum smelting plants at KITIMAT and in Quebec. The Kitimat smelter and the town around it were built during 1951–54 at the head of DOUGLAS CHANNEL on the North Coast. Alcan chose the site because of its deep-water access and proximity to HYDROELEC-TRIC power. The company constructed the KEN-NEY DAM in the Nechako Canyon to divert the headwaters of the NECHAKO R westward through a tunnel in the COAST MTS to KEMANO, where electricity is generated at a powerhouse. The electricity is then carried by transmission lines 75 km northwest to Kitimat to power the smelter. Taken together, the dam, powerhouse, smelter and

townsite, with associated structures, was the largest construction project in BC history to that time and Kitimat continues to be one of BC's major industrial sites. In 1987 Alcan won approval from the federal and provincial governments to build the second stage of its hydroelectric development, the so-called Kemano Completion Project, but it was opposed by environmentalists and in 1995 the provincial government cancelled the project.
Reading: Bev Christensen, *Too Good to be True: Alcan's Kemano Completion Project,* 1995.

ALDER, a member of the BIRCH family (Betulaceae), occurs in 3 species in BC. Of these, only the red alder (*Alnus rubra*) occurs as a tree. The other two, mountain alder and Sitka alder, seldom grow taller than shrubs. The red alder

*Red alder.
Kim LaFave drawing*

inhabits a narrow band along the coast and is one of the most important hardwoods. FIRST NATIONS people used it extensively for utensils and as fuel, and extracted a red dye from the inner bark. One of the first trees to reforest a burned-over or logged-over area, it has nitrogen-fixing bacteria in its roots that replenish vital nutrients in the soil. Many people are allergic to pollen released in spring from the alder's catkins. The tallest red alder in Canada (41 m) grows in STANLEY PARK, VANCOUVER. *See also* FOREST FIRES; FOREST PRODUCTS; LOGGING.

ALDERGROVE, pop 9,600, is one of several increasingly urban areas in the district municipality of LANGLEY. Located in the FRASER VALLEY, south of the TRANS-CANADA HWY and about an hour's drive east of VANCOUVER, it developed as a rural community known particularly for chicken and DAIRY FARMING and production of BERRIES.

ALDERMERE, a farming community 13 km southeast of SMITHERS, was the earliest non-aboriginal settlement in the BULKLEY R valley. It was established about 1904 and had several stores and a hotel. The GRAND TRUNK PACIFIC RWY considered putting a divisional point there but settled on Smithers instead. Most residents ended up moving 1 km west to TELKWA, at the confluence of the Bulkley and Telkwa rivers, which had better water access. By 1920 Aldermere had disappeared. AS

ALDERSON, Sue Ann, writer (b 11 Sept 1940, New York City). After graduate work at the Univ of California (Berkeley) she arrived in VANCOU-VER in 1967 to teach at SFU. Later she moved to Capilano College (*see* COMMUNITY COLLEGES) and then in 1980 to UBC to begin a writing-for-children program in the creative writing department. Her first book for young readers was *bonnie mcsmithers, you're driving me dithers* (1974), which became a series. As well, she has published picture books, verse and juvenile novels.

ALERT BAY, village, pop 612, is on CORMORANT ISLAND off the northeast coast of VANCOUVER ISLAND, about 290 km north of VANCOUVER. The area was a seasonal gathering place for the Namgis (Nimpkish), a KWAKWA̱KA̱'WAKW nation,

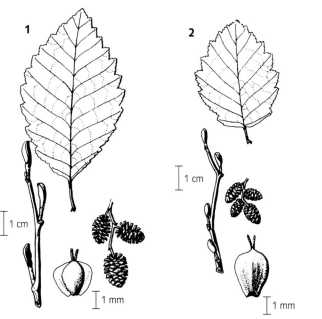

Leaves, twigs, fruit and fruiting catkins of the red alder (1), mountain alder (2) and Sitka alder (3). © *T.C. Brayshaw*

Totem poles at Alert Bay, c 1900. UBC 1291/50

when it was named for the British warship HMS *Alert*, which was engaged on a naval survey of the coast. In 1870 A.W. Huson and his partners built a store and a saltery for preserving SALMON. They encouraged Rev A.J. Hall to relocate his mission from FORT RUPERT in order to encourage their aboriginal labour force to settle permanently near the saltery. Rev Hall arrived in 1880 and the Namgis moved their village from the mouth of the Nimpkish R. Soon there was a SAWMILL, a hospital, St Michael's RESIDENTIAL SCHOOL, a SALMON CANNERY and the headquarters of the government Indian agency. During the 1960s and 1970s the village declined somewhat with the rapid growth of competing centres on Vancouver Island. It is still a commercial FISHING and marine service centre, with summer TOURISM a growing industry. There is a RESERVE, the U'mista Cultural Centre and a notable collection of TOTEM POLES, one of which at 53 m is the world's tallest.

ALEXANDER, Richard Henry, businessman (b 26 Mar 1844, Edinburgh, Scotland; d 29 Jan 1915, Vancouver). He joined a group of OVER-LANDERS who crossed Canada in 1862 to try their luck in the Cariboo goldfields (*see* GOLD RUSHES). After working at a variety of jobs he joined the HASTINGS MILL as an accountant in 1870 and in 1882 became mill manager. He was a member of the committee that drafted the bill of incorporation for VANCOUVER and he ran unsuccessfully in the city's first mayoralty campaign in 1886. Later he served as a city alderman and was twice president of the Board of Trade. His son Henry (1873–1920) was the first white child born in what became Vancouver.

ALEXANDER MACKENZIE HERITAGE TRAIL (the Grease Trail, est 1985) runs 420 km from the confluence of the FRASER and BLACKWATER (West Road) rivers between PRINCE GEORGE and QUESNEL to DEAN CHANNEL west of BELLA COOLA. The first heritage trail in BC, it follows part of the route traversed by Alexander MACKENZIE on his overland trek to the Pacific in 1793. Prehistorically it was part of a network of TRAILS used by the FIRST NATIONS as trade routes connecting coastal and Interior peoples. It takes at least 18 days and extensive preparation to hike the entire trail. *See also* EULACHON.

ALEXANDRA BRIDGE crosses the FRASER R in the canyon, 20 km north of YALE on the TRANS-CANADA HWY. The original bridge was built slightly north of the present site by Joseph TRUTCH in 1863 as part of the CARIBOO WAGON ROAD. It was the first suspension bridge west of the ROCKY MTS in Canada and continued to be used until it was washed out in 1894. It was not replaced until 1926; the second bridge, now abandoned, is the focus of Alexandra Bridge Provincial Park. The third, and present, Alexandra Bridge was built in the 1960s south of the site of the first crossing. It is named for Alexandra, Princess of Wales.

ALEXIS CREEK, pop 164, is on the Chilcotin Hwy (*see* ROADS & HWYS) 112 km west of

The original Alexandra Bridge, c 1869.
Frederick Dally/UBC BC80

WILLIAMS LAKE. Alex Graham, a pioneering settler, established a ranch here in 1891. Located on a bench overlooking the CHILCOTIN R and named for a TSILHQOT'IN chief, it has been the focal point of the mid-CHILCOTIN since 1912, when ranchers built a hospital here. Following WWI the village became the headquarters for various government agencies, including the FOREST SERVICE, highways department and police. It has one of the best growing climates in the Chilcotin.

ALEZA LAKE was a SAWMILL community and station on the GRAND TRUNK PACIFIC RWY 50 km northeast of PRINCE GEORGE. It was named after a DAKELH (Carrier) woman who lived in the area. The settlement, which dates from about 1915, reached a peak population of 200 and was famed throughout the region for its moonshine production. Only a handful of rugged individualists still live in the area today. An experimental forestry station (now a research forest and ECO-LOGICAL RESERVE) operated here from 1924 to 1963. *AS*

ALGAE; *see* SEAWEED.

ALICE ARM is a 15-km-long FJORD at the top of OBSERVATORY INLET in the COAST MTS 150 km north of PRINCE RUPERT, as well as the name of a small community at the head of the fjord. Both were named for the wife of Robert TOMLINSON, an ANGLICAN CHURCH missionary. Sited at the mouth of the Kitsault R, the community was the service centre for the Dolly Varden SILVER mine (1916–21) located 25 km north up the river and connected to the fjord by a narrow-gauge railway. When the mine closed, most of the population moved away. On the opposite side of the arm was the community of Kitsault, which serviced a nearby MOLYBDENUM mine until it also closed in the early 1980s.

ALKALI LAKE RANCH, 50 km south of WILLIAMS LAKE, is believed to be the first beef cat-

tle ranch in western Canada and is one of the largest in BC. Founded in 1861 by the German-born Herman Otto Bowe, the ranch remained in his family until 1910; that year it was sold to an Englishman, Charles Wynn Johnson, who added to the holdings over the next 30 years. Mario Reidemann, an Austrian business magnate, purchased the ranch in 1939 and his son Martin took over the operation in 1963. Under his management it became a model of efficiency and productivity. Following Martin Reidemann's accidental death in 1975, the ranch was sold to a KELOWNA couple, Doug and Marie Mervyn, who are known throughout the CATTLE INDUSTRY for their innovative management practices and ENVIRONMENTAL consciousness. Alkali Lk itself, on the ranch, is a bird sanctuary dedicated to Martin Riedemann. It is a feeding place for white PELICANS.

The Esketemc, a nation of about 600 SECWEPEMC (Shuswap) people, formerly called the Alkali Lake band, have their main RESERVE on a bench overlooking the ranch. They are well known for their progressive treatment of alcohol and drug addiction, spearheaded by Chief Andy Chelsea and his wife Phyllis during the 1970s. In addition to her work as a social worker and educator, Phyllis Chelsea was the first First Nations person elected to the Cariboo Chilcotin School Board and received the Order of Canada and an honorary degree from UBC.

ALL RED LINE was a steamship company that ran a regular passenger service between VANCOUVER and POWELL RIVER with stops along the SUNSHINE COAST from 1911 to 1917. The line's fleet consisted of 2 steamers, the *Selma* and the *Santa Maria*. The company also owned the SELMA PARK resort south of SECHELT. The UNION STEAMSHIP CO purchased the All Red Line in Oct 1917.

ALLAN, ROBERT LTD is a leading firm of naval architects founded in VANCOUVER in 1930 by Robert Allan Sr. Allan had immigrated to BC from his native Scotland in 1919 to work at Wallace Shipyards (*see* BURRARD DRY DOCK), where he designed the *PRINCESS LOUISE*, the first steel passenger steamer built in the province.

Under the direction of the senior Allan, his son Robert F. Allan and grandson Robert G. Allan, the firm grew and the Allans became known as the foremost designers of modern tugs and barges on the Coast. Among their innovative designs were the first modern twin-screw steel tug on the coast, the *Lorne Yorke*; the first ocean-going deck cargo barges; numerous self-dumping LOG BARGES; ice-breakers for Arctic oil exploration; and the Z-drive tractor tugs used by CATES TOWING in Vancouver harbour. From its Vancouver offices, the firm designs a wide range of specialized vessels for a world-wide client base.

ALLCO, halfway between HANEY and ALOUETTE LK on the north side of the FRASER R, was a large RAILWAY LOGGING camp. The name is an abbreviation for Abernethy Lougheed Logging Co, which ran an extensive operation here from 1921 to 1931 before a major fire (*see* FOREST FIRES) destroyed much of the area's FORESTS. AS

ALLEN, Bruce Norman, talent manager (b 19 May 1945, Vancouver). After studying economics at UBC for 3 years he dropped out to manage his first band, Crosstown Bus. He joined forces with Sam FELDMAN, a doorman at a local club, and together they built a prosperous booking agency. In 1972 Allen met Randy Bachman and became manager of the guitarist's new band, BACHMAN-TURNER OVERDRIVE. By 1974 BTO was topping the charts in N America and the UK, and Allen relinquished the booking agency to Feldman to concentrate on artist management. His company, Bruce Allen Talent Promotions, has managed such bands as LOVERBOY and PRISM, as well as Olympic boxing medallist Dale WALTERS, and his stable of clients includes the singers Martina McBride, Kim Stockwood and Anne Murray. But he is best known for his 20-year association with the VANCOUVER rocker Bryan

Bruce Allen, manager and rock promoter.
Courtesy Bruce Allen Talent

ADAMS. Trade magazines have named Allen one of the world's top managers. His recognizably abrasive verbal style is featured on a regular radio show, "Sound Off With Bruce Allen."

ALLIED INDIAN TRIBES OF BC (1916–27) was a FIRST NATIONS organization formed at a meeting on the SQUAMISH Nation RESERVE in N VANCOUVER. The association, led by Andrew PAULL and Peter KELLY, represented 16 tribal groups from all parts of the province. It was formed to pursue aboriginal land claims in the courts and it became the voice of BC aboriginal people on many issues. In 1927 a special parliamentary committee in Ottawa considered the Allied Tribes' arguments and ultimately rejected them. Soon after, the *Indian Act* was amended to prohibit the FIRST NATIONS from pursuing their claims without government approval. This legislation forced the collapse of the Allied Tribes. *See also* ABORIGINAL RIGHTS.

ALLIFORD BAY, 12 km west of SANDSPIT, on the south shore of Skidegate Inlet in the QUEEN CHARLOTTE ISLANDS, was selected by Sir George Doughty, president of BC Fisheries Ltd, as the site of a "model cannery town" in 1911. The project attracted workers from Britain but went into receivership in 1913 and was taken over by Maritime Fisheries Ltd, which operated a smaller cannery until 1927. An RCAF seaplane station was established in 1939; Shark and Canso aircraft were flown on anti-submarine patrols and base staff reached a peak of 700. The station was dismantled after WWII. The bay is now the southern terminus for the BC FERRIES run between Graham and MORESBY islands. AS

ALLISON, A.P., logger (b 1883, London, England; d 1947, Vancouver). He came to Canada as a child in 1892 and took his first job at the VICTORIA LUMBER & MANUFACTURING CO sawmill at CHEMAINUS in 1900. Five years later he started his own LOGGING company in Chatham Channel, before opening a large RAILWAY LOGGING camp and shingle mill at GREENE POINT RAPIDS in 1908, which sent the first cargo of BC shingles through the Panama Canal. In 1936 he opened a SPRUCE logging operation on the QUEEN CHARLOTTE ISLANDS, which he sold to the government-owned Aero Timber Co in 1942. That year he built the Lions Gate Lumber mill in N VANCOUVER. He was president of the TRUCK LOGGERS' ASSOCIATION at the time of his death.

Ken Drushka

ALLISON, John Fall, prospector, rancher (b 1825, Leeds, England; d 28 Oct 1897, Princeton), and **Susan (Moir)**, rancher, writer. He emigrated to the US with his parents in 1837. After leaving home in 1849 to go prospecting in California he migrated to BC in 1858 to take part in the GOLD RUSH on the FRASER R. In 1860 he investigated the SIMILKAMEEN R valley for the government, reporting that gold was plentiful. In the process he located Allison Pass, now used by the HOPE–PRINCETON HWY to cross the CASCADE MTS. He took up land near PRINCETON and began

John Fall Allison, pioneer rancher in the Princeton area. BC Archives A-01961

farming, then ranching, eventually accumulating more than 2,000 ha. He married Susan Moir in 1868; her reminiscences of their life together were published in 1976 as *A Pioneer Gentlewoman in British Columbia*. The couple went to live on the west side of OKANAGAN LK 30 km north of PENTICTON in 1872 but returned to Princeton in 1881. After John's death, Susan continued to manage what was left of the ranch for a few years, then moved into town. In 1928 she moved to VANCOUVER, where she died in 1937.

ALLISON HARBOUR, established about 1927, was a LOGGING camp and UNION STEAMSHIP CO port of call, named after Allison Logging Co (see A.P. ALLISON). It was located 35 km north of PORT HARDY just east of Bramham Island near the south entrance to Schooner Passage. AS

ALOUETTE LAKE, 16.44 km², forms the southern edge of GOLDEN EARS PROVINCIAL PARK east of VANCOUVER. It was used originally by FIRST NATIONS people for FISHING and hunting. During the 1920s loggers established a vast RAILWAY LOGGING operation on the surrounding slopes until a devastating FOREST FIRE put an end to it in 1931. Accessible by car, the lake is popular with campers, boaters, fishers and hikers. Originally called Lillooet Lk, it became Alouette in 1914 to avoid confusion with the other Lillooet Lk. The Alouette R, draining southwest through MAPLE RIDGE and PITT MEADOWS to the Pitt R, is a BC HERITAGE RIVER. *See also* LAKES.

ALSEK RIVER, 255 km, rises in Kluane National PARK in the Yukon and flows south through the ST ELIAS MTS across the northwest corner of BC to its confluence with the TATSHENSHINI R, before passing into Alaska and emptying into Dry Bay on the Gulf of Alaska. This isolated area of spectacular MOUNTAIN scenery is in the territory of the Champagne and Aishihik FIRST NATIONS, who fished for SALMON along the banks of the river. In 1993 it became part of the 9,580 km² Tatshenshini–Alsek Wilderness Provincial PARK and in 1994 the UN designated the park a WORLD HERITAGE SITE. The upper part of the river in Kluane National Park has been designated a Canadian Heritage River. *See also* RIVERS.

ALTA LAKE, 99.6 ha, 120 km north of VANCOUVER, is the highest LAKE in the CHEAKAMUS Valley. It was completely isolated in 1912, when Myrtle and Alex Philip hiked in from SQUAMISH. Two

Russell Jordan's Alta Lake Hotel, one of the earliest hotels in the Whistler area, c 1920.
VPL 53922

years later, when the Pacific Great Eastern Rwy (*see* BC RAIL) arrived, they opened Rainbow Lodge. A popular summer resort, it offered FISHING, hiking, sailing and trail riding. The Philips retired in 1948; their lodge remained in operation until it burned in 1978. With the completion of a paved highway (*see* ROADS AND HIGHWAYS) in 1964, ski facilities (*see* SKIING) boomed at nearby WHISTLER, a resort of which Alta Lk became a part. *See also* LAKES.

ALTONA is a tiny agricultural community in the PEACE R district 70 km north of FORT ST JOHN on the Beatton R. It was settled by MENNONITES in the late 1960s and has close ties with PRESPATOU. A post office opened in 1976. *AS*

ALVASTON was a farming community located at the south end of Wood Lk, 18 km north of KELOWNA, near present-day WINFIELD in the OKANAGAN VALLEY. Alvaston was known for its unusual post office. Because the stagecoach driver refused to detour to pick up mail, it was left in a packing case at the side of the road along with stamps and money. The system operated from 1909 to 1919 without any thefts being recorded. Both Alvaston and Wood Lk were named after Thomas Alva Wood, an early resident. *AS*

ALVENSLEBEN, Gustav Constantin Alvo von, financier (b 25 July 1879, Westphalia, Germany; d 1965, Seattle, WA). The son of a Prussian count, he embarked on a trip around the world and arrived in VANCOUVER in 1904. He was penniless but real estate investments soon made him wealthy; in the pre-WWI period he was one of Vancouver's most flamboyant busi-

nessmen, playing a key role in encouraging German investment in BC. His Kerrisdale estate, staffed by 13 servants, is now CROFTON HOUSE SCHOOL. Alvensleben was visiting Berlin when the war began. Unable to return to Canada, where a depression had wiped out much of his fortune and the government had confiscated the rest, he relocated to the US. He was interned in 1917, then lived in Seattle for the rest of his life though he was involved in business speculation in BC from time to time. He was rumoured to have been a wartime spy for the Germans, a calumny he steadfastly denied.

ALVIN, a remote community on the Pitt R 7 km north of the north end of PITT LK, 50 km northeast of VANCOUVER, was homesteaded in the early 1900s by a group of 22 families. It is now the site of a LOGGING camp. *AS*

AMPHIBIAN; *see* FROG; SALAMANDER.

AMSBURY was a stop on the GRAND TRUNK PACIFIC RWY 15 km west of TERRACE on the SKEENA R near Amsbury Crk. A SAWMILL operated here from 1917 to 1928 cutting Sitka SPRUCE for airplane construction. Capt S.J.R. Amsbury was a pioneer local settler. *AS*

ANACONDA, established in 1896, was a MINING townsite in the BOUNDARY DISTRICT south of GREENWOOD, 20 km east of GRAND FORKS. The BC Copper Co operated a SMELTER here from 1901 to 1918 for ore from its DEADWOOD and Mother Lode mines. The site was named after the Anaconda Smelter in Bute, MT. *See also* COPPER. *AS*

ANAHIM LAKE, pop 522, is on the Chilcotin Hwy (*see* ROADS & HWYS) 315 km west of WILLIAMS LAKE. Named for a FIRST NATIONS chief, Anaham, it is the westernmost community in the CHILCOTIN and the last to be settled. Anaham and his people were moved east to the Anaham RESERVE in the valley of the CHILCOTIN R following the CHILCOTIN WAR, and the spelling of the community's name was changed by the first postmaster, Stan Dowling, to avoid confusion between the 2 places. Dowling, who took the first motor vehicle into Anahim Lake, was responsible for starting the now famous Anahim Lake Stampede (*see* RODEO). The community has been the centre of a vast ranching (*see* CATTLE INDUSTRY), guiding and trapping area since the 1930s. In the 1940s a group of DAKELH (Carrier) people moved here from their remote villages so that the children could attend school. Most of the Dakelh now live on reserves in the surrounding area. Along with numerous ranches, there are resorts and a growing arts community. LOGGING has also become important to the economy.

ANARCHIST MOUNTAIN (el 1,233 m), on Hwy 3 east of OSOYOOS, is named for Richard Sidley, an Irish pioneer, whose radical political views cost him the job as local postmaster. He took up ranching (*see* CATTLE INDUSTRY) on the summit.

ANDERSON, Alexander Caulfield, fur trader (b 10 Mar 1814, Calcutta, India; d 8 May 1884, Saanich). The son of a plantation owner in India, he joined the HBC in 1831 and came to Canada. After a year at Lachine outside Montreal, he moved to Fort Vancouver on the COLUMBIA R. From 1835 to 1848 he served the company primarily in the Interior of northern BC. In 1846–47, Anderson made 3 important overland expeditions seeking a practicable supply route between KAMLOOPS and FORT LANGLEY that avoided the impassable rapids of the Fraser Canyon (*see* FRASER R). He pioneered several trails, one of which, via the Coquihalla R, was used by FUR BRIGADES for several years (*see also* COQUIHALLA TRAIL). Another route via SETON, ANDERSON and HARRISON lakes later became an important wagon road to the Interior (*see* DOUGLAS TRAIL). From 1848 to 1854 he worked at posts in what is now Washington state. After retiring he settled on the lower Columbia, then moved in 1858 to VICTORIA, where he lived the rest of his life, holding various government posts and managing his business interests.

ANDERSON, David Alexander Hebden, politician (b 16 Apr 1937, Victoria). He was an accomplished athlete as a student, and won a silver medal in rowing at the 1960 Olympics. After graduating from UBC law school, he worked in the Canadian foreign service from 1963 to 1967, then won election as a Liberal Member of Parliament for VICTORIA in 1968. While in Ottawa he developed a reputation as an ENVIRONMENTALIST and garnered headlines for criticizing his own government's oil transport policies (*see* OIL AND GAS INDUSTRY). He returned to BC in 1972 to take on the leadership of the provincial LIBERAL PARTY. The party held only 5 seats in the legislature and, after 3 of these members defected to the SOCIAL CREDIT PARTY in 1975, he resigned the leadership. In his years out of politics he worked mainly as an environmental consultant, particularly on oil issues. He returned to Ottawa as a Liberal MP in 1993 and joined Prime Minister Chretien's cabinet as minister of revenue. Following the 1996 election he served as transport minister, then minister of fisheries, then minister of the environment, becoming BC's most powerful voice in the government.

ANDERSON, Glenn, hockey player (b 2 Oct 1960, Vancouver). After a season with the Bellingham Blazers of the BC JUNIOR HOCKEY LEAGUE he played at the Univ of Denver 1978–79. He was drafted in 1979 by the NHL Edmonton Oilers sixty-ninth overall but played for the Canadian National team before joining Edmonton in 1980. His speed and grit at right wing made him an integral component of the Oilers dynasty of the 1980s and in 11 seasons he twice scored more than 50 goals, 3 times scored more than 100 points, and helped the team to win 5 Stanley Cups. When general manager Glen Sather dismantled the dynasty in the early 1990s Anderson was sent to Toronto where he helped the Maple Leafs reach the 1993 Stanley Cup semifinals. The next season he was traded to the

New York Rangers and in the 1994 Stanley Cup finals he scored 2 game-winning goals against his hometown VANCOUVER CANUCKS to help the Rangers win their first league championship in 54 years. He divided his last three seasons, 1994–97, playing with Edmonton, St Louis, the Canadian National team and clubs in Finland, Germany and Switzerland. He left the NHL in 1996 with the most goals (498) and points (1,099) scored by a player born and raised in BC. *See also* HOCKEY.   *SW*

ANDERSON, H.H. "Torchy," journalist (b 1894, Victoria; d 1982, Ganges). His roots grew deep in the history of the province: both grandfathers were HBC fur traders, an uncle was Alexander Caulfield ANDERSON, and his father Henry was the police officer who arrested Robert SPROULE for the murder of Thomas Hammill at the Blue Bell mine site. "Torchy" began his career in journalism in 1910 after Bob Edwards, of Calgary *Eye Opener* fame, got him a job at the *Calgary Herald*. He first earned notice for his coverage of the 1911 federal "reciprocity election," during which the burning issue was a proposed agreement on trade with the US. During WWI he served as a cavalry officer and after the war he returned to the *Herald*. In 1928 he joined the Vancouver PROVINCE, where he established himself as a prominent political journalist. After a stint in Ottawa covering national politics and the founding of the United Nations for the Southam Group, he returned to the *Province* as editor-in-chief in 1946. He is credited with using the phrase "no shirt too young to stuff" in a description of CONSERVATIVE leader Arthur Meighen, but he always claimed that his peak experience as a reporter was covering 9 bank robberies in one afternoon, then going to drink champagne at a black-tie reception that evening.   *Stephen Hume*

P.B. Anderson (second from left) with one of his logging crews, 1920s. UBC

ANDERSON, Peter Bodward "P.B.," logger (b 1 June 1866, Ansjo Looro, Sweden; d 10 Dec 1959, Vancouver). As a teenager he moved to Minnesota and logged there until 1889. Then he moved to Bellingham, WA, where he set up a SAWMILL. In 1911 he moved to BC and logged at PENDER HARBOUR, West THURLOW ISLAND, Loughborough Inlet and JERVIS INLET. With his sons Dewey and Clay, he founded the Green Point and Salmon River logging companies, which he operated until 1945. P.B. Anderson was a widely respected logger during the pioneering days of the industry.   *Ken Drushka*

ANDERSON LAKE, 28.3 km², lies in the COAST MTS, 44 km northeast of PEMBERTON. From 1858 to 1863 it was part of the DOUGLAS TRAIL, the first route used by miners to reach the Interior goldfields (*see* GOLD RUSH). In 1861 BC's first railway linked the east end of the lake with neighbouring SETON LK using horse-drawn cars on wooden rails. Named for the FUR TRADER A.C. ANDERSON, the lake is still on a rail route; the BC RAIL main line was built along its west shore. The southern end of the lake is accessible by a paved ROAD at the small community of D'ARCY. *See also* LAKES.

ANDERSON-DARGATZ, Gail, writer (b 1964, Salmon Arm). After working as a journalist in her native SALMON ARM, she studied creative writing at UNIV OF VICTORIA, where she was encouraged by the novelist Jack HODGINS. She won a CBC literary competition in 1992 and her first book, a short-story collection, *The Miss Hereford Stories* (1994), was nominated for the Stephen Leacock Award for humour. But it was the publication of her first novel, *A Cure for Death by Lightning* (1996), that propelled her into the ranks of Canada's best young writers. The story of rural domestic life, with a twist, won a BC BOOK PRIZE and a nomination for the prestigious Giller Prize. It was followed in 1998 by another novel, *A Recipe for Bees*, which also garnered a Giller nomination.

ANDERSON LEE, Pamela, actress, model (b 1 July 1967, Ladysmith). At the end of the 20th century she could claim to be the most widely recognized Canadian in the world. Raised in LADYSMITH, she became an immediate sensation when a Jumbotron camera focussed on her at a 1989 BC LIONS football game. Clad in a Labatt's t-shirt, her figure caught the attention of the beer company's advertising executives, who signed her to do commercials. She subsequently appeared on the cover of *Playboy* magazine 6 times, more than any other woman in the magazine's history. In Los Angeles, a minor role in the television sitcom *Home Improvement* led to a role as a lifeguard on *Baywatch* and international fame. She became a favourite of the tabloid press, especially after her marriage to the rock musician Tommy Lee.   *SW*

ANDERSON MILL, the first export SAWMILL in BC, was built at the head of ALBERNI INLET in 1860 by the British sea captain Edward STAMP, on behalf of the Anderson family of London. The first substantial steam-driven sawmill in the

Pamela Anderson Lee, 1998.
© *Columbia TriStar Television Distribution*

province, it milled DOUGLAS FIR logs cut from land granted to Stamp on the present site of PORT ALBERNI. Logging operations using oxen were supervised by Jeremiah ROGERS. Lumber was exported to various ports in Australia, China, Hawaii, S America and Great Britain during the approximately 4 years the mill operated. A lack of mechanical equipment to haul logs to the mill resulted in its closure in 1864.   *Ken Drushka*

ANDREWS, George Lloyd "Porky," basketball player (b 18 Sept 1917, Victoria; d 26 May 1999). One of BC's finest BASKETBALL players, he first attracted national attention playing alongside Doug PEDEN and Art and Chuck CHAPMAN on the VICTORIA Blue Ribbons, the 1935 Canadian amateur champions. After being recruited by the Univ of Oregon to play football, basketball and baseball he was part of the university's 1939 NCAA championship basketball team. However, he spent the NCAA's inaugural Final Four tournament on the bench due to a rule restricting play by freshmen. He was captain of the U of O Ducks 1941–42 and was named to the all-coast team and received all-American mention in 1942. He continued to play basketball while serving with the RCAF and when WWII ended he rejoined the Chapmans, Peden and Norm BAKER on the undefeated Victoria Dominoes, the 1946 Canadian champions. In 1947 he played and coached professionally for the short-lived Vancouver Hornets before building the PORT ALBERNI Athletics into national contenders. He returned to Victoria to embark on a long career of teaching and coaching at Victoria High School.   *SW*

ANDREWS, Sybil, artist (b 1898, Bury St Edmonds, England; d 21 Dec 1992, Victoria). After taking a correspondence course in art during WWI she studied formally at Heatherly's School of Fine Art. She then worked as a secretary at another art school in London, where she met Claude Flight, an instructor who encouraged her choice of the linocut print medium. Flight led a group of artists influenced by Futurism, a short-lived Italian movement that glorified war and machinery and emphasized speed and motion. Andrews's work reflects a Futurist emphasis on dynamic movement but eschews the political in favour of the more everyday aspects of life. Andrews and her husband Walter Morgan immigrated to BC in 1947 and settled in CAMPBELL RIVER, where she taught art classes for most of the rest of her life. She held her first exhibition of linocuts at the VANCOUVER ART GALLERY in 1948 and enjoyed a measure of critical success, but it was a 1982 retrospective of her prints organized by the Glenbow Museum in Calgary that revived her reputation for a modern audience. *Shannon Emmerson*

ANEMONE; *see* SEA ANEMONE.

ANGLEMONT, pop 400, is a LOGGING and summer recreation community on the north shore of SHUSWAP LK, 30 km northeast of SALMON ARM. It was named in 1914 by the first postmaster, W.A. Hudson, after nearby Angle Mt, which had earlier been named by G.M. DAWSON after the angle formed by SEYMOUR ARM and Shuswap Lk.

ANGLICAN CHURCH of Canada is part of the worldwide Anglican family of churches under the spiritual leadership of the Archbishop of Canterbury in England. In BC the 1991 census indicated that there were 328,600 people identifying themselves as Anglicans. The church is made up of lay people, deacons, priests and bishops, organized into regional groupings called dioceses. In BC there are 5 dioceses, each led by a bishop: the original diocese of British Columbia, established in 1858 (cathedral in VICTORIA), which once comprised the entire province and is now confined to VANCOUVER ISLAND; Caledonia (1879, cathedral in PRINCE RUPERT), which comprises the area north of PRINCE GEORGE; New Westminster (1879, cathedral in VANCOUVER), which stretches from the US border to the SUNSHINE COAST (with the addition of KINGCOME INLET) and from Vancouver to HOPE; Kootenay (1899, cathedral in KELOWNA), which includes the area from the 120th meridian east to the Alberta border; and Cariboo (1914, cathedral in KAMLOOPS), which includes the Yale, Cariboo and Similkameen districts. These 5 dioceses, along with the diocese of Yukon (1891, cathedral in Whitehorse), form the Ecclesiastical Province of BC, established in 1910. Each diocese is divided into parishes, which are geographic areas with defined boundaries in which a group of worshippers gather together into a congregation. In rural areas several congregations may form a multi-point parish. In 1999 there were 286 Anglican congregations in BC. Parishes are grouped into regional deaneries, which in turn are grouped into archdeaconries. The governance of a diocese is the charge of the synod,

St Saviour's Anglican Church, Barkerville. Built in 1869, it was one of the first churches constructed in BC. Roy Luckow photo

made up of elected lay people, and the priests and bishop of that diocese.

The Anglican Church established a presence on the West Coast in 1836, when the HBC appointed Herbert Beaver to be the chaplain and schoolmaster at Fort Vancouver on the COLUMBIA R. Relations between Beaver and chief factor John MCLOUGHLIN were strained, and Beaver returned to England in 1838. In 1849, Robert Staines arrived in FORT VICTORIA to serve as HBC chaplain and schoolmaster. He fell out with Chief Factor James DOUGLAS and was dismissed from the school in 1854. In his place the HBC appointed Edward CRIDGE, who arrived in Victoria in 1855. Missions to FIRST NATIONS peoples began the following year when Capt James Prevost of the Royal Navy strongly recommended that a missionary be sent to the North Pacific. The cause was taken up by the Church Missionary Society (CMS), which chose William DUNCAN, a fervent young Evangelical schoolmaster. Duncan arrived at ESQUIMALT in June 1857, and after a 4-month wait obtained permission to go north to FORT SIMPSON. He remained there until 1862, when he established the Christian TSIMSHIAN community of METLAKATLA.

Meanwhile, in 1858, as word spread of the GOLD RUSH on the FRASER R, there were concerns in England that the influx of miners would lead to the Americanization of the colony. The Church of England argued that it could best provide a steadying British presence through formal ecclesiastical structures. The colonial diocese of Columbia was established with George HILLS as its first bishop. Hills arrived in Victoria in Jan 1860 and immediately started to organize missionary work in the diocese. Between 1860 and 1865 a total of 12 missions funded by the Society for the Propagation of the Gospel (SPG) were added to the diocese, as well as two private schools in Victoria. Missionaries were sent to preach to First Nations peoples, and to minister to miners and settlers on Vancouver Island and the mainland. However, by the late 1860s the early promise of the diocese had been challenged by economic recession and a fluctuating population, and Hills was forced to retrench. The stability of the diocese was further challenged by serious tensions between Hills and Edward Cridge, who had been made dean of Christ Church Cathedral in Victoria. The doctrinal differences between the men eventually resulted in 2 court cases in 1874, and Cridge's departure from the Anglican Church. Hills had argued for the division of the Diocese of Columbia since the mid 1860s. In 1879, three dioceses—British Columbia, Caledonia, and New Westminster—were created from the old diocese of Columbia. Two new bishops were appointed: William RIDLEY for Caledonia, and Acton Windeyer SILLITOE for New Westminster.

The new Bishop of Caledonia, William Ridley, faced a difficult problem at Metlakatla. William Duncan was a strong-minded man, who was seemingly unwilling or unable to work with many of the other missionaries sent by the CMS to the North Pacific. Ridley grew increasingly opposed to the Metlakatla system, and in 1882 came into open conflict with Duncan. The situation was resolved in 1887 when Duncan and some 500 of his Tsimshian converts moved to a new Metlakatla in Alaska. The CMS supported aboriginal missions at HAZELTON (1880), KITWANGA (1882), Aiyansh (1883), KINCOLITH (1886), and KITKATLA (1887). The CMS and the SPG both stressed the importance of translation, and the missionaries who served aboriginal communities were active in translating portions of the Bible and Prayer book into various indigenous languages. Day schools for the education of aboriginal children were built on or near RESERVES throughout the province. The Ridley Home was established at Metlakatla, All Hallows School for girls was founded at Yale, and larger industrial schools at ALERT BAY and

Anglican Church leaders and guests at the chapel on the ski slopes of Sun Peaks, BC. The chapel was built in 1999 with donated funds and consecrated on 15 Jan 2000. Anglican Diocese of Cariboo

LYTTON were built in partnership with the federal government. In the north, the focus of mission in the diocese of Caledonia gradually changed. As commercial canneries at the mouth of the SKEENA and NASS rivers developed, missions among European settlers at PORT ESSINGTON and Port Simpson were established. Aboriginal missions continued to be supported, but the decision in 1907 to move the cathedral from Metlakatla to the new railway town of Prince Rupert was emblematic of an ongoing change. Gradually, as CMS money was withdrawn, the church focussed increasingly on its mission to British immigrants.

ANGLICANS IN BC

Year	Members	% of BC Population
1881	10,913	22.1
1891	24,196	24.7
1901	41,457	23.2
1911	101,582	25.9
1921	161,494	30.8
1931	206,867	29.8
1941	246,191	30.1
1951	315,469	27.1
1961	367,096	22.5
1971	386,670	17.7
1981	374,055	13.4
1991	328,580	10.0

Bishop Sillitoe arrived in New Westminster in 1880, just as work on the new CPR link to eastern Canada was starting in the west. Initially there were only a few priests in the diocese, concentrated in established communities in the Lower Mainland and FRASER VALLEY. The major aboriginal mission in the diocese was centred at Lytton. As Vancouver grew in prominence, new urban parishes and services multiplied. Theological training was provided by St Mark's College and Latimer Hall, both founded in Vancouver in 1909. In 1920, the two schools merged into the Anglican Theological College (incorporated in 1915 and from 1971 part of the Vancouver School of Theology) and in 1927 moved into a new facility on the UBC campus. Throughout the 20th century the church sought to provide religious services for workers in MINING and LOGGING camps, for people engaged in commercial FISHING and for the workers constructing transcontinental rail links. Sailors arriving in the PORT OF VANCOUVER were made welcome at the Mission to Seamen (est 1904). Remote logging camps and settlements on the coast were served by the COLUMBIA COAST MISSION (est 1904), with its system of hospital and mission ships, churches and hospitals. Religious education in remote communities was provided by the Sunday School Caravan Mission, founded by Eva Hasell. Night schools and evangelistic missions to CHINESE, JAPANESE and SOUTH ASIAN workers were established under the direction of

lay and ordained workers like Deaconess Hilda Hellaby. During WWII several women church workers accompanied Japanese Canadians into the internment camps in the Interior, and provided support to families and education for their children (*see* JAPANESE, RELOCATION OF).

The church in BC was initially dependent on funding from England. The constraints of two world wars and the growing economic self-sufficiency of the province gradually released the church from dependence on the English church, although many rural and isolated mission parishes continued to rely on external support from the Canadian church. As links between the ecclesiastical provinces in Canada became stronger, the church gradually shifted from being the Church of England in Canada to the Anglican Church of Canada, and officially changed its name in 1952. As the population boomed in the 1950s, many new suburban parishes were built in anticipation of church growth, which levelled off and then declined in the 1970s and 1980s. By the end of the 1990s the members of the Anglican Church in BC reflected the ethnic diversity of the wider population. Indigenous ministries have been nurtured, at the same time that the church struggles with the legacy of the RESIDENTIAL SCHOOL system. Anglican parishes work with other community groups on social justice issues, and dioceses engage in inter-faith dialogue with people from other religious traditions.　　*Gail Edwards*
Reading: Frank A. Peake, *The Anglican Church in British Columbia*, 1959.

ANGLO-BC PACKING CO owned SALMON CANNING operations on the FRASER R and up the coast. It was established in 1891 by the VANCOUVER financier Henry Ogle BELL-IRVING, who used British capital to buy several canneries. Within 2 years it was the largest producer of canned sockeye in the world. Three generations of Bell-Irvings led the company before it sold its assets and closed in 1969.

ANGLO-RUSSIAN TREATY, signed on 28 Feb 1825, described the border between Alaska and British territory, in dispute since 1821 when Tsar Alexander I of Russia had claimed the coast of N America between Bering Strait and latitude 51°N (everything north of VANCOUVER ISLAND). Not surprisingly, Great Britain and the US disputed the Russian claim. In 1824, following negotiations with the US, the Russians gave up any claim to territory south of 54°40'N (just north of PRINCE RUPERT). The following year Russia and Great Britain agreed on the line that became the Alaska boundary, in effect the border between the territories of the HBC and the RUSSIAN–AMERICAN CO. The boundary between Alaska and the Yukon was fixed at the 141st meridien of longitude. Russia retained a coastal strip as far south as the end of Prince of Wales Island, extending up Portland Canal (*see* PORTLAND INLET) to 56°N and then along the summit of the mts paralleling the coast. This strip, known as the Alaska Panhandle, later became the cause of another boundary dispute between the US, and Britain

and Canada, not settled until 1903 (*see* ALASKA BOUNDARY DISPUTE).

ANGUS, Henry Forbes "Harry," economist (b 19 Apr 1891, Victoria; d 17 Sept 1991, Vancouver). After studies at McGill and Oxford Univs and military service during WWI, he joined the economics department at UBC in 1919 and taught there with distinction for the next 37 years. He served as head of the department 1930–56 and first dean of graduate studies 1949–56. He was a member of the Royal Commission on Dominion-Provincial Relations (Rowell-Sirois) and during WWII worked in the federal Dept of External Affairs, where he was one of the few people who spoke out against the Japanese internment (*see* JAPANESE, RELOCATION OF). In retirement he chaired the 1965 Royal Commission on Electoral Redistribution in BC. His books include *British Columbia and the United States* (1942, with F.W. HOWAY and W.N. Sage) and *Canada and the Far East 1940–53* (1953).

ANIAN, STRAIT OF, was a legendary waterway separating Asia and N America, supposedly the western entrance to the Northwest Passage. The name probably refers to the Chinese province of Ania, which appeared on maps of the early 1560s. Francis DRAKE was seeking the strait in 1579 when he sailed north from California, as was James COOK 2 centuries later. In the meantime more than one mariner, including Juan de FUCA, claimed to have sailed through it. George VANCOUVER finally disproved the existence of the strait with his coastal surveys of 1792–94.

ANMORE, village, pop 961, is a suburban community on the north side of BURRARD INLET, on the eastern outskirts of VANCOUVER adjacent to PORT MOODY. Incorporated in 1987, it expanded in 1997 to include the popular recreational area surrounding BUNTZEN LK. The village hall is the original homestead of the legendary newspaperwoman "Ma" MURRAY and her husband George.

ANNACIS ISLAND in DELTA lies in the south arm of the FRASER R near the east end of LULU ISLAND. Originally used as a FISHING site by FIRST NATIONS people, it was called Annance's Island after the METIS fur trader Francis ANNANCE. Starting in 1953 a large part of the island was developed as an industrial park by the Duke of Westminster. Deep-sea SHIPPING port facilities were built in the 1970s, along with a major sewage treatment plant.

ANNANCE, Francis Noel, fur trader (b 1789, St Francis, QC; d there circa 1851). Part Abenaki, part French Canadian, he joined the NWC and moved to the Columbia District to work as a trapper (*see* FUR TRADE). Following the 1821 merger with the HBC he stayed on as a clerk and later served as postmaster. In 1824 he visited the lower FRASER R as part of a reconnaissance mission for the HBC and in 1827 helped to establish FORT LANGLEY on the river. He left the Pacific slope in 1833 for a tour of duty on the

Mackenzie R. After 16 years in the trade he got on the wrong side of his HBC superiors and was dismissed in 1835. He retired to his birthplace, where he farmed and taught school. ANNACIS ISLAND ("Annance's Island") is named for him.

ANNIEVILLE, now known as Gunderson Slough, is in N DELTA on the south arm of the FRASER R opposite ANNACIS ISLAND. It was the site of the first successful SALMON CANNING facility on the river, opened in 1871, and continued to be a canning centre for many years. Originally a FIRST NATIONS village site, it has been occupied for millennia, and in the 1990s was still home to hundreds of boats.

ANNIS, on the south shore of SHUSWAP LK, 16 km northeast of SALMON ARM, was a CPR station and later the site of a LOGGING camp and SAWMILL. It was named after the mill's owner. *AS*

ANSCOMB, Herbert, politician (b 1892, Maidstone, England; d 1972, Victoria). He immigrated to BC in 1911 and found work in VICTORIA as an office clerk. Eventually he became a chartered accountant and long-time manager of the Victoria Phoenix Brewery Co. He began his political career as reeve of OAK BAY from 1925 to 1927 and served as mayor of Victoria from 1929 to 1931. Anscomb was active in the provincial CONSERVATIVE PARTY, and though his run for leader in 1938 was unsuccessful, he was an influential member of the opposition in the legislature (*see* LEGISLATIVE ASSEMBLY); when the wartime COALITION GOVERNMENT formed at the end of 1941 he joined John HART's CABINET as minister of mines, trade and industry, and later public works. In 1946 he became the Coalition's minister of finance, then won the Conservative leadership later that year, soundly defeating W.A.C. BENNETT. As minister of finance in 1948, still with the Coalition, he brought in BC's first sales tax. A rabid anti-socialist, he was considered on the right wing of the Tory Party. In 1950 Bennett again challenged him for the Conservative leadership, backed by younger, slightly more progressive elements in the party. Anscomb won handily and the party fractured. Meanwhile he was growing increasingly critical of the Coalition and in Jan 1952 Premier Byron JOHNSON dismissed him from Cabinet. When other Tory members followed him, the Coalition dissolved. Later in the year he was defeated in a provincial election that marked the demise of the Conservative Party as a force in provincial politics.

ANTLE, John, Anglican missionary (b 1865, Harbour Grace, NF; d 3 Dec 1949, Vancouver). Known as the Wilfred Grenfell of the West Coast, he was born and raised in Newfoundland, where at age 18 he became a teacher on the rugged north coast. After studying theology in St John's he returned to a remote parish to minister to isolated fishing families. In 1897 he moved to Washington state, where his wife's family lived, and 2 years later he took over a parish in VANCOUVER. Disturbed at the lack of social and reli-

John Antle, founder of the Columbia Coast Mission, 1933. CVA Port.P1295

gious amenities in camps and villages along BC's West Coast, Antle conceived the idea of a seagoing ministry and in 1904 he persuaded the ANGLICAN CHURCH to launch the COLUMBIA COAST MISSION. He served as superintendent of the mission until 1936, travelling the coast by boat delivering medical care and spiritual support to LOGGING camps, FIRST NATIONS villages and isolated settlements. Always the seafarer, he celebrated his retirement by embarking at age 73 on a 2-year ocean cruise and afterwards lived aboard ship. He was buried at sea off BOWEN ISLAND.

ANVIL ISLAND, located in HOWE SOUND 30 km north of Vancouver, was used as a campsite by the SQUAMISH NATION long before it was named by George VANCOUVER after its shape; a line drawn from its peak through PASSAGE ISLAND helped him to avoid the FRASER R's dangerous mud flats. The south end of the island was settled as early as 1874. In 1887 Thomas J. Keeling discovered deposits of clay at Irby Point and the Columbia Clay and Anvil Island Brick companies operated factories here from 1897 to 1917. Anvil Island was a UNION STEAMSHIP CO stop and had a post office for many years. *AS*

ANVIL PRESS, a VANCOUVER publisher, was founded in 1988 by Brian Kaufman and Dennis Bolen to publish the literary magazine *sub-TERRAIN*. In 1991 the company began publishing books and a year later took over the international THREE-DAY NOVEL WRITING CONTEST from ARSENAL PULP PRESS. Anvil is interested in discovering and publishing new literary talent.

ANYOX was the site of a huge COPPER mine and SMELTER on Granby Bay near the head of OBSER-

VATORY INLET north of PRINCE RUPERT. The name comes from a TSIMSHIAN word for the bay. A townsite took shape after Granby Consolidated Mining, Smelting & Power Co began developing the copper deposits in 1912. At its peak the mine was one of the most productive in the British Empire and the town had a population of 2,700. Copper prices fell during the Depression and in 1935 the mine closed. In 1942 fire destroyed the last homes and the site was deserted.

APICULTURE, or beekeeping, is carried out in BC by 2,200 registered beekeepers who raise honeybees (*Apis mellifera*) that pollinate more than $100 million worth of crops annually. As well, BC hives produce $4.2 million worth of honey every year, most of it gathered by 300 commercial apiarists. Other hive products include beeswax, bee pollen, royal jelly and propolis.

The blossoms of clover and canola fields in the PEACE R district, berry farms (*see* BERRIES) in the FRASER VALLEY and orchards (*see* TREE FRUITS) in the OKANAGAN VALLEY and the KOOTENAY are important sources of nectar converted by the bees into honey. Long hours of daylight and abundant nectar make the Peace R region especially productive; the 60,000–80,000 worker bees in an average Peace R hive produce up to 90 kg of honey per year, well above the 22 kg world average. One of the largest operators is North Peace Apiaries at Mile 42 on the ALASKA HWY. Owned by Ernie Fuhr, the firm overwinters 1,200 hives, transports them in the spring to orchards in the south, then takes them back to the Peace country for summer clover blooms.

Many fruit, berry and seed producers rent honeybee hives to ensure good pollination. Babe's Honey Farm of VICTORIA, operated by Charlie and Babe Warren since 1945, maintains 3,000 hives on VANCOUVER ISLAND and elsewhere and is an important source of queens and nuclei for other operators. Wild Mountain Honey Farms, one of 13 members of the BC Bee Breeders Assoc, is a mid-sized breeding business in ARMSTRONG that starts up to 250 nucleus hives annually, providing pollinators for Interior apple, pear and cherry farmers.

Since 1987 the importation of US bees has been banned to control diseases, resulting in increased demand for BC-bred bees and encouraging the construction of overwintering facilities. The Varroa mite, a Southeast Asian parasite, arrived in BC during the 1990s and has killed up to 66% of the bees belonging to some keepers. During that period, agricultural needs were met by expanding the use of other bee species, including the alfalfa leafcutter bee, bumblebee and orchard mason bee. Nature's Alternative Insectary Ltd, established at NANOOSE BAY in 1989, is a BIOTECHNOLOGY firm that mass-produces biologically beneficial INSECTS and provides greenhouse pollinators. *See also* AGRICULTURE. *Robert Allington*

APPLEDALE, 15 km south of SLOCAN on the Slocan R in the W KOOTENAY, is a farming settlement named for the area's extensive orchards.

Many DOUKHOBORS moved here in the early 1900s. There is a golf course nearby. *See also* TREE FRUITS. AS

APRIL POINT LODGE is a sport FISHING and TOURIST resort on QUADRA ISLAND, across DISCOVERY PASSAGE from CAMPBELL RIVER. It was founded in 1945 by Phil and Phyllis Peterson, an American couple who visited the area on holiday and stayed to develop one of the leading fishing resorts in the world. Under the management of the Petersons and their sons Warren and Eric, April Point was a popular retreat with entertainers, politicians and SALMON fishers of all types. In 1998, after 53 years in the Peterson family, it was sold to OAK BAY MARINE GROUP, a VICTORIA company.

AQUACULTURE, FIN FISH, refers to the cultivation of fin fish in a controlled environment, such as tanks, ponds or net cages. Commonly called fish farming, it is carried on in BC by both the public and private sectors and is limited almost exclusively to salmonids and TROUT. Other fin fish species being cultured in limited or experimental quantities in BC include SABLEFISH (black cod), HALIBUT, STURGEON, Arctic CHAR and carp. The government's primary role is to culture salmonids in their early life stages, releasing fry into river systems or lakes to enhance wild populations. Many non-profit clubs and associations also are involved in the operation of salmonid enhancement facilities. The private sector operates hatcheries at the first stage of fish farming, where fish are held in captivity throughout their lives. When ready to enter salt water, salmon fry are transferred to net pens rather than being released. Fish are fed fish meal and reared to market size, then harvested as they reach adulthood. BC fish farmers raise coho and

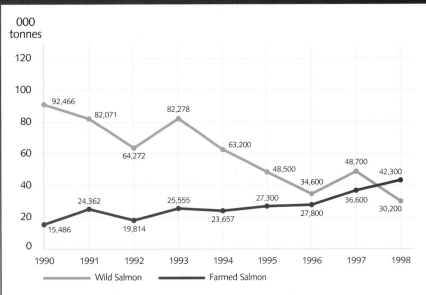

BC WILD & FARMED SALMON PRODUCTION LANDED WEIGHT 1990–98

Salmon farm, Sunshine Coast, 1980s.
Rick Blacklaws photo

chinook (*see* SALMON, PACIFIC) and Atlantic Salmon (*see* SALMON, ATLANTIC), as well as a small quantity of rainbow trout.

Commercial salmon farming began on the West Coast in the mid-1970s, when several applicants were granted licences to raise fish in salt water net pens on the SUNSHINE COAST and in ALBERNI INLET. In the early 1980s dozens of facilities opened on the South Coast, particularly in JERVIS and SECHELT inlets. In the late 1980s a series of HARMFUL ALGAL BLOOMS (which use the available oxygen in the water and clog the fish's gills), heavy storms and low market prices precipitated an industry-wide reorganization as small farms closed, amalgamated with others or were purchased by large multinational companies. The centre of the industry shifted north and west, into colder water where algal blooms were less frequent. By the mid-1990s salmon farms were concentrated from QUADRA ISLAND north along the INSIDE PASSAGE to the islands around JOHNSTONE STRAIT and on the west coast of VANCOUVER ISLAND near TOFINO. In 1998 there were 104 active farm sites, about half of which were owned by 3 companies: HERITAGE AQUACULTURE LTD, STOLT SEA FARM INC and the OMEGA SALMON GROUP LTD. BC farms produced 42,300 tonnes of farmed salmon that year, the first time that farmed salmon production exceeded commercial wild salmon production. Of these, 78% were Atlantics, 16% were chinook and 6% were coho. Together they generated a wholesale value of $298 million and supported 1,675 direct and 1,460 indirect jobs. Of the total production, 86% was exported, making farmed salmon BC's largest agricultural export crop. The US was the largest customer, buying 94% of the export value. Chief market competitors are the wild salmon fishery, as well as farmed product from Chile and Norway.

There is controversy concerning the salmon farming industry and its ENVIRONMENTAL impact, particularly in relation to the siting of farms, the

transmission of diseases, the use of antibiotics and the mixing of farmed fish and wild salmon stocks. But in 1999, after a prolonged review, the provincial government lifted a 5-year moratorium on new farms and gave approval to limited expansion of the industry.

Trout farming is another aspect of fin fish aquaculture in BC. The majority of BC trout farms consist of tanks or ponds on private property. Most trout growers in the North and Interior of the province have a limited growing season. They purchase fry in the spring and sell fish weighing 500 g–1 kg in the fall. On Vancouver Island and in the FRASER VALLEY, growers are able to maintain their ponds all year round. Fry are supplied to BC growers from a handful of operators who maintain brood fish and hatcheries.
Reading: Betty C. Keller and Rosella M. Leslie, *Sea-Silver: Inside BC's Salmon-Farming Industry,* 1996.

AQUACULTURE, SHELLFISH, refers to the culturing, or farming, of shellfish. In BC the industry centres around CLAMS and OYSTERS, though smaller experimental and commercial culturing takes place for GEODUCKS, SCALLOPS, MUSSELS, ABALONES and PRAWNS. (Because prawns have a tough chitinous exoskeleton they are commonly classified as shellfish.) In 1998 the BC shellfish culture sector produced 6,100 tonnes of cultured products with a wholesale value of $12 million. This represented less than 10% of total wild and cultured shellfish landings.

Shellfish farming began in BC around the turn of the century, when the Atlantic oyster (*Crassostrea virginica*) was introduced to BOUNDARY BAY and ESQUIMALT and LADYSMITH harbours. A second species, the Pacific oyster (*Crassostrea gigas*), was introduced from Japan to Ladysmith harbour around 1912. Oyster farming was largely unregulated until 1949, and bottom culture (when beach areas are seeded) was the technique used in commercial production. In the 1970s, oyster farmers began to experiment and adapt Japanese off-bottom culture techniques—suspending oysters on strings from floats—to BC conditions. At the same time, initial experiments with blue mussel culture were conducted, and in the 1980s the Japanese scallop was imported and research into culture methods began. In the 1990s declining landings in the wild manila clam and geoduck fisheries prompted research into culture techniques for these species as well.

Shellfish farming is centred in the BAYNES SOUND area, which produces 39% of BC's oysters and 55% of manila clams. Other areas of active shellfish culture include the SUNSHINE COAST, the QUADRA–CORTES islands area and VANCOUVER ISLAND's west coast. Industry proponents see huge growth potential in shellfish culture and in 1998 the provincial government committed to doubling the amount of Crown land available for shellfish aquaculture to 42.3 km² within 10 years.

Carol Swann

AQUARIUM, VANCOUVER; *see* VANCOUVER AQUARIUM MARINE SCIENCE CENTRE.

ARBUTUS (*Arbutus menziesii*), also known as the madrona, is the only broad-leafed evergreen tree native to Canada. It is the largest member of the Heather (Ericaceae) family. Usually found close to the ocean on rocky bluffs, the species is confined to a narrow coastal habitat in southern BC and, in the southernmost portion of its range in BC, is

Arbutus.
Kim LaFave drawing

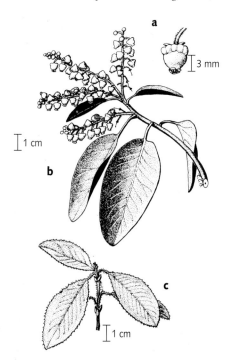

Flower (a), flowering branch (b) and seedling foliage (c) of the arbutus. © *T.C. Brayshaw*

usually found with DOUGLAS FIR and garry OAK. The trunk twists and leans and the tree seldom grows taller than 20 m, but may grow to 35 m. Distinctive red-brown, paper-thin bark peels off each summer to reveal the bright green young bark underneath. The large, shiny dark green leaves remain green all winter and are shed in small amounts all through the year when new ones form to replace them. The small clustered flowers are waxy-white or greenish; they mature into orange-red berries, which are a favourite food of many birds.

Archaeological excavations at the Pender Canal site on N Pender Island. This site, excavated under the auspices of Simon Fraser Univ during 1983–86, is very important for documenting Middle Period archaeology and prehistory.
Roy Carlson photo

ARCHAEOLOGY, the discovery of physical evidence of the human past, in BC relates overwhelmingly to the pre-European remains of indigenous peoples and cultures. Archaeologists have worked in BC for more than a century, but research only recently resulted in a fair understanding of the remains found throughout the province. Pioneering work was done by Charles HILL-TOUT, a BURNABY schoolteacher, who published *Later Prehistoric Man in British Columbia* in 1895, and by Harlan I. Smith, who from 1901 to 1903 described artifacts and excavations in BC in the *Memoirs* of the American Museum of Natural History. Both researchers paid particular attention to the site of the MARPOLE MIDDEN in S VANCOUVER. Further work at this site was done by Herman Leisk for the VANCOUVER MUSEUM in the 1930s and by Charles BORDEN in the late 1940s and 1950s. Borden, who was based at UBC and whose work marks the beginning of modern archaeology in BC, was the only archaeologist working in the province from the late 1940s until Roy Carlson was appointed to develop a program in Pacific Northwest archaeology at SFU when it opened in 1965. In the early 1950s Borden excavated a number of sites on the Lower Mainland. He also undertook the first salvage archaeology in the province with the survey and excavation of sites in the area of central BC about to be flooded by construction of the KENNEY DAM on the NECHAKO R. Later that

decade he excavated several important sites on the FRASER R above YALE, and established a 9,000-year-long chronology for that locality. In 1960 Borden and Wilson DUFF were instrumental in drafting the provincial *Archaeological and Historic Sites Protection Act*, which superseded the earlier *Historic Objects Preservation Act*, established the Archaeological Sites Advisory Board, and provided a measure of protection for sites on Crown land. This legislation was in turn superseded in 1979 by the *Heritage Conservation Act*, covering all non-federal land in BC. It led to the establishment of the Archaeology Branch, the provincial agency responsible for issuing excavation permits and for maintaining a master file of all excavation and survey reports and a roster of all archaeological sites in the province. This act was amended in 1994 to provide automatic protection to sites (including shipwrecks) that pre-date 1846, and to make consultation with aboriginals mandatory regarding permits for archaeological work in their traditional territories. Up to that point, consultation had been a matter of policy rather than law.

Archaeology blossomed in BC in the late 1960s and 1970s. Following a series of lectures on BC archaeology by Roy Carlson, a group of lay people formed the Archaeological Society of British Columbia in 1967. The society began to meet monthly at the Vancouver Museum; their official publication, *The Midden*, became a highly significant source of information on ongoing research. Affiliated societies in the FRASER VALLEY and VICTORIA were subsequently organized. The archaeology program at SFU established by Roy Carlson and Philip Hobler evolved into the Department of Archaeology in 1970. In the late 1960s and 1970s, field research undertaken by a number of archaeologists from various institutions expanded to the more remote parts of the province, and by 1980 some archaeological data had been recovered from all regions. Technical reports on excavations have been published by Archaeology Press at SFU since 1972, and by the National Museum in Ottawa since 1973. A workshop on underwater archaeology in 1975 led to the formation of the Underwater Archaeological Society of BC, which actively promotes conservation and research on shipwrecks.

The first general book synthesizing BC archaeology, *British Columbia Prehistory*, by Knut Fladmark, appeared in 1986. UBC PRESS published its first book on BC archaeology, *Early Human Occupation in British Columbia*, in 1996.

In the 1990s aboriginal people became increasingly involved in local archaeology; other developments in this decade were the development of professional consulting archaeologists who contract with FIRST NATIONS bands, government and industry to undertake impact assessments and inventories before LOGGING or other developments that could adversely affect archaeological sites, and the expansion of archaeology courses in colleges and universities. In 1989 a collaborative educational program involving archaeology and other First Nations studies was initiated between the Secwepemc Cultural Education Society and SFU on the SECWEPEMC (Shuswap) Reserve in KAMLOOPS. Many aboriginal students take university courses there and participate in the archaeological field school. The BC Association of Professional Consulting Archaeologists, which sets professional standards, was organized in 1995. All 4 provincial universities and many of the COMMUNITY COLLEGES now offer archaeology courses, although SFU has the only Department of Archaeology.

Over the years hundreds of sites have been excavated in BC. Some of the more important are briefly summarized here. The Milliken site on the Fraser R above Yale, excavated from 1958–61, provided the first long sequence of human occupation. Other Early Period (pre-5,000 years ago) sites excavated since include NAMU on the Central Coast, which shows continuous occupation for 10,000 years; CHARLIE LAKE CAVE near FORT ST JOHN with sporadic occupation beginning 10,500 years ago; GLENROSE at the Glenrose Cannery on the Fraser R in DELTA and Bear Cove on Hardy Bay on northern VANCOUVER ISLAND with occupations beginning about 8,000 years ago; Tsinni Tsinni on the ATNARKO R and several sites on the QUEEN CHARLOTTE ISLANDS dating to 9,300 years ago. The most important Middle Period (5,000–2,000 years ago) coastal site is the PENDER CANAL site on northern PENDER ISLAND, excavated from 1984 to 1986, demonstrating that most major aspects of coastal aboriginal culture had developed by

Simon Fraser Univ archaeological excavations at Tsinni-Tsinni, situated high above the Atnarko R valley. The site dates to the end of the Ice Age, when sea levels were much higher than today. Roy Carlson photo

3,500 years ago. The Blue Jackets Creek site in the Queen Charlottes and several sites around PRINCE RUPERT Harbour excavated in the 1960s and early 1970s show some of the same cultural complexes. In the Interior the most extensively excavated Middle Period site is the KEATLEY CREEK pithouse village known from a series of excavations beginning in 1970. Excavated Late Period (2,000 years ago to European contact) sites occur throughout the province. Excavations have also been undertaken at a number of FUR TRADE posts, including FORT LANGLEY on the Fraser R and Fort Epinette on the PEACE R. *Roy L. Carlson*

Readings: Roy L. Carlson and L. Dalla Bona, eds, *Early Human Occupation in British Columbia*, 1996; G.P. Nicholas and T.D. Andrews, eds, *At a Crossroads: Archaeology and First Peoples in Canada*, 1997.

ARCHIPELAGO MARINE RESEARCH LTD, established in VICTORIA in 1978, is a company specializing in fisheries monitoring and marine environmental assessment. It also provides aquatic habitat evaluation and site assessment to mitigate the impact of development on fish habitat. AMR, owned and operated by Howard McElderry (president), Brian Emmett and Shawn Stebbins, has more than 150 employees based in Victoria and along the Coast. *See also* FISHING, COMMERCIAL.

ARCHITECTURE in BC tells a story of material growth and expanding commercial networks. Pre-colonial structures were constrained by the limits of technology and materials, as exhibited in the massive timber framed "big houses" of aboriginal peoples (*see* ARCHITECTURE, ABORIGINAL). A similar use of materials is found in the restored HBC trading posts at FORT ST JAMES (1806) and FORT LANGLEY (1827) and at the HBC farms such as CRAIGFLOWER (1856) on VANCOUVER ISLAND. Large logs, either end-notched or piled "pièce-sur-pièce" within a timber frame, used abundant timber resources. However, in the hands of their Québécois (*see* FRANCOPHONES), METIS or HAWAIIAN carpenters, the forms of the fort structures were drawn from 18th-century house types of Quebec, and ultimately France and Britain. These defensive and utilitarian building types gave way to the more ephemeral frontier settlement architecture. Such buildings defined the small towns and farming communities established in the wake of the FRASER R and CARIBOO GOLD RUSHES of the 1850s and 1860s. Timber remained the essential building material, but water- and steam-powered SAWMILLS allowed for the quick adaptation of Chicago wood frame construction methods and the application of mass-produced detailing. While towns like HOPE, LYTTON, YALE and BARKERVILLE sported false-front "boomtown" commercial structures, manufacturing technologies also allowed for the more serious application of "style" to mark institutions. The ANGLICAN CHURCH distinguished its small "Gothic" mission churches with pointed windows; the Catholics (*see* ROMAN CATHOLIC CHURCH) marked theirs in the round arched "Roman" manner.

The Marine Building in downtown Vancouver, designed by Townley & Matheson and completed in 1930. Roy Luckow photo

Burgeoning wealth and its display created the necessary conditions for the professionalization of development. Institution of the Crown colonies of BC and Vancouver Island consolidated direct British rule and the ROYAL ENGINEERS arrived to take on the role of road builders, town planners and architects. Col Richard MOODY's Government House (1860) in NEW WESTMINSTER and the engineers' church at their camp in Sapperton (1860) were "Carpenter Gothic" wooden buildings with vertical proportions, but set within an ambitious grid-block town plan marking major and minor axial streets, crescents, public squares, parks and church reserves. The building boom of the developing colony consolidated the building professions and trades. Nowhere was this more evident than in VICTORIA, capital of the Vancouver Island colony, and ESQUIMALT, port for the British Pacific fleet and point of entry for maritime trade to both colonies. Imperial connections were important, as is evident in the first major structures: for example, in the built-to-standard brick buildings erected at Esquimalt for the Admiralty and the bungalow-style colonial administration buildings (1858) overlooking JAMES BAY, which owed much to the hill town retreats of British India for their inspiration. However, it was American west coast money and trade that underpinned early development in Victoria. Commercial "iron front" buildings on Wharf St, along with other building materials from bricks to fretted details, originated from San Francisco foundries and sawmills but were soon made locally. Early architects such as the firm Wright & Sanders (which arrived from Upper Canada in 1858), John TEAGUE and Singapore-born Edward MALLANDAINE produced commercial, institutional and domestic buildings that would have been common in any of the developing American west coast towns of the day.

Little changed when BC joined CONFEDERATION in 1871, although the red-brick Customs House (1876) introduced the Dominion gov-

Provincial legislative buildings in Victoria, designed by Francis Rattenbury and opened in 1898. Roy Luckow photo

ernment's Second Empire style (named after the French Renaissance-inspired Parliament Buildings in Ottawa) to Victoria, a national signal that was picked up by Teague in his design of the Masonic Lodge and Victoria City Hall (both 1878) with their distinctive mansard-roofed top floors. It was the building and completion of the CPR that brought significant change. The CPR created VANCOUVER, which came to overtake Victoria as the province's economic and communications hub, and it opened the Interior for the transportation of resources, people, ideas—and building supplies. Rails brought a new class of international TOURIST, business person and even labourer. The nascent CHINATOWN in Victoria emerged as port of entry and home for many of the thousands of workers brought in to build the CPR. Centred on Fisgard St, elegant tong buildings with their distinctive streetfront balconies stood out against mundane tenement blocks. A high point of this development remains the Chinese Consolidated Benevolent Association School (1908). There was also a Chinatown adjacent to GASTOWN on BURRARD INLET and, after a disastrous fire in 1886 (*see* DISASTERS) levelled the wooden boomtown, both grew rapidly into the core of present-day Vancouver. As the city rose from the ashes, local architectural companies emerged (eg E.H. Fisher, R. MacKay Fripp and Parr & Fee) to build the Italianate commercial fronts, marked by their bracketed cornices, and Romanesque retail-warehouse structures distinguished by the use of heavy masonry and arched windows.

With the arrival of 2 English architects the stage was set for the powerhouse architectural practices of the pre-war period of stupendous growth. Thomas SORBY, trained in London, designed the first generation of stations and railway hotels for the CPR's western division, while Francis RATTENBURY, born in Leeds, came "on spec" and in 1892 won the competition for the

province's largest building project, the highly symbolic Parliament Buildings in Victoria. Both men quickly adapted to the N American building environment. The ponderous Renaissance Revival LEGISLATIVE BUILDINGS, reminiscent of the classical architecture of 16th-century Rome and Florence, owed more to the contemporary American state capitol building program than any English precedents. Sorby's shingle-style chalets in the ROCKY MTS and his Italianate and Romanesque Vancouver and Victoria buildings were similarly American in inspiration. Rattenbury became architect for the CPR western division in 1901 and ultimately primary architect to the provincial government. He brought the CPR's picturesque Chateau style to the province, notably with the EMPRESS HOTEL in Victoria (1903–8), then applied variants of this style to a series of courthouses and banks.

Along with Rattenbury, 2 other Victoria firms dominated the provincial landscape. In 1889 Thomas HOOPER, trained in Ontario, opened his Victoria office, and in 1892 Samuel MACLURE moved from New Westminster to the capital. Together these 3 architects led the movement toward a unique blending of British and American elements and the creation of a West Coast voice that ultimately influenced even the regional Modern Expressionist architecture of the 1950s and 1960s. Hooper, through his practices in Victoria and Vancouver, adopted the Richardsonian Romanesque style marked by heavy masonry elements and arched forms. Post-1900, he and Rattenbury utilized a more refined Greek or Roman classicism ("Beaux Arts") for a series of LIBRARIES, banks and courthouses throughout the province. Hooper's red-brick schools, inspired by those of E.R. Robinson for the Inner London Education Authority, still dominate the skylines of many small BC towns. The late-Victorian picturesque styles, whether Chateauesque, Queen Anne or Italianate, stamped a mark on the communities of the resource-based economy—NELSON, ROSSLAND, TRAIL, REVELSTOKE, NANAIMO, LADYSMITH, POWELL RIVER—that remains to this day.

Samuel Maclure was a more studied practitioner. His shingle-style and half-timber decorated ("Tudor Revival") houses for the province's power-broker families adopted the communal central hall of the British colonial bungalow to larger scale domestic designs. Around these halls he adapted the forms of alpine chalets, English manor houses or cottage bungalows. These finely crafted wood-finished homes were clad in shingle or unbarked slab, or half-timbered. Maclure's busy Victoria and Vancouver offices literally defined the tenor of the 2 cities' prestigious residential developments of the late Victorian and Edwardian periods: Rockland, OAK BAY and the Uplands in Victoria; Shaughnessy, Kitsilano and Point Grey in Vancouver. Hooper, Rattenbury and Maclure gave BC an indigenous style adapted from international building trends but suited to its unique CLIMATE, PHYSICAL GEOGRAPHY and multinational outlook. Other architects, including C.E. Watkins, brothers Douglas and Percy JAMES and J.C.M. Keith in Victoria, and Ross Lort, G.L.T. Sharp, C.J. Thompson, Honeyman & Curtis and Townley & Matheson in Vancouver, followed in the footsteps of these pioneers.

Town planning allowed for grandiose gestures during this period. In contrast to Edward Mallandaine's modest but picturesque Victoria cemetery layouts of the 1870s and 1880s, or John BLAIR's BEACON HILL PARK in Victoria (1886), whole towns and suburbs were planned on English and American "City Beautiful" principles. New towns for the GRAND TRUNK PACIFIC RWY at PRINCE GEORGE and PRINCE RUPERT were laid out by the Boston planning and landscape architecture firm Brett & Hall. They also laid out the HATLEY PARK estate for James DUNSMUIR (1908). The upscale residential garden suburb of Uplands in Victoria was developed by the Seattle office of Olmsted Bros beginning in 1908. The hilltop Shaughnessy Heights subdivision in Vancouver was the product of Montreal land-

Vancouver Public Library, main branch, designed by Moshe Safdie and opened in 1995. Oi-Lun Kwan photo/VPL

scape architect Frederick G. Todd. Thomas Mawson, an English town planner and landscapist, also operated a Vancouver office, from which he developed a Beaux Arts plan for downtown Vancouver and collaborated on large garden estates in Point Grey.

The economic doldrums of the interwar years was reflected in an architectural conservatism. Vancouver's answer to the Empress Hotel in Victoria, the Chateau-style Hotel Vancouver (1928–39), was left unfinished during the Depression. The consolidation of economic influence in Vancouver meant that lead architectural monuments of international Art-Deco and Moderne movements happened there. The buildings themselves were symbolic of this. A Montreal architect, S.G. Davenport, designed the stepped-back skyscraper Royal Bank (1929–31) on Hastings St, the first bank to substitute a tower for the traditional temple-form banking chamber. Townley & Matheson's sumptuously ornate Marine Building (1929–30), with its west coast maritime-inspired decorative motifs, towered over the harbourfront. It housed the Vancouver Merchants (Stock) Exchange and bankrupted it; the project had to be salvaged by the Guinness family of Britain. Townley & Matheson also designed the city's monument to itself, Vancouver City Hall (1936–37). This massive Deco-style pile, intended to rejuvenate Vancouver's south side, was a million-dollar Depression make-work project. Characteristically the stripped-down streamlined design ethic of the Moderne movement had even less impact, although traces of the style can be discerned in the St James ANGLICAN CHURCH (1935–37) on Cordova St in Vancouver (designed by the English architect A. Gilbert Scott), in Victoria apartment blocks such as Tweedsmuir Manor (designed by W.J. Semeyn, 1936), and in tract housing in Interior towns such as Trail and CRESTON.

The return of young architects after WWII, the founding of the UBC School of Architecture in 1946 and the arrival of several British architects profoundly influenced the post-war building boom, which was characterized by the popularization of the minimal, clean-lined and functional International style along with the materials-conscious Expressionist movement. Anchor buildings in cities and towns throughout the province were prompted by a concentration on social services and social housing to accommodate the post-war baby boom. Bert BINNING, artist–architect and UBC professor, had designed and built a radically new, open-plan, flat-roofed post-and-beam house for himself in 1941. Around Binning clustered a group of architects pushing Expressionist design principles, their residential work drawing heavily on Japanese screen and landscape principles. Ned PRATT, John Porter, Duncan McNabb and Peter Thornton experimented with small-house designs. They were joined in the early 1950s by Ron THOM, Arthur ERICKSON, Fred Hollingsworth, Bob BERWICK and C.B.K. VAN NORMAN. Out of this group emerged one of Vancouver's largest offices: Sharp, Thompson, Berwick, Pratt, which

alone designed some 190 schools throughout the province. The minimalist post-and-beam formula for these schools drew on the earlier domestic experiments using new wood technologies, particularly sheet plywood modules and laminated truss systems. The provincial architect, W.H. Whittaker, and after 1950 his partner in a Victoria practice, Don WAGG, produced several hospitals, first in a late streamlined Moderne style, then as European-influenced Expressionist forms. In Victoria an abrupt change to Modern Expressionism styles occurred

The central atrium at the University of Northern BC at Prince George. The facility opened in 1998. UNBC

with the design team brought together for Mayor Biggerstaff Wilson's creation of a new civic centre on Centennial Square. Working with city planner Rod Clack, the group included John DI CASTRI, Alan Hodgson, Bob Siddall, Clive Campbell, Wagg and John Wade. The resulting combination of heritage conservation, urban renewal and contextual modern infill around a pedestrian amenity set the stage for urban design in Victoria for the next 40 years. The architectural monuments of this period in Victoria and Vancouver illustrate symmetrical themes. In 1953, Thompson, Berwick, Pratt designed new office towers in both cities for BC HYDRO AND POWER AUTHORITY; both illustrated a dramatic new use of glass curtain walls with colour schemes by Binning. The tall, translucent structure in Vancouver set the stage for the redevelopment of downtown. Frank MUSSON's Bentall Centres in Victoria (1963) and Vancouver (1965) transported a contemporary though scaled-down New York look to both cities, while Peter KAFFKA's Imperial Apartments in the West End of Vancouver (1962–63) and Eng & Wright's Orchard House (1969) in James Bay presaged the soaring slab apartment blocks that transformed the historic neighbourhoods of both cities during the 1960s and 1970s. The crowning

achievements of the decade, however, were 2 vast educational projects: Erickson-Massey's SFU atop Burnaby Mt, and the GORDON HEAD campus of the UNIV OF VICTORIA, coordinated by Siddall.

It was essentially the maturation of these architectural offices that so altered BC's urban landscape during the 1970s and 1980s. Erickson's Brutalist MACMILLAN BLOEDEL Building on Georgia St (1968–69) provided the impetus both for the Robson Square Law Courts complex and the MUSEUM OF ANTHROPOLOGY at UBC, built simultaneously during 1973–76, which set new standards for design in the city's business core and on the university campus. Victoria took a different turn at this juncture. In the reconstruction of Government House after a fire in 1957, Peter COTTON and Hodgson worked with the department of public works to rebuild the house and reconstruct some of the main Maclure and Rattenbury-era rooms. Cotton went on to pioneer drawing and recording techniques for the Canadian Historic Sites and Monuments Board, then developed the province's foremost historic restoration practice. Hodgson undertook the complete restoration of Rattenbury's Parliament Buildings, a vast and complex 20-year project that began in 1973. Elsewhere in the province, resource industries were creating new modernist towns, for instance at CASSIAR and KITIMAT.

It was heritage conservation, particularly in Vancouver with the provincial designation of Gastown and Chinatown in 1971, the recycling of industrial buildings on GRANVILLE ISLAND (1973–76) and some of Cotton's neo-historic works, that opened up the regional design vocabulary in the forefront of Post Modernism. This freeing of form and style led to an explosion of creative activity, including the symbolic gesturalism of John and Patricia PATKAU (Salish people's SEA ISLAND School, 1991, and Strawberry Vale Elementary School, 1996); the CHINESE Cultural Centre in Vancouver, a contemporary interpretation of forms from old China (Jim Cheng,

1978); and the Pompidou Centre-inspired functionalism of Russell Vandiver's high-tech research facility at Discovery Park (1979–82). The contemporary mood can be summarized by the finely textured Queen Ann Revival townhouse schemes of the Victoria architect Bas Smith, which fit the textural detail of their neighbourhoods, and the stridently structuralist main buildings (1995) for the UNBC at Prince George, which seek landmark monumentalism and dramatic viewscapes, just as Rattenbury's CPR hotels did some 100 years earlier.   *Martin Segger*

ARCHITECTURE, ABORIGINAL, refers to the FIRST NATIONS houses that were the earliest man-made structures in BC. They reflected successful adaptations to particular environmental factors and to cultural beliefs and lifestyle practices. At their simplest, First Nations houses were temporary and portable, adapted to a nomadic lifestyle. At their most complex, they achieved an impressive monumentality, requiring a sophisticated use of construction techniques. Some housing types in BC were common to those used by First Nations elsewhere, such as teepees and pole-framed lodges, but 2 forms in particular were unique to the province. The **pit house** was used by First Nations of the central plateau region: the SECWEPEMC (Shuswap), the TSILHQOT'IN (Chilcotin), the ST'AT'IMX (Lillooet) and the NLAKA'PAMUX (Thompson). During the summer months these people occupied light pole-framed shelters covered with woven reeds or grass mats, suited to their seasonal movements to food-gathering sites. In the winter, however, they gathered at permanent hamlets of pit houses, semi-subterranean dwellings capable of accommodating up to 30 inhabitants. These houses, usually referred to as *kekuli* from the CHINOOK JARGON word for "underneath," varied in size, configuration and building methods. Some were circular; others were elongated or square. Construction began with the excavation of the pit, which was 1–1.2 m deep with outward-sloping walls. A rounded superstructure of posts, beams, poles

and a layer of bark, PINE needles or grass was covered with earth. Entry was via a ladder through a smoke hole cut in the roof. The pit house was an efficient conserver of heat and required only a central fire to warm the interior. When grass began to sprout in the earth, the structure seemed to be a living part of the landscape.

The **plank house** was used by the various First Nations living along the Pacific coast. Forms differed in style but all employed post-and-beam construction that exploited the large dimensions of the western red CEDAR. Salish-speaking people in the south (*see* SALISHAN FIRST NATIONS) developed a shed-roofed variant of the plank house, characterized by a single roof pitch sloping from front to back, a "longhouse." Massive roof beams spanned the width of the house, supported by 2 rows of posts. Overlapping roof planks were laid over pole rafters attached to the beams. Walls were clad with wide split-cedar planks tied horizontally between upright poles. Salish plank houses varied in size. Sometimes they stood alone; sometimes an entire village consisted of houses attached lengthwise to form a continuous line that might extend 450 m. This modular system created a stockade-like wall useful for defence. KWAKW<u>A</u>KA'WAKW (Kwakiutl) people of the central coast inhabited winter villages that often contained a dozen or more plank houses arranged, according to social rank, in rows facing the water. The facades of these houses were decorated with paintings, and carved poles stood at the entrance (*see* ART, NORTHWEST COAST ABORIGINAL; TOTEM POLES). Houses were believed to possess spiritual power. Kwakw<u>a</u>ka'wakw traditional "big houses" had gable roofs and were essentially square, with sides ranging from 12 to 18 m. Vertical wall planks and roof planks were laid over a subframe of poles lashed to the frames. Gable ends facing the water typically were covered with vertical plank facades that sometimes rose above the roof line. In the north, the HAIDA, TSIMSHIAN, NISGA'A and GITKSAN people built smaller, more tightly fitted houses than their

Cedar plank house at Haina, a Haida village, 1888. Richard Maynard/RBCM PN701

southern neighbours. Usually about 12 m², Haida plank houses were built in 2 primary forms. The most common type was a 6-beam house framed with 6 large longitudinal beams that projected beyond the gable wall ends. The Haida also built a 2-beam variant, as did the Tsimshian. External ornamentation was limited to carved house posts and frontal totem poles. More than simple dwellings, these houses were regarded as expressions of their owners' prestige, family history and supernatural ancestry. They were used for mid-winter ceremonies, including the POTLATCH. Houses were named and their construction and decoration was a significant cultural event, inaugurated with ceremonial potlatches.   *Ted Mills*

ARGENTA, pop 150, is a community overlooking the northeast corner of KOOTENAY LK north of KASLO. It developed as an AGRICULTURAL centre in the early 20th century, producing fruit and vegetables for nearby MINING camps. For many years it was accessible only by steamboat. A Quaker community dates back to 1952.

ARGENTA, Nancy, singer (b 17 Jan 1957, Nelson). Raised in the KOOTENAY, she is one of the world's leading sopranos specializing in baroque repertoire. She was born Nancy Herbison, but in her mid-20s she took the name of a KOOTENAY LK community to avoid being confused with another Canadian singer. After

Restored pit house (kekuli) on the banks of the Thompson R. Keith Thirkell photo

Nancy Argenta, one of the world's leading sopranos. *Nicky Johnston photo*

graduating from Univ of Western Ontario in 1980, she studied in W Germany for a year, then moved to London, where she studied under famous New Zealand singer Dame Kiri Te Kanawa. Argenta made her professional opera debut in 1983 and has since performed worldwide with major orchestras and at major festivals. She later made her home in England.

Shannon Emmerson

ARGILLITE is a dense black shale used by the HAIDA of the QUEEN CHARLOTTE ISLANDS to make stone carvings for sale. The carvings have been much imitated, but authentic Haida argillite comes only from Slatechuck Mt near SKIDEGATE. The first carvings were tobacco pipes made for trade early in the 19th century. Later carvers produced an array of objects, including human figures, bowls, animals, tableware and small TOTEM POLES. Although the quality of the artistry deteriorated after 1910, numerous carvers maintained the tradition through to the 1960s, when a resurgence of the art form began. *See also* ART, NORTH-WEST COAST ABORIGINAL.

ARMSTRONG, city, pop 3,906, is located in the N OKANAGAN VALLEY, surrounded by the district municipality of SPALLUMCHEEN. The first settlers lived 5 km away at Lansdowne until 1892, when the SHUSWAP & OKANAGAN RWY bypassed Lansdowne's hilly location and caused the town to relocate to its present site. Many houses, commercial buildings and the ANGLICAN CHURCH were moved and most remain standing. The new site was named for William Heaton-Armstrong, a London banker who helped to finance the railway. It prospered as the business and shipping centre for a growing AGRICULTURAL district and incorporated as a city separate from Spallumcheen on 26 Mar 1913. Armstrong, formerly known as the "Celery City," is noted for the Interior Provincial Exhibition and the railway bisecting its main thoroughfare, as well as cheese production: the Armstrong Cheese Co-

operative Assoc operated from 1939 to 1961 and at one point was the second-largest cheese producer in Canada; Armstrong cheese is still produced by DAIRYWORLD. Chicken processing and the milling of plywood and other wood products are also important to the local economy. Armstrong is home to the CARAVAN FARM THEATRE.

ARMSTRONG, Jeannette Bonneau, writer (b 1948, Penticton). A member of the OKANAGAN First Nation, she grew up on a RESERVE at PENTICTON and later graduated from the UNIV OF VICTORIA. She has studied traditional teachings with Okanagan elders and co-founded the aboriginal

Jeannette Armstrong, Okanagan First Nations writer.

WRITING school at the EN'OWKIN CENTRE in Penticton, where she has served as director. She has written children's books, a novel (*Slash*, 1985), a collection of poetry (*Breath Tracks*, 1991) and a book on the aboriginal creative process.

ARMY & NAVY Department Store has been a downtown VANCOUVER institution for more than 80 years. Founded in 1919 on West Hastings St by three Cohen brothers, Sam, Joe and Harry, the army-surplus business grew to a chain of 5 stores known for their variety of merchandise sold at bargain basement prices. Sam bought out his brothers and ran the business until his death in 1966; control left the family's hands at that time. In 1998 Sam's granddaughter Jacqui Cohen reassumed family control of the company and relaunched the downtown store.

ARRANDALE was the site of a SALMON cannery overlooking PORTLAND INLET at the mouth of the NASS R. It began SALMON CANNING operations in 1904 and remained in business under a series of owners until 1942, employing a workforce made up mainly of NISGA'A people from villages on the Nass. There were also immigration buildings, a PROVINCIAL POLICE post and a second cannery, the Port Nelson, next door.

ARRAS, pop 160, is a small agricultural community and service centre in the PEACE R district, 20 km west of DAWSON CREEK on the Kiskatinaw R and Hwy 97. It was named in 1923 by the first postmaster, R. Soutes, who fought in the battle of Arras during WWI.   AS

ARROW LAKES, 499 km², are part of the COLUMBIA R system in southeast BC. They form an elongated reservoir stretching 232 km from REVELSTOKE to CASTLEGAR. Originally 2 LAKES connected by a river, they merged in 1969 when the KEENLEYSIDE DAM near Castlegar backed up water to its present levels, drowning several small lakeside communities. A lock carries boat traffic around the dam. Upper Arrow Lk (301 km²) was part of the late 19th-century MINING boom and PADDLE-WHEEL STEAMERS operated for several years. The lakes were named by FUR TRADERS for the FIRST NATIONS practice of shooting arrows into the crevices of a huge rock on the shore.

ARROW PARK is a farming and LOGGING settlement and former steamship landing on the west bank of the COLUMBIA R between Upper and Lower ARROW LKS. Arrow Park and East Arrow Park, a settlement on the other side of the lake, were established before WWI. Although most of Arrow Park was submerged in the late 1960s after the KEENLEYSIDE DAM was built, a few people continue to live here. A free cable ferry runs between Arrow Park and East Arrow Park, as it has since the 1920s.   AS

ARROWHEAD, a community at the north end of the ARROW LKS 40 km south of REVELSTOKE, was the terminus of a CPR branch line from Revelstoke completed in 1896, but the area is mostly submerged today after the KEENLEYSIDE DAM raised water levels in the 1960s. The rail line connected with sternwheelers such as the *Rossland* and the *Minto*, which ran to NAKUSP and ROBSON. Steamer service ended in 1954. *See also* ARROWHEAD & KOOTENAY RWY.   AS

ARROWHEAD & KOOTENAY RAILWAY was a small CPR branch line serving the SILVER mining district of the LARDEAU. The line, connecting GERRARD on Trout Lk with steamships at Lardeau on KOOTENAY LK, opened in June 1902 and briefly stimulated an economic boom in the area. But it was never completed through to Upper ARROW LK and the boom collapsed before WWI. The tracks were pulled up in 1942.

ARSENAL PULP PRESS is a VANCOUVER literary and trade book publisher, founded in 1971 as Pulp Press by a collective of young writers disenchanted with what they perceived to be the academic pretensions of Canadian literature at the time. As well as books, the press published broadsheets and pamphlets and *3-Cent Pulp*, a monthly literary magazine that sold for 3 cents. Pulp also initiated the THREE-DAY NOVEL WRITING CONTEST in 1978. In 1982 Pulp became Arsenal Pulp Press and since that time has become increasingly interested in publishing non-fiction, particularly history and aboriginal studies, and books on gay and lesbian subjects. It is owned jointly by Brian Lam, publisher, and one of the founders, Stephen Osborne. *See also* BOOK PUBLISHING.

ART, NORTHWEST COAST ABORIGINAL, is the rich, visual, cultural expression of the FIRST NATIONS people living in the coastal area of the Northwest portion of N America from Alaska in the north to the COLUMBIA R in the south. Archaeological discoveries provide evidence of thriving communities in large permanent villages up and down the coast dating back more than 8,000 years. Decorated tools and ceremonial items made of bone, stone, shell and wood and dating back about 2,000 years provide insight into the origins of classic Northwest Coast art. The mild climate, plentiful rainfall and wealth of food resources resulted in the development of stable communities where an elaborate and sophisticated culture thrived. Art of the Northwest Coast is an expression of spirituality, social status and ceremony. Iconographic images represent ancestral crest figures—KILLER WHALES, grizzly BEARS, WOLVES, EAGLES, thunderbirds, etc—from which a lineage descended. These are represented on TOTEM POLES, housefront paintings, talking sticks, ceremonial blankets, heirloom feast dishes and other eating utensils. The art also serves to make the supernatural world visible and is related to theatre, where powerful spirits are manifest in song and dance through the use of masks and other stage properties. The tendency in non-aboriginal, European society to distinguish between artistic and utilitarian concerns is absent from aboriginal culture, where art and spiritual ceremony pervaded every aspect of life. Even the most utilitarian objects were wonderfully wrought and decorated.

Northwest Coast art reflects the close relationship between the indigenous people and their environment. The great stands of red CEDAR in the coastal RAIN FORESTS were used to make masks, rattles, feast dishes and bentwood boxes, as well as houses, totem poles and CANOES. Yellow cedar, YEW, ALDER and MAPLE were used for

Speaking Great Silence *by Susan Point.*
Kenji Nagai/Spirit Wrestler Gallery

Man/frog transformation by Doug Cranmer, 1976. MOA Nb3.1483

ceremonial items, while HEMLOCK, DOUGLAS FIR and other species were used for a variety of implements and tools. Women made basketry items, capes, skirts, blankets, hats and mats from cedar bark, roots and branches, spruce root, bulrushes and SEAGRASSES. Decorative features also came from nature. Objects were decorated or inlaid with ABALONE shell, opercula, SEA LION whiskers, feathers, ermine skins, antler, teeth, bone and hooves.

The iconography of the art is bound to both this natural environment and the supernatural worlds of the different First Nations groups. Within the natural and supernatural are the distinct worlds of the sea, sky, land and spirit world. Supernatural beings interact with characters of the natural world. The recurring theme of transformation, linking the supernatural and natural planes of existence, is a key concept in the iconography of the art. Ceremonies, such as the Hamatsa of the KWAKWA̲KA̲'WAKW (Kwakiutl) or Tloquana of the NUU-CHAH-NULTH (Nootka), portray and dramatize the philosophies, spirituality and social structure of the specific group by calling on a well-known pantheon of characters. Such ceremonies demonstrate the significant relationship between art and belief systems. The rights to certain privileges are inherited or acquired through marriage. These privileges include stories, songs, dances and crests and ceremonial objects such as masks, rattles, blankets, feast dishes, etc.

Impact of Contact

The continuity of Northwest Coast cultures was disrupted by contact with Europeans. The post-contact period generally dates from the 1770s, when SPANISH and British explorers arrived on the coast. The material culture since that time reflects the profound changes, both positive and negative, brought about by the introduction of European materials, tools and values. From ear-

liest contact First Nations artists incorporated commercial trade goods into their culture and artistic output. With the advent of the maritime FUR TRADE, iron became a popular trade item. Iron tools facilitated the carving process. The most popular trade good, textiles—particularly blankets—evolved quickly into ceremonial button blankets in which crest and other decorative border designs were sewn onto the blanket and outlined with trade buttons made of mother of pearl. Dance aprons were decorated with everything from deer hooves to thimbles.

Following the decline of the maritime fur trade due to the near extinction of the SEA OTTER, a second wave of newcomers arrived on the coast during the 19th century in the form of administrators, missionaries, industrialists, entrepreneurs and settlers. This new guard often deliberately sought to change the customs and beliefs of the First Nations people. The majority of missionaries and government officials promoted radical changes in lifestyle and sought to suppress the POTLATCH ceremonies, which were perceived as being diametrically opposed to their own economic views and spiritual beliefs. In 1862 the worst of a series of SMALLPOX epidemics swept through the population of the Northwest Coast, destroying whole villages and decimating the aboriginal population (*see* ABORIGINAL DEMOGRAPHY). On the heels of the smallpox epidemic came the official banning of the potlatch in 1884. For countless generations the potlatch had provided one of the main contexts for artistic production. At the same time, contact was a stimulus to artistic production, providing improved technology in the form of metal blades and new sources of wealth. As well, artists began producing items for sale to Euroamerican sailors, collectors and travellers. Early examples include ARGILLITE objects made by HAIDA carvers on Haida Gwaii (QUEEN CHARLOTTE ISLANDS). Religious icons commissioned by missionaries and model totem poles and canoes commissioned by ethnographers were the origins of the now flourishing art market. Along with the ethnographers of the late 19th and early 20th centuries came the TOURISTS. Steamboats plied the waters between Seattle and Alaska with frequent stops in First Nations villages. Northwest Coast artists responded to the tourist market and art was adapted to new purposes and new expectations, while maintaining links to the age-old artistic heritage.

Style

The style of Northwest Coast art is highly formalized and subtle, whether it is the two-dimensional flat designs on boxes, chests, bowls and screens or the carved designs on sculptured objects such as masks, poles and headdresses. Scholars usually distinguish between three style "provinces," each of which had distinctive stylistic similarities: the northern province (including the TLINGIT, Haida, TSIMSHIAN, GITKSAN, NISGA'A and HAISLA); the central province (including NUXALK, HEILTSUK, Kwakwaka'wakw and Nuu-chah-nulth); and the southern province of the SALISHAN-speaking groups. The style of Northwest Coast art was analyzed by the artist and art historian Bill Holm in his landmark study *Northwest Coast Art: An Analysis of Form* (1965). Holm identified certain essential design elements: the formline, a continuous flowing line that outlines the creature being represented; the ovoid, a slightly-flattened oval

shape; and the u-form, lines drawn in the shape of the letter *U*. These elements are most strongly associated with the 2-dimensional arts of the northern groups. Southern groups share some characteristics of style with their northern neighbours, but they also employ their own graphic motifs. While these elements are present in most of the art, their use varies from group to group and from artist to artist. Styles in sculpture also differ from group to group, chiefly in the manner in which facial features—human, animal and mythical—are carved. Historically, 2 or more artists often collaborated. For example, pattern boards were prepared by male artists, then used by women artists who transferred the design to the weaving of the treasured CHILKAT BLANKETS in the north. Similarly, with Tsimshian and Kwakwaka'wakw button blankets, a male artist created the design while the female artist executed it. With Haida clan or chief hats, the weaving was completed by a woman, then passed on to a male artist for hand-painted decoration. By the close of the 20th century these gendered artistic boundaries were blurring.

Resurgence

The production of aboriginal art for ceremonial purposes, and for the curio trade, managed to survive the negative impact of contact with

Europeans and the repressive government policies epitomized by the ban on the potlatch during 1884 to 1951. During the first half of the 20th century, several important artists were at work, including Charles EDENSHAW, a Haida man, and the Kwakwaka'wakw artists Charlie JAMES, Willie SEAWEED and Charlie G. Walkus, to name just a few. The legacy of knowledge and skills passed on by these masters enjoyed a resurgence beginning in the 1950s. In 1950 the Kwakwaka'wakw carver Mungo MARTIN was hired to restore totem poles at UBC's Totem Park. Martin later moved to the ROYAL BC MUSEUM to carry out a similar project, and he trained apprentices to repair and replicate totem poles. In 1967 the VANCOUVER ART GALLERY staged the "Arts of the Raven" show, a major exhibition that presented Northwest Coast aboriginal art as art instead of artifact. In 1970 the Kitanmaax School of Northwest Coast Indian Art opened at 'KSAN, providing an opportunity for young artists to develop. Amidst all this activity, a new generation of carvers and artists emerged, including Bill REID, Robert DAVIDSON and Freda Diesing (Haida), Doug CRANMER and Henry and Tony HUNT (Kwakwaka'wakw), Dempsey Bob (TAHLTAN-TLINGIT), Norman TAIT (Nisga'a), Joe DAVID, Ron Hamilton, Tim Paul and Art Thompson (Nuu-chah-nulth), Susan Point (Coast Salish), Walter Harris (Gitksan) and many others. Whether they are producing for ceremonial or community purposes, or for sale in the wider marketplace, aboriginal artists are recognized as being among the leading contemporary artists in BC.

Reading: Roy Carlson, *Indian Art Traditions of the Northwest Coast*, 1983; Wilson Duff, *The Indian History of British Columbia*, 1965; Marjorie Halpin, *Totem Poles: An Illustrated Guide*, 1981; Bill Holm, *Northwest Coast Indian Art: An Analysis of Form*, 1965; Peter Macnair et al, *The Legacy: Continuing Traditions of Canadian Northwest Coast Art*, 1980; Hilary Stewart, *Looking at Indian Art of the Northwest Coast*, 1979.

ART, VISUAL in BC marks an immigrant history of people and ideas. As settlers and visitors to a new land, artists have sought to accommodate a vast and diverse landscape, its gradual urbanization and a particular cultural given, the arts of its First Peoples (*see* ART, NORTHWEST COAST ABORIGINAL). First were the colonial documentarists, beginning with the meticulous sketches of John WEBBER, the artist on James COOK's expedition to NOOTKA SOUND in 1778. Webber's sketches of aboriginal life and coastal scenery, like those of later sojourners such as the Ontario "Indian painter" Paul KANE and the British ethnologist W.G.R. HIND, were intended for publication as engraved illustrations. In general, they owed much to the English Romantic tradition of landscape painting, a tradition continued in the topographical sketches of the GOLD RUSH period by ROYAL ENGINEERS and Royal Navy surveyors such as Edward Parker Bedwell (1836–1919), Henry James Warre (1819–98) and John Clayton WHITE. Small watercolour sketches of

Thunderbird headdress by Richard Hunt.
Bob Matheson photo

Westward Drift *by Jack Shadbolt, 1989.*
Courtesy Doris Shadbolt/Bau-Xi Gallery

life in VICTORIA by local amateurs, such as Sarah Lindley Crease (*see* Henry P.P. CREASE), exhibit the same technical and aesthetic grounding. However, by the end of the 19th century the role of documentarist was being overtaken by PHOTOGRAPHY, traced in BC through the work of Richard and Hannah MAYNARD, Edward CURTIS, Harry KNIGHT and Harold MORTIMER-LAMB. The early photographs of FIRST NATIONS people no doubt provided the impetus and background to the vast art nouveau-style mural scheme for the ballroom of Victoria's new Government House (*see* CARY CASTLE). The house, completed in 1903, was designed by architects Samuel MACLURE and Francis RATTENBURY and the paintings were executed by artist James BLOMFELD in what the press of the day called a "historicoethnological plan."

The Great Eagle, Skidegate, *a watercolour painting by Emily Carr, 1929.*
Art Gallery of Greater Victoria

William Van Horne promoted the newly completed CPR by offering free passes to artists, an offer that attracted major eastern Canadian landscape painters who specialized in large canvases featuring the high drama of the ROCKY MTS and the massively treed forests of the West Coast. Lucius O'Brien (1832–99) and Frederick Arthur Verner (1836–1928) were typical of these, and a generation of landscape artists such as Mower Martin (1838–1934) and F.M. Bell-Smith (1846–1923) sold well in Victoria and VANCOUVER. Early scientific artists such as Webber and Hind started a tradition for the visual documentation of BC's flora and fauna, typically illustrated in the early work of the amateur naturalist and wildlife artist Allan BROOKS. This interest found later expression in the 20th century with, for example, the meticulous botanical drawings of the Austrian-trained Victoria artist Richard Ciccimarra (1924–73), the renowned ornithological artist J. Fenwick LANSDOWNE or the international wildlife artist Robert BATEMAN. On the other hand, BC's WILDFLOWERS served more as inspirational subject matter for Elizabeth Duer's (d 1948) series of Japanese-style watercolours, or Molly Lamb BOBAK's colourful watercolour sketches that flirt with free-form western abstraction.

In Victoria and Vancouver artists congregated around exhibition societies. Sam Maclure (trained in Philadelphia), his wife Margaret, James Blomfeld and Emily CARR founded the Arts and Crafts Society in 1909. Members of the Victoria society drew inspiration from the English movement pioneered by the British socialist and artist William Morris. In particular within Morris's eclectic interests, Japanese orientalism found resonance as the West Coast developed its PACIFIC RIM connections. The soft, unfocussed impressionism of Maclure, Carr, Thomas FRIPP (who founded the BC Society of Fine Arts in Vancouver in 1908) and the English-born painter Charles John COLLINGS, who lived in the SHUSWAP LK area, emulated the effects found in Japanese

woodblock prints. By the 1920s a powerful Canadian presence was felt through both exhibitions and visits by members of the Group of Seven. An exhibition by the Group in Vancouver in 1922 attracted wide attention. A.Y. Jackson (1882–1974) was painting coastal Indian villages in 1926; Fred VARLEY came west to teach at the Vancouver School of Decorative and Applied Arts (see EMILY CARR INSTITUTE OF ART & DESIGN) in 1926 under the direction of Charles H. SCOTT; Lawren HARRIS lived in Vancouver for the last 30 years of his life. Varley and his colleague Jock MACDONALD founded the ill-fated British Columbia College of Arts (1933–35). Professionalization of the art scene was confirmed with construction of the VANCOUVER ART GALLERY (VAG) in 1931. In Victoria a splinter group of the Arts and Crafts Society, including Carr, Max MAYNARD, Jack SHADBOLT and Ina Uhthoff (1889–1970), held their own exhibition, "The Modern Room," in 1932, itself reflecting Vancouver currents of the day. These artists, with their interests in bold, expressive landscape painting, theosophy, oriental religion and aboriginal arts, formed the backdrop against which Carr developed her own highly personal style of West Coast expressionism. They were supported by the gritty, hard-edge photography of Mortimer-Lamb and John VANDERPANT. It was this milieu that grounded Vancouver's war artists: Orville FISHER, E.J. HUGHES, Molly Lamb Bobak and Shadbolt. Meanwhile, Katharine Emma Maltwood (1878–1961), antiquarian, theosophist and London-trained sculptor, moved to Victoria in 1939 and established her own salon with immigrant artists such as the illustrator Stella Langdale (1880–1976) and Elizabeth Duer.

Mural painting enjoyed a brief flowering during the 1930s. In 1932 George H. Southwell (1865–1961) had been commissioned to produce 4 historical pageant murals for the rotunda of the LEGISLATIVE BUILDINGS. Fisher, Hughes and Paul Goranson (b 1911) collaborated on a Renaissance-style 6-panel biblical commission for the First United Church (1938), while Jock Macdonald produced a cubist-inspired First Nations village for the Hotel Vancouver in 1939. But the largest commission of the decade was a mural series commissioned for the BC exhibition at the 1939 Golden Gate Exposition in San Francisco, carried out by Hughes, Goranson and Fisher; it depicted the industries of BC executed in a social realism style.

During wartime the VAG adopted an outspoken social program with the Labour Arts Guild's 1944 exhibition "British Columbia at Work," followed in the immediate post-war period with a trend-setting exhibition of modern movement ARCHITECTURE, "Design for Living" (1949). However, artistic leadership moved to UBC's newly formed Faculty of Fine Arts and its gallery, which opened in 1948. At UBC, Bertram BINNING, Roy KIYOOKA, Don JARVIS and Gordon SMITH brought New York abstract expressionism, particularly its minimalist variant, to the West Coast. In 1951 the Art Gallery of Greater Victoria was founded under Colin Graham, the director,

(continued on page 35)

Gallery of BC Painters & Printmakers

View of English Bay Looking at Point Grey, *William Ferris, watercolour. Courtesy Uno Langmann*

Pond Painting F.S. IV, *Gordon Smith, 1996, acrylic on canvas, 150x120 cm. Private collection/Courtesy Equinox Gallery*

Chief Moody Humchitt, *Mildred Valley Thornton, c 1940, oil on board, 60x50 cm. Courtesy Heiltsuk Nation Collection, Heiltsuk Cultural Education Centre, Bella Bella*

Marbled Murrelets, *Robert Bateman, 1992, hand pulled lithograph, 22.5x30 cm. © Robert Bateman. Reproduction rights courtesy of Boshkung, Inc.*

Mount Rundle, *Frederick Bell-Smith. Courtesy Art Gallery of Greater Victoria*

Haida Dog Salmon, *1974 silkscreen by Bill Reid. Courtesy Martine Reid.*

In the Mineral Regions, a Prospector's Hut, *Charles John Collings, watercolour. Courtesy Uno Langmann*

First Narrows Looking West, *James Blomfield, 1905, watercolour. Courtesy Uno Langmann*

Odalisque, *Maxwell Bates. Courtesy Art Gallery of Greater Victoria*

Yale in the Morning, *William Brymner, 1886, oil on canvas.*
Courtesy Uno Langmann

Blue Sky, *Emily Carr, 1932–34, oil on canvas, 95.3x66.14 cm.*
Courtesy Art Gallery of Greater Victoria

Mt Cheam, Fraser Valley, *George Southwell, oil on canvas.*
Courtesy Uno Langmann

Final Break, *Jack Shadbolt, 1993, acrylic on linen.*
Photo by Tien Huang/Courtesy Doris Shadbolt

Hermit Thrush, *J.F. Lansdowne. Courtesy the artist*

Leaves of a Box, *Jock Macdonald. Courtesy Art Gallery of Greater Victoria*

Farm Northeast of Chilliwack, *E.J. Hughes, 1959, oil, 63.5x81 cm.*

and the early 1950s saw the arrival of Herbert Siebner (b 1925), trained in Berlin, and the Austrian-born Jan Zach (1914–86), both of whom introduced expressionist art to Victoria. In 1969 artistic life in Victoria was further reinforced with the creation of the Faculty of Fine Arts at the UNIV OF VICTORIA. Founding teachers included the American-educated abstractionist John Dobereiner (1920–85) and Donald Harvey (b 1930), trained in England. In 1971 Siebner, along with Max BATES, founded the influential LIMNERS group of artists in the capital.

In 1967 the VAG hosted Vancouver Print International. A printmaking tradition was

Dress with Insects by Gathie Falk, 1998.
Courtesy Equinox Gallery

already in place from the pioneer work of Alistair BELL, the linocuts of the CAMPBELL RIVER printmaker Sybil ANDREWS, the woodblock prints of First Nations coastal villages by Walter J. Phillips (1884–1963), and the 1950s block-print illustrations of George CLUTESI. During his career as head of graphics at the Vancouver School of Art, Orville Fisher perfected his intaglio and drypoint techniques. Pat Martin Bates (b 1927), teaching at the Univ of Victoria in the 1960s, expanded the genre with her multi-media monoprints. Later lithographic production houses such as Potlatch Press (founded by Bud Mintz, a Langley College instructor) and Vincent Rickard's Pacific Editions in Victoria set the standard for screenprint editions by aboriginal artists. Prior Editions, founded by the printmaker Torry Groening, has provided a co-operative production facility in a wide range of print media for Vancouver artists.

While travel and study were a part of almost every BC artist's education, geographical isolation finally lost its hold by the late 1960s. The influence of the international art journals was complemented by radio and television. A new teaching institution, the Kootenay School of Art,

opened in NELSON in 1960. In 1965 SFU founded the Centre for Communications and the Arts. Artists' centres in Vancouver became the focus of emerging multi-media explorations. In 1966 Iain and Ingrid Baxter founded the N.E. THING CO and produced their *Bagged Place* exhibit at UBC. INTERMEDIA operated from 1967 to 1972, followed by the WESTERN FRONT, Video Inn (started by Michael Goldberg) and Pumps Centre for the Arts (1976), an operating centre for punk generation artists. At SFU Jeff WALL was producing monumental backlit cibachrome tableaux. Two artist-run centres were established in Victoria during this period: Exchanges Artist Gallery and Studio (1967) and Open Space (1972). Back in Vancouver, Stan DOUGLAS was working with slide-dissolve and soundtracks; Gathie FALK moved from ceramics to large-scale environmental installations; and Anna BANANA championed performance and mail art. By this time contemporary aboriginal art was also joining the mainstream. A landmark exhibition, *Arts of the Raven*, organized by Doris SHADBOLT, the curator, brought this revival to the Vancouver Art Gallery in 1967, and the Kitanmaax School of Northwest Coast Indian Art at 'KSAN near HAZELTON was founded. Bill REID, Tony Hunt (*see* Henry HUNT), Robert DAVIDSON and Beau Dick (b 1955) were just 4 of many First Nations artists who began exhibiting prints and sculptures in their highly personalized styles at the new MUSEUM OF ANTHROPOLOGY at UBC and at the relocated VAG.

At the end of the 20th century the BC art scene had absorbed the neo-conservatism that was prevalent internationally. The Vancouver Art Gallery had moved into its renovated courthouse location and its show of the 1990s, *The New Spirit*, was actually a retrospective of Vancouver's modern-style architects of the 1950s. The ROYAL BC MUSEUM hosted a successful exhibition on Leonardo da Vinci. Jack Shadbolt, perhaps the leading BC artist of his generation, returned to aboriginal icons and environmental themes. Toni ONLEY also adopted an ecological stance for

a major cycle of work. Vicki Husband (b 1940), a Victoria painter, and Nina Raginsky (b 1941), an avant-garde photographer in Vancouver, both gave over their careers in favour of environmental activism (*see also* ENVIRONMENTAL MOVEMENT). Joe PLASKETT returned from a long exile in Paris to sketch the QUEEN CHARLOTTE ISLANDS (Haida Gwaii) in the 1980s, then the OKANAGAN VALLEY; by the late 1990s his exhibited work demonstrated a retreat from three-dimensional figurative work to a flat, elementary formalism reminiscent of the 1950s. By the end of century the BC art world had lost many members of its first generation of pioneer heroes: Bell, Reid, Shadbolt, Bates, Bob DeCastro (1923–86), Nita Forrest (1926–99), Robin SKELTON and Sylvia Skelton (1927–99). The largest artistic commission of the decade, for the newly reconstructed Vancouver Airport terminal buildings, was awarded to an innovative SALISHAN FIRST NATIONS artist, Susan Point (b 1952). *Martin Segger*

ARTS CLUB THEATRE opened in 1964 above a downtown VANCOUVER autobody shop. Productions have ranged from light comedy to contemporary drama, with strong emphasis on Canadian material. Bill Millerd began serving as artistic director in 1972, the year the theatre staged its first hit show, *Jacques Brel is Alive and Well and Living in Paris*, starring Ann MORTIFEE, Leon BIBB, Ruth Nichol and Pat Rose. The show sold out its entire run, becoming a legend in Vancouver THEATRE history; in 1997 it was remounted for a brief run with the original cast. The theatre moved to a 460-seat GRANVILLE ISLAND site in 1979 and opened a smaller Arts Club Revue Theatre next door for cabarets and revues in 1983. A third stage opened in the renovated Stanley Theatre, an old vaudeville house and movie theatre on S Granville Street, in 1998.

ASAHI was an amateur BASEBALL team composed of members of VANCOUVER's JAPANESE community. Founded in 1914, it routinely won

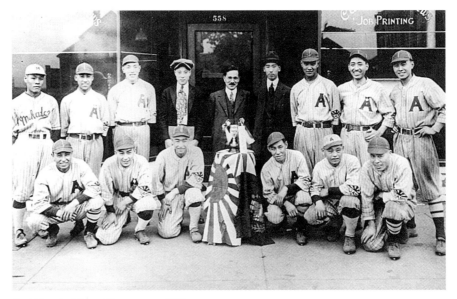

Asahi baseball team, Vancouver, c 1925.
Japanese Canadian National Museum

the championship of whatever senior league it joined. The best known of several local Japanese baseball clubs, it toured Japan in 1921 and was a source of pride for the city's beleaguered Japanese Canadian community. The team played its last game in 1941; it disbanded with the relocation (*see* JAPANESE, RELOCATION OF) that occurred the following year. Asahi means "morning sun."

ASBESTOS, a fibrous mineral used for fire-proofing and insulation and in a variety of products, was produced in BC from 1952 to 1991 at a mine on McDame Mt north of DEASE LK. The community of CASSIAR, which developed as a townsite for the mine, was abandoned and sold off when the mine closed.

ASHCROFT, village, pop 1,858, overlooks the THOMPSON R 8 km south of CACHE CREEK. The settlement was known by several names until 1884, when the CPR arrived; it then became Ashcroft. After a bridge was built across the river in 1886 and the BC EXPRESS CO made headquarters here in 1887, it became the "Gateway to the CARIBOO." A disastrous fire in 1916 and the extension of the Pacific Great Eastern Rwy (*see* BC RAIL) to QUESNEL in 1919 brought hard times. Ashcroft was incorporated as a village on 27 June 1952. It is known as an oasis in the surrounding arid ranch country (*see* CATTLE INDUSTRY); almost anything will grow here. Known also for its heritage buildings, it has become popular as a retirement community. The nearby Ashcroft Ranch was established on the CARIBOO WAGON ROAD by Clement CORNWALL and his brother Henry, who named the ranch for their family home in Gloucester, England. The Cornwalls developed the ranch along with a popular roadhouse later known as Ashcroft Manor. They also built a racetrack (*see* HORSE RACING) and entertained themselves and guests by hunting COYOTES with foxhounds imported from England. Henry later owned the Cherry Creek Ranch near Cache Creek. The Ashcroft Ranch was owned by Allan Cameron from the 1930s to the mid-1970s. As of 1999 it was owned by Wicklow West Holdings Ltd.

ASIA PACIFIC ECONOMIC CO-OPERATION (APEC) is an organization formed in 1989 to promote trade and economic co-operation among 21 member countries around the PACIFIC RIM including Canada. BC has particular interest in APEC affairs because of its extensive trade with Pacific Rim countries. Other members are Australia, Brunei Darussalam, Chile, China, Hong Kong, Indonesia, Japan, Korea, Malaysia, Mexico, New Zealand, Papua New Guinea, Peru, Philippines, Russia, Singapore, Chinese Taipei, Thailand, the US and Vietnam. Canada hosted the 5th annual meeting of leaders of APEC countries in VANCOUVER in Nov 1997. The meeting was disrupted by protesters who particularly objected to the presence of Indonesian president Suharto, because of alleged human rights abuses in his country. Confrontations between protesters and police led to several arrests and an official inquiry into police conduct.

Police pepper-spray demonstrators at meeting of APEC, Vancouver, 1997.
Stuart Davis/Vancouver Province

ASIATIC EXCLUSION LEAGUE (AEL) was formed in VANCOUVER in Aug 1907. Initiated by the Trades and Labour Council, it had loose affiliations with the Japanese and Korean Exclusion League founded in San Francisco 2 years earlier. The initial meeting included labour leaders and prominent LIBERAL and CONSERVATIVE politicians. The AEL proposed a legislated end to all Asian immigration to Canada. A rally in support of the league was held on 7 Sept in Vancouver and it became a riot when thousands of hotheads marched through CHINATOWN and the JAPANESE district destroying property. When the Japanese fought back, the mob dispersed. Branches of the AEL formed in VICTORIA, NEW WESTMINSTER and N VANCOUVER, but it faded into inactivity by the end of 1908. The league was revived briefly in Vancouver during 1921–22.

ASPELL, Peter Noel Lawson, artist (b 1918, Vancouver). He studied at the Vancouver School of Art (*see* EMILY CARR INSTITUTE OF ART & DESIGN) and the Ghent Academy in Belgium. His first exhibition was a critically successful showing of figurative paintings at the VANCOUVER ART GALLERY in 1946. This launched a career characterized by experimentation with a variety of styles and approaches. During the 1950s he experimented with still life paintings; with Jack SHADBOLT, Takao TANABE and Gordon SMITH he was part of a "school" of Vancouver painters that acquired a national reputation for modernism. In 1959 he was included in the landmark "7 West Coast Painters" show that toured Canada. In the 1960s he switched to metal collage and in the late 1970s became known for his abstract "T-forms." In the late 1980s he made another shift in style, working with layers of colour and a palette-scraping technique. He taught at the Vancouver School of Art from 1947 to 1972, then at UBC and at his own Peter Aspell Art Studios.

ASPEN GROVE, 22 km southeast of MERRITT, was a stop on the old stagecoach road from

Merritt to PRINCETON and a centre for ranchers (*see* CATTLE INDUSTRY) and prospectors. It is named for the region's bountiful trembling aspen trees. About 1900 the area was thought to be rich in COPPER, but large-scale MINING never took place. A coffee shop and gas station are located here.

ASSU, Billy, Kwakwaka'wakw chief (b 1867; d 1965). A fisher for most of his life, he became chief of the Cape Mudge (now We Wai Kai) Nation in 1891 when he was 24 years old. He

A portrait of Billy Assu of Cape Mudge, taken by the photo-historian Henry Twidle, c 1915.
MCR 9105

built the first modern house in the village in 1894 and during the 1920s organized the replacement of all the traditional longhouses with modern housing (*see* ARCHITECTURE, ABORIGINAL). He bought the first gas fish boat at CAPE MUDGE, and during the Depression he helped to create the Pacific Coast Native Fishermen's Assoc, which later merged with the NATIVE BROTHERHOOD OF BC. His son Harry succeeded him as the first elected chief of the Cape Mudge band (1954–70). **Harry Assu** (b 14 Feb 1905, Cape Mudge; d 1 Feb 1999) began FISHING for the SALMON CANNERY in QUATHIASKI COVE when he was a teenager, dividing his time between the fishery and LOGGING during the winter. He fished for BC PACKERS LTD for 49 years and his seiner *BCP NO 45* was pictured on the Canadian 5-dollar bill. His memoirs, *Assu of Cape Mudge*, were published in 1989. Other Assus also were fishers; they are one of the most prominent families in the history of the coast SALMON fishery. *See also* FISHING, COMMERCIAL; KWAKWAKA'WAKW.

ATCHELITZ is a farming community (*see* AGRICULTURE) in the FRASER VALLEY, 6 km southwest of CHILLIWACK. The name is a HALKOMELEM word for "bottom," which perhaps derives from the way Atchelitz Crk skirts the base of Chilliwack Mt.

Atchelitz school dates from 1892. A nearby museum of antique agricultural equipment is open in the summer.   AS

ATHABASCA PASS (el 1,748 m) is in the ROCKY MTS on the BC–Alberta border in the remote southwest corner of Jasper National Park. The explorer David THOMPSON made the first recorded crossing in Jan 1811, guided by an Iroquois trapper, on his way to the COLUMBIA R and the Pacific for the NORTH WEST CO. He opened a FUR TRADE supply route into NEW CALE-DONIA, which was popular with Nor'westers until it was eclipsed by easier routes. As a result it has been called the "first trans-Canada highway" over the mountains. A small lake at the summit draining both east and west was named the Committee's Punch Bowl, in honour of the governors of the HBC, by George SIMPSON on his way over the pass in 1824. Today the pass is accessible only to hikers.

ATHABASCAN First Nations are aboriginal FIRST NATIONS that originally spoke tongues related within the Athabascan language family, sometimes spelled Athapaskan. These nations originally spoke 8 different related tongues, some with considerable regional dialectal variation. They all descended from a single, original "proto-Athabascan" community, the ancestors of peoples that occupied territories extending from Alaska, the Yukon and the Northwest Territories all the way to the Navajo and their relatives in the American Southwest. It is now accepted that TLINGIT relates distantly to these Athabascan groups. The Taku people came to be called Inland Tlingit (later Taku Tlingit) since they assimilated culturally to the Tlingit, who had risen in influence and power as a result of their early access to trade goods during the period of exploration and the FUR TRADE. The Athabascans in BC reflect Interior and subarctic cultural patterns. *See also* FIRST NATIONS LAN-GUAGES.   *Jay Powell*

ATHALMER is a community at the north end of Windermere Lk in the Columbia Valley, 130 km north of CRANBROOK. An early wagon road between GOLDEN and FORT STEELE forded the COLUMBIA R at this point, and a store, tavern and SAWMILL were built around 1900. Athalmer is now a suburb of INVERMERE. The name means "noble lake" in Anglo-Saxon; F.W. Aylmer, who laid out the townsite, chose it in homage to his own surname.   AS

ATHANS, George Demetrie, diving champion, (b 4 Jan 1921, Vancouver). He joined the front ranks of Canadian divers in 1936 when he won the Canadian championship and went to the Berlin Olympics at age 15. He was Canadian champion for 4 more years as well as western US and US Pacific coast intercollegiate champion while attending the Univ of Washington 1938–42 and earning a degree in medicine. At the 1938 British Empire Games he won bronze medals in the springboard and highboard competitions, and at the 1950 Games he won a gold

in the springboard and a silver in the tower contest. After retiring from competition, Athans turned to his medical practice and coaching and was largely responsible for the success of Ontario diver Irene MacDonald. He married Irene Hartzell, an important builder of SYNCHRONIZED SWIMMING in BC, and their son George ATHANS Jr became a world champion water-skier and joined his father in the BC SPORTS HALL OF FAME. Another son, Greg, was a 3-time Canadian water-ski champion and a world champion professional freestyle skier and a third son, Gary, was a Canadian alpine-ski champion and 5-time national water-ski champion.   SW

ATHANS, George Stanley, water-ski champion (b 6 July 1952, Kelowna). The son of champion diver George ATHANS, he was the Canadian senior water-skiing champion 1965–74 and the

George Athans Sr returning home from the British Empire Games in New Zealand, 1950. VPL 59391

world champion 1971–74. He was also a 2-time World Cup winner and the first foreigner to capture the US masters crown. He set and broke the world slalom record in 4 consecutive years, 1969–72. Athans was BC athlete of the year in 1971, Canadian amateur athlete of the year in 1972 and 1973, and is a member of the Order of Canada, the Canadian Sports Hall of Fame, the World Water Skiing Hall of Fame and the BC SPORTS HALL OF FAME. An excellent alpine skier, he declined an invitation to join Canada's national team in 1969. When a knee injury ended his career at 23 he became involved in television, doing sports commentary for CBC-TV and forming Athans Communications to produce watersports shows for TV. His book *Water Skiing* was published in 1975.   SW

ATKINSON, POINT, at the west end of W VAN-COUVER, guards the northern entrance to BUR-RARD INLET. The present LIGHTHOUSE, now automated and designated a National Historic Site, was erected in 1912, replacing the original wooden structure dating from 1875. It is surrounded by Lighthouse Park (75 ha) with spectacular views of VANCOUVER across the inlet. The point was named in 1792 by George VANCOUVER after Thomas Atkinson, a British naval officer. The mournful drone of the foghorn, nicknamed "Old Wahoo," was such a familiar part of the city soundscape that when it was silenced in 1996 the Coast Guard was accused of "cutting the vocal chords of Vancouver."

ATLIN, pop 499, lies on the eastern shore of Atlin Lk, at 735.5 km² (BC portion only) the largest natural lake in BC, in the remote mountainous northwestern Interior. The name derives from an aboriginal word meaning "big (or stormy) water." GOLD was discovered in the area in 1898, touching off what has been called BC's "last GOLD RUSH." Within a year the population in the area swelled to 6,000. Though the rush faded, MINING has been a principal activity ever

Llewellyn Glacier, Atlin, 1905. UBC BC49

since. The community was a terminus on the 375-km Telegraph Trail running north from TELEGRAPH CREEK on the STIKINE R. A small PADDLEWHEEL STEAMBOAT, the *Scotia*, worked the lake 1899–1918, succeeded by the propeller-driven *Tarahne* 1917–36. These boats served the scattered MINING camps and carried TOURISTS attracted by the wilderness scenery. There has been a highway connection to Whitehorse since 1949. The southern end of the lake is Atlin Provincial Park (2,327 km²), inaccessible by road (*see* PARKS, PROVINCIAL).
Reading: Christine Frances Dickinson and Diane Solie Smith, *Atlin: The Story of British Columbia's Last Gold Rush,* 1995.

ATNARKO RIVER, 100 km, originates in Charlotte Lk in the western CHILCOTIN and flows northwest through Lonesome Lk and TWEEDSMUIR PROVINCIAL PARK to its junction with the Talchako R and the beginning of the BELLA COOLA R. For most of its route it follows a steep-sided valley teeming with wildlife, including grizzly and black BEAR and MOUNTAIN GOAT. The river supports an active sport fishery (*see* FISHING, SPORT) as well as an aboriginal food fishery (*see* FISHING, ABORIGINAL). Atnarko is a DAKELH (Carrier) word meaning "river of strangers," a reference to the NUXALK (Bella Coola) from the coast. It has been designated a BC HERITAGE RIVER. *See also* RIVERS.

AUDITOR GENERAL is an independent officer of the legislature who monitors management of public money. The auditor general reports annually to the legislative assembly—not to the government or CABINET—on the government's financial statements, indicating whether the statements fairly present the province's financial position. The auditor general also monitors government compliance with legislation and assesses whether its programs are implemented efficiently and effectively. The Select Standing Committee on Public Accounts examines these reports in detail. *Russ Francis*

AUKLET is a small, dark grey seabird. Auklets nest in island colonies, in long burrows excavated in the soft ground; they feed out at sea by diving for fish and planktonic shrimp. Two species are present in BC. About 80% of all the world's Cassin's auklets (*Ptychoramphus aleuticus*) nest along the outer coast, about 1 million on TRIANGLE ISLAND alone. The rhinoceros auklet (*Cerorhinca monocerata*) is a larger bird, more like a PUFFIN. In breeding season it has a distinctive upright "horn" at the base of its yellow bill.

AUSTRALIAN, 27 km south of QUESNEL on the east side of the FRASER R, is a farming settlement and site of a former Pacific Great Eastern Rwy station (*see* BC RAIL). It is named after the Australian ranch and roadhouse, founded in the early 1860s by settlers who had worked earlier in the Australian gold rush. *AS*

AUTO RACING started in BC at the Langford Speedway northwest of VICTORIA on VANCOUVER

The Molson Indy, Vancouver.
Brian Gauvin photo

ISLAND, which opened in the early 1920s and claimed to be Canada's first paved track. Since 1954 the Western Speedway has operated a racing oval and drag strip at Langford. Billy Foster of Victoria, one of BC's first internationally successful drivers, developed his skills at the Western, which under the management of Reg Midgley was once considered one of the top short tracks on the west coast of N America. Foster raced in the NASCAR circuit in the mid-1960s and competed in the Indianapolis 500 race in 1965 and 1966. He died during a NASCAR race at Riverside, CA, on 29 Jan 1967. Victoria also produced Grant King, a mechanic who designed and built Indy cars for top American professional drivers from the early 1960s to 1984; he himself owned cars that finished 4th at the 1973 Indy and 3rd in 1974. Western Speedway driver Roy Smith qualified 3 times for the Daytona 500, finishing 10th in 1982, and he won the west coast's NASCAR Winston West points championship from 1980 to 1982. BC's most successful racer was Greg MOORE from MAPLE RIDGE, who was considered one of the most promising young drivers in the sport when he was killed during a race in 1999. The Sports Car Club of BC got Westwood Motorsport Park, a Euro-style race circuit, rolling in COQUITLAM in 1959 and operated it for 30 years until the land was sold to make way for a housing development and GOLF course. In 1990 IndyCar professional racing arrived in downtown VANCOUVER, on the streets surrounding BC PLACE STADIUM, and the race has become a familiar part of Labour Day weekend in the city. In 1994 the MISSION Raceway added a road track to its older drag strip and began running a regular schedule of formula, production and sports races. As well, there are a number of smaller raceways around BC.

AVALANCHES are sudden slides of snow common in BC's alpine areas. They consist either of loose snow rolling down a slope or slabs of snow that fracture and fall as a mass. (Avalanches of rock or soil are more properly called LANDSLIDES or rockslides.) When the snow is dry, avalanches move very quickly and may be accompanied by billowing powder clouds and strong ground winds. Dry snow avalanches have been clocked at speeds of up to 50 m per second. Wet snow avalanches are slower and more akin to mudslides.

Avalanche, Rocky Mts. Duane Sept photo

There are 200,000 significant avalanches a year in BC. While most occur away from travel routes and populated places, a few cause destruction and claim human lives. Between 1900 and 1979, 267 avalanche deaths were recorded, more than for any other natural hazard, and the number of fatalities is rising. During the 1990s about 10 people died in avalanches in BC annually. This danger was brought dramatically to public attention in Nov 1998 when Michel Trudeau, son of former Prime Minister Pierre Trudeau and Margaret (Trudeau) KEMPER, died in KOKANEE GLACIER PROVINCIAL PARK. Like the young Trudeau, who was backcountry skiing, most people who die in avalanches are caught while engaged in hiking, skiing, snowshoeing or snowmobiling. As the popularity of backcountry recreation grows, so will the number of avalanche fatalities. But the worst snow avalanche in BC occurred 4 Mar 1910 in ROGERS PASS, when 62 railway workers died (see DISASTERS).

The main economic impact of avalanches is felt when they close roads and rail lines. In its program of avalanche control the Ministry of Transportation and Highways uses explosives and special guns ("avalaunchers") to bring down potentially dangerous snow under controlled circumstances. As well, snowsheds are built over stretches of road and rail particularly prone to avalanche activity.

AVALON DAIRY LTD began in 1906 when Jeremiah Crowley and his wife Maud arrived from Newfoundland and bought a farm in S VANCOUVER. Jeremiah (1875–1950) worked as an iron moulder and Maud (1876–1956) ran the farm and its growing herd until 1913, when the Crowleys turned to DAIRY FARMING full-time. In 1931 the business lost all its cows to bovine tuberculosis; since then Avalon has bottled and delivered milk produced elsewhere. As Jeremiah and Maud grew older the dairy was managed by their sons, chiefly Everett (1909–84). In 2000, still owned by the family, Avalon was the oldest continuously operating dairy in BC.

AVIATION began in BC when the American aviator Charles Hamilton took off in a Curtiss biplane at the Minoru Park race track at RICHMOND on 25 Mar 1910. There had been earlier hot-air balloon flights, and a dirigible flew above NEW WESTMINSTER in 1909, but Hamilton's was the first heavier-than-air controlled flight. A few months later, on 8 Sept 1910, William Wallace GIBSON became the first person in Canada to design, build and fly his own aircraft when he took to the air at Mt Tolmie near VICTORIA and flew 61 m. Aviation was introduced to the Interior on Dominion Day 1912 when William Stark, a stunt pilot and the first licensed pilot in BC, made the inaugural flight at ARMSTRONG. Stark had already made history that April at Minoru when he and James Hewitt, a journalist, made a brief flight that marked the first time 2 people had flown in a single plane in western Canada. On the same occasion Stark took his wife Olive aloft, making her the first woman in

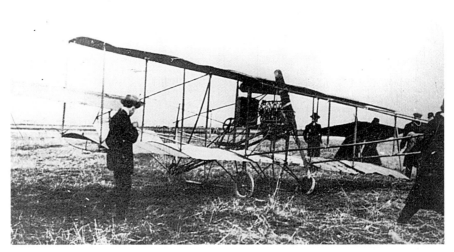

First airplane flight in BC, Lulu Island, 25 Mar 1910. *City of Richmond Archives*

Canada to fly as a passenger. All of these flights attracted crowds of people eager to get a first look at, and perhaps a short ride in, the new flying machines.

By 1914 the novelty was wearing off but the outbreak of war gave a great impetus to aviation. Canadians distinguished themselves as members of Britain's Royal Flying Corps and Royal Naval Air Service and airfields were opening in Ontario to train pilots for the front. In 1915 a group of Vancouver businessmen formed the Aero Club of BC; they funded a flying training school at Minoru Park and hired Stark as instructor. In 1917 the British War Office authorized the formation of the Royal Flying Corps, Canada, and several bases and aerodromes opened in Ontario. After the war, aviation began to be adapted for peacetime purposes. On 13 May 1919 two members of the Aerial League of Canada made the first flight from VANCOUVER to Victoria, followed 3 months later by the first flight across the ROCKY MTS—from Vancouver to Calgary in 16 1/2 hours—and then in Oct 1920 the first transcontinental flight from Halifax to Vancouver. The federal government created the Canadian Air Board in 1919 to regulate the growth of civil aviation. It established bases across the country, including a seaplane base at JERICHO BEACH in Vancouver that opened in

One of the Canso amphibians built in BC and used for coastal patrol during WWII. *RCAF photo/Courtesy Jack Schofield*

1920. The Jericho base pioneered bush flying in BC. By the 1920s private companies had become involved in flying. The pioneer airline in BC was Vancouver Island Aerial Service, founded by Harry BROWN in 1920 in Victoria; it folded in 1922 when its plane crashed. Meanwhile, in 1920, Eddie Hubbard, a Seattle pilot, began fly-

Carl Agar, a founder of Okanagan Helicopters Ltd (later Canadian Helicopters), on an early crop-spraying job, c 1950. *Courtesy Jack Schofield*

ing mail between Seattle and Victoria with a service that eventually led to the creation of United Air Lines. In 1925, Donald MACLAREN, a wartime flying ace who had settled in Vancouver, and Ernest Rogers of BC SUGAR founded Pacific Airways Ltd (PAL). PAL was headquartered at SWANSON BAY, where it flew fishery patrols. In

Boeing assembly plant, Coal Harbour, Vancouver, 1932.

The de Havilland Beaver, the workhorse of backcountry aviation, Clayoquot Sound, 1996.
Peter A. Robson photo

1928 it sold out to Western Canada Airways, which in turn was absorbed in 1930 by Canadian Airways Ltd, a new consortium of several regional airlines organized by James Richardson with additional funding from both national railways, CNR and CPR.

The first regular scheduled passenger service between Victoria, Vancouver and Seattle was initiated by BC Airways with a Ford Trimotor in 1928, but the operation was short-lived: the Trimotor crashed in fog off Port Townsend, WA, after 10 days of service. Canadian Airways initiated a scheduled service between Vancouver and Victoria in 1932. The first national airline, Trans Canada Airlines, was organized in 1937 and commenced service between Vancouver and eastern Canada on 2 Mar 1939. Trans Canada later became Air Canada. In 1942 Canadian Pacific Air Lines (later CP Air) was created out of Canadian Airways and several other companies as a subsidiary of CPR. It played a leading role in the construction of the ALASKA HWY and in 1947

moved headquarters to Vancouver, where it developed into a major international airline. In 1987 it was acquired by PACIFIC WESTERN and moved to Alberta. Meanwhile several smaller regional airlines appeared, including Dominion Airways (1927–32), CENTRAL BC AIRWAYS (1945–53), West Coast Air Services (1954–80) and QUEEN CHARLOTTE AIRLINES (1946–55), until one by one they either merged with their rivals or went out of business. In 1980 Air BC emerged as a dominant regional carrier after a merger of several smaller operations. Skyway Air Services was another important company. It began as a small flying club in 1945 and expanded into Canada's largest crop spraying and firebombing operation by the 1960s. Eventually it sold off much of its business to Conair Aviation and returned to being a Langley-based flying school. By the end of the 1990s Conair was operating a fleet of 50 fixed-wing aircraft and 40 helicopters, including land-based and water-scooping air tankers and bird-dog planes to guide tankers to their drop sites. Also in the 1990s several small airlines offered floatplane service to communities and camps along the coast. Chief among them was Inland

Air Charters, Nanaimo's Baxter Aviation Ltd, and Vancouver's Harbour Air Ltd, the largest all-seaplane scheduled airline in Canada. As well, Pacific Coastal Airlines, operated by the Smith family, has flown the BC coast for 40 years. With the 1998 acquisition of another coastal carrier, Wilderness Airlines, Pacific Coastal had a fleet of 23 planes providing regular service to a variety of regional terminals.

AVISON, John Henry Patrick, musician (b 25 Apr 1915, Vancouver; d 30 Nov 1983, Vancouver). He was a prodigy as a young pianist, and went on to study at UBC, the Univ of Washington and the Juilliard School. He was 23 years old in 1938, when Ira DILWORTH hired him to lead the newly formed CBC VANCOUVER ORCHESTRA, a position Avison held for the next 42 years until his retirement in 1980. He was named to the Order of Canada in 1978.

John Avison conducts the CBC Vancouver Orchestra. BC Entertainment Hall of Fame

AVOCET, American (*Recurvirostra americana*), is a large, long-necked shorebird with a thin, upturned bill and long, blue-grey legs for wading. It has a pale brown head and neck with black wings and white underparts. It feeds on insects and small aquatic animals by sweeping its bill scythe-like through the water and disturbing the bottom mud. This bird appeared infrequently until the 1960s, when it began to be seen in southern BC and the PEACE lowland; now it breeds regularly on alkaline lakes in the KELOWNA area.

AVOLA, pop 160, established in 1913 as a CANADIAN NORTHERN RWY station, is a picturesque log cabin community beside the N THOMPSON R on the Yellowhead Hwy (*see* ROADS AND HWYS), 185 km north of KAMLOOPS. It is a centre for the area's FOREST INDUSTRY, railway and farm workers. The original name, Stillwater Flats, was changed when it was discovered a STILLWATER post office already existed. The current name is after the town in Sicily. *AS*

Martin Mars water bomber, Sproat Lk.
Courtesy Graeme Wragg

B

BABCOCK, John Pease, public servant (b 1855, St Paul, MN; d 1936). As a young man he joined the California Fish and Game Commission, where he became an expert on SALMON. After moving to BC he became the province's first commissioner of fisheries in 1901 and began conducting surveys of salmon spawning grounds in the FRASER R watershed. It is said that he travelled the entire watershed on foot and horseback. His 1908 book, *The Game Fishes of British Columbia*, is a classic. He was a proponent of FISH HATCHERIES as a way to replenish salmon stocks. His concern for depleted sockeye runs contributed to the creation of the INTERNATIONAL PACIFIC SALMON FISHERIES CONVENTION in 1937, the year after his death.

BABINE BARRICADES were a network of fish traps and weirs used by DAKELH (Carrier) fishers near the north end of BABINE LK and in the Babine R, a tributary of the SKEENA R. The system produced large quantities of sockeye SALMON, which the Dakelh had utilized for centuries for their own consumption and for trade. As the commercial fishery expanded during the last quarter of the 19th century, salmon canners on the lower Skeena blamed declining runs on the barricades and persuaded the government to enforce regulations against them in 1904–05. The ban caused considerable hardship among the Dakelh. In 1906 they defied the government by rebuilding the barricades and refusing to take them down, even in the face of armed threats. A delegation of chiefs went to Ottawa to negotiate a solution to the standoff. Under the terms of the 1906 Barricades Agreement, the government promised to provide nets, to allow the Dakelh to sell surplus fish and to enlarge the local reserve in return for destruction of the barricades. *See also* ABORIGINAL RIGHTS; FISHING, ABORIGINAL; FISHING, COMMERCIAL; SALMON CANNING.

BABINE LAKE, 36 km north of BURNS LAKE in central BC, is the longest (177 km) and largest (495 km²) natural lake entirely in the province. It is part of the traditional territory of the Nat'oot'en people, a branch of the DAKELH (Carrier) First Nation. *Babine* is a French word for "large lip," a reference to the aboriginal practice of wearing labrets in the lower lip, though the Nat'oot'en call it Na-taw-bun-kut, "long lake." The Babine R, which drains northwest 100 km into the SKEENA, and other streams are important SALMON spawning RIVERS that the Nat'oot'en have fished for many generations. Traders reached the lake in 1812 and the HBC operated a post at the entrance to the lake's north arm for 50 years (1822–72), chiefly to provide salmon to the trade (*see* FUR TRADE, LAND-BASED). Subsequently the post, called FORT BABINE, relocated to the north end of the lake. A dispute over the so-called BABINE BARRICADES resulted in a 1906 agreement that severely hampered the aboriginal fishery. COPPER mining took place near GRANISLE on the west shore from the mid-1960s to 1992. There are two Nat'oot'en communities on the lake. The Babine R is a BC HERITAGE RIVER.

BABY DUCK is a sparkling, lower-alcohol wine launched in 1971 by Andre's Wines Ltd, then based in PORT MOODY. Cheaper than most wines of its type, it was for a time the best-selling domestic Canadian wine, though its sweet flavour earned the ridicule of connoisseurs.

BACHMAN, Talmage "Tal," singer, songwriter (b 13 Aug 1970, Winnipeg). Raised as a MORMON in WHITE ROCK, he was attending university in Utah when his father, Randy Bachman of the band BACHMAN-TURNER OVERDRIVE, encouraged him to drop out and start a music career in VANCOUVER. He teamed up with Bob Rock to produce his self-titled first album featuring the international hit "She's So High," one of North America's most frequently played radio tracks of 1999. After touring with fellow British Columbian Bryan ADAMS, he released his second hit single, "If You Sleep." In 2000 he earned Juno awards for best producer (with Rock) and for best new solo artist.   SW

BACHMAN-TURNER OVERDRIVE (BTO) is a hard-rock band that achieved international success in the 1970s with guitar-laden hits such as "Takin' Care of Business," "You Ain't Seen Nothing Yet" and "Roll On Down the Highway."

Bachman-Turner Overdrive (l to r): Robin Bachman, C.F. Turner, Randy Murray, Blair Thornton, 1998. Nic Sieflow photo

The band, originally named Brave Belt, was founded in Winnipeg by 2 alumni of the Guess Who, Randy Bachman (vocals and guitar) and Chad Allan (vocals and guitar), along with Randy's brother Robbie (drums) and Fred Turner (vocals and bass). When Allan left the band in 1972 to pursue a solo career he was replaced by a third Bachman brother, Tim. The band changed its name to Bachman-Turner Overdrive, moved to VANCOUVER, and after releasing 2 albums, captured the 1973 Juno Award for most promising group. Soon after, Vancouver's Blair Thornton replaced Tim Bachman on guitar. The band's third album, *Not Fragile*, released in 1974, sold millions of copies worldwide, reached number one on Canadian and American radio charts and won 3 Juno Awards. The band's success continued with the 1975 album *Four Wheel Drive*, but later albums were less successful. Randy's departure in 1977 led to a series of personnel changes. Over the years several incarnations of the band have toured using the BTO name, including a few occasions when Randy reunited with the group. In 1992 Randy Murray, a Vancouver guitarist, joined the BTO lineup. The band has continued to perform concerts worldwide. Its music also remains popular due to airplay on classic rock radio stations and the use of "Takin' Care of Business" as an advertising jingle for a large American office supply chain. *Mike Harling*

BADEN-POWELL TRAIL is a 48-km hiking TRAIL meandering across the lower slopes of the North Shore mountains opposite VANCOUVER, from HORSESHOE BAY to DEEP COVE. It was built in 1971 by Boy Scout and Girl Guide troops and is named for Lord Baden-Powell, the British founder of the Boy Scouts. It is easily accessible at a number of points along its length.

BADGER (*Taxidea taxus*), a member of the WEASEL (Mustelidae) family of mammals, is a medium-sized carnivore inhabiting the GRASS-LANDS and open woodlands of the southern Interior. Active mainly at night, it grows to about 80 cm in length and up to 13 kg in weight. The badger has short, powerful legs and large, clawed feet, which it uses to dig burrows for hibernating and raising young, and to capture its prey, which includes ground SQUIRRELS, mice, and INSECTS. Its burrows were important nest sites for the bur-

The badger, found in the southern Interior of BC. Mike Steele photo

rowing OWL, but this bird is no longer found nesting naturally in BC, due in large part to agricultural activity, which has put the badger itself at risk of extirpation. Badgers are Red-listed by the Conservation Data Centre (*see* ENDANGERED SPECIES).

BADMINTON was first played in Canada in the late 1890s by military personnel at the Imperial Opera House in VANCOUVER. In 1900 play commenced at the Beatty Street Drill Hall, which served as the city's main badminton club until 1928. Once VICTORIA became a competitive badminton centre as well, the two cities began holding matches, the first one taking place on 2 Dec 1913. In 1920 the Vancouver club joined the Canadian Badminton Assoc and two BC men, McTaggart Cowan and G.H. Gorges, dominated the Dominion Championships in Ottawa. In Feb 1925 the BC Badminton Assoc was formed, with clubs in towns such as ALERT BAY, ANYOX, KELOWNA, DUNCAN, KAMLOOPS and NELSON.

Badminton champions Brent Olynyk (l) and Darryl Yung. Jeff Vinnick/Vancouver Sun

Cowan and the husband-wife tandem of Jack and Eileen (George) Underhill dominated BC's early provincial tournaments and all won national singles and doubles championships as well. The Underhills were the first husband-and-wife team inducted to the BC SPORTS HALL OF FAME (1970). Other British Columbians to succeed at the national level included singles champions Anna Kier, Margaret Taylor, Lois Reid, Claire Lovett (twice) and 3-time winners Dick Birch and Johnny Samis. Through the 1940s and '50s, Daryl Thompson and Jean Bardsley each won 7 Canadian titles in singles, doubles and mixed competition. Bardsley was a member of one of Vancouver's foremost sporting families with husband Jim (see BASKETBALL) and TENNIS-playing sons Tony and Bob. Future GREENPEACE International president David MCTAGGART won 3 consecutive national singles titles 1956–58. The

BC player of the 1960s was undoubtedly Wayne Macdonnell, the winner of the Canadian singles title a record 6 times. In 1966 he shared a US mixed-doubles title. Rolf Paterson established himself as Canada's best doubles player of the day by collecting 7 doubles (some with his brother Eddy) and mixed titles between 1964 and 1974. In the mid-60s, two best friends from Victoria, Alison Daysmith and Judy (Humber) Rollick, hit the national scene with Daysmith winning 3 Canadian singles titles and the 1975 North American women's singles championship and Rollick capturing singles, doubles and mixed national crowns. Her husband Bruce Rollick took Macdonnell's place as BC's top men's player by capturing 5 Canadian singles titles and an Open Canadian championship. He also won mixed national titles with Judy and another partner, Mimi Nilsson, who went on to win over 30 Canadian titles in various Masters and Seniors competitions.

Badminton entered the Commonwealth Games in 1964 and Vancouver's Sharon Whittaker won BC's first badminton medal with a silver in singles. Claire Backhouse-Sharpe made a name for herself internationally by winning one gold medal (women's doubles) and 5 silvers in a Canadian record 5 Commonwealth Games over the late 1970s and 1980s. She also played for Canada in 5 World Championships and collected 11 various national titles. During the same period, Jane Youngberg won 10 national titles and added a Commonwealth doubles silver and 2 team silvers. As a doubles team, she and Sharpe were semi-finalists in the 1978 All England tournament (world championships). Sandra Skillings, a national doubles champion, joined Sharpe and Youngberg on the 1982 Commonwealth silver-medal Canadian women's team. At the 1994 Commonwealth Games in Victoria, Vancouver's Sian Deng won a silver in singles. She also won 8 various national titles and competed in the Olympics in 1996, only the second time the event was held. Other early BC Olympians were team manager Bert Fergus (1992) and national doubles and mixed champions Anil Kaul (1992, 1996) and Darryl Yung (1996). In Pan Am Games competition, W Vancouver's Brent Olynyk combined with 2 Ontario partners to win men's doubles gold and mixed silver in 1999. *SW*

BAHA'I FAITH began in Persia (Iran) in 1844 when a young merchant known as the Bab ("the Gate") proclaimed his own prophetic mission and predicted the coming of another divine prophet. Although the Bab was executed as a heretic, his message spread throughout Persia and Iraq. In 1863 a Persian noble known as Baha'u'llah ("Glory of God") revealed that he was the Promised One foretold by the Bab, then spent the rest of his life a prisoner of the Turks for teaching his faith. Baha'i belief centres on the idea of oneness: oneness of God, oneness of religion, oneness of humankind. Principles include equality between men and women, eliminating extremes of poverty and wealth, and establishing universal education.

The Baha'i Faith took root in BC when Marian Jack, from New Brunswick, successfully promoted the religion in VANCOUVER. Jack brought prominent Baha'i scholar Jenabi Fadil to the city in 1921, and by 1927 Vancouver had more than enough Baha'is to establish the first Spiritual Assembly in BC. Vancouver Baha'is then launched radio programs and organized youth groups to spread their ideas. Soon after WWII, Baha'i communities were established in VERNON, VICTORIA and W VANCOUVER, and in 1948 BC Baha'is took part in elections for the first National Spiritual Assembly of the Baha'is of Canada. By the 1990s Baha'is in about 100 BC localities annually elected Spiritual Assemblies, and immigration had brought Baha'is from Iran to BC after the Islamic Revolution of 1979 renewed suppression of religious freedoms there. Since the mid-1990s members of the BC Baha'i Spiritual Assemblies have participated in annual elections for the BC/Yukon Baha'i Council, which coordinates the teaching and administrative work of the Faith here. In 2000 there were close to 4,000 Baha'is in BC.

Dianne Mackay

BAILEY, Byron, football player (b 12 Oct 1930, Omaha, NE; d 18 Jan 1998, Winfield). After graduating from Washington State Univ he began his FOOTBALL career as a professional in 1952 at fullback with the NFL Detroit Lions. The Lions won the league championship but he was traded to Green Bay for the next season. He came to Canada to join the BC LIONS for their inaugural season in 1954. Bailey scored the Lions' first touchdown in their first game. Six games later he scored the only touchdown in the franchise's first win. He played both fullback and defensive back until he retired after the team won its first Grey Cup in 1964. After football he had a management career with CROWN ZELLERBACH. He is a member of the BC SPORTS HALL OF FAME and the CFL Hall of Fame.

By Bailey, one of the original BC Lions. BCSHF

BAILEY, Nathaniel Ryal "Nat," restaurateur (b 31 Jan 1902, St Paul, MN; d 27 Mar 1978, Vancouver). His mother was a cook in railway eating houses; his father worked in carnivals. In 1911 the Baileys moved to VANCOUVER from Seattle. By age 12 Nat was selling newspapers on city streets. Later he sold peanuts, and at age 18 he moved his peanut stand to Athletic Park and added hot dogs and beverages. In his early 20s

Nat Bailey, founder of White Spot Restaurant.
Courtesy White Spot

he made a name for himself as "Caruso Nat" announcing local ball games. When laryngitis struck, he turned his 1918 Ford Model T truck into a travelling kitchen, serving Sunday drivers at Lookout Point on SW Marine Drive. It was a shout from a customer—"Why don't you bring it to us?"—that inspired him to open his first drive-in, in 1928, on Granville Street at 67th Avenue in Marpole. In 1930 he was joined by his second wife Eva (Ouellette), who helped him run the business until the early 1960s. Known for its hamburgers with Triple-O (triple oozy) sauce, WHITE SPOT's 13 outlets and related business interests were sold to General Foods in 1968 for $6.5 million. Bailey then dedicated himself to his real love, supporting local BASEBALL; Nat Bailey Stadium, long home to Vancouver's minor professional baseball franchise, is named after him.

BAILLIE-GROHMAN, William Adolphe, sportsman, land developer (b 1 Apr 1851, London, England; d 27 Nov 1921, Austria). Raised in Austria and Ireland by well-to-do parents, he became a big game hunter, mountain climber and world traveller. He came to BC in 1882 on a hunting expedition and later embarked on a scheme to reclaim the flatlands at the south end of KOOTENAY LK for agriculture. Backed by British capital, he planned to build a canal to divert the upper KOOTENAY R into the COLUMBIA R. In 1884 he became the first person

to launch a steamboat on the lower Kootenay navigation system. His schemes were unsuccessful and he returned to Europe in 1893. He spent WWI in England but returned to Austria in 1919; at his death he was engaged in post-war relief efforts there. Baillie-Grohman's failed reclamation effort on the Kootenay Flats was taken over by the Alberta & BC Exploration Co under the management of George Alexander.

BAIRD, Irene, writer (b 1901, Cumberland, England; d 1981). She came to VANCOUVER with her parents in 1919 and worked for many years as a newspaper journalist there. Her first novel, *John,* appeared in 1937. It was followed by her best-known work, *Waste Heritage* (1939), a novel about political protest in Depression-era Vancouver. In 1942 she moved east to join the federal public service, where she worked until retirement. During the the same time she published 2 more novels, *He Rides the Sky* (1941) and *Climate of Power* (1971).

BAKER was a ranching (*see* CATTLE INDUSTRY) and SAWMILLING settlement and a CPR station in the E KOOTENAY, 15 km east of CRANBROOK. Gypsum was quarried nearby. Formerly known as Mayook after a prominent local KTUNAXA (Kutenai) family, the name was changed in 1905 to honour Colonel James BAKER, a local landowner and politician.

BAKER, Francis Russell, aviation pioneer (b 31 Jan 1910, Winnipeg, MB; d 15 Nov 1958, Vancouver). He quit school after grade 8 and learned to fly while still a teenager, though he did not become a full-time pilot until the mid-1930s after he moved to BC. In 1938 he joined Canadian Airways, based at PRINCE GEORGE, flying people and supplies to Interior communities and MINING camps. Baker continued with the company, which became Canadian Pacific Air Lines in 1942, until 1945; then he and Walter GILBERT founded CENTRAL BC AIRWAYS. Two years later he became the most famous bush pilot in Canada after Pierre BERTON wrote a series of articles for the VANCOUVER SUN about their trip into the S Nahanni R, the "Headless Valley" of legend. Baker oversaw the expansion of CBCA into PACIFIC WESTERN AIRLINES, which at his death was one of the leading airlines in Canada.

BAKER, James A., founder of Cranbrook (b 6 Jan 1830, London, England; d 31 July 1906, Inglewood, England). A graduate of Cambridge Univ and a retired lieutenant colonel from the British army, he emigrated to BC with his family in 1884, settling first at SKOOKUMCHUCK on the KOOTENAY R. In 1886 he bought land at Joseph's Prairie and named the site Cranbrook Farm after a town in England. He developed a ranch and a trading post and promoted railway and COAL developments in the CROWSNEST PASS area. Elected MLA for KOOTENAY in 1886, Baker held his seat for 14 years while he developed his business interests and the CRANBROOK townsite. He retired from the legislature and returned to live in England in 1900.

BAKER, Michael Conway, composer (b 13 Mar 1937, West Palm Beach, FL). The son of an American vaudeville comedian, he had an itinerant childhood in the US and Canada. He taught himself the basics of musical theory, then studied at the London College of Music, UBC and Western Washington State College. He has lived in VANCOUVER, his mother's hometown, since 1958, and he is a prolific composer. He has written symphonic works, film scores, ballets, chamber music and songs. He also teaches and writes music for young people. Baker wrote the fanfare for EXPO 86 and his "Piano Concerto (Op. 38)" won a 1992 Juno Award. He was awarded the ORDER OF BC in 1997.

BAKER, MOUNT (el 3,285 m) is a familiar sight from much of the Lower Mainland on clear days. Its snow-covered sides shimmer in the sunshine to the southeast of VANCOUVER just

Mount Baker, as seen from Mt McGuire, just across the border in BC. Len Mackave photo

across the Canada–US border in Washington state. It is the most northerly and isolated of 11 volcanoes in the CASCADE MTS that have erupted in the past 250 years. After Mt Rainier it is the most heavily glaciated peak in the range (*see also* GLACIATION). At about 30,000 years old Baker is still a young volcano; it erupted several times between 1820 and 1870 and is thermally very active. In 1975–76, increased heat emissions at the crater caused melting, steam jets and fumaroles (crevices through which hot vapour is vented). *AS*

BAKER, Norman, basketball player (b 17 Feb 1923, Victoria; d 23 Apr 1989). He developed his skills in NANAIMO before winning the Canadian BASKETBALL championship with the VICTORIA Dominoes in 1939 when he was only 16. He led the Dominoes to 2 more Canadian championships in 1942 and 1946, and in 1943 he won the championship with the Patricia Bay RCAF club, scoring a record 38 points in one

game of the series. He turned professional in 1946 with the Chicago Stags and later was a standout player for the New York Celtics, Boston Whirlwinds and VANCOUVER Hornets. In 1950 he toured Europe as the only non-American on a team billed as the Stars of the World. He was voted the greatest basketball player in Canada in the first half of the 20th century by the Canadian Press news agency, and Abe Saperstein, famed as manager of the Stars as well as the Harlem Globetrotters, called him "one of the greatest natural basketball players I have ever seen." An all-around athlete, Baker was a member of the NEW WESTMINSTER Adanacs LACROSSE team that won the Mann Cup in 1947. In retirement he worked as a police officer and coached basketball and lacrosse in SAANICH. He was inducted into the BC SPORTS HALL OF FAME in 1966 and the Canadian Basketball Hall of Fame in 1979. *SW*

BAKER, Simon, Squamish leader (b Jan 1911, N Vancouver). The grandson of Joe CAPILANO, he grew up on the Capilano Reserve in N VANCOU-

Simon Baker, an elder of the Squamish Nation. Gary Fiegehen photo

VER. After attending St George's RESIDENTIAL SCHOOL at LYTTON from 1918 to 1926, he worked as a fisher, then as a stevedore on the VANCOUVER waterfront from 1935 to 1976. At the same time, he was a leading member of the SQUAMISH Band Council and an ambassador for aboriginal culture in Canada and abroad. In 1990 he received an honorary Doctorate of Laws from UBC, where he was an Elder at the First Nations House of Learning. He published his autobiography *Khot-La-Cha* ("Man With a Kind Heart") in 1994 and was named to the Order of Canada in 1997.

BALCOM, George Washington Sprott, seal and whale hunter (b 19 Sept 1851, Sheet Harbour, NS; d 21 Dec 1925, Victoria). Descended from a New England sea-going family, he entered the sealing trade, making voyages into the S Atlantic. In 1892 he rounded Cape Horn and eventually arrived in VICTORIA, where he settled and continued his involvement in sealing (*see* FUR SEAL). On one expedition into the N Atlantic he was taken prisoner by the Russians and escaped by boat to Japan, an incident that formed the basis of Rudyard Kipling's story "The Devil and the Deep Sea." (Balcom and Kipling met when the author visited Victoria.) On a visit to Newfoundland, Balcom learned about the modern WHALING industry and in 1905 created Pacific Whaling Co. It began operations at SECHART in BARKLEY SOUND and later built other stations near NANAIMO (1907), at Kyuquot (1906) (*see* KYUQUOT SOUND) and on the QUEEN CHARLOTTE ISLANDS (1910–11). In 1913 Balcom retired in Victoria, where he invested in steamships and real estate.

BALCOMO was a fruit-growing settlement in the OKANAGAN VALLEY, 15 km northwest of PENTICTON, and a flag station on the KETTLE VALLEY RWY. The first homesteader was R.H. Agur in 1904. The area is now known as Prairie Valley and is part of SUMMERLAND. *AS*

BALDONNEL is an AGRICULTURAL settlement, service centre and BC RAIL stop on Hwy 97, 10 km east of FORT ST JOHN near the AIRPORT. An experimental farm here demonstrated that alfalfa could be grown successfully as a fodder crop in the PEACE R region. Baldonnel was named in 1923 by J.W. Abbott, an early settler and justice of the peace, after his home in Ireland. *AS*

BALDRY, "Long" John (b 12 Jan 1941, Bakewell, England). A legendary figure in the development of British pop music, he served as mentor to some of rock'n'roll's biggest stars before moving in the early 1980s to VANCOUVER, where he continued his music career. As a blues bandleader in the 1960s Baldry was responsible for recruiting Rod Stewart and Reginald Dwight, a pianist who later adopted Baldry's and another bandmate's names to become Elton John. Baldry is best known in Canada for the songs "Don't Try To Lay No Boogie Woogie on the King of Rock and Roll," "You've Lost That Lovin' Feelin'" and "A Thrill Is a Thrill." He played popular live shows in Vancouver while continuing to record and tour N America and Europe. In 1997 Baldry received a Grammy nomination for his spoken-word recording of A.A. Milne's *Winnie the Pooh*, and his voice can be heard regularly on commercials and animated television series.

BALDY HUGHES, 35 km south of PRINCE GEORGE, was the site of a Canadian Forces long-range radar facility from 1955 to 1988, part of the Pinetree Line. The base was named after Mt Baldy Hughes, which was earlier named after Baldy Hughes himself, a former CARIBOO WAGON ROAD stage driver, who operated a remount station at the base of the mountain for many years.

AS

BALFOUR, pop 524, overlooks the entrance to the west arm of KOOTENAY LK 34 km east of NELSON. Founded in 1889 and named for British Prime Minister Arthur James Balfour, it was a port for steamboats on the lake. In 1911 the CPR opened a 50-room resort hotel here, and during WWI the hotel was used as a veterans' hospital; it closed in 1920. Today Balfour is a small resort community and terminal for the car ferry across the lake to KOOTENAY BAY.

BALKIND, Alvin, art curator, writer (b 28 Mar 1921, Baltimore, MD; d 21 Dec 1992, Vancouver). Educated at Johns Hopkins Univ and the Sorbonne, he served in the US navy during WWII. After moving to VANCOUVER in 1955, he and Abraham Rogatnick opened the New Design Gallery, which became a centre of contemporary art. Balkind was a co-founder of the Arts Club of Vancouver, which evolved into the present ARTS CLUB THEATRE. In 1962 he became curator of the Fine Arts Gallery at UBC, where he was appointed associate professor. His innovative program of exhibitions, plus his course in "creative curatorship," helped to launch the careers of several Canadian artists and curators. In 1973 he moved to Toronto as curator of contemporary art at the Art Gallery of Ontario. After returning west in 1975 he became chief curator of the VANCOUVER ART GALLERY. He remained there until 1978, when he resigned to become a freelance curator and writer. Head of the Visual Arts Studio at the Banff Centre in 1985–87, he was awarded an honorary diploma from the EMILY CARR INSTITUTE OF ART & DESIGN in 1991 and in 1992 received the first $50,000 VANCOUVER INSTITUTE FOR VISUAL ARTS award for his contribution to the arts in BC.

BALLARD POWER SYSTEMS INC is a Burnaby-based manufacturer of non-polluting fuel-cell technology. Fuel cells convert hydrogen fuel into electricity for powering vehicles without the polluting emissions of internal combustion engines. Ballard, the world leader in the development of this technology, was co-founded by Geoffrey Ballard, Keith Prater and Paul Howard in N VANCOUVER in 1979. In 1997 both the Ford Motor Co and Daimler-Benz AG, the German car manufacturer, bought into the company.

THE BALLARD FUEL CELL

PEM (Proton Exchange Membrane)
Oxidant flow field plate
Exhaust water vapour
Heat (90 c) water cooled
Single Ballard fuel cell
Fuel flow field plate
Fuel to recirculate
Air
Fuel (Hydrogen)

Detail of a Ballard© fuel cell showing the flow field plates, which supply the bodies of fuel and air to either side of the proton exchange membrane. Stacking together more cells increases the voltage produced; increasing the surface area increases the current produced.
Drawing by Kim LaFave

Ballard reported 1999 revenues of $33.1 million. Fuel cells have been used in bus, car and minivan prototypes, and mass manufacturing is expected to make the technology cost-competitive for the consumer market.

BALLET BC is a VANCOUVER ballet company formed originally as Pacific Ballet Theatre by

Ballet BC dancers Isabelle Itri and Sylvain Senez perform "There, Below." David Cooper/Ballet BC

Maria Lewis in 1969. In 1985 the company reorganized and changed its name to Ballet BC. It tours provincially, across Canada and internationally as well as presenting visiting companies to the Vancouver audience. The company's dancers perform a mixture of modern and classical ballets. Artistic directors have been Annette av Paul (1985–87), Reid Anderson (1987–89), Patricia Neary (1989–90) and Barry Ingham (1990–92). In Apr 1992 John Alleyne, former first soloist and resident choreographer with the National Ballet of Canada, took over as artistic director. *See also* DANCE.

BALSAM; *see* FIR.

BALTZLY, Benjamin F., photographer (b 5 Apr 1835, Tuscarawas City, OH; d 10 July 1883, Cambridge, MA). Already trained as a photographer when he moved to Montreal in 1866–67, he joined the firm of William Notman and came to BC in 1871 as part of a Geological Survey of Canada expedition to gather information about possible routes for the planned transcontinental railway. During several months in the province he travelled by boat and pack animal up the FRASER and N THOMPSON rivers almost to the YELLOWHEAD PASS, taking photographs along the way. Later he returned to the US, where he spent the rest of his life.

BAMBERTON overlooks the west side of SAANICH INLET 37 km north of VICTORIA, just off the Malahat Hwy (*see* MALAHAT DRIVE). In 1912 the BC Cement Co opened a cement plant at the site, an expansion of its original plant across at TOD INLET. (BUTCHART GARDENS later developed at the original quarry site.) The Bamberton facility closed during WWI but reopened in 1921 and at its peak employed 180 workers. After many years of production the cement plant closed, and by the 1980s the community that had grown up around it was abandoned. During the 1990s plans to develop the property as a residential complex for up to 12,000 people met with vocal opposition and were shelved.

BAMFIELD, pop 516, is a village on BARKLEY SOUND on the west coast of VANCOUVER ISLAND. It was originally a NUU-CHAH-NULTH (Nootka) settlement. Its name is a corruption of "Banfield," after William Eddy BANFIELD, a trader and Indian agent who came to live here in 1859. In 1902 it became the terminus for the trans-Pacific underwater telegraph cable, part of a circumglobal communications network known as the All-Red Route linking countries of the British Commonwealth. The cable station, designed by Francis RATTENBURY, operated until 1959, when it was bypassed by a line directly to PORT ALBERNI. Surviving station buildings now house a marine sciences facility. In 1963 a road connected the village with the outside world for the first time.

BANANA, Anna (Frankham), conceptual artist (b 1940, Victoria). She first used her *nom d'art* in 1972 when she appointed herself VICTORIA's town fool. In VANCOUVER she was active in the performance art scene and undertook various publishing and mail art projects throughout the 1970s and 1980s; in 1986 she changed her name legally. The co-founder of *Vile Magazine*, she has held Banana Olympics in San Francisco and Vancouver as well as staging performances at the WESTERN FRONT and elsewhere. She moved

Village of Bamfield, 1910. Leonard Frank/VPL 9246

to ROBERTS CREEK in 1995 and continued work on her magnum opus, the *Encyclopedia Bananica*.

BANCROFT, Hubert Howe, bookseller, historian (b 1832, Granville, OH; d 1918, San Francisco, CA). He began selling books for his brother-in-law in Buffalo, NY, and remained in the business for the rest of his life. In 1856 he moved to San Francisco, where he ran a bookshop and a printing and publishing company. After amassing a large collection of books on the American West, he embarked on his own prodigious history of the area, including Central America and BC. With the aid of assistants who did research and much of the writing, he produced a set of 39 volumes during 1874–90. Three volumes are among the first histories of BC: *History of the Northwest Coast I, 1543–1800* (1884), *History of the Northwest Coast II, 1800–1846* (1884) and *History of British Columbia, 1792–1887* (1887). The books are no longer widely read by the public, but remain a useful reference work for other historians. Bancroft sold his library and archives in 1906 to the Univ of California; the collection remains an important repository of western Americana and of important sources for the early history of BC.

BANFIELD, William Eddy, trader and Indian agent (date and place of birth unknown; d 20 Oct 1862, Barkley Sound). He arrived in VICTORIA in 1846 as a carpenter on a British naval vessel. After leaving the navy in 1849, he began trading from a boat along the west coast of VANCOUVER ISLAND. In 1861 Gov James DOUGLAS appointed him an Indian agent based in BARKLEY SOUND near the site of what would be BAMFIELD, making him the first settler in the sound. He explored the sound and nearby ALBERNI INLET, got to know the local FIRST NATIONS people well and encouraged economic activity on the coast. Apparently he drowned in a canoeing accident; suspicions that he was murdered were never proved.

BANK OF BC was created in 1862 by a group of financiers in London, England. With headquarters in VICTORIA, the bank opened branches throughout BC and in San Francisco, Portland, Seattle and Tacoma. In 1886 the bank moved into a new, 3-storey brick building at the corner of Government and Fort streets in Victoria. Considered the finest bank building in BC, it is now a heritage site. At the same time it opened a branch in VANCOUVER, the city's first formal bank. The Bank of BC merged with the Canadian Bank of Commerce in 1901. A new Bank of BC, with headquarters in Vancouver, was chartered in 1966. By 1986, when it was purchased by the HONGKONG BANK OF CANADA (now HSBC Bank Canada), it had 1,410 employees and assets of $2.7 billion.

BANKEIR is a tiny settlement 35 km northeast of PRINCETON on Hayes Crk and the KETTLE VALLEY RWY. A post office operated here from 1934 to 1963. A store and guest house cater to fishers and a growing number of hikers and bikers exploring the route of the disused railway. AS

BANKS, Charles Arthur, mining entrepreneur, lt gov 1946–50 (b 18 May 1885, Thames, New Zealand; d 28 Sept 1961, Vancouver). Trained in mine management, he worked for various MINING companies around the world before settling in BC in 1912 with his French-born wife, Jean. During WWI both he and his wife served overseas. After returning to VANCOUVER he became manager of the British Columbia Silver Mines Ltd. In 1925 he co-founded the Placer Development Co, which had mining properties in several countries. His wife was also a prospector and explorer and a Fellow of the Royal Geographical Society. Gold mines in New Guinea and Colombia made the couple extremely wealthy and they moved between homes in Vancouver, London and San Francisco. During WWII, as a representative of the federal government in London, he was responsible for the shipment of military supplies between England and Canada. Partly as a reward for his war service he was appointed LT GOV on 1 Oct 1946. Banks was not an enthusiastic lt gov. He

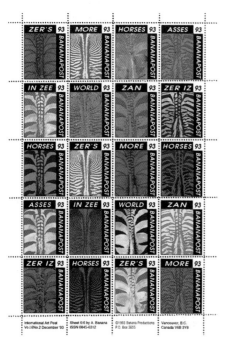

A sheet of Anna Banana's "BananaPost" stamps

did not enjoy pomp and ceremony, and he remained active in his own business affairs and did as little as the job allowed. As a result he was not popular with the public. In the summer of 1950 he resigned from the post, a year early. He and his wife continued to live in VICTORIA until he retired from his company in 1959 when the couple moved to W VANCOUVER.

BANKS ISLAND, 855 km², BC's sixth-largest ISLAND, is located on the east side of HECATE STRAIT opposite the QUEEN CHARLOTTE ISLANDS, 80 km south of PRINCE RUPERT. Separated by Principe Channel from PITT and McCauley islands, it is exposed and uninhabited and lies in the traditional territory of the KITKATLA First Nation, whose village is just north on Dolphin Island. It was named after the British naturalist Sir Joseph Banks (1743–1820), who accompanied Capt James COOK on his first voyage to the S Pacific. *AS*

BANTOCK, Nick, writer, artist (b 14 July 1949, Stourbridge, England). Raised in London, he attended the Art College of Maidstone in Kent. He immigrated with his wife and family to BC in 1987 and settled on BOWEN ISLAND, where he began designing and writing elaborate pop-up books and teaching at the EMILY CARR INSTITUTE. In 1991 he achieved international success with the appearance of his epistolary art-novel *Griffin and Sabine*. The second volume of what turned out to be a trilogy, *Sabine's Notebook* (1992), won a BC BOOK PRIZE and the third volume, *The Golden Mean*, appeared in 1993. All 3 books feature interactive elements and an unusual combination of text and illustrations. The trilogy has sold about 3 million copies altogether. Bantock's other books include *The Venetian's Wife* (1996) and *The Forgetting Room* (1997), as well as several books for young readers. Along with author and illustrator Barbara Hodgson, he operates Byzantium, a book-packaging company in VANCOUVER. *Shannon Emmerson*

BARBEAU, Marius, anthropologist (b 5 Mar 1883, Ste-Marie-de-Beauce, QC; d 27 Feb 1969, Ottawa). He was the first native-born anthropologist to work in the field in Canada. After studying law at Laval Univ he won a Rhodes scholarship to Oxford, where he became interested in anthropology. On his return to Canada in 1910 he got a job as an ethnologist in the anthropology division of the Geological Survey of Canada, later the National Museum of Man and still later the Canadian Museum of Civilization. During his career he pursued 3 distinct areas of research: Quebec folklore, Huron culture and the FIRST NATIONS of the Pacific Coast, particularly the TSIMSHIAN. He made his first field trip to BC in 1914. During the 1920s he made several more trips to the SKEENA and NASS R areas, relying on the assistance of William BEYNON as his interpreter and field researcher. Barbeau was involved in a project to preserve and restore TOTEM POLES in the Skeena villages. His 2-volume study of totems helped to make the monuments known to the outside world. In it he theorized that First

Nations people did not start carving poles until after contact, a theory that was later disproved. Barbeau also wrote widely for the general public; his 1928 novel *The Downfall of Temlaham* deals with the people of the Skeena. He retired from the museum in 1948, though he continued to study and publish until his death. He was one of the first Companions of the Order of Canada, when it was created in 1967.

BARKER, William "Billy," prospector (b June 1817, March, England; d 11 July 1894, Victoria). As a young man he worked as a boatman on the canals of Norfolk, England. With the arrival of railways in the 1840s, prospects for canal workers diminished and he emigrated to the US, leaving his wife and daughter destitute. He sought his fortune in the goldfields of California, then came to BC in 1858 when the GOLD RUSH began. By 1861 he was in the CARIBOO, prospecting

along Williams Crk. In the summer of 1862 he and his partners struck pay dirt and he became very rich. He spent that winter in VICTORIA and married for a second time, then returned to the Cariboo with his wife and continued prospecting. By this time a town, BARKERVILLE, was springing up in the area of his big strike. He soon went through his fortune and spent the rest of his life in the bush, unsuccessfully attempting to repeat his success. He died a virtual pauper in the Old Men's Home in Victoria.

BARKERVILLE HISTORIC TOWN is a heritage site in the CARIBOO MTS 88 km east of QUESNEL. Founded in 1862 after a prospector named Billy BARKER struck GOLD below the canyon on Williams Crk, it quickly grew into the largest community in BC, with a floating population that peaked at about 5,000. In Sept 1868 it was largely destroyed by fire. Rebuilt, it settled into its

Top: Cariboo gold escort at Barkerville, 1863. UBC BC400
Bottom: Miners at the Mucho Oro gold mine near Barkerville, 1868. Frederick Dally/UBC BC389

Government Assay Office and Hotel de France, Barkerville, 1860s. *Frederick Dally/UBC BC59*

role as a supply centre to the mines of the Cariboo. The Barkerville area boomed 3 times: 1862–72, 1898–1910 and 1932–42. Declared a heritage site in 1958, the 100 original and 20 reconstructed buildings house over 110 display rooms celebrating BC HISTORY and it has become one of the province's most popular visitor destinations.

BARKLEY, Charles William, sea captain, trader (b 1759; d 16 May 1832, Hertford, England), and **Frances Hornby (Trevor)** (b 1769; d 1845). He arrived at NOOTKA SOUND in June 1787 in command of the *Imperial Eagle* on a trading voyage. With him was his 18-year-old wife Frances, whom he had married the previous autumn. Frances was the first white woman known to have seen the coast of BC. Barkley traded widely with the aboriginals on the west coast of VANCOUVER ISLAND and during a visit named BARKLEY SOUND after himself. He sold his furs in China; in 1792 he paid a return visit to the coast as commander of his own small trading brig, the *Halcyon*, again in company with his wife. Little is known about his later years. Frances's reminiscences were published in 1978 as *The Remarkable World of Frances Barkley: 1769–1845*, edited by Beth Hill.

BARKLEY SOUND is a maze of ISLANDS, bays and inlets on the west coast of VANCOUVER ISLAND just south of LONG BEACH. About 24 km wide, it is broken into 3 channels by 2 major island groups—the BROKEN GROUP and the Deer Islands. The Broken Group are part of PACIFIC RIM NATIONAL PARK. Six narrow inlets—ALBERNI, Effingham, Pipestem, UCLUELET, Uchucklesit and Useless—radiate from the sound. It is the rainiest spot in Canada: in 1997 HENDERSON LK at the head of the sound received a record 8,997.1 mm of precipitation. The sound supports a wide variety of bird species and is one of the major bald EAGLE habitats on the coast. Five NUU-CHAH-NULTH (Nootka) nations claim territory in the sound—the Toquaht, Sheshaht, Ucluelet, Ohiaht and Uchucklesaht—though at contact many more separate groups lived here, subsist-

ing on the abundant marine resources. There are 23 RESERVES in the sound. Named by the British sea captain Charles William BARKLEY after his visit to trade for SEA OTTER pelts in 1787, the sound attracted the attention of maritime FUR TRADERS, then fell back into obscurity. In the 1850s traders began arriving to barter DOGFISH oil with the FIRST NATIONS and stayed to establish small stores. There was a WHALING station at SECHART from 1905 to 1917. In the 1930s fish plants and CANNERIES flourished at several locations, but most closed by WWII. Commercial FISHING, LOGGING and TOURISM became the economic mainstays. The 2 main communities are Ucluelet at the western entrance to the sound and BAMFIELD on the east.

BARNACLE belongs to the group of marine invertebrates known as crustaceans. The young animal swims freely near the water surface, growing rapidly until it develops a shell and adheres permanently to a hard surface or, with some species, to a larger animal. Barnacles generally occur in large quantities bunched together. There are 2 common species. Acorn barnacles (*Balanus glandula*) are small, white, volcano-shaped creatures. Their hard outer shell consists of a set of rigid plates and 2 pairs of movable plates; these are used to close off the top of the "volcano" to protect the animal inside. The goose barnacle (*Pollicipes polymerus*) attaches itself to a rock or piling by a long, fleshy stalk. Once attached, it uses its legs as antennae to sweep the water in search of food, which it entraps and delivers to the mouth. This is why the barnacle is said to be an animal that stands on its head and, like SHRIMP, kicks food into its mouth. Individuals have both male and female sex organs but do not fertilize their own eggs. They are considered a nuisance by mariners because they cover the bottoms of boats so swiftly and thoroughly. A small commercial fishery for goose barnacles began in 1987. Most of the harvest was exported to Spain. The fishery closed indefinitely in 1999 to protect other species from inadvertent damage during harvesting. *See also* FISHING, COMMERCIAL.

The thatched barnacle is the most recognizable of the acorn barnacles. *Rick Harbo photo*

BARNARD, Francis Jones, stage line operator (b 18 Feb 1829, Quebec City; d 10 July 1889, Victoria). Son of a Quebec harness maker, he came west to join the GOLD RUSH in 1859. After failing to make a strike, he settled in YALE. In 1861 he began carrying mail between Yale and BARKERVILLE, and the next year he organized an express company, Barnard's Express & Stage Line, to deliver mail to the CARIBOO. Within 2 years Barnard was making regular mail and express deliveries up the CARIBOO WAGON ROAD and had started a stagecoach line to carry gold, mail and passengers from Yale to SODA CREEK. By 1867 he

Francis Jones Barnard, owner of the longest stage line in N America, 1868. *BC Archives G-00385*

controlled all transport between VICTORIA and Barkerville, with several coaches and hundreds of horses, most of them bred at his Okanagan ranch. He was elected to the legislative council from 1867 to 1869 and served as MP from Yale from 1879 to 1887. He actively supported union with Canada and dreamed of creating a transport company that would span the continent, a dream that was dashed when the federal government promised to build a railway to the Pacific coast. Barnard's company went by different names, including BC EXPRESS CO, but it was known popularly as the BX and was considered the longest stage line in N America. He suffered a severe stroke in 1880 and by 1883 was an invalid. His company survived under various owners until the advent of auto transport in 1913.

BARNARD, Francis Stillman, businessman/politician, lt gov 1914–19 (b 16 May 1856, Toronto; d 11 Apr 1936, Victoria). He was brought west to the CARIBOO in 1861 by his father, Francis Jones BARNARD, who ran a stage line between the Lower Mainland and the Interior. The younger Barnard was educated in VICTORIA and London, ON, then returned to BC and took control of the family business when his father suffered a disabling stroke in 1880. He expanded his business investments into steamboats, land development, MINING, ranching and STREET RAILWAYS to become one of the wealthiest men in the province. In 1897 he was one of the founders of the BC ELECTRIC RWY CO and became its first managing director. A member of Victoria city council from 1886 to 1887, he was a CONSERVATIVE MP for the Cariboo from 1888 to 1896. He continued to be an active Conservative behind the scenes and it was no surprise when he became LT GOV on 17 Dec 1914. Anti-German sentiment was strong, especially after several Victorians died in the sinking of the *Lusitania* in May 1915, and an angry mob marched on Government House because Barnard's wife, Martha Loewen, was a member of a German family. Troops were called out, but feelings cooled and Barnard served out his term as a popular lt gov. He was knighted in 1919, the same year he retired from office.

BARNES, Emery Oakland, social worker, politician (b 15 Dec 1929, New Orleans, LA; d 1 July 1998, Vancouver). A high jumper on the 1952 US Olympic team, he came to VANCOUVER in 1957 to play football for the BC LIONS. At the same time he studied social work at UBC, and when he retired from football in 1964 he became a social worker. He also ran a nightclub in HARRISON HOT SPRINGS. In 1972 he was elected to the legislature for the NDP for the riding of Vancouver–Burrard, and he served as an MLA for the next 24 years. He was Speaker prior to his retirement in 1996. He and Rosemary BROWN were the first BLACKS elected to the BC legislature. As a member of the Lions team that won the Grey Cup in 1964 he was inducted into the BC SPORTS HALL OF FAME.

Emery Barnes, the first black man elected to the BC Legislative Assembly.

BARNET was the site of one of the largest SAWMILLS in the British Empire, on the south shore of BURRARD INLET just west of PORT MOODY. Built in 1889 by James MacLaren and Frank Ross, the North Pacific Lumber Co was on the CPR line connecting VANCOUVER and Port Moody. The small community of millworkers and their families was given MacLaren's wife's maiden name. The mill closed in 1929, then reopened as Barnet Lumber Co and operated until 1964. The site is now Barnet MARINE PARK.

BARNETT, Cunliffe, lawyer, judge (b 1936, Vancouver). A graduate of the Massachusetts Institute of Technology in geophysics and business administration, he worked briefly in the OIL AND GAS and FOREST INDUSTRIES before returning to school to study law. After graduating from UBC law school in 1966 he practised in PRINCE RUPERT and VANCOUVER; in 1973 he became a provincial court judge in WILLIAMS LAKE. During 23 years on the bench he was famous for taking his court to the people, holding sessions in schools and community halls across the CHILCOTIN. His even-handed decisions in cases involving aboriginal people more than once embroiled him in controversy with the non-aboriginal community and he ruled on several cases with important implications for ABORIGINAL RIGHTS. He retired from the bench in 1996.

BARNHARTVALE is 14 km east of KAMLOOPS on Campbell Crk, which was the original name for the area. P.A. Barnhart, conductor of the first CPR transcontinental to reach Kamloops, and later a homesteader and postmaster here, bestowed his own name on the settlement in 1909. AS

BARNSTON ISLAND is a small island in the FRASER R, just east of the mouth of the Pitt R. It is accessible from SURREY by a short ferry ride. Named for the HBC trader George Barnston, it is primarily AGRICULTURAL.

BARR, David, golfer (13 Apr 1952, Kelowna). He has won more money on the professional GOLF tour than any other Canadian. After attending Oral Roberts Univ in Oklahoma, where he earned second-team all-American honours, he turned professional in 1974 and earned his first important win the next year at the BC Open. He qualified for the PGA tour in 1978 and waited 3 years for his first tour victory, which came at the 1981 Quad Cities Open in Coal Valley, IL. In 1985 he won the Canadian PGA championship and missed winning the US Open by a stroke, the best finish by a Canadian to that point. His most profitable year on the tour was 1994, when he won more than $300,000, enough to place him among the top 50 money earners. During the same year he was a member of the Dunhill Cup team that won the Scottish tournament for Canada for the first time. Barr continued to golf professionally through the late 1990s but back problems limited his performance. The Dunhill Cup team of which he was a member was inducted into the BC SPORTS HALL OF FAME in 1999.

BARRETT, David, social worker, politician, premier 15 Sept 1972–22 Dec 1975 (b 2 Oct 1930, Vancouver). He grew up in an east VANCOUVER Jewish working-class home; both parents were politically active leftists. After attending Seattle Univ in 1948–53 he did graduate work in social work at St Louis Univ in 1954–56, and returned to BC to work at the Haney Correctional Institute. His experience in corrections led him to seek the provincial CCF nomination in Dewdney in 1959. This cost him his job with the province, but he was elected to the legislature in 1960 and held his seat through 4 subsequent elections. He became known for his ability as a

Dave Barrett and his wife Shirley celebrate Barrett's re-election to the legislature, June 1976. Ross Kenward/Vancouver Province

public speaker and his emotional, plain-spoken personal style. In 1969 he ran for the provincial NDP leadership, but lost to Tom BERGER. Later that year Berger lost his seat in an election and Barrett became leader early in 1970. Taking advantage of public disenchantment with the aging SOCIAL CREDIT government of W.A.C. BENNETT, Barrett led the provincial NDP to its first election victory in Aug 1972. Determined to be an activist PREMIER while he had the chance, he introduced a spate of legislation, including an increase to the minimum wage, new labour laws, a freeze on development of agricultural land, the creation of BC Petroleum and the INSURANCE CORPORATION OF BC, and a controversial royalty on mineral production. In 1975 he broke with NDP tradition by imposing back-to-work legislation to end labour strife. Many observers believed Barrett to have tried to do too much in too short a time. He was defeated by a revitalized Social Credit Party in the Dec 1975 election. He lost his own seat but won a by-election in June 1976 and remained NDP leader through 2 more elections. In Oct 1983, during debate over government spending restraints, he was physically removed from the legislature and banned for several months. He finally gave up the party leadership in 1984. After stints as a talk show host and academic, Barrett returned to politics and ran successfully for the federal NDP in Esquimalt in the 1988 election. In 1989 he ran for the national party leadership, narrowly losing to Audrey McLaughlin. When he lost his seat in the 1993 election he retired from politics for the second time. In 1999 he headed a public commission investigating the "leaky condo" problem on the coast.

BARRETT LAKE, 45 km southeast of SMITHERS near the confluence of the Morice and BULKLEY rivers, was named after Charlie Barrett, who moved into the area about 1900 and later established the Barrett Ranch. Barrett Lake was also a station on the GRAND TRUNK PACIFIC RWY.   AS

BARRIERE, pop 1,653, is on the N THOMPSON R 63 km north of KAMLOOPS. It was named by FUR TRADERS either for the rocks in the river that blocked navigation or because it was a place where FIRST NATIONS people built fish weirs (*see* FISHING, ABORIGINAL). LOGGING and AGRICULTURE are the mainstays of the local economy.

BARROW, Francis John, coastal pioneer (b 1876, London, England; d 1944). He came to BC in 1903 to visit his brother, then returned in 1905. In England the next year he married Amy Bradford; together they moved to a small farm near SIDNEY and began their summer excursions along the INSIDE PASSAGE in their boat the *Toketie*. The Barrows were familiar figures along the coast for many years, where they located and recorded Native ROCK ART for the provincial archives. Their voyages are the subject of *Upcoast Summers* (1985) by Beth Hill.

BASEBALL was probably brought to BC by California prospectors during the 1858 GOLD RUSH. The earliest reported game took place in NEW WESTMINSTER in 1862, but VICTORIA emerged as the hotbed of the game. One of the earliest organized teams was the Victoria Olympics, later the Amity Base Ball Club, which beat Seattle for the Pacific Northwest Championship in 1885. With the arrival of the transcontinental railway in the 1880s, teams appeared in the construction camps and rail towns of the Interior, particularly DONALD and KAMLOOPS, the site of the first provincial championship in 1888. In VANCOUVER the game blossomed in the 1890s and early 1900s at Larwill Park (named for Al Larwill, a kind-hearted eccentric who lived on the site in a shed full of sports equipment) and the Powell St Grounds. The inter-city BC Amateur League, consisting of Vancouver, Victoria, NANAIMO and New Westminster, lasted 4 years but folded in 1903. The following year Vancouver's first professional team joined the Oregon State League but only lasted a season, as long as earlier pro clubs in Victoria and ROSSLAND. The city's first successful pro squad was the Vets, also known as the Horse Doctors, later renamed the Beavers. Members of the Northwestern League (along with a team from Victoria), they played at Recreation Park and won the league championship in 1908, 1911 and 1913–14. Bob BROWN bought the team

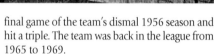

Nat Bailey Stadium, Vancouver, considered one of the most beautiful minor league ballparks in N America. Len Mackave photo

in 1910 and 3 years later built Athletic Park on the south side of FALSE CREEK, which remained the home of pro ball in Vancouver until 1922, when the Beavers broke up. At the same time there were many amateur and semi-pro teams and leagues. Players often received jobs in return for playing, or they received surreptitious payments. Between the 2 wars there were 9 leagues in the province, meeting in playoffs to determine a champion. One of the best teams was the ASAHI from Vancouver's JAPANESE community. Vancouver became the first city in Canada to feature night baseball in 1930 when Brown installed lights at Athletic Park. Amateur players of note during the 1930s included third baseman Johnny Nestman; Coley HALL, future owner of the VANCOUVER CANUCKS; and Ralph Stong of Stong's Market.

The pro game returned to Vancouver in 1937, when Con JONES entered the Maple Leafs in the Western International League. In 1939 Brown bought the team and renamed it the Capilanos after a local brewery sponsor. The brewery bought Athletic Park and the Vancouver club won the league championship in 1942, 1947 and 1954, the year the league folded. The first outstanding BC players to play pro ball in the city, Sandy ROBERTSON and Reg CLARKSON, both starred for the Capilanos. In 1951 the team moved to Capilano Stadium, later named Nat BAILEY Stadium, on the edge of Little Mountain. Meanwhile Victoria had joined the Western International League in 1946 as the Athletics, originally a farm team of the New York Yankees, and won the pennant in 1952. In 1956 pro ball resumed when the Vancouver Mounties fielded a team in the triple-A Pacific Coast League. Before they folded in 1962, the Mounties featured standouts George Bamberger, Jim Marshall and Ron Hansen, as well as a stint by Hall of Fame third baseman Brooks Robinson in 1959. Another personality of note was manager "Lefty" O'Doul, who went to bat as a 59-year-old in the

final game of the team's dismal 1956 season and hit a triple. The team was back in the league from 1965 to 1969.

In 1978 the Vancouver franchise in the Pacific Coast League was revived as the Canadians, the most successful pro baseball team in BC history. It attracted fans to Nat Bailey Stadium in unprecedented numbers and won the league championship in 1985, 1989 and 1999. The Canadians helped to develop a long list of major leaguers, including Tom Candiotti, Jose Lind, Jack McDowell, Lance Johnson and Sammy Sosa. After the 1999 season, which culminated in a Triple A World Series championship, the team's California owners moved the franchise to Sacramento.

Over the years a handful of British Columbians have appeared in the major leagues, including Ted BOWSFIELD, Dave McKay, Kevin REIMER and Paul Spoljaric. The greatest BC player ever is MAPLE RIDGE outfielder Larry WALKER, who established himself as one of the best all-around players in the sport and won the National League MVP award in 1997. By the late 1990s more young British Columbians than ever were being recruited by major league teams, notably GIBSONS pitcher Ryan Dempster breaking in with the Florida Marlins in 1998 and Jeff ZIMMERMAN joining the Texas Rangers in 1999. Several of these players were produced by SURREY's National

Vancouver Canadians celebrate their 1999 Triple A World Series championship. Chris Relke/Vancouver Province

Baseball Institute, a training program for young players started by John Haar and Wayne Norton. WHALLEY, near Surrey, is famous for producing young talent, as is Dave Empey's North Shore Twins. Other successful developers of BC talent include Little League coaches Andy Bilesky, who coached his TRAIL teams to 11 BC championships and 5 national championships to represent Canada in the Little League World Series, and Kathy Bernard, who became the first female head coach to participate in the World Series after she led her Lynn Valley team to the Canadian championship in 1993. Behind the plate, Doug Hudlin from Victoria was the only non-American, and one of only a handful of people ever to umpire the LLWS twice (1967, 1974). *SW*

BASKETBALL began in BC, one story goes, in 1897 when Carey Pope returned from Portland, OR, to VICTORIA to spread the word of a new sport developing in the US. Pope and other enthusiasts turned a building on Belleville St into BC's first basketball court by lining the windows with chicken wire, marking the floor and setting up iron hoops. However, historic photographs of a Victoria "BC Basketball Champions" team dating back to 1893–94 suggest even earlier origins for the game in BC. Regardless, it was in 1897 that the first known league was formed in Victoria, featuring games every Saturday night at the old Drill Hall on Menzies St. The first recorded women's game was played in 1903 when the Seattle High School girls met a team of girls from Vancouver College. One of Canada's finest basketball players in the early days of the sport was Roy Phipps of VANCOUVER, who led his local YMCA clubs and McGill Univ College (the precursor to UBC) to city championships and was a longtime player and coach for the Native Sons of BC. BC's first national men's title was captured in 1929 by the NEW WESTMINSTER Adanacs. Adanacs star Wally Mayers was an original inductee to the BC SPORTS HALL OF FAME. The national crown was won by the Adanacs again in 1930 and then by the UBC Varsity club in 1931. In fact, teams from BC dominated the national championships during the 1930s and early 1940s, taking home the title 12 times in the period from 1930 to 1943. Among these remarkable teams were the Victoria Blue Ribbons, featuring Art and Chuck CHAPMAN, Lynn and Muzz PATRICK, Doug PEDEN and Porky ANDREWS, and the 1936–37 UBC Varsity, led by the "Gold Dust Twins," Jim Bardsley and Art Willoughby. On the women's side, a team from UBC won the world championships in Prague in 1930 (*see* UBC WOMEN'S BASKETBALL TEAM).

At the administrative level, coach Ken Wright, a former star with the Adanacs, organized the first successful BC High School Boys tournament in 1946 (the BC Girls Provincials started 2 years later), and Wink Willox pioneered modern officiating with his cross-province clinics and new BC Rules Examination. Willox disciples Bob Hall and Harold Cronk extended his officiating-development legacy through to the 1990s. Wright's tournament emerged as the most popular event in BC high school sport and celebrated its 50th anniversary in 1995. Wright

SFU women's basketball team in a practice session, 1993. Rick Loughran/Vancouver Province

was involved every year to 1996 and the championship trophy was eventually named for him. Former UBC star Ken Winslade took over from Wright as the main organizer in the 1960s and ran the tournament for over 30 years.

Victoria produced "BC's team of the century" and perhaps the most talented fully Canadian basketball team of all time, the 1945–46 Dominoes, a club that included the Chapman brothers, Peden, Andrews and Norm BAKER. After winning the national championship that year, the team folded and Art Chapman, Peden, Andrews, Baker and Ritchie Nichol went on to play on BC's first professional basketball team, the Vancouver Hornets, which played 2 seasons in the PNE Forum from 1946 to 1948. Led by Baker, the Hornets posted winning records in both seasons.

As the Meralomas in 1947, and the Clover Leafs in 1948, 1949 and 1951, Vancouver clubs featuring Sandy ROBERTSON, Norm Gloag, Jack POMFRET and Bardsley took over the national title. In 1948, the UBC team were also considered national champs for defeating the Clover Leafs in an Olympic Elimination Tournament. Other Canadian champions included the Alberni Athletics, led by Elmer Speidel, in 1955; the BC Totems in 1957; the Vancouver Eilers in 1958; the Vancouver IGA Grocers, featuring star Billy Joe Price, from 1966 to 1968; and SFU in 1970. John Kootnekoff, a teenage spare on the 1955 Alberni team, went on to play for Seattle Univ in the 1958 NCAA Championship. Bob Houbregs, born in Vancouver in 1932, learned his basketball in Seattle and went on to become a 1953 All-American and NCAA Player of the Year with Washington state, the first overall NBA draft pick and a Basketball Hall of Famer. Meanwhile, between 1940 and 1970, women's teams from BC won 25 national championships, including the Vancouver Eilers, who won from 1950 to

1958. Off the court, coach Ruth WILSON and players Rita Bell and Shirley Topley were all top-notch softball players who competed internationally. Bell was such a talented basketball player she was asked by the Globetrotters' Abe Saperstein to play on his professional women's team.

BC basketball extended its Canadian domination to the national program as Bob Osborne led his UBC men's team, with some added Montreal players, to the 1948 Olympics. UBC coach Jack Pomfret was an assistant coach on a 1956 Olympics squad that included 9 British Columbians, among them Bob Pickell and John McLeod, while Ruth Wilson was manager of the women's national team in 1959 and later coach. At the collegiate level, UBC Thunderbirds, with standouts Ron Thorsen and Derek Sankey, won the Canadian Univ Championship in 1970 and 1972, and coach Ken SHIELDS, with help from players Joannne Sargent, Bev Bland, Bev Barnes, Liz Silcott and Kathy Williams (Shields's future wife), took the UBC women to 4 CIAU crowns from 1971 to 1974. One of BC's great all-around athletes, Bob Burrows of Victoria was drafted by the NBA's Seattle SuperSonics in 1969 before pursuing a baseball career in the Kansas City Royals organization. A star of Canada's 1976 Olympic fourth-place basketball entry was flashy guard Billy Robinson of CHEMAINUS, a former SFU standout and a pro player in Europe and Mexico. He was joined on the Olympic team by Sankey and Lars Hansen of COQUITLAM, the first player from BC to appear in the NBA. Hansen played 15 games for the SuperSonics in 1978 and 1979 and was a member of the team during their 1979 NBA championship win. He was the most successful BC native in the NBA until Steve NASH became the first local player to become an NBA regular during the 1990s with the Phoenix Suns and the Dallas Mavericks.

In university level basketball, Jay TRIANO of Niagara Falls entered SFU in 1977 and became one of the most successful athletes in the school's history, breaking virtually every basket-

Ron Thorsen of the UBC Thunderbirds, winners of the Canadian University Championship in 1970. UBC Athletic Dept

ball record while starring internationally for the national team. He was joined on the Canadian team by Eli Pasquale, a Sudbury native who led the UNIV OF VICTORIA Vikings to the first 5 of 7 consecutive Canadian university national championships (1980–86). The Vikings, who once posted a 63-game winning streak and had only one loss in 4 years of intercollegiate play, boast one of the most successful records in all competitive sports. Under the tutelage of future national team coach Ken Shields, top Vikings included VANCOUVER ISLAND players Gerald Kazanowski, Kelly Dukeshire and Greg Wiltjer. Pasquale, Kazanowski and Wiltjer were all NBA draft picks and national-team starters. Wiltjer went on to become Spain's highest-paid basketball player. Ken Shields's wife Kathy began coaching the Vikettes women's basketball team in 1977 and led them to 8 national championships through the 2000 season.

Coach Allison McNeill arrived at SFU in 1988 and led the women's team into 9 consecutive NAIA championship tournaments, also capturing honours as NAIA, Pacific Northwest, US Women's Basketball Coaching Assoc and SPORT BC coach of the year. Major contributions by star players Nikki Johnson, Joby McKenzie, Andrea Schnider and Michelle Hendry of TERRACE, the school's all-time leading scorer, also led to the team's success. Coached by Canada's best-ever female basketball player, Bev SMITH of SALMON ARM, Hendry led Team Canada to Pan Am Games silver in 1999. In men's play, SFU has produced more pro players, mostly in Europe,

than UBC and Univ of Victoria combined. Mike Jackel of N VANCOUVER, an All-American who led the NAIA in scoring in 1980 and 1981, went on to become a legend as the all-time leading scorer in German pro basketball, the highest paid Canadian in Europe, the captain of the German national team and a European sports celebrity. SFU product Mark Staley was the only BC player to make the Vancouver Nighthawks, a professional club that played a season in the late 1980s in a league that had a height restriction of 6'5". The professional game returned in 1995 when Vancouver was granted an NBA franchise and the GRIZZLIES took to the floor at GENERAL MOTORS PLACE for the first time, the culmination of a long history of basketball in the province.   SW

BASS occurs in BC in two species of freshwater fish: smallmouth bass (*Micropterus dolomieu*) and largemouth bass (*M. salmoides*). Both species are introduced. The smallmouth was introduced in 1901 as a game fish to both mainland and VANCOUVER ISLAND waters and is now found on Vancouver Island and SALTSPRING ISLAND and in the OKANAGAN VALLEY. The smallmouth has a deep, compressed body, two dorsal fins and a mouth that contains many small teeth. Body colour ranges from almost black to green and dark brown with olive-coloured blotches and noticeable tall vertical brown-green bars, and the fish can change the colour of its upper body to match its surroundings. It spawns in late spring. Smallmouth bass average .9 kg, but fish of 1.5 kg are not uncommon.

Largemouth bass are found primarily in the lakes of the Okanagan, in the COLUMBIA R and the KOOTENAY, though the species is appearing with greater frequency in the Lower Mainland south of the FRASER R, in ABBOTSFORD and LANGLEY. The largemouth spawns in late spring and can grow much larger than the smallmouth, but averages 1 to 1.4 kg. The largemouth is most readily distinguished from the smallmouth by its upper jawbone, which extends back beyond the eye. As well, the largemouth's upper body is dark green to olive and its sides are green to yellow; unlike the smallmouth, it cannot change its colour.

BAT is a member of the mammal order Chiroptera ("hand-wing"). BC's bats are mostly small, furry, nocturnal creatures, usually brown, black or grey in colour, with large ears and well-developed teeth for chewing insects. The bat is the only mammal capable of sustained flight. Of the more than 1,000 known species worldwide, 16 are native to BC, all belonging to the family Vespertilionidae, which feed on insects. BC has a greater diversity of bats than any other province: 8 species are found nowhere else in Canada, and the OKANAGAN VALLEY, with 14 species, has the greatest density and variety in the country.

For the most part, bats inhabit lower elevations in the southern portions of the province, but 3 species are known to occur as far north as ATLIN and FORT NELSON, and 5 occur in the Sub-Boreal Interior ecoprovince (*see* ECOREGION CLASSIFICATION SYSTEM) from the headwaters of

the NASS and SKEENA rivers south to PRINCE GEORGE.

Bats mate in the autumn, but females ovulate and give birth only after emerging from hibernation in the spring. Bats' wings are actually thin, double-layered membranes of skin stretched over arms, hands and elongated fingers. At rest they fold the wings at their sides. Bats do not walk on their hind legs, which are relatively small; they hang upside down by their feet. Bats navigate at speeds up to 36 km/h, often in total darkness. They emit high-pitched sound pulses and listen for the echo with their large ears, thus producing a sonic image of their surroundings (echolocation). They also have the ability to lower body temperature to conserve energy during periods of rest and winter hibernation.

Bats are protected and may not be killed without permit. Half of BC's 8 bat species are endangered or threatened, due to human activity such as LOGGING and pesticide spraying. Of these, 3 are Red-listed by the Conservation Data Centre (*see* ENDANGERED SPECIES): Keen's long-eared myotis (*Myotis keenii*), a rare bat occurring in coastal forests, whose only known breeding colony is on the QUEEN CHARLOTTE ISLANDS; western red bat (*Lasiurus blossevillii*), characterized by red-orange fur and very rare in BC; and pallid bat (*Antrozous pallidus*), the second largest BC bat and a rare species, found at low elevations only in the southern Okanagan Valley. Five species are Blue-listed: western small-footed myotis (*Myotis ciliolabrum*), the smallest bat in BC; northern long-eared myotis (*M. septentrionalis*), a rare species apparently confined to the eastern edge of the province; fringed myotis (*M. thysanodes*), which occurs in the dry southern Interior; spotted bat (*Euderma maculatum*), distinguished by its white patches and large pink ears; and Townsend's big-eared bat (*Plecotus townsendii*, also listed as *Corynorhinus townsendii*), which has huge ears and 2 swellings on its nose.

The remaining 8 species are western long-eared myotis (*Myotis evotis*), one of the few species found at high elevations; little brown myotis (*M. lucifugus*), the most widespread species in BC; long-legged myotis (*M. volans*); Yuma myotis (*M. yumanensis*), a species associated with water that congregates in large maternity colonies of many hundred animals (a colony on the First Nations reserve near SQUILAX is the largest in BC); hoary bat (*Lasiurus cinereus*), the largest species in BC, sometimes called the tree bat because of its fondness for roosting in trees; silver-haired bat (*Lasionycteris noctivagans*), another species that likes to roost in trees; and big brown bat (*Eptesicus fuscus*), a species with an affinity for buildings that often appears in the provincial legislature in Victoria.
Reading: David W. Nagorsen and R. Mark Brigham, *Bats of British Columbia*, 1993.

BATEMAN, Robert McLellan, artist (b 24 May 1930, Toronto). He grew up in Toronto, where he became fascinated with the natural world and began drawing animal subjects from a young age. After studying geography at the Univ of Toronto he became a schoolteacher in

Spirits of the Forest, Totems and Hermit Thrush, *a painting by Robert Bateman, 1983, acrylic on board, 40x53 cm. © Robert Bateman. Reproduction rights courtesy of Boshkung, Inc.*

1955 and for 20 years taught in Toronto and Burlington, taking time out to travel all over the world. Although he is known as a naturalist painter, he was early influenced by impressionism and abstract expressionism. It was during a teaching sojourn in Africa (1963–65) that he found his way to the realist style for which he is now internationally admired. By the mid-1970s he had left teaching and was painting full-time. In 1980 *American Artist* magazine acclaimed him as Artist of the Year and 1984 he was made an Officer in the Order of Canada. In 1985 he moved with his family to SALTSPRING ISLAND. His artistic interest in the natural world is mirrored in his support for a variety of ENVIRONMENTAL

Robert Bateman, Saltspring Island.
Birgit Freybe Bateman photo

causes and in 1998 the US National Audubon Society named him one of the 20th century's 100 Champions of Conservation. Books of his paintings include *The Art of Robert Bateman* (1981), *The World of Robert Bateman* (1985), *Robert Bateman: An Artist in Nature* (1990) and *Robert Bateman: Natural Worlds* (1996).

BATES, Maxwell, artist, architect (b 14 Dec 1906, Calgary; d 14 Sept 1980, Victoria). After studying art in Alberta he lived in England during the 1930s. He joined the British army and spent most of WWII as a German prisoner of war. Back in Calgary after the war he practised ARCHITECTURE as well as continuing to paint as an influential member of the Calgary Group. He moved to VICTORIA in 1962 to recover from a stroke and spent the final productive years of his life there. As founding president of the LIMNERS he played a leading role in the city's cultural life. His paintings, figurative and expressionist in style, were mainly satirical social commentaries; they have been called pessimistic and cynical, as well as whimsical and observant.

BAWLF, Nicholas R., architect (b 18 Feb 1938, Winnipeg, MB). After graduating from the UBC School of Architecture in 1963, he worked in England, Denmark and Ireland before returning to VANCOUVER, where he worked with the leading architectural firms Thompson, Berwick and Pratt and Erickson Massey. He was designer with TB&P on the CBC Building in Vancouver and with Arthur ERICKSON on the Bank of Canada Building in Ottawa. In 1972 he established a practice in VICTORIA in association with the Vancouver firm of Cooper, Tanner Associates. In 1978 this became Bawlf Cooper Associates. Major projects include restorations (Market Square, St Andrew's Cathedral and the Jewish synagogue), heritage rehabilitation (Belmont Building), contemporary contextual work (Victoria Conference

Centre, which won a LT GOV's Medal for Excellence) and historical restoration at BARKERVILLE, COTTONWOOD, HAT CREEK and YALE. *See also* ARCHITECTURE. *Martin Segger*

BAXTER, Robert, architect (b 7 Sept 1936, Bralorne). After completing a B Arch at UBC in 1960, he pursued a dual specialty in institutional design and heritage restoration. Restoration work has included the BC LEGISLATIVE BUILDINGS, FORT STEELE Heritage Town, St Andrew's Presbyterian Church, CRAIGDARROCH, and Lampson St and Victoria High schools. He moved to VICTORIA in 1973 and worked on numerous institutional projects, including renovations to Royal Jubilee and Victoria General hospitals and completion of Christ Church Cathedral. His work on the Pacific Forestry Centre in Victoria with Wade Williams earned a Gov Gen's Medal. *See also* ARCHITECTURE.

BAYNES, Robert Lambert, naval officer (b 1796, England; d 1869, England). The son of a commander in the Royal Navy, he entered the navy himself when he was 14 years old. After a distinguished career he became commander of the Pacific Station, based at Valparaiso, Chile. When the FRASER R gold rush began in 1858 (*see* GOLD RUSH, FRASER R), he was sent north in the warship *Ganges* to maintain law and order and British sovereignty. During the squabble over SAN JUAN ISLAND in 1859 he took a conciliatory approach, refusing Gov James DOUGLAS's request to land a military force on the island (*see* PIG WAR). He recommended moving Pacific station headquarters from Valparaiso to ESQUIMALT, a step the admiralty took in 1862. Meanwhile, he returned to England in 1860. Several of his watercolour paintings of coastal scenes are in the provincial archives.

BAYNES LAKE is a farming and resort community 50 km southeast of CRANBROOK in the E KOOTENAY, site of a weekly farmers' market. The 8-km-long lake was named after Andrew Bain, who settled in the area in 1896. Frederick Adolph operated a large SAWMILL here from the early 1900s until 1923, and the settlement, which was also a station on the CROWS NEST SOUTHERN RWY, reached a peak population of about 250. *AS*

BAYNES SOUND separates the east coast of VANCOUVER ISLAND from DENMAN ISLAND, extending 40 km south from COMOX to DEEP BAY. The waters of the sound are rich with crustaceans and other sea life that attract a large number of seabirds, several species of which stay for the winter months. Large schools of Pacific HERRING spawn here in March, supporting a commercial fishery and attracting birds, SEA LIONS and SEALS. The shores are lined with OYSTER leases and shellfish AQUACULTURE is a major employer in the area. The sound produces 39% of BC's cultured oysters and 55% of its manila CLAM harvest. It was named for Robert BAYNES, commander of the Pacific naval station from 1857 to 1860. Sandy Island Provincial MARINE PARK lies off the north end of Denman Island; off the south end the Chrome Island LIGHTHOUSE marks the entrance to the sound.

BAYONNE was a MINING camp on the CPR line, 32 km northwest of CRESTON on the west side of KOOTENAY LK. This stretch of rail between PROCTER and Kootenay Landing at the south end of the lake was not built until 1930 because of the difficulty and cost of construction. When completed, it opened the country to mining but spelled the end of the Kootenay Lk PADDLEWHEEL STEAMBOATS. The Bayonne GOLD-COPPER mine, which operated from 1936 to the mid-1950s, was 37 km southwest of the camp on John Bull Mt. *AS*

BC AMBULANCE SERVICE provides public ambulance service under the authority of the Emergency Health Services Commission of the provincial Ministry of Health. The service was created in 1974 to rationalize emergency pre-hospital health services that were being supplied by a variety of commercial operators. As of 1999 the BCAS handled about 390,000 calls annually and employed some 3,200 full- and part-time personnel, many of whom were trained at the Paramedic Academy at the JUSTICE INSTITUTE OF BC. The BCAS also provides air ambulance service and transfers patients between medical facilities.

BC ARTS COUNCIL is an independent agency created by the provincial government in 1996 to administer public support programs for the arts and cultural community. The council consists of a maximum of 15 members appointed by the government. The founding chair of the council was Mavor MOORE (1996–98), followed by Ann MORTIFEE.

BC ASSESSMENT AUTHORITY, known as BC Assessment, is an independent, publicly funded corporation responsible for administering the real property assessment procedures on which the provincial property tax system is based. Created in 1974, BC Assessment produces annual rolls assessing the market value of property and sends an assessment notice to every property owner. The province uses the assessment to establish property taxes. BC Assessment is governed by its CEO—the assessment commissioner—and a board of governors, both appointed by the LIEUTENANT GOVERNOR on the advice of CABINET.

BC BOOK PRIZES, established in 1985 and first awarded to books published in 1984, are awarded annually to the best books written by BC authors and/or published by BC companies during the previous year. In the first year there were 4 prizes; now there are 6: the Sheila EGOFF Children's Literature Prize, the Hubert EVANS Non-Fiction Prize, the Roderick HAIG-BROWN Regional Prize, the Dorothy LIVESAY Poetry Prize, the Ethel WILSON Fiction Prize and the Bill DUTHIE Booksellers' Choice Award. The prizes are administered by the West Coast Book Prize Society, which is composed of representatives from different segments of the writing and publishing community. *See* list of winners opposite.

BC CATTLEMEN'S ASSOCIATION has been the official voice of BC ranchers since 1929. With a membership of almost 2,000, the BCCA is a grassroots organization representing the interests of beef cattle producers. The 56 local stockmen's groups combine to form 15 regional associations, which elect the executive. The BCCA publishes the magazine *Beef in BC* 7 times a year. *See also* CATTLE INDUSTRY. *Diana French*

BC CENTRE FOR DISEASE CONTROL is the centre of excellence for the prevention, detection and control of communicable disease in BC. It was originally known as Special Health and Treatment Services, but in 1955 the various service divisions operating in VANCOUVER were brought together under one roof, although they continued to operate independently. In 1977 the name was changed to the Vancouver Bureau and the divisions began operating under a single administrative structure. In 1986 the name was changed to its current form to reflect its primary focus. In 1997, BCCDC was established as a society and its governance devolved from the Ministry of Health to the Vancouver–RICHMOND Health Board (*see* HEALTH POLICY). Today BCCDC integrates 4 key divisions: epidemiology services, laboratory services, sexually transmitted diseases/AIDS control, and tuberculosis control. *Claire Sowerbutt*

BC CENTRE FOR EXCELLENCE IN HIV/AIDS was established in 1992 by the BC Ministry of Health and Providence Health Care, a group of Lower Mainland ROMAN CATHOLIC hospitals. It operates in VANCOUVER from St Paul's Hospital, which provides care to more than 65% of the seropositive people in the province. The centre provides education to health care providers, conducts natural history and observational studies, develops innovative laboratory tests and carries out clinical trials. Its drug program is at the core of its activities. HIV-positive persons living in BC receive their anti-retroviral drugs free of charge when enrolled in this program. The centre was the first in Canada to use viral load testing and combination therapy, and is one of the few clinics in the world to provide drug resistance testing. *See also* AIDS; HEALTH POLICY. *Claire Sowerbutt*

BC COALITION OF PEOPLE WITH DISABILITIES is an advocacy organization whose mandate is to promote independence among people with disabilities, to bring about their full participation in all aspects of society and to break down physical and attitudinal barriers through political lobbying and public education. Programs include the Advocacy Access Program, which assists people with disabilities in securing information, disability benefits and support services, and which encourages individuals to share self-help skills; the Individualized Funding (IF) Project, in which public funding for services such as home care, personal care, vocational and recreational programs is administered by consumers themselves rather than government workers; and the Community and Residents Mentors Association (CARMA) Project, in which people with disabilities who leave care facilities and re-establish themselves in the larger community are paired with those who have already made the transition, as they learn how to plan and how to get information and support. The coalition also founded *Transition* magazine, a print and on-line forum published 8 times a year.

BC ELECTRIC RAILWAY CO was an electrical utility and transit company incorporated on 15 Apr 1897. Francis S. BARNARD, a local promoter, and Robert Horne-Payne, a British financier, organized the company using capital raised in England, and went on to take over STREET RAILWAY service in VICTORIA, VANCOUVER and NEW WESTMINSTER. As well as being the largest provider of electricity in the province, it expanded its urban rail lines dramatically before WWI, began build-

A 1936 Ford Tri-Coach bus in Vancouver. With a front end that swivelled, it was the forerunner of the modern articulated buses. Vancouver Sun

LIST of BC BOOK PRIZE WINNERS

2000

Ethel Wilson Fiction Prize: Michael TURNER, *The Pornographer's Poem*
Haig-Brown Regional Prize: Margaret Horsfield, *Cougar Annie's Garden*
Hubert Evans Non-Fiction Prize: Rita Moir, *Buffalo Jump: A Woman's Travels*
Dorothy Livesay Poetry Prize: Lorna CROZIER, *What the Living Won't Let Go*
Sheila Egoff Children's Prize: Vivien Bowers, *WOW Canada! Exploring This Land from Coast to Coast to Coast*
Bill Duthie Booksellers' Choice: Derek Hayes, *Historical Atlas of British Columbia and the Pacific Northwest*

1999

Ethel Wilson Fiction Prize: Jack HODGINS, *Broken Ground*
Haig-Brown Regional Prize: Mark Hume, *River of the Angry Moon: Seasons on the Bella Coola*
Hubert Evans Non-Fiction Prize: Peter C NEWMAN, *Titans: How the New Canadian Establishment Seized Power*
Dorothy Livesay Poetry Prize: David Zieroth, *How I Joined Humanity at Last*
Sheila Egoff Children's Prize: Ron and Sandra Lightburn, *Driftwood Cove*
Bill Duthie Booksellers' Choice: Tom Henry, *Westcoasters: Boats That Built BC*

1998

Ethel Wilson Fiction Prize: Marilyn BOWERING, *Visible Worlds*
Haig-Brown Regional Prize: Richard Bocking, *Mighty River*
Hubert Evans Non-Fiction Prize: Suzanne Fournier & Ernie Crey, *Stolen From Our Embrace*
Dorothy Livesay Poetry Prize: Patricia YOUNG, *What I Remember From My Time on Earth*
Sheila Egoff Children's Prize: James Heneghan, *Wish Me Luck*
Bill Duthie Booksellers' Choice: Ian & Karen McAllister with Cameron Young, *The Great Bear Rainforest*

1997

Ethel Wilson Fiction Prize: Gail ANDERSON-DARGATZ, *The Cure for Death by Lightning*
Haig-Brown Regional Prize: Alan Haig-Brown and Rick Blacklaws, *The Fraser River*
Hubert Evans Non-Fiction Prize: Catherine Lang, *O-bon in Chimunesu*
Dorothy Livesay Poetry Prize: Margo Button, *The Unhinging of Wings*
Sheila Egoff Children's Prize: Sarah Ellis, *Back of Beyond*
Bill Duthie Booksellers' Choice: Richard and Sydney CANNINGS, *British Columbia: A Natural History*

1996

Ethel Wilson Fiction Prize: Audrey THOMAS, *Coming Down From Wa*
Haig-Brown Regional Prize: Ken Drushka, *HR: A Biography of H.R. MacMillan*
Hubert Evans Non-Fiction Prize: Claudia Cornwall, *Letters from Vienna*
Dorothy Livesay Poetry Prize: Patrick LANE, *Too Spare, Too Fierce*
Sheila Egoff Children's Prize: Nan Gregory & Ron Lightburn, *How Smudge Came*
Bill Duthie Booksellers' Choice: Bill Richardson, *Bachelor Brothers' Bed and Breakfast Pillow Book*

1995

Ethel Wilson Fiction Prize: Gayla Reid, *To Be There With You*
Haig-Brown Regional Prize: Howard WHITE, *Raincoast Chronicles*
Hubert Evans Non-Fiction Prize: Lisa Hobbs Birnie, *Uncommon Will*
Dorothy Livesay Poetry Prize: Linda Rogers, *Hard Candy*
Sheila Egoff Children's Prize: Lillian Boraks-Nemetz, *Old Brown Suitcase*
Bill Duthie Booksellers' Choice: Ulli Steltzer & Robert Davidson, *Eagle Transforming*

1994

Ethel Wilson Fiction Prize: Caroline Adderson, *Bad Imaginings*
Haig-Brown Regional Prize: Alex Rose, *Nisga'a*
Hubert Evans Non-Fiction Prize: Sharon Brown, *Some Become Flowers*
Dorothy Livesay Poetry Prize: Gregory Scofield, *The Gathering: Stones for the Medicine Wheel*
Sheila Egoff Children's Prize: Julie Lawson, *White Jade Tiger*
Bill Duthie Booksellers' Choice: Alan Haig-Brown, *Fishing for a Living*

1993

Ethel Wilson Fiction Prize: W.D. Valgardson, *The Girl With The Botticelli Face*
Haig-Brown Regional Prize: Harry Robinson & Wendy Wickwire, *Nature Power: In The Spirit of an Okanagan Storyteller*
Hubert Evans Non-Fiction Prize: Lynne Bowen, *Muddling Through*
Dorothy Livesay Poetry Prize: Bill BISSETT, *inkorrect thots*
Sheila Egoff Children's Prize: Shirley Sterling, *My Name is Seepeetza*
Bill Duthie Booksellers' Choice: Nick BANTOCK, *Sabine's Notebook*

LIST of BC BOOK PRIZE WINNERS *continued*

1992

Ethel Wilson Fiction Prize: Don Dickinson, *Blue Husbands*
Haig-Brown Regional Prize: Herb Hammond, *Seeing the Forest Among the Trees*
Hubert Evans Non-Fiction Prize: Rosemary Neering, *Down the Road*
Dorothy Livesay Poetry Prize: Barry MCKINNON, *Pulplog*
Sheila Egoff Children's Prize: Alexandra Morton, *Siwiti: A Whale's Story*
Bill Duthie Booksellers' Choice: Robert BRINGHURST & Ulli Steltzer, *The Black Canoe*

1991

Ethel Wilson Fiction Prize: Audrey THOMAS, *Wild Blue Yonder*
Haig-Brown Regional Prize: Paul Tennant, *Aboriginal People & Politics*
Hubert Evans Non-Fiction Prize: Scott Watson, *Jack Shadbolt*
Dorothy Livesay Poetry Prize: Jeff Derksen, *Down Time*
Sheila Egoff Children's Prize: Nancy Hundal, *I Heard My Mother Call My Name*
Bill Duthie Booksellers' Choice: Michael Kluckner, *Vanishing Vancouver*

1990

Ethel Wilson Fiction Prize: Keith MAILLARD, *Motet*
Haig-Brown Regional Prize: WESTERN CANADA WILDERNESS COMMITTEE, *Carmanah*
Hubert Evans Non-Fiction Prize: Philip Marchand, *Marshall McLuhan*
Dorothy Livesay Poetry Prize: Victoria Walker, *Suitcase*
Sheila Egoff Children's Prize: Paul Yee, *Tales from Gold Mountain*
Bill Duthie Booksellers' Choice: Western Canada Wilderness Committee, *Carmanah*

1989

Ethel Wilson Fiction Prize: Bill Schermbrucker, *Mimosa*
Haig-Brown Regional Prize: Celia Haig-Brown, *Resistance and Renewal*
Hubert Evans Non-Fiction Prize: Robin Ridington, *Trail to Heaven*
Dorothy Livesay Poetry Prize: Charles LILLARD, *Circling North*
Sheila Egoff Children's Prize: Mary Ellen Collura, *Sunny*
Bill Duthie Booksellers' Choice: Michael M'Gonigle & Wendy Wickwire, *Stein*

1988

Ethel Wilson Fiction Prize: George McWhirter, *Cage*
Haig-Brown Regional Prize: W.A. Hagelund, *Whalers No More*
Hubert Evans Non-Fiction Prize: P.K. PAGE, *Brazilian Journal*
Dorothy Livesay Poetry Prize: Patricia Young, *All I Ever Needed was a Beautiful Room*
Sheila Egoff Children's Prize: Nicola Morgan, *Pride of Lions*
Bill Duthie Booksellers' Choice: Hilary STEWART, *The Adventures and Sufferings of John R. Jewitt*

1987

Ethel Wilson Fiction Prize: Leona Gom, *Housebroken*
Haig-Brown Regional Prize: Ruth Kirk, *Wisdom of the Elders*
Hubert Evans Non-Fiction Prize: Doris SHADBOLT, *Bill Reid*
Poetry Prize: Diana Hartog, *Candy From Strangers*
Sheila Egoff Children's Prize: Sarah Ellis, *The Baby Project*
Bill Duthie Booksellers' Choice: Doris Shadbolt, *Bill Reid*

1986

Ethel Wilson Fiction Prize: Keath FRASER, *Foreign Affairs*
Haig-Brown Regional Prize: Donald Graham, *Keepers of the Light*
Hubert Evans Non-Fiction Prize: Bruce HUTCHISON, *The Unfinished Country*
Poetry Prize: Joe ROSENBLATT, *Poetry Hotel*
Bill Duthie Booksellers' Choice: Cameron Young, et. al., *The Forests of BC*

1985

Ethel Wilson Fiction Prize: Audrey Thomas, *Intertidal Life*
Haig-Brown Regional Prize: Hilary Stewart, *Cedar*
Hubert Evans Non-Fiction Prize: David Ricardo WILLIAMS, *Duff: A Life in the Law*
Bill Duthie Booksellers' Choice: Islands Protection Society, *Islands at the Edge*

ing its own cars at a plant in New Westminster and also operated a network of INTERURBAN trains on the SAANICH PENINSULA, from Vancouver to RICHMOND and through the FRASER VALLEY as far as CHILLIWACK. The 102-km Chilliwack line was crucial to the economic development of the valley, providing farmers with a way to get their produce to market and also encouraging LOGGING operations. As highways improved in the inter-war period, BCER branched out into intercity bus service through its PACIFIC STAGE LINES subsidiary. In 1928 ownership of the company passed into Canadian hands as a group of eastern investors took control. BCER continued to operate transit services under a new parent company, the BC Power Corporation. In the late 1940s and early 1950s, the street railways were converted to bus lines. One by one the interurban lines closed during the 1950s, but the company continued to operate urban transit in the Lower Mainland and Victoria.

The other side of the company's operations was the provision of HYDROELECTRIC power. Its first plant, and the first hydro plant on the coast, was built at Goldstream north of Victoria in 1897–98, providing electricity to the capital until another plant at JORDAN RIVER became the main provider for southern VANCOUVER ISLAND in 1912. Another huge project was at BUNTZEN LK, where from 1902 to 1904 the BCER constructed a plant to produce power for Vancouver. Over the years the company added plants around the province, culminating in the completion of the BRIDGE R project in 1960, the largest source of electricity in BC prior to the mammoth dams built on the PEACE and COLUMBIA rivers in the 1960s. It was to pursue those projects that the provincial government suddenly expropriated the BCER on 1 Aug 1961, merging it with the BC POWER COMMISSION the next year to form BC HYDRO.

BC ENVIRONMENTAL NETWORK (est circa 1977) is one of the oldest and largest of 11 regional and affiliate networks under the umbrella of the Canadian Environmental Network. BCEN provides communications services, facilitates activities and links more than 250 provincial member groups with some 1,500 member groups in the CEN. Members include community, environmental, FIRST NATIONS, labour and church groups active in promoting environmental responsibility, community stability, human health and biological diversity. The BCEN provides liaison services between government, business and industry, First Nations and environmental organizations with the overall goals of facilitating environmental awareness and capacity-building for member groups. An 8-member elected board of directors provides the governance structure. Issues are dealt with through various caucuses (issue-based working groups) that facilitate information sharing and build strategies for joint action. The BCEN has 12 caucuses: Atmosphere & Ozone, Communications Outreach, Environmental Assessment, Forests, Health & Toxics, Indigenous Peoples Liaison, International Affairs, Parks & Wilderness,

Pesticides, Transportation, Waste Stewardship and Water. BCEN assists members of these caucuses in developing unified policy statements, becoming more effective in liaising with governments, and in public and organizational education. Like the CEN, the BCEN does not take positions on environmental issues, but member groups and caucuses may do so. BCEN has a foundation arm, the BCEN Educational Foundation, which sponsors conferences, seminars and workshops, and raises funds to provide for scientific research and public environmental education. *See also* ENVIRONMENTAL MOVEMENT. *Maggie Paquet*

BC EXPRESS CO, known as the "BX," at one time operated the longest stagecoach line in N America. Founded in 1862 as Barnard's Express and Stage Line by Francis J. BARNARD, the company hauled mail, passengers and freight along the CARIBOO WAGON ROAD between YALE and BARKERVILLE and eventually controlled most of the traffic between the coast and the CARIBOO. The company raised most of its horses at the BX Ranch near VERNON. The distinctive red and yellow stages were a familiar sight on the road until they were phased out by motor transport after 1910. The company also operated a pair of PADDLEWHEEL STEAMBOATS on the upper FRASER R from 1910 to 1920. After 1920 the company lost its mail and freight contracts to competitors and went out of business.

Stagecoach on the Cariboo Wagon Road, c 1890. BC Archives A-09775

BC Express Co stage going south on the Cariboo Wagon Road, 51 Mile Post, c 1897. Stephen Tingley is driving. Leonard Frank/UBC BC390

BC FEDERATION OF LABOUR, an affiliation of labour unions representing about 450,000 workers, is the dominant voice of organized labour in BC. The 20-member executive includes representatives from the 14 largest affiliated unions plus 6 chosen to meet affirmative action and sectoral requirements. The "Fed" was founded in 1910 as an alliance of radical unions. It published the *Federationist* newspaper and at the height of post-WWI labour unrest it had 18,000 members. It endorsed socialism and industrial unionism and played a leading role in the creation of the One Big Union at the 1919 Calgary Convention. The OBU disbanded the Fed the next year. It was resurrected in 1944 as the provincial arm of the industrial unions grouped in the Canadian Congress of Labour. When the CCL merged with the other national labour council, the Trades and Labour Congress, to become the Canadian Labour Congress in 1956, the Fed was left as the central provincial labour organization. *See also* LABOUR FORCE; LABOUR MOVEMENT.

BC FERRY CORP originated in 1958 during a labour dispute that shut down the privately owned ferry service between VANCOUVER ISLAND and the mainland. Premier W.A.C. BENNETT announced that his government would be going into the ferry business, and two vessels were built. Designed by Phillip Spaulding of Seattle and T. Arthur MCLAREN of VANCOUVER, the *Sidney* and the *Tsawwassen* were put into service 9 June 1960 between terminals at Swartz Bay, north of VICTORIA, and TSAWWASSEN, south of VANCOUVER. Late in 1961 the government purchased the BLACK BALL LINE and took over the HORSESHOE

ordered several larger vessels, the 137-m "C" Class ferries, which were the largest double-ended ships in the world at that time. Initially a branch of the Ministry of Highways, BC Ferries, as it is known, was reorganized as a CROWN CORP on 1 Jan 1977; it has grown to become one of the world's largest ferry systems. The corporation runs 41 vessels on 26 routes and handles about 22 million passengers and close to 8 million vehicles annually. The longest route is the 491-km run through the INSIDE PASSAGE between PORT HARDY at the north end of Vancouver Island and PRINCE RUPERT (inaugurated from the

The PacifiCat Explorer, *which went into service in 1999. Courtesy BC Ferry Corp*

A Spirit Class *"superferry," added to the BC Ferry Corp fleet in 1994. Allison Eaton photo*

BAY–NANAIMO run as well. The early BC ferries were among the most efficient traffic movers in the world; this, combined with the fact that freight was being moved increasingly by truck rather than barge, led to a higher demand for ferry service. By 1965, 7 more vessels had been launched; then some ships were modified to accommodate more vehicles and passengers. In the 1970s and early 1980s the corporation

original terminus at KELSEY BAY in 1966). Two Spirit Class ferries (the "superferries") were added to the fleet in 1994; each is 167.5 m long and capable of carrying 470 vehicles and 2,100 passengers. The vessels were built by a consortium of BC shipbuilders. These new ships were so much larger than the earlier vessels that the ferry terminals had to be upgraded to accommodate them. In 1996 BC Ferries launched the Discovery Coast Passage service, offering car ferry service from Port Hardy to BELLA COOLA with stops at coastal communities along the

way. The latest addition to the fleet was the PacifiCat high-speed ferry ("fast ferry"), a 122.5-m aluminum catamaran vessel with a maximum speed of 70 km/h. The PacifiCat, with a capacity of 1,000 passengers and 250 vehicles, is the second largest catamaran in the world. Three of these vessels were built by Catamaran Ferries International Inc, a wholly-owned subsidiary of BC Ferry Corp; the first began service in 1999. Subsequent revelations about construction cost overruns and operational deficiencies led to one of the major controversies of Glen CLARK's term as PREMIER, and in 2000 the government announced it would sell the fast ferries. *See also* SHIPBUILDING; TOURISM.

BC FILM is a provincial government agency that uses public money to promote BC-controlled movie and television production in the province. In 1997 it supported 112 productions with a total budget of $75 million, of which the agency contributed $4.2 million. This included 7 television series and several feature films. *See also* FILMMAKING INDUSTRY.

BC FILM COMMISSION, an agency of the provincial Ministry of Small Business, Tourism and Culture, was created in 1977 to promote BC production services to the international film and television industry. It also keeps an extensive library of locations that might be of interest to production companies, and it acts as a liaison between filmmakers working on location and local residents. Thanks in part to the efforts of its commissioners, Wolfgang Richter (1977–78), Justis Greene (1978–82), Dianne Neufeld (1982–95) and Peter Mitchell (1995–99), the FILMMAKING INDUSTRY grew by 21% per year from the late 1970s, bringing more than $1 billion into the province in 1999.

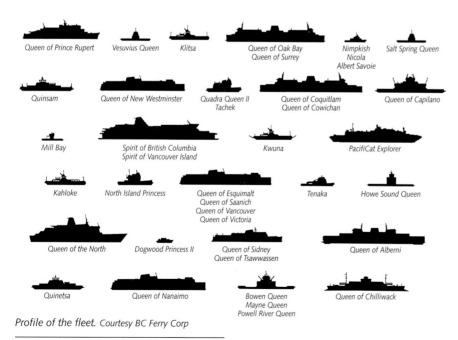

Profile of the fleet. Courtesy BC Ferry Corp

BC FISHERMEN'S UNION was founded in 1899 with locals in NEW WESTMINSTER and VANCOUVER, then spread to fishing communities along the coast. It led the famous FRASER RIVER FISHERMEN'S STRIKES of 1900–01, when fishers attempted to negotiate a higher price for SALMON from the STEVESTON canners. The 1900 strike ended with a negotiated settlement, but the 1901 strike was broken when fishers were intimidated into breaking ranks. The union had attempted to unite all fishers regardless of ethnic background but after 1901 it was badly divided. After failing to get support for a strike call in 1907 it faded away. *See also* FISHING, COMMERCIAL; LABOUR MOVEMENT; SALMON CANNING; UNITED FISHERMEN AND ALLIED WORKERS' UNION.

BC FOREST PRODUCTS LTD (BCFP) was established in 1946 by the Toronto industrialist E.P. Taylor with the purchase and amalgamation of several established coastal lumber companies. During its first 7 years of operation the company was managed and its lumber sold by the H.R. MACMILLAN Export Co. At the same time, the company acquired more timber and consolidated its holdings. In 1955 BCFP acquired a Forest Management Licence at TOFINO, an agreement that included the construction of a PULP mill at CROFTON, financed by sale of a one-third interest in the company to SCOTT PAPER LTD. BCFP was implicated in a scandal involving Minister of Forests Robert Sommers, who was convicted of accepting bribes in exchange for issuing Forest Management Licences—including the one at Tofino. During the trial Hector Munro, the company president, died suddenly. BCFP was found not guilty on some charges; other charges were dropped (*see* SOMMERS AFFAIR).

Throughout the 1960s and '70s the company expanded steadily, acquiring extensive timber rights, forest land and production capacity. In the late 1960s BCFP built an integrated forest complex at MACKENZIE in northeastern BC, including a townsite, 3 SAWMILLS and a pulp mill. The project was undertaken in co-operation with the Mead Corp, which acquired an interest in BCFP, as did Noranda Mines in 1969. In partnership with Donohue Inc, the company built a pulp mill complex at St-Félicien, QC, in 1975. Two years later it made its first foreign purchase with the acquisition of Blandin Paper in Minnesota. In 1980 BCFP bought Elk River Timber, consisting of a large tract of old- and second-growth timber and an extensive LOGGING operation at CAMPBELL RIVER. The company also bought an interest in Finlay Forest Industries, including a pulp and sawmill complex at Mackenzie and a one-third interest in Western Forest Products, which owned 2 pulp mills, 3 sawmills and extensive coastal timber rights. During the recession of the early 1980s, the company ran into financial difficulties and was taken over by two Toronto investment firms. In 1987 it was purchased by a New Zealand company, Fletcher Challenge, at which time it merged with Crown Forest Industries and was renamed FLETCHER CHALLENGE CANADA LTD. In 1991 several former BCFP holdings on the BC coast were sold to INTERNATIONAL FOREST PRODUCTS. *See also* FOREST INDUSTRY.   *Ken Drushka*

BC FRUIT GROWERS' ASSOCIATION is a producers' CO-OPERATIVE formed in VANCOUVER in 1889 as an information exchange and lobby group for orchardists. Most of its efforts over the next half-century were spent organizing and expanding an effective fruit marketing system. This led in 1939 to the creation of BC Tree Fruits Ltd, a co-operative selling agency based in KELOWNA that still markets most of the fruit produced in the province. The BCFGA also created SUN-RYPE PRODUCTS LTD in 1946 to develop and market processed fruit products and to use up cull apples, which were wasted at that time. During the 1990s the BCFGA relinquished control of both BC Tree Fruits and Sun-Rype and focused on growers' problems and government–grower relations.

BC GAS INC, a shareholder-owned company with headquarters in VANCOUVER, was incorporated in 1988 when INLAND NATURAL GAS acquired the Mainland Gas Division of BC HYDRO AND POWER AUTHORITY. One of its 3 principal subsidiaries is BC Gas Utility, which distributes 90% of the natural gas consumed in the province, serving some 750,000 customers in more than 100 communities through a pipeline system exceeding 36,000 km in length. BC Gas Utility purchases natural gas from various suppliers whose gas comes primarily from wells in Alberta and northeastern BC.

The other 2 major subsidiaries of BC Gas Inc are TRANS MOUNTAIN PIPE LINE CO LTD, a petroleum PIPELINE transportation company, and Inland Pacific Enterprises Ltd, which offers energy and utility marketing and consulting services. BC Gas Inc also operates a wood-burning power plant at WILLIAMS LAKE; the electricity produced at the plant is sold to BC Hydro. In 1998 BC Gas Inc had revenues of $925 million. *See also* OIL AND GAS INDUSTRY.

BC GAS LIFETIME ACHIEVEMENT AWARD is given annually to a BC writer who has made an extraordinary contribution to the literary arts. The $5,000 award includes the addition of the recipient's name to the "Walk of Fame" in the concourse of the main branch of the VANCOUVER Public Library. The award is co-sponsored by VPL and *BC BookWorld* magazine. Inaugurated in 1995 when the branch's new building was officially opened, the award has gone to Paul ST PIERRE (2000), Phyllis WEBB (1999), Christie HARRIS (1998), Barry BROADFOOT (1997), Jane RULE (1996) and Eric NICOL (1995).

BC GOLF HOUSE, located in VANCOUVER at the original UBC golf clubhouse at 10th Ave and Blanca St, is western Canada's only GOLF museum. Started in 1987, it is dedicated to preserving the history of BC golf by displaying artifacts and memorabilia and collecting information on BC golfers and events. The BC Golf House Society is a nonprofit organization dependent on financial and volunteer contributions.   *SW*

BC GOVERNMENT AND SERVICE EMPLOYEES' UNION is the largest public-sector union in the province with 60,000 members. It was founded as the BC Government Employees' Assoc in 1968 in response to a rapid expansion in government services and in the number of people working in the public sector. Until 1985 it was led by Norman Richards, the founding president. In 1973 the union won full collective bargaining rights for government employees. With more than 400 bargaining units, the union represents most public service providers, including social workers, tradespeople, clerks and administrators, corrections officers, liquor store clerks, health care workers and many employees of CROWN CORPS. It also represents some workers in the private sector, including in theatres, child care centres and hotels.

BC HERITAGE RIVERS SYSTEM was established in 1995 to identify BC RIVERS that are of particular natural, cultural or recreational significance, and to promote greater awareness and stewardship of provincial rivers. The selection process incorporates considerable public involvement and is overseen by the BC Heritage Rivers Board, an appointed volunteer advisory board under the aegis of BC Parks, which nominates rivers to the provincial government for designation. The first 7 rivers to inaugurate the system in Sept 1995 were the ADAMS, Babine, BLACKWATER, COWICHAN, FRASER, SKAGIT and STIKINE rivers. In 1996, the ATNARKO, BELLA COOLA, KECHIKA and KETTLE rivers were added. The Alouette, COLUMBIA, MIDDLE, MISSION, PEACE, PROPHET and STUART rivers were added in 1997. The BC Heritage Rivers System is only partially analogous to the older, nation-wide Canadian Heritage Rivers System program. To become a Canadian Heritage River, the province must nominate a candidate river; the CHRS board decides whether to accept it. By 1999, 4 BC rivers have received consideration for designation as a Canadian Heritage River: Fraser, Stikine, Cowichan, and TATSHENSHINI. The Fraser River was designated; it became BC's first Canadian Heritage River. The province also nominated the Cowichan and stated its intention to nominate the Stikine when the land use management process for that river has been completed. In 1999 negotiations were pending for nomination of the Tatshenshini R.

BC's HERITAGE RIVERS	
ADAMS	KECHIKA
ALOUETTE	KETTLE
ATNARKO	MIDDLE
BABINE	MISSION
BELLA COOLA	PEACE
BLACKWATER	PROPHET
COLUMBIA	SKAGIT
COWICHAN	STIKINE
FRASER	STUART

BC HISTORICAL FEDERATION was organized in 1922 as the BC Historical Association to record and publish provincial histories, to mark and preserve historic sites and to collect and display artifacts. It began producing a quarterly publication in 1927: originally *BC Historical Quarterly*, then a newsletter, and since 1980 the magazine *BC Historical News*. It also sponsors an annual writing competition and conference, hosted each year by a different community. In 1983 the name changed to BC Historical Federation.   *Naomi Miller*

BC HOUSE is the headquarters of BC's government representative in London, England. The province's first representative, Gilbert M. SPROAT, began as an emigration agent and later assumed the title agent general, which has been used ever since. The present BC House, built in 1914, is at 1 Regent St. Since 1872 there have been 23 agents general. Five other provinces have an agent general in London.

BC HYDRO AND POWER AUTHORITY, the largest of the provincial CROWN CORPORATIONS and third-largest electric utility in Canada, generates and delivers electricity to more than 1.5 million customers. In 1997 the corporation generated 54,484 gigawatt-hours of electricity. Most of this power is produced by 32 hydroelectric generating stations around the province; the rest is produced at steam, gas turbine and stationary diesel plants. In 1999 BC Hydro earned revenues of $3 billion and in 1998 it had 5,819 employees. It is regulated by the BC Utilities Commission.

BC Hydro was created in 1962 when the provincial government merged the recently expropriated BC ELECTRIC RWY CO with the BC POWER COMMISSION in order to have a utility large enough to undertake massive hydroelectric developments on the PEACE and COLUMBIA rivers. Largely because of these developments BC Hydro more than quintupled the electrical capacity of the province between 1962 and 1980. The corporation also built a vast network of transmission lines to carry power to markets, principally in the Lower Mainland. At the same time small utilities were purchased and integrated into the system. Along with power dams the corporation operates the Burrard Thermal Generating Station at PORT MOODY. Completed in 1963, the station uses natural gas to produce steam to drive turbines that produce electricity for the VANCOUVER area. When the province

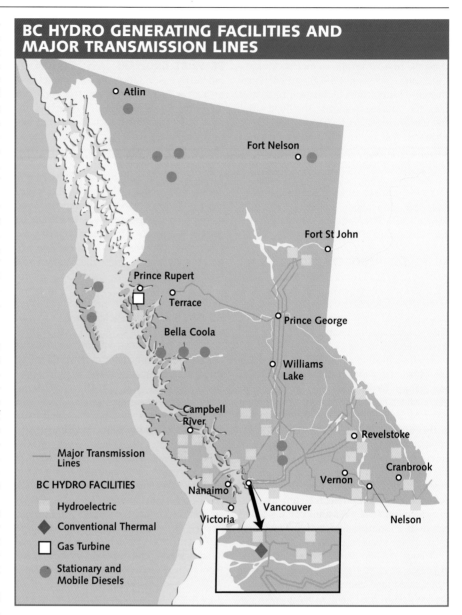

BC HYDRO GENERATING FACILITIES AND MAJOR TRANSMISSION LINES

Atlin

Fort Nelson

Fort St John

Prince Rupert

Terrace

Bella Coola

Prince George

Williams Lake

Campbell River

Revelstoke

Cranbrook

Nanaimo

Vernon

Victoria

Vancouver

Nelson

— Major Transmission Lines

BC HYDRO FACILITIES

▨ Hydroelectric

◆ Conventional Thermal

☐ Gas Turbine

● Stationary and Mobile Diesels

Some of the 72,000 km of transmission and distribution lines maintained by BC Hydro.
Rick Blacklaws photo

acquired BC Electric it took possession of a gas company and a variety of transit lines. BC Hydro began shedding these operations in 1979; by the end of the 1980s it was purely an electrical utility. During the 1980s Hydro's emphasis also shifted from construction of new production facilities to conservation and improved efficiency. The Power Smart program, initiated in 1989, is considered a model of energy conservation through public education. *See also* HYDROELECTRICITY; OIL AND GAS INDUSTRY.

BC INSTITUTE OF TECHNOLOGY (BCIT), the province's inaugural technical training school, welcomed the first 700 students to its $7-million BURNABY campus in 1964. The first principal was Cecil Roper, a MINING engineer. BCIT expanded rapidly and by the late 1990s the main campus occupied 55 buildings with satellite campuses on SEA ISLAND, in N VANCOUVER and downtown VANCOUVER where a $35-million complex opened in 1996. Billed as western Canada's first "smart building," the downtown campus has labs connected by fibre optics, conference rooms equipped with cable video access, and lights that

turn on and off as people enter and leave rooms. BCIT offers programs in business, computing, electrical and electronic technology, engineering, health sciences and trades to about 40,000 full- and part-time students.

BC JUNIOR HOCKEY LEAGUE, BC's junior A HOCKEY league, is an important developmental stage for many of western Canada's best hockey players and the most popular sports draw in many communities. The league began in 1961 as the Okanagan Junior A League with teams in KELOWNA, VERNON, KAMLOOPS and PENTICTON. It became the BCJHL with the addition of NEW WESTMINSTER and VICTORIA in 1967. In 1972 the league welcomed the Bellingham Blazers as members and became the first international junior A league in the world. The BCJHL continued to go through lineup changes; by the late 1990s it had 14 franchises spanning the province in centres such as NANAIMO, POWELL RIVER, QUESNEL and PRINCE GEORGE. The Penticton Knights became the first BCJHL team to win the Centennial Cup for national junior A hockey supremacy in 1986 and BC's national success continued with the 1987 RICHMOND Sockeyes under coach Orland Kurtenbach, the 1990 and 1991 Vernon Lakers and the 1993 Kelowna Spartans. The Centennial Cup was renamed the Royal Bank Cup and was won by the Vernon Vipers in 1996 and 1999. Through the turn of the 21st century, the BCJHL continued to lead all junior A leagues in Canada in the number of graduates to US college hockey and the NHL. SW

BC LAKE & RIVER SERVICE was a fleet of inland sternwheelers, tugs and barges operated by the CPR from 1897, when it purchased and renamed the COLUMBIA & KOOTENAY STEAM NAVIGATION CO. The CPR expanded the fleet with vessels and barges working on KOOTENAY, Trout, SLOCAN, ARROW and OKANAGAN lakes, and BOAT-BUILDING and repair facilities at NELSON, ROSEBERY, NAKUSP and OKANAGAN LANDING until the operation was second to none in the freshwater steamboating annals of the Pacific Northwest. Following WWI the development of highways and railways caused a gradual decline in both express sternwheeler and railcar barging service. The post-WWII era saw the retirement of the last two sternwheelers, the Arrow Lks steamer *Minto* in 1954 and the Kootenay Lk vessel *Moyie* in 1957, while the last railcar barge service, on Slocan Lk, ended in 1988. *See also* ROADS AND HIGHWAYS; PADDLEWHEEL STEAMBOATS.

Edward Affleck

BC LIONS is the name of the CFL franchise awarded to VANCOUVER in 1954. Annis STUKUS was brought from Toronto to coach, manage and promote the FOOTBALL team and he quickly signed up 8,500 season-ticket holders. He also lured Arnie Weinmeister, a future NFL Hall of Fame lineman, from the New York Giants. BC's first touchdown, by fullback Byron BAILEY, was the lone highlight of their first game, a loss to Winnipeg on 28 Aug 1954. The next 7 years were plagued by more losses and ineffective management and in 1961 season-ticket holder Sam Salloum organized a petition for a review. The McPherson Report limited the operation of the club to a small committee and success on the field followed. General manager Herb Capozzi and coach Dave Skrien built around quarterback Joe KAPP, running back Willie FLEMING, lineman Tom Hinton and linebackers Tom Brown and

Norm FIELDGATE a team that made it to the Grey Cup finals in 1963, then won the trophy the next year. Brown captured defensive player of the year honours both years and was MVP of the west in 1964. During the 1970s the Lions didn't often win but featured gate attraction Carl Weathers (who played "Apollo Creed" in the *Rocky* films) and star players Jim Evenson, Ted Gerela (*see* GERELA BROTHERS), Jim YOUNG, Ray Nettles and Bill Baker.

Led by quarterbacks Joe Paopao and Roy DeWalt and receiver Ty Grey the team enjoyed more consistent success in the early 1980s. In 1983 the franchise moved from its original home, Empire Stadium, to BC PLACE STADIUM and lost the Grey Cup to Toronto by 1 point. The Lions won their second Grey Cup in 1985 under coach Don Matthews with DeWalt, defensive star James "Quick" Parker, key receivers Mervyn Fernandez and Jim Sandusky, DUNCAN native Al WILSON and Lui PASSAGLIA, pro football's scoring king and the most popular Lion of them all. Fernandez became the first Lion to win CFL most-outstanding-player honours but after one more season left to join the LA Raiders. After finishing first again in 1987 the Lions acquired quarterback Matt Dunigan, who led them to an emotional 22-21 loss to Winnipeg in the Grey Cup final.

In the early 1990s new owner Murray PEZIM signed quarterbacking legend Doug Flutie and former NY Jets star Mark Gastineau but the Lions didn't win their third Grey Cup until after Pezim sold the team to Bill Comrie. Passaglia was responsible for perhaps the most dramatic moment in club history when he kicked a game-winning field goal to win the 1994 Cup over Baltimore, the first non-Canadian city represented in the CFL championship. In the rest of the 1990s ownership of the team passed from Comrie to a group led by Nelson SKALBANIA to David Braley, who rescued the franchise from folding in 1996. Highlights included running back Corey Philpot's CFL touchdown record (22) in 1995, Passaglia's continued inspiring performance and a 13-5 record in 1999 to top the Western Conference.

BC LIVESTOCK PRODUCERS CO-OPERATIVE ASSOCIATION was established in 1943 by livestock industry pioneers who believed in

the CO-OPERATIVE movement and were determined to improve marketing opportunities in BC. Before they united there was no exchange of marketing information among BC ranchers, who were convinced buyers were taking advantage of them. Since 1990 the association has been managed by a team of elected directors and stockyard staff. The co-op currently operates stockyards at OKANAGAN FALLS, KAMLOOPS and WILLIAMS LAKE. *See also* CATTLE INDUSTRY. *Diana French*

BC MILLS TIMBER & TRADING CO was organized in 1889 by the pioneer lumberman John HENDRY. He combined his operations at NEW WESTMINSTER with the HASTINGS MILL on the VANCOUVER waterfront and later the MOODYVILLE SAWMILL CO across BURRARD INLET at N VANCOUVER to create what soon became the largest lumber manufacturer in BC. The newly expanded company produced lumber, doors, sashes and moulding using wood from its extensive coastal LOGGING operations. Much of its success was based on the booming pre-war construction market in western Canada. In 1904 BC Mills began producing unique pre-fabricated houses for new settlers in the West. When Hendry died in 1916, his son-in-law Eric HAMBER became president, but following WWI the company went into a decline. It sold its logging operations during the 1920s and closed the Vancouver mill before the onset of the Depression. *See also* FOREST PRODUCTS.

BC MOUNTAINEERING CLUB held its inaugural meeting in VANCOUVER on 18 Nov 1907 as the Vancouver MOUNTAINEERING Club, but changed its name on 29 Mar 1909. In the early years a cabin on the slopes of GROUSE MT was the focus of the club and activities centred on the North Shore mountains. The BCMC also had a close relationship with the Garibaldi area and put a great deal of effort into advocating the creation of a provincial park there (*see* GARIBALDI PROVINCIAL PARK). In later years the club played a major role in explorations throughout the COAST MTS and built several huts, most notably the Plummer Hut near Mt WADDINGTON. Many of BC's finest mountaineers have been active members, including Tom FYLES, Neal Carter, Don and Phyllis MUNDAY, Ralph Hutchinson, Martin and Esther Kafer, Werner Himmelsbach and Dick CULBERT. *Chic Scott*

BC PACKERS LTD was the largest fish processing company on the coast until the late 1990s. Its predecessor, the BC Packers Assoc, was formed in 1902 and purchased several SALMON CANNING operations accumulated by Henry DOYLE and Aemilius Jarvis. Originally incorporated in 1903 under a New Jersey charter, it was reincorporated as a BC Special Act company in 1910. In 1920 a reorganization resulted in the BC Fishing & Packing Co Ltd becoming the operating company. Following another reorganization and expansion in 1928, BC Packers Ltd was incorporated as an amalgamation with several other canning companies and became the dominant processing company on the coast. Its can-

BC Lions celebrate their 1994 Grey Cup victory.
Mark van Manen/Vancouver Sun

nery in PRINCE RUPERT was once the largest in the world. The company was controlled by the Toronto food conglomerate George Weston Ltd from the late 1950s and became a wholly owned subsidiary of that company in 1985. Besides SALMON, the company processed and marketed a variety of seafood products and was involved in salmon farming (*see* AQUACULTURE, FIN FISH). Its farm operations were subsequently transferred to another Weston subsidiary, Connors Bros Ltd, operating as HERITAGE AQUACULTURE LTD. In 1999 BC Packers' branded canned seafood distribution business under the Clover Leaf and Paramount trademarks was sold to International Home Foods Inc of New Jersey and substantially all of its fishing and processing assets were sold to the CANADIAN FISHING CO, a division of Jim PATTISON Enterprises Ltd. *See also* FISHING, COMMERCIAL.

BC PENITENTIARY, the first federal penal institution west of Winnipeg, opened 28 Sept 1878 on the north bank of the FRASER R in NEW WESTMINSTER. Additions were made to the original building over the years and the inmate population rose to 756 in the 1950s. After a decade-long series of violent disturbances, it closed 15 Feb 1980. The remains of the original building became a heritage site. *See also* PRISONS.

BC PLACE STADIUM in downtown VANCOUVER was the first covered stadium in Canada when it opened on 19 June 1983. Built at a cost of $126 million, it is home to the BC LIONS football team and is used for concerts, consumer shows and special events. The roof is 60 m high

BC Place Stadium, Vancouver. Roy Luckow photo

and the stadium covers an area of 10 ha. With seating for 60,000 it is the world's largest air-supported domed stadium.

BC POWER COMMISSION was a public utility created in 1945 by the John HART government to provide electricity to rural areas ignored by the province's main electrical producer, BC ELECTRIC RWY CO. BC Power built and operated several plants around the province including the Puntledge R near COURTENAY and the John Hart development near CAMPBELL RIVER. By 1961 it served over 200 communities, some with small diesel generators. In 1962 it was merged with the recently nationalized BC Electric to become the BC HYDRO AND POWER AUTHORITY. *See also* HYDRO-ELECTRICITY.

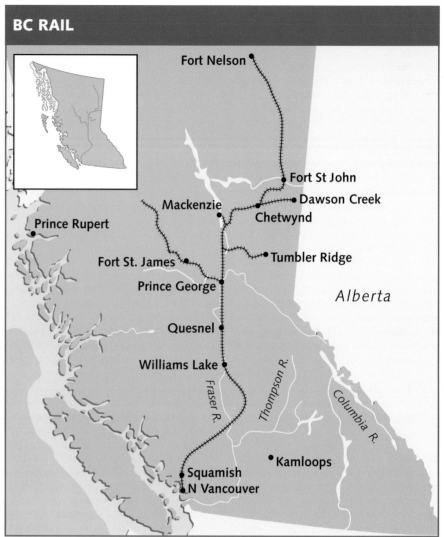

BC RAIL

Fort Nelson
Fort St John
Dawson Creek
Mackenzie
Chetwynd
Prince Rupert
Tumbler Ridge
Fort St. James
Alberta
Prince George
Quesnel
Williams Lake
Fraser R.
Thompson R.
Columbia R.
Kamloops
Squamish
N Vancouver

BC RAIL LTD, a CROWN CORPORATION, was incorporated as the Pacific Great Eastern (PGE) Railway on 27 Feb 1912 during the optimistic railway-building era that preceded WWI. The new line was intended to run from VANCOUVER north to PRINCE GEORGE; there it would connect with the GRAND TRUNK PACIFIC RWY, then being completed to the Pacific Ocean at PRINCE RUPERT. Most of the money for the project came from Britain and the name was chosen to remind British investors of their own Great Eastern Railway. The company managed to complete a

BC Rail diesel engine carrying freight from the Interior to Vancouver. David Larson/BC Rail

passenger line between N VANCOUVER and WHYTE-CLIFFE (1914) and a main line from SQUAMISH as far as CLINTON (1916) before the economic boom collapsed. In 1918 the provincial government took over the bankrupt railway and completed the line to QUESNEL by 1921. For several decades the PGE was something of a laughingstock. Known variously as the Please Go Easy, the Prince George Eventually and "the railway from nowhere to nowhere," it was starved of cash and neglected. Then in the 1950s Premier W.A.C. BENNETT made the railway a key instrument for developing the economy of the north. He wrote off its debt and undertook to complete construction all the way to the PEACE R. In 1952 it finally reached Prince George; in 1956 track was laid along the HOWE SOUND section; in 1958 the line reached FORT ST JOHN. By 1971 track ran all the way to FORT NELSON. But the company continued to lose money. In 1972 the name changed to BC Rail and in 1977 a Royal Commission into the operations of the railway issued a report critical of its management. During the 1980s the railway became profitable for the first time.

BC Rail operates 2,952 km of track and is the third largest railway in Canada. As well as hauling freight, it offers passenger service from North Vancouver to Prince George, including the popular excursion along Howe Sound to Squamish using the vintage ROYAL HUDSON steam locomotive. A 129-km electrified line opened in 1984 to haul COAL from the mines at TUMBLER RIDGE to the main track north of Prince George. At the time it was one of only three 50-kV railways in the world. The corporation is also involved in real estate development, telecommunications and transportation consulting worldwide.

BC RESEARCH INC is a scientific research company situated in Pacific Spirit Park adjacent to the UBC campus. The company specializes in consulting and applied research and development in the areas of plant BIOTECHNOLOGY, environment, health and safety, process and analysis, and ship dynamics. Originating in 1944 as the non-profit BC Research Council, it incorporated in 1993 as a private company. It spun off Silvagen Inc (clonal reforestation) and Azure Dynamics Inc (hybrid vehicle systems) and is actively engaged in technology innovation partnerships.

BC RESOURCES INVESTMENT CORP was created in 1977 by the SOCIAL CREDIT government. It had its origins in BC Cellulose, a CROWN CORP created earlier by the NDP government to manage 4 forestry companies it had rescued from insolvency. BCRIC privatized 3 of these companies along with some other public resource assets. Shares were offered for sale, and in 1979 the government offered every BC citizen 5 free shares. BCRIC soon became an operating company with large ambitions rather than the holding company it was originally intended to be. In 1980 it bought a controlling interest in Kaiser Resources, a COAL-mine operator, at what critics claimed was an inflated price. This investment went sour, and with it so did the prospects for BCRIC. The company was renamed Westar

A share in BC Resources Investment Corp. Every British Columbian received 5 free shares in 1979. *Courtesy Sage Wright*

Industries in 1982, and the remains of its holdings were taken over by Jim PATTISON in 1995.

BC SECURITIES COMMISSION, established in 1987, is responsible for regulating securities markets in the province. Since 1995 it has been a CROWN CORP. Members of the commission are government-appointed. *See also* VANCOUVER STOCK EXCHANGE.

BC SPORTS HALL OF FAME AND MUSEUM was founded in 1966 and located in the BC Pavilion on the grounds of the PNE in VANCOUVER. It moved to BC PLACE STADIUM in 1991. Sports columnist Eric Whitehead was instrumental in developing the facility during its early years and legendary ROWING coach Frank READ was the founding chair. Hall of Fame member and former BC LIONS president Jack Farley led a fundraising drive that brought in $5 million to make the hall the most interactive sports museum in N America. By the year 2000, the hall had inducted over 250 athletes, teams, coaches, media personalities and administrators for their contribution to sports in the province. The museum preserves photographs, trophies, scrapbooks, film and other memorabilia of BC's dynamic sporting history.

BC STUDIES is a quarterly journal of scholarly writing about the province. It was founded in 1969 by its original co-editors, Margaret Prang, a historian, and Walter Young, a political scientist. Based at UBC since its inception, it is an interdisciplinary journal, publishing articles on a range of political, economic and cultural subjects, past and present, as well as poetry, reviews and a bib-liography. From time to time it devotes an entire issue to a single theme. Other editors have included Allan Smith (1983–95) and co-editors Jean Barman and R. Cole Harris (1995–present).

BC SUGAR; *see* ROGERS SUGAR.

BC TEACHERS' FEDERATION was formed in Vancouver in 1916 as a federation of local teacher associations with the dual aim of improving public education and representing the interests of the province's 2,064 teachers. Membership grew slowly until the 1930s, when the federation expanded to include two-thirds of the teacher population. In 1940 it converted from a federation of local associations to an association of individual teachers and in 1948 membership became automatic for all teachers in the province. Over the years the BCTF has expanded its involvement in curriculum development, continuing education for members and lobbying for improvements to the education system generally. In 1999 it represented about 44,000 public school teachers.

BC TELEPHONE CO; *see* TELUS COMMUNICATIONS INC.

BC TRANSIT is a provincial CROWN CORPORATION operating a fleet of buses in VICTORIA and 44 other communities around the province. It also operates handyDART service for the physically disabled and paratransit in sparsely populated areas. The corporation has a board of directors appointed by CABINET and responsible to a cabinet minister. Greater Victoria has its own regional transit commission to regulate service in the capital region. The commission consists of locally elected representatives from the municipalities in the region and the chair is a member of the corporation's board of directors. In 1999, transit in the VANCOUVER area came under the control of the Greater Vancouver Transportation Authority, known as TransLink, consisting of 12 members appointed by the GREATER VANCOUVER REGIONAL DISTRICT and 3 members of the legislature. TransLink is responsible for buses, including SEABUS, SKYTRAIN and the West Coast Express commuter train from MISSION, along with AirCare (a program that monitors vehicles to control harmful exhaust emissions) and major ROADS and bridges.

Transit became a responsibility of the provincial government in 1961 when the BC ELECTRIC RWY CO was expropriated, then merged with the BC POWER COMMISSION to create BC HYDRO. In 1973 the government created a separate Bureau of Transit Services and greatly expanded services. Finally, in 1978, transit was completely separated from BC Hydro and transferred to a new Crown corporation, the Urban Transit Authority, which became BC Transit in 1982. The Corporation spent $667.8 million in 1997–98.

BC TREATY COMMISSION is an independent body created in 1993 to coordinate and oversee the negotiation of treaties with FIRST NATIONS people. The 5 commissioners are appointed jointly by the federal and provincial governments and the First Nations Summit, an umbrella organization of First Nations groups. The commission determines when negotiations will begin and provides a means of dispute resolution. In Nov 1998 the HAIDA leader Miles Richardson was appointed chief commissioner, the first aboriginal person to hold the post.

BC WATERFOWL SOCIETY, created in 1961, is devoted to the welfare of waterfowl and the preservation of their habitat. The society's major accomplishment was the creation, in 1963, of the George C. REIFEL MIGRATORY BIRD SANCTUARY on the foreshore at WESTHAM ISLAND in the ESTUARY of the FRASER R. The sanctuary now encompasses 6.5 km² of WETLANDS where waterfowl are viewed and studied. *See also* ENVIRONMENTAL MOVEMENT.

BC WILD is a coalition of ENVIRONMENTAL groups established in 1993 to coordinate research on and support for environmental issues. In 1996 it had a budget of $2 million, most of which came from American charitable organizations. Activities include preparing maps and research reports and planning youth education programs.

BC WILDLIFE FEDERATION (BCWF) is the largest and one of the oldest voluntary conservation organizations in BC. A number of fish and game clubs, some of which had been in existence since the beginning of the 20th century, formed a provincial organization under the name of BC Sportsman's Council in 1947. Ten years later (1957), the name was changed to the BC Wildlife Federation. A major purpose was to meet annually with the government's Game Commissioner to establish hunting and fishing seasons and bag limits, and to discuss issues relating to the health of wildlife populations. The federation has clubs in all areas of the province and is involved with land use issues, along with other conservation organizations. BCWF initiated the Hunter Training Program (a requirement for all first time hunting licence applicants) and the "Observe, Record, Report" program to help stem poaching. It was at the urging of the BCWF that government instituted the Habitat Conservation Trust Fund in which a percentage of all hunting and fishing licences and fees are placed in the fund and distributed to public and private projects, which are open to all applicants and are administered by an advisory board. The NEW WESTMINSTER club was formed in 1894, the FERNIE club celebrated its centennial in the late 1990s, and the NANAIMO club is 100 years old as of 2002. In 1999 the BC Wildlife Federation had over 30,000 members from 140 fish and game clubs. *See also* ENVIRONMENTAL MOVEMENT.

BCP No 45 is a 14.3-m wooden fish boat, a table seiner, made famous by its appearance on the old Canadian 5-dollar bill. Built for BC PACKERS LTD by Burrard Shipyard in Coal Harbour, VANCOUVER, in 1927, it was owned by Harry ASSU of QUADRA ISLAND from 1941 to 1959 and skippered by his son Mel. The 5-dollar note featuring the photograph of the *BCP No 45* was in circulation between 1972 and 1986. In 1996 the boat, sometimes called the West Coast's answer to Nova Scotia's *Bluenose*, was donated to the VANCOUVER MARITIME MUSEUM, where it remains on display. *See also* FISHING, COMMERCIAL.

BEACHCOMBERS was the most successful television show ever made in BC. Filmed at GIBSONS, north of Vancouver, from 1971 to 1991, it depicted life in a "typical" coastal community. Its focal point was Molly's Reach cafe, actually Gibsons' old liquor store. Regular cast members included Bruno GERUSSI, Robert CLOTHIER, Pat John, Rae Brown and Jackson Davies, all of whom are now familiar to viewers in the many countries around the world where the series has been rebroadcast.

Bruno Gerussi and Pat John, 1980. They starred in the TV series Beachcombers *for many years. Roy Luckow photo*

Top: George Hunter's 1958 photograph of the seiner BCP No 45, taken near Ripple Rock, a rendering of which eventually appeared on the Canadian $5 bill. VMM

BEACON HILL PARK, 74 ha, VICTORIA's largest urban park, overlooks JUAN DE FUCA STRAIT and is named for the beacons that were once lit to warn ships about the dangerous shoals offshore. The area was a natural meadow, where local FIRST NATIONS harvested CAMAS, when Governor James DOUGLAS set it aside as a park reserve in 1858. The province transferred it to the city in 1882. Later in the decade the city laid out a formal civic park on a design by John BLAIR, a Scottish landscape architect, though much of the wildness was preserved. The park features winding paths, gardens planted with tens of thousands of flowers, stands of Garry OAK, a petting zoo, playgrounds, streams and ornamental ponds and a TOTEM POLE, once the world's tallest at 38.9 m, carved by Mungo MARTIN.

BEAGLE, Mickey, union organizer (b 1907, Vancouver; d 1999 Vancouver). After living for many years in the US, she and her husband returned in 1945 to VANCOUVER, where she worked as local union secretary for the INTERNATIONAL WOODWORKERS OF AMERICA (IWA). In 1949 she went to work in the FISHING industry, joining the UNITED FISHERMEN AND ALLIED WORKERS' UNION. She first served on the union executive in 1951 and became second vice-president in 1954. A dedicated Communist and the union's first woman organizer, she was made an honorary life member on her retirement.

BEAR, BLACK (*Ursus americanus* spp), inhabits virtually all of BC and is thought to number between 120,000 and 160,000, a quarter of all black bears in Canada. Six subspecies range through the distinct colour morphs of black, brown, cinnamon, creamy white (*see* BEAR, KERMODE) and blue-grey (the "glacier bear" found in Tatshenshini-Alsek Provincial Park). This genetic diversity likely reflects the diverse habitats and environmental conditions in the province. Bears have heavy bodies, small eyes, short tails and flat feet with short, curved claws for climbing trees. Forests are their natural habitat and they can move through the bush at amazing speeds. Their size varies depending on quality and abundance of food: adult males weigh 60–300 kg while females generally weigh 40–100 kg. The largest black bears are on VANCOUVER ISLAND and the QUEEN CHARLOTTE ISLANDS. Unlike grizzly bears (*see* BEAR, GRIZZLY), the black bear has no shoulder hump and its muzzle is straight and tapered, where a grizzly's face is flatter and rounder.

Black bears are omnivorous, eating different foods according to the season, although SALMON is a critically important pre-winter food for bears inhabiting watersheds that contain salmon. While they consume mainly vegetation, roots, BERRIES, INSECTS, fish and carrion, they will prey on small mammals and newborn DEER, ELK, MOOSE and CARIBOU. Black bears learn to take advantage of feeding opportunities in their environment, including garbage, orchards, backyard barbecues and campgrounds, so urban development places them in increasing conflict with people. Attacks on humans are infrequent, but black bears can be dangerous and should be treated cautiously.

The female becomes sexually mature at 3–4 years and gives birth to 1–4 cubs every second year depending on the abundance of food. Birthing takes place during hibernation from late autumn to Apr. While populations are stable overall, black bears are vulnerable to poaching, sloppy waste management and agricultural practices, human intolerance and increasing alienation of their habitats. Hunting of black bears is regulated by the Wildlife Branch and reflects

Black bear. A quarter of Canada's black bears live in BC. Mark Newman/Image Makers

their numbers and distribution. The number killed annually in the allowable hunt, however, does not compare with the hundreds killed by conservation officers responding to public complaints and by poachers to supply an illicit international trade in body parts. *Maggie Paquet*

BEAR, GRIZZLY (*Ursus arctos horribilis*) once ranged throughout the BC mainland. In the late 1990s it was still found in many northern parts of the province and in pockets of coastal and mountain wilderness, but in greatly reduced numbers. An estimated 10,000–13,000 grizzlies live in BC, roughly half the Canadian population and a quarter of the number found in all N America. Larger than the black BEAR, the grizzly weighs 170–360 kg, though larger males weigh 500 kg or more. The average grizzly reaches a nose-to-tail length of 1.8 m, but individuals have been known to attain 2.7 m. A grizzly bear's size often depends on its diet, which is determined by the location and quality of its habitat. Despite its bulk, this bear is a quick, agile hunter, capable of running up to 65 km/h over most terrain.

The grizzly bear differs from the black bear in several ways. It has a pronounced shoulder hump and a large, rounded head with a dished facial profile. Its ears are small and rounded and set well apart. The long outer guard hairs of a grizzly's coat are often tipped with white, silver or cream, giving the bear the grizzled appearance from which it gets its name. Coat colour can be various shades of blond, brown, black or a combination of all of these.

Grizzlies are omnivorous, feeding mainly on vegetation, roots, BERRIES, INSECTS, grubs and, in season, nuts and fish, notably SALMON. Research in the 1990s showed important links between SALMON, grizzly bears, and forest health and diversity (*see* BIODIVERSITY). Grizzlies also prey on small and large mammals; in areas such as SPATSIZI PLATEAU WILDERNESS PROVINCIAL PARK they are significant predators of MOUNTAIN SHEEP and CARIBOU. Like black bears, grizzlies are also attracted to garbage, orchards, campsites and fish farms, all of which may bring them into conflict

A family of grizzly bears.
Mark Newman/Image Makers

Grizzly bear catching a salmon.
Mark Newman/Image Makers

with humans, which usually results in their being shot, as relocation has been shown to be largely ineffective.

Grizzly bears require a large home range and have a low reproductive capacity. The female reaches sexual maturity at 4–8 years and breeds once every 3 years, sometimes less frequently, giving birth to 1–3 cubs each time. Cubs are born and nursed about halfway through hibernation, which lasts from autumn until about Apr. They then emerge with their mothers, who are hungry for new plant growth to replenish lost fat reserves. The grizzly rarely lives longer than 25 years.

Though grizzlies have a reputation for ferocity, they are reclusive and solitary. Attacks on humans occur infrequently, and usually when people have failed to take precautions to avoid encounters. Humans are much more of a threat to grizzlies than vice versa. Threats to grizzlies include more access into backcountry and more people spending time in wilderness areas; loss and fragmentation of habitat due to LOGGING, MINING and recreational developments; and poaching. As well, about 500 bears are killed each year as a result of animal control strategies and a Limited Entry Hunt. The KHUTZEYMATEEN Grizzly Bear Sanctuary, designated by the province in 1992 as a first step in a provincial conservation strategy, is Canada's first grizzly bear sanctuary and protects about 50 grizzlies. In the late 1990s other protected areas and management zones were being planned to help conserve habitat for these remarkable animals.

Maggie Paquet

BEAR, KERMODE (*Ursus americanus kermodei*) is a subspecies of black BEAR that may be white or black in colour. Kermodes in their white coloration are known as spirit bears or snow bears. They are generally found in a 400 km² range of

coastal forest from PRINCESS ROYAL ISLAND north to STEWART and inland as far as HAZELTON, though some have been found as far away as the LIARD R. It was named in 1905 after Dr Francis Kermode, director of the provincial museum (*see* ROYAL BC MUSEUM), who collected the first white pelts that led to its identification. A single Kermode, confiscated from a smuggler, lived in a cage in Victoria's BEACON HILL PARK during 1924–48. Hunting Kermodes has been illegal since 1965; the population appears to be stable but could be compromised if logging takes place on large north coast islands. TERRACE has adopted the Kermode as the town symbol.

Kermode bear, a subspecies of black bear.
Ian McAllister photo

BEAR CREEK was a railway station located on the original CPR tracks 7 km north of ROGERS PASS in the SELKIRK MTS. It was bypassed in 1916 by the CONNAUGHT TUNNEL.   AS

BEAR FLAT is a tiny farming and stock-raising settlement 25 km west of FORT ST JOHN on the north shore of the PEACE R. A post office operated here from 1924 to 1950. Alexander MACKENZIE saw "2 grissly and hideous bears" here on his historic 1793 journey to the West Coast.   AS

BEAR LAKE, pop 300, 65 km north of PRINCE GEORGE on the HART HWY, developed around the site of the Polar Forest Industries SAWMILL, established in the early 1960s and sold to CANADIAN FOREST PRODUCTS in 1989. Crooked River Provincial Park, with its fine sandy beach on Bear Lk, is nearby (*see* PARKS, PROVINCIAL).   AS

BEATON, now a ghost town, was founded on the Northeast Arm of Upper ARROW LK to serve as a transfer point for traffic on the wagon roads to Camborne, TROUT LAKE CITY and FERGUSON during the LARDEAU SILVER-mining boom of the 1890s. Originally called Thomson's Landing, it was renamed in 1902 at the height of the boom, after a local entrepreneur. As MINING faded there was little to sustain the settlement except subsistence farming; after several brief revivals it became overgrown and deserted. Much of the site was flooded in 1969 upon completion of the High Arrow Dam. Beaton's early years are recorded in the photographs of Mattie GUNTERMAN.

BEAUTIFUL BC is a glossy BC scenic and travel magazine based in VICTORIA. Founded in 1959 as a publication of the provincial government, it is now owned by Great Pacific Industries, one of the companies owned by Jim PATTISON. With a paid circulation of 244,000 in 173 countries, it is BC's most widely read MAGAZINE.

BEAVEN, Robert, businessman, politician, premier 13 June 1882–29 Jan 1883 (b 28 Jan 1836, Leigh, England; d 18 Sept 1920, Victoria). He emigrated with his family to Toronto as a child and after graduating from Upper Canada College came west with friends. After trying his luck in the goldfields, he settled in 1866 in VICTORIA and became a successful insurance broker and importer. He was drawn into politics by the debate over union with Canada and became secretary of the pro-union CONFEDERATION LEAGUE. In the first provincial election he won a seat in the legislature for Victoria, and he remained a member for 23 years, serving in the cabinets of Amor DE COSMOS and George WALKEM as chief commissioner of lands and works in 1873–76 and minister of finance in 1878–82. When Walkem was elevated to the BC Supreme Court, Beaven became PREMIER. His term was not lengthy; he lost an election shortly after taking office, and though he tried to retain power, he was finally defeated in a non-confidence vote and had to step down. He remained in the legislature as leader of the opposition until 1894, during which time he also served two terms as mayor of Victoria (1892–93). He was elected mayor once more, in 1896, before the voters ended his career. In a strange turn of events, the lt gov asked him to try to form a government following the 1898 election, though he had no seat.

Robert Beaven, premier of BC 1882–83, shown here in 1883. BC Archives A-01990

"In the whole province," one observer noted, "he could not be said to represent anyone but himself." Negotiations failed and Charles SEMLIN became premier instead.

BEAVER (*Castor canadensis*) is a large brown mammal of the order Rodentia (RODENTS) weighing up to 35 kg and inhabiting forested areas across the province, including VANCOUVER ISLAND and introduced to the QUEEN CHARLOTTE ISLANDS. Beavers spend much of their time in the water; their broad black tails are scaly and paddle-shaped, their large hind feet are webbed for swimming and their red-brown fur is insulated for warmth. Beaver fur has 2 surfaces: an outer layer of long, coarse "guard" hair and an under layer of fine, smooth "wool." FIRST NATIONS used the pelts for clothing, but it was the underfur that Europeans used to make felt hats, making the animal valuable to the FUR TRADE. Beavers live in LAKES and streams (*see* RIVERS), where they build their lodges out of logs, branches and mud. Though the opening to the lodge is built

beneath the water, the inside remains dry and warm. The pile is hollowed (or gnawed) out above the high-water mark so that the animals can live inside. They also build dams to maintain the water level around their lodges. Beavers have large front teeth for gnawing on wood and collecting the material they need for their elaborate constructions. They have a varied diet of leaves and bark of aspen, willows, roots and stems of pond lilies and other pond weeds, cattails and some sedges. Beavers mate for life and the female gives birth to 3–4 young in the spring. Two-year-olds leave the colony in midsummer and pair up to build new lodges. They may travel widely during this period. Although beavers are preyed upon by all large carnivores, their most serious enemy is disease, notably tularemia. Along with their historical economic importance, beavers play a crucial role in maintaining their forest aquatic ecosystem.

BEAVER was the first steamboat on the north Pacific coast. Built in 1835 near London, England, for the HBC, it was 31 m long with a pair of 35 hp engines powering paddlewheels on either side. It arrived at Fort Vancouver on the COLUMBIA R on 10 Apr 1836 after sailing from England, and the paddles were installed at the fort. The HBC used the ship to supply posts, collect furs and explore the coast. In Nov 1858 it carried dignitaries to FORT LANGLEY to officiate at the ceremonies marking the founding of BC as a colony. From 1858 to 1862 it mainly plied the waters between VICTORIA and the mainland, then worked as a naval survey ship with a swivel gun mounted on the bow. The HBC sold the *Beaver* in 1874, but it remained in use as a coastal freighter and towboat until it was wrecked on 26 July 1888, off Prospect Point at the entrance to

The steamboat Beaver, in a later reincarnation as a coastal freighter and towboat, c 1870. BC Archives A-00009

VANCOUVER harbour. In 1898 a second notable vessel named *Beaver* was built at ALBION IRON WORKS in Victoria for the CANADIAN PACIFIC NAVIGATION CO. A sternwheeler originally intended for service on the STIKINE R, this ship was the first steel-hulled vessel wholly built in BC. It was completed too late for the brief Stikine boom, so instead it served on the FRASER R. In 1913 it was forced out of business by the INTERURBAN rail service, and later became a ferry for the BC government. The *Beaver* was finally stricken from the Registry of Ships in 1930.

BEAVER, later known as Beavermouth, 80 km northeast of REVELSTOKE near the confluence of the Beaver and COLUMBIA rivers, was an important CPR depot established in 1884. A SAWMILL produced the vast amounts of timber needed to build snowsheds in the mountains, and "helper" locomotives were based here to push passenger and freight trains along the steepest sections of line. With the opening of the MICA DAM in 1973, the area was flooded by KINBASKET LK.   *AS*

Beaver, Canada's national animal. Duane Sept photo

John Innes's painting of the steamboat Beaver, trading for furs along the coast. VPL 800

BEAVER COVE is on the east coast of VANCOU-VER ISLAND, at the top of JOHNSTONE STRAIT just south of PORT MCNEILL at the mouth of the Kokish R. It has been a LOGGING centre since 1917, when the Nimpkish Timber Co began operations. The community that developed was called ENGLE-WOOD. The cove eventually became a saltwater dump for a huge RAILWAY LOGGING operation in the Nimpkish Valley, owned by CANADIAN FOREST PRODUCTS LTD. As of 1999 the last logging rwy in BC continued to work out of the cove, which is named for the HBC steamer *BEAVER*.

BEAVER CREEK, 10 km northwest of PORT ALBERNI on VANCOUVER ISLAND, is at the centre of a rich farming district (*see* AGRICULTURE) beside the Stamp R. The area was settled and cleared in the 1880s and became important to the development of Port Alberni. AS

BEAVER First Nation; *see* DUNNE-ZA.

BEAVER LAKE, 43 km northeast of WILLIAMS LAKE, was the site of an early CARIBOO roadhouse established by Peter DUNLEVY in 1861. The Hamilton family later operated a ranch and post office here. From Beaver Lake a road runs northwest to QUESNEL past the picturesque farms and log cabin homes of the Beaver Valley AS

BEAVER POINT, on the southeast corner of SALTSPRING ISLAND in the GULF ISLANDS (40 km north of VICTORIA), was first settled about 1860. Henry Ruckle arrived in 1872, built a wharf, established a post office in 1884 and developed the largest farm on the island (4.86 km²). Still operating, it is the oldest family farm in BC and is part of Ruckle Provincial Park (*see* AGRICUL-TURE; PARKS, PROVINCIAL). AS

BEAVERDELL, pop 280, is a farming community (*see* AGRICULTURE) and former station on the KETTLE VALLEY RWY 35 km east of PENTICTON. The Highland Bell SILVER mine operated nearby on Wallace Mt from 1901 to 1991. The hotel, opened in 1904, has one of the longest continuously operated pubs in BC. Two neighbouring settlements, Beaverton and Rendell, merged and adopted the current name around 1905. Beaverdell hosts a High Water Days festival in early June. AS

BEAVERLEY was the centre of a farming and ranching district 15 km southwest of PRINCE GEORGE and just south of the Yellowhead Hwy. A school opened here in 1919 and a post office was in operation from 1922 to 1948 AS

BECHER, Frederick, pioneer rancher (b 1862, India; d 1936, Riske Creek). He was a former HBC employee who started a trading post at RISKE CREEK with a partner, George Dester. Dester returned to England but Becher went on to develop a landmark stopping place, store, ranch and saloon. Many CHILCOTIN ranchers got their start at Becher Place. Becher's prairie, a vast track of land at Riske Creek, was named for him, as was Becher's Dam. The hotel and store are long

gone, but the ranch, now the Bar M7, was still operating in 1999.

BECK, Barry, hockey player (b 3 June 1957, Vancouver). He was one of the best, and most intimidating, HOCKEY defencemen from BC to play in the NHL. As a junior he starred with the NEW WESTMINSTER BRUINS of the WHL 1974–77. In each of his 3 junior seasons the team went to the Memorial Cup finals, eventually capturing the national title in 1977. In his final year he won league MVP honours. Drafted second overall in 1977, he entered the NHL with the Colorado Rockies and scored 22 goals in his first season, a record for rookie defencemen that stood for 11 years. After another season in Colorado he was traded to the NY Rangers where he was captain until shoulder problems forced his retirement in 1986. After a brief comeback with the LA Kings 1989–90, he left the league permanently and became part owner of a Vancouver nightclub. He retired with the most points (65, in 1979–80) and the most goals (22) ever scored in one season by an NHL defenceman from BC SW

BEDAUX SUB-ARCTIC (CITROEN) EXPEDI-TION was an attempt by the French-American adventurer Charles Bedaux to cross northern BC by motor vehicle. Bedaux (1886–1944), who had made his fortune as an industrial efficiency expert, led the first motor vehicle crossing of the Sahara in 1930 using Citroen half-tracks, the same vehicle he intended to drive across BC. The expedition left Edmonton amid great fanfare 6 July 1934, then proceeded up the PEACE R and into the mountains. Along with advance parties to clear the trail, the expedition consisted of 5 half-tracks and 16 people (including Bedaux's wife, his mistress and a Spanish maid) and carried a mountain of unnecessary gear. The wilderness soon overwhelmed the vehicles, which were abandoned in the HALFWAY R, and the party continued on horseback up the Juskwa and Kwadacha rivers as far as Sifton Pass, about 660 km northwest of FORT ST JOHN. They then aban-

Bedaux Subarctic Expedition vehicles in Peace R country, 1934. BC Archives I-33249

doned the project and returned by boat to the Peace. During WWII the Americans arrested Bedaux as a spy. Before the case could be proven he committed suicide; later it appeared likely he was unjustly accused.

BEEKEEPING; *see* APICULTURE.

BEGBIE, Matthew Baillie, judge (b 9 May 1819, Cape of Good Hope; d 11 June 1894, Victoria). He was raised on the Isle of Guernsey, then attended Cambridge Univ, where he studied classics and mathematics. He then studied

Matthew Baillie Begbie, chief justice of BC 1870–94. Langley Centennial Museum

law in London and practised there for several years. When the mainland colony of BC was created in 1858, he won appointment as judge. He arrived in VICTORIA in November of that year and spent the rest of his life in BC. He lived in NEW WESTMINSTER from 1860 to 1870, then in Victoria, but spent a large part of each year presiding over courts throughout the Interior. Begbie was a sociable, witty man of imposing size and appearance who spoke French and Italian and established himself as a patron of the arts. His central role in introducing British law to a rough frontier made him the subject of many legends. Although he gained a posthumous reputation as a "hanging judge," the imputation of callousness is unfair: he was severe but just, often taking the side of the underdog. At the union of the colonies in 1866 he remained chief justice of the mainland until 1870, when he became chief justice of the entire colony, then the province, a position he held until his death. His Victoria home, where he lived as a bachelor and entertained freely, had spacious grounds that accommodated a croquet pitch and 3 grass tennis courts. He was knighted in 1875 for his contributions to the BC JUDICIAL SYSTEM.
Reading: David Ricardo Williams, *The Man for a New Country: Sir Matthew Baillie Begbie*, 1977.

BELCARRA, village, pop 665, is a residential waterfront community at the mouth of INDIAN ARM in BURRARD INLET, opposite DEEP COVE. It was incorporated on 22 Aug 1979 as a member of the GREATER VANCOUVER REGIONAL DISTRICT and much of it comprises Belcarra Regional Park (11.48 km²). Once a winter village site of the TSLEIL WAU-TUTH NATION, it is named for a place in Ireland and means "fair land on which the sun shines."

BELFORD, 8 km west of NELSON on the south shore of the KOOTENAY R, and Granite, its neighbour 1 km to the north on the CPR, formed a MINING and AGRICULTURE district that flourished in the 1910s. Granite, site of an early quarry and lime kiln, was surrounded by mining claims   AS

BELIZE INLET is a long (40 km), narrow finger of water on the mainland coast just south of Cape Caution, entered via NAKWAKTO RAPIDS. During the initial naval survey of the inlet in 1865 by the steamer *BEAVER*, it was named after the capital of the British Honduras, where Frederick SEYMOUR had served prior to being appointed governor of BC in 1864. The steep-sided shores have undergone extensive LOGGING.

BELL, Alistair Macready, artist (b 21 Oct 1913, Darlington, England; d 12 Oct 1997, Vancouver). He emigrated to VANCOUVER in 1929 and later studied at the Vancouver School of Art (*see* EMILY CARR INSTITUTE OF ART & DESIGN), where he developed his talent as a printmaker. While earning his living as a draftsman in a steel plant, he produced work in a variety of media, including lithographs, wood engravings and woodcut prints. From 1967 he was able to devote himself full time to his art and exhibited in galleries and museums around the world. He is especially known for his prints of birds, animals and West Coast scenes. A large number of his prints belong to the permanent collection of the Art Gallery of Greater VICTORIA.

Alistair Bell, artist. Eliza Massey photo

BELL, Jack, farmer, philanthropist (b 28 Feb 1913, Montreal). Sometimes called "the Cranberry King," he planted BC's first commer-

cial CRANBERRY crop in RICHMOND in 1946 and is credited with founding the local industry. Very successful in his agricultural enterprises, he became one of the province's leading philanthropists. Projects he has funded wholly or in part include the Jack Bell Research Centre at Vancouver General Hospital (1978), a new School of Social Work building at UBC (1992), the FIRST NATIONS Longhouse at UBC (1993), shelters for women and the homeless, and a carpooling program aimed at reducing traffic congestion and air pollution in the VANCOUVER area. Among his many awards are Freeman of the City of Vancouver, membership in the FRASER RIVER Hall of Fame, an honorary degree from UBC, the Order of Canada (1996) and the ORDER OF BC (1991).   *Shannon Emmerson*

BELL-IRVING, Duncan, businessman, military aviator (b 28 Aug 1894, Vancouver; d 24 Apr 1965, Vancouver). As a young man from a privileged family, straight out of boarding school, he enlisted in the Seaforth Highlanders when WWI began and was among the first contingent of Canadian troops to go overseas. He was one of 6 brothers to join up, sons of the cannery owner Henry BELL-IRVING. He fought in the trenches of northern France, then transferred to the Royal Flying Corps in the fall of 1915. After training, he first saw action as an observer in Sept. He was wounded in Dec but recovered and obtained his pilot's wings in May 1916. From June to Nov he took part in raids across the front lines until he was again wounded. During this time he was credited with shooting down 6 enemy planes and a balloon, more than any other Canadian pilot to that time. Unable to resume flying because of his injuries, he became chief instructor at the famous Gosport School of Special Flying. After the war he was married to Elizabeth "Pye" Keith-Falconer Pybus. He was involved in business in VANCOUVER and eventually managed Bell-Irving Insurance Ltd, a family company. An energetic supporter of the RCAF, he was recalled to active service in WWII and commanded the Central Flying School at Trenton, ON. He served on many civic and military committees and kept in touch with aviation policy matters until his death.

BELL-IRVING, Henry Ogle "H.O.," businessman (b 26 Jan 1856, Lockerbie, Scotland; d 19 Feb 1931, Vancouver). After his father died, the family moved to Germany where he trained as a civil engineer. He emigrated to Canada in 1882 to work on the survey for the CPR. When the track reached SALMON ARM in 1885 he decided to quit and walk to GRANVILLE (Vancouver), but along the way he was set upon and robbed, and when he arrived at the coast he was destitute. Nevertheless he was impressed by the tiny community, and after returning briefly to England to marry he settled in VANCOUVER with his wife and founded an import business. In 1891 he and his partner, R.G. TATLOW, later minister of finance, used British capital to form the ANGLO-BC PACKING CO, which owned fish canneries on the FRASER R and up the coast. In time ABC Co became the largest exporter of tinned

SALMON to markets around the world. The Bell-Irvings had 10 children, most of whom married and settled in Vancouver, creating one of the city's dynastic families. The family lived in a palatial home in the West End called The Strands and developed Pasley Island as a summer retreat. During WWI Bell-Irving supported the training of Canadian pilots for the Royal Flying Corps.

BELL-IRVING, Henry Pybus, real estate executive, lt gov 1978–1983 (b 21 Jan 1913, Vancouver). A grandson of H.O. BELL-IRVING, he grew up in VANCOUVER a scion of one of the city's leading families. After studies at UBC he joined the Seaforth Highlanders in 1932 and retired as a brigadier in 1945. During WWII he was decorated for his service in Italy and the Netherlands, and he commanded the first Canadian troops to enter Amsterdam at the liberation. After returning to Vancouver, he joined the family real estate firm, Bell-Irving Insurance Agencies, which merged with A.E. LePage in 1972. He was a senior executive with the company when he was appointed LT GOV. During his time in office he was recognized as a citizens' voice for aboriginal land claims (*see* ABORIGINAL RIGHTS). After retiring from the vice-regal post he lived in W VANCOUVER. He was awarded the Order of Canada (1985) and the ORDER OF BC (1990).

Shannon Emmerson

BELLA BELLA, pop 1,211, is on Campbell Island (166 km²) overlooking Lama Passage, about 520 km north of VANCOUVER via the INSIDE PASSAGE. It takes its name from the HEILTSUK (Bella Bella) nation. The community originated as the FUR TRADE centre of FORT MCLOUGHLIN, operated by the HBC from 1833 to 1843. The HBC reopened a trading store in 1868 and Heiltsuk people moved to the community from outlying areas. METHODIST CHURCH missionaries arrived in 1880 and built a mission and a school. During the 1890s the community outgrew its location and moved 3 km north to a more open site. The original site is called Old Town. New Bella Bella, later renamed Waglisla, developed as a LOGGING and FISHING centre. The Heiltsuk band operates a hotel, store, school and cultural centre. Across Lama Passage is an old SALMON CANNERY settlement known as East Bella Bella.

View of the village of Bella Bella.
Les Bazso/Vancouver Province

Bella Coola, at the head of the Bella Coola River. Ian McAllister photo

BELLA COOLA, pop 873, is at the head of N Bentinck Arm, an extension of Burke Channel at the mouth of the BELLA COOLA R about 400 km north of VANCOUVER. It is named for the original inhabitants, people of the NUXALK (formerly known as Bella Coola) nation, who live at settlements near the townsite. The first outsiders arrived in 1793 when a party of British sailors attached to Capt George VANCOUVER's expedition explored to the head of N Bentinck Arm in longboats. A few weeks later Alexander MACKENZIE arrived overland, seeking a navigable route to the Pacific Ocean. He proceeded by CANOE about 60 km into DEAN CHANNEL, where he wrote his famous message on a rock, now Alexander Mackenzie Provincial PARK. The HBC built a post at BELLA BELLA in 1833 to serve the area and the company had another post at Bella Coola from 1868 to 1882. Both were purchased from the HBC by John Clayton, the most influential businessman on the Central Coast for many years. AGRICULTURE began in the valley in 1894 with the arrival of a colony of NORWEGIAN settlers, mainly from Minnesota. Led by Rev Christian Saugstad, they located up the valley around HAGENSBORG. Commercial FISHING became important early in the 20th century, with the construction of first one, then a second cannery. They closed in the 1930s but Bella Coola remains a base for the fishery, both sport and commercial. Another mainstay of the local economy has been LOGGING, which began on a large scale during WWII. Various large companies have been active, along with many small independents. The Mid-Coast Forest District office is located here. Accessible only by air and water for most of its history, Bella Coola was linked to WILLIAMS LAKE by land in 1953 with the completion of Hwy 20, the famous Chilcotin Hwy.

BELLA COOLA First Nation; *see* NUXALK.

BELLA COOLA FISHERIES LTD, established in BELLA COOLA in 1977 by W.R. Bingham and T.W. Turyk, is one of BC's largest fishing and fish products companies. Privately owned, with its head office and main processing plant on the FRASER R in DELTA, the company is involved in catching, processing, marketing and worldwide distribution of Pacific seafood products including fresh, frozen and canned SALMON, salmon roe, sujiko (full skeins of salmon roe) and caviar, HERRING roe and DOGFISH. In 1999 the company had 150 employees and working arrangements with about 150 fishing vessels, it processed an average of 9 million kg of fish annually, and it operated 2 plants in Delta and a small facility in PRINCE RUPERT. *See also* FISHING, COMMERCIAL; SALMON CANNING.

BELLA COOLA RIVER, 70 km, flows from the junction of the ATNARKO R and Talchako R on the eastern edge of TWEEDSMUIR PROVINCIAL PARK down a deep valley to empty through a broad ESTUARY into N Bentinck Arm at BELLA COOLA. A mild CLIMATE and heavy rainfall nurtures a verdant RAIN FOREST in the valley. In the territory of the NUXALK (Bella Coola) people, the river provided a TRAIL to the Interior for coastal FIRST NATIONS and was part of the route taken by Alexander MACKENZIE out to the coast in 1793. From about 1900 farm settlers occupied the lower valley, which is connected to the CHILCOTIN by The Hill, an infamous 9-km stretch of unpaved switchbacks with a grade of up to 18%. Well stocked with SALMON and STEELHEAD, the river was considered one of the finest in the world for sport FISHING until the early 1990s, when the steelhead fishery collapsed. It has been designated a BC HERITAGE RIVER. *See also* RIVERS. *Reading:* Mark Hume, *River of the Angry Moon*, 1998.

BELLEROSE was a FRASER VALLEY farming settlement and station on the BC ELECTRIC RWY east of Sumas Lk and 17 km southwest of CHILLIWACK. It was named after George Bellerose, who took up residence there in 1895 and served as local postmaster until his death in 1918, when the post office closed. The district still maintains a quiet, rural character.

BELTED KINGFISHER; *see* KINGFISHER, BELTED.

BEN-MY-CHREE was an unusual tourist destination at the south end of Taku Arm in Tagish Lake. Otto Partridge, manager of a steamboat company at Bennett Lake, invested in a GOLD mining property at the site in 1911. The mine was abandoned but Partridge and his wife Kate moved to the site, built a log cabin and developed a beautiful English garden in the middle of the wilderness. Visitors came down the lake aboard excursion steamers from Carcross in the Yukon to visit and take tea and homemade wine. When the Partridges both died in 1930, the WHITE PASS & YUKON Rwy took over the property and operated tours until 1955. Ben-My-Chree meant "Girl of My Heart" in Manx, the language of the Isle of Man where Otto Partridge grew up.

BEND was a SAWMILL settlement and station on the CNR and the FRASER R, 110 km east of PRINCE GEORGE and just west of DOME CREEK. A school and post office operated here in the 1930s. It was named for the 90-degree turn the railway tracks take at this location. *AS*

BENE, John, plywood manufacturer, engineer, community activist (b 1910, Vienna, Austria; d 1986, Vancouver). He was educated in Hungary, where his family was in the plywood business and where he earned degrees in mechanical and electrical engineering. In 1938 he moved to VANCOUVER and with Poldi Bentley and John Prentice founded Pacific Veneer Co in NEW WESTMINSTER. He served as managing director until 1944 when he sold his interest to his partners and formed Western Plywood Co, which later became WELDWOOD OF CANADA. He was the first Canadian director of US Plywood, Weldwood's parent company. In 1964 Bene became a special adviser on international development to the Canadian government and assisted in projects in many underdeveloped countries. He served terms as a director of the Children's Foundation, the BC Research Council, UNICEF Canada and the BANK OF BC. In 1981 he became the chief federal negotiator on NISGA'A land claims (*see* ABORIGINAL RIGHTS) and was named to the Order of Canada in 1984. In 1986, a few weeks before his death, he was awarded an honorary degree by SFU.

Ken Drushka

BENNETT was the terminus of the CHILKOOT TRAIL at the south end of Bennett Lk, which straddles the BC–Yukon border in the far northwest corner of the province. Prospectors on their way to the Klondike goldfields during 1897–98 paused here to build boats to carry them the rest of the way to Dawson City (*see* GOLD RUSHES). Several SAWMILLS produced lumber for boat construction, and the area had hotels, saloons, stores and a church. A townsite was surveyed in 1898 and named, like the lake, for the New York newspaper publisher James Gordon Bennett. Activity peaked in 1899 with the arrival of the WHITE PASS & YUKON RWY, and the population rose to 2,000. Once the railway passed on to Whitehorse, most of the people and businesses left and by 1902 the town was abandoned. The site was used subsequently by FIRST NATIONS people for trapping and hunting.

BENNETT, William "Ol' Bill," labour journalist (b 1881, Greenock, Scotland; d 31 Dec 1949, Vancouver). He immigrated to BC in 1907 and opened a barber shop in downtown VANCOUVER. He was a member of the Socialist Party of Canada and contributed regularly to the party paper, the *Western Clarion.* Following WWI he joined the Communist Party and was a founding member of its affiliate, the Workers Party of Canada. In the mid-1930s he began writing his "Short Jabs" column, which appeared in several party publications and made him one of the best-known communist propagandists of the era. He also wrote a labour history, *Builders of British Columbia* (1937).

BENNETT, William Andrew Cecil, merchant, politician, premier 1 Aug 1952–15 Sept 1972 (b 6 Sept 1900, Hastings, NB; d 23 Feb 1979, Kelowna). Born on a small farm in New Brunswick, he emerged from poverty to become a successful hardware merchant. He moved in 1919 to Alberta and in 1930 to BC, where he bought a hardware business in KELOWNA. During the Depression he was active in the provincial CONSERVATIVE PARTY and won election to the legislature in 1941. In 1946 he failed in his bid to win the Conservative leadership. Bennett temporarily abandoned provincial politics to run in a federal by-election in 1948. He lost and returned to the legislature in 1949, a member of the anti-socialist COALITION GOVERNMENT, which had formed during the war. In 1950 Bennett failed in his second attempt to win the Conservative leadership. He crossed the floor to sit as an independent early in 1951, by which time his career seemed to be stalled. But later that year he joined the SOCIAL CREDIT PARTY, and when the Socreds won a surprise victory in the 1952 election they chose him leader of their minority government. Bennett became the longest-serving PREMIER in BC history. His 20-year term was marked by rapid economic growth based on resource development, much of it financed by out-of-province investment, and his government initiated the building of highways, power dams and railways at an energetic pace. While all of this activity took place, Bennett claimed to be eliminating the provincial debt; in 1959 he celebrated this feat with a huge bonfire of cancelled bonds on a barge in OKANAGAN LK. A fervid supporter of free enterprise, he nevertheless nationalized the ferry system, expanded post-secondary education and created BC HYDRO, a CROWN CORPORATION, in 1961. At the same time, Bennett held social spending and labour unions in check. A volatile campaigner (one journalist described "the fixed neon smile, the bustling salesman's assurance, the ceaseless torrent of speech"), Bennett retained power with fierce attacks on the "socialism" of the CCF-NDP. He won re-election 6 times, but finally lost to his NDP archfoes, led by Dave BARRETT, in 1972. He resigned the next year and his son Bill BENNETT took over as leader of the Social Credit Party.
Reading: David Mitchell, *W.A.C. Bennett and the Rise of British Columbia,* 1983.

W.A.C. Bennett, premier of BC 1952–72.
Kelowna Museum

BENNETT, William Richards "Bill," businessman, politician, premier 22 Dec 1975–6 Aug 1986 (b 14 Apr 1932, Kelowna). The son of longtime premier W.A.C. BENNETT, he went into business directly after high school and made a substantial fortune in real estate and other investments. Following his father's retirement from politics in 1973, he won election to the legislature in the same S Okanagan seat and ran successfully in Nov 1973 for leadership of the SOCIAL CREDIT PARTY. As leader of the opposition, and with the help of his father, he regained support for the party and in the 1975 election he led the Socreds back to power. His first term culminated in the creation of the BC RESOURCES INVESTMENT CORPORATION, a massive privatization of public assets. Re-elected in 1979, he ran head-

long into a severe economic recession; his government responded with an austerity program of wage restraint and budget cutting. At the same time he launched a series of megaprojects designed to stimulate the economy, including EXPO 86 in Vancouver, a huge coal development in the north, a rapid transit system (SKYTRAIN) for the Lower Mainland, and the COQUIHALLA HWY. All these measures were highly controversial, especially combined with cuts to social services and government spending. Nonetheless Bennett was re-elected to a third term in May 1983; soon after that he announced dramatic spending cuts, layoffs and changes in bargaining practices that workers believed to threaten job security. So began the most tumultuous period of political protest in recent BC history. In summer 1983 labour unions and community groups formed the SOLIDARITY coalition to fight the government program, while Bennett tried to force his mea-

*Outgoing Premier Bill Bennett at the 1986
Social Credit leadership convention.*
Brian Kent/Vancouver Sun

sures through the legislature in unprecedented all-night sittings. In the end he introduced his program with only minor concessions, but his confrontational style cost him voter support and he resigned in 1986 assuming that he could not win another election. He returned to private business and remained out of the public eye until the early 1990s when insider-trading charges against Bennett, his brother Russell and Herb Doman of DOMAN INDUSTRIES LTD led to prolonged legal proceedings. A provincial court acquitted the plaintiffs but in Aug 1996 a separate BC SECURITIES COMMISSION investigation found them guilty. *See also* PREMIER.

BENNETT (W.A.C.) DAM is located at the canyon of the PEACE R 24 km west of HUDSON'S HOPE. Along with its associated Gordon M. SHRUM Generating Station, named for a former chair of BC HYDRO, it has a generating capacity of 2,730,000 kilowatts, more than any other HYDROELECTRIC plant in BC. The dam was constructed by BC Hydro from 1962 to 1967 and the generating station, the largest underground powerhouse in the world at the time, came on line in 1968. The complex flooded the upper Peace, FINLAY and PARSNIP river valleys to create WILLISTON RESERVOIR, the largest reservoir in BC. The Bennett Dam is 183 m high and 2 km long across the top. A second, smaller power station, the Peace Canyon Dam, is located 23 km downstream at the bottom of the canyon. Completed in 1980, it has a capacity of 700,000 kilowatts.

BENTALL, Barney, singer, songwriter (b 10 Mar 1956, Toronto). The grandson of the VANCOUVER construction magnate Charles BENTALL, he began his recording career using the name Brandon Wolf in an attempt to disguise his connection to the prominent family. After playing for several years in Vancouver clubs, he and his band recorded a 1988 album, *Barney Bentall and the Legendary Hearts*, and captured the Juno Award for most promising group. Through the 1990s they recorded several more albums,

including *Lonely Avenue* (1990), *Ain't Life Strange* (1992), and *Gin Palace* (1995). In 1997 Bentall collaborated with the Canadian novelist Guy Vanderhaeghe to write lyrics for the album *Till Tomorrow*. *Mike Harling*

BENTALL, Charles, engineer (b 16 June 1882, Felsted, England; d 6 Nov 1974, Vancouver). He left school at age 13 to train as an engineer in his native England before immigrating to Ontario in 1907. He moved west to VANCOUVER the next year and in 1911 joined Dominion Construction. By 1920 he owned the company, and over the next 3 decades he made it the leading builder in the city (*see* BENTALL CORP). Bentall was active in the Baptist Church and was a founder of the local Kiwanis Club and the Vancouver Better Business Bureau. He retired from Dominion in 1955, handing control to his sons Clark and Bob. In 1986 he was named to the Canadian Business Hall of Fame.

BENTALL CORP is a VANCOUVER real estate company focussed on the acquisition, development, leasing and management of office properties. Its assets, valued in excess of $1.5 billion (1999), are principally in Vancouver, Seattle and southern California. The business was founded by Charles BENTALL, a structural engineer who arrived in Vancouver from Britain in 1908. He joined the Dominion Construction Co and by 1920 he owned it. At times referred to as "the company that built Vancouver," Dominion's landmarks include HMCS *Discovery* (a naval cadet training school on DEADMAN'S ISLAND), the STANLEY PARK causeway, PORT ALICE townsite, the TELUS (BC Tel) building in BURNABY and the 4-towered Bentall Centre in downtown Vancouver. Bentall retired in 1955 and his sons Clark and Robert ran the company until 1988; at that time the assets of the construction business carried on by Dominion were transferred to a group of Bentall family members while the newly formed Bentall Corp retained ownership of the real estate portfolio. In mid-1996 control of the company was sold to the *Caisse de dépôt et placement du Québec*. In June 1997 the company completed an initial public offering and was listed on the Toronto, Montreal and Vancouver stock exchanges. Its revenues were $213.3 million in 1999.

BENTINCK ISLAND is a small piece of rock off the southern tip of VANCOUVER ISLAND between the island and RACE ROCKS. In 1924 the leper colony on D'ARCY ISLAND closed and a new facility opened here. It was not until 1956 that the last leper died. The department of defence assumed ownership of the island, which has been used as a demolition range.

BENTLEY, Peter John Gerald, forestry executive (b 17 Mar 1930, Vienna, Austria). He is chairman of Canfor Corp (*see* CANADIAN FOREST PRODUCTS), a company his father Poldi founded after immigrating to BC from Austria in 1938. He is also on the board of several major corporations. An avid sportsman, he was one of the

people who won an NHL franchise for the VANCOUVER CANUCKS. A fundraiser for and significant donor to the BC SPORTS HALL OF FAME, he received the hall's W.A.C. Bennett Award in 1999 for his devotion to BC sports.

BERGER, Mitch, football player (b 24 June 1972, Kamloops). Raised in N DELTA, he was drafted as a punter and kickoff man out of the Univ of Colorado by the NFL's Philadelphia Eagles in 1994. After being cut from the team, he tried out for the Chicago Bears and Indianapolis Colts before earning a starting position with the Minnesota Vikings in 1996. In Minnesota he developed into one of FOOTBALL's best kickers. In 1998 he set an NFL record by forcing 40 touchbacks from his kickoffs, and in 1999 he led the league in punting average (45.4 yards), net average (38.4 yards) and longest single punt (75 yards), earning a Pro Bowl selection. In 2000 he became the highest-paid punter in NFL history.
SW

BERGER, Thomas Rodney "Tom," lawyer, jurist (b 23 Mar 1933, Victoria). After graduating from UBC law school, he practised law in VANCOUVER from 1957 to 1971. One of his notable cases was representing the NISGA'A in the landmark CALDER CASE. Active in the NDP, he served a term as MP for Vancouver–Burrard in 1962–63, then won election as an MLA in 1966. In Apr 1969 he defeated Dave BARRETT for the NDP leadership and led the party into a provincial election later that year. After a stunning defeat in which he lost his own seat, he retired from politics. A judge on the BC Supreme Court in 1971–83, he jumped to national prominence as commissioner of the Mackenzie Valley Pipeline Inquiry in 1974–77, when he toured the North

Tom Berger, former BC Supreme Court judge, 1999. Barry Peterson & Blaise Enright-Peterson

listening to the views of aboriginal inhabitants. His bestselling report *Northern Frontier, Northern Homeland* (1977) halted PIPELINE construction. Following his resignation from the Supreme Court because of a disagreement over his freedom to express opinions on public issues, he taught at UBC's law faculty in 1983–86; during this time he also headed the Alaska Native Review Commission. He then returned to private practice. He was named to the Order of Canada in 1990 and has received a dozen honorary degrees. *See also* FIRST NATIONS; JUDICIAL SYSTEM; OIL AND GAS INDUSTRY.

Reading: Carol Swayze, *Hard Choices: A Life of Tom Berger*, 1987.

BERGMANN, Art, musician (b 1954, Vancouver). A pioneer of VANCOUVER's punk music scene, Bergmann joined his first band, the Schmorgs, in 1977. A year later he started the K-Tels, later renamed the Young Canadians. Their 1979 recording of his satire of college spring break, "Hawaii," remains a local punk anthem. In the 1980s Bergmann was a member of Los Popularos and Poisoned. In 1988 he recorded his first solo album, *Crawl With Me*, produced by Velvet Underground legend John Cale. The album was certified gold in Canada and the song "Our Little Secret," about child abuse, received considerable airplay. In 1989 Bergmann released *Sexual Roulette*, an album for which he received a Juno Award nomination for most promising male vocalist. In 1993 he recorded *What Fresh Hell Is This?*, an album paying tribute to his victory over a long-time heroin habit. He has also appeared in two Bruce McDonald films, *Highway 61* and *Hard Core Logo*. *Mike Harling*

BERING SEA DISPUTE, 1886–1911, pitted Canadian pelagic sealers against American conservationists and sealing interests. The hunt for the northern FUR SEAL began with Pacific coast FIRST NATIONS, who used the animals for food and then for pelts to trade with the HBC. In 1866 white traders inaugurated a pelagic hunt with the help of aboriginal hunters, who were transported with their canoes to the sealing grounds some distance off the west coast of VANCOUVER ISLAND. By the 1880s the sealing fleet was following the migrating fur seals north to the Gulf of Alaska and into the Bering Sea, where the animals congregated each spring and summer, mainly on the Pribilof Islands, to breed. American hunters conducted a land-based seal hunt on the Pribilofs following the purchase of Alaska by the US in 1867. The Americans grew alarmed at the decline in the seal population and blamed the pelagic fleet. In 1886 a US cutter seized 3 Canadian vessels, claiming they were in violation of US territorial waters and touched off an international dispute that continued for 25 years. While diplomats negotiated, VICTORIA became the main port of the pelagic fleet, supplying provisions, crews and winter moorage. In 1893 an international tribunal ruled that the Bering Sea did not fall under American jurisdiction, but it did place several restrictions on the seal hunt, which the hunters

Pribilof Islands sealers, c 1900. They were involved in the Bering Sea dispute, which was resolved in 1911. BC Archives F-01264

ignored. Canada remained adamant that the hunt should not end without compensation for its sealers. In 1911 Britain (on behalf of Canada), the US, Russia and Japan signed the NORTH PACIFIC FUR SEAL CONVENTION banning the pelagic hunt in the region. In return, Canadians received a share of the proceeds from the land-based hunt on the Bering Sea islands. The Convention was renewed in 1957 and Canada continued to share in profits from the sale of pelts from a managed hunt.

BERKELEY, Edith (Dunington), biologist (b 6 Sept 1875, Tulbagh, S Africa; d 25 Feb 1963, Nanaimo) and **Cyril**, chemist (b 2 Dec 1878, London, England; d 25 Aug 1973, Nanaimo). After meeting as undergraduates at London Univ, where Edith had a scholarship, they married in 1902 and moved to India; there she aided Cyril's research into indigo culture and processing. In 1914 they immigrated to BC to farm in the OKANAGAN VALLEY. After 2 years they took teaching positions at UBC, then located in the Fairview Shacks near the Vancouver General Hospital. Following WWI the couple went to work at the PACIFIC BIOLOGICAL STATION in NANAIMO. There Edith began research on marine polychaetes (marine worms), and Cyril soon gave up his own research to help her. Together they became world authorities on the subject. In recognition of their work, a number of organisms have been named after them. *Shannon Emmerson*

BERRIES are grown commercially in BC mainly in the FRASER VALLEY, the most productive berry growing area in Canada. Along with the CRANBERRY, the most important commercial berries are blueberries, strawberries and raspberries. The annual harvest totals 13.6 million kg, about 40% of which is consumed fresh while the rest is frozen or canned or used in a variety of processed foods. BC is one of the top 3 blueberry producing regions in the world. About 100 producers grow strawberries in the Fraser Valley. All the berries are hand-picked during a 3-week harvest period in June. The ABBOTSFORD area produces 90% of Canada's raspberries, an annual harvest of 11.3 million kg.

A wide variety of wild berries are found in BC and have been utilized as food by FIRST NATIONS people, particularly SALAL and Canada buffaloberry or SOOPOLLALIE. Other native fruit-bearing shrubs include the saskatoon (*Amelanchier alnifolia*), a tall shrub that can reach an impressive 5 m in height; the bog blueberry (*Vaccinium uliginosum*); black raspberry (*Rubus leucodermis*); bog cranberry (*V. oxycoccus*); red huckleberry (*V. parvifolium*); black huckleberry (*V. membranaceum*); and black gooseberry (*Ribes lacustre*). The Himalayan blackberry (*Rubus discolor*) is a common introduced species popular with berry pickers throughout the Pacific Northwest, who use the fruit to make wine, pies, jams, jellies and other preserves. Pickers should beware, however, because there are several species of poisonous berries in BC.

Reading: Nancy J. Turner and Adam F. Szczawinski, *Edible Wild Fruits and Nuts of Canada*, 1988.

BC BERRY FARMS by area (hectares)

	1971	1981	1991	1996
Strawberries	1,045	1,317	649	613
Raspberries	882	-	2,107	2,056
Grapes	974	1,247	590	833
Blueberries	-	-	1,655	2,068
Cranberries	-	-	963	1,187
Other berries	1,082	3,015	134	131
Total area in berries & grapes	3,983	5,579	6,098	6,888

BERTON, Pierre, writer (b 12 July 1920, Whitehorse, YT). A widely read popularizer of Canadian history, as well as a journalist and media personality, he was raised in Dawson City, YT, and spent his teen years living in VICTORIA. He began his career in NEWSPAPER journalism as a student at UBC from 1939 to 1941; there he worked on the student paper, the *Ubyssey*, and

Pierre Berton, Canada's foremost popular historian, 1998. Thies Bogner/Random House

was the campus correspondent and summer reporter for the *News-Herald*, a VANCOUVER daily. After graduating from university he went to work full-time at the *News-Herald* and within months, at age 21, was made city editor. He served in the army from 1942 to 1945, then returned to Vancouver, where he joined the *SUN* newspaper early in 1946. Under Hal Straight, the editor, the *Sun* was at that time carrying on a heated competition with the PROVINCE to be the city's leading paper and Berton was one of its most energetic reporters. He achieved international attention in 1947 with a series of stories about the so-called "Headless Valley" of the South Nahanni R. *Maclean's* magazine hired him away from the *Sun* and in May 1947 he left Vancouver for Toronto where he spent the rest of his career. After *Maclean's* he wrote for the *Toronto Star* and was a panelist on the long-running television quiz show *Front Page Challenge*, as well as hosting his own show. His first book of history, *Klondike*, appeared in 1958; it was followed by a succession of popular histories about a variety of subjects, including the building of the CPR, the settling of the West, the War of 1812, the Great Depression and Arctic exploration. A 3-time winner of the GOV GEN'S LITERARY AWARD for nonfiction, he was made a companion in the Order of Canada in 1986.

BERWICK, Robert A.D., architect (b 1909, Shelbourne, ON; d 1974, Vancouver). After completing his B Arch at the Univ of Toronto in 1938, he worked at the VANCOUVER firm of Sharp & Thompson until joining the air force in 1941. When he returned from the war, he joined Vancouver's most influential post-war firm, Sharp & Thompson Berwick Pratt, first as an associate (1946–56), then as a partner in Thompson Berwick & Pratt (1956–68). Among his notable buildings that set trends in modern expressionist design are the Vancouver Vocational Institute (1948–49), the BC HYDRO Building (1955–57) and various buildings on the UBC campus. *See also* ARCHITECTURE.

Martin Segger

BERYL G was a fish packer used to haul liquor illegally across the border into the US during Prohibition in the 1920s (*see* RUM-RUNNERS). On 16 Sept 1924 it was discovered floating near SIDNEY ISLAND. No one was on board and the cabin was smeared with blood. A police investigation led to charges against 3 Americans known to be involved in the liquor traffic and suspected of murdering the vessel's captain, William Gillis, and his teenage son. The accused were found guilty; 2 of them were hanged and the third received a life sentence. The *Beryl G*, renamed the *Manzetta*, continued to work the South Coast until it sank in the SAN JUAN ISLANDS in 1929. The *Beryl G* incident was one of the most notorious of the rum-running era on the coast from 1920 to 1933.

The Beryl G, *whose skipper and crew were murdered in the most ruthless crime of the rum-running era.*

BESSBOROUGH is a small farming district (*see* AGRICULTURE) 18 km west of DAWSON CREEK in the PEACE R region. Originally known as Willowbrook, it was renamed after a former gov gen of Canada when the post office was opened in 1935. The first homesteader was Joe Frederickson in 1928. *AS*

BESTWICK is a ranching settlement (*see* CATTLE INDUSTRY) 20 km southeast of KAMLOOPS near CAMPBELL LK. It was named after R. Bestwick, who served as the first postmaster in 1911. *AS*

BEVAN was a coal mining town north of CUMBERLAND in the COMOX Valley. A company town, it was built during 1911–12 by Canadian Collieries near one of its mines. As the mine began to deteriorate at the end of WWI so did the town, though it enjoyed a brief revival from 1937 to 1953, when #8 mine nearby was productive. *See also* COAL MINING, VANCOUVER ISLAND.

BEYNON, William, TSIMSHIAN ethnographer (b 1888, Victoria; d 1958). Raised in VICTORIA, he was the son of a high-ranking Tsimshian woman and a Welsh steamer captain. He returned to the North Coast, where he inherited a chieftainship from an uncle and became an important authority on Tsimshian culture for most of the anthropologists who visited the coast, including Franz BOAS, Marius BARBEAU and Philip Drucker.

BIBB, Leon, singer, entertainer (b 7 Feb 1922, Louisville, KY). He worked on Broadway and as a folksinger in New York for 20 years, appearing in 2 films with his friend Sidney Poitier and making 3 appearances on the *Ed Sullivan Show*. He performed with Paul Robeson, another friend, at Carnegie Hall and has recorded 9 albums. In 1970 he moved with his family (his son Eric is also a singer and musician) to VANCOUVER, where he performed in the ARTS CLUB THEATRE's wildly successful *Jacques Brel is Alive and Well and Living in Paris* and quickly became part of the city's entertainment scene. Since 1992 his interactive anti-racist musical show has toured BC secondary schools. He was an inaugural member of the BC ARTS COUNCIL created in 1996. *AS*

BICYCLING; *see* CYCLING; TRANSPORTATION ALTERNATIVES.

BIG BAR CREEK is a ranching area (*see* CATTLE INDUSTRY) on the east shore of the FRASER R northwest of CLINTON in the south CHILCOTIN. In about 1862 Joseph Haller opened a roadhouse, known as the Red Dog Saloon; other early settlers included the Grinder and Kostering families. In later years the well-known OK Ranch was located here. A ferry that crosses the Fraser at the mouth of Big Bar Crk has operated since 1894. The current-driven "reaction ferry," also known as a friction ferry, runs on cables and is carried back and forth by the movement of the river; the operator shifts the angle of the hull as necessary to adjust

The reaction ferry at Big Bar Creek.
Rick Blacklaws photo

to the current. There is a backup aerial tramway for winter use. The ferry at Big Bar is the most isolated in BC. Several nearby guest ranches plus Big Bar Lk Provincial Park (*see* PARKS, PROVINCIAL) attract TOURISTS to the region.   AS

BIG BAY, once known as Asman Bay and Yaculta Landing, is a maritime community on the northwest side of STUART ISLAND near the mouth of BUTE INLET, 45 km north of CAMPBELL RIVER. The first reported settler in the area was Anderson Secord in 1907. A school opened in 1928. The bay is home to fishers and loggers, and supports a pub, store, marina and sport fishing resort.   AS

BIG BEND GOLD RUSH; *see* GOLD RUSHES.

BIG BEND HIGHWAY, connecting GOLDEN and REVELSTOKE via the Big Bend of the COLUMBIA R, was the final link in the original trans-provincial highway. Funded jointly by the provincial and federal governments, the 305-km stretch was built from 1929 to 1940, largely as a Depression relief project. Officially opened on 29 June 1940, it was used for 2 decades until it was replaced by the ROGERS PASS section of the TRANS-CANADA HWY in 1962. The old route was partially flooded during dam construction in the 1970s. *See also* ROADS AND HIGHWAYS.

BIG CREEK is a ranching community (*see* CATTLE INDUSTRY) in the CHILCOTIN south of HANCEVILLE. The creek itself rises in the COAST MTS and drains north into the CHILCOTIN R, flowing through well-watered rangeland where cattle have been raised since 1896. LOGGING and TOURISM have also become important industries. Big Creek Provincial PARK (659.82 km²) at the headwaters is an isolated preserve for BEAR, MOOSE and bighorn sheep (*see* MOUNTAIN SHEEP).

BIG EDDY, 3 km west of REVELSTOKE on the CPR, was a small settlement named after a turbulent current nearby in the COLUMBIA R. It was the site of an early SAWMILL, built in 1893 by Dan Robinson and J.C. Steen, that manufactured ties and timbers for the railway until 1910, when it burned down.   AS

BIG LAKE is a historic ranching district (*see* CATTLE INDUSTRY) 50 km northeast of WILLIAMS LAKE

in the CARIBOO. The area was first settled in the 1890s by William Parker, who established Big Lake Ranch and operated an early stagecoach express service. Big Lake Ranch no longer exists, except as the post office name, which has been retained by popular demand despite attempts by postal authorities in the 1980s to change it to Big Lake.   AS

BIGG, Michael, marine mammalogist (b 1939; d 18 Oct 1990). He was the pioneer of modern research into the life habits of the KILLER WHALE of the West Coast. A graduate of UBC, he went to work at the PACIFIC BIOLOGICAL STATION in NANAIMO, where early in his career he studied harbour SEALS and FUR SEALS and helped plan the relocation of SEA OTTERS to the BC Coast. In the early 1970s he turned his attention to the killer whale, developing a technique for identifying individual whales by the markings on their bodies. This led to a reliable photographic census of coastal killer whales and a better understanding of their population distribution. The ECOLOGICAL RESERVE at ROBSON BIGHT is named for Bigg. He co-wrote *Killer Whales: A Study of their Identification, Genealogy and Natural History in British Columbia and Washington* (1987) as well as several scientific papers.

BILLINGS BAY, on the west side of NELSON ISLAND in Malaspina Strait, 90 km northwest of VANCOUVER, was equipped with a government float, freight shed and post office from 1950 to 1970 to serve the 70-odd people who lived in the area and in neighbouring BLIND BAY. The decline of the Nelson Island LOGGING and quarrying industries in the 1960s prompted many residents to move away. William Thomas Billings was a Royal Navy surgeon who served on the BC coast in the 1840s.   AS

BINNING, Bertram Charles, artist (b 10 Feb 1909, Medicine Hat, AB; d 16 Mar 1976, Vancouver). He studied at the Vancouver School of Art (see EMILY CARR INSTITUTE OF ART & DESIGN) under Fred VARLEY and in New York and London, England. After teaching at the VSA from 1934 to 1949 he joined the school of ARCHITECTURE at UBC. In 1955 he founded the fine arts department at the university, where he remained until his retirement in 1973. He took up oil painting in 1948 and is best known for his abstract paintings. His mosaics and murals in Vancouver include the BC Hydro Building, among others. One of the first modernist painters in western Canada, he was made a member of the Order of Canada in 1971. The W VANCOUVER house he built in 1941, with his wife Jessie, became a prototype of domestic modernism.

BIODIVERSITY is a three-fold term, referring simultaneously to life in all its forms, the habitats it occupies and the natural processes that support it. The term encompasses genetic variation within a species, the number and variety of species in a given area, and the variety of habitats available. Because of our highly varied topography, BC has the greatest number of habitats and

BIOGEOCLIMATIC ZONES (14) of any Canadian province. For comparison, the Yukon has 8 zones and is the second most diverse jurisdiction in Canada. This means BC has Canada's greatest biological diversity and a level of biodiversity of international and global significance. To 1999, 1,086 species of vertebrates have been identified in BC, comprised of 454 bird species, 450 fish species, 143 mammal species, 20 amphibian species and 19 reptile species. As well, the province has an estimated 2,073 native vascular plants, about 1,000 bryophytes (MOSSES and liverworts), 1,600 lichens, 522 species of algae (*see* SEAWEEDS), well over 10,000 species of fungi and between 50,000 and 70,000 invertebrate species, including about 35,000 species of INSECTS. Because of the isolating influence of mountains and islands, species in BC tend to show a very high genetic diversity. Undoubtedly there are organisms that have not yet been discovered or classified. At the same time, existing and unnamed species are disappearing as a result of human activities and population growth. *See also* ECOREGION CLASSIFICATION SYSTEM; ENDANGERED SPECIES; PLANTS, NATIVE.   *Maggie Paquet*

BIOGEOCLIMATIC ZONES are areas that represent a distinctive combination of CLIMATE, physiography, vegetation and soil. Each is named for a dominant tree, shrub, herb or moss, plus a geographical modifier, such as "Interior" or "Coastal." There are 14 major biogeoclimatic zones in BC. This system of classifying complex interrelationships was developed by Vladimir KRAJINA, a plant ecologist at UBC, and refined by Del Meidinger and others in the Ministry of Forests Research Branch. Each zone is extensively subdivided into subzones and variants. This system, in combination with the ECOREGION CLASSIFICATION SYSTEM, is the ecological basis of most forest and land use planning in BC (*see* FOREST SERVICE; FORESTRY).   *Maggie Paquet*

BIOGEOCLIMATIC ZONES (% area of BC covered)

Alpine tundra	19.6%
Boreal white and black spruce	16.3%
Engelmann spruce–subalpine fir	14.7%
Coastal western hemlock	11.3%
Sub-boreal spruce	10.4%
Spruce–willow–birch	7.8%
Interior cedar–hemlock	5.3%
Interior Douglas fir	4.6%
Mountain hemlock	3.8%
Montane spruce	2.8%
Sub-boreal pine–spruce	2.5%
Bunchgrass	.3%
Coastal Douglas fir	.3%
Ponderosa pine	.3%

BIONDA, Jack, lacrosse player (b 18 Sept 1933, Huntsville, ON; d 3 Nov 1999, London, ON). Perhaps the best box LACROSSE player in the history of the game, he came to BC in 1954 to play

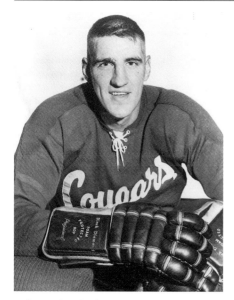

Jack Bionda in his lacrosse gear, 1950s.
Vancouver Sun

for the VICTORIA Shamrocks, winning the league scoring title and leading them to the BC championship. In every full season he played Bionda was the league's scoring champion, winning the accompanying Dennis Huddlestone Trophy 6 times. His best season was in 1959 when he was named league MVP and scored 74 goals and 144 points, 71 more points than the runner-up. He played in 5 Mann Cup national championship tournaments, winning in 1958, 1959 and 1962 with the NEW WESTMINSTER SALMONBELLIES and losing with the 1955 Shamrocks and the 1960 NANAIMO Timbermen. Bionda also had a 93-game career in the NHL with the Toronto Maple Leafs and Boston Bruins. He was inducted into the Canadian Sports Hall of Fame and the BC SPORTS HALL OF FAME. *SW*

BIOTECHNOLOGY refers to the use of biological processes and living organisms to manufacture medical, agricultural and consumer products. In BC it is a growing part of the HIGH TECHNOLOGY sector; the province is the third-largest centre in Canada in terms of the number of people involved. More than 80 companies are engaged in biotechnology in various areas of the economy, including HEALTH care, FORESTRY, AGRICULTURE, FISHERIES and AQUACULTURE, as well as environmental and waste management. The industry is very young; most BC companies have been founded since the mid-1980s. In forestry, Silvagen Inc of VANCOUVER is the first commercial user of somatic embryogenesis (a tissue culture process for producing synthetic seed) and introduced genetically identical, high-yield DOUGLAS FIR to the FOREST INDUSTRY. TerraGen Discovery Inc was founded by Dr Julian Davies, whose research with cloned plasmids helped elaborate how pathogens acquire and use resistance genes from other biota. The company maintains one of the world's largest genomic libraries of rare fungi, bacteria and lichens. Micrologix Biotech Inc in Vancouver manufactures cationic peptide variants.

BIRCH is a tree occurring in BC in 2 varieties. White birch, also known as paper birch (*Betula papyrifera*), is distributed throughout most of the province. It is distinctive for its smooth white paper-like bark, which Interior FIRST NATIONS used for making CANOES, containers, and a host of other items. More recently the wood has been used for PULP stock and veneer (*see also* FOREST PRODUCTS). Western birch, or water birch (*Betula occidentalis*), is a more shrubby tree. It grows across western Canada from the BC Interior to the Ontario border and has no commercial value.

Paper birch.
Kim LaFave drawing

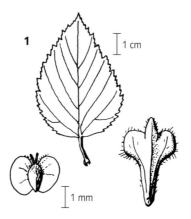

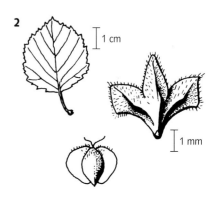

Leaves, bracts and fruits of the white birch (1) and western birch (2). © T.C. Brayshaw

Birch forest near Chilliwack. *Roy Luckow photo*

BIRCH ISLAND, pop 250, is a farming (*see* AGRICULTURE) and LOGGING community 105 km north of KAMLOOPS and was a station on the CANADIAN NORTHERN RWY. Established about 1917, it was named after an island in the N THOMPSON R. A massive uranium deposit was discovered nearby but in 1978, after some site preparation and much debate had taken place, the development was postponed indefinitely. *AS*

BIRCHBANK was a farming settlement (*see* AGRICULTURE) and CPR station 10 km north of TRAIL on the west bank of the COLUMBIA R. Birchbank Ranch overlooked the river and a post office operated from 1912 to 1929. *AS*

BIRKEN, pop 109, a station on the Pacific Great Eastern Rwy (*see* BC RAIL) 30 km north of PEMBERTON, was named by the early explorer A.C. ANDERSON after HMS *Birkenhead*, as were a nearby lake and provincial PARK. The soldiers on this famous British troop ship, commanded by Anderson's relative, Lt Col Alexander Seton, died heroically to save women and child passengers. Today farming (*see* AGRICULTURE), LOGGING and TOURISM support the community. *AS*

BIRLEY, S. Patrick, architect (b 1904, Manchester, England; d 1962, Victoria). He articled with the VICTORIA architects K.B. Spurgin and J. Graham Johnson from 1931 to 1934. After serving in the Canadian navy during WWII he formed a brief partnership with D.C. Frame, then in 1946 became a partner in the Victoria firm Birley Wade and Stockdill. He set up a private practice in VANCOUVER in 1952 before becoming a partner in Birley Simpson Wagg in 1958. His early work in Victoria, especially the Sussex Building (1938) and the Athlone Apartments (1947–48), represents the high point and end of the Moderne movement just prior to the post-war transition to modern expressionist styles. *Martin Segger*

BIRNEY, Alfred Earle, writer, teacher (b 13 May 1904, Calgary; d 3 Sept 1995, Toronto). His family moved from Alberta to a fruit ranch near CRESTON when he was 12, and he went to school there. In 1922 he left for VANCOUVER to study chemistry at UBC. After graduate studies in Toronto and Berkeley, CA, he taught at the Univ of Utah and then completed a PhD at the Univ of London with a thesis on Chaucer. From 1936 to 1942 he taught at the Univ of Toronto, while editing the literary and political journal *Canadian Forum*. Following wartime military service and a stint at the CBC, he returned to Vancouver, where he taught literature at UBC during 1948–65 and founded Canada's first department of creative writing. Birney's first collection of poetry, *David and Other Poems*, won a 1942 GOV GEN'S LITERARY AWARD; he won again in 1945 for *Now Is Time*. His first novel *Turvey* (1949), a comic satire on life in the army, won a Leacock Medal for Humour. *Down The Long Table*, a 1955 novel, is an account of leftist political activity during the 1930s. Birney published more than 30 books,

Earle Birney, twice a winner of the Gov Gen's literary award for his poetry.

including essays, fiction and drama, but his main contribution was his poetry, much of it experimental in form and presentation.

BISHOP, Kenneth James, film producer (b 20 Apr 1893, Surrey, England; d 6 Sept 1941, Vancouver). He had been a small-time film producer in New York and Hollywood when he came to VICTORIA in 1932, determined to create a feature film industry based on Great Britain's quota legislation (*see* FILMMAKING). Backed by Kathleen Dunsmuir, heiress to part of the DUNSMUIR family fortune, he established Commonwealth Productions, later Northern Films, at Willows Park in OAK BAY. His films were undistinguished and the company went bankrupt. He made 12 more films in BC under the auspices of Columbia Pictures, two of which starred a young Rita Hayworth, before that venture also petered out in 1938.

BISHOP BAY, 65 km south of KITIMAT on the east side of Ursula Channel opposite Gribbell Island, was the site of a floating LOGGING camp, store and post office in the 1930s. A HOT SPRINGS and picnic area are located at the head of the bay. AS

bissett, bill, poet, painter, singer (b 23 Nov 1939, Halifax). As a young teenager he ran away from home with his boyfriend and eventually settled in VANCOUVER. There he became a central figure in the counterculture movement, as a poet and as publisher of *BLEWOINTMENT* magazine, which evolved into blewointmentpress, a BOOK PUBLISHER. bissett's poetry, distinctive for its use of lower case and phonetic spelling, and his sound poetry performances in cities across North America and in Europe have won him an international following: Jack Kerouac once

called him "the greatest living poet today." bissett has published more than 70 books of poetry, including *inkorrect thots* (1992), *th influenza uv logik* (1995) and *b leev abul char ak trs* (2000). His work was attacked in the House of Commons in 1978 and became the subject of a lengthy debate on public funding for the arts in Canada. bissett won the Milton ACORN People's Poet Award in 1990 and a BC BOOK PRIZE in 1993. He was a singer and lyricist with the Luddites, an alternative rock band in London, ON, and went on to work with the composers Chris Miloche and Bill Roberts. His album *rainbow mewsik* was released in 2000. bissett is also a prolific painter in many media and has had hundreds of exhibitions, including a major retrospective at the VANCOUVER ART GALLERY in 1985.

BITTERN, American (*Botaurus lentiginosus*), is a long-legged, long-necked wading bird related to the HERON. It has a long, straight bill and stands up to a metre in height. Its yellow and brown markings blend perfectly with surrounding marsh grasses, and it has a distinctive booming call. American bitterns occur along the South Coast as far north as CAMPBELL RIVER, in the FRASER VALLEY lowlands and in the south-central Interior, where most of them breed. They prefer wet, marshy habitat with tall vegetation, where they feed on small fish, INSECTS, crustaceans, amphibians and reptiles.

BLACK, David Kenneth McKenzie "Ken," golfer (b 23 July 1912, Montreal; d Nov 1995). He grew up on the Shaughnessy GOLF course under the tutelage of his golf-professional father Davie BLACK and became Canada's top amateur golfer of the 1930s. Ken won the BC Open in 1932 and the Canadian Western Open in 1941. He was BC amateur champion 3 times, BC closed champion in 1945 and in 1939 became the first British Columbian to win the Canadian amateur championship. He played on 9 Willingdon Cup teams and helped BC win the trophy 3 times. In 1936 he won his most memorable victory, over top American PGA professionals including Byron Nelson, at Shaughnessy's Jubilee Open with a course record 63. He was inducted into the BC SPORTS HALL OF FAME in 1966 and the Canadian Golf Hall of Fame in 1987. SW

BLACK, David Lambie "Davie," golfer (b 1883, Troon, Scotland; d 26 Mar 1974, Vancouver). He came to Canada in 1905 and became a fixture at VANCOUVER's old Shaughnessy GOLF course, where he acquired a reputation as one of the top professional golfers in Canadian history and one of the game's finest putters. He won the Canadian professional championship in 1913, 1919, 1920 and 1921, the Pacific North West Open in 1920 and 1922, the Washington State Open in 1924 and the BC Open in 1928 and 1929. He was inducted into the BC SPORTS HALL OF FAME in 1966 and the Canadian Golf Hall of Fame in 1972. His son Ken BLACK was one of Canada's top amateur golfers. SW

BLACK, Sam, painter (b 1913, Ayrshire, Scotland; d 23 Apr 1998, N Vancouver). He came to Canada in 1958 and taught painting and art education at UBC; after his retirement in 1978, he was a professor emeritus. He was elected to the Royal Canadian Academy of Arts in 1977. Primarily a watercolourist of coastal scenes, he lived and worked in his later years at a studio/home on BOWEN ISLAND.

BLACK, Samuel, fur trader (b 3 May 1780, Pitsligo, Scotland; d 8 Feb 1841, Kamloops). He came to Canada in 1802 and served for many years with the NORTH WEST COMPANY at trading posts in the Athabasca District. Stopping at nothing to defeat his HBC competitors, he was a notorious ruffian and bully. When the HBC absorbed the NWC in 1821, Black was refused a job in the reorganized company because of his history. But in 1823 he was taken on as officer in charge at FORT ST JOHN on the upper PEACE R. The next year he explored the FINLAY R for the HBC; his journal of that expedition has been published. He moved posts regularly until 1830, when he was stationed at Thompson's River Post (KAMLOOPS). In 1837 he became chief factor in charge of all the posts in the district. Black was never much of a diplomat, and his relations with the aboriginal people were poor. It was not unexpected when a dispute with a SECWEPEMC (Shuswap) chief ended in Black's murder.

BLACK BALL LINE operated ferry service on the South Coast between 1951 and 1961. It was formed by the PUGET SOUND NAVIGATION CO when many of that company's ferry routes in Puget Sound were taken over by the state of Washington. Black Ball routes connected HORSESHOE BAY with NANAIMO and Langdale, on the western shore of HOWE SOUND, and in 1952 crossed JERVIS INLET to link POWELL RIVER to the Sechelt Peninsula. A labour dispute in the summer of 1958 on both the Black Ball and PRINCESS ferries brought marine service to VANCOUVER ISLAND to a halt. During the strike the provincial government formed the BC FERRY CORP to operate a ferry fleet of its own; late in 1961 it bought the vessels of the Black Ball Line. Black Ball Transport Inc operates the ferry MV *Coho* between Port Angeles, WA, and VICTORIA.

BLACK CREEK, pop 1,950, 28 km south of CAMPBELL RIVER on the Island Hwy (*see* ROADS AND HWYS), is a farming and LOGGING community and a service centre for the region. A number of MENNONITES settled here in the 1930s. A farmers' market operates in summer and nearby Miracle Beach Provincial Park attracts tourists. AS

BLACK PINES is a rural area of hobby farms and small acreages on the west side of the N THOMPSON R, 30 km north of KAMLOOPS. It was the site of an early ranch owned by Alex McLean from 1873 to 1909 (*see* CATTLE INDUSTRY). Just to the north is Whispering Pines, pop 48, a village founded in 1972 by a group of SECWEPEMC (Shuswap) people who moved from the CLINTON area to avoid BC HYDRO development. AS

BLACK PRESS LTD, owned by David Black, is one of BC's largest publishers of community NEWSPAPERS. The purchase of 33 western Canadian publications early in 1997 brought the company's total to 80 papers, mainly in BC but also in Alberta and Washington. Black Press began in 1969, when Black's father Alan purchased a newspaper in WILLIAMS LAKE. David took over the paper in 1975 and with the purchase of the ASHCROFT *Journal* in 1980 began building a chain. In 1998 the company had revenues of $160 million.

BLACK TUSK, 2,315 m, is a protruding finger of bare rock towering above the meadows surrounding Garibaldi Lk in the mts of GARIBALDI PROVINCIAL PARK north of SQUAMISH. Thought to be the lava plug of an extinct volcano that has weathered away, it is accessible by hiking trail via Rubble Crk.

Hikers in Garibaldi Park, below Black Tusk, 1930. Leonard Frank/VPL 8181

BLACKBIRD is the common name for several medium-sized songbirds usually found congregated in large, noisy flocks. They have sharp, pointed beaks and feed primarily on grain, seeds, fruit and INSECTS. Four species occur in BC. Red-winged blackbirds (*Agelaius phoeniceus*) inhabit colonies in cattail marshes where the male has a harem of nesting females and raucously defends a particular breeding territory. Male red-wings are black with bright red shoulders, while females have brown plumage. Yellow-headed blackbirds (*Xanthocephalus xanthocephalus*), with their yellow heads and necks, share the marshy habitat with their smaller, red-winged relatives. Brewer's blackbirds (*Euphagus cyanocephalus*) prefer drier, more open habitat, where they nest on or near the ground and forage for seeds and insects. Males have iridescent black plumage; females are grey-brown. The rusty blackbird (*E. carolinus*) is found near swamps and bogs, mainly in the northern half of

Brewer's blackbird, one of 4 blackbird species in BC. R. Wayne Campbell photo

the province. Two other species are related to the blackbird. Brown-headed cowbirds (*Molothrus ater*), usually found near grazing horses or cattle, are infamous for laying eggs in the nests of other species. The male cowbird is black with a brown head; the female is brown-grey. Common grackles (*Quiscalus quiscula*), with entirely black plumage, are found east of the ROCKY MTS in the northeast corner of the province. They nest in small colonies in conifer forests.

BLACKCOD; *see* SABLEFISH.

BLACKLOAM is a farming area and suburb of KAMLOOPS 5 km southeast of the city on the slopes of Rose Hill. Named for the quality of the soil in the area, it was settled in the early 1900s.

AS

BLACKPOOL, 100 km north of KAMLOOPS on the west side of the N THOMPSON R, was named about 1910 by J.H. Miller, an early settler, after Blackpool, England. By the late 1990s the community had a store, gas station, pub and golf course. AS

BLACKS began arriving in BC in 1858 from California, where discriminatory laws were making their lives intolerable. An advance party sailed to VICTORIA aboard the *Commodore*; they received a positive welcome and more followed until about 800 newcomers had settled in the colony. They were ordinary settlers, not fugitives from slavery, and by and large they received equal treatment. A few ventured to the goldfields but most opened businesses in Victoria or took up land elsewhere on the Island (*see* Mifflin GIBBS). A sizable number chose to locate on SALTSPRING ISLAND. As time passed racial antagonism grew, and after the American Civil War many

Blacks returned to the US until the number in BC fell below 300. Prejudice was not formalized, however; Blacks were not barred from holding public office or from public institutions and they enjoyed formal legal and political equality with other colonists.

Prior to WWI immigration policy discouraged Blacks and the population grew slowly. The 1951 census counted only 438. The BC Association for the Advancement of Coloured People was founded in 1958 as an advocacy group in VANCOUVER. One of its founders was Frank Collins, who was the city's first Black bus driver. His sister-in-law, Eleanor Collins, was a jazz singer who in 1955 hosted her own show on CBC television: she was the first woman with a national TV series in Canada. With liberalized immigration laws in the 1960s, Black immigration increased dramatically, especially from the Caribbean region. Most Caribbean immigrants came from the former British colonies of Jamaica, Guyana, Trinidad-Tobago and Barbados. Another significant source was Haiti. Then, during the 1980s, large numbers of people began arriving directly from Africa for the first time, particularly Ghana, Nigeria, Ethiopia and Somalia.

With the increased immigration, Blacks became more prominent in all walks of life. In 1969 in Vancouver a Black theatre company was created, the Sepia Players, later Black Theatre West. In politics, Emery BARNES and Rosemary BROWN were the first Blacks elected to the BC legislature in 1972. By 1996 there were about 10,000 Blacks—African, American and Caribbean—living in BC. A Caribbean Day festival takes place annually in N VANCOUVER, organized by the Trinidad and Tobago Society. *Reading:* Crawford Kilian, *Go Do Some Great Thing: The Black Pioneers in British Columbia*, 1978.

BLACKWATER RIVER, 227 km, rises in the ILGACHUZ RANGE near TWEEDSMUIR PROVINCIAL PARK and flows east through deep valleys and canyons of black volcanic rock to its confluence with the FRASER R between QUESNEL and PRINCE GEORGE. Also known as the West Road R, it formed part of the Grease TRAIL used by FIRST NATIONS people as a trading route between the coast and the Interior. Alexander MACKENZIE followed the river on his way to the Pacific in 1793 and today it is part of the ALEXANDER MACKENZIE HERITAGE TRAIL. It has been designated a BC HERITAGE RIVER. *See also* RIVERS.

BLADES, Ann, writer, artist (b 16 Nov 1947, Vancouver). After graduating from UBC in 1967 she taught elementary school, then went back to school to qualify as a nurse. At the same time she became a leading author/illustrator of books for children. Her first book, *Mary of Mile 18* (1971), is based on her experiences as a teacher in the BC Interior and won the Canadian Library Assoc's Book of the Year for Children Award. *A Salmon for Simon* (1978), which she illustrated, won a Canada Council children's literature prize. Other titles include *A Boy of Tache* (1973), *The Cottage* at *Crescent Beach* (1977) and *By the Sea* (1986). Since 1982 she has exhibited her art work in galleries as well.

BLAEBERRY RIVER, 60 km, is a swiftly flowing stream descending out of the ROCKY MTS from the vicinity of HOWSE PASS to join the COLUMBIA R 10 km north of GOLDEN. It was part of a well-used route across the Rockies pioneered by David THOMPSON in 1807. The name refers to the huckleberries found along the valley bottom.

BLAIR, John, landscaper (b 8 Aug 1820, Callander, Scotland; d 28 May 1906, near Duncan). Trained as a landscape gardener in his native Scotland, he emigrated to Ontario in 1851, then moved to Chicago, where he became superintendent of parks in the 1860s. During the 1870s he was based in Colorado, where he designed several parks and housing developments. In 1881 he returned to Canada, this time to VICTORIA. When control of BEACON HILL PARK passed from the province to the city, Victoria held a design competition and Blair's proposal was accepted in 1889. His award-winning design, carried out with the help of his foreman, the horticulturist George FRASER, featured the artful arrangement of rocks, water and trees to create natural-looking landscapes in a park setting. Blair eventually settled at Sahtlam near DUNCAN.

BLAKEBURN is an abandoned COAL mining town on Granite Crk northwest of PRINCETON. The mine was established in 1911, and coal was carried by aerial tramway to the railhead at nearby COALMONT. The camp at the mine was named for the principal owners, W.J. Blake-Wilson and Pat Burns, the meat-packing king and senator. In 1930 an explosion in the mine killed 45 men, one of the worst mine DISASTERS in BC history. After operating through the Depression, the mine closed in 1940 and residents moved away.

BLANCHET, Muriel Wylie (Liffiton) "Capi," writer (b 1891, Lachine, QC; d 30 Sept 1961, Sidney). Educated at St. Paul's private school in Montreal, she married Geoffrey Blanchet, a banker, when she was 18 years old. The Blanchets lived in Sherbrooke, QC, and Toronto before Geoffrey became ill and took early retirement. In 1922 the couple and their children moved to Curteis Point, near SIDNEY on VANCOUVER ISLAND, and bought the 7.6-m wooden cruiser *Caprice*. Blanchet's husband died in 1927, leaving her with 5 children to raise. That year she rented the family home, and she and the children boarded the *Caprice* and spent the summer exploring the West Coast. Over the next 15 summers they travelled the INSIDE PASSAGE as far as Cape Caution and retraced the voyage of Capt George VANCOUVER. Blanchet wrote about these trips in her book *The Curve of Time*, which was published shortly before her death in 1961 and which has since become a classic of BC literature. She also wrote the children's book *A Whale Named Henry*.

BLANSHARD, Richard, governor of Vancouver Island 1849–51 (b 19 Oct 1817, London, England; d there 5 June 1894). The son of a wealthy merchant, he obtained an MA from Cambridge Univ and was admitted to the bar but did not practise law, preferring to travel. When Vancouver Island became a colony (*see* VANCOUVER ISLAND, COLONY OF) in 1849, he was named its first governor. He arrived at FORT VICTORIA in Mar 1850 and almost immediately came into conflict with James DOUGLAS, the HBC chief factor. Blanshard's term in office was a disaster. He had nowhere to live, no salary and no authority over the HBC, and his health was poor. In a high-handed show of force he ordered 2 KWAKWA̱KA'WAKW (Kwakiutl) villages near FORT RUPERT destroyed following the apparent murder of 3 British naval deserters. Blanshard despised life in the colony. He resigned in disgust and in Sept 1851 left for home and retirement at his country estate in England.

Richard Blanshard, first governor of Vancouver Island, c 1870. BC Archives A-01113

BLASER, Robin, writer, teacher (b 18 May 1925, Denver, CO). He has been an influential critic, editor and poet since arriving in VANCOUVER in 1966 to teach in the English department at SFU. Before coming to Canada he was part of the literary movement known as the San Francisco Renaissance and his writing remained centred in his US experience. He retired from SFU in 1985, becoming professor emeritus. He has published several books of verse and his collected poems, *The Holy Forest* (1993), nominated for a GOV GEN'S LITERARY AWARD, was the focus of an international conference in Vancouver in 1995.

BLAYLOCK, Selwyn Gwillym, metallurgist, COMINCO executive (b 1879, Paspébiac, QC; d 1945). After graduating from McGill Univ in 1899 he came west to the KOOTENAY to work at the TRAIL smelter owned by the CPR. In 1906, when Canadian Pacific created Cominco, he was the new company's chief metallurgist. He

worked on a team that developed a successful method of separating the complex ores of the SULLIVAN MINE, enabling it to expand rapidly during the 1920s despite a slump in world metal prices. By 1919 he was general manager of Cominco and remained a senior executive until his death. A paternalistic employer, he introduced a form of company unionism that lasted to WWII. At the same time, he was no friend of radical unionists and was rumoured to have had a hand in running Ginger GOODWIN out of town by having him reclassified fit for military service.

BLENKINSOP, George, HBC trader, Indian agent (b 1822, Penryn, England; d 2 June 1904, Fort Rupert). He joined the HBC in 1840 and served his entire term west of the ROCKY MTS in Alaska, VANCOUVER ISLAND, Oregon and the BC mainland. He helped to build FORT RUPERT on the north end of Vancouver Island near PORT HARDY in 1850 and remained there to the end of 1856. After a brief sojourn on the COLUMBIA R he took charge at FORT LANGLEY in 1860. He took advantage of private business opportunities, which brought him into conflict with the HBC at Langley, so in 1861 he resigned. After a series of failed enterprises he went to work for the federal Department of Indian Affairs in 1874, identifying RESERVES and carrying out the first census of aboriginal people in BC (*see also* ABORIGINAL DEMOGRAPHY). From 1881 to 1886 he was Indian agent at Fort Rupert and after his retirement he remained there. He was an important informant on FIRST NATIONS culture for anthropologists and government.

BLESSING'S GRAVE, BC's smallest provincial historic site, is on the road to BARKERVILLE 44 km east of QUESNEL. Charles Morgan Blessing was an Ohioan who came to the CARIBOO in the 1860s during the GOLD RUSH. On 31 May 1866 he was murdered by another prospector, James Barry, who stole his gold tiepin and a large amount of cash. Thanks to the efforts of Blessing's friend, Wellington Moses, a barber in Barkerville, Barry was arrested while fleeing south by stagecoach. He was tried by Judge Matthew BEGBIE, convicted by a jury and hanged. Moses erected the headstone and fence that now surround the grave.

BLEWETT, Peter, architect, artist (b 28 Sept 1932, Swansea, Wales; d 25 Nov 1999, Vancouver). He studied industrial design and ARCHITECTURE at the Canterbury School of Architecture and graduated in 1954. After immigrating to Canada in 1957, he settled in VANCOUVER. He joined the VICTORIA firm of Wade Stockdill & Armour in 1960 and set up a Vancouver office with John Armour; in 1965 he became a partner. The firm was reorganized as Armour Blewett & Partners, including Selwyn Dodd, in 1977, then as Blewett Dodd Ching Lee, with offices in Hong Kong, in 1987. The partnership became a corporation, Blewett Dodd Canada (Architecture) Ltd (1993–96), then a partnership again, Blewett Dodd Architecture.

Projects included SAANICH Municipal Hall (1964), Oakridge Centre expansion in Vancouver (1984) and Long Fu Commercial City in Beijing (1998). Blewett also painted, mostly in acrylics, and his work was exhibited widely.

David R. Conn

blewointment was a literary magazine founded in VANCOUVER by the poet bill BISSETT in 1963. The magazine, characterized by bissett's unconventional spelling and left-wing politics, appeared irregularly as a crude mimeograph until 1978. Contributors over the years constitute a veritable who's who of Canadian writing. bissett launched blewointment press in 1967 to publish books. He sold it in the mid-1980s and it continued as Nightwood Editions.

BLIND BAY, pop 454, on the south shore of the main arm of SHUSWAP LK 22 km north of SALMON ARM, is a popular summer resort community reached via SORRENTO. The bay, with several marinas and a public picnic and swimming area, got its name from the fact that the lakeshore hides it from view from most angles. *AS*

BLIND CHANNEL is a harbour village in the jumble of islands on the Mid-Coast between VANCOUVER ISLAND and the mainland. It is situated on W THURLOW ISLAND overlooking Mayne Passage between W and E Thurlow Islands near the south end of JOHNSTONE STRAIT. It was a thriving community through the 1920s, with SALMON CANNING and SAWMILLING operations. The sawmill burned, and in 1935 the cannery became a saltery that closed when its JAPANESE owners were interned during WWII (*see* JAPANESE, RELOCATION OF). The tiny community picked up again in 1970 with the development of a tourist resort by Edgar and Annemarie Richter. It is a regular stop for boaters waiting to navigate nearby GREENE POINT RAPIDS.

BLISS LANDING in Turner Bay 30 km northwest of POWELL RIVER on Malaspina Peninsula, was established at the close of WWI. Steamships once stopped regularly at this small settlement; today a private marina operates here. Formerly known as Bishop Landing after an early settler, the landing is named after Joe Blissto, a pioneer handlogger. *AS*

BLOEDEL, a VANCOUVER ISLAND logging camp 16 km northwest of CAMPBELL RIVER on the south side of Menzies Bay, was named after the FOREST INDUSTRY pioneer J.H. BLOEDEL. Established in 1925, it was the terminus of an extensive RAILWAY LOGGING operation by BLOEDEL, STEWART & WELCH ltd for 30 years, and had a peak population of about 400. Menzies Bay was home to several other LOGGING camps in the 1920s and 1930s and is still a sorting and booming ground. *AS*

BLOEDEL, Julius Harold, pioneer lumberman (b Mar 1864, Fond du Lac, WI; d 20 Sept 1957, Seattle, WA). After graduating from the Univ of Michigan in the late 1880s he moved to

Bellingham, WA, where he managed a sawmill, a mine and a bank. In 1898 he joined Peter Larson, a prominent railway contractor, and J.J. Donovan, an engineer, to form Lake Whatcom Logging Co, with Bloedel as manager. The partners later formed several other forest product companies. In 1911 Bloedel came to BC to buy standing timber and formed a company with railway contractors John STEWART and Patrick Welch. Initially the company, BLOEDEL, STEWART & WELCH, logged timber that was cut by other mills to provide lumber for Stewart and Welch's contract to build the GRAND TRUNK PACIFIC RWY from Edmonton to PRINCE RUPERT. Bloedel's first priority was to acquire timber on the southern BC coast and VANCOUVER ISLAND and on this base the company went on to build an integrated SAWMILLING and PULP MILL operation at various coastal locations. In 1942 his son Prentice BLOEDEL took over as head of the company and in 1951 Bloedel, Stewart & Welch merged with the H.R. MACMILLAN Export Co to form MacMillan & Bloedel Ltd. (later MACMILLAN BLOEDEL LTD). Bloedel remained active in company affairs until his death. *Ken Drushka*

BLOEDEL, Prentice "Bing," lumberman (b 1900, Bellingham, WA; d 15 June 1996, Seattle, WA). After graduating from Yale Univ he intended to become a schoolteacher but instead entered the family logging business at his father's request. He began work at BLOEDEL, STEWART & WELCH, one of the largest logging/sawmilling companies on the BC coast, in 1929 and was president from 1942 to 1951. The company merged in 1951 with the H.R. MACMILLAN Export

Prentice Bloedel, pioneer BC lumberman and philanthropist. Courtesy MacMillan Bloedel

Co to form the timber giant MACMILLAN BLOEDEL LTD. He served briefly as vice-chair of the new company (he remained a director until 1972), then retired with his wife to an estate on Bainbridge Island near Seattle to pursue an interest in gardening. The 60-ha Bloedel Reserve he developed there is open to the public. Bloedel donated money to several Seattle institutions and made possible the construction of the Bloedel Conservatory in QUEEN ELIZABETH PARK in VANCOUVER. He was made a freeman of the city in 1971.

BLOEDEL, STEWART & WELCH (BS&W) was formed in 1911 by the Bellingham lumberman Julius BLOEDEL and two railway builders, Patrick Welch and John STEWART. The company began LOGGING on a 40.5 km² tract of leased timber at MYRTLE POINT near POWELL RIVER, under the direction of Sidney Smith, the logging superintendent. A second logging operation opened in 1920 at UNION BAY on VANCOUVER ISLAND. The next year BS&W entered the SAWMILLING business, taking over the bankrupt Shull Lumber & Shingle mill on the north arm of the FRASER R in VANCOUVER. In 1925 major timber purchases at Menzies Bay, north of CAMPBELL RIVER, and in the Alberni Valley made the company one of the largest logging operations in BC. A new mill and townsite at GREAT CENTRAL LK were built in partnership with the King-Farris Lumber Co. In 1934 the company built the Somass sawmill at PORT ALBERNI to mill timber from the Franklin R area down ALBERNI INLET. The following year BS&W established FRANKLIN CAMP, the largest logging camp in the world. A shingle mill built at Port Alberni in 1937 made the company the largest shingle producer in BC.

In the late 1930s the company began reforesting logged lands, one of the first companies in BC to do so (*see* SILVICULTURE). During WWII Julius's son Prentice took over as company president and in 1947 a pulp mill was opened at Port Alberni. On 10 April 1951, BS&W merged with H.R. MacMillan Export Co to form MACMILLAN BLOEDEL in the largest corporate merger in BC history. *See also* FOREST INDUSTRY. *Ken Drushka*

BLOMFELD, James, stained-glass designer (b 1872, Maidenhead, England; d 1951, Toronto). In 1889 he arrived in BC, where his father Henry Bloomfield established a plumbing and art glass business in NEW WESTMINSTER with his two sons, James (who later altered his last name as a tribute to his English ancestors) and Charles. From the first, James provided the design talent. He pursued art glass studies in New Orleans and England during 1894–98 and returned to BC just months before the family business premises were destroyed by the great New Westminster fire of 1898. The firm moved to new studios in VANCOUVER, and for the next 7 years Blomfeld produced some of the finest glass art in turn-of-the-century Canada. Among his many commissions were Holy Trinity Cathedral in New Westminster, the Jubilee Window in the LEGISLATIVE BUILDINGS, Government House in VICTORIA, B.T. ROGERS's splendid home in Vancouver's West

End, and a series of courthouses around the province. He was also a skilled painter, with a particular interest in portraying FIRST NATIONS culture. He left BC in 1905 when Bloomfield & Sons closed. After a period of itinerancy he settled in Toronto in 1921 where he lived the rest of his life. *Robert D. Watt*

BLOODY SUNDAY, 19 June 1938, ended a peaceful occupation of three downtown VANCOUVER buildings by protesters hoping to pressure the government into improving conditions for unemployed people. In Apr the provincial government had closed its winter RELIEF CAMPS for lack of funds and cut single men off relief. As a result hundreds of destitute transients converged on Vancouver. They were organized into brigades

Protestors being forced from the Vancouver post office by tear gas, Bloody Sunday, June 1938. VPL 12751

by Steve BRODIE, a Communist who had taken part in the ON-TO-OTTAWA TREK, and on May 20 about 1,200 men occupied the federal post office, the Georgia Hotel and the VANCOUVER ART GALLERY. Brodie wanted the police to arrest the protesters, which would tie up the courts and fill the jails to overflowing. Instead the situation developed into a standoff. The group occupying the hotel soon gave up, but the others remained. Finally the federal government lost patience. Early in the morning of "Bloody Sunday," troops of RCMP evicted the protesters. At the art gallery the men went peacefully, but at the post office police drove the men brutally into the streets with clubs and tear gas. Hundreds were injured. Outraged protesters rampaged through the downtown streets, breaking store windows and causing thousands of dollars' damage. Later in the day 10,000 angry citizens gathered at an outdoor meeting to protest police violence and demand Premier Duff PATTULLO's resignation.

BLUBBER BAY, pop 75, a community at the northern end of TEXADA ISLAND, is the terminus

of a BC FERRIES route from POWELL RIVER, 10 km northeast. Limestone has been exported from the area since before WWI and a very visible quarry above the village ships out almost 2 million tonnes a year. The ruins of old lime kilns can be seen nearby. The bay is named for a short-lived WHALING operation run by Elijah Fader in the late 1880s. *AS*

BLUCHER HALL was a farming settlement (*see* AGRICULTURE) located between the N THOMPSON R and ADAMS LK 50 km northeast of KAMLOOPS. Donald Fraser, who had worked on the construction of the CPR, then settled in 1895 at Forest Lake, opened a post office and store and named his farm Blucher Hall after an estate he had inherited in England but did not claim. *AS*

BLUE RIVER, pop 283, on the N THOMPSON R 230 km north of KAMLOOPS, just outside WELLS GRAY PROVINCIAL PARK, is a LOGGING and TOURISM centre. A helicopter-SKIING operation in the CARIBOO and MONASHEE Mts attracts skiers from around the world. The community is named for the colour of the surrounding hills.

BLUEBERRY RIVER, pop 205, is a FIRST NATIONS community, predominantly DUNNE-ZA (Beaver) and Cree, on the Blueberry R northwest of FORT ST JOHN. The people moved here from Fort St John following WWII, when the federal government took back their original reserve for agricultural settlement.

BLUEBIRD is a perching songbird, a member of the thrush family, about the size of a large SPARROW. It feeds on INSECTS and small fruit. The male has mainly blue plumage all over; the female tends to be more greyish in colour. Bluebirds nest in natural cavities and birdhouses. Of 3 Canadian species, 2 occur in BC. The western bluebird (*Sialia mexicana*) is identifiable by red colouring on its breast. The south coastal population has essentially disappeared, but it is still common in ponderosa PINE woodlands in the southern Interior. A small number overwinter in

Mountain bluebird. R. Wayne Campbell photo

the OKANAGAN VALLEY, but most migrate south. The mountain bluebird (*S. currucoides*) occurs in open, grassy areas throughout the province east of the CASCADE and COAST MTS. The male of this species is a beautiful sky-blue colour all over.

BLUNDEN HARBOUR was a coastal village on the mainland opposite the north end of VANCOUVER ISLAND, occupied by the Gwa'sala and 'Nakwaxda'xw groups of the KWAKWA̲KA̲'WAKW people. They resettled here in the mid-19th century from older villages around SMITH and SEYMOUR inlets to be closer to commercial FISHING. The village was the subject of a famous painting by Emily CARR in 1930. In the 1960s the people moved again, this time to the Tsulquate reserve at PORT HARDY. A tiny SAWMILL settlement and steamship landing called Port Progress was also established here about 1918 and lasted until the early 1930s.

BOAS, Franz, anthropologist (b 9 July 1858, Minden, Germany; d 21 Dec 1942, New York). He went on his first field trip as a geographer to Baffin Island in 1883–84; his close encounter with the Inuit redirected his interests toward anthropology. When a party of NUXALK from BELLA COOLA visited Germany, he met them and became fascinated with West Coast FIRST NATIONS cultures. In 1886 he made his first research trip to BC, visiting various groups on VANCOUVER ISLAND. Boas returned 6 times between 1888 and 1897, sponsored by the British Assoc for the Advancement of Science, and gathered artifacts, stories and information for his many publications. In 1894 at FORT RUPERT, the KWAKWA̲KA̲'WAKW named him Heiltsakuls, "the one who does not speak." Boas, who became a US citizen, was the first professor of anthropology at Columbia Univ and the most influential American anthropologist of his generation.

BOATBUILDING in coastal BC has its roots in the dugout canoes carved by FIRST NATIONS people from a single CEDAR log. This versatile craft was the only vessel built on the coast until the arrival of the colonists in the mid-1800s (with the exception of the NORTH WEST AMERICA, a 36-tonne sloop built by John MEARES at YUQUOT in 1788). Before there were ROADS and steamship service, the earliest settlers relied on borrowed canoes, scows and rowboats to get around, often travelling hundreds of kilometres for supplies. The first boatyards were established at FORT VICTORIA in the 1850s, expanding over the next decade to NEW WESTMINSTER and VANCOUVER. By the late 1860s many of these yards were building simple, sturdy schooners for the sealing fleet (*see* FUR SEAL, NORTHERN); among the first was the 21.5-m *Favorite*, launched by the John MUIR family at SOOKE in 1868. Among the immigrants to the province were skilled mechanics and shipwrights, who brought the expertise required for a boatbuilding industry. Joseph Spratt, from England, founded ALBION IRON WORKS in VICTORIA in 1872, the largest machine shop supplying engines north of San Francisco. SAWMILLS provided the high quality edge-grain FIR and yellow cedar planking used in traditional boat construction.

Although the first boats built were tugs for the lumber carriers (*see* TOWBOATING), by far the biggest demand came from the developing fisheries industry (*see* FISHING, COMMERCIAL), beginning around 1870 with the gillnetters that serviced the SALMON CANNING industry. Early gillnetters, called Fraser River skiffs, were flat-bottomed double-enders with oars and a canvas sprit sail. A more seaworthy boat later emerged, the larger, round-bottomed Columbia River type. At northern canneries, stacking dory skiffs were used. Steam-powered tenders towed thousands of skiffs out to the fishing grounds and carried the SALMON back in scows. During the 1890s, Coal Harbour in Vancouver became the heart of the boatbuilding industry, with yards set up by Captain William Watts, Andy Linton and Andy WALLACE, the main supplier of Columbia River boats who went on to become extremely successful building commercial vessels of all sizes and types.

By the early 1900s, boatbuilders were found all along the coast. Some, such as the THULIN brothers at LUND and the Rodd brothers at Victoria, lasted for a few decades, while others, such as the McLean family at PRINCE RUPERT, have remained in business for 4 generations. JAPANESE builders—including the Tasakas on the north coast and the Nakade, Kishi and Atagi families at STEVESTON—became well known for their fishing boats, as did Gunderson, Wahl and Frostad, all NORWEGIAN immigrants. Builders developed their own designs or relied on naval architects, including A.C. Hanson, Edwin Monk, Robert ALLAN, William Garden, Alan McIlwain, John Brandlmayr and Arthur MCLAREN, who founded Allied Shipbuilders in 1948. Coal Harbour yards, particularly larger ones such as W.R. Menchions and A.C. Benson's, continued to produce the majority of the commercial fleet until the latter part of the 20th century, when resource industries went into decline.

With the introduction of gas engines around 1910, boats became bigger and more complex. By the 1920s purse seiners had evolved from open skiffs with a platform (table) aft for storing the net to 15-m vessels produced by the dozens for fishing companies such as BC PACKERS. Trollers, originally rowboats with lines towed astern, developed into deep-draught vessels with distinctive poles. Ice-carrying packers greatly increased the range and viability of the fishing fleet in the 1920s and 1930s. The next transition was to more reliable and efficient diesel engines; by the late 1930s, almost all new seiners had diesel power and had increased in size to over 20 m in length.

During WWII, both yachts and fishing vessels were modified for use as navy patrols. Builders gained experience with wartime steel ship construction, which led to improved welding techniques and marine-grade alloys (*see* SHIPBUILDING). Steel, then aluminum and fibreglass, gradually replaced wood as labour costs rose and good lumber became harder to find. The Matsumoto family at DOLLARTON pioneered alu-

Bent Jesperson maintains the traditions of fine wooden boatbuilding at his Sidney yard.
Don Morison photo

minum seiner construction during the 1960s, and many aluminum boats launched in the 1970s and 1980s came from Al Renke's RICHMOND yard. The Gooldrups of PENDER HARBOUR experimented with fibreglass over plywood, then produced seiners from fibreglass moulds. Barrie Farrell on VANCOUVER ISLAND was among the first to use moulded hulls for his gillnetter designs.

The ANGLICAN CHURCH mission delivered medical and spiritual care by boat to isolated settlements (*see* COLUMBIA COAST MISSION); their 30-m *Columbia II*, built by Dawes Shipyard in 1910, served the coast for 50 years. The SHANTYMEN'S CHRISTIAN ASSOC also operated a series of vessels bearing the name *Messenger*. The BC FOREST SERVICE maintained a large number of patrol boats, including 6 built by the Hinton Electric Co of Victoria in 1912. The first of numerous boats built at the THURSTON BAY base on SONORA ISLAND was the 9.75-m *Sitka Spruce*, in 1917. Forest Service construction shifted in 1941 to the Marine Station on the FRASER R, where the last wooden-hulled boat was built in 1966.

There were few private yachts until the early 1900s, although families took outings in small launches and sloops. Vancouver Shipyard built the 10.5-m *Rhinegold* for a city businessperson in 1911, and by the 1920s Henry and Jim HOFFAR in Coal Harbour had orders for 60 power cruisers, in addition to their custom designs. When the Boeing family bought out Hoffar's in 1929, one of the first yachts commissioned was their own 38-m *Taconite*. The waters off southwestern BC were very active during PROHIBITION in the late 1920s and early 1930s when "mother ships" off-loaded cargo worth millions of dollars to high-speed yachts, known as RUM-RUNNERS, many of them built in Victoria and Vancouver and outfitted with WWI surplus Liberty engines. One of

Menchions Shipyard in Coal Harbour, Vancouver, c 1990. Alan Haig-Brown photo

these mother ships was the former lumber carrier MALAHAT, later converted into the world's first self-propelled LOG BARGE. After WWII there was a surge of interest in pleasure boating, with builders taking advantage of new materials such as marine plywood and waterproof glues. Engines became more compact and economical, and synthetic fibres like nylon improved the quality of ropes and sails. The introduction of fibreglass revolutionized the industry in the 1950s, allowing the mass production of small craft. Davidson, in Vancouver, began building dinghies and lifeboats that are still popular; companies such as Hourston Glasscraft, K&C Thermoglass and Double Eagle were among the first to manufacture sport FISHING and utility boats. Spencer and others produced cruising sailboats out of fibreglass, a material that also proved well suited to lightweight racing designs, including Carl Petersen's Star class and the popular Martin series. Continuing prosperity through the 1960s led to faster hulls with twin engines, stylish interiors and an increasing array of navigation equipment. McQueen Boat Works of Vancouver started off in the 1950s building modest wooden power boats designed by Ed Monk, progressing to ever-larger sizes, filling the docks at local yacht clubs. Thornton GRENFELL became renowned for his lapstrake planing hull cruisers, in addition to writing a newspaper column encouraging ama-

A state-of-the-art aluminum seiner constructed by Shore Boatbuilders. *Alan Haig-Brown photo*

teurs to build their own boats. Philbrook's at SIDNEY on Vancouver Island launched a variety of yachts, many designed by Bill Garden, while nearby Canoe Cove built hundreds of power cruisers and workboats between 1958 and 1994.

Other individuals who have made significant contributions include Frank Fredette of Victoria, a designer-builder best known for his sailing fish boats; James HUTCHISON of Vancouver, famous for his "Teaser" hydroplaning race boats in the 1950s and 1960s; and John Samson, a pioneer of inexpensive ferro-cement construction. Following the launch of his 61-m wooden schooner in Victoria in 1920, Christian Cholberg moved to northeastern Vancouver Island to build trollers. George Bruigom at COMOX built rugged sailboats, and Sidney shipwright Peter London specialized in workboats. Edward Painter developed the "tyee" rowboat for catching chinook around CAMPBELL RIVER, while Alan

A mega-yacht under construction at McQueen's Boat Works, Richmond. *Rob Morris photo*

and Sharie FARRELL lived aboard and cruised in their unique hand-built sailboats for 50 years.

Toward the end of the 1990s, as BC's commercial fleet became more modern and specialized, retired FOREST INDUSTRY and fisheries vessels were being converted for pleasure use. Maritime-based industries from fish farms (*see* AQUACULTURE) to sport fishing lodges create a steady need for heavy duty, rigid inflatable or welded aluminum service vessels: water taxis, fireboats, patrol boats, tenders and charter boats. The growing ecotourism industry has been a boon for canoe and kayak builders since the 1970s. Meanwhile, favourable market conditions have given rise to at least 10 major boatyards producing large, luxury yachts for an international clientele. West Bay SonShip Yachts Ltd in DELTA was Canada's biggest yard in the year 2000, with more than 300 employees. McQueen's continues to build custom motor yachts with fibreglass hulls, supervised by Doug McQueen (son of George McQueen, who founded the company) and designed by Ed Monk Jr. Since 1982, Waterline Yachts has launched a number of steel sailboats over 21 m. A few yards still use traditional methods, particularly for refit and repair. Phil Barron at Sooke built several fir-planked power cruisers in the early 1990s. Bent Jespersen, from Denmark, became a leader in cold-moulded yacht construction, a new approach to working with wood. The Jespersen yard at Sidney was still in the family by 2000, an example of the merging of old-world craftmanship with innovative technique that has made boatbuilding in BC such a success for the past 150 years.   *Bet Oliver*

BOBAK, Molly (Lamb), artist (b 25 Feb 1922, Vancouver). The daughter of the photographer Harold MORTIMER-LAMB, she grew up in BURNABY and at age 16 entered the Vancouver School of Art (*see* EMILY CARR INSTITUTE OF ART & DESIGN) where she studied with Jack SHADBOLT, among other teachers. In Nov 1942 she enlisted in the Canadian Woman's Army Corps and before the war was over became Canada's only official woman war artist. Her diaries and sketches from this period have been published as *Double Duty* (1992), ed. by Carolyn Gossage. At the end of the war she married Bruno Bobak (b 1923), a fellow war artist. The couple moved to VANCOUVER, where both taught at the art school and

Molly worked in radio and television. In 1960 Bruno was appointed artist-in-residence at U of New Brunswick and the couple left BC for Fredericton. Molly continued to teach, both at the university and on television, and to paint. She is known for her watercolours of flowers and for oil paintings that capture the events of everyday life.

BOBCAT (*Lynx rufus*) is one of 3 types of wildcats in BC (the others are COUGAR and LYNX). It is a tawny-coloured (greyish or red-brown) animal with some dark spotting, distinguishable from the other cats by its small feet, stubby tail and lack of ear tufts. Bobcats occur on the mainland throughout the southern two-thirds of the province, in a variety of habitats that give good mixed ground cover from valley bottoms to timberline. They feed on RODENTS, hares, ground SQUIRRELS, birds and sometimes young DEER. Males, which weigh up to 18 kg, are larger than females. The female gives birth to a litter of 1–7 young in the spring, and a second litter in the same year is not uncommon.

Bobcat. *Mark Newman/Image Makers*

BODEGA Y QUADRA, Juan Francisco de la, naval explorer (b 22 May 1744, Lima, Peru; d 26 Mar 1794, Mexico City). After early education in Lima, he entered the Naval Academy in Cádiz and graduated as a midshipman in 1767. He arrived in New Spain (Mexico) in 1774 among other young officers selected and trained for Pacific Northwest Coast exploration. From San Blas in 1775 he made an epic voyage to Alaska in the tiny schooner *Sonora*; he reached Kruzov Island and charted the first realistic delineation of the coast to 58°. In 1779, in the *Favorita*, he explored the entrances to Prince William Sound and Cook Inlet and reached Kodiak Island. He returned from Spain to the Pacific in 1789 as commandant of the San Blas naval department. He assisted the MALASPINA expedition and planned and managed other voyages searching for the Northwest Passage. In 1792, serving in a diplomatic role as Spanish commissioner, he met with George VANCOUVER at Friendly Cove in an attempt to settle the terms of the Nootka Convention under which Spain had agreed to cede to England its establishment at NOOTKA (*see*

NOOTKA SOUND CONTROVERSY). He was a generous host, entertaining aboriginal leaders and fur traders in the commandant's house. Bodega Bay in California and QUADRA ISLAND in BC are named for him. *See also* NUU-CHAH-NULTH; SPANISH EXPLORATION. *Freeman Tovell*

BOLD POINT was a FISHING community and UNION STEAMSHIP CO stop on the east coast of QUADRA ISLAND, 20 km northeast of CAMPBELL RIVER. The famed timber cruiser (*see* FOREST INDUSTRY) Moses IRELAND established a hotel and ranch here in 1901 and there was also a store and post office (est 1911), but the settlement was abandoned by the 1960s. AS

BOLIDEN (WESTMIN) CANADA LTD is a Toronto MINING company with a ZINC-COPPER mine at Myra Falls near CAMPBELL RIVER on VANCOUVER ISLAND and two copper projects in Chile. The Myra Falls mine above BUTTLE LK in STRATHCONA PROVINCIAL PARK began shipping ore in 1967 and touched off furious protests from conservationists objecting to the dumping of mine tailings in the lake, the source of drinking water for Campbell River. The company was later convicted of releasing heavy metals into the water and switched to a land-based disposal system. Founded in 1951 as Westmin Resources, it was the object of a successful 1998 takeover by Boliden Ltd, a Swedish company.

BONAPARTE PLATEAU is a 1,000 km² area of rolling subalpine FOREST northwest of KAMLOOPS between the N THOMPSON R and FRASER R. It is part of the traditional territory of the SECWEPEMC (Shuswap) people but was largely isolated from outside contact until post-WWII, when sport fishers, hunters and loggers began arriving in greater numbers. The plateau is known for its many productive FISHING lakes, the largest being Bonaparte Lk. Hwy 24 across the north of the plateau is sometimes called the "Fishing Highway." Portions of the plateau have been protected as recreational reserves, though LOGGING has continued. The Bonaparte R loops west and south out of Bonaparte Lk through CACHE CREEK to empty into the S Thompson R near ASHCROFT.

BONNER, Robert, lawyer, politician (b 10 Sept 1920, Vancouver). He served overseas with the Seaforth Highlanders during WWII and was the first officer wounded in the invasion of Italy. Following the war he was among the first graduates of UBC's law school in 1948. An active CONSERVATIVE, he backed W.A.C BENNETT in his failed bid for the party leadership in 1950. When Bennett became SOCIAL CREDIT PARTY leader and PREMIER in 1952, he asked Bonner to join his CABINET as attorney general; at age 32 Bonner became the youngest attorney general in BC history. He had never run for office, but he agreed and was elected in a by-election. He served as attorney general for 16 years, during which time he was one of the most powerful ministers in the Socred government and one of the premier's closest advisors. As well, he served as minister of

Bob Bonner, one of the most powerful cabinet ministers in W.A.C. Bennett's Social Credit government. *CVA 136-51*

education (1953–54) and of industrial development, trade and commerce (1957–64). After being defeated in the 1966 election, Bonner again won a by-election, but he retired from the cabinet in 1968 to join MACMILLAN BLOEDEL as vice-president. He was chairman and CEO of MacBlo from 1972–76, then chairman of BC HYDRO until his retirement in 1985.

BONNINGTON FALLS, on the KOOTENAY R 18 km west of NELSON, is the site of 4 dams (Corra Linn, Upper Bonnington, Lower Bonnington and South Slocan) operated by WEST KOOTENAY POWER & LIGHT CO. This stretch of water has produced HYDROELECTRIC power since 1898, when the longest electrical transmission line then known carried power to the LeRoy Mine at ROSSLAND and later to COMINCO operations at TRAIL and KIMBERLEY. The city of Nelson owns a power plant at the Upper Bonnington dam and generates a portion of its power there; the rest it purchases from West Kootenay Power. The area has been occupied by the KTUNAXA (Kutenai) FIRST NATION for at least 4,000 years. It was named after Bonnington Linn, a waterfall on the Scottish estate of Sir Charles Ross, a president of the power company and the inventor of the Ross Rifle.

BOOK PUBLISHING in BC is a $50 million industry, producing about 500 new book titles each year and accounting for about 3% of total sales in Canada. Its origins date back to 1858, when Alfred Waddington wrote and published the first book to appear in the colony, *The Fraser Mines Vindicated; or, A History of Four Months*. About 110 more books appeared before 1900, a mixture of regional travel and information books, political and social commentary, fiction

and poetry. Not much has been recorded about BC publishing between 1900 and 1950. For the most part, it seems to have been an offshoot of the printing business, an extension of regional, literary and/or historical societies, and occasional temporary partnerships with Ontario firms. S.J. Clark published Frederic HOWAY's seminal 4-volume history *British Columbia From the Earliest Times to the Present*, in VANCOUVER in 1914, a major undertaking for the time. The Vancouver *Province* published some very handsome books by staff writers, such as B.A. McKelvie's *Tales of Conflict* (1949), and in the same era the *Sun* published Edith Adams recipes and books of cartoons by Len NORRIS. Self-publishing was also widespread, particularly by groups writing community and family histories. This is a tradition that continues strongly to the present day: the author Joe GARNER, for example, sold some 70,000 copies of his self-published memoirs. School textbooks were brought into the region mostly by Toronto subsidiaries of British and US firms. J.M. Dent and Sons were particularly successful in BC, partly because they operated a Vancouver office run by Gordon Stephen, the brother of the novelist and activist A.M. STEPHEN.

The modern era of book publishing in BC began with the 1958 Centennial, which encouraged a burst of publishing activity. Two of the most influential books appearing that year were actually published in Toronto—Margaret Ormsby's *British Columbia: A History* (Macmillan) and *British Columbia: A Centennial Anthology* (McClelland & Stewart), edited by Reginald Watters and designed by Robert Reid—but they were developed in BC for a BC audience. These and many other centennial books demonstrated the appetite for regional non-fiction and laid the foundation for the kind of book that has become the mainstay of the industry. Partly in response to this emerging market, Mitchell Press, a printing company, published its first book in 1959. The 1960s saw a lively publishing scene that provided books to BC readers alongside titles published in the UK, US and Ontario. The most notable BC-published book to follow the 1958 breakthrough was *Wagon Road North* (1960) by Art DOWNS, which is still in print and is among the top 5 all-time BC bestsellers. The book publishing operation it sparked, which was run by Downs until 1995, is still in business under the name Heritage House, taken over by Rodger and Pat Touchie in the 1990s. Other important books of this era include Alan Morley's *Mill Town to Metropolis* (Mitchell, 1961), *Far Pastures* by R.M. Paterson (Gray's, 1963), *The Pacific Gardener* by Art Willis (Gray's, 1962), *Son of Raven, Son of Deer* by George CLUTESI (Gray's, 1967), *The Salmon People* by Hugh McKervill (Gray's, 1967), *Curve of Time* by M. Wylie BLANCHET (Gray's, 1968) and *The Pathless Way* by Justin de Goutiere (Graydonald Graphics, 1969). Nor was publishing confined to Vancouver and Victoria. F.W. Lindsay of QUESNEL and N.L. Barlee of PEACHLAND were also making a commercial success of publishing popular history books in the BC Interior. The largest BC publisher of trade books prior to the 1970s, though, was the Provincial Museum (*see* ROYAL

BC MUSEUM) with its 50-title list of natural history handbooks and anthropology memoirs. Some of these titles, like Wilson DUFF's *Indian History of BC* and Nancy J. TURNER's *Food Plants of BC Indians*, are BC classics still in use.

The 1970s brought another surge of publishing activity. In 1971 James J. Douglas, then the western sales representative for the Toronto company McClelland & Stewart, founded J.J. Douglas, a firm that evolved into DOUGLAS & MCINTYRE, BC's largest trade book publisher in 2000. Douglas's activities, in part, provided the foundation for sales and distribution activities by others including Mark Stanton, Scott McIntyre and Allan MacDougall. McIntyre took over D&M on Douglas's retirement, while Stanton and MacDougall provided sales and distribution services, first through their firm, Stanton and MacDougall, and after 1979, through RAINCOAST BOOKS. In 1979 they also formed the wholesaler Book Express, as an attempt to raise sales of BC books in the rest of Canada. Book Express grew to become the largest national wholesaler and Raincoast added its own publishing program, which included the internationally successful *Griffin and Sabine* series by Nick BANTOCK. In 1991 Raincoast sold off its sales and publicity activities to Kate Walker, a former employee, who formed Kate Walker & Co. Douglas's daughter, Diana Douglas, also became an active publisher. INTERNATIONAL SELF-COUNSEL PRESS was founded by Jack James, Vancouver's original storefront lawyer, but it was Diana Douglas who made the firm one of BC's 3 largest publishing companies active in international markets.

BC has been an active centre of literary book publishing. This aspect of the industry also traces its roots back to 1958, when William MCCONNELL founded KLANAK PRESS. Throughout the 1960s and 1970s McConnell published such notable writers as Jane RULE, Robert HARLOW, Henry Kreisel, Raymond HULL, Saint-Denys Garneau, Anne Hébert, and F.R. Scott in fine editions with artwork by Takao TANABE, Don JARVIS, and Ben Lim. In the 1960s literary publishing expanded with the arrival of bill BISSETT's BLEWOINTMENT press, followed by Seymour Mayne and Patrick LANE's Very Stone House, David Robinson and Jim Brown's TALON BOOKS LTD, and in 1969 the GEORGIA STRAIGHT Writing Supplement, edited by Dan MacLeod, Dennis Wheeler and Stan PERSKY, which in 1974 evolved into NEW STAR BOOKS. The 1970s also saw the establishment of Pulp Press (1971, now ARSENAL PULP PRESS), HARBOUR PUBLISHING (1974), Oolichan Books (1974), PRESS GANG PUBLISHERS (1975), SONO NIS PRESS (1976) and Caitlin Press (1977), while POLESTAR BOOK PUBLISHERS (1981), Exstasis Editions (1982) and ANVIL PRESS (1988) followed in the 1980s. Apart from Talon, Exstasis and Anvil, most of these houses had evolved by the mid-1990s into regular trade publishers relying on mainstream nonfiction titles to sustain reduced poetry and fiction lists.

In 1972, when Basil Stuart-Stubbs called western Canadian publishers together to discuss common cause, some 50 operators attended, mostly from BC. In addition to those listed above, the active firms of the period included Hancock House, Fforbez, November House, Cloudburst, Gordon Soules, Saltaire, Whitecap Books, UBC PRESS, Press Porcépic, and Discovery Press. Two years later the BC Publishers' Group was formed. It was renamed the Association of Book Publishers of BC in 1978 and became the most active regional trade association in Canada.

The market for books in BC is healthy, especially for books about BC. Surveys indicate that British Columbians read slightly more books in general than other Canadians, while the consumption of regional books is far greater than in any other province except Quebec. The market for regional fiction is modest; regional non-fiction is the mainstay of the local publishing industry.

BC's book publishers are beneficiaries of federal assistance through programs of Heritage Canada and the Canada Council for the Arts. The former supports the development of book publishers as businesses while the latter provides subsidies for publishers to diminish the risk of losing money on cultural titles. In 1990, following a consultant's report, the BC government created a $500,000 program of grants to assist BC book publishers and authors. This program complemented 2 smaller programs, one supporting the production of books on BC heritage and another funding purchases for school libraries. The BC government has not, except in one instance, seen the wisdom of working with the province's book publishers to create school textbooks or other learning materials. Consequently that sizable market is dominated by foreign-owned branchplants located in Ontario.

The state of the book publishing industry might be described as stable, and at the same time precarious. The continuity of firms and their cultural contributions suggest that most are here to stay. The marginal profitability of most companies suggests that they owe their continued existence to literary, ideological and cultural commitments rather than to financial reward.

Rowland Lorimer

BORDEN, Charles E., archaeologist (b 15 May 1905, New York City; d 25 Dec 1978, Vancouver). He came to VANCOUVER in 1939 as an assistant professor of German at UBC, where he taught until his retirement. He took up local ARCHAEOLOGY in 1945 and until 1965 was the only archaeologist working in BC. He received many official honours and in 1970 was appointed professor of archaeology at UBC in recognition of his research, teaching and publications. He worked on excavations at MARPOLE and other Fraser delta sites and in the Interior, and at the Milliken site near YALE, where he established a 10,000-year-long sequence of cultures. He was instrumental in drafting the *Archaeological and Historic Protection Act* passed by the legislature in 1960. *Roy Carlson*

BORRADAILE, Osmond, cinematographer (b 1898, Winnipeg, MB; d 1998, Vancouver). He began his career in Hollywood in 1914 and gradually worked his way up to cameraman. It was the era of the silent movies and Borradaile worked with such directors as Cecil B. DeMille and stars such as Rudolph Valentino and Gloria Swanson. In the 1930s he went to England and worked with London Films, Alexander Korda's production team, shooting some of the great classics of film history, including *Elephant Boy* (1937), *The Scarlet Pimpernel* (1934), *The Four Feathers* (1939) and *Foreign Correspondent* (1940). A veteran of WWI, Borradaile also served in the British Army during WWII as a military photographer. In 1950 he moved to a farm in the FRASER VALLEY, where he lived for the rest of his life. His 1951 National Film Board documentary about the royal visit of Princess Elizabeth won a British Academy Award. He was an officer in the Order of Canada and was inducted as a Chevalier de la Légion d'honneur for his WWI service in France.

Osmond Borradaile, Hollywood cinematographer.
Eliza Massey photo

BORSOS, Phillip, filmmaker (b 5 May 1953, Hobart, Tasmania; d 2 Feb 1995, Vancouver). He moved to PITT MEADOWS with his family as a youngster and became interested in FILMMAKING when he was in high school. His first films were theatrical shorts on industrial subjects. All 3—*Cooperage* (1976), *Spartree* (1977) and *Nails* (1979)—won Canadian Film Awards, and *Nails* earned an Academy Award nomination. He turned to feature films with his movie about the train robber Billy MINER, *The Grey Fox* (1982), which is considered one of the best Canadian films ever made. The film won a Golden Globe nomination and 5 Genies, including best picture and best director. Subsequent features included *The Mean Season* (1985), *One Magic Christmas* (1985) and the controversial *Bethune* (1991). Borsos completed his final film, *Far From Home: The Adventures of Yellow Dog*, shortly before he died of leukemia.

BOSSIN, Bob, folk singer (b 5 Jan 1946, Toronto). In the early 1970s he was a founder of the legendary Canadian folk group Stringband and in 1974 he wrote its biggest hit, "Dief Will Be the Chief Again," a paean to Canada's 13th prime minister, John Diefenbaker. Bossin left Ontario in 1980 to reside in VANCOUVER, and when Stringband dissolved in the mid-1980s he concocted Bossin's Home Remedy for Nuclear War, a satirical one-man musical revue. He moved to GABRIOLA ISLAND in 1991 and in 1994 recorded *GABRIOLA V0R1X0*, an album that included his song "Sulphur Pass," urging that VANCOUVER ISLAND's old-growth rain forest be preserved. The song and its promotional video, featuring vocals by Bossin and several other like-minded BC artists, won several international awards.   *Mike Harling*

BOSTOCK, Hewitt, rancher, journalist, politician (b 31 May 1864, Surrey, England; d 28 Apr 1930, Monte Creek). A graduate of Cambridge Univ, he was a lawyer in England but took up ranching near KAMLOOPS when he immigrated to BC in 1888. In 1894 he founded the *PROVINCE* as a weekly newspaper in VICTORIA. Along with his partner Walter NICHOL, who later served as lieutenant governor, he moved the paper to VANCOUVER in 1898 and made it a daily. At the same time he was a successful politician, serving as LIBERAL MP for Yale–Cariboo from 1896 to 1904. As his political career developed, Bostock sold his share in the *Province*. He was appointed to the Senate in 1904, where he served as Liberal leader and eventually Speaker. He was also minister of public works in Mackenzie King's government 1921–22.

BOSTON was an American-owned sailing vessel that arrived in NOOTKA SOUND on the west coast of VANCOUVER ISLAND on a trading voyage on 12 Mar 1803. Capt John Salter and his 26-man crew met the local NUU-CHAH-NULTH people, led by their chief MAQUINNA. As trading and refitting progressed, a misunderstanding developed between the traders and the local people, and on 22 March Maquinna and his followers attacked the ship, killing all hands except John JEWITT and John Thompson. The *Boston* was beached and three weeks later it was accidentally burned. Jewitt and Thompson remained captives of the Nuu-chah-nulth for two and a half years.

BOSTON BAR, pop 733, 42 km north of YALE, overlooks the top end of HELLS GATE in the Fraser Canyon (*see* FRASER R). During the 1858 GOLD RUSH a MINING camp grew up near the NLAKA'PA-MUX (Thompson) village of Kwi.owh.um, or Koia'um ("to pick berries"). Once the gold rush passed, the population dwindled. Due to flooding in 1894 the community was relocated to higher ground north of the original site. An aerial tramway that crossed the canyon to NORTH BEND in 1940–86 has been replaced by a bridge. The name refers to "Boston Men," as local FIRST NATIONS people referred to American miners.

BOSTON PIZZA INTERNATIONAL is a RICH-MOND-based chain of restaurants with 125 locations across Canada and in the US. It was founded as a single restaurant in Edmonton in 1964 by Konstantinos Agioritus, a Greek immigrant, who chose the name Boston simply because he liked it. The franchise operation was bought by a group of BC investors in 1983. The company had 1998 revenues of $170 million.

BOSWELL, pop 200, is a LOGGING and resort community on the east shore of KOOTENAY LK, 43 km northwest of CRESTON. It was formerly a steamship landing and fruit-growing area. Gov Gen Earl Grey bought land here for his son Lord Howick in 1906 and named it the Boswell Ranch after the surveyor he had employed for the property transfer. Boswell hosts an East Shore Craft Faire in Aug. It is also the site of an unusual house built with 600,000 embalming fluid bottles, by the late David Brown, who once worked as an undertaker.   AS

BOUCHIE LAKE is a ranching settlement (*see* CATTLE INDUSTRY) in the north CARIBOO, 8 km northwest of QUESNEL on Bouchie Crk. It was named after Billy Boucher, son of one of Simon FRASER's boatmen on his journey through BC. Boucher operated an early ferry across the FRASER R near here.

BOULDING, James "Jim," outdoor educator (b 1932, Calgary; d 7 May 1986). He grew up in PENTICTON and attended UBC, where he met his future wife Myrna Baikie. After marrying in 1955, the Bouldings taught school in NANAIMO, then moved north in 1957 to teach in CAMPBELL RIVER. Soon afterward they took over STRATHCONA PARK LODGE, on upper Campbell Lk; the lodge had been rescued from flooding by Myrna's family. They quit teaching in 1972 to devote their time to developing the lodge into a combined resort and wilderness education centre that pioneered programs in outdoor training for youth. Many thousands of schoolchildren from around the province have visited the lodge to take part in activities devised by the Bouldings. In 1986 they received the prestigious Heaslip Award for their ENVIRONMENTAL work.

BOUNDARIES separate BC from the American states of Washington, Idaho and Montana to the south, from Alberta on the east, from the Northwest Territories and the Yukon on the north and from Alaska in the northwest. The southern boundary with the US stretches 640 km from AKAMINA PASS in the ROCKY MTS along the 49th parallel of latitude to the Pacific just south of TSAWWASSEN. There are 22 border crossings used by motor vehicles along the border with the US. The border continues westward out into GEORGIA STRAIT, where it veers south through the GULF ISLANDS and HARO STRAIT around the bottom of VANCOUVER ISLAND and out through the middle of JUAN DE FUCA STRAIT. The 49th parallel was accepted as the border in the OREGON TREATY (officially, the Treaty of Washington) in 1846 and was mapped by the British Boundary Commission from 1858 to 1862. The line through the Gulf Islands remained in dispute until it was settled by international arbitration in 1872 (*see* PIG WAR). Because of the border's southern dip, insisted on by British negotiators in order to keep southern Vancouver Island in British hands, ferries crossing Georgia Strait between ACTIVE PASS and Tsawwassen actually cut across American territory. The boundary with Alberta, 1,545 km long, snakes northwestward along the height of land in the ROCKY MTS until it meets the 120th meridian of longitude, at which point it turns directly north up the meridian as far as the 60th parallel of latitude. When BC was created as a colony in 1858 its northern border was defined rather vaguely by the STIKINE R and FINLAY R. A short-lived GOLD RUSH to the Stikine in 1862 prompted Britain to create the STIKINE TERRITORY north of the river to the 62nd parallel and east to the 125th meridian. The governor of BC was given jurisdiction. Then, in 1863, the boundary of the colony was extended to its present limits, absorbing most of the Stikine Territory. This border extends 1,062 km along the 60th parallel west to the extreme northwest corner of the province where Alaska, the Yukon and BC converge at Boundary Peak. The border with the Alaska Panhandle, 893 km long, was resolved in 1903 after many years of negotiation between Great Britain, Russia and the US (*see* ALASKA BOUNDARY DISPUTE).

BOUNDARY BAY, south of DELTA and west of SURREY, is bisected by the Canada–US border. Thousands of years ago it was the mouth of the FRASER R before silt deposits filled in the area between POINT ROBERTS and Delta and forced the river farther north. The low, marshy shoreline attracts many types of birds; the bay and its adjacent wetlands are a critically important stop along the PACIFIC FLYWAY of North America for hundreds of thousands of migrating waterfowl. The shallow water provides several warm-water beaches. At the north end, dikes protect Delta farmland from tidal flooding. In the northeast corner, at the mouths of the Serpentine and NICOMEKL rivers, are MUD BAY and CRESCENT BEACH. The region was formerly a summer cottage area and is now a residential suburb of VANCOUVER. OYSTERS were raised here from 1904 to the 1960s, when pollution became too great. Until then, this area produced over 50% of all the oysters cultured in BC.

BOUNDARY DISTRICT is the mountainous region of south-central BC along the US border between the OKANAGAN VALLEY and the KOOTENAY. It extends from BRIDESVILLE east along Hwy 3 to Paulson Pass 35 km beyond CHRISTINA LK, and north from the border roughly 70 km. The name derives from Boundary Crk, where many discoveries of minerals in the area were initially made. The main waterway is the KETTLE R, which loops through almost the length of the district. Christina Lk is the largest lake and the centre of summer recreation. GRAND FORKS (pop 3,944) is the only community of any size. The region was occupied by groups of OKANAGAN FIRST NATIONS when prospectors began arriving in the mid-19th century. Gold was discovered near Rock

Farmland at Anarchist Mt Pass, Boundary District. *Walter Lanz/Image Makers*

Creek (*see* ROCK CREEK WAR) in 1857, sparking an intense GOLD RUSH. The DEWDNEY TRAIL was extended into the district by 1861, but by the middle of the decade the rush had petered out; it was not until copper ore was discovered in the 1890s that outsiders began arriving in large numbers. GREENWOOD, MIDWAY and PHOENIX all began as COPPER mining centres, and while the Granby smelter was in operation at Grand Forks (1900–19) it was the second largest copper smelter in the world. DOUKHOBORS began arriving in 1908 and these settlers' distinctive homesteads are a feature of the district. The prosperous mines encouraged railway construction and by 1916 the famed KETTLE VALLEY RWY linked Midway via PENTICTON to the CPR main line at HOPE. The mining boom collapsed immediately after WWI, population growth stalled and many communities disappeared. Since then the district has come to rely on forestry and farming and, around Grand Forks, fruit growing.

BOUNDARY FALLS was a COPPER MINING community in the BOUNDARY DISTRICT, 18 km east of GRAND FORKS on the CPR. A hotel, store and post office were in place by 1895. The Montreal and Boston Copper Co built its Sunset SMELTER here in 1902, but ceased operations in 1908 for lack of ore.   AS

BOWEN ISLAND, 52.6 km², is located at the mouth of HOWE SOUND, 15 minutes from HORSE-SHOE BAY by ferry and less than an hour from downtown VANCOUVER. It is named for the British naval officer James Bowen. Steep and heavily wooded, the island is dominated by Mt Gardner (el 762 m). The earliest settlers were loggers and farmers. A brickyard in Snug Cove produced bricks used to build Vancouver's first city hall. When steamer service began after 1900, the main

appeal became recreational. In 1920 the UNION STEAMSHIP CO took over the Snug Cove–Deep Bay area, including the Hotel Monaco, owned since 1900 by John Cates, a tugboat captain (*see* CATES TOWING). Union Steamship renamed the resort the Bowen Inn and made the island the most popular destination on the lower coast for excursions and summer holidayers, featuring TENNIS courts, a swimming pool, a putting green, horse stables and the largest dance pavilion in BC. The advent of car-ferry service in 1958 brought rapid population growth but marked the end for Union Steamships, which closed the hotel. By the late 1990s the permanent population was about 3,000, many of whom commute to the city. Since the 1970s residents have fought to protect the rural atmosphere of the island from large development schemes. The island was administered by the GREATER VANCOUVER REGIONAL DISTRICT and the ISLANDS TRUST until 4 Dec 1999, when it became a municipality with its own mayor and district council.

BOWERING, George, writer (b 1 Dec 1936, Okanagan Falls). While studying at UBC he belonged to a group of writers influenced by the American Black Mountain poets Robert Creeley, Robert Duncan and Charles Olson. In 1961 he helped to found the poetry magazine TISH, which gave voice to a new poetics in VANCOUVER. He taught at SFU for many years. A prolific and varied writer, he has published more than 40 books, including collections of short fiction, poetry, novels, criticism and memoir. He won a GOV GEN'S LITERARY AWARD for poetry in 1969 for *Rocky Mountain Foot* and *The Gangs of Kosmos*, and another in 1980 for his novel about George VANCOUVER, *Burning Water*. He returned to the subject of BC history in *Shoot*, his 1994 novel about the MCLEAN GANG and his idiosyncratic history of the province, *Bowering's BC: A Swashbuckling History* (1996).
Reading: Eva-Marie Kröller, *George Bowering: Bright Circles of Colour*, 1992.

BOWERING, Marilyn, writer (b 13 Apr 1949, Winnipeg, MB). She grew up in VICTORIA and graduated with an MA from the Univ of Victoria in 1973, the same year that her first book of poetry, *The Liberation of Newfoundland*, appeared. Since then she has published steadily, her works including several more books of poetry, a story collection and 2 novels. Among the poetry collections are *Grandfather Was A Soldier* (1987) about the WWI combat experience, *Autobiography* (1996), which won the Pat LOWTHER Award and was nominated for a GOV GEN'S LITERARY AWARD and *Human Bodies: New and Collected Poems 1987–1999* (1999). Her first novel, *To All Appearances a Lady* (1989), is set in CHINATOWN in Victoria around 1900. Her second novel, *Visible Worlds* (1997), won a BC BOOK PRIZE and was shortlisted for the prestigious Orange Prize in Britain. SOOKE has been her home since 1979, though she has spent extended sojourns in Europe.

Marilyn Bowering, poet and novelist.
Barry Peterson & Blaise Enright-Peterson

BOWES, Sarah, teacher, temperance advocate (b 28 June 1834, Milton, ON; d 12 Sept 1911, Milton, ON). A schoolteacher and activist with the Women's Christian Temperance Union (WCTU), she moved west to VANCOUVER in 1886. She became a home visitor for the METHODIST CHURCH and a teacher at a church-run school for CHINESE people, as well as continuing her involvement in the WCTU. She was an organizer for the Union from 1889 to 1893, then its provincial superintendent of missionary work from 1894 to 1900 in VICTORIA. At the same time she took part in a variety of activities related to the welfare of women and children until 1910, when she returned to her native Ontario.

BOWRON LAKE PROVINCIAL PARK, 1,232 km², lies in the heart of the CARIBOO MTS east of BARKERVILLE, an area with spectacular mountain scenery and varied wildlife. The park's outstanding feature is a wilderness canoe circuit: a 116-km chain of 11 LAKES, RIVERS and portages in the shape of a rectangle. The area was occupied by the SECWEPEMC (Shuswap) and DAKELH (Carrier) FIRST NATIONS for at least 2,000 years before being visited by whites during the Cariboo GOLD RUSH of the 1860s. Bowron Lake is named for John Bowron, an OVERLANDER who came to the goldfields in 1862 and stayed in the CARIBOO, where he worked as a public servant until his death in 1906 (among other things, he established the first LIBRARY in the Cariboo). The area was popular for fishing, trapping and hunting; as more visitors arrived and more lodges and cabins appeared, local conservationists began to raise questions about depletion of wildlife. In 1925 the area inside the chain of lakes was set aside as a game reserve, and in 1961 an expanded area was designated a provincial PARK. A number of Secwepemc archaeological sites, most notably pit house depressions (kekuli), have been located in the area.

BOWSER, pop 130, is a community on the east side of VANCOUVER ISLAND looking into GEORGIA STRAIT 66 km north of NANAIMO. It is named for William J. BOWSER, BC premier 1915–16. The ESQUIMALT & NANAIMO RWY arrived in 1914 and a post office was established in 1915. LOGGING sustained the local economy for many years; now it is a commercial centre catering to TOURISM and the surrounding rural area. The local hotel in the 1930s boasted a dog named Mike who was trained to deliver beer to tables.

Mike the bartending dog, in a photo that appeared in Life *magazine in 1940.*
Courtesy Rita Levitz and Leah Willott

BOWSER, William John, lawyer, politician, premier 15 Dec 1915–23 Nov 1916 (b 3 Dec 1867, Rexton, NB; d 25 Oct 1933, Vancouver). After graduating from Dalhousie Univ in Halifax, he moved to VANCOUVER in 1891 and began practising law. He won a Vancouver seat in the provincial legislature in 1903 as a CONSERVATIVE and held it for the next 21 years. He was attorney general and the most important cabinet member in Richard MCBRIDE's government in

William Bowser, premier of BC 1915–16.
CVA Port.P1066

1907–15. In 1914 he sent the militia to the Vancouver Island coal mines to put down civil disturbances during the drawn-out strike by coal miners (see COAL MINING, VANCOUVER ISLAND). He also attempted to derail WOMEN'S SUFFRAGE and PROHIBITION by promising referenda on both issues, which he personally opposed. Bowser had a reputation as a politician who lacked personal warmth but was skilled at dispensing favours and getting out the vote. He inherited a divided party from McBride. C.H. TUPPER, a prominent Tory, lobbied publicly against him, calling him a "little Kaiser." This, combined with Liberal charges of corruption, brought down the government in the 1916 election. Bowser held his own seat and remained leader of the opposition until his defeat in 1924. He gave up the Conservative leadership in Nov 1926. He came out of retirement to lead a non-partisan group into the 1933 election but died during the campaign; only two of the movement's candidates won seats. *See also* PREMIER.

BOWSFIELD, Edward Oliver "Ted," baseball pitcher (b 10 Jan 1935, Vernon). One of BC's first major league BASEBALL players, he was recruited by the Boston Red Sox straight out of his PENTICTON high school. He signed a contract with the team in 1954 and played in the minor leagues before being called up to Boston in 1958. He won 4 games for the Red Sox, 3 against the powerful NY Yankees, earning him the team's rookie-of-the-year award. Bowsfield's powerful fastball soon began to wear down his arm, but he logged 5 more seasons in the major leagues with the Cleveland Indians, California Angels and Kansas City Royals. Appearing in 215 major league games, he had a 4.34 earned run average and a record of 37 wins, 39 losses. He ended his playing days with the Pacific Coast League VANCOUVER Mounties in 1965, then started a successful career in stadium management.

He was named first manager of Seattle's Kingdome stadium in 1974.   *SW*

BOWYER ISLAND lies on the east side of HOWE SOUND 4 km north of HORSESHOE BAY. Herbert Bingham purchased it in 1926 and made the south end into an estate with gardens, farm animals and a large house. His wife Annie called it her "Treasure Island." In 1999 Bingham descendants still owned the southern section; numerous part-time residents owned the rest. The island was named for British Admiral Sir George Bowyer by Capt G.H. RICHARDS during his 1859 survey.   *Doreen Armitage*

BOXING was the spectator sport of choice during the 1860s GOLD RUSH in the CARIBOO, but fans became disillusioned after Cariboo champion George Wilson was caught staging a fixed match with VICTORIA's Joe Eden. In 1884 world heavyweight champion John L. Sullivan brought boxing back to the province without throwing a punch; fight fans who filled Victoria's Philharmonic Hall were disappointed when the local coal miner scheduled to face the champion backed out. The crowd enjoyed the rest of the bill, however, and professional boxing continued to be a draw at the hall. At the turn of the century, "bare-knuckle" fighters began to be replaced by boxers wearing fist-protecting gloves. The second world heavyweight champion to come to BC, Jack Johnson, soundly defeated Victor McLaglen at the VANCOUVER Athletic Club in 1909 (McLaglen later became a Hollywood actor, winning an Oscar for his supporting role in *The Informer* in 1935).

Other world champs to fight in Vancouver were lightweight Freddy Welsh in 1913 and Jack Dempsey, who faced 3 challengers in one night at the Calvary Club on Granville St in 1931. Two world-renowned fighters came to BC in 1936—Barney Ross defeated local favourite Gordon Wallace (who once beat Billy TOWNSEND in an amateur match) on 11 Mar in Vancouver and Max Baer, who earlier fought his own brother in TRAIL, appeared on a bill at the Denman Arena on 19 Aug, the night before it burned down. Joe Louis fought exhibition matches in Vancouver and Victoria in 1945. Willie Pep, Joey Maxim and Archie Moore came to Vancouver in the 1950s and the most famous boxer of the modern era, Muhammad Ali, fought an exhibition in Vancouver in Jan 1972, returning in May to defeat Canadian George Chuvalo in a memorable 12-round decision. Vancouver's last world title bout of the 20th century was light-heavyweight champ Michael Spinks's 1983 knockout of Oscar Rivandeneyra.

BC's only world champion is Jimmy MCLARNIN, who won the world welterweight crown in 1933 and earned approximately half a million dollars over his career. Hector McDonald, a close friend of McLarnin's, won the Pacific coast lightweight championship in 1930 and also faced top locals such as Mickey Gill and Billy Townsend. Tommy Paonessa dominated the local bantamweight division in the 1920s and 1930s but turned down an offer from

McLarnin's coach "Pop" Foster to join them on the US professional circuit. He remained in Vancouver to build a 60-year legacy as a coach, manager, referee and builder. Victoria's Wes Byrnell built up a 136-0 amateur record in the 1930s before becoming a world-ranked light welterweight and later the trainer of the Montreal Canadiens, Toronto Maple Leafs and Canadian national SOCCER team. Vancouver's Vic Foley, a Canadian featherweight champ, faced world champion Tony Canzoneri in a 1936 non-title match in Montreal. Foley, Townsend and Gordon Wallace were managed by former Alaska bootlegger Jack Allen. He and Al Princepe were Vancouver's most prominent promoters, responsible for organizing many of the city's world-class bouts.

Oral Campbell, a local fighter, poses with Jack Dempsey (r) in the ring of the Calvary Club, Vancouver, 1931. Courtesy Tommy Paonessa

Kenny Lindsay had title fights in the early 1940s with world bantamweight champions Lou Salica and Manuel Ortiz, losing to both in 10-round decisions. Jackie Turner, a N VANCOU-VER shipyard worker, was an 8-time Golden Glove winner and a world-ranked flyweight for almost a decade. He lost two 10-round decisions to world champ Dado Marino in the 1940s before retiring to CAMPBELL RIVER. Amateur fighter Gordie Woodhouse was expected to succeed at the 1940 Olympics, but when the games were cancelled because of WWII he travelled overseas as a soldier and defeated some of the top boxers in Europe and in the service. In amateur boxing, the "Golden Boy" award for the province's top amateur boxer was inaugurated in 1939 with Phil Vickery taking the first honours. Frank Almond won the Lou Marsh Trophy as Canada's Athlete of Year after he edged his brother Stan in a 1946 match for the Portland Golden Gloves.

Eddie Haddad, the Canadian amateur light-weight champion based in ESQUIMALT, was a favourite in the 1948 London Olympics but was disqualified in the quarterfinals on a highly questionable decision. Vancouver fighter Bill Brenner, a national amateur champion who later went to the New York pro ranks, also participated in the 1948 Olympics.

Canada's most successful international showing in boxing came at the 1954 British Empire Games (*see* BRITISH EMPIRE AND COMMONWEALTH GAMES) in Vancouver. When the national team coach from eastern Canada couldn't make it to the Games, assistant coach Paonessa unofficially took charge and led the boxers to 2 golds, 1 silver and 2 bronzes, one of which was captured by BC light heavyweight William Misselbrook. Canadian champions from BC included Angelo BRANCA, Phil Palmer, Buddy Palmer, Al Chabot and Harold Mann. Mann's most outstanding achievement was winning the light middleweight gold medal at the 1962 British Empire Games in Perth, the only gold medal ever won by a BC boxer in a major international competition. He later started the successful Spruce Capital Boxing Club in his native PRINCE GEORGE, where he coached national champions including his son, Laurie, voted best boxer in Canada on 3 occasions, Jack Meda, the heavyweight bronze medallist at the 1970 Commonwealth Games, and Roger Adolf, future Lillooet chief. He also coached Marjan Kolar, an Edmonton light heavyweight who moved to Prince George and won the 1967 Pan Am bronze. The trophy for greatest contribution to BC amateur boxing, inaugurated in 1971, is named for Harold Mann, who was also a national team coach and a referee. One of the first winners of the trophy was Irving Mann, Harold's own coach and father. Perhaps BC's most important boxing builder was Bert Lowes, a national

team coach who developed Vancouver's South Hill and Firefighters' boxing clubs in the 1950s and 1960s and became one of the world's top-ranked referees, overseeing matches at 3 Olympics. Lowes' top boxers included Canadian champions Winnie Schelt, Dave Wiley, Dick Findlay, Freddy Fuller, Franky Scott, Wayne and Tommy Boyce and Ignatz "Lindy" Lindmoser. The Boyce brothers won over a dozen Pacific Northwest gold gloves between them. Scott won a bronze medal at the 1966 British Empire Games and Fuller, who logged 339 amateur matches, was also expected to win a medal at the Games before sustaining a broken arm. Dave Brown ran a Vancouver club in the early 1950s that featured Canadian champions Lenny Walters, Jimmy Walters (no relation), Bobby Shires, Norm Jorgenson, Jerry Boucher, Hugh Meikle and Buddy Pearson. Brown went on to become the director of BC boxing in the Canadian Boxing Federation, a top-ranked referee and a World Boxing Council judge for 17 world title bouts. A top club during the 1960s was the North Shore Eagles, run by Elio Ius, a coach of the national team and patriarch of the family that included coaching brother Mel and 1970s Canadian champions Chris and David Ius. Chris joined fellow-Eagle and national champ Les Hamilton at the 1972 Munich Olympics. In the late 1970s, Vancouver's Astoria Club and New Westminster's Queensborough Club became dominant. Astoria, primarily run by George Angelomatis, produced Dale WALTERS, Tony PEP, Jimmy Worral, 1990 Commonwealth Games silver medallist Geronimo Bie and Manny Sobral, a Canadian welterweight champion and successful pro. With help from his wife Margaret, Pat O'Reilly ran the Hastings Community Centre Boxing Club from 1959-85, producing several successful boxers including his sons Patrick and Michael, both Canadian champions, but mainly focusing on less competitive concerns in getting kids off the streets. The early 1980s saw the emergence of BC's ultimate back-woods brawler, Gordy RACETTE. After Vancouver manager Tony Dowling taught him how to box, he became a successful pro, fighting Jimmy Young and Trevor Berbick, and was briefly bankrolled by Sylvester Stallone. Welterweight Jamie Ollenberger was a 2-time Golden Boy (1980-81) who posted a remarkable amateur career and fought for a professional ISBA title. Michael OLAJIDE had a chance at the IBF world middleweight title in 1987 and also fought top US pros Thomas Hearns and Iran Barkley. Olajide had won the Canadian middleweight crown in Vancouver in 1985, on the same bill as Tony Pep's Canadian featherweight championship win. The most popular BC boxer of the 1980s was Dale Walters, who took the bronze medal in the bantamweight division at the 1984 Los Angeles Olympics. His father Len, a member of the BC SPORTS HALL OF FAME, had been a BC, Pacific Northwest, Canadian and US amateur champion in the 1950s. Nanaimo's Shane Sutcliffe became BC's next great hope by winning the Canadian professional heavyweight title in 1998 though he lost it a year later. *SW*

BOYD, Denny, journalist (b 18 June 1930, Anyox). After leaving the northern MINING community of ANYOX, he grew up in VANCOUVER and VICTORIA and began his career in NEWSPAPERS as a teenager, contributing freelance sports stories to the *Victoria Colonist*. In 1951 he joined the staff of the *Victoria Times* as a sports reporter during the heyday of the paper when Stu KEATE was publisher and Bruce HUTCHISON editor. Boyd moved across to the *VANCOUVER SUN* in 1957 and worked there as a sports writer until 1970. After a brief stint with CJOR radio (*see* BROADCASTING, COMMERCIAL) he returned to the *Sun* in 1978 and wrote a daily column until his retirement in 1995. He has also written 2 books about HOCKEY, a cookbook, and a memoir, *In My Own Words* (1995), chronicling his struggle with alcoholism. He continued to write columns for the *Sun* following his retirement.

BOYD, Rob, downhill skier (b 15 Feb 1966, Vernon). He grew up in VERNON and WHISTLER and joined the Canadian national ski team in 1985. The following year he won his first World Cup race at Val Gardena, Italy, at 20 the youngest male winner of a World Cup event in more than a decade. He won 2 more World Cup races in 1987 and 1989 before injuries slowed his pace. After an 11-year career he retired from competitive SKIING in 1997 to coach with the Canadian alpine ski team in Whistler.

BRABANT, Augustin Joseph, Roman Catholic missionary (b 23 Oct 1845, Rolleghem, Belgium; d 1912, Victoria). After studies at the American College of Louvain he was ordained a priest in 1868 and left Europe for BC and a life as a missionary to the NUU-CHAH-NULTH (Nootka) people on the remote west coast of VANCOUVER ISLAND. In 1875 he founded a ROMAN CATHOLIC mission at HESQUIAT at the north end of CLAYOQUOT SOUND, the first mission on the Island's outer coast. His book, *Vancouver Island and its Missions* (1900), is important as a historical record. Brabant helped establish the Christie RESIDENTIAL SCHOOL at KAKAWIS in 1900. In 1908 he was appointed to an administrative position in VICTORIA.

Augustin Brabant, West Coast Catholic missionary, c 1860. BC Archives A-01432

BRACKENDALE, pop 1,100, is a residential community beside the SQUAMISH R, 10 km north of SQUAMISH. It is named either for John Bracken, an early settler, or for the bracken FERN that grows in abundance. Hop farming (*see* AGRICULTURE) was important early in the century, along with LOGGING. During the winter, one of the world's largest populations of bald EAGLES congregate here to feed on SALMON in the river. A 6 km^2 provincial reserve was created in 1996 to protect the eagles' habitat.

BRADNER is a community in the FRASER VALLEY about 15 km west of downtown ABBOTSFORD and now part of that city. It was a stop on the BC ELECTRIC RWY CO's INTERURBAN line to CHILLIWACK. Since the 1920s it has become the centre of the largest bulb-growing area in BC and is known as the Daffodil Capital of Canada (*see* AGRICULTURE). An annual spring flower show has been held here since 1928. One of the early growers was William Vander Zalm Sr, father of former premier Bill VANDER ZALM.

BRAID, Kate, carpenter, poet (b 1947, Calgary). She was a member of the VANCOUVER Industrial Writers' Union from 1987 to 1995 and a founding member of Women in Trades. Her first collection of poems about her working experience, *Covering Rough Ground*, won the 1992 Pat LOWTHER Award from the League of Canadian Poets. In 1995 she published a set of poems inspired by Emily CARR, *To This Cedar Fountain*. She returned to the subject in 1998 in *Inward to the Bones*, imagining a friendship between Carr and the American painter Georgia O'Keefe in a collection that won the VANCITY BOOK PRIZE. She has also co-written an oral history of the INTERNATIONAL UNION OF MINE, MILL AND SMELTER WORKERS.

BRALORNE, pop 78, is a former GOLD MINING company town in the BRIDGE R country about 160 km north of VANCOUVER in the COAST MTS. The mine was originally called the Lorne mine, then renamed Bralorne when Austin TAYLOR and his associates took control in 1931. The Bralorne mine operated until 1971, yielding more than 2.8 million oz of gold. At its peak during the 1930s it had a population of about 1,000.

BRANCA, Angelo Ernest, criminal lawyer, judge (b 21 Mar 1903, Mt Sicker, Vancouver Island; d 3 Oct 1984, Vancouver). He was the son of an immigrant Italian miner who moved to VANCOUVER and became a successful grocer/food importer. Branca studied law and began practising in the city in 1926. To keep fit he took up BOXING and he eventually won the Canadian amateur middleweight championship. This combative style carried over to the courtroom, where he developed a reputation as a top defence lawyer. He pleaded the cases of 61 murderers during his career (only 2 were hanged), as well as defending high-profile gamblers and well-known cabinet ministers. Active in the backrooms of the LIBERAL PARTY, he was also a leader in the BC ITALIAN community and

during WWII an outspoken critic of Benito Mussolini and fascism. In Oct 1963 he was appointed to the BC Supreme Court, then in Jan 1966 he joined the BC Court of Appeal, where he served until his retirement from the bench in Mar 1978. Two years after his death the Vancouver Italian community erected a bronze statue of Christopher Columbus in his honour. *See also* JUDICIAL SYSTEM.

BRANDYWINE FALLS, at 61 m the fourth-highest WATERFALL in BC, is the centrepiece of Brandywine Falls Provincial PARK (1.43 km^2), nestled between the highway to WHISTLER and the BC RAIL track 37 km north of SQUAMISH. The story goes that 2 members of a railway survey crew in 1910 wagered a bottle of brandy against a bottle of wine over the height of the falls. The loser lost his brandy but won the right to name one of the most scenic roadside attractions in southern BC.

Brandywine Falls, on the road to Whistler.
Roy Luckow photo

BRECHIN was a tiny settlement 3 km north of NANAIMO that had a school, church and post office by 1905. Today it is part of Nanaimo. Brechin Road runs from the Island Hwy down to the BC FERRIES terminal at the south end of Departure Bay. *AS*

BREEZE, Claude, artist (b 9 Oct 1938, Nelson). He was raised in Saskatoon and studied painting with Ernest Lindner before graduating from the U of Saskatchewan in 1958. After a year at the Vancouver School of Art (*see* EMILY CARR INSTITUTE OF ART & DESIGN), he moved to the West Coast permanently. His first solo exhibition was at the New Design Gallery in 1965. One of his paintings, *Sunday Afternoon: From an Old American Photograph*, created a public uproar for its graphic depiction of a lynching in the

American South. Other works have commented on the depiction of violence in the media, presenting violent images as though framed by a television screen. In 1972 he moved to London, ON, to teach; in 1976 he joined the fine arts faculty at York Univ in Toronto.

BREM RIVER was a large LOGGING camp that operated from the late 1940s to the mid-1960s. It was located near Brem Bay, where the Brem R runs into TOBA INLET, 65 km north of POWELL RIVER on the mainland coast. Remains of the abandoned camp can still be seen.   AS

BRENTWOOD BAY, pop 3,200, is on the east side of SAANICH INLET, north of VICTORIA on VANCOUVER ISLAND. It was named for a village in Essex, England, home of the president of the BC ELECTRIC RWY CO, which operated the SAANICH INTERURBAN line and maintained a powerhouse here. Early settlements in the area, all with post offices by the 1890s, were known as Sluggett, Hagan and Heal. John Sluggett settled immediately east of Brentwood Bay in the 1870s; James Hagan took up land just to the north, Fred Heal just to the south. A ferry crosses the inlet to MILL BAY and BUTCHART GARDENS is nearby. In recent years the picturesque waterfront community has been transformed by suburban residential development.

BRENTWOOD COLLEGE is a co-educational private secondary school at MILL BAY, north of VICTORIA. It began in 1923 as a boys' boarding school nearer Victoria, founded by a group of wealthy, mainly English-born lawyers and businessmen, to provide education on the English public school model. The original school closed in 1948 after fire destroyed the premises. It revived at the present location in 1961 on the initiative of several alumni. Girls have been admitted since 1972. *See also* EDUCATION, PRIVATE.

BREW, Chartres, first chief inspector of PROVINCIAL POLICE (b 31 Dec 1815, County Clare, Ireland; d 31 May 1870, Richfield). A veteran of the Royal Irish Constabulary and the Crimean War, he was asked to become chief inspector of police for the new colony of BC in 1858. When he arrived, Gov James DOUGLAS also appointed him chief gold commissioner. Along with Douglas, Chief Justice Matthew BEGBIE and Col Richard MOODY of the ROYAL ENGINEERS, Brew was one of the four most important COLONIAL GOVERNMENT officials. Although never able to create the professional police force he envisioned, he played an important role in all of the major conflicts with miners and aboriginals that marked the early years of the colony. In 1859 Brew became chief magistrate at NEW WESTMINSTER; in 1862–64 he was the colony's treasurer. From 1864 to 1868 he served in the Legislative Council. In 1868 he became a county court judge based at Richfield in the CARIBOO gold district. That year he supervised the rebuilding of BARKERVILLE after its devastation by fire. At his death he was praised for his honesty and diligence.

BREWSTER, Harlan Carey, salmon canner, premier 23 Nov 1916–death (b 10 Nov 1870, Harvey, NB; d 1 Mar 1918, Calgary). His father owned a shipyard, and as a young man Brewster earned his mate's ticket in deep-sea navigation. He arrived in BC in 1892 and worked as a purser for the CP NAVIGATION CO. He later managed a cannery and grew wealthy as owner of the

Harlan Brewster, premier of BC 1916–18, shown here c 1916. BC Archives A-01105

Clayoquot Sound Canning Co. In 1907, running as a LIBERAL, he won the Alberni seat in the legislature. Re-elected in 1909, he became the lone Liberal in the house when his colleague defected to the Conservatives. In 1912 he became Liberal leader but failed to unseat Premier Richard MCBRIDE in VICTORIA a few weeks later. At this point the Liberals had no MLAs, but Brewster sparked a rebirth of his party. Early in 1916, after McBride retired, Brewster won the Victoria seat in a by-election; he led the Liberals to an overwhelming victory in the general election later that year. His short-lived reformist government gave women the vote (*see* WOMEN'S SUFFRAGE), introduced PROHIBITION, streamlined the civil service and attempted to end patronage. But Brewster was not a strong leader and his term was marked by squabbling within his party. He died from pneumonia on his way back from consulting with PM Borden in Ottawa. *See also* PREMIER.

BREXTON was a tiny GOLD MINING community in the BRIDGE R country, 175 km north of VANCOUVER. Originally known as Fish Lake, the settlement was renamed after Bridge River Exploration Co and BRX Gold Mines Ltd, owner of the surrounding claims. It was active in the 1930s and 1940s.   AS

BRIAR RIDGE is a farming (*see* AGRICULTURE) and DAIRY FARMING area in the PEACE R district, 12

km east of DAWSON CREEK, near the Alberta border. The area is sometimes referred to as E POUCE COUPE. The first settlers, Sam and Jack Suffern, arrived in 1914, and many WWI veterans took up land here from 1918 to 1919.   AS

BRIDAL FALLS, a small resort community in the FRASER VALLEY 15 km east of CHILLIWACK on the TRANS-CANADA HWY, is the site of a provincial park that features 25-m-high Bridal Veil Falls. Julius Warneboldt built the Bridal Falls Lodge here in the mid-1930s. MINTER GARDENS, a 9-hole GOLF course and driving range and other TOURIST attractions are nearby.   AS

BRIDESVILLE, pop 66, is a community near the US border east of OSOYOOS. First called Maud after the wife of the first settler, Hosie Edwards, it was just a stop on the wagon road between ROCK CREEK and Osoyoos until the GREAT NORTHERN RWY arrived in 1905. Two years later a customs post opened. The station was renamed after David McBride, who opened the post office and the grand Bridesville Hotel in 1910. For 2 decades it was a lively railway town, then the rail service shut down and the hotel closed. The community survived as a service centre for the surrounding AGRICULTURAL area.

BRIDGE LAKE, pop 278, east of 100 MILE HOUSE in the CARIBOO and 95 km north of KAMLOOPS, is the main service centre on Hwy 24, which connects the Cariboo and Yellowhead highways (*see* ROADS AND HWYS). The village hosts a RODEO in June and has recreational facilities for summer visitors. Nearby Bridge Lk Provincial Park has a walking trail around the lake.   AS

BRIDGE RIVER, 142 km, flows east out of the COAST MTS to join the FRASER R just north of LILLOOET. Its mid-section is a spectacular 16-km steep-walled canyon and the area has gained popularity with hikers and climbers. There is an important ST'AT'IMX (Lillooet) FISHING site on the Fraser above the junction. Prospectors moving north up the Fraser Canyon arrived here in 1858 and found enough GOLD in the Bridge R to spark a brief GOLD RUSH. The name refers to a toll footbridge built across its mouth by the local FIRST NATIONS. After 1900 MINING activity centred farther west at Cadwallader Crk, where the Bend 'Or gold mine went into production in 1899. Beginning in the 1930s the BRALORNE and PIONEER mines were important gold producers; MINING continued until Bralorne's closure in 1971. The Bridge R mines produced a total yield of just over 4 million ounces. Between 1946 and 1960, as part of a HYDROELECTRIC power scheme, 2 dams were built, creating Downton and CARPENTER lakes, with water from the latter diverted through tunnels and penstocks to powerhouses at SETON LK. Several communities, including MINTO CITY, were drowned as a result of the flooding. *See also* RIVERS.

BRIDGMAN, Mel, hockey player (b 28 Apr 1955, Trenton, ON). He was the first BC HOCKEY

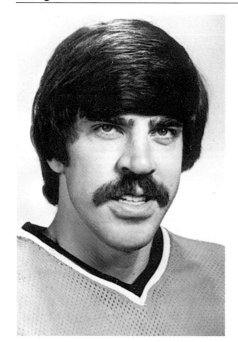

Mel Bridgman, hockey player, 1979.

player drafted first overall in the NHL entry draft. Raised in VICTORIA, he played a season for the BC JUNIOR HOCKEY LEAGUE's NANAIMO Clippers before joining the VICTORIA COUGARS of the WHL in 1973. In his second season he led the league with 157 points and tied Bryan Trottier as its all-star centre. The Philadelphia Flyers selected Bridgman in the 1975 entry draft and he joined their lineup the next season. He was captain of the team 1979–81. While scoring a career-high 87 points in the 1981–82 season, he was traded to the Calgary Flames. He also played for the New Jersey Devils, Detroit Red Wings and VANCOUVER CANUCKS before retiring during the 1988–89 season. In 1992 he returned to the NHL as the first general manager of the expansion Ottawa Senators but was replaced at the end of the season.   *SW*

BRIGADE LAKE is in the heart of a ranching district (*see* CATTLE INDUSTRY), 20 km south of KAMLOOPS. Because there was good pasturage for horses there, the lake became the first camping spot south of Kamloops on the HBC's 19th-century FUR BRIGADE trail to HOPE, hence the name.   *AS*

BRIGHOUSE, Samuel, pioneer settler (b 13 Jan 1836, Lindley, England; d there 31 July 1913). He arrived in NEW WESTMINSTER in 1862 with his cousin John MORTON and their friend William Hailstone, the so-called THREE GREEN-HORNS. They took up land in what became VANCOUVER's West End, built the first cabin there and tried their hand at raising cows and making bricks. Brighouse moved to a farm on LULU ISLAND but later returned to Vancouver and when it was incorporated as a city he was elected to city council. With the arrival of the CPR the Greenhorns sold their land and made a fortune. Brighouse returned to England in 1911 and died there.

BRILL, Debbie, high jumper (b 10 Mar 1953, Mission). From 1969 to the mid-1980s she was Canada's leading female high jumper and one of the best in the world. Using her unique reverse roll, the "Brill Bend," she won gold medals at the 1970 and 1982 Commonwealth Games, the 1971 Pan American Games and the 1979 World Cup, a silver medal at the 1978 Commonwealth Games and a bronze at the 1979 Pan Am Games. In 1971 she was co-winner of Canada's award for top female athlete. She was the first woman in N America to clear 6 ft and in 1982 held the world indoor record. After a break to recover from injuries and parent her children she returned to jumping and set a masters indoor world record in 1995. She is a member of the BC SPORTS HALL OF FAME and the Order of Canada. *See also* TRACK AND FIELD.
Reading: Debbie Brill, *Jump*, 1986.

Debbie Brill demonstrating her unique "Brill bend." Vancouver Sun

BRILLIANT, near CASTLEGAR, was an abandoned GOLD MINING camp named Waterloo in 1908 when DOUKHOBORS from Saskatchewan relocated here and established a community, renaming it for the waters of the KOOTENAY R. The newcomers established SAWMILLS, a jam factory and several other enterprises. The tomb of Doukhobor leader Peter VERIGIN is nearby. The 100-m steel and concrete Brilliant Suspension Bridge, constructed by the Doukhobors in 1913, is a national historic site.

BRIND'AMOUR, Rod, hockey player (b 9 Aug 1970, Ottawa). He is one of the best HOCKEY players to come from VANCOUVER ISLAND and one of the most complete NHL players of the 1990s. He was brought west by his parents to PRINCE RUPERT and then to CAMPBELL RIVER where he first learned to play the game. At age 15 he travelled to Saskatchewan to attend Notre Dame College, notable for producing many NHL stars. After leading the school to a national midget championship, he was drafted ninth overall by the St Louis Blues and recorded an exceptional season at Michigan State Univ before joining the Blues in 1989–90. In 1991 he was traded to the Philadelphia Flyers where he became an integral forward on one of the league's premier teams before he was dealt to the Carolina Hurricanes in 2000. His versatility and work ethic earned him key roles on Canada's 1996 World Cup and 1998 Olympic teams.   *SW*

BRINGHURST, Robert, writer (b 16 Oct 1946, Los Angeles, CA). He came to Alberta with his parents when he was 6 years old and moved to BC to study at UBC in the 1970s. A full-time writer and sometime teacher, he has published several volumes of poetry characterized by its erudition and complexity. An interest in aboriginal culture resulted in a collaboration with the HAIDA artist Bill REID, *The Raven Steals the Light* (1984), and another book, *The Black Canoe* (1991), about Reid's sculpture *Spirit of Haida Gwaii*. In 1999 he published a monumental study of Haida literature, *A Story as Sharp as a Knife: The Classical Haida Mythtellers and Their World*. He is also an expert on typography and book design.

BRISCO, pop 138, lies on the COLUMBIA R 75 km south of GOLDEN. It is a small service centre and entry point for the nearby BUGABOO Provincial Park (136.47 km²). Originally known as Columbia Valley, it was renamed for Arthur Brisco, a hero of the British army's famed Charge of the Light Brigade in the Crimean War and an officer with the Palliser Expedition to western Canada 1857–60.

BRITANNIA MINES was a complex of 4 adjoining COPPER mines and associated mills on the east side of HOWE SOUND, 50 km north of Vancouver. Discovered in 1888 by Dr. Alex Forbes, a local doctor and keen prospector, the copper deposits of the Britannia Mts were staked in 1897 by the trapper Oliver Furry. Mining began in 1905 by the Britannia Mining and Smelting Co, an arm of the Howe Sound Co. By WWI the operation included two concentrators, a townsite at the water (Britannia Beach) and another at the entrance to the main mine. Ore was transported by aerial tramway from the mines down to the beach, where it was concentrated before shipping. By 1929 the operation had survived fluctuating copper prices, flood, fire and AVALANCHE to become the largest copper producer in the British Commonwealth. But copper prices declined during the late 1950s and the mines faltered. In 1963 the Anaconda Mining Co bought the operation, which continued production on a reduced scale until it finally closed in 1974. The following year the BC Museum of Mining opened at the site and in 1988 the mines were declared a National Historic Site. The museum includes a concentrator building dating from 1923 and part of the undergound tunnel system. During the 1990s part of the abandoned mine site was found to be releasing large quantities of toxic effluent into Howe Sound, stimulating plans for a cleanup.

BRITISH COLUMBIA was chosen as the name for the new colony created on 19 Nov 1858. The mainland area comprising the colony had been known as NEW CALEDONIA to the FUR TRADERS active there and at first it was suggested that this name be given to the new jurisdiction. In a letter to Sir Edward Bulwer Lytton, the British colonial secretary, Queen Victoria gave her reasons for choosing British Columbia instead. "If the name of New Caledonia is objected to as being already borne by another colony or island claimed by the French, it may be better to give the new colony west of the Rocky Mountains another name. New Hanover, New Cornwall and New Georgia appear from the maps to be names of subdivisions of that country, but do not appear on all maps. The only name which is given to the whole territory in every map the Queen has consulted is 'Columbia,' but as there exists also a Columbia in South America, and the citizens of the United States call their country also Columbia, at least in poetry, 'British Columbia' might be, in the Queen's opinion, the best name." Following the merger of the mainland with VANCOUVER ISLAND in 1866, British Columbia was retained as the name of the united colony.

BRITISH EMPIRE AND COMMONWEALTH GAMES were first held in BC in VANCOUVER in 1954. Sports administrator Stanley Smith was general chairman of the British Empire Games from 1949 to the event itself, overseeing the construction of the $1.5 million, 32,000-seat Empire Stadium, the swimming pool at UBC and the Empire Oval yellow CEDAR cycling track in China Creek Park, as well as the damming of the

The townsite at Britannia Beach in its heyday, 1915. BC Museum of Mining

Vedder Canal (*see* CHILLIWACK/VEDDER R) for rowing. Even after all these expenditures, the Games made a profit of $30,000 and international officials called it the most successful in history. The Vancouver Games is most famous for the MIRACLE MILE, one of the most memorable events in track and field history. BC accomplishments included Tommy Paonessa coaching Canada to its best BOXING performance, Doug HEPBURN's heavyweight weightlifting gold medal, Frank READ's UBC/VANCOUVER ROWING CLUB rowing 8 winning a gold, and Bruce Springbett and Harry Nelson participating in Canada's 440-yard relay gold.

The games returned to BC in 1994 when VICTORIA hosted the event, renamed the Commonwealth Games in 1978. The successful 1994 bid, engineered by newspaper publisher David Black (*see* BLACK PRESS LTD), track coach Ron Bowker, former LACROSSE star Whitey Severson, lawyer George Jones and others, made Victoria one of the smallest cities ever to win the games. Held Aug 18–28, the Victoria games were most notable for the inclusion of South Africa, which had rejoined the Commonwealth earlier that year following the end of apartheid. Events took place at the Juan de Fuca Velodrome, the SAANICH Commonwealth Place Pool, Memorial Arena and Centennial Stadium. Angela CHALMERS's 3000 m gold performance highlighted accomplishments by British Columbians. *SW*

BRITISH PROPERTIES are 16 km² of view property in W VANCOUVER, on the slopes of Hollyburn Mt overlooking VANCOUVER west of the CAPILANO R. The land was purchased in 1931 by British Pacific Properties, a company controlled by the Guinness brewing family, and was developed as expensive residential lots. The company built LIONS GATE BRIDGE to connect the development to the city, and also built the Park Royal shopping centre.

BROADCASTING began in BC with the licensing of the first radio stations in Mar 1922. The first 3 stations to go on air were all in VANCOUVER and all owned by NEWSPAPERS: CJCE, which evolved over the years into CFUN, was owned by the *VANCOUVER SUN* and the Sprott-Shaw School of Commerce; CKCD, owned by the *PROVINCE*;

and CFYC, owned by the *World*. Other early radio stations included CFDC in NANAIMO, which went on the air in 1923 and 4 years later moved to Vancouver and became CKWX; CFXC, started in NEW WESTMINSTER by Fred HUME in 1924, then sold to George Chandler and moved to Vancouver as CJOR; CFCL, later CJVI, a religious station started in VICTORIA in 1923 by Rev Clem DAVIES; CFJC KAMLOOPS (1926), the first station in the Interior; CKOV KELOWNA (1931), the first station in the OKANAGAN; and CJAT TRAIL (1935), the first station in southeastern BC. These early stations only operated for a few hours daily and were conceived as a vehicle for selling radio equipment or newspapers, not as commercially viable enterprises on their own. Programming was largely live broadcasts of musical performances (it was quite usual for a radio station to have its own house orchestra), dramas, and children's and variety programming. News broadcasts began to make their appearance in the late 1920s; one of the Canadian pioneers in this area was Earle Kelly, a *Province* reporter who began giving nightly news summaries on different Vancouver stations. Kelly, known as "Mr Good Evening" (his sign-off was "A restful good evening"), is considered to be Canada's first personality newscaster. During the 1930s CJOR was the main station in Vancouver, with such broadcasters as Ross and Hilda Mortimer, Dorwin Baird and Vic Waters. CJOR pioneered sports broadcasting in the province in the mid-1930s by airing box LACROSSE games. Public broadcasting began in Canada during the 1930s with the creation of the Canadian Radio Broadcasting Commission, which became the CBC in 1936. The Vancouver CBC station was CBR, managed by Ira DILWORTH from 1938 to 1946. Vancouver also became known for generating some of the best radio drama in Canada, epitomized by the work of Andrew Allan, a producer, at the CBC from 1939 to 1943. Still, much of the programming in this era originated in the US. CKNW joined the ranks of local stations in 1944 when Bill Rea, the founding owner, took it on the air in New Westminster with a format of country music and news. In 1947 it became the first BC station to broadcast 24 hours a day. NW also took the leadership in sports broadcasting, airing lacrosse, BASEBALL, HOCKEY, BASKETBALL and HORSE RACING. In 1956 Frank GRIFFITHS, an accountant, and 2 partners bought the station and built it into a broadcasting empire, (WIC) WESTERN INTERNATIONAL COMMUNICATIONS; by 1991 it was the largest private broadcaster in Canada. More than 50 years later, with a format of all-talk, CKNW is the most listened-to station in Vancouver. In 1953 Red ROBINSON pioneered the playing of rock 'n' roll with his afternoon program for teens on CJOR. Soon pop music filled the airwaves as private radio began catering to its youthful target audience. Meanwhile the CBC launched BC's first FM station, CBU-FM, in Vancouver in 1947, followed by CHQM-FM, the first private FM station, specializing in "easy listening" music. Canada's first radio phone-in show was *The Pastor's Study*, a short-lived program on CKNW in 1946 featuring Rev John W. Smith answering callers' questions. But the talk-radio format really had its origins with Jack WEBSTER, who brought his hard-hitting style and Scottish brogue to CJOR in 1953 as host of a program called *City Mike*. This evolved in the early 1960s into the caller phone-in format that exploded in popularity with the appearance on CJOR of Pat BURNS and his *Hotline* program. By the 1990s, phone-in shows were a staple of many stations, with CKNW's Rafe MAIR leading the ratings. Unusual fixtures on the radio scene since 1975 include VANCOUVER CO-OPERATIVE RADIO (CFRO-FM), a non-profit, community-based station broadcasting an eclectic mix of non-mainstream music, news and feature programs; CITR, an alternative pop/rock station based at UBC; and a more specialized outlet, CHMB, an ethno-cultural station broadcasting in 15 languages.

Television began broadcasting in BC in Dec 1953, when CBC launched CBUT in Vancouver, though American programs from Washington state were available earlier. The BRITISH EMPIRE AND COMMONWEALTH GAMES that took place in Vancouver the following summer were the first international sports event broadcast live on television to all of N America. The first made-in-BC television drama was CARIBOO COUNTRY, which ran on CBUT from 1958 to 1966. Private television arrived in 1957 with the launch of CHBC Kelowna, co-owned by the owners of the radio stations in VERNON, Kelowna and PENTICTON. It was another 3 years before the launch of Vancouver's first private station, CHAN-TV (now BCTV, a CTV affiliate) in 1960. Although the schedule was freighted with American programs, some locally produced shows did make it to air, including Ted PECK's *Tides and Trails*, and *All-Star Wrestling*. The Lower Mainland's first community cable channel arrived in 1969. In 1976 Daryl DUKE and his partner Norm Klenman shook up the local television scene when they founded CKVU, a small, independent station with some innovative programming that eventually became part of the CanWest Global network. And in Jan 1981 the provincial educational channel, KNOWLEDGE NETWORK, premiered. Later still, Vancouver Television (VTV) premiered in 1997. By 1999 there were 12 television stations broadcasting in the province, including stations that broadcast in Asian languages (*see* FAIRCHILD MEDIA GROUP), and 84% of households subscribed to a cable service offered by one of the 2 major providers, Rogers Communications Inc

and Shaw Communications Inc. (In 2000 Rogers and Shaw completed an asset swap in which Shaw became the only cable provider for BC's 921,000 subscribers.)

The broadcasting world underwent a shake-up in 1998 when the Griffiths family sold its interest in (WIC) Western International Communications. After extensive negotiations, the company's assets were divided between Calgary-based Shaw Communications and CanWest Global Communications Corp, based in Winnipeg. WIC's radio stations, including CKNW, went to Shaw, along with its specialty television channels. CanWest Global took over WIC's television stations, including stations in Vancouver (BCTV), Victoria (CHEK) and Kelowna (CHBC). Another major change occured in 1999 when the largest media company in western Canada, the Vancouver-based Okanagan Skeena Group, owner of 31 radio stations, 2 TV stations and 12 cable-TV systems in small communities in the West, was purchased by the eastern Canadian media giant Telemedia Communications Inc. Another important owner is the Vancouver entrepreneur Jim PATTISON; his business empire includes a TV station in Kamloops and 6 radio stations in the Interior and the Lower Mainland.

BROADFOOT, Barry Samuel, writer (b 21 Jan 1926, Winnipeg). After wartime infantry service he graduated from the Univ of Manitoba in 1949. His career with various Canadian NEWSPAPERS began at the Winnipeg *Tribune*, culminating in many years with the VANCOUVER SUN. In 1972 he started his bestselling series of oral histories, among them *Ten Lost Years* (1973) about the Depression, *Six War Years* (1974) about WWII, *The Pioneer Years* (1976) about homesteading the west and *Years of Sorrow, Years of Shame* (1977) about the wartime internment of Japanese Canadians (*see* JAPANESE, RELOCATION OF). His

Barry Broadfoot, writer and oral historian, 1998.
Barry Peterson & Blaise Enright-Peterson

awards include an honorary degree from the Univ of Manitoba, the Order of Canada and a BC GAS LIFETIME ACHIEVEMENT AWARD.

BROADWATER was a farming settlement (*see* AGRICULTURE) in southeast BC on the east shore of Lower ARROW LK, 35 km northwest of CASTLE-

GAR. It was named for the width of the lake before the KEENLEYSIDE DAM was built in 1965. The site was flooded by the dam construction and the lake became even wider. AS

BROBDINGNAG, the imaginary kingdom of giants in Jonathan Swift's classic *Gulliver's Travels* (1726), appears to be situated along the BC coast. Gulliver is travelling in the South Pacific when his ship is blown off course by a storm and ends up far to the east "so that the oldest sailor on board could not tell in what part of the world we were." The map accompanying the story indicates that Brobdingnag is north and west of Francis DRAKE's supposed landfall, which may

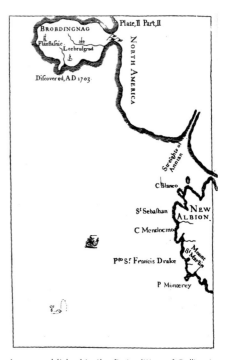

A map published in the first edition of Gulliver's Travels.

well put it off the north coast of BC. Gulliver has many adventures among this land's gigantic inhabitants before returning safely home. His sojourn in Brobdingnag may be the earliest representation of BC in European literature.

BROCKTON POINT in STANLEY PARK juts out into VANCOUVER's inner harbour east of the LIONS GATE BRIDGE at the entrance to Coal Harbour. It is named for Francis Brockton, a British naval engineer and member of the crew that surveyed the harbour in 1859. The HASTINGS MILL logged the point in the 1860s. A LIGHTHOUSE was built in 1902 to guide vessels in and out of the harbour. The present seawall and light tower were built in 1914. Brockton Point has had recreational facilities since 1890, when the athletic centre at Brockton Oval was built; a CRICKET pitch was added adjacent to the centre and for a brief period there was a GOLF course as well.

BRODIE, Robert "Steve," relief-camp activist (b 8 June 1910, Falkirk, Scotland; d 6 Dec 1997, Victoria). He came to Canada as an orphan sponsored by the Red Cross in 1924. He lost his job as a farm labourer when the Depression hit and he ended up in one of the BC RELIEF CAMPS for unemployed men. After participating in the ON-TO-OTTAWA TREK in 1935 he joined the Communist Party and was back in VANCOUVER in 1938 when another demonstration of unemployed men was being organized. He led a group of protestors occupying the downtown post office. On 19 June, "BLOODY SUNDAY," the police forcibly evicted the demonstrators. Brodie was singled out and given a beating by police, suffering permanent damage to one eye. During WWII he was in the merchant marine; after the war he worked in the shipyards in ESQUIMALT until his retirement in 1968.

BROKEN GROUP ISLANDS is a group of more than 100 islands scattered across BARKLEY SOUND on the west coast of VANCOUVER ISLAND south of UCLUELET. The islands, part of PACIFIC RIM NATIONAL PARK, cover an area of 130 km² and are a favourite spot with canoers and kayakers. They are in the territory of the Tseshaht, a NUU-CHAH-NULTH (Nootka) nation, who used them each summer to fish, collect shellfish and hunt SEAL and SEA LION.

BROOKMERE, located just off the COQUIHALLA HWY 46 km northwest of PRINCETON on Brook Crk, was a divisional point on the KETTLE VALLEY RWY. It was named after Harry Brook, who ranched here before WWI. Some relics of the railway era, including a plum red wooden water tower and handcar shed, can still be seen.   AS

BROOKS, Allan Cyril, artist, naturalist (b 15 Feb 1869, Uttar Pradesh, India; d 3 Jan 1946, Comox). Raised in England and on an Ontario farm after his family immigrated in 1881, he came to BC in 1887 when his family moved to a farm near CHILLIWACK. For the rest of his life, he divided his time between OKANAGAN LANDING and VANCOUVER ISLAND. Before WWI he roamed the province trapping and hunting. During the war he served overseas for 4¹/₂ years, distinguishing himself as a sniper. Afterward he gained prominence as an amateur naturalist, museum collector and wildlife artist. His illustrations, which appeared in many books and magazines including *National Geographic*, were familiar to a large audience.

BROOKS PENINSULA PROVINCIAL PARK, 516.3 km², encompasses the Brooks Peninsula, which juts nearly 16 km into the Pacific Ocean from the northwest coast of VANCOUVER ISLAND south of QUATSINO SOUND. First established as a recreation area in 1986, it was enlarged and upgraded to a Class A provincial PARK 10 years later in recognition of its high BIODIVERSITY values. Additions include an average 2-km boundary extension into the surrounding offshore waters and islands (including Solander Island ECOLOGICAL RESERVE), the entire Nasparti watershed, streams draining into Johnson Lagoon, west-facing slopes along Nasparti Inlet, the Power River and Battle Creek watersheds, and

The Broken Group Islands.
Courtesy Ucluelet Chamber of Commerce

the Mount Seaton area. Checleset Bay Ecological Reserve, protecting a population of endangered SEA OTTERS, abuts the southern shoreline of the peninsula, encompasses the Bunsby Islands and extends along the coast to Kyuquot. A narrow ribbon of beaches surrounds the peninsula, backed by steep cliffs and high rocky headlands. The mountainous spine of the peninsula is known as the Refugium Range because its peaks escaped the last Pleistocene GLACIATION. Botanical exploration here has yielded evidence of a continuous succession of plant species for more than 13,000 years. The peninsula boasts old-growth RAIN FORESTS of Sitka SPRUCE, western HEMLOCK and western red and yellow CEDAR, and supports a variety of wildlife, including over 120 bird species and Roosevelt ELK. WETLANDS provide habitat for a variety of amphibians, notably SALAMANDERS. Numerous sea birds, SEA LIONS, SEALS and SEA OTTERS inhabit the coastal waters. At the time of European contact the peninsula was the boundary between the territories of the NUU-CHAH-NULTH (Nootka) and KWAKWAKA'WAKW (Kwakiutl) First Nations. A number of archaeological sites are recorded, including a major village site. While most of the shoreline is subject to strong winds and high seas, and a number of shipwrecks have occurred in these waters, the area is increasingly used by sea kayakers. The park has no facilities; hikers and campers are urged to use "no-trace" standards.
Maggie Paquet

BROTHER XII; *see* WILSON, EDWARD ARTHUR.

BROUGHTON ARCHIPELAGO is a group of islands on the Mid-Coast between the mainland and the north end of VANCOUVER ISLAND, near the entrance to KINGCOME INLET. It stretches from Drury Inlet southeast to KNIGHT INLET. The 2 largest islands are Broughton and GILFORD, among many others, but local residents refer to the area as "the mainland." It is part of the tradi-

tional territory of several KWAKWAKA'WAKW (Kwakiutl) tribes and some village sites date back thousands of years. In the historic period there have been several communities, supporting themselves on the FOREST INDUSTRY and FISHING, including SULLIVAN BAY, SIMOOM SOUND and Echo Bay. Many of the smaller islands are part of Broughton Archipelago MARINE PARK (116.79 km²). It is named for Lt William Robert Broughton, one of Capt George VANCOUVER's officers.

BROUSE is a farming (*see* AGRICULTURE) and fruit-growing settlement and former station on the CPR's Nakusp & Slocan Rwy, 4 km east of NAKUSP near Upper ARROW LK. Now the site of the Nakusp Golf Club, it was named after Dr J.E. Brouse, a CPR medical officer at NEW DENVER.   AS

BROWN, Audrey Alexandra, poet (b 1904, Nanaimo; d 1998). She was the first important BC-born poet and the last important representative of romantic poetry in Canada. She wrote 5 volumes of poetry, *A Dryad in Nanaimo* (1931), *The Tree of Resurrection and Other Poems* (1937), *Challenge to Time and Death* (1943), *V-E Day* (1946) and *All Fool's Day* (1948). A prose work, *The Log of a Lame Duck* (1938), was written after Brown spent 10 months in a solarium at Malahat Beach for the treatment of a rheumatic illness. In 1944 she was awarded the Royal Society's Lorne Pierce Medal for distinguished contributions to Canadian letters.
Howard White

BROWN, Harry, aviator (dates not available). He was a bank clerk in VICTORIA when WWI began. He enlisted in the infantry and saw action at the front. Later he transferred to the Royal Flying Corps, where he served as a fighter pilot; he was awarded the Military Cross for shooting down several enemy planes. After returning to BC, he took up stunt flying and on 18 May 1919 made the first flight between Victoria and Seattle, in a small 2-seater biplane. With Norman Goddard he founded Vancouver Island Aerial Service, BC's first commercial airline and the first to operate seaplanes on the coast. After the company failed in 1921 he joined the JERICHO BEACH Air Station, then moved to California and opened a flying school. He lived there for the rest of his life. *See also* AVIATION.

BROWN, Peter, business executive (b 15 Dec 1941, Vancouver). "The most interesting and exciting money man in town" is how Peter C. NEWMAN described him, the town being VANCOUVER, where during the 1970s and early 1980s Brown headed Canarim Investment Corp, the leading underwriter of resource stocks on the VANCOUVER STOCK EXCHANGE. His 70 pairs of Gucci loafers and flamboyant exploits made him an icon of this high-living, free-spending era in the city's financial district. Brown also served as vice-chair of EXPO 86, and chair of the Vancouver Exchange (now the Canadian Venture Exchange), as well as on the boards of numerous corporations. Brown subsequently settled into a more sedate middle age and became chair and CEO of the Vancouver-based Canaccord Capital Corp, the largest independent investment firm in Canada, with offices across the country and in Europe.

BROWN, R.A. "Volcanic," prospector (b 1849; d 1930, north of Pitt Lk). His prospecting career in the BOUNDARY DISTRICT began in 1891, when he staked a claim at Volcanic Mt north of GRAND FORKS. Shifting his attention westward to COPPER MT, he established the Sunset Mine with more success. When he sold his interest he was able to buy a mouthful of gold teeth. Brown spent 40 years in the mountains of southern BC looking for his big strike and became something of a legend. He was also known as "Doc," because reportedly he financed his prospecting by performing abortions. In 1930 he set off in search of the famous SLUMACH MINE north of PITT LK. Searchers found his camp on the upper Stave R, but Brown was never seen again.

BROWN, Robert, botanist, explorer (b 23 Mar 1842, Camster, Scotland; d 26 Oct 1895, London, England). He arrived in VICTORIA from Scotland in May 1863 with a commission as seed collector for the BC Botanical Assoc of Edinburgh. After a year travelling on VANCOUVER ISLAND and the mainland, he was named leader of the VANCOUVER ISLAND EXPLORING EXPEDITION. He saw the expedition as an opportunity to gather scientific information and he was discouraged to find that other members saw it chiefly as an excuse to hunt for gold. Once the expedition ended, Brown continued his travels on behalf of the Botanical Assoc until he was recalled in Aug 1866. He wrote about his experiences on the Pacific coast for both scholarly and popular audiences. Frustrated by unsuccessful attempts to launch an academic career, he became a journalist in London.

BROWN, Robert Paul "Bob," a.k.a. Mr Baseball (b 5 July 1876, Scranton, PA; d 17 June 1962, Vancouver). He was a professional BASEBALL player in the US in 1910 when he bought

Bob Brown, Vancouver's "Mr. Baseball." BCSHF

the VANCOUVER Beavers of the Northwestern League and then managed and played for the team. In 1913 he built Athletic Park on the south side of FALSE CRK, the home of professional baseball in Vancouver for almost 40 years. He later owned the Vancouver Capilanos of the Western International League during and after WWII. He served terms as league president and as a major-league scout. One of Vancouver's favourite citizens, he is remembered for initiating the first nighttime baseball in Canada in 1931. He was the first inductee to the BC Baseball Hall of Fame and is a member of the BC SPORTS HALL OF FAME.

BROWN, Rosemary (Wedderburn), politician, social activist (b 17 June 1930, Kingston, Jamaica). She came to Canada in 1950 to attend McGill Univ in Montreal. After graduation she followed her fiancee Bill Brown to VANCOUVER, where he was studying medicine. They married

Rosemary Brown, 1991. She was the first black woman elected to the BC Legislative Assembly.
Denise Howard/Vancouver Sun

in 1955 and had 3 children. She studied social work at UBC and was working for the counselling service at SFU when she won the Vancouver-Burrard riding for the NDP in the 1972 provincial election. The first black woman ever elected to public office in Canada, she remained in the legislature for 14 years before retiring in 1986. In 1975 she ran for the leadership of the federal NDP, surprising many in the party by finishing a strong second to Ed Broadbent. After leaving politics she moved to Ottawa to become executive director of MATCH International Centre, a development agency working with women in developing nations. A recipient of the ORDER OF BC (1995) and the Order of Canada (1996), she served as head of the Ontario Human Rights Commission from 1993 to 1996.
Reading: Rosemary Brown, *Being Brown: A Very Public Life*, 1989.

BROWNSVILLE, across the FRASER R from NEW WESTMINSTER, was the site of a hotel and saloon built by Ebenezer Brown, a pioneer farmer, in 1861. Marshall ENGLISH opened a fish cannery in 1877 (*see* SALMON CANNING). Before the construction of the first bridge it was connected to New Westminster by ferry.

BRUCE, Robert Randolph, engineer, mine owner, lt gov 1926–31 (b 16 July 1861, St Andrew-Lhanbryde, Scotland; d 21 Feb 1942, Montreal). The son of a clergyman, he studied engineering at the Univ of Glasgow and in 1887 emigrated to the US, then to Canada where he worked for the CPR. He came to BC briefly in 1895 to survey a rail line near CROWSNEST PASS. In 1897 he returned to set up a stamp mill near FORT STEELE, then turned to prospecting and with a partner started the Paradise Mine, a lead/silver property near Windermere Lk (*see* MINING). After purchasing a block of CPR land on the lake, he promoted the area in England as prime fruit land and attracted many immigrant settlers pre-WWI. Following the war his business affairs faltered but he was managing to maintain his properties when he was appointed LT GOV on 24 Feb 1926. The choice of Bruce remains a mystery. He was not wealthy and had no background in politics. Nonetheless, he carried out his duties efficiently and was popular with the public. After retiring from office he tried to launch a political career as a federal Liberal MP but was defeated in the general election of 1935. After serving as ambassador to Japan from 1936 to 1938, he retired to live in Montreal.

BUCK RIDGE, 25 km south of QUESNEL on the west side of the FRASER R on the old W Fraser Rd, is the centre of a farming and ranching district (*see* AGRICULTURE; CATTLE INDUSTRY), site of a store and community hall. A post office operated here from 1948 to 1961. AS

BUCKLEY BAY, on the northwest shore of Masset Inlet in the QUEEN CHARLOTTE ISLANDS, was the site of a large SAWMILL from 1918 to 1924. Sitka SPRUCE, valued for its lightness and strength, was cut here during WWI and used to build Mosquito fighter-bombers and other planes. The mill initially employed 400 people, but demand for spruce fell after the war. Named after Frank Buckley of the Masset Timber Co, the bay is now deserted.   AS

BUDDHISM is a world religion founded in India about 500 BC. It subsequently spread throughout Asia, dividing into several different strands. There are some 36,500 Buddhists in BC, mostly followers of the Jodoshinshu school, a form of Mahayana Buddhism developed in Japan and brought to BC by JAPANESE immigrants late in the 19th century. The first regular meetings of Jodoshinshu Buddhists in BC were held in NEW WESTMINSTER in 1901. In 1905 Rev Senju Sasaki arrived from Japan to begin teaching; the following year a religious centre, called a bukkyo-kai, opened in VANCOUVER. This temple later became the Vancouver Buddhist Church. During the 1920s Rev Takunen Nishimoto developed the Young Buddhists' Assoc and carried out extensive missionary work around Vancouver and on VANCOUVER ISLAND. By 1939 bukkyo-kais had been established at several locations. Buddhism was dealt a blow by the internment of Japanese Canadians in 1942 (*see* JAPANESE, RELOCATION OF) and the subsequent sale by the government of all the bukkyo-kais in BC. Following the war, centres were re-established and in 1955 they joined in a formal union, the BC Buddhist Churches Federation. Other Buddhist groups include the Reiyukai Society of BC, the Universal Buddhist Church (a Chinese

BUDDHISTS IN BC

Year	Members	% of BC Population
1901	15,050	8.4
1911	22,435	5.7
1921	30,317	5.8
1931	32,917	4.7
1941	29,215	3.6
1951	6,928	0.6
1961	7,893	0.5
1971	7,080	0.3
1981	11,820	0.4
1991	36,555	1.1

congregation established in 1986 in Vancouver), the International Buddhist Society with its remarkable Kuan Yin Temple in RICHMOND, several Zen Buddhist centres, different varieties of Tibetan Buddhism and several Theravada Buddhist societies.

BUFFALO CREEK is a tiny farming (*see* AGRICULTURE) and recreational settlement in the CARIBOO lake district, 80 km southeast of WILLIAMS LAKE on Bridge Crk. A school opened here in 1923, a post office in 1934. It was named after an ox team used by a freighter on the old CARIBOO WAGON ROAD.   AS

BUGABOOS are a set of soaring granite spires in a spectacular glacier region of the northern PURCELL MTS, south of GOLDEN. The area, known worldwide for its spectacular backcountry SKIING and MOUNTAINEERING, was first explored in 1910. Some of the taller spires (the tallest is 3,400 m) were first climbed in 1916 by a party guided by Conrad KAIN. BC Parks maintains a hut named

Bugaboo Provincial Park in the Purcell Mountains, south of Golden.
Walter Lanz/Image Makers

after him as a base for climbers. Bugaboo Glacier Provincial PARK (136.47 km²), established in 1969, is accessible only by TRAIL and helicopter. Heli-skiing was pioneered in the area by Hans Gmoser in the mid-1960s.

BUICK, pop 100, is a small farming settlement and BC RAIL station 60 km north of FORT ST JOHN in the PEACE R district and the site of BC's northernmost grain elevator. North of this point, farming is not possible except on a small scale (*see* AGRICULTURE). The community was established in 1964 when Miro Fibich opened a store and gas station. Ranching (*see* CATTLE INDUSTRY), trapping and LOGGING are also important in the area.   AS

BULKLEY RIVER, 257 km, the main tributary of the SKEENA R, rises in Bulkley Lk about 40 km west of BURNS LAKE and loops north and west through the central Interior to join the Skeena at HAZELTON. The river is followed by the Yellowhead Hwy most of the way. Its lower portions are narrow and steep-sided, tumbling through canyons at HAGWILGET and MORICETOWN where FIRST NATIONS have fished the plentiful SALMON runs for thousands of years (*see also* FISHING, ABORIGINAL). Above Moricetown the river widens into a broad valley. It is the main corridor through the territory of the WET'SUWET'EN (Carrier) people whose ancient capital, Dzilke, was near Moricetown. The Wet'suwet'en know the river as Wa Dzun Kwuh; the English name refers to

Charles Bulkley, an American engineer in charge of building the COLLINS OVERLAND TELEGRAPH, which was strung through the valley in the 1860s. That project collapsed but the dominion telegraph line was installed during 1899–1901. Ranching (*see* CATTLE INDUSTRY) began in the valley in 1898 and TELKWA developed as the main population centre until construction of the GRAND TRUNK PACIFIC RWY through the valley (1913–14) shifted most activity to SMITHERS. MINING and AGRICULTURE have been important as economic mainstays of the valley, though both have been eclipsed by the forest industry. There is SKIING on Hudson Bay Mt at Smithers and excellent camping and sport FISHING.

BULL RIVER, pop 18, lies on the east shore of the KOOTENAY R, where it is joined by the Bull R 23 km east of CRANBROOK. It was the site of a major CPR SAWMILL and horse LOGGING operation from 1912 to 1928. Railway construction required huge volumes of timber, and the Bull R show was the largest in the BC Interior at the time. A hotel and a few houses are the only reminders of this era. The river was named after J. Bull, an early prospector.   AS

BULLION, at Dancing Bill's Gulch, 62 km northeast of WILLIAMS LAKE on the road to LIKELY, was one of the world's largest hydraulic MINING sites. From 1892 to 1898 John Hobson and the CPR-controlled Cariboo Hydraulic Mining Co used high-pressure monitors to recover GOLD worth $1.25 million. Later large-scale operations, which ceased in 1942, diverted water from distant lakes and created the vast man-made pit that exists today. A tiny settlement nearby is known as Hydraulic. Independent prospectors still try their luck here.   AS

BUNGEE JUMPING describes diving from a high platform with an elastic cord tied to the ankles. The first legal bungee jumping operation in N America is located at the Nanaimo R gorge south of NANAIMO on VANCOUVER ISLAND. Patrons leap from a bridge headfirst into the gorge, plummeting 43 m at speeds up to 50 km/h before the cord snaps them back just before they touch the water.

BUNTING is a SPARROW-like bird, of which 2 species breed regularly in BC. The lazuli bunting (*Passerina amoena*) is found in open habitats in the southern Interior and more rarely in the Lower Mainland. It is related to cardinals and GROSBEAKS. The male has a metallic sky-blue head and back and orange breast; the female is a drab brown colour. The snow bunting (*Plectrophenax nivalis*), related to native SPARROWS, breeds only on the mountain tundras in the northwest corner of the province. This species is white with black markings in summer and white and brown in winter.

BUNTZEN LAKE, 1.82 km², is a 30-minute drive east of downtown VANCOUVER, near PORT MOODY at the head of BURRARD INLET. According to Coast Salish (*see* SALISHAN FIRST NATIONS) tra-

Buntzen Lake, east of Vancouver.
Duncan McDougall/Image Makers

Palaeontology students at work in the Burgess Shale fossil bed, Yoho National Park.
Nick Procaylo/Vancouver Province

dition, the lake was a refuge for the aboriginals during a great flood. In 1903 the Vancouver Power Co, a subsidiary of BC ELECTRIC RWY CO, built HYDROELECTRIC facilities at the north end of the lake to supply electricity to the city. About 90% of the water for the Buntzen generating station comes via a tunnel from COQUITLAM LK. BC HYDRO AND POWER AUTHORITY developed the south end for recreation in 1970 and the lake now features a sand beach, FISHING, boating and manicured trails. Originally called Lk Beautiful, it was named for Johannes Buntzen, general manager of BC Electric from 1897 to 1905. *See also* LAKES.

BURBOT (*Lota lota*), also known as freshwater lingcod, is the only member of the order Gadiformes (482 species) that dwells in fresh water. The burbot is COD-like in appearance with a flat, pointed head that extends almost a quarter of the length of the fish. Its body is very narrow at the anterior (front) end. It has small eyes, barbels (fleshy filaments) on its chin and near each nostril, and fine scales covered by a thick layer of mucus, which makes the body extremely slimy. The burbot is heavily mottled, with colour ranging from light brown to dark brown to dark olive and sometimes even yellow. Its main prey is other fish, but it will devour almost anything else it can find. It is one of the few Canadian freshwater fish that spawns in the winter under the ice. To spawn, males and females gather in a communal mass; a million or more eggs are ejected and fertilized. In BC, burbot are found in larger freshwater lakes, away from the coast.

BURDETT-COUTTS, Angela, British philanthropist (b 21 Apr 1814, London, England; d 30 Dec 1906, London, England). At the age of 23 she inherited a vast fortune from her banker grandfather and became one of the richest women in Victorian England. She used the money to embark on a career of philanthropy, much of it in partnership with the writer Charles Dickens. Among her many causes was the endowment of ANGLICAN CHURCH bishoprics overseas, including VANCOUVER ISLAND, where in 1860 Rev George HILLS arrived as the first bishop in BC. She also endowed an Anglican girls' school, Angela College, built in VICTORIA in 1865, paid for the famous "Iron Church" that stood in Victoria from 1860 to 1912, and sponsored the brideship TYNEMOUTH.

BURE, Pavel, hockey player (b 31 Mar 1971, Moscow, USSR). He was a teenage phenomenon playing in the Russian Elite League when the VANCOUVER CANUCKS drafted him in the sixth round of the 1989 NHL entry draft. Because of a bookkeeping error concerning his eligibility for the draft, a league controversy erupted. The dispute was settled in VANCOUVER's favour and Bure signed a multimillion-dollar contract, taking to the ice at right wing partway through the 1991–92 season. He amazed fans with his speed and stickhandling ability and despite starting the season late he earned the Calder Trophy as the NHL rookie of the year. The next year he became the first Canuck to score 50 goals in a season; in fact he scored 60 goals and 110 points, eclipsing the previous team points record by 19. During 1993–94 he scored 60 goals again to lead the league, then led all scorers in the playoffs as the Canucks reached the Stanley Cup final. Injuries began to plague him, though he rebounded with 51 goals in

Pavel Bure on his way to a 60-goal season, 1992–93. Steve Bosch/Vancouver Sun

1997–98. After that season he announced he would not play again for the team, later citing conflicts with management, and he was traded in Jan 1999 to the Florida Panthers. *See also* HOCKEY. SW

BURGESS SHALE, a quarry in the ROCKY MTS high above FIELD in YOHO NATIONAL PARK, contains one of the most important fossil finds in history. Discovered by the American palaeontologist Charles Walcott in 1909, the shale contains the FOSSILS of 140 species of marine invertebrates, many of them soft-bodied and most previously unknown. The remains of the small creatures were embedded in the silt on the floor of an ancient sea 530 million years ago. Named for nearby Burgess Pass, the shale is about a city block long and 3 m high. It and the surrounding

ROCKY MTS national parks were named WORLD HERITAGE SITES by UNESCO in 1980.
Reading: Stephen Jay Gould, *Wonderful Life: The Burgess Shale and the Nature of History,* 1989.

BURGOYNE BAY, 42 km north of VICTORIA on southern SALTSPRING ISLAND in the GULF ISLANDS, is at the west end of a gentle, fertile valley. John Maxwell and James Lunney established a cattle ranch (*see* CATTLE INDUSTRY) here in 1860 and other settlers soon followed. There was a wharf by 1869 and a post office by 1880. The bay served as the island's log sort (*see* LOGGING) into the 1990s. Hugh Talbot Burgoyne was stationed on the coast from 1857 to 1860 as commander of the British naval vessel HMS *Ganges*. AS

BURKEVILLE is a residential community next to VANCOUVER INTERNATIONAL AIRPORT on SEA ISLAND in RICHMOND. It emerged during WWII when the federal government built 328 houses for workers at the nearby Boeing plant, and it was named for Stanley Burke, president of Boeing. After the war, houses were sold to veterans. The community survives, though it is surrounded by airport development.

BURNABY adjoins the eastern edge of VANCOUVER between BURRARD INLET on the north and the FRASER R to the south. It is the 3rd most populous municipality in BC and in the GREATER

VANCOUVER REGIONAL DISTRICT after Vancouver and SURREY. The area was surveyed by the ROYAL ENGINEERS in 1859 and named for Robert BURNABY, who led the survey. A naval reserve was set aside in western Burnaby and the engineers cut masts and spars there for British warships. The area is now Central Park. The 1891 construction of the INTERURBAN tram line connecting NEW WESTMINSTER and Vancouver via Burnaby led to incorporation in 1892. Burnaby was originally a rural area (only 400 inhabitants in 1900) with an active LOGGING industry, then evolved gradually into a mainly working-class suburb. During the 1930s the weight of unemployment relief forced the municipality into bankruptcy; until 1943 its affairs were managed by a provincially appointed commissioner. Since WWII it has been heavily urbanized and the economy evolved into a mix of commercial and industrial enterprises, including steel fabricating, truck manufacturing, lumber and fish processing. A healthy HIGH-TECHNOLOGY sector (mostly communication and computer technologies) developed through the 1980s and 1990s. Metrotown Centre, served by one of the city's 5 SKYTRAIN stations, emerged as the main commercial centre during the 1980s. Burnaby Lake Regional Park is a 3 km² nature park and wildlife sanctuary. Another landmark is Burnaby Mt (365 m), on top of which SFU was established in 1965. The BC INSTITUTE OF TECHNOLOGY is another important educational facility. Cultural amenities include Burnaby Heritage Village, an Ismaili Mosque, the SHADBOLT Centre for the Arts and Burnaby Art Gallery, along with one of the world's largest indoor ice rink complexes. Burnaby received city status exactly 100 years after its incorporation.

Population: 179,209
Rank in BC: 3rd
Population increase since 1981: 31%
Date of incorporation: district 22 Sept 1892; city 22 Sept 1992
Land area: 106.74 km²
Location: Greater Vancouver Regional District
Economic base: manufacturing, refineries, wholesale and retail services, railways

BURNABY, Robert, businessman (b 30 Nov 1828, Leicestershire, England; d 10 Jan 1878, Loughborough, England). He was a member of the English civil service when he learned about the FRASER R gold strike (*see* GOLD RUSHES) and decided to come out to VANCOUVER ISLAND. He arrived in VICTORIA in Dec 1858 and secured an appointment as secretary to Col Richard MOODY, head of the ROYAL ENGINEERS contingent. He was involved in the survey of NEW WESTMINSTER; Burnaby Lk and subsequently the municipality of BURNABY were named for him. After leaving government service, he dabbled in coal prospecting in BURRARD INLET, then set up in business in Victoria, where he promoted several ventures aimed at developing the colonial economy. He was also active in local theatre and the Freemasons. He won election to the LEGISLATIVE ASSEMBLY in 1860 and served until 1865, when he resigned his seat to return to England on business. Back in Victoria the next year he resumed a leading role in the affairs of the colony until his

health began to fail. He was forced to return to England for good in 1874. It is said that more BC landmarks are named for him than any other pioneer.

BURNS, Patrick, broadcaster (b 6 Apr 1921, Montreal; d 8 June 1996, Vancouver). He broke into BROADCASTING with the BBC in London, England, in 1949, then moved to VANCOUVER, where he worked in radio and served as a N VANCOUVER alderman. In 1962 he pioneered the talk radio format with his *Hotline* program on station CJOR, where his ratings soared. He was notorious for phoning up prominent personalities and putting them on air without warning. His manner was loud and brash; his voice, said one colleague, sounded "like anthracite coal sliding down a tin chute." In 1965 when the station owners fired him, a downtown farewell rally attracted thousands of supporters. He moved to Montreal, where his outspoken announcing style provoked several death threats. He returned to Vancouver in the 1970s but never regained the notoriety of his heyday. He was inducted posthumously into the Canadian Broadcast Hall of Fame.

BURNS BOG is an unusual WETLAND located in DELTA, south of RICHMOND on the way to the US border, between the FRASER R and BOUNDARY BAY. Thousands of years old, it is composed primarily of sphagnum moss that forms layers of peat—slowly decaying plant material—when it dies. It is 40 km² in size, the largest domed peat bog in N America, and provides a home to 24 species of mammals and 150 species of birds. It is named for Dominic Burns of the Alberta meat packing family, who once owned the land. Commercial peat harvesting began in the bog in the 1930s and continued until the 1970s. A GREATER VANCOUVER REGIONAL DISTRICT landfill site, the largest garbage dump west of Toronto, occupies one corner of the bog, more than half of which is now owned privately. Recurring proposals to develop at least part of the bog are opposed by conservationists who wish to preserve it as a unique ecosystem. *See also* ENVIRONMENTAL MOVEMENT.

BURNS LAKE, village, pop 1,793, lies on the Yellowhead Hwy (*see* ROADS & HWYS) 225 km west of PRINCE GEORGE near the geographical centre of the province. It was settled in the 1860s during construction of the aborted COLLINS OVERLAND TELEGRAPH to Alaska and is named for Michael Byrnes, a surveyor for the telegraph line. Little development occurred until the arrival of the GRAND TRUNK PACIFIC RWY in 1914. The construction of the KENNEY DAM on the NECHAKO R in 1952 gave a boost to the local economy, as did 4 major MINING discoveries between 1964 and 1981: to the east the MOLYBDENUM mine at ENDAKO, to the north the GRANISLE and Bell COPPER mines, and to the southwest the Equity SILVER/copper/GOLD mine. The establishment of 2 large mills nearby in the 1970s made the FOREST INDUSTRY the major employer. Most AGRICULTURE is based on the

CATTLE INDUSTRY and there is a campus of the College of New Caledonia (*see* COMMUNITY COLLEGES). The village is located at the centre of a lake district and is the northern gateway to TWEEDSMUIR PROVINCIAL PARK.

BURR, Raymond William Stacey, actor (b 21 May 1917, New Westminster; d 12 Sept 1993, Dry Creek, CA). One of the most famous actors born in BC, he left the province at age 6 when his parents divorced and he moved to California with his mother. As a teenager he performed in radio dramas, then took to the stage in Toronto, in England, and eventually in New York, where he appeared on Broadway and taught drama at Columbia Univ. After serving in the navy during WWII he went to Hollywood and appeared in about 70 movies, usually as a villain. His most famous role was the killer in Alfred Hitchcock's *Rear Window* (1954). He is better known for his television roles: as star of the *Perry Mason* hit series that ran from 1957 to 1966 and then was resurrected in the late 1980s, and as a disabled police detective in *Ironside* (1967–75). Plans are underway to create a Raymond Burr Performing Arts Centre in NEW WESTMINSTER.

Raymond Burr, most famous for his TV role as Perry Mason. Courtesy Raymond Burr Performing Arts Society

BURRARD DRY DOCK was founded as Wallace Shipyards by Alfred "Andy" WALLACE on FALSE CREEK in VANCOUVER in 1894, and it relocated to N VANCOUVER DISTRICT in 1906. The operation changed its name to Burrard Dry Dock in 1921 and the harbour's first large dry dock began operations 4 years later. Clarence WALLACE became head of the company on his father's death in 1929. Among the company's significant projects were the *PRINCESS LOUISE* and the *ST ROCH*. During WWII the shipyard turned out a third of all the cargo ships produced in Canada; at the peak of production 14,000 people were employed. With the acquisition of Yarrows Ltd in VICTORIA in 1946 and Pacific Dry Dock in 1951, Burrard became the largest shipbuilder in Canada. As the international market expanded the company lost ground to competitors, and in 1971 the Wallaces sold to Cornat Industries for $10 million. Cornat amalgamated with Versatile Manufacturing in 1978 and the name changed to Versatile Pacific Shipyards Inc 7 years later. When it lost a sizeable contract to build the government icebreaker *Polar 8*, the company ceased to be viable. The last employees were laid off in 1992. *Francis Mansbridge*

BURRARD INLET is the convoluted body of water forming VANCOUVER's waterfront. It extends from Point ATKINSON along the base of the North Shore mts, through Vancouver harbour into INDIAN ARM and as far east as PORT MOODY, around STANLEY PARK into ENGLISH BAY and FALSE CRK and along Kitsilano, JERICHO BEACH and Spanish Banks to Point Grey, a total shoreline of 152.6 km. The sand beaches of the inlet were formed by silt from the FRASER R carried by the TIDES around Point Grey. The same process warms the water in the inlet during the summer, making it popular with swimmers. Much of the shoreline has been fringed by seawalls and pedestrian walkways. The entrance to the central harbour is via First Narrows; the inner harbour stretches from Second Narrows to Port Moody. Both narrows are spanned by bridges and the harbour as a whole is ringed by shipping facilities. Ferry service between the North Shore and downtown began in 1900 and is now provided by BC TRANSIT's SEABUS passenger service. The inlet was home to the SQUAMISH and MUSQUEAM nations, who occupied several seasonal villages sites. It was explored in June 1792 by Capt George VANCOUVER's expedition, then ignored by outsiders until 1859 when Capt G.H. RICHARDS surveyed it aboard the HMS *Plumper*. During the 1860s LOGGING began, and the earliest non-aboriginal communities took root at MOODYVILLE on the north side of the harbour and GRANVILLE on the south side. With the decision to make the inlet the western terminus of the CPR in 1886, its future as a major shipping centre was assured and activity in the inlet grew along with the new city of Vancouver. In all seasons the inlet presents a busy scene of boats of all descriptions, from large freighters and CRUISE SHIPS to the smallest sailboats and windsurfers.

BURRELL, Arnold Alfred, artist (b 19 Feb 1924, Winnipeg; d 9 May 1991, Maple Bay). He graduated from the Vancouver School of Art (*see* EMILY CARR INSTITUTE OF ART & DESIGN) in 1956, then spent 2 years in northern BC living among and painting FIRST NATIONS people. In 1960 he moved to VANCOUVER ISLAND, where he lived for the rest of his life. While setting up outreach art classes through the Art Gallery of VICTORIA, he developed his own post-abstract impressionist style, participating in solo and group shows throughout BC and in eastern Canada. In the mid-1970s he withdrew from teaching and exhibitions to paint in solitude. Most of his work is in private and corporate collections. *Ellen Mackay*

BURTON, pop 162, originally established as a MINING settlement, is on the east bank of Lower ARROW LK, 30 km south of NAKUSP. It was named after Reuben Burton, who settled here in 1893 and was the community's first postmaster. The village was moved to its present site after the opening of the KEENLEYSIDE DAM in the 1960s. Arrow Lakes Provincial Park is located nearby. *AS*

BUSH MILLS were small portable SAWMILLS used extensively throughout the Interior from the 1930s until the 1960s. It was easier to take a mill to the logging site and cut rough lumber in the woods than to transport logs to stationary sawmills. The lumber was then sold to planing mills in larger centres, where it was finished and dried. Bush mills were phased out with the growth of the Interior pulp industry: the need to utilize sawmill waste for pulp mill feedstock required the consolidation of sawmills in central locations. Many of the large Interior forest companies evolved from simple bush mills. *See also* FOREST INDUSTRY; PULP AND PAPER. *Ken Drushka*

BUSHTIT (*Psaltriparus minimus*) is a tiny, nondescript grey bird common in the Georgia Basin region of southwestern BC, where flocks of 30 or more drift through shrubbery in open habitat. They are often found with KINGLETS, WARBLERS, CHICKADEES and red-breasted NUTHATCHES. Bushtits increased in BC during the last century as the lowland FORESTS of the South Coast were cleared, providing more bushtit habitat. Bushtit nests, woven from MOSSES and lichens, look like socks hanging in shrubs and trees. *Kim Goldberg*

Sunken gardens in spring, at Butchart Gardens north of Victoria. Courtesy Butchart Gardens Ltd

BUTCHART, Robert Pim, industrialist (b 30 Mar 1856, Owen Sound, ON; d 27 Oct 1943, Victoria). After working in the family hardware business he established the first Portland cement company in Canada in 1888. He and his wife Jennie (1868–1950) moved west in 1903 to establish a cement plant in TOD INLET on the SAANICH PENINSULA north of VICTORIA. Jennie developed BUTCHART GARDENS in the limestone quarry associated with the plant. Robert also had interests in cement plants across Canada and in the US. During WWI he was in charge of SHIPBUILDING on the west coast for the Imperial Munitions Board. In 1921 cement production ceased at the original site and moved across SAANICH INLET to BAMBERTON. In his retirement Robert helped his wife develop the gardens into a world-famous tourist attraction.

BUTCHART GARDENS is a 20-ha landscaped garden 21 km north of VICTORIA, open to the public. The gardens feature 700 varieties of flowering plants, as well as seasonal fireworks, concerts and displays of coloured lights. Work on the gardens began in 1904 when Robert BUTCHART, a wealthy cement manufacturer, and his wife Jennie established a home, Benvenuto, next to a limestone quarry at TOD INLET. As Butchart's company used up the stone, Jennie decided to beautify the quarry site by laying down soil and planting a sunken garden. Over the years the Butcharts added a Japanese garden, an Italian garden and an English rose garden. By the 1920s the property had become a major TOURIST attraction. Robert Butchart died in 1943, his wife in 1950, but the gardens remained in the family under the management of a grandson, Robert Ian Ross (1918–1997).

BUTE INLET is one of the long, narrow FJORDS indenting the Mid-Coast 50 km north of CAMPBELL RIVER. It doglegs through the COAST MTS 66 km from STUART ISLAND at its mouth to the ESTUARIES of the HOMATHKO and Southgate rivers, which drain into the top end. The steep-walled inlet, a natural wind tunnel, is notorious for its "Bute Winds," strong outflows sweeping down from Mt WADDINGTON, and for "Bute wax," a

Bute Inlet, a dramatic coastal fjord.
Philip Stone photo

mysterious oily substance that periodically appears in large balls on the surface of the water. It was via Bute Inlet that Alfred WADDINGTON made his ill-fated attempt to build a road across the Interior that ended in the so-called CHILCOTIN WAR in 1864. Later Bute was touted as a possible Pacific terminus for the transcontinental railway. Originally occupied by the HOMALCO nation, the inlet has been home to a scattering of trappers, loggers and fishers, including August SCHNARR, but later was largely deserted.

BUTEDALE is a North Coast SALMON CANNERY site on the east side of PRINCESS ROYAL ISLAND in the heart of the INSIDE PASSAGE. The cannery operated, under different owners, from 1909 to 1952. Until 1976 Butedale was a regular stop for coastal steamers, and during the 1960s it was the base for a UNITED CHURCH mission ship. Until the mid-1980s the site was a supply centre for passing pleasure boats. It was abandoned for a decade, but the Butedale Founders Assoc purchased it in 1994 and reopened some facilities.

BUTTERFLY, SKIPPER and **MOTH** are INSECTS in the order Lepidoptera, which are characterized by having scaled ("lepido") wings ("ptera"). Butterflies and skippers have two antennae, each of which is a straight shaft that expands near the tip. In contrast, moths have

antennae that are hair-like, formed of bead-like segments, feathery, or otherwise unlike those of butterflies and skippers. The few moths in BC that have antennae similar to those of butterflies and skippers (family Sphingidae) also have a frenelum (spine) on the base of the hindwing that fits into a retinaculum (hook) on the forewing to hold the wings together. Butterflies and skippers, except for one Australian skipper, lack a frenelum and retinaculum. Skippers always have 3 pairs of legs that are functional for walking, and forewings with 12 veins unbranched from base to outer margin of the

wing. In contrast, butterflies frequently have the first pair of legs reduced in size and used for tasting and smelling, rather than walking. Butterflies that do have 3 fully functional pairs of legs also have some of the forewing veins branched. These distinguishing characteristics make it clear that there is only a small difference between butterflies, skippers and moths.

Butterflies belong to the superfamily Papilionoidea, which includes the families Papilionidae (swallowtails and apollos), Pieridae (whites, sulphurs and marbles), Lycaenidae (coppers, hairstreaks and blues), Riodinidae (metalmarks) and Nymphalidae (brushfoots). There are 188 species of butterflies in BC. Of the 11 Papilionidae, the western tiger swallowtail (*Papilio rutulus*) is the most abundant on the South Coast and in the extreme southern Interior. From the southern Interior northward the Canadian tiger swallowtail (*P. canadensis*) is abundant. Anise swallowtail (*P. zelicaon*) caterpillars are sometimes found feeding on garden parsley and carrot leaves in all but the most northern part of BC.

Among the 28 Pieridae, the clouded sulphur (*Colias philodice*) and pink-edged sulphur (*C. interior*) are commonly seen in the Interior, along with other sulphurs. The introduced cabbage white (*Pieris rapae*) and the native pine white (*Neophasia menapia*) are the most commonly seen whites. The cabbage white is introduced from Europe and is the only significant pest butterfly in BC.

The 43 species of coppers, hairstreaks and blues in BC are small and mostly unnoticed. The western spring azure (*Celastrina echo*) in southern BC and the boreal spring azure (*C. ladon*) in central and northern BC are the most commonly noticed because of the bright blue wings of the males and their early spring flight period. The one species of Riodinidae in BC, the Mormon metalmark (*Apodemia mormo*), is known only from a few small populations near KEREMEOS.

The 74 Nymphalidae are mostly brown or grey, and range in size from small to moderately large. The migratory monarch (*Danaus plexippus*) is the most famous species, and breeds in BC on native milkweed plants in the southern Interior and occasionally on garden milkweeds on the South Coast. The Committee on the Status of Endangered Wildlife in Canada (COSEWIC)

Butterflies (clockwise from top left): Baird's swallowtail, callippe fritillary, monarch, Mormon metalmark. Cris Guppy photos

considers it vulnerable, in part due to habitat degradation in Canada (*see* ENDANGERED SPECIES). Fritillaries (*Speyeria* spp) are abundant in the Interior, while anglewings (*Polygonia* spp) are the most commonly seen group on the coast. Large numbers of painted ladies (*Vanessa cardui*) migrate into BC from the south in some years.

Skippers are in the superfamily Hesperioidea, which includes only the family Hesperiidae. Skippers are frequently lumped in with butterflies in conversation because both are day-flying except for some tropical species. The most abundant of the 27 skippers in BC is the woodland skipper (*Ochlodes sylvanoides*), a brown species that flies in mid- to late summer.

Moths are in many superfamilies, each of which includes one or several families. There are well over 2,000 species of moths in the province, including both day-flying and night-flying species. Most moths go unnoticed because of their nondescript brown and grey colours. The families Noctuidae (noctuids) and Geometridae (inchworms) include most of the larger moths in BC, and the families Tortricidae (tortricids) and Pyralidae (pyralids) include most of the smaller species. These families, as well as others, include many forest and garden pests. However the overwhelming majority of moths are of little or no economic signficance. Of particular note are the families Sphingidae (hawkmoths or hummingbird moths) and Saturniidae (silkmoths), which include the largest moths in BC.

Most of BC's rare and endangered butterflies and moths occur on the South Coast and in the OKANAGAN VALLEY, where human development is the most extensive. Other critical areas include the SIMILKAMEEN R valley, the southern KOOTENAY and the PEACE R canyon. The coastal subspecies of the silver-spotted skipper (*Epargyreus clarus californicus*) no longer migrates into BC, the coastal subspecies of the large marble (*Euchloe ausonides* undescribed subspecies) is apparently extirpated from BC, the viceroy (*Limenitis archippus*) is extirpated, and the VANCOUVER ISLAND subspecies of greenish blue (*Plebejus saepiolus insulanus*) is apparently globally extinct.

There are 13 other endangered or threatened species and subspecies of butterflies, and another 44 that are sufficiently rare to be vulnerable to

the adverse effects of future human development. The Dione copper (*Lycaena dione*, also known as the grey copper, *L. xanthoides*) in CRANBROOK is the most endangered butterfly in BC, and may be lost to the province due to habitat degradation. There are as many as several hundred endangered, threatened or vulnerable species of moths in BC, and many will be lost from the province before their status is known. There is at present no protection for endangered butterflies and moths, and adequate protection of their habitats was not forthcoming by the year 2000. On the South Coast, the spraying of "BtK" (*Bacillus thuringiensis* K) to eliminate GYPSY MOTH introductions is a major threat to the non-target butterflies and moths of the area.   *Crispin Guppy*
Reading: Crispin S. Guppy and Jon H. Shepard, *Butterflies of British Columbia*, 2000.

BUTTLE LAKE, 31 km², is a long (29 km), narrow lake surrounded by mountains in the central interior of VANCOUVER ISLAND, west of CAMPBELL RIVER in STRATHCONA PROVINCIAL PARK. It is named for John James Buttle, a ROYAL ENGINEER who was part of the 1864 VANCOUVER ISLAND EXPLORING EXPEDITION. He was thought to have been the first white person to visit the lake, in 1865, though later it appeared unlikely that he did so. In 1956 a power dam on neighbouring upper CAMPBELL LK raised the water level 5 m, despite protests by environmentalists, "the Battle of the Buttle," led by the writer Roderick HAIG-BROWN.

BUZZ-BOMB, the most successful sport FISHING lure developed in BC, was invented in 1964 by Rex Field, a COMOX Valley maker of plastic fishing plugs. By observing feeding SALMON, he came up with a lure that imitated the actions of wounded HERRING. Renowned for enabling fishers to catch any species, it fundamentally changed how people fished. As the lure descends on a slack line, it rotates on its axis, giving off a hydrosonic vibration that attracts fish and agitates them into biting. The lure was developed, manufactured and marketed by Rex's son Doug Field, who operates the company Buzz-Bomb and Zzinger Lures Inc. The company has diversified its product line over the years and besides producing variants of the Buzz-Bomb it manu-

factures Zzinger, Spinnow and Zelda Jig lures and many other fishing products that are sold around the world.   *Peter A. Robson*

BYRNES, James Thomas Kevin "Jim," musician, actor (b 22 Sept 1948, St Louis, MO). He settled in BC in the early 1970s, bringing a blues music heritage from St Louis; as an underaged teen he had learned his craft there by sneaking into clubs. He became a regular on the BC blues circuit, playing with Al Foreman in the

Jim Byrnes, Vancouver blues musician.
S.L. Feldman & Associates

Foreman–Byrnes Band and later in the Jim Byrnes Band. He has released 3 albums, including *That River*, which won the 1996 Juno Award for best blues or gospel recording. He has also worked as an actor since his teenage years, and he took full advantage of the growth in movie and television production in BC (*see* FILMMAKING), landing starring roles in the TV series *Wiseguy* and *Highlander* and recurring roles in *Neon Rider* and *The Net*. He has appeared in several movies and his voice has become familiar in commercials and animated TV series. *The Jim Byrnes Show*, a TV variety show, began in 1998. He was inducted into the BC Entertainment Hall of Fame in 1995.   *Mike Harling*

CAAMANO, Jacinto, Spanish naval officer (b 8 Sept 1759, Madrid, Spain; d after 1820, Guayaquil, Ecuador). He entered the Spanish navy as a teenager and went to New Spain (Mexico) with other young officers in 1789 to strengthen the naval establishment at San Blas, which supplied the California settlements, and to explore the Northwest Coast. Commanding the *Princesa*, he was part of the expedition that established the Spanish settlement in NOOTKA SOUND in 1790. In 1792, as a member of BODEGA Y QUADRA's expedition, commanding the *Aránzazu*, he charted the coast north and south of DIXON ENTRANCE, finally destroying the myth of the Strait of Fonte (*see* FONTE, Bartholomew de). George VANCOUVER used his chart in 1793 and retained a number of the Spanish place names. Caamaño's journal is noteworthy for its detailed descriptions of aboriginal peoples he encountered. He later served in the Philippines and Mexico and as captain of the port of Guayaquil in Ecuador. *See also* SPANISH EXPLORATION.   *Robin Inglis*

CABINET, formally known as the executive council, is composed of members of the LEGISLATIVE ASSEMBLY elected as representatives of the majority political party. Cabinet members are selected by the PREMIER; each is a minister responsible for at least one government department, or ministry, sometimes more. They also serve on a variety of cabinet committees. The cabinet is the principal decision-making body in the government. It determines policy, and individual members are held responsible for the affairs of their departments, or portfolios. On occasion ministers serve in the cabinet with no direct responsibility for a department; they are known as ministers without portfolio. Very rarely a cabinet minister is chosen from outside the legislature; in such a case it is expected that the minister will seek election as soon as possible, because it is an established principle that cabinet ministers should be available in the legislature to explain and defend government policy. Once a decision is made by cabinet after full discussion, all members are expected to endorse it. When a member feels unable to keep cabinet solidarity, he or she is expected to resign: one may not publicly criticize the government from within the cabinet.

Government ministries have changed in scope and number over the years. In 1999 the cabinet consisted of ministers responsible for the following departments: finance; attorney general; energy and mines; northern development; health; children and families; education; employment and investment; advanced education, training and technology; intergovernmental relations; fisheries; municipal affairs; aboriginal affairs; labour; human resources; forests; agriculture and food; multiculturalism, human rights and immigration; small business, tourism and culture; transportation and highways; environment, lands and parks; and women's equality.

CACHALOT, on the south shore of Cachalot Inlet in KYUQUOT SOUND, 85 km southeast of PORT HARDY on VANCOUVER ISLAND, was a WHALING station from 1907 to 1924 established by Sprott BALCOM and the Pacific Whaling Co. In 1926 it was converted to a pilchard (*see* SARDINE, PACIFIC) reduction plant by the Wallace Bros and operated for another 10 years. More WHALES were landed here than anywhere else in BC.   *AS*

CACHE CREEK, village, pop 1,115, lies at the junction of the TRANS-CANADA and CARIBOO hwys (*see also* ROADS & HWYS) in the semi-arid southern Interior, 85 km west of KAMLOOPS. It originated during the GOLD RUSH of the 1860s as a stopping point on the CARIBOO WAGON ROAD. Ranching (*see* CATTLE INDUSTRY), MINING, LOGGING and AGRICULTURE (particularly forage crops and GINSENG) all contribute to the local economy, though much economic activity still depends on passing travellers. It was incorporated on 28 Nov 1967.

CADBORO was the first sailing vessel brought to the coast by the HBC to conduct trading and supply voyages under the command of Lt Aemilius SIMPSON. It arrived at Fort Vancouver on the COLUMBIA R in 1827, just in time to transport a party to establish FORT LANGLEY on the FRASER R. It also assisted at the founding of Fort Nass in 1831. It was a 2-masted schooner weighing 63 tonnes, with a crew of up to 35. The HBC sold it in 1860 to new owners, who used it to haul COAL and lumber until it was wrecked in a gale in 1862. Cadboro Bay near VICTORIA is named after it.

CADBOROSAURUS is BC's own sea monster, believed to inhabit the coastal waters between VANCOUVER ISLAND and the mainland. One of the province's most famous mythic beasts and on a par with OGOPOGO and SASQUATCH, "Caddy" is named for Cadboro Bay in VICTORIA, where the first reported sighting occurred in 1933. Since then there have been nearly 200 alleged encounters, but no hard evidence of the monster's existence. It is reputed to be a speedy, serpent-like aquatic reptile, 15–20 m in length, with 2 pairs of flippers and a head resembling a horse.

Drawing of Cadborosaurus that appeared in the Victoria Daily Times *26 Oct 1933.*

CAETANI, Sveva, artist (b 6 Aug 1917, Rome, Italy; d 27 Apr 1994, Vernon). She was a member of an aristocratic Italian family; her father, the Duke of Sermoneta, brought Caetani, her mother and a family assistant, Miss Jüül, to the OKANAGAN VALLEY. The duke died in 1935 when Sveva was 18 years old, and her mother required Sveva to live in seclusion with her and Miss Jüül at their VERNON home. For the next 25 years Sveva did not venture alone beyond the confines of the property. This remarkable period of isolation ended with her mother's death in 1960. Left with a house but no income, Sveva took up teaching in Vernon, finally earning the opportunity to study at UNIV OF VICTORIA, where she was encouraged to resume her love of painting. She continued to teach until 1983, and her driving passion became a series of paintings and writings entitled *Recapitulation* (1975–89). Representing a summary of her perspective on life and her unusual experiences, it is expressed as a visionary journey with links to Dante's *Divine Comedy*. The work has been exhibited in various Canadian centres; it was donated to the Alberta Foundation for the Arts and published in book form in 1995. After Caetani's death, the family home and library went by arrangement to the City of Vernon and it is now the Caetani Cultural Centre for the arts.

CAHILTY was a remote AGRICULTURAL settlement established in the early 1900s on LOUIS CRK at the mouth of Cahilty Crk, 40 km northeast of KAMLOOPS. In later years, the Tod Mt ski resort, now known as Sun Peaks, built a recreational housing project called Whitecroft on this site.   AS

CALDER, Frank Arthur, Nisga'a chief, politician (b 3 Aug 1915, Nass Harbour). A graduate of the Anglican Theological College at UBC (1946), he worked in fish canning and forestry,

Frank Calder, the Nisga'a chief who initiated the historic land claims case. Gary Fiegehen photo

and as an entrepreneur. He was elected to the provincial legislature for the CCF in 1949, the first aboriginal person elected to a Canadian legislature. He held his ATLIN seat for the CCF/NDP until 1956 and again from 1960 to 1975. With the NDP victory in 1972 he joined the cabinet as minister without portfolio, the first aboriginal cabinet minister in Canadian history, but he was dismissed in 1973 after a policy disagreement. He left the NDP to join the SOCIAL CREDIT PARTY and was re-elected in 1975 but lost his seat in 1979 and retired from politics. Meanwhile he was a respected activist in the struggle for aboriginal land rights (*see* ABORIGINAL RIGHTS) as founding president of the Nishga Tribal Council during 1955–74. Under his leadership the NTC initiated the landmark CALDER CASE in the courts. His awards include the Order of Canada (1988) and membership in the FIRST NATIONS Hall of Fame (1967). *See also* NISGA'A.

CALDER CASE was a landmark legal case launched in 1969 by the Nishga Tribal Council and its lawyer, Tom BERGER, and named for NISGA'A chief Frank CALDER. The NTC sought a court

ruling that the Nisga'a (then called Nishga) people of the NASS R had aboriginal title to their traditional territory and had never given it up. The BC Supreme Court rejected the NTC's arguments, ruling that there was no aboriginal title. This decision was upheld by the BC Court of Appeal, but the NTC persevered and took its case to the Supreme Court of Canada. In 1973, 6 of the 7 justices ruled that the Nisga'a did have a pre-existing aboriginal title based on the longtime occupation and use of their traditional territory (the seventh justice ruled against the NTC on a technicality). On the matter of whether or not this title had been extinguished when BC joined CONFEDERATION, the 6 justices divided evenly, leaving that aspect moot. By finding that aboriginal title had existed, and by raising at least the possibility that it still existed, the court encouraged the federal government to begin negotiating the land claims issue. *See also* ABORIGINAL RIGHTS; FIRST NATIONS.

CALONA WINES LTD, BC's oldest winery still in business, was launched in KELOWNA in 1932 by a syndicate of investors that included Giuseppe Ghezzi, "Cap" CAPOZZI and W.A.C. BENNETT. Bennett, a teetotaller, was company president until his election to the legislature in 1941. Originally called Domestic Wines and By-Products Co, it produced apple wines until switching to grapes in 1935 and taking the new name, suggested by customers. After a slow start the winery, under Capozzi family management in the 1960s, became the largest in BC. In 1971 the Capozzis sold the company to Standard Brands of New York, which introduced better-quality table wines. The Vancouver-based International Potter Distilling Corp, now Cascadia Brands, purchased the company in 1989. *See also* WINE MAKING.

CALORI, Angelo, miner, hotelier (b 1861, Italy; d 7 May 1940, Vancouver). He arrived in BC from Italy via California in 1882 and found work in the coal mines in NANAIMO. After moving to the mainland, he worked on the construction of the CPR. Following the 1886 fire in VANCOUVER he purchased one of the surviving buildings and went into the hotel business. In 1908 he financed the first reinforced concrete building in the city, the flatiron Hotel Europe at the edge of GASTOWN. In its heyday it was one of Vancouver's poshest hotels, and Calori was one of the city's best-known hoteliers. A co-founder of the Sons of Italy (*Figli d'Italia*) in 1905, he was a leading member of the city's ITALIAN community. His landmark building still stands as the Europe Hotel Apartments.

CALVERT ISLAND is a large, mountainous island on the Central Coast opposite RIVERS INLET. It is separated from the mainland by FITZ HUGH SOUND, a busy section of the INSIDE PASSAGE. The northern half of the island is part of HAKAI RECREATION AREA. Before the arrival of Europeans, the HEILTSUK (Bella Bella) and OWEEKENO nations used the shores of the island for food gathering, and there was a village site at

the north end in Kwakshua Inlet. Calvert Island was named by the FUR TRADE captain Charles DUNCAN in 1788; Safety Cove on the west side was as far north as Capt George VANCOUVER reached on his 1792 survey of the coast. Early in the 1900s there was a small community and LOGGING camp in the cove, which was later deserted.

CAMAS, a member of the lily family, is a blue (and occasionally white) flowering plant with a sizable bulb that was a staple food item for FIRST NATIONS people, who harvested them from May to July and steamed them in large pits. The sweet-tasting bulbs were traded as a delicacy amongst some aboriginal groups. The camas occurs in BC in 2 species. The great camas (*Camassia leichtlinii*) is found only on southeastern VANCOUVER ISLAND south from NANAIMO. It is recorded that fields of great camas once occupied much of the present site of VICTORIA's BEACON HILL PARK. The common camas (*C. quamash*) occurs across southern BC and south into Montana and Utah. A distant relative is the extremely poisonous death camas (*Zygadenus* spp), differentiated from the edible species by its cream-coloured flowers and its more compact flowering head.

Common camas. Dean van't Schip photo

CAMBIE, Henry John, railway engineer (b 25 Oct 1836, Tipperary, Ireland; d 23 Apr 1928, Vancouver). He moved to Canada in 1852 and settled in Nova Scotia, where he studied engineering and became a railway builder. In 1874 he came to BC and was put in charge of surveying a route to the Pacific for the proposed CPR. He backed the Fraser Canyon–Burrard Inlet route and later was chief engineer during construction of the canyon section. Upon completion of the railway in 1885 he became chief engineer for the western division. He remained with the CPR to 1920. Cambie St in VANCOUVER is named for him.

CAMEL was used briefly as a pack animal in the Interior in 1862–63. The animals had been used successfully by the military in the American southwest and in 1862 Frank Laumeister imported 24 of them from San Francisco. They went to work packing supplies across the DOUGLAS TRAIL to LILLOOET and up the CARIBOO

One of the two dozen camels used by packers in the BC Interior, 1888. VPL 9944

WAGON ROAD to BARKERVILLE. But their feet proved too soft for the rocky terrain and they spooked the other pack animals, causing several accidents. As a result the camels were sold or turned loose. A mother and calf lived in BEACON HILL PARK in VICTORIA for many years. The last surviving camel on the open range died in 1905. The building used to stable the animals still stands in Lillooet, where for many years it was the town movie theatre.

CAMERON, Agnes Deans, educator, writer (b 20 Dec 1863, Victoria; d 9 May 1912, Victoria). She graduated from Victoria High School and began teaching school in VICTORIA while still a teenager. During a long career in Victoria, COMOX and VANCOUVER, she was BC's first female high school teacher (1890) and first female principal (1894). At the same time she pursued a part-time career as a journalist, publishing stories and articles in the popular press. Her support for women's equality put her at odds with school administrators and in 1906 she was dismissed from her principal's job for a minor infraction. The case became a *cause célèbre* that led to a royal commission and an outpouring of public support for her, but ultimately she lost her licence to teach. To earn a living she turned full time to journalism, writing mainly about the settlement boom in western Canada. In 1908 she travelled down the Mackenzie R to the Arctic with her

niece; they were the first white women to reach the Arctic overland. She chronicled the trip in her book *The New North* (1910). The federal government sent her on a lecture tour of Britain in 1910 to promote emigration to Canada. At her death, from complications after appendicitis, she was one of the most famous writers in the country.

CAMERON, Anne, writer (b 20 Aug 1938, Nanaimo). Her first books and scripts, written under the name Cam Hubert, centred on aboriginal themes. Among them was her TV script *Dreamspeaker*, directed for the CBC by Claude

Anne Cameron, bestselling writer of fiction, poetry, screenplays and books for children. Alan Twigg photo

Jutra, which won 7 film awards; it also won a first novel award when it was published in book form in 1979. Cameron has also written other film scripts, collections of FIRST NATIONS legends, poetry and fiction, including *Daughters of Copper Woman* (1980), *The Journey* (1983), *A Whole Brass Band* (1992), *Wedding Cakes, Rats and Rodeo Queens* (1994) and *Aftermath* (1998). She is an outspoken lesbian feminist and one of the best-selling contemporary writers working in BC.

CAMERON, John "Cariboo," prospector (b 1 Sept 1820, Glengarry County, Upper Canada; d 7 Nov 1888, Barkerville). He came to BC to join the Cariboo GOLD RUSH in 1862. The discovery of gold on his claim at Williams Crk made him a rich man. When his wife died, Cameron decided to return her body to Ontario. His business partner helped him haul the corpse by toboggan to VICTORIA; there he placed the body in an alcohol-filled coffin to preserve it. He then headed back to the CARIBOO to work his claim, and later shipped the coffin by boat via Panama to New York and on to Glengarry County, where he buried it. Cameron settled down in his former home, married again and spent his money lavishly. Stories began to circulate that perhaps the coffin did not contain the body of his first wife. It was rumoured that he had sold her to a FIRST NATIONS chief. Finally, in 1873, Cameron had the coffin dug up and opened to expose the face of his wife, almost perfectly preserved in alcohol. Eventually he exhausted his fortune, and he returned to BARKERVILLE shortly before his death.

CAMERON LAKE, a recreational community at the east end of 12-km-long Cameron Lk, 50 km west of NANAIMO on the way to PORT ALBERNI, was also a station on the ESQUIMALT & NANAIMO RWY. The lake, which is popular with sailboarders, was named for Hon David Cameron, chief justice of VANCOUVER ISLAND from 1853 to 1863. Most of the lakeshore is part of Little Qualicum Falls Provincial Park. *AS*

CAMOSUN was a UNION STEAMSHIP CO vessel, built in Scotland and launched in 1905. The next year it pioneered the company's run to PRINCE RUPERT and the SALMON CANNERIES of the North Coast, a route it worked for 30 years carrying workers and supplies to the fish plants and returning to VANCOUVER loaded with cases of SALMON. The ship was 58.7 m long with a gross weight of 1,232 tonnes and room for 199 passengers and 270 tonnes of cargo. In 1907 it became the first vessel on the coast to be equipped with Marconi wireless. The company scrapped it in 1936. The *Camosun* name appeared on two later vessels—a 1,210-tonne ship in service during 1940–45 and a 1,652-tonne ex-corvette in service during 1946–58—but neither matched the record of the original.

CAMP McKINNEY was a settlement of a few hundred people associated with the CARIBOO Amelia GOLD mine in the mountains about 50

km east of OSOYOOS. Named for Al McKinney, a prospector, it sprang into existence in 1887 and lasted until the early 1900s. The mine played out after producing more than $1 million in gold and became a ghost town. It is located near the Mt Baldy ski area.

CAMPAGNOLO, Iona, politician (b 18 Oct 1932, Galiano Island). Raised in PRINCE RUPERT, she got her start in politics at the local level while working in BROADCASTING. She was chair of the Prince Rupert school board from 1966 to 1972, then a city alderman for a term before winning election as a Liberal MP in 1974. During 5 years in Ottawa as a member of Pierre Trudeau's government, she served as minister of state for fitness and amateur sport from 1976 to 1979. She was defeated in the 1979 election but remained active in the LIBERAL PARTY; in 1982 she became the first woman elected president of the party, a position she held until 1986. Campagnolo is a member of the Order of Canada and the ORDER OF BC (1998) and served as the founding chancellor of UNBC from 1992 to 1998. She is chair of the Fraser Basin Council, created in 1997 to find solutions to environmental problems in the FRASER R watershed.

CAMPBELL, Avril Phaedra "Kim," politician, prime minister of Canada 25 June–4 Nov 1993 (b 10 Mar 1947, Port Alberni). She grew up in VANCOUVER, where her father was a well-known lawyer and city prosecutor. After graduating from UBC in political science, she did graduate work at the London School of Economics. She then returned to Vancouver and worked as a college teacher, and launched her political career in 1980 by winning election to the school board. In 1983, the year she graduated from law school, she became chairperson of the board and ran unsuccessfully for a seat in the provincial legislature for the SOCIAL CREDIT PARTY. She left her law firm in 1985 to join the staff of PREMIER Bill BENNETT and in 1986, when Bennett resigned as party leader, she ran to succeed him. She finished last in the race but made enough of an impression to win election to the legislature soon after.

In 1988 Campbell left VICTORIA to run successfully as a Progressive Conservative in the federal election in the riding of Vancouver Centre. In Ottawa she quickly became a key member of Brian Mulroney's cabinet, first as junior minister for Indian Affairs, then in 1990 as justice minister. Early in 1993 she became defence minister. Although considered on the left wing of the Conservative Party, she was criticized by feminists for not going far enough with changes to gun control and abortion legislation. When Mulroney announced early in 1993 that he was stepping down as prime minister, Campbell immediately became front-runner in the race to succeed him. Conservatives agreed that she would best satisfy voter demand for a fresh face. She won the party leadership in June 1993, becoming Canada's first female prime minister and the only native of BC ever to become PM. She was unable to overcome the unpopularity of

Kim Campbell, prime minister of Canada, 1993.

the party, however, and in a fall election she led the Conservatives to one of the worst defeats in Canadian history. She lost her own seat and shortly afterwards gave up the leadership and politics. Later she served as Canadian consul general in Los Angeles.

CAMPBELL, Gordon Muir, politician (b 12 Jan 1948, Vancouver). Raised on the west side of VANCOUVER, he graduated from Dartmouth College and taught school for 2 years in Nigeria with CUSO before returning home. He began his political career at age 24 as assistant to Vancouver mayor Art Phillips. During a break from politics from 1976 to 1984 he worked for Marathon Realty. Campbell was elected for the first time in 1984 as a Vancouver alderman, then

Gordon Campbell, leader of the BC Liberal Party from 1994.

won the mayor's job 2 years later. During 3 terms (1987–93) he presided over a prolonged building boom in the city. He became leader of a rejuvenated provincial LIBERAL PARTY in 1994 and by the late 1990s was favoured to defeat the incumbent NDP government, which had been discredited by scandal. He positioned the Liberals on the right, promising to slash public spending and stimulate the economy with tax cuts. Working against him was his own persistent lack of popularity with the public. In the 1996 election the Liberals narrowly failed to unseat the NDP, winning a plurality of the popular vote but fewer seats in the legislature. Campbell won his own riding and became leader of the opposition, promising to remain for at least one more election. *See also* ELECTION RESULTS.

CAMPBELL, Gray, book publisher (b 1912, Ottawa, ON; d 10 June, 2000, Victoria). He was BC's first full-time BOOK PUBLISHER. Fresh out of high school he worked at a stock brokerage firm in Ottawa, then joined the RCMP, serving with the force in western Canada from 1932 to 1939. During WWII he served overseas in the Royal Air Force. He and his new wife Eleanor took up ranching in Alberta after the war, an experience he wrote about in his 1953 memoir *We Found Peace*. In 1959 the couple moved to VANCOUVER ISLAND. Campbell continued his writing and in 1962 encouraged a neighbour, John Windsor, a veteran blinded in action during the war, to write his memoirs. The Campbells published the book, *Blind Date*, using money won on a television game show; Gray's Publishing was born. During 12 years in business Gray's published many books that have become classics of BC LITERATURE, including *Far Pastures* by R.M. Patterson (1963), *The Salmon People* by Hugh McKervill (1967), *Son of Raven, Son of Deer* by George CLUTESI (1967) and a second edition of the perennial bestseller *The Curve of Time* by Muriel Wylie BLANCHET.
Reading: Gray Campbell, *Butter Side Up*, 1994.

CAMPBELL, R. Wayne, ornithologist (b 1942, Edmonton). After working as a naturalist with the BC PARKS branch, he became curator of Cowan Vertebrate Museum at UBC in 1969. In 1973 he moved to VICTORIA to become curator of ornithology at the ROYAL BC MUSEUM, and then a survey biologist with the Ministry of Environment, Lands and Parks. A graduate of UNIV OF VICTORIA and the Univ of Washington, he has written hundreds of scientific papers and reports and co-authored 40 books, most notably the monumental 4-volume *The Birds of British Columbia*, published in 1990–99. One of BC's leading biologists, Campbell was appointed to the ORDER OF BC in 1992.

CAMPBELL, Robert, fur trader (b 21 Feb 1808, Glenlyon, Scotland; d 9 May 1894, MB). He was one of the most resourceful overland travellers of the FUR TRADE era. After joining the HBC in 1831 he was assigned to a company sheep farm at the Red River Settlement. In 1835 he entered the fur trade proper, taking command at Fort Liard in the North-Western Territory, from where he began a series of explorations of northern BC and the Yukon. In 1838 he followed the LIARD and Dease rivers to DEASE LK, where he established a trading post and explored the headwaters of the STIKINE R. He was the first white person to reach the area. After a desperate winter at DEASE LAKE POST he returned to the Liard and took command at FORT HALKETT. He then commenced a series of expeditions to the headwaters of the Liard, where he built the first trading post in the Yukon. After several years exploring the watershed of the Yukon R he left the area in 1852 and spent the rest of his career east of the ROCKY MTS. Dismissed from the HBC in 1871 for disregarding regulations, he settled on a farm in Manitoba.

CAMPBELL, Thomas, lawyer, property developer, politician (b 5 Oct 1927, Vancouver). He was one of VANCOUVER's most controversial mayors. Raised on the city's east side, he became a lawyer and also owned several apartment buildings in the city. He was elected to the first of 3 terms in 1967 and became known as a pro-development mayor ("Tom Terrific"), supporting the construction of a hotel at the entrance to STANLEY PARK and a freeway through CHINATOWN, both initiatives that were blocked by an emerging urban reform movement. His strong law-and-order platform (he suggested using the War Measures Act, invoked in 1970 to deal with political terrorism in Quebec, to "clean up" city streets) brought him into conflict with the youth movement of the period and culminated in the GASTOWN "riot" on 7 Aug 1971, when police overreacted violently to a gathering of young protesters. Campbell retired from the mayor's chair in 1972 and returned to his development business.

CAMPBELL LAKE and Upper Campbell Lk on north-central VANCOUVER ISLAND are part of the Campbell R system that empties into DISCOVERY PASSAGE at the city of CAMPBELL RIVER. After WWII the BC government chose the Campbell R for a large HYDROELECTRICITY project (see also BC POWER COMMISSION). The John HART Dam near Elk Falls was built in 1947 and 2 more dams followed, on Campbell and Upper Campbell lakes. The dams raised the level of BUTTLE LK, deep in STRATHCONA PROVINCIAL PARK, and they were hotly protested by citizens' groups, led by the writer Roderick HAIG-BROWN and others. See also ENVIRONMENTAL MOVEMENT. AS

CAMPBELL RIVER is about halfway up the east coast of VANCOUVER ISLAND at the top of GEORGIA STRAIT, 152 km north of NANAIMO via the Island Hwy. It is the sport FISHING capital  of BC, famous for its TYEE. There is also excellent freshwater fishing in area LAKES and streams. The mouth of the Campbell R has been occupied by aboriginal people for thousands of years, most recently the KWAKWA̱KA̱'WAKW (Kwakiutl). Non-

native settlement began in the early 1880s. Charles and Fred THULIN came over from LUND in 1904, bought what is now downtown Campbell River and opened a store and the Willows Hotel, a coastal landmark until it burned in 1963. Loggers also arrived early in the 20th century and the FOREST INDUSTRY has been a mainstay of the local economy ever since: by 1999 FLETCHER CHALLENGE's Elk Falls PULP mill, established in 1952, was the community's largest employer. In July–Aug 1938 a large FOREST FIRE, the Bloedel Fire (GREAT SAYWARD FIRE), which started in a LOGGING camp, destroyed 300 km² of timber between Campbell River and COURTENAY. HYDROELECTRIC development at Elk Falls dates from 1948. Another major employer has been the nearby Myra Falls GOLD–COPPER–ZINC–SILVER mine owned by BOLIDEN (WESTMIN) CANADA LTD. The municipality is thought to have been named by Capt George RICHARDS for Dr Samuel Campbell, surgeon aboard his British naval survey vessel *Plumper*. A ferry runs from Campbell River across DISCOVERY PASSAGE to QUADRA ISLAND. The Museum at Campbell River, opened in 1994, is one of the finest local museums in the province.
Reading: Jeanette Taylor, *River City: A History of Campbell River and the Discovery Islands*, 1999.

Population: 28,851
Rank in BC: 25th
Population increase since 1981: 82%
Date of incorporation: village 24 June 1947; district 17 Dec 1964
Land area: 148.98 km²
Location: Comox-Strathcona Regional District
Economic base: forest industry, fishing, aquaculture, silviculture, mining, tourism

CANADA GOOSE; see GOOSE.

CANADIAN BROADCASTING CORPORATION (CBC), the national public broadcasting system, was created in 1936 and the next year VANCOUVER radio station CBU officially joined the national network. The local station, managed by Ira DILWORTH from 1938 to 1946, quickly established itself as a source of quality programming, epitomized by the radio drama department and the creation in 1938 of the CBC VANCOUVER ORCHESTRA under the direction of John AVISON. During the 1940s, CBC radio introduced *Hot Air*, BC's JAZZ show, the longest running radio program in Canada; it is still broadcast from the Vancouver studios. Other national music programs originating with the local station include *Disc Drive*, *RadioSonic* and *Radio Escapade*. French-language radio came to BC in 1967 with the opening of the French CBC outlet, CBUF-FM, and in 1998 CBC Radio opened a station in VICTORIA, servicing the entire population of VANCOUVER ISLAND.

CBC Television began broadcasting in BC in Dec 1953 when station CBUT went on the air in Vancouver. CBUT was the public network's fourth TV station—Canadian television was just a year old at the time—and the first in western Canada. In 1954 CBUT was the host broadcaster

for the BRITISH EMPIRE AND COMMONWEALTH GAMES in Vancouver, the first "live" sports coverage across N America. The first "made-in-BC" television dramatic series was CARIBOO COUNTRY, which ran from 1958 to 1966. It was followed up by one of the great success stories of Canadian television, the BEACHCOMBERS, filmed on the SUNSHINE COAST and shown for a remarkable 20 seasons (1971–91) and sold around the world. In 1976 French-language regional news launched its first program, *Edition Pacifique*, which eventually established itself as the award winning *Ce Soir*. Another award-winner on the French-language side was *Courant du Pacifique*, a weekly cultural magazine show that won the Rogers Communications Award for Arts Coverage in 1997. Meanwhile, the CBC won an Academy Award nomination in 1994 for the documentary "The Broadcast Tapes of Dr Peter," which began as a series of diaries by a young Vancouver doctor, who was also an AIDS patient, broadcast on the Vancouver CBC news. Other award-winning programs include *DaVinci's Inquest*, a gritty Vancouver-based crime drama that won a 1999 Gemini Award for best dramatic series. During the 1990s CBC Television British Columbia was confirmed as one of 2 network production centres to remain outside of Toronto providing news, information, children's and drama programming. CBC BC has launched or advanced the careers of many well-known radio and television personalities and producers, including Michael J. FOX, Bill Richardson, Chief Dan GEORGE, Ian Tracy, Daryl DUKE, the comedy duo of Double Exposure, the Irish Rovers, David FOSTER, Vicki GABEREAU, and Jason PRIESTLEY.

From 1953, CBC Vancouver radio studios operated out of the Hotel Vancouver, and the television studio was a converted garage and automobile showroom in the city's West End. All that changed in 1975, when the new CBC Regional Broadcasting Centre opened opposite the Queen Elizabeth Theatre in downtown Vancouver.

CANADIAN FISHING CO LTD (Canfisco) was a small HALIBUT fishing company in VANCOUVER in 1906 when it was purchased by the New England Fish Co. The new owner kept the original name and installed Alvah HAGER to expand operations. In 1918 the company bought its first SALMON cannery in Vancouver, then spread aggressively to the North Coast in the 1920s. It grew to become, with BC PACKERS LTD, one of the 2 industry giants. The parent New England Fish Co went bankrupt in 1980, forcing its subsidiary to sell many of its northern holdings to BC Packers and to concentrate its BC operations at its Vancouver plant. In 1984 the Jim PATTISON group purchased the company, which markets its products in Canada and around the world under the Gold Seal and Tea Rose Brands labels as well as several independent labels. In 1999 Canfisco purchased most of BC Packers' operating assets, including fishing vessels, licences and processing plants, to become the largest seafood company in BC. See also FISHING, COMMERCIAL; SALMON CANNING.

CANADIAN FOREST PRODUCTS LTD

(Canfor) was started in 1938 by John Prentice and Poldi Bentley, two textile manufacturers fleeing Nazi-occupied Austria. It began as Pacific Veneer Co in NEW WESTMINSTER and manufactured BIRCH and SPRUCE plywood for the construction of fighter planes. In 1940 the company acquired Eburne Sawmills in VANCOUVER and soon after switched to production of DOUGLAS FIR plywood. By the end of the war it had purchased several small LOGGING companies in the FRASER VALLEY, along with the timber they owned, and the BEAVER COVE Timber Company, which had extensive holdings on northern VANCOUVER ISLAND. In 1947 the company name was changed to Canadian Forest Products Ltd. A hardboard plant was built in 1948; 3 years later control of the Howe Sound Pulp Co mill at PORT MELLON was acquired.

During the late 1950s and '60s several plywood, SAWMILL and timber operations were added in northwest Alberta and northeast BC. In 1966, with a British partner, Canfor opened the Prince George PULP AND PAPER mill. A second PRINCE GEORGE pulp mill, Intercontinental, was established in 1968, this time in partnership with a German company. In the 1970s, with the acquisition of Balco Industries, a KAMLOOPS-area lumber and plywood operation, the company diversified into equipment manufacturing and financial services.

In the following decade Canfor sold its non-forest interests and acquired more sawmill and woods operations in northern BC. During the late 1980s and early '90s many of the company's plants were extensively upgraded, among them the Howe Sound Pulp mill, which underwent a $1-billion modernization and expansion. In 1999 Canfor completed purchase of Northwood Inc to become the largest producer of lumber in Canada and the largest locally-owned forest products company in the province, controlling 11% of the total timber harvest. *See also* FOREST INDUSTRY; FOREST PRODUCTS. *Ken Drushka*

CANADIAN GOVERNMENT MERCHANT MARINE LTD

was created by the federal government in 1919 to engage in the export trade and support the Canadian SHIPBUILDING industry. The first Pacific sailing was in Jan 1920, when the *Canadian Raider* left VANCOUVER with a cargo of lumber for Australia. Operated under the management of the CNR, the fleet eventually

The Canadian Highlander, *one of the fleet of Canadian Merchant Marine vessels. Courtesy S.C. Heal*

grew to 68 vessels and 2,000 sailors. In the Pacific it connected Vancouver and PRINCE RUPERT with Australia, New Zealand and the Orient. Trade declined during the Depression and the government sold the ships in 1936. *Reading:* S.C. Heal, *Conceived in War, Born in Peace,* 1992.

CANADIAN HELICOPTERS LTD

(Okanagan Helicopters Ltd) began in 1947 as Okanagan Air Services, founded in PENTICTON by three RCAF veterans, pilots Carl AGAR and Barney Bent and engineer Alf STRINGER. The company provided aerial spraying from a Bell 47-B3 and the initial flight in Aug 1947 was the first commercial helicopter flight in BC. The difficulties of flying in

Alf Stringer (l) and Carl Agar, co-founders of Canadian Helicopters Ltd, Penticton Airport, 1947. Stocks family collection/Interior Photo Bank

mountainous terrain had to be overcome as the company pioneered the use of helicopters for MINING exploration, forestry surveys, mapmaking, heavy construction—anything that required access to remote locations. Its success was assured with its involvement in the ALCAN project at KITIMAT in the early 1950s. By late in the decade it had a fleet of 35 helicopters and more than 100 staff. It became Okanagan Helicopters Ltd in 1952, and by the 1970s it was one of the foremost commercial helicopter operations in the world. In 1989 it became Canadian Helicopters Ltd.

CANADIAN LACROSSE HALL OF FAME

opened in 1967 in the Centennial Community Centre in NEW WESTMINSTER. Because LACROSSE has such a successful history in New Westminster, in 1964 enthusiasts of the game selected it as the best location for the hall, then worked to incorporate it and to select charter members. Photographs, sweaters, sticks, plaques, trophies and medals dating back to the origins of organized lacrosse are displayed there. By the end of the 20th century it had honoured about 360 inductees. *SW*

CANADIAN LITERATURE,

founded at UBC by George WOODCOCK in 1959, is a quarterly journal of literary commentary and reviews, the first devoted to Canadian writing. It also publishes poetry in each issue. Woodcock, the original editor, was succeeded in 1977 by William New, who was followed by Eva-Marie Kröller in 1995. Over the years several anthologies of articles from the magazine have been published.

CANADIAN MEMORIAL CHAPEL

is a UNITED CHURCH on 16th Ave at Burrard St in VANCOUVER, constructed in 1927–28 as a memorial to WWI dead. The chapel was the inspiration of Rev George Fallis, a chaplain during the war, who also raised most of the money for the building and was minister until 1933. It features a set of 10 stained-glass windows, one for each of the 9 provinces (Newfoundland was not yet a part of the federation) and the Yukon. Each window depicts a biblical scene and 2 events from the sponsoring province's history. An all-Canada window above the chapel entrance depicts important scenes from national history. The chapel opened on Remembrance Day in 1928.

CANADIAN MUSEUM OF FLIGHT

was incorporated in 1977 by a group of AVIATION enthusiasts. The museum restores and exhibits early aircraft dating back to the 1920s and has a large collection of historic photographs. Originally located on the SURREY property of Ed and Rose Zalesky, who founded it, the museum moved in 1996 to a hangar at the AIRPORT in LANGLEY.

Sandy Tinsley of the Canadian Museum of Flight, in the nose of a Handley Page Hampden bomber, 1998. The aircraft crashed off Vancouver Island in 1942 and the museum is restoring it. Ian Smith/Vancouver Sun

CANADIAN NATIONAL RAILWAYS

(CN) is a transcontinental railway system formed from the nationalization and merger of several financially troubled private railways following WWI. In 1918 Canadian National absorbed the CANADIAN NORTHERN RWY, which ran from Winnipeg to VANCOUVER via the YELLOWHEAD PASS, and in 1919 it took over the GRAND TRUNK PACIFIC line that ran from Winnipeg to PRINCE RUPERT. The organization of the new, government-owned company was complete by 1923. CN also took over the Grand Trunk Pacific's coastal steamship service, the PRINCE LINE, renamed it Canadian National Steamships and operated it until 1975. On VANCOUVER ISLAND, CN took control of the Canadian Northern line running between VICTORIA and Patricia Bay that had opened in 1917, and the partially built line from Victoria to PORT ALBERNI that eventually (1924) opened as far as COWICHAN LAKE. The Patricia Bay line closed in 1935 but the Cowichan line played an important role in supporting the logging industry at the lake from the 1920s to the 1950s. The CNR was a major transportation route across central BC. It was key to the development of PRINCE GEORGE

CANADIAN NATIONAL & CANADIAN NORTHERN RAILWAYS

Prince Rupert

Fort St James

Prince George

Quesnel

Williams Lake

Alberta

Yellowhead Pass

Thompson R.

Columbia R.

Fraser R.

Kamloops

Vancouver

Hope

┿┿┿┿ Canadian National Railway ⋯⋯⋯ Canadian Northern Railway

and Prince Rupert as regional centres, and it promoted AGRICULTURE, LOGGING, SAWMILLING and settlement along its northern route. Prince Rupert became an important port for export of wheat from the prairies and COAL from northeast BC and Alberta. CN also built branch lines from KAMLOOPS to KELOWNA in the 1920s and to KITIMAT in the 1950s. It provided transcontinental passenger service that connected Prince Rupert and Vancouver with Edmonton on its route across the northern prairies to eastern Canada. With the decline of passenger traffic, all passenger rail service devolved in 1977 to a new CROWN CORPORATION, VIA Rail, and in Vancouver the CN terminal at the head of FALSE CREEK became the terminus for this traffic. The CNR continued to operate freight service on its main lines into Vancouver and Prince Rupert. In 1995 the company was sold to private interests for $2.2 billion; in 1999 it completed a takeover of the historic US railway, Illinois Central, giving CN a 30,000-km network of track linking the Atlantic and Pacific coasts in Canada to the Gulf of Mexico.

CANADIAN NORTHERN RAILWAY was founded in 1899 in Manitoba by 2 entrepreneurs, William Mackenzie and Donald Mann. It expanded across the prairies and in 1909 announced its intention to build all the way to the Pacific, using the YELLOWHEAD PASS through the ROCKY MTS and descending to VANCOUVER via the THOMPSON and FRASER river valleys. The BC section was officially called the Canadian Northern Pacific Rwy. The railway was strongly supported by the provincial government of Richard MCBRIDE, which guaranteed the compa-

ny's bonds. The company agreed not to employ any Asians on the project. Construction began at PORT MANN in June 1910 and proceeded up the Fraser Canyon. During the summer of 1912, work in the canyon was disrupted by a strike involving several thousand labourers protesting low wages and poor living conditions in the camps. Joe Hill, balladeer of the INDUSTRIAL WORKERS OF THE WORLD, visited the strike and wrote a famous song, "Where the Fraser River Flows," about it. Special police eventually forced the men back to work and the last spike was driven south of ASHCROFT on 23 Jan 1915. The first passenger train from the east arrived in Vancouver on 28 Aug. The railway also built lines on southern VANCOUVER ISLAND. One of these, running north from VICTORIA to Patricia Bay, went into service in 1917. The other, intended to run from Victoria to PORT ALBERNI, was not completed before the Canadian Northern—debilitated by cost overruns, insufficient traffic and the impact of WWI—was nationalized by the federal government in 1918 and folded into the publicly owned CANADIAN NATIONAL RAILWAYS. *See also* LABOUR MOVEMENT.

CANADIAN ORTHODOX MONASTERY of All Saints of N America, with the Centre for Canadian Orthodox Studies, is nestled in the mountains east of MISSION. This is the first skete (small monastery) in Canada to focus its work on the indigenization of Orthodox Christian tradition in Canada (*see* ORTHODOX CHURCHES). It has established Orthodox parishes that include people of various cultural origins, has translated and written liturgical texts with Canadian ele-

ments, and has established the first Canadian Orthodox feast day (the feast of the Theotokos, Joy of Canada, held on the first Sunday in August). The monastery has a publishing house, Synaxis Press, which publishes 2 theological journals. The initiative for the foundation of the monastery came from Lev Puhalo and Vasili Novakshonoff in discussions in 1968 with the monks of Mt Athos, Greece. They founded their initial skete near CHILLIWACK, moved in 1973 to a cabin in the mountains in the Chilliwack Valley, then in 1991 purchased the present site. Fr Lazar Puhalo was consecrated bishop in 1990, when the monastery entered the Ukrainian Orthodox Church of Kiev (*see* UKRAINIANS). In 1994 Bishop Lazar became archbishop and Novakshonoff became bishop of VANCOUVER.

David J. Goa

CANADIAN PACIFIC NAVIGATION CO was created in 1883 when Capt John IRVING merged his PIONEER LINE of FRASER R steamboats with the fleet of vessels owned by the HBC. Irving directed the company, which ran vessels between VANCOUVER and VICTORIA, up the Fraser, south to Puget Sound and along the west coast of VANCOUVER ISLAND. During the Klondike GOLD RUSH, service expanded to the North Coast. In 1901 the CPR purchased the CPN fleet of 14 vessels. CPN continued to operate as a separate entity until May 1903, when it was absorbed into the CPR as its British Columbia Coast Steamship Service.

CANADIAN PACIFIC RAILWAY (CPR) began construction in BC on 15 May 1880 at YALE. A rail link to eastern Canada had been a condition of BC's entry into CONFEDERATION in 1871 and the CPR was a fulfilment of that promise. Prime Minister John A. Macdonald had initially said that ESQUIMALT on VANCOUVER ISLAND would be

CPR freight train running alongside the Thompson R near Spences Bridge.
Walter Lanz photo/Image Makers

CANADIAN PACIFIC RAILWAY MAINLINE 1886

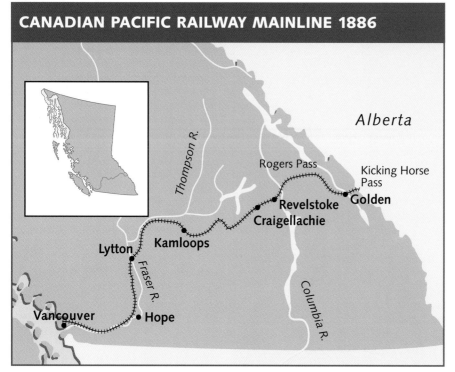

the western terminus of the line. When the impracticality of that decision became clear, the terminus was changed to PORT MOODY. In 1879 Andrew ONDERDONK, an engineer representing an American syndicate, won the contract from the federal government to build the Fraser Canyon section of the line, the first section to be built in BC. Onderdonk needed a huge labour force, which he acquired first from California and then from China. CHINESE workers were favoured because they accepted lower pay and worked diligently at even the most dangerous tasks. Several thousand Chinese worked on CPR construction (6,500 were employed in 1883) and an estimated 600 of them died. Along with the canyon section, Onderdonk received the contract to build west to the coast and east to EAGLE PASS. Rail construction from the east reached KICKING HORSE PASS on the Alberta border in 1883. On the west side of the pass the line descended the "Big Hill" to FIELD on a 4.5% temporary grade. Extra locomotives were required to get trains up the hill and very strict precautions were necessary to prevent runaways on the downhill slope. Finally the CPR built the Spiral Tunnels between 1907 and 1909 to eliminate the Big Hill, reducing the grade to 2.2% by looping tracks through long tunnels bored through the mountains. Meanwhile construction continued over ROGERS PASS during 1885 and in November met Onderdonk's crew from the west at CRAIGELLACHIE, just west of REVELSTOKE; there, on 7 Nov 1885, the last spike was driven. The first scheduled passenger train from Montreal arrived at Port Moody on 4 July 1886. It took 5 days, 19 hours to complete the trip. A spur line to NEW WESTMINSTER opened later that year. Port Moody's celebration was short-lived, however. The CPR decided to relocate its terminus farther down BURRARD INLET at GRANVILLE, which quickly incorporated as VANCOUVER, and where the

province granted the railway 24.3 km² of land. The first train arrived there on 23 Feb 1887, though the formal first arrival was celebrated on 23 May. The presence of the railway virtually guaranteed that Vancouver would develop into the commercial and transportation capital of the province. It also secured the futures of the several southern Interior communities through which it passed. In return for building the railway the CPR received 45,000 km² of public land in BC, consisting of a 32-km-wide belt straddling the main line. Later the company also received many more large parcels of land along its southern route.

In the KOOTENAY, the discovery of SILVER at NELSON in 1887 sparked a MINING rush. At first, transportation to and from the area was by steamboat (*see* PADDLEWHEEL STEAMBOATS) on KOOTENAY LK and KOOTENAY R connecting south to the US. The CPR tried to divert traffic north by opening a small line, the COLUMBIA & WESTERN RWY, between Nelson and ROBSON in 1891. Combined with steamers on the ARROW LKS, this line, the first in southeast BC, connected the mining area to the CPR main line at Revelstoke. But growing competition from J.J. Hill's GREAT NORTHERN RWY to the south convinced the CPR that it had to build a line across the south of the province. In 1897 it negotiated the Crow's Nest Pass Agreement with the federal government. In return for a subsidy of $3.3 million, the CPR promised to maintain reduced freight rates on key commodities in the west (the infamous Crow Rate) and to build a rail line from Fort Macleod, AB, across the CROWSNEST PASS to the south end of Kootenay Lk. The 400-km line was completed in 1898, leaving a gap between the bottom of the lake and Nelson that was filled by sternwheelers, tugs and barges until track was laid up the west side of the lake between 1929 and 1931. The CPR also extended its C&K Rwy from Robson south to TRAIL and ROSSLAND in 1898 by purchasing the COLUMBIA & WESTERN RWY and SMELTER operations of F. Augustus HEINZE. These later formed the basis of the CPR-owned mining giant, COMINCO. The Columbia & Western was extended west as far as MIDWAY by 1900. The CPR finally completed its line across southern BC in 1916, when it opened the KETTLE VALLEY RWY from Midway to the main line at HOPE.

On the coast, the CPR branched into steamship service in 1901 with the purchase of the CANADIAN PACIFIC NAVIGATION CO and the subsequent introduction of its PRINCESS LINE. On Vancouver Island, it purchased the ESQUIMALT &

Celebration of the formal arrival of the first CPR passenger train in Vancouver, 23 May 1887.
Harry Devine/UBC BC288/8

NANAIMO RWY from the DUNSMUIR family. The CPR also built the Vancouver Hotel (1887) and Victoria's EMPRESS HOTEL (1908) to anchor its chain of railway hotels, which included Mount Stephen House at Field (1886), Fraser Canyon House at NORTH BEND (1887), GLACIER HOUSE (1887), Revelstoke Hotel (1896) and Hotel Sicamous (1898). The railway was the largest landholder in Vancouver, owning about 50% of the real estate, and was a significant force in the development of the city for many years to come.

Until the 1950s CPR trains were powered by steam locomotives. Following WWII the railway began converting to diesel-electric power, which was less expensive to operate. The first section to become diesel powered was the Esquimalt & Nanaimo, which converted in 1949. By the mid-1950s, diesel locomotives were in use everywhere in BC on the CPR. At the same time, passenger service continued its inexorable decline. Early in 1964 CPR passenger service was discontinued along the southern route to the Crowsnest Pass. Then, in 1977, passenger service for both the CPR and the CANADIAN NATIONAL RWY was combined in a new CROWN CORPORATION, VIA Rail Canada. VIA took over operation of the Canadian, the CPR's remaining transcontinental train, and the E&N passenger service on Vancouver Island. In 2000 CP Rail was still operating freight service across southern BC. Major commodities carried include grain, COAL, sulphur and potash. Much freight was carried by intermodal trains moving trailers and containers.

Reading: Robert D. Turner, West of the Great Divide: An Illustrated History of the Canadian Pacific Railway in BC, 1880–1986, 1987.

CANADIAN WESTERN LUMBER CO, initially Ross Maclaren Co, built its first SAWMILL at MILLSIDE on the FRASER R, just upstream from NEW WESTMINSTER, in 1889. James Maclaren, an Ottawa Valley lumberman, and Frank Ross, a Quebec lumber merchant, headed the company, which built a second mill at BARNET on BURRARD INLET. The company obtained a large tract of timber in the CULTUS LK area, but ran into difficulty during its early years due to depressed lumber markets.

In 1902 the Millside mill was acquired by Lester David, a Seattle lumber broker involved in several early BC lumber and pulp developments. He acquired large stands of timber near COMOX and on the Stave R, and renamed the company Fraser River Saw Mills Ltd in 1906. When David's American backers declined to finance further expansion, he obtained backing from Canadian investors, and in 1907 A.D. MCRAE, a Winnipeg land agent for the CANADIAN NORTHERN RWY, was appointed president. Two years later the company began bringing in mill workers from Quebec to replace Asian labourers. They were accommodated in company-built housing, on the site of what later became MAILLARDVILLE. In 1910 additional investment was secured to build a CEDAR mill, a veneer plant and a door factory (*see also* FOREST PRODUCTS). David sold his interests and several principals of Canadian Northern, includ-

ing William Mackenzie, Donald Mann, David Hanna and Robert HORNE-PAYNE, were appointed directors. McRae became general manager and a young New Yorker, Henry Mackin, sales manager. The company name was changed to Canadian Western Lumber Co; the mill became known as Fraser Mills. BC's first plywood plant was built at the mill site in 1913. The timber and logging operations on VANCOUVER ISLAND were brought under a subsidiary, Comox Logging & Railway Co. Under this organization the mill became one of the largest and most modern in the world, while Comox Logging became the biggest woods operation in BC.

Canadian Western Lumber was headed by McRae during its development phase, and then by Mackin, while Comox Logging was headed by Robert FILBERG. A second subsidiary, Canadian Tugboat Co, towed logs from the timber operations to the mill. The company was sold to CROWN ZELLERBACH in 1953; in 1991 it was sold again to INTERNATIONAL FOREST PRODUCTS LTD.

Ken Drushka

CANAL FLATS, pop 753, occupies flatland between the south end of Columbia Lk and the KOOTENAY R. The site was named McGillivray's Portage by David THOMPSON when he visited in 1808. The present name derives from William BAILLIE-GROHMAN's canal-building scheme of the late 1880s. A canal with a lock was dug between the river and the lake but it was hardly ever used. In the 1970s BC HYDRO & POWER AUTHORITY revived the water diversion idea, this time to expand the HYDROELECTRICITY potential of the COLUMBIA R system, but local opposition put the plans on hold. The FOREST INDUSTRY is the main employer.

CANFORD, 15 km west of MERRITT beside the NICOLA R, was the site of the Nicola Valley Lumber Co SAWMILL, established about 1906. The mill was on the CPR's Nicola branch, which later became part of the KETTLE VALLEY RWY, and was a major supplier of lumber to the railway. It burned in 1919, was rebuilt and taken over by Nicola Valley Pine Mills, and operated into the 1950s. The community was named by a local rancher after Canford Manor near Bournemouth, England. *AS*

CANIM LAKE, 56 km², 37 km long, nestles in the mountains 35 km east of 100 MILE HOUSE. Its eastern end touches the edge of WELLS GRAY PROVINCIAL PARK. The name means "canoe" in CHINOOK JARGON. It is a popular recreational lake with good FISHING and boating and many resorts and summer homes. The area is traditional Secwepemc (Shuswap) territory and the home of the Canim Lake Nation, centred at Tsq'escen'. *See also* LAKES.

CANNERIES; *see* SALMON CANNING.

CANNINGS, Richard J. "Dick," biologist, and **Sydney**, zoologist (b 31 Mar 1954, Penticton). Twin brothers from the OKANAGAN VALLEY, they have made major contributions to their special-

ties while also helping to inform the public about the natural world of BC. Dick Cannings was curator of the Cowan Vertebrate Museum at UBC from 1980 to 1995, when he left to become a consulting biologist out of his home in NARAMATA. His specialty is the conservation of ecosystems and wildlife species in the southern Interior, and he is BC program coordinator of Bird Studies Canada, developing volunteer programs to monitor bird populations. Sydney Cannings, former curator at the Spencer Entomological Museum at UBC, is a provincial government zoologist. In 1996 the brothers co-authored *British Columbia: A Natural History*, which won a BC BOOK PRIZE, a Lt Gov's Award for best book on BC HISTORY and an award from the Canadian Science Writers Assoc. Each has written extensively on the natural environment for a more academic audience. *See also* NATURAL HISTORY.

CANOE, a farming, fruit-growing and LOGGING community on the CPR and SHUSWAP LK, was established in the early 1900s and is now a suburb of SALMON ARM. A SAWMILL was built here in 1925 by R.W. Bruhn; today Federated Co-operatives Ltd owns a plywood plant. Dugout CANOES were once common on the lake. *AS*

CANOE, DUGOUT, was brought to a high degree of functionality on the BC coast by FIRST NATIONS people, who constructed canoes in a variety of sizes for many different purposes. The HAIDA built BC's largest ocean-going dugouts—up to 24 m in length, though 10 to 15 m was more common—for WHALING, sealing, trading and raiding (*see also* FUR SEAL; FUR TRADE, MARITIME). Each canoe was carved from a single log,

18-m canoe on the shore of Nitinat Lk, c 1914.
Courtesy Angela Newitt

Edward S. Curtis photograph of a Kwakwaka'wakw canoe under sail, 1914. *BC Archives D-08356*

Secwepemc women paddling cottonwood dugout canoes—traditional in parts of the BC Interior—at Enderby, 1908. *Enderby Museum 220*

an enormous red CEDAR trunk. It was first shaped and hollowed out with hand adzes. The wood was then made pliable with hot water and the canoe was widened with wooden stretchers. Several styles prevailed: northern designs favoured a rounded hull and high bow and stern extensions while southern hulls were often V-shaped and had less pronounced prows. Both types of canoe were prized trade items. Dugouts were often elaborately painted and incised and have inspired artists such as Bill REID (*see also* ART, NORTHWEST COAST ABORIGINAL). They had mostly disappeared by the 1900s. In recent years a number of coastal aboriginal groups have paddled replica canoes (usually made of fibreglass) on lengthy journeys. *See also* LOOTAS.　　　AS

CANUCKS; *see* VANCOUVER CANUCKS.

CANYON, a small fruit-growing and farming community 6 km east of CRESTON, formed around a SAWMILL and pole yard operated by Canyon City Lumber Co from the early 1900s to the mid-1920s. It was named for the nearby GOAT RIVER Canyon. There is a school, community hall, general store and post office.　　　AS

CANYON CITY, or Gitwinksihlkw as it is known to its NISGA'A residents, pop 220, is the smallest of the 4 Nisga'a villages on the NASS R in northeastern BC. It has been linked by road to the outside world only since 1995. Commercial FISHING and LOGGING are the main employers.

CAPE MUDGE, village, pop 189, located at the south end of QUADRA ISLAND, looks across DISCOVERY PASSAGE to CAMPBELL RIVER about halfway up VANCOUVER ISLAND's east coast. It was established in the mid-19th century by members of the Lekwiltok, a KWAKWAKA'WAKW (Kwakiutl) nation, as they moved south into territory formerly held by the Coast Salish (*see* SALISHAN FIRST NATIONS), and became the main village of the We-Wai-Kai nation. It is named for Zachary Mudge, a naval officer with Capt George VANCOUVER. A METHODIST CHURCH mission was established here in 1892 and by the 1920s most of the traditional big houses had been replaced by modern housing. Commercial FISHING is the main economic activity. The Kwagiulth Museum contains a historic collection of POTLATCH regalia seized by the federal government earlier in the century and repatriated for the museum's opening in 1979.

CAPE SCOTT is a wilderness provincial PARK (est 1973; 218.49 km²) at the northwest tip of VANCOUVER ISLAND. It is named for David Scott, a merchant who backed a voyage there in 1786. Long stretches of rocky coast are broken by a series of sandy beaches. The area is exposed to wind and storm and heavy rainfall (an average of 425 cm annually). The terrain is low and rolling, rising to the highest point at Mt St Patrick (el 422 m). Occupied by the KWAKWAKA'WAKW (Kwakiutl) at contact, the area was settled between 1896 and 1897 by a group of Danish (*see* DANES) pioneers led by Rasmus Hansen. The colonists intended to support themselves by AGRICULTURE, commercial FISHING and DAIRY FARMING, but most had moved away by 1907. A second wave of settlement peaked in 1913 but dissipated again during WWI. The automated LIGHTHOUSE was erected in 1959. It is accessible by trail or boat, though facilities were undeveloped by the end of the 20th century.

CAPILANO, Joe (Su-a-pu-luck), Squamish leader (b circa 1840 near Squamish; d 11 Mar 1910, N Vancouver). He grew up at SQUAMISH villages in HOWE SOUND, then moved to the ROMAN CATHOLIC mission RESERVE near CAPILANO R in N Vancouver. A sawmill labourer and stevedore, he became chief of the Squamish Nation in 1895 and a leading political activist on FIRST NATIONS issues. In 1906 he led a delegation of elders to England to meet King Edward VII and inform him about the struggle for aboriginal title (*see* ABORIGINAL RIGHTS).

Experiment Bight, Cape Scott Provincial Park. *Philip Stone photo*

Joe Capilano, at centre with robe over his arm, with delegation of chiefs leaving for London to meet with the King, 1906. CVA In.P41

Many of the stories in Pauline JOHNSON's *Legends of Vancouver* (1911) were based on the stories he told her. His wife Mary (1836–1940) was a noted orator, storyteller and genealogist. Their son Mathias Joe (circa 1885–1966) was a well-known carver and political activist; in 1949 he and his wife Ellen were the first aboriginal people in BC to vote.

CAPILANO RIVER, 35 km, rises in the mountains north of VANCOUVER and flows south to empty into BURRARD INLET near the First Narrows. Its turbulent stream cuts a deep valley through the North Shore Mts, forming a natural boundary between N VANCOUVER and W VANCOUVER. The mouth of the river was the site of a SQUAMISH village and a productive fishing station since before the earliest explorers arrived (*see* FISHING, ABORIGINAL). The river was dammed in 1888 to supply water to the new city of Vancouver via pipes running beneath Burrard Inlet. The original dam was replaced farther downstream by the present Cleveland Dam in 1954, creating Capilano Lk, a 5.6-km-long reservoir that now supplies 40% of the Lower Mainland's water. LOGGING took place in the watershed from 1904 to 1934, and a SALMON hatchery was built below the dam in 1971. The CAPILANO SUSPENSION BRIDGE is one of the Lower Mainland's main tourist attractions. The river is named for a Squamish chief. *See also* RIVERS.

CAPILANO SUSPENSION BRIDGE is a privately owned tourist attraction crossing the CAPILANO R in N VANCOUVER. The original rope bridge across the canyon was built by George Grant Mackay, a land developer, in 1889. It was replaced in 1903 by a steel-cable bridge. Edward Mahon, an Irish-born mine promoter, purchased the site in 1910 and added a teahouse and public garden. During the 1950s, under the ownership of Rae Mitchell, a banquet hall, restaurant and gift shop opened. The 137-m bridge, the longest suspended footbridge in the world, has been rebuilt over the years; under the ownership of Mitchell's daughter Nancy Stibbard, the bridge remains a favourite destination for tourists.

Capilano Suspension Bridge, N Vancouver.

CAPOZZI, Pasquale "Cap," grocer, winemaker (b 1887, Santo Stephano del Sole, Italy; d 1976). He arrived in Canada in 1906 and worked as a railway labourer and store manager before opening his own store in the MINING town of PHOENIX in 1917. Two years later he moved to KELOWNA, where he opened a grocery store. In 1932 he helped raise money to launch CALONA WINES LTD. During the 1960s, under the management of Capozzi and his sons, Calona became the largest winery in BC (*see* WINE MAKING). He retired in 1971.

CARAVAN FARM THEATRE is a THEATRE company based on a farm near ARMSTRONG since 1978. Paul Kirby and Nans Kelder founded it in 1969 as Caravan Stage Co and toured from place to place in horse-drawn wagons. The troupe settled at the farm while Nick Hutchinson was artistic director from 1976 to 1993. In 1983 it split into the resident Caravan Farm Theatre and the touring stage company. The Farm Theatre presents summer productions and a popular winter production for which it moves the audience by sleigh from scene to scene through the woods.

CARDENA was a member of the UNION STEAMSHIP CO fleet of coastal passenger/freight vessels. Built in Scotland in 1923, it serviced the upcoast camps and SALMON CANNERIES for 35 years. At 69 m, it was the largest of the Union ships to that time, with a gross weight of 1,403 tonnes and capacity for 250 passengers and 350 tons of cargo. Navigators considered it the best sea-going ship on the coast. It was sold with the rest of the fleet to NORTHLAND NAVIGATION CO LTD in 1959 and sunk as part of the breakwater in KELSEY BAY.

CARDERO, Manuel José Antonio, sailor, artist (b 20 Oct 1766, Ecija, Spain; d after 1810, in Spain). In 1789 he was a cabin boy on Alejandro MALASPINA's round-the-world expedition. A talented artist, he began making sketches during the trip. The expedition reached Mexico and was diverted north in 1791 to seek the famed Strait of ANIAN. His ship visited NOOTKA SOUND in mid-Aug; there he made some of the earliest drawings of BC. In 1792, when Dionisio ALCALA-GALIANO and Cayetano VALDES were sent to explore JUAN DE FUCA STRAIT in the *Sutil* and the *Mexicana*, Cardero went along as artist. This was the expedition that met with Capt George VANCOUVER and explored much of the southern INSIDE PASSAGE. Cardero's two dozen surviving drawings of the trip make him the most important artist of the early contact and exploration period. He sailed back to Mexico in fall 1792, then returned to Spain and served in the Spanish navy. *See also* SPANISH EXPLORATION.

CARELESS, Ric, environmental activist (b 1951, Toronto). As a student attending the UNIV OF VICTORIA in 1970, he launched a public campaign to halt LOGGING in the Nitinat Triangle, an area of ancient RAIN FOREST located inland from the WEST COAST TRAIL on southwestern VANCOUVER ISLAND. The success of that campaign led ultimately to the inclusion of the Triangle in PACIFIC RIM NATIONAL PARK RESERVE and launched Careless on a career of full-time ENVIRONMENTAL activism. As an early activist with the Sierra Club in BC, one of the founders of Tatshenshini Wild and executive director of the Wilderness Tourism Council, he led campaigns to protect several wilderness areas, including the central PURCELL MTS, the Schoen Valley on northern Vancouver Island, the Babine R, the SPATSIZI PLATEAU and the TATSHENSHINI R. A member of the ORDER OF BC (1994), he is executive director of BC Spaces for Nature and an advocate of partnerships between environmentalists and industry to create a sustainable economy.

CARIBOO is the name applied to the Interior plateau spreading east of the FRASER R to the CARIBOO MTS and south from just north of QUESNEL to south of CLINTON. (The region is often said to include the CHILCOTIN country west of the Fraser.) The name seems to have originated in about 1860 as a reference to the woodland CARIBOU found in the area. The topography varies from the open ranges of the Fraser benchlands through the undulating PINE and SPRUCE forests

Cariboo ranching country. Rick Blacklaws photo

of the Quesnel Highlands to mountain peaks soaring over 2,500 m. There are many LAKES well stocked for sport FISHING. The eastern flank of the region comprises BOWRON LAKE and WELLS GRAY PROVINCIAL PARKS. The CLIMATE is warm and dry in the summer; winters may be long and harsh. The northern part of the region is the traditional territory of the DAKELH (Carrier) people, and the middle and southern area is the territory of the SECWEPEMC (Shuswap). FUR TRADERS were active here but it was really the search for GOLD that attracted the first influx of outsiders. Discoveries were made in the creeks and mountains east of Quesnel beginning in 1859 and peaking in 1865. The main GOLD RUSH community was BARKERVILLE, which has been restored as a provincial historic site. Early prospectors followed the FUR BRIGADE trails until the CARIBOO WAGON ROAD was built from YALE to the goldfields in 1863, pioneering a route along the Fraser R that was subsequently followed by Hwy 97, known as the Cariboo Hwy. The CATTLE INDUSTRY developed with the gold rush and became the principal activity when MINING waned. The Cariboo is still considered cattle country and many of the original ranches remain in business. The Pacific Great Eastern Rwy (*see* BC RAIL) from the coast was completed to Quesnel in 1920. Since the 1950s the FOREST INDUSTRY has dominated the economy, with major lumber complexes at WILLIAMS LAKE, 100 MILE HOUSE and Quesnel. The Cariboo is home to a large number of artists, artisans and craftspeople. The Cariboo Art Society, based in Williams Lake, is said to be the oldest continuing art society in BC.

CARIBOO COUNTRY was the first television drama series made in BC. Using scripts by Paul ST PIERRE and produced and directed by Philip Keatley, the program premiered on the VANCOUVER CBC television station CBUT in 1958 and continued until 1966. Stories were set in the fictional community of Namko and strongly reflected the character of the CHILCOTIN ranching region. The show was styled as "fictional documentary" and filmed at RISKE CREEK. It featured a cast that included Chief Dan GEORGE.

CARIBOO MOUNTAINS are a northern range of the COLUMBIA MTS forming the eastern edge of the CARIBOO district, dividing the Interior plateau from the ROCKY MT TRENCH. The FRASER R swings in a great arc north around the top of the range before flowing south via PRINCE GEORGE toward the coast. The range, which contains the headwaters of many of the most productive creeks of the GOLD RUSH era, lies along the eastern side of BOWRON LAKE and WELLS GRAY PROVINCIAL PARKS. These parks are connected by Cariboo Mts Provincial PARK (1,134.70 km²); together they form a vast area of protected wilderness 7,600 km² in size. The highest peak in the range is Mt Sir Wilfrid Laurier (el 3,505 m).

CARIBOO WAGON ROAD was built between YALE and BARKERVILLE to provide access to the CARIBOO goldfields during the rush of prospectors to the area in the early 1860s (*see* GOLD RUSH, CARIBOO). The road was built by a combination of ROYAL ENGINEERS and private contractors. Construction of the Fraser Canyon section began at Yale, the head of steamboat navigation on the river, in the spring of 1862. Much of the road was blasted out of the sheer rocky sides of the canyon. It crossed to the east side via the ALEXANDRA BRIDGE (which was actually not in place until 1863) and reached LYTTON by the autumn of 1862. There it left the FRASER R and followed an overland route north via CLINTON and 100 MILE HOUSE to rejoin the river at SODA CREEK, north of present-day WILLIAMS LAKE, by the end of 1863. In 1864 the road continued on to QUESNEL and made a turn eastward to Cottonwood, leaving the final stretch across the rocky highlands to Barkerville to be completed in the summer of 1865. The finished road was 5.5 m wide and 492 km long. Its construction added greatly to the colony's debt. A series of roadhouses sprang up to provide accommodations for travellers who arrived by freight wagon and stagecoach. Today a paved highway follows approximately the same route. *See also* ROADS AND HIGHWAYS; TRAILS.

Freight wagons pulled by mules at Spences Bridge, 1867. UBC BC380

CARIBOO WAGON ROAD

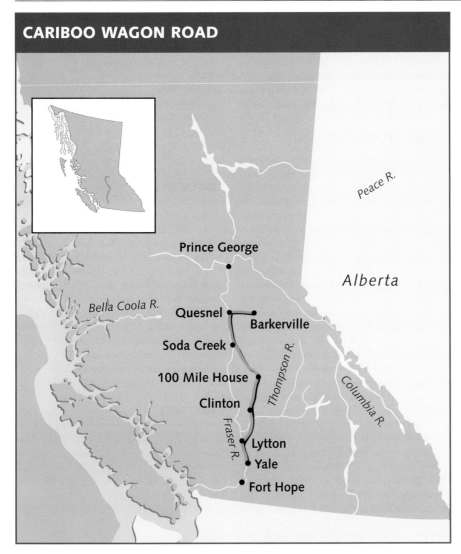

Prince George

Alberta

Peace R.

Bella Coola R.

Quesnel • — • Barkerville

Soda Creek •

100 Mile House •

Clinton •

Thompson R.

Columbia R.

Fraser R.

Lytton
Yale
Fort Hope

region known as the Interior Wet Belt, encompassing the COLUMBIA MTS and adjacent foothills and highlands across the southeast and east-central part of the province. Almost all the world's population of mountain caribou (2,500 animals) live in BC, where they are considered to be at risk and are Blue-listed (*see* ENDANGERED SPECIES). The boreal ecotype occupies the comparatively flat boreal lowlands, or taiga plains, of the northeast. The population of northern and boreal caribou is estimated to be about 16,000.

The most important food source for all caribou is lichens. The northern ecotype feeds primarily on terrestrial lichens and other plants and shrubs year-round. Winter forage is available on terrain that is open and windswept, enabling them to obtain food by cratering (or digging with their large hooves) in shallow snow. Once the snowpack builds up, the mountain ecotype depends heavily on tree-growing lichens, such as common witch's hair, which is why these caribou are so dependent on (mostly old-growth) forests that contain sufficient amounts of these slow-growing plants.

All caribou are social, gregarious animals but unlike barren ground caribou, the 3 BC ecotypes do not aggregate into large migratory herds. Northern caribou herds are the largest. Mountain caribou come together only in small groups that do not migrate over great distances but that do migrate extensively from valley bottoms to alpine areas, depending on the time of year. Boreal caribou are found in small bands that may remain in one area throughout the year. Caribou breed in late autumn and the female usually produces a single calf in late May or early June. Calves must be up and travelling with their mothers almost immediately to avoid

CARIBOU (*Rangifer tarandus*) is a medium-sized member of the DEER family (Cervidae), somewhere between mule deer and ELK in size and uniquely adapted to living in a cold climate. The woodland caribou (*R. tarandus caribou*) is a subspecies of which 3 ecotypes occur in BC: mountain, northern and boreal. How they are classified is based primarily on behaviour and habitat use.

Caribou are dull brown in colour, although in winter some may look whiter. In males the head and neck are often greyish-white, with a mane on the underside of the neck. The tail and surrounding area, as well as a band around each hoof, are also whitish. The body is elongated and cylindrical, with a short tail and large hooves, which enable the animal to inhabit snow-covered areas impossible for moose and deer to use. Unique among the deer family, both males and females have antlers, although some females are antlerless or have only one antler.

In BC, woodland caribou are found east of the COAST MTS. The northern ecotype is the largest; it is found in the north, west and central portions of the province from TWEEDSMUIR PROVINCIAL PARK to MT EDZIZA and SPATSIZI PLATEAU WILDERNESS PARKS, northward to the Yukon border and east across the northern plateaus into the ROCKY MTS. Distribution of the mountain ecotype corresponds roughly to the

Woodland caribou. Ken Bowen photo

predation. Wolves are the main predators; grizzly BEAR and COUGAR are also significant. Industrial developments (LOGGING, MINING, GAS AND OIL exploration and road building) and recreational activities pose significant additional threats.

One other type of woodland caribou is Dawson's caribou (*Rangifer tarandus dawsoni*), named for the geologist George DAWSON, who first reported the animal. It was unique to the QUEEN CHARLOTTE ISLANDS, but no specimen has been seen since 1920 and it is assumed to be extinct.

Maggie Paquet

CARL, G. Clifford, marine biologist (b 1908, Vancouver; d 27 Mar 1970, Victoria). He earned his Master's degree from UBC in 1932 and a PhD from the Univ of Toronto in 1937. After spending a few years conducting research on shellfish and freshwater fisheries for the Fisheries Research Board of Canada, he joined the Provincial Museum of Natural History and Anthropology (now the ROYAL BC MUSEUM) in 1940. As director of the museum from 1942 to 1969, he oversaw its expansion into its new building in 1968. He was an active member of the Audubon Wildlife Society and wrote a series of handbooks on reptiles, amphibians and marine life in BC. Not long before his death he stepped down from his director's position to concentrate on establishing a Hall of the Sea exhibit at the museum.

Dianne Mackay

CARLIN was a settlement on the CPR 15 km north of SALMON ARM. It was named after Michael B. Carlin, manager of Columbia River Lumber Co, which had a RAILWAY LOGGING operation here in the early 1900s. The community hall still stands and the old Carlin school is preserved at THREE VALLEY GAP.

AS

CARMANAH VALLEY, on the west side of VANCOUVER ISLAND, is named for Carmanah Crk, which crosses the WEST COAST TRAIL just south of NITINAT LAKE. The name comes from a former Ditidaht (*see* NUU-CHAH-NULTH) village at the creek mouth and means "canoe landing in front." The Carmanah watershed contains an ancient old-growth RAIN FOREST of towering Sitka SPRUCE, western HEMLOCK and western red CEDAR. Some of the cedars are 1,000 years old, and the Carmanah Giant (95.8 m) is considered the world's tallest Sitka spruce and the tallest tree in Canada (*see also* TREES, GIANT). The Carmanah rain forest contains nearly twice the biomass of tropical rain forests. A number of "new" insects were discovered in its canopy by Dr Neville Winchester, and marbled MURRELET nests have also been documented here. In 1988 the valley was the centre of a controversy between government and environmentalists who wished it preserved from LOGGING. In 1990 the province created Carmanah Pacific Provincial PARK to preserve the lower portions of the watershed. More of the Carmanah Valley and the lower part of the adjacent WALBRAN VALLEY were added in 1995 to form Carmanah–Walbran Provincial Park (164.5 km²). *See also* ENVIRONMENTAL MOVEMENT.

CARMI, pop 44, a GOLD MINING settlement on the KETTLE VALLEY RWY 50 km southeast of KELOWNA, was named after Carmi, IL, home of postmaster J.C. Dale. Dale staked a claim here and laid out a townsite. A mine operated intermittently from 1900 to 1934; a concentrator was built in 1920. LOGGING took place in the 1950s. Carmi was mostly abandoned by the 1970s.

AS

CARNARVON TERMS were a set of proposals submitted in 1874 by the British colonial secretary Lord Carnarvon in an attempt to resolve the dispute between BC and the federal government over the construction of the transcontinental railway. BC had been promised a rail link as a precondition of its entry into CONFEDERATION in 1871. When the Liberal administration of Prime Minister Alexander Mackenzie weakened its commitment to the project, British Columbians grew impatient. In London BC's agent general Gilbert SPROAT persuaded Carnarvon to arbitrate. Both Ottawa and VICTORIA agreed at least to consider a proposal. The resulting Carnarvon Terms suggested that BC agree to an extension of the rail deadline to 1890 in return for an immediate beginning of construction on a rail line between NANAIMO and ESQUIMALT, a wagon road and telegraph line from Red River to the Pacific and a promise by Ottawa to spend $2 million annually on rail construction. These terms were not acceptable to the federal Liberals, who instead offered to pay BC $750,000 as compensation for the delay. BC refused, and in Jan 1876 the legislature voted to secede from Canada. Cooler heads prevailed and the railway was eventually completed in 1885. The $750,000 was paid in the form of a cash bonus to the syndicate that built the ESQUIMALT & NANAIMO RWY. *See also* CPR, FEDERAL–PROVINCIAL RELATIONS.

CARNEY, Patricia "Pat," economist, journalist, politician (b 26 May 1935, Shanghai, China). Her grandparents were homesteaders in the OKANAGAN VALLEY and she grew up in NELSON. After studying economics at UBC she graduated with an MA in regional planning and worked as a journalist for local NEWSPAPERS. In 1970 she started her own consulting business in the Northwest Territories. She served as Conservative MP for Vancouver Centre from 1980 to 1988; after the Conservatives were elected in 1984 she was minister of energy, mines and resources; minister for international trade; and president of the treasury board. She was deeply involved in negotiations leading to free trade agreements with the US. In 1990 she was appointed to the Senate. Her memoirs, *Trade Secrets*, were published in 2000.

CAROUSEL THEATRE CO, founded in VANCOUVER in 1974 by Elizabeth Ball, its first artistic director, specializes in presenting Shakespeare and other classical works to young audiences. It is based at the Waterfront Theatre on GRANVILLE ISLAND where it operates the city's oldest and largest THEATRE school. The company visits schools and tours productions throughout western Canada.

CARP LAKE PROVINCIAL PARK (193.4 km²) lies in boreal forest on the Nechako Plateau 150 km north of PRINCE GEORGE, just west of MCLEOD LAKE. The park was established in 1973 and is popular for camping and FISHING. Fur traders, including Simon FRASER, used the LAKE as an important source of food fish in the early 1800s. A historic fur trade trail connected old Fort McLeod (now McLeod Lake) and FORT ST JAMES; parts of it can still be found in the park. *See also* FUR TRADE, LAND-BASED; PARKS, PROVINCIAL.

CARPENTER LAKE, 46 km², is a reservoir created between 1955 and 1960 by the construction of the Terzhagi Dam on the BRIDGE R, west of LILLOOET. The narrow lake, rimmed by mountains, stretches 64 km behind the dam west to GOLD BRIDGE. It was created to regulate the flow in the river to the HYDROELECTRIC development at SHALALTH on SETON LK. The dam is named for Karl Terzhagi, the project engineer; the lake is named for the American engineer who designed much of the power project. Three tiny MINING communities—Wayside, Congress and MINTO CITY—were submerged by the creation of the lake, as were many hunting and FISHING sites belonging to the ST'AT'IMX (Lillooet) people. *See also* LAKES.

CARR, Emily, artist, writer (b 13 Dec 1871, Victoria; d 2 Mar 1945, Victoria). She began her art studies in VICTORIA and in 1891 went to San Francisco to study painting at the California School of Design. After returning to Victoria 2 years later, she made a living teaching art. In the summer of 1898 she visited UCLUELET, where her sister Lizzie was becoming a missionary. This seems to be where her fascination with aboriginal subjects began, drawing the local NUU-CHAH-NULTH (Nootka), who named her Klee Wyck ("the one who laughs"). From 1899 to 1904 she studied at the Westminster School of Art in London, England, where ill health led to a stay in a sanatorium. Once again back in BC, she

Emily Carr in her studio, 1936.
Harold Mortimer-Lamb/BC Archives D-06009

moved to VANCOUVER in 1906 and lived there for the next few years teaching painting. She also resumed her summer visits to coastal villages. In 1907 she travelled to Alaska, where she was impressed by the TOTEM POLES at Sitka. An encounter with the American artist Theodore Richardson confirmed her desire to make aboriginal cultures the focus of her art. After a sojourn in Paris from 1910 to 1911 she returned to Vancouver to teach and show her paintings. However, she failed to gain support for her work and in 1913 she abandoned her attempts to be a professional artist; she returned to Victoria and began earning a living as a boardinghouse keeper, an occupation that preoccupied her for the next 15 years. In 1927 the National Gallery in Ottawa was preparing to mount a major exhibition of West Coast art. Eric Brown, the gallery director, visited Victoria and saw Carr's paintings; later he accepted some for the exhibit. In November she travelled east for the opening. In Toronto she met members of the Group of Seven and was so encouraged, particularly by Lawren HARRIS, that she resumed painting and making summer excursions along the coast. Under Harris's influence she began to concentrate less on aboriginal subjects and more on the brooding coastal landscape. During the 1930s she began to gain the reputation that has since moved her into the front ranks of Canadian painters. As her health declined following a heart attack in 1937, she turned to writing. Her first book of short non-fiction pieces, *Klee Wyck*, appeared in 1941 and won a GOV GEN'S LITERARY AWARD. It was followed by 2 more books published before her death—*The Book of Small* (1942) and *The House of All Sorts* (1944)—and four collections published posthumously: *Growing Pains* (1946), *Pause* (1953), *The Heart of a Peacock* (1953) and *Hundreds and Thousands* (1966).

CARRALL, Robert William Weir, doctor, politician (b 2 Feb 1837, Woodstock, ON; d 19 Sept 1879, Woodstock, ON). He received his medical degree from McGill Univ in Montreal in 1859 and served as an army surgeon with the Union forces during the American Civil War. In 1865 he moved west to BC. He settled in NANAIMO, then established a medical practice in BARKERVILLE in 1867. He got involved in politics as a proponent of CONFEDERATION with Canada. Elected to the legislative council in 1868 he was one of 3 delegates from BC chosen by Gov Anthony MUSGRAVE to travel to Ottawa in 1871 to discuss the terms of union. He was also one of BC's first 3 federal senators, remaining a member of the Upper House until his death. Shortly before he died, he introduced the bill making July 1 the anniversary of Confederation, Canada's national holiday.

CARRIER; *see* DAKELH.

CARROLLS LANDING, a fruit and vegetable farming (*see* AGRICULTURE) settlement 25 km south of NAKUSP on the east side of the COLUMBIA R between Upper and Lower ARROW LKS, was submerged when the KEENLEYSIDE DAM raised water levels. It was named for Mike Carroll, a local landowner. A post office operated here from 1938 to 1968. *AS*

CARSON, a tiny settlement and crossing at the US border 5 km southwest of GRAND FORKS, was established on the Vancouver, Victoria & Eastern Rwy (*see* GREAT NORTHERN RWY) in the 1890s. Named after Isabella Carson McLaren, mother of local MP J. Carson, it was formerly known as Kettle River. *AS*

CARTER-COTTON, Francis Lovett, journalist, politician (b 11 Oct 1843, London, England; d 20 Nov 1919, Vancouver). Fleeing from creditors in Colorado, he arrived in VANCOUVER in 1886 and secured a job with the *Advertiser* newspaper. The next year he bought the paper and merged it with a competitor, the *News*, continuing as editor and owner of the *Daily News-Advertiser* until 1910. It was one of the leading papers in the city, later becoming part of the merger that created the VANCOUVER SUN. He was elected to the provincial legislature for Vancouver in 1890 as an independent, though he was a federal Conservative. Carter-Cotton has been described as a middle-class reformer opposed to the granting of public resources to private companies. He was minister of finance in Charles SEMLIN's government (1898–1900) and was involved in a bitter feud in CABINET with Attorney General Joseph MARTIN. His political career was interrupted by a defeat in the 1900 election, but he was re-elected in RICHMOND in 1903 and served as president of the Executive Council in Richard MCBRIDE's cabinet from 1904 to 1910. He left the cabinet to concentrate on business affairs, retiring from politics completely in 1916. Carter-Cotton served as the first chancellor of UBC (1912–18) and the first chair of the Vancouver Harbour Commission. *See also* NEWSPAPERS.

CARTIER, MOUNT (el 2,608 m) looms over the site of a former settlement and station with the same name on the CPR's ARROWHEAD branch 11 km south of REVELSTOKE. Many UKRAINIAN farmers moved into the district in the early 1900s and operated DAIRY FARMS and ranches (*see* CATTLE INDUSTRY), providing dairy and meat products for Revelstoke and surrounding communities. The area is now underwater as a result of the KEENLEYSIDE DAM. The mountain was named for Sir George-Etienne Cartier, one of the "fathers of Confederation." *AS*

CARVER, Brent, actor (b 17 Nov 1951, Cranbrook). He is one of the most acclaimed stage performers to come out of the BC Interior. He came to VANCOUVER to attend UBC but dropped out after his third year in 1972 to join a children's THEATRE troupe at the VANCOUVER PLAYHOUSE. After tackling a variety of roles in film, stage and television—one of his early parts was in the CBC sitcom *Leo and Me* with Michael J. FOX in 1976—he established his national reputation performing in the classics at the Stratford Festival in Ontario during the 1980s. He has won 4 Dora Awards for best actor and a Gemini Award for his television work. In 1992 he went to Broadway in New York, starring in the hit musical *Kiss of the Spider Woman*, for which he won a Tony Award. He has continued to compile a long list of credits, both stage and film, that highlight his great versatility as an actor–singer–dancer.

CARY, George Hunter, politician (b 16 Jan 1832, Essex, England; d 16 July 1866, London, England). A lawyer in London, he was appointed attorney general for the new gold colony of BC in 1859. When he arrived in VICTORIA, Gov James DOUGLAS made him attorney general for VANCOUVER ISLAND as well. Within 4 months of his arrival he defeated Amor DE COSMOS in an election and entered the House of Assembly as the representative from Victoria. From 1860 to 1863 he served capably as the Island's minister of finance as well as attorney general. In 1861 new regulations required that he resign his post as attorney general on the mainland because he did not live there. Cary was a vain, outspoken man who was widely disliked in the colony. His term of office was marked by financial irregularities that led to his resignation as attorney general of Vancouver Island in 1864. By the next year his eccentricity had become mental illness, and he left Victoria with his wife to return to England in September. While he lived in Victoria, Cary spent more lavishly than his resources allowed; one of his indulgences was CARY CASTLE, a large mansion overlooking JUAN DE FUCA STRAIT. The government purchased it in 1865 and it was subsequently used as the residence of LIEUTENANT GOVERNORS until it was destroyed by fire in 1899. *See also* VANCOUVER ISLAND, COLONY OF and COLONIAL GOVERNMENT.

CARY CASTLE was the original name for Government House, the official residence of the LIEUTENANT GOVERNOR in VICTORIA. The first Cary Castle was built in the 1860s as the home of George Hunter CARY, attorney general of VANCOUVER ISLAND. It was sold to the Crown in 1865 as a residence for the colonial governor, and when BC became a province in 1871 it became the home of the lt gov. Destroyed by fire in 1899, it was replaced by a new residence, which became known officially as Government House. It too was destroyed by fire, in 1957, and was replaced by the third building to stand on the site.

CARY FIR is a mythical giant tree said to have been harvested in 1895 in Lynn Valley on the north shore of BURRARD INLET by George Cary, a local logger. The story began as a hoax in 1922, supported by a photograph of a very large tree and by fake statistics: overall length 417 feet (127.2 m), diameter of stump 25 feet (7.6 m), height to first limb 300 feet (91.5 m), diameter of bole at first limb 9 feet (2.75 m), thickness of bark 16.5 inches (41.9 cm), age 1,800 years. The claim was debunked by J.S. MATTHEWS, the VANCOUVER archivist, and by George Cary himself; but British Columbians' desire to believe they once possessed the world's tallest tree is such that the myth has proved difficult to arrest. For

George Cary poses on a ladder in the famous 1922 photograph that launched the hoax of the world's tallest fir tree. VPL 1236

many years the Cary Fir was listed in the *Guinness Book of World Records*. In fact the alleged dimensions of the tree were not so exaggerated as to be beyond belief and may have been based on the Lynn Valley Tree, an actual tree that rivalled the Cary Fir. (*See also* TREES, GIANT).   *A.C. Carder*
Reading: A.C. Carder, *Forest Giants of the World*, 1995.

CASCADE is a border crossing south of CHRISTINA LK on the KETTLE R, 20 km east of GRAND FORKS. From 1895 it was a key stopping place on the wagon road linking Marcus, WA, and the Spokane Falls & Northern Railroad with settlements on the Canadian side of the border. The construction of the COLUMBIA & WESTERN RWY between CASTLEGAR and MIDWAY (1898–99) raised false hopes that a SMELTER would be constructed. A power dam at the river gorge supplied HYDROELECTRICITY to early COPPER mining camps in the BOUNDARY DISTRICT. Successive fires destroyed most of the old business area.

CASCADE MOUNTAINS extend roughly from CULTUS LK east to the SIMILKAMEEN R and north from the US border to LYTTON. They consist of 3 ranges: the Skagit on the west, the Hozameen and the Okanagan. Dividing the FRASER R canyon from the OKANAGAN VALLEY, they are the northern end of an American range that runs south to California and includes several volcanic peaks, among them Mt BAKER and Mt St Helens. There are no active volcanoes in the BC section. The COQUIHALLA HWY and the HOPE–PRINCETON HWY run through the Cascades, which mark a transition from the wet coastal forests to the drier Interior ranges and plateaus. MANNING, Skagit Valley and CATHEDRAL PROVINCIAL PARKS along the US border are all in the Cascades.

CASCADIA has two meanings. It is first of all a geographical region (*see* PHYSICAL GEOGRAPHY), encompassing BC, Washington, Oregon, Idaho and northern California. The region has characteristics that differ from the rest of the continent, making it a distinct geographical, economic, cultural and ecological unit. Some people argue that landscape is more important than political boundaries, and believe that all parts of the region share a common identity arising from a shared geography. The name comes from the CASCADE MTS that join the US and Canadian sections. It began to be applied to the region in the 1970s, and has found limited support among ENVIRONMENTALISTS and business people who wish to create common economic opportunities. Cascadia is also a term applied by geologists to a chain of volcanic mountains running along the west side of N America from northern California to the top end of VANCOUVER ISLAND. This unstable zone contains such familiar peaks as Garibaldi and Meager in BC and Mt BAKER across the border in Washington. It is characterized by a slab of ocean crust known as the Juan de Fuca Plate, slowly subducting below the continent and triggering EARTHQUAKES and volcanic activity as it does so.

CASCARA (*Rhamnus purshiana*), one of the largest of the buckthorn family of deciduous trees and shrubs, occurs on the South Coast, on VANCOUVER ISLAND and in the COLUMBIA R basin. The fruit is purplish-black and cherry-like. Spanish missionaries called the tree cascara sagrada, "holy bark," a reference to the fact that aboriginal people used the bark medicinally as a laxative. Today the bark is the source of the drug cascara.

Cascara.
Kim LaFave drawing

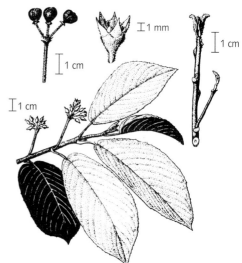

Clockwise from top left: Fruit, flower, winter twig and flowering branch of the cascara.
© T.C. Brayshaw

CASPACO, 18 km southeast of PRINCE RUPERT on the north shore of Inverness Passage at the mouth of the SKEENA R, was the site of the Cassiar Cannery, which operated from 1903 to 1983 and had the longest continuous existence of any cannery on the BC coast (*see* SALMON CANNING). The name is an abbreviation for Cassiar Packing Co.   *AS*

CASSIAR is an abandoned townsite in the mountainous northwestern Interior 130 km south of the Yukon, just off the STEWART–Cassiar Hwy (*see also* ROADS & HWYS). It was also the name given to a MINING district centred on DEASE LK farther south, the scene of a frenetic GOLD RUSH in the 1870s (*see also* LAKETON; CENTREVILLE). Cassiar townsite, which reached a peak population of 1,500, grew up around an ASBESTOS mine that opened in 1952. Forty years later, when the mine closed, everything in the town was sold or moved and Cassiar disappeared. The name derives from the aboriginal name for nearby McDame Crk (*see* MCDAME, HENRY).

CASSIAR was a wooden-hulled UNION STEAMSHIP CO vessel, built by Wallace Shipyards (*see* BURRARD DRY DOCK) in FALSE CREEK, VANCOUVER, and

The steamer Cassiar, the loggers' palace.
CVA Bo.P451

launched in Sept 1901. Known familiarly as the "loggers' palace," it was used mainly to transport loggers between their isolated coastal camps and the saloons of Vancouver. The vessel itself was equipped with a barroom, and it made many raucous voyages. It was 36.5 m long and had a gross weight of 537 tonnes and capacity for 144 passengers. The *Cassiar* retired in 1923 after cruising almost 1.4 million km, and eventually became a floating dance hall in Washington state.

CASSIDY is an abandoned COAL mining town 13 km south of NANAIMO on VANCOUVER ISLAND. It was built in 1918 by the Granby Consolidated Mining, Smelting & Power Co, the same year the company opened a mine at the site to produce coal to fuel its COPPER SMELTER at ANYOX. Unlike most MINING camps, it was a planned community with company-built bungalows on wide lots, parks and landscaped roadways. The mine closed in 1932. A few years later the buildings were auctioned. *See also* COAL MINING, VANCOUVER ISLAND.

CASTILLOU, Henry, jurist (b 1896, Merritt; d Apr 1967). He was born on his family's Coldwater Ranch and was running his own packtrain when he was 17 years old, but he took up law as a profession. As one of the first lawyers in BC to work on ABORIGINAL RIGHTS, he was advisor to the N American Indian Brotherhood and represented BC bands before the Indian Claims Commission. He capped his legal career by serving as a County Court judge for the CARIBOO during 1950-60, based in WILLIAMS LAKE. An amateur anthropologist, he owned a large collection of aboriginal artifacts, most of which were donated to UBC after his death. He also had a great interest in RODEO and often acted as master of ceremonies or judge at Cariboo events, including the WILLIAMS LAKE Stampede. Known as the Cowboy Judge, he invariably wore cowboy boots and hat and a fringed buckskin jacket.

CASTLE ROCK is the centre of a small ranching district on the west bank of the FRASER R, 50 km northwest of WILLIAMS LAKE in the CARIBOO. A post office operated here between 1916 and 1951, and a school was opened in 1922. AS

CASTLEDALE, formerly known as Beard Crk, was a farming settlement 45 km southeast of GOLDEN on the COLUMBIA R. It had a school by 1914, a post office from 1914 to 1944, and a population of 60 in 1930. The site is deserted today. AS

CASTLEGAR, city, pop 7,027, is in the KOOTENAY near the south end of ARROW LK at the confluence of the KOOTENAY and COLUMBIA rivers about halfway between Calgary and VANCOUVER. The name is a combination of the Gaelic word *gar*, meaning rock, and *castle*, after the shape of a large rock formation nearby. The FUR TRADE explorer David THOMPSON camped on the site in 1811 on his return from the mouth of the

Columbia. The community got its start in the 1890s as the GOLD mining centre of W Waterloo, now S Castlegar. In 1902 the CPR built a railway bridge across the Columbia and laid track to TRAIL. The station, located here, was called Kinnaird after a prominent CPR shareholder. The site developed as a service centre and later as a focus of the FOREST INDUSTRY. The Celgar pulp mill (*see* PULP & PAPER) was built in 1959 and modernized in the 1990s; a SAWMILL has also contributed to the economy. DOUKHOBORS had a large community called Ootischenia ("valley of consolation") where the AIRPORT opened in 1945. The Doukhobor Village Museum is nearby, as is Zuckerberg Island Heritage Park with its unusual Russian house; Alexander Zuckerberg was a Russian engineer who arrived in 1931 to teach school for the Doukhobors. On 1 Jan 1974 the town of Castlegar amalgamated with Kinnaird to become a city. A campus of Selkirk College (*see* COMMUNITY COLLEGES) is located here, and in the winter there is excellent SKIING at nearby RED MT and WHITEWATER.

CATBIRD; *see* MIMIC THRUSH.

CATES TOWING, formally C.H. Cates and Sons Ltd, is a major tugboat company founded on the waterfront in N VANCOUVER by Charles Henry Cates (1859–1938). Cates arrived in VANCOUVER during the 1880s and built the first wharf on the north shore of BURRARD INLET. He used his fleet of tugboats to haul stone from quarries at GIBSONS and SQUAMISH. After Vancouver was destroyed by fire in 1886, Cates's tugboats transported the construction materials needed to rebuild the city. He incorporated the tug company under his own name in 1913; it took its present name in 1921, when his sons joined the firm. The fleet of pug-nosed little tugs—with "Cates" emblazoned in large white letters along each hull—specialized in assisting ships while docking and became one of the most recognizable images of the Vancouver harbour. The 3 boys—John Henry, Charles Warren and James—were all certified sea captains. John Henry Cates (1896–1986) served in the merchant marine during WWI and was elected to the legislature as a member of the COALITION GOVERNMENT in 1945. He served in the legislature for 7 years, 3 of them as labour minister. John Henry's wife Carrie Cates (1905–77) was also active in politics, serving as a 3-term mayor of N Vancouver during the 1960s. Charles Warren Cates (1899–1960) was also a mayor of N Vancouver and served as president of the BC Tugboat Owners Association. James Cates (1909–67), the youngest son, became vice-president of the family firm and served briefly as a N Vancouver alderman in the 1960s. Cates Park in N Vancouver is named for the family. In 1992 C.H. Cates and Sons was bought by Dennis Washington, a Montana businessman and owner of WASHINGTON MARINE GROUP. Washington retained the Cates name and the company continues to operate from its original N Vancouver location. *See also* TOWBOATING.

Capt Charles Henry Cates, founder of Cates Towing. CVA Port.P741

CATHEDRAL GROVE is a small remnant stand of western red CEDAR and DOUGLAS FIR 16 km east of PORT ALBERNI, bisected by Hwy 4. The trees survived a FOREST FIRE that ravaged the area 300 years ago. Some of them are more than 800 years old and 75 m tall. The grove attracts some

Cathedral Grove, Vancouver Island. Roy Luckow photo

200,000 visitors annually. It was donated to the public by H.R. MACMILLAN and forms part of the 1.36 km² MacMillan Provincial PARK (est 1947).

CATHEDRAL PROVINCIAL PARK (332.7 km²) is in the CASCADE MTS adjacent to the US border southwest of KEREMEOS. The park features 5 turquoise alpine LAKES: Quiniscoe, Pyramid, Glacier, Lake of the Woods and Ladyslipper. The park also contains interesting rock formations, including a jumble of columnar basalt formations known as the Devil's Woodpile and a wind-eroded granite formation called Stone City. There are extensive blooms of WILDFLOWERS in summer. The park is named for Cathedral Mt (2,800 m); the core of the park is accessible by hiking trails. Part of the movie *Clan of the Cave Bear* was filmed in the park. *See also* PARKS, PROVINCIAL.

CATTLE INDUSTRY in BC contributes about $700 million to the economy and supports an estimated 12,000 jobs. In 1995 there were 268,000 beef cows in the province.

The HBC first brought cattle to NEW CALEDONIA in the 1830s to feed employees at its trading posts in the Interior, but the cattle industry did not begin until the wholesale importation of cattle, mainly from Oregon, during the GOLD RUSH years, 1858–68. Cattle in western Oregon were a mix of California cattle, some of which were the small Spanish black (though not necessarily longhorn), with Durhams and shorthorns driven over the Oregon Trail from the East. As the demand for beef dwindled with the waning of the gold rush, many of the drovers, especially those whose British origins qualified them to pre-empt land, decided to remain in BC. The government made it as easy as possible to acquire land for ranching and made Crown land available for pastoral leases. The excellent bunch grass ranges of the CARIBOO and the THOMPSON and OKANAGAN valleys were enthusiastically acquired by those intending to stay on as ranchers, and by the late 1870s the MERRITT and

Cattle roundup in the N Okanagan, fall 1888.
Vernon Museum 5021

CHILCOTIN areas were also being settled for ranching. The post-gold rush economic doldrums of the 1870s made ranching a difficult proposition and many small ranchers struggled to survive, but those who did so were able to take advantage of the demand for beef created by the construction of the CPR in the 1880s. The opportunity to feed construction crews, and the potential access to distant markets once the railway was completed, stimulated the formation of large enterprises such as the DOUGLAS LAKE CATTLE CO and the GANG RANCH. These companies had large amounts of capital and their own butcher shops in the large urban centres.

The completion of the railway brought widespread immigration to BC and expanding markets for beef. This took some pressure off the bunch grass ranges, which by the 1890s were becoming severely overgrazed. In order to supply the new markets, especially the year-round demand for beef, ranchers began to grow more extensive forage crops, principally alfalfa, to facilitate stall feeding for the winter market. At the same time the imposition of 90-day quarantine for all beef coming from the US between 1890 and 1897 assured local ranchers of a near monopoly in the expanding cities on the coast.

Increased immigration also put pressure on ranchers to subdivide their holdings to open up the land for settlement. As a result, in the Okanagan Valley and to a lesser extent in the Thompson, many large ranches were sold off for orchard lands. The construction of the Pacific Great Eastern Rwy (*see* BC RAIL) from QUESNEL to SQUAMISH in 1912 and the Canadian Northern Rwy line through the N Thompson River valley to VANCOUVER in 1915 provided new districts with easy access to coastal markets. By the end of WWI all ranching areas except the east Chilcotin were within reach of rail transportation. As well, the advent of motor vehicles made it possible to truck cattle to markets and to regional centres such as WILLIAMS LAKE, KAMLOOPS and ASHCROFT.

During WWI the number of cattle in BC increased to about 190,000 head, and soon after the war, almost all the land suited for cattle raising had been acquired. The larger ranches consolidated their holdings by buying up smaller ones, particularly land that had been granted to returned soldiers. By 1956 there were 332,702 head of cattle in the province. Up until the mid-1950s, almost all the cattle raised in the Interior were shipped to the Lower Mainland. But in 1956, thanks to a surplus of grain on the prairies, about half of all BC cattle were shipped across the ROCKY MTS for finishing. This marked a change: from cattle finished on grass and shipped directly to market, to cattle finished on grain at feedlots. The trend continued, and by the end of the 20th century cow/calf raising was the mainstay of the BC cattle industry, while much of the backgrounding and finishing were done outside the province. *Ken Mather*

CAUX, Jean "Cataline," packer (b 1832, Oleron, France; d Oct 1922, Hazelton). He arrived in the Fraser Canyon with a pack train from Oregon in 1858, and for the next 54 years he ran supply trains into the MINING camps of the Interior, first from ASHCROFT, then QUESNEL and finally from HAZELTON. Caux was illiterate but was a shrewd businessman who conducted his affairs in a mix of Spanish, French, English and various aboriginal tongues. In 1912 he sold his business and retired to a cabin overlooking the BULKLEY R.

CAVENDISH, Nicola, actor (b 11 Nov 1952, Cirencester, England). She accompanied her parents to Canada at age 6 and grew up in PENTIC-

Beef cattle, 100 Mile House, 1994.
Roy Luckow photo

TON. A graduate of the THEATRE program at UBC, she has established herself as a leading BC actor since launching her professional career in 1975 at the VANCOUVER PLAYHOUSE. In the 1980s she appeared in many plays, including *Pygmalion* at the prestigious Shaw Festival in Niagara-on-the-Lake, ON, and she starred in the CBC television series *Red Serge*. In 1986 she went to Broadway with a production of *Blithe Spirit* and starred in the popular show *Shirley Valentine* across Canada in 1990–92. She won a Montreal Critics Award for best actress for her performance in the English-language premiere of *For the Pleasure of Seeing Her Again*, by the Quebec playwright Michel Tremblay, in which she toured Canada in 1999–2000. Her film credits include *The Grocer's Wife*, which earned her a Genie in 1993, *My American Cousin* (1985) and the 1993 television production of *The Diviners*. She also wrote two popular ARTS CLUB Christmas productions, *It's Snowing on Saltspring* and *Blowin' on Bowen*.

Shannon Emmerson

CAVES; *see* KARST FORMATIONS.

CAVOUKIAN, Raffi, musician (b 8 July 1948, Cairo, Egypt). He went to Toronto with his family in 1958. He began his singing career on the coffee house circuit but gained success in the 1970s as a writer and performer of children's music. The appearance of his first record, *Singable Songs for the Very Young* (1976), contributed to a boom in the N American children's music market. In 1990 he moved to VANCOUVER; there he continued his musical career (he recorded 13 albums) and devoted much of his time to ENVIRONMENTAL issues. He was made a member of the Order of Canada in 1983 and has won many awards for his music.
Reading: Raffi Cavoukian, *Raffi: The Life of a Children's Troubador*, 1998.

CAWSTON, pop 420, is on the SIMILKAMEEN R 5 km southeast of KEREMEOS. The HBC opened a store here in 1860 in the home of the original homesteader, R.L. Cawston, and experimented with growing wheat. In 1864 F.X. RICHTER, a rancher, began raising cattle (*see* CATTLE INDUSTRY) in the area. Orcharding began in 1911 and today fruit growing is the main economic activity (*see* TREE FRUITS).

CAYCUSE is a former LOGGING centre on the south shore of COWICHAN LK at the mouth of Nixon Crk, about 55 km from DUNCAN on VANCOUVER ISLAND. It was the site of a logging camp from 1927 to 1998, making it the longest-operating logging camp in Canada; it may be preserved as a heritage site. The Caycuse Fir was a giant DOUGLAS FIR cut down by loggers in 1959; it turned out to be 1,266 years old. With a diameter of 3.6 m it was the third largest tree found in BC to that point (*see also* TREES, GIANT).

CBC; *see* CANADIAN BROADCASTING CORP.

CBC VANCOUVER CHAMBER ORCHESTRA is the only regularly performing radio orchestra

in N America. Founded in 1938 by Ira DILWORTH, it was led by John AVISON for its first 42 years. He was succeeded by the English conductor John Eliot Gardiner (1980–83); Mario Bernardi took over in 1983. A chamber orchestra consisting of 35 musicians drawn from other local ensembles, it is supported by CBC Radio, on which it is regularly heard across Canada. It also gives live concerts and is the most recorded orchestra in the country.

CECIL LAKE, 18 km northeast of FORT ST JOHN in the PEACE R district at the south end of Cecil Lk, is a farming community and service centre for the region settled in the 1930s. Many MENNONITES settled here. The lake itself, named for Maj Cecil M. Roberts, a federal government draughtsman and surveyor, is the site of much conservation activity by Ducks Unlimited.   *AS*

CEDAR tree is an evergreen belonging to the cypress family. The western red cedar (*Thuja plicata*) occurs along the coast and the western slopes of the ROCKY MTS and is distinguished by scale-like needles. At high altitudes it is stunted in size, but in other areas individual trees

Western red cedar.
© *T.C. Brayshaw*

are gigantic. The largest known specimen in Canada, 59.1 m tall and 6 m across, overlooks Cheewhat Lk in PACIFIC RIM NATIONAL PARK RESERVE on the west coast of VANCOUVER ISLAND. The yellow cedar (*Chamaecyparis nootkatensis*), also known as the cypress, is smaller and occurs in cold, wet areas of higher elevation. The name refers to the light, creamy colour of the soft, pungent wood. Coastal FIRST NATIONS used the yellow cedar for carving and making paddles, and prepared the soft inner bark for use in weav-

Yellow cedar in the Caren range, Sunshine Coast. Dean van't Schip photo

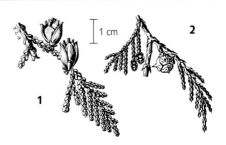

Branches of the western red cedar (1) and yellow cedar (2). © *T.C. Brayshaw*

ing clothing. It is a very long-lived species: one tree cut down on the SECHELT Peninsula was calculated to be almost 1,700 years old and there are a few specimens still standing in CYPRESS

Top: U'Mista Centre, a cedar longhouse at Alert Bay built in 1979. Vickie Jensen photo
Bottom: A modern home incorporating cedar decking, siding, shingles and railings.
Peter A. Robson photo

PROVINCIAL PARK that are over 1,200 years old. Western red cedar is highly valued in foreign lumber markets, especially Japan. Aboriginal people used it for TOTEM POLES, dugout CANOES and houses, as well as many types of containers and in weaving. Because the wood is resistant to decay it has been used commercially for BOATBUILDING and in many types of wood construction. In 1988 the western red cedar was named BC's official tree. *See also* ARCHITECTURE, ABORIGINAL; FOREST PRODUCTS.
Reading: Nancy J. Turner, *Plants in British Columbia Indian Technology*, 1979.

CEDAR, at the heart of a rural agricultural district 12 km southeast of NANAIMO on VANCOUVER ISLAND, was settled in the 1880s. By 1999 the area was still pleasantly bucolic, with rolling fields, farm animals at pasture, galleries, pubs, and bed and breakfast operations. *AS*

CEDARVALE, on the SKEENA R 72 km north of TERRACE, was a non-sectarian Christian village founded in 1888 by Robert TOMLINSON, an ANGLICAN CHURCH missionary. The mission, where FIRST NATIONS converts ran a SAWMILL and farmed, was modelled on METLAKATLA and was called Meanskinisht. The community divided after the death of its founder and the site was virtually abandoned.

CEEPEECEE is a former fish plant site at the head of ESPERANZA INLET not far from TAHSIS on the west coast of VANCOUVER ISLAND. The name refers to the Canadian Packing Corp Ltd, which built a reduction plant at the site in 1926 to take advantage of the appearance of swarms of pilchard (*see* SARDINE, PACIFIC) on the coast. NELSON BROS FISHERIES LTD bought the plant in 1934 and added a cannery 4 years later. A multi-ethnic community housed in shacks and bunkhouses developed, with a post office, a store and regular steamer service. Medical and spiritual help was available 2 km west at Esperanza, where a chapel, a hospital and a hotel were located. The fish plant closed in 1951 and almost all the buildings were destroyed by fire in 1954. By the close of the 20th century, only a small marine boat ways marked the site.

CELISTA, pop 950, on the north shore of SHUSWAP LK 28 km north of SALMON ARM, was named after Celesta Creek on SEYMOUR ARM (Selesta is a prominent SECWEPEMC ancestral name). Settled by British immigrants in the early 1900s, this quiet farming and LOGGING community has developed into a popular summer resort. *AS*

CENTRAL BC AIRWAYS was founded in 1945 by Russell BAKER, a bush pilot with Canadian Pacific Air Lines, and his partner Walter GILBERT. The new airline, based at PRINCE GEORGE and FORT ST JAMES, initially carried out surveys for the BC FOREST SERVICE, carried mail and supplied remote camps in the BC Interior. It got a flurry of welcome publicity in 1947 when Pierre BERTON hired Baker to fly him to the legendary "Headless Valley" of the S Nahanni R and wrote about it for the *VANCOUVER SUN*. CBCA shifted headquarters south to KAMLOOPS in 1949, then to VANCOUVER, where it prospered flying supplies to the ALCAN construction project at KITIMAT in the early 1950s. In 1953 CBCA began a period of rapid growth; the name was changed to PACIFIC WESTERN AIRLINES and the company bought up several regional carriers. As PWA it went on to become a major national airline and the core of Canadian Airlines International.

CENTREVILLE was a MINING camp on McDame Crk about 150 km north of DEASE LK. It

appeared in the fall of 1874 after Henry MCDAME, a prospector, struck GOLD and sparked a rush to what turned out to be the most productive creek in the CASSIAR district. In 1877 a miner washed out a 73-oz nugget, the largest ever found in BC. By the 1890s the gold was exhausted and the site abandoned.

CHALMERS, Angela, runner (b 6 Sept 1963, Brandon, MB). The daughter of a Scottish father and Sioux mother, she moved with her family to NANAIMO and later to VICTORIA. She won a spot on the 1984 Canadian Olympic team and in 1990 won gold medals in the 3,000 m and 1,500 m at the Commonwealth Games. Her most celebrated accomplishment was winning a bronze medal for Canada in the 3,000 m at the 1992 Barcelona Olympics. After winning another Commonwealth 3,000-m gold in 1994 (*see* BRITISH EMPIRE AND COMMONWEALTH GAMES), she finished fourth in the 1,500 m at the 1995 world championships, then set a women's record in the 10 km *VANCOUVER SUN* Run in 1996. Her career was interrupted in 1996 when a calf injury prevented her from competing at the Atlanta Olympics but she attempted a comeback 2 years later. Throughout her involvement in track and field, Chalmers acted as a spokesperson for aboriginal empowerment and anti-drugs and alcohol campaigns. *See also* TRACK AND FIELD. *SW*

CHAMBERLIN, James Arthur, aerospace designer (b 23 May 1915, Kamloops; d 8 Mar 1981, Houston, TX). After a childhood in KAMLOOPS, SUMMERLAND and VICTORIA, he moved with his family to Toronto. A graduate engineer from the Univ of Toronto and the Imperial College of Science and Technology in London, England, he joined Avro Canada, where he became chief technical designer on the ill-fated and controversial CF-105 Avro Arrow. When the Arrow project was cancelled in 1959 he joined the US space program. He designed the Gemini spacecraft and also played key roles in the Mercury program and the Apollo program, which landed the first humans on the moon.
Chris Gainor

CHANDLER, William, marathon runner (b 10 Feb 1883, Beautiful Plains, MB; d 1957). Running for the VANCOUVER Athletic Club he became one of N America's top marathoners. Almost unbeatable over distances of between 5 and 15 miles (8-24 km), he won the Pacific Coast Championship 4 times and consistently defeated the best runners the USA offered. The highlight of his career occurred in 1913 at the San Francisco International Race when he easily beat 15 marathoners dubbed the best on the continent. Also that year he set a Canadian 5-mile record in Vancouver. He was selected as an inaugural member of the BC SPORTS HALL OF FAME in 1966. *See also* TRACK AND FIELD. *SW*

CHAPMAN, Charles Winston "Chuck," basketball player (b 21 Apr 1911, Vancouver). He and his brother **Arthur "Art"** (b 28 Oct 1912,

Victoria; d 4 Feb 1986) grew up in a vibrant sporting environment in VICTORIA, training under Archie MCKINNON at the YMCA, playing FOOTBALL, LACROSSE and SOCCER and developing into the best Canadian BASKETBALL-playing siblings of the 20th century. In 1933 with Chuck as captain they led the Victoria Blue Ribbons/Dominoes basketball team to the first of 5 (1933, 1935, 1939, 1942 and 1946) national amateur championships. In 1936 the team lost the title to the Windsor Fords but the Chapmans and Doug PEDEN joined the Ontario team as Canadian representatives at the Berlin Olympics and played integral roles in securing the silver medal. The 1946 Dominoes, which also included Peden, Norm BAKER and Porky ANDREWS, was undefeated and is often cited as the best amateur club team in Canadian history. Chuck, widely considered after Baker the finest Canadian player in the first half of the 20th century, retired from playing at age 35. Art then coached, managed and played for the short-lived professional VANCOUVER Hornets for the 1947–48 season. Both brothers are members of the BC SPORTS HALL OF FAME. *SW*

CHAR (*Salvelinus* spp) belong to the Salmonidae family of fish, which includes SALMON (*Oncorhynchus* spp) and TROUT (*Salmo* spp). Like some trout, char have both freshwater and sea-run (anadromous) varieties. They are distinguished from trout by their smaller, brighter scales and light spots on a dark background (whereas trout have dark spots on a light background). Also they spawn primarily in fall,

Dolly Varden char. Phil Edgell photo; drawing courtesy Fisheries & Oceans Canada

while trout spawn in spring. There are 4 types of char. Dolly Varden (*Salvelinus malma*), widespread in coastal waters, seldom exceeds 3.5 kg in weight. Named for a character in a Charles Dickens novel, it is easy to catch; it was once shunned by anglers but has become quite highly regarded as a game fish. Bull trout (*S. confluentus*) primarily inhabit the Interior of the province, though distribution does extend to the coast in some of the larger watersheds. It is similar in appearance to Dolly Varden but can grow larger and has a flattened head. Brook trout (*S. fontinalis*) is a species transplanted from eastern Canada in 1908. The smallest char, it usually does not grow much beyond 2 kg, though it is a spirited game fish and delicious to eat. Lake trout (*S. namaycush*) is the largest species. It lives in some larger Interior lakes and remains in fresh water for life. It is not particularly popular with FLY FISHERS because it often inhabits waters that are too deep to be reached effectively with a fly and it is not widely available.

CHARLIE LAKE CAVE is an archaeological site in a rocky outcrop 9 km northwest of FORT ST JOHN, just off the ALASKA HWY. Stone artifacts and animal remains found in 1983 date back 11,500 years, making this the oldest dated human occupation in BC. The earliest occupants were bison hunters. (*See also* ARCHAEOLOGY.) The nearby community of Charlie Lake, a small service centre, was the site of a major Alaska Hwy construction camp during WWII. The lake, with good fishing for walleye, yellow perch and northern pike, was named for Charlie Chok or Big Charlie, father of Charlie Yahey, a DUNNE-ZA (Beaver) prophet. Yahey died in the early 1970s.

CHASE, village, pop 2,460, is at the west end of Little SHUSWAP LK on the TRANS-CANADA HWY, 58 km east of KAMLOOPS. It is named for Whitfield Chase, a carpenter from New York who began ranching and farming there in 1865. A townsite was developed in 1908 by the Adams River Lumber Co, which built what was at that time the largest SAWMILL in the Interior. The flourishing community was dealt a blow in 1925 when the mill closed; many families moved away. LOGGING continued to be a mainstay of the local economy, along with summer TOURISM. The ADAMS R, which has been known for its spectacular run of sockeye SALMON every 4 years, is nearby.

CHASE RIVER was a farming (*see* AGRICULTURE) and COAL MINING settlement at the mouth of the Chase R, 5 km south of NANAIMO on VANCOUVER ISLAND. A post office operated here from 1910 to 1919. Its name supposedly derives from an incident in 1852, when colonial authorities chased after a group of HALKOMELEM people. The location is now within Nanaimo city limits. AS

CHATHAM SOUND is a broad channel on the North Coast off PRINCE RUPERT, between the mainland and Dundas and several smaller islands. It connects the north end of HECATE STRAIT with PORTLAND INLET. It is named for John Pitt, second Earl of Chatham and First Lord of the British Admiralty from 1788 to 1794. The LIGHTHOUSE on Green Island in the sound, constructed in 1906, is the most northerly light on the coast.

CHEAKAMUS RIVER flows out of the lake of the same name located in GARIBALDI PROVINCIAL PARK north of VANCOUVER. The river snakes down out of the high mountains, then swings south to flow via Daisy Lk and Paradise Valley to its confluence with the SQUAMISH R near BRACKENDALE. Highway 99 and the BC RAIL main line both follow the river for much of the way between SQUAMISH and WHISTLER. Its clear, turbulent flow

makes it a popular destination for whitewater sports enthusiasts, as well as with anglers (*see* FISHING, SPORT). Every winter the banks of the river attract a large number of bald EAGLES, which congregate to feed on spawning salmon. Water levels in the lower river are controlled by a hydro dam at the outlet to Daisy Lk. The name means "salmon weir place" in the language of the SQUAMISH NATION, who formerly inhabited the river's banks.

CHEAM PEAK (el 2,107 m) towers over the upper FRASER VALLEY east of CHILLIWACK. One of the most prominent peaks in the valley, it was named from the STO:LO word meaning "wild strawberry place." The local people also know it as Lhilheqey, "the mother mountain," believed to have been the wife of nearby Mt BAKER. The surrounding smaller peaks are her children. According to legend, the local Sto:lo are descendants of the Mountain Goat People, who once lived inside the mountain. The community of Cheam was a crossroads and farming settlement on the old Yale Rd 5 km east of Chilliwack. The brothers Cory and John Ryder homesteaded in the area around 1870 and Cory Ryder operated a store. A post office operated here from 1891 to 1911. Cheam View is another small community, 17 km northeast of Cheam, on the banks of the FRASER R, where a post office operated from 1914 to 1957.

North face of Cheam Peak. Len Mackave photo

CHEE KYE, 10 km north of SQUAMISH, was a tiny LOGGING and farming settlement on the Pacific Great Eastern Rwy (*see* BC RAIL) where the Cheekye R joins the CHEAKAMUS R. The name—Squamish for "dirty place"—was originally applied to Mt Garibaldi and may refer to the appearance of the old snow on the mountainsides. AS

CHELOHSIN was a member of the UNION STEAMSHIP CO fleet of coastal freight/passenger vessels, built in Ireland in 1911. It initially serviced PRINCE RUPERT, but it was on the LOGGING camp run that it became one of the most familiar vessels on the coast during the inter-war period. It was 53.5 m long, had a gross weight of 1,021 tonnes and carried 191 passengers and 150 tons of freight. Its career ended one foggy night in Nov 1949 when, coming through the First Narrows into BURRARD INLET, it ran onto the rocks. It was salvaged and sold for scrap.

CHEMAINUS, town, pop 3,900, overlooks Stuart Channel on the east side of VANCOUVER ISLAND, between DUNCAN and NANAIMO. It is the main community in the district municipality of NORTH COWICHAN. The first farm settler, J.A.

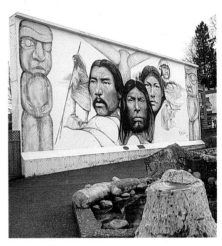

Mural in Chemainus. Walter Lanz/Image Makers

Grahames, arrived in the area in 1858; several others followed the next year. LOGGING became important and several SAWMILLS have operated here since 1862. COPPER mines at nearby Mt SICKER and a SMELTER at CROFTON boosted the local economy in the early 1900s. When its only sawmill closed in 1983 the town was threatened with devastation, but Chemainus launched a successful revitalization program, centred on a series of outdoor murals depicting the area's history. These became a major TOURIST attraction, drawing as many as 300,000 visitors a year. MACMILLAN BLOEDEL opened a new sawmill in 1985 and the FOREST INDUSTRY continued as an economic mainstay. A ferry connects Chemainus to THETIS and KUPER islands.

CHENEY, Nan (Lawson), artist (b 22 June 1897, Windsor, NS; d 3 Nov 1985, Vancouver). After studying in the US she became the first medical illustrator in Canada. She worked in Montreal from 1922 to 1924; there she met and married Dr Hill Cheney. The couple moved to Ottawa and she began painting landscapes. It was in Ottawa that she met Emily CARR in 1927 and began a correspondence that lasted many years. In 1937 she moved to VANCOUVER, where her husband joined the staff of the General Hospital and she continued painting and exhibiting her work. In 1951, then a widow, she joined the medical school at UBC as BC's first medical illustrator. Her correspondence with Carr was published in 1990 as *Dear Nan*, edited by Doreen Walker.

CHERRYVILLE, pop 500, 37 km east of VERNON in the foothills of the MONASHEE MTS, began in the 1860s to attract prospectors looking for GOLD in the rugged tributaries of the Shuswap R. A group of English immigrants attempted to establish a fruit-growing community named Camagna before WWI, but it failed and the site was abandoned temporarily. LOGGING and small ranches (*see* CATTLE INDUSTRY) have supported the local economy. The community is named for the wild cherries that grew in abundance.

CHESLATTA, 50 km south of BURNS LAKE between Cheslatta and FRANÇOIS lakes, is a rural agricultural district settled in about 1940 by MENNONITES from the prairies. The Cheslatta lakeshore, traditional territory of the Cheslatta Carrier people, was flooded in 1952 for ALCAN's KEMANO power project. The name is a DAKELH word and refers to a "small mountain." AS

CHETWYND, district municipality, pop 2,980, on the HART HWY in the Pine R Valley, 310 km north of PRINCE GEORGE, was known as Little Prairie by the first settlers who arrived in 1912. Development really began in the 1950s with the arrival of BC RAIL (then the Pacific Great Eastern Rwy) and the community was renamed after SOCIAL CREDIT Minister of Railways Ralph Chetwynd. It incorporated as a village in 1962 and as a district municipality in 1983. The local economy relies on SAWMILLING, a pulp mill (*see* PULP AND PAPER) and WESTCOAST ENERGY INC's Pine River gas plant (*see* OIL AND GAS INDUSTRY).

CHEZACUT, north of PUNTZI LAKE 140 km west of WILLIAMS LAKE, is a remote ranching and trapping district in the CHILCOTIN. The TSILHQOT'IN people lived here until the 1930s, when they moved to REDSTONE. The name means "birds without feathers," referring to Chilcotin Lk, where geese go to moult. AS

CHICKADEE is a small, plump, excitable bird with a short, strong bill and fluffy plumage. It nests in cavities in trees or stumps; one batch of up to 9 eggs hatches each year. Chickadees feed on INSECTS and seeds and often congregate in flocks of different species. In several areas of the south and central Interior, all 4 of BC's chickadee species may be found together. The black-capped chickadee (*Poecile atricapillus*) is the most widespread. With its solid black cap and grey back, it is a familiar visitor to bird feeders in winter and quickly learns to take feed from people's hands. In the southern Interior it overlaps with the mountain chickadee (*P. gambeli*), distinguishable in appearance by a white eyebrow line. The boreal chickadee (*P. hudsonicus*), a brown bird, occurs mainly in the north and at higher elevations elsewhere. The chestnut-backed chickadee (*P. rufescens*), with its red-brown back and sides, is the principal species along the coast and on VANCOUVER ISLAND.

CHILANKO FORKS, pop 123, a ranching settlement on the Chilanko R and CHILCOTIN Hwy 55 km west of ALEXIS CREEK, dates from the early 1900s. The Nygaard family founded the original ranch and sold it to Arthur Knoll in 1912. Part of the PUNTZI LAKE air base was built on the property. Today Ducks Unlimited have turned much of it into a WETLANDS reserve for waterfowl. Chilanko, also spelled Chilanco, is a TSILHQOT'IN word meaning "many beaver river." AS

CHILCOTIN, also known as the Chilcotin Plateau, lies in central BC, spreading west 300 km from the FRASER R to the COAST MTS. To the north it merges into the NECHAKO Plateau; to the south it is bounded by the BRIDGE R country. Because it lies in the lee of the Coast Mts, which block the flow of moisture-laden Pacific air, it has a drier CLIMATE than the coast and experiences greater extremes of temperature, which ranges from the occasional -40°C in winter to 20°C in summer. The land is undulating GRASSLAND and FORESTS dominated by lodgepole PINE. TWEEDSMUIR PROVINCIAL PARK sprawls along the western edge of the plateau, while Ts'ylos Provincial Park protects the mountainous wilderness in the south around CHILKO LK, the area's largest lake. The plateau drains east into the Fraser via the Chilcotin R (235 km) and its tributaries. Alexander MACKENZIE crossed the north end of the region in 1793 on his way to the Pacific but the FUR TRADE was not important here, nor was the GOLD RUSH, so the plateau remained isolated from the rest of the province until settlers began arriving on the eastern plateau in the early 1870s, principally ranchers attracted by the vast stretches of grassland. The plateau has been known as cattle country ever since (*see* CATTLE INDUSTRY), and BC's last frontier. Since the 1960s LOGGING has become important to the economy. Sport FISHING is excellent in the many LAKES well stocked with TROUT. The Chilcotin is the traditional territory of the TSILHQOT'IN nation, who over the years have congregated in 6 communities. Most of the relatively small population is clustered along Hwy 20, the Chilcotin Road, which bisects the plateau from WILLIAMS LAKE to the Pacific at BELLA COOLA. The road was built largely by private citizens because the government decided the terrain was impossible and the project too costly. At its western end the road descends from the plateau into the valley of the BELLA COOLA R down The Hill, a precipitous 9-km stretch of unpaved switchbacks with a steep dropoff to one side and a grade of up to 18%.

CHILCOTIN First Nation; *see* TSILHQOT'IN.

CHILCOTIN WAR was not a war at all, but an isolated outbreak of violence in Apr 1864 by a group of TSILHQOT'IN people against a work party cutting a road through their territory. The exact cause of the attack is not known. It occurred in an atmosphere of increasing unrest as survey parties and pack trains penetrated the CHILCOTIN plateau in the wake of the Cariboo GOLD RUSH. The newcomers did not ask the aboriginals' permission to cross their land and did not always treat the Tsilhqot'in with respect; the attack may have been an act of retaliation. Fourteen roadbuilders died in the assault. Two parties of troops were dispatched to bring in the fugitives. The hunt continued all summer, and 5 more white people were killed (among them Donald MCLEAN). Finally the Tsilhqot'in agreed to come to a parley. Instead they were seized and put on trial. Five Tsilhqot'in were found guilty by Judge Matthew BEGBIE and hanged in Oct 1864. Another was later hanged for one of the murders. The road was never built. More than a century later the provincial government officially apologized for the incident and in 1999 a plaque commemorating the graves of the 5 men hanged at QUESNEL was unveiled.

CHILD CARE MOVEMENT in BC goes back more than a century. The first recorded institution devoted exclusively to the care of children in the province was the Alexandra Orphanage, founded in 1894 in VANCOUVER. The first child care centre was opened at Cambie and Pender streets, also in Vancouver, and operated from 1910 to 1932. Known as the "City Creche," it accommodated groups of children of all ages for daytime care. It was organized by women who employed other women to do domestic work, and as such it functioned as both a child care service and an employment service for the working mothers. With the onset of the Depression the government of Vancouver closed the City Creche in 1932, and the Vancouver Day Nursery took over services for unemployed women and established a system of family homes where care was provided for the children of working mothers. In 1941 the National Employment Services assumed responsibility for assisting women with employment, leaving welfare institutions to take responsibility for regulating child care.

WWII had a huge impact on the child care movement throughout the 1940s, when a large number of women worked outside the home. Between 1943 and 1945 the federal government and the provinces set up child care centres under a cost-sharing plan in which 75% of the women receiving child care had to be employed by war industries in order for the centre to qualify for the federal funds. At war's end the number of working mothers grew, but many of them were no longer employed by the war industry, and federal funding was withdrawn.

To support the growing numbers of women entering the workforce, the Women's Voluntary Services in 1944 established a child care centre in Vancouver, and 2 more centres were financed entirely by contributions from the Women's Auxiliary to the Armed Forces. During this time, child care services also began to become available in smaller BC communities. The first places outside Vancouver to open licensed centres included SIDNEY (1943), OCEAN FALLS (1945) and PORT ALBERNI (1945). The 1940s brought the need for child care services to the public eye and drew attention to the alarming number of welfare organizations that had sprung up to protect abused and neglected children. Education of workers and licensing standards became fundamental principles in improving child care services in BC. In 1952 a committee to develop preschool education courses was established. Licensed centres began to flourish and spread under the direction of Mrs Whittaker, a member of the Haddon Play Group. This group provided opportunities for parents to discuss common concerns and for parents and children to socialize. In 1972, with a membership of 2,700, these play groups changed the name of their organization to the Council of Parent Participation Preschools of BC.

The 1950s–60s was a time of dedicated lobbying efforts by mothers and other women to institute formal training for early childhood educators. They persuaded UBC, the Vancouver School Board and the health and welfare ministry to provide such programs. Dr Neville Scarfe, Dean of the Faculty of Education, established the Education of Young Children Studies Program at UBC in 1956, and, in co-operation with Dean McCleary of the Faculty of Medicine, the Child Study Centre at UBC in 1961. UBC then began offering more courses in rural areas. The Northwest COMMUNITY COLLEGE established in TERRACE was the first smaller centre to offer a program in early childhood education.

Until 1966, eligibility for startup grants and assistance to parents seeking child care services was dependent on "the lessening, removal, or prevention of the causes and effects of poverty, child neglect," as stated in the regulations of the time. The child care movement that has been active since the 1970s has worked diligently to change such attitudes, which have prevailed in spite of much personal experience and public education to the contrary. Several advocate organizations have developed over that time. In the early 1970s the BC Child Care Federation—a coalition of day care workers, parents and community organizers—began requesting collective bargaining between community and province for a community-based child care service. The federation also produced a newsletter and organized province-wide conferences and political lobbying groups. In 1986, 2 societies, the NELSON District Child Care Society and the Nelson Family Daycare Society, amalgamated services to form the W KOOTENAY Family and Childcare Services Society. Other organizational efforts have been directed toward developing child care services that fulfill the needs of FIRST NATIONS communities in BC. By the start of the 21st century, programs were established in the Capilano, COWICHAN VALLEY, WILLIAMS LAKE, CARIBOO–CHILCOTIN, OKANAGAN VALLEY and SUNSHINE COAST regions.

In Nov 1999 the BC government released a discussion paper, "Building a Better Future for BC Kids," to generate public response to the issue of subsidized child care. Never in the history of the child care movement has the message been made clearer: 10,000 people responded, calling for a publicly funded system of care for all children, with the emphasis on families with young children. On 27 Mar 2000, the BC government made a commitment to begin to develop a publicly funded child care system in BC that entitled all children and families to affordable care. The spirit of the child care movement in BC has remained one of optimism tempered with caution. As the expectations of parents and other workers have evolved, the child care issue has become a growing priority, but policy changes at both the federal and provincial levels have been small, slow in coming and easily eroded. *Charmaine Saulnier*

CHILKAT BLANKET, or robe, is a unique form of Northwest Coast FIRST NATIONS weaving used as the regalia of high-ranking men and women. It is fringed on 4 of its 5 sides and woven by women from MOUNTAIN GOAT wool, which is spun into yarn and wrapped around strands of yellow CEDAR bark for strength. Representations of crests and more abstract figures are woven into the robes following pattern boards painted by men. The robe is worn like a cape on ceremonial occasions. According to tradition, Chilkat weaving originated with the TSIMSHIAN people and spread to the TLINGIT. The term *Chilkat blanket* was used by Europeans because, by the time trading began, such robes were mostly obtained from the Chilkat, a subdivision of the Tlingit. *See also* ART, NORTHWEST COAST ABORIGINAL.
Reading: Cheryl Samuel, *The Chilkat Dancing Blanket*, 1982.

CHILKO LAKE, 185.4 km², 83 km long, south of Hwy 20 in the CHILCOTIN, is the centrepiece of Ts'yl-os Provincial PARK (est 1994; 2,332.4 km²), a wilderness park jointly managed by the province and the TSILHQOT'IN First Nation. At 1,171 m elevation, Chilko is the highest major LAKE in BC. Its frigid blue-green waters drain north via the Chilko R, which has BC's third largest sockeye SALMON run. The river, flowing 107 km to join the Chilcotin R near ALEXIS CREEK, is a favourite with RIVER RAFTERS, especially the turbulent Lava Canyon section.

CHILKOOT PASS (el 1,067 m), on the border with Alaska in the far northwest corner of BC, was the main overland route to the Klondike goldfields. As many as 30,000 people struggled up the Chilkoot Trail from Dyea, AK, across the pass to BENNETT, BC, in 1897–98. After the GOLD RUSH the route fell into disuse until the 1960s, when it was rebuilt as a 53-km historic hiking trail, managed by Canadian Parks Service and the US National Park Service. The pass and trail draw their names from the Chilkat people, a TLINGIT nation, who used the route to trade with Interior groups.

CHILLIWACK is on the south side of the FRASER R, 100 km east of VANCOUVER. The name derives from the local Ts'elxwiqw people and is thought to mean "going back up," or returning to  the Chilliwack R from a visit to the Fraser. It is a growing retirement centre with an economy based on AGRICULTURE, service industries, food processing and lumber re-manufacturing. A Canadian Forces Base, established in 1942, was the largest single employer for many years until it closed in 1996. Farm settlement began in the 1860s. The townsite was originally known as Five Corners because of its location at a crossroads of several transportation routes. Incorporation of the area began with the Township of Chilliwhack in 1873 (the third oldest in BC). In 1883 the site at Five Corners was renamed Centreville and it was incorporated in 1908 as the City of Chilliwack. The two municipalities merged in 1980 to form the District of Chilliwack, which also includes smaller communities at SARDIS, VEDDER CROSSING, Promontory, YARROW, ROSEDALE and Greendale. The BC ELECTRIC RWY CO's INTERURBAN to Vancouver (1910–50) integrated Chilliwack into the region-

Summit of Chilkoot Pass, 1898. UBC BC713

al economy of the Lower Mainland and the city developed as a commercial centre for a rural farming district. Nearby CULTUS LK is a popular recreation area. Chilliwack's museum is located in the old city hall, a national historic site.

Population: 60,186
Rank in BC: 16th
Population increase since 1982: 47%
Date of incorporation: town 26 Apr 1873; city 26 Feb 1908; district 1 Jan 1980
Land area: 265.33 km²
Location: Fraser Valley Regional District
Economic base: agriculture, forestry, tourism

CHILLIWACK was one of BC's most successful pop-rock bands. The group began as the Classics in the mid-1960s and became the house band on CBC TV's *Music Hop* broadcast from VANCOUVER. Members were Howie Vickers (vocals), Glenn Miller (bass), Claire Lawrence (keyboards and saxophone) and Gary Taylor (drums). In 1967 Bill Henderson, guitarist and singer, and Ross Turney, a replacement for Taylor, joined the group, which became the Collectors. Their first album, *The Collectors*, recorded on Tom NORTHCOTT's New Syndrome label, was a major psychedelic hit on the West Coast in 1968 and earned the band opening slots for Frank Zappa,

The rock band Chilliwack, 1970 (l to r): Robbie King, Claire Lawrence, Bill Henderson, Ross Turney. Deni Eagland/Vancouver Sun

the Doors, Iron Butterfly, the Grateful Dead and Jefferson Airplane. Their second and last album was *Grass and Wild Strawberries*. By late 1969 the band was known as Chilliwack. During the next 2 decades it recorded 12 albums and had numerous national and international hits. As members came and went, only the leader, Bill Henderson, remained constant. The group received just one Juno Award, for producer of the year in 1982, shared by Brian "Too Loud" MacLeod and Henderson. During a break in the band's activities in the 1980s, Henderson expanded his production credits to acts such as Long John BALDRY, the Nylons, the Irish Rovers and the West End Girls, featuring his daughter Camille. In 1990 he

won a Genie Award for best original song, "When I Sing," from the movie *Bye Bye Blues*. In 1989 he formed UHF, an acoustic trio, with Shari ULRICH and Roy FORBES. In 1998 he and Forbes resurrected Chilliwack for several concert dates.   *Mike Harling*

CHILLIWACK LAKE, 12.1 km², is nestled in the CASCADE MTS next to the US border southeast of CHILLIWACK. It drains west through the VEDDER and Chilliwack rivers to the FRASER R. Originally occupied by the STO:LO First Nation, the valley was first visited by outsiders when fur traders arrived from FORT LANGLEY in 1828 (*see* FUR TRADE, LAND-BASED). The area has undergone extensive LOGGING since the 1920s. The river appeals to whitewater enthusiasts and the valley is a popular destination for anglers, campers and hikers. There is a small (1.62 km²) provincial PARK here. *See also* LAKES.

CHINA CREEK is on the east side of ALBERNI INLET, 14 km south of PORT ALBERNI on the road to BAMFIELD. With the presence of a marina and a small provincial PARK, it is a convenient staging area for sport FISHING in the inlet; winds funnelling down the inlet also make it popular with windsurfers. There has been extensive LOGGING in the watershed of the creek itself.

CHINATOWNS are urban enclaves of CHINESE Canadians' homes, businesses and associations. They formed partly because Chinese newcomers preferred to congregate together in familiar surroundings but mainly because discrimination ostracized them to their own communities. For example, in VANCOUVER Chinese were restricted from buying property outside Chinatown until the 1930s. As a result, Chinatowns became virtually self-sustaining, providing all the social, cultural and economic needs of their residents. They came into existence wherever Chinese settled, whether in large urban centres or in small MINING camps and farming communities. BARKERVILLE, for example, had a Chinatown that is now part of the reconstructed historic town, while COAL MINING centres such as NANAIMO and CUMBERLAND had Chinese neighbourhoods that were destroyed or abandoned after the mining era ended.

The Gates of Harmonious Interest, Chinatown, Victoria. Konstantin Ahrndt/Image Makers

By the 1960s outsiders had a new perception of Chinatowns as interesting ethnic districts with potential for TOURISM and urban redevelopment. After immigration restrictions were relaxed in 1967, Chinese immigrants increasingly settled outside the Chinatowns, most notably in RICHMOND, though the original neighbourhoods remain vital commercial and cultural centres for Chinese Canadians. The 2 most significant BC Chinatowns are in Vancouver and VICTORIA.

Victoria's is the first and oldest surviving Chinatown in Canada. Located on either side of Government St, it began with the arrival of Chinese miners in 1858 and it was the largest Chinese community in Canada until 1910. It dwindled during the 1960s and 1970s and almost disappeared before a rehabilitation program in 1979 began reviving it as a historic tourist district. Landmarks include a permanent arch over Government St, Fan Tan Alley and many heritage buildings, including the Chinese Consolidated Benevolent Assoc (1885), the first major Chinese-owned building in Canada.

Chinese began to settle in Vancouver in 1886 following completion of the CPR. Many of them had worked on railway construction and drifted to the coast looking for jobs. Originally they congregated along Dupont (now Pender) St. Since then Chinatown has grown to encompass an area of the Downtown Eastside roughly bounded by Hastings, Union, Carrall and Gore streets. In 1967 the community mobilized successfully to oppose a freeway that the city wanted to route through the neighbourhood. In 1971 the province designated the Chinatown core a historic area. Landmarks include the SAM KEE Building (the narrowest commercial building in the world), the Dr SUN YAT-SEN Classical Chinese Garden and the Chinese Cultural Centre, opened in 1980.
Reading: David Chuenyan Lai, *Chinatowns: Towns Within Cities in Canada*, 1988.

CHINESE first arrived in BC at NOOTKA SOUND aboard British fur-trading vessels in 1788–89. They were mostly artisans, brought by John MEARES to build a trading post, then settle a small colony near YUQUOT. They also helped build the NORTH WEST AMERICA, the first sailing vessel launched on the coast. The fate of these 120 or so people is not known, but it is known that a small number of Chinese were present in the crews of vessels engaged in the maritime FUR TRADE. The next arrivals were several hundred merchants and miners who hurried north from California in 1858 to join the GOLD RUSH to the FRASER R. A few of the newcomers opened businesses in VICTORIA, which by 1859 had a small CHINATOWN. The first Chinese baby born in Canada was Won Alexander CUMYOW, at PORT DOUGLAS in 1860. At the height of the gold rush the Chinese population reached almost 7,000, but it declined as the rush petered out and the 1871 census recorded just 1,548 Chinese, all but 53 of whom were men. The Chinese referred to BC as Gold Mountain. Chinese prospectors specialized in reworking the diggings abandoned by white miners. The tolerance that characterized

Chinese labourers arriving at William Head quarantine station during WWI.
BC Archives G-01591

relations between whites and Chinese during the gold rush period gave way to antipathy after 1871. Early Chinese colonists faced discrimination on many fronts. They received lower wages than white workers in the COAL mines; in 1875 they lost the right to vote provincially (municipally in 1876); they were barred from certain professions; for the most part they were confined to low-paying manual labour. Even so, residents feared that the Chinese, by their willingness to work for lower wages, would monopolize the job market. Mainly they worked clearing land, in SALMON CANNERIES, coal mines, laundries and restaurants, and as domestic servants. During construction of the CPR through the mountains (1880–85), about 6,500 Chinese labourers were imported by the railway. They were given the most dangerous jobs and at least 600 men died. Afterwards many of them remained in the province, but it was difficult for them to send for their families because in 1885 the federal government began imposing a HEAD TAX on Chinese immigrants. On 23 Feb 1887 a mob of about 300 men attacked a camp of Chinese land clearers at Coal Harbour in VANCOUVER and forced them to leave the city. It was the first organized violence against the Chinese in Canada and was repeated in Sept 1907 when a mob rampaged through Vancouver's Chinese and Japanese quarters. Nonetheless, by 1911 there were 20,000 Chinese in BC, most of them single men imported as labourers by special contractors. Discrimination continued; it reached a low point in 1923 with the publication of the viciously racist novel *The Writing on the Wall*, by Hilda GLYNN-WARD. On 1 July 1923, the head tax was revoked and replaced by the *Chinese Immigration Act*, which halted virtually all immigration from China. During WWII several hundred Chinese Canadians fought on the Allied side in Europe. Following the war BC restored the vote to Chinese who had fought in the world wars. Then in 1947 Ottawa repealed the Chinese Immigration Act, and all Chinese Canadians

regained the federal and provincial vote. (The municipal vote in Vancouver was granted in 1949.) Some restrictions on immigration were also lifted, but it was not until the introduction of the point system in 1967 that the Chinese were treated like anyone else. Post-1967 Chinese immigrants as a rule were better educated and wealthier than those who arrived pre-1923. They also came from a wider variety of places, including Taiwan, Singapore, Hong Kong and Vietnam, and they settled to a greater extent in parts of Canada other than BC. In 1901, 86% of Chinese Canadians lived in BC; by 1991 that figure had declined to 31%, second to Ontario. Within BC, many of the newcomers settled outside the traditional Chinese communities, most notably in RICHMOND, which during the 1990s became a suburban "Chinatown"; it became known, for example, for its Asian-themed shopping malls. SUCCESS (the United Chinese Community Enrichment Services Society), formed in Vancouver in 1973, is an important immigrant assistance agency in the city. In the late 1980s, immigration from Hong Kong increased in anticipation of the colony's return to China in 1997; it fuelled an economic boom in BC which was the envy of the rest of the country.

While there is evidence of continued racism, Chinese Canadians, both native-born and immigrants, now have unprecedented access to leadership positions in BC, symbolized by the 1957 election of Douglas JUNG as a Vancouver MP and the appointment of David LAM as LT GOV (1988–95). The artistic community has been enriched by writers such as Paul Yee, Evelyn LAU, Jim Wong-Chu and Wayson CHOY, the pianist Alexina LOUIE, the visual artist Paul WONG and the filmmaker Mina Shum; other prominent members of the community include the Olympic gymnast Lori FUNG, former UBC chancellor Robert Lee and many others.

The major community festival is Chinese New Year, celebrated in January or February with a colourful parade through Chinatown. Another is the Mid-Autumn, or Moon, Festival, held in late summer when special moon cakes are prepared. In the Greater Vancouver area there are Chinese-language NEWSPAPERS and BROADCAST-

ING outlets (*see* FAIRCHILD MEDIA), and since 1986 the annual Dragon Boat Festival has become a major cultural event for all residents and visitors (*see* DRAGON BOAT RACES). At the 1996 census 312,330 people in BC claimed Chinese ethnic origin, almost 9% of the provincial total. An overwhelming majority of these people, about 93%, live in the LOWER MAINLAND, where the community comprises almost 15% of the total population.
Reading: James Morton, *In The Sea of Sterile Mountains: The Chinese in British Columbia*, 1977; Edgar Wickberg et al, eds, *From China to Canada: A History of Chinese Communities in Canada*, 1982.

CHINESE CEMETERY in OAK BAY is one of a very few CHINESE cemeteries established in Canada between the 1880s and the 1920s. Located at the end of Harling Pt overlooking the mouth of Gonzales Bay, it contains over 1,000 individual graves and 13 communal graves. It was established in 1903 by VICTORIA's Chinese community, which employed the ancient principles of *feng shui* to determine a propitious site. The last individual burials at the site occurred in 1950, though the bones of 849 Chinese pioneers that had been awaiting shipment to China were interred in a special ceremony in 1961. The oldest Chinese cemetery in Canada, it has been designated a National Historic Site.

CHINOOK COVE, a CANADIAN NORTHERN RWY station originally named Genier on the N THOMPSON R 64 km north of KAMLOOPS, sounds as if it should be located on the ocean. Its name is a reminder that chinook SALMON travel great distances from the sea in order to reproduce before they die. *AS*

CHINOOK JARGON is a pidgin language that was used on the west coast of N America, roughly from California to Alaska, to facilitate communication between FIRST NATIONS groups, and between First Nations and non-aboriginals. Sometimes incorrectly referred to as simply "Chinook," this lingua franca consists of words and phrases borrowed from different aboriginal languages, including NUU-CHAH-NULTH (Nootka), Lower Chehalis and the Chinook language spoken by the people who formerly occupied the mouth of the COLUMBIA R. It also contains French and English words. During the 1880s, the OBLATE missionary Jean-Marie Le Jeune used a French shorthand system as an orthography, and later instituted the Jargon's "golden age" with a short-lived publication called the KAMLOOPS WAWA. The language, which has a small vocabulary of about 700 words, was spoken by 250,000 people at its peak but by 2000 was known by only a few. Familiar words include *tyee* ("chief"), *skookum* ("strong"), *tillikums* ("friends"), *klahowyah* ("greetings"), *cheechako* ("newcomer"), *saltchuck* ("ocean"), and *potlatch*, an adaptation of the Nuu-chah-nulth word for "giving." See also FIRST NATIONS LANGUAGES.
Reading: Charles Lillard and Terry Glavin, *A Voice Great Within Us*, 1998.

CHIPMUNK is a tiny ground-dwelling RODENT belonging to the SQUIRREL family. Alert and quick-moving, chipmunks dart about with their bushy tails erect, scampering up trees but nesting in burrows in rockpiles or under root tangles or buildings. They have brown to red fur with 5 dark stripes down the back, and they seldom grow longer than 13 cm. These busy little creatures stock their food caches with seeds, nuts and

Yellow pine chipmunk. Ken Bowen photo

fruit pits. While relatively inactive in winter, they wake every once in a while to snack on their horde. Four types occur in BC: the least chipmunk (*Tamias minimus*), a boreal species found principally in the north; its slightly larger relative of the central and southern parts of BC, the yellow pine chipmunk (*T. amoenus*); the red-tailed chipmunk (*T. ruficauda*) in the southern KOOTENAY and ROCKY MTS; and Townsend's chipmunk (*T. townsendii*), the largest, found in the coastal lowlands and coastal mountains of southwestern BC. No chipmunks occur on VANCOUVER ISLAND. Two subspecies of the least chipmunk and 2 subspecies of the red-tailed chipmunk are on the province's Red-list of ENDANGERED SPECIES.

CHITON is an ancient marine MOLLUSC belonging to the class Polyplacophora. Of several hundred species worldwide, at least 20 are found in the intertidal zone along the BC coast, including

Giant Pacific chiton, also known as the gumboot chiton. Rick Harbo photo

the giant Pacific or gumboot chiton (*Cryptochiton stelleri*), the largest in the world (to 33 cm). Chitons are slow-moving, oval animals protected by 8 overlapping plates, or shells. Nearly all species roll up into a ball when disturbed. The chiton is typically sedentary, attaching itself to a rock or any solid object, where it browses by scraping food with a rasp-like radula. Chitons were a food resource for FIRST NATIONS people, especially the giant Pacific and the smaller black Katy chiton (*Katharina tunicata*).

CHIWID, TSILHQOT'IN drifter (b June 1903, Redstone; d 1986, Stone Reserve). She was a mixed-blood woman, baptized Lily Skinner but better known by her aboriginal name, which means "chickadee." When she was in her twenties her husband beat her severely. She left him and lived most of the rest of her life outdoors, summer and winter, wandering the CHILCOTIN, surviving by FISHING and trapping SQUIRRELS. Along with her amazing hardiness, she developed a reputation for having spiritual powers and was well known to—and sometimes feared by—residents of the Chilcotin.
Reading: Sage Birchwater, *Chiwid*, 1995.

CHOATE, 11 km north of HOPE on the FRASER R, was named after James Z. Choate, a CPR bridge construction foreman. The station is still called Choate but residents in the small community here were able to persuade authorities to change its name to Dogwood Valley in 1972.   AS

CHONG, Thomas "Tommy," guitarist, comedian (b 24 May 1938, Edmonton). Best known as one half of the popular 1970s comedy duo Cheech and Chong, he began his career as a pro-

Rae Dawn Chong with her father Tommy Chong, 1982.

fessional entertainer in VANCOUVER nightclubs in the mid-1960s. He was the lead guitarist in the rhythm & blues band Little Daddy and the Bachelors, a band that is best remembered for offending local sensibilities by changing its name to Four Niggers and a Chink. Bowing to public pressure, the band assumed a third identity, Bobby Taylor and the Vancouvers, and was discovered at the Elegant Parlour by Diana Ross and Berry Gordy Jr, the president of Detroit's Motown Records. The band's first single in 1968, "Does Your Mama Know About Me," co-written by Chong, was a Top 20 hit on the American Billboard chart. The Vancouvers broke up soon

after (Taylor is credited with discovering Michael Jackson and the Jackson Five) and Chong turned his attention to comedy. With partner Cheech Marin, he made a career out of a unique brand of drug-related humour. The duo performed stand-up comedy and recorded comedy albums, and wrote and starred in several movies. After their breakup in 1985, Chong settled in N VANCOUVER and continued writing and performing for film.   *Mike Harling*

CHOY, Wayson, writer, teacher (b 1939, Vancouver). He was raised in CHINATOWN in VANCOUVER and studied creative writing at UBC, then moved to Ontario and became a college English instructor. In 1996 he and Margaret Atwood shared Ontario's Trillium Award, she for her novel *Alias Grace* and he for his first book, also a novel, *The Jade Peony*. His next book, *Paper Shadows*, a memoir about his childhood, was nominated for a 1999 GOV GEN'S LITERARY AWARD.

CHRISTINA LAKE, 26 km², 19 km long, 21 km east of GRAND FORKS in the MONASHEE MTS of the W KOOTENAY, is one of the warmest LAKES in BC, a benefit that draws thousands of summer visitors. Pictographs on the east side are evidence of early FIRST NATIONS occupation (*see* ROCK ART). The lake was named for Christina McDonald, daughter of a chief factor of the HBC at Fort Colville in Washington state. Its southern end is intersected by the DEWDNEY TRAIL. The southern line of the CPR reached the lake in the late 1890s, initiating a modest settlement boom. LOGGING was economically important and the lake attracted tourists from the beginning. The north end is in Gladstone Provincial PARK (393.2 km²), and there is a small park at the south end. The lake drains south via the KETTLE R into the US.

CHRISTY, Jim, writer (b 14 July 1945, Philadelphia, PA). After extensive travels through the US and Mexico he moved to Canada in 1968 at the height of the Vietnam War. Settling first in Toronto, he founded the underground newspaper, *Guerilla*, and began writing. His first book, *The New Refugees*, appeared in 1972 and he has published steadily ever since, producing 16 books, including poetry, stories and 2 novels. His non-fiction includes a biography of the French adventurer Charles Bedaux, *The Price of Power* (1984) (*see* BEDAUX SUBARCTIC EXPEDITION) and a study of boxing, *Flesh and Blood* (1990). He became a Canadian citizen in 1974 and in 1981 moved west to BC, where he has lived ever since. His book *The Long, Slow Death of Jack Kerouac* (1998) evokes a generation of writers, the Beats, with whom he strongly identifies. In 1999 he published a collection of travel writings, *Between the Meridians*.

CHU CHUA, pop 231, is a small SECWEPEMC (Shuswap) settlement and former CANADIAN NORTHERN RWY station on the east side of the N THOMPSON R, 75 km north of KAMLOOPS. There is a SAWMILL here. The name is the plural form of a Secwepemc word for "creek."   AS

CHU LAI, merchant (b circa 1847, Guangdong Province, China; d 4 June 1906, Victoria). He arrived in BC in the 1860s and established himself as a merchant in the CARIBOO goldfields (*see* GOLD RUSH, CARIBOO). In 1876 he opened a company in VICTORIA, Wing Chong, selling general merchandise and conducting business of various kinds. He became the wealthiest Chinese merchant in the city and was active in the CHINESE community, helping immigrants, funding Chinese-language schools and speaking out against government restrictions. He was also one of the organizers in 1884 of the Chinese Consolidated Benevolent Assoc, an influential community group.

CHUKAR (*Alectoris chukar*) is a chicken-sized game bird introduced from eastern Europe to the south-central Interior during 1950–55. It is grey in colour with a black and white barred chest, red bill, white face and black eyeband. Chukars inhabit the rocky hillsides and dry GRASSLANDS of the THOMPSON, NICOLA and S OKANAGAN valleys. Attempts to introduce them elsewhere in the province have failed.

CHUNLAC is an ancient village site of the DAKELH (Carrier) people at the confluence of the STUART and NECHAKO rivers 55 km west of PRINCE GEORGE. Evidence of occupation dates back 2,000 years. The site was apparently abandoned in the 1600s after a war with the neighbouring TSILHQOT'IN. *See also* ARCHAEOLOGY.

CHURCH HOUSE is a tiny village on the mainland coast near the mouth of BUTE INLET. Originally it was a main village of the HOMALCO First Nation and was located across the channel on MAURELLE ISLAND, where missionaries built a church. Around 1900 a gale destroyed most of the buildings so the village was moved to its present site. All residents subsequently moved away.

CHURN CREEK Protected Area, 360 km², is on the west side of the FRASER R south of the GANG RANCH. Established in 1994, it includes the historic EMPIRE VALLEY RANCH, purchased by the province in 1998. The preserve protects a unique GRASSLANDS ecosystem along with the habitat of several threatened animal species.

CHUTE LAKE, 20 km south of KELOWNA in the OKANAGAN VALLEY, was a stop on the KETTLE VALLEY RWY in the 1920s. The Chute Lake Resort now occupies the site but remnants of the station can still be found. Chute is French for "waterfall" or "rapid" and describes the lake's outflow creek.   *AS*

CINEMA, a small settlement 28 km north of QUESNEL in the north CARIBOO, was named by Dr Lloyd Champlain, an early settler. There are several explanations for why he chose this name; one local history suggests it was to celebrate a journey he made to Hollywood in the 1920s.   *AS*

CITY OF AINSWORTH was a small sternwheeler built in AINSWORTH HOT SPRINGS in

1892 by a local business consortium. They were concerned that the settlement should have a means of shipping to the railhead at Bonners Ferry, ID. Most of its service life was spent on a run between NELSON and the north head of KOOTENAY LK. On 29 Nov 1898 the vessel foundered in a gale off CRAWFORD BAY and was blown onto the rocks. Two passengers and 7 crew drowned when a lifeboat capsized. In 1990 the wreck was located in 110 m of water near the mouth of the bay; it was later designated a provincial historic site.

CITY OF VANCOUVER BOOK AWARD is an annual prize of $2,000 for the year's best book—fiction or non-fiction—about VANCOUVER, as chosen by a panel of judges from the book WRITING and PUBLISHING community. Inaugurated in 1989, the prize is presented at the opening ceremonies of the Vancouver International Writers' (& Readers) Festival each Oct. See list of winners above.

CLALLUM First Nation are a Central Coast Salish people (*see* SALISHAN FIRST NATIONS) who speak a language closely related to the NORTHERN STRAITS dialects of the T'Sou-ke (Sooke), Saanich, LEKWAMMEN (Songhees) and Lummi. The Clallum (spelled Clallam in the US, or S'Klallam) occupy the Olympic Peninsula along the south side of JUAN DE FUCA STRAIT, with RESERVES at Elhwa, Jamestown and Little Boston, WA. By about 1850 some had crossed the strait

to occupy villages at Becher and Parry Bays on the southern tip of VANCOUVER ISLAND. The Clallum were the only Central Coast Salish group to hunt WHALES, presumably HUMPBACK that entered the strait (*see* WHALING). At first contact with Europeans the Clallum population numbered 3,200; including those in the US, it was about the same in 2000.

CLAM is a marine MOLLUSC belonging to the class Bivalvia. It consists of a soft body enclosed by a hinged shell with 2 halves (valves). Clams inhabit burrows in the substrate, intertidally and subtidally, and most species feed by filtering microscopic plants and animals from the water they take in through their siphons, or necks. The butter clam (*Saxidomus gigantea*), the Pacific, or native, littleneck clam (*Protothaca staminea*), the manila, or Japanese, littleneck clam (*Venerupis japonica*), and the GEODUCK all support significant commercial FISHING operations. Other important edible species include horse clams and cockles. The razor clam (*Siliqua patula*) is found only on exposed sandy beaches; a recre-

BC's 3 most popular edible clam species (from top): butter, Japanese littleneck (Manila), Pacific littleneck. Rick Harbo photos

ational fishery for this species exists in the QUEEN CHARLOTTE ISLANDS. An exotic species, the varnish, or dark mahogany, clam (*Nuttallia obscurata*) was unknowingly introduced to the coast in the late 1980s and by the 1990s had become abundant in GEORGIA STRAIT and BARKLEY SOUND.

Clam shell MIDDENS several metres thick have been discovered throughout the coast area, indicating the importance of clams as a historical food source for many aboriginal people. The clam is also significant in HAIDA legend, as reflected in Bill REID's large sculpture at the MUSEUM OF ANTHROPOLOGY at UBC, showing Raven releasing the first people from a clam shell.

During the 1980s the commercial clam fishery grew rapidly, mainly for natural manila and native littleneck clams. Landings peaked at 4,360 tonnes in 1988 before declining due to overharvesting. Area licensing was introduced in 1989, and as these stocks continued to decline, shellfish farmers began to produce manila clams to meet market demands (*see* AQUACULTURE, SHELLFISH). In 1998 landings for wild clams totalled 1,300 tonnes, with a wholesale value of $6.2 million, while farmed production was 700 tonnes. Landings were composed almost entirely of manila clams, a species that was introduced to the coast along with the Pacific OYSTER. BAYNES SOUND on the east coast of VANCOUVER ISLAND is BC's most productive shellfish growing area, accounting for 55% of the farmed manila clam production. To culture manila clams, farmers spread tiny "seed" clams on a beach that has been cleared of large rocks and predators. Each tiny clam burrows into the substrate using its foot, and the farmer covers the seeded area with a plastic netting to keep out predators such as CRABS and diving DUCKS. The clams grow to marketable size in 2–3 years and are harvested manually. Like other bivalves that are filter feeders, clams are susceptible to the toxic effects of HARMFUL ALGAL BLOOMS, notably paralytic shellfish poisoning. Butter clams are particularly hazardous because their siphons may retain the neurotoxin for up to 2 years.

CLARK, Catherine (Anthony), writer (b 5 May 1892, London, England; d 24 Feb 1977, Victoria). Raised and educated in England, she immigrated to Canada in 1914 and she and her family settled at KOOTENAY LK in the southern Interior of BC. After marrying Leonard Clark, a rancher, she wrote for the *Prospector*, a community newspaper in NELSON. She was 58 years old before she published her first book, *The Golden Pine Cone*, in 1950. Other books include *The Sun Horse* (1951), *The One-Winged Dragon* (1955), *The Silver Man* (1958), *The Diamond Feather* or *The Door in the Mountain: A Magic Tale for Children* (1962), and *The Hunter and the Medicine Man* (1966). She was well known as an accomplished writer of juvenile fantasy whose works portray western Canada through a successful combination of aboriginal legends and fantastical elements, set against a backdrop of the mountains of BC. *Heidi Brown*

CLARK, Glen David, politician, premier 22 Feb 1996–25 Aug 1999 (b 22 Nov 1957, Nanaimo). He grew up on the east side of VANCOUVER and graduated from UBC with an MA in community planning. As an organizer for the Ironworkers Union, he became active in the provincial NDP and was first elected to the provincial legislature in 1986. He became minister of finance—at age 33 the youngest in BC history—when the party took office in 1991. Later he was minister of employment and investment. When Mike HARCOURT resigned due to revelations about a charity bingo scandal involving the party (*see* NANAIMO COMMONWEALTH HOLDING SOCIETY), Clark was selected NDP leader and became PREMIER. He was 38 years old—the youngest BC premier since Richard MCBRIDE in 1903. The NDP seemed headed for defeat in the

Glen Clark, premier of BC 1996–99.

1996 election campaign, but Clark won back enough support to squeeze out a narrow victory (*see* ELECTION RESULTS). When revenue figures in the pre- and post-election budgets were shown to be overly optimistic, Clark faced charges that he had misled voters about the state of the province's finances. He won kudos for maintaining funding for health and education (his government froze university tuition fees), but his popularity suffered from economic woes tied to a slump in the FOREST INDUSTRY, the collapse of the SALMON fishery and a general decline in other resource industries. Clark backed large infrastructure programs, including construction of the Island Highway (*see* ROADS AND HIGHWAYS), new ferries (*see* BC FERRY CORP) and a new section of the SKYTRAIN. These efforts alienated many ENVIRONMENTAL supporters of the NDP, despite Clark's extension of the policy on creating new provincial PARKS. He led the fight to pass the NISGA'A TREATY, BC's first modern-day aboriginal land claims treaty (*see* ABORIGINAL RIGHTS), against strong opposition from the provincial LIBERALS. Highly publicized attempts to RECALL NDP MLAs during Clark's tenure were all unsuccessful, but the party's popularity sank so low in the polls (to 11%) that Clark was given no chance to win re-election. Amid public concern over revelations of major cost overruns on the construc-

tion of the BC Ferry Corp's "fast ferries," the RCMP raided Clark's home in search of evidence related to an investigation of a friend's application for a gambling licence (*see* GAMING). When it was revealed that Clark himself was under police investigation, he resigned the premiership and leadership of the party, according to political custom. Clark's tenure as premier was characterized by a highly centralized and polarized style of government that alienated even some staunch NDP supporters.

CLARK'S NUTCRACKER; *see* NUTCRACKER, CLARK'S.

CLARKE, John, mountaineer (b 25 Feb 1945, Dublin, Ireland). He moved with his parents to VANCOUVER when he was 13 and in the mid-1960s began exploring the remote regions of the COAST MTS, making forays into the wilderness for weeks at a time and often alone. He has made hundreds of first ascents and his love of the mountains has led him to become active in protecting the remaining old-growth forests by giving educational talks and forest tours. He was made an honorary member of the Alpine Club of Canada in 1988 and is the subject of a 1995 film, *Child of the Wind*. *See also* MOUNTAINEERING.
Chic Scott

CLARKSON, Reginald Louis, athlete (b 19 Aug 1925, Victoria). One of BC's greatest all-round athletes, he was a standout in BASEBALL, BASKETBALL, FOOTBALL, SOCCER and LACROSSE. He started his professional baseball career with the VANCOUVER Capilanos in 1946 and worked his way up to first-team all-star status the next year on the Brooklyn Dodgers class A team in Pueblo, CO. In 1949 he went to Edmonton to play pro football with the Eskimos while also starring for the Edmonton Motor Cubs baseball team and acting as player-coach for a senior amateur basketball club. He returned to Vancouver in 1950 to play for the Capilanos and the Clover Leafs, the Canadian amateur basketball champions that year. While playing semiprofessional baseball and pro football with the Calgary Stampeders in 1951 he was diagnosed with a threatening heart ailment and ended his sports career at age 26. He dedicated himself to community service and GOLF and was inducted into the BC SPORTS HALL OF FAME in 1974. *SW*

CLAXTON, 30 km southeast of PRINCE RUPERT on Telegraph Pass, was the first of the SKEENA R canneries built beyond the protected waters of the river mouth and closer to the fishing grounds. It was established by Royal Canadian Packing Co in 1892 and later owned by Wallace Bros and BC PACKERS; it closed in 1944. A SAWMILL, built in 1893, made boxes for several Skeena canneries. *See also* FISHING, COMMERCIAL; SALMON CANNING. *AS*

CLAYBURN is a historic village south of the FRASER R on the northern edge of ABBOTSFORD. Charles Maclure (with his sister Sara MCLAGAN, and helped by brother Samuel MACLURE) established a brick factory here in 1905 using clay mined from nearby Sumas Mt and developed a private townsite for employees. Brick from Clayburn was used in many notable BC buildings, including the Hotel Vancouver, OAKALLA PRISON and Royal Jubilee Hospital in VICTORIA. In the 1920s the plant moved to KILGARD, but the small community of tidy brick buildings survived.

CLAYHURST, 50 km east of FORT ST JOHN near the Alberta border in the PEACE R district, was named after William Clay, who took up land here in 1930. Many UKRAINIAN farmers settled in this rich agricultural area. A ferry, now replaced by a bridge, operated on the Peace R for many years due south of Clayhurst. *AS*

CLAYOQUOT, on Stubbs Island in CLAYOQUOT SOUND, 2 km northwest of TOFINO on the west coast of VANCOUVER ISLAND, was the sound's commercial centre for many years. William E. BANFIELD, after whom BAMFIELD is named, built a fur-trading post here in 1855. Another store was run by Frederick Thornberg from 1874 to 1885. By the 1890s several businesses operated, as well as a hotel, school and post office. In the 20th century, the village gradually lost ground to Tofino; eventually, only the hotel remained. Most of it was demolished in the early 1990s. *AS*

CLAYOQUOT SOUND on the west coast of VANCOUVER ISLAND extends from ESTEVAN POINT on the HESQUIAT Peninsula in the north to PACIFIC RIM NATIONAL PARK in the south. It encompasses 9 major watersheds, several large islands—including FLORES, VARGAS and MEARES—and 2,440 km² of lush rain forest nurtured by dense fogs and heavy annual precipitation. It is considered one of the most spectacular wilderness areas on the continent. Most of it is accessible only by water. People of the Tla-o-qui-aht First Nation (NUU-CHAH-NULTH), after whom the sound is named, have occupied the area for many generations. TOFINO is the commercial and TOURISM centre of the sound. There are HOT SPRINGS at HOT SPRINGS COVE and AHOUSAT.

Clayoquot Sound encompasses one of the largest tracts of temperate rain forest remaining in N America. Intensive LOGGING occurred from early in the 1900s; about a quarter of the forest had been logged by the late 1990s. In the mid-1980s the area became the focus of a protracted dispute between loggers and environmentalists. In April 1993 the provincial government released a compromise land use plan that permitted controlled logging in parts of the sound. Many environmentalists did not accept the compromise; that summer logging roads were blocked in a protest that resulted in the largest mass arrest in Canadian history. More than 900 people were arrested for violating an injunction banning the blockade and 857 were charged with contempt of court. Some received suspended sentences; others were fined and jailed. In March of the following year, the Nuu-chah-nulth signed a resource management agreement with the government that gave them a role in the economic development of the sound. Numerous solutions have been sug-

Shoreline of Clayoquot Sound.
Adrian Dorst/WCWC

gested to resolve the situation, including the Clayoquot Biosphere Reserve under the UN's Man and Biosphere Program, and the Central Region Board, a unique government–Nuu-chah-nulth body under which a development corporation, Ma-Mook, was established to undertake agreements with large forest companies. As well, in 1995 the government announced strict guidelines for logging companies operating in the watershed; but the controversy continued to simmer. *See also* ENVIRONMENTAL MOVEMENT; FOREST INDUSTRY; PARKS, PROVINCIAL.

CLAYTON, 15 km southeast of NEW WESTMINSTER, was an early settlement in SURREY. John George opened a store where the old Yale Rd crossed the CLOVER VALLEY Rd. In 1889 he added a post office and named it after his Ontario hometown. The spot became a station on the NEW WESTMINSTER SOUTHERN RWY in 1891. Growth elsewhere in Surrey made Clayton's section of track obsolete and the community had faded into obscurity by WWI. *AS*

CLEARBROOK is a residential and farming suburb within the City of ABBOTSFORD in the FRASER VALLEY. Many MENNONITES settled in this area. The post office was originally named Pinecrest in 1952 after a certain Pinecrest Auto Court. Local residents complained so the name was changed to North Clearbrook and finally, in 1957, to Clearbrook. *AS*

CLEARWATER, pop 4,976, on the N THOMPSON R 122 km north of KAMLOOPS, is the gateway to WELLS GRAY PROVINCIAL PARK. The Simpcw people, a division of the SECWEPEMC (Shuswap) nation, have a long history in the area. The settlement was founded around the turn of the century by John Smith, a prospector, and named Raft River. Nearby Dutch Lake was homesteaded by GERMANS at about the same time. Steamboats worked the river south to Kamloops until WWI; in 1916 the CANADIAN NORTHERN RWY was con-

structed through the valley. The community was incorporated in 1968 as an improvement district. It prides itself on its clean water, which is bottled for sale around the world (*see* WATER EXPORTS). The FOREST INDUSTRY has been the major employer.

CLEMENT, Douglas Bruce, athlete, sports medicine pioneer (b 15 July 1933, Montreal). He was an outstanding track athlete while growing up in VANCOUVER and later at the Univ of Oregon and UBC. He took part in the 1952 and 1956 Olympics with the Canadian track team and was a member of the team that won a silver medal in the 4 x 440 relay at the 1954 British Empire Games (*see* BRITISH EMPIRE AND COMMONWEALTH GAMES) in Vancouver. He earned his medical degree in 1959 and in 1962 he and his wife Diane began the RICHMOND Kajaks, eventually one of Canada's top track clubs. In 1964 the couple organized the first Achilles International Games, precursor to the Harry JEROME Track Classic. Increasingly Clement focussed his medical practice on sports and exercise and in 1979 at UBC he began the Allan McGavin Sports Medicine Centre, the premier facility of its kind in Canada. He is recognized around the world as an innovator in sports medicine and has earned the Sports Medicine Council Lifetime Achievement Award and the Order of Canada. As a running coach he has guided more than 10 athletes to the Olympics, including 1984 bronze medallist Lynn WILLIAMS. *See also* TRACK AND FIELD. *SW*

CLEMRETTA is a small agricultural and summer resort settlement 43 km southwest of BURNS LAKE on the northwest shore of FRANÇOIS LK. It was named in 1939 by H.S. Cowan, the first postmaster, after two cows, Clementine and Henrietta. The post office had apparently rejected all his other suggestions for place names. *AS*

CLEXLIXQEN, Louis "Chief Louis," Secwepemc chief (b 1828, Kamloops; d 12 Apr 1915, Kamloops). He was a guide, trader and farmer and one of the wealthiest members of the

KAMLOOPS First Nation of the SECWEPEMC (Shuswap) people. After becoming chief in 1852 he converted to Catholicism and was active in supporting schools and other church activities on the RESERVE. He also played a leading role in asserting Secwepemc land claims and in trying to create an alliance among the Interior FIRST NATIONS to pursue the land issue. He took part in a delegation to Great Britain to see Queen Victoria and in 1909 was a founding member of the Interior Tribes of BC. *See* ABORIGINAL RIGHTS.

CLIFF, Leslie, swimmer (b 11 Mar 1955, Vancouver). At age 16 she won 3 gold and 2 silver medals at the 1971 Pan American Games in Colombia. The next year she earned silver in the 400-m individual medley at the Munich Olympics. In 1973 she won gold at the US Amateur Athletic Union Championships and picked up 2 more golds in her specialties—the 200-m and 400-m individual medleys—at the Commonwealth Games in New Zealand. She was 1971 junior BC athlete of the year and overall BC athlete of the year, 1972 BC junior athlete of the year, and is a member of the Order of Canada, Canada's Aquatic Hall of Fame and the BC SPORTS HALL OF FAME. *SW*

CLIFTON, Heber Louis, hereditary Tsimshian chief (b 1872; d 1 Jan 1964). He was raised in the village of METLAKATLA where he was educated by William DUNCAN. When the Gitga'ata people left Metlakatla and built HARTLEY BAY in their traditional territory, he emerged as their leader. He was a well-known fisher and tugboat captain on the North Coast and one of the founders of the NATIVE BROTHERHOOD OF BC in 1931. An active organizer for the brotherhood, he donated the services of his seine boat *Kwatsu* to travel the coast building membership. *Ken Campbell*

CLIMATE varies widely in BC for 2 principal reasons: the diverse topography and the proximity to the Pacific Ocean. The main elements of climate—precipitation and temperature—are affected by factors such as elevation, latitude, air flow and particularly whether a location is coastal or inland. Generally speaking, moist Pacific air affects coastal regions by making them cooler in summer and warmer in winter than Interior regions, which are subject to what are called continental influences. Coastal regions enjoy the longest frost-free periods in Canada: up to 280 days a year in some years and in some southern areas. Average winter temperatures on the coast remain above 0°C and are the mildest in Canada, while average summer temperatures are 18°C or less. Coastal winters are cloudy and wet as a result of Pacific air masses dumping their load of moisture as they rise over the COAST MTS. Even so, there is wide variation within the region. VICTORIA, which is subject to more wind coming up the STRAIT OF JUAN DE FUCA, averages only 619 mm of precipitation annually, while VANCOUVER receives 1,113 mm, and OCEAN FALLS, the wettest populated place in the country, gets 4,386 mm. The absolute wettest spot in N America is HENDERSON LK on the southwest coast

SELECTED BC WEATHER STATISTICS

Most rain in one year	Henderson Lk	8997.1 mm (1997)
Least rain in one year	Ashcroft	71 mm (1938)
Most rain in one day	Ucluelet	489 mm (6 Oct 1967)
Longest period of rainfall of any Canadian city	Victoria	33 days (Apr–May 1986)
Lowest temperature	Smith R	-58.9°C (31 Jan 1947)
Highest temperature	Lytton	44.4°C (16 July 1941)
Most sun in a year	Victoria	2,426 hours (1970)
Annual average sun (high)	Cranbrook	2,244 hours
Annual average sun (low)	Stewart	949 hours
Most snow in one day	Lakelse Lk	118.1 cm (17 Jan 1974)*
Most snow in a year	Revelstoke	2,446 cm (1972)*
Frost-free periods of selected places:	Victoria	287 days
	Cape St James	272 days
	Estevan Pt	228 days
	Chilliwack	216 days
	Vancouver	216 days
	Lytton	186 days
	Kamloops	149 days
	Penticton	148 days
	Fort St John	115 days
	Golden	115 days
	Fort Nelson	106 days
	Smithers	91 days
	Prince George	85 days

Canadian record
Source: Environment Canada

of VANCOUVER ISLAND, in from BARKELY SOUND. Despite the coast's reputation as "the Wet Coast," Vancouver is just the 6th wettest major city in Canada and Victoria receives 2,100 hours of sunshine per year, as much as any place in the southern prairies. Most of the precipitation falls as rain. The coast, especially in the south, gets very little snow; in fact, annual averages are the lowest in southern Canada. According to Environment Canada's Climate Severity Index, the South Coast has the best climate in Canada in terms of human comfort and well-being.

The Interior of the province has a completely different climate; it is much drier and, since it is not modified by the fairly constant temperature of the Pacific, is subject to greater temperature extremes. Summers are hot, particularly in the south, where LYTTON, OLIVER and OSOYOOS are often the hot spots in the country, reaching temperatures well in excess of 30°C. Winters, on the other hand, are much colder than on the coast, though the cold is broken by periodic mild Pacific storms that work their way through the mountains. The western part of the southern Interior is the driest part of the province because it is in the rainshadow of the CASCADE MTS. The OKANAGAN VALLEY, for example, receives a mere 250 mm of precipitation annually. Much of the eastern part of the southern Interior lies in what is called the Interior Wet Belt and receives considerably more precipitation. This occurs because warm, dry air over the Okanagan, for

instance, picks up moisture as it passes over the large LAKES of the southern Interior and drops it again as it hits the CARIBOO, MONASHEE, and SELKIRK mountains on the west side of the ROCKY MT TRENCH. The central and northern Interior are also wet (PRINCE GEORGE receives 628 mm of precipitation), colder in the winter and not as hot in the summer. Annual snowfall ranges from 50 to 100 cm in the dry valleys of the south to 400 cm around REVELSTOKE and in the north. The northeast corner of the province has its own climate, which is an extension of the continental prairie climate. It is colder in winter than the rest of the north (but enjoys considerably more winter sunshine than coastal areas) and it enjoys warm summer temperatures and an extended frost-free period that allows AGRICULTURE to flourish.

Despite the general trends described, BC's climate is characterized by many local anomalies that defy generalization. The "pocket desert" near Osoyoos, a northern extension of the Great Basin, is one of these. TELEGRAPH CREEK, on the middle STIKINE R in the northwest of the province, has much drier weather than the rest of the river corridor and is hot enough in the summer to support many fruits and vegetable crops that don't grow well in the northwest generally. Another is the GULF ISLANDS, which, despite their coastal location, enjoy a comparatively drier Mediterranean-like climate because they lie in the rainshadow of the mountains on Vancouver Island and the Olympic Peninsula.

CLIMATE DATA FOR SELECTED BC STATIONS

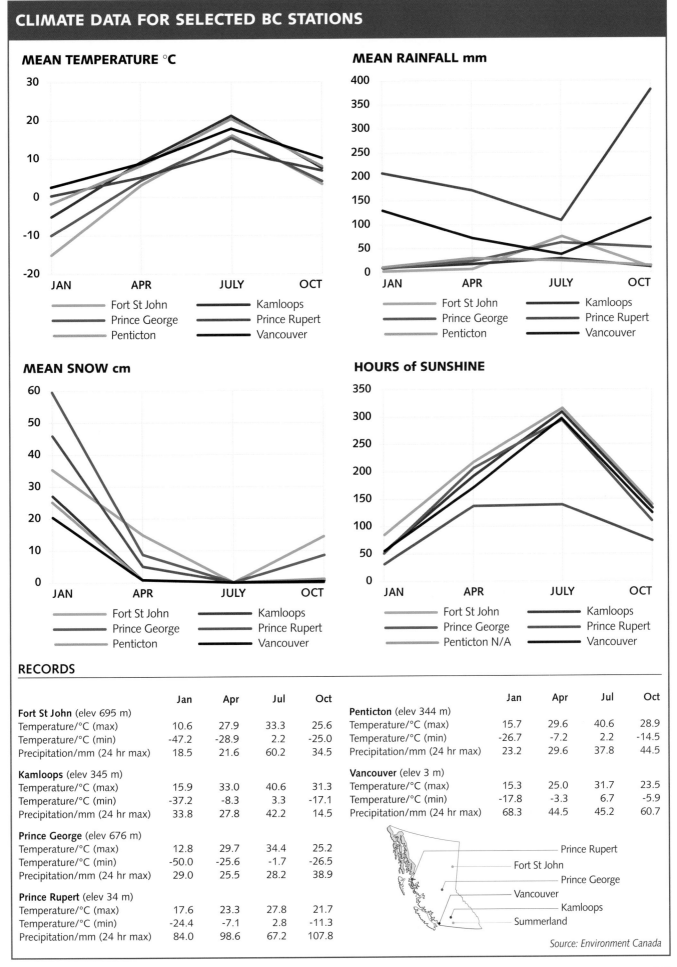

MEAN TEMPERATURE °C

Legend: Fort St John, Kamloops, Prince George, Prince Rupert, Penticton, Vancouver

MEAN RAINFALL mm

Legend: Fort St John, Kamloops, Prince George, Prince Rupert, Penticton, Vancouver

MEAN SNOW cm

Legend: Fort St John, Kamloops, Prince George, Prince Rupert, Penticton, Vancouver

HOURS of SUNSHINE

Legend: Fort St John, Kamloops, Prince George, Prince Rupert, Penticton N/A, Vancouver

RECORDS

	Jan	Apr	Jul	Oct
Fort St John (elev 695 m)				
Temperature/°C (max)	10.6	27.9	33.3	25.6
Temperature/°C (min)	-47.2	-28.9	2.2	-25.0
Precipitation/mm (24 hr max)	18.5	21.6	60.2	34.5
Kamloops (elev 345 m)				
Temperature/°C (max)	15.9	33.0	40.6	31.3
Temperature/°C (min)	-37.2	-8.3	3.3	-17.1
Precipitation/mm (24 hr max)	33.8	27.8	42.2	14.5
Prince George (elev 676 m)				
Temperature/°C (max)	12.8	29.7	34.4	25.2
Temperature/°C (min)	-50.0	-25.6	-1.7	-26.5
Precipitation/mm (24 hr max)	29.0	25.5	28.2	38.9
Prince Rupert (elev 34 m)				
Temperature/°C (max)	17.6	23.3	27.8	21.7
Temperature/°C (min)	-24.4	-7.1	2.8	-11.3
Precipitation/mm (24 hr max)	84.0	98.6	67.2	107.8

	Jan	Apr	Jul	Oct
Penticton (elev 344 m)				
Temperature/°C (max)	15.7	29.6	40.6	28.9
Temperature/°C (min)	-26.7	-7.2	2.2	-14.5
Precipitation/mm (24 hr max)	23.2	29.6	37.8	44.5
Vancouver (elev 3 m)				
Temperature/°C (max)	15.3	25.0	31.7	23.5
Temperature/°C (min)	-17.8	-3.3	6.7	-5.9
Precipitation/mm (24 hr max)	68.3	44.5	45.2	60.7

Map labels: Prince Rupert, Fort St John, Prince George, Vancouver, Kamloops, Summerland

Source: Environment Canada

CLINTON, village, pop 729, is on the GOLD RUSH road 40 km north of CACHE CREEK at the entrance to the CARIBOO–CHILCOTIN. Originally it was part of the territory of the SECWEPEMC (Shuswap) people. A townsite began in 1862 at the junction of the DOUGLAS TRAIL and the CARIBOO WAGON ROAD, the 2 earliest routes to the Interior goldfields. Known as 47 Mile House, Cut Off Valley, or simply The Junction, in 1863 it was named for the retiring British colonial secretary Henry Clinton, 5th Duke of Newcastle. One of the earliest buildings was the Clinton Hotel, where the Clinton Ball was held annually from 1868 until the hotel burned in 1958. The tradition continues at another hall in the village. Since its inception Clinton has been the centre of a ranching (*see* CATTLE INDUSTRY) district and it retains a frontier atmosphere, though many of the spreads became working guest ranches. Indeed, by the late 1990s Clinton could lay claim to being the Guest Ranch Capital of the world.

Ox team at Clinton Hotel, c 1870. UBC BC416

CLOAK BAY is on the west side of Langara Island, the most northerly of the QUEEN CHARLOTTE ISLANDS, facing out into the Pacific. The first European trader in the Charlottes, Capt George DIXON, arrived in the bay 2 July 1787, finding the HAIDA eager to trade. His trader, William Beresford, described how they "fairly quarrelled with each other about which should sell his cloak first." Maritime traders visited the bay regularly for the next 2 decades. There were 3 Haida villages in the vicinity—Kiusta, Yaku and Dadens—all subsequently abandoned.

CLO-OOSE was a small settlement on the west coast of VANCOUVER ISLAND, at the mouth of the Cheewhat R south of NITINAT LK. It was in the territory of the Ditidaht, a NUU-CHAH-NULTH (Nootka) nation. A trading store opened at the site in the late 1880s and in 1894 David Logan and his wife Sarah became the first white settlers. Logan ran the store and post office and worked as a linesman on the west coast telegraph line; his family was associated with the spot for many years. The METHODIST CHURCH established a mission and school in 1894. Most white residents had left by 1964, when the local Ditidaht moved to a new reserve on Nitinat Lk.

CLOTHIER, Robert Allan, actor, sculptor (b 22 Oct 1921, Prince Rupert; d 10 Feb 1999, N Vancouver). He was a pilot in the RAF during WWII until an accident in 1945 left him with a broken back. After convalescing for nearly 2 years, he began architecture studies at UBC, then

departed for England to pursue training in both theatre and sculpture. After returning to VANCOUVER in 1954 he worked steadily as an actor in THEATRE, radio, television and feature films for almost 40 years, all the while pursuing a parallel career as a sculptor. He is best known for his role in the *BEACHCOMBERS* television series in which he appeared for 19 seasons, earning ACTRA and Gemini awards for his portrayal of the irascible Relic. Film credits include *One's a Heifer* (1984), *The Journey of Natty Gann* (1985) and *North of Pittsburgh* (1992).   *Shannon Emmerson*

CLOVER VALLEY, 20 km southeast of NEW WESTMINSTER, was one of SURREY's earliest settlements. The three Shannon brothers moved here in 1874–75 and it became the site of Surrey's town hall in 1883. The community drifted 2 km away to the west, however, to the NEW WESTMINSTER SOUTHERN RWY line and became known as CLOVERDALE.   *AS*

CLOVERDALE is one of the 5 main townships comprising the city of SURREY in the FRASER VALLEY east of VANCOUVER. Centrally located, it was the original business and government centre of Surrey and the site of the municipal hall from 1912 to 1962. It profited from the arrival of the BC ELECTRIC RWY CO's Fraser Valley INTERURBAN rail line that ran out to CHILLIWACK from 1910 to 1950. The CLOVERDALE RODEO has been held annually since 1945 and is the second largest in Canada after the Calgary Stampede.

CLOVERDALE RODEO & EXHIBITION began as a fair on the SURREY Municipal Hall and Surrey Centre grounds in Sept 1888—without a RODEO. In 1938 the fair moved to CLOVERDALE and rodeo events began in 1945. The rodeo became a professional competition in 1948 but was postponed for 4 months that year because of FRASER R flooding; when it opened in September it attracted a record crowd of 7,000. The first Rodeo Queen was crowned in 1950, which was also the first year the rodeo's results counted toward standings on the World Champion All-around Cowboy circuit. The rodeo gradually grew to be the second-largest community rodeo in Canada and in 1983 attracted 20,000 spectators for the first time. The next year it was voted the top performance rodeo in N America by the Professional Cowboy's Assoc. The original fair continued separately as the fall exhibition but was integrated into the rodeo weekend in 1996. *See also* COWBOYS.   *SW*

CLOWHOM LAKE lies in the COAST MTS at the head of Salmon Inlet north of SECHELT. The lake is divided from the inlet at its west end by Clowhom Falls and is accessible only by boat and seaplane. There was a shingle mill at the falls from 1906 to 1931; when it went bankrupt, new owners converted it into a resort, which continues in business. Another FISHING lodge operated toward the other end of the lake from 1943 to 1956. The BC POWER COMMISSION built a HYDROELECTRICITY dam at the falls between 1950 and 1952. The facility was later upgraded and still provides power to the SUNSHINE COAST. *See also* LAKES.

CLUTESI, George, writer, artist (b 1905, Port Alberni; d 27 Feb 1988, Victoria). A member of the Sheshaht Nation (NUU-CHAH-NULTH), he grew up on VANCOUVER ISLAND. He worked for 20 years as a pile driver; then, while convalescing from an injury, he took up drawing and writing. He was encouraged to draw by Emily CARR, who left him her artist's supplies when she died. He painted one of the murals at the Canada pavilion at Expo 67. His book *Son of Raven, Son of Deer* (1967) was the first published collection of aboriginal stories by an aboriginal person. It was followed by *Potlatch* (1969). Clutesi appeared in two motion pictures and in 1973 was named to the Order of Canada. *See also* ART, NORTHWEST COAST ABORIGINAL.

George Clutesi, writer and artist, c 1960. UBC BC1019

CLYNE, John Valentine, jurist, forestry executive (b 14 Feb 1902, Vancouver; d 22 Aug 1989, Vancouver). He graduated from UBC, studied at the London School of Economics and was called to the BC Bar in 1927. Clyne specialized in maritime law and was appointed chair of the Canadian Maritime Commission in 1947. He was a judge of the BC Supreme Court from 1950 to 1957, a position he resigned to become chair and later CEO of MACMILLAN BLOEDEL LTD. He was instrumental in transforming MacBlo from a large forest company into a diversified multinational operation. He was made a member of the Order of Canada in 1972 and retired the next year. A member of the UBC Senate from 1951 to 1960, he also served as chancellor of the university. *See also* FOREST INDUSTRY.
Reading: J.V. Clyne, *Jack of All Trades*, 1987.

COAL is the most valuable mineral produced in BC. In 1998 coal accounted for revenues of nearly $1.1 billion, about 30% of the province's total mineral output, excluding petroleum and natural gas. Coal also accounts for about 40% of BC's MINING employment. In 1999, 8 coal mines were operating in BC: Quinsam on VANCOUVER ISLAND near CAMPBELL RIVER, Bullmoose and Quintette

BC COAL 1860–1998: VALUE & PRODUCTION

	$ Million	Tonnes
1860	0.1	14,475
1870	0.1	30,322
1880	0.8	271,889
1890	2.0	689,020
1900	4.7	1,615,688
1910	11.1	3,007,074
1920	13.5	2,587,763
1930	9.4	1,809,364
1940	7.1	1,507,758
1950	10.1	1,427,907
1960	5.2	715,455
1970	19.6	2,398,635
1980	461.5	10,823,530
1990	979.9	24,366,481
1995	987.7	24,515,000
1998	1,087.9	27,711,000

mines near TUMBLER RIDGE in the northeast (Quintette was slated to close mid-2000), and Elkview, Line Creek, Coal Mountain, Greenhills and Fording River in the ELK R Valley in the southeast corner of the province.

Coal mining began on Vancouver Island in the middle of the 19th century under the auspices of the HBC (see COAL MINING, VANCOUVER ISLAND). On the mainland, significant development of coal deposits came in the 1890s, with the construction of railways into the southeast corner of the province by the CPR and its American rivals. Mines opened near FERNIE (Coal Creek), MICHEL–NATAL, MORRISSEY and HOSMER, all in the valley of the Elk R. The addition of these CROWSNEST PASS-area mines, along with deposits at MERRITT and northwest of PRINCETON, doubled the province's coal output and by WWI, coal accounted for 25% of the total value of BC mineral production. Following the war, as first ships, then railways, converted to oil as their main fuel, coal mining went into a slump and from the 1930s its contribution to the provincial economy was small. Then, in the late 1960s, coal mining rallied as operations expanded into new deposits in the southeast corner of the province. This was followed by development of the northeast coalfields at Tumbler Ridge in the 1980s. Most of the coal was exported for use by the Japanese steelmaking industry and for generating electric power. The Asian economic crisis of the 1990s, and the consequent decline in Japanese demand for BC coal, forced the commodity price down; the future of BC mines was put in jeopardy and it became obvious how dependent on international economic conditions the industry had become.

COAL HARBOUR, pop 290, overlooks Holberg Inlet, an arm of QUATSINO SOUND 15 km south of PORT HARDY on northern VANCOUVER ISLAND. Founded by COAL miners in the 1880s, it was a Royal Canadian Air Force FLYING BOAT STATION during WWII. In 1947 the base was converted to

a shore WHALING station; whales killed offshore were towed here for processing. The station closed in 1967. Commercial FISHING has been important to the area.

COAL MINING, VANCOUVER ISLAND,

began at Beaver Harbour near the north end of the Island, where the HBC and Royal Navy ships traded coal from the local KWAKWAKA'WAKW. The HBC established FORT RUPERT in 1849, installing a party of 7 Scottish miners to put the operation on a more professional footing. The company was ill-prepared for the miners and their families, however. Food was inadequate and housing non-existent. Moreover, the underground coal deposits could not be reached without extensive work. Instead of mining, the miners were sinking shafts, prospecting for coal and doing general

Miners working underground at the No 5 Mine, Cumberland. Cumberland Museum C-165-30

labourers' work. As a result they could not earn the bonuses for coal production they had been promised in Scotland, and the company would not renegotiate their contracts. Equally frustrating was the fact that the miners were used to being treated as tradesmen—skilled workers who controlled the pace and process of the work. HBC treated them as servants, as it did its own employees, who worked as hard and as long as the company dictated. In the end, the miners refused to work. Most of them left the colony for the California goldfields. They were replaced by new workers, but the mine was unsuccessful and closed in 1852. Meanwhile, in 1849 the SNUNEYMUXW (Nanaimo) people told the HBC about coal deposits in their territory. The company purchased 24 km² from the Crown and put the Snuneymuxw to work collecting surface coal. Colliers from Fort Rupert moved south to NANAIMO in 1852 and began digging shafts. A decade later, HBC sold out to Vancouver Coal

Mining and Land Co, which built BC's first railway in 1863, a short line linking the mines to the wharf at Nanaimo.

In 1869 Robert DUNSMUIR purchased property at WELLINGTON, north of Nanaimo, and developed another major mine. The third important island coal centre was the COMOX Valley. Coal was discovered at Comox in 1853 but serious development did not begin until the 1880s, when Dunsmuir acquired claims at CUMBERLAND and created the Union Colliery Co. The Cumberland mines were linked to UNION BAY by rail. By the mid-1890s the best coal at Wellington was played out and the operation was phased out by 1900. The town moved to LADYSMITH, on Oyster Harbour, which had become the trans-shipment centre for new mines developed by the Dunsmuir company at

the small community of EXTENSION. By 1900 this mine was producing 360,000 tonnes a year. In 1910 James Dunsmuir sold the mines at Extension and Cumberland to 2 railway promoters, Donald Mann and William Mackenzie, for $7 million. In turn they reorganized the operation and sold it to British entrepreneurs, who created Canadian Collieries (Dunsmuir) Ltd.

Meanwhile the other major player, Vancouver Coal Mining, was prospering at Nanaimo; the mines reached peak production in 1922 when over 1.25 million tonnes were shipped. It eventually changed its name to Western Fuel Corp of Canada and in 1928 sold to Canadian Collieries, giving that company a virtual monopoly on Island coal mining. During the Depression years there was a steady decline in production, which continued in the post-war period as OIL AND GAS rapidly replaced coal as a fuel. The Extension mines closed in 1931, followed by the last large-scale Nanaimo-area mines in the early 1950s. Mining continued at Cumberland until 1960. When the Tsable River mine south of Union Bay closed in 1966, it marked the end of 80 years of coal mining in the area. In 1999 the Quinsam mine near CAMPBELL RIVER was the Island's last coal producer.

The mine workforce was polyglot, consisting mainly of British immigrants with large numbers of CHINESE, JAPANESE and BLACK labourers, all paid less than their white comrades and all segregated in separate districts of the various mining communities. Underground mining was extremely dangerous work. Fires, flooding and cave-ins were all common. On 3 May 1887 an explosion and fire in the Vancouver Coal Co mine at Nanaimo killed 148 men. In 1888 another 77 men died in an explosion at Wellington. These were the worst accidents; there were many others. Chinese miners were blamed for the accidents and mine owners agreed not to hire Chinese labour underground (though they continued to work at Cumberland). Nanaimo miners were unionized, but attempts to organize unions at the Dunsmuir mines met with strong opposition; the struggle culminated in a strike in 1890–91, which the miners lost.

In 1911 miners invited in the United Mineworkers of America (UMWA). A bitter strike began in Sept 1912 and lasted 2 years, spreading from Cumberland and Ladysmith to all the island mines. By this time there were 4 owners: Canadian Collieries at Cumberland and Extension, Western Fuel at Nanaimo, Pacific Coast Collieries with a single mine at S Wellington, and Vancouver and Nanaimo Coal Co (VNCC), owner of the Jingle Pot Mine at Nanaimo. The VNCC settled with the miners and resumed production in 1913, but the other owners firmly opposed unionization, predicting it would raise their costs and drive them out of business. They brought in strikebreakers and evicted workers from company-owned houses. Police arrived to maintain peace and allow the mines to operate. At Cumberland, Chinese and Japanese miners were threatened with deportation if they did not sign a contract. They did sign, exacerbating racial tension in the mines. During the summer of 1913 frustration boiled over in clashes with police and strikebreakers in Cumberland, Nanaimo, Extension and Ladysmith. In response to the violence, Attorney General William BOWSER sent militia units into the mining towns; they stayed there until the following summer, when the strike petered out with the outbreak of WWI. Troops were withdrawn and many strikers enlisted. The strike was a defeat for the union and cost hundreds of miners their jobs. It was not until the 1930s that union organizing resumed in the Island mines with the appearance of the Communist-backed Mine Workers Union of Canada. Later in the decade the UMWA returned. *See also* LABOUR MOVEMENT.

COALITION GOVERNMENT of CONSERVATIVES and LIBERALS held power in BC's provincial legislature from 1941 to 1952. The Coalition was intended to reduce political partisanship during the war and to keep the socialist CCF out of power when it refused to join.

The Liberal Party, led by Duff PATTULLO, was reduced to a minority in the 1941 election. Seeing their opportunity, supporters of coalition within the party held a special convention in December endorsing the idea, also supported by the Conservative Party under its leader, Royal MAITLAND. Pattullo, who opposed coalition, resigned as party leader and PREMIER, and a new government was installed, led by John HART. With the most seats in the legislature, the Liberals were the senior partner in the Coalition. As a result, Premier Hart (1941–47) and Premier Byron JOHNSON (1947–52) and most Coalition CABINET members were Liberals, while the Conservatives formed a minority.

The Coalition was able to take advantage of the wartime economic boom and won the 1945 election with a solid majority. It was re-elected 4 years later by an even larger majority. Indeed, the 61.4% of the popular vote it won in 1949 is the highest recorded by any provincial government since the party system was introduced. Among the Coalition's achievements were major improvements to ROADS AND HIGHWAYS, the creation of the BC POWER COMMISSION to extend rural electrification, and the introduction of the province's first retail sales tax and a controversial hospital insurance plan (*see* HEALTH POLICY).

After 1949, animosity between Liberals and Conservatives intensified until finally in 1952 the Conservative leader, Herbert ANSCOMB, engineered his own dismissal from cabinet. He was followed by other Conservatives and the Coalition dissolved. During the 1952 election, which introduced the preferential ballot, both

Conservatives and Liberals were trounced by the CCF and the emergent SOCIAL CREDIT PARTY. BC did not have another Liberal or Conservative administration in the 20th century.

COALMONT is a small cluster of houses on the TULAMEEN R, 17 km northwest of PRINCETON on the old stagecoach route to MERRITT. It was founded after COAL was discovered in the surrounding hills in 1906. An aerial tramway was built to carry the coal from the mines at BLAKEBURN down to a rail line here to be shipped out. Since the last mine closed in 1940, Coalmont has been home to only a few residents.

COAST MOUNTAINS are an immense chain of rugged peaks sweeping 1,600 km along the BC coast from VANCOUVER to the Alaskan Panhandle. Formed about 45 million years ago as a result of collisions between pieces of the earth's crust, they rise abruptly from the ocean and are intersected by deep FJORDS created by GLACIATION. Remnants of the glaciers are still present, notably around Mt WADDINGTON, at 4,019 m the highest peak entirely in the province. Other major summits are Mt Combatant, Mt Tiedemann, Monarch Mt, Mt Silverthrone and Mt Gilbert. The first ascents in this chain were made between the 1930s and 1950s. More recently mountaineers (*see* MOUNTAINEERING) have sought challenging secondary routes. About 300 km wide, the Coast Mts have a profound effect on BC's CLIMATE by forcing moisture-laden air off the ocean to rise, dropping precipitation on the lush FORESTS of the western

Summit of Serra 2 in the Waddington range of the Coast Mts. John Baldwin photo

slopes. As a result, parts of the coast have the heaviest rainfalls in N America, nurturing a lush growth of temperate RAIN FOREST dominated by FIR, HEMLOCK, CEDAR and SPRUCE. The eastern slopes descending to the Interior Plateau are less steep and comparatively dry. The range is bisected by 2 main transportation corridors: Hwy 20 across the CHILCOTIN to BELLA COOLA, and the SKEENA R Valley to PRINCE RUPERT.

Reading: John Baldwin, *Mountains of the Coast,* 1999.

COAST SALISH; *see* SALISHAN FIRST NATIONS.

COASTLINE of BC stretches 7,022 km from JUAN DE FUCA STRAIT north to Alaska. The total length when the shorelines of ISLANDS are included is 27,200 km. The continental shelf, a platform of relatively shallow water less than 365 m deep, runs along the edge of the continent. Off VANCOUVER ISLAND it extends up to 50 km offshore, narrowing to the north until, at the QUEEN CHARLOTTE ISLANDS, it drops away quite dramatically from the west coast. Most of the important commercial FISHING takes place in this shallow zone. Almost all of the mainland coast is protected by islands lying a short distance offshore; the tops of a sunken chain of MOUNTAINS, they create the sheltered passages and straits that have been used as coastal transportation corridors. The CLIMATE is mild and wet, influenced by Pacific currents that circulate warm water along the outer coast. When moisture-laden air off the ocean hits the COAST MTS it rises, dumping its load of precipitation as it does so. As a result, the coast is one of the wettest places on earth. HENDERSON LK on the west side of Vancouver Island gets more rain than any other spot in N America. Aside from the occasional warm pockets, water temperatures are chilly. Beaches are scarce and in many places the land rises steeply out of the water. The coast emerged from beneath the last ice sheets 12,000 to 15,000 years ago and, with the weight of ice removed, the land has risen relative to the sea level since that time. The major islands and deep-water FJORDS all were formed by the action of the glaciers (*see* GLACIATION).

Because of the steepness of the landscape and absence of arable soil there is little AGRICULTURE on the coast. Mountain slopes are cloaked in lush temperate RAIN FOREST, at least in those areas that have not been logged (*see* LOGGING). North of Vancouver Island the forest is dominated by HEMLOCK and CEDAR; in the southern region DOUGLAS FIR predominates. Balsam (*see* FIR) and Sitka SPRUCE are also common.

Occupied for at least 9,000 years, the coast had the highest concentration of aboriginal population in N America before contact with Europeans (*see* ABORIGINAL DEMOGRAPHY). It was surveyed during the last half of the 18th century by Spanish and British explorers seeking an entry to the fabled Northwest Passage (*see* SPANISH EXPLORATION). The SEA OTTER trade flourished from 1785 to 1820, after which the HBC established several trading posts, the first settlement by Europeans. SALMON CANNERIES were established at the mouths of major RIVERS and up some of the inlets at the end of the 19th century and the coast became one of the richest salmon-producing areas in the world. SALMON continue to be the mainstay of the fishery, though many other species are also harvested commercially. Logging began in the late 19th century and has continued to the present. By WWI there were many small communities scattered along the coast, linked by regular steamboat service. The period between the world wars is sometimes called the "Golden Age of the Coast," when the population reached its widest distribution and economic activity was decentralized enough to support a network of communities (*see* ECONOMY). Consolidation of the major industries in the post-WWII period dramatically reduced economic opportunities and population became centralized in a few larger centres. The coastline is accessible by road and rail from the Interior at only 4 points: VANCOUVER, BELLA COOLA, KITIMAT and PRINCE RUPERT. BC FERRY CORP operates a regular service from the north end of Vancouver Island to Prince Rupert and to Bella Coola, and CRUISE SHIPS ply the INSIDE PASSAGE during the summer. Otherwise, most of the coast is still remote, accessible only by boat or seaplane.

COAT OF ARMS for BC features a central shield flanked by 2 supporters above a scrolled motto. It was designed by Rev Arthur Beanlands, adopted in 1895 and confirmed by King Edward VII on 31 Mar 1906. The shield shows a Union Jack, below which 3 wavy bars signify the Pacific Ocean and a setting sun signifies BC's location as the most westerly province. Atop the shield is a lion, garlanded with DOGWOOD flowers, and a royal crown. The supporter on the left is a wapiti stag (*see* ELK) and on the right a bighorn-sheep ram (*see* MOUNTAIN SHEEP). The scrolled MOTTO *Splendor sine occasu* ("Splendour without diminishment") is entwined with Pacific dogwood flowers, since 1956 the official floral emblem of the province. On 20 June 1960 the design of the central shield was adopted as the provincial FLAG.

Provincial coat of arms. Roy Luckow photo

The earliest BC municipalities to adopt coats of arms were NEW WESTMINSTER (1860), VICTORIA (1862) and VANCOUVER (1886). Since about 1950 the number of municipal coats of arms has grown dramatically, incorporating a wide variety of emblems, including the black diamonds for COAL in the arms of NANAIMO (1951), the waters of OKANAGAN LK for KELOWNA (1954), the thunderbird for ESQUIMALT (1956), the first appearance in heraldry of the COUGAR for NELSON (1958), the Coast Salish (*see* SALISHAN FIRST NATIONS) spindle whorl for N VANCOUVER (1982), the PEACE ARCH for SURREY (1987) and the CARIBOO WAGON ROAD for 100 MILE HOUSE (1992). ROSSLAND's arms feature a female skier, OLIVER's apples and horseshoes, CASTLEGAR's a castle and railway references, and the arms of SAYWARD and PRINCE GEORGE celebrate the FOREST INDUSTRY. Among educational institutions, UBC was the first university in Canada to receive arms (1915); it has been joined by SFU, UNIV OF VICTORIA and UNBC.

COBBLE HILL, a rural village on the ESQUIMALT & NANAIMO RWY 35 km northwest of VICTORIA on VANCOUVER ISLAND, is the site of one of BC's longest-running fall fairs, held each August. The origin of the name is uncertain; it may refer to a place in England, a visiting naval officer or the proximity of a quarry.   AS

COBURN, 17 km south of NANAIMO on VANCOUVER ISLAND, was a station on the ESQUIMALT & NANAIMO RWY. It was named after John W. Coburn, who operated the Ladysmith Lumber Co SAWMILL at this location in the early 1900s and became the first mayor of LADYSMITH.   AS

COCCOLA, Nicolas, missionary (b 12 Dec 1854, Coccola, Corsica; d circa 1940, Smithers). He spent 60 years working as an Oblate missionary (*see* OBLATES OF MARY IMMACULATE) among BC's FIRST NATIONS. He arrived from France in 1880 and initially was posted to KAMLOOPS, where his missionary field included the NICOLA Valley. In 1887 he moved to the ST EUGENE MISSION north of CRANBROOK, where he played an important role in the MINING boom then sweeping the KOOTENAY. Not only did he grubstake the founder of the SULLIVAN MINE, he also had a share in the St Eugene Mine, a valuable lead-ZINC mine near Moyie Lk. When he sold his share he used the proceeds to build a church at the mission, a church that is still standing. Known by this time as "the miner priest," he was transferred in 1905 to the Our Lady of Good Hope Mission near FORT ST JAMES, where he ministered to the DAKELH (Carrier) and SEKANI peoples. Later he was principal of the RESIDENTIAL SCHOOL at LEJAC. In 1934 he retired from the school and moved to SMITHERS.

COD, PACIFIC (*Gadus macrocephalus*), also known as true cod or grey cod, grows to a length of more than 115 cm and a weight of 22.7 kg. Distinguished by 3 separate dorsal fins and a prominent barbel (fleshy filament) below the lower jaw, it lives from southern California north around the PACIFIC RIM and south to Japan and Korea. In the winter and spring, Pacific cod dwell along the ocean's shelf edge and upper slope at depths of 100–200 m. Here they overwinter; they spawn between Jan and Apr and later move to shallower waters for the summer. The female is highly fertile and can produce more than a million eggs. Pacific cod prey on other sea creatures such as worms, CRABS, MOLLUSCS, SHRIMP

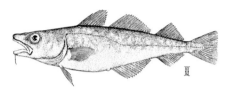

Pacific cod. Phil Edgell photo; drawing courtesy Fisheries & Oceans Canada

and smaller fish and in turn are preyed upon by HALIBUT, SHARK, seabirds and marine mammals. This species has an estimated maximum life span of 19 years. Pacific cod stock is commercially harvested in GROUNDFISH fisheries, principally by trawl nets and in smaller amounts by hook and line fisheries. Jigging is the favoured method of sport FISHING. The Atlantic or northern cod (*Gadus morhua*) is a member of the same family.

CODY was a SILVER mining settlement 13 km east of NEW DENVER between SLOCAN and KOOTENAY lakes near SANDON. Founded by Henry Cody and the Noble Five MINING Co, it was the terminus of the KASLO & SLOCAN RWY and site of a concentrator mill. Cody had 150 residents, 3 hotels, 3 laundries, a livery and blacksmith shop, and a dressmaker in 1897, but was abandoned by the early 1900s. A few ruins can still be seen.　AS

CODY CAVES are located inland from the west side of KOOTENAY LK, 15 km northwest of AINSWORTH HOT SPRINGS. Discovered in the 1880s by Henry Cody, a prospector, they were rumoured to be lined with GOLD, but none was ever found. They do contain wonderful calcite formations, which make them a favourite with spelunkers. The caves, 800 m deep, are part of Cody Caves Provincial PARK (63 ha), created in 1966 (*see* KARST FORMATIONS).

COE-JONES, Dawn, golfer (b 19 Oct 1960, Campbell River). The daughter of a COWICHAN LAKE logger, she was BC junior women's GOLF champion in 1978–79, BC amateur champion

in 1982–83 and Canadian amateur champion in 1983. After golfing at Lamar Univ in Texas, where she was an all-American in 1983, she turned professional and joined the LPGA tour. By 1990 she was among the tour's top 20 players, finishing eleventh in earnings that year with $240,000. Her first tour victory came 2 years later when she won the $75,000 Kemper Open. In 1994 she won the HealthSouth Palm Beach Classic and in 1995 the LPGA Tournament of Champions in Lake Buena Vista, FL. Such successes weren't repeated in the rest of the 1990s, but by 1999 her career earnings were more than $2.3 million US.　SW

COGHILL, Joy, actor, director (b 13 May 1926, Findlater, SK). Born in Canada, she lived in Scotland until wartime conditions forced her return to Canada in 1941. She studied THEATRE at UBC after the war and received an MA in fine arts from Goodman Theatre in Chicago in 1951. Back in VANCOUVER, she joined Sydney RISK's EVERYMAN THEATRE as a director. When the company folded in 1953 she helped establish Holiday Theatre, Canada's first professional theatre for children. In 1967 she became the first woman artistic director at VANCOUVER PLAYHOUSE; during her tenure the Playhouse staged George RYGA's landmark play *The Ecstasy of Rita Joe*. In the early 1970s she lived in eastern Canada and was director of the English acting section at the National Theatre School, but she returned to Vancouver to continue her career as actor, producer and director. She has also written plays and in 1995 directed Benjamin Britten's opera *Noye's Fludde* to celebrate the UN's 50th anniversary. She received the Order of Canada in 1990 and has honorary degrees from both SFU and UBC.　*Shannon Emmerson*

Joy Coghill, actor, 1991. Les Bazso/Vancouver Province

COGHLAN is an AGRICULTURAL and former LOGGING settlement in the FRASER VALLEY, 19 km northwest of ABBOTSFORD in LANGLEY municipal-

ity. It grew up in 1911 around a stop on the BC ELECTRIC RWY. A huge concrete electrical substation building was erected here. The site was named after early homesteaders H. and N. Coghlan.　AS

COLDSTREAM, district municipality, pop 8,975, occupies a long, narrow valley in the north OKANAGAN VALLEY 5 km southeast of VERNON. Most of the population is clustered at the western end close to KALAMALKA LK. The first settler was Charles F. HOUGHTON, an Irish army officer who acquired a military grant in 1863 that became Coldstream Ranch (*see* CATTLE INDUSTRY). The ranch was subsequently owned by Forbes and Charles VERNON, who sold it to Lord Aberdeen in 1891. Aberdeen developed the orchards (*see* TREE FRUITS) and subdivided some of the land for settlement, mostly by British gentlefolk. Incorporated on 21 Dec 1906, the district grew slowly as a ranching and fruit-growing area. Since WWII and especially since the 1960s, housing development has transformed it into a residential suburb of Vernon. Glass and lumber manufacturing became the main industries (*see* FOREST PRODUCTS), though most residents work in Vernon. In 2000 the Coldstream Ranch still owned agricultural land.

COLE, Douglas Lowell, historian (b 9 Dec 1938, Mason City, WA; d 18 Aug 1997, N Vancouver). A graduate of George Washington Univ and the Univ of Washington, he came to BC in 1966 to teach history at SFU and he spent the rest of his career there. He became a Canadian citizen in 1974. His research came to focus on the history of white–aboriginal relations on the coast. His books include *Captured Heritage* (1985), the story of how outsiders collected artifacts among coastal FIRST NATIONS, and *An Iron Hand Upon the People* (with Ira Chaikin, 1990), a controversial history of the suppression of the POTLATCH. At his death he had completed the first volume of a long-awaited biography of the anthropologist Franz BOAS.

COLLEGES; *see* COMMUNITY COLLEGES.

COLLEYMOUNT is a farming and cattle-raising (*see* AGRICULTURE; CATTLE INDUSTRY) settlement on the north shore of FRANÇOIS LK 35 km southwest of BURNS LAKE. It was named after nearby Mt Colley, which commemorates Edward P. Colley, who worked as a surveyor here from 1905 to 1906 and later went down with the *Titanic*.　AS

COLLIER, Eric, trapper, writer (b 1903, Northampton, England; d 15 Mar 1966, Riske Creek). He arrived in BC from England in 1920 to work at an uncle's homestead near CLINTON, then moved to RISKE CREEK and worked for Frederick BECHER. In 1930 he, his wife Lillian and young son Veasy moved north to an isolated area near MELDRUM CRK, where he was instrumental in returning BEAVER to the area. A guide and conservationist, he wrote about his life in many magazine articles and his best-selling book *Three*

Against the Wilderness (1959). A classic of BC LIT-ERATURE, the book was condensed by *Reader's Digest* and translated around the world.

COLLINGS, Charles John, artist (b 1848, Chudleigh, England; d 1931). As a young man he worked as a solicitor's clerk and in business, learning to paint in his spare time. He did not begin exhibiting until he was middle-aged and initially his watercolour landscapes did not sell well enough to provide an income. In 1910 he immigrated to Canada with his family and settled at SEYMOUR ARM on the north side of SHUSWAP LK, where he intended to take up fruit farming and continue painting. A 1912 exhibition in London of his paintings of the BC Interior met with great success, and though he was not well known locally he enjoyed a moderate reputation in England. His gentle watercolours, a unique blend of English and Japanese traditions, were in stark contrast to the more vivid oil paintings of contemporaries such as Emily CARR and the Group of Seven.

COLLINS OVERLAND TELEGRAPH CO was an attempt to create a communications link between N America and Europe by running a telegraph line from San Francisco through BC and Alaska and across Bering Strait to Siberia. The project was initiated by an American promoter, Perry Collins, and financed by the Western Union Telegraph Co. Construction began in 1865 under the direction of Charles Bulkley, a Civil War veteran. During the first season crews strung line from NEW WESTMINSTER up the FRASER VALLEY and along the CARIBOO WAGON ROAD as far as QUESNEL. When work resumed the next year, VICTORIA was added to the line. Meanwhile crews of mainly CHINESE and aboriginal people were pushing through extremely rugged terrain toward the SKEENA R. "Banishment in Siberia is a paradise in comparison to this place," lamented one engineer. Nevertheless surveys had reached as far as TELEGRAPH CREEK when word arrived that an underwater telegraph cable had been laid successfully across the Atlantic. The overland line was no longer needed; work was stopped. The operating line that remained between New Westminster and Quesnel was the beginning of telecommunications in BC. Local FIRST NATIONS used some of the abandoned materials to build the famous suspension bridge at HAGWILGET.

COLLISHAW, Raymond, WWI air ace (b 22 Nov 1893, Nanaimo; d 29 Sept 1976, W Vancouver). He grew up in NANAIMO and as a teenager joined the Fishery Protective Service, working out of NEW WESTMINSTER as a mate on a fisheries patrol boat. After being rejected 3 times for the air service, he paid for his own flying lessons, earned his wings and was accepted as a Royal Naval Air Service pilot. He was posted to France in Aug 1916 and served on the western front where his 60 kills made him the third-leading Allied air ace and the fifth-leading ace in the war. He was highly decorated, winning most major decorations except the VICTORIA CROSS.

Following the war he accepted a permanent commission in the Royal Air Force, fighting against the Bolsheviks in southern Russia and northern Persia. During WWII he commanded the RAF's Egypt Group, which became the Desert Air Force. Under his command the RAF devastated the Italian air force in the western desert. He became air vice-marshal in 1941 but retired in 1943 after a confrontation with senior commanders. At the end of the war he returned to BC, where he retired but stayed active in mineral exploration.
Ken Macleod

COLLISON, William Henry, Anglican missionary (b 1846, Ireland; d 1922, Kincolith). A schoolteacher in Cork, he arrived at METLAKATLA in 1873 with his wife, Marion Goodwin, an experienced nurse. After 3 years working there with William DUNCAN, the couple established the first permanent mission to the HAIDA at MASSET on the QUEEN CHARLOTTE ISLANDS. Collison was ordained a priest in 1878; shortly afterward he returned to Metlakatla and took a key role in mitigating the tensions that had developed between the Church Missionary Society and Duncan. In 1880 he ascended the SKEENA R to open a mission church at HAZELTON. In 1884 he transferred to the mission village of KINCOLITH on the NASS R. There he supervised the erection of a new church in 1891. Two years later this building burned and Collison spent the winter of 1895–96 in Ireland raising money for another church, which still stands. He worked among the NISGA'A until his death, serving 49 years in the missions altogether. His memoir *In the Wake of the War Canoe* was published in 1915.

COLNETT, James, maritime fur trader (b 18 Oct 1753, England; d Sept 1806, London, England). An experienced mariner who had sailed on James COOK's second voyage to the Pacific in 1772–75, he traded on the northern BC and Alaskan coasts in 1787 and 1788 in command of the *Prince of Wales* and the *Princess Royal*, sponsored by the KING GEORGE'S SOUND CO. Colnett sold his furs in China, then joined John MEARES in a new commercial enterprise aimed at establishing trading posts on the coast. In the spring of 1789 he arrived at NOOTKA SOUND in the *Argonaut* with 29 Chinese artisans. The Spanish, under Estéban José MARTINEZ, were already established in Friendly Cove, claiming sovereignty over the sound. The two men quarrelled; Colnett was arrested and his ships impounded, and he was sent to New Spain (Mexico). This incident brought Spain and Britain to the brink of war (*see* NOOTKA SOUND CONTROVERSY). Colnett meanwhile won his release and continued trading on the coast. He later served in both the merchant marine and the Royal Navy before retiring from the sea in 1805.

COLONIAL GOVERNMENT on mainland BC began with creation of a colony separate from VANCOUVER ISLAND in 1858 (*see* VANCOUVER ISLAND, COLONY OF). James DOUGLAS, already governor of Vancouver Island, was appointed governor of the new jurisdiction. Initially

Douglas received temporary power to legislate by proclamation on the mainland to establish British jurisdiction quickly during the GOLD RUSH, when there was a sudden and large influx of American miners. He formed an informal council to advise him but it had no constitutional status. In 1863 Britain established a 15-member appointed legislative council consisting of 5 senior officials, 5 magistrates and, in a form of representation, 5 members selected to represent 5 districts of the colony. It met for the first time in 1864. The same year the new governor, Frederick SEYMOUR, swore in a formal executive council of advisors. When the mainland absorbed the colony of Vancouver Island in 1866, the legislative council was expanded to a maximum of 23 members, but the mainland government remained otherwise intact; there was no elected assembly. In 1870 Britain replaced the legislative council with a partially elected body. Elections for 9 members took place in Nov; the governor appointed another 6. This new legislature first met in Jan 1871. With CONFEDERATION later that year, the new province's legislature became completely elective and achieved responsible government.

COLUMBIA, a short-lived community on the north side of the KETTLE R just southwest of GRAND FORKS, was originally known as Upper Grand Forks. It was established in 1897 to compete with Grand Forks by siphoning off passenger and freight traffic from the US. At its peak, Columbia had 6 streets and 4 hotels and was also a station on the CPR's COLUMBIA & WESTERN RWY. It lost the contest with its neighbour, however, and had mostly disappeared by WWI. *AS*

COLUMBIA & KOOTENAY STEAM NAVIGATION CO was formed in 1890 by a syndicate including John MARA, John IRVING and others to work steamers on the COLUMBIA R–ARROW LKS run between Little Dalles, WA, 13 km south of the border, and the CPR railhead at REVELSTOKE. The maiden voyage of the sternwheeler *Lytton* in the summer of 1890 coincided with a surge of interest in GOLD prospects in the ROSSLAND–TRAIL area. From this propitious beginning, the CKSN extended its field of operation to KOOTENAY LK in 1891 and steadily expanded its fleet on both lakes. The company was purchased by the CPR early in 1897 and became the BC LAKE & RIVER SERVICE. *Edward Affleck*

COLUMBIA & WESTERN RAILWAY was a narrow-gauge line, completed in 1896, connecting the mines at ROSSLAND with the SMELTER at TRAIL. A standard-gauge line was built between Trail and CASTLEGAR the following year. In 1898 the CPR bought it and the Trail smelter from Frederick Augustus HEINZE and rebuilt the narrow-gauge section as a standard-gauge line, thus connecting Rossland via NELSON and KOOTENAY LK to the CPR's CROWSNEST PASS line and eastern Canada. Using the C&W's charter, the CPR built west from ROBSON until the line reached MIDWAY in 1900, opening the southern MINING centres of GRAND FORKS, PHOENIX and GREENWOOD.

COLUMBIA BASIN TRUST was created in 1995 to bring some of the revenue from sales of HYDROELECTRIC power on the COLUMBIA R back into the W KOOTENAY (*see* COLUMBIA RIVER TREATY). Based in NAKUSP, the trust is governed by an 18-person board made up of residents of the region; their mandate is to invest in economic and ENVIRONMENTAL developments in the basin.

COLUMBIA COAST MISSION was established in 1904 by the ANGLICAN CHURCH to provide seagoing medical care and assistance to isolated camps and settlements on the BC coast north of VANCOUVER as far as KINGCOME INLET. The mission was the brainchild of John ANTLE, who served as superintendent from 1904 to 1936. Other superintendents were Alan GREENE

The Columbia, *built in 1905, one of the Columbia Coast Mission fleet.*
BC Archives B-05475

(1936–59), Patrick Ellis (1960–65), and John Forth (1965–70). Along with a small fleet of vessels, the mission operated hospitals at ROCK BAY (1905–45), VAN ANDA (1907–20), ALERT BAY (1909–46), Carriden Bay (1920–28) and PENDER HARBOUR (1930–52), and published a magazine, *Log of the Columbia*. In 1944 the Mission opened the first of its Aged Folks' Guest Houses for indigent retired pioneers at Pender Harbour. The work of the missionary Eric POWELL at Kingcome was the inspiration for Margaret CRAVEN's classic 1967 novel, *I Heard the Owl Call My Name*. During the 1970s the Mission began making visits by air. Increasingly, services offered by the Mission were taken over by other agencies and it disbanded in 1982.
Reading: Michael L. Hadley, *God's Little Ships: A History of the Columbia Coast Mission*, 1995.

COLUMBIA GARDENS, a settlement on the COLUMBIA R and the GREAT NORTHERN RWY 12 km southeast of TRAIL, was named for a large orchard planted here to demonstrate that SMELTER smoke was no danger to fruit trees.   AS

COLUMBIA ICEFIELD, 225 km², is an immense ice cap straddling the BC–Alberta border south of Jasper on the Icefields Parkway. It is composed of a central névé of snow and ice up to 365 m thick, from which glaciers radiate into the surrounding valleys. The icefield was located in 1898 by British mountaineers Norman Collie and Hermann Wooley. The highest mountain in the region, Mt Columbia, was first climbed on 19 July 1902 by James Outram and his Swiss guide Christian Kaufmann. Snowdome (3,520 m) is the hydrographic apex of N America and from here meltwater flows west via the COLUMBIA R to the Pacific Ocean, east via the Saskatchewan R to Hudson Bay and the Atlantic Ocean and north via the Athabasca and Mackenzie rivers to the Arctic Ocean.

COLUMBIA MOUNTAINS are a complex group of mountains occupying most of southeast BC from the Interior Plateau and the Okanagan Highlands east to the ROCKY MT TRENCH. About 600 km in length, it is composed of 4 separate ranges: the SELKIRKS, PURCELLS, MONASHEES and CARIBOOS. The highest peak in the Columbia Mts is Mt Sir Sandford at 3,530 m. Other major peaks are Mt Sir Donald, Mt Adamant, Bugaboo Spire and Mt Sir Wilfrid Laurier. These ranges are largely metamorphic and granitic in nature and a wide variety of rock types are found. Meltwater drains into the COLUMBIA R, hence the name.

COLUMBIA RIVER, 2,000 km (763 km in BC), originates in Columbia Lk in the southern ROCKY MT TRENCH. After flowing north along the floor of the trench past GOLDEN, it enters KINBASKET LK, a reservoir created in the 1970s when the river was flooded and the MICA DAM was constructed. The reservoir drowned what was formerly known as the Big Bend of the Columbia, where it made an abrupt U-turn around the north end of the SELKIRK MTS and began to flow south. This route was followed by the BIG BEND HWY, which opened in 1940 and provided the shortest ROAD connection through the Interior

until it was replaced by the ROGERS PASS section of the TRANS-CANADA HWY in 1962. Since construction of the dam, the river flows south out of Kinbasket through a series of long, narrow reservoirs: Lk Revelstoke and the ARROW LKS. Near CASTLEGAR it is joined by the KOOTENAY R, its major tributary, and continues its southward flow past TRAIL to cross the US–Canada border at WANETA. In the US it winds south through Washington state, then veers west, forming the border with Oregon until it reaches the Pacific Ocean at Astoria. The Columbia drains a total area of 155,000 km², of which 102,800 km² are in BC. Named by Capt Robert GRAY, who sailed his ship *Columbia Rediviva* into the mouth of the river in 1792, it is the largest N American river by volume flowing into the Pacific Ocean and the third longest river in N America after the Mississippi and the Mackenzie. The upper reaches of the river were located by the FUR TRADE explorer David THOMPSON in 1807. In 1811 he travelled by CANOE down the river to the Pacific, hoping to establish a fur trade post for the NORTH WEST CO at its mouth. He arrived to find American traders already installed in Fort Astoria. He returned east and followed the river all the way to its headwaters, the first person known to have travelled its length. Later the river was used by the HBC as a link in the main fur trade transport route connecting the BC Interior with the Pacific (*see also* FUR BRIGADES; NEW CALEDONIA). Until 1846 the Columbia was the southern BOUNDARY of British territory in the Pacific Northwest. With the signing of the OREGON TREATY, the British withdrew north of the 49th parallel of latitude and the southern Columbia was absorbed into the US.

The Columbia is one of the world's greatest sources of HYDROELECTRIC power. The Americans began development in the 1930s with the construction of the Grand Coulee and Bonneville dams. Eventually 11 dams were built on the American side of the border and another 3 dams in BC—the DUNCAN, KEENLEYSIDE and MICA dams—as part of the COLUMBIA R TREATY (1964). Along with the production of electricity, the dams were used for flood control and irrigation. As a result of the development, SALMON stocks in the river, once plentiful, were drastically reduced when land and communities in BC were flooded to create reservoirs. In 1995 the COLUMBIA BASIN TRUST was established to bring some of the revenue from sales of hydroelectric power on the Columbia R back into the W KOOTENAY. *See also* RIVERS.

COLUMBIA RIVER TREATY, signed in 1964 between Canada and the US, provides HYDROELECTRIC power and flood control on both sides of the border. Negotiations were initiated by the Americans, who needed more hydro power for the growing cities of the Pacific Northwest and improved flood control along the lower reaches of the river. After years of talks, the 2 sides agreed in 1961 to a plan calling for the construction of 3 dams in BC: the DUNCAN DAM north of KASLO, the KEENLEYSIDE DAM near CASTLEGAR and the MICA DAM north of REVELSTOKE. In return Canada received a share of the extra power produced in the US as a result of the treaty—the so-called downstream benefits. Implementation of the treaty was delayed by a dispute between the federal government and W.A.C. BENNETT's provincial government over the use of downstream benefits. Ottawa believed it had authority in the matter and wanted the power returned to Canada, but Bennett asserted the province's right to sell the benefits back to the US for cash. Bennett eventually prevailed and the treaty was signed on 16 Sept 1964. The downstream benefits were sold to a group of US electric utilities for 30 years at a cost of $273 million, money with which Bennett then built the dams from 1968 to 1973. The treaty was highly controversial: critics argued that BC had sold the power at too low a price, and at the risk of ENVIRONMENTAL damage to watersheds in southeast BC. In 1998 a share of the downstream benefits began returning to BC, and by 2003 all 1,400 megawatts of downstream power will belong to the province.

COLWOOD, city, pop 13,848, is a residential suburb of VICTORIA overlooking JUAN DE FUCA STRAIT 18 km west of the capital. It originated as one of the farms established by the  PUGET'S SOUND AGRICULTURAL CO and run by Capt Edward Langford in the 1850s, and was named for Langford's home in England. A SAWMILL, tannery and shoe factory were established in the area in the 1870s. FORT RODD HILL, built in the 1890s to defend ESQUIMALT harbour and now a national historic park, is within the city's boundaries, as are other naval facilities associated with the Esquimalt base. ROYAL ROADS UNIV, formerly a military college, occupies the heart of Colwood. During the 1970s, as the population of Victoria expanded, Colwood began to develop a distinctly residential flavour. It incorporated as a city in 1985.

COMINCO (formerly Consolidated Mining and Smelting Co of Canada Ltd), based in VANCOUVER, was created in 1906 by the merger of assorted MINING interests with the TRAIL smelter owned by the CPR. The new company, dominated by the CPR, also owned rail lines and power facilities

The Cominco smelter at Trail, 1980.
Roy Luckow photo

but its main asset was the SMELTER, which had been upgraded to handle output from most of the mines in the booming KOOTENAY district. In 1910 Cominco purchased the SULLIVAN MINE at KIMBERLEY. Using ore from this mine the company began producing ZINC; with the development in 1919 of the differential flotation system—an ore-treatment process using the capacity of various constituents of ore to float on liquid— the company became the largest lead-zinc producer in the world. Cominco also produced COPPER at a refinery in Trail, until prices fell and the company abandoned this side of the business in 1930. During the 1930s, Cominco also became a major producer of sulphuric acid and fertilizers. In 1986 CPR sold its interest to a group headed by TECK CORP in Vancouver. In 1998 the mining giant had revenues of $1.63 billion.

The principal source of feed for the Trail smelter is the Cominco-operated Red Dog deposit in Alaska. Along with the Sullivan Mine, scheduled to close in 2001, Cominco also has interests in the Highland Valley copper mine near KAMLOOPS, the Polaris lead-zinc mine in the Canadian Arctic and a zinc refinery in Peru.

COMMANDO BAY, 16 km north of NARAMATA on the east side of OKANAGAN LK, was the site of a training camp for commandos during WWII. Between May and Sept 1944 the Special Operations Executive of the Canadian military trained volunteers, many of them CHINESE Canadians (including Douglas JUNG, later a VANCOUVER MP), in the skills of subversion, sabotage and guerrilla warfare, preparing them to infiltrate behind enemy lines. The force, known as the Oblivion group, was honoured with a historic plaque unveiled at the site in 1988. Originally called Dunrobin's Bay, Commando Bay is now part of Okanagan Mt Provincial Park. *See also* PARKS, PROVINCIAL.

COMMISSION ON RESOURCES AND THE ENVIRONMENT (CORE) was appointed by the NDP government in Jan 1992 to bring together interested parties—ENVIRONMENTALISTS, FIRST NATIONS, industry, TOURISM and community groups—to develop a long-term land use strategy for the province. Headed by Stephen Owen, a lawyer and former provincial OMBUDSMAN, CORE convened three regional round tables (VANCOUVER ISLAND, CARIBOO–CHILCOTIN and KOOTENAY–BOUNDARY) to develop comprehensive land use plans. The objective was to identify areas for protection from industrial activity, especially LOGGING, and areas available for exploitation. The plans eventually produced by CORE provoked stiff opposition—from environmentalists for allowing too much development, from industry for protecting too much land, and from the public for sacrificing too many jobs— and were modified by the government before they were implemented. The process was highly influential on public policy. As a result of CORE's work, the government granted protected status to between 11% and 16.5% of the land in the affected regions. CORE was declared a success and dismantled in Mar 1996.

COMMODORE BALLROOM has been a downtown VANCOUVER landmark for over 70 years. It opened on Granville St as the Commodore Cabaret in Dec 1929 and quickly established itself as the most popular nightclub in the city, principally because of its spring-loaded maple dance floor. Through the 1930s and 1940s it featured a mix of local and touring bands, including all the big names of the swing era: Tommy Dorsey, Cab Calloway and Count Basie, to name just three. The ballroom closed in July 1996, but reopened in 1999 under new management.

COMMONWEALTH GAMES; *see* BRITISH EMPIRE AND COMMONWEALTH GAMES.

COMMONWEALTH NATURE LEGACY is a network of PARKS, TRAILS and green spaces north and west of VICTORIA on southern VANCOUVER ISLAND. It was inaugurated in 1994 and named for the Commonwealth Games, hosted that year by Victoria. Its components include Gowlland Tod Provincial PARK (12.21 km²), overlooking the bottom of SAANICH INLET, the 49-km JUAN DE FUCA MARINE TRAIL and several other preserves both rural and urban.

COMMUNITY COLLEGES were established as part of a general expansion of POST-SECONDARY EDUCATION in the 1960s. They are primarily 2-year institutions offering programs in 4 fields of education: academic (university transfer); career/technical, to train students for specific employment with programs ranging in duration from a few weeks to 2 or more years; vocational, offering short applied programs of a year or less; and adult basic education to prepare those without high school graduation for other post-secondary programs or for employment. The first college to open (1965) was Vancouver City

College, renamed Vancouver Community College in 1974. Its Langara campus separated into an independent college in 1994. Along with the 2 VANCOUVER colleges there are 9 other community colleges around the province: College of New Caledonia in PRINCE GEORGE, Northwest Community College in TERRACE, Capilano College in N VANCOUVER, Douglas College in NEW WESTMINSTER, Camosun College in VICTORIA, College of the Rockies (formerly East Kootenay Community College) in CRANBROOK, North Island College in COURTENAY, Northern Lights College in DAWSON CREEK and Selkirk College in CASTLEGAR. Most of these colleges operate subsidiary campuses in neighbouring communities. Enrolment of full- and part-time students in 1996 averaged 5,090, ranging from 12,000 (VCC) to 1,300 (Northwest). In 1989 the province began upgrading several colleges to the status of university-colleges, offering upper-level courses and granting bachelor degrees. There are now 5 of these: Okanagan Univ College in KELOWNA, Univ College of the Cariboo in KAMLOOPS, Malaspina Univ College in NANAIMO, Univ College of the Fraser Valley in ABBOTSFORD and Kwantlen Univ College in RICHMOND/SURREY, with an average 1996 enrolment of 6,400. Unionized college faculty associations coordinate their efforts through the College-Institute Educators Assoc, while administrators work through corresponding bodies such as the Advanced Education Council of BC and the Presidents' Council.

COMMUNITY DEVELOPMENT (CD), a term that came into wide use after WWII, refers to efforts undertaken by people in a community—defined by geography or shared interests—to gain more control over their lives and to improve their situation. CD involves a democratic approach to change or progress, and the emphasis is on community control and self-reliance, though it is sometimes initiated or supported by government to promote social development or economic renewal. As CD has evolved in N America, it has also come to embody values such as equity and social justice.

Community development was first practised in BC at the beginning of the 20th century and evolved to take many forms as people worked to improve rural life, develop social infrastructure in urban and rural communities, and establish economic tools such as consumer CO-OPERATIVES and CREDIT UNIONS. In the 1960s CD began to be used as a tool for conscious social change. The first urban community development work was undertaken in 1964, in Woodland Park in east VANCOUVER, with a paid CD worker. In 1968 the city established the Department of Social Planning and Community Development (unique in Canada at the time), which teamed up with the United Way (then the Community Chest and Councils) to create the "local area approach." A special CD unit was set up by the Neighbourhood Services Association (NSA), an organization of neighbourhood houses. Citizens held local elections to form Area Councils that worked together on local issues, and a CD worker from NSA pro-

vided staff support. Area Services Teams were set up, composed of staff from community service agencies; they were assisted by city Social Planning staff. Councils and teams worked together on improving the quality of neighbourhood life. During this same period in Vancouver (1968–75), city-wide citizens' groups organized around particular issues, among them tenants' rights (Vancouver and District Public Housing Tenants' Association); training, VOLUNTEER placement and employment for people on social assistance (Vancouver Opportunities Program); and unemployment advocacy (the Unemployed Citizens' Welfare Improvement Council). In nonmetropolitan areas the federal Company of Young Canadians (CYC) agency funded rural as well as urban workers to undertake projects. One of the first CYC projects in Canada was with aboriginal people in ALERT BAY.

By the 1980s, institutional support and public funding for community development had fallen off. The economy was much less buoyant and some CD work had challenged the policies and practices of governments and vested interests. But the values and practices of CD continued, especially in the burgeoning self-help and ENVIRONMENTAL MOVEMENTS, whose participants drew on the skills, experience and confidence of themselves and their peers rather than that of paid organizers. In the context of BC's economic downturn, CD workers shifted their focus from social issues to economic ones. Community economic development (CED) emerged to help communities and regions build greater economic self-reliance, especially in the many resource-dependent towns in BC whose mainstays had suddenly disappeared. Through the early to mid-1980s, the Social Planning and Research Council of BC (SPARC) provided leadership in stimulating the CED movement in BC, through regional skills training and published information. In 1995 it also funded a provincial Community Development Institute.

In the 1990s, interest in environmental and land use issues rose to prominence for both the BC public and the newly elected NDP government. With the publication of the UN Brundtland Commission's report on Environment and Development in the late 1980s, the term *sustainable development* came into broad use. People involved in CED activity were mobilized in the early 1990s under the umbrella of the BC Working Group on Community Economic Development, a broad coalition of community organizations, co-operatives, educational institutions, employment training groups, credit unions and others. During the same period government played a larger role than ever before in promoting CD. The NDP administration instituted consultative practices that involved citizens in planning for environment, land use, FOREST management and health and social services (*see also* COMMISSION ON RESOURCES AND THE ENVIRONMENT; HEALTH POLICY; HUMAN CARE SERVICES). In 1999 the BC government created the first-ever ministry focussed on community development, the Ministry of Community Development, Co-operatives and Volunteers, which supports co-ops

and other CED projects throughout the province with an emphasis on promoting economic alternatives for resource communities.

Michael Clague & Leslie Kemp

COMOX, town, pop 11,069, overlooks GEORGIA STRAIT on the east side of VANCOUVER ISLAND, 4 km east along Comox Harbour from COURTENAY. The name derives from a Kwakwala (see KWAKWA̲KA̲'WAKW) word meaning "plenty." The site was used by the Royal Navy as a training location from the 1850s. Farm settlement began in 1862; the construction of a wharf in 1874 brought steamer traffic and the development of a small community. It grew as a service centre for the Comox Valley and incorporated on 14 Jan 1946. Comox became a bedroom suburb of Courtenay and attracted a number of retired people. AGRICULTURE, especially potato and DAIRY FARMING and fruit growing, remains important to the district. The Mt WASHINGTON ski area is nearby and the town is surrounded by spectacular mountain views. Canadian Forces Base Comox, a major employer, opened in 1942; it specializes in air–sea rescue and maritime patrol (*see also* SEARCH AND RESCUE). Up to 2,000 trumpeter SWANS congregate in the area each winter and a Trumpeter Swan Festival is held in early Feb. A ferry runs from Comox across Georgia Strait to POWELL RIVER.

COMOX, or Island Comox, are a FIRST NATION of the Northern Coast Salish people (*see* SALISHAN FIRST NATIONS). Before contact with Europeans they occupied the east coast of VANCOUVER ISLAND from KELSEY BAY south almost to COMOX, and the adjacent islands, including QUADRA ISLAND. There were at least 5 subgroups inhabiting different villages throughout the territory. By 1800 the Lekwiltok, a tribe of the KWAKWA̲KA̲'WAKW (Kwakiutl), were expanding southward down JOHNSTONE STRAIT and they displaced the Comox, forcing them south to the area of Comox Harbour; there they subsequently absorbed their neighbours, the PENTLATCH people. Over time the Comox intermingled with the Lekwiltok, and Kwak'wala (see KWAKWA̲KA̲'WAKA) replaced the Island Comox language, which is now all but extinct (*see* FIRST NATIONS LANGUAGES). The descendants of this intermingling now comprise the Comox Nation at their RESERVE in Comox Harbour. There are about 300 registered band members. The name *Comox* derives from a Kwak'wala term meaning "plenty" or "abundance."

CONFEDERATION with the Dominion of Canada occurred on 20 July 1871. Faced with a growing public debt and the end of the GOLD boom, British Columbians had been considering their options, including annexation to the US. In 1868 Amor DE COSMOS and others had formed the CONFEDERATION LEAGUE to promote union with Canada, while opposition to the idea was led by a coterie of government officials and some American residents. By 1869 the two factions were deadlocked. Britain, which favoured union, appointed Anthony MUSGRAVE as governor to press for Confederation. Popular support swung behind union and in 1870 BC presented its terms, including assumption by the Dominion of BC's debt, a road link to Manitoba leading eventually to a railway, federal per capita subsidies based on highly inflated population figures, plus 4 senators and 8 MPs in the federal Parliament. Three negotiators went to Ottawa to represent the colony: R.W.W. CARRALL, J.W. TRUTCH and J.S. HELMCKEN. Their terms were accepted with slight modifications. BC would receive 3 senators and 6 MPs and the per capita grants would be based on a population figure of 60,000, still many times the actual figure. As well, the federal government agreed to take over BC's debt and to complete a railway within 10 years. To facilitate railway construction, BC agreed to give to the Dominion government a 32-km-wide strip of land on either side of the track, the so-called "Railway Belt." (In the end BC turned over almost 58,500 km² of Crown Land for the railway.) BC accepted the terms in Jan 1871, after which the colonial legislative council agreed that the new provincial government would consist of a 25-seat legislative assembly from which a LT GOV would choose 5 executive councillors. From the outset confederation represented an economic arrangement more than a sentimental attachment to Canada. During the 1870s, when the railway appeared to be in question, BC threatened to leave the union, earning a reputation as "the spoilt child of confederation." "Ottawa bashing," whether deserved or not, has been a mainstay of provincial politics ever since, but there has never been a serious popular movement to withdraw from confederation. *See also* FEDERAL–PROVINCIAL RELATIONS.

CONFEDERATION LEAGUE, formed in May 1868 in VICTORIA, was a group of activists in favour of BC's union with Canada. Leading members of the League included Amor DE COSMOS, John ROBSON and Robert BEAVEN, all future PREMIERS. They convened the YALE CONVENTION in Sept 1868 to promote the idea, along with responsible government and freer trade with the US.

CONFLICT OF INTEREST COMMISSIONER is an independent officer of the provincial legislature responsible for administering the Members' Conflict of Interest Act, passed in 1990 and strengthened in 1992. The Act governs the separation of MLAs' official duties from their private interests, prohibiting them from performing official tasks if there is either a conflict of interest or an apparent conflict of interest. The Act also bans MLAs from accepting fees or gifts connected with the performance of their duties, and restricts the CABINET from giving contracts to former cabinet ministers or parliamentary secretaries within 24 months of their holding office. Under the Act, MLAs are required to file annual disclosure statements with the commissioner,

listing their assets, liabilities and financial interests and those of their spouses and minor children. The commissioner also advises MLAs on possible conflicts and conducts inquiries into allegations of violations of the Act.   *Russ Francis*

CONGREGATION EMANUEL TEMPLE, BC's first synagogue, was built in VICTORIA in 1863, just 5 years after the arrival of the first members of the city's Jewish community (*see* JEWS) during the FRASER R GOLD RUSH. The building was designed in the Romanesque style by the local firm Wright and Saunders. It has been restored and is the oldest surviving synagogue in Canada.
Ted Mills

CONNAUGHT TUNNEL is an 8-km railway tunnel beneath ROGERS PASS. From the time the CPR laid its main line over the pass in 1885, AVALANCHES were a constant problem. The worst accident occurred in 1910 when 62 CPR employees on a plow train were buried—the most railway-related fatalities in a single accident in BC history. The company responded by boring the tunnel, then the longest in N America. The new tunnel also increased the capacity of the railway through the mountains. Named for the gov gen, it was completed in 1916 and allowed trains to avoid the hazardous pass. In the 1980s the CPR built an even longer tunnel, the 14.7-km Mt Macdonald Tunnel, which further improved this section of track.

CONNELL, Grant, tennis player (b 17 Nov 1965, Regina, SK). Raised in N VANCOUVER, he didn't begin playing TENNIS seriously until he was 15. After attending Texas A&M Univ where he was an all-American, he turned professional in 1985 and in a 12-year career developed into one of the most successful tennis players Canada has produced. He was ranked the best doubles player in the world in 1993 and won the 1995 world championship with American partner Pat Galbraith. Connell reached the doubles finals at

Grant Connell, N Vancouver tennis star.
Courtesy Tennis Canada

Wimbledon 3 times and won a total of 22 tournament doubles titles. By the finish of his career he had accumulated more prize earnings than any Canadian before him, topping $2.9 million. In national play he won 7 Canadian doubles titles and the 1991 singles championship. Connell was a key member of the only Canadian Davis Cup team to earn a place in the elite World Group (1990). He retired from the pro tour in 1997 and went on to teach tennis. He is a member of the Canadian Tennis Hall of Fame and the BC SPORTS HALL OF FAME (1999).

CONNELL, Robert, Anglican cleric, first CCF leader (b 1871, Liverpool, England; d 13 Nov 1957, Victoria). He came to Canada in 1888, went into the Anglican ministry and settled in VICTORIA. He was one of 7 members of the new CCF elected to the provincial legislature in 1933. Selected house leader over Ernest WINCH, he was later confirmed as the first leader of the provincial party. Connell was a poor debater and his politics were not far enough to the left for a large faction of the party; he was deposed as leader in 1936 and subsequently was expelled from the party. He then organized his remaining supporters as the Social Constructive Party and finished the legislative session as the leader of the official opposition. In the 1937 election, however, his party was wiped out and Connell retired from politics.

CONNOLLY, William, fur trader (b circa 1786, Lachine, QC; d 3 June 1848, Montreal). A veteran of the NORTH WEST COMPANY, he joined the newly organized HBC in 1821 as a chief trader and in 1824 took command in NEW CALEDONIA (the central Interior of BC). During the next 7 years he managed the business of the district, developing new transportation routes to the coast and extending the trade west and north toward the Russian traders in Alaska. In 1828 his daughter Amelia married James DOUGLAS, then a FUR TRADE clerk, later governor of VANCOUVER ISLAND and BC. In 1831 Connolly left New Caledonia and spent the rest of his career in Quebec.

CONSERVATIVE PARTY was one of BC's 2 dominant political parties, along with the LIBERALS, until the 1950s. It faded as a political force after the 1952 provincial election, eclipsed by the new SOCIAL CREDIT PARTY, and had become moribund by the late 1990s.

The party emerged formally at a 1902 convention in REVELSTOKE; led by Richard MCBRIDE, it came to power in an election the following year. Previously MLAs had not formally identified themselves with parties, instead uniting in shifting legislative factions bound by personal relationships and self-interest rather than principles or policies. This arrangement was highly unstable; MLAs accepted party discipline in an attempt to bring order to government. McBride, a very successful politician, remained PREMIER to 1915, when his attorney general William BOWSER broke with him over railway policy and threatened to divide the party. McBride resigned and

Bowser took over as party leader and premier. Bowser led the Conservatives to disastrous defeat in 1916 and remained leader through two more losing elections before retiring in 1926.

Simon Fraser TOLMIE replaced Bowser and led the Tories back to power with a landslide victory in the 1928 election, but he was the province's last Conservative premier in the 20th century. His inadequate response to economic crisis in the Depression squandered Conservative electoral support and badly fractured the party. In 1933 the Conservatives elected only 3 MLAs belonging to splinter groups; 2 were Non-Partisan Independents and one was a Unionist. Dr F.P. Patterson took over a reunited party in 1936 and doubled the popular vote in the next year's election. He was succeeded as leader in 1938 by Royal MAITLAND, a Vancouver lawyer. Following the 1941 election, in which the Conservatives ran a respectable third, Maitland pressed for a COALITION GOVERNMENT of the 3 major parties. The CCF declined, but the Tories and Liberals formed a coalition. Maitland was attorney general in Premier John Hart's cabinet. After he died in 1946, Herbert ANSCOMB, another senior cabinet minister, succeeded him. Anscomb twice fought off challenges to his leadership from W.A.C. BENNETT; these fractured the party. When the coalition broke up, Anscomb led the Conservatives to a disastrous showing in the 1952 election. Reduced to 4 seats in the legislature, the party was never again a serious contender for power, superseded as a right-wing party by the Social Credit Party. Deane Finlayson, a Nanaimo insurance agent, replaced Anscomb in 1953. During the decade of his leadership, the party lost all of its seats in the assembly. In 1963 E. Davie FULTON left federal politics to take over the provincial party leadership but failed to win even his own seat and resigned in 1965. The party had an acting leader for several years and fielded only 3 candidates in the 1966 election.

Subsequent leaders were John DeWolfe, Derril Warren, Scott Wallace, Vic Stevens, Brian Westwood and Peter POLLEN, none of whom re-established the party as a credible alternative to Social Credit. Even when the Socreds faded in the 1990s, their support moved to a resurgent Liberal Party and an emergent REFORM PARTY rather than back to the Conservatives.

CONSERVATIVE PROTESTANTISM is a term referring to Protestant Churches that subscribe to a fundamentalist interpretation of the Bible and to the concept of evangelism, the belief that salvation, or spiritual rebirth, comes through faith. Conservative Protestants generally accept that humans are inherently sinful and believe the virgin birth, miracles and the resurrection and divinity of Christ to be historical facts. On social issues they tend to emphasize conservative family values and are reluctant to adapt their beliefs to modern social trends. Conservative Protestant Churches in BC experienced a dramatic increase in membership during the 1980s and by the 1990s there were more than 1,150 Conservative Protestant Churches of various denominations in

the province. The main denominations, among which there is considerable variety in beliefs and practices, include the SALVATION ARMY, Pentecostalists, Baptists, the Christian and Missionary Alliance, the Plymouth Brethren, the Evangelical Free Church, the Seventh-Day Adventists, the Dutch Reform Churches and the Vineyard Christian Fellowship.

Pentecostalism, which originated in Los Angeles in 1906 when the entire congregation at a revival meeting began speaking in tongues, arrived in BC in 1912 with the formation of a small Pentecostal mission in VANCOUVER. (The denomination has been identified with speaking in tongues since its origin.) By 1923 the congregation had grown large enough to establish its own church, the Sixth Avenue Pentecostal Tabernacle. That same year Charles Price, a convert of the popular evangelist Aimee Semple McPherson, held healing crusades in Vancouver and VICTORIA, resulting in the creation of new churches in both cities. The 1920s was a period of rapid expansion for Pentecostalism in BC, and 10 churches joined together to form the BC district of the Pentecostal Assemblies of Canada (PAOC). By 1953 there were 100 congregations in BC and by the 1980s Pentecostalism had reached out successfully to various ethnic communities, establishing 22 aboriginal (*see* FIRST NATIONS) congregations, 2 CHINESE churches, 6 GERMAN churches and single congregations in the Korean, FINNISH and UKRAINIAN communities. In 1974 the Western Pentecostal Bible College opened in ABBOTSFORD. The PAOC is the largest denomination but there are other Pentecostal organizations, including the International Church of the Foursquare Gospel, the United Pentecostal Church, the Glad Tidings Christian Fellowship and the Apostolic Church of Pentecost.

Baptists take their name from the practice of total immersion in water as the only form of baptism. To join the church, initiates personally accept Christ as their saviour and acknowledge their faith in public. The first Baptists in BC were Americans who arrived during the GOLD RUSH. When the First Baptist Church was formed in Victoria in 1876, more than half the congregation consisted of American BLACKS. By 1897 there were 11 Baptist Churches in the province, enough to form the Convention of Baptist Churches of BC. Numbers continued to grow until the 1920s, when a schism developed over theological teaching and church financial policies, and about a third of the membership left the Convention of Baptist Churches and founded the Convention of Regular Baptists. The Regular Baptists thrived following WWII, establishing the Northwest Baptist Theological College in 1945 and developing congregations all over the province. Other denominations include the Baptist Union of Western Canada (the successor organization to the Convention of Baptist Churches), the Southern Baptist Convention, General Conference Baptists and affiliated German Baptist Churches.

Christian and Missionary Alliance was founded in the eastern US by a Canadian-born PRESBYTERIAN minister, A.B. Simpson. It began as a mis-

sionary society but has been recognized as an independent denomination since the 1970s. It emphasizes the importance of evangelizing among the poor. The first permanent CMA Church in BC was established in Victoria in 1928; a home for returning missionaries opened in Vancouver 2 years later.

Plymouth Brethren, founded in England as an offshoot of the ANGLICAN CHURCH, is Calvinist in nature and believes in "dispensationalism," a form of prophetic teaching popularized by early Brethren leader, John Nelson Darby. In BC most adherents are Open Brethren who seek fellowship with a variety of Christian groups. In 1968 the Open Brethren established REGENT COLLEGE at UBC, providing evangelical graduate training to students from a range of Conservative Protestant denominations. There are also several assemblies of Exclusive Brethren who are less ecumenical.

Evangelical Free Church began in the US as splinter groups of disaffected Scandinavian Lutherans (*see* LUTHERAN CHURCH). Two of these groups, the Swedish Evangelical Free Church and the Norwegian-Danish Evangelical Free Church, operated as separate entities until they merged as the EFC in 1950. "Free" churches have been present in BC since the 1930s. In 1962 the EFC founded Trinity Western Junior College, now TRINITY WESTERN UNIV, in LANGLEY.

Seventh-Day Adventist Church originated in Michigan in 1863 under the leadership of Ellen White. Its theology is based on a prophetic body of doctrines (many written by White herself) and a literal reading of the Bible, and the church is unique in its emphasis on the Ten Commandments as guidelines for daily living. Adventists also stress the imminent second coming of Christ. The first Seventh-Day Adventists in BC were missionaries from Oregon who began visiting the province in 1886. Four years later the first Adventist Church was organized in Victoria, and by the outbreak of WWII there were churches in most major centres. The church also operates nursing homes, senior citizen centres, health education centres, dental clinics and schools.

Dutch Reform Churches arrived in BC with the large numbers of DUTCH immigrants who came to Canada following WWII. Originating in Holland in 1834, the Reformed Church divided into 3 different strands in Canada: the Christian Reformed Church, the Reformed Church of America and the Canadian Reformed Church. The Christian Reformed Church has the largest membership in BC with the greatest concentration of members in the FRASER VALLEY. Many of its members send their children to schools established by the church.

Vineyard Christian Fellowship was started by John Wimber, a former Quaker from California. The church emphasizes expressive forms of worship that demonstrate the power of the Holy Spirit in Christian life. It arrived in BC in 1986 and grew quickly after Wimber spoke at a series of conferences. There were an estimated 3,300 members of the Vineyard in BC in 1991.

Reading: Robert Burkinshaw, *Pilgrims in Lotus Land*, 1995.

CONTEMPORARY VERSE was a "little" poetry magazine founded by Alan CRAWLEY in W VANCOUVER in 1941. At the time it was one of a very few outlets for Canadian poets and Crawley published most of the best work being written. The lead poem in the first issue, "Hands," was one of the early published works by Earle BIRNEY, and was accompanied by work by P.K. PAGE, Floris McLaren (who became associate editor), Leo Kennedy, Dorothy LIVESAY, A.J.M. Smith and Anne MARRIOTT. Except for the jumbo 10th anniversary edition which contained 28 pages, the quarterly consisted of 24 staple-bound pages set on an office typewriter and priced at 35 cents, yet it was hailed by Toronto critic Nathan Cohen for playing "an important part in the development of Canadian writing." Crawley closed the magazine in 1952, after 39 issues.

CONTIMCO was a LOGGING camp near COWICHAN LK on VANCOUVER ISLAND and a station on the Cowichan branch of the CNR. It was named for the Continental Timber Co and flourished briefly in the late 1920s. *AS*

COOK, James, British naval officer (b 27 Oct 1728, Marton, England; d 14 Feb 1779, Hawaiian Islands). After apprenticing as a sailor with a commercial shipowner, he enlisted in the Royal Navy in 1755. He rose quickly through the ranks and served as master of a gunship during the battle for Louisbourg in 1758. Cook was an accomplished surveyor and took part in the mapping of the St Lawrence R that allowed the British fleet to besiege Quebec in 1759. He later charted the coast of Newfoundland. From 1768 to 1775 he commanded the *Endeavour* on 2 long voyages of exploration in the S Pacific, sailing farther south than anyone before him. These voyages established his reputation as the most accomplished naval explorer in Europe. In 1776 he embarked on a third voyage in search of the Pacific entrance to the fabled Northwest Passage. With 2 ships, *Resolution* and *Discovery*, he rounded Africa and crossed the Pacific, and arrived off the coast of Oregon in Mar 1778. He then proceeded north and anchored in Resolution Cove in NOOTKA SOUND on the west coast of VANCOUVER ISLAND on 29 Mar. His contacts with the local NUU-CHAH-NULTH (Nootka) were the first interactions between the British and FIRST NATIONS people on the BC coast. After spending a month taking on wood and water, trading with the local people and repairing his vessels, Cook left Nootka Sound on 26 Apr. He did not see land again until he approached the coast of Alaska, where he explored Prince William Sound and Cook Inlet. He penetrated Bering Strait before being driven back by ice. He then returned to the Sandwich Islands (Hawaii), where he was killed by natives. Accounts of Cook's last voyage opened the northwest coast of America to the outside world and drew attention to its wealth of furs, leading to the maritime FUR TRADE.

COOK, Wendy (Hogg), swimmer (b 15 Sept 1956, Vancouver). She trained at the Canadian Dolphins Swim Club in VANCOUVER and took part in her first major international competition at the 1972 Munich Olympics, where she finished fifth in her specialty, the 100-m backstroke. In 1973 she took the bronze medal in the same event at the world championships in Belgrade. Competing at the 1974 Commonwealth Games she won the 100-m and 200-m backstroke races and helped Canada's relay team to the gold in the 400-m medley, in which she also set a world record of 1:04:78 in her 100-m backstroke leg.

Cook placed fourth in the individual 100-m at the 1976 Montreal Olympics and helped the medley relay team win bronze. She set more than 30 Canadian records before retiring in 1979. She was inducted into the Canadian Aquatic Hall of Fame in 1983 and the BC SPORTS HALL OF FAME in 1990. *SW*

COOMBS, pop 840, is on the east side of VANCOUVER ISLAND near PARKSVILLE. It began in 1910 with the arrival of 100 farm settlers from Leeds, England, sponsored by the SALVATION ARMY as part of its program to resettle poor Britons in Canada. Coombs was named for Thomas Coombs, the organization's Canadian commissioner. It is a quiet rural community with a series of TOURIST attractions, including a country market where goats graze on the sod-covered roof..

COOP, Jane Austin, pianist (b 18 Apr 1950, Saint John, NB). She studied with the pianists Anton Kuerti and Leon Fleischer while obtaining a BMus from Univ of Toronto in 1971 and an MM from Peabody Conservatory of Music in Baltimore in 1974. Winner of the 1970 CBC Talent Festival, she gave her performance debut in 1973 at St Lawrence Centre in Toronto. She performed with various orchestras during the 1970s, during which time she won the

Jane Coop, pianist, 1984.
Rob Draper/Vancouver Sun

Washington International Piano Competition and took top prize at the New York Artists' Guild. She began teaching at Univ of Toronto in 1976 as Kuerti's assistant, then moved to VANCOUVER in 1980 to join the UBC music faculty. Coop also maintains a busy performance schedule, appearing with chamber ensembles and most of the world's major orchestras. Two of her recordings have been nominated for Juno Awards. In the 1990s her touring schedule included appearances in the Orient, and her performances included the complete cycle of Beethoven sonatas for piano and violin (with Andrew Dawes). *Shannon Emmerson*

Captain Cook's Arrival in Nootka Sound, 1778, an illustration by Robert John Banks, 1970.
BC Archives PDP-00494

CO-OP RADIO; *see* VANCOUVER CO-OPERATIVE
RADIO.

COOPER, Michael, aboriginal leader (b Nov
1865, San Juan Island; d 10 Jan 1936, Victoria).
His father was an English military officer stationed on SAN JUAN ISLAND (*see also* PIG WAR); his
mother was a LEKWAMMEN (Songhees) woman
from the VICTORIA area. Cooper worked for 27
years at a fish cannery owned by J.H. TODD. In
1894 he became the first chief of the
Lekwammen elected under the provisions of the
Indian Act, and he remained chief until he
resigned because of ill health in 1935. A prominent resident of the capital, he was chief when
the Lekwammen were pressured by the government to move from their main village across the
harbour from downtown Victoria to their present location west of downtown.

**CO-OPERATIVE COMMONWEALTH FED-
ERATION** (CCF) in BC was the provincial
branch of the national socialist party formed in
Calgary in 1932. In Oct 1932 the SOCIALIST PARTY
OF BC affiliated with the new national party and
joined with the provincial branch of the League
for Social Reconstruction to become the CCF in
BC. It was joined in 1933 by several small
Associated CCF Clubs of BC; W.A. PRITCHARD
was president. That fall the first convention
endorsed a platform advocating nationalization
of financial institutions and natural resources,
socialized medicine, free education (including
university), and other radical policies. In the Nov
election, the first time the CCF ran candidates
anywhere in the country, the new party won 7
seats in the legislature and almost a third of the
popular vote, becoming the official opposition.
The leader was Rev Robert CONNELL.

The new party was a fractured coalition of
hard-line socialists, labour activists, social
reformers and middle-class intellectuals. Discord
surfaced during 1936 when Connell was
expelled for not being radical enough. The result
was a loss of support in the 1937 election. Party
discipline took hold, however, and in each of 7
elections from 1941 to 1960, the CCF won
enough seats to serve as the official opposition.
(The party also succeeded modestly at the
municipal level in Vancouver: several CCF candidates won seats on council during the 1930s,
and Lyle TELFORD served as mayor in 1939–40.)

Under Harold WINCH, CCF leader from 1939
to 1953, the party twice came close to forming
the provincial government. In 1952 it won the
highest percentage of popular vote but lost to the
SOCIAL CREDIT PARTY under the new system of
transferable balloting. In Mar 1953, when the
minority Socreds lost a legislative vote, the LT
GOV did not ask the CCF to form a government
but allowed Premier W.A.C. BENNETT to call an
election. Before that election, Winch resigned
and the party chose Arnold WEBSTER as leader. He
was succeeded in 1956 by Robert STRACHAN. For
the rest of its existence, the party was denied
power by Social Credit's portrayal of the CCF
platform as dangerously socialist. In 1961 the
CCF was reborn as the NEW DEMOCRATIC PARTY.

*Sointula, site of some of the earliest
co-operatives in BC. Rick James photo*

CO-OPERATIVES are associations of people
who pool their money and time to provide
themselves with a fair way of marketing or purchasing products or services. For example, prairie
grain farmers organized to sell their grain
through wheat pools, while in BC fishers combined to sell their own fish. Co-operative grocery shoppers invest their resources—a share
purchase and sometimes their occasional voluntary labour—to provide themselves with goods.
Worker co-operatives pool their resources to provide a way for each member to own and operate
the business, and each member owns a piece of
the co-op and has a say in how it is run, usually
through an elected representative. Each member
of a co-op has one vote regardless of the amount
of money invested. Surpluses are shared or rein-
vested in the co-op by members as they determine.

One of the earliest co-operatives in BC was
established in 1902 at SOINTULA, on MALCOLM
ISLAND, by a community of Finnish settlers.
Isolated from commerce and what they perceived as cutthroat private enterprise, they promoted a philosophy of helping one another by
sharing resources. The commune they founded
collapsed but the co-operative spirit continued;
in 1929 FINNS at Sointula set up the first fishing
co-op in BC to give themselves bargaining power
with the canning companies (*see also* FISHING,
COMMERCIAL; SALMON CANNING). This endeavour
had foundered by 1932 but the idea attracted
other fishers. In 1944, the Fishermen's Co-operative Federation united fishing co-ops into a
complete co-operative fishing enterprise that
eventually encompassed packing houses, marine
insurance and CREDIT UNIONS to help finance
boats and equipment. The fishers were not
alone: in 1913 DAIRY FARMERS in the FRASER VALLEY
had begun their own milk-producing enterprise,
the Fraser Valley Milk Producers' Association,

which evolved over the years into DAIRYWORLD
FOODS, now Canada's largest dairy company.

The economic climate during the 1930s and
early 1940s fostered a wave of co-operative formation. Organizers from the UBC Extension
Department, under the direction of Gordon
SHRUM, assisted local groups to create credit
unions, a form of co-operative bank. During the
jobless years, the desperate situation of 16,000
BURNABY relief recipients prompted the formation of the "Army of Common Good" under the
visionary guidance of D.G. MacDonald. In 1936,
the Common Good Co-operative started food
stores, a bakery and a wood chopping group.
Members also established their own savings and
lending "credit unit," becoming the first credit
union in the province (though not chartered
until 1939). This enterprise later evolved into the
Pioneer Credit Union. For decades the co-op
store has been the mainstay of small rural towns,
often serving as the major feed supplier. One
example was the Surrey Co-op, BC's largest,
which closed its doors in 1982 after operating
for nearly 60 years. Federated Co-operatives Ltd,
with 337 member co-ops in the western
provinces, continues to be one of the strongest
wholesalers of goods, hardware, feed, groceries,
clothing and petroleum products.

Consumer co-ops, such as co-op stores, generally provide wholesale or retail goods to members. In BC the consumer co-op with the largest
membership is MOUNTAIN EQUIPMENT CO-OP.
Over the past 25 years, VANCOUVER CO-OP RADIO
(CFRO), a non-commercial station that invites
listeners to become shareholding members, has
also acquired a huge membership.

In the 1970s some co-ops, such as those in
NANAIMO, introduced the direct charge co-op, in
which goods are sold to members at cost with a
weekly fee added. This innovation attracted hundreds of new members to the co-op system. The
formation of the Amor de Cosmos Food Co-op
in VICTORIA in 1971 heralded an era of grassroots
co-operative growth known as the "new wave co-

ops." In the 1970s a network of over 50 small food co-ops and buying clubs flourished throughout the province, using their Vancouver distributor, Fed-Up Co-operative. Members favoured the purchase of natural health foods and pioneered selling in bulk to eliminate excess packaging. They emphasized democratic principles such as the rotation of leadership, and they required members to donate labour occasionally. In order to provide co-operatively produced goods and to provide employment to themselves, a Vancouver workers' co-op was founded and later became a model for others. Owned and operated by its employees, CRS Workers' Co-op, incorporated in 1976, was still going strong as CRS Holdings (no longer structured as a co-operative) in the year 2000. Its operations have included a cannery, a beekeeping co-op, a food wholesaler (Horizon Distributors) and a bakery (Uprising Breads). Other worker co-ops in BC are associated with FOREST PRODUCTS, printing and construction.

Housing co-ops flourished in the 1970s and 1980s, when housing prices rose dramatically. Because co-op homes are designed to be affordable and may not be bought or sold for a profit, they are seen as a way for lower income people to own a quality home. Residents/members buy shares in the co-op and share in decision-making and management. By 1997 there were 253 housing co-ops (13,962 units) in BC.

A provincial government co-op department in the Ministry of Small Business, Tourism and Culture offers advice and technical assistance to developing co-ops. In 1997 the BC co-operatives Agrifoods International (the parent company of DAIRYWORLD FOODS) and Lilydale (a poultry processor in BC and Alberta) rated among the top 500 businesses named by the *Financial Post*. Co-operative growers selling produce through the BC TREE FRUIT Marketing Board account for the largest fruit and vegetable co-op marketing activity in Canada. In 1999 there were 1.8 million co-op members in BC employing 13,000 staff with a business volume of $1 billion.

Jan Degrass

COOTE, Russell L. "Ginger," bush pilot (b 1899, Chilliwack; d Jan 1970, Chilliwack). A fighter pilot during WWI, he later came to personify the dashing, intrepid bush pilot of the 1930s. After acquiring a private pilot's licence in 1929 he flew for Wells Air Transport, one of the pioneering aviation companies of the early 1930s that serviced the GOLD MINING camps in the BRIDGE R area. In 1933 he became part owner of Bridge River & Cariboo Airways, based at SETON LK. Within 2 years he was president and in 1938 the company became Ginger Coote Airways, ferrying prospectors to the MINING camp at ZEBALLOS. Margaret Fane Rutledge, one of the famous FLYING SEVEN, joined the company as radio operator and co-pilot. In 1941 Coote sold his airline and it was absorbed into Canadian Pacific Air Lines the following year (*see* AVIATION). During WWII he was an instructor with the British Commonwealth Air Training Plan.

Ginger Coote, legendary bush pilot.
BC Archives C-04907

COPP, Douglas Harold, physiologist (b 16 Jan 1915, Toronto; d 17 Mar 1998, Vancouver). He studied medicine at the Univ of Toronto and biochemistry at the Univ of California at Berkeley, where he taught during WWII. As an atomic energy researcher he was asked to take a loyalty oath in 1950, but instead moved to VANCOUVER and the new medical school at UBC. There he headed the physiology department for 30 years and became interested in regulation of calcium in the body. His research led to the 1961 discovery of calcitonin, a hormone effective in the treatment of osteoporosis, arthritis and other medical conditions. A companion in the Order of Canada (1980) and winner of the coveted Gairdner Award (1967), he was one of 10 original inductees into the Canadian Medical Hall of Fame. *See also* MEDICAL PROFESSION.

COPPER has been one of the most valuable minerals mined in BC since the beginning of the 20th century. In 1998 it was the second most valuable mineral produced in BC (after COAL), earning revenues of $681 million. Revenues were in decline during the 1990s, however, as copper prices fell internationally. Active mines include Myra Falls near CAMPBELL RIVER on VANCOUVER ISLAND, Mount Polley near WILLIAMS LAKE, Huckleberry south of HOUSTON, Highland Valley north of MERRITT and Kemess just outside TATLA-TUI PROVINCIAL PARK in the northern Interior.

Copper mining began with discoveries in the BOUNDARY DISTRICT in the 1890s. The Granby Consolidated Mining, Smelting and Power Co operated the largest copper SMELTER in the British Empire at GRAND FORKS from 1900 to 1919, processing ore from mines at GREENWOOD, PHOENIX and MIDWAY. Thanks to production from these ore bodies, copper accounted for 35% of all minerals produced in BC by the beginning of WWI. At the end of the war, the centre of copper

mining shifted to ANYOX up OBSERVATORY INLET on the North Coast, where the Granby company operated a mine and smelter until 1935; to BRITANNIA in HOWE SOUND, the most productive mine during the 1930s; and to COPPER MOUNTAIN near PRINCETON. Nevertheless, copper's share of the total value of mineral production began to decline during the 1930s and did not rally until the 1960s, with the beginning of a series of huge open-pit developments, including the Craigmont mine near MERRITT (1961–82), the Brenda mine west of KELOWNA (1970–90), the ISLAND COPPER MINE near PORT HARDY (1971–95), the Gibraltar mine at MCLEESE LAKE (1972–98) and the Lornex mine (1971) southeast of KAMLOOPS. By 1999 only the last of these, operating under the Highland Valley name, was still in production.

COPPER MOUNTAIN towers above the SIM-ILKAMEEN R between MANNING PROVINCIAL PARK and PRINCETON on the HOPE-PRINCETON HWY. Copper ore was found here in the 1880s and the site was originally known as Voigts Camp. From 1920 to 1957 the Copper Mt mine was one of the most productive in the British Commonwealth. Ore was shipped to a concentrator at nearby Allenby. In 1971, after the original mine had closed, an open-pit operation began on a new discovery on the opposite side of the river, which required re-routing of part of the highway. The mine was eventually bought by Princeton Mining Co, which closed the site. *See also* COPPER.

COPPER RIVER is a small rural LOGGING settlement and former riverboat landing on the south side of the SKEENA R southwest of the mouth of the Zymoetz R, 8 km east of TERRACE. It was named for the COPPER stains that colour the riverbed. A post office operated here from 1909 to 1956. *AS*

COPPERS were large pieces of hammered natural copper, symbolizing wealth and status to the FIRST NATIONS people of the coast. Shaped like shields and often decorated with designs significant to the owner, they were precious possessions that gained value each time ownership was transferred. The prestige of their history resulted in their ceremonial use. In a gesture of superiority, a person sometimes broke a copper and threw

Coppers, symbols of wealth, at Village Island.
Vickie Jensen photo

away a piece of it. Coppers carried names and were inherited or transferred along with other symbols of rank and wealth in aboriginal society. *See also* ART, NORTHWEST COAST ABORIGINAL.

COQUIHALLA HIGHWAY is the newest route connecting the Lower Mainland to the Interior. Completed in 1987, it runs 210 km from HOPE over the CASCADE MTS via the Coquihalla Pass (el 1,674 m) to MERRITT and KAMLOOPS. Much of the route follows the old KETTLE VALLEY RWY line. It is BC's only toll highway. The SOCIAL CREDIT government was accused of misleading the public about the costs of construction, which were

Cavalcade organized in 1972 to prove that the Coquihalla was a feasible route for a highway. *Bob Egby/Vancouver Province*

much higher than projected, and in Dec 1987 the MacKay Commission report revealed serious deficiencies in the administration of the Coquihalla project. In 1990 the 106-km Okanagan Connector between Merritt and PEACHLAND opened. Construction included a 100-km chain-link fence, the longest in N America, to prevent wildlife from crossing the highway.

COQUIHALLA TRAIL was a route used by early ranchers to drive their cattle from the NICOLA Valley south to HOPE. Originally a packhorse trail, it was improved by the government in 1876 for use by cattle drivers. The COQUIHALLA HWY follows almost the same route between Hope and MERRITT. After reaching Hope, cattle were taken by boat down the FRASER R to the coast. The trail was eclipsed by the completion of the CPR in 1885 and the emergence of KAMLOOPS as a transshipment centre; it was destroyed during 1913–16 by the construction of the KETTLE VALLEY RWY through Coquihalla Pass. *See also* TRAILS.

COQUITLAM surrounds PORT COQUITLAM on the north side of the FRASER R east of BURNABY and PORT MOODY. The name derives from a SALISHAN word for "small red salmon." In its early days, Coquitlam was centred on the large SAWMILL at Fraser Mills (*see* MILLSIDE). A community of French-Canadian millworkers developed north of the mill at MAILLARDVILLE, which continued to be BC's largest French-speaking enclave. RIVERVIEW Psychiatric Hospital (Essondale) opened in 1910 with its associated gardens known as Colony Farm. Port Coquitlam disengaged as a separate city in 1913. Much of southern Coquitlam was inundated by the great Fraser R flood of 1948. After the opening of the Lougheed Hwy in 1953, the district grew rapidly as a residential suburb of VANCOUVER and incorporated as a city in 1992. The Coquitlam Centre, a large regional shop-

ping mall, opened in 1979. Coquitlam's urban core, still in the process of development in 2000, is known as Town Centre. A city hall, cultural centre, stadium, pool, municipal buildings and Douglas College campus are located here, and it was scheduled to be linked to Vancouver by SKYTRAIN in 2003. North of Town Centre is Westwood Plateau, a residential suburb of approximately 15,000 people. Green space has been preserved in Mundy, MINNEKHADA and Colony Farm parks, Widgeon Marsh and the southern part of Pinecone Burke Provincial PARK, all of which fall within city boundaries.

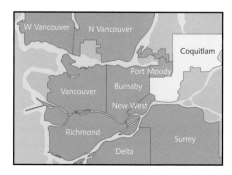

Population: 101,820
Rank in BC: 6th
Population increase since 1981: 67%
Date of incorporation: district 25 July 1891; city 1 Dec 1992
Land area: 152.50 km²
Location: Greater Vancouver Regional District
Economic base: wholesale, retail and transportation services, gravel and wood products, warehousing

COQUITLAM LAKE, 12.5 km², a narrow LAKE in the COAST MTS east of VANCOUVER, drains via the Coquitlam R to empty into the FRASER R just east of the PORT MANN Bridge. The river's lower reaches form the boundary between COQUITLAM and PORT COQUITLAM. The name is a corruption of Kwikwetl'em, the FIRST NATION that originally occupied the area. The lake was dammed at its lower end in 1903 and water was diverted via a 3.5-km tunnel to neighbouring BUNTZEN LK for HYDROELECTRIC purposes. At the time it was the longest hydro tunnel in the world. The lake also provides water to the GREATER VANCOUVER REGIONAL DISTRICT. LOGGING and gravel operations seriously degraded the river, which was once plentiful with SALMON. Reclamation efforts undertaken since the 1970s have reversed some of the ill effects, but it is still considered one of the most endangered rivers in BC.

CORAL is a member of the phylum Cnidaria (sea nettles), an invertebrate related to the SEA ANEMONE and the JELLY (jellyfish). It is characterized by many small polyps, each having a mouth surrounded by a ring of tentacles, which contain stinging capsules. Familiar tropical corals are colonial structures, that is they grow in interdependent colonies, which form large branching growths. Coral reefs are formed as hard corals die and new corals grow on the hard skeletons.

Coquihalla Lk, along the route of the historic Coquihalla Trail. *Roy Jackson/Image Makers*

White sea pen, one of several corals found in BC waters. Rick Harbo photo

BC's cold waters host more than 30 coral species. The hydrocorals, of the class Hydrozoa, include the pink hydrocorals, which form encrusting patches and low branching growths. Among the corals in the class Anthozoa (which also includes anemones and jellies) are the octocorals (gorgonians, sea pens, sea whips, soft corals), named for the 8 tentacles surrounding the mouth, and the cup corals. The fan, or gorgonian, corals with their branching core of tough, horny material, inhabit the shallow subtidal and deeper waters of BC. The most commonly encountered is the pink candelabrum coral (*Paragorgia pacifica*). The structure of the white sea pen, the sea whip and the common orange sea pen (*Ptilosarcus gurneyi*) is a stalk of many branches, each bearing numerous polyps; these species are found anchored in sand-mud. The soft corals, in the order Alcyonacea, do not have hard skeletons. Among them is the white to pink to red soft coral, also called the sea strawberry (*Gersemia rubiformis*), which forms fleshy masses in current-swept passages. The cup corals, of the subclass Zoantharia, order Scleractinia, are related to the well-known reef-building corals of the tropics. They are solitary rather than colonial, but they sometimes form clumps. At least 3 species of cup corals are found in the intertidal waters to depths of 90 m. The most common is the orange cup coral (*Balanopyllia elegans*); its bright orange polyp has nearly transparent tentacles. It sits in a calcareous cup growing to 1 cm high and 1 cm in diameter.   *Rick Harbo*

CORBIN is an abandoned COAL mining community south of SPARWOOD in the CROWSNEST PASS area. The mine, founded by Daniel Corbin, an American railway promoter, went into production in 1908 and was linked by the EASTERN BC RWY to the CPR's Crowsnest line. The mine

closed in 1935 after a strike. The town dwindled away, though MINING continued at the Byron Creek Collieries nearby.

CORDILLERA, literally Spanish for "mountains," is a term applied to the physiographic region of mountain ranges and their associated valleys and plateaus that comprise almost all of BC from the coast to the ROCKY MTS. It is one of 6 geological regions in Canada. The Cordillera was formed millions of years ago by the repeated accretion of exotic terranes that moved east and north across the earth's crust and welded onto the western edge of N America, in the process crumpling the landscape into a series of long mountain ranges. Subsequently the land was shaped to its present contours by uplift, GLACIATION and other forms of erosion. The Cordillera, extending north into the Yukon and along the western edge of Alberta, comprises about 16% of Canada.

COREN, Stanley, psychologist, author (b 1942, Philadelphia). A graduate of the Univ of Pennsylvania and Stanford Univ, he is a professor of psychology at UBC and one of BC's most successful popular science writers. Widely published in academic circles, he is better known to the general public as the author of bestselling books about dogs, including *The Intelligence of Dogs* (1994), which has been translated into 18 languages. He has also published two other books of popular psychology, *The Left-Hander Syndrome* (1992), about lefthandedness, and *Sleep Thieves* (1996), about sleep deprivation in modern life.

CORFIELD was an early AGRICULTURAL settlement on the flats near the mouth of the COWICHAN R 5 km southeast of DUNCAN on VANCOUVER ISLAND. G.T. Corfield opened a general store here and operated a post office from 1887 to 1911.   AS

CORMORANT is a large, black water bird, roughly the size of a GOOSE. It has a long, slim bill, hooked at the end, and a slender head and long, S-shaped neck. Cormorants nest in colonies on cliff faces and rocky islets near the water, where they feed by diving for fish. They appear awkward on land as they are adapted for an aquatic habitat: they have large webbed feet and can remain underwater for more than 2 minutes at a time. Of 28 species worldwide, 3 occur in BC, all on the coast. The double-crested cormorant (*Phalacrocorax auritus*) is the only species that nests inland, though in BC it is commonly only along the South Coast in GEORGIA and JUAN DE FUCA straits. Brandt's cormorant (*P. penicillatus*) is common in winter all along the coast. Most go south in spring to nest in California, but a few stay to breed along the west and south coast of VANCOUVER ISLAND. This bird has a blue chin in the spring. The pelagic cormorant (*P. pelagicus*), the smallest of the 3 BC species, is far more widespread. It nests along the inner and outer coast as far north as the QUEEN CHARLOTTE ISLANDS.

Cormorant. Ken Bowen photo

CORMORANT ISLAND, 3.2 km², lies at the top of JOHNSTONE STRAIT opposite PORT MCNEILL on the northeast end of VANCOUVER ISLAND, 290 km north of VANCOUVER. Long a traditional gathering spot for the KWAKWA̱KA̱'WAKW (Kwakiutl) people, this small (4 km long), crescent-shaped island is named for HMS *Cormorant*, a British naval survey ship. The FISHING village of ALERT BAY sprawls along its inner shore. Ever since 1870, when a SALMON saltery was established, it has been a centre for the commercial fishery. There is a fine collection of TOTEM POLES, including the tallest in the world (52.7 m), and the U'Mista Cultural Centre (1980) with its display of FIRST NATIONS ceremonial objects. A ferry connects the island to Port McNeill.

CORNWALL, Clement Francis, lawyer, politician, lt gov 1881–87 (b 18 June 1836, Gloucestershire, England; d 15 Feb 1910, Victoria). The son of an Anglican cleric, he emigrated to BC with his brother Henry Pennant Cornwall in 1862. The brothers headed for the Cariboo goldfields (*see* GOLD RUSH, CARIBOO), but instead claimed a parcel of land at what became ASHCROFT and began farming in the style of English country gentlemen. They built a large home, operated a sawmill, a roadhouse and a gristmill, raised livestock and kept foxhounds and race horses. Clement, who was trained as a lawyer, also practised law. In 1864 he was elected for a term to the legislative council and in 1870 was a member of the last colonial assembly before CONFEDERATION. In 1871 he became one of BC's 3 representatives in the federal Senate, a position he held until 20 July 1881, when he was sworn in as LT GOV. After his term expired he returned to live at Ashcroft, where he was a county court judge from 1889 until he retired to VICTORIA in 1906.

CORTES ISLAND, 125 km², one of numerous small islands between VANCOUVER ISLAND and the mainland at the north end of GEORGIA STRAIT, was originally occupied by Coast Salish (*see* SALISHAN FIRST NATIONS). It was explored in 1792 by the Spanish mariners Dionisío ALA-CALÁ-GALIANO and Cayetano VALDÉS, who named it after the Spanish conqueror of Mexico. A shore WHALING station operated at Whaletown between 1869 and 1870 and is now the site of a small ferry terminal. The first permanent settlers were Michael and Jane Manson, who arrived in 1886 on the west side of the island in the area now called Manson's Landing; there is a small (1 km²) provincial MARINE PARK here. Other small settlements were established at Seaford and Cortes Bay on the eastern shore. LOGGING and farming (*see* AGRICULTURE) became the main occupations. The population in 1999 numbered around 550, most of whom lived on the south half of the island. Squirrel Cove on the east coast, where the KLAHOOSE First Nation has a reserve, is a popular refuge with boaters, as is Gorge Harbour on the western side and Von Donop Provincial MARINE PARK (12.77 km²)—jointly managed by the BC government and the people of Klahoose—on the north. Smelt Bay Provincial PARK, on the southern tip of Cortes, has some significant archaeological sites. Several resorts and retreats, including Hollyhock Farm, have become popular. Cortes Island is connected to Vancouver Island by ferry, via QUADRA ISLAND.

COTTON, Peter Neve, architect (b 1918, Merritt; d 1978, Victoria). He was BC's first architectural historian and first serious restoration architect. After serving in Egypt and Italy during WWII he enrolled at UBC, where he was instrumental in pressuring the administration to establish the School of Architecture (from which he graduated in 1955). He apprenticed with Col W. Ridgeway-Wilson, then joined the design section of the provincial department of public works, where he was architect-in-charge of interior design for the Government House reconstruction project (*see* CARY CASTLE). One outcome of this work was his book, *Vice Regal Mansions*, published posthumously. He returned to private practice in 1960. He helped to found the North West Chapter of the Society of Architectural Historians and published many articles relating to the architectural history of BC. FORT LANGLEY, FISGARD LIGHTHOUSE and CRAIGFLOWER Manor are just a few of the province's early restoration projects to pass through his office. *See also* ARCHITECTURE. *Martin Segger*

COTTONWOOD HOUSE, 30 km east of Quesnel, opened in 1865 as a roadhouse on the old CARIBOO WAGON ROAD leading to the goldfields at BARKERVILLE (*see* GOLD RUSH, CARIBOO). It was owned by John and Janet Boyd and their children from 1874 to 1950. The provincial gov-

Boat day at Cortes Island, early 1900s.
MCR 19332

ernment purchased the property in 1961 and turned it into a historic park: the buildings have been restored so that the area has the look of the 1870s.

COUGAR (*Felis concolor*), the largest member of the cat family native to BC, is a speedy, solitary predator whose range extends across most of the province. Also called mountain lion, it has red-brown to grey-brown fur and a long tail. The average adult male weighs 57 kg, though weights up to 95 kg have been recorded. Kittens, usually 2 per litter, are born after a 3-month gestation period. About 4,000 cougars live in BC, a fifth of these inhabiting VANCOUVER ISLAND. Their princi-

pal prey is DEER; to a lesser extent they hunt wild sheep, ELK, MOUNTAIN GOAT, smaller game and even domestic pets. Attacks on humans are rare but do occur when a cougar mistakes a child for another animal, or is starving or defending its young. A bounty was offered on cougars in BC until 1957 and many thousands were killed by hunters. Today cougar hunting is still legal but regulated; about 400 are killed by licensed hunters and wildlife officers each year.

COUGAR ANNIE; *see* RAE-ARTHUR, ADA ANNIE.

COULTHARD, Jean, composer (b 10 Feb 1908, Vancouver; d 9 Mar 2000, Vancouver). She was one of Canada's leading modern composers and the first composer from BC to achieve national recognition. She studied first with her mother,

Cougar. Ken Bowen photo

Jean Coulthard, composer.

then in England at the Royal College of Music in the 1920s with, among others, Ralph Vaughan Williams. In 1947 she began teaching at UBC, an association that lasted to her retirement in 1973. A prolific worker, she created about 400 pieces of music for various instruments and in several genres. Her work is more accessible than that of many modern composers and several of her pieces are heard regularly in concert and broadcast. She was named to the Order of Canada in 1978, the same year she was made a freeman of the City of VANCOUVER, and in 1994 she received the ORDER OF BC.

COUNCIL OF FOREST INDUSTRIES OF BC

(COFI) was established in 1960 to represent most of the associations in the province's FOREST INDUSTRY: BC Loggers' Assoc, BC Lumber Manufacturers' Assoc, Cariboo Lumber Manufacturers' Assoc, BC Division of Canadian Pulp and Paper Assoc, Consolidated Red Cedar Shingle Assoc, and Plywood Manufacturers' Assoc of BC. Initially COFI's duties were to present briefs to government on behalf of these associations, publicize the forest industry and coordinate safety campaigns. One of its early successes was a drive to prevent a US tariff on BC lumber (*see* SOFTWOOD LUMBER AGREEMENT). In 1966 member associations disbanded and their member companies became members of COFI. In 1970 COFI undertook an overseas market development program, funded in part by the provincial and federal governments, and expanded its staff and influence considerably. In subsequent years, under President Mike Apsey, it played a major role representing the industry during confrontations between forest companies and environmentalists (*see also* ENVIRONMENTAL MOVEMENT). In 1989 COFI was taken to court by a PRINCE GEORGE member and SAWMILL owner and convicted of being part of a fraudulent lumber grading scheme. Since then many of the functions it once performed have been reassigned to other organizations and it has reduced its operations considerably. *Ken Drushka*

COUNTY LINE is an AGRICULTURAL settlement in the FRASER VALLEY, 17 km northwest of ABBOTSFORD in LANGLEY municipality. Formerly named Rand after an early realtor, it got its start in 1911 when a BC ELECTRIC RWY station was established there. A SAWMILL was located nearby at Beaver R.
AS

COUPLAND, Douglas Campbell, writer (b 30 Dec 1961, Baden-Solingen, Germany). He was born on a NATO base and moved to W VANCOUVER as a youngster with his Canadian parents. A graduate of the EMILY CARR INSTITUTE, he was a sculptor, graphic designer and magazine journalist before leaping to prominence in 1991 with his first novel, *Generation X*. Heavy with irony, the novel satirizes N American consumer culture from the viewpoint of 3 young "Genxers" and was widely thought to have described the outlook of a generation. In subsequent novels he continued to use an unconventional style and minimalist plotting to explore his interest in

Douglas Coupland, bestselling author.

the ironies of modern life. *Shampoo Planet* appeared in 1992, followed by *Life After God* (1994), *Microserfs* (1995), *Polaroids from the Dead* (1996), *Girlfriend in a Coma* (1998), *Miss Wyoming* (1999) and *City of Glass* (2000).

COURTENAY, city, pop 17,335, the commercial centre of the Comox Valley, lies on a low plain on the east side of VANCOUVER ISLAND, 220 km north of VICTORIA. It is named for Capt  George W. Courtenay, who surveyed the area during 1846–49 aboard HMS *Constance*. Laid out as a townsite in 1891, it was incorporated on 1 Jan 1915. The site was used by Central Coast Salish people (*see* SALISHAN FIRST NATIONS) long before the first whites arrived. In the 1850s the HBC opened a store, and permanent settlement began in the 1860s. Two of the earliest settlers were Reginald Pidcock, who later owned most of QUATHIASKI COVE, and Joseph McPhee. LOGGING was a significant factor in the growth of the local

The waterfront at Courtenay. Keith Thirkell photo

economy along with MINING and commercial FISHING. These activities, as well as AGRICULTURE, TOURISM and the Canadian Forces Base at nearby COMOX, have continued to be important. The road from Victoria arrived in 1910 and since 1914 the city has been the northern terminus of the ESQUIMALT & NANAIMO RWY. Some of the best SKIING on Vancouver Island is available at nearby Mt WASHINGTON and FORBIDDEN PLATEAU. Each summer the community hosts the Courtenay Youth Music Centre and in 1992 North Island College (*see* COMMUNITY COLLEGES) opened a campus here. The ESTUARY of the Courtenay R is the world's most important wintering site for the trumpeter SWAN.

COURTNALL, Geoff (b 18 Aug 1962, Duncan) and **Russ** (b 2 June 1965, Duncan), hockey players. Raised in VICTORIA, Russ played his high school HOCKEY at Notre Dame College in Saskatchewan before joining his older brother in the lineup of the hometown VICTORIA COUGARS. Both forwards scored well at the WHL level but only Russ was drafted, seventh overall in 1983 by the Toronto Maple Leafs in the NHL entry draft. The same year Geoff signed as a free agent with the Boston Bruins and spent the next 3 years

The hockey-playing Courtnall brothers, Russ (l) and Geoff.
Courtesy Vancouver Canucks Photo Archives

commuting between the big-league club and its farm team. By the time he had proved himself as an NHL forward he was traded to the Edmonton Oilers, arriving just in time to help them win the 1988 Stanley Cup. Geoff was then dealt to Washington, where he collected a career-high 80 points in 1988–89. After starting 1990–91 in St. Louis he was sent to the VANCOUVER CANUCKS in a move that contributed to the team's most successful seasons. Russ enjoyed an easier transition to the NHL, quickly becoming a top forward with the Leafs. He was traded to the Montreal Canadiens in 1989 and then to the Minnesota North Stars, moving with them to Dallas. After equalling Geoff's 80 points while in a Dallas uniform, he was reunited with his brother on the Canucks for part of the 1994–95 season, before Geoff signed with St. Louis as a free agent. The brothers remained active in VANCOUVER as owners of a sports bar across from BC PLACE STADIUM. While Russ faded out of the league in the late 1990s with the New York Rangers and Los Angeles Kings, Geoff continued to play and score regularly but was forced to retire in 1999 due to concussions.   *SW*

COUTLEE, in the NICOLA Valley 3 km northwest of MERRITT, was the site of the Coutlee Ranch, founded in 1873 by Alexander Coutlee, a former GOLD seeker. He also ran a hotel and store here and his establishment became a stop on the KETTLE VALLEY RWY.   *AS*

COWAN, George, lawyer, politician (b 1858, Watford, ON; d 25 Sept 1935, Vancouver). After graduating from the Univ of Toronto and Osgoode Hall, he moved west in 1893 to VANCOUVER and established a law practice. While acting as city solicitor, he was also active in the CONSERVATIVE PARTY and served one term (1908–11) as Vancouver's MP in Ottawa. He wrote an anti-Asian pamphlet called *The Chinese Question in Canada* that helped raise the level of the infamous HEAD TAX. In 1899 he bought 4 km² on BOWEN ISLAND in an area now known as Cowan's Pt, where he built cottages for visitors and raised cattle. *See also* ASIATIC EXCLUSION LEAGUE; CHINESE.
Shannon Emmerson

COWAN, John Lawrence "Jack," soccer player (b 6 June 1927, Vancouver). He began playing SOCCER in VANCOUVER's Grandview area as a youngster and emerged as the first BC player to play first-division soccer in the UK. While starring for UBC, Cowan impressed an international referee from Scotland and was offered a tryout with the Scottish League's Dundee United. After struggling to make the club for 6 months, he played 2 spectacular games in the Scottish Cup and was signed to a 5-year contract in 1949. He developed into a star fullback as the team toured the world and twice captured the Scottish Cup. The Scottish national team tried to add Cowan to its roster but failed to find any Scottish ancestry in his family. When his contract was up Dundee wanted him to re-sign but he chose to return to Vancouver, where he led his amateur Vancouver club to a dominion championship and played in several international games before retiring at age 29. He was inducted into the BC SPORTS HALL OF FAME in 1974.   *SW*

COWBOYS in BC have a history that is distinctive from their counterparts east of the ROCKY MTS, combining, it is said, the skills, equipment and clothing styles of the Mexican and Californian *vaqueros* with the British sense of law and order, the know-how of the FIRST NATIONS and the manners of the English gentleman. The BC CATTLE INDUSTRY originally obtained livestock from Oregon and California, and along with the cattle came the men who worked them. The original drovers (the term *cowboy* did not come into use until the late 1870s) were strongly influenced by the Mexican/Californian way of working cattle. Hispanic *vaqueros* (from which the term *bucka-*

roo derives) used whips and long, braided rawhide ropes and rode single-cinched saddles with thick saddle horns. They wore distinctive leather overpants called *chaparreras* to protect them from rain and brush. As the industry moved north, Hispanic clothes and equipment were modified to suit the different climate and terrain. Thus "chaps" were adapted for the cold BC climate by adding pelts of various kinds, making the "woolies" seen throughout the province; the short Mexican bolero vest was exchanged for the longer English vest; the Mexican wide-brimmed hat was redesigned by John Stetson of Philadelphia in 1870 to make the more familiar cowboy hat. No matter what else they modify, cowboys always wear blue jeans, invented by Levi Strauss of California in 1859, and a fancy silver belt buckle.

The widespread use of Spanish loan words in the BC cowboy vocabulary showed the influence of the *vaquero*. From the earliest days RODEO referred to the roundup of cattle; hackamore (from the Spanish *jaquima*) bridles were used; silver conchos (from *concha*, meaning "a shell") decorated the cowboy's saddle and hat; and even the term *rancherie* led to the use of "rancherie" for aboriginal villages in BC. Added to the strong *vaquero* influence was the Anglo influence, which began in California in the 1840s and spread to Oregon with the drovers who brought cattle over the Oregon Trail. From them came the practice of fencing pasture lands, irrigating and cutting hay lands, and the close herding of cattle. By the 1880s, with Alberta and Montana cowboys crossing the Rockies to work on BC ranches, the distinctive features of BC cowboys began to blend with the Texas influence east of the mountains, making their appearance and techniques more homogeneous. Nonetheless, because of the mountainous terrain and sagebrush slopes, cowboys in BC continued to wear chaps and use "taps" (leather hoods over stirrups, from the Spanish *tapaderas*). Although BC cowboys came from all over the world, including China, First Nations cowboys were employed extensively and continue to play a significant role in the modern

Cowboy carrying young calf, Nicola, 1998. Rick Blacklaws photo

ranching scene, adding to the blend of cultures that has made the BC cowboy unique in the world.

A working cowboy's job was, and still is, to take care of the beef herd. This involves acting as midwife during calving; branding, dehorning and castrating bull calves; turning cattle out in the spring; and riding the range in summer to protect the animals from predators and to keep them on the move to prevent overgrazing. The cowboy ensures the breeding program is proceeding as it should and keeps an eye out for any sick or injured cattle. In the fall the cattle are rounded up and returned to the ranch, where calves are weaned, cows are tested for pregnancy and animals are separated into sale units. Most cowboys break or train their own horses and dogs. Some are involved in rodeo, and most larger stampedes feature ranch team events such as cattle penning on horseback or with dogs.
Diana French and Ken Mather

Chilcotin cowgirl. Rick Blacklaws photo

COWICHAN BAY, pop 2,795, at the mouth of the COWICHAN R on the east coast of VANCOUVER ISLAND south of DUNCAN, was a traditional gathering place for the COWICHAN First Nation. The first white settlers arrived in the late 1850s. Along with AGRICULTURE, LOGGING and FISHING have been important to the economy. The CNR operated a railway car barge to the mainland from here for many years. The S Cowichan Lawn Tennis Club, founded in 1888, is the second oldest lawn tennis club in the world after the All England Club at Wimbledon. For many years it had the only public grass courts on the west coast of the continent; its facilities are now a BC heritage site.

COWICHAN FIRST NATION is a Coast Salish group (*see* HALKOMELEM; SALISHAN FIRST NATIONS), the largest First Nations group in BC with a population close to 3,000. The Cowichan own 9 RESERVES along the COWICHAN R near DUNCAN on the east coast of VANCOUVER ISLAND. They also used to inhabit several summer villages near the mouth of the FRASER R on LULU ISLAND, where they went to fish. The name derives from *Quw'utsum'*, meaning "warmed by the sun." On the outskirts of Duncan the Cowichan Native Village welcomes visitors wishing to learn about the history and culture of the Cowichan people.

Fish weir, c 1860. Weirs were used on the Cowichan R by aboriginal fishers until the 1930s. BC Archives H-06525

COWICHAN LAKE, 62 km², lies on south-central VANCOUVER ISLAND about 100 km north of VICTORIA. The area was first occupied by the COWICHAN First Nation, who called it Kaatza, which means "lake." First surveyed in 1857, it was too isolated to attract many settlers until the end of the 1800s. The first LOGGING took place in 1890; logs were driven down the COWICHAN R to SAWMILLS on the coast until 1908. A branch of the ESQUIMALT & NANAIMO RWY arrived in 1912 and logging expanded dramatically through the 1920s, when as many as 300 million board ft of timber were taken out in a year. Several logging camps and mill sites developed around the lake,

including YOUBOU, CAYCUSE, HONEYMOON BAY and MESACHIE LAKE. The principal business centre is the town of Lake Cowichan (inc 1944; pop 2,856; called Sutton Green in the 1880s after the lumberman James Sutton) at the east end of the lake. The area was also a summer resort and a popular sport FISHING destination. In 1910 the federal government opened the first sport fish hatchery in Canada at the lake. Cowichan Lk drains via the Cowichan R, a BC HERITAGE RIVER and candidate Canadian Heritage River, into COWICHAN BAY at DUNCAN. *See also* FISHING, SPORT; LAKES.

COWICHAN RIVER runs 47 km from COWICHAN LK in the south-central part of VANCOUVER ISLAND past the city of DUNCAN and empties into COWICHAN BAY. It is home to the COWICHAN First Nation. The valley of the river was first explored by outsiders in 1851 and farm settlement (*see* AGRICULTURE) began later in the decade. The river was used for driving logs from the lake to tidewater between 1890 and 1908 (*see* LOGGING). It is popular with outdoor recreationists and is known to sport fishers for its plentiful TROUT, SALMON and STEELHEAD. It is one of very few BC rivers with brown TROUT, introduced in the 1930s. Coho and chum salmon spawn in the fall. The ESTUARY is a wintering ground for trumpeter SWANS and many species of waterfowl, including the rare green HERON. The Cowichan River Footpath, constructed in the 1960s, runs for 19 km beside the stream. In 1996 the Cowichan River was designated a BC HERITAGE RIVER and in 1999 became the second BC river to be nominated to the national Canadian Heritage River System.

COWICHAN SWEATER, named for the COWICHAN First Nation of VANCOUVER ISLAND, is a bulky sweater hand-knitted from sheep's wool in natural colours of white, grey, brown and black. Before contact with Europeans, the Cowichan wove blankets and clothing from MOUNTAIN GOAT wool and the hair of a specially bred woolly breed of dog. They were introduced to knitting by white settlers after 1850 and a distinctive sweater style gradually emerged: it has a shawl collar, and the maker uses a 2-colour Fair Isle technique in which the unused colour is carried along the back of the work between design units. In 1999 about 2,000 Coast Salish (*see* SALISHAN FIRST NATIONS) knitters were active, mainly on the Cowichan RESERVES around DUNCAN, and the sweater has become a distinctive symbol of BC for TOURISTS and locals alike.

COYOTE (*Canis latrans*) is found across the province (though not on VANCOUVER ISLAND or the QUEEN CHARLOTTE ISLANDS) and increasingly in urban areas, where individuals are often mistaken for large dogs. Distinguished by pointed ears and snout, long bushy tail and a thick coat of grey to yellow-brown fur, the coyote feeds mainly on rabbits, small rodents, berries and birds, though it will eat virtually anything. It prefers open prairie, parkland, alpine meadows and desert habitats and has become adapted to

Coyote. Duane Sept photo

urban suburbs, where it is thought to be a threat to small domestic animals. The coyote lives about 10 years in the wild and the average adult weighs 13 kg. It usually mates for life; it breeds annually and produces 5–6 young in an underground den. Coyotes are often blamed for killing livestock, but the animal's reputation as a predator is exaggerated.

CRAB is a member of the crustacean branch of the phylum Arthropoda. It is a shelled invertebrate with a segmented body and an exoskeleton. "True" crabs (*Brachyurans*), including spider crabs and the well-known Dungeness and red rock crab, have 10 jointed appendages, the front two ending in pincers used for feeding. Crabs crawl along the sea bottom eating algae and small marine animals. To grow, a crab must periodically shed its exoskeleton, expand, then form a new, larger one. When the time comes, it backs

Dungeness crab, an important commercial species. Rick Harbo photo

out of the old shell, then goes into hiding until the new covering hardens. Large numbers of shedded carapaces, or moults, are washed ashore and may be erroneously reported as crab kills. Crabs are able to grow, or regenerate, limbs and pincers that have been torn or lost. There are

4,500 species of crab worldwide, ranging in size from the tiny ones seen scuttling under rocks in tidal pools to large, commercially significant types. Of the 35 species found in BC waters, one of the largest is the Dungeness crab (*Cancer magister*). The male of this orange-brown species grows to 25 cm across and has large, meaty legs and claws. It dwells on sandy bottoms, often hiding in eelgrass beds. Dungeness crab is the major recreational and commercially harvested crab species and is fished using traps. In 1996 the commercial catch amounted to 4,932 tonnes, worth $23.2 million. The fishery is licensed and only males of greater than a minimum size may be taken. Another edible crab is the red rock crab (*Cancer productus*), which is smaller and has less meat than the Dungeness. The purple shore crab (*Hemigrapsus nudus*) and the hairy shore crab (*H. oregonensis*) are the species most familiar to beachcombers, who find these small creatures lurking along the rocky shoreline. Despite their names, they come in a variety of colours. More unusual crabs include the lithodid and hermit crabs. The lithodid crabs, which appear to have only 3 pairs of walking legs, include the king crabs, caught occasionally in OBSERVATORY INLET and off the coast of Alaska, and box crabs. Hermit crabs are sometimes hairy in appearance with long antennae and usually have one claw larger than the other. Hermit crabs have soft, unprotected abdomens and the common name "hermit" refers to their habit of using empty snail shells as shelter. *See also* FISHING, COMMERCIAL; FISHING, SPORT.

CRABAPPLE (*Pyrus fusca*) is a small deciduous tree growing wild in moist habitat along the coast. It bears small, sour-tasting oval fruit from which excellent jelly is made. Crabapples were an important food item for all coastal FIRST NATIONS, who ate the fruit, sometimes mixing it with EULACHON grease, and traded it extensively. The bark was used for medicine by some coastal groups and the wood, being hard and resilient, was used to make implement handles, wedges, digging sticks and pegs for use in wood construction.

CRACROFT ISLAND, 233 km² (40 km long), 100 km northwest of CAMPBELL RIVER between JOHNSTONE STRAIT and KNIGHT INLET, is really 2 islands, E and W Cracroft, barely separated by a gorge that dries at low tide. Cracroft is traditional KWAKWAKA'WAKW territory but has also been the location of several 20th-century settlements: at Growler Cove; at Bones Bay, where the CANADIAN FISHING CO LTD operated a cannery from 1920 to 1949 (*see* SALMON CANNING); at Port Harvey, site of a hotel; and on the south shore, where a large LOGGING camp was active for many years. Cracroft and nearby Sophia Island were named for Sophia Cracroft (a niece of the Arctic explorer Sir John Franklin), who visited BC in 1861 with Lady Franklin. AS

CRAFT ASSOCIATION OF BC (CABC) is a coordinating organization for professional craftspeople in the province. Founded in 1973 as the Craftsmen's Association of BC (it took its present name in 1984), the CABC operates the Crafthouse Shop and Gallery on GRANVILLE ISLAND in VANCOUVER. The association emerged from a slow flowering of the crafts in BC following WWII. By this time crafts such as ceramics and textiles were being taught in university and art school by a pioneering generation of artists that included Grace Melvin, Mollie Carter, Hilda Ross, Reg Dixon and David Lambert. The counterculture of the 1960s, with its enthusiasm for the "handmade" object, gave an additional boost; by the early 1970s crafts artists saw a need for an organization to share information and coordinate group exhibitions of their work. The result was the CABC. The association moved onto Granville Island and into Crafthouse in 1986. (The Island is also home to the Circle Craft Co-op, a co-operative gallery and store, and several leading craftspeople have studios there.) The high level of achievement of BC crafts was exemplified during the 1970s and 1980s, when the Canadian Craft Council established the annual Saidye Bronfman Award for Excellence in the Crafts, and artists from BC were regular winners, including: Robin Hopper (1977), Wayne NGAN (1983) and Walter Dexter (1992), potters; Carole SABISTON (1987), a VICTORIA fibre artist; Lutz HAUFSCHILD (1988), a glass artist; Bill REID (1986), a carver; and Joanna Staniszkis (1981), a textile artist. The status of crafts in the province was affirmed in 1992 when the Canadian Craft Museum opened in downtown Vancouver.

CRAIGDARROCH is an elaborate mansion in VICTORIA, built for the industrialist Robert DUNSMUIR. Known also as Dunsmuir Castle, it was designed by Warren H. Williams, a Portland architect, and is reputed to be the most expensive residence ever built in western Canada.

Construction began in 1887. Dunsmuir himself died before his fairy-tale castle was finished, but his wife Joan moved into it in the summer of 1890. When she died in 1908 the contents of the house were sold at auction and the large estate was subdivided. The castle stood empty until 1919, when the federal government turned it into a hospital for veterans. Over the years it also served as home to Victoria College (1921–46), the Victoria school board (1946–67) and the Victoria School of Music (1967–79). It later became a museum open to the public.

CRAIGELLACHIE, pop 71, 45 km west of REVELSTOKE on the TRANS-CANADA HWY, is the site of the "Last Spike," driven in on 7 Nov 1885 to commemorate the completion of the transcontinental CPR. The name, meaning "stand fast," comes from a rocky crag near the Scottish birthplace of Donald Smith, Lord Strathcona, a financial backer of the CPR and the person who drove in the spike. The CPR had a station and a water fuelling stop at the site until the late 1950s. Later it was made a historic site and park.

Driving the last spike of the CPR, Craigellachie, 7 Nov 1885. BC Archives E-02200

CRAIGFLOWER was one of the large farms established by the PUGET'S SOUND AGRICULTURAL CO near VICTORIA at the head of ESQUIMALT harbour in the 1850s. It was also called Mr McKenzie's Farm after Kenneth McKenzie, leader of the group of colonists who arrived from England in 1853 to develop the property. McKenzie's 1856 house, Craigflower Manor, and an 1855 schoolhouse, the oldest school in western Canada on its original site, are National Historic Sites and have been refurbished for public visits. Craigflower was named for the English estate of Andrew Colville, an HBC governor.

CRAIGS CROSSING, 27 km northwest of NANAIMO on VANCOUVER ISLAND, where the old and new Island highways diverge, was a station on the ESQUIMALT & NANAIMO RWY. It was named after J. Craig, early settler and first postmaster, and eventually became known simply as Craig. A number of local 19th-century buildings have been moved here to Craig Heritage Park.   AS

CRAMOND, Mike, journalist (b 1913, AB; d 1998, Vancouver). He was the outdoors editor at the Vancouver PROVINCE newspaper from 1956 to 1978, as well as the author of more than a dozen books and countless magazine articles about sport FISHING and the outdoors. While establishing himself as one of the leading outdoor writers in N America, he wrote and broadcast *The Fishing and Hunting Club of the Air*, a radio show aired on CKNW in the 1950s, that was the first of its kind in Canada. His book *Killer Bears* (1981) sold more than 50,000 copies and is still a standard reference on bear attacks. His knowledge was practical; before becoming a full-time writer he had been a member of the BC PROVINCIAL POLICE, a game warden and a hunting guide. The winner of 2 National Newspaper Awards, he was also a staunch conservationist, an early advocate of catch-and-release fishing and FISH HATCHERIES and an active member of various wildlife societies. *See also* ENVIRONMENTAL MOVEMENT.

Roger M. Brunt

CRANBERRY (*Vaccinium macrocarpon*) is one of 3 fruits native to N America supporting a commercial harvest (the others being blueberries and Concord grapes). About 50 BC growers produce 17 million kg of berries, worth $25 million. BC supplies 95% of the Canadian crop and the province is the third-largest producer in the world after Massachusetts and Wisconsin. Most of the crop is sold to Ocean Spray, an American grower co-operative. Growers are concentrated in the FRASER R delta on the outskirts of VANCOUVER, where flat land, acidic soils and an abundance of water provide the essential requirements. The tart red berries grow on low vines and are harvested in the fall by flooding the bogs, causing berries to float to the surface where they are scooped up. *See also* BERRIES.

Harvesting cranberries in the Fraser Valley, 1999. Brian Gauvin photo

CRANBERRY JUNCTION is a tiny community off the STEWART–CASSIAR Hwy (Hwy 37), 62 km northwest of HAZELTON. The Cranberry R drains into the NASS R and is part of the traditional territory of the NISGA'A people. The Junction was on an important aboriginal trade route (*see also* TRAILS) leading to the east and north. In the last few years it has become the centre of an annual autumn harvest of wild matsutake (pine) MUSH-ROOMS, considered a delicacy in Japan.

CRANBROOK, city, pop 18,131, the largest city in the E KOOTENAY, lies at the southern end of the ROCKY MT TRENCH on a broad plain between the PURCELL MTS on the west and the ROCKY

MTS to the east. People of the KTUNAXA nation called the place "where two horns lie," but the first white settlers knew it as Joseph's Prairie, after a Ktunaxa chief. The townsite, with its spectacular mountain views, was surveyed in 1897 and named Cranbrook after the English home of Col James BAKER, an early rancher. The town's future was assured with the arrival of a CPR line

Clock tower, Cranbrook.
Walter Lanz/Image Makers

in 1898; it later became a divisional point for the railway. With the development of MINING, the FOREST INDUSTRY and the CATTLE INDUSTRY, Cranbrook became an important regional service centre. It was incorporated on 1 Nov 1905. The Canadian Museum of Rail Travel houses the "Trans Canada Ltd," a 1929-vintage CPR train, while the city's performing arts centre, the Key City Theatre, seats 600. East Kootenay COMMUNITY COLLEGE, later renamed College of the Rockies, opened in 1975. FORT STEELE Heritage Town, a major TOURIST attraction, is 16 km away and there are several popular ski hills in the area.

CRANE, SANDHILL (*Grus canadensis*) is the only crane species present in BC. It is a tall, long-legged, long-necked wading bird with slate grey plumage and a red crown. It is distinguished from the HERON by its distinctive call and by its habit of flying with neck outstretched. Cranes mate for life, though each spring they "renew their vows" by engaging in an elaborate dance-like performance in which they bow, leap and call while tossing sticks and grass into the air with their beaks. They nest in shallow WETLANDS where they forage for INSECTS, seeds, roots, RODENTS and amphibians. They are migrants to the province, spending winters in California and Mexico. They breed at scattered locations throughout BC, and thousands migrate through the Interior each fall and spring on their way to and from major breeding grounds in Alaska.

Sandhill cranes. Roy Luckow photo

CRANMER, Douglas, artist (b 1927, Alert Bay). A member of the 'Namgis (KWAK-WAKA'WAKW) First Nation, Cranmer is the son of Dan Cranmer, who hosted a POTLATCH at VILLAGE ISLAND on Christmas Day 1921 that resulted in jail terms for 26 FIRST NATIONS people and the confiscation of ceremonial regalia. As a young man, Doug Cranmer worked in LOGGING and commercial FISHING until the mid-1950s, when he began carving in VICTORIA under the tutelage of Mungo MARTIN. In 1958 he joined Bill REID in constructing the HAIDA-style houses and poles at Totem Park at UBC, a 3-year project that launched Cranmer's career as a full-time carver. From 1960 to 1965 he was part owner of the Vancouver gallery, the Talking Stick, an early attempt by First Nations people to market Northwest Coast art. He helped to build and paint the housefront for the U'mista Cultural Centre at ALERT BAY, which houses some of the artifacts seized at his father's 1921 potlatch, and he was involved in building displays at EXPO 86 and the Canadian Museum of Civilization in Hull, QC. His work, which includes paintings as well as TOTEM POLES and other carvings, is found in museums and private collections around the world.

Doug Cranmer, 'Namgis artist. *Vickie Jensen photo*

CRAVEN, Margaret, writer (b 1901, Helena, MT; d July 1980). Raised in Washington state, she put herself through Stanford Univ in California and determined to be a writer. She worked as a journalist and wrote magazine fiction for 37 years before publishing her first book, the wildly successful *I Heard the Owl Call My Name*, in 1967. Based on the work of the missionary Eric POWELL at KINGCOME INLET, which Craven visited, it tells the story of a young priest's encounter with FIRST NATIONS culture. The book was followed by a CBC television version directed by Daryl DUKE. Craven later wrote *Walk Gently This Good Earth* and the autobiographical *Again Calls the Owl*. *Shannon Emmerson*

CRAWFORD BAY, on the east side of KOOTENAY LK 75 km north of CRESTON, was a port of call in the steamship era. The landing, Port Crawford, was at the head of the bay, but the main settlement, called Crawford Bay, developed just inland in the early 1900s. Today the community, pop 312, is home to such innovative cottage industries as an authentic blacksmith's forge; Kokanee Springs golf resort is nearby. A fall fair has been held here since 1910. James Crawford, or "White Man Jim," was an early trapper and prospector. The wreck of the sunken sternwheeler *CITY OF AINSWORTH*, a provincial historic site, lies off the head of the bay. *AS*

CRAWLEY, Alan, lawyer, literary editor (b 23 Aug 1887, Coburg, ON; d 26 July 1975, Victoria). As a lawyer in Winnipeg he developed an interest in poetry, and in England during WWI he was a regular at Harold Munro's Poetry Bookshop, a popular meeting place for British writers. In Winnipeg after the war he attended writers' gatherings, reciting and discussing poetry. In 1933 he lost his sight to illness and the following year he moved to VICTORIA with his wife

Jean. There they met the poets Dorothy LIVESAY, Anne MARRIOTT and Doris Ferne, who wanted to create a literary MAGAZINE for Canadian writers. They asked Crawley to be its editor, and the first edition of CONTEMPORARY VERSE appeared in 1941 in VANCOUVER, where he now lived. It consisted of 14 lithographed pages and 9 poems. For 39 issues Crawley published most of the best Canadian poets in one of the few literary periodicals in Canada at the time. After he closed the magazine in 1952, he and his wife moved to the PENTICTON area before returning to VANCOUVER ISLAND. *Shannon Emmerson*

CREASE, Henry Pering Pellew, jurist (b 20 Aug 1823, Plymouth, England; d 27 Nov 1905, Victoria). After legal training in England, he went to live briefly in Ontario in 1849, then returned to England and managed a tin mine in Cornwall. In 1858 he immigrated to VANCOUVER ISLAND, where he set up as the colony's first qualified lawyer. He was elected in 1860 to the House of Assembly (*see* COLONIAL GOVERNMENT) and in 1861 became BC attorney general, a position he retained following union of the colonies. He joined the BC Supreme Court in 1870 and remained a member until 1895, when he resigned in disappointment at not being named chief justice to succeed Matthew BEGBIE. On his retirement he was knighted. His wife Sarah Lindley (1826–1922) was an accomplished watercolourist whose views of VICTORIA were the first to be exhibited in England. Their beautiful Italianate house, Pentrelew, was a gathering spot for Victoria's social elite.

Henry Crease, 1853. He served as BC Supreme Court judge 1870–95. *BC Archives F-07698*

CREDIT UNIONS are co-operative financial institutions offering loans and other financial services to member-owners. They are considered local alternatives to the major banks. In 1999 there were 85 credit unions in BC, with assets totalling $21 billion. Many credit unions, especially the earlier ones, were of the closed-bond

type, with membership restricted to people sharing a particular affiliation such as workplace, ethnicity, religion or neighbourhood. With mergers and expansion, however, only a small number of closed-bond credit unions remain. The dominant model, including the larger credit unions, is now the open-bond type, or "community credit union": anyone within a geographic area is eligible to join. VANCOUVER CITY SAVINGS (VanCity), the largest credit union in Canada, is an open-bond type, as is Surrey Metro Savings, the second largest in the country, and most other credit unions in BC.

The first credit unions in Canada were the *caisses populaires*, established in Quebec after 1900. In English Canada credit unions did not catch on until the 1930s, beginning in Atlantic Canada. The first credit union in BC was the Common Good Credit Unit in Burnaby in 1936, but it was another two years before provincial legislation provided for the formal chartering of credit unions. The first charter went in June 1939 to the Powell River Credit Union, which was still operating 60 years later, and many others followed in various parts of BC. VanCity, formed in 1946, led the way in pioneering the idea of a credit union open to residents at large. By 1963 it was the biggest credit union in the province. The number of credit unions in BC peaked in 1961 at 328; later the trend was toward consolidation into larger units. Six of the 10 largest credit unions in Canada are based in BC, and the province's credit unions together represent 40% of the industry's assets outside Quebec.

CREEPER, brown (*Certhia americana*), is a small forest-dwelling bird, widely distributed and breeding throughout southern BC and distributed more sparsely in the north. Its small size (13 cm long) and brown-and-white-streaked plumage makes the creeper difficult to spot when it sits motionless on a tree trunk. When feeding, it creeps up a tree in a spiral pattern, using its stiff tail feathers for support while prying INSECTS and larvae from beneath the bark with its decurved bill.

CREO PRODUCTS INC, one of BC's leading HIGH-TECHNOLOGY companies, was founded in 1983 by two engineers, Dan Gelbart and Ken Spencer. Beginning as a small electro-optical developer, the BURNABY-based company integrated its strengths in electronics, optics, precision mechanics and software to become a pioneer in the field of digital print-production technology, producing systems that transfer computer files directly onto printing plates. By 1999 more than 1,400 of Creo's imaging systems had been installed around the world. Popular magazines such as *Time*, *Scientific American* and *Sports Illustrated* are printed using Creo technology.

CRESCENT BEACH is a small seaside community in SURREY, south of VANCOUVER overlooking BOUNDARY BAY. Archaeological evidence suggests habitation dating back several thousand years (*see also* ARCHAEOLOGY). It was originally called Blackie's Spit after an early settler. At one time a popular summer cottage resort area, it later became a suburb of Vancouver. OYSTER farmers were active until pollution put them out of business in 1963.

CRESCENT SPUR, 140 km east of PRINCE GEORGE on the CNR, was the site of a SAWMILL established in 1917 by Ole Olson Leboe and Helmar Johnson and later operated by Bert Leboe. The mill closed in the late 1960s and a fire consumed most of the settlement in 1971. The original GRAND TRUNK PACIFIC RWY station, located near a crescent-shaped oxbow lake formed by the FRASER R, was called Loos after the famous WWI battle. Today about 70 people make a living from AGRICULTURE, LOGGING, TOURISM and the CATTLE INDUSTRY.   *AS*

CRESCENT VALLEY, 20 km west of NELSON on the CPR and the east side of the SLOCAN R, was the site of one of the largest SAWMILLS in the KOOTENAY, built in 1907 by Joe Patrick, father of the HOCKEY legends Lester and Frank PATRICK. Logs were driven to the mill down the Little Slocan R. A crescent-shaped hill behind the valley gave the settlement its name.   *AS*

CRESTBROOK FOREST INDUSTRIES LTD began life as Cranbrook Sash & Door in 1898. The company grew steadily with the acquisition of several SAWMILLS, LOGGING operations and timber rights in southeastern BC. In 1956 Cranbrook Sash & Door was acquired by the newly formed Crestbrook Timber Ltd. Over the next 10 years the company expanded steadily, acquiring several mills throughout the region. In 1967 a joint venture with 2 Japanese firms, Honshu and Mitsubishi, financed construction of a pulp mill at SKOOKUMCHUCK, north of CRANBROOK. At this time the company name changed to Crestbrook Forest Industries. During the late 1960s lumber production was consolidated at new sawmills in Cranbrook and CANAL FLATS. In 1983 Crestbrook bought Crows Nest Forest Products from Shell Canada, which included a large sawmill at ELKO and extensive timber rights and timberlands. In 1991 Crestbrook, along with Mitsubishi and the Kanzaki Paper Manufacturing Co of Japan, began constructing the Alberta Pacific pulp mill at Athabasca in northern Alberta, but Crestbrook sold its stake in the mill in 1998. In 1999 the Ontario-based firm Tembec Inc purchased the company and its main asset, the Skookumchuck mill, for $270 million.   *Ken Drushka*

CRESTON, town, pop 4,816, in the valley of the KOOTENAY R south of KOOTENAY LK, is the centre of an AGRICULTURAL and TREE FRUIT-growing area made possible by land reclamation along the river, first proposed by William BAILLIE-GROHMAN in the 1880s. Located on the Crowsnest Hwy (Hwy 3), it became a distribution centre for the Kootenay Flats following completion of the SOUTHERN RWY OF BC from CROWSNEST PASS to Kootenay Landing in 1898. The only grain elevators in southern BC are here, along with the only important grain fields south of the PEACE R. LOGGING, SAWMILLING, brewing, food processing

and TOURISM are also important to the local economy, and the community attracts many retirees. The Creston Valley Wildlife Management Area nearby supports more than 250 bird species, including the highest concentration of breeding OSPREYS in Canada and significant colonies of TERNS. The town is named for Creston, IA, home of a pioneer settler, and was incorporated 14 May 1924.

CRICKET was one of BC's first sports, starting in 1849 when a captain of the Royal Navy introduced cricket equipment to FORT VICTORIA. The formation of the Victoria Pioneer Cricket Club followed a few years later and huge crowds regularly showed up at BEACON HILL PARK to take in games. Matches between locals and clubs from visiting naval fleets were particularly competitive and popular. By the 1860s, the ROYAL ENGINEERS had become active in the cricket scene and the first mainland club had formed in NEW WESTMINSTER. Former Victorians who had moved to

Playing cricket in Stanley Park, 1994.
Vancouver Sun

California initiated BC's first international tournament, a home-and-home series that called for a Victoria team to travel south in 1869 and a San Francisco team to come north in 1872. Also in 1872, the BC Cricket Club was formed; its administrators in Victoria included Judge Matthew BEGBIE and Lt Gov Joseph TRUTCH. By 1880 New Westminster had a thriving cricket scene, and in 1888 the Vancouver Cricket Club formed and later held matches at Brockton Oval in STANLEY PARK, a venue later described by the Australian legend Sir Donald Bradman as "the most beautiful cricket ground I know." In 1912 the BC Cricket Association formed to administer the first BC representative club to compete interprovincially; 2 years later league play began in the BC Mainland Cricket League. Clubs from

Australia, New Zealand and England all visited BC, and a Vancouver team was the only North American club to defeat the visiting Australian side on their 1932 North American tour. The most celebrated team to visit the province was the Hollywood side that came to Brockton Oval in 1936, featuring C. Aubrey Smith, Errol FLYNN, Boris Karloff and Nigel Bruce. The same year, 3 BC players were involved in the Canadian national team's first tour of England. Perhaps BC's best player ever was Victoria's Reg Wenman, who starred locally and for BC teams in the 1920s and 1930s. Among the outstanding BC players in the 1940s was Bill Hendy, who set a world record in a 1945 match by scoring 125 not out and then taking 10 wickets for 12 runs. BC tied for first at the first senior national tournament in 1947. The provinces competed for the Bob Quinn Trophy, named for the builder of junior cricket in BC. After WWII, BC cricket went through a rebuilding stage but was bolstered in the 1950s by an influx of West Indian players, particularly at UBC. Also during this period the game spread as clubs formed in places such as W VANCOUVER, LANGLEY and PITT MEADOWS, and in 1959 the Vancouver Women's Cricket Assoc was formed. Teams from other nations continued to visit Canada throughout the last half of the 20th century, and BC players contributed to a surge by the Canadian national team to become international contenders.   *SW*

CRIDGE, Edward, Anglican cleric (b 17 Dec 1817, Devonshire, England; d May 1913, Victoria). After graduating from Cambridge Univ, he was ordained an Anglican minister and served for several years as rector of a London church. He came out to FORT VICTORIA in 1855 as a chaplain employed by the HBC. He built the colony's first ANGLICAN CHURCH in 1856 and his wife Mary ran the first Sunday school. He also played a leading role in creating the city's first hospital and orphanage and served as inspector of schools during 1856–65. In 1872, as dean of the new Christ Church Cathedral, he engaged in a heated dispute with George HILLS, the Anglican bishop whose high church practice he opposed, over the form of the cathedral service. At one point Cridge barred Hills from the cathedral. The matter ended in court, which ruled against Cridge. He was dismissed, and he formed a new church backed by James DOUGLAS. The Reformed Episcopal Church opened in 1875; Cridge served there until he retired in 1902.

CRIME; *see* POLICING.

CRISS CREEK, 45 km northwest of KAMLOOPS, was a grain and cattle-raising (*see* CATTLE INDUSTRY) settlement named after Christopher Pumpmaker, a rancher here in the 1870s. The district was most active between 1910 and 1960. Criss Crk itself flows into the Deadman R northwest of Kamloops Lk.   *AS*

CROATIANS first came to BC during the 1858 GOLD RUSH. One early settler, Samuel Miletich, arrived in VICTORIA from San Francisco and opened the Adelphi Saloon, which became the focus of a block of downtown buildings known as the Adelphi Block. In 1883 Dominic Bussanich and Antonio Cosulich established a small fish cannery on WESTHAM ISLAND and the community of PORT GUICHON (now part of LADNER) was established as the first permanent Croatian settlement in Canada. By the 1890s a steady stream of Croatians was immigrating to BC from Washington and California. Many entered commercial FISHING and Croatians continue to be associated with the fishing industry; others became involved in MINING. They settled in many small communities, including POWELL RIVER, CAMPBELL RIVER, CUMBERLAND, LADYSMITH, NANAIMO and PORT ALBERNI, and by 1937 there were more than 4,000 living in the Lower Mainland. Because Croatia was an ally of Germany during WWII, as many as 200 BC Croatians were interned for the duration of the war. Many of those who immigrated following the war were urban professionals escaping the Communist regime in Yugoslavia; in the 1990s, others were fleeing the ravages of the war associated with the dismemberment of Yugoslavia. The Croatian population in BC, about 10,000 strong, has worked to promote its heritage through schools, associations and cultural centres. The community was also involved in the Croatian struggle for independence, achieved in 1991, staging rallies in VANCOUVER and organizing support for Croatians in Europe. The twin centres of the BC community are the Croatian Catholic Church and the Croatian Cultural Centre in Vancouver. *Dianne Mackay*

CROFT, Henry, engineer, politician (b 15 Jan 1856, Sydney, Australia; d 28 July 1917). Trained as a civil engineer in England, he returned to his native Australia in 1879, then immigrated in 1882 to BC. Here he got involved in the lumber business and married a daughter of Robert DUNSMUIR. In 1898 he developed the Lenora Mine on Mt SICKER, north of VICTORIA, and in 1902 built a SMELTER on the east coast of VANCOUVER ISLAND to process COPPER ore from the mine. The settlement that grew up around the smelter was named CROFTON in his honour.

CROFT, Peter, rock climber (b 18 May 1958, Ottawa, ON). He grew up in NANAIMO, where he was introduced to the outdoors by his father. He

Peter Croft, rock climber, at Smoke Bluffs near Squamish, 1987. Mark Van Manen/Vancouver Sun

took up ROCK CLIMBING in his teens and became one of the world's leading climbers, noted for amazing free solo ascents. Among his many accomplishments are a free climb of the University Wall on the STAWAMUS CHIEF with Hamish Fraser in 1982; a free solo ascent of 4 major routes in a single day in the BUGABOOS in 1983; a complete traverse of the WADDINGTON Range with Greg Foweraker and Don SERL in 1985; ascents of the Nose on El Capitan and the northwest face of Half Dome in Yosemite, CA, in 1 day; and in 1987 a free solo ascent of Astroman on the east face of Washington Column, also in Yosemite. He is one of the few Canadian climbers with an international reputation.

CROFTON, pop 2,500, overlooks Osborne Bay on the east coast of VANCOUVER ISLAND 74 km north of VICTORIA. An instant community, it got its start in 1902 as the townsite for a COPPER SMELTER processing ore from nearby Mt SICKER. Named for Henry CROFT, owner of one of the mines, it languished when the smelter closed in 1908, and the advent of WWI put an end to plans to construct a large SAWMILL. The town's prospects revived after 1958 when BC FOREST PRODUCTS LTD built a pulp mill, later owned by FLETCHER CHALLENGE CANADA LTD, which became the mainstay of the local economy (*see also* PULP AND PAPER). Crofton is part of the district of NORTH COWICHAN. There are local parks at Osborne Bay and Maple Mt, and a museum in the old school building. A ferry runs from Crofton to VESUVIUS BAY on SALTSPRING ISLAND.

CROFTON HOUSE SCHOOL is a private school for girls located in the Kerrisdale neighbourhood of VANCOUVER. Founded in 1898 by Jessie Gordon, a 27-year-old governess, in the billiard room of her parents' home in the city's West End, it is the oldest private school in Canada west of Ontario that is still operating. Jessie Gordon, supported by her sisters Edith and Mary, served as headmistress until 1937. The school moved to its own West End building in 1901 and again to its present location in 1942. It is named for some cottages in Cambridge, England, where Jessie Gordon attended university. *See also* EDUCATION, PRIVATE.

CROMIE, Donald Cameron, newspaper publisher (b 16 Oct 1915; d 17 Mar 1993, Vancouver). The son of Robert CROMIE, who took over the VANCOUVER SUN newspaper in 1917, he became publisher of the paper in 1942 and ran it until he sold it to FP Publications in 1963. An eccentric individual, Cromie ran a paper that was aggressive, flashy and outspoken, and as unpredictable as its publisher. During his tenure the *Sun* passed the PROVINCE in circulation. After he sold the *Sun* he published MAGAZINES and, in the 1970s and 1980s, developed real estate.

CROMIE, Robert James, newspaper publisher (b 4 July 1887, Scotstown, QC; d 11 May 1936, Victoria). He came to VANCOUVER in 1906 to work for FOLEY, WELCH & STEWART, a large railway-building company. He was put in charge of

one of its properties, the VANCOUVER SUN newspaper, and by 1917 he owned it himself. As publisher he absorbed his main competitors, the *News-Advertiser* and the *World*, and built the *Sun* into one of the city's two leading dailies. When he died suddenly of a heart attack, his sons Donald, Peter and Samuel took over the paper. Donald CROMIE, who became publisher in 1942, was in charge when the *Sun*, the last locally owned paper in Vancouver, was sold to FP Publications of Winnipeg in 1963. *See also* NEWSPAPERS.

CROSBY, Thomas, Methodist missionary (b 21 June 1840, Pickering, England; d 13 Jan 1914, Vancouver). He emigrated to Canada with his parents when he was 16 and settled in Woodstock, ON. In 1858 he joined the Wesleyan Methodist Church after a revivalist meeting. He became a preacher and in 1862 responded to a request for missionaries in BC. After teaching at a mission school in NANAIMO he became an itinerant preacher, carrying the Wesleyan message along the coast of VANCOUVER ISLAND and up the

Thomas Crosby, coastal missionary. CVA Port.P976

FRASER VALLEY, where he held emotional camp meetings. In 1874 he became a missionary at FORT SIMPSON. He remained there for 23 years, working among the TSIMSHIAN people and touring the coastal settlements in the mission boat *Glad Tidings*. Crosby believed that in order to accomplish a spiritual rebirth, FIRST NATIONS people had to abandon all vestiges of their traditional culture and adopt a western mode of living. At the same time he supported Tsimshian land claims (*see* ABORIGINAL RIGHTS) and helped the people cope with the negative influences of white society. In 1897 he was appointed chair of the BC Conference of the METHODIST CHURCH and left Fort Simpson, which was now called Port Simpson. He later ran missions at SARDIS and CHILLIWACK until his retirement in 1907. His autobiography *Up and Down the North Pacific*

Coast by Canoe and Mission Ship was published the year of his death.

CROW is the common name for a number of large black squawky birds occurring in abundance across BC both in rural areas and in populated places. They are familiar, and omnivorous, scavengers. Many people consider them pests; early in the 20th century there were government-sponsored bounties placed on them, but their numbers have not suffered. Crows are considered highly intelligent and they are certainly adaptable, having made themselves at home in almost every habitat. They exhibit a daily pattern of dispersing at dawn to forage, then reassembling, sometimes in large numbers,

Northwestern crow. R. Wayne Campbell photo

at their roosting sites at the end of the day. Two species occur in BC. The northwestern crow (*Corvus caurinus*) lives along the length of the coast, never far from tidewater. It forages along the shoreline and preys on eggs in seabird nesting colonies. BC is home to most of the world's population of this species. Across the COAST MTS in the south and central Interior is the closely related but slightly larger American crow (*C. brachyrhynchos*).

CROWN CORPORATIONS (provincial) are corporate entities established or acquired by the provincial government to provide services not furnished by the private sector. Though accountable to the relevant government department, they are not subject to direct government control and enjoy greater administrative autonomy than a government department. Some Crown corporations are financially independent, generating revenues from the sale of services and paying their own operating expenses, while others receive a degree of government financial assistance.

Crown corporations are responsible for many of the public services British Columbians have come to take for granted, including the generation and transmission of electricity (BC HYDRO), the retail distribution of liquor (LIQUOR DISTRIBUTION BRANCH of BC), the operation of

TOP 5 BC CROWN CORPORATIONS & AGENCIES AND THEIR 1999 REVENUES

1	BC HYDRO AND POWER AUTHORITY	$3.0 billion
2	INSURANCE CORPORATION OF BC	$2.8 billion
3	WORKERS' COMPENSATION BOARD	$1.73 billion
4	LIQUOR DISTRIBUTION BRANCH	$1.64 billion
5	BC Lottery Corporation	$1.26 billion

Other major Crown corporations:

BC ASSESSMENT AUTHORITY	BC Transportation Financing Authority
BC Buildings Corp	Columbia Power Corp
BC FERRY CORP	FOREST RENEWAL BC
BC Housing Management Commission	Okanagan Valley Tree Fruit Authority
BC Pavilion Corp	Provincial Capital Commission
BC RAIL LTD	PACIFIC NATIONAL EXHIBITION
BC TRANSIT	Provincial Rental Housing Corp

the provincial railway (BC RAIL) and the provision of auto insurance (INSURANCE CORPORATION OF BC), public transit (BC TRANSIT) and ferry service (BC FERRY CORP).

CROWN OF THE CONTINENT is the name given to the extreme southeast corner of BC and the neighbouring parts of Alberta and the US. A region of high, alpine-glaciated mountains (*see* GLACIATION), it includes Waterton Lakes National Park in Alberta, Glacier National Park in Montana and the AKAMINA–Kishinena Recreation Area (109.22 km²) in BC. This is an extremely important continental transition zone, with watersheds draining from the area to the Arctic, Pacific and Atlantic oceans. Rare wildlife species abound, and the area is home to 50% of the rare and ENDANGERED SPECIES of plants in BC.

CROWN ZELLERBACH CANADA LTD was formed in 1954 by Crown Zellerbach of San Francisco, a successor company to Crown Willamette, a Portland forest company. When it was established, CZ Canada consisted of the Pacific Mills Co PULP AND PAPER mill at OCEAN FALLS, which CW had acquired in 1914; CANADIAN WESTERN LUMBER CO, which owned the British Commonwealth's largest SAWMILL at Fraser Mills in NEW WESTMINSTER and BC's largest LOGGING and timber company, Comox Logging on VANCOUVER ISLAND; and the new Elk Falls pulp mill at CAMPBELL RIVER. Between 1965 and 1970 CZ acquired sawmills in the OKANAGAN VALLEY; these were centralized during the 1970s at ARMSTRONG and KELOWNA. CZ also operated a chain of building supply stores and retail lumberyards, later sold to Beaver Lumber. The Ocean Falls mill was sold to the BC government in 1973 and closed a few years later. In 1983 CZ Canada was sold to

FLETCHER CHALLENGE LTD of New Zealand and its name was changed to Crown Forest Industries Ltd. *Ken Drushka*

CROWS NEST SOUTHERN RAILWAY was a branch line of James J. Hill's GREAT NORTHERN RWY, running north from the Montana border along the KOOTENAY R and up the ELK R almost to FERNIE. Opened to traffic in 1902, it was built to carry COAL from area mines south to the US market, though it also offered passenger service. In 1908 the line was extended farther up the Elk R to MICHEL. During the 1920s coal shipments declined and the CNSR reduced service, first abandoning the line between Michel and ELKO in 1925 and then in 1937 closing altogether.

CROWSNEST PASS (el 1,357 m), on the BC–Alberta border 40 km north of US, is the southernmost of the ROCKY MT railway passes. The KTUNAXA (Kutenai) used it to reach the plains to hunt buffalo, though the name derives from a story about a group of Crow warriors who were attacked and killed in their camp, or "nest," by pursuing Blackfoot. In 1873 Michael PHILLIPPS, a prospector and trader, became the first white person to cross the pass. The CPR built a line through the pass between 1897 and 1898 to develop the rich COAL deposits of the area. The railway received a public subsidy to build the line in return for reduced freight rates for western farmers. The so-called Crow Rate was considered a vital part of the western Canadian economy; it remained in effect, with changes, until 1995.

CROYDON STATION, west of TETE JAUNE CACHE on the CNR and upper FRASER R, was the site of a SAWMILL established by Etter & McDougall Lumber Co at the end of WWI. It employed 80 people in 1920 but was moved to SHERE the next year; by 1928 the population had dropped to 15. An ANGLICAN CHURCH, St John in the Wilderness, was built here with contributions from the town of Croydon in England, after which Croydon Station was named. The site was later deserted.

AS

CROZIER, Lorna, poet, teacher (b 24 May 1948, Swift Current, SK). After graduating from the Univ of Saskatchewan, she taught high school in her native province. Her first book of poems, *Inside Is the Sky*, appeared in 1976 and has been followed by close to a dozen more. Twice nominated for a GOV GEN'S LITERARY AWARD, in 1986 and 1988, she won the award in 1992 for *Inventing the Hawk*. That book also won the Canadian Authors' Assoc Award and the Pat LOWTHER Award. Her next book, *Everything Arrives at the Light*, also won the Pat Lowther Award. In 1992 she moved to VANCOUVER ISLAND, where she began teaching creative writing at the Univ of Victoria. In 1996 she published a volume of poems, *A Saving Grace: the Collected Poems of Mrs Bentley*, inspired by Sinclair Ross's classic 1941 novel *As For Me and My House*. In 1999 her collection *What the Living Won't Let Go* was published; it won a BC BOOK PRIZE.

CRUISE SHIP INDUSTRY in the PORT OF VANCOUVER carries passengers on luxurious vessels north through the INSIDE PASSAGE to Alaska during summer. From its origins in the 1970s the industry has grown to become a major contributor to the Lower Mainland economy, particularly since terminal facilities were opened at Canada Place for EXPO 86. Nearby Ballantyne Pier is also used to berth the vessels. In 1999 there were 309 cruise ship sailings, carrying a total of 947,659 passengers who collectively spent an estimated $300 million in the VANCOUVER area. There are also a number of small companies running

short-hop excursions to locales on the South Coast. The modern industry is a continuation of a passenger vessel service that began with the CANADIAN PACIFIC NAVIGATION CO and the UNION STEAMSHIP CO.

CUCKOO is a long-tailed, slender bird. Two of the three species found in North America occur very rarely in British Columbia. The Yellow-billed Cuckoo (*Coccyzus americanus*) is considered accidental in this province, while Black-billed Cuckoos (*Coccyzus erythropthalmus*), which breed from Alberta to Nova Scotia, are infrequently seen or heard singing in the BC interior in the late spring and summer, particularly in the Creston and Revelstoke areas.

Kim Goldberg

CULBERT, Dick, mountaineer (b 1940, Winnipeg, MB). When his father was killed in WWII his family moved to W VANCOUVER. During the late 1950s and early 1960s he made several extended exploratory trips into the COAST MTS and made dozens of first ascents, most notably Serra V in the Waddington Range with Glenn Woodsworth in 1964. In 1969 he made the first winter ascent of Mt WADDINGTON with a large team. He made first ascents of the east ridge of Devil's Thumb in 1970, the Cat's Ears Spire in 1972 and also that year the east face of Mt Colonel Foster on VANCOUVER ISLAND. All 3 climbs were with Fred Douglas and Paul Starr. A professional geologist and diligent researcher, Culbert wrote *A Climber's Guide to the Coastal Ranges of British Columbia* (1965) and *Alpine Guide to South Western British Columbia* (1974). *See also* MOUNTAINEERING.

CULHANE, Claire Eglin, social activist (b 18 Sept 1918, Montreal; d 28 Apr 1996, Vancouver). As a young woman she was a member of the Communist Party and supported the Mackenzie-

Papineau Battalion in Spain. She worked in the trade union movement before temporarily retiring from activism to raise her 2 children. During the 1960s she worked in a hospital in Vietnam and became an outspoken opponent of Canada's involvement in the war there, once chaining herself to the public gallery in the House of Commons. In 1974 she came to live in VANCOUVER, where she was active in the prisoners' rights movement. For more than 20 years she worked tirelessly as an unofficial ombudsperson and thorn in the side of the government on behalf of prisoners and favoured the ultimate abolition of PRISONS. She also wrote 4 books. Culhane was named to the Order of Canada in 1995.

CULLEN, John Francis "Jack," radio broadcaster (b 1922, Vancouver). An avid record collector as a teenager, he served as a wireless operator in the navy during WWII, then began his radio career on station CKMO hosting VANCOUVER's first all-night radio show. In 1947 he launched the program that made him famous, *The Owl Prowl*, a late-night blend of music, humour and chat. He switched to CKNW in Aug 1949 and remained there for the next 50 years. Based on his personal archive of music, vintage radio shows and movies, his knowledge of show business was unmatched. In 1999 when CKNW dropped the *Prowl*, Cullen moved it to a rival station and kept on BROADCASTING.

CULTUS LAKE, 6.3 km², 15 km south of CHILLIWACK in the FRASER VALLEY, is the centre of a resort community and one of the most popular summer recreation spots in BC. There is a provincial PARK (6.5 km²) and a variety of campgrounds, trails, beaches and picnic sites. Cultus is a CHINOOK JARGON word meaning "bad," possibly a reference to the angry winter squalls that descend on the lake or to the supernatural creature that was believed to inhabit the area. *See also* LAKES.

CULVER, Daniel George, mountaineer (b 12 June 1952, Vancouver; d 7 July, 1993). The fifth Canadian to reach the top of Mt Everest and one of the first Canadians (with Jim HABERL) to climb K2, he became the only Canadian to have reached the summits of Earth's 2 highest mountains. Culver grew up in N VANCOUVER, studied at UBC and joined a white-water rafting company before starting his own tour operation. In 1989 he formed Blue Heron Adventure Experiences, taking company executives into the BC wilderness. A lover of the natural environment, he dedicated his Everest climb of 4 Oct 1990 to the threatened KHUTZEYMATEEN and Tsitika valleys. Culver made his K2 climb for awareness of the TATSHENSHINI valley, later preserved as a provincial PARK. He fell to his death on the way down from the K2 summit and, as his will instructed, his estate was put toward the preservation of the BC coast as a portion of the funds used to purchase JEDEDIAH ISLAND for a provincial MARINE PARK. Haberl, whose book of photographs *K2: Dreams and Reality* documents the K2 feat, was killed in an Alaska avalanche on 29 Apr 1999.

SW

A cruise ship on its way through the Inside Passage to Alaska. Ken Bowen photo

CUMBERLAND, village, pop 2,548, is located on the east side of VANCOUVER ISLAND near Comox Lk, 6 km south of COURTENAY. It was founded in 1888 by Robert DUNSMUIR in the middle of a rich COAL mining district. The original townsite was called Union Camp; a newly developed area, named Cumberland after the English county, became the overall name in 1898. In its heyday (1900–14) Cumberland had a mixed population of 13,000 people, including JAPANESE, BLACK, ITALIAN, Slavic and British miners and the second largest CHINATOWN north of San Francisco. It was a centre of a bitter coal mine strike during 1912–14. Production fell as markets diminished during the 1920s and the last of its mines closed in 1966. By then the local economy was relying on LOGGING and AGRICULTURE, and the town was reduced to village status as the population fell. Many of the original buildings burned but others have been restored in an effort to reclaim the history of this important community. *See also* COAL MINING, VANCOUVER ISLAND.

CUMYOW, Won Alexander, interpreter (b 24 Mar 1861, Port Douglas; d 6 Oct 1955, Vancouver). He was the first CHINESE born in Canada. After attending high school in NEW WESTMINSTER, he studied law and became a court interpreter and labour contractor. He was an interpreter in the VANCOUVER police court from 1904 to 1936. He voted for the first time in 1890, then not again until 1947 when the franchise was returned to residents of Asian background. Active in the city's Chinese community, he was founder of the Empire Reform Assoc, an organization of overseas Chinese in support of the emperor, and a president of the Chinese Benevolent Assoc. His son, Gordon Won Cumyow, was the first Chinese notary public in Canada.

Won Alexander Cumyow, the first Chinese born in Canada. UBC BC1848/5

Chinatown in Cumberland, 1910.
Courtesy Cumberland Museum

CUNNINGHAM, George Torrance, druggist (b 1889, ND; d 7 Mar 1965, Palm Springs, CA). He grew up in NEW WESTMINSTER and went to work as an apprentice druggist at WOODWARD'S when he was 15 years old. Later he studied pharmacy in Ontario and the US, then returned to VANCOUVER to open his first Cunningham Drug Store in the city's West End in 1911. By WWII the chain had grown to 35 stores. A well-known community leader, he served on city council from 1955 to 1957 and was chair of the UBC board of governors.

CUNNINGHAM, Jimmy, stonemason (b 1878, Isle of Bute, Scotland; d 29 Sept 1963, Vancouver). More than any other person he was responsible for the construction of the STANLEY PARK seawall, though it was not completed until after his death. He came to VANCOUVER in 1910 and served overseas during WWI. He worked as a mason on a wide variety of projects in the province, including the EMPRESS HOTEL and UBC, but is best known for his work on the seawall. The Vancouver parks board named him master stonemason in 1931 and he supervised the ongoing construction of the wall even after his retirement in 1955. By the time he died, about 5 km of the wall was built. The whole 8.5 km was finished in 1980.

CUNNINGHAM, Robert, missionary, fur trader, salmon canner (b 1 Jan 1837, Tullyvally, Ireland; d 8 Apr 1905, Victoria). The son of a Protestant farmer, he studied at the Church Missionary Society (CMS) college in London and in 1862 came to BC to assist William DUNCAN's mission at METLAKATLA. After he married a FIRST NATIONS woman the CMS expelled him in July 1867. He was employed by the HBC from 1867 to 1870 and eventually took charge of FORT SIMPSON, but he resigned over a salary dispute. In partnership with Thomas Hankin he pre-empted several lots on the SKEENA R, out of which grew the towns of PORT ESSINGTON and HAZELTON. When the partnership dissolved in 1877, he kept control of Port Essington, establishing a SALMON CANNERY there in 1883. His other commercial ventures included a hotel, a SAWMILL, a dogfish oil refinery, a store in Hazelton and real estate. As well, he was a leader in transportation ventures on the North Coast. After his death, R. Cunningham & Son continued under his son George until 1926. *Kenneth Campbell*

CURLING had been a popular sport in eastern Canada for about 90 years when GOLDEN organized BC's first curling club in 1894. Four years later the province's first recorded bonspiel was held by 18 KOOTENAY Curling Assoc rinks from ROSSLAND, NELSON, SANDON, KASLO and REVELSTOKE. In 1906 the provincewide BC Curling Assoc formed, though the game continued to be centred in the MINING towns of the Kootenay. During the next few decades it spread to other parts of BC including VANCOUVER, KAMLOOPS and the OKANAGAN VALLEY and when TRAIL hosted a bonspiel in 1937 it attracted 65 rinks, the largest curling competition in BC to that date. Trail also produced BC's first winners of the MacDonald Brier Canadian men's curling championship when Theo "Frenchy" D'Amour skipped Robert McGhie, Fred Wendel and Jim Mark, all employees of the Trail smelter, to national supremacy in 1948. Frank Avery, a member of the BC SPORTS HALL OF FAME, was instrumental in introducing the sport to Vancouver by coming up with the concept for the city's first curling club. Avery belonged to 5 rinks that won the BC men's championship. By 1952 the BC Ladies Curling Assoc had held its first provincial championship and the men's BC Curling Assoc had 46 clubs and more than 1,000 members. The Pacific Coast Curling Assoc (another Avery initiative) formed in 1960 and the BCCA changed its name to the BC Interior Curling Assoc in 1981.

Since being held for the first time in 1936, the men's provincial championships have featured several standout performers. Bernie

Greg McAulay (standing), at a Richmond bonspiel. He skipped the third BC rink to win the men's world curling championship in 2000.
Arlen Redekop/Vancouver Province

Sparkes, a winner of 3 world championships with a rink from Calgary, came to BC in the early 1970s and helped his rinks win 8 BC championships. The Stone brothers from Trail, Reg and Roy, won 7 BC Consol Championships and represented the province in the Brier 6 times. Thirty BC rinks have won Canadian championships in various categories including the Brier and the women's national championship now known as The Scott Tournament of Hearts. Lyall DAGG's rink captured BC's first men's world championship in 1964 and Rick FOLK duplicated the feat 30 years later. The 1985 Linda MOORE and 1987 Pat SANDERS rinks both won women's world championships. Moore's rink also won a demonstration gold at the 1988 Calgary Olympics while Julie Sutton's team, the 1991 Canadian champions, accepted an Olympic bronze in 1992. Prior to Moore, Sanders and Sutton, the KIMBERLEY rink skipped by Ina Hansen won the Canadian Women's Championship in 1962 and 1964, and Lindsay (Davie) Sparkes claimed the title in 1976 and 1979. Flora Martin, a member of the Canadian Curling Hall of Fame, dominated senior women's curling in the late 1970s, winning 4 national championships. BC broadcaster Bill Good Sr attended more Briers than anyone as the official voice of the sport from 1946 to 1990. Curl BC, which was inaugurated as the Curling Council of BC in 1971, assumes responsibility for promoting and administering the sport in the province. At the turn of the century, Curl BC estimated that approximately 130,000 British Columbians were involved in the sport and 115

rinks were active around the province. The entire curling community was electrified early in 2000, when BC rinks scored an unprecedented triple-play in world competition: the Greg MCAULAY rink from New Westminster won the men's world championship, the Kelley LAW rink from Richmond won the women's world title and the Brad Kuhn rink from Kelowna won the world junior crown. *SW*

CURRIE, Arthur William, soldier (b 5 Dec 1875, Strathroy, ON; d 30 Nov 1933, Montreal). He was Canada's greatest military hero, distinguishing himself in WWI by becoming the first Canadian to command the Canadian Expeditionary Force in 1917–19. Before the war he had been a teacher in the VICTORIA area (1894–1900) and an insurance salesman and realtor (1900–14). He joined the militia in 1897 and was promoted to command the 5th BC Garrison of Artillery in 1909. His troops were sent to quell striking coal miners at NANAIMO in 1913 (*see* COAL MINING, VANCOUVER ISLAND). At the outbreak of WWI he commanded the newly formed 50th Regiment (Gordon Highlanders) and was soon promoted to brigadier general to command the 2nd Canadian Infantry Brigade. Appalled at the losses resulting from the war of attrition, Currie was ingenious at devising new strategies that helped to break the deadlock on the western front. The capture of Vimy Ridge in Apr 1917 was one result of his innovations. For his role at Vimy, Currie was knighted and promoted to lieutenant general to command the Canadian Corps. Following the war he served until his death as president of McGill Univ in Montreal.

During the latter years of the war and the 1920s, Currie faced a campaign by Sir Samuel Hughes, former federal minister of militia and defence, to discredit him over pre-war debts and needless casualties prior to the Armistice. Currie sued for libel and was vindicated in court. *See also* MILITARY HISTORY. *Ken Macleod*

CURRIE, MOUNT; *see* MOUNT CURRIE.

CURTIS, Edward S., photographer (b 19 Feb 1868, WI; d 21 Oct 1952, CA). A self-taught photographer, he began his career in St Paul, MN, before moving with his father to Washington state when he was 19 to homestead. In 1891 he joined a photographic firm in Seattle and soon came to own it. He took his first portrait of a Native in 1896 and began to develop his ambitious plan to make a photographic record of N American aboriginal people before they vanished, as he believed they were destined to do. He began work on this project about 1903 and it consumed all his energy for the next three decades. The results were published as a series of 20 volumes, *The North American Indian*, published 1907–30. Included in the collection were many photographs of BC FIRST NATIONS people. As well, he made a film about the KWAKWAKA'WAKW (Kwakiutl), *IN THE LAND OF THE HEAD HUNTERS*, which premiered in New York and Seattle in 1914. When Curtis finished his project in 1930 he was broke and in poor health. He spent the rest of his life in California. When he died he was virtually forgotten, but his work, which conveys a romantic image of precontact aboriginal life, has enjoyed a revival since the 1970s. *See also* PHOTOGRAPHY.

General Arthur Currie (centre) at practice attack near Vimy Ridge, Sept 1917. NAC PA2004

A classic Edward S. Curtis photograph, "The Wedding Party," 1914, likely a still from his film In the Land of the Head-hunters. *The newlyweds stand on a painted "bride's seat" in the stern of the canoe. BC Archives D-08291*

CUTLER, David, football player (b 17 Oct 1945, Biggar, SK). He grew up in VICTORIA, then attended SFU 1965–68 and joined the FOOTBALL team as an unknown. When the regular kicker played poorly in the team's first game of the season, Cutler stepped into the role and went on to set all the school's kicking records. He was drafted third overall in the CFL but signed with the NFL's Green Bay Packers. In 1969 he returned north to Edmonton, where he played for the Eskimos for 16 seasons, a key component in Edmonton's 9 Grey Cup final appearances in 10 years and 5 consecutive wins (1978–82). He led the league in scoring 7 times and once held 26 CFL records including most points (2,337), most conversions (627), most field goals (464), most field goals in a season (50) and longest field goal (59 yds). These records lasted until Lui PASSAGLIA broke them in the mid-1990s. After retiring in 1984 Cutler returned to Victoria, where he joined an internet company. He is a member of the SFU Sports Hall of Fame and CFL Hall of Fame. *SW*

CYCLING was introduced to BC when the first shipment of velocipedes, the earliest bicycles, arrived in VICTORIA from Paris in Feb 1869. Velocipedes were initially unpopular because they required more physical work to ride than did horses. In one year the price of a unit dropped from $150 to $10 and Victoria's *British Colonist* newspaper published an obituary for the new machine. By 1888 only two bicycles had arrived in VANCOUVER, one owned by Prince Edward Island champion cyclist Sam Mason, who promoted cycling by beating a horse in a race down Water St. Victoria's Island Wanderers Club became BC's first cycling organization in 1889 and Vancouver cyclists formed the Terminal

City Cycling Club in 1892 to compete on the new cinder cycling track at BROCKTON POINT in STANLEY PARK. By 1894 Vancouver women had taken up cycling despite the protests of some men that such behaviour was "undignified."

Bicycle competition thrived in Vancouver and Victoria during the 1890s and other BC communities such as NANAIMO and KAMLOOPS started cycling clubs. The Burrard Bicycle Club, later the Vancouver Bicycle Club, formed as part of the Canadian Wheelmen's Assoc in 1896 and soon became the largest club in the province. In 1901 the Vancouver Good Roads Assoc began to construct cycling paths in Vancouver and the next year the city hosted the Dominion Bicycle Meet, attracting 7,000 spectators.

The automobile was introduced to BC in 1906 but it was extremely expensive and the bicycle "craze" continued. In 1920 the *Vancouver Daily PROVINCE* Bicycle Road Races were first held and 3 years later the *TIMES-COLONIST* sponsored a similar event in Victoria. Top racers included Dave Mercredy, Don Sutherland, Charlie Staples, William "Torchy" PEDEN, his brother Doug

YWCA cyclists on an outing. UBC BC1509/9

PEDEN and Jim Davies, winner of the first Canadian cycling championship in 1927. Davies and Torchy Peden represented Canada at the 1928 Amsterdam Olympics though they brought home no medals. But Peden swept the Canadian indoor championships, turned professional the next year and established a world speed record that stood for 12 years. Aside from

The start of the Test of Metal mountain bike race in Squamish. Craig Hodge/Vancouver Sun

touring the world competing in popular 6-day races, Peden coached 5 top amateurs from BC at the 1932 Los Angeles Olympics: Lew Rush, Glen Robbins, Frank Elliot, Stan Jackson and Leo Marchiori. Peden, Davies, Staples, Rush, Elliot and Jackson all appeared in the international 6-Day Bicycle Races that Vancouver hosted in the early 1930s. Morris Robinson of Vancouver emerged in the late 1930s to break most of the racing records in BC and to race for Canada at the 1938 British Empire Games.

Lorne "Ace" Atkinson was the next top cyclist to emerge in BC, winning provincial and national events at distances up to 50 miles (80 km)and competing in the 1948 London Olympics and the 1950 and 1954 British Empire Games. He then embarked on a long coaching career, developing the 1967 Pan American Games team and training and advising more BC riders than anyone else over the next 40 years. Vancouver's China Creek Velodrome, a world-class cycling oval built with yellow CEDAR, was constructed for the 1954 British Empire Games (*see* BRITISH EMPIRE AND COMMONWEALTH GAMES). It fell into neglect several years after the Games but was restored in 1973 and used until it was demolished in 1980 to make room for Vancouver Community College (*see* COMMUNITY COLLEGES). Forty years after the construction of the first velodrome, Victoria had the concrete-surfaced Juan de Fuca Velodrome built for the 1994 Commonwealth Games.

After a difficult transition period for cycling in the 1950s and 1960s, bike sales boomed in 1970 and a new criterium road race in Vancouver, the Gastown Grand Prix (1973–92), attracted top riders from around the world including 1991 winner Lance Armstrong, who won the 1999 Tour de France. John Hathaway of

Vancouver attracted unprecedented interest in RANDONNEURING distance cycling by riding 80,000 km around the world in 100 weeks between 1974 and 1976. In Victoria, the Wheelers Cycling Club was established by Don Fawthorpe and Tom Morris, a Canadian champion and 2-time Olympic cyclist. Led by Vancouver's Ron Hayman, a new generation of competitive cyclists bloomed. Hayman rode in the Olympics in 1972 and 1976 and as a founding member and leader of the professional 7-11 team, he was an important figure in the re-emerging N American pro ranks. He later became the national team's coach, attending another Olympics in 1988. Hayman paved the way for 1984 Olympian Martin Willock, brother Bernie Willock, a 1979 Pan Am Games bronze medallist, and Alex STIEDA, the first N American ever to lead the Tour de France. BC's first world-level women's cyclist was Sara Neil, a national champ who competed 1985–90 and appeared in the 1988 Olympics.

In the mid-1980s mountain bike racing spread out of California and quickly became popular in BC. The province has led Canada in recreational and competitive mountain biking with successful riders such as Leslie Tomlison, Roland Green and Alison SYDOR, a silver medallist at the 1992 Olympics and 3-time world champion (1994–96). In track racing, Brian WALTON of DELTA was a 1996 Olympic silver medallist in the points race and 2-time Pan Am gold medallist (1995, 1999). Recreational cycling grew rapidly in the late 1990s as bicycle tours of areas such as the ROCKY MTS and GULF ISLANDS became increasingly popular. Bicycle commuting also continued to increase. Cycling BC, formed in 1974 as a provincial umbrella organization, promoted and administered the sport.   *SW*

CYPRESS PROVINCIAL PARK, 30.12 km², is located in the North Shore mountains above W VANCOUVER. Designated a park in 1975, it is one of the most popular recreation areas in the Lower Mainland. It encompasses the Mt Hollyburn ski area, operated under lease by Cypress Bowl Recreations Ltd, part of the BADEN-POWELL TRAIL and the HOWE SOUND CREST TRAIL.

The Cypress Bowl recreation area, overlooking Vancouver. Keith Thirkell photo

Skiing began on Hollyburn (el 1,324 m) in the 1920s with skiers hiking up the mountain from the ferry dock at Ambleside. Access improved in 1950 with the construction of a chairlift. When the lift closed in 1965, use of the mountain declined until the government created the park and built road access. Cypress contains some of the largest and oldest trees in BC.

Dave Wood, Saltspring Island cheese maker.
John Yanyshyn/Vancouver Sun

DAGG, Lyall, curler (b 27 July 1929, Tisdale, SK; d 14 May 1975, Kelowna). One of the most competitive and intense athletes in BC history, he was the coach and skip of the successful Vancouver CURLING Club of the 1960s. Dagg began curling with his family at VANCOUVER's Pacific Curling Rink in 1953. By 1961 he had put together his rink of Leo Hebert, Fred Britton and Barry Naimark and in 1964 they won the Canadian Brier title in Charlottetown and the world title in Calgary. With Terry Paulsen replacing Britton, the rink won the BC championship for a second time in 1970 but finished third at the Brier. Dagg worked as a sports reporter and in public relations for CROWN ZELLERBACH. He died at age 45 of a rare blood disease and was inducted into the BC SPORTS HALL OF FAME in 1977. His daughter, Elaine Dagg Jackson, coached the Julie Sutton rink to 1992 Olympic bronze and later became the head coach of the Japanese national team. *SW*

DAIRY FARMING is one of the largest components of the AGRICULTURE industry in BC, employing about 11,000 people and contributing more than $1 billion to the provincial ECONOMY, including more than $330 million annually in farm gate receipts. There are 785 producers in the province, concentrated in the lower FRASER VALLEY, on southern VANCOUVER ISLAND and in the northern OKANAGAN VALLEY–Shuswap where winters are mild and there is plentiful pasture land. Smaller concentrations of herds are found near SMITHERS in the Bulkley Valley, in the PEACE R area and in the KOOTENAY and the CARIBOO. In 1998 the total BC herd numbered 85,000 cows, the fourth-largest provincial herd in Canada after Quebec, Ontario and Alberta. BC cows produce about 570 million litres of milk annually, 8% of the national total. Production is regulated by the BC Milk Marketing Board. There are about 20 dairy processors in BC; the largest, DAIRYWORLD FOODS, formed in 1913 as a CO-OPERATIVE of

Holstein dairy cattle at Sardis, 1991.
Roy Luckow photo

Fraser Valley producers, handles more than two-thirds of the total milk production. Island Farms, a long-standing co-operative of Vancouver Island farmers, is another important processor. Two-thirds of the milk produced in BC is sold as fluid milk; the rest is used to manufacture other products such as cheese, yogurt, ice cream and cottage cheese. *See also* AVALON DAIRY LTD.

DAIRYWORLD FOODS, known for its Dairyland brand of products, began in 1913 as a

CO-OPERATIVE of FRASER VALLEY dairy farmers (*see* DAIRY FARMING), called the Fraser Valley Milk Producers Assoc. The original association involved 90% of the valley's producers. Over the years it grew from a bargaining agent for farmers to an owner and operator of creameries, a milk condensory, an ice cream maker and a milk distributorship. In 1992 it merged with 2 Alberta dairy co-operatives to form Agrifoods International Co-operative Ltd, the parent company of Dairyworld. In 1996 it added a Saskatchewan dairy to become Canada's largest dairy company and western Canada's largest food company. Among its products is Armstrong cheese, pro-

BC DAIRY FARMS				
	1971	**1981**	**1991**	**1996**
No of dairy farms	1,637	1,345	1,158	1,184
No of dairy cows (000s)	80	89	75	82
		1993	**1996**	**1998**
Dairy farming revenues ($ millions)		268.1	302.0	336.0

duced in ABBOTSFORD, named the finest cheddar in the world in 1994. The company had 1998 revenues of $1.2 billion.

DAKELH are a FIRST NATIONS people, formerly known as the Carrier, who inhabit the mountainous north-central Interior from the FRASER R west to the COAST MTS. In the local language Dakelh means "people who travel on the water," a reference to the many LAKES and waterways in their territory. The name *Carrier* was from the traditional practice of a widow carrying the cremated remains of her dead husband in a bundle on her back.

About 7,000 registered Dakelh live in more than 2 dozen modern communities. Long ago the people are said to have inhabited a large village, DIZKLE, on the banks of the BULKLEY R near MORICETOWN. Today the main groups include the NAZKO of the Nazko R area west of QUESNEL, the Lheidli T'enneh (formerly Fort George) at PRINCE GEORGE, the Nak'azdli (Necoslie) at FORT ST JAMES, the Tl'azt'en of Stuart and Trembleur Lakes, the Nadleh Whut'en on FRASER LK, the Stellat'en along the Stellako R, the Ulkatcho near ANAHIM LK, the Nat'oot'en (Lake Babine) of BABINE LK, the Cheslatta of the lake country south of BURNS LK, and the WET'SUWET'EN in the Bulkley Valley.

Before contact with Europeans the Dakelh were hunters and fishers, relying in particular on SALMON runs in the major RIVERS. They lived in small groups based on extended families. The Great Road, or NUXALK–Carrier Grease TRAIL, stretched across the southern part of the territory connecting the Fraser R to the Pacific (it is now part of the MACKENZIE HERITAGE TRAIL). Trade with coastal aboriginal groups via this road led some of the Dakelh to adopt the POTLATCH and hierarchical systems of social ranking. The FUR TRADE became established in their territory early in the 19th century with the arrival of NORTH WEST CO traders. Fort St James, established on Stuart Lk in 1806, became the trading centre for a vast area known as NEW CALEDONIA. After 1860, miners, farmers and ranchers moved into the area (*see* MINING; AGRICULTURE; CATTLE INDUSTRY), accelerating the pace of economic change. As well, OBLATE missionaries attempted to eradicate traditional customs. With the completion of the GRAND TRUNK PACIFIC RWY in 1914, the LOGGING industry flourished, creating wage employment for the Dakelh but damaging the natural environment on which their traditional economy had depended. The damming of the NECHAKO R in the 1950s also had a serious impact on subsistence patterns. Though the Dakelh participate in the wage economy, FISHING, hunting and trapping continue to be important. The Yinka Dene Language Institute at VANDERHOOF is concerned with preserving the culture and traditions of the Dakelh. *See also* FIRST NATIONS LANGUAGES.

DALLY, Frederick, photographer (b 29 July 1838, Southwark, England; d 28 July 1914, Wolverhampton, England). He arrived in VICTORIA in 1862 and went into business as a dry goods merchant; 4 years later he opened a pho-

tographic studio. His subjects included prominent Victoria citizens as well as some of the earliest images of the CARIBOO WAGON ROAD, Interior goldfields and aboriginal people. He briefly had a studio in BARKERVILLE but it was destroyed by the 1868 fire. He left Victoria in 1870 for Philadelphia where he trained to be a dentist, then returned to live in England. *See also* PHOTOGRAPHY.

DALSKOG, Carl Einar "Ernie," logger, union activist (b Sweden, date unknown; d 1992, Fanny Bay). He immigrated to BC from Sweden in 1923 and went to work in the woods. He became involved in union activity with the radical LUMBER WORKERS' INDUSTRIAL UNION at a time when union organizers were routinely fired and blacklisted by forest companies. After the creation of the International Woodworkers of America (IWA) (*see* INDUSTRIAL, WOOD AND ALLIED WORKERS OF CANADA) in 1937 he served the union in various capacities, eventually as president of the BC district council. In 1945 he was instrumental in organizing workers at SAWMILLS across the Interior. Along with other Communist IWA leaders he was expelled for life by the International union in 1948. *See also* FOREST INDUSTRY; LABOUR MOVEMENT.

DANCE in BC has a distinguished history, but until well into the second half of the 20th century the province's main contribution was as a breeding ground for talented performers who went on to pursue careers elsewhere. Edna Malone, from NELSON, was one of the first: she danced with the US modernist pioneers Ruth St Denis and Doris Humphrey following WWI, and performed with their company in VANCOUVER in 1919. In the 1930s June Roper, an immigrant teacher from Texas, sent more than 60 BC

dancers to New York and Hollywood. Among them were 2 Vancouver teenagers, Rosemary Deveson and Patricia Meyers, who became, respectively, Natasha Sobinova and Alexandra Denisova with the Ballet Russe; Ian Gibson of VICTORIA and Duncan Noble and Robert Lindgren of Vancouver (all to New York's Ballet Theatre); and Peggy Middleton of Vancouver, who became renowned in Hollywood as Yvonne DE CARLO. The tradition was maintained by dancers such as Lois Smith, a founding star of the National Ballet of Canada (NBC) in 1951; Lynn Springbett of Port Moody, who as Lynn Seymour became a principal with the Royal Ballet of London; Reid Anderson, who made a distinguished career in Germany before he returned to Canada as artistic director of BALLET BC and later of the NBC; and most recently Chan Hon Goh, who left her father's Goh Ballet in Vancouver in the early 1990s to become a principal with the NBC.

While the first N American production of the classic ballet *Coppelia* was staged by an amateur troupe directed by Dorothy Wilson (and starring Ian Gibson) in Victoria in 1936, until very recently dancers with hopes of a professional future had no choice but to leave the province. Local audiences have always had a taste for visiting dance companies, but it was more difficult to root the art in the pioneer soil of the province. Several unsuccessful attempts were made during the 1940s, '50s and '60s to establish a resident professional ballet company in Vancouver, but funding was always uncertain and it was not until the creation of Pacific Ballet Theatre by Maria Lewis in 1969 that ballet found a footing. Renamed Ballet BC in 1985, it has become one of the country's top 5 ballet companies. Under John Alleyne, who was appointed artistic director in 1992, it forged a distinctive creative identi-

Karen Jamieson, dancer and choreographer, with members of her troupe.
Mark Van Manen/Vancouver Sun

ty that eschewed the big, expensive classics in favour of a repertoire of sleek, European-style modernity.

Modern dance, less expensive than ballet to produce and perhaps more in tune with the individualistic character of the West Coast, established a footing in the late 1950s under 2 immigrant teachers from Bohemia, Gertrud and Magda Hanova. By the early 1960s, Norbert VESAK of PORT MOODY returned to BC after several years of study abroad to establish Western Dance Theatre (1970), and what followed was a golden decade for modern dance. Its spirit of revolution and freedom of artistic expression reflected the mood of optimism and experiment that permeated Canadian society at the time. Fuelled by new government funding and serious attention at the university level, modern dance became, during the late 1960s and 1970s, the darling of the arts world. SFU and to a lesser extent UBC turned out a generation of young choreographers eager to test their creative powers, and a number of leading BC modernist companies date from that period, among them the Karen JAMIESON Dance Co and Special Delivery Dance Theatre (now called Vancouver Moving Theatre). The 2 most influential companies in those years were directed by Paula ROSS, a former itinerant showgirl, who founded the Paula Ross Dancers in 1965, and Anna WYMAN, a European immigrant whose Anna Wyman Dance Theatre gave its first performance in 1971.

In the 1970s, with diminished funding for dance companies, dancers and choreographers began experimenting with new forms of organization and administration, as well as new forms of dance. One of the most influential groups, EDAM (Experimental Dance and Music), was founded in 1982 by Karen Jamieson with Peter Bingham, Peter Ryan, Lola MacLaughlin, Jennifer Mascall, Barbara Bourget, Jay Hirabayashi and Ahmed Hassan. With its own studio theatre at the WESTERN FRONT, EDAM has grown into an internationally respected company, known for its work in contact improvisation and collectivism. Peter Bingham took over as artistic director in 1989. EDAM has inspired a number of other acclaimed companies that have remained active, including Mascall Dance, Lola Dance and KOKORO DANCE (founded by Bourget and Hirabayashi). These activities and the establishment of the Vancouver Dance Centre, as well as the creation of 2 high-profile annual showcase venues—Judith MARCUSE's Kiss Project and the Firehall Arts Centre's Dancing on the Edge Festival—have provided the dance community with solidity and self-confidence.

By the start of the 21st century, dance in BC had begun to reflect the province's cultural diversity, with Indo-Canadian-inspired and Asian Canadian-led companies (such as Battery Opera, under the guidance of Lee Su-Feh and David McIntosh), flamenco and fusion dance, and other bold new works. In the 1990s as in the 1960s, modern independent dance companies in BC are known for developing unique forms in spite of minimal resources. Unlike ballet, modern dance has almost as many styles as it has practitioners. A host of choreographers experimenting with new forms of self-expression and regularly winning national awards have made BC one of the country's most exciting choreographic hotbeds, and BC dancers are among the most accomplished in Canada. While audiences are still sometimes sparse, BC dance at the turn of the millennium has reached a stage of maturity and achievement that belies its comparative youth.

Max Wyman

DANES began arriving in BC as part of the huge migration of Europeans to N America at the end of the 19th century. In 1896–97 a group of Danish pioneers from Denmark and from the US, led by Rasmus Hansen, established itself at the north end of VANCOUVER ISLAND in the CAPE SCOTT area, hoping to found a co-operative agricultural colony in this wild neck of the woods. The colony boasted a SAWMILL and a newspaper, but before long it ran out of money; by 1907 the settlers had moved away, many to the nearby communities of HOLBERG and SAN JOSEF BAY. By the 1920s Danish immigrants had arrived in the more populous Lower Mainland in sufficient numbers to establish the first Danish LUTHERAN Church (in 1923). By 1931 there was a chapter of the Danish Brotherhood in America and a mutual aid society, and other community institutions followed. The Danish Community Centre was established in SURREY in 1962 and there are Danish churches (the Danish Lutheran Church in BURNABY resembles a 12th-century Danish church), senior citizens' homes and cultural organizations. According to the 1996 census, 47,845 British Columbia residents claimed Danish heritage.

DANIELLS, Roy, teacher, poet (b 6 Apr 1902, London, England; d 13 Apr 1979, Vancouver). He arrived in VICTORIA with his family in 1910. After graduating from UBC and the Univ of Toronto he became a professor of English. Most of his career until his retirement in 1974 was spent at UBC, where he was head of the English department. His main scholarly interest was 17th-century English poetry but he also wrote extensively about Canadian literature. He published two books of poetry—*Deeper into the Forest* (1948) and *The Chequered Shade* (1963)—and a biography of the explorer Alexander MACKENZIE. He was inducted into the Order of Canada in 1971.

DANSKIN is a farming (*see* AGRICULTURE) and LOGGING settlement 30 km south of BURNS LAKE on the south side of FRANÇOIS LK. A group of MENNONITES moved here in the late 1930s and still exert a strong cultural influence on the community.

AS

DARBY, George Elias, medical missionary (b 27 Oct 1889, Everton, ON; d 1 Sept 1962, Vancouver). After studying medicine at the Univ of Toronto, where he graduated as a silver medallist in 1913, he moved to VANCOUVER to intern at the General Hospital. In 1914 he married his college sweetheart, Edna Matthews, a tennis champion, and together they undertook a METHODIST medical mission to a widely scattered population of aboriginal people, loggers, fishers and cannery workers from RIVERS INLET to NAMU, BELLA BELLA, KLEMTU and HARTLEY BAY on the North Coast. For 40 years he brought high quality medical care to these isolated communities. A Canadian Coast Guard vessel was named in his honour.
Reading: Hugh McKervill, *Darby of Bella Bella*, 1964.

Adam Waldie

DARCUS, Jack Winston, filmmaker (b 22 Feb 1941, Vancouver). He was already established as a painter and art instructor in 1969 when he wrote and directed his first film, *Great Coups of History*. An independent feature made with the help of the UBC Film Society, it offered a portrait of an irrepressible single mother and represented a vision of low-budget, personal cinema to which Darcus has remained faithful. He has divided his time between painting and feature filmmaking, producing a distinctive body of work that includes *Proxyhawks* (1970), *Wolfpen Principle* (1974), *Deserters* (1984), *Kingsgate* (1989), *The Portrait* (1993) and *Silence* (1997), all made in VANCOUVER, and *Overnight* (1984), shot in Toronto. He has taught at UBC, the EMILY CARR INSTITUTE OF ART & DESIGN and the Vancouver Film School. *See also* FILMMAKING INDUSTRY.

Michael Walsh

D'ARCY, pop 60, is a farming (*see* AGRICULTURE) and Lil'wat (Lillooet) FIRST NATION community at the south end of ANDERSON LK, 110 km northeast of SQUAMISH. In the 1920s the Pacific Great Eastern Rwy (*see* BC RAIL) made a lunch stop here at D'Arcy Lodge, which was popular also with TOURISTS visiting the lake and nearby beach. It was named after D'Arcy Tate, vice-president of the PGE from 1912 to 1918.

AS

D'ARCY ISLAND, 82 ha, is one of many small GULF ISLANDS just north of the San Juan archipelago off the SAANICH PENINSULA. In 1891 it became the site of a lazaretto, or leprosarium. The original inhabitants were CHINESE immigrants who had contracted leprosy in China. The island was basically a quarantine station, where lepers were supplied with provisions and left to fend for themselves. There was no medical treatment until 1906, when the federal government took over, hired a medical officer and began to regulate care. In 1924 the lazaretto moved to BENTINCK ISLAND closer to VICTORIA and D'Arcy was left uninhabited. Named for John D'Arcy, a British naval officer, it later became a MARINE PARK accessible only by boat.

DARFIELD, 72 km north of KAMLOOPS on Hwy 5 and the west side of the N THOMPSON R, is a small farming (*see* AGRICULTURE) community. The name has two sources: Darfeld, the German home of resident Hubert Janning, and nearby Darlington Crk.

AS

DAVID, Joe, artist (b 30 June 1946, Opitsat). Born to the Tla-o-qui-aht (Clayoquot) nation of the NUU-CHAH-NULTH, he credited his father Hyacinth David as his main teacher of cultural tradition. He was raised at Opitsat on MEARES ISLAND and in Seattle, and studied graphic design in Texas. He began to explore Northwest Coast ART in museums, attending classes at the Univ of Washington taught by the art historian Bill Holm, and he apprenticed to the carver Duane Pasco. In 1969 he received the name Ka-Ka-Win-Chealth from his father's family. In 1975 he moved back to BC and in 1984 he raised a welcoming figure at the LEGISLATIVE BUILDINGS in VICTORIA in support of a protest against LOGGING on Meares Island. Fluent in a range of media, he helped to revitalize the Tla-o-qui-aht style of sculpture and painting.

Karen Duffek

Joe David at work on a totem pole, 1974

DAVID THOMPSON UNIVERSITY CENTRE; *see* NOTRE DAME UNIV OF NELSON.

DAVIDSON, Florence (Edenshaw), Haida elder (b 15 Sept 1896, Masset; d Dec 1993, Masset). Her father was the HAIDA artist Charles EDENSHAW. At age 14 she married Robert Davidson Sr, a logger, fisher and trapper, and together they had 13 children. In the 1950s she began making button blankets, the first Haida woman in the modern period to resume this craft, and weaving traditional baskets and hats. She shared her knowledge of Haida culture with many anthropologists, historians and filmmakers and acted as a respected ambassador for her people in the wider world. One of her grandsons is Robert DAVIDSON, the distinguished artist. *See also* ART, NORTHWEST COAST ABORIGINAL.
Reading: Margaret Blackman with Florence Davidson, *During My Time: Florence Edenshaw Davidson, a Haida Woman*, 1982.

Florence Edenshaw Davidson, Haida elder, 1983. Ralph Bower/Vancouver Sun

DAVIDSON, John "Botany John," botanist (b 6 Aug 1878, Aberdeen, Scotland; d 10 Feb 1970, Vancouver). As a teenager he went to work as an assistant in the botany department at Univ of Aberdeen where he remained for 18 years. During that time and despite his lack of formal education he became curator of the university's botanical museum. Seeking a milder climate for his health he immigrated to BC in 1911. He was appointed the first provincial botanist, charged with conducting a survey of native flora (*see* PLANTS, NATIVE) and collecting specimens in a botanical garden. The garden, the first of its kind in western Canada, was established on the grounds of RIVERVIEW, the new mental hospital in COQUITLAM, then moved in 1916 to VANCOUVER, to the Point Grey site of UBC. Davidson was a professor of botany at the university until his retirement in 1948. The original garden at Riverview is the Davidson Arboretum.

DAVIDSON, Robert Charles, artist (b 4 Nov 1946, Hydaburg, AK). He grew up in MASSET on the QUEEN CHARLOTTE ISLANDS, where he began carving as a teenager, working in wood and ARGILLITE under the instruction of his HAIDA father and grandfather. He moved to VANCOUVER in 1965 to complete high school, then apprenticed with the carver Bill REID. Davidson attended the Vancouver School of Art 1967–70 (*see* EMILY CARR INSTITUTE OF ART & DESIGN). In Masset in 1969 he carved his first TOTEM POLE, the first pole raised in the village in more than 90 years. He also began carving masks and making jewellery and prints. Among his major commissions

are the housefront for the Charles EDENSHAW Memorial Longhouse at Masset (1977–78); a talking stick presented to Pope John Paul II during his Vancouver visit in 1984; a trio of poles in the International Sculpture Garden in Purchase, NY; and poles in Dublin, Montreal and Toronto. In 1993 a major retrospective of his work opened at the VANCOUVER ART GALLERY and travelled to the Canadian Museum of Civilization in Ottawa. Davidson is a member of the ORDER OF BC (1995).
Reading: Ian Thom, ed, *Robert Davidson: Eagle of the Dawn*, 1993.

Robert Davidson, Haida carver, 1998. Ulli Steltzer photo

DAVIE, Alexander Edmund Batson, lawyer, politician, premier 1 Apr 1887–death (b 24 Nov 1847, Somerset, England; d 1 Aug 1889, Victoria). He immigrated to BC in 1862 and articled as a lawyer in VICTORIA. Called to the bar in 1873, he became the first lawyer to obtain his complete legal education on VANCOUVER ISLAND. He established a practice in the capital and in the CARIBOO; in 1875 he was elected to the provincial legislature as an independent. Two years later Premier A.C. ELLIOTT invited him into the cabinet, but Davie lost the necessary by-election. Discouraged, he returned to practising law full-time. In 1882 he was elected a second time and in Jan 1883 joined the cabinet of Premier William SMITHE as attorney general. When Smithe died in 1887 Davie took over as PREMIER, but ill health limited his effectiveness. Less than 6 months after assuming office, he left BC to convalesce in the US for several months. In his absence John ROBSON ran the government. Davie returned in May 1888 in poor health and died the following year. His brother Theodore DAVIE later served as premier from 1892 to 1895.

DAVIE, Theodore, lawyer, premier 2 July 1892–2 Mar 1895 (b 22 Mar 1852, Brixton, England; d 7 Mar 1898, Victoria). He came to VICTORIA in 1867 to join his father and elder brother A.E.B. DAVIE. After studying law, he practised in the CASSIAR area and in NANAIMO. He then returned to Victoria, where he became a leading criminal lawyer. Davie launched his political career in the 1882 provincial election, supported his brother when he was PREMIER in 1887–89 and served as attorney general in John ROBSON's government in 1889–92. When Robson died suddenly, Davie became premier. His government's most lasting achievement was construction of the present parliament buildings. He resigned to succeed Matthew BEGBIE as provincial chief justice, a position he held at his death.

DAVIES, Clem, radio preacher (b 1890, England; d 1951, Los Angeles, CA). He arrived in VICTORIA in 1922 after studying at an American bible college and launched radio station CFCL (later CJVI) to broadcast his brand of prophetic evangelism. In 1937 he moved to VANCOUVER, where he held fervent outdoor meetings for crowds of 10,000 faithful. Davies was strongly anti-Catholic: he claimed that the Duke of Windsor had abdicated the British throne because he was drugged by Jesuits. During WWII he moved to Los Angeles where he continued his ministry.

DAVIS, Chuck, broadcaster, writer (b 1935, Winnipeg). During a varied journalism career in VANCOUVER, begun in 1956, he was a broadcaster, quizmaster and newspaper columnist. The author of more than a dozen books, including histories of N VANCOUVER and PORT COQUITLAM and of radio station CKNW (*see also* BROADCASTING, COMMERCIAL), he is best known as editor of the ultimate urban compendium *The Vancouver Book*, which appeared first in 1976 and then in a greatly expanded and updated version, *The Greater Vancouver Book*, in 1997. This encyclopedic collection of information, which won the 1998 CITY OF VANCOUVER BOOK AWARD and a distinguished-achievement award from SFU, affirmed his reputation as "Mr Vancouver."

DAVIS, Henry Fuller "Twelve Foot," prospector, trader (b 1818, VT; d 13 Sept 1900, Lesser Slave Lake, AB). He came to BC from California to take part in the GOLD RUSH in the CARIBOO. Though he was unable to read or write, he discovered an error that had left unclaimed a rich, 12-ft strip of GOLD-bearing gravel next to the Discovery claim, thus earning his nickname. After joining the Omineca gold rush, he established a small post at HUDSON'S HOPE and began trading along the PEACE R, where his many feats and long tenure, not to mention his pumpkin pies, established him as a regional icon.

Howard White

DAVIS, John "Jack," engineer, economist, politician (b 31 July 1916, Kamloops; d 28 Mar 1991, Vancouver). After graduating from UBC in 1938 he went on to graduate studies at McGill Univ in Montreal and Oxford Univ in England. He then settled in VANCOUVER, where from

1955 to 1957 he served as senior economist with the Royal Commission on Canada's Economic Prospects, then became director of research and planning for BC ELECTRIC RWY CO and BC HYDRO until 1962. At that time he went into politics, running successfully for Parliament as a Liberal. He represented his Capilano riding from 1962 to 1974 and served in Prime Minister Pierre Trudeau's cabinet as minister of fisheries and forestry and minister of the environment. While minister of fisheries, he was responsible in 1969 for implementing the Davis Plan to reduce the size of the west coast fishing fleet (*see* FISHERIES POLICY). In 1975 he ran provincially for the SOCIAL CREDIT PARTY. He won election and joined PREMIER Bill BENNETT's CABINET as minister of energy, transportation and communications. His career was blighted in 1978 when he was convicted of fraud involving the misuse of airline tickets, and he left the cabinet. Davis remained an MLA, however, rejoining the cabinet in 1986 as Premier Bill VANDER ZALM's minister of energy. He retired from politics in 1990. A talented BASKETBALL player in his youth, he is a member of the BC SPORTS HALL OF FAME.

DAVIS, Wade, ethnobotanist, writer (b 1953). Raised in BC, he attended Harvard Univ and obtained a PhD in ethnobotany. He has conducted fieldwork in S America and Haiti, much of it related to the hallucinogenic properties of plants. His books describing this work are a unique combination of botany, anthropology and personal adventure story. *The Serpent and the Rainbow* (1985), about voodoo in Haiti, was made into a motion picture. Other books include *One River: Explorations and Discoveries in the Amazon Rain Forest* (1996), which was nominated for a GOV GEN'S LITERARY AWARD, and the essay collections *Shadows in the Sun* (1992) and *The Clouded Leopard* (1998). He has hosted a television series on the ENVIRONMENT and carried out ethnographic fieldwork in northern Canada.

DAVIS RAFT was a LOG BOOM devised by G.G. Davis, a logger, at PORT RENFREW in 1911. The rafts were used to transport logs across the exposed waters off the west coast of VANCOUVER ISLAND and QUEEN CHARLOTTE SOUND, where conventional booms—used to transport logs on protected waters—could not withstand the larger swells and rougher waves of the open ocean. A Davis raft consisted of a 40-m-long mat of logs woven together with steel cables; logs were piled on in layers. The entire raft was wrapped securely with cable and a TOWBOAT hauled it to a SAWMILL. Davis rafts were used extensively during WWI to transport SPRUCE logs from the Queen Charlotte Islands to VANCOUVER and PRINCE RUPERT for use in aircraft construction. The rafts were also used to move heavy HEMLOCK logs to coastal pulp mills. A similar raft using a different cable system, known as the Gibson raft, was designed and used by Gordon GIBSON to transport logs from NOOTKA SOUND to Vancouver. *See also* LOG BARGES.

Ken Drushka

A Davis raft under tow by the tug Ivanhoe. *VMM*

DAWSON, George Mercer, geologist (b 1 Aug 1849, Pictou, NS; d 2 Mar 1901, Ottawa). Dawson was one of the leading Canadian geologists of his generation, and his field trips through BC made major contributions to our understanding of the geographic complexities of BC and to economic development in the province. As a youngster he was bedridden for several years with tuberculosis of the spine and was left with a permanent spinal deformity. Nonetheless, he was able to complete studies abroad at the Royal School of Mines in London between 1869 and 1872, and carry out many seasons of arduous field work in the far-flung reaches of the North and West. After taking part in the survey of the US–Canada border across the West, he joined the Geological Survey of Canada, came to BC and spent the period from 1875 to 1878 examining the geology of the central and southern Interior, northern VANCOUVER ISLAND and the QUEEN CHARLOTTE ISLANDS. He also gathered ethnological data, publishing studies of the KWAKWAKA'WAKW (Kwakiutl), SECWEPEMC (Shuswap) and HAIDA First Nations, photographing their villages and collecting many artifacts for Canadian museums. After leaving BC he rose through the ranks of the Geological Survey, serving as director from 1895 to 1901.

DAWSON CREEK, city, pop 11,125, lies among the rolling hills of the fertile PEACE R district, near the Alberta border 412 km northeast of PRINCE GEORGE. It is named for George

Mercer DAWSON, who explored the area for the Geological Survey of Canada in 1879 and named the creek after himself. The first farm settler took up land in 1907 and settlement became steady after WWI. In 1931 the Northern Alberta Rwy arrived; when it built its station on the outskirts of the community, many people moved to create a new townsite around the station. It was incorporated as a village on 26 May 1936 and as a city on 6 Jan 1958. It was still a sleepy hamlet of about 500 people early in 1942, when a large contingent of US troops arrived to begin construction of the ALASKA HWY, on which Dawson is Mile 0. Following WWII the HART HWY arrived from Prince George (1952) and BC RAIL extended its track (1957). Located at the hub of several transportation networks, Dawson became the distribution centre of the Peace R country. The local economy also came to rely on a variety of natural resources developed since the war, including OIL AND GAS development (it was the first town in BC to use natural gas), COAL mining at TUMBLER RIDGE, AGRICULTURE (it is considered the wheat capital of BC), and FOREST INDUSTRY activities. It is the site of the main campus of Northern Lights College (*see* COMMUNITY COLLEGES).

Grain elevators at Dawson Creek, 1977.

DAWSON'S LANDING is a small floating community on the west side of RIVERS INLET. Established in 1924 as a fisheries department station, it became the supply centre for canning, trapping and LOGGING operations in the inlet. Named for Jimmy and Jean Dawson, the original storekeepers, it remains a local commercial centre. *See also* FISHING, COMMERCIAL; FLOATHOUSES.

DE CARLO, Yvonne (b 1922, Vancouver). Born Peggy Yvonne Middleton, she was one of June Roper's dance students but made her mark in films after moving to Hollywood with her mother. She made her movie debut in 1942 and appeared in many popular westerns, comedies

Yvonne de Carlo, Hollywood star, 1954.

and adventure films. A list of her leading men reads like a Hollywood Who's Who: it includes Victor Mature, Clark Gable, David Niven and Rock Hudson. In the mid-1960s she starred on television as Lily Munster in the comedy series *The Munsters*.

DE COSMOS, Amor, journalist, politician, premier 23 Dec 1872–11 Feb 1874 (b 20 Aug 1825, Windsor, NS; d 4 July 1897, Victoria). Born William Alexander Smith, he left Nova Scotia at age 26 and went to California, where he became a photographer. In 1854 he changed his name to Amor de Cosmos, "lover of the universe." At the beginning of the Fraser R GOLD RUSH four years later, he moved to VICTORIA and founded the *British Colonist* NEWSPAPER. As editor,

Amor de Cosmos, premier of BC 1872–74.
CVA P1592

he was an outspoken critic of Gov James DOUGLAS and the colony's leadership. He then entered politics and was elected to the assembly in 1863 after two unsuccessful attempts; he sold his newspaper and devoted his full attention to public affairs. As a member of the Legislative Council in 1867–71, De Cosmos advocated responsible government and union with Canada. Following CONFEDERATION in 1871 he was elected to the new provincial legislature and also to the federal House of Commons as one of 2 MPs from Victoria. He became PREMIER at the end of 1872 but his undistinguished administration lasted only 14 months. Re-elected MP early in 1874, he resigned his BC seat and the premiership as the law then required. In Ottawa he voiced provincial grievances and once introduced a resolution calling for BC to secede from the country. De Cosmos's increasingly extreme racial bigotry eventually cost him support and in July 1882 he lost his seat in Parliament. He retired to private life and became steadily more eccentric, until in 1895 a court ruled him incompetent to manage his own affairs and his brother became his legal guardian. *See also* COLONIAL GOVERNMENT.
Reading: George Woodcock, *Amor de Cosmos: Journalist and Reformer*, 1975.

DE COURCY ISLANDS are a string of low islands tucked between VANCOUVER ISLAND and GABRIOLA and VALDES islands, south of NANAIMO. They are among the most northerly of the GULF ISLANDS. The largest of the group are Mudge, Link, Ruxton, Pylades and De Courcy islands. Michael De Courcy was commander of HMS *Pylades*, a British naval vessel on the coast from 1859 to 1861. The other islands in the group are named for his fellow officers. The infamous Brother XII (Edward Arthur WILSON) based his religious cult at the south end of De Courcy Island. Since 1966 the site has been part of Pirate's Cove MARINE PARK (38 ha). The islands are inhabited and popular with boaters, but they are not serviced by a ferry.

DE GOEDE, Hans, rugby player (b 13 Feb 1953, Amsterdam). The son of DUTCH immigrants, he joined the JAMES BAY Athletic Assoc RUGBY club while still in high school in 1971 and led it for 20 years as it became one of the best teams in N America. In 1974 he played in his first international match for Canada. In his long career he captained Canada in the first World Cup of rugby in 1987, and with All-World selections in 1976 and 1980 he was recognized as a top international player. He spent a year in Wales playing for Cardiff, one of the legendary teams in rugby history. *SW*

DE ROO, Remi, Catholic bishop (b 24 Feb 1924, Swan Lake, MB). Ordained a priest in 1950, he received a doctorate in theology from the Angelicum Univ in Rome in 1952. He arrived in BC at the end of 1962 from Manitoba as the new bishop of VANCOUVER ISLAND. The author of several books, including *Cries of Victims—Voices of God* (1986) and *A Cause de*

L'Evangile (1988), he has been an outspoken activist on issues of world peace and social justice, and his influence spread far beyond his diocese. A defender of liberation theology, he criticized the free-enterprise economy for failing to provide for the disadvantaged. He was a founding member of the World Conference of Religions for Peace and also served as chair of the BC HUMAN RIGHTS Commission. When he retired in 1999 he was the longest-serving Catholic bishop in Canada.   *Shannon Emmerson*

DEADMAN'S ISLAND is a small island in Coal Harbour in VANCOUVER, connected to STANLEY PARK by a short causeway. Originally a FIRST NATIONS burial ground, it was used for a SMALLPOX isolation hospital during the 1890s. In 1908 a LOGGING company claimed to have the right to cut timber on the island and the city had to intervene with police in the so-called "Battle of Deadman's Island." The parks board took over the island and it remained home to a group of squatters until WWII, when the defence department took possession and built HMCS *Discovery*, a naval cadet training school, which opened in 1944 and still occupies the site.

DEADWOOD, 22 km west of GRAND FORKS near GREENWOOD in the BOUNDARY DISTRICT, was the site of the Mother Lode Mine, staked in 1891 and in production from 1900 to 1918. A townsite, complete with hotels and stores, was laid out at the mine to serve the workforce of 200, a SAWMILL was built, and the CPR's COLUMBIA & WESTERN RWY ran in a branch line. Deadwood was abandoned by early 1920s.   AS

DEAN CHANNEL is one of the long (97 km), narrow passages winding through the maze of offshore islands on the Mid-Coast east of BELLA BELLA. An extension of Fisher Channel, it reaches from Cousins Inlet northeast along the top of KING ISLAND deep into the snow-capped COAST MTS. OCEAN FALLS, the former PULP mill town, is located at the head of Cousins Inlet. On the north side of the channel at Elcho Harbour is Sir Alexander Mackenzie Provincial PARK; on 21 July 1793, the explorer Alexander MACKENZIE, the first person to travel overland across N America, reached this point, the westernmost on his journey. A cairn commemorates the event. Part of the traditional territory of the NUXALK (Bella Coola) people, the channel is on the BC FERRY route to BELLA COOLA.

DEAN RIVER, 241 km, originates in the CHILCOTIN and flows north and west across the rugged wilderness of TWEEDSMUIR PROVINCIAL PARK and through the COAST MTS to empty into the head of DEAN CHANNEL, north of BELLA COOLA. It was named by Capt George VANCOUVER in 1793 after Rev James King, dean of Raphoe, Ireland, and father of a fellow naval officer. Alexander MACKENZIE crossed the river on his 1793 overland passage to the coast. The Dean is an important SALMON spawning river and is world-famous for its summer STEELHEAD and TROUT fishing. *See also* RIVERS.

DEAS, John Sullivan, salmon canner (b circa 1838, Charleston, SC; d 22 July 1880, Portland, OR). Trained as a tinsmith, he travelled west to the California gold rush, then moved north to VICTORIA in 1862. He was at YALE from 1866 to 1868, and began canning SALMON in 1871 on the FRASER R at Sapperton for Edward STAMP. In 1873 he built his own cannery on what was named DEAS ISLAND. It was the pioneer phase of SALMON CANNING and Deas was an industry leader, the only BLACK man working as a canner on the river. When his wife bought a rooming house in Portland he sold the cannery in 1878 and moved south.

DEAS ISLAND, 70 ha, is in the south arm of the FRASER R between RICHMOND and DELTA. It is named for John Sullivan DEAS, who operated a SALMON CANNERY on the island from 1873 to 1877. Today it comprises Deas Island Regional Park, with trails, picnic sites and 3 heritage buildings, and is joined to the mainland by a causeway. The George Massey Tunnel carries Hwy 99 under the Fraser R via Deas Island.

George Massey tunnel, Deas Island, under construction, 1958. Don LeBlanc/Vancouver Sun

DEASE LAKE, 62.8 km², is in the traditional territory of the KASKA people in northwest BC. It is long (40 km) and narrow, linked by the Dease and LIARD rivers to the Mackenzie R drainage. In 1838 Robert CAMPBELL of the HBC established DEASE LAKE POST on the east side. In the 1870s the area was at the heart of the short-lived but intense GOLD RUSH in the CASSIAR district; the MINING town of LAKETON flourished briefly on the lake's west shore. The modern community of Dease Lake is at the south end of the lake and the STEWART–Cassiar Hwy (Hwy 37) runs along the east side (*see also* ROADS AND HWYS).   AS

DEASE LAKE POST was an HBC trading post at Sawmill Point on the east side of DEASE LK, established by Robert CAMPBELL in 1838. The post was the base for Campbell's exploration of the upper STIKINE R that summer. After a winter marked by food shortages, the traders abandoned the post. The present community (pop 700) at the south end of the lake is near the site of the old fort. It began as a MINING centre with the GOLD RUSH to the CASSIAR district in the 1870s, and mining continued to be important to the economy.

Dease Lake is the centre of regional government and a staging area for outdoor recreation in the Stikine R watershed.

DEBECK family, originally from France, migrated to the US and then to New Brunswick as United Empire Loyalists. In 1867 George DeBeck, along with 4 sons, 3 daughters and their husbands, moved to BC and homesteaded on LULU and SEABIRD islands at the mouth of the FRASER R. When farm income proved inadequate, George and his sons Ward, Warren and Clarence all went HANDLOGGING in BURRARD INLET for the MOODYVILLE SAWMILL CO. From there the family spread out through the pioneer coastal FOREST INDUSTRY. In 1877 the 3 sons started the Brunette Sawmill in NEW WESTMINSTER. Ward's son E.K. "Ned" DeBeck was a well-known coastal timber cruiser (*see* FORESTRY) early in the 20th century and later was appointed clerk of the BC legislature. The family name was still well known in the coastal forest industry in the late 1990s.

Ken Drushka

DECKER LAKE, 8 km northwest of BURNS LAKE on the Yellowhead Hwy (Hwy 16), was the site of a 1913 post office established to serve the GRAND TRUNK PACIFIC RWY gangs. Sivert "Bull River Slim" Anderson and 3 partners set up a substantial operation here cutting ties for the CNR and other railways in the mid-1920s. The lake was named after the foreman of the COLLINS OVERLAND TELEGRAPH party, which passed through here in 1866.   AS

DEELEY, Frederick Trevor, motorcycle racer/dealer (b 15 Mar 1920, Vancouver). His grandfather, Fred Sr, was an English bicycle dealer who came to VANCOUVER in 1914 and with his son Fred Jr established a successful bicycle, motorcycle and eventually car dealership. Trevor quit school at 15 to go to work in the family business. He raced competitively in Alberta and the Pacific Northwest and by the early 1950s was pretty much in charge of the motorcycle division of Fred Deeley Ltd. In 1958 he became the first distributor of Honda motorcycles in the English-speaking world and later was the pioneer Yamaha distributor in Canada. His own company, Fred Deeley Imports Ltd, dealt in Harley-Davidsons. In 1993 he opened the Trev Deeley Motorcycle Museum in Richmond, the largest museum of its kind in Canada. In 2000 he was inducted into the BC SPORTS HALL OF FAME. *Reading:* Frank Hilliard, *Deeley: Motorcycle Millionaire*, 1994.

DEEP BAY is on the east side of VANCOUVER ISLAND, 70 km north of NANAIMO opposite DENMAN ISLAND. Aboriginal people have fished here for 5,000 years. The Canadian Robert DOLLAR Co ran a LOGGING operation from a camp on the bay during 1917–31 and there was a fish processing plant from 1917 to 1951. Today it is a small resort community.

DEEP COVE is a bay on the southwest shore of INDIAN ARM, named by British naval surveyors in

1859–60. Formally the community consists of the Neighbourhood Community of Deep Cove, pop 1,995, and the Community of Cove Cliff, pop 1,349, to the south. The area was primarily a summer recreation spot with annual regattas, a dance hall and roller skating rink until after WWII; then many full-time residents moved here and several small businesses opened. Today it is a suburban village with beach, marinas, public wharf and Panorama Park.

Doreen Armitage

DEEP CREEK is a small AGRICULTURAL community 11 km south of SALMON ARM, just west of Gardom Lk. A variety of crops are grown in the rich valley soil and DAIRY FARMING is also important here. A school was established here in 1894 but later closed. There is a park at Gardom Lk and the Deep Creek Tool Museum has an array of pioneer implements and farm equipment.   AS

DEER belong to the same family (Cervidae) of hoofed mammals as ELK, MOOSE and CARIBOU. Pale brown to red-brown in summer, deer become grey-brown during the winter. They are graceful, long-legged creatures that browse on a variety of trees, shrubs and vegetation. Only the males grow antlers, which are shed annually. Two species occur in BC. White-tailed deer (*Odocoileus virginianus*) are found in the southeastern Interior, while mule deer (*O. hemionus*)

Mule deer. R. Wayne Campbell photo

are more widespread, occurring to the east of the COAST MTS as far north as the valley of the LIARD R. A subspecies of mule deer, the black-tailed deer (*O. h. columbianus*), inhabits the coastal rain forest. Another subspecies, the Sitka black-tailed deer (*O. h. sitkensis*), was introduced to the QUEEN CHARLOTTE ISLANDS early in the 20th century. White-tailed and mule deer can be distinguished by their movement: mule deer bound through the woods as if on springs, while their white-tailed relatives swing their hind legs ahead of their front ones. Their principal predators, aside from humans, are domestic dogs, COUGARS and WOLVES, likely in that order.

DEER PARK, on the southeast shore of ARROW LK, was one of the communities flooded out in 1969 by the construction of the KEENLEYSIDE DAM near CASTLEGAR. The settlement dated from

1896; after a brief railway-building boom it settled into a quiet existence as a lakeside hamlet accessible only by steamboat. A group of MENNONITES chose to settle there in 1912. The arrival of a road in 1954 brought few changes, and since the flooding the site has been used by locals as a park.

DEERHOLME, 45 km northwest of VICTORIA on VANCOUVER ISLAND, is a rural AGRICULTURAL district, settled in the early 1900s, that grew up around the early store and post office of Justus E. Williams. When the CNR's Cowichan branch line reached this area in the early 1920s, LOGGING became important. Another branch line, later abandoned, was built from Deerholme to COWICHAN BAY in 1924 so that wood products could be shipped more easily.   AS

DEIGHTON, John "Gassy Jack," mariner, saloon keeper (b Nov 1830, Hull, England; d 29 May 1875, Vancouver). At age 14 he went to sea and became an officer on an American clipper ship. After joining the tail end of the gold rush in California, he moved north to BC in 1858 to join the Fraser R GOLD RUSH. Eventually he tired of prospecting; he became a customs agent, then a steamboat pilot on the FRASER from 1859 to 1864. Deighton retired from the river in 1865 and purchased a saloon in NEW WESTMINSTER. The business failed in 1867 and he moved to the south shore of BURRARD INLET and built the Globe Saloon next door to Edward STAMP's new sawmill. As a talkative saloon keeper he earned the nickname Gassy Jack, and the ramshackle community that grew up around him became known as GASTOWN, the core of what became VANCOUVER. He built the Deighton House hotel

Gassy Jack Deighton, Vancouver pioneer and saloonkeeper, c 1870. BC Archives D-07873

in 1870 and ran it with his young wife, a SQUAMISH woman, until his death. The hotel burned in the 1886 fire.

DELASALLE, Philip Lawrence Emmanuel, gymnast (b 18 July 1958, Victoria). One of Canada's greatest male gymnasts, he went to his first Canada Winter Games at age 13 and became the provincial and national junior champion and Canada's outstanding junior athlete in 1973. As Canadian senior champion he went to the 1976 Montreal Olympics where he finished 22nd, the highest standing a Canadian had received to that date. In 1977 Delasalle was the first Canadian invited to the World Cup where he finished 8th overall and the next year he was all-round champion at the Commonwealth Games. His 12th-place finish at the 1979 World Gymnastic Championships was also a high for Canadian men. He retired in 1980 after winning his 5th straight Canadian championship. In his best event, the pommel horse, he scored three perfect 10s over his career and introduced a move that is officially referred to as "the Delasalle" all over the world. The Canadian national senior all-round championship is awarded in his name. In 1994 Delasalle was named to the BC SPORTS HALL OF FAME.   SW

DELGAMUUKW CASE is a landmark legal case involving the GITKSAN and WET'SUWET'EN people whose hereditary chiefs sued the provincial and federal governments in 1984 for ownership of and jurisdiction over 58,000 km[2] of their traditional territory in northwest BC. The name of the case is derived from the traditional name of one of the chiefs who initiated the claim. The trial before the BC Supreme Court began on 11 May 1987 and lasted until 30 June 1990. On 8 Mar 1991, Chief Justice Allan McEachern dismissed the claim in a controversial decision. The BC Court of Appeal in 1993 also dismissed the claim for jurisdiction, but acknowledged that the Gitksan-Wet'suwet'en have "unextinguished non-exclusive ABORIGINAL RIGHTS, other than a right to ownership," and said that these should be negotiated with government. The case went forward to the Supreme Court of Canada, which in Dec 1997 acknowledged aboriginal title and ordered a new trial. The court ruled that oral history, which played a crucial role in the plaintiffs' case, should be accepted by the court, a decision that contradicted Justice McEachern's flat rejection of such testimony in the original case. The Supreme Court also encouraged the 2 sides to seek a negotiated settlement outside the courts. The decision affected ongoing BC land claims cases and caused insecurities on the part of businesses operating on land claimed by FIRST NATIONS.

DELLA FALLS, 440 m, the highest WATERFALL in Canada and the tenth highest in the world, tumbles in 3 cascades into the valley of Drinkwater Crk in STRATHCONA PROVINCIAL PARK on central VANCOUVER ISLAND. The base of the falls can be reached by a hiking trail 16 km from the head of

GREAT CENTRAL LK north of PORT ALBERNI. The falls are named for the wife of Joe Drinkwater, a trapper who came upon them in 1899.

DELTA lies south of VANCOUVER across the south arm of the FRASER R from RICHMOND. It is bounded on the south by the US border and on the east by SURREY. The best-known pioneers  are the brothers William and Thomas LADNER, who arrived in 1868 and began farming on the site of the riverside community named for them. LADNER is the business and administrative centre of the district. Delta's two other population centres are TSAWWASSEN, in the southwest corner of the municipality, and North Delta, which has strong ties to Surrey. Both are primarily residential. Farming, especially DAIRY FARMING, has remained an important part of the local economy, despite the rapid population growth of the last few decades that has made Delta a major residential suburb of Vancouver. The George Massey Tunnel, opened in 1958, contributed to this expansion by making the district more accessible to automobile traffic. BC FERRY CORP has one of its largest terminals at Tsawwassen and the AIRPORT at BOUNDARY BAY serves private and charter planes. Industrial development is centred on ANNACIS and Tilbury islands, and at the ROBERTS BANK superport, which expanded during the 1990s to ship wheat as well as COAL. Natural attractions include BURNS BOG, which occupies a quarter of the district, and the REIFEL BIRD SANCTUARY on WESTHAM ISLAND.

Population: 95,930
Rank in BC: 8th
Population increase since 1981: 28%
Date of incorporation: district 10 Nov 1879
Land area: 180.46 km²
Location: Greater Vancouver Regional District
Economic base: agriculture, fishing, manufacturing, warehousing, boatbuilding, railways, port

DEMERS, Modeste, Catholic bishop (b 11 Oct 1809, St Nicolas, QC; d 21 July 1871, Victoria). He received his ordination as a priest in 1836 and 2 years later came west to BC, where he and Norbert Blanchet were the first Catholic missionaries in the Pacific Northwest

(*see* ROMAN CATHOLIC CHURCH). Demers passed the Big Bend of the COLUMBIA R in Nov 1838 and became the first priest to celebrate Mass on the BC mainland. He made excursions to the FRASER R in 1841–42 and up the FUR BRIGADE TRAIL through the OKANAGAN VALLEY in 1842. He then moved west to VICTORIA in 1847 and became the first bishop of VANCOUVER ISLAND. Among his many projects he imported a printing press and in Sept 1858 established the colony's second newspaper, *Le Courrier de la Nouvelle Calédonie*. Also in 1858 he recruited the SISTERS OF ST ANN to come to Victoria and open their first school. He was one of the mainstays of the colony until his death.

DEMOGRAPHY; *see* ABORIGINAL DEMOGRAPHY; PEOPLES OF BC.

DENE-THAH, formerly known as Slavey, are an ATHABASCAN-speaking FIRST NATIONS people living in the extreme northeast corner of the province in the vicinity of FORT NELSON. At contact with Europeans their population was about 1,250. Until the late 20th century their society was based on small extended-family hunting groups that dispersed in winter to harvest MOOSE, CARIBOU and small game and congregated during the year for FISHING, hunting and socializing. With the arrival of the FUR TRADE, commercial trapping became important. They adhered to TREATY NO 8 in 1910. During WWII the ALASKA HWY was built through their territory and contacts with the outside world increased. Many Dene-thah participate in the wage economy; others continue to fish, hunt and trap.

DENISON, Francis Napier, meteorologist (b 19 Apr 1866, Toronto; d 24 June 1946, Victoria). He worked as a weather observer and electrical engineer in Toronto before being transferred to VICTORIA in 1898. He was widely respected for his research on weather cycles and studies of seismic disturbances. He helped to design Victoria's Gonzales Observatory and served as its director from 1914 to 1936. His daily weather forecasts and frequent musings in local newspapers endeared him to Victoria residents, who referred to him as "our weatherman." After retiring in 1936, Denison produced several inventions, including a seismograph and a cleaning device for use in hospitals.

Dianne Mackay

DENMAN ISLAND, 50 km², is one of the 2 most northerly of the GULF ISLANDS in GEORGIA STRAIT between VANCOUVER ISLAND and the mainland. Rear Admiral Joseph Denman was commander of the Pacific Station at ESQUIMALT from 1864 to 1867. Long used by FIRST NATIONS for hunting and clam digging, the island welcomed its first settlers in 1874. Many of the early residents came from the Orkney Islands. From 1878 to 1892 the post office was named Quadra. Aside from a quarry and some small-scale LOGGING, mixed farming has been the main occupation of the permanent population, which in 1999 numbered about 800. Ferry service to

Vancouver Island began in 1930, but the population did not show a rapid increase until 1980.

DENNISON was a station on the BC ELECTRIC RWY 11 km northwest of ABBOTSFORD in the FRASER VALLEY. It was named after J. Dennison, the first storekeeper at the tiny settlement that grew up there. A post office operated from 1912 to 1923.   AS

DENTISTRY in BC is organized and governed by the College of Dental Surgeons of BC through the BC Dentistry Act. The college registers accredited dentists and certified dental assistants and enforces standards of education, practice and conduct. Once dentists are registered, they become members of the Assoc of Dental Surgeons; certified dental assistants have their own association. As well, dental hygienists have their own college. In 1999 there were 2,750 dentists in BC and about 4,500 dental assistants.

The first step toward organizing the dental profession in BC was taken by Dr Thomas A. Jones, who opened a dental practice in VICTORIA in 1884. Formerly the president of the Ontario Dental Assoc, Dr Jones proposed what became BC's first *Dental Act*, passed by the provincial government in 1885. At the same time he organized the BC Dental Society and as its founding president organized the first dental convention held in the province. In 1907 a new Dentistry Act authorized the formation of the College of Dental Surgeons. Prior to 1962 there was no dental school in BC. Practitioners had to graduate from an out-of-province facility, then pass the BC Board before establishing a practice. In 1962 the faculty of dentistry was established at UBC under Dean S.W. Leung. It was the third dental faculty west of Ontario. It graduates dentists, dental specialists and dental hygienists.   *William Hastings*

DERBY, named for the 14th Earl of Derby, Edward Stanley, prime minister of England, was the original site of FORT LANGLEY, on the south bank of the FRASER R. Construction began in 1827 and the post remained here until it was moved to a more convenient location 5 km away in 1839. In 1858 Gov James DOUGLAS designated Derby as the capital of the new colony of British Columbia. The ROYAL ENGINEERS began building log barracks and land parcels were sold at public auction. Early in 1859 Richard MOODY, commander of the engineers, decided that Derby was too vulnerable to American attack and moved the capital to a new site that became NEW WESTMINSTER. The Derby townsite was gradually abandoned, but it was later bought by the GVRD, who in the 1990s planned to construct a fort-to-fort trail that will link this historic place to the present site of Fort Langley.

DEROCHE is a hamlet on the north side of the FRASER R 19 km east of MISSION. It is named for Joseph Deroche (1824–1922), a teamster who hauled supplies to the Cariboo GOLD RUSH before settling here on a farm. Nearby Nicomen Slough is a wintering area for EAGLES, trumpeter SWANS and other waterfowl.

DESOLATION SOUND is a network of inlets and passages on the coast 30 km north of POW-ELL RIVER. Capt George VANCOUVER visited the area in July 1792 and named it for what he believed was its dreary aspect and lack of food resources. Modern boaters and SEA KAYAKERS disagree; they flock to the sound each summer to enjoy its protected waters and spectacular scenery. The area is accessible by boat and by car to Okeover Arm. Desolation Sound Provincial Marine Park, BC's largest MARINE PARK, comprises 82.56 km² of islands and mainland.

DEVERELL, William H., lawyer, writer (b 4 Mar 1937, Regina). He worked as a journalist in Montreal, VANCOUVER and Saskatoon, where he was an editor at the *Star Phoenix* newspaper while attending law school at the Univ of Saskatchewan. As a member of the BC, Alberta and Yukon bars he was involved in more than 1,000 criminal cases as defence counsel or prosecutor. He is a founding director, former president and honorary director of the BC Civil Liberties Assoc. While on sabbatical from his law practice, he wrote his first novel, *Needles*, which won the $50,000 Seal prize in 1979. He has since published several more crime novels and has become one of the bestselling writers in Canada. His 1997 book, *Trial of Passion*, won the Hammett Prize for best crime novel in N America. Deverell also writes radio plays and screenplays and created the long-running television series *Street Legal*. He served as president of The Writers' Union of Canada from 1994 to 1995 and again on an interim basis in 1999.

Desolation Sound, a favourite cruising area for coastal boaters. *Ian Douglas photo*

William Deverell, mystery writer, 1998.
Barry Peterson & Blaise Enright-Peterson

DEVINE, pop 35, a BC RAIL flag station 105 km northeast of SQUAMISH on the Gates R, was once the site of the Blackwater Timber Co SAWMILL. It was named after A. Devine, the first postmaster.
AS

DEWDNEY, a small community on Nicomen Slough east of MISSION in the FRASER VALLEY, was an early riverboat stop originally known as Johnson's Landing after N.C. Johnson, a local farmer. By the mid-1880s a school, several stores and the CPR line served the area's farmers and their families. The Dewdney Trunk Rd, first thoroughfare on the north side of the FRASER R, was completed through here in 1900. The route was surveyed by Edgar DEWDNEY, a well-known politician and LT GOV of BC from 1892 to 1897.   AS

DEWDNEY, Edgar, engineer, politician, lt gov 1892–97 (b 5 Nov 1835, Bideford, England; d 8 Aug 1916, Victoria). Trained as an engineer, he emigrated to BC in 1859 and got a job surveying the townsite for NEW WESTMINSTER. The following year he won a contract to build a road from HOPE eastward to WILD HORSE CREEK, the so-called DEWDNEY TRAIL. His first foray into politics was in 1868, when he was elected to the legislative council. Following the union with Canada he was elected to the House of Commons, where he remained a member until 1879. A strong supporter of John A. Macdonald, Dewdney lobbied strenuously for the completion of the transcontinental railway (*see* CPR). In 1878 he was named commissioner of Indian Affairs and in 1881 he became lt gov of the North-West Territories (as Alberta and Saskatchewan were then known). One of the most powerful officials in the West, he imposed measures to pacify the aboriginal people and force them onto reserves. In 1888 he returned to the House of Commons and became minister of the interior and superintendent general of Indian Affairs, a position he held until he was named LT GOV of BC on 2 Nov 1892. After an uneventful term of office he returned to private life and tended to his business interests until his death. *See also* ABORIGINAL RIGHTS.

Edgar Dewdney, lt gov of BC 1892–97, shown here in a painting by Victor Albert Long, 1915.
BC Archives PDP-02243

DEWDNEY TRAIL, 576 km long, was built from 1860 to 1865 across southern BC to provide access to GOLD mining areas. It was named for Edgar DEWDNEY, the engineer in charge of the project. The original portion of the trail, completed in 1861, ran from HOPE to PRINCETON and the SIMILKAMEEN R. In 1861 it was extended as far as ROCK CRK; in 1865 it reached WILD HORSE CRK, a tributary of the KOOTENAY R, near the present FORT STEELE. By this time the goldfields were played out, however, and the eastern portion of the trail was not much used. Parts of the trails were eventually restored for use by hikers. *See also* GOLD RUSHES; TRAILS.

DI CASTRI, John A., architect (b 26 July 1924, Victoria). He articled with the provincial department of public works in 1942 and worked briefly in the office of Birley Wade and Stockdill (*see* BIRLEY, S. Patrick). In 1949 Di Castri left VICTORIA to attend the Univ of Oklahoma, where he studied under Bruce Goff. Back in Victoria, he started his own practice in 1952 and played a seminal role in establishing modern ARCHITECTURE in the city. His Canadian Trend House design still stands as built. He chaired the Community Planning Assoc of Canada from 1958 to 1968 and the Canadian Housing Design Council from 1976 to 1980. Major examples of his work in Victoria include the Institute for the Blind, the Students' Union and Cornett buildings and the Chapel at UNIV OF VICTORIA, the entrance foyer addition to the ROYAL BC MUSEUM and several churches. One of his largest projects was the planning and building designs for NOTRE DAME UNIV OF NELSON. *Martin Segger*

DIAMOND, Charlotte, musician (b 31 July 1945, Vancouver). She is one of the most popular children's performers in Canada. After graduating from UBC and Laval Univ, she taught junior high for 12 years before turning to music full-time. Her first album was *10 Carrot Diamond*, produced independently with money she withdrew from her pension fund; it went gold and won a Juno Award. After that initial success she went on to make 9 more albums and 2 videos and to establish herself as a leading family enter-

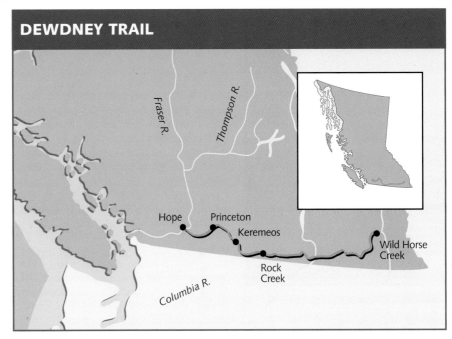

DEWDNEY TRAIL

Charlotte Diamond, children's performer, at Burnaby Heritage Village, 1996.
Bill Keay/Vancouver Sun

tainer with concerts across N America. She performs in French and Spanish as well as in English and is an active spokesperson for UNICEF.

DIAMOND, Jack, entrepreneur (b 9 Apr 1909, Lubience, Poland). He immigrated to Canada in 1926 to join his brother Dave in VANCOUVER. From his first job peddling potatoes door-to-door he moved quickly into the meat business. He and Dave bought a butcher shop in 1928 and expanded it into a chain of stores, along with a wholesale operation. Jack also purchased Pacific Meat Co; during his ownership (1939–64) it became the largest independent meat packer in western Canada. During WWII he served in Ottawa as a "dollar-a-year" man advising the government on meat supply. After selling Pacific Meat he was involved in property development and founded West Coast Reduction, a rendering business later run by his son Gordon.

Diamond's great love was horseracing, from the 1930s, when he bought his first thoroughbred, to 1993, when he gave up his involvement in managing HASTINGS PARK. He was a leader in the city's Jewish community and he contributed to countless charitable causes as a fundraiser and through his own charitable foundation, one of the largest in Vancouver. He raised more than half the money necessary to stage the 1954 BRITISH EMPIRE AND COMMONWEALTH GAMES in Vancouver and also helped to speed construction of Empire Stadium in time for the games. He was a member of the SFU board of governors from 1967 to 1978 and chancellor from 1975 to 1978. He is a member of Canada's Horse Racing Hall of Fame (1977), a Freeman of the City of Vancouver (1979), an Officer of the Order of Canada (1980) and a member of the ORDER OF BC (1991).

DIAMOND HEAD is a peak in southern GARIBALDI PROVINCIAL PARK near Mt Garibaldi. In 1946 Emil and Ottar Brandvold, two brothers,

joined Joan Matthews (later Mrs Ottar Brandvold) to open a ski lodge below the peak beside the Elfin Lakes, the first private SKIING lodge in BC. It was a popular destination with hikers and skiers from around the world until it closed in 1972. The building was still standing in 1999.

DICKIE, Francis, writer (b 1890, Carberry, MB; d 1976). He left school at age 16 and worked on railway survey parties across the West, at the same time writing stories for the popular press. In 1911 he began a career as a journalist with the *Calgary Herald*. At the end of WWI he was living in VANCOUVER and working as a freelance writer. In 1923 he and his Parisian wife Suzanne purchased a home at HERIOT BAY on QUADRA ISLAND, where they settled more or less permanently. Dickie was a noted eccentric, who liked to garden in the nude and boast about his friendship with Somerset Maugham. He owned one of the largest libraries on the coast and published dozens of magazine stories along with several novels.

DILWORTH, Ira, broadcaster (b 25 Mar 1894, High Bluff, MB; d 23 Nov 1962, Vancouver). He grew up in the OKANAGAN VALLEY and VICTORIA, where he was a schoolteacher from 1915 to 1926 and a high school principal from 1926 to 1934. While in Victoria he befriended the artist Emily CARR, whose career as a writer he later promoted and for whom he acted as literary trustee. He moved to VANCOUVER to teach English at UBC from 1934 to 1938, then joined CBC Radio, where he directed BC operations from 1938 to 1946. In 1956 he became director of the English-language network. Dilworth founded the CBC VANCOUVER ORCHESTRA in 1938; in 1999 it was the only regularly performing radio orchestra in N America.

DINOSAURS lived in abundance in BC during the Mesozoic Era 250 million to 65 million years ago. Only a few bones have been found, but

Dinosaur footprint in Peace R canyon.
Courtesy BC Hydro Information Services

many fossilized footprints and trackways have turned up. The first dinosaur tracks discovered in Canada were found in 1922 near HUDSON'S HOPE. Subsequently the PEACE R area proved very productive of tracks until they were destroyed by flooding associated with HYDROELECTRIC dam construction in the 1960s and 1970s. Other tracks were discovered along the Narraway R in eastern BC (now destroyed) and in the southeast corner of the province. As well, the tooth of a terrestrial dinosaur, a meat-eating theropod, was found in 1992 in the Trent R south of COURTENAY on VANCOUVER ISLAND. *See also* FOSSILS.

DIPPER, American (*Cinclus mexicanus*), is a small unmarked grey bird that is typically found along clear rushing streams from sea level to the timberline throughout most of the province. It breeds in southern BC, and is the only N American songbird that flies underwater and walks on stream bottoms in search of aquatic INSECT larvae, FISH eggs and other food. The loud, bubbling song of the dipper can be heard year-round.   *Kim Goldberg*

DISABILITIES; *see* COALITION FOR PEOPLE WITH DISABILITIES.

DISASTERS include both catastrophic accidents and natural disasters that claim a large number of lives or are otherwise significant. BC is particularly prone to certain types of natural disasters because of the nature of its CLIMATE and terrain (*see* PHYSICAL GEOGRAPHY). Coastal areas experience heavy rainfall and severe Pacific storms that imperil shipping. The Interior is characterized by steep mountain slopes, high snowfall and unstable rock formations, all of which contribute to LANDSLIDES and AVALANCHES. Seismic activity regularly occurs in the coastal MOUNTAINS, and shifting tectonic plates both on- and offshore pose the threat of a massive EARTHQUAKE, perhaps the greatest natural disaster of all. Disaster response activities are coordinated by the provincial gov-

ernment's Provincial Emergency Program (*see also* SEARCH AND RESCUE).

The list that follows is only a sampling of some of the worst disasters that have occurred in BC.

Avalanches

4 March 1910, a snow avalanche in ROGERS PASS kills 62 men working to clear the CPR main line of an earlier blockage. It was the highest number of lives lost in a single railway accident in BC history and led to the construction of the CONNAUGHT TUNNEL.

9 Jan 1965, avalanche of rock buries a 3-km stretch of the HOPE–PRINCETON HWY, killing 4 motorists (*see* HOPE SLIDE).

Mining

3 May 1887, an explosion and fire at a NANAIMO coal mine kills 148 men, the worst mining disaster in BC history (*see* COAL MINING, VANCOUVER ISLAND).

1888, another explosion at a WELLINGTON coal mine kills 77 miners (*see* COAL MINING, VANCOUVER ISLAND).

22 May 1902, an explosion at Coal Creek mine near FERNIE kills 130 miners; BC's worst 20th-century mine disaster (*see* COAL MINING).

1930, an explosion in a coal mine at BLAKEBURN claims 45 lives (*see* COAL MINING).

Transportation

26 May 1896, a street railway plunges through the POINT ELLICE BRIDGE in VICTORIA, killing 55 people. It was the worst transit disaster in Canadian history to 2000.

Jan 1906, the steamer *VALENCIA* breaks up on the rocks on the west coast of VANCOUVER ISLAND near PACHENA POINT, claiming the lives of 126 passengers and crew.

1913–14, railway construction through the Fraser Canyon (*see* FRASER R) causes the HELLS GATE BLOCKADE.

25 Oct 1918, the CPR coastal steamer *PRINCESS SOPHIA* breaks up on a reef in Lynn Canal; all 343 people aboard are lost.

9 Dec 1956, a Trans-Canada Airlines plane smashes into Mt SLESSE near CHILLIWACK, killing all 62 people on board in BC's worst AVIATION disaster. The wreckage was not discovered until the following May.

8 July 1965, a Canadian Pacific Airlines flight explodes in mid-air near 100 MILE HOUSE on its way to PRINCE GEORGE from VANCOUVER, killing all 52 people on board. The cause of the explosion was never determined, though it was believed to be a bomb.

11 Feb 1978, a PACIFIC WESTERN AIRLINES flight crashes on landing at CRANBROOK, killing 43 people.

Construction

17 June 1958, the new Second Narrows Bridge (*see* IRONWORKERS MEMORIAL SECOND NARROWS CROSSING) in Vancouver collapses while under construction, killing 18 workers.

Earthquakes

27–28 March 1964, the largest recorded TSUNAMI on the BC coast, created by an earthquake in Alaska, surges up ALBERNI INLET and smashes into PORT ALBERNI, causing $10 million in property damage.

Epidemics

See INFLUENZA; SMALLPOX.

Fires

13 June 1886, clearing fires burn out of control and in less than an hour claim at least 8 lives and destroy almost every building in the young VANCOUVER townsite.

July–Aug 1938, the GREAT SAYWARD FIRE destroys 300 km² of FOREST between CAMPBELL RIVER and COURTENAY on VANCOUVER ISLAND.

6 Mar 1945, fire touches off an explosion on

Flooding at Chilliwack, 1894. UBC BC411/1

Debris from the 1965 mid-air explosion of a CP Air plane en route from Vancouver to Prince George. *Vancouver Province*

board the freighter GREEN HILL PARK, killing 8 people, in Vancouver's worst waterfront disaster.

Floods

May–June, 1894, the FRASER R floods, drowning the entire valley west of Chilliwack and washing away homes and businesses, causing millions of dollars' worth of damage and leading the government to begin diking the river.

May 1948, the Fraser R overflows its banks, resulting in $15 million worth of property damage in the valley.

DISCOVERY, or Pine City, was a GOLD mining camp on Pine Crk just east of ATLIN. It was founded in 1898 when prospectors flooded into the Atlin district. In 1899 there were as many as 3,000 miners on the creek and the town was booming. By 1915 the gold was gone and the town was virtually abandoned.

DISCOVERY was Capt George VANCOUVER's ship during his epic survey of the BC coastline from 1792 to 1794. Launched in England in 1789, it was 29 m long, weighed only 303 tonnes and carried a crew of 86, plus 14 marines. It sailed to the West Coast in company with the smaller *Chatham*. After it returned to England in 1795 *Discovery* was armed with heavy guns and took part in the attack on Copenhagen under Admiral Nelson in 1801. Later it was a convict hulk in the Thames R until its demolition in 1834.

DISCOVERY ISLAND lies at the junction of HARO and JUAN DE FUCA straits east of VICTORIA. Capt E.G. Beaumont lived on the island from WWI until his death in 1967, sharing his property with a variety of youth organizations. He left 60 ha to the province and it was designated a MARINE PARK in 1972. The northern part of the island, which is named for George VANCOUVER's ship, is a FIRST NATIONS reserve. During the SMALLPOX outbreak in 1862 the LEKWAMMEN (Songhees) people were quarantined on the island. A LIGHTHOUSE has been in operation since 1886.

DISCOVERY PASSAGE is a narrow tidal surge channel (*see* TIDES) running between VANCOUVER ISLAND and QUADRA ISLAND north from CAMPBELL RIVER. At its top end around ROCK BAY it merges into JOHNSTONE STRAIT. The area attracts thousands of seabirds, SEA LIONS and SEALS, especially during winter HERRING season, and is known internationally for its SALMON fishing. RIPPLE ROCK, a treacherous obstacle to navigation in SEYMOUR NARROWS at the south end of the passage, was destroyed by explosives in 1958. The passage is named for Capt George VANCOUVER's vessel.

DIVE FISHERIES, COMMERCIAL, in BC employ more than 250 divers annually and had a commercially landed value estimated at $45–50 million in 1999. Limited commercially to invertebrates, divers harvest GEODUCK clams, horse CLAMS, red and green SEA URCHINS, SEA CUCUMBERS, pink and spiny SCALLOPS and OCTOPUS. Commercial use of diving gear to spear fish was prohibited in 1978. Divers are also employed in the AQUACULTURE industry, inspecting and maintaining pens and sites. Some divers use scuba gear, which allows for mobility in special situations. Many vessels are now equipped with "surface supplied air" systems, using compressors and tanks on the vessel and long umbilical hoses to tether divers and supply them with air and communications.

Commercial harvesting by divers dates back to the early 1900s, when ABALONE were harvested by the JAPANESE in the QUEEN CHARLOTTE ISLANDS by "diving" and "long poles" (their techniques were not described in detail). The first commercial dive fishery by scuba divers was for abalone in the 1950s; by the 1970s as many as 78 divers from 25 vessels were harvesting up to 433 tonnes annually. Abalone fisheries (aboriginal, commercial and recreational) closed in 1990 due to conservation concerns. Initially hardhat divers from Japan harvested red sea urchins in TOFINO during 1970–1972. A small fishery by scuba divers followed in GEORGIA STRAIT during 1973–74. In 1978 the fishery began again, using scuba gear and surface-supplied air; in 1992 it peaked at 12,983 tonnes landed on a year-round basis by 110 vessels and 291 divers. Fishing for green sea urchins is a winter activity that began in 1987 and generally employs scuba divers. This fishery too peaked in 1992 with landings of 1,042 tonnes from 49 vessels and as many as 191 divers. Diving for geoduck clams and to a minor extent horse clams began in BC waters in Georgia Strait in 1978. Divers with surface-supplied air harvest geoducks by grasping the exposed siphon and using a jet of high pressure water from a nozzle or "stinger" to loosen the sand or mud surrounding the clam body. The harvest of geoducks peaked coastwide in 1987 at 5,789 tonnes, landed by 56 vessels and 186 divers. The commercial harvest of California sea cucumber by divers has been licensed since 1980. Quantities peaked in 1988 at 1,422 tonnes, landed by 79 vessels and 150 divers. Octopus have been harvested commercially for HALIBUT bait and food markets. A high market demand for bait led to peak landings of 209 tonnes in 1990. Pink and spiny scallops are harvested by scuba divers, primarily in the protected waters of Georgia Strait. Landings peaked in 1994 at 101 tonnes, gathered by 17 vessels and 37 divers.

Rick Harbo

DIVING, an outgrowth of aerial acrobatics and tumbling rather than swimming, was not an accessible sport in BC until springless wooden planks were replaced and more towers were built, particularly in VANCOUVER, in the 1930s. Art Stott of VICTORIA, a springboard diver who was afraid of heights, won BC's first diving medal in international competition with a bronze in the 1930 British Empire Games. Lynda Adams (Hunt), a pupil of Percy NORMAN, became BC's first diving star when she won 2 Empire Games silvers in 1938 and a bronze in 1950. George ATHANS, long considered to be Canada's all-time best male diver, emerged as Canadian men's champion in 1936 and won a gold in springboard and a silver in tower diving at the 1950 Empire Games. Athans' coaching skills lured Irene MacDonald, an Ontario diver, to BC to train in KELOWNA during her summers.

The *Discovery*, grounded in Queen Charlotte Sound, 1792, in a drawing by Zachary Mudge. *VMM*

She won the bronze medal at the 1956 Melbourne Olympics and bronze and silver, respectively, at the 1954 and 1958 British Empire Games. Bill Patrick joined her in 1954, winning gold at tower in front of his hometown Vancouver crowd and in 1958 capturing a silver in the 3 m.

Tom Dinsley was national diving champion from 1962 to 1965 and won a silver in the 3-m event at the 1962 BRITISH EMPIRE AND COMMONWEALTH GAMES and a gold in the 3 m at the 1963 Pan American Games. MacDonald settled in BC at the end of her career and coached Dinsley. Her other protégés included Carol-Ann Morrow, a 1964 Olympic finalist, and Kathy MacDonald, Ken Sully and Teri York, all international medal winners. Vancouver natives and Commonwealth Games medal winners Kathy Keleman (tower bronze in 1982) and John Nash (tower bronze and 3 m silver in 1986) were BC's most successful divers in the 1980s. In the 1990s the Vancouver Aquatic Centre produced Paige Gordon, who competed in the 1992 and 1996 Olympics and won 2 silver medals at the 1994 Commonwealth Games in Victoria, and Blythe Hartley, who earned a 1 m silver at the 1998 Commonwealth Games and a 10 m silver and 3 m bronze at the 1999 Pan Am Games. *SW*

DIXON, George, fur trader (active 1776–91). He was an armourer on board the *Discovery* during James COOK's 1778 visit to the Northwest Coast of America. That voyage initiated the maritime FUR TRADE for SEA OTTER pelts and in 1785 Dixon and partners formed the KING GEORGE'S SOUND CO. He commanded the *Queen Charlotte*, one of 2 vessels that sailed on the company's first expedition and operated during 1786 mainly in Alaskan waters with limited success. In 1787, during his second summer on the BC coast, he encountered and named the QUEEN CHARLOTTE ISLANDS and traded with the HAIDA as he cruised along the coast. He proceeded to NOOTKA SOUND and then on to China, where he sold his furs; he then returned to England.

DIXON ENTRANCE is the broad (65 km wide) passage north of the QUEEN CHARLOTTE ISLANDS leading from the open Pacific into HECATE STRAIT and the INSIDE PASSAGE. It was named for Capt George DIXON, one of James COOK's crew and the first European to trade with the HAIDA during a visit to the Charlottes in 1787.

DIZKLE (or Dzilke) was a large prehistoric village of CEDAR plank houses (*see* ARCHITECTURE, ABORIGINAL) on the banks of the BULKLEY R north of the modern community of MORICETOWN. According to oral tradition, the WET'SUWET'EN people shared the village with the GITKSAN and other groups, all of whom spent at least the summer there FISHING for SALMON. The name Dizkle meant "dead trees all pointing in one direction." Acting on an omen of disaster, inhabitants abandoned the site suddenly, dispersing to other villages. Archaeologists have found evidence of occupation dating back at least 4,000 years (*see* ARCHAEOLOGY; PREHISTORY).

DOA was the premier band of the punk rock era in VANCOUVER in the late 1970s. The band was founded in 1978 by Joe Keithley, whose stage name was Joey Shithead (vocals, guitar), Randy Rampage (bass), and Chuck Biscuits (drums). Through the years the band's lineup has changed and Keithley is the only remaining original member. The band's politics have always been front and centre in its music, and it forged an ardent following amongst leftist punkers in N America and Europe. The closest it got to mainstream success was when it recorded Randy Bachman's "Takin' Care of Business" (*see* BACHMAN-TURNER OVERDRIVE). In 1998 DOA celebrated its 20th anniversary with a reunion concert featuring many of its former members.

Mike Harling

DODD, Charles, ship's captain, trader (b 29 Nov 1808, New Buckenham, England; d 2 June 1860, Victoria). He joined the HBC in 1833 and two years later became second mate on the steamship BEAVER, travelling with the vessel on its inaugural voyage from England to the Pacific coast. Until 1842 he served as mate on different HBC ships plying the FUR TRADE along the coast as far north as Alaska. After briefly taking charge at FORT STIKINE, he returned to the *Beaver* and was captain of the vessel from 1852 to 1856. He later was put in charge of a larger HBC coasting vessel, the *Labouchere*. At the time of his death of a kidney infection, he was a chief factor in the company.

Captain Charles Dodd of the Hudson's Bay Co. VMM

DOE RIVER, 30 km northeast of DAWSON CREEK near the Alberta border, is a pioneer PEACE R AGRICULTURAL and ranching (*see* CATTLE INDUSTRY) community. It was opened to settlement in 1911, though most homesteaders arrived after WWI. A school (1921), store (1928) and SAWMILL (1932) soon operated; the first Doe River stampede (*see also* RODEO) was held in 1941. The old community hall still stands. *AS*

DOG CREEK, pop 116, is on a back road east of the FRASER R about 80 km south of WILLIAMS LAKE, across from the GANG RANCH. It was originally a SECWEPEMC (Shuswap) village, Xqet'em, and FIRST NATIONS people continue to live here and at nearby Sexqeltqin (Canoe Creek). The earliest white settlers arrived in the Dog Crk Valley in the 1850s, and the community grew as the centre of the surrounding CARIBOO farming and ranch country (*see* AGRICULTURE; CATTLE INDUSTRY). Sheila WATSON taught school here in the mid-1930s and used the community as a setting for her classic novel *The Double Hook* (1959). Dog Creek House, a famous hotel founded by J.S. Place, a community pioneer, and owned for many years by members of the Place family, burned in 1966.
Reading: Hilary Place, *Dog Creek: A Place in the Cariboo*, 1999.

DOGFISH, spiny (*Squalus acanthias*) is the most common SHARK species found on the BC coast. The animal is long and slender, growing to about 1.5 m. It is grey-brown above and dirty white below, with a pointed snout and a long spine in front of each dorsal fin. The spines secrete a painful venom. After copulation, the female takes almost 2 years to produce a litter of 7–8 pups, which at birth are already at least 25 cm long. The name dogfish refers to their habit of pack hunting. A commercial fishery (*see* FISHING, COMMERCIAL) began in the 1850s, when traders began acquiring dogfish oil from coastal FIRST NATIONS fishers. It was used as a lubricant in the FOREST INDUSTRY and, less importantly, as an illuminant. Later, dogfish were reduced for animal fodder and their livers were extracted to obtain vitamin A. About 1950 the fishery declined significantly due to the introduction of synthetic products and the importation of vitamin A oils from Japan. Due to concerns about dogfish competing with other more valuable commercial species, government subsidies were implemented from 1959 to 1962 to reduce stocks. During the 1990s landings increased again, partially in response to the scarcity of SALMON. In 1996 the dogfish fishery produced 3,523 tonnes, primarily as food fish. Dogfish tagged in BC have migrated considerable distances; some have been recovered from as far away as northern Japan and Mexico.

Spiny dogfish. Phil Edgell photo; drawing courtesy Fisheries & Oceans Canada

DOGWOOD tree has been the floral emblem of BC since 1956 and appears on the official COAT OF ARMS. The largest of the 4 dogwood species in BC is the Pacific, or western flowering, dogwood (*Cornus nuttallii*), which occurs in

Pacific dogwood. Kim LaFave drawing

the southwest corner of the province, south of KNIGHT INLET and across most of VANCOUVER ISLAND. Its showy white or pink flowers appear from Apr to June and occasionally in Sept. The wood is very hard and has been used for piano keys and for skewers—or "dags," hence "dagwood," later dogwood. The Dogwood Act forbids cutting or removing a Pacific dogwood tree from Crown lands. During the 1940s the Pacific variety was crossed with the eastern dogwood to produce a hardier hybrid known as the white wonder. Since the 1960s this hybrid has found wide use as an ornamental in gardens and parks. Two dogwood types are creeping perennials: the dwarf dogwood (*C. canadensis*), also called the bunchberry, and *C. suecica*. The fourth species is the red-osier dogwood (*C. stolonifera*), a shrub found throughout the province.

Pacific dogwood in bloom, official floral emblem of BC. Roy Luckow photos

DOHERTY, Charles Edward, hospital administrator (b 29 Nov 1873, Peel Country, ON; d 14 Aug 1920, New Westminster). After taking medical training in Toronto he moved to BC in 1900. Almost all of his career was spent as an administrator rather than a practitioner. He worked as superintendent of the hospital in NELSON. Then, in 1905, after failing to establish a private practice, he became medical superintendent of the Public Hospital for the Insane (WOODLANDS) in NEW WESTMINSTER, where he introduced several

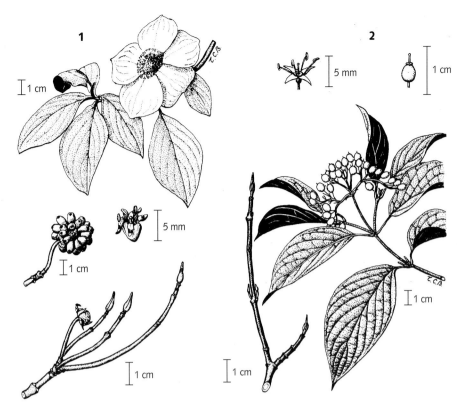

1

2

Flowering branch, fruiting head, flower and winter branch of the Pacific dogwood (1); flower, fruit, winter branch and fruiting branch of the red-osier dogwood (2). © T.C. Brayshaw

treatment innovations and oversaw construction of a sister facility, Essondale. During WWI he served overseas in the Canadian Army Medical Corps, then returned to BC. He was demobilized shortly before his death.

DOIG RIVER, pop 120, is a FIRST NATIONS community 30 km northeast of FORT ST JOHN at the confluence of the Doig and Beatton rivers. The Doig River people moved here from Fort St John following WWII when the federal government took back their original reserve (*see* RESERVES) for AGRICULTURAL settlement. Trapping and the CATTLE INDUSTRY are the main economic activities.

DOLLAR, Robert S., lumberman, shipowner (b 1844, Falkirk, Scotland; d 16 May 1932, San Rafael, CA). At age 14 Dollar moved to Ottawa with his father; 2 years later he began working in logging camps on the Gatineau R. There he taught himself to read and write, and at age 21 he was made foreman. Later he acquired his own LOGGING operation but went bankrupt and took several years to pay off his debts. In the early 1880s the family moved to Michigan, where Dollar started another logging company, this time successfully. In 1887 he moved to California and began logging on the west coast. So few ships were available that he bought one of his own, and gradually he acquired more vessels. In 1911 his shipping company opened an office in VICTORIA; in 1916 it acquired timber rights and built a SAWMILL at N VANCOUVER,

around which the community of DOLLARTON developed. From his BC base, Dollar developed a large trans-Pacific lumber trade with an emphasis on China. His BC interests were managed by his son Melville, who started his own shipping company, the Canadian-American Shipping Co. The company went into decline after Dollar's death, and in 1942 the BC timber and mill assets were sold.   *Ken Drushka*

DOLLARTON is a small community on the north shore of BURRARD INLET at the mouth of INDIAN ARM. There was already one SAWMILL, the VANCOUVER Cedar Mill, on the site in 1916 when the Canadian Robert DOLLAR Co erected a second mill and laid out a village site for its employees. Initially the community was accessible only by boat. In 1918 a rough road was pushed through from N VANCOUVER, and in 1930 the Dollarton Hwy opened. Sawmilling here ended when the Depression forced the closure of both mills in 1929, but the Dollar mill reopened in 1932 and operated until 1943 when new owners dismantled it. From the 1930s to the 1950s squatters' shacks lined the foreshore; among the occupants were the writers Malcolm LOWRY, Earle BIRNEY and Dorothy LIVESAY. Since WWII the area has developed as a residential suburb, and SHIPBUILDING companies have continued to operate along the waterfront since 1930.

DOLPHIN is a toothed WHALE belonging to the family Delphinidae. The largest species is the KILLER WHALE, or orca. Smaller species are distinguished by long, slender bodies, beaks clearly demarcated from their foreheads, and usually a prominent dorsal fin. Dolphins are highly social animals; some species congregate in groups of

Pacific white-sided dolphin.
Martin Nichols illustration; Brian Gauvin photo

up to a thousand or more individuals. They may leap playfully and ride the bow waves of vessels. They use an elaborate echolocation system to manoeuvre through the water and to find their food, which consists mainly of fish. They are widely distributed throughout the world's oceans and usually stay in deep water away from the coast. The most common species in BC waters is the Pacific white-sided dolphin (*Lagenorhynchus obliquidens*), which grows to 140 kg and to 2.4 m in length. It has a black back, white belly and grey flanks with white stripes ("suspenders") down the sides. These dolphins, which travel in schools of several hundred animals, are very animated and acrobatic and may be seen year-round.

DOMAN INDUSTRIES LTD began in 1955 as a trucking and building supplies retailer in DUNCAN, owned by the Doman family. In 1964 the company began LOGGING and SAWMILLING on southern VANCOUVER ISLAND, and in 1967 it built a sawmill at LADYSMITH. Three more sawmills were built on Vancouver Island during the 1970s. In 1980 Doman was one of 3 companies to acquire the operating assets of Rayonier Ltd, a large New York–based firm, which included pulp mills at PORT ALICE and SQUAMISH, 3 sawmills and extensive timber rights. The new company was called Western Forest Products; by 1992 Doman had acquired control of it. In 1999 Doman's net revenues were $873.6 million. During the early 1990s CEO Herb Doman, former premier Bill BENNETT and Bennett's brother

Russell were embroiled in extended legal proceedings involving alleged insider trading. A provincial court acquitted the three men, but in Aug 1996 a BC SECURITIES COMMISSION investigation found them guilty of the charges and issued sanctions.   *Ken Drushka*

DOME CREEK, pop 80, named after nearby Dome Mt, is the largest settlement between PRINCE GEORGE and MCBRIDE on the upper FRASER R. Originally a construction camp for building a GRAND TRUNK PACIFIC RWY bridge over the river, it once supported 3 SAWMILLS, which closed in the late 1960s when logs could be hauled to Prince George via the Yellowhead Hwy. LOGGING is still important to the area, as is ranching and drinking coffee at the Dome Diner. River sternwheelers (*see* PADDLEWHEEL STEAMBOATS) were once laid up here for the winter.   *AS*

DOMINION ASTROPHYSICAL OBSERVATORY on Little Saanich Mt north of VICTORIA was established in 1918 by the federal government. Its 1.85-m telescope was the largest in the world at that time and was used to collect important data about the Milky Way. A 1.2-m telescope was

Dominion Radio Astrophysical Observatory, near Penticton. Roy Luckow photo

added in 1962. The first director of the observatory was J.S. PLASKETT. The telescopes are used for research on binary stars, star clusters, quasars, black holes and dark matter in the universe. The federal government also operates a radio telescope at the Dominion Radio Astrophysical Observatory near PENTICTON.

Chris Gainor

DONALD, or Donald Station, pop 101, was originally called First Crossing. It lies 28 km west of GOLDEN, at the point at which the CPR crosses the COLUMBIA R. Donald is named for the railway executive Donald Smith, Lord Strathcona (*see* CRAIGELLACHIE). When the CPR moved its divisional point to REVELSTOKE in 1899, most of the community's residents and buildings moved as well.

DORISTON, originally known as Shaw Cove after the first settler, is an isolated settlement on the west shore of SECHELT INLET on the SUNSHINE COAST, 28 km north of SECHELT. Herbert Whitaker built a SAWMILL here at the turn of the century and a school opened in 1918. LOGGING, commercial FISHING and AGRICULTURE supported residents, most of whom had moved elsewhere by the 1960s.   *AS*

DORR, 50 km southeast of CRANBROOK, was a SAWMILL settlement and CROWSNEST SOUTHERN RWY station on the KOOTENAY R. Its heydays were the 1920s and 1930s. Today it is submerged beneath the waters of KOOCANUSA LK.   *AS*

DORREEN, a tiny settlement on the CNR and the west side of the SKEENA R 41 km northeast of TERRACE, was named after E.J. Dorreen, a GRAND TRUCK PACIFIC RWY construction engineer from New Zealand. A school opened here in 1924 and a post office operated from 1925 to 1967.

DOSANJH, Ujjal, lawyer, politician, premier Feb 24, 2000– (b 1947, Dosanjh Kalan, Punjab, India). He left India at age 17 to move to England, then immigrated to BC in 1968. While working in a VANCOUVER SAWMILL he injured his back and decided to pursue his education. Eventually he graduated with a BA from SFU, followed by a law degree from UBC. In 1979 he established a private law practice in Vancouver. A long-time HUMAN RIGHTS activist, he spoke out against the use of violence by SIKH nationalists in India in the mid-1980s, earning the enmity of some members of the BC Sikh community. A secular Sikh himself, he was assaulted and injured during this period for his outspokenness. After running unsuccessfully for the provincial legislature as an NDP candidate in 1979 and 1983, he won the Vancouver–Kensington seat in 1991 and in 1995 joined the CABINET as government services minister, then attorney general. There he earned a reputation as a low-key, moderate "law-and-order" minister. He was chosen leader of the party at a convention on 20 Feb 2000; a few days later, when he was sworn in as PREMIER, he became the first Canadian of Indian descent to serve as premier of a province. His

Ujjal Dosanjh, chosen premier of BC in Feb 2000. Wayne Leidenfrost/Vancouver Province

wife Raminder is a prominent feminist and political activist in the BC Indo-Canadian community. *See also* SOUTH ASIANS; WOMEN'S MOVEMENT.

DOT, 26 km northwest of MERRITT on the NICOLA R, was a flag station on the KETTLE VALLEY RWY. Dot was the nickname of Dalton P. Marpole, a local property owner; his father, Richard MARPOLE, had served as manager of CPR operations in BC.   AS

DOUG AND THE SLUGS was a nationally popular rock 'n' roll band noted for its live performances and hit songs in the 1980s. The group—Doug Bennett (vocals), Simon Kendall (keyboards), Rick Baker (guitar), John Burton (guitar), Steve Bosley (bass) and John Wally Watson (drums)—was formed in the late 1970s and developed a cult following in VANCOUVER nightclubs. Buoyed by its club success, the band released its first album, *Cognac & Baloney*, on its own Ritdong label in 1980. In 1983 it released its third—and most successful—record, *Music for the Hard of Thinking*, featuring the hit "Making it Work"; the band received a Juno Award nomina-

Doug and the Slugs, Vancouver band, 1986

tion for most promising group. Much of its appeal can be attributed to its singer, the multi-talented Doug Bennett, who wrote most of the songs and created an irreverent and charismatic on-stage persona. The group continued recording into the early 1990s, but never realized the commercial promise of its earlier works. In 1998 "Making it Work" resurfaced as a television-ad jingle for BC Tel (*see* TELUS CORPORATION).

Mike Harling

DOUGLAS, Amelia (Connolly), governor's wife (b 1812, Fort Assiniboine, Rupertsland; d 1890, Victoria). She was the daughter of William CONNOLLY, a NORTH WEST CO (NWC) trader, and his Cree wife Miyo Nipiy. They raised her at FUR TRADE posts in the northwest, and when she was 9 years old the NWC merged with the HBC and the family moved to NEW CALEDONIA, where her father was a chief factor with the reorganized HBC. At FORT ST JAMES in 1828 she married one of her father's clerks, James DOUGLAS. The marriage was later solemnized in a church ceremony. As James Douglas rose through the company ranks, the couple lived at Fort Vancouver, then FORT VICTORIA. In 1851 he became governor of VANCOUVER ISLAND. She lived between two worlds, remembering her aboriginal traditions and trying to pass them on to her children while moving in settler society as the "governor's lady." By all accounts she was a shy but gracious person who avoided as much as possible the social occasions that were an inevitable part of her official role.

DOUGLAS, Clifford Hugh, engineer, originator of Social Credit (b 20 Jan 1879, Stockport, England; d 1952). He developed the theory of SOCIAL CREDIT during WWI and spent the rest of his life trying to spread his ideas. A critic of capitalism, he argued that increasing individual spending power would improve the system. To this end he proposed putting public money, or "social credit," directly into the hands of consumers. During the Depression his theory attracted a following in Canada, especially in Alberta, which elected William Aberhart's Social Credit Party in 1935, but also in BC. Major Douglas, as he was known, visited BC once on his way to Alberta in 1934. The Social Credit government that eventually came to power in BC in 1952 adopted the name but virtually ignored the content of Douglas's doctrine. Douglas later developed paranoid tendencies and was dismissed as a "funny money" crank.

DOUGLAS, David, scientist (b 25 June 1799, Scone, Scotland; d 12 July 1834, HI). He was the son of a stonemason who grew up in Scotland, where as a youngster he developed an interest in plants and wildlife. He studied at the Glasgow Royal Botanical Garden and in 1823 was hired as a collector by the Horticultural Society of London. The society sent Douglas to Upper Canada and New York to gather specimens. The trip was a great success and in 1824 Douglas left on a similar expedition to the Pacific Northwest. He was based at Fort Vancouver on the COLUMBIA

R for the next 3 years. The huge collection of plants and seeds he brought home made him a scientific celebrity. In 1829 Douglas again departed for Fort Vancouver; he spent another 3 years collecting from California to Puget Sound. His plans to return to England via Siberia were thwarted and instead he sailed to Hawaii, where he remained for several months. Douglas died on a remote mountain trail, apparently gored by a bull, though at least one biographer has argued that he committed suicide. Aboriginal people called Douglas "the Grass Man" and respected him for his endurance and his knowledge of the wilderness. He introduced to England about 7,000 new species of plants, more than any other person. The DOUGLAS FIR is named after him.

DOUGLAS, Gilean, writer, naturalist (b 1 Feb 1900, Toronto; d 31 Oct 1993, Cortes Island). Raised in a prosperous professional family, she began her writing career at age 19 as a Toronto newspaper reporter. Through 4 marriages and recurring health problems, she made her living as an independent writer. She moved to BC in 1938 and lived in a cabin on the Coquihalla R northeast of HOPE, then moved in 1949 to CORTES ISLAND, where she lived for the rest of her life. Douglas published 7 books of poetry but is remembered best for her nature writing, collected in 3 books: *River for My Sidewalk* (1953) and *Silence is My Homeland* (1978), both about the CASCADE MTS, and *The Protected Place* (1979) about her life on Cortes. Over the years her articles, short stories and poems appeared in many N American magazines and newspapers, and for 31 years (1961–92) she wrote a nature column for the Victoria *Daily Colonist*, later the TIMES-COLONIST.

DOUGLAS, James, fur trader, governor of Vancouver Island 1851–63, of BC 1858–64 (b 15 Aug 1803, Demerara, British Guiana; d 2 Aug 1877, Victoria). He was the most influential person in the history of colonial BC. The son of a Creole woman and a Scottish merchant, he was educated in Scotland and apprenticed to the NORTH WEST COMPANY at age 16. His time as a Nor'wester was spent in eastern Canada. Following the 1821 merger of the NWC with the HBC, he joined the reorganized HBC and came out to NEW CALEDONIA to FORT ST JAMES in 1825. Three years later he married Amelia Connolly, daughter of Chief Factor William CONNOLLY (*see* Amelia DOUGLAS). Douglas had a strong temper and was not always diplomatic with his FIRST NATIONS customers. On one occasion he ordered the execution of a local DAKELH (Carrier), who had been implicated in the murder of 2 HBC men. A party of angry Dakelh came to the post and threatened Douglas's life; only his wife's quick-witted intervention saved him. As a result of this incident, Douglas was transferred to Fort Vancouver in 1830. He was a chief factor by 1839 and in 1842 he chose the site for FORT VICTORIA at the southern tip of VANCOUVER ISLAND. The following summer he returned to supervise construction of the post and he moved there

James Douglas, first governor of the colony of BC, 1858–64. BC Archives HP-2652

himself in 1849, when it replaced Fort Vancouver as the headquarters of the trade on the Pacific coast. In 1851 he became governor of the colony of Vancouver Island and then, when the separate mainland colony of British Columbia was created in 1858, he became its governor as well, resigning his position with the HBC. When the discovery of gold (see GOLD RUSH, FRASER RIVER) sparked an influx of American miners, he took decisive steps to secure the area for British rule. He also opened roads to the Interior (*see* DOUGLAS ROAD, CARIBOO WAGON ROAD) and made treaties with Vancouver Island First Nations (*see* DOUGLAS TREATIES). Despite a stern, even autocratic manner (he was known as "Old Squaretoes"), he was a capable, energetic administrator. He retired in 1864, the same year he was knighted. *See also* COLONIAL GOVERNMENT.

DOUGLAS, Stan, artist (b 1960, Vancouver). A 1982 graduate of the EMILY CARR INSTITUTE OF ART & DESIGN in VANCOUVER, he is one of Canada's leading multimedia artists, producing innovative work that combines PHOTOGRAPHY, video and sound recording. His pieces explore such themes as the effect of technology on culture, the relationship between viewer and viewed, and historical narrative and memory. He has had several solo exhibitions internationally, including in England, France, Spain, Switzerland and the US. A show he curated in 1988 for the VANCOUVER ART GALLERY, *Samuel Beckett: Teleplays*, later toured N America and travelled to Australia and Europe. In 1990 he organized a series of lectures on contemporary art that were published the next year as *Vancouver Anthology: the institutional politics of art*. He is a recipient of a VANCOUVER INSTITUTE OF THE VISUAL ARTS award and the 1999 Gershon Iskowitz Prize, awarded annually by the Canada Council for the Arts.

DOUGLAS & McINTYRE LTD (D&M) is BC's largest BOOK PUBLISHER. Founded in 1971 by Scott McIntyre and J.J. Douglas, it is a "regional" publisher that has developed a national and international reputation. In 1996 the company had revenues close to $11 million, making it the largest Canadian publisher outside Toronto. Under McIntyre, president of the company, D&M publishes books on a variety of subjects; it is perhaps best known for high-quality art books and books about aboriginal culture and natural history. D&M also has a children's division, Groundwood Books, based in Toronto.

DOUGLAS CHANNEL is a long (72 km), narrow passage on the North Coast reaching from the TSIMSHIAN community of HARTLEY BAY at its mouth, deep into the COAST MTS, to KITIMAT at its head. The interior of the channel was home to the HAISLA (Kitimat) people, now congregated at the village of Kitamaat. Named for the colonial governor James DOUGLAS, the channel is used by deep-water vessels approaching the ALCAN SMELTER and other industrial sites at Kitimat. LOGGING has taken place here and the area is a popular sport FISHING spot.

DOUGLAS FIR (*Pseudotsuga menziesii*) grows generally along the BC coast but is dominant in the southwest corner of the province on the east side of VANCOUVER ISLAND and the adjacent coastal mainland, where summers are dry and warm and winters mild and wet. The coastal variety reaches heights of more than 90 m; a shorter variety (to 42 m) inhabits the south-central Interior. The long cylindrical trunk made Douglas fir a favourite with loggers and it has been one of the world's most important trees for the LOGGING industry, used for construction lumber and PULP AND PAPER stock. Creosote-protected piles and decking made of this wood are used extensively along the coast in marine structures. By the end of the 20th century most of the large trees had disappeared and the species was less important to the FOREST INDUSTRY. Of the remaining giants, most are found in the NIMPKISH valley on Vancouver Island, though the tallest Douglas fir in Canada (94 m) grows in COQUITLAM (*see* TREES, GIANT). The oldest known Douglas fir, thought to be

Douglas fir.
© *T.C. Brayshaw*

Douglas fir at Serenity Creek, Stoltmann Wilderness, 1998. Kerry Dawson/WCWC

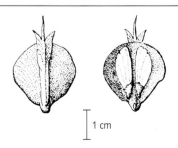

Cone scale with bract (2 views) and branch with cone of the Douglas fir. © T.C. Brayshaw

Top: Giant Douglas fir. Dean van't Schip photo
Bottom: Douglas fir cone. Duane Sept photo

more than 1,700 years old, is near LADYSMITH, while a grove of 1,350-year-old trees stands beside the Elaho R north of WHISTLER. The Douglas fir is named for the British scientist David DOUGLAS, though Archibald MENZIES, the naturalist who accompanied George VANCOUVER in 1792–94, collected the first specimens. It is not a true FIR tree; its cones have 3-pronged bracts and its bark is deeply furrowed and very fire-resistant. *See also* FOREST PRODUCTS.

DOUGLAS LAKE CATTLE CO is in the NICOLA Valley east of MERRITT. The largest ranch in Canada, stretching nearly 100 km from corner to corner, the ranch controls 2,025 km² of GRASSLAND and runs about 19,000 head of Hereford and crossbreed cattle. The ranch operates under an Integrated Management Plan, using all its resources through such diverse activities as selective timber harvesting (*see* LOGGING), TOURIST and recreation programs, a movie set and sales of ranch supplies and equipment. The nucleus of the ranch was pre-empted in 1872 by John Douglas at the north end of Douglas Lk. Aggressive new owners incorporated as the Douglas Lake Ranch in 1884 and dramatically expanded the size of the operation. The Douglas Lake Cattle Co, incorporated in 1886, is the fifth oldest corporation in BC. Subsequent owners

Ranch buildings and corral, Douglas Lake Ranch, 1994. Roy Luckow photo

have included the department store owner Victor SPENCER and Frank ROSS, former LT GOV of BC. From 1959 to 1998 the ranch was owned by Charles "Chunky" WOODWARD and his family; it was sold in 1998 to the Alberta-born telecommunications entrepreneur Bernard Ebbers. *See also* CATTLE INDUSTRY.

DOUGLAS TRAIL, named for Gov James DOUGLAS, ran from PORT DOUGLAS at the head of HARRISON LK to LILLOOET on the FRASER R via Lillooet, SETON and ANDERSON lakes. The route, explored by the HBC trader A.C. ANDERSON in 1846, allowed travellers to the Interior to avoid the impassable rapids of the Fraser Canyon. Construction began in Aug 1858 and a rough trail was finished in Oct. The workforce consisted of unemployed miners who received food and shelter for their labour, but no pay. Douglas hoped the project would keep the men away from VICTORIA, where they might stir up trouble. During 1860–61 the ROYAL ENGINEERS widened and improved the trail to accommodate wagons.

Steamers were used on the main lakes and 5 km of narrow-gauge track and horse-drawn rolling stock connected Seton and Anderson lks. The road was eclipsed as the main route into the Interior with the completion of the CARIBOO WAGON ROAD in the mid-1860s. *See also* TRAILS.

DOUGLAS TREATIES, or the Vancouver Island Treaties, were a series of 14 land purchases (1850–54) by the HBC, acting as agent for the British government, from several FIRST NATIONS on VANCOUVER ISLAND. The treaties were negotiated by James DOUGLAS, HBC chief factor and governor of the island. In 1849 Vancouver Island became a Crown colony, and before settlement could proceed the issue of land ownership had to be decided. The first treaties were made around FORT VICTORIA in 1850, followed by similar agreements at FORT RUPERT (1851), SAANICH (1852) and NANAIMO (1854). A total of 927 km² was purchased, about 3% of the area of the island. In return the people received a few blankets, small RESERVES surrounding their village sites, and hunting and fishing rights on adjacent unoccupied land. Historians disagree about whether Douglas's commitment to the principle of aboriginal title later changed. Regardless, there were no more treaties, and subsequent governments explicitly denied aboriginal title. Until the NISGA'A TREATY in 1998, the only other treaty affecting First Nations in BC was TREATY NO 8 in the northeast corner of the province. The Douglas land purchases have been upheld as treaties by the courts. *See also* ABORIGINAL RIGHTS.

DOUKHOBORS are a religious sect of Russian Christians dating back to the 18th century. The term means "spirit wrestlers" or heretics and was adopted by the sect as a proud emblem of their spiritual struggle. Persecuted at home for their pacifism and unorthodox theology, about 7,500 Doukhobors came to Canada in 1899 in search

Protest by the Sons of Freedom, a radical group of Doukhobors, Agassiz, 1962.

of religious freedom. The government granted them land in present-day Saskatchewan and Manitoba, exempted them from military service and tolerated the development of their own distinctive settlement patterns. Within a few years, however, the government took steps to regain some of the land it had granted and required the Doukhobors to swear allegiance to the British Crown and to break up their communal holdings into individual properties. Objecting to the new conditions, about 5,000 Doukhobors led by Peter ("Peter the Lordly") VERIGIN migrated west beginning in 1908 to the KOOTENAY and the BOUNDARY DISTRICT of southeastern BC; there they formed settlements at BRILLIANT, Pass Creek, Glade, SHOREACRES, Ootischenie, Champion

Creek and GRAND FORKS. They continued to follow a communal lifestyle, living an austere, isolated life engaged in community enterprises. In 1917 the Doukhobors incorporated as the Christian Community of Universal Brotherhood Ltd (CCUB), later the Union of Spiritual Communities of Christ. When Verigin died in a train explosion in 1924 he was succeeded as leader by his son, Peter Petrovich Verigin (1880–1939). During the Depression the CCUB lost its lands to creditors and the communal system disintegrated, but in the 1950s the provincial government sold properties back to individual Doukhobors. The outside world looked upon the Doukhobors with suspicion, in part because of their pacifism and their resistance to government registration. As animosity developed, public schools became the focus of Doukhobor resistance to government authority and some members of the community withheld their children. In 1923 the first schools were burned as a protest and clashes within the community and between the community and the authorities continued for the next 40 years. Doukhobors were denied the federal and provincial vote from 1931 to 1956 because they were conscientious objectors, and during the 1950s about 170 Doukhobor children were removed from their families and sent to a government boarding school. On the prairies the sect had developed 2 dissident elements: Independents, who favoured varying degrees of accommodation with mainstream society, and Sons of Freedom, a radical fundamentalist element that sometimes employed the nude march as a form of protest against western secularism. From the 1920s the Sons of Freedom carried on what amounted to a guerrilla war against assimilation into Canadian society, especially in BC. It is this minority that was responsible for most of the incidents of arson, bombing and public nudity that lasted to the 1960s, peaking with the Great Trek of protestors to VANCOUVER in 1963. The protest finally exhausted itself, as did overt

Doukhobor houses, Grand Forks.
Len Mackave photo

attempts to force the Doukhobors to assimilate. Today about 15,000 Doukhobors live in BC, mainly at CASTLEGAR, Grand Forks and in Vancouver. *See also* PIERS ISLAND.
Reading: George Woodcock and Ivan Avakumovic, *The Doukhobors*, 1968.

DOVE; *see* PIGEON.

DOWNS, Arthur, writer, publisher (b 21 June 1924, England; d 13 Aug 1996, Aldergrove). He was a key figure in establishing modern BC MAGAZINE and BOOK PUBLISHING. After serving in the merchant marine during WWII, he began submitting historical articles to *Cariboo Digest*, a pioneer BC magazine published in QUESNEL by Alex Sahonovitch. Downs purchased the magazine in 1955, renaming it *Northwest Digest* and later *BC Outdoors*. Under his editorship, *BC Outdoors* became one of BC's most important consumer magazines, often reaching beyond the confines of its outdoor themes to publish important articles on BC HISTORY and issues. In 1960 Downs wrote and published *Wagon Road North*, a popular history of the CARIBOO WAGON ROAD, followed by the equally successful *Paddlewheels on the Frontier*. He was also a committed environmentalist, serving as president of the BC WILDLIFE FEDERATION and on the PACIFIC SALMON COMMISSION. After selling *BC Outdoors* to Maclean Hunter Ltd of Toronto in 1979, Downs and his wife Doris concentrated on publishing books through their firm Heritage House Publishing until failing health forced his retirement in 1995. *Howard White*

DOWNS, Barry Vance, architect (b 19 June 1930, Vancouver). After obtaining a B Arch from the Univ of Washington in 1954, he worked with leading VANCOUVER architects Thompson, Berwick Pratt & Partners. He was in partnership with Fred Hollingsworth from 1964 to 1966, then worked independently until 1969 when he founded Downs/Archambault & Partners with architect Richard Archambault. The company has been responsible for several well-known buildings and renovations including the Carnegie Community Centre, the Britannia Community Centre, Canada Place and Langara College in VANCOUVER, the N VANCOUVER Civic Centre, and the Museum at CAMPBELL RIVER. Downs was awarded a Massey gold medal in 1964 and won an Eaton's book prize for his 1980 book *Sacred Places*, a celebration of BC's early churches and church sites. His own cliffside W VANCOUVER home is a design landmark. *See also* ARCHITECTURE. *Shannon Emmerson*

DOWNTOWN EASTSIDE RESIDENTS' ASSOCIATON (DERA) is a grassroots community organization in VANCOUVER's historic central core. Formed in 1973 by a group of neighbourhood activists led by Bruce ERIKSEN, the group represents the interests of some of the city's poorest residents, many of them living in the area's hotels and rooming houses. Among other accomplishments, DERA has been active in getting improved street lighting and safer living conditions in rental accommodation in the area. It was also instrumental in developing low-cost CO-OPERATIVE housing and in creating the Carnegie Community Centre, located in a heritage building given to the city by Andrew Carnegie in 1903, for use as a LIBRARY. During the mid-1980s, DERA led the opposition to the social disruption caused in the community when EXPO 86 was under construction: longtime local residents were displaced as inexpensive accommodations and other facilities in the area were upgraded to take advantage of Expo tourist traffic. The association is known for pioneering innovative social programs that involve residents in the evolution of their own community. *See also* COMMUNITY DEVELOPMENT.

DOYLE, Henry, businessman (b 8 Sept 1874, Paterson, NJ; d 1961, Hollywood). His father began a fishing supply and packing company in San Francisco and he joined the firm as a salesperson. In 1895 he came to VANCOUVER to manage a new branch office. When his father died, he took over the entire firm at age 24. In 1902 he led attempts to eliminate competition and control costs in the SALMON CANNING industry by merging several companies into the British Columbia Packers Assoc, later BC PACKERS LTD. He was the first general manager of the association, which owned 35 canneries. In 1904 he resigned in a dispute with directors and went on to own and manage several canneries on the North Coast, often in partnership with R.V. WINCH. Hit hard by the post-WWI depression, he lost his properties to the bank in the early 1920s and left the business. He compiled an extensive archive on the canning industry, part of which resides at UBC.

DRABEK, Jan, writer (b 5 May 1935, Prague, Czechoslovakia). In his teens he left his native Czechoslovakia, where his father had been active in the underground during WWII, and lived for several years in the US, India, Austria and Germany. He arrived in VANCOUVER in 1965, decided to stay, and taught high school for 10 years before becoming a full-time writer. The author of several novels, he took advantage of his position as an émigré to alert N Americans to the dangers of east European dictatorships. When the Berlin Wall came down in 1989 he returned to Czechoslovakia, where he taught English and later was named ambassador to Kenya and Albania. He also served as director of protocol at the Czech foreign ministry before returning to Vancouver late in 1998 to resume his writing career.

DRAGON BOAT RACES take place each June in FALSE CREEK in VANCOUVER. Dragon boats are long, teak-hulled CANOES; each is propelled by 20 paddlers. Racing dates back hundreds of years in China but was introduced to Vancouver during EXPO 86. It became an annual event the next year when leaders of the local Asian community launched the Canadian International Dragon Boat Festival as a way to promote good relations with the non-Asian majority. In 1996 the

Dragon boat racers, False Creek, Vancouver.
Larry Scherban/Image Makers

Dragon Boat World Championships were held in Vancouver.

DRAGONFLY is a large, colourful, spiny-legged flying INSECT, of the order Odonata, commonly seen swooping low across the surface of a pond or perching elegantly on vegetation beside the water. There are 85 species in BC, divided into 2 suborders, the true dragonflies (Anisoptera) and the damselflies (Zygoptera). True dragonflies have large, compound eyes that occupy almost

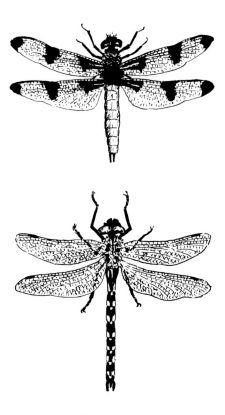

The ten-spot libellula (top) and green darner dragonflies. Illustrations by Philip Croft

the entire head, an elongate abdomen and a biting mouth; as aquatic larvae, they breathe through gills located near the tail end. Adults are active mainly in sunlight, when they dart about feeding on small flying insects. Mating occurs in flight with the female curled beneath the male. The female deposits her fertilized eggs in water or on aquatic plants, where they hatch into larvae. The larval stage may last from a few weeks up to a few years in some species. During this time larvae live among submerged plants or on the bottom of ponds or streams. When the time is right, they emerge from the water to transform into adults: this is the stage at which they are most visible to humans, but it usually lasts for only 5–10 weeks before the insect dies. True dragonflies are characterized by 2 pairs of long, net-veined wings that remain extended even when the insect is not flying. Damselflies fly more slowly than dragonflies and when they are at rest they hold their wings together above their bodies. Dragonflies and damselflies rely on WETLANDS for their survival and the gradual disappearance of these ecosystems accounts for a reduction in the number of aquatic insects in general.

DRAKE, Francis, mariner (b circa 1540, Devonshire, England; d 28 Jan 1596, on board ship off Panama). An English sea captain and privateer, he commanded a fleet of 5 ships during 1577–80 on a voyage around Cape Horn into the Pacific. The crew explored the coast of S America, harassed the Spanish there and tried to locate a northern sea passage back to the Atlantic. By the time Drake reached the Pacific, only one ship remained, his own *Golden Hinde*. After looting the Spanish he sailed north, but how far north is a matter of conjecture. He may have reached the west coast of VANCOUVER ISLAND during the summer of 1579; the NUU-CHAH-NULTH recount stories of an encounter with a mystery ship that may have been the *Hinde*. Others conclude he got no farther than Oregon. Drake completed a circumnavigation of the globe by sailing home across the Pacific. He was knighted for his accomplishments and went on to play an important role in the defeat of the Spanish Armada in 1588. He died of yellow fever while engaged in yet another expedition against his lifelong enemies.

DUCHARME CASE was one of VANCOUVER's most bizarre murder cases. In 1949 Roger Ducharme, a repeat sex offender who suffered from penile giantism, was charged in a sex-related homicide and tried before Justice Alexander MANSON. Although Ducharme's physical deformity was material to the case, sensitivities of the time prevented its mention in evidence or media coverage. The trial took place in a charged atmosphere with rowdy overflow crowds disrupting the proceedings. Ducharme was convicted by an all-male jury and hanged on 14 July 1950 at the BC PENITENTIARY. In retrospect it is clear the case said more about the sexual squeamishness of the 1950s than issues at law.

Howard White

Roger Ducharme, convicted sex offender, Vancouver, 1940s.

DUCK is a small waterfowl with short legs, webbed feet, flat bill and highly varied plumage. Ducks are among the most common shorebirds in the province. Most species are strong flyers and migrate each year from their northern and Interior nesting grounds to winter along the milder coast. They inhabit a variety of WETLANDS—sloughs, marshes, ponds, lakeshores, ESTUARIES and streams—and inshore waters along the coast. Strictly speaking the females are ducks; males are called drakes. Conventionally ducks are divided into 3 groups according to feeding habits: the dabbler, the most colourful, feeds on the surface or by submerging its head and body in shallow water until only its upright tail remains visible; the diver plunges completely below the surface; the merganser dives to pursue fish. Of the 30 species occuring in BC, mallards (*Anas platyrhynchos*) are the most widespread and abundant, breeding almost everywhere there is open water. The female has nondescript mottled brown plumage; the male is marked by its iridescent green head and chestnut breast. Mallards are the most important game ducks for hunters, and their adaptability to changes in their habitat makes them familiar denizens of urban areas. Other dabblers include 3 species of teal, the smallest duck: green-winged teal (*Anas crecca*), cinnamon teal (*A. cyanoptera*) and blue-winged teal (*A. discors*); the wood duck (*Aix sponsa*); the northern pintail (*Anas acuta*), vast numbers of which migrate down the coast from

Male wood duck. Ken Bowen photo

From top: female hooded merganser, male mallard (R. Wayne Campbell photos), male Barrow's goldeneye, male northern pintail (Ervio Sian photos).

Alaska every year; the northern shoveler (*A. clypeata*); the gadwall (*A. strepera*); and two species of wigeon, the Eurasian wigeon (*A. penelope*) and the American wigeon (*A. americana*), one of the most abundant winter visitors to the coast, especially in the FRASER R delta. Diving species include the large canvasback (*Aythya valisineria*), the redhead (*A. americana*)—the only species that winters more in the Interior than along the coast, the ring-necked duck (*A. collaris*), the tufted duck (*A. fuligula*), the greater scaup (*A. marila*), the lesser scaup (*A. affinis*), the quite rare king eider (*Somateria spectabilis*), the

harlequin duck (*Histrionicus histrionicus*), the oldsquaw (*Clagnula hyemalis*), the black scoter (*Melanitta nigra*), the surf scoter (*M. perspicillata*), the white-winged scoter (*M. fusca*), the common goldeneye (*Bucephala clangula*), the Barrow's goldeneye (*B. islandica*), the bufflehead (*B. albeola*) and the ruddy duck (*Oxyura jamaicensis*). Mergansers are identifiable by their slender, round bills, hooked at the tip, and their tufted heads. They include the hooded merganser (*Lophodytes cucullatus*), common merganser (*Mergus merganser*) and red-breasted merganser (*M. serrator*).

DUCK RANGE, a ranching district 35 km east of KAMLOOPS, was named after the pioneering Duck family, early settlers and landowners in the area. A post office operated here from 1908 to 1943 and a rural school was established in 1913.   *AS*

DUDOWARD, Alfred, Tsimshian leader (b 1848, Port Simpson; d unknown). He was the son of a ranking Lax Kw'aalams woman, Elizabeth Diex, and a French Canadian trader named Dudoier. Dudoward lived for a time in VICTORIA with his mother, then returned to Port Simpson (*see* FORT SIMPSON) to be chief. He married Katharine Holmes in 1871 and the couple were converted to Methodism during a visit to Victoria. At that time Port Simpson was occupied by about 500 Tsimshian who had rejected the ministry of the ANGLICAN William DUNCAN when he was among them 10 years earlier. On their return, the Dudowards used their influence to spread the METHODIST gospel and petitioned their church to send them a Christian teacher. The church sent Thomas CROSBY; in league with the Dudowards, he succeeded in converting the majority of Port Simpson Tsimshian and over the next 23 years helped them create a model Christian village that rivalled Duncan's fabled METLAKATLA. The Dudowards' status as founders of this new order consolidated their influence and they continued to advocate for the church, ensuring the popularity of Methodism among the FIRST NATIONS of the North Coast. The Dudoward family still thrives in the region.

Howard White

DUFF, Wilson, anthropologist (b 23 Mar 1925, Vancouver; d 8 Aug 1976, Vancouver). Educated at UBC and the Univ of Washington, he was curator of anthropology at the provincial museum (*see* ROYAL BC MUSEUM) between 1950 and 1965 and was involved during that time with the reclamation of TOTEM POLES at abandoned HAIDA village sites on the QUEEN CHARLOTTE ISLANDS. He moved to the Department of Anthropology at UBC in 1965. He chaired the provincial Archaeological Sites Advisory Board (*see* ARCHAEOLOGY) from 1960 to 1966 and was a member of the Indian Advisory Committee from 1963 to 1976. Later in his career he was particularly interested in the analysis of coastal FIRST NATIONS art forms. He wrote *The Indian History of British Columbia*, vol. 1 (1964), *Arts of the Raven: Masterworks by the Northwest Coast Indians* (1967)

Wilson Duff, anthropologist. Vickie Jensen photo

and *Images:Stone:BC* (1975).

DUKE, Daryl, film director-producer (b 8 Mar 1929, Vancouver). After graduating from UBC in 1950, he began working for the National Film Board in Ottawa as a film editor, writer and director. In 1953 he produced some of the first shows on CBUT, CBC's VANCOUVER television station, and went on to produce and direct many successful CBC programs, including *Close Up*, *Quest* and *Explorations*. In 1968 he produced *The Steve Allen Show* and later directed made-for-television movies such as *I Heard the Owl Call My Name*, a 1973 adaptation of the classic Margaret CRAVEN novel, as well as the highly popular TV miniseries *The Thorn Birds* (1983) and *Tai-Pan* (1986). In 1978 he won a Canadian Film Award (now the Genie) for his feature film *The Silent Partner*. Back in Vancouver, he founded CKVU-TV in 1976 and remained with the station until 1987. He was inducted into the BC Entertainment Hall of Fame in 1997 and is a member of the board of directors of BC FILM and of the steering committee of the Friends of Canadian Broadcasting.

Shannon Emmerson

DUNCAN, city, pop 4,583, lies in the Cowichan Valley on the east side of VANCOUVER ISLAND about halfway between VICTORIA and NANAIMO. In 1864 William Chalmers Duncan, a native of Sarnia, ON, settled on 40 ha of land near COWICHAN BAY, most of which now comprises downtown Duncan. In 1887 the ESQUIMALT & NANAIMO RWY built a station on his land and a village named Alderlea developed around it. When a post office opened in 1891 it was called Duncan's Station, later shortened to Duncan. Between 1898 and 1908 there was a flurry of MINING activity at nearby Mt SICKER and the community boomed. It was incorporated as a city on 4 Mar 1912, when it separated from the district of NORTH COWICHAN. Once described as "the

Potlatch in Duncan, 1911. BC Archives E-04017

Most English Town in Canada," it had a preponderance of British residents who felt strong ties to the old country. When WWI began, so many young men enlisted for overseas service that Duncan earned a reputation for contributing more soldiers per capita to the war than any other community in Canada. Following the war the city grew slowly as the business centre for AGRICULTURE and LOGGING activities in the Cowichan Valley; gradually Duncan's British flavour blended with others. Since 1985, TOTEM POLES have been erected around the city, which began to call itself the City of Totems.

DUNCAN, Charles, maritime fur trader (active 1786–92). He was in the Royal Navy prior to joining the KING GEORGE'S SOUND CO, organized in 1785 to trade for SEA OTTER pelts on the Northwest Coast. He commanded the *Princess*

William Duncan, coastal missionary, c 1867. BC Archives A-01175

Royal in 1786 as part of the company's second expedition. In 1788, during a second summer of trading, he sailed through HECATE STRAIT and DIXON ENTRANCE, proving that the QUEEN CHARLOTTE ISLANDS were not connected to the mainland. He spent most of that summer in the north; PRINCESS ROYAL ISLAND is named for his ship. He returned to England a firm believer in the existence of a Northwest Passage and from 1790 to 1792 was engaged on the west side of Hudson Bay in a fruitless search for an entrance to the passage. *See also* FUR TRADE, MARITIME.

DUNCAN, William, missionary (b 3 Apr 1832, Bishop Burton, England; d 30 Aug 1918, New Metlakatla, AK). He was a leather salesman with experience in business, then trained for mission work at the ANGLICAN CHURCH Missionary Society's Highbury College. In 1857 the society sent him to the North Coast to serve as a lay missionary to the TSIMSHIAN people living at FORT SIMPSON, an HBC post. He decided after 4 years that the disadvantages of life at the post were not conducive to his success. Overcrowded conditions, exacerbated by alcoholism and disease, made it impossible for him to establish the stable environment he needed for his work. During the SMALLPOX epidemic of 1862, he convinced some of his followers that the disease was a warning from God and he led 400 Tsimshian away from the post to METLAKATLA, an ancestral village site 25 km down the coast. Together they built a European-style village that at its peak had 1,200 residents, a large church, a school, a SAWMILL and SALMON CANNERY, its own newspaper and several other enterprises. Metlakatla became famous worldwide as a model Christian village. But the Anglican hierarchy was unhappy with Duncan's lack of co-operation and in 1879 sent a bishop, William RIDLEY, to represent the church's interests. A schism developed and in 1887 Duncan led 823 Tsimshian followers north to Annette Island in Alaska, where they founded New Metlakatla. Once again his strong personality provoked division. In 1915 the US government stepped in to seize all the property at the

site. Duncan remained there until his death, isolated and almost friendless.
Reading: Peter Murray, *The Devil and Mr Duncan*, 1985; Jean Usher, *William Duncan of Metlakatla*, 1976.

DUNCAN DAM, located 42 km north of KASLO at the south end of Duncan Lk, was the first of 3 dams constructed by BC HYDRO as a result of the COLUMBIA R TREATY. Construction of the earth-filled water storage dam began in Sept 1964 and was completed by Aug 1967. The structure is 40 m high and extends 800 m across the Duncan R valley. The river flows south 10 km to KOOTENAY LK. *See also* HYDROELECTRICITY.

DUNLEVY, Peter Curran, prospector (b 21 Oct 1834, Pittsburgh, PA; d 15 Oct 1904, Soda Creek). He is credited with making the initial discovery that sparked the Cariboo GOLD RUSH. In the spring of 1859 he was among a party of prospectors looking for GOLD on the FRASER R when they met a SECWEPEMC (Shuswap) man named Baptiste. He led them to Little Horsefly Crk, where they found nuggets in great quantity. It was rumoured that the find was worth $1 million, and when word got out, another rush was on. Dunlevy invested his earnings in several roadhouses and a ranch and hotel at SODA CREEK, where he lived for many years. The Dunlevy Ranch was still in operation in the late 1990s.

DUNNE-ZA, formerly known to outsiders as the Beaver, are an ATHABASCAN-speaking FIRST NATIONS people living in the boreal forest of the PEACE R drainage in northeast BC and neighbouring Alberta. Dunne-za means "real people." At contact with Europeans they lived in nomadic hunting groups consisting of 2 or more related families. The group size was flexible, changing according to the availability of food supplies. Groups congregated during the year for socializing and ceremonies. Unlike most other northern hunters, the Dunne-za used horses. They depended for subsistence on fish and large game: MOOSE, wood bison, ELK, CARIBOU and DEER. They ate the meat of the animals and used the hides and bones for clothing, tenting and utensils. European trade goods began reaching the Dunne-za early in the 18th century through trade with neighbouring groups. Direct contact began with the establishment of trading posts on the upper Peace R by the NORTH WEST CO in the 1790s. At contact the population may have been 1,000 people but this number declined sharply due to disease and other factors, reaching a low of less than 300 people. The population recovered and by the late 1990s was estimated to be approximately what it was at contact. FUR TRADERS were followed by GOLD-seekers who passed through Dunne-za territory at the end of the 19th century on their way to the Klondike (*see* GOLD RUSHES). The encroachment of outsiders worried the Dunne-za; in the hopes of protecting their lands they signed TREATY NO 8, which the federal government negotiated with Peace R aboriginal groups between 1899 and 1910. The treaty created RESERVES where the people subsequently tended to congregate. With the construction of the ALASKA HWY and the development of the FOREST INDUSTRY and the OIL AND GAS INDUSTRY, the Dunne-za became involved in the wage economy, though trapping and hunting continued to be important. Communities include HALFWAY RIVER, PROPHET RIVER, DOIG RIVER and BLUEBERRY RIVER. Dunne-za have a complex spiritual life based on the solitary vision quest and the interpretation of dreams. Prophets are special dreamers who use their knowledge to advise the group.

DUNSMUIR, James, industrialist and politician, premier 15 June 1900–21 Nov 1902, lt gov 1906–09 (b 8 July 1851, Fort Vancouver, WA; d 6 June 1920, Cowichan). The son of the COAL mine operator Robert DUNSMUIR, he entered and

James Dunsmuir, premier of BC 1900–02, shown here in a portrait painted by Victor Albert Long in 1920. BC Archives PDP-02234

eventually took charge of the family business. Like his father he was a tyrannical employer who became identified with brutal labour practices, and his mines were considered the most dangerous in the world. He won election to the legislature in 1898. Two years later the lt gov named him PREMIER as the only person with enough support to form a government: at this politically unsettled time, party allegiance was weak and no leader commanded a strong following in the legislature. Dunsmuir's conservative, business-oriented administration was marked by continual squabbling, exacerbated by his leadership style, which was autocratic and intolerant of opposition. He was glad to step down after 2 turbulent years in office. After his brother Alexander's

death in 1900, he was involved in lawsuits with other family members over the will and the vast family fortune. In 1906 the issue was resolved in his favour, but he suffered much embarrassing publicity and a permanent rift with his mother Joan. Dunsmuir became LT GOV 26 May 1906. Once again he did not enjoy public office, and he retired before his full term expired. In 1910 he sold the family collieries to Donald Mann and William Mackenzie for $10 million, adding to his already substantial fortune. He lived in ostentatious splendour at HATLEY PARK, his 2.4 km² estate near VICTORIA.

DUNSMUIR, Robert, industrialist, politician (b 31 Aug 1825, Hurlford, Scotland; d 12 Apr 1889, Victoria). He arrived on VANCOUVER ISLAND in 1851 to work at the HBC COAL deposits at FORT RUPERT and later in NANAIMO. When his contract with the company expired he stayed on as a mine manager and became extremely wealthy with his own coal properties at WELLINGTON. During the 1880s he twice won election as an MLA from Nanaimo. In 1883 he contracted to build the ESQUIMALT & NANAIMO RWY, in return for a cash subsidy and land grants totalling a quarter of Vancouver Island. By this time he was the richest man in BC and also one of the most detested, primarily because of the ruthless labour practices at his mines. He built CRAIGDARROCH CASTLE as a monument to his wealth and power but died before it was completed. *See also* COAL MINING, VANCOUVER ISLAND; LABOUR MOVEMENT.

Robert Dunsmuir, Vancouver Island industrialist. BC Archives D-03608

DUNSTER, 225 km southeast of PRINCE GEORGE, has preserved one of the last GRAND TRUNK PACIFIC RWY stations on the lonely "East Line." SAWMILLS boosted the population to 200 in the 1920s; by the 1990s far fewer people lived here. AGRICULTURE, LOGGING and the CATTLE INDUSTRY are the main employers. The community straddles the upper FRASER R; a ferry operated between

1915 and 1921 until a bridge was built. It was named by a Grand Truck Pacific Rwy inspector after his hometown in England.

DUN-WATERS, James Cameron, gentleman farmer (b 28 Nov 1864, Torguay, England; d 24 Oct 1939, Fintry, Okanagan Lk). He was raised on his family's estate at Fintry in Scotland and became extremely wealthy through inheritance. He visited BC in 1908 on a hunting trip. Impressed by the north OKANAGAN VALLEY, he sold his British estate and bought a large plot of undeveloped ranchland on the northwest shore of OKANAGAN LK. He lived there from 1910 until his death, developing the estate, which he called Fintry, and replicating the life of a Scottish country squire (hence his nickname, the Laird of Fintry). In 1914, at age 50, he joined the Middlesex Yeomanry as a captain and saw action in Italy, Gallipoli and Africa. Back at his estate, Dun-Waters planted orchards, built a large manor house, imported Ayrshire cattle and indulged his twin passions—hunting and CURLING.

DURIEU, 60 km east of VANCOUVER north of the FRASER R, was an AGRICULTURAL community that grew up on fertile HATZIC prairie. Site of an early school and post office, it was named after Father Paul DURIEU, the pioneer OBLATE missionary who in 1869 took over ST MARY'S MISSION, 10 km to the south, and went on to become bishop of NEW WESTMINSTER. The Oblates encouraged French-speaking farmers from Quebec to move to this location in the late 1860s. *AS*

DURIEU, Paul, Roman Catholic missionary (b 4 Dec 1830, Saint-Pal-de-Mons, France; d 1 June 1899, New Westminster). He entered the order of the OBLATES OF MARY IMMACULATE in 1848 in France and was ordained a priest in 1854. Later that year he arrived in the Pacific Northwest to begin his missionary career in what is now Washington state; he remained there until 1859, when most of the Oblates moved north to their new headquarters at ESQUIMALT. After serving on VANCOUVER ISLAND and at SECHELT, KAMLOOPS and NEW WESTMINSTER, he became director of ST MARY'S MISSION in the FRASER VALLEY in 1867. While at St Mary's he translated the Bible into CHINOOK JARGON. He then rose through the hierarchy, becoming bishop of New Westminster and vicar apostolic of BC in 1890. He was famous for refining the so-called Durieu system, a strict system of social control aimed at Christianizing the aboriginals and eradicating most vestiges of their traditional culture. However, Durieu and other Oblates also encouraged temperance and education among the FIRST NATIONS and supported their claims for more land from the government (*see* ABORIGINAL RIGHTS).

DUTCH began arriving in Canada in significant numbers in the 1920s when the Canadian government, faced with a shortage of farm LABOUR, established a special program to encourage Dutch agriculturalists to emigrate. Most of the newcomers settled in Ontario but some made their way west to BC, and by 1926 there were sufficient Dutch living in the lower FRASER VALLEY to support the first Christian Reformed Church (*see* CONSERVATIVE PROTESTANTISM). In the 1930s a group of Noord-Dutch arrived in the province and settled in the Bulkley Valley, but generally during the Depression and the WWII era immigration was curtailed.

Beginning in the late 1940s a wave of Dutch immigrants came to Canada seeking to escape the disruption of post-WWII Europe. Entire families moved to the Fraser Valley under the "Netherlands Farm Families Movement." This migration was encouraged by the Dutch government, which was anxious to alleviate overcrowding in the homeland, and by a Canadian government wishing to provide farm labour (*see* AGRICULTURE). During this period PITT POLDER was reclaimed and settled by Dutch DAIRY FARMERS. These newcomers strengthened the Dutch Reform Church and established many private "Christian" schools for their youngsters (*see* EDUCATION, PRIVATE). By the 1960s Holland was experiencing economic prosperity and immigration decreased.

By the year 2000 the Dutch community in BC included people from a wide range of occupations, though agriculture continued to attract Dutch Canadians and their largest concentration in BC was in the agricultural areas of the lower Fraser Valley. Communities were also found in PRINCE GEORGE, on VANCOUVER ISLAND and in the OKANAGAN VALLEY. In 1996, 176,235 people in BC claimed Dutch heritage. Several associations serve the Dutch community and a Dutch newspaper and radio program are available to people living in the Lower Mainland. Prominent British Columbians of Dutch heritage include Bill VANDER ZALM, BC premier from 1986 to 1991, Dorothy Biersteker STEEVES, a leading CCF politician, Allard de Ridder, an early conductor of the VANCOUVER SYMPHONY ORCHESTRA, and the photographer John VANDERPANT.   *Dianne Mackay*

DUTHIE, Wilfred John "Bill," bookseller (b 8 Apr 1920, Weston, ON; d 7 Apr 1984, Vancouver). He came to VANCOUVER in 1952 and opened his first bookstore in 1957 at the corner of Hornby and Robson streets where, for many years, the legendary Binky Marks ran the paperback "cellar." Duthie expanded in 1962, opening a store on West 10th Ave (near UBC) that his brother David (1921–1998) managed for many years. Other stores followed, and by 1998 the chain, under the management of his daughter Celia since his death, numbered 10 outlets. Duthie was the most respected bookseller in the city; in his memory the Canadian Booksellers' Assoc sponsors an annual lecture to close the Vancouver International Writers (& Readers) Festival. The Booksellers' Choice award, one of

Bill Duthie, Vancouver bookseller, in his Robson Street store, 1977. Steve Bosch/Vancouver Sun

the annual BC BOOK PRIZES, is also named for him. By 1999, competition had forced the chain of Duthie's stores to the brink of bankruptcy; after restructuring, Duthie Books was reduced to a single store in the Kitsilano neighbourhood of Vancouver.

E

EAGLE is a large bird commonly seen soaring gracefully in the sky or perched high in a treetop searching out its prey. The eagle is extremely powerful, with a 2-m wingspan, curved talons and a hooked beak for tearing flesh. Eggs, which are laid in spring, take 35–45 days to hatch and the young are usually out of the nest by the end of Aug. Two eagle species occur in BC. The bald eagle (*Haliaeetus leucocephalus*) is distinguished by dark plumage and a prominent white head and tail. It builds its stick nest (the largest of any bird species in the world) high in a tree with a good view of the surrounding area. Bald eagles feed on water birds and fish and are seen mainly close to water, especially in winter when they

congregate at SALMON spawning rivers. Thousands of bald eagles can be seen between Nov and Feb at Harrison R and BRACKENDALE on the SQUAMISH R, among other locations. Two provincial reserves were created in 1996 in the Brackendale area to protect the eagles' habitat from LOGGING.

Golden eagles (*Aquila chrysaetos*) are brown in colour with tawny heads and legs feathered to the talons. They feed on meat and nest most frequently high on cliff ledges. They are most common in the Interior but since the 1950s have been seen more often on the South Coast. Golden eagles were once actively hunted by ranchers and farmers, who claimed they preyed on livestock, but they are no longer hunted and the population is stable.

EAGLE BAY, pop 500, is a resort and residential community on the south shore of SHUSWAP LK 26 km north of SALMON ARM. It is the site of a church summer camp. Swimming and picnicking are popular at nearby Shannon Beach. *AS*

EAGLE CREEK, 38 km northeast of 100 MILE HOUSE in the CARIBOO, is a small rural community on the northwest shore of CANIM LK. AGRICULTURE, TOURISM and the CATTLE INDUSTRY are important and there are many recreational properties in the area. WELLS GRAY PROVINCIAL PARK lies just to the east. A small provincial PARK is nearby. *AS*

EAGLE PASS (el 561 m) slices through the MONASHEE MTS 20 km west of REVELSTOKE. It was found by the surveyor Walter MOBERLY in 1865, when he noticed EAGLES flying through it, and the CPR used the pass in the 1880s as the route for its main line. The TRANS-CANADA HWY was also built through this pass.

EARLY CHILDHOOD EDUCATION; *see* CHILD CARE MOVEMENT.

Adult bald eagle. Duane Sept photo

EARTHQUAKES occur as a result of movement in the earth's crust. Pieces of the crust, called plates, float atop the earth's mantle, which is viscous and very slowly moving. This mantle carries the plates in various directions, and when they meet, plates slide past or over and under each other. Occasionally they lock, movement stops and pressure builds up. When at length the pressure is great enough to rupture the snag, shock waves are created that ripple through the rock, causing shaking and sometimes cracking on the earth's surface. This is an earthquake. When two plates move suddenly sideways along a break or fault, a strike-slip quake is the result. When plates move suddenly over and under each other, the result is a subduction quake. Earthquakes also occur along faults within plates, as well as at their boundaries. Shock waves can turn soil temporarily to liquid in a process called liquefaction, causing the ground to become jelly-like and structures to sink and collapse. For this reason, structures built on rock may survive earthquakes with less damage than those built on dirt. Seismic activity is greatest along the fault line where the rupture takes place, but seismic waves travel great distances and may cause damage hundreds of kilometres away.

The southwestern and northwestern corners of BC are both areas of high seismic activity. About 200 quakes a year are registered in the south, almost all too small to be felt, but there have been 9 magnitude 6–7 quakes (on the 10-point Richter scale) in this area and adjacent northern Washington during the past 130 years. The biggest quake to shake BC in recorded history occurred off the coast of the QUEEN CHARLOTTE ISLANDS in Aug 1949. It registered 8.1 on the Richter scale. A smaller 7.3 quake, the largest on-shore quake in Canadian history, occurred 3

Aftermath of the earthquake of 1946, near Courtenay.

SOME MAJOR EARTHQUAKES IN BC, ALASKA & WASHINGTON

DATE	LOCATION	RICHTER SCALE
1700	Northern Washington	9+
1872	Northern Washington	7+
1899	Alaska	8.3 & 8.6
1909	Gulf Islands	6
1910	Queen Charlotte Islands	6.8
1918	West Coast, Vancouver Island	7
1918	Revelstoke	6
1920	Gulf Islands	5.5
1929	South of Queen Charlotte Islands	7
1946	Courtenay	7.3
1949	Queen Charlotte Islands	8.1
1949	Puget Sound, Washington	7
1958	Alaska	7.9
1964	Alaska	8.6
1970	South of Queen Charlotte Islands	7.4
1972	West Coast, Vancouver Island	7.2
1976	Pender Island (Gulf Islands)	5.3

years earlier (23 June 1946) near COURTENAY on VANCOUVER ISLAND, causing one death and extensive property damage. Any tremor over 5 is large enough to do damage, depending on where it occurs. An 8.6 quake struck the coast of Alaska in Mar 1964, creating a huge TSUNAMI that surged up ALBERNI INLET and crashed into PORT ALBERNI. The most recent significant quake in the Lower Mainland occurred beneath PENDER ISLAND in 1976. It measured 5.3 but did only minor damage. Scientists believe that seismic pressure is now building beneath coastal BC toward a large quake that will occur sometime in the next 100 years.

BC is part of the North American plate that is moving slowly west at a speed of about 2 cm per year and is overriding the Juan de Fuca plate beneath the ocean bottom. The line of contact is called the CASCADIA subduction zone. It stretches all the way to California and it is along this line that the largest quake is expected, perhaps the equal of the force 9 quake believed to have struck the west coast of Vancouver Island in the early 1700s. However, before this happens the area will probably experience a smaller but still very damaging quake on a fault that cuts across the North American plate. During the past few years efforts have been made to upgrade bridges, dams and public buildings in an attempt to minimize potential earthquake damage. Regardless, a major quake is expected to cause billions of dollars' worth of damage and perhaps claim many lives. When "The Big One" comes, it could likely be the worst natural disaster in Canadian history. *See also* PHYSICAL GEOGRAPHY.

EAST PINE, is a small ranching (*see* CATTLE INDUSTRY) settlement 63 km west of DAWSON CREEK, in the foothills of the ROCKY MTS in the PEACE R district. It is situated in a terraced valley near the confluence of the Murray and Pine rivers and is on the HART HWY and the BC RAIL line. East Pine Provincial PARK is located here. The Pine R is a tributary of the Peace. AS

EASTERN BC RAILWAY was built in 1908 by Daniel Corbin, a US railway promoter, to link his new COAL mine in the CROWSNEST PASS area to the CPR line. The mine closed in 1935 and the track was ripped up in 1939.

EASTHOPE BROTHERS manufactured boat engines on the coast for 7 decades. Ernest Easthope and his family immigrated to NEW WESTMINSTER from England in 1889. He and his son Vincent began making primitive 2-cycle gas engines with make-and-break ignition in 1900.

TECTONIC SETTING OF COASTAL BC

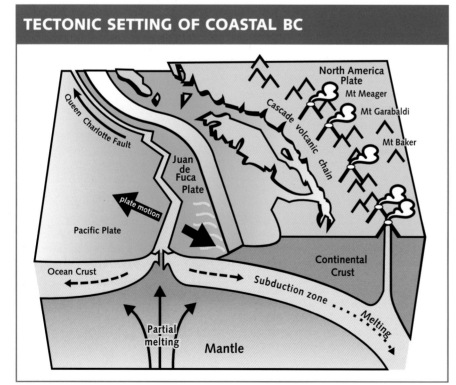

Kim LaFave illustration

The Easthope Standard, the engine that powered coastal fishing fleets into the 1950s.
Courtesy Joe Holmes

The Easthope 2-cycle ran rough and was unreliable, but it was popular because it offered fishers the first available and affordable means of powering their gillnet skiffs. The original company, Easthope and Son, got into financial trouble and was sold in about 1910, but 2 other sons, George and Percy ("Peck"), started up again as Easthope Brothers, this time using a smoother-running, more reliable 4-cycle design. Heavy-duty, slow-turning and simple to repair, this series of engines with their distinctive putt-putt sound became ubiquitous on the coast. Nicknamed "Last Hope" and "Jesus, Light of the World" (after a slogan the evangelical brothers used in advertisements), the humble engine became a maritime legend in BC during the company's heyday through to the 1950s. By the 1960s, however, high-speed engines from American manufacturers were taking over the market. Easthope made its last engine in 1968. *See also* FISHING, COMMERCIAL.

Howard White

ECOFORESTRY, or ecosystem-based forestry, refers to a system of FOREST planning and management that leaves forest ecosystems intact and fully functioning. Some basic principles of ecoforestry are: retain the diversity of plants, animals and microorganisms; retain many of the oldest and tallest trees; let the forest reseed itself naturally; protect snags and fallen trees; prohibit slash burning and chemicals (fertilizers, pesticides, herbicides); prohibit clearcutting; use low-impact LOGGING systems; minimize road building; protect watercourses, shorelines and other ecologically sensitive sites; leave organic debris to preserve topsoil; manage for the many non-timber products in the forest, not just logs; and protect the non-monetary forest values (aesthetic, spiritual, genetic, recreational, wilderness) as much as the marketable FOREST PRODUCTS. Ecoforestry also tends to be labour-intensive and locally based in contrast to industrial forestry, which is capital-intensive and corporate-based.

Ecoforestry has been practised by a few woodlot owners in BC and elsewhere for decades, and earlier by many FIRST NATIONS cultures that took what they needed from the forest without disrupting the ecosystem. In the 1990s the argument for ecoforestry gained considerable prominence in BC in response to dwindling jobs in the forest sector and increasing public opposition to the industrial practice of clearcut logging. Consumer pressure for ecologically harvested forest products has led to the related development of forest certification, in which logging operations using ecoforestry practices can seek eco-certification from a recognized certifier. BC's first eco-certified forest, a 6.7 km² woodlot east of WILLIAMS LAKE, was announced in Mar 1999 by Herb Hammond, an ecoforester and certifier, of the Silva Forest Foundation in SLOCAN PARK. Other prominent practitioners and advocates of ecoforestry in BC include Merv Wilkinson, who has applied ecoforestry techniques to his VANCOUVER ISLAND woodlot since 1945, and the Victoria-based Ecoforestry Institute Society of Canada, which publishes the journal *Ecoforestry*. *See also* ENVIRONMENTAL MOVEMENT; FOREST INDUSTRY.

Kim Goldberg

Reading: Alan Drengson and Duncan Taylor, eds, *The Art & Science of Sustainable Forest Use*, 1997.

ECONOMY OF BC

Overview

John M. Munro

The 1999 population of BC is estimated to be just over 4 million people. At the time of CONFEDERATION in 1871, the population was about 36,000, including the First Nations (*see* ABORIGINAL DEMOGRAPHY; PEOPLES OF BC). Getting from then to the present has involved economic development on a large and continuous scale.

The Gold Rush to the Modern Era
Before the GOLD RUSHES that began in 1858, the small European population of BC was located at a few fur-trading posts, the largest of which was FORT VICTORIA. The gold rushes brought relatively large, but short-lived, population increases to southwestern BC and to the CARIBOO. When the first comprehensive census was taken in 1881, about one-half of BC's population lived in the Lower Mainland and VANCOUVER ISLAND, with another 20% in the southern Interior and 30% elsewhere. The regional distribution of the population fluctuated considerably between 1881 and 1911, but by the outbreak of WWI the current distribution of about 70% on the Southwest Coast, 20% in the southern Interior and less than 10% in the rest of the province had been established.

The aboriginal economy, prior to contact with Europeans, was based on the use and exchange of products from the natural environment. While it is impossible to calculate the total product of this economy, it is noteworthy that the highest aboriginal population density in the Americas north of Mexico was along the Northwest Coast. Interior FIRST NATIONS populations in BC were smaller, reflecting the less abundant resource base found there. Once Europeans began arriving, the initial economic activity was the FUR TRADE. European interest in exchanging manufactured products for furs, matched by the First Nations' interest in acquiring new products through the processes of commodity exchange, brought the modern commercial economy to BC. Since fur production was antithetical to extensive settlement, there was little development of BC so long as it was a protected preserve

SELECTED ECONOMIC STATISTICS FOR BC 1986–96

	Units	1986	1991	1996
Gross domestic product (GDP)	$millions	55,527	81,453	103,631
Personal income	$millions	48,876	74,947	91,970
Capital investment	$millions	9,576	17,216	18,571
Business incorporations	number	17,064	18,528	23,237
Labour force	thousands	1,548	1,762	1,982
Employment	thousands	1,354	1,585	1,806
Unemployment rate	percent	12.5	10.0	8.9
Average weekly earnings	$	440.43	531.80	607.54
Wages & salaries	$millions	27,288	41,132	51,126
Manufacturing shipments	$millions	20,240	23,259	32,916
Retail sales	$millions	17,416	23,537	31,252
Housing starts	number	20,687	31,875	27,641
Non-residential building permits	$millions	912	1,803	1,957
BC product exports	$millions	13,179	15,215	25,199
Electric power generated	GW.h	50,759	62,981	70,733

BC HOUSEHOLD INCOME 1996

Under $10,000	105,370	7.4%
$10,000-$19,999	213,660	15.0%
$20,000-$29,999	184,390	12.9%
$30,000-$39,999	171,145	12.0%
$40,000-$49,999	156,925	11.0%
$50,000-$59,999	141,030	9.9%
$60,000-$69,999	116,335	8.2%
$70,000-$79,999	91,695	6.4%
$80,000-$89,999	68,210	4.8%
$90,000-$99,999	48,385	3.4%
$100,000 and over	127,480	9.0%
Total private households	1,424,625	100.0%
Average household income ($)50,667		
Median household income ($)42,160		

of the HUDSON'S BAY CO, which it was until the gold rush of 1858 changed BC forever.

The story of the FRASER R and Cariboo gold rushes is familiar. Fortuitously timed to catch a lull in the much richer and larger California gold rush, the discovery of significant quantities of gold along the Fraser caused a huge increase in population within a few months. The newcomers had little intention of remaining, and few of the more than 20,000 would-be miners who poured into BC in the summer of 1858 saw beyond their own personal fortune-hunting. Yet the gold rush did leave behind a political structure and a sense of great economic potential that had been absent to that time. This potential was slow to be realized. The end of the gold rush and the continuing decimation of aboriginal populations by epidemic disease brought a decline in economic activity. Yet the economy was more diverse than before. Commercial salmon FISHING, AGRICULTURE and lumber production for export all began in the 1860s and early 1870s (see SALMON CANNING; LOGGING; SAWMILLING). These industries, along with base metal and coal MINING, boomed in the 30 years before WWI. Tens of thousands of people migrated to BC each year as the population grew from 49,000 in 1881 to almost 400,000 in 1911. Annual rates of population growth averaged over 6% for this period. Large inflows of investment capital from the US and the UK accompanied the interest of entrepreneurs from those countries in developing the province's natural wealth.

Normal economic life returned after the war, but it was a different normalcy than had existed before 1914. BC never again received the enthusiastic attention of British investors. The economy's growth slowed and annual population growth dropped to an average of less than 3% in the 1920s and less than 2% in the 1930s. The Great Depression was felt intensely because of its negative effect on export markets, but people in other Canadian provinces still decided to move to BC. The main structural elements of the economy remained the same—between 30% and 40% of provincial output consisted of primary and manufactured resource products destined for markets

outside the province. Within this group, the FOREST INDUSTRY continued to garner an increasing share of exports.

WWII caused a sudden burst of diversification in the manufacturing sector because of the creation and expansion of factories to build war products. After the war the world economy behaved very differently than it had following WWI, and the differences were important for BC. Demands for resource products surged as the world economic environment focussed on rebuilding war-damaged countries and took a more internationalist perspective on trade and investment. In the 1940s and 1950s BC's population grew by an average of almost 3.5% annually, and while it was a slower rate of growth than earlier in the century, the base for the growth was larger. New government policies encouraged use of the province's FOREST resources and large investments in various resource industries resulted. Typical were the expansion of PULP AND PAPER manufacturing and the ALCAN ALUMINUM project built at KITIMAT during 1951–54. And just as another resource boom was underway, the growing size and prosperity of the economy encouraged the development of the service sector as consumer and government services expanded rapidly. Total output growth in the services was over 5 times as large in the 1950s as growth in the resource-dominated goods sector.

1960 to the Present

As the 20th century drew to a close, most British Columbians seemed to believe that good economic times had ended some years earlier. They were correct: the postwar boom ended around 1980. The recession of the early 1980s was deep and prolonged in BC. It took until 1985 for Gross Domestic Product to recover its 1981 level, and the rate of population growth during the 1980s was second-lowest to the 1930s. Yet this slowdown needs to be viewed in context with the rapid development of the resource industries that had preceded it, an expansion that was bound to end as world markets began to be served by competing suppliers and the environmental and social consequences of continued rapid economic growth became problematic.

BC now has over 25 times the population and 90 times the real output of 100 years ago, a considerable economic achievement by any standard. Yet as the century turned, uncertainty about future prospects for the economy was rampant and the need for restructuring almost an article of faith. Of course, the economy was already restructuring itself as the resource industries steadily lost their share of total output and employment while new economic activity in TOURISM and technology flourished. Neither of these sectors was as important as the resource industries, but both grew rapidly in the last 2 decades of the century. Importantly, in an era of environmental consciousness, both promise less impact on a natural environment perceived by many British Columbians to be more and more at risk (see ENVIRONMENTAL MOVEMENT). Also, both match the expectations of the large number of immigrants who have come from Asia to the Lower Mainland in the last 15 years expecting good urban employment opportunities. Increasingly, the attention of policy-makers in both the private sector and government will be directed away from the industries that have played such a large role in shaping BC.

BC MANUFACTURING REVENUES

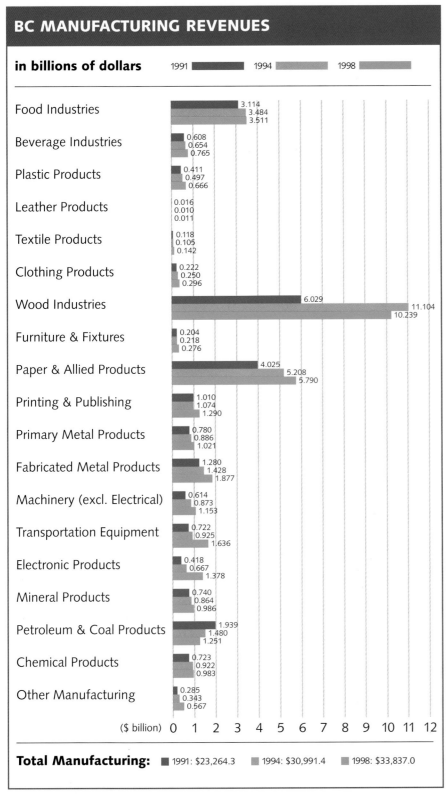

in billings of dollars   1991 ▮   1994 ▮   1998 ▮

Industry	1991	1994	1998
Food Industries	3.114	3.484	3.511
Beverage Industries	0.608	0.654	0.765
Plastic Products	0.411	0.497	0.666
Leather Products	0.016	0.010	0.011
Textile Products	0.118	0.105	0.142
Clothing Products	0.222	0.250	0.296
Wood Industries	6.029	11.104	10.239
Furniture & Fixtures	0.204	0.218	0.276
Paper & Allied Products	4.025	5.208	5.790
Printing & Publishing	1.010	1.074	1.290
Primary Metal Products	0.780	0.886	1.021
Fabricated Metal Products	1.280	1.428	1.877
Machinery (excl. Electrical)	0.614	0.873	1.153
Transportation Equipment	0.722	0.925	1.636
Electronic Products	0.418	0.667	1.378
Mineral Products	0.740	0.864	0.986
Petroleum & Coal Products	1.939	1.480	1.251
Chemical Products	0.723	0.922	0.983
Other Manufacturing	0.285	0.343	0.567

($ billion) 0 1 2 3 4 5 6 7 8 9 10 11 12

Total Manufacturing: ▮ 1991: $23,264.3   ▮ 1994: $30,991.4   ▮ 1998: $33,837.0

Together, these industries directly employed almost 10% of BC's labour force in 2000, and still accounted for almost 80% of exports to other countries.

BC has 5 important industries based on its natural resource endowment: forestry, agriculture, mining, energy and fishing. Arguably, two other industries also rely on the natural environment: tourism and the footloose HIGH-TECHNOLOGY industries, whose success seems to rely on attracting and retaining highly skilled employees whose decisions about where to live are influenced by the quality of the natural environment. The forest industry indirectly employed just over 100,000 people in 1997, not far off its historic peak a few years earlier. However, the industry's share of total employment has been falling for decades and during the 1990s declined from 6.5% to 5.5%. Its share of total provincial GDP has shown a similar downward trend. The timber harvest peaked in 1989 and by 1999 was almost 30% below that peak. The reduction is partly the result of new land-use priorities that reserve a larger part of the forest for non-timber use such as PARKS, and partly the natural effect of having logged mature forests before the replacement second-growth forest was ready for harvest. The decline in this industry is not just cyclical; it represents a long-term trend. Nonetheless, forestry is still BC's most important industry and it is especially important in dozens of forest-based communities. Its impact on employment and output across the whole economy is made larger through indirect employment and output that are dependent on harvesting and processing timber. This indirect employment may be twice as large as the forest industry's direct employment. Government policy is of immense importance to the industry given that most forest land is Crown-owned.

Agriculture in BC is diverse and scattered across much of the province. Specialization in different regions reflects differences in climate and soils. Of the total $1.8 billion in farm cash receipts in 1997, about $1 billion was from animal products (split about evenly between DAIRY, eggs and poultry, and livestock) and about $800 million in crops, led by floral and nursery products. TREE FRUITS account for less than 10% of total crop receipts as new crops such as GINSENG are introduced. Economists do not include illegal activities in

BC's economic dependence on the resource industries has been declining for decades. This process is not unusual—it has happened in many regional economies in N America—and it need not be viewed with alarm. Nevertheless, the path of this adjustment is not smooth and its effects are felt unevenly across communities and labour groups. That said, the traditional resource industries are not at the disappearing point and will be influential in the provincial economy for many years to come.

BC EXPORTS 1989–98 & IMPORTS 1998 ($ millions)

	1989 Exports	% of Total	1998 Exports	% of Total	1998 Imports	% of Total
United States	7,815	42.6	16,406	63.0	12,509	48.7
Japan	5,094	27.8	4,532	17.4	4,997	19.4
United Kingdom	789	4.3	303	1.2	236	0.9
South Korea	682	3.7	678	2.6	820	3.2
Germany	576	3.1	395	1.5	310	1.2
Australia	359	2.0	226	0.9	319	1.2
Taiwan	325	1.8	399	1.5	667	2.6
China	218	1.2	465	1.8	1,892	7.4
Hong Kong	116	0.6	270	1.0	242	0.9
India	44	0.2	85	0.3	202	0.8
Mexico	32	0.2	60	0.2	351	1.4
Other	2,285	12.5	2,242	8.6	3,166	12.3
Total	18,335	100.0	26,061	100.0	25,711	100.0
Summary:						
Pacific Rim	7,156	39.0	6,952	26.7	—	—
Western Europe	2,843	15.5	2,041	7.8	—	—
South America	155	0.8	224	0.9	—	—
Africa & Middle East	177	1.0	200	0.8	—	—
All other regions	8,003	43.7	16,645	63.8	—	—

their calculations but media reports suggest that cultivation of illegal drugs may be larger in terms of market value of output than all other crops (*see* MARIJUANA).

After the fur trade, mining was BC's first basic industry. BC has a very diverse geological profile and, while some of the province is not highly mineralized, much of it is, and a wide variety of minerals have been exploited. COAL has been mined in BC since the 1850s and in the late 1990s the industry in the E KOOTENAY and the PEACE R district was larger than ever before. Gold was another big mineral discovery in the 1850s and was soon followed by SILVER, COPPER, lead, ZINC and several other metals. The industry is heavily influenced by world prices and by the perceived advantages of mining in BC as compared to mining elsewhere. Since most of BC's deposits of metallic minerals are low-grade, economic mining has to be based on large-scale operations and efficient mining and preparation of concentrates. Markets for mineral concentrates are now centred in E Asia. Mining in BC in recent years has not been associated with a SMELTER industry producing metals from concentrates. There are only 2 smelter operations (Kitimat and TRAIL), and only the Trail smelter processes concentrates from BC mines (*see* COMINCO). Periodically suggestions are made that the HYDROELECTRIC resources that brought the aluminum smelter to Kitimat should be exploited to bring other metal smelters to the province, but environmental concerns about the building of new power dams and the pollution associated with metal smelting have so far prevailed over these proposals.

BC is a significant producer and exporter of electricity and of natural gas (*see* OIL AND GAS INDUSTRY). Major hydroelectric dams have been built on the Peace and COLUMBIA rivers, and the province is connected to a comprehensive electric grid. Natural gas is available as a domestic, commercial and industrial fuel in most places in BC and has become an important export. While BC does produce petroleum, consumption is far larger than can be supplied from BC oil wells. Two potential energy-related activities are currently prohibited by government policy: the offshore exploration for petroleum and natural gas and the mining of uranium.

Fur trapping aside, the smallest natural resource industry is fishing. This fact surprises many people because of the amount of media attention paid to the SALMON fishery, but the interest in this industry follows from its historical and cultural significance, not its economic importance. The salmon fishery used to be more important, but changing habitat and poor management of this complex and sensitive natural resource necessitated closure of many fishing opportunities and curtailment of others. There are, however, many other fisheries which are not being utilized at their potential and the future of FISH production and processing in BC may well lie with these or with AQUACULTURE, both shellfish and fin fish.

In BC, as in other advanced economies, about 80% of the economy is in the service sector. The production of goods has declined partly as a result of statistical classifications that bias these calculations against the goods-producing sector as companies contract for business and professional services that were previously provided in-house, but the major impetus for the increased service sector share comes from rising consumer demand for such services as education, financial services, HEALTH care and travel. The 7 largest service industries in BC are, in order of direct employment, retail trade, health and welfare, accommodation and food, education, wholesale trade, government administration, and transportation. Together they account for 43% of total employment. Much of this employment is driven by purchases or consumer spending from what economists call "basic" (export) industries. Retail trade employment in particular communities depends in large measure on employment and output in a community's export industries. When the pulp mill closes, for example, retail business shuts down in its wake and jobs are lost. Service industries can be basic industries in their own right. Successive BC governments have sought to promote service-type economic activity that can be a successful export as the province experiences the transition away from reliance on natural resource commodities and products. For example, spending by a family on vacation from outside BC is just as much an export as a carload of lumber sold in Chicago. Tourism, which is split between about 30% spending by British Columbians on vacation in the province and 70% spending by visitors from elsewhere, is a large industry in BC, directly accounting for about two-thirds as much GDP as the forest industry. Other efforts to find an export base in the service sector have centred on financial services and the high-technology sector. While the statistical FIRE ("finance, insurance and real estate") classification is the largest single sector in provincial GDP, its employment share of about 5% is a more useful measure of its importance. Also, despite efforts to make VANCOUVER an "international financial centre," Canada already has one (Toronto) and the emergence of a second will be a slow process. As of the year 2000, most economic activity in the FIRE sector is directed at the provincial economy, not on export markets. BC's exports of transportation services, such as those provided by the PORT OF VANCOUVER, are 4 times larger than its exports of financial services. High technology, which involves the application of knowledge-intensive processes to the production of goods or the delivery of services, may offer more potential. Computers are an important sign of high technology, but not all high tech is based on computers; BIOTECHNOLOGY and pharmaceuticals are counter-examples. BC's interest in promoting this sector is shared by every other jurisdiction in N America, however. Everyone would like to have BC's low pollution, high wages and growth potential. Our neighbours to the south in California, Oregon and Washington have been much more successful than BC in developing this sector, but the attraction of natural and civic amenities which have been important there should be within the reach of BC. As the century ended, high tech was about half the size of tourism, but its recent growth was much faster.

In BC, preoccupation with government politics and policies often seem to swamp consideration of the economy. Government is important: total spending by all 3 levels of government accounts directly for about 25% of GDP; government directly accounts for 5% of provincial employment; and taxation and general policies are important across all other sectors,

particularly for the resource sector. Nevertheless, many major influences on provincial economic activity are beyond the purview of the 3 levels of government. The largest and most important level is provincial: federal government policies are rarely determined with an eye to their effects on BC (our 13% share of Canada's population ensures that) and many municipal government policy areas are strongly influenced, if not controlled, by provincial decisions. In the provincial economic accounts, government appears in 3 categories: health and welfare, education and government services. Spending on health has been growing more rapidly than population, while spending on education has matched increases in population and government services spending has, at least since 1993, been decreasing in relation to population (*see also* EDUCATION, PUBLIC). Government is also important through the provincial government's role as the owner of CROWN CORPS. There are dozens of provincially owned Crown corps, and annual revenues of the 8 largest totalled about $10 billion in 1998. Debt of Crown corps

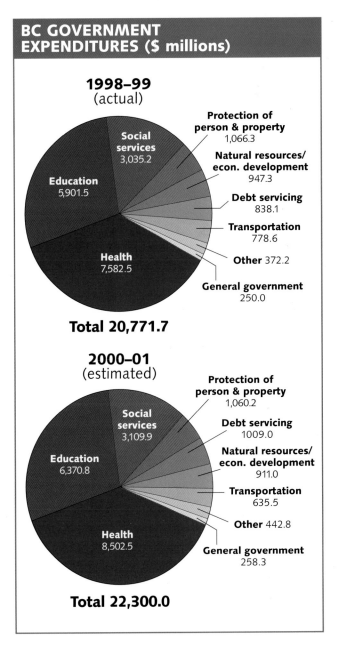

BC GOVERNMENT EXPENDITURES ($ millions)

1998–99 (actual)

- Social services 3,035.2
- Education 5,901.5
- Health 7,582.5
- Protection of person & property 1,066.3
- Natural resources/econ. development 947.3
- Debt servicing 838.1
- Transportation 778.6
- Other 372.2
- General government 250.0

Total 20,771.7

2000–01 (estimated)

- Social services 3,109.9
- Education 6,370.8
- Health 8,502.5
- Protection of person & property 1,060.2
- Debt servicing 1009.0
- Natural resources/econ. development 911.0
- Transportation 635.5
- Other 442.8
- General government 258.3

Total 22,300.0

THE TOP 20 PRIVATE AND PUBLICLY TRADED CORPORATIONS WITH HEAD OFFICES IN BC (1999 figures)

Company	Industry	Revenue ($ millions)	Net Income ($ millions)	Assets ($ millions)	Employees (in BC)
WESTCOAST ENERGY INC	energy	6,265	267.0	11,777	1,447
TELUS COMMUNICATIONS	telecomm	5,872	349.7	7,811	12,992
Jim PATTISON Group	holding co	4,600	n/a	2,900	13,100
H.Y. Louie	wholesale	2,500	n/a	n/a	n/a
FINNING INTERNATIONAL INC	equipment	2,230	59.6	2,026	1,450
WEST FRASER TIMBER CO LTD	forestry	2,204	147.4	2,265	7,805
FUTURE SHOP	retail	1,960	-82.2	339	n/a
HSBC Bank Canada	financial	1,877	165.0	25,100	2,600
CANADIAN FOREST PRODUCTS LTD	forestry	1,750	102.6	2,348	5,200
Placer Dome	mining	1,726	52.0	4,842	150
COMINCO	mining	1,645	159.0	2,964	2,497
WESTERN STAR TRUCKS	vehicles	1,356	29.8	817	1,390
Agri Foods International	dairy co-op	1,209	n/a	n/a	n/a
WEYERHAEUSER CANADA	forestry	1,192	n/a	3,636	5,524
Chevron Canada	petroleum	1,159	n/a	353	362
WELDWOOD OF CANADA LTD	forestry	1,088	91.2	1,213	3,200
SLOCAN FOREST PRODUCTS LTD	forestry	1,086	108.4	789	4,000
FLETCHER CHALLENGE CANADA	forestry	1,047	37.5	2,526	2,696
BC GAS	energy	1,041	81.2	2,451	1,869
METHANEX CORP	chemicals	1,033	-222.8	2,443	207

n/a: (not available for some private corporations)
(source: BC Business; figures compiled by PriceWaterhouseCoopers)

and similar agencies used to finance investment in ROADS AND HIGHWAYS and public buildings amounted in 1998 to about two-thirds of the total provincial debt of $32 billion.

The role of the federal government includes policy responsibility for areas of direct provincial interest, such as oceans and ocean fisheries, areas such as defence and foreign affairs in which British Columbians share a common interest with other Canadians, and TRANSFER PAYMENTS to individuals, such as old age security and employment insurance. In 1997 transfers to the provincial government through the Canada Health and Social Transfer (*see* HEALTH POLICY) returned to the provincial government about $1.6 billion of the $19 billion in federal revenues collected in BC.

Conclusion

As the 20th century ended, popular conversation about the BC economy usually focussed on the difficulty of present economic times. It seemed many years since British Columbians exuded much optimism or satisfaction with the way the economy was functioning. Yet over the long sweep of history, the economy is much better than it was. Not only is it larger in absolute terms (simple evidence is the quadrupling through migration of BC's population in barely 50 years), but the spending power of per capita income has grown even faster: the "average" British Columbian has 2.5 times as much to spend as he or she would have had in 1948. Admittedly, during the 1990s this economic progress stalled. Many wondered whether the province had reached the limits of desirable or sustainable economic growth. Others blamed the slowdown on misguided government policies, or temporary economic setbacks in the economies of overseas trading partners. Certainly the provincial economy has been experiencing a restructuring. Whether or not that process will result in a return to stable, sustainable economic growth, the 21st century will reveal.

Readings: Ministry of Finance and Corporate Affairs, *British Columbia Financial and Economic Review,* published annually.

ECOLOGICAL RESERVES are generally small marine or terrestrial areas of the province designated for protection because of their representative, unique or vulnerable species or ecosystems. While most are open to the public for non-consumptive uses, they are not created for outdoor recreation; their primary functions are for research, conservation and education. They are intended to preserve rare, unique or ENDANGERED SPECIES, ecosystems or natural phenomena. In some cases, permits must be obtained before exploring them. The first 29 reserves were established under the *Ecological Reserves Act* in May 1971, and the number had climbed to 141 reserves by late 1999. BC was the first jurisdiction in Canada to establish an ecological reserves program and in the year 2000 continued to have the largest such program in North America.

ECONOMY OF BC; *see* essay on p. 193.

ECOOLE, 37 km southwest of PORT ALBERNI on VANCOUVER ISLAND, is a former NUU-CHAH-NULTH (Nootka) village site and FISHING settlement on the southeast side of Seddall Island near the head of BARKLEY SOUND. The name can be translated as "bushes on hill." A trading post was established here in the 1850s. BC PACKERS had a pilchard reduction plant here in the 1920s and 1930s, but the site was later abandoned. *AS*

ECOREGION CLASSIFICATION SYSTEM was developed by Dennis Demarchi and adopted by the BC Wildlife Branch of the Ministry of Environment in 1985 as a framework for systematic descriptions of ecosystems in BC. The classification is based on CLIMATE and landforms and is used to stratify the complexities of our terrestrial and marine ecosystems into discrete geographical units at 5 levels: ecodomain, ecodivision (both of which are very broad and place BC globally), ecoprovinces, ecoregions and ecosections (which are progressively more detailed and narrow in scope). They describe areas of similar climate, physiography, oceanography, hydrology, vegetation and wildlife potential. As an indication of the tremendous diversity in the province, there are only 4 ecodomains in North America, all of which occur in BC (Cool Oceanic, Humid Temperate, Dry and Polar). The province has 7 ecodivisions, 10 ecoprovinces, 46 ecoregions and 116 ecosections. The Ecoregion Classification System is used jointly with the BIOGEOCLIMATIC ZONE classification system at the ecoregion and ecosection levels to further describe smaller-scale sites. Together they are powerful tools that help describe the diversity of BC.

Ecodivisions of BC
Sub-Arctic Pacific
Northeast Pacific
Humid Maritime and Highland
Coast and Mountains
Georgia Depression
Humid Continental Highlands
Central Interior

Ecoprovinces
Sub-Boreal Interior
Southern Interior Mountains
Semi-Arid Steppe
Southern Interior
Boreal
Boreal Plains
Sub-Arctic
Taiga Plains
Sub-Arctic Highlands
Northern Boreal Mountains

Maggie Paquet

Reading: Dennis A. Demarchi, *An Introduction to the Ecoregions of British Columbia*, 1996.

ECSTALL RIVER empties into the SKEENA R from the south, not far from its mouth. It drains a lushly forested 840 km² watershed and supports major runs of SALMON. PORT ESSINGTON, once a booming cannery town, sat at its confluence with the Skeena. *See also* RIVERS; SALMON CANNING.

Aerial view of the Ecstall R, the largest intact unprotected coastal watershed in BC.
Ian McAllister photo

EDDY was a LOGGING and farming (*see* AGRICULTURE) settlement and former CNR station southwest of MCBRIDE on the upper FRASER R. G.U. Ryley, land commissioner for the GRAND TRUNK PACIFIC RWY, named it in 1910 for a natural feature of the river. In 1999 Eddy had only 2 households. *AS*

EDENSHAW, Charles (Tahaygen), artist and Haida chief (b circa 1839, Skidegate; d 12 Sept 1920, Masset). He was one of the first professional HAIDA artists, an innovator with a distinctive style that set him apart from his contemporaries. He lived for many years at villages on the northern end of the QUEEN CHARLOTTE ISLANDS (Haida Gwaii), then moved to MASSET in 1882, where he was baptized and chose his English name. He learned to carve from his uncle Albert Edward Edenshaw (circa 1815–94), a prominent Sta'stas Eagle clan chief, and produced works in precious metals, wood and especially ARGILLITE. He painted many articles woven by his wife Isabella (1858–1926), a renowned basket maker. Edenshaw also worked with numerous anthropologists and collectors and was considered an important authority on Haida language and culture. *See also* ART, NORTHWEST COAST ABORIGINAL; FIRST NATIONS LANGUAGES.

EDGEWATER, pop 518, next to the COLUMBIA R in the Columbia Valley near KOOTENAY NATIONAL PARK, 93 km south of GOLDEN, was founded pre-WWI as a farm community. During the war many of the settlers returned to England and the community floundered, but it revived in the 1920s and now relies on AGRICULTURE and the FOREST INDUSTRY.

EDGEWOOD, 62 km northwest of CASTLEGAR, was a sternwheeler (*see* PADDLEWHEEL STEAMBOATS) landing on the west side of Lower ARROW LK south of NEEDLES, until the CPR abandoned the route in 1954. The village was re-established on higher ground in the mid-1960s when the KEENLEYSIDE DAM was built. AGRICULTURE, LOGGING and MINING are all important to the local economy. *AS*

EDMONDS, Henry Valentine, land speculator, government official (b 14 Feb 1837, Dublin, Ireland; d 14 June 1897, Vancouver). After arriving in BC in 1862 he plunged into a variety of business ventures in and around NEW WESTMINSTER. In 1867 he was appointed deputy sheriff, the first of a series of government positions he held, including GOLD commissioner and justice of the peace. In 1883 he became mayor of New Westminster. Meanwhile he speculated in real estate—he was the original developer of the Mt Pleasant district of VANCOUVER—and promoted railway development, mainly as a means of raising the value of his property. He was one of the principals behind the Westminster and Vancouver Tramway Co, which opened an INTERURBAN electric railway between the 2 cities—the first in N America—in 1891. When the Interurban went bankrupt he lost most of his money; 2 years later he died.

EDUCATION, POST-SECONDARY began in the 1890s, when local schools affiliated with eastern universities to offer courses toward a degree. In 1892 the METHODIST CHURCH opened Columbian College in NEW WESTMINSTER. It was affiliated with Univ of Toronto and was the first institution to turn out university graduates in BC. In 1898 Vancouver High School began offering first-year university courses in affiliation with McGill Univ, as did Victoria High School in 1903. In VANCOUVER the relationship was formalized as McGill Univ College, which moved into separate buildings in 1912. In 1915 it changed its name to the UNIVERSITY OF BC, which moved to its present site in Point Grey in 1925. With the opening of UBC in 1915, Victoria College closed, but it reopened in 1920 as an affiliate of the provincial university. This was the extent of post-secondary education in BC until the 1960s, when there was a sudden expansion of facilities, including a system of COMMUNITY COLLEGES, the creation of the UNIV OF VICTORIA (1963) and NOTRE DAME UNIV OF NELSON (1963), and the construction of SIMON FRASER UNIV in BURNABY (1965). Another flurry of university openings began in 1985 with the elevation of TRINITY WESTERN to university status, followed by the upgrading of several 2-year community colleges to 4-year degree-granting institutions, the

Royal Roads University, 1998.

opening of the UNIV OF NORTHERN BC in PRINCE GEORGE in 1994 and the transformation of the military college at ROYAL ROADS into a public university in 1996. Other post-secondary educational opportunities are provided by the OPEN LEARNING AGENCY, the BC INSTITUTE OF TECHNOLOGY, the EMILY CARR INSTITUTE OF ART & DESIGN and the TECHNICAL UNIV OF BC. In 1997–98 there were about 150,000 students enrolled in BC's post-secondary educational institutions. Of these, 72,389 were enrolled at one of the 6 universities, either full- or part-time. In total, 23% of BC residents aged 18–24 attended a university, college or technical program full-time, well below the national average of 35% and the lowest of any province.

EDUCATION, PRIVATE, dates back to colonial times when the HBC and different religious denominations opened the first schools in BC. The demand for education that came with the growth of the European population was met mainly by a system of public schools established by the provincial government (*see* EDUCATION, PUBLIC), but there has also been a parallel network of private schools, both religious and non-sectarian, supporting themselves through fees paid by students. The ROMAN CATHOLIC CHURCH has been particularly active. Among the first schools in the colony were the ones established by the SISTERS OF ST ANN in VICTORIA and NEW WESTMINSTER. Their original schoolhouse, dating to 1858, is now the oldest building in Victoria. Early Anglican schools included Collegiate School for boys and Angela College for girls, both in Victoria. These particular schools did not survive the turn of the century, but religious schools continued to offer a parochial education for a significant minority of the province's children. By 1960, for example, there were about 65 Catholic schools in BC.

A second strain of private education was provided by independent schools based on the model of the British "public" school. They were established and patronized by pre-WWI British immigrants wishing to reinforce their class position and to replicate Old World social standards. Anglicanism was invariably emphasized although the church was not always formally involved in the foundation of the schools (*see* ANGLICAN CHURCH). Many schools came and went over the years. Examples of successful schools of this type for boys include: VERNON PREPARATORY SCHOOL (1914–72), founded by Austin C. Mackie, an Anglican cleric, at COLDSTREAM outside VERNON; ST MICHAEL'S UNIV SCHOOL in Victoria, created in 1971 from a merger of 2 pre-WWI prep schools; BRENTWOOD COLLEGE, originally (1923–48) a boarding school for boys near Victoria, then revived at MILL BAY (1961–present); SHAWNIGAN LAKE SCHOOL on VANCOUVER ISLAND, founded in 1916 by Charles W. Lonsdale, who remained headmaster for 36 years; and ST GEORGE'S SCHOOL, established in 1931 in VANCOUVER. Major private schools for girls include CROFTON HOUSE, BC's oldest independent girls' school, established in Vancouver in 1898 as Miss Gordon's School after the founder, Jessie Gordon; YORK HOUSE, also in Vancouver, founded in 1932 by 6 female teachers; and 4 schools on Vancouver Island: St Margaret's (1908) and Norfolk House (1913) in Victoria, QUEEN MARGARET'S in DUNCAN (1921) and Strathcona Lodge at SHAWNIGAN LK (1927). Following WWII private schools of the British type accommodated themselves to a changing society. They became non-profit, were more focussed on educating a Canadian business and social elite, and welcomed students who more accurately reflected BC's cultural diversity. Beginning in the 1970s many of these schools became co-educational.

A third strain of private schools are the conservative, Christian schools that have sprung up since the 1950s. Originally they were associated with the post-WWII influx of DUTCH Calvinist immigrants, especially to the FRASER VALLEY. These newcomers were unhappy with the public schools and established their own Christian alternatives. Schools with a conservative Christian orientation have subsequently gained popularity, appealing to parents who believe that educational and moral standards in the public schools have declined.

Private schools have always catered to a small minority of students; in the 1970s more than 95% of BC children attended the public system. At first private schools received no public funding and were more or less ignored by public policy. As a result of a strong lobbying effort, the government passed legislation in 1977 that provided for partial funding of private schools. Schools are still free to operate without accepting public money and the requirements that come with it, although beginning in 1989 all private schools had to register with the province, submit to inspection and provide the same basic curriculum as public schools. Public funding revitalized private education, which was faltering at least in part because of financial constraints, and since 1977 the percentage of students attending private schools has risen. In 1999 there were 350 independent schools in BC, with an enrolment of about 56,000 students. The Federation of Independent Schools Assoc, formed in 1966, is the most important organized voice for private education.

Private education has also been available at the post-secondary level (*see* TRINITY WESTERN UNIV).

EDUCATION, PUBLIC, originated with the *Free School Act* of 1865 on VANCOUVER ISLAND, which established the first system of non-denominational, free public schools in the colony. The act created a General Board of Education, appointed by the governor, and provided for local school boards, also appointed. These first public schools supplemented private, fee-paying institutions organized by one or other of the churches (*see* EDUCATION, PRIVATE). The public system ran into financial troubles and was replaced in 1869 with a *Common School Ordinance* that abolished the general board and placed control of public education directly into the hands of the governor. Fees were reintroduced, but the education system continued to experience financial problems and served only a minority of school-age children. At CONFEDERATION the new province strengthened the education system with the passage of the *Free Public School Act of 1872*, creating free, non-sectarian public schools for children ages 6–16. The act re-established a central Board of Education and provided for the election of local school boards within school districts. The first superintendent under the new act was John JESSOP. The system was reasonably successful in urban areas, but in the sparsely inhabited Interior many children lived beyond the reach of a school. In response the government in 1874 established a central boarding school at CACHE CREEK that remained open until 1890, by which time the spread of local day schools through the Interior had made it unnecessary. Until the 1880s some FIRST NATIONS children attended the public schools but with the creation of reserve day schools and RESIDENTIAL SCHOOLS they were streamed into their own facilities. School attendance was made compulsory from 1901 for urban children ages 7–14 and from 1921 for all children, though enforcement of this requirement was lax for many years. The first high schools were established in VICTORIA (1876), NEW WESTMINSTER (1884), NANAIMO (1886) and VANCOUVER (1890). By 1920 there were 53 high schools around the province, organized into grades 9–12. Students wishing to attend high school were required to pass entrance examinations until the examinations were abolished in 1938.

BC EDUCATION STATISTICS 1996

TOTAL POPULATION AGED 15+ BY HIGHEST LEVEL OF SCHOOLING

Total population aged 15+	2,954,700	100.0%
Less than Grade 9 education	218,780	7.4%
Grades 9–13, without graduation certificate	699,545	23.7%
Secondary school graduation certificate	381,725	12.9%
Trade certificate or diploma	103,550	3.5%
Other non-university education, without diploma	217,455	7.4%
Other non-university education, with diploma	580,685	19.6%
University, without certificate, diploma or degree	167,600	5.7%
University, with certificate or diploma	183,640	6.2%
University, with bachelor's degree or higher	401,720	13.6%

TOTAL POPULATION AGED 15–24 BY SCHOOL ATTENDANCE

Total population aged 15–24	483,070	100.0%
Not attending school	187,160	38.7%
Attending school full-time	252,040	52.2%
Attending school part-time	43,870	9.1%

POPULATION WITH POST-SECONDARY QUALIFICATIONS BY FIELD OF STUDY

Total with post-secondary qualifications	1,269,585	100.0%
Educational, recreational & counselling services	136,040	10.7%
Fine & applied arts	74,545	5.9%
Humanities & related fields	74,645	5.9%
Social sciences & related fields	112,220	8.8%
Commerce, management & business administration	272,230	21.4%
Agricultural & biological sciences/technologies	66,380	5.2%
Engineering & applied sciences	53,335	4.2%
Engineering & applied science technologies & trades	287,545	22.7%
Health professions, sciences & technologies	153,160	12.1%
Mathematics & physical sciences	37,790	3.0%
No specialization & all other categories	1,695	0.1%

Teachers at all levels were certified by the Board of Education, but there was no formal teacher training until the Vancouver Normal School opened in 1901. It was followed by a second normal school in Victoria in 1915. Before this time most teachers were simply high school graduates who qualified by examination for their certificates. During the 1920s UBC began offering summer courses for teachers; in 1956 the normal schools closed and the job of educating the province's teachers passed to UBC and Victoria College. By 1962 BC had a higher proportion (37%) of teachers with university degrees than any other province. In 1988 teachers organized their own professional organization, the BC College of Teachers, with responsibility for certification, discipline and professional development. *See also* BC TEACHERS' FEDERATION.

Meanwhile the provincial government was reorganizing its administration of education. More responsibility for operating the schools was shifted to the local boards, along with responsibility for providing funding. In 1920 a formal Department of Education was created, with a bureaucracy of superintendents and inspectors. The number of school districts grew rapidly from the initial 25 in 1872 until by 1924 there were 760 districts and a student population of 96,204. In 1924 the government decided it was time to assess the education system. Schools were becoming overcrowded and rural schooling in particular was thought to be inadequate. "Progressive" ideas about education were spreading across the continent. A 2-person Royal Commission was appointed to carry out a study. In its report the PUTMAN-WEIR COMMISSION suggested a series of reforms, several of which were adopted by the government, including the introduction of junior high schools for grades 7–9. The next major administrative change occurred in 1946 following a report by Max Cameron, a UBC professor. At Cameron's suggestion hundreds of school districts were consolidated into 74 large administrative units. A provincial Royal Commission chaired by S.N.F. Chant, UBC dean of arts, produced a well-received report in 1960 that led to other changes in the system, none of them very radical. It recommended the creation of BCIT, for example, and favoured the creation of kindergartens. It was not until 1973 that the province made kindergartens mandatory in all school districts, though many had been providing pre-school classes since the 1940s. Another Royal Commission on Education, chaired by Barry Sullivan, reported in 1988. Its recommendations, some of which were embodied in the "Year 2000" changes subsequently proposed by the government, were overtaken by a more conservative public temper and eventually withdrawn in favour of changes that emphasized a more structured school environment and a job-directed curriculum.

In 1998 there were about 1,600 public schools in the province and 608,000 high school and elementary students. Close to 70% of children entering kindergarten were completing grade 12. The schools were spread across 59 school districts, each administered by a board chosen at local elections. During the 1980s the SOCIAL CREDIT government initiated an overhaul of education financing. Up to that time individual boards raised a portion of their annual budget from local property taxes. The rest came from the provincial government. Facing a revenue shortage in the 1980s, the government removed the commercial–industrial share of the property tax from school boards and took control of the amount of money each board received. A maximum annual funding level was established—in 1997–98 it was $3.47 billion, an average of $5,756 per pupil—and each district got a portion of this amount. The new policy permitted a school board to raise more money for a specific purpose through a referendum, though this process is cumbersome. The province also centralized contract negotiations with teachers, a responsibility that used to rest with the individual boards. *See also* EDUCATION, POST-SECONDARY.

Kinnikinnick School, an elementary school that opened in Sechelt in 1999.

EDWARDS, Ralph A., pioneer homesteader, conservationist (b 1891, NC; d 1977, Prince Rupert). As a teenager he travelled west to Oregon and California. In 1907 he arrived in BC, where he worked on the construction of the GRAND TRUNK PACIFIC RWY. He then returned to California but came back to BC in 1912 and took

Ralph Edwards, the "Crusoe of Lonesome Lake."
VPL 60427

up land at LONESOME LK in the valley of the ATNARKO R in what is now southern TWEEDSMUIR PROVINCIAL PARK. Along with his wife Ethel Hober, whom he married in 1923, and their 3 children, he carved a farm out of the wilderness. During the 1920s the family began working to preserve the trumpeter SWANS that winter at the lake. Their life was chronicled in the bestselling book *Crusoe of Lonesome Lake* (1956) by Leland Stowe. Their daughter, Trudy Edwards Turner, established her own nearby homestead called Fogswamp Farm and played an active role in the conservation of the swans. Edwards left the lake in 1966 to take up commercial FISHING at OONA R on PORCHER ISLAND. He was inducted into the Order of Canada in 1972.

EDWARDS, Roger Yorke, wildlife biologist (b 22 Nov 1924, Toronto). After completing a FORESTRY degree at the Univ of Toronto in 1948 and an MS in biology at UBC in 1950, Yorke Edwards moved to VICTORIA to work as a wildlife biologist with the provincial PARKS branch. There he took a leading role in establishing natural history interpretation centres. A former president of the BC Museums Assoc and an editor of the newsletter *Museum Round-Up* in the mid-1960s, he moved to Ottawa in 1967 to work for the Canadian Wildlife Service. After returning to BC, he became director of the BC Provincial Museum (now the ROYAL BC MUSEUM) in 1974 and held the post until his retirement in 1984. He published many scientific articles and several books, including *The Mountain Barrier* and *The Land Speaks.* *Dianne Mackay*

EGMONT, pop 119, is a waterfront community straddling the entrance to SECHELT INLET, not far from the ferry terminal at Earls Cove on the SUN-SHINE COAST. Its first settler was Joseph Sylvia Simmonds, better known as Joe SILVEY, a VANCOUVER saloonkeeper who moved here in the 1870s. Later settlers engaged mainly in LOGGING and commercial FISHING. A road was built in 1956.

EGOFF, Sheila A., librarian, writer (b 20 Jan 1918, Auburn, ME). Born in Maine but raised and educated in Galt (now Cambridge), ON, she graduated from the Univ of Toronto and worked as a children's librarian in Galt (1939–42) and Toronto (1942–57). In 1962 she came west to join the new library school at UBC, where she taught until her retirement in 1983, specializing in writing and librarianship for young people. A much admired figure in her field, Egoff has written several influential books, including *The Republic of Childhood* (1967, revised as *The New Republic of Childhood* 1990), the first critical survey of Canadian writing for children; *Thursday's Child* (1981); and *Worlds Within* (1988). She is the recipient of many awards, and is a professor emerita at UBC and an officer in the Order of Canada (1994). The annual BC BOOK PRIZE for children's literature is named in her honour.

EGOYAN, Atom, filmmaker (b 19 July 1960, Cairo, Egypt). He grew up in VICTORIA, where he moved with his parents when he was a youngster. After finishing high school he attended the Univ of Toronto, where he became interested in theatre and FILMMAKING. His first feature, *Next of Kin,* premiered at the 1984 Toronto International Film Festival. Later films—*Speaking Parts* (1989), *The Adjuster* (1991), *Exotica* (1994) and *Felicia's Journey* (1999)—were all invited to the Cannes Film Festival in France; *Exotica* won the festival's Critics' Prize. His 1997 drama *The Sweet Hereafter,* based on a novel by the American writer Russell

Atom Egoyan, director and filmmaker.
Nick Didlick/Vancouver Sun

Banks, earned an Oscar nomination and unprecedented attention for a made-in-Canada movie. He was named to the Order of Canada in 1999.

EGRET is a type of HERON, typically white, of which 2 species are found in BC. The cattle egret (*Bubulcus ibis*) is a small, stocky bird occasionally seen in winter in cow pastures and other open habitats, primarily in southern BC including VANCOUVER ISLAND. The great egret (*Casmerodius albus*) is a rare visitor to the Lower Mainland, southeast Vancouver Island and the southern Interior. *Kim Goldberg*

EHOLT was a community near the summit of the COLUMBIA & WESTERN RWY line between GRAND FORKS and GREENWOOD in the BOUNDARY DISTRICT of southern BC. It was a divisional point where the railway also headed south 15 km to a COPPER mine at PHOENIX. When the pre-WWI MINING boom in the Boundary faded, residents moved away and Eholt became a ghost town. It is named for a rancher who lived in the area.

EL NINO (pronounced "El NEEN-yo") is a variation in the usual climate system over a large part of the globe. Occurring about every 5 years, El Niño originates on the equator in the Pacific Ocean. Its effects are particularly strong in BC, where the CLIMATE is influenced by Pacific ocean currents.

Under normal conditions at the equator, winds blow along the surface of the ocean, causing an upward tilt to the water surface in the direction of Asia, with airflow returning aloft. Air

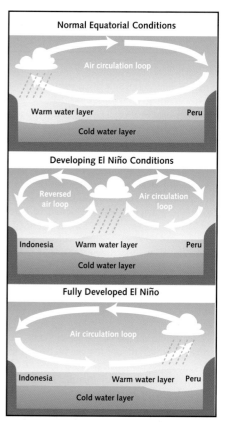

Kim LaFave drawing

circulation is completed with rising moist air over Asia (where there are some of the world's great rain forests) and sinking dry air over Peru (site of one of the driest deserts in the world). This normal air flow is called the Walker circulation. Every autumn a small air reversal occurs near Indonesia. Most years it goes away, but occasionally the reversal is strong enough to push the warm water bulge back along the equator toward Peru, which can strengthen the reversed wind pattern. This is called "positive feedback" and ends with reversed winds in the Walker circulation and a thick layer of warm water off the coast of Peru. On these occasions it rains in the Atacama desert and the Asian monsoons fail. As well, fisheries may fail catastrophically as the warm water layer becomes so thick that the supply of nutrient-rich cold water on which the fish depend is cut off.

The earth's climate may be viewed as a series of interlocking circulation systems, similar to a system of gears: one gear cannot be reversed without affecting the movement of the other gears. When the Walker circulation changes and the flow of air on the equator reverses, airflow over the rest of the earth is affected. The effects are strongest closest to the source, so PACIFIC RIM locations feel the changes first and most intensely. Waves of warm water move up the coast of the Americas affecting the sub-tropical areas first, then California, Oregon, Washington and eventually BC. During a large El Niño, sea levels off BC stand up to 40 cm above normal for up to 4 months. The surface ocean may become as much as 4°C warmer than usual, affecting the behaviour of all living things that have evolved to expect cooler conditions. The following occurrences in BC have been attributed to El Niño activity:

- invasion of BC waters by exotic species of fish, especially predatory species such as MACKEREL

- changes in the migration paths of sockeye SALMON

- reduced supply of nutrients in the ocean because of warmer water

- starving seabirds and reproductive failures in seabird populations

- unusually warm and comfortable winters

- reduced snowpack in mountains

- reduced water flow in the FRASER R

The opposite phase to El Niño, usually called La Niña, also occurs in some years, but the climate system does not oscillate regularly between the 2 phases. La Niñas are not as common as El Niños and the timing of both phenomena is irregular: El Niños can occur in consecutive years or 9 years apart. The name El Niño, first used by Peruvian workers, means roughly "the Christ-child," a reference to the fact that these events typically appeared at Christmas time and workers saw rain on the desert as a miracle. El Niño is not a modern phenomenon. It has certainly been occurring since the 16th century, and fossil evidence suggests that it may have occurred since the last Ice Age. But it was not until the late 1960s that an international oceanographic expedition, called CUEA for Coastal Upwelling Ecosystem Analysis, discovered that El Niño was not exclusively a Peruvian phenomenon. The coastal waters of Peru merely offered a particularly clear window on an oscillation that was affecting the entire equatorial Pacific region. Over the subsequent decade it became evident that El Niño had global influence.   *Howard Freeland*

ELASMOSAUR is an extinct marine reptile (a swan lizard) that lived in BC during the Cretaceous era (65–140 million years ago). In 1988 the fossil bones of a 10-m long specimen were found in rocks exposed along the PUNTLEDGE R near COURTENAY on VANCOUVER ISLAND. These Upper Cretaceous rocks have been dated at about 80 million years old. The fossil remains of 2 other types of ancient marine reptiles have been found in the same general area: a sea turtle (chelonioid) and a large crocodile-like sea lizard (mosasaur). The area has been declared a provincial heritage site.

ELECTION RESULTS, from 1903 when party politics was formally introduced to the legislature, are shown on page 204.

ELECTORAL SYSTEM selects members of the provincial LEGISLATIVE ASSEMBLY. The province is divided into 79 electoral districts, known also as constituencies or ridings (up from 75 at the 1996 election); eligible voters in each district elect one representative MLA to the provincial legislature. Anyone may run for election after meeting certain basic requirements (a candidate must be at least 18 years old and a resident of BC for at least 6 months; nomination papers must be signed by at least 25 qualified voters; candidates must pay a deposit of $100), but candidates are usually nominated by one of the main political parties at meetings within the ridings.

Elections are held at least every 5 years and the party winning the most seats in the election forms the government. Formally elections are held at the discretion of the LT GOV; in practice they invariably occur when the PREMIER wants one. Advance polls are held for voters unable to vote on election day, and results of advance polls are counted along with other votes on election day. The voting age for provincial elections is 18 years or older.

Elections are administered by Elections BC, an independent office of the legislature headed by the chief electoral officer. The Election Act requires candidates and parties to file statements

Reconstructed cast of the Puntledge elasmosaur.
Courtenay & District Museum & Archives

BC PROVINCIAL ELECTION RESULTS from 1903

Party	Votes	%	Seats
1903 (Oct 3)			
Conservatives	**27,913**	**46.4**	**22**
Liberals	22,715	37.8	17
Socialist Party BC	4,787	7.9	2
Labour Party	4,421	7.4	1
Others	284	.5	0
Totals	60,120		42
1907 (Feb 2)			
Conservatives	**30,871**	**48.7**	**26**
Liberals	23,481	37.1	13
Socialist Party Can	5,603	8.9	3
Others	3,340	5.3	0
Totals	63,295		42
1909 (Nov 25)			
Conservatives	**53,074**	**52.3**	**38**
Liberals	33,675	33.2	2
Socialist Party Can	11,665	11.5	2
Others	3,001	3.0	0
Totals	101,415		42
1912 (Mar 28)			
Conservatives	**50,423**	**59.6**	**39**
Liberals	21,443	25.4	1
Socialist Party Can	9,366	11.1	1
Others	3,297	3.9	1
Totals	84,529		42
1916 (Sept 14)			
Conservatives	72,842	40.5	9
Liberals	**89,892**	**50.0**	**36**
Socialist Party Can	2,106	1.2	0
Others	14,304	8.3	2
Totals	179,144		47
1920 (Dec 1)			
Conservatives	110,475	31.2	15
Liberals	**134,167**	**37.9**	**25**
Federated Labour	32,230	9.1	3
Socalist Party Can	12,386	3.5	0
Soldier–Farmer/ Labour	10,780	3.0	0
Others	54,050	15.3	4
Totals	354,088		47
1924 (June 20)			
Conservatives	101,765	29.5	17
Liberals	**108,323**	**31.3**	**23**
Provincial Party Canadian	83,517	24.2	3
Labour Party	39,044	11.3	3
Socialist Party Can	4,364	1.3	0
Others	8,593	2.4	2
Totals	345,606		48
1928 (July 18)			
Conservatives	**192,867**	**53.3**	**35**
Liberals	144,872	40.0	12
Independent Labour	17,908	5.0	1
Others	6,167	1.7	0
Totals	361,814		48
1933 (Nov 2)			
Liberals	**159,131**	**41.7**	**34**
CCF	120,185	31.5	7
Non-Partisans	38,836	10.2	2
Unionists	15,445	4.1	1
Independent Conservatives	7,114	1.9	0
Independent	29,506	7.7	2
Others	11,006	2.9	1
Totals	381,223		47

Party	Votes	%	Seats
1937 (June 1)			
Conservatives	119,521	28.6	8
Liberals	**156,074**	**37.3**	**31**
CCF	119,400	28.6	7
Independent	7,341	1.8	1
Social Credit League	4,812	1.2	0
Others	10,781	2.5	1
Totals	417,929		48
1941 (Oct 21)			
Conservatives	140,282	30.9	12
Liberals	**149,525**	**32.9**	**21**
CCF	151,440	33.4	14
Independents	1,638	.4	0
Others	11,008	2.4	1
Totals	453,893		48
1945 (Oct 25)*			
Coalition	**261,147**	**55.8**	**37**
CCF	175,960	37.6	10
Labour Progressives	16,479	3.5	0
Social Credit	6,627	1.4	0
Independent	1,532	.3	0
Others	5,896	1.3	1
Totals	467,641		48
1949 (June 15)			
Coalition	**428,773**	**61.4**	**39**
CCF	245,284	35.1	7
Social Credit Party	8,464	1.2	0
Social Credit League	3,072	.4	0
Independent	5,163	.7	1
Others	8,067	1.2	1
Totals	698,823		48
1952 (June 12)			
Conservatives	65,285	9.6	4
Liberals	170,674	25.3	6
CCF	231,756	34.3	18
Social Credit Party	**203,932**	**30.2**	**19**
Others	4,007	.6	1
Totals	675,654		48
1953 (June 9)			
Conservatives	7,362	1.1	1
Liberals	154,090	23.4	4
CCF	194,414	29.5	14
Social Credit	**300,372**	**45.5**	**28**
Others	3,361	.5	1
Totals	659,563		48
1956 (Sept 19)			
Conservatives	25,373	3.1	0
Liberals	177,922	21.8	2
CCF	231,511	28.3	10
Social Credit	**374,711**	**45.8**	**39**
Others	7,880	1.0	1
Totals	817,397		52
1960 (Sept 12)			
Conservatives	66,943	6.7	0
Liberals	208,249	20.9	4
CCF	326,094	32.7	16
Social Credit	**386,886**	**38.8**	**32**
Communist Party	5,675	.6	0
Independent	2,557	.3	0
Totals	996,404		52
1963 (Sept 30)			
Conservatives	109,090	11.3	0
Liberals	193,363	20.0	5
NDP	269,004	27.8	14
Social Credit	**395,079**	**40.8**	**33**
Others	1,139	.1	0
Totals	967,675		52

Party	Votes	%	Seats
1966 (Sept 12)			
Conservatives	1,409	.2	0
Liberals	152,155	20.2	6
NDP	252,753	33.6	16
Social Credit	**342,751**	**45.6**	**33**
Others	2,808	.4	0
Totals	751,876		55
1969 (Aug 27)			
Conservatives	1,087	.1	0
Liberals	186,235	19.0	5
NDP	331,813	33.9	12
Social Credit	**457,777**	**46.8**	**38**
Others	1,444	.2	0
Totals	978,356		55
1972 (Aug 30)			
Conservatives	143,450	12.7	2
Liberals	185,640	16.4	5
NDP	**448,260**	**39.6**	**38**
Social Credit	352,776	31.1	10
Others	2,046	.2	0
Totals	1,132,172		55
1975 (Dec 11)			
Conservatives	49,796	3.9	1
Liberals	93,379	7.2	1
NDP	505,396	39.2	18
Social Credit	**635,482**	**49.3**	**35**
Others	6,398	.5	0
Totals	1,290,451		55
1979 (May 10)			
Conservatives	71,078	5.1	0
Liberals	6,662	.5	0
NDP	646,188	46.0	26
Social Credit	**677,607**	**48.2**	**31**
Others	3,542	.3	0
Totals	1,405,077		57
1983 (May 5)			
Conservatives	19,131	1.1	0
Liberals	44,442	2.7	0
NDP	741,354	44.9	22
Social Credit	**820,807**	**49.8**	**35**
Western Canada Concept	14,185	.9	0
Others	9,614	.6	0
Totals	1,649,533		57
1986 (Oct 22)			
Conservatives	14,074	.7	0
Liberals	130,505	6.7	0
NDP	824,544	42.6	22
Social Credit	**954,516**	**49.3**	**47**
Others	11,814	.7	0
Totals	1,935,453		69
1991 (Oct 17)			
BC Reform	2,673	.2	0
Liberals	486,208	33.2	17
NDP	**595,391**	**40.7**	**51**
Social Credit	351,660	24.0	7
Others	26,535	1.9	0
Totals	1,462,467		75
1996 (May 28)			
BC Reform	146,734	9.27	2
Liberals	661,929	41.8	33
NDP	**624,395**	**39.5**	**39**
Progressive Democratic Alliance	90,797	5.7	1
Others	58,849	3.7	0
Totals	1,582,704		75

For mathematical reasons, percentages total 99.9% rather than 100%

BC PROVINCIAL & FEDERAL ELECTORAL DISTRICTS

Provincial *(set in 1999 for use in the next election)*

Abbotsford–Clayburn
Abbotsford–Mt Lehman
Alberni–Qualicum
Bulkley Valley–Stikine
Burnaby Edmonds
Burnaby North
Burnaby Willingdon
Burquitlam
Cariboo North
Cariboo South
Chilliwack–Kent
Chilliwack–Sumas
Columbia River–Revelstoke
Comox Valley
Coquitlam–Maillardville
Cowichan–Ladysmith
Delta North
Delta South
East Kootenay
Esquimalt–Metchosin
Fort Langley–Aldergrove
Kamloops
Kamloops–North Thompson
Kelowna–Lake Country
Kelowna–Mission
Langley
Malahat–Juan de Fuca

Maple Ridge–Mission
Maple Ridge–Pitt Meadows
Nanaimo
Nanaimo–Parksville
Nelson–Creston
New Westminster
North Coast
North Island
North Vancouver–Lonsdale
North Vancouver–Seymour
Oak Bay–Gordon Head
Okanagan–Vernon
Okanagan Westside
Peace River North
Peace River South
Penticton–Okanagan Valley
Port Coquitlam–Burke Mountain
Port Moody–Westwood
Powell River–Sunshine Coast
Prince George–Mt Robson
Prince George North
Prince George–Omineca
Richmond Centre
Richmond East
Richmond–Steveston
Saanich North and the Islands
Saanich South

Shuswap
Skeena
Surrey–Cloverdale
Surrey–Green Timbers
Surrey–Newton
Surrey–Panorama Ridge
Surrey–Tynehead
Surrey–Whalley
Surrey–White Rock
Vancouver–Burrard
Vancouver–Fairview
Vancouver–Fraserview
Vancouver–Hastings
Vancouver–Kensington
Vancouver–Kingsway
Vancouver–Langara
Vancouver–Mt Pleasant
Vancouver–Point Grey
Vancouver–Quilchena
Victoria–Beacon Hill
Victoria–Hillside
West Kootenay–Boundary
West Vancouver–Capilano
West Vancouver–Garibaldi
Yale–Lillooet

Federal

Lower Mainland

Burnaby–Douglas
Delta–South Richmond
Dewdney–Alouette
Fraser Valley
Langley–Abbotsford
New Westminster–Coquitlam–Burnaby
North Vancouver
Port Moody–Coquitlam
Richmond
South Surrey–White Rock–Langley
Surrey Central
Surrey North
Vancouver Centre
Vancouver East
Vancouver Kingsway
Vancouver Quadra
Vancouver South–Burnaby
West Vancouver–Sunshine Coast

Vancouver Island

Esquimalt–Juan de Fuca
Nanaimo–Alberni
Nanaimo–Cowichan
Saanich–Gulf Islands
Vancouver Island North
Victoria

Interior

Cariboo–Chilcotin
Kamloops
Kelowna
Kootenay–Columbia
Okanagan–Coquihalla
Okanagan–Shuswap
Prince George–Bulkley Valley
Prince George–Peace River
Skeena
West Kootenay–Okanagan

disclosing election contributions and expenses. Elections BC also has responsibility for administering RECALL and initiative campaigns. Constituency boundaries are re-evaluated after every second election by an independent government-appointed electoral boundaries commission. By law the commission must include a retired or sitting judge of the provincial Supreme Court or court of appeal, the chief electoral officer and a third person nominated by the speaker of the legislature. The commission has a mandate to hold public hearings and recommend changes to constituency boundaries based on changes in population. Ideally each district has an equal number of people (about 50,000, according to the 1996 census) but the commission allows deviation up to 25%. In 1996 the most populous constituency was Surrey–Newton with 85,861 people; the least populous was Prince George–Mt Robson with 31,401. The largest constituency by area is Bulkley Valley–Stikine (200,274 km²); the smallest is Victoria–Beacon Hill (8 km²).

Residents of BC at least 18 years old also vote for representatives to the federal Parliament in Ottawa. BC is divided into 34 single-member federal constituencies. Each constituency is divided into polling divisions, and voters must cast their ballots in their designated divisions.

See p. 205 for a list of electoral districts. *See also* GOVERNMENT, LOCAL.

ELEWONIBI, Mohammed "Moe," football player (b 16 Dec 1965, Lagos, Nigeria). At age 11 he moved with his mother and his brother to her hometown, VICTORIA. He started playing FOOTBALL at age 15; after relocating with his family to KAMLOOPS he was awarded a football scholarship to Snow College in Utah. In his junior year he transferred to Brigham Young Univ and in 1989 he won the Outland Trophy as the top lineman in US college football. The next year he started for the NFL's Washington Redskins. After winning the Super Bowl with Washington in 1991 and playing briefly for the Buffalo Bills, he abandoned an NFL career plagued by injuries. He joined a World Football League team in Spain for a season, then signed with the BC LIONS of the CFL in 1997. While with the Lions he was a CFL all-star (1998) and also became known for his charitable contributions to the community, including the establishment of the "Moe-Zone," a program that helps troubled youths and provides them with seats at Lions games. In 2000 he was traded to Winnipeg.   *SW*

ELGIN, at the mouth of the NICOMEKL R, 17 km south of NEW WESTMINSTER in the FRASER VALLEY, was established as an "Out-port of Customs" in 1880. The Semiahmoo Rd crossed the river here and both land and water traffic from the US could be controlled. In the railway era, the customs house was moved to the border and Elgin declined. Named after the Earl of Elgin, gov gen of Canada from 1846 to 1854, it is now a semi-rural suburb of SURREY and site of a historic farm and heritage park.   *AS*

ELIZA Y REVENTA, Francisco de, Spanish naval officer (b 1759, Puerto de Santa Maria, Spain; d 19 Feb 1825, Cádiz, Spain). He arrived in Mexico in 1789 among other young officers to strengthen the naval base at San Blas and Spain's maritime presence in the N Pacific. After the NOOTKA SOUND CONTROVERSY he established a settlement and fort at YUQUOT in 1790; he maintained this outpost through 2 winters until handing it over to BODEGA Y QUADRA in 1792. He oversaw exploration by Salvador Fidalgo to Alaska and Manuel QUIMPER into JUAN DE FUCA STRAIT, and himself entered the strait in 1791. His reports to Mexico City provided detailed information about the Mowachaht of NOOTKA SOUND (*see* NUU-CHAH-NULTH). He initiated the practice of purchasing aboriginal children, ostensibly for their own good. *See also* SPANISH EXPLORATION.

Robin Inglis

ELK is a large member of the DEER family (Cervidae). Also known as wapiti, an aboriginal word meaning "white deer," elk were misnamed by early settlers who thought they were moose, which in Europe are called elk. This statuesque animal, with its long legs, neck and head, is tawny coloured with a dark brown mane and a buff-coloured rump patch. During the fall rut, bulls have a distinct mating call, or bugle, that warns off other males and attracts females. Bull elk are polygamous; each has a harem of up to 20 cows. Only males have antlers, and those of older males can weigh up to 12 kg and span more than 1 m. Antlers are important for mating behaviour; without them the bull cannot keep females in his harem. The female generally has one calf, born in early spring.

Elk are both grazers (like sheep) and browsers (like moose). They spend the summer in high alpine meadows, then migrate down to the forest for winter. Their preferred habitat is open parkland, where they have clumps of trees for shelter and shrubs and grasses for forage. Normally their diet is about 80% grass and herbs but they can survive on a diet of up to 80% browse. While habitat loss has caused population decline in some areas, because of their versatility elk have been reintroduced successfully into historic range. The BC population is estimated at about 43,000 animals.

Elk occur in BC in 2 subspecies. Rocky Mountain elk (*Cervus elaphus nelsoni*) inhabit the Interior, particularly the KOOTENAY and the northern ROCKY MTS. Roosevelt elk (*Cervus elaphus roosevelti*), larger and darker than the Rocky Mountain subspecies, inhabit VANCOUVER ISLAND and the SUNSHINE COAST. The antlers of the Roosevelt elk are less spreading than those of the Rocky Mountain elk and may be cupped on the ends, possibly an adaptation for travelling through dense coastal RAIN FOREST.

COUGAR, WOLF and grizzly BEAR are the chief predators. Roosevelt elk were hunted aggressively in the early 1900s until the hunt was banned before WWI. The ban was later lifted, then reimposed in 1987 on the south Island, where the population is estimated at 500 animals. On the north Island, where the population is about 2,500, a limited hunt is allowed. Logging continues to present a threat to the Island elk population and in certain watersheds its survival may be endangered. Roosevelt elk are Blue-listed by the Conservation Data Centre (*see* ENDANGERED SPECIES).

Maggie Paquet

Male Rocky Mountain elk, Yoho National Park.
Ken Bowen photo

ELK CREEK was a tiny AGRICULTURAL and LOG-GING settlement 8 km east of CHILLIWACK in the FRASER VALLEY and the site of an early SAWMILL established by James TRETHEWEY. A post office operated here from 1908 to 1912.   AS

ELK LAKES PROVINCIAL PARK, 172.4 km², is nestled high in the Front Ranges of the ROCKY MTS south of Banff, contiguous to Alberta's Peter Lougheed (Kananaskis) Provincial Park. Established in 1973, it contains the headwaters of the ELK R. Much of the park is above treeline and features outstanding panoramic mountain scenery, including numerous large alpine glaciers. Some wildlife can be observed in the alpine areas, notably grizzly BEARS and Rocky Mountain bighorn sheep (*see* MOUNTAIN SHEEP). The lower elevation areas have populations of ELK, MOOSE and smaller mammals. *See also* LAKES; PARKS, PROVINCIAL.

ELK RIVER originates in ELK LAKES PROVINCIAL PARK high in the ROCKY MTS in the southeastern corner of the province. The river flows south to the KOOTENAY R system, emptying into KOOCANUSA Lk south of ELKO. It is named for the herds of Rocky Mountain ELK that inhabit the area. The Elk R Valley was used seasonally by the KTUNAXA First Nation as a corridor to travel across the mountains to hunt bison on the plains. By the time outsiders arrived, the Ktunaxa had shifted westward into the COLUM-BIA R Valley, where food resources were more plentiful. In 1898 the CPR built its southern main line through the CROWSNEST PASS and down the river; COAL MINING also began in the Elk R Valley at this time. Four years later the American rail promoter James J. Hill built a competing railway into the valley from Montana. Both these lines provided transport for the mines that opened near FERNIE, MICHEL-NATAL, MORRISSEY and HOSMER (*see* MINING). In the 1970s, other coal mines opened farther north in the ELKFORD area. In 1999 there were 5 mines operating in the Elk R Valley, producing coal mainly for Japanese markets. As well as mining, LOGGING has sustained valley communities. A curse is said to have been placed on the valley by a Ktunaxa woman whose granddaughter was jilted by William FERNIE. The floods, fires and mine accidents that subsequently occurred were all blamed on the curse until it was lifted in 1964 at a special Ktunaxa ceremony. *See also* RIVERS.

ELKFORD, district municipality, pop 2,729, lies in the Elk R Valley in the E KOOTENAY 60 km north of FERNIE. At elevation 1,299 m it is the highest community in Canada. The land was purchased from Mathias Baher, a legendary Elk R Valley trapper and guide, and was incorporated 16 July 1971 as a townsite for the FORDING INC open-pit COAL mine. Since then other mines have opened and the population has grown. Coal mining is the major economic activity in the area but TOURISM has grown in importance. Elkford is the gateway to spectacular ELK LAKES PROVINCIAL PARK and maintains many kilometres of hiking and biking trails, a golf course and a ski hill within its boundaries.

ELKO, pop 519, is a community on the ELK R, 31 km south of FERNIE in the southeast corner of the province. The first post office and school opened at the site in 1899. It is on the main line of the CROWSNEST PASS route of the CPR and is the southern gateway to the Elk R Valley COAL country. There is a HYDROELECTRIC power plant nearby and SAWMILLING has been the main industry.

ELLERSLIE LAKE, 25.8 km², lies at the head of Spiller Channel on the central coast 43 km north of BELLA BELLA in the traditional territory of the HEILTSUK First Nation. Surrounded by the forested slopes of the KITIMAT ranges of the COAST MTS, it drains into Spiller Channel over a 40-m WATER-FALL. Environmentalists and the Heiltsuk hope to preserve the area from LOGGING. *See also* ENVI-RONMENTAL MOVEMENT; LAKES.

ELLIOTT, Andrew Charles, lawyer, politician, premier 1 Feb 1876–25 June 1878 (b circa 1828, Ireland; d 9 Apr 1889, San Francisco). A lawyer in London, he came to practise in BC in 1859. He was appointed a county court judge for YALE and HOPE, then a GOLD commissioner and magistrate at LILLOOET. After the colonies of VANCOU-VER ISLAND and British Columbia united in 1866, he became high sherriff, then police magistrate in VICTORIA. Elliott was elected to the legislature in 1875 and became leader of the opposition. Early the next year he was called on to form a government. As PREMIER he was able to stabilize the province's finances and add a moderate voice to disputes with Ottawa over railway policy, but he was irresolute and unable to manage the political alliances necessary to survival. After his government was defeated in the legislature, then at the polls, he retired from public life. In 1886 he settled in San Francisco for health reasons. *See also* COLONIAL GOVERNMENT.

ELLIS, Thomas, rancher (b 26 April 1845, Tyrone, Ireland; d 1 Feb 1918, Victoria). He arrived in BC early in 1865 and was placed in

Thomas Ellis, Penticton rancher, c 1890.
BC Archives G-00394

charge of stores for the construction of the DEWDNEY TRAIL east of OSOYOOS. The next year he pre-empted 2.6 km² at the south end of OKANA-GAN LK, the first step in amassing a ranching empire that at one point totalled 120 km² and 20,000 head of cattle. He also planted one of the earliest orchards in the OKANAGAN VALLEY. He sold his estate in 1905 to the syndicate that founded PENTICTON and retired to VICTORIA. *See also* CATTLE INDUSTRY.   *Peggy Imredy*

EMERALD LAKE is in YOHO NATIONAL PARK in a spectacular mountain setting northwest of FIELD. Drained by the Emerald R, a tributary of the KICKING HORSE R, it was visited in 1882 by the famed mountain guide and outfitter Tom Wilson, who named it for its brilliant colour. In 1902 the CPR, as part of its attempt to attract tourists to the mountains, built a chalet that is still in operation. The lake was featured on the back of the Canadian 10-dollar bill from 1954 to 1971. *See also* LAKES; PARKS, NATIONAL.

EMILY CARR INSTITUTE OF ART & DESIGN (ECIAD) in VANCOUVER, the leading art school in BC, had its origins in the Vancouver School of Decorative and Applied Arts, founded in 1925. It became the Vancouver School of Art in 1933 with Charles SCOTT serving as principal, and in 1978 it was renamed the Emily CARR College of Art, after the VICTORIA-born artist. The college moved to its present site on GRANVILLE ISLAND in 1980. Since 1994, when it took its present name, it has offered bachelor's degrees in fine arts and design. It has an enrolment of 700 full-time students and more than twice that number part-time.

EMISSARIES OF DIVINE LIGHT is a quasi-religious sect founded in 1940 by Lloyd Meeker, an American spiritualist. Meeker's philosophy attracted the wealthy British aristocrat Lord Martin Cecil (b 1909), who had come to 100 MILE HOUSE in 1930 to manage the Bridge Creek Ranch owned by his family. Cecil became a follower and in 1948 established a community on his property. Following Meeker's death in 1954, Cecil took over as leader of the order, which operated several businesses in 100 Mile House and had a strong influence on the town. Branches sprang up in PRINCE GEORGE, VANCOU-VER, KAMLOOPS and elsewhere as the order grew to about 1,000 BC members by the mid-1980s. As well it had extensive membership and activities worldwide. When Cecil died in 1988 his son took over leadership of the Emissaries, but the order declined and is now a shadow of its former self, though still in existence.

EMORY CITY is an abandoned MINING town on the FRASER R, 18 km north of HOPE. It was first settled in the winter of 1858–59 by prospectors looking for gold (*see* GOLD RUSH) on nearby Emory's Bar. Named for one of the miners, the townsite flourished briefly, then was eclipsed by YALE. It boomed again during the railway construction of the 1880s. In the 1930s the government established training camps here for the unemployed; by the 1990s only remnants of the camps remained. The area became a provincial PARK in 1956.

EMPIRE VALLEY RANCH is one of the oldest and once one of the largest ranches in BC. Located on the west side of the FRASER R south of the GANG RANCH, it began on a small scale in the 1880s and expanded in the 1920s under the ownership of Henry Koster Sr. Koster consolidated the Empire Valley land with the Canoe Creek Ranch on the east side of the river as the BC Cattle Co Ltd. At that time the ranch ran 3,000 head of cattle on 202.5 km². The properties were divided in 1953. Empire Valley Ranch had several owners until 1998, when the provincial government purchased it and added it to the 360 km² CHURN CREEK Protected Area. *See also* CATTLE INDUSTRY.

EMPRESS HOTEL in VICTORIA is one of a chain of chateau-style hotels built across Canada by the CPR. The name refers to Queen Victoria, Empress of India, and to the fleet of CPR Empress ocean liners. The hotel was designed by Francis RATTENBURY and built on a landfill site in JAMES BAY next to the LEGISLATIVE BUILDINGS. Since opening in 1908 it has come to symbolize the opulence of high-Victorian gracious living, and "tea at the Empress" is still a special occasion for visitors to the capital. The hotel was extensively renovated in 1989. Behind it is the Crystal Garden, designed by Rattenbury and Percy L. JAMES for the CPR and opened as a SWIMMING pool and indoor garden in 1925. Until 1954 the pool was filled with sea water. The city took over the Crystal Garden building in 1964 and closed it in 1971, but it has been restored and now offers shops and a botanical garden.

EMPRESS LINE of ocean-going steamships was owned by the CPR and provided service between BC and the Orient (Japan, China and the Philippines) from 1891 to 1941. The line began as an extension across the Pacific of the transcontinental railway. Service actually began in 1886 using chartered sailing vessels; in 1887 it used 3 charter steamships formerly owned by the Cunard Line, *Abyssinia*, *Parthia* and *Batavia*. The first 3 Empress liners were purpose-built for the trans-Pacific service by the CPR after it won a mail contract from the British government. The first, the *Empress of India*, arrived in VANCOUVER on 28 Apr 1891. There were 8 Pacific Empress liners in all, no more than 4 of them in service at one time: *Empress of India*, *Empress of Japan*, *Empress of China*, *Empress of Russia*, *Empress of Asia*, *Empress of Canada*, *Empress of Australia*, and a second *Empress of Japan*, which was renamed the *Empress of Scotland*. Elegant and speedy, they set the highest standards of luxury accommodation and fast, reliable service. During both world wars the vessels were requisitioned for military work. All but one of the liners were destroyed during or shortly after WWII, and the service was not resumed following the war.
Reading: Robert D. Turner, *The Pacific Empresses*, 1981.

Empress Hotel, on the Inner Harbour of Victoria, 1996. Allison Eaton photo

ENDAKO, pop 102, is a community on the Yellowhead Hwy (*see* ROADS & HWYS) about 170 km west of PRINCE GEORGE. Once the GRAND TRUNK PACIFIC RWY was finished in 1914, the town became a divisional point, and the railway has always been a major employer, along with the FOREST INDUSTRY. In 1965 a huge open-pit MOLYBDENUM mine opened 8 km south of town. At one time it was the largest producer of molybdenum in Canada and the second largest in the world, employing 600 people. In 1997 Placer Dome Inc sold the mine to Thompson Creek Mining Co of Denver, CO.

ENDANGERED SPECIES are species of plants, animals and plant communities considered to be in imminent danger of extinction or extirpation in BC. BC has no endangered species act, but there are some existing laws that could legally protect some species: the *Wildlife Act*, the *Ecological Reserves Act*, the *Fish Protection Act* and the *Forest Practices Code Act*. Only once in the past 20 years has BC's *Wildlife Act* been used to designate critical habitat for an animal species (the Vancouver Island MARMOT); less than 20% of ENDANGERED SPECIES in the province are protected by PARKS and protected areas.

There is also no specific legislation at the federal level, although an endangered species act for Canada was introduced in Parliament early in 2000. A national body, the Committee on the Status of Endangered Wildlife in Canada (COSEWIC), was established in 1977 to determine the status of species suspected of being at risk. As of 1999, COSEWIC listed 339 species at risk throughout the country. Another national initiative is RENEW (committee on the Recovery of Naturally Endangered Wildlife), established in 1988 by provincial wildlife ministers from across the country to work for the protection and recovery of endangered species.

Species become endangered because growing human populations are putting ever greater demands on natural resources and the environment; specifically, a number of human activities cause significant changes to ecosystems and direct loss of habitats. These include road building and other forms of access and disturbance; LOGGING, MINING, urban, recreational and HYDROELECTRIC developments; grazing and AGRICULTURE; the introduction of exotic or alien species that displace native species (*see* KNAPWEED, for example); poaching; human-caused fires; widespread air and water pollution; and CLIMATE change. Provincial wildlife authorities consider access and loss of habitat to be the 2 most important factors in the decline of wildlife populations.

Vancouver Island marmot, one of the most endangered species in the world.
Ken Bowen photo

ENDANGERED, THREATENED & VULNERABLE SPECIES OF BC

	ENDANGERED	THREATENED	VULNERABLE
Mammals	right WHALE Vancouver Island MARMOT American BADGER	humpback whale Pacific water SHREW Townsend's MOLE SEA OTTER wood bison woodland CARIBOU	blue whale fin whale grizzly BEAR WOLVERINE Queen Charlotte ermine pallid BAT spotted bat fringed myotis Keen's long-eared myotis Nuttall's cottontail western harvest mouse
Birds	Anatum peregrine FALCON burrowing OWL spotted owl sage thrasher	marbled MURRELET white-headed WOODPECKER yellow-breasted chat	Peale's peregrine falcon Queen Charlotte goshawk ferruginous HAWK Pacific great blue HERON long-billed curlew Caspian TERN ancient murrelet barn owl flammulated owl short-eared owl
Reptiles	leatherback TURTLE		
Amphibians	northern leopard FROG tailed frog (mountain)		Pacific giant SALAMANDER Coeur d'Alene salamander Great Basin spadefoot toad tailed frog (coast)
Fish	Nootsack dace Salish sucker	Enos Lake stickleback shorthead SCULPIN Texada stickleback	Pacific SARDINE white STURGEON green sturgeon Charlotte unarmoured stickleback giant stickleback Cultus pygmy sculpin lake LAMPREY speckled dace Umatilla dace Columbia mottled sculpin
Molluscs	hotwater physa		
Butterflies			monarch
Plants	southern maidenhair FERN deltoid balsamroot prairie lupine seaside birds-foot lotus seaside centipede lichen water-plaintain buttercup bearded owl-clover	Mexican mosquito fern golden paintbrush small-flowered lipocarpha white-top aster yellow montane violet western blue flag apple MOSS	Macoun's meadowfoam giant helleborine coastal wood fern phantom orchid cryptic paw lichen oldgrowth specklebelly lichen seaside bone lichen

Source: Committee on the Status of Endangered Wildlife in Canada

While only 4 animal species in BC are listed as endangered under the Wildlife Act—burrowing OWL, Vancouver Island marmot, white PELICAN and SEA OTTER—the province's Conservation Data Centre has devised a system of keeping track of endangered species: plants, plant associations and animals considered to be at risk are placed on the Red and Blue lists. Species (and plant associations) on the Red List are considered candidates for endangered or threatened status. These species occur in low abundance and are threatened with imminent extinction or extirpation throughout all or a significant portion of their range in BC. Threatened species are any indigenous species likely to become endangered if factors affecting their vulnerability are not reversed. The Blue List denotes species at risk and sensitive or vulnerable species. Indigenous species are placed on the Blue List when their populations are low or declining, when they occur at the fringe of their range (because some factor has driven them from their optimum range), or when they occur in restricted areas (areas that serve to enclose or isolate populations and prevent natural movements of genes and species). Population viability is a major concern for Blue-listed species because there is a downward trend in their population, or a downward trend in available or suitable habitat, or both. This category also includes species that are generally suspected of being vulnerable but about which there is not enough information to allow designation in another category.

In BC, 208 vertebrate species are Red- and Blue-listed, including ermine, wood bison, BADGER, all 4 populations of white STURGEON, bull TROUT, northern leopard FROG, Pacific giant SALAMANDER, western GREBE, upland SANDPIPER, Ferruginous HAWK, marbled MURRELET, northern spotted owl, purple martin, trumpeter SWAN, mountain CARIBOU, grizzly BEAR and 2 subspecies of WOLVERINE.

Native vascular plants on the lists number 595 species, 30% of the total vascular plants in the province, including yellow montane violet, pink sand verbena, southern maidenhair fern, riverbank anemone, deltoid balsamroot, 3 species of evening primrose, giant helleborine and wild licorice.

In addition to individual species, plant associations may also be Red- and Blue-listed. A plant association, analogous to a species, is a unit of vegetation with a relatively uniform species composition and physical structure, tending to have characteristic environmental features. These associations provide habitat for many rare plants and animals; most important, they perform functions that influence their environment and set the stage for complex interactions between organisms. Losing plant associations not only harms the species that depend on them, it also has far-reaching effects that are not fully understood. In 1999 there were 241 Red- and Blue-listed plant associations, including these on the Red-list: Douglas FIR/SALAL, Douglas fir/Garry OAK–oniongrass, DOUGLAS fir/ARBUTUS, ponderosa PINE/black cottonwood–Nootka rose–poison ivy, water birch–red osier DOGWOOD, ponderosa pine/black cottonwood–snowberry, and certain GRASSLAND plant associations such as bluebunch wheatgrass–junegrass. *Maggie Paquet*

ENDEAVOUR HOT (HYDROTHERMAL) VENTS

ENDEAVOUR HOT (HYDROTHERMAL) VENTS are openings in the earth's crust located on the ocean floor at a depth of 2,250 m, 250 km southwest of VANCOUVER ISLAND. The vents were discovered in 1982, along with a rich surrounding ecosystem: numerous unique species of animals are supported by microbes whose life processes are fuelled by chemical energy from the vents. The area has become a focus of Canadian and international research in which manned and unmanned submersibles are used.

In 1998 it was designated as a pilot marine protected area to encourage science, technology and education activities. *Rick Harbo*

ENDERBY, city, pop 2,754, lies in the rolling hills of the Shuswap Valley about halfway between VERNON and SICAMOUS. First settled in 1866, the tiny community was known variously as Belvedere; Little Prairie; Fortune's Landing, after A.L. Fortune, the first settler; and Lambley's Landing, after 2 brothers who owned most of the original townsite. In 1887 it adopted its present name, taken from a place mentioned in a poem by Jean Ingelow, "High Tide on the Coast of Lincolnshire." The city was incorporated on 1 Mar 1905 and AGRICULTURE and LOGGING have been its economic mainstays. While the Columbia Flour Mill was in operation (1887–1923) the most important crop was grain; DAIRY FARMING took precedence later. SAWMILLING and wood products have also been important, along with a range of small manufacturing.

ENGEN, a farming (*see* AGRICULTURE) and LOGGING settlement 100 km west of PRINCE GEORGE on the CNR and the Yellowhead Hwy (Hwy 16), was named after Fred Engen, a local pioneer. The Plateau SAWMILL was founded here by Dave Martens in the 1940s. Owned since 1993 by SLOCAN FOREST PRODUCTS LTD, the mill is one of BC's largest producers of dimension lumber (350 million board ft/yr). *AS*

ENGINEER, a GOLD MINING camp in northwestern BC, was established 32 km west of ATLIN on the southeast shore of TAGISH Lk's Taku Arm in the 1920s. Engineer Gold Mines Ltd operated here for several years, but the site was abandoned in the 1930s. *AS*

ENGLEWOOD was a SAWMILLING community in BEAVER COVE on the east side of VANCOUVER ISLAND, south of PORT MCNEILL. The name refers to the original mill owners, Fred Wood and E.G. English, who started LOGGING in the Nimpkish Valley in 1917 and built the mill in 1924. CANADIAN FOREST PRODUCTS LTD took over the operation during WWII. Though the community no longer exists, logging continues and Englewood is the site of one of the last RAILWAY LOGGING operations in N America.

ENGLISH, Marshall Martin, pioneer fish canner (b 8 Apr 1840, Charleston, VA; d not available). He was among the first generation of SALMON CANNERS who established the industry at the mouth of the FRASER R. He arrived in BC from California and in 1877 built his first cannery at BROWNSVILLE, opposite NEW WESTMINSTER. In 1882 he moved closer to the mouth of the river and built the English Cannery (later the Phoenix), the first cannery at STEVESTON. He sold to the ANGLO-BC PACKING CO in 1891 and became a manager for the new consortium. The English School at London's Landing, established in 1897, was named for him.

ENGLISH BAY is the inner portion of BURRARD INLET on the south side of VANCOUVER's downtown peninsula leading into FALSE CREEK. It encompasses a popular strip of sand beach extending along the north side of the bay near the entrance to STANLEY PARK. Originally a SQUAMISH fishing camp (*see* FISHING, ABORIGINAL), the beach developed in the 1890s as a summer swimming spot for residents of the city's West End. Initially development was unregulated and buildings of all sorts fringed the beach. The city parks board took over in 1905 and began reclaiming the beach for the public by buying up all waterfront property, a process that was not complete until 1981. Attractions at the beach have included a long pier with a dance hall at the end (1907–38) and an aquarium featuring an octopus in the bathhouse (1939–56). Joe FORTES was the guardian of the beach from 1901 to 1922. The beach continues to attract summer sun worshippers and strollers and has been the site of annual events such as the Polar Bear Swim on New Year's Day, the Sea Festival in July and the *Symphony of Fire* fireworks competition through July and August.

Polar bear swim, English Bay, Vancouver, New Year's Day 2000. Craig Hodge/Vancouver Sun

EN'OWKIN CENTRE is a unique FIRST NATIONS training centre and gathering place at PENTICTON, established in 1981 by several nations of the OKANAGAN people. The centre, which includes a resource library focussing on Okanagan culture, carries out a variety of programs including a school of writing, language-teacher training, adult education and COMMUNITY DEVELOPMENT initiatives. It is also associated with THEYTUS BOOKS, a First Nations BOOK PUBLISHER. The word *en'owkin* refers to a process of consensual decision-making.

ENTERTAINERS, EXPATRIATE, have been an important BC export over the years. Many famous and accomplished people in the arts were either born or grew up in BC but achieved their greatest success elsewhere in Canada or in the US. Some moved with their families when they were young; others left BC as adults to take advantage of better opportunities in the entertainment capitals of Toronto, New York and especially Hollywood. Among the most famous are Nell SHIPMAN, Raymond BURR, Michael J. FOX, Brent CARVER, Jeff HYSLOP, Jason PRIESTLEY, Nancy ARGENTA, Ben HEPPNER, Richard MARGISON and Pamela ANDERSON LEE, but there are a host of others, including:

Bell, Donald (b 1934, Burnaby), an opera singer who won international honours and appeared regularly in the leading opera houses of Europe.

Bellows, Gil (b 1969, Vancouver), an actor who drew attention for his portrayal of a prison inmate in the critically acclaimed movie *The Shawshank Redemption* (1994) before co-starring in the popular late-1990s television series *Ally McBeal*.

Bosustow, Stephen (b 1912, Victoria), an animator who won 4 Oscars for his cartoon work and created the memorable character "The Near-sighted Mr Magoo."

Broadfoot, Dave (b 1925, N Vancouver), a longtime member of the *Royal Canadian Air Farce* comedy troupe who is best known for his comic characters: the long-winded Member for KICKING HORSE PASS, HOCKEY star Big Bobby Clobber and the dimwitted Mountie Corporal Renfrew.

Cattrall, Kim (b 1956, Liverpool, England), an actor who grew up on VANCOUVER ISLAND and since 1975 has appeared in a variety of feature films and TV movies, including *Police Academy* (1984), *Midnight Crossing* (1988), *Bonfire of the Vanities* (1990) and *Star Trek IV: The Undiscovered Country* (1991). In 1999 she starred in the hit TV series *Sex in the City*.

Day, Richard (1896–1972), a VICTORIA-born movie set designer who won 7 Oscars, including one for his work on the classic 1954 film *On the Waterfront*. He worked with such famous directors as Erich Von Stroheim, Fritz Lang, John Ford and Elia Kazan.

Dmytryk, Edward (b 1908, Grand Forks), a director who began in films as a 15-year-old messenger at Paramount Studios in Hollywood and eventually became director of such classics as *The Caine Mutiny* (1954), *Raintree Country* (1957) and *The Carpetbaggers* (1964). In 1949, during the post-WWII Communism scare in the US, he was convicted as one of the celebrated Hollywood 10 and spent a year in jail.

Doohan, James (b 1932, Vancouver), an actor who appeared in hundreds of stage plays and in movies but is famous worldwide as "Scotty," chief engineer aboard the USS *Enterprise* in the original *Star Trek* TV series.

Greenwood, Bruce (b 1960, Vancouver), an actor who starred in the short-lived TV series *The Nowhere Man* but is better known for a series of accomplished film roles, including Atom EGOYAN's award-winning drama *The Sweet Hereafter* (1997) and the 1999 thriller *Double Jeopardy*.

Griff, Ray (b 1940, Vancouver), a singer–songwriter who has written more than 500 tunes for the top performers in the country and western field.

Hines, Mimi (b circa 1925, Vancouver), a singer–comedian who was performing in CHINATOWN in VANCOUVER when she met Phil Ford; she married him and the two became the popular stage act Ford and Hines.

Hylands, Scott (b 1943, Vancouver), an actor who after studying at UBC went on to land roles in a number of movies and TV shows, most notably as the lead in the mid-1980s CTV series *Night Heat*.

Ireland, John (1914–92), a Vancouver-born actor (brother of Willard Ireland, the provincial archivist) who began his movie career in 1945 and appeared in more than 200 films. He worked for leading directors, including Howard

John Ireland, 1966. Vancouver Sun

Hawks and John Ford, and won an Oscar nomination as best supporting actor for *All the King's Men* (1949). Later he turned to TV, where he became best known for his role as Ben Cartwright's brother on *Bonanza: The Next Generation*.

Ito, Robert (b 1931, Vancouver), an actor and former dancer with the National Ballet of Canada, who is best known for his role as the laboratory associate in the TV series *Quincy*, starring Jack Klugman.

Jackson, Joshua Carter (b 1978, Vancouver), an actor whose first major Hollywood role was in the 1992 hockey movie *The Mighty Ducks*; he became an internationally known teen idol in 1998 as Pacey in the TV series *Dawson's Creek*. In 2000 he appeared in 2 films: *Skulls* and *Gossip*.

Kidder, Margot (b 1948, Yellowknife), an actor who began her career appearing on CBC-TV while a student at UBC in the 1960s, she went to Hollywood and appeared in a string of films, most notably as Lois Lane in the 4 *Superman* movies (1979–87). Ill health left her hospitalized and bankrupt but she bounced back to become a mental-health advocate and resume her acting career.

Margot Kidder, 1987.
Colin Price/Vancouver Province

King, Allan (b 1930, Vancouver), a film director who worked for the CBC in Vancouver during the 1950s before making 2 path-breaking documentary films, *Warrendale* (1966) and *The Married Couple* (1969). He directed many TV movies and in 1977 directed the feature film adaption of W.O. Mitchell's classic novel *Who Has Seen the Wind*.

Livingstone, Mary (b circa 1906, d 1983), born Sadie Marks, an actress who met the comedian Jack Benny on one of his visits to Vancouver, later married him and played his partner for 21 years on his hugely popular radio show.

Moss, Carrie-Anne (b 1970, Vancouver), a model turned actor whose first feature film role was opposite Keanu Reeves in the 1999 science fiction thriller *The Matrix.*

Ontkean, Michael (b 1946, Vancouver), an actor who began his career playing opposite Raymond Burr in the TV drama *Ironside* and became a familiar face in dozens of dramatic roles, most notably the sheriff in David Lynch's unusual TV series *Twin Peaks.*

Owens, Patricia (b 1935, Golden), a film actor in the 1950s whose screen credits include *Island in the Sun* (1957) and *Sayonara* (1957).

Parkins, Barbara (b 1945, Vancouver), an actor whose career peaked in the 1960s when she starred in the scandalous TV series *Peyton Place* (1964–69) and the 1967 movie *Valley of the Dolls.*

Barbara Parkins, 1967. Vancouver Sun

Pepper, Barry (b 1971, Vancouver), a veteran of the TV series *Madison;* he landed a leading role in Steven Spielberg's 1998 war epic *Saving Private Ryan.*

Qualen, John (1899–1987), born John Oleson in Vancouver, a character actor who appeared in more than 100 movies, including *His Girl Friday* (1940) and *The Grapes of Wrath* (1940). During the 1930s he was famous for playing the role of the father of the Dionne quintuplets in the movies in which the quints appeared.

Sabiston, Andrew (b 1965, Victoria), an actor who was one-half of *The Edison Twins,* a hit 1984 TV series that aired in 30 countries.

Sasso, Will (b 1976, Ladner), an actor who graduated from the TV series *Madison* to a leading role as "the larger-than-life average citizen" on MAD-TV.

Seymour, Lynn (b 1939, Wainwright, AB), born Lynn Springbett, a ballerina who moved to the Vancouver area as a child and became a principal dancer with the Royal Ballet in London.

Shaw, Bernie (b 1956, Victoria), a musician who was lead singer with the British pop group *Uriah Heep,* the first western rock band to tour the then-Soviet Union.

Singer, Marc (b 1947, Vancouver), son of Polish conductor Jacques Singer (director of the VANCOUVER SYMPHONY ORCHESTRA 1947–1950), an actor best known for his starring role in the 1983 TV science fiction series *V.*

Smith, Alexis (1921–93), a PENTICTON-born actress who was discovered by a Hollywood talent scout while she was attending college in Los Angeles. She appeared in many movies during the 1940s and 1950s before retiring. She made a comeback in the 1970s, winning a Tony for her work in the Broadway musical *Follies* (1971) and also appearing in the popular TV prime-time soap opera *Dallas.*

Stratten, Dorothy (1960–80), born Dorothy Hoogstratten, a Vancouver beauty who was a *Playboy* magazine centrefold and a movie actor described as "the next Marilyn Monroe" before she was murdered by her estranged husband, Paul Snider. Her life and death inspired several books and movies.

Dorothy Stratten, 1980 Playmate of the Year. Deni Eagland/Vancouver Sun

Thomas, Audree, a ballerina who at age 14 danced with the Russe de Monte Carlo troupe using her "Russian" stage name Anna Istomina. Her parents homesteaded at Ballet Bay on NELSON ISLAND; they named the bay in honour of their daughter.

Thomson, Norman, a dancer trained in ballet by Frieda Shaw in POWELL RIVER before he went on to dance with the San Francisco Touring Co. He later became director of the State Opera House in Vienna.

Tilly, Meg (b 1960, Los Angeles), an actress who grew up in ESQUIMALT and the GULF ISLANDS and played leading roles in the 1983 hit movie *The Big Chill* and the 1985 feature *Agnes of God.* Her younger sister Jennifer Tilly followed in her footsteps, winning kudos for her role in Woody Allen's 1994 comedy *Bullets Over Broadway.*

Meg Tilly, 1992.

Tyson, Ian (b 1933, Victoria), a country singer who left BC for Toronto, where he met and married Sylvia Fricker; as Ian and Sylvia they became the most popular country duo in Canada. Since they broke up in the mid-1970s Tyson has had a successful solo singing career while also running a cattle ranch in Alberta.

Ian Tyson, country singer. Stony Plain Records

White, Onna, a ballerina trained by Frieda Shaw in POWELL RIVER, joined the San Francisco Touring Co in 1939 and in 1969 won an Oscar for her choreography work on the movie *Oliver*.

Young, Alan (b 1919, Northumberland, England), an actor and former disc jockey who appeared in the first season of THEATRE UNDER THE STARS in 1940 and went on to achieve fame as the voice of the horse in the TV series *Mr. Ed* from 1961 to 1966. *Ed Gould*

ENVIRONMENTAL MOVEMENT in BC emerged in its modern form in the 1950s with protests over HYDROELECTRICITY development. The writer Roderick HAIG-BROWN and other conservationists objected to dam building on BUTTLE, CAMPBELL and Upper Campbell lakes on the grounds that valuable wildlife habitat would be lost to rising waters and the pristine wilderness of STRATHCONA PROVINCIAL PARK would be sullied. Although these efforts were largely unsuccessful, future environmentalists took heart from the fact that protestors were able to effect small changes (the dam proposed for Buttle Lk was built on Upper Campbell instead, resulting in less flooding of Strathcona Park) and influence government policy with their actions. From this period onwards, environmental groups objected to numerous hydroelectric projects in BC. In the 1970s they succeeded in halting the expansion of Ross Lk, a reservoir created by US dams, which straddles the BC–Washington border and which would have flooded the SKAGIT R valley. One of their most dramatic successes was the cancellation in 1995 of the so-called Kemano Completion Project, a vast scheme to supply the ALCAN ALUMINUM CO's SMELTER at KITIMAT with additional power; the plan would have reduced the flow of the NECHAKO R, already depleted by the KENNEY DAM.

The preservation of wilderness areas, especially old-growth FORESTS, has provided much of

Military police preparing to arrest anti-nuclear protestor during visit of US submarine to Nanoose Bay, 1991. Courtesy Society for Promoting Environmental Conservation

the impetus behind BC's modern environmental movement. Groups such as the Sierra Club of BC and WESTERN CANADA WILDERNESS COMMITTEE have worked tirelessly to protect significant or vulnerable sites in the province. Bitter fights have taken place over MORESBY ISLAND in the QUEEN CHARLOTTE ISLANDS (1974–87), the VALHALLA MTS (1976–83) and the STEIN (1976–88) and CARMANAH (1988–90) valleys, to name just a few. Other wilderness regions, including TATSHENSHINI, KHUTZEYMATEEN and KITLOPE, were the sites of less intense conflicts. FIRST NATIONS groups have played instrumental roles in many of these struggles. Civil disobedience reached a peak in CLAYOQUOT SOUND in 1993, when over 800 anti-logging protestors were arrested and charged.

All the sites mentioned above are now protected or partially protected by parks. Many BC environmental leaders, including David SUZUKI, Colleen MCCRORY, Paul George, Joe Foy, Ric CARELESS, Tzeporah Berman, Adriane Carr and Vicky Husband, rose to prominence during these campaigns. In the face of relentless pressure from the public, the BC government developed a Protected Areas Strategy in 1992 with the goal of doubling parkland from 6% to 12% of the province's total area. A crusade by GREENPEACE and the Rainforest Action Network to boycott old-growth timber products from BC has had enough success in Europe and the US that in 1995 the BC government adopted the Forest Practices Code, a tough set of regulations on FOREST INDUSTRY practices, and in 1998 MACMILLAN BLOEDEL announced its intention to phase out clearcut logging in old-growth forest areas. Environmental activism has failed so far, however, to force serious change on provincial FOREST POLICY.

Some of BC's earliest environmental protests concerned nuclear radiation dangers. Greenpeace, now an international organization based in Amsterdam, was founded in VANCOUVER in 1970 to oppose weapons testing in the Aleutian Islands. Led in the 1970s by Bob HUNTER, it became world-famous for its anti-WHALING exploits (see also Paul WATSON, Patrick MOORE) and for protests against the North Atlantic seal harvest. Greenpeace's anti-nuclear activism was echoed in the late 1990s in BC by protests over the possible appearance of nuclear-capable submarines at the NANOOSE BAY naval testing range.

The protection of wildlife and wildlife habitat in BC has gone hand in hand with efforts to preserve wilderness and old-growth forests. Ironically, much of the initial energy behind the environmental movement came from hunting and sport FISHING organizations such as the BC WILDLIFE FEDERATION and Steelhead Society of BC, which sought to enhance recreational opportunities for members. Important habitat restoration

The Raging Grannies protesting logging in Clayoquot Sound, 1993. WCWC

projects in the province have been undertaken by these and other groups, including Ducks Unlimited and the FEDERATION OF BC NATURALISTS.

Aquatic habitats are a particular environmental worry in BC, which has 24,000 LAKES, RIVERS and streams and a 27,200-km coastline. Conservationists have prevented the OIL AND GAS INDUSTRY from exploring offshore since 1972. The PULP AND PAPER industry, targeted by the environmental movement for its toxic discharges, spent large amounts in the 1990s to clean up effluents. Acid drainage from current and obsolete BC mines (*see* MINING) is a related issue; environmental protests have erupted over future developments by Redfern Resources (Tulsequah Chief), Princeton Mining (Huckleberry), Royal Oak (Kemess South) and Manalta Coal (Telkwa). AQUACULTURE is the latest BC industry to come under scrutiny: environmentalists are demanding that salmon farms use tanks or "closed" farming systems instead of open pens and that they be banned from sensitive parts of the coast. The Living Oceans Society has lobbied BC and Canadian governments for a system of marine protected areas similar to those now established on land; other groups seek reductions in sport and commercial FISHING quotas. The destruction of ESTUARIES, especially that of the FRASER R, through urban development is another major concern for environmentalists.

In urban areas the environmental movement has directed its energies toward issues such as air pollution from automobile emissions; traffic congestion; water quality and usage; transportation options, including rapid transit and bicycle lanes; sewage treatment and garbage disposal; the loss of AGRICULTURAL land to development; and spraying to exterminate GYPSY MOTHS.

By the year 2000 hundreds of BC-based environmental organizations were active, with tens of thousands of members. Many groups, such as the Georgia Strait Alliance or the Friends of Clayoquot Sound, focus their energies on a particular area. Others, including the David Suzuki Foundation, BC WILD, West Coast Environmental Law Association, Canadian Earthcare Society, BC ENVIRONMENTAL NETWORK, Land for Nature, SIERRA LEGAL DEFENSE FUND and the Land Conservancy of BC, have a broad outlook. BC's GREEN PARTY reflects the environmental movement's political aspirations. While the party has yet to come close to electing a provincial MLA, it has had success on the municipal level; members were elected to Vancouver's parks board and Victoria's city council for the first time in 1999. *See also* AGRICULTURAL LAND RESERVE; BIODIVERSITY; COMMISSION ON RESOURCES AND THE ENVIRONMENT; ENDANGERED SPECIES; SOCIETY PROMOTING ENVIRONMENTAL CONSERVATION. *AS*

EQUESTRIAN SPORTS date back to the early settlement of the province, when horses were used extensively for travel and manual labour but were also ridden recreationally. Early RODEOS included horse events. Organized equestrian riding under international rules was taken up seriously in BC in the late 1950s; Jean McKenzie and Inez Profpe-Credo became the first British

Stav Adler riding Scotch Chocolate at the Richmond Riverside Equestrian Centre, 1998.
Bill Keay/Vancouver Sun

Columbians to succeed on the international level by winning a dressage-team bronze in the 1967 Pan American Games. Profpe-Credo also joined Robin Hahn, a BC 3-day rider, at the 1968 Mexico Olympics. Other competitors who have succeeded at the international level include show jumpers Barbara Simpson Kerr and Laura Tidball Balisky, dressage riders Leslie Reid and Shannon Oldham-Dueck and 3-day rider Therese Washtock. Equestrian riders in BC also participate in *English, Western* (rodeo) and *Driving* disciplines. Orville Unrau of ROCK CREEK emerged as BC's most successful driving competitor, when he made a strong showing at the 1998 World Singles Combined Driving Championship. BC holds many annual equestrian competitions throughout the province, including the PACIFIC NATIONAL EXHIBITION Horse Show, Milner Downs in LANGLEY, the western events at the CLOVERDALE RODEO and 3-day riding at the Chase Creek Event.

In 1998, there were approximately 90,000 horses in BC and the horse industry—including breeding, racing and feeding—generated $771 million of economic activity. The non-profit Horse Council of BC, initiated in 1980, fosters and promotes all horse-related activities in the province. *See also* HORSE RACING.

ERICKSON, 4 km east of CRESTON, is in a fertile valley of farms and orchards (*see* AGRICULTURE) on Hwy 3 (also called the Crowsnest Hwy), which is lined at this point with fruit and vegetable stands. LOGGING is also important to the area. The community was named for E.G. Erickson, CPR superintendent at CRANBROOK from 1904 to 1908. *AS*

ERICKSON, Arthur Charles, architect (b 14 June 1924, Vancouver). After studying at UBC and McGill Univ, he began practising in VANCOUVER in 1953. No other architect has done as much to shape the face of the city, and he is international-

ly renowned for his work in Vancouver and elsewhere. His notable Lower Mainland projects include SFU, the Robson Square Complex (comprising Robson Square, Law Courts and the VANCOUVER ART GALLERY), the MUSEUM OF ANTHROPOLOGY and Central Library at UBC, and the MACMILLAN BLOEDEL office tower, as well as award-winning private homes, experiments in work-live housing structures, and the Portland Hotel development for homeless and indigent people. Notable projects beyond BC include Roy Thomson Concert Hall in Toronto; the Univ of Lethbridge; the Canadian embassy in Washington, DC; the Canadian Pavilion at Expo 70 in Osaka, Japan; the Univ of Arizona business

Arthur Erickson, Vancouver architect.

school; the convention centre in San Diego, CA; and the International Glass Museum in Tacoma, WA. Erickson has received many prestigious civic and architectural honours, including a Molson Prize for outstanding contributions to Canadian culture (1967); the Royal Bank of Canada gold medal and award for contributions "to human welfare and the common good" (1971); the gold medal of the French Academy of Architecture and the Royal Architectural Institute of Canada. He is a companion in the Order of Canada (1981) and the only Canadian to receive the American

Institute of Architecture's gold medal (1986). During the economic recession of 1987–92 he closed offices in Toronto and Los Angeles, and in 1992 he filed for personal bankruptcy. When a real estate developer planned to purchase his home and remove his remarkable garden, which gives an illusion of endless country landscape on 2 city lots, a grassroots movement sprang up and succeeded in saving the property. The Arthur Erickson Garden Foundation was established to preserve the residence as a heritage site, which permits him to live there for his lifetime. Erickson has continued to design buildings for clients around the world, and to be an outspoken commentator on the future of his native city.

Edith Iglauer

Readings: Arthur Erickson, *The Architecture of Arthur Erickson*, 1975; Edith Iglauer, *Seven Stones: A Portrait of Arthur Erickson, Architect*, 1981.

ERIE, 34 km south of NELSON on Hwy 3B at Erie Crk, was a MINING settlement on the NELSON & FORT SHEPPARD RWY founded in the 1890s to serve the nearby Relief and Arlington GOLD mines. By 1903 Erie had 2 hotels and a population of 200. Mining took place intermittently in the area until the 1950s, by which time the community had waned. Today there are just a few buildings beside the highway.   AS

ERIKSEN, Bruce Gordon, social activist (b 21 Mar 1928, Winnipeg; d 16 Mar 1997, Vancouver). Raised in an orphanage from the age of 5, by 14 he was on his own riding the rails. At 16 he shipped aboard a grain freighter to China, then returned to BC and worked as a logger, construction worker and ironworker. In VANCOUVER in 1973 he was a founder and first president of the DOWNTOWN EASTSIDE RESIDENTS ASSOCIATION (DERA), a community group seeking to improve living conditions for residents of that inner-city neighbourhood, one of the poorest in Canada. Eriksen was elected to city council in 1980 and was re-elected 5 times before retiring in 1993. His widow Libby Davies, also a council member, later served as Member of Parliament for Vancouver East.

ERRINGTON, a tiny community 34 km northwest of NANAIMO on VANCOUVER ISLAND, got its start in the early 1890s when J.A. McCarter built a roadhouse on the route to PORT ALBERNI. A general store, restaurant and weekend crafts and produce market are located here. At the end of the Errington Road is Englishman River Falls Provincial PARK. AGRICULTURE, LOGGING and some TOURISM are the economic mainstays. Errington is named after a village in Northumberland, England, mentioned in Sir Walter Scott's poem, "Jock of Hazeldean."   AS

ESPERANZA INLET is a narrow channel on the west coast of VANCOUVER ISLAND connecting the outer coast to Zeballos Inlet and TAHSIS Inlet, both at the north end of Nootka Island. Traditionally it was occupied by the Nuchatlaht and Ehattesaht, two NUU-CHAH-NULTH nations, and both still have villages in the area. Capt

James COOK named it Hope Bay during his 1778 visit; it was later renamed by the Spanish mariner Alejandro MALASPINA. During the heyday of the PILCHARD fishery (1925–45), 5 reduction plants were in operation. ZEBALLOS, at the head of Zeballos Inlet, was a GOLD MINING centre from 1936 to 1948. LOGGING later became the main economic activity, but TOURISM, sport FISH-ING and AQUACULTURE have grown in importance. The Nootka Mission Hospital was built in 1937 at the east end of the inlet at a site known as Esperanza; the mission now uses the buildings for retreats. Inhabitants of the inlet are supplied by the MV *UCHUCK III*, which operates out of GOLD RIVER.

ESQUIMALT, district municipality, pop 16,151, overlooks a natural harbour at the southern tip of VANCOUVER ISLAND adjacent to VICTORIA. Originally the territory of Coast Salish  people (*see* SALISHAN FIRST NATIONS), it was visited in 1790 by Manuel QUIMPER, a Spanish naval officer who was exploring JUAN DE FUCA STRAIT. The name Esquimalt derives from a Salish word meaning "place of gradually shoaling water," a reference to the tidal flats at the head of the harbour. In 1843 HBC Chief Factor James DOUGLAS surveyed the area preparatory to establishing a trading post at Victoria; most of the site was used subsequently as farmland (*see* AGRICULTURE) by the PUGET'S SOUND AGRICULTURAL CO. The British navy used the harbour from 1846; in 1865 it created the Royal Naval Establishment to replace Valparaiso as the headquarters of its Pacific Squadron. Naval developments continued with the opening of a graving dock in 1887. Since 1910 the Royal Canadian Navy has maintained its principal west coast base and training establishments here. Civilian SHIPBUILDING has been important too; the Esquimalt Marine Rwy,

founded in 1893, evolved into Versatile Pacific Shipyards. The ESQUIMALT & NANAIMO RWY began operation in 1888 and a garrison of soldiers has been based at the historic Work Point Barracks since 1887. Incorporated on 1 Sept 1912, the municipality is one of the major residential suburbs of the capital area.

ESQUIMALT & NANAIMO RAILWAY (E&N), linking the 2 VANCOUVER ISLAND communities, was completed on 13 Aug 1886 when Prime Minister Sir John A. Macdonald, on his only visit to BC, drove the last spike at Cliffside near SHAWNIGAN LAKE. It was the partial fulfillment of a promise by Macdonald that ESQUIMALT would be the terminus of the transcontinental railway. The line was built by a syndicate headed by the COAL baron Robert DUNSMUIR, under Chief Engineer Joseph Hunter. In return, the builders received $750,000 and a land grant of 8,000 km^2, about one-fifth of the entire island. In 1905 the CPR acquired the E&N and all its lands. The line eventually ran from VICTORIA to COURTENAY

The Esquimalt & Nanaimo Railway has connected Courtenay and Victoria since 1914.
Robert Turner photo

E & N RAILWAY

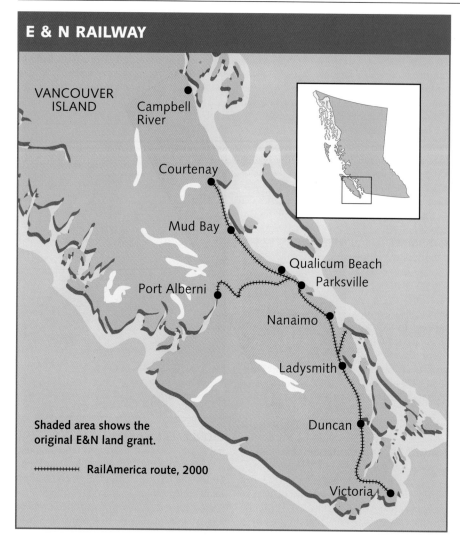

VANCOUVER ISLAND

Campbell River

Courtenay

Mud Bay

Qualicum Beach
Parksville

Port Alberni

Nanaimo

Ladysmith

Duncan

Victoria

Shaded area shows the original E&N land grant.

++++++++ RailAmerica route, 2000

The estuary of the Lockhart Gordon Creek on the Central Coast of BC. Ian McAllister photo

(1914), with branches to PORT ALBERNI (1911) and Lake Cowichan (1911). It provided the major north–south transportation link on the island until ROADS were expanded after the 1920s, and it was very important for the FOREST INDUSTRY, especially in the Cowichan Valley and at Port Alberni. VIA Rail, a CROWN CORPORATION, was created in 1977 and took responsibility for passenger service on the Island. VIA tried to end passenger service in 1989 as part of the cutbacks to Canada's rail system but opposition from the BC government led to a decision to retain the service. In 1999 the CPR turned the freight portions of the E&N over to RailAmerica Inc, a Florida-based rail company. VIA continues to operate passenger service between Victoria and Courtenay.

ESTEVAN POINT is at the tip of rugged HESQUIAT Peninsula at the north end of CLAYOQUOT SOUND on the west coast of VANCOUVER ISLAND. It was named in 1774 by Spanish explorer Juan PEREZ after one of his officers, Estéban José MARTINEZ. The LIGHTHOUSE, built in 1908–09, is the tallest on the coast (38.7 m). Some claim that on 20 June 1942 a Japanese submarine fired on the light; if it is true, Estevan Point is the only place in Canada to come under enemy fire during either world war.

ESTUARIES occur where rivers empty into the sea. They are transition zones between the fresh water of RIVERS and the salt water of the ocean. Like all transition ecosystems, they are places of tremendous BIODIVERSITY. Nutrients wash down

the river to mix with and enrich the near-shore marine environment. Estuaries are among the richest, most productive, most diverse ecosystems on earth. But they are also among the most endangered: just as sediments and nutrients flow downstream, so do pollutants from industrial, agricultural and settlement activities. Estuaries not only bear the brunt of human waste and contamination, they often suffer physical alteration from diking and industrial and settlement developments.

Estuaries perform a number of ecological functions. A variety of habitat types are found in and around estuaries, including shallow open waters, freshwater and salt marshes, sandy beaches, mud and sand flats, rocky shores, OYSTER reefs, river deltas, tidal pools, SEAGRASS and KELP beds, and wooded swamps. The WETLANDS adjacent to many estuaries filter out sediments, nutrients and pollutants. Because of the richness of life in estuaries—from myriad microscopic organisms to many types of large specialized plants and animals—they provide permanent and seasonal habitat for numerous plants, animals and fish. They provide critical staging and

The light station at Estevan Point, c 1950.

nesting habitat for hundreds of thousands of migratory birds and waterfowl. Their often sheltered tidal waters are safe places for spawning fish and shellfish; in this way they are regarded as nursery grounds. The seaward boundaries of estuaries—whether reefs, barrier islands or fingers of land, mud or sand—help to diminish the full brunt of the ocean's force and act as buffers against storm surges.

Estuaries also provide important economic and cultural benefits. Most commercial species of fish and shellfish either have their beginnings in estuaries or are nurtured in one at some point (*see* FISHING, COMMERCIAL). Estuaries of large sediment-laden rivers like the FRASER R are major places of deposition where extensive areas of rich AGRICULTURAL lands build up. Harbours and ports are often built on estuaries, and they provide a wealth of TOURISM and recreation opportunities.

Estuaries are found along less than 3% of BC's 7,000-km-long indented, island-dotted coastline, yet they are used by about 80% of all coastal wildlife.   *Maggie Paquet*

EULACHON (*Thaleichthys pacificus*), also known as oolichan and by a variety of other spellings, is a member of the SMELT family. Eulachon are thin, elongated, silvery fish that spawn in large numbers each spring in the lower reaches of several major coastal RIVERS from Alaska to northern California. Upon hatching they are immediately flushed out to sea. Little is known about their larval or juvenile stages. During their 3- to 4-year lifespan they grow to a length of 20 cm. Eulachon have been an important food resource for FIRST NATIONS for thousands of years. They were rendered to produce oil, or grease, which was used as a condiment, a preservative, a medicine and a valuable trade item. They are so oily that a dried fish will burn like a candle, which accounts for their nickname, candlefish. Ancient trade routes known as grease TRAILS linked coastal fishing sites to Interior groups. A commercial gillnet fishery began on the NASS R in 1877 and by the early 1900s the fishery was the 5th most valuable in BC. Spawning returns began to fluctuate greatly in the 1990s and most runs have shown a marked decrease from historical levels. In 1994 concerns over low and declin-

Eulachon. Phil Edgell photo;
drawing courtesy Fisheries & Oceans Canada

Eulachon drying on racks at the Nass R, 1882.
BC Archives G-09232

ing abundance closed the eulachon fishery on the FRASER R. *See also* FISHING, ABORIGINAL; FISHING, COMMERCIAL.

EUPHAUSIID, also known as krill, is a tiny crustacean arthropod bearing a superficial resemblance to SHRIMP. Among other differences, euphausiids (order Euphausiacea) have 6–8 pairs of 2-branched legs, while shrimp have 5 pairs of unbranched legs. Approximately 85 species of euphausiid occur throughout the world's oceans and 23 have been reported in BC waters, with *Euphausia pacifica* apparently making up most of the biomass. This krill species has a life span of about 19 months for males and 22 months for females. Krill body length ranges in size from 5–150 mm, depending on the species, but most are between 10 and 30 mm long. Euphausiids are a major food source for many species of adult fish, SEALS, WHALES and marine birds. Larval and immature fish may also feed on the smaller juvenile euphausiids. By day, many euphausiids live in the dark depths of the ocean at 100 m or more. At night they migrate to the surface and feed on phytoplankton. Commercial TRAWLING of *Euphausia pacifica* began in 1970 in GEORGIA STRAIT and adjacent mainland inlets. Most of the harvested krill are frozen for use in the manufacture of fish food for AQUACULTURE. A small portion of the catch is freeze-dried and used as aquarium pet food. Because of concerns that euphausiids are a forage species upon which SALMON and other finfish depend, only a limited number of commercial licences have been issued and a very conservative annual quota has been set. The total catch quota is estimated to be less than 0.1% of the annual euphausiid production in exploited areas.

EVANGELISM; *see* CONSERVATIVE PROTESTANTISM.

EVANS, Arthur Herbert "Slim," labour activist (b 24 Apr 1890, Toronto, ON; d 13 Feb 1944, Vancouver). After training as a carpenter he moved to western Canada in 1911. There he got involved in radical labour politics as a member of the INDUSTRIAL WORKERS OF THE WORLD. He was working in the mines in KIMBERLEY when the One Big Union formed in 1919 and he became an organizer in the coalfields at Drumheller, AB. During the 1920s he served 3 years in prison for using United Mineworkers funds without permission to fund a wildcat strike at the mines. Unrepentant, he moved to BC on his release and became an organizer for the Communist Party. He was one of the leaders of the ON-TO-OTTAWA TREK in 1935, and when the trek stalled in Regina he was chair of the delegation invited to Ottawa by Prime Minister R.B. Bennett. During the heated meeting, Bennett called him a thief and he called Bennett a liar. Back in Regina he was among the trekkers arrested, then released. Later he organized miners in TRAIL and shipyard workers on the coast. He died from injuries sustained when he was struck by a car. *See also* LABOUR MOVEMENT; MINING.

EVANS, Hubert, writer (b 9 May 1892, Vankleek Hill, ON; d 17 June 1986, Sechelt). Before completing high school he dropped out to begin a career as a NEWSPAPER reporter, which brought him to BC. During WWI he served in the trenches of France and was wounded at Ypres. After returning to BC, he worked as a fisheries officer. He sold his first freelance article to *The New Yorker* magazine and by the mid-1920s he was writing full-time. His career spanned 60 years, during which time he produced a steady stream of books, stories, plays, poems and arti-

Hubert Evans, Sunshine Coast writer.

cles, most for juvenile readers, from his home at ROBERTS CRK. He wrote three adult novels: *The New Front Line* (1927), about a war veteran homesteading in BC; *Mist on the River* (1954), the first Canadian novel to depict aboriginals realistically as central characters; and *O Time in Your Flight* (1979), written in his eighties, about a boy in Ontario in 1899. In 1984 he received an honorary degree from SFU.

EVELYN, 12 km northwest of SMITHERS on the GRAND TRUNK PACIFIC RWY, was named after Evelyn Smithers, daughter of GTP chairman Sir Alfred Waldron Smithers. In 1999 only the community hall (a former school) remained of this small farming settlement. *AS*

EVERYMAN THEATRE, VANCOUVER's first permanent professional THEATRE company, was formed in 1946 by the actor/teacher Sydney RISK to provide work and training for young Canadian actors. The company performed works in repertory, toured BC and Canada and put on school productions. Several members went on to distinguished careers in the theatre, including Murray Westgate, Ted Follows, Arthur Hill, Bruno GERUSSI and Joy COGHILL. But the company was plagued by financial problems and differences over artistic direction. In 1953 it mounted a production of *Tobacco Road* that was closed by the police in mid-performance for being "lewd and filthy." Subsequent court cases added to the company's problems and it closed later that year.

EWEN, Alexander, pioneer salmon canner (b 22 Nov 1832, Aberdeen, Scotland; d 8 July 1907, New Westminster). His father was a SALMON fisher and he became foreman of several fishing stations on the coast of his native Scotland. In 1864 he arrived in BC to manage a FRASER R salmon-curing operation owned by Alexander Annandale. When the enterprise failed after one season, Ewen continued fishing and salting salmon for export. In 1871 he opened his first cannery at ANNIEVILLE in partnership with Alexander Loggie and others. This was the beginning of uninterrupted SALMON CANNING on the river. When Loggie withdrew, the operation became Ewen and Wise and, after 1878, Ewen and Co. In 1884 Ewen built what was then the largest cannery on the Fraser R at LION ISLAND, and he emerged at the end of the decade as one of the leading independent firms in the business. He managed to maintain his success during the booming 1890s, when the number of canneries tripled. Along with his business interests, he was an active LIBERAL and served several terms on NEW WESTMINSTER council. By 1901 the elderly Ewen welcomed the chance to merge his canneries with a newly formed conglomerate, the BC Packers' Assoc (*see* BC PACKERS), of which he was the president until his death.

EWINGS LANDING is a rural AGRICULTURAL settlement and former sternwheeler (*see* PADDLE-WHEEL STEAMBOATS) stop on the west side of OKANAGAN LK, 20 km southwest of VERNON. It is named after R.L. Ewing, who settled here in the early 1900s, opened a store and served as postmaster. *AS*

EXPO 86 was an international transportation and communications exposition in VANCOUVER timed to celebrate the city's centennial. It opened 2 May 1986 and ran 165 days to 13 Oct, attracting 22,111,577 visitors. The single-day attendance record was 341,806. Criticized as a giant make-work project that diverted public money from much-needed social programs, it was promoted by its boosters as a way of putting Vancouver on the map as a world-class city; it was also touted as a source of economic spin-offs. The main site on the north shore of FALSE CREEK contained 65 pavilions, along with theatres, restaurants, rides, plazas and a 5.4-km monorail. Canada Place, the federal government pavilion, was built across town from the main site on BURRARD INLET. It later became a convention centre and CRUISE SHIP terminal. Other prominent facilities that stayed in place after the fair include BC PLACE STADIUM, SCIENCE WORLD BC and the SKYTRAIN. A total of 54 countries participated, along with 7 provinces, 2 territories, 3 American states and 41 corporations, making it the largest special-category exposition ever held. It was managed by Expo 86 Corp, a non-profit agency chaired by the entrepreneur Jim PATTISON. The fair's commissioner general was Patrick Reid, a diplomat. The total cost of $1.5 billion was shared by federal and provincial governments and corporate participants. The $311-million deficit was picked up by provincial lottery revenues. In 1988, the provincial government sold the 82.5-ha site on False Creek to Concord Pacific Developments, a company owned by the Hong Kong billionaire LI KA-SHING, which began building a vast commercial–residential complex known as Concord Pacific Place.

EXTENSION, a small residential community southwest of NANAIMO, was the site of one of the DUNSMUIR family's COAL mines. After MINING began in 1897, coal was shipped by rail to the wharves at LADYSMITH. Much of the town was wrecked by rioters during the 1913 strike, but it rallied and survived until 1931; that year the mine closed and most residents moved away. *See also* COAL MINING, VANCOUVER ISLAND.

Fireworks at Expo 86, Vancouver.
Larry Scherban/Image Makers

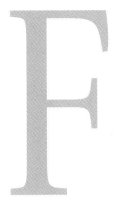

and broadcasts in Mandarin, Korean and Vietnamese. Fairchild also has radio stations in Vancouver, Toronto and Calgary.

FAIRMONT HOT SPRINGS, pop 364, between Columbia and Windermere lakes, about 100 km north of CRANBROOK, were used by FIRST NATIONS people long before the earliest settlers arrived in the 1880s. TOURISM facilities were established at the springs in 1909. *See also* HOT SPRINGS.

FAIRVIEW is an abandoned GOLD MINING town in the south OKANAGAN VALLEY west of OLIVER. It began in 1890 with the discovery of the Stemwinder mine. As several more mines opened they provided business for a growing number of hotels and saloons. The population grew to 500 before the gold suddenly gave out in 1906. The mines closed, and by the 1920s the site was deserted.

FAIRWEATHER, MOUNT (el 4,663 m) is the highest peak in BC. It is in the ST ELIAS MTS of the Outer Mountains System at the top end of the Alaska Panhandle, where it straddles the BC–Alaska border near TATSHENSHINI–ALSEK Provincial Park (Mt WADDINGTON is the highest peak wholly within BC). Rising almost directly from the water, it has a massive appearance. It was named by James COOK in 1778 to commemorate the "fair weather" he was encountering. The mountain was first climbed in 1931 by the American mountaineers Terris Moore and Allen Carpe. A Canadian party made the second ascent in 1958 to mark the BC Centennial. After climbing a new route, Fips Broda, Paul Binkert, Joseph Hutton and Walter Romanes reached the summit on 26 June. The following day Denis Moore, Russell Yard, David Blair and Paddy Sherman, the team leader, reached the top. Despite its name, the mountain is often wrapped in clouds and receives enormous amounts of snow.

FALCON is a speedy bird of prey with long, pointed wings, long tail and a notched beak that

Merlin, or pigeon hawk, a small species of falcon. Ervio Sian photo

FAHRNI, Mildred (Osterhout), peace activist (b 2 Jan 1900, Rapid City, MB; d 12 Apr 1992, Vancouver). The daughter of a METHODIST minister, she moved with her family to BC in 1914. After graduating with an MA from UBC she taught school in VANCOUVER, but the classroom did not satisfy her social activism so she left BC to do graduate studies at Bryn Mawr College in Pennsylvania and the London School of Economics. By the time she returned to Vancouver in the early 1930s, she had met and been deeply influenced by Mahatma Gandhi and the Fabian Socialists. She was a leading influence in the CCF after it was formed in 1932 and ran successfully for a term on the city school board (1936–37). Her already high profile was enhanced by her weekly radio program, *The Woman's Point of View*. With the outbreak of WWII her dedication to pacifism came to the fore. She was active in the Fellowship of Reconciliation and the WOMEN'S INTERNATIONAL LEAGUE FOR PEACE AND FREEDOM (WILPF) and made a lecture tour of Canada opposing the war. She continued to be a leading international peace activist for the rest of her life.

FAIR HARBOUR is in KYUQUOT SOUND and up Tahsish Inlet, south of BROOKS PENINSULA on the west coast of VANCOUVER ISLAND. A LOGGING camp was active at the head of the harbour in the 1960s, and GOLD and iron ore have also been mined in the area (*see* MINING). A wharf and FOREST SERVICE campground at this site allow access into Kyuquot Sound. *AS*

FAIRBAIRN, Bruce, record producer (b 30 Dec 1949, Vancouver; d 17 May 1999, Vancouver). An urban planning graduate from UBC, he joined an R&B/funk/jazz ensemble, Sunshyne, as a trumpet player in the mid-1970s. By 1976 Sunshyne had evolved into PRISM; when Prism entered the studio to record its first album, Fairbairn began his career as a record producer.

He won the 1980 Juno Award for producer of the year for the album *Armageddon*. He also began producing the hard rock acts Blue Oyster Cult and LOVERBOY, whose album *Get Lucky* sold more than 3 million copies in the US and earned Fairbairn his second Juno. He was then hired to produce *Slippery When Wet*, the breakout album of the New Jersey rocker Bon Jovi, and Aerosmith's 1987 album, *Permanent Vacation*. Following his success with Aerosmith—he received his third production Juno for their 1989 album, *Pump*—Fairbairn worked with AC/DC, Van Halen, Kiss and INXS. Most of his records were made at the Little Mountain Sound Studio in Mount Pleasant until 1994, when he purchased Kitsilano's Armoury Studios from Jim VALLANCE, a former bandmate. In the late 1990s Fairbairn ventured beyond his usual hard rock boundaries, making records with bands such as the Cranberries, Atomic Fireballs and Yes. He was inducted posthumously into the Canadian Music Hall of Fame. *Mike Harling*

FAIRBRIDGE FARM SCHOOL was a residential school for underprivileged British youngsters, established in 1935 near DUNCAN on VANCOUVER ISLAND. It was named for Kingsley Fairbridge (1885–1924), a Rhodes scholar from Rhodesia who founded the Child Emigration Society in 1913 to create a series of farm schools in the British dominions. The Duncan school, intended to train young agriculturalists, remained in operation through WWII but closed soon after the war ended in 1945, and the property became a dairy.

FAIRCHILD MEDIA GROUP is a CHINESE-language BROADCASTING company owned by Thomas Fung of VANCOUVER. It operates 2 television networks: Fairchild TV, the only national Chinese-language pay TV network, with stations in Vancouver, Edmonton, Calgary and Toronto; and Talentvision, which is based in Vancouver

ends in a hook. It nests in trees or high on rock ledges close to open areas, where it prefers to hunt. Five species occur in BC. The American kestrel, sometimes called the sparrow hawk (*Falco sparverius*), is a robin-sized bird common throughout the province in summer, which feeds on mice and large INSECTS. The female is mottled brown; the male has blue wings. The merlin, or pigeon hawk (*Falco columbarius*), is another small species occurring widely across BC in most habitats and feeding on small birds. The peregrine falcon (*F. peregrinus*), about the size of a CROW, is present mainly along the coast; it breeds on cliff ledges, trees or headlands in close proximity to populations of shorebirds, seabirds or other waterfowl, which are its main prey. There is a high concentration in the QUEEN CHAR-LOTTE ISLANDS. The gyrfalcon (*F. rusticolus*), a northern species, occurs in small numbers across BC, hunting PTARMIGAN and waterfowl. It breeds in the northwest corner of the province and migrates south for winter. The prairie falcon (*F. mexicanus*) is a brown, crow-sized bird common in the southern Interior from the FRASER R east; it feeds on birds and ground SQUIRRELS. Like other large falcons it nests on steep cliff faces next to the open GRASSLAND areas in which it hunts.

FALK, Agatha "Gathie," artist (b 31 Jan 1928, Alexander, MA). Her parents were MENNONITE immigrants from Russia and she grew up in the Manitoba Mennonite community. Forced by economic circumstance to go to work at the age of 16, she completed high school by correspondence. In 1947 she moved to VANCOUVER, where she worked in a luggage factory. While studying to be a schoolteacher she developed an interest in art, and after 12 years as a teacher she became a full-time artist in 1965. Initially she concentrated on painting, then she switched to ceramic sculpture, bringing a careful but whimsical approach to sculptures of shirts, shoes, tele-

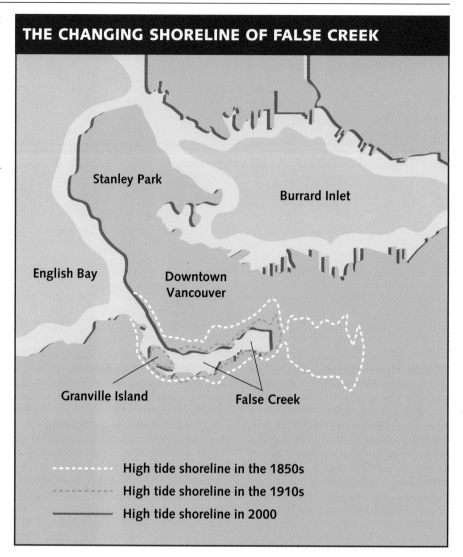

THE CHANGING SHORELINE OF FALSE CREEK

Stanley Park

Burrard Inlet

English Bay

Downtown Vancouver

Granville Island

False Creek

- - - - - - - High tide shoreline in the 1850s

- - - - - - - High tide shoreline in the 1910s

————— High tide shoreline in 2000

Gathie Falk, artist.

phones, fruit and other everyday objects. Through her involvement with INTERMEDIA she also engaged in performance art. By the 1970s her work was being purchased by major galleries and she was receiving important commissions for public installations. A quilt maker, sculptor, muralist and painter, and a recipient of the Order of Canada, she is recognized as one of the country's leading multimedia artists. The VANCOUVER ART GALLERY mounted a major touring retrospective of her work in 2000. *See also* ARTS, VISUAL.

FALKLAND, pop 620, is a small community in the SALMON R valley 45 km northwest of VERNON. The valley was on the FUR BRIGADES route running northwest from OKANAGAN LK and later attracted farm settlers, one of whom was Falkland Warren, a retired English colonel. It was the site of the largest gypsum mine in BC, in full production from 1925 to 1956 and still used occasionally by the late 1990s. LOGGING, mixed AGRICULTURE and the CATTLE INDUSTRY are the main economic activities. Falkland hosts a popular international stampede (*see* RODEO) every May. It has received national attention for the huge Canadian flag on the face of a hill overlooking the town and for the patriotic fervour of its Canada Day celebrations.

FALSE CREEK is a saltwater inlet of ENGLISH BAY extending around the south side of downtown VANCOUVER. Originally 5 times its present area, it was occupied seasonally by SQUAMISH people long before Europeans arrived. It was named by Capt George RICHARDS of the British navy, who surveyed it in 1859 and was disappointed that it did not lead through to BURRARD INLET. After Vancouver was established in 1886, the area attracted SAWMILLS, rail yards and SHIPBUILDING operations, and became the industrial heart of the city. During WWI and after, most of the east end was filled in to provide land for railways and other industrial development. By the 1950s it was polluted, congested with mills and factories, and was considered an eyesore. Civic politicians launched a reclamation effort and the south shore was transformed into a residential area focussed on GRANVILLE ISLAND. The province took over the north side for the site of EXPO 86. After the Expo buildings were removed, the site was sold to the Hong Kong billionaire LI KA-SHING, whose Concord Pacific company began redeveloping the north shore of False Creek as a residential community for some 15,000 people. False Creek is crowded with marinas and spanned by 3 major bridges: Burrard, Granville and Cambie Street.

The Burrard Bridge spanning False Creek, Vancouver, 1991. *Roy Luckow photo*

FANNIN, John, shoemaker, naturalist, first curator of the provincial museum (b 27 July 1837, Kemptville, ON; d 20 June 1904, Victoria). In 1862 he joined the group of OVERLANDERS led by Thomas MCMICKING and trekked west across the Plains and the ROCKY MTS to the goldfields of BC (*see* GOLD RUSH, CARIBOO). After years of fruitless prospecting he settled in NEW WESTMINSTER in 1870 as a shoemaker. An experienced hunter and outdoorsman, he was hired by the government during the 1870s to conduct resource surveys of the FRASER VALLEY and the headwaters of the STIKINE R. In 1877 he moved to BURRARD INLET, where he plied his trade as a shoemaker in the tiny settlement that later became VANCOUVER; he well known as a hunting guide and taxidermist. The province appointed him the first curator of the new provincial museum in 1886 (*see* ROYAL BC MUSEUM) and his own collection of stuffed animals formed the core of the museum's natural history collection. He remained curator until shortly before his death.

FANNY BAY, pop 110, is a waterfront community on BAYNES SOUND, 83 km north of NANAIMO on the east side of VANCOUVER ISLAND. The Island Hwy drops down next to the beach, offering excellent views of the SEA LIONS and waterbirds that frequent the sound. The Fanny Bay Inn is an Island landmark.

FARDON, George, photographer (b. 1807, Birmingham, England; d. 20 Aug 1886, Victoria). After emigrating to New York he went to California in 1849 during the gold rush, then moved north to VICTORIA in about 1858. By 1861 he was in business as one of the first professional photographers in the colony, specializing in portraits and also making some of the first images of BC aboriginal people. He retired in the early 1870s. *See also* PHOTOGRAPHY.

FARLEY, Lilias, painter, sculptor (b 1907, Ottawa; d Aug 1989, YT). She moved to VANCOUVER with her family when she was 17 and attended the Vancouver School of Decorative and Applied Arts (later EMILY CARR INSTITUTE OF ART & DESIGN) from 1925 to 1930. Following graduation she painted and taught at the BC College of Art from 1933 to 1935, founded by Fred VARLEY and J.W.G. MACDONALD. She also worked in theatrical design. In 1937 she designed the stewardess uniform for Trans-Canada Airlines (now Air Canada). During WWII she worked for Neon Electric Co, which was manufacturing depth sounders for the British navy. She moved to the Yukon in 1948 and taught school until her retirement in 1972, while continuing to exhibit her sculpture in Vancouver. In 1967 she was awarded a Centennial Medal for service in the arts.

FARMER'S DAUGHTER is an all-female country vocal group consisting of Angela Kelman, Shauna Rae Samograd and Jake Leiske. The 3 women, who hail from the Canadian prairies, began singing together in VANCOUVER in the early 1990s. The albums *Girls Will Be Girls* (1994), with its single "Borderline Angel," and *Makin' Hay* (1996), featuring "Cornfields or Cadillacs," earned them 11 BC Country Music Assoc awards. In 1997 the Canadian Country Music Assoc named them group of the year and the Pacific Music Industry recognized them for video of the year and country album of the year. In 1998 the women released *This is the Life*, capturing 2 more BCCMA awards and a Juno Award for country group of the year. A *Best of Farmer's Daughter* album was released in 2000. *SW*

FARMING; *see* AGRICULTURE.

FARMINGTON, pop 79, is a small AGRICULTURAL community 25 km northwest of DAWSON CREEK in the PEACE R district. There's a golf course here and a store and gas station. Just to the north, the ALASKA HWY's last original wooden bridge has been preserved on a loop of old roadway near Kiskatinaw Provincial Park. *AS*

FARRELL, Alan, boatbuilder, coastal mariner (b 12 May 1912, Vancouver). He was born Jasper Mallory Daniels and was known as Mallory for the first 33 years of his life. He grew up in a homestead on Powell Lk near POWELL RIVER and in VANCOUVER, and at age 17 went to sea on a freighter bound for China. Back in BC he worked at a variety of jobs while building wooden boats and pursuing an ambition to live on the water. Influenced briefly by KABALARIAN ideas, he took the name Alan Farrell in 1945 and his new companion, Gladys Nightingale (b 22 Apr 1922, Woodstock, ON), took the name Sharie Farrell. The couple subsequently lived together on a series of boats they built and at different locations on the South Coast. They made several long-distance trips across the Pacific and their boat, *China Cloud*, a distinctive 12.8-m junk-rigged sailboat, is a familiar sight to coastal boaters. *See also* BOATBUILDING.
Reading: Dan Rubin, *Salt on the Wind*, 1996.

Alan and Sharie Farrell aboard their boat, the China Cloud. *Maria Coffey photo*

FARRELL CREEK is a farming (*see* AGRICULTURE) and trapping settlement 45 km west of FORT ST JOHN on Hwy 29 beside the PEACE R. It was named after Henry W. Farrell, a homesteader who took up land in 1913. The area is known locally as Red R. The creek itself joins the Peace 12 km farther west. Many FOSSILS have been found here. *AS*

FARRIS, Evlyn Fenwick (Kierstead), education activist (b 21 Aug 1878, Windsor, NS; d 5 Nov 1971, Vancouver). She graduated with an MA from Acadia Univ in 1899 and taught school in Connecticut until 1905, when she married John Wallace deBeque FARRIS, a VANCOUVER lawyer, and moved to BC. In 1907 she organized the University Women's Club, a social club for university-educated women, the second in Canada. The club encouraged the founding of a provincial university and promoted a variety of socially progressive causes. Farris was appointed to the UBC Senate in 1912; later, as a member of the Board of Governors, she played a significant role in persuading the government to begin construction of the Point Grey campus. For this and other accomplishments she received an honorary law degree from Acadia Univ in 1923, the third such degree presented to a woman in Canada. UBC presented her with the same degree in 1942. Farris's husband was a leading LIBERAL politician and they were a socially prominent couple in the city for many years.

FARRIS, John Wallace deBeque, lawyer, politician (b 3 Dec 1878, White's Cove, NB; d 25 Feb 1970, Vancouver). After attending university in Nova Scotia and Pennsylvania he arrived in VANCOUVER in 1903 to become the city's first Crown prosecutor. He became a power in the local LIBERAL PARTY and in 1916 was elected MLA for Vancouver. He served as attorney general and labour minister in Harlan BREWSTER's cabinet. When Brewster died suddenly, Farris contested the party leadership but lost narrowly to John OLIVER. He resumed his post as attorney general in Oliver's government. Under increasing criti-

John W. deB. and Evlyn Farris at UBC, 1955.
UBC 1.1/10397

cism for his enforcement of liquor legislation, and alienated from Oliver, he resigned from the cabinet in late 1921. He lost his seat in the 1924 election and subsequently was named to the federal Senate. He received an honorary degree from UBC in 1938. His brother Wendell Farris was chief justice of the BC Supreme Court, and his wife Evlyn FARRIS was a prominent social activist.

FARWELL CANYON, on the CHILCOTIN R 20 km south of RISKE CREEK, is a spectacular bad-

lands area of hoodoos, sand dunes and sagebrush. A bridge crosses the canyon where FIRST NATIONS people have been netting SALMON for as long as memory records. There are pictographs on the rock walls. The canyon is named for Gordon Farwell, a CHILCOTIN pioneer, who established the Pothole Ranch in 1912. *See also* FISHING, ABORIGINAL; ROCK ART.

FAUQUIER, pop 159, a lakeside community 57 km south of NAKUSP, has been the eastern terminus for a ferry across Lower ARROW LK since 1913. The hamlet was flooded out in 1969 when HYDROELECTRIC dam construction raised water levels in the lake, but it relocated on higher ground. It is named for F.G. Fauquier, a rancher and fruit grower.

FAWCETT, Brian, writer (b 13 May 1944, Prince George). Raised in PRINCE GEORGE, he moved to VANCOUVER in 1965 to attend SFU and write poetry. He later switched to fiction and essays. Fawcett worked as an urban planner in Vancouver and a teacher in federal prisons before turning to writing full-time; his published books began appearing in 1971. *Cambodia: A Book for People Who Find Television Too Slow* (1986), *Public Eye: An Investigation into the Disappearance of the World* (1990) and *Gender Wars* (1994) are experimental combinations of fiction and non-fiction. In 1992 Fawcett moved to Toronto, where he continued to write.

FEDERAL-PROVINCIAL RELATIONS are the relations between the national government in Ottawa and the provincial government in VICTORIA. Over the years this relationship has been more or less strained depending on the issue, the economic climate, the political parties in power and a number of other factors. BC is not unique in this regard: from time to time every province, most notably Quebec, has expressed displeasure with the federation. In BC's case an attitude of ambivalence was established early. The terms by which the colony joined CONFEDERATION and became a province in July 1871 included the construction of a railway across the continent to the Pacific coast, along with other promised benefits. British Columbians took these terms seriously, to the degree that in 1874 when Premier Amor DE COSMOS suggested easing the terms in return for federal funding of a drydock in ESQUIMALT, an angry mob of 800 people invaded the legislature in VICTORIA, sending the premier scurrying for cover. Apparently the public would brook no compromise over the terms, an attitude for which the eastern Canadian press labelled BC "the Spoilt Child of Confederation." De Cosmos took the lesson to heart and in 1876, as anger grew in the province over perceived delays in the completion of the railway, he introduced a resolution in Parliament (he was by this time a federal MP) calling for BC to secede from Canada. Secession was not widely supported in the province, and never has been, but policies demanding more out of Confederation were. This antagonism toward the government in Ottawa was exacerbated by a general resentment

against the Toronto and Montreal economic elites who were believed to be denying BC entrepreneurs the capital they required to develop the local economy. In other words, from the beginning Confederation was seen in BC as an arrangement for economic benefit and evaluated according to economic criteria.

With the completion of the railway in 1885, freight rates became a bone of contention (*see* CROWSNEST PASS) but the main area of federal-provincial disagreement shifted from transportation to immigration. (Freight rates became a contentious issue again in the 1920s and 1940s.) Concerned about an influx of newcomers from China, Japan and India, white British Columbians wanted laws restricting the inflow, and thereby protecting their hegemony (*see* CHINESE, HEAD TAX, JAPANESE, PEOPLES OF BC; SOUTH ASIANS). Restrictions were eventually imposed by the federal government, which had jurisdiction in this area, but not soon or thoroughly enough for many British Columbians, who blamed Ottawa for being indifferent to their concerns. More generally, BC has had a sense of itself as Canada's window on the PACIFIC RIM and there has been a persistent suspicion that Ottawa does not understand the uniqueness this confers on the province.

Early in the 20th century the focus of federal-provincial relations shifted once again, to BC's attempts to gain "better terms" from Ottawa. Simply put, "better terms" meant larger federal subsidies. The provincial case was based on a series of contentions: that BC's mountainous geography made the provisions of basic government services uniquely difficult, and expensive; that the federal government collected tax revenues in the province in excess of what it spent there; that high tariffs caused BC consumers to pay more for foreign goods; that freight rates discriminated against the province's resource-based economy; that BC's dependence on foreign markets for its products made it particularly vulnerable to low-cost foreign competition. These arguments eventually were examined by the Royal Commission on Dominion-Provincial Relations, better known as the Rowell-Sirois Commission after its 2 chief commissioners. In its 1940 report, the commission rejected BC's arguments, seeing no reason why the province should have any unique claims on the federal treasury. Indeed, Rowell-Sirois demonstrated that BC was one of 3 "have" provinces in the country, along with Alberta and Ontario.

During the SOCIAL CREDIT government of Premier W.A.C. BENNETT (1952–72), contention between Ottawa and Victoria reached a peak over the COLUMBIA RIVER TREATY and sale of power benefits to the US; Bennett eventually prevailed, much to the satisfaction of British Columbians, who have always been suspicious that Ottawa wanted more than a fair share of the province's most valuable asset, its rich natural resources. Later, during the 1990s, BC's relations with the national government deteriorated once again, this time over commercial FISHING and lumber disputes with the US (*see* SOFTWOOD LUMBER AGREEMENT), when once again the province felt its interests were not being backed by Ottawa. Basically BC expects Ottawa to support it in any trade disputes with its neighbours and feels betrayed when it does not. Antagonism between the federal government and the NDP government of Glen CLARK came to head with the federal expropriation of the missile testing range at NANOOSE BAY in 1999. That dispute ended in defeat for the province, but on another matter, the decision to destaff LIGHTHOUSES along the coast, BC was able to persuade Ottawa to rescind its policy and leave some of the lighthouses occupied. Whatever the issue, it does not take much to remind British Columbians of the truth of the jibe, variously attributed, that Vancouver is 2,500 miles from Ottawa but Ottawa is 25,000 miles from Vancouver.

To the extent that there has been a lack of communication between BC and Ottawa, political scientists argue that part of the reason has been the absence of conventional political ties through the party system. Whatever political party has held power in Ottawa invariably had a BC spokesperson in its cabinet, but the province seldom has had a politician of stature expressing its viewpoint in Ottawa. (Two exceptions have been James SINCLAIR, who was touted as possible prime ministerial material in the 1950s, and E. Davie FULTON, a member of John Diefenbaker's cabinet.) No BC-born politician led a national political party until Kim CAMPBELL took the reins of the Conservative Party in 1993, and her brief tenure as prime minister was the only time a BC native has ever held that position. This sense of political impotence has combined with a series of economic issues to maintain the wary mistrust that usually characterizes federal-provincial relations in BC.

FEDERATED LABOUR PARTY was a socialist party created in 1918 by the BC FEDERATION OF LABOUR. It absorbed members of the old Socialist Party of Canada and the Social Democratic Party, united mainly by dislike of Russian-style communism. In 1924 it affiliated with the new Canadian Labour Party, a loose alliance of provincial labour parties, and 2 years later disappeared into the INDEPENDENT LABOUR PARTY. *See also* LABOUR MOVEMENT.

FEDERATION OF BC NATURALISTS was established in 1963 under the name BC Nature Council, a collection of 7 nature clubs. In 1969 the group received federation status and began to evolve into an umbrella organization concerned with nature conservation and education. The federation is primarily concerned with BC environmental issues; national and international issues are left to the larger Canadian Nature Federation, with which the provincial federation is affiliated. With some 50 member clubs representing over 5,300 individual members, the Federation has undertaken many tasks, including organizing bird counts, working on park stewardship and habitat restoration projects, lobbying to restore marshes and create protective barriers, and monitoring bird species, most notably bald EAGLES and peregrine FALCONS.

Federation members include birdwatchers, hikers, botanists and outdoor enthusiasts of all types. *Dianne Mackay*

FELDMAN, Samuel Leon "Sam," music agent (b 14 Mar 1949, Shanghai, China). A talent agent who began booking rock bands into VANCOUVER nightclubs in the early 1970s, he built his entertainment agency, S.L. Feldman and Associates, into the largest in Canada. He was working as a doorman at a Kitsilano nightspot when he met the band manager Bruce ALLEN, and the two became partners in a booking agency. In 1972 Allen set up an affiliated company to manage the burgeoning success of BACHMAN-TURNER OVERDRIVE. Feldman took over management of the booking agency and oversaw the expansion of its scope from local to regional to national. As Vancouver's status as an entertainment centre grew, Feldman branched out into the television and FILMMAKING industry, providing services such as a talent agency that represents actors, screenwriters and directors. In addition he became the personal manager of Diana KRALL, the Chieftains and Joni Mitchell, and was instrumental in organizing Sarah MCLACHLAN's Lilith Fair tours. In 1998 Feldman won the Walt Grelis Industry Builder Juno Award. He and Allen remained business partners, sharing interests in nightclubs, an apparel company and Ayotte Drums, a world-class drum manufacturer. *Mike Harling*

FEMINISM; *see* WOMEN'S MOVEMENT.

FERGUSON is an abandoned townsite in the LARDEAU country east of Upper ARROW LK. One of several communities founded during the SILVER mining boom of the 1890s, it was a supply centre for MINING high in the mountains north of Trout Lk. When the boom collapsed before WWI, most residents moved away.

FERGUSON, John Bowie, hockey player (b 5 Sept 1938, Vancouver). He played left wing for the legendary Montreal Canadiens of the 1960s, earning a reputation as one of the roughest players in HOCKEY. Ferguson played minor hockey in VANCOUVER before moving east to play junior in Melville, SK, and minor pro for the Cleveland Barons. He also played senior LACROSSE for the NANAIMO Timbermen and won the league's MVP title in 1963. Coaching icon Toe Blake recruited him to play for the Canadiens in 1963 and Ferguson led all NHL rookies in scoring; he checked ferociously and fought anyone who dared to face him. Over his 8 seasons with the Canadiens the team won 5 Stanley Cups. He played in 2 all-star games, led the league in penalty minutes (177) in 1966–67, and set a league record for penalty minutes in the playoffs with 80 in 1969. After his retirement from playing, he worked as an assistant coach for Team Canada in the 1972 Canada Cup, coach and general manager of the NY Rangers and Winnipeg Jets, and director of player personnel for the Ottawa Senators. He was inducted into the BC SPORTS HALL OF FAME in 1979. *SW*

FERN is a vascular plant, which means it has true roots, stem and leaves, and takes in fluid through a system of tubes rather than absorbing it through the surface. Ferns reproduce by spores instead of seeds. In fact, ferns are in between the more simple, primitive plants, such as liverworts and MOSSES, and the later evolving seed-producing plants. They are very ancient; ancestors of modern species were the dominant vegetation

Branching bracken fern. Dean van't Schip photo

on the planet 350 million years ago. All ferns have leaves that usually divide into many smaller leaflets, or pinnae. Spores are usually produced on the backs of the leaflets. Of the 114 species recorded in Canada, about 40 occur in BC; of these, 18 are on provincial Red and Blue lists (*see* ENDANGERED SPECIES). Most grow in moist, wooded areas, though some species prefer drier, open habitat. Among the most common are the ostrich fern (*Matteucia struthiopteris*), which grows in the Interior and is best known for its edible (in spring) fiddleheads, or tightly coiled leaf blades; the branching bracken fern (*Pteridium aquilinum*), possibly the most widespread fern in the world; the western sword fern (*Polystichum munitum*), a large fern that grows along the coast and in moister regions of the southern Interior; and deer fern (*Blechnum spicant*), another coastal species found on the wet forest floor. Fiddleheads are often gathered for eating but not all species are edible; in fact, some may be poisonous or carcinogenic.

FERNIE, city, pop 4,877, has been a COAL mining centre since it was founded in 1898. Located in the Elk Valley of southeastern BC and nestled among the snow-capped ROCKY MTS, it is 52 km from the Alberta border in the CROWSNEST PASS area. William FERNIE, the founder, was a prospector, railway promoter and one of the organizers of the Crow's Nest Pass Coal Co. Coal from nearby Coal Creek mine fed the steam railways that were spreading across the west and the townsite grew along with the success of the mine, earning the nickname "Pittsburgh of the West." But prosperity had a price. In 1902 an explosion at Coal Creek killed 130 men, while another explosion in 1917 killed 35 miners. Incorporated as a city in 1904, Fernie was almost completely destroyed by fire in Aug 1908. But the city rebuilt, this time in brick, and for years was the hub of the Elk Valley coal industry. Following WWII, as railways switched to diesel, the demand for coal waned; in 1958 Coal Creek closed. In the 1990s the Japanese steel industry has been a steady customer for Elk Valley coal and the city continued to be a service centre for the Michel Creek MINING region. The nearby Snow Valley Ski Resort is popular with skiers.

FERNIE, William, prospector (b 2 Apr 1837, Kimbolton, England; d 15 May 1921, Victoria). After travelling extensively in Australia and N and S America, he arrived in BC in 1860 and headed for REVELSTOKE to prospect for GOLD. His search took him to the CARIBOO and then to the BOUNDARY DISTRICT, where he worked on the construction of the DEWDNEY TRAIL. He established himself in the KOOTENAY, where he became gold commissioner and he and his brother Peter took part in the development of mining COAL deposits in the ELK R valley in the 1880s. He was involved in the Crow's Nest Pass Coal Co. The city of FERNIE, established in 1898, was named for him. In 1906 he retired to OAK BAY.

FERRARO, Ray, hockey player (b 23 Aug 1964, Trail). Among the most prolific goal scorers in

Canadian junior HOCKEY, he became an accomplished NHL scorer and grinder. Ferraro played minor hockey in TRAIL and junior A hockey with the PENTICTON Knights before joining the Portland Winter Hawks of the WHL in 1982. Alongside MAPLE RIDGE scoring star Cam NEELY Ferraro helped Portland win the Memorial Cup major junior championship in his rookie year. He played the next season with the Brandon Wheat Kings, accumulating 108 goals and 192

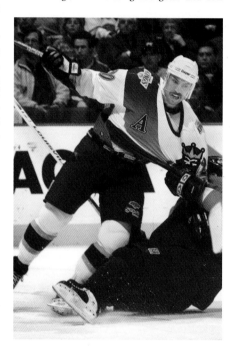

Ray Ferraro, playing for the LA Kings.
Peter Battistoni/Vancouver Sun

points. He was the only player ever to score 100 goals in the WHL and the third-highest single-season scorer in Canadian junior history behind Mario Lemieux and Guy Lafleur. His NHL career took him to the Hartford Whalers, New York Islanders, New York Rangers, Los Angeles Kings and Atlanta Thrashers. In his best season in the NHL, 1991–92, he earned 40 goals, 80 points and an all-star appearance.   *SW*

FERRIES; *see* BC FERRY CORP; BIG BAR CREEK.

FERRON, singer/songwriter. An internationally acclaimed lesbian feminist singer/songwriter who grew up in RICHMOND as Debby Foisy, she is known for her powerful and thoughtful lyrics. Her recordings have garnered remarkable critical and popular success, drawing favourable comparisons with top international songwriters such as Bob Dylan and Leonard Cohen. In 1980 she financed and recorded her breakthrough album, *Testimony*, released on her own label, Lucy Records. Her next record, *Shadows on a Dime* (1984), received critical praise from *Rolling Stone* magazine. The *New York Times* called her 1994 album, *Driver*, one of the year's 10 best. A former resident of SATURNA ISLAND, Ferron resides with her family on Vashon Island, WA, in Puget Sound. She continues to record and perform.
Mike Harling

Ferron, singer and songwriter, performing at the Vancouver Folk Music Festival, 1996.
Mark van Manen/Vancouver Sun

FIELD, pop 237, is a mountain-ringed community beside the Kicking Horse R on the TRANS-CANADA HWY, 16 km west of the Alberta border. Named for Cyrus Field, the American promoter of the trans-Atlantic telegraph cable, it began as a CPR construction camp in the 1880s and remained a railway centre for many years. In 1886 the CPR built Mount Stephen House, a rest stop that expanded in 1902 into a full hotel designed by Francis RATTENBURY; it later was operated by the YMCA before being demolished in 1954. As mountain TOURISM expanded, Field developed as the headquarters for YOHO NATIONAL PARK. The community's spectacular location attracts a growing number of hikers and climbers (*see* MOUNTAINEERING).

FIELD HOCKEY started in Canada in the late 19th century with the inception of the VANCOUVER Hockey Club in 1895 and the Vancouver Ladies Hockey Club in 1896. Competition took place between teams from Vancouver, VICTORIA, NANAIMO, NEW WESTMINSTER and WELLINGTON and a men's BC championship was awarded as early as 1903. McGill Univ College, the forerunner of UBC, formed its first women's team around 1910. The first international match was likely between a Victoria men's team (featuring future BC premier John HART) and Seattle in 1907. The Challenge Cup was inaugurated in 1911 for competition within the BC Grass Hockey Assoc composed of men's teams from Vancouver, Victoria, the ESQUIMALT Garrison, JAMES BAY and N VANCOUVER. Between the world wars the Challenge Cup was awarded to champions of the Mainland Grass Hockey Assoc, while the separate Vancouver Island & Gulf Island Hockey Assoc competed for another trophy. Representative teams from each league met every year to compete for the O.B. Allen Cup. The Women's Lower Mainland Grass Hockey Assoc, started by Marjorie McKay, in its first season 1929–30 played a handful of games with teams from Victoria, DUNCAN and GANGES.

High school girls' field hockey, Comox, 1996.
Don MacKinnon/Vancouver Province

Vancouver, Duncan and Victoria formed the Triangle League in 1939 but women's hockey did not have provincewide organized competition until the BC Women's Field Hockey Federation started in 1966.

International competition came to the fore when an Australian women's team visited Vancouver and Duncan in 1936 and women's and men's clubs from Vancouver participated in tournaments against California teams. In 1938 Con JONES (later Callister) Park hosted a Los Angeles side in N America's first grass hockey match under floodlights. The first major tournament held in Canada, the Pacific Northwest Field Hockey Conference, took place in Vancouver in 1950. In 1956 the Greater Vancouver Women's Grass Hockey Assoc sent a team to Sydney, Australia, to represent Canada at an International Federation of Women's Hockey tournament. The Vancouver club, featuring future BC Sports Hall of Fame members Eleanor Whyte and Moira Colbourne, went on a 1959 tour that included the world championships in Amsterdam. Vancouver women represented Canada again at the 1960 US National Tournament.

It was not until the early 1960s that field hockey organizations across the country were united. Harry WARREN put together the Canadian Field Hockey Assoc and assisted a women's group chaired by Barbara Schrodt in the formation of the Canadian Women's Field Hockey Assoc. The 2 associations eventually merged into Field Hockey Canada in 1992. In 1964 the CFHA sent a men's team to the Tokyo Olympics. Vancouver was the location for both the CFHA's first men's national championship in 1964 and the inaugural CWFHA nationals in

1965. The city later hosted 2 international tournaments: the 1979 IFWHA Tournament and the 1985 Junior Men's World Cup.

BC dominated the national game right through the turn of the century, winning more Canadian championships than any other province and providing a large proportion of the top talent on both the men's and women's national teams. In the early 1980s, the Canadian women's team became one of the world's best. BC's Nancy Charlton, Heather Benson, Jody Blaxland, Alison Palmer, Diane Mahy (Virjee) and Shelley Winter helped the team reach the podium at the 1983 and 1986 World Cups and at the 1987 Pan Am Games. Lynne Beecroft, a star mid-fielder from Duncan, joined Winter and Charlton for the 1983 World Cup silver and Canada's 5th-place finish in the 1984 Los Angeles Olympics. UBC has had a very successful women's field hockey program, winning 5 CIAU championships in the period 1978–91 under coach Gail Wilson. Wilson's replacement Hash Kanjee and team captain Jen Dowdswell led UBC to another CIAU title in 1998. In 1999, UBC won again in the second consecutive all-BC final with Univ of Victoria.

Prominent BC men to play the game in recent years include Lee Wright, Kelvin Wood, Alan Hobkirk, David Bissett, Ross Rutledge, Bubli Chohan, Chris Gifford, Peter Milkovich and Mike Mahood. The Canadian men's team qualified for the Olympics several times starting in 1964 and captured Pan Am gold medals in 1983, 1987 and 1999. Chohan participated in every major event from 1974 to the 1998 World Cup qualifying rounds, accumulating a Canadian record 288 international caps. Warren and Schrodt have both been inducted into the BC SPORTS HALL OF FAME for their outstanding achievements as builders. *SW*

FIELDGATE, Norman, football player (b 12 Jan 1932, Regina, SK). He travelled west to join the BC LIONS for their inaugural season in the CFL in 1954 and in 14 seasons with the team he played linebacker, defensive end and offensive lineman. He was the Western Conference all-star linebacker in 1959 and 1960, a member of the all-Canadian team in 1963 and a key player in the Lions' 1964 Grey Cup win. He is a founding member of the CFL Players Association and in his second career as a VANCOUVER businessman was active in the administration of the BC SPORTS HALL OF FAME, of which he is also a member. His number 75 is retired by the Lions. *SW*

FIFE, a small AGRICULTURAL settlement 18 km west of GRAND FORKS near CHRISTINA LK on the COLUMBIA & WESTERN RWY, was formerly known as Sutherland Siding. COMINCO had a quarry here that supplied limestone for its TRAIL smelter. It was named after a local resident. *AS*

54•40 is an internationally successful rock band with roots in the punk rock movement of the late 1970s. The band's founders, Neil Osborne and Brad Merritt, met in 1978 at South Delta High in TSAWWASSEN, and 54•40 debuted on 31 Dec 1980 at the legendary birthplace of VANCOUVER punk rock, the Smilin' Buddha Cabaret. In 1984, 54•40 released its first full-length record, *Set The Fire*, and since that time has recorded 7 more albums. In 1995 the band had its greatest commercial success when the song "I Go Blind"—from *The Green Album* (1986)—was a major hit in the US for Hootie and the Blowfish. The group's name derives from US President James Polk's 1844 expansionist cry, "54°40' or Fight!" *Mike Harling*

Members of the rock band 54•40

FIGURE SKATING began in an organized way in BC with the formation of the Connaught Figure Skating Club in VANCOUVER, the province's first, in 1914. The mild CLIMATE prevented figure skating from becoming very popular until the first public rinks were built: Kerrisdale Arena in Vancouver in 1949 and the Capilano Winter Club on the North Shore in 1955. International figure skating stars Barbara Ann Scott and Sonja Henie both performed in Vancouver in the early 1950s, helping to raise the profile of the sport. BC figure skaters first

Shae-Lynn Bourne and Victor Kraatz practising before the Canadian figure skating championships, Burnaby, 1997.
Jon Murray/Vancouver Province

participated in the Winter Olympics at Innsbruck, Austria, in 1964. Early builders of the sport included Granville Mayatt and Billie Mitchell. From the late 1960s to the early 1970s Barry and Louise Soper of Vancouver became the first Canadians to win pairs dance titles in senior, junior and novice categories. The most successful BC figure skater of the 20th century, Karen MAGNUSSEN, won the Olympic silver medal in Sapporo, Japan, in 1972 and the World Figure Skating Championships in Bratislava, Czechoslovakia, in 1973. Her coach Linda Scharfe Brauckmann trained many champions at the North Shore Winter Club and the Figure Skating Centre of Excellence. Tracy WILSON of COQUITLAM combined with Robert McCall of Nova Scotia to hold the Canadian ice dance title from 1982 to 1988 and to win 3 consecutive world championship bronze medals from 1986 to 1988. After becoming the first Canadians to win the international "Skate Canada" event in 1983, and capturing it again in 1987, they won a bronze medal at the 1988 Calgary Olympics. Victor Kraatz of QUALICUM BEACH paired with Shae-Lynn Bourne of Ontario in the early 1990s to win 7 consecutive senior national championships and 4 consecutive world championship bronze medals through 1999. They finished fourth at the 1998 Winter Olympcs in Nagano, Japan. *SW*

FIJIANS began immigrating to BC in 1908 when a group of 5 Indo-Fijians arrived in VANCOUVER. They were among the many labourers who moved from India to Fiji in the early 1900s to work in the sugar fields there. Because Canadian law at the time restricted Indian immigration, the 5 Fijians were deported to Fiji; no other immigration occurred until the late 1940s, when the first Fijian to reside in BC arrived from India, followed by a handful of native Fijians who jumped ship in Vancouver in the early 1950s. These were isolated incidents and Fijian

population did not grow in a meaningful way until Canada liberalized its immigration laws in 1962. The first 4 officially recognized Fijian immigrants arrived in Vancouver in the winter of 1962–63 and by 1968 there were 300 living in the city. The number continued to grow and in the late 1990s Vancouver had the largest Fijian population in the world outside Fiji. Most members of the community are of Indian descent. Two organizations, the Fiji Canada Assoc and the Sangam Educational and Cultural Society of BC, have been formed to serve the community and Fijian Canadians also have their own television program. In 1996 there were 14,800 people of Fijian background living in BC. *Dianne Mackay*

FILBERG, Robert Joseph, lumberman (b 1890, Sweden; d 1977, Honolulu). His family moved to Colorado when he was a child and he came to BC in 1909. He soon became chief engineer of Comox Logging Co and eventually became president of that company as well as CANADIAN WESTERN LUMBER CO. In 1954 he became a director of CROWN ZELLERBACH. During WWII Filberg served as president of Aero Timber, a company set up by the federal government to log SPRUCE on the QUEEN CHARLOTTE ISLANDS for aircraft construction. He was an active participant in several COMOX-area service and community organizations and made large charitable donations through the VANCOUVER FOUNDATION. *Ken Drushka*

FILIPINOS began immigrating to BC in the 1880s as crew members aboard the sailing vessels that visited VANCOUVER. Some of these early immigrants found work at the HASTINGS MILL in BURRARD INLET. Filipino immigration did not begin in significant numbers, however, until 1958, when a small group of migrants arrived in Vancouver. By the mid-1960s Canada's liberalized immigration laws allowed more immigrants to move to BC. Many people in this second wave of Filipino immigration were well-trained, educated people, including women who came to Canada to work as domestics or nurses. With the rise of the regime of Ferdinand Marcos in the Philippines came groups of political immigrants from many walks of life, a trend that accelerated after Marcos declared martial law in 1972 and public discontent with his administration grew. By the mid-1980s the Philippines was among the top 5 source countries of immigrants to BC. The controversial leadership of Marcos in the Philippines brought disunity to the BC Filipino community, which divided into pro- and anti-Marcos factions; tensions between the 2 groups dissipated with the end of the Marcos presidency in 1986. Since that time, immigration from the Philippines has increasingly been spurred by poor economic conditions in the islands and by the popularity of Filipino domestic workers in Canada. Filipino organizations in Vancouver include the BC Committee for Human Rights in the Philippines and the Filipino Diamonds Society of BC. The community publishes 2 newspapers and a directory, and television and radio programs are available for

Filipinos living in Vancouver. The Philippines National Day is celebrated on 12 June. In 1996 there were 49,185 people of Filipino origin living in BC. *See also* PEOPLES OF BC. *Dianne Mackay*

FILMMAKING INDUSTRY has enjoyed such a boom in BC since the 1970s that the long-cherished dream of a "Hollywood North" has been realized in the form of Canada's largest feature film and television production centre. In 1999 the film industry generated direct spending of $1,069,871,000—62% of that spent by foreign producers—for a net impact of nearly $3 billion on the BC economy. A labour-intensive enterprise, the industry was the province's third-largest in 1999, employing more than 25,000 British Columbians and generating 198 productions, including 54 feature films, 60 television movies and 30 TV series.

BC's first recorded cinematic enterprise was the exhibition of a US prize fight film in Mar 1897, when viewers packed the Trilby Music Hall on Broad Street, VICTORIA, to watch Bob Fitzsimmons defeat Jim Corbett. In Oct 1902 Canada's first permanent movie house, the Electric Theatre, was opened by John Albert Schulberg, an itinerant showman, at 38 Cordova Street in VANCOUVER. Its premiere attraction was Edison's *Mount Pelée in Eruption*.

Film realized its first commercial value as a promotional medium. To entice travellers to its Canadian destinations, the CPR became an advertising movie pioneer by producing the first film shot in BC: views of the ROCKY MTS filmed from the front of a CPR locomotive by Billy Bitzer, of the American Mutoscope and Biograph Company, in 1899. The railway also commissioned Warwick Trading Co, a British firm owned by Charles Urban, to produce films featuring BC scenery (1901) and US Edison Manufacturing Co to make a series of short travel comedies (1910). A CPR-sponsored travelogue was the first colour film shot in BC (1911). In 1908, the Urban company sent James Ferrens to shoot promotional films for BC's provincial government, which was the first in Canada to involve itself directly in movie sponsorship. The government took note of the exhibition business in 1913: it enacted the BC Motion Picture Act and established a Board of Censorship of Theatres and Film with C.L. Gordon, a former newspaperman, as its chief censor. In 1920, following Ottawa's creation of the Exhibits and Publicity Bureau—the world's first government film unit—BC set up its own production unit, the BC Patriotic and Educational Picture Service (PEPS). Exhibitors protested when it took the politically controversial step of imposing a quota, requiring cinemas to show 15 minutes of PEPS films every day. Although it existed in law until 1970, little funding and less enforcement effectively dispatched PEPS by 1925.

Coincidentally, the consolidation of Canada's exhibition business in US hands also began in 1920. In Jan of that year, with the incorporation of Famous Players Canadian Corp, the US film mogul Adolf Zukor established a theatre chain to show the features made by his Famous

Filming the television series Poltergeist, *1998.*
Ward Perrin/Vancouver Sun

Both generated commissions for Shelley's company, Vancouver Motion Pictures Ltd.

In Apr 1941 a new force in the exhibition business made its debut in Vancouver, when N.L. Nathanson, former managing director of Famous Players, opened the Vogue Theatre. It was the first link in his new Odeon Theatres chain, a circuit that Britain's Rank Organization acquired in 1946. By that time BC filmmakers were optimistic. Jack Bowdery of Vancouver identified a market niche in the network of 16mm cinemas that had grown during the war years. He formed North American Pictures and produced 4 short features before his market disappeared. In expectation of a post-war film boom, Leon Shelley relocated to Toronto; his production manager, Lew Parry, stayed in BC and founded Trans-Canada Films (1946), then sold it to Don Coltman and Wally Hamilton (1948). Lew Parry Productions was formed

Players (later Paramount Pictures) production company. In Feb 1920 it acquired its first 2 BC cinemas, and by 1926 it dominated the market. US producers began shooting features on BC locations in 1921 with *The Conflict* and continued with a series of films shot throughout the 1920s, films that were assured theatrical bookings. There was no such assurance for Canadian producers, as the story of A.D. (Cowboy) KEAN illustrates. Kean became the first British Columbian to be known as a filmmaker. He incorporated Kean's Canada Films in 1915 to produce newsreels, but when theatres refused to book them he turned to industrial films. In 1920 he became chief cameraman for PEPS. He then returned to private production and in 1927 completed *Policing the Plains*, a feature-length romance paying tribute to the North-West Mounted Police, but was unsuccessful in his efforts to have it distributed. Kean was in debt when he finally left the film business, which was institutionally inhospitable to Canadians.

In Dec 1927 the British Parliament adopted the British Cinematograph Films Act, which had a significant impact on BC filmmaking. Designed to protect the UK's indigenous film industry from US predation by imposing a quota on exhibitors, the Act generously defined Commonwealth-produced films as British. In July 1932 the British-born Kenneth BISHOP responded to this incentive by incorporating Commonwealth Productions Ltd in Victoria. With the backing of Kathleen Dunsmuir Humphries, an OAK BAY heiress with acting ambitions, Bishop leased studio space at Willows Park and produced BC's first sound feature, *The Crimson Paradise*. Although Victoria society turned out for the film's premiere in Dec 1933, Bishop was not able to find a distributor for his picture and Commonwealth went broke before

completing its second feature. With the backing of Columbia Pictures, Bishop rebounded to form Central Films in 1935, producing 12 low-budget "quota quickies" in 3 years. His efforts did not go unnoticed: in 1938 Britain revised its legislation to exclude such Hollywood-backdoor products.

In Apr 1931 the report of the White inquiry, *An Investigation into an Alleged Combine in the Motion Picture Industry in Canada*, was released. The federal royal commission had heard months of testimony from Canadian film professionals and had found that "a combine exists...and has existed since the year 1926," and that 2 US companies, Famous Players Canadian Corp and Motion Picture Distributors and Exhibitors of Canada, controlled the Canadian film market. Encouraged by White's findings, Ontario, BC, Alberta and Saskatchewan charged 15 distribution companies with offences under the Combines Investigation Act. In 1932, following a 6-month trial, the Ontario Supreme Court upheld the status quo by finding the defendants not guilty. That same year BC amended its Moving Pictures Act to give the government power to implement a quota system for films "of British manufacture," but the power was never used, and the amendment was quietly dropped from the Act in 1971. It was business as usual in 1936, the year the Vancouver Film Society was founded and the Gaumont British Company went on location in REVELSTOKE to film *Silent Barriers*, the story of the building of the CPR.

BC filmmakers who were excluded from theatrical feature production, including Leon Shelley and others, created a regional industry based on documentaries and sponsored short subjects. The pattern of government agencies taking responsibility for a significant portion of production in the province was set in 1939 when BC's Government Travel Bureau established a Photographic Branch and the federal government set up the National Film Board of Canada.

The Hollywood legend Charlton Heston working on the 1981 film Mother Lode, *the first feature film made at the Dominion Bridge Sound Stage in Burnaby. Helcermanas-Benge photo*

when Parry bought out North American Productions (1948), and the company remained the core of BC's commercial film community into the 1960s. Economists predicted that Ottawa would impose a quota on US films to stem the alarming flow of dollars out of the country. Instead, in Jan 1948, federal officials sat down to lunch with US film industry lobbyists and signed on to the Canadian Co-operation Project—essentially a promise by Hollywood studios to include more references to Canada in their films.

Television changed the economic and social dynamic of the film industry. CBUT, the Vancouver CBC-TV station, went on the air in Dec 1953. Its 16mm Film Unit, whose members included Stan Fox, Allan King, Daryl DUKE and

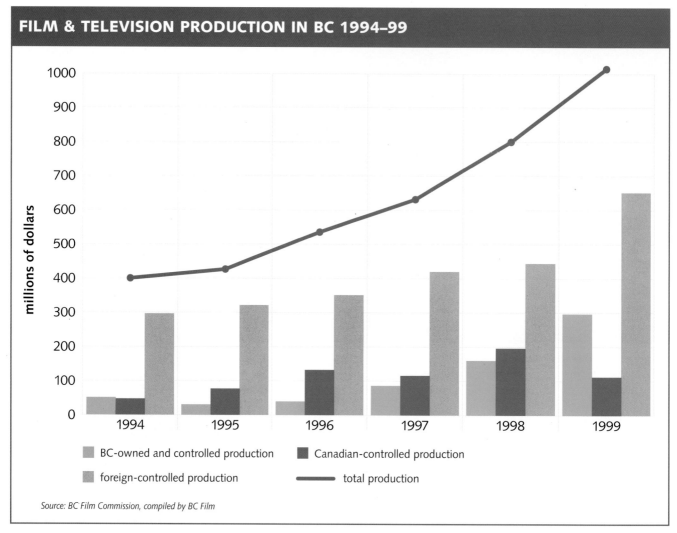

FILM & TELEVISION PRODUCTION IN BC 1994–99

millions of dollars

■ BC-owned and controlled production   ■ Canadian-controlled production

■ foreign-controlled production   —— total production

Source: BC Film Commission, compiled by BC Film

Ron Kelly, helped shape BC's sense of itself as a creative centre. CBUT documentaries such as King's *Skidrow* (1957) were recognized nationally for their excellence. *CARIBOO COUNTRY*, a tele-play produced in 1958, evolved into a mini-series (1960), then a full series (1963). By 1962 the CBC was operating 6 stations in BC. When the privately owned CHAN-TV (later BCTV)

Jean-Jacques Annaud in BC, directing Wings of Courage, *the first dramatic feature made in IMAX 3-D, 1994. Doane Gregory photo*

went on the air in Oct 1960, its main competition was the border station KVOS, located in Bellingham, WA. KVOS had been on the air since June 1953 and Vancouver was its major market. To serve its commercial clients it established offices on Burrard St and its film unit, set up in 1960 under Jack Gettles and Vic Spooner, became Canawest Film Productions in 1963. By 1965 its Vancouver animation studio was a major subcontractor for Hanna-Barbera in the production of television cartoon series. Canawest incorporated as an independent company in 1967. The broadcasters brought a sense of new opportunity to the market that was reflected in Lew Parry's decision to build a $100,000 studio in N VANCOUVER for his Parry Film Productions (1956). When Oldrich Vaclavek founded Panorama Productions Ltd to make feature films (1956), his initiative resulted in the construction in 1961 of Panorama Studios (later Hollyburn Film Studios) in W VANCOUVER. In 1958, a year after the creation of the Canada Council for the Arts, Al Sens set up BC's first animation studio. The theatrical exhibitions mix was enriched by the founding of the original VANCOUVER INTERNATIONAL FILM FESTIVAL, and in 1962 the regional office of Odeon Theatres organized the first Varsity Festival of International Films, a 2-week foreign-film showcase that ran annually until 1982. In expectation of feature

Nelson Eddy and Jeannette MacDonald in the 1936 film Rose Marie, parts of which were filmed on the North Shore of Vancouver.
Metro-Goldwyn-Mayer

Mel Gibson and Goldie Hawn in the 1990 comedy/mystery Bird on a Wire.
Universal City Studios

Everett McGill and Rae Dawn Chong in the 1981 film Quest for Fire. © Royal Bank of Canada

Mariel Hemingway as Dorothy Stratten in the 1983 film Star 80.
Ladd Company

Publicity poster for My American Cousin, directed by Sandy Wilson and filmed in the Penticton area in 1985. Spectrafilm

Publicity poster for the Vancouver-made thriller Intersection, 1994.
Paramount Pictures

Chief Dan George starring in the television show The Bears and I.
Walt Disney

Jason, the villain in the Friday the 13th series of films, 1989.
Paramount Pictures

Publicity poster for Needful Things, a Stephen King thriller filmed in Gibsons.
Castle Rock Entertainment

Sylvester Stallone in the boxing classic Rocky IV, 1985.
United Artists

Warren Beatty in the Robert Altman film McCabe & Mrs Miller, made in the Vancouver area in 1970. Warner Brothers

Richard Farnsworth (l) and Wayne Robson in
Phillip Borsos's 1982 film The Grey Fox.
United Artists

productions, Local 891 (motion picture production technicians) of the International Alliance of Theatrical Stage Employees (IATSE) was chartered in 1962, the year James Clavell directed *The Sweet and the Bitter*, Vancouver's first sound-era feature, for Vaclavek's much-restructured Commonwealth Films. At UBC, where the CBC's Stan Fox had conducted production workshops, the student film society supported one of their own, Larry KENT, in the making of 3 low-budget features: *Bitter Ash* (1963), *Sweet Substitute* (1964) and *When Tomorrow Dies* (1965). The National Film Board, perhaps recalling that the Vancouver-made *Herring Hunt* had been a 1953 Academy Award nominee, opened its first regional production office in Vancouver in 1965. The BC Film Industry Association, founded in the same year, saw renewed hope for BC filmmaking in the Anglo-Canadian co-production *The Trap* (1965), the American director Robert Altman's "discovery" of Vancouver with *That Cold Day in the Park* (1967), and the CBC's first made-for-TV movie, *Waiting for Caroline* (1967).

In Feb 1968, Bill C-204 created the Canadian Film Development Corporation (renamed Telefilm Canada in 1984). Although its mandate was to "foster and promote the development of a feature film industry," it favoured Montreal and Toronto as production centres, offering only token support in other regions. The policy was made explicit in 1972 by its first director, Michael Spencer: "Vancouver is never going to be the Hollywood of Canada and although there will likely be films made here, hopes are dim

that BC will ever have what can be called a feature film industry." Undeterred, independent filmmakers from the student and fine arts communities—Jack DARCUS, Tom Shandel, Byron Black, Boon Collins, Peter Bryant—all completed features. In 1972, Pacific Cinematheque was established to promote and exhibit non-commercial films. The CBC created BEACHCOMBERS, an international hit series (1972–89), and the service industry attracted US projects such as Bob Rafelson's *Five Easy Pieces* (1969), Altman's *McCabe and Mrs Miller* (1970) and Mike Nichols's *Carnal Knowledge* (1971).

Having produced *The Groundstar Conspiracy* (1972) on location for Universal, the British-born studio executive Trevor Wallace formed his own BC-based company and made the features *Christina* (1974) and *Journey into Fear* (1975). The Canadian government amended the Income Tax Act in 1974 to offer a 100% Capital Cost Allowance (CCA) for "certified feature films," and the emphasis shifted from domestic directors to producers. The tax-shelter production boom that followed (1977–81) occurred largely in Toronto and Montreal. The single significant BC beneficiary was the award-winning documentary director Phil BORSOS, whose superlative feature debut, *The Grey Fox* (1982), was his ticket to a Hollywood career.

In 1975 BC's animation community grew with the addition of Marv Newland's International Rocketship studio. Also in 1975 the federal government made a timid attempt to deal with the long-standing question of exhibition: it negotiated a "voluntary quota" agreement with Famous Players and Odeon Theatres, who agreed to play Canadian films in each of their cinemas for a minimum of 4 weeks a year. The plan was quietly abandoned 2 years later,

just as the era of the multiplex arrived with the opening of Famous Players' Capitol 6 on Granville Street in downtown Vancouver. In July 1975 the BC Film Industry Association recognized the need for more local initiatives and petitioned Victoria to establish an office to promote the industry. In Aug 1977 Wolfgang Richter was hired to head a BC Film Promotion Office (later BC FILM COMMISSION).

By the late 1970s all the important infrastructure was in place for an industry to provide full-service location support. The Canadian dollar had begun a decline that would reach 72 cents US in 1986—an economic reality that made it possible for US producers working in BC to realize irresistible savings. A significant increase in the production of features, TV movies, series pilots and series episodes created the need for new facilities. In 1981 a Dominion Bridge Co building in Burnaby was pressed into service as a movie sound stage for the Charlton Heston feature *Mother Lode*. It remained busy and opened officially as the provincially owned Bridge Studios in 1987, the same year Stephen Cannell brought his 3 television series—*Wiseguy, JJ Starbuck* and *21 Jump Street*—to BC. In 1989, together with Paul Bronfman, Cannell built the North Shore Studios (renamed Lions Gate Studios in 1997) in N Vancouver. The growth of the service sector was reflected in an annual industry directory, *The Reel West Film and Video Digest*, first issued in 1980. Its publishers, Sandy Flanagan and Martin Borycki, spun off the bimonthly *Reel West Magazine* in Apr 1985, and it became a vocal advocate for the BC industry. TV producers, meanwhile, were sufficiently impressed with BC to bring ever more sophisticated series into the province. By the mid-1990s, so many special-effects-dependent shows were based in Vancouver that BC became known as Hollyweird. The Vancouver International Film Festival, revived in 1982, added a Trade Forum in 1986, and a year later the privately owned Vancouver Film School opened. All of this activity contributed to the parallel growth of indigenous filmmaking. In 1987 the provincial government set up BC FILM, with Wayne Sterloff as president, to provide funding for local productions. Some BC-based producers, including Lloyd Simandl and James Shavick, prospered by making direct-to-video features. Others, including Peggy THOMPSON, Charles Wilkinson, Sandy WILSON and the fearless documentarian Nettie Wild, developed independent theatrical features. In 1991 John Pozer, a UBC film student, produced as his Master's thesis a feature film, *The Grocer's Wife*, that brought together Bruce Sweeney, Mina Shum, Kathy Garneau, Gregory Wild and Lynn Stopkewich, all of whom were also UBC film students and all of whom went on to direct their own features. The visibility of filmed-in-BC TV shows such as X-FILES (1993–97) and such blockbuster features as *First Blood* (1982), *The Accused* (1987), *Legends of the Fall* (1994) and *Double Jeopardy* (1999), have established BC as a major N American production centre, rivalling New York for the number 2 position (after Los Angeles). *Michael Walsh*

FINCH is the common name for a diverse family of perching songbirds that includes crossbills, GROSBEAKS, siskins and redpolls. The finch has a strong, conical bill that it uses to extract seeds from the cones of conifer trees, its favourite food. It also eats BERRIES and INSECTS. In most types the males are bright red; females' plumage is more subtle in colour. Two of the most unusual finches are the red crossbill (*Loxia curvirostra*) and the white-winged crossbill (*L. leucoptera*). Both are named for the distinctive beak that crosses at the tip, forming an effective tool for prying open cones. Crossbills often hang upside down from branches while feeding. Males are red or pinkish

Purple finch. Tim Zurowski photo

in colour; females are yellowish. The white-winged variety has white wing bars and is particularly partial to spruce cones. Other finches include the common redpoll (*Carduelis flammea*), a streaky bird with a red cap and black chin that appears in the winter from its northern breeding grounds; the house finch (*Carpodacus mexicanus*), common in populated areas of southern BC, where it nests near human dwellings and is a regular visitor to backyard feeders; Cassin's finch (*C. cassinii*) and the purple finch (*C. purpureus*), which prefer forest habitat in southern BC; the pine siskin (*Carduelis pinus*), a gregarious bird that travels in large groups from tree to tree and feeds in the canopy; and the American goldfinch (*Carduelis tristis*), yellow with black wings, forehead and tail, which prefers to feed on the seeds of thistles and dandelions. The grey-crowned rosy finch (*Leucosticte tephrocotis*) is an alpine species, occurring above the treeline and nesting in rocky crevices; it feeds on windblown seeds and INSECTS at the edges of snowfields.

FINLAY FORKS, 180 km west of FORT ST JOHN, was where the PARSNIP and FINLAY rivers joined to form the PEACE R before the area was flooded when the BENNETT DAM was built. It was the territory of the SEKANI First Nations. Trading posts were established here before WWI and a tiny settlement of trappers and prospectors formed. Now beneath WILLISTON RESERVOIR, the Forks

temporarily became a LOGGING centre in the 1960s when salvage operations clearcut the doomed forests. The Finlay R is named after John Finlay of the NORTH WEST CO, who explored this region in 1797.   AS

FINLAY RIVER, 306 km, is an important tributary of the PEACE R in northeast BC, flowing east and south from Thutade Lk near TATLATUI PROVINCIAL PARK in the Skeena Mts, through a 19,040 km² drainage area. Much of its southern valley was flooded by the WILLISTON RESERVOIR, created in 1968 after the building of the BENNETT DAM at HUDSON'S HOPE.   AS

FINLAYSON, Roderick, fur trader (b 16 Mar 1818, Loch Alsh, Scotland; d 20 Jan 1892, Victoria). He immigrated to New York as a young man, then joined the HBC as an apprentice clerk. In 1839 he came out to the Columbia District and took part in the effort to penetrate the Alaska FUR TRADE. He served in the north at Taku R, FORT STIKINE and FORT SIMPSON; in 1843 he was recalled to work on the construction of FORT VICTORIA. The next year he took command of the post, a position he held until 1849, when VICTORIA became the principal HBC post on the coast and James DOUGLAS arrived to take control. Finlayson was chief accountant at the post from 1849 to 1862. During this time he acquired valuable lands on the island and served on the colonial council (1852–63). In 1862 he became HBC superintendent in the mainland Interior.

Roderick Finlayson, fur trader.
BC Archives PDP-02246

He retired in 1872 to farm and manage his estates. He was a prominent Victoria business leader and served a term as mayor in 1878.

FINLAYSON ARM is a long, finger-like southern extension of SAANICH INLET north of VICTORIA. The forested shoreline is protected in GOLDSTREAM PROVINCIAL PARK at the head of the arm and Gowlland-Tod Provincial PARK (12.2 km²) along its eastern side. BAMBERTON overlooks the entrance to the arm on the west side. It is named for the HBC trader Roderick FINLAYSON. During WWII it stood in for the coast of Norway during the filming of the Hollywood feature *The Commandos Strike at Dawn*.

FINMOORE, 56 km west of PRINCE GEORGE on the CNR, is a farming (*see* AGRICULTURE) settlement beside the NECHAKO R named after P. Moore, early settler and first postmaster. Formerly known as Stuart River, it is just west of where this tributary joins the Nechako at the former site of CHUNLAC, a historic DAKELH (Carrier) village.   AS

FINNING INTERNATIONAL INC is the largest Caterpillar heavy equipment dealer in N America. It was founded in 1933 by Earl B. Finning, an American from Salinas, CA, as Finning Tractor & Equipment Co, selling and servicing Caterpillar machines mainly for the construction, MINING and FOREST INDUSTRIES. It took its present name in 1987. With 5,400 employees worldwide, Finning operates in the United Kingdom, Poland and Chile, as well as in western Canada. Revenues were $2.23 billion in 1999.

FINNS began arriving in BC in significant numbers as part of the great wave of European migration to N America in the final decades of the 19th century. Some of these newcomers worked on the construction of the CPR, then remained in the province to take up commercial FISHING or to work at other types of manual labour. A settlement of Finnish coal MINING families at WELLINGTON, near Nanaimo, was dubbed "Finn Town" and had a population large enough to support a church, a brass band, a theatre group and a temperance society (*see also* COAL MINING, VANCOUVER ISLAND). Some of these miners joined the utopian socialist experiment at SOINTULA on MALCOLM ISLAND when it was established there in 1901. The utopia collapsed in 1905 but many of the settlers remained on the island, which developed into an important fishing centre, and Finns are still associated with Sointula. Other Finnish communities developed at White Lake near SHUSWAP LK and at Chase River on VANCOUVER ISLAND. Finnish immigration slowed to a trickle during the Depression of the 1930s and did not pick up again until the 1950s, when many Finns sought to escape their war-ravaged nation. Out-migration dropped off again after 1960 as the economic situation in Finland improved. The post-war immigrants tended to be better educated than their predecessors and better able to prosper in BC at a wide variety of occupations. BC's Finnish community, which by the late 1990s numbered about 10,000, is served by the Finlandia Club in BURNABY, a monthly Finnish-language newspaper (*West Coast News*) and radio and television programs. The Finnish Canadian Rest Home Assoc operates 2 care facilities in the Lower Mainland.

FINTRY, on the west side of OKANAGAN LK at Shorts Point 30 km north of KELOWNA, was a pioneer AGRICULTURAL and ranching (*see* CATTLE INDUSTRY) settlement named in 1909 by James DUN-WATERS after his family estate in Scotland. The property was once home to Capt T.D. SHORTS, who operated the lake's earliest commercial boats. In the 1890s the CPR's fine PADDLE-WHEEL STEAMBOAT, the *ABERDEEN*, stopped just to the north at Bruce's Landing, named after J.B. Bruce, an early homesteader. Fintry Provincial Park is nearby. *AS*

FIR, also known in the LOGGING industry as balsam, is a tree occurring in BC in 3 types. Grand fir (*Abies grandis*) is the largest type, with individual trees reaching heights up to 73 m on VANCOUVER ISLAND. It inhabits lower elevations in the southern part of the province, usually mixed with other tree species. Alpine fir (*A. lasiocarpa*) grows at higher elevations through most of BC. Trees vary from shrub size in exposed areas to 35 m in height. Amabilis fir (*A. amabilis*) is also called Pacific silver fir because of the silvery

Grand fir.
© *T.C. Brayshaw*

Alpine fir on mountain slope. Duane Sept photo

streaks on the undersides of its needles. Its habitat does not extend far inland from the coast. Individual trees of great height are found at CAPE SCOTT on Vancouver Island. Wood from fir species has been used mainly for general construction and PULP AND PAPER stock. The boughs of the fir have a pleasant scent thanks to an

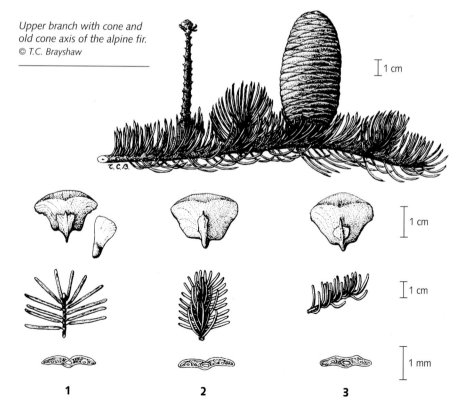

Upper branch with cone and old cone axis of the alpine fir.
© *T.C. Brayshaw*

I 1 cm

I 1 cm

I 1 cm

I 1 mm

1   **2**   **3**

Top to bottom: Cone scale, foliage and leaf section of the grand fir (1), amabilis fir (2), alpine fir (3). © *T.C. Brayshaw*

abundance of resin, and firs make popular Christmas trees. DOUGLAS FIR is not closely related to the true firs. *See also* FOREST PRODUCTS.

FIRESIDE, 275 km northwest of FORT NELSON at Mile 543 of the ALASKA HWY in northern BC, was named by US Army members in 1942 after a large circular fireplace in the officers' mess building, later an inn. The Eg fire destroyed over 4,000 km² of forest and half the settlement in 1982. There is a highway maintenance depot here. *See also* FOREST FIRES. *AS*

FIRST NATIONS OF BC; *see essay opposite.*

FIRST NATIONS LANGUAGES are more prevalent in BC than in any other province in Canada. Approximately half of Canada's 60 FIRST NATIONS languages are native to BC. Of the 32 native tongues originally spoken in the province, 3 (Nicola, TSETSAUT and PENTLATCH) are extinct and several others are *in extremis*, spoken only by a few elders. Each of these languages is a distinct idiom but may be spoken over a large area in several mutually intelligible dialectal forms. Linguists sometimes disagree as to whether the usage of related peoples should be considered separate tongues (ie not mutually understandable by speakers) or dialects of the same language. Oweekyala-Heiltsuk and Nass-Gitksan are examples of this.

Two of BC's First Nations languages (HAIDA and Kutenai) are isolates, not known to be related to any other tongues. The rest belong to 5 language families as follows (for reference purposes, group names customarily used in the past have been indicated, with more appropriate and preferred contemporary usage in parentheses):

ATHABASKAN:
Beaver (DUNNE-ZA), Carrier (including DAKELH and WET'SUWETEN), Chilcotin (TSILHQOT'IN), Nicola, SEKANI, Slavey (DENE-THAH), TAGISH, TAHLTAN, Taku, TSETSAUT; and TLINGIT is considered to be distantly related.

SALISHAN:
Coast Salish: COMOX (including Island and Mainland Comox or SLIAMMON), HALKOMELEM (including Island, Downriver and Upriver Halkomelem), PENTLATCH, SECHELT (Shishalh), SQUAMISH, NORTHERN STRAITS (including Sooke [T'sou-ke], Saanich and Songhees [LEKWAMMEN]), CLALLUM, and the coastal outlier, Bella Coola (NUXALK); *Interior Salish:* Lillooet (ST'AT'IMC), OKANAGAN, Shuswap (SECWEPEMC), and Thompson (NLAKA'PAMUX).

WAKASHAN:
Northern branch: Kwakiutl (KWAKWAKA'WAKW), Oweekyala-Heiltsuk, and HAISLA; *Southern branch:* Nootka (NUU-CHAH-NULTH) and Nitinat (Ditidaht).

TSIMSHIAN:
Coast Tsimshian, Southern Tsimshian and Nass-GITKSAN (including East and West Gitksan and NISGA'A).

ALGONKIAN:
Cree.

Many groups now prefer and officially use phonetic renderings of their own group names, and a group may use a different term for its language. First Nations languages (except Cree) share a sound system that has fascinated linguists, including a series of snapped (ejective) consonants, back (uvular) and rounded (labialized) consonants and syncopated pronunciation caused by glottal stops. The languages are called polysynthetic, a reference to their feature of adding prefixes and suffixes to a word-root, often resulting in words of great length. Bella Coola is remarkable for having words composed only of consonants. In order to assert distinct ethnic identity, communities speaking related dialects occasionally characterize their usage as a distinct language. None of these languages is being transmitted as mother tongue to children. The prospect of impending language extinction has inspired nearly all First Nations communities in BC to implement programs for documenting and teaching their heritage tongues. However, despite a variety of techniques and approaches, the trend toward language loss continues and in many communities the native language is used almost exclusively in ceremonial contexts. A hybrid trade language, CHINOOK JARGON (composed primarily of loanwords from Chinook, Nuu-chah-nulth, Chehalis, French and English), was widely used in BC during the period of settlement but died out when English became broadly known among First Nations people. Today the BC landscape reflects the province's heritage of First Nations languages and Chinook Jargon in hundreds of anglicized place names. *Jay Powell*

FIRVALE, 32 km east of BELLA COOLA on the north shore of the BELLA COOLA R, was a farming (*see* AGRICULTURE) and LOGGING community, formerly known as Sloan. It was established by Seventh Day Adventist settlers in 1912, but most moved away after WWI. *AS*

FISGARD LIGHTHOUSE at the entrance to ESQUIMALT Harbour was built in 1860 after a design by John WRIGHT. Named for a Royal Navy vessel, it was the first LIGHTHOUSE on the coast, beginning operation on 16 Nov 1860. It was automated in 1928 and joined to the mainland by a causeway in 1951. Fisgard was designated a National Historic Site in 1972 and was still in operation in 2000.

Fisgard lighthouse, the first light station on the coast. VPL 3274

FIRST NATIONS OF BC

Overview

Charles R. Menzies

FIRST NATIONS OF BC societies, cultures and languages are among the most varied and developed in the world. Their antiquity predates the rise of civilization in Europe by several millennia (*see* PREHISTORY). Prior to the arrival of Europeans, between 80,000 and 250,000 people lived in villages and communities spread across BC (*see* ABORIGINAL DEMOGRAPHY). For the most part they derived their livelihood from the land, hunting, FISHING, tending and collecting fruits and other PLANTS. Understandings of the environment, other beings and animals, and how people became human, are key aspects of the cultures of the indigenous peoples.

Social Complexity

Many early European theories of social evolution argue that the development of AGRICULTURE is the key that opens the door to civilization. In fact, until recently Euro-centric theories of social evolution assumed that development of social complexity, the process of civilization, was intrinsically bound with the development of Indo-European-style agriculture. We now know that the development of human cultures is far more complex and multifaceted than a simplistic unilineal evolution from small unorganized bands of hunters to late-20th-century capitalist society.

In what we now know as BC, highly complex cultures emerged that were based on hunting and gathering, not agriculture. There was great knowledge of plant husbandry among the indigenous peoples of BC—in fact, recent evidence suggests that the first people understood principles of plant husbandry quite well—but these societies were able to generate social surpluses without having to resort to agricultural modes of production. Harvesting technologies and ecological knowledge, refined over the course of several millennia, permitted extensive and sustainable harvesting and processing of natural resources until the industrial resource exploitation was implanted in the late 19th and early 20th centuries. It is important to recognize that hunting and fishing are about more than just subsistence. They are a

Petroglyph of the "Man who fell from the Sky," Prince Rupert Harbour. The Tsimshian tell the story that relates to this rock carving. Roy Carlson photo

FIRST NATIONS OF BC

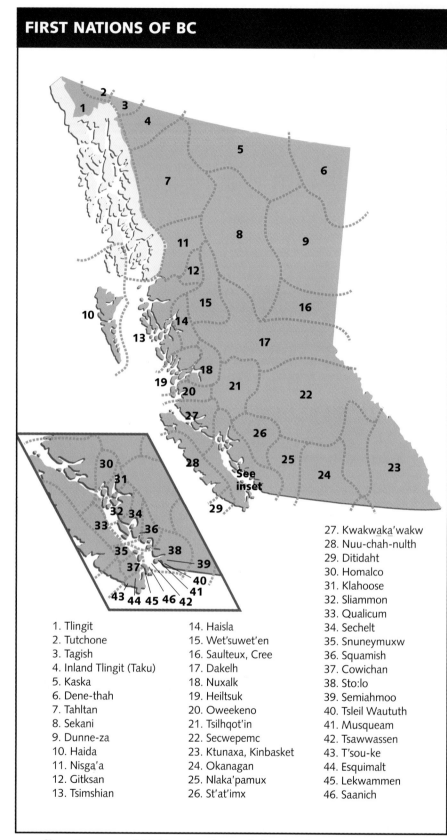

27. Kwakwaka'wakw
28. Nuu-chah-nulth
29. Ditidaht
30. Homalco
31. Klahoose
32. Sliammon
33. Qualicum
34. Sechelt
35. Snuneymuxw
36. Squamish
37. Cowichan
38. Sto:lo
39. Semiahmoo
40. Tsleil Waututh
41. Musqueam
42. Tsawwassen
43. T'sou-ke
44. Esquimalt
45. Lekwammen
46. Saanich

1. Tlingit
2. Tutchone
3. Tagish
4. Inland Tlingit (Taku)
5. Kaska
6. Dene-thah
7. Tahltan
8. Sekani
9. Dunne-za
10. Haida
11. Nisga'a
12. Gitksan
13. Tsimshian
14. Haisla
15. Wet'suwet'en
16. Saulteux, Cree
17. Dakelh
18. Nuxalk
19. Heiltsuk
20. Oweekeno
21. Tsilhqot'in
22. Secwepemc
23. Ktunaxa, Kinbasket
24. Okanagan
25. Nlaka'pamux
26. St'at'imx

monly shared culture traits and environment): Northwest Coast, Sub-Arctic, and Plateau. Each area was also typified by a unique form of social organization. Even though these types of models tend to ignore the historical processes of colonization, they are useful in organizing cultures and societies for the purpose of comparative analysis.

The Northwest Coast extends from the delta of the COPPER R in the Gulf of Alaska to the mouth of the Chetco R on the southern Oregon coast. Practically two-thirds of the indigenous population of BC lived along the coast zone. This was a region of abundance well known for its SALMON streams and RIVERS and temperate RAIN FORESTS. The typical form of social organization on the coast was the chiefdom, in which the political authority of the group is vested in chiefs or chiefly families. Most of these societies were divided into 3 basic classes: chiefly families, commoners and slaves (*see* SLAVERY). Membership in the family groups, essentially multigenerational kin groups that lived in the classic plank longhouse (*see* ARCHITECTURE, ABORIGINAL), was determined differently in northern than in southern BC. Membership in household groups of North Coast peoples, such as the TSIMSHIAN and the HAIDA, was determined through matrilineal descent (calculated through one's mother). On the Central and South coasts—among the HEILTSUK, SALISHAN and Kwak'wala-speaking peoples, for example—household membership was based on a bilateral kinship system (calculated through mother and father). The societies that developed along coastal BC were highly complex, sedentary hunting-gathering societies. Coastal peoples maintained permanent winter villages for thousands of years before the present, with populations ranging from 100 to 500 people. Effective political authority was vested at the household level. Each household maintained a set of territories in the surrounding region. House territories were clearly demarcated collective property that contained fish, animal, plant and spiritual resources. Access to and use of these resources was strictly controlled. In effect, no area of the coast was not property at the time Europeans arrived.

The peoples of the Plateau, or southern Interior, made up about 25% of BC's aboriginal population. The region, bounded

way of knowing, a way of thinking about human beings in relation to other beings. This is a fundamental difference between the resource-extractive way of living that defines modern capitalist societies and the indigenous modes of subsistence.

Anthropological models normally divide the indigenous societies of BC into 3 culture areas (defined in terms of com-

Grade 8 and 9 students at St Mary's residential school, Mission, c 1950.
Bert Clifford/Mission Community Archives

on the west by the COAST MTS and on the east by the ROCKY MTS, is made up of a series of connected north–south valleys and plateaus. The region is environmentally diverse, containing zones ranging from sagebrush deserts to sub-boreal SPRUCE forests (*see also* BIOGEOCLIMATIC ZONES; ECOREGION CLASSIFICATION SYSTEM). The peoples of the Plateau maintained semi-permanent winter villages. Typically these villages were located near key salmon-fishing sites. Unlike on the coast, however, social organization was not hierarchical. Political authority was vested in extended household groups and leadership relied upon persuasion, not force or heredity. Membership in these kin-based groups was far more fluid and contingent than it was on the coast. Because kinship was determined bilaterally, people could (and often did) change allegiances. This mobility militated against the institutionalization of hereditary leadership. Essentially, chiefs and headmen were managers of specific activities for which they had specialized knowledge.

People of the northern Interior lived in the least populated region of aboriginal BC, with less than 10% of the population. The region was defined by northern boreal forests of spruce, FIR and PINE. Little rain falls in the region (less than 40 cm per year). The ground is snow-covered for 6 months of the year (*see* CLIMATE). Yet the peoples living in this region developed a detailed ecological knowledge of their environment and of the wildlife they relied upon that enabled them to prosper as nomadic hunter-gathers. They developed social strategies characterized by flexibility and informal institutional arrangements. The basic social unit in the northern Interior was the small, self-

sufficient group of 20 to 30 (rarely more than 50) related people. These groups were dispersed over the land during winter to hunt and trap. In the summer, larger encampments of up to several hundred gathered near LAKES and rivers for fishing. A key aspect of this form of social organization was egalitarianism. There were no formal inherited leadership positions. Leaders were people who knew something, not bosses. Thus leadership shifted from task to task in accordance with individual skill and knowledge. Following the arrival of Europeans, all of these societies went through major periods of disruption, crisis and transformation. Despite being alienated and displaced within their own territories, the First Nations of BC maintained a deep-rooted connection with their pasts and it is this strength that they draw upon in their current struggle for self-determination (*see* ABORIGINAL RIGHTS).

Origins: Sacred Histories and Western Science

There is a major epistemological difference underlying the origin stories of indigenous peoples in BC and the scientific theories of the peopling of the Americas. First Nations are less concerned about "where" people come from than with "how" people came to be fully human, how they have learned to share power with other animals and other humans. Western science begins with the questions of when and how did people arrive in the Americas. While this is an interesting and theoretically useful question, it also reflects the colonial past (and present) of the Americas, whether intended or not. The focus on how people first arrived reinforces the notion of the Americas as "new lands" into which successive waves of migrants have come. The oral traditions of indigenous peoples, however, shed light on the process that transformed their ancestors into fully human beings. In essence, Euro-American science presents the

Coast Salish potlatch in the Fraser Valley.

history of the Americas as a history of migration and population dynamics. Aboriginal history explores the birth of human culture.

Bill REID, the Haida artist, recounts through sculpture the story of RAVEN and the first humans. In this story Raven, the trickster and creator, spots a large CLAM shell full of frightened creatures left on the beach after the retreat of the waters of the great flood. Raven swoops down to investigate and, upon finding the terrified creatures, coaxes and coerces them to come out and explore the new world. Realizing that there are no women among them, Raven flies the creatures to North Island (also known as Langara Island) where he cajoles them into a sexual experience with CHITONS. Later, the chitons give birth to the original Haidas. Raven also figures in Tsimshian stories of origins. One of Raven's, or Tx'msm's, accomplishments was the freeing of the sun from a box in the Sky Chief's house. He also brought the people fire and taught them how to catch EULACHON. The people of the Interior Plateau (ST'AT'IMX, SECWEPEMC, TSILHQOT'IN, Nicola, etc) explain their origin in terms of the separation of people from the rest of nature. They received mortality as the price for guaranteed salmon runs and sunlight. Among the NUXALK (Bella Coola) there is a sequence of family histories for each of the "ancestral families" from which present-day Nuxalk reckon their family lineage. Each family history, or *symayusta*, describes the descent to Earth of one of the first ancestors. In these stories, groups of brothers and sisters are brought to life by a creator, then dropped on a mountaintop to populate the world. They arrive dressed in the cloaks of birds or animals and carry with them some food, tools and special knowledge for the world's future inhabitants. The first ancestors built villages at the foot of the MOUNTAINS and took territory from the surrounding region for subsistence activities. All of these traditions focus on "becoming" human. This is not simply a biological process; it is an important social and cultural process in which the ancestors become self-conscious of their place in an already existing world. The key figures in this transformation are typically tricksters, such as Raven or COYOTE, who act more as midwife than creator.

Euro-American scientific models, on the other hand, focus on when and how people arrived in the Americas. It is widely accepted within anthropological and archaeological circles that the first people in the Americas came from Asia. They are believed to have travelled across the Bering Strait during periods when intensification of the Ice Ages lowered the sea level and transformed the strait into a grassy steppe called Beringia. Evidence used to date the movement of people into the Americas includes physiological, linguistic and archaeological data. Physiological data, primarily relating to teeth, has been used to link populations of indigenous Americans to populations from northeast Asia. According to the physical anthropologist Christy Turner, indigenous Americans share a tooth pattern (sinodont) with prehistoric and contemporary peoples of China. This evidence suggests that indigenous Americans have inhabited the Americas for at least 20,000 years (*see* ARCHAEOLOGY). Linguistic data are used to determine what one might think of as a conceptual history of a language. Using vocabulary and grammatical structures, linguists try to determine the degree of similarity between languages. The underlying assumption is that language diversification proceeds slowly. Thus the existence of a high degree of linguistic diversity in the Americas would suggest a fairly profound time depth to human habitation (*see* FIRST NATIONS LANGUAGES). It is difficult if not impossible to actually determine how long it might take for a common ancestral language to diversify into distinct languages. Even so one anthropologist, Joseph H. Greenberg, has argued that the indigenous languages of the Americas all stem from 3 macrofamilies. Suggesting that all the indigenous languages of the Americas stem from a small group of proto-languages pushes back the time of first occupation beyond 20,000 years to nearly 50,000 years BP (Before Present). Archaeologists generally agree that people have inhabited the Americas for at least 12,000 years. This is a rather conservative date given recent archaeological data that could push the earliest date back several tens of thousands of years. In BC, the earliest archaeological date of human occupancy is 11,500 BP (+/- 120 years) at the CHARLIE LAKE CAVE site in the PEACE R district. Evidence from coastal sites also shows dates approaching 10,000 years BP (NAMU, 9,800 BP; GLENROSE, 8,250 BP; QUEEN CHARLOTTE ISLANDS 9,300 BP).

From the perspective of Euro-American science, the antiquity of aboriginal cultures is no longer in question. Even the most conservative estimates of first arrival are truly beyond the ability of human imagination. The notion that indigenous peoples have been here since time immemorial is no less fantastic than academic debates over stone shards and the remains of fire sites. The reality is that Europeans arrived in the Americas to find a complex variety of highly developed societies. The process by which indigenous lands were expropriated and the people displaced is called colonialism.

Colonialism and Resource Appropriation

The history of relations between non-aboriginal newcomers and First Nations has revolved around the exploitation and appropriation of the natural resources of BC. Initially resource extraction was organized by First Nations groups themselves. Resources were exchanged for commodities such as iron tools, blankets or other trade goods. However, the development of industrial resource extraction in the form of commercial FISHING, MINING and the FOREST INDUSTRY fundamentally altered relations between non-aboriginal newcomers and First Nations. No longer valued as trading partners, First Nations were slotted into the developing resource economy as a subordinate part of a growing industrial LABOUR FORCE segregated by race, ethnicity and gender. The early maritime-based FUR TRADE structured first contacts between Europeans and First Nations (from 1774 to 1858). In this period a European-based mercantile capitalism articulated with an indigenous kin-ordered mode of production, a system of production in which the control over labour power and the production of trade goods remained under the control of the aboriginal American traders who were for the most part "chiefs." They mobilized their followers and personal contacts to deliver SEA OTTER pelts, and their power grew with

Annual powwow in Kamloops, 1999. Aboriginal people from all over N America attend the gathering. Keith Thirkell photo

the development of the trade. The merging of these 2 modes of production—one based on the family and one based on European capitalism—produced new wealth and intense inflation for both First Nations and Europeans.

As Europeans prospered from the fur trade and developed industrial enterprises, First Nations people lost control over trade and were displaced by a settler-based industrial capitalism. The change from colonies in which Europeans exploited indigenous labour power to colonies of settlement followed the discovery of GOLD in the 1850s. By the early 1860s mining, forestry and fishing had supplanted the fur trade to become the backbone of BC's settler economy. Indigenous control of commercially valuable land and resources was almost completely destroyed by the 1880s through a variety of legal (and extra-

legal) measures introduced by Canada and the provinces. One of the most insidious changes was the creation of the legal category of "food fishing" in the 1880s under the provisions of the *Canada Fisheries Act* (*see* FISHERIES JURISDICTION; FISHERIES POLICY). Under the provisions of the Act, aboriginal fishers were prohibited from selling fish caught within their traditional fisheries. Despite having never been universally applied (many First Nations have continued to sell fish caught under the so-called food fish permits), the intention and result of this regulation was to shift ownership of the resource from traditional and customary ownership by First Nations into the hands of industrial capitalist fishing firms (owned and operated by US and British financial interests), which were then able to distribute fishing "rights" to fishers loyal to the companies. At the same time as First Nations' control over their resources and territories were being usurped, First Nations people were being integrated into every major resource industry in BC as workers and owner-operators.

The Legacy of Colonialism

The impact of BC's colonial relationship with indigenous peoples is starkly revealed in basic social indicators such as income, health and interactions with the criminal justice system. Often the dramatic gaps between First Nations and other Canadians is presented as though this were the problem. In reality this is a symptom of a far bigger problem: the disruption, degradation and destruction of aboriginal societies by an encroaching settler state. The average income of First Nations people is only 70% of the average income of other Canadians. The household income of First Nations families is 40% lower than the national average ($21,800 for First Nation families versus $38,000 for other Canadian families). The source of income is also a good indicator of social inequalities. In BC, aboriginal people (especially those living on RESERVES) receive a higher portion of their income in government transfer payments (employment insurance, PENSIONS or social assistance) than from earned income (wages, salaries or self-employed income). Health is another area in which significant differences exist between aboriginal people and members of mainstream society. Illnesses resulting from poverty, overcrowding and poor housing have led to chronic and acute respiratory diseases, which take a heavy toll among aboriginal people. The standardized death rate for BC's aboriginal population is more than double that of the general population (15.9 versus 6.6 deaths per 1,000 population). The average age of death is more than 20 years below that of the average non-aboriginal Canadian. The rate of infant mortality, though improved, is still nearly 3 times the Canadian average (17.5 versus 7.9 per 1,000). More than 33% of all aboriginal deaths are related to violence (compared with 8% in mainstream society). These statistics highlight a significant discrepancy between non-aboriginal and aboriginal Canadians.

Interactions between First Nations and the criminal-law system of Canada also reveal structural inequalities. This occurs at both a collective and an individual level. On the collective level, the right to vote in federal elections was denied to all status Indians until the early 1960s. Land claims activity was criminalized between 1927 and 1951 (*see* ABORIGINAL RIGHTS). And aboriginal children were forcibly removed from their home com-

Masked Natives block Douglas Lake Road in a protest against fishing regulations on Douglas Lake Ranch, 1995. *Ian Smith/Vancouver Sun*

munities and placed in RESIDENTIAL SCHOOLS. The result of criminalizing indigenous forms of social organization, combined with the expropriation of First Nations' territories, is reflected in the disproportionate number of aboriginal people incarcerated in Canada. As of 1996 aboriginal people accounted for slightly less than 3% of the total Canadian population. However, they accounted for 12% of federal and 20% of provincial admissions to PRISONS. Each stage of the judicial process is marked by a disproportionate number of aboriginal people. Careful studies of the judicial process have clearly demonstrated that if an individual is aboriginal, his or her chance of being incarcerated is higher than among any other group of Canadians.

Facing the Future

Confronting the problems faced by aboriginal peoples will require a commitment on the part of mainstream Canada to settle their outstanding claims and to recognize in practice their existing aboriginal rights. An important first step is to accelerate the process of treaty negotiations, thereby beginning the process of dismantling the colonial apparatus of the Canadian state. Serious negotiations between First Peoples and the governments of BC and Canada began only in 1992, following the election of the NDP. For most of BC's history the government has refused to recognize aboriginal rights, let alone negotiate treaties. Gov James DOUGLAS signed 14 treaties with First Nations on VANCOUVER ISLAND during the period from 1850–54 (*see* DOUGLAS TREATIES). However, upon joining CONFEDERATION the provincial government refused to recognize aboriginal rights, essentially stalling the resolution of claims until 1992, when the BC TREATY COMMISSION Agreement was signed by representatives of the First Nations Summit and the provincial and federal governments. That agreement set in motion a process of negotiation that continues.

The final passage of the NISGA'A TREATY between BC, Canada and the NISGA'A in 1999 signals a new beginning for the people of BC. Though this treaty was completed outside the BC Treaty Commission process, it has the potential to transform relations between First Peoples and other British Columbians. In light of recent court cases, such as the 1997 DELGAMUUKW decision, the Nisga'a Treaty may well come to be seen as a rather conservative document. Nonetheless it is an undeniably important step toward the development of aboriginal self-determination. While the treaty process and self-determination are not panaceas for all the past wrongs, they are an important place to start, though most people agree that if they are going to have any meaningful remedial effect on the experience of First Nations social inequality, they must be built upon a solid economic and resource base.

The 1997 Supreme Court of Canada ruling in the Delgamuukw case lays the basis for a fundamental change in Canadian law that could vastly improve the economic situation of First Nations. The court found that aboriginal people have a right to fair compensation for lands expropriated by the Canadian state, that they have a right to use their traditional lands as they see fit, and that their oral traditions should be accorded the same evidentiary weight as written sources in legal cases concerning aboriginal rights and title. This decision may well usher in a new era of economic and political co-operation between First Nations and the non-aboriginal peoples of BC. At the very least it can be read as the beginning of a process of reconciliation in which mainstream BC (and, by extension, Canada) finally accepts its complicity in the process of colonialism.

Jane Stewart, federal minister of aboriginal affairs, Chief Joe Gosnell and Premier Glen Clark at signing of historic Nisga'a Treaty, 1998. *Gary Fiegehen photo*

FIRST NATIONS of BC

PEOPLE	BANDS	HISTORIC NAMES	LOCATION
ATHABASCAN			
DAKELH (Carrier)	Alexandria	-	north of Williams Lake
	Burns Lake	-	Burns Lake
	Cheslatta	-	south of Burns Lake
	Kluskus	-	west of Quesnel
	Lheidli T'enneh	Fort George	Prince George
	Nadleh Whut'en	Fraser Lake	Fraser Lake
	Nak'azdli	Necoslie	Fort St James
	Nat'oot'en	Lake Babine	Babine Lake
	Nazko	-	west of Quesnel
	Red Bluff	Quesnel	Quesnel
	Stellat'en	Stellaquo	Fraser Lake
	Sai Kuz	Stoney Creek	south of Vanderhoof
	Takla Lake	-	Takla Lake
	Tl'azt'en	Stuart-Trembleur L	Stuart Lake
	Ulkatcho	-	Anahim Lake
	Yekooche	-	Fort St James
WET'SUWET'EN	Broman Lake	Omineca	Decker Lake
	Hagwilget	-	New Hazelton
	Moricetown	-	Moricetown
	Nee-Tahi-Buhn	Omineca	François Lake
DENE-THAH (Slavey)	Fort Nelson	Slave Indian Band	Fort Nelson
	Prophet River	Slave Indian Band	south of Fort Nelson
DUNNE-ZA (Beaver)	Blueberry River	-	northwest of Fort St John
	Doig River	-	northeast of Fort St John
	Halfway River	-	north of Fort St John
	Prophet River	-	south of Fort Nelson
	West Moberley Lake	-	north of Chetwynd
KASKA	Dease River	-	Good Hope Lake
SEKANI	Doig River	-	Fort St John
	McLeod Lake	-	McLeod Lake
	Fort Ware	Finlay River Band	north of Williston Lake
	Tsay Keh Dene	Ingenika	Finlay River
	Prophet River	-	south of Fort Nelson
TAHLTAN	Iskut	-	Eddontenajon Lake
	Tahltan	-	Telegraph Creek
Taku	Taku Tlingit	Inland Tlingit	Atlin
TSILHQOT'IN (Chilcotin)	Alexis Creek	-	Alexis Creek
	Anaham	-	west of Williams Lake
	Stone	-	Hanceville
	Toosey	-	Riske Creek
	Xeni Gwet'in	Nemiah	Nemiah Valley
HAIDA			
	Old Masset Village Council	-	Queen Charlotte Islands
	Skidegate	-	Queen Charlotte Islands
KUTENAI (Ktunaxa)			
	Kinbasket	-	Invermere
	Columbia Lake		
	Lower Kootenay	-	Creston
	St Mary's	-	Cranbrook
	Tobacco Plains	-	Cranbrook

FIRST NATIONS of BC *continued*

PEOPLE	BANDS	HISTORIC NAMES	LOCATION
SALISHAN			
NUXALK		Bella Coola	Bella Coola
Coast Salish Northern:	Comox	Island Comox	Comox
	Homalco	Mainland Comox	Bute Inlet
	Klahoose	Mainland Comox	Cortes Island
	Qualicum	-	-
	Sliammon	Mainland Comox	Powell River
	Shishalh	Sechelt	Sechelt
	Pentlatch	-	Qualicum
Coast Salish Central:			
Island HALKOMELEM	Chemainus	-	Chemainus
	Cowichan	-	Duncan
	Cowichan Lake	-	Cowichan Lake
	Halalt	-	near Duncan
	Lyackson	-	Valdes Island
	Malahat	-	Saanich Inlet
	Snuneymuxw	Nanaimo	Nanaimo
	Nanoose	-	Nanoose Bay
	Penelakut	-	Kuper Island
Downriver Mainland			
Halkomelem	Chehalis	-	Harrison River
	Katzie	-	Fraser Valley
	Kwayhquitlim	Coquitlam	Coquitlam River
	X'muzk'i'um	Musqueam	south Vancouver
	New Westminster	-	Poplar Island
	Semiahmoo	-	south of Vancouver
	Tsawwassen	-	south of Vancouver
Upriver Mainland			
Halkomelem (STO:LO)	Yale	-	Yale
	Aitchelitz	-	Chilliwack
	Chawathil	Hope	Hope
	Cheam	-	Chilliwack
	Kwantlen	Langley	Langley
	Kwaw Kwaw A Pilt	-	Chilliwack
	Lakahahmen	-	Deroche
	Matsqui	-	-
	Peters	Squawits	Upper Fraser Valley
	Popkum	-	Upper Fraser Valley
	Scowlitz	Harrison River	Harrison River
	Seabird Island	-	-
	Shxw'ow'hamel	Ohamil	Laidlaw
	Skawahlook	-	Upper Fraser Valley
	Skowkale	Skulkayn	
	Skwah	Chilliwack	Chilliwack
	Skway	Chilliwack	Chilliwack
	Soowahlie	-	Chilliwack River
	Squiala	Chilliwack	
	Sumas	-	-
	Tzeachten	-	-
	Union Bar	Tait	north of Hope
	Yakweakwioose	-	-
	Tsleil Waututh	Burrard Band	Burrard Inlet
	Squamish	-	Burrard Inlet/Howe Sound
	Nooksack	-	-

FIRST NATIONS of BC *continued*

PEOPLE	BANDS	HISTORIC NAMES	LOCATION
NORTHERN STRAITS	Beecher Bay	-	Becher Bay
	Esquimalt	-	Esquimalt
	Pauquachin	-	Saanich
	Songhees	-	Victoria
	Tsartlip	-	Gulf Islands/Saanich
	Tsawout	-	Gulf Islands/Saanich
	Tseycum	-	Gulf Islands/Saanich
	T'Sou-ke	Sooke	Sooke
	Clallum	Clallam	Olympic Peninsula
Interior Salish			
NLAKA'PAMUX (Thompson)	Ashcroft	-	Ashcroft
	Boothroyd	Chomok	Fraser Canyon
	Boston Bar	-	Fraser Canyon
	Cook's Ferry	-	Spences Bridge
	Kanaka Bar	-	Fraser Canyon
	Lytton	-	Lytton
	Nicomen	-	Thompson R
	Oregon Jack Creek	-	Ashcroft
	Siska	-	Lytton
	Skuppah	-	Lytton
	Spuzzum	-	Fraser Canyon
SCE'EXMX	Coldwater	-	Merritt
	Lower Nicola	-	Merritt
	Nooaitch	-	Nicola Valley
	Shackan	-	Nicola Valley
	Spaxomin	-	Douglas Lake
OKANAGAN	Lower Similkameen	-	Keremeos
	Okanagan	-	Vernon
	Osoyoos	-	Osoyoos
	Penticton	-	Penticton
	Upper Nicola	-	Nicola Valley
	Upper Similkameen	-	Keremeos
	Westbank	-	Kelowna
SECWEPEMC (Shuswap)	Adams Lake	-	Chase
	Bonaparte	-	Cache Creek
	Canim Lake	-	Canim Lake
	Canoe Creek	-	Fraser River
	Esketemc	Alkali Lake	south of Williams Lake
	High Bar	-	Fraser River
	Kamloops	-	Kamloops
	Little Shuswap	-	Chase
	Neskonlith	-	Chase
	North Thompson	-	Barrière
	Skeetchestn	Deadman's Creek	Savona
	Soda Creek	-	Williams Lake
	Spallumcheen	-	Enderby
	Ts'kw'aylaxw	Pavilion	Pavilion
	Whispering Pines	Clinton	Clinton
	Williams Lake	-	Williams Lake
ST'AT'IMX (Lillooet)	Anderson Lake	-	Anderson Lake
	Bridge River	-	Lillooet
	Cayoose Creek	-	Lillooet
	Douglas	-	Harrison Lake
	Lillooet	Fraser River	Lillooet
	Mount Currie	-	Pemberton
	Samahquam	-	Lillooet River
	Seton Lake	-	Shalalth
	Skookum Chuck	-	Lillooet River
	Xaxli'p	Fountain	Lillooet

FIRST NATIONS of BC *continued*

PEOPLE	BANDS	HISTORIC NAMES	LOCATION
TSIMSHIAN			
GITKSAN	Gitanmaax	-	Hazelton
	Gitanyow	Kitwancool	Kitwancool
	Gitsegukla	Skeena Crossing	west of Hazelton
	Kispiox		
	Sikokoak	Glen Vowell	Glen Vowell
	Gitwangak	-	Kitwanga
NISGA'A	Gitlakdamix	-	New Aiyansh
	Gitwinksihlkw	-	Canyon City
	Kincolith	-	Kincolith
	Lakalzap	-	Greenville
TSIMSHIAN	Kit'k'a'ata	Hartley Bay	Hartley Bay
	Kitasoo	Klemtu	Klemtu
	Kitkatla	-	Dolphin Island
	Kitselas	-	Terrace
	Kitsumkalum	-	Terrace
	Lax Kw'aalams	-	Port Simpson
	Metlakatla	-	Metlakatla
WAKASHAN			
NORTHERN WAKASHAN			
HAISLA	-	Kitamaat	Kitimat
HEILTSUK	Heiltsuk	Bella Bella	central coast
	Haishais	-	Milbanke Sound
	Oweekeno	-	Rivers Inlet
KWAKWA̱KA'WAKW **(Kwakiutl)**	Gwa'sala-Nak'waxda'xw	Smith Inlet	Tsulquate (Port Hardy)
	Kwakiutl	-	Fort Rupert
	Mamaleleqala-QweqwaSot'Enox	Village Island	Gilford Island
	'Namgis	Nimpkish	Alert Bay
	Da'naxda'xw	New Vancouver	Alert Bay
	Tlowitsis-Mumtagila	Turnour Island	Alert Bay
	Gusgimukw	Quatsino	Quatsino
	Gwat'sinuxw	Winter Harbour	Quatsino
	Tlatlasikwala	Cape Scott	Quatsino
	Dzawada'enuxw	-	Kingcome Inlet
	We Wai Kai	Cape Mudge	Quadra Island
	We Wai Kum	-	Campbell River
	Kwiakah	Kweeha	Campbell River
Southern Wakashan			
NUU-CHAH-NULTH **(Nootka)**	Ahousaht	-	Flores Island
	Ehattesaht	-	Esperanza Inlet
	Hesquiaht	-	Hesquiat Harbour
	Huu-ay-aht	Ohiaht	Bamfield
	Ka:'yu:'K't'h/Che:K'tles7et'h'	Kyuquot	Kyuquot Sound
	Mowachaht	Nootka	Gold River
	Nuchatlaht	-	Espinoza Inlet
	Opetchesaht	-	Port Alberni
	Tla-o-qui-aht	Clayoquot	Clayoquot Sound
	Toquaht	-	Barkley Sound
	Tseshaht	-	Port Alberni
	Uchucklesaht	-	Alberni Inlet
	Ucluelet	-	Ucluelet
Nitinat	Diitiidaht	Nitinat	Nitinat Lake
	Pacheedaht	Pacheenat	Port Renfrew

FISH is a cold-blooded vertebrate (having a backbone), typically possessing paired fins, gills and, usually, scales. These characteristics separate fish from warm-blooded mammals and the cold-blooded reptiles and amphibians. Fish are generally grouped as primitive jawless fish, such as the hagfish and LAMPREY; fish with cartilaginous skeletons, including SHARK, ray and ratfish; and the common bony fish, including STURGEON, SALMON, TUNA and many others. Of the approximately 21,000 species of fish worldwide, more than 850 occur in Canadian waters. BC hosts more than 75 freshwater species and more than 325 marine species, ranging from the tiny tidepool SCULPIN to the largest BC fish, the basking shark, the second largest fish in the world after the whale shark. Anadromous fish, such as salmon, STEELHEAD trout and EULACHON, spawn in fresh water but spend much of their adult life in marine waters. Marine fish such as the HERRING and Pacific sand lance are important sources of food for seabirds, other fish such as salmon, ROCKFISH, HALIBUT and LINGCOD, and marine mammals such as the SEAL, SEA LION and WHALE. Common freshwater fish of LAKES and RIVERS include the TROUT, sturgeon, CHAR, BASS, WHITEFISH, sunfish, sucker, catfish, SHINER, minnow, northern pike, freshwater sculpin and lamprey. The 3-spined stickleback is found in marine waters and in lakes a short distance inland. Species of trout, char and sturgeon are found mostly in fresh water or non-tidal waters, but some are found occasionally in estuarine and marine waters. Fish of many varieties have been an important commercial product in BC since the HBC began exporting salmon in the 1850s. *See also* AQUACULTURE; FISH HATCHERIES; FISHING, ABORIGINAL; FISHING, COMMERCIAL; FISHING, SPORT and individual species. *Rick Harbo*

FISH HATCHERIES are generally government- and community-run facilities intended to rebuild SALMON and TROUT populations and to conserve and rebuild threatened fish stocks. Hatcheries are also used to provide stock for the fish farming industry (*see* AQUACULTURE, FIN FISH).

In BC fresh waters, the earliest government hatchery efforts, dating back to the 1880s, primarily enhanced sockeye salmon at 17 hatcheries. This early program was discontinued in 1936, with the last hatchery closing in 1941. An enhancement program was re-established in the early 1960s with the use of spawning channels, expanding into hatchery technology. Initially the culture of salmon and trout was the responsibility of the federal government, but in 1938 responsibility for management of freshwater species was delegated to the province (*see* FISHERIES JURISDICTION). The provincial Ministry of Fisheries coordinates the inspection and licensing of all aquaculture sites, including hatcheries. The Ministry of Environment, Lands and Parks (MELP) is responsible for management of freshwater fish, including sea-going trout (cutthroat and STEELHEAD), within BC LAKES and streams and determines which areas are to be stocked with freshwater fish. The fish are then raised by the Fish Culture Section of the Ministry of Fisheries.

Hatchery tanks at Sunshine Coast fish farm, c 1989. Rick Blacklaws photo

Many parts of BC have a long legacy of stocking. Some early stocking programs involved the use of exotic and non-native species, such as the brown trout. However, most fisheries agencies across N America now emphasize the culture of native stocks. To avoid ecological and genetic impacts on wild stocks, the provincial hatchery program is guided by a number of conservative policies. Stocking is only undertaken if it can be carried out without compromising wild stocks, or if there has been a previous history of stocking in a lake. The lakes chosen for stocking generally are closed systems—that is, they have no inflow or outflow streams—with little capability of sustaining a population of trout. The lake stock program is largely for "put-and-take" fisheries: fish are put in the lake so they can be taken out by sport fishers. The fish are not marked, and there is little or no "wild" component. In the mid-1990s, close to half of the freshwater angling effort in BC was on stocked lakes. The MOF operates 5 hatcheries and releases about 10 million trout (rainbow, steelhead, cutthroat, KOKANEE and brook trout) annually into 1,100 lakes and streams.

Another form of hatchery rearing focusses on supplementation programs, in which hatchery fish supplement a naturally spawning population. The hatchery fish may be clipped for a hatchery-selective sport fishery; that is, adipose fins are removed to distinguish hatchery fish from wild fish. Fisheries and Oceans Canada (known as DFO after its former name, Department of Fisheries and Oceans), a federal agency, oversees salmonid hatcheries participating in the SALMONID ENHANCEMENT PROGRAM. Projects are operated by DFO staff or contracted

to community and aboriginal groups, as well as by volunteers with some DFO support. As many as 10,000 volunteers participate in the program in any given year. A number of cutthroat and steelhead hatchery programs are administered jointly by DFO, MELP and Ministry of Fisheries.

Yet another form of enhancement is known as Lake Enrichment (fertilization). These programs are designed to stimulate higher levels of food organisms and accelerate growth rates for the sockeye fry rearing in specific lakes. DFO also contributes financial and technical support to projects to improve and create freshwater spawning and rearing habitat throughout BC. *See also* FISHING, ABORIGINAL; FISHING, COMMERCIAL; FISHING, SPORT. *Peter A. Robson*

FISHER (*Martes pennanti*), a member of the WEASEL (Mustelids) family of mammals, is a medium-sized carnivore that may reach 1 m in length and weigh between 2 and 4 kg. Males are about 20% larger than females. Fishers are larger than martens and are in the same genus. The fisher has rich, dark brown to black fur, often with white tips on some of the hairs, and a small white throat patch. It dwells in mixed coniferous and deciduous forests, is seldom found above treeline and is distributed widely across the mainland and absent from VANCOUVER ISLAND and the QUEEN CHARLOTTE ISLANDS. Despite its name, the fisher rarely eats fish; it feeds mainly on GROUSE, hare, SQUIRREL and mouse, and is one of the few predators able to kill PORCUPINE. INSECTS, fruits and BERRIES are also sometimes eaten. Solitary in their habits, fishers travel in hunting circuits that may extend to 100 km in length. Mating occurs in the spring and the female gives birth to a litter of 1–4 young in Mar of the following year. Fishers are Blue-listed by the Conservation Data Centre (*see* ENDANGERED SPECIES).

FISHER, Orville, artist (b 1911, Vancouver; d 1999, Langley). He studied at the Vancouver School of Art (*see* EMILY CARR INSTITUTE OF ART & DESIGN) in the 1930s under Fred VARLEY and Lawren HARRIS. After graduating, he joined E.J. HUGHES and Paul Goranson, who worked as commercial artists. Together they executed several mural projects, including one at the BC Pavilion at the 1938 San Francisco World's Fair. During WWII he was an official artist for the Canadian army. In June 1944 he accompanied the forces landing in Normandy and was the only Allied painter to record on canvas what it was like on the beaches during D-Day. One of his paintings was chosen for a D-Day commemorative medallion in 1994. After the war he founded the graphic arts department at the Vancouver School of Art and ran it until his retirement in 1976. He continued painting until he was incapacitated by illness shortly before his death.

FISHERIES JURISDICTION in BC is divided between the federal and provincial governments. The federal government (Fisheries and Oceans Canada) has constitutional responsibility for conservation and management of the fisheries resource. The department sets allowable harvest levels and establishes and enforces rules and regulations to ensure that these harvest levels are not exceeded. It also makes policy and operational decisions with respect to fisheries licensing, catch regulation and harvest allocation that directly affect recreation, commercial and FIRST NATIONS fisheries along the coast and throughout the Interior of the province. Some aspects of commercial fisheries and the management of freshwater species have been delegated to the provincial BC Ministry of Fisheries and/or the Ministry of Environment, Lands and Parks (MELP). BC Fisheries is responsible for the inland commercial fisheries (except SALMON),

Federal fisheries patrol boat Tanu *during the herring fishery on the west coast of Vancouver Island, c 1985. Rick Blacklaws photo*

the commercial harvest of marine plants, the management and commercial harvest of wild OYSTERS, licensing and monitoring AQUACULTURE and licensing fish processing, fish buyers and vendors and brokers. BC Fisheries and MELP are jointly responsible for managing all freshwater fish in BC, including anadromous TROUT and CHAR (STEELHEAD, cutthroat trout and Dolly Varden) and non-tidal recreational fisheries (except for salmon). The use of water for FISH HATCHERIES and the regulation of waste discharges are regulated by MELP, while foreshore tenures are managed by the BC Assets and Lands Corporation. *See also* FISHING, ABORIGINAL; FISHING, COMMERCIAL; FISHING, SPORT.

FISHERIES POLICY refers to government policies affecting the management of the fisheries resource: the timing of the harvest, the size of the catches and the benefits deriving from them (*see* FISHING, COMMERCIAL). Although the province has enjoyed substantial fisheries on other species, particularly HERRING and HALIBUT, the story of fisheries management in BC is basically the story of the SALMON fishery. Fish purchased from aboriginal harvesters supported a profitable salted salmon operation at FORT LANGLEY, the HBC post on the lower FRASER R, from the

early 1830s until the Fraser R GOLD RUSH in 1858, but it was not until the rise of the modern SALMON CANNING industry, with its reliance on high-volume, low-cost supplies of fish harvested by growing numbers of non-aboriginal gillnet fishers, that public authorities saw a need to intervene in fisheries management.

Government management of fisheries resources in BC began in 1874 with a letter to Ottawa from the pioneering BLACK canner John Sullivan DEAS, who was seeking the exclusive right to gillnet in a lucrative stretch of the Fraser R. Although the salmon canning industry was then less than 10 years old—the first canning occurred in 1864 and Alexander EWEN did not establish a sustained cannery business until

1871—the enormous profits available from the fishery had already produced intense competition for fish. Following Deas's letter, Ottawa appointed the former FUR TRADER A.C. ANDERSON as the province's fisheries inspector that same year. The federal Fisheries Act was not extended to cover BC until 1875, however, and no regulations were implemented for the BC commercial fishery until 1878. These regulations—offal was not to be dumped in the river, and a 36-hour weekend closure was imposed on cannery gillnetters—were routinely ignored, and their impact would have been negligible even if they had been enforced.

While the new regime did little to affect the canning industry, it did begin the century-long process of dismantling the legal basis for the aboriginal fisheries. In 1877 the *Fisheries Act* was amended to allow Natives only the "privilege" of fishing for food purposes, an implicit restriction on the FIRST NATIONS' commercial right to fish. Anderson initially advocated firm legal protection for aboriginal FISHING rights, but ultimately was forced to create this regulatory distinction between subsistence fishing and commercial harvest to satisfy canners' demands to suppress any commercial harvest they did not control. In doing so, the government planted the seeds of a conflict that has haunted the fishery down to the modern era.

No serious attempt to regulate commercial fishing was undertaken until 1888, when Fraser

R canners lobbied Ottawa to control both the number of canneries and the number of boats by allotting a certain number of gillnet licences to each cannery. Although advanced as a measure to reduce "overfishing," this initiative was intended to reduce costs, eliminate competition from new entrants to the canning industry and reduce the bargaining power of fishers. Despite an increase in the number of boats on the Fraser from 65 in 1874 to more than 900 just 15 years later, the number of fish caught had fluctuated and even declined during some cycles. Efforts by the federal government to implement the canners' regime in 1889 met stiff resistance from an emerging class of "free fishermen." These fishers lived along the river and built their own gillnetters. They used their political clout to force a 1-year moratorium on implementation of licence limitation and campaigned for much tougher conservation measures. But the government ultimately created 2 classes of licences, one open on an unlimited basis to white, "free" fishers and another restricted class tied to canneries and issued, in practice, to fishers of JAPANESE descent. The Japanese Canadians, fishing on contract and (like aboriginals) denied the right to vote, were locked for the next half-century in this regulatory ghetto.

The main features of the modern salmon industry fell into place with Henry O. BELL-IRVING's organization in 1893 of the ANGLO-BC PACKING CO, a sprawling cannery combine that controlled 70% of the Fraser pack. This new company, superseded by the forerunner of the modern-day BC PACKERS in 1903, was confronted in 1900 and 1901 by bitter strikes by fishers; these actions established a pattern of labour–management conflict that persisted for almost 90 years, with serious consequences for fisheries management (*see* FRASER RIVER FISHERMEN'S STRIKES). During this period, canners worked tirelessly to intensify their fishing effort, lobbying successfully to expand the Japanese contract fleet and adding the destructive power of fish traps, particularly on the American side, to the pressure on the stocks. To compensate for their enormous catches, they demanded public investment in FISH HATCHERIES as an alternative to conservation measures. In 1901, angry that federal authorities had created only 4 hatcheries to sustain the Fraser R runs and disturbed at Ottawa's failure to prevent devastating MINING on critical salmon rivers like the Horsefly, the provincial government appointed John Pease BABCOCK, an American, as the province's first fisheries commissioner. Subsequent attempts to create a provincial licensing authority led to repeated negotiations and court challenges in Ottawa. The federal authority was confirmed in a reference to the Privy Council in the United Kingdom in 1914, but BC did create its own fisheries legislation and, through Babcock, played an important role in mobilizing public opinion in favour of improved conservation (*see* FISHERIES JURISDICTION). It was Babcock who in 1913 sounded the alarm about the HELLS GATE BLOCKADE, when slides of rock and debris in the Fraser Canyon choked salmon runs and devastated the resource. The destruction of so many salmon prompted a complete closure of aboriginal fisheries in the canyon, and stopped further investment in hatcheries. It also caused canners to intensify their fisheries on every inlet and creek of the coast, targeting all 5 salmon species. This renewed rush for access to salmon stocks triggered its own crisis of overexpansion in 1928, when a second major round of corporate consolidation was accompanied by government action to eliminate the beach or drag seine operations of coastal First Nations. Although depicted as a conservation measure, the elimination of the drag seines effectively transferred fish—and the jobs that went with it—to the growing fleet of purse seiners deployed by canners. The 1928 crisis did, however, precipitate government investment in improved monitoring of catches and spawning escapements, which laid the basis for fisheries management in the modern era.

It was not until 1937, with the negotiation of a sockeye treaty with the US which provided for the elimination of American traps targeting Fraser runs, that actual management of the salmon runs to achieve conservation objectives became a possibility (*see* INTERNATIONAL PACIFIC SALMON FISHERIES CONVENTION). By agreeing to share the Fraser runs with the Americans, Canada secured a measure of control over the catch. Comprehensive research into the life cycle of salmon was undertaken for the first time and plans were laid to eliminate the blockade at Hells Gate. It took a further 10 years to complete construction of the first fishways at Hells Gate, but the subsequent management of Fraser salmon fisheries by the International Pacific Salmon Fisheries Commission led to a major recovery of Fraser runs in the 1950s and 1960s. Returning

runs were protected right through coastal waters and assured safe passage through the Fraser Canyon. The result was a dramatic increase in sockeye and pink returns, particularly after the treaty was extended to Fraser pink salmon in the 1950s. In the case of the Horsefly sockeye run, a few thousand spawners in the 1940s were built up to several million by the 1980s.

WWII brought profound changes to the fishery. Fishers saw their bargaining power strengthened because of their vital role in coastal protection and food production. New technology had a growing impact on the harvest. Race-based licensing had been eliminated at the end of the war and the creation of the UNITED FISHERMEN AND ALLIED WORKERS' UNION (UFAWU) in 1945 allowed fishers a strong voice in management and price negotiations. The union's leadership overcame strong resistance from some members to ensure that Japanese Canadian fishers returned to the industry as equals, free of the discriminatory licensing and housing of the pre-war era. Direct union action in 1946 even forced a change in the allocation of catches between seine and gillnet fleets. A series of successful strikes drove up the price paid to fishers and the union began a campaign for a licence limitation scheme to protect fishers' incomes. Increased public investment in fisheries led to the development of a new generation of fisheries managers who combined unprecedented research resources with a sense of independence from corporate priorities. The International Pacific Salmon Commission's research supported a growing conservation ethic among British Columbians, epitomized by successful opposition to the proposed Moran hydroelectric dam across the Fraser R (*see also* ENVIRONMENTAL

MOVEMENT). Fisheries managers were confident that they could not only protect the salmon runs, but restore them to unprecedented strength. Their objective was maximum sustained yield, the regular and predictable harvest of exactly that amount of fish which would generate maximum harvests without impairing survival of the stock.

By the end of the 1960s, however, BC fisheries managers found themselves confronting new challenges on several fronts. Some economists complained that protection of fish habitat to sustain salmon runs was holding back more valuable investment in HYDROELECTRICITY, LOGGING and other industries. The fishing industry, they argued, suffered from the "tragedy of the commons"—the dissipation of economic rent from a resource that occurs when access to the resource is unlimited. The value of the fishery appeared to be equal to the cost of harvest and management. The large increase in the number of fishers and their stagnant earnings appeared to support this analysis. The UFAWU had long advocated licence limitation, to protect both the fish and the fishers. The union believed the government should protect the public interest in the resource by limiting the number of fishers to as many as could make a decent living from the available harvest, admitting new entrants as veterans retired or moved to other jobs. But resource economists led an assault against a fisheries management system that had conservation as its only goal. Unless it could show a profit greater than other economic activity, they argued, fisheries management was a waste of time. The lines of a renewed conflict were drawn. In 1969 the federal government introduced the Davis Plan, a licence limitation and reduction program named for Jack DAVIS, the Liberal fisheries minister. Under the plan, a new fishing privilege was attached to the boat, not to the fisher. Rather than limit labour, the government limited capital by limiting the number of boats in the fishery and allowing their licences to be bought and sold like any other commodity. Government funds were used to eliminate boats from the fleet and to invest in a new round of hatchery construction. Despite vocal and prolonged opposition from the UFAWU and the NATIVE BROTHERHOOD (the main bargaining agent for aboriginal fishers), both of whom warned of a new round of capital investment, tighter corporate control and more intense fishing pressure, the plan was implemented. The Davis Plan marked a radical restructuring of fisheries management. Although the number of vessels was reduced, overall capital investment in boats and gear skyrocketed, creating a much more efficient fleet and an enormous new financial burden that could only be paid for with more fish. Within 4 years, the Davis Plan was pronounced a failure. Rather than reducing effort and raising profit, it sparked speculative investment in boats and licences. But a remarkable 7-year boom during the 1970s disguised these effects. A strong economy and Canada's extension of its maritime economic zone out to the 200-mile (320 km) limit provoked a greater demand for fish, as well

Protestors demonstrating against the federal government's Aboriginal Fisheries Strategy, 1992. Colin Price/Vancouver Province

as higher prices and new investment in the industry. For a time, revenues outpaced costs.

The economic bubble burst in 1980, when fish prices collapsed and a general economic recession drove interest rates up. Debt-ridden fishers, still trying to pay off huge loans incurred to buy licences and build more efficient boats, faced bankruptcy. Peter PEARSE, a UBC resource economist, was appointed to conduct a Royal Commission into the Pacific fishery to tackle its problems once and for all. Pearse concluded that the failure of the Davis Plan was that it allowed remnants of an open-entry, common property fishery to remain. His final report in Sept 1982 declared flatly that "common property is repugnant to the principles of a market economy" and set out a 10-year program to privatize all of the province's fisheries. He recommended that all fisheries resources be parcelled up and auctioned to the highest bidder so that private interests could force efficiency into the industry. A key element of his proposals was the creation of private, for profit, salmon hatcheries, or ocean ranches, which would eliminate the necessity for any fleet at all by harvesting returning runs in traps at river mouths. No fish stocks, including salmon, would exist as a common property resource, only as private property subject to management by market forces. Determined resistance from coastal communities and fisheries organizations stalled the passage of legislation to implement this plan until the defeat of the Liberal government in 1984. But the newly-elected Conservatives proceeded to advance the privatization scheme through policy changes. The Mulroney government's determination to cut government spending and regulation produced a series of dramatic budget cuts at the Department of Fisheries and Oceans (DFO), which reduced the ministry's research and management capability. Public investment in SALMONID ENHANCEMENT was cut back and then almost eliminated. Ottawa accelerated the privatization policy on several fronts, moving to create transferable quotas in fisheries like SABLEFISH and halibut and raising licence fees to pass more of the cost of management back to fishers. Both the federal and provincial governments undertook a crash program to introduce salmon farming (*see* AQUACULTURE, FIN FISH) in the province and a new "no net loss" habitat protection policy, designed by Pearse, made it possible for developers to trade artificial or man-made habitat for natural salmon-rearing areas slated for destruction. A ruling under the General Agreement on Tariffs and Trade in 1989 marked a turning point in the process of restructuring by allowing, for the first time since the start of the 20th century, the export of unprocessed salmon from the province. Although Canada had long benefited from Alaskan salmon imported for processing in BC when Alaskan plants were oversupplied, the ban on the export of unprocessed salmon from BC had fostered a strong canning sector. The loss of this protection further reduced the economic benefits to Canada of salmon management. Seven canning lines left the province during the next 4 years.

The GATT ruling inaugurated a decade of unprecedented changes in salmon management. A 1990 Supreme Court of Canada decision known as the SPARROW DECISION found that the aboriginal right to fish for food, society or ceremonial purposes was a communal right protected by Section 35 of the Charter of Rights and Freedoms. This right can only be interfered with for reasons of conservation and after due consultation with affected First Nations. In response to the Sparrow decision, and to lay the groundwork for a transition to negotiated treaties in the province, the federal government inaugurated the Aboriginal Fisheries Strategy. This change in fisheries management provoked outraged protests from non-aboriginal fishers. Racial tensions on the Fraser reached unprecedented levels, amid charges of rampant poaching. The turmoil reached a peak in 1994, when all sectors of the industry hoped to reap the return of record numbers of Fraser R sockeye to the spawning grounds. But hope turned to bitter disappointment and conflict when the run, forecast to be as many as 30 million fish, apparently "disappeared." A subsequent inquiry determined that the beleaguered federal fisheries department, its infrastructure weakened by years of budget reductions, made critical errors in the management of JOHNSTONE STRAIT seine fisheries, which nearly caused the destruction of the run.

The 1994 crisis occurred against the backdrop of efforts by the federal government to secure a renewed salmon treaty with the US (American fishers continued to intercept large numbers of Canada-bound fish). An overarching agreement achieved in 1984 had been beneficial to Canada, but attempts to extend its provisions beyond their original term proved futile. Negotiations failed, and the inability of the government to resolve the problems plaguing the industry generated renewed calls for restructuring, this time against a growing public anxiety about sustainable management of all resources. Worldwide overproduction of farmed salmon had driven prices for wild fish to all-time lows. Fleet capitalization and operating costs remained unacceptably high, despite nearly 20 years of buybacks and licence limitation. The Mifflin Plan, introduced in 1996 and named for then federal Fisheries Minister Fred Mifflin, sought to resolve the crisis with a 50% reduction in the salmon fleet, yet more concentration of ownership and higher fees for those who remained. The plan and the resistance it produced became a provincial election issue, and conflict between Victoria and Ottawa over the direction of fisheries management and the content of a renewed salmon treaty continued for 2 years. But Mifflin's successor, David ANDERSON, won the day with a radical recommitment to conservation as the fundamental principle of fisheries management. His emphasis on a new "risk averse" management philosophy mandated complete closures for any salmon fishery in which there was a risk of harvesting weak coho stocks. Anderson gave sport FISHING a higher management priority and required an emphasis on "selective harvest techniques," including fish

traps and wheels, to allow abundant runs to be harvested while weaker ones escaped. These goals were substantially achieved by the end of decade.

At the beginning of the 21st century, the fishing industry remained an important part of the BC economy, generating nearly $900 million a year in wholesale value. But the wild salmon fishery was a much smaller part of the picture than it had been, with farmed salmon making up most of the difference. All fisheries were under some form of licence limitation and many were operated by private quota holders who paid royalties for the privilege. Fishers were increasingly sharecropping for shore-based quota or licence holders, often major processors. In the salmon fishery, total fishing closures were the main management tool of a fisheries department seeking to protect weaker runs without the research or enforcement capability of the past. The salmon treaty, which had done so much to rebuild Fraser stocks, had been converted into a mechanism to allow the US to oversee Canadian management of all salmon stocks. Canada's long-sought goal of equity—the right to a harvest equivalent to our production—was abandoned. For all intents and purposes, both salmon management and salmon processing were conducted as a continental exercise, without regard to the Canadian boundary. Habitat destruction, especially by logging, continued apace and new environmental concerns, particularly global warming and growing destruction of streams by urban development and pollution, cast a shadow over the resource. The century-long struggle over whether fisheries resources should be privately owned or held in common had largely been settled in favour of private ownership in all but the salmon fishery, where government policy, at least, respected the deeply held public conviction that fisheries resources are a common trust. *Geoff Meggs*

FISHERIES RENEWAL BC is a government agency established in 1997 to deal with problems affecting the BC FISHING industry. Directed by a board of representatives from government, FIRST NATIONS, fishing communities and the industry, the agency was granted $22.5 million for its first 3 years. Responsibilities include restoring fish habitat, developing seafood markets, planning community-based fisheries and advising governments on fishing issues. *See also* FISHERIES JURISDICTION; FISHERIES POLICY.

FISHERMEN'S INDUSTRIAL UNION was a militant organization of fishery workers on the coast formed in VANCOUVER early in 1932. Affiliated with the Communist Party through the Workers Unity League, it attempted to present an industry-wide united front to cannery owners. To this end it reorganized in 1934 as the Fishermen and Cannery Workers' Industrial Union (FCWIU). Two years later it led a bitter strike on the Central Coast, focussed on RIVERS INLET, with the objective of obtaining higher prices for fish from the canners (*see* SALMON CANNING). Owners moved replacement workers into the canneries under police guard and the strike ended in a stalemate. Soon after, the FCWIU dissolved as fishers decided to consolidate with other unions. The Rivers Inlet strike proved to be a catalyst for later organization, however, because it demonstrated the renewed potential of strike action in the fishing industry. The strike had enjoyed wide support, including that of JAPANESE Canadian fishers, and the losses suffered by Rivers Inlet canners caused them to agree to price arbitration in 1937. *See also* FISHING, COMMERCIAL; LABOUR MOVEMENT.

FISHING, ABORIGINAL, predates the arrival of Europeans in BC by many centuries. FIRST NATIONS on the coast and in the Interior relied on many different types of marine plants and animals as traditional sources of food and as trade goods. Coastal people had access to a wide variety of marine resources, including SALMON, different types of GROUNDFISH (HALIBUT, LINGCOD, ROCKFISH and others), shellfish (ABALONE, CLAMS, SEA URCHINS, CRABS and others), STURGEON, EULACHONS, HERRING and herring roe. Historically, WHALING and the harvest of marine mammals such as SEA OTTERS, SEALS and SEA LIONS were also important, and many marine plants and animals were used in the making of tools, weapons, medicines and other items. Interior groups inhabiting the inland watersheds were particularly reliant on the salmon that migrate up the province's many rivers and streams to spawn. Using a variety of ingenious weirs, traps, nets and spears, the First Nations intercepted the salmon on their migration paths. When the first FUR TRADERS arrived in the region early in the 19th century, they relied on salmon caught by the First Nations to provision the trading posts, and ultimately as an item of trade in its own right. Salmon became so important a commodity in the frontier economy that it was accepted as a form of currency.

Aboriginal fishery on the Fraser R, 1993.
Roy Luckow photo

The establishment of SALMON CANNERIES at the mouth of the FRASER R in the 1870s marked the beginning of the Euro-Canadian commercial fishery in BC (*see* FISHING, COMMERICIAL). Initially the commercial fishery relied on local aboriginal labour, with the men employed in fishing and the women in processing. As competition for the resource became acute, the Canadian government severely restricted the upriver weir and trap fisheries of the aboriginal groups. Government fishery managers, concerned first and foremost with the interests of the canners, decided to protect the Euro-Canadian fishery at the expense of the aboriginal fishery. Regulations introduced in 1888 confined First Nations to a "food fishery" for their domestic use and prohibited them from selling salmon. They were also prohibited from using their efficient traps and weirs and confined to less efficient fishing methods (*see* BABINE BARRICADES). These prohibitions were most serious for First Nations inhabiting the watersheds of the 2 great salmon rivers, the Fraser and the SKEENA; most of them lived too far from the ocean to join the commercial fishery, in which many coastal aboriginal people participated. Indeed, aboriginal fishers have always comprised a significant portion of the regular commercial fishery; since the early 1900s about one-third of the BC commercial fleet has been owned and/or crewed by aboriginal fishers. However, a series of developments in the commercial fishery during the 20th century, and especially after WWII, conspired to reduce the participation of aboriginal people.

At the same time, the food fishery was also in decline as industrial developments and government regulation tended to compromise the aboriginal economy. This trend began to be reversed in the 1990s, however. First Nations have a constitutional right to fish for food and for social and ceremonial purposes in accordance with Section 35 of the *Constitution Act, 1982*. The aboriginal right to fish for these purposes is second in priority only to conservation. This right was confirmed by the Supreme Court of Canada in the 1990 SPARROW DECISION. Demands by First Nations for greater access to the resource have been part of the land claims process (*see* ABORIGINAL RIGHTS), pursued in part by court appeals and in part by negotiations in the ongoing treaty-making process that began during the 1990s. The NISGA'A TREATY, for example, contains important fisheries provisions. In response to the Sparrow decision, the federal government, which has jurisdiction over the salmon fisheries (*see* FISHERIES JURISDICTION), implemented the Aboriginal Fisheries Strategy (AFS) in 1992. In agreements with a number of First Nations, the government started to allocate more fish to the aboriginal food fishery. The sale of fish from these negotiated allocations was also permitted.

Aboriginal salmon traps on Vancouver Island, as shown in an illustration in the Canadian Illustrated News in 1873.

Aboriginal fisher netting salmon at Lillooet, 1993. Roy Luckow photo

In return, aboriginal groups agreed to a negotiated cap on the amount of fish allocated to them, which helped to restore government control over aggregate catch levels. The AFS was opposed by many stakeholders in the commercial fishery on the grounds that the government was creating a separate fishery based on race, but in general the policy was intended to enhance aboriginal participation in the province's fisheries. At the end of the 20th century, aboriginal food fisheries were estimated to account for about 8% of the total fish catch in BC.

FISHING, COMMERCIAL, in BC dates back to the FUR TRADE era of the early 19th century, when the HBC began buying SALMON from FIRST NATIONS people to feed its employees and for export. The fishery expanded dramatically when SALMON CANNING began at the mouth of the FRASER R in the early 1870s and near the mouth of the SKEENA R shortly afterwards. Gillnetting (*see below*) was the primary salmon fishing method at this early stage, when the commercial fishery was almost exclusively a salmon fishery. Until the 1920s salmon accounted for two-thirds of the dollar value of the industry. HALIBUT was next in importance, followed by HERRING and COD. A SARDINE (pilchard) fishery flourished between 1925 and 1946. By the late 1990s, over 80 different species of fin fish, shellfish and aquatic plants were harvested commercially in BC. In 1998, 259,000 tonnes of seafood products from wild and farmed sources were harvested, with a wholesale value of over $877 million. Seafood is the province's number one food export, with an export value of $813 million in 1998, when it accounted for 25% of the total value of all seafood exports from Canada. Despite its historic importance, the commercial fishery accounts for less than 1% of the provincial gross domestic product. Nonetheless, many coastal communities rely on the fishery for their livelihood; they were being seriously threatened by its decline as the 20th century ended.

Between 1996 and 2000, the number of salmon licences was reduced by 50%, largely due to government licence buyback schemes (*see*

FISHERIES POLICY). Wild salmon harvests declined as well. The 1998 harvest of 30,200 tonnes was the lowest in 50 years. This was due in part to the severe curtailment of BC's salmon harvest in order to protect and conserve salmon stocks. BC's share of the world market for salmon amounted to less than 4% in 1998. Competition has come in recent years from Russia, Japan, Alaska and farmed salmon. In 1998 BC's farmed salmon industry produced 42,300 tonnes of salmon with a wholesale value of $245 million, exceeding the wild salmon harvest for the first time (*see* AQUACULTURE, FIN FISH). Declining yields of wild species have caused fishers to become more and more concerned about interception of Canadian-origin salmon in US fisheries and has touched off several confrontatons with the US (*see* PACIFIC SALMON TREATY). Meanwhile, federal government policy was aimed at reducing the catch of the fleet by reducing the number of fishing vessels. Other threats to the industry during the decade included the rising temperature of the Pacific Ocean and continued habitat destruction along rivers and streams.

Six gear types are used in commercial fishing in BC: seine, gillnet, hook and line (including longline, troll and jigging), trawl, trap and dive (*see* DIVE FISHERIES). The major fishing gears for Pacific salmon are seine, gillnet and troll. There are several methods for capturing HERRING, including seining, gillnetting and ponding. A variety of gear is employed in the shellfish harvest. Hand tools are used in the intertidal zone to gather CLAMS, OYSTERS and goose BARNACLES. Traps are used to land CRAB and some SHRIMP species, especially prawns. Shrimp are also harvested by beam trawls and otter trawls. Small trawl fisheries take place for EUPHAUSIIDS, or krill, and for pink swimming SCALLOPS. Many shellfish species are harvested by divers, including GEODUCKS and horse clams, SEA URCHINS, SEA CUCUMBERS, scallops, OCTOPUS and, before the fishery was closed, ABALONE.

Trolling

Trolling is a salmon fishing method in which fish are caught on hooks towed on lines behind the vessel. The first commercial trolling in BC was done by aboriginal people fishing from dugout CANOES using baited barbs and handlines. European immigrants became involved in commercial handlining from rowboats and skiffs in the 1910s, and the handline fishery remained viable into the 1940s. Gasoline-powered boats were introduced in the early 1900s. The gas boat had tall trolling poles, spread open at the top to form a *V*, so that multiple lines could run through the water without tangling. The gas boat could be crewed by a single fisher. In about 1912 the gurdy (powered reel) was introduced, eliminating the need for hand-hauling. In the 1930s

Dave Reid gillnetting for sockeye salmon aboard the Meg, Barkley Sound, Vancouver Island, 1998. Brian Gauvin photo

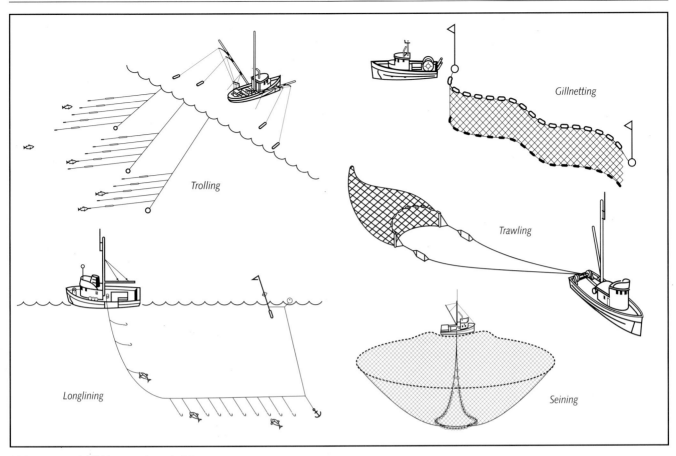

Major commercial fishing gear types in BC.
Drawings by Kim LaFave and Roger Handling

fishers began to take ice aboard, allowing them to work farther offshore and to stay out for several days; many of them took a crew member to help. By the 1960s, compact freezing systems allowed trollers to freeze their catch at sea, extending their trips even further. In the 1950s and 1960s, the BC troll fleet consisted of approximately 1,600 vessels. By the year 2000, largely due to government buyback programs, the fleet had shrunk to 544 boats. Conservation concerns for coho, chinook and sockeye stocks have severely curtailed the troll fishery. As of 1999, a BC troller fished for an average of 30 days a year. Modern trolling vessels can have as many as 120 lures in the water at once, at depths of 10 to 60 fathoms. Troll-caught salmon bring in top prices because they are cleaned and iced or frozen immediately after being caught and are not scarred by net marks.

Troller at work off Dundas Island on the North Coast, 1994. Peter A. Robson photo

Gillnetting

Gillnetting is one of the oldest forms of fishing, practised around the world for thousands of years. A gillnet is a long, horizontal mesh sheet with floats along the upper edge. It is set perpendicular to the path of the fish and designed so that incoming fish can get their heads but not their bodies through the mesh; thus the term *gillnet*. First Nations fishers used gillnets made of nettles, CEDAR and sometimes hemp with wood floats and stone weights. In BC waters, gillnets are used primarily in the commercial salmon fishery, but also in the herring roe, EULA-CHON and recreational SMELT fisheries. Most gillnets are set on the surface but they can be set on the seabed or at any depth in between. A form of gillnet known as a setnet is set from shore. Setnets are most commonly used by First Nations fishers along the banks of major salmon rivers. In shallow inshore waters and small rivers, gillnets are often worked by hand: crew members wade in the water or work from canoes and small skiffs. In deeper waters and in large rivers, gillnets are operated from larger vessels, typically 10 to 13 m long. A typical large gillnetter has the net stored on a hydraulic drum on the afterdeck, and the net is set and retrieved over the stern. Fish are picked out of the net as it comes aboard. Another type of gillnetter is the bow-picker, in which the drum and rollers are at the forward end of the vessel and the net is set from the bow while the vessel backs away. The size of the netting used in a gillnet is determined by the type of fish targeted. Typical mesh sizes include 50 mm for herring, 100–175 mm for cod and 130 mm for salmon. Gillnets vary

dramatically in size; an individual net may span 30 to 75 m.

BC's commercial salmon gillnet fishery began on the Fraser R in about 1865 to supply the many canneries that were being built near the mouth of the river. The typical gillnet vessel of the late 1800s was open, double-ended and 6–9 m long. Many had gaff rigs for sailing. The gillnetter was crewed by 2 people: one rowed while the other set and retrieved the net. Nets were made of linen and measured up to 200 fathoms long, and hauling them in was backbreaking work. The gillnet fishery expanded upcoast as canneries were built on the Skeena and NASS rivers, along RIVERS INLET and many other locations. Most early gillnet skiffs were owned by the canneries and rented daily to fishers. By 1900 there were approximately 3,700 gillnet boats in BC, most of them crewed by JAPAN-ESE fishers. Gas engines were in widespread use on the lower coast by the 1910s and fishers began adding small cabins as protection from the elements. This was when the rounded, classic "west coast" cabin with vertical tongue-and-groove planking became common. In the early 1930s, Laurie JARVIS, a SOINTULA fisher, pioneered the powered gillnet drum. After the war, high-speed 6-cylinder motors were available and speedier boats were able to fish over a wider area. In the 1950s synthetic net materials were introduced and nets became stronger, more durable and more elastic. During the 1970s and 1980s, fibreglass and aluminum vessels became common. Limited entry programs began to be introduced in the 1980s, a measure designed to control the number of boats in the industry.

New vessels had to be built to an equal or lesser length than boats they replaced. To build more room into the same length of vessel, the bow-picker was introduced from the US. A vessel of this design had crew accommodations over the engine and left the forward half of the vessel for the drum and storage. This allowed for the installation of larger, faster engines, and wide, roomy accommodations aft. Many of these vessels travelled at speeds up to 40 knots, which meant they could travel almost the entire coast in a day, fishing more openings and moving quickly to areas where fish were most plentiful.

In the early 1990s, when a dramatic decline in fish stocks reduced the number of legal fishing days, many people were forced to leave the industry. By the end of the decade gillnetting was tightly regulated; fishers were restricted to specific fishing zones and opening times in an effort to conserve the remaining fish. Between 1996 and 2000, the coastal gillnet fleet was reduced through government buyback programs from 2,269 vessels to 1,411.

Seining

Seining is a method of fishing in which a net is used to encircle fish. Two types of seines are used in BC: the purse seine and the drag, or beach, seine.

The earliest seines were the drag type. Up to 200 m long, they were set from the shore, usually at a river mouth, in a large circle around schooling fish. The net was then dragged ashore full of fish. In the early 1900s, only First Nations people, sometimes working in conjunction with nearby canneries, were allowed to use drag seines. Government policy eventually eliminated most drag seine operations, and the harvest transferred to the purse seine fishery. Drag seining was still being used in the 1990s in the eulachon fishery, and as an experimental selective fishing method and as a way to collect brood stock for salmon hatcheries.

Seiners at work during the herring roe fishery, Barkley Sound. Brian Gauvin photo

A purse seine is designed so that rings, bridles and a purse line are used to gather ("purse") a net along its bottom edge, forming a pouch in which the fish are trapped until they can be hauled aboard. Purse seines are set and retrieved from seine boats, or seiners. Purse seining was introduced to BC from the US in the early 1900s. Early purse seines were set using a pair of rowed boats, the crew of each boat holding half the net. When a school of fish was detected, the 2 boats encircled it in a pincer movement and the net was hand-pursed. Another method, using skiffs and small scows with manual winches, was perfected by the Japanese Canadian fishers who carried on a WWI-era herring seine fishery in GEORGIA STRAIT. With the introduction of the gas engine in about 1905, the setting and pursing operations were brought together on a single, larger vessel. The typical seiner was about 15 m long with a graceful-looking shape. The first of

these was built in BC in 1913; by 1920 the purse seiner had become a major force in the coastal fishery, not only for salmon (usually chum, pink and sockeye) and herring, but in the new SARDINE fishery as well. They set and retrieved their nets using a system known as table seining. The net was set from a large, square platform in the stern called a turntable. A small skiff known as a tow-off boat was tied to one end of the net and was used to help pull the net off the stern as the seiner moved away. The seiner then turned in a circle, gradually drawing the net around the fish. The table was turned 90° and the net was pursed and retrieved manually from the side. The skiff also played an important role in towing the seiner sideways so that it did not pull itself into the body of the net as it pursed. The body of the net was hauled aboard by tying a line around a portion of the web and winching it with a line running from the deck winch through a pulley at the masthead.

Early purse seine nets were made of cotton, with different mesh sizes depending on which species of salmon the seiner was catching. The top edge of the net—the corkline—was hung with floats. The bottom edge of the net—the lead line—was made of manila and weighted with lead. Hanging from the lead line were bridles and heavy rings through which ran the purse line. An average seine was 200 fathoms in length and about 15 m deep, large enough to capture 20,000 or more salmon (close to 70 tonnes) in one set. The advent of synthetic fibres led to nets that were lighter, stronger, more durable and easier to maintain. A series of technological innovations greatly improved the productivity of the seine fishery following WWII. The seine drum was introduced in the 1950s, allowing the net to be wound on and off the vessel more easily than with a table. In 1953 the Puretic power block was introduced. This was a hydraulically powered block mounted high above the deck with which the crew could bring the net aboard. During the following decade, tow-off skiffs were replaced by motorized "power" skiffs, where allowed by regulation. In the 1960s wood hulls began to give way to fibreglass and metal hulls. Concerns about overcapacity of the fleet led the

Halibut longlining aboard the Summer Wind, *Queen Charlotte Islands, 1994. L to r: Dale Erickson, Corey Erickson, Todd Vick. Peter A. Robson photo*

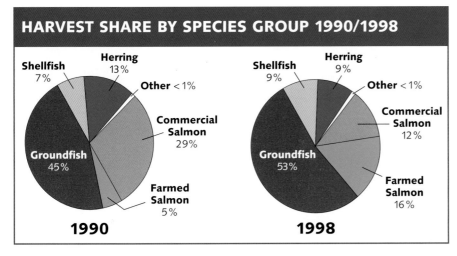

HARVEST SHARE BY SPECIES GROUP 1990/1998

1990
- Shellfish 7%
- Herring 13%
- Other <1%
- Commercial Salmon 29%
- Groundfish 45%
- Farmed Salmon 5%

1998
- Shellfish 9%
- Herring 9%
- Other <1%
- Commercial Salmon 12%
- Groundfish 53%
- Farmed Salmon 16%

government to limit the number of seine licences beginning in the 1970s. New regulations also prohibited licence holders from building new vessels larger than the boats they were replacing, a restriction that led to significant design changes. As with gillnetters, new seine vessels were much wider, often with blunt noses, allowing a dramatic increase in the carrying capacity while staying within length requirements.

Between 1996 and the year 2000, the number of salmon seine licences on the coast was reduced from 536 to 276, largely due to government licence buyback schemes designed to reduce the fish-catching capacity of the seine sector of the commercial salmon fishery. At the same time, Pacific sardine stocks rebounded and a fishery for this species was once again undertaken by seiners.

Longlining

Longlining is a hook-and-line fishery in which long lengths of baited hooks are laid on the ocean floor to catch HALIBUT, SABLEFISH, ROCKFISH, DOGFISH and other species of GROUNDFISH. To set longline gear, a buoy topped with a marker flag is tossed overboard. Attached to it is a length of line (buoy line) at least as long as the depth of water into which the gear is being set. When enough line has been set out, an anchor is tied onto the buoy line, a skate (or fixed length) of groundline is secured to the anchor and the groundline begins running over the stern. At set intervals along the groundline, baited hooks are attached by shorter lengths of line—a metre or so—known as gangions. These are either tied to the longline or attached by removable snaphooks. Several skates are usually joined together. When enough line has been set out, another anchor and buoy are attached, making a "string" of gear. Further strings are set out as required. Gear is allowed to "soak" several hours, or sometimes all night, before being hauled back aboard. To retrieve the gear, modern longliners use a powered davit mounted amidships. As the boat steams along the track of the gear, fish are gaffed aboard while the longline is spooled back onto a revolving drum or carefully coiled into piles on deck. In the late 1990s, a typical longline trip lasted 4–8 days, with the fish cleaned and iced at sea to preserve freshness.

Until the late 1980s, longline fisheries were known as a derby-style fisheries. A certain portion of the coast was opened by fisheries officials for a set length of time. Longline vessels then crowded together for the best areas and crews scrambled to fish as much gear as they could to maximize their catch before the fishery closed. Vessels fished regardless of weather, and prices were often low because markets were flooded at the close of the fishery. In the late 1980s, management of the halibut and sablefish fisheries changed to a quota system, where the annual quota is divided among the licence holders and each may fish at almost any time of the year until his quota is met.

Trawling

Trawling, or dragging, is a commercial fishing method in which a trawl vessel (trawler or dragger) drags a cone-shaped net with a rectangular opening through the water to trap fish. Trawling is used to take a wide variety of species in a number of separate fisheries including shrimp, euphausiids, scallops and groundfish. As of 2000, the trawl fishery was the largest commercial fishery, by volume, in BC.

Two types of trawling systems are used, the otter trawl and the beam trawl. The otter trawl is the standard method for harvesting groundfish, while the beam trawl is used primarily in the shrimp fishery. The otter trawl was introduced to BC in about 1910 and is used for both bottom trawling and mid-water trawling (fishing off the sea bottom). The bottom trawl has rollers along its bottom edge, while floats on the top edge keep the net open. The wings of the net are spread by large wood or steel "otter boards," or "doors," which are connected to the winch drum on the vessel and keep the doors straining outwards from the wings. Mid-water trawls do not require rollers because they do not come into contact with the bottom, but they do use weights, floats and doors to keep the net open. Mid-water trawling accounts for more than 76% of the groundfish catch by volume, mostly hake and turbot. Otter trawl fishers estimate that only 6% of the coastal waters of BC are suitable for bottom trawling. This is due to the abundance of underwater obstacles such as pinnacles, rocks and steeply sloped bottoms that cannot be

fished. With either net, the trapped fish accumulate in the narrow end of the cone, known as the cod end, which is the last part of the net hauled aboard. The crew then release a special knot at the cod end, the chain knot, and the fish spill out. Otter trawlers are sturdy, powerful vessels, 10.5 m to 45 m long; many of them are constructed from steel. The introduction of depth sounders, synthetic nets and the powered net drum in the 1950s have been the major innovations in the fishery. Since 1997 the groundfish trawl fishery (excluding shrimp) has been managed on an individual vessel quota system for each species. Most groundfish trawlers must carry government-approved observers to gather data needed to manage the fishery and comply with regulations. The groundfish trawl fleet consists of 142 licence holders (of which about 80 were active in 1999); during the 1990s they landed an average of 140,000 tonnes annually with an estimated wholesale value of $133 million.

The beam trawling vessel is 9 to 13.5 m long, smaller than the otter trawler. The 2 are similar in shape and function but the beam system does not incorporate doors. Instead the wings and mouth of the net are held open by a long pole, or beam, about the same length as the vessel. A beam trawl net does not have rollers. In 2000, there were 200 vessels actively fishing for shrimp using this method. Beam trawlers estimate that only 2% of the BC ocean bottom is suitable for beam trawling.

Both beam and otter trawling raise concerns about bycatch: unwanted species, undersize species or incidental species that the trawler is not allowed to keep. Experimental projects have been underway for many years to reduce bycatch. There is also concern about the ecological effects of trawl nets dragging along the ocean bottom.

Trawler hauling a huge catch of turbot aboard the Caledonian, Queen Charlotte Sound, *1989.*
Peter A. Robson photo

Brailing fish from a salmon trap, 1907.
BC Archives B-06318

Weirs and traps

Weirs and traps are devices that were employed traditionally by First Nations fishers to catch salmon and trout migrating through tidal waters or travelling upstream to spawn. A weir is a fence-like structure constructed from rocks and/or posts and latticework set across a stream to block the passage of fish. Rock weirs at river mouths allowed fish to pass over the barrier on the incoming tide, then become stranded when the tide receded. A stake weir was built across a creek,

Steven Malcolm grading prawns aboard the
Gladiator, 1998. Brian Gauvin photo

blocking the passage of the fish, which were speared or netted as they bunched up against the barrier. Some stake weirs incorporated fish traps. The fish passed through a single opening in the weir and into the trap—a device constructed from wood that allowed the fish to swim in but not out. In the late 1800s, cannery owners began constructing large commercial fish traps up to 1 km long. These were located in salt water in areas where major migratory routes of salmon passed close to shore; eg, at SOOKE and BOUNDARY BAY. Such a trap consisted of a row of pilings strung with net, set perpendicular to the shoreline and designed to lead fish into a series of compartments; the last of these was a "spiller," where the fish were trapped. When enough fish accumulated, they were hauled from the trap spiller into scows and towed to a cannery for processing. This type of trap was extremely profitable to the canneries. At one point there were 21 such traps in the Boundary Bay–POINT ROBERTS area (19 were American). During the 1940s and 1950s traps became less and less viable due to restrictive opening times, competition from seiners and rising costs of operation. The trap nets at Sooke, the last remaining device of this sort, closed after the 1958 season.

However, small-scale weirs and traps were again being used and tested in the 1990s as a live capture method, allowing the release of non-target species as part of a more selective and responsible fishery. These methods can also be used to enumerate fish and to collect brood stock for salmonid enhancement.

Small, portable box-type traps have been used throughout the world for thousands of years. In BC they are used to catch shellfish in both the sport and commercial fisheries, usually for crab and shrimp. The commercial fishery also uses traps to catch sablefish. Most traps are a rectangular or circular box shape with a metal frame covered with mesh. Some form of bait is placed within the net. When set, the trap sits on the ocean bottom with a line and a float running

to the surface. Prey are drawn by the smell of the food and enter through funnel-shaped openings in the trap. Once inside, they are unable to find the narrow opening again and become trapped.

Selective fishing

The catch of non-target (and sometimes threatened) stocks is a characteristic of most mixed-stock fisheries, particularly those that pursue salmon, groundfish and shellfish. Compounding the problem is uncertain environmental conditions that are causing unpredictable stock abundance and making it extremely difficult to predict the composition and size of fish stocks. Therefore, the ability of fishers to fish selectively by avoiding non-target species and stocks, or releasing them unharmed, is increasingly important. Selective fishing is also seen as part of a long-term conservation strategy for rebuilding the resource. Selective fishing allows fishers to continue to harvest more abundant stocks while protecting weaker ones.

Selective fishing strategies include: minimizing encounters with stocks of concern, experimenting with alternative fishing gear, modifying existing fishing gear, employing new fishing methods, and improving existing gear and practices that reduce fish mortality and injury when releasing fish. Some of the experimental gear and methods that have shown promise are brailing and sorting techniques, revival tanks, fish wheels, traps, weirs and nets, weedlines, tooth tangle nets, Alaska twist web, hot picking, different mesh sizes, and proper catch and release and fish handling techniques. In 1998 Fisheries and Oceans Canada introduced selective fishing as a fundamental and permanent change to the way commercial fishing is carried out in BC.

Peter A. Robson

Reading: Alan Haig-Brown, *Fishing for a Living*, 1993; Mark Hume, *The Mystery of the Adams River Sockeye*, 1994; Peter Robson and Michael Skog, eds, *Working the Tides: A Portrait of Canada's West Coast Fishery*, 1996.

Gillnet fishers at Steveston on the Fraser River,
c 1910. BC Archives B-08416

FISHING, DIVE; *see* DIVE FISHERIES.

FISHING, SPORT, has long been one of the most popular recreational activities in BC. Saltwater sport fishing takes place everywhere along the coast. In the Interior there are thousands of LAKES and RIVERS that provide freshwater fishing opportunities. In the late 1990s more than 600,000 people—residents and visitors—bought sport fishing licences annually. Saltwater anglers spent an average of 7 days fishing per year; freshwater fishers spent an average of 11 days angling. Sport fishing annually generates more than $1 billion in business through lodges and fish camps, hotels/motels, angling guide/charter services, fishing licences and sales of fishing gear and tackle, boating equipment, and sundries.

Saltwater Sport Fishing

BC is known as one of the world's greatest saltwater sport fishing destinations. This is due to an abundance of fish, in particular the giant TYEE (a chinook SALMON weighing more than 13.5 kg, though tyee ranging from 22 to 27 kg are caught frequently). The records for coho salmon (15.4 kg) and STEELHEAD (19 kg) were set in BC waters and HALIBUT of over 18 kg are also regularly landed on jigs. The primary saltwater sport fisheries are for salmon (coho and chinook, and to a lesser extent chum, pink and sockeye), halibut, LINGCOD and ROCKFISH, as well as FLATFISH such as FLOUNDER and SOLE. There are 150 saltwater fishing lodges along the coast. Several "ship" or floating lodges specialize in "following the fish," and other private lodges operate exclusively as company retreats for executives and guests (*see also* APRIL POINT LODGE, PAINTER'S LODGE, OAK BAY MARINE GROUP).

Angler expenditures in the saltwater fishery grew steadily through the 1970s and 1980s and peaked at $611 million in 1994; then the numbers declined primarily because of reduced salmon catch limits, new salmon catch-and-release-only regulations and closures of many areas for certain species. These measures were adopted for reasons of conservation and in 2000 were expected to continue (*see* FISHERIES POLICY). In 1999, approximately 5% of the total salmon catch in BC was caught by the sport sector, the balance by the commercial fishery (87%) and the FIRST NATIONS fisheries (8%). That year the federal government modified its allocation policy. After providing for conservation of stocks and access by First Nations (*see also* FISHING, ABORIGINAL), Fisheries and Oceans Canada gave sport fishers access to chinook and coho salmon all along the coast, and access to 5% of sockeye, pink and chum salmon in years of abundance.

Freshwater Sport Fishing

BC has 80 freshwater fish species, of which about 24 are of interest to the freshwater fishery, primarily TROUT (STEELHEAD, rainbow, cutthroat, brown) and CHAR (Dolly Varden, bull trout, brook trout, lake trout), STURGEON, KOKANEE, BURBOT and WHITEFISH. Steelhead are probably the most sought-after sport fish in BC, though

Don Johnson with a steelhead on the Nicola R near Merritt. Rick Blacklaws photo

various conservation measures have been put in place to protect stocks. Several RIVERS are world-famous for these hard-fighting fish, including the Stamp, Gold and COWICHAN rivers on VANCOUVER ISLAND and the VEDDER, THOMPSON, SKEENA and BULKLEY rivers on the mainland and their tributaries. BC has approximately 25,000 lakes and 4,600 streams from which fishers may choose; in the 1990s more than 300,000 anglers were fishing these waters every year. While many LAKES have wild fish stocks, about 1,100 lakes and streams are enhanced with approximately 10 million fish each year. This stocking program supports 50% of angling

David Dustan (l) and George Nichols with a day's catch of salmon caught in Alberni Inlet, 1994. Martin Nichols photo

effort and a substantial portion of the catch (*see also* FISH HATCHERIES). More than 200 lakes have fishing resorts, ranging from rustic to luxurious, and many have campsites. Some of the best fishing can be found at wilderness lakes that cannot be reached easily by car or can be reached only by float plane. There is no significant commercial fishery for freshwater game fish. *See also* FLY FISHING.

FITZ HUGH SOUND is a narrow channel that connects QUEEN CHARLOTTE SOUND 65 km north to Fisher Channel, and lies between the Central Coast and CALVERT and HUNTER islands. It is part of the protected INSIDE PASSAGE route that carries ferries and CRUISE SHIPS along the coast. Named in 1786 by James Hanna, a FUR TRADE captain, it was surveyed by George VANCOUVER on his 1792–93 trip. At that time it was used by members of the HEILTSUK First Nation, who had village sites in the area. A LIGHTHOUSE was established on Addenbroke Island in 1914. The tiny, historic community of NAMU is the only populated place in the sound, though HAKAI Provincial Recreation Area along the west side attracts kayakers and sport FISHING enthusiasts for its world-famous SALMON fishing and wilderness environment.

FJORDS are steep, magnificently scenic inlets that occur the length of the mainland BC coast and on the west side of the QUEEN CHARLOTTE ISLANDS and VANCOUVER ISLAND. Originally U-shaped valleys scoured by glaciers during the Pleistocene ice ages, a fjord characteristically has steep sides falling dramatically to and below the water; a RIVER, often with a spectacular WATERFALL, flows into the top end. Many fjords have shoaling along the mouth produced by a ridge or sill; this was caused when the glacier eroded well below sea level, creating a basin that was then invaded by sea water as the ice retreated. Depths are generally greater farther up the inlet than at the mouth. Most fjords contain at least one right angle, or dogleg, somewhere along their length. Some are extremely long, allowing deep-water vessels to penetrate far inland.
Reading: Stuart S. Holland, *Landforms of British Columbia*, 1976.

BC's LONGEST FJORDS

GARDNER CANAL	114 KM
KNIGHT INLET	113 KM
PORTLAND INLET	100 KM
DEAN CHANNEL	97 KM
Burke Channel	90 KM
JERVIS INLET	77 KM
DOUGLAS CHANNEL	72 KM
OBSERVATORY INLET	66 KM
BUTE INLET	66 KM
ALBERNI INLET	60 km

FLAG was adopted by provincial order-in-council 20 June 1960. It features the central shield from the provincial COAT OF ARMS, adopted in 1895. The Union Jack on top evokes the British connection; the setting half-sun symbolizes BC's location as Canada's westernmost province; and the 3 wavy bars suggest the Pacific Ocean. There seems to have been another flag that predated the official one. Featuring a BEAVER surrounded by a wreath of maple leaves in the middle of the Union Jack, it was designed in the 1860s by Joshua Spencer Thompson, a BARKERVILLE newspaper publisher and politician, and is reputed to have been used in the CARIBOO before it was supplanted by the official Union Jack. There was also, very briefly, an official flag of VANCOUVER ISLAND, adopted in 1865 just a year before the Colony of Vancouver Island merged with the mainland to form BC. The Island flag was a blue ensign featuring the colony's badge: a beaver sitting on an island below Neptune's trident, Mercury's wand and a pine cone.

The provincial flag. Roy Luckow photo

FLATFISH is a general fisheries term, inclusive of FLOUNDER, HALIBUT, SOLE and TURBOT. In descending order of abundance, commercial TRAWL flatfish catches include Dover sole, arrowtooth flounder (turbot) and rock sole. Pacific halibut are landed primarily by hook and line in the commercial fisheries. There are also recreational fisheries for flatfish. *See also* FISHING, COMMERCIAL; FISHING, SPORT.

FLEMING, Willie, football player (b 3 Feb 1939, Detroit). Among the best running backs to play Canadian FOOTBALL, he joined the BC LIONS in 1959 after growing up in Detroit and winning the US college Rose Bowl with the Univ of Iowa. By the time he retired in 1967 he had rewritten the Lions' record book and established himself as a CFL legend. He gained more than 1,000 yards in rushing and receiving for 7 straight seasons and in 1963 he recorded pro football's highest seasonal rushing average of the 20th century with 9.7 yards per carry. In 1960 he scored a career-high 18 touchdowns for 109 points. He helped the Lions to reach the league championship Grey Cup finals in 1963, the year he was a Canadian all-star, and to win the trophy in 1964. He is a member of the CFL Hall of Fame and BC SPORTS HALL OF FAME.   *SW*

Willie Fleming, BC Lions all-star.

FLETCHER CHALLENGE CANADA LTD (FCC) is a N American FOREST PRODUCTS company formed in 1988 by the New Zealand-based Fletcher Challenge Ltd (FCNZ). The new company was created by changing the name of BC FOREST PRODUCTS LTD and merging its management and operations with another long-established BC forest company, Crown Forest Industries Ltd. FCNZ had purchased Crown in 1983, when it was called CROWN ZELLERBACH CANADA LTD, and BC Forest Products in 1987. During the first 5 years of its existence, FCC invested close to $1 billion in plant modernization and expansion and disposed of several operations. In the period 1989–93 the company's interests in 3 large integrated operations—Western Forest Products and Finlay Forest Industries in BC and Donohue St-Felicien Inc in Quebec—were sold, as were several mills in BC, Alberta and the US. Part of the company's timber rights and forest lands in BC were sold, and the VICTORIA sawmill and the MACKENZIE stud mill were closed. Ownership of the Crown Forest assets, including the Elk Falls pulp mill and associated timber rights and forest lands, were transferred to FCC in 1993. In the same year FCC's FORESTRY, LOGGING and lumber operations on the BC coast and at WILLIAMS LAKE were transferred to a new subsidiary company, TimberWest Forest Ltd, 52% of which was owned by FCC. In 1996 FCC sold TimberWest to an investment syndicate in order to concentrate on paper making. In 1997 FCC's revenues were $1.35 billion.   *Ken Drushka*

FLOATHOUSES are a unique adaptation to seaside life implemented by the coastal pioneers of BC, particularly those involved in FISHING and LOGGING. Because the shoreline where they wished to locate was steep and heavily wooded, these innovators found it more practical to construct their dwellings and outbuildings on rafts

of floating logs, which could be easily moved to a new tie-up when the adjacent timber was logged or the local SALMON run was finished. Western red CEDAR, which had low market value but possessed superior buoyancy and resistance to SHIPWORMS, provided cheap and abundant float logs. As logging became mechanized and larger crews were required, the floathouse evolved into the float camp, with a variety of larger buildings including cookhouses and shops arranged around a floating steam donkey, which yarded timber from the hillsides using an "A-frame" consisting of 2 raised logs standing 50 m or more in the air. These floating "A-frame camps" (*see* LOGGING, A-FRAME) became a coastal trademark and sometimes developed the complexity of more traditional villages. SIMOOM SOUND near KINGCOME INLET had a store, community hall, post office and school complete with fenced playground, all perched on logs. Even the larger floating villages remained portable, and occasionally moved *en masse* from one sheltered cove to another. Simoom Sound moved and subdivided several times. When it was finally abandoned, the floating post office was towed to Echo Bay on GILFORD ISLAND, which had been denied its own postal service. Echo Bay still receives its mail under the name of Simoom Sound, technically the name of a geographical feature many kilometres distant. Another floating village built up in the 1940s at Claydon Bay near Drury Inlet and later moved to SULLIVAN BAY on Sutlej Channel, where some of the original buildings continue floating into the third millennium as a supply centre for pleasure boats and float planes. Some of the largest float camps, such as BC FOREST PRODUCTS' Camp 6 on COWICHAN LK, were located in the large LAKES on Vancouver Island. Other BC lakes, such as SHUSWAP LK and Powell Lk, are notable for having large populations of summer cottages on floats. Float camps used in commercial fishing often included small stores or "commissaries," along with cold storage facilities and net floats for mending nets, but tended to be small and transitory. An exception was DAWSON'S LANDING in RIVERS INLET, which developed into a permanent supply base and was still an official postal address at the turn of the millennium. Dwellings on floats were also favoured as a form of low-cost

Modern floathouse community, Sullivan Bay. Ian Douglas photo

The Reynolds family's floathouse at Claydon Bay on the Central Coast, 1939. MCR 14141

shelter for transients in larger coastal communities, where they sometimes accumulated in backwaters to form floating shacktowns. VANCOUVER had a sizeable floathouse community in FALSE CREEK from 1920 to 1950, as did many sloughs of the FRASER R, the most enduring being at Finn Slough near STEVESTON. By the 1970s the old style of floathouse was forced out of existence by sanitary regulations and cleanup campaigns, and was replaced by a new generation of fashionable architect-designed structures that hook up to municipal utilities and pay taxes.

Howard White

FLOOD, or Floods, 5 km west of HOPE on the FRASER R, was a flag station on the CNR named after W.L. Flood, an early FRASER VALLEY builder who operated the Hope SAWMILL here in the 1910s. A post office was open from 1913 to 1960.

AS

FLORES ISLAND, 155 km², in CLAYOQUOT SOUND 20 km north of TOFINO on the west coast of VANCOUVER ISLAND, was named by Spanish explorers in 1791 after Don Manuel Antonio Flores, a viceroy of Mexico. The NUU-CHAH-NULTH community of AHOUSAT is on the southwest coast, near a popular sulphur spring that is part of Gibson MARINE PARK (1.42 km²). Ahousat Wild Side Heritage Trail links the community to the sand beaches and RAIN FOREST along the southern shore. Flores Island Provincial PARK (71.13 km²) encompasses much of the island's western shore. Wild and remote, the island is linked to Tofino by float plane and water taxi.

FLOUNDER is a general name for a family (Pleuronectidae) of FLATFISH, the right-eyed flounder. It is also a common name used for some specific flatfishes. This family has 19 species that live in BC waters, including the arrowtooth flounder or TURBOT, the starry floun-

der, the Pacific HALIBUT and a variety of SOLE. There are both commercial and sport fisheries for the flounder. *See also* FISHING COMMERCIAL; FISHING, SPORT.

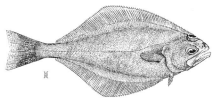

Starry flounder (top), arrowtooth flounder.
Rick Harbo photo; drawing courtesy Fisheries & Oceans Canada

FLY FISHING was transplanted to BC in the 1850s from Britain by colonial officials using tackle and techniques proven effective on TROUT and sea trout in Britain. It was generally agreed that Pacific SALMON would not take a fly in the ocean. Otherwise, flies of British origin found great success with native stocks of cutthroat and rainbow trout and STEELHEAD. With the completion of the CPR in 1886, the Interior LAKES became more accessible to fly fishers. In 1890 H.W. Seton Karr led some of the first fly rod excursions into the Interior and other anglers soon followed, most notably A. Brian Williams, who was provincial game warden from 1905 to 1918 and game commissioner from 1929 to 1934. Williams wrote 2 books—*Rod and Creel in British Columbia* (1919) and *Fishing in British Columbia* (1935)—and his observations of INSECT activity resulted in the production of the first locally inspired dry flies for Interior lakes. Observations on the coast also began to produce original flies, as well as local angling techniques. Notable anglers included Roderick HAIG-BROWN in CAMPBELL RIVER and Gen Noel MONEY, long-time manager of the QUALICUM BEACH Hotel. Both men began tying flies that imitated natural foods of the local cutthroat and steelhead species. Artist Tommy Brayshaw and Bill NATION also helped to popularize the sport and globally more anglers looked to BC as an angling destination. During WWII fly fishing developments slowed, but the 1950s saw the introduction of glass rods as replacements for the traditional split cane rods. Soon synthetic materials replaced the silk lines used since the previous century. Fly patterns became increasingly localized. Anglers attempted to take steelhead on the dry fly on coastal RIVERS and used experimental saltwater flies to dispel the notion that Pacific salmon would not take flies. Meanwhile still-water technique expanded to include a vast battery of dry and wet flies. As the popularity of fly fishing grew, more areas of the province became known for their exemplary stocks of wild fish. Since the 1960s the northern waters of the SKEENA R system and the DEAN R watershed have added to the already intense variety of Interior lakes and streams, particularly in the KAMLOOPS area. At the same time, organizations such as the BC Steelhead Society, the Totem Flyfishers and the Haig-Brown Kingfisher Creek Society have taken the lead on issues of habitat conservation and public education.

Chad Brealey

Fly fishing in the early morning at Watch Lake near Lone Butte, 1996. Peter A. Robson photo

FLYCATCHER is a small perching bird belonging to the diverse family Tyrannidae. The bird has a hooked bill with stiff bristles at the base. There are more than a dozen types of flycatchers, including their near relatives the wood-pewee, the phoebe and the kingbird. All types are summer visitors to BC, attracted to the province by the plentiful numbers of flying INSECTS on which they feed. Several belong to the genus *Empidonax*; small, dull-coloured birds with light eye-rings and pale bars of plumage on the wings. These include the alder flycatcher (*Empidonax alnorum*) and the yellow-bellied flycatcher (*E. flaviventris*), both concentrated in the northeast part of the province; the willow flycatcher (*E. traillii*); least flycatcher (*E. minimus*); Hammond's flycatcher (*E. hammondii*); dusky flycatcher (*E. oberholseri*); the grey flycatcher (*E. wrightii*), restricted to the S OKANAGAN VALLEY; the Pacific-slope flycatcher (*E. difficilis*); and the cordilleran flycatcher (*E. occi-*

Western kingbird, a species of flycatcher.
R. Wayne Campbell photo

dentalis). The largest member of the family in BC is the olive-sided flycatcher (*Contopus borealis*). Two other species are very rare visitors to southern BC: the ash-throated flycatcher (*Myiarchus cinerascens*) and the scissor-tailed flycatcher (*Tyrannus forficatus*), named for its long tail feathers. The western wood-pewee (*Contopus sordidulus*) is a sparrow-sized flycatcher lacking the eye-ring common to the *Empidonax* birds. Two types of phoebe occur in BC. The eastern phoebe (*Sayornis phoebe*) lives across the ROCKY MTS in the northeast corner of the province, while Say's phoebe (*S. saya*), resembling a small ROBIN, is concentrated in open country in the Interior. Kingbirds are small grey birds with white/yellow chests, occurring in the southern Interior east of the COAST MTS. The most widespread is the western kingbird (*T. verticalis*). The eastern kingbird (*T. tyrannus*) is distinguished by a band of white across the tip of the tail. The tropical kingbird (*T. melancholicus*) is a very rare visitor to the southern GEORGIA STRAIT.

FLYING BOAT STATIONS were situated along the West Coast for use by the Royal Canadian Air Force to conduct aerial patrols and to protect against Japanese invasion. The original station was at JERICHO BEACH (1920) but when WWII began, another 5 stations were established for the duration of the war: UCLUELET (1940–44); ALLIFORD BAY in Skidegate Inlet on the QUEEN CHARLOTTE ISLANDS (1940–45); Seal Cove near PRINCE RUPERT (1941–44); Coal Harbour in QUATSINO SOUND on VANCOUVER ISLAND (1941–45); and BELLA BELLA (1941–45).

FLYING SEVEN were a group of women aviators who met at the AIRPORT in VANCOUVER in 1936. They got together regularly to organize activities that would promote flying among women across Canada, and they led the drive to establish the first aviation training centre for women in Canada, which opened in Vancouver in 1941. Members were Margaret Fane, an Edmonton pilot and the world's first woman radio operator; Betsy Flaherty, a department store buyer who took up flying in 1931; Quebec-born Alma Gaudreau, who came to BC in 1927, earned a commercial licence and ferried aircraft during WWII; Rolie Moore, the first BC woman to qualify as a flying instructor; Elianne Roberge, who worked for the British Air Commission during WWII; Tosca Trasolini, who later moved to California, maintained her business career and continued flying; and Jean Pike, the youngest member of the group.

The Flying Seven, a pioneer group of women aviators (l to r): Jean Pike, Tosca Trasolini, Betsy Flaherty, Alma Gilbert, Elianne Roberge, Margaret Fane, Rolie Moore.
Courtesy Jack Schofield

FLYNN, Errol, film actor (b 1909, Tasmania; d 14 Oct 1959, Vancouver). He was famous for his roles as a swashbuckling romantic lead in a series of Hollywood adventure films in the 1930s. He was 50 years old and much dissipated by alcohol when he arrived in VANCOUVER in Oct 1959 to negotiate the sale of his yacht to a W VANCOUVER stockbroker. He was undergoing treatment for back problems at a doctor's West End apartment when he dropped dead of a heart attack, his third. His 17-year-old female companion was unable to revive him. The story became associated with the local reporter Jack WASSERMAN, who had an exclusive in the pages of the VANCOUVER SUN.

FOCH was an isolated farming (*see* AGRICULTURE) and LOGGING settlement 30 km north of

POWELL RIVER near the Theodosia R and Olsen Lk. The Olson family first homesteaded there in 1913; the lake is probably named for them despite the spelling difference. The post office, originally Olsen Lk, changed to Foch at the end of WWI in honour of the Allied leader Marshall Ferdinand Foch. The community was abandoned by the mid-1950s.   AS

FOLEY, WELCH & STEWART was the largest railway construction company in N America before WWI. It was created in 1908 as a reorganization of a prior company, Foley Bros & Larson. Principal partners in the new concern were John W. STEWART and his brothers-in-law Tim Foley and Patrick Welch. The company carried out most of the major railway projects in BC, including construction of the famous CONNAUGHT TUNNEL for the CPR, the western section of the GRAND TRUNK PACIFIC RWY and the Fraser Canyon section of the CANADIAN NORTHERN RWY. Stewart was also the first president of the Pacific Great Eastern Rwy in 1912; his company began construction of the line between SQUAMISH and PRINCE GEORGE and operated the railway until it was taken over by the province in 1918 (*see* BC RAIL). The onset of WWI marked the end of the company's glory years; following the war Stewart formed his own contracting firm.
Reading: Geoffrey W. Taylor, *The Railway Contractors*, 1988.

FOLK, Rick, curler (b 5 Mar 1950, Saskatoon). Already a world champion in CURLING, he moved to BC in the late 1980s and won the BC championship in 1989 and 1993. He led his KELOWNA team of Pat Ryan, Bert Gretzinger, Gerry Richard and alternate Ron Steinhauer to another BC championship in 1994 and on to the Labatt Brier in Red Deer, where they became only the third BC rink to win the Canadian men's championship. In Apr 1994 they travelled to Oberstdorf, Germany, where after losing their

Rick Folk, curler, at the 1994 Labatt Brier.

first match they won 10 straight games to bring home Canada's 22nd world title in 36 years. The Folk rink repeated as BC champion in 1995 and was inducted into the BC SPORTS HALL OF FAME later that year. *SW*

FONCIE; *see* PULICE, ALFRED.

FONTE, Bartholomew de, a mysterious "Admiral of New Spain and Prince of Chile" credited in a 1767 London publication with a voyage to the N Pacific coast in 1640. There he reportedly discovered a navigable sea passage across N America at about the latitude of DIXON ENTRANCE (54°). Influential French cartographers promoted the existence of the passage and it was widely accepted until disproved officially by the voyages of Jacinto CAAMANO in 1792 and George VANCOUVER in 1793. Reports of Fonte and his expedition were a hoax to promote interest in a trade route from Europe to China.

FONYO, Stephen Charles, runner (b 29 June 1965, Montreal). He lost most of a leg to cancer at age 12. He was a teenager living in the OKANAGAN VALLEY when Terry FOX ran his Marathon of Hope; inspired by Fox, he organized his own cross-Canada marathon run to raise funds for cancer research. The Journey For Lives began on 31 Mar 1984 at St John's, NF, and ended 14 months later on 31 May 1985 at VICTORIA. The run covered 7,924 km and raised $13 million. In 1986–87 he ran the length of Britain to raise money for cancer research there. After retiring from running he was plagued by legal and personal problems.

FOOD BANKS are food distribution agencies that provide groceries free of charge to people in need, in both households and "soup kitchens." According to HungerCount 98, a survey by the Canadian Association of Food Banks, in 1998

BC had 111 food banks, located in communities of all sizes. These facilities dispense food to about 65,500 British Columbians, about 26,000 of whom are children. In BC, as in other provinces, the average household gets 1 food hamper per month, containing enough groceries to feed them for 3 to 5 days. Social assistance is the main source of income for most recipients, though food banks report that working poor people comprise a growing proportion of those served. Some food banks accept government funding but many choose not to; organizations of both types consider their services to be emergency assistance, not a cure for poverty or a substitute for public policy.

FOON, Dennis, writer (b 18 Nov 1951, Detroit, MI). After attending the Univ of Michigan he came to VANCOUVER in 1973 to study creative writing at UBC. As co-founder and artistic director of GREEN THUMB THEATRE from 1975 to 1988, he helped push the company to the forefront of innovative, socially engaged THEATRE for young people, revolutionizing youth drama in the country. As well as directing productions, he wrote several plays, notably *Skin* (1988), which won a gold medal at the New York International TV Festival, and *Invisible Kids*, winner of a 1986 British Theatre Award. *Feeling Yes, Feeling No*, about sexual abuse, was made into a series of films by the National Film Board. Since leaving Green Thumb he has worked primarily in film and television. *Little Criminals*, a drama about youth street crime, aired on CBC television in 1996, followed by *White Lies*, a look at the neo-Nazi movement, in 1998.

FOOTBALL in Canada began to emerge as a modified form of RUGBY in the 1880s. Rugby games had taken place in BC for approximately 10 years before the influence of American rugby—with no scrum, a single line of forwards and the snap of the ball to the backs—could be seen in the Canadian game following a match between Toronto Varsity and Harvard in 1879. The rules of English rugby continued to be altered until the game known as "Canadian rugby" or "rugby football" fully diverged from the original sport in the late 19th century.

In 1911 the Western Canada Rugby Football Union was formed. The only two clubs in BC, both in VANCOUVER, were not allowed into the league because other western teams were not willing to make the long and expensive trips out to the coast. Many more squads formed in BC, including UBC's first team in 1924, and by 1926 arrangements had been made for the province to compete for the Western Canadian Championship. By the time BC high schools began playing the sport in 1933, the forward pass had been introduced to the game. Vancouver's Big Four league, made up of UBC, the Meralomas, the Vancouver Athletic Club and the North Shore Lions, played during the 1930s but disappeared at the outbreak of WWII. The Vancouver Grizzlies, BC's first professional team, only lasted one season (1941) but pro football came to Vancouver permanently in 1954 when

the BC LIONS joined the Western Interprovincial Football Union (which became part of the new Canadian Football League in 1958). Empire Stadium hosted Vancouver's first Grey Cup final, between Edmonton and Montreal, in 1955. The Lions made it to their first championship final in 1963 and won their first Grey Cup in 1964. By the 1960s, UBC had started playing by Canadian rules again (they had joined an American conference during the 1940s) and competed in the first Shrum Bowl against SFU in 1967. The UBC Thunderbirds won their first Vanier Cup as national collegiate champions under coach Frank Smith in 1982, the same year former Lions' CFL rookie-of-the-year and future Lions' assistant coach Dave Easley led the Renfrew Trojans to BC's second Canadian Junior Football National Championship (the first was won by the Vancouver Blue Bombers in 1947). Smith took the T-Birds to their second cup in 1986 and his son Casey coached the team to its third CIAU championship in 1997. The Lions made it to the Grey Cup again 3 times during the 1980s, winning the championship in 1985, and they won again in 1994. During this period the team featured BC-raised stars such as Easley, team captain Al WILSON and all-time professional leading scorer Lui PASSAGLIA. Other CFL stars from BC include early pioneer Paul ROWE, former pro scoring champion Dave CUTLER, offensive lineman Gerry Hornett, defensive lineman Doug Peterson and kickers Don Sweet, Tom Dixon, Paul Osbaldiston and Tony Martino. SFU, playing American football in the National Association of Intercollegiate Athletics for small US colleges, has provided over 150 players to the CFL—more than any other university in Canada. The most successful BC football family act has been the GERELAs from POWELL RIVER: Ted kicked for the Lions, Roy went south to boot for the Pittsburgh Steelers and Metro had a tryout with the Philadelphia Eagles. Other BC players to follow Roy to the NFL include Eddie MURRAY, Harald Hasselbach, Mitch BERGER, Moe ELEWONIBI, Doug Brown and Jerome Pathon. *SW*

FORBES, Roy, singer, songwriter (b 13 Feb 1953, Dawson Creek). He is one of BC's favourite folk entertainers. His first group was the Beatles-influenced Crystal Ship, formed in 1968 in DAWSON CREEK. In early 1971 he opened for the group Spring during its northern BC tour and was encouraged to move to VANCOUVER, where he recorded 4 albums over the next decade as "Bim," a childhood nickname. *Kid Full of Dreams* (1975) earned him a Juno Award nomination for best new male artist. In the early 1980s he discarded his nickname and began an independent recording career that revealed his talent for songwriting and accentuated his distinctive voice. His songs have been recorded by many leading artists and he has produced records for singers such as Connie Kaldor, Susan Crowe and Mark Perry. He also hosted a CBC Radio show, *Snap, Crackle, Pop*. In 1989 he formed the acoustic trio UHF with Shari ULRICH and Bill Henderson. As a solo artist Forbes continued to be a popular attraction on the N American folk music festival circuit. His 1998 album *Crazy Old Moon* received a Juno Award nomination for best roots traditional recording.   *Mike Harling*

Roy Forbes, singer/songwriter, surrounded by record memorabilia, 2000.
Wayne Leidenfrost/Vancouver Province

FORBES LANDING on Lower Campbell Lk, west of CAMPBELL RIVER on VANCOUVER ISLAND, was the site of a popular wilderness vacation resort. Established by Jim and Elisabeth Forbes in 1912, Forbes Landing Lodge offered hunting, sport FISHING and horseback expeditions into nearby STRATHCONA PROVINCIAL PARK, as well as an idyllic hideaway for many BC honeymooners. It was destroyed by the GREAT SAYWARD FIRE during the summer of 1938.

FORBIDDEN PLATEAU is a year-round recreation area on the lower slopes of Mt Becher in STRATHCONA PROVINCIAL PARK on central VANCOUVER ISLAND. According to aboriginal legend, the COMOX people sent their women and children there to be safe during an attack by their enemies, the COWICHAN people. But the fugitives vanished, supposedly devoured by evil spirits, and the region became taboo. This did not stop skiers, who began using the slopes in the 1920s, making this the first SKIING area on the Island. In the summer it is well used by hikers and mountaineers (*see* MOUNTAINEERING).

FORDING INC was created in Dec 1969 to develop COAL properties in the ELK R valley in southeast BC. A subsidiary of CPR, the company began shipping coal in 1972. Its initial market was the Japanese steel industry; later it began selling to other countries as well. The largest coal exporter in Canada, Fording operates 3 open-pit mines in BC—Coal Mountain, Fording River and Fording Greenhills. In 1998 it exported 11.16 million tonnes of coal, earning revenues of $769 million.

FOREST ALLIANCE OF BC was organized in 1991 by a group of BC forest companies to pro-

vide a forum for discussion of, and public education on, FORESTRY issues. It has 10,000 members from a wide range of occupations and interests and is supported by most forest companies and about 300 other organizations, including municipal governments, boards of trade and chambers of commerce. Its first president was Jack MUNRO, former head of the INDUSTRIAL, WOOD AND ALLIED WORKERS OF CANADA. During the mid-1990s the Alliance engaged in a vigorous defence of the BC FOREST INDUSTRY, then the target of an international boycott campaign by GREENPEACE. *See also* FOREST POLICY.

FOREST FIRES, also known as wildland fires, burn an average of 300 km² of forest in BC annually. Each year the province spends about $40 million on forest fire preparedness and an equal amount on fire fighting. On average 2,800 fires occur in BC annually, a little over one-third of the national total. The worst year on record was 1958, when 8,358.76 km² of timber went up in smoke. The greatest number of fires (4,068) occurred in 1994, but they burned over a smaller area.

The forest fire protection system has two components:

Detection. A fire weather network uses data from meteorological stations around the province to compute fire hazards at different locations on an hourly basis. Forecasts are used to allocate fire-fighting crews and equipment, regulate FOREST INDUSTRY operations and control access to provincial FORESTS. A lightning strike location system uses electronic locaters in various parts of the province to automatically map every lightning strike, one of the most common causes of fires, and to provide foresters with a continuous report. In times and areas of high fire hazard, fire lookout towers are staffed and regular air and ground patrols are carried out.

Suppression. Historically, LOGGING and SAWMILL crews constituted the mainstay of BC's wildland fire-fighting force, as did untrained citizens hired as needed during busy fire seasons. In times of desperate need forest officers conscripted citizens to fight fires, often selecting patrons from the nearest bar. Since the mid-1980s the trend has been toward more highly trained and increasingly mobile crews. The min-

istry of forests seasonally employs 800 to 900 fire fighters stationed at bases throughout the province. Forest industry crews continue to fight fires when needed and a network of volunteer fire wardens provide valuable assistance through their knowledge of local terrain and conditions. When a fire is reported it is fought by one or more 3-person "initial attack" crews, which may include "Rapattack" teams who rappel into difficult terrain from helicopters. In 1999 and 2000 the province experimented with a "Parattack" unit, composed of fire fighters trained to parachute into particularly remote locations in northern BC. Fires that grow beyond the initial attack stage are fought by 20-person unit crews overseen by teams of experienced fire specialists.

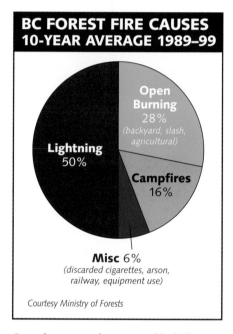

BC FOREST FIRE CAUSES
10-YEAR AVERAGE 1989–99

Lightning 50%
Open Burning 28% (backyard, slash, agricultural)
Campfires 16%
Misc 6% (discarded cigarettes, arson, railway, equipment use)

Courtesy Ministry of Forests

Ground crews may be supported by helicopters and planes dropping water or fire-retarding chemicals. The largest company providing aerial fire suppression in BC is Conair Group Inc of ABBOTSFORD (*see also* AVIATION). Undoubtedly the highest-profile fire-bombing aircraft are 2 Martin Mars bombers operated by Fire Industries Flying Tankers Ltd, based at SPROAT LK near PORT ALBERNI (*see also* Dan MCIVOR).

Fire destroying Port Neville, 25 June 1925.

Martin Mars bomber fighting a fire on the Mid-Coast, 1996. Courtesy Weyerhaeuser

Although the damage to commercial timber, human lives and property justifies the cost and effort of fighting forest fires, fire is a natural part of the forest ecology. Some BC forest ecosystems are dependent on regular fires. The open Interior PINE forests that have grass ground cover require periodic fires to burn off dried grass and brush to prevent a buildup of inflammable materials that would also burn the trees. Other forests, such as those of coastal DOUGLAS FIR, require mineral soil seedbeds and exposure to sunlight to regenerate, or they will be replaced over time by species such as western HEMLOCK or western red CEDAR that can grow in the shade of established forests. Without periodic fires these types of forests would disappear. Like the Douglas fir, species such as pine and western LARCH require occasional fires to survive and have thick bark that enables them to survive the heat of groundfires. Lodgepole pine cones need the heat of a fire to open and release their seeds. The management of forest fires involves much more than attempting to extinguish all the fires that begin; increasingly foresters are concerning themselves with the long-term ecological effects of fire. *See also* ECOFORESTRY; FORESTRY; GREAT SAYWARD FIRE.

Some Forest Fire Facts:

Largest forest fire in BC history: the 1958 Kech fire, which burned 2,860 km² in the remote wilderness of north-central BC. It eventually burned out naturally.

Largest fire ever fought in BC: the 1982 Eg fire (1,827.22 km²), which was left largely unfought for weeks and finally blew into an inferno that overran the ALASKA HWY hamlet of FIRESIDE, destroying a hotel, a service station and 6 homes. At its peak the fire's front was estimated to be 25 km long and 200 m high. Most fire fighting occurred around the evacuated community of Coal River.

Largest fire to start in BC: the 1950 Wisp fire, which began north of FORT ST JOHN and burned 900 km² in BC before crossing into Alberta and the Northwest Territories. Its final size was 14,000 km², nearly half the size of VANCOUVER ISLAND.

Most expensive suppression effort: the 1998 SILVER CREEK (SALMON ARM) fire, which cost approximately $10 million to fight. Sixteen homes were destroyed, making this fire the second most destructive to human habitation in BC history. (The most destructive was the 1994 Garnett fire in PENTICTON, which burned 18 homes.) The Silver Creek blaze also caused BC's largest evacuation: 7,500 people fled their homes in anticipation of a firestorm that could have burned over the town of Salmon Arm.

FOREST GROVE, pop 837, is a spirited ranching (*see* CATTLE INDUSTRY) and recreational village 20 km northeast of 100 MILE HOUSE on the road to CANIM LK in the CARIBOO lake district. It has a number of stores and community facilities and is a business centre for the surrounding area. *AS*

FOREST INDUSTRY is usually considered to include those economic activities related to the growing, harvesting and utilization of timber.

They include the LOGGING, SAWMILLING, PULP AND PAPER, panelboard, SILVICULTURE and secondary manufacturing sectors. It is BC's largest industrial sector, directly and indirectly employing about 275,000 people during the 1990s. The industry was also the province's first. It began in 1788 with the production and export of masts by John MEARES, and in 1999 the BC industry accounted for about one-half of the entire Canadian forest industry, providing 8% of the world's exports of FOREST PRODUCTS. Most forest products produced in BC are exported, accounting for about 50% of all provincial exports. The major customers, in order of importance, are the US, the rest of Canada, Japan and Europe. The forest industry experienced maximum production in 1987–88 when it cut a record 89.1 million m³ of timber. During the last quarter of the 20th century it came under heavy criticism for its impact on the environment, and by the end of the century the timber harvest had been reduced to about 65 million m³ (*see also* ENVIRONMENTAL MOVEMENT). Non-timber commercial use of the forests includes livestock grazing, trapping, collection of botanical products, outdoor recreation and TOURISM.
Reading: M. Patricia Marchak, *Green Gold: The Forest Industry in BC*, 1983; M. Patricia Marchak, *Logging the Globe*, 1995.

FOREST POLICY, until 1910, was concerned only with the means by which Crown-owned timber and forest land was made available for private use. Under colonial governments, outright grants of forest land were made to provide timber for industrial purposes. In 1865 a land ordinance introduced the principle of granting rights for use of timber only, with ownership of the land and other resources remaining with the Crown. When BC entered CONFEDERATION in 1871 the province assumed jurisdiction over all

Logging truck being unloaded at Stillwater, near Powell River, 1994. The stiff-leg crane to which the grapple is attached is the largest in the world. Keith Thirkell photo

natural resources, including forests. In return for railway construction financed by the federal government, extensive areas of land were given to the Dominion, which in turn granted the right to harvest timber from them in exchange for royalty payments. In 1896 timber lands were defined and the sale of forest land prohibited. Governments used various forms of leases and licences to make timber available to encourage industrial development. In 1905, anxious to increase revenues, the government of Richard MCBRIDE introduced a new form of licence granting a 21-year right to harvest timber from a square mile of land. Licences were transferable and required fluctuating annual payments. Within 3 years, 15,000 of these licences were issued on 36,000 km² of the most valuable timberland in the province.

The staking frenzy provoked by the McBride leases, combined with the rising incidence of FOREST FIRES caused by railway and LOGGING operations, and a growing N American conservationist movement, led to the formation of a Royal Commission on forestry conducted by F.J. Fulton, which reported in 1910. The commission's recommendations led to the Forest Act of 1912, which created a FOREST SERVICE to oversee protection of the province's forests and collection of revenues from the sale of timber. A primary objective of the new policies was to develop and maintain a FOREST PRODUCTS industry. Further alienation of Crown forests was prohibited, with small, short-term Timber Sales introduced to meet minor needs. This basic policy framework prevailed until the end of WWII. In 1942 Chief Forester C.D. Orchard sent a confidential memo to the government proposing major changes in forest policy. His suggestions led to the establishment of a second Royal Commission on forestry under Chief Justice Gordon Sloan, who reported in 1945. The major change stemming from this report was the decision to regulate the annual timber harvest in the province to provide a steady, perpetual flow of timber, with the objective of stabilizing the economic base of timber-dependent communities. This policy was called "sustained yield."

At the same time as it brought in these changes, the government introduced a new form of licence on designated forest land granting the right to harvest timber and the responsibility to manage forests for future crops. These Forest Management Licences provoked a great deal of controversy and were bitterly opposed by much of the established FOREST INDUSTRY, which feared they would lead to monopoly control over timber rights and fail to encourage good forest management. Another Royal Commission under Chief Justice Sloan reported in 1956, endorsing Forest Management Licences. Shortly thereafter, Minister of Forests Robert Sommers (see SOMMERS AFFAIR) was jailed for accepting bribes in the issuance of these licences; few of them were issued after this.

The policies established following the 2 Sloan commissions prevailed until 1978, by which time the industry had become concentrated in the hands of a few corporations that had

obtained Forest Management Licences, now known as Tree Farm Licences (TFLs). During the same period the use of Timber Sales had become widespread and extensive, and when timber shortages began to occur, administrative measures restricted the use of Timber Sales to established operators in each supply area. By the mid-1970s, the large TFL companies had acquired most of these short-term cutting rights as well. A fourth Royal Commission under Peter PEARSE reported in 1976 and recommended extensive policy changes. Pearse's major proposals concerned measures to halt the concentration of control over timber rights, warnings about impending timber shortages and the recognition of non-timber forest rights and values. In 1978 the government passed a new Forest Act, including only minor changes in tenure rights. The effect was to entrench the power of major holders of cutting rights; most volume-based leases and licences were consolidated into Forest Licences granting forest companies a specified volume of timber for a 15-year period. The 1978 act also introduced numerous changes to recog-

Protestors attempting to stop logging in the Carmanah Valley. Forest policy is often controversial in BC. WCWC

nize non-timber forest values, but no attempt was made to restrict timber harvests, which grew steadily over the next decade or more.

In 1989 a government attempt to convert volume-based Timber Licences into area-based Tree Farm Licences provoked widespread public opposition, leading to the formation of the Forest Resources Commission (FRC) to examine broad issues of forest policy. The FRC issued a report in 1991 recommending radical changes in forest tenure, but the proposals received little support. That same year an NDP government was elected; during its term the government introduced numerous measures to restrict the annual timber harvest, to resolve land use disputes and to regulate FORESTRY practices. *See also* COMMISSION ON RESOURCES AND THE ENVIRONMENT.

Ken Drushka

Reading: Ken Drushka, *In the Bight,* 1999; M. Patricia Marchak, *Falldown: Forest Policy in BC,* 1999.

FOREST PRODUCTS sector of the BC economy is focussed on the primary manufacturing of lumber, PULP AND PAPER, and plywood and other panel boards, most of which are exported. Since early in the 20th century, the export of logs cut

A stack of lumber, one of many BC forest products, ready for export to markets around the world. Roy Luckow photo

on Crown land has been restricted to encourage the province's manufacturing industries, and in 1997 more than 98% of the 68.6 million m³ of logs harvested were processed in BC. The FOREST INDUSTRY sector had total sales of over $13 billion in 1998, making it the single most important component of the economy. In the late 1990s, exports of forest products accounted for about 50% of the province's exports.

The first SAWMILL began operating near VICTORIA in 1848 to supply local needs, and by 1900 several large export mills had been established in VANCOUVER and on VANCOUVER ISLAND. During construction of the CPR, a large sawmill industry developed in southeastern BC, providing much of the lumber used during the first decades of the 20th century to develop the prairie provinces. Today most coastal lumber production occurs in the Greater Vancouver area, with the majority of Interior milling taking place at various centres. In 1997 BC sawmills produced 13.9 billion board feet of softwood lumber, about half of Canada's output. Three-quarters of this was milled in the Interior of the province at some of

Martin Blackwell, Sechelt guitar maker, with 2 of his guitars made from BC wood.
Ian Lindsay/Vancouver Sun

PRODUCTION & VALUE OF BC FOREST PRODUCTS 1998

Production:

Lumber	30,240,000 m³
Plywood	1,390,000 m³
Pulp shipments	4,450,000 tonnes
Newsprint, paper & paperboard	2,750,000 tonnes

Value ($ million) and percentage of total forest products:

Lumber	6,437	47.8%
Pulp	2,768	20.6%
Paper & paperboard	1,204	8.9%
Value-added wood products	918	6.8%
Newsprint	786	5.8%
Cedar shakes & shingles	248	1.8%
Plywood	202	1.5%
Other	898	6.7%
Total	**13,461**	**99.9%** *

* For mathematical reasons, percentages total 99.9% rather than 100%

the most modern and efficient sawmills in the world, utilizing relatively small logs of uniform size. The older coastal mills, built to cut big logs (which are now in short supply), accounted for 25% of provincial lumber production.

Plywood production began at the Canadian Western Lumber Co plant in NEW WESTMINSTER in 1913. Several other coastal mills were built to utilize high-grade, old-growth DOUGLAS FIR; these operated until supplies of suitable timber began to run out in the 1980s. The first Interior plywood plant opened at NELSON in 1927. Several Interior mills built in the 1970s and 1980s utilize SPRUCE to make sheathing-grade plywood. In 1997 plywood plants produced the equivalent of 207 million m² of ³/₈" plywood, resulting in $760 million in sales.

BC's first pulp mills began operating in 1909 at SWANSON BAY and PORT MELLON. (A paper mill using rags had opened at PORT ALBERNI in 1894 but it failed.) Today most coastal pulp and paper production occurs on Vancouver Island, in HOWE SOUND and at PRINCE RUPERT. Interior pulp and paper mills are scattered, with the largest concentration at PRINCE GEORGE. Market pulp production in the province in 1997 was 4.1 million tonnes; 1.5 million tonnes of newsprint and about 1 million tonnes of fine papers, cardboard and other paper products were manufactured. Pulp and paper operations employed 10,700 people in 26 operating mills. *Ken Drushka*

FOREST RENEWAL BC is a provincial CROWN CORPORATION created in Apr 1994 to retrain and employ displaced forest workers in forest rehabilitation, enhancement and value-added manufacturing jobs. It is funded by a special stumpage levy on Crown timber. In its first 5 years the corporation invested about $2 billion in retraining forest workers, in secondary manufacturing and in forest enhancement. *See also* FOREST INDUSTRY.

FOREST SERVICE, BC, was established as a branch of the Department of Lands in 1912 under its first chief forester, H.R. MACMILLAN. The primary responsibilities of the service included protecting the province's forests from fire, promoting the commercial use of forests and collecting revenues for the government. The branch also administered rangelands. In the late 1930s the Forest Service took on SILVICULTURAL responsibilities, opening nurseries and planting trees in areas damaged by FOREST FIRES on VANCOUVER ISLAND.

From its inception, one of the Forest Service's most important functions has been to take inventory of the provincial forests. For administrative purposes the province was divided into several districts, each of which was further divided into ranger districts under the authority of individual forest rangers. A chief forester oversaw the entire organization. This structure was retained until 1978, when the Forest Service underwent an extensive reorganization.

By the year 2000 the province was divided into 6 forest regions; these were divided into forest districts under district managers. The chief forester, responsible for the forestry division, shares administrative duties with a deputy minister, regional managers and several assistant deputy ministers.

In 1978 a Ministry of Forests Act was passed, assigning the Forest Service the additional task of managing fisheries, wildlife, water and recreation resources. In 1993 it assumed responsibility for regulating forest practices on Crown and private forest lands. *See also* FOREST INDUSTRY; FOREST POLICY; FORESTRY. *Ken Drushka*

FORESTDALE, 75 km southeast of SMITHERS, was homesteaded in the early 1900s and originally known as South Bulkley. GRAND TRUNK PACIFIC RWY workers settled here after 1914; by the 1920s a school, store and church had opened. AGRICULTURE and LOGGING were the

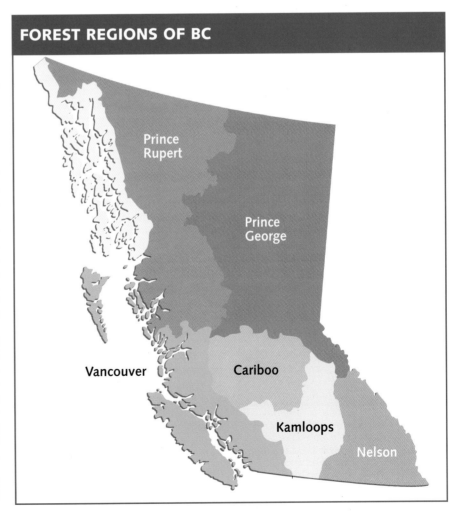

FOREST REGIONS OF BC

main occupations. The post office closed in 1965 and by 1999 the settlement had mostly dispersed. AS

FORESTRY is a broad field of activity comprising the art, science and practice of managing forested landscapes for both consumptive and non-consumptive uses. Its major divisions include inventory (counting and measuring FOREST attributes), engineering (planning and executing harvest), protection (preventing and treating damage from diseases, pests and fire) and SILVICULTURE (establishing and managing new forests). These activities are usually conducted under the direction of professional foresters who, since 1947, have been registered by the Association of BC Professional Foresters. In the past, forestry focussed on timber harvesting and processing, but now it is concerned with a broader range of forest values, including fish, wildlife, water, recreation and forest diversity.

Ken Drushka

Reading: Hammond, Herb, *Seeing the Forest Among the Trees*, 1991; Working Forest Project, *The Working Forest of BC*, 1995.

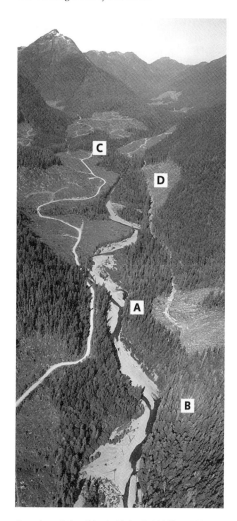

Experimental cutblock, Nahmint Valley, 1994, showing buffer zone left to protect salmon habitat (A), intact old-growth forest area (B), wildlife corridor (C), irregular cutblock (D). Forestry in the 1990s involves much more than timber extraction. Courtesy Working Forest Project

Temperate rain forest near Squamish. About a quarter of the world's remaining temperate rain forest is located in BC. Keith Thirkell photo

FORESTS in BC grow in a great range of types and habitats, and the temperate RAIN FORESTS along the coast are among the most biologically rich and diverse forests in N America. Much of BC is covered with a series of MOUNTAIN ranges running north and south, which become progressively higher moving eastward from the Pacific. This terrain shapes the 2 major climatic influences—warm, moist air sweeping east from the ocean and dropping precipitation as it rises over the mountain ranges, and cold Arctic air flowing southward down the valleys between the mountain ranges—creating a wide variety of regional conditions. BC forests have evolved in the 10,000 years since the last GLACIERS began their retreat. As the ice melted, flora and fauna repopulated the scoured land from unglaciated refugium to the south, on the QUEEN CHARLOTTE ISLANDS, and the BROOKS PENINSULA on the northwest coast of VANCOUVER ISLAND. Today about 450,000 km², almost one-half of the province's land area, is forested. More than two-thirds of Canada's bird and land mammal species are found here (*see* BIODIVERSITY). For many species, such as the grizzly BEAR, BC forests have become the last refuge in N America. The forests also maintain a large network of WETLANDS, LAKES, RIVERS and streams that contain large populations of fish. Prior to the development of HYDROELECTRIC dams on some rivers and excessive exploitation in other areas, all the major river systems west of the ROCKY MTS flowing into the Pacific supported huge populations of SALMON.

For the sake of simplicity, scientists have identified 12 forest types in BC (*see* BIOGEOCLIMATIC ZONES). The major division is between coastal and Interior forest zones. Coastal forests contain several tree species that grow to an enormous size (*see* TREES, GIANT). On the South Coast surrounding GEORGIA STRAIT is the coastal DOUGLAS FIR zone, where trees of that species have been known to grow to a height of 120 m and to an age of more than 1,000 years. Other species in this zone include western HEMLOCK, western red CEDAR, yellow cedar, Sitka SPRUCE, red ALDER, bigleaf MAPLE, Garry OAK and Pacific DOGWOOD. At higher elevations in the south and along the remainder of the coast is the coastal western hemlock zone, the most productive forest zone in BC. Cooler and wetter than the fir zone, it also contains Douglas fir in drier sites, amabilis FIR,

Boreal forest, which stretches across northern N America. Rick Blacklaws photo

western red and yellow cedar. At higher elevations along the entire coast lies the mountain hemlock zone, also containing significant amounts of amabilis fir and yellow cedar. The hot, dry South-Central Interior has a ponderosa PINE zone at low elevations, consisting of a relatively open forest interspersed with areas of bunchgrass and scrub sage. The mid-elevation slopes of this area and other areas to the north, as well as valley bottoms in the E and Central KOOTENAY, make up an Interior Douglas fir zone. It also contains lodgepole and ponderosa pine, aspen, BIRCH, western red cedar, Engelmann and white spruce, western LARCH and grand fir. Low and middle elevation slopes in southeastern BC, and a smaller area in the valleys of the SKEENA and NASS rivers in the northwest, host the Interior cedar–hemlock zone. This is the second most productive forest zone in the province. Because it is the wettest Interior zone, western red cedar and hemlock dominate, with several species of spruce, western larch, grand and Douglas fir, aspen, birch and black COTTONWOOD also present. Central BC, in a large area surrounding PRINCE GEORGE, is dominated by the sub-boreal spruce zone. It is populated mostly by Engelmann and white spruce and subalpine fir; lodgepole pine, Douglas fir and black cottonwood are also present. The far northern and northeastern portions of the province are part of the boreal forest that stretches from Alaska to Newfoundland in North America. This is known as the boreal white and black spruce zone, and its major species also include lodgepole pine and aspen. The mid-elevation slopes of northwestern and north-central BC are in the spruce–willow–birch zone, a mostly scrub forest that contains scattered stands of white spruce, subalpine fir and lodgepole pine. Most of the higher elevations in the Interior occupy the Engelmann spruce–subalpine fir zone, where these species grow in scattered stands interspersed with alpine tundra and alpine meadows. Where this zone overlaps in mid-elevation slopes with the Interior Douglas fir zone, there exists a small montane spruce zone dominated by lodgepole pine and containing a mixture of species from the other 2 zones. High mountain slopes throughout the province have an alpine tundra zone consisting of a sparse growth of stunted subalpine fir, Engelmann spruce, mountain hemlock and whitebark pine.

In the past 140 years about 95,000 km² of BC's forests have been logged, and about the same amount have been burned by fire. *See also* ENDANGERED SPECIES; FOREST FIRES; FOREST POLICY; FOREST PRODUCTS; LOGGING.

Reading: Cameron Young, *The Forests of British Columbia*, 1985. *Ken Drushka*

FORST, Judith (Lumb), mezzo-soprano (b 7 Nov 1943, New Westminster). She is one of the most acclaimed opera voices to emerge from BC. After graduating from high school in COQUITLAM she obtained a BMus from UBC in 1966. She studied with Bliss Hebert in New York and Robert Keys in London and made her operatic debut with the VANCOUVER OPERA in 1967 as Lola

Judith Forst, mezzo soprano.
Columbia Artists Management Inc

in *Cavalleria Rusticana*. The following year she won the CBC Talent Festival and an exclusive 3-year contract with the Metropolitan Opera of New York. She has since performed often with the Canadian Opera Company and with leading opera companies around the world. She is an Officer in the Order of Canada (1992) and returns periodically to BC to perform.

Shannon Emmerson

FORT ALEXANDRIA, opened in 1814, was the last trading post built by the NORTH WEST CO (NWC) before it merged with the HBC in 1821. Originally it was located on the FRASER R about 30 km north of SODA CREEK; after the merger the NWC operation moved north up the river to a local DAKELH (Carrier) fishing site. Named for the explorer Alexander MACKENZIE, the fort was an important way station along the HBC's overland brigade trail from the coast during 1826–47 (*see* FUR BRIGADES). Peter Skene OGDEN built the first flour mill in BC here. The fort moved across to the west side of the river in 1837, in the hopes of attracting the TSILHQOT'IN to trade, and may have moved again before it closed in 1867.

FORT BABINE was an HBC trading post founded in 1822 at the entrance to the north arm of BABINE LK. Originally named Fort Kilmaurs after the Scottish birthplace of Chief Trader William Brown, it was established mainly to supply SALMON as food for company servants. It closed temporarily in 1829 but reopened and operated until 1872, when it moved to the north end of the lake. The tiny settlement of Old Fort is near the original site. The modern community of Fort Babine is home to about 250 Nat'oot'en (DAKELH) people.

FORT CHILCOTIN was a FUR TRADE post established by the HBC at the confluence of the Chilko and CHILCOTIN rivers in 1829. It relied on trade from the surrounding TSILHQOT'IN people, who were not enthusiastic participants in the fur trade. The fort operated intermittently until 1844.

FORT CONNOLLY was an HBC trading post established in 1827 at the north end of Bear Lk (19.7km²) in the mountainous Interior north of BABINE LK. The lake drains via the Sustut R into the headwaters of the SKEENA R and is rich in SALMON; the post was expected to supply food as well as furs. A traditional meeting place of DAKELH (Carrier), GITKSAN and SEKANI people, all of whom traded here, Fort Connolly closed in the 1890s.

FORT DEFIANCE was a short-lived log fort built in the fall of 1791 by the American trader Robert GRAY in Adventure Cove, on the west side of MEARES ISLAND in CLAYOQUOT SOUND. Gray and his men remained at the site for the winter refitting their vessel, the *Columbia*, and building a small sloop. But before leaving in the spring the sailors attacked the nearby NUU-CHAH-NULTH (Nootka) village of Opitsat. The fort was torn down and the site was not relocated until 1966.

FORT FRASER, pop 370, is a town at the east end of Fraser Lk on the Yellowhead Hwy (*see* ROADS AND HWYS) about 140 km west of PRINCE GEORGE, in the territory of the DAKELH (Carrier). It was the site of a trading post established by Simon FRASER for the NWC in 1806. After 1821 the fort was run by the HBC. All that is left of the fort, where some of BC's earliest AGRICULTURE took place, is pieces of the rock foundation. The last spike of the GRAND TRUNK PACIFIC RWY was driven in here in 1914 and the town boomed briefly. Later the FOREST INDUSTRY became the main employer.

FORT GRAHAME was a trading post established in 1890 by the HBC on the east side of the FINLAY R north of its confluence with the PEACE R. The post, named after the senior HBC official James A. GRAHAME, served the local SEKANI people until its closure in 1948. In the 1960s flooding behind the BENNETT DAM created WILLISTON RESERVOIR and drowned the site.

FORT HALKETT was an HBC trading post established in 1829 on the LIARD R near the Fort Nelson R, then moved farther west on the Liard to its confluence with the Smith R in 1832. The post traded furs with the KASKA, SEKANI and DENE-THAH (Slavey) nations. It closed in 1875.

FORT LANGLEY was a trading post established in 1827 by the HBC on the FRASER R about 50 km from its mouth at the site now known as DERBY. It was named for Thomas Langley, an HBC official. In 1839 a new post was built 5 km upriver, closer to suitable farmland. When this fort burned in 1840 its replacement was relocated close by on the present site. BC was declared a colony here on 19 Nov 1858, by which time the post was a jumping-off point for miners heading to the Interior goldfields (*see* GOLD RUSHES). It remained in operation until 1886; for most of that time it was an important provisioning post, producing AGRICULTURAL products and cured SALMON. In 1955 the site was declared a

Fort Langley, 1971. Deni Eagland/Vancouver Sun

National Historic Park and several buildings were reconstructed. The village itself, with its array of antique shops, sidewalk cafés and historic buildings, caters to an ever-increasing flow of TOURISTS. In the 1990s the GREATER VANCOUVER REGIONAL DISTRICT and LANGLEY Township began building a fort-to-fort trail linking the Historic Park with the old Derby site.

FORT McLOUGHLIN, established in May 1833, was an HBC trading post in McLoughlin Bay on Campbell Island, about 520 km north of VANCOUVER along the INSIDE PASSAGE. Named for Dr John MCLOUGHLIN, it was built in the territory of the Bella Bella, now the HEILTSUK, people; they acted as intermediaries in the FUR TRADE with groups up and down the coast and deep into the Interior. With the arrival of the steamship *BEAVER* on the coast, George SIMPSON, an HBC governor, decided that northern trade could be conducted by boat and in 1843 the fort closed. The community that grew up around the post was called BELLA BELLA.

FORT NELSON, town, pop 4,401, is located in the northeast corner of BC on the ALASKA HWY, 483 km north of DAWSON CREEK. A FUR TRADE fort named for the British naval hero Lord Nelson was first established in the region by the NORTH WEST CO in 1805. The HBC built a post in 1865 near the confluence of the Fort Nelson and MUSKWA rivers, where the AIRPORT is today, an area once known as Otter Park. It was rebuilt farther east in 1890, and became known as Old Fort Nelson. The construction of the Alaska Hwy during WWII contributed to economic development, as did the arrival of a BC RAIL extension in 1971. The economy is based on resource industries, chiefly the FOREST INDUSTRY, including a plywood plant, and the OIL AND GAS INDUSTRY. Until 1997 the town also had the world's largest chopstick factory. WESTCOAST ENERGY INC has N America's largest gas processing facility here. Incorporated in 1987, the town is a stopover point for travellers on the highway and for other visitors attracted by the surrounding wilderness. A campus of Northern Lights COMMUNITY COLLEGE is located here.

FORT RODD HILL is a set of coastal defences on the southern tip of VANCOUVER ISLAND built between 1895 and 1900 to defend the entrances to VICTORIA and ESQUIMALT harbours. Esquimalt in particular was an important Pacific base for the Royal Navy until the early years of the 20th century. The defences at Fort Rodd Hill consisted of 3 gun batteries manned by a permanent garrison of British troops. In 1906 the British garrison withdrew and Canadian forces took over the fort. It remained an active military station until 1956, by which time modern weapons had made the coastal defences obsolete. Today it is a National Historic Park.

FORT RUPERT was built in 1849 by the HBC in Beaver Harbour, at the north end of VANCOUVER ISLAND near the site of COAL deposits in the territory of the KWAKWAKA'WAKW (Kwakiutl) people. The company imported 7 miners from Scotland, but with the discovery of coal more conveniently located at NANAIMO, mining ceased at Fort Rupert by 1852 (*see* COAL MINING, VANCOUVER

ISLAND). The post continued to supply furs and shingles until 1883, when the company sold it to its factor, Robert Hunt. He operated a store on the site. The buildings partly burned in 1889 and by the late 1990s all that remained was a crumbling chimney.

FORT ST JAMES, district municipality, pop 2,046, lies at the southeast corner of Stuart Lk, 62 km north of VANDERHOOF. Founded as a FUR TRADE post for the NORTH WEST CO by Simon FRASER in 1806, it is the second-oldest continuously inhabited non-aboriginal community in BC. The post was in the territory of the DAKELH (Carrier), who still live at the nearby village of Nak'azdli, and it was considered the "capital" of NEW CALEDONIA for many years. Fort St James National Historic Park uses some of the old buildings to depict life at the post as it was in 1896. Incorporated in 1952, the community got an economic boost from the arrival of BC RAIL in the late 1960s. SAWMILLING has been the main economic activity, as well as some MINING.

FORT ST JOHN, city, pop 15,021, at Mile 47 on the ALASKA HWY, is near ROCKY MT FORT, the first white settlement in mainland BC, established in 1794 on the PEACE R by Alexander MACKENZIE  for the NORTH WEST CO. The fort moved several times between 1794 and 1823, when it was closed. It reopened in 1860. While the Alaska Hwy was being built during WWII the population swelled to several thousand, then it contracted again with the completion of the project. Permanent growth came with the development of the OIL AND GAS INDUSTRY in 1951. BC RAIL

Downtown Fort St John, 1962. Vancouver Sun

arrived in 1957 and the city now bills itself as the Energy Capital of BC. AGRICULTURE and the FOREST INDUSTRY are also important. It is the largest community north of PRINCE GEORGE and the centre of government for the Peace R area. There is a campus of Northern Lights COMMUNITY COLLEGE and of the UNBC. CHARLIE LAKE CAVE, 9 km to the north, is the oldest site of human occupation in BC.

FORT SHEPHERD was a FUR TRADE post built in 1856 by the HBC just north of the US border on the west side of the COLUMBIA R opposite its junction with the Pend d'Oreille R. Known as Fort Pend d'Oreille for 3 years, it was renamed after John Shepherd, a governor of the HBC. The post was never very profitable; it closed in the mid-1860s and burned down in 1872. The customs house that had been located adjacent to the fort moved across the Columbia to the south bank of the Pend d'Oreille R, but was closed in 1896 when WANETA on the north bank was designated the Canadian Customs port.

FORT SIMPSON was first established in 1831 by the HBC as Fort Nass on the NASS R to counter Russian and American fur trade competition on the North Coast. That same year it was renamed for the company trader Aemilius SIMPSON. In 1834 it was relocated to the TSIMSHIAN location known as Lax Kw'alaams to allow supply ships easier access. In its early years the post was tremendously productive, a result of high volumes of beaver furs traded from TLINGIT, NISGA'A, HAIDA and especially Tsimshian people. By the 1840s, about 2,000 Tsimshian had moved their winter villages to the fort site. During the 1880s the name changed to Port Simpson. The fur trade declined; the trading post burned in 1914 but was not rebuilt, though the HBC operated a store there from 1934 to 1954. By WWI PRINCE RUPERT, 55 km to the south, was emerging as the regional entrepôt and white settlers drifted away. At the start of the 21st century Fort Simpson was a Tsimshian community of about 1,200 people. *Reading:* Helen Meilleur, *A Pour of Rain,* 1980.

FORT STEELE Heritage Town is a reconstructed frontier settlement located at the junction of WILD HORSE CREEK and the KOOTENAY RIVER, 16 km northeast of CRANBROOK in the E KOOTENAY. The original settlement, Galbraith's Ferry, named after John and Robert Galbraith, sprang up during the GOLD RUSH to the area during 1863–66. A second rush 20 years later led to friction between the KTUNAXA (Kutenai) people and white miners and settlers. In 1887 a troop of North-West Mounted Police arrived, led by Superintendent Sam STEELE, who was able to reach a peaceful understanding with the Ktunaxa. The NWMP built a log post, which they named Fort Steele. Two years later the police left and the post reverted to the province. Another MINING boom, this time SILVER–lead, took place in 1892 and the fort and surrounding town became a business and administrative centre for the region. But by the end of the century the railway had bypassed Fort Steele in favour of Cranbrook, and the settlement

Fort Steele. Duncan McDougall/Image Makers

became a ghost town. During the 1960s the province designated the fort a historic site and restored it as an 1890s frontier town.

FORT STIKINE was an HBC trading post at the mouth of the STIKINE R on Wrangell Island. Built by the Russians in 1834 and called Fort St Dionysius, it became HBC property in 1840 following Russian agreement to lease the Alaska Panhandle to the HBC. In Apr 1842 the officer in charge, John McLoughlin Jr, was murdered by his men. Gov George SIMPSON, who arrived at the post not long after, blamed the tragedy on the deceased—wrongly, as it turned out—and the incident further soured relations between Simpson and John MCLOUGHLIN Sr. The HBC abandoned the post in 1844.

FORT TAKU, also known as Fort Durham, was built by the HBC in 1840, south of where the TAKU R flows into Taku Inlet on the Alaska Panhandle, near the present site of Juneau, AK. Construction of the trading post followed Russia's agreement to lease the Panhandle to the HBC. It turned out to be cheaper to conduct trade by periodic ship visits, and the fort closed in 1843.

FORT VICTORIA, built in 1843, was an HBC trading post overlooking a fine harbour at the south end of VANCOUVER ISLAND. The site was chosen by Chief Factor James DOUGLAS, who said it resembled "a perfect Eden in the midst of the dreary wilderness." The fort was meant to replace HBC headquarters at Fort Vancouver on the COLUMBIA R once the Oregon Territory was ceded to the US; this took place in 1846 (*see* OREGON

Hudson's Bay Co warehouses and stockade, Fort Victoria, 1860. BC Archives A-04100

TREATY). The site, now in downtown VICTORIA, is bounded by the modern Government, Broughton, Wharf and Bastion streets. Charles Ross was in command for the first year, followed by Roderick FINLAYSON. Fields surrounding the fort grew wheat and other produce, and the little community that sprang up soon outgrew the fort, which was overwhelmed by the arrival of a flood of prospectors heading for the goldfields in 1858 (*see* GOLD RUSHES). The walls and buildings were demolished between 1859 and 1864, and the land was sold for development.

FORT WARE, pop 222, is a remote SEKANI community on the FINLAY R, north of WILLISTON RESERVOIR about 800 km north of PRINCE GEORGE. A group of Sekani moved here in 1917 and shortly after the HBC established a trading post, also called WHITEWATER. Most residents are hunters and trappers; some work in LOGGING.

FORTES, Seraphim "Joe," lifeguard (b 1865, Barbados; d 4 Feb 1922, Vancouver). He arrived in VANCOUVER as a deckhand on a sailing ship in 1885 and found work as a porter and bartender at the Sunnyside Hotel in GASTOWN. By the 1890s he was a familiar figure on the beach at ENGLISH BAY, where he swam daily and taught children to swim. The city appointed him its first official lifeguard and special constable for the beach in

Joe Fortes plunging into English Bay, c 1906. Philip Timms/CVA 677-591

1901. Originally his squatter's shack stood on the beach opposite the Sylvia Hotel, but in 1905 it was moved into Alexandra Park near the bandstand. He is credited with saving more than 100 lives, and in 1986 the Vancouver Historical Society named him Citizen of the Century.

FORTUNE, William, farmer, businessman (b 1838, Yorkshire, England; d 1 Dec 1914, Kamloops). After immigrating to Ontario, he joined the party of OVERLANDERS who travelled

across the continent in 1862 to join the CARIBOO GOLD RUSH. He worked for the HBC in KAMLOOPS, then moved west to settle at TRANQUILLE, where he developed a ranch and farm and built the first flour mill in the Interior. In 1878 he built the sidewheel steamer *Lady Dufferin* to haul supplies on the THOMPSON and SHUSWAP waterways. He sold his property for use as a tuberculosis sanitarium in 1907 and returned to Kamloops, where he was prominent in business until his death.

FOSSILS are at once fascinating and richly informative. They are used to date rock units and to gauge the passage of geologic time. Fossils furnish direct evidence about the nature of ancient environments and about the composition of past animal and plant communities. The fossil record provides the best information possible about the history of life and the course that evolution has followed. Moreover, to many people, fossils are natural images and sculptures of great beauty. Fossils have been collected for many years in the CORDILLERA. A trilobite on a rock wafer that could only have come from Cambrian shale east of CRANBROOK was found in a Coast Salish (*see* SALISHAN FIRST NATIONS) archaeological site in the FRASER Canyon. Likely picked up by aboriginal people a few thousand years ago, it must have been carried or traded 500 km across the Interior.

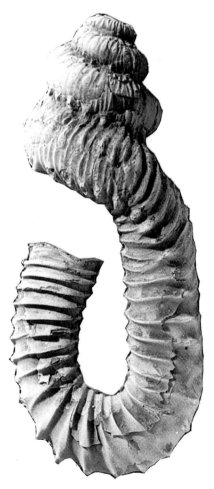

Upper Cretaceous ammonite Nostoceras, *14 cm high, from Hornby Island. Rolf Ludvigsen photo*

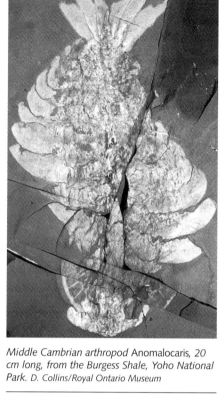

Middle Cambrian arthropod Anomalocaris, *20 cm long, from the Burgess Shale, Yoho National Park. D. Collins/Royal Ontario Museum*

Significant fossils occur in BC in sedimentary rock assigned to each of the 13 geological systems from Vendian through Quaternary (650 million years ago to 10,000 years ago; see chart). Some sites preserve truly spectacular fossils of cardinal importance for charting the development of life on the planet. Middle Cambrian rocks on Mt Field in YOHO NATIONAL PARK include the celebrated BURGESS SHALE assemblages of exquisitely preserved arthropods, worms, SPONGES, MOLLUSCS, brachiopods and other groups, most with preserved soft tissues (*see also* WORLD HERITAGE SITES). Triassic strata near WAPITI LK south of TUMBLER RIDGE contain diverse assemblages of complete fossil fishes (including a coelacanth) and many extinct marine reptiles (ichthyosaurs and thalattosaurs). Fossil localities on eastern VANCOUVER ISLAND and the GULF ISLANDS have some of the most diverse faunal associations known from Upper Cretaceous rocks—ammonites, cuttlefish, bivalves, gastropods, crustaceans, marine reptiles (mosasaurs, ELASMOSAURS, turtles), sharks, crinoids, corals, INSECTS, a bird and a DINOSAUR, plus well-preserved fossil plants. Lower Paleogene lake beds in the PRINCETON, CACHE CREEK and WILLIAMS LAKE areas include superbly preserved FISH, INSECTS, SPIDERS, birds, flowers, leaves and permineralized aquatic plants preserved in 3 dimensions.

Organized investigations of geology and systematic collection of fossils began when BC entered CONFEDERATION in 1871 and the Geological Survey of Canada (GSC) started its work in the Cordillera. The initial emphasis was on the geology and age of mineral-bearing regions on Vancouver Island, the QUEEN CHARLOTTE ISLANDS and the Interior. In the 19th cen-

SIGNIFICANT FOSSIL SITES IN BC

System (age in years)	Site or Area	Fossils Present
QUATERNARY (2m)	SAANICH PENINSULA	mammoth, bison, muskox
	Kamloops Lk	salmon
NEOGENE (25m)	QUESNEL	angiosperms, diatoms
PALEOGENE (65m)	Flathead R	rodents, rabbit, marsupial
	HORSEFLY	fishes, insects, angiosperms, diatoms
	McAbee	conifers, angiosperms, flowers, bird, insects, fishes
	SIMILKAMEEN R	aquatic angiosperms, turtle
CRETACEOUS (140m)	HORNBY ISLAND	ammonites, bivalves, sharks, bird, monasaurs
	Trent R	theropod dinosaur, sharks, turtle
	Duke Pt	angiosperms, palms, flowers
	Puntledge R	elasmosaur, turtle, ammonites, crustaceans
	PEACE R	dinosaur trackways
	TUMBLER RIDGE	ferns, cycads, conifers
JURASSIC (210m)	Skidegate Inlet	ammonites, bivalves, radiolarians
	Graham Island	ammonites, radiolarians, ichthyosaur
TRIASSIC (250m)	Kennecott Point	ammonites, conodonts, radiolarians
	WILLISTON RESERVOIR	ammonites, conodonts, ichthyosaurs
	WAPITI LK	coelacanth, ichthyosaurs, thalattosaurs
PERMIAN (290m)	Marble Range	fusilinids, conodonts
	STRATHCONA PROV PARK	brachiopods, bryozoans
CARBONIFEROUS (360m)	Mt Harper	brachiopods, corals, conodonts
	Mt Spencer	brachiopods, trilobites
DEVONIAN (410m)	Monkman Pass	brachiopods
	MUNCHO LK	agnathans
SILURIAN (440m)	Toad R	brachiopods, corals
	Mt Tegart	trilobites, graptolites, conodonts
ORDOVICIAN (500m)	TOP OF THE WORLD PROV PARK	stromatoporoids, brachiopods
	Kicking Horse R	graptolites
CAMBRIAN (550m)	BULL R	trilobites
	MT FIELD	Burgess Shale soft-bodied animals
	FORT STEELE	olenellid trilobites
VENDIAN (650m)	CARIBOO MTS	vendozoans

tury, fossils collected from these areas by James Richardson, George M. DAWSON and Alfred Selwyn were described by the GSC paleontologist J.F. Whiteaves and the McGill Univ paleobotanist Sir J.W. Dawson. In the 20th century, GSC paleontologists published major works on

Upper Cambrian trilobite Labiostria, *3 cm long, found in the Fraser Canyon. Rolf Ludvigsen photo*

Paleogene plants and insects, Cretaceous molluscs and plants, and on Triassic and Jurassic ammonites of the Cordillera. West Coast paleontology became an academic discipline in 1921 with the appointment of M.Y. Williams as UBC professor of paleontology. The subject is now studied at 3 BC universities, at the GSC, at a few museums and increasingly by amateur paleontologists and fossil collectors belonging to the BC Paleontological Alliance. Many important BC fossils are studied outside the province by paleontologists at the Royal Tyrrell Museum at Drumheller, AB, the Univ of Alberta, the Univ of Saskatchewan, Cambridge Univ in England and the Royal Ontario Museum in Toronto, as well as the Canadian Museum of Nature in Ottawa. Major collections of BC fossils reside outside the country. The Smithsonian Institution alone holds 65,000 specimens from the Burgess Shale, while the American Museum of Natural History has many Triassic fishes from Wapiti Lk. Within the province there are modest or specialized collections at the ROYAL BC MUSEUM, Princeton Museum, COURTENAY Museum,

KELOWNA Museum, HUDSON'S HOPE Museum, Vancouver Island Paleontological Museum (QUALICUM BEACH), Queen Charlotte Islands Museum and the Fraser Centre for Eocene Research (CHILLIWACK). Many of the museums display fossils. *Rolf Ludvigsen*

Readings: Rolf Ludvigsen, ed., *Life in Stone: A Natural History of British Columbia's Fossils*, 1996; Rolf Ludvigsen and Graham Beard, *West Coast Fossils: A Guide to the Ancient Life of Vancouver Island*, 1998.

FOSTER, David Walter, musician, record producer (b 1 Nov 1949, Victoria). After growing up in VICTORIA, he moved to England when he was still in his teens to pursue a career in pop music. When he returned to Canada he played briefly with Rompin' Ronnie Hawkins, then moved to VANCOUVER and played in the band Skylark, which had a huge success with its song "Wildflower." He moved to Los Angeles in 1972, then went from being a studio session musician to an award-winning record producer for a string of big-name pop stars, including

Barbra Streisand, Celine Dion, Whitney Houston, Natalie Cole, Michael Jackson and Paul McCartney. He wrote the music for "Tears Are Not Enough," the 1985 song for Ethiopian famine relief featuring Canadian performers, and has won more than a dozen Grammy Awards. As well he has written many theme songs for successful movies, and he runs his own record company. *See also* SOUND RECORDING INDUSTRY.

FOSTER, William Wasborough "Billy," public servant, mountaineer (b 1875, Bristol, England; d 2 Dec 1954, Vancouver). He participated in the first ascents of Mt ROBSON, the highest peak in the Canadian ROCKY MTS (1913), and Mt Logan, the highest mountain in Canada (1925), 2 of the greatest achievements in the history of Canadian MOUNTAINEERING. Educated as an engineer in his native England, he came to Canada as a young man. He worked for the CPR in REVELSTOKE and in 1910 became provincial deputy minister of public works. He was elected to the legislature as a CONSERVATIVE member from VANCOUVER ISLAND in 1913; during WWI he went overseas, where he was wounded twice and rose to the rank of brigadier. While away at the front he lost his seat as an MLA. He served as VANCOUVER's chief of police from 1935 to 1939, having been brought in by Gerry MCGEER to "clean up" the city and its police force. Foster returned to active service in the army during WWII and was promoted to major general. Following the war he was a member of the BC POWER COMMISSION. Mt Colonel Foster on Vancouver Island is named for him.

FOTHERINGHAM, Allan, journalist (b 31 Aug 1932, Hearne, SK). After graduating from UBC in 1954, he joined the *VANCOUVER SUN* as a sports reporter. In 1968 he began writing a daily column that quickly became the liveliest, most controversial reading in the paper, mixing an acid wit with solid political reporting. In 1975 he also

began contributing a regular column to *Maclean's* magazine. Ambitious and not always tactful, he fell out with *Sun* management and left the NEWSPAPER in 1979; he then moved to Ottawa to write for FP News Services and later Southam News Service. In 1984 he became a panelist on the long-running CBC television quiz show *Front Page Challenge*. His books include *Malice in Blunderland* (1982), *Look Ma...No Hands* (1983), *Capitol Offences: Dr Foth Meets Uncle Sam* (1986), an account of his time as Southam's correspondent in Washington, DC, and *Last Page First* (1999). He makes his home in eastern Canada but maintains a residence in BC.

FOX, red (*Vulpes vulpes*), a small member of the dog family (Canids), is the only fox species found in BC. Rust red or silver-black, the red fox has prominent black ears, blackish lower legs and feet, and white underparts, chin and throat.

Young red fox. Duane Sept photo

Allan Fotheringham (second from left) with fellow journalists Robert Lewis (l), Marjorie Nichols and Jack Webster, Vancouver, 1986. Vancouver Sun

The species occurs throughout the province in a variety of habitats, preferring open parklands and alplands where meadows are interspersed with shrubs and trees. It preys on birds, FROGS and small mammals (especially rodents), and also eats INSECTS, seeds and fruit. The female gives birth in the spring to as many as 10 kits. Foxes were unsuccessfully introduced on VANCOUVER ISLAND in the 1930s.

FOX, Michael J., actor (b 9 June 1961, Edmonton). He moved to BURNABY with his family in the early 1970s and at age 15 began his acting career on the CBC television program *Leo and Me* (Brent CARVER also appeared on the show). After moving to Hollywood in 1979, he shot to fame playing the conservative teenager Alex Keaton in the hugely successful television sitcom *Family Ties* (1982–89). At the same time he emerged as a motion picture star in the hit comedy *Back to the Future* (1985). After roles in a series of movies, some more successful than others, he returned to television in 1997 in another sitcom, *Spin City*. In 1998 he revealed publicly that he was ill with Parkinson's disease; in 2000 the illness forced his departure from *Spin City*. A theatre in Burnaby is named for him.

Michael J. Fox, actor, 1988.
Deni Eagland/Vancouver Sun

FOX, Terrance Stanley "Terry," runner (b 28 July 1958, Winnipeg; d 28 June 1981, New Westminster). He moved to PORT COQUITLAM as a youngster with his family and after losing a leg to bone cancer in 1977 he decided to run across Canada to raise money for cancer research. His "Marathon of Hope" began at St John's, NF, on 12 Apr 1980 and continued until Sept 1, when he reached Thunder Bay, ON, a distance of 5,373 km. The run ended when cancer was discovered in his lungs but his marathon raised $1.7 million and an additional $23 million was donated by Canadians inspired by his efforts. His legacy continues in the annual fundraising Terry Fox Run. He is commemorated with Mt Terry Fox (el 2,651 m) north of VALEMOUNT and

Terry Fox during his Marathon of Hope, 1980.
Gail Harvey/Terry Fox Foundation

in 1984 a memorial to him was installed outside BC PLACE STADIUM in VANCOUVER. He was named a Companion of the Order of Canada.

FOX, TERRY, LABORATORY; *see* TERRY FOX LABORATORY.

FRAME, Statira, artist (b 1870, Waterloo, QC; d 1933, Vancouver). Largely self-taught as a painter, she attended modelling classes at the Vancouver School of Art (*see* EMILY CARR INSTITUTE OF ART & DESIGN) and travelled to California to study briefly with Arnim Hansen in 1921. She was a member of the Vancouver Studio Club, the Vancouver Sketch Club and an early vice-president of the BC Society of Fine Arts. She was a close friend of Emily CARR; the 2 women shared a studio and worked together following Carr's return to Vancouver from France. Frame exhibited frequently in VANCOUVER as well as at the National Gallery in Ottawa (1932–33) and in Montreal (1934) and she was recognized as a BC pioneer of modernism. Her oil paintings exhibit an expressive post-impressionist technique utilizing strong, vibrant colours. *See also* ART, VISUAL.

FRANCIS, William John, entertainer, bon vivant (b 1881; d 16 Apr 1954, Vancouver). Known as "The Professor," he was an habitué of VANCOUVER's nightlife for 30 years. Around 1900 he ran a professional musical troupe in the East. He came to Vancouver in the 1920s and became well known in THEATRE and media circles as an affable eccentric who forced himself on visiting celebrities and into public performances. A gaunt, silver-haired figure, dressed in ragged clothes and looking like an unmade bed, he hung about hotel and theatre lobbies cadging meals and free tickets. Late in his life he could be heard regularly on local radio, chatting about his adventures. He died of a heart attack while beating out a song on a nightclub piano. Several of the city's best-known media personalities were pallbearers at his funeral.

FRANCKS, Donald, actor (b 28 Feb 1932, Burnaby). A versatile entertainer, he began his career in the 1950s doing stand-up comedy in nightclubs, and progressed to star turns in Broadway musicals and roles in a host of feature films and television series. In the 1960s he abandoned show business to live on a reserve in Saskatchewan, where he was made an honorary Cree and given the name Iron Buffalo. After returning to acting in the late 1970s, he won a pair of ACTRA Awards for dramatic roles on CBC-TV and appeared in several movies. He also performed and recorded with his own JAZZ group.

FRANÇOIS LAKE, in central BC south of BURNS LAKE, is in the traditional territory of the DAKELH (Carrier) First Nations. The region around the narrow, 98-km-long LAKE is important for AGRICULTURE, TOURISM and the CATTLE INDUSTRY. The east/west-oriented body of water is known by the Dakelh as Nitapoen, or "lip lake," because of its shape. *Nita* was mistaken by early settlers for *neto*, or "white man," and the name of the lake was wrongly translated as Lac des Français, as most white men in the area at that time were French Canadian voyageurs. Français was then corrupted to François. At the settlement of François Lake, on the north shore of the lake and 20 km south of BURNS LAKE, a ferry crosses to SOUTHBANK, a 20-minute ride. AS

FRANCOPHONES were the among the first non-aboriginal people in BC. Six French Canadians accompanied Alexander MACKENZIE on his 1793 trek across the ROCKY MTS to the Pacific. French Canadian voyageurs were also part of the expeditions of Simon FRASER (among them Jules-Maurice QUESNEL) and David THOMPSON. In 1827 a group of 16 French Canadians travelled with James MCMILLAN north from Fort Vancouver to the lower FRASER R, where they established FORT LANGLEY. By 1850, a total of 800 French Canadians had worked west of the Rockies in the FUR TRADE and some of them had taken up permanent residence. In 1851 a military corps was established to protect FORT VICTORIA. Called the Voltigeurs and consisting largely of francophones, this corps served Victoria for 7 years until the arrival of the ROYAL ENGINEERS. The Fraser R GOLD RUSH attracted francophones to BC, not only from Quebec but from France as well. Many of these French immigrants had taken part in the California gold rush and travelled north to BC from the US. There were enough French-speaking people in VICTORIA by 1858 to warrant the appearance of a French newspaper, *Le Courrier de la Nouvelle Calédonie*. The ROMAN CATHOLIC CHURCH, under the leadership of Bishop Modeste DEMERS, played an important role in bringing French culture to BC. The SISTERS OF ST ANN, for example, established a school in Victoria as early as 1858. Construction of the CPR attracted groups of French Canadian workers to the province in the 1880s; some of them later became farmers in the FRASER VALLEY at Hatzic Prairie, which remained a French-speaking centre until WWI. The francophone presence was also felt in the Lower Mainland. In

1909 the Fraser Mills Lumber Co near NEW WESTMINSTER (*see* MILLSIDE) imported 40 families from Quebec to replace its Asian workforce. The families were provided with a school and a church, Notre Dame de Lourdes, and by 1913 the small community of MAILLARDVILLE had emerged. A second francophone community developed in VANCOUVER following WWII, centred around Blessed Sacrament Church. Although francophones maintained a strong presence in the Lower Mainland prior to the 1950s, changes in immigration patterns curtailed the community's growth. Maillardville, for example, increasingly became populated by English-speaking people. Nonetheless, the francophone community continues to be active in both Victoria and Vancouver and has also developed a presence in the OKANAGAN VALLEY. Organizations such as Alliance Française and La Federation des Franco-Columbiens were established to promote francophone culture. There is a French newspaper, *Le Soleil de Colombie*, and French-language radio and television. In Vancouver, La Maison de la Francophonie provides a home for several French-language organizations. An estimated 65,000 francophones live in BC. *Dianne Mackay*

FRANK, Leonard Juda, photographer (b 3 July 1870, Berne, Germany; d 23 Feb 1944, Vancouver). His father was one of Germany's earliest professional photographers. Frank immigrated to the US in 1892 and 2 years later arrived in BC, intending to prospect for GOLD. He worked for a merchandising firm on VANCOUVER ISLAND, then in 1898 ended up in PORT ALBERNI. He settled there and opened a general store and continued to prospect. He also began taking photographs of the surrounding country; eventually PHOTOGRAPHY became his profession. Frank was an active outdoorsman and carried his camera with him on excursions around the

Leonard Frank, photographer, 1923.

Island, but it was chiefly as a photographer of LOGGING, FISHING and MINING activities that he made his reputation. He moved to VANCOUVER in 1917 and soon became the leading commercial/industrial photographer in the city. His photographs provide a vivid visual record of the growth of the city between the wars, and his logging photographs in particular are considered the finest taken anywhere. Following his death his company was purchased by Otto LANDAUER. *Reading:* Cyril Leonoff, *An Enterprising Life,* 1990.

FRANKLIN CAMP, 60 km west of NANAIMO and about halfway between PORT ALBERNI and BAMFIELD on VANCOUVER ISLAND, was established in 1934 by BLOEDEL, STEWART & WELCH and became the base for extensive RAILWAY LOGGING operations until 1957, when trucks took over. The camp was run by MACMILLAN BLOEDEL for years, until WEYERHAEUSER CANADA LTD bought that company. The Franklin R, which is actually 12 km north of the camp, was named after Selim Franklin, a VICTORIA realtor and power broker who backed the 1864 VANCOUVER ISLAND EXPLORING EXPEDITION.   AS

FRASER, Alexander Vaughn "Alex," politician (b 22 June 1916, Quesnel; d 1989, Victoria). A partner in a CARIBOO trucking company, he was mayor of QUESNEL for 20 years before winning election to the legislature as a SOCIAL CREDIT PARTY member from the Cariboo in 1969. He held the seat for the next 20 years until his death. Re-elected 5 times, he was known widely as "the King of the Cariboo." He joined Bill BENNETT's CABINET in 1975 as minister of highways and kept the portfolio until 1987. Improvements to the Chilcotin Hwy and the construction of the COQUIHALLA HWY were the major projects carried out during his tenure. The Alex Fraser Bridge across the FRASER R from DELTA to ANNACIS ISLAND is named for him. *See also* ROADS AND HWYS.

FRASER, D.M. "Don," writer (b 1946, NS; d 1985, Vancouver). He settled in VANCOUVER in 1967 and lived there until his death. He was a founder and editor of Pulp Press (*see* ARSENAL PULP PRESS), and his 2 collections of stories, *Class Warfare* and *The Voice of Emma Sachs*, were published to great critical acclaim. Fraser was renowned as a prose stylist and a literary character whose great promise was cut short by his early death. For some years he lived in the railroad flat above Morris's Junk Store on Main Street, which, as the "Vancouver Least Cultural Centre," became a focus of literary life in Vancouver.   *Stephen Osborne*

FRASER, George, horticulturalist (b 25 Oct 1854, Lossiemouth, Scotland; d 1944, Port Alberni). Already an experienced gardener when he emigrated to Canada in 1883, he arrived in VICTORIA 5 years later and became foreman in charge of BEACON HILL PARK. RHODODENDRONS he planted there in 1889 are still flourishing. In 1894 he moved to UCLUELET, where he established a plant nursery and became an internationally known hybridizer of rhododendrons. In 1990 he became the first non-American to win a Pioneer Achievement Award from the American Rhododendron Society.

FRASER, Hugh, jazz musician (b 1958, Victoria). After graduating from ST MICHAEL'S UNIV SCHOOL, studying trombone under Dave Robbins at Vancouver COMMUNITY COLLEGE and spending a term at the Creative Music Studio in Woodstock, NY, Fraser, a trombonist and pianist, organized the Vancouver Ensemble for Jazz Improvisation (VEJI, pronounced "veggie") in 1980. With the release of its debut album, VEJI won widespread acclaim for the vigour and originality with which Fraser embraced a world of influences within the standard jazz orchestra format. In addition, the Hugh Fraser Quintet has won Juno and West Coast Music awards and issued a number of recordings, and has toured Canada, the US, Europe, South America and Cuba. Fraser went on to residencies in New York and teaching positions at the Banff Centre for the Arts, the Royal Academy of Music in London and the Univ of Ulster in Northern Ireland. In VICTORIA he founded his own Boathouse Records label and has continued to compose, tour and record.   *David Lee*

FRASER, Keath, writer (b 25 Dec 1944, Vancouver). After completing a PhD at the Univ of London, he taught literature at the Univ of Calgary for 5 years, then returned to VANCOUVER in 1978 to become a full-time writer. His first book of stories, *Taking Cover* (1982), was followed by a second, widely acclaimed collection of fiction, *Foreign Affairs* (1986), nominated for a GOV GEN's LITERARY AWARD. His first novel, *Popular Anatomy* (1995), a large, complex book, won the Chapters/*Books in Canada* First Novel Award. He followed it with another collection of interconnected stories, *Telling My Love Lies* (1997). He has also written a memoir about his relationship with the writer Sinclair Ross, *As For Me and My Body* (1997), and edited 2 anthologies of travel writing.

FRASER, Simon, fur trader (b 20 May 1776, Mapletown, VT; d 18 Aug 1862, St Andrews West, ON). He came to Canada with his widowed mother as part of the Loyalist migration in 1784. The family settled near Cornwall, ON, and

Aboriginal guides lead Simon Fraser and his crew along the precipitous cliffs of the Fraser Canyon, as shown in a painting by John Innes. VPL 13315

SIMON FRASER'S TRAVELS

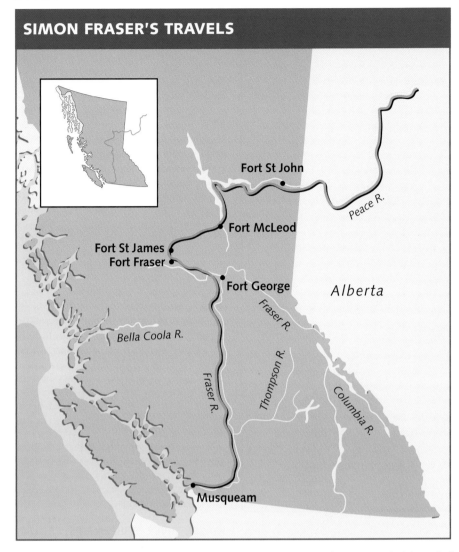

Fort St John

Peace R.

Fort McLeod

Fort St James
Fort Fraser

Fort George

Alberta

Bella Coola R.

Fraser R.

Fraser R.

Thompson R.

Columbia R.

Musqueam

in 1792, through a relative, he joined the NORTH WEST CO (NWC) in Montreal as an apprentice clerk. After becoming a partner in 1801, he was assigned the task of opening up the trade beyond the ROCKY MTS. In 1805 he led an expedition up the PEACE R through the mountains and built Fort McLeod on MCLEOD LK, the first permanent European settlement west of the Rocky Mts in what is now BC. The next year he reached Stuart Lk, the territory of the DAKELH (Carrier) people, where he established FORT ST JAMES and, a bit to the south, FORT FRASER. The NWC was seeking a navigable water route to the Pacific; in 1807 Fraser built Fort George at the present site of PRINCE GEORGE as a base for exploring the FRASER R, which at that point he believed was the COLUMBIA R. On 22 May 1808 he began his famous descent of the river, embarking from Fort St James in 4 canoes with 21 NWC employees and 2 aboriginal guides. His account of the trip through the turbulent waters of the Fraser Canyon and out to the coast, edited by W. Kaye LAMB (1960), is a classic of BC LITERATURE. Fraser's party reached the village of MUSQUEAM at the mouth of the river early in July, and the crew met a hostile reception. Already discouraged that the river was obviously not the Columbia, and of no use to the NWC as a transportation route, Fraser turned back and arrived at Fort George on

Aug 6. His descent of the river marked the end of his explorations in the territory he called NEW CALEDONIA. Subsequently he served at posts in the Mackenzie R and Athabasca districts before retiring from the FUR TRADE in 1818. He married and lived the rest of his life quietly as a farmer and miller near Cornwall.

FRASER INSTITUTE is a private, non-profit research and educational organization committed to the view that the competitive market system offers the best solution to social and economic problems. It promotes this opinion in publications and seminars and through lobbying. Founded in 1974 by the executive director, Michael WALKER, and T. Patrick Boyle, a MACMILLAN BLOEDEL executive, its aim was to propagandize against continued government growth. Under Walker the institute has become an influential public policy think tank, associated with conservative, market-oriented ideas. It also operates the National Media Archive, which collects and analyzes national news and public affairs programming.

FRASER LAKE, village, pop 1,344, is near the western end of Fraser Lk (54.6 km²) on the Yellowhead Hwy (*see* ROADS AND HWYS) about 160 km west of PRINCE GEORGE. A community

was established in 1914 with the arrival of the GRAND TRUNK PACIFIC RWY. It grew slowly as a SAWMILLING town until 1965, when a huge MOLYBDENUM mine opened south of ENDAKO and Fraser Lake became home to many mine families. The village was incorporated on 27 Sept 1966. The other major employer is Fraser Lake Sawmills at nearby LEJAC. There is excellent hunting and sport FISHING in the area. The turbulent Stellako R links Fraser Lk to FRANÇOIS LK and is famous for its FLY FISHING, its annual SALMON run and its whitewater canoeing.

FRASER MILLS; *see* MILLSIDE.

FRASER RIVER, at 1,399 km the longest river wholly within BC, rises in the ROCKY MTS near Mt ROBSON at Moose Lk. It flows northwest to the ROCKY MOUNTAIN TRENCH, flows along the Trench to SINCLAIR MILLS, then dips to the southwest toward PRINCE GEORGE, where it turns south and continues through the centre of the province; it takes a right turn at HOPE, then heads west to empty into the GEORGIA STRAIT at VANCOUVER. The Fraser drains an area of 231,510 km², about a quarter of BC. Nearly 65% of the provincial population lives in its basin, most between Hope and Vancouver. The basin produces an estimated two-thirds of BC's income. Many different FIRST NATIONS have lived along its banks, attracted by the plentiful runs of migrating SALMON.

The Fraser was descended by Simon FRASER, after whom it is named, in 1808 (*see also* FUR TRADE, LAND-BASED; NORTH WEST CO). He reported the canyon section between Hope and LILLOOET as being virtually impassable, so it was never used as a fur trade route to the Interior. The discovery of gold on the sandbars of the canyon in 1857 attracted the first influx of outsiders to

The Fraser River near Clinton.
Rick Blacklaws photo

FRASER RIVER BASIN

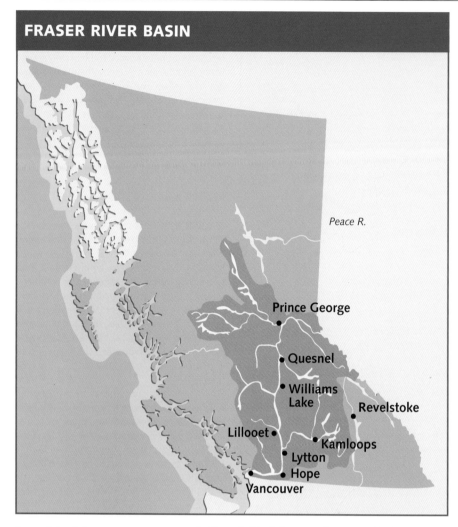

Peace R.

Prince George

Quesnel

Williams Lake

Revelstoke

Lillooet

Kamloops

Lytton

Hope

Vancouver

the mainland (*see* GOLD RUSH, FRASER R). The CARIBOO WAGON ROAD was constructed between 1862 and 1864 and the river has been a major road and rail corridor connecting the coast to the Interior ever since.

The Fraser supports 5 species of salmon, some of which migrate over 1,300 km from the sea to their spawning grounds, and accounts for

half of the annual provincial salmon catch. During construction of the CPR in 1913–14, rock slides in HELLS GATE blocked the salmon runs and caused serious depletion of all upriver salmon stocks. Not until 1941 did the US and Canada provide funds to alleviate the damage; in 1946 the first salmon ladders were completed to allow migrating salmon to get around the obstruction.

The Fraser River, looking east from New Westminster, with a view of working vessels and the Port Mann Bridge. Rick Blacklaws photo

The river basin contains 48% of BC's farmland, most of it in the broad, fertile valley between CHILLIWACK and the coast. The main stem of the Fraser has never been dammed, though there has been extensive diking and industrial development. Over the years the river has been polluted by agricultural and industrial waste and poorly treated sewage; by the mid-1990s it was among the 10 most endangered rivers in BC. The flow of water has been reduced over the years by dam construction on its tributaries, and the temperature of the river has risen, threatening fish stocks. The biggest polluters are Greater Vancouver's 3 sewage treatment plants, which in 1996 discharged more than 2 million m³ of waste into the river every day. Many efforts have been made to clean up the river, but rapid population growth along its banks, especially in the Lower Mainland, has made the situation worse.

The lower river is susceptible to heavy spring flooding resulting from rapid snowmelt in the watershed. The worst flooding on record occurred in 1894, but another serious flood in 1948 caused more property damage because the valley was more populated. The Fraser system has 600 km of flood-control dikes between Chilliwack and the mouth of the river; nevertheless a 1996 report warned that communities in the lower valley and at the mouth remain in danger from serious flooding and called for several million dollars' worth of flood control projects. The Fraser has been designated as a BC HERITAGE RIVER and is one of Canada's newest Canadian heritage rivers. *See also* AGRICULTURE; DISASTERS; FISHING, ABORIGINAL; LAKES.

FRASER RIVER FISHERMEN'S PROTECTIVE AND BENEVOLENT ASSOCIATION, formed 20 May 1893, was the first union of fishers in BC. They organized to secure a wage increase, maintain the price paid for fish by the canners, ban American boats from the FRASER R and exclude JAPANESE fishers from the industry. When canners ignored their demands, members of the association tied up their boats on 14 July, and the strike lasted 10 days. Canners brought in strikebreakers and forced the fishers back to work, but they also agreed to maintain fish prices and increase wage rates. The FRFPBA soon faded away but it was followed by other similar organizations. *See also* FISHING, COMMERCIAL; LABOUR MOVEMENT; SALMON CANNING.

FRASER RIVER FISHERMEN'S STRIKES, 1900–01, were attempts by fishers supplying salmon to the canneries at the mouth of the FRASER R to fix a minimum price for their catch. As the 1900 season began, the employers, organized as the Fraser River Canners Assoc, offered 20 cents per fish, the price to fall as the size of the catch increased. Fishers were divided by race: FIRST NATIONS had their own organizations; the JAPANESE formed the Japanese Fishermen's Benevolent Society; whites created a separate union, the BC FISHERMEN'S UNION, led by Frank ROGERS, a prominent socialist. Initially all the 5,000 fishers supported the demand for a constant price of 25 cents per fish. Anyone attempting to fish during the strike was forced from the river, but violence was minimal. Owners prevailed on the government to send special constables to STEVESTON, the centre of the strike; Rogers was arrested but the strikers held firm until 22 July, when Japanese fishers accepted an offer and returned to work. Two days later, fearing retaliation against the Japanese, the owners brought in a force of militia, the Duke of Connaught's Own Rifles, known derisively as the "Sockeye Fusiliers," to maintain order. White and aboriginal fishers continued to strike until 30 July, when both sides agreed on a price of 19 cents, a slightly better deal than the Japanese had received, and the dispute ended. The following season, 1901, was a peak year in the sockeye cycle. Canners offered 12.5 cents per fish, to fall to 10 cents when a certain quantity of fish was caught. Fishers held out for a constant price of 15 cents. A strike began 1 July, and once again white and aboriginal fishers stayed off the water but some Japanese were pressured into fishing. Union and employers sent out patrol boats, fishers began carrying weapons and violence escalated. Rogers and other union members were arrested but not convicted of any wrongdoing. On 21 July negotiations ended the strike and fishers agreed to the canners' offer. The Fraser R strikes mark the beginning of effective unionism in the BC fishing industry. *See also* FISHING, COMMERCIAL; LABOUR MOVEMENT; SALMON CANNING.

FRASER VALLEY refers to the broad floodplain of the lower FRASER R extending 140 km westward from HOPE, where the river bursts out of the mountains, to the Pacific Ocean. Between Hope and the coast, the river loses 40 m of elevation. The valley lies between the COAST MTS on the north and the CASCADE MTS and US border on the south. Home to almost a third of BC's population, the Valley encompasses 25,000 km², most of it rich alluvial soil perfectly suited for farming. It is the most productive AGRICULTURAL area in BC, responsible for half of the province's farm income. Important products include berries, vegetables, flowers, chickens, pigs, mushrooms and DAIRY products.

The valley is the traditional territory of the Mainland HALKOMELEM, a group of Coast Salish (*see* SALISHAN FIRST NATIONS) that include the KATZIE, MUSQUEAM, Kwikwetl'em, Tsawwassen and STO:LO peoples. Archaeological evidence indicates that their ancestors lived beside the river for thousands of years. The first Europeans to travel through the valley were Simon FRASER and his companions on their canoe trip from the Interior to the coast in 1808 (*see* FUR TRADE, LAND-BASED; NORTH WEST CO). Fur traders made their first permanent establishment at FORT LANGLEY in 1827. Owned by the HBC, the fort not only served as a fur trade centre but also sponsored the first commercial salmon FISHING and the earliest agriculture.

Farm settlement followed the GOLD RUSH era (1858–63), and a number of communities developed as commercial centres for their surrounding agricultural areas, notably CHILLIWACK and

Fraser Valley farmland near Chilliwack, 1991.
Roy Luckow photo

ABBOTSFORD. The Fraser R flooded each spring, spreading fertile silt across the valley floor and rejuvenating the WETLANDS that supported so much wildlife. As settlement increased, so did the damage caused by the annual flooding, until diking and reclamation projects more or less confined the river to its main stem. The largest drainage project in the valley was the Sumas Reclamation Scheme of the 1920s, when Sumas Lk was drained to create SUMAS PRAIRIE, more than 130 km² of fertile crop land. From Chilliwack to the mouth of the river there are 600 km of flood control dikes on the Fraser system.

The Fraser Valley is the main access route connecting the Pacific coast to the BC Interior and the rest of Canada. First steamboats, then railways and ROADS, took advantage of its flat terrain. The HBC's famous paddlewheeler, the *BEAVER*, was used to supply Fort Langley. During the gold rush other paddlewheelers went into operation and steamboats plied the valley from 1858 until the last one was retired in 1925 (*see* PADDLEWHEEL STEAMBOATS). Meanwhile the railway arrived in the 1880s with the construction of the CPR along the north side of the river. This stimulated LOGGING, which became a major industry during the 1880s; the valley floor and then the slopes of the mountains were gradually stripped of their forest cover. The CPR was followed by the CANADIAN NORTHERN RAILWAY, later absorbed into the CNR, which built a line along the south side of the river just before WWI. A more local railway was the electric INTERURBAN line, which opened in 1910 and ran between New Westminster and Chilliwack. For 40 years, until its closure in 1950, this line carried passengers, mail, milk, fresh produce, fish and other freight to and from valley communities. In the end, it was superseded by the extension of a network of roads, culminating in the construction of the TRANS-CANADA HWY in the early 1960s; this inaugurated a new era of suburban expansion.

The character of the valley has changed markedly since the 1960s. Most of its residents have arrived since that time, and if they took up agriculture it was as hobby farmers, not commercial operators. In the late 1990s the ambience remained rural, which is why many new residents have been attracted to the area, but the economy was growing increasingly industrial and commercial. The AGRICULTURAL LAND RESERVE has protected some farmland from urban development, but much of the agriculture and wetland habitat has been eliminated to make way for highways and housing developments. At the turn of the millennium the valley faced serious problems associated with rapid population growth, including suburban sprawl, municipal and industrial pollution, and increasing environmental degradation.

FREDRICKSON, Frank, hockey player (b 11 June 1895, Winnipeg; d 28 Apr 1979). A prolific scorer, he was captain of the Winnipeg Falcons when they won the 1920 Allan Cup for Canadian amateur HOCKEY supremacy and the Olympic gold medal in Antwerp. He came to BC in 1921 to play for Lester PATRICK's VICTORIA Aristocrats (later VICTORIA COUGARS) and led the PACIFIC COAST HOCKEY ASSOCIATION in scoring in 1921 and 1923. Under his leadership the club reached the Stanley Cup finals twice and won the trophy in 1925. He played in the NHL for Detroit, Boston and Pittsburgh, for whom he was the playing coach, and reached the Stanley Cup finals with the Bruins in 1929. He then coached at Princeton Univ before returning to BC in 1934 and coaching the UBC Thunderbirds for 7 years. He also served as a VANCOUVER school trustee and later a city alderman. He was elected to the Hockey Hall of Fame in 1958 and to the BC SPORTS HALL OF FAME in 1983. *SW*

FREE SPEECH CAMPAIGNS were protests by militant labour unionists against attempts by authorities to ban public speaking in the streets of VANCOUVER and VICTORIA. The first campaign occurred in Vancouver in Apr–May 1909 after city police tried to stop members of the INDUSTRIAL WORKERS OF THE WORLD (IWW) and the SOCIALIST PARTY OF BC from addressing crowds. Fines and jail sentences were imposed; in response, outdoor protest rallies grew in intensity. Finally the authorities decided to back away from a confrontation and the situation cooled. Similar events took place in Victoria in July–Aug 1911 when city officials attempted to ban socialist speakers from downtown streets. In the face of angry protests, the city backed down. The action returned to Vancouver in early 1912. With unemployment running high, the city launched a crackdown on vagrancy and also banned all outdoor meetings. The IWW and others immediately breached the ban and police broke up protest gatherings with clubs and whips, arresting dozens of people. On one occasion a group of speakers rented a boat, took it just off STANLEY PARK and addressed a crowd using a megaphone. They were arrested when they landed. Eventually a compromise was worked out, speaking was permitted in certain locations and protests faded. The free speech campaigns are notable for being one of the IWW's most successful militant actions during its brief presence in BC. *See also* LABOUR MOVEMENT.

FREEDOM OF INFORMATION refers to a citizen's right to obtain access to records held by governments and other public bodies. The BC *Freedom of Information and Protection of Privacy Act* was proclaimed on 4 Oct 1993 and hailed as one of the strongest in the world. Initially it applied to government ministries, agencies and CROWN CORPORATIONS. On 2 Nov 1994 it was extended to apply to local public bodies, including municipalities, school boards, hospitals, police departments, colleges and universities. Then on 6 Nov 1995 it was extended again to include all self-governing professional bodies. By 1999 the act covered more than 2,200 public bodies and 33 self-governing professional organizations. The right to obtain records is not infinite: for example, there are limits to disclosure of information gathered during law enforcement activity and to revealing information that might harm the business interests or personal privacy of a third party. Applicants request records by writing to the information and privacy office of the public body. In most circumstances a response is required within 30 days. An applicant who is unhappy with the result of a request may ask for a review by the office of the information and privacy commissioner, the official responsible for administering the process. The commissioner, an officer of the LEGISLATIVE ASSEMBLY, is appointed to a 6-year non-renewable term. The first commissioner was David Flaherty. *Russ Francis*

FRENCH CANADIANS; *see* FRANCOPHONES.

FRENCH CREEK, 80 km north of REVELSTOKE, was the site of rich discoveries during the Big Bend GOLD RUSH, and a small settlement sprang up briefly in the 1860s. The creek, named for numerous French Canadian miners, is a tributary of the Goldstream R, which runs into the COLUMBIA R. A different French Creek, 37 km northwest of NANAIMO on VANCOUVER ISLAND, started as an AGRICULTURAL community with many French Canadian homesteaders in the 1880s, and has become the terminus for a passenger ferry to LASQUETI ISLAND, with a marina and plenty of TOURISM facilities. *AS*

FRESCHI, Bruno Basilio, architect (b 18 Apr 1937, Trail). After graduating with a BArch from UBC in 1961, he did postgraduate studies at the Architectural Association in London, England. He then returned to VANCOUVER, worked with Erickson/Massey Architects (*see also* Arthur ERICKSON and Geoffrey MASSEY) from 1964 to 1970, and set up his own practice. Freschi was an associate professor at the UBC School of Architecture from 1968 to 1978 before becoming dean of the School of Architecture and Planning at the State Univ of New York in Buffalo. He was chief architect of EXPO 86, where he designed the spherical Expo Centre, now SCI-

Bruno Freschi, architect. Eliza Massey photo

ENCE WORLD BC. Other notable designs include Burnaby Municipal Centre, MacMillan Bloedel Research Centre, the Wall Centre in Vancouver, Whistler Village and the Burnaby Jamatkhana. Freschi won a gov gen's medal in 1983, and became an officer of the Order of Canada in 1987. *David R. Conn*

FRESHWATER BAY, 60 km east of PORT HARDY on the south side of Swanson Island, was the site of a remote Blackfish Sound store and post office in the 1930s and 1940s. A fish-buying station here was run by the Proctor family until 1962. *AS*

FRIGON, Edouard "Ned," homesteader (b 28 March 1834, St Prosper, QC; d 16 June 1917, Port Alice). He carried the voyageur spirit of his ancestors all the way to VANCOUVER ISLAND. In 1855 he travelled west to the California goldfields via Panama. Three years later he joined the GOLD RUSH to BC and spent many years searching for gold in the Interior. After the Omineca rush petered out in the early 1870s, he became the first white settler on the north end of Vancouver Island, building trading posts and stores at FIRST NATIONS villages from HOPE ISLAND to Koprino Sound. In 1895 he opened a hotel and saloon on Limestone Island, opposite the village of Quatsino. By 1912 he had closed his saloon and moved to a Crown grant near PORT ALICE, where he lived for the rest of his life. The nearby Frigon Islets are named for him. *Wendy Scott*

FRIPP, Thomas William, artist (b 23 Mar 1864, London, England; d 30 May 1931, Vancouver). Following in the footsteps of his father, a watercolourist of the Victorian era, Fripp studied to become a painter. In 1893 he immigrated to BC and settled on a homestead at HATZIC, but farming proved to be too strenuous for him. He and his new wife Gertrude moved in 1904 to VANCOUVER; there he established himself as a successful painter of landscapes and a pho-

tographer (*see also* PHOTOGRAPHY). In 1909 he became founding president of the BC Society of Fine Arts, the first chartered art society in the province, and he played a leading role in a variety of other arts organizations, helping to create public interest in the arts in what was in many ways still a frontier society. His brother, R. Mackay Fripp, was a prominent Vancouver architect (*see* ARCHITECTURE). *See also* ART, VISUAL.

FROG is a freshwater amphibian: it starts life in water, hatching from an egg to a larval form (such as a tadpole), complete with gills; then it metamorphoses so that it can live on land; then it must return to water to reproduce. Frogs and toads are both in the order Anura, which contains 5 families found in BC: Leiopelmatidae (bell toads), Bufonidae (true toads), Pelobatidae (spadefoot toads), Hylidae (treefrogs), Ranidae (true frogs). Most frogs are adapted for a more aquatic life and have smooth skin, streamlined shape and webbed feet; toads are adapted to spending more time on land and generally have tough, warty skin and a stouter body. Both are small, squat, tailless, neckless animals with long, muscular hind legs, shorter forelegs and well-developed eyes. Unlike most fish, all reptiles and birds, and most mammals, amphibians do not have any protective covering for their skin, which is thin, moist, generally smooth and vulnerable to drying out. Many, however, have poison glands that secrete toxic, slimy, bitter-tasting or sticky substances to deter predation.

Pacific tree frog. Duane Sept photo

Males are extremely vocal and each species has distinctive calls. The frog does not drink but absorbs water through its skin. It can also breathe through its skin, which it does when hibernating beneath the mud at the bottom of a pond during the winter. The adult eats mainly insects, which it captures by unfurling a long, sticky tongue at lightning speed. Eggs are laid in water and fertilized externally in every species except the tailed frog. They hatch into fish-like tadpoles that, in the BC region, are vegetarian and live in freshwater ponds for several months, slowly metamorphosing into little frogs. There are 11 species of frogs in BC. The tailed frog (*Ascaphus truei*) is a brown-grey animal with a pink belly. It is the only N American species to have tail-wagging muscles and ribs, making it one of the most ancient frogs in existence. The common name refers to the unique tail-like organ used by the male during mating. Tailed frogs occur mainly along the coast and in the lower FRASER VALLEY, where they are Blue-listed (*see* ENDANGERED SPECIES), and in the KOOTENAY, where they are Red-listed. Great Basin spadefoot toads (*Scaphiopus intermontanus*) are nocturnal creatures, preferring to spend their days burrowed into the ground extracting moisture from the soil. They inhabit the dry GRASSLANDS of the OKANAGAN, THOMPSON and NICOLA valleys. These toads are Blue-listed. Western toads (*Bufo boreas*), another burrowing species, are found widely throughout BC and are the only amphibian native to the QUEEN CHARLOTTE ISLANDS. Pacific treefrogs (*Hyla regilla*), one of the smallest of the province's frogs, are found across southern BC, VANCOUVER ISLAND and introduced to the Queen Charlottes. They are the only amphibians in BC with adhesive toe-pads, which they use to climb in trees and shrubs. Their colour changes in response to surrounding humidity and temperature. Northern chorus frogs (*Pseudacris triseriata*) are the smallest frogs and are found mainly in the PEACE R area. The male has a balloon-like throat pouch that helps him make loud calls. Red-legged frogs (*Rana aurora*), a large species, inhabit forest ponds on Vancouver Island, along the Central Coast and the Lower Mainland. Spotted frogs (*R. pretiosa*) are similar in appearance to their red-legged relatives but occur throughout the Interior, except in the Peace district. Northern leopard frogs (*R. pipiens*) are brown-green in colour with solid dark spots on their backs and legs. When students dissect frogs in biology class, this is the species they are usually handling. Northern leopard frogs once occurred in the Kootenay, across the southern Interior and at COOMBS on Vancouver Island, but now are found only around CRESTON. Both *R. pretiosa* and *R. pipiens* are Red-listed. Wood frogs (*R. sylvatica*) are the only N American amphibian to live north of the Arctic Circle. In BC they are found throughout the Interior to the east of the COAST MTS from the CARIBOO north. Bullfrogs (*R. catesbeiana*), the largest N American species, occur in the lower Fraser Valley, on eastern Vancouver Island and in the south Okanagan. Bullfrogs are an introduced species and are likely responsible for out-competing, and outright eating, a large number of native amphibians. Another introduced species is the green frog (*R. clamitans*), a smaller variety found in the Fraser Valley, in Vancouver and on eastern Vancouver Island. *Reading:* C.C. Corkran and C. Thoms, *Amphibians of Oregon, Washington and British Columbia,* 1996.

FRUITS; *see* AGRICULTURE; BERRIES; TREE FRUITS.

FRUITVALE, village, pop 2,117, is situated in the picturesque Beaver Valley, in the W KOOTENAY near the US border. It began as a stop on the GREAT NORTHERN RWY called Beaver Siding and took the name Fruitvale in 1906, when land developers thought it might be more appealing to potential settlers. Incorporated in 1952, it has developed as a residential community for TRAIL, 14 km west.

FRY, Alan, writer (b 1931, Lac La Hache). Raised on a ranch near LAC LA HACHE, he joined the federal Department of Indian Affairs in 1954 and eventually became superintendent of an Indian agency on the Mid-Coast. His 1970 exposé of the squalid conditions on a coastal RESERVE, *How a People Die*, was acclaimed by some FIRST NATIONS leaders for its unflinching realism and denounced by others for its comment that BC aboriginals "are the hardest damn people in the world to help." Fry, the grandson of the British dramatist Christopher Fry, wrote a number of popular books about BC and the Yukon, including *Ranch on the Cariboo, The Revenge of Annie Charlie, Come a Long Journey* and *The Burden of Adrian Knowle.* *Howard White*

FUCA, Juan de, sailor (b Valeriano, Greece; d circa 1602, Valeriano, Greece). He worked as a pilot for the Spanish on the Pacific Coast and claimed to have been sent north from Mexico in 1592 to seek the fabled Strait of ANIAN, the entrance to the Northwest Passage. In an unverified account, he said that he entered the strait at about 47°N, sailed into it for 20 days and reached a large inland sea before turning back. In 1787, when the English trader Charles BARKLEY located a broad strait south of VANCOUVER ISLAND about where Juan de Fuca said he had been, Barkley named it for him. *See also* SPANISH EXPLORATION.

FULFORD HARBOUR, 40 km north of VICTORIA on southern SALTSPRING ISLAND in the GULF ISLANDS, is a picturesque hamlet at the east end of the fertile Burgoyne–Fulford valley (*see* AGRICULTURE). A ferry runs between here and Swartz Bay on VANCOUVER ISLAND. A number of HAWAIIAN families settled in the area in the 1860s and 1870s and helped build St Paul's Catholic church from 1880 to 1885. The local post office was called South Salt Spring from 1900 to 1924. The harbour was named after Capt John Fulford of HMS GANGES, who served on the BC coast from 1858 to 1860. *AS*

FULMAR, northern (*Fulmarus glacialis*), is a pelagic seabird common along the outer coast and in the QUEEN CHARLOTTE ISLANDS, especially in winter. It resembles a medium-sized GULL, but it is stockier and has a rounded yellow bill with tube-like nostrils and a distinctive stiff-winged way of flying. Its colour ranges from white to dusky grey. There are 3 distinct subspecies, all of which breed in the North. The one that visits BC comes from Siberia and Alaska; the other subspecies migrate into the north Atlantic. The northern fulmar has been observed breeding on TRIANGLE ISLAND off the north end of VANCOUVER ISLAND. Fulmars are surface feeders; they follow boats and pick up food scraps.

FULTON, Edmund Davie, lawyer, politician (b 10 Mar 1916, Kamloops, d 22 May 2000, Vancouver). As a UBC student he won a Rhodes scholarship (1937) to study at Oxford. During WWII he served overseas with the Seaforth Highlanders, then returned to KAMLOOPS to practise law. First elected to Parliament as a Conservative in 1945 before he was 30 years old, he contested the national party leadership in 1956 at the convention that chose John Diefenbaker. When the Tories formed a minority government the next year, he served in the cabinet as minister of justice from 1957 to 1962. During this period he was the chief federal negotiator for the COLUMBIA RIVER TREATY. In 1962 he also served briefly as minister of public works. Highly regarded as a minister, he left federal politics in Jan 1963 to take over leadership of the BC CONSERVATIVE PARTY, which held no seats in the legislature. In that year's election the party failed to improve its situation; Fulton did not win even his own seat. He returned to federal politics in 1965 for one term, then became the first chair of the BC Law Reform Commission. From 1973 he served as a judge on the BC Supreme Court, until an impaired driving charge forced his resignation in 1981. He was inducted into the Order of Canada in 1992.

FUNDAMENTALISM; *see* CONSERVATIVE PROTESTANTISM.

FUNG, Donna "Lori," gymnast (b 21 Feb 1963, Vancouver). She emerged as a leading Canadian rhythmic gymnast in 1981, when she won the western Canadian all-around championship. She went on to become the national

Lori Fung, Olympic gymnast. She was national grand champion 7 years in a row.
Ian Lindsay/Vancouver Sun

grand champion 7 years in a row. She capped her career at the 1984 Summer Olympics in Los Angeles when she won the first gold medal ever awarded in rhythmic gymnastics. After retiring from competition she became a national team coach and co-owner of a Vancouver gymnastics club. She is a member of the Canadian Sports Hall of Fame, BC SPORTS HALL OF FAME, the ORDER OF BC (1990) and the Order of Canada.

FUR BRIGADES were the means by which fur trading companies carried furs from, and supplies to, their trading posts in the BC Interior, known as NEW CALEDONIA. The principal brigade route connected the posts in the upper FRASER R watershed with Fort Vancouver on the lower COLUMBIA R. This route, via KAMLOOPS and the OKANAGAN VALLEY, was discovered in 1811 by David Stuart of the PACIFIC FUR CO. In 1813 John STUART of the NORTH WEST CO led the first brigade to use the route to carry furs out of New Caledonia. Initially the route proved too lengthy to allow a round trip between FORT ST JAMES and Fort Vancouver in a single season; traders preferred the more familiar route across the ROCKY MTS to the east via the headwaters of the PEACE R. Then in 1826, after the HBC took control of the trade in New Caledonia, the route was reactivated. The brigade began at Fort St James on Stuart Lk, where the previous season's fur returns were assembled. As soon as the ice melted, usually late Apr, a flotilla of up to 5 boats and CANOES travelled via the STUART and NECHAKO rivers to Fort George, then down the Fraser to FORT ALEXANDRIA. At Alexandria goods were transshipped to horses, and the caravan of up to 100 animals continued overland southeast to the N THOMPSON R following roughly the route of modern Hwys 97 and 24. After descending the N Thompson, the pack train reached Fort Kamloops, then followed the S Thompson, MONTE CREEK and the SALMON R to the north end of OKANAGAN LK. Following a trail on the west side of the lake, it continued south through the valley and down the Okanagan R to its confluence with the Columbia at Fort Okanogan. Once again goods were transshipped, this time onto 9-m boats for the final leg of the journey down the Columbia to Fort Vancouver. After a brief rest, the brigade returned with a year's worth of supplies and trade goods along the same route to New Caledonia, usually reaching Fort St James by mid-Sept. This supply route was used continuously until 1847, when the HBC, having withdrawn from the Oregon Territory north to VANCOUVER ISLAND, no longer needed it. *See also* FUR TRADE.
Reading: James R. Gibson, *The Lifeline of the Oregon Country*, 1998.

FUR SEAL, NORTHERN (*Callorhinus ursinus*), is a carnivorous marine mammal. Males annually migrate between their breeding grounds in the N Pacific and the coast of California. The migration occurs many kilometres offshore, but sometimes animals are seen in JUAN DE FUCA STRAIT. Dark brown or grey in colour, with large shoul-

ders and front flippers, fur seals breed in the summer at only a few rookeries, mostly on the Pribilof Islands but also on Robben Island and the Commander and Kurile Islands. Males grow to 270 kg in weight and 2.5 m long; females are much smaller—45 kg on average. (The only mammal species with a larger size difference between male and female is the elephant seal.) Fur seals feed on fish and squid and spend nearly all of the non-breeding season at sea.

Their rookeries were discovered in 1786, and Russian sealers began to harvest them without restriction. Tens of thousands of the animals were killed every year for their plush pelts, and the population fell dramatically from an estimated 3 million. After Alaska was sold to the US, a consortium of American sealing interests secured exclusive rights to pursue a land-based hunt. From 1866 there was also a pelagic (sea-going) hunt with a base in VICTORIA. American and Canadian pelagic hunters sailed to the sealing grounds in large schooners, then launched CANOES whose crews—mostly FIRST NATIONS people from the west coast of VANCOUVER ISLAND—did the actual killing with guns or spears. The pelagic hunt peaked in the 1890s, when more than 100 vessels were involved. Most of the major BC owners combined in 1891 to form the Victoria Sealing Co. The international pelagic hunt had a devastating impact on the size of the seal population, which declined rapidly to a low of about 300,000. American land-based hunters responded in 1886 by seizing Canadian sealing vessels, precipitating a controversy that dragged on until it was resolved by the NORTH PACIFIC FUR SEAL CONVENTION in 1911 and pelagic sealing was banned. The US placed a 5-year moratorium on the land-based hunt in 1913, after which time a regulated hunt resumed. Canada is a member of the North Pacific Fur Seal Commission, which continues to manage the stock. *See also* SEAL.

FUR TRADE, LAND-BASED, was a trade for animal pelts carried on between aboriginal peoples and European traders. In Canada it began along the Atlantic coast in the early 16th century when visiting fishers from Europe came ashore to dry their catch, encountered the indigenous peo-

ple and began to barter with them. Gradually the trade spread across the continent as European colonists established settlements and explorers mapped the waterways of the Interior. The staple fur of the trade was the BEAVER pelt, used by Europeans to manufacture felt hats and other garments, though the skins of many other fur-bearing animals, including MINK, MARTEN, muskrat, FOX, BEAR, LYNX, WOLVERINE and WOLF, were also traded. Actual trapping of the animals was done by aboriginal hunters, who brought their furs to trading posts and exchanged them for guns, metalware, blankets and other imported items. Traders then transported the year's trade to tidewater by CANOES and by ship to Europe.

For many years, trade in the Interior was dominated by the HBC, based in London, England. After Britain defeated France in the Seven Years War and took possession of its Canadian colonies in 1763, other groups of merchants based in Montreal launched an aggressive campaign to rival the HBC. By 1780 these merchants were organized into the NORTH WEST CO (NWC) and were expanding their trading activities as far west as the foothills of the ROCKY MTS. It was at this point that the fur trade reached BC.

A trade in SEA OTTER pelts began along the coast of BC following the visit of Capt James COOK in 1778 (*see* FUR TRADE, MARITIME) and goods exchanged in this trade made their way to FIRST NATIONS groups in the Interior, but a land-based trade similar to the one being conducted east of the Rockies did not become established on the Pacific slope until the early years of the 19th century. In 1793 aboriginal guides led the NWC trader and explorer Alexander MACKENZIE up the PEACE R, across the Rocky Mts, down the FRASER R and overland to the Pacific at the mouth of the BELLA COOLA R. It was the first crossing of the northern half of the continent by a European. Mackenzie was looking for a plausible trading route linking the Interior to the Pacific and he began to develop plans to exploit the commercial possibilities of the Northwest Coast.

The NWC followed up these plans in 1805 by sending Simon FRASER across the Rockies into the area he christened NEW CALEDONIA, now the central Interior of BC. Fraser and his men built

Old fur trade factor's house, Fort St James.

Trading room at historic Fort Langley.
Rick Blacklaws photo

several trading posts: Fort McLeod on MCLEOD LK (1805), FORT ST JAMES on Stuart Lk (1806), FORT FRASER on FRASER LK (1806) and Fort George (later PRINCE GEORGE) at the confluence of the Fraser and NECHAKO rivers (1807). These posts mark the real beginning of the land-based fur trade in BC, and until the discovery of gold in the 1850s (*see* GOLD RUSHES) fur was the area's most significant export. Fraser sought the same route to the Pacific as Mackenzie; in 1808 he descended the river that now bears his name but the ruggedness of the terrain convinced him that traders could not make use of it. Fraser was followed by David THOMPSON, another NWC "Nor'wester." In 1811 he followed the COLUMBIA R to its mouth, where he found the PACIFIC FUR CO already installed. Two years later the NWC bought out the Pacific Fur Co and took sole possession of the trade west of the Rockies.

The Nor'westers based their Columbia trade at a second Fort George, this one located at the mouth of the Columbia. At first, trading posts in the northern district, the area Simon Fraser called New Caledonia, continued to be supplied by canoe brigades from the east. In 1813 a party of Nor'westers led by John STUART pioneered the FUR BRIGADES route connecting the lower Columbia and the upper Fraser posts via the THOMPSON R and the OKANAGAN VALLEY, but the NWC chose not to use this route to supply New Caledonia. The NWC had limited involvement in the maritime fur trade along the coast and was not able to achieve Mackenzie's dream of a sustained trading link with China. It did, however, establish a network of 6 trading posts in what is now BC. Along with the 4 posts mentioned above, these included Fort Kamloops (1813) and FORT ALEXANDRIA (1821).

In 1821, after a period of spirited and sometimes violent competition, the NWC merged with the HBC, which to that point had no presence west of the mountains. The new company retained the HBC name and took over all the NWC posts on the Columbia and in New Caledonia. Under Governor George SIMPSON the HBC reorganized the trade, cutting manpower, readjusting supply routes and encouraging economy. In 1825 the headquarters of the Columbia District moved to Fort Vancouver, farther up the river, from where traders communicated with their inland empire to the north via the Okanagan Valley brigade route pioneered a dozen years earlier. The company also expanded north up the coast, establishing trading posts at FORT LANGLEY (1827), FORT SIMPSON (1831) and FORT MCLOUGHLIN (1833). In 1836 the first steam vessel on the northwest coast, the BEAVER, arrived and was put to work supplying posts and collecting furs. In anticipation of the impending border settlement between Great Britain and the US, the HBC opened FORT VICTORIA at the south end of VANCOUVER ISLAND in 1843. Later, after the signing of the OREGON TREATY in 1846, this fort became the headquarters of the company's BC trade.

By the mid-19th century the fur trade was not the sole attraction offered by BC to Europeans. The trade continued, but it contributed progressively less to the provincial ECONOMY as gold, COAL, timber and fish resources began to be exploited. The HBC itself diversified into a range of other economic activities. When the British decided to colonize Vancouver Island in 1849, the company received proprietorial rights to the Island in return for which it was expected to encourage land settlement. This arrangement lasted until 1859, when Great Britain took direct control of the colony. Meanwhile the gold rush of 1858 led to the creation of the mainland colony of British Columbia. The HBC lost its exclusive right to trade and the company now functioned like any other private enterprise. It continued to dominate the fur trade by virtue of its long experience and established infrastructure, but technically the field was open to competitors. By 1870 furs had declined to just 13% of BC's exports, a trend that continued. In time the trading posts either closed or evolved into general stores and the barter trade evolved into the trapping economy.

The impact of the fur trade on BC HISTORY was profound. The presence of traders constituted effective British occupation of the Pacific slope and held the region until the British government was willing to extend formal control in the mid-19th century. Under the auspices of the trade much of the Interior and the West Coast was explored and mapped. The trade's impact on aboriginal people was more equivocal. All evidence suggests that aboriginal people willingly engaged in the trade and welcomed the useful material goods it provided. They had long trad-

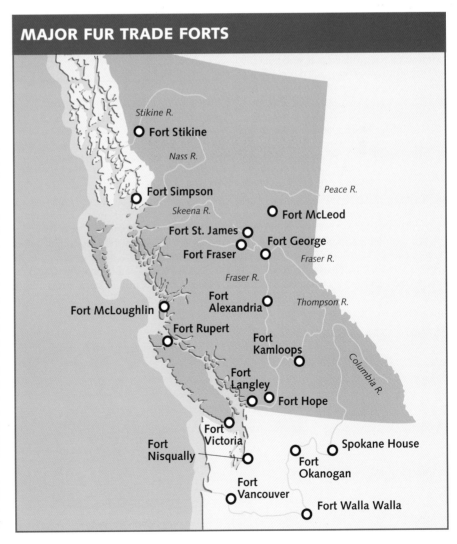

MAJOR FUR TRADE FORTS

Stikine R.
Fort Stikine
Nass R.
Fort Simpson
Skeena R.
Peace R.
Fort McLeod
Fort St. James
Fort George
Fort Fraser
Fraser R.
Fraser R.
Fort McLoughlin
Fort Alexandria
Thompson R.
Fort Rupert
Fort Kamloops
Fort Langley
Fort Hope
Columbia R.
Fort Victoria
Fort Nisqually
Spokane House
Fort Okanogan
Fort Vancouver
Fort Walla Walla

ed among themselves and were experienced negotiators who managed to establish a more or less equitable relationship with the European traders. It has also been argued that the wealth produced by the fur trade, along with the access to iron tools, contributed to a cultural flowering among coastal First Nations, as evidenced by an increase in wood carving and an elaboration of the POTLATCH. However, contact with outsiders brought tragic side effects—principally epidemic diseases, and especially SMALLPOX—that sharply reduced the aboriginal population (*see* ABORIGINAL DEMOGRAPHY).
Reading: Richard Somerset Mackie, *Trading Beyond the Mountains: The British Fur Trade on the Pacific, 1793–1843,* 1997.

FUR TRADE, MARITIME, began with the arrival of Russian traders in the Gulf of Alaska in the 1740s. The Spanish sent naval expeditions from California and Mexico to forestall the Russian advance in the 1770s, but the heyday of the trade on the BC coast dates from the publication of accounts of James COOK's 1778 visit to the coast. Cook's men had traded for SEA OTTER pelts and exchanged them in China. The first British trader to arrive was Capt James Hanna with his brig the *Sea Otter* in 1785. He traded furs in NOOTKA SOUND that fetched over $20,000 in Canton, and the rush was on. The first American in the trade was Robert GRAY, who arrived in 1789. By 1800 American traders, mainly from Boston, dominated the trade. Furs from the coast were taken to Canton and exchanged for tea, silk, porcelains and sugar. In the peak years from 1790 to 1812 there were as many as 2 dozen vessels on the coast, trading tens of thousands of pelts. Coastal FIRST NATIONS people were experienced traders who drove a hard bargain. In exchange for their furs they obtained guns, metalware, cloth and liquor. Relations between traders and aboriginals were often strained by ignorance and suspicion, and there were instances of violence on both sides. The trade expanded the wealth of the coastal people and seems to have stimulated their ceremonial and artistic lives. But it also introduced diseases such as SMALLPOX, which eventually led to drastic population decreases. By the 1820s trade was in decline and the HBC was taking over from American traders and establishing forts on the coast (*see* FUR TRADE, LAND-BASED).
Reading: James R. Gibson, *Otter Skins, Boston*

Haida canoes carrying sea otter pelts, gathering around an American trading vessel, Queen Charlotte Islands, 1791, *in an illustration by Gordon Miller.*

Ships and China Goods: The Maritime Fur Trade of the Northwest Coast, 1785–1841, 1992.

FUTURE SHOP LTD is Canada's leading chain of computer and consumer electronics stores. It was founded in VANCOUVER in 1982 by Hassan Khosrowshahi (b 1940), a member of a prominent Iranian business family who immigrated to Canada in 1981 and made a fortune in Vancouver land development. One of the richest people in BC, he is the president of Inwest Investments Ltd, the holding company for his various interests. Future Shop went public in 1993 and by 1998 had 81 stores across Canada and annual revenues of $1.76 billion. The com-

pany also owned the Computer City retail chain. An attempt to expand into the US did not meet with success, and in 1999 the company sold its money-losing American outlets.

FYLES, Tom, mountaineer (b 1887; d 1979, Vancouver). While working all his life as a mail carrier in VANCOUVER, he was the leading MOUNTAINEER in the South Coast area from WWI to the mid-1930s. He made first ascents of the Table and the North Peak of BLACK TUSK in GARIBALDI PROVINCIAL PARK; Dione, Pelops and Omega peaks in the TANTALUS RANGE; American Border Peak in the CASCADE MTS; and Widgeon Peak and Mt Judge Howay in the FRASER VALLEY, as well as several peaks at the head of BUTE INLET and up the headwaters of the LILLOOET and Toba rivers. He played a major role for many years in the BC MOUNTAINEERING CLUB. Mt Fyles near BELLA COOLA is named in his honour.

G

GABEREAU, Vicki Frances, broadcaster (b 31 May 1946, Vancouver). She joined CBC Radio in Toronto in 1976 and spent the next 21 years at CBC, taking time off in 1978 and 1982 to run unsuccessfully for mayor of Toronto disguised as Rosie the Clown. From 1981 to 1986 she hosted *Variety Tonight*, then moved back to VANCOUVER and hosted a popular afternoon radio talk show, *Gabereau*, from 1988 to 1997. When Baton Broadcasting launched a new television station in Vancouver in 1997 she was hired to host a national talk show.

GABRIOLA ISLAND, 59 km², is one of the GULF ISLANDS in GEORGIA STRAIT, opposite NANAIMO. It was visited in 1792 by the Spanish explorers ALCALA-GALIANO and VALDES, and the name apparently derives from the Spanish word for "seagull." The SNUNEYMUXW (Nanaimo) First Nation had a village here. The earliest settlers were miners from the Nanaimo coalfields (*see* COAL MINING, VANCOUVER ISLAND) who wanted land to farm. For several decades a sandstone quarry and a brickyard provided local employment. During the 1920s summer cottagers discovered the island and the permanent population (about 2,600 in 1999) still swells with seasonal visitors. An interesting landmark is the Malaspina Galleries near Descanso Bay, a wide, overhung rock ledge running 75 m along the shoreline cut into the sandstone by wave action. Silva Bay at the east end of the island is a favourite anchorage with coastal boaters.

GABRIOLA PASSAGE, between GABRIOLA and VALDES islands east of NANAIMO, is the smallest of 3 main passages leading from GEORGIA STRAIT into the calmer inner waters of the GULF ISLANDS (PORLIER PASS and ACTIVE PASS are the others). Tidal currents run up to 8 knots through the channel. Drumbeg Provincial PARK (20 ha) is on the south end of Gabriola Island; at the entrance to Degnen Bay there is a unique petroglyph etched in the rock (*see also* ROCK ART).

An illustration of the Malaspina Galleries, published in Spain in 1802.

GAGLARDI, Philip Arthur, evangelist, politician (b 13 Jan 1913, Silverdale; d 23 Sept 1995, Vancouver). Raised on a homestead near MISSION, he left home at age 14 to earn his living as a mechanic in LOGGING and construction camps. Through the influence of Jennie Sandin, whom he later married, he converted to Pentecostalism, attended bible college and in 1938 became a pastor for the Pentecostal Assemblies of Canada (*see* CONSERVATIVE PROTESTANTISM). In 1944 he became pastor at Calvary Temple in KAMLOOPS, a position he held until 1972. His work at the Temple, and his daily radio ministry, made him a local celebrity and in 1952 he was elected to the provincial legislature for the fledgling SOCIAL CREDIT PARTY. For the next 20 years he was a leading member of CABINET, often touted as a likely successor to Premier W.A.C. BENNETT.

Phil Gaglardi at the N Thompson Fall Fair, 1971. Doug Struther/Barrière and District Heritage Society

As minister of public works, and later minister of highways, from 1952 to 1968 he oversaw an ambitious program of highway building during which most of the province's major roads and bridges were completed. His aggressive energy and flamboyant style seemed to personify this expansive period of economic prosperity. As he rushed about the province checking on highway projects, he earned the nickname "Flyin' Phil" for his frequent use of government aircraft and his many speeding tickets.

After years of dodging claims of patronage by opposition MLAs, Gaglardi was forced to resign from the highways portfolio in 1968 over charges that he flew relatives on the government jet. But he remained in cabinet as minister without portfolio (1968–69) and minister of rehabilitation and social improvement (1969–72). He lost his seat in the 1972 Socred election defeat, which some people blamed on his questioning of Bennett's leadership during the campaign. Gaglardi retired to private business and resumed public life briefly as mayor of Kamloops from 1988 to 1990. *See also* ROADS AND HIGHWAYS.

GAIT, Gary and Paul, lacrosse players (b 5 Apr 1967, Victoria). Growing up in BRENTWOOD BAY the twin brothers amazed local LACROSSE fans with their combination of size, speed and deft stickhandling. They led their ESQUIMALT Legion team to 4 straight BC Junior Lacrosse League titles before winning the Canadian junior championship Minto Cup in 1988. Paul won Minto Cup MVP honours in 1985 and 1987 and Gary took the trophy in 1986. They played college field lacrosse at Syracuse, NY, and turned it into a popular spectator sport on the east coast college circuit, once attracting 23,000 fans to a game. While leading Syracuse to 3 consecutive NCAA championships Gary broke almost all US college-lacrosse scoring records. After graduation they played senior box lacrosse in Ontario; in 1996 Paul returned to BC to play with the North Shore Indians of the Western Lacrosse Assoc. Gary joined the league a year later with the Victoria Shamrocks and was Mann Cup MVP in the Shamrocks' 1997 national championship win. For winter play the brothers suited up for the professional Major Indoor Lacrosse League in the US and Gary was its MVP 1994–98. While still playing, Gary became coach of the field lacrosse team at the Univ of Maryland and Paul opened a lacrosse equipment company in Syracuse. Together again in VICTORIA in 1999 they led the Shamrocks to another Mann Cup before announcing their retirement from Canadian amateur play. They continued to win accolades and break records in the American Indoor League through the turn of the millennium. *SW*

Gary (l) and Paul Gait (r), brothers and lacrosse players, with Grant Hamilton, a fellow player, Victoria, 1997. *Arlen Redekop/Vancouver Province*

GALDIKAS, Biruté, anthropologist (b 1946 Wiesbaden, Germany). Her family was Lithuanian and she was born in occupied Germany after the war. With her parents she came to Canada in 1947, settling first in Toronto, then in Elliot Lake, ON, and VANCOUVER. After a year of studies at UBC she moved to Los Angeles in 1965. She was doing graduate studies in anthropology at UCLA when she met the renowned African anthropologist Louis Leakey, who supported her plans to make a study of orangutans in the wild. In 1971 she went to southern Borneo, where she has been closely observing these wild primates in their natural habitat ever since. Along with Dian Fossey and Jane Goodall, she is world famous as one of the 3 scientists who have pioneered the study of the great apes. She returns for a portion of every year to BC to teach at SFU.
Reading: Biruté Galdikas, *Reflections of Eden: My Years with the Orangutans of Borneo*, 1995.

Biruté Galdikas, orangutan expert, 1993.
Nick Didlick/Vancouver Sun

GALIANO, Dionisio Alcalá; *see* ALCALA-GALIANO, DIONISIO.

GALIANO ISLAND, 57 km², is the driest of the GULF ISLANDS between southern VANCOUVER ISLAND and the mainland. It is named for Dionisio ALACALA-GALIANO, a Spanish naval commander who explored the area in 1792. Evidence from shell middens at MONTAGUE HARBOUR (established as BC's first MARINE PARK in 1959) suggests that human occupation goes back at least 3,000 years. Whites began settling in the area in the 1870s, but AGRICULTURE was impeded by the lack of good farmland and a shortage of water. Small communities also formed at Retreat Cove and at the northern tip of the island (North Galiano), where a HERRING saltery once employed a number of JAPANESE workers. A large part of the long (25 km), narrow island was owned by the large FOREST PRODUCTS company MACMILLAN BLOEDEL until it sold off most of its property during the 1990s. BC FERRIES vessels travelling between TSAWWASSEN and Swartz Bay and to the southern Gulf Islands go through ACTIVE PASS at the southern end of Galiano. Its approximately 950 permanent residents have included many artists and writers, among them Jane RULE, Audrey THOMAS and Elisabeth HOPKINS.

GALLOWAY, 43 km southeast of CRANBROOK, is a LOGGING community and a station on the CPR's Crowsnest branch and Hwy 3. It was named after a place in Scotland. The Galloway Lumber Co runs a SAWMILL and pole yard here and owns other mills in the area. Two early sawmill settlements, Hanbury and Manistee, flourished close by prior to WWI, but have since disappeared. *AS*

GAMBIER ISLAND, 58.3 km², the largest island in HOWE SOUND, is named after British Admiral Lord Gambier. It is high and rugged, and dominated by a trio of mountains. Until recently, West, Centre and Long bays on the south shore were popular booming grounds (*see* LOG BOOMING) for the coastal LOGGING industry. In 1922 the ANGLICAN CHURCH established Camp Artaban in Long Bay. The island is linked to the mainland at Langdale by ferry service and there is a provincial MARINE PARK in Halkett Bay. Two tiny communities—New Brighton, the ferry terminus, and Gambier Harbour, once known as Grace Harbour—are located on the southwest part of the island. A settlement at the southeast corner formed briefly in the 1910s around Hope Point post office and school. The population of the island in 1999 was 120. *Doreen Armitage*

GAMING in BC is regulated by 3 government agencies. The BC Gaming Commission, established in 1987, manages charitable gaming. It licenses charities to conduct bingos, ticket raffles, social casinos and gaming at fairs and exhibitions. It also awards gaming revenue to eligible charitable and religious organizations. The 7-member commission reports to the minister of labour. The BC Lottery Corp, created in 1985 with headquarters in KAMLOOPS, is a CROWN CORP managing commercial gaming, including lotteries, casinos and electronic gaming. Provincial lottery sales totalled $1.26 billion in 1998–99; after expenses the province netted $449 million. It devotes 50% of the revenue from lottery ticket sales to health care programs and 50% to general revenues. The third agency, the BC Racing Commission, regulates HORSE RACING.

GANG RANCH, on the west side of the FRASER R 80 km south of WILLIAMS LAKE in CHILCOTIN country, was started in 1874 by 2 brothers, Thaddeus and Jerome Harper. In 1876–77 Thaddeus drove a herd of cattle from the Chilcotin to California via Washington state, the longest drive ever made from Canada. Eventually the ranch was taken over by British financial interests, who made extensive improvements; for a time it was the largest cattle spread in N America with more than 16,000 km² of GRASSLAND. Since 1988 it has been owned by a

Gang Ranch, 1999. Rick Blacklaws photo

Saudi Arabian sheik, Ibrahim Afandi. It is often said that the name of the ranch comes from the multi-bladed gang plow used by the Harpers, but there is also evidence that "gang" may refer to the labourers, many of them CHINESE, who helped run the operation in the early days.

GANGES, the largest community in the GULF ISLANDS, is on SALTSPRING ISLAND overlooking Ganges Harbour. It is the Gulf Islands' primary service centre and in 1999 had their only hospital, high school and courthouse. Its busy commercial centre has marinas, restaurants and stores, providing a wide range of products and services, as well as many shops featuring the work of local artists and craftspeople. Along with the village's popular Saturday market, Ganges' many shops and services have been an important centre for the thousands of TOURISTS who visit each year. The community is named for HMS *Ganges*, a British naval vessel stationed on the coast from 1857 to 1860.

GARCIA, Jesus, packer, rancher (b 1846, Mexico; d Jan 1916, Merritt). After working as a mule packer in California he arrived in BC about 1861 and began running pack trains on the CARIBOO WAGON ROAD between YALE and the CARIBOO goldfields (*see* GOLD RUSH, CARIBOO). He wintered his animals in the NICOLA Valley and in 1872 he pre-empted land at the site of what is now MERRITT. He and his wife Qwayntko (Mary), a NLAKA'PAMUX (Thompson) woman from SPUZZUM, established one of the earliest ranches in this part of the valley. *See also* CATTLE INDUSTRY.

GARDEN BAY is a small community in PENDER HARBOUR, north of SECHELT on the SUNSHINE COAST. It is named for a BC surveyor general. In 1930 the COLUMBIA COAST MISSION opened St Mary's Hospital on the waterfront; it operated until 1965, when hospital services were centralized in Sechelt, and the building later became a restaurant and inn. A MARINE PARK and a variety of services for boaters are located here.

GARDNER CANAL is a narrow, steep-sided coastal inlet extending 192 km from Otter Pass at the outer coast to deep into the COAST MTS south of KITIMAT. It is the longest of the many FJORDS indenting the coast. The canal was explored by George VANCOUVER in 1793 and named after his friend and fellow naval officer Alan Gardner. One of Vancouver's sailors described it as being "one rude mass of almost naked rocks, rising into rugged mountains more lofty than any he had before seen." The inlet was home to the Henaaksiala people, who lived at KEMANO and Kitlope. Both groups had amalgamated with the HAISLA at Kitamaat by the 1950s. The KITLOPE R empties into the top end of the inlet while Kemano, the source of HYDROELECTRIC power for the aluminum SMELTER at Kitimat, is about halfway along.

GARDOM, Garde Basil, lawyer, politician, lt gov 1995–2000 (b 17 July 1924, Banff, AB). First elected to the provincial legislature as a LIBERAL in 1966, he held his VANCOUVER constituency for the next 20 years. He was one of 3 Liberal MLAs who crossed the floor of the legislature in 1975

Garde Gardom, 1972. He was appointed lt gov of BC in 1995. Ray Allan/Vancouver Sun

to join the SOCIAL CREDIT PARTY. As a Socred he served in Bill BENNETT's cabinet as attorney general (1975–79), then minister of intergovernmental affairs (1979–86). He retired from politics in 1986 and was BC's agent general in London before being named LT GOV in 1995.

GARE, Daniel Mirl "Danny," hockey player (b 14 May 1954, Nelson). The best HOCKEY player of the 20th century to be raised in the KOOTENAY and the first British Columbian to score 50 goals in the NHL, Gare played his minor hockey in NELSON and his junior hockey for the Calgary Centennials. His rugged, combative style combined with a natural scoring touch earned him a place on the WHL all-star team in 1974. Drafted and signed by the Buffalo Sabres, he had an outstanding rookie year. He was captain of the Sabres for more than 4 years, had two 50-goal seasons with them and in 1979–80 set a long-standing team goal-scoring record of 56. Soon after appearing in the 1981 all-star game he was traded to the Detroit Red Wings but a back injury limited his play for Detroit and after a brief stint with the Edmonton Oilers he retired in 1987. He owned a restaurant in Buffalo, NY, worked in broadcasting, and later worked as an assistant coach for the Tampa Bay Lightning. *SW*

GARIBALDI was a recreational community and BC RAIL station, originally called Daisy Lk, 80 km north of VANCOUVER on the CHEAKAMUS R. Before WHISTLER was established, Garibaldi was the main access point to GARIBALDI PROVINCIAL PARK. In the 1970s residents were relocated farther north on Hwy 99 due to fears of LANDSLIDES. Daisy Lk, popular for sport FISHING and boating, formed in 1855 when one such slide blocked the Cheakamus; a BC HYDRO dam raised water levels in 1964. *AS*

GARIBALDI PROVINCIAL PARK, 1946.5 km², is a wilderness of volcanic mountains, subalpine meadows and glacial LAKES 65 km north of VANCOUVER. Mt Garibaldi (el 2,678 m) was named in 1860 for the 19th-century Italian patriot Giuseppe Garibaldi by the British naval officer G.H. RICHARDS, as the latter surveyed HOWE SOUND. Members of the SQUAMISH Nation called the peak *Chuckigh* (Cheekye), meaning "dirty snow"; it was first climbed in 1907 and became a mecca for MOUNTAINEERING enthusiasts, who lobbied for the creation of a provincial park. Established in 1920, the park has several extraordinary volcanic features, including the weathered cone of BLACK TUSK and a natural lava dam, the Barrier, created when Mt Price erupted 12,000 years ago. Garibaldi Lk formed behind the dam. Garibaldi Chalet, the first lodge in the park and the first private ski lodge in BC, opened at DIAMOND HEAD in 1946 and operated until the 1970s. The park is readily accessible from Hwy 99 between SQUAMISH and PEMBERTON. The WHISTLER and Blackcomb ski resorts are adjacent to the northwest corner of the park.

GARNER, Joe, logger, contractor (b 11 Feb 1909, Saltspring Island; d 27 Oct 1998,

A view of Garibaldi Provincial Park.
Len Mackave photo

Nanaimo). He began LOGGING for his father when he was a youngster. Later he worked as a longshoreman and construction worker and owned a fleet of float planes and helicopters. He was an entertaining storyteller with a wide knowledge of BC, and in 1980 he was ready to publish his memoirs. Garner decided that he could do the job better than any publisher (*see* BOOK PUBLISHING), so he created Cinnabar Press and released 4 books of reminiscences as well as a critique of forest management policies. *See also* FOREST POLICY.

GARRY OAK; *see* OAK.

GASTOWN was the informal name of the original settlement of VANCOUVER. It appeared in 1867

Landmark steam clock in Gastown, Vancouver.
Mike Steele photo

on the south shore of BURRARD INLET just west of Stamp's Mill (later HASTINGS MILL), when Gassy Jack DEIGHTON opened a saloon–hotel to cater to the millhands. The site was officially surveyed and christened GRANVILLE in 1870. As Vancouver expanded, Gastown became a commercial centre, then a warehouse district. By the late 1960s it had fallen on hard times; it was refurbished as a historic neighbourhood of brick streets, restaurants and shops catering to TOURISTS. Gastown was the scene on 7 Aug 1971 of the infamous "Gastown Riot," when police violently overreacted to a gathering of street people and hippies.

GAULTIER, Marie-Angele, missionary (b 9 Feb 1828, Vaudreuil, QC; d 25 May 1898, Duncan). Raised on a farm in Lower Canada (QC), she entered the congregation of the SISTERS OF ST ANN in 1849 and took the name Sister Marie-Angele. She trained as a teacher and arrived in VICTORIA in 1858 with 3 other women religious, the first Christian nuns on VANCOUVER ISLAND, to start a mission. They established the convent and school of St Ann's Academy in VICTORIA. She spent the following 40 years serving at schools and hospitals in Victoria, Vancouver, the FRASER VALLEY (ST MARY'S MISSION) and DUNCAN.

GAY AND LESBIAN RIGHTS in BC have been secured gradually and amid heated controversy, despite the fact that homosexual men and women have a continuous—if often hidden—presence in BC history. Canada's first homophile group, the Association for Social Knowledge (ASK), was formed in the Kitsilano neighbourhood of Vancouver in 1964, followed by The Gay Alliance Towards Equality (GATE) in 1971 and the Society for Education, Action, Research and Counselling on Homosexuality (SEARCH) in 1973. GATE was responsible for one of the first gay rights cases ever considered by the Supreme Court of Canada when it took

the *VANCOUVER SUN* to court over its refusal to publish an ad for its newspaper, *Gay Tide*. In 1973 GATE organized BC's first annual Gay Pride Week, which later expanded into a major cultural festival that hosts the largest annual parade in Vancouver. Pride Days later came to be celebrated in KELOWNA, NANAIMO, PRINCE GEORGE, VERNON, NELSON, Victoria and the OKANAGAN VALLEY.

In 1979 SVEND ROBINSON of Burnaby became Canada's first openly gay Member of Parliament and throughout the 1980s dozens of gay organizations sprung up in response to the special interests of their members. In 1980 the Vancouver Gay and Lesbian Community Centre (VGLCC) was founded to provide meeting space, legal and medical information and other services. In 1984 the Vancouver Lesbian Centre became the first of its kind in Canada, presaging other centres in the Lower Mainland, the Interior and the Island. Sports leagues formed for gay athletes, leading to Vancouver's selection in 1990 Vancouver to host the third International Gay Games. In the arts high-profile activists like journalist STAN PERSKY and novelists JANE RULE and ANNE CAMERON contributed to a new sense of cohesion, maturity and visibility for the gay community.

In 1981 AIDS began to make inroads in BC's gay community and AIDS Vancouver (AV) was incorporated to provide public information, offer support services and advocate to governments. AV was the first of its kind in Canada, and a template for AIDS services across the continent. Its pioneering efforts were acknowledged when Vancouver was chosen as the host of the 1996 International Conference on AIDS.

The 1990s saw increasing acceptance of homosexuality by mainstream BC society with the establishment of gay churches and gay businesses. In the 1990s there was also a steady increase in legal protections for gays and lesbians in BC. In 1992 the BC Human Rights Act was amended to include homosexuals as a group explicitly protected against discrimination. In 1996 the federal government passed legislation to make it illegal to discriminate against Canadians on the basis of sexual orientation and in 2000 the BC government prepared an omnibus bill in 2000, intended to extend the same-sex protections of the *Human Rights Act* to other provincial legislation.

GELLATLY, an AGRICULTURAL settlement 12 km southwest of KELOWNA near WESTBANK, was once a landing for PADDLEWHEEL STEAMBOATS on the west side of OKANAGAN LK. It was named after David E. Gellatly, the "Tomato King of the Okanagan," who arrived in 1893 and championed the development of market farming. *AS*

GENELLE, pop 900, is a growing residential and light industrial community 12 km south of CASTLEGAR on the west side of the COLUMBIA R. In about 1900 it was the site of a SAWMILL established by Peter Genelle to supply lumber for the Consolidated Mining and Smelting Co (now COMINCO) plant at TRAIL. It includes the area known as CHINA CREEK, a stopping place on an early wagon ROAD from Trail to ROBSON, where CHINESE miners once panned for GOLD. AS

GENERAL MOTORS PLACE is a 20,000-seat arena in downtown VANCOUVER, home to both the VANCOUVER CANUCKS hockey team and the VANCOUVER GRIZZLIES basketball team. Built at a cost of $163.5 million by ORCA BAY SPORTS AND ENTERTAINMENT, then controlled by the Griffiths family (*see* Frank GRIFFITHS), the arena opened in Sept 1995. It was purchased in 1996 by John McCaw Jr, a Seattle entrepreneur, as part of a deal in which McCaw took complete control of Orca Bay.

GENOA BAY is a small harbour on the north side of COWICHAN BAY, east of DUNCAN on southern VANCOUVER ISLAND. It was named in 1858 by Giovanni Ordano, a maritime trader and early settler, after his Italian birthplace. From the 1870s to 1925 a SAWMILL operated, cutting timber from COWICHAN LK; at one time it was the largest mill in the Cowichan Valley. A small seaside community now sits in the shadow of Mt Tzuhalem, named for a fearsome COWICHAN warrior chief, and a marina welcomes boaters.

GENOME SEQUENCE CENTRE, located in VANCOUVER at the BC Cancer Research Centre, is the first gene science program in Canada devoted to cancer research and treatment. Established in 1999 under the direction of Dr Michael SMITH, a 1993 Nobel Prize laureate, the centre is part of the Human Genome Project, a global team of scientists and research centres working to discover the location of genes and their specific roles in illness and health. *Claire Sowerbutt*

GENTILE, Charles, merchant, photographer (b 1835, Italy; d 1893, Chicago). He arrived in VICTORIA in 1862 and lived there for 4 years. Initially he operated a "fancy goods" store, then added a PHOTOGRAPHY studio. He took some of the earliest photographs of BC aboriginals, as well as of the GOLD mining camps of the Interior. He left BC for San Francisco in 1866.

GEODUCK (*Panopea abrupta*), pronounced "gooey-duck," is the largest CLAM species living on the BC coast. Individuals may grow to a weight of 5 kg and live up to 150 years. A geoduck is so large that the animal cannot retract its entire body into its shell. A large shell may be 20 cm long and the clam's neck, or siphon, may extend up to 25 cm beyond it. Geoducks are now scarce in the intertidal zone and live mainly at depths of 20–30 m, though some have been found as deep as 120 m. They are seldom harvested recreationally (*see* FISHING, SPORT) as they can bury themselves up to 75 cm deep in a mud, sand or gravel bottom. The name geoduck, or "gueduc," is said to derive from the Nisqually phrase for "dig deep." Like other filter-feeding bivalves, geoducks can become toxic to humans through HARMFUL ALGAL BLOOMS. The commercial fishery (*see* FISHING, COMMERCIAL) is regulated through licensing and quota management. In

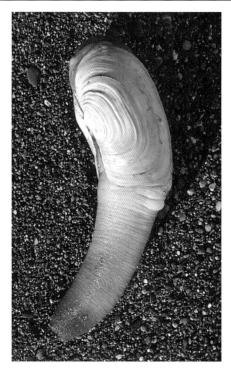

Pacific geoduck. Duane Sept photo

commercial DIVE FISHERIES, divers harvest geoducks by holding onto the exposed siphon and using a jet of pressurized water to loosen the sand or mud surrounding the shell. Geoduck landings peaked in 1987 at 5,789 tonnes, then

declined to an average of 1,800 tonnes a year during the late 1990s. This represented 30% of the provincial total landed value of all shellfish. Most geoducks are shipped live to mainland China and Hong Kong. In 1993 Fan Seafoods Ltd of COURTENAY began experimental geoduck culture, building on research and techniques pioneered in Washington state. Results from outplants of juvenile clams, or "seed," were encouraging, indicating a strong AQUACULTURE potential for the species.

GEOGRAPHY; *see* PHYSICAL GEOGRAPHY.

GEOLOGY; *see* PHYSICAL GEOGRAPHY.

GEORGE, Dan (Teswahno), Squamish chief, actor (b 24 July 1899, N Vancouver; d 12 Sept 1981, Vancouver). A stevedore and logger, he was chief of the TSLEIL WAUTUTH (known also as the Burrard band) of the SQUAMISH First Nation from 1951 to 1963. At age 60 he began acting in television, stage and feature film productions, usually portraying a wise Elder. He appeared on the CBC's *Cariboo Country* and in the original production of George RYGA's play *The Ecstasy of Rita Joe* (1967). His performance in the Hollywood film *Little Big Man* (1970) earned him an Academy Award nomination. Other film appearances included *Harry and Tonto* (1974) and *The Outlaw Josey Wales* (1975). He also wrote 2 books of prose and poetry, *My Heart Soars* (1974) and *My Spirit Soars* (1982).

Chief Dan George at a potlatch, 1966. VPL 44651

GEORGE, Gloria Mary Maureen, aboriginal activist (b 24 July 1942, Hubert). Born of DAKELH (Carrier), Lil'wat (*see* ST'AT'IMX), Cree, Welsh and French heritage, she has pursued a variety of political and social initiatives to promote understanding between aboriginal and non-aboriginal communities. She has participated in numerous federal and provincial organizations, including the BC Council for the Family, BC Rural and Remote Housing, Canadian Association in Support of the Native Peoples, Canadian Red Cross Society, Helping Spirit Lodge, Indigenous Bar Association, the John Howard Society of BC, and the United Church Land Claims Education Campaign. Among the first to join the BC Association of Non-Status Indians (BCANSI), she became its secretary-treasurer in 1971, and also served as secretary-treasurer (1972), vice-president (1974) and president (1975-76) of the Native Council of Canada (NCC), making her the first woman to head a major aboriginal political organization. She also served as commissioner for both the Canadian Human Rights Commission (1978–80) and BC Human Rights Commission (1980–82). As a mature student she attended law school at the Univ of Saskatchewan Native Law Program and graduated from UBC law school in 1989. *See also* ABORIGINAL RIGHTS.

Gloria George, 1982.

GEORGE, Ron, Wet'suwet'en Hereditary Chief (b 30 May 1945, Smithers). After working in the LOGGING and building industries, he became involved in aboriginal politics as a board member of the BC Assoc of Non-Status Indians (BCANSI) in 1970 and was founding vice-president of its successor organization, the United Native Nations (UNN), in 1976. Later elected president of the UNN (1985–91), he actively supported the establishment in BC of the National Indian Veterans Association (now the National Aboriginal Veterans Association), and

Ron George, Wet'suwet'en chief, admiring a carving with Doreen Jensen, 1990.
David Clark/Vancouver Province

helped lobby to establish both Bill C-31, which ended discrimination against aboriginal women in the *Indian Act*, and the Family Reunification Program, which assisted aboriginal people who had been "adopted out" to find their birth families. As president of the UNN he was also one of the founding members of the Vancouver Aboriginal Child and Family Services Society. From 1991 to 1994 he was president of the Native Council of Canada (NCC). *See also* ABORIGINAL RIGHTS; FIRST NATIONS; WET'SUWET'EN.

Heidi Brown

GEORGETTI, Kenneth "Ken," labour leader (b 12 May 1952, Trail). He began working at the COMINCO smelter in TRAIL in 1971, a year after graduating from high school. Trained as a pipefitter, he rose quickly through the ranks of his union, the United Steelworkers of America Local 480, to become president of the local in 1981. At the end of 1986 he was elected leader of the BC FEDERATION OF LABOUR. During 12 years as head of the federation he played an important role in rallying the LABOUR MOVEMENT around the provincial NDP, support that was crucial to NDP election victories in 1991 and 1996. Generally considered to be a pragmatic moderate within the labour movement, Georgetti left the BC Fed in 1999 to become leader of the Canadian Labour Congress. He was named to the Order of Canada in 2000.

GEORGIA, STRAIT OF (known as Georgia Strait), separates southern VANCOUVER ISLAND from the mainland coast. It extends 220 km from the SAN JUAN ISLANDS in the south to CAMPBELL RIVER in the north and is 20–40 km wide.

The water has an average depth of 155 m and a maximum depth of 420 m south of TEXADA ISLAND. The east coast is indented by a series of long, steep-walled inlets (*see* FJORDS) formed by GLACIATION, the same force that gouged out the floor of the strait millions of years ago. About 200 GULF ISLANDS are scattered through the strait, many of them inhabited and almost all frequented by boaters. Water flows into and out of the strait via JUAN DE FUCA STRAIT in the south and JOHNSTONE STRAIT in the north; numerous RIVERS and streams also flow in, most notably the silt-laden water of the FRASER R, which washes a light brown stain deep into the blue-green waters at the southeastern edge of the strait.

Inhabited for thousands of years by aboriginal people, the strait was visited by the Spanish mariner José Maria NARVAEZ in 1791, then more fully explored the following year by Dionisio ALCALA-GALIANO, Cayetano VALDES and George VANCOUVER. It was Vancouver who named the waterway after the British king, George III. Subsequent British naval surveys in the mid-19th century completed mapping the strait and many place names date from these surveys. With the beginning of a SALMON CANNING industry at the mouth of the Fraser R in the 1870s, the strait was established as the most important commercial FISHING ground in BC.

More than 70% of BC's population lives around the shores of the Strait of Georgia. A great deal of industrial activity takes place here, including 7 PULP AND/OR PAPER mills (at Campbell River, CROFTON, NANAIMO, POWELL RIVER, NEW WESTMINSTER, WOODFIBRE and PORT MELLON), 35 fish farms (*see* AQUACULTURE) and 6 deep-water ports (VANCOUVER/ROBERTS BANK, the Fraser R, Campbell River, Powell River, Nanaimo and SQUAMISH). The strait is also one of the province's main recreational areas. As a result of all this use, huge quantities of industrial and domestic waste have been emptied into the water and have seriously threatened fisheries and wildlife habitats.

The strait is the busiest overwintering spot for migrating waterfowl in Canada, with more than 130 species of waterbirds visiting the area. A wide variety of marine plant and animal species are found here, many of which have declined in number because of pollution and habitat destruction. Some types of fish—coho SALMON, LINGCOD and red snapper are notable examples—have nearly disappeared and it is not uncommon for shellfish harvesting to be interrupted by waterborne pollutants. Steps have been taken to reverse this trend, including cleanup and new technologies at pulp mills, which have significantly reduced the amount of chlorine-based (such as dioxins) and sulphur-based (which causes acid rain) emissions. There are about 30 provincial terrestrial and MARINE PARKS and ECOLOGICAL RESERVES in the strait, protecting 64 km^2 of land. In 1995 the provincial and federal governments began assembling land under the Pacific Marine Heritage Legacy agreement for an expanded network of protected areas and for a new national park in the southern Gulf Islands.

GEORGIA STRAIGHT is a news and entertainment weekly, published in VANCOUVER and distributed free through various outlets. It first appeared on 5 May 1967 as a voice of the city's "underground" community (at a cost of 10 cents) and immediately outraged conservative civic leaders with articles about sex, drugs and rock 'n' roll. Mayor Tom CAMPBELL and the police repeatedly tried to shut it down, but the paper defended itself successfully in court and survived to become a city legend. By the end of the 1990s it was still being published by its founder, Dan McLeod, but had evolved over the years into a more middle-of-the-road paper featuring entertainment news and reviews mixed with award-winning coverage of environmental, cultural and political issues. McLeod began a sister publication, the *Calgary Straight*, in 1998.

GERELA, Ted (b 13 Mar 1944, Sarrail, AB) and **Roy** (b 2 Apr 1946, Sarrail), football players. Raised in POWELL RIVER, Roy became the first British Columbian to star in the NFL and Ted was a star with the BC LIONS. After playing FOOTBALL at Washington State Univ, Ted opened his first season with the Lions in 1967 by tying the CFL record of 5 field goals in one game, a feat he accomplished 5 times in his career. He proved to be a dangerous long-range kicker and won Western Conference rookie-of-the-year honours. In his sophomore year he set a short-lived professional record of 30 field goals in one season and led the CFL with 115 points. In 1970 Ted was named to the CFL all-star team. He retired from the Lions in 1974 and settled into a business career in LANGLEY after a stint as the local GOLF pro in PORT ALBERNI. Roy, after playing college football at New Mexico State Univ, was drafted in the fourth round by the NFL Houston Oilers and signed with them in 1969. During his rookie season he equalled his brother's accomplishment of kicking 5 field goals in a game, an Oilers record. After 2 years in Houston he joined the Pittsburgh Steelers and starred as a kicker for 9 more seasons, becoming the team's career scoring leader and the longest-serving Canadian NFLer before Eddie MURRAY. Roy was named an all-pro 4 times, played in the Pro Bowl twice, won the NFL scoring title once and helped the Steelers win 3 Super Bowls (1974–75, 1979). No other Canadian has as many Super Bowl rings. He settled in the US after retiring from football.
SW

GERMANS were among the first Europeans to arrive in BC, beginning with Heinrich Zimmerman, a coxswain serving on James COOK's ship *Resolution* in 1778. Among the most prominent colonists of the FUR TRADE era was John S. HELMCKEN, a member of the first provincial LEGISLATIVE ASSEMBLY and one of the delegates who negotiated BC's entry into CONFEDERATION. Several German naturalists made visits to BC during the 19th century: the writings of Berthold Seemann, A.E. Johann and Aurel Klaus heightened Europeans' interest in BC. The Cariboo GOLD RUSH attracted many German immigrants, some to prospect for GOLD, others to work as packers, merchants and ranchers. It was German-born Frank Laumeister who imported the CAMELS that were used briefly as pack animals on the CARIBOO WAGON ROAD. At the height of the gold rush, dancing girls were brought from Berlin to work in the saloons that opened in the CARIBOO. The main centre for the German population at this time was VICTORIA, where German JEWS established a cemetery and synagogue in the 1860s. In the years leading up to WWI, one of the most prominent investors in the province was Alvo von ALVENSLEBEN. Germans were the object of suspicion during the war. German Canadians naturalized since 1902 lost the right to vote and many German-language associations and publications were suppressed and people of German origin interned. When the British passenger liner *Lusitania* was sunk in May 1915, Victoria was the scene of 2 days of anti-German rioting, including threats against Lt Gov Francis BARNARD, whose wife was German (*see* LUSITANIA RIOTS). During WWII a small number of German Canadians were again interned. In general, though, Germans integrated easily into Canadian society during peacetime. Four distinctly German settlements were established in BC. One was Edelweiss, a small community of Swiss-German mountaineers built near GOLDEN by the CPR in 1912 (*see* SWISS GUIDES). CHILLIWACK and VANDERHOOF were settled by German MENNONITES who came to BC from the prairies in 1925. Chilliwack continues to have a high concentration of German Canadians, but the German population of Vanderhoof has largely dispersed. Another group of immigrants, the Sudeten Germans, arrived at the beginning of WWII as they fled Nazi rule over their former region of Czechoslovakia; in BC they founded the community of TOMSLAKE. Following the war, restrictions on German immigration were lifted; between 1947 and 1967 about 300,000 Germans arrived in BC, making them the second-largest group of Europeans in the province after the British. It was during this period that several German businesses opened in the West End of VANCOUVER and Robson St, with its German restaurants, delicatessens and shops, became known as "Robsonstrasse." BC is home to many German associations (Vancouver's Alpen Club and the Goethe Institute, which closed in 2000, have been 2 of the most prominent), German radio and television programs and 2 German-language newspapers. In 1996 there were 498,380 people of German origin living in BC. The community has always been very diverse, including Germans from several different countries and having several different religious affiliations.
Dianne Mackay

GERMANSEN LANDING, pop 44, is a community on the Omineca R, 207 km north of FORT ST JAMES by unpaved road. It is named for James Germansen, an American prospector whose gold discovery here in 1870 helped sustain the Omineca GOLD RUSH.

GERRARD, 85 km southeast of REVELSTOKE at the south end of Trout Lk in the LARDEAU area, was the terminus of the CPR's ARROWHEAD & KOOTENAY RWY, built in 1902 into what was expected to be a rich MINING area. The Canadian Pacific Timber Co had a SAWMILL here in the 1910s. PADDLEWHEEL STEAMBOAT service was available on the lake between 1902 and 1921, but mining activity declined and the railway was abandoned in 1942. Named after G.B. Gerrard, a KASLO bank manager, the deserted townsite later became a campground in Goat Range Provincial Park.
AS

GERUSSI, Bruno, actor (b 7 May 1928, Medicine Hat, AB; d 21 Nov 1995, W Vancouver). The son of immigrant ITALIANS, he grew up in NEW WESTMINSTER, where he began acting right out of high school. From 1949 to 1954 he was one of VANCOUVER's leading stage performers. He moved east to join the Stratford

Bruno Gerussi appearing in the Beachcombers, *1980. Roy Luckow photo*

Festival in 1954, its second season, and became one of the leading Shakespearean actors of his generation. In the mid-1960s he began a second career as a radio announcer. *Words and Music*, the highly successful show he hosted for the CBC from 1969 to 1972, was the forerunner of *Morningside*. In 1972 he began the role of Nick Adonidas on the *BEACHCOMBERS* TV series. Filmed on the SUNSHINE COAST, the show ran for 19 years and was carried in 38 countries. It was one of the most popular programs ever produced by Canadian television and made Gerussi one of the country's few TV stars.

GETHING, MOUNT (el 1,827 m), 100 km west of FORT ST JOHN in the PEACE R district, and nearby Gething Crk are named after members of the Gething family. Jim Gething was a pioneer COAL mine developer in the HUDSON'S HOPE area, and his civic-minded son Quentin "King" Gething followed in his footsteps. Gething was also the name of one of the enormous construction camps that sprang up in the 1960s to build the BENNETT DAM. *AS*

GIBBS, Mifflin Wistar, merchant (b 17 Apr 1823, Philadelphia; d. 11 July 1915, Little Rock, AR). Born a free black man, he went to California during the gold rush and prospered as a merchant. He came north to VICTORIA in 1858 as part of a group of American BLACKS who were sick of racial discrimination in the US. He later wrote: "I cannot describe with what joy we hailed the opportunity to enjoy that liberty under the 'British lion' denied to us beneath the pinions of the American Eagle." After accumulating some money selling supplies to miners, he opened a general store in competition with the HBC. A spokesperson for the local black community, he helped to organize the VICTORIA PIONEER RIFLES; in 1866 he won election to the town council, on which he headed the finance committee and served as acting mayor. He moved to SALTSPRING ISLAND, where he was a pro-Confederation delegate to the YALE CONVENTION. He spent 1869–70 on the QUEEN CHARLOTTE ISLANDS overseeing the operations of a COAL mine, after which he returned to the US. Gibbs became a lawyer in Arkansas and was the first black person in the US to be elected a judge.

Mifflin Gibbs, entrepreneur. BC Archives B-01601

GIBBS, Rufus, fishing lure maker (b 1882, Vancouver; d 11 Dec 1968, Vancouver). He pioneered BC sport FISHING and the making of metal lures for western waters. Many of his designs are still in use decades after his death. Gibbs stamped his first spoons in 1908 at his Gibbs Tool and Stamping Works in VANCOUVER. He co-invented lures with Bert Clendon, notably the brass Clendon Stewart line, a favourite with both sport and commercial fishers, and produced several other equally famous lures, including Tom Mac spoons and Gibbs Mortin plugs. He was a regular participant in fishing competitions, and his 29-kg (64-lb) chinook, caught in 1964, still holds the record for the Tyee Club in CAMPBELL RIVER. He was also a 4-term president of the Vancouver Gun Club. *Rikk Taylor*

GIBSON, George S., sculptor (b 1867, Edinburgh, Scotland; d 1942, Shawnigan Lk). He and Charles MAREGA were among BC's major architectural sculptors from 1910 to 1940. After apprenticing in his native Scotland, he moved to New York in the early 1890s. He returned to Edinburgh to marry and in 1908 brought his family to NELSON. The following year the family moved to VANCOUVER and finally, in 1910, to SHAWNIGAN LK. He was employed by both Samuel MACLURE and Francis RATTENBURY. Among his major commissions were HATLEY PARK, Miraloma for W.C. NICHOL and the P.J. Angus home. For Rattenbury he supplied carved ornament for the library and the Speaker's chair in the LEGISLATIVE BUILDINGS and the heads of Neptune in carved stone for the CPR marine terminal. Throughout his career Gibson indulged a special interest in ecclesiastical work and was responsible for most of the sculptural program for Christ Church Cathedral as well as ornamentation for small Anglican mission churches across the province. *See also* ARCHITECTURE. *Martin Segger*

GIBSON, James Gordon, logger, politician (b 28 Nov 1904, Goldbottom Creek, YT; d 18 July 1986, Vancouver). Born in a log cabin in the Klondike, he was raised in VANCOUVER. After dropping out of school at age 13, he went LOGGING with his father, William F. Gibson, on the west coast of VANCOUVER ISLAND. From 1918 to the 1930s the family business was based at AHOUSAT on FLORES ISLAND, one of many hand-to-mouth logging operations on the coast. Along with logging and milling, he and his brothers diversified into commercial FISHING, coastal freighting, construction and WHALING. In 1945

Gordon Gibson, logging pioneer, known as the "Bull of the Woods," 1966. Vancouver Province

they built a large SAWMILL at TAHSIS and operated it until 1952, when they sold out to their partners, the East Asiatic Co. In 1953 Gibson won election as a LIBERAL to the provincial legislature, principally to protest government FOREST POLICY. His charges of corruption in 1955 touched off an investigation that led to the imprisonment of CABINET minister Robert Sommers (*see* SOMMERS AFFAIR). He lost his seat in a subsequent by-election, but was re-elected in N VANCOUVER in 1958 and served as MLA until retiring in 1966. Known for a hard-drinking, outspoken style and a large personal fortune, the "Bull of the Woods" was a leading member of a generation of pioneer loggers who opened up the coast.
Reading: Gordon Gibson, *Bull of the Woods*, 1980.

GIBSON, William, writer (b 17 Mar 1948, Conway, SC). He moved to Toronto when he was 18 years old to avoid the US military draft and came to VANCOUVER in 1972. After attending UBC he began writing science fiction and sold his first story in 1981. His first novel, *Neuromancer* (1985), which won several awards, introduced the grim, computer-generated world of cyberspace; this world was revisited in 2 subsequent novels, *Count Zero* (1986) and *Mona Lisa Overdrive* (1988). Other books include *Virtual Light* (1993), *Idoru* (1996) and *All Tomorrow's Parties* (1999). Gibson's books have won him an international following; he is one of the most successful science fiction writers of his generation.

GIBSON, William Wallace, aviation pioneer (b 1876, Dalmellington, Scotland; d Dec 1965, San Francisco). He grew up in Saskatchewan, where he became a blacksmith and hardware merchant and indulged an interest in building model airplanes. After going bankrupt in a failed railway construction venture, he arrived in VICTORIA in 1907 and used the proceeds from the sale of a GOLD claim to manufacture the first Canadian-built aircraft. On 8 Sept 1910, on the slopes of Mt Tolmie north of the city, he made the first manned flight in BC, all of 61 m. The plane's engine, with propellers at both ends of the crankshaft rotating in opposite directions, is in the collection of the National Aviation Museum in Ottawa. Having used up all his resources, Gibson returned to MINING, then moved to the US, where he lived the rest of his life. The 1998 film documentary *Birdman*, produced by Sask Film/Harmony Entertainment, was based on his life. *See also* AVIATION.

GIBSONS, town, pop 3,732, climbs the hillside overlooking the northern entrance to HOWE SOUND, a short ferry ride north of VANCOUVER. Part of the traditional territory of the SQUAMISH Nation, it was named for its original white settler, George Gibson, a retired British naval officer who arrived in 1886. The community was known as Gibson's Landing but in 1892, when it was time to name a post office, many residents preferred Elphinstone. Gibson, the first postmaster, liked Georgetown. The authorities decided on Howe Sound, which was changed to Gibson's Landing in 1907 and to Gibsons in 1948. A community took shape with the arrival of a group of FINNISH colonists in 1905. Jam canning was important between the world wars but later the economy came to rely on FISHING, TOURISM and the nearby pulp mill at PORT MELLON (*see also* PULP AND PAPER). Gibsons is known to television viewers around the world as the setting for the *BEACHCOMBERS*, a series filmed here from 1971 to 1991.

William Gibson on the first flight of his Gibson twinplane, Mt Tolmie, 24 Sept 1910, in a painting by Graham Wragg.

GIFFORD, a station on the BC ELECTRIC RWY CO'S INTERURBAN line 7 km northwest of ABBOTSFORD in the FRASER VALLEY, was probably named after Thomas Gifford, NEW WESTMINSTER MLA in 1910 when the railway was built. The area was previously known as Glenmore. A post office operated here from 1912 to 1948.　　　　AS

GILBERT, Jim, sport fisher, artist (b 8 Apr 1932, Victoria). He grew up around his father's marina business in BRENTWOOD BAY on VANCOUVER ISLAND, and from the age of 13 he was guiding and operating his own charter business. He attended the UNIV OF VICTORIA and UBC, where he obtained a degree in marine biology. Using his knowledge of fish attractants, he developed (with Jack Robertson) the famed "Kripple Minnow" lure for SALMON. A founding member of the Sport Fishing Institute, he is a member of the BC Sport Fishing Hall of Fame. After giving up his charter and guide business in 1972 he wrote fishing books, gave lectures and became an accomplished artist and jewellery carver. Using aboriginal themes learned from KWAKW̱A̱KA̱'WAKW artists, he carves in precious metals, wood, ivory, bone and stone. *See also* ART, NORTHWEST COAST ABORIGINAL; FISHING, SPORT.

Rikk Taylor

GILBERT, Walter Edwin, aviator (b 8 Mar 1899, Cardinal, ON; d 18 Oct 1986). He joined the Royal Flying Corps during WWI and saw action in France. Following the war he worked as a commercial pilot, mainly in northern Canada. He spent much of his career as a bush pilot along the Mackenzie R and the Arctic coast, experiences he recorded in his 1939 memoir, *Arctic Pilot*. In 1938 he moved to VANCOUVER as BC superintendent of Canadian Airways, later Canadian Pacific Air Lines. Then, in 1945, he

joined Russell BAKER to form CENTRAL BC AIRWAYS, the forerunner of PACIFIC WESTERN AIRLINES. Gilbert left CBCA in 1947. He opened a sport FISHING resort on CHILLIWACK LK, and later moved to Washington state. In 1933 he won the McKee Trophy for his contributions to Canadian AVIATION, and in 1973 he was inducted into the Canadian Aviation Hall of Fame.

GILFORD ISLAND, 388 km², is located on the Mid-Coast between northern VANCOUVER ISLAND and the mainland at the entrance to KNIGHT INLET. It is named for Richard James Meade, Viscount Gilford, a British naval officer who served on the coast from 1862 to 1864. Part of the BROUGHTON ARCHIPELAGO, Gilford Island has been inhabited for thousands of years by peoples of the KWAKW̱A̱KA̱'WAKW First Nations and their ancestors. LOGGING began in the 1880s and was still being done in the 1990s. There is a small community at Echo Bay named SIMOOM SOUND.

GILLIES BAY, on the west side of TEXADA ISLAND 18 km south of POWELL RIVER, developed as an AGRICULTURAL and LOGGING settlement in the 1910s and 1920s. Nearby iron ore deposits were identified in 1871 and worked sporadically, but not mined on a large scale until 1952 (*see* MINING). Texada Mines Ltd ran open-pit and underground operations until 1976, employing 200 people and shipping ore to Japan. By the 1990s TOURISM had become more important and the community had many retired residents. The bay is supposedly named after an unpleasant captain whose crew mutinied and tossed him overboard here.　　　　AS

GILLIS, Duncan, athlete (b 28 Dec 1882, Cape Breton, NS; d 1963, Vancouver). He was BC's first Olympic medallist and international sporting star. Gillis arrived in VANCOUVER in 1904 and found a job with the police force. He developed a reputation as an excellent athlete in various

Gibsons waterfront, the setting for the long-running television series the Beachcombers.
Keith Thirkell photo

events at track (*see* TRACK AND FIELD) meets throughout the Pacific Northwest, once defeating Native American legend Jim Thorpe in the hammer throw. In 1909 Gillis set a Canadian record for throwing the 16-pound shot. He was selected as Canada's flag-bearer at the 1912 Olympics in Stockholm, where he won a silver medal in the 16-pound hammer throw. Later he became Canadian heavyweight WRESTLING champion and nearly beat the USA's Marin Plestina for the $25,000 world championship. Gillis held a BC record for the hammer throw that stood until 1967, the year he was inducted into the BC SPORTS HALL OF FAME. *SW*

GILLNETTING; *see* FISHING, COMMERCIAL.

GINSENG, a leafy plant with gnarled roots valued for its medicinal and nutritional properties, became one of BC's most lucrative crops after it was planted for the first time at LYTTON in 1982. The industry peaked in 1994, when there were 128 growers around the South-Central Interior. They produced a crop worth about $30 million, making BC the third-largest growing area in N America after Wisconsin and Ontario. Throughout the rest of the decade, production declined as the international price of ginseng plummeted. In the late 1990s the largest BC producers were Chai-Na-Ta Corp and Imperial Ginseng Products Ltd. Most of the roots are sold in Asia, though the N American health-food market is expanding rapidly.

GINTER, Benjamin George, contractor, brewer (b 10 Feb 1923, Wolyn, Poland; d 17 July 1982, Richmond). Raised on a farm near Swan River, MB, he left home at age 14 to make his

Bottles of Uncle Ben's beer, bearing the image of Ben Ginter, the company founder, 1971. *Vancouver Province*

way as an itinerant labourer. Following WWII he began a construction company, working for contractors in western Canada. In 1949 he moved to PRINCE GEORGE, his base for the next 2 decades, where his company helped to build the Pacific Great Eastern Rwy (*see* BC RAIL) and later the ALCAN project at KITIMAT. During the 1950s Ginter made his fortune building roads for the

SOCIAL CREDIT government. He became a local tycoon, living in opulence at an impressive home on the outskirts of the city, where he raised Arabian horses. In 1962 he bought a defunct Prince George brewery and began Tartan Brewing, later Uncle Ben's Brewery, which waged a running battle with the large national breweries. His extensive business interests ran into difficulty in the mid-1970s and he fought to hold onto the remnants of his brewing and construction empire until his death. Ginter was an ambitious and often abrasive man, whose manner won him few friends, but he was one of BC's leading post-war entrepreneurs.

GISCOME, 30 km northeast of PRINCE GEORGE and 20 km southeast of GISCOME PORTAGE, was a station on the GRAND TRUNK PACIFIC RWY. A settlement formed here around the Eagle Lake SAWMILL, which was one of the largest in the Interior in the 1930s and the focus of an extensive truck LOGGING operation. It was dismantled in 1975.

GISCOME PORTAGE is just off the HART HWY, about 40 km north of PRINCE GEORGE. It connects the FRASER R to SUMMIT LK across the height of land between the Arctic and Pacific drainages. It was used by FIRST NATIONS people, who showed it in 1863 to John Robert Giscome, a BLACK prospector from Jamaica on his way to the PEACE

R. During the 1870s a wagon road was built across the portage. In 1904 Albert Huble and Edward Seebach, trappers from Ontario, opened a trading post and rebuilt the portage TRAIL. They both developed homesteads that attracted a number of other settlers. The Huble homestead later became a historic park.

GITANYOW, pop 408, is a GITKSAN village 20 km north of the SKEENA R on the STEWART–CASSIAR Hwy (*see* ROADS AND HWYS). It was formerly called Kitwancool, "people of a small village," referring to the terrible impact of disease and warfare on the population (*see also* ABORIGINAL DEMOGRAPHY). There is a fine display of TOTEM POLES here.

GITKSAN, or Gitxsan, are a FIRST NATIONS people whose territory encompasses the upper valley of the SKEENA R, from its headwaters in the mountainous Interior west to KITSELAS CANYON near TERRACE. They are closely related linguistically and culturally to their TSIMSHIAN neighbours. Gitksan means "people of the Skeena River." They divide their land into 63 "house territories," each represented by a hereditary chief. Many generations ago, according to their traditions, they lived together in a huge village, TEMLAXHAM (also known as Dimlahamid), southwest of HAZELTON. It was destroyed in an upheaval and the people dispersed. Today they number about 7,000,

Gitksan women picking berries near Hazelton, c 1900. *RBCM PN2479*

many living in 6 main communities: GITWANGAK, GITANYOW (Kitwancool), KITSEGUECLA, Gitanmaax (Hazelton), Sikokoak (GLEN VOWELL) and Anspayakws (KISPIOX). The traditional subsistence activity was FISHING for SALMON, supplemented by other fishing, hunting and gathering. Winter villages were substantial communities of CEDAR plank houses (see ARCHITECTURE, ABORIGINAL); during spring and summer the people migrated to a variety of resource sites. The POTLATCH and other ceremonies validated a complex hierarchical social system and the Gitksan achieved a superior level of artistic output, including TOTEM POLES and other elaborate carved and woven items (see ART, NORTHWEST COAST ABORIGINAL). They were active traders; it was via their neighbours that they first made contact with European trade goods. Direct contact with whites did not occur until the construction of the COLLINS OVERLAND TELEGRAPH through their territory in the 1860s. Since that time the Gitksan have become involved in LOGGING and commercial FISHING, but they have consistently resisted encroachments on their land by outsiders. Their system of 4 matrilineal clans (Frog, Wolf, Fireweed and Eagle) is maintained through the li'ligit (potlatch), in which traditional names are passed from one generation to the next, memorial "obligations" are fulfilled by heirs, and marriage and other events are put on record. In 1970 'KSAN, modelled on a 19th-century Gitksan village, was opened as a cultural centre and exhibit site in Hazelton, fostering a flourishing of traditional carving and art. Most recently the Gitksan joined the WET'SUWET'EN people of the Bulkley Valley in a land claims case that went all the way to the Supreme Court of Canada (see DELGAMUUKW CASE). See also ABORIGINAL RIGHTS.

Reading: Terry Glavin, A Death Feast in Dimlahamid, 1998.

GITLAKDAMIKS ("people of the ponds") was a NISGA'A village at the head of navigation on the NASS R, about 75 km from the mouth. Important grease TRAILS radiated from here inland. The Anglican missionary James B. McCullagh (1862–1921) established a mission nearby in 1883, calling it Aiyansh ("early leaves"), or Upper Nass. The Nisga'a divided their time between the 2 places until 1917, when the mission was flooded out and the population gathered back at Gitlakdamiks. In 1961 another flood inundated the community and it moved again, this time across the Nass to the present site of New Aiyansh (pop 800), the administrative centre of Nisga'a territory.

GITNADOIX RIVER flows 100 km from Alastair Lk north to its confluence with the SKEENA R 50 km west of TERRACE. It drains a 580 km² watershed that is protected as the Gitnadoix River Recreation Area. The name derives from a TSIMSHIAN word meaning "people of the swift water." The river is considered to be of outstanding recreational and environmental significance. It is an important SALMON river. MOUNTAIN GOATS, BEARS, trumpeter SWANS and harbour SEALS

are among the wildlife that inhabit the area. *See also* RIVERS.

GITWANGAK, pop 481, is a quiet GITKSAN village on the north side of the SKEENA R near the Hwy 37 turnoff about 75 km northeast of TERRACE. Until recently it was known as Kitwanga. Some outstanding TOTEM POLES here date from 1875; an ANGLICAN CHURCH with a detached bell tower was built in 1893. The name means "place of rabbits." There is a National Historic Site here called KITWANGA FORT. AS

GLACIATION occurred in BC over a period, known as the Pleistocene, that lasted for about 2 million years. Then, as now, the earth experienced alternating warming and cooling trends. During the colder periods, great glaciers covered BC, grinding out valleys, sculpting the mountains and bulldozing large amounts of sediment. The last major glaciation, known as the Fraser Glaciation, began about 25,000–30,000 years ago and reached its maximum extent about 14,000 years ago when the Cordilleran Ice Sheet (see CORDILLERA) covered most of BC to a thickness of 2 km. (The northeast corner of the province was covered by the separate Keewatin Ice Sheet that spread west from Hudson's Bay.) Only the highest peaks were ice-free; these are called nunataks. The QUEEN CHARLOTTE ISLANDS and VANCOUVER ISLAND may have developed their own ice caps that merged with the main ice sheet for different lengths of time. The final ice age ended quite quickly; by about 10,000 years ago the glaciers had withdrawn from the lower elevations, allowing the recolonization of BC by plants and animals. The ice was very heavy and compressed the land beneath it. When it melted, sea

Bear Glacier near Stewart.
Bernie Pawlik/Image Makers

water inundated the coastal plain, inlets and river valleys, and rose in some places at least 200 m above what it is today. Slowly the land rebounded and as it did, the sea withdrew to present levels. Remnants of the last great glaciation are visible in mountain icefields at several locations around the province, such as the Homathko Icefield near Mt WADDINGTON, the Iskut Icefield south of the lower STIKINE R, the Llewellyn Icefield west of ATLIN LK and the Columbia Icefield in the ROCKY MTS, straddling the BC–Alberta border south of Jasper. Other evidence of glaciation on the landscape includes

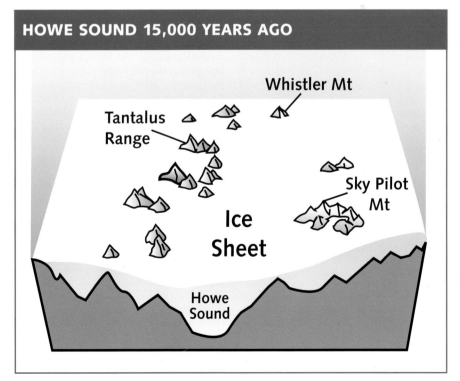

HOWE SOUND 15,000 YEARS AGO

Whistler Mt

Tantalus Range

Sky Pilot Mt

Ice Sheet

Howe Sound

7,000 feet of ice covered Howe Sound 15,000 years ago. Kim LaFave illustration

characteristic U-shaped valleys, alpine cirques, coastal FJORDS, drumlins, eskers, pothole lakes, striations on exposed bedrock and ground moraines. In the mid-15th century alpine ice-fields began advancing again during a cooling episode that has been called the Little Ice Age. This continent-wide trend lasted until about 1850, when average temperatures once again began to rise. Much more recently the warming trend has accelerated dramatically; Sentinel Glacier in GARIBALDI PROVINCIAL PARK, for example, decreased in area by 10% between 1965 and 1992. A few areas in BC are believed to have escaped the last major glaciation; these are called glacial refugia. One notable glacial refugium is at BROOKS PENINSULA PROVINCIAL PARK, on the northwestern side of Vancouver Island, where elevations above 600 m were likely untouched by glacial periods over the last 25,000 years, making possible the existence of rare species. On a much more localized scale are nunataks, which are mountain peaks that protruded above glaciers and icesheets and so were not subject to the typical alpine erosion effects of glaciers.

GLACIER HOUSE was an early hotel on the CPR mainline at the foot of the ILLECILLEWAET GLACIER near ROGERS PASS. Built on the model of a Swiss chalet, it opened as a traveller's dining room in 1886, then expanded into a full hotel. It is widely regarded as the birthplace of Canadian MOUNTAINEERING. In 1899 the CPR brought SWISS GUIDES to the hotel to lead guests to the surrounding summits. Over the years the glacier receded, and after the CONNAUGHT TUNNEL rerouted the track in 1916 the CPR closed the hotel in 1926. It was torn down in 1929, although in the 1990s a trail still led to the site.

Glacier House hotel near Rogers Pass, c 1900. UBC BC1291/44

GLACIER NATIONAL PARK, 1,350 km², was established as a national park reserve in 1886. Together with YOHO NATIONAL PARK, it was the second national park to be established after Banff. Initially the park reserve extended just 74 km² along the recently completed CPR main line across ROGERS PASS; the park now includes the original reserve and representative portions of the SELKIRK and PURCELL ranges of the COLUMBIA MTS.

A view of an arm of the Illecillewaet Glacier, Glacier National Park. E. Dafoe/© Parks Canada

The rugged, steep-sided mountains and valleys covered by glaciers enticed early railway passengers to stop and explore the landscape; the park became known as the birthplace of recreational MOUNTAINEERING in N America. In 1886 the CPR opened GLACIER HOUSE at the ILLECILLEWAET GLACIER to attract climbers to the area. By the 1990s most visitors arrived via the TRANS-CANADA HWY, which opened in 1962. *See also* PARKS, NATIONAL.

GLAVIN, Terry, writer (b 20 May 1955, England). After 15 years with the VANCOUVER SUN as a reporter and editor, he left daily journalism to write books and magazine articles and to work as a consultant on fisheries and ABORIGINAL RIGHTS issues. His first book, *A Death Feast in Dimlahamid* (1990, revised 1998), investigates the background to the famous DELGAMUUKW land claims case. *This Ragged Place: Travels Across the Landscape* (1996) is a collection of articles that was nominated for a GOV GEN'S LITERARY AWARD. Other books include *Nemiah: the Unconquered Country* (1992) and *A Voice Great Within Us* (with Charles LILLARD, 1998) about CHINOOK JARGON. The winner of several awards for magazine writing, Glavin is also the editor of the *Transmontanus* series of books about BC published by NEW STAR BOOKS.

GLEN VALLEY, 32 km east of NEW WESTMINSTER in LANGLEY municipality, is a former steamship landing on the south shore of the FRASER R and the CNR. This prosperous DAIRY FARMING district, located in a rich pocket of alluvial soil left by an age-old turn of the river, was first settled (and named) by Gilbert McKay in 1877. A regional park is located nearby. *AS*

GLEN VOWELL, pop 306, is a GITKSAN community on the SKEENA R 5 km north of HAZELTON. It was created in 1898 by members of a dozen families who had become adherents of the Salvation Army and wanted to live apart from the main community at KISPIOX. It was named for A.W. Vowell, commissioner of Indian Affairs at the time.

GLENEMMA, 24 km northwest of VERNON in the SALMON R valley, is a N OKANAGAN VALLEY farming (*see* AGRICULTURE) and ranching (*see* CATTLE INDUSTRY) settlement. Its name was to have been *Kenemma*, after the early settlers Ken and Emma Sweet, but it somehow got mangled. A nearby CNR station is called Sweetsbridge. Kenneth Sweet was the first postmaster here in 1895. *AS*

GLENORA, 400 km north of PRINCE RUPERT and 145 km west of DEASE LAKE by road, was a GOLD MINING boom town on the STIKINE R 20 km below the head of navigation at TELEGRAPH CREEK. It was the site of a customs port and HBC post during the McDame Crk and CASSIAR GOLD RUSHES of the 1870s, when thousands of miners and tonnes of freight passed through on their way to Dease Lake and points north. Glenora received another jolt of energy from 1898 to 1902 during the Klondike gold rush. In 1898 an estimated 10,000 people landed on the Glenora flats and its population grew to about 5,000. The name means "valley of gold." Glenora is located in TAHLTAN First Nation territory; SALMON fishing stations and smokehouses and a BC FOREST SERVICE campsite are nearby. The landing at Glenora, which once saw regular riverboat service from Wrangell, showed no evidence of its history by the 1990s. In the 1960s and 1970s, homesteaders were attracted to the area because of its favourable climate. Warmer and drier than areas to the east and west, Glenora supports some fruit- and vegetable-growing that otherwise would not be possible in this part of northern BC. Several homesteader families on the terraces above Glenora have carved out local businesses in TOURISM and AGRICULTURE. The HBC post, a designated heritage building, was barged upriver to TELEGRAPH CREEK, where it became a general store and lodge run by a local homesteader family.
Reading: R.M. Patterson, *Trail to the Interior*, 1993.

GLENROSA, a farming district (*see* AGRICULTURE) 14 km southwest of KELOWNA on the west side of OKANAGAN LK, is on the hillside above WESTBANK. It was first settled in the early 1900s. Curtis and Louis Hitchner established a SAWMILL and store and sold real estate here in the 1910s. They picked this name for their property after postal authorities turned down Glencoe, their first choice. *AS*

GLENROSE is an archaeological site in DELTA, on the south shore of the FRASER R opposite ANNACIS ISLAND. Excavated in the 1970s, the site revealed evidence of the oldest human occupation in the Greater VANCOUVER area, dating back at least 8,000 years. At that time the delta had not yet formed and the site was at the river's mouth. Glenrose also produced one of the oldest art objects found in BC, a 4,500-year-old figure carved from an antler and used as a tool handle. In the historic period the site was used for the Glenrose SALMON CANNERY. *See also* ARCHAEOLOGY; PREHISTORY.

GLENWOOD, a small FRASER VALLEY AGRICULTURAL settlement 28 km southeast of NEW WESTMINSTER, was named by the district's first homesteaders after Glenwood, MN. In 1899 it had a store, a church and a school. Campbell Valley regional park later occupied this area and Glenwood was absorbed by the municipality of LANGLEY. *AS*

GLYNN-WARD, Hilda (pseudonym for Mrs Hilda Williams Howard), writer (b 1887, Wales; d 1966). Educated in her native Wales, she came to Canada in 1910 and spent most of the rest of her life in the VICTORIA area. In 1920 she began writing as a freelance journalist. Her novel *The Writing on the Wall*, published in 1921 by the *VANCOUVER SUN*, was a virulently racist diatribe against Asian immigration. (It was reissued as a historical artifact in 1974 by Univ of Toronto Press.) In the apocalyptic conclusion of the novel, Glynn-Ward envisions a future war between JAPANESE and CHINESE for control of BC, while the white population dies off in a typhoid epidemic. She also wrote a travel book, *The Glamour of British Columbia* (1926).

GOAT HARBOUR, 80 km south of KITIMAT on the east side of Ursula Channel opposite Gribbell Island, was a supply centre for a dozen LOGGING camps in the 1920s. The logs were sent south to OCEAN FALLS. There is a HOT SPRINGS in the bay noted by George VANCOUVER's surveyors. A post office operated here briefly in the late 1930s. *AS*

GOAT RIVER, on the CNR line 150 km southeast of PRINCE GEORGE, was a SAWMILLING and railway settlement just west of where the Goat R joins the FRASER. There was a small GOLD MINE nearby. By 1978 only one dwelling, occupied by a CNR maintenance man, remained. *AS*

GODFREY, Albert Earl, aviator (b 27 July 1890, Killarney, MB; d 1 Jan 1982). He grew up in VANCOUVER. At age 12 he got involved in the military and became bugler for a local regiment. During WWI he was decorated for his exploits as a pilot with the Royal Flying Corps; he destroyed 17 enemy planes and 2 observation balloons. Back in Vancouver, he joined the Canadian Air Force in 1922 and took command of the base at JERICHO BEACH. From 1925 to 1944 he served in eastern Canada and abroad, aside from a brief stint at Jericho during WWII. He made history in Sept 1926, when he and James McKee made the first cross-Canada seaplane flight. In 1928 he carried the first trans-Canada air mail from Ottawa to Vancouver. He retired in 1944 as an air vice-marshal. A member of the Canadian Aviation Hall of Fame, he was awarded the McKee Trophy in honour of the 1926 flight. *See also* AVIATION.

GODFREY, David, teacher, writer (b 9 Aug 1938, Winnipeg) and **Ellen (Swartz)**, businessperson, writer (b 1942, Chicago). After attending university, David Godfrey served with CUSO in Ghana, then returned to Canada to teach literature and creative writing at Univ of Toronto and York Univ. He was a leading member of a new generation of cultural nationalists who vitalized Canadian publishing in the 1960s and 1970s. He co-founded House of Anansi Press in 1967, New Press in 1969 and Press Porcepic (later renamed Beach Holme Publishing) in 1973. Godfrey's only novel, *The New Ancestors*, won a GOV GEN'S LITERARY AWARD in 1970. In 1978 he moved to the writing department at UNIV OF VICTORIA. Since the appearance of 2 short story collections in the late 1970s, his writing has concentrated on the impact of the new electronic technologies. Ellen Godfrey was a co-founder of Press Porcepic and later undertook to operate a software firm in VICTORIA. She has written several mystery novels; her non-fiction account of the murder of VANCOUVER English professor Betty Belshaw, *By Reason of Doubt* (1982), won the prestigious Edgar Award and was made into a television movie.

GOLD mining played an all-important role in the historical development of BC and remains a significant part of the modern MINING industry in the province. In 1998 revenue from gold production totalled $304 million, making it the most valuable metallic mineral after COPPER. During the GOLD RUSH era of the 19th century, most gold was mined from surface deposits using placer methods. By 1900 placer mining had given way to lode mining, which requires extensive diggings. Gold is also produced as a by-product of other mineral production. BC is the third largest producer of gold in Canada after Ontario and Quebec.

Gold was first mined at Gold Harbour on the QUEEN CHARLOTTE ISLANDS by the HBC in 1851–52, though not in any significant quantity. More important, this discovery led to the extension of British sovereignty over the islands and the adoption of the first gold-mining regulations by the colonial government. It was the gold rushes on the FRASER R and in the CARIBOO in the late 1850s and 1860s that established gold mining as the cornerstone of the early BC economy. Subsequent rushes into the FORT STEELE (1863–66), Big Bend (1865–66), Omineca (1870–72) and CASSIAR (1870s) areas were less productive, but gold remained the most valuable mineral produced in the province until 1884. Later in the century, mining began at CAMP MCKINNEY (1887), the Bullion Pit Mine at LIKELY (1892), ATLIN (1898), HEDLEY (1899) and most significantly at the LeRoi, War Eagle and Centre Star mines near ROSSLAND, which produced about half of the gold mined in the province from 1900 to 1916. The development of industrial minerals such as copper and ZINC eclipsed the importance of precious metals after 1900, and production in BC more or less stabilized in the decade leading up to WWI. There was a second gold-mining boom during the 1930s; the most productive mines dating from this period were the BRALORNE and PIONEER mines in the BRIDGE R Valley, the Cariboo Gold Quartz Mine at WELLS and the Privateer Mine at ZEBALLOS. Lode gold production in BC peaked in 1939, then began another decline that continued to a low point in 1971. After that the sector rallied again, reaching production levels in the late 1990s that matched those of the heyday of the late 1930s. In 1999, producing mines included Blackdome near CLINTON, Table Mountain in the Cassiar area, Eskay Crk and Snip north of STEWART and Golden Bear west of DEASE LK. Gold was also produced along with other minerals at Myra Falls on VANCOUVER ISLAND and at the Mount Polley and Kemess copper mines.

GOLD BAR was a remote settlement of homesteaders, trappers and prospectors 125 km west of FORT ST JOHN where Carbon Crk joined the PEACE R. Jim Beattie established a ranch in the vicinity in 1914. The whole area disappeared beneath the waters of WILLISTON RESERVOIR in 1968. *AS*

GOLD BRIDGE, pop 68, is a hamlet at the head of CARPENTER LK, 100 km west of LILLOOET. It developed in the 1930s to service the GOLD mining communities of the BRIDGE R country. After the last mine closed in 1971 it continued to be a service centre for the area.

GOLD RIVER, village, pop 2,041, is on the west coast of VANCOUVER ISLAND, 12 km upriver from the head of MUCHALAT INLET. It began as a LOGGING community at the mouth of the river when the Tahsis Co established a camp there in 1955. Road access to CAMPBELL RIVER was complete in 1958. Gold River was incorporated at its present location on 26 Aug 1965, when it moved to make way for a pulp mill under construction on the original townsite, a joint venture of the Tahsis Co and Canadian International Paper (CIP) (*see also* PULP AND PAPER). A newsprint mill was added in 1989 but closed in 1993. The town was carefully planned with all the amenities to house the pulp workers. The mill produced pulp for world markets until its new owner, Bowater

Inc, closed it in 1999, putting the future of the community in question.

GOLD RUSH, BIG BEND, began in 1865 on the banks of the COLUMBIA R, where it reaches its northernmost point and loops back to the south. Prospectors, mainly Americans, made their way to the site by river steamer or overland from SEYMOUR ARM at the head of SHUSWAP LK. Within 2 years the gold petered out and the rush collapsed.

GOLD RUSH, CARIBOO, was an extension of the gold rush in the Fraser Canyon from 1858 to 1860 (*see* GOLD RUSH, FRASER R). As prospectors worked their way north up the Fraser R looking for gold, they entered CARIBOO country. The first major gold find occurred at HORSEFLY in the summer of 1859. Thousands of miners flooded into the area from 1860 to 1861, pressing the search north through the CARIBOO MTS from Keithley Crk on Cariboo Lk down into Antler Crk and then Williams Crk, where BARKERVILLE sprang into existence in 1862. That spring, work began on the CARIBOO WAGON ROAD, eventually linking

Main street of Barkerville, the centre of the Cariboo gold rush, early in 1868.
BC Museum of Mining

the Interior goldfields to the outside world. The rush peaked in 1863 with an estimated production of 10 tonnes of gold. Soon the surface diggings were depleted and replaced by underground shafts, a type of MINING that required more capital and labour. Well-financed companies took over the mines and hired crews at daily wages. Banks opened to value and receive the

A painting of Bill Dietz discovering gold on Williams Crk in the Cariboo, 1861. VPL 13314

A Cariboo miner sluicing for gold with a rocker box. BC Museum of Mining

gold, which was shipped to the coast by express companies using pack trains and stagecoaches. The government tried to establish an armed gold escort but it was not popular with miners and was discontinued after just 2 seasons. An estimated $30 million worth of gold came out of the Cariboo during the 1860s, but by the next decade the gold had petered out and most miners had departed.

Miners at the Neversweat Mine at Williams Crk, in the Cariboo. BC Museum of Mining

GOLD RUSH, FRASER RIVER, began in 1858 when some 25,000 to 30,000 prospectors, mainly Americans, flocked to the FRASER R. Aboriginal people had found traces of GOLD on the upper Fraser R near FORT ALEXANDRIA in 1853 and on a tributary of the THOMPSON R in 1856, and the HBC outfitted them with equipment and encouraged them to seek more. Fearing an influx of outsiders, James DOUGLAS, HBC chief factor and governor of VANCOUVER ISLAND, attempted to keep the discoveries secret but in 1857 word leaked south, touching off a stampede of gold seekers the following spring. The rush came mainly through VICTORIA, where miners arrived by steamboat, then headed across GEORGIA STRAIT and toward the mouth of the Fraser by any means possible. As they travelled upriver they discovered gold on the gravel bars in the river below HOPE and all the way up the Fraser Canyon. Attempts to improve access to the goldfields led to construction of the DOUGLAS TRAIL and, eventually, the CARIBOO WAGON ROAD. The presence of so many American miners led to skirmishes with FIRST NATIONS along the river and to the assertion of British sovereignty over the mainland, which became a separate colony on 19 Nov 1858. In 1859 prospectors worked their way along the upper Fraser as far as QUESNEL, and by 1860 the bars of the canyon were abandoned to CHINESE and aboriginal miners while the focus of the rush shifted to the CARIBOO (*see* GOLD RUSH, CARIBOO).

GOLD RUSH, OMINECA, occurred from 1870 to 1872 on the tributaries of the Omineca R in the mountainous North-Central Interior west of WILLISTON LK. Having heard exaggerated accounts of a GOLD discovery the previous year on Vital Crk east of TAKLA LK, prospectors began pouring into the area early in 1870. The rush peaked in 1871 when the main camps at GERMANSEN LANDING and Manson Crk swelled with about 1,200 miners. One of the main supply routes ran from the headwaters of the SKEENA R east via BABINE LK. What gold there was to find was gone within a couple of years and the miners drifted away.

GOLD RUSHES, a phenomenon of the mid- to late 19th century, were sudden frenetic, short-lived bursts of MINING activity. Several occurred in western N America from California (1848–49) to Alaska (1896–99), and there were others in Australia (1851, 1886), New Zealand (1857) and S Africa (1886). The stampede attracted large numbers of prospectors and an equally large number of "camp followers" who took advantage of the mining activity: merchants, packers, saloonkeepers, gamblers, dance-hall girls, prostitutes and others. Gold rush mining was placer mining; that is, it relied on surface deposits that did not require a great deal of

One of the dry goods merchants that flourished in Vancouver outfitting miners on their way to the Klondike goldfields in 1898. CVA Bu.P311

equipment, capital or know-how to exploit (*see* GOLD). Gold rush communities tended to appear almost overnight, flourish for a brief period, then decline as the surface gold played out and prospectors moved on in search of the next strike. In some cases, however, gold camps grew into permanent settlements; many an Interior community in BC owes its origins to one of the rushes.

In BC, gold was first mined at Gold Harbour on the QUEEN CHARLOTTE ISLANDS by the HBC in 1851–52, but the first real rush of gold seekers occurred in 1858 when tens of thousands of prospectors, mainly Americans, arrived in the canyon of the FRASER R (*see* GOLD RUSH, FRASER R). These newcomers worked their way north up the river and entered the CARIBOO country, where the first major gold find occurred in the summer of 1859. The search extended north and east through the CARIBOO MTS, became centred at BARKERVILLE in 1862, and peaked the following year when an estimated 10 tonnes of gold left the area (*see* GOLD RUSH, CARIBOO). Subsequent stampedes into the WILD HORSE CREEK (1863–66), Big Bend (1865–66), Omineca

TO THE DIGGINGS AND FROM THE DIGGINGS.

Engraving from the 1860s depicting the typical gold prospector, before and after. UBC BC439

(1870–72) and CASSIAR (1870s) areas (*see also* GOLD RUSH, BIG BEND; GOLD RUSH, OMINECA) were less productive than the Fraser R and Cariboo rushes, but gold remained the most valuable mineral produced in BC until 1884, by which time placer techniques had given way to lode mining. Although the dream that drove a gold rush was to "get rich quick," most prospectors returned home with empty pockets. Still, gold rushes had a profound impact on BC. The Fraser R rush led to the creation of the mainland colony of British Columbia in 1858 and much of the early government and transportation infrastructure was put in place to service and regulate the miners (*see* CARIBOO WAGON ROAD). Gold brought the first sizable number of non-aboriginal people into BC, including small but significant numbers of CHINESE and BLACKS. The mining camps provided a market for foodstuffs and supplies that expanded opportunities for farmers, ranchers, loggers, bankers and merchants. In other words, gold was the foundation on which a diversified ECONOMY began to develop. The influx of miners also led to clashes with aboriginal people that heralded a new, more antagonistic attitude to BC's indigenous people than had existed during the FUR TRADE period (*see* FIRST NATIONS; CHILCOTIN WAR).

The world's last great gold rush was to the Klondike in 1896; though these goldfields were located in the Yukon, this rush too had an important impact on BC. Many thousands of "stampeders" passed through the province on their way north, spending money on supplies, hotel rooms and steamer tickets. Businesses profited greatly from this traffic, which pulled BC out of an economic recession and fuelled a growth spurt in which VANCOUVER surpassed VICTORIA as BC's economic metropolis.

GOLDEN, town, pop 3,968, nestles in the mountains at the junction of the COLUMBIA and Kicking Horse rivers, on the TRANS-CANADA HWY east of ROGERS PASS. When the CPR arrived in 1883 the site was known as The Cache, or Kicking Horse Flats; the railway changed the name to Golden City, later simply Golden. In 1899 the CPR began bringing mountaineers from Switzerland to guide tourists (*see* SWISS GUIDES) and in 1912 it built a small village of chalets for the guides at Golden. Known as Edelweiss, the cluster of buildings is still standing. The railway has continued to play a prominent role in the community; in 1987 it built a major rail car repair shop. The town was incorporated in 1957. The FOREST INDUSTRY is the mainstay of the local economy and there are 2 silica mines (*see* MINING). The 5 nearby national PARKS attract a growing number of TOURISTS in all seasons and Kicking Horse Canyon offers some of the best whitewater river rafting in BC.

GOLDEN EARS PROVINCIAL PARK, 556 km², extends from the southern boundary of GARIBALDI PROVINCIAL PARK almost to the FRASER R, about 50 km east of VANCOUVER. Sandwiched between PITT and ALOUETTE lakes, this wilderness of mountain and valley offers a nearly complete example of COAST MTS landscape. During the 1920s it was the site of a vast RAILWAY LOGGING operation, though today the park is given over entirely to hikers, horseback riders and campers. Originally part of Garibaldi Park, it was established separately in 1967 in recognition of the high wall of mountains dividing the two. It is named for the snow-capped twin peaks of Mt Blanshard, which glisten like gold in the setting sun. *See also* PARKS, PROVINCIAL.

GOLDEN HINDE (el 2,200 m), the highest mountain on VANCOUVER ISLAND, is in STRATHCONA PROVINCIAL PARK near the centre of the island. It was known as Rooster's Comb until 1939, when it was renamed for the ship in which

A view of the Golden Hinde, the highest peak on Vancouver Island. Philip Stone photo

Francis DRAKE circumnavigated the globe. Golden Hinde was first scaled in 1914 by the survey photographer W.R. Kent and his young guide Einer Anderson. *See also* PARKS, PROVINCIAL.

GOLDSTREAM PROVINCIAL PARK straddles the Island Highway, 16 km north of VICTORIA. Established in 1958, the park celebrates a long history of use by FIRST NATIONS and local settlers, and features 3.88 km² of luxuriant forest and coastal ESTUARY habitats. The name derives from a minor GOLD RUSH in the 1860s. The Goldstream R was the site of a HYDROELECTRIC plant from 1897 to 1957. The annual fall SALMON spawning season in the river is a major attraction.

GOLF as an organized sport began in BC in 1892 with the formation of the VANCOUVER Golf Club. Soon after, the 14-hole VICTORIA Golf Club course in OAK BAY (Nov 1893) and the VGC's 9-hole course at JERICHO BEACH were constructed as official courses. When the Oak Bay course expanded in 1895 it became BC's first 18-hole course and it remains the third-oldest course in N America at its original location. The Jericho course had to be abandoned when it was damaged by a winter storm and it was not permanently re-established until 1907. Meanwhile the first course opened in the Interior at KELOWNA (1899), followed by others at TRAIL (1900) and HEDLEY (1909), and on VANCOUVER ISLAND at KOKSILAH (1908) and at COLWOOD (1913). Major prewar courses in the Vancouver area were the Vancouver Golf Club at COQUITLAM (1910) and Shaughnessy Heights (1911), where the CPR built a course to complement its upscale residential suburb. Interest in the game spread rapidly in the 1920s, including the opening of BC's first public course at HASTINGS PARK in 1924 (it closed in 1953). The most important course designer in

Pacific Northwest golf history was Arthur "Mac" Macan, a 2-time BC amateur men's champion based in Victoria whose innovative designs shaped the development of golf in BC, Washington and Oregon from the 1920s onward.

The first provincial amateur golf championships were held in 1894 for both men and women. Victoria's Harvey Combe won the BC championship 9 times between 1897 and 1909 and his wife captured the first 4 women's titles and another in 1907. Violet (Pooley) Sweeny, also from Victoria, was the best female golfer in BC pre-WWI; she has been called the finest female player never to win the national championship, though she won the Pacific Northwest Golf Assoc title 7 times and the BC Ladies Championship 9 times. British ex-patriot Vera Hutchings moved to BC in the early 1920s and captured the PNGA 5 times and the Canadian Closed title twice. She was followed by Victoria's Margaret (Sutcliffe) Todd, a 3-time BC women's champion who represented Canada internationally 4 times but made more of an impact as a teacher and administrator.

The BC Open championship was inaugurated in 1928 and first won by Davie BLACK, the pro at Shaughnessy Heights 1920–45 and 4-time winner of the Canadian PGA title. In 1927, interprovincial team competition for the Willingdon Cup began. Through 1998, BC won the trophy 20 times. Davie Black's son Ken BLACK, the top amateur player in Canada during the 1930s, became the first amateur ever to win an official PGA tournament when he captured the Vancouver Jubilee Open in 1936. The first Canadian Open west of Toronto was at Shaughnessy in 1948 and was won by Chuck Congdon from Tacoma. The last Canadian to win the Canadian Open was Victoria's Pat Fletcher in 1954. Ken Black was succeeded as BC's top amateur by 2 fellow Vancouverites. Walter McElroy won the Canadian men's tournament in 1951, twice defeated the world's top amateur, Frank Stranahan, and helped BC win 3 Willingdon Cups. Bill Mawhinney also beat Stranahan, starred in Willingdon Cup play in the early 1950s and won both the Canadian Junior (1948) and Canadian amateur (1950) titles. Over the next decade and a half, John Johnston duplicated Mawhinney's feat by winning every major city, regional and provincial title, as well as the Canadian amateur crown (1950). He also played a major role in 3 of BC's Willingdon Cup wins and took the Mexican Amateur tournament in 1967.

During the period 1965–89, Marilyn Palmer O'Connor of Kamloops tied Violet Sweeny's record of 9 BC amateur titles. O'Connor, who was the first BC-born Canadian amateur champion (1986) and national closed champion (1966), won an additional 7 provincial amateur titles in Alberta and one in Saskatchewan. Canada's Outstanding Female Amateur Golfer in 1981, she also won the PNGA title once (1973) and represented Canada in the world amateurs 5 times. Gail Hitchens also emerged during the 1960s, winning 2 Canadian junior championships, a BC

Amateur title and the province's first Women's Amateur Championship, before relocating to Ontario.

In 1996 the Northview Golf & Country Club in SURREY hosted the inaugural Greater Vancouver Open, BC's first regular stop on the N American PGA tour. BC's most successful PGA golfer was Stan LEONARD, who won 3 PGA titles, finished in the top 10 at the Masters 4 times and was the 1959 Golf Writers' Assoc player of the year. Other BC golfers who made it to the professional tour include Dave BARR, Jim Nelford, Richard ZOKOL, Ray Stewart, Dawn COE-JONES, Lisa (Young) WALTERS, Gail GRAHAM (Anderson), Jennifer Wyatt and A.J. Eathorne. Rick Gibson and Brent Franklin enjoyed success on the professional Asian and Japanese tours, while Jim Rutledge played pro in Japan and Europe. One of the high points in professional BC golf history occurred in 1994 when Barr, Stewart and Gibson combined to win the Dunhill Cup, a major team event held at St Andrew's in Scotland. The Cup-winning team was inducted into the BC SPORTS HALL OF FAME in 1999. On the amateur side, Doug ROXBURGH collected 13 BC championships to surpass Harvey Combe's old record of 9.

Dawn Coe-Jones on the LPGA tour.
Vancouver Sun

One particularly remarkable BC golfer was C. Arthur Thompson, who is recognized in the *Guinness Book of World Records* as the oldest player ever to score his age or less in an 18-hole round; in 1973, age 103, Thompson shot 103 on the Uplands course in Victoria. Another BC golfer to appear in *Guinness* is Kelly Murray, who hit one of the longest recorded drives, 682.2 m,

at FAIRMONT HOT SPRINGS in 1990. Golf continues to enjoy growing popularity; during the 1990s, 75 new courses opened around the province. The history of the sport is recorded at Vancouver's BC GOLF HOUSE, the only golf museum in western Canada.   SW

GOOD HOPE LAKE, pop 150, 628 km north of GITWANGAK (Kitwanga) on the Stewart-Cassiar Hwy (Hwy 37), is a community of KASKA people closely related to those living at LOWER POST at the confluence of the DEASE and LIARD rivers 90 km northeast. They originally moved to the area to be close to a mission and HBC trading post established nearby on McDame Crk, which was one of the major strikes during the Cassiar GOLD RUSH.   AS

GOODLOW, a pioneer farming settlement (*see* AGRICULTURE) 45 km east of FORT ST JOHN in the PEACE R district, was named after J. Good and A. Low, early homesteaders. First settled in the late 1910s, it sits in the heart of a vast natural gas producing region (*see* OIL AND GAS INDUSTRY).   AS

GOODWIN, Albert "Ginger," miner, union activist (b 10 May 1887, Treeton, England; d 27 July 1918, Comox Lk). He immigrated to Canada in 1906 to work in the Cape Breton coal mines, then moved west in 1910 to the mines at CUMBERLAND on VANCOUVER ISLAND. He was a member of the Socialist Party and a local organizer for the United Mineworkers. During the 1912–14 strike he was blacklisted and could not get work. He moved to MERRITT in 1915, then to the mines near FERNIE, then to TRAIL to work in the COMINCO smelter. He ran as a Socialist Party candidate in the 1916 provincial election and became a leader of the local LABOUR MOVEMENT. Goodwin opposed conscription but was refused exemption in 1917 despite his obvious poor health (some believe the government wished to dispose of a union troublemaker). He refused to report, and in the summer of 1918, back in Cumberland, he disappeared into the woods around Comox Lk. There he was shot to death by Special Constable Dan Campbell, who was with a PROVINCIAL POLICE detail searching for draft evaders. The shooting occurred just 6 days before the declaration of conditional amnesty for draft evaders. A grand jury later decided not to send the case to another court and Campbell went free, but many people at the time and since have raised questions about the incident. Goodwin became a martyr to anti-conscriptionists. A 24-hour work stoppage in VANCOUVER on 2 Aug 1918 to protest his death is considered Canada's first general strike. *See also* COAL MINING, VANCOUVER ISLAND.
Reading: Susan Mayse, *Ginger: The Life and Death of Albert Goodwin*, 1990.

GOOSE is a waterfowl midway in size between a DUCK and a SWAN. It is related most closely to the swan, showing a long neck and identical male and female plumages. The goose uses a short, thick bill to forage for the plant roots that provide the bulk of its diet. Geese mate for life,

Ginger Goodwin, labour martyr, Cumberland, 1911. Cumberland Museum C-110-2

nest close to water singly or in colonies, and raise their young as a couple. Males are called ganders; youngsters are known as goslings. Six species occur in BC. The most familiar is the Canada goose (*Branta canadensis*), the largest variety, familiar for its honking call and V-formation flight pattern. It is distinguishable by its black neck and head, white throat patch and grey-brown body plumage. Found widely throughout the province on its annual migration, the Canada goose has also taken up permanent residence in many urban parks, a marked change: as recently as the 1940s, it was still primarily a summer visitor. Another familiar species is the snow goose (*Chen caerulescens*), about the size of the Canada goose and brilliant white in colour with pink legs and bill and black wing tips. Snow geese breed in the summer in the Arctic, then fly south in the fall. They congregate by the thousands in WETLANDS throughout the Lower

A pair of Canada geese and their goslings.
Roy Luckow photo

Mainland but especially in the FRASER R delta and along the Serpentine R. A few are sometimes seen in the Interior. After wintering farther south, they return to BC in the spring on their way back to their Siberian breeding grounds on Wrangel Island. The brant (*Branta bernicla*) is a noisy sea goose, dark-coloured, about the size of a large duck. It used to overwinter in BC in large numbers but later became mainly a seasonal visitor; in spring about 140,000 brant pause to feed on eelgrass, ALGAE and HERRING roe along the tidal flats and sheltered beaches of the coast. In late Feb, large flocks begin arriving at the PARKSVILLE–QUALICUM area of VANCOUVER ISLAND; they stay until early May. Since 1991 the area has hosted an annual Brant Festival and in 1993 the provincial government created a 17-km-long wildlife management area along the foreshore to protect the habitat for the migrating birds.

The greater white-fronted goose (*Anser albifrons*) breeds in Alaska and the western Arctic and visits BC in spring and fall on its migrations to and from wintering grounds in the US. It keeps mainly to the coast, though it is seen occasionally in the South-Central Interior and PEACE R area. Recently the Somenos Marsh on Vancouver Island north of DUNCAN has become a popular spring stopover for birds heading north. Other species are Ross's goose (*Chen rossii*) and the emperor goose (*C. canagica*), both of which are seen only very rarely in BC.

GORDON, Jean, bowler (b 28 Aug 1951, Vancouver). One of Canada's least-known world champions, she was working as a laboratory technologist in VANCOUVER when she won the 1980 Women's World Cup of 10-pin bowling in Jakarta, Indonesia. She bowled for a 603 average over the 3-game finals. To get to Jakarta she stepped up her bowling routine of one night per week to win citywide, provincial, national and zone qualifying rounds. Gordon also qualified for the 1983 and 1987 world championships. SW

GORDON HEAD, a former farming and fruit-raising district (*see* AGRICULTURE) in what is now the northeast corner of VICTORIA, was named after Capt John Gordon, commander of the British naval vessel HMS *America* in 1845 and brother of the Earl of Aberdeen, British foreign secretary. AS

GOSDEN, Robert Raglan, labour activist (b 1882, Surrey, England; d 11 Apr 1961, Gibsons). After leaving his native England he worked at a variety of labouring jobs in a number of places. In 1910 he was in PRINCE RUPERT, where he was imprisoned during a strike, and he was arrested again in 1912 during free speech protests in San Diego, CA. He was back in BC during the bitter coal miners' strike in the NANAIMO area from 1912 to 1914 (*see* COAL MINING, VANCOUVER ISLAND) and led the Miners' Liberation League to aid imprisoned miners. A tough-minded leftist, he nonetheless went to work raising support for the LIBERAL PARTY in VANCOUVER in 1916, an involvement that implicated him in a vote-rigging scandal and two perjury trials involving the province's leading politicians. But he is most notorious for his role as "Agent 10," an RCMP informant who spied on the 1919 Western Labour Conference that led to the formation of the One Big Union. His career as a police spy was short-lived and he never again played an important role in the labour politics of the province.
Reading: Mark Leier, *Rebel Life: The Life and Times of Robert Gosden*, 1999.

GOSNELL, a tiny travellers' stop and CNR station 175 km northwest of REVELSTOKE at the confluence of the N THOMPSON and Albreda rivers, was originally Thompson Crossing. It was renamed after R.E. GOSNELL, a journalist and the first provincial librarian (1893–98) and first provincial archivist (1908–10). A Japanese internment camp (*see* JAPANESE, RELOCATION OF) was located here during WWII. AS

GOSNELL, Joseph Jr "Joe," Nisga'a leader (b 21 June 1936, New Aiyansh). A former commercial fisher, he was elected president of the NISGA'A Tribal Council in 1992 and twice won re-election. He was lead negotiator for the landmark NISGA'A TREATY, which took almost 25 years to complete. Initialled in New Aiyansh (GITLAKDAMIKS) on 4 Aug 1998, the treaty was passed by the provincial legislature on 22 Apr 1999. Gosnell's dramatic speech to the legislature on 2 Dec 1998 has been widely anthologized: "Under the treaty we will no longer be wards of the state, no longer beggars in our own lands." He is a member of the ORDER OF BC and the recipient of honorary doctorates from ROYAL ROADS UNIV and the OPEN LEARNING AGENCY. His elder brother James Gosnell (1924–88), a commercial fisher and Nisga'a chief, galvanized a generation of Nisga'a to fight for ABORIGINAL RIGHTS in the 1950s and 1960s through his involvement in the famous CALDER CASE. *Alex Rose*

Joe Gosnell, Nisga'a chief. Gary Fiegehen photo

GOSNELL, Richard Edward, journalist, public servant (b 1860, Lac Beauport, QC; d 1931). He came to BC in 1888 and worked as a reporter on the VANCOUVER *News*. He was secretary to the provincial Bureau of Information and the first provincial librarian. Later he was the first provincial archivist. In 1897 he prepared the original *BC Year Book*, an "encyclopedia of Provincial information," which became a standard source until after WWI. An influential advisor to Premier Richard MCBRIDE, he moved to eastern Canada during WWI and did not return to BC until his retirement. Gosnell, a tiny settlement and CNR station 175 km northwest of REVELSTOKE, was named for him.

GOSS, Wayne, lacrosse player (b 13 Mar 1947, New Westminster). The most complete box LACROSSE player ever to play in BC, he excelled at every aspect of the game during his 14-year career with the NEW WESTMINSTER SALMONBELLIES. A league all-star 11 times, he also was rookie of the year in 1968, MVP 4 times, playoff MVP 3 times, and Mann Cup MVP in 1981. When he retired in 1981 he held or shared 45 league records. The holder of 2 BC scoring titles, he ended his career with 812 goals and 1,852 points (the highest career total in BC lacrosse) in 465 games. Goss has been inducted into both the CANADIAN LACROSSE HALL OF FAME and the BC SPORTS HALL OF FAME. *Stan Shillington*

GOSSE, Josiah, mariner (b 1 Sept 1865, Harbour Grace, NF; d 1938, Victoria). He left home at age 13 as a sailor on a merchant ship trading from NF to Europe and the West Indies. In 1886 he sailed around Cape Horn to BURRARD INLET. He returned by rail the following year to stay. After a summer of fishing he joined the CANADIAN PACIFIC NAVIGATION CO and worked on coastal steamers. He obtained his master's ticket, becoming BC's first licensed coastal pilot, and commanded a series of vessels operating between VICTORIA and VANCOUVER and up the INSIDE PASSAGE to Alaska. Appointed a government pilot in 1903, Gosse guided vessels along the coast for the next 32 years until his retirement in 1935. His son Walter Gosse (1900–64) was also a prominent coastal pilot.

GOVERNMENT, LOCAL, provides and maintains essential services at the community level. Services include water, sewage, garbage collection, roads and sidewalks, street lighting, fire and police and may include LIBRARIES, parks and recreational facilities.

Communities are organized as either municipalities or regional districts. There are 4 types of municipalities: villages, with population under 2,500; towns, 2,501–5,000; cities, more than 5,000; and district municipalities, which are large geographic areas with low population. (Villages and towns may grow larger without altering their corporate status.) In 1998 BC had 43 cities, 53 districts, 15 towns and 40 villages. About 83% of the population lives within municipalities, though municipalities account for less than 1% of the total land area in the province. In 1998 there was also one Indian government district at SECHELT.

In the late 1960s, REGIONAL DISTRICTS were created to deliver services to the approximately 15% of the population living outside municipal areas, and to allow municipalities to provide shared services. There are 28 regional districts, ranging from the GREATER VANCOUVER REGIONAL DISTRICT (pop 2 million), to the Central Coast Regional District (pop 3,200). The largest in area is Peace River, 120,000 km².

The provincial Ministry of Municipal Affairs, Recreation and Culture is responsible for the Municipal Act, which regulates the creation and operation of local government. Municipalities are governed by mayors and elected councils. Regional district boards are partly elected, partly appointed by municipalities within the district from among their elected officers. Property taxes provide about 60% of the money local government uses to pay for its services. The rest comes from grants from other levels of government (about 10%) and special user charges.

Reading: Robert L Bish, *Local Government in British Columbia*, 2nd ed, 1990.

GOVERNMENT HOUSE; *see* CARY CASTLE.

GOVERNOR GENERAL'S LITERARY AWARDS are presented annually to writers in 6 categories (both French and English): fiction, non-fiction, poetry, translation, drama and children's literature. They are considered Canada's highest literary honour. Established by the Canadian Authors Assoc in 1937 (for the year 1936), the awards have been administered by the Canada Council since 1959. Winners receive $10,000 and a medal. See list of BC winners on p. 298.

GOWARD, Trevor, natural scientist (b 18 Oct 1952, Vancouver). While working as a naturalist in several BC PARKS, he became interested in botanical research; beginning in 1982 he devoted his career to the study of lichens. In 1986 he became curator of lichens of UBC. He has published more than 70 books and articles on the subject and is responsible for the identification of several new BC lichen species. He is also one of the founders of the Wells Gray Education Research Centre, an environmental study institute established in the early 1990s. *Dianne Mackay*

GRAHAM, Gail (Anderson), golfer (b 16 Jan, 1964, Vanderhoof). Raised in Winnipeg, she attended Lamar Univ in Texas (which also developed BC golfers Dawn COE-JONES and Jennifer Wyatt) on a GOLF scholarship and won several provincial amateur titles in Manitoba before relocating to KELOWNA, where she turned professional in the mid-1980s. She qualified for the LPGA tour in 1989. In 1997 she worked her way up to 32nd on the earnings list and won her second tournament, the Australian Ladies Masters Championship. *SW*

GRAHAM, Rodney, artist (b 1949, Matsqui). He belongs to a group of VANCOUVER conceptual artists (others are Stan DOUGLAS, Jeff WALL and Ian WALLACE) who have achieved international reputations for their film- and photo-based installations. Graham studied fine arts at UBC during 1968–72 and has been exhibiting his complex works, filled with references to intellectual and literary figures, since the late 1970s. While serious in intent, his work is often playful in presentation, causing one newspaper critic to label him "a serious goofball." Two of his recent works are *Halcion Sleep*, in which the artist films himself, dressed in pajamas and apparently on drugs, riding through the Lower Mainland in the back of a car, and *Vexation Island*, another short film in which the artist plays a desert island castaway, complete with parrot. The latter was exhibited at the 1997 Venice Biennale, and Graham's work is regularly featured in major exhibitions around the world.

GRAHAM CENTRE, on Masset Inlet in the QUEEN CHARLOTTE ISLANDS, was a hopeful Graham Island townsite promoted between 1911 and 1916 by Charlie Adam, who ran a store and post office there. Nearby Queenstown, later PORT CLEMENTS, competed more successfully for settlers; Graham Centre disappeared. Graham Island was named after Sir James Robert Graham, British politician and First Lord of the Admiralty from 1852 to 1855. *AS*

GRAHAM LANDING was an AGRICULTURAL community and former port of call for PADDLE-WHEEL STEAMBOATS 80 km north of CASTLEGAR, on the west side of the COLUMBIA R between Upper and Lower ARROW LKS. It disappeared after the KEENLEYSIDE DAM raised water levels in 1968. Settled in the 1890s, it was named after A.J. Graham, who ran a small SAWMILL here and became the first postmaster. *AS*

GRAHAME, James Allan, fur trader, chief commissioner of HBC 1874–84 (b 22 Dec 1825, Edinburgh, Scotland; d 19 June 1905, Victoria). He joined the HBC as an apprentice clerk in 1842 and arrived on the COLUMBIA R 2 years later. He rose rapidly through the ranks and was in charge of the company's Oregon affairs by 1858. In 1860 he moved to VICTORIA, where he was made a chief factor and transferred to Manitoba for several years. Back in BC in 1867, he served in the CARIBOO and in 1870 took charge of the Western Department, a job he shared with Roderick FINLAYSON, his brother-in-law. When Finlayson retired 2 years later, Grahame took sole charge; in 1874 he succeeded Donald Smith as chief commissioner of the HBC in North America, based in Winnipeg. This was a period of transition for the HBC. No longer enjoying its trading monopoly, it was adjusting to the influx of settlers into the West by becoming more of a retail operation. His superiors thought Grahame was not pursuing these new directions aggressively enough and in 1884 they asked for his resignation. He retired to Victoria. *See also* FUR TRADE, LAND-BASED.

GRAINGER, Martin Allerdale, author, lumberman, public servant (b 17 Nov 1874, London, England; d 15 Oct 1941, Vancouver). As

Martin Allerdale Grainger, 1920s.
BC Archives G-08669

GOVERNOR GENERAL'S LITERARY AWARDS

Writers associated with BC who have won awards are:

Joyce Anne MARRIOTT	poetry	1941	*Calling Adventurers!*
Emily CARR	non-fiction	1941	*Klee Wyck*
Earle BIRNEY	poetry	1942	*David, and Other Poems*
		1945	*Now Is Time*
Bruce HUTCHISON	non-fiction	1942	*The Unknown Country*
		1952	*The Incredible Canadian*
		1957	*Canada: Tomorrow's Giant*
Pierre BERTON	non-fiction	1958	*Klondike*
	non-fiction	1971	*The Last Spike*
Dorothy LIVESAY	poetry	1944	*Day and Night*
		1947	*Poems for People*
P.K. PAGE	poetry	1954	*The Metal and the Flower*
Wilfred WATSON	poetry	1955	*Friday's Child*
Malcolm LOWRY	fiction	1961	*Hear Us O Lord From Heaven Thy Dwelling Place*
Al PURDY	poetry	1965	*The Cariboo Horses*
		1986	*Collected Poems*
George WOODCOCK	non-fiction	1966	*The Crystal Spirit*
George BOWERING	poetry	1969	*Rocky Mountain Foot* and *The Gangs of Kosmos*
	fiction	1980	*Burning Water*
Dave GODFREY	fiction	1970	*The New Ancestors*
Joe ROSENBLATT	poetry	1976	*Top Soil*
Patrick LANE	poetry	1978	*Poems New and Selected*
Alice Munro	fiction	1978	*Who Do You Think You Are?*
	fiction	1986	*The Progress of Love*
Jack HODGINS	fiction	1979	*The Resurrection of Joseph Bourne*
Maria Tippett	non-fiction	1979	*Emily Carr: A Biography*
Stephen SCOBIE	poetry	1980	*McAlmon's Chinese Opera*
Phyllis WEBB	poetry	1982	*The Vision Tree*
John MacLachlan GRAY	drama	1982	*Billy Bishop Goes to War*
Fred WAH	poetry	1985	*Waiting for Saskatchewan*
Kim LaFave	children's illustration	1988	*Amos's Sweater*
Joan MacLeod	drama	1991	*Amigo's Blue Guitar*
Robert HUNTER (and Robert Calihoo)	non-fiction	1991	*Occupied Canada*
Sarah Ellis	children's writing	1991	*Pick-up Sticks*
Lorna CROZIER	poetry	1992	*Inventing the Hawk*
Ron Lightburn	children's illustration	1992	*Waiting for the Whales*
Guillermo Verdecchia	drama	1993	*Fronteras Americanas*
Morris PANYCH	drama	1994	*The Ends of the Earth*
Kit PEARSON	children's writing	1997	*Awake and Dreaming*
Jan Zwicky	poetry	1999	*Songs for Relinquishing the Earth*

an infant he moved to Australia when his father was appointed a colonial official. He then returned to England to attend Cambridge Univ, where he obtained a BA in 1896. He passed through BC on his way to the Klondike, and later returned after serving in the Boer War. After several years' placer mining around ATLIN and DEASE LAKE, he moved south and worked as a logger in the MINSTREL ISLAND area. When his wife-to-be, Mabel Higgs, went to London, he followed her there; in 1908 he published the classic novel about his LOGGING experiences, *Woodsmen of the West*, to finance his marriage and trip back to BC. The book is considered one of the best novels

about the province ever published. In 1910 he served as secretary to the Royal Commission on forestry (*see* FOREST POLICY) and was instrumental in having H.R. MACMILLAN appointed chief forester in 1912. When MacMillan took on the task of timber commissioner in 1915, Grainger served as acting chief forester, and he assumed the position permanently the next year. In 1920 he resigned and entered the timber trade, forming a management company with Aird Flavelle and Frank Pendleton. He spent much of the late 1920s and 1930s travelling in the area now known as MANNING PROVINCIAL PARK, and writing at a cabin he built near PRINCETON. His written

work during this period was published posthumously under the title *Riding the Skyline*. One of his chief interests during his later years was to lobby for the creation of Manning Park. Grainger earned a reputation as a brilliant, eccentric visionary.

Ken Drushka

GRAND FORKS, city, pop 3,994, is named for its location in a broad valley at the confluence of the Granby and KETTLE rivers in the BOUNDARY DISTRICT, about 100 km west of CASTLEGAR. Aboriginal people inhabited the site for at least 9,000 years. The pace of settlement quickened in 1895 with completion of wagon roads (*see*

TRAILS) north from Marcus, WA, and east from PENTICTON. The construction of the COLUMBIA & WESTERN RWY from Castlegar through Grand Forks to MIDWAY in 1898–99, promising a steady supply of smelting COAL from the Crowsnest fields, prompted the Granby Mining & Smelting Co to construct a smelter at Grand Forks to treat copper ore from PHOENIX. In Aug 1900, 3 years after incorporation of the city, the smelter was blown in. Successive improvements to the smelter, which operated until 1919, made it the largest COPPER smelter in the British Empire and the second largest in the world. In 1909 DOUKHOBORS from the prairies moved to an area known as W Grand Forks, joining earlier settlers who were engaged in fruit growing and mixed farming (see AGRICULTURE; TREE FRUITS). In the early 1990s it was the fastest growing community in the KOOTENAY–Boundary area.

GRAND HAVEN, 4 km west of FORT ST JOHN, was a pioneer farming settlement (see AGRICULTURE) in the PEACE R district, site of an early school and outpost hospital in the 1920s. The area became increasingly residential through the 1990s and served as a base for a number of OIL AND GAS INDUSTRY-related businesses. It was named after Grand Haven, N Dakota, home of Thor Thorsen, a storekeeper.   AS

GRAND TRUNK PACIFIC RAILWAY (GTP) was incorporated by the Grand Trunk Rwy in 1903 to build a rail line across western Canada. The line was to run from Winnipeg via Edmonton, the YELLOWHEAD PASS and PRINCE GEORGE to PRINCE RUPERT, the western terminus. Construction began at the eastern end in 1905 and at the Prince Rupert end in 1908. At any one time as many as 6,000 men worked on the line as it made its way across the mountainous Interior. One of 2 transcontinental lines built during an orgy of pre-war railway construction, it was plagued by financial difficulties and construction delays and was completed largely through the determination of C.M. HAYS, president of Grand Trunk Rwy, who died on the

Titanic before the project was finished. The last spike was finally driven 7 Apr 1914 at Finmoore, near FORT FRASER, 665 km east of Prince Rupert. Within a few years the line faced bankruptcy; the federal government nationalized it in 1919, joining it with the rival CANADIAN NORTHERN RWY line to form CNR.
Reading: Frank Leonard, *A Thousand Blunders: The Grand Trunk Pacific Railway and Northern British Columbia*, 1996.

GRANISLE, village, pop 446, is on the west side of BABINE LK, about 55 km east of SMITHERS. Established in 1965 with the opening of an open-pit COPPER mine on nearby Sterret Island, it got a further boost in 1972 when Noranda Mines opened the Bell copper mine. In 1981 Noranda took over the original mine as well. The economy, which is totally dependent on MINING, suffered a severe shock in 1992 when Noranda closed the Bell mine, putting the future of the community in question.

GRANITE BAY is an almost landlocked basin on the northwest corner of QUADRA ISLAND, north of CAMPBELL RIVER. LOGGING began at the end of the 19th century and the camp was one of the major coastal operations of the BC MILLS TIMBER & TRADING CO. Logging attracted a number of Finnish settlers, several of whom moved down from the colony at SOINTULA after it collapsed. From 1910 to 1925 the Lucky Jim Mine was in operation not far away. A school and a well-known coastal hotel operated here for several years.

GRANITE CITY is an abandoned MINING town 19 km west of PRINCETON on Granite Crk. In July 1885 a cowboy named John Chance found GOLD nuggets in the creek and within 3 months a town sprang up. For a short time it was the third-largest community in BC, but when it became clear that gold was not abundant, the hotels and saloons closed and the miners drifted away. The town survived as a tiny service centre for local mining camps until 1907, when fire destroyed most of the buildings.

GRANT, Dorothy, fashion designer (b Mar 1955, Hydaburg, AK). A member of the Kaigani HAIDA nation with roots in the QUEEN CHARLOTTE ISLANDS, she grew up in Ketchikan, AK, and began making button blankets in the 1970s under the tutelage of her grandmother, Florence DAVIDSON. In 1986 she began designing clothing; she soon emerged as Canada's leading aboriginal fashion designer. Designs and materials of her clothing, from casual wear to high fashion, reflect her Haida background. She opened a retail store in VANCOUVER in 1994, and museums and art galleries around the world have collected her work. In 1999 she received an Aboriginal Achievement Award and she holds an honorary degree from UNBC.

Dorothy Grant, Haida designer.

GRANT, Maria Pollard, suffrage activist (b Quebec City). Dedicated to securing the vote for BC women, she circulated the first petition for the franchise in 1885 on behalf of the Women's Christian Temperance Union and almost every year thereafter presented a petition or led a delegation to the legislature. Elected to the VICTORIA school board in 1895, she was the first female school trustee in BC. In 1910 she was a founding member of the Political Equality League, formed to lobby for WOMEN'S SUFFRAGE. Once the vote was secured in 1917, she became more involved in religion and was a minister in the Unity Church.

GRANT, Walter Colquhoun, pioneer settler, founder of Sooke (b 27 May 1822, Edinburgh, Scotland; d 27 Aug 1861, India). In 1848 he left the British Army and purchased 80 ha of land near FORT VICTORIA from the HBC. He agreed to establish settlers on the land and the HBC hired him as a surveyor to make maps of VANCOUVER ISLAND. In Aug 1849 he arrived at Fort Victoria to join the 8 colonists who had preceded him. They began clearing a farm on the shores of Sooke Basin about 40 km from the fort, and in 1850 Grant installed a SAWMILL to produce lumber. He resigned from his surveying job to devote all his

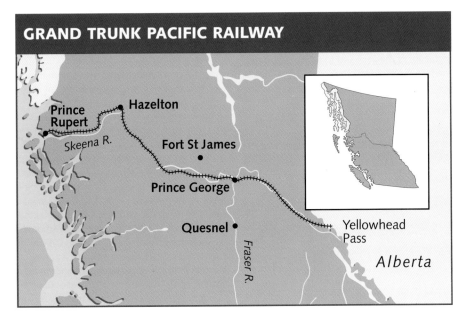
GRAND TRUNK PACIFIC RAILWAY

Prince Rupert · Hazelton · Skeena R. · Fort St James · Prince George · Quesnel · Fraser R. · Yellowhead Pass · Alberta

energy to the settlement scheme, but when his money ran low he went to Oregon to prospect for gold. In 1853 he sold his property at SOOKE and left the island for good. He did not get on well with the HBC and was not an effective colonizer, but the Scottish settlers he brought to the island were the earliest white inhabitants independent of the HBC. He is also credited with introducing broom to the Island. Grant returned to the British Army and was serving in India at his death.

GRANT, William, sea captain (b 22 June 1835, Grantville, NS; d 1916, Victoria). He went to sea at age 16 and 6 years later was captain of his own vessel. In 1873 he married a young school-teacher, Helen Smith (1853–1943), and together they embarked on a life at sea that took them around the world on many adventurous voyages. In 1886 they settled permanently in VICTORIA, where Grant became involved in the FUR SEAL industry. He was a founding member of the Victoria Sealing Co, a merger of most of the major shipowners, and was also prominent in the Pacific Whaling Co with G.W. Sprott BALCOM. Helen assisted her husband in the business as well as serving on the Victoria school board and being active in the Women's Christian Temperance Union and many other women's organizations.

GRANTHAM was an early VANCOUVER ISLAND farming community (*see* AGRICULTURE) 10 km north of COURTENAY on Portuguese Crk. Tom Beech settled in the area in 1862. The post office was named in 1889 after a local DAIRY FARMING family; GRANTHAMS LANDING on the SUNSHINE COAST is named after the same family. *AS*

GRANTHAMS LANDING, 35 km northwest of VANCOUVER, is a small residential and recreational community and former steamship stop on the west shore of HOWE SOUND between GIBSONS and the ferry terminal at Langdale. Frederick C. Grantham, a Vancouver lime-juice maker, bought land here in 1909; he then subdivided it, put in roads, sidewalks, water lines and a wharf and marketed his property as the Howe Sound Beach resort. *AS*

GRANVILLE, the original name for VANCOUVER, was a tiny LOGGING community on the south shore of BURRARD INLET. A townsite was surveyed

Granville, as it looked in the early 1880s. CVA Dist.P30

in 1870 next door to the HASTINGS MILL sawmill and named for Lord Granville, the colonial secretary, though locals continued to use its informal name, GASTOWN. In 1885 the CPR announced that Granville would be the western terminus of the transcontinental railway. The next year the burgeoning community was incorporated as the City of Vancouver.

GRANVILLE ISLAND is a 17-ha island in FALSE CRK in VANCOUVER, beneath the Granville St Bridge. Originally a large sandbar used by the SQUAMISH Nation for fishing, the island was created in 1916 when dredges cleared the shipping channel and greatly expanded the size of the sandbar. It was already joined to the south shore by a narrow bridge (erected in 1889) and it

Sailboats at Granville Island. David Cooper/CMHC

quickly attracted a variety of large industries. By the mid-1920s the island, owned by the government of Canada, was one of the city's busiest industrial sites. Its character changed dramatically during the 1970s, when the city began to develop the surrounding False Crk area and the federal government invested $25 million in the project. The objective was to keep the industrial ambience of the area, and to add a large public market, shops, artists' studios, theatres, restau-

rants, parks and marinas. Granville Island is one of the success stories of urban renewal: by the 1990s it was attracting more than 6 million visitors a year.

GRANVILLE ISLAND MUSEUMS is a complex of 3 museums (sport FISHING, model ships and model trains) in one building on GRANVILLE ISLAND in VANCOUVER. It opened in 1997 and is owned by John Keith-King, an architect and passionate fisher who operated the Maritime Market and the Granville Island Marina and Boatyard from 1978 to 1998. The Sport Fishing Museum highlights the BC sport fishing industry. It contains an extensive BC and international collection of historic and contemporary artifacts, artwork and fishing memorabilia for both saltwater and freshwater fishing. It also houses the largest collection of Hardy fishing reels on public display in the world. The Model Ships Museum contains many large-scale models of BC-made tugs (*see* TOWBOATING), fish boats and other coastal working vessels, as well as of famous warships (including an 11-m version of HMS *Hood*, at one time the largest battleship in the world) and a collection of model submarines. The Model Trains Museum presents the largest international collection of model and toy trains on public display in the world.

GRASMERE, pop 147, 70 km southeast of CRANBROOK near the Montana border, is a small LOGGING and ranching (*see* CATTLE INDUSTRY) community in the E KOOTENAY. Originally called McGuire after an early settler, it was renamed in 1922 from choices submitted by local schoolchildren. The Tobacco Plains KTUNAXA (Kutenai) reserve, so named because tobacco was grown in the area for ceremonial use, is nearby, as was Flagstone, a former settlement on the CROWS NEST SOUTHERN RWY. The town is also close to KOOCANUSA LK and the site of the Rock Crk Lumber Co SAWMILL. *AS*

GRASSLANDS large and small occur throughout BC where conditions allow, but primarily in the dry valleys and adjacent plateaus of the southern Interior, including the KETTLE, OKANAGAN, SIMILKAMEEN, THOMPSON, NICOLA, FRASER and CHILCOTIN river valleys, with generally smaller grasslands in the KOOTENAY and COLUMBIA river valleys of southeast BC. They are characterized by a relative absence of trees and an abundance of various grasses. Grasslands occur where summers are hot and dry and winters are cold with minimal precipitation. The grasslands of the southern Interior are dominated by bunchgrasses. At the lowest elevations of the Thompson and Okanagan valleys, sagebrush and bluebunch wheatgrass predominate. A little higher, in the Nicola Valley for example, Sandberg bluegrass, common rabbitbrush, junegrass and prairie sagewort are more common. In the moister upper grasslands, bluebunch wheatgrass and a variety of fescues occur. Beginning in Mar and lasting through June, grasslands may be dominated by a burst of many species of WILDFLOWERS. Patches of grassland can be found in northern BC, usually on south-facing slopes, and on the coast, where meadows associated with Garry OAK woodlands are among the most endangered ecosystems in Canada. Much of BC's original grassland cover has disappeared due to the over-grazing of livestock and other agricultural uses, and to urban development.

GRASSY PLAINS, 30 km south of BURNS LAKE on the south side of FRANÇOIS LK, is a LOGGING, AGRICULTURAL and ranching (*see* CATTLE INDUSTRY) community first settled in 1905 by farmers from BELLA COOLA and HAZELTON. The area is strongly influenced by the DAKELH (Carrier) First Nations and a number of CHESLAT-TA people live on a nearby reserve. MENNONITES moved into the region about 1940.   AS

GRAUER, Albert Edward "Dal," hydro executive (b 21 Jan 1906, Sea Island; d 28 July 1961, Vancouver). His parents Jacob and Marie Grauer were pioneer settlers on SEA ISLAND. After graduating from UBC he won a Rhodes scholarship and took a BA in jurisprudence at Oxford.

Dal Grauer, president of BC Electric Railway Co 1946–61.

He completed his studies with a PhD in economics from the Univ of California. Grauer belonged to Canada's Olympic LACROSSE team in 1928. He was called to the bar in VANCOUVER in 1930 and articled, but then decided to teach economics at the Univ of Toronto, where he became head of the Department of Social Sciences. He returned to BC in 1939 as general secretary of BC ELECTRIC RWY CO; in 1946 he became president and reigned over a period of dynamic expansion of HYDROELECTRICITY. He also served as chair of Vancouver General Hospital, president of the VANCOUVER SYMPHONY ORCHESTRA and chancellor of UBC in 1957. Grauer died of leukemia at age 55. The provin-

cial government nationalized BC Electric to create BC HYDRO on the day of his funeral.

GRAY, John Hamilton, politician, judge (b 1814, St George, Bermuda; d 5 June 1889, Victoria). He was a New Brunswick delegate to both the Charlottetown and Quebec conferences that led to CONFEDERATION. As a reward, Prime Minister John A. Macdonald appointed him to the BC Supreme Court in 1873. Gray came west reluctantly but he served with distinction. As a member of the 1885 Royal Commission on Chinese Immigration he praised the industriousness of the CHINESE and pointed out their importance to the economic development of the province, though he did not go so far as to acknowledge their equality with white residents. He is the only "Father of Confederation" to be buried west of Ontario.

GRAY, John MacLachlan, writer, musician (b 26 Sept 1946, Ottawa). Raised in Truro, NS, he came to VANCOUVER to study THEATRE at UBC and helped found TAMAHNOUS THEATRE. He has written screenplays, drama and a novel, *Dazzled* (1984), but he is best known for his musicals, which include *18 Wheels* (1976), about trucking; *Billy Bishop Goes to War* (1978), about the WWI flying ace; *Rock and Roll* (1982), based on his own experience in a teenage rock band; *Health, The Musical* (1989), about health issues; and *Amelia* (1993), about the American aviatrix Amelia Earhart. *Billy Bishop* won a GOV GEN'S LITERARY AWARD for drama in 1982 and enjoyed a brief run on Broadway in 1980. It was remounted for a Canadian tour in 1998 with the original cast, Gray and the actor Eric Peterson. An outspoken nationalist, Gray regularly contributes his deft satire to magazines and CBC television and writes a regular column in the *VANCOUVER SUN*. His book *Lost in North America* (1995), was a witty essay on Canadian identity. He was named to the Order of Canada in 2000.

GRAY, Robert, trader (b 10 May 1755, RI; d 1806 at sea). During 1788–90 he commanded one of the ships in the first American expedition to trade SEA OTTER pelts on the Northwest Coast. He sailed the length of the coast and proved the insularity of the QUEEN CHARLOTTE ISLANDS. He then took the *Columbia Rediviva* to China and back to Boston, making it the first American ship to sail around the world. On his second trading expedition, Gray wintered on MEARES ISLAND at FORT DEFIANCE. In the spring of 1792 he suspected the NUU-CHAH-NULTH people at CLAYOQUOT SOUND of plotting against him and ruthlessly burned their village at Opitsat. He sailed south, crossed the bar on 11 May and entered the COLUMBIA R, which he named after his ship. He returned to Boston via China, and spent the rest of his career sailing the east coast.

GRAY CREEK, pop 150, is a community on the east side of KOOTENAY LK, 65 km north of CRESTON. It was the site of considerable orchard development during 1908–13 (*see* TREE FRUITS) and it served as the eastern terminus of the Kootenay Lk ferry from 1931 to 1947. The wreck of the *CITY*

OF AINSWORTH, a sternwheeler that foundered in 1898, was located offshore in 1990 and later became a provincial heritage site.

GREASE TRAILS; *see* TRAILS.

GREAT CENTRAL LAKE, 53.76 km², is a deep, narrow, sinuous lake surrounded by mountains northwest of PORT ALBERNI on VANCOUVER ISLAND. It drains via the Stamp and SOMASS rivers into the top of ALBERNI INLET. The lake is part of the traditional territory of the Opetchesaht Nation of the NUU-CHAH-NULTH, and the area is sparsely populated. LOGGING began in the 1860s to supply SAWMILLS at Port Alberni, then expanded dramatically in the 1920s with the arrival of a branch line of the ESQUIMALT & NANAIMO RWY. BLOEDEL, STEWART & WELCH ran a sawmill and large logging camp at the lake from 1926 to 1952. DELLA FALLS, the highest WATERFALL in Canada, is accessible by trail along Drinkwater Crk from the head of the lake. Great Central Lk and its outflow rivers are noted for sockeye, coho and chinook SALMON. The Robertson Creek FISH HATCHERY opened near the outlet in 1959 and produces millions of salmon smolts annually. In the same year, BC HYDRO opened a generating station nearby to provide power to the Port Alberni forestry complex. *See also* LAKES.

GREAT NORTHERN RAILWAY (GNR) was the creation of James Jerome Hill, a Canadian-born entrepreneur who transformed a small Minnesota rail line into a transcontinental giant. After his main line was built west across the US to Seattle (the last spike was driven in 1893), Hill carried on a fierce rivalry with the CPR by extending lines north into BC. A GNR subsidiary, the NEW WESTMINSTER SOUTHERN RWY, opened in 1891 between Blaine, WA, and NEW WESTMINSTER and in 1904 extended into VANCOUVER via another subsidiary, the Vancouver, Westminster & Yukon (VW&Y). The GN station was originally on Pender St in CHINATOWN, Vancouver; in 1917 it moved to the east end of FALSE CREEK beside the CNR station (now Pacific Central Station), where it stood until 1965. Meanwhile, in 1895 Hill financed the KASLO & SLOCAN RWY, which he ran through 1910, and built several lines into the KOOTENAY district in an attempt to divert traffic to the US. The GNR also owned the VICTORIA & SIDNEY RWY on VANCOUVER ISLAND from 1901 to 1919. In 1909 the GNR began using a new route into Vancouver via WHITE ROCK, replacing the original VW&Y line. Following WWI the GNR began to abandon much of its BC trackage and eventually concentrated on its Vancouver–Seattle run. In 1947 it was the first railway in BC to introduce diesel power on its passenger trains. Three years later it introduced a new thrice-daily service to Seattle, The International, which was popular with travellers until the opening of the I-5 highway. The International was discontinued in 1971, by which time the GNR had merged with other lines to become the Burlington Northern. Passenger service was later resumed on the route by Amtrak.

G

The Great Northern Rwy arrives at Hedley, Dec 1909. BC Archives A-08679

GREAT SAYWARD FIRE burned out of control on VANCOUVER ISLAND for 6 weeks in July–Aug 1938. It began 5 July in tinder-dry conditions when sparks from a train ignited a pile of logs at a LOGGING camp operated by BLOEDEL, STEWART & WELCH northwest of CAMPBELL RIVER. As the blaze grew, all available young men in the district and 211 unemployed men brought in from VANCOUVER were put to work trying to stop it. Naval vessels waited off Campbell River and prepared to evacuate the residents, but the fire skirted the community and headed south toward COURTENAY. Before it died away, as it approached the FORBIDDEN PLATEAU area, the fire burned 300 km² of terrain and spewed smoke and ash as far south as Seattle. A massive tree-planting project took place in the burned area. *See also* DISASTERS; FOREST FIRES.

Burned-out area in the wake of the Great Sayward Fire, 1938. BC Archives NA-06497

GREATER VANCOUVER REGIONAL DISTRICT (GVRD) is one of 29 regional governments created in 1967 to coordinate local services to Lower Mainland municipalities. It now encompasses 20 municipalities and 2 electoral districts with a total population of 2 million and a total area of 2,820 km². The GVRD includes ANMORE, BELCARRA, BURNABY, COQUITLAM, DELTA, LANGLEY city and district, LIONS BAY, MAPLE RIDGE, NEW WESTMINSTER, NORTH VANCOUVER city and district, PITT MEADOWS, PORT COQUITLAM, PORT MOODY, RICHMOND, SURREY, VANCOUVER, WEST VANCOUVER and WHITE ROCK. Its responsibilities include transportation and land use management, solid waste and air quality management, regional parks, regional housing, drinking water quality and distribution, collection and treatment of waste water, and the 911 emergency phone system. The board of directors consists of representatives from each of the elected local councils; the electoral districts elect their directors sepa-

rately. In 1999 the GVRD operating budget was $354.6 million.

GREBE is a tailless water bird that breeds on Interior LAKES and mostly winters on the coast. It is highly adapted to swimming and diving in search of food, principally fish and INSECTS. Its wings are small and it uses mainly its legs and feet for underwater propulsion. Grebes appear clumsy on land. They build floating nests on the surfaces of freshwater ponds and lakes. Many species engage in excited, noisy mating rituals, most notably "running" upright in pairs across the water. The young often ride on their parents' backs, tucked safely among the feathers. Of about 20 species worldwide, 6 occur in BC. The pied-billed grebe (*Podilymbus podiceps*), found most often on inland marshes, is recognized in summer by the black ring around its bill. It is a squat, brown bird with a stubby beak and a short neck, quite different in appearance from the other species. The horned grebe (*Podiceps auritus*) has a small, rust-coloured body and golden "horns" on a black face in summer. In winter it

Red-necked grebe. R. Wayne Campbell photo

is white and black. The red-necked grebe (*P. grisegena*) is a dull grey-brown when it appears along the coast in winter, but in summer it has silver cheeks and a vermilion neck. The western grebe (*Aechmophorus occidentalis*), at 1.5 kg the largest of the family, has a long swan-like neck and a slim, pointed yellow bill. Thousands of individuals winter in the vicinity of VANCOUVER. The eared grebe (*Podiceps nigricollis*) breeds in colonies on some Interior marshes but is not often seen on the coast. The Clark's grebe (*Aechmophorus clarkii*) is very rare in BC.

GREEKS began arriving in BC during the 1850s when George Kapiotis, the first Greek known to have settled here, arrived from California. He prospered in the Fraser R GOLD RUSH and lived in VICTORIA, where he married an aboriginal woman. Another early Greek immigrant was John Nicholas Giannaros, who in 1878 became the first Greek fisher on the FRASER R. He later developed a fish processing business in LADNER with George Kontrafilla, a fellow Greek. (The earliest Greek of all to visit BC may have been Juan de FUCA: in 1592, sailing for Spain, he claimed to have discovered the fabled Strait of Anian, but his account has never been verified.)

A wave of Greek newcomers came to BC from the US in the decades prior to WWI, most of them settling in VANCOUVER, where Greek merchants operated several businesses in GASTOWN. Among the prominent early immigrants was Peter Pantages, who in 1921 inaugurated the first Polar Bear Swim in ENGLISH BAY on New Year's Day. By 1930, when St George's Greek Orthodox Church was built in Kitsilano, the centre of the city's Greek community had shifted to the west side. The high point of Greek immigration to Canada occurred following WWII when many newcomers arrived, anxious to leave their war-torn homeland. By 1970 the Vancouver community had outgrown its church and a new St George's Cathedral was built in Kerrisdale. Immigration has declined since then, but Vancouver retains a strong Greek presence, encouraged by the Hellenic Canadian Congress of BC, an umbrella organization for some 30 Greek social and cultural associations. According to the 1996 census there are 9,335 Greek speakers in BC. *See also* PEOPLES OF BC.   *Dianne Mackay*

GREEN, Howard Charles, lawyer, politician (b 5 Nov 1895, Kaslo; d 26 June 1989, Vancouver). After graduating from Osgoode Hall law school in Ontario, he was called to the BC bar in 1922 and began practising in VANCOUVER. He was first elected to the federal House of Commons for the Conservatives in 1935 and held his seat for the next 28 years. In 1942 he ran for the leadership of the party, finishing well behind the winner, John Bracken; he did not try again, content to be a prominent front bencher in opposition and then a senior cabinet minister. With the election of the Diefenbaker minority government in 1957, Green became minister of public works. In 1959 he was named minister of external affairs, a post he held for the duration of

Howard Green, shown here in the early 1960s when he was minister of external affairs.
National Film Board 90497

the Conservative government. A proponent of disarmament, he was suspicious of American power and infuriated the Kennedy administration with his perceived neutrality in Cold War crisis situations. During the final tumultuous days of the Diefenbaker government he remained a loyal confidant to the beleaguered prime minister. Defeat in the 1963 election ended his political career.

GREEN HILL PARK was a 9,679-tonne freighter that exploded and burned on 6 Mar 1945, in VANCOUVER's worst waterfront disaster. Eight men died in the accident. It started when fire broke out between decks while the freighter was loading at the CPR dock near the foot of Burrard St. The flames touched off the explosion, which blew out the sides of the vessel, shattering thousands of windows in the downtown area and hurling pieces of cargo as far as LUMBERMAN'S ARCH in STANLEY PARK. The burning freighter was towed away from the dock and beached at Siwash Rock. It was later refitted and sold.

The Green Hill Park *burning in Vancouver Harbour, 1945. BC Archives E-03974*

GREEN MOUNTAIN HOUSE, 15 km southwest of PENTICTON, was the site of a ranch (*see* CATTLE INDUSTRY) and roadhouse established by L.A. Clark and named after the Green Mts in Vermont, where Clark grew up. He settled in the area after being contracted in 1900 to build a road from Penticton to the Nickel Plate Mine (*see* HEDLEY). Apex Mountain Provincial Park and the Apex SKIING area are nearby. Green Mt post office was moved 2 km northeast in 1908, renamed Allen Grove after E.F. Allen, a rancher, then closed in 1931.

GREEN PARTY, BC, is the provincial wing of the national Green Party of Canada. Founded in 1983, the BC Green Party is part of a network of Green Parties around the world. Since receiving

.19% of the popular vote in the 1983 provincial election, the party has expanded its support: it got 2% of the vote in the 1996 election. The party was led by Stuart Parker until 2000, when a group of environmental activists ousted him at a party annual meeting and forced a leadership race. Since 1990 the BC Greens have elected several candidates in municipal elections. A coalition of environmentalists and social justice activists, the party advocates the introduction of a proportional representation system of elections and supports policies that encourage sustainable economic growth. *See also* ENVIRONMENTAL MOVEMENT.

GREEN THUMB THEATRE FOR YOUNG PEOPLE was founded in Vancouver in 1975 by Dennis FOON and Jane Howard Baker. The company is well known for presenting THEATRE works about social and personal issues of interest to young people; for example, family violence in *Mirror Game* (1987), pollution in *Land of Trash* (1991), AIDS in *Co$t of Living* (1991) and immigration in *New Canadian Kid* (1982). *Skin*, Foon's play about racism in schools, won a Chalmers Award in 1988. The company tours schools throughout BC and the rest of Canada and internationally; theatre groups worldwide have performed its original productions.

GREENE, Alan, missionary (b 1889, Orillia, ON; d 10 Oct 1972, Sechelt). While he was a student at Wycliffe College in Toronto in 1911 he was asked to work with the COLUMBIA COAST MISSION during his summer holiday. After 3 summer tours with the mission, and service as a chaplain during WWI, he returned to BC permanently in 1919 to minister to the LOGGING camps and isolated homesteads along the coast. He worked with the CCM for his entire career, serving as its second superintendent from 1936 until his retirement in 1959. His elder brother Heber also served with the mission from 1943 to 1958.

Nancy Greene, Olympic skier, on the slopes, 1969. Chuck Diven/Vancouver Province

GREENE (Raine), Nancy Catherine, skier (b 11 May 1943, Ottawa). She was raised in ROSSLAND, where she began ski racing as a teenager. Between 1960 and 1968 as a member of Canada's national SKI team she was a leading competitor on the international circuit. Her career included 13 World Cup victories and the overall World Cup titles in 1967 and 1968 and culminated in 2 medals at the 1968 Grenoble Olympics, gold in the giant slalom and silver in the slalom. She was Canada's female athlete of the year for 1967 and 1968. Greene was also Canadian alpine champion 7 times, US champion 3 times and the FIS world combined champion in 1968. Following her retirement from competition she and husband Al Raine were key players in the development of the WHISTLER ski resort. In 1995 the Raines moved to KAMLOOPS to assist in the development of Sun Peaks Resort. Nancy Greene Lk near Rossland is named for her. She has been inducted into the Order of Canada, the Canadian Sports Hall of Fame and the BC SPORTS HALL OF FAME. In 1999 she was declared Canada's female athlete of the century.

GREENE POINT RAPIDS, 55 km north of CAMPBELL RIVER, are in Cordero Channel between W THURLOW ISLAND and the mainland. A.P. ALLISON had a LOGGING camp near here in the early 1900s and eventually one of the largest shingle mills on the BC coast. *AS*

GREENPEACE is an environmental group, originally called the Don't Make a Wave Committee, formed in VANCOUVER in 1970 to oppose American nuclear weapons-testing in the Aleutian Islands. The founders were Jim Bohlen and Irving Stowe, 2 expatriate Americans active in the Sierra Club, and Paul Cote, a law student. In the fall of 1971 the group sent the 24-m fishing vessel *Phyllis Cormack* into the testing range near Amchitka, hoping to halt the blast. The crew of that historic voyage included Capt John Cormack, engineer Dave Birmingham, and Jim Bohlen, Bob HUNTER, Ben Metcalfe, Bob Cummings, Bob Keziere, Patrick MOORE, Bill Darnell (credited with originating the Greenpeace name), Dr Lyle Thurston, Terry Simmons and Richard Fineberg. By 1975 the group was led by Hunter and headquartered in an office on West 4th Ave in Vancouver. That year Greenpeace took up the anti-WHALING cause, launching voyages to harass whaling fleets on the high seas. These efforts, combined with protests against sealing in the north Atlantic, brought Greenpeace worldwide attention. Membership boomed but growth brought problems too. In 1977 Hunter was replaced as leader by Moore, and groups in Europe and the US resented his attempts to assert Canadian control. Eventually the group reorganized as Greenpeace International and leadership shifted away from Vancouver headquarters. Greenpeace is now one of the largest environmental groups in the world, famous for its nonviolent direct action against polluters and other threats to wildlife and the environment. *See also* ENVIRONMENTAL MOVEMENT.

GREENVILLE, pop 588, is one of the main NISGA'A villages on the NASS R known to local people as Laxqalts'ap ("dwelling place comprised of other dwelling places"). Traditionally it was a popular EULACHON fishing spot. The English name refers to Alfred Green, a METHODIST missionary who based his activities here from 1877 to 1890. He was a controversial figure because he sided with the Nisga'a in their land disputes with the government (*see also* ABORIGINAL RIGHTS). By 1904 the Nisga'a had converted to Anglicanism. Greenville became accessible by road in 1984.

Crew of the Phyllis Cormack *on their historic voyage to Amchitka to protest US nuclear testing, 1971. At top (l to r): Bob Hunter, Patrick Moore, Bob Cummings, Ben Metcalfe, Dave Birmingham; bottom (l to r): Richard Fineberg, Lyle Thurston, Jim Bohlen, Terry Simmons, Bill Darnell, John Cormack. Bob Keziere/Greenpeace*

GREENWOOD, Canada's smallest city, pop 784, is located on Boundary Crk 18 km west of GRAND FORKS in the BOUNDARY DISTRICT. It was founded in 1895 by Robert Wood, a merchant, and incorporated as a city in 1897. Greenwood prospered during the ensuing MINING boom, and the population grew to 3,000. The BC Copper Co blew in a SMELTER at nearby ANACONDA in 1901 to treat COPPER ore from its DEADWOOD and Mother Lode deposits; the brick smelter stack was still visible a century later. Following WWI and the collapse of mining, Greenwood almost became a ghost town. During WWII JAPANESE Canadians from the coast were interned here (*see* JAPANESE, RELOCATION OF) and many stayed on. Several buildings dating from the early 1900s have been restored; the FOREST INDUSTRY has become the major employer.

Downtown Greenwood, 1995.
Len Mackave photo

GRENFELL, Thornton, boatbuilder (b Nov 1911, N Vancouver; d 2 Nov 1971, Vancouver). He designed some of the finest wooden power boats on the coast. Raised on VANCOUVER ISLAND, where his father was a COAL miner, he quit school after grade 10 but later obtained certification as a naval architect. He began building boats at age 16, but it was after he opened an office as a marine architect in VANCOUVER in 1945 that his reputation began to grow. Grenfell specialized in speedy runabouts although he designed everything from fishing vessels to large cabin cruisers. In 1958 he opened his own boat yard, Grenfell Yachts Ltd, and built elegant lapstrake cruisers, many of which were still active on the coast in the late 1990s.

GRENVILLE CHANNEL is a 72-km-long, extremely narrow passage dividing PITT ISLAND from the mainland south of PRINCE RUPERT. It is the final leg of the INSIDE PASSAGE navigation route much travelled by CRUISE SHIPS and coastal ferries. A dramatically scenic passage, with WATERFALLS tumbling down the steep side walls and mountain ranges towering into the clouds, it was explored by Capt George VANCOUVER, who named it after William Grenville, a British politician. Lowe Inlet on the mainland side has long been a TSIMSHIAN fishing site, and a fish cannery operated there from 1890 to 1934. It is now a

provincial MARINE PARK, as is Klewnuggit Inlet farther north up the channel. *See also* FISHING, ABORIGINAL; SALMON CANNING.

GRIFFIN, Harold "Hal," labour journalist (b 1912, London, England; d 1998, Vancouver). He began his career on Fleet Street and moved to Canada during the Depression. He joined the Communist Party and spent his life reporting for the political left. A longtime editor of the UNITED FISHERMEN AND ALLIED WORKERS' UNION newspaper *The Fisherman* (1966–78), he wrote 4 books, including *BC: A People's Early History* (1958), *A Ripple, A Wave* (1974), a labour history of the BC FISHING industry and *Radical Roots: The Shaping of British Columbia* (1999). *See also* LABOUR MOVEMENT.

GRIFFITH, Henry Sandham, architect (b 1865, Oxfordshire, England; d 1944, Vancouver). Educated at Oxford Univ and trained in his native England, he immigrated to Canada in the early 1890s. He worked in Winnipeg and Saskatoon, then established a practice in VICTORIA. He operated one of the quality firms in the capital from 1900 to 1912 and was responsible for several large commercial commissions, including the Times Building and the Stobart-Peas Building. He then expanded to VANCOUVER, closing his Victoria office in 1918. One of his most impressive works was his own Victoria home, known as "Spencer's Castle" after he sold it to the Spencer family of department store renown. *See also* ARCHITECTURE.

GRIFFITHS, Frank Armathwaite, broadcasting executive (b 17 Dec 1916, Burnaby; d 7 Apr 1994, Vancouver). After studying accounting, he joined his father's firm, Griffiths and Griffiths, in 1939. In 1956 he and 2 partners purchased the

Frank Griffiths and his wife Emily, 1994.
Malcolm Parry photo

radio station CKNW, which became the first major holding in a BROADCASTING empire, Western Broadcasting, later (WIC) WESTERN INTERNATIONAL COMMUNICATIONS. WIC grew to include other radio stations, television and cable services. Griffiths bought the VANCOUVER CANUCKS hockey team in 1974, kept it through a record 15 consecutive losing seasons and was majority owner until his death. He is a member of the Hockey Hall of Fame, the Canadian Business Hall of Fame and the Canadian Broadcasting Hall of Fame. His son Arthur (b 1958) concentrated on the sports side of the family's business empire. Along with his sister Emily, Arthur founded Northwest Entertainment Group, which owned the Canucks, the Vancouver GRIZZLIES of the NBA, and GENERAL MOTORS PLACE, an arena in downtown Vancouver. With the expansion of their sports activities the Griffiths operation became overextended, and they sold out to John McCaw, a Seattle entrepreneur, early in 1995. Arthur Griffiths remained CEO of the company, which changed its name to ORCA BAY SPORTS AND ENTERTAINMENT, until McCaw acquired complete ownership in 1996.

GRINDROD, pop 421, is an AGRICULTURAL, DAIRY FARMING, LOGGING and retirement community 14 km southeast of SALMON ARM on the Shuswap R. Originally known as N ENDERBY, it was a station on the SHUSWAP & OKANAGAN RWY and site of a SAWMILL and early pole yard. The post office, opened here in 1911, was named after Edmund H. Grindrod, first CPR telegraph inspector in BC in 1886, who settled near KAMLOOPS. *AS*

GRIZZLIES; *see* VANCOUVER GRIZZLIES.

GRIZZLY BEAR; *see* BEAR, GRIZZLY.

GROSBEAK is a chunky, bright-coloured songbird related to FINCHES or SPARROWS. With its strong, stubby bill it cracks open the hard seeds that form a significant part of its diet. Four species occur in BC. The black-headed grosbeak (*Pheucticus melanocephalus*) is yellow-brown in

Evening grosbeak. Ken Bowen photo

colour with a black head and wings. It occurs in wooded valleys in the southern half of the province. The rose-breasted grosbeak (*P. ludovicianus*) is found most commonly in deciduous forests in the northeast corner of the province. Males are striking-looking white and black birds with large white beaks and red breast patches; females have the characteristic white beak and dull brown plumage. Evening grosbeaks (*Coccothraustes vespertinus*) are denizens of coniferous forests. The male is lemon yellow with a brown head, black tail and wings and white wing patches; females' colour is more subtle. Pine grosbeaks (*Pinicola enucleator*), the largest of the BC species, are found in 3 varieties along the coast, in the southern Interior and in the north. The male is pinkish red with grey wings barred white; the female is grey with a yellow head. The 2 species groups are actually quite unrelated: *Pheucticus* grosbeaks are related to cardinals, while evening and pine grosbeaks are types of finches.

GROUNDBIRCH, a small AGRICULTURAL community on the HART HWY and BC RAIL, 45 km west of DAWSON CREEK in the PEACE R district, no longer has a wheat elevator to serve local farmers but in 1999 was still the site of an RV park and general store. It was first settled about 1920 by Ivor Benterud and Ole Martinsen, and was originally known as Stewart Flats. The Bruce Groner Memorial Museum is located here.   AS

GROUNDFISH is a fisheries term that refers to a variety of fish that are usually caught at or near the ocean floor. There are more than 50 species, including ROCKFISH, FLATFISH (SOLE, HALIBUT, FLOUNDER) and an assortment of other species: COD, DOGFISH, HAKE, LINGCOD, pollock, SABLEFISH (blackcod), SKATE and others. Trawling, trapping, and hook and line are used in the commercial harvest of these species (*see* FISHING, COMMERCIAL). There are also recreational fisheries for many groundfish species (*see* FISHING, SPORT).

GROUSE is a chicken-sized game bird. It nests on the ground and feeds primarily on conifer needles, tree buds and insects. Adaptations to the cold include feathered legs and, in some species, feather-covered feet and nostrils. Of 9 species in Canada, 4 occur in BC. Ruffed grouse (*Bonasa umbellus*) are widely distributed, especially in the south. Much sought after by hunters, this species has brown plumage and a fan-like tail with many bars. The male attracts females by drumming—standing on a log and producing a low sound by beating his wings. Blue grouse (*Dendragapus obscurus*) is the largest species. Individuals are widely distributed, especially in the southern half of the province. In winter they inhabit coniferous forests and are rarely seen. In spring they emerge to frequent forest edges, slopes and lowlands. Spruce grouse (*Falcipennis canadensis*) are so tame that they are sometimes called "fool hens." They have dark plumage with white-tipped tail feathers and bright red eye combs. They are not present on the coast but are widely distributed in Interior SPRUCE forests. Sharp-tailed grouse (*Tympanuchus phasianellus*)

Ruffed grouse. Duane Sept photo

are a GRASSLAND species with brown plumage, a short pointed tail and underparts marked by dark Vs. In spring males congregate at dawn to perform an elaborate mating dance characterized by stamping feet, ruffling feathers and emitting low, booming vocalizations. They occur in the E KOOTENAY, the South-Central Interior and the northeast corner of the province, though numbers are declining due to habitat destruction and overhunting. The sage grouse once inhabited the south OKANAGAN VALLEY but the last ones were extirpated by hunters around the turn of the 20th century.

GROUSE CREEK WAR was a conflict over MINING rights on a GOLD-rich creek 5 km south of BARKERVILLE in 1867. Despite an existing claim to the property, a group of promoters called the Canadian Company began mining a strip of land along the creek. When the local gold commissioner swore in special constables to enforce the original claim, the Canadian Co rounded up a small army of miners to resist the police and drive away the rival claimants. The company then tried to take as much gold as possible before the dispute could be settled against it. Early in Aug, Gov Frederick SEYMOUR arrived to mediate the dispute; it was the first visit by a governor to the CARIBOO. He ordered the Canadian Co to surrender the land, but his jail sentences were so lenient that the dispute still simmered. Finally, after a trial, Chief Justice Joseph Needham ordered the Canadian Co to turn over the land and the gold to the court and the "war" ended.

GROUSE MOUNTAIN (el 1,211 m), overlooking N VANCOUVER and BURRARD INLET, is one of the most popular SKIING areas and visitor destinations in the Lower Mainland. It was named in 1894 by a party of climbers after a blue grouse they shot. A ski chalet opened in 1924, and the area became even more popular with skiers in 1949 with the construction of the first double chairlift in N America. The lift was subsequently replaced by the Skyride gondola, which carries visitors up to the ski runs, hiking trails, Grouse Nest restaurant and other facilities at the summit. The illuminated ski runs have become a familiar Vancouver nighttime landmark. A 3-km hiking trail up the side of the mountain, known as the Grouse Grind, is a popular workout.

The skyride on Grouse Mountain.
Keith Thirkell photo

GROWERS' WINES LTD, one of BC's earliest wineries, was founded in 1923 in VICTORIA by farmers on the SAANICH PENINSULA. Initially the company specialized in loganberry products. It was managed by the CONSERVATIVE politician Herbert ANSCOMB from 1927 until 1955, when it was sold to a VANCOUVER syndicate. Imperial Tobacco bought the company in 1965 and changed the name to Ste-Michelle. Then, after Jordan Wines of Ontario bought it, the name changed to Jordan & Ste-Michelle Cellars Ltd. The winery in Victoria closed in 1977 and the company moved to a new facility in SURREY; T.G. Brights took over in 1990 and closed the Surrey operation.

GUICHON FAMILY are a pioneer family of NICOLA R valley ranchers. Joseph Guichon (1848–1921) arrived in BC in 1864 and worked as a packer before settling with his brothers in the Nicola Valley, where they acquired several ranches. In 1918 Joseph's children assumed management, operating as a partnership; in 1933 the holdings—121.5 km^2 of land, 4,000 head of cattle and 500 horses—were incorporated as the Guichon Ranch Ltd. One son, Lawrence, received an honorary doctorate of science from UBC and was recognized as the "Dean of BC ranchers." In 1947, 3 shareholders sold their shares to the remaining 4, who formed the Guichon Cattle Co Ltd. Lawrence's son Gerard served as general manager until 1957, when the ranch was divided and sold. Joseph's grandson Guy Rose purchased the QUILCHENA property, while Gerard purchased the north section, which

Guichon family ranch, Nicola Valley.
Rick Blacklaws photo

became Gerard Guichon Ranch Ltd. Gerard, who died in 1991, received the Order of Canada for his community activism and his participation in national, provincial and local stockmen's organizations. In 1972 his son Lawrence and daughter-in-law Judith joined the ranch; they took over management in 1979. Lawrence, who died in a car accident in 1999, was a leader in the movement to preserve the GRASSLANDS habitat. *See also* CATTLE INDUSTRY.

GUILLEMOT, PIGEON (*Cepphus columba*), a member of the family Alcidae, is a PIGEON-sized seabird abundantly present on the rocky shorelines of the coast. It is black with white wing patches, red legs and red mouth lining. In winter its plumage is mottled grey. Like other alcids, it feeds by diving and "flying" underwater in pursuit of fish. Pigeon guillemots have demonstrative summer courting rituals, including peering down each other's throats, and nest singly in a variety of locales along the coast, usually in rock cavities or other nooks and crannies on the ground.

GULF ISLANDS are a scattering of more than 200 islands and islets situated in GEORGIA STRAIT. Technically the term encompasses all islands in the strait, but commonly it refers to those on the southwestern side, from DENMAN ISLAND south to DISCOVERY ISLAND in JUAN DE FUCA STRAIT. The main Gulf Islands are TEXADA (the largest), SALTSPRING, GABRIOLA, GALIANO, MAYNE, N and S PENDER, SATURNA, HORNBY, THETIS and LASQUETI. The islands were once part of VANCOUVER ISLAND but were detached by glacial erosion. They are well wooded, with a rugged topography and uneven coastlines attractive to recreational boaters. Located in the rainshadow of Vancouver Island, they enjoy more sunshine than almost any other place in Canada.

Human occupation dates back at least 5,000 years. The islands were used extensively by Coast

Salish groups (*see* SALISHAN FIRST NATIONS) for resource harvesting. The first Europeans in the area were SPANISH mariners, who explored in 1791, and British naval vessels surveyed the islands in 1858 and 1859. Many topographical features are named for these navigators. The earliest non-Native settlers, who arrived in the 1860s and 1870s, were farmers and fishers. AGRICULTURE remained important, and over the years other industries have included fish reduction plants, quarrying, brickmaking and LOGGING, which was still taking place in the 1990s but on a smaller scale.

Since the 1960s the islands have become a favourite spot for retirees and refugees from the urban rat race, including many artists. In 1999 the permanent population was about 11,500—65% of them residents of Saltspring—but the numbers swell each summer as seasonal visitors are attracted by the pleasant weather, convenient ferry access and beautiful scenery. Popularity has

A view of the Gulf Islands from Mt Galiano on Galiano Island. Keith Thirkell photo

a price: rapid population growth, rising land costs and environmental degradation have all become concerns. These and other matters are dealt with by the ISLANDS TRUST, which has administered the islands since 1974. In 1995, the provincial and federal governments agreed to purchase land in the Gulf Islands as part of the Pacific Marine Heritage Legacy to create a new national PARK.

GULF OF GEORGIA CANNERY is a national historic site on the STEVESTON waterfront near the mouth of the FRASER R. Built in 1894 by the Gulf of Georgia Canning Co, it was expanded by new owners in 1895 to become the second-largest cannery in BC. The CANADIAN FISHING CO bought it in 1926. During the Depression, the company stopped canning SALMON, although it continued to buy fish and operate a net loft for net construction and repair. In 1940 the complex began canning HERRING and added a herring reduction plant to produce oil and meal. Canning ceased in 1947, but the reduction plant operated until 1979. The federal government has owned the site since 1977. In 1984 Parks Canada took over and began to develop a historic park, which opened to the public in 1994. *See also* SALMON CANNING.

Historic Gulf of Georgia Cannery at Steveston, c 1994. Rick Blacklaws photo

GULF OF GEORGIA TOWING CO LTD was one of the top 5 TOWBOATING companies on the BC coast before the industry was reorganized in the 1970s. Founded in VANCOUVER during WWI by George WALKEM, it grew to have the largest fleet of wooden barges or scows in the industry. Sometimes known as the Hertz of the tug and barge business, it supplied scows on daily rentals or monthly charters to other tugboat companies and had a repair yard in FALSE CRK to maintain its fleet. James S. Byrn took over the company in the early 1960s and began phasing out the wooden scows and replacing them with larger steel barges and more powerful tugs. The largest tug owned by Gulf of Georgia was the *Gulf Joan*, which ran at over 3,000 hp. The company was sold to SEASPAN INTERNATIONAL in 1977. *See also* LOG BARGES.

GULL is a stout waterbird with long, pointed wings, webbed feet and a square tail. Adults are usually white and grey in colour; juveniles are more brownish. In flight they glide and soar effortlessly and are a familiar sight to coastal mariners, but while they are thought of as seabirds ("sea gulls"), most species nest inland. Whether on the coast or in the Interior, they are found close to water; they subsist on fish and invertebrates and by scavenging. More than a dozen species are found in BC. The glaucous-winged gull (*Larus glaucescens*) is a large bird with grey wingtips. It is the most common gull on the coast, where it nests on rocky islets. The glaucous gull (*L. hyperboreus*) is an Arctic species seen only in small numbers in BC in winter. Two other species of large gulls are the herring gull (*L. argentatus*), which breeds across the central Interior, then migrates to the coast and southern LAKES for the winter, and the Thayer's gull (*L. thayeri*), which visits the coast in winter from its Arctic nesting grounds. These are the 4 largest

Mew gull. R. Wayne Campbell photo

gull species. Four medium-sized gulls are the California gull (*L. californicus*), breeding mainly on the prairies and found in the BC southern Interior and around VANCOUVER ISLAND in the spring and fall (there is also a small nesting colony in OKANAGAN LK); the ring-billed gull (*L. delawarensis*), which nests in Okanagan and FRASER lakes and is distinguishable by its yellow legs and a black band around its bill; the mew gull (*L. canus*), common along the coast, where it breeds in forested lakes; and Heermann's gull (*L. heermanni*), a dark-coloured species. Smaller gulls include Bonaparte's gull (*L. philadelphia*), a black-headed gull that breeds near fresh water in the central and northern Interior and is found in abundance on the South Coast on migration; the dark-headed Franklin's gull (*L. pipixcan*), a transient in BC as it migrates to and from S America; and the western gull (*L. occidentalis*), another dark-coloured species. Finally, 2 species that usually stay offshore in their migrations are the black-legged kittiwake (*Rissa tridactyla*) and the Sabine's gull (*Xema sabini*).

GUMBOOT NAVY was the informal name for the Fishermen's Reserve, a reserve unit of fishers within the Royal Canadian Navy formed to patrol the BC coast during WWII. It was established early in 1939 as the threat of war loomed, and expanded to a maximum size of 42 boats

The Gumboot Navy, a fleet of converted fishing vessels, Esquimalt, 1943. NAC DND RCN E-4810

and 975 men in 1942 after the attack on Pearl Harbor. Recruits used their own fish boats outfitted by the navy with guns and equipment. The unit disbanded in May 1944 as the fear of Japanese invasion passed. *See also* FISHING, COMMERCIAL.

GUNANOOT, Simon, Gitksan trapper, storekeeper (b circa 1874, Gitanmaax; d Oct 1933, near Stewart). He is the most famous fugitive in BC history. The son of a GITKSAN chief, he was accused of the murder of 2 men, Alex McIntosh and Max Leclair, near HAZELTON in June 1906. He did not know Leclair and no evidence linked

Simon Gunanoot at Hazelton, following his acquittal on charges of murder, 1920.
BC Archives A-07788

him to that killing, but he had been fighting with McIntosh and had been heard to threaten him. Rather than risk trial before a white jury, Gunanoot and his brother-in-law Peter Himadan, also accused in the McIntosh murder, fled into the bush with other members of their family. Despite efforts by police to catch them they eluded their pursuers for an astonishing 13 years, becoming legendary for their ability to survive in the wilderness. They were protected by aboriginal people and were seen from time to time, but it was not until 24 June 1919 that Gunanoot surrendered to authorities. He stood trial for the deaths and with the help of a Vancouver lawyer, Stuart Henderson, he was acquitted. Hi-madan gave himself up soon after and was also discharged.

GUNDY, 20 km southeast of DAWSON CREEK near Swan Lk on the Alberta border, was the site of the Tate Creek Ranch (*see* CATTLE INDUSTRY) and also a Northern Alberta Rwy station. Many Sudeten German WWII refugees settled here in 1939 (*see* TOMSLAKE). The ranch was renamed after the Gundy brothers, who were part of a Toronto syndicate that owned the property. It was acquired by the CPR in the 1930s. The Gundy post office was moved to Alberta in 1961. AS

GUNTERMAN, Ida "Mattie" (Warner), camp cook, photographer (b 1872, La Crosse, WI; d 18 June 1945, Beaton). As a youngster she learned PHOTOGRAPHY from an uncle before moving to Seattle in 1889. She married William Gunterman and in 1898 the couple moved north to the LARDEAU valley, east of Upper ARROW LK in the W KOOTENAY. Based at Thomson's Landing (later BEATON), the Guntermans worked in MINING and LOGGING camps, Mattie primarily as a cook. When the Lardeau mining boom

Mattie Gunterman (centre), pioneer photographer, hamming it up with Ann (l) and Rose Williams at the Nettie L Mine, Ferguson, 1902. VPL 2276

ended she became an itinerant camp cook, trapper and subsistence farmer. Meanwhile she continued to indulge her interest in photography. Her glass-plate negatives, rediscovered 15 years after her death, provide a record of life on the Kootenay mining frontier.
Reading: Henri Robideau, *Flapjacks and Photographs: A History of Mattie Gunterman, Camp Cook and Photographer,* 1995.

GURR, Donna-Marie, swimmer (b 18 Feb 1955, Vancouver). She made her first impact on the national SWIMMING scene in 1969 when she won 5 gold medals at the British national championships, 4 golds and a silver at the Canadian National Games and 5 golds and a silver at the Canada Summer Games. She followed this up in 1970 with a gold and 2 silvers at the Commonwealth Games, then collected 3 golds and a silver at the 1971 Pan American Games. Next came the highlight of her career, the 1972 Munich Olympics, where Gurr won bronze for Canada in the 200-m backstroke, coming on strong in the last length to finish only 2 places behind Melissa Belote's world record. Gurr also won a silver and a bronze at the 1974 Commonwealth Games. She is a member of Canada's Aquatic Hall of Fame and the BC SPORTS HALL OF FAME.   *SW*

GUSTAFSEN LAKE lies at the end of a dirt road in rolling ranch land west of 100 MILE HOUSE in the CARIBOO. It burst into the headlines in Aug 1995 when a group of aboriginal activists and sympathizers occupied property belonging to a local rancher beside the lake, insisting it had spiritual significance and claiming ownership. The dispute escalated into an armed confrontation with RCMP and came to symbolize the tense relations between aboriginals and non-aboriginals in BC. People were shot at by both sides and one person was wounded. In mid-Sept, after a tense standoff closely watched by the media, a dozen people remaining in the camp surrendered. Later a 10-month trial of 18 people on a variety of charges arising from the incident resulted in 21 convictions and 39 acquittals. Those convicted received prison terms ranging from 6 months to 4$^{1/2}$ years.

GUTTERIDGE, Helena Rose, political activist (b 8 Apr 1879, London, England; d 3 Oct 1960, Vancouver). She left home at age 13 and worked to put herself through school. She was already a suffragette when she immigrated to VANCOUVER in 1911 and became involved in the local movement for WOMEN'S SUFFRAGE, forming the BC Woman's Suffrage League soon after her arrival. She was also active in the labour movement as an organizer and agitator for the rights of working women. From 1921 to 1932 she was a poultry farmer in the FRASER VALLEY, then returned to Vancouver and re-immersed herself in politics. Prominent in the newly formed CCF, she became the first woman elected to Vancouver city council in 1937. She was defeated in 1940 because the CCF had alienated voters by making anti-war speeches in the provincial legislature. During the war she worked as a welfare officer in one of the camps for displaced JAPANESE Canadians and afterwards remained active in the peace movement.

Defiant lookouts at Gustafsen Lake, 1995. Aboriginal people and their supporters occupied buildings during a land dispute. Mark van Manen/Vancouver Sun

GUTTMAN, Irving Allen, artistic director (b 27 Oct 1928, Chatham, ON). Widely considered to be the father of opera in western Canada, he was educated in Toronto and Montreal and began his stage-directing career in Montreal in 1953. He became the founding artistic director of the VANCOUVER OPERA in 1960 and occupied that position until 1974. He also served as artistic director of the Manitoba Opera, Opera Saskatchewan and the Edmonton Opera. He has directed performances across Canada and the US and in Brazil, Taiwan, Puerto Rico and Spain, and he has worked with such famous singers as Maureen Forrester, Marilyn Horne, Luciano Pavarotti, Beverly Sills, Joan Sutherland and Jon Vickers.   *AS*

GWAII HAANAS NATIONAL PARK RESERVE AND HAIDA HERITAGE SITE, 1,470 km², encompasses about 15% of the QUEEN CHARLOTTE ISLANDS. The magnificent archipelago contains about 138 islands, including S Moresby, Lyell, Burnaby, Kunghit and Anthony islands, and extends about 90 km from north to south. The area contains ancient FORESTS of giant Sitka SPRUCE and western red CEDAR. The park reserve was established in 1987 after a long struggle by HAIDA elders, more than 75 of whom were arrested during the blockades, and environmentalists (*see* ENVIRONMENTAL MOVEMENT) to protect some of the rich Haida culture and to prevent LOGGING. The Haida had occupied the area until the late 19th century, when epidemic diseases dramatically reduced the population and the survivors congregated at villages to the north. Over 500 archaeological and historic sites have been identified, including villages, shelters, caves and burial sites. At the abandoned villages of Skedans and NINSTINTS, decaying TOTEM POLES still stand on their original sites. Ninstints was declared a UNESCO WORLD HERITAGE SITE in 1981. The reserve, sometimes called the Galapagos of the North, is a breeding ground for 750,000 seabirds. It is accessible only by air and sea and is managed by the Haida and the federal government pending the resolution of a land claim. Important heritage sites are patrolled by Haida caretakers.

Intertidal edge at Burnaby Narrows, Gwaii Haanas National Park Reserve. Duane Sept photo

Gwaii Haanas is Haida for "islands of wonder and beauty." *See also* PARKS, NATIONAL.

GYPPO LOGGING originally referred to contract LOGGING work undertaken by small, underfinanced firms that relied on resourcefulness and ingenuity to compete. The term "gyppo" was first applied to contract labour crews who built short sections of railway grades and competed, or "gypped," by working long hours, cutting corners and otherwise establishing themselves in this highly competitive business. After "gyppo" began to refer to small, independent logging contractors, many of whom evolved into substantial operations, the term gained respectability; for many loggers it became a designation to be proud of. In modern usage it refers to an attitude or an approach to logging that applies entrepreneurial skill and mechanical ingenuity rather than elaborate planning and substantial capital.   *Ken Drushka*

GYPSY MOTH (*Lymentria dispar*) is native to Europe and Asia and is a major INSECT pest in eastern N America, where caterpillars (moth larvae) have defoliated millions of hectares of trees and shrubs. European gypsy moth egg masses attached to vehicles migrated from eastern Canada to BC and introduced the insect to the VICTORIA and VANCOUVER areas, and on occasion to the OKANAGAN VALLEY. Asian gypsy moths, the females of which are able to fly (females of the European variety are flightless), are occasionally introduced to Vancouver from eggs on Russian freighters. It is feared that if they are allowed to get established they will become a major garden and forest pest, so the bacterial spray BtK (*Bacillus thuringiensis* K) is used to combat new infestations. Many populations of non-target BUTTERFLY, SKIPPER AND MOTH species are reduced or eliminated by the spray and, while there are no officially acknowledged adverse effects on humans of BtK used in normal concentrations, the spraying program has attracted opposition from health and ENVIRONMENTAL activists.   *Cris Guppy*

H

HABERL, James Edward, mountaineer, photographer, writer (b 28 Feb 1958, Montreal; d 29 Apr 1999, University Range, AK). He started climbing early and scaled Mt McKinley at age 24. He and Dan CULVER were the first Canadians to reach the summit of K2 (1993), the world's second-highest peak (8,616 m). Haberl taught recreation management at Capilano College, ran MOUNTAINEERING tours and led a well-publicized trek up Mt Kilimanjaro in 1998 to raise funds for research into Alzheimer's disease. A long-time WHISTLER resident, he was the author of *K2: Dreams and Reality* (1994), which detailed his historic climb and Culver's subsequent death, and *Risking Adventure: Mountaineering Journeys around the World* (1997). Haberl died in an AVALANCHE while climbing in Alaska. *AS*

HABITAT, the United Nations Conference on Human Settlements, opened in VANCOUVER on 31 May 1976. The largest UN conference to that time, it drew 10,000 people from more than 150 countries and focussed international attention on the city. A parallel gathering of non-governmental organizations, Habitat Forum, was organized by the community activist Alan Clapp at the former army base at JERICHO BEACH and thousands of volunteers and many local artists transformed the site into an extraordinary "happening." Habitat II took place in Ankara, Turkey, in 1996.

HACKING, Norman "Norm," journalist, marine historian (b 12 Feb 1912, Vancouver; d 18 Sept 1997, N Vancouver). He studied history at UBC, where he edited the *Ubyssey* student newspaper. During WWII he served on convoys in the N Atlantic with the Canadian naval reserve. During his time as marine editor of the Vancouver PROVINCE newspaper (1947–77) he wrote about all aspects of BC shipping. In retirement he continued to write regularly for local publications and to publish books about maritime history. His books include *Annals of the Royal Vancouver Yacht Club* (1971), *The Two Barneys* (1984), *The Princess Story* (with W. Kaye LAMB, 1974) and *Prince Ships of Northern BC* (1995). He was an honorary commodore of the PORT OF VANCOUVER. His interest in boats was not solely academic; he was a keen sailor with a solo crossing of the Atlantic to his credit.

HAGAN, Michael, pioneer newspaper publisher, farmer (b 1831; d 2 Nov 1896, Kelowna). He was already an experienced NEWSPAPER publisher of the *Thunder Bay Sentinel* when he moved to BC in 1880. Believing that EMORY CITY in the Fraser Canyon (*see* FRASER R) would become an important railway centre, he located there and began publishing the *Inland Sentinel* on a French hand press that was brought to BC in 1853. He moved the paper to YALE and then to KAMLOOPS before selling it in 1886 and taking up farming at KELOWNA. Aside from a brief stint as superintendent of the Kamloops Indian Industrial School (*see* RESIDENTIAL SCHOOLS), he continued farming and contributing articles to various BC newspapers for the rest of his life. *Peggy Imredy*

HAGENSBORG, pop 606, in the Bella Coola Valley about 20 km east of BELLA COOLA, was established in 1894 by a group of NORWEGIAN colonists. They had settled first in Minnesota but followed their pastor, Rev Christian Saugstad, to the new site and settled well up the valley, where the government granted them land. The colonists built a road from Bella Coola, cleared the land for AGRICULTURE and erected a school and a church. The settlement, which retains some of its Norwegian flavour, took its name from Hagen Christensen, who owned the store and post office.

HAGER, Alvah L., fishing executive (b 19 Nov 1877, Oelwein, IA; d 1948, Vancouver). He entered the fishing business in Boston, then moved to Washington state and opened a processing plant that specialized in COLUMBIA R chinook (*see* SALMON, PACIFIC). In 1908 he moved to VANCOUVER as general manager of local operations for the New England Fish Co, which took over the CANADIAN FISHING CO LTD and built it into one of the major processors on the coast. Hager became president of the company in 1931. A committed conservationist, he was a commissioner on the first INTERNATIONAL PACIFIC HALIBUT COMMISSION in 1923 and a commissioner of the INTERNATIONAL PACIFIC SALMON FISHERIES CONVENTION from 1937 to his death. *See also* FISHING, COMMERCIAL; SALMON CANNING.

HAGWILGET, pop 262, is a WET'SUWET'EN community on the south bank of a narrow canyon in the BULKLEY R near its confluence with the SKEENA R. Originally it was the site of an ancient GITKSAN village, Tse Kya. In about 1820 a rock blocked the annual SALMON run through the canyon and

Suspension bridge over the Bulkley R at Hagwilget, c 1895. BC Archives A-00783

Wet'suwet'en people from upstream moved down to the area to fish. There is a famous suspension bridge across the canyon. *See also* FISHING, ABORIGINAL.

HAIDA are the FIRST NATIONS people of the QUEEN CHARLOTTE ISLANDS, which they call Haida Gwaii, where human occupation dates back at least 7,000 years (*see* ARCHAEOLOGY). Their language, spoken in 2 main dialects (Skidegate and Masset), is an isolate, not known to be related to any other language (*see* FIRST NATIONS LANGUAGES). One group of Haida migrated across DIXON ENTRANCE, probably in the 18th century, to the southern Alaska Panhandle, where they are now centred at Hydaburg on Prince of Wales Island. The population of Haida before contact with Europeans has been estimated at 6,000 to 9,000. Exposure to disease following contact took a heavy toll, especially during the SMALLPOX

Haida celebration at Skidegate, 1987.
Ken Bowen photo

epidemic of 1862–63 when several villages were abandoned. (One of these, NINSTINTS, is now a UNESCO WORLD HERITAGE SITE.) By 1915 the Haida population had fallen to 588. The decline was reversed in the 1920s and 1930s; in the late 1990s the population numbered about 3,500. Traditionally the Haida subsisted on abundant food resources, chiefly FISH, shellfish, SEAL, SEA LION, SEA OTTER, BEAR and edible PLANTS. They lived in villages of CEDAR plank houses (*see* ARCHITECTURE, ABORIGINAL) and followed a seasonal round of subsistence activities. Haida are known for their TOTEM POLES and other examples of monumental art, as well as the ARGILLITE carving that flourished in the 19th century to meet the European demand for curios (*see also* ART, NORTHWEST COAST ABORIGINAL). Traditional society was hierarchical. Social position was inherited. Individuals still belong to one of 2 clans, or moieties—Eagle or Raven. They reckon their

identity through the mother's lineage and marry members of the opposite clan. Individuals also belong to one of several lineages that trace their origins far back in time. Lineages controlled property, house sites, the right to fish and hunt in certain areas, even dances, stories, crests and names. Each lineage was headed by a hereditary chief, who was trustee of the lineage properties. Prestige was maintained by feasting and the POTLATCH. Much of the work was done by slaves, who were war captives and children of captives (*see* SLAVERY). Haida came into contact with Europeans in 1774 when they encountered the Spanish explorer Juan PEREZ at Langara Island. Trade for sea otter pelts began in 1787 and lasted until about 1830. In 1834 they began trading at FORT SIMPSON, the HBC post on the mainland. As disease depleted the population, the Haida congregated in 2 main villages, MASSET and SKIDEGATE. The HBC operated a post at Masset from 1869 to 1898, though the Haida continued to visit Fort Simpson annually to interact with other North Coast tribes. An ANGLICAN missionary arrived in Masset in 1876, while the METHODIST CHURCH established itself at Skidegate in 1883; the 2 denominations agreed to divide their efforts to Christianize the people. Missionaries did much to suppress traditional customs and encourage the adoption of European lifestyles. RESERVES were surveyed in 1882.

In the 20th century wage labour in canneries, at LOGGING camps and in fish boats supplanted the seasonal subsistence economy. In the 1950s Masset had one of the finest seine-boat fleets (*see* FISHING, COMMERCIAL) on the coast, while at Skidegate logging was the main activity. Since the 1960s the Haida have experienced a cultural florescence, reflected in the revival of traditional carving led by Bill REID and Robert DAVIDSON,

and in the forceful assertion of their right to control events in their homeland of Haida Gwaii (*see also* ABORIGINAL RIGHTS). The Council of the Haida Nation consists of representatives from the 2 communities.
Reading: George F. MacDonald, *Haida Monumental Art,* 1983.

HAIDA GWAII; *see* QUEEN CHARLOTTE ISLANDS.

HAIG-BROWN, Roderick Langmere, writer (b 21 Feb 1908, Lancing, England; d 19 Oct 1976, Campbell River). He went to Washington state in 1926 to work as a logger and later transferred to a camp on VANCOUVER ISLAND. Seeking more free time to write, he took up trapping, guiding and beachcombing to make a living and began selling articles to sporting magazines. In 1929 he went back to England determined to make a literary career, but returned to BC late in 1931, and settled in CAMPBELL RIVER in 1934. His first books were about animals, but with the publication of *The Western Angler* in 1939 he found his true subject, FLY FISHING, and turned out a series of books that established his reputation as one of the most popular writers about the outdoors on the continent. His 25 books include *Return to the River* (1941), *A River Never Sleeps* (1946) and *A Primer of Fly Fishing* (1964). He also wrote several novels and books for young readers, winning a GOV GEN'S LITERARY AWARD and two Canadian Library Assoc awards for his juvenile fiction. From 1942 to 1975 he was a magistrate in Campbell River. His fame as a writer and his position in the community gave him a platform to speak out publicly on conservation issues (*see also* ENVIRONMENTAL MOVEMENT). He was chancellor of UNIV OF VICTORIA from 1970 to 1972.

Roderick Haig-Brown, writer and naturalist,
Campbell River, 1965. John Ough/National Film Board

HAIHAIS, or XaiXais, First Nation traditionally occupied the complex network of inlets and passages leading north out of Milbanke Sound on the Central Coast. Their language is Oowekyala-Heiltsuk, the central language of Northern WAKASHAN people (*see also* FIRST NATIONS LANGUAGES), and they are usually grouped with the OWEEKENO and the Heiltsuk (Bella Bella) First Nations as the HEILTSUK people. They migrated seasonally to different resource sites in their territory to take advantage of plentiful supplies of SALMON, sea mammals, shellfish, MOUNTAIN GOAT, DEER and BEAR. Main villages of CEDAR plank houses (*see* ARCHITECTURE, ABORIGINAL) were occupied more or less permanently during the winter, the season for elaborate ceremonies conducted by dancing societies. The basic social unit was the local group, comprised of related families with their own chief, names, village sites and so on. One or more local groups might congregate in a winter village but each retained its autonomy. Society was divided into chiefs, commoners and slaves (*see* SLAVERY), who were usually war captives. Traditional villages were situated at the heads of the inlets, but in the 1870s the people moved to KLEMTU on Swindle Island to take advantage of economic opportunities provided by coastal steamers. Later they took jobs at the cannery that operated from 1927 to 1968. By the late 1990s FISHING was the main activity. *See also* FIRST NATIONS.

HAINES HIGHWAY, 256 km, runs from Haines Junction in the Yukon south across the northwest corner of BC to Haines, AK, at the top of Lynn Canal. It was built during 1942–45 by US Army engineers to connect the ALASKA HWY to tidewater. It roughly follows the Dalton Trail, an old route to the Klondike established in 1897 by Jack Dalton, an Alaska guide. Pre-contact it was a trade route between coast and Interior FIRST NATIONS. The highway, which crosses Chilkat Pass (el 1,065 m), was upgraded in the 1970s and is mainly paved. *See also* ROADS AND HIGHWAYS.

HAISLA are a FIRST NATIONS people occupying the inner North Coast in the KITIMAT–KEMANO region south of the SKEENA R. Their language, sometimes called Xaisla, belongs to the northern subgroup of the WAKASHAN people and the term Northern Kwakiutl (*see* KWAKWA̱KA̱'WAKW) is sometimes inappropriately applied to them (*see also* FIRST NATIONS LANGUAGES). Haisla derives from an aboriginal word meaning "those living at the rivermouth." Formerly there were 2 main tribal groupings: the Kitamaat (from the TSIMSHIAN, meaning "people of the falling snow") of DOUGLAS CHANNEL, and the Kitlope (from the Tsimshian, meaning "people of the rock") in GARDNER CANAL. Disease almost wiped out the Kitlope and the survivors merged with the Kitamaat in the 1930s. The Haisla subsisted on abundant supplies of SALMON, EULACHON, MOUNTAIN GOAT, DEER and BEAR. BERRIES and CRABAPPLE were also important. The basic social unit was the matrilineal clan; there were 6 of these, allied into 3 ceremonial sets: Raven,

Haisla village of Kitamaat, 1954.
Bill Dennett/Vancouver Sun

Beaver, Crow, Killer Whale, Salmon and Eagle. Clans had hereditary chiefs and owned territories, names and so on. People married outside their clan, though within their social caste, either noble, commoner or slave (*see* SLAVERY). The POTLATCH was practised, along with feasts and dance ceremonies conducted by a well-established set of secret societies. First contact with European naval expeditions occurred in the 1790s. The Haisla became involved in the FUR TRADE, travelling to FORT MCLOUGHLIN when it opened in 1833. The first missionary arrived in 1883 and a METHODIST mission was established among the Kitamaat in 1893. Missionary activities, along with a government ban on ceremonies and the drastic effect of epidemic diseases, amounted to an all-out assault on traditional society. From the 1890s LOGGING, commercial FISHING and cannery work were the main economic activities. With the growth of the town of KITIMAT in the 1950s, the aluminum complex and the town became sources of employment. In 1999 the Haisla numbered about 1,400.

HAKAI RECREATION AREA, 1,229.98 km², created in 1987, is the largest MARINE PARK on the West Coast. It consists of an archipelago of islands south of BELLA BELLA, including all or part of CALVERT, Hecate and HUNTER islands. There is evidence of ancient habitation; at least 130 archaeological sites have been recorded, including middens, pictographs (*see* ROCK ART), fish traps and winter village sites. Hakai Pass is world famous for its SALMON fishing. The remote area, accessible only by boat or plane, features long beaches, rugged headlands, many delightful coves and inlets, and a wide variety of animal life. It preserves one of the most scenic wilderness environments on the coast for camping, kayaking, boating and fishing. *See also* FISHING, ABORIGINAL; FISHING, SPORT.

HAKE, Pacific (*Merluccius productus*), or Pacific whiting, is a slim, silvery fish that schools in the open ocean along the outer coast. Closely related to the Pacific COD, it grows up to 1 m in length. Recreational fishers (*see* FISHING, SPORT) consider the hake a nuisance fish, but it has been

taken offshore commercially since the mid-1970s. Prior to the establishment of the 200-mile (320-km) fishing limit in 1978, hake found off the coast was caught primarily by Russian and Polish factory trawlers and frozen at sea. In 1979 the Canadian government began to regulate the fishery, establishing an experimental joint venture fishery and setting an annual catch ceiling. The Hake Consortium was established to manage the joint venture fishery. Hake is difficult to process as its flesh breaks down almost immediately after being caught. Foreign factory ships could process the hake while at sea, so the new regulations allocated a portion of the allowable catch to them, but the fish had to be caught by Canadian vessels and transferred at sea to the factory vessels. The balance of the allowable catch was both caught and processed by the foreign factory trawlers. Looking for ways to utilize hake, BC vessels discovered that by cooling the catch immediately using ice and refrigerated salt water, the crew could bring it to shore plants before it broke down. This, combined with the construction of processing plants in UCLUELET, meant that hake could be processed in BC. New regulations were introduced that stipulated that Canadian processors had priority access to as much of the allowable catch as they could use. Foreign vessels received the balance, but it all had to be caught by Canadian trawlers. Offshore hake products are mostly used as a component of surimi, the paste used to make artificial CRAB meat and other seafood products. In the late 1990s the total allowable catch of offshore hake for commercial uses was 80,000–100,000 tonnes and the stocks were considered to be healthy.

Pacific hake. Phil Edgell photo; drawing courtesy Fisheries & Oceans Canada

An "inside" commercial hake trawl fishery also takes place in GEORGIA STRAIT. This fishery is for the same species of hake, but for a different stock, somewhat smaller than the offshore hake. The annual quota ranges between 10,000 and 15,000 tonnes. This stock is utilized primarily as a filleted or head-off and gutted frozen product destined for the US domestic market. *See also* FISHING, COMMERCIAL.
Peter A. Robson

HALCYON HOT SPRINGS are the HOT SPRINGS on the east side of Upper ARROW LK, 35 km north of NAKUSP, known to the FIRST NATIONS from early times as "the Great Medicine Waters." Robert Sanderson staked the springs in 1889 and formed a consortium to develop the property. The partially completed spa passed into the hands of Mr & Mrs Macintosh, who erected a solarium and bottling works in 1898. In 1924 Brigadier General Frederick Burnham acquired the property and managed it until he perished in a fire that destroyed the facility in 1955; only a year earlier, the CPR had withdrawn the steamer service that had served the spa since it opened. The site stood vacant until 1999, when a new resort and health spa opened for business.

Edward Affleck

HALFMOON BAY, pop 1,656, is a small waterfront community on the SUNSHINE COAST, 10 km north of SECHELT. Established in the mid-1890s, it was originally named Welcome Pass after the channel that separates the bay from a group of offshore islands. Well protected by the largest of these, S THORMANBY ISLAND, it offers good anchorage and a variety of services to passing boaters. A popular summer resort, Redrooffs, was located here and gave its name to the main access road. The Merry Island light station, located offshore, began operating in 1902 and in 1999 was one of 27 coastal BC LIGHTHOUSES to have a keeper in residence.

HALFWAY RIVER, pop 137, is a predominantly DUNNE-ZA (Beaver) community in the TREATY NO 8 area northwest of FORT ST JOHN. It was formed in 1977 following a division of the Hudson Hope band into the W Moberley and Halfway River bands. The Halfway R is a tributary of the PEACE R. The FOREST INDUSTRY is the main employer.

HALIBUT (*Hippoglossus stenolepsis*) is the largest of the marine FLATFISH found off the coast of BC and Alaska. An important traditional food fish for the FIRST NATIONS, it has been fished commercially from the 1880s. Fishers used longlines, heavy lines set on the bottom to which a series of shorter hooked and baited lines are attached. Initially fishers worked from small dories or canoes associated with a large schooner. During the 1920s there was a shift to longlining directly from larger fish boats. The classic halibut schooner was powered by a gas or diesel engine but was also rigged with sails for increased speed and stability. The catch was either frozen or sold fresh; it was not canned. The arrival of railways made VANCOUVER and PRINCE RUPERT the principal halibut shipping ports. The catch peaked in 1912 and overfishing resulted in the stocks being depleted rapidly, especially in inshore waters. In 1923 Canada and the US signed a treaty to regulate the fishery and create the International Fisheries Commission (from 1953 the INTERNATIONAL PACIFIC HALIBUT COMMISSION). Stocks then stabilized until the late 1960s, when they began to dwindle again, largely due to foreign trawling activity, and in 1979 halibut fishers came under

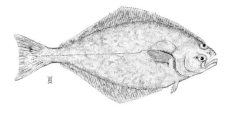

Pacific halibut. Phil Edgell photo; drawing courtesy Fisheries & Oceans Canada

licence limitation. By this time halibut accounted for less than 2% of the wholesale value of all BC fish, down from 20% a decade earlier. The IPHC's conservative management policies helped stocks rebound in the 1980s, and by the late 1990s they had returned to near historic highs. In the late 1990s halibut fishers had individual quotas, which they filled during the Mar–Oct halibut season. In 1998 BC fishers harvested 5,300 tonnes of halibut with a wholesale value of $68 million. *See also* FISHING, COMMERCIAL; FISHING, SPORT; HALIBUT TREATY.

HALIBUT TREATY (formally the Convention for the Preservation of the Halibut Fishery of the Northern Pacific Ocean) was an agreement between the US and Canada signed on 2 Mar 1923. A milestone in the development of Canadian autonomy, it was the first time that Canada alone negotiated and signed an international treaty on its own behalf. The convention provided for a 3-month closed winter season for HALIBUT fishing, created a 4-member International Fisheries Commission (IFC) and authorized a study of the life history of the fish. The treaty was ratified by both countries in 1924. It was replaced in 1930 by a new agreement that gave the IFC expanded powers to limit the halibut catch and to regulate vessels and gear. It was revised again in 1937, then replaced in 1953 by the establishment of the INTERNATIONAL PACIFIC HALIBUT COMMISSION (IPHC), which had 6 members. In 1979 a renewed convention stipulated an end to the US fishery off the BC coast and the BC fishery in American waters, in keeping with the earlier introduction of 200-mile (320-km) limits by both countries. The IPHC continued as a research and advisory group.

HALKOMELEM are Central Coast Salish people (*see* SALISHAN FIRST NATIONS) with Island and Mainland branches, the latter divided into Upriver and Downriver. Halkomelem is a single language comprised of mutually understandable dialectal forms spoken by groups along the lower FRASER R and across GEORGIA STRAIT on VAN-

COUVER ISLAND (*see also* FIRST NATIONS LANGUAGES).

Island Halkomelem FIRST NATIONS (also known as Hul'qumi'num) include the Malahat (pop 215) of SAANICH INLET, the COWICHAN of the Cowichan Valley (3,000), the Chemainus of LADYSMITH Harbour (817), the Halalt (181) near DUNCAN, the Penelakut (650) on KUPER ISLAND, the Lyackson (200) on VALDES ISLAND, the SNUNEYMUXW (formerly Nanaimo; pop 1,200) at NANAIMO and the Snaw naw as (formerly Nanoose; pop 177) at NANOOSE BAY. Traditionally each group occupied several villages throughout its territory, subsisting on SALMON, shellfish, DEER and CAMAS. They visited the lower Fraser R for the summer salmon run, mingling there with their Mainland Halkomelem-speaking relatives and, in the FUR TRADE era, trading at FORT LANGLEY. At the end of the 19th century they found seasonal employment in SALMON CANNERIES at the mouth of the Fraser. Today the different groups are represented by 3 tribal councils: the Mid-Island at Chemainus, the Alliance at DELTA and the First Nations of South Island at SAANICHTON.

The Mainland, or River, Halkomelem occupy the banks of the Fraser R from YALE down to the mouth. There are 30 First Nations communities in the territory, many of which belong to the STO:LO Nation. Along with the Sto:lo, they include the Kwayhquitlam (formerly Coquitlam), KATZIE, X'muzk'i'um (MUSQUEAM) and Tsawwassen First Nations. The X'muzk'i'um (pop 890) inhabited the mouth of the Fraser and around Point Grey into BURRARD INLET and FALSE CRK; in other words, much of modern VANCOUVER. The Tsawwassen (pop 158) lived along the coast south of the river near the site of the modern BC FERRY CORP terminal at TSAWWASSEN. All groups subsisted by hunting, gathering and FISHING for the salmon that was the mainstay of their livelihoods. They did not participate in the SEA OTTER trade but became involved in the land-based fur trade after the HBC established Fort Langley in 1827. The discovery of gold in the Fraser Canyon in 1858 touched off an influx of white miners (*see* GOLD RUSH, FRASER R), followed by settlers and missionaries. By the end of the century salmon canneries at the mouth of the river were providing seasonal employment for the people, and non-aboriginal fishers were competing for the fish upon which the Halkomelem had relied for centuries. The fishery continues to be a contentious issue on the river.

HALL, an early W KOOTENAY MINING camp on the Salmo R and NELSON & FORT SHEPPARD RWY 13 km south of NELSON, was named for Oscar and William Hall, who discovered rich SILVER and COPPER deposits on nearby Toad Mt in 1886. They developed the Silver King mine, which was connected by a 14-km tramway to the Hall SMELTER in Nelson, at one time the largest copper blast furnace in the world. *AS*

HALL, Coleman E. "Coley," hockey executive (b 6 Dec 1906, Vancouver). After trying out as a professional BASEBALL pitcher he went into the lumber business, then owned a series of hotels in VANCOUVER including the York. During WWII he sponsored a senior amateur HOCKEY team named after his St Regis Hotel. Following the war he leased the Forum from the PNE and in 1945 he and co-owner Paul Thompson started the VANCOUVER CANUCKS franchise in the Pacific Coast League, which became a minor-league professional organization in 1948 and changed its name to the Western Hockey League in 1951. Hall remained owner/manager of the Canucks until he sold the club to the PNE in 1959 and went to San Francisco to operate the WHL Seals team 1961–64. Back in Vancouver he was a member of the board of directors of the NHL Canucks from their first season in 1970 to the late 1980s. *SW*

Coley Hall, hockey executive, 1995.
Ralph Bower/Vancouver Sun

HALLIDAY brothers, William and Ernest, took up land in the estuary of the Kingcome R at the head of KINGCOME INLET in 1895 and established one of BC's most isolated cattle ranches. William became Indian agent for the Central Coast region and played a controversial role in implementing the federal government's ban on the POTLATCH. He wrote about his experiences in *Potlatch and Totem* (1935). The Halliday ranch remained in the family until the 1990s, and became a coastal landmark. *See also* ABORIGINAL RIGHTS; FIRST NATIONS. *Howard White*

HALLS PRAIRIE was an early FRASER VALLEY farming (*see* AGRICULTURE) settlement 26 km southeast of NEW WESTMINSTER in SURREY. Sam Hall, a trapper who traded with the HBC at FORT LANGLEY, lived here in the early 1860s. The first homesteaders arrived the next decade and by the 1880s a road, post office and school were in place. *AS*

HALPERN, Ida (Ruhdorfer), musicologist (b 17 July 1910, Vienna, Austria; d 7 Feb 1987, Vancouver). She was a talented musician and scholar. With her husband Georg, a chemist, she joined the exodus of Jews from Austria following the 1938 invasion by Germany. The couple

fled to Shanghai, then immigrated to VANCOUVER in 1939. Halpern became a music teacher and an active force in the local music scene. She was founding president of the Friends of Chamber Music, a director of the symphony orchestra and the Academy of Music, and a music critic with the Vancouver PROVINCE from 1952 to 1957. Her main scholarly interest was the music of the coastal FIRST NATIONS; she was virtually the first non-Native person to study this music seriously. She collected hundreds of songs from cultural authorities such as Billy ASSU, Mungo MARTIN and Tom Willie, and between 1967 and 1987 produced 4 double record albums of material. An independent researcher with no regular university affiliation, she earned widespread respect for her work, 2 honorary degrees and membership in the Order of Canada.

Ida Halpern, musicologist, 1962. VPL 60953

HAMBER, Eric Werge, businessman, lt gov 1936–41 (b 21 Apr 1879 Winnipeg; d 10 Jan 1960, Vancouver). The son of a schoolmaster at St John's School in Winnipeg, he was an all-around athlete as a youth, excelling at ROWING, RUGBY, FOOTBALL and HOCKEY. He began a career in banking as a junior clerk with the Dominion Bank and moved to VANCOUVER to open a branch in 1907. Five years later he married Aldyen Hendry, daughter of the prominent mill owner John HENDRY. The newlyweds moved into their Shaughnessy mansion, Greencroft, and he went to work for his father-in-law at BC MILLS TIMBER & TRADING CO. At Hendry's death in 1916 Hamber became president of the company. Other directorships followed. Active in HORSE RACING and yachting, he and his wife supported many charitable causes and were one of the most prominent couples in the city. Hamber succeeded J.W.F. JOHNSON as LT GOV on 1 May 1936. He filled the position with flair and was popular

Eric Hamber, lt gov of BC 1936–41, on his polo pony, 1936. Leonard Frank/VPL 10304

with the public. In 1939 he welcomed King George VI to the province as part of that year's royal tour. Resisting pressure to take another term, he left office in 1941 and returned to Vancouver. Among other positions, he was chancellor of UBC from 1944 to 1951.

HAMBER PROVINCIAL PARK, 245 km², lies adjacent to Jasper National Park in the ROCKY MTS west of the Continental Divide. When it was established in 1941, it spanned the distance along the Rockies from Mt ROBSON Provincial Park to YOHO NATIONAL PARK, but the boundaries were redrawn in response to commercial pressure, largely from the LOGGING industry. The park is named after Eric HAMBER, a former LT GOV. Accessible only on foot or by float plane, the park caters to experienced hikers and MOUNTAINEERS. *See also* PARKS, PROVINCIAL.

HAMERSLEY, Alfred St George, lawyer (b 8 Oct 1848, Oxfordshire, England; d 25 Feb 1929, Bournemouth, England). He was educated in British public schools, then went to New Zealand and practised law, fought the Maoris and apparently introduced RUGBY, one of his passions. He came to VANCOUVER in 1888. He was the city's first solicitor, an advisor to the CPR and first president of the BC Rugby Union. He developed the lower Lonsdale area of N VANCOUVER in 1905, then returned to England the next year. Every inch the English gentleman, he was a British MP from 1910 to 1918.

HANCEVILLE, pop 68, 90 km west of WILLIAMS LAKE on the Chilcotin Hwy (*see* ROADS AND HWYS), is named for Tom Hance (d 1910), a pioneer FUR TRADER and rancher (*see* CATTLE INDUSTRY) who arrived in 1875. A post office opened at his TH Ranch in 1889, and there was a store and stopping place. Subsequently the post office moved to nearby Lee's Corner, named for another pioneer rancher, Norman LEE, and took the name with it, so that Lee's Corner is now Hanceville. One of the Hance children, Rene, was BC's longest serving coroner. The ranch remained in the family until 1966.

HANDLOGGING was practised on the banks of many protected waterways of the BC coast, beginning in the 1860s. On areas of steep shoreline, loggers selected trees that would fall or slide into the water when cut. Trees that did not reach the water were moved with hand jacks, after the tops and limbs were removed. The first handloggers worked in BURRARD INLET, supplying timber to HASTINGS MILL, which later grew into the city of VANCOUVER, and MOODYVILLE SAWMILL on the North Shore. After 1906, regulations prohibited the use of machinery to skid handlogged timber into the water. Many early handlogging operations evolved into much larger, successful LOGGING and SAWMILLING companies. Handlogging licences, granting the right to cut timber on Crown land, were still being issued in the BELLA COOLA area in 2000. The early handlogging era is documented in the novel *Woodsmen of the West*, by Martin Allerdale GRAINGER, BC's second chief forester. *Ken Drushka*

HANEY is a riverside community on the north side of the FRASER R, in MAPLE RIDGE east of VANCOUVER. It was established by and named for Thomas Haney; he arrived in 1876 and established a successful brickyard that remained in business until 1977. In 1878 he and his wife Annie built Haney House, later opened to the public. Haney, or Port Haney as it was originally called, developed as a commercial centre and then formed the downtown of Maple Ridge.

HANSARD, a SAWMILLING community 62 km east of PRINCE GEORGE on the FRASER R and the CNR, was named after Hugh Hazen Hansard, the GRAND TRUNK PACIFIC RWY's solicitor. It was the site of a post office from 1924 to 1957. Hansard Lk is located 8 km west. *AS*

HANSEN, Rick, a.k.a. the Man in Motion (b 26 Aug 1957, Port Alberni). He became a paraplegic at age 15 when he was involved as a passenger in a motor vehicle crash near his hometown of WILLIAMS LAKE. He became a competitor in wheelchair sports, winning 19 international marathons, including 3 world championships, and competing for Canada in an exhibition race at the 1984 Olympics. On 21 Mar 1985 he launched his Man in Motion World Tour, and pushed his wheelchair around the globe to raise money for spinal cord injury research and rehabilitation and to celebrate the abilities of people with disabilities. He travelled 40,163 km through 34 countries and ended back in VANCOUVER on 22 May 1987 having raised $24 million. The first person with a disability to graduate in physical education from UBC, he has returned to his alma mater as head of the Rick Hansen Institute dedicated to helping find a cure

Rick Hansen during his Man in Motion world tour, Australia, 1986. Courtesy NIKE International

for paralysis and continuing to improve the quality of life of people with spinal cord injuries. The story of his world tour is told in *Rick Hansen: Man in Motion* (1987). He is a Companion of the Order of Canada (1987), a member of the ORDER OF BC (1990) and has generated $100 million in support of the disabled in Canada.

HAPPY VALLEY, a farming (*see* AGRICULTURE) district 13 km west of VICTORIA, became home to a group of BLACK settlers from the US in about 1860. There are various explanations for the name. According to an early postmaster, one of the settlers, Isaac Mull, named the valley for the joy he felt at being a free man in Canada. Happy Valley is a suburb of COLWOOD, along with the neighbouring communities of METCHOSIN, Luxton and Glen Lake. *AS*

HARBLEDOWN ISLAND, 36 km², is one of a jumble of islands near the northern entrance to JOHNSTONE STRAIT east of ALERT BAY between VANCOUVER ISLAND and the mainland. Heavily forested and mostly uninhabited, it was the site of one or more KWAKWAKA'WAKW villages. A small LOGGING and FISHING settlement existed on the north shore from the early 1900s to the 1920s. *AS*

HARBOUR PUBLISHING CO LTD is a BOOK PUBLISHER founded 1974 by Howard and Mary WHITE in PENDER HARBOUR. It started as an offshoot of the Whites' regional journal *RAINCOAST CHRONICLES*; by the turn of the 21st century the company had published some 350 books in almost every genre, from poetry chapbooks to full-colour coffee table books, mostly by BC authors and virtually all on BC subjects. Some of Harbour's best-known titles are *Raincoast Chronicles First Five*, ed Howard White; *Between the Sky and the Splinters* by Peter TROWER, *Now You're Logging* by Bus Griffiths, *Unborn Things* by Patrick LANE, *O Time in Your Flight* by Hubert EVANS, *Going for Coffee* ed Tom WAYMAN, *Fishing with John* by Edith IGLAUER, *Spilsbury's Coast* by

Joe Fitzgerald, a Denman Island logger, using a Gilchrist jack to roll a log into the water at Henry Bay, 1906. Courtenay & District Museum & Archives D500c

Howard White and Jim SPILSBURY, *A Whole Brass Band* by Anne CAMERON, *Beyond Remembering: The Collected Poems of Al Purdy* by Al PURDY, and the *Encyclopedia of British Columbia*, ed Daniel Francis.

HARCOURT, Michael Franklin, lawyer, politician, premier 5 Nov 1991–22 Feb 1996 (b 6 Jan 1943, Edmonton). Raised in VANCOUVER, he studied law at UBC in the 1960s and emerged in 1968 as a left-leaning activist lawyer, one of the first to practise from a storefront. He began his political career as a city alderman in 1972–80, then served 3 successful terms as mayor in 1980–86, capping his tenure with EXPO 86. Elected to the legislature as an NDP member in 1986, he was acclaimed leader of the party in Apr 1987. He served 4 years of effective opposition, then defeated the scandal-plagued SOCIAL CREDIT government of Bill VANDER ZALM to become BC's second NDP PREMIER. Land use planning, treaty negotiations with FIRST NATIONS (*see* ABORIGINAL RIGHTS) and park creation were among his government's accomplishments, but they were overshadowed by controversy. Harcourt's preference for pragmatic, moderate government earned him the disapproval of both the left and the right. Despite BC's strong economy, business leaders painted him as a hapless servant of labour interests while his attempts to cut budgetary deficits by reducing costs of health care, education and social programs alienated his traditional supporters. So did a decision to allow limited logging in CLAYOQUOT SOUND on VANCOUVER ISLAND, which provoked the ENVIRONMENTAL MOVEMENT to vigorous anti-government protest. Harcourt's attempts to navigate a middle course through these conflicting interests were dealt a fatal blow by a charity-bingo scandal involving his party (see NANAIMO COMMONWEALTH HOLDING SOCIETY). Early in 1996 he stepped down as leader and left politics to work at UBC on sustainability issues. It was widely believed that he had failed to translate his personal decency into an effective leadership style.

Michael Harcourt, premier of BC 1991–96.

HARDIN, Herschel, writer (b 17 Aug 1936, Vegreville, AB). He has been at different times a playwright, broadcaster, journalist, arts critic and social activist. After graduating from Queen's Univ in Kingston, ON, and travelling for a couple of years, he moved to BC in 1960 and wrote his first plays, most notably *Esker Mike and his Wife, Agiluk*. In the 1970s he began writing about economics and broadcasting from a Canadian nationalist point of view. His books include *A Nation Unaware: The Canadian Economic Culture* (1974), *Closed Circuits: The Sellout of Canadian Television* (1985), *The Privatization Putsch* (1989) and *The New Bureaucracy: Waste and Folly in the Private Sector* (1991). Hardin's work combines journalistic inquiry with economic and political iconoclasm, reflecting his CCF roots and a keen sense of how Canada differs from the US. In 1995 he ran unsuccessfully for the leadership of the federal NDP. *Working Dollars: The VanCity Story* (*see* VANCOUVER CITY SAVINGS CREDIT UNION) was published in 1996; a political work for THEATRE, *The New World Order*, was produced in 1999.

HARDWICKE ISLAND, 78 km², one of numerous small and medium-sized islands between northern VANCOUVER ISLAND and the mainland, lies across JOHNSTONE STRAIT from KELSEY BAY 70 km north of CAMPBELL RIVER. It was named in 1792 by Capt George VANCOUVER after Philip Yorke, 3rd Earl of Hardwicke, a British politician. Yorke Island, off the western tip, was fitted with gun emplacements during WWII to defend against an anticipated Japanese invasion of the coast. The first permanent settlers were the logger William Kelsey and his wife in 1911. They were followed by Hans Bendickson, who settled with his family in 1918 and developed a substantial LOGGING business in the area. The Bendickson family has been associated with the island ever since.

HARDY ISLAND lies at the mouth of JERVIS INLET north of NELSON ISLAND. It is named after a British naval hero from the Battle of Trafalgar. During WWI it was the site of a granite quarry. From 1930 to 1951 it was owned by LeRoy Macomber, a Seattle financier; Macomber's caretaker, Tom Brazil, turned the island into a DEER sanctuary. Since the 1950s it has been logged extensively by a series of owners.

HARLOW, Robert, writer, teacher (b 19 Nov 1923, Prince Rupert). He was raised in PRINCE GEORGE and while still a teenager joined the RCAF and flew as a bomber pilot during WWII, earning a DFC. After the war he attended UBC and then the famous Writers' Workshop at the Univ of Iowa, where he acquired an MFA in 1951. From 1951 to 1965 he worked for CBC Radio in VANCOUVER, for most of that time as director of radio for the BC region. At the same time he wrote his first novel, *Royal Murdoch*, which appeared in 1962. It was followed by 2 others, *A Gift of Echoes* (1965) and *Scann* (1972); together they make up the Linden trilogy, named for their setting, an imaginary town modelled on Prince George. Harlow succeeded Earle BIRNEY as

head of the creative writing department at UBC in 1965, a post he held until 1977. He remained at the university until his retirement in 1988 and is a professor emeritus. Meanwhile he published 4 more novels: *Making Arrangements* (1977), *Paul Nolan* (1983), *Felice: A Travelogue* (1985) and *The Saxophone Winter* (1988).

HARMAC PACIFIC INC, a Vancouver-based pulp producer, was spun off from MACMILLAN BLOEDEL in 1994 to operate a pulp mill in NANAIMO. The mill was built in 1950 by the H.R. MacMillan Export Co, forerunner of Macblo. In 1997 it added mills in Pictou County, NS, and Terrace Bay, ON, along with associated timberlands, and became the largest producer of pulp in Canada with revenues of $226.4 million. In 1998 Pope & Talbot Inc of Portland bought a controlling interest in the company. *See also* PULP AND PAPER.

HARMFUL ALGAL BLOOMS, or HABs, are blooms of phytoplankton, or algae, that build up to a large enough number that they are harmful to other forms of life. The rate of reproduction is so rapid compared to other species that they may discolour the ocean over a wide area. Red Tide is the popular name for this phenomenon. One type of HAB is caused by a tiny, single-celled dinoflagellate called *Alexandrium*, which produces a poison called saxitoxin. When filter-feeding shellfish—principally bivalves such as CLAMS, OYSTERS, SCALLOPS and MUSSELS—ingest large quantities of this algae they concentrate the toxin, which can be fatal when eaten by fish, seabirds and mammals, including humans. Saxitoxin in very small quantities blocks nerve impulses, causing muscle paralysis and sometimes death. This condition, known as Paralytic Shellfish Poisoning (PSP), has caused 5 recorded fatalities on the BC coast since 1942. Mild symptoms include tingling of the extremities (lips, face, neck, fingers and toes), headache and dizziness. There may also be gastrointestinal symptoms such as nausea, vomiting, diarrhea and abdominal pain. Higher levels of poisoning may result in paralysis of the respiratory muscles and death within 2½ hours of consumption. Onset of symptoms is usually within 5–30 minutes. Many people inaccurately term any discoloration of the sea caused by algae as "red tide"; in fact most red discolorations are not toxic.

Demoic acid, another toxic compound produced by algae, causes Amnesic Shellfish Poisoning (ASP). It produces intestinal and neurological symptoms, including memory loss, and in large quantities may be fatal. Time for onset of symptoms is usually ½–6 hours. Other types of HABs are caused by species of algae such as *Heterosigma* and *Pfisteria*, which primarily affect fin fish. Non-toxic to humans, some of these blooms have had a severe impact on SALMON farms by either poisoning the fish or suffocating them by plugging their gills (*see* AQUACULTURE, FIN FISH). The Canada Food Inspection Agency monitors levels of toxicity and periodically recommends closures of parts of the coast to shellfish harvesting.

HARMON, Daniel Williams, fur trader (b 19 Feb 1778, Bennington, VT; d 23 Apr 1843, near Montreal). He joined the FUR TRADE in Montreal in about 1800 and served with the North West Co (NWC) for 2 decades. After stints at posts in Saskatchewan and northern Alberta, he crossed the ROCKY MTS into NEW CALEDONIA in 1810. Stationed at FORT ST JAMES and FORT FRASER, he remained in the district for 9 years before returning to eastern Canada. When the NWC and the HBC merged, he retired to Vermont. Later he tried to develop a farm north of Montreal, but he died in poverty. Harmon kept a journal for many years; it is one of the most interesting accounts of daily life in fur country.

HARO STRAIT, between the SAANICH PENINSULA on southern VANCOUVER ISLAND and the San Juan Islands of the US, extends 30 km from JUAN DE FUCA STRAIT north to the main GULF ISLANDS and GEORGIA STRAIT. The Canada–US border runs down the middle of Haro Strait. This section of the border was left ambiguous by the OREGON TREATY of 1846. The British argued that the line passed east of the San Juan Islands down Rosario Strait, while the Americans claimed the islands and wanted the border drawn through Haro Strait. The matter led to the so-called PIG WAR and was not resolved in favour of the Americans until 1872. Haro Strait was located by the Spanish explorer Manuel QUIMPER in 1790; he named it for his first mate Gonzalez Lopez de Haro. Islands in Haro Strait are important stopovers for migratory birds; MANDARTE ISLAND, 2 km due east of the north end of SIDNEY ISLAND, supports the largest seabird colony on the South Coast.

HARRIS, Christie Irwin, writer (b 21 Nov 1907, Newark, NJ). Raised on a BC homestead, she became a schoolteacher and turned to writing after her marriage in 1932. She wrote hundreds of radio scripts but did not begin publishing books for young readers—for which she is best known—until she was 50. Since then she has written 20 children's books, most notably *Raven's Cry* (1966), *Mouse Woman and the Vanished Princesses* (1976) and *The Trouble with Princesses* (1980). Her work promotes respect for nature and for FIRST NATIONS cultures. A member of the Order of Canada (1980), Harris has won several major book awards.

HARRIS, Lawren Stewart, artist (b 23 Oct 1885, Brantford, ON; d 29 Jan 1970, Vancouver). The acknowledged leader of the Group of Seven, he was an influential figure in Canadian art for half a century. After studying painting in Berlin from 1904 to 1908, he returned to Ontario and spent the next few years developing his talents as a painter of the northern shield country. He was joined by a group of young painters who shared his commitment to the Canadian landscape and in 1920 they formed the Group of Seven. The group formally lasted until 1931, then merged into the larger Canadian Group of Painters. During the 1930s Harris developed a more abstract spiritual approach to painting, influenced by his interest

Lawren Harris, artist, at age 74.
Brian Kent/Vancouver Sun

in theosophy. From 1934 to 1940 he lived in the US, then moved to VANCOUVER, where he remained for the rest of his life, developing his cerebral abstract style. He was an influential leader in the art community, both locally at the VANCOUVER ART GALLERY and nationally with the National Gallery. *See also* ART, VISUAL.

HARRISON, Lance Easton, musician (b 23 June 1920, Vancouver). The father of traditional and Dixieland JAZZ in VANCOUVER, he began playing saxophone professionally when he was in his teens. A self-taught musician, he was inspired by the clarinet playing of Benny Goodman and picked up the clarinet before focussing on the sax. He began playing locally in the 1930s with Trevor Page's Big Band. He then played briefly with the Dal RICHARDS Orchestra before a 5-year stint in the RCAF band during WWII. After the war he led his own Dixieland bands and hosted several CBC Radio shows. During the 1950s he was part of the house band at the legendary Palomar Supper Club. In the 1960s and 1970s he was a regular at Frank Baker's Attic restaurant in W VANCOUVER and later at the Troller in HORSESHOE BAY. He made 3 records over his career and continued to perform through the 1990s.

Mike Harling

HARRISON HOT SPRINGS, village, pop 898, is a waterfront resort community at the south end of HARRISON LK, about 100 km east of VANCOUVER. Hot, mineral-rich water from nearby springs was believed to be healthful, especially for arthritis and rheumatism sufferers, and the community has been a popular year-round resort since the first hotel, the St Alice, opened in 1886. It has also been a supply centre for LOGGING around the lake. Incorporated on 27 May 1949, the community is named for Benjamin Harrison, an official with the HBC. An annual sand-castle building competition takes place here each summer, attracting visitors from around the world.

HARRISON LAKE, 224.7 km², 55 km long, lies in the mountains north of the FRASER R about 100 km east of VANCOUVER. It is the largest LAKE in the FRASER VALLEY, and drains by the Harrison R 18 km into the Fraser. The area was originally the territory of 3 Coast Salish nations: Sts'a'i:les (Chehalis), Sq'ewlets (Scowlitz) and Xa'xtsa (Douglas) (*see* SALISHAN FIRST NATIONS). The waterway was explored by HBC traders in search of a route to the Interior and named for the HBC official Benjamin Harrison. The HBC operated a SALMON saltery near the mouth of the river from 1848 to 1858 (*see also* FUR TRADE, LAND–BASED). From 1858 it was an important route used by prospectors heading for GOLD diggings, until the CARIBOO WAGON ROAD became available in the mid-1860s (*see also* DOUGLAS TRAIL). HARRISON HOT SPRINGS developed after 1886 as a tourist resort at the thermal springs at the south end of the lake. LOGGING began at the end of the 19th century and was the main activity in the area for several decades. In the late 1990s logs from around the lake were still boomed and towed out to the mills along the lower Fraser. The Harrison R supports a salmon population; as a result, EAGLES are plentiful during late autumn and winter. The Sts'a'i:les occupy a village (pop 785) on the north shore of the river and the Sq'ewlets (pop 198) live on Harrison Bay.

HARRISON MILLS was a SAWMILLING centre on Harrison Bay near the confluence of the Harrison and FRASER rivers about 50 km west of HOPE. Originally the site of a Scowlitz (*see* STO:LO) village, it was named Carnarvon during the GOLD RUSH period when it was little more than a stopping place for miners. Henry Cooper opened the first mill here in 1870. It was joined by a second, larger mill in 1887; in 1903 this second mill became the Rat Portage mill and for a brief period was the centre of a small company town. The Rat Portage mill ceased operation in 1911, though it was not dismantled until 1923. A third mill, at one time the largest shingle mill in BC (*see* FOREST PRODUCTS), operated from 1901 to 1948. Following the mill closures the area continued to be used by loggers, chiefly as a dump site. The KILBY GENERAL STORE museum recalls the early days.

HARROGATE, pop 37, on the east side of the COLUMBIA R 50 km southeast of GOLDEN, is a farming (*see* AGRICULTURE) and LOGGING settlement. It got its start as a roadhouse in the stagecoach era and was named—with a bold eye to the future—after Harrogate, a grand English resort.

AS

HARROP, a quiet rural settlement 20 km northeast of NELSON, on the CPR and the south shore of the West Arm of KOOTENAY LK, is connected to Longbeach on Hwy 3A by a cable ferry (*see also* BIG BAR). A ferry of one sort or another has operated here since 1925; before that the area was served by PADDLEWHEEL STEAMBOATS. It is named after Ernest Harrop, who moved here in 1905 and became the first postmaster.

AS

HART, John, businessman, politician, premier 9 Dec 1941–29 Dec 1947 (b 31 Mar 1879, Mohill, Ireland; d 7 Apr 1957, Victoria). He arrived in VICTORIA in 1898 and was running his own finance business when he was elected a LIBERAL MLA for Victoria in 1916. The next year he became finance minister in Harlan BREWSTER's government and occupied the post continuously until becoming PREMIER, aside from an absence from politics in 1924–33. In fall 1941 Hart endorsed a wartime COALITION GOVERNMENT. Liberal Premier Duff PATTULLO, who opposed the idea, resigned; Hart became party leader and premier as well as finance minister. He immediately formed a coalition ministry with the CONSERVATIVES. The provincial Liberal Party did not form another government on its own in the 20th century. Hart ran a businesslike, middle-of-the-road government notable mainly for its aggressive highway-building policies, creation of the BC POWER COMMISSION (1945) to undertake rural electrification, and promotion of northern economic development. At the end of the war the coalition continued as a means of denying power to the increasingly popular CCF, a tactic that worked in the 1945 provincial election. In 1947 Hart resigned as premier, citing ill health. The Senate seat he expected did not materialize and he returned to private life in Victoria.

John Hart, premier of BC 1941–47, shown in a painting by F. Aveline. BC Archives PDP-00362

HART HIGHWAY (Hwy 97) runs 406 km northeast from PRINCE GEORGE across the ROCKY MTS to DAWSON CREEK in the PEACE R country. Construction began in 1945 and after many delays was completed on 1 July 1952. The highway is named for John HART, who was premier from 1941 to 1947. *See also* ROADS AND HIGHWAYS.

HARTLEY BAY, pop 155, is a coastal FISHING community at the mouth of DOUGLAS CHANNEL, 125 km south of PRINCE RUPERT. It was occupied originally by the Gitga'ata, a southern TSIMSHIAN nation. They moved north to William DUNCAN's settlement at METLAKATLA in the 1860s and 1870s, but many returned to their traditional territory in 1887 and founded a new community, Hartley Bay, not far from their original village site. It is an isolated waterfront village linked by elevated wooden roads.

HASTINGS, Oregon Columbus, photographer (b 26 Apr 1846, Pontoosuc, IL; d 5 Aug 1912, Victoria). He came to VICTORIA in the 1870s and entered the photographic business, eventually opening his own studio. Mainly a portrait photographer, he was also official photographer aboard a naval survey of coastal FIRST NATIONS villages in 1879; in the 1890s he made images for the famed anthropologist Franz BOAS during Boas's visits to VANCOUVER ISLAND aboriginal communities. Hastings was also an amateur astronomer and had a homemade observatory in his house. *See also* PHOTOGRAPHY.

HASTINGS MILL, built in 1865, was the first SAWMILL to operate on the south shore of BURRARD INLET, at the foot of Heatley St in what is now VANCOUVER. It was built by Capt Edward STAMP to cut lumber for the export market, using wood logged at JERICHO BEACH by Jeremiah ROGERS. In 1870 the mill was sold to Heatley & Co of London, with Capt J.A. Raymur appointed manager. The settlement that grew around the mill was known as GRANVILLE, or GASTOWN. It became the western terminus of the CPR when the railway moved from PORT MOODY in 1887. In about 1890 the mill was sold to John HENDRY, who merged it with his Royal City Planing Mills in NEW WESTMINSTER to form BC MILLS TIMBER & TRADING CO. Hendry doubled its capacity, developing the company's LOGGING operations in the JOHNSTONE STRAIT area, and building a fleet of TOWBOATS to haul logs to the mill. Just after 1900, Hendry purchased the MOODYVILLE sawmill across the inlet from the Hastings Mill, making his company one of the biggest lumber producers in the Pacific Northwest. The company prospered until after WWI, when it went into a long decline. In the early 1920s its logging operations were sold and the mill closed before the onset of the Depression. *Ken Drushka*

HASTINGS PARK RACECOURSE is a thoroughbred HORSE RACING track, formerly known as Exhibition Park, in HASTINGS PARK on the east side of VANCOUVER. A racetrack of some kind has been on the site since 1889. From 1909 the track was operated by the Vancouver Exhibition Assoc; in 1923 it leased the half-mile (0.8-km) facility to the Westminster Thoroughbred Assoc, later the Ascot Jockey Club, owned by Sam RANDALL. This arrangement lasted until 1960, when the Randall family and Vancouver entrepreneur Jack DIAMOND created the BC Jockey Club, which took over the lease and concentrated all thoroughbred racing in the Lower Mainland at Hastings Park. Since 1993 the track has been managed by the Pacific Racing Association.

HAT CREEK is a historic ranch 11 km north of CACHE CREEK. It began as a cattle ranch, and a roadhouse and store were established in 1860

Historic Hat Creek Ranch.
Walter Lanz/Image Makers

Hastings Mill on the Vancouver waterfront, c 1890. UBC BC288/4

on the old CARIBOO WAGON ROAD by Donald MCLEAN, an HBC trader. Gradually Hat Creek House expanded into a full-service hotel. The ranch was owned from 1910 by Charles Doering, president of BC Brewing Co, and his descendants who sold it to BC HYDRO in the 1970s. The old roadhouse and adjacent buildings were acquired by the provincial government in 1981, restored as a heritage site and opened to the public in 1987 as the Historic Hat Creek Ranch. The property is said to be haunted: guests and caretakers have reported sounds from the blacksmith shop that used to operate here, and according to local legend a man committed suicide in the roadhouse.

HATLEY PARK is a large medieval castle built by James DUNSMUIR, one-time premier (1900–02) and lt gov (1906–09), where he and his family emulated the life of the English landed gentry. Construction of the palatial home was completed in 1908 on 2.4 km² of land overlooking Esquimalt Lagoon outside VICTORIA. It was designed by Samuel MACLURE, the city's leading architect, and was known for its fine gardens. The Department of National Defence purchased the property in 1940 and made it part of Royal Roads Military College. When the government closed the college in 1994 it was resurrected as ROYAL ROADS UNIV; the castle now serves as the university administration building.

HATZIC, 65 km east of VANCOUVER on the north shore of the FRASER R, is in the municipality of MISSION. A former HBC employee named La Croix had a trading post here in the 1860s; Ralph Burton cleared the first homestead. The fertile land attracted many early settlers and fruit-growing became important. Hatzic was originally known as Well's Landing after a local pioneer. The name is HALKOMELEM and may mean "shore" or "beach."   AS

HATZIC ROCK is a huge boulder near HATZIC, 2 km east of MISSION on the north side of the FRASER R. The rock is held sacred by the STO:LO

Nation. Archaeologists digging in the vicinity have uncovered the oldest human dwellings in BC, dating back 5,200 years. The site, which is now Xa:ytem National Historic Site, was the main village of the Xat'suq' (Hatzic) Nation of the Sto:lo, until it was infected by SMALLPOX and abandoned. *See also* ARCHAEOLOGY.

HAUFSCHILD, Lutz, artist (b 1943, Breslau, Germany). He has practised as an independent sculptor and stained glass artist in VANCOUVER since 1969. His work constitutes some of the largest architectural stained glass ever executed in N America. His traditional use of colour and glass at Westminster Abbey in the FRASER VALLEY is representative of his ecclesiastical work, while the vast skylights at Coquitlam Centre and windows for Sunridge Mall in Calgary demonstrate a more expressionist style. His masterpiece remains the Ismaili Prayerhouse in BURNABY (Bruno FRESCHI, Architects). At the Robson Court in VANCOUVER he moved beyond stained glass, creating a composition of crystal prisms and flowing areas of painted glass. In 1988 he won the annual Saidye Bronfman Award for Excellence in the Crafts.   *Martin Segger*

HAWAIIANS arrived on the Pacific coast of N America between the late 18th and mid-19th centuries as crew members with the earliest maritime traders. From 1811 they were recruited directly for the FUR TRADE by the trading companies and served the NORTH WEST CO and the HBC at posts throughout the Pacific slope. About 400 Hawaiians were employed in the land-based trade and several hundred more visited the coast as crew aboard trading vessels. Known colloquially as Kanakas, a Polynesian word meaning "human being," they were employed mainly at coastal trading posts. Instead of returning to Hawaii, some married FIRST NATIONS women and settled in BC, principally along the lower FRASER R, at MOODYVILLE on the north side of BURRARD INLET, and on SALTSPRING ISLAND. In VICTORIA, Kanaka Row was a small shantytown on

the present site of the EMPRESS HOTEL; in VANCOUVER, several Hawaiians lived at Kanaka Ranch in what is now STANLEY PARK. As Hawaiians intermarried they tended to merge with either local aboriginal or white society, losing their distinctive ethnic identity. Nevertheless there are still many people who trace their ancestry back to the original Hawaiian pioneers. *See also* William NAUKANA.

HAWK is a bird of prey, smaller than an EAGLE. Most types feed on small mammals and birds, using their hooked beaks and curved talons to catch and tear their prey. Along with eagles, they have the keenest eyesight of any living animal. The plumage is usually a blend of greys, browns and whites. Nine species breed in BC. The northern harrier, or marsh hawk (*Circus cyaneus*),

Northern goshawk. Ervio Sian photo

occurs throughout the province, preferring open country, where it nests on the ground in marshes and shrubbery. It also hunts close to the ground, listening for meadow mice, on which it preys. The sharp-shinned (*Accipiter striatus*) and Cooper's hawk (*A. cooperii*) nest in forested areas, hunting small birds. The northern goshawk (*A. gentilis*) is an extremely aggressive species, swooping down on its prey—usually SQUIRRELS, hare (*see* RABBIT) or GROUSE—at speeds up to 60 km/h. Slate grey in colour with a distinctive white line above each eye, it nests in northern and mountain forests. The rare broadwinged hawk (*Buteo platypterus*) is seen mainly in

Linnea Battel at Hatzic Rock, a sacred site for the Sto:lo Nation, 1991.
Jean Konda-Witte/Abbotsford Times

Red-tailed hawk with its prey.
R. Wayne Campbell photo

the PEACE R lowlands and is a recent arrival in BC. The Swainson's hawk (*B. swainsoni*) occurs mainly in the grasslands of the South-Central Interior, though in much smaller numbers than earlier in the century; it migrates to Argentina for the winter. The red-tailed hawk (*B. jamaicensii*) is one of the most common species, especially in winter in the FRASER R lowlands. Its distinctive brick-red tail colouring appears at age 2 or 3. The ferruginous hawk (*B. regalis*) is an extremely rare summer visitor to the South-Central Interior, where it prefers open parkland terrain. It is the largest species, almost the size of an eagle. The rough-legged hawk (*B. lagopus*) also inhabits open, treeless areas and winters mainly in the Fraser R lowlands and southern valleys.

HAWTHORN is a small deciduous tree occurring across Canada in more than 2 dozen species. Three species are native to BC, the most widespread being the black hawthorn (*Crataegus douglasii*), which is distributed across the southern half of the province. Hawthorn is distinguished by thorny branches, lovely white blossoms and black-purple or red fruit, called haws, which resemble tiny apples.

HAWTHORN, Harry, anthropologist (b 15 Oct 1910, Wellington, NZ); and **Audrey**, sociologist, museum curator (b 25 Nov 1917). The couple met at graduate school in the US and in 1947 moved to VANCOUVER, where Harry had been offered a position at UBC's new department of anthropology. Together they established the MUSEUM OF ANTHROPOLOGY, initially in the basement of the Main Library on the UBC campus. Harry served as museum director while Audrey became the first curator, in 1949. She attracted worldwide attention for the museum by publishing *Art of the Kwakiutl Indians* (1967) (*see* KWAKWAKA'WAKW) and exhibiting part of the collections at Montreal's Man and his World exhibition (1969–70) She was subsequently responsible for choosing Arthur ERICKSON to design a new museum building; it opened in 1976, at the same time she retired as curator. In 1948 Harry organized a conference on BC FIRST NATIONS arts and crafts (*see* ART, NORTHWEST COAST ABORIGINAL), the first of its kind, and invited aboriginal delegates to represent themselves. He established himself as an authority on aboriginal affairs in BC and Canada through the publication of 2 landmark reports that had a profound effect on public policy: *The Indians of British Columbia* (1958, with Cyril Belshaw and Stuart Jamieson) and *A Survey of the Contemporary Indians of Canada* (1966). Both Hawthorns have been inducted into the Order of Canada.

Shannon Emmerson

Harry and Audrey Hawthorn. *Eliza Massey photo*

HAWTHORNTHWAITE, James Hurst, labour politician (b 1869, Ireland; d 1926, Victoria). After immigrating to BC in 1885, he worked as a colliery clerk at the NANAIMO coal mines, where he was a supporter of the local labour politician Ralph SMITH. Smith defected to the federal Liberal Party in 1900, and Hawthornthwaite took over his seat in the provincial legislature as a member of the Nanaimo INDEPENDENT LABOUR PARTY. Eventually he joined the Socialist Party of Canada, and even though he was instrumental in the passage of Canada's first Workmen's Compensation Act in 1902, he was mistrusted by militants who did not like his qualified support for Premier Richard MCBRIDE, a CONSERVATIVE. Indeed, McBride relied so much on his support from 1903 to 1907 that the press called Hawthornthwaite the "premier-in-fact." In the 1908 federal election Hawthornthwaite ran against Smith in Nanaimo; it was a close contest but Hawthornthwaite lost. He was re-elected to the provincial legislature in 1909, but came under fire from militants in his own constituency. In 1911 he resigned his seat and went to England, where he engaged in a series of business ventures. He then returned to BC and won re-election to the legislature as an independent socialist-labour candidate in a 1918 by-election. His long political career ended after he lost in the 1920 election. *See also* COAL MINING, VANCOUVER ISLAND; LABOUR MOVEMENT.

HAYES MANUFACTURING CO LTD was a major BC manufacturer of LOGGING trucks for over 50 years. Established in 1922 by Douglas Hayes and W.E.Anderson, a QUADRA ISLAND businessman, the company began building trucks specially designed for conditions in the Pacific Northwest. In 1928 the company moved to a new plant on 2nd Ave in VANCOUVER, where it remained for 47 years. It amalgamated with Lawrence Manufacturing in 1946 and became known as Hayes-Lawrence; by the late 1960s it had 600 employees in 3 Vancouver plants. Mack Trucks acquired the company in 1969, then sold to Paccar, a Seattle outfit, which shut Hayes down in 1975. Hayes vehicles were a testament to industrial-strength reliability: hundreds of them were active in the woods a quarter century after they were made. Classic Hayes vehicles from early in the century are in museum collections.

Robert Allington

HAYNES, John Carmichael, public official, rancher (b 6 July 1831, Landscape, Ireland; d 6 July 1888, Princeton). He came to BC in 1858 to join the new PROVINCIAL POLICE force. After serving in the force, he became a justice of the peace and collector of customs in the Interior, and eventually a GOLD commissioner and district court judge. At the same time, he was acquiring land around OSOYOOS; he established a cattle ranch there. By 1882 he owned 90 km² of ranchland, lived in a fine house overlooking OSOYOOS LK and was known as "the Cattle King of the South Okanagan." He died suddenly on his way home from VICTORIA. *See also* CATTLE INDUSTRY.

John Carmichael Haynes, Osoyoos rancher, c 1880. *BC Archives A-01337*

HAYSPORT is an abandoned townsite on the north side of the SKEENA R near its mouth. Established in 1910 as part of the building boom surrounding construction of the GRAND TRUNK PACIFIC RWY to PRINCE RUPERT, it was named for Charles Hayes, president of the railway. A fish cold-storage plant and a SALMON CANNERY were the mainstays of the economy, but by the 1930s both had closed and residents gradually moved away.

HAZELMERE, a farming (*see* AGRICULTURE) settlement in the FRASER VALLEY 24 km south of NEW

WESTMINSTER, was also a station on the NEW WEST-MINSTER SOUTHERN RWY and the site of a SAWMILL. Henry Thrift, who became one of SURREY's early civic leaders, took up land here in 1884 and named his farm Hazelmere.   AS

HAZELTON, village, pop 347, lies at the confluence of the BULKLEY and SKEENA rivers, 290 km east of PRINCE RUPERT. Long inhabited by the GITK-SAN people, it is the site of KSAN, a reconstructed Gitksan village. A townsite was laid out in 1871 next to the village of Gitanmaax and named for the plentiful hazelnuts. In 1879 the HBC purchased a store and began operating a trading post supplied by canoe brigades up the Skeena. The community developed as the head of steamboat navigation on the river and a supply centre for trappers and prospectors. Downtown buildings have been restored to reflect this period. The arrival of the GRAND TRUNK PACIFIC RWY in 1914 diverted development to the opposite side of the river where NEW HAZELTON (pop 822) and S Hazelton (pop 654) grew up. By the 1990s LOGGING and SAWMILLING were the major employers. Sport FISHING for STEELHEAD and SALMON attracts visitors from around the world.

HEAD TAX was a tax imposed in 1885 on CHINESE immigrants to Canada by the federal government's Act to Restrict and Regulate Chinese Immigration. The tax began at $50, rose to $100 in 1900 and was set at $500 from 1903 to 1923. The Chinese were the only group ever taxed to enter Canada. The tax was removed in 1923 and replaced by a virtual ban on all Chinese immigration. During the years it was in force the tax was paid by 82,380 Chinese, producing $22.5 million in public revenue. *See also* PEOPLES OF BC.

HEADQUARTERS was a small LOGGING community on the Tsolum R, north of COURTENAY on VANCOUVER ISLAND. It was established in 1911 by the Comox Logging & Rwy Co as the centre of its FOREST INDUSTRY operations. When the company centralized its activities in 1958, the town was auctioned off.

HEALTH POLICY in BC over the past century has concerned itself with ensuring that all residents have access to adequate medical and hospital care. The province has been in the vanguard of health care reform, introducing both hospital and medical insurance prior to the national adoption of such plans. In 1998 BC became the second province to provide registered midwife services. BC also provides some chiropractic, naturopathic, optometric, orthoptic, podiatric, massage and physiotherapy services under the BC Medical Services Plan (MSP), and PHARMACARE pays for drugs for selected groups. In 1998–99 health services accounted for 36.5% of the provincial government's total expenditures. Health costs rose from $6.3 billion in 1993 to $7.6 billion in 1999, an increase of 20%. This increase in health spending, not only in absolute terms but also relative to the population, distinguished BC from most other provinces, where health budgets shrank during the 1990s.

The history of health policy in BC begins in 1888 with the first *Health Act*. It dealt with general issues of public health, including the collection of morbidity and mortality statistics, the investigation of diseases and epidemics and the monitoring of conditions likely to affect people's health. It also regulated food inspection and handling. Although physicians were regulated under a separate *Medical Act*, it was not until 9 years later that the first *Hospital Act* was legislated. Following WWI health care became an important topic of debate. In 1919 the provincial government appointed a Royal Commission on Health Insurance. Two years later it recommended a plan of limited health insurance but no action was taken. In 1929 another provincial Royal Commission was appointed to report on health insurance. As a result of this commission a medical insurance plan was almost put into place in 1937, but because of opposition from physicians the government did not implement it. In its place a non-profit society, the Medical Services Association (MSA), was created in 1938 with the support of the doctors. MSA was a voluntary plan involving contributions collected by employers. Public medical insurance for those not covered by a private plan was introduced in 1965 as the BC Medical Plan. In 1967 all medical insurance plans were brought under a single Medical Services Commission and the following year universal public medical insurance was introduced in BC. MSA (the private society) continued in areas such as dental insurance until 1996, when it merged with the other non-profit dental insurer, CU&C, to form Pacific Blue Cross.

In 1948 BC introduced provincial hospital insurance. The plan was originally financed with premiums heavily weighted against single people. Financial difficulties were quick to appear as premiums were not paid. In 1954 the premium system was eliminated for provincial hospital insurance and universality was introduced, funded in part by a 2% increase in the sales tax. When medical insurance was introduced in BC, it too was financed in part with a premium system. In 1999 BC and Alberta remained the only provinces that used premiums to finance part of their provincial health insurance. For the fiscal year 1998–99 premium revenues amounted to about $898 million.

Following the introduction of medicare the costs of health services increased dramatically. For example, during 1967–97 physician costs rose from 2.5% to 8.5% of the entire provincial budget, and hospital costs increased from 12% to 14.5%. In 1972 the newly elected NDP government commissioned a major review of BC's health care system. Dr Richard Foulkes' report, *Health Security for British Columbians*, released on 17 Jan 1974, called for a massive reorganization of health care. It recommended the creation of locally elected, provincially funded community human resources and health centres and regional health district boards. Decentralization, service integration and public involvement were the major themes. Six pilot centres were established but none of the other major recommendations of the report were acted on. In 1989 the provincial

Social Credit government appointed a royal commission under Justice Peter Seaton to investigate the issue of escalating health costs, and in the Seaton report, *Closer to Home* (1991), the Foulkes recommendations resurfaced: the report called for decentralized health services and a greater emphasis on home-based care. In response the NDP government announced a restructuring of the health care system. The province created 11 regional health districts for urban areas, each with its own board, and 34 community health councils and 7 community health services societies for rural areas. These bodies are responsible for the delivery of health care services in their jurisdictions. Physician services, Pharmacare, supplementary benefits and the BC AMBULANCE SERVICE continued to be funded centrally. Similar changes to the organization of health services occurred during the 1990s across Canada.

Discussions of health policy tend to focus on services provided by physicians and hospitals because they are the big-budget items. In fiscal year 1996–97 the province's 123 hospitals received a budget of almost $2.9 billion while the budget for the Medical Services Commission was over $1.7 billion. Those 2 items accounted for 64% of the budget of the Ministry of Health. MENTAL HEALTH, community health, public health and the many auxiliary services usually receive less attention. One of the objectives of the new governance structure for health care was to allow community boards to manage the entire range of health services and funding so as to achieve the best outcomes.

The federal government started funding hospital services on roughly a 50% basis with the provinces under the authority of the Hospital Insurance and Diagnostic Services Act of 1957. Medical services also received 50% federal funding when provinces qualified under the Medical Care Act of 1966. The 50% federal sharing was changed in 1977 with the introduction of the Established Programs Financing Act (EPF), covering cost sharing for both health and advanced education. In order to obtain provincial agreement to the change, funding on a per capita basis for extended health care was added, resulting in increased provincial coverage of nursing homes. Under EPF, federal funding was to increase according to a formula tied to the growth of the population and the economy, but with no ties to actual provincial spending on health care. By the early 1980s some provinces, though not BC, were experiencing increased "extra billing" by physicians. (Extra billing is when physicians ask their patients for money in addition to what the provincial plan pays.) Canada responded by adopting the Canada Health Act, which restored the federal government's authority to financially penalize provinces that failed to meet certain national standards. In BC this resulted in the end of user fees for standard ward acute care hospital beds. In 1996 federal funding was further changed with the implementation of the Canada Health and Social Transfer (CHST) to replace EPF. CHST combines federal funding for health, education and social services in one block grant (*see* TRANSFER PAYMENTS).

Hospital Services and Medical Care

Hospital services in BC are funded, on a non-profit basis, by the Regional Programs of the Ministry of Health (MOH). The Medical Services Plan (MSP) is administered and operated on a non-profit basis by the Medical Services Commission (MSC). The Commission is responsible to the provincial government for the administration and operation of the Plan. Regional programs and the MSC are subject to audit of their accounts and financial transactions by the AUDITOR GENERAL of BC. All residents, excluding members of the Canadian Forces and the RCMP, inmates of federal penitentiaries and refugee claimants, and those eligible for compensation from another source, are entitled to hospital and medical care insurance coverage. Enrolment in the MSP is mandatory and payment of premiums is ordinarily a requirement for coverage. However, failure to pay premiums is not a barrier to access to care for those who meet the basic enrolment eligibility criteria. Residents of limited means are eligible for premium assistance. The Medical Care Plan provides for all medically required services of medical practitioners' claims and specified dental/oral surgery when it is necessary for it to be performed in hospital by a dental/oral surgeon. Services not insured are those covered by the Workers' Compensation Act or by other federal or provincial legislation. Payment for medical services delivered in the province is made through the MSP to individual physicians, based on billings submitted. The patient is not normally involved in the payment system. Compensation for medical practitioners is based on a fee schedule established by the MSC, with the advice of the BC Medical Association. Other health-care practitioners offering insured services have individual fee schedules approved by the appropriate co-managed tripartite special committees. The MSC also funds certain medical services through alternative payment arrangements. An Alternative Payments Branch provides funding to some 300 health-care agencies that retain physicians to deliver approved programs. Approximately 1,800 physicians have voluntarily entered into alternative payment arrangements with these agencies and receive part or all of their income through salaries, sessions or service agreements.

The Regional Programs of the MOH fund a comprehensive range of community-based supportive care services to assist people whose ability to function independently is affected by long-term health-related problems or who have acute care needs that can be met at home. Continuing Care services are not federally mandated services and are funded at the sole discretion of the provincial government, through the MOH. Services are delivered at the community level through the health authorities.

Public Health

The Public Health Protection Branch consists of 2 program areas—Food Protection and Environmental Health Protection—and is responsible for the development and implementation of legislation, policies and programs. This activity supports regional health authorities that are responsible for the delivery of these programs and the prevention of disease that may arise from unsanitary practices or exposure to environmental health and safety hazards. Public health protection programs are administered locally by medical health officers and environmental health officers, who are responsible for direct service delivery in health authorities throughout the province. Environmental health officers provide surveillance and monitoring of specific activities and premises that may affect the public's health, and provide appropriate interventions to minimize health and safety hazards. Among its services are a food safety program, including inspection of food service (in restaurants, for example) and other food-processing and food-sale facilities (food stores, butcher shops, dairy plants, schools, hospitals, etc); food safety advice and information to the public and industry; communicable disease investigations related to drinking water, food and other vectors; on-site sewage disposal monitoring, assessments and permits; recreational water inspection and sampling (at public pools, beaches, etc); public drinking-water supply inspection and monitoring; institutional environmental health inspection (at summer camps, schools, etc); tobacco sales enforcement; personal services facilities monitoring (at tattoo parlours, tanning salons, hairdressing salons, etc); and other public health-related activities such as rodent control and investigation of unsanitary conditions. The Preventive Health Branch is responsible for the development of provincial standards, policies and priorities for public health and for prevention issues. These include population health and adult services for public health NURSING, speech, audiology, nutrition, dental, tobacco reduction, heart health, injury prevention, non-communicable disease epidemiology and health services for community living programs. *See also* COMMUNITY DEVELOPMENT; HUMAN CARE SERVICES; MEDICAL PROFESSION.

HECATE, on the north coast of Nootka Island in ESPERANZA INLET, 110 km across VANCOUVER ISLAND from CAMPBELL RIVER, is the former site of a NUU-CHAH-NULTH (Nootka) village. It sat at the entrance to McBride Bay, which had a SALMON CANNERY and SAWMILL in the 1920s and 1930s; LOGGING continued to be a mainstay. Hecate was named after the survey ship commanded by Capt G.H. RICHARDS during 1860–62.   AS

HECATE STRAIT is a stormy passage separating the QUEEN CHARLOTTE ISLANDS from the BC mainland. Ranging in width from 50 to 130 km, it is quite shallow and susceptible to high winds, especially in winter. Swells as high as 8 m are common and because of its shallow depth, seas can build up quickly. These factors combine to make the strait one of the most dangerous bodies of water in the world for boaters. That did not stop the HAIDA from venturing across in their great cedar CANOES, nor does it stop commercial fishers, for whom the strait is an important FISHING ground for a variety of species. It was first explored by the Spanish mariner Jacinto CAAMANO in 1792 and is named after the *Hecate*, a British naval survey vessel that was on the coast from 1860 to 1862.

Stormy seas in Hecate Strait aboard the trawler Caledonian, 1989. Peter A. Robson photo

HECTOR, James, doctor, naturalist (b 16 Mar 1834, Edinburgh, Scotland; d 5 Nov 1907, Wellington, NZ). He graduated from medical school in 1856 and immediately was appointed natural scientist to the Palliser Expedition to explore western Canada. In Aug 1858 he travelled on horseback into the ROCKY MTS, passing the present site of Banff and crossing via Vermilion Pass into BC. He and his small party followed the Vermilion R south through what is now KOOTE-NAY NATIONAL PARK, then turned north up the KOOTENAY R and crossed over to the Kicking Horse R where, on 29 Aug, he was seriously injured by a kick in the chest from a packhorse. The celebrated incident gave its name to the river and to

James Hector, naturalist and explorer.
CVA 371-1634

the pass by which Hector's party travelled back across the mountains out of BC. Before returning to England he toured the FRASER R goldfields (*see* GOLD RUSH, FRASER R) and explored VANCOUVER ISLAND, including the COAL deposits at NANAIMO. In 1862 Hector went to New Zealand, where he became head of the Geological Survey; he stayed there for the rest of his life. In 1903, accompanied by his son Douglas, he made one more visit to BC, touring some of the places he had visited earlier. During the visit Douglas died of appendicitis in REVELSTOKE.

HEDDLE, Kathleen, rower (b 27 Nov 1965, Trail). She teamed with fellow BC native Marnie MCBEAN to win the straight pair race at the 1991 world rowing championships. Both rowers also competed on the first-place Canadian eight team at the same competition. The following year at the Barcelona Olympics the pair won gold medals in the same 2 events. Heddle gave up rowing after the 1992 Olympics but she came out of retirement in 1994 to row with McBean again and the pair won world championship and Commonwealth championship silvers that year. After winning another gold at the 1995

world championships the duo captured their third Olympic gold in 1996 in Atlanta. Heddle also succeeded with her quad sculls team, winning a 1995 world championship silver and a 1996 Olympic bronze. She retired for good at the end of 1996 and later received the ORDER OF BC. Their 3 gold medals make Heddle and McBean the most successful Canadian Olympians of the 20th century.

HEDLEY, pop 402, nestles at the base of the steep face of Nickel Plate Mt in the SIMILKAMEEN R Valley 40 km east of PRINCETON. Mineral claims were staked at several locations on the mountain in the 1890s but the Nickel Plate mine became the most productive. The camp that serviced the mine was named Hedley Camp after Robert R. Hedley (1863–1940), the SMELTER manager at NELSON who had grubstaked one of the early prospectors. A townsite was laid out in 1900 and in 1902–03 the mine added a stamp mill for processing ore. By 1906 the community had 6 hotels, a bank, a newspaper and an orchestra. The Vancouver, Victoria & Eastern Rwy, a subsidiary of the GREAT NORTHERN RWY, arrived in 1909. MINING continued until the mid-1950s when GOLD petered out and the mines closed, but the community survived as a retirement and local service centre. In the 1990s the province began developing the abandoned Mascot mine as a historic site.

HEFFLEY CREEK, 20 km north of KAMLOOPS on the CNR and N THOMPSON R, is an AGRICULTURAL and LOGGING settlement named after Adam P. Heffley, pioneer rancher (*see* CATTLE INDUSTRY), in 1862. Heffley was a partner of Frank Laumeister, who brought 2 dozen CAMELS to BC and tried to use them as pack animals during the GOLD RUSH in the CARIBOO. Bert Balison built a SAWMILL in 1951 (it was later closed) and

added a plywood plant in the 1970s, which was sold to Tolko Industries and employed 190 people in 1999. *AS*

HEILTSUK First Nation, or Bella Bella people, traditionally occupied the Central Coast along FITZ HUGH SOUND and up Burke Channel and DEAN CHANNEL. Their language is Oowekyala-Heiltsuk (*see* FIRST NATIONS LANGUAGES) and they are related to the KWAKWAKA'WAKW (Kwakiutl) and HAISLA within the Northern subgroup of the WAKASHAN family. They migrated seasonally to different resource sites to take advantage of the territory's abundant supplies of FISH, shellfish, sea mammals and land animals. Winters were spent in semi-permanent villages, where they engaged in POTLATCHING and elaborate ceremonies conducted by dancing societies. A distinctive artistic tradition produced CANOES, boxes and utensils made of CEDAR that were prized by outsiders for their workmanship (*see* ART, NORTHWEST COAST ABORIGINAL). The basic social unit was the community group, comprised of related families with their own chief, names, village sites and so on. Society was divided into chiefs, commoners and slaves, who were mainly war captives (*see* SLAVERY). Direct contact with Europeans occurred in 1793 with both Capt George VANCOUVER's expedition and Alexander MACKENZIE's overland party. The Heiltsuk were actively involved in the SEA OTTER trade, and following the establishment of FORT MCLOUGHLIN on Campbell Island in 1833 they became important intermediaries in the FUR TRADE. In 1835 their population was estimated at 1,598, belonging to 5 tribal divisions. As a result of epidemic diseases, the number sank to 204 by 1890 and the 5 original tribes merged. Subsequently the population recovered and in the late 1990s the Heiltsuk numbered about 1,900. The presence of METHODIST missionaries and a trading store at

Heiltsuk workers processing fish for export, Bella Bella. Ian McAllister photo

Campbell Island attracted the people and BELLA BELLA became their main settlement after 1880. During the 1890s the village moved to its present site, now called Waglisla, where the local group operates a hotel, store, school and cultural centre. In 1977 the first potlatch in more than 50 years was held in Waglisla, evidence of the resurgence of traditional culture. The word Heiltsuk means "to speak or act correctly."
Reading: Michael Harkin, *The Heiltsuks*, 1998.

HEINE, Harry, artist (b 1928, Edmonton). He is a watercolourist specializing in the FISHING grounds and FORESTS of the great Northwest, capturing them in romantic settings of mist-shrouded mountains and deep forest. A self-taught painter who moved from his native Alberta to VANCOUVER ISLAND in 1970, he was a founding member of the Canadian Society of Marine Artists and is a senior member of the Federation of Canadian Artists and the only Canadian member of the Royal Society of Marine Artists.

Martin Segger

HEINZE, Frederick Augustus, industrialist (b 5 Dec 1869, Brooklyn, NY; d 1914). A graduate MINING engineer, he was already owner of a COPPER smelter in Montana when he arrived in BC in 1895 looking to invest in the ROSSLAND mining boom. He purchased property at the future site of TRAIL and in 1896 built a SMELTER, still one of the province's major industrial facilities. He also built the COLUMBIA & WESTERN RWY linking his smelter to the mines. Two years later he sold his interests to the CPR, which in 1906 combined them with other holdings to create the Consolidated Mining & Smelting Co, now COMINCO. Heinze left the province to continue his mining career in Montana.

Heli-logging at Khartoum Lk near Powell River, in a Canadian Air Crane S-64, 1996.
Keith Thirkell photo

HELI-LOGGING involves the use of helicopters to log difficult or sensitive terrain. Helicopters function as aerial yarders to haul logs short distances from the stump to nearby landings, reducing the need to build roads or disturb sensitive sites. The first heli-logging operation in BC, on REDONDA ISLAND in 1975, was an experiment by a group that included Okanagan Helicopters Ltd (see CANADIAN HELICOPTERS LTD). Two years later Jack Erickson, a veteran US logger, undertook the first large-scale heli-logging operation in the KHUTZEYMATEEN VALLEY, north of PRINCE

RUPERT, under the name Silver Grizzly Logging. By the late 1990s, when as much as 25% of coastal logging was done with helicopters, the most experienced company was Helifor, a subsidiary of INTERNATIONAL FOREST PRODUCTS LTD (Interfor), which began working with helicopters in 1978. Other successful companies include Coulson Aircrane Ltd of PORT ALBERNI, Air Log Canada and VIH Logging, a subsidiary of VANCOUVER ISLAND HELICOPTERS LTD, which introduced the Russian Kamov heavy-lift helicopter to coastal skies. *See also* LOGGING.   *Ken Drushka*

HELLS GATE is a narrow (34 m) gorge in the Fraser Canyon, about 30 km north of YALE, bursting with turbulent rapids. Simon FRASER had to portage around what he called the "gates of hell" during his descent of the river in 1808. In 1882 the *Skuzzy*, owned by the CPR, became the only STEAMBOAT to pass upriver through the rapids. Railway construction in 1913–14 caused rock slides that blocked the river and depleted the runs of SALMON and the situation was not improved until 1946 (*see* HELLS GATE BLOCKADE). Visitors view the gorge from an aerial tramway, and river rafting through the "gate" has been popular since it began. At the river's peak flow, 908 million litres of water roar through the gorge every minute.

Hells Gate in the Fraser Canyon.
Rick Blacklaws photo

HELLS GATE BLOCKADE occurred in 1913–14 when debris from rail construction nearly blocked the FRASER R at HELLS GATE, north of HOPE. It is one of the greatest environmental DISASTERS in BC history. The CANADIAN NORTHERN RWY was building its main line through the canyon and to save time and money was illegally dumping rock into the river. The debris narrowed the channel and altered the flow pattern of the water, making it impossible for most of the SALMON migrating up the river to pass through. In Feb 1914 the situation worsened following a rock slide caused by construction work. Local aboriginal people used dipnets to carry some of the fish across the blockage and ineffectual steps were taken to remove some of the debris, but millions of fish died, causing starvation among the Interior FIRST NATIONS people, who relied on salmon for most of their food. The average annual catch of Fraser R salmon fell to one quarter what it had been prior to the blockage. The damage was not counteracted until 1944–46, when the International Pacific

Harry Heine painting of Steveston Harbour, 1994.

Salmon Commission constructed concrete fishways at Hells Gate to help the fish pass up the river (*see* INTERNATIONAL PACIFIC SALMON FISHERIES CONVENTION). *See also* FISHING, ABORIGINAL; FISHING, COMMERCIAL.

HELMCKEN, John Sebastian, doctor, politician (b 5 June, 1824, London, England; d 1 Sept 1920, Victoria). He arrived in VICTORIA in 1850 as the HBC surgeon for VANCOUVER ISLAND, and for the next 70 years he was one of the city's leading citizens. In 1852 he married Cecilia, daughter of Gov James DOUGLAS, confirming his close ties to the colony's elite. He entered politics in 1856, winning election to the Island's first legislative assembly. He served as speaker from 1856 to 1871. He supported the union of Vancouver Island and the mainland but was dubious about the value of joining CONFEDERATION. Nonetheless, as the most experienced politician in BC, he was part of the 3-man delegation sent to Ottawa in 1870 to negotiate union with Canada. The economic advantages of union overcame his reluctance and in the end he supported Confederation. He then turned down a chance to be premier of the new province: he retired from politics and resumed his medical practice. In 1885 he was the first president of the BC Medical Society (*see* MEDICAL PROFESSION). His house on Elliot St is now restored as part of the ROYAL BC MUSEUM complex.

HELMCKEN FALLS, 137 m, is a spectacular WATERFALL on the Murtle R in WELLS GRAY PROVINCIAL PARK, the fifth-highest falls in BC and one of the main attractions of the park. A government surveyor came upon it in 1913 and named it for J.S. HELMCKEN, first Speaker of the LEGISLATIVE ASSEMBLY. In winter it sometimes freezes into a massive ice cone. It has been featured on the cover of telephone books.

Helmcken Falls, Wells Gray Provincial Park.
Walter Lanz/Image Makers

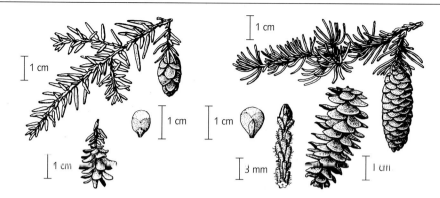

Branch, open cone, cone scale and bract of the western hemlock. © *T.C. Brayshaw*

HEMLOCK trees occur in BC in 2 species. Western hemlock (*Tsuga heterophylla*) is the most common tree species along the coast and also inhabits wetter parts of the southern Interior. Its distinguishing marks are feathery foliage, small cones and a top that droops limply to one side. It was once considered commercially worthless, in part because of a high moisture content in its wood. During WWII, Walter KOERNER and his brothers, timber merchants from Czechoslovakia, developed a technique for drying hemlock in kilns. They marketed the wood as quality lumber under the name Alaska pine. Various parts of the tree supplied medicines and dyes for FIRST NATIONS people, who also used the boughs to collect HERRING spawn. The tallest known western hemlock (75.6 m) is near the mouth of the Tahsish R on the west coast of VANCOUVER ISLAND. Mountain hemlock (*Tsuga mertensiana*), a species adapted to heavy winter snowpack, grows at sea level on the North Coast and dominates subalpine forests on the South Coast. *See also* FOREST INDUSTRY; FOREST PRODUCTS.

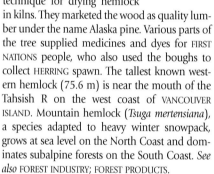

Western hemlock. © *T.C. Brayshaw*

HEMMINGSEN, Mathias "Matt," logger (b July 1876, WI; d 1967, Victoria). He began logging in Wisconsin in 1894 as a cant-hook man, piling logs for river driving (*see* LOGGING). He later became a riverman and went to work for J.A. Humbird in 1902. Soon after, Humbird sent him to BC to drive logs down the Puntledge and Tsolum rivers, near COURTENAY. He stayed on to become the logging superintendent of Humbird's VICTORIA LUMBER & MANUFACTURING CO at CHEMAINUS. There he developed several modern logging methods, including high-lead yarding. In 1913 he went to work for Empire Logging and 2 years later set up his own logging company. In 1938, with J.O. Cameron, he founded Hemmingsen Cameron Co, a major RAILWAY LOGGING operation at PORT RENFREW, which was later purchased by BC FOREST PRODUCTS LTD in 1946. Hemmingsen earned a reputation as one of BC's best pioneer loggers.

Ken Drushka

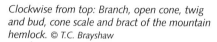

Clockwise from top: Branch, open cone, twig and bud, cone scale and bract of the mountain hemlock. © *T.C. Brayshaw*

HENDERSON LAKE, 15.45 km², on south-central VANCOUVER ISLAND between PORT ALBERNI and BARKLEY SOUND, is the rainiest spot in N America. In 1997 it received a record 8,997.1 mm of precipitation, the wettest spot on the continent that year and an all-time record for Canada. The boomerang-shaped LAKE, surrounded by mountains, has a SALMON hatchery at one end operated by the Uchucklesaht First Nation.

Joanne and Bruce Hepburn at Henderson Lake, the rainiest spot in N America. They measure rainfall and operate a fish hatchery.
Don MacKinnon/Vancouver Sun

HENDRIX LAKE is in the CARIBOO district 90 km east of WILLIAMS LAKE. Noranda Mines operated the nearby Boss Mountain MOLYBDENUM mine between 1965 and 1983, and a townsite for the workers was built at the lake. It is named for "Slim" Hendrix (1870–1938), a local trapper.

HENDRY, John, pioneer lumberman, railway builder (b 20 Jan 1843, Belledune, NB; d 17 July 1916, Vancouver). After early training in the SAWMILLING business, he came to VANCOUVER in 1872, then went to Washington state and worked as a millwright for 2 years. In 1874 he was hired to oversee reconstruction of the burned-out MOODYVILLE SAWMILL, and stayed to work as night superintendent. In 1876, in partnership with David McNair, he built a sawmill at

NANAIMO, which eventually relocated to NEW WESTMINSTER as the Royal City Planing Mills Co, with Hendry as president and general manager. He also served a term as mayor, built a second mill in Vancouver and bought the Dominion Sawmill Company of New Westminster. In 1889 Royal City Planing took over the HASTINGS MILL and a new company, BC MILLS TIMBER & TRADING CO, formed, with Hendry at its helm. This company prospered and grew to become the largest lumber company in BC. In addition, Hendry headed the companies that built the KASLO & SLOCAN RWY and the Vancouver, Westminster & Yukon Rwy, and he served with several business associations, including the Canadian Forestry Assoc, the Canadian Manufacturers' Assoc and in 1910 the Vancouver Board of Trade. He retired from BC Mills in 1913, leaving the presidency to his son-in-law Eric HAMBER. *Ken Drushka*

HENDRYX BROS was a syndicate of American capitalists formed by a successful CT brass manufacturer, Andrew Hendryx, and his brother Wilbur to mine and process the large low-grade galena (lead ore) deposits on the site of present day RIONDEL. The Bluebell mine was worked by the brothers from 1885 to 1896 and stockpiled ore was barged 11 km south to the Hendryx SMELTER, blown in at PILOT BAY in 1895. The smelter went bankrupt in 1896 and the Hendryx name virtually disappeared from the KOOTENAY LK area. *See also* MINING. *Edward Affleck*

HENSHAW, Julia (Henderson), writer (b 1869, Durham, England; d 18 Nov 1937, W Vancouver). After arriving in VANCOUVER in 1890, she worked as an editor and columnist with several city NEWSPAPERS, as well as writing novels (under the name Julia Durham) and 3 books on mountain WILDFLOWERS. She was mar-

ried to an investment broker, Charles Grant Henshaw, and was a leading member of elite society, but her adventurous spirit took her far beyond the polite confines of tea parties and society balls. From 1910 to 1911 she mapped the interior of VANCOUVER ISLAND; in 1914 she and her husband drove the first motor car across the ROCKY MTS; and during WWI she won the Croix de Guerre for her work as an ambulance driver in France.

HEPBURN, Douglas, weightlifter (b 16 Sept 1927, Vancouver). As a youth he was scrawny and handicapped by a withered leg, the result of an operation to correct a clubfoot. He began weightlifting in school and although he was entirely self-taught he won the US championship at Los Angeles in 1949. By that time he weighed

Julia Henshaw, writer, 1911. CVA Port.P1073

Doug Hepburn, World Heavyweight Weightlifting champion, prepares to lift several Vancouver Canucks hockey players, 1953. Vancouver Sun

125 kg and was competing in the heavyweight division. Still a relative unknown, he raised money by performing feats of strength in public and paid his way to the world championship in Sweden in 1953, which he won. Back in VANCOUVER he finally attracted public support. The

mayor hired him as a bodyguard so that he could train for the 1954 British Empire Games (*see* BRITISH EMPIRE AND COMMONWEALTH GAMES) where he won the heavyweight gold medal. An eccentric who claimed to be the first of the hippies, he tried his hand at a variety of jobs after his weightlifting career ended, including wrestler, nightclub singer, gym manager, writer and inventor. *SW*

HEPPNER, Ben, singer (b 14 Jan 1956, Murrayville). Youngest of 9 children in a MENNONITE farm family in the PEACE R district, he gained recognition as a promising heldentenor ("heroic tenor") in 1979 when he won first prize at the CBC Talent Festival. His first professional role was as Roderigo in the 1981 VANCOUVER OPERA production of Verdi's *Otello*. After completing music studies at UBC and the Univ of Toronto, he joined the Canadian Opera Company's Ensemble Studio in 1982–84. His international career began in 1987, when he sang the role of Bacchus in Strauss's *Ariadne auf Naxos* in Australia, followed by performances in

Ben Heppner, tenor.
Columbia Artists Management Inc

Stockholm, Vienna, Cologne and Marseilles. In 1988 he swept top honours at the Metropolitan Opera auditions in New York, winning the prestigious Birgit Nilsson Prize. He has performed in several Canadian productions, including the VANCOUVER OPERA's 1995 production of *Peter Grimes*. In 1998 he performed the male lead in Seattle Opera's production of Wagner's *Tristan und Isolde*. A member of the Order of Canada, he is an international superstar of the opera world. *Shannon Emmerson*

HERBOMEZ, Louis-Joseph d', Catholic missionary (b 17 Jan 1822, Brillon, France; d 3 June 1890, New Westminster). A member of the OBLATES OF MARY IMMACULATE, he was ordained a priest in 1849 and the following year came out to the missions in the Oregon Territory. In 1858 the Oblates moved their headquarters to ESQUIMALT, where they enjoyed better relations with government officials. D'Herbomez was by this time missionary vicar; under his direction missions were established on the FRASER R and in the OKANAGAN VALLEY. In 1864 he became vicar apostolic for BC, based in NEW WESTMINSTER. During the next 2 decades, under his energetic direction, the Oblates established several schools and model villages on the mainland, including ST MARY'S MISSION in the FRASER VALLEY. He was a promoter of planned agricultural settlements where aboriginals would live under the tutelage of Catholic priests. He was buried at St Mary's Mission. *See also* ROMAN CATHOLIC CHURCH.

HERIOT BAY is a small community on the southeast side of QUADRA ISLAND facing Rebecca Spit. It began in the 1890s as a LOGGING centre; commercial FISHING has also been important. A ferry connects Heriot Bay to WHALETOWN on CORTES ISLAND. The Heriot Bay Inn is a descendant of the original hotel, built in the 1890s and operated for many years by Hosea Bull and his first wife Cordelia and second wife Helen. The community was named for F.L.M. Heriot, a relative of a British naval officer.

HERITAGE AQUACULTURE LTD (West Coast) is one of the top 3 fish farming companies in BC. It is a Canadian company owned by George Weston Ltd. Primarily a grocery operation, Weston has fishing interests through its subsidiary, Connor Bros Ltd. Heritage Aquaculture owns SALMON farms in BC, New Brunswick, Maine and Chile and sells about $300 million in farmed salmon annually, mainly in the US. In 1999 Heritage operated 2 hatcheries and 8 salmon farms in BC, raising some $25 million worth of salmon a year. *See also* AQUACULTURE, FIN FISH.

HERITAGE RIVERS SYSTEM; *see* BC HERITAGE RIVERS SYSTEM.

HERNANDO ISLAND, in GEORGIA STRAIT 30 km northwest of POWELL RIVER, is flat and wooded, with many beautiful beaches. It was originally settled in the 1880s and had a population of 40, mostly farmers, in 1892. RAILWAY LOGGING by the Campbell River Lumber Co took place in the 1910s. Unsuccessful development plans over the years have included several major resorts. The island is privately owned and subdivided into about 50 large lots, many of which sport luxurious summer beach homes. The island was named in 1792 by the explorers Dionisio ALCALA-GALIANO and Cayetano VALDES after Hernando Cortes, conqueror of Mexico. AS

HERON is a long-legged, long-necked wading bird distributed widely across southern BC from VANCOUVER ISLAND to the KOOTENAY. It stands over a metre in height. The heron prefers a wet, marshy habitat such as tidal flats, riverbanks, sloughs and lakeshores. It feeds in the water using its long, straight bill to catch fish, crus-

Great blue heron. Dean van't Schip photo

taceans, INSECTS and other small animals. Herons nest in colonies in trees, where they build large nests of sticks. They resemble CRANES but in flight they fold their necks back into their shoulders, while cranes fly with necks extended. Three heron species occur in BC. The most common is the great blue heron (*Ardea herodias*), blue-grey in colour with a black strip above the eyes that tapers into black plumes at the back of the head. In winter, great blues are found mainly on the coast; a few winter in the Interior in the OKANAGAN VALLEY. The black-crowned night heron (*Nycticorax nycticorax*) is a squatter bird, seen rarely during the summer in southern BC; a few winter each year at the REIFEL MIGRATORY BIRD SANCTUARY in DELTA. Its name refers to its habit of being active mainly at night. The smallest species is the green heron (*Butorides virescens*), which has only been reported in the province since the 1950s. It occurs almost entirely along the South Coast and in the lower FRASER VALLEY.

HERRIDGE, Herbert W. "Bert," politician (b 1895, Ramsdean, England; d 19 Oct 1973, Nakusp). He came to Canada as a youngster with his parents, who settled at NAKUSP in 1907. After attending agricultural college in Ontario he returned to the family property. During WWI he was wounded in France and never regained full use of one arm. In England he married his nurse, Ella Leppingwell, and the couple lived at Nakusp, developing a fruit farm and eventually a small LOGGING business. Herridge joined the CCF when it was created and ran unsuccessfully in 3 elections before winning a seat in the provincial legislature in 1941. In 1945 he gave up his seat to run federally; the CCF leadership opposed the move, believing Herridge to be a communist sympathizer. Nevertheless he won his KOOTENAY West riding and held it for the next 23 years. Eventually he was reconciled with the party, though he opposed the creation of the NDP in 1961 because he feared it would be dominated by labour unions. He retired from politics in 1968.

HERRING, Frances, teacher, writer (b 23 Dec 1851, King's Lynn, England; d 16 Nov 1916, New Westminster). She emigrated to BC in 1874, married a cousin and settled in LANGLEY, where she taught school from 1876 to 1878. The following years were devoted to raising her 8 children, but as they grew she turned to journalism, charitable work and the WOMEN'S SUFFRAGE movement. Between 1900 and 1914 she published 6 novels, mostly dealing with immigrant themes. Her books include *Among the People of British Columbia* (1903) and *In the Pathless West with Soldiers, Pioneers, Miners and Savages* (1904).

HERRING, PACIFIC (*Clupea harangus pallassi*) is a small pelagic fish found on the continental shelf in the eastern Pacific from Baja in Mexico north to the Beaufort Sea and in the western Pacific along the coast of Asia. It is a member of the family Clupeidae, which includes Pacific SARDINES (pilchards) and American shad. Herring

Pacific herring. Phil Edgell photo; drawing courtesy Fisheries & Oceans Canada

congregate in vast schools that can cover several square kilometres. They migrate from offshore summer feeding areas in the late fall and early winter to shallow bays and inlets, where they overwinter in preparation for spawning season between Feb and Apr. Spawning occurs in the intertidal and subtidal zones, where the eggs are attached in clusters to SEAWEED and other underwater vegetation. Spawning herring attract large numbers of seabirds, SEA LIONS, even WHALES, which feed on both the herring and the eggs.

Aboriginal people harvested herring with dip nets and rakes and collected the roe for eating. Herring are commercially very important as well as being a major food for larger fish and marine mammals. The commercial fishery began in BC on a small scale in 1877, when 67.5 tonnes were caught and sold for food. Annual output increased steadily during the early part of the 20th century, especially after 1913, when purse seining for herring became legal. A dry-salted fishery aimed at Asian markets flourished from 1904 to 1935. Catches during this period reached a peak in 1927 when 76,500 tonnes were landed. As the salt fishery declined during the 1930s, there was a corresponding increase in the use of herring for reduction into fish meal, fertilizer and oil. The peak catch during this fish-

Herring being pumped aboard a fish packer.
Rick Blacklaws photo

ery occurred in 1962–63, when 237,600 tonnes were landed. The reduction fishery in its turn ended abruptly in 1967, when an extremely high rate of exploitation, combined with changing environmental conditions off the coast, resulted in low survival of young fish. When the fishery resumed in 1972 it was chiefly to supply roe for the Japanese market. The catch is now closely regulated: 29,230 tonnes were harvested in 1999, with a wholesale value in excess of $100 million. Participants are both seiners and gillnetters (see FISHING, COMMERCIAL). A valuable commercial harvest of roe-on-kelp (also called spawn-on-kelp) is carried on mainly by FIRST NATIONS fishers: herring spawn directly on kelp and the roe is then harvested. Most of this product is exported to Japan.   *Dennis Chalmers*

Harvesting herring roe on kelp.
Rick Blacklaws photo

HESQUIAT, pop 141, is a Hesquiaht First Nation (NUU-CHAH-NULTH) village on Hesquiat Harbour, 125 km west of PORT ALBERNI on the west coast of VANCOUVER ISLAND. The name refers to the sound made by eating HERRING spawn off eelgrass, a delicacy. The early ROMAN CATHOLIC mission of Father A.J. BRABANT was located here in 1875. The shores of Hesquiat Harbour and HESQUIAT PENINSULA are now provincial parkland and a destination for hikers and kayakers. At the head of the harbour is the tiny settlement and landing spot of Boat Basin.   AS

HIGGINS, David Williams, journalist, politician (b 30 Nov 1834, Halifax, NS; d 30 Nov 1917, Victoria). He was raised in New York City and trained as a printer, then moved to San Francisco in 1856 and founded a NEWSPAPER. In 1858 he followed the lure of GOLD to BC, where he became a prospector and ran a store in YALE. He moved to VICTORIA in 1860 and joined the *British Colonist*, recently founded by Amor DE COSMOS. Later he purchased the paper and turned it into a forum critical of de Cosmos; it became an advocate of CONFEDERATION and the most influential paper in the city. Higgins was elected to the legislature for ESQUIMALT in 1886 and served as speaker of the assembly from 1890 to 1898. His political career ended with electoral defeat in 1900. He was also a director of the National Electric Tramway and Lighting Co, operator of Victoria's first electric streetcars, in 1889 (see also STREET RAILWAYS). In retirement he wrote 2 popular books of reminiscences: *The Mystic Spring and Other Tales of Western Life* (1904) and *The Passing of a Race and More Tales of Western Life* (1905). His home on Fort Street has been restored.

HIGH-TECHNOLOGY INDUSTRIES utilize and depend on advanced scientific and engineering applications; for example, aerospace, BIOTECHNOLOGY, computers, pharmaceuticals, SUBSEA TECHNOLOGY and telecommunications. In BC during the 1990s the "high-tech" sector of the economy grew faster than any of the traditional export sectors. By 1996 the sector

employed 41,850 people and contributed about $2 billion to the province's total economic output. Of the 5,700 high-tech companies operating in BC, over 95% had fewer than 50 employees and the majority were locally owned. The sector is heavily concentrated in the Greater VANCOUVER area (65%) with secondary concentrations in Greater VICTORIA (10%) and the southern Interior (9%).

HILL-TOUT, Charles, anthropologist (b 28 Sept 1858, Buckland, England; d 30 June 1944, Vancouver). He is known as BC's leading amateur ethnologist. In 1890 he moved to VANCOUVER, where he worked as a private-school teacher. He later moved to a farm in the FRASER VALLEY, and he carried out studies of SALISHAN FIRST NATIONS groups and surveyed the famous MARPOLE MIDDEN. He was elected to the Royal Society of Canada in 1913. His publications include *Later Prehistoric Man in British Columbia* (1895), *The Native Races of British North America: the Far West* (1907) and *The Salish People* (1978).

HILLE, Veda, musician (b 11 Aug 1968, Vancouver). One of the strongest voices to emerge on the alternative music scene in VANCOUVER in the 1990s, she began writing music while studying film and sculpture at art school. Her first album, *Songs About People and Buildings*, appeared in 1992 and was followed by 5 more records during the decade. The album *Here Is A Picture* (1998) was inspired by the work of the artist Emily CARR. Hille also composes for modern DANCE and has written for films and other commissions. She has toured alone and with her band in Canada, the US and Europe.

HILLIERS, a small farming (see AGRICULTURE) and SAWMILL settlement and ESQUIMALT & NANAIMO RWY station 42 km northwest of NANAIMO on VANCOUVER ISLAND, was originally known as Hilliers Crossing. Named after Thomas Hellier, an early local settler, it was the site of a small RAILWAY LOGGING operation between 1919 and 1936. In the 1940s and 1950s, a DOUKHOBOUR community here was led by Michael "The Archangel" Verigin.   AS

HILLS, a stop on the CPR's Nakusp & Slocan Rwy originally known as Hills Siding, is 70 km north of NELSON at the north end of SLOCAN LK. Alfred and Wilson Hills arrived in the region in 1892 and set up a SAWMILL, long since disappeared, on Bonanza Crk.   AS

HILLS, George, Anglican bishop (b 26 June 1816, Eythorne, England; d 10 Dec 1895, Parham, England). He was a prominent ANGLICAN vicar in England, and in 1859 was named first bishop of the new diocese of Columbia, which included VANCOUVER ISLAND and the mainland. Charged with establishing the church on the Pacific Coast, he recruited clergy, built churches, schools and mission outposts, and raised money. His term of office was disrupted by a doctrinal dispute with Edward CRIDGE, the dean of the VICTORIA cathedral, which ended in court in 1874 when Cridge refused to allow Hills into the cathedral. In 1879 the mainland was divided into two new dioceses; Hills remained bishop of Vancouver Island until he returned to England in 1892.

HILTON, a farming (*see* AGRICULTURE) and LOGGING district 50 km east of VERNON near the MONASHEE MTS, got its start during a brief GOLD mining frenzy on nearby Cherry Crk. The first strike was in the 1860s but a number of CHINESE miners continued to work the area until much later. Hilton was named after J. A. Hiltz, an early homesteader. The settlement's original name was Jackman, after N. Jackman, another pioneer. AS

HIND, William George Richardson, artist (b 12 June 1833, Nottingham, England; d 18 Nov 1889, Sussex, NB). He came to Canada in 1851 to join his older brother Henry, a teacher and naturalist. After settling in Toronto he began to develop a small reputation as a painter. In 1861 he accompanied his brother on an expedition into Labrador that provided subjects for some of his best-known paintings. When news of GOLD discoveries in the CARIBOO reached the east in 1862, he joined the group of OVERLANDERS led by Thomas MCMICKING (*see also* GOLD RUSH) and later recorded the transcontinental trip in a series of watercolour paintings. During a 7-year sojourn in BC he painted many local scenes, including a set of pictures depicting MINING life in the Cariboo that are well known today. After leaving BC in 1869 he lived briefly in Winnipeg, then settled permanently in Atlantic Canada. His work was virtually ignored until 1967, when an exhibition brought it to the attention of a modern audience.

HISPANICS first came to BC in 1774 when the Spanish mariner Juan PEREZ navigated his frigate up the west coast of N America as far north as the QUEEN CHARLOTTE ISLANDS (*see* SPANISH EXPLORATION). In 1789 Estéban José MARTINEZ established a Spanish colony at NOOTKA SOUND on the west coast of VANCOUVER ISLAND. The colony became the centre of a territorial dispute between Spain and Great Britain as both countries struggled for control of the Pacific Northwest. In the end the Spanish abandoned their claim and their colony in Nootka Sound (*see* NOOTKA SOUND CONTROVERSY). For the most part Hispanics were absent from BC for the next century, except for a small number of Mexicans who arrived with the GOLD RUSH and worked mainly as packers. In the late 1800s a small group of Chilean sailors arrived in BURRARD INLET. Many of these sailors worked at the MOODYVILLE SAWMILL CO and some married into local FIRST NATIONS communities, where their descendants still bear Hispanic names. Large-scale Hispanic immigration did not begin until after WWII with the liberalization of Canadian immigration laws. Spain, Argentina, Uruguay, Mexico and Colombia accounted for most of BC's Hispanic immigrants in the 1950s and 1960s. The 1970s brought a wave of Chilean refugees seeking asylum from the brutal regime

of General Augusto Pinochet. By 1992 an estimated 1,538 Chilean immigrants lived in BC, about 6% of the national total. During the 1980s and 1990s thousands of Central Americans arrived, escaping the civil wars raging in El Salvador and Guatemala.

BC's Hispanic community is very diverse, encompassing a wide range of people from more than 20 Spanish-speaking countries, including Hispanic JEWS from Mexico and Mayan Indians from Central America. Most of the province's 40,000 Hispanics are from Latin America and have settled in the Lower Mainland. The Hispanic community is one of the most socially active groups in VANCOUVER. Umbrella organizations such as the Latin American Community Council and the Canadian Hispanic Congress coordinate Spanish-speaking services and organize social and political events. Local community groups such as the Chilean Housing CO-OPERATIVE have been established to help meet the day-to-day needs of Hispanics. Vancouver is also home to the Hispanic Community Centre, several Hispanic cultural groups, radio stations and magazines, and it is the site of an annual Latin American fair. *See also* PEOPLES OF BC. *Dianne Mackay*

HISTORY OF BC; *see* opposite.

HIXON, pop 191, is a ranching (*see* CATTLE INDUSTRY), horse-raising and LOGGING community on the BC RAIL line 55 km south of PRINCE GEORGE and east of the FRASER R. There are several stores and motels here, plus a pub and gas station; many residents work at the SAWMILL in nearby STRATHNAVER. Hixon was named after Joseph Foster Hixon, a prospector who searched for GOLD in the area in 1866. AS

HOBSON, Richmond, rancher, author (b 1907, Washington, DC; d 1966, Vanderhoof). When his life's savings were wiped out in the stock market crash in 1929, he moved west to Wyoming and met "Pan" PHILLIPS; in 1934 they and another companion came north to explore the Interior of BC. Hobson and Phillips formed the Frontier Cattle Co and established the Home Ranch north of ANAHIM LAKE in the CHILCOTIN. Hobson left the partnership in the 1940s but he and his wife Gloria continued to ranch in the VANDERHOOF area. His books about his pioneering experience—*Grass Beyond the Mountains* (1951), *Nothing Too Good for a Cowboy* (1955) and *The Rancher Takes a Wife* (1961)—are BC classics. *See also* CATTLE INDUSTRY; COWBOYS.

HOCKEY had been played in central Canada for half a century before the organized game began in BC in the early 1900s. Easterners came west to work in LOGGING and MINING camps in the Interior and brought the game with them, particularly to GRAND FORKS, PHOENIX and GREENWOOD. The 3 towns built covered rinks and started the Boundary Hockey League in 1908. Farther east in the KOOTENAY, teams were started in ROSSLAND, TRAIL and NELSON. SANDON, the birthplace of Hockey Hall of Fame goaltender Tiny Thompson, claims BC's first covered rink, circa

1896. In 1907 Joe Patrick, a Montreal businessman, moved to Nelson to start a lumber company with his sons Lester and Frank PATRICK. When Joe sold the company in 1911, Frank suggested using the proceeds to build Canada's first artificial-ice arenas in VANCOUVER, VICTORIA and NEW WESTMINSTER to bring professional hockey to the West Coast. One of the 3 new venues, Denman Arena in Vancouver, became the largest sports facility in Canada and the second largest in N America after Madison Square Gardens in New York. On 2 Jan 1912, the first game of the Patricks' PACIFIC COAST HOCKEY ASSOC was played in Victoria and the league went on to enjoy immense success, signing eastern stars Cyclone TAYLOR, Frank FREDRICKSON, Mickey MACKAY, Newsy Lalonde, Frank Boucher, Frank Nighbor and Jack Adams. The PCHA produced 2 Stanley Cup winners, the 1915 VANCOUVER MILLIONAIRES and 1917 Seattle Metropolitans, and truly established hockey as Canada's coast-to-coast national sport. After the league merged into the professional Western Hockey League in 1924, the VICTORIA COUGARS won the Stanley Cup in 1925, the last time the cup was won by a West Coast team. (Also during the 1920s, the Denman Arena hosted the Cyclone Taylor-coached Vancouver Amazons, BC's most famous women's team.)

The Patrick family sold the Pacific Coast League's players to the emerging NHL in 1926 and major-league pro hockey did not return to BC until 1970. In the meantime, BC hockey fans settled for watching amateur and minor-pro teams. About half a dozen Vancouver teams competed for the men's national amateur championship, the Allan Cup, but the BC teams successful in capturing the Cup were not from urban centres. The KIMBERLEY DYNAMITERS won BC's first Allan Cup in 1936, going on to capture the 1937 world amateur championship. The PENTICTON VS, led by the Warwick brothers, followed the same path in 1954–55, and Trail, BC's most successful hockey centre, saw its TRAIL SMOKE EATERS win the cup in 1938 and 1962, and the world championships in 1939 and 1961. BC Sports Hall of Fame members from Trail include Jim Morris, an all-around athlete who played for the 1938 and 1939 Smoke Eaters, goaltender Seth MARTIN, who led Trail to the 1961 world title and later played for the Canadian national and Olympic teams, and Cesare Maniago, who played his amateur hockey in Ontario and later played in the NHL. Smoke Eater star Mike Buckna played an important role in building the Czechoslovakian national program in the 1930s. Larry KWONG, a Smoke Eater in the early 1940s, played a game for the New York Rangers in 1947–48, becoming one of the earliest BC players and the first Asian player to appear in the NHL. Soon after the Smokies became Canada's last club team to win a world championship, in 1961, Fr David Bauer moved from Toronto to UBC to execute his concept of building a true national team. Featuring players from across the country, the national team made its first major appearance at the 1964 Olympics in Innsbruck, where it finished 4th. Bauer remained at UBC as an adviser to the university and national hockey programs until the 1980s. With the implementation of the national program and the boom in professional hockey, senior amateur hockey lost much of its significance but it continued, and the 1956 VERNON Canadians, 1978 Kimberley Dynamiters and 1997 POWELL RIVER Regals won additional Allan Cups for BC.

In pro hockey, the Pacific Coast League, later renamed the Western Hockey League (1951), started as a major amateur league in 1945 and turned into a minor-professional league in 1948. In their first year, the VANCOUVER CANUCKS won the 1946 US senior amateur championship. The Canucks, owned by Coley HALL until 1959, topped the PCHL/WHL in 1946, 1948, 1958, 1960, 1969 and 1970. The New Westminster Royals, owned by Hockey Hall of Famer Fred HUME, played in the league from 1945 to 1959 and captured the championship under playing coach Babe PRATT in 1950. Lester Patrick returned to Victoria in 1949 to operate a new PCHL franchise that won league championships in 1951 and 1966. Hume bought the Canucks from the PNE in 1962 and helped to organize the construction of the PACIFIC COLISEUM. Another member of the Hall of Fame, Jim ROBSON, began calling the play-by-play for Canucks' games in 1960 and continued straight through the team's leap to the NHL and into the late 1990s. Notable individuals who passed through the minor-league Canucks included coaches Max McNab, Bert Olmstead and Joe Crozier, and players Emile Francis, Gump Worsley, Johnny Bower, Maniago, Tony Esposito, Andy Bathgate, Larry Popein, Lou Fontinato, Jackie McLeod, Allan Stanley, future NHL Canucks captain and coach Orland Kurtenbach and 12-year stalwart and future team coach and general manager Phil Maloney. With the financial backing of Medicor American Co of Minnesota and the construction of the Coliseum, Vancouver secured its NHL franchise in 1969 and began play in 1970. Vancouver's only other pro franchise, Jimmy PATTISON's VANCOUVER BLAZERS, played in the World Hockey Assoc for 2 unspectacular seasons from 1973 to 1975.

The lack of natural ice surfaces in BC, and the relatively late start of organized hockey in the province, meant that the eastern provinces supplied most of the talent to the NHL during the league's early history. Until the mid-1970s, the only BC-born players to star in the pros were Lynn and Muzz PATRICK and John FERGUSON. But more artificial-ice rinks were built around BC, and coaches and administrators such as Ivan Temple, who coordinated Minor Hockey Week in Canada, built BC minor hockey to a strong level. Since the 1970s many of the NHL's top players have developed their skills in BC, including Joe and Jimmy WATSON, Danny GARE, Barry BECK, Ryan WALTER, Glenn ANDERSON, Andy MOOG, Cam NEELY, Brett HULL, Joe SAKIC, Mark RECCHI, Rod BRIND'AMOUR, Scott NIEDERMAYER and Paul KARIYA. In 2000, the Vancouver Griffins semi-professional women's team began playing as one of the first National Women's Hockey League franchises. *See also* BC JUNIOR HOCKEY LEAGUE; NEW WESTMINSTER BRUINS; WESTERN HOCKEY LEAGUE. *SW*

HISTORY OF BC

Overview

Jean Barman

Human beings have inhabited the place we call British Columbia for about 10,000 years. Unfortunately, far less information survives about the early centuries than about the last two. Men and women did not leave the kinds of records making it possible to reconstruct their lives in more than the broadest outlines. It was the arrival of newcomers with a penchant for record keeping that is usually seen to mark the beginning of the "history" of BC. The name BRITISH COLUMBIA is itself an artifact emanating out of these last 200 years. Apart from the Pacific Ocean to the west and the ROCKY MTS to the east, the place BC is as much constructed as is the "history" that we attribute to it. All the same, some boundaries, both literal and illusory, are essential to any story. BC has existed as a political entity—and increasingly also as an economic and social unit—only since the 1860s.

Some aspects of the lives of aboriginal peoples prior to the European intrusion are generally known (*see* FIRST NATIONS). A broad division existed between peoples living along the coast and those inland. The generally harsh nature of the Interior terrain meant that people there had to spend much of their time obtaining food and shelter. For the most part they did not develop the complex social organization and rich ceremonial life associated with coastal people, who lived in a more bountiful environment symbolized by the 2 basic staples of SALMON for food and CEDAR for most everything else. Coastal peoples divided the year into 2 parts, the summer given over to securing a livelihood and the winter to cultural and spiritual activities. At their heart lay the POTLATCH, a highly regulated ceremony at which goods were distributed to confirm or assert status or to commemorate important events. The complexities of tribal groupings across what is now BC are indicated by the existence of 30 different languages, each as distinctive from the others as is English from German (*see also* FIRST NATIONS LANGUAGES).

BC's location on the far edge of N America kept it from being visited by Europeans long after most other areas of the world were claimed by them. It was Russian exploitation of present-day Alaska to the north and Spanish colonization of Mexico to the south that brought the first intrusions. Vitus Bering, a Danish sea captain in the Russian naval service, may have reached as far south as BC during a 1740 expedition intended to determine whether N America was a separate continent from Asia. Spanish expansion resulted in 3 expeditions between 1774 and 1779, which nominally claimed the coast for Spain. Britain had long sought to locate a water route, a Northwest Passage, to facilitate its lucrative trade with Asia. Attempts to do so from eastern N America failed, and so the English national hero Capt James COOK was dispatched to find a route inland from the West Coast. Cook anchored near NOOTKA SOUND on the west coast of VANCOUVER ISLAND in the spring of 1778 and then sailed north along the coast before turning away toward Asia. Although he did not find a Northwest Passage (not surprisingly, since none existed), his voyage had 2 important consequences. Most immediately, Cook's expedition triggered the first economic intrusion into the Pacific Northwest. His men acquired a few SEA OTTER pelts in trading with local people, and these found a ready market in China. A maritime FUR TRADE quickly developed in which New England merchants from the newly independent United States soon beat out their competitors. More than 170 ships from several countries visited the coast during the peak years of exploitation between 1785 and 1825, by which time the sea otter was essentially trapped out. The future BC's first resource-based boom collapsed, much as would a series of others over the next 2 centuries. The second consequence of Cook's visit was a growing controversy with Spain over the sovereignty of Nootka, perceived as the entryway to the BC coast. A diplomatic resolution of 1790–94 gave trading rights to both countries without determining ownership. Each country sought to support its position by acquiring as much information as possible, and it was in this connection that Capt George VANCOUVER mapped much of the coast for Britain in 1792–94. Thereafter Spain turned its attention elsewhere (*see also* NOOTKA SOUND CONTROVERSY).

The future BC faced east as well as west. The first intrusions from this direction were by fur traders also in search of a water route, in their case one through which the NORTH WEST CO based in Montreal could take furs to market. In 1793 Alexander MACKENZIE travelled Interior rivers to the inlet at BELLA COOLA. In 1808 Simon FRASER reached the mouth of the river that bears his name, and David THOMPSON was exploring areas to the south at about the same time. Although none of these men located the much-sought water route, several small trading posts were established. The agreement ending the War of 1812 between Britain and the US established a loose joint occupation of the Pacific Northwest, which still did not much interest any country apart from the immediate economic advantages to be got from trading for pelts.

A land-based FUR TRADE developed in the early 19th century across the central Interior of today's BC, an area dubbed NEW CALEDONIA, and south to the COLUMBIA R in Washington and Oregon. In 1821 the HBC, based in London, took over the last of its rivals and thereafter managed the Pacific Northwest fur trade through a series of posts at which newcomers lived year-round while trading with local peoples for pelts. Overall this trade was a minor intrusion into aboriginal societies. Trade goods entered local economies and a few women cohabited with newcomers, but for the most part lives continued much as they always had. The fundamental shift for aboriginal peoples came when Europeans decided to stay and thereby to compete for land and resources rather than merely exploit a specific resource and then move on. This shift began in the 1830s, at a time when Americans increasingly believed they had a "manifest destiny" to occupy the continent from ocean to ocean. Trekking overland, American families settled near the principal HBC trading post of Fort Vancouver, sited near the mouth of the Columbia R, in such growing numbers that the HBC decided, in order to ensure its future well-being, to establish a new post on Vancouver Island to the north. FORT VICTORIA was built in 1843 under the supervision of an HBC fur trader named James DOUGLAS. Agitation by American settlers caused the US and Britain to sign the Treaty of Washington in 1846 (*see* OREGON TREATY), extending the existing international boundary of 49°N west from the Rocky Mountains circling around the southern tip of Vancouver Island to the Pacific Ocean.

The Treaty of Washington not only gave the future BC its southern boundary, it ceded the territory to Britain. In 1849 Britain officially colonized Vancouver Island. A governor, Richard BLANSHARD, was appointed, but that was about all. Britain was not much interested in this remote corner of N America, and handed over everyday administration of its new possession to the HBC on condition that it encourage colonization. The HBC moved its centre of operations north to Fort Victoria, put James Douglas in charge, and gradually closed its posts in American territory. On Blanshard's departure in 1851, Douglas took on the additional responsibility of governor, which ensured that the links would remain close between colony and fur trade. In practice, as Douglas recognized, "the interests of the Colony, and the Fur Trade will never harmonize." To the extent that newcomers took up land, they altered the existing order of things, making it less likely that local First Nations would continue to collect furs. The HBC's encouragement of colonization was never more than lukewarm, the minimum needed to keep the British government from revoking the agreement. The HBC did get into the business of mining COAL, and brought over a handful of English miners to settle at NANAIMO. The few newcomers and the unwillingness of Great Britain to spend much money on its fledgling colony meant that little attention was given to making treaties with aboriginal people. Douglas did negotiate 14 small treaties covering the area around VICTORIA and the coal mines in the years 1850–54, but thereafter lacked the resources to do more (*see* DOUGLAS TREATIES). Britain became briefly interested in Vancouver Island with the outbreak of the Crimean War in 1854, whereupon its Royal Navy contingent stationed on the west coast of N America was moved north from Chile to ESQUIMALT. As of 1855 the non-aboriginal population of Vancouver Island did not much exceed

Cayetano Valdes. Museo Naval, Madrid A-676

John Innes painting. UBC BC1060

John Innes painting. Native Sons of BC/SFU

1774, July: Spanish explorers arrive off the West Coast.

1778, March: Capt James Cook arrives in Nootka Sound.

1792: Capt George Vancouver begins his 3-year survey of the coast.

1793, July: Alexander Mackenzie is first European to cross N America.

1795, March: Spanish withdraw from Nootka Sound and the coast.

700, with another handful at the various posts scattered across the mainland.

There matters stood until news leaked out in 1857 of the discovery of GOLD in sandbars on the FRASER R. The gold rush of 1849 to California had transformed that territory, only recently acquired by the US from Spain. Now it was BC's turn. The first newcomers to make it north to Victoria in the spring of 1858 were almost all experienced miners and merchants. As news spread, others came from farther away, including the US, Great Britain and China. Some estimates put the number at 30,000 in 1858 alone, followed by additional thousands over the next 6 years. Most men—and they were almost all men—left almost as soon as they came, for the difficulties of getting to the goldfields were enormous. New finds moved up the Fraser River north into the CARIBOO, meaning that travel was never easy. By 1865 the early trails relying as much as possible on water gave way to the newly constructed CARIBOO WAGON ROAD, which extended north to the boom town of BARKERVILLE. The GOLD RUSH made it imperative that authority be regularized. The long time it took to communicate with Great Britain forced James Douglas to act largely on his own initiative to establish control over the goldfields. His actions were confirmed by Britain's decision to declare the mainland a separate colony of British Columbia on 2 Aug 1858, the name being selected personally by Queen Victoria. Douglas was given the additional responsibility of governing the mainland colony on condition that he sever his HBC ties. Great Britain sent out a contingent of ROYAL ENGINEERS to construct basic infrastructure and, for strategic reasons, they selected NEW WESTMINSTER on the north bank of the Fraser R as the mainland colony's capital. Vancouver Island became wholly a British colony on 30 May 1859 when the HBC lease expired. In 1863 BC's present BOUNDARIES were essentially put in place when, following the discovery of gold in the far north, Britain asserted the mainland colony's sovereignty north to 60° and east to the 120th meridian.

Much like other British possessions around the world, the two colonies were governed by a combination of appointed and elected men (*see* COLONIAL GOVERNMENT). A legislative assembly with 7 elected members existed on Vancouver Island from 1856, together with an appointed council that had to approve all laws

enacted. At first BC had no legislative bodies whatsoever, likely because Britain lacked confidence in its largely transient MINING population. In 1863 the mainland colony was granted a legislative council intended to have a gradually increasing proportion of elected as opposed to appointed members. The minority eligible to participate in political life by virtue of being male, British subjects, and property holders divided on several bases. Newcomers, particularly those from within British North America, resented the privileges enjoyed by senior officers associated with the HBC, whose position was buttressed by more recent arrivals from Britain to staff the colonial bureaucracies. Douglas was accused of favouring their interests, as well as that of Vancouver Island over the mainland. The 2 principal protagonists were Amor DE COSMOS, a Nova Scotian, in Victoria and John ROBSON, an Ontarian, in New Westminster, both of whom used the NEWSPAPERS they edited to make their points.

On Douglas's retirement in 1864, Britain appointed separate governors to the 2 colonies. They were replaced by a single governor in 1866, when the colonies were joined into the United Colony of British Columbia. The decline of the gold rush had decreased governmental revenues whereas the construction of the Cariboo Wagon Road left a large debt. Victoria became the capital of the new colony, but it was the mainland's legislative council, mostly appointed, that replaced Victoria's elected legislative assembly. BC's long-term status became much debated. The contingent allied with Britain was content with the existing situation, whereas newcomers from within British North America looked to entry into the new Dominion of Canada, created in 1867 (*see also* CONFEDERATION). The lack of representative and responsible government was deemed unacceptable. Yet others sought annexation to the US. Relationships with the self-confident nation to the south had never been easy. In 1859 disagreement over the location of the "main channel" dividing Vancouver Island from the US had led to an open confrontation over SAN JUAN ISLAND, dubbed the PIG WAR. The matter was sent to an arbitrator, who eventually awarded the island to the Americans. In 1867 the expansionist US purchased Alaska, making it appear almost inevitable to some that the British colony would become its next possession. A leading BC politician, John Sebastian HELMCKEN, later recalled how local

BC Archives PDP-02258

John Innes painting. VPL 13315

BC Archives PDP-01891

1805: Simon Fraser establishes Fort McLeod, the first permanent European settlement west of the Rockies.

1808, May–July: Fraser makes the first descent of the Fraser R.

1811: David Thompson travels the entire length of the Columbia R.

1821: HBC takes over fur trade west of the Rockies.

1827: Fort Langley is established.

Americans "boasted that they had sandwiched B. Columbia and could eat her up at any time!!!" Sympathetic merchants in Victoria prepared 2 petitions requesting annexation and sent them to the US Congress, which debated the matter briefly. It was likely the presence of the Royal Navy base at Esquimalt that kept Britain from bargaining away its remote and not much wanted possession.

Britain favoured BC's becoming part of Canada and in 1869 named a new governor, Anthony MUSGRAVE, with a mandate to achieve that option. The handful of men who dominated local politics had to be convinced, and the formal proposal that Musgrave cajoled out of the legislative council in Apr 1870 contained such bold demands for entry into Confederation that they were considered likely to be rejected. It was events elsewhere that caused them to be accepted. Britain had already arranged for the large territory located between BC and Ontario that was loosely under HBC supervision to be transferred to the new Dominion. Canada's control over the fur trade colony at Red River, which became the province of Manitoba in 1870, was soon challenged by local Metis under the leadership of Louis Riel. These factors made the BC delegation's demands that a wagon road be built and that Canada pick up the colony's large debt and assume a larger population base for future per capita grants than actually existed, appear not preposterous but quite reasonable. The wagon road was even upgraded to a railway to be constructed within the decade, as much to ensure control over the prairies as to appease BC. The delegation had no choice but to accept the terms of union, and on 20 July 1871 BC joined the Canadian Confederation. The British North America Act that had created Canada in 1867 was extended to BC. The Act was intended to ensure a strong central government. Only matters considered of local significance were left to the provinces, including health and education services, maintenance of law and order, development of physical infrastructure, and management and sales of public Crown lands. BC received 3 seats in the Senate and 6 in the House of Commons, the small numbers being diminished further by the distance, both real and psychological, that then and thereafter separated the far west province from the capital at Ottawa. As a rule, BC's representatives did not distinguish themselves at the federal level or rise to national prominence. Shortly after entry into Confederation, elections were held for members of Parliament and for the 25 members of the new provincial legislature. The Canadian gov gen, acting on behalf of the British Crown, appointed a LT GOV for BC. It was his obligation to request one of the elected MLAs to form a government and so become PREMIER. The concept of responsible government was formally acknowledged when the first premier, John Foster MCCREIGHT, resigned after losing a non-confidence vote in the legislature. McCreight was replaced by Amor de Cosmos, a long-time political activist, and then by a sequence of men selected not as leaders of parties, which did not yet exist in BC, but as heads of loose, shifting coalitions of like-minded persons. The legislature's representative character was restricted in 1874 with the removal of the franchise from CHINESE and aboriginal people, but was extended 2 years later, so far as male British subjects were concerned, by removing property holding as a requirement for voting. Overall the provincial government was a fairly passive affair, apart from dispensing patronage and encouraging resource exploitation. A system of free non-denominational elementary schooling was enacted in 1872, but little else was done in the way of social services.

The relative ease with which political structures became responsible and representative, from the perspective of white males, obscured the fragile demographic and economic bases of the new province. Alongside 25,000 or more aboriginal persons, 1,500 Chinese and about 500 BLACKS were just 8,000 whites. Not surprisingly, given the character of the gold rush, 3 out of every 4 non-aboriginal adults were men. Even though the availability of land gave newcomers a reason to stay, many soon discovered that multiple occupations were necessary in order to survive economically. Gold and coal were mined and some lumbering went on (*see also* LOGGING), but for many their principal interest lay in waiting for the railway with its promise of prosperity. The impact of entry into Confederation fell on aboriginal peoples, perhaps more than on any other group. As governor, Douglas had expressly prohibited the pre-emption of aboriginal settlements, but in practice the situation became chaotic once the gold rush erupted. Waves of European disease, and in particular a devastating SMALLPOX epidemic in 1862–63, led to sharp numerical

VPL 800

BC Museum of Mining

BC Archives HP-2652

1836: *Beaver*, first steamboat on the West Coast, arrives.

1843: Fort Victoria is established.

1846, June: 49th parallel becomes southern boundary of BC.

1849: First coal is mined on Vancouver Island, at Fort Rupert.

1849: British create the colony of Vancouver Island.

1850: James Douglas makes the first of 14 land purchases from Island First Nations.

decline even as social Darwinian notions of "survival of the fittest" convinced many newcomers that indigenous populations were in any case destined to disappear. Under the terms of the BNA Act, responsibility for aboriginal peoples was transferred to the Dominion government when BC joined Canada. According to the terms of union, they would be treated as generously as had previously been the case. In practice it was the interests of newcomers that won out. Aboriginal peoples were increasingly confined to small, remote RESERVES even as no more treaties were signed, or indeed even contemplated. The sole exception was TREATY NO 8, one of several numbered treaties negotiated by the federal government on the prairies; it was signed in 1899 and included the northeast region of BC.

Construction of the promised rail line was repeatedly postponed for political and financial reasons. In 1878 Prime Minister John A. Macdonald launched a new National Policy intended to encourage economic development through higher tariffs, immigration and a transcontinental railway. The National Policy echoed the imperialist sentiment of the day in viewing the role of the periphery, be it colonies or western Canada, as strengthening the economy of the centre through providing raw materials to be returned as manufactures. Not only did value added in the form of jobs and industrial growth rightfully accrue to the centre (Ontario and Quebec), but the imposition of differential freight rates and tariffs on manufactured imports ensured that the periphery would not develop independent of the centre. While detrimental to BC over the long term, the National Policy did get rail construction underway. The Montreal syndicate that won the right to build the CPR received considerable government assistance, including large land grants. Much of the labour was provided by Chinese, over 15,000 of whom entered the country through Victoria for that purpose. The syndicate sought to maximize profits by putting the western terminus in a location where the best land could still be had, and so chose BURRARD INLET. With the arrival of the first scheduled passenger train on 4 July 1886, the small lumbering community at GASTOWN was almost overnight transformed into the new city of VANCOUVER. Britain now lay just over 2 weeks away, and very soon the CPR extended its reach west to Asia by steamship. In little more than a decade Vancouver replaced Victoria as the province's principal commercial centre and port through which goods moved to world markets. Stops along the new rail line also quickly developed into communities, as at KAMLOOPS and REVELSTOKE.

The CPR energized the province's economy, whose base in natural resources was consistent with the National Policy. Lumbering continued apace. COAL MINING grew on Vancouver Island and gold mining still went on across the Interior. Hard rock mining expanded into the KOOTENAY. SMELTERS proliferated, notably at TRAIL in the W Kootenay. A new industrial process permitting very thin, uniform sheets of metal to be rolled out made possible the canning of salmon, an abundant resource that had not yet been much exploited. Soon seasonal canneries, largely financed by external investment, dotted the coast (see SALMON CANNING). Salmon from BC became a staple of many British households. The paucity of arable land meant that AGRICULTURE never acquired the hold it exercised elsewhere in Canada, where at least half of all employed males were working in agriculture. In BC the proportion was less than 1 in 5. Another effect of the railway was population growth. The line encouraged migration from within Canada, with which the province now for the first time had a direct link. The number of BC residents born elsewhere in Canada mushroomed from 3,500 in 1881 to 20,000 by 1891. The Chinese who had helped to construct the new line were not, as promised, provided transportation back home. Many put down roots where last employed, others made their way to the CHINATOWNS that were growing up in Victoria, Vancouver and other communities. The number of residents born in Asia approached 10,000 by 1891 and doubled by the end of the century. The province's population rose from about 50,000 in 1881 to 100,000 a decade later and almost 180,000 by 1901 (see PEOPLES OF BC).

BC's growth as a settler society altered provincial politics. The number of eligible voters rose sharply from about 3,000 in the mid-1870s to 44,000 in the 1900 election. Provincial life was more impersonal, making it less acceptable to be governed by small cliques and by premiers whose prestige rested on personal contacts who tended to reward their friends in order to stay in power. By the end of the century, ministries fell so quickly that potential investors were being scared away. The introduction of

Grouse Creek, 1868. BC Archives A-00351

1856, Aug: BC's first elected assembly meets.

1858: Fraser River gold rush, the first of several rushes, begins.

1858, 2 Aug: The mainland colony of British Columbia is created.

1859: Townsite of New Westminster is laid out as the first capital of BC.

1860: First export sawmill in BC opens at Port Alberni.

party labels, such as existed elsewhere in Canada, began to be discussed. One of the enthusiasts was young Richard MCBRIDE, a lawyer born in New Westminster. McBride was elected an MLA in 1898 and became premier in 1903 under the banner of the CONSERVATIVE PARTY. When his opponents banded together as LIBERALS, also in emulation of federal practice, political parties became a fact of life in BC. Previous premiers had held office at most 3 or 4 years before being replaced by the next clique; McBride broke the pattern by remaining in charge for 12 years. He inherited a large provincial debt and considerable doubt as to the province's future course. Many British Columbians, including McBride and the Conservatives, considered that the ordinary business of government could not be carried on under the terms of union with Canada. The province's size, difficult terrain and scattered population made for exceptionally high routine costs of administration. A lack of manufacturing obliged BC to buy goods from central Canada at highly protected prices, whereas the province's chief products—minerals, fish, timber— had to be sold in world markets in direct competition with all other nations. McBride sought "better terms" with the federal government. The compromise that was reached provided a short-term annual subsidy in exchange for the provincial government raising taxes and reducing expenses in an attempt to balance the provincial budget. The apparent ease with which the quest for "better terms" resolved itself was deceptive, for BC was entering another of its periodic boom periods. Across Canada and beyond, economies were expanding. Growing world demand for BC commodities obscured the fundamental issue of the province's status in Confederation. McBride soon became caught up in the new spiral of growth. Keen to open up more of the province to resource exploitation, he encouraged rail construction and financially supported the CANADIAN NORTHERN and Pacific Great Eastern lines (*see* BC RAIL). As well, the federal government subsidized a second transcontinental line, the GRAND TRUNK PACIFIC, which opened up the prairies and then the BC central Interior to agricultural settlement. PRINCE RUPERT got its beginnings as the western terminus of this new line.

Complementing the provincial government's encouragement of rail construction was its promotion of external investment. The capital that could be generated within BC was extremely limited, so expansion came primarily through outside impetus, as had already occurred with salmon canning and mining. Two Ontarian entrepreneurs, William Mackenzie and Donald Mann, were particularly active, not only in rail construction but also in coal and lumbering. Both Britons and Canadians engaged in land speculation, in which parcels oftentimes located near the new rail lines were divided into small plots and sold to newcomers. Irrigation transformed the interior OKANAGAN VALLEY from ranching (*see* CATTLE INDUSTRY) to small-scale fruit growing. British pounds entering BC tended to be unobtrusive, many taking the form of portfolio investment in government-guaranteed bonds underwriting new physical infrastructure or public utilities. American dollars expanded the COPPER industry in the Kootenay and Boundary regions and financed a large PULP AND PAPER mill on the South Coast at POWELL RIVER. American investment also caused lumbering to grow phenomenally, in part because the allocation of timber leases on Crown land long remained unregulated. By the time a provincial Royal Commission finally raised the alarm in 1910, about 80% of FOREST land owned by the Crown had been leased, mostly to large syndicates (*see* FOREST POLICY). Boom conditions were fuelled by population growth. As part of the National Policy, the Dominion government in 1896 launched an immigration campaign intended to attract the agricultural settlers needed to produce raw materials and purchase manufactures. BC also benefited. Britons in particular found the province attractive, in part because of its earlier colonial status. The number of British-born grew from just 6,000 in 1881 to 116,000 by 1911. BC's population more than doubled in the first decade of the 20th century to almost 400,000, and swelled to half a million by the beginning of WWI, which effectively curtailed large-scale immigration into Canada until mid-century. BC, alone among the Canadian provinces, continued to attract immigrants from Asia because of physical proximity. SIKHS from India often arrived with lumbering experience and tended toward that occupation, just as JAPANESE were most likely to become fishers or small-scale farmers. The number of British Columbians born in Asia approached 30,000 by WWI. In sharp contrast, numbers of aboriginal men, women and children declined to a nadir of 20,000 by 1911. The racism that confined aboriginal peoples to reserves and their

BC Museum of Mining

Dry dock, Esquimalt. BC Archives F-08452

UBC 361/1

1862: Barkerville appears as the centre of the Cariboo gold rush.

1862: Royal Navy moves its Pacific headquarters to Esquimalt.

1862: Smallpox epidemic ravages First Nations population.

1864: "Chilcotin war" occurs, inflaming Native–white relations.

1865: Cariboo Wagon Road reaches Barkerville.

children to segregated schools affected all newcomers who were perceived to be non-white (*see also* RESIDENTIAL SCHOOLS). Provincial disenfranchisement was extended in 1895 to the Japanese and in 1907 to East Indians (*see* SOUTH ASIANS). The number of Japanese allowed to enter Canada—in practice, BC—was restricted by a "gentlemen's agreement" between the 2 countries. Chinese immigration was initially controlled through a HEAD TAX on new arrivals and then, in 1923, legally prohibited by the federal government. The *KOMAGATA MARU* incident in 1914 symbolized the commitment of politically and economically dominant groups to a "white" BC.

The benefits of growth were increasingly filtered through Vancouver, which acted as service centre to an ever-expanding hinterland, one that eventually encompassed almost the entire province. By 1911 almost half the population lived in the Lower Mainland region extending from Vancouver through the FRASER VALLEY. Wherever British Columbians resided across the vast province, the tremendous expansion of capitalism during the early 20th century had an enormous impact on their lives. Changing patterns of residence and employment heightened, and made more visible, inequities in conditions of work and quality of life. Agitation for reform extended from the workplace into the home. The nature of resource exploitation threw men together in work that was often tedious, dirty and hard, and at the same time poorly paid. As early as 1877 coal miners went on strike on Vancouver Island after the mine owner, Robert DUN-SMUIR, cut their wages by a third. The ruthlessness with which the men were forced back to work, with the co-operation of the provincial government, set a pattern for employer–employee relations in BC. While some workers sought change through the ballot box, direct action held greater appeal. Membership in trade unions reached over 22,000, or 12% of the non-agricultural LABOUR FORCE, by 1911. During these years more strikes broke out in BC than in any other province (*see also* LABOUR MOVEMENT). Activism was not confined to men or to the workplace. The movement for social reform was a largely female, white, middle-class enterprise in which women's traditional role within the home was extended outward to the community. Their authority to do so was sanctioned by the Protestant churches, which increasingly felt under an obligation to improve this

world as well as prepare their adherents for the next one. Two of the issues that most agitated social reformers, in BC and more generally, were temperance and WOMEN'S SUFFRAGE. The first branch of the Women's Christian Temperance Union began in Victoria in 1882 and the first suffrage association was formed in 1910. Sensing the winds of change, the opposition Liberals backed female suffrage 2 years later.

Even as reform was gaining impetus, the economic boom ran its course. By 1912 those with capital were pulling back in the realization that much of the dynamism was little more than the rhetoric of boosterism. The political situation in Europe was deteriorating, culminating in Britain's declaration of war against Germany in Aug 1914. The war affected everyone as patriotism became the order of the day. BC had the highest per capita volunteer rate in Canada at just over 90 per 1,000 population. The province's uneven sex ratio played a role, as did its renewed British ethos. British Columbians of every background volunteered for service, including members of the province's aboriginal, Japanese and Sikh communities, and they all contributed to the successful conclusion of the war in 1918 (*see also* MILITARY HISTORY). It was during the war that McBride's premiership finally ended. A combination of factors, ranging from his ill health to charges of patronage and corruption, brought his resignation at the end of 1915. Within months his successor went down to defeat by the Liberals, which then governed for 12 years. The most significant of the 3 Liberal premiers was John OLIVER, who held office from 1918 to his death in Aug 1927. Oliver's long tenure rested as much on internal dissension within the opposition Conservatives as it did on his image as a self-made sage. In 1922 a right-wing splinter group led by Vancouver businessmen joined with dissatisfied farmers to attempt a return to the older coalition style of politics. Their choice of name, the PROVINCIAL PARTY, pointed up their dissatisfaction with the mainstream parties, which they viewed as a federal imposition. The change in ruling parties from Conservative to Liberal worked to the advantage of social reformers. The patriotism unleashed by the war led to women being given the right to vote in Manitoba in 1915, and the other prairie provinces followed in short order. The provincial Liberals made PROHIBITION and suffrage part of their successful 1916 election campaign. The ballot included referen-

BC Archives A-00934

VPL 13448

BC Archives E-02200

1866: BC and Vancouver Island merge to form a single colony.

1868: Victoria becomes capital of BC.

1871: First successful salmon cannery opens on the Fraser River.

1871, 20 July: BC becomes a province of Canada.

1885, 7 Nov: Last spike completes the CPR at Craigellachie.

1886: Vancouver is incorporated as a city.

dums on both issues, which were approved. Legislation soon followed to prohibit the sale of liquor and to give women the right to vote provincially and to be elected to the legislature. The first female MLA was Mary Ellen SMITH, who in 1918 ran in a Vancouver by-election to succeed her late husband. WWI also set the stage for what in retrospect can be seen as the culmination of labour's thrust of the previous 2 decades. Unrest became widespread, particularly after the federal government enacted conscription legislation in 1917. The concept of One Big Union, a single organization of all workers, was gaining appeal even as a general strike broke out in Winnipeg in May 1919. Support was widespread for both initiatives across BC, but neither succeeded. Within the year it became clear to most observers that the brute power of the state in support of capitalism was superior to that which could be marshalled by workers, even under favourable conditions. Trade unions continued to exist across BC but the movement as a whole became fragmented by issues of personality and race. The limits to reform of the workplace were paralleled in social activism in the case of Prohibition. The law was openly flouted, and in 1920 a Prohibition plebiscite passed. The first English-Canadian province to repeal Prohibition, BC became the source of much of the liquor smuggled illegally into the US before it too finally repealed its legislation in 1933 (*see also* RUM-RUNNERS). On the other hand, the Liberal government had caught the reform mood and enacted a spate of legislation that created a civil service, initiated workmen's compensation, provided for neglected children, gave pensions to needy mothers, established public LIBRARIES and expanded public schooling. The limit to reform, in or out of the workplace, was its equation with the dominant society to the almost total disregard of aboriginal and other non-white British Columbians.

The war's end in 1918 did not return BC to its earlier economic self-confidence, but rather heralded a recession across the western world that only lifted in 1923. BC's considerable growth during the remainder of the decade built on existing strands in the province's development. International demand for staples, particularly lumber and minerals, once again set the pace. The Panama Canal, which opened in 1914, made Vancouver an important transshipment point for a wide range of commodities. These included not only products from BC but also prairie grain previously sent east by the CPR. By the end of the decade, fully 40% of Canada's grain exports were going through Vancouver. BC's economy still depended on the vagaries of international markets, which collapsed following the stock market crash of Oct 1929. What first appeared to be only another recession soon became a full-blown depression. The phenomenon had world-wide causes and consequences, but that in no way diminished the effect on individual British Columbians. Every component of the economy moved down. Net value of production fell by almost 60%. So did exports of Canadian products from BC, including prairie grain. Almost all wages fell. Vancouver was hard hit, in particular elderly people and residents of modest means. Initially provincial politicians seemed unable to grasp the seriousness of the Depression. The Conservatives returned to power in 1928, due not as much to their better policies as to the force of personality. Simon Fraser TOLMIE, like his predecessor Richard McBride, had strong roots in BC. Descended from HBC fur traders, he had been an MP and federal minister of agriculture. The Conservatives promised "the application of business principles to the business of government," which rebounded to their disadvantage once the Depression hit. By 1931, when unemployment reached 28%, the highest in Canada, Tolmie was finally forced to act. RELIEF CAMPS were set up, mostly at remote locations safely out of sight of the general populace, where single unemployed males built ROADS and other public facilities in exchange for room, board and a small cash payment. The next year the federal government took over the relief camps, which eventually housed 8,000 men in over 200 camps. The Conservative party became entrapped by its commitment to "business principles." In 1931 Tolmie acceded to the request of a deputation of Vancouver businessmen that he establish a committee to propose solutions to the increasingly desperate financial situation. The KIDD REPORT, issued in 1932, recommended such sharp cuts to social services that mainstream British Columbians were enraged. They had come to expect more from their provincial government than its traditional functions of maintaining law and order, providing physical infrastructure and encouraging private enterprise. The growing sentiment in favour of more government was reflected at the national level, when in 1932 a new political party, the CO-OPERATIVE COM-

CVA Wat.P83

UBC 518/6

1889: Union Steamship Co is created.

1896: Trail smelter goes into operation.

1903: Party politics is introduced to BC.

1907, Sept: Anti-Asian riots occur in Vancouver.

1913: Hells Gate slides block salmon runs on the Fraser River.

1914: Grand Trunk Pacific Rwy is completed to Prince Rupert.

MONWEALTH FEDERATION, was established. The CCF brought together reformist strands in Canadian society with the goal of forming a socialist government by democratic means.

The next provincial election in 1933 was won handily by the Liberals, who captured 42% of the vote. The principal opposition came from the newly formed CCF with fully 32% of the vote. It was once again the force of personality that made the difference. The new premier was Duff PATTULLO. As well as having a strong hinterland base as a Prince Rupert businessman and mayor, Pattullo exuded self-confidence. The Liberal Party, long identified with social reform, now also committed itself to a more activist role for the state in dealing with social inequalities and unbridled capitalism. The CCF's shadow may have spurred on the enactment of legislation reforming taxation, restoring social programs and initiating public works. Pattullo's background led him to look northward at the immense area of the province that was still largely an aboriginal preserve, in the hopes of initiating economic development. Depressed conditions persisted, intensified in BC by unemployed men from across Canada who drifted west in the belief that at least they would not freeze to death. Often "riding the rails," they tended to congregate in "jungles," communities along the tracks, and repeatedly protested their circumstances. So did men dissatisfied with their lot in the relief camps, who were prone to march through Vancouver. In the spring of 1935, after getting no federal government response to their demands, unemployed men began a mass trek to Ottawa. The ON-TO-OTTAWA TREK, by then 25,000 men strong, was halted in Regina, where a riot ensued after negotiations broke down. These events finally persuaded the federal government to act. Nonetheless, numbers of unemployed grew in BC, and after the provincial government in desperation restricted relief to all but provincial residents, confrontation ensued on 19 June 1938, BLOODY SUNDAY, when about 1,000 jobless men occupying the Vancouver post office were forcibly evacuated. Pattullo increasingly came to believe that the province could only do so much and, like his predecessor Richard McBride, increasingly spoke out for "better terms" with the federal government. Federal acknowledgment of regional disparities came with the 1937 appointment of a Royal Commission on Dominion–Provincial Relations (the Rowell-

Sirois Commission). Pattullo informed the commission in no uncertain terms that in 1938 "approximately 80% of the manufactured commodities imported into the Province of British Columbia is imported from Eastern Canada, while approximately 75% of our main primary products, apart from agriculture is sold in open competition in the world markets." Concluding in 1940 that disparities did exist, the commission recommended that the federal government exercise greater authority in relationship to the provinces. BC and some other provinces expressed their opposition, but by then WWII had intervened to postpone the debate.

The declaration of war in Sept 1939 once again put lives on hold, or so it seemed. The painter Emily CARR reflected in her journal how "war halts everything, suspends all ordinary activities." In reality the war initiated fundamental changes. The outbreak of hostilities finally ended the Depression. The value of production in BC doubled over the 6 war years. Manufacturing took off, owing particularly to SHIPBUILDING and aircraft construction. Northern BC was opened up dramatically after the bombing of Pearl Harbor in Dec 1941 convinced the Americans that a highway was essential for them to protect Alaska in case of attack. The BC portion of the Alaska Highway ran from DAWSON CREEK through the PEACE R country in the province's northeast. Prince Rupert became an important supply centre for American bases. By the end of the war the north had, in a psychological sense, become part of BC. The war also brought a measure of political stability. In part to ward off the CCF, which won a plurality in 1941 although not the majority of elected of MLAs, the mainstream parties joined forces in a governing COALITION. Pattullo's strong advocacy of provincial rights contrasted sharply with a shift in public opinion toward a stronger federal government once the war broke out. Pattullo resigned in 1941, and the new coalition government was headed by Liberal leader John HART. The war put at particular risk Canadians of Japanese descent, almost all of whom lived in BC. After WWI many males had brought over "picture brides," women courted by correspondence and married by proxy. In sharp contrast to the declining numbers of Chinese and South Asians, British Columbians of Japanese descent numbered more than 22,000 by 1941. More than half were Nisei, born in the province and

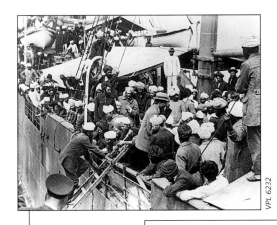

VPL 6232

BC Archives F-01220

1914, May–June: *Komagata Maru* and its S Asian passengers are refused entry to Canada.

1917: Women win the right to vote in BC.

1925: UBC moves to its present site in Point Grey.

1925: Victoria Cougars win the Stanley Cup.

1927, Nov: Emily Carr has major exhibition in Ottawa.

1928: Percy Williams wins 2 gold medals at the Olympic Games.

very much integrated into BC life. But in most people's minds there was little difference between Nisei and Japanese nationals, particularly as Japanese foreign policy became more aggressive during the 1930s. The province's geographical position made some people fear that British Columbians of Japanese descent, in particular fishers along the coast, might act against Canada's interests. Almost immediately after Pearl Harbor in Dec 1941, Canada declared war against Japan and, by federal action, seized some 12,000 fishing boats owned by residents of Japanese ancestry. A growing public outcry led first to male "enemy aliens" being rounded up, then to all persons of Japanese descent being expelled from the coast and from the Trail area, where the smelter was critical to the war effort. Men, women and children were sent to internment camps. Their property was sold off, sometimes far below fair value. About 4,000 evacuees, over half of them Canadian-born, accepted a federal offer to be repatriated to Japan. The others were only in 1949 allowed to return to the coast (*see also* JAPANESE, RELOCATION OF).

In sharp contrast to the treatment accorded British Columbians of Japanese descent, working people reaped the benefits of war. Full employment from 1941 accelerated the movement toward unionization, particularly in the FOREST INDUSTRY. Union membership among BC's non-agricultural labour force, which had reached a low of 7% in 1934, approached 30% by 1943. The next year the federal government established compulsory collective bargaining and the right of employees to form and join unions and the right to strike. By war's end in 1945, trade unions had become generally accepted by the population at large. WWII also brought some attention to aboriginal peoples. Individuals such as the Squamish chief Joe CAPILANO and groups like the NISGA'A had long spoken out for aboriginal rights to the land, but in general the dominant society had been unwilling to listen. Awareness now grew among veterans and others that aboriginal men had volunteered and fought valiantly in both wars, only to return home to segregation and racism. In 1946 the Senate and House of Commons established a Select Joint Committee to examine laws relating to aboriginal people. As recommended by its report, separate schooling (residential schools) gave way to children's attendance at the same schools as other British Columbians. The ban on the potlatch,

which had never entirely kept aboriginal peoples from practising their traditional ways, was removed in 1951. So were prohibitions against political fundraising and the consumption of alcohol in public places. All the same, such measures were partial; for the most part aboriginal people remained confined to small reserves without the resources necessary to lead independent, self-confident lives.

As WWII drew to a close, many British Columbians feared another recession. Their worries were groundless: Canada entered a period of economic stability that with only a brief recessionary break from 1958 to 1962 extended into the early 1970s. The need to rebuild Europe, together with industrial expansion occurring around the world, increased demand for primary resources. BC was well placed to take advantage of economic opportunities. Forest industry activity expanded away from the coast into the central Interior, precipitating the growth of PRINCE GEORGE. OIL AND NATURAL GAS began to be exploited in the northeast, as it was on a larger scale in northern Alberta. The smelter at Trail was expanded, and ASBESTOS mining began in the far northwest. In 1951 the provincial government signed an agreement with the Aluminum Company of Canada (ALCAN) to construct a large smelter southwest of Prince Rupert at what would become the new town of KITIMAT. The next year the long-dormant Pacific Great Eastern Railway was finally completed to Prince George (later it was extended farther north). The province's capacity to capitalize on opportune economic conditions was enhanced by political realignment. The governing coalition continued after the war even as a new political force was emerging in the person of W.A.C. BENNETT. The consummate small businessman, Bennett rose to power under the banner of SOCIAL CREDIT, a populist political party that had originated on the prairies during the Depression, come to power in Alberta in 1935, and migrated westward as part of a movement of peoples. The number of British Columbians born on the prairies grew to over 1 in 5 by 1951. Among the newcomers was Bennett himself, a maritimer who moved first to Alberta and then to the Okanagan Valley. Unable to gain acceptance within the Conservative party, whose power base lay in the Vancouver establishment, Bennett was soon vitalizing BC's fledgling Social Credit movement. By the time of the provincial election of 1952,

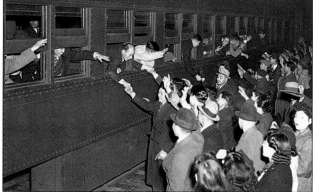

VPL 1384

1938, 19 June: "Bloody Sunday" ends unemployed protests in Vancouver.

1941, Dec: Coalition government takes power in Victoria.

1942: Japanese Canadians are relocated away from the coast.

1947: British Columbians of Asian descent receive the right to vote.

1952, June: First Social Credit government is elected.

policy and personal differences had splintered the governing coalition. A transferable ballot had been put in place, intended to keep out the CCF, which was viewed as the common enemy. The result indicated how fully the 2 mainstream parties had fallen out of favour with voters. The CCF received the plurality of votes, but Social Credit ended up with one more seat. Called upon to form a government, Bennett made clear his sensitivity to the province's growing diversity by including in his cabinet the first woman to hold a portfolio, a trade unionist, persons of non-British descent, evangelical Christians, hinterland British Columbians and former Albertans. To resolve the political stalemate, Social Credit called a new election just a year later. The party benefitted from CCF disarray and won a decisive victory. In the next election, by which time the province had returned to a straight ballot, the Social Credit coalition was entrenched. The force of personality continued to be decisive even after the CCF reorganized itself federally in 1961 as the NEW DEMOCRATIC PARTY. Intended to be more moderate and inclusive, particularly of organized labour, the NDP proved incapable of getting more than a third of the popular vote, compared with Social Credit's 40–47%. Only in 1972, by which time Bennett had been in power a full 2 decades, did the balance shift.

Social Credit built on initiatives already underway and capitalized on generally rising wages, material prosperity and growing self-confidence existing across much of the western world. Much like his predecessors, Bennett also tended to blame the federal government for his failures and take personal credit for the successes. He promised British Columbians what he liked to term "the good life," and for a time he largely succeeded. Material progress through rapid resource development became almost a secular faith within Social Credit. The key to expansion lay in attracting large amounts of outside capital, and American dollars in particular arrived at unprecedented rates. By the mid-1950s over half the investment in a rapidly expanding forest industry came from the United States. A government policy favouring long-term leaseholders of Crown land as being more dependable and profitable encouraged corporate concentration. Much of the expansion centred on pulp, and this too encouraged the forest industry's consolidation into a handful of large integrated multinationals. The value of Canadian products exported from BC grew 5 times over the 2 decades from 1952 to 1972. A focus during the 1950s on infrastructure creation facilitated the big development projects, especially in HYDROELECTRIC power, that followed in the next decade. During the first 6 years of Bennett's tenure, more money was spent building roads than in the entire history of the province. Air and water transport also expanded during these years. The COLUMBIA RIVER TREATY signed in 1961 with the US initiated the construction of 3 storage dams in southern BC in exchange for a lump-sum payment by the US for the downstream hydroelectric benefits that would result. The Peace R in the northeast was harnessed with the construction of the BENNETT DAM. BC was finally becoming an integrated economic unit.

The more active role taken by the state extended into social services. Both the provincial and federal governments facilitated health insurance and special provisions for the young and the old in the form of family allowances and pensions. Educational opportunities became more equitable at the post-secondary level. A 2-year college was upgraded into the UNIV OF VICTORIA in 1963 and SFU opened in BURNABY 2 years later. COMMUNITY COLLEGES offering both vocational training and 2 years of university transfer courses were established around the province.

By the beginning of the 1970s, enthusiasm for Social Credit was finally waning. As it became obvious that even Bennett could not make the good times last forever, many had difficulty reconciling themselves to a harsher reality. In 1972 the NDP, led by David BARRETT, a youthful social worker, squeaked out a victory with 40% of the popular vote compared with Social Credit's 31%. The NDP immediately enacted numerous reform measures, which in retrospect can be seen as an attempt to do too much too fast during an economic downturn. The NDP government called an election in 1975, well before the end of its mandate, and was defeated by a revived Social Credit coalition headed by Bennett's son, William "Bill" BENNETT. The younger Bennett, who was identified with free enterprise and government restraint, headed a more austere administration than had his father. Under Bennett, then Bill VANDER ZALM and, briefly, BC's first woman premier, Rita JOHNSTON, Social Credit stayed in power as a free enterprise coalition until internal disorganization and lack of vision caused it to implode. A revived Liberal Party

1954: CBC launches BC's first television station.

1958: BC celebrates its centennial.

1960: Aboriginals receive the right to vote.

1961: BC Hydro is established.

1965: Simon Fraser Univ opens in Burnaby.

was unable to stop the NDP, which in 1991, led by Vancouver's popular former mayor Michael HARCOURT, narrowly won the provincial election with 40% of the popular vote. The NDP was returned to power in 1996 under Glen CLARK, despite losing out in the popular vote—39% to 43%—to the Liberal Party, led by former Vancouver mayor Gordon CAMPBELL and very deliberately non-aligned with its federal counterpart.

It was not only politics that kept BC out of skew with the rest of Canada. A provincial economy based on natural resources, much as it had been since the first intrusions of outsiders, ensured an erratic pattern of economic growth. Shifts in world prices and in world demand rebounded as sharply as ever on provincial coffers. Vancouver continued to garner most of the benefits, although the provincial capital of Victoria and regional service centres of Kelowna, Nanaimo and Prince George all acquired their own much smaller hinterlands. It was increasingly evident that natural resources, whether lumber, fish or minerals, were finite. Moreover, attitudes toward exploiting these resources were shifting dramatically. The provincial government was repeatedly pressed into managing, protecting and conserving resources more actively. Particularly during Harcourt's tenure as premier, protection of the environment over the long term began to take precedence over immediate financial gain. TOURISM and the growth of the service sector moderated the situation to some extent.

Demographics also remained distinctive. Some newcomers had been permitted into Canada in the aftermath of WWII, but it was only in 1967 that a new federal policy once again encouraged immigration. Immigration, migration from elsewhere in Canada, and natural increase combined to put BC at the forefront of growth. By 1971 the province's population surpassed 2 million, having more than doubled since the end of the war. Over the next 2 decades it continued to grow, reaching almost 3.3 million by 1991. Unlike everywhere else in Canada, BC was still a province most of whose residents had been born elsewhere. It remained a land of newcomers who in adapting also refashioned the status quo. British Columbians who were Asian by descent once again became a sizable component of the province's population. The proportion born in Asia, which had fallen to 1% by 1961, approached 8% by 1991. Growing num-

bers of people from Hong Kong and elsewhere, many bringing with them considerable wealth and sophistication, erased forever the image of the Chinese as menial labourers. Their influence was particularly felt in the Lower Mainland, where most of them settled. As other British Columbians grew more tolerant, there were more opportunities for equality in all aspects of provincial life. In 1988 David LAM, a Chinese immigrant, was named the province's lt gov, and British Columbians of Chinese and South Asian descent were elected to public office both provincially and federally. No group of British Columbians occupied a more contradictory position than did aboriginal peoples. Social activism from the 1960s onwards contributed to a new dynamic, growing numbers. By 1991 almost 120,000 British Columbians, just under 4% of the population, so described themselves. Land claims, more than any other issue, rallied aboriginal peoples (*see* ABORIGINAL RIGHTS). The lack of treaties in all but small parts of the province could no longer be ignored. Shortly before Social Credit lost power, the provincial government declared its willingness to negotiate in partnership with the federal government. The process of doing so proved to be enormously complex. The Supreme Court decision handed down in the DELGAMUUKW case at the end of 1997 and the signing of a draft treaty with the Nisga'a the next summer began, finally, to indicate the direction negotiations would take.

At the start of the 21st century BC remained as enigmatic a place as it had ever been. Provincial politics still depended more on personality and on populist coalitions than on loyalty to parties emulating their federal counterparts. Busts still followed booms as the province continued to rely on resource exploitation as the base of its economy. Not just politics and economics, but progressive approaches to issues of racial equality, continued to set the province apart even though newcomers of the past century and a half had not yet learned to live comfortably with BC's first peoples. Vancouver and the Lower Mainland dominated social and economic life much as they had throughout the century. Yet even the glitz of Vancouver, which is ever imagining itself a city-state on a world stage, could not disguise the province's increasingly fragile economic base. BC remained an exciting, if at times exasperating, place in which to live and work.

Bob Keziere/Greenpeace

Larry Scherban/Image Makers

Gary Fiegehen

1971: Greenpeace is founded in Vancouver.

1972: First NDP government in BC is elected.

1986: Expo 86 takes place in Vancouver.

1993: Provincial government begins treaty negotiations with First Nations.

2000: Nisga'a Treaty is ratified by Canadian government.

HODGES, Nancy (Austin), politician, journalist (b 28 Oct 1888, London, England; d 15 Dec 1969, Victoria). She graduated from London Univ and married the journalist Harry Percival Hodges in 1910. The couple moved to KAMLOOPS in 1912; there they published the *Inland Sentinel* for 4 years. After moving to VICTORIA they both began successful careers at the *Daily Times* NEWSPAPER. As women's editor for 26 years, then a daily columnist, Nancy was a strong advocate for women's causes (*see also* WOMEN'S SUFFRAGE). An active Liberal, she ran unsuccessfully in Victoria in the 1937 provincial election but was elected in 1941 and held her seat until 1953. She gave key support that helped Byron JOHNSON win the LIBERAL PARTY leadership and the premiership in 1947. On 14 Feb 1950 she was elected Speaker of the legislature, becoming the first female Speaker in the British Commonwealth. She held the post until Johnson's government was defeated in the 1952 election. After she lost her own seat in the 1953 election, she became the first woman from BC appointed to the federal Senate. *See also* LEGISLATIVE ASSEMBLY.   *Chris Gainor*

HODGINS, Jack Stanley, writer (b 3 Oct 1938, Comox). He grew up in the VANCOUVER ISLAND community of MERVILLE and after graduating from UBC he moved to NANAIMO, where he taught high school from 1961 to 1980. Much of his fiction is set on the Island. His first book, *Spit Delaney's Island*, appeared in 1976. It was followed by *The Invention of the World* (1977), *The Resurrection of Joseph Bourne* (1979), which won a GOV GEN'S LITERARY AWARD, *The Barclay Family Theatre* (1981), *The Honorary Patron* (1987), *Innocent Cities* (1990), *The Macken Charm* (1995), and *Broken Ground* (1998). His work has been honoured with several awards, including a 1986 Canada–Australia Prize, a 1988 Commonwealth Literary Prize and a BC BOOK PRIZE for *Broken Ground*. Since 1983 he has taught writing at the UNIV OF VICTORIA.

Jack Hodgins, writer. Barry Peterson & Blaise Enright-Peterson

HODGSON, Tommy, freighter (b 1885, Yorkshire, England; d 1945, Williams Lake). After arriving in BC in 1897 he worked as a ranch hand, then as a driver for Inland Express, the company that hauled freight and passengers on the CARIBOO WAGON ROAD. In 1912 he moved to 150 MILE HOUSE, where he took the weekly mail run to the CHILCOTIN, first with horses, later with motor vehicles. He took over the mail contract—at one time the longest mail run in the British Empire—and except for one year held it until his death, hauling mail and freight over some of the roughest roads anywhere. His sons Wilf and Pat and son-in-law Joe Gillis continued the service, known as "Chilcotin's lifeline," until 1962, and subsequent owners kept the Hodgson name.   *Diana French*

HOFFAR, Henry, boatbuilder (b 1888, Vancouver; d 1976, Vancouver). He built more than 2,000 vessels at his VANCOUVER yard, from simple fishing boats to elegant yachts. At age 13 he quit school to apprentice at a sash and door factory, and he built his first boat in the family basement when he was 17. (His father, Nathaniel Hoffar, was Vancouver's first important architect.) In 1916 the Hoffar Motor Boat Co, which he started with his brother Jim, built the first Vancouver-made aircraft, a seaplane, based on photographs they had seen in a British magazine. It made a successful test flight the following year. In 1925, when Jim started his own engine manufacturing facility, Henry took on a new partner and renamed the shipyard Hoffar-Beeching. He sold it to Boeing, the Seattle-based aircraft manufacturer, in 1929 and began making flying boats at his Coal Harbour plant. During 1929–30 he built the *Taconite II* for William Boeing, at 38 m the largest yacht ever built in Coal Harbour. It continues to cruise coastal waters as a charter vessel. Hoffar retired from BOATBUILDING in 1935 and turned full-time to inventing. Following WWII he lived near SIDNEY on VANCOUVER ISLAND.

HOFFMEISTER, Bertram Meryl, soldier, forest executive (b 15 May 1907, Vancouver; d 4 Dec 1999, Vancouver). He was one of Canada's outstanding battlefield commanders in WWII. In 1930 he joined Canadian White Pine Co as a salesperson, beginning a long career in the FOREST INDUSTRY and a long association with the owner of the company, H.R. MACMILLAN. During WWII Hoffmeister served with distinction with the Seaforth Highlanders, an outfit he joined as a 12-year-old cadet. He commanded the Seaforths before the invasion of Italy in 1943, when he was promoted to Brigadier to command the 2nd Canadian Infantry Brigade. Following the Battle of Ortona he was promoted to major general and took command of the 5th Canadian Armoured Division, becoming the youngest Canadian divisional commander. In the final months of the war he commanded the division during the liberation of Holland. He was one of Canada's most decorated soldiers in the war and was known as a talented battlefield strategist who never risked the lives of his men

Bert Hoffmeister, as commander of the 5th Canadian Armoured Division and 6th Canadian Division, Pacific Force, 1945. NAC PA115880

unnecessarily. After returning to VANCOUVER a war hero, he resumed his career in the forest industry and in 1949 was appointed president of the H.R. MacMillan Export Co, soon to be MACMILLAN BLOEDEL. He became chair of the company in 1956 and was expected to succeed MacMillan, but was suddenly dismissed at the end of 1957. He served as BC agent general in London during 1958–61, and from 1961 to 1968 he was president of the COUNCIL OF FOREST INDUSTRIES OF BC. He was made an officer in the Order of Canada in 1982.

HOLBERG is a tiny community at the head of Holberg Inlet, one of the arms of QUATSINO SOUND near the northern tip of VANCOUVER ISLAND, 36 km west of PORT HARDY. Early Danish settlers located in this area after a colony they established at CAPE SCOTT failed; they named their new community after the 18th-century Danish writer Baron Ludwig Holberg. The settlement became a LOGGING centre; for many years most of its buildings were on floats (*see* FLOATHOUSES). A historic TRAIL links Holberg to Cape Scott. A radar station, CFS Holberg, also known as San Josef, was located 5 km farther west from 1954 to 1991.

HOLLINGSWORTH, Margaret, playwright. She trained as a librarian in England before immigrating to Canada in 1968. She came west to VANCOUVER in 1971 to study THEATRE and creative writing at UBC. A professor of writing at the UNIV OF VICTORIA since 1992, she is a prolific author of drama for the stage, radio and television. Her plays have been performed around the world and in Canada have won several awards. Some of her plays have been published in 2 collections: *Willful Acts* (1985) and *Endangered Species* (1988). She has also published a collection of short stories, *Smiling Under Water* (1989), and has been active in political issues related to writers.

HOLT, Simma, journalist (b Mar 1922). After graduating from the Univ of Manitoba she joined the VANCOUVER SUN in 1944 and was a reporter with the NEWSPAPER for the next 30 years. She won dozens of awards for her coverage of the VANCOUVER waterfront, major crime stories, the DOUKHOBOR demonstrations in the Interior and issues related to juvenile crime and abuse. Of her 4 books the best known is *Terror in the Name of God* (1964), about the Doukhobors. After retiring from journalism she was a one-term Liberal Member of Parliament (1974–79) and served on the National Parole Board. She was inducted into the Canadian News Hall of Fame in 1996 and received the Order of Canada in 1997.

Simma Holt, writer.
Kim Gallagher/Random House Canada Ltd

HOMALCO people, a First Nation of the Northern Coast Salish (*see* SALISHAN FIRST NATIONS) and formerly known as Mainland COMOX, occupied the shores of BUTE INLET and the islands near its mouth at the top of GEORGIA STRAIT. At contact with Europeans their main villages were situated at the mouth of the HOMATHKO, Southgate and Orford rivers, all in Bute Inlet. These villages were later abandoned. By the end of the 20th century the registered Homalco population was about 400, many of whom were living at the village of Sliammon, north of POWELL RIVER (*see also* SLIAMMON), and at CAMPBELL RIVER. The name means "swift water."

HOMATHKO RIVER, 137 km, flows out of the CHILCOTIN via Tatlayoko Lk south through the COAST MTS to empty into the Pacific Ocean at the head of BUTE INLET. It was chosen in the 1860s by Alfred WADDINGTON to be the route for his wagon road to the Interior (*see* CHILCOTIN WAR), and railway surveyors touted it as a possible terminus for the transcontinental rail line (*see* CPR). But these ambitious schemes did not come to fruition and the river was left to loggers, who have been active in the lower watershed, and trappers such as August SCHNARR who visited the valley for 50 years. The river is fed by vast glaciers and flows beneath the looming presence of Mt WADDINGTON, the highest peak in the Coast range. *See also* RIVERS.

HOMOSEXUALITY; *see* GAY AND LESBIAN RIGHTS.

HONEYMOON BAY, 34 km west of DUNCAN on the southeast shore of COWICHAN LK, was first settled in 1886 by Henry March, a farmer who used rafts and ox-teams to get his produce to market at Duncan, a 3-day trip. Another early local settler went to England to find a bride and never returned, but his intentions gave the bay its name. LOGGING has always been a mainstay in the area; TOURISM later became important as well. There is a golf course nearby, as well as Gordon Bay Provincial Park and an ECOLOGICAL RESERVE that protects a VANCOUVER ISLAND concentration of very rare pink fawn lilies (*Erythronium revolutum*) and other WILDFLOWERS.

HONG, Wong Mon "Bill," miner, merchant (b 28 Aug 1901, Van Winkle; d 20 Apr 1985, Quesnel). Raised in the N CARIBOO, he was steeped in MINING lore and made his living from mining and operating grocery and general stores at STANLEY, BARKERVILLE and WELLS. A sociable, generous man, he saved many from destitution by extending "credit," much of it never repaid. He was a keen collector of memorabilia and made significant contributions of historical artifacts to museums at QUESNEL and Barkerville. His book *And So...That's How It Happened* (1978) documented 20th-century mining activity in the Barkerville area. Five generations of Bill Hong's family have lived in the N Cariboo.

HONGKONG BANK OF CANADA is owned by HSBC Group of London, England. In Canada its operations are based in VANCOUVER. The bank received its charter in 1981 and after purchasing the assets of the BANK OF BC in 1986, it began to develop a national presence, both commercial and retail. By 1995 it had 109 branches across the country and in 1998 its assets were worth $24.8 billion. In 1999 it changed its name to HSBC Bank Canada.

HOOK AND LINE FISHERIES; *see* FISHING, COMMERCIAL.

HOOPER, Thomas, architect (b 1857, Devonshire, England; d 1935, Vancouver). In 1871 he immigrated to London, ON, where he worked as a joiner and apprenticed as an architect. He moved west and lived in Manitoba from 1878 to 1886, then moved to VANCOUVER, where he worked as a supervisory architect for the provincial government. In 1889 he moved to

The abandoned village of Church House, at the mouth of Bute Inlet, 1974. It was formerly a Homalco settlement. Dorothy Kennedy photo

VICTORIA and entered private practice. It was Hooper, together with John TEAGUE, who was responsible for the majority of nondescript commercial buildings constructed in the capital during the boom years of the late 19th and early 20th centuries. Many of these structures line lower Johnson, Yates and Wharf streets. Hooper operated offices in Victoria and Vancouver (and briefly in Edmonton) and by 1907 had designed a large percentage of BC's public ARCHITECTURE. The Carnegie Library in Victoria and civic buildings in REVELSTOKE and VERNON date from this era, during which the predominant style progressed from a rugged Arts and Crafts blend to a severe Edwardian classical revival. During WWI Hooper moved his practice to New York, although he returned to Vancouver to retire. In Vancouver his more notable buildings include the Winch Building, the Spencer Building on Cordova St and the rear addition to the Vancouver courthouse (now the VANCOUVER ART GALLERY). *Martin Segger*

HOPE, district municipality, pop 6,247, nestles in the mountains at the mouth of the Fraser Canyon (*see* FRASER R), 150 km east of VANCOUVER. It began as Fort Hope, a trading post established for the HBC by Henry Newsham Peers during 1848–49 near the ancient STO:LO nation village of Ts'qo:ls. When the GOLD RUSH began in 1858 it became a stop for miners heading up the river, and a townsite was laid out. The name refers to the HBC's hope that the fort would form part of an all-British supply route to the Interior. It continued to be the gateway to the Interior as first the CPR main line and then the HOPE–PRINCETON and TRANS-CANADA highways passed through. It also lies at the south end of the COQUIHALLA HWY. Christ Church, built in 1859, is the oldest church on its original site in BC. LOGGING and MINING have been the mainstays of the local economy.

A photograph of the Hope slide, taken hours after it occurred, Jan 1965. BC Archives H-04745

HOPE ISLAND, off the northern tip of VANCOUVER ISLAND, was occupied at contact by the Nahwitti, one of the KWAKWA̱KA̱'WAKW First Nations. The island was popular with maritime FUR TRADERS. Bull Harbour, which gets its name from the numerous bull SEA LIONS found in the area, was the site of a Nahwitti village burned in 1850 by the British navy in retaliation for the suspected murder of 3 HBC deserters. There is now a small Coast Guard SEARCH AND RESCUE station; most of the island is a Kwakwa̱ka̱'wakw reserve.

HOPE-PRINCETON HIGHWAY (Hwy 3) winds across the CASCADE MTS 136 km from HOPE to PRINCETON. It follows the SKAGIT and SIMILKA-MEEN rivers for much of its route, crossing the height of land via Allison Pass (el 1,342 m), named for the pioneer rancher John Fall ALLISON. It also cuts through the heart of MANNING PROVINCIAL PARK. The government promised to build the highway in 1929 but the Depression intervened. In the 1930s some construction was done by RELIEF CAMP workers, and during WWII Japanese Canadian internees at TASHME laboured on the road (*see* JAPANESE, RELOCATION OF), but construction did not begin in earnest until 1946. The highway opened on 2 Nov 1949, providing a link between the southern Interior and the coast. In Jan 1965 a portion was buried by the HOPE SLIDE; it took 21 days to rebuild the road over top of the rubble. *See also* ROADS AND HIGHWAYS.

HOPE SLIDE occurred on 9 Jan 1965 at about 7:00 am, in the Nicolum Valley east of HOPE. A minor EARTHQUAKE dislodged more than 46 million m³ of earth, snow and stone from the mountain ridge on the north side of the valley. Debris buried the valley floor to a depth of 70 m, including a 3-km stretch of the HOPE–PRINCETON HWY. The slide smothered 3 vehicles, killing 4 people; 2 bodies were never found. The new highway is built about 55 m above former ground level. *See also* DISASTERS; LANDSLIDES.

HOPKINS, Elisabeth, nurse, artist (b 21 Apr 1894, England; d 22 Apr 1991, Ganges). She immigrated to VANCOUVER ISLAND in 1954. In 1964 she retired from NURSING and moved to GALIANO ISLAND, where she began to paint. Specializing in watercolours, she studied with Molly BOBAK and developed a charming, child-like style infused with humour. She also wrote and illustrated a children's book, *The Painted Cougar* (1977). *See also* ART, VISUAL.

HOPKINS LANDING, 35 km northwest of VANCOUVER on the west shore of HOWE SOUND between the ferry terminal at Langdale and GIBSONS, is a tiny residential community that swells in summer with recreational traffic. A former

Hope, 1872. BC Museum of Mining

UNION STEAMSHIP CO port of call, it was named after George H. Hopkins, a retired engineer who built a cottage here in 1907 and later ran a successful marine TOWBOATING business with his sons. *AS*

HOPKINSON, William Charles, police official (b 16 June 1880, Delhi, India; d 21 Oct 1914, Vancouver). His father was an officer in the British Indian army and his mother was Indian. He was a member of the Calcutta police when he came to BC on leave in 1908. Because of his background and his knowledge of Hindi, he became useful to the immigration department and the Royal Northwest Mounted Police, both of which engaged him to spy on political activists in the local SOUTH ASIAN community. It was an open secret that he ran a string of informers; following the *KOMAGATA MARU* incident he was assassinated by Mewa Singh in the halls of the VANCOUVER courthouse.

HORNBY ISLAND, 30 km², pop 900, is one of the 2 most northerly GULF ISLANDS lying in GEORGIA STRAIT between southern VANCOUVER ISLAND and the mainland (the other is Denman Island). It was a seasonal home for SALISHAN FIRST NATIONS. The first settlers arrived to begin farming in the 1860s, and a shore WHALING station operated at Whaling Station Bay from 1870 to 1872. The island is well known as an arts and crafts centre, with many galleries and studios. AGRICULTURE and commercial FISHING are also important, and summer TOURISM provides a seasonal boost to the local economy. The sand beach at Tribune Bay is one of the few in the Gulf Islands. Hornby also has the largest grove of ancient Garry OAKS in BC. Rear Admiral Phipps Hornby was the British naval commander of the Pacific Station from 1847 to 1951.

HORNE, Adam Grant, trader (b 1831, Edinburgh, Scotland; d 10 Aug 1901, Nanaimo). He came to BC in 1851 to take charge of the HBC store at NANAIMO. In May 1856 he and a party of aboriginal guides opened a TRAIL across VANCOUVER ISLAND from QUALICUM BEACH to the head of ALBERNI INLET, initiating trade with the NUU-CHAH-NULTH (Nootka) there. HORNE LK, the headwaters of Qualicum R, is named for him. He married Elizabeth Bate, whose brother Mark was Nanaimo's first mayor. From 1868 to 1878 he operated the HBC store at COMOX; later he served as an alderman in Nanaimo.

HORNE, James Welton, land promoter, founder of Mission (b 3 Nov 1853, Toronto, ON; d 21 Feb 1922, Vancouver). He made a fortune speculating on land in Manitoba prior to the arrival of the CPR, then moved west to VANCOUVER in 1885 planning to do the same there. He bought land in the city and at MISSION, where a townsite was laid out in 1890. He became one of Vancouver's biggest landowners and a promoter of the city's first STREET RAILWAY. He was also involved in politics as a member of city council (1889–90) and of the provincial legislature (1890–94).

HORNE LAKE, 9.61 km², is on VANCOUVER ISLAND 40 km northwest of PARKSVILLE. It is the headwaters of the QUALICUM R and is a good trout fishing site (*see* FISHING, SPORT). The lake is named for Adam Grant HORNE, a trader who came across it in 1856. The area around the lake has been logged extensively since the 1920s. Horne Lake Caves Provincial Park (1.2 km²), at the west end, protects a network of 7 underground caves, 3 of which are open to visitors. *See also* KARST FORMATIONS; LAKES.

HORSE RACING began in BC at BEACON HILL PARK in VICTORIA in the mid-1850s. The park held a Queen's Plate race open to all horses and in the 1860s featured the horse Wake Up Jake, namesake of the famous Wake-Up-Jake Saloon in BARKERVILLE. Horse racing in early BC towns often took place through the main streets. One of the first recorded races in VANCOUVER, for instance, ran along Granville St from Beach Ave to Georgia St, approximately three-quarters of a mile (1.2 km), for a $100 first-place and $50 second-place prize, and was followed by a ball at the Hotel Vancouver. Dominion Day races in 1889 involved a 5-lane track of similar length on Howe St from Drake St to Georgia St in front of a makeshift grandstand.

The first official racetrack in Vancouver was at HASTINGS PARK and opened in 1892. Originally known as East Park, then Hastings Driving Park and later Exhibition Park, the track faced competition from Minoru Park, later named Brighouse Park (1909–41), and Lansdowne Park (1924–61), both in RICHMOND. In Victoria the main tracks were The Willows in OAK BAY and COLWOOD Park. The racing season ran from May to Sept with each track staging its own meet. Two wealthy horsemen of note were Eric HAMBER, who was LT GOV from 1936 to 1941 and raised thoroughbreds at his Greencroft Stable, and Austin TAYLOR, whose horse Indian Broom ran third in the 1936 Kentucky Derby. When betting declined in the late 1950s, BC Turf Ltd and the Sam RANDALL family of Lansdowne Park merged operations with the Ascot Jockey Club and the Jack DIAMOND family at Exhibition Park under the BC Jockey Club. After acting as the "father" of BC thoroughbred racing by operating Hastings,

Lansdowne and The Willows, Randall had passed the reins of the company to his son Bill.

Jack Short, N America's longest serving race announcer, started in 1934 and was a fixture at Hastings until 1976; he called the 1965 race in which Johnny Longden became the first jockey ever to reach 6,000 wins. The greatest BC-bred horse of all time was George Royal, who set a N American record with 9 stakes victories in one season (1964), won the San Juan Capistrano at Santa Anita twice, and won the Canadian Championships twice. George Royal and Travelling Victor are the only BC-bred horses named Canadian Horse of the Year. The top BC jockey was Vancouver's Hedley Woodhouse, who compiled 2,600 victories including 67 stakes, all over N America during his long career (1940–71). More recent legends at the course include Chris Loseth, the first Canadian to be named top apprentice (1976) and outstanding rider (1984) and the fourth to amass 3,000 wins, and Harold Barroby, the winner of 7 trainer's titles and the all-time top stakes-winning trainer. After the BC Jockey Club began experiencing difficulty in the early 1990s, the BC government and the racing industry formed the non-profit Pacific Racing Assoc to take over the Hastings track in 1994. *SW*

HORSEFLY, pop 426, is located near the west end of Horsefly Lk (59 km²), 50 km east of WILLIAMS LAKE and the Cariboo Hwy (*see* ROADS AND HWYS). It is the site of the first gold discovery in the CARIBOO in 1859 (*see* GOLD RUSH, CARIBOO) and originally was named Harper's Camp after Thaddeus Harper, one of the brothers who founded the GANG RANCH. The present name, adopted in the 1920s, refers to the annual arrival of flying INSECTS. MINING, trapping and later LOGGING have supported the community; the CATTLE INDUSTRY is also important. The Horsefly R, a key SALMON spawning stream, originates in the Quesnel Highlands near WELLS GRAY PROVINCIAL PARK and flows 98 km west into QUESNEL LK. It has been designated a BC HERITAGE RIVER.

HORSESHOE BAY is a small community (pop about 1,000) on HOWE SOUND, 20 km north of downtown VANCOUVER. Called Chai-hai by the

Horse racing action at Hastings Park Racecourse, Vancouver, 1998.

original inhabitants, it was developed as a summer resort by a land company in 1909. In 1914 the Pacific Great Eastern Rwy (see BC RAIL) arrived and the number of summer residents grew. One of the earliest was the Roedde family of Vancouver, who built a home here in the early 1900s. By 1931 Dan Sewell Sr had bought the Roedde property and was operating a marina and hotel. The bay became a major destination for sport FISHING and the Sewell family continued to own and operate the marina (see SEWELL'S MARINA). Troll's Restaurant, founded by Joe and Dorothy Troll, was established in 1946 and was still thriving in the late 1990s. BLACK BALL ferries began car ferry service from the bay to GIBSONS in 1951 and to NANAIMO in 1953. BC FERRY CORP took over the service in 1961 and began operating ferries to BOWEN ISLAND and Nanaimo, and to Langdale on the SUNSHINE COAST.

HOSMER, pop 380, is on the ELK R, 11 km north of FERNIE, in the COAL belt of the E KOOTENAY. The CPR, through its subsidiary the Pacific Coal Co, began MINING here in 1908, but the town's future was cut short in 1914 when the mine shut down due to poor-quality coal. Hosmer was named for Charles R. Hosmer, a former CPR executive and one of the founders of the WEST KOOTENAY POWER & LIGHT CO.

HOT SPRINGS occur when surface water seeps deep into the earth, is heated, and rises back to the surface through fractures in the rock. There are 95 identified hot springs in BC, along the coast and throughout the mountainous Interior. The heated water contains dissolved minerals that are considered healthful. As a result several springs have been developed as tourist and health resorts. These include HARRISON HOT SPRINGS, NAKUSP, AINSWORTH HOT SPRINGS, RADIUM HOT SPRINGS, HALCYON HOT SPRINGS, LAKELSE HOT SPRINGS and FAIRMONT HOT SPRINGS. Others,

especially on the coast, are more isolated and are visited only by more intrepid outdoor enthusiasts. Among many others, these include HOT SPRINGS COVE and FLORES ISLAND in CLAYOQUOT SOUND, MEAGER CRK near PEMBERTON, Hotspring Island in the QUEEN CHARLOTTE ISLANDS, The Grotto south of ATLIN and Liard River Hot Springs Provincial Park (see also PARKS, PROVINCIAL) on the ALASKA HWY.
Reading: Jim McDonald, *Hotsprings in Western Canada,* 1991.

HOT SPRINGS COVE is located on a peninsula of land within Maquinna Provincial PARK (est. 1955; 23 km²) opposite FLORES ISLAND at the north end of CLAYOQUOT SOUND, 37 km north of TOFINO. The springs consist of 6 rocky pools containing mineralized water. The site is accessible by boat or seaplane from Tofino. Across the inlet is the HESQUIAHT village of Hot Springs Cove.

HOUGHTON, Charles Frederick, soldier (b Kilkenny, Ireland; d 13 Aug 1898, Victoria). A close friend of the VERNON brothers, he accompanied them from Ireland to BC in 1863. He settled on land near the north end of OKANAGAN LK at COLDSTREAM, where he was a prominent gentleman farmer. In 1872 he served briefly as an MP in Ottawa before resigning his seat. He sold his share of the Coldstream property to the Vernons in 1873 and joined the Canadian militia. He was deputy adjutant general for BC and in 1877 led troops against striking coal miners near NANAIMO (see COAL MINING, VANCOUVER ISLAND). Two years later he married Marion Dunsmuir, daughter of the mine owner Robert DUNSMUIR. He was stationed in Winnipeg during 1881–88 and saw action in the North West Rebellion; then he served in Quebec City from 1888 to 1897. He was ill with cancer when he retired and returned to VICTORIA to die.

C.F. Houghton, Okanagan pioneer, c 1885.
BC Archives F-06864

HOUSTON, district municipality, pop 3,934, lies at the confluence of the BULKLEY and Morice rivers on the Yellowhead Hwy (see ROADS AND HWYS), 320 km west of PRINCE GEORGE. Originally known as Pleasant Valley, it was renamed for John HOUSTON, a local newspaperman. The townsite developed before WWI with the construction of the GRAND TRUNK PACIFIC RWY. Lumber manufacturing expanded in the 1940s, then again in the 1970s with the construction of 2 SAWMILLING complexes. In 1980 one of the largest SILVER producers in the world, the open-pit Equity mine, opened nearby; it was later exhausted. Along with the FOREST INDUSTRY, the CATTLE INDUSTRY and TOURISM are important to the economy. Incorporated as a village in 1957, it became a district on 31 Jan 1969.

HOUSTON, John, journalist, politician (b Nov 1850, Caledon, ON; d 8 Mar 1910, Quesnel). An itinerant newspaperman in the US in his younger years, he arrived in BC in 1888 and founded a NEWSPAPER, *The Truth,* in DONALD. For the next 2 decades he ran a series of papers around the province that were often critical of the railways and other corporate interests. In 1897 he was elected the first mayor of NELSON. His tenure was notable for the city's purchase of the Nelson Electric Light Co, in which Houston held an interest. He lost his bid for re-election in 1899 but in 1900 was elected both mayor and MLA. In the legislature his hard drinking and outspokenness got him on the wrong side of Premier Richard MCBRIDE and the LT GOV, and his ambitions were thwarted. He lost interest in provincial politics; in 1905 he regained the mayor's chair in Nelson, but he resigned later that year. He returned to journalism and continued to lock horns with the railway companies.

Paddlers enjoying the hot springs at Hotspring Island, Queen Charlotte Islands. Greg Shea photo

HOWAY, Frederic William, jurist, historian (b 25 Nov 1867, London, ON; d 4 Oct 1943, New Westminster). He moved west as a youngster with his family, and settled eventually in NEW WESTMINSTER in 1874. After teaching school for several years, he enrolled in law school at Dalhousie Univ in Halifax in 1890. He returned to BC to open a practice with his friend Robie Reid. Appointed a county court judge in New Westminster in 1907, he served on the bench until his retirement 30 years later. He was also active in public affairs: he belonged to the UBC Senate from 1915 to 1942, was a New Westminster school trustee and ran unsuccessfully for the legislature as a LIBERAL. His first book of history, which he wrote with E.O.S. Scholefield, was a 4-volume compendium, *British Columbia from the Earliest Times to the Present* (1914). It remained the standard work on the subject for several decades. He wrote 2 other books and many articles, but his greatest influence was as a collector of historical material, a leading member of various historical associations, and western representative on the Historic Sites and Monuments Board of Canada (1923–43). During his life he was considered the leading authority on BC HISTORY.

HOWE SOUND, north of VANCOUVER, extends 42 km from GEORGIA STRAIT to the mouth of the SQUAMISH R. The broad, outer sound is studded with islands, the largest being BOWEN and GAMBIER. The inner sound is a narrow, steep-sided FJORD. The sound is in the territory of the SQUAMISH First Nation, who at one time had several camps and village sites around its shores. Spanish explorers visited in 1791 and named it Boca del Carmelo ("entrance to Carmel") after the biblical Mt Carmel. The following year, George VANCOUVER surveyed the sound and named it after Admiral Earl Howe, a British naval hero. Many locations in the sound were named for ships and officers who served with Howe. LOGGING operations began at several sites during the 1870s, and a shore-WHALING station operated on PASLEY ISLAND between 1868 and 1871. In 1877 a trail opened from the head of the sound to PEMBERTON, which was intended to be used for driving cattle from the CARIBOO, but it quickly fell into disuse. The SEA-TO-SKY HWY along the east side of the sound opened as far as Squamish in 1958. Substantial industrial activity has taken place in the sound, including LOGGING, pulp mills at WOODFIBRE and PORT MELLON (*see also* PULP AND PAPER), and MINING at BRITANNIA. Effluents from these activities, together with municipal sewage from Squamish and other communities, have damaged water quality in Howe Sound. It has been closed to commercial FISHING since 1989, though it remains a popular location for sport FISHING. Shellfish harvesting also has been restricted at a number of times and in various locations throughout the sound.

HOWE SOUND CREST TRAIL is a rugged hiking trail following the ridge of mountains that parallel the east side of HOWE SOUND north of VANCOUVER. The trail begins in CYPRESS PROVINCIAL PARK above W VANCOUVER and winds its way 29 km northward to PORTEAU COVE, offering spectacular views of Howe Sound and the LIONS.

Overlooking Howe Sound. Dean van't Schip photo

HOWSE PASS (el 1,524 m) is on the BC–Alberta border in the ROCKY MTS north of KICKING HORSE PASS. It is reached from the east via the headwaters of the Howse R and from the west by following the BLAEBERRY R to its source. Named after Joseph Howse, the HBC fur trader who crossed it in 1810, it was first used in 1807 by David THOMPSON on his expedition to establish KOOTENAE HOUSE on the COLUMBIA R. In the 1870s it was suggested as a possible route for the transcontinental railway, but Kicking Horse Pass was chosen instead and Howse Pass has never been a major transportation route.

HOWSER, 80 km northeast of NELSON on the west side of Duncan Lk in the W KOOTENAY, was supposed to be the terminus of a GREAT NORTHERN RWY push into the LARDEAU MINING district. The line was not completed and the short-lived boomtown, originally called Duncan City after a prospector named Jack Duncan, soon lost steam. Because of confusion with DUNCAN on VANCOUVER ISLAND, the name was changed to Hauser in 1900, after another early prospector, but the post office misspelled it Howser. A quiet rural settlement developed; it had to be moved in 1967 when the DUNCAN DAM raised the lake's level. AS

HOY, Chow Dong, entrepreneur, photographer (b 2 July 1883, Sui Soon Lee, China; d Mar 1973, Quesnel). He came to BC in 1902 and worked as a houseboy in VANCOUVER. Three years later he moved to the CARIBOO, where he worked at a variety of jobs. While living in BARKERVILLE in 1909 he taught himself PHOTOGRAPHY, and when he moved to QUESNEL in 1911 he became the town's first professional photographer. He also operated a store, C.D. Hoy & Co, and became one of the area's leading entrepreneurs. His collection of photographic portraits is a rich storehouse of images of Cariboo people.
Reading: Faith Moosang, *First Son: Portraits by C.D. Hoy*, 1999.

HUDSON'S BAY CO (HBC), Canada's oldest corporation, was formed in 1670 when a group of merchant-traders in England received by royal charter the exclusive right to trade in northern N America. HBC competed with French merchants for dominance in the FUR TRADE until 1763, when Great Britain won control of Canada. After 1763 the French were replaced by Montreal traders, who carried on a spirited competition under the banner of the NORTH WEST CO until 1821, when HBC absorbed its rival. As part of the merger, HBC took over the fur trade in BC. The company inherited several trading posts in NEW CALEDONIA, along with Fort George, then the headquarters of trade on the COLUMBIA R. In 1825 the headquarters moved to Fort Vancouver farther up the river, from where traders communicated with their inland empire to the north via the Columbia and the OKANAGAN VALLEY (*see* FUR BRIGADES). The company also expanded up the coast, establishing trading posts at FORT LANGLEY in 1827, FORT SIMPSON in 1831 and FORT MCLOUGHLIN in 1833. In anticipation of the impending border settlement between Great

The first Hudson's Bay Co store at Vernon, built in 1887. BC Archives H-00250

Britain and the US, HBC opened FORT VICTORIA at the south end of VANCOUVER ISLAND in 1843. This fort subsequently became the headquarters of the company's BC trade after the OREGON TREATY of 1846. When the British decided to colonize Vancouver Island they turned to HBC and in 1849 granted the company proprietorial rights to the island. In return HBC was expected to encourage land settlement. This arrangement lasted until 1859, when Great Britain took direct control of the colony (*see* VANCOUVER ISLAND, COLONY OF). Meanwhile, the gold rush of 1858 (*see* GOLD RUSH, FRASER R) forced the creation of the mainland colony of British Columbia. When HBC Chief Factor James DOUGLAS was appointed gov of the new colony he was required to give up his position with the company. The British government did not renew HBC's right to exclusive trade in the colony and the company now functioned like any other private enterprise. HBC continued to dominate the fur trade by virtue of its long experience and established infrastructure, but technically the field was open to competitors. As the colony filled with settlers the fur trade became just one aspect of the HBC's business and gradually it phased out its trading forts and opened the general retail stores for which it subsequently became known—and which continue to do business in communities throughout the province.

HUDSON'S HOPE, district municipality, pop 1,122, lies beside the PEACE R in the foothills of the ROCKY MTS, 90 km west of FORT ST JOHN. In 1805 Simon FRASER established ROCKY MT PORTAGE HOUSE here as a jumping-off spot for the NORTH WEST CO's expansion across the mountains into the Interior of BC. The post was located at the head of a portage trail running west around the turbulent Peace Canyon. The site attracted a series of FUR TRADERS and prospectors.

In the pre-WWI period homesteaders began taking up land in the area. During the 1960s the community boomed as the centre for the construction of the nearby W.A.C. BENNETT DAM, which began generating power in 1968; the dam created WILLISTON RESERVOIR, the largest body of fresh water in BC. AGRICULTURE and wilderness TOURISM have been major economic activities. The district was incorporated in 1965.

HUGHES, Edward John, artist (b 17 Feb 1913, N Vancouver). Raised in NANAIMO and N VANCOUVER, he studied during the Depression at the Vancouver School of Decorative and Applied Arts (*see* EMILY CARR INSTITUTE OF ART & DESIGN), where he encountered Fred VARLEY and J.W.G.

MACDONALD. In 1934 he formed a partnership with the muralists Paul Goranson and Orville FISHER in a commercial art firm. When WWII began he enlisted and served as a war artist. Afterwards he settled on VANCOUVER ISLAND with his wife Fern, determined to become a full-time artist. During the 1950s his reputation grew, especially after he began to be represented by Max Stern, owner of the famous Dominion Gallery in Montreal. In 1954 he was one of 18 artists asked by the CPR to contribute murals for cars on the transcontinental train. He received other corporate commissions and was elected to the Royal Canadian Academy in 1968. A reclusive artist, he is known for his ordered BC coastal landscapes that often depict the human presence; they are distinctive in their clarity of form and colour. In 1992 Canada Post used one of his images on a stamp commemorating 125 years of Confederation. Hughes's paintings are held in galleries and private collections around the world. *See also* ART, VISUAL.

HUGHES, Howard, American industrialist (b 1905, Houston, TX; d 1976 in flight from Mexico to Houston). After making a fortune from the Hughes Tool Co, founded by his father, he formed Hughes Aircraft and eventually took over Trans World Airways. He was also a major Hollywood film producer during the 1930s. Hughes was a noted eccentric; for the last 25 years of his life he lived in seclusion, hardly ever seen in public, so he set VANCOUVER abuzz in Mar 1972 when he arrived in the city and holed up on the 20th floor of the Bayshore Inn. During a stay lasting several months, he was never seen, but it was later revealed that the newspaper publisher Stuart KEATE had interviewed him by phone before he left town. The episode gave the Bayshore new stature in the folklore of the city.

Echo Bay, Gilford Island, *a 1963 oil painting by E.J. Hughes*

HUGHES, Jane, swimmer (b 30 June 1948, Vancouver). One of many successful swimmers coached by Howard Firby at VANCOUVER's Dolphin Swim Club, she set herself apart in 1964 by setting a world record in the 880-yard freestyle. Hughes was a member of the Canadian national team 1964–67, finishing 5th in the 400-m freestyle at the 1964 Tokyo Olympics and winning a bronze medal in the 440-yard individual medley and gold in the 440-yard medley relay at the 1966 British Empire Games. The gold-medal relay performance, set with a team that included Elaine TANNER, was another world record. Hughes won the 1964 Beatrice Pines Trophy as Canada's top female swimmer and was named to the Canadian Aquatic Hall of Fame in 1972. *See also* SWIMMING.   SW

HUI, Terry, entrepreneur (b 1964, Hong Kong). The son of K.M. Hui, a Hong Kong business tycoon, he came to N America as a teenager and graduated from university in California as an electrical engineer. He moved to VANCOUVER in 1985 to work on his father's development projects, and when he was 29 *Vancouver* magazine dubbed him "the most powerful man in town." As CEO of Concord Pacific Holdings he was in charge of the massive redevelopment of the former EXPO 86 lands along FALSE CRK. He subsequently became president and CEO of Concord Adex Developments Corp, a related company that undertook a huge real estate development on the Toronto waterfront. He was also head of Multiactive Software Inc, a HIGH-TECHNOLOGY firm.

Terry Hui, Vancouver entrepreneur.

HULATT was a LOGGING and railway settlement on the GRAND TRUNK PACIFIC RWY and the NECHAKO R 66 km west of PRINCE GEORGE. It was named after Henry Hulatt, manager of the Grand Trunk Pacific Telegraph Co.   AS

HULL, Brett, hockey player (b 9 Aug 1964, Belleville, ON). He was raised in Chicago and Winnipeg, the cities where his famous father Bobby played HOCKEY, before his parents sepa-

Brett Hull, in action with the Dallas Stars.
Jeff Vinnick/Vancouver Canucks

rated and he moved to N VANCOUVER with his mother in 1979. Too lethargic even to make his midget team's top line, he considered giving up hockey in 1982, but made the PENTICTON Knights of the BC JUNIOR HOCKEY LEAGUE because the team felt his lineage would sell tickets. Under the influence of coach Rick Kozuback, Hull improved his play enough to be the Knights' rookie of the year. The next season, as rightwinger, he scored 105 goals, shattering Cliff RONNING's league record by 22, and also set the points record with 188. Hull starred for Minnesota–Duluth in the NCAA and for the minor pro Moncton Golden Flames before being called up to the NHL by the Calgary Flames. Traded to St. Louis in 1988, he became one of the best goal scorers in hockey history, scoring 70 or more goals in 3 seasons and being awarded a Hart Trophy as league MVP, a Lady Byng Trophy for sportsmanship and 3 first-team all-star selections. His 86 goals in 1990–91 were the third-highest total ever in one season and the most anyone other than Wayne Gretzky had ever scored. In the summer of 1998 Hull signed as a free agent with the Dallas Stars and played a leading role in their run to the 1999 Stanley Cup.   SW

HULL, Raymond, writer (b 27 Feb 1919, Shaftesbury, England; d 6 June 1985, Vancouver). He was one of BC's most successful and prolific professional writers. He worked as a public servant in his native England before immigrating to BC and settling in VANCOUVER in 1947. He continued to work at a variety of jobs until committing himself to full-time writing in 1957. The bulk of his work was non-fiction, often done with a collaborator. His first book was *The Art of Making Wine* (1968), with Stanley Anderson, and his most successful was the international bestseller *The Peter Principle* (1968) with Laurence Peter. In total he produced more than 25 books and plays and many magazine

articles. When he died he left most of his substantial estate to the Vancouver Public Library (*see* LIBRARIES), the Canadian Writers Foundation and the Canadian Authors Assoc.

Shannon Emmerson

HULLCAR, 20 km south of SALMON ARM in the municipality of SPALLUMCHEEN, is a farming (*see* AGRICULTURE) district settled in the 1870s by James Steele, who brought the first thoroughbred horses to BC from eastern Canada. Fruit was grown until the 1920s, then grain and cattle (*see* CATTLE INDUSTRY). A school (1892–1921), SAWMILL (1911–26) and community hall were established. The name comes from an OKANAGAN word that refers to a nearby bluff, though the exact meaning is unclear.   AS

HUMAN CARE SERVICES in early BC were provided informally within families, institutions and tribal groups. When BC joined Confederation in 1871, the BNA Act made the province responsible for "The Establishment, Maintenance and management of Hospitals, Asylums, Charities and Eleemosynary [charitable] Institutions in and for the Province, other than Marine Hospitals." Between 1871 and 1900 the BC government passed the *Municipalities Act*, which made it "the duty of every city and municipality to make suitable provision for the poor and the destitute"; established a public school system (1872) (*see* EDUCATION, PUBLIC); and established the Destitute, Poor and Sick Fund in 1880. During this period the first formal private charities appeared in VANCOUVER: the YMCA in 1886, the SALVATION ARMY in 1887 and the YWCA and the Victorian Order of Nurses in 1897. Following passage of the *Infants Act*, the Children's Aid Society (CAS) incorporated in 1901 to provide care for Vancouver children; later it assumed guardianship responsibility as well. The Catholic Children's Aid Society was formed in 1905. In 1920 the BC government introduced the first Mothers' Pension for widows and wives who had been separated or deserted. During the 1930s, the devastating effects of the Great Depression provoked major provincial and federal legislative initiatives. Growth in the number of charities resulted in the formation of the Vancouver Council of Social Agencies (1930), the predecessor of the United Way. The BC government presented a comprehensive Social Assistance Act in 1945 and by 1946 BC had a full-fledged Department of Health and Welfare. In 1947 the provincial government assumed 80% of the responsibility for municipal welfare costs.

The "welfare state" reached its peak in BC in the late 1960s and early 1970s. Costs for health and welfare had risen from 15% of the provincial budget in 1930 to nearly 70% 30 years later. In 1972 the new NDP government introduced major system reforms. The *Community Resources Boards Act* and the Vancouver Resources Board (VRB) (1974) changed the face of social services. In 1978 the SOCIAL CREDIT government abolished resources boards but continued to expand some social programs, notably long-term care for the elderly. Growing conservatism in the 1980s combined with a slowing local economy to set the Bill BENNETT government on a course of privatization and cuts to social services. The budget was stabilized when the NDP returned in 1991 to launch a new round of reforms emphasizing integration, decentralization and local accountability. Health services were reorganized into a single, comprehensive system administered by regional health boards. In 1996 a new Ministry of Children and Families was formed and a new income support program, BC Benefits, was introduced. As the 20th century ended, human care services still made up the largest portion of the provincial budget, although the idea of the welfare state was being questioned on many fronts. *See also* COMMUNITY DEVELOPMENT; HEALTH POLICY.

Michael Clague

HUMAN RIGHTS in BC are governed by the Human Rights Code, introduced by the provincial government in 1996 to replace the 1984 Human Rights Act. The Code prohibits discrimination on the basis of race, colour, ancestry, place of origin, political belief, sexual orientation, religion, marital status, family status, sex, physical or mental ability or age. On 1 Jan 1997 the government created the Human Rights Commission and the Human Rights Tribunal to administer the code. The commission's 3 members—the chief commissioner, deputy chief commissioner and commissioner of investigation and mediation—and their staff investigate and mediate complaints of discrimination. In some instances the commission refers cases to the tribunal, a quasi-judicial body that holds public hearings at which complainants present their cases for adjudication. *Dianne Mackay*

HUME, Frederick John, electrical contractor, municipal politician (b 2 May 1892, New Westminster; d 17 Feb 1967). He began in NEW WESTMINSTER with a small radio shop and expanded it into western Canada's largest electrical contracting business, Hume & Rumble. In 1924 he founded CFXC, one of the first radio stations in BC, in the back of his shop. The station later moved to VANCOUVER as CJOR (*see* BROADCASTING). As a young man Hume played

Frederick Hume (r), mayor of Vancouver 1951–58, shown here in 1964 during his tenure as president and owner of the Vancouver Canucks, with Max McNab, team general manager (centre) and Carl "Buddy" Boone, team captain. *Courtesy Fred Hume II*

LACROSSE with the NEW WESTMINSTER SALMONBELLIES, and he went on to become an enthusiastic promoter of sports in his native city. He owned the Salmonbellies as well as SOCCER and HOCKEY teams, and was the owner of the VANCOUVER CANUCKS from 1962 until his death. He served as mayor of New Westminster from 1933 to 1942, then moved to Vancouver, where he was mayor from 1951 to 1958. By then he was a wealthy philanthropist, and he donated his mayor's salary to charity. As mayor he was instrumental in bringing the BRITISH EMPIRE AND COMMONWEALTH GAMES to Vancouver in 1954. In 1972 Hume & Rumble became the electrical division of Commonwealth Construction. Hume is a member of the BC SPORTS HALL OF FAME, as well as the Canadian Lacrosse and Hockey Halls of Fame. New Westminster's Hume Park is named for him.

HUMMINGBIRD is a tiny bird with iridescent plumage and a long, slender bill with which it sucks nectar from flowers, its main source of food. The hummingbird darts and hovers on rapidly beating wings, giving off the humming sound from which its name derives. At night it achieves a state of torpor akin to hibernation, to conserve energy. Four species are found in BC, 3 of which are summer visitors from their winter-

Rufous hummingbird. Dean van't Schip photo

ing grounds in Mexico and the southern US. By far the most widespread is the rufous hummingbird (*Selasphorus rufus*), distinguishable by its bright throat patch. Much rarer is the black-chinned hummingbird (*Archilochus alexandri*), found mainly in the OKANAGAN VALLEY and KOOTENAY region. The calliope hummingbird (*Stellula calliope*) of the southern Interior is the smallest bird in N America. The fourth species, Anna's hummingbird (*Calypte anna*), found mainly in residential gardens, is entirely nonmigratory and relies on hummingbird feeders to make it through the winter.

HUMPHREYS, Thomas Basil, politician, (b 10 Mar 1840, Liverpool, England; d 26 Aug

1890, Victoria). He came to BC in 1858 to join the GOLD RUSH but instead served as a police constable at HOPE and PORT DOUGLAS until 1860. He then became a miner and auctioneer at LILLOOET, but politics became his primary activity. As a member of the legislative council in 1868–71, he was a strong advocate of union with Canada. At CONFEDERATION, Humphreys won election to the provincial legislature, representing Lillooet in 1871–75 and a VICTORIA riding in 1875–82. He served as minister of finance and agriculture in the cabinet of Premier A.C. ELLIOTT in 1876 and as provincial secretary and minister of mines in G.A. WALKEM's government in 1878–82. Outspoken and opinionated, he was frequently at odds with his colleagues. After defeat in the 1882 election, he tried unsuccessfully to return to the legislature; finally in 1887 he won a by-election in COMOX and held the seat until his death.

HUNGARIANS began arriving in BC following WWI. Most came not from Hungary itself but from the US and the Canadian prairies, where Hungarians have lived since the 1880s. By 1921 about 400 Hungarians lived in BC, a total that had climbed to more than 2,000 by the outbreak of WWII. The majority of these early immigrants settled around ABBOTSFORD, though Hungarian communities also developed in VANCOUVER, TRAIL and the OKANAGAN VALLEY. But the largest influx occurred in 1956–57 following the Soviet invasion of Hungary and the subsequent arrival of some 37,000 refugees in Canada. In BC, hundreds of refugees passed through the temporary reception camp at the Abbotsford AIRPORT. Many were highly educated and had been politically active in their homeland. For example, almost the entire faculty and student body of the school of FORESTRY at the Univ of Sopron ended up in Vancouver, where they continued their studies at UBC. (The dean of the forestry school, Kalman Roller, who emigrated with his students, was awarded an honorary degree by UBC in 1999.) The Hungarian community in VANCOUVER annually marks the Soviet invasion and, with organizations such as the Hungarian Cultural Society of Greater Vancouver, maintains a cultural presence through festivals, a radio show and a Hungarian-language MAGAZINE. In 1996 there were 40,535 people in BC claiming Hungarian origin. *Dianne Mackay*

HUNGERFORD, George William, rower (b 2 Jan 1944, Vancouver). Raised in VANCOUVER, he attended UBC, where he joined Frank READ's UBC–VANCOUVER ROWING CLUB ROWING dynasty. Hungerford planned to go to the 1964 Tokyo Olympics as a member of the 8-man UBC team but was forced to withdraw when he came down with mononucleosis. Instead he began working out with Toronto native Roger Jackson, and the 2 men managed to qualify for Tokyo as a pairs team. At the Olympics they astonished the rowing world, first by making it to the final heat of their event (2,000 m without coxswain), then by edging out the Dutch to win the gold medal. Back home they shared the Lou Marsh Trophy as

Canadian athletes of the year. A Vancouver lawyer, Hungerford has served as chairman of the BC SPORTS HALL OF FAME, of which he is a member. He was inducted into the Order of Canada in 1984 and is a member of the UBC Sports Hall of Fame.   SW

HUNGRY WOLF, Adolf, writer (b 16 Feb 1944, Heidenheim, Germany). He was born Adolf Gutohrlein to a Swiss father and a Hungarian mother; the family emigrated to California in 1954. He graduated from the Univ of California, and in 1969 he moved to Canada, where he has worked as a writer and publisher ever since. In 1973 he moved with his wife Beverly to land on the KOOTENAY R near SKOOKUMCHUCK in southeastern BC. Together the couple homesteaded, raised a family and launched a publishing company, Good Medicine Books, specializing in publications about railways and aboriginal life. During this time he collected a wealth of information about Blackfoot culture and traditions. *See also* BOOK PUBLISHING.

HUNT, Edmund Arthur "Ted," athlete (b 15 Mar 1933, Vancouver). He is one of the best RUGBY players and all-around athletes BC has ever produced. Raised in VANCOUVER, he starred in several sports at UBC, captaining the varsity rugby club, going undefeated as a BOXER for 4 years and competing as a SKI-jumper in the 1952 Oslo Olympics and 1954 world championships. After completing his doctorate he played for the Vancouver Kats rugby dynasty that won 12 straight provincial championships. He was also captain of the Canadian national team in matches with England and the British Isles and participated in victories over the US, Japan, Australia and the British Lions. Hunt returned punts and kicked field goals for the BC LIONS in the CFL for 3 years, winning the team's 1957 rookie-of-the-year and 1958 top-Canadian honours. He also played LACROSSE for the Vancouver Burrards in 1954–64, helping the team win the Mann Cup as Canadian champions in 1961 and 1964. In 1957 he was named BC athlete of the year and has been inducted into the BC SPORTS HALL OF FAME (1972) and UBC Sports Hall of Fame (1994). After retiring from competitive sport he turned his energies to working as a school administrator in Vancouver and supporting junior GOLF.   SW

HUNT, George, ethnographer, collector (b 14 Feb 1854, Fort Rupert; d Sept 1933, Fort Rupert). His father was an HBC factor at FORT RUPERT; his mother a TLINGIT woman from Alaska. He was raised among the KWAKWAKA'WAKW (Kwakiutl), spoke their language and was married twice, both times to aboriginal women. Because of his knowledge of FIRST NATIONS LANGUAGES and culture he became a valued interpreter and collector of artifacts on the coast for European anthropologists and museums. From 1888 until his death he was associated with Franz BOAS, and from 1911 to 1914 he assisted Edward S. CURTIS during the filming of *IN THE LAND OF THE HEAD-HUNTERS*. Much of what the academic world learned about the Kwakwaka'wakw depended on Hunt's work.

HUNT, Henry, artist (b 16 Oct 1923, Fort Rupert; d 13 Mar 1985, Victoria). A member of the KWAKWAKA'WAKW (Kwakiutl) nation, he worked as a logger and fisher. When he was in his 30s he began carving at the provincial museum (see ROYAL BC MUSEUM), where he apprenticed with his father-in-law, Mungo MARTIN. In 1962 Hunt succeeded Martin as the museum's chief carver, a position he held until 1974. He carved many impressive TOTEM POLES and trained 3 of his sons, Tony, Richard and Stanley. Tony Hunt (b 1942, Alert Bay) worked at the museum as assistant to his father from 1962 to 1972, then left to devote full attention to his Arts of the Raven Gallery, which markets Northwest Coast art and trains young carvers. He is one of the leading Kwakwaka'wakw artists of his generation. **Richard Hunt** (b 1951, Alert Bay) followed in his father's footsteps by becoming chief carver at the Royal BC Museum and is known particularly for creating cultural property for ceremonial use. *See also* ART, NORTHWEST COAST ABORIGINAL.

Kingfisher model poles by Richard Hunt (l) and Henry Hunt. Bob Matheson photo

HUNTER, Robert, journalist, "eco-warrior" (b 13 Oct 1941, St Boniface, MB). In the 1960s he moved west from Winnipeg, where he had worked as a reporter for the *Tribune*. As a columnist for the *VANCOUVER SUN* he became the voice of the counterculture and a strong advocate of environmentalism. He was a member of the crew of the *Phyllis Cormack*, the fishing vessel sent to Alaska in 1971 to protest American nuclear testing. This adventure led to the formation of the environmental group GREENPEACE, which Hunter led until 1977. He then left BC and in 1988 joined the Toronto television station CityTV as an environmental specialist. His

Bob Hunter, journalist and former president of the environmental group Greenpeace.

books include the experimental novel *Erebus* (1968), *Warriors of the Rainbow: A Chronicle of the Greenpeace Movement* (1979) and, with Robert Calihoo, *Occupied Canada: A Young White Man Discovers his Unsuspected Past*, winner of the 1991 GOV GEN'S LITERARY AWARD for non-fiction. *See also* ENVIRONMENTAL MOVEMENT.

HUNTER ISLAND, 334 km², is a large island on the Mid-Coast 500 km north of VANCOUVER, just south of BELLA BELLA. It is separated from the mainland by FITZ HUGH SOUND, a busy shipping lane used by Alaska CRUISE SHIPS and the ferry to PRINCE RUPERT. The shores of the island were used for food gathering by people of the HEILTSUK First Nation. Icelandic settlers began arriving in 1912 and eventually formed a colony that at its peak numbered about 70 people, most of whom made their living FISHING or LOGGING. By the mid-1920s, most of the Icelanders had left; by the late 1990s the island had only a few scattered homes. The HAKAI Recreation Area (1,230 km²) comprises about half the island, together with CALVERT ISLAND immediately south of it.

HUNTINGDON, 5 km south of ABBOTSFORD, is an AGRICULTURAL community in the FRASER VALLEY named after Huntingdon, QC, home of Benjamin Douglas, the first settler in the area. The CPR built a branch line from MISSION to the US in 1889. Douglas and a partner laid out a townsite at the border, which became a port of entry with a hotel and customs office. Sumas, its neighbour on the US side, saw more growth than Huntingdon, though on some weekends during American Prohibition (1919–33) Huntingdon played host to as many as 3,000 thirsty visitors, who strayed across the border to wet their whistles in the community's saloons.

HUPEL, 55 km northeast of VERNON on the north side of the Shuswap R just west of MABEL LK, was a ranching (*see* CATTLE INDUSTRY) and

LOGGING settlement with a store and post office. It was named after Herman Hupel, who homesteaded here in the 1890s and became the first postmaster. *AS*

HURD, Dennis, engineer (b 11 Jan 1942, Timmins, ON). As the president of VANCOUVER-based Atlantis Submarines International Inc, he heads a company that has taken more than 7 million passengers on undersea adventures all over the world. The company's fleet of 28-, 48- and 64-passenger SUBMARINES is larger than that of many national navies. The *Atlantis XIV* operating off Waikiki Beach in Hawaii is the world's largest passenger submarine. Hurd came up with the idea of recreational submarines when he was working at International Hydrodynamics Co Ltd in the 1970s. Later he ran Offshore Engineering Corp, operating small oil-industry subs in the Gulf of Mexico, and used the profits from that venture to form Sub Aquatics Development Corp, now Atlantis Submarines International. His first submarine, *Atlantis I*, was launched in 1985 in the Cayman Islands. In 1998 the company bought Shorex International, adding semi-submersible TOURIST boats to its product line. *See also* SUBSEA TECHNOLOGY. *Vickie Jensen*

HUTCHISON, Bruce, journalist and author (b 5 June 1901, Prescott, ON; d 14 Sept 1992, Victoria). His family moved to BC when he was a baby. He began his long career in journalism as a sports reporter with the *Victoria Times* in 1918. He went to Ottawa to cover national politics for the first time in 1925, then returned to become

The legendary journalist Bruce Hutchison, 1991.
John Yanyshyn/Vancouver Sun

editor of the *Times*. In 1927 he moved to VANCOUVER to join the *PROVINCE* and in 1938 went to work for the *VANCOUVER SUN*. In 1944 he left BC to become associate editor of the *Winnipeg Free Press*, but he returned to VICTORIA in 1950, and in partnership with the publisher, Stuart KEATE, he

made the *Times* one of the leading NEWSPAPERS in the province, winning 3 National Newspaper Awards in the process. In 1963 Hutchison rejoined the *Sun* and worked there for the rest of his life, first as editorial director, then, after 1979, as editor emeritus and regular columnist. Hutchison was recognized as one of the leading political reporters in Canada. He lived in BC but had impeccable sources in the nation's capitals. His writing mixed stylistic eloquence with down-to-earth common sense and self-deprecating humour. As well as politics, he wrote feelingly about his love of nature and the wilderness long before it was fashionable. He is credited with coining the term LOTUS LAND to describe the relaxed lifestyle of the West Coast. Besides daily journalism and magazine articles, Hutchison wrote 15 books, including three GOV GEN'S LITERARY AWARD winners: *The Unknown Country* (1943), *The Incredible Canadian* (1953) and *Canada: Tomorrow's Giant* (1958). Shortly before his death he was appointed to the Privy Council.

HUTCHISON, James Hay, hydroplane builder and racer (b 10 May 1909, England; d 1995, Vancouver). A self-taught designer and builder, in 1939 he became the first Canadian to build a 3-point hydroplane. From 1946–64, during the heyday of hydroplane racing locally, he set Canadian speed records with his "Teaser" hydroplanes and won the Northwest Gold Cup 4 times. He helped to found the Vancouver Power Boat Assoc, which held its first meeting in his workshop. In 1969 he designed and constructed his most famous hydroplane, *War Canoe*. Driven by Ron Derrickson, it set a world record for the most competitive points awarded in a single year of racing. Hutchison is the only boat racer in the BC SPORTS HALL OF FAME. *See also* BOATBUILDING. *SW*

HUTTON, Ralph, swimmer (b 6 Mar 1948, Ocean Falls). The "iron man" of Canadian SWIMMING joined the national team at age 15 with legendary OCEAN FALLS coach George Gate. Hutton won a bronze in the 1,500-m freestyle and a silver and bronze in relays at the 1963 Pan American Games. He didn't bring home a medal from the 1964 Tokyo Olympics but he and Ocean Falls teammate Sandy Gilchrist performed better than any Canadian male swimmers since the 1920s. At the 1966 British Empire Games Hutton won an unprecedented 5 individual medals (3 silver and 2 bronze) and 3 medals in relays. He won 5 more medals at the 1967 Pan Am Games: Canada's first gold in Pan Am men's swimming history in the 200-m backstroke, silvers in the 200-, 400- and 1,500-m freestyle and silver in the 800-m freestyle relay. He was favoured to win gold in the 400-m freestyle at the 1968 Mexico City Olympics, having established the world record earlier that year, but had to settle for silver. He won 4 silvers at the 1970 Commonwealth Games and 3 more medals at the 1971 Pan Am Games, and ended his career, after a disappointing 1972 Munich Olympics, with 11 Canadian records to his name. He became a VANCOUVER police officer

and is a member of the International Swimming Hall of Fame, Canadian Aquatic Hall of Fame, Canadian Sports Hall of Fame and BC SPORTS HALL OF FAME. *SW*

HUTTON MILLS, 75 km east of PRINCE GEORGE on the FRASER R, was established as a tie camp in 1912 during the construction of the GRAND TRUNK PACIFIC RWY. Several large SAWMILLS were built during the decade, including one by United Grain Growers, a prairie co-op that required vast quantities of lumber for its elevators. The community had a hospital and a population of 800 by the 1920s. During WWII it produced BIRCH plywood, used in aircraft construction, but the last mill closed in the 1950s and the community died. *AS*

HYDAH, 10 km north of SKIDEGATE on Graham Island in the QUEEN CHARLOTTE ISLANDS, was a tiny homesteading settlement with a brief life prior to WWI. It was centred on the store of William Leary, former manager of the Skidegate oil works. Hydah is an alternative spelling of HAIDA, which simply means "the people" in the Haida language. *AS*

HYDROELECTRICITY is electricity generated by moving water, usually at power plants in dams on major RIVERS. Water is backed up in reservoirs by the dams to obtain a steady flow and to increase the head (the height the water falls to the turbines). Because of the abundance of running water in BC, hydro quickly replaced other energy sources, principally steam. Electricity now supplies 20% of BC's energy requirements, 92% generated by hydro.

In 1897 a group of entrepreneurs formed the WEST KOOTENAY POWER & LIGHT CO to provide electrical power to MINES in ROSSLAND. The power dam it put into operation at lower BONNINGTON FALLS on the KOOTENAY R in 1898 was the first hydroelectric facility in BC. It was followed closely by a plant on the GOLDSTREAM R north of VICTORIA, owned by the BC ELECTRIC RWY CO (BCER); the facility went into operation later that same year, as the first hydro plant on the coast. The BCER next built a generation plant at BUNTZEN LK, which began supplying electricity to VANCOUVER at the end of 1903, and in 1911 it opened a plant at JORDAN R, which eventually replaced the Goldstream plant as the main power supplier to Victoria. There were other private developments on rivers around the province, mainly to supply power for industrial projects of one kind or another, but over the next 50 years BC Electric became by far the largest supplier of electricity to homes and industries, especially in the densely populated Lower Mainland. In response to BC Electric's dominance, the provincial government created the Public Utilities Commission (PUC) in 1938, to supervise and regulate utilities. (In 1973 the PUC was reconstituted as the BC Energy Commission and then in 1980 as the BC Utilities Commission.) Post-WWII, the demand for electricity grew dramatically and the province's main producers responded by expanding their generating capacity. The provin-

The Mica Dam north of Revelstoke, 1976.
Vancouver Sun

cial government created the BC POWER COMMISSION to provide electricity to rural customers not being served by other suppliers. Meanwhile BC Electric began in 1948 to produce power from an expanded BRIDGE R development; it remained the largest hydro development in BC for the next 20 years. Another huge development was the KEMANO project, built in the early 1950s by ALCAN ALUMINUM CO. The company constructed the KENNEY DAM on the NECHAKO R to divert its headwaters westward through a tunnel in the COAST MTS to Kemano. There it was used to generate electricity that was carried by transmission lines 75 km north to power the aluminum smelter at KITIMAT.

In the 1960s the SOCIAL CREDIT government of W.A.C. BENNETT embarked on its TWO RIVERS POLICY of hydroelectric development, which saw the construction of large power dams on the PEACE and COLUMBIA rivers, dramatically increasing electrical output in the province. In 1961 Bennett announced the nationalization of BC Electric; the following year he merged it with the BC Power Commission to form BC HYDRO AND POWER AUTHORITY, the government's chosen instrument for carrying out its ambitious plans. With the signing of the COLUMBIA RIVER TREATY in 1964, Bennett was able to proceed with the construction of a series of power and storage dams, including the BENNETT DAM on the Peace R (1968) and the DUNCAN (1967), KEENLEYSIDE (1968) and MICA (1976) dams on the Columbia R. By 1980 Hydro was capable of producing almost 8 million kilowatts of power, 5 times its 1962 capacity. In 1998 the utility had a capacity of over 10 million kilowatts, 90% of it hydroelectric, and shared the market with only a handful of private companies producing for primarily industrial needs.

HYNDMAN, Cecil, bird enthusiast (b 11 Oct 1911, Edmonton; d 17 Apr 1997, Victoria). After brief stints at agricultural college and medical school, he joined the CBC in 1932 as a sound effects specialist, the network's first. During WWII he worked for the National Film Board, then moved to VICTORIA with his new wife Adele. In 1946 the couple established a bird interpretative centre called Featherland outside the city, where they observed and photographed birds, conducted public tours and cared for injured animals. Based on his observations, Hyndman published articles on avian psychology and physiology. His 1968 book *The Grasp* describes the habits of a golden EAGLE, who lived at the centre.

HYSLOP, Jeff, actor, dancer (b 1957, Vancouver). He is one of the most successful entertainers to emerge from that breeding ground of BC talent, THEATRE UNDER THE STARS. As a teenager he appeared in the classic *Anne of*

Jeff Hyslop, actor and dancer, 1995.
Bill Keay/Vancouver Sun

Green Gables at Charlottetown in 1972 and 1973, and as the lead dancer in Norman Jewison's film *Jesus Christ Superstar* (1973). His other film credits include *The Wars* (1983), and during the 1980s he was a lead character in the children's television series *Today's Special*. He also starred in the international touring production of *A Chorus Line*. But it was the title role in *Phantom of the Opera* on Broadway in New York in 1991 that rocketed him to stardom, followed by the lead role opposite Chita Rivera in the award-winning *Kiss of the Spider Woman* (1993). A versatile actor/singer/dancer, he has performed on stages across N America.

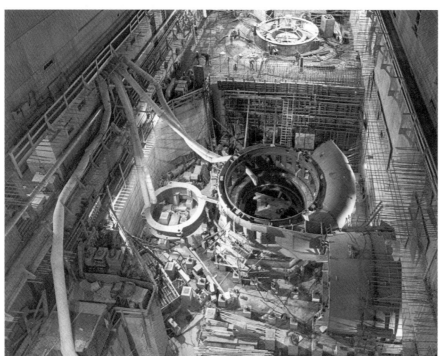

Inside the powerhouse at BC Hydro's Revelstoke Dam project on the Columbia R, 1983. The generating units are under construction. Vancouver Sun

most closely associated. Her work brought her to Canada on several occasions, notably to write articles about the North and profiles of Pierre Trudeau and Arthur ERICKSON. In 1966 she was divorced from Hamburger; in 1976 she married John Daly, a fisher on the SUNSHINE COAST, and moved to GARDEN BAY. After Daly's death in 1978 she wrote a memoir of their life together, *Fishing With John* (1987), which became a bestseller, was nominated for a GOV GEN'S LITERARY AWARD and was later made into a feature film. Iglauer is still on staff at *The New Yorker*, and she is the author of *Denison's Ice Road* (1975); *Seven Stones: A Portrait of Arthur Erickson* (1981); *The Strangers Next Door* (1991), a 50-year retrospective of her work; and a revised and updated edition of *Inuit Journey: The Co-operative Adventure in Canada's North* (2000).

Edith Iglauer, writer, 1998.
Barry Peterson and Blaise Enright-Peterson

I

ICE CLIMBING is the sport of climbing frozen WATERFALLS using specialized tools, including ice axes, crampons and ice screws. It has evolved dramatically since the mid-1960s due to advances in equipment design and climbers' technical ability, among them the *Terrodactyl* ice hammer, a downward-angled ice pick, and rigid crampons, which enable climbers to ascend steeper ice. While much climbing activity centred initially on the Alberta side of the ROCKY MTS, in BC the sport began in FIELD. The winter of 1974 saw several significant ascents in the Field area. Bugs McKeith and Dick Howe conquered the 140-m Nemesis, while McKeith teamed up with Jack Firth, Rob Wood and John Lauchlan to climb TAKAKKAW FALLS. Firth and Lauchlan climbed two other significant routes in 1974: Pilsner Pillar and Carlsberg Column. Garry Brace, John Knight and Don Serl teamed up to climb the difficult Icy BC and Deeping Wall in Marble Canyon near LILLOOET in 1976. Ice climbing continued to grow in popularity through the 1980s and 1990s. The canyons around Lillooet were the site of many new ascents. Other popular areas include the PINE PASS north of MACKENZIE, the MCBRIDE area, along Hwy 16 between TERRACE and PRINCE RUPERT, the WHISTLER/PEMBERTON and BELLA COOLA corridors, and in the KOOTENAY. *Lyle Knight*
Reading: Don Serl and Bruce Kay, *The Climbers' Guide to West Coast Ice*, 1993.

IDAHO PEAK MEADOWS are alpine meadows 25 km east of NEW DENVER near the ghost town of SANDON in the SELKIRK MTS. They are considered one of the best places in BC to view mountain WILDFLOWERS. The view from the lookout takes in a spectacular vista of SLOCAN LK and the VALHALLA MTS. SILVER–lead ore was found on Idaho Peak (el. 2,280 m) in 1891, causing frenzied MINING activity until about 1910.

IGLAUER, Edith Theresa, writer (b 1917, Cleveland, OH). She earned her BA from Wellesley College and her MS from the graduate school of journalism at Columbia Univ. During WWII she worked for the Office of War Information, in the radio newsroom and as a member of Eleanor Roosevelt's circle of women journalists at the White House. She married the writer Philip Hamburger in 1942; in 1945 she joined him abroad and worked as a war correspondent for the *Cleveland News* (he was on assignment for *The New Yorker*). After the war she began a long career as a freelance writer in New York City, writing for *Harper's*, the *Atlantic Monthly* and other publications, while raising 2 young sons. In 1961 she began contributing to *The New Yorker*, the magazine with which she is

Ice climber scaling a frozen Shannon Falls near Squamish, 1995.
Gerry Kahrmann/Vancouver Province

ILGACHUZ RANGE is a distinctive mountain massif about 25 km in diameter that looms above the CHILCOTIN north of ANAHIM LAKE. It is a shield volcano formed in the late Miocene about 10 million years ago. The Ilgachuz is on the Fraser Plateau near the eastern edge of the southern section of TWEEDSMUIR PROVINCIAL PARK. Much of the range is in Itcha–Ilgachuz Provincial Park (1,120 km²). It is the home range of the Itcha–Ilgachuz population of woodland CARIBOU, whose survival is threatened by LOGGING activity: for much of the year the animals depend on arboreal and terrestrial lichens, which reach sufficient volume only in old-growth forests. The headwaters of the BLACKWATER R rise in the Ilgachuz Range. *See also* ENDANGERED SPECIES; PARKS, PROVINCIAL.

ILLECILLEWAET GLACIER lies high in the SELKIRK MTS in GLACIER NATIONAL PARK west of ROGERS PASS. The name comes from an OKANAGAN Nation word meaning "rushing water." The

Base of the Illecillewaet Glacier, 1920.
UBC BC193

CPR ran GLACIER HOUSE at the base from 1886 to 1925. The site is visible from the TRANS-CANADA HWY and accessible by trail. The ice sheet is the source of the Illecillewaet R, which flows 77 km west to join the COLUMBIA R at REVELSTOKE. Illecillewaet was also the name of a MINING settlement and CPR station 40 km northeast of Revelstoke, where a 19th-century lead–ZINC smelter operated briefly. *See also* PARKS, NATIONAL.

IMMIGRATION; *see* PEOPLES OF BC.

IMPERIAL PARKING LTD (Impark), the largest parking lot operator in Canada, was founded in VANCOUVER in 1962. In 1998 it managed more than 1,500 parking lots in 60 cities in N America and Asia. Annual revenues exceeded $200 million.

IMREDY, Elek, sculptor (b 13 Apr 1912, Budapest; d 22 Oct 1994, Vancouver). He immigrated to VANCOUVER in 1957 following the 1956 uprising in his native Hungary. Besides his church sculpture in BC and across Canada, he is known for his likenesses of public figures, including Matthew Baillie BEGBIE in NEW WESTMINSTER, Charles Melville Hayes at PRINCE RUPERT's city hall, a bust of archivist J.S. MATTHEWS at the Vancouver city archives and Prime Minister Louis St Laurent at the Supreme Court in Ottawa. In the end, though, his most famous work is *Girl in a Wetsuit* located on a rock along the STANLEY PARK seawall.

IN THE LAND OF THE HEAD-HUNTERS was a film about the KWAKWAKA'WAKW (Kwakiutl) people, made between 1911 and 1914 at FORT RUPERT by the American photographer Edward S. CURTIS. It was the first full-length documentary motion picture made about aboriginal N Americans. The film used Kwakwaka'wakw actors and costumes to depict aspects of ceremonial and social life. The title was chosen for its shock appeal; the Kwakwaka'wakw were not "head-hunters." The film premiered in New York and Seattle in 1914, then disappeared. A damaged copy appeared in Chicago in 1947; it was restored during the 1970s as *In the Land of the War Canoes.*

INDEPENDENT LABOUR PARTY (ILP), formerly the FEDERATED LABOUR PARTY, was an alliance of the non-communist left formed in 1926 largely through the efforts of Angus MACINNIS. At the onset of the Depression, the ILP attracted increased support; MacInnis was elected to the House of Commons on its platform in 1930. As the Depression deepened, the party moved further left and in 1932 renamed itself the Socialist Party of Canada. Leading figures included Ernest and Harold WINCH, Lyle TELFORD and Wallis Lefeaux. The ILP–SPC affiliated with the CCF on its formation in 1933 and officially merged into the CCF in 1935.

INDIAN ARM is a 17-km-long FJORD running north from upper BURRARD INLET to the Indian R estuary. The traditional territory of the TSLEIL WAUTUTH First Nation, it was first explored by the Spanish in 1792. It has been a popular recreation area since the 1870s, and though close to VANCOUVER, some homes along its shores remain accessible mainly by water. For years the MV *Scenic* delivered passengers, freight and mail from the city. WIGWAM INN was built in 1910 at the top end of the inlet. On the northeast shore, a stone quarry operated from the 1890s. South of the old quarry site 2 power plants at BUNTZEN LK intermittently provide electricity to parts of the Lower Mainland. DEEP COVE on the southwest shore is the main community. Much of the west side is part of or adjacent to Mt SEYMOUR Provincial Park; Indian Arm Provincial Park (6.8 km²) is on the east side; and Raccoon and Twin Islands in the middle of the arm make up Indian Arm Provincial MARINE PARK. Since 1910, there have been 3

unsuccessful proposals to span the entrance to the inlet with a bridge or causeway.

Doreen Armitage

INDIAN HOMEMAKERS' ASSOCIATION (IHA), established in 1969, is a provincially organized network of aboriginal women's clubs. The association acts as an advocate for aboriginal women living on and off reserve, provides a variety of social services from its office in VANCOUVER and holds an annual conference that brings together members from IHA clubs across the province. Originally reserve-based, Indian Homemakers clubs evolved from a mid-1930s initiative of the Department of Indian Affairs, which also provided the name. The department undertook to offset the effects of growing poverty on prairie reserves during the Depression by providing resources, such as shared sewing machines, and "homemaking" instruction to women on reserves. Indian Homemakers' Associations were then set up across Canada; from the mid-1960s onward, many of them formed the basis for a new and more political aboriginal women's movement focussing on the right of aboriginal people and women. IHA of BC was at the forefront of these movements in the 1970s and 1980s. Because of its political stance, the association's charitable status was withdrawn by the federal government in the late 1980s. In the 1990s the association has been less visible provincially and nationally. *See also* ABORIGINAL RIGHTS; FIRST NATIONS; WOMEN'S MOVEMENT.

INDO-CANADIANS; *see* SIKHISM; SOUTH ASIANS.

INDUSTRIAL, WOOD AND ALLIED WORKERS OF CANADA was formerly known as the International Woodworkers of America, which was formed in 1937 to represent the interests of loggers and millworkers in the Pacific Northwest. Led by Harold PRITCHETT, the first Canadian to lead an international union, the IWA was a left-leaning industrial union; it was embroiled in disputes with the American Federation of Labour and more conservative unions for all of its existence. The IWA staged and won its first major strike in the SPRUCE logging camps of the QUEEN CHARLOTTE ISLANDS in 1943 and the following year negotiated its first master agreement with the BC Loggers' Assoc. It emerged from WWII as the largest union in BC, with 27,000 members. During the anti-Communist hysteria of the Cold War period Pritchett was forced out of the presidency; in 1948 in BC the IWA split, with the leftist faction voting to disaffiliate and create its own Woodworkers Industrial Union of Canada. Bitter rivalry between the factions led to violence, and before long the WIU faded away. In the late 1950s the IWA reorganized itself into regions and BC, with 30,000 members, became Region 1. The union was strongest on the coast but during this period it spread into the Interior. Jack MUNRO led the union from 1973 to 1991 and in 1987 he spearheaded the creation of an independent Canadian union, IWA-Canada. At the start of the 21st century, the Industrial, Wood

and Allied Workers was still the largest private-sector union in BC, and it drew a significant portion of its membership from occupations outside the primary FOREST INDUSTRY. *See also* LABOUR MOVEMENT; LOGGING.
Reading: Jerry Lembcke and William M. Tattan, *One Union in Wood,* 1984.

INDUSTRIAL WORKERS OF THE WORLD

(IWW) was a radical syndicalist union founded in Chicago in 1905. The IWW spread rapidly across the American West and into BC, where it appealed mainly to workers in LOGGING, MINING and construction industries. Members of the IWW—known popularly as Wobblies after a Chinese restaurateur mispronounced the initials "Eye Wobbly Wobbly"—advocated worker control of industry and general strikes as a means of direct action. By 1907 at least 8 IWW locals were active in BC. For a time it was the largest union in BC and took a leading role in important labour protests, including the FREE SPEECH CAMPAIGN in VANCOUVER in 1909–12 and the 1912 strike of more than 8,000 construction workers on the CANADIAN NORTHERN RWY line between HOPE and KAMLOOPS. (The IWW martyr Joe Hill memorialized this strike in his song "Where the Fraser River Flows.") IWW influence in BC peaked during the CN strike, and faded because of employer hostility, discord within the LABOUR MOVEMENT and the end of rail construction.

INFLUENZA EPIDEMIC of 1918, the deadliest

flu outbreak in recorded history, claimed about 21 million lives worldwide, including 50,000 Canadians. Known as the Spanish flu, it appeared in the spring of 1918 and was spread by troops returning from WWI. It reached eastern Canada with the troopships in June and by early Oct the first cases were reported in VANCOUVER and VICTORIA. The MEDICAL PROFESSION was powerless to halt the disease and fought its spread mainly by quarantine and closure of public places. The flu was carried into the Interior along rail lines and up the coast on steamships, and it thrived in LOGGING and MINING camps. FIRST NATIONS communities were particularly hard hit; at least 1,150 aboriginal people died, a much higher death rate than in the non-aboriginal population. The epidemic ran its course early in 1919, having claimed about 4,000 lives in BC.

INLAND NATURAL GAS was created in 1951

by John McMahon and Norman Whittall to supply BC Interior communities with natural gas acquired from the Westcoast Transmission pipeline (*see* WESTCOAST ENERGY INC). In 1988 Inland purchased the Mainland Gas Division of BC HYDRO and formed a successor company, BC GAS INC, which now supplies customers throughout the province. *See also* OIL AND GAS INDUSTRY; PIPELINES.

INOUYE, Kanao "the Kamloops Kid,"

war criminal (b 1916, Kamloops; d 25 Aug 1947, Hong Kong). After growing up in KAMLOOPS, he went with his mother to Japan in 1935; during the war he worked as a prison camp interpreter and for the Japanese secret service. Harbouring strong resentment against whites who had picked on him when he was a boy in Canada, he sought revenge by brutalizing prisoners under his control. He was directly responsible for the deaths of at least 3 POWs. After the war he was charged with 27 counts of cruelty and appeared before a war crimes tribunal. Because he was a Canadian citizen he was tried for treason and executed.

INSECTS are a group of invertebrates (Phylum

Arthropoda) belonging to the class Insecta, which is larger than all other animal groups combined. As a group, insects are of great ecological significance. While our knowledge about insects and their roles is incomplete, we know that insects are vital in maintaining ecosystems. Two-thirds of all flowering plants are dependent upon insects for pollination; the principal pollinators are bees, wasps, flies, BUTTERFLIES AND MOTHS. Insects are critical components of food webs, controlling other invertebrate and plant populations and providing food for a variety of animals from birds to BEARS; they are of tremendous importance as food for SALMON. Insects are important because of their roles in decomposition, in creating productive soil, and in associations with fungi; many plants, including forest species, are dependent on insect–fungal associations. Insects are also of great economic importance, notably to AGRICULTURE, the FOREST INDUSTRY and human health, and vast sums of money are spent on their control. Termites, carpenter ants and other insects infest buildings, and weevils infest stored food, especially grains. Lice, fleas and a host of flies, including MOSQUITOES, not only contribute directly to human misery, some are direct and indirect vectors of diseases affecting humans and domesticated plants and animals.

All adult insects have segmented bodies made up of 3 parts: head, thorax and abdomen. The head typically bears a single pair of antennae and a pair of compound eyes. Three pairs of legs (and usually 2 pairs of wings or related structures) grow from the thorax; the thorax and the abdomen generally contain the reproductive and gas exchange structures. Insects have an external skeleton (exoskeleton). Development from egg to adult is of 2 principal types: homometabolous and hemimetabolous, formerly called complete and incomplete metamorphosis. In the first type, the individual develops from egg to adult in 4 stages: egg, larva (feeding stage), pupa (quiescent stage), and adult. Metamorphosis generally occurs during the pupal stage and the adult looks nothing at all like the larva. Insects that experience this process include butterflies and moths, beetles, flies and ants. Hemimetabolous insects do not undergo a pupal stage. In some of these, the nymphs, or immatures, look much like the adults. This group includes grasshoppers, cockroaches and crickets. In others, the adults may be radically different from the larvae; these include aquatic insects, such as DRAGONFLIES and mayflies.

Over 33,000 insect species have been identified in Canada, and a conservative estimate allows that more than twice that many remain to be discovered. Because of its high diversity of ecosystems, BC probably has the most diverse insect fauna in Canada. The province is estimated to have at least 40,000 species. Over 1.4 million specimens (representing about 10,000 species) were collected in the CARMANAH forest canopy studies between 1992 and 1997 by Dr Neville Winchester of the UNIV OF VICTORIA. While most of these are still not catalogued, so far 500 are new to science and are still not named.

Insects were the first animals to develop flight; they occupy all environmental niches on land and in fresh water, and to a limited extent in surface and tidal ocean waters. Insects occur in all habitats in BC and exhibit a fascinating range of behaviours, from ants farming aphids for their honeydew to dragonflies patrolling their territories, challenging interlopers as large as humans. Fierce predators are found in lakes and rivers, such as the water boatman and the upside-down backswimmer. Our largest aquatic insect is the giant water bug: also called the toe-biter, it is the size of a small frog and can capture small fish. Specialized insects occur at HOT SPRINGS, such as the vivid dancer, an intense blue damselfly. The plains forktail damselfly occurs at LIARD R Hotsprings and nowhere else in BC. Some insects are found in the inhospitable environments on the tops of mountains: flying ants feed on aerial plankton that drop onto the surface of

Top: Large marble butterfly captured by a crab spider. Bottom: Canadian swallowtail caterpillar. Crispin Guppy photos

glaciers and icefields. The OKANAGAN VALLEY, which has some of Canada's most endangered ecosystems, is also home to some of BC's rarest insects, including the ground mantid (*Litaneutria minor*), Canada's only native praying mantis. It is also the only place in BC where the introduced (from Europe) praying mantis (*Mantis religiosa*) is found.

The largest insect in BC is the polyphemus moth (*Antheracea polyphemus*), with a wingspan of 12–13 cm. The heaviest is our largest beetle, the spiny woodborer (*Ergates spiculatus*), which measures 6–7 cm long, not counting its long antennae. The smallest insect is likely one of the hundreds of species of tiny trichogramma wasps, which are about 0.2 mm long. These wasps are parasites of insect eggs and are important as biological controls in FORESTRY and agriculture.

There are many rare insects in the province; most live in threatened or disappearing habitats. In addition to those already noted is the Edith's checkerspot butterfly, found nowhere in the world but on HORNBY ISLAND, where there is a small population. The river jewelwing is a spectacular metallic green damselfly known in BC from only one short stretch of stream near CHRISTINA LAKE. A number of insects are no longer found in BC, including the viceroy butterfly. This monarch mimic used to be a rare inhabitant of the southern Interior, but none has been seen for many years. The island marble butterfly used to live in Garry OAK woodlands around Victoria and the GULF ISLANDS, but it is now found only on SAN JUAN ISLAND in Washington state.

Maggie Paquet (with help from Dr Robert Cannings)
Reading: Cannings, Richard and Sydney, *British Columbia: A Natural History*, 1996.

INSIDE PASSAGE is the corridor of protected water between the mainland coast of BC and its offshore ISLANDS. The passage extends about 1,600 km from Puget Sound in Washington state to Skagway, AK. In the south it passes the Lower Mainland with its teeming population and continues north through GEORGIA STRAIT into the jumble of islands between VANCOUVER ISLAND and the mainland. After leaping across the open waters of QUEEN CHARLOTTE SOUND, the northern passage plunges once again into a network of narrow channels leading all the way to the northern terminus at PRINCE RUPERT. This northern section is what many people mean when they use the term Inside Passage. For most of its length it is sparsely populated and accessible only by water or float plane. First charted by Capt George VANCOUVER in the 1790s, the passage became the coastal "highway" along which marine vessels of every description plied the coast. BC FERRY CORP vessels use the northern passage to provide year-round service between Prince Rupert and PORT HARDY at the north end of Vancouver Island, and summer service to BELLA COOLA. While offering shelter from the heaviest seas and weather, the route is strewn with perilous currents, reefs and channels that have claimed many an unwary vessel. *David Lee*

The ferry Queen of the North *steaming through the Inside Passage. Courtesy BC Ferries*

INSURANCE CORPORATION OF BC (ICBC) is a commercial CROWN CORP, based in N VANCOUVER, which administers Autoplan, the compulsory provincial automobile insurance program. Established in 1973 by the NDP government of Dave BARRETT, ICBC operates on a non-profit basis: insurance premiums collected from motorists are expected to pay for all insurance claims. Under the terms of Autoplan, every motorist is required to have basic insurance. Private insurance companies may compete with ICBC in offering extended coverage, and private agencies take care of premium collection. ICBC also issues drivers' licences and vehicle licences and registration, and carries out a variety of safe-driving initiatives. In 1999 ICBC had revenues of $2.8 billion, making it the fourth-largest corp in BC and the second-largest Crown corp.

INTERMEDIA (1967–72) was a loose association of artists working in VANCOUVER in a variety of media who combined to exchange ideas and stage events. The idea grew out of a series of meetings initiated by Jack SHADBOLT and others in 1967; it became a more official entity the following year when it moved to a building on Beatty St and appointed Werner Aellen as director. Intermedia Nights at the VANCOUVER ART GALLERY were an important part of the gallery's attempt to reach a broader audience. Artists associated with Intermedia were interested in expanding popular notions of what constitutes art and in exploring new technologies through experimental film, performance art, correspondence art and other media. The organization dissolved in 1972, though several other artist groups rose from its ashes. *See also* ART, VISUAL.

INTERNATIONAL FOREST PRODUCTS LTD (Interfor) originated in 1933 as a small SAWMILL, the Tidewater Lumber Co, at WHONNOCK on the north shore of the FRASER R near MISSION. As ownership changed over the years, the company acquired a shake and shingle mill at STAVE LK and additional timber holdings in the FRASER VALLEY. In 1971 a sawmill and timber rights at Adams Lk were added and the company was renamed Whonnock Industries. In 1976 the Pacific Pine sawmill at NEW WESTMINSTER was purchased, along with the McDonald Cedar mill at FORT LANGLEY the following year, when control of the company was acquired by Sauder Industries, a VANCOUVER door and molding manufacturer owned by W.L. Sauder. Rapid expansion followed as the company added sawmills in

Vancouver and PITT MEADOWS, along with a third of the assets of Rayonier Canada Ltd. In the late 1980s the name changed to International Forest Products and a major small-log sawmill was opened in New Westminster. In 1991 extensive cutting rights on VANCOUVER ISLAND, a sawmill at MAPLE RIDGE and the historic Fraser Mills (*see* MILLSIDE) at COQUITLAM were bought from FLETCHER CHALLENGE CANADA LTD, making Interfor the second largest LOGGING operator on the BC coast. By 1993 the company accounted for two-thirds of SEABOARD LUMBER SALES business and absorbed Seaboard, a 60-year-old co-operative sales organization. In 1995 it purchased the coastal operations of WELDWOOD OF CANADA LTD, including sawmills at PORT MOODY and SQUAMISH. Sales in 1998 totalled $597 million. *See also* FOREST INDUSTRY.

INTERNATIONAL PACIFIC HALIBUT COM-MISSION (IPHC), established in 1923 as the International Fisheries Commission by a convention between Canada and the US, is a body that oversees the management and preservation of the HALIBUT resource of the north Pacific Ocean and the Bering Sea. The convention was the first international agreement that provided for the joint management of a marine resource. Each country pays half of the commission's annual expenses as required by the HALIBUT TREATY. Three IPHC commissioners are appointed by the governor general of Canada and 3 by the president of the US. The commissioners appoint the director who supervises the scientific and administrative staff; these people collect and analyze the statistical and biological data needed to manage the halibut fishery. The commission meets annually to review all regulatory proposals, including those made by the scientific staff; the conference board, which represents fishers and vessel owners; and a processors advisory group. The measures recommended by the commission are submitted to the 2 governments for approval. Upon approval the regulations are enforced by the appropriate agencies of both governments. The IPHC headquarters and laboratory are located on the campus of the Univ of Washington in Seattle, WA. *See also* FISHING, COMMERCIAL.

INTERNATIONAL PACIFIC SALMON FISH-ERIES CONVENTION (IPSFC), 4 Aug 1937, was a treaty between the US and Canada regulating sockeye and pink SALMON stocks in the FRASER R. Fishing interests had been worried for years about an apparent decline in the stocks, especially since the HELLS GATE BLOCKADE of 1913-14. Negotiations had resulted in the Fraser River sockeye salmon convention of 1930; this agreement had been approved by Canada but not by the US Senate. Finally, in 1937, the last American opposition was overcome and the Convention was signed. Half of the Fraser R sockeye was assigned to each country, and the International Pacific Salmon Fisheries Commission was established to restore and conserve salmon stocks in convention area waters. The Commission consisted of 6 members, 3

from each country, plus an advisory committee of representatives from industry groups. Among other things, the Commission built fishways at Hells Gate during 1944-46. In 1956 the convention was amended to include pink salmon. Overall the Commission was successful in rebuilding the Fraser R salmon population. In 1985, the Fraser River sockeye and pink convention was replaced by the PACIFIC SALMON TREATY, and the Commission was replaced by a new PACIFIC SALMON COMMISSION. *See also* FISHING, COMMERCIAL.

Reading: John F. Roos, *Restoring Fraser River Salmon: A History of the International Pacific Salmon Fisheries Commission, 1937–1985,* 1987.

INTERNATIONAL SELF-COUNSEL PRESS is a N VANCOUVER book publisher founded in 1971 by Jack James, a law student, and Diana Douglas, who operated a bookstore. The company's first book, *Divorce Guide for BC,* was very successful and the press developed a niche as a publisher of legal self-help books. The company has since published a series of books covering a wide range of legal and business subjects, including wills, landlord–tenant rights and corporate practices. James left the company in the early 1980s and Douglas became the sole owner and CEO. By the late 1980s the press had expanded into US and overseas markets. By the late 1990s it was selling some 200 titles in 19 countries and maintaining offices in N Vancouver, Brampton, ON, and Bellingham, WA. *See also* BOOK PUBLISHING.

Dianne Mackay

INTERNATIONAL UNION OF MINE, MILL & SMELTER WORKERS was founded in 1916 as a successor union to the WESTERN FEDERATION OF MINERS. Concentrated in BC, among hardrock KOOTENAY miners and workers in the COMINCO smelter at TRAIL, it was one of the most militant labour groups in Canada. The union, known familiarly as Mine Mill, was weakened by a disastrous strike in Trail in 1917 but re-emerged during the 1930s as one of the founders of the Congress of Industrial Organizations, a radical offshoot of the American Federation of Labour and a proponent of industrial unionism. Following WWII the BC union was led by Harvey Murphy, a prominent Communist labour leader, and was embroiled in the Cold War struggle over "red" unionism. One of the legendary events of BC labour history occurred in 1952 after Murphy had invited Paul Robeson to sing at the union's annual convention. Because of his supposed connection to the US Communist Party, Robeson was not allowed to cross the border so the union organized an outdoor concert at the PEACE ARCH on 18 May that attracted a crowd of 40,000 people. In 1967, after more than 50 years of activity, Mine Mill merged with the United Steelworkers. *See also* Albert KING; MINING.

INTERNATIONAL WOODWORKERS OF AMERICA; *see* INDUSTRIAL, WOOD AND ALLIED WORKERS OF CANADA.

INTERURBANS were electric railways connecting communities in two areas: southern VANCOUVER ISLAND and the Lower Mainland. The first Interurban in BC was also the first in N America. It opened in 1891, running between NEW WESTMINSTER and downtown VANCOUVER through then-unsettled BURNABY. Known as the Central Park Line, it became part of the new BC ELECTRIC RWY CO in 1897. In the decade before the outbreak of WWI, the BCER expanded its network of Interurbans, building lines through RICHMOND to STEVESTON, from Marpole along the FRASER R to New Westminster, and a second line from New Westminster to Vancouver via Burnaby Lk. On Vancouver Island, a line running from VICTORIA to the tip of the SAANICH PENINSULA opened in 1913. But the most ambitious line, opened in 1910, ran 100 km into the FRASER VALLEY from Vancouver to CHILLIWACK. As well as passengers, the Interurbans carried mail, milk, fresh produce, fish and other freight. With the

BC Electric Railway Co interurban streetcar leaving Kitsilano Station in Vancouver, bound for Minoru Park races in Richmond, 1909. VPL 2137

exception of the Saanich line, which closed in 1924, the Interurbans played a vital role in the economic development of the region. By the 1950s, however, trucks and motor buses were proving more efficient. The Fraser Valley line closed in 1950, followed by the others. The last Interurban made its final run between Marpole and Steveston on 28 Feb 1958. Vancouver's SKY-TRAIN rapid transit system, started in 1986, follows much of the same route pioneered by the Central Park Interurban; the West Coast Express, started in 1995, restores commuter rail service to the Fraser Valley.

INTRAWEST CORP is a VANCOUVER resort developer and operator with 1997–98 revenues of $601.7 million. Founded by Joe Houssian in 1979 as a real estate development company, it purchased Blackcomb Mt in 1986, then added ski resorts at Panorama Mt in BC, Mont Tremblant in QC, Blue Mt in ON and at several locations across the US. In 1997 it added

WHISTLER Mt to its holdings and is now the leading mountain resort developer in N America. It also has an interest in Alpine Helicopters Ltd, owner of Canadian Mountain Holidays, the largest heli-SKIING operation in the world. Several of the resorts are being developed as all-season travel destinations.

INVERMERE, district municipality, pop 2,687, lies in the COLUMBIA R Valley at the north end of Windermere Lk, 130 km north of CRANBROOK. With the ROCKY MTS on one side and the PURCELL MTS on the other, the site was used for fishing by the KTUNAXA nation. David THOMPSON built KOOTENAE HOUSE nearby in 1807. In 1890 a MINING boom resulted in the creation of a townsite, Copper City. This name changed in 1900 to Canterbury, after the English cathedral town, and eventually to Invermere, a name chosen by R. Randolph BRUCE, lt gov of BC from 1926 to 1931, who developed an estate on the shores of the lake. His home, Pynelogs, was still standing at the end of the 20th century. The FOREST INDUSTRY became the mainstay of the area; TOURISTS are attracted to the HOT SPRINGS at nearby RADIUM and FAIRMONT and to the SKIING at Panorama Ridge.

Rural church near Invermere.
Walter Lanz/Image Makers

INVERNESS, 14 km south of PRINCE RUPERT at the mouth of the SKEENA R, was the first SALMON CANNERY north of the FRASER R. It was built by North Western Commercial Co on the site of Woodcock's Landing, an early inn and trading post, and subsequently owned by Turner, Beeton and J.H. Todd. Operations began in 1876. Twice the cannery burned to the ground and was rebuilt. Linked to the GRAND TRUNK PACIFIC RWY in 1914, the plant closed in 1950 and was destroyed by fire in 1973. Its peak year was 1938 when 62,271 cases of salmon were produced. *See also* FISHING, COMMERCIAL. *AS*

IOCO, located west of PORT MOODY on the north side of BURRARD INLET, is an Imperial Oil distribution terminal. It began its long history as a centre for oil refining in 1909, when the BC Refining Co opened a small facility. A much larger refinery owned by Imperial Oil began production in 1915. A townsite for employees opened in 1920, taking its name from the company's initials. In 1953 the TRANS MOUNTAIN PIPE LINE CO LTD connected major oil reserves in Alberta to Ioco, resulting in a $12-million expansion; during the 1980s the refinery employed more than 200 people and had a capacity of 40,000 barrels a day. On 31 July 1995 the refinery closed and the facility became an asphalt plant and a bulk storage plant for bunker oil from Alberta. The community has been phased out gradually since 1953; 14 homes remained in 1998. *See also* OIL AND GAS INDUSTRY. *Doreen Armitage*

IRANIANS began arriving in BC in significant numbers in the early 1970s, many as political refugees fleeing Iran during the reign of Shah Reza Pahlevi. After Iran became an Islamic republic in 1979, the number of refugees rose dramatically. This second wave of immigrants were generally well educated and many came from wealthy backgrounds. Most came to BC to escape the theocracy of the Ayatollah Khomeini but some came seeking educational opportunities for their children; others, especially members of the BAHA'I FAITH, came to escape religious persecution in Iran. Vancouver's North Shore became a centre of the Iranian population, partly because of its physical resemblance to northern Tehran. The Lonsdale area of N VANCOUVER now boasts a wide range of Iranian shops and businesses. By 1996 BC had welcomed about 11,000 Iranian immigrants and was home to a quarter of the total Iranian-Canadian population. Several Iranian organizations are active in Vancouver, including the Iranian Community Association of BC. The community supports a Persian-language radio show, a newspaper and a television program. *Dianne Mackay*

IRELAND, Moses Cross, timber cruiser (b 1830, Piscataquis, ME; d May 1913, Valdes Island). He began his LOGGING career as a 14-year-old in the Maine woods before crossing the continent to join the California gold rush in 1851. In 1861 he followed the gold trail to the CARIBOO (*see* GOLD RUSH, CARIBOO) but a year later he was in NEW WESTMINSTER. He met Sewell MOODY and went into business with him, first importing cattle from Oregon, then buying a SAWMILL on the north shore of BURRARD INLET at what later became MOODYVILLE. A few months later Ireland sold his share in the mill to go gold prospecting in the Cariboo. He returned to the coast and resumed his career as a logger and timber cruiser; he became one of the legendary characters of the pioneer days of the industry. He lived for many years at BOLD POINT on QUADRA ISLAND. *Ken Drushka*

IRON CHINK was the name given to the Smith Butchering Machine, a tool for butchering SALMON that was introduced in BC canneries in 1906. Developed in Seattle by E.A. Smith, it greatly accelerated the SALMON CANNING process. The name is a reference to the many CHINESE cannery workers made redundant by the machine.

The iron chink, the machine that revolutionized the salmon canning industry. VMM

IRONWORKERS MEMORIAL SECOND NARROWS CROSSING across BURRARD INLET in VANCOUVER was completed in 1960. A bridge across this part of the inlet was first erected in 1925 to handle both car and rail traffic. After a series of accidents, the original bridge was knocked out by the log barge *Pacific Gatherer* in 1930 and was not replaced until 1934. The present bridge was built as the Second Narrows Bridge from 1956 to 1960. During construction, on 17 June 1958, the partially completed span collapsed into the water, killing 18 workers and injuring 20 others. A diver also died while looking for bodies. A government inquiry by Chief Justice Sherwood LETT attributed the accident to an engineering mistake. The 2 men found responsible for the mistake had died in the collapse. The new bridge opened in 1960. On 17 June 1994 it was renamed.

IROQUOIS were a confederacy of FIRST NATIONS tribes originally occupying northern New York state. Many Iroquois moved to Canada and settled in Ontario and Quebec; there, from the late 18th to the 19th century, they were recruited into the FUR TRADE as voyageurs, guides, interpreters and trappers. As employees of the NORTH WEST CO and the HBC, several hundred Iroquois made their way into the Canadian West. Some remained after their contracts expired, marrying local women and making a living as "free" (self-employed) trappers. About 200 Iroquois came west of the ROCKY MTS during the fur trade era. In time those who stayed were absorbed into other aboriginal communities, and no identifiable Iroquois population exists any longer in BC.

IRVINES LANDING, on the SUNSHINE COAST 85 km northwest of VANCOUVER, was the first non-aboriginal settlement on PENDER HARBOUR. Charles Irvine opened a store and hotel at the harbour's north entrance in the 1880s; his wharf became the local port of call for UNION STEAMSHIPS. Joe Gonsalves and Theodore Dames built a larger hotel in the early 1900s and various stores, resorts and boatyards have operated there over the years. Today the landing is the site of a marina and pub.   AS

IRVING, John, steamboat captain (b 24 Nov 1854, Portland; d 10 Aug 1936, Vancouver). In 1872, when he was still a teenager, he took over the PIONEER LINE of FRASER R steamboats founded by his father William IRVING. Over a 30-year career he was the leading captain on the river operating the most successful navigation company in the province. He merged the Pioneer Line with the HBC fleet of steamers in 1883 to form the CANADIAN PACIFIC NAVIGATION CO which he managed until it was sold to the CPR in 1901. He was also a member of the legislature for CASSIAR from 1894 to 1900. After the sale of his company he retired from the steamboat business but continued to use his lifetime free pass on the CPR vessels to travel up and down the coast. He exhausted a large fortune, which included a mansion in VICTORIA, and ended his days living

Collapse of the Second Narrows Bridge (later renamed Ironworkers Memorial Second Narrows Crossing), Vancouver, 1958.
Bill Cunningham/Vancouver Province

in a converted store in VANCOUVER. He died, as one writer put it, "poor in everything but friends."

IRVING, William, steamboat captain (b 3 Mar 1816, Annan, Scotland; d 28 Aug 1872, New Westminster). He went to sea as a young boy and was a veteran of steamboating in New Brunswick and Oregon when he arrived in VICTORIA in 1859. There he established a navigation company operating a fleet of PADDLEWHEEL STEAMBOATS on the FRASER R and HARRISON LK. He sold this operation in 1862 but immediately launched another company, the PIONEER LINE. It operated boats on the Fraser between NEW WESTMINSTER and YALE and made Irving one of the leading steamer captains on the river. He ran the line until his death, after which his son John IRVING took over. His house in New Westminster, built in 1864, is now a museum.

ISKUT are a group of about 300 FIRST NATIONS (ATHABASCAN) people centred at Eddontenajon Lk, south of the STIKINE R in northwest BC. They are closely affiliated with their neighbours the TAHLTAN people. In the 19th century the Iskut lived at BEAR LK, where they traded at FORT CONNOLLY. When the fort closed they drifted west to the TELEGRAPH CREEK area; in the 1960s they moved again to their present location.

ISLAM is one of the 3 major monotheistic religions (the others are Christianity and Judaism), with an estimated 930 million adherents worldwide. It is the dominant religion throughout N Africa, the Middle East and central and south Asia. Followers of Islam, known as Muslims, are

expected to submit themselves to the word and will of God (Allah in Arabic), and consider the teachings of the prophet Muhammad, collected in the *Qur'an*, or Koran, to be holy scripture. The Five Pillars of the Faith require Muslims to make a formal declaration of their faith (*shahadah*), to prostrate themselves before Allah 5 times a day, to provide generously for the poor, to fast between dawn and sunset during the month of Ramadan, and to make at least one pilgrimage (*hajj*) to Mecca. The fundamental division of Islam into Sunni (the majority) and Shiite dates back several centuries.

The first Muslim immigrant to BC was a retired British soldier named Salamat Khan, who settled in NEW WESTMINSTER in 1923. He was followed during the 1920s and 1930s by other individuals, most of whom congregated in New Westminster and found work in the lumber industry. In the wake of the liberalization of Canadian immigration laws in the 1960s (*see also* PEOPLES OF BC), the number of Muslims, mostly Sunnis, grew more dramatically and the Lower Mainland community became very diverse, including people from India, Pakistan, Egypt, Turkey and a wide variety of other countries. An Islamic Centre was built in Vancouver in 1964 and the BC Muslim Association was established in 1966. By the early 1980s mosques had been built in SURREY, RICHMOND and Vancouver. BC also has a sizeable Shiite Muslim community, largely made up of Isma'ilis who arrived in the 1970s after being expelled from Uganda by Idi Amin. Isma'ilis differ from other Shiites in that they take their leadership from the Aga Khan family, whom they believe to be direct descendents of Ali, for Shiites the legitimate successor to Muhammad. The Isma'ili community established the Isma'ili Jamatkhana Centre in 1982; it serves as a place of worship and also houses the headquarters of the Isma'ili National Council for Canada. Sixteen other jamatkhanas had been organized in the Lower Mainland by the mid-1980s. According to the 1991 census there were 24,930 Muslims in BC.

ISLAND COPPER MINE

ISLAND COPPER MINE, at one time the third- largest COPPER mine in Canada, was built at the north end of VANCOUVER ISLAND near PORT HARDY. Owned by BHP Copper (formerly Utah Construction and Mining Ltd), it went into production in 1971 and closed at the end of 1995. During its life it produced about 1.4 million tonnes of copper, as well as MOLYBDENUM, GOLD, SILVER and rhenium. Its massive open pit, 402 m below sea level, was the lowest open-air point on earth. The pit has since been turned into a giant lake.

The open pit at the Island Copper Mine near Port Hardy.

ISLAND TUG & BARGE LTD was one of the main TOWBOATING companies on the BC coast. Founded by Harold Elworthy (1901–75) in VICTORIA in 1925, it provided towing services to a variety of local industries, then expanded after WWII into deep-sea towing and salvage with the famous tug SUDBURY and later, *Sudbury II*. The company also pioneered the use of self-dumping LOG BARGES. In 1960 Elworthy sold controlling interest in his company to 2 international firms. He remained president until 1970, then gave up ownership completely. In 1971 Island Tug merged with Vancouver Tug to form the company now called SEASPAN INTERNATIONAL.

Harold Elworthy, founder of Island Tug & Barge.
Seaspan International

ISLAND WEAVERS was a VICTORIA company producing handwoven tweeds and tartans between 1933 and 1974. It was founded by Maj Robin Murray, a retired British Army officer, and his wife Enid after they moved to Victoria in 1932. Mrs Murray studied weaving at Galasheils College in Scotland, only the second woman ever to apply to the renowned college, and her husband ran the business side of the operation. They began production using hand looms in a former high school in ESQUIMALT and opened retail outlets in Victoria and VANCOUVER. From 1935 to WWII they also operated a factory in Seattle for the American market. Maj Murray died in 1973, by which time the cost of yarn was rising and competition from synthetics and mechanical looms was increasing, so Mrs Murray closed the business.

ISLANDS, coastal, are actually the tops of a chain of submerged mountains lying off the coast of BC. They were formed as sea levels rose following the retreat of the glaciers that once covered most of the province. There are approximately 6,500 islands along the 7,022 km of coastline.

THE 10 LARGEST BC ISLANDS

Vancouver	31,284 km²
Graham	6,436 km²
Moresby (Queen Charlottes)	2,787 km²
Princess Royal	2,274 km²
Pitt	1,373 km²
Banks	855 km²
King	824 km²
Porcher	531 km²
Nootka	526 km²
Aristazabal	425 km²

ISLANDS TRUST provides local government for the islands in southern GEORGIA STRAIT and HOWE SOUND. It was established by the province in 1974 as a planning agency to regulate development in the area, which was experiencing rapid population growth and its attendant economic and environmental pressures. The area, approximately 5,178 km² in size, includes 12 major GULF ISLANDS and more than 450 smaller ones. The major islands are N and S PENDER, SALTSPRING, SATURNA, MAYNE, GALIANO, THETIS, GAMBIER, GABRIOLA, LASQUETI, HORNBY and DENMAN. In 1990 the Trust became an autonomous local government with land-use planning and regulation authority. It is administered by a 26-member elected council with a 4-person executive committee carrying out daily business.

ISLE PIERRE, 35 km west of PRINCE GEORGE on the NECHAKO R and the CNR, was first settled by homesteaders from Saskatchewan in the 1920s. CANADIAN FOREST PRODUCTS operates a SAWMILL here. The community is named for a rocky island in the river's rapids.   AS

ITALIAN immigration to BC began with the arrival of Father Giovanni Nobili and other Jesuit missionaries who worked in the OKANAGAN VALLEY in the 1840s. They were not the first Italians to set foot in the province, however. That distinction belongs to the mariner Alejandro MALASPINA; sailing in the service of Spain, he arrived at NOOTKA SOUND in 1791. Large-scale immigration of Italians commenced at the end of the 19th century, and newcomers settled throughout BC wherever the opportunity for work existed in construction, MINING, AGRICULTURE, commercial FISHING, the FOREST INDUSTRY and on railway gangs. In the pre-WWI era, only about 25% of Italians settled in Vancouver. The majority went to smaller communities such as TRAIL, for example, where jobs were available in the COMINCO SMELTER, and POWELL RIVER, where the PULP AND PAPER complex was a major employer. Prominent members of this first generation of Italian immigrants included the Vancouver hotelier Angelo CALORI; "Cap" CAPOZZI, the founder of CALONA WINES LTD; the Arduini brothers in KAMLOOPS and Charles MAREGA, the first professional sculptor in the province.

The influx of Italians declined dramatically during the 1930s, then ceased altogether at the outbreak of WWII. During the war an estimated 40 BC Italians were arrested and interned as enemy aliens. After the war and the repeal of enemy alien legislation in 1947, immigration resumed. In general, this second wave of Italian immigrants possessed more skills, education and wealth than their predecessors. By 1996 there were 46,525 people in BC who listed Italian as their ethnic origin, with an additional 71,365 claiming to be part Italian. This amounted to 10% of the Italian-Canadian population. Italian was the language spoken at home by 10,516 BC residents. The majority of these people came to live in Vancouver, where Little Italy developed on the east side of the city near the Commercial Drive area. Another focus for the community has been the Sacred Heart Catholic Church, established in 1905 as just the second ROMAN CATHOLIC CHURCH in Vancouver. The social hub of this urban community is the Italian Cultural Centre, opened in 1977 and offering language classes, library, daycare centre, banquet facilities and a full calendar of social and cultural events. The *Casa Serena*, a 90-apartment seniors' retirement home, is next door. Other *Casa d'Italia* facilities are active in Kamloops, NEW WESTMINSTER, Trail, PORT ALBERNI, VICTORIA, NANAIMO and KELOWNA. Prominent members of BC's Italian community include Justice Angelo BRANCA, the soccer star Bob LENARDUZZI, Supreme Court of Canada Justice Frank Iacobucci, and the labour leader Ken GEORGETTI. In Vancouver the Italian-language newspaper *L'Eco d'Italia* has published weekly since 1956 and from May 1988 Telitalia has provided local and international programming on the Rogers multicultural television channel.

Ray Culos

A large bear made of jade, BC's official stone.
Ian Smith/Vancouver Sun

JACKS, Terry, producer, singer/songwriter (b 29 Mar 1944, Winnipeg). He grew up in VANCOUVER and was a member of the Chessmen in the mid-1960s, making appearances with the group on CBC TV's *Music Hop*. He met Susan Pesklevits, a Saskatoon singer, on the show; they married and became the Poppy Family. Their song "Which Way You Goin' Billy?" reached number 1 on the international charts in 1970. It cost just $125 to record at Vancouver's R & D Studio and it sold more than 3 million copies and received 2 Juno Awards. The Poppy Family released several more singles but did not recapture the success of "Billy"; they broke up when Jacks and his wife divorced. In 1974 Jacks scored a worldwide number 1 hit with a rewritten English version of the Jacques Brel song

Terry Jacks (l) sharing a meal with the French songwriter Jacques Brel, Brussels, 1974.

"Seasons In The Sun." The single sold more than 13 million copies and captured Juno Awards for bestselling single in both 1974 and 1975; Jacks also received Junos for best Canadian male vocalist in both years. By early 2000, "Seasons In The Sun" remained the bestselling single ever released by a Canadian artist. Jacks continued to record but his attention gradually turned to environmental issues and FILMMAKING. He became

an outspoken critic of PULP mill pollution on the BC coast and was honoured for his efforts with the 1992 United Nations Association-Western Canada Wilderness Environment Award. *See also* SOUND RECORDING INDUSTRY. *Mike Harling*

JACKSON BAY, 65 km northwest of CAMPBELL RIVER, is a northerly arm of Topaze Harbour between KNIGHT and Loughborough inlets. The area was the site of at least one KWAKWA̱KA̱'WAKW village. Homesteaders arrived in the 1910s and a settlement formed around a store and boat landing that lasted into the 1950s. LOGGING and FISHING were the main employment; fruit, vegetables, poultry (*see* AGRICULTURE), and cattle (*see* CATTLE INDUSTRY) were raised and sold to local logging camps. *AS*

JACOBSON, Sybil (Atkinson), artist (b 29 July 1881, London, England; d 4 Nov 1953, Vancouver). After studying under John Singer Sargent at London's Royal Academy Schools, she continued her art studies in Paris, where she met her first husband, also an artist. Together they immigrated to a homestead in Saskatchewan in 1912. Her husband suffered a mental breakdown, the couple divorced and Sybil remarried. It was after the death of her second husband that she moved to BC in 1936. Despite a hard life blighted by poverty she never stopped painting and managed to eke out a living doing portraits and teaching art. In VANCOUVER she exhibited with some of the leading artists of the day, including Emily CARR, Jack SHADBOLT and B.C. BINNING, though she herself was not a modernist, preferring to paint landscapes, portraits and still lifes.

JADE was designated the official provincial stone of BC in 1967. The same material prized by Chinese and Maori cultures for millennia, nephrite jade was used by aboriginal people in BC as early as 3,000 years ago. Jade is a blend, or

aggregate mineral. Its fibrous nature makes it extremely tough and useful as a tool. In thin section it is translucent so that carvings and sculptures appear to glow when backlit. There are 2 types: nephrite belongs to the amphibole family and has been known since ancient times; jadeite is a pyroxene and was identified in 1784 in Burma. BC produces about 100 tonnes of nephrite annually, supplying most of the world's requirements.

During the GOLD RUSH on the FRASER R, CHINESE prospectors recognized jade boulders in the river and sent them to China. The story goes that rather than pay an export tax they filled the coffins of their dead compatriots being sent home for burial. For a century the source of the material was elusive and it was found only as pebbles or boulders in rivers. Then, in 1960, a small deposit was located in the basin of the Yalakom R, a tributary of the Bridge R, northwest of LILLOOET. More extensive discoveries in the Omineca, DEASE LK and CASSIAR areas followed. Jade is still found on the gravel bars of the Yalakom, Bridge, Coquihalla and lower Fraser rivers. In 1960 a 1.5-tonne boulder found near GOLD BRIDGE was sold in New York for $30,000. In 1967 a 6-tonne boulder from the Bridge R area was donated by the O'Keefe Brewing Co to SFU, where it sits in the Academic Quadrangle. A 23-tonne boulder was shown at the BC Pavilion at Expo 70 in Osaka, Japan, and in 1990 a 13-tonne specimen was carved into the world's largest jade Buddha and placed in a Bangkok monastery. In Jan 1968 Premier W.A.C. BENNETT's government created the Fraser River Jade Reserve, which extends from the bridge at HOPE to the suspension bridge at Lillooet, allowing anyone to collect jade below the mean high water mark for personal use without the need for a free miner's certificate. *Rick Hudson*

JAEGER is a falcon-like GULL, graceful and speedy, recognized by its elongated central tail feathers. It nests on the Arctic tundra and spends the rest of the year in the air at sea. With its dark head and back and its white underparts, the jaeger is most commonly seen on the offshore banks and around fishing vessels. On breeding grounds, these birds feed on smaller birds and LEMMINGS, but once at sea they feed by forcing other birds to drop their food, then pouncing on it in mid-air. The pomarine jaeger (*Stercorarius pomarinus*) is the largest of the 3 species found in summer off the BC coast. It is distinguished by central tail feathers that twist into a vertical position. The parasitic jaeger (*S. parasiticus*) is the most common species on the coast. The long-tailed jaeger (*S. longicaudus*) is the smallest species with long, streaming tail feathers. It is rarely seen from land in BC. A related species, the south polar skua (*Catharacta maccormicki*), is dark brown in colour and larger than a jaeger. It is another ocean wanderer, visiting the outer coast in its summer migration around the Pacific basin from Antarctica.

JAFFRAY, pop 375, is 35 km southeast of CRANBROOK on the CPR's Crowsnest branch. Two SAWMILLS were built here in the early 1900s and some RAILWAY LOGGING took place. The mills have since closed but the FOREST INDUSTRY still supports the local economy, along with TOURISM and the CATTLE INDUSTRY; MINING was important in the early days. The community was named after Senator Robert Jaffray of Toronto, president of the Crows Nest Pass Coal Co. AS

JAMES, Charlie (Yakuglas), artist (b circa 1870, Fort Rupert; d 1938). He produced TOTEM POLES, house posts and ceremonial objects for the use of the KWAKWAKA'WAKW and was best known outside his community for the many model totem poles he produced for sale. He was the progenitor of a line of Kwakwaka'wakw artists, including his stepson Mungo MARTIN and Henry and Tony HUNT. *See also* ART, NORTHWEST COAST ABORIGINAL.

JAMES, Colin, musician (b 1965, Regina). After spending his youth in Saskatchewan, he settled in VANCOUVER in the early 1980s and played in several bands. In 1984 he was discovered by the late blues guitar virtuoso Stevie Ray

Colin James, rock musician, performing at the Juno Awards, 1991. Craig Hodge/Vancouver Sun

Vaughan, who took him on as his opening act for a US tour. In 1987 James released an independent single, "Five Long Years," that was successful enough to secure a SOUND RECORDING deal with Virgin Records. For his first album, *Colin James* (1988), he received the Juno Award for most promising male vocalist. In 1990 he won Juno Awards for male vocalist of the year and single of the year ("Just Came Back"). During the 1990s he recorded two albums of swing tunes, as well as *National Steel* (1997), a collaboration with fellow Canadian bluesman, Colin Linden. James has had moderate commercial success and he enjoys great respect from his peers. He has toured as an opening act for such groups as The Rolling Stones, ZZ Top and the Fabulous Thunderbirds. *Mike Harling*

JAMES, Percy Leonard, architect (b 1878, London, England; d 1970, Victoria). The son of Samuel James, a well-known artist, Percy was educated in London and articled with his uncle, John Elford, architect and engineer to the city of Poole. In 1906 Percy immigrated to Canada. He settled in Edmonton, where he opened a partnership with M.A. Magoon and E.C. Hopkins. Two years later he moved to VICTORIA and was joined there in 1910 by his brother Douglas, also a London-trained architect. The brothers founded the firm of James and James, for many years second only to Samuel MACLURE as designers of prestigious Victoria residences. Percy was closely associated with Francis RATTENBURY on a number of projects in the capital, including the CPR Steamship terminal and Crystal Gardens. *See also* ARCHITECTURE. *Martin Segger*

JAMES BAY is the eastern end of VICTORIA Harbour and the location of the provincial PARLIAMENT BUILDINGS and the EMPRESS HOTEL. Much of the original bay was filled in from 1903 to 1904 to provide a site for the construction of the Empress. The name also refers to the peninsula south of downtown overlooking JUAN DE FUCA STRAIT and the outer entrance to the harbour. Originally owned by the HBC and known as Beckley Farm, the peninsula was subdivided and developed as Victoria's first fashionable residential district. Many of the old buildings remain. BEACON HILL PARK runs along one edge.

JAMES ISLAND, 3.2 km², lies off the east coast of the SAANICH PENINSULA 25 km north of VICTORIA. Named for Gov James DOUGLAS, it was settled originally by farm families in the 1870s. Later it was a private hunting ground for Victoria sportsmen, including Premier Richard MCBRIDE. In 1913 Canadian Explosives Ltd, later Canadian Industries Ltd, purchased the island and built an explosives plant. During WWI it was producing 900 tonnes of TNT a month. TNT from James Island was aboard the vessel that exploded in Halifax Harbour in 1917. At its peak, the plant had 800 employees, most of whom lived in a small village on the island. In 1962 the company closed the village and removed the buildings. In 1979 most of the manufacturing shut down and the plant was demolished. In 1999 the

island was primarily a residential area, owned by a Seattle businessman.

JAMIESON, Karen, choreographer (b 10 July 1946, Vancouver). After graduating from UBC with a BA in philosophy and anthropology, she trained in DANCE at SFU. She then moved to New York, where she studied classical modern dance techniques and began to develop her own choreography. She returned to VANCOUVER in the mid-1970s and co-founded Terminal City Dance, where she continued to develop her reputation as a choreographer and dancer. In 1980 Jamieson received the Jean A. Chalmers award for choreography. She founded the Karen Jamieson Dance Company in 1983 and has devoted her attention to exploring dance as mythic thinking and to creating a cross-cultural dialogue with FIRST NATIONS artists. As well as leading her own company, she has choreographed pieces for others, including Dancemakers and Winnipeg Contemporary Dancers. *Dianne Mackay*

JAMIESON, Laura Emma (Marshall), judge, politician (b 29 Dec 1883, Park Head, ON; d 29 June 1964, Vancouver). A graduate of the Univ of Toronto, she married J. Stewart Jamieson, a lawyer, and moved to VANCOUVER in 1911. There she worked at the forefront of the WOMEN'S SUFFRAGE movement through her work for the University Women's Club and the Local Council of Women. She was also a peace activist and in 1921 co-organized the Vancouver branch of the WOMEN'S INTERNATIONAL LEAGUE FOR PEACE AND FREEDOM. Her husband was a juvenile court judge in BURNABY, and when he died she succeeded him on the bench and served from 1926 to 1938. In 1939 she entered provincial politics, winning a by-election for the CCF. She represented Vancouver Centre from 1939 to 1945 and again from 1952 to 1953, and was a city alderman from 1948 to 1950.

JAPANESE immigration to BC began in 1877 with the arrival of Manzo Nagano, a sailor who jumped ship in NEW WESTMINSTER. Nagano, who later owned a store and hotel in VICTORIA, was followed by a small number of mostly male Japanese sojourners who remained temporarily. In 1891, for example, a group of 100 labourers came to work in the COAL mines at CUMBERLAND. In 1895 Japanese residents, whether or not they were Canadian citizens, were denied the provincial vote and, as a result, the federal and municipal vote as well. They were also denied the right to hold public office and to take jobs in most professions. This was followed by other discriminatory legislation aimed at stemming the inflow of immigrants, though the federal government felt obliged to disallow most of it because it violated international agreements between Britain and Japan. By 1901 there were 4,600 Japanese living in BC, 97% of all Japanese in Canada. Many were single males who had intended to return home. When they could not, they turned to the picture-bride system of arranged marriages. They found work mainly in FISHING, MINING and

Cooking up delicacies at Oppenheimer Park, Vancouver, during the annual Powell Street Festival, 1981. Powell Street was the centre of the Japanese Canadian community in Vancouver before WWII. Rob Draper/Vancouver Sun

the FOREST INDUSTRY, and in railway construction, where employers paid them less than other workers. In about 1914 many Japanese began moving onto farms in the FRASER VALLEY around MISSION and HANEY and in the OKANAGAN VALLEY, where they grew BERRIES and TREE FRUITS (*see* AGRICULTURE).

Anti-Asian sentiment in the population boiled over in Sept 1907 when a mob rampaged through Japanese and CHINESE quarters in VANCOUVER (*see* ASIATIC EXCLUSION LEAGUE). Japan then agreed to restrict emigration to BC and the number of new arrivals dropped sharply. Those who did come were mainly women and children joining their men, initiating what has been called the "family-building phase" of Japanese immigration. The growth of the community was dealt a blow in 1928 when Japan agreed to restrict emigration to Canada to 150 individuals annually. Also during the 1920s Japanese fishers were increasingly excluded from the coastal fishery by government regulation. The provincial franchise was extended to Japanese Canadian veterans of WWI in 1931, but the rest of the community remained excluded from government.

Despite the discrimination, the first generation of Japanese in Canada (the Issei) established themselves in the fishing industry, on farms in the Lower Mainland and the Fraser Valley and in the main urban neighbourhood around Powell St in Vancouver, known as *Nihonjinmachi*—"Japanese town," or "Little Tokyo." The second, Canadian-born generation, the Nisei, accounted for over half the people of Japanese ancestry in BC by WWII. But discrimination peaked during the war, when some 22,000 people of Japanese ancestry were removed from coastal BC and relocated to Interior camps and to other provinces east of the Rocky Mts (*see* JAPANESE, RELOCATION OF). By 1947 the number of people of Japanese descent living in BC was reduced to 6,776. For the first time, more people of Japanese ancestry lived in the rest of Canada than in BC. Not until 1949 were evacuees allowed to return to the coast.

Japanese Canadians received the federal franchise in June 1948 (effective Apr 1949) and the provincial vote in Mar 1949; governments had recognized at last that they were citizens like any

others. Still, restrictions on immigration to Canada from Japan were not all lifted until 1967. Since that time only a comparatively small number of Japanese have immigrated to BC. A third generation of Japanese Canadians—the Sansei, born since the war—encountered less discrimination than earlier generations and moved more easily into professions and jobs once closed to them. Many married non-Japanese people; a substantial number achieved positions of influence and authority. In 1988 the federal government formally apologized and compensated the Japanese Canadian community for the WWII relocation policy. At the 1996 census there were 33,245 people of Japanese origin living in BC. Most live in Vancouver, and while the large central Powell St community was never restored, a major Japanese Canadian cultural event, the Powell Street Festival, is held the first weekend of Aug each year. There is a significant Japanese Canadian population in STEVESTON, where a Japanese Canadian Cultural Centre opened in 1992. Prominent members of the Japanese Canadian community in BC have included the environmentalist David SUZUKI, the writers Roy MIKI, Joy KOGAWA and Roy KIYOOKA, the artist Takao TANABE, the photographer Tamio Wakayama and the architect Raymond Moriyama.
Reading: Ken Adachi, *The Enemy that Never Was: A History of the Japanese Canadians,* 1976.

JAPANESE, RELOCATION OF, was the forced removal of people of JAPANESE descent from coastal BC during WWII. The Japanese attack on Pearl Harbor on 7 Dec 1941 raised the question of an invasion of the Pacific coast of Canada. The authorities saw all people of Japanese descent in

NOTICE

TO ALL PERSONS OF JAPANESE RACIAL ORIGIN

Having reference to the Protected Area of British Columbia as described in an Extra of the Canada Gazette, No. 174 dated Ottawa, Monday, February 2, 1942:-

1. EVERY PERSON OF THE JAPANESE RACE, WHILE WITHIN THE PROTECTED AREA AFORESAID, SHALL HEREAFTER BE AT HIS USUAL PLACE OF RESIDENCE EACH DAY BEFORE SUNSET AND SHALL REMAIN THEREIN UNTIL SUNRISE ON THE FOLLOWING DAY, AND NO SUCH PERSON SHALL GO OUT OF HIS USUAL PLACE OF RESIDENCE AFORESAID UPON THE STREETS OR OTHERWISE DURING THE HOURS BETWEEN SUNSET AND SUNRISE;

2. NO PERSON OF THE JAPANESE RACE SHALL HAVE IN HIS POSSESSION OR USE IN SUCH PROTECTED AREA ANY MOTOR VEHICLE, CAMERA, RADIO TRANSMITTER, RADIO RECEIVING SET, FIREARM, AMMUNITION OR EXPLOSIVE;

3. IT SHALL BE THE DUTY OF EVERY PERSON OF THE JAPANESE RACE HAVING IN HIS POSSESSION OR UPON HIS PREMISES ANY ARTICLE MENTIONED IN THE NEXT PRECEDING PARAGRAPH, FORTHWITH TO CAUSE SUCH ARTICLE TO BE DELIVERED UP TO ANY JUSTICE OF THE PEACE RESIDING IN OR NEAR THE LOCALITY WHERE ANY SUCH ARTICLE IS HAD IN POSSESSION, OR TO AN OFFICER OR CONSTABLE OF THE POLICE FORCE OF THE PROVINCE OR CITY IN OR NEAR SUCH LOCALITY OR TO AN OFFICER OR CONSTABLE OF THE ROYAL CANADIAN MOUNTED POLICE.

4. ANY JUSTICE OF THE PEACE OR OFFICER OR CONSTABLE RECEIVING ANY ARTICLE MENTIONED IN PARAGRAPH 2 OF THIS ORDER SHALL GIVE TO THE PERSON DELIVERING THE SAME A RECEIPT THEREFOR AND SHALL REPORT THE FACT TO THE COMMISSIONER OF THE ROYAL CANADIAN MOUNTED POLICE, AND SHALL RETAIN OR OTHERWISE DISPOSE OF ANY SUCH ARTICLE AS DIRECTED BY THE SAID COMMISSIONER.

5. ANY PEACE OFFICER OR ANY OFFICER OR CONSTABLE OF THE ROYAL CANADIAN MOUNTED POLICE HAVING POWER TO ACT AS SUCH PEACE OFFICER OR OFFICER OR CONSTABLE IN THE SAID PROTECTED AREA, IS AUTHORIZED TO SEARCH WITHOUT WARRANT THE PREMISES OR ANY PLACE OCCUPIED OR BELIEVED TO BE OCCUPIED BY ANY PERSON OF THE JAPANESE RACE REASONABLY SUSPECTED OF HAVING IN HIS POSSESSION OR UPON HIS PREMISES ANY ARTICLE MENTIONED IN PARAGRAPH 2 OF THIS ORDER, AND TO SEIZE ANY SUCH ARTICLE FOUND ON SUCH PREMISES;

6. EVERY PERSON OF THE JAPANESE RACE SHALL LEAVE THE PROTECTED AREA AFORESAID FORTHWITH;

7. NO PERSON OF THE JAPANESE RACE SHALL ENTER SUCH PROTECTED AREA EXCEPT UNDER PERMIT ISSUED BY THE ROYAL CANADIAN MOUNTED POLICE;

8. IN THIS ORDER, "PERSONS OF THE JAPANESE RACE" MEANS, AS WELL AS ANY PERSON WHOLLY OF THE JAPANESE RACE, A PERSON NOT WHOLLY OF THE JAPANESE RACE IF HIS FATHER OR MOTHER IS OF THE JAPANESE RACE AND IF THE COMMISSIONER OF THE ROYAL CANADIAN MOUNTED POLICE BY NOTICE IN WRITING HAS REQUIRED OR REQUIRES HIM TO REGISTER PURSUANT TO ORDER-IN-COUNCIL P.C. 9760 OF DECEMBER 16th, 1941.

DATED AT OTTAWA THIS 26th DAY OF FEBRUARY, 1942.

Louis S. St. Laurent,
Minister of Justice

To be posted in a Conspicuous Place

Order-in-Council calling for the removal of "all persons of Japanese racial origin" from the coast, Feb 1942.

Japanese internment camp, Tashme, 1942.
BC Archives E-09913

BC—whether or not they were Canadian-born citizens, naturalized Canadians or citizens of Japan—as a possible fifth column sympathetic to the enemy. As a first step the government closed Japanese-language newspapers and impounded FISHING vessels belonging to Japanese fishers. Then, on 14 Jan 1942, the federal government passed Order-in-Council PC365 creating a 160-km-wide "protected area" along the coast. All Japanese nationals aged 18–45 were removed to work camps near Jasper, AB. Late in Feb another Order-in-Council authorized the removal of all persons "of the Japanese race," whether they were Canadians or not, from the coastal zone. It also imposed a dusk-to-dawn curfew on Japanese and allowed police to search premises and remove belongings without warrant. On 4 Mar 1942 a BC Security Commission was established to supervise the relocation of the people removed from the coast. Chaired by Austin TAY-LOR, a Vancouver financier, it included RCMP Assistant Commissioner Frederick Mead and BC PROVINCIAL POLICE Assistant Commissioner John Shirras. A Custodian of Enemy Property was named to manage property belonging to the evacuees. People of Japanese ancestry living in the zone were required to congregate at Hastings Park in east VANCOUVER. The majority were sent to communities in the BC Interior selected as relocation centres: GREENWOOD, SLOCAN, SAN-DON, KASLO and NEW DENVER. Settlements at Rosebery, Bay Farm, Popoff, Lemon Creek and TASHME consisted mainly of buildings constructed specifically for the purpose. Other people were sent to work on sugar beet farms in Alberta, Manitoba and Ontario. Men who refused to be relocated, in protest at being separated from their families, were interned in prisoner-of-war camps in Ontario until the Security Commission relented and arranged for family reunification. A total of nearly 22,000 people were relocated by Nov 1942. Early in 1943 the Custodian of Enemy Property was authorized to sell off property belonging to the internees. This was done ostensibly to pay for the cost of their relocation;

in other words, they were required to pay for their own involuntary removal. In the spring of 1945, as the war wound to its conclusion, the federal government offered internees a choice between deportation to Japan and permanent relocation to provinces east of the Rockies. In the end, deportation was cancelled in the face of public protest, though not before 3,964 people were sent to Japan. Relocation went ahead, however, and the BC camps emptied as internees were uprooted a second time and moved across the mountains, mainly to Ontario, which by 1947 had as large a population of Japanese Canadians as BC. At war's end there were 6,776 Japanese Canadians living in BC, down from a pre-war population of about 22,000. Not until 1949 were people of Japanese ancestry allowed to return to live on the BC coast.

In 1947, in response to demands from the Japanese Canadian community for compensation for the property seized during the war, the federal government established the Royal Commission to Investigate Complaints of Canadian Citizens of Japanese Origin, known as the Bird Commission after its chair, BC justice Henry Irving Bird. The commission was mandated only to investigate economic losses from the wartime sale of property by the Custodian. Bird's 1950 report resulted in payments totalling $1.2 million to individuals who had submitted claims. From the government's point of view this closed the book on the relocation, but the Japanese Canadian community did not forget. In 1984 the National Association of Japanese Canadians launched a campaign seeking redress for the events of the war. On 22 Sept 1988, following protracted negotiations, the federal government formally apologized for "past injustices" and offered a compensation package including a payment of $21,000 to every evacuee still living, $12 million to the Japanese Canadian community and $24 million to create a national race relations foundation.

Historians differ in their explanations for the relocation. At the time the government insisted it was motivated by security concerns, though senior military and police officials advised that the relocation was unnecessary. No Japanese

Canadian was ever charged with disloyalty. The most widely held interpretation of events is that racist politicians in BC used the war as an excuse to attempt to remove the province's Japanese population permanently. A minority view takes more seriously the state of panic that prevailed at the time and argues that the government, however mistakenly, was motivated by a desire to protect the evacuees from British Columbians made suspicious and vengeful by the war. According to this view, authorities worried that if Japanese in Canada were harmed, the government of Japan might retaliate against Canadian prisoners-of-war in that country. Whatever the government's motivation, the relocation is now recognized to have been a deplorable violation of HUMAN RIGHTS, one of the worst in BC's history.

JARVIS, Donald, artist (b 1923, Vancouver). He studied at the Vancouver School of Art (*see* EMILY CARR INSTITUTE OF ART & DESIGN) with B.C. BINNING and Jack SHADBOLT, and after graduating in 1948 continued his studies with Hans Hofmann in New York. Returning to VANCOUVER, he was one of a small group of abstract painters who led the burgeoning visual ARTS scene in the 1950s. In 1951 he joined the faculty at the Vancouver School of Art and taught there until his retirement in 1986. He has exhibited widely in Canada and abroad, notably as part of the landmark 1959 touring exhibition *7 West Coast Painters* as well as in a solo retrospective at the VANCOUVER ART GALLERY in 1977 and as part of a 1993 National Gallery of Canada exhibition titled *The Crisis of Abstraction in Canada, 1950s.* His work is represented in many private and public collections.

JARVIS, Laurie, fisher (b 2 Mar 1892, Helsinki, Finland; d 1965). Born Laurie Mattias Jarvelainnen, he immigrated from Finland to the planned utopian community at SOINTULA on MALCOLM ISLAND in 1901, changing his surname because most people couldn't pronounce it. After working as a logger he joined the gillnetting fleet and in the off-season operated a small boatyard on the Sointula waterfront (*see* BOAT-BUILDING; FISHING, COMMERCIAL). At this time gillnets were still pulled laboriously by hand. Drawing on his LOGGING experience with cable spools, he came up with the idea of winding in gillnets on a drum. In 1931 he built his first gillnet drum and after many failures and much experimentation he perfected a design and began manufacturing drums at his boatyard. He patented his concept but later dissolved the patent, recognizing that the concept was too simple to make the patent enforceable. The gillnet drum is now used worldwide.

JAY is a medium-sized member of the CROW family. The Steller's jay (*Cyanocitta stelleri*) was adopted as BC's provincial bird in 1987. Known for its raucous call and iridescent blue colouring, it inhabits coniferous and mixed forests from Alaska to California. It feeds on acorns, seeds, fruit, INSECTS, eggs and nestling birds. The name refers to Georg Wilhelm Steller, a Russian

Steller's jay, the official bird of BC.
Roy Luckow photo

naturalist who observed this jay on Kayak Island, Alaska, during the Vitus Bering expedition in 1741. Two other jay species occur in BC. The grey jay (*Perisoreus canadensis*) mainly inhabits the forests of the southern Interior mountains. The blue jay (*Cyanocitta cristata*) has only started appearing in BC since WWII; it is found mainly east of the ROCKY MTS in the PEACE R region.

JAZZ music generally has benefitted greatly from BC talent. Phil Nimmons (b 1923, Kamloops), a clarinetist, is a highly original composer-arranger whose music was prominent on CBC Radio for many years. His group, Nimmons 'N' Nine Plus Six, included Dave McMurdo (b 1944, Vancouver), a trombonist who later formed his own acclaimed jazz orchestra. Don Thompson (b 1940, Powell River), a bassist-pianist, is also a Juno Award-winning composer and multi-instrumentalist, and Ed Bickert (b 1932, Hochfeld, MB; raised in Vernon) is a world-renowned guitarist. All of these musicians moved east to Toronto in order to pursue greater musical opportunities; Terry Clarke (b 1944, Vancouver), a drummer, and Ingrid Jensen (b 1966, N

Fraser MacPherson, jazz musician, 1989.
Ian Smith/Vancouver Sun

Vancouver), a trumpeter, moved to New York City, as did pianist/singer Diana KRALL.

Jazz activity in BC is concentrated in VAN-COUVER, often the last stop for musicians touring west across Canada or north from California. The city has a proud history of innovative musicians' co-operatives, including the Cellar Club (1950s–1960s) and the New Orchestra Workshop (NOW) in the 1970s and 1980s. In the 1990s the NOW Orchestra was revived to perform original work by its members and by guest composers such as Barry Guy, George Lewis and Rene Lussier. Vancouver's distance from other Canadian centres makes touring difficult, so the city's resident musicians have developed a jazz microcosm of their own. A busy nucleus of traditional (Lance HARRISON, Linton Garner), mainstream (Oliver Gannon, Alan Matheson), fusion (Skywalk, Pacific Salt) and avant-garde (Al NEIL, Paul Plimley) artists produce consistently outstanding work. At EXPO 86 the Coastal Jazz and Blues Society, under artistic director Ken Pickering, launched an annual jazz festival that has acquired an international reputation. In recent years jazz festivals have sprung up in small communities such as HEDLEY, GIBSONS and PENDER HARBOUR, and jazz is increasingly part of music programs at colleges and universities. *David Lee*

JEDEDIAH ISLAND, 2.6 km², lies in GEORGIA STRAIT between LASQUETI ISLAND and the south end of TEXADA ISLAND. Privately owned for many years, it was made available for sale by its last owners, Al and Mary Palmer, as a provincial PARK. In 1995 the BC government purchased the island, with substantial funds raised from private sources—including the estate of the environmentalist and MOUNTAINEER Dan CULVER—and designated it a MARINE PARK. It is named for Jedediah Tucker, son of a British naval officer. *Reading:* Mary Palmer, *Jedediah Days*, 1998.

JEDWAY is an abandoned MINING community on the east coast of MORESBY ISLAND in the QUEEN CHARLOTTE ISLANDS. It began in the early 1900s as a centre for COPPER mining, faded during WWI, then flourished briefly as an iron mining centre from 1961 to 1968.

JEHOVAH'S WITNESSES belong to a religious movement founded in 1872 in Pittsburgh by Charles T. Russell, a businessman. He developed a unique theology based on the belief that Christ's presence would be revealed only to the righteous few who understood His message. Russell taught that the world's religious, political and economic institutions were corrupted by Satan and would be destroyed at Christ's second coming, originally expected to occur before the generation of people born before 1914 died out. (Witnesses are no longer so specific about the timing of Armageddon.) In 1881 Russell founded the Watchtower Society to spread his views. He was succeeded as leader in 1916 by Joseph Rutherford, who adopted the name Jehovah's Witnesses and introduced the practice of house-to-house evangelism for which the movement is

known. The first meetings in VANCOUVER were held in 1889 and congregations grew steadily in the face of public antagonism to their pacifism, their rejection of blood transfusions and their practice of shunning former followers. The movement has experienced rapid growth since WWII. According to the 1991 census there were 33,665 Witnesses in BC, making it one of the largest Christian sects in the province.

JELLY, popularly but erroneously referred to as jellyfish, is a free-swimming invertebrate belonging to the phylum Cnidaria, which also includes marine animals such as SEA ANEMONES. Jellies are structurally primitive animals, possessing no circulatory or respiratory systems. They absorb oxygen from the water directly through cell tissue and move by pulsing their bodies. Their only sense organs are photo receptors, which respond to light. A single body opening leads to a central stomach; waste is ejected through that opening. A jelly has tentacles suspended from the edges of its saucer-shaped body, and many species also possess oral lobes surrounding the mouth, which may flutter in the water like long ribbons. The animal is equipped with small stinging cells called nematocysts, with which it attacks its prey (mostly small zooplankton) and protects itself. In most species these "stingers" do not pose a serious threat to humans, though the sting of the brightly coloured lion's mane, or sea blubber

Lion's mane, the largest species of jelly in the world. Duane Sept photo

(*Cyanea capillata*), is strong enough to cause discomfort. This is the largest jelly in the world, measuring up to 2.5 m across. Common along the BC coast is the water jelly (*Aequorea victoria*), a small, colourless species seen drifting in the current near the surface. At night its luminescence is obvious. Another common species is the moon jelly (*Aurelia labiata*), large aggregations of which sometimes swarm in bays and harbours. As large as a side plate or as small as a coin, the moon jelly has a short fringe of tentacles and 4 horseshoe-shaped sex organs, which are clearly visible in the middle of the bell. The male produces sperm and releases it into the water, fertilizing eggs produced by the female. The tiny larvae settle on the bottom and develop into white, vase-shaped polyps. As each polyp grows, it divides crosswise until it resembles a stack of small saucers; one by one these separate and float off to become new jellies.

JERICHO BEACH, in the Point Grey neighbourhood of VANCOUVER on the south shore of BURRARD INLET, became the site of a military Air Station for FLYING BOATS in 1920. Planes from the base engaged in a variety of civilian activities, including forest and fishery patrols, geological surveys, aerial photography, firefighting and general coast surveillance. It was run by the Canadian Air Board until the RCAF took over in 1924. During WWII the army located at the site as well and post-war Jericho became a permanent army establishment. The city lobbied to take over the land until 1969, when the federal government surrendered most of it for a public park. Jericho is believed to be named for the pioneer logger Jeremiah ROGERS.

JEROME, Harry Winston, sprinter (b 30 Sept 1940, Prince Albert, SK; d 7 Dec 1982, Vancouver). He moved to BC with his family when he was 12 and began running at N VANCOUVER High School. After equalling the world 100-m record (10 secs) he went to the Olympic Games in Rome in 1960 but had to pull up in a qualifying heat with a pulled muscle. In 1962 he tied the world record for the 100 yards (9.2 secs), becoming the first male sprinter to share records at both distances. Later that year at the Commonwealth Games he suffered a torn thigh muscle that almost ended his career but he bounced back in 1964 to win a bronze medal at the Tokyo Olympics. He added to his gold medal collection at the 1966 Commonwealth Games and the 1967 Pan American Games. With an MA in physical education from the Univ of Oregon he retired from racing after the 1968 Mexico City

Harry Jerome, sprinter, running in the colours of the Optimist Striders, his Vancouver track and field club. BCSHF

Olympics to a career of teaching and promoting athletics among the young. A member of the Canadian Sports Hall of Fame and the Order of Canada, he died of a brain tumour. *See also* TRACK AND FIELD.

JERVIS INLET is a majestic FJORD that doglegs 77 km into the COAST MTS on the north end of the SECHELT peninsula. It is part of the territory of the SECHELT FIRST NATION, who had important villages at the head of the inlet and at Deserted Bay. Capt George VANCOUVER explored here in 1792 and named it after Admiral John Jervis. A later survey named many of the places after events in the career of Admiral Horatio Nelson. The inlet, with a maximum depth of 732 m, is the deepest fjord on the coast. It is a funnel for a fierce wind known to mariners as the Jervis Express. The scenic highlight is PRINCESS LOUISA INLET near the top end and the 40-m drop of Chatterbox Falls at its head. Only the occasional early settler attempted to homestead these isolated shores, though extensive LOGGING has taken place on the mountain slopes. Fin fish AQUACULTURE began in the 1970s, boomed during the 1980s, then collapsed in 1989.

JESMOND, 55 km northwest of CLINTON in the south CHILCOTIN, is a ranch (*see* CATTLE INDUSTRY), originally called Mountain House, established by Phil Grinder in 1870. The Coldwell family bought it in 1911 and ran a post office until 1960 and a store until 1970. Today the ranch house is a private residence. Ottawa turned down Mountain House as a post office name so Henry Coldwell chose Jesmond, after his English birthplace. AS

JESSICA, 16 km northeast of HOPE beside the Coquihalla R, was a station on the KETTLE VALLEY RWY named by Andrew MCCULLOCH, the railway's chief engineer and a Shakespeare enthusiast, after a character from *The Merchant of Venice*. A number of stations on this section of line have been named for characters in Shakespeare's plays. Jessica was important enough to have a post office between 1918 and 1942, but the line was abandoned in 1959. AS

JESSOP, John, educator, BC's first superintendent of education (b 29 June 1829, Norwich, England; d 30 Mar 1901, Victoria). He immigrated to Ontario with his parents in 1846. After working as a printer, he became a schoolteacher. In 1859 he joined the OVERLANDERS, who crossed the continent to BC. He failed to make a fortune in the Cariboo goldfields (*see* GOLD RUSH, CARIBOO) and found work as a printer, first in NEW WESTMINSTER then in VICTORIA. In Sept 1861 he returned to teaching and opened a private school, which in 1865 became part of a newly organized public school system. In 1870, when the Victoria district was unable to pay them, Jessop and the city's other teacher withdrew their services, an episode that has been called Canada's first teachers' strike. Following CONFEDERATION and the creation of a new public school system, he was named the first superintendent of

education, a position he held from 1872 to 1878. During his tenure he administered a dramatic expansion of the system, but he eventually resigned in protest against the government's policies and was never involved in education again. In 1883 he became an immigration agent, a position he held until his death. *See also* EDUCATION, PUBLIC.

JEUNE LANDING, 33 km south of PORT HARDY on Neroutsos Inlet, is just north of PORT ALICE on VANCOUVER ISLAND. Western Forest Products Ltd maintains an office here and a dryland timber sort nearby. This former LOGGING settlement was named after the Jeune brothers, pioneer VICTORIA sailmakers who also produced canvas tents and tarpaulins for BC's resource industries, and later for the recreation market. AS

JEWETT, Pauline, academic, politician (b 11 Dec 1922, St Catharines, Ont; d 5 July 1992, Ottawa). Educated at Queen's Univ, Harvard and the London School of Economics, she was a member of Carleton Univ's political science department from 1955 to 1974 and director of its Institute of Canadian Studies from 1969 to 1971. As president of SFU from 1974 to 1978, she

Pauline Jewett, Apr 1974, during her tenure as president of SFU.

was the first woman to head a major Canadian university. She was an admirer of Lester B. Pearson and began her political career as a Liberal, sitting in the House of Commons for an Ontario riding from 1963 to 1965. But she grew disenchanted with the Liberals under Pierre Trudeau, partly because of his handling of the October Crisis of 1970, and in 1972 she joined the NDP. She won re-election to Parliament for the riding of New Westminster–Coquitlam in 1979 and served until 1988. For all her academic achievements, Jewett had an unpretentious personal style that proved popular with voters on the campaign trail. She was a lifelong feminist, nationalist and social activist, and an inspiration to many women who followed her into public life. On her retirement from politics she became chancellor of Carleton Univ. She won appointment to the Privy Council just a few days before her death.

JEWITT, John Rodgers, blacksmith (b 21 May 1783, England; d 7 Jan 1821, Hartford, CT). The son of a blacksmith, he took up his father's trade and in 1802 sailed as an armourer aboard the trading vessel BOSTON bound for the Northwest Coast. On 22 Mar 1803 the vessel was attacked in NOOTKA SOUND by a group of local NUU-CHAH-NULTH led by Chief MAQUINNA, perhaps in revenge for insults he had suffered. The attackers killed the entire crew, except for Jewitt and a sailmaker, John Thompson, whom they took captive. The two men were treated well by their captors and eventually became Maquinna's bodyguards. Jewitt kept a journal that was later published as *Narrative of the Adventures and Sufferings of John R. Jewitt* (1815). The book was a unique early account of the Nuu-chah-nulth people based on first-hand experience, and has been republished many times. The captives were rescued in 1805 by another trader, who held Maquinna hostage until they were released. Jewitt travelled with this vessel to New England, where his book made him a celebrity. But he soon sank into obscurity and died poor and unnoticed.

JEWS have been living in BC since the beginning of non-aboriginal settlement. During the 1858 GOLD RUSH, many Jews arrived from California while others came from Australia, Great Britain and Europe. Some worked as miners; others established themselves as traders, merchants and wholesalers. Most of these newcomers settled in VICTORIA; within 5 years there was a community of about 100 Jews there. In 1860 they opened BC's first Jewish cemetery and in 1863 they built CONGREGATION EMANUEL TEM-PLE, the oldest surviving synagogue in Canada. Selim Franklin became the first Jew elected to political office in Canada when he became a member of BC's LEGISLATIVE ASSEMBLY in 1860. The first Jew in the House of Commons was another British Columbian, Henry Nathan, elected in Victoria in 1871. NANAIMO, PRINCE RUPERT, ROSSLAND, TRAIL and PRINCE GEORGE soon had small Jewish communities and Jewish business people played leading roles in many of the province's early economic ventures, including the Union Brewery in Nanaimo, BRITANNIA MINES on HOWE SOUND and the SMELTER at Trail. David OPPENHEIMER, a Jew of German descent, was known as the "father of VANCOUVER" because of his involvement in so many civic projects; he was the city's second mayor. Vancouver became the centre of BC's Jewish population when a wave of East European Jews settled in the city between 1880 and the early 1920s. By the outbreak of WWI the community was large enough to support a synagogue, a cultural society and a business association. Vancouver's Jewish population almost doubled during the 1920s, though the Depression and WWII brought a halt to immigration from Europe. Following the war the Canadian Jewish Congress lobbied persistently for the liberalization of Canadian immigration laws; as a result a large number of Holocaust survivors settled in Canada. About 400 moved to Vancouver and assumed influential roles in the local community. Since WWII the city's Jewish population has grown sharply, doubling about every decade. Numbering some 25,000, Vancouver's Jewish community is the third largest in Canada (after Toronto and Montreal) and the Lower Mainland is home to 95% of the provincial Jewish population (30,700 in 1996). The community has produced many prominent citizens, including Justice Samuel Davies Schultz, Canada's first Jewish judge, Dave BARRETT, the first Jewish premier in the country, and Nathaniel NEMETZ, BC chief justice from 1978 to 1988. There are many Jewish organizations in Vancouver and Victoria, including the Jewish Federation of Greater Vancouver and the Jewish Historical Society of BC. In 1994 the community opened a Holocaust Education Centre in Vancouver.
Dianne Mackay
Reading: Cyril Leonoff, *Pioneers, Pedlars and Prayer Shawls: the Jewish Communities in BC and the Yukon*, 1978.

JOHN, Mary, Dakelh elder (b June 1913, near Prince George). She grew up in the DAKELH (Carrier) village of STONEY CREEK, south of VANDERHOOF, and on traplines and in hunting camps in the vicinity. After attending RESIDENTIAL SCHOOLS at FORT ST JAMES and LEJAC, at age 16 she entered an arranged marriage that lasted for 66 years. As well as having 12 children, she was a hospital worker, Dakelh-language teacher (*see* FIRST NATIONS LANGUAGES) and a community activist. UNBC awarded her an honorary degree in 1996 and she received the Order of Canada in 1997.
Reading: Bridget Moran, *Stoney Creek Woman*, 1988.

Mary John, Dakelh elder (seated), with her collaborator Bridget Moran, 1989.
Ian Lindsay/Vancouver Sun

JOHNSON, Byron Ingemar, merchant, politician, premier 29 Dec 1947–1 Aug 1952 (b 10 Dec 1890, Victoria; d 12 Jan 1964, Victoria). Following WWI he and his brothers ran a building supply company in VICTORIA. He entered politics in 1933 when he was elected to the provincial legislature as a LIBERAL. He lost in the 1937 election and returned to his business until 1945, when he was again elected to the legislature as a member of the COALITION GOVERNMENT led by John HART. Two years later he narrowly defeated Gordon WISMER for the Liberal leadership and became PREMIER. His term was short but productive. His government extended the Pacific Great Eastern Rwy (see BC RAIL) beyond QUESNEL, invested in highway expansion (*see* ROADS AND HIGHWAYS) and introduced a controversial hospital insurance scheme (*see* HEALTH POLICY) and the retail sales tax. He won re-election in 1949, but the coalition broke up in 1952 and he was

Byron Johnson, premier of BC 1947–52.
BC Archives B-07943

JEWS IN BC

Year	Members	% of BC Population
1881	104	0.2
1891	277	0.3
1901	554	0.3
1911	1,384	0.4
1921	1,654	0.3
1931	2,666	0.4
1941	3,244	0.4
1951	5,969	0.5
1961	7,816	0.5
1971	9,715	0.4
1981	14,680	0.5
1991	16,565	0.5
1996	30,700	0.8

defeated in that year's election. Johnson's nickname was "Boss," not because he resembled an old-style political boss but as a corruption of his family nickname "Bjosse."

JOHNSON, John William Fordham, business executive, lt gov 1931–36 (b 28 Nov 1866, Spalding, England; d 28 Nov 1938, Vancouver). A bookkeeper by training, he emigrated in 1888 to Portland, where he took a job in the branch office of the BANK OF BC. In 1898 he transferred to the VANCOUVER office. Two years later he left the bank and joined BC SUGAR as an accountant; he rose through the ranks of the company to become president in 1920. He was a director of several other companies and a member of the city's business elite. He remained with BC Sugar until he became LT GOV on 1 Aug 1931. Johnson was not a popular or a particularly effective lt gov. His term coincided with the Depression, when public opinion was intolerant of conservative business leaders like himself. Ill health hastened his departure from office and he retired to Vancouver.

JOHNSON, Pauline, poet, stage performer (b 10 Mar 1861, near Brantford, ON; d 7 Mar 1913, Vancouver). She was born on the Six Nations Reserve, the daughter of a Mohawk chief and a Quaker Englishwoman. She began writing in her teens and her first poem was published in a New York magazine in 1884. Early in 1892 she took part in a public reading in Toronto that launched her stage career. For the next 18 years she toured Canada, the US and England, performing her works dressed as an "Indian princess." Called by one critic "the most popular figure in Canadian literature," she enthralled audiences with her

unique stage presence and poems about aboriginal life. Late in 1909 Johnson retired from touring and settled in VANCOUVER, where she lived the rest of her life. She published 3 books of poems, 2 books of stories and a collection of aboriginal tales, *Legends of Vancouver* (1911). A memorial to her was erected near Third Beach in STANLEY PARK in 1922.

JOHNSONS LANDING, 70 km northeast of NELSON on the east shore of KOOTENAY LK, is a tiny farming (*see* AGRICULTURE) and LOGGING community first settled in the early 1900s. Until a road arrived in 1954, residents were connected to KASLO by PADDLEWHEEL STEAMBOAT. A Johnson's Landing is located on the north shore of the FRASER R (*see* DEWDNEY).   AS

JOHNSTON, Rita Margaret (Leichert), politician, premier 2 Apr–5 Nov 1991 (b 22 Apr 1935, Melville, SK). She came to BC as a child and began her political career as an alderman in SURREY in 1969, the same year that Bill VANDER ZALM became mayor. In 1983 she entered provincial politics when she was elected SOCIAL CREDIT MLA for Surrey. A strong Vander Zalm supporter,

Rita Johnston, premier of BC 1991.
Denise Howard/Vancouver Sun

she joined his cabinet as minister of municipal affairs following his election as PREMIER in 1986. She also served as minister of transportation and highways in 1989–91. When Vander Zalm resigned following a scandal in 1991, a Socred convention chose her party leader and the first female premier in Canadian history. However, the party was devastated in an election later that year: only 6 MLAs were elected. Johnston lost her own seat and retired to private business.

JOHNSTON, Robert "Bob," rower (b 1868, Elmsville, NB; d 1951). One of the most prominent VANCOUVER sports personalities of the 19th century, he dominated amateur and professional sculling in the Pacific Northwest in the 1890s.

Johnston came to Vancouver in 1888 and began work as a boat builder (*see* BOATBUILDING). His ROWING career started with the BURRARD INLET Rowing Club in 1890 and he compiled 4 BC amateur championships 1891–94. He turned professional in 1896 and 2 years later, in one of the most famous sporting events of early Vancouver history, he became the first BC athlete to challenge for a world title by inviting world sculling champion Jake Gaudaur to race him over a 3-mile course in Vancouver harbour. Gaudaur retained his title by only 2 boat lengths and took home the $2,500 prize purse put up by the city. After narrowly losing to Gaudaur again in NELSON and then winning his final race against former world champion John L. Hackett, Johnston retired in 1900. He later coached many VANCOUVER ROWING CLUB oarsmen including 1932 Olympic bronze medallists Ned Pratt and Noel de Mille. He was among the first inductees into the BC SPORTS HALL OF FAME in 1966.   SW

JOHNSTONE STRAIT is a narrow corridor extending 110 km along the northeast side of VANCOUVER ISLAND from ROCK BAY and DISCOVERY PASSAGE in the south to ALERT BAY and Broughton Strait in the north. It is the main shipping route through the maze of islands at the north end of GEORGIA STRAIT and an important SALMON fishing ground, especially in years when migrating FRASER R sockeye return from the open ocean via the north end of Vancouver Island, rather than the southern route through JUAN DE FUCA STRAIT. It is also a favourite KILLER WHALE watching area. The strait was named by Capt George VANCOUVER in 1792 after James Johnstone, master of the *Chatham*. Its shores, which are in the territory of the KWAKWA̱KA̱'WAKW First Nations, have been extensively logged.   *David Lee*

Killer whales in Johnstone Strait. Greg Shea photo

JOLY DE LOTBINIERE, Henri-Gustave, lawyer and politician, lt gov 1900–06 (b 5 Dec 1829, Epernay, France; d 15 Nov 1908, Quebec City). Raised in Lower Canada and educated in Paris, he practised law in Quebec and managed his family's seigneury. A lifelong Liberal, he sat in the Canadian Assembly from 1861 to 1867, the Quebec legislature from 1867 to 1885, and the House of Commons from 1867 to 1874. He served briefly as premier of Quebec from 1878 to 1879. In 1885, disillusioned by the Riel affair,

Pauline Johnson, dressed for one of her stage performances, c 1904. BC Archives A-09684

he left politics. He was knighted in 1895 and the next year re-entered the House of Commons and joined Wilfrid Laurier's cabinet. On 22 June 1900 Laurier appointed him LT GOV of BC. It was a turbulent period in BC politics and the new lt gov was chosen as an outsider who had no affiliations with any of the local factions. His term of office saw the return of stability to the political arena. He lived out his retirement on his estate in Quebec.

JONES, Con, sports entrepreneur (b Australia; d 1942, Vancouver). The ex-bookie came to VANCOUVER at the turn of the century and became one of the city's most flamboyant sports and business personalities. He opened a chain of tobacco stores/pool halls named "Don't Argue!" and one of them boasted Vancouver's first neon sign: "Don't Argue Con Jones Sells Fresh Tobacco." In 1907 Jones attracted 12,000 people to his heavily promoted BROCKTON POINT Sports Show, largely a SOCCER exhibition, to raise funds for Vancouver General Hospital. He co-founded the Pacific Coast League of soccer the same year. Jones also owned the Vancouver LACROSSE Club, a semi-pro field lacrosse team that won the 1911 Minto Cup national championship. The next year he fielded the team in his new 10,000-seat Con Jones Park in east Vancouver. Jones also started a short-lived professional lacrosse league, BC's first. In 1937 he bought a class B Western International League BASEBALL franchise, named the Vancouver Maple Leafs, but Con Jones Park was too small for baseball and he sold the team to Bob BROWN in 1939. After Brown died in 1962 the park was renamed Callister Park, continuing to serve as a soccer venue until the city tore down the stands in 1971 to create an open park and playground.   *SW*

JONES, Effie, political activist (b 1889, England; d 1985, Vancouver). During the 1930s she was a principal leader of the Housewives League, a women's organization that lobbied on women's rights, the cost of living and other issues. Following WWII she organized the Civic Reform Assoc (CRA) which for many years monitored the activities of VANCOUVER city council. In 1946 she ran unsuccessfully for mayor as a CRA candidate. Particular targets of her activism were BC ELECTRIC RWY CO and BC Telephone Co (*see* TELUS). One lawyer claimed that in the upper echelons of BC Electric she was known as "Public Enemy No 1."

JONES, Jemmy, captain, coastal mariner (b 1830, Wales; d 1882). He went to California in 1849 and 5 years later moved north to Puget Sound, where he acquired a boat and began trading between the Sound and VANCOUVER ISLAND. He was a regular visitor to the South Coast for almost 30 years. Early in 1865 he was imprisoned in VICTORIA for debt. He escaped, and dressed as a woman he canoed across JUAN DE FUCA STRAIT in pursuit of his ship, which had been seized by creditors. He then proceeded to steal his own vessel and sail it all the way around the north end of Vancouver Island, then south to

Mexico. He later sold the boat, resolved his troubles with the law and returned to BC to re-enter the coasting trade. Jemmy Jones Island at the mouth of Cadboro Bay in Baynes Channel east of Victoria is named for him.

JORDAN RIVER, pop 284, is a LOGGING community at the mouth of the Jordan R on the west coast of VANCOUVER ISLAND, 60 km from VICTORIA. A powerhouse generated HYDROELECTRICITY for southern Vancouver Island from 1911 to 1971, and there was an army camp here to protect the power complex during WWII. The river mouth is a popular SURFING spot. The community is named for Alejandro Jordan, a Spanish chaplain at NOOTKA in the 1790s.

JOWETT, Alice Elizabeth, hotel keeper, prospector (b 5 Nov 1853, Bradford, England; d 1955, Kelowna). She arrived in VANCOUVER in 1889, a 26-year-old widow with 3 young children. After running a bakery in the city for 7 years she moved to Trout Lake City in the LARDEAU east of ARROW LK, where a SILVER-mining boom was in progress. For almost 50 years she operated the Windsor Hotel and prospected in the surrounding hills long after the boom had collapsed. Others moved away from Trout Lake City, but not Mrs Jowett, whose hotel remained a local landmark. Finally, advancing years forced her to sell out and she retired to a convalescent home in KELOWNA.

JOY, Greg, high jumper (b 23 Apr 1956, Portland, OR). Raised in VANCOUVER, he won the high jump at the Canada Games in BURNABY at age 16 and broke the 7-ft mark in Athens, Greece 2 years later. He was a student at the Univ of Texas at El Paso when he travelled to Montreal for the 1976 Olympic Games. Despite poor track conditions and a foot injury that interfered with his training he cleared 7'3¾" to win the silver medal, Canada's first medal in the high jump since Duncan MCNAUGHTON's gold in 1932. Joy

was further rewarded with a Gov Gen's medal and titles as BC and Canadian male athlete of the year. In 1978 he set a world indoor record with a jump of 7ft 7 in and won another silver medal at Edmonton's Commonwealth Games. Major knee problems plagued him in the last years of his career. After retiring from competition in 1984 he became executive director of the Ottawa Food Bank and ran provincially for the Ontario Progressive Conservative Party in 1995. He was inducted into the BC SPORTS HALL OF FAME in 1986. *See also* TRACK AND FIELD.   *SW*

JUAN DE FUCA MARINE TRAIL runs 47 km along the north side of JUAN DE FUCA STRAIT from China Beach near JORDAN RIVER to Botanical Beach near PORT RENFREW. Opened in 1995, it is a more accessible southern extension of the WEST COAST TRAIL. The trail, which takes 3–4 days to hike, winds through mostly second-growth forest following an old telegraph trail much of the way. Highlights include some of the best SURFING beaches in Canada, SEAL colonies at Parkinson Crk and tidal pools at Botanical Beach Provincial Park. *See also* TRAILS.

JUAN DE FUCA STRAIT, 160 km, the southern entrance to GEORGIA STRAIT, separates VANCOUVER ISLAND from Washington's Olympic Peninsula and forms part of the international BOUNDARY. Heavily travelled by vessels bound for VICTORIA, VANCOUVER and Puget Sound, it was named by Capt Charles BARKLEY in 1787 after a Greek mariner who claimed to have discovered it in 1592. For 200 years the strait was considered the possible entrance to a Northwest Passage. De Fuca's claims have always been doubted, but the name remains. The strait is susceptible to heavy weather and the Vancouver Island shoreline has been called "the Graveyard of the Pacific" because of the large number of vessels that have foundered there. The first person to swim the Strait was Bert Thomas, a logger from Tacoma who made the crossing in 1955.

Sombrio Beach, on Juan de Fuca Strait. Philip Stone photo

JUDICIAL SYSTEM in BC consists of 3 courts: the Court of Appeal, the Supreme Court and the Provincial Court, which includes Adult Criminal Court, Small Claims Court, Family Court and Youth Court. The court of last resort is the Supreme Court of Canada but only a small number of cases from BC are referred to it. Locally the court of last resort is the BC Court of Appeal, created in 1911, consisting of a chief justice and 13 justices, all appointed by the federal government. (Supernumerary justices, who must have reached the age of 65 and have at least 15 years' experience on a superior court, have reduced responsibilities.) Appeals are heard by at least 3 justices selected by the chief justice. The other superior court is the Supreme Court of BC, the province's superior trial court. There are 102 Supreme Court judges, all appointed by the federal government, sitting in 13 centres around the province. There are also 14 Supreme Court Masters who deal with pretrial matters. The Supreme Court hears the most serious criminal cases and all civil cases where a claim exceeds $10,000. Most trials are conducted by judges alone, but in cases where the defendant faces a PRISON term of at least 5 years the defendant may choose a jury trial. Provincial Court deals with less serious criminal offences, civil cases involving less than $10,000, disputes arising out of family law such as adoption and child custody, and offences under the *Young Offenders Act*. (Divorce is a matter for the Supreme Court because it involves the division of property.) Provincial Court consists of a chief judge and about 130 judges, formerly called magistrates, all appointed by the LT GOV on advice from the provincial CABINET and particularly the attorney general. It sits at more than 100 locations around the province.

JUDO was brought to BC by Shigetake "Steve" Sasaki in 1924 when he opened the VANCOUVER Judo Club, the first in Canada, 2 years after immigrating from Japan. In the 1930s Sasaki taught judo to the RCMP and in 1936 he joined the founder of the martial art on a European outreach tour. During WWII Sasaki was interned (*see* JAPANESE, RELOCATION OF) but in the internment camps he continued to teach judo. Settling in ASHCROFT after the war he started the Canadian Kodokan Black Belt Assoc, the forerunner of Judo Canada, in 1955. He travelled to Japan in 1958 to arrange for Canadian membership in the International Judo Federation. Before his death in 1993 he opened more judo clubs in Vancouver, was honoured with an 8th level black belt standing and was inducted into the Canadian Amateur Sports Hall of Fame and Japan's Order of the Rising Sun. The Steve Sasaki Award is presented annually to the top male and female judoka demonstrating excellence in the spirit of the sport. Canada's most successful judoka of the 20th century was Vancouver's Doug ROGERS, who won a silver medal at the

Doug Rogers, judo silver medalist at the 1964 Tokyo Olympics. Dave Paterson/Vancouver Province

1964 Tokyo Olympics. In 1999 Judo BC had 58 clubs with 1,981 members and 260 black belts among them.   *SW*

JULIETTE, stage name of Juliette Augustina Sysak, singer, television star (b 26 Aug 1927, St Vital, MB). One of the first performers from the BC music scene to gain national attention, she began her career as a 13-year-old singing at the Kitsilano Showboat in VANCOUVER, where Ivan ACKERY, a local theatre manager, heard her and spoke of her to Dal RICHARDS. The next year, 1940, she began fronting Richards' orchestra at the Hotel Vancouver's Panorama Roof ballroom. She starred on radio and television, when it went on the air in the early 1950s, and is best known as the host of her own CBC show, called simply *Juliette*. The show was broadcast on Saturdays right after *Hockey Night in Canada*; it aired from 1956 to 1966 and made "your pet, Juliette" a national institution. Juliette also hosted *Juliette and Friends* from 1973 to 1975. In the 1980s she reduced her performance schedule and retired to Vancouver.

JUNCO is a small SPARROW with a characteristic black hood and white outer tail flashes. The dark-eyed junco (*Junco hyemalis*), the only species found in BC, occurs in two types: the slate-coloured junco in the northern half of the province, with a dark grey head, back and sides; and the Oregon junco in the south, with a black or grey head, brown back and buff sides. Juncos breed in forests throughout the province, then migrate south in the winter to lower elevations, where they are common backyard feeder birds.

JUNG, Douglas, politician (b 25 Feb 1924, Victoria). After serving in the S Pacific as a mem-

ber of the Allied Intelligence Bureau during WWII, he returned to Canada and earned his law degree from UBC. In 1957 he was elected Conservative MP for Vancouver Centre, becoming the first CHINESE-Canadian to hold elected federal office in Canada. During his term as an MP, Jung served as Canada's representative to the UN, helped to establish the National Productivity Council (now the Economic Council of Canada) and initiated the creation of the Canadian Coast Guard Service. After his electoral defeat in 1962, he became an immigration appeal board judge. He later opened his own law practice in VANCOUVER. In 1979, the Chinese Benevolent Association of Vancouver presented Jung with its Citizenship Award, and he was named to the Order of Canada in 1990.

Dianne Mackay

JUNIPER occurs worldwide in many species, but in BC only the Rocky Mountain juniper (*Juniperus scopulorum*) reaches tree size. It inhabits the southern Interior, the GULF ISLANDS and scattered parts of VANCOUVER ISLAND, appearing most notably on rock ledges and in crevices close by the ocean. Its round blue cones resemble berries and carry the distinctive smell of gin, which they are used to flavour. The tree is too small and scattered to be commercially significant.

JURA, 11 km northeast of PRINCETON, was a small railway and LOGGING settlement on a section of the KETTLE VALLEY RWY completed in 1915. The steep grade eased here and "helper" engines could be turned. It was named after the mountain range on the French–Swiss border. By the 1990s, only a few deserted barns and red railway sheds remained.   *AS*

JUSKATLA, in Juskatla Inlet on Graham Island, is headquarters of MACMILLAN BLOEDEL's substantial LOGGING operations in the QUEEN CHARLOTTE ISLANDS. The camp was established in 1941 by Pacific Mills, then taken over by Aero Timber, a CROWN CORPORATION that cut Sitka SPRUCE for wartime airplane construction. After the war, Aero's assets were acquired by the POWELL RIVER CO, which later merged with MacBlo. The name is a modification of a HAIDA word that may refer to a tidal rapid.   *AS*

JUSTICE INSTITUTE OF BC is the central training institution for firefighters, police and corrections officers and other public safety workers. The institute also offers training in mediation and negotiation, and programs for community and social service workers. Established in 1978, it was originally located in the former Jericho Hill School for the Deaf in west Point Grey in VANCOUVER, then moved in 1995 to its own purpose-built campus in NEW WESTMINSTER. It is administered by the Ministry of Advanced Education, Training and Technology, which also provides core funding.

He joined the family enterprise, Kaiser Steel Corp, in 1970 and came to BC to run its COAL operations, Kaiser Resources, at FERNIE. In 1979 he took over a floundering Kaiser Steel and·rescued it in part by selling Kaiser Resources to the BC RESOURCES INVESTMENT CORP at a huge profit. He became a Canadian citizen in 1980, the same year he left Kaiser Steel. He was president of the BANK OF BC from 1984 to 1986. Active in a variety of philanthropic organizations, he is also an avid amateur aviator and has held several speed-over-distance records for jet aircraft.

KAKAWIS, on the west side of MEARES ISLAND in CLAYOQUOT SOUND 5 km north of TOFINO, was the site of the Christie RESIDENTIAL SCHOOL, which left its mark on 8,000 FIRST NATIONS children between 1900 and 1971. It burned down in the 1980s and was replaced by a drug and alcohol recovery centre. The name is a NUU-CHAH-NULTH (Nootka) word meaning "many berries."   AS

KALAMALKA LAKE, 2.78 km², is in the OKANAGAN VALLEY south of VERNON. Once part of a vast glacial sea—Penticton Lake—that filled the entire valley, it is an exceptionally deep lake with ever-changing colours, hence its nickname, the "lake of many colours." Originally called Long Lake by Europeans, it apparently got its present name from HAWAIIAN recruits employed in the FUR TRADE. The lake is bordered on the north and west by orchards and residential development, and the beach at the north end is the most popular in the N Okanagan. Kalamalka Lake Provincial Park (90 ha) on the eastern shore shows a fine example of GRASSLANDS and is known for its population of RATTLESNAKES at Rattlesnake Point. Kekuli Bay Provincial Park is on the west side of the lake. *See also* GLACIATION; PARKS, PROVINCIAL.

KABALARIAN SOCIETY was founded in VANCOUVER in 1930 by Alfred J. Parker (1897–1964) to promote a philosophy of personal fulfilment based on a belief in mathematical cycles. Practices include vegetarianism, physical exercises and a belief in the mystical influence of numbers and number combinations. On his death, Parker was succeeded as leader by Ivon Shearing, under whose leadership the society grew to about 1,500 Canadian members. In 1995 Shearing was accused of sexually assaulting female members of the society and handling its funds improperly. He was convicted of several sexual offences and sent to prison. The society was shattered by the scandal.

KAFFKA, Peter, architect (b 1899, Budapest, Hungary; d 1992, Vancouver). A graduate of the Royal Hungarian Joseph Polytechnical Univ in his native Budapest, he immigrated to Canada at the end of WWII. After 5 years in Ontario he moved to VANCOUVER in 1950 and worked for W.K. Noppe and Sharp & Thompson Berwick Pratt before establishing his own practice in 1954. The Imperial Apartments on Bidwell St and the GROUSE MOUNTAIN Chalet are two of his most prominent designs. He retired in 1983. *See also* ARCHITECTURE.

KAIN, Conrad, mountaineer (b 10 Aug 1883, Nasswald, Austria; d 2 Feb 1934, Cranbrook). He began guiding as a young man in Austria to help support his widowed mother and 6 siblings. In 1909 the Alpine Club of Canada hired him as its first official guide to lead climbers in the ROCKY MTS. Widely considered to be the greatest of all Canadian mountain guides, he made many first ascents including Mt ROBSON, highest peak in the Canadian Rockies (1913); Mt Farnham, highest in the PURCELL Mts (1914); Bugaboo Spire in the BUGABOOS (1916); and Mt Louis (1916). During WWI he visited New Zealand three times and made 29 first ascents

there. He married and in 1920 settled on a ranch near WILMER on Windermere Lk, where he and his wife raised pack horses and ran a fur farm. During the climbing season he guided mainly in the Purcells. Following the death of his wife early in 1933 his health declined and he died a year later. *See also* MOUNTAINEERING.

KAISER, Edgar Fosburgh Jr, business executive (b 5 July 1942, Portland). He comes from a line of prominent American industrialists. After studying at Stanford and the Harvard School of Business, he served in Vietnam during the war, then went to work as a White House advisor to presidents Lyndon Johnson and Richard Nixon.

Edgar Kaiser (r), Vancouver entrepreneur, with the pop singer John Denver, 1993. Malcolm Parry photo

KALEDEN, pop 1,246, is a community on the west side of SKAHA LK in the OKANAGAN VALLEY, 13 km south of PENTICTON. The site was a camping ground for passing FUR BRIGADES. A townsite was established in 1909 as the centre of an orchard area (*see* TREE FRUITS) and a contest was held to name it. The winning entry, suggested by Rev Walter Russell, combines *kalos*, Greek for "beautiful," and Eden.

KAMLOOPS lies at the confluence of the N and S THOMPSON rivers, 325 km from VANCOUVER. It is both the commercial and administrative centre of the south-central Interior and the third-largest community outside the Lower Mainland. The name is a variation of *T'kumlups*, a SECWEPEMC (Shuswap) word meaning "meeting of the waters." The Secwepemc were the original inhabitants. In 1811 David Stuart, a FUR TRADER with the PACIFIC FUR CO (PFC), arrived from the coast to trade. The following year he returned to establish a post. He was joined that fall by a party of NORTH WEST CO (NWC) traders, led by Joseph Larocque. In 1813 the NWC bought out the PFC and its post, Fort Thompson, became the centre of the trade. In 1821 the HBC took over the post, moved it from time to time, then closed its fort in 1893 and moved to a downtown store. A community began to develop during the GOLD RUSH period of the 1860s. The CATTLE INDUSTRY was established to feed the miners and subsequently the railway camps. With the arrival of the CPR in 1885, and the designation of Kamloops as a railway divisional point, the community boomed. Incorporated as a city in 1893, Kamloops expanded in 1967 and again in 1973 to include the surrounding suburbs. Fruit and vegetable growing flourished on the fertile flatlands next to the river (*see also* AGRICULTURE), and from WWI, canning, especially of tomatoes, was an important industry. A period of prosperity

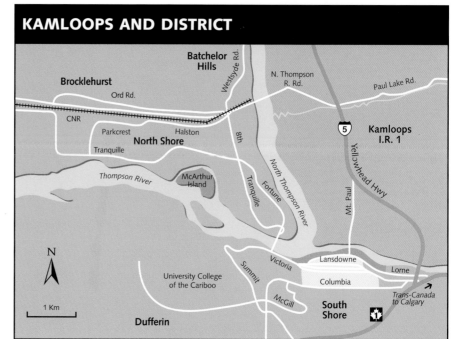

KAMLOOPS AND DISTRICT

Overlooking Kamloops. Walter Lanz/Image Makers

followed WWII, symbolized by the flamboyant career of Rev Phil GAGLARDI, local MLA and minister of highways in the SOCIAL CREDIT government. By the 1970s growth had slowed. At the end of the 20th century Kamloops remained the centre of the province's ranching industry, but MINING and the FOREST INDUSTRY had become more important, and the city had a PULP mill and a COPPER SMELTER. Long known for its TROUT fishing, Kamloops attracts a growing number of TOURISTS in all seasons, especially since the completion of the COQUIHALLA HWY in 1986 reduced driving time to the coast. A campus of Cariboo University College is located here.

Population: 76,394
Rank in BC: 12th
Population increase since 1981: 19%
Date of incorporation: city 1 July 1893
Land area: 311.42 km²
Location: Thompson–Nicola Regional District
Economic base: transportation, lumber, agriculture, tourism, cattle ranching, mining, manufacturing

KAMLOOPS BLAZERS joined the WHL in 1981 as the Junior Oilers, owned by the NHL Edmonton Oilers. In 1984 they took their present name and since then have been the most successful team in the junior league. They won the national championship Memorial Cup in 1992, 1994 and 1995, the only team to win it 3 times in 4 years. Four consecutive coaches—Bill LaForge, Ken Hitchcock, Tom Renney and Don Hay—became head coaches in the NHL and the team developed many professional players including Doug Bodger, Greg Hawgood, Jarome Iginla, Mark RECCHI, Daryl Sydor, Corey Hirsch and Scott NIEDERMAYER.

KAMLOOPS WAWA was a monthly NEWSPAPER published for BC FIRST NATIONS from 1891 to 1917 by the OBLATE missionary Jean Marie Le Jeune. Called "the Queerest Newspaper in the World" by its contemporary rivals, but later collected by the Smithsonian Institution and the British Museum, the *Wawa* had many unusual qualities, the strangest of which was the language it was written in. After Father Le Jeune despaired of teaching his parishioners how to read and write English, he hit on the idea of creating a simplified written language using CHINOOK JARGON words written in a script adapted from Duployan shorthand. Soon hundreds of aboriginal people were using Le Jeune's shorthand Chinook throughout the CARIBOO, the lower FRASER R and on the coast, and he decided to publish the *Wawa* to serve them. (*Wawa* is Chinook jargon for "talk.") The paper typically had 16 mimeographed pages and sold on subscription for a dollar a year to whites and 25 cents to aboriginals. Contents included "news from the surrounding villages and teepees, notices of births, marriages and deaths, plus news from the outside world." Native readers contributed letters to the editor and Le Jeune added lengthy sermons proffering moral instruction and denouncing infidels. The *Wawa* was avidly read with printings running to 3,000 copies at its peak, but it declined when RESIDENTIAL SCHOOLS improved Native literacy in English, and after 1904 it appeared only in occasional special editions. Surviving copies have become some of the most highly prized BC memorabilia.   *Howard White*

KANAKAS; *see* HAWAIIANS.

KANE, Paul, artist (b 3 Sept 1810, Cork, Ireland; d 20 Feb 1871, Toronto). The famous "Indian painter" crossed the continent in 1846 and descended the COLUMBIA R to arrive at Fort Vancouver on 8 Dec. It was the first time a professional artist had gathered material along the FUR TRADE routes of the West. In Mar of the following year, Kane embarked on a sketching trip in a canoe with aboriginal guides to FORT VICTORIA on VANCOUVER ISLAND. He arrived on 8 Apr. As well as making sketches at a nearby village, he traded for masks, pipes and a blanket, all to be used later as models in his studio. He also visited villages north of Victoria, in the southern GULF ISLANDS and on the Olympic Peninsula before leaving on 9 June to return to Fort Vancouver. He left the Columbia early in July to retrace his steps across the continent to Toronto. He related his adventures in a memoir, *Wanderings of the Artist among the Indians of North America*, published in 1859. Most of Kane's paintings and sketches are in the Royal Ontario Museum and the National Gallery of Canada. His artifacts are at the Manitoba Museum of Man and Nature, Winnipeg.

KAPP, Joe, football player (b 19 Mar 1938, Santa Fe, NM). After leading the Univ of California to the Rose Bowl in 1958 he played 2 seasons with the CFL's Calgary Stampeders. He joined the BC LIONS in 1961 in a 4-for-1 player trade. As quarterback and undisputed leader he led the Lions to the Grey Cup final in 1963 and to the championship the following year. After 6 years with BC he joined the NFL's Minnesota Vikings in 1967 and led them to the 1968 Super Bowl, losing to the Kansas City Chiefs. In 1982 he became head FOOTBALL coach at the Univ of California but after 19 wins and 32 losses in 5 years he was fired. He rejoined the Lions as president and general manager under team owner Murray PEZIM in 1990 but was fired before the season was over. As of 2000 he was the only person to have played in the Rose Bowl, Super Bowl and Grey Cup.
Archie McDonald

KARIYA, Paul, hockey player (b 16 Oct 1974, Vancouver). His father was born in an internment camp for Japanese Canadians (*see* JAPANESE RELOCATION) during WWII and raised his family on the Lower Mainland, where Paul played HOCKEY at the BURNABY Winter Club. With the PENTICTON Panthers in 1991–92 he tore through the BC JUNIOR HOCKEY LEAGUE, scoring 132 points

Paul Kariya, star hockey player with the Anaheim Mighty Ducks.
Jeff Vinnick/Vancouver Canucks

PROMINENT BC CAVING AREAS

On Vancouver Island
HORNE LK Caves Provincial Park near QUALICUM BEACH
Upana Caves Recreation Site near GOLD RIVER
Little Hustan Caves Regional Park near NIMPKISH LK
Karst Creek Trail in STRATHCONA PROVINCIAL PARK

In the Interior
CODY CAVES Provincial Park near KOOTENAY LK
NAKIMU CAVES near ROGERS PASS
Arctomy's Cave in Mt ROBSON Provincial Park
TOP OF THE WORLD PROVINCIAL PARK east of KIMBERLEY

in 40 games and earning honours as Canada's top junior A hockey player. The next season he led the Univ of Maine Black Bears to the NCAA national championship, was the first freshman to win the Hobey Baker award as the top player in US college hockey and joined a team of NHL players to represent Canada at the 1993 world hockey championships. He was drafted 4th overall in the 1993 NHL entry draft by the expansion Anaheim Mighty Ducks but opted not to sign with Anaheim. Instead he started the 1993–94 season with Maine and then joined the Canadian Olympic team, leading it to the silver medal at the 1994 Olympics in Lillehammer. Playing at the world championships again later that year, he won top forward and all-star leftwinger honours while helping Canada win gold. Signing with Anaheim, he led the team in scoring and finished 2nd in rookie-of-the-year voting. In 1995–96 he scored 50 goals and 108 points, 7th in the league in both categories, and was honoured as the league's most sportsmanlike player and all-star leftwinger. In his third season he finished 2nd in league scoring with 99 points and again was the most sportsmanlike player and an all-star. Concussions threatened his career in 1997-98, but he bounced back the next season to find his way back near the top of the scoring charts. In 1999-00, his younger brother Steve entered the NHL with the VANCOUVER CANUCKS.
SW

KARST FORMATIONS occur in areas of carbonate bedrock—usually limestone, dolomite or marble—when groundwater dissolves the rock, creating a variety of subsurface features including sinkholes, disappearing streams, springs and, most notably, underground caves. In BC, karst is found extensively in the ROCKY MTS and on VANCOUVER ISLAND, where plentiful rainfall and large units of limestone create ideal conditions. Karst formations are usually associated with abundant plant and animal life; some wildlife species live intermittently in the caverns, using them for shelter, nesting or hibernation. Karst caves have yielded several important archaeological finds and some of the most notable karst formations have been protected in public parks. Caving, or spelunking, has become increasingly popular with outdoor recreationists. Some prominent caving areas are shown at the top of the page.

KASKA are a group of FIRST NATIONS people occupying the LIARD R and Dease R watersheds in north-central BC and the southern Yukon. They speak a dialect of ATHABASCAN. Traditionally they lived in small family groups subsisting on wild game, food PLANTS and FISH. The FUR TRADE extended into their territory in the 1820s but outsiders began arriving in significant numbers only with the GOLD RUSHES in the Cassiar (1874) and the Klondike (1898). A ROMAN CATHOLIC mission was established at McDame Crk in 1926. The construction of the ALASKA HWY (1942) produced jobs and another influx of outsiders. Today the 200 Kaska in BC live mainly at Dease River on GOOD HOPE LK.

KASLO, village, pop 1,063, lies on the west side of KOOTENAY LK, 71 km northeast of NELSON. First settled in 1888–89 by SAWMILL operators, it boomed following the discovery of SILVER–lead–ZINC ore in the SLOCAN area in 1891. It may have been named after John Kasleau, a prospector. In 1895 it was connected to the MINING area by the narrow-gauge KASLO & SLOCAN RWY. Incorporated as a city in Aug 1893, it chose village status in 1958. Over the years mining declined and LOGGING became the main economic activity. The beautiful mountain scenery and fine FISHING attract many visitors. A reminder of the steamship days on Kootenay Lk is the partly restored PADDLEWHEEL STEAMBOAT *Moyie*, a national historic site. There is also a museum commemorating the JAPANESE Canadians interned here during WWII (*see also* JAPANESE, RELOCATION OF.
Martin Lynch

KASLO & SLOCAN RAILWAY (K&S) ran 53.5 km between KASLO on KOOTENAY LK and SANDON and Cody in the mountains above SLOCAN LK. Financed by James J. Hill of the GREAT NORTHERN RWY, this narrow-gauge railway was constructed in 1895 to carry ore from the LEAD, ZINC and SILVER mines (*see* MINING) down to Kootenay Lk for transshipment via steamers. When the CPR attempted to extend a rival line into Sandon late in 1895, the K&S sent a party of men to tear down the CPR station and rip up the track. After this high-spirited beginning the line remained in operation to the end of 1910, when, damaged by LANDSLIDES and fire, most of it closed. Parts of it were operated by a local syndicate until it was taken over in 1912 and rebuilt to standard gauge by the CPR, which operated it from 1914 to 1955.

Reading: Robert D. Turner and David S. Wilkie, *The Skyline Limited*, 1994.

KATHAUMIXW is a unique international choral festival, staged every 2 years in POWELL RIVER. It was originated by Don James, founder of the Powell River Academy of Music, and was held for the first time in 1984. More than 1,000 singers from Europe, Africa and Asia attend the event, which has brought international fame to the host community. *Kathaumixw* is a Salish word meaning "a gathering together of different peoples."

KATHLYN LAKE, 5 km northwest of SMITHERS in the BULKLEY VALLEY, was originally called Chickens Lake after Jimmy Chickens, an elderly DAKELH (Carrier) man who sold GROUSE, or "chickens," to the early settlers. Photographs of this beauty spot were used in GRAND TRUNK PACIFIC RWY brochures and officials renamed it after the daughter of W.P. Hinton, general manager of the railway. *AS*

KATZIE are a Downriver Mainland HALKOMELEM First Nation occupying 3 RESERVES in PITT MEADOWS, BARNSTON ISLAND and LANGLEY. Their traditional territory encompasses PITT LK and the valley of the Pitt R. In 1998 there were 422 Katzie, about half of whom lived on the reserves. They are closely related to the STO:LO NATION of the FRASER VALLEY. The name *Katzie* derives from *Q'eyts'I*, the aboriginal word for a type of MOSS. *See also* FIRST NATIONS OF BC.

KEAN, Arthur David "Cowboy," rodeo promoter, pioneer filmmaker (b 26 Feb 1882, Emerson, MB; d 1961, Toronto, ON). The son of a US Army horse broker, he spent most of his childhood in the western American states. In 1897 he returned to Canada with his family and became a hunter, trapper and transporter in the BC Interior. He participated in the first Calgary Stampede in 1912. Soon after, he settled in VANCOUVER where he combined RODEO promotion with motion picture production (*see* FILMMAKING INDUSTRY). Drawing on his own wide experience of BC, he made newsreels and documentary features about local subjects. His most ambitious film project was *Policing the Plains*, about the history of the RCMP. In 1928 he moved to Toronto, where he became a freelance writer and radio cowboy celebrity; he remained active until his death.

KEARNEY, Jim, journalist (b 1922, Victoria). His NEWSPAPER career began at the VICTORIA Times as a copy runner fresh out of high school. He quickly graduated to general news reporting and in 1943 moved across GEORGIA STRAIT to the VANCOUVER SUN. After a short stint writing general features, he transferred to the sports department and sports was where he remained. He worked in Toronto for the Canadian Press and London with Reuters before returning to VANCOUVER in the 1950s to join the *PROVINCE*. In 1963 he was back at the *Sun* writing a daily sports column that last-

ed close to 18 years and earned him a reputation as one of the finest sports writers in the country. During that time he won a National Newspaper Award for a 2-part series on drugs in sport. After leaving the *Sun* he was media relations director for SPORT BC. In semi-retirement he published *Champions: A British Columbia Sports Album* (1986) and continued to contribute columns to local media outlets. He was inducted into the Canadian Football and BC SPORTS HALLS OF FAME, and the CBC named its CBC Radio Student Journalism Award for Commentary after him.

KEARNS, Lionel, teacher, writer (b 16 Feb 1937, Nelson). While studying at UBC in the 1960s he became involved in the TISH movement of poets and published his first books of verse, *Songs of Circumstance* (1962) and *Listen, George* (1964). After further studies in England and Trinidad he returned to VANCOUVER in 1966 to join the English department at SFU, where he remained until his retirement in 1986. During this period he published several more books of poetry, including *Convergences* (1984) about Capt James COOK's arrival on the West Coast. After his retirement he became involved in on-line education via the electronic media.

KEATE, James Stuart "Stu," journalist (b 13 Oct 1913, Vancouver; d 1 Mar 1987, Vancouver). He grew up in Pt Grey and attended UBC, where he was editor of *The Ubyssey* student newspaper. After graduating in 1935 he joined the Vancouver PROVINCE as a sports reporter. He remained at the *Province*, with an interlude at the Toronto *Star* from 1938 to 1939, until the war, when he served in the navy as an information officer. After the war he joined the staff of *Time* magazine, first in New York and then as bureau chief in Montreal. In 1950 Max Bell, a financier, hired him to take over as publisher of the *Victoria Times*. With the help of Bruce HUTCHISON, the editor, Keate turned the paper into one of the leading dailies in BC (*see* NEWSPAPERS). Bell later created a chain of papers, FP Publications, which added the *VANCOUVER SUN* to its stable in 1963. Keate moved over from VICTORIA to be publisher the next year. During his tenure, which lasted until 1978, the *Sun* grew to become the second largest paper by circulation in Canada.

Reading: Stuart Keate, *Paper Boy*, 1980.

KEATING, 16 km north of VICTORIA on the SAANICH PENINSULA, is an AGRICULTURAL and residential district established in the early 1890s and named for a local landowner. It was originally called Young, after Henry Young, a pioneer settler and the first postmaster. *AS*

KEATLEY CREEK is an archaeological site overlooking the FRASER R north of LILLOOET. It contains the remains of a village of more than 100 semi-subterranean houses (*see* ARCHITECTURE, ABORIGINAL) dating back at least 2,500 years. At its peak the population of the village was about 1,500, making it one of the largest prehistoric village sites in western Canada. The people who lived here subsisted on SALMON, meat and PLANT

food and traded with other people who came great distances to acquire salmon. The village was abandoned suddenly in the year 850. *See also* ARCHAEOLOGY; PREHISTORY.

KEATS ISLAND, pop 63, lies in southwest HOWE SOUND opposite GIBSONS and is part of the SUNSHINE COAST Regional District. During his 1859 survey, Capt George RICHARDS named it for British Admiral Sir Richard Goodwin Keats. The Keats Island Baptist Camp established in 1926 still operates as Keats Camps. Eastbourne community developed on the east side and the Barnabas Family Ministries camp is on the north. Plumper Cove Marine Park is located near a dock that services a ferry link to the mainland.

Doreen Armitage

KECHIKA RIVER, 230 km, originates near Sifton Pass north of FORT WARE and flows north in the ROCKY MT TRENCH through a spectacular mountain wilderness to join the LIARD R at about Mile 540 of the ALASKA HWY. The wild valley of the Kechika, mainly undisturbed by human activity, supports a variety of wildlife including populations of woodland CARIBOU, Stone's sheep (*see* MOUNTAIN SHEEP), MOUNTAIN GOATS, WOLVES, BEARS and ELK. Used by the North West Mounted Police as a route to the Klondike during the GOLD RUSH, it is in the traditional territory of the KASKA First Nation and has been designated a BC HERITAGE RIVER.

KEEFERS, on the west side of the Fraser Canyon (*see* FRASER R) 72 km north of HOPE, was a CPR station and workers' depot with a post office (1895–1965), general store and school that made it a centre for surrounding ranchers and loggers (*see* CATTLE INDUSTRY; LOGGING). It was named after George A. Keefer, construction engineer for this section of the rail line, who lived here with his family. *AS*

KEENLEYSIDE, Hugh Llewellyn, diplomat, public servant (b 7 July 1898, Toronto; d 27 Sept 1992, Saanich). He moved to BC with his family, attended school in VANCOUVER and graduated from UBC in 1920. After graduate work in the US he taught history at various American universities before returning to UBC. He tired of academic life and in 1928 joined Canada's Department of External Affairs. In 1929 he opened Canada's first legation in Japan and served in Tokyo until 1936. During the war he was secretary to the Canadian section of the Permanent Joint Board of Defence and opposed the internment of the Japanese (*see* JAPANESE, RELOCATION OF) on the West Coast, calling it "a cheap and needless capitulation to popular prejudice." After the war he served as ambassador to Mexico (1944–47), then left the diplomatic corps to become deputy minister of mines and commissioner of the Northwest Territories (1947–50). During the 1950s he was director general of the UN Technical Assistance Administration. In 1959 he returned to BC to become chairman of the BC POWER COMMISSION; in 1961 he became co-chairman of BC HYDRO.

An opponent of nuclear power, he was influential in negotiations surrounding the COLUMBIA R TREATY. The KEENLEYSIDE DAM on the river at CASTLEGAR is named for him. He retired from Hydro in 1969 when he became chancellor of NOTRE DAME UNIV OF NELSON until it closed. Author of 5 books and numerous articles, Keenleyside was made a companion in the Order of Canada in 1969 and won the Pearson Peace Medal for outstanding contributions to foreign affairs in 1982.

KEENLEYSIDE DAM, located 8 km west of CASTLEGAR, was the second of 3 dams constructed by BC HYDRO as a result of the COLUMBIA R TREATY. Also known as the Arrow Dam, it is named for Hugh KEENLEYSIDE, chairman of BC Hydro during the 1960s. Completed in Oct 1968, the dam holds back a storage reservoir, the ARROW LAKES, stretching 232 km north to REVELSTOKE. Several smaller communities were drowned when the reservoir was flooded, and 3 communities—FAUQUIER, BURTON and EDGEWOOD—were relocated. A navigation lock carries river traffic around the 52-m-high dam.

KEITHLEY CREEK was an early MINING camp and supply centre 85 km northeast of WILLIAMS LAKE on Cariboo Lk. It was named after W.R. "Doc" Keithley, who hit the jackpot here with several companions in 1860 and started the Cariboo GOLD RUSH. The creek itself was soon played out and most miners moved farther north, but a roadhouse and store flourished here for many years and a number of ranchers (*see* CATTLE INDUSTRY) and homesteaders settled in the district. *See also* CARIBOO.   AS

KELESI, Helen, tennis player (b 15 Nov 1969, Victoria). Her parents moved to BC in 1968 when the USSR invaded their native Czechoslovakia and she grew up in RICHMOND. She broke into the international scene in 1985, winning her first TENNIS tournament the next year in Japan. Known for her fiery intensity, she won 3 more singles and 2 doubles championships (one of them paired with Monica Seles) and beat some of the world's top players. In 1989 she was ranked the 13th-best women's singles player in the world, the highest-ever sin-

Helen Kelesi, tennis player, 1996.
Arlen Redekop/Vancouver Province

gles ranking by a player from BC. She represented Canada on the Federation Cup team (1986–90, 1992) and at the 1988 Seoul Olympics and was top Canadian female athlete in 1989 and 1990. Bouncing back from life-threatening brain surgery, she began a second career as a broadcaster and fitness educator. In 1998 she was appointed national women's tennis coach.

KELLY, Peter Reginald, Methodist (later United Church) minister, Haida leader (b 21 Apr 1885, Skidegate; d 2 Mar 1966, Nanaimo). After studying at the Coqualeetza Institute, a Methodist-run school at SARDIS, he returned to SKIDEGATE in the QUEEN CHARLOTTE ISLANDS and taught school for 5 years. In 1910 he became a lay preacher in the METHODIST CHURCH and was posted to HARTLEY BAY. He attended Columbian College in NEW WESTMINSTER from 1913 to 1916 and on graduation was ordained a Methodist minister. He served in NANAIMO and BELLA COOLA and in 1933 moved to OCEAN FALLS to take charge of the mission boat *Thomas Crosby III*. For 16 years he toured the North Coast, visiting

Rev Peter Kelly, aboriginal rights activist, 1958.
Vancouver Sun

remote villages, LOGGING camps and canneries. Meanwhile he was acknowledged as a spokesperson for the HAIDA and he was active in attempts by coastal FIRST NATIONS to persuade government to recognize their land claims (*see* ABORIGINAL RIGHTS). In 1916 he co-organized a meeting of aboriginal leaders that led to the formation of the ALLIED INDIAN TRIBES OF BC, an organization he led for several years. He visited Ottawa on many occasions to present the First Nations point of view, and in the 1940s and 1950s he was a leading voice in the NATIVE BROTHERHOOD OF BC. In 1949 he left the maritime mission and spent the rest of his church career in and around Nanaimo, where he retired in 1962.
Reading: Alan Morley, *Roar of the Breakers*, 1967.

KELLY, Robert, wholesale grocer (b 1862, Russell, ON; d 22 June 1922, Vancouver). He came to VANCOUVER in 1890, and he and his partner Frank Douglas co-founded the large wholesale grocery business Kelly Douglas Ltd. The firm prospered during the boom associated with the Klondike GOLD RUSH. Its own brand name, Nabob, became a household word in BC. Originally located in a huge warehouse in GASTOWN (now The Landing), the company moved to BURNABY in 1946. Kelly was a prominent LIBERAL PARTY member during the Laurier era.

KELLY LAKE, BC's only METIS community, lies on the lake of the same name (2.02 km²) astride the BC–Alberta border south of DAWSON CREEK. Founded by a group of trapper families in 1893, the community survived by hunting, trapping and FISHING. By the late 20th century, local resources had been depleted due in part to MINING and LOGGING activity by outside interests, and the community was economically depressed with chronic high unemployment, substandard housing and inadequate facilities. Residents marked the centennial of their community by registering a land claim (*see* ABORIGINAL RIGHTS) with the provincial government.

KELOWNA is located on the east side of OKANAGAN LK halfway between PENTICTON and VERNON, about 395 km from VANCOUVER via the COQUIHALLA HWY. It is BC's most populous city outside the Lower Mainland (VICTORIA is larger only if its metropolitan area is counted; SAANICH has more residents but is incorporated as a district rather than a city). The name derives from an aboriginal word meaning "grizzly BEAR." The first outsider to visit the area was the fur trader David Stuart in 1811, and the valley became a transport route to the Interior used by

Lakefront at Kelowna, 1998. Keith Thirkell photo

KELOWNA AND DISTRICT

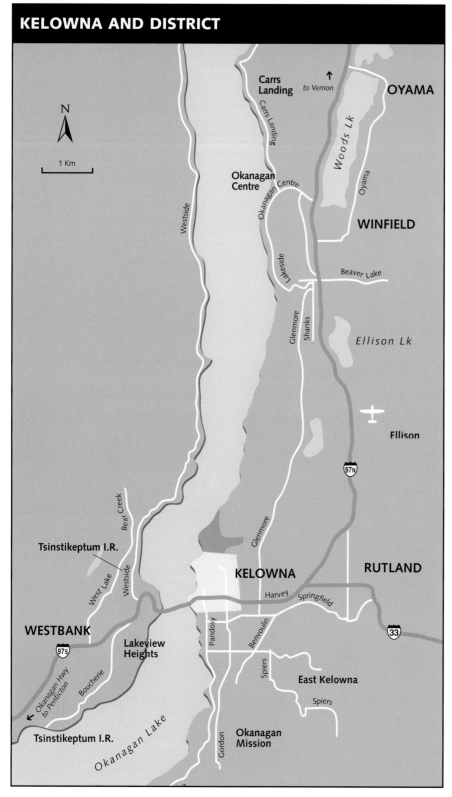

largest winery in the province and SUN-RYPE PRODUCTS LTD is a major employer. The Floating Bridge, which opened in 1958, was the first of its kind in Canada. Okanagan Univ College (*see* COMMUNITY COLLEGES) opened its doors in 1963. The mild, sunny climate (366 mm annual precipitation) attracts both TOURISTS and retirees and during the 1980s Kelowna was the fastest growing community in BC.

Population: 89,442 (metropolitan population approx. 140,000)
Rank in BC: 9th
Population increase since 1981: 49%
Date of incorporation: city 4 May 1905
Land area: 228.4 km²
Location: Central Okanagan Regional District
Economic base: fruit growing and packing, lumber, manufacturing, wineries, tourism

KELP is the common name for a number of species of large brown SEAWEED. It grows thickly on the rocky Pacific shore in the subtidal and intertidal zones. In BC the 2 largest types are giant kelp (*Macrocystis integrifolia*), also known as small perennial kelp, which grows on the outer coast, and bull kelp (*Nereocystis luetkeana*), which is common on both the inner and outer coasts. Both types grow in thick beds, or "kelp forests," that shelter a wide variety of marine life.

Bull kelp, with its long, hollow, rubbery stem, or stipe, is attached to the sea bottom by holdfasts and ends on the surface in a round float with long brown blades, or fronds, trailing across the water. It is predominantly an annual plant, with much of the biomass removed by winter storms each year. Before it dies it disperses a huge number of zoospores that settle on the ocean floor and begin to grow into microscopic, filamentous male and female gamete-producing plants (gametophytes). In spring the male plantlets produce sperm cells that swim to and fertilize the females. The fertilized kelp then begins to grow rapidly—up to 60 cm a day—and reaches a length of 20 m or more by summer's end. Bull kelp is harvested in BC for use as compost, or to be dried and marketed mainly as a health food.

Giant kelp, a perennial plant, is even bigger: its main stipe may grow to more than 33 m in length. As well, it has long, leaf-like blades with pointed tips. Giant kelp is harvested for use in the lucrative HERRING roe-on-kelp fishery each spring. Most of that product is exported to Japan. Small amounts are harvested at other times of the year for fertilizer. Giant kelp is often called small perennial kelp to distinguish it from the related giant kelp (*Macrocystis pyrifera*), which is harvested in California and used in the production of kelp tablets and other products.

Kelp was once much more abundant on the BC coast than it is today. In the early decades of the 19th century, when maritime fur traders hunted SEA OTTERS almost to extinction, SEA URCHINS, the favoured food of the otter, expanded in population. Urchins feed on kelp; as they spread they laid waste to the vast forests of kelp

the FUR BRIGADES. Father Charles PANDOSY, an OBLATE missionary, built a mission near the site in 1860 and 2 years later planted the area's first fruit trees. However, the CATTLE INDUSTRY remained the mainstay until the first large commercial orchards were planted in the 1890s (*see* TREE FRUITS). A townsite was laid out in 1892, the same year the SHUSWAP & OKANAGAN RWY reached VERNON, linking the lake to the CPR mainline at SICAMOUS. Steamboats began appearing on the lake and the valley began to boom. Kelowna

became a city in 1905 and expanded quickly in the pre-war period as the valley became the leading fruit-producing region in BC. The Kelowna Regatta, which included canoe and boat races, aquatic sports, a beauty contest and other events, began in 1906 and grew to become BC's major summer festival. Unruly mobs disrupted the regatta in 1986–87 and it was discontinued. Today Kelowna is the business centre of the OKANAGAN VALLEY. Fruit growing is still important. CALONA WINES LTD, started in 1932, is the

Bull kelp. Rick Harbo photo

that once grew on the coast. Following the reintroduction of sea otter and the subsequent depletion of urchins, many kelp beds have recovered. The commercial DIVE FISHERY for red sea urchins has also led to the expansion of kelp beds.

KELSEY BAY lies at the mouth of the SALMON R on the east side of VANCOUVER ISLAND, 75 km north of CAMPBELL RIVER. Before WWI a government wharf was built and UNION STEAMSHIP CO vessels began making regular calls. Kelsey Bay is named for William Kelsey and his wife, early settlers who opened a store and post office in 1922. Across the river is the site of Hkusam, an ancient KWAKWA̱KA̱'WAKW (Kwakiutl) village. It was the southern terminus of the ferry to PRINCE RUPERT from 1966 until the terminal was moved north to PORT HARDY in 1979. LOGGING and commercial FISHING have sustained the local economy.

KEMANO, on the Kemano R near where it drains into the GARDNER CANAL on the North Coast, is an ancient village site of the Henaaksiala people. Residents amalgamated with the HAISLA (Kitamat) at Kitamaat in 1953 but still return annually to harvest EULACHON from the river. Nearby is a massive generating station (*see* HYDROELECTRICITY) that was built to provide power for the ALCAN ALUMINUM CO smelter at KITIMAT 75 km to the north; it began generating electricity in 1954. The project was made possible by damming the NECHAKO R and diverting its headwaters westward through a 16-km tunnel drilled under the mountains. A second stage of the diversion, the so-called Kemano Completion Project, was initially approved in 1987 by the provincial government, then cancelled in 1995 because of anticipated environmental damage; under a 1997 agreement between Alcan and the government, BC HYDRO AND POWER AUTHORITY will supply power at below market value to the company for a proposed new SMELTER at Kitimat. In 1999 Alcan announced that it was closing the

small townsite at Kemano, leaving only a camp for fly-in workers.

KEMPER, Margaret (Sinclair) Trudeau, homemaker, writer, television host (b Sept 1948, Vancouver). A daughter of James SINCLAIR, a former Liberal cabinet minister, she stunned Canadians in March 1971 when, as a 22-year-old "flower child" from N VANCOUVER, she married Prime Minister Pierre Trudeau, 51 years old and considered a confirmed bachelor. Beautiful and free-spirited, she brought youthful informality to the grey world of Canadian politics. During the 1970s she gave birth to 3 sons, Justin, Sacha and Michel (the first 2 both born on Christmas Day). But by 1977 the fairytale romance had broken down. Margaret was involved in a series of notorious escapades involving drugs and show business celebrities; the Trudeaus separated. She further scandalized the public by writing 2 books about her life with the prime minister, *Beyond Reason* (1979) and *Consequences* (1982). In 1984 the couple divorced. She married Fried Kemper, an Ottawa businessman, and had 2 more children. In 1998 her youngest son, Michel Trudeau, died in a skiing accident near NELSON.

Margaret Trudeau, later Margaret Kemper, leaving the church with Pierre Trudeau on their wedding day, March 1971.
Bill Cunningham/Vancouver Province

KENDRICK, John, maritime fur trader (b circa 1740, Harwich, MA; d 12 Dec 1794, Hawaii). A veteran New England sea captain, he was placed in command of a trading expedition to the BC coast from Boston in 1787. He arrived in NOOTKA SOUND in Sept 1788 and wintered there, ingratiating himself with Chief MAQUINNA. The following spring he built a small base, Fort Washington, at Marvinas Bay north of YUQUOT. When a Spanish expedition under MARTINEZ arrived, Kendrick befriended the Spanish and was in a position to profit from the hostilities that later erupted between trading factions (*see* NOOTKA SOUND CONTROVERSY). That summer he traded along the coast as far north as Anthony Island, where he humiliated KOYAH, a HAIDA chief. After a visit to China to sell his furs, he returned to the coast in 1791 and at Anthony Island the Haida attacked his vessel, unsuccessfully seeking revenge. Kendrick then went south to VANCOUVER ISLAND to trade; between 1793 and 1794 he made 2 more visits to the coast before his accidental death in Hawaii.

KENNEDY, Arthur Edward, third and last governor of Vancouver Island (b 5 Apr 1809, County Down, Ireland; d 3 June 1883, at sea). A veteran of 20 years in the British army, he became an official in the colonial service and was appointed governor of VANCOUVER ISLAND after successful terms in Sierra Leone and Western Australia. He arrived in VICTORIA in Mar 1864. Kennedy had little good to say about the colony, once complaining that it consisted of just 2 groups, "those who are convicts and those who ought to be convicts." Understandably he was disliked by the populace, and the elected assembly was antagonistic from the start. As well, many of his plans were thwarted by a severe recession. In 1866, when mainland BC and Vancouver Island merged as one colony, Frederick SEYMOUR became the governor and Kennedy lost his job. Nevertheless, when he returned to England he won a knighthood and went on to serve as colonial governor in West Africa, Hong Kong and Queensland. *See also* COLONIAL GOVERNMENT.

KENNEDY LAKE, 69.2 km², connected by the Kennedy R to CLAYOQUOT SOUND, is the largest lake on VANCOUVER ISLAND. It lies within the traditional territory of the Tla-o-qui-aht, a FIRST NATION of the NUU-CHAH-NULTH (Nootka) people, who launched a major SALMON restoration project there in 1998. An iron-ore mine operated nearby from 1961 to 1969 and reopened in 1998 for quarrying (*see* MINING). The area has undergone heavy LOGGING. Two small provincial PARKS are located on the lake.   AS

KENNEY, Herbert Martin "Mart," musician (b 7 Mar 1910, Tweed, ON). He moved west to BC with his mother when he was a baby and began playing the saxophone when he was a teenager. He made his first professional appearance in VANCOUVER at age 18. Three years later, in 1931, he formed a dance band that evolved into the legendary Mart Kenney and his Western

Gentlemen. The next year it became the first Canadian band to broadcast a weekly live music program on radio. Called "Sweet and Low," the radio show lasted to 1942 and was heard internationally. During WWII the band headlined Coca-Cola's Victory Parade and toured the country entertaining Canadian forces and war workers. From 1949 to 1969 the group was based at "Mart Kenney's Ranch," a dance hall near Woodbridge, ON, but it continued to tour widely and to some Canadians its theme song, "The West, A Nest and You," was as familiar as the national anthem. Kenney received the Order of Canada in 1980 and in 1992 was named BC's senior citizen of the year. Despite being "retired" since 1969, he performs regularly across Canada with big bands and symphony orchestras reprising the sounds of an earlier era.

KENNEY DAM, in the Grand Canyon of the NECHAKO R 95 km south of VANDERHOOF, was built in 1952. It impounded the water draining from a huge area, flooding several major lakes, creating a reservoir 925 km² in size and redirecting water west through the COAST MTS to the KEMANO hydroelectric generating station. This plant produces power for the SMELTER at ALCAN ALUMINUM at KITIMAT. At the time of construction the Kenney Dam was the largest rock-filled, clay-core dam in the world, standing 96.6 m tall and measuring 457 m long and 12 m wide at the top. It was named for Edward Kenney, minister of lands and forests in the COALITION GOVERNMENT.

KENSINGTON PRAIRIE was an AGRICULTURAL district in SURREY, 20 km southwest of NEW WESTMINSTER just north of the area now known as Sunnyside. It was named by H.T. Thrift, a Surrey pioneer, after Kensington, England, and first logged (see LOGGING) and settled in the 1880s. A ditch was dug to the NICOMEKL R so that timber could be floated to booming grounds (see LOG BOOMING) in MUD BAY.　　　　AS

KENT, district municipality, pop 4,844, occupies the north side of the FRASER R in the upper FRASER VALLEY between the Harrison R and HOPE. The main communities are AGASSIZ, site of a Dominion Experimental Farm, and HARRISON HOT SPRINGS. The district, which is in the traditional territory of the STO:LO people, was settled by farmers in the mid-19th century. Hop growing was particularly important; the name was chosen because Kent in England was also known for its hops. DAIRY FARMING and mixed crops have been predominant, and 2 federal PRISONS contribute to the local economy.

KENT, Larry, filmmaker (b 16 May 1937, Johannesburg, S Africa). He was the most notorious of the handful of independent filmmakers at work in BC in the 1960s. While he was a student at UBC, he made his first feature film at a cost of $5,000 using a cast of fellow students. *The Bitter Ash* (1963) was a *succès de scandale* for its sex scenes—screenings were banned in several places—but was not a critical success.

Nevertheless he recouped his investment and went on to make 2 more films in VANCOUVER: *Sweet Substitute* (1964) and *When Tomorrow Dies* (1965), his first film with a paid cast and crew and winner of the grand prize at the 1966 VANCOUVER INTERNATIONAL FILM FESTIVAL. Kent then moved to Montreal and continued to make films, including *High* (1967), *Fleur Bleue* (1971), *Yesterday* (1981) and *Mothers and Daughters* (1992). In the mid-1980s he made a return visit to Vancouver to film *High Stakes* (1987), an action comedy featuring the broadcasting legend Jack WEBSTER. *See also* FILMMAKING.

Shannon Emmerson

KEREMEOS, village, pop 1,167, is a community on the SIMILKAMEEN R, 42 km southwest of PENTICTON. The site was a PREHISTORIC aboriginal village and the name derives from the Salish (*see* SALISHAN FIRST NATIONS) for "wind channel in the mountains." First visited by FUR TRADERS in 1813, it was the site of an HBC post from 1864 to 1872. The CATTLE INDUSTRY got its start here in 1864 when Francis X. RICHTER arrived with a herd of cattle. In 1877 Barrington Price built a gristmill that has been restored as a historic site and in the same year a post office opened. The mill is the only example of a pioneer BC mill with its original machinery in place. Since the early 1900s the main industry as been fruit growing, though MINING and LOGGING have also been important. In the past the village had 2 SAWMILLS and a fruit-

Restored gristmill at Keremeos.
Glen Fulton/Image Makers

packing plant, but these have closed. An adjacent community 3 km to the north, Keremeos Centre, flourished from 1907 to 1917.

KEREMEOS COLUMNS are a spectacular volcanic monument, 30 m high, of vertically hexagonal columns, formed by the relatively slow cooling of molten basalt (which causes this columnar jointing) some 30 million years ago. The columns are north of KEREMEOS; they can be

viewed from Keremeos Columns Provincial Park, though they are not within the park boundary.

KERMODE BEAR; *see* BEAR, KERMODE.

KERSLEY, pop 283, 18 km south of QUESNEL and east of the FRASER R, is a farming (*see* AGRICULTURE) settlement on the BC RAIL line and Hwy 97. It was named after Charles Kersley, who was a merchant during the Cariboo GOLD RUSH and then pre-empted land here in 1867.　　　AS

KETTLE RIVER (336 km from the head of its east fork) originates as twin forks in the MONASHEE MTS east of OKANAGAN LK. The west fork flows south out of the mountains past the former MINING centre of CARMI and the village of BEAVERDELL to WESTBRIDGE, where it joins the east fork flowing down from Holmes Lk in the north. From Westbridge the combined river loops south and east through the BOUNDARY DISTRICT, sometimes on the BC side of the border, sometimes on the American side, before disappearing into the US south of CHRISTINA LK. The valley of the Kettle—main stem and west fork—was the route followed by the KETTLE VALLEY RWY from MIDWAY to PENTICTON; much of the abandoned right-of-way is now a hiking and biking TRAIL. It has been designated a BC HERITAGE RIVER and is a favourite trout stream with anglers. *See also* RIVERS; FISHING, SPORT.

KETTLE VALLEY RAILWAY, a subsidiary and later a division of the CPR, crossed southern BC from HOPE to MIDWAY via the Coquihalla Pass and the KETTLE R valley. The line was one of a network of railways constructed by the CPR to reach the rich mineral deposits in the mountainous southeast (*see* MINING). It originated with the Kettle River Valley Rwy, incorporated in 1901, a short line running north and south from GRAND FORKS. In 1910 the CPR took over this line, changed its name to the Kettle Valley Rwy, and used the charter to build west from Midway to

One of the great trestles on the Kettle Valley Rwy, over West Fork Canyon Creek, between Penticton and Midway, 1915. *Kelowna Museum*

link up with its own line at Hope. Under the direction of Andrew MCCULLOCH, the line was completed from Midway to MERRITT via PENTICTON and PRINCETON in May 1915. In the same year the CPR's NICOLA Valley branch line from Nicola Lk to the main line at SPENCES BRIDGE, which opened in 1907, was added to the KVR. During 1916 McCulloch extended the line south through the difficult terrain of the Coquihalla Pass and Canyon to Hope. The KVR was the central link in a CPR line connecting VANCOUVER to NELSON and on to Alberta. The Coquihalla sec-

KETTLE VALLEY RAILWAY

Spences Bridge • Merritt

Kelowna

Hope

Vancouver •

Princeton

Penticton • Osoyoos

• Midway

++++++++ Mainline   ++++++++ Branch line

tion remained in operation until late 1959; the CPR abandoned passenger traffic on the rest of the line early in 1964. Freight traffic continued until 1980 when track between Midway and Penticton was torn up. (Sections of the abandoned right-of-way became a bike trail.) That left the section west of Penticton to Spences Bridge, which closed in 1989. One portion of the line is in operation at SUMMERLAND, where a steam engine pulls tourist trains over a 16-km stretch of track.

Reading: Barry Sanford, *McCulloch's Wonder: The Story of the Kettle Valley Railway*, 1977.

KHAHTSAHLANO, August Jack, Squamish elder (b 16 July 1876, False Creek; d 14 June 1967, Vancouver). He was a resident of SNAUQ, or Sun'ahk, a SQUAMISH Nation village on the south shore of FALSE CRK in VANCOUVER, roughly between Kitsilano Point and today's Burrard Street Bridge. Prior to WWI the provincial government forced Squamish people to leave the site, then took it over for industrial development. August Jack was a SAWMILL worker and later in his life an important informant about the history of the area. The Kitsilano neighbourhood of Vancouver is named after his grandfather, Chief Khahtsahlano.

August Jack Khahtsahlano, Squamish elder (r), with his brother Sewhultun in 1946.

KHORANA, Har Gobind, scientist (b 9 Jan 1922, Raipur, India). After growing up in an impoverished family, he won scholarships to school and eventually earned degrees in organic chemistry at Punjab Univ and a PhD from Univ of Liverpool in 1968. He grew frustrated at being denied advancement in England because of racial prejudice and in 1952 accepted an invitation to pursue his research in organic chemistry at the BC Research Council at UBC. After 8 years at UBC he moved to the US; he was living there when he won the Nobel Prize for medicine in 1968 for his work with DNA and synthesizing genes. At the time he acknowledged the role his VANCOUVER research played in his work.

Shannon Emmerson

KHUTZEYMATEEN VALLEY, 443 km², is a wilderness watershed north of PRINCE RUPERT in the COAST MTS. It is part of the traditional territory of the TSIMSHIAN First Nation. The name derives from a Tsimshian word meaning "in valley." LOGGING has occurred in the watershed, but in 1992 the government designated part of the estuary and valley a grizzly BEAR reserve, off-limits to hunting and logging, the only grizzly bear sanctuary in Canada. It became a provincial PARK on 17 Aug 1994.

KICKING HORSE PASS (el 1,622 m) is on the BC–Alberta border 10 km west of Lake Louise. It was named by Dr James HECTOR, the naturalist with the Palliser Expedition, who was kicked in the chest by one of his pack horses in Aug 1859 while exploring the river, which was later named the Kicking Horse River. The CPR built its main line through the pass in 1883–84. As it descended down the west side to FIELD, the railway had the steepest grade of any line in N America. This section of track, known as the "Big Hill," was replaced in 1908 by the Spiral Tunnels. The TRANS-CANADA HWY also follows the pass, which connects YOHO and Banff national PARKS.

Kicking Horse Pass in the Rocky Mts.
Keith Thirkell photo

KIDD REPORT was the response of a group of business leaders to the economic chaos of the Great Depression. In Apr 1932 a delegation representing 22 business groups and service clubs went to VICTORIA to present their complaints about the way the provincial government was handling the economy. As a result of this meeting the government approved the creation of a committee of business executives to look into provincial finances. Members of the committee were George Kidd, former president of the BC ELECTRIC RWY CO; W.L. Macken and Austin TAYLOR, both financiers; A.H. Douglas, a VANCOUVER lawyer; and R.W. Mayhew, a Victoria manufacturer. In its report, made public in Aug 1932, the group recommended slashing the provincial

budget by cutting public service salaries, reducing the size of the legislature, capping spending on social services and curtailing support for public EDUCATION, including cutting off funding for UBC. The report blamed the party system for failing to rein in public spending and called for a non-partisan COALITION GOVERNMENT. The Kidd Report reflected the disillusionment of business with party government, but its recommendations were not supported by the public and were not implemented.

KILBY GENERAL STORE, located at the mouth of the Harrison R where it joins the FRASER R 16 km west of AGASSIZ, opened for business in 1906 to serve the small company town at the Rat Portage SAWMILL at HARRISON MILLS. Thomas Kilby operated the store until 1922, when his son Acton took over. The provincial government purchased the store in 1972 and turned it into a museum, re-creating the ambience of a country store in the 1920s.

KILDONAN is an abandoned cannery village in Uchucklesit Inlet, an arm of BARKLEY SOUND on the west coast of VANCOUVER ISLAND. The original cannery was built in 1903 and acquired in 1910 by Wallace Bros, whose owners named it after their hometown in Scotland. The cannery and associated buildings stood on pilings next to the shore and during the heyday of the pilchard fishery in the 1920s and 1930s (*see* SARDINE, PACIFIC), the population reached 300. The last owners, BC PACKERS, closed the HERRING reduction plant in 1960; 2 years later they demolished the buildings. Kildonan later became the site of a marine resort.

KILGARD is a small community 7 km west of ABBOTSFORD in the FRASER VALLEY. SUMAS Clay Products, a brick factory formerly located at CLAYBURN, has been based here since 1920. It was purchased in 1979 by the Kilgard STO:LO nation, who now operate it.   AS

KILIAN, Crawford, teacher, writer (b 7 Feb 1941, New York City). Raised in the US and Mexico, he moved to VANCOUVER in 1967. He is a prolific author of both fiction and non-fiction, producing fantasies, science fiction and adventure novels as well as a highly regarded history of BLACKS in BC, *Go Do Some Great Thing* (1978). He began teaching at Capilano College (*see* COMMUNITY COLLEGES) in N VANCOUVER in 1968 and has written extensively on educational issues (*see also* EDUCATION), including the book *School Wars* (1985).

KILKERRAN, 10 km north of DAWSON CREEK in the PEACE R district, originally known as Saskatoon Crk, was settled by the Piper family in 1912. The first PROVINCIAL POLICE officer in the district was based here in 1914, and a school opened the following year. Kilkerran was named after Rev John Kerr, who built a rural church at the site in 1919.   AS

KILLER WHALE (*Orcinus orca*), also known as orca or blackfish, is the largest member of the DOLPHIN family of WHALES. Males and females are white and black in colour. The adult male grows to 7 tonnes and to 10 m in length; it has the tall, pointed dorsal fin that distinguishes the species. Killer whales are very sociable, living together in groups of related individuals called

The cannery at Kildonan, 1940s.
BC Archives D-00594

Killer whale. Martin Nichols drawing

pods. There are 3 known "types" in BC waters. The most common, known as residents, travel in larger groups and eat fish. The second type, known as transient whales, travel in smaller groups; they range more widely and sometimes attack and eat other marine mammals, giving rise to the name killer whale. The third type, known as offshores, live in larger groups much farther away from the coastline and are believed to eat fish. In 1999 the BC coast was home to 300 resident killer whales, about 200 transients and at least 200 offshores.

The first live killer whale was captured by the VANCOUVER AQUARIUM in 1964. Named Moby Doll, it survived almost 3 months and became a "goodwill ambassador" for killer whales, which had previously been feared and detested as vicious predators. Public opinion changed quickly, and commercial fishers began netting the animals to supply aquariums and theme parks around the world. At the end of the 1990s,

one killer whale, Bjossa, was on display at the Vancouver Aquarium (a second, Finna, died in 1997), but there were plans to move it.

In 1971 scientists using cameras and underwater microphones began to study BC killer whales, compiling a census of the local population and learning a good deal about their social organization and means of communication. Today the animals in JOHNSTONE and GEORGIA STRAITS are the focus of a booming WHALE WATCHING industry. ROBSON BIGHT, a favourite resort of the killer whales, was made a marine ECOLOGICAL RESERVE in 1982, now called the Robson Bight (Michael BIGG) Ecological Reserve, after a pioneer of killer whale study in the province. *Reading:* Michael R. Bigg et al, *Killer Whales: A Study of Their Identification, Genealogy & Natural History in BC and Washington State*, 1987.

KIMBERLEY, city, pop 6,738, in the PURCELL MTS overlooking the KOOTENAY R valley, 30 km by road from CRANBROOK, is Canada's second-highest city (el 1,200 m). It was named after the

diamond mining town in S Africa. It flourished in the 1890s as a MINING centre and grew with the success of the North Star and SULLIVAN MINES. The Sullivan, once the largest lead–ZINC–SILVER mine in the world, was still producing ore for its owner, COMINCO, in 2000, but was expected to play out before long. Iron and tin were also processed here until 1974, and Cominco operated a fertilizer plant from 1951 to 1987. The city was incorporated on 29 Mar 1944, then re-incorporated on 1 Nov 1968 with the addition of 2 adjacent villages, Chapman Camp and MARYSVILLE. With the decline in mining, Kimberley has been planning the transition to a more diversified economy. TOURISM has become important: part of the downtown was developed on a Bavarian theme in the 1970s and Kimberley Ski and Summer Resort is popular with skiers. Every July the city hosts the largest old-time accordion championship in N America.

KIMBERLEY DYNAMITERS was the first BC HOCKEY team to win the Allan Cup as Canadian amateur champions in 1936 and went on to win the International Ice Hockey Federation amateur championship in 1937. The Dynamiters appeared in the West Kootenay League in 1931 and first dislodged the TRAIL SMOKE EATERS from BC hockey dominance in 1934. They were undefeated in league play 1935–36 and their Allan Cup win over Sudbury qualified them for the 1937 world championship where, led by Ken Campbell, Ralph Redding, James "Puffy" Kemp, Harry Brown, brothers Hugo and Art Mackie and coach John Achtzener, they outscored their opposition 60-4 while winning 9 straight games in London, England. In the following decades the Dynamiters' stars included Frank "Sully" Sullivan and the potent line of Walt Peacosh, Dick Vincent and Ken McTeer. The team was particularly successful in the mid-1960s and won another Allan Cup in 1978. *SW*

KIMSQUIT, 55 km north of BELLA COOLA on the east side of DEAN CHANNEL at the mouth of the DEAN R, was the site of Nut'l, the largest of several ancient NUXALK (Bella Coola) villages in the area. LOGGING was important and BC PACKERS operated a fish cannery here in the 1910s and 1920s. Across the channel, where many JAPANESE fishers settled and also operated a SAWMILL, the CANADIAN FISHING CO built another cannery. Kimsquit was briefly considered as a possible terminus for various transcontinental railway schemes, as was Bella Coola. The Kimsquit R runs into the head of the inlet. *AS*

KINBASKET RESERVOIR (529 km²) the second-largest reservoir entirely in BC (after WILLISTON Reservoir), is a long (216 km) narrow stretch of the COLUMBIA R in the ROCKY MT TRENCH north of GOLDEN that reaches all the way to VALEMOUNT. It was created in the 1970s by construction of the MICA DAM, North America's highest earth-filled dam. Surrounded by spectacular mountain scenery, it takes its name from Kenpesq't, a SECWEPEMC (Shuswap) chief.

Killer whale breaching. Chris Hopkins/Image Makers

KINCOLITH, or Gingolx ("the place of skulls") as it is known to its NISGA'A residents, pop 318, is a FISHING village at the mouth of the NASS R, 80 km north of PRINCE RUPERT. Accessible only by boat or plane, it was founded in 1867 by ANGLI-CAN CHURCH missionaries Robert Doolan and Robert TOMLINSON and a group of Nisga'a who wished to live apart from the other villages upriver. Following Tomlinson were Henry Schutt (1878–81), David Leask (1881–82), Thomas Dunn (1882–84) and William COLLISON, who stayed 38 years (1884–1922). The community was based on a similar experiment at METLAKAT-LA. Its economy relied for many years on the SALMON CANNERIES that operated in nearby Nass Bay until the 1940s. The Anglican Church still had a strong presence here by the end of the 20th century.

KING, Albert Lorenzo "Al," union leader (b 3 Mar 1915, Manchester, England). He was brought to Canada in 1928 by his parents, who settled on a homestead in northern Saskatchewan. He dropped out of school at age 13 to help support the family. In the middle of the Depression he left home to find work and ended up in TRAIL, where in Mar 1937 he was hired on at the COMINCO smelter. One of the first members of Local 480 of the INTERNATIONAL UNION OF MINE, MILL & SMELTER WORKERS, he organized for several years to get the union certi-fied in Trail. He was president of the local from 1950 to 1960, a time when the union was under attack from the employer and from the right wing of the LABOUR MOVEMENT. In 1960 he moved to VANCOUVER to become secretary of the union's BC District and after the IUMMSW merged with the United Steelworkers in 1967 he stayed on as an organizer until his retirement in 1980. During a long career in the labour move-ment, King was known for his fierce commit-ment to improving job conditions for miners and SMELTER workers. *See also* MINING.
Reading: Al King with Kate Braid, *Red Bait: Struggles of a Mine Mill Local*, 1998.

KING GEORGE'S SOUND CO, also known as Richard Cadman Etches and Co, was a business syndicate formed in London, England, in 1785 to carry on the trade for SEA OTTER pelts on the BC coast. Its name refers to James COOK's origi-nal name for NOOTKA SOUND. Two of the com-pany's principal investors, Nathaniel PORTLOCK and George DIXON, spent the summers of 1786 and 1787 on the coast; in 1786 the company dispatched a second expedition under Charles DUNCAN. In 1789 the company merged with another group of British traders led by John MEARES.

KING ISLAND, 824 km², is a mountainous island at the north end of FITZ HUGH SOUND on the middle coast east of BELLA BELLA. It is separat-ed from the mainland by DEAN CHANNEL to the north and Burke Channel to the south, both routes used by marine traffic to reach BELLA COOLA. It was named by Capt George VANCOUVER in 1793 after the father of his friend and fellow

Kincolith on the Nass R, early 1920s. UBC BC123

officer James King. People of the NUXALK (Bella Coola) and HEILTSUK (Bella Bella) First Nations used the shores of the island for food gathering. James Codville and his family homesteaded from 1890 to 1899 in Evans Inlet. Codville became keeper of the LIGHTHOUSE on Pointer Island across Fisher Channel; when he died, his son Ben staffed the light until 1945. Codville Lagoon Provincial MARINE PARK (7.55 km²) on King Island commemorates this pioneer family. Wild and uninhabited, the island has undergone extensive LOGGING.

KINGCOME INLET is a deep FJORD about 500 km north of VANCOUVER. The Kingcome R flows out of the mountains through a grassy delta at the head of the inlet. The delta was settled in 1895 by two brothers, Ernest and William HALL-IDAY, who planned to graze cattle on the wild meadows. They were joined by a handful of other settlers. Loggers moved into the inlet prior to WWI, and a fish cannery operated at Charles Creek between 1903 and 1933 (*see* SALMON CAN-NERIES). Regular steamship service linked the community to the outside world. A KWAK-WAKA'WAKW village belonging to the Tsawataineuk First Nation is located 5 km up the river. The inlet is named after Rear Adm John Kingcome, a British naval commander on the coast between 1863 and 1865.

KINGFISHER, BELTED (*Ceryle alcyon*), is the only species of kingfisher in Canada. In BC it occurs widely along the coast and throughout the Interior, perching high above the water look-ing for prey. It feeds by plunging head first into the water after small FISH, FROGS and INSECTS, which it carries back to its perch to devour. It nests in burrows excavated in dirt banks. It is a stocky, short-legged bird with a large head and a pointed black bill. Plumage is white below and blue-grey above with a white collar around the neck and a dark, crested head. The female has a brownish-red belly band.

Belted kingfisher. Ervio Sian photo

KINGLET is a tiny, plump bird found in conif-erous forest habitat. Kinglets are seen flitting actively from branch to branch in search of INSECTS. The two N American species, the gold-en-crowned kinglet (*Regulus satrapa*) and the ruby-crowned kinglet (*R. calendula*), occur throughout BC. Golden-crowned kinglets are most abundant in the southwest corner of the province, including southeast VANCOUVER ISLAND, year-round. Ruby-crowned kinglets (whose red crown is not always visible) are most common in southwest BC in the winter, and in the central Interior of the province and farther north in the summer. *Kim Goldberg*

KINGSGATE is a tiny settlement and customs office on the Moyie R, 26 km southeast of CRESTON. A spur of the CPR's CROWSNEST PASS branch connects here with the Union Pacific Rwy at Eastport, ID. *AS*

KINSELLA, William Patrick, writer (b 25 May 1935, Edmonton). He was raised on a remote homestead near Darwell, AB, and did not take up writing until middle age. He graduated from the UNIV OF VICTORIA with a degree in creative writing in 1974 and, after doing graduate work at the Univ of Iowa, he taught at the Univ of Calgary from 1978 to 1983. Since then he has

W.P. Kinsella, writer.

resided in WHITE ROCK. The main subjects of his fiction are aboriginal people and baseball. His first book was a collection of stories, *Dance Me Outside* (1977), set on the Hobbema reserve in Alberta. This and subsequent books have been criticized for containing negative images of aboriginals, but they enjoy wide readership. In 1987 one of his "Indian" collections, *The Fencepost Chronicles*, won the Leacock Medal for Humour. His first novel, *Shoeless Joe* (1982), a magical story about the American baseball legend Shoeless Joe Jackson, was adapted to film and became the hit movie *Field of Dreams*. Kinsella has published over a dozen books and is one of BC's most commercially successful writers. He was awarded the Order of Canada in 1994.

KISPIOX, pop 553, lies at the junction of the Kispiox and SKEENA rivers, 13 km north of HAZELTON. It is the site of a traditional GITKSAN village, Anspayaxws, and there are 15 TOTEM POLES on display. The area is renowned for STEELHEAD fishing; LOGGING has been the main industry.

KITCHENER, pop 218, is a community 13.5 km east of CRESTON in the E KOOTENAY near the GOAT R. The townsite was surveyed in 1899 and named for Earl Kitchener, the British Imperial war hero. MINING and the FOREST INDUSTRY have been important to the economy, though it is mainly a residential community.

KITIMAT, district municipality, pop 11,136, is at the mouth of the Kitimat R near the head of DOUGLAS CHANNEL on the North Coast. It lies 60 km by highway and rail south of

TERRACE, its nearest neighbour. The name is from the TSIMSHIAN word *Kitamaat*, meaning "people of the snow," a reference to the area's heavy annual snowfall. Long the site of a HAISLA village based on FISHING, it attracted its first white settlers in the 1890s. In about 1906 the GRAND TRUNK PACIFIC RWY considered putting its western terminus here and a townsite was laid out. When the railway instead chose PRINCE RUPERT 110 km to the west, most settlers left. The modern community dates from 1950, when the Aluminum Company of Canada (*see* ALCAN ALUMINUM CO), attracted by the deep-water access and the HYDROELECTRICITY potential, chose the site for a SMELTER. The city was incorporated on 31 Mar 1953. Alcan was still the main employer in 2000 but by then it had been joined by Eurocan PULP & PAPER, which manufactures unbleached packaging paper at its mill, and METHANEX CORP (formerly Ocelot Chemicals), a petrochemical company manufacturing methanol and ammonia. A large FISH HATCHERY and TOURISM have also contributed to the economy. The Haisla occupy an adjacent village, Kitamaat, pop 558, which is sometimes called Haisla and was formerly known as Kitimat Mission.

KITKATLA, pop 451, is a TSIMSHIAN fishing village on Dolphin Island about 65 km south of PRINCE RUPERT. The Kitkatla were the first group of Tsimshian to meet the maritime FUR TRADERS, probably in 1787. *See also* FISHING, ABORIGINAL.

KITLOPE VALLEY is a majestic coastal RAIN FOREST 100 km southeast of KITIMAT at the head of GARDNER CANAL. The name comes from the TSIMSHIAN, meaning "people of the rock." The area was occupied by the Henaaksiala First Nation until the 1930s, when surviving members moved to Kitamaat. The watershed is rich in all 5 species of Pacific SALMON and a wide variety of wildlife. The valley contains the largest intact coastal temperate rain forests still in existence. LOGGING began in the 1970s, but after a historic agreement between WEST FRASER TIMBER CO LTD,

The Kitlope Valley, declared a protected area in the mid-1990s. Ian McAllister photo

the province and the HAISLA people, 3,172.91 km² of the valley were set aside as Kitlope Provincial PARK in 1995.

KITSEGUECLA (Gitsegukla), pop 506, is a GITKSAN community located at the junction of the SKEENA and Kitseguecla rivers, about 40 km

Totem poles at Kispiox. Rick Blacklaws photo

southwest of HAZELTON. The name means "people living under the precipice," though locals often refer to the area as Skeena Crossing. It was the site of a blockade of the Skeena R in 1872 when the village was destroyed by a campfire, presumed to have been set by whites, that burned out of control. The Gitksan refused to allow passage of freight up the river until they met with Lt Gov TRUTCH and were compensated. In about 1900, residents divided into followers of the SALVATION ARMY and those of the METHODISTS, and the community disintegrated. It was reconstituted at about the same place in 1926 when Gitsegukla people began returning.

KITSELAS CANYON, about 2 km long, is a narrowing of the SKEENA R 150 km upstream from the mouth, just east of TERRACE. It is near the boundary between the coastal TSIMSHIAN and the GITKSAN First Nations and has been occupied for at least 5,000 years. The Kitselas people believe their ancestors migrated to the foot of the canyon from the ancient capital of Tam Lax Aamid (Dimlahamid) and established the village of Tsunyow. There were other villages in the canyon, all now abandoned. Kitselas village boomed between 1909 and 1912 with the arrival of the GRAND TRUNK PACIFIC RWY, then dissolved. Some Kitselas people occupy New Kitselas on the outskirts of Terrace and still fish the river.

KITSILANO BOYS BAND was founded in 1928 at General Gordon School in VANCOUVER. Led by the trumpeter Arthur Delamont (1892–1982) it became one of the finest amateur junior bands in the world. Under Delamont's direction, the band toured internationally, made recordings and won more than 200 competitions. It played at the Chicago World's Fair (1933), at the opening of the Golden Gate Bridge in San Francisco (1937), at the NY World's Fair (1939) and at Expo 67 in Montreal. Several of its alumni went on to have successful professional music careers, including Dal RICHARDS and Bobby Gimby. The band ceased operations in 1975.

KITSUMKALUM, pop 207, is a TSIMSHIAN village at the confluence of the Kitsumkalum and SKEENA rivers just west of TERRACE. It was the site of a bitter disagreement with the GRAND TRUNK PACIFIC RWY over a right-of-way through an aboriginal graveyard. A neighbouring non-aboriginal settlement called Eby's Landing, with its early hotel and store, became part of Terrace. The name means "people of the plateau." *AS*

KITWANGA FORT was an imposing group of plank homes surrounded by a palisade atop a large mound near the SKEENA R between TERRACE and HAZELTON. The fort, which was destroyed in the early 1800s, was located on an important trading route used by the GITKSAN people. Battles were fought to control this route and its attendant fishing spots (*see* FISHING, ABORIGINAL). The site is associated with the story of Nekt, a legendary warrior who was the fort's last defender. It is now a National Historic Site. The small com-

Tourists viewing totem poles at Kitwanga, 1920s. UBC BC677/2

munity of Kitwanga, with a sawmill and services for travellers, is located nearby.

KIYOOKA, Roy Kenzie, artist, poet (b 18 Jan 1926, Moose Jaw, SK; d 8 Jan 1994, Vancouver). He grew up in Calgary and attended art school there, in Mexico and at the highly regarded workshop at Emma Lake, SK. He came to VANCOUVER in 1960 to teach at the Vancouver School of Art (*see* EMILY CARR INSTITUTE OF ART & DESIGN) and from 1973 to his retirement in 1991 he was a member of the fine arts department at UBC. During the 1960s he was known for his abstract paintings; by the 1970s he had turned to poetry and PHOTOGRAPHY. Involved with the *TISH* group of poets and the WESTERN FRONT, he became increasingly interested in the experience of JAPANESE Canadians (*see also* JAPANESE, RELOCATION OF). His 1988 collection, *Pear Tree Pomes*,

Roy Kiyooka, writer and artist, early 1980s. Courtesy Catriona Jeffries Gallery/Estate of Roy Kiyooka

was nominated for a GOV GEN'S LITERARY AWARD. Other books of poetry include *StoneDGloves* (1970), *transcanadaletters* (1975) and *The Fontainbleau Dream Machine* (1977). *See also* ART, VISUAL.

KLAHOOSE (Mainland COMOX) people, a FIRST NATION of the Northern Coast Salish (*see* SALISHAN FIRST NATIONS), occupied the shores of TOBA INLET and the islands at its mouth at the top of GEORGIA STRAIT. Their traditional villages were at the head of Toba Inlet. Following contact with Europeans they expanded onto CORTES ISLAND and founded a village at Squirrel Cove, their main community for many years. Today there are about 275 members, living on Cortes and at SLIAMMON, north of POWELL RIVER. The name *Klahoose* derives from their term for a type of SCULPIN.

KLANAK PRESS was founded in VANCOUVER in 1958 by William MCCONNELL and Alice McConnell (1913–82). The aim of this award-winning private press was to publish poetry and prose in limited edition books with handsome design and typography. Klanak's authors included Marya Fiamengo, Ralph Gustafson, Anne Hébert, Robert HARLOW, Henry Kriesel and Jane RULE. Klanak published one book of stories, 9 books of poetry and a reprint of an 1862 CARIBOO settler's guide. Most of the books were designed by Takao TANABE, some by Charles Morriss and one by Ben Lim. *Klanak* is Salish for "a gathering of people for the purpose of good talk." The press's emblem, a human head, was designed by the Haida artist Bill REID. Klanak ceased operations in 1978.   *Sheryl Salloum*

KLATSASSIN, Tsilhqot'in (Chilcotin) chief (d 26 Oct 1864, Quesnel). He was the leader of the party of TSILHQOT'IN who precipitated the so-called CHILCOTIN WAR in the spring of 1864. Apparently fearing that European road builders would bring SMALLPOX into their territory, the Tsilhqot'in attacked a supply depot and then a work camp on the HOMATHKO R, killing 14 men. The Tsilhqot'in, about 20 in number, continued to terrorize the country for several months, killing another 4 people before Klatsassin and some others gave themselves up in Aug 1864. Five aboriginals, including Klatsassin, were sentenced to hang by Judge Matthew BEGBIE.

KLEECOOT was a LOGGING settlement and NUU-CHAH-NULTH (Nootka) village 11 km northwest of PORT ALBERNI on the northeast shore of SPROAT LK on VANCOUVER ISLAND. Kleecoot is Sproat Lk's aboriginal name and means "wide open." *AS*

KLEENA KLEENE, 180 km west of WILLIAMS LAKE in the CHILCOTIN, is a ranching (*see* CATTLE INDUSTRY) district on the Klinaklini R, which flows into KNIGHT INLET. The first residents, Pat McClinchy, Frank Render and Sam Colwell, arrived in the early 1900s. James Mackill opened a resort at nearby One Eye Lk in 1927. Today the Brink and Dowling ranches are located here. The name comes from a Kwakwala word for "EULACHON grease." *AS*

KLEMTU, pop 311, is a FISHING village on Swindle Island in the heart of the INSIDE PASSAGE, halfway between PORT HARDY and PRINCE RUPERT. It was founded in the 1870s by TSIMSHIAN and HAIHAIS families to take advantage of the growing number of steamers passing through Finlayson Channel needing wood and supplies. Originally called China Hat after the shape of a nearby island, it became Klemtu in 1902. It was the site of a SALMON cannery (*see also* SALMON CANNING) from 1927 to 1968 and is now occupied by both HEILTSUK speakers and Kitasoo people, a branch of the Tsimshian.

KLONDIKE GOLD RUSH; *see* GOLD RUSHES.

KNAPWEED is a thistle-like plant accidentally introduced to N America in the late 1880s. With no natural enemies to keep it in check, it invaded different regions of the continent, including BC, where it has displaced native PLANTS and caused considerable environmental deterioration and economic loss to the CATTLE INDUSTRY. Over 600 km² of the Interior is infested and the economic impact from lost hay production alone is estimated to be over $400,000 annually. As well, the widespread growth of this drought-resistant plant has resulted in the loss of already precious few GRASSLANDS for native wildlife. Because it secretes substances into the soil surrounding its roots that makes the soil unfavourable for other plants (allelopathy), it has altered the characteristics of the habitats where it is found, creating a change in ecosystem conditions that affects other plants and animals. Knapweed has large, prickly seeds and is easily spread by the tires and undercarriage of vehicles, by wild and domestic animals, and in hay being moved from infested areas. Biological methods (two species of fly larvae and one species of beetle) have been tested to bring this plant under control.   *Diana French*

KNIGHT, Harry Upperton, photographer (b 6 July 1873, Tillington, England; d 28 Dec 1973, Victoria). Prior to immigrating to Canada in 1910 he operated a portrait studio in Cranleigh, England. He sold real estate in VANCOUVER until 1917, when he moved to VICTORIA and established a commercial portrait studio at 715 Fort St. For the next 47 years he documented the capital's early history and citizens in his "camera sketches and camera portraits" (*see* PHOTOGRAPHY). Knight favoured soft-focus pictorial moodiness in his prints and inspired John VANDERPANT to experiment with pictorialism. The H.U. Knight Collection at the Victoria city archives houses 3,000 prints and 30,000 negatives.
Sheryl Salloum

KNIGHT INLET, 113 km long, 250 km north of VANCOUVER, is one of the major FJORDS indenting the mainland coast. It was named by Capt George VANCOUVER in 1792 after John Knight, a British naval officer. Like all visitors to the inlet, Vancouver was impressed by the "high stupendous mountains rising perpendicularly from the water's edge." Mt WADDINGTON, the highest peak

The wharf at Klemtu. Ian Douglas photo

entirely within BC, towers over the upper end. The Klinaklini R forms an elaborate ESTUARY where it drains into the head of the inlet. Thousands of FIRST NATIONS people, both coastal and Interior, gathered here in the territory of the KWAKW<u>A</u>K<u>A</u>'WAKW to fish for EULACHON each spring. There was a SALMON CANNERY at Glendale for several years and a failed attempt to establish a farm colony during the 1890s. The inlet was also the focus of several GYPPO LOGGING operations, glorified in the pages of M. Allerdale GRAINGER's coast classic *Woodsmen of the West*. Otherwise, Knight Inlet has been largely unpopulated except for the occasional hardy pioneers, like Jim and Laurette STANTON. They made a living fishing, trapping and logging here from 1919 to 1971; their story is told in *Grizzlies in Their Backyard* (1957) by Beth Day.

KNIGHTS OF LABOR was an early labour organization that originated in Philadelphia in 1869. It arrived in BC at the end of 1883; the first local was formed in NANAIMO. Locals subsequently were founded in several places across the province and membership peaked at about 450, mainly miners and rail workers. As much a fraternal organization as a union, the Knights organized CO-OPERATIVES, engaged in political campaigns (they were largely responsible for electing VANCOUVER's second mayor), lobbied for a shorter work day and tried to pressure government and employers to exclude low-paid Asian workers from BC. In Vancouver they helped to form the Trades and Labour Council in 1889 and organized printers, stevedores and labourers. Knights thought that all workers should belong to a single organization and they were supplanted by the rise of craft unionism in the early 1890s.

Abandoned log dump in Knight Inlet.
Ian McAllister photo

KNOUFF LAKE, 40 km northeast of KAMLOOPS, is just north of Sullivan Lk; local people know Sullivan Lk as Knouff Lk, and Knouff Lk as Little Knouff Lk. A recreational community called Knouff Lake, which started life as a LOGGING settlement, has grown up at the south end of Sullivan Lk. FISHING and horseback riding are popular here and Knouff Lake Resort, at the north end of Sullivan Lk, dates back to the 1930s. James Knouff and Michael Sullivan, after taking part in the Cariboo GOLD RUSH, both settled in the area in the 1860s. *See also* VINSULLA.

AS

KNOWLEDGE NETWORK is a provincial public educational television service that went on the air in Jan 1981. It is now part of the OPEN LEARNING AGENCY. It provides general educational programming for all ages as well as full-credit courses for college and university. It is funded by the provincial government, corporate donors and individual supporters.

KNUTSFORD, on Peterson Crk 6 km south of KAMLOOPS, is a cattle and grain farming (*see* CATTLE INDUSTRY; AGRICULTURE) district that has grown more residential, with many small acreages and hobby farms. It was named after Knutsford, England, former home of Robert Longbridge, an early storekeeper and postmaster. The area was first settled in 1872 by James Mellors; a horse breeder named Archie McConnell was another pioneer. An agricultural showground was established in 1914. AS

KOERNER, John, artist (b 1913, Czechoslovakia). He was a law student in his native Czechoslovakia when he moved in 1937 to Paris to pursue studies in art. In 1939, as war approached, he left Europe and came to VANCOUVER, where he worked in the family lumber business (*see* KOERNER BROTHERS) until 1951. That year he left the business world to paint full-time. He also taught, first at the Vancouver School of Art (later EMILY CARR INSTITUTE OF ART &

DESIGN) from 1953 to 1958, then at UBC from 1958 to 1962. He was active in the city's burgeoning cultural scene during the 1950s and belongs to the pioneering group of BC modernist painters that included Jack SHADBOLT, B.C. BINNING and Gordon SMITH, among others. While he was not a landscape painter, Koerner's work strongly evokes the landscape of his adopted province.

KOERNER BROTHERS, Leon (1892–1972), **Otto** (d 1946) and **Walter** (1898–1995), were members of a wealthy fourth-generation European lumber dynasty; they fled Czechoslovakia during the Munich Crisis of 1938 shortly before the country was occupied by Nazi troops. Leon and his wife Thea, a celebrat-

Leon Koerner, lumberman and philanthropist, 1955. Vancouver Sun

ed actress, were in VANCOUVER on the N American leg of a six-month world tour at the time and were unable to continue their journey. Within weeks he arranged to buy a small defunct SAWMILL in NEW WESTMINSTER. He was joined by Otto, and Walter, who had made his way to London to set up a marketing office. The Koerners gained a position in the lumber business by discovering a means of curing Western HEMLOCK lumber, not considered very valuable at the time, so it could be exported and sold in the UK and Europe. They called this wood Alaska pine and their business ALASKA PINE CO LTD. The venture was enormously successful and in 1954 was sold to Rayonier Inc of New York. After Otto's death, Leon and Walter were appointed directors of numerous companies and social agencies. Leon, with Thea, and Walter, with his wife Marianne, bestowed most of their large fortunes on public institutions in BC, particularly UBC. Leon and Thea set up one of the

province's major charitable foundations, the Leon and Thea Koerner Foundation. Both Leon and Walter were awarded 2 honorary degrees and the Order of Canada. *Ken Drushka*

KOEYE RIVER empties through a small bay into FITZ HUGH SOUND on the Central Coast just south of NAMU, opposite HUNTER ISLAND. The name is a HEILTSUK (Bella Bella) word meaning "bird sitting on the water." The spot was inhabited originally by the Koey, a division of the Heiltsuk, who gradually abandoned the area after contact. Homesteaders tried their luck without success. There was a limestone quarry on the banks of the river from 1935 to 1967. The 186.25 km² watershed is slated for LOGGING, but environmentalists and some Heiltsuk want the old-growth rain forest and grizzly BEAR populations protected.

KOGAWA, Joy, writer (b 6 June 1935, Vancouver). Her family was interned by the Canadian government in 1942 during the relocation of JAPANESE Canadians from the West Coast. They lived first in the SLOCAN district, then on the prairies. Kogawa has written several books of poetry but is best known for her novels: *Obasan* (1981), about the internment, winner of the *Books in Canada* First Novel Award; *Itsuka* (1992), set against the background of the redress movement; and *The Rain Ascends* (1995). She also wrote the children's book *Naomi's Road* (1986). She is a member of the Order of Canada.

Joy Kogawa, writer.

KOKANEE (*Oncorhynchus nerka*) is a sockeye salmon (*see* SALMON, PACIFIC) that spends its entire life in fresh water. It occurs throughout much of the range of anadromous sockeye and in some landlocked headwater lakes. The kokanee is a popular freshwater game fish, quite widely distributed over the south central and coastal portions of the province. It is prized for its table quality; smoked kokanee is delicious.

John Koerner, artist, 1991.
Jeff Vinnick/Vancouver Sun

Spawning kokanee near Chilliwack.
Roy Luckow photo

The kokanee is similiar in most regards to the anadromous sockeye but it is much smaller, averaging about 500 g and sometimes reaching 1.3 kg. Like the sockeye it has a lifespan of 4 years, though some individuals live as long as 8 years. In BC spawning takes place in the fall and the fish dies after spawning once.

KOKANEE CREEK empties into the west arm of KOOTENAY LK 21 km east of NELSON. During Aug and Sept it is the site of a huge run of bright red spawning KOKANEE. Kokanee Creek Provincial PARK (2.6 km²) is at the mouth of the creek. A large number of OSPREYS congregate here.

KOKANEE GLACIER PROVINCIAL PARK (est 1922), 320.35 km², is one of BC's oldest parks. It is located in the SELKIRK MTS north of

View of Kokanee Glacier Provincial Park.
Len Mackave photo

NELSON, west of KOOTENAY LK. The area was well picked over by prospectors in the late 19th century and several lead, SILVER and ZINC mines were formerly in production (*see* MINING). The terrain features high granitic peaks intersected by several deep valleys. There are 3 glaciers—Kokanee, Caribou and Woodbury—feeding many LAKES and creeks. The park contains prime grizzly BEAR habitat.

KOKISH, 52 km southeast of PORT HARDY near BEAVER COVE on VANCOUVER ISLAND, was a truck LOGGING camp situated on the Kokish R and run by CROWN ZELLERBACH CANADA LTD. In operation from 1955 to 1985, the camp boasted a school and post office and had a peak population of more than 200 people. The name may derive from a Kwakwala term for "broken or notched beach." *AS*

KOKORO DANCE is a Vancouver-based dance troupe co-founded in 1986 by Barbara Bourget and Jay Hirabayashi. It combines western dance techniques with butoh, a dance form developed in post-WWII Japan and characterized by raw, emotional movement that expresses interior states of being. Kokoro Dance has appeared across N America and in Europe, performing original choreography to original musical scores. The name of the company is the Japanese word for heart, soul and spirit.

KOKSILAH is a LOGGING and AGRICULTURAL community beside the Island Hwy and ESQUIMALT & NANAIMO RWY, south of DUNCAN on VANCOUVER ISLAND. The origin of the Hul'qumi'num (*see* HALKOMELEM) name is uncertain but may mean "place of snags." Bright Angel Provincial PARK lies south of here on the Koksilah R. *AS*

KOMAGATA MARU was a Japanese steamer chartered in 1914 for $66,000 by Gurdit Singh Sarhali, a SIKH entrepreneur, to bring a group of prospective SOUTH ASIAN immigrants, mainly Sikhs, to Canada from the Far East. The venture was intended to challenge restrictive Canadian immigration policies requiring new arrivals from India to take direct passage to Canada; in practice no direct passage from India was available. When the vessel arrived in VANCOUVER harbour on 23 May 1914, officials refused to allow the 376 passengers to disembark, except for 22 returning to Canada. The South Asian community was adamant that the newcomers be allowed to land, but public sentiment was mostly against them and the authorities insisted that the ship should return to India.

Conditions on board deteriorated as supplies of food and drinking water dwindled. On 28 June a case was heard in court to test the regulations; it upheld the government, which ordered the ship out of the harbour. When the *Komagata Maru* failed to leave, Malcolm Reid, a local immigration official, led 125 armed police officers and 35 ex-military men on the tug *Sea Lion* in an unsuccessful attempt to board the ship. Finally the federal government called in the naval cruiser *Rainbow*; with its appearance the *Komagata Maru* departed on 23 July. When the ship arrived in Calcutta, British officials attempted to arrest Gurdit Singh, touching off a riot in which 20 people died and many more were arrested.

In Vancouver the incident divided and angered the South Asian community and led to a series of shootings as individuals took revenge on police informants. In Oct a member of the Sikh community, Mewa Singh, assassinated William HOPKINSON, an immigration inspector. Singh was executed for the murder; the Sikh community still honours him as a martyr.

In 1989 a stone lion was installed in Portal Park, Vancouver, to mark the 75th anniversary of the incident.
Reading: Hugh J.M. Johnston, *The Voyage of the Komagata Maru,* 1979.

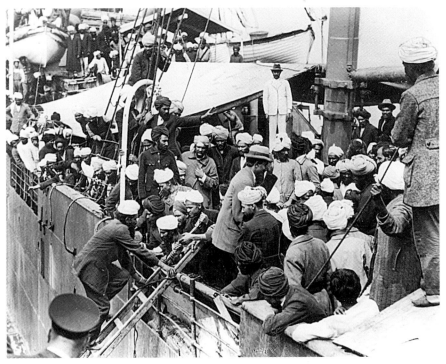

Passengers aboard the Komagata Maru in Vancouver Harbour, awaiting immigration clearance, 1914. VPL 6232

KOOCANUSA RESERVOIR, 273.9 km², straddles the Canada–US border in the E KOOTENAY south of FERNIE. It is a widening of the KOOTENAY R formed in 1973 when the Libby Dam was built on the river near Libby, MT. The reservoir extends 110 km south from WARDNER. Of its total area, 141.3 km² are in BC. The name comes from Koo(tenay), Can(ada), and USA.

KOOTENAE HOUSE was a short-lived trading post established in 1807 by David THOMPSON with the help of his KTUNAXA (Kutenai) guides for the NORTH WEST CO near the present site of INVERMERE at the north end of WINDERMERE Lk. It was the first FUR TRADE post in the COLUMBIA Valley. Thompson spent 2 winters there while he traded and explored the surrounding area. The post consisted of a 3-sided log stockade backing onto a cliff above the water. Only the chimneys survive, marked by a cairn.

KOOTENAY is the name applied to the mountainous southeast corner of BC, extending eastward from the OKANAGAN VALLEY all the way to the Alberta border and from the US border north to the TRANS-CANADA HWY. The region takes its name from the KTUNAXA (Kutenai) First Nation. It has an area of 59,500 km², which is 6.7% of the total land area of the province, and a population of 153,400. Unofficially the region is divided into West Kootenay, between the MONASHEE and PURCELL MTS and including the SELKIRK MTS, and East Kootenay, which is dominated by the ROCKY MT TRENCH between the Purcells and the ROCKY MTS. (Increasingly the southwest corner of the Kootenay region, between ROCK CREEK and CHRISTINA LK, is known as the BOUNDARY DISTRICT and has its own separate identity.) For purposes of government the area is subdivided into 3 REGIONAL DISTRICTS: East Kootenay, Central Kootenay and Kootenay–Boundary.

The rugged topography features a series of roughly north–south mountain ranges separated by deep valleys and long, narrow LAKES. The two main rivers are the COLUMBIA and the KOOTENAY; both have major dams that have created large reservoirs, including KOOTENAY, Upper and Lower ARROW, SLOCAN, KOOCANUSA and Duncan (*see* DUNCAN DAM) lakes. CRANBROOK (pop 18,131) and NELSON (9,585) are the largest cities. The region was occupied by the SINIXT and the Ktunaxa peoples when traders arrived early in the 19th century. First explored by David THOMPSON, it did not play a major role in the fur trade, so it was not until a MINING boom erupted later in the century that outsiders arrived in any number. GOLD was discovered on WILD HORSE CRK near Cranbrook in 1864, followed by major COPPER, lead–ZINC, gold, COAL and SILVER discoveries at different locations in the 1880s and 1890s. A network of small towns sprang into existence to service the mines. PADDLEWHEEL STEAMBOATS appeared on the larger lakes and a flurry of railway building, culminating with the arrival of the CPR's CROWSNEST PASS line in 1898, linked the region to outside markets. The hardrock mining boom collapsed by the

MacBeth Icefield in the Kootenay.
Keith Thirkell photo

1920s—though the SULLIVAN MINE at KIMBERLEY, owned by COMINCO, remained productive—and the regional population decreased from a high of 18% of the provincial total in 1900 to 4% by 1996. With the decline of mining, the FOREST INDUSTRY became the most important employer in the region and has continued to be the economic mainstay of many communities. Coal mining re-emerged in the late 1960s as a significant factor in the regional economy. Coal from mines in the ELK R valley is sent by rail to ROBERTS BANK and exported principally to Japan. The mountainous topography has confined AGRICULTURE to a few locations, mainly around CRESTON and in the Rocky Mt Trench. Though HYDROELECTRIC power has been generated on the Kootenay R since 1898 (*see* WEST KOOTENAY POWER & LIGHT CO), the region was affected profoundly by the COLUMBIA RIVER TREATY and subsequent dam construction in the 1960s. The Hugh KEENLEYSIDE DAM at CASTLEGAR raised the level of the Arrow Lks in 1969, drowning several small communities in the process. The COLUMBIA BASIN TRUST was formed in 1995 to ensure that the benefits of hydroelectric development are fed back into the region.

Along with a rich endowment of natural resources, the Kootenay is blessed with a dramatic natural landscape that attracts a growing number of visitors for hiking, camping, fishing and SKIING in the winter (*see* TOURISM). Along with KOOTENAY and YOHO NATIONAL PARKS, there are several major PROVINCIAL PARKS, including VALHALLA, KOKANEE GLACIER, TOP OF THE WORLD, Height of the Rockies, MT ASSINIBOINE, Gladstone, Granby, Goat Range, AKAMINA–Kishenina and PURCELL WILDERNESS CONSERVANCY. The BURGESS SHALE area in Yoho National Park is a UNESCO WORLD HERITAGE SITE. The Kootenay is also known for its thriving artistic community composed of writers, visual artists and artisans who appreciate the region's beauty and relative isolation and contribute to its distinctive character.

KOOTENAY BAY, pop 38, on the east side of KOOTENAY LK 79 km north of CRESTON, is a former steamship landing, now the eastern terminus for the car ferry across the lake from BALFOUR. LOGGING and TOURISM have been important to the area.　　　　　　　　　　　　AS

KOOTENAY LAKE, 407 km², is a long (105 km), narrow lake lying in a deep trough between the PURCELL and SELKIRK Mts in southeast BC. After BABINE LK, it is the second-largest natural lake completely within the province. (ATLIN Lk is larger but about 5 km extends into the Yukon.) From the north, Kootenay Lk is fed by the DUNCAN R; from the south by the KOOTENAY R. It drains westward through the 30-km-long West Arm, on which the city of NELSON is located, eventually narrowing into the lower section of the Kootenay R. *See also* HYDROELECTRICITY.

The KTUNAXA (Kutenai) First Nation occupied the southern end of the lake long before the arrival of Europeans and travelled the lakeshore to their various camping sites to hunt and fish. The first outsiders began arriving with the lead–ZINC–SILVER mining boom of the late 19th century. MINING activity began on both sides of the lake in the mid-1880s. A townsite was laid out in 1883 at AINSWORTH HOT SPRINGS on the west shore. Mining began in 1885 across the lake at Big Ledge, later RIONDEL, the site of the famous Bluebell lead–zinc discovery. The Riondel property eventually was owned by COMINCO and was productive to 1971. In the 1890s both KASLO and LARDEAU flourished as lakeside termini for railways leading to productive mining areas.

The mining boom provided business for a fleet of PADDLEWHEEL STEAMBOATS that plied the lake for several decades. The first steamboat on Kootenay Lk, the *Midge*, owned by William A. BAILLIE-GROHMAN, arrived in 1884. It was followed in 1891 by the first paddlewheeler, the *Nelson*, built by the COLUMBIA & KOOTENAY STEAM NAVIGATION CO. This company was acquired by the CPR in 1897 and renamed the BC LAKE & RIVER SERVICE. From 1898 to 1930, sternwheelers linked the CPR railhead at Kootenay Landing at the south end of the lake to Nelson. Famous Kootenay Lk sternwheelers include the *MOYIE*, the *CITY OF AINSWORTH*, the *Kuskanook* and the *NASOOKIN*, the largest sternwheeler in BC. Passenger steamers served the lakeside communities until the 1930s, when only the *Moyie* remained in regular service. It was retired in 1957. A free car ferry crosses the lake between BALFOUR and Kootenay Bay.

With the collapse of the hardrock mining boom by the 1920s, LOGGING became the primary economic activity on the lake, along with AGRICULTURE on the flatlands at the southern end. More recently, the mountain wilderness on both sides of the lake has attracted a growing number of TOURISTS, especially to the 4 large provincial PARKS in the area: Goat Range, KOKANEE GLACIER, West Arm and PURCELL WILDERNESS CONSERVANCY. There has never been a commercial fishery in the lake but it has a well established sport fishery for KOKANEE, WHITEFISH, BURBOT and TROUT, especially the famous Gerrard trout (*see* FISHING, SPORT).

Kootenay National Park. Walter Lanz/Image Makers

KOOTENAY NATIONAL PARK, 1,406 km², is on the western slope of the Continental Divide west and south of Banff National Park. The park encompasses the mountain ranges on either side of the Vermilion and KOOTENAY rivers, and contains an abundance of glacial features, including hanging valleys (*see* GLACIATION). It was transferred from the province to the federal government in 1920 in return for construction of the Banff–Windermere Hwy, which bisects the park north–south from Vermilion Pass (el 1,651 m) to RADIUM HOT SPRINGS. The park has populations of Rocky Mountain bighorn sheep (*see* MOUNTAIN SHEEP), MOUNTAIN GOATS, ELK, and both grizzly and black BEARS. Other attractions include the HOT SPRINGS, Sinclair Canyon and the Paint Pots, where heavily mineralized springs bubble to the surface, staining the ground with reddish iron deposits. There is considerable ARCHAEOLOGICAL evidence showing thousands of years of use, including pictographs near the hot springs (*see* ROCK ART). The park contains more than 150 species of birds and migratory waterfowl. Along with YOHO, Banff and Jasper national parks, it comprises a UNESCO WORLD HERITAGE SITE designated in 1985 as the Four Mountain Parks.

KOOTENAY RIVER rises in the ROCKY MTS west of Banff and flows south into and along the floor of the ROCKY MT TRENCH. At CANAL FLATS it passes within 2 km of Columbia Lk, the headwaters of the COLUMBIA R. Over the years numerous schemes have been promoted to divert the Kootenay into the Columbia system at this point, including one notable but foolhardy scheme promoted by William BAILLIE-GROHMAN in the 1880s; none has been successful. The river continues south past FORT STEELE and widens into KOOCANUSA RESERVOIR, which straddles the Canada–US border. South of the border the Kootenay loops through Montana and Idaho before re-entering BC south of CRESTON. It meanders through the fertile Creston Valley, then empties into the south end of KOOTENAY LK. The river exits the lake near NELSON, on the West Arm, then continues its southwesterly flow to CASTLEGAR, where it merges with the Columbia R. This lower stretch of the river was dammed by the WEST KOOTENAY POWER & LIGHT CO beginning in 1898; 4 dams (South Slocan, Lower BONNINGTON, Upper Bonnington, and Corra Linn) continue to provide electricity to the region. In total, the Kootenay R is 780 km long, 508 km of which run in BC, where it drains a watershed of 37,685.73 km². *See also* HYDROELECTRICITY; PADDLEWHEEL STEAMBOATS; COLUMBIA RIVER TREATY.

KOOTENAY SCHOOL OF WRITING (KSW), the first writer-run centre in Canada, was founded in 1983 in response to the closure of the David Thompson University Centre in NELSON (*see* NOTRE DAME UNIV OF NELSON) and began operating in VANCOUVER the next year. Writers associated with the creation of the school included Tom WAYMAN, Jeff Derksen, Gary Whitehead, Calvin Wharton, Peter Cummings and Colin Browne. KSW offered courses in writing and other subjects in a workshop format, as well as publishing *Writing* magazine (*see* MAGAZINES, LITERARY) and sponsoring readings and talks. For 2 years the Artspeak Gallery was associated with the school. Despite chronic difficulties obtaining funding, the KSW continued to provide a focus for literary experimentation outside the cultural mainstream.

KOPAS, Cliff, storekeeper, writer, outdoorsman (b 1911, Nanton, AB; d 1978). He was raised on a farm in Alberta. As a teenager he undertook long pack trips in the wilderness. Later he and

Cliff Kopas at Bella Coola wharf, 1955.
Courtesy John Morton

his first wife Ruth used packhorses to traverse Alexander MACKENZIE's route to the Pacific; they arrived in BELLA COOLA in 1933. There he worked as a packer, writer and photographer before opening a general store that was still in business at the end of the 20th century. Ruth died in 1935. With his second wife Mae, Kopas took an active role in community development, including the

Bonnington Dam and monolith, lower Kootenay River. Len Mackave photo

completion of the "Freedom Road" portion of the CHILCOTIN HWY (*see* ROADS & HWYS) in 1953. His books include *Bella Coola* (1970), *Packhorses to the Pacific* (1976) and *No Path But My Own* (1996, completed by his son Leslie).

KOYAH, Haida chief (d 21 June 1795). He was a combative leader of the Kunghit HAIDA at NINSTINTS during the early years of the maritime FUR TRADE. His people traded peacefully with George DIXON and Charles DUNCAN in 1787 and 1788, but in 1789 an American captain, John KENDRICK, became angry at the disappearance of some personal items and humiliated Koyah by tying him up, whipping him and cutting his hair. Two years later when Kendrick reappeared at Ninstints his vessel was attacked by Koyah's people; they were driven off with the loss of many lives. Apparently Koyah lost his position after this defeat and, perhaps to regain it, he began attacking trading vessels. During one of these attacks, at Ninstints against the American vessel *Union*, Koyah was killed.

KRAJINA, Vladimir, botanist (b 30 Jan 1905, Slavonice, Czechoslovakia; d 31 May 1993, Vancouver). Educated at Charles Univ in Prague, he taught at the university until 1948. During WWII he was a leader in the Czech underground resistance to the Germans. He won election to the Czech parliament after the war, but in 1948, when the Communists took power, he and his family fled to Canada. They settled in VANCOUVER, where he taught in the botany department at UBC until his retirement in 1973. He is best known for developing a system of BIOGEOCLIMATIC ZONES for classifying ecosystems. He also directed the creation of the first ECOLOGICAL RESERVES in BC in 1971 and played a lead role in the creation of SPATSIZI PLATEAU WILDERNESS PROVINCIAL PARK in 1975. He was made a Member of the Order of Canada in 1981.

KRALL, Diana Jean, jazz musician (b 16 Nov 1964, Nanaimo). As a teenager she moved from her home on VANCOUVER ISLAND to Boston, where she attended the Berklee College of Music on a Vancouver Jazz Festival scholarship. She was later discovered by the legendary jazz bassist Ray Brown—Ella Fitzgerald's husband—at a NANAIMO restaurant. She spent 10 years studying piano in Los Angeles, Toronto, Boston and New York. Early in her career she was known mainly as a jazz pianist, but this changed when she moved to New York in 1990 and began to concentrate more on singing. She released 2 CDs featuring her vocals—*Steppin' Out* (1993) and *Only Trust Your Heart* (1995)—but it was her Nat King Cole tribute CD, *All For You* (1996), that garnered her international recognition and a Grammy nomination. Her fourth CD, *Love Scenes*, appeared in 1997 and received Grammy and Juno Award nominations. It was followed in 1999 by *When I Look In Your Eyes*, which won a Juno and an American Grammy Award for best jazz vocal album of the year. Krall was inducted into the ORDER OF BC in 2000. *See also* SOUND RECORDING INDUSTRY. *Shannon Emmerson*

Diana Krall, jazz musician, 1999.
Jane Shirek/S.L. Feldman & Associates Ltd

KROMM, Bobby, hockey player, coach (b 8 June 1928, Calgary). He moved to BC at age 19 to play for the KIMBERLEY DYNAMITERS and stayed in the senior amateur Western International League until 1965, also playing for the TRAIL SMOKE EATERS and the NELSON Maple Leafs. Frequently one of the league's top scorers, he played briefly for the minor-professional Western Hockey League's NEW WESTMINSTER Royals in the late 1950s. While still playing, he began coaching in Trail in 1959 and led the Smoke Eaters to a 1961 world championship and the 1962 Allan Cup. He also reached the cup finals with Trail in 1960 and with Nelson in 1965. Kromm left BC to pursue a professional coaching career. In 1976 he coached the Winnipeg Jets, led by Bobby Hull, to the World Hockey Association championship, then joined the Detroit Red Wings where he became the first rookie NHL coach to win the Jack Adams Trophy as coach of the year. After 2 more seasons with the Red Wings he retired from HOCKEY. *SW*

'KSAN is a reconstructed GITKSAN village at HAZELTON, at the confluence of the SKEENA and BULKLEY rivers. Opened in 1970, it was developed by Gitksan and non-Gitksan to promote local aboriginal culture and to provide an economic stimulus to the area. It features TOTEM POLES, traditional houses (*see* ARCHITECTURE, ABORIGINAL), a museum, summer performances by Gitksan artists and the Kitanmaax School of Northwest Coast Indian Art (*see* ART, NORTHWEST COAST ABORIGINAL).

KTUNAXA–KINBASKET are 2 related groups of FIRST NATIONS people occupying the mountainous southeast corner of BC from the ARROW LKS east to the ROCKY MTS. The Ktunaxa, also known as the Kutenai people, are related to Kootenai tribes in Idaho and Montana. Their language, Kutenai, is a linguistic isolate, not known to be related to any other language (*see* FIRST NATIONS LANGUAGES). The Kinbasket are a First Nation of SECWEPEMC (Shuswap) who arrived in the INVERMERE area in the 1850s and became allied with the Ktunaxa. They are centred at ATHALMER. From spring to fall the Ktunaxa dispersed throughout their territories in small, mobile groups to hunt, fish and gather food. Those groups without access to SALMON runs relied more heavily on hunting DEER, MOUNTAIN SHEEP, BEAR and ELK. They also crossed the MOUNTAINS to hunt bison on the plains and to trade with other groups. In the winter they congregated in larger villages for ceremonials and socializing. They began acquiring horses in the early 1700s and became active breeders and traders of these animals. The explorer David THOMPSON arrived in Ktunaxa territory in 1807; he established KOOTENAE HOUSE and drew the people into the FUR TRADE. In the 1860s the discovery of valuable minerals sparked the first of several MINING rushes into the area and the establishment of permanent settlements. In 1874 one group congregated at an Oblate mission, ST EUGENE (*see also* OBLATES OF MARY IMMACULATE), on the ST MARY R near CRANBROOK. When outsiders began to encroach on their land the Ktunaxa complained. Fearing violence, the government sent a detachment of North-West

Ktunaxa people at Windermere Lk, 1922. UBC BC188/22

Mounted Police, who established FORT STEELE, named for their commander, Sam STEELE. In 1888 the Ktunaxa received RESERVES on Windermere Lk and around Cranbrook. In the late 1990s the population numbered about 1,000, divided into 4 First Nations: Columbia Lake near WINDERMERE, Lower Kootenay at CRESTON, St Mary's, and Tobacco Plains at GRASMERE.

KU KLUX KLAN is a secret anti-Catholic, white-supremacist organization based in the southern US but active in Canada briefly during the 1920s and 1930s. A local of the Klan opened in BC in 1925, headquartered at a VANCOUVER mansion in Shaughnessy Heights once owned by William Tait, a lumber baron. The Klan managed to attract 500 supporters to its first Vancouver meeting and in 1927 claimed a provincial membership of 13,000. It targeted Asian people in particular and called for a complete ban on Asian immigration and the expropriation of property owned by residents of Asian background. When

Members of the Ku Klux Klan hand out literature on Hastings St, Vancouver, 1982.

the city passed a bylaw outlawing the wearing of masks in public and the national organizer absconded with the treasury, the Klan faded, but it continued to function locally, however ineffectually, until 1932. There was a brief revival of Klan activity in BC in the early 1980s but it failed to attract support. The Klan's Shaughnessy "Imperial Palace" now houses Canuck Place, a hospice for terminally ill children.

KUALT, on SHUSWAP LK 12 km north of SALMON ARM near present-day TAPPEN, was an early SAWMILLING settlement and CPR station that had

disappeared by WWI. In 1886 Joseph Genelle built a sawmill here that employed 50 people. The Columbia River Lumber Co, a subsidiary of CANADIAN WESTERN LUMBER CO, opened another mill in the 1900s. *Kualt* is a SECWEPEMC (Shuswap) word meaning "east" and refers either to a nearby village or a neighbouring tribal group. *AS*

KUPER ISLAND, 8.66 km², pop 185, opposite CHEMAINUS, is one of the GULF ISLANDS between southern VANCOUVER ISLAND and the mainland. It is named for Capt Augustus Kuper, who commanded a British naval vessel on the coast from 1851 to 1853. In Apr 1863 a British gunboat fired on the First Nations village of Lamalcha on the island in retribution for the earlier murders of 3 whites, a key incident in the history of aboriginal–white relations on Vancouver Island. This incident ended with the public hanging of 4 aboriginal men in Victoria. The island was connected to THETIS ISLAND until a canal was dredged to separate them in 1905. The island is part of the territory of the Penelakut, a Coast Salish group (*see* SALISHAN FIRST NATIONS), who used to hunt SEA LIONS here. A RESIDENTIAL SCHOOL run by the ROMAN CATHOLIC CHURCH operated on the island from 1890 to 1978; it has been replaced with an adult learning centre.

KURIKKA, Matti, Finnish community leader, journalist (b 24 Jan 1863, Tuutari, Russia; d 1 Oct 1915, Westerly, RI). He was a socialist journalist and playwright in his native Finland when he founded the Kalevan Kansa ("the people of Kaleva") Colonization Company in 1899 to establish a utopian community in Australia. The community failed and he arrived in BC in 1900 at the invitation of a group of Finnish miners near NANAIMO, who wanted to establish their own idealistic community. They set him up as editor of the first Finnish-language NEWSPAPER in Canada, *Aika* (Time), and in 1902 he moved to

Matti Kurikka, leader of the Finnish utopian colony at Sointula, 1899.

SOINTULA on MALCOLM ISLAND, site of the new settlement. Kurikka was a charismatic visionary who inspired people with his idealism, but he held controversial ideas, notably about free love and marriage, and as an administrator he was a failure. The commune fractured under his leadership and in 1904 he departed with some of his followers to establish another community in the FRASER VALLEY near Webster's Corners. It collapsed almost immediately. He returned to Finland, then moved with a new wife and daughter to the US, where he settled on a farm in Rhode Island, but he never gave up the idea of creating his ideal society.

KUSKONOOK, pop 43, is a recreational and farming (*see* AGRICULTURE) settlement near the south end of KOOTENAY LK, 25 km northwest of CRESTON. Originally known as Armstrong's Landing, it became the terminus during 1900–13 for the Bedlington & Nelson Rwy, a GREAT NORTHERN RWY subsidiary from Idaho. Kootenay Rwy & Navigation Co steamboats, including the fast and elegant *Kaslo*, ran from here to NELSON and KASLO. The name is a KTUNAXA word meaning "end of the lake." *AS*

KWADACHA WILDERNESS PROVINCIAL PARK, 1,584.75 km², is in the northern ROCKY MTS, 160 km southwest of FORT NELSON. It was established in 1973. The park takes its name from an aboriginal word meaning white water, a reference to the milky colour of the Kwadacha R. This milkiness comes from the finely ground rock flour suspended in the water that is scoured by the glaciers at the river's headwaters. The huge Lloyd George Icefield, the largest in the Rocky Mts north of 54°N, feeds the 2 main rivers, the Kwadacha and the MUSKWA. The park is a favourite with birdwatchers and trail riders.

KWAH, Carrier (Dakelh) chief (b circa 1755, Stuart Lake; d summer 1840, Fort St James). When FUR TRADERS arrived to build FORT ST JAMES on Stuart Lk in 1806, he was chief of the nearby village and became one of the principal suppliers of furs and fish to the post. He was involved in 1828 when a group of DAKELH invaded Fort St James and threatened to kill James DOUGLAS. The incident stemmed from the murder by 2 Dakelh people of 2 HBC men several years earlier. Douglas and a party of HBC men had violated the sanctuary of Kwah's house and killed one of the suspects. As a result, Kwah and his followers attacked the post. But Kwah realized it was dangerous to harm the traders. When gifts were offered in compensation, the Dakelh withdrew.

KWAKIUTL First Nation; *see* KWAKWA̱KA̱'WAKW.

KWAKWA̱KA̱'WAKW (Kwakiutl, or Kwagiulth) are a WAKASHAN First Nations people on northern VANCOUVER ISLAND, the adjacent mainland coast and the islands between. They speak the Kwakwala language (Kwakwa̱ka̱'wakw means "those who speak Kwakwala") and share a cultural orientation to the sea. The people were organized socially in small family groups, called

Native canoes and seine boats filled with chiefs and well-wishers arriving at Alert Bay to celebrate the opening of the new Big House, 1999.
Vickie Jensen photo

numayms. Each numaym had its own chief, resource sites, crests and privileges. Several numayms from an area congregated in a tribe that might inhabit a central winter village and perform social and economic activities together. Following winter ceremonies, the people moved to their EULACHON fishing stations in Apr and May, then spent the period from June to Nov FISHING for SALMON, gathering shellfish and BERRIES, hunting and engaging in other subsistence activities. Some of the Kwakwaka'wakw engaged in the SEA OTTER trade, especially at the north end of Vancouver Island (*see* FUR TRADE, MARITIME). This was their first contact with Europeans. With the decline of the otter trade during the 1820s, the land-based FUR TRADE became more important. The HBC used the steamer *BEAVER* to visit the villages of the INSIDE PASSAGE, which now became centres of trade. The first permanent trading settlement in Kwakwaka'wakw territory was FORT RUPERT, established by the HBC in 1849 to exploit local COAL resources. The non-aboriginal population grew slowly until the 1880s, when economic activity—LOGGING, fishing, SALMON CANNING, MINING—began to increase sharply. At the same time diseases took a terrible toll on the Kwakwaka'wakw. From a population estimated at 19,000 at contact with Europeans, the number fell to a low point of only 1,000 people in the 1920s, a decline of close to 95%. The number of tribes also declined from more than 2 dozen to about 15 as villages were abandoned and groups amalgamated. By WWI the

Kwakwaka'wakw were no longer the majority in their own territory. The survivors began to engage in the commercial economy, working in the fishery, the canneries, the SEAL hunt, hop picking and logging. Since the 1920s the population has recovered; by the 1990s it had reached about 4,500.

Social organization depended on the POT-LATCH and other ceremonies, so the prohibition of the potlatch in 1884 was another serious blow to the culture. People continued to hold potlatches secretly until 1921, when Dan Cranmer held a large ceremony on VILLAGE ISLAND and the authorities enforced the law. Participants were arrested and ceremonial objects were confiscated. Some of these objects were returned in 1979 and are now housed in the U'Mista Cultural Centre at ALERT BAY and in the Kwagiulth Museum at CAPE MUDGE on QUADRA ISLAND. Each tribal group is associated with a particular territory, though there are fewer tribes today than formerly. The Lekwiltok are the most southerly group, occupying Quadra Island and the CAMP-BELL RIVER area. They were known as the "Vikings of Vancouver Island" for their fierce attacks on the SALISHAN FIRST NATIONS along GEORGIA STRAIT. A group of 4 tribes known collectively as the Musgamagw occupied GILFORD ISLAND and the principal village of Gwayasdums. One of these tribes, the Tsawatainuk, is associated with KING-COME INLET and the ancient village of Gwa'yi. Two tribes occupied the upper reaches of KNIGHT INLET where each spring thousands of people congregated at Tsawatti village for the eulachon run. Three tribes associated with lower Knight Inlet are the Mamaleleqala of Village Island, the Matilpi and the Tlowitsis. The 'Namgis First Nation, or Nimpkish, used to occupy the Nimpkish R watershed. Their main village at the

mouth of the river was Whulk (Xwalkw), called Cheslakee by Capt George VANCOUVER when he visited in 1792. The 'Namgis are now centred at Alert Bay. The Kwakiutl First Nation are the 4 related tribes that congregated around Fort Rupert after it was built. Four tribes occupied QUATSINO SOUND; they later amalgamated and moved to a site near COAL HARBOUR. Other tribes or tribal groups include the Nahwitti, who occupied the northern tip of the Island, and the Gwa'sala and 'Nakwaxda'xw, whose descendants moved to the PORT HARDY area in 1964.

KWONG, Larry, hockey player (b 17 June 1923, Vernon). Known as the "China Clipper," he was the first CHINESE Canadian to play in the NHL. After playing midget HOCKEY in VERNON he joined the legendary TRAIL SMOKE EATERS for the 1941–42 season. All the other players worked at the COMINCO smelter but the company would not hire him because he was Chinese. After playing in NANAIMO and VANCOUVER and serving in the army he rejoined the Smoke Eaters in 1945–46, helping them to become BC senior champions. The New York Rangers recruited him in 1946 and he played for their farm team and had one appearance in an NHL game in 1947. Returning to Canada he played for a team in Valleyfield, QC, coached by Toe Blake, that won the Canadian senior championship in 1951. He finished 2nd to Jean Beliveau in the league scoring race. When his career in N America ended Kwong went to Europe where he played and coached hockey and TENNIS for 15 years. In 1972 he returned to Calgary to join the family retail business.

KYUQUOT SOUND is one of the 5 major sounds indenting the west coast of VANCOUVER ISLAND south of the BROOKS PENINSULA. Accessible only by air and water, it is scattered with islands and rocky shoals. The inner sound divides into 5 narrow inlets. It is the traditional territory of the Kyuquot First Nation of the NUU-CHAH-NULTH (Nootka), who now occupy their principal village at Houpsitas (Kyuquot Village) near the northern entrance to the sound. Maritime FUR TRADERS visited Kyuquot sporadically from 1785 to 1800, but sustained outside interest did not occur until the 1850s, when traders arrived to barter for DOGFISH oil. By the 1870s local people were hiring on to work in the northern FUR SEAL hunt. In 1880 a ROMAN CATHOLIC mission was established, including a school and a church. A WHALING station operated at CACHALOT from 1907 to 1925; when it closed, many of the Scandinavian employees settled in WALTER'S COVE and took up commercial SALMON fishing. The cove, with its fish camps, boat ways and store, became the business centre of the sound. Commercial FISHING, and to a lesser extent LOGGING, remain important economic activities.

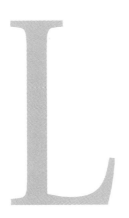

employ comparatively fewer people they have a significant impact on a community dependent on them. Nonetheless, employment in the service industries is increasing at a rapid rate (by almost 34% in the period 1986–96) while resource employment falls. A result of the increasing importance of the service sector is the corresponding concentration of employment in urban areas, particularly in the Lower Mainland, where a large proportion of British Columbians now live.

The second trend is the increase in the number of self-employed individuals. In 1996 alone there was a 12.5% increase in this sector and in 1999 it accounted for 20% of total employment. The third important change has been the growth in the number of women in the paid labour force. At the end of WWII women accounted for 18% of the labour force; by 1997 that number had risen to 45.4%. Of all females aged 15 and over, 58.2% were in the labour force in 1997 (compared with 71.8% of men), an increase of 36.5% in the previous decade alone. *See also* LABOUR MOVEMENT.

LABOUR FORCE in BC in 1999 (ie, the number of people available for employment) numbered 2,079,000. Of these, 1,906,000 were actually employed, leaving an unemployment rate of 8.3%. Most jobs, about 75%, were provided by service-producing businesses, while the goods-producing sector (utilities, primary resource extraction, construction and manufacturing) accounted for the rest. About 20% of the labour force was employed in public service, either at some level of government, in CROWN CORPORATIONS or in teaching, POLICING, or NURSING. Thirty-two percent of the paid workers were members of labour unions. The three largest unions were the Canadian Union of Public Employees (68,102 members), BC Government and Service Employees' Union (60,000) and BC TEACHERS' FEDERATION (44,000).

Three trends stand out in the evolution of the labour force in BC since WWII. The first is the decline in employment in primary industries such as MINING, FISHING and the FOREST INDUSTRY, and an increase in the number of people employed in the service industries. Resource jobs usually pay more and they contribute to job creation in other sectors, so that although they

LABOUR MOVEMENT originated in BC with the appearance of the HBC. It was a trading company and FIRST NATIONS people who swapped furs for manufactured goods were not employees but traders (*see* FUR TRADE, LAND-BASED). This relationship changed over time, however, as the HBC required people to perform other tasks. First Nations people were soon hired for wages to do a variety of jobs, ranging from supplying food to gathering coal from surface outcroppings. In addition the HBC hired men from Britain and the Canadas to collect furs, build and maintain forts, load and sail ships, chop wood and hunt for food. Even at this early stage, employees (who were referred to as servants) organized to assert their claims against the company. They did not form unions but they did resist, by refusing to obey orders and even going on strike. These disputes were sporadic and ill-organized, as workers struggled to find effective ways to fight the company, but they were early examples of the clash between bosses and workers that has characterized labour history in BC ever since.

As the HBC diversified into MINING, farming (*see* AGRICULTURE) and other industries, its workforce also diversified. Conflict between the company and its employees persisted in the new industries, most obviously in COAL mining. When the HBC began mining coal at FORT RUPERT on northern VANCOUVER ISLAND in the 1840s, it needed skilled miners. The company advertised in Great Britain; John MUIR and 7 other miners came out to the colony. The miners soon grew discontented with working and living conditions and in 1850 refused to work until the situation improved. The company responded by arresting 2 of the miners and clapping them in irons. In protest, all the miners downed tools and contacted the chief factor of the HBC, James DOUGLAS. Douglas, Magistrate John HELMCKEN and Governor Richard BLANSHARD all refused to deal with the grievances, so the miners "voted

CHARACTERISTICS OF THE BC LABOUR FORCE, 1987–97

	1987		1997	
	000's	%	000's	%
Labour force size	1,579	100	2,012	100
Sex				
Male	903	57.2	1,099	54.6
Female	677	42.8	913	45.4
Age				
15-24	331	20.9	312	15.5
25-44	848	53.7	1,076	53.5
45-64	382	24.2	599	29.8
65+	19	1.2	25	1.3
Educational attainment				
0-8 years	100	6.3	52	2.6
9-13 years	833	52.8	720	35.7
some secondary	-	-	266	13.2
high school graduation	-	-	454	22.5
some post-secondary	205	12.9	242	12.0
post-secondary certificate/diploma	222	14.1	649	32.3
university degree	220	13.9	351	17.4

Source: Statistics Canada

BC EMPLOYMENT BY INDUSTRY, 1911–96

	1911	1931	1951	1971	1996
Agriculture and related industries	24,000	43,600	28,400	23,100	44,865
Forestry	11,800	12,900	19,200	27,700	39,390
Fishing & trapping	4,600	9,400	5,300	3,800	8,850
Mining, oil & gas	15,500	10,300	7,600	14,700	15,935
Manufacturing	21,300	35,000	74,500	146,900	198,235
Construction	59,300	60,800	60,800	63,900	142,160
Transportation & communication	15,800	30,300	51,400	86,600	142,300
Trade, finance, real estate & insurance	18,000	30,900	52,000	189,000	440,310
Business, educational, health, social & tourism services	33,500	72,800	139,000	225,600	601,160
Government services	-	-	-	57,100	111,420
Miscellaneous	-	100	6,200	71,700	159,880
Total	203,800	306,100	444,400	910,100	1,904,505

Source: Statistics Canada

with their feet" and left for California. To replace them the HBC brought over another group of miners in 1850. One of these newcomers was Robert DUNSMUIR. By Sept 1855, when another strike broke out in the coalfields, Dunsmuir had decided to throw in his lot with the company rather than his fellow miners. Now a subcontractor for the HBC, Dunsmuir did not take part in the strike, and soon became an employer himself. He proved himself the equal of the HBC as a ruthless employer determined to squeeze profits and blood from the workers in his hire. Strikes against Dunsmuir's company broke out in 1877 and 1888. Robert Dunsmuir died in 1889, leaving a legacy of wealth and labour strife to his son James, who fought the miners in vicious strikes in 1890 and 1903. Between 1850 and 1912, miners were forced to go on strike over union recognition, safety concerns, better wages, control over the weigh scales and high prices at the company store. Dunsmuir's refusal to deal fairly with workers created chaos in the coalfields. To protect themselves, miners formed unions and took an active part in politics. By 1877, Vancouver Island miners had formed the Miners Mutual Protective Association; by 1890 they had elected two MLAs, Thomas Forster and Keith Thomas, in the ridings of NANAIMO and Nanaimo City. By 1901, the miners had moved further to the left and were electing members of the Socialist Party of Canada to represent them.

Coal miners were not the only workers to organize in early BC. The GOLD RUSHES of the 1850s and 1860s attracted thousands of prospectors who hoped to strike it rich on their own, but GOLD mining soon became big business and miners became employees working for wages. At the same time, a variety of other groups organized to protect themselves. In VICTORIA, bakers formed a union to secure better wages and to end work on Sundays. By 1862, printers and shipwrights had also formed protective societies.

These organizations were rarely called unions: technically, unions formed to obtain higher wages were illegal in Canada until 1872. Mutual aid societies, benevolent associations and protective associations performed many of the same functions as unions, but under different names. As the colony grew and became a province, its economy diversified. More and more people had to work for wages in the frontier; the dream of independence was more often than not replaced with the grim reality of wage work under harsh conditions.

As the economy grew, so did the labour movement. Increasingly, BC workers chose not to form small local unions but instead to join larger established Canadian, British or American unions. Whether national or international, these unions gave workers more security and power, as their strikes and organizing efforts could be supported by union members in other regions. Workers organized into 2 types of unions: craft unions and industrial unions. Craft, or trade, unions organized workers by their craft: printers, carpenters and plasterers, for example, were among the first workers in VANCOUVER to form unions. Other craft unions included longshoremen, printers and the "running trades" on the railways—engineers, conductors, firemen and brakemen. Craft unions soon recognized the need to work together to press their demands. In 1889 they formed a federation of unions, the Vancouver Trades and Labour Council (VTLC), and in 1910 the BC FEDERATION OF LABOUR. Craft unions, like employers, followed the rule of supply and demand. By restricting employment in the trades to a relatively small number of workers, they were able to demand higher wages. Thus craft unions tried to control apprenticeship programs, insisted on the union shop, enforced limits to the amount of work done in a day, established strict controls over the type of work performed by each trade and restricted entry to

the trade. This often led to higher wages and improved conditions for these workers. It also meant that unions organized only the minority of craft workers and did not attempt to organize women, so-called unskilled workers and immigrant workers, whom they regarded as a threat to their ability to control and limit jobs.

As a result, workers outside the trade unions formed their own organizations. Instead of organizing by craft, they organized by industry. These industrial unions were often led by socialists, such as Frank ROGERS and William McClain, who organized Fraser R fishermen in 1900 and 1901 (see FRASER R FISHERMEN'S STRIKES). They met with hostility from the established trade unions. The KNIGHTS OF LABOR, an early effort to organize workers regardless of skill, helped created the VTLC in 1889, but was purged from the labour council a few years later. The most tragic clash with trade unions occurred on the CPR in 1903, when the running trades refused to support the freight handlers, baggage carriers and other workers who joined the industrial union, the United Brotherhood of Railroad Employees. The running trades did not respect the UBRE picket lines, and the company was able to avoid bargaining with the union. One UBRE supporter, Frank ROGERS, was murdered by CPR thugs and the strike was broken.

More successful was the INDUSTRIAL WORKERS OF THE WORLD, or the Wobblies. Formed in Chicago in 1905, the IWW sought to organize all workers, regardless of craft, skill, gender or ethnicity, into one big union. At the same time, the Wobblies insisted that the exploitation of workers could only be ended if the capitalist system was destroyed. In BC, Wobblies organized loggers, city labourers, longshoremen and railway construction workers. Wobblies also fought for the right to freedom of speech in Victoria and Vancouver (see FREE SPEECH CAMPAIGNS) and played an important role in the Vancouver Island coal strike of 1912 (see COAL MINING, VANCOUVER ISLAND). WWI led to government repression of radicals, however, and IWW members were harassed, arrested and deported. Other unions were more successful during the war, as labour shortages made it easier to win strikes and the government encouraged employers to settle with workers to keep war production from stalling. The rapidly growing economy was soon wracked with inflation, and workers had to organize to keep up with the increase in the cost of living. As a result, union membership and strike activity climbed during the war and workers experimented with new forms of organization, such as joint bargaining committees, sympathy strikes and general strikes.

By the end of the war, workers were more militant than ever. BC socialists and unionists were instrumental in forming the One Big Union in 1919. Similar to the IWW in its organization, but with less emphasis on revolution, the OBU quickly organized thousands of BC loggers into the LUMBER WORKERS' INDUSTRIAL UNION. Employers and the government soon fought back. The RCMP was reorganized, and charged with spying on labour and the left. Employers launched the open shop movement and used blacklists to keep suspected union organizers from working. By 1924, the OBU was, for all practical purposes, dead and other unions were under attack. Membership fell dramatically: the percentage of organized workers in BC dropped from more than 20% in 1919 to about 7% by 1934. Most union organizing carried out in the 1930s was done by men and women connected to the Communist Party of Canada. Formed in 1921, the CPC was dedicated to organizing unions; in the 1930s it took on the difficult task of creating new industrial unions under the umbrella of the Workers' Unity League. Communists organized workers in mining, LOGGING, FISHING, longshoring, seafaring and other industries (*see also* STEVENS, Homer). Unlike the more conservative trade unions, they believed that the strike was labour's best weapon. They also organized unemployed and relief camp workers, and led the famous ON-TO-OTTAWA TREK in 1935 and the Vancouver post office occupation in 1938 (*see* BLOODY SUNDAY).

Communists were joined in 1935 by other unionists who believed that industrial unionism and progressive politics were crucial if organized labour was going to survive. In the US, the passage of the Wagner Act made union organizing easier, and the Congress of Industrial Organizations (CIO) was created. In BC, the government of Duff PATTULLO passed the Industrial Conciliation and Arbitration Act. While it guaranteed the right to organize, it discriminated against real unions in favour of company unions and initially forbade international industrial unions from collective bargaining. Despite the anti-labour law, workers continued to join unions. Loggers and SAWMILL workers, for example, were quick to join the International Woodworkers of America (IWA) and elected a Canadian Communist, Harold PRITCHETT, as the union's first president. Ironically, the union's first strike was not by loggers, but by lime quarry workers at BLUBBER BAY on TEXADA ISLAND in 1937. Though the strike was lost, it established the IWA as a force in the provincial labour movement.

By 1939, more than 12% of BC's workers were unionized, far fewer than the 1919 level but a substantial increase since the beginning of the decade. Real gains came during WWII and by the end of the war, nearly 30% of BC's workers belonged to unions. Changes in the law made organizing easier. The federal government realized that unions had become a permanent part of industry. It also realized that strikes disrupted production and ultimately hurt profits. Since most strikes were over union recognition, the government passed a series of laws during the war, notably Privy Council Order 1003 in 1944, aimed at easing restrictions on union activity. Unions were granted the check-off, so that union dues were collected directly from the paycheque, and in 1946 the Rand formula required all employees to pay union dues even if they chose not to belong to the union. These measures gave unions more security and stability.

With employers forced to accept unions, labour was on a slightly more level playing field.

An early success was the organization of COMINCO's smelter workers in TRAIL into the INTERNATIONAL UNION OF MINE, MILL & SMELTER WORKERS, formerly the WESTERN FEDERATION OF MINERS. Led by Harvey Murphy, a Communist, Mine-Mill finally succeeded in unionizing the smelter in 1944, after more than 25 years of organizing drives. But labour paid a heavy price for the protection offered by PC 1003 and subsequent legislation. The right to strike was limited because new contracts required workers to promise not to strike during the life of the collective agreement and to give ample notice before any strike action took place. Complex grievance procedures, arbitration and conciliation, rather than union militancy, became the new way of resolving conflict—which meant that labour's main weapon, the right to stop work, could rarely be used, and could only be used when contracts expired. This condition allowed employers to prepare for strikes, by stockpiling, running extra shifts, moving production to other plants, and/or stalling negotiations until workers were no longer able to muster enthusiasm for militant action. Unions were also restricted in what they could bargain for, and sympathy strikes, boycotts, secondary picketing and other tactics were prohibited. If labour had won the right to exist, it was now stripped of much of its ability to force employers to come to terms. For a time, this did not seem to matter. The era of post-war prosperity and the creation of the welfare state provided benefits and protection undreamed of a generation earlier. Unionization rates climbed steadily: in 1958, more than half of BC's workers were in unions. Not all workers gained, however. Women, government workers and the growing service sector did not do as well as male workers in the traditional resource sector.

By the 1960s, a new wave of militancy infused the labour movement. Government workers fought and won the right to organize and to strike, often by engaging in illegal strikes. New union members brought new concerns to the bargaining table and to union meetings. Many resented the transfer of union dues to international headquarters in the US, especially when the international refused to release the money for strike pay. Dues collected by the check-off allowed unions to hire permanent, paid officers, necessary now that bargaining and grievance procedures were complex and legalistic. But high union salaries, and officers who turned the union into a career, led many workers to believe that some union leaders were little more than bureaucrats—or, in labour slang, "porkchoppers." Pay equity and patriarchal policies that excluded women or failed to address their concerns were vital issues taken up by the large number of women now entering the workforce and the union movement. To address these new issues of nationalism, democratization and the proper representation of women, new unions were created. Among these were the Canadian Association of Industrial and Mechanical and Allied Workers (CAIMAW) and the Service, Office, and Retail Workers Union of Canada (SORWUC). Though never more than a

	Strikes/ lockouts	Workers involved	Worker days lost
1901	11	10,194	190,318
1911	12	8,221	312,800
1921	18	2,298	38,147
1931	11	2,322	79,310
1941	8	1,408	7,594
1951	26	3,326	74,722
1961	17	1,638	34,659
1971	110	53,368	275,580
1981	159	120,817	3,232,817
1991	57	69,630	283,983
1996	33	38,750	340,880

WORK STOPPAGES in BC

Compiled by John Henry-Harter

small part of the labour movement, their commitment to social issues, democracy and feminism helped rejuvenate a labour movement that had grown sluggish and complacent. Teachers and nurses became more militant, and the labour movement was crucial to the NDP's success in the 1972 provincial election. A new labour code brought in by that government gave BC workers and their unions better protection.

These successes faded in the 1970s and 1980s. In BC, employers began demanding concessions from unions: insisting that workers give up wages, benefits and protections won in earlier rounds of bargaining. Successive SOCIAL CREDIT governments under Bill BENNETT and Bill VANDER ZALM brought in changes to the labour code that made union organizing more difficult and made it easier for employers to break unions, contract out and forestall organizing drives. The percentage of union workers began to decline again, slipping below 43% in 1981 and below 40% in 1987, its lowest rate since 1948. In 1983, when the labour movement launched Operation SOLIDARITY to oppose Bill Bennett's restraint policies, it had little experience in fighting back and few leaders able to mobilize union members effectively.

Since then, the labour movement has been changing yet again. It has devoted more time and money to political action, and was a key factor in the election of NDP governments in 1991 and 1996. It has also lobbied for changes to the labour code. But the economy has changed significantly and labour has had to adapt. Jobs in the resource sector, long the preferred territory for trade unions in BC, have been declining, while the service sector has been expanding. The new industries are comprised of smaller workplaces, often employing only a few people. Organizing is time-consuming and expensive, and employers have been able to stall drives and lobby to prevent laws enabling sectoral bargaining and other measures that would help unions organize in the new economy. The labour movement has adapted by merging smaller unions into larger ones, notably the Canadian Auto Workers and the BC Government Employees'

Union (BCGEU), and devoting new resources to organizing in the service sector. A symbolic measure of this change was the decision to change the name of the International Woodworkers of America to the INDUSTRIAL WOOD AND ALLIED WORKERS OF CANADA, indicating its commitment to organize workers outside its traditional sphere and its decision in 1986 to leave the parent union and become an independent Canadian union. Similarly, the BCGEU changed its name to the BC GOVERNMENT AND SERVICE EMPLOYEES' UNION. Much has changed, but much remains the same. At the outset of the 21st century, BC workers need unions as much as they did in Robert Dunsmuir's time, for they continue to face similar conflicts. The labour movement continues to evolve as BC workers in fast-food chains, coffee bars and convenience stores join the ranks of labour beside workers in more traditional occupations. *See also* LABOUR FORCE.

Mark Leier

LABOUR RELATIONS BOARD (LRB), established in 1993, is a dispute resolution agency of the provincial government. It operates under the Labour Relations Code, which governs all aspects of collective bargaining in the province. The chair of the board monitors all labour disputes in the province, may be asked to adjudicate the disputes, and informs the government when a dispute may require the designation of essential services. The LRB consists of a mediation division and an adjudication division. The mediation division provides mediation services to all parties in the collective bargaining process. It is also responsible for joint consultation processes, the administration of last-offer votes and the administration of provisions for first collective agreements and essential services. More than 300 mediation processes are overseen by the LRB every year. The adjudication division rules on a range of labour-related complaints. Typical applications include disputes over labour practices, strikes, lockouts, picketing and replacement workers. *See also* BC FEDERATION OF LABOUR; LABOUR MOVEMENT. *Dianne Mackay*

LAC LA HACHE, pop 420, began in the 1860s as a stopping place on the CARIBOO WAGON ROAD 25 km north of 100 MILE HOUSE. Known as "the longest town in the CARIBOO," it stretches along the shores of the lake of the same name ("lake of the axe"), so named by early FUR TRADE voyageurs. The lake is still a favourite sport FISHING spot, and there are several lodges around its perimeter.

LAC LE JEUNE is a small lakeside resort 35 km south of KAMLOOPS. It is named for the OBLATE missionary Jean-Marie Le Jeune (1855–1930), who served at WILLIAMS LAKE and Kamloops. There is a provincial PARK beside the lake, which offers excellent sport FISHING for rainbow TROUT.

LACROSSE was first played in BC during the 1880s. In 1886 BEACON HILL PARK in VICTORIA hosted the first inter-city game, a 3–1 win for a team from VANCOUVER. Two years later KAMLOOPS

Field lacrosse action between the Victoria Shamrocks and Ladner Footmen in New Westminster, 1999. Peter Battistoni/Vancouver Sun

was the site of the first provincial championships, and in 1890 the BC Amateur Lacrosse Assoc was incorporated, marking the official beginning of organized lacrosse in the province. The game was played outdoors, by professionals, and contests between Vancouver, NEW WESTMINSTER and Victoria drew huge crowds. Con JONES, a sports promoter, built a park for field lacrosse in Vancouver and started professional lacrosse in the city. The Minto Cup was established in 1901 for the top senior lacrosse team in the country, and the NEW WESTMINSTER SALMONBELLIES won it for the first time in 1908, the same year the 'Bellies won gold in the Olympics. Jones engineered a Vancouver Minto Cup win in 1911 by importing Ontario stars Newsy Lalonde and Billy Fitzgerald, and Vancouver won again in 1920. Otherwise the 'Bellies won the Cup every year it was competed for between 1908 and 1934, the year it was turned over to the Canadian Lacrosse Association. The amateur Salmonbellies represented Canada when lacrosse was a demonstration sport at the 1928 and 1932 Olympics. Players such as Alex "Dad" Turnbull and brothers Cliff "Doughy" and Gordon "Grumpy" Spring starred for the Salmonbellies in the early field lacrosse days. At the time, lacrosse offered the highest salaries and

attracted the largest crowds, regularly drawing 15,000 people out of a Lower Mainland population of 60,000 for New Westminster–Vancouver matches. In 1925 the first organized women's league started up, consisting of 4 Lower Mainland clubs including the RICHMOND Milkmaids; the team lasted 15 years, until World War II. Wishing to return the game to its amateur roots, the CLA repackaged the trophy as a junior championship in 1937. The Mann Cup, which had rewarded Canadian amateur supremacy since the railway tycoon Donald Mann inaugurated it in 1910, had by then become the most-coveted trophy.

Men's field lacrosse died out in 1920s but was revived as amateur box lacrosse, an indoor version, in 1933. The 1930s represented BC's golden age of lacrosse: amateur games were played at Queens Park Arena in New Westminster and at the PNE Forum in Vancouver and were broadcast live on radio by Leo Nicholson and Jim Cox until 1954. Merv Ferguson, a tireless sports administrator, led the BC Lacrosse Association out of debt, served as president of the Canadian Lacrosse Association in 1969 and was later inducted to the Canadian Lacrosse and BC SPORTS HALLS OF FAME. Along with the Salmonbellies, teams in the Senior A Inter-City League included the North Shore Indians, Vancouver Burrards, Richmond Farmers, New Westminster Adanacs and Bluebirds in the formative years; Army, Navy and Wallaces during the war years; and after 1950, the Victoria Shamrocks, NANAIMO Timbermen and COQUITLAM Adanacs. The Indians, led by coach Andy PAULL, the Baker brothers, Stan Joseph Sr. and many other Native stars from across the country such as Hubie Smith, Russell Smith and Stu Bomberry, were the most exciting and colourful team of the 1930s but never won the Mann Cup. Since the Mann Cup began play in 1910, the Salmonbellies have captured the national title 24 times (3 times under the "O'Keefes" name), and the Adanacs were champions twice. In Vancouver, the legendary Dot Crookall and the Athletic Club took the trophy from 1911 to 1914 in the early field lacrosse days, the Coughlans held it in 1918, the box-lacrosse Burrards earned it in 1945, 1949, 1975 and 1977, and 4 more times in the 1960s under the "Carlings" name. VANCOUVER ISLAND boasts several Mann Cup champions: the 1919 Victoria Foundation Club, 1956 Nanaimo Timbermen, and the 1955, 1957, 1979, 1983 (under the name Payless) and 1997 Victoria Shamrocks. In 1980 a world championship tournament between box lacrosse teams from Australia, the USA and Canada was initiated by the International Federation of Amateur Lacrosse and the Coquitlam Adanacs won the right to represent western Canada. Led by Don Wilson's MVP performance, they swept 4 round-robin games and then defeated the North American Warriors Native all-star side at PACIFIC COLISEUM in Vancouver to claim the world championship.

Great box lacrosse players in BC have included Bill Dickinson, Jim Douglas, Jack BIONDA, Fred "Whitey" Severson, Archie Browning, Arnie Ferguson, speedy brothers Ranjit and Nirmal Dillon, Paul Parnell (the all-time leading goals scorer among BC players with 921 goals in 587 games), Cliff Sepka, Dave Durante, Kevin Alexander, Geordie Dean, Wayne GOSS (BC's career points leader), and the fabulous twins Gary and Paul GAIT. Lacrosse has dwindled in popularity with the rise of professional sport franchises in Vancouver, but it continues to attract a loyal following; along with southern Ontario, BC remains a hotbed of the sport. The CANADIAN LACROSSE HALL OF FAME is located in New Westminster.

LADNER is the business and administrative centre of the district municipality of DELTA. Originally Ladners Landing, it is located on the south shore of the FRASER R opposite LULU ISLAND. It is named for William and Thomas LADNER, pioneer settlers who arrived in 1868. Ladner developed both as a farming (see AGRICULTURE) community and a commercial FISHING port. Friendly rivalry has always prevailed between residents of STEVESTON and Ladner, who were referred to by their FRASER VALLEY neighbours as "mud-flatters."

LADNER, Leon Johnson, lawyer, politician (b 29 Nov 1884, Ladner; d 12 Apr 1978, Vancouver). The son of Thomas LADNER, he graduated in law from Univ of Toronto and began

practising in VANCOUVER in 1912. His company, Ladner Downs, remains one of the city's most prestigious law firms. Ladner was an active Conservative; he sat as a federal MP for Vancouver South from 1921 to 1930. In 1926 he narrowly missed winning the leadership of the provincial CONSERVATIVE PARTY. After a long association with UBC as a member of the senate and the board of governors, he donated the carillon and clock tower that stands outside the old library at UBC.

LADNER, Thomas Ellis, farmer, fish canner (b 8 Sept 1837, Cornwall, England; d 24 Apr 1922, Vancouver). He went to the US in 1851 to join his father and his brother William LADNER, who earlier had settled in Wisconsin. The following year, after the death of their father, the brothers crossed the Great Plains by wagon train to California, where they prospected for gold for several years. In 1858 they moved north to BC with news that gold had been discovered on the FRASER R (see GOLD RUSHES). In 1859, having tired of the fruitless quest for gold, they began freighting supplies by mule train north from YALE to the CARIBOO. On their way to the gold-fields the brothers had been impressed by the fertile land on the DELTA peninsula; in 1868 they were the first settlers to pre-empt land there, on the site of the present town of LADNER, and begin farming. Thomas became involved in the SALMON CANNING industry in 1878, when he and some partners built a cannery at Ladner. Later he was prominent with R.P. RITHET in the Victoria Canning Co, which owned canneries up and down the coast. For health reasons he sold out his cannery interests and in 1900 moved his family to California, but a year later, his health restored, he returned to the farm at Ladner. In 1909 he moved into VANCOUVER,

where he remained active in business ventures until his death.

LADNER, William Henry, farmer, politician (b 28 Nov 1826, Cornwall, England; d 1 Nov 1907, Ladner). He emigrated to the US in 1848 to join his father in Wisconsin. His father died in 1851; he and his younger brother Thomas LADNER then travelled by wagon train to California, where they prospected for gold in the Grass Valley for several years. They moved north to the FRASER R goldfields (see GOLD RUSHES) in 1858. By the following year, having failed to find gold, they began freighting supplies by mule train north from YALE to the CARIBOO. William ran into financial difficulties and in 1868 moved to DELTA, where he and his brother were the first farm settlers on the present site of LADNER. His farm was called Frogmore. He launched a political career in 1880, when he was elected first reeve of the new municipality of Delta. He served as reeve for a total of 15 years, and from 1886 to 1890 was a member of the provincial legislature.

LADY ALEXANDRA was a 68.5-m steam vessel built in Scotland in 1923 for the UNION STEAMSHIP CO. It arrived in BC the next year to become the flagship of an expanded fleet of excursion vessels primarily servicing the company's property at BOWEN ISLAND. For 30 years the "Lady Alex" ran day excursions and moonlight cruises out of VANCOUVER, sometimes carrying as many as 2,000 passengers to dances and picnic spots. For much of this time it was commanded by Bill "Cappy" Yates (1889–1966). The vessel retired in 1952. In 1959 it was converted into a floating restaurant in Coal Harbour, Vancouver, and was towed to California in 1972 to serve as a nightclub. The ship was wrecked in a storm in 1980.

The Lady Alexandra, *its decks crowded with passengers, departing the Union Steamship Co dock in Vancouver, c 1935.* VMM

LADY FRANKLIN ROCK is a large obstacle in the Fraser Canyon (*see* FRASER R) just north of YALE. It blocked PADDLEWHEEL STEAMBOAT traffic from going any farther upstream and so was largely responsible for Yale becoming the head of navigation on the river. It was named in 1861 to mark the visit of Lady Jane Franklin, widow of the British naval explorer John Franklin, who had disappeared in the Arctic 16 years earlier.

LADY ROSE is a 31-m cargo and passenger vessel serving camps and communities in ALBERNI INLET and BARKLEY SOUND on the west coast of VANCOUVER ISLAND. Built in Glasgow in 1936 for the UNION STEAMSHIP CO, it was first used in HOWE SOUND; during WWII it served as an armed forces carrier in Alberni Inlet. After the war it returned to the south coast and was operated by Union Steamship until 1951, when it was sold to

in 1931 but the town rebounded later in the decade as a LOGGING and milling centre. SAWMILLING continued to be a major employer, along with commercial FISHING. In the mid-1980s the town restored its downtown historic district and emerged as a popular destination for boaters. *See also* COAL MINING, VANCOUVER ISLAND.

LAIDLAW is a FRASER VALLEY farm settlement (*see* AGRICULTURE) and former steamship landing on the south side of the FRASER R, 14 km southwest of HOPE. W.F. Laidlaw, an early storekeeper, demanded that the CANADIAN NORTHERN RWY name its station after him in return for crossing his property. Residents of the tiny community, previously known as St Elmo after Laidlaw's St Elmo Hotel (and a novel by Augusta J. Evans), were outraged.   *AS*

Arthur Laing, c 1970. He was leader of the BC Liberal Party 1953–56. UBC 5.1/4139

The Lady Rose, *built for the Union Steamship Co in 1936 and still operating on the BC coast in 2000.*

Harbour Navigation Co. In 2000 the *Lady Rose* was the only former Union Steamship vessel still in operation, running between PORT ALBERNI, BAMFIELD and UCLUELET.

LADYSMITH, town, pop 6,456, overlooks Oyster Harbour on the east coast of VANCOUVER ISLAND halfway between DUNCAN and NANAIMO. It was founded in 1901 by Premier James DUNSMUIR as a residential suburb for workers at his COAL mine at EXTENSION, 11 km north. It was also a shipping port for coal. It was named for the town in S Africa that was relieved by the British after a long siege during the Boer War; this event occurred while the townsite was being developed and many streets are named for British generals who took part. The town was incorporated on 3 June 1904. The mine closed

LAING, Arthur, politician (b 9 Sept 1904, Vancouver; d 13 Feb 1975, Vancouver). After graduating from UBC in 1925, he went to work for the Vancouver Milling and Grain Co and then for Buckerfield's Ltd. His political career began in 1949, when he was elected to the House of Commons as a Liberal in the riding of Vancouver South. He resigned his federal seat in 1953 to become leader of the BC LIBERAL PARTY. In that year's provincial election he won his own seat, but his party finished with only 4 seats, well behind SOCIAL CREDIT and the CCF. After another disappointing result in the 1956 election, when he lost in his own riding, he stepped down as leader in 1959. He returned to the House of Commons in the 1962 election, joined Lester Pearson's cabinet as minister of northern affairs and natural resources (1963–66) and later served as minister of Indian affairs and northern development (1966–68). When Pierre Trudeau took over as prime minister, Laing became minister of public

works (1968–72) and briefly minister of veterans affairs (1972) before he was appointed to the Senate. The bridge between VANCOUVER and SEA ISLAND is named for him.

LAING, David Hamilton Mack, naturalist (b Feb 1883, Hersall, ON; d Feb 1982, Comox). He was raised on a dairy farm in Manitoba. As a young rural teacher he became avidly interested in wildlife, especially birds. In 1911 he gave up teaching and went to study art in New York. He also wrote many magazine articles over the next 3 decades. He wrote books about the birds of Manitoba, *Out With the Birds* (1913), and about wildlife artist Allan BROOKS. During WWI he served as an instructor with the Royal Flying Corps. In 1922 he moved to COMOX, where he established a farm, Baybrook, and lived for the rest of his life. He took part in many scientific expeditions in BC and elsewhere in the country, collecting museum specimens and writing about his work.

LAKE COUNTRY, district municipality, pop 9,007, is located between KELOWNA and VERNON on the east side of OKANAGAN LK. Spread over 167.09 km², it comprises the communities of WINFIELD, OYAMA, OKANAGAN CENTRE and SUNNYWOLD (Carr's Landing) and was incorporated on 2 May 1995. TOURISM and fruit growing and packing (*see* TREE FRUITS) underpin the local economy.   *AS*

LAKE ERROCK, a rich AGRICULTURAL district 7 km northwest of CHILLIWACK on the north side of the FRASER R, was originally known as Squakum Lake after a type of SALMON. A.W. Ross, who had a major orchard (*see* TREE FRUITS) and fruit canning operation here in the 1890s, came up with Loch Errock (derived from Loch Ericht in Scotland) as a name for the post office, and Loch later became Lake.   *AS*

LAKELSE HOT SPRINGS are south of TERRACE on the way to KITIMAT in Lakelse Lk Provincial PARK (3.62 km²). TOURIST facilities were established here in 1910 and the sport FISHING is excellent. More than 100 bird species visit the lake, including trumpeter SWANS, EAGLES, OSPREY and OWLS. Williams Crk is a sockeye SALMON spawning area. On 17 Jan 1974 the lake received 118.1 cm of snow, a Canadian record for a 24-hr period.

LAKES cover 18,000 km² of BC, or just shy of 2% of the province. This is far less than in Canada as a whole, 7.6% of which is covered by fresh water. BC has 861 lakes larger than 3 km².

BC's 10 LARGEST LAKES

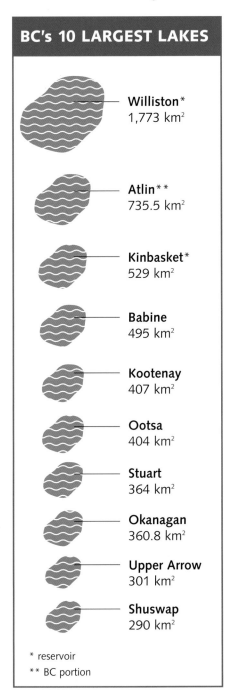

Williston* 1,773 km²

Atlin** 735.5 km²

Kinbasket* 529 km²

Babine 495 km²

Kootenay 407 km²

Ootsa 404 km²

Stuart 364 km²

Okanagan 360.8 km²

Upper Arrow 301 km²

Shuswap 290 km²

* reservoir
** BC portion

LAKETON, or Laketown, was a MINING camp established in 1874 on the west side of DEASE LK at the mouth of Dease Crk. It was the capital of

BC's 10 DEEPEST LAKES

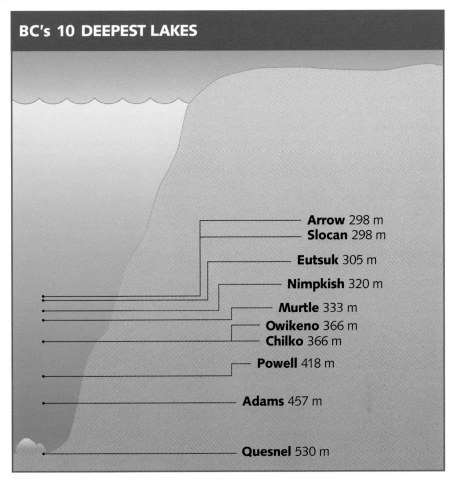

Arrow 298 m
Slocan 298 m
Eutsuk 305 m
Nimpkish 320 m
Murtle 333 m
Owikeno 366 m
Chilko 366 m
Powell 418 m
Adams 457 m
Quesnel 530 m

A view of Chilko Lk. Rick Blacklaws photo

the GOLD RUSH into the CASSIAR district in the mid-1870s, and a post office operated here from 1874 to 1880 under the name Cassiar. At its peak it had a population of 500, several hotels and saloons, a courthouse and a jail. By 1900 the GOLD was exhausted and the site was abandoned. Another short-lived mining settlement, Porter Landing, was at the north end of the lake.

LAM, David See Chai, real estate developer, philanthropist, lt gov 1988–95 (b 25 July 1923,

Hong Kong). He was the first CHINESE-Canadian to serve as a provincial LT GOV. During WWII his family had to relocate from Hong Kong to Macao, where at age 19 he went into his father's coal-importing business. Following the war he came to the US to study at Temple and New York universities. He then returned to Hong Kong in 1950; he became manager of a family-owned bank and engaged in a variety of other businesses. He immigrated to BC with his wife and children in 1967 and started a new career in real estate. He prospered, and in 1975 formed his own development company, Canadian International Properties. As his personal wealth grew, so did his involvement in a variety of community and charitable activities. On retirement in 1982, he and his wife Dorothy created their own charitable foundation, which has given millions of dollars to many organizations, including UBC, SFU, the UNIV OF VICTORIA, the VANCOUVER AQUARIUM and many hospitals and churches. In 1988 he was made a member of the Order of Canada, the same year he became BC lt gov. After retiring from the vice-regal post he returned to private business. He became a member of the ORDER OF BC in 1995.

LAMB, William Kaye, historian, librarian (b 11 May 1904, New Westminster; d 24 Aug 1999, Vancouver). After studying at UBC he pursued graduate work in Paris at the Sorbonne and at the London School of Economics. In 1933 he returned to UBC to teach in the history department. The following year he moved to VICTORIA to become provincial librarian, a position he held until 1940 when he returned again to UBC, this time as the university librarian. In 1948 he was appointed dominion archivist at the National Archives in Ottawa and from 1953 was also in charge of the newly created National Library of Canada. He was a member of the Historic Sites and Monuments Board from 1949 to 1957. He retired in 1969, the same year he was made a member of the Order of Canada. Lamb published extensively on the early history of BC and is known particularly for his edited versions of historical documents relating to the careers of explorers Daniel HARMON (1957), Simon FRASER (1960), Alexander MACKENZIE (1970) and George VANCOUVER (1985).

LAMBERT, Betty Lee, writer (b 23 Aug 1933, Calgary; d 4 Nov 1983, Burnaby). She was raised in urban poverty, and in her writing she dealt with social injustice, violence and oppression. She moved to VANCOUVER in 1951 to attend UBC. Her work as a copywriter at a radio station led her to begin writing radio plays, of which she produced dozens during her career. Many of her plays were for children, including *The Riddle Machine*, performed at Expo 67 in Montreal. *Grasshopper Hill*, about a love affair between a Canadian woman and a Holocaust survivor, won an ACTRA award for best radio play in 1980. Lambert taught English at SFU from 1965 until her death. Among her best known stage plays are *Sqrieux-de-Dieu* (1975) and *Jennie's Story* (1981). Her one novel, *Crossings*, appeared in 1979. She finished writing her last play, *Under the Skin*, based on a true story of kidnap and rape, just 3 months before she died of cancer.

LAMMING MILLS, 180 km southeast of PRINCE GEORGE on the upper FRASER R and the CNR line, was a SAWMILLING town established by the 4 Lamming brothers, who moved here from Alberta in the mid-1940s. The mill operated until the 1960s and the village at one time had a population of 250. By the end of the 20th century only a handful of families lived in the area.

AS

LAMPREY is a speedy, eel-like animal, 30–90 cm in length, inhabiting the cool depths of coastal waters. It migrates up rivers and streams to spawn in fresh water, and it constructs small nests by moving rocks with its mouth. The lamprey has no jaws but attaches itself to its prey—HERRING and SALMON are preferred—with a sucker mouth surrounded by teeth. With its rasping tongue the lamprey creates a raw wound, through which it draws sustenance from its host. Of 30 known species, 4 occur on the coast: Pacific lamprey (*Lampetra tridentata*), the largest; western brook lamprey (*L. richardsoni*), the smallest; and the mid-sized river lamprey (*L. ayresi*), the least common of the anadromous species. A lake lamprey (*L. macrostoma*) spends its entire life in fresh water, never migrating to the sea; in BC this species is confined to COWICHAN LK and nearby Mesachie Lk on VANCOUVER ISLAND.

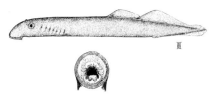

Pacific lamprey. Phil Edgell photo; drawing courtesy of Fisheries & Oceans Canada

LAND CLAIMS; *see* ABORIGINAL RIGHTS.

LANDAUER, Otto, commercial photographer (b 3 Oct 1903, Munich, Germany; d 19 Sept 1980, Vancouver). The son of a Munich carpet merchant, he went to work in his father's store at age 16 and took over the business in 1928. He was an avid mountaineer who took up PHOTOGRAPHY as a hobby on his mountain excursions. Faced with growing anti-Semitism in Germany, he left in 1937, ending up in Oregon for the duration of the war. He arrived in VANCOUVER in 1947, where he purchased Leonard FRANK's photography business and ran it for the next 33 years, specializing in commercial/industrial projects. Upon his death Leonard Frank Photos closed after 63 years in business.

LANDSLIDES are one of the most common geological hazards in BC and have been recorded in all mountainous regions of the province. They occur when gravity pulls a mass of earth, rocks or other debris down a slope. Depending on the materials involved and the manner in which these materials move during a slide, geol-

ogists classify different kinds of landslides as rockfalls, AVALANCHES, slumps; earthfalls, flows and topples; mudflows; and debris flows, torrents and slides. While most landslides affect wilderness or undeveloped areas, a number have occurred on inhabited sites and caused serious damage and casualties. At the BRITANNIA MINE in 1915, a rock avalanche killed 56 men; at Britannia Creek in 1921, 37 people died in a debris torrent. BC's most famous landslide occurred in 1965 near HOPE, where a rock slide killed 4 motorists and damaged a major highway (*see* HOPE SLIDE). Landslides are frequently caused by EARTHQUAKES and severe weather, but there are also human-generated causes and the risk to life and property increases as urban areas, recreational sites and resource extraction expand into landslide zones. *See also* DISASTERS.

Guy Robertson

LANE, Patrick, writer (b 26 Mar 1939, Nelson). During the 1960s and 1970s he worked at many jobs in western Canada, from ditchdigger to logger, catskinner and industrial accountant. His early poetry placed the Interior and the high country of the North in the Canadian literary imagination. His *Selected Poems* (1974) garnered a national audience for his poetry. In 1978 he won a GOV GEN'S LITERARY AWARD for *Poems New and Selected*. In 1992 he published a collection of short fiction, *How Do You Spell Beautiful?* Lane has been an editor, critic, commentator, gadfly and recluse. A resident writer at various Canadian universities, he returned to BC in 1991 with his companion, the poet Lorna CROZIER, to live on VANCOUVER ISLAND. His poetry collection *Too Spare, Too Fierce* won the BC BOOK PRIZE for poetry in 1996, and his *Selected Poems 1977–1997* was published in 1998.

Patrick Lane, 1998.
Barry Peterson & Blaise Enright-Peterson

LANG BAY, on the west side of Malaspina Strait 17 km southeast of POWELL RIVER, was the site of oxen LOGGING by Edward STAMP and RAILWAY

LOGGING by BC MILLS TIMBER & TRADING CO in the 19th century. The Lang family arrived in 1911. The bay remains an active LOG BOOMING and sorting ground. TOURISM has become important to the area, which has many fine beaches, and residential development has expanded. AS

LANGFORD, district municipality, pop 18,225, is located west of VICTORIA at the south end of VANCOUVER ISLAND. It is part of the Capital REGIONAL DISTRICT and was incorporated on 8 Dec 1992. The PUGET'S SOUND AGRICULTURAL CO, which helped the HBC colonize southern Vancouver Island, established one of its farms here. Capt Edward E. Langford, the bailiff, named the farm COLWOOD after his home in England. Rural for most of its history, the district has grown rapidly over the past 2 decades and is becoming the commercial and industrial centre of the group of communities clustered just to the west of Victoria. Thetis Lk and Mill Hill parks are located nearby, as is an AUTO RACING facility, the Western Speedway. AS

LANGLEY is located on the TRANS-CANADA HWY about 40 km east of VANCOUVER. The district municipality stretches from the FRASER R on the north to the US border and is bounded by MATSQUI on the east and SURREY on the west. It has always been an AGRICULTURAL area and 75% of the land remained rural by 1999. Farming has been a major economic activity, with vegetable, DAIRY, poultry, beef, BERRY and greenhouse products all important. Langley has more horses than any other municipality in BC, and equestrian centres and the artificial insemination and breeding of domestic animals is big business here. At the start of the 21st century it was also the largest MUSHROOM-producing area in Canada. Urban development is focussed in several communities, including ALDERGROVE, Brookswood, FORT LANGLEY, Willoughby, Willowbrook, MURRAYVILLE and WALNUT GROVE. Population rose dramatically following WWII as part of the suburbanization of the lower FRASER VALLEY. In 1955 the City of Langley (pop 22,523), which had long been the district's trade and service centre, was created as a separate entity. In the 1960s, with the building of the Trans-Canada Hwy, a residential and industrial construction boom commenced; warehousers, wood remanufacturers, an estate winery, machine shops, meat packers and HIGH-TECHNOLOGY companies flourish. The largest single employer is the OVERWAITEA FOOD GROUP, which has its head offices and distribution centre here. Fort Langley National Historic Park is near the site of the original HBC trading post, established in 1827. TRINITY WESTERN UNIV is the largest private university in western Canada. Willowbrook Shopping Centre on the edge of Langley City is a focus of commercial development.

Langley Prairie, 1940s.
Langley Centennial Museum

Population: 80,179
Rank in BC: 11th
Population increase since 1981: 80%
Date of incorporation: district 26 Apr 1873; city 15 Mar 1955
Land area: 317.65 km²
Location: Greater Vancouver Regional District
Economic base: farming, manufacturing, retail services, lumber

LANGLEY PRAIRIE, a rich AGRICULTURAL district in the FRASER VALLEY, in the municipality of LANGLEY, was first cultivated by FORT LANGLEY employees in the 1830s. Produce from their 8.1 km² farm was sold to Russian forts in Alaska in the 1840s. The HBC subdivided the land in 1877 and sold lots to newly arrived settlers. A commercial centre named Langley Prairie (originally Innes' Corners) developed where the BC ELECTRIC RWY CO line crossed Yale Road, a location now in the heart of the City of Langley. AS

LANGUAGES, FIRST NATIONS; *see* FIRST NATIONS LANGUAGES.

LANSDOWNE, J. Fenwick, artist (b 8 Aug 1937, Hong Kong). He came with his mother from China to live in VICTORIA in 1940. Earlier he had contracted polio; it was during the long

hours of convalescence that he developed an interest in birds. Despite his physical disabilities, he taught himself to draw and to paint. The first exhibition of his work was in 1952 at the ROYAL BC MUSEUM, where he often went to study the ornithological collections. He came to national attention in 1956 when, not yet 20 years old, he exhibited some watercolours at the Royal Ontario Museum in Toronto. Exhibitions in New York (1958) and London (1961) firmly established him as one of the foremost bird painters in the world. Many of his paintings were produced for a series of books that he began

Fenwick Lansdowne, wildlife artist.
Kate Williams photo

publishing in 1966. Because of his subject matter he is sometimes considered outside the artistic mainstream, but his work is extremely popular with a wide audience. He has been commissioned to produce paintings for the British Royal Family. He was inducted into the Order of Canada in 1977 and the ORDER OF BC in 1995. *See also* ART, VISUAL.

LANTZVILLE, pop 408, overlooks GEORGIA STRAIT 10 km north of NANAIMO on the east side of VANCOUVER ISLAND. Nanoose Collieries opened a COAL mine here in 1917. It was purchased by a Seattle company in 1920 and the townsite that grew up around the mine was named after a director of the company. Coal MINING continued through the 1930s. By the end of the 20th century Lantzville was a residential seaside community known for its winter population of SEA LIONS.

LAPEROUSE, Jean-François Galaup, Comte de, naval officer (b 23 Aug 1741, Albi, France; d June 1788, Melanesia). He joined the French navy at age 15 and served with distinction for the rest of his life, taking part in many naval operations during the long years of conflict between France and England during the last half of the 18th century. One of his most notable adventures was the successful raid on English trading posts in Hudson Bay in 1782. Inspired by Capt James COOK's explorations, the French in 1785 mounted an expedition to continue the work of scientific discovery in the Pacific Ocean, placing Lapérouse in command of 2 ships. After arriving in the Pacific via S America, he visited the coast of Alaska in July 1786, seeking a Northwest Passage. The 2 vessels left Alaska and sailed down the BC coast, where Lapérouse sighted the QUEEN CHARLOTTE ISLANDS but missed NOOTKA SOUND in the fog. He left BC waters without making a landfall and continued his exploration of the Pacific basin for another 2 years. In June 1788 both French vessels were wrecked at Vanikoro Island and every member of the expedition died.

LARCH trees are conifers occurring in BC in 3 native species. The largest species, western larch (*Larix occidentalis*), flourishes in the southeast corner of the province. It is an important timber-producing tree. Tamarack (*Larix laricina*) inhabits the northeast corner of the province and around PRINCE GEORGE. It prefers a cold, wet climate and usually grows in boggy ground. Its tough roots were prized by aboriginal people, who used them to sew their bark CANOES. More recently tamarack has been used as PULP AND PAPER stock. Alpine larch (*Larix lyallii*) grows at high altitudes in the southern Interior, sometimes forming the upper treeline in the CASCADES and ROCKY MTS. Larch are the only deciduous conifers in Canada; their soft green needles turn a brilliant gold before dropping in fall.

Western larch. © *T.C. Brayshaw*

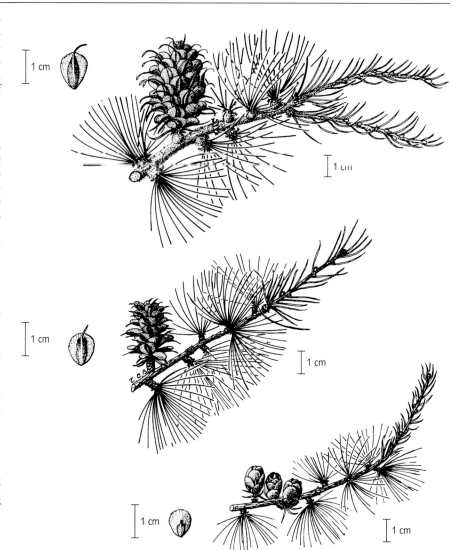

From top: Branches and cones, scales and bracts of the alpine larch, western larch, tamarack.
© *T.C. Brayshaw*

LARDEAU refers to the mountainous country northeast of upper ARROW LK in the W KOOTENAY, encompassing Trout Lk and the Lardeau, Duncan and Incomappleux rivers. It was the site of a SILVER mining boom in the 1890s, when several small MINING towns appeared: Thomson's Landing (later BEATON), TROUT LAKE CITY and FERGUSON. Camborne flourished briefly as a GOLD mining centre. At the height of the boom in 1902 there were about 100 silver mines, the Nettie-L being the most productive. LOGGING was also important; large SAWMILLS at Comaplix and ARROWHEAD exported lumber to the prairies. By WWI most of the mines and mills had closed. There was a brief mining revival in the 1930s, but most of the pioneer communities have become ghost towns. The town of Lardeau, pop 59 (formerly spelled Lardo), once a terminus for the ARROWHEAD & KOOTENAY RWY, is a tiny logging community on the shores of KOOTENAY LK.

LARGE, Richard Geddes, doctor (b 21 Oct 1901, Bella Bella; d 26 Apr 1988, Prince Rupert).

The son of the medical missionary R.W. LARGE, he studied medicine at the Univ of Toronto, then returned to the North Coast to work at mission hospitals in BELLA BELLA and HAZELTON. He was superintendent of the Port Simpson General Hospital (*see* FORT SIMPSON) from 1926 to 1931, then operated a private practice in PRINCE RUPERT from 1931 to 1982. Active in civic affairs, he was chair of the city school board from 1945 to 1956, served on city council and was president of the Museum of Northern BC for 25 years. He also found time to publish several local histories, including *Skeena: River of Destiny* (1957), *Prince Rupert, A Gateway to Alaska* (1960) and *Drums and Scalpel* (1968).

LARGE, Richard Whitefield, medical missionary (b Feb 1873, Orangeville, ON; d 20 Aug 1920, Prince Rupert). After working for a year as a schoolteacher in Ontario he attended medical school in Toronto, then came west to BC in 1898 to work at a hospital in STEVESTON. At the end of the year he transferred to BELLA BELLA and shortly afterwards was ordained a minister in the METHODIST CHURCH. He was the first long-term missionary at Bella Bella and the first permanent doctor on the central coast. During 12 years among the HEILTSUK (Bella Bella) people he made a large collection of their art and cultural artifacts, now in the Royal Ontario Museum in Toronto. At the end of 1910 he left Bella Bella to become superintendent of the hospital at Port Simpson (see FORT SIMPSON), where he remained until his death.

LARK is a ground-dwelling, SPARROW-sized bird inhabiting large fields and foraging for INSECTS and small seeds. Two species occur in BC. The horned lark (*Eremophila alpestris*) is found throughout the province and breeds over much of that range. In winter the highest numbers are found in the southern Interior, and in summer in the central Interior. The sky lark (*Alauda arvensis*) is a Eurasian species that was intentionally released at various points in BC's Lower Mainland and southeast VANCOUVER ISLAND (from VICTORIA to DUNCAN) in 1903. Their numbers and range grew for decades. But today, due to habitat loss, the sky lark is mainly limited to the Victoria International Airport and three other locations on the SAANICH PENINSULA of southern Vancouver Island.   *Kim Goldberg*

LARKIN, Peter Anthony, biologist (b 11 Dec 1924, Auckland, NZ, d 10 July 1996, Vancouver). He was one of Canada's leading fisheries experts. After graduating from the Univ of Saskatchewan in 1946, and attending Oxford Univ as a Rhodes Scholar, he worked as a fisheries biologist with the BC government and taught at UBC from 1948 to his retirement in 1989, when he became a professor emeritus. He was a member of the Science Council of Canada from 1971 to 1977 and served on a variety of national and international organizatons related to fisheries and marine management. Among many awards, he was named a Distinguished Canadian Biologist and a member of the Order of Canada (1995). *See also* FISHING, COMMERCIAL.

LASQUETI ISLAND, 68 km², pop 350, lies at the north end of GEORGIA STRAIT between VANCOUVER and TEXADA islands. It is the least developed of the GULF ISLANDS. Occupied by First Nations people at least seasonally for hundreds of years, it was named by a SPANISH expedition in 1791 after Juan Maria Lasqueti, a naval officer. The first settler was A.G. Tranfield, who began raising sheep at False Bay in the 1860s. Loggers began cutting the stands of red CEDAR in 1898 and some LOGGING has continued to the present. A cannery operated in False Bay from 1915 to 1926. In the 1950s local residents formed a commercial FISHING company that was still operating in 1999. Cultivation of MARIJUANA has become a significant economic activity.

LATIMER, Frank Herbert, irrigation engineer (b 23 May 1860, Kincardine, ON; d 10 Feb 1948). He was responsible for designing and constructing the irrigation systems that allowed the development of the TREE FRUIT industry in the OKANAGAN VALLEY. He was brought to BC in 1891 by Lord Aberdeen, who had just acquired the Coldstream Ranch and wished to plant orchards. Latimer designed a system to obtain water from Aberdeen Lk via the Grey Canal. He also designed irrigation systems at PEACHLAND, SUMMERLAND and NARAMATA as they were laid out, and in the post-WWI period he took charge of the lands project that opened up the OLIVER–OSOYOOS area to soldier settlement.

LAU, Evelyn, writer (b 2 July 1971, Vancouver). At age 14 she left her parents' home and spent 2 years on the streets in VANCOUVER. She wrote about her experiences with drugs and prostitution in her first book, *Runaway: Diary of a Street Kid* (1989), later made into a television movie. Her first volume of poetry, *You Are Not Who You Claim*, appeared in 1990 and won the Milton ACORN People's Poet Award. It was followed in 1992 by *Oedipal Dreams*, for which she was nominated for a GOV GEN'S LITERARY AWARD: she was the youngest poet ever to be so recognized. She has also published 2 volumes of stories, *Fresh Girls and Other Stories* (1993) and *Choose Me* (1999), and a novel, *Other Women* (1995). Much of her work deals with themes of eroticism and power.

LAUMANN, Silken Suzette, rower (b 14 Nov 1964, Mississauga, ON). She began ROWING at age 17 and joined the Canadian national team in 1983. After winning an Olympic bronze medal in double sculls in 1984 (with her sister Danielle) she moved to VICTORIA and in 1991 became the first Canadian woman to win a world championship in single sculls. That year

Silken Laumann displays the bronze medal she won for rowing in the 1992 Olympics in Barcelona.

she was named Canada's outstanding athlete. While preparing for the 1992 Barcelona Olympics she suffered a leg injury that threatened to end her career but she rebounded to win a bronze medal in the 2,000 m single sculls. Again she was chosen Canada's top female athlete. In 1995 she was disqualified from the Pan American Games following a positive drug test brought about by the mistaken use of cold medication. Undeterred, she won a silver medal at the 1996 Atlanta Olympics. Retired from rowing since 1999, she is a member of Canada's Sports Hall of Fame.

LAVEROCK, Lily, journalist, impresario (b 1890, Edinburgh, Scotland; d 2 Dec 1969, Duncan). After graduating with a philosophy degree from McGill Univ in Montreal, she returned to VANCOUVER, where she had earlier gone to school, and began work with the *World* NEWSPAPER as its first woman reporter. She was later women's editor of the *News-Herald*. In 1921 she began bringing theatrical acts to the city and during the inter-war years she booked many of the world's leading performers. She was the first of several Vancouver impresarios, including Hugh PICKETT and David Y.H. Lui.

LAVINGTON, a ranching (see CATTLE INDUSTRY) and LOGGING settlement on the CNR line 14 km east of VERNON, was named after Lavington Park, home of James Buchanan, a wealthy Scottish distiller who owned land here in the early 1900s and later acquired the Coldstream Ranch. Harold Thorlakson and his sons established a SAWMILL in the 1960s; it expanded to become a much larger and more diversified forest company, Tolko Industries, with interests across western Canada.   *AS*

LAW, Kelley, curler (b 11 Jan 1966, Burnaby). In 2000 she was skip of the Richmond Winter Club rink, consisting of lead Diane Nelson, second Georgina Wheatcroft and third Julie Skinner, which captured BC's third women's world CURLING championship. After qualifying for the worlds by winning the national Scott Tournament of Hearts championship, the rink travelled to Glasgow, Scotland, where in the finals it defeated the Swiss team in a tight 3-hour match. Law joined Linda MOORE (1985) and Pat SANDERS (1987) as world women's champions from BC and men's champion Greg MCAULAY of NEW WESTMINSTER and junior men's champion Brad Kuhn of KELOWNA to achieve a BC "triple crown" of world titles in 2000.   *SW*

LAWN HILL, on the east coast of Graham Island, 18 km north of SKIDEGATE in the QUEEN CHARLOTTE ISLANDS, was an AGRICULTURAL district that developed before WWI. Robert Scharfee and his wife operated a store and post office; the East Coast Farmers' Institute established an experimental farm, and there was a hotel. Most residents had moved away by the 1930s. The origin of the name is uncertain, though the 130-m hill itself was originally known as Long or Lone Hill.   *AS*

LAZO, an AGRICULTURAL district 6 km north of COMOX on VANCOUVER ISLAND, was settled in the 1890s by DAIRY and poultry farmers. Charlie Piggott ran a store and post office here from 1910 to 1920. Nearby Little River is the terminus for ferries to POWELL RIVER. Much of this area is now occupied by Canadian Forces Base Comox. Lazo is also the name of the nearby cape that extends eastward into GEORGIA STRAIT.   AS

LEAR, 9 km northeast of HOPE beside the Coquihalla R, was a station on the KETTLE VALLEY RWY named by Andrew MCCULLOCH, the railway's chief engineer, and his enthusiam for the plays of William Shakespeare is also reflected in the names of a number of stations on this section of the railway—Othello, JESSICA, Portia, Iago, Romeo, Juliet. The line was opened in 1916 and abandoned in 1959.   AS

LEE, Norman, rancher (b 1862, England; d Mar 1939, Lee's Corner). He went to the CHILCOTIN in 1884 to establish a ranch west of HANCEVILLE, in partnership with Hugh Bayliff. In 1898 he tried to drive a herd of 200 cattle 2,400 km to the Klondike to feed the miners during the GOLD RUSH. The drive bogged down at TESLIN LK, where Lee butchered the herd, loaded the meat onto scows and continued by water. A storm destroyed the scows and all the meat was lost. He returned to his ranch and rebuilt his herd. When Bayliff bought him out, Lee took over the store at Lee's Corner from Dan Nordberg. Following his death Lee's widow Agnes continued to run the store almost until her death in 1958. Their son Dan (d 1979) was a successful rancher for 50 years. *See also* CATTLE INDUSTRY.

LEE, Ronald Bick (Yat Yee), entrepreneur, community leader (b 1892, Toisan, China; d 22 Dec 1994, Vancouver). When he arrived in VICTORIA as a teenager he worked as a dishwasher. He then founded Foo Hung Co and prospered as an importer of Asian goods. He was also a philanthropist and leader in Vancouver's CHINESE community. His son, Robert H. Lee, a successful developer, was UBC chancellor from 1993 to 1996 and was named to the Order of Canada in 1999.

LEE-GARTNER, Kerrin, skier (b 21 Sept 1966, Rossland). She learned to ski while very young and joined Canada's national team by age 17. She participated in the 1988 Winter Olympics in Calgary and in World Cup competition placed 3rd and 5th in downhill races in 1990–91 and had a consistent 1991–92 season. But her SKIING career was marred by injuries and she was a 13th-seeded underdog at the 1992 Albertville Olympics when she shocked everyone by capturing the gold medal, Canada's first Olympic downhill gold. She continued to succeed throughout the 1992–93 season and finished 12th at the 1994 Olympics. She retired immediately after the Olympics and was inducted into the BC SPORTS HALL OF FAME later that year.   SW

Kerrin Lee-Gartner, 1988.
Les Bazso/Vancouver Province

LEECH, Peter John, surveyor (b circa 1828, Dublin, Ireland; d 6 June 1899). He came to BC in 1858 as a surveyor with the ROYAL ENGINEERS and, when the engineers were recalled in 1863, he took his discharge and remained in the colony. In 1864 he was second-in-command of the VANCOUVER ISLAND EXPLORING EXPEDITION, which discovered GOLD on a tributary of the Sooke R. The stream and the MINING camp were named for him (*see* LEECHTOWN). After serving on other surveying expeditions, including the attempt to string a telegraph line through BC to Siberia, he worked for the HBC from 1868 to 1883, rising in the company to take charge of the ESQUIMALT post. Subsequently he was VICTORIA city surveyor (1884–92), then went into private business. He made an important contribution to the early mapping of the province.

LEECHTOWN was a MINING camp on a tributary of the Sooke R, 40 km west of VICTORIA. Peter LEECH, a former ROYAL ENGINEER and member of the VANCOUVER ISLAND EXPLORING EXPEDITION, discovered GOLD on the creek in July 1864, sparking a rush of prospectors to the area. At its peak there were 3 hotels and 30 saloons, but the rush petered out and by 1875 the site was abandoned.

LEGAL AID, legal services for people who cannot afford to pay for them, is provided in BC by the Legal Services Society (LSS), created by the provincial government in 1979 as a merger of Legal Aid Society and Legal Services Commission. Legal aid is provided by lawyers and paralegals working in LSS offices (there are 59 throughout BC) or by lawyers in private practice on a referral basis. The LSS also funds the provision of services to aboriginal people and provides education and information about the law through a variety of programs. It is an independent, non-profit organization managed by a 15-member board; it is required to report financially to the legislature. LSS receives most of its funding from the province ($81.5 million in 1997–98), and additional funds from the federal government, the Law Foundation and the Notary Foundation. The demand for legal aid has risen dramatically since the creation of the LSS. In 1981 there were 34 offices with a staff of 161. Tariff costs for work billed that year came to $6.9 million. There were 50,726 applications for legal aid; 50% were referred to private bar lawyers. Total expenditures for the organization were $15.5 million. By 1997–98 there were 59 offices with the equivalent of 450 full-time staff. Tariff costs came to $52.8 million for the year, and there were 102,336 applications, 51% of which were referred to either staff or private bar lawyers. Total expenditures for the year were $85.2 million—down $12.9 million from the previous year—and the LSS had an accumulated deficit of $16.1 million.

LEGISLATIVE ASSEMBLY is the supreme law-making body in BC. Its members, Members of the Legislative Assembly (MLAs), are elected from constituencies throughout the province. The legislature is required to meet annually. It has become customary to convene a session in mid-Mar and continue sitting into June, but the time frame is flexible. The assembly meets in the LEGISLATIVE BUILDINGS overlooking the inner harbour in downtown VICTORIA. The first assembly in 1871 consisted of 25 MLAs; in the 1996 election voters selected 75 members and in the subsequent election that number increases to 79. Terms are for up to 5 years. Party distinctions have existed in the legislature since 1903. The party electing the most MLAs forms the government; the party with the next largest number of seats is the official opposition.

Legislation is devised in CABINET and the civil service, then debated and approved in the assembly. Proceedings are directed by the Speaker of the House, who is chosen by members in a secret vote. BC added a daily question period to assembly proceedings in 1973; it was the last province to do so. A written *Hansard* was introduced in 1970, and sessions have been televised since 1989. Six officers report directly to the assembly: the AUDITOR GENERAL; the chief electoral officer; the child, youth and family advocate; the CONFLICT OF INTEREST COMMISSIONER; the information and privacy commissioner; and the OMBUDSMAN. *See also* COLONIAL GOVERNMENT.

LEGISLATIVE BUILDINGS overlooking VICTORIA Harbour were constructed in stages from 1893 to 1916. They replaced the original colonial buildings, known as the Birdcages, which had housed the BC government since 1859. Designed by Francis RATTENBURY, the buildings utilized many BC materials, including granite from NELSON ISLAND and roofing slate from JERVIS INLET. A 2-m gilded statue of Capt George VANCOUVER graces the top of the central dome. Critics of the building project complained at its cost; mainlanders suspected it was an excuse to

The BC legislative buildings at night.
Roy Luckow photo

"anchor" the capital on the Island just as Victoria was being eclipsed by Vancouver. The first stage of the project opened on 10 Feb 1898; the Parliamentary Library was added in 1916. The building is outlined at night by 3,300 light bulbs. It went through extensive modernization and restoration in 1974.

LEHMAN, Jane (Bryant), nurse (b 1913, Absartee, MT; d 1983, Williams Lake). She arrived in BC in 1919 with her parents and 3 siblings; the family settled at SODA CREEK, then moved to the CHILCOTIN. Surmounting many obstacles, she trained as a nurse at Royal Inland Hospital and after graduation returned to ANAHIM LAKE, where her family was living. There she worked for the Department of Indian Affairs. For years she made monthly trips alone on horseback, in all weather, to the village of Ulkatcho 80 km away. She also took patients to hospital in BELLA COOLA, a 160-km ride over the MOUNTAINS. A dedicated nurse, "on call" to whomever needed help, she is credited with saving many lives. When she married and had twins she put the babies in baskets on either side of a packhorse and took them with her on her rounds. She refused any recognition when she was alive but was posthumously awarded the Red Cross Florence Nightingale Medal for outstanding service. *See also* NURSING. *Diana French*

LEJAC is a Nadleh Whut'en (*see* DAKELH) RESERVE on the south shore of FRASER LK, 50 km west of VANDERHOOF. It was the site of a RESIDEN-

TIAL SCHOOL operated by the ROMAN CATHOLIC CHURCH from 1922 to 1976, named for Father Jean Marie Lejacq, an OBLATE missionary. A large SAWMILL is the main employer. The grave site of Rose PRINCE attracts many pilgrims annually.

LEKWAMMEN (Songhees) are a group of NORTHERN STRAITS First Nations people who live at the south end of VANCOUVER ISLAND in the vicinity of VICTORIA. Traditionally they fished for SALMON and harvested CAMAS, an edible root-bulb traded along the coast. With the arrival of FUR TRADERS in the 1840s many of the

Lekwammen congregated in a large village near FORT VICTORIA, which they helped to build. This group became known as Songhees. They moved across the harbour in 1844 to a site known now as Old Songhees Village; they lived there until 1911, when they were pressured to move to their present location (pop 315) west of downtown. Another Lekwammen group established itself on the site of the Parliament Buildings (*see* LEGISLATIVE BUILDINGS). They were the Kosapsom, or Esquimalts, who later moved to their present site on ESQUIMALT Harbour (pop 135). The Lekwammen speak a Coast Salish language known as Northern Straits, which is a continuum of mutually understandable dialects and was also spoken by the Semiahmoo (pop 41) who live south of WHITE ROCK. *See also* FIRST NATIONS OF BC; FIRST NATIONS LANGUAGES; SALISHAN FIRST NATIONS.

LEMMING is a large mouse with very short ears and tail, inhabiting the tundras of the northern hemisphere. BC's most common species, the brown lemming (*Lemmus sibiricus*), is found in mountain tundras north from TWEEDSMUIR PROVINCIAL PARK. It is recognizable by its orange rump. Lemmings are herbivorous and forage

Northern bog lemming. R. Wayne Campbell photo

Old Songhees Village on Victoria Harbour, 1880s. The Songhees are now known as the Lekwammen. Richard Maynard/UBC BC650

beneath the snow during the winter. They are prone to rapid population explosions, followed by equally rapid population declines. This has given rise to the mistaken notion that they commit mass suicide by marching over cliffs into the sea. In fact their population cycle is regulated by breeding habits and predation.

LEMPRIERE, a former CNR station 170 km northwest of REVELSTOKE on the west side of the N THOMPSON R, was named after Capt Arthur R. Lemprière of the ROYAL ENGINEERS. He helped survey the CARIBOO WAGON ROAD and also designed Holy Trinity Church in NEW WESTMINSTER. An internment camp was located here during WWII (*see* JAPANESE, RELOCATION OF). AS

LENARDUZZI, Robert Italo "Bob," soccer player, coach (b 1 May 1955, Vancouver). He grew up in a SOCCER family in east Vancouver and became Canada's top player. He played semiprofessional for the Vancouver Spartans in 1969 before being recruited by England's Reading Club, with which he played for 5 years. He joined the new VANCOUVER WHITECAPS N American Soccer League franchise with his brother Sam in 1974 and remained with them

Bob Lenarduzzi, soccer star, playing for the Vancouver Whitecaps in the early 1980s.

for their 10-year existence. In 1978, playing midfield, he became the first Canadian to be named N American Player of the Year. The next year he had a major role in the Whitecaps' NASL Soccer Bowl victory over the Tampa Bay Rowdies. He was selected to the NASL all-star team in 1979, 1981 and 1984 and when the league folded in 1984 he had played more NASL games (312) than any other player. Internationally he was a

key member of Canada's national team 1973–86, helping it to qualify for the 1984 Los Angeles Olympics and the 1986 World Cup in Mexico, the only time in the 20th century that Canada appeared in the event. After the Whitecaps folded in 1984 he played professional indoor soccer in Tacoma, WA, then in 1987 became player-coach of the VANCOUVER 86ERS of the Canadian Soccer League. When he retired as a player in 1989 he became the team's general manager and the most successful coach in Vancouver professional sports history, leading the 86ers to 4 consecutive league championships (1988–91). He was named CSL Coach of the Year in 1988 and 1989. He left the team in 1993 to coach the Canadian national team but returned as general manager in 1998. SW

LENNIE, Beatrice, artist (b 16 June 1904, Nelson; d 1 June 1987, Vancouver). She moved to VANCOUVER with her family as a youngster and attended the Vancouver School of Decorative and Applied Arts (*see* EMILY CARR INSTITUTE OF ART & DESIGN) from 1925 to 1929. After further studies in San Francisco, she taught from 1933 to 1935 at the BC College of Art founded by Fred VARLEY and J.W.G. MACDONALD. She was both a painter and a sculptor and was involved in the THEATRE, designing sets and particularly masks. In the late 1930s she ran a school of sculpture in Vancouver, then taught art at CROFTON HOUSE SCHOOL from 1940 to 1975. She completed a variety of commissioned murals, sculptures and reliefs during her long career. *See also* ART, VISUAL.

LEO CREEK, a LOGGING camp and SAWMILL 95 km north of BURNS LAKE at the south end of TAKLA LK, was active in the 1970s and 1980s and was served by the DEASE LK branch of BC RAIL. The original name of Leo Crk was Leon, after Leon Prince, member of a prominent DAKELH (Carrier) family at FORT ST JAMES. AS

LEONARD, Stan, golfer (b 2 Feb 1915, Vancouver). As a youngster he caddied at Shaughnessy Heights GOLF Club and honed his game on VANCOUVER's public courses. At 17 he won the BC amateur championship with homemade clubs. He turned professional in 1937 and in 1942 became the pro at Marine Drive Golf Club in Vancouver. He was a prodigious driver with a fluid swing—and a strong temper when his game was not going well. During the 1950s he was among the best golfers in the world. He won the Alberta Open 9 times, the BC Open 5 times and the Canadian PGA championship 8 times, a record. In 1955 at age 40 he decided to join the PGA tour full-time and he won 3 titles: the Greater Greensboro Open in 1957, the Tournament of Champions in 1958 and the Western Open in 1960. In 4 of his 12 appearances in the Masters, he finished in the top 10. In 1959 he became the only Canadian ever voted player of the year by the Golf Writers' Assoc, but he won no major titles after 1960. Leonard made his last tournament appearance in a 1982 seniors event.

Stan Leonard, golfer, 1997.
Leita Cowart/Vancouver Sun

LESBIAN AND GAY RIGHTS; *see* GAY AND LESBIAN RIGHTS.

LESTER B. PEARSON COLLEGE OF THE PACIFIC is a private boarding school offering a 2-year international baccalaureate program to 200 senior high school students selected from countries around the world. Named for the former Canadian prime minister, it was established in 1974 in Pedder Bay west of VICTORIA. It is one of 8 United World Colleges, whose curricula emphasize public service and international understanding.

LETT, Sherwood, lawyer (b 1 Aug 1895, Iroquois, ON; d 2 July 1964, Vancouver). Raised in the Ottawa Valley, he arrived in VANCOUVER in 1912 with his family. He attended McGill Univ College (the forerunner of UBC) from 1912 to 1915 and on graduation enlisted in the army, seeing action in France from 1917 to 1918. When he returned to Vancouver he began articling as a lawyer, then won a Rhodes scholarship to study at Oxford from 1920 to 1922. He was admitted to the BC bar in 1922 and joined a Vancouver firm, where he specialized in corporate law. He took an active interest in UBC all his life, serving on the senate from 1924 to 1957, on the board of governors and as chancellor from 1951 to 1957. During WWII he again served overseas, where he was wounded twice, once at Dieppe in 1942 and once during the Normandy campaign in 1944. After the war he was one of the leading corporate lawyers in Vancouver. He served as Canadian representative on the Vietnam truce commission from 1954 to 1955 and became chief justice of the BC Supreme Court in 1955, a position he held until his death. His most controversial decision was to declare the expropriation of BC ELECTRIC RWY CO by the BC government illegal, forcing a renegotiation of the deal. His wife Evelyn Story Lett (1896–1999) was one of the first women graduates of UBC, where she received a BA in 1915 and an MA in 1926. For 60 years she was active in a wide variety of volunteer community work, including the SALVATION ARMY, the United Way, UBC, the VANCOUVER ART GALLERY and the Vancouver General Hospital.

Chief Justice Sherwood Lett (l) swearing in Fred Hume as mayor of Vancouver, Jan 1957. CVA Port.P.1427

LEWIS, Glenn, artist (b 1935, Chemainus). He graduated from the Vancouver School of Art (*see* EMILY CARR INSTITUTE OF ART & DESIGN) in 1958 and after living in England for several years, where he studied pottery with Bernard Leach, he returned to BC and during the mid-1960s taught ceramics at UBC. One of the founders of INTERMEDIA and the WESTERN FRONT, he was a pioneer in the creation of artist-run spaces. A conceptual artist who sometimes worked under the *nom d'art* Flakey Rose Hip, Lewis made porcelain sculptures, performed in DANCE theatre, made films and multimedia installations and even created a SYNCHRONIZED SWIMMING troupe, the New York Corres Sponge Dance School of Vancouver, whose members wore shark-fin bathing caps. He has been the subject of major retrospectives and his work is in the collections of the VANCOUVER ART GALLERY, the National Gallery of Canada and a variety of other public and private collections.

LI KA-SHING, entrepreneur (b 23 June 1928, Chaozhou, China). His family fled to Hong Kong in 1940 to escape Japanese invaders and on the death of his father 2 years later he was forced to leave school and go to work. In 1950 he established his own plastics company, and eventually specialized in plastic flowers, the basis of his enormous fortune. Li invested his profits in real estate and by 1979 he was the largest private landlord in Hong Kong. His first investment in BC was an apartment building in the West End of VANCOUVER in 1968. Other deals followed, including a Toronto hotel and a share of Husky

Oil in Alberta, but his largest investment was the 1988 purchase of the 84-ha site of EXPO 86 on FALSE CRK in Vancouver. His company, Concord Pacific Holdings, redeveloped the site into a multi-billion dollar downtown residential community. One of the richest people in the world, he remained in Hong Kong and delegated responsibility for his BC holdings to his sons. At the beginning of 1999 he turned over control of all his enterprises to his eldest son, Victor Li, and retired to devote time to charity.

LIARD HIGHWAY (Hwy 77) runs straight north from a point on the ALASKA HWY 27 km west of FORT NELSON, 137 km to the border between BC and the Northwest Territories. It continues another 260 km north to FORT SIMPSON on the Mackenzie R, following the LIARD R for most of its length. Construction began from the northern end in 1969 and the provincial government began building the BC section in 1972, but the entire road was not open to traffic until 1984. It is unpaved and isolated with only scattered facilities for travellers.

LIARD RIVER, 1,115 km long, originates in the Yukon's Pelly Mts and flows into BC just southeast of Watson Lake. The BC section, about 250 km long, is followed by the ALASKA HWY for much of its route before winding eastward around the top of the ROCKY MTS and north into the Northwest Territories. Eventually it joins the Mackenzie R at FORT SIMPSON. Its main tributaries in BC include the Dease, KECHIKA, Coal, Toad, and Fort Nelson rivers. The Liard flows through the territory of the KASKA First Nations, draining a watershed in BC of 1,434.07 km². The FUR TRADE arrived on the river in 1829 when the HBC established FORT HALKETT. It was surveyed for the Geological Survey by R.G. McConnell in 1887 and used by prospectors heading for the Klondike GOLD RUSH in 1897 and 1898, but it was not until construction of the Alaska Hwy during WWII that outsiders in any number had access to the river. Liard River Hotsprings Provincial Park (9.76 km²) is located where the highway meets the river from the south. It is named for a species of poplar growing on its banks.

Reading: Ferdi Wenger, *Wild Liard Waters*, 1998.

LIBERAL PARTY was one of the two dominant political parties, along with the CONSERVATIVE PARTY, in BC during the first half of the 20th century. It faded as a political force following the 1952 provincial election and did not regain a significant amount of electoral support until 1991.

The party emerged formally at a 1902 convention, and in an election the following year legislators in BC began identifying openly with particular parties. Prior to that time MLAs had divided themselves into shifting factions held together by personal relationships and self-interest rather than policies and/or principles. This arrangement proved highly unstable and party labels were accepted in an attempt to bring a semblance of order to government. The first Liberal leader was James A. MacDonald, a cor-

porate lawyer from ROSSLAND, who led the party with little success until he resigned to become BC Chief Justice just before the 1909 election. He was succeeded by John OLIVER, but when Oliver lost his seat in 1909 the party drifted without a leader, and with only two, then one, then no MLAs. Harlan BREWSTER took over in 1913 and led the Liberals to a stunning victory over a tired Conservative government in 1916, beginning 12 years of Liberal Party rule under Brewster (1916–18), Oliver (1918–27) and J.D. MACLEAN (1927–28). During this period, electoral support for the Liberals peaked at 50% of the popular vote, an all-time high. The Liberals finally lost power in the 1928 election; having lost his own seat, the uncharismatic Maclean resigned as leader and was succeeded by House Leader Duff PATTULLO in 1930. Pattullo managed to lead the party back to power in 1933 and thereafter moved it steadily leftward in response to the Depression and in an attempt to undercut support for the new CO-OPERATIVE COMMONWEALTH FEDERATION. Liberals were reduced to a minority in 1941 and at a special convention voted to form a COALITION GOVERNMENT with their Conservative rivals. Pattullo did not agree; he resigned and John HART took over as party leader and premier at the end of 1941. Because they held the most seats, the Liberals remained the senior partners in the coalition, naming the premier and senior cabinet ministers. When Hart resigned in 1947 he was succeeded by Byron JOHNSON, who remained premier until 1952. By this time coalition partners were divided on more and more issues and many Liberals began to believe the party could succeed electorally on its own, so no one objected when the coalition broke up. What few had counted on was the sudden appearance of SOCIAL CREDIT, which emerged from the 1952 election with more seats than any other party. The Liberals, who had effectively been in power for two decades, were reduced to 6 seats. It turned out that the 1952 election was a watershed for the party as it did not form another government during the 20th century. Byron Johnson lost his seat, so E.T. Kenney filled in as the party House Leader until Arthur LAING took over as leader in time for the 1953 election. Laing, who served from 1953 to 1959, and his successors Ray PERRAULT (1959–68) and Pat MCGEER (1968–72), managed to garner about 20% of the popular vote in successive elections, but none could muster more than a handful of seats in the legislature, as the middle-of-the-road Liberals were eclipsed by the bitter polarization between Social Credit and the CCF-NDP. The situation worsened during the 1970s. Under David ANDERSON's leadership (1972–75) the Liberals managed to hang on to 5 seats in the 1972 election, which was won by the NEW DEMOCRATIC PARTY; but the Liberal Party was devastated by the defection of 3 of its MLAs to the Socreds in 1975. Clearly Social Credit was the "free enterprise" alternative to the NDP and most of the Liberal electorate deserted the party. In the subsequent 4 elections the party managed to elect only one MLA, Gordon Gibson, who took over from Anderson just before the 1975 election. Gibson was followed by 3 equally ineffective leaders: Jev Tothill (1976–81), Shirley McLoughlin (1981–85) and Art Lee (1985–86). In 1987 the party acclaimed Gordon WILSON as new leader. Wilson made a remarkable impression during the 1991 election campaign and the party staged a surprising comeback, winning 33% of the popular vote, 17 seats and official opposition status in the legislature. Wilson was unable to consolidate this success, however. Weakened by personal scandal and party infighting, he was forced to step down and in 1993 lost the leadership to former Vancouver mayor Gordon CAMPBELL. Under Campbell the party actually won a plurality of the popular vote in the 1996 election but with 6 fewer seats than the NDP it had to be content to continue in opposition. The Liberals then staked out a position on the centre-right of the political spectrum, advocating tax cuts, government downsizing and balanced budgets while maintaining social spending.

LIBRARIES have operated in BC since the days of the FUR TRADE, when the NORTH WEST CO and the HBC provided libraries for traders stationed at remote posts. As the province developed and many immigrants and FIRST NATIONS people followed the resource industries from place to place, libraries or reading rooms were established in MINING, LOGGING, SAWMILLING and FISHING communities.

The first recorded library in BC belonged to John McKay, the surgeon aboard the ship *Experiment*, whose crew explored the NOOTKA SOUND area in 1786. The first circulating library, founded by William Fraser TOLMIE in Fort Vancouver in 1833, operated until 1843, when the HBC moved its operations to FORT VICTORIA. Within a decade the ROYAL ENGINEERS had established a reading room in NEW WESTMINSTER and stocked it with a collection chosen in England by the novelist and dramatist Edward Bulwer-Lytton. The materials, which included donations from Queen Victoria, were valued at £500.

But many communities in BC were small, remote and accessible only by sea or rail. Shipping books, magazines and NEWSPAPERS to them was prohibitively expensive, so John Bowron, one of the OVERLANDERS, who in 1864 established the first library in the CARIBOO, persuaded the government to absorb these costs, thereby obtaining BC's first postal subsidy.

In 1898 E.O.S. Scholefield, the parliamentary librarian in Victoria, established the "travelling libraries," boxes of books that schools or communities could borrow for several months at a time. Each library cost $6 and 18 of them were in circulation by 1900. Designed especially for BC's rugged terrain and scattered settlements, this system was unique in North America. It grew steadily for the next 15 years, aided by the CPR's willingness to ship books for free and by the hiring of Herbert Killam (later the superintendent of the Public Library Commission) to oversee the project from the provincial library (later the legislative library) in Victoria. There were 100 libraries circulating by 1918 and more than 1,100 in use by 1959. During the 1960s and

Fraser Valley bookmobile, c 1930.
Fraser Valley Regional Library

1970s the travelling libraries were phased out: bookmobiles had begun operating, and the Public Library Commission (later the BC Library Development Commission, and still later the Library Services Branch) was focussing on building facilities and formally training library staff.

In 1934 the FRASER VALLEY Union Library District was established to provide library services to a number of towns in the area, in a pilot project sponsored by Andrew Carnegie, the American philanthropist who built libraries all over North America, including 3 in BC. He funded the construction of buildings and the development of collections with the proviso that the community maintain them ever after. The Carnegie branch of the VANCOUVER Public

Library was built in 1903 with a $50,000 grant from the Carnegie Foundation; it was the first of 22 branches eventually opened throughout the city. In the late 1990s a small, vital branch library still thrived in the building, now the Carnegie Community Centre, in the Downtown Eastside area.

BC's need for library services grew through the 1930s and 1940s, and so did the development of services. By the 1950s, residents of most cities and towns had access to publicly owned reading materials. At the end of the 20th century the Fraser Valley Regional District administered 22 library branches throughout the valley, and 5 other public, federated/integrated/regional library systems were in place in BC. Bookmobile services, introduced in the Fraser Valley in about 1930, are still essential for many British Columbians living in remote areas and

The Carnegie Community Centre, Vancouver, built as the Carnegie Library in 1903. Philip Timms/UBC BC720

Vancouver Public Library, main branch, completed in 1995. *Jennifer Echols photo*

The BC Library Association (est 1911), an independent association of libraries and interested groups and individuals, listed 486 libraries in BC in 1999, about half of which are public libraries and the other half government, academic, school and special (non-governmental) libraries and archives. There are many more collections in both the private and the non-profit sectors. The Library Services Branch calculated that in 1998, public libraries in BC had a total income of $105 million, of which 83% came from local or municipal governments, 8% from the province and 9% from fundraising and other sources. The branch also calculated that 98% of BC residents were served by libraries in 1998, and that British Columbians were among the most literate people in North America, borrowing more than 45 million items—11.63 per capita, or about 50% more than any other region on the continent. *Karen Schendlinger*

LIDSTONE, Dorothy Carole (Wagar), archer (b 2 Nov 1938, Wetaskiwin, AB). She moved to VANCOUVER in 1955 and started shooting in 1962, developing into the best female archer in the world. She competed in her first Canadian championship in 1963 and set national points records while winning the Canadian title in 1969. Later that year she won the women's world championship in Valley Forge, PA, with a record-breaking score of 2,361 points, 110 more than the previous women's record and only 62 below the men's. She won the Canadian championship twice more, in 1970 and 1971. She was named senior athlete and overall athlete of the year in BC and was elected to the Canadian Sports Hall of Fame in 1970 and the BC SPORTS HALL OF FAME in 1982. *SW*

LIEUTENANT GOVERNOR is the Crown's representative in BC and therefore, theoretically at least, is the ultimate authority in the province. The lt gov is appointed by the gov gen on the prime minister's advice and originally acted as the eyes and ears of the federal government in the province. Today the appointment includes informal consultation with the premier and the lt gov is no longer considered a creature of Ottawa. The lt gov appoints the government; convenes, prorogues and dismisses the assembly; reads the Speech from the Throne; gives royal assent to all legislation; and has a variety of other responsibilities. However, most duties other than the purely ceremonial are exercised on the advice of the premier and assent to legislation is taken for granted. The lt gov's power to dismiss a premier was last used in 1903, before the emergence of identifiable political parties in the legislature. The lt gov last played an important role in selecting a premier in 1952 when Clarence WALLACE chose to allow W.A.C. BENNETT to form a government. The usual term of office runs 5 years, during which time the lt gov occupies Government House, the official residence. *See also* CARY CASTLE and entries for individual lt govs.

LIGHTHOUSES are aids to marine navigation operated by the Canadian Coast Guard. They warn of treacherous rocks, guide vessels into the proper navigation channels, mark entrances to harbours, help in SEARCH AND RESCUE and pro-

Sisters Rocks, the light station at Sisters Islets near Lasqueti Island.

vide weather information and tidal-wave warnings. There are 45 light stations on the BC coast, of which 18 were operating automatically and the rest were staffed by lightkeepers in 1999. The two earliest lighthouses—FISGARD and RACE

temporary working communities. They are also important in the Lower Mainland. The Vancouver Bookmobile service was inaugurated in 1956, when the city had only 7 library branches, and before long it was circulating some 13,000 items every month. It stopped operating in 1990 despite lobbying efforts by residents; Outreach Services continued taking library materials to seniors and disabled people in their homes.

In 1977 BC's public libraries initiated the BC Union Catalogue project to automate their catalogues. By 1981, with the participation of academic libraries and the provincial Library Services Branch, they established an online catalogue of over 1 million records, standardized for all libraries in the province. Automation became widespread; the internet and inter-library loan system provided even better access to library materials for residents of large and small communities.

BC LIEUTENANT GOVERNORS 1871–2000

Joseph Trutch	1871–76	J.W.F. Johnson	1931–36
A.N. Richards	1876–81	Eric Hamber	1936–41
Clement F. Cornwall	1881–87	William C. Woodward	1941–46
Hugh Nelson	1887–92	Charles Banks	1946–50
Edgar Dewdney	1892–97	Clarence Wallace	1950–55
T.R. McInnes	1897–1900	Frank M. Ross	1955–60
Henri-Gustave Joly de Lotbinière	1900–06	George Pearkes	1960–68
James Dunsmuir	1906–09	John R. Nicholson	1968–73
T.W. Paterson	1909–14	Walter Owen	1973–78
F.S. Barnard	1914–19	Henry Bell-Irving	1978–83
E.G. Prior	1919–20	Robert G. Rogers	1983–88
W.C. Nichol	1920–26	David Lam	1988–95
Robert Bruce	1926–31	Garde Gardom	1995–

LIGHTHOUSES OF BC

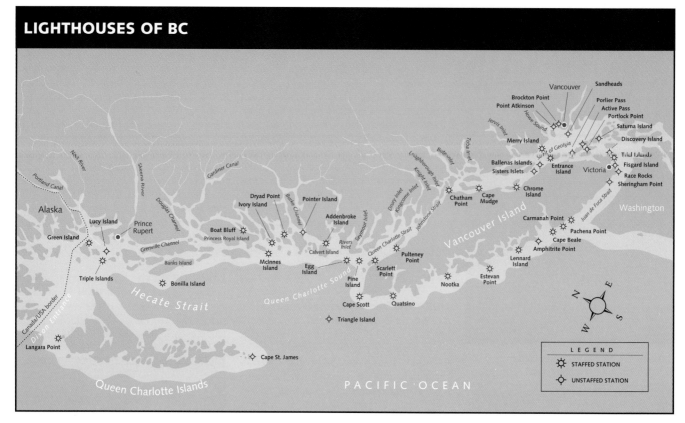

Cape Beale light station, shown in a painting by Buzz Walker.

Bob Noble, lightkeeper. Many BC boaters owe their lives to vigilant lighthouse staff.
Jim Ryan photo

ROCKS, both guarding the entrance to ESQUIMALT Harbour at the south end of VANCOUVER ISLAND—began operation in 1860. They were followed by several others built to guide marine traffic safely into the major ports: VICTORIA, VANCOUVER, NANAIMO and PORT ALBERNI. Beginning in the 1890s a series of lights were constructed along the west coast of Vancouver Island, including ESTEVAN POINT, at 38.7 m the tallest lighthouse on the Pacific coast. Light stations are also located in the GULF ISLANDS and up the INSIDE PASSAGE as far as Green Island, the most northerly light on the coast, at the entrance to CHATHAM SOUND. The last light to be added to the chain is on Bonilla Island in HECATE STRAIT, built in 1960. In the early 1990s the federal government, wanting to reduce costs, announced a policy of automation by which all stations eventually would be destaffed and visited only periodically for maintenance. Stiff opposition from coastal mariners worried about safety issues forced the government to cancel this policy early in 1998 and to maintain keepers at 27 lights.

LIGNUM LTD is an independent SAWMILL company in the BC Interior. It was started in 1946 by Leslie Kerr, the founding president of the Cariboo Lumber Manufacturers' Assoc. After operating several small mills in the CARIBOO and Shuswap areas, the company concentrated its operations in WILLIAMS LAKE, where its mill was a pioneer in the use of modern computerized equipment. Leslie Kerr's son John later became chairman. The company had sales of $204 million in 1997. *See also* FOREST INDUSTRY.

LIKELY, pop 375, located 94 km east of WILLIAMS LAKE where the Quesnel R enters QUESNEL LK, was a GOLD mining camp named for John Likely (1842–1929), a prospector with a taste for philosophy. During the 1920s he lectured his fellow miners on the philosophy of Plato and Socrates. The nearby Bullion Pit mine (1892–1942) left a crater 3 km long, washed out by hydraulic operations; it is considered the world's largest gold MINING pit. Another minor GOLD RUSH occurred during 1922–23 at nearby Cedar Creek, and the Mt Polley gold–COPPER mine opened in 1997.

LILLARD, Charles Marion "Red," writer (b 26 Feb 1944, Long Beach, CA; d 27 Mar 1997, Victoria). He grew up in Alaska, then moved to BC in the mid-1960s and studied creative writing at UBC. A poet, historian, teacher, editor, translator and sometime NEWSPAPER columnist, he published his first book of poetry, *Cultus Coulee*, in 1971 and went on to publish more than 25 other books while making varied contributions to the VICTORIA literary community. His history of VANCOUVER ISLAND, *Seven Shillings a Year*, won a LT GOV's Medal in 1986; a volume of poetry, *Circling North*, won a Dorothy LIVESAY poetry prize in 1989 (*see also* BC BOOK PRIZES); and his last book of poetry, *Shadow Weather: Poems, Selected and New* (1996), was shortlisted for a GOV GEN'S LITERARY AWARD. His last book, a history of CHINOOK JARGON co-written with Terry GLAVIN, was published posthumously.

Charles Lillard, writer.

LILLOOET, district municipality, pop 1,988, occupies the benchlands beside the FRASER R 325 km northeast of VANCOUVER, 65 km north of LYTTON. It was originally known as Cayoosh Flat because the body of a dead horse (a "cayuse") was found here. The present name comes from the local FIRST NATIONS people, the ST'AT'IMX (Lillooet). To the north, the confluence of the Fraser and BRIDGE rivers at the Six-Mile Rapids was a popular SALMON-fishing site, not only for the St'at'imx but for First Nations from all over the province (*see* FISHING, ABORIGINAL). The community boomed in the 1860s with the discovery of GOLD on the Fraser and in the CARIBOO. It was the terminus of the DOUGLAS TRAIL from HARRISON LK, used by miners to avoid the steep, narrow canyons of the Fraser. With the building of the CARIBOO WAGON ROAD, Lillooet became Mile 0, but once the GOLD RUSH waned the population declined. The Pacific Great Eastern Rwy (*see* BC RAIL) arrived in 1912 and during WWII JAPANESE Canadians from the coast were interned here (*see* JAPANESE, RELOCATION OF). By the late 1990s the largest employer was the FOREST INDUSTRY. Incorporated as a village on 20 Dec 1946, Lillooet is a centre for GINSENG growing and shares with Lytton the distinction of being the hottest spot in Canada: on 16 July 1941 the temperature reached a record 44.4°C. With the paving of the Duffey Lake Road from PEMBERTON, the community has become a popular destination with regional travellers.

LILLOOET First Nation; *see* ST'AT'IMX.

LILLOOET RIVER, 145 km, originates with meltwater from the Lillooet Glacier high in the COAST MTS north of VANCOUVER and flows south and east past the towns of PEMBERTON and MOUNT

View of Lillooet and surrounding area.
Rick Blacklaws photo

CURRIE to empty into the north end of HARRISON LK. A widening of the river near Pemberton forms Lillooet Lk (35.3 km²). The lower river valley from Harrison Lk north was part of the DOUGLAS ROAD to the Interior, used between 1858 and 1862. Since that time most of the watershed has undergone LOGGING. The river encompasses the traditional territory of the Lil'wat First Nation, a branch of the ST'AT'IMX. Aside from Mount Currie, there are 3 small Lil'wat communities along the river between Harrison and Lillooet lakes (*see* SKOOKUMCHUCK).

LIMNERS is a group of VICTORIA visual artists, founded in 1971, who meet socially and sometimes exhibit together. The name refers to the itinerant artists in Europe who painted portraits and illuminated manuscripts in the Middle Ages. The group's original members were the painters Maxwell BATES, Herbert Siebner (b 1925), Myfanwy PAVELIC, Richard Ciccimarra (1924–73), and Nita Forrest (b 1926); the sculptors Elza Mayhew (b 1916) and Robert deCastro (1923–86); the collagist and writer Robin SKELTON; the calligrapher Sylvia Skelton; the mixed media artist Karl Spreitz (b 1927); and a non-exhibiting member, Nikola Pavelic. The group has survived the deaths of several founders and has added new members: Colin Graham and Jack Wilkinson, painters; Walter Dexter, Jan Grove and Helga Grove, ceramists; Carole SABISTON, a textile artist; and Pat Martin Bates, a printmaker.

LIMPET is a small (to 50 mm across) marine MOLLUSC belonging to the gastropod class. Its soft body is protected by a single cone-shaped shell. It inhabits inshore waters along the coast, where it attaches to rocks, other solid objects and SEAWEED. Limpets are primarily herbivores. Many species are present in BC. Members of one family, known as keyhole limpets, have a hole at the top of the shell, which distinguishes them from so-called "true" limpets. They are prey for birds, SEA STARS and SNAILS. FIRST NATIONS harvested limpets for food but there is no commercial harvest.

LINDELL BEACH, a recreational community 20 km east of ABBOTSFORD at the south end of CULTUS LK, was named for Andrew F. Lindell, a Swedish settler who had a farm here in the 19th century. The agricultural district south of the beach to the US border was served by a post office called Lindell but is better known as the Columbia Valley.   AS

LINGCOD (*Ophiodon elongatus*) belongs to a family of FISH called greenlings, and it is the only Canadian greenling whose large mouth is filled with canine-like teeth. Other defining characteristics are small scales and a long single dorsal fin. Its colour varies with its surroundings, but it is mainly dark mottling over brown, grey, green or

Lingcod. Rick Harbo photo; drawing courtesy Fisheries & Oceans Canada

blue shades. Lingcod grow up to 150 cm long and weigh up to 45 kg, with females attaining a much larger average size than males. Their range extends from California through BC to Alaska. Lingcod live on the rocky ocean floor and are often found along shorelines and around reefs subject to strong current flows. Peak spawning occurs from Dec to Mar when the female deposits her eggs under a rock or in a crevice. The male uses his large pectoral fins to fan water over the eggs and guard them from predators. Lingcod are voracious carnivores, feeding on other fish, crustaceans, OCTOPUS and even smaller lingcod.

Lingcod are prized by sport fishers (*see* FISHING, SPORT) and are harvested along the BC coast by commercial GROUNDFISH trawlers and by hook and line. In 1998 the coastwide commercial fishery landed 2,000 tonnes with a wholesale value of $5 million. Due to a severe population crash attributed to overfishing, the commercial fishery in GEORGIA STRAIT was closed in 1990 and severe restrictions were placed on the sport fishery. *See also* FISHING, COMMERCIAL.

LION ISLAND lies in the south arm of the FRASER R in the channel south of LULU ISLAND and west of ANNACIS ISLAND. It was the site of an early

SALMON CANNERY owned by Alexander EWEN, an industry pioneer (*see also* FISHING, COMMERCIAL). In 1902 a colony of JAPANESE fishers and their families settled on the island and on neighbouring Don Island under the leadership of Jinsaburo Oikawa, an entrepreneur. The colonists exported salted salmon and salmon roe, produced soy sauce and sake, cleared farms and worked at the fishery. Oikawa returned to Japan in 1917 and the colonists gradually abandoned the islands. They are owned by the GREATER VANCOUVER REGIONAL DISTRICT and in the late 1990s were slated for development as parkland.

LIONS are twin peaks in the North Shore mountains overlooking BURRARD INLET and downtown VANCOUVER. Symbolic guardians of the entrance to Vancouver's harbour, known as the Lions' Gate, the Lions were known as Chee-Chee ("Twins") to the SQUAMISH people. The present name was suggested in about 1890. The first recorded ascent of the West Lion (el 1,646 m) took place in 1889 by a party led by Joe CAPILANO, a Squamish chief. The first recorded climb of the East Lion (el 1,599 m) was in 1903 by 3 brothers, William, John and Robert Latta. The West Lion, accessible from GROUSE MT or the HOWE SOUND CREST TRAIL, is still a popular, though arduous, hiking trail. The East Lion is in Vancouver's water supply watershed and is out of bounds to recreationists.

LIONS BAY, village, pop 1,347, is a residential community perched on the steep side of HOWE SOUND, 11 km north of HORSESHOE BAY. The name refers to the famous twin mountain peaks, the LIONS, which loom above it. Originally a collection of summer cottages, Lions Bay developed a more permanent population after the completion in 1958 of Hwy 99, the SEA TO SKY HWY. Lions Bay was incorporated as a village in 1971.

In 1983 flooding killed 2 teenagers and destroyed 5 homes; water-control structures were built to protect the community.

LIONS GATE BRIDGE spans the First Narrows at the entrance to BURRARD INLET and connects VANCOUVER to its North Shore suburbs, NORTH VANCOUVER and WEST VANCOUVER. The bridge was built during the depths of the Depression by a financial consortium, organized by engineer Alfred James Towle TAYLOR and backed by Guinness, the British brewing family, who wished to provide access to its BRITISH PROPERTIES residential development in West Vancouver. It is a suspension bridge, modelled on the Golden Gate Bridge in San Francisco. The proposal to build it encountered stiff opposition because it would be necessary to construct a roadway through the heart of STANLEY PARK, but it was finally approved because it offered jobs to unemployed workers. The span opened to pedestrians on 12 Nov 1938 and to vehicles 2 days later, and the owners of the bridge collected a toll from drivers. The provincial government purchased the bridge in 1955; tolls were discontinued in 1963. In 1986, as part of Vancouver's centennial, the bridge was illuminated with decorative lighting, nicknamed "Gracie's Necklace" after MLA Grace MCCARTHY, whose idea it was to approach the Guinness family to pay for the lights. By the 1990s the bridge had deteriorated and the provincial government, after much public debate, decided to renew the structure rather than replace it.
Reading: Lilia D'Acres and Donald Luxton, *Lions Gate*, 1999.

LIQUOR DISTRIBUTION BRANCH (LDB) was established as the Liquor Control Board (LCB) in 1921 by the *Government Liquor Act*, the same legislation that abolished PROHIBITION. The

South end of Lions Gate Bridge, 1938. VPL 15015-14

3-person board was set up to regulate the sale of liquor through government stores, making BC the first province to choose government control of liquor distribution. The first stores opened on 15 June 1921. Following a 1924 plebiscite, the government began allowing sales of beer by the glass in licensed premises; hotel beer parlours began opening the next year. These were the parlours familiar to patrons until the 1970s—no food, no entertainment and separate sections for women. After a decade of corruption and patronage, the LCB was reduced in 1932 to one person, W.F. Kennedy, who remained liquor commissioner until 1951. He was succeeded by Lt Col Donald McGugan, who held the job to 1969. Known to journalists as the "liquor czar," McGugan was an aloof administrator who ran the LCB as his own personal fiefdom. For the most part, the SOCIAL CREDIT government (1952–72) followed a restrictive liquor policy. During the short-lived NDP administration (1972–75), policy grew more liberal. Neighbourhood pubs were allowed, along with entertainment in beer parlours. This trend continued in the 1980s with the appearance of brew pubs, cottage breweries, Sunday drinking and private beer and wine stores.

In the early 1970s the LCB became the Liquor Administration Branch, which divided in two in 1975: the Liquor Distribution Branch, a CROWN CORPORATION, took responsibility for liquor stores, while the Liquor Control and Licensing Branch looked after licensing. In 1999 the LDB reported total revenues of $1.64 billion from 223 government stores and 142 agency stores that operate privately but share revenues with the LDB. There are also about 350 private retail outlets (cold beer and wine stores, wine stores and duty-free stores) in the province. As of 1999 there were 7,628 licensed premises and 101 licensed manufacturers of alcoholic beverages, including wineries, breweries and distillers.

LISTER, formerly known as Camp Lister, 6 km southeast of CRESTON in the Creston Valley, was the site of a WWI soldier resettlement program. A farming community (*see* AGRICULTURE) developed, named after Col Fred Lister, who administered the project and later became a local MLA. This rural district has a community hall and a demolition derby grounds.   AS

LITERARY MAGAZINES; *see* MAGAZINES, LITERARY.

LITERATURE; *see* essay at right.

LITTLE FORT, pop 175, 85 km north of KAMLOOPS, was the site of an HBC fur-trading outpost during 1850–52. Known for many years as Mt Olie, after the pioneer Olie Oleson, it was originally settled by ranchers in the 1890s (*see* CATTLE INDUSTRY). A hotel opened in 1913. LOGGING and TOURISM have become the important economic activities. One of BC's few remaining current-driven ferries crosses the N THOMPSON R here, backed up by an aerial passenger tramway.   AS

LITERATURE OF BC

Overview

Howard White

Literature has a long history in BC. The province traditionally leads the nation in per capita book purchases and LIBRARY use, and has the strongest market for regional books in English-speaking Canada. It is not unusual for favourite local titles such as *The Curve of Time, Raincoast Chronicles First Five* or *Never Fly over an Eagle's Nest* to sell in excess of 50,000 copies—enough to be ranked as national bestsellers in many larger countries.

Aboriginal Literature

The first BC literature, that of the aboriginal peoples, has been largely lost but enough fragments survive to indicate a highly developed oral tradition with a great variety of forms. Some work was sacred or ritualistic and some was secular and functional. Poetry, song, drama and prose were all present. Creativity was protected and encouraged by a highly developed concept of intellectual property. Among the sacred texts, some works gave explanations of the origins of various family rights and told of the encounters of ancestors with power-giving supernatural beings; these were recited within the family to pass on the historical knowledge to new generations, or used in public to validate claims to certain privileges. Another class of sacred texts was the songs and chants used by shamans for curing the ill and casting spells, or by individuals to summon personal powers. Such sacred works were considered to be some of the owner's most valuable private property. Secular works were often considered common property, being used for general entertainment and instruction. Some of these were lengthy origin myths rivalling Norse sagas in their complexity, while others were short, humorous tales improvised to entertain children. They often featured the trickster figures raven and mink on the West Coast, and coyote in the Interior. Certain legends like the story of the salmon boy, copper woman, the snot boy, the wild woman of the woods and the thresher myth were widely distributed but modified with local details by individual groups.

The most methodical and prodigious collector of aboriginal literature was the German-American anthropologist Franz BOAS, whose main compilations include *The Mythology of the Bella Coola Indians* (1898), *Kwakiutl Texts* (1905–6), *Tsimshian Mythology* (1916) and *Kutenai Tales* (1918). Boas extended his work by training local ethnographers to carry on in his absence, resulting in *Mythology of the Thompson Indians* (1898) and *Traditions of the Thompson Indians* (1912) by James TEIT and *Ethnology of the Kwakiutl* (1921) with the KWAKWAKA'WAKW collector George HUNT. Hunt was the first aboriginal author to publish his own traditional

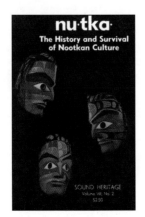

literature in written form, although he worked under Boas's close supervision. Among the TSIMSHIAN Henry Wellington Tate performed a similar role for Boas, collecting most of the material in his *Tsimshian Mythology*. Some of Tate's work was republished in 1993 as *The Porcupine Hunter and Other Stories: The Original Tsimshian Texts of Henry Tate* (ed Ralph Maud). William BEYNON (1888–1958), a native Tsimshian, collected literary artifacts for the Canadian government under the direction of the ethnographer Marius BARBEAU and wrote an unpublished history, *Ethnical and Geographical Study of the Tsimsiyaen Nation*. Other early texts of importance are *Haida Texts and Myths* by

John Swanton (1905) and Charles HILL-TOUT's monographs on the SQUAMISH (1897), Thompson (1899) Lillooet (1905), HALKOMELEM (1902) and SECHELT (1904). Later ethnographies that contain some transcribed aboriginal literature are *The Bella Coola Indians* (1948) by Thomas F. MCILWRAITH and *Tsimshian Myths* (1961) and *Totem Poles* (1950) by Marius Barbeau.

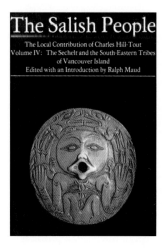

As more aboriginal people became fluent in English, popular "as-told-to" accounts of traditional literature became more common, though the total remains disappointingly small. *Legends of Vancouver* (1911) is a sentimentalized but enduringly popular rendering of a group of origin myths given to the celebrated MÉTIS poet Pauline JOHNSON by Chief Joe CAPILANO (1840–1910). *Men of Medeek* is a tribal history of the Kitselas band by Chief Walter Wright rendered with some of the art of the aboriginal teller by Will Robinson (1935); and *Conversations with Khahtsahlanough* (1955) by August Jack KHAT-

SAHLANO (1876–1967) and J.S. MATTHEWS, is a collection of legends and accounts by Khatsahlano, a Squamish elder. Transcribed collections of traditional stories by later informants include *Lillooet Stories* (1977) by Dorothy Kennedy and Randy Bouchard and *Write it on your Heart: The Epic World of an Okanagan Storyteller* (1988) by Harry ROBINSON and Wendy Wickwire. In a class by themselves are traditional works written directly in English by aboriginal writers, the most outstanding being George CLUTESI, the NUU-CHAH-NULTH (Nootka) author of *Son of Raven, Son of Deer* (1967) and *Fables of the Tse-Shaht* (1994). Clutesi, an artist and actor as well as author, also wrote *Potlatch* (1969), a view of Nuu-chah-nulth ceremonial life, and *Stand Tall My Son* (1990), a statement of his philosophy.

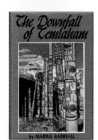

Many other storytellers departed from the traditional to offer their own views and tell their own life histories, both with the aid of ghost writers and on their own. One of the earliest and also one of the most entertaining is *Smoke From Their Fires* (1968), a memoir of Charles James Nowell (b 1870), a Kwakwaka'wakw elder, as told to Clellan Ford. Of similar vintage is "The Faith of a Coast Salish Indian" (1955), a biographical study of KATZIE shaman Xa'xc'elten (b 1855) by the anthropologist Diamond Jenness. Later autobiographical works include *Guests Never Leave Hungry* (1972) by James SEWID with James Spradley (1972); *The Days of Augusta* (1973) by the SECWEPEMC (Shuswap) elder Mary Augusta Tappage with Jean Speare; *During My Time: Florence Edenshaw Davidson, A Haida Woman* (1982) by DAVIDSON as told to Margaret Blackman; *Assu of Cape Mudge* (1989) by the Lekwiltok elder Harry ASSU with Joy Inglis; and *Bella Coola Man* (1994) by the NUXALK elder Clayton MACK with Harvey Thommasen. Among the most popular of all books featuring aboriginal personalities was the oratorical *My Heart Soars*, by the celebrated Squamish actor Chief Dan GEORGE and his speechwriter, Father Herbert Dunlop.

From the 1970s onward a new generation of aboriginal BC writers began to publish novels and poetry that draw on the traditions of English literature to render contemporary Native experience. These writers include Lee MARACLE, Skyros Bruce, Jeannette ARMSTRONG and Richard Van Camp. Traditional literature has had a strong influence on such non-aboriginal writers as Howard O'HAGAN, Christie HARRIS, Catherine Anthony CLARK, Robert BRINGHURST and others. *A Guide to Indian Myth and Legend* by Ralph Maud provides a useful overview of the Northwest Coast tradition and in *A Story Sharp as a Knife* (1999) Robert Bringhurst argues that its greatest achievements deserve to be ranked among the classics of oral literature.

Euro-Canadian Literature

The earliest Euro-Canadian writers in BC were the first European explorers, most of whom considered it an important part of their duties to keep detailed diaries for later publication as books. The journals of James COOK, George VANCOUVER,

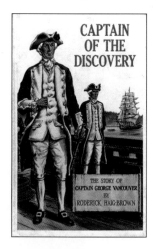

Alexander MACKENZIE, Simon FRASER and David THOMPSON in particular stand out as some of the best exploration literature and did much to form the world's mental image of the region, a role they continue to serve in modern editions. The FUR TRADE era produced a considerable literature owing to the British appetite for books about remote corners of Empire and to the formidable diary-keeping habits of 19th-century traders like Alexander Caulfield ANDERSON, Daniel HARMON, Dr John MCLOUGHLIN, Peter Skene OGDEN and John WORK.

The first opportunity for BC residents to read and write about themselves was provided by early NEWSPAPERS. *The British Colonist* was founded in VICTORIA on 11 Dec 1858 by Amor DE COSMOS, while John ROBSON founded the NEW WESTMINSTER *British Columbian* on 13 Feb 1861. Voters were sufficiently

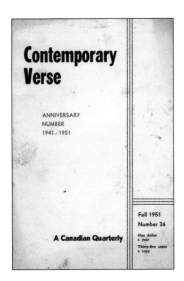

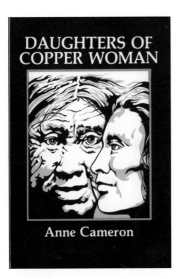

appreciative of this enhancement to colonial life that both de Cosmos and Robson were later elected premier. Settlers' hard struggle for survival left little time for writing, and 19th-century pioneer literature was limited mostly to diaries and letters, with the occasional memoir such as "Recollections of a Pioneer of the Sixties" by Susan ALLISON (reprinted as *A Pioneer Gentlewoman in BC*, 1976). Alfred WADDINGTON, the tireless pioneer entrepreneur, found time to write a book chiefly notable for being the first one actually published within the province, *Fraser Mines Vindicated, Or the History of Four Months* (1858). Gilbert Malcolm SPROAT, another gentleman entrepreneur, wrote several books reflecting his energetic travels and broad interests, including *Scenes and Studies of Savage Life* (1868). Missionaries were particularly diligent writers, the most outstanding being the OBLATE Father A.G. MORICE (1859–1938) whose *History of the Northern Interior of British Columbia* (1904), *History of the Catholic Church in Western Canada* (1904) and *The Carrier Language* (1932) remain important works in their fields. Father J.M. Le Jeune earned special distinction by publishing a newspaper in CHINOOK JARGON, the *KAMLOOPS WAWA*, from 1891 to 1917.

British Columbia, 1792–1887, published in 1887 by Hubert Howe BANCROFT, served notice that the brevity of BC history would not prevent its becoming the most popular subject of local readers. Bancroft's work was followed by a long series of histories including those by Father Morice, and Captain John T. WALBRAN's *British Columbia Place Names 1592–1906* (1909), still serving as the province's de facto maritime history. Alexander Begg's 3-volume *History of the North-west* appeared in 1894, only to be superseded by the 4-volume *British Columbia from the Earliest Times to the Present*

(1914) by Judge F.W. HOWAY and E.O.S. Scholefield, the standard reference until *British Columbia: A History* (1958) by Margaret ORMSBY and *The West Beyond the West* (1991) by Jean Barman. BC's passion for history has also been reflected in a long series of journals, including *The British Columbia Historical Quarterly* (1937–58), *Sound Heritage, Canada West, RAINCOAST CHRONICLES, BC Historical News* and BC STUDIES.

Although BC was not known for poetry until the emergence of the "West Coast scene" in the 1960s, a literary MAGAZINE, *Westminster Hall*, was being published as early as 1911, and when the poet Pauline Johnson died in 1913, thousands of people lined the streets of VANCOUVER to honour her. Isabel Ecclestone MACKAY (1875–1928) tried to follow in Johnson's footsteps,

giving dramatic readings to full houses at the Pender Auditorium and publishing 4 books of verse between 1904 and 1930. Tom MacInnes (1867–1951), son of BC Lt Gov Thomas MCINNES (their names were spelled differently), published the first of his 8 books of highly mannered verse, *A Romance of the Lost*, in 1908, and went on to achieve the kind of mass popularity today's poets can only dream of. Audrey Alexandra BROWN, the first important BC poet born in BC, began a distinguished career with publication of *A Dryad in Nanaimo* in 1931 and Floris McLaren introduced a more modern note with *Frozen Fire* in 1937, followed by Anne MARRIOTT's *Calling Adventurers* (1941), which earned BC its first GOV GEN'S LITERARY AWARD for poetry. Robert SWANSON's chapbooks of spirited LOGGING ballads sold an estimated 80,000 copies during the 1940s and 1950s, exclusively along the BC coast.

The first BC novels appeared around the turn of the 19th century and in 1906 Martin Allerdale GRAINGER published one that came to be recognized as a BC classic, *Woodsmen of the West*. Grainger also anticipated the experience of later novelists by seeking more remunerative work and published no further books during his lifetime. Hubert EVANS (1891–1976), having earned only $400 from *The New Front Line*, his sturdy 1927 novel about a WWI veteran returning to do battle with the BC wilderness, turned to other forms and didn't write another novel about BC for 27 years. Howard O'Hagan's fanciful reworking of the Yellowhead legend, *Tay John*, became a critical sensation when reprinted in 1974, but was so unsuccessful in its original British publication (1939)

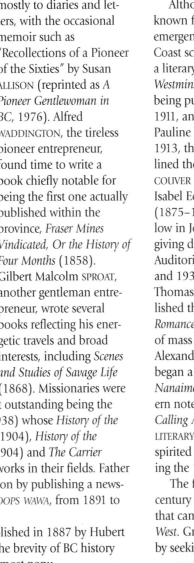

George Ryga's The Ecstasy of Rita Joe

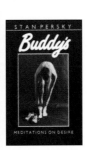

that O'Hagan didn't publish another novel for 44 years.

Evans learned he could make his stories saleable by replacing BC place names with US ones, though he reverted to authentic names in *Mist on the River* (1954), a superb novel of Native white cultural conflict on the SKEENA. R. Frederick NIVEN

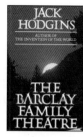

(1878–1944) began writing about Canada for Scottish newspapers and published some 30 novels about Scotland and Scottish-Canadians. Bertrand W. SINCLAIR (1881–1976) first moved from Ontario to Montana, where he established a US following writing COWBOY stories, then moved to BC and continued to mix popular novels of the wild west with novels like *Poor Man's Rock* (1920) and *The Inverted Pyramid* (1924), written in

the same pulp magazine style about BC fishers, loggers and settlers. His US publishers were unenthusiastic about his BC material and in 1936 Sinclair gave up writing to become a SALMON troller. Two novels of international reputation were linked with BC during the 1940s: *Under the Volcano* (1947) by the visiting English writer Malcolm LOWRY and *By Grand Central Station I Sat Down and Wept*, written during a 1949 stopover in PENDER HARBOUR by the Ottawa writer Elizabeth Smart. *Under the Volcano* was not written on BC soil, only revised, and neither book owed or offered much to BC experience, but both have been lionized by local scholars eager to seize upon links to the world stage.

Some writers refused to angle their BC focus to suit foreign taste, and generally time has been kinder to them. Chief among these was Roderick HAIG-BROWN (1908–76), who came to BC from England when he was 19 years old and published his first book, *Silver*, in 1931. Over the next 4 decades he went on to publish 25 books on cougars, salmon, whales, homesteading, angling, commercial FISHING, trapping, logging and Capt George Vancouver, pioneering almost every major theme in BC literature—especially environmentalism. His lifelong effort to forge environmental awareness was crucial in making BC one of the world's breeding grounds of environmental activism (*see* ENVIRONMENTAL MOVEMENT). Haig-Brown's 2 adult novels,

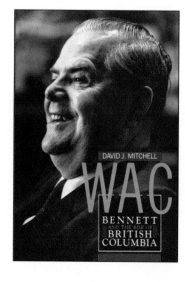

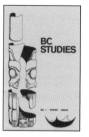

Timber (1942) and *On the Highest Hill* (1955), are unsatisfying artistically but the brilliance of his essay style in books like *Measure of the Year* and the breadth of his overall achievement make him the major BC writer up to the mid-century and arguably longer. If he had a shortcoming it may be that, much as he tried to achieve the voice of a native British Columbian, he never completely stopped sounding like a man whose sensibilities were formed at a good English public school. This is not as true of the BC-born Emily CARR (1871–1945), even though she came out of Victoria's faux-English enclave and studied in Paris and London. *Klee Wyck* (1941), her Gov Gen's award-winning collection of vignettes about travelling around BC, has a relaxed humour that marks it as the work of a writer perfectly at home in her world. *The Book of Small* (1942), *The House of All Sorts* (1944) and her autobiography *Growing Pains* (1946)—all written when she was in her 70s—confirm her status as an important BC writer. The novels of Ethel WILSON (1888–1980) derive from an urban middle-class world circumscribed by its characters' inner preoccupations in a way that subdues locale, though West Coast nature flavours them all. Having previously written only occasional short stories, Wilson had a remarkable burst of cre-

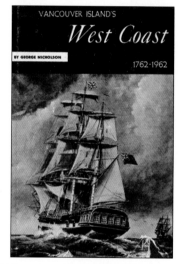

ativity upon reaching late middle age, producing 5 major novels between the ages of 59 and 68; among these, *Swamp Angel* (1954) is generally considered the best. Her plots are quiet and her characterizations etched in low relief, but her writing has an assured elegance that makes it one of the fine achievements of BC fiction. At the opposite end of the stylistic spectrum, *The Double Hook* (1959) by Sheila WATSON, raised in New Westminster, explores the life of a rustic CARIBOO town in fragmentary, jarring images interspersed with mythic invocations that echo the modernist experiments of Joyce and Faulkner.

Both Hubert Evans and Roderick Haig-Brown wrote successful books for children set in BC during the 1930s and 1940s, opening the way for such writers as Catherine Anthony CLARK, whose fantasy classic the *Golden Pine Cone* (1950) paralleled the many works of Christie Harris in its imaginative use of aboriginal myth. In *The Republic of Childhood* (1964), the librarian and critic Sheila EGOFF helped to define the role of children's literature both in BC and across Canada.

Most British Columbians, asked to name a BC writer they admired at any time up to the 1970s, would not have named a poet or novelist but a leading journalist like Margaret "Ma" MURRAY, Bruce HUTCHISON, Pierre BERTON, Jack WEBSTER, Paul ST PIERRE, Eric NICOL, Barry BROADFOOT or Allan FOTHERINGHAM. Far more than mere reporters, such writers helped define BC's place in the nation, while others like Nancy HODGES, Helena GUTTERIDGE, Jack SCOTT, Bob HUNTER, and more recently Terry GLAVIN, Ben Parfitt, and Stephen Hume, helped establish concepts like universal suffrage, the welfare state and environmentalism to their central place in BC culture. Starting in the 1940s under the influence of Ira DILWORTH, CBC radio also began to provide an

important forum for BC writing, with such producers as Robert HARLOW, Phyllis WEBB and Don Mowat playing key roles in airing poetry, drama and prose. In the 1960s CBC television also began to play a role in developing BC subject matter with *CARIBOO COUNTRY*, produced by Philip Keatley, and the long-running adventure series the *BEACHCOMBERS*, which did much to establish BC as a leading centre for film and new media production (*see also* FILM-MAKING INDUSTRY).

The appearance of the new poetry magazine *CONTEMPORARY VERSE* in 1941 helped to coalesce a group of BC poets led by

Earle BIRNEY (1904–95), winner of the Gov Gen's Literary Award for *David and Other Poems* in 1942 and Dorothy LIVESAY, Gov Gen's Award winner for *Day and Night* in 1944. Birney expressed a stronger sense of the West Coast in works like "David," "The Condemnation of Vancouver" and "November Walk Near False Creek Mouth," and nurtured a circle of younger writers like Marya Fiamengo, Rona Murray and Daryl Hine as head of Canada's first creative writing school at UBC. His genteel mentorship was interrupted in the late 1950s by another UBC English professor, Warren TALLMAN, who encouraged exchanges between young BC writers and avant-garde American poets, including members of the San Francisco renaissance and the Black Mountain group. This cross-fertilization produced a rich flowering of new talent, including George BOWERING, Frank Davey, Fred WAH, Daphne MARLATT, David Dawson, David Bromige, Jamie Reid, George Stanley, Lionel KEARNS and Barry MACKINNON, as well as prose writers Gladys Hindmarch and Stan PERSKY, whose modernist American flavouring

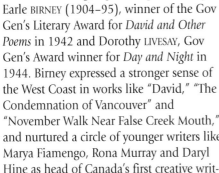

turned West Coast poetry sharply away from the humanist and nationalist tradition coming down through Birney and Livesay.

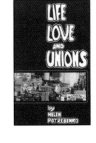

Loosely identified as the "*TISH* group" after a magazine founded by Davey and Bowering, it collided noisily in the late 1960s with a faction marshalled by another assertive American teaching at UBC, J. Michael YATES, resulting in the so-called "poetry wars." Yates led a contingent of "West Coast surrealists" of which he was himself the most energetic practitioner, but which also involved such writers as Andreas SCHROEDER, Michael Bullock, Charles LILLARD, John Skapski, George MCWHIRTER, Michael Finlay, George Amabile, Stanley Cooperman, Derk Wynand and the novelist

George Payerle. In addition to these divisions, the disputatious BC writing scene of the 1960s and 1970s harboured a number of poets including Patrick LANE, Red Lane, Tom WAYMAN, Pat LOWTHER, John Pass, Ken Belford, Peter TROWER, David (then known as Dale) Zieroth, and John Newlove, who generally followed the humanist and nationalist lead of Birney and Livesay, bolstered by the later arrival of Milton ACORN and Al PURDY. Adding their unique spice to the "West Coast scene" were the idiosyncratic figures of bill BISSETT, Seymour Mayne and Joe ROSENBLATT. During the 1970s and 1980s on VANCOUVER ISLAND the *Malahat Review*, edited by the expatriate British poet and UNIV OF VICTORIA professor Robin SKELTON, served as the focal point for a distinct community that at various times included Derk Wynand, Doug Beardsley, Charles Lillard, Susan MUSGRAVE, Marilyn BOWERING, Sharon THESEN, David Day, Stephen SCOBIE, Theresa Kishkan, Patricia YOUNG and Linda Rogers. In NELSON, Tom Wayman, Colin Browne, Jeff Derksen, Gary Whitehead, Calvin Wharton and others started the KOOTENAY SCHOOL OF WRITING; later they relocated it to Vancouver, where it became associated with the l=a=n=g=u=a=g=e poetry movement. The ferment that made BC Canada's poetry hot spot in the 1970s gradually died down but enjoyed a resurgence in the 1990s with

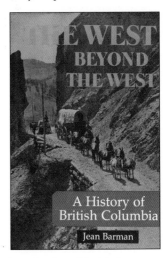

the appearance of a new generation of writers like Mark Cochrane, Tim Bowling, Evelyn LAU, Thea Bowering, Kevin Paul and Shannon Stewart.

A new generation of BC-born fiction writers began publishing in the 1960s and 1970s, among them Robert Harlow, Joy

KOGAWA, George Bowering, Alan FRY, Anne CAMERON and Jack HODGINS. Harlow produced a series of dense, intellectual novels brooding on his PRINCE GEORGE roots, while Kogawa fashioned her heart-rending evocation of the JAPANESE RELOCATION, *Obasan*. Bowering pursued an experimental course, mixing myth, history and post-modernism in the Gov Gen's Award-winning *Burning Water*, while Fry continued the BC preoccupation with aboriginal issues in his controversial docu-novel *How a People Die* (1970). But it was in the work of Hodgins that the flame of BC identity burned most brightly. Beginning with *Spit Delaney's Island* (1976) and continuing through *Invention of the World* (1977) to *Broken Ground* (1998), no novelist has pursued the grail of BC character as self-consciously as Hodgins. Anne Cameron's work taps the same Vancouver Island material, but with her the evocation of regional character takes second place to her rage for feminist social criticism, which runs undiminished through more than 30 published books, from *The Dreamspeaker* (1978) to *Aftermath* (1999). Children's writing recovered its momentum during the 1980s in the hands of such writers as Sue Anne ALDERSON, Diane Swanson, Betty Waterton, Kit PEARSON, Mary Razzell and Sarah Ellis. Writing for the THEATRE, on the other hand, had fewer successes, mainly in the work of George RYGA, John MacLachlan GRAY, Morris PANYCH, Dennis FOON and Margaret HOLLINGSWORTH. Beginning in the 1980s, BC writing belatedly began to shed its all-white coloration, with works reflecting its Pacific Rim heritage from Kogawa, Roy MIKI, Wayson CHOY, Sky Lee, Larissa Lai and Jim Wong-Chu. Modern aboriginal writing also began to appear in the work of George Clutesi, Jeannette Armstrong and Lee Maracle. All worked in their own way at solving the riddle of BC experience, and their books are British Columbian in the sense that no reader could mistake them as being from anywhere else.

The emergence of truly indigenous voices could hardly be said to have dominated the scene, as BC continued to serve as a literary crossroads. It provided a home not just to writers from other parts of Canada like Ryga, W.D. VALGARDSON, W.P. KINSELLA and D.M. FRASER, but also to many expatriate writers like Jane RULE (US), Audrey THOMAS (US), William GIBSON

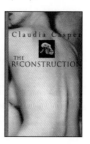

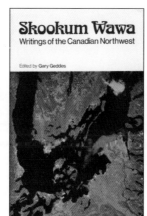

(US), Keith MAILLARD (US), David WATMOUGH (UK), Kevin Roberts (Australia), Bill Schermbrucker (Kenya), Jan DRABEK (Czech Republic), and later, Anita Rau Badami (India) and Goh Poh Seng (Singapore). Some, like Rule, Thomas and Roberts, followed Malcolm Lowry's example by gradually merging their former identities into the new to develop a hybrid voice; others such as Gibson, Watmough and Drabek found BC a congenial retreat from which to continue engaging their former cultures. In the 1990s the roster of fiction writers was augmented by a wave of new names like Douglas COUPLAND, Linda Svendsen, Marilyn Bowering, Gail ANDERSON-DARGATZ, Carol Windley, Michael TURNER, Shani Mootoo, Zsuzsi Gartner, and Anne Fleming, while a strong cadre of new First Nations writers like Eden ROBINSON, Gregory Scofield and Richard Van Camp built on the work of Clutesi, Armstrong and Maracle.

The upsurge of Canadian nationalism and the arrival of indigenous BOOK PUBLISHING in the 1960s had a particularly liberating affect on writers of non-fiction books about BC history, places and issues, who were finally freed from having to submit to out-of-province editors who judged manuscripts not according to their interest in BC, but according to their interest in Toronto and London. The result was an increase in BC-authored books from a mere handful to 500 a year by the end of the 20th century. The author who best exemplified this era was George WOODCOCK, a scholar, critic and all-purpose man of letters whose prodigious output of more than 150 books on every imaginable topic from the Third Century BC to the future of electronic communications mirrored the rise of the non-fiction book in BC. A partial list of his fellow authors attests to the remarkable strength of the genre: Helen and Philip Akrigg, M. Wylie BLANCHET, Lynne Bowen, Ken Coates, David Cruise, Wade DAVIS, Gilean DOUGLAS, Ken Drushka, Wilson DUFF, Brian FAWCETT, Robin Fisher, Daniel Francis, Alison Griffiths, Alan Haig-Brown, Lynn Hancock, Herschel HARDIN, Cole Harris, Tom Henry, Raymond HULL, Stephen Hume, Adolf HUNGRY WOLF, Edith IGLAUER, Vickie Jensen, Michael Kluckner, Rolf Knight, W. Kaye LAMB, C.P. LYONS, Susan Mayse, Bridget MORAN, Rosemary Neering, Peter C. NEWMAN, Margaret Ormsby, Stephen Osborne, T.W. Paterson, R.M. Patterson, Stan PERSKY, Bill Richardson, Andreas Schroeder, Martin Segger, Doris SHADBOLT, Hilary STEWART, David SUZUKI, Robert TURNER, Alan TWIGG and Paul Yee. The vast majority of the books produced are on BC subjects, anchoring the province's claim to having one of the most supportive environments for regional writing in the English-speaking world.

LIVESAY, Dorothy, poet, social worker (b 12 Oct 1909, Winnipeg; d 29 Dec 1996, Victoria). One of the finest poets of her generation, she began writing as a teenager and published her first book of poems, *Green Pitcher*, in 1928. After studying in France she returned to Canada in 1932 and became a social worker. During the 1930s she was drawn increasingly to social activism, and her poetry explored political and feminist themes as well as personal, emotional ones. She came to VANCOUVER in 1936; there she met and married Duncan McNair. During the 1940s she won 2 GOV GEN'S LITERARY AWARDS for

Dorothy Livesay, poet. *Eliza Massey photo*

Day and Night (1944) and *Poems for People* (1947). When her husband died in 1959 she left Canada to teach with UNESCO in Zambia. She returned to Vancouver in 1963 and published several more poetry collections as well as volumes of memoirs. In 1987 she was appointed to the Order of Canada. She held honorary degrees from several universities including SFU, UBC and the UNIV OF VICTORIA.

LIZARD is a 4-legged, elongate reptile with a long tail that in some species can be shed and regenerated. Most species worldwide occur in warm, dry climates, but the 2 most common BC species are also found in forest habitat. Both are insectivores and comparatively small, given that the giant Komodo dragon of Indonesia, the largest lizard in the world, grows to 3 m long. The western skink (*Eumeces skiltonianus*) is a smooth, shiny, egg-laying species found in south-central and southeastern BC. The northern alligator lizard (*Elgaria coerulea*) is live-bearing, producing broods of up to 15 young. It occurs across southern BC from VANCOUVER ISLAND to the KOOTENAY. A third species, the short-horned lizard (*Phrynosoma douglassi*), a squat, spiny creature, is found only near OSOYOOS.

Northern alligator lizard. *Dean van't Schip photo*

LOCKEPORT, on the east coast of MORESBY ISLAND in the QUEEN CHARLOTTE ISLANDS 60 km south of SKIDEGATE, began as a settlement of prospectors in 1907. Steamships called and a store opened, run by Harry Morgan, who was also involved with the area's main COPPER mines, Apex and Copper Belle. By 1918 the mines were closing and a cannery was established that operated intermittently until 1928. Lockeport was named after the Nova Scotia hometown of Capt Louis Locke, who ended his days as skipper of the ill-fated *PRINCESS SOPHIA*. *AS*

LOG BARGES were first used in the 1920s to transport logs along the coast from cutting sites to southern SAWMILLS. The earliest barges were old ships' hulls converted for the purpose. One of these was the *MALAHAT*, a former rum-runner converted by Gordon GIBSON in 1935 into the world's first self-propelled, self-loading log carrier. Self-dumping barges were introduced in 1954, and by the 1960s cranes had been added for self-loading and barges had replaced DAVIS RAFTS as the main log transporters on the coast. Modern barges, some of them self-propelled, are able to carry 4 million board ft of wood. The *Seaspan Forester*, a 138-m behemoth owned by SEASPAN INTERNATIONAL, was the world's largest barge in 1999.

LOG BOOMING is the sorting of floating logs into rafts, or booms, for transport from a LOGGING camp to a mill. In earlier usage it referred to the sorting of logs driven down rivers. In early coastal logging camps, logs were hauled, or skidded, from the stump to the salt water ("salt chuck") and dumped into a general holding area, or bullpen, defined by a string of logs

Randy Arden booming logs with pike pole and heavy chain. *Rick Blacklaws photo*

attached end-to-end with "boom chains." In all but the smallest camps, a special boom crew sorted the logs: using pike poles (a long pole with a point and a hook), workers fit the logs into square sections circumscribed by 20-m "boom sticks," which were attached at the corners with boom chains. Several sections of logs

Seaspan Forester, *the largest log barge in the world*. Seaspan International

were chained together into large "flat booms" and towed by tugboats to mills, mostly in VAN-COUVER; to large sorting grounds in Howe Sound; and to storage areas on the FRASER R. Because logs could not be kept in salt water for more than a few weeks before they were attacked by teredos (*see* SHIPWORMS), they were stored for longer periods in fresh water. Flat booms were suitable for use in protected waters, where log losses were relatively low and any strays could be recovered by "beachcombers," people who collect loose logs and return them to their owners. When logging began in less protected parts of the coast, DAVIS RAFTS were used, as were "bundle booms," sections of bundled logs of approximately one truckload each, held together by wire cables. Bundles were easier to contain within booms than single logs. In the 1950s, LOG BARGES became the preferred method of transporting logs. The first barges were old ship hulls; later purpose-built barges were produced. Hand sorting of logs ended with the development of "boom boats," small, manoeuvrable steel-hulled boats designed for moving logs and bundles in the water. Kingcome Navigation, the log-towing arm of MACMILLAN BLOEDEL LTD, pioneered the development of self-loading, self-propelled log barges: these vessels could dump their loads by flooding internal holds and tipping the logs into the water. The use of barges dramatically reduced the number of logs lost, depleted the ranks of beachcombers who made their living in log salvage, and diminished the hazard to navigation caused by loose floating logs. In the 1970s all coastal log sorting was done on land (in "dryland sorts") to avoid contaminating aquatic areas with bark and other debris. In the logging operations of the late 20th century, machines sort logs into species and grades; then the logs are bundled, weighed or "scaled" to obtain a volume measurement, and loaded directly onto barges or dumped in the water to be loaded.

Ken Drushka

LOG CABIN, 660 km north of PRINCE RUPERT, in northwestern BC near the Alaska border, was a remote and lonely station on the WHITE PASS & YUKON ROUTE. Passengers arriving during the Klondike GOLD RUSH could alight here and take a rough 80-km overland trail to ATLIN. Log Cabin had a hotel, customs house and police post, and a post office from 1899 to 1909. *AS*

LOGAN LAKE, district municipality, pop 2,492, is situated in the Highland Valley between MERRITT and KAMLOOPS west of the COQUIHALLA HWY. It was an instant community created in 1971 as a residential base for workers at the Lornex Copper Mine, later Highland Valley Copper; at 160 km² this was the largest open-pit COPPER mine in N America and one of the largest open-pit mines in the world. A slump in the price of copper led to the temporary closure of the mine during 1999, but it later resumed production. The community attracts a significant number of retirees who appreciate its picturesque setting and recreational opportunities.

LOGGING, as a distinct branch of the FOREST INDUSTRY, began at the head of ALBERNI INLET in 1860. The work was done under the direction of the head logger, Jeremiah ROGERS, to supply wood to the province's first major SAWMILL. With axes to fell the giant DOUGLAS FIR trees and oxen to skid the logs to the mill, it was a short-lived operation: the accessible timber supply was soon consumed. Within a few years the mill closed and its founder, Capt Edward STAMP relocated with Rogers at HASTINGS MILL on the site of what later became VANCOUVER. The first Interior mill opened in the CARIBOO, near BARKERVILLE, in 1860. The earliest west coast loggers discovered that logging methods used in eastern N America were of limited use in the wet coastal rain forests with their enormous trees and soggy ground, and their wild RIVERS that were unsuited to log driving. Coastal BC loggers and their American counterparts in the Pacific Northwest devised entirely new systems and equipment to harvest the valuable timber that would be milled into lumber and exported to the rest of the world.

Felling a Douglas fir in Kitsilano, Vancouver, c 1885. CVA Tr.37

In the Interior, with its smaller trees and drier, colder CLIMATE, logging techniques were similar to those used in the East. Much of the work was done in the winter. Logs were loaded on sleds pulled by horses, either to nearby BUSH MILLS or to LAKES and rivers on which they were

BC LOGGING HARVEST 1912–98

	Total cut (m³)	Coast	Interior
1912	3,000,000	n/a	n/a
1920	9,000,000	n/a	n/a
1930	12,000,000	n/a	n/a
1940	18,000,000	n/a	n/a
1950	22,000,000	n/a	n/a
1955	29,300,000	63%	37%
1965	43,400,000	56%	44%
1976	69,500,000	46%	54%
1983	77,664,000	37%	63%
1994	78,013,000	32%	68%
1998	70,713,000	32%	68%

towed to bigger mills. In some locations, such as Adams Lk, long wooden flumes were built to carry logs. These methods prevailed in the Interior until mechanized equipment appeared in the 1920s and 1930s.

The earliest method of moving felled trees was with oxen and horses along skid trails made of cross-logs. Once the timber within skidding range of the mills was cut, other means had to be devised. The first indigenous form of coastal logging was called HANDLOGGING. Trees along the steep shoreline were felled; with the aid of jacks they were moved into the water, where they were cut into logs and towed to the mills. Beginning about 1890 many radical changes in equipment were introduced. In that year crosscut saws were first used to fall and buck trees. In the late 1880s a small steam-powered locomotive known as OLD CURLY, used on construction of the CPR, was put to work logging in SURREY. In 1892 the first steam-powered yarder was acquired by the VICTORIA LUMBER & MANUFACTURING CO in CHEMAINUS. With these innovations trees could be cut much more easily, far inland from the mill and the water. The winch, known as the "donkey," dragged logs to the water or the railway, from where they were hauled to the mill. This form of hauling, or "yarding," was called ground-lead logging, because logs were dragged on the ground or along skid roads. It was the main system used for almost 30 years. In 1909 the Comox Logging Co imported the first of half a dozen Lidgerwood skidders, huge machines designed for logging Louisiana swamps. They had 27-m steel towers mounted on large rail cars

Yarding logs along a skid road with oxen, c 1885.

River driving, early 1900s.

Illustrations by Kim LaFave, based on "Bull Cats" by Bert Bushell

Yarding with a steam (spool) donkey, 1902.

Steam donkey hauling logs along a skid road to the water, 1908.

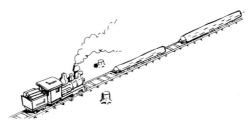

Skidding logs with a roader, 1920s.

Victoria Lumber & Manufacturing Co crew and steam donkey at Cowichan Lake, 1926. *VPL 1433*

However, until the late 1940s the main means of hauling logs from roadside landings was the steam railway (*see* RAILWAY LOGGING). During WWII a shortage of skilled fallers contributed to the rapid development of gasoline-powered saws. By the end of the war one of the world's major power saw manufacturers, Industrial Engineering Ltd, was located in Vancouver, producing saws developed by coastal BC loggers.

During the economically buoyant post-war period, several changes were introduced in logging systems. Wooden spar trees were replaced with portable steel spars, complete with their own winches on self-propelled frames, that could be moved to new locations easily and quickly. Bigger and more powerful trucks gradually replaced railways in almost all operations, travelling on roads built with a variety of new

Bear Creek flume, built by Adams River Lumber, c 1910. *BC Archives F-73475*

and several winches. Similar set-ups using limbed and topped trees or spars, instead of steel towers, later became popular. A heavy skyline ran from the skidder to the top of the spar, and then to the back end of the area being logged, where the trees were already felled and bucked into logs. Another line, the mainline, pulled a carriage hanging from the skyline. The carriage was pulled out over the logs with a haulback line. A set of tongs on the end of the mainline were attached to the log and the winch hauled in the line, lifting the log off the ground in the process. This was known as skyline logging. At about the same time another system, called

high-lead logging, was developed. A mainline ran from the winch through a block at the top of a tall spar tree and out to the logs without the use of a skyline. The logs were dragged in over the ground, and could be lifted over obstacles by applying a brake on the haulback line while pulling on the mainline. Cable logging systems were used only rarely in the Interior.

In the 1920s, gasoline engines began to replace steam engines on yarders and loading machines. Diesel engines came into use somewhat later. Trucks were used to haul logs in the early 1920s, but because suitable road-building equipment was not available they had to operate on log or plank roads. In the 1930s Caterpillar tractors appeared and were quickly adopted by loggers to skid logs and build roads for trucks.

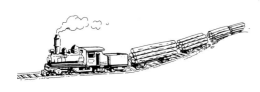

Shay logging locomotive.

Steel tower skidder and cold deck, late 1920s.

Logging truck, 1930s.

Skidding logs with a cat and arch.

Balloon logging, 1990s.

Helicopter logging, 1990s.

Fleetwood Forest Products grapple yarder, yarding logs on the Sunshine Coast, 2000.
Keith Thirkell photo

Wooden skyline spar tree working near Chemainus, 1940s. A boom is being used to load the rail cars. *Jack Cash/UBC BC1930/547*

Falling a spruce. *Courtesy Western Forest Products*

One of the most versatile pieces of equipment introduced has been the hydraulic excavator. As originally designed, it became the primary piece of road-building equipment. When the bucket is replaced with other devices, it can be used for loading logs, tossing them toward the road in a method called "hoe chucking." It can also be used to operate feller-bunchers and tree processors, and for a host of other tasks. On the coast, until the 1990s, the favoured yarding system used grapple yarders. Cables were strung from the yarder, which moved along a road, to a stump or another heavy machine at the back end of the area being logged. A grapple tong was hauled out along the cable and dropped on a log, which it grabbed. Another line hauled the grapple and log to roadside. Later, in order to minimize road building and to avoid environmental damage, skyline yarding systems began replacing grapple yarders. Since 1975 a growing number of heavy-lift helicopters have been used on the coast to haul logs from the woods to landings or drop them into nearby bodies of water (*see* HELI-LOGGING). Another semi-aerial system uses a large helium-filled balloon to hold up a skyline, along which logs are hauled. In the early 1980s a variety of sophisticated machines began to appear in forests throughout the province to selectively log the relatively small coastal second-growth and Interior forests. These feller-processors and forwarders were manufactured and first used in Europe. They will likely be complemented by many other types of new machines as harvesting of second-growth forests becomes more widespread. In the late 20th century, operations in some parts of BC were using horses once again in selective logging.

road-building machinery. Rubber-tired skidders, equipped with a small winch and capable of travelling over rough, off-road terrain came into widespread use in the Interior and on the coast. They could winch logs short distances, and then drag a turn of several logs over much longer distances than skyline or high-lead systems could yard. After the mid-1960s several new types of machines were introduced. By the late 1990s feller-bunchers were being used extensively in the Interior and to a lesser degree on the coast. The feller-buncher is a large, tracked or wheeled machine with a power saw and a hydraulic clamp on the end of a boom. It falls and stacks trees in piles; these are skidded to the road with rubber-tired skidders equipped with large grapples.

Loading a sleigh at a Columbia River Lumber show, Horse Thief Creek, 1910.
BC Archives D-03623

Feller buncher at work.
Courtesy Western Forest Products

A-frame logging, Knight Inlet, 1930s.

In 1997 about 29,150 loggers were employed harvesting more than 68.6 million m³ of timber—two-thirds of it in the Interior. Logging is the most dangerous job in BC: in the 1990s about 40 loggers died each year on the job and many more suffered injury when they were struck by trees or maimed by equipment. Between the time logging began in BC and 1997, about 95,000 km² were logged. Since 1906 there have been restrictions on log exports, and almost all the logs harvested in BC are processed in the province.

In the mid-1970s an enormous and heated controversy arose over the extent of logging in BC and the practices loggers use. As a result, an increasing amount of the forest land base has been protected from logging and regulations restricting the way logging is done have been adopted. *See also* FOREST INDUSTRY.   *Ken Drushka*

Reading: Ken Drushka, *Working in the Woods,* 1992; Ken Drushka, *Tie-Hackers to Timber Harvesters,* 1998; Bus Griffiths, *Now You're Logging,* 1978.

LOGGING, A-FRAME, was a method of cutting waterfront timber, in use from 1920 to 1950. Unlike land-based systems, which yarded logs into a central "landing" and transported them to water by road, rail, chute or cable, A-frame loggers used a yarder floating on the water to pull logs down to it. The A-frame yarder was mounted on a large raft of floating logs and the lines were threaded through blocks hung at the apex of 2 log spars hung in an "A" configuration. This arrangement provided lift to keep the timber from fouling as it was pulled down the slope into the water. A typical A-frame operation was a small affair using a handful of workers to harvest limited patches of timber located near the water in steep coastal inlets; these were most common before WWII, when good timber was still to be found near tide water. KNIGHT INLET in particular

was renowned for the number of A-frame "shows" it supported. A-frame operations were also used in large LAKES such as COWICHAN, NIMP-KISH, GREAT CENTRAL and Lois. *See also* LOGGING.
Howard White

LONDON DRUGS is a drugstore chain established in 1945 when Sam Bass (1915–90), a Winnipeg-born pharmacist, bought a store at the corner of Main and Union streets in VANCOUVER and created the first modern drugstore in BC. Bass opened more stores before selling to the American company Daylin Corp in 1968. Daylin opened the chain's first Alberta store in 1975, then sold to the Vancouver-based H.Y. Louie Group in 1976. By 1999 the chain operated 50 stores in Alberta and BC. *See also* LOUIE, Tong.

LONE BUTTE, a DAIRY farming and ranching (*see* CATTLE INDUSTRY) settlement and BC RAIL station 12 km southeast of 100 MILE HOUSE in the

CARIBOO, is named for a prominent flat-topped outcrop of basalt just to the east. A heritage log-cabin hotel and one of the last wooden water towers from BC Rail's steam era are found here; several guest ranches operate nearby. The post office for this area was named Fawn for many years and was located 8 km east.   *AS*

LONESOME LAKE; *see* EDWARDS, RALPH.

LONG BEACH is part of a 20-km-long stretch of sandy shore between TOFINO and UCLUELET on the west coast of VANCOUVER ISLAND, 195 km from NANAIMO by road. Part of the territory of the NUU-CHAH-NULTH (Nootka) First Nations, it was for many years accessible only by dirt road from PORT ALBERNI until the road was paved early in the 1970s. Long Beach was popular with campers, surfers, hermits and "hippies," some of whom lived on the beaches in communities of driftwood shanties. There were also businesses and a scattering of residences. This all ended with the creation of PACIFIC RIM NATIONAL PARK

Long Beach, Pacific Rim National Park Reserve, 1985. Roy Luckow photo

RESERVE in 1971, when Long Beach became one of the park's 3 components (the WEST COAST TRAIL and BROKEN GROUP ISLANDS are the other two). Although this section of the park is called Long Beach, there are actually several beaches of which Long Beach is one. The area attracts thousands of visitors every year, but cars no longer roar up and down the hard-packed sand and camping is confined to designated sites. A small FIRST NATIONS reserve (Esowista) lies at the north end of the beach and an interpretation centre has been established at WICKANINNISH Beach.

LONGLINING; *see* FISHING, COMMERCIAL.

LONGSHOREMEN'S STRIKES, 1923 and 1935, were among the most important labour actions of the inter-war period. The 1923 strike began on 8 Oct when 1,400 dock workers, members of the International Longshoremen's Assoc, struck for higher wages. Employers, represented by the BC Shipping Federation, responded by locking out the workers; instead of negotiating they imported strikebreakers, who were housed for their own protection in ships on the waterfront, guarded by armed patrols. Employers organized strikebreakers into a new company union, the Vancouver & District Waterfront Workers Assoc (WWA), without the right to strike. On 7 Dec strikers voted to go back to work, though only men approved by the employers were allowed to return. Many others never worked on the docks again.

During the Depression the WWA was radicalized, and in the spring of 1935 it staged a series of job actions on the VANCOUVER waterfront. In May, city dock workers refused to handle a cargo of paper from POWELL RIVER, where police had clashed with strikers and the PULP AND PAPER company had locked out the workers. Strike action spread to other BC ports and once again the Shipping Federation formed its own company union. On 18 June in Vancouver, after strike leaders had been refused a chance to speak to strikebreakers, a crowd of 1,000 strikers, led by Mickey O'Rourke, a VICTORIA CROSS winner, marched on Ballantyne Pier. A riot ensued, the so-called "Battle of Ballantyne Pier," in which local police and RCMP greeted marchers with tear gas and batons. When peace was restored, 28 people had been injured and 24 arrested. An inquiry into the dispute blamed it on union leadership. Amid renewed anti-Communist scaremongering the strike dragged on until 9 Dec, when it ended with the WWA in tatters. *See also* LABOUR MOVEMENT.

LONGSPUR is a SPARROW-like bird found in open GRASSLANDS and tundras. Two species are found regularly in BC. The Lapland longspur (*Calcarius lapponicus*) breeds on Arctic tundras around the world and migrates through BC; Smith's longspur (*C. pictus*) breeds in shrubby tundras across northern N America, including the northwest corner of BC.

LONGWORTH is a tiny LOGGING and ranching settlement (*see* CATTLE INDUSTRY) and VIA Rail station on the FRASER R 85 km east of PRINCE GEORGE. Longworth Lumber Co used oxen in its LOGGING operations here as late as the 1930s, and the Berg SAWMILL operated into the 1960s. It was one of the few communities in BC with road access that was still without telephone service at the end of the 20th century. *AS*

LOON is a large swimming bird usually seen on the open water along the coast, where it migrates for the winter from breeding grounds on Interior LAKES. Loons are aquatic predators whose bodies

Common loon at Tahla Lake, south of Merritt, 1998. Roy Luckow photo

are highly specialized for diving in search of food, principally fish. They cannot walk on land and come to shore only to nest, and like other waterfowl they cannot fly during moult. There are 5 types of loons, 4 of which are found in BC. The common loon (*Gavia immer*) is, as the name suggests, the most common. This is the type whose haunting call is so often identified with the Canadian wilderness. The Pacific loon (*G. pacifica*) is the most gregarious, appearing along the South Coast in flocks of hundreds or even thousands. The small red-throated loon (*G. stellata*) is distinctive for its red throat patch in summer, while the yellow-billed loon (*G. adamsii*), identified by its large straw-coloured bill, is a rare winter visitor.

LOOTAS ("Wave Eater") is a 15-m dugout CANOE designed and built under the supervision of HAIDA carver Bill REID for EXPO 86. It was made at SKIDEGATE on the QUEEN CHARLOTTE ISLANDS from a single red CEDAR tree, the first large dugout canoe carved there in 70 years. In Oct 1989 it was taken to Europe and paddled up the Seine R to Paris, where it was the centrepiece of an exhibition of Reid's work at the Musée de l'Homme. When Reid died in 1998 his ashes were carried in *Lootas* to the abandoned village site of Tanu, where his mother was from, for scattering. The canoe is stored at the museum in Skidegate.

LORANGER, Clancy, journalist (b 30 Sept 1921, Cutknife, SK). A popular VANCOUVER personality, he started his career in NEWSPAPERS in 1939 as a copy boy with the PROVINCE, earning $7 per week. He gradually worked his way into the sports department, becoming a full-fledged sports writer in 1941. Two years later he moved to the Vancouver *News-Herald*, where he served 5 years as sports editor and 1 year as city editor before returning to the *Province* in 1951. He became a regular columnist in 1965 and wrote 5 columns a week until his retirement in 1986. He was best known for his coverage of BASEBALL and HOCKEY; Clancy Loranger Way near Nat BAILEY Stadium is named for him.

Clancy Loranger, sportswriter, with the Stanley Cup, 1968. John Helcermanas photo

LORD, John Keast, naturalist (b 1818, Cornwall, England; d 9 Dec 1872, Brighton, England). After training as a veterinarian and practising briefly, he left England to follow a series of adventurous pursuits in different parts

Lootas, the 15-m dugout canoe designed and built under the supervision of Bill Reid, Skidegate, 1986. J.L. Gijssen/UBC/MOA

of the world. He arrived in BC in 1858 as assistant naturalist to the Northwest Boundary Commission marking the border along the 49th parallel from the coast to the ROCKY MTS (see BOUNDARIES). His main job was to acquire and care for the commission's pack animals. His account of this experience was published in 2 vols as *The Naturalist in Vancouver Island and British Columbia* (1866), one of the earliest books about the province. When the commission completed its work in 1862 he returned to England. After a sojourn in Egypt, he became manager of an aquarium in Brighton, England, shortly before his death.

LORNE CREEK, a former riverboat landing and GRAND TRUNK PACIFIC RWY flag station on the west side of the SKEENA R, 50 km northeast of TERRACE, was a rich GOLD placer-mining site in the 1880s. Just upstream where the river swirls round a bend is the Devil's Elbow, a danger to navigation. *AS*

LOST LAGOON, 16.6 ha, is the freshwater lake at the causeway entrance to STANLEY PARK in VANCOUVER. Originally a part of Coal Harbour, the lake was created in 1916 when construction of the traffic causeway to the LIONS GATE BRIDGE divided the 2 bodies of water. Stocked with TROUT in 1929, the lake became a popular spot with fishers and boaters. Many species of birds and waterfowl seek food and shelter along its muddy shores, and boating was eventually banned to protect the wildlife. The fountain was added in 1936 as part of the city's 50th anniversary celebrations. The name probably came from Pauline JOHNSON's poem "The Lost Lagoon" ("It is dusk on the Lost Lagoon, / And we two dreaming the dusk away").

LOTUS LAND is a phrase used by some writers to characterize BC—especially southern BC—as a place where life is slower-paced and people are more self-absorbed than in the rest of Canada. The reference is drawn from the episode in Homer's *Odyssey* where an atmosphere of languid indolence in the land of the lotus-eaters saps the will of Ithacan soldiers to continue their mission. The comparison to BC was first made by the journalist Bruce HUTCHISON, who used the phrase "The Lotus Eaters" as a chapter title in his celebrated book on Canadian identity, *The Unknown Country* (1943). Interestingly this chapter dealt only with VANCOUVER ISLAND, not the entire province, and not even the whole of the Island but only the "happy never-never land" south of NANAIMO, where an English culture-in-exile produced "the final perfection of country life everywhere." Other writers, notably Allan FOTHERINGHAM, put a significantly different twist on the lotus land reference by using it to evoke the sybaritic lifestyle of an overdeveloped modern leisure class, primarily in suburban Vancouver, "the hot tub capital of North America." Against this view of leisure-centred urban BC society, such writers as Tom WAYMAN and Patrick LANE emphasize the hardships of rural and working-class life in BC. *Howard White*

LOUIE, Alexina Diane, composer (b 30 July 1949, Vancouver). One of Canada's leading contemporary composers, she was born in CHINATOWN in VANCOUVER and began playing the piano at age 7. After studying composition at UBC and the Univ of California at San Diego she lived in Los Angeles for several years before moving to Toronto in 1980 to teach at the Royal Conservatory of Music. In 1983 her composition *O Magnum Mysterium: In Memoriam Glenn Gould* brought her to the attention of the concert-going public. She composed the opening music for EXPO 86 and *Three Fanfares for the Ringing Earth* that opened the new National Gallery in Ottawa in 1988. Her expressive compositions are a unique combination of Asian and Western musical influences. In 1999 she won the Jules Léger Prize, Canada's foremost award for composition and in 2000 her composition *Shattered Night, Shivering Stars* won a Juno Award.

LOUIE, Tong, entrepreneur (b 1 Mar 1914, Vancouver; d 28 Apr 1998, Vancouver). He was the son of Hok Yat Louie, founder of a VANCOUVER grocery. When his father died suddenly in 1934, Tong interrupted his education to join the family business. Under his leadership H.Y. Louie Group grew and diversified. In 1955 it purchased the franchise for IGA grocery stores in BC, adding Dominion stores in 1968 and LONDON DRUGS in 1976. Louie's son took over pres-

Tong Louie, Vancouver entrepreneur.

idency of the company in 1987. Louie took a leading role in Vancouver's CHINESE and business communities and donated generously to various causes, including SFU, St Paul's Hospital, youth groups and health charities. He had an honorary degree from UBC, was inducted into the Order of Canada in 1989 and was a member of the ORDER OF BC (1991).

LOUIS CREEK, pop 95, 53 km north of KAMLOOPS on the east bank of the N THOMPSON R, is a SAWMILL community originally settled in 1886 by the BLACK prospector and storekeeper John Fremont Smith. It was the site of a ranch and hotel, and trapping, LOGGING and some GOLD mining all took place in the early days. It was named after either Chief Louis, a SECWEPEMC (Shuswap) leader (see Louis CLEXLIXQEN), or Louis Barrie, a prospector who found gold here in 1860. *AS*

LOVERBOY was a VANCOUVER rock band that achieved international success in the early 1980s with hits such as "The Kid is Hot Tonite," "Turn Me Loose" and "Working for the Weekend." Founded at a Calgary nightclub managed by Lou Blair, the group moved to Vancouver in 1979

The Vancouver rock band Loverboy, 1982.

when Blair struck a co-management deal with Bruce ALLEN. The band consisted of Paul Dean (guitar), Mike Reno (Rynoski) (vocals), Matt Frenette (drums), Doug Johnson (keyboards) and Scott Smith (bass). In Nov 1979 Loverboy debuted at the Pacific Coliseum as the opening act for the American glam-rockers Kiss. The 1980 debut album, *Loverboy*, sold more than 800,000 copies in N America and captured a record 6 Juno Awards. In 1981 the band released its second and most successful album, *Get Lucky*, which sold more than 3 million copies in the US. The third album, *Keep It Up* (1983), was the first of several records that failed to match the group's earlier successes and Loverboy eventually limited its activity to the occasional reunion tour. *See also* SOUND RECORDING INDUSTRY. *Mike Harling*

LOWE INLET cuts into the mainland shore of GRENVILLE CHANNEL, the northerly stretch of the INSIDE PASSAGE. The TSIMSHIAN call it Kmodo. The head of the inlet around Verney Falls has been an aboriginal FISHING site for centuries and is now part of a RESERVE belonging to the KITKATLA First Nation. A fish cannery operated in the inlet from 1890 to 1934 and there was some LOGGING during the 1930s. Lowe Inlet MARINE PARK is a favourite anchorage for coastal boaters. It is named for Thomas Lowe, an HBC employee.

LOWER MAINLAND; *see* GREATER VANCOUVER REGIONAL DISTRICT.

LOWER NICOLA, pop 494, is an old SCE'EXMX village, also known as Shulus, in the NICOLA Valley northwest of MERRITT. A large community-owned cattle herd ranges just west of here (*see* CATTLE INDUSTRY). There is a new health centre in the village, as well as several arts-oriented businesses and a golf range. AS

LOWER POST, pop 150, at Mile 620 of the ALASKA HWY near the Yukon border, is a settlement of KASKA people, who are related to those living at GOOD HOPE LAKE 90 km to the southwest. It was the site of a large RESIDENTIAL SCHOOL from 1953 until the 1970s. The HBC established a trading post here, where the Dease R joins the LIARD; it was lower on the river than the post at McDame Crk, a tributary of the upper Dease, hence the name. AS

LOWERY, Robert Thornton, editor, publisher (b 12 Apr 1859, Halton County, ON; d 20 May 1921, Grand Forks). Only a little over 5 ft tall (152 cm), "Colonel" Bob nevertheless loomed large on the KOOTENAY newspaper scene for more than 27 years. His feisty publications appeared all over the Kootenay, SLOCAN and BOUNDARY districts. His famous tombstone edition of the *Kaslo Claim* (25 Aug 1893) identified merchants with delinquent accounts by displaying advertisements upside down (unpaid) or sideways (partially paid). *Lowery's Claim*, his journal devoted to "Truth, Humour and Justice," was boycotted by the CPR and the post office. With the collapse of this paper in 1906, his passion for and involvement with a variety of publishing endeavours diminished. *See also* NEWSPAPERS.

Ron Welwood

LOWRY, Clarence Malcolm, novelist (b 28 July 1909, Birkenhead, England; d 27 June 1957, Ripe, England). One of England's most notorious expatriate writers, he moved to BC in 1939 and lived in a shack at DOLLARTON from 1940 to 1954, where he finished his most celebrated

Malcolm Lowry, writer, at his Dollarton shack, 1953. UBC BC1614/107

novel, *Under the Volcano* (1947). Lowry graduated from Cambridge Univ in 1932, then rejected his middle-class family and left England to begin a life of wandering, writing and drinking. His most productive years were spent in BC, where he completed his masterwork and also did much of the work on 2 more novels, *October Ferry to Gabriola* (1970) and *Dark as the Grave Wherein My Friend is Laid* (1968); a story collection, *Hear Us O Lord From Heaven Thy Dwelling Place* (1961); and a large number of poems, some of which were published in *Selected Poems of Malcolm Lowry* (1962). Not long after his death the shack in Dollarton was razed, but his years spent there with his second wife Margerie are memorialized by Malcolm Lowry Walk, a trail in Cates Park at DEEP COVE. Many of his letters were published in *Sursum Corda: The Collected Letters of Malcolm Lowry* (2 vols, 1995–96), and the main archive of his papers and writings is at the UBC Library Special Collections.

LOWTHER, Patricia Louise (Tinmuth) "Pat," poet (b 29 July 1935, Vancouver; d 24 Sept 1975, Vancouver). At age 16 she quit school to work and write. She produced 4 volumes of poetry: *This Difficult Flowering* (1968), *The Age of*

Pat Lowther, poet, 1970.
Peter Hulbert/Vancouver Sun

the Bird (1972), *Milk Stone* (1974) and *A Stone Diary* (1977). She was an activist in the NDP and in 1974 served as co-chair of the League of Canadian Poets. She was murdered by her husband Roy, a schoolteacher, who was convicted and later died in prison. The League of Canadian Poets annually presents the Pat Lowther Award in her memory. *Time Capsule*, another volume of poems, including some discovered in the mid-1990s, was published in 1997.

LUCERNE (or Lucerne Station) was a divisional point on the CANADIAN NORTHERN RWY, 32 km west of Jasper on Yellowhead Lk just inside the BC–Alberta border. The station was built in 1912 and a lively railway community grew up around it; its peak population was 300, but it was abandoned in the 1920s when the railway shifted operations to Jasper. A camp of Japanese Canadian internees (*see* JAPANESE, RELOCATION OF) was located here during WWII to help construct the Yellowhead Hwy. AS

LUKACS, Attila Richard, artist (b 1962, Calgary). A graduate of the EMILY CARR INSTITUTE OF ART & DESIGN, he was associated in VANCOUVER with a group of artists known as the Young Romantics. He began to gain an international reputation during the mid-1980s for his provocative tableaux of naked male skinheads. After moving to Berlin in 1988, he continued to produce large figurative paintings, notably a 6-painting cycle collectively titled *E-Werk*. He moved to New York in 1996.

LULU ISLAND is one of the large islands formed by silt deposits at the mouth of the FRASER R directly south of VANCOUVER. It is now occupied by the city of RICHMOND. Surveyed in 1859, the low-lying, boggy island was designated Island No. 1 until 1863, when it was christened after the visiting American actress Lulu Sweet. The earliest farm settlers arrived soon after (*see* AGRICULTURE) and the island was incorporated, along with neighbouring SEA ISLAND, as the Corporation of Richmond in 1879. STEVESTON began developing as a SALMON CANNING centre on the south arm of the Fraser in the 1880s. Most of the fertile agricultural land has been developed for housing, but the island still has 48 km² of farmland preserved in the AGRICULTURAL LAND RESERVE. Flooding used to be a major problem but has largely been prevented with dikes. The island is connected to Vancouver on the north by the Knight St and Oak St bridges and to NEW WESTMINSTER by the Queensborough Bridge. To the south, the George Massey Tunnel carries traffic between Lulu Island and DELTA.

LUMBER WORKERS' INDUSTRIAL UNION (LWIU) was formed in 1929 by the Communist-backed Workers Unity League to organize FOREST INDUSTRY workers in BC. Its first major action was to stage a strike in 1931 at the CANADIAN WESTERN LUMBER CO mill at MILLSIDE. Led by 27-year-old Harold PRITCHETT, the strike ended after 3 months with a wage increase for millworkers. Subsequently the LWIU led job actions in other SAWMILLS and LOGGING camps in the province, notably in 1934 on VANCOUVER ISLAND, where a bitter strike prompted the provincial government to introduce a minimum wage for FOREST INDUSTRY workers. In 1936 the LWIU merged with the United Brotherhood of Carpenters and Joiners to form the Lumber and Sawmill Workers' Union of BC, based in Vancouver, a step that led the next year to the creation of the International Woodworkers of

America (*see* INDUSTRIAL WOOD AND ALLIED WORKERS OF CANADA). *See also* FOREST INDUSTRY; LABOUR MOVEMENT.

LUMBERMAN'S ARCH in STANLEY PARK overlooking VANCOUVER's inner harbour was erected originally by the BC Lumber and Shingle Manufacturers to celebrate the 1912 visit to the city by the Canadian gov gen, the Duke of Connaught. Following the Duke's visit it was moved from its downtown location to the park; it stood there until the early 1950s, when it was replaced by a simpler structure. The arch stands on the site of a FIRST NATIONS village, Khwaykhway, that was burned after an outbreak of SMALLPOX in 1888. The village stood on a shell MIDDEN that indicated human occupation going back many generations.

LUMBERTON is an abandoned mill town 13 km southwest of CRANBROOK in the E KOOTENAY. It was founded in 1910 as Wattsburg after A.E. Watts, the original owner of the SAWMILL. In 1922 he sold the mill to BC Spruce Mills Ltd; the operation was expanded into the largest in the Interior, supporting a population of 250. In 1941 the mill closed and the town gradually disappeared.

The BC Spruce Mills flume at Lumberton, 1920s. BC Archives F-08769

LUMBY, village, pop 1,689, 25 km east of VERNON on Hwy 6 in the rolling foothills of the MONASHEE MTS. Quebec forest workers settled the area in the 1870s and gave it the name White Valley. Louis Morand and Quinn Faulkner laid out a townsite in 1888; it became the trading centre for the surrounding FOREST INDUSTRY and ranching (*see* CATTLE INDUSTRY) districts of Echo, Sugar and MABEL lakes and Cherry Creek, Creighton Valley and Trinity Valley. It was renamed in 1892 after Moses Lumby (1842–93), government agent and vice-president of the SHUSWAP & OKANAGAN RWY. The forest industry continued to be the major economic activity.

The historic Lund Hotel, 1996.
Allison Eaton photo

LUND, pop 204, is a coastal hamlet at the end of the SUNSHINE COAST Hwy (Hwy 101), 25 km north of POWELL RIVER. Long a winter camping ground for FIRST NATIONS people, the settlement was founded in 1889 by 2 young brothers, Charles and Frederick THULIN, recent immigrants from Sweden. They named the spot Lund, Swedish for "forest grove." By 1892 the community had a wharf, a store, a post office and regular steamship service. Two years later the brothers built the first licensed hotel north of VANCOUVER. Commercial FISHING and LOGGING were the mainstays of the local economy for many years. Later, marine TOURISM became important as well. Highway 101 was paved in 1954. It is part of the longest highway in the world, which runs from Tierra del Fuego to Lund.

LUSITANIA RIOTS were public outbursts of anti-German sentiment in VICTORIA following the sinking of the British passenger liner *Lusitania* off the coast of Ireland by a German submarine on 7 May 1915. Feelings ran high because among the 1,195 fatalities were 15 people from Victoria, including James Dunsmuir, son of the former LT GOV. When word spread that local GERMANS were celebrating the sinking, an angry crowd smashed up German-owned businesses while the police watched. The mayor was forced to read the Riot Act and call out troops to maintain the peace. On 10 May, anger bubbled to the surface once again and another mob marched on Government House (*see* CARY CASTLE), home of then Lt Gov Francis BARNARD: Barnard's wife Martha Loewen was a member of a prominent German family. Once again troops had to be deployed at the residence. There was no more rioting, but the incidents culminated in public calls for the internment of BC's German population.

LUTHERAN CHURCH is a Protestant church founded by Martin Luther in the early 16th century. Considered the "mother church" of Protestantism, it accepts the Bible as the word of God and emphasizes that sinners receive forgiveness from God alone through faith in Jesus Christ. In addition to the Bible, Lutherans look to the Book of Concord (1580) for doctrinal guidance. Local congregations hold the seat of authority.

The first Lutherans came to BC during the GOLD RUSH in 1858. A second influx arrived in the 1880s to work on construction of the CPR. Although most of these newcomers came from the US, many also came from eastern Canada and Europe. GERMANS, Scandinavians and eastern Europeans were among the most prominent Lutheran groups who settled in BC. Early Lutheran churches tended to be exclusive, built to serve the needs of particular national groups. The first Lutheran church built in BC was founded by a group of Icelandic settlers in VICTORIA in 1889. Later the site was acquired by some German Lutherans and became St Paul's Evangelical Lutheran Church. German Lutherans also built churches in Vancouver and the OKANAGAN VALLEY in the early 1900s. VANCOUVER became a centre for Scandinavian Lutherans in 1890, when the

LUTHERANS IN BC

Year	Members	% of BC Population
1881	632	1.3
1891	2,129	2.2
1901	5,395	3.0
1911	19,483	5.0
1921	17,709	3.4
1931	36,938	5.3
1941	41,884	5.1
1951	60,641	5.2
1961	100,393	6.2
1971	120,355	5.5
1981	122,395	4.5
1991	108,190	3.3

First Scandinavian Lutheran Church was constructed. Norwegian, Swedish and Danish Lutherans later established separate congregations in the city. The first Finnish Lutheran church was established in NANAIMO in 1893, but it was abandoned as Finnish settlers migrated to the Lower Mainland and to SOINTULA. Lutheran immigrants from eastern Europe, notably Estonia and Latvia, also established congregations in Vancouver. After WWII the Lutheran Church experienced rapid growth in BC, quickly developing a presence in most major cities. A radio show, *The Lutheran Hour*, has been broadcast throughout BC since 1930.

There are 2 Lutheran jurisdictions in Canada: the Evangelical Lutheran Church in Canada (ELCC) and Lutheran Church-Canada (LCC). The ELCC, formed in 1986, is an amalgamation of the Lutheran Church of America and the Evangelical Lutheran Church of Canada and has headquarters in Winnipeg. The LCC consists of the districts of the Lutheran Church Missouri Synod in Canada. There are 54 congregations of the LCC in BC, and at the 1991 census a total of 108,190 Lutherans lived in the province.

Dianne Mackay

LYNN CREEK is a turbulent stream flowing south out of the North Shore mountains between GROUSE MT and Lynn Peak, emptying into BURRARD INLET west of the IRONWORKERS MEMORIAL SECOND NARROWS CROSSING. The creek is named for John Linn, a member of the ROYAL ENGINEERS, who built the first home on its banks. The residential suburb of Lynn Valley developed in the early 1900s around J.M. Fromme's SAWMILL. LOGGING began in the upper watershed in the 1890s and continued until 1929, when it was closed to the public and used as a municipal water supply for N VANCOUVER. The water supply was shifted to other watersheds in 1983, and Lynn Headwaters Regional Park (46.85 km²) opened in the upper reaches of the creek in 1986. Lynn Canyon Park (2.5 km²) is a smaller park encompassing a particularly scenic and dangerous middle stretch of the creek, where a suspension bridge was built in 1912.

LYNX (*Lynx canadensis*) is one of 3 wildcats in BC (the others are the COUGAR and BOBCAT). They inhabit the Interior forests, where they prey mainly on snowshoe hare, though they also eat RODENTS and birds. The lynx weighs up to 18 kg and is characterized by a short tail, large feet, tawny fur and long black ear tufts, which improve hearing. The female bears up to 4 kits in

the early summer and the young remain with their mother for about a year. Lynx are speedy, agile predators that hunt over large areas. The size of the BC population is uncertain, probably between 20,000 and 80,000. Lynx pelts are valued by trappers.

LYONS, C.P. "Ches," naturalist (b 1915, Regina, SK; d 20 Dec 1998). He moved to PENTICTON with his family when he was 4 years old and grew up in the OKANAGAN VALLEY. After graduating in forest engineering from UBC in 1939, he went to work for the BC Parks Branch, a brand new organization at the time (*see* PARKS, PROVINCIAL). In his role as parks engineer he was involved in the development of most of the major provincial parks. He was also one of the people responsible for the restoration of BARKERVILLE and managed the site for its first 4 years. After leaving government he became a popular lecturer, wildlife filmmaker, television producer and author, well known for his appearances on the CBC television program *Klahanie*. The WEST COAST TRAIL, PACIFIC RIM NATIONAL PARK RESERVE (*see also* PARKS, NATIONAL) and BOWRON LAKE PROVINCIAL PARK were all brought to public attention by Ches Lyons. His books include *Milestones on the Mighty Fraser* (1950), *Trees, Shrubs and Flowers to Know in BC* (1952), *Milestones on Vancouver Island* (1958) and *Milestones in Ogopogo Land* (1957).

LYONS, Thaddeus Sylvester "Teddy," transit worker (b 1887, Portage la Prairie, MB; d 27 Feb 1955, Vancouver). From 1911 to 1950 he worked

as a conductor on one of BC ELECTRIC RWY CO's 2 open-air observation cars touring downtown VANCOUVER. He was a master of the corny one-liner who entertained passengers with a steady stream of jokes and stories. He was one of the city's most popular characters; BC Electric even published a book of his patter. The observation cars retired in 1950 and Lyons followed the next year.

LYTTON, village, pop 322, sprawls along the benchlands above the confluence of the THOMPSON and FRASER rivers, 258 km northeast of VANCOUVER. The northern gateway to the Fraser Canyon, it was the site of a NLAKA'PAMUX (Thompson) village called Kumsheen long before the arrival of the first outsiders. Settlers arrived with the GOLD RUSH and the site was named in 1858 after Edward Bulwer-Lytton, the British colonial secretary and a popular novelist remembered for his immortal opening line: "It was a dark and stormy night…" The CARIBOO WAGON ROAD, 2 transcontinental railways and the TRANS-CANADA HWY all passed through the community, which incorporated on 3 May 1945. AGRICULTURE and the railways were the mainstays of the local economy for many years. In the 1960s the FOREST INDUSTRY became important and GINSENG became a valuable cash crop. The STEIN Valley is nearby, and whitewater rafting attracts many visitors. Lytton and nearby LILLOOET share the distinction of being the hottest spot in Canada; on 16 July 1941 the mercury reached a record 44.4°C.

View of Lytton, 1895. Lytton Museum & Archives

McBRIDE, village, pop 740, on the Yellowhead Hwy (*see* ROADS AND HWYS) 207 km west of PRINCE GEORGE, was founded during the construction of the GRAND TRUNK PACIFIC RWY (1906–14) and named for Premier Richard MCBRIDE. The local economy relies on AGRICULTURE and the FOREST INDUSTRY, and McBride is the service centre for the surrounding ROBSON VALLEY.

McBRIDE, Richard, lawyer, politician, premier 1 June 1903–15 Dec 1915 (b 15 Dec 1870, New Westminster; d 6 Aug 1917, London, England). He graduated in law from Dalhousie Univ in Halifax and practised mainly in NEW WESTMINSTER. First elected to the legislature in 1898, he

Richard McBride, premier of BC 1903–15, in a painting by Victoria Albert Long, 1929. BC Archives PDP-02261

joined James DUNSMUIR's cabinet in 1900 as minister of mines, but resigned the following year and sat as leader of the opposition. When E.G. PRIOR resigned, McBride took over as PREMIER, the first born in the province and, at 32, the youngest in BC history. In the ensuing election he ran under the CONSERVATIVE PARTY banner, thus introducing party lines to BC politics. Despite a slim majority he rode a booming economy to unprecedented electoral success: he won re-election 3 times, held office longer than any other premier until W.A.C. BENNETT and became the only BC premier to be knighted (1912).

Early in his tenure, when he needed the support of Labour MLAs, McBride introduced an 8-hour work day in the COAL mines. He also tried to ban Asian immigration, but the federal government consistently overturned his legislation. In the 1909 and 1912 elections he virtually eliminated the opposition and no longer needed to consider anyone's agenda but his own. A charming, sociable politician, he was popular with voters, earning the nicknames "Handsome Dick" and "The People's Dick." He presided over an era of unprecedented resource giveaways as he

MABEL LAKE is a farming (*see* AGRICULTURE) and LOGGING community on the Shuswap R, 35 km east of VERNON and 12 km south of the lake itself, which was named for Mabel Hope Charles, daughter of William Charles, HBC manager at Fort HOPE. A major log drive occurred for many years on the river. When the timber reached Mabel Lk, it was collected in a boom and winched to the outlet by horses working on a raft. Today there is a provincial PARK on the lake. *AS*

MACALISTER, on the east side of the FRASER R, 40 km north of WILLIAMS LAKE, was at the heart of a small farming and ranching district (*see* AGRICULTURE; CATTLE INDUSTRY). Named after James M. Macalister, an early settler, it was a station on the BC RAIL line and had a post office from 1914 to 1953. *AS*

McAULAY, Greg, curler (b 2 Jan 1960, Winnipeg). Skipping the Royal City CURLING rink from NEW WESTMINSTER, he led third Brent Pierce, second Brian Miki and lead Jody Sveistrup to the 2000 men's world championship in Glasgow, Scotland. After triumphing at the provincial championships and the national Brier tournament, the foursome, along with coach Glen Pierce, defeated the Swedish team 9–4 in the finals to win the world title. The win marked BC's third men's world title; the others were won by Lyall DAGG in 1964 and Rick FOLK in 1994. The McAulay rink's triumph was actually the third world championship of 2000 for BC curlers, after wins by Kelley LAW's Richmond Winter Club team in the women's competition and by Brad Kuhn's team from KELOWNA in the world juniors. *SW*

McBEAN, Marnie, rower (b 28 Jan 1968, Vancouver). She grew up in VANCOUVER but moved to Toronto as a teenager and learned to row there. She teamed with Vancouver's

Kathleen HEDDLE to win the straight pair races at the 1991 world championships. Both women were also part of the championship-winning Canadian 8 team at the same competition. The following year at the Barcelona Olympics the pair won gold medals in the same 2 events. Competing in single sculls, McBean won a silver at the 1993 world championships, a gold at the Commonwealth championships and an overall standing of first at the 1994 World Cup competition. Heddle came out of retirement to rejoin McBean as a double-sculls pair and they won sil-

Marnie McBean (l) with her rowing partner Kathleen Heddle, displaying their 1996 Olympic gold medals. Arlen Redekop/Vancouver Province

ver medals at the 1994 world and Commonwealth championships, gold at the 1995 world championships and their third Olympic gold in 1996 in Atlanta. After her partner retired for a second time, McBean won a silver in the 4s and a bronze in the 8s at the 1998 world championships and resumed her single-sculls ROWING, winning at the 1999 Pan American Games. With their 3 gold medals she and Heddle are the most successful Canadian Olympians of the twentieth

attracted investment to the province with large land grants to railways (including the CANADIAN NORTHERN RWY and the Pacific Great Eastern Rwy, later BC RAIL) and preferential deals with timber and MINING companies. At the same time he launched a campaign for "Better Terms" within Canada, arguing that BC deserved more out of CONFEDERATION. His success in BC gave him considerable stature on the national scene, where there was a move to draft him as a successor to Prime Minister Robert Borden. However, following the 1912 election his popularity was eroded by a pre-war economic depression, growing public suspicion about his railway grants, and his indifference to emerging issues such as workers' rights (*see* LABOUR MOVEMENT), WOMEN'S SUFFRAGE and PROHIBITION. With his government beset by fiscal problems and by demands for reforms he did not want to make, McBride resigned and took over the post of BC agent general in London, where he died of Bright's disease soon after.

McCARTHY, Grace Mary (Winterbottom), politician (b 14 Oct 1927, Vancouver). She opened Grayce Florists in 1944 and was a successful businessperson when she launched her political career by winning election to the VANCOUVER parks board in 1960. After 6 years on the board she switched to provincial politics, running successfully for SOCIAL CREDIT in the 1966 election. She was minister without portfolio in W.A.C. BENNETT's last government, then lost her seat in the 1972 election that brought the NDP to

Grace McCarthy, prominent Social Credit politician, 1997. David Clark/Vancouver Province

power. As president of the Social Credit Party she played a key role in rebuilding under its new leader, Bill BENNETT, and when the Socreds returned to power in 1975 she won re-election and rejoined the CABINET as provincial secretary, minister of tourism and deputy premier. When Bennett retired in 1986 she ran for the party leadership but lost to Bill VANDER ZALM. She resigned from her cabinet post of economic development minister in 1988 over differences with Vander Zalm. When he retired she ran again for the leadership, but lost to Rita JOHNSTON. On

a third try in 1993 she finally won the leadership, but by this time the party was virtually nonexistent; when she lost a by-election she retired from politics and began devoting her time to charitable work.

McCONNELL, William C. "Bill," lawyer, writer, editor (b 12 Feb 1917, Vancouver). After serving in the Canadian Army during WWII he was among the first graduates from UBC's law school and was called to the bar in 1949. In addition to a busy law practice, he published many short stories in the major literary MAGAZINES from the 1940s to the 1970s. He founded KLANAK PRESS in 1958 and published early work by important BC writers, including Jane RULE and Robert HARLOW. He was a close friend and legal advisor to Malcolm LOWRY, whose novel *October Ferry to Gabriola* is dedicated to him. A selection of McConnell's own fiction, *Raise No Memorial*, was published in 1989. He lives and continues to write in W VANCOUVER.

McCREIGHT, John Foster, lawyer and first premier 14 Nov 1871–23 Dec 1872 (b 1827, Caledon, Ireland; d 18 Nov 1913, Hastings,

John McCreight, premier of BC 1871–72. BC Archives A-01449

England). After practising law in Australia he arrived in VICTORIA in 1860; there he earned a reputation as an effective lawyer. In 1871, after the province entered CONFEDERATION, he was one of 25 members elected to the first provincial legislature, and Lt Gov Joseph TRUTCH asked him to become PREMIER. By all accounts bad-tempered and obstinate, McCreight proved a disappointing premier. He resigned a year later and retired from the assembly altogether in 1875. Named a justice of the provincial Supreme Court in 1880, he served in the CARIBOO, then in NEW WESTMINSTER until his retirement in 1897, when he returned to England.

McCRORY, Colleen, environmentalist (b 5 Jan 1950, New Denver). She is one of the leading

activists in the BC ENVIRONMENTAL MOVEMENT, and since 1976 has been chair of the Valhalla Wilderness Society. Her initiation into the movement was a successful 8-year campaign for the creation of Valhalla Provincial PARK (1983) near her hometown, NEW DENVER. She was also involved in QUEEN CHARLOTTE ISLANDS protests that led to the creation of the national park reserve (*see* PARKS, NATIONAL) on S Moresby Island (1987). She has since been active in a variety of campaigns to conserve Canadian FORESTS.

McCULLOCH, Andrew, railway engineer (b 16 June 1864, Lanark County, ON; d 13 Dec 1945, Penticton). Raised on a farm in eastern Ontario, he attended business college in Kingston and in 1889 struck out for the West Coast on the CPR. For several years he worked in sawmills and on rail construction in the US and western Canada, and eventually settled in as a chief engineer with the CPR. He was in charge of the construction of many CPR lines in eastern Canada from 1907 to 1910, but he is primarily known for his work as chief engineer during construction of the KETTLE VALLEY RWY from MIDWAY to HOPE via the Coquihalla Pass from 1910 to 1916. He is the one who named the stations on the Coquihalla line after characters from Shakespeare's plays. When construction of the KVR (known colloquially as "McCulloch's Wonder") was completed, he became superintendent, a job he held until his retirement on 31 Jan 1933.

McDAME, Henry, prospector (b Bahamas; d circa 1900). He was a BLACK man who was attracted to BC in 1858 by the GOLD RUSH to the FRASER R; he then pursued his search for GOLD in the CARIBOO in the 1860s and the Omineca in 1870. In the Omineca he had a hand in discovering the rich deposits on Germansen Crk. By 1874 he had moved on to DEASE LK. Travelling north, he made his way up the Dease R and followed the creek that now bears his name, where he found evidence of gold. His discovery touched off a frantic rush to what turned out to be the most productive creek in the CASSIAR district. The details of his life are sketchy, though he appears to have been prospecting on the SKEENA R in 1884.

MACDONALD, Blanche (Brillon), entrepreneur, aboriginal activist (b 11 May 1931, Faust, AB; d 8 June 1985, Vancouver). She came to VANCOUVER as a teenager from Edmonton with her Cree mother. After her mother remarried they moved to Alaska, but Blanche returned to Vancouver to attend secretarial school. She began modelling and in 1952 was crowned Miss ENGLISH BAY in a beauty pageant. In the mid-1950s she taught modelling in Los Angeles, but returned to Vancouver in 1960 with her new husband, Jack Macdonald, to launch her own modelling agency and self-improvement school. A generation of young women learned their self-presentation skills at Blanche Macdonald's. She was also an advocate for ABORIGINAL RIGHTS; the year of her death she received a Woman of Distinction award from the YWCA.

MACDONALD, James W.G. "Jock," artist (b 31 May 1897, Thurso, Scotland; d 3 Dec 1960, Toronto). He was teaching commercial design in England when he was appointed to the VANCOUVER School of Decorative and Applied Arts (*see* EMILY CARR INSTITUTE OF ART & DESIGN) in 1926. For the next 20 years he was a leading exponent of modern art in the city. He began to paint under the influence of Fred VARLEY, with whom he co-founded the short-lived but influential BC College of Arts (1933–35). When the college went bankrupt he moved with his family to Friendly Cove (*see* YUQUOT) in NOOTKA SOUND, on VANCOUVER ISLAND, to pursue his attempts to capture the spiritual essence of the natural world on canvas. His experiments with colour and "automatic" painting made him one of the first abstract artists in Canada. At the end of 1936 he returned to Vancouver broke and in poor health. Eventually he found work as a high school art teacher. Meanwhile he found encouragement for the spiritual content of his paintings in his friendship with Emily CARR and, after 1940, with Lawren HARRIS, and in the influence of surrealism. In 1946 he left Vancouver to take a teaching post in Calgary, and in 1947 he moved to the Ontario College of Art in Toronto, where he played a key role in the abstract group Painters Eleven. He lived there for the rest of his life.

MacDONALD, Ranald, adventurer (b 3 Feb 1824, Fort George, OR; d 24 Aug 1894, Toroda, WA). His father was a Scottish fur trader working for the HBC; his mother was a Chinook woman, the daughter of a chief. Ranald was raised at FORT LANGLEY and Fort Colville and educated in Red River. At age 17 he embarked on a life of adventure, working first as a deckhand on Mississippi riverboats, then shipping out of New York as a sailor. In 1848, while serving on a WHALING ship, he arrived in Japan claiming to be shipwrecked. Japan was closed to foreigners at the time; MacDonald was imprisoned and during his confinement became the first teacher of English in Japan. After his release he visited the Australian goldfields before rejoining his family in Montreal. In 1858 MacDonald returned to BC and lived for 20 years in the BONAPARTE area, engaged in a variety of ventures. He ran a ferry across the FRASER R; he explored for minerals and for alternative pack routes to the Interior; and he ranched. In 1864 he was a member of the VANCOUVER ISLAND EXPLORING EXPEDITION. In the early 1880s he returned to Fort Colville, where he lived the rest of his life.
Reading: Ranald MacDonald, *The Narrative of his Early Life on the Columbia under the Hudson's Bay Company's regime; of his experiences in the Pacific Whale Fishery; and of his Great Adventure to Japan; with a sketch of his later life on the Western Frontier 1824–1894,* 1990.

MacDONALD, DETTWILER AND ASSOCIATES LTD (MDA), based in RICHMOND, is a world-class provider of information services and technology. Founded in 1969 by Dr John S. MacDonald, a PRINCE RUPERT native, the company is diversified across international space,

Internet systems development and information product markets. In 1999 the company acquired the robotics division of Spar Aerospace (now MD Robotics), developers of the Canadarm, the mechanical arm attached to the US space shuttle. It also acquired RADARSAT International, worldwide distributors of satellite imagery for mapping, environmental monitoring and disaster management applications. MDA is partially owned by Orbital Sciences Corp of Virginia.

McFARLANE, James "Jim," engineer (b 20 June 1934, Winnipeg). A mechanical engineer, naval architect and marine engineer, he was introduced to submersibles in 1966, when he was an officer in the Canadian navy and got involved in submarine construction in England. After returning to Ottawa, he assumed responsibility for program management for new underwater systems. He left the navy in 1971 to come to BC to work for International Hydrodynamics Ltd as director of engineering and later director of engineering and operations. In 1974 he formed his own company, International Submarine Engineering, in PORT MOODY, specializing in the production of Remotely Operated Vehicles (ROVs). Starting with just 2 employees, ISE grew to become the largest SUBSEA TECHNOLOGY company in Canada and one of the largest in the world. A company subsidiary, International Submarine Engineering Research, deals primarily with Autonomous Underwater Vehicles (AUVs) while the parent company focuses on ROVs and robotics. *Vickie Jensen*

McGEER, Gerald Grattan, lawyer, politician, mayor of Vancouver (b 6 Jan 1888, Winnipeg; d 11 Aug 1947, Vancouver). One of the most prominent, flamboyant politicians in VANCOUVER's history, he is described by his biographer as "the most successful failed politician of his time." He moved to Vancouver in his youth with his family and quit school at age 14 to become an iron moulder. As a member of the union he developed into a skilled debater and decided to

Gerry McGeer, mayor of Vancouver 1934–36 and 1946–47. CVA Port.P967

become a lawyer. After studies in Halifax and Vancouver he was called to the bar in 1915. McGeer was an active LIBERAL PARTY member and won election to the provincial legislature in 1916. The next year he married Charlotte Spencer, daughter of the department store owner David SPENCER. In accordance with her wish that he not run for re-election, he retired from politics temporarily. During the 1920s McGeer represented BC in freight-rate negotiations with the railways and the federal government, helping to win lower rates and stimulating the development of the PORT OF VANCOUVER.

During the Depression, McGeer conceived his own unique analysis of the financial system, which he trumpeted from podiums across the country and later published as *The Conquest of Poverty* (1935). His speeches earned him public notoriety, and in the 1933 provincial election he re-entered the legislature as a Liberal. Surprisingly, Premier Duff PATTULLO did not ask him to join the CABINET and McGeer proved to be a renegade MLA, attacking his government as often as he supported it.

In 1934 he decided to run for mayor of Vancouver and won easily in Dec of that year. Despite the Depression, McGeer managed to improve the city's debt situation, lead a campaign against police corruption, launch construction of a new city hall and host a lavish celebration of the Golden Jubilee in 1936. However, he is probably most remembered for his militant response to unemployed demonstrators in Apr 1935 when he read the Riot Act in Victory Square.

Before his term was up McGeer won election to the federal parliament, and he did not seek re-election as mayor. As a federal MP he once again ran afoul of his leader, Prime Minister Mackenzie King. When he retired from parliament in 1945, he was appointed to the Senate. A year later he was elected mayor again, but his health was deteriorating, due in part to his heavy drinking, and he died midway through the first year of his term.
Reading: David Ricardo Williams, *Mayor Gerry,* 1986.

McGEER, Patrick, medical scientist, politician (b 29 June 1927, Vancouver), and **Edith (Graef)** (b 18 Nov 1923, New York City). Educated at UBC and Princeton Univ, he joined the faculty of medicine at UBC in 1959 and established a reputation as a leading researcher in the area of neurobiology. He retired in 1992 and became professor emeritus at the university. A noted athlete in his youth, McGeer was inducted into the BC SPORTS HALL OF FAME in 1996. First elected to the legislature as a LIBERAL in a 1962 by-election, he became party leader in 1968 but failed to improve its standing and gave up the leadership in 1972. In 1975 he crossed the floor to join the SOCIAL CREDIT PARTY, then led by Bill BENNETT, who became PREMIER late that year. McGeer went on to serve as minister of education (1976–79), minister of universities, science and communications (1979–86) and minister of international trade (1986). His political career ended in 1986 and he returned to medical research in partnership with his wife Edith. Also a professor emerita at UBC, she joined the university as a researcher in 1954. The McGeers are both officers in the Order of Canada and have conducted important research related to Alzheimer's disease and associated disorders.

MacGILL, Helen Gregory, journalist, judge (b 7 Jan 1864, Hamilton, ON; d 27 Feb 1947, Chicago). The first woman graduate of Trinity College, Univ of Toronto, she moved to California with her first husband in 1892. In San Francisco she worked as a journalist and co-edited a suffragist newspaper (*see* WOMEN'S SUFFRAGE). After her husband died, she married

Helen MacGill, BC's first woman judge.
CVA Port.P1140

James MacGill and moved to VANCOUVER in 1901. Active in various women's, business and social welfare organizations, in 1917 she accepted appointment as judge of the juvenile court, the first woman judge in BC; she served on the bench in 1917–28 and in 1934–45. She wrote several books on legal and social issues and in 1938 was the first woman to receive an honorary law degree from UBC.
Reading: Elsie MacGill, *My Mother the Judge*, 1981.

McGILLIVRAY FALLS is a summer resort area 105 km northeast of SQUAMISH on BC RAIL and the north shore of ANDERSON LK. It was named after nearby McGillivray Crk, which probably honours William McGillivray, chief director of the NORTH WEST CO in the early 1800s.   AS

McGOWAN, Edward "Ned," prospector (b 1813; d 1893). He was superintendent of police in Philadelphia, where he was implicated in a bank robbery, and a judge in California, where he was acquitted on a murder charge, before he came to the FRASER R in 1858 to mine at Hill's Bar, near Fort YALE (*see* GOLD RUSH, FRASER R). Late in Dec 1858, P.B. Whannell, the justice of the

peace in Yale, ordered the arrest of 2 Hill's Bar men on charges of assault. The Hill's Bar magistrate arrested the men, but decided they would stand trial in his court. The petty dispute escalated: Whannell, furious, imprisoned a police constable from Hill's Bar, then Ned McGowan led a gang to Yale to release the constable and arrest Whannell. Fearing an outbreak of violence in the goldfields, Gov James DOUGLAS dispatched a force of ROYAL ENGINEERS, led by R.C. MOODY, to keep the peace. McGowan stood trial and after lecturing the miners, mainly Americans, on the virtues of British law, Judge Matthew BEGBIE fined him a small amount for assault. Both sides in the dispute were satisfied; despite comic overtones the incident, which became known as "Ned McGowan's War," is considered a turning point toward the peaceful development of the MINING frontier. McGowan returned to California soon after.

McGREGOR, a LOGGING settlement 63 km east of PRINCE GEORGE on the FRASER R and the VIA Rail line, was abandoned in about 1970. The McGregor R, named after Capt James McGregor, a well-known VICTORIA land surveyor killed in WWI, runs to the north through the McGregor model forest, where research is done on sustainable LOGGING. Various area SAWMILLS, including the Cornell mill at nearby Dewey, operated over the years. By 1999 only a few CNR employees lived at McGregor.   AS

McGREGOR, Donald Alexander, journalist (b 25 Aug 1879, Kincardine, ON; d 31 Oct 1970, Vancouver). After graduating from Queens Univ in 1905, he taught school briefly before joining the *Montreal Herald* as a police reporter. He moved to VANCOUVER in 1910 and joined the PROVINCE, where he worked for the next 45 years, gaining a reputation as one of the country's best editorial writers. He was also a historian who wrote widely about BC's commercial history. His book about the LT GOVS, *They Gave Royal Assent*, appeared in 1967. *See also* NEWSPAPERS.

McGUIGAN, a siding on the KASLO & SLOCAN RWY 58 km north of NELSON, was named for a local prospector, as was nearby McGuigan Crk. A townsite was laid out in 1892 and a number of mines (*see* MINING) were soon served by a store and 3 hotels. The K&S abandoned the section of line near McGuigan in 1909 and a FOREST FIRE destroyed much of the area the following year.
      AS

McILWRAITH, Thomas Forsyth, anthropologist (b 9 Apr 1899, Hamilton, ON; d 29 Mar 1964, Toronto). A student of the NUXALK (Bella Coola) people, he first came to the Pacific coast in 1922 as a young researcher sent by the Victoria Memorial Museum (now the Canadian Museum of Civilization). He lived among the Nuxalk for a year, though his authoritative book about them, *The Bella Coola Indians*, was not published until 1948. In 1925 he joined the Univ of Toronto, where he headed the department of anthropology for many years.

McINNES, Thomas Robert, doctor, lt gov 1897–1900 (b 5 Nov 1840, Lake Ainslie, Cape Breton Island; d 19 Mar 1904, Vancouver). The son of Scottish immigrants to Nova Scotia, he studied medicine in the US and after serving in the Civil War returned to Canada to settle in Dresden, ON. In 1874 he moved his family to NEW WESTMINSTER, where he built a successful medical practice and indulged an interest in politics. After serving as mayor from 1877 to 1878, he won election as a federal MP (1878–81) and was named to the Senate in 1881. On 1 Dec 1897 he began his term as BC's most controversial LT GOV. The period was marked by an unstable political situation. Parties were ill-defined and none of the leaders commanded a strong majority in the legislature. By deposing and appointing premiers without popular support, McInnes alienated the politicians and the public, forcing Prime Minister Laurier to dismiss him on 20 June 1900. McInnes is the only lt gov in BC history to have lost his post in mid-term. In 1903 he attempted a political comeback, running for election to a federal seat for the new Provincial Progressive Party, a very short-lived alliance, but he lost badly and died a year later.

MacINNIS, Angus, streetcar conductor, politician (b 2 Sept 1884, Glen William, PEI; d 2 Mar 1964, Vancouver). He came to BC in 1908 to work on an uncle's dairy farm on LULU ISLAND. Largely self-educated, he became a streetcar conductor in 1910 and later worked for the Street Railwaymen's Union (*see* STREET RAILWAYS). He won election to the VANCOUVER school board in 1922, the beginning of a long political career. After serving on city council in 1926–30, he was federal MP for Vancouver East from 1930 to 1956, first as a Labourite (*see* INDEPENDENT LABOUR PARTY), then as a member of the CCF, a party he helped to organize. He married Grace Woodsworth in 1932 (*see* MACINNIS, Grace). When he retired because of ill health, he was the longest-serving MP in the House of Commons and one of the most respected. UBC granted him an honorary doctorate in 1956.

MacINNIS, Grace Winona (Woodsworth), politician (b 25 July 1905, Winnipeg, MB; d 10 July 1991, Vancouver). The daughter of J.S. Woodsworth, founding father of the CCF, she was raised in a highly political environment. In 1931 she became her father's secretary in Ottawa and the following year she married Angus MACINNIS, a Labour MP from VANCOUVER. She became a leading organizer for the newly formed CCF and in 1941 won election to the BC LEGISLATIVE ASSEMBLY. In 1945 she lost her seat but remained a strong force within the party. A moderate social democrat, she resisted all attempts to carry the party too far to the left. In 1953 she published a biography of her father, *J.S. Woodsworth: A Man to Remember*. When Angus died in 1964, Grace returned to electoral politics, winning the Vancouver–Kingsway seat for the NDP in the 1965 federal election, thus becoming BC's first female MP. She held the seat until 1974, when poor health forced her

Grace MacInnis, CCF and NDP politician.

resignation. As a politician she was particularly interested in women's equality, consumers' rights and poverty issues.

McINTOSH, James, Kamloops entrepreneur (b 1842, Ottawa; d 23 June 1901, Kamloops). He came west to BC in 1862 and tried his luck at GOLD mining in the CARIBOO and on VANCOUVER ISLAND, then moved to KAMLOOPS in 1864. In partnership with William FORTUNE he built a flour mill and SAWMILL at TRANQUILLE, then became part of a partnership that built the Shuswap Milling Co on the Kamloops waterfront in 1877. Over the next several years there was hardly a development in town in which McIntosh was not involved, including the waterworks, the electric light company and the first hospital. As a result he became known as the "King of Kamloops." *Peggy Imredy*

McINTYRE BLUFF is a steep rock face rising 260 m above the valley floor at the south end of VASEUX LK just north of OLIVER in the OKANAGAN VALLEY. A prominent landmark, it was the site of a famous battle between OKANAGAN and SECWEPEMC (Shuswap) war parties in the days before white settlement. It is named after Peter McIntyre, an early settler who came to BC in 1862 with a party of OVERLANDERS.

McIVOR, Daniel, aviation pioneer (b 30 Aug 1911, Killarney, MB). He was working as a pilot for the FOREST INDUSTRY giant MACMILLAN BLOEDEL when he came up with the idea of fighting FOREST FIRES from the air. In 1957 he doused a small fire near PORT ALBERNI by dropping water-filled bags out of a Grumman Goose—the first time a plane had been used to extinguish a fire in BC. Seeking a more effective aircraft, he persuaded MacBlo to purchase the last 4 Martin Mars flying boats from a California naval station. He became chief pilot of Forest Industries Flying Tankers Ltd, a consortium of BC forest companies, and supervised the conversion of the Mars

into water bombers. The giant planes, capable of filling their 22,700-litre tanks in just 21 seconds, proved a great success and revolutionized the fighting of forest fires in BC. In 1963 McIvor moved to PACIFIC WESTERN AIRLINES, where he remained until his retirement in 1973. During his long career (he logged a total of 11,571 hours) he not only pioneered firefighting but also served as one of the original DEW Line pilots, participated in the KEMANO project at KITIMAT and helped to bring scheduled air service to the West Coast.

MACK, Clayton, Nuxalk hunter, guide (b 7 Aug 1910, Nieumiamus Creek; d Apr 1993, Bella Coola). His grandfather was the BELLA COOLA storekeeper John Clayton and his father Willie Mack was an influential NUXALK (Bella Coola) chief. Clayton Mack worked as a fisher, logger and a rancher in the CHILCOTIN before becoming one of the legendary trackers and hunting guides

Clayton Mack, Nuxalk guide. Hank Winning photo

on the coast. He claimed to have seen more than 300 grizzly BEARS killed during almost 50 years as a guide. His stories are collected in the books *Grizzlies and White Guys* (1993) and *Bella Coola Man* (1994).

MacKAY, Duncan McMillan "Mickey" a.k.a. the Wee Scot, hockey player (b 25 May 1894, Chelsey, ON; d 21 May 1940, Nelson). He came to BC in 1913 to play HOCKEY in GRAND FORKS and joined the VANCOUVER MILLIONAIRES of the PACIFIC COAST HOCKEY ASSOC the following year. He had a spectacular rookie year, leading the league in goals and points and playing a major role in the Millionaires' 1915 Stanley Cup victory. He skated with VANCOUVER for 11 seasons, helping it to 6 league championships, winning the goal-scoring title 3 times and finishing his PCHA career with 198 goals in 247 games. His 290 career points stand as the highest in the PCHA. After the league folded in 1926 he played 3 seasons in the NHL, leading the Chicago Blackhawks in scoring in 1927–28 and winning

the Stanley Cup with the Boston Bruins in 1929. Only a year after being named an all-time all-star by Maple Leaf Gardens in Toronto, he died in a car accident in the KOOTENAY. He was elected to the Hockey Hall of Fame in 1952 and to the BC SPORTS HALL OF FAME in 1989. *SW*

MACKAY, Isabel Ecclestone (Macpherson), writer (b 25 Nov 1875, Woodstock, ON; d 15 Aug 1928, Vancouver). She moved to VANCOUVER in 1909 with her husband and was an active member of various writers' groups. Well-connected to the major Canadian writers of her day, she was close to Pauline JOHNSON and in 1911 helped to raise money to publish Johnson's *Legends of Vancouver*. During her life she was best known for her poetry, of which 5 volumes were published. She also wrote 5 novels: *The House of Windows* (1912), *Up the Hill and Over* (1917), *Mist of Morning* (1919), *The Window-Gazer* (1921) and *Blencarrow* (1926).

McKAY, Joseph William, fur trader, businessman (b 31 Jan 1829, Rupert's House, QC; d 21 Dec 1900, Victoria). He was born to mixed-blood parents at a remote fur trade post on James Bay and joined the HBC himself in 1844, when he was 15 years old. After two years at Fort Vancouver on the COLUMBIA R he transferred to FORT VICTORIA, where he rose to second-in-command. A trusted subordinate of James DOUGLAS, he helped to negotiate treaties with the local FIRST NATIONS and began the development of COAL MINING at NANAIMO (*see also* COAL MINING, VANCOUVER ISLAND). In 1856 he won election to VANCOUVER ISLAND's first House of Assembly. After 1860 he served the HBC at several Interior posts, but by 1878 his outside business interests were so extensive that the company released him. He became a cannery manager and then an Indian agent. At the time of his death he was the assistant superintendent of Indian Affairs in BC.

McKELVIE, Bruce Alistair, journalist, historian (b 1889, Vancouver; d 1960). He was apprenticed to a printer when he was 10 years old and later became one of BC's leading journalists as managing editor of the *Victoria Colonist* (later *TIMES-COLONIST*) and feature writer for the Vancouver *PROVINCE*. He was also recognized as an early authority on BC history, writing books that were among the first to appear on the subject. These include *The Early History of the Province of British Columbia* (1926), *Maquinna the Magnificent* (1946), *Fort Langley: Outpost of Empire* (1947) and *Pageant of BC* (1955). A prolific popular writer, McKelvie also published a novel, *Huldowget: A Story of the North Pacific Coast* (1926), and several books for boys. Mt McKelvie on VANCOUVER ISLAND is named for him. *Shannon Emmerson*

McKENNA–McBRIDE COMMISSION (1913–16) was established under the terms of a 1912 federal-provincial agreement settling outstanding matters relating to aboriginal affairs. The agreement created a Royal Commission on Indian Affairs to adjust the size of BC RESERVES. The 5-person

Alexander Mackenzie recording his arrival at the Pacific, 1793. Painting by John Innes.
SFU & Native Sons of BC

commission was named for Premier Richard MCBRIDE, who was not a member, and J.A.J. McKenna, a federal Department of Indian Affairs official, who was. Both governments promised that changes to reserves would take place only with FIRST NATIONS' consent. After 3 years of extensive consultations the commission reported in June 1916. It recommended that 353.53 km² of land be added to existing reserves or used to create new ones, and that 190.58 km² be removed. The land "cut off" from the reserves was much more valuable than the additions and aboriginal groups objected. Nevertheless the governments violated their own guarantees and approved the changes. In 1924 the recommendations of the commission were officially implemented.

MACKENZIE, district municipality, pop 5,997, nestles in the ROCKY MT TRENCH at the south end of WILLISTON RESERVOIR, in 1999 the largest artificial lake in N America, 193 km north of PRINCE GEORGE. Named for the FUR TRADE explorer Alexander MACKENZIE, this was an instant community created in 1966 with the development of a FOREST INDUSTRY complex on the shores of the lake. This industry continued to be the main employer, with pulp mills (*see* PULP AND PAPER), a newsprint mill and several SAWMILLS.

MACKENZIE, Alexander, fur trader, explorer (b 1764, Stornoway, Isle of Lewis, Scotland; d 12 Mar 1820, Dunkeld, Scotland). At age 10 he went to the US with his widowed father, who subsequently died fighting on the loyalist side in the Revolutionary War. Young Alexander's aunts sent him to Montreal to go to school, and in 1779 he entered the FUR TRADE firm of Gregory, McLeod, one of the companies that later amalgamated to form the NORTH WEST CO. At that time Mackenzie became a partner and went to winter at a post on the Athabasca R, where he developed a plan to seek out the great river rumoured to flow westward into the Pacific. In 1789 he travelled north down the river that now

bears his name, as far as the Arctic Ocean. He was the first European to explore the Mackenzie R to its mouth but he was disappointed that it had not taken him in the direction he expected. He set out again in 1793, this time following a route up the PEACE R, across the ROCKY MTS, down the FRASER R and overland with the help of FIRST NATIONS guides to reach the Pacific at the mouth of BELLA COOLA R on North Bentinck Arm. He and his party continued by CANOE and reached DEAN CHANNEL, where he painted on a rock in Elcho Harbour the famous message "Alex Mackenzie, from Canada, by land, 22nd July 1793," before returning the way he had come. Parks Canada has erected a plaque at the site to commemorate the first known crossing of N America by a non-aboriginal person. Mackenzie was unaware that just 6 weeks earlier George VANCOUVER had rowed through these same waters as part of his survey of the coast. The next year Mackenzie went to Montreal, where he became a lightning rod for discontent within the NWC. In 1799 he quit the Nor'westers and joined the rival XY Co, which embarked on a bitter competition for control of the trade. The rivalry proved ruinous, and in 1804 the two companies combined. Mackenzie returned to England, where the publication of the journals of his expeditions, *Voyages from Montreal* (1801), had made him a celebrity and won him a knighthood. In 1812 he married and retired to a Scottish estate.

MACKENZIE, ALEXANDER, HERITAGE TRAIL; *see* ALEXANDER MACKENZIE HERITAGE TRAIL.

MACKENZIE, Ian Alistair, lawyer, politician (b 27 July 1890, Assynt, Scotland; d 2 Sept 1949, Banff, AB). After graduating in law from Edinburgh Univ he immigrated to BC in 1914. During WWI he served in France with the Seaforth Highlanders. His political career began in 1920 with his election to the provincial legislature as a LIBERAL. He lost his VANCOUVER seat in 1928 but switched to federal politics in 1930, winning election as Liberal MP for Vancouver Centre, a seat he held for the next 18 years. When the Liberals formed the government in 1935 he

joined the CABINET, first as defence minister (1935–39), then as minister of pensions and health (1939–44) and finally as veterans affairs minister (1944–48). An outspoken racist who opposed Asian immigration to BC, he was a key figure in the government's decision to relocate people of Japanese ancestry away from the coast during WWII (*see* JAPANESE, RELOCATION OF). By 1946 he had lost his influence in cabinet; early in 1948 Prime Minister Mackenzie King elevated him to the Senate.

MacKENZIE, Norman Archibald MacRae "Larry," lawyer, UBC president 1944–62 (b 5 Jan 1894, Pugwash, NS; d 26 Jan 1986, Vancouver). He survived 4 years in the trenches during WWI, then studied law at Dalhousie Univ in Halifax. After graduate work at Harvard and Cambridge, he was called to the NS bar in 1926. He entered academic life as a professor of international law at the Univ of Toronto from 1926 to 1940, at the same time advising several world organizations. In 1940 he became president of the Univ of NB and 4 years later moved across the country to VANCOUVER to take up the presidency of UBC. During his 18-year tenure the student population more than quadrupled and several professional faculties were established. He was a member of the Royal Commission on National Development in the Arts, Letters and Sciences (1949–51), commonly known as the Massey Commission, which led to the creation of the Canada Council for the Arts.
Reading: P.B. Waite, *Lord of Point Grey: UBC's Larry Mackenzie*, 1987.

MACKEREL is a sleek fish with a finely forked tail fin and recessible dorsal and pectoral fins for fast swimming. It belongs to the family Scombridae, which also includes TUNA, and like tuna it is a wide-ranging fish of the open seas.

Chub mackerel. Fisheries & Oceans Canada

Five species have been found in coastal BC waters but only 2 are regular visitors: the chub mackerel (*Scomber japonicus*) and the larger jack mackerel (*Trachurus symetricus*). The more numerous chub mackerel is steel-blue on the dorsal surface and silvery below and is characterized by a variable number of black diagonal stripes across the upper part of the body and 5–6 rayed finlets behind the dorsal and anal fins. Chub mackerel can grow to 63 cm but average 40 cm and live up to 12 years. They are believed to be part of a single migratory stock. Chub mackerel appear in Canadian waters when a high stock abundance and anomalous warm ocean temperatures coincide. Voracious feeders, they grow very rapidly and are significant predators of juvenile SALMON and HERRING stocks, especially off the west coast of VANCOUVER

ISLAND. The appearance of large schools of mackerel in BC waters since the early 1990s has caused concern over their impact. In 1999, plans were underway for commercial fishing of mackerel.

McKINNON, Archibald "Archie," sports coach (b 19 Aug 1896, Govan, Scotland; d 25 Dec 1984, Victoria). He arrived in VICTORIA in 1913 to become its premier sports personality and one of its most popular citizens. As physical education director at the YMCA he built a successful program that produced many champions. He coached DIVING at the 1932 Los Angeles Olympics, TRACK AND FIELD at the 1936 Berlin Olympics and SWIMMING at the 1948 (London) and 1952 (Helsinki) Olympics. Every Olympic team from 1928 to 1960 included at least one of his athletes. He worked with Doug and Torchy PEDEN, Chuck and Art CHAPMAN, Norm BAKER, Peter and Inez Salmon, Bill Parnell, Bruce Humber, Bill Dale and for 3 decades with the athletic PATRICK family. When he retired, Victoria honoured him with a night of tribute and made him a freeman of the city. He was among the first inductees to the BC SPORTS HALL OF FAME in 1966.
SW

McKINNON, Barry, teacher, poet (b 13 Oct 1944, Calgary). He came to BC to complete an MA at UBC and in 1969 began teaching at the College of New Caledonia in PRINCE GEORGE. He began publishing his own poetry in 1967. One of his books, *The the*, was nominated for a 1980 GOV GEN'S LITERARY AWARD, his 1991 collection *Pulp Log* won a BC BOOK PRIZE and another collection, *Arrhythmia*, won the 1994 bp Nichol Chapbook Award. A mentor and inspiration to northern BC writers, he also operates Gorse Press.

McLACHLAN, Sarah, pop singer (b 28 Jan 1968, Halifax). She was discovered in 1985 by NETTWERK Productions and moved to VANCOUVER

Sarah McLachlan, singer.
BC Entertainment Hall of Fame

to sign with the local record company. Her first 2 albums, *Touch* (1988) and *Solace* (1991), were successful in Canada but it was her 1993 album, *Fumbling Towards Ecstasy*, that propelled her to international stardom, selling more than 4 million copies worldwide. In 1997 she released the even more successful *Surfacing*, for which she received 4 Juno Awards and 2 Grammys. It was followed in 1999 by *Mirrorball*, for which she won an American Grammy Award for best female pop vocal performance. She was the originator of the highly successful all-women summer festival Lilith Fair, which made its last tour in 1999. McLachlan is one of a handful of BC-based musical performers who have established an international following. *See also* SOUND RECORDING INDUSTRY.

McLACHLIN, Beverley, lawyer, judge (b 7 Sept 1943, Pincher Creek, AB). After attending law school at the Univ of Alberta, she was called to the Alberta bar and practised 2 years in Edmonton before moving to FORT ST JOHN in 1971. She then went to VANCOUVER, where she entered private practice, and in 1974 she joined the faculty of the UBC law school. She became a Vancouver County Court judge in 1981, moved quickly to the BC Supreme Court and joined the BC Court of Appeal in 1985 (*see* JUDICIAL SYSTEM). Named the first female chief justice of the BC Supreme Court in 1988, she was elevated to the Supreme Court of Canada just 6 months later, in March 1989. She became first female chief justice of the Supreme Court of Canada in Jan 2000.

McLAGAN, Sara Ann (Maclure), journalist, publisher (b 1856, Ireland; d 20 Mar 1924, Vancouver). She arrived in NEW WESTMINSTER in 1859 when her father, a member of the ROYAL ENGINEERS, was dispatched to the new colony. The family moved to MATSQUI, where her father worked as a telegrapher; at age 13 Sara qualified as a telegraph operator herself. She left home in 1875 to move to VICTORIA, where she became manager of the Western Union telegraph office. In 1884 she married John McLagan, publisher of the *Victoria Times*, and helped him run the newspaper. Four years later they established the *Daily World* in VANCOUVER. As her husband's health failed, Sara took over management of the paper, becoming the first female daily NEWSPAPER publisher in Canada. She was active in the WOMEN'S SUFFRAGE movement and gave voice to the concerns of the city's poor and underprivileged. After she sold the *World* in 1905 she and her brothers (one of whom was the architect Samuel MACLURE) started the successful brickworks at CLAYBURN. During WWI, despite being in her 60s, she went to France to work for the Red Cross. After returning to Vancouver she was appointed superintendent of the city's Old People's Home.
Reading: John Cherrington, *Vancouver at the Dawn: A Turn-of-the-Century Portrait*, 1997.

McLAREN, Donald Roderick, aviator (b 28 May 1893, Ottawa; d 4 July 1988, Burnaby). He was raised in the PEACE R district, where his parents ran a trading post. In 1917 he joined the

Royal Flying Corps and, in just 8 months of action at the front, shot down 48 enemy planes and 6 observation balloons, an incredible record that won him several medals. He finished the war as Canada's third-ranked flying ace. After returning to civilian life he moved to VANCOUVER, where in 1925 he and Ernest Rogers of BC SUGAR founded Pacific Airways Ltd, a pioneer commercial airline (*see* AVIATION). Eventually he became a senior executive with Canadian Airways and then Trans-Canada Airlines. He retired in 1957.

McLAREN, Thomas Arthur, shipbuilder (b 1919, Montrose, Scotland; d 19 Feb 1999, N Vancouver). His father, William Dick McLaren, was managing director of the Scottish company that built the *LADY ALEXANDRA* for the UNION STEAMSHIP CO in 1923. The family emigrated to VANCOUVER in 1928. His father managed West Coast Shipbuilders, established in FALSE CREEK at the outbreak of WWII. The company built 55 10,000 dwt freighters over a 4-year period. Arthur graduated in engineering from UBC in 1941 and joined West Coast, where in 1946 he replaced his father as general manager. In 1948 he launched his own company, Allied Builders Ltd (later renamed Allied Shipbuilders Ltd), and over the next 5 decades built more than 250 vessels, from fishing boats to tugs, barges and ice-breakers. McLaren served as president of the Association of Professional Engineers of BC and was a fellow of both the Society of Naval Architects & Marine Engineers and the Royal Institution of Naval Architects, among many other professional activities. He and his wife Dorothy Irene Baxter raised 3 sons, James, Douglas and Malcolm, who continue with Allied Shipbuilders.

McLARNIN, Jimmy "Baby Face," boxer (b 19 Dec 1907, Belfast, Ireland). He arrived in VANCOUVER as a youngster with his family and at 12 began BOXING under the coaching of ex-longshoreman Charles "Pop" Foster. At 16 McLarnin moved to California and turned professional, winning his first 19 bouts. He then moved on to New York, where he became known as "the Irish Hero" and the most popular boxer of his era. On 29 May 1933 McLarnin won the world welterweight championship by knocking out Young Corbett III in the first round. Over the next 2 years he lost his crown, regained it, then lost it again in a series of title bouts with Barney Ross that became one of the greatest rivalries in the history of boxing. McLarnin retired at age 28 with a career record of 63 wins, 11 losses and 3 draws. "Pop" Foster acted as his manager and surrogate father throughout his career and settled down near Jimmy and his family in California. In 1950 McLarnin was named Canada's boxer of the half century.

MacLEAN, Alexander, sealing captain (b 15 May 1858, Cape Breton, NS; d 26 Aug 1914, Vancouver). He was already an experienced seafarer when he arrived in VICTORIA in 1881. Along with his brother Dan he became one of the most successful captains in the pelagic FUR SEAL hunt

M

based in Victoria Harbour that flourished in the 1890s. His name was linked, probably incorrectly, with the hero of Jack London's famous novel *The Sea-Wolf* (1904), and his many adventures were celebrated by the press from California to the Yukon. After the sealing industry was closed down, he continued to be involved in maritime life on the coast until his death by drowning in FALSE CREEK.

McLEAN, Donald, fur trader (b 1805, Tobermory, Scotland; d 17 July 1864 near Chilko Lk). He joined the HBC in 1833 and served in the Oregon Territory until he transferred to FORT ALEXANDRIA on the upper FRASER R in 1842. For the next 18 years he rose through the ranks, serving at different posts in NEW CALEDONIA until he was put in charge of Fort Kamloops in 1855. He was an effective trader known for harsh treatment of his FIRST NATIONS clients. In 1860 he resigned from the HBC rather than accept a transfer out of BC. With his family he settled at HAT CREEK south of CLINTON, where he farmed, raised livestock and ran a stopping place on the CARIBOO WAGON ROAD. In 1864, during the so-called CHILCOTIN WAR, he joined the pursuit of the fugitive TSILHQOT'IN and was shot and killed by one of them. His sons were members of the notorious MCLEAN GANG of outlaws.

McLEAN, Ernie "Punch," hockey coach (b 3 Nov 1932, Estevan, SK). A legend of Canadian junior HOCKEY, he was among the most colourful personalities ever involved in the game. Scotty Munro became his mentor while McLean was playing for Munro's Humboldt Indians in the Saskatchewan Junior Hockey League in the 1950s and the pair had many successful seasons running the Estevan Bruins, first in the SJHL and then in the WHL, which they played a major role in organizing. In 1971 McLean moved the Bruins to BC, where they became one of the most intimidating teams in the history of Canadian junior hockey, the brawling NEW WESTMINSTER BRUINS. McLean won coach-of-the-year honours in 1976 but is remembered just as well for escapades that included removing a referee's toupée, being hauled away in handcuffs from a fight-filled game in Portland, OR, and allegedly hypnotizing the president of an opposing fan club to root for the Bruins. Following the 1979–80 season he sold the team to VANCOUVER entrepreneur Nelson SKALBANIA. McLean returned briefly to the Bruins in the mid-1980s, then retired in 1987 to work a small GOLD MINE near ATLIN. *SW*

McLEAN, Herman Alexander, missionary doctor (b 10 May 1896, Killarney, MB; d 17 Oct 1975, Victoria). After graduating in medicine from the Univ of Manitoba in 1928 he worked for several years at BELLA COOLA, then attended bible school in Alberta. He and his wife Hester were in VANCOUVER in 1937 when he was invited by the SHANTYMEN'S CHRISTIAN ASSOC to make a medical tour up the west coast of VANCOUVER ISLAND. Impressed by the obvious need, he built a small hospital at ESPERANZA INLET and ran it for

35 years until his retirement in 1972. The hospital, operated by the Nootka Mission Assoc, closed in 1973 but the mission, which was taken over by the Shantymen in 1989, still operated a facility at the site in the late 1990s.

MacLEAN, John Duncan, teacher, doctor, politician, premier 20 Aug 1927–20 Aug 1928 (b 8 Dec 1873, Culloden, PEI; d 28 Mar 1948, Ottawa, ON). A schoolteacher by training, he was principal in ROSSLAND when he decided to study medicine. He graduated from McGill Univ in 1905, then ended up back in BC. He was practising in GREENWOOD when he entered politics, first as mayor, then in 1916 as a LIBERAL member of the provincial legislature. In John OLIVER's CABINET he served successively and competently as provincial secretary and minister of education, railways and finance. He became interim party leader when Oliver's health failed and took over as PREMIER when "Honest John" died. The Liberal government was losing popularity and the businesslike but uncharismatic MacLean did little to reverse the trend during his tenure. He and his party were defeated in the 1928 election. After running unsuccessfully for the Liberals federally, he became chair of the Canadian Farm Loan Board in Ottawa and served there until his death.

McLEAN, Kenny, rodeo champion (b 17 May 1939, Penticton). The king of Canadian RODEO won his first buckle in 1956 and went on to dominate Canadian bronc riding, calf roping, steer wrestling and team roping. He was Canadian saddle bronc champion 5 times (1959–61, 1968–69), all-around Canadian champion 4 times (1967–69, 1972), and in 1972 also won in calf roping and steer wrestling. On the US professional circuit he was rookie of the year in 1961 and national bronc riding champion in 1964, 1968 and 1971. Internationally, in 1962 he was world saddle bronc champion and he is the only Canadian who has won the international points crown (1967, 1969). He is a member of the Order of

Canada and the BC SPORTS HALL OF FAME. The National Film Board of Canada has made a documentary about his career. *SW*

MACLEAN, Malcolm Alexander, real estate promoter, first mayor of Vancouver (b 14 July 1844, Tiree, Scotland; d 4 Apr 1895, Vancouver). As a small boy he immigrated to Upper Canada with his parents. He taught school briefly, moved to New York City to work for the Cunard Steamship Co, then went back to Ontario and set up as a storekeeper. In 1878 he and his wife moved to Winnipeg, where his fortunes went up and down with the boom-and-bust cycle of the real estate market. He intended to move to Hawaii, but when passing through GRANVILLE early in 1886 he decided to stay. He quickly became involved in real estate and with a group petitioning for the incorporation of Granville as the city of VANCOUVER; that spring he was elected the new city's first mayor. After 2 terms he retired from the mayoralty and later served as a police magistrate and an immigration commissioner in the US. At his death he had returned to Vancouver, where he had just been made a stipendiary magistrate.

McLEAN GANG was a quartet of young COWBOYS whose encounters with the law in the NICOLA Valley south of KAMLOOPS during the late 1870s have become the stuff of frontier legend. Allen, Charles and Archie McLean were sons of Donald MCLEAN, a FUR TRADER with the HBC, and his mixed-blood wife Sophia; the fourth member of the gang was Alex Hare. On 8 Dec 1879, while being questioned about the theft of a horse, they shot and killed John Ussher, a member of the BC PROVINCIAL POLICE from Kamloops. They then killed a second man, a shepherd named Jim Kelly, while fleeing from a posse. Settlers feared that the "gang" intended to spark an uprising by local aboriginal people, but if this was their plan it found no support. Instead they holed up in a cabin on Douglas Lk; there, after a siege, they surrendered on 13 Dec. They were found guilty of murder twice (the first trial was voided on a

The McLean gang (l to r): Alexander Hare, Allen McLean, Archie McLean, Charley McLean; 1880. UBC BC818/1-4

technicality) and were hanged together at NEW WESTMINSTER on 31 Jan 1881. Archie McLean, 16 years old at the time of the killings, was the youngest murderer executed in BC.

McLEAN MILL is a 1920s-era steam SAWMILL located 10 km northwest of PORT ALBERNI on VANCOUVER ISLAND. Opened in 1926 by the R.B. McLean family, it remained in operation until 1965. Later it was designated a National Historic Site and was opened to visitors.

McLEESE LAKE, 50 km north of WILLIAMS LAKE on the CARIBOO Hwy, is a small resort and ranching (*see* CATTLE INDUSTRY) community named for Robert McLeese, a SODA CREEK hotelier and politician. The nearby Gibraltar open-pit COPPER–MOLYBDENUM mine operated from 1972 to 1998.

McLEOD LAKE, pop 135, on the HART HWY 140 km north of PRINCE GEORGE, is the site of the first European settlement west of the ROCKY MTS and the longest continually occupied European settlement in BC. In 1805 Simon FRASER established a trading post here in the territory of the SEKANI, leaving James MacDougall in charge for the winter. Originally called Trout Lake Post, it was renamed McLeod's Lake Post, or Fort McLeod, after the trader A.R. McLeod. It remains a Sekani community; the FOREST INDUSTRY is the economic mainstay. The trading post remained open to 1952 and since 1990 there has been a campaign to restore the 4 remaining buildings. McLeod Lk itself is 22.9 km² in size.

McLOUGHLIN, John, physician, fur trader (b 19 Oct 1784 near Rivière du Loup, QC; d 3 Sept 1857, Oregon City). He was licensed to practise medicine but in 1803 he joined the NORTH WEST CO as an apprentice fur trader. Serving mainly at Fort William, he became a partner in the company in 1814. This was a period of intense, often violent, rivalry between the NWC and the HBC.

John McLoughlin, pioneer fur trader and physician. *BC Archives PDP-00291*

Gabriola, a mansion designed in 1900 by Samuel Maclure for Benjamin Rogers, a Vancouver sugar magnate. VPL 7161

McLoughlin grew tired of it and led a group of partners who wished the competition to end. When it did, and the HBC absorbed the NWC in 1821, he became a chief factor. In 1825 he arrived at Fort Vancouver on the COLUMBIA R to take charge of the Columbia District for the HBC, a position he held for 2 decades. McLoughlin was temperamental but competent. He disagreed with the HBC governor, George SIMPSON, about 2 fundamental issues. While Simpson believed the FUR TRADE along the northern coast should be carried out by visiting ships, such as the steamer *BEAVER*, McLoughlin favoured building posts at strategic locations, which he did during the 1830s. And while Simpson believed that the HBC should not cooperate with settlers coming into the Oregon Territory, McLoughlin preferred to do business with them. Relations between the 2 men broke down completely after the murder of McLoughlin's son, John Jr, at FORT STIKINE in 1842. Simpson blamed John Jr for the incident and chose to hush it up. In vain McLoughlin tried to get the HBC to investigate the affair, turning it into a personal vendetta against the governor. In 1846 he retired to Oregon, where he lived the rest of his life, running various businesses. He is known as "the Father of Oregon."

McLURE, pop 273, on the CNR 44 km north of KAMLOOPS, was named after John McLure (1849–1933), a settler who arrived in the area in 1906. Residents are involved in ranching (*see* CATTLE INDUSTRY), LOGGING and TOURISM. Small current-powered reaction ferries (*see* BIG BAY) have crossed the N THOMPSON R here since 1919, when the site was known as Fishtrap. *AS*

MACLURE, Samuel, architect (b 11 Apr 1860, Sapperton; d 8 Aug 1929, Victoria). He is probably the most notable of VICTORIA's architects for the quality and originality of his work produced during a 40-year practice in BC. The first white child born in NEW WESTMINSTER, he was the son of John Maclure, a ROYAL ENGINEER, who was later a surveyor and telegraph operator. It was while studying art in Philadelphia from 1884 to 1885 that Sam discovered an interest in ARCHITECTURE. Financial difficulties cut short his stay in the US and he returned to BC, where he supported himself as a telegrapher for the ESQUIMALT & NANAIMO RWY, while studying architecture at home. In 1887 he began his career in New Westminster with C.H. Clow. In 1892 he opened his own practice in Victoria, concentrating initially on designing small Shingle Style bungalows. The Robin Dunsmuir house of 1900, since destroyed, marked his successful breakthrough to the patronage of the city's commercial and political elite that later brought him the commission for HATLEY PARK. In 1903 he was joined by Cecil Croker Fox, who ran the VANCOUVER office of the firm. This office closed in the early days of WWI, when Fox was killed; it was reopened after the war with Ross Lort as partner in charge. The period from 1900 to 1914 was the high point of Maclure's practice. It was during these years that he popularized the English half-timber idiom that is an essential element of Victoria's present-day character. He was also an avid watercolourist and boasted a fine library; particularly interesting is his correspondence with the American architect Frank Lloyd Wright.

McMAHON, Francis Murray Patrick "Frank," industrialist (b 2 Oct 1902, Moyie; d 20 May 1986, Bermuda). He was raised in KIMBERLEY and attended university in Spokane, WA, before dropping out and becoming a hardrock driller in the KOOTENAY mines. After moving to VANCOUVER in 1926, he began his career in the energy business, drilling without success for natural gas in the FRASER R delta. He had better luck drilling for oil in Alberta during the 1930s, and in 1939 he organized Pacific Petroleum Ltd, a leading player in the petroleum business for 40 years. He next found natural gas in the PEACE R area of BC; in 1949 he founded Westcoast Transmission to build a gas pipeline to Vancouver. The line, completed in 1957, was the first major gas pipeline in Canada. McMahon was also deeply involved in thoroughbred racing; in 1969 his horse Majestic Prince came within a race of winning the coveted Triple Crown. He retired in 1970 and was inducted into the Canadian Business Hall of Fame in 1980. *See also* OIL AND GAS INDUSTRY; WESTCOAST ENERGY.

McMICKING, Robert Burns, mechanic, engineer (b 7 July 1843, near Queenston, ON; d 27 Nov 1915, Victoria). An employee of a telegraph company in Queenston, he joined the OVERLANDERS, a party of gold seekers who in 1862 trekked across the western Interior to the CARIBOO (*see* GOLD RUSH, CARIBOO). His elder brother Thomas MCMICKING was the expedition leader. When they failed to strike it rich, the brothers descended the FRASER R to NEW WESTMINSTER and settled there. Robert worked in a grocery store, then resumed his career in the telegraph business by joining COLLINS OVERLAND TELEGRAPH. In 1870 he moved to VICTORIA as manager of the Western Union office. He left the telegraph service in 1880 to manage the Victoria and Esquimalt Telephone Co. A skilled mechanic, he later helped to establish the first electric light company in Victoria. He owned one of the first 2 telephones in BC.

McMICKING, Thomas, leader of the Overlanders (b 16 Apr 1829, Stamford, ON; d 25 Aug 1866, near New Westminster). A former schoolteacher and general merchant in Queenston, ON, he helped to organize and lead the main party of OVERLANDERS who travelled from Ontario across the western Interior to the CARIBOO goldfields in the summer of 1862 (*see* GOLD RUSH, CARIBOO). After failing to strike it rich as a prospector, he descended the FRASER R to NEW WESTMINSTER, where he found work in a shingle

mill. He sent for his wife and children to join him and was soon a prominent member of his adopted community. He died in an unsuccessful attempt to save his son, who had fallen into the Fraser R.

MacMILLAN, Harvey Reginald, forester, industrialist, philanthropist (b 9 Sept 1885, Pleasantville, ON; d 9 Feb 1976, Vancouver). After his father's death, he was raised by his grandparents and attended school in Aurora, ON. He went on to obtain a BSc at Ontario Agricultural College in Guelph and an MA in Forestry at Yale Univ in the US in 1908. While working as a forester for the federal government he contracted tuberculosis and spent 2½ years in sanatoriums. After his recovery he was appointed in 1912 the first chief forester of BC. Three years later he left on a round-the-world mission to find customers for BC lumber. After a brief stint in the private sector, he spent the rest of WWI with the Imperial Munitions Board, overseeing SPRUCE production for aircraft construction. In 1919 he founded H.R. MacMillan Export Co to sell BC lumber abroad, a highly successful venture from the outset, and in 1926 he bought his first SAWMILL. He was elected president of the Vancouver Board of Trade in 1933, as well as president of BC PACKERS LTD, a large west coast commercial FISHING company. During WWII MacMillan served as timber controller, chairman of the Wartime Requirements Board and president of Wartime Merchant Shipping, the federal government's emergency shipbuilding effort. Through the 1940s and 1950s his companies experienced steady growth. In 1951 he was appointed Canadian representative on

the NATO Defence Production Board and he retired as chairman of MacMillan & Bloedel Ltd (later MACMILLAN BLOEDEL) in 1956. The recipient of several honorary degrees, he was appointed a Commander of the Order of the British Empire in 1943 and a Companion of the Order of Canada in 1970. MacMillan's philanthropic activities included a founding contribution to the VANCOUVER FOUNDATION, a gift of the H.R. MACMILLAN SPACE CENTRE to the city, and numerous large gifts to UBC. He was an ardent hunter and fisher, an enthusiastic and well-read collector of books, and for several years the owner of VANCOUVER ISLAND's largest farm, Arrowsmith, near PARKSVILLE. MacMillan was also the leading member of a group of BC businessmen who, beginning in the 1920s, brought a large measure of the province's business interests under local control.
Ken Drushka

MacMILLAN, H.R., SPACE CENTRE was established in Vanier Park, VANCOUVER, in 1969 with money donated by the FOREST INDUSTRY magnate H.R. MACMILLAN. Originally called the H.R. MacMillan Planetarium, it became the Pacific Space Centre in 1997, then took its present name in 2000. The building's unique shape was inspired by the traditional hats worn by the HAIDA. It features a 20-m domed screen used to display multimedia shows about space, along with a theatre, learning stations and a virtual voyage simulator. A large stainless steel fountain sculpture, *The Crab*, by the artist George Norris, stands in front of the building.
Dianne Mackay

McMILLAN, James, fur trader (b circa 1783, Scotland; d 1858, Perth, Scotland). He led the expedition that founded FORT LANGLEY for the HBC in 1827, then commanded the post for its first 2 years. McMillan was originally a member of the HBC's great rival, the NORTH WEST CO (NWC). He came to BC with David THOMPSON's 1808 expedition across the ROCKY MTS and was one of the Nor'westers who purchased Astoria from the PACIFIC FUR CO in 1813. When the HBC absorbed the NWC in 1821 he joined the new company as a chief trader. In 1824 he led a party of 36 men sent by the HBC from the COLUMBIA R to scout the lower reaches of the FRASER R. Three years later he returned to establish a fort. In 1830 he became superintendent of the farming operation at the Red River Colony. He retired in 1839 to his native Scotland. McMillan Island in the Fraser R opposite Fort Langley is named for him.

MacMILLAN BLOEDEL LTD, BC's largest forest company, was formed by a merger of three older companies and numerous small ones. The H.R. MacMillan Export Co was established in 1919 by H.R. MACMILLAN, a former chief forester, to market BC lumber abroad. The business was an enormous success and in 1924 a shipping company, the Canadian Transport Co, was established to carry lumber to foreign buyers. In 1926 the company acquired its first SAWMILL, Canadian White Pine in VANCOUVER, and two years later it began operating several portable mills on VANCOUVER ISLAND to cut railway ties.

H.R. MacMillan, founder of the forestry giant MacMillan Bloedel. *Courtesy MacMillan Bloedel*

MacMillan Bloedel off-highway logging truck.

That year most of the mills supplying the company formed their own marketing agency, SEABOARD LUMBER SALES. When this group attempted to cut off MacMillan's source of supply in the 1930s, he acquired more sawmills, beginning with Ðominion Mills in Vancouver. In 1935, in partnership with Blake Ballentine, he opened a plywood plant; the following year he bought the Alberni Pacific Lumber Co in PORT ALBERNI, along with large timber stands in the area owned by the Rockefeller family. By 1938 he was the largest lumber producer on the coast, and during WWII he acquired extensive timber holdings on Vancouver Island and built a plywood plant in Port Alberni. Near the end of the war he took over the VICTORIA LUMBER & MANUFACTURING CO's CHEMAINUS mill and its large timber holdings on Vancouver Island, and in 1949 he opened a pulp mill at Harmac, near NANAIMO (*see also* PULP AND PAPER).

In 1951 the company merged with BLOEDEL, STEWART & WELCH, MacMillan's major competitor, founded in 1911 by J.H. BLOEDEL, a Bellingham lumberman. By aggressively acquiring timber rights, BS&W had come to control 1,210 km² of timber on Vancouver Island and operated sawmills and a pulp mill at Port Alberni. The new company, MacMillan and Bloedel Ltd, spent the next few years modernizing its mills and acquiring additional timber rights. In 1960 M&B merged with the POWELL RIVER CO, operator of the world's biggest newsprint mill in POWELL RIVER. This company was set up in 1909 by the Brooks, Scanlon & O'Brien Lumber Co, which had acquired huge areas of pulp leases originally granted for the construction of other pulp mills that were never built. After 50 years of successful operation it was the leading newsprint producer in BC and still held extensive timber rights. At the time it joined M&B it was headed by Harold Foley, who became vice-chairman of the new company, MacMillan, Bloedel and Powell River Co. His brother Joseph was president and J.V. (Jack) CLYNE, a former BC Supreme Court judge, was chairman. Within a few months the upper echelons of the new company were engaged in the most intense internal corporate bloodbath in Canadian business history. When it was over, the Foley brothers had resigned and the company name had been changed to MacMillan Bloedel Ltd. During the 1960s and early 1970s, under Clyne, the company was transformed into a diversified multinational corporation, with forestry operations around the world and investments in many non-forestry businesses, including aircraft and electronics manufacturing, real estate and pharmaceutical equipment. By 1975 the company was in serious financial trouble, largely the result of losses incurred by turning the Canadian Transport Co into a general shipping company. That year, a few months before H.R. MacMillan died, MacBlo recorded the first loss in its 56-year history. MacBlo was later restored to its original business as a FOREST PRODUCTS company, with all of its operations in N America. In 1998 the company operated several sawmills, panel board and container board plants and dozens of FORESTRY and LOGGING operations in various parts of the US and Canada, most of them in BC. The company suffered a serious downturn in the mid-1990s; early in 1998 it responded by slashing its staff by 20% (1,300 jobs in BC alone), selling its paper mills to a new company, PACIFICA PAPERS INC, and closing some other operations. MacBlo also stunned the FOREST INDUSTRY by announcing that it would no longer use clear-cut techniques in its logging operations. In 1999 there was another, even greater surprise: MacMillan Bloedel was purchased by the American timber giant Weyerhaeuser Co (*see also* WEYERHAEUSER CANADA LTD), based in Washington state.   *Ken Drushka*

McMURDO, a LOGGING and farming settlement (*see* AGRICULTURE) on the COLUMBIA R 24 km southeast of GOLDEN, was also a station on the CPR's KOOTENAY branch. It was named after Archie McMurdo, a local prospector who became the first settler.   *AS*

McMURPHY, an abandoned farming settlement (*see* AGRICULTURE) on the N THOMPSON R and the CNR line 115 km northeast of KAMLOOPS, was named for a CANADIAN NORTHERN RWY engineer who died in a construction accident near here.   *AS*

McNAUGHTON, Duncan Anderson, high jumper (b 7 Dec 1910, Cornwall, ON). Raised in VANCOUVER and KELOWNA, he enrolled at the Univ of Southern California in 1930 to train for the high jump and study geology. With the help of teammate and close friend Bob Van Osdel he perfected the western-roll jumping style that won him the California state championship. When the Olympics were held in Los Angeles in 1932 he was named to the Canadian team, in part because he lived in California and had no travel expenses. At the Games he jumped 6 ft 5⅝ in, shocking the world and winning the gold over Van Osdel. It would be 60 years before a Canadian again won Olympic gold in TRACK AND FIELD. McNaughton, who later served in the RCAF before working as a petroleum geologist in Texas, was inducted into the BC SPORTS HALL OF FAME in 1966.   *SW*

MacNEILL, Mary, medical doctor (b circa 1859, Bruce County, ON; d unknown). At the death of her father she inherited enough money to undertake medical studies at Women's Medical College of Chicago from 1887 to 1891. She moved to California, then in 1893 to VICTORIA, where she was the first woman registered to practise medicine in BC. In 1907 she returned to Ontario to care for a widowed brother. A devout Baptist, she gave up medicine at that time in favour of religious work.

McNEILL, William Henry, sea captain (b 1801, Boston, MA; d 1875, Victoria). An experienced trader on the Northwest Coast, he entered the service of the HBC in 1832 when his brig, the *Lama*, was purchased by the company to supply its coastal posts. Later he commanded the steamer *BEAVER*. In 1837 he located the harbour on the southern tip of VANCOUVER ISLAND that later became the site of VICTORIA. He became master at FORT RUPERT when it was built in 1849 and was promoted to chief factor in 1857. McNeill remained with the HBC until his retirement in 1863. PORT MCNEILL is named for him.

MacPHERSON, Fraser J., musician (b 1928, Winnipeg, MB; d 28 Sept 1993, Vancouver). He moved to BC as a boy and after a short stint at UBC and 18 months studying music in New York he became, in his early 20s, the bandleader at the Cave Supper Club in downtown VANCOUVER. An accomplished tenor and alto saxophonist, he formed the Fraser MacPherson Trio JAZZ group in 1975 after years of studio and radio work. He recorded 7 albums and made a number of international tours, including several to Russia. His album of duets with the guitarist Oliver Gannon,

I Didn't Know About You, won a Juno Award in 1983. He became a member of the Order of Canada in 1987. *AS*

McRAE, Alexander Duncan, soldier, politician (b 17 Nov 1874, Glencoe, ON; d 26 June 1946, Ottawa). He arrived in VANCOUVER in 1907 after making a fortune in land speculation in Saskatchewan. He then invested in lumber and fish canning and became one of the city's leading industrialists. His Shaughnessy mansion, Hycroft, was the scene of an annual costume ball for the social elite. McRae went overseas with the Canadian Expeditionary Force in 1915 and became a senior officer in the Allied Ministry of Information. During the 1920s he became interested in politics and for a brief period was touted as a future PREMIER. He was president and financial backer of the PROVINCIAL PARTY and unsuccessfully contested the 1924 provincial election under its banner. When the party dissipated, he ran federally for the Conservatives, winning a Vancouver seat in Parliament in the 1926 election. Following his defeat in 1930 he was named to the Senate. During WWII he donated Hycroft to the federal government for use as a convalescent home for veterans and retired to QUALICUM BEACH. The mansion was later taken over by the University Women's Club.

McTAGGART, David, environmentalist (b 30 June 1932). Raised in VANCOUVER, he first attracted attention as Canadian national BADMINTON champion (1956–58). He was back in the headlines in 1972, this time as an environmental protestor, when he sailed his boat deliberately into a French nuclear testing zone and was rammed by French authorities. When he repeated the act a year later, members of the French military boarded his boat and assaulted him. He became an ENVIRONMENTAL MOVEMENT icon when photographs of the beating hit international newswires. More significant, France ceased its testing operation, the last atmospheric tests in the world. In 1978 McTaggart was responsible for the merger of N American and European GREENPEACE groups into Greenpeace International, of which he became president. He resigned his position in 1991 for health reasons but remained with the organization as honorary chair. He spent much of the 1990s establishing an organic olive oil company from his olive farm in Italy. *SW*

McTAGGART-COWAN, Ian, zoologist (b 25 June 1910, Edinburgh, Scotland). He came to BC with his family at age 3 and grew up in N VANCOUVER. After graduating from UBC in 1932, he studied at Univ of California at Berkeley and in 1935 joined the staff of the provincial museum (now ROYAL BC MUSEUM), where he played an important part in reviving a flagging institution. He moved to UBC in 1940 to teach zoology and became zoology department head in 1953 and dean of graduate studies in 1964. He retired in 1975. As well as being a scholar, McTaggart-Cowan is an activist in the cause of wildlife conservation. He became an officer of the Order of

Canada in 1972 and a member of the ORDER OF BC in 1991; he has won many other awards and served on various conservation boards and committees. He was chancellor of the UNIV OF VICTORIA in 1979–84.

Ian McTaggart-Cowan, at work in the lab.
UBC 1.1/12670/2

McTAGGART-COWAN, Patrick Duncan, meteorologist, university president (b 31 May 1912, Edinburgh, Scotland; d 11 Oct 1997, Bracebridge, ON). He came to BC as a baby with his family and grew up in N VANCOUVER. A Rhodes Scholar from UBC, he graduated from Oxford in 1936, then went to Newfoundland, where he organized the provincial meteorological service. During WWII he was responsible for deciding if weather conditions permitted planes delivering supplies to Europe to venture across the Atlantic Ocean. After the war he joined the Canadian Meteorological Service and was director from 1959 to 1963. Chosen the first president of SFU in 1963, he was responsible for starting the new university. When the doors opened in 1965, McTaggart-Cowan was immediately caught up in controversies surrounding student radicalism and academic freedom. In 1968 he was dismissed. He returned to Ottawa to become head of the Science Council of Canada until his retirement. In 1970 he directed the cleanup of Canada's first major oil spill in Chedabucto Bay, NS. He became an officer in the Order of Canada in 1979.

McWHIRTER, George, writer, teacher (b 26 Sept 1939, Belfast, N Ireland). After teaching high school in his native Ireland, he immigrated to BC in 1966. He lived first in PORT ALBERNI, where he taught school, then in VANCOUVER. He began teaching at UBC in 1970 and was head of creative writing there from 1983 to 1993. His first book of poetry, *Catalan Poems*, appeared in 1971, won the Commonwealth Poetry Prize and announced a lifelong interest in Spain and Latin America. His *Selected Poems of José Emilio Pacheco* won the 1997 F.R. Scott Prize for translation. He has published several collections of poetry, 5

books of stories and 3 novels, including *Cage* (1987) which won a BC BOOK PRIZE. In 1998 *Ovid in Saskatchewan* won the League of Canadian Poets' chapbook competition and McWhirter was awarded a Killam Prize for teaching by UBC.

MADEIRA PARK, pop 1,100, is the commercial centre of PENDER HARBOUR, 75 km northwest of VANCOUVER on the SUNSHINE COAST. It has a shopping mall, a marina and government wharf, several resorts and cultural and other community facilities. Madeira Islander Joe Gonzalves operated a hotel at IRVINES LANDING in the early 1900s. *AS*

MADSEN, Nels, logger, union activist (b 1899, Denmark; d 1977, Vancouver). He immigrated to BC during the 1920s and was active in the LUMBER WORKERS' INDUSTRIAL UNION and in the International Woodworkers of America (IWA) (*see* INDUSTRIAL, WOOD AND ALLIED WORKERS OF CANADA) after it was formed in 1937. As a member of the Mackenzie-Papineau Battalion during the Spanish Civil War, he saw front-line action and was taken prisoner by Nationalist forces in 1938. A lifelong Communist, he was expelled for life from the IWA by the International Union in 1948, in compliance with the US Taft Hartley Act.

MAGAZINE PUBLISHING in BC began in the early 1900s with the appearance of such general interest periodicals as *Western Ho!* (1907), *British Columbia Home Magazine* (1907–15) and *Canada West Magazine* (1907–18). The industry remained small as local publishers found it difficult to compete with eastern Canadian and American magazines and, later, weekend NEWSPAPER supplements. *British Columbia Magazine* (1911–27) was one of the few general interest publications to flourish before WWII, though several trade and business periodicals were founded during this period (one of them, *Harbour and Shipping Journal*, established in 1918, is the oldest continuously published magazine in BC). In the post-war period *BC Outdoors* (established 1944) and *Western Homes and Living* (1950–66) led a Vancouver-based magazine renaissance that soon included such significant titles as *Pacific Yachting*, BEAUTIFUL BC, *Western Living*, GEORGIA STRAIGHT, *WestWorld*, *Vancouver*, *Vancouver Calendar*, *BCBusiness*, *Business in Vancouver*, *TV Week*, *Geist*, *BC Report*, *Where*, *Westcoast Fisherman*, ADBUSTERS, *Woman to Woman*, *Playboard*, *Equity*, *V*, *Step*, *West*, *Common Ground*, *CityFood*, *Xtra West*, *Reel West* and VICTORIA'S *MONDAY MAGAZINE*. One unusual venture was *Sound Heritage*, launched in 1972 as a quarterly publishing oral history and reminiscences on every conceivable aspect of BC history and culture. Forty volumes were produced before the magazine ceased operations. As of 2000, more than 200 magazines were published in the province. The Western Magazine Awards annually recognize the finest magazine journalism in the western provinces. *See also* BC HISTORICAL FEDERATION; BC STUDIES; CANADIAN LITERATURE; MAGAZINES, LITERARY; RAINCOAST CHRONICLES. *AS*

MAGAZINES, LITERARY, publish original literary texts, reviews and criticism. In BC one of the earliest examples was *BC Argonaut*, which published 2 issues in the 1930s. A more successful publication was CONTEMPORARY VERSE, edited by Alan CRAWLEY in W VANCOUVER from 1941 to 1952, which featured the work of leading modern Canadian poets. The efflorescence of WRITING and BOOK PUBLISHING in BC during the 1960s was matched by a proliferation of "little magazines," many of them associated with a particular writer or group of writers. TISH, for example, was published from 1961 to 1969 by young writers at UBC who were influenced by the American Black Mountain poets, while *BLEWOINTMENT* was published by the VANCOUVER poet bill BISSETT irregularly from 1963 to 1978. Jim Brown and David Robinson's *Talon*, Gerry Gilbert's *BC Monthly*, John Marshall's *Island* in LANTZVILLE, John Harris' *Repository* in PRINCE GEORGE, and Paul de Barros and Daphne MARLATT's *periodics* (which was devoted to prose with a focus on language use), were just a few of the dozens of ephemeral publications that flourished for a time. *Iron* and *NMFG* (no money from the government) appeared in the 1970s from SFU-connected writers, including Brian FAWCETT. The writers associated with Pulp Press (*see* ARSENAL PULP PRESS) published *3-Cent Pulp* and sold it for 3 cents. Sheila WATSON and her husband Wilfred WATSON produced *White Pelican* in NANAIMO during 1971–78. In 1988, *sub-TERRAIN* was founded by Brian Kaufman and Denis Bolen, who later established ANVIL PRESS. Several literary magazines are associated with a college or university. *CANADIAN LITERATURE*, founded by George WOODCOCK at UBC in 1959, has comprehensive national coverage. *The Malahat Review* at UNIV OF VICTORIA began under Robin SKELTON with a deliberately international perspective, then focussed more on Canadian writers. *Prism International* at UBC emphasizes student editorial involvement. *The Capilano Review*, founded by Pierre Coupey at Capilano College, mixes writing with visual art. *West Coast Line*, an amalgamation of *West Coast Review* and *Line*, is based at SFU and features themed issues. *Event: The Douglas College Magazine* has a special interest in promoting and redefining "creative non-fiction." *Writing* promotes the KOOTENAY SCHOOL OF WRITING. *Room of One's Own* is a feminist quarterly published by The Growing Room Collective. The established Ontario quarterly *Canadian Fiction Magazine* began publication in Prince George and Vancouver before moving east. The Vancouver Edgewise Electrolit Centre publishes the *EEC E-Zine*, a quarterly multimedia on-line magazine of Canadian poets, writers and artists.

Bill Schermbrucker

MAGNA BAY, pop 225, on the north shore of SHUSWAP LK 30 km north of SALMON ARM, is a recreational and retirement community. The wide bay here (magna is Latin for "great") was formerly called Steamboat Bay. AS

MAGNUSSEN, Karen Diane, figure skater (b 4 Apr 1952, N Vancouver). Raised in N VANCOU-

Karen Magnussen, 1973 world figure skating champion. Canadian Figure Skating Hall of Fame

VER, she began winning FIGURE SKATING competitions when she was 7 years old. A dramatic free-style skater, she won her first Canadian women's championship in 1968. After recovering from leg injuries, she regained the national championship in 1970 and held the crown through 1973. Silver medals at the 1972 Olympics and world championships were followed by gold at the 1973 worlds. She was named BC athlete of the year in 1972 and Canada's female athlete of the year in 1971 and 1972. After turning professional in 1973, she skated in the Ice Capades, then retired to coach and operate a chain of skating schools. A skating arena in N Vancouver is named for her and she is a member of the Canadian Figure Skating, Canadian Sports and BC SPORTS HALLS OF FAME and the Order of Canada (1973).

MAGPIE, black-billed (*Pica pica*), is the only type of magpie found in Canada. In BC it is most common in the southern Interior. A member of the CROW family, it is a large, long-tailed, short-winged bird with black plumage above and a white belly. Magpies build large nests in trees; the nest consists of a hooded mound of sticks and other material surrounding a mud base. It has more than one entrance and takes up to 6 weeks to build. Early in the 20th century magpies were considered a nuisance and hunted for bounty.

MAHATTA RIVER was a remote Western Forest Products Ltd LOGGING camp on the south side of QUATSINO SOUND, 38 km southwest of PORT HARDY on VANCOUVER ISLAND. Established on an ancient Koskimo (KWAKWAKA'WAKW) summer village site, it was dismantled in the late 1980s after a road was finally punched in from PORT ALICE. The company still maintains a yard and log

dump here. The name is a Kwakwala word that means "having sockeye salmon." AS

MAHOOD FALLS is a resort community 90 km southeast of WILLIAMS LAKE, near the east end of CANIM LK in the CARIBOO. The spectacular 23-m falls are on the Canin R between Canim and Mahood Lks; Mahood Lk forms part of the southern boundary of WELLS GRAY PROVINCIAL PARK and is named after James A. Mahood, who led a CPR survey party in the area in 1872. *See also* WATERFALLS. AS

MAILLARD, Keith, writer (b 28 Feb 1942, Wheeling, WV). After being active in the underground-press movement in Boston in the late 1960s he immigrated to VANCOUVER in 1970. He began publishing fiction in 1976, the year he became a Canadian citizen. His 1989 novel *Motet* won a BC BOOK PRIZE and his eighth novel, *Gloria* (1999), earned a GOV GEN'S LITERARY AWARD nomination. He has also published a book of poetry, *Dementia Americana* (1994), for which the League of Canadian Poets gave him the Gerald Lampert Award for the best first book of poetry. He has worked extensively in radio and he joined the department of theatre, film and creative writing at UBC in 1989.

MAILLARDVILLE is a FRANCOPHONE settlement northeast of NEW WESTMINSTER, created in 1909 when Fraser River Saw Mills imported 150 workers from Quebec to replace Asian employees at its MILLSIDE operations. More French-speaking workers followed, and a community developed around the parish of Notre Dame de Lourdes Church (1910). It is named for Rev Edmond Maillard, first priest at the church. Maillardville later became part of COQUITLAM. It lies just north of the FRASER R and is bounded by

Black-billed magpie. Roy Luckow photo

M

Brunette, Schoolhouse, Rochester and Blue Mountain streets.

MAIN, Lorne, tennis player (b 9 July 1930, Vancouver). He won the national junior TENNIS championship in 3 consecutive years, then the Canadian senior title before reaching the age of 20. He joined the world professional tour in the early 1950s, reached the third round at Wimbledon and won the Monte Carlo and Belgian singles titles in 1954. He also won doubles tournaments in Florida, Jamaica and Ireland that year. Main represented Canada in Davis Cup play from 1949 to 1958 and as nonplaying captain in 1959–61. He continued his involvement in tennis as a coach and administrator and was inducted into the BC SPORTS HALL OF FAME in 1974.   *SW*

MAIR, Rafe, lawyer, politician, broadcaster (b 31 Dec 1931, Vancouver). After graduating from UBC law school he was called to the bar in 1961 and practised law in VANCOUVER and KAMLOOPS from 1961 to 1975. He entered politics as a Kamloops alderman in 1973 and in 1975 won

Rafe Mair, outspoken talk show radio host.
CKNW/98

election to the provincial legislature as a SOCIAL CREDIT PARTY member for that city. He held 3 posts in Premier Bill BENNETT's CABINET: minister of consumer and corporate affairs (1975–78), environment (1978–79) and health (1979–81). During much of this period he also handled the constitutional portfolio for the province. In 1981 he retired from politics to become host of his own radio talk show on CJOR in Vancouver (*see* BROADCASTING, COMMERCIAL). In 1984 he switched to CKNW, where he emerged as one of the liveliest, most outspoken broadcasters in Canada. His show became the highest rated single-market talk show in the country, and he was credited with influencing opinion on major public issues such as the constitutional referendum debate in 1992, the KEMANO completion project and the NISGA'A TREATY.

Reading: Rafe Mair, *Canada: Is Anyone Listening?*, 1998.

MAITLAND, Royal Lethington "Pat," lawyer, politician (b 1889, Ingersoll, ON; d 28 Mar 1946, Vancouver). A leading lawyer in VANCOUVER, he was elected to the legislature for the first time in the CONSERVATIVE landslide of 1928 and joined Simon Fraser TOLMIE's CABINET as a minister without portfolio. He lost his seat when the Conservatives were routed in the 1933 election, but was re-elected in 1937 and the next year took over leadership of the party. Following the 1941 election, in which the Conservatives ran a respectable third, Maitland pressed for a COALITION GOVERNMENT of the 3 major parties. The CCF declined to join but the Tories and the LIBERALS did form a coalition in Dec 1941; Maitland joined the cabinet as deputy PREMIER and attorney general. He remained Conservative leader and attorney general until his death 5 years later.

MAJORITY MOVEMENT was an attempt to create a single, anti-socialist political party in the wake of the NDP electoral victory in 1972. With the SOCIAL CREDIT PARTY defeated, business interests in the province believed that a realignment of the opposition into a new unity party was necessary. The Majority Movement for Freedom and Private Enterprise, founded in 1973 by Jarl

The Malahat, launched in 1917. The ship went on to work as a lumber carrier, rum-runner and self-propelled log barge. BC Archives D-01777

Whist, a KAMLOOPS entrepreneur and Arnold Hean, a BURNABY lawyer, briefly touted Robert BONNER as possible leader of the new party. However, when the Socreds rallied behind their new leader Bill BENNETT, and proved able to mobilize anti-socialist forces themselves, the new movement died out.

MAKELA, Augusti Bernhard "Austin," Finnish socialist, community leader (b 12 July 1863, Finland; d 28 Feb 1932, Sointula). He was a schoolteacher in his native Finland, where he was prominent in the socialist movement.

Eventually he became a journalist and associate of Matti KURIKKA. In 1901 he came to BC to join Kurikka at his utopian community at SOINTULA. Makela became joint editor of the Finnish-language newspaper *Aika* (Time) and secretary of the Kalevan Kansa Colonization Co. More practical and responsible than Kurikka, he soon broke with his friend over Kurikka's management of the community. When Kurikka left in 1904, Makela took over leadership but he had no greater success and the company dissolved in 1905. Afterwards he remained on MALCOLM ISLAND, working as a LIGHTHOUSE keeper and writing for various periodicals.

MAKINSON, a fruit and poultry farming settlement (*see* AGRICULTURE) and former steamship stop on the east side of the COLUMBIA R between Upper and Lower ARROW LKS, 85 km north of CASTLEGAR, was submerged under rising water levels when the KEENLEYSIDE DAM was built in 1968. Tom Makinson, a pioneer, used salvaged materials from the wrecked sternwheeler *Lytton* to build his home.   *AS*

MALAHAT was a 75-m wooden-hulled schooner built at VICTORIA in 1917 as a coastal lumber carrier. During Prohibition in the US it was employed as a "mother ship," supplying liquor to smaller vessels that ran the illicit cargo to shore (*see* RUM-RUNNERS). With the end of

Prohibition in 1933 the *Malahat* was converted again, this time by the logger Gordon GIBSON, into the world's first self-propelled, self-loading log carrier. After 9 years hauling logs along the coast it sank in 1944 in BARKLEY SOUND.

MALAHAT DRIVE is a 16-km stretch of the Island Hwy (part of the TRANS-CANADA HWY) across Malahat Mt on VANCOUVER ISLAND. It begins at GOLDSTREAM PROVINCIAL PARK about 20 km north of VICTORIA. Originally a TRAIL made in 1862 for driving livestock, it was improved to a wagon road 2 years later and then paved in 1911. The summit, 31 km north of Victoria, offers splendid views of SAANICH INLET. The local Salish people (*see* SALISHAN FIRST NATIONS) know the summit as Yos and consider it a sacred site.

MALAKWA, pop 400, is an AGRICULTURAL settlement on the CPR line and the Eagle R, 43 km west of REVELSTOKE. The Eagle Valley, which burrows into the MONASHEE MTS here, is a rich farming district for DAIRY, meat, fruit, vegetable and grain products. Several SAWMILLS, the first established by Sinclair McLean in 1949, have operated over the years. The name is a CHINOOK JARGON word for "mosquito."   AS

MALASPINA, Alejandro, Spanish naval officer (b 5 Nov 1754, Mulazzo, Italy; d 9 Apr 1810, Pontremoli, Italy). He entered the navy in 1774 and served in the Mediterranean, Atlantic and Pacific before leading an expedition around the world in 1784–88 in the frigate *Astrea*, proving himself a highly competent navigator and leader. On his return to Spain he proposed an investigation of Spanish colonies as part of another round-the-world voyage and recruited a group of

Alejandro Malaspina in the uniform of a brigadier of the Spanish navy, 1795.
Museo Naval, Madrid

brilliant officers and scientists to accompany him. At Acapulco, the expedition was diverted by royal order to the NW coast to search for the rumoured Northwest Passage linking the Atlantic and Pacific oceans. Malaspina explored Yakutat Bay, AK, but found no passage. He then visited NOOTKA SOUND in mid-Aug 1791, meeting Chief MAQUINNA and compiling an important documentary and artistic record of the area's geography and aboriginal inhabitants (*see also* NUU-CHAH-NULTH). Malaspina's experiences and liberal ideas gained during the expedition led to political trouble once he returned home. A year later he was arrested, jailed and finally exiled to his native Parma. Although Malaspina was a Spanish subject, and Italy as a nation did not then exist, he was probably the first "Italian" to visit BC. *See also* SPANISH EXPLORATION. *Robin Inglis*

MALCOLM ISLAND, 83 km², lies at the south end of QUEEN CHARLOTTE STRAIT off the east coast of VANCOUVER ISLAND opposite PORT MCNEILL. Petroglyphs and shell MIDDENS are evidence of

prior use by the local KWAKWAKA'WAKW First Nations (*see* ROCK ART). The earliest settlers arrived in 1883. A British temperance society attempted unsuccessfully to establish a commune in 1895. In 1901 a party of FINNS from NANAIMO founded SOINTULA, the island's main community, as a utopian socialist commune. This experiment collapsed in 1905, but many Finns remained, making their living by LOGGING, FISHING, and FARMING. In 1996 the island was home to a mixed population of 938 people, among whom the Finnish presence remains strong. It was named in 1846 by a British survey after Sir Pulteney Malcolm, an admiral in the Royal Navy. A ferry connects Sointula with Port McNeill. Changes to the commercial fishing industry in the 1990s led island residents to explore alternate means of making a living, such as TOURISM and value-added wood and seafood industries.

MALKIN, William Harold, merchant (b 30 July 1868, Burslem, England; d 11 Oct 1959, Vancouver). He immigrated to Canada in 1884 and came west to VANCOUVER in 1895 with his 2 brothers. They established a wholesale grocery business, W.H. Malkin & Co, which flourished during the days of the Klondike GOLD RUSH. Increasingly he left management of the company to his brothers while he indulged his interest in arts and politics. He served a term as mayor from 1929 to 1930, during which Vancouver absorbed S Vancouver and Point Grey and construction began on the Burrard St Bridge. When his wife died in 1933, Malkin donated money in her memory for the construction of Malkin Bowl in STANLEY PARK. During the 1940s he was president of Neon Products Ltd.

MALLANDAINE, Edward, architect (b 1827, Singapore; d 1905, Victoria). After training and working as an architect in England, he came to BC for the first time during the 1858 GOLD RUSH and later returned to teach in a private school for boys (*see* EDUCATION, PRIVATE). In 1866 he opened an architectural practice in VICTORIA. His major commission was the old Customs House and Post Office on Government St. He also designed hotels, churches—of which St Luke's on Cedar Hill and St John's at COWICHAN BAY are still standing—residences and commercial blocks in VANCOUVER, Victoria and NANAIMO. In 1869 he co-compiled the first directory of Victoria and BC. *See also* ARCHITECTURE.

MALLARD, Gwen, environmental activist (b 1917, Fernie; d 13 Nov 1999, E Sooke). In 1968, while living in COQUITLAM, she was one of the founders (along with her husband Derrick) of the VANCOUVER-based SOCIETY FOR PROMOTING ENVIRONMENTAL CONSERVATION (SPEC), Canada's first citizens' environmental advocacy group. Often called the "mother of Canadian environmentalism," she led campaigns against strip MINING in the ELK R valley, oil tanker traffic along the coast, the use of herbicides by BC HYDRO and other dangers to the environment. In 1972 she and her husband moved to VANCOUVER ISLAND,

where she operated a well-known vegetarian restaurant, at the same time continuing her work as an environmental activist. In 1993 she received an Environmental Lifetime Achievement Award from the federal government. *See also* ENVIRONMENTAL MOVEMENT.

MAMALILACULLA is a KWAKWAKA'WAKW (Kwakiutl) village on the west side of VILLAGE ISLAND, one of the jumble of islands in the INSIDE PASSAGE between VANCOUVER ISLAND and the mainland at the entrance to KNIGHT INLET. It is the main village site of the Mamaleleqala people and in 1921 was the site of a famous POTLATCH, hosted by the Cranmer family, which resulted in several arrests by the authorities. From 1920 to 1945 the missionary Kathleen O'BRIEN operated a school and small tuberculosis sanatorium here. The site was abandoned in the 1960s, but in the late 1990s some buildings were still standing and former residents were returning for visits.

MAMIT LAKE, originally spelled Mamette, 45 km southwest of KAMLOOPS on Guichon Crk, was the centre of a ranching (*see* CATTLE INDUSTRY) district settled as early as 1873 by the French Canadian pioneers Joseph and Pierre GUICHON, Louis Quenville and Jean and François Rey. Mamit is an OKANAGAN First Nation word for "whitefish."   AS

MANDARIN ORANGES have been a BC tradition since the first shipment of the small, seedless citrus fruit arrived from Japan in 1884. Legend has it that they were intended as a reminder of home for JAPANESE people living in the province, but they have long since been adopted by non-Japanese residents and now they are as much a part of the Christmas season as candy canes, poinsettias, even Santa Claus himself. Mandarins are grown in other places, including Morocco and China, but the Japanese variety remains most popular in BC, making Canada the largest market for Japanese mandarins in the world. Mandarin season lasts from mid-Nov until the end of Dec.

MANDARTE ISLAND, a bare white rock in HARO STRAIT east of SIDNEY ISLAND off the SAANICH PENINSULA, supports the largest seabird colony in GEORGIA STRAIT. More than 8,000 birds nest on the island, which is a FIRST NATIONS reserve. It is the only place in BC where rhinoceros AUKLETS and tufted PUFFINS breed in protected waters and has more CORMORANTS and pigeon GUILLEMOTS than any other place in the province.

MANDRAKE, Leon, "Leon Mandrake the Magician" (b 11 Apr 1911, New Westminster; d 27 Jan 1993, Surrey). He began performing on stage at age 11 and began touring in 1927. Eventually he became one of the most famous performing magicians in the world. He had his own television show and was an inspiration for the cartoon strip "Mandrake the Magician." He performed professionally for more than 50 years, the last 40 of these with Velvet, his wife and partner.

MANNING, Ernest Callaway, forester, "the father of BC conservation" (b 1890, Selwyn, ON; d Feb 1941, Armstrong, ON). He was raised in Toronto, and after graduating in FORESTRY from the Univ of Toronto he took a job in the natural resources department of the CPR. From his base in Calgary he spent much of his time cruising timber in the E KOOTENAY, and in 1918 he joined the BC FOREST SERVICE. By 1927 he was assistant chief forester, and at the end of 1935 he became chief forester, the senior public servant in charge of FOREST POLICY. Recognizing that the province's FORESTS were not inexhaustible, he was an early advocate of conservation and reforestation. He also encouraged the creation of more parks, and in 1939 the provincial PARKS system became the responsibility of the Forest Service. He played a key role in the development of VANCOUVER's North Shore SKIING areas. When WWII began he became assistant timber controller for BC. On his way home from a war-related business trip to Ottawa he died in the crash of a Trans Canada Air Lines plane. MANNING PARK is named after him.

MANNING PROVINCIAL PARK, 658.84 km², is situated in the northern end of the CASCADE MTS along the US border 30 km east of HOPE and is bisected by the HOPE–PRINCETON HWY. It is the northern terminus of the Pacific Crest Trail, which traverses the CORDILLERA of N America to

Manning Provincial Park.
Roy Jackson/Image Makers

Mexico and has sections of the TRANS-CANADA and Centennial TRAILS. Established in 1941, the park offers superb hiking, backcountry skiing and horseback riding. Lying in the transition zone between the moist coast and the dry Interior, Manning contains a tremendous variety of landscapes. Blackwall Peak Meadows are ablaze with one of BC's finest displays of WILD-FLOWERS during the summer. As the POPULATION of the FRASER VALLEY and Lower Mainland expands, the park faces overcrowding in the

summer season; it had about 1.4 million visitors in 1995. The park is named for former Chief Forester Ernest C. MANNING. *See also* PARKS, PROVINCIAL.

MANNION, Joseph, hotelier (b 17 Mar 1839, County Mayo, Ireland; d 12 Sept 1918, Lillooet). He arrived in BC in 1862 and after an abortive attempt at GOLD prospecting went to work for the COLLINS OVERLAND TELEGRAPH. He was at BUR-RARD INLET in 1875 helping to build the HASTINGS MILL, and by the mid-1870s he was a prospering hotelier, owner of the Granville Hotel in GAS-TOWN and the Gladstone Hotel on the trail between NEW WESTMINSTER and the inlet. Known as the "unofficial mayor of GRANVILLE," he was elected an alderman when VANCOUVER officially became a city in 1886. But he retired soon after to BOWEN ISLAND, where he lived the life of a country squire and operated a brickyard in partnership with David OPPENHEIMER. He returned with his family to the city in 1898, after selling his lovely island home to John Cates, who developed it as a hotel. Later Mannion moved to the Interior for his health.

MANSON, Alexander Malcolm, lawyer, politician (b 7 Oct 1883, St Louis, MO; d 1964). Born in the US, he was raised by grandparents in Quebec. After studying law at Osgoode Hall in

Toronto, he moved west to PRINCE RUPERT and began practising in 1905. He was elected to the legislature as a LIBERAL from Omineca in 1916, and in 1921 Premier John OLIVER appointed him attorney general. He was a bright star in the Liberal government, an efficient administrator and a rousing orator; during the mid-1920s he was considered a likely successor to Oliver. However, he was also arrogant and irascible and a bit of a maverick, and his political promise was not fulfilled. He survived the Liberal defeat of 1928 but when his party returned to power in 1933, led by Duff PATTULLO, Manson was not asked to join the CABINET. In 1935 he resigned

his provincial seat to run federally, but lost. He was then appointed to the BC Supreme Court, where he remained until he left the bench in 1961 at age 77.

MANSON CREEK, 230 km northwest of PRINCE GEORGE, was a focal point of the OMINECA GOLD RUSH in the early 1870s, when more than 1,000 miners rushed to the region. The settlement lingered as a tiny centre for local prospectors; over the years it was the site of an HBC trading post, a motel, a museum, a restaurant and a gas station, but later it was abandoned. It was named for the HBC's Donald Manson, who ruled the NEW CALEDONIA district from FORT ST JAMES from 1844 to 1857. *AS*

MANUEL, George, Secwepemc (Shuswap) activist (b 17 Feb 1921, Neskonlith; d 15 Nov 1989, Kamloops). Raised by grandparents, he attended Kamloops RESIDENTIAL SCHOOL until he fell sick with tuberculosis at age 12. He worked as a busboy, fruit picker and logger and, inspired by Andrew PAULL, got involved in aboriginal politics as an organizer. From 1970 to 1976 he was president of the National Indian Brotherhood, now the Assembly of First Nations, and led the organization in its activist role. He was a tireless worker who travelled the world, promoting the concept of a "Fourth World" of indigenous peoples, and brought international attention to Canada's FIRST NATIONS and ABORIGINAL RIGHTS issues. Manuel's book *The Fourth World: An Indian Reality* appeared in 1974; in 1975 he became founding president of the World Council of Indigenous Peoples, a position he held until 1981. Largely self-educated, he received an honorary degree from UBC and was made an officer in the Order of Canada in 1986. His son Robert (1947–98) led the UNION OF BC INDIAN CHIEFS in the 1980s. *See also* SECWEPEMC.

MAPES, a small farming and ranching settlement 75 km west of PRINCE GEORGE, was named after a local pioneer. A post office operated here from 1911 to 1952, and in the late 1990s an elementary school was still serving approximately 40 families in the area. *AS*

MAPLE, Canada's national tree, occurs in BC in 3 species. The largest, bigleaf maple (*Acer macrophyllum*), commonly grows along the coast south of ALERT BAY. It has the largest leaf of any Canadian tree and its hard wood has some commercial uses, including furniture, panelling and

Broadleaf maple.
Kim LaFave drawing

musical instruments. FIRST NATIONS used it to make CANOE paddles. The largest specimen in Canada (31.7 m tall) grows in STANLEY PARK above Third Beach. Rocky Mountain, or Douglas, maple (*Acer glabrum*) grows mainly in the Interior, along streams and in sheltered

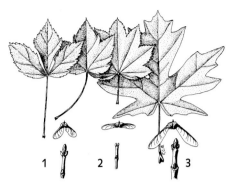

Leaf, fruit (containing seed) and twig of Rocky Mountain (1), vine (2) and bigleaf (3) maple. © T.C. Brayshaw

Rural Maple Ridge, with Golden Ears Provincial Park in the background. *BC Archives HP-63627*

Maquinna, chief of the Mowachaht, at time of first European contact. *BC Archives HP-7931*

ravines, and on VANCOUVER ISLAND. It is often no larger than a tall shrub, which is also true of the third species, the vine maple (*Acer circinatum*), a gnarled, crooked tree confined to the southern mainland coast. The leaves of the vine maple may turn bright scarlet in the fall.

MAPLE BAY is a seaside community east of DUNCAN, looking onto Sansum Narrows between SALTSPRING ISLAND and VANCOUVER ISLAND. Known as Hwtlupnets to its COWICHAN First Nation inhabitants, it was the site of a great battle in about 1840, when a large group of Coast Salish (*see* SALISHAN FIRST NATIONS) warriors defeated their dreaded enemies the Lekwiltok, a group of KWAKWA̲KA̲'WAKW from the north. This battle marked the end of large-scale invasions into the south by northern peoples. A townsite was laid out in 1864 and it became the main port for the surrounding farms. The bay is ringed with upscale homes and is a moorage popular with passing boaters.

MAPLE LEAF is a 28.3-m schooner built at Vancouver Shipyards in 1904 as an ocean racer for a local lumber magnate. The vessel was seized during WWI and its lead keel was melted for bullets. In 1916 it was converted to a HALIBUT schooner, first called *Constance B*, then *Parma*. It left the fishery during a buyback in the 1970s and was fully restored with its original name, then used for cultural and natural history tours on the Central Coast. *See also* FISHING, COMMERCIAL; SHIPBUILDING.   *Bet Oliver*

MAPLE RIDGE is located on the north shore of the FRASER R, 45 km east of VANCOUVER. One of a series of suburban districts in the lower FRASER VALLEY that have enjoyed explosive growth since WWII, it is bounded on the west by PITT MEADOWS and COQUITLAM and on the east by MISSION. To the north are the mountains of GOLDEN EARS PROVINCIAL PARK. White habitation began in 1827 when the HBC built FORT LANGLEY across the river. The first settler was Samuel Robertson, an HBC carpenter, who in 1858 planted an orchard in the area now known as

ALBION. The next year another HBC employee, John McIvor, began clearing land for a DAIRY farm, which he called Maple Ridge. The GOLD RUSH into the CARIBOO provided a market for produce, and other farmers followed. Thomas Haney arrived in 1876 to establish a brickworks. The community named for him later came to be considered Maple Ridge's downtown (*see* HANEY). In 1881 construction of the CPR began in the district, encouraging settlement. During this period, St John the Divine ANGLICAN CHURCH was moved across the river from DERBY. Built in 1859, it remained the oldest functioning church in BC by the start of the 21st century. Farming has been the main occupation but LOGGING has also been important to the local economy. Loggers were active around the shores of ALOUETTE LK, and there was a large mill at RUSKIN for many years, owned by E.H. Heaps. Wood processing remains a significant part of the local manufacturing sector and the huge mill at WHONNOCK has traditionally contributed much to local employment. Maple Ridge has a diversified economy; many of its residents commute to Vancouver. Outside of BC it is probably best known as the home of sports superstars Cam NEELY, Larry WALKER and Greg MOORE.

Population: 56,173
Rank in BC: 17th
Population increase since 1981: 74%
Date of incorporation: district 12 Sept 1874
Land area: 267.1 km²
Location: Greater Vancouver Regional District
Economic base: forest industry, wood manufacturing, fishing, high technology, retail services

MAQUINNA, Mowachaht chief (b circa 1760, Nootka Sound; d date unknown, Nootka Sound). He was the principal chief in NOOTKA SOUND on the west coast of VANCOUVER ISLAND during a period of intense activity in the earliest days of the maritime FUR TRADE and Spanish settlement in the 1780s and 1790s. Because the

name Maquinna was, and continues to be, held by successive Mowachaht chiefs (the Mowachaht being a FIRST NATION of the NUU-CHAH-NULTH), it is unclear whether the same Maquinna who apparently met Capt James COOK in 1778 also attacked the *BOSTON* and captured John JEWITT in 1803. The Maquinna whose well-known portrait was drawn by the artist Tomás Suria in 1791 (see above; now in the Museo Naval in Madrid) seems to have gained his superior rank through primogeniture, maintenance of respect through wealth gained in the fur trade and diplomatic acumen. Maquinna had a winter village at TAHSIS and suffered the occupation of his summer village at YUQUOT by the Spanish from 1789 to 1795. He had extensive dealings with most of the principal visitors to Nootka Sound at the end of the 18th century.   *Robin Inglis*

MARA, an AGRICULTURAL community on the west bank of the Shuswap R, 14 km east of SALMON ARM, is just south of Mara Lk, a popular summer recreation spot lined with resorts and campgrounds. A stagecoach stop between SICA-MOUS and VERNON, it was later a station on the SHUSWAP & OKANAGAN RWY. A WWI internment camp for enemy aliens was located nearby in 1915–17. The lake is named after John A. MARA, who was among the OVERLANDERS of 1862 and who later became an entrepreneur and served as both MLA and MP. *AS*

MARA, John Andrew, merchant, politician (b 21 July 1840, Toronto; d Feb 1920, Victoria). He arrived in BC with a party of OVERLANDERS from Ontario in 1862 to join the Cariboo GOLD RUSH. Instead he settled at KAMLOOPS, where he worked as a packer, then commenced a successful business career. He owned a series of steamboats on the Thompson–Shuswap system as well as a general store. A proponent of CONFEDERATION, he was elected to the provincial legislature in 1871 and served as Speaker from 1883 to 1886. He was a Conservative MP (*see* CONSERVATIVE PARTY) from 1887 until his defeat in the 1896 election. After selling his store he moved to VICTORIA in 1900. Mara Lk south of SICAMOUS is named for him.

MARACLE, Lee, writer (b 1950, N Vancouver). Her first novel, *Bobbie Lee: Indian Rebel* (1975), published when she was 25 years old, is a memoir of her life on the road and her anger at the racism and injustice suffered by aboriginal people and especially aboriginal women. She continued to engage with these themes in her essay collection *I am Woman* (1988). Other novels include *Sundogs* (1991) and *Ravensong* (1993). She also co-edited a collection of conference papers, *Telling It: Women and Language Across Cultures* (1988). A member of the STO:LO NATION, she has taught at the EN'OWKIN CENTRE in PENTICTON.

MARCHAND, Leonard Stephen "Len," scientist, politician (b 16 Nov 1933, Vernon). A graduate of UBC (1959) and the Univ of Idaho (1964), he was an agricultural research scientist at the KAMLOOPS Research Station from 1960 to 1965. He worked as special assistant to 2 federal cabinet ministers in Ottawa, then was elected Liberal MP for Kamloops–Cariboo in 1968—the first aboriginal elected to Parliament since Louis Riel. In 1976 he became the first aboriginal to serve in the federal cabinet when he was named minister of state for small business by Prime Minister Pierre Trudeau. He also served as minister of state for the environment (1977–79). After his defeat in the 1979 election, Marchand became administrator for the Nicola Valley Indian Administration in MERRITT. He was named to the Senate in 1984, the same year he became honorary chief of the OKANAGAN NATION, and served until retiring in 1997. In 1999 he was named to the Order of Canada.

MARCUSE, Judith Rose (Margolick), dancer, choreographer (b 13 Mar 1947, Montreal). After training as a dancer in Montreal and at London's Royal Ballet School from 1962 to 1965, she danced with several companies,

Charles Marega, Vancouver sculptor. *CVA Port.P358*

including Les Grands Ballets Canadiens (1965–68), Bat-Dor Dance Co in Israel (1970–72) and Ballet Rambert in London (1974–76). In 1976 she came to VANCOUVER and 4 years later she began her own company, now known as DanceArts Vancouver. Marcuse is a choreographer of modern DANCE and her works have been performed widely across Canada and internationally. She has won several prestigious awards for her work. In 1994 she founded the Kiss Project, an annual festival of dance, video and theatre held on GRANVILLE ISLAND in Vancouver.

Judith Marcuse, Vancouver choreographer and dance producer. *Peter Battistoni/Vancouver Sun*

MAREGA, Charles (Carlos), sculptor (b 24 Sept 1871, Lucinico, Italy; d 27 Mar 1939, Vancouver). He was the first professional sculptor to work in BC. After studying sculpture in Italy, Vienna and Zurich, he arrived in VANCOU-VER in 1909 on his way to California. He remained in Canada when he received a commission for a sculpture of David OPPENHEIMER. His many works in the city include the Harding Memorial, Joe FORTES Memorial in Alexandra Park, the sculpture on the Burrard St Bridge, Capt George VANCOUVER at city hall, and his final work, the lions at the south end of the LIONS GATE BRIDGE. He also did much of the plaster work in elegant Shaughnessy homes. Marega taught night school after his arrival, then at the Vancouver School of Art (*see* EMILY CARR INSTITUTE OF ART & DESIGN) during the Depression, when private commissions were scarce. He collapsed and died shortly after one of his art school classes. *Peggy Imredy*

MARGISON, Richard, singer (b 15 July 1953, Victoria). One of the world's leading lyric tenors, he began his career singing and strumming guitar in coffee houses around VICTORIA. After studies at the Victoria Conservatory of Music and performances with a variety of local musical groups ranging from Pacific Opera to Gilbert & Sullivan, he debuted with the VANCOUVER OPERA in 1985. He first appeared with the Canadian Opera Co in 1989, the same year he made his European debut in London with the English National Opera. Since then he has sung with leading opera companies in Europe and N America, including a New York debut with the Metropolitan Opera in 1995, singing Pinkerton in *Madama Butterfly*.

MARGUERITE, a ranching district (*see* CATTLE INDUSTRY) in the CARIBOO, is the site of a tiny reaction ferry (*see* BIG BAY) across the FRASER R 46 km north of WILLIAMS LAKE. An aerial passenger tramway runs when the river freezes. The settlement, located on the BC RAIL line and Hwy 97, was named after a local TSILHQOT'IN woman. AS

MARIJUANA (*Cannabis sativa*) has had a significant role in the culture and economy of BC. Its popularity as both a recreational drug and a cash crop dates from the 1960s, when the counterculture movement brought thousands of young people, many of them marijuana users, into the province. In the extensive areas of LOGGING slash in rugged mountain terrain, growers found garden sites that were open to the sun, yet remote enough to provide some security from police and thieves. Cannabis thrived in the warm, dry summers characteristic of the southern Interior and Georgia Basin, though quality and prices remained low and markets small and local for nearly 2 decades. In the 1980s plant breeding and horticultural innovation revolutionized the fledgling industry. By crossbreeding strains of *Cannabis sativa* with the more northerly *C. indica*, growers created scores of early-flowering varieties adapted to local conditions. Potency was further increased by weeding out male plants so that females produced only seedless flowers. Finally, in the latter half of the 1980s, cultivators moved their operations indoors, growing year-round under powerful lights. As producer prices peaked at about $3,200 a pound in the early 1990s, thousands of people were attracted to the trade by the promise of tax-free profits that commonly exceeded $100,000 a year. Thanks to the international reputation of "BC Bud" for exceptional quality, new export markets in the US

RCMP removing marijuana from an illegal grow operation. Ward Perrin/Vancouver Sun

absorbed much of the increased production.

The BC cannabis harvest is believed to be worth at least $1 billion a year with some estimates ranging as high as $10 billion, making it the economic mainstay of many small towns hit hard by the 1990s downturn in the forest and fishing industries. Marijuana has been outlawed in Canada since 1923, though the law is enforced with widely varying severity across the country. BC is the most lenient province: jail sentences are rare and discharges are common for simple possession. All convictions, however, still leave the

offender with a criminal record. *Michael Poole*
Reading: Michael Poole, *Romancing Mary Jane,* 1998.

MARILLA is a scattered AGRICULTURAL district 60 km south of BURNS LAKE on northeast shore of OOTSA LK. It was first settled in the early 1900s by the Horr family, who got their supplies from BELLA COOLA, 165 km southwest, by pack train. George Henson opened a store in the 1920s. AS

MARINE PARKS are provincial PARKS designated to facilitate marine recreation and/or conservation. They are meant for boaters and only a

Octopus Islands Marine Park, Quadra Island.
Ian Douglas photo

few have road access. The vast majority are on the coast but there are also some on large Interior lakes, notably Upper and Lower ARROW, KOOTENAY and SHUSWAP lakes. The first marine park was established at MONTAGUE HARBOUR on GALIANO ISLAND in 1959. Since then, more than 50 marine parks of varying sizes have been established, from DISCOVERY ISLAND near VICTORIA to Kitson Island near PRINCE RUPERT. Some were established on vacant Crown land, others were purchased by the government, still others were gifts from private individuals.

MARITIME MUSEUM OF BC was established as a naval museum on Signal Hill in ESQUIMALT in 1954. It moved to its present site in the former VICTORIA Law Courts Building on Bastion Square in downtown Victoria in 1965. There is a legend that the court building—designed by H.O. TIEDEMANN, opened in 1889 and remodelled by Francis RATTENBURY in 1900—is haunted by a convict who was imprisoned by Judge Matthew BEGBIE. Part of the building is again being used for court cases. The museum presents the marine history of BC from early exploration to the Royal Canadian Navy.

MARLATT, Daphne (Buckle), writer (b 11 July 1942, Melbourne, Australia). She came to VANCOUVER as a child. As a student at UBC in the 1960s she was involved with the TISH group of post-modernist poets. After graduate studies at the Univ of Indiana, she returned to live in BC and during the 1970s published several books of poetry. At the same time she conducted 2 oral history projects with the provincial archives, and produced books about STEVESTON and the Strathcona neighbourhood of Vancouver. During the 1980s her work became more explicitly feminist and lesbian in such poetry collections as *How Hug a Stone* (1983), *Touch to My Tongue* (1984) and *Salvage* (1991). She then turned to prose and published her first novel, *Ana Historic*, in 1988; it is considered a classic of BC LITERATURE. A second novel, *Taken*, was published in 1996. Some of her earlier work was revisited in *Ghost Works* (1993). A collection of her feminist essays on Canadian women's writing, gathered over a period of 15 years, appeared in 1998 as *Readings from the Labyrinth*. As an editor she has worked on several literary MAGAZINES, including the *Capilano Review, Periodics, Island* and the feminist magazine *Tessera.*

MARMOT is a burrowing rodent resembling the woodchuck in size and appearance. It inhabits subalpine meadows, where it feeds on grasses and wildflowers. Its distinctive whistling call signals danger. (The resort community of WHISTLER is named for this sound.) During the winter the marmot hibernates in burrows beneath the snow and rock. Of 14 species worldwide, 3 occur in BC. The Vancouver Island marmot (*Marmota vancouverensis*), one of the rarest mammals in N America, has been officially endangered since 1980; only an estimated 100–200 survive, mostly in a mountainous area southwest of NANAIMO. It has a dark brown coat, a white nose and a white streak down its belly. In 1996 scientists

Hoary marmot. R. Wayne Campbell photo

began moving individuals to preferable habitat elsewhere on the island in an attempt to rebuild the population. Mainland species are the hoary marmot (*M. caligata*) and the yellow-bellied marmot (*M. flaviventris*).

MARPOLE, Richard, railway engineer (b 8 Oct 1850, Wales; d 8 June 1920, Vancouver). After coming to Canada to work on rail construction he joined the CPR in the 1880s and succeeded Henry ABBOTT as the company's superintendent of the western district from 1897 to 1907. On behalf of the CPR he planned the development of the upscale VANCOUVER residential suburb of Shaughnessy Heights and built the first home there in 1909. The south Vancouver neighbourhood of Marpole was named for him in 1916.

MARPOLE MIDDEN is a vast archaeological site that covered 1.8 ha on the north bank of the FRASER R at the foot of Granville St in VANCOUVER, opposite the eastern end of SEA ISLAND. The site, now built over, was occupied at least 2,500 years ago during the late middle period of BC's PREHISTORY. Stone tools, carvings and copper ornaments were recovered from the site, whose occupants are believed to be the direct ancestors of the Coast SALISHAN peoples encountered by the earliest explorers. The items unearthed at the site were given to the VANCOUVER MUSEUM. Marpole Midden is also called the Eburne Mound and the Great Fraser Midden. The major excavation was by Charles BORDEN in the late 1940s and early 1950s. *See also* MIDDENS; ARCHAEOLOGY.

MARRIOTT, Joyce Anne, writer (b 5 Nov 1913, Victoria; d 10 Oct 1997, Vancouver). Her first book of poetry, *The Wind Our Enemy* (1939), describes prairie farm life during the Depression. Her second book, *Calling Adventurers*, won a GOV GEN'S LITERARY AWARD for poetry in 1941. (Emily CARR won the Gov Gen's Award for fiction that year—the first time writers from BC had ever won the award.) Marriott was a co-founder of the poetry magazine CONTEMPORARY VERSE. Following WWII she worked as a scriptwriter for the CBC and the National Film Board in Ottawa, and during the 1950s she was a NEWSPAPER journalist in PRINCE GEORGE. She married Gerald McLellan in 1947 and her literary career took a back seat to raising a family. Her husband died in 1974 and as their 3 children grew up she began publishing more regularly. She produced 8 books of poetry, including *The Circular Coast: Poems New and Selected*, which won a Gov Gen's Literary Award nomination in 1981, and a collection of short fiction, *A Long Way to Oregon*. Her work is widely anthologized.

MARRON VALLEY, including Marron Lk and the Marron R, is a ranching district (*see* CATTLE INDUSTRY) 14 km southwest of PENTICTON, part of a large OKANAGAN First Nation RESERVE. The Marron was probably the "river of wild horses" mentioned by botanist David DOUGLAS in 1833.

AS

MARSH, Leonard Charles, social scientist (b 24 Sept 1906, London, England; d 10 May 1982, Vancouver). An important architect of the Canadian welfare state, he went to Montreal in 1930. He directed a research program at McGill Univ and belonged to the League for Social Reconstruction, influential in formation of the CCF during the 1930s. He was a major contributor to the League's *Social Planning for Canada* (1935), a groundbreaking analysis of the need for progressive social reform. During WWII he advised the government on post-war reconstruction. He moved to VANCOUVER in 1948 to become director of research at UBC's school of social work, and he was professor of educational sociology at UBC from 1964 until his retirement in 1973. His books include *Canadians In and Out of Work* (1940) and *Report on Social Security for Canada* (1943).

MARTEN (*Martes americana*), a member of the WEASEL family (Mustelids) of mammals, occurs widely in forested areas across BC from sea level to the subalpine and on VANCOUVER ISLAND, the QUEEN CHARLOTTE ISLANDS and several other large ISLANDS. The marten (or pine marten, as it is sometimes known) is a small carnivore of weasel-like shape similar to a MINK in size but with longer legs, a longer and bushier tail and more prominent ears. It may grow to 70 cm in length and weigh up to 1 kg. Its fur, which has been highly valued by trappers, is a rich, dark brown above and lighter beneath, often with a distinctive yellow or orange patch on the throat and chest. Martens are skilled climbers that scramble up trees in search of SQUIRRELS and bird's eggs, hunt on the ground for rodents and INSECTS, and prey on marine crustaceans in coastal areas. They are solitary animals and the sexes mix only during the mid-summer mating season. The female produces a litter of 2–6 kits and rears them alone.

MARTIN, Joseph, lawyer, politician, premier 28 Feb 1900–14 June 1900 (b 24 Sept 1852, Milton, ON; d 2 Mar 1923, Vancouver). He first earned his political reputation in Manitoba where he served as attorney general in the government of Thomas Greenway (1888–1900) and played a key role in the infamous Manitoba Schools Question, a political crisis involving the withdrawal of public funding for Catholic schools. After sitting as an MP for Winnipeg in 1893–96 he moved to VANCOUVER and was elected to the provincial legislature in 1898. The legislature was highly factionalized; no one commanded enough of a following to keep a secure grip on the premiership. Lt Gov Thomas MCINNES appointed Charles SEMLIN premier and Martin joined the CABINET as attorney general.

Joe Martin, premier of BC, 1900.
CVA Port.P1746

Martin was a fiery orator who represented himself as an enemy of vested interests. He was intelligent, headstrong, ambitious and incapable of getting along with anyone for very long. In July 1899 he was dismissed from the cabinet. He continued to be an outspoken figure in the legislature, and when the Semlin government fell early in 1900 McInnes asked Martin to form an administration. Amid stormy protests, Martin cobbled together a cabinet and attempted to conduct business. Before he met the legislature he was forced to call an election. He won his seat but lost most of his support, and he was replaced as PREMIER. Martin remained a loose cannon in the legislature, however, and at one point got into a scuffle with Richard MCBRIDE over who had the right to occupy the leader of the opposition's chair. When the LIBERAL PARTY was organized provincially in 1902, Martin was chosen first leader, but he lost the election of Oct 1903. He then practised law in Vancouver and made a fortune developing the Hastings Manor subdivision on the city's eastern edge. After moving briefly to England he sat as an MP from 1910 to 1918. At the same time he maintained a residence in Vancouver, where he ran for mayor unsuccessfully in 1915.

MARTIN, Mungo (Naka'pankam), Kwakwaka'wakw artist (b circa 1881, Fort Rupert; d 16 Aug 1962, Victoria). A member of a noble family, he apprenticed as a carver to his stepfather Charlie JAMES and became one of the best-known carvers on the coast. He played a major role in preserving KWAKWAKA'WAKW (Kwakiutl)

Mungo Martin (r), master Kwakwaka'wakw carver, 1961. BC Archives I-26830

artistic traditions during the prohibition of the POTLATCH and bringing Northwest Coast art to wide public attention. UBC hired him in 1950 to restore and carve TOTEM POLES for its Totem Park. He also recorded many traditional songs with the musicologist Ida HALPERN. In 1952 he became resident carver at the provincial museum (*see* ROYAL BC MUSEUM), where he trained his son-in-law Henry HUNT and grandson Tony Hunt. He constructed a new version of his ancestral community house at the museum and dedicated it with a potlatch in 1953. One of his poles, once the world's tallest (38.9 m), stands in BEACON HILL PARK in VICTORIA.

MARTIN, Seth, hockey goaltender (b 4 May 1933, Rossland). He joined the TRAIL SMOKE EATERS of the amateur Western International League in 1953 after playing junior HOCKEY in Lethbridge, AB, and remained with Trail for 9 years, leading it to the world amateur championship in 1961. With the legendary Jacques Plante he pioneered the use of goaltenders' masks, designing and making his own and introducing the concept to Europe at the 1961 tournament. After taking the team to the international championships again in 1963 (this time it was eliminated), he joined Father David Bauer's new Canadian national team. Martin played for Canada at the 1964 Innsbruck Olympics and continued goaltending for the national team while with the WIHL's ROSSLAND Warriors in 1966–67. At age 34 he played 30 games for the NHL St Louis Blues, with a stellar 2.59 goals-against average. He returned to the Smoke Eaters the next season, then led the 1969–70 Spokane Jets to the WIHL title and the Allan Cup amateur championship before ending his career after the 1972–73 season. The holder of several Western International League records, he was inducted into the BC SPORTS HALL OF FAME in 1998.

Fred Hume

MARTINEZ, Estéban José, naval officer (b 9 Dec 1742, Seville, Spain; d 28 Oct 1798, Baja California, Mexico). He entered the Spanish navy as a teenager and was posted to the naval base of San Blas, Mexico; from there he accompanied Juan PEREZ on his 1774 voyage to the QUEEN CHARLOTTE ISLANDS to investigate rumours of Russian expansion. He returned in 1775–88 to regular naval service between Spanish ports in Mexico and California, then in 1788 made his second voyage north to investigate Russian activity. On his advice, the viceroy decided in 1789 to establish a base in NOOTKA SOUND under his command. His seizure of several trading vessels during the summer of 1789 touched off the NOOTKA SOUND CONTROVERSY. He was back at Nootka in 1790, then served out his career in Spain and Mexico. *See also* SPANISH EXPLORATION.

MARYSVILLE was a MINING community on the ST MARY R 6 km south of KIMBERLEY. It was the site of a SMELTER from 1903 to 1908, then developed as a bedroom community for the nearby SULLIVAN MINE after it was taken over by COMINCO. Since 1968 the community has been part of Kimberley.

MASSET, village, pop 1,293, on the north shore of Graham Island, is the largest community on the QUEEN CHARLOTTE ISLANDS. Also known as New Masset, it was established in 1907 as Graham City, but changed its name to Masset in 1909 when it obtained a post office. It became the first incorporated village on the islands in 1961. Commercial FISHING has been an important employer. The HAIDA community of Old Masset (pop 692) is 2 km away on the site of 3 ancient villages. It was one of 2 villages where the Haida congregated at the end of the 19th century after epidemics had depleted their population (*see also* ABORIGINAL DEMOGRAPHY). The HBC operated a post at the site (1869–98) and

the ANGLICAN CHURCH established a mission in 1876. The name Masset derives from nearby Maast Island.

MASSEY, Geoffrey "Geoff," architect (b 29 Oct 1924, London, England). After graduating from the Harvard School of Design in 1952 he moved to VANCOUVER, where he worked for the architectural firm of Thompson, Berwick & Pratt. In 1957 he began a long association with Arthur ERICKSON and was a partner in Erickson/Massey from 1963 to 1972. The firm designed such familiar Vancouver area landmarks as SFU (1963–65), the MacMillan Bloedel Building (1968–69) and the Ross St Sikh Temple (1969–70). He subsequently had his own practice and was a partner in the Coal Harbour Architectural Group from 1975 to 1985.

David R. Conn

MATHIAS, Joe, Squamish leader (b 1944, Vancouver; d 10 Mar 2000, N Vancouver). He grew up on the Capilano RESERVE in N VANCOUVER and at age 22 succeeded his grandfather as a chief of the SQUAMISH Nation. From 1969 to his death he was the political spokesperson for the Squamish people. During the 1980s he was the leading aboriginal politician in BC, serving as chair of the Aboriginal Peoples Constitutional Conference and BC chief of the Assembly of FIRST NATIONS. A powerful speaker, much admired both within and beyond the aboriginal community, he was a guiding force in the First Nations Summit, established in 1991 to promote a negotiated resolution to the BC land claims question. *See also* ABORIGINAL RIGHTS.

MATSQUI was a rural municipality in the central FRASER VALLEY, 70 km east of VANCOUVER. The name derives from a STO:LO Nation word meaning "stretch of higher ground," a reference to a portage between the FRASER R and Sumas Lk. The

Aerial view of Masset, the largest community in the Queen Charlotte Islands.

earliest settlers arrived in the 1860s and the local economy relied on AGRICULTURE, principally DAIRY FARMING, eggs, poultry, vegetables and BERRIES. From the 1970s the district experienced rapid urban growth centred mainly in CLEAR-BROOK, the town centre. Commercial expansion spilled over into ABBOTSFORD; on 1 Jan 1995 the 2 merged to form the City of Abbotsford, the largest municipality between Vancouver and KAMLOOPS.

MATTHEW GOOD BAND started as a folk band touring bars in western Canada. Matthew Good (b 29 June, 1971, Burnaby), a guitarist, singer and songwriter, decided to reinvent his band as a rock incarnation with his fellow Lower Mainland natives Ian Browne (drums), Dave Genn (guitar & keyboards) and Geoff Lloyd (bass). In 1995 they released *Last of the Ghetto*

Matthew Good Band, 1999. The band won a Juno Award in 2000. J. Blakesberg/S.L. Feldman

Astronauts, which attracted heavy airplay on VAN-COUVER radio and became one of the bestselling independent recordings in Canadian music history. After making a 5-song EP, *Raygun*, in 1997, the band released their second album, *Underdogs*, in 1998. The record earned platinum sales status; the band won 4 Juno nominations and Best New Group honours at the Canadian Music Awards. Rich Priske replaced Lloyd in 1999, the year the band released their third album, *Beautiful Midnight*, which earned a pair of Junos, best group and best rock album, at the 2000 awards. *SW*

MATTHEWS, James Skitt, archivist (b 7 Sept 1878, Newton, Wales; d 1970, Vancouver). After attending school in New Zealand, he immigrated to California. In 1899 he reached VANCOUVER, where he went to work for Imperial Oil. Active in the militia, he served overseas during WWI. He achieved the rank of major and was known as Major Matthews the rest of his life. After his retirement from business in 1924 he pursued his interest in Vancouver history. His documents, records and memorabilia filled up his home; when he transferred the collection to an attic room in city hall in 1931, the City Archives was born. After a dispute over ownership of the material was resolved in 1933, he was appointed city archivist and held the position until he retired in 1969, at age 91. Idiosyncratic in his approach to history and irascible by nature, Matthews was continuously embroiled in con-

Major J.S. Matthews, founder of the Vancouver City Archives, 1968. Vancouver Province

troversy with the city and the academic establishment, but his passion for collecting historical records—at a time when there was little official support—was undeniable, and his work inspired much excellent work that followed.

MAURELLE ISLAND, 54 km², is located in the INSIDE PASSAGE between QUADRA ISLAND and the mainland. Hole in the Wall, a rapids familiar to coastal boaters, lies along the north coast. Known originally as Middle Valdes Island, it was renamed in 1903 after Francisco Antonio Maurelle, a Spanish naval officer who visited the coast in 1775. The earliest inhabitants were loggers and most of the island was logged by 1916. The terrain is rocky and broken, and though some farming took place in the south, FISHING and LOGGING have been the main occupations. Only a few people inhabit the island.

MAXWELL, George Ritchie, Presbyterian minister, politician (b 11 Jan 1857, Stonehouse, Scotland; d 17 Nov 1902, Vancouver). He was a COAL miner by the age of 11, but he managed to complete his schooling and in 1880 graduated from theological college an ordained minister. Five years later he immigrated to Quebec; in 1890 he took charge of the First PRESBYTERIAN CHURCH in VANCOUVER. As a social gospel clergyman, his concerns for the working class led naturally to politics. In 1894 he helped create BC's first labour party, the NATIONALIST PARTY, and in 1896 he was elected to the House of Commons on a Liberal–Labour platform for the riding of Burrard. He was re-elected in 1900 and died in office.

MAYNARD, Hannah (Hatherly), photographer (b 17 Jan 1834, Bude, England; d 15 May 1918, Victoria) and **Richard James**, shoemaker, photographer (b 22 Feb 1832, Stratton, England; d 10 Jan 1907, Victoria). The couple immigrated

to Ontario in 1852 and settled in Bowmanville, where Richard opened a boot and shoe business and Hannah learned PHOTOGRAPHY. Richard joined the GOLD RUSH to BC in 1859 and in 1862 the family moved to VICTORIA. Hannah opened a photographic studio, one of the first in the city, and Richard re-established his shoe business. Richard appears to have learned photography from his wife and by the 1870s the couple were engaged in commercial photography of all sorts. Hannah specialized in portrait and other studio work and was the more experimental of the two, working with montage and double exposure and creating surreal domestic tableaux; Richard was mainly a landscape photographer. In 1873–74 he accompanied the Indian commissioner on a tour of coastal villages and in 1884 was official photographer on a government expedition to the QUEEN CHARLOTTE ISLANDS. The Maynards rarely travelled together but they photographed throughout the province for 4 decades.

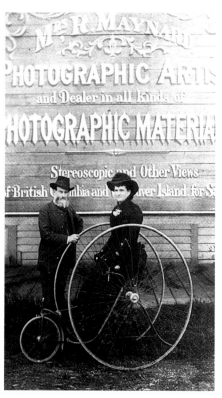

Self-portrait of Richard and Hannah Maynard, Victoria photographers, c 1880. BC Archives C-08673

MAYNARD, Max Singleton, artist (b 30 Dec 1903, India; d 1982, Victoria). He moved with his parents, who were missionaries, to VICTORIA in 1912. There he earned his teaching certificate and taught elementary school until 1938. At the same time he developed his skill as a painter, principally of landscapes, and became a vigorous exponent of modernism. Early influences included Emily CARR and the Group of Seven. After teaching at the Univ of Southern California from 1938 to 1939 he returned to Victoria, then taught literature at the Univ of Manitoba from 1941 to 1945. He then moved to the Univ of New Hampshire and taught until his retirement in 1973. At age 74 he returned to Victoria, where he continued to paint.

MAYNE ISLAND, 23.27 km², is one of the GULF ISLANDS between southern VANCOUVER ISLAND and the mainland. It is named for the British naval officer Lt Richard C. Mayne, who served on the coast from 1857 to 1861. There is evidence that aboriginal settlement by Coast Salish (*see* SALISHAN FIRST NATIONS) goes back at least 5,000 years. The earliest white visitors were gold miners who passed by on their way to the FRASER R during the 1858 GOLD RUSH. They were followed during the 1860s by farmers who were attracted by the island's gently rolling landscape and raised sheep and fruit, as well as other crops (*see* AGRICULTURE). With the construction of a government wharf in 1878, steamboats began calling at Miners Bay. From 1880 to 1900 the post office here was named Plumper Pass, an old name for ACTIVE PASS. JAPANESE Canadian settlers first arrived in the 1890s, hired to cut cordwood for the Fraser R SALMON CANNERIES. By 1938 they made up a third of the island population. Their removal and internment during WWII was a severe blow to the island's economic and social life (*see* JAPANESE, RELOCATION OF). TOURISM has always been important on Mayne. Springwater Lodge in Miners Bay, built in 1895, is BC's oldest continuously operating hotel; the island welcomes many summer visitors to augment the permanent population, about 1,000 people in 1999.

MAYSE, Arthur William Caswell, writer (b 1912, St James Mission, MB; d 21 Mar 1992, Campbell River). He grew up in NANAIMO and VANCOUVER and was only 12 years old when he sold his first short story; poetry prizes paid for his tuition at UBC. He wrote for Vancouver NEWSPAPERS before going east, where he was fiction editor at *Maclean's* magazine until 1948. After returning to VANCOUVER ISLAND in 1951, he published many short stories about coastal life in the *Saturday Evening Post* and other magazines, as well as working at the Victoria *Daily Times*. Among his published novels are *Perilous Passage* (1949), *Desperate Search* (1952), *Morgan's Mountain* (1960) and the juvenile novel *Handliner's Island* (1990). He also wrote television scripts, notably for the BEACHCOMBERS, filmed in GIBSONS in the 1970s.
Reading: Arthur Mayse, *My Father, My Friend*, 1993. *Susan Mayse*

MAZAMA, a ranching and farming district (*see* CATTLE INDUSTRY; AGRICULTURE) 53 km northwest of PENTICTON, was first settled in 1913 by John S. Chapman, a British lawyer, who ran a ranch here with his sons until the 1950s. Located where an old trail from PRINCETON to the OKANAGAN VALLEY crossed Trout Crk, the site was first known as Princeton Crossing. More settlers arrived after the KETTLE VALLEY RWY passed through in 1914; a station was built 3 km west at Osprey Lk. AS

MEADOW CREEK, north of KOOTENAY LK and 85 km northeast of NELSON, is a small rural settlement with a store, service station, café and community hall. A nearby KOKANEE spawning channel has compensated for some of the fish habitat lost during the construction of the nearby DUNCAN DAM. AS

MEADOWLARK, western (*Sturnella neglecta*), is a plump, ROBIN-sized bird known for its beautiful flute-like song. Meadowlarks occur predominantly in Interior GRASSLANDS habitat, where they build their nests on the ground, camouflag-

Giant cedar on Meares Island.
Leo Degroot/ WCWC

ing them beneath canopies of woven grass. Their backs are mottled brown-grey in colour and their fronts are a bright lemon yellow. With their long, pointed bills, they feed mainly on INSECTS and seeds.

MEAGER CREEK lies in the COAST MTS northwest along the LILLOOET R from PEMBERTON. Nearby Mt Meager was the site of a volcanic eruption in about 450 BC. HOT SPRINGS on the creek make it a popular destination for backroaders, and since the creation of a FOREST SERVICE recreation site in 1979, concerns have grown about the impact of LOGGING and recreational overuse.

MEARES, John, fur trader (b circa 1756; d 1809). After serving in the Royal Navy, he made his first trading voyage to the Northwest Coast in 1786. He spent a horrible winter in Prince William Sound, where 23 of his men died, but was rescued by 2 rival traders, Nathaniel PORTLOCK and George DIXON. In 1788 he was in NOOTKA SOUND, where he established a trading post and built a 40-ton schooner, *NORTH WEST AMERICA*, the first vessel of European design built on the coast. In 1789, operating from China, he sent trading vessels to the sound; they were seized by the Spanish, precipitating a diplomatic showdown between Spain and Britain (*see* NOOTKA

SOUND CONTROVERSY). Meares returned to England, where he stirred up anti-Spanish feeling by exaggerating events at Nootka Sound. Eventually he won reparations, but the published account of his activities on the coast was criticized by his contemporaries for being unreliable.

MEARES ISLAND, 84.77 km², lies at the south end of CLAYOQUOT SOUND off TOFINO on the west coast of VANCOUVER ISLAND. It is part of the traditional territory of the Tla-o-qui-aht FIRST NATION of the NUU-CHAH-NULTH and the site of their main village, Opitsat (pop 151). Heavily forested with western red CEDAR and HEMLOCK, the island was logged beginning in 1905. During the 1980s it was the scene of massive protests against LOGGING plans by MACMILLAN BLOEDEL LTD. Aboriginals declared it a "tribal park" in 1984 and by the 1990s the fate of the trees still awaited the outcome of land claims negotiations. The island is named for John MEARES, the British trading captain who stirred up the NOOTKA SOUND CONTROVERSY.

MEDICAL PROFESSION in BC is organized and governed by 2 provincial bodies, the College of Physicians and Surgeons of BC and the BC Medical Assoc (BCMA). The college is a regulatory body established by the *Medical Practitioners Act* to protect the public from unqualified, incompetent or unscrupulous medical practitioners. The Act empowers the college to register physicians, establish and enforce standards of physician education, maintain standards of physician practice and conduct, and enforce the Act's provisions against medical practice by unregistered persons. The college also accredits diagnostic and non-hospital medical and surgical facilities throughout the province. The BCMA, a division of the Canadian Medical Assoc (CMA), is responsible for negotiating physicians' fees with the government and in general acts as an advocacy body for the profession. It also runs a number of scientific, educational and community health programs through its numerous committees and specialty sections and produces a scholarly publication, the *BC Medical Journal*. In addition to these provincial organizations, there are 33 local societies that represent the views of community physicians through 16 district representatives elected to the board of directors of the BCMA.

The first step toward organizing the medical profession in BC was taken with the passage of the Medical Ordinance in 1867 providing for the appointment of a registrar responsible for registering physicians. In 1885 Dr John Sebastian HELMCKEN founded the BC Medical Society, which drafted the essentials of the *Medical Act* of 1886. This Act provided for the establishment of the Medical Council of BC, later renamed the College of Physicians and Surgeons of BC, which assumed responsibility for registering physicians, setting examinations for prospective registrants, and prosecuting offences against the Act. The college continued to be responsible for setting examinations until 1920, when this function was taken over by the Medical Council of Canada.

The rise of local medical associations designed to serve the needs of local practitioners occurred spontaneously in larger communities late in the 19th century. Members of these associations realized the need for a provincial body that could, among other things, represent the interests of the profession to the provincial government. Several of the larger associations therefore joined to form the BCMA in 1900, with Dr Robert E. McKechnie as president. The BCMA's activities were curtailed, however, by the onset of WWI. The association was revived in 1921 under the presidency of Dr A.S. Munroe, but financial difficulties, particularly during the 1930s, prompted a strong reliance on the College of Physicians and Surgeons for most of its funding. Its importance was also diminished by the presence of the vibrant Vancouver Medical Assoc, which published a medical journal, the *VMA Bulletin*, managed a medical LIBRARY and ran the VMA Summer School, a continuing medical education program for physicians. During these years, the college was responsible for medical economics, which included setting minimum fees for the profession and regulating contracts and private insurance schemes. From 1945 to 1950, however, the college and the BCMA shared responsibility for economics through a Joint Committee on Medical Economics. In 1951 physicians voted in a referendum to have responsibility for medical economics assumed entirely by the BCMA.

At this time the BCMA was reorganized under the leadership of Dr Frank Turnbull and Dr Russell Palmer; in addition to its new economic role, a new emphasis was placed on public relations and community health programs. The *VMA Bulletin* was taken over by the BCMA and became the *BC Medical Journal*; the VMA Medical Library became the Provincial Medical Library Service, run by the college; and the summer school was absorbed by the UBC Continuing Education Department following the establishment of the UBC Faculty of Medicine in 1950. The once powerful VMA returned to its role as a local society and the BCMA's provincial powers grew rapidly. Its status was also enhanced by the formation of an "Action Committee" under Dr E.C. (Tim) McCoy in the late 1950s. This committee travelled extensively, gathering information on health care plans in other parts of the world, with the result that the BCMA played a strong role in the development of universal health care in BC in the 1960s. In the 1970s the BCMA became more aggressive in its fee negotiations with the provincial government. At the same time, the leadership of the association became more representative of physicians outside the Lower Mainland, due in part to the emergence of a reform movement within its ranks.

The practice of medicine in the province in the first half of the 20th century was taken up largely with the control of infectious diseases. Of these, one of the greatest challenges was presented by tuberculosis. In 1907 a group of VANCOUVER doctors took the initiative and, under the leadership of Dr C.J. Fagan, established an open-air TB sanatorium at TRANQUILLE near KAMLOOPS. After the introduction of penicillin and other antibiotics beginning in the 1940s, attention turned away from infectious diseases and focused on chronic illnesses, such as rheumatoid arthritis and medical conditions of the elderly. Physicians also took the lead in developing an infrastructure for the treatment of cancer, establishing the BC Cancer Society in 1935. Radiation therapy for treatment of cancer was pioneered in BC by Dr Ethlyn TRAPP, who became the first chief of radiotherapy at the BC Cancer Clinic in 1939. Surgical advances in the latter half of the century led to the performance of joint replacements, open heart surgery, organ transplantation and other complex procedures at hospitals in the major urban centres, and the presence of the Faculty of Medicine at UBC has stimulated the development of research activities within hospitals. In the 1990s the province became a national leader in AIDS research with the establishment of the BC CENTRE FOR EXCELLENCE IN HIV/AIDS at St Paul's Hospital in Vancouver.

C.E. McDonnell and Evelyn Peters McLellan

MEEKER, Howard William "Howie," hockey commentator (b 4 Nov 1923, New Hamburg, ON). One of HOCKEY's most famous personalities, he moved to PARKSVILLE in 1977. The former player and coach for the Toronto Maple Leafs opened a popular hockey school in BC and continued his famous "golly-gee-whiz" television colour commentary. His high-pitched enthusiasm and controversial frankness on TSN, BCTV and CBC-TV's *Hockey Night in Canada* maintained a powerful love-him-or-hate-him reputation with hockey fans. In 1998, he retired to Parksville permanently and was inducted into the Hockey Hall of Fame in the media category.

SW

MELDRUM CREEK is a ranching community (*see* CATTLE INDUSTRY) on the west side of the FRASER R, just north of the Chilcotin Hwy (*see* ROADS AND HWYS) 14 km west of WILLIAMS LAKE. The area was pioneered by Thomas Meldrum (1828–89) who came from Ontario in the mid-19th century; Meldrums have lived here ever since. The community was located on a TRAIL that became a road leading north up the west side of the Fraser to QUESNEL after being well used by early settlers coming into the CHILCOTIN. For many years it was the home of Eric COLLIER, guide, conservationist and author of the best-selling book *Three Against the Wilderness* (1959).

MELLON, Henry Augustus, naval captain and financier (b 1840, Nottingham, England; d 1916, Vancouver). As a member of the Royal Navy he saw action in India during the Sepoy Rebellion of 1857–1858. He later worked his way up to the rank of captain on vessels of the Dominion Steamship Co. In 1880 he immigrated to Canada, settling first in Manitoba, then late in 1886 in VANCOUVER, where he built the first home in the West End after fire destroyed the city. He was involved in various marine-related businesses and in 1907 was a principal investor in the British–Canadian Wood PULP AND PAPER Co, the short-lived company that built the first mill at PORT MELLON. The mill only operated for 4 months, then closed. Mellon lost much of his fortune in the Vancouver real estate slump of 1913–15.

MENGHI, Umberto, restaurateur (b 24 Oct 1946, Pontedera, Italy). He began working in restaurants in his native Italy when he was 12. After 3 years at hotel college he went to work in London, then came to Canada for Expo 67 to work at a Montreal hotel. When the fair ended he moved west to VANCOUVER and opened his first restaurant, Umberto's, in 1973. According to one legend he financed the venture with money earned from selling Italian sweaters to WOODWARD'S department store. His operation grew

Howie Meeker, hockey legend, 1996.

from there until he was managing 8 businesses, including restaurants in Vancouver and WHISTLER and the Villa Delia Cooking School, opened in 1995 in Tuscany. Menghi became a cult sensation on Australian television and starred in his own American Express commercial. He has also written 4 cookbooks, including *Umberto's Kitchen: The Flavours of Tuscany* (1995).

Shannon Emmerson

MENNONITES are members of a Protestant religious group originating in Germany and the Netherlands in the 16th century. In 1999 about 39,000 Mennonites lived in BC. The name originates with Menno Simons, an early leader of the group. Members began emigrating to N America in response to persecution, and the first Mennonites in Canada settled in Ontario in 1786. Another wave of immigrants came from Russia during the 1870s and colonized southern Manitoba, then spread across the West. The Mennonites who began arriving in BC in 1928 were refugees from Russia, where civil war and collectivization had ravaged their colonies. They settled at YARROW, near CHILLIWACK, on land reclaimed from Sumas Lk, and around ABBOTSFORD and CLEARBROOK. There was also a settlement at BLACK CREEK on VANCOUVER ISLAND. These early settlers were particularly successful at DAIRY FARMING and raising BERRIES. They tended to live in self-sufficient communities, apart from mainstream culture, and to worship at their own churches, open their own schools and shun worldly activities. Their communities prospered; in the post-war period the segregation dissolved as a new generation began to use English instead of German and to move into urban areas in increasing numbers. To facilitate this transition, 2 Mennonite Girls' Homes (Madchenheims) were established by the Mennonite Church in VANCOUVER to provide support for hundreds of young women who came to the city as domestic workers beginning in the 1930s. The homes operated from 1931 to 1961 and functioned as employment agencies and hostels for orphans and immigrant women.

MENTAL HEALTH POLICY in BC up to the 1970s was concerned almost exclusively with mental hospitals. The first institution in the province to be used for the mentally ill was Royal Hospital in VICTORIA; the facility was taken over by the provincial government in 1872 and renamed the Provincial Lunatic Asylum. Its inmates were moved to the new Provincial Asylum for the Insane (*see* WOODLANDS) when it opened in NEW WESTMINSTER in 1878. A hospital at Essondale, now RIVERVIEW, opened in 1913 and facilities for elderly patients were later established at VERNON (1948) and TERRACE (1950), though mental health policy focussed on Essondale. Facilities for the mentally ill were reorganized into the Provincial Mental Health Services in 1950. From the 1970s the focus of care began to shift from Essondale's large psychiatric complex to psychiatric units in general hospitals and to community care. Deinstitutionalization was not matched by cor-

responding resources in the community, however, and the policy was carried out with mixed success. Much of the load continued to be taken by diminishing facilities at Riverview. It was only at the end of the 1990s that services began expanding to accommodate the needs of the mentally disabled living in the community. The 204-bed Forensic Psychiatric Institute in PORT COQUITLAM is the province's only hospital for mentally disordered criminals (though the federal government maintains psychiatric facilities at its PRISONS). In addition there is a 13-bed forensic assessment unit at the VANCOUVER Pretrial Services Centre. These facilities are operated by the Forensic Psychiatric Services Commission, the agency responsible for the assessment, treatment and clinical case management of mentally disordered persons who are in conflict with the law. The institute admits persons who are remanded by the courts for a psychiatric assessment to determine whether they are fit to stand trial, or whether at the time of an alleged offence they were suffering from a mental disorder rendering them not criminally responsible. The courts can remand a patient to the institute for treatment to restore fitness, or for treatment if found to be not criminally responsible on account of a mental disorder (NCR-MD). Persons found unfit to stand trial, or NCR-MD, fall under the jurisdiction of the BC Review Board, which makes decisions as to their disposition. The board can order a person detained in custody in the institute, or released on conditions into the community. The institute will also admit inmates who become acutely mentally ill while in the custody of a provincial correctional facility. Services are provided on an outpatient basis through community services clinics in Vancouver, Victoria, NANAIMO, PRINCE GEORGE, KAMLOOPS and SURREY. These clinics are responsible for the supervision and monitoring of NCR-MD persons living in the community, and for any persons who are found unfit to stand trial and granted a conditional discharge by the BC Review Board. The clinics also conduct assessments ordered by the provincial courts (fitness to stand trial, NCR-MD, pre-sentence and mental status), as well as provide assessment and treatment services for offenders on bail and probation/parole.

Claire Sowerbutt

MENZIES, Archibald, botanist and naval officer (b 15 Mar 1754, Weem, Scotland; d 15 Feb 1842, London, England). A trained botanist and physician, he joined the Royal Navy in 1782 as an assistant surgeon. Wherever he travelled on naval expeditions he collected seeds and specimens of native plants and made botanical drawings. He arrived on the Pacific Coast in 1787 as surgeon on a trading ship commanded by James COLNETT and spent a month at NOOTKA SOUND collecting plants. During 1792–94 he was back on the coast as naturalist with Capt George VANCOUVER's survey expedition, continuing his collecting. He is credited with introducing the MONKEY PUZZLE TREE from Chile to England and with collecting the first specimen of DOUGLAS FIR. Menzies served in the Royal Navy until 1802,

Archibald Menzies, naturalist with George Vancouver's coastal survey crew 1792–94. BC Archives PDP-05374

when he resigned to practise medicine in London and to pursue his scientific work.

MERAW, Annabelle "Ann" (Mundigel), swimmer (b 23 Feb 1917, Powell River). She began distance SWIMMING at Britannia Beach at age 10, when she swam across HOWE SOUND and back. She won the high school division of the PNE's BURRARD INLET swim at 13 and was signed up next day by the Vancouver Amateur Swim Club. She turned professional in 1934, started competing in marathons and in 1938 became the first person to swim the 22 km from VANCOUVER to BOWEN ISLAND. Because of WWII she had to abandon plans to swim the English Channel, but at home she became Canada's first female lifeguard and the founder of the Canadian "Water Babies" swimming program. Between 1956 and 1958 she made 3 attempts to swim across OKANAGAN LK, setting a new world

Ann Meraw, long-distance swimmer. VPL 62388

endurance record of 25 hrs 1 min and a world speed record of 51.2 km in 16 hrs 14 mins. On her third bid she made it across the lake, swimming 88 km in 32 hrs 12 mins. She attempted crossings of JUAN DE FUCA STRAIT as well. She turned to coaching full-time in 1961, retired in 1982 and was inducted into the BC SPORTS HALL OF FAME in 1985. *SW*

MERCHANT MARINE; *see* CANADIAN GOVERNMENT MERCHANT MARINE LTD.

MERRICK, Paul, architect (b 1938, Vancouver). A graduate of UBC, he worked with Ron THOM in Toronto during the 1960s, then returned to VAN-

Paul Merrick, Vancouver architect, 1976.
George Diack/Vancouver Sun

COUVER to join Thompson, Berwick & Pratt in 1969. In 1979 he was a founding partner in Merrick Chandler Kennedy Architectural Group, and in 1984 he established his own firm, Paul Merrick Architects Ltd. His designs are found throughout downtown Vancouver; they include the CBC Building (1973–75), renovations to the Marine Building (1989), the Cathedral Place and Canadian Craft Museum complex that replaced the Georgia Medical/Dental Building in 1991, and City Square (1989).

MERRIMAN, Alec Robert, journalist (b 21 Apr 1920, Victoria). The son of Tom Merriman, a long-time writer with the *Victoria Times* newspaper, he joined the staff of the Victoria *Colonist* (*see* TIMES-COLONIST) in 1953 after 8 years as editor of *Island Events* MAGAZINE. He became the paper's outdoors writer in 1960 and wrote a daily column until his retirement in 1985. Along with his colleague Jim Tang he organized the *Colonist*'s first King Fisherman Contest in 1956 and ran the popular event from 1960 to 1985. He wrote several books, including *Outdoors with Alec Merriman*, an overview of salt- and freshwater sport FISHING on VANCOUVER ISLAND. He

worked with LOGGING companies to open many Island logging roads to the public and was a tireless advocate for wildlife conservation measures.
Ken MacLeod

MERRITT, city, pop 7,631, lies at the confluence of the NICOLA and Coldwater rivers between HOPE and KAMLOOPS on the COQUIHALLA HWY, 270 km northeast of VANCOUVER. It is the commercial centre of the Nicola Valley. Inhabited by the NLAKA'PAMUX (Thompson) and OKANAGAN nations, the valley was used as part of a FUR TRADE supply route between Fort Kamloops and the FRASER R during 1848–60. During the GOLD RUSH into the CARIBOO, a market for cattle devel-

oped (*see* CATTLE INDUSTRY) and lush grazing lands in the area encouraged livestock raising. DOUGLAS LAKE CATTLE CO, in 1999 the largest ranch in Canada, is nearby. The townsite was laid out in 1893 following the discovery of COAL

deposits. Originally called Forksdale, it was renamed after William Hamilton MERRITT III, who promoted the construction of a railway from SPENCES BRIDGE in 1906, the same year the Middlesboro Collieries produced the first coal. When it opened in 1908, the Coldwater Hotel was considered the finest hotel in the Interior (later it was restored). The city developed quickly and was incorporated on 1 Apr 1911. The FOREST INDUSTRY became important during the 1920s but the city, hit hard by the Depression, went into receivership in 1933 and the province ran its affairs until 1952. Following WWII, coal MINING dwindled until it ceased altogether in 1963, but meanwhile the local economy was reviving with the recovery of SAWMILLING and the opening of 2 large COPPER mines. Though the Craigmont copper mine closed in 1982, the Highland Valley mine, 65 km away, provided many jobs. The forest industry continues to be the main employer.

MERRITT, Charles Cecil Ingersoll, soldier, lawyer (b 10 Nov 1908, Vancouver; d 12 July 2000, Vancouver). He was one of 5 BC-born recipients of the VICTORIA CROSS for military valour. A lawyer, he joined the 72nd Seaforth Highlanders at the beginning of WWII. In 1942 he transferred to the South Saskatchewan Regiment, which he commanded during the ill-fated Dieppe raid on 19 Aug 1942. For his leadership during the raid he received Canada's first Victoria Cross of the war. Taken prisoner, he spent the rest of the war in POW camps, including the notorious camp at Colditz. After the war he returned home and was elected Conservative MP for Vancouver Burrard in 1945–49, then returned to his law practice.

MERRITT, William Hamilton III, mining engineer (b 8 June 1855, St Catharines, ON; d 26 Oct 1918, Toronto). The city of MERRITT is named after him. Grandson of W.H. Merritt, the promoter of the Welland Canal, he grew up in Ontario and studied mining engineering in

Nicola Lake, near Merritt.
Bernie Pawlik/Image Makers

England. He was impressed by the potential of the NICOLA Valley in the 1880s and in 1891 organized the Nicola, Kamloops and Similkameen Coal and Railway Co in the hopes of exploiting COAL deposits near what was then called Forksdale. When, in 1905–6, the CPR did build a railway from SPENCES BRIDGE to the site, it used Merritt's franchise to do so, and the settlement that developed took his name although he never lived there. An ardent member of the militia, he fought in the Northwest Rebellion (1885) and the Boer War and commanded the gov gen's bodyguard from 1903 to 1908. The author of 3 books on minerals and prospecting, he died in the Spanish INFLUENZA EPIDEMIC at the end of WWI. *See also* MINING.

MERVILLE, pop 865, is an AGRICULTURAL community on the east side of VANCOUVER ISLAND, 14 km north of COURTENAY. It was established in 1919 as a settlement of returned veterans and named for a town in France where Canadian soldiers had been headquartered. In 1922 it was hit by a fire that destroyed many of the farms, and it never prospered. The childhood home of the novelist Jack HODGINS, who placed it at the centre of his 1998 novel *Broken Ground*, it remains a rural hamlet.

MESACHIE LAKE was a thriving LOGGING centre on the south shore of COWICHAN LK. Established in 1943 by the Hillcrest Lumber Co, it was the site of a SAWMILL and timber operations until the supply of wood ran out in 1968. A BC Forest Research Station is nearby (*see* FORESTRY). *Mesachie* is a CHINOOK JARGON word meaning "ill-tempered."

METCHOSIN, district municipality, pop 4,709, is on southern VANCOUVER ISLAND overlooking JUAN DE FUCA STRAIT, west of VICTORIA between COLWOOD and SOOKE. It is part of the Greater Victoria region. Once an AGRICULTURAL area, it has become a residential suburb of the capital while retaining some of its rural characteristics. The name derives from a SALISHAN word meaning, roughly, "smelly fish." The LESTER B. PEARSON COLLEGE OF THE PACIFIC is located at Pedder Bay.

METHANEX CORP, based in VANCOUVER, is the world's largest producer of methanol, with production facilities at KITIMAT and in Alberta, the US, Chile and New Zealand. The plant at Kitimat manufactures methanol and ammonia, using natural gas from northeastern BC (*see* OIL AND GAS INDUSTRY). Methanol is a chemical raw material used in the manufacture of a wide variety of other products and may have potential for use in fuel cells. The company was founded in Alberta in 1968 and built its Kitimat plant in 1982. In 1999 it had revenues of $1.03 billion and supplied about 23% of the total world market for methanol.

METHODIST CHURCH, which had its origins in the 18th-century Church of England, encouraged its followers to live a life of personal holiness, striving for spiritual perfection and publicly witnessing to their experience of God. The Methodist Church in BC existed as a denomination from 1859 until 1925, at which time distinctive Methodist churches joined in organic union with the PRESBYTERIAN and Congregational churches at the formation of the UNITED CHURCH of Canada.

The governance of the Methodist Church was structured through an elected hierarchy of conferences. Members were organized into worshipping communities, or preaching points, led by an ordained minister who was usually stationed for a period of 1–3 years, though some mission congregations were led by a lay preacher or probationer for ministry. As well, members some-

The Methodist church in Ladner, in a painting by Rudi Dangelmaier. The church served Methodists from 1880 to the 1930s, and has been demolished.

times met in small weekly "class meetings" for prayer and self-examination under the guidance of a lay class leader. One or more congregations were bound together into a circuit, which were usually expected to be at least partially self-supporting. Areas where the majority of funding was received from the national missionary society were known as mission fields. Circuits and mission fields were grouped by geographic region into districts, consisting of ministers and elected lay representatives, who were responsible for assigning ministers and probationers, overseeing the work in each field, and directing the finances of the district. Districts were grouped into Annual Conferences, consisting of all ministers within its boundaries, and elected lay representatives, who were responsible for the work of the church in a particular region. In turn, Annual Conferences sent ministerial and lay representatives to the national General Conference, which met every 4 years under the supervision of the general superintendent. At union in 1925, there were 151 circuits with 166 preaching points.

The first active member of the Methodist Church in BC, Cornelius Bryant, was a young schoolteacher who led the first religious service in NANAIMO in 1857. The first 4 ordained Wesleyan Methodist missionaries were sent to BC from Ontario. Ephraim Evans, Edward White, Arthur Browning and Ebenezer Robson and their families arrived in Jan 1859 with partial funding from the English Wesleyan Methodist Missionary Society. The majority of support for BC missions, however, came from the Missionary Society of the Methodist Church of Canada, centred in Toronto, and from funds raised by individual congregations in Ontario. The first missionaries established congregations in VICTORIA and Nanaimo, and on the Lower Mainland in NEW WESTMINSTER and HOPE. From the beginning the Methodists particularly focussed on the mission field, preaching the need for personal conversion, strict temperance and the rigorous observation of the Sabbath. Missionaries travelled extensively to hold camp meetings, preach to the miners and settlers, and evangelize aboriginal peoples. Evening school and an evangelical mission for CHINESE workers were established in New Westminster, Victoria and Nanaimo. In 1862 Thomas CROSBY arrived in Nanaimo and started a school for aboriginal children and adults, then travelled north to FORT SIMPSON in 1874 to institute a mission to the TSIMSHIAN. In the same year the various branches of Canadian Methodism merged into the Methodist Church of Canada, at which time the BC mission became a district, although the work continued to be supervised by the Toronto Conference. In 1887, 3 years after the final amalgamation of the Methodist Church, Canada, the British Columbia Conference held its first meeting in Victoria and took over responsibility for supervising the work in the province. In time, an extensive network of mission fields served remote FISHING and MINING settlements. A marine mission was developed, and the mission boats *Glad Tidings* and *Thomas Crosby* provided religious services to isolated coastal communities. Major aboriginal missions were established on the NASS R, at Port Simpson, SKIDEGATE, PORT ESSINGTON, Kitamaat, BELLA COOLA and BELLA BELLA, and an industrial school at Coqualeetza in CHILLIWACK, with funds and direction provided by the national church. Medical missions were

M

developed in northern BC to provide help to aboriginal and European communities, and hospitals opened in Port Simpson, Bella Bella and HAZELTON. Funding for specific projects that served women and children was provided by the Woman's Missionary Society, which established several boarding schools for aboriginal girls and a rescue home for Chinese and JAPANESE girls and young women in Victoria. Missions to Chinese and Japanese workers were established at the canneries on the SKEENA and FRASER rivers. In 1892 Columbian College was opened in New Westminster to provide education from high school through the first 2 years of university and theological training for probationers for ordination. As the immigrant population grew in the years following the arrival of the railway, established Methodist congregations multiplied. Many Methodist and Presbyterian congregations worked closely together to serve new communities, focussing on the social needs of their congregations as inspired by the Social Gospel movement.   *Gail Edwards*

METIS are people of mixed aboriginal and European background, formally recognized as an aboriginal people in Section 35 of the *Constitution Act 1982.* Historically Metis were "children of the FUR TRADE," offspring of European traders and FIRST NATIONS women. In BC an indigenous Metis population began with the establishment of the first trading posts in the Interior after 1805. It was augmented over the years by the arrival of Metis employees of the major trading companies. Following the suppression of the 1885 Northwest Rebellion in Manitoba, many Metis dispersed across the West, including into northern BC; there they made their living by trapping and hunting. In 1991, 22,290 people of Metis ancestry were recorded as living in the province, though the Metis National Council estimated the BC population to be closer to 70,000. Beginning in the 1950s increasing numbers of Metis moved to the cities, principally to VANCOUVER, where they took whatever jobs they could find. According to one estimate, approximately 20,000 Metis migrated to the LOWER MAINLAND during the 1970s and 1980s. A 1996 report by Howard Adams for the Vancouver Metis Assoc (VMA) found unemployment to be very high (62%) among these urban Metis, most of whom were surviving on very low incomes. Metis began organizing politically in 1969 as part of the BC Assoc of Non-Status Indians (*see* SMITHERAM, Henry) where they took a leading role. The association became the United Native Nations in 1976, but by that time most Metis had left to found their own organizations, the largest of which, the VMA, promotes Metis customs and values. The VMA operates a pre-school program for Metis children and a youth training program for teaching computer and business skills. There is also a Circle of Metis Women organization and a Metis Housing Project for the elderly and families in critical need. There is a Louis Riel Metis Council in SURREY and several other associations around the province.

Buildings at Metlakatla, 1870s.
BC Archives 55798

METLAKATLA is an ancient TSIMSHIAN village site on Venn Passage, opposite PRINCE RUPERT on the North Coast. In 1862 the ANGLICAN CHURCH missionary at FORT SIMPSON, William DUNCAN, decided to move here with some of his Tsimshian converts to establish a model Christian community away from what he considered to be the corrupting influences of the FUR TRADE post. The new village featured wood frame houses, a huge church, a newspaper, school, SAWMILL and cannery. At its peak it numbered 1,200 residents and attracted worldwide interest. When Duncan fell out with his church superiors he and some of his followers moved north in 1887 to establish New Metlakatla on Annette Island near Ketchikan, AK. In 1901 a fire destroyed most of the original village. It survived as a small (pop 120) Tsimshian community.

MEZIADIN LAKE, 210 km north of PRINCE RUPERT, where the highway to STEWART diverges from the Stewart–CASSIAR Hwy (Hwy 37; *see* ROADS AND HWYS), is a tiny roadside stop with a gas station, store, motel and seasonal information centre. Meziadin Lake Provincial PARK is nearby. The name is from the now extinct TSETSAUT language and supposedly means "beautiful fishing."   *AS*

MICA DAM, near the Big Bend in the COLUMBIA R 135 km north of REVELSTOKE, was the last of the

Spillway gates at the Mica Dam, 1977.
John Denniston/Vancouver Province

HYDROELECTRIC power dams built by BC HYDRO under the terms of the COLUMBIA R TREATY. The dam began storing water in 1973 and flooded the river valley to create KINBASKET RESERVOIR; the plant began generating electricity in 1976. Mica Creek was the townsite established for dam workers 8 km to the south. At 242 m, Mica Dam is the highest earth-filled dam in N America, with a generating capacity of 1,736,000 kilowatts. Only the Revelstoke development downstream of Mica and the Gordon SHRUM Generating Station at the W.A.C. BENNETT DAM produce more electricity.

MICHEL was a COAL mining town in the ROCKY MTS 40 km north of FERNIE. It began in 1898 and miners lived here until the 1960s, when residents were relocated to the new community of SPARWOOD and the Michel site was demolished. Only 1 original building remained in 1999, serving as shops and offices for TECK CORP, owner of the nearby open-pit Elkview mine. Michel was named for a local KTUNAXA chief. *See also* MINING.

MIDDENS are mounds of refuse. Shell middens that contain layers of discarded CLAM and MUSSEL shells are common on the coast of BC, where

Prehistoric shell midden on Quatsino Sound, Vancouver Island. *Roy Carlson photo*

they are archaeological sites. During the middle period of coastal PREHISTORY they were widely used as cemeteries for burying the dead. It is likely some groups believed animal bones and shellfish remains deposited in the middens would be reincarnated in the land of the dead for the benefit of the humans buried there. *See also* MARPOLE MIDDEN; ARCHAEOLOGY.

MIDDLE RIVER flows between TAKLA and Trembleur lakes northwest of FORT ST JAMES in the north-central Interior. It is in the territory of the Tl'azt'en FIRST NATION, a group of DAKELH (Carrier) people, whose village, Dzitl'ainli, lies at the mouth of the river on Trembleur Lk. Rich in SALMON and other animal life, it is a BC HERITAGE RIVER. *See also* RIVERS.

MIDWAY, village, pop 686, is on the KETTLE R just north of the US border about halfway between the ROCKY MTS and the Pacific Ocean and between HOPE and WILD HORSE CREEK on the old DEWDNEY TRAIL. However, the name may refer to the midway at the Chicago World's Fair in 1893, the year the townsite was laid out. Midway became the western terminus of the COLUMBIA & WESTERN RWY, built from CASTLEGAR in 1898–99. During the MINING boom in about 1900, there was a COPPER SMELTER at nearby BOUNDARY FALLS but it failed to compete successfully with smelters at ANACONDA and GRAND FORKS. The FOREST INDUSTRY became the main economic activity, though irrigation projects have greatly assisted AGRICULTURE. The KETTLE VALLEY RWY station (1900) on the outskirts has been restored as a museum; passenger service on the line ended in 1964.

MIDWIFERY was practised unregulated in BC for many years. In Mar 1995 the provincial legislature proclaimed the Midwives Regulation under the *Health Professions Act* and the College of Midwives of BC (CMBC) was established as the regulatory body for the profession. The first midwives were registered to practise in BC on 1 Jan 1998. They offer primary care to healthy pregnant women and their normal newborn babies from early pregnancy through labour and birth and up to six weeks postpartum. The college has detailed standards of practice and guidelines for physician consultation and transfer of care. Individual midwives must be registered with the college and as independent practitioners are regulated by the college. Levels of public funding for registered midwives were determined by the Ministry of Health and the Midwives Assoc of BC; only college registrants are funded, through the ministry. To ensure that their services are integrated with those of other health professions—physicians, nurses and emergency personnel in particular—the ministry endorsed a model under which midwives are incorporated into the medical staff of hospitals and have systems of consultation that encourage co-operation. *See also* MEDICAL PROFESSION.

Claire Sowerbutt

MIKI, Roy, writer (b 10 Oct 1942, Winnipeg, MB). He was born to parents who had just been relocated by the government from HANEY to a sugar beet farm in Manitoba. This wartime experience marked his life. He was a leader of the redress movement, which in 1988 succeeded in winning compensation for interned and relocated JAPANESE Canadians. He told the story in *Justice in Our Time* (1991, with Cassandra Kobayashi). He also edited *This Is My Own:*

Letters to Wes and Other Writings on Japanese Canadians, 1941–1948 by Muriel Kitagawa (1985). Miki is an English professor at SFU, where he edited the literary journal *West Coast Line*. His critical works include *The Prepoetics of William Carlos Williams* (1983), *A Record of Writing: A Bibliography of George Bowering* (1990) and a book of essays, *Broken Entries* (1998). His own poetry has been published in *Saving Face: Poems Selected, 1976–1988* (1991) and *Random Access File* (1995).

Members of the BC Regiment of Garrison Artillery, No 1 Company, New Westminster, 1892. Museum of the Royal Westminster Regiment Historical Society

MILITARY HISTORY OF BC

Early History to 1914

Prior to 1858, the HBC administered the territory that would become BC and relied on the Royal Navy for military support. The HBC established a number of trading posts, including FORT VICTORIA on VANCOUVER ISLAND in 1843. The Royal Navy sent HMS *Pandora* to Fort Victoria during the Oregon boundary dispute in 1846 (*see* OREGON TREATY), and in 1848 HMS *Constance* used ESQUIMALT harbour as a temporary base. To allay the security concerns of settlers on Vancouver Island, Gov James DOUGLAS established in 1851 the Victoria Voltigeurs, a small unit of volunteers, mostly French-Canadian voyageurs. In 1852, and again in 1854, the unit accompanied Royal Navy sailors and marines on punitive actions against aboriginal villages on the coast.

Following the discovery of GOLD on the FRASER R in 1857 (*see* GOLD RUSH, FRASER R), the British took direct control of Vancouver Island and the mainland from the HBC. The Voltigeurs were disbanded and the British sent out 2 detachments (225 men) of ROYAL ENGINEERS under Col Richard MOODY. The Engineers estab-

lished the new capital of NEW WESTMINSTER and constructed parts of the CARIBOO WAGON ROAD from YALE to the CARIBOO goldfields (*see* GOLD RUSH, CARIBOO) before they were withdrawn at the end of 1863. Meanwhile, in 1862, the Royal Navy moved the headquarters of its Pacific Squadron from Chile to Esquimalt, where it remained until the Canadian government took over in 1906.

In 1860 the VICTORIA PIONEER RIFLES was formed by 45 former black slaves who had taken refuge on Vancouver Island; it disbanded in 1864. In Nov 1863 the New Westminster Volunteer Rifles (NWVR), formed largely from Royal Engineers who had remained in the colony, was established to defend the capital and the mainland against invasion and to keep peace among miners, settlers, traders and aboriginals. A corresponding unit, the Victoria Rifle Corps, was created the following summer on the Island. During the so-called CHILCOTIN WAR, the NWVR were called out to bring in the fugitives. Trouble of a different kind was anticipated in 1866 when Irish Americans seeking the independence of Ireland, known as Fenians, threatened British possessions in N America and carried out attacks on the Canadas and the Maritime colonies. On the Pacific Coast, George Train urged Fenians in San Francisco to take over BC. Reacting to the threat, New Westminster municipal council authorized on 16 June 1866 the formation of the Home Guards to support the NWVR. On the same day the Seymour Artillery Company was formed and several former Royal Engineers with artillery training were recruited. By 1867 armaments and supplies had arrived from Britain to train these volunteers. However, the Fenian threat soon died away.

In 1871 BC entered CONFEDERATION and came under the authority of Military District 11. The Canadian government had decided to establish militia units instead of maintaining a standing army. Under the Militia Act of 1868, provision was made to pay members 50 cents a day for training 8–16 days a year. Uniforms, guns and funds were all in short supply and dependent on local leaders and initiatives. The emphasis of defence policy shifted from rifle units to artillery to protect harbours and vital locations such as New Westminster, Victoria and NANAIMO (a source of COAL for the Royal Navy). By 1883 the BC Provisional Regiment of Garrison Artillery, a brigade of artillery with headquarters in Victoria, had been established on the coast, including the Seymour Battery in New Westminster, the oldest continuous militia unit in BC. With the completion of the CPR in 1885, gun batteries were placed in BURRARD INLET to protect the railway.

In 1893 the BC Battalion of Garrison Artillery became the 5th BC Regiment of Garrison Artillery (BCRGA). Then in July 1899 the 2nd Battalion of the 5th BCRGA was con-

Regiment, Gordon Highlanders (1913); and the 5th Field Regiment (artillery). Elsewhere in the province, the 102nd Rocky Mountain Rangers was formed, moving from NELSON to KAMLOOPS by 1912, and there were the Okanagan Mounted Rifles, the 30th BC Horse, Earl Grey's Own Rifles in PRINCE RUPERT and various rifle companies in the KOOTENAY.

By 1914, 3 naval vessels were stationed at Esquimalt: HMCS *Rainbow* and 2 smaller vessels, the *Alberine* and the *Shearwater*. On 3 Aug 1914, the rumoured presence of 2 German cruisers off Cape Flattery caused Premier Richard MCBRIDE to purchase 2 SUBMARINES from a Seattle shipbuilding company. Three days later the province transferred the submarines to federal control, but they remained on the West Coast until June 1917. The Admiralty also leased 3 fishing boats, equipping them with torpedoes to patrol coast waters.

Interior of munitions factory, Vancouver, WWI.
UBC BC1759

verted to a rifle battalion, the 6th Battalion Duke of Connaughts Own Rifles (DCORs) with 2 companies in New Westminster and 4 companies in VANCOUVER. That same year, 24 DCOR members fought with the Royal Canadian Regiment in the Boer War as part of the first Canadian contingent to S Africa. Two other contingents later saw service there with the Lord Strathcona Horse and the South African Constabulary.

During and after the Boer War, militia units sprang up all over BC. In 1910 the 104th Regiment, Westminster Fusiliers of Canada, was formed from 2 companies of the DCORs. Militia units in Vancouver included the DCORs, 72nd Seaforth Highlanders of Canada (1911); 11th Regiment, Irish Fusiliers (1913); 6th Field Engineers (North Vancouver); and the 18th Field Ambulance. In Victoria there were the 88th Regiment, Victoria Fusiliers (1912); the 50th

British Columbians in WWI: 1914–18

WWI began in Aug 1914 when Germany marched into neutral Belgium. Britain declared war against Germany on 4 Aug and 2 days later Canadian Prime Minister Robert Borden offered to send an expeditionary force overseas to aid Britain. Sir Sam Hughes, minister of militia and defence, called for 25,000 volunteers, but outraged by reported German atrocities against the Belgians, 33,000 Canadians enlisted within a month. These early recruits were gathered at Valcartier, QC, and formed into battalions of soldiers from various militia units.

The first contingent overseas in 1914 included 2 predominantly BC battalions. The 7th Battalion, commanded by Lt Col Hart-McHarg of the Duke of Connaught's Own Rifles (DCORs), with Maj Victor ODLUM of the 11th Irish Fusiliers second-in-command, contained units from the DCORs, the 11th Fusiliers from Vancouver, the 88th Fusiliers from Victoria, the 102nd Rocky Mountain Rangers, the 104th Fusiliers from New Westminster, MISSION and

CHILLIWACK and the W Kootenay detachment. Meanwhile, half of the 16th Canadian Scottish Battalion, and its commander Lt Col (later Maj Gen) R.G.E. Leckie, came from the 72nd Seaforth Highlanders of Canada based in Vancouver. The 50th Gordon Highlanders in Victoria, commanded by Arthur CURRIE at the outbreak of the war, contributed another 25% to the 16th Battalion. Both battalions served with the 1st Canadian Infantry Division, Canadian Expeditionary Force (CEF), that went into action in Apr 1915 at the Second Battle of Ypres where the Germans first used poison gas. The 16th, along with the 10th Battalion (Calgary), took part in the counterattack against German positions at Kitchener Wood on 22 Apr, for which members of both battalions were rewarded with the symbol of an oak cluster. They were the only Canadian battalions to win this honour during the war.

The 2nd Canadian Mounted Rifles (Okanagan Mounted Rifles and 30th BC Horse) went overseas in June 1915, while the 29th Battalion of the 2nd Canadian Infantry Division, known as "Tobin's Tigers" after its commander Henry TOBIN, was formed with drafts of men from the 11th Irish Fusiliers, the DCORs, the Seaforths and the 104th Westminsters. The 29th first saw action in Apr 1916 at St Eloi near Ypres, where the Allies tunnelled under the German lines and blew huge craters, then tried to occupy them. The craters filled with water and the 29th spent a miserable time trying to hold them before relief arrived. The 29th distinguished itself at the Somme in Sept 1916 with the capture of Sugar Trench and Courcelette.

The 4th Canadian Division, containing the 47th (Westminster) Battalion, the 54th (Kootenay) Battalion, the 72nd (Seaforths) Battalion and the 102nd (Northern BC) Battalion, first saw action at the Somme in Oct 1916. The 102nd captured sections of Regina Trench on 11 Nov. Several other BC battalions went overseas as distinct units or were broken up to provide reinforcements for other battalions. The 104th Westminster Fusiliers, for example, raised 6,500 men from New Westminster and the FRASER VALLEY and supplied drafts of recruits to other battalions. Men who were too old or too young for overseas service stayed home to guard bridges, railways, reservoirs and other strategic points, and to patrol the 24 internment camps established throughout BC for the incarceration of "enemy aliens," mostly German and Austro–Hungarian immigrants. Other local units supplying men to the front included the 6th Canadian Field Company (N VANCOUVER), Royal Canadian Engineers, the 18th Field Ambulance (Vancouver), and the 8 Provost (military police) from Vancouver, along with 3 artillery regiments. British Columbians also served in railway (see STEWART, John W.), tunnelling and forestry battalions. The Canadian Forestry Corps provided timber for building railways and trenches. On one occasion the 250 men of the 70th Company from REVELSTOKE cut more lumber in a 10-hour day—156,000 board ft—than any other company during the war.

Canada had no air force, but 22,800 Canadians served in the Royal Flying Corps and the Royal Naval Air Service (RNAS). Canadians dominated the list of top air aces out of all proportion to their numbers. Of the 27 Allied aces who had 30 or more hits, 10 were Canadians. Lt Col Raymond COLLISHAW from Nanaimo, serving with the RNAS, ranked third with 60 hits. An unknown number of British Columbians served in the Royal Navy, mostly on convoy duty protecting merchant ships from German U-boats in the Atlantic. About 300 CHINESE and 225 JAPANESE served in the CEF, many from Vancouver and Victoria. Most served in battalions from Alberta and Ontario because they were refused entry to BC-raised battalions. An unknown number of Chinese from BC served overseas with the Chinese Labour Corps, which performed tasks such as digging trenches and carrying supplies to the front. About 4,000 aboriginal men from across Canada served overseas, including every eligible male between 20 and 35 from the OKANAGAN Head of the Lake band. Several BC women served as nurses and in the Red Cross and other volunteer agencies.

The Battle of Vimy Ridge in Apr 1917 was Canada's most memorable victory in WWI and the first major Allied victory of the war. All 4 Canadian divisions participated in the attack on Vimy Ridge, which dominated the Douai Plain near Arras and was considered impregnable. The 1st Canadian Division had been commanded since Sept 1915 by Maj Gen Arthur Currie, a SIDNEY real estate developer considered the best divisional commander on the Western Front by British Prime Minister Lloyd George. The Canadian Corps was commanded by Lt Gen Sir Julian Byng, who along with Currie and Brig Gen Andrew McNaughton, in command of the artillery, used aircraft observation and reconaissance patrols to pinpoint enemy guns and neutralize them by counter-battery fire. Currie and McNaughton also perfected the creeping barrage in which artillery and machine gun fire moved steadily ahead of the advancing infantry. Most of Vimy Ridge was taken on 9 Apr, Easter Monday. However, the 4th Division, including the 54th (Kootenay), the 72nd (Seaforths) and the 47th (Westminsters) suffered heavy casualties from a section of trench at Hill 145, which guns had spared in the expectation that it be used later as headquarters by the Canadians. Hill 145 finally was taken on 13 Apr in a blinding snowstorm. Canada achieved international recognition with the capture of Vimy Ridge. Currie was knighted and promoted to lt gen to become the first Canadian commander of the Canadian Corps.

Currie's first battle as Corps Commander was at Hill 70, Lens, in Aug 1917 where the Canadians captured the hill and beat back 17 German counterattacks, at the cost of many casualties. The Canadians' next major battle was at Passchendaele, Third Battle of Ypres, in Oct–Nov 1917, which came to epitomize the horrors of WWI. Broken drainage systems combined with autumn rains to create a sea of mud where unburied bodies littered the battlefield and wounded men and horses drowned in the mire.

The 72nd (Seaforths) captured the strongly held Crest Farm on 30 Oct and the 7th Battalion (1st BC) captured one of the final objectives on 10 Nov. The Canadians suffered 15,654 casualties at Passchendaele.

Canada's last major offensive of the war, known as the "Hundred Days," began on 18 Aug 1918, referred to by German Gen Ludendorff as "the Black Day of the German Army in the history of this war." The Canadians advanced over 12 km, taking numerous prisoners and enemy guns. Currie had developed a fighting force second to none on the Western Front. "Wherever the Germans found the Canadian Corps coming into their line," wrote Lloyd George, "they prepared for the worst." The Canadians broke the heavily defended Hindenburg Line near Arras on 2 Sept, a day on which 7 Canadians won the VICTORIA CROSS (VC), a record unmatched by any other country in the British Empire. Canadians continued to distinguish themselves at several more engagements throughout the autumn; early on the morning of 11 Nov, the 13th Brigade, commanded by Brig Gen J.A. Clark, former commander of the 72nd (Seaforths), liberated Mons, Belgium and at 11 am, an armistice ended the war. Since late Aug Canadians had fought 37 km through the toughest German defences, suffering 30,000 casualties while capturing 19,000 prisoners, 370 guns and 2,000 machine guns. The 16th Canadian Scottish were awarded 4 VCs, more than any other battalion in the CEF; the 7th (1st BC Battalion) won 3 VCs. Of the 620,000 Canadians who served with the CEF, 55,570 came from BC, the highest per capita rate of enlistment in the country. Canada suffered close to a quarter of a million casualties in the war. Of the 61,661 deaths, 6,225 were British Columbians.

Between the Wars

Following WWI Canada's armed forces once again had primarily a militia role. The numbered battalions of wartime were disbanded and replaced by the non-permanent militia units that existed before the war. The regular army was represented in the West by the Princess Patricia's Canadian Light Infantry (PPCLI), of which one company was stationed at the Work Point Barracks at Esquimalt. The 16th Canadian Scottish, in Victoria after the war, became in 1920 the Canadian Scottish (Princess Mary's) Regiment, perpetuating the 50th Gordon Highlanders and the 88th Victoria Fusiliers. The Vancouver elements of the 16th Scottish and the 72nd Battalion reverted to the Seaforth Highlanders of Canada, while the 54th Kootenay Battalion was redesignated as artillery with various batteries in the Kootenay region. The 7th Battalion, 1st BC Regiment, and the 104th Regiment (Westminster Fusiliers of Canada) were reorganized as the 1st BC Regiment (Duke of Connaught's Own Rifles) with 6 battalions. In 1924 these 6 battalions were re-organized into 3 separate regiments: the 1st BC Regiment (Duke of Connaughts), the Vancouver Regiment and the Westminster Regiment. The BC Regiment was later designated

as an armoured unit as was the BC Dragoons (VERNON and KELOWNA), formerly the 2nd Canadian Mounted Rifles. The 15th Brigade, Canadian Field Artillery, was authorized in Feb 1920 with one battery in Victoria and 5 in Vancouver. In 1924 the Royal Canadian Air Force was formed with Western Air Command headquarters at JERICHO BEACH air station in Vancouver.

In 1937, 400 BC men volunteered to fight with the International Brigades in the Spanish Civil War against Gen Francisco Franco and his fascist forces.

Warren Bernard, age 5, saying goodbye to his father, Pvt Jack Bernard of the Duke of Connaught's Own Rifles, leaving for Europe, New Westminster, June 1940. VPL 8616

British Columbians in WWII: 1939–45

Six BC regiments fought as distinct units in WWII: the Seaforth Highlanders of Canada (Vancouver) fought with the 1st Canadian Division as part of the British 8th Army in Sicily and Italy (July 1943–Mar 1945) and with the 1st Canadian Army in the Netherlands (Mar–May 1945). The Princess Patricia's Canadian Light Infantry (Esquimalt) also served with the 1st Canadian Division. The Royal Westminster Regiment and the BC Dragoons, 9th Armoured Regiment, fought in Italy and northwest Europe as part of the 5th Canadian Armoured Division. The Canadian Scottish Regiment (3rd Canadian Division) and the BC Regiment (4th Canadian Armoured Division) also fought in northwest Europe.

The first major action for the Canadian Army took place at Dieppe on 19 Aug 1942. The raid across the English Channel was a disaster; 907 Canadians died and another 3,100 were wounded or taken prisoner. Lt Col Cecil MERRITT, a former Seaforth, commanded the South Saskatchewan Regiment (SSR) during the raid and won Canada's first Victoria Cross of the war. "C" Company of the SSR was the only Canadian unit

Lt Colonel Bert Hoffmeister of the Seaforth Highlanders, leading his battalion in Sicily, Aug 1943. Terry F. Rowe/NAC PA136216

to capture its objective during the raid.

The Canadian Army did not see action again until 10 July 1943 when the 1st Canadian Division took part in the invasion of Sicily. The Seaforths, under the command of Lt Col Bert HOFFMEISTER, excelled in the capture of Agira and a model infantry-tank action at Adrano. After capturing Sicily, Allied troops crossed the Messina Straits into Italy and began a long, difficult advance up the peninsula. The 2nd Canadian Infantry Brigade, by this time commanded by Hoffmeister and including the Seaforths, Loyal Edmontons and the Patricias, engaged in very heavy fighting at the Moro R in early Dec 1943. After crossing the Moro they fought their way north to Ortona, the eastern end of the Gustav Line, where the Seaforths and the Edmontons, using a technique called mouse-holing to move from house to house, eventually took the town. The Battle of Ortona took 7 days and became known as "Little Stalingrad."

On 23 May 1944 the 1st Canadian Division, led by the Seaforths, cracked the heavily defended Hitler Line south of Rome. The 2nd Brigade suffered the heaviest single-day losses (162 killed) of any Canadian brigade in the Italian campaign. Only 77 Patricias were left to continue the fighting at the end of the day. Following the breach in the Hitler Line, the 5th Armoured Division, commanded by Maj Gen Hoffmeister, saw its first major action. "A" Company of the Westminster Regiment, led by Maj Jack Mahoney (a Victoria Cross winner), succeeded in establishing a bridgehead across the Melfa R which helped open the door to Rome. In late Aug 1944 the Canadians moved over to attack the heavily defended Gothic Line on the Adriatic coast. The 5th Armoured Division, by this time known as

"Hoffie's Mighty Maroon Machine," pulled off in a surprise attack one of the biggest Allied victories of the war by getting behind the enemy's defences. The BC Dragoons, despite heavy losses, proved to be a first-class tank regiment at the Gothic Line and later fighting at Pozzo Alto Ridge, the Lamone Crossing and Conventello–Comacchio. The Royal Westminster Regiment, known as "Corbould Force" after their commander Lt Col Gordon Corbould, was highly successful in every engagement in the war, including Coriano Ridge, Naviglio Canal, Piangipane and the liberation of the Netherlands. (Two of the Westminsters, Sgts Gino Bortolussi and Ron Hurley, were Canadian Armed Forces sprint champions and if not for the war, potential Olympic champions.)

Major General R.F.L. Keller, commander of the 3rd Canadian Infantry Division in Normandy, on D-Day, 6 June 1944. Frank L. Dubervill/NAC PA115544

On 6 June 1944, D-Day, the Allies landed in Normandy—the largest invasion in history. "B" Company of the Canadian Scottish, Princess Mary's Regiment (Victoria and Vancouver) landed with the first wave at Juno Beach and advanced farther inland than any other Allied

regiment that day. The Canadian Scots fought through Caen to Falaise, suffering over 600 casualties in Normandy, then participated in the clearing of the Channel ports, the Scheldt estuary and the Rhineland and the liberation of the Netherlands. Meanwhile, the BC Regiment went into action on 8–9 Aug and suffered a disaster. Its tanks became disoriented in the dark near Estrées-la-Campagne and ran into a German ambush, losing 47 tanks and 39 men. The regiment eventually recovered to participate in the Battles of the Scheldt and the Rhineland, as well as the liberation of the Netherlands. Other BC units playing a vital role in northwest Europe included the 6th Field Company, Royal Canadian Engineers (North Vancouver), No. 11 Divisional Signals, the No. 12 Light Field ambulance and No.16 General Hospital, both from Vancouver. Many engineers and other special forces were trained at Camp Chilliwack (est 1942), including a special unit of Chinese Canadians deployed in 1945 as airborne troops in Burma. Other personnel were trained at Camp Vernon and GORDON HEAD in Victoria. Close to 21,000 British Columbians served in the RCAF, mostly in Bomber Command, as fighter pilots and ground crews, and almost all these airmen received training as part of the British Commonwealth Air Training Plan in Canada. Wing Commander Vernon "Chunky" Woodward of Victoria, rejected by the RCAF, served with the RAF in N Africa and the Mediterranean, becoming BC's leading fighter pilot with 21 confirmed hits. Almost 2,000 British Columbians also served in the Royal Canadian Navy, escorting convoys of merchant ships across the N Atlantic, and many others served in the Canadian Merchant Marine. Many women from BC volunteered for service in the war: 2,308 served in the RCAF, Women's Division; 2,541 in the Canadian Women Auxiliary Corps; 762 in the Women's Royal Canadian Naval Service; 44 in the RCN nursing service; and 32 in the RCAF nursing service. By the end of the war, about 85,000 BC men between 18 and 45 had served in the war, the highest proportion of the population of any province in Canada.

On the home front, defence of the West Coast was a top priority, especially following the Japanese attack on Pearl Harbor on 7 Dec 1941 and the appearance offshore of Japanese submarines, one of which was believed to have fired on ESTEVAN POINT lighthouse in June 1942. Prior to Pearl Harbor, 3 minesweepers, a few auxiliary vessels and the boats of the Fishermen's Reserve (*see* GUMBOOT NAVY) patrolled the coast. By early 1942 they had been supplemented by 3 converted passenger liners from the PRINCE LINE of Canadian National Steamships and another 15 minesweepers. (The 3 Prince liners were later used in the landings in Europe.) To bolster west coast defences the Pacific Coast Militia Rangers was formed. It was an auxiliary corps of about 14,000 men (115 companies), mainly farmers, loggers, fishers and trappers, many of them WWI veterans, who kept watch for subversive activity and provided information to the regular forces.

Three RCAF squadrons and the 13th Canadian Infantry Brigade, Pacific Command, were sent to the Aleutian Islands in 1942 to counter the Japanese occupation of Kiska. However, the Japanese withdrew from Kiska before the scheduled attack. By mid-1943 there were 3 divisions—21 infantry battalions consisting of 34,316 troops—training in BC and manning coast stations under the command of Maj Gen George PEARKES. In Sept 1942 following the disastrous Dieppe Raid, which he had opposed, Pearkes was transferred back to Canada to take charge of Pacific Command. Regiments such as the Rocky Mountain Rangers and the 11th Irish Fusiliers did not fight overseas as units but trained soldiers for overseas reinforcements and contributed to defence of the coast. Western Air Command, at Jericho Beach, had 18 operational squadrons by Nov 1943 and was used for anti-submarine and bombing reconnaissance along the coast. Training took place at BOUNDARY BAY, ABBOTSFORD, SEA ISLAND and Pat Bay. These planes also shot down Japanese balloons packed with explosives and incendiaries to terrorize civilians and set forest fires. The RAF also opened FLYING BOAT STATIONS along the coast, using the air base at Pat Bay (established in 1939) and later the COMOX base (established in 1944) as training centres.

Brigadier John Rockingham briefing his commanders on arrival in Korea, 7 Oct 1951.
Paul E. Tomelin/NAC PA128875

The Korean War

On 25 June 1950, hostilities broke out in Korea when Communist N Korea crossed the 38th parallel and invaded the Republic of Korea, capturing Seoul 3 days later. Canada supported action by the United Nations to halt the N Korean aggression by dispatching 3 destroyers from Esquimalt, assigning an air force squadron to transport duties and recruiting a Canadian Army Special Force (CASF) to be part of UN forces. The CASF was commanded by Brig John ROCKINGHAM, who chose Lt Col Jim Stone to lead the 2nd Battalion Princess Patricia's Canadian Light Infantry (PPCLI). Stone, one of the heroes of Ortona, had served with the Loyal Edmonton Regiment during WWII and settled in BC after the war. He held the distinction of being the only soldier in the Canadian Army to rise during the war from the rank of private to commanding officer of his own regiment. Stone's leadership was put to the test in Apr 1951 when

the 2nd PPCLI, heavily outnumbered and exposed on both flanks, stopped a major attack by the Communist Chinese at Kapyong. As a result, the battalion received the US Presidential Citation, the only Canadian unit to receive such an honour. The Korean conflict turned static until a truce was signed on 27 July 1953, preserving the border at the 38th parallel. Almost 27,000 Canadians served there at a cost of 309 killed. Three of the highest decorations were won by BC soldiers: Sgt Dick Buxton of the 2nd PPCLI won a Distinguished Conduct Medal, as did Sgt John Richardson of Victoria and Pte Wayne Mitchell of Vancouver, both members of the 1st Battalion PPCLI.

Present Organization of the Militia in BC

With a reduction in military spending in Canada in the 1990s, BC lost its last major contingent of regular land forces in 1996 as both the PPCLI and the Royal Canadian Engineers moved to Edmonton from Chilliwack. Except for a skeleton staff, Canadian Forces Base Chilliwack, which had housed the A6 Canadian Engineer Training Centre and the Royal School of Military Engineering for 50 years, was closed. That left the reserve army, in Mar 1997 redesignated the 39th Canadian Brigade Group, with 14 units totalling about 2,400 reservists: the BC Regiment (Duke of Connaught's Own), the BC Dragoons, 5 Field Regiment (Royal Canadian Artillery), 15 Field Regiment (Royal Canadian Artillery), 6 Field Engineer Squadron, 44 Field Engineer Squadron, Rocky Mountain Rangers, Royal Westminster Regiment, Seaforth Highlanders, Canadian Scottish Regiment (Princess Mary's), 11 (Victoria) Service Battalion, 12 (Vancouver) Service Battalion, 11 (Victoria) Medical Company, and 12 (Vancouver) Medical Company. Most of these units include cadets who attend Camp Vernon's Western Canada Army Cadet Summer Training Centre for 2 weeks each summer. Reserve units from BC have contributed substantially to peacekeeping missions abroad.

The Royal Canadian Navy on the West Coast is centred at Maritime Forces Pacific Headquarters Esquimalt, along with 2 reserve units—HMCS *Malahat* (Esquimalt) and HMCS *Discovery* (Vancouver)—and a sea cadet summer training centre at HMCS *Quadra* (Comox). During the Cold War, the main responsibility of the RCAF (19 Wing, Comox) on the coast, in addition to SEARCH AND RESCUE, was to conduct anti-submarine aircraft patrols and to monitor Russian missiles. Since 1991 patrols have been reduced, though not abandoned completely. Air cadets receive summer training at ALBERT HEAD and Comox. *Ken MacLeod*

Reading: Douglas Harker, The Dukes: The story of the men who have served in Peace and War with the British Columbia Regiment (DCO): 1883–1973, 1974; Peter Moogk and Maj R.V. Stevenson, Vancouver Defended: A History of the Men and Guns of the Lower Mainland Defences: 1859–1949, 1978; R.H. Roy, Ready for the Fray: The History of the Canadian Scottish Regiment (Princess Mary's) 1920–55, 1958; R.H. Roy, The Seaforth Highlanders of Canada: 1919–65, 1969; R.H. Roy,

Sinews of Steel: The History of the British Columbia Dragoons, 1965; Jeffery Williams, Princess Patricia's Canadian Light Infantry, 1914–84: Seventy Years Service, 1992.

MILL BAY, pop 953, is a waterfront community at the mouth of Shawnigan Crk on the west side of SAANICH INLET, 42 km north of VICTORIA on VANCOUVER ISLAND. It is named for a SAWMILL built there in 1861 and operated for several years by William SAYWARD. It has been home to BRENTWOOD COLLEGE since 1961. A ferry crosses the inlet to BRENTWOOD BAY.

MILLER, Daniel Arthur, millwright, politician, premier 25 Aug 1999–24 Feb 2000 (b 24 Dec 1944, Port Alice). After completing high school in N VANCOUVER and a year of university study, he moved in 1964 to PRINCE RUPERT, where he became a millwright at the pulp mill (*see* PULP AND PAPER). During the NDP government's tenure from 1972 to 1975 he worked as

Dan Miller, premier of BC 1999–2000, at a Nisga'a pole raising. Gary Fiegehen photo

an assistant to a CABINET minister, then resumed his work at the mill. His own career in elected politics began in 1977 when he was elected to Prince Rupert city council. He switched to provincial politics in 1986, winning the Prince Rupert seat in the legislature for the NDP. When the party returned to power in 1991 he joined Premier Mike HARCOURT's cabinet as minister of forests. Between 1991 and 1999 he also served as minister of labour, of municipal affairs, of employment and investment, of energy and mines and of northern development. In cabinet he was known for controversial policies such as the "fast ferry" construction program (*see* BC FERRY CORP), expanded GAMING and the financial rescue of SKEENA CELLULOSE INC in Prince Rupert. He became BC's 32nd PREMIER after Glen CLARK resigned in the midst of a police investigation and the NDP caucus designated Miller as leader. He served in an interim capacity until a new party leader was chosen in Feb 2000. The new leader and premier, Ujjal DOSANJH, then named him to the cabinet in his former position as minister of energy and mines and minister responsible for northern development.

MILLSIDE, or Fraser Mills, was a company town on the FRASER R northeast of NEW WESTMINSTER, centred on the Ross Maclaren SAWMILL built in 1889. The mill became Fraser River Saw Mills in 1906 and began importing FRANCOPHONE workers from Quebec to replace its Asian workforce. The newcomers established a separate community, MAILLARDVILLE, and at Millside SOUTH ASIANS, other Asians and white millworkers lived in different sections of the community. The area has been part of COQUITLAM since 1971.

MILLSTREAM is an AGRICULTURAL and residential suburb of VICTORIA 13 km northwest of the city. Mill Stream itself flows south into ESQUIMALT Harbour and was the site of the first SAWMILL on VANCOUVER ISLAND, built in 1847 by Roderick FINLAYSON of the HBC. A lime kiln also operated in the region in the early 1890s.   AS

MILNER, a DAIRY FARMING settlement 22 km southeast of NEW WESTMINSTER in the municipality of LANGLEY, was named after Viscount Milner, a British colonial administrator. The area is known for its honey (*see also* APICULTURE). Langley's fairgrounds and AGRICULTURAL hall were built here in 1918. Milner was also a station on the BC ELECTRIC RWY CO INTERURBAN line.   AS

MIMIC THRUSH belongs to a family of long-tailed birds including catbirds, mockingbirds and thrashers that are somewhat drab in appearance but have loud and varied songs. Some mimic the songs of other species. The grey catbird (*Dumetella carolinensis*) breeds throughout BC's southern mainland and is most abundant in the OKANAGAN VALLEY and in the valleys of the SIMILKAMEEN and S THOMPSON rivers. Its catlike "mew" can be heard coming from dense thickets in deciduous woodlands or along riversides. The northern mockingbird (*Mimus polyglottos*) has been expanding its range north from the US and was first observed in BC in 1931. Its numbers have grown steadily ever since, particularly in the southern part of the province. It mimics other birds as well as non-avian sounds such as those of barking dogs, squeaky gates, pianos, etc. Two species of thrasher occur in BC, the sage thrasher (*Oreoscoptes montanus*) and the brown thrasher (*Toxostoma rufum*). The sage thrasher breeds in the arid sagebrush of the Okanagan and Similkameen valleys. The larger brown thrasher is rare throughout western N America and has been sighted infrequently in BC from the southern border up to TERRACE and TUMBLER RIDGE. With more than 1,100 types of songs, the male brown thrasher has the largest song repertoire of all N American birds.   *Kim Goldberg*

MINER, Bill, outlaw (b circa 1847, Bowling Green, KY; d 2 Sept 1913, Covington, GA). He left home at age 16, went west and began robbing stagecoaches. Before he was 20 he was doing time in the notorious San Quentin

Bill Miner, gentleman train robber, 1906.
BC Archives HP-77284

Penitentiary. He spent most of the next 30 years in prison, where he worked at hard labour and suffered abusive maltreatment in the penal system. His final term was for 20 years; undaunted, he turned to robbing trains after his release. Once again on the run, he crossed into Canada in 1904 and settled in the NICOLA Valley south of KAMLOOPS, posing as George Edwards, gentleman rancher. On 13 Sept 1904 he held up a CPR train at MISSION, then on 8 May 1906 he struck the CPR again, east of Kamloops. A massive search followed and Miner and his gang were captured near Douglas Lake. Sentenced to life imprisonment in the NEW WESTMINSTER Penitentiary, he escaped in Aug 1908, fled across the border and was not seen in Canada again. He was arrested in 1911 in Georgia, where he died in prison. Miner became a folk hero in BC for his gentlemanly ways and the fact that he targetted the unpopular CPR. It is said that he originated the phrase "Hands up!" An award-winning 1983 film by Philip BORSOS, *The Grey Fox*, dramatized his career.

MINING is the third largest industry in BC in dollar value after the FOREST INDUSTRY and TOURISM. In 1998 mineral output was worth $3.2 billion (excluding petroleum and natural gas; *see* OIL AND GAS INDUSTRY). Net COAL revenues were $1.19 billion; COPPER revenues $681 million; GOLD revenues $304 million; ZINC revenues $231 million; SILVER $119 million. There were 22 producing mines in the province, down from 30 major mines in operation at the beginning of the 1990s, a decline that companies blamed on taxes and new ENVIRONMENTAL regulations. However, mining is highly dependent on international commodity prices and that decade was marked by a slump in world metal prices. In 1997 profits in the mining sector fell to $154 million from $208 million the year before. Mining employs about 9,400 people in BC, 40% in the coal sector.

BC is one of the world's major mining regions, thanks to its location in the mineral-rich CORDILLERA of western N America. The first mining in the province was undertaken by the HBC in search of coal on northern VANCOUVER ISLAND in 1849 and NANAIMO in 1852 (*see* COAL MINING, VANCOUVER ISLAND). Gold discoveries during the 1850s led to the GOLD RUSH on the FRASER R in 1858, extending into the CARIBOO in the early 1860s. This rush led to the creation of the mainland colony of British Columbia and to the construction of the first roads into the Interior. This was placer mining, for the most part producing

BC MINERALS 1890–1998: PRODUCTION

(*kg*=kilogram, *t*=tonne)

	Gold(*kg*)	Silver(*kg*)	Copper(*t*)	Lead(*t*)	Zinc(*t*)	Molybd(*t*)
1890	904	2,191	-	-	-	-
1900	7,539	123,113	4,534	28,738	-	-
1910	9,314	76,211	17,347	15,721	1,897	-
1920	4,140	105,063	20,360	17,840	21,413	-
1930	5,281	352,343	41,895	145,967	113,615	-
1940	19,364	383,436	35,371	211,758	141,529	-
1950	9,428	295,773	19,197	128,831	131,697	-
1960	6,514	231,613	14,998	151,322	182,978	2
1970	3,151	202,521	96,330	97,449	125,005	14,187
1980	7,477	203,802	264,675	76,709	67,481	11,180
1986	9,392	395,850	332,215	91,784	137,583	11,574
1990	16,035	631,084	325,320	19,556	57,436	12,285
1995	19,325	462,259	278,330	59,282	135,912	9,113
1998	21,736	451,000	277,078	31,333	153,612	7,563

gold recovered from stream deposits either on the surface or in deep buried channels, requiring little equipment or organization. Subsequent gold rushes into the Omineca and CASSIAR areas were less productive, but until 1884 gold was the leading mineral produced in BC in terms of value.

The next important mining area was the KOOTENAY, where hardrock, or lode, mining required processing to remove metals from the ores and a transportation network to carry material to SMELTERS and then to market—in other words, capital and organization on a scale not known to the gold prospectors of the Cariboo. The first major discovery was the Silver King mine near NELSON (1887), followed by copper–gold near ROSSLAND (1890), silver–lead in the SLOCAN (1891), lead–zinc near KIMBERLEY (1892) and the silver–lead St Eugene Mine near MOYIE (1893). In the neighbouring BOUNDARY DISTRICT, copper was the basis of the industry, with mines at GREENWOOD, MIDWAY and PHOENIX supplying a smelter at GRAND FORKS; while it was in operation (1900–19), it was the second-largest copper smelter in the world. During the mining boom from 1886 to 1900 more than 1,300 mining companies were formed. Initially much of the interest and financing came from the western US, where mining had been booming since the 1860s, while Ontario and Quebec

Open-pit mining at the Island Copper Mine near Port Hardy, c 1980. Courtesy Island Copper

were as yet unaware of their tremendous mineral potential. In 1896 F.A. HEINZE, a smelter owner from Butte, MT, opened a smelter at TRAIL, later acquired by the CPR and merged into its mining subsidiary COMINCO in 1906. Mining in this area benefited from intense competition for traffic between the CPR and its American rivals, chiefly James J. Hill's GREAT NORTHERN RWY. Not only

did the railways carry product to market, they also created a demand for fuel that, along with the need for coke at the new metal smelters, led to the first coal mining in the southeast corner of the province in the valley of the ELK R. By WWI, precious metals (gold and silver) accounted for 36% of the value of mineral production while

Coal mining at the Extension mine near Nanaimo, c 1908. BC Archives E-02768

copper accounted for 35% and coal 25%. Hardrock mining in the Kootenay led to much of the first formal labour organization in BC and helped to establish the province's tradition of labour militancy (*see* INTERNATIONAL UNION OF MINE, MILL & SMELTER WORKERS; LABOUR MOVEMENT; WESTERN FEDERATION OF MINERS).

Following WWI, as first ships, then railways, converted to oil as their main fuel, coal mining went into a slump. But the market for other minerals—lead, zinc and copper—remained healthy. By the 1930s the copper mines at BRITANNIA were the most productive in the British Empire, supplemented by the Granby copper mine at ANYOX until it closed in 1935. At the same time the SULLIVAN MINE, owned by Cominco, was the world's largest lead–zinc producer and the BRALORNE and PIONEER mines in the BRIDGE R country were important gold producers. Prior to the 1950s nearly all mining in BC was underground. After mid-century, open-pit production became feasible and several huge copper mines opened, including the Craigmont Mine near MERRITT (1961–82), Highland Valley Copper, the largest

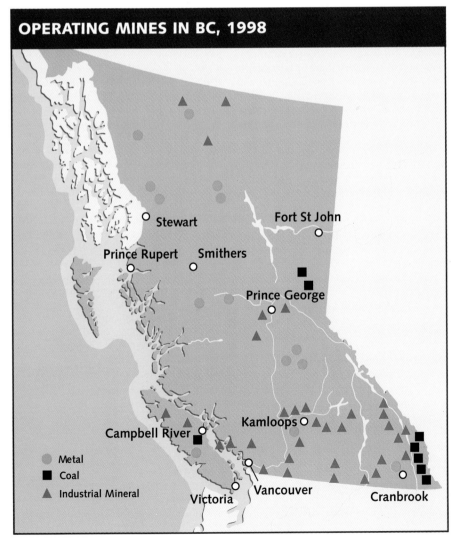

OPERATING MINES IN BC, 1998

Stewart
Fort St John
Prince Rupert   Smithers
Prince George
Kamloops
Campbell River
Victoria   Vancouver   Cranbrook

● Metal
■ Coal
▲ Industrial Mineral

open-pit operation in N America at LOGAN LAKE near KAMLOOPS, and the ISLAND COPPER MINE (1971–95) near PORT HARDY. Likewise ASBESTOS was mined at Cassiar (1952–92), MOLYBDENUM at ENDAKO starting in 1965 and silver at the Equity mine near HOUSTON. Coal mining rallied in the late 1960s with the development of fields in the southeast corner of the province, principally to fuel the Japanese steel industry. This was followed by development of the northeast coalfields at TUMBLER RIDGE; in 1998 there were 8 coal mines in production in BC and coal was the leading mineral export. Mine openings during the 1990s include the Huckleberry molybdenum–copper mine south of Houston (1997), the Mount Polley gold–copper mine northeast of WILLIAMS LAKE (1997) and the Kemess gold–copper mine 350 km north of PRINCE GEORGE (1998). Several mines closed during the 1990s, including the Nickel Plate, Equity, Gibraltar, Quinsam and Island Copper mines, and early in 2000 the Quintette coal mine at Tumbler Ridge announced that it was closing. None of these developments changed a fundamental fact about the BC mining industry: that it has prospered as an exporter of raw materials but with the exception of the smelters at Trail and KITIMAT, it has failed to develop related manufacturing industries in the province.

MINK (*Mustela vison*) is a small semi-aquatic member of the WEASEL family (Mustelids) inhabiting Interior WETLANDS, the banks of RIVERS, LAKES and streams, and the seashore. Adult mink grow to about 60 cm in length and weigh up to 2 kg. Excellent swimmers with partially webbed hind feet, mink feed on fish, invertebrates, reptiles, amphibians, birds, muskrats and young BEAVERS. Coastal mink feed largely on marine crustaceans, notably CRABS. Mink are not unknown to prey on domestic fowl. They dig dens near water or occupy abandoned beaver lodges or bank burrows. Mink are dark brown with white on the chest and abdomen; they have been trapped for their dense, glossy fur, though most mink used in the fur industry today are raised in mink ranches.

MINNEKHADA LODGE is a historic Scottish-style hunting lodge built in 1934 by the lumber tycoon Eric HAMBER on a large estate he owned in COQUITLAM overlooking the Pitt R. Hamber, who was BC LT GOV in 1936–41, used the property for private hunting parties and to stable his string of polo ponies. The shipbuilder Clarence WALLACE, also a lt gov, purchased the property in 1958 and continued to use it as a hunting retreat until 1975, when he sold it to the province. The lodge is now part of Minnekhada Regional Park (219 ha), owned by the GVRD, and is open intermittently to visitors.

MINSTREL ISLAND is a small island at the mouth of KNIGHT INLET on the lower Central Coast. The region is rich in KWAKWAKA'WAKW (Kwakiutl) history, and this particular island is famous as the bustling centre of the lower coast's golden age of LOGGING. From 1907, when the

general store and hotel opened, until the 1960s it was a steamer stop and watering hole for hundreds of HANDLOGGERS and GYPPO outfits carving a living out of the maze of islands they called "The Jungle." The Minstrel Island Hotel had the reputation for selling more beer than any other

Minstrel Island waterfront, c 1968.

licensed establishment in BC. The island is a setting in novels by Martin Allerdale GRAINGER (*Woodsmen of the West*) and Peter TROWER (*Grogan's Cafe*). It is named for crew members of HMS *Amethyst*, who performed black-face minstrel shows in the area when their ship was bringing Gov Gen Lord Dufferin up the coast to METLAKATLA in 1876.   *David Lee*

MINTER GARDENS is a 10-ha public show garden located at BRIDAL FALLS, east of CHILLIWACK in the FRASER VALLEY. Developed by Brian Minter on the site of an old farm, it opened in 1980 and grew to include 11 theme gardens, a maze, aviaries and the largest floral flag in Canada. Minter is a well-known author and media commentator on gardening.

MINTO CITY was established on the BRIDGE R east of GOLD BRIDGE in 1934 as a townsite for miners at the nearby Minto GOLD mine. At its peak the community had 800 residents. The mine closed in 1942 but a group of JAPANESE Canadians who were moved from the coast (*see* JAPANESE, RELOCATION OF) kept the town alive until the end of WWII. Then it dwindled to a handful of residents, the last of whom left in 1959; that year Minto and its sister communities, Wayside and Congress, were drowned by the damming of the river that created the artificial CARPENTER LK.

MIOCENE, 33 km northeast of WILLIAMS LAKE on the road to HORSEFLY, is a tiny AGRICULTURAL and LOGGING settlement that probably got its start as a roadhouse during the GOLD RUSH to the CARIBOO. It was named for the old Miocene mine on the Horsefly R. The Miocene is a geological epoch that lasted from 26 to 12 million years ago.   *AS*

MIRACLE MILE took place at Empire Stadium in VANCOUVER on 7 Aug 1954 at the British Empire Games (*see* BRITISH EMPIRE AND COMMON-

Roger Bannister (l) passes John Landy near the finish line to win the Miracle Mile, Vancouver, 1954. BCSHF

WEALTH GAMES). The race pitted Australian John Landy against Englishman Roger Bannister, the first direct competition between the only runners in the world who had covered a mile in under 4 minutes. It ended in a dramatic finish when Landy, in the lead, glanced over his left shoulder at the very second Bannister surged past him on the right. The moment was captured in one of the most famous photographs in sports history. Final times were Bannister 3:58.8, Landy 3:59.6. It was the first time two runners had broken the 4-minute barrier in the same race and it created enormous excitement globally. The first international sports event broadcast live on television to all of N America, it also became the lead story in the first issue of *Sports Illustrated*. Often forgotten is BC runner Bill Parnell, who held the British Empire Games record before Bannister.

MIRROR LAKE, a community on the west shore of KOOTENAY LK, 50 km northeast of NELSON, was the site of an early shipyard. Several PADDLEWHEEL STEAMBOATS, including the *International*, *Kaslo* and *Argenta*, were built here during 1896–1900. The Mirror Lake Ice Co, incorporated in 1895, supplied the area with block ice. Fruit growing, especially apples and cherries (*see* TREE FRUITS), was also important. *AS*

MISSION is located on the north side of the FRASER R, about 70 km east of downtown VANCOUVER, across the river from ABBOTSFORD and MATSQUI. It is named for ST MARY'S MISSION, established

on the banks of the river in 1862 by the OBLATE missionary Leon Fouquet. The mission included

Westminster Abbey, in the hills above Mission.

a school—the first RESIDENTIAL SCHOOL for aboriginals in BC—as well as a church and a grist mill used by local farmers. With the arrival of the CPR in 1885, James Welton HORNE, a real estate developer, anticipated a land boom. He developed a townsite, Mission City, and sold lots at auction; in 1892 the area incorporated as a municipality. The townsite was incorporated as a separate village in 1922, then as a town in 1958; in 1969 the town and the municipality merged to form the district municipality. Within the district there are 2 main communities, Mission and HATZIC, and 4 smaller ones: Steelhead, Stave Falls, RUSKIN and SILVERDALE. The central FRASER VALLEY is known for its fertile soil and mild climate and AGRICULTURE has always been important, principally DAIRY FARMING and fruit and vegetable production. Many of the berry farms were owned by JAPANESE producers until the internment of 1942 (see JAPANESE, RELOCATION OF). LOGGING was also significant. An iron railway bridge across the Fraser R is as far upstream as commercial SALMON fishers may operate. The district is served by a campus of Univ College of the Fraser Valley (see COMMUNITY COLLEGES). Westminster Abbey, a Benedictine monastery built in 1954, overlooks the valley from a hillside to the east.
Population: 30,519
Rank in BC: 24th
Population increase since 1981: 52%
Date of incorporation: original district 2 June 1892; village 22 Dec 1922; town 1 Jan 1958, current district 1 Nov 1969
Land area: 253.33 km²
Location: Fraser Valley Regional District
Economic base: logging, lumber, manufacturing

MISSION HILL VINEYARDS INC is an OKANAGAN VALLEY winery established in 1966 by a KELOWNA business syndicate. In 1970 the original owners sold to Ben GINTER, who ran the company until 1981; then new owners took over and began to upgrade the winery. An aggressive marketing campaign established it as one of BC's leading wine makers, a position solidified in 1994 when one of its wines won a prestigious international competition in London. *See also* WINE MAKING.

MITLENATCH ISLAND, 1.55 km², is a low-lying rock at the north end of GEORGIA STRAIT south of CAMPBELL RIVER. A provincial nature PARK, it is a refuge for a variety of nesting seabirds, including GULLS, pigeon GUILLEMOTS and pelagic CORMORANTS. SEALS and SEA LIONS disport themselves on the rocky shores. Volunteer naturalists are in residence from April through the summer, when there is a profuse display of WILDFLOWERS. FIRST NATIONS people once gathered gull eggs here. The name is a corruption of a Salish word meaning "calm back end," a reference to the safe anchorages for visiting boats. Today it is popularly known to naturalists as "the Galapagos of Georgia Strait."

MIYAZAKI, Masajiro, doctor (b 24 Nov 1899, Hikone City, Japan; d 24 July 1983, Kamloops). He arrived in VANCOUVER in 1913 and worked as a domestic servant before enrolling at UBC in 1923. Because Asians were not allowed to study medicine there, he went to Missouri and obtained a degree in osteopathy, then returned to Vancouver to practise. During the Japanese internment in 1942 (see JAPANESE, RELOCATION OF), he went to the BRIDGE R area to provide medical services to camp internees. In 1944 he moved to LILLOOET, where he practised for the rest of his life. When he was elected alderman in 1950, after Asian Canadians got the vote, he became the first JAPANESE Canadian in public office in Canada. Also active in the Boy Scouts, he was awarded the Order of Canada in 1977. His home was restored as a historic site after his death. *See also* MEDICAL PROFESSION.

MOBERLY, Walter, engineer (b 15 Aug 1832, Steeple Aston, England; d 14 May 1915, Vancouver). He arrived in BC a trained civil engineer in 1858 and helped to lay out NEW WESTMINSTER the next year. He was involved in the construction of the DEWDNEY TRAIL from 1859 to 1865. As assistant commissioner of lands and works from 1864 to 1866 he located EAGLE PASS,

built a trail from SHUSWAP LK to the GOLD diggings at Big Bend (see GOLD RUSH, BIG BEND) and surveyed the first road into BARKERVILLE. After a sojourn in the US he returned to BC in 1871 as engineer in charge of the surveys for the CPR east of Shuswap Lk. He quit in 1873, disappointed that the route he favoured was not adopted, and moved to Winnipeg. His memoir, *The Rocks and Rivers of British Columbia*, appeared in 1885.

Walter Moberly, pioneer surveyor, c 1870.
BC Archives A-01814

MOBERLY LAKE, pop 242, is a community on the north shore of the lake of the same name (29.43 km²), 20 km north of CHETWYND. It is named for Henry Moberly, who lived in a cabin here from 1865 to 1868. The brother of the surveyor Walter MOBERLY, Henry lived for many years in the PEACE R country as a trapper, trader and prospector and wrote a book of reminiscences, *When Fur Was King* (1929). DUNNE-ZA (Beaver) people live at W Moberly Lake.

MOCKINGBIRD; *see* MIMIC THRUSH.

MOHA, at the confluence of the Yalakom and BRIDGE rivers northwest of LILLOOET, is a scattered AGRICULTURAL and MINING district set in dry sagebrush country. A post office operated at this lonely spot from 1912 to 1947, and the site later became a ranch.

MOLE is a small burrowing mammal, a member of the order Insectivore, inhabiting the Lower Mainland and lower FRASER VALLEY. It has short legs with shovel-like feet for digging, a long snout and short velvety hair, grey to dark brown in colour. The mole spends much of its time underground: its small eyes see very poorly and it functions mainly by touch. Moles feed on earthworms and are themselves preyed upon mainly by OWLS. The female produces one litter annually of 1–4 young. Of 142 mole species worldwide, 3 occur in BC. The shrew-mole (*Neurotrichus gibbsii*) is completely blind, but is nevertheless the most active species above ground. The coast mole (*Scapanus orarius*) is

M

considered a pest for digging up lawns, gardens and golf courses. Townsend's mole (*S. townsendii*), the largest mole in N America, occurs only in a small area north of the US border near ABBOTSFORD and is considered endangered in BC.

MOLLUSC (or mollusk) is the term for members of the huge invertebrate phylum Mollusca. Only the phylum Arthropoda contains more species. There are more than 50,000 living species of molluscs, including the bivalves, or CLAM, GEODUCK, MUSSEL, OYSTER, SCALLOP and SHIPWORM (class Bivalvia); the gastropods, or ABALONE, SNAIL, and NUDIBRANCH (class Gastropoda); the CHITON (class Polyplacophora); and the OCTOPUS and SQUID (class Cephalapoda).
Reading: Rick M. Harbo, *Shells & Shellfish of the Pacific Northwest*, 1997; J. Duane Sept, *The Beachcomber's Guide to Seashore Life in the Pacific Northwest*, 1999.

MOLLY GIBSON, 28 km northeast of NELSON in what is now KOKANEE GLACIER PROVINCIAL PARK, was a MINING camp near the headwaters of KOKANEE CRK. A productive lead–ZINC–SILVER mine owned by COMINCO operated here from the early 1900s until about 1915. Ore was transported to a steamship/barge landing named Kokanee on the north shore of the west arm of KOOTENAY LK.   AS

MOLYBDENUM is a metal used as an alloying agent in steel fabrication and in the lubricant industry. In BC, the only province producing molybdenum, it is mined at ENDAKO, 170 km west of PRINCE GEORGE. Opened in 1965, the Endako mine was at one time the second-largest producer in the world. Molybdenum is or has been a by-product at some COPPER mines, including Brenda at PEACHLAND, Highland Valley northwest of MERRITT, the ISLAND COPPER MINE near PORT HARDY and Huckleberry south of HOUSTON. It was also mined at the Boss Mountain Mine at HENDRIX LK from 1969 to 1983. In 1998 total production was valued at $82 million.

MONASHEE MOUNTAINS are one of 4 ranges (the others are the CARIBOO, PURCELL and SELKIRK Mts) in south-central BC that form the COLUMBIA MTS. They extend about 400 km from north of REVELSTOKE to the US border, creating a natural boundary between the OKANAGAN VALLEY on the west and ARROW and Revelstoke lakes on the east. In general the range is low with an average height of 2,100 m, but in the north some peaks soar close to 3,000 m. Hwy 3 traverses the southern part of the range, where communities such as GRAND FORKS, PHOENIX and GREENWOOD sprang up during a MINING boom at the end of the 19th century. Hwy 6 bisects the lushly forested central section between Lower Arrow Lk and LUMBY; in this area LOGGING is the mainstay of the economy. In the north the TRANS-CANADA HWY crosses the range between Revelstoke and SICAMOUS. A small, high-elevation region is protected in Monashee Provincial PARK. The name is a corrup-

tion of a Gaelic phrase, "mountain peace."

MONDAY MAGAZINE is a VICTORIA weekly newspaper founded in 1975 by Bill Barringer and Gene Miller. It focusses on urban issues, the BC government, the environment and arts and entertainment, and has developed a reputation as a feisty, leading-edge journal of news and opinion about important local and regional issues. In its early days it was the only alternative news weekly in Canada. *Monday* is operated by Island Publishers, owned by David Black of BLACK PRESS LTD in Victoria. It had a circulation of 41,000 in 1999.   *Sid Tafler*

MONEY, Noel, soldier, sportsman (b 1867, Montreal, QC; d 30 May 1941, Qualicum Beach). Raised in England, he alternated service in the British Army in India and South Africa with extended overseas hunting and fishing trips. He was a land agent in England before WWI, then in 1914 immigrated with his family to QUALICUM BEACH on VANCOUVER ISLAND after a sport FISHING excursion there. During the war he rejoined the British Army and served with distinction in the Middle East. After returning to BC, he became manager of the Qualicum Beach Hotel in 1923, a position he held until 1939. The hotel attracted many celebrity guests under his gracious management. An expert fisher ("the wisest and the best" in BC, according to Roderick HAIG-BROWN) and an avid golfer, he was a well-known character in sporting circles.

MONKEY PUZZLE TREE (*Araucaria araucana*) is a large evergreen imported from Chile and Argentina. It is characterized by hard, scaly, pointed leaves that cover the trunk and limbs, and its appearance is sufficiently unusual to attract attention. This tree was especially popular with urban landscapers in the 1920s and 1930s. British Columbians may remember that sighting a tree gave a youngster permission to pinch his neighbour and exclaim, "Monkey tree, can't pinch me."

MONKMAN PROVINCIAL PARK, 320 km², is a mountain wilderness park in the Hart Ranges on the eastern flanks of the ROCKY MTS, southwest of TUMBLER RIDGE along the Murray R. A number of interesting geological features can be seen throughout the park, and it is replete with aquamarine lakes and tumbling streams. Kinuseo Falls (69 m), on the Murray R, is one of the highest WATERFALLS in northern BC. The park is named for Alex Monkman, a homesteader in the area. *See also* PARKS, PROVINCIAL.

MONTAGUE HARBOUR is a protected bay on southwest GALIANO ISLAND. Occupied by Coast Salish for at least 3,000 years (*see* SALISHAN FIRST NATIONS), it is known for its shell middens and white shell beach. In 1959 it was established as BC's first MARINE PARK (97 ha). *See also* ARCHAEOLOGY; PARKS, PROVINCIAL.

MONTE CREEK, pop 65, is a community on the TRANS-CANADA HWY, 30 km east of KAMLOOPS

in the ranching (*see* CATTLE INDUSTRY) High Country. Originally it was named Duck and Pringles after the pioneers Jacob Duck and Alex Pringle, who established a ranch here in 1862 and built a hotel, Brunswick House, which operated from 1884 to 1909. In 1888 Duck's much expanded holdings were purchased by Hewitt BOSTOCK, who developed them into the largest spread in the valley of the S THOMPSON R. In 1906 the CPR station was the scene of a holdup by the notorious train robber Billy MINER.

MONTE LAKE, pop 68, is a farming (*see* AGRICULTURE) and LOGGING community 40 km southeast of KAMLOOPS at the north end of Monte Lk. Wilf Hanbury established the Ponderosa Pine Lumber Co SAWMILL here in the 1920s; it was sold to CROWN ZELLERBACH CANADA LTD and closed in the 1970s. Henry Buff operated another mill at the south end of the lake during 1952–80. The name derives from the French word *montée*, meaning "height of land," because it was in this area that the early FUR BRIGADES of the HBC crossed over from the THOMPSON R valley to the OKANAGAN VALLEY.   AS

MONTNEY, 23 km north of FORT ST JOHN, is a small AGRICULTURAL settlement in the PEACE R district. It was named after Montaigné, chief of the main DUNNE-ZA (Beaver) tribe at Fort St John, who died in the INFLUENZA EPIDEMIC of 1919. AS

MONTROSE, village, pop 1,137, is situated in the Beaver Valley, 11 km east of TRAIL in the W KOOTENAY. Formerly known as Beaver Falls, the area was developed during WWII as a residential community by A.G. Cameron, a Trail lawyer, and the Columbia Mining & Smelting Co, now COMINCO. The name refers to a popular place in Cameron's native Scotland. The community was managed by an improvement association until it was incorporated as a village on 22 June 1956.

MOODY, Richard Clement, military engineer (b 13 Feb 1813, Barbados; d 31 Mar 1887, Bournemouth, England). A graduate of the Royal Military Academy at Woolwich, he joined the ROYAL ENGINEERS in 1830 and served in Ireland and the West Indies, and as a professor at Woolwich. In 1841 he went to the Falkland Islands as lt gov, later governor, and stayed until 1849. He continued to serve with distinction in the Royal Engineers until 1858, when he was appointed chief commissioner of lands and works and LT GOV of the new colony of BRITISH COLUMBIA. He also received command of a corps of Royal Engineers sent to the colony to keep peace in the goldfields (*see* GOLD RUSHES), lay out a capital and other townsites, build roads (*see* ROADS AND HIGHWAYS) and report on the local resources. Moody arrived in VICTORIA by ship on Christmas Day 1858, then journeyed up the FRASER R to FORT LANGLEY. When he arrived word spread of trouble in the MINING camps near YALE and he was forced to intercede (*see* MCGOWAN, Edward). When he returned to the coast he chose the site of NEW WESTMINSTER for the new capital and by the summer of 1859 a town was

Richard C. Moody, commander of the Royal Engineers. Langley Centennial Museum

taking shape. The engineers also built 2 roads connecting the capital to BURRARD INLET, improved the DOUGLAS TRAIL and surveyed townsites at Yale and HOPE. Moody himself purchased a large lot near New Westminster, which he transformed into a model farm, Mayfield. In 1862 his engineers began work on the CARIBOO WAGON ROAD northward from Yale through the Fraser Canyon, though much of the road was built by private contractors. In 1863 the Royal Engineers were withdrawn from BC. Many elected to remain as settlers, but Moody returned to England. He retired in 1866 and lived for another 20 years in Lyme Regis.

MOODY, Sewell Prescott, pioneer lumberman (b circa 1835, Hartland, ME; d 4 Nov 1875, at sea near Victoria). He came to BC as a young man and began working in a local SAWMILL before opening a butcher shop in NEW WESTMINSTER. He built the first significant sawmill there,

Sewell Moody, pioneer lumberman, c 1870. CVA Port.P861

and in 1865 bought Pioneer Mills on the north shore of BURRARD INLET. He expanded the capacity of the mill and became the first large-scale exporter of lumber in BC. The settlement that built up around the mill was called Moodyville (*see* MOODYVILLE SAWMILL CO), the beginning of N VANCOUVER. Moody was active in developing the community, building a LIBRARY and community centre, and banning liquor sales. He disappeared when the SS *Pacific* was rammed and sank off Cape Flattery en route to San Francisco. Several days after the sinking, a piece of wood washed up on the beach near VICTORIA on which was engraved: "All lost, S.P. Moody." *Ken Drushka*

MOODYVILLE SAWMILL CO was built in 1863 at the present site of N VANCOUVER by T.W. Graham, a NEW WESTMINSTER contractor. It was called Pioneer Mills and cut lumber for the local market. After going through two bankruptcies, it was purchased in 1865 by Sewell MOODY and operated as an export mill. The company name was changed to S.P. Moody and Co, and the settlement that grew up around the mill was called Moodyville. Two partners, Hugh NELSON and G.W. Dietz, joined the firm in 1866 and it was renamed Moody, Dietz & Nelson. Moody was active in the growing community: among other things he banned liquor and started the Moodyville Mechanic's Institute, which opened BURRARD INLET's first LIBRARY, organized lectures and concerts, and held church services. In 1875 Moody drowned. Three years later the company was reorganized as the Moodyville Sawmill Co. In 1890 it was sold to the Moodyville Lands & Sawmill Co, a subsidiary of John HENDRY's BC MILLS TIMBER & TRADING CO. The mill closed in 1901; the remains were destroyed by fire in 1916. *See also* FOREST INDUSTRY. *Ken Drushka*

MOOG, Donald Andrew "Andy," hockey player (b 18 Feb 1960, Penticton). After playing junior HOCKEY in KAMLOOPS, PENTICTON and Billings, MT, he was drafted by the Edmonton Oilers in 1980 and moved up to the NHL team in 1982. For the next 5 years he and former VICTORIA COUGARS goaltender Grant Fuhr formed one of the best netminder duos in hockey history, helping the Oilers to 3 Stanley Cups and twice appearing together in league all-star games. But Moog grew tired of sharing the job in Edmonton and in 1987 he joined the Canadian national Olympic team. When the 1988 Calgary Olympics were over, Edmonton traded him to the Boston Bruins and he spent 6 seasons there, reaching the Stanley Cup finals once and the semifinals twice. He and fellow Bruin goalie Reggie Lemelin won the Jennings Trophy for allowing the fewest goals in the league in 1989–90. In 1993 Moog went to the Dallas Stars for 4 seasons, then to the Montreal Canadiens in 1997–98 before ending his career. In 1999 he returned to BC to become goaltending coach with the VANCOUVER CANUCKS. *SW*

MOORE, Douglas L. "Buzz," rugby player (b 20 Apr 1921, Regina). He was one of the most durable players in Canadian RUGBY history and

the first Canadian to be given the coveted international title of "Honorary Barbarian." Moore was brought to BC by his mother in 1925 and he grew up playing many sports, joining the senior Meraloma Rugby Club at the age of 16. He played or coached on every BC and Canadian representative rugby team from 1938 to 1966, not missing a single match as Canada's captain between 1948 and 1964. In 1948 he was selected as the winner of the Howie McPhee trophy by the Vancouver Rugby Union for his outstanding sportsmanship, playing ability and leadership. In 1962 the legendary Barbarians rugby club made Moore the second player in the world to be named an Honorary Barbarian, the highest international recognition for dedication to the game. His administrative career included terms on the executives of the BC and Vancouver Rugby associations and a posting in the UBC Department of Athletics and Recreation starting in 1964. He has been elected to the UBC Sports Hall of Fame and the BC SPORTS HALL OF FAME.

MOORE, Greg, race-car driver (b 22 Apr 1975, Maple Ridge; d 31 Oct 1999, Fontana, CA). He started competing at age 11 when his father bought him a go-kart to race at Westwood Motorsport Park. After winning the USAC Formula 2000 West title at 17, Greg joined the

Greg Moore, race car driver, 1995. Firestone Indy Lights

Indy Lights developmental series and won a record 10 of 12 races in 1995, quieting critics who had said he was too young for professional racing. He replaced Jacques Villeneuve on the World IndyCar circuit's Player's Forsythe team and he ended his rookie season (1996) 9th in overall points. He improved in 1997, becoming the youngest driver ever to win a CART race and finishing 7th in the points standings. In 1998 he posted two more victories, and in 1999 added another for a career total of 5 victories in 4 seasons on the CART circuit. He died, age 24, during the final race of the 1999 season when his car smashed into a wall. He was inducted into the BC SPORTS HALL OF FAME in 2000. *SW*

MOORE, James Mavor, writer, producer, actor, teacher (b 8 Mar 1919, Toronto). While still a philosophy student at the Univ of Toronto, he was a pioneer in Canadian radio drama and documentary and, after overseas service in Army Intelligence, became active with his mother Dora Mavor Moore in the post-war revival of professional THEATRE. His early Canadian premieres included *Spring Thaw* (1948–67), in its time the longest-running annual revue in the world. He has directed and acted on television and in theatres across Canada and appeared in some 60 feature films. He was the first production chief for CBC Television (1950–54), first chair of the Canadian Theatre Centre and founding head of the Charlottetown Festival. In 1967 he co-chaired Canada's 1967 Centennial Committee. Moore taught theatre at York Univ from 1970 to 1984 and was the first artist to chair the Canada Council for the Arts (1979–83). He has lived in BC since 1984, and began teaching at the UNIV OF VICTORIA in 1990. From 1996 to 1998 he was founding chair of the BC ARTS COUNCIL and has served on the boards of SCIENCE WORLD BC, the VANCOUVER SYMPHONY and the Canadian Music Centre. In 1998 his musical *Johnny Belinda* (with composer John Fenwick) had its fifth revival at the Charlottetown Festival and his musical version of Dickens' *A Christmas Carol* appeared in 7 US states in addition to its annual production by the CAROUSEL THEATRE CO. He is professor emeritus at York Univ, a Companion in the Order of Canada, winner of the Molson Prize (1986) and recipient of the ORDER OF BC as well as honorary degrees from 6 universities.
Reading: Mavor Moore, Reinventing Myself, 1994.

MOORE, Linda, curler (b 24 Feb 1954, Vancouver). After forming a CURLING team that

Linda Moore (centre) throwing stone at 1988 Calgary Winter Olympic Games. Her teammates Penny Shantz Ryan (l) and Debbie Jones Walker (r) sweep. Doug Shanks photo

included second Debbie Jones, third Lindsay Sparkes, lead Laurie Carney and coach Rae Moir in 1983, Moore skipped the N VANCOUVER rink to the 1985 world women's curling championships, winning the BC provincials and going undefeated in the Scott Tournament of Hearts national championship along the way. The rink won 7 of 9 round-robin games and beat host Sweden and then Scotland in the final playoff rounds to capture the world title. Three years later, with Edmonton's Penny Ryan taking the place of Carney, Moore's rink captured the gold medal in demonstration women's curling at the Calgary Olympics. *SW*

MOORE, Patrick Albert, ecologist (b 15 June 1947, Port Alice). He grew up in a float camp in QUATSINO SOUND where his father, Bill Moore, was a logger. While doing graduate studies at UBC, he took part in protests against American nuclear testing in the N Pacific that led to the founding of GREENPEACE in 1971. He was president of Greenpeace in 1977–79 and a director until he left the organization in 1986; he felt that it had served its purpose and that the time had come to make change by co-operating with industry. He has operated a salmon farm near his home in WINTER HARBOUR (*see* AQUACULTURE, FIN FISH) and has been active in the FOREST ALLIANCE OF BC. Moore is considered to be an articulate and resolute defender of modern FOREST INDUSTRY practices; as such he became a special target of environmentalists who claimed that he had betrayed the ENVIRONMENTAL MOVEMENT. He aired his views on FORESTRY in his 1995 book *Pacific Spirit: The Forest Reborn*.

MOORE, William, steamboat captain (b 30 Mar 1822, Hanover, Germany; d 29 Mar 1909, Victoria). At an early age he sailed the North Sea and eventually arrived in New Orleans. He served in the war with Mexico in 1848, then moved to San Francisco and on to BC, where he was a leading captain and owner of PADDLEWHEEL STEAMBOATS on the FRASER R during the GOLD RUSH era. In the 1860s he pioneered steam navigation on the STIKINE R and was involved as a supplier to the gold rushes in Omineca and CASSIAR. In the 1880s he returned to the lower Fraser R, where he went bankrupt competing against John IRVING. Shifting his activities back north, he began exploring overland routes into the Yukon, where he delivered mail and became convinced that a gold strike would soon take place. He had the foresight in 1887 to buy property at Skagway and, when the Klondike gold rush began, he prospered. *Peggy Imredy*

MOOSE (*Alces alces*) is the largest member of the deer family; males can weigh 400–700 kg depending on the subspecies and on local conditions. Moose are distinguished by a number of unique physical attributes, including (on the males) palmate antlers—the largest of all N American ungulates; a dewlap, or bell, that hangs under the lower jaw; and a pendulous upper lip. The animal is long-legged and heavy-bodied, with large front quarters, a short neck

and a large shoulder hump. This body structure gives it speed and an ability to swim strongly and plow through deep snow. Scent glands occur on the inside of the hind legs, below the tail and between the hooves; these secrete pheromones that other moose detect with their keen sense of smell. The female gives birth to 1 calf, occasionally 2, annually. Principal predators are the BEAR, WOLF and COUGAR.

Bull moose feeding in water. Duane Sept photo

Three subspecies of varying size and coloration occur in BC: northwestern moose (*A. alces andersoni*), Alaska moose (*A. alces gigas*) and Rocky Mountain moose (*A. alces shirasi*). Before 1900 moose were absent from most of the southern part of BC. Since then they have dramatically expanded their range, in part due to changing climate and vegetation patterns, but also due to landscape-altering industrial and settlement activities. By 1991 the BC population was estimated to be 165,000. Moose are browsers, inhabiting mixed forests of coniferous and deciduous trees where they eat the leaves, twigs and buds of woody plants. Preferred food includes willow, aspen, red osier dogwood, birch and balsam fir. They also prefer WETLAND complexes around rivers and lakeshores and eat a variety of aquatic plants.

MORAN, Bridget, social worker, writer (b 1923, Northern Ireland; d Aug 1999, Prince George). Raised in Success, SK, she served in the Women's Royal Canadian Naval Service during WWII, then attended the Univ of Toronto and studied social work. She came to BC in 1951 to work as a social worker for the provincial government. From 1977 to her retirement in 1989 she was employed by the PRINCE GEORGE school district. Toward the end of her social work career she began writing. Her first book, *Stoney Creek Woman* (1988), about DAKELH (Carrier) elder Mary JOHN, has become a BC classic. It was followed by 3 more books. She received honorary degrees from UNBC and the UNIV OF VICTORIA.

MORESBY ISLAND, 6.5 km², located between the SAANICH PENINSULA and the 2 PENDER ISLANDS, is one of the smallest GULF ISLANDS. It is named after Admiral Fairfax Moresby, naval commander-in-chief on the BC coast from 1850 to 1853 (as is one of the main islands in the QUEEN CHARLOTTE ISLANDS). It has been settled since 1863 and has had some lively owners. One of these was Horatio Robertson, who retired from a successful merchant career in China and built an extravagant island home. He developed a reputation for mistreating his CHINESE workers, who were sometimes seen pulling him by rickshaw through the streets of VICTORIA. Another owner was Thomas PATERSON, who served as LT GOV of BC from 1909 to 1914. A prosperous DAIRY FARM was established on Moresby in the 1910s. The island is still privately owned.   AS

MORGAN, Nigel, labour politician (b 1913, Galiano Island; d 1978, Vancouver). As a union organizer in the FOREST INDUSTRY, he negotiated and signed the first collective agreement between the International Woodworkers of America (later renamed INDUSTRIAL, WOOD AND ALLIED WORKERS OF CANADA) and an employer (Batco). Later he

The Bulkley R, near Moricetown.
Walter Lanz/Image Makers

was BC member on the IWA's international board and first president of the Committee of Industrial Organization in BC. In 1945 he resigned his position in the union to become provincial leader of the Labour Progressive Party, the legal wing of the Communist Party, a position he held until his retirement in 1977.

MORICE, Adrien Gabriel, Catholic missionary (b 27 Aug 1859, Mayenne, France; d 21 Apr 1938, St-Boniface, MB). He joined the Oblate order (*see* OBLATES OF MARY IMMACULATE) in 1879 and came to BC the next year. Following his ordination as a priest in 1882 he rebelled against his posting as a schoolteacher and the order sent him to FORT ST JAMES as punishment. He remained there until 1905, working among the DAKELH (Carrier) people. He invented a syllabic script for the Dakelh and imported a printing press on which he published his own writings. A

domineering personality, he often came into conflict with other missionaries and with aboriginal spiritual leaders. He was an energetic explorer and a pioneer ethnographer of the Central Interior; he wrote the first history of the area, *History of the Northern Interior of British Columbia* (1904), based on oral accounts he collected from the local people. Morice Lk, Morice R and MORICETOWN are all named for him. After leaving Fort St James he transferred to Manitoba but continued his studies of the Dakelh. In 1932 he published his groundbreaking study, *The Carrier Language*, in 2 vols.
Reading: David Mulhall, *Will to Power: The Missionary Career of Father Morice*, 1986.

MORICETOWN, pop 259, is located on the BULKLEY R, where it plunges through a narrow canyon 31 km north of SMITHERS on the Yellowhead Hwy (Hwy 16; *see* ROADS AND HWYS). The site has been an important FISHING camp (Kyah Wiget) for WET'SUWET'EN people for thousands of years. It is named for the OBLATE missionary A.G. MORICE.

MORIGEAU, François, pioneer settler (b 1793, St Martin, QC; d 31 Mar 1870, Fort Colville, WA). He is considered to be the first white settler in the WINDERMERE valley and possibly the first anywhere in the KOOTENAY. He arrived in BC about 1818 and set up as an independent fur trader in the upper COLUMBIA R valley. A missionary once called him "the monarch who rules at the source of the Columbia." In the mid-1840s he moved south to a farm near Colville, WA. He had 2 FIRST NATIONS wives and his descendants still live in the E Kootenay and the western US. The best-known child was Sophie Morigeau (circa 1835–1915), a pioneer mixed-race entrepreneur in the Kootenay. During the GOLD RUSH to WILD HORSE CRK Sophie ran her own pack trains and sold supplies to hungry miners. Later she set up as a storekeeper, first near Windermere Lk, then at Tobacco Plains near the US border. See also FUR TRADE, LAND-BASED.

MORMON CHURCH has about 20,000 members in BC. The vast majority belong to the

Church of Jesus Christ of Latter-day Saints (LDS), the principal Mormon denomination. A few hundred belong to a second denomination, The Reorganized Church of Jesus Christ of Latter Day Saints (RLDS).

The Mormon Church was founded in 1830 in New York State by Joseph Smith. Smith preached that a great apostasy had taken place shortly after Christ's death, that the Bible represented only part of the Gospel of Christ, and that he had received the rest directly from God. The *Book of Mormon* is a written account of these divine revelations. Widely persecuted in New York, Mormons made their way to Illinois; there Smith was murdered by an angry mob. His death divided his followers. Brigham Young led the majority of the faithful to Utah, where they established Salt Lake City as their religious base and became known as the Church of Jesus Christ of Latter-day Saints. Meanwhile Joseph Smith's own family resisted Young's leadership and formed an alternative Mormon church, the Reorganized Church, based in Iowa and later Missouri. The denominations differ slightly in doctrine and practice.

Before travelling to Utah, the LDS briefly considered establishing their settlement at NOOTKA SOUND on VANCOUVER ISLAND. A group of LDS Mormons in Britain actively petitioned the government for the right to colonize Vancouver Island until it was placed under the stewardship of the HBC in 1849. During the 1880s the LDS again considered moving to BC when they were persecuted in Utah for their practice of polygamy. John Taylor, Young's successor as leader of the LDS, sent Charles Ora Card to the OKANAGAN VALLEY and the BOUNDARY DISTRICT in 1886 to look for possible settlement sites, but in the end the church chose southern Alberta instead.

The first Mormons to live in BC were the Copley family, who moved to VICTORIA from Utah in 1875. In 1887 A. Maitland Stenhouse, a member of the provincial legislature, surprised his constituents by abruptly resigning his seat and converting to the LDS; eventually he moved to Card's settlement in Alberta. He was the first Mormon convert in BC. By the early 1900s individual LDS families were moving to BC from Utah. LDS churches were established in VANCOUVER in 1925 and in Victoria in 1942. Following WWII the LDS experienced rapid growth in BC, eventually forming congregations in every major centre in the province. The RLDS got established in BC largely through the efforts of Alex McMullen and Daniel McGregor, who organized small congregations in CHILLIWACK and NEW WESTMINSTER in 1900. Joseph Smith III, president of the RLDS, visited BC in 1905 and by 1912 there were enough RLDS members in Vancouver to organize a congregation. It now has congregations in every major centre in BC, though it has a much smaller membership than the LDS.

MORRIS, Joseph, labour leader (b 14 June 1913, Lancashire, England; d 11 Oct 1996, Victoria). His family immigrated to LADYSMITH when he was a teenager and shortly after he went to work in the woods as a scaler (*see* LOGGING). He became an organizer for the International Woodworkers of America (*see* INDUSTRIAL, WOOD AND ALLIED WORKERS OF CANADA), then rose to become president of the western district from 1953 to 1962. After joining the executive of the Canadian Labour Congress, he became president in 1974; two years later he shot to public prominence when he led one million trade unionists on a one-day (Oct 14) national political strike to protest the federal government's policy of wage and price controls. During his tenure as CLC president (1974–78), he promoted the idea of tripartism by which labour would share economic decision-making with government and business. The idea, which came to be known as corporatism, was ultimately rejected. He was also active internationally, serving a term as chair of the International Labour Organization in 1977. He became a companion of the Order of Canada in 1984.

MORRIS, Michael, artist (b 1942, Saltdean, England). He moved to VICTORIA with his family as a child. After graduating from the Vancouver School of Art (*see* EMILY CARR INSTITUTE OF ART & DESIGN) in 1964 and further studies in England, he became a leading figure in VANCOUVER's avant-garde arts scene in the 1960s and 1970s. Under his own name and sometimes his *nom d'art*, "Marcel Idea," he was involved in INTERMEDIA, helped to found the WESTERN FRONT and, along with his partner and fellow artist Vincent Trasov ("Mr Peanut"), ran the Image Bank. Along with his painting, he engaged in a variety of activities that expanded the boundaries of what constitutes "art." He moved to Berlin in the 1980s.

MORRISSEY, 60 km east of CRANBROOK in the valley of the ELK R, had a brief but vivid life as a COAL mining centre in the early 1900s. The collieries—Morrissey, Tonkin and Carbonado—were owned by the Crow's Nest Pass Coal Co, a subsidiary of the GREAT NORTHERN RWY. The coal company had its own line, the Morrissey, Field & Michel, to serve its mines here and at Coal Creek (*see* FERNIE; CROWS NEST SOUTHERN RWY). The coal was not suitable for making coke, however, and the MINING was abandoned by 1909. A large WWI internment camp for enemy aliens was located here. Morrissey was also the name of a station on the Crowsnest branch of the CPR just northwest of the mines on the Elk R. James Morrissey was a local settler who pioneered TRAILS between ELKO and CROWSNEST PASS. AS

MORROW, Patrick Allan, mountaineer, photographer (b 18 Oct 1952, Invermere). A native of KIMBERLEY, he began climbing as an outdoors photographer and became the second person, after American Dick Bass, to scale the highest peaks on each of the 7 continents: Mts Everest (Asia), McKinley (N America), Aconcagua (S America), Elbrus (Europe), Kilimanjaro (Africa) and Kosciusko (Australia), and Vinson Massif (Antarctica). He was the first British Columbian and second Canadian to reach the summit of Everest. In May 1986 he climbed Carstenz

Pyramid in New Guinea, the highest peak in Australasia and twice the height of Kosciusko, to add a footnote to Bass's MOUNTAINEERING "grand slam." His first book, *Beyond Everest: Quest for the Seven Summits*, appeared in 1986 and over the next 13 years 4 more volumes of photographs followed. He has won many national magazine awards for PHOTOGRAPHY and is a Member of the Order of Canada (1987). SW

MORTIFEE, Ann, singer, songwriter (b 30 Nov 1947, Zululand, S Africa). She began her musical career while studying English at UBC, performing as a folk and blues singer-guitarist in VANCOUVER clubs. Her association with the George RYGA play *The Ecstasy of Rita Joe* brought her to national attention. She co-composed its score in 1967,

Ann Mortifee, singer/songwriter, c 1999.
BC Arts Council

revised it for a ballet in 1971 and released the album in 1972. Mortifee has recorded 7 other albums on her Jabula Records label, written several scores for ballet, film and television and performed in many plays and one-woman shows. She gives workshops and talks on creativity and spiritual healing. She received the Order of Canada (1992) and in 1998 was appointed chair of the BC ARTS COUNCIL.

MORTIMER-LAMB, Harold, journalist, photographer (b 21 May 1872, Leatherhead, England; d 25 Oct 1970, Burnaby). After immigrating to VICTORIA in 1889 he worked as a journalist and editor of several NEWSPAPERS. In 1896 he became editor of *BC Mining Review*, the beginning of a lifelong involvement in the MINING industry. From 1905 to 1919 he edited *Canadian Mining Review*, based in Montreal, then returned to BC and continued to write about mining. Mortimer-Lamb had a second career as an accomplished pictorialist photographer whose work was exhibited widely in BC, eastern Canada and England. A founding member of the Arts and Letters Club in VANCOUVER in 1921, he was active in local artistic circles in the 1920s

and 1930s. In 1926 he cofounded the VANDER-PANT GALLERIES with fellow photographer John VANDERPANT. He married the artist Vera WEATHER-BIE in 1942 and gave up PHOTOGRAPHY in favour of painting. His daughter is the painter Molly Lamb BOBAK.

MORTON, John, pioneer settler (b 16 Apr 1834, Lindley, England; d 18 Apr 1912, Vancouver). He was one of the THREE GREEN-HORNS—himself, his cousin Sam BRIGHOUSE and their friend William Hailstone—who originally settled what is now VANCOUVER's West End in 1862. Morton heard that a British naval survey had found COAL in BURRARD INLET and persuaded the others to go and have a look. He built a cabin, the first in Vancouver, and a brickyard. When the CPR arrived in Vancouver it bought most of the Greenhorns' property; Morton moved to MISSION but returned to the city in his later years.

MOSQUITO is a small fly notorious for its irritating bite. About 50 species occur in BC, distributed in 5 genera. They all have a long, slender proboscis, or beak; both male and female use it to feed on plant nectar, and females use it to puncture the skin of animals to suck blood. Mosquitoes pass through 4 life stages: eggs hatch into worm-shaped larvae that moult and become pupae from which adults emerge. Eggs are laid directly on water or in areas that will be flooded. They hatch in spring and are aquatic during the larval stage of development. Mosquitoes mate in swarms; males die shortly afterwards while females set off to find the blood they require to provide protein to their eggs prior to laying them. Humans consider mosquitoes to be obnoxious. In BC at least they are not responsible for any harmful diseases, though they may transmit western equine encephalitis which, as the name suggests, affects horses. In the past century the number of mosquitoes in the province has been much depleted by urban and AGRICULTURAL development and by the destruction of breeding areas by drainage and flood control. *Reading:* Peter Belton, *The Mosquitoes of British Columbia*, 1983.

MOSS is a small green plant usually growing in dense clumps or carpets. Mosses are found throughout BC, blanketing the damp forest floors, covering rocks and stumps, coating the branches and trunks of trees and invading the lawns of suburban homeowners. They require water for fertilization, and because they lack complex vascular systems they absorb water and nutrients through the stem and leaves, which are usually only one cell layer thick. During periods when rainfall is low, some species are capable of drying up and becoming dormant until re-wetting sparks a resumption of biological activity. Moss life cycles consist of two parts: the sporophyte, or spore-producing stage, and the gametophyte, or growth stage. The sporophyte is attached to and dependent on the leafy green gametophyte. Mosses grow from tiny spores that are released into the air to be transported by

Moss draping a tree in the coastal temperate rain forest. Dean van't Schip photo

Mt Assiniboine, sixth-highest peak in the Rocky Mts. David Wirzba/Image Makers

wind or water to a spot where they will germinate into new plants. Many mosses also reproduce vegetatively by fragmentation when a part of the plant breaks off and grows into a new plant. Peat mosses, or *sphagnum* mosses, are important commercially for gardening and other agricultural uses. There are 965 moss species in Canada, more than 3/4 of which occur in BC, including 160 species that are found nowhere else but BC. Of these, 117 species are considered critically imperilled, mainly by LOGGING, AGRICULTURE, urban developments and changes in climate. *See also* ENDANGERED SPECIES; PLANTS, NATIVE.

MOTH; *see* BUTTERFLY; GYPSY MOTH.

MOTTO, PROVINCIAL, is *splendor sine occasu* ("splendour without diminishment"). The words are engraved beneath BC's official shield, which was designed by Rev Arthur Beanlands in 1895 and adopted that year by the provincial government. The design was not confirmed by Britain's royal College of Arms until 1906, however, and other elements of the provincial COAT OF ARMS were not granted until 1987. Some other official BC emblems include the Pacific DOGWOOD (flower), the Steller's JAY (bird), the western red CEDAR (tree) and JADE (mineral). BC also has an official tartan. AS

MOUNT ASSINIBOINE PROVINCIAL PARK, 390.5 km², nestles in the ROCKY MTS on the Alberta border, 48 km south of Banff. This wilderness park is dominated by Mt Assiniboine (el 3,618 m), a Matterhorn-like peak, the sixth highest in the Rockies and first scaled in 1901. The park started as a camp for the Alpine Club of Canada and became BC's seventh provincial PARK in 1922. The CPR built an alpine lodge there in 1928, which was the first cross-country ski lodge in western N America. Now a heritage site, the lodge still welcomes guests attracted by the spectacular setting for hiking and SKIING. The park is only accessible by air or trail.

MOUNT CURRIE, pop 1,060, is a Lil'wat RESERVE near the northern end of Lillooet Lk, on the BC RAIL line 5 km east of PEMBERTON. The Lil'wat are a division of the ST'AT'IMX (Lillooet) people. The reserve population is spread between a newer residential subdivision named Xitolacw, the older community that dates from the 1870s, and a number of homes along Lillooet Lake Road. Originally named Creekside, the village has become known for its annual RODEO. The Lil'wat regard nearby Mt Currie (el 2,590 m) as sacred. John Currie, a gold seeker from Scotland who married a Lil'wat woman, was one of the first settlers in the Pemberton Valley.

MOUNT EDZIZA PROVINCIAL PARK, 2,327 km², is a high-elevation volcanic wilderness southeast of TELEGRAPH CREEK in the Tahltan Highlands between the STIKINE and Iskut rivers. Created in 1972, the park features a number of cinder cones atop and along the flanks of Mt Edziza (el 2,787 m), a shield volcano that last erupted about 1,300 years ago. Spectacular adjacent volcanism at Hoodoo Mtn southwest of Mt Edziza on the north side of the Iskut R is estimated to have occurred as recently as 300 years ago. The name Edziza, from the TAHLTAN language, may mean "ice mountain" or may refer to the crunching sound made by people walking on the hardened lava. For thousands of years FIRST NATIONS people obtained obsidian here for making tools and weapons, and ancient trade TRAILS have been located. The first Europeans into the area were fur traders arriving from the north and east (*see* CAMPBELL, Robert; FUR TRADE, LAND-BASED). The park contains critical wildlife habitat, notably for woodland CARIBOU, MOUNTAIN GOATS and BEARS. Access is by hiking trails, horseback and float plane. *See also* PARKS, PROVINCIAL.

MOUNT LEHMAN is a rural community on elevated ground in the lower FRASER VALLEY between LANGLEY and MATSQUI. The pioneer settler was Alben Hawkins, who took up farmland in 1874, though it is named for a later settler, Isaac Lehman. When the BC ELECTRIC RWY CO opened its INTERURBAN line to CHILLIWACK in 1910, it placed a station at Mount Lehman that became a focus for the community, which is now part of the City of ABBOTSFORD.

MOUNT REVELSTOKE NATIONAL PARK, adjacent to the city of REVELSTOKE, was established in 1914 at the insistence of the city's residents, who wanted a dominion park to protect the natural beauty of Mt Revelstoke's (el 1,830 m) rolling meadows of WILDFLOWERS and surrounding snow-capped peaks. The park contains 260 km² of the Clachnacudainn Range in the SELKIRK MTS. In the early days visitors had to hike for hours to visit the summit, but by 1927 a 29-km gravel road to Balsam Lk made the meadows accessible to vehicles. Heather Lake Lodge operated at the lake from 1936 to 1966. For much of the year the mountainous wilderness park is snow-covered. The park is in the Interior wet belt and its lower-elevation FORESTS, with their giant CEDARS and lush understorey, are similar to coastal RAIN FORESTS. *See also* PARKS, NATIONAL.

MOUNTAIN EQUIPMENT CO-OP is a member-owned VANCOUVER co-operative producing and selling products for outdoor recreation. The business was hatched when a spring snowstorm trapped a party of hikers on Mt BAKER one weekend in 1970. They discussed their frustration with the lack of MOUNTAINEERING stores in Vancouver and decided to start their own. By 2 Aug 1971 Mountain Equipment Co-op was incorporated with 6 original members. Starting from an inventory closet in GASTOWN, the co-op expanded to include a flagship store in Vancouver and other outlets across Canada selling equipment for mountaineering, ROCKCLIMBING, ski touring, hiking, paddling and bicycle touring. The millionth share was sold 17 May 1997. Revenues in 1998 were $130,374,000. *SW*

Mountain goat in the Rocky Mts.
Duane Sept photo

MOUNTAIN GOAT (*Oreamnos americanus*) is a hoofed mammal widespread in the mountainous Interior of the province, where it subsists on a wide variety of plants. About 60% of the world population is found in BC, an estimated 55,000 animals. Adult males weigh 80–135 kg; females are smaller. A thick coat of fine white hair makes mountain goats visible high up on cliffsides, where they scramble with amazing agility. They have short, curved black horns, but unlike MOUNTAIN SHEEP, whose habitat they share, they do not engage in head-butting. The female gives birth to a single kid in late spring after a 6-month gestation period. Hair from the goat was used by aboriginal people to weave blankets and clothing (*see* CHILKAT DANCING BLANKET).

Rocky mountain bighorn sheep. Duane Sept photo

MOUNTAIN SHEEP is a stocky, hoofed mammal inhabiting alpine and subalpine habitats throughout BC. The animal is remarkable for its heavy curling horns, with which the rams butt heads during rutting season in aggressive displays of dominance. Mountain sheep are surefooted scramblers that evade predators by escaping onto cliff faces and rock formations where they cannot be followed. Otherwise they forage for plants in open areas. Four types occur in BC. Stone's sheep (*Ovis dalli stonei*) are thinhorn sheep indigenous to northern BC and neighbouring parts of the Yukon, where they mingle with their near-relatives, the all-white Dall's

sheep (*O. dalli dalli*). Dall's sheep only occur in the TATSHENSHINI R region in the extreme northwest of the province. Stone's sheep are black-grey in colour with white faces and rumps. They were named for the American hunter/collector Andrew J. Stone in 1897 and are associated in particular with the SPATSIZI R plateau and the route of the ALASKA HWY. Two other types are bighorn sheep and are found in the southern half of the province. Brown in colour, they are the California bighorn (*Ovis canadensis californiana*) in the mountainous south-central Interior, and the slightly larger and paler Rocky Mountain bighorn (*Ovis canadensis canadensis*) in the Rockies. A group of 500 California bighorns, the world's largest non-migratory herd, is protected in Junction Sheep Range Provincial PARK (4,573 ha) at the confluence of the FRASER and Chilcotin rivers.

MOUNTAINEERING began in BC when the completion of the CPR in 1885 made the mountains of the BC Interior accessible to mountaineers from around the world. Soon British and American climbers, often led by Austrian or SWISS GUIDES, were reaching the summits of the ROCKY and COLUMBIA MTS. The first climber of note was a Canadian surveyor from Aylmer, QC, James Joseph McArthur. In 1887 he and an assistant climbed Mt Stephen near FIELD while sur-

Climbers on Mt McGill in Glacier National Park, c 1920. Revelstoke Museum & Archives P996.1

veying for the Dominion Land Surveys. The following year two Britons, Rev William Spotswood Green and his cousin Rev Henry Swanzy, visited GLACIER HOUSE near the summit of ROGERS PASS in the SELKIRK MTS. Their finest ascent was Mt Bonney, and during their stay they made a map

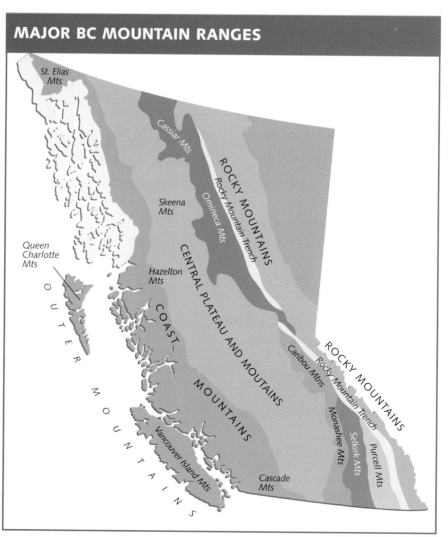

MAJOR BC MOUNTAIN RANGES

St. Elias Mts

Cassiar Mts

ROCKY MOUNTAINS

Rocky Mountain Trench

Skeena Mts

Omineca Mts

Queen Charlotte Mts

Hazelton Mts

OUTER MOUNTAINS

CENTRAL PLATEAU AND MOUNTAINS

COAST MOUNTAINS

Vancouver Island Mts

Cariboo Mtns

Rocky Mountain Trench

ROCKY MOUNTAINS

Monashee Mts

Selkirk Mts

Purcell Mts

Cascade Mts

of the region. In 1890 Emil Huber and Carl Sulzer, two Swiss amateurs, accompanied by a Canadian woodsman named Harry Cooper, climbed Mt Sir Donald near Rogers Pass, an outstanding feat for its time. The CPR brought Swiss-trained mountain guides to Glacier House in 1899 to promote TOURISM along the mountain portion of the railway. The first to come were Edouard Feuz Sr and Christian Haesler Sr; that summer they led two American climbers, Charles Fay and Herschel Parker, to the summit of Mt Dawson. Swiss guides also led the first parties to the top of Mt ASSINIBOINE (1901) and Mt Sir Sandford (1912), the highest peak in the Selkirks. One of the most active mountain guides was Conrad KAIN, born in Austria. In 1913 Kain led Albert H. MacCarthy and W.W. "Billy"

FOSTER to the summit of Mt ROBSON, the highest peak in the Canadian Rockies. This may or may not have been a first ascent; Rev George Kinney claimed to have reached the Robson summit in 1909 with Donald "Curly" Phillips. Their ascent was later discredited and the truth remains uncertain. In 1916 Kain made what was perhaps the most difficult ascent of the era when he led John Vincent and Albert MacCarthy and his wife Elizabeth to the summit of Bugaboo Spire in the PURCELL MTS.

Climbing in the COAST MTS did not get its start until 1907, when the BC MOUNTAINEERING CLUB was founded and a party of 6 climbers scaled Mt Garibaldi north of VANCOUVER. In 1911 Basil Darling, Allan Morkill and Stanley Davies climbed both Mt Tantalus and Mt Serratus (*see*

TANTALUS RANGE). Throughout the 1920s and early 1930s the leader of the coast climbing community was Tom FYLES, a Vancouver mail carrier whose regular climbing companions included Alec Dalgleish, Neal Carter and Mills Winram. In 1925 Don and Phyllis MUNDAY spotted what they called "Mystery Mountain" (Mt WADDING-TON); the following year they went in search of the peak. For 8 years they mapped and explored the Waddington area but never succeeded in reaching the summit. That honour went to two Americans, Fritz Wiessner and William House, in 1936. Throughout the 1930s and 1940s the Mundays continued to explore the Coast Mts, making many first ascents including Combatant Mt (1933), Silverthrone Mt (1936), Mt Grenville (1941), Mt Queen Bess (1942) and Reliance Mt

MOUNTAIN RANGES IN BC

Mountains	Ranges	Length (km)	Location	Highest peak
ST ELIAS	Fairweather	-	Alaska-BC border	Mt FAIRWEATHER 4,663 m
	Icefield	-	Alaska-Yukon-BC border	Mt Logan, YT 5,950 m
	Alsek	-	south of Alsek R	-
QUEEN CHARLOTTE		-	west side of Queen Charlottes	Newcombe Peak 1,050 m
VANCOUVER ISLAND		-	-	Golden Hinde 2,200 m
COAST MTS	Pacific	480 km	Fraser R to Bella Coola	Mt WADDINGTON 4,019 m
	Kitimat	320 km	Bella Coola to Nass R	Atna Peak 2,757 m
	Boundary	-	BC-Alaska border	Mt Ratz 3,136 m
CASCADES	Skagit	-	Cultus Lk east to Skagit R	Welch Peak 2,360 m
	Hozameen	-	Manning Park	Mt Outram 2,438 m
	Okanagan	-	west of Similkameen	Haystack Mt 2,605 m
SKEENA MTS	Eaglenest	-	Spatsizi Plateau	Nation Peak 2,359 m
	Oweegee	-	southwest of Spatsizi	Oweegee Peak 2,300 m
	Tatlatui	-	Tatlatui Park	Melanistic Peak 2,350 m
	Sicintine	-	-	Shelagyote Peak 2,466 m
	Atna	-	Babine R	Kisgegas Peak 2,347 m
	Babine	-	northwest of Babine Lk	Netalzul Mt 2,330 m
HAZELTON MTS	Nass	48 km	between Skeena & Nass rivers	-
	Bulkley	-	between Skeena & Bulkley valleys	Seven Sisters 2,790 m
	Kispiox	30 km	Nass Basin	Kispiox Mt 2,696 m
	Tahtsa	64 km	north of Eutsuk Lk	-
CASSIAR MTS	Stikine	440 km	Yukon south to Spatsizi Plateau	-
	Kechika	-	north of Sifton Pass	-
	Sifton	-	Finlay R	-
OMINECA MTS	Swannell	320 km	west of Williston Lk	Mt Cushing 2,469 m
	Finlay	200 km	Finlay R	-
	Hogem	225 km	Takla Lk to Thutade Lk	Sustut Peak 2,469 m
COLUMBIA MTS	CARIBOO	200 km	east of Wells Gray Park	Mt Sir Wilfrid Laurier 3,505 m
	MONASHEES	400 km	Mica Crk south to US border	Hallam Pk 3,219 m
	SELKIRKS	350 km	east of Arrow Lakes	Mt Sir Sandford 3,530 m
	PURCELLS	300 km	east of Kootenay Lk	Mt Farnham 3,457 m
ROCKY MTS	Border	-	southeast corner of BC	-
	Continental	640 km	central area	Mt ROBSON 3,954 m
	Hart	290 km	south from Peace R	Sentinel Pk 2,499 m
	Muskwa	420 km	between Peace & Liard rivers	Mt Churchill 2,819 m

M

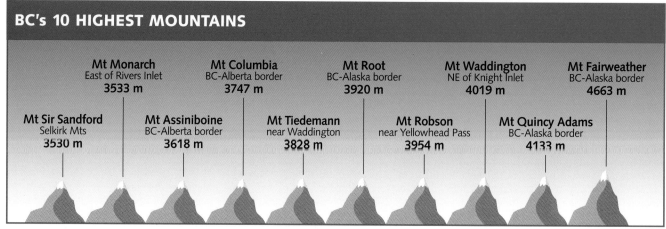

BC's 10 HIGHEST MOUNTAINS

Mt Monarch
East of Rivers Inlet
3533 m

Mt Columbia
BC-Alberta border
3747 m

Mt Root
BC-Alaska border
3920 m

Mt Waddington
NE of Knight Inlet
4019 m

Mt Fairweather
BC-Alaska border
4663 m

Mt Sir Sandford
Selkirk Mts
3530 m

Mt Assiniboine
BC-Alberta border
3618 m

Mt Tiedemann
near Waddington
3828 m

Mt Robson
near Yellowhead Pass
3954 m

Mt Quincy Adams
BC-Alaska border
4133 m

(1946). An American man, Henry Hall, and his Swiss guide Hans Fuhrer were also very active during these years, often in the company of the Mundays. During the 1950s climbers such as John Dudra, Fips Broda, Neal Carter, Paddy Sherman, Ralph Hutchinson, Elfrida Pigou, Leon Blumer, Adolph Bitterlich, John Owen and Werner Himmelsbach made the last major first ascents in the Coast Mts, including Mt Saugstad (1951), Mt Monmouth (1951), Mt Gilbert (1954), Mt Homathko (1955), Mt Essex (1955), Mt Howson (1958) and Mt Raleigh (1959). In 1958 the first Canadian ascent of Mt

John Clarke, mountaineer, traverses a narrow ridge during the first ascent of an unnamed summit at the head of the Toba Glacier in the Coast Mts. John Baldwin photo

Waddington was made by Adolph Bitterlich, Ulf Bitterlich, John Owen, Arno Meier and Christian Schiel.

The 1960s was the era of a Vancouver climber, Dick CULBERT. During the early years of the decade he made extended exploratory trips into the Coast Mts, often accompanied by Glenn Woodsworth, and unravelled the secrets of many ranges. In 1965 he published *A Climber's Guide to the Coastal Ranges of British Columbia*, which finally revealed the extent and complexity of the Coast Mts. In the latter part of his career Culbert made several difficult climbs with Paul Starr and Fred Douglas: the East Ridge of Devil's Thumb

(1970), Cats Ear's Spire (1972) and the east face of Mt Colonel Foster (1972). During the 1960s ROCK CLIMBING began on and around the STAWA-MUS CHIEF. In the 1970s and 1980s the leading figures in coast mountaineering were Don SERL and John CLARKE. Serl pioneered many difficult secondary routes throughout the Coast Mts on the great unclimbed faces and ridges. Clarke specialized in long expeditions to remote regions, often alone, travelling for up to a month at a time across icefields and along high ridges. Perhaps the finest achievement of the era was the complete traverse of the Mt Waddington Range in 1985 by Serl, Greg Foweraker and Peter CROFT. During the 1990s great climbs in the Coast Mts continued to be discovered by Canadians such as Michael Down and Jim HABERL and Americans such as Carl Diedrich and Jim Nelson. Although not well-known internationally, the Coast Mts of BC offer some of the great mountain climbing challenges in the world.   *Chic Scott*
Reading: Chic Scott, *Pushing the Limits: The Story of Canadian Mountaineering,* 2000.

MOUNTAINS are the most characteristic physiographic feature in BC. With their associated valleys and plateaus, mountains cover about 75% of the province. The main ranges are listed on the previous page. *See also* CORDILLERA.

MOYIE, pop 617, overlooks Moyie Lk in the E KOOTENAY, 31 km south of CRANBROOK. David THOMPSON passed by in 1808. From 1893 to 1929 it was the site of the St Eugene lead–SILVER mine discovered by a local KTUNAXA man, Pierre Ironhead, or Indian Pete, and developed by James Cronin. The CPR's Crowsnest line arrived in 1898 and the town had a population of more than 800, most of whom drifted away when the mine closed. The name derives from *mouille,* a French word meaning "wet" or "soggy."

MOYIE is the oldest surviving passenger sternwheeler steamboat in the world and the oldest surviving member of the CPR's large fleet of freshwater steam vessels in its BC LAKE & RIVER SERVICE. Launched at NELSON in 1898, the vessel first

SS Moyie, the oldest surviving passenger sternwheeler in the world, Kaslo, c 1898.
BC Archives A-00321

M

worked on a run linking that city with the south head of KOOTENAY LK at Kootenay Landing, the western terminus of the SOUTHERN RWY OF BC (the CROWSNEST PASS route). In 1906 the 49-m vessel was reassigned to general service and in 1931, after the cessation of most of the CPR's express runs, it maintained service to the more remote points at the north head of the lake. When the *Moyie* was retired in 1957 it was the last operating passenger sternwheeler in Canada and the western US. Berthed at KASLO, it is a National Historic Site, open to the public. *See also* PADDLEWHEEL STEAMBOATS.
Reading: Robert D. Turner, *S.S.* Moyie: *Memories of the Oldest Sternwheeler*, 1991.

MOZINO, José Mariano, scientist (b Sept 1757, Temascaltepec, Mexico; d May 1820, Barcelona, Spain). A member of a royal botanical expedition to New Spain, holding university degrees in theology, medicine, mathematics and botany, he was appointed as a scientist on BODEGA Y QUADRA's 1792 expedition to NOOTKA SOUND. During his summer on the coast he compiled *Noticias de Nutka*, an important early description of the Nootka area and its Mowachaht inhabitants (*see also* NUU-CHAH-NULTH). The book was not published until 1913 and in English translation in 1970. Back in Mexico he continued to participate in botanical expeditions throughout Central America. Later he returned to Spain, where he taught medicine and was director of the royal museum of natural history. *See also* SPANISH EXPLORATION.

MUCHALAT INLET is a long FJORD starting in NOOTKA SOUND at the north side of Hesquiat Peninsula on the west coast of VANCOUVER ISLAND. Hwy 28 runs from the village of GOLD RIVER, near the head of the inlet, through STRATHCONA PROVINCIAL PARK across the Island, to CAMPBELL RIVER. Various NUU-CHAH-NULTH First Nations originally occupied the inlet. Reduced by war and disease, some of the groups came together as the Muchalaht First Nation with a main village at the mouth of the Gold R. In the 1890s most of the Muchalaht moved to YUQUOT on Nootka Island and later merged with the Mowachaht First Nation there. The traditional village at Gold R later became a RESERVE. Outside interest in the inlet began in the 1890s when a SALMON CANNERY operated briefly. Active LOGGING began in the 1930s, and by 1950 the largest operator was the Tahsis Co, a partnership of the Gordon GIBSON family and East Asiatic Co. In 1955 the company moved its main camp to the mouth of the Gold R, where it was replaced by a pulp mill complex (*see* PULP AND PAPER) in 1965 and the new, "instant" town of Gold River sprang up. Because of pollution from the mill, the Mowachaht moved upriver to a new reserve in 1994. The mill complex was sold to Bowater and closed in 1999. The MV UCHUCK III runs regular boat service to camps along the inlet.

MUD BAY, a shallow, silty extension of BOUNDARY BAY 25 km southeast of VANCOUVER, was also the name of an adjacent AGRICULTURAL district in

SURREY first settled in the 1860s. William Woodward arrived in 1873; his farmhouse became a stagecoach stop on the SEMIAHMOO Trail and the site of an early post office in 1881. When the GREAT NORTHERN RWY built its line from PORT GUICHON through CLOVERDALE in 1903, the station here was named Alluvia after the rich soil. The area is still semirural. AS

MUD RIVER, 25 km southwest of PRINCE GEORGE, is a LOGGING and ranching (*see* CATTLE INDUSTRY) settlement on the Chilako R first settled in the early 1910s. It had a rural school, and a post office operated from 1922 to 1949. The Arbour family moved its SAWMILL here from MCBRIDE in the early 1950s. AS

MUIR, John, miner, Sooke pioneer (b 28 May 1799, Ayrshire, Scotland; d 4 Apr 1883, Sooke). He was hired by the HBC to oversee the development of COAL properties on VANCOUVER ISLAND. After arriving with his family at VICTORIA in May 1849, he travelled to FORT RUPERT where he began digging with 7 other miners. Relations between the miners and the local HBC post were poor and in July 1850, after an altercation, all the miners deserted, including Muir's son and nephew. He left the HBC's employ when his contract expired the following year, and he settled on a farm at SOOKE. He returned to supervise the HBC mine at NANAIMO from 1852 to 1854, then retired permanently to his farm, Woodside, where he established the island's first steam SAWMILL. In 1860 Muir and Co opened a lumberyard in Victoria. The company remained in business until 1892. Muir served in the colony's legislative council from 1862 to 1866 and his son Andrew was the island's first sheriff. *See also* COAL MINING, VANCOUVER ISLAND; COLONIAL GOVERNMENT.

MUNCHO LAKE, 149 km², lies beside the ALASKA HWY at the top end of the spectacular northern ROCKY MTS 175 km west of FORT NELSON. It is the centrepiece of Muncho Lake Provincial PARK (884.16 km²) and one of the best spots in BC for viewing Stone's sheep (*see* MOUNTAIN SHEEP). The water's distinctive emerald colouring is caused by copper dioxides on the lake bottom. A small community beside the lake caters to travellers. The name comes from the KASKA for "big lake." *See also* LAKES.

Muncho Lake Provincial Park. Ken Bowen photo

MUNDAY, Phyllis (James), mountaineer (b 24 Sept 1894, Ceylon; d 11 Apr 1990, Nanaimo). After arriving in VANCOUVER in 1901, she climbed her first mountain, GROUSE, when she was just 10 years old. As a member of the BC MOUNTAINEERING CLUB, she met and married **Don Munday**, a journalist and mountaineer (b 16 Mar 1890, Portage la Prairie, MB; d 12 June 1950, Vancouver). Together they scaled many of the province's highest peaks, some for the first time; more than anyone else they were responsible for early explorations in the COAST MTS. In 1925, while climbing on VANCOUVER ISLAND, they spotted a high mountain across GEORGIA STRAIT on the mainland, beginning a long love affair with what they called Mystery Mt, later named Mt WADDINGTON. They led several expeditions to Waddington between 1926 and 1934, and although they never reached the highest point they did climb the lower northwest summit in 1928. They climbed many other peaks in the region as well, thoroughly mapping and exploring the area. They also made many notable first ascents throughout the province, including Mt Silverthrone (1936), Mt Sir John Thompson (1925) and Mt Grenville (1941). In 1924 Phyllis became the first woman to climb Mt ROBSON (an honour shared with her rope-mate Annette Buck). She outlived her husband by 40 years and was greatly honoured during her career: she received honorary memberships in the Alpine Club of Canada and the American Alpine Club, and she was awarded the Centennial Medal and the Order of Canada (1973). Mt Munday near Mt Waddington was named in the couple's honour. *See also* MOUNTAINEERING.
Reading: W.A. Don Munday, *The Unknown Mountain*, 1948.

MUNDELL, Robert, Nobel prize-winning economist (b 1932, Kingston, ON). He won the 1999 Nobel Prize for economics for work he did in the 1960s on exchange rates and international trade. A prophet of globalization, he expressed ideas that influenced the development of common currency in Europe (the "euro") and underpinned the supply-side economic policies of US President Ronald Reagan in the 1980s. As a teenager Mundell moved to BC with his parents and graduated from Maple Ridge High School in 1949. After completing an undergraduate degree at UBC in 1953, he took graduate studies at the Univ of Washington and MIT. At age 29 he was chief international economist at the International Monetary Fund in Washington. The author of several books, he has taught mainly in the US, from 1974 at Columbia Univ in New York City.

MUNRO was a FRASER VALLEY farming district 10 km east of CHILLIWACK. Its original name—Camp Slough, after a temporary STO:LO Nation stopping place—was considered too mundane by early settlers as a post office designation. Gilbert Munro, who first took up land in the area in 1877, was commemorated instead. AS

MUNRO, Jack, labour leader (b 28 Mar 1931, Lethbridge, AB). Raised in poverty in rural

Jack Munro, former labour leader and retired chair of Forest Alliance of BC. FABC

Alberta, he dropped out of school in grade 10 and became an apprentice machinist with the CPR. In 1959, after being laid off in NELSON, he went to work in a SAWMILL. It was the beginning of a long involvement in the FOREST INDUSTRY. Munro joined the International Woodworkers of America (IWA) (*see* INDUSTRIAL, WOOD AND ALLIED WORKERS OF CANADA) and was soon a full-time official with the union. In 1966 he ran as an NDP candidate for election to the provincial legislature, but was unsuccessful. He moved to VANCOUVER in 1968 to join the executive of the IWA and continued his climb through the ranks until he won election as president in 1973. The IWA is BC's largest private-sector union, and Munro was one of the most important labour leaders not just in the province but nationally: in 1976 he became vice-president of the Canadian Labour Congress. Large in stature, loud and profane in manner, proud of his working-class roots, he is considered one of the last of the old-time labour leaders. He played a key role in the events of July–Nov 1983 when the SOLIDARITY protest movement against Bill BENNETT's government brought the province to the verge of a general strike. Munro believed that the members of his union, which was negotiating a contract at the time, would suffer if the protest escalated, and he intervened to work out a settlement with the government, the so-called Kelowna Accord. As a result he was accused by many Solidarity supporters of selling out the movement. In 1987 he played a leading role in the creation of an independent Canadian IWA. He left the union presidency in 1992 and served as chair of the FOREST ALLIANCE OF BC, an industry lobby group, until 1999. That year he also became a member of the Order of Canada. *See also* LABOUR MOVEMENT. *Reading:* Jack Munro with Jane O'Hara, *Union Jack*, 1988.

MUNRO, James Alexander, ornithologist (b 1883, Kildonan, MB; d 1959). Raised in Toronto, he moved to BC in 1910, settling on property at OKANAGAN LANDING, where he worked as an orchardist. He also began to work as a professional field collector, gathering bird specimens for museums throughout N America. He developed an impressive reputation as a collector and in 1920 was appointed Chief Federal Migratory Bird Officer for the western provinces, a post he held for 13 years. By the early 1930s Munro was concentrating his attention on the study of BC waterfowl. He actively promoted wildlife study in schools and became a recognized authority on BC birds, publishing 175 articles on the subject. He also co-authored *A Review of the Bird Fauna of British Columbia* (1947) with Ian MCTAGGART-COWAN. Munro's exhaustive research in southeastern BC led to the creation of the CRESTON Valley Wildlife Management Area.

Dianne Mackay

MURPHY, Cal, football coach, general manager (b 12 Mar 1932, Winnipeg). He moved to VANCOUVER at an early age and established himself as an outstanding athlete, particularly in FOOTBALL and BASEBALL. After coaching at Notre Dame and Vancouver College high schools he moved into the US college system as a football coach before returning to Vancouver in 1974 to become offensive-line coach for the BC LIONS. He became head coach in 1975 but was fired at the end of the 1976 season. He then won 6 straight Grey Cups as an assistant, the first one with Montreal and 5 in Edmonton. Hired as head coach of the Winnipeg Blue Bombers in 1983, he became general manager later that year. Over the next 14 years the Bombers made it to the Grey Cup 5 times, winning 3. Murphy had a heart transplant in 1992 but returned to coaching before the end of the season. Twice named the CFL's coach of the year, he became head coach of the Saskatchewan Roughriders in 1999.

Archie McDonald

MURRAY, David "Dave," skier (b 5 Sept 1953, Abbotsford; d 24 Oct 1990, Vancouver). Named to the Canadian national alpine ski team in 1971, he emerged as the unofficial leader of the "Crazy Canucks," the daredevil group of Canadian skiers that included Dave Irwin, Ken Read and Steve Podborski. After winning the 1978 Europa Cup in Italy and twice placing 2nd during the 1978–79 season, Murray was ranked as the 3rd-best downhill skier in the world. He was overall Canadian alpine champion in 1978 and BC athlete of the year in 1979. At the 1976 Olympic Games in Innsbruck he was 18th in the downhill and at the 1980 Lake Placid Olympics he placed 10th. He retired in 1982 and became director of SKIING at WHISTLER where he started the popular Masters racing series and chaired several World Cup events. He was named to the BC SPORTS HALL OF FAME 5 years before he died of cancer at age 37. Whistler's World Cup downhill course is named for him.

SW

MURRAY, Edward "Eddie," football player (b 29 Aug 1956, Halifax, NS). He is one of the most successful Canadians ever to play in the NFL. He and his mother moved to VICTORIA when he was 15. When he attended the BC LIONS training camp straight out of high school, coach Cal MURPHY recommended that he go to a US college to work on his game. At Tulane Univ in New Orleans Murray broke enough school records to impress the Detroit Lions, who made him their 7th-round draft pick in 1980. He became their top place-kicker and by 1986 his .749 field goal accuracy was second only to contemporary Nick Lowery in NFL history. He helped Detroit win the 1991 conference championship, was selected to the Pro Bowl all star team twice and was the Lions' all-time leading scorer by the time they released him in 1992. He joined the Dallas Cowboys and booted them to their 1994 Super Bowl win. After spending the 1997 season with the Minnesota Vikings, he retired as the longest-serving Canadian to play in the NFL.

SW

MURRAY, Margaret "Ma" (Lally), newspaper editor (b 3 Aug 1888, Windy Ridge, KS; d 25 Sept 1982, Lillooet). After leaving school at age 13 she worked as a hired girl in rural Kansas, then graduated from a business course and came north in 1912 to VANCOUVER, where she went to work for George Murray (b 1890, Woodstock, ON; d 19 Aug 1961, Vancouver), a newspaper

Ma Murray at Fort St John, 1952. Wilfred Doucette/Fort St John–North Peace Museum Archives

publisher. They married in 1913. While George worked at a variety of NEWSPAPERS around town, Margaret published *Country Life* magazine. In 1933 they moved to LILLOOET and founded the *Bridge River–Lillooet News*. During WWII they left that paper in the hands of their son and moved to FORT ST JOHN to establish a second weekly, the *Alaska Highway News*. Meanwhile George carried on an intermittently successful career as a politician, sitting as a LIBERAL MLA for Lillooet during 1933–41 and a federal MP for CARIBOO during 1949–53. The couple returned to Lillooet in 1959 and once again took over the daily operations of the *News*, where Margaret consolidated her reputation as an opinionated, no-nonsense journalist who never let the rules of correct syntax stand in the way of a good story. Her own daughter perhaps described her best as "part ham and part crusader." Margaret was made a member of the Order of Canada in 1971.

MURRAYVILLE, formerly Murray's Corners, is an AGRICULTURAL and residential suburb of LANGLEY municipality 25 km southeast of NEW WESTMINSTER. It was named after Paul Murray, who settled here in 1874 and built a hotel on the old YALE Road. A SAWMILL and store were established in the 1880s. The community was the commercial centre of Langley in the early 1900s and site of the municipal hall and high school before economic power shifted to LANGLEY PRAIRIE.   AS

MURRE is a medium-sized, short-necked seabird related to the auk. On land it struts about, much like a penguin. It has a dark head and back and a snow-white belly. Murres come to land only to breed in dense colonies on coastal cliffs and islets; otherwise they congregate on their marine feeding grounds, where they fish by diving. A murre beats its short wings rapidly in flight and beneath the water. There are 2 species. Common murres (*Uria aalge*) breed at several sites and are generally abundant along the coast. Thick-billed murres (*U. lomvia*), a more northerly species, are much rarer on the BC coast; they are known to breed only on TRIANGLE ISLAND.

MURRELET, a member of the auk family, is a small, chubby seabird. It flies low over the water with rapid wing beats; like other alcids it can also "fly" underwater in pursuit of fish, crustaceans and other food. Two species are present on the outer coast. The marbled murrelet (*Brachyramphus marmoratus*) is usually found close to shore or, very rarely, on coastal lakes. It is the only auk species to nest in trees, laying its single

The marbled murrelet, an endangered species. R. Wayne Campbell photo

egg on a mossy branch high in an old conifer of the coastal RAIN FOREST. The mottled brown and white plumage provides excellent cover, so much so that a murrelet nest was not discovered until 1990. Murrelets are considered threatened as more and more of their habitat is reduced by LOGGING. Ancient murrelets (*Synthliboramphus antiquus*) nest in ground burrows on forested islands, mainly the QUEEN CHARLOTTE ISLANDS,

where since about 1960 rats and RACCOONS have drastically reduced the population.

MUSEUM OF ANTHROPOLOGY is located near the cliff edge at the tip of Point Grey on the UBC grounds. Established in 1947 in the basement of the Main Library at UBC, it was directed

Museum of Anthropology at UBC, designed by Arthur Erickson. Len Mackave photo

for many years by Harry and Audrey HAWTHORN. It moved to its present location in 1976 when Prof Michael Ames became director. The building was designed by Arthur ERICKSON and inspired by the post-and-beam ARCHITECTURE of the northwest coast FIRST NATIONS. Displays focus on the First Nations people of BC and include large sculptures, TOTEM POLES, a variety of utensils and ceremonial items. The main doors, carved from red CEDAR, were made by artists at 'KSAN. Another highlight is a monumental yellow cedar sculpture by Bill REID, *The Raven and the First Men*, presented by Walter and Marianne KOERNER in 1980. The Koerner Ceramics Gallery, also donated by the Koerners, opened in 1990. Ruth Phillips became the third director in 1997.

MUSGRAVE, or Musgrave's Landing, 38 km north of VICTORIA on the southwest coast of SALTSPRING ISLAND in the GULF ISLANDS, was settled in 1874 by the 4 Pimsbury brothers, who ran a large sheep ranch and built a wharf. Edward Musgrave bought the property in 1885. Other homesteaders also raised sheep. The landing was not connected to the rest of the island by road until 1926. There was a LOGGING camp of JAPANESE workers nearby in the 1930s and adventurers Miles and Beryl SMEETON farmed here from 1946 to 1955.   AS

MUSGRAVE, Anthony, governor of BC from 1869 to 1871 (b 31 Aug 1828, St John's, Antigua; d 9 Oct 1888, Brisbane, Australia). He had an English education and in 1854 he was appointed colonial secretary in Antigua, where his family had deep roots. It was the first of a series of appointments in Britain's Caribbean possessions.

In 1864 Musgrave became governor of Newfoundland, where he argued—unsuccessfully it turned out—for union with the mainland colonies. He succeeded Frederick SEYMOUR as governor of BC and once again made union with Canada his top priority. He threw the prestige and influence of his office behind the CONFEDER-

Anthony Musgrave, governor of the colony of BC 1869–71. UBC BC742

ATION scheme, persuading many of its opponents to change their minds and lobbying for a transcontinental rail connection to win over the rest. BC's entry into Confederation in 1871 was in large part a result of his efforts. Despite this diplomatic success he turned down the chance to become the province's first LT GOV and departed in 1871. He was later knighted and went on to serve as governor in Africa, Jamaica and Australia. *See also* COLONIAL GOVERNMENT.

MUSGRAVE, Susan, writer (b 12 Mar 1951, Santa Cruz, CA). She was raised on VANCOUVER ISLAND and at age 19 published her first book of poetry, *Songs of the Sea-Witch* (1970). She has since published 13 volumes of poetry, several books for children and 2 novels, *The Charcoal*

Susan Musgrave, writer. Anne Bayin photo

Burners (1980) and *The Dancing Chicken* (1987). In 1991 she won the bp Nichol Chapbook Award for *In the Small Hours of the Rain* and in 1996 the CBC national literary competition for poetry. Her NEWSPAPER columns have also been collected in book form. Musgrave's flamboyant personality and colourful private life have contributed to her prominence in the West Coast literary community. She has taught creative writing at several universities and colleges and served as chair of the Writers' Union of Canada (1997–98). Her much-publicized 1987 prison marriage to Stephen Reid, a writer and convicted bank robber, made headlines again in 1999, when Reid was convicted of attempted murder and other charges related to a failed bank holdup.

MUSHROOMS are the fruiting bodies of fungi, primitive plants that reproduce by spores and obtain nutrients from a root-like mycelium (a threadlike vegetative part of the plant). Many mushrooms have the familiar gills and rounded top, but they come in a wide array of shapes and colours and in both edible and poisonous varieties.

Cultivated mushrooms are BC's most valuable vegetable cash crop and the second most valuable edible product after apples. The annual farm gate value of production is $47,250,000. Mushrooms are grown commercially mainly in the Lower Mainland but also in KELOWNA, PRINCE GEORGE and on VANCOUVER ISLAND. The most common variety are button mushrooms (*Agaricus bisporus*), though shiitake, oyster and wild pine varieties are also produced. The total annual crop is 15 million kg, 25% of all the mushrooms grown in Canada. The average British Columbian consumes about 3 kg of mushrooms a year, more than in any other province. Mushrooms are grown commercially in beds of specially prepared compost in insulated houses under carefully controlled conditions.

They are either sold fresh or used to manufacture a variety of food products. BC mushrooms are exported to Japan, the US and the rest of Canada. By far the largest producer is Money's Mushrooms, which markets 35 million pounds a year. Money's, the largest mushroom producer in Canada, traces its origins to a CO-OPERATIVE of FRASER VALLEY growers formed in 1931. In the 1950s the co-operative began branding its product under the name Money's, after W.T. Money, a founding member. In 1993 the member grower co-operative gave way to a corporate structure, Money's Mushrooms Ltd. The company has facilities in several provinces and is expanding internationally; in 1998 it had revenues of $109.8 million.

BC provides an ideal habitat for many species of wild mushrooms, some of which are edible. The yellow morel (*Morchella esculenta*), with distinctive ribs on its cap, is collected in the

Chanterelle mushrooms, a BC delicacy.
Peter Battistoni/Vancouver Sun

spring. Other edible species are found in the autumn, including the king boletus (*Boletus edulis*), with its spongy cap resembling the top of a muffin; the fan-shaped oyster mushroom (*Pleurotus ostreatus*), white or yellow to brown in colour, which grows on logs and dead trees; the distinctive puffball (*Lycoperdon* sp.) with a leathery pouch containing firm, white flesh; and the coral mushroom (*Hericium* sp.), easily identified because of its coral-like shape. Two other wild species, the pine mushroom (*Tricholoma magnivelare*) and the golden chanterelle (*Cantharellus cibarius*), form the basis of a multimillion-dollar gathering operation for sale overseas. However, many species of wild mushrooms in BC are poisonous—for example, the deadly red-capped fly agaric (*Amanita muscaria*)—and caution is advised.

MUSIC FESTIVALS date back to 1913 in BC when A.E. Waghorne organized the first competitive festival in N VANCOUVER, consisting entirely of choral music. The BC (VANCOUVER) Musical Festival was founded in 1923 with the support of the Knights of Pythias and continued until 1960, when it was renamed the Vancouver Kiwanis Festival. Initially adjudicators were hired from Britain. By 1930 the festival had grown to 11,000 participants and 130 school choirs. Elsewhere in the province, the OKANAGAN VALLEY Festival began holding competitions in KELOWNA in 1926, followed a year later by the VICTORIA Music Festival, then by the Upper Island Music Festival at NANAIMO (1927), the West KOOTENAY Music Festival (1928) and the YALE–CARIBOO Music Festival in KAMLOOPS (1930). In 1929 the BC Federation of Music Festivals was formed to coordinate local festivals.

For many years the Kiwanis Festival was a competitive one. Burton Kurth, supervisor of music from 1939 to 1955, was largely responsible for the growth of choral singing in Vancouver schools. Excellent choirs from John Oliver High School, led by Ifor Roberts, Sherwood Robson and Teo Repel, dominated the festival to 1980. Repel's choirs won 2 national awards and second place at the 1970 World Choir Festival in Wales. The Kiwanis Festival has since been divided into 3 parts—concert band, choral and individual— and the band and choral sections are adjudicated for educational purposes only. In the early years bands were an important part of community musical life, though not in schools. In 1938 Fred Turner became the first certified band teacher in BC and was instrumental in developing band programs in NEW WESTMINSTER and BURNABY and later as supervisor of music in Vancouver schools. Gar McKinley initiated many music programs in Okanagan schools from 1939 to 1974. Beginning with conductors such as Arthur Delamont (*see* KITSILANO BOYS BAND) and Joseph and Gordon Olsen, bands were started in several schools around Vancouver. Other prominent band leaders whose bands have won national awards over the years include Art and

Ron Smith in N Vancouver, A.N. McMurdo in Kamloops, C.H. Rowles in Victoria and Peter Stigings in Vancouver. The ABBOTSFORD International Music Festival boasts the largest participation by out-of-province groups (*see also* KATHAUMIXW).

The BC Music Festival Assoc, an umbrella organization formed in 1964 to coordinate the many festivals in the province, became the BC Assoc of Performing Arts Festivals in 1982 and oversees 31 regional organizations, each of which hosts an annual performing arts festival. Approximately 80,000 students participate in these festivals. Competitors also take part in the provincial and national finals of the Canadian Federation of Music Festivals in Toronto. The Pacific Coast Music Festival Assoc is another umbrella organization of 16 independent festivals, mostly for large ensembles. Several prominent BC musicians have come up through the ranks of the music festivals, including David FOSTER, Ben HEPPNER and the Vancouver gospel singer Connie Scott.

Several music festivals are operated by non-profit societies involving both amateur and professional musicians, including the VANCOUVER FOLK MUSIC FESTIVAL, the Vancouver Jazz Festival, Music West and various country music, instrumental and ethnic music festivals, including Dixieland JAZZ festivals at CHILLIWACK, Victoria and PENTICTON. *Ken Mcleod*
Reading: Dale McIntosh, *History of Music in British Columbia: 1850–1950*, 1989.

MUSKWA RIVER rises in the Muskwa Ranges of the northern ROCKY MTS just east of the ROCKY MT TRENCH. Feeding off the vast Lloyd George Icefield in KWADACHA PROVINCIAL PARK, the Muskwa flows east and north to merge with the PROPHET R before joining the Fort Nelson R, a tributary of the LIARD R. Its watershed, traditional territory of the SEKANI and DENE-THAH (Slavey) First Nations, is a largely roadless unlogged wilderness. Much of the Muskwa watershed was protected in 1997 in the Northern Rockies Protected Area (6,450 km²), and is considered the heart of the greater Muskwa-Kechika Management Area. The watershed is rich with wildlife. Among its large mammals are black BEARS, grizzly BEARS, MOUNTAIN SHEEP, MOUNTAIN GOATS, MOOSE, ELK, woodland CARIBOU, LYNX, WOLVES and WOLVERINES. The word *Muskwa*—Cree for "black bear"—is also associated with the town of FORT NELSON and was a post office name there in the 1940s and 1950s. *See also* RIVERS. AS

MUSQUEAM (X'muzk'i'um) are a Coast SALISHAN FIRST NATIONS group (*see* HALKOMELEM) who have lived on the north shore of the FRASER R near its mouth for at least 3,000 years. The site of their main village is now a reserve in VANCOUVER. The Musqueam took advantage of the rich fishery resources of the Fraser and also used other resource sites at least seasonally in BURRARD INLET, throughout the Fraser Delta, up the river and on the GULF ISLANDS. It was the Musqueam who met the earliest coastal explorers, including Dionisio ALCALA-GALIANO, George VANCOUVER

and Simon FRASER. The Musqueam were not involved in the FUR TRADE for SEA OTTER pelts, but from the 1870s they were involved in SALMON CANNING and LOGGING. Their numbers were seriously depleted by early SMALLPOX epidemics, which periodically swept up the coast beginning in the 1780s. Like other First Nations groups they experienced a rebound in population during the 20th century; there were 900 registered members of the band in 1998.

Although they were traditionally fishers, the Musqueam became interested in land development in the 1940s, when they leased large tracts of their land to CHINESE farmers. Subsequently they arranged to lease some of their holdings along the Fraser R to timber companies in need of a place to store log booms. Many members of the community began working as stevedores as a result of these arrangements. Using the federal government as an agent, the band leased land to a golf club in 1957 and developed upscale housing subdivisions during the 1960s. These arrangements have embroiled the band in contentious legal squabbles with tenants and the federal government but the courts have upheld the Musqueams' right to manage their lands.

MUSSALLEM, Helen Kathleen, nursing educator (b Prince Rupert). She began her career as a nurse at VANCOUVER General Hospital and during WWII served overseas in the Royal Canadian Army Medical Corps. After the war she attended Columbia Univ in New York, then taught at the VGH School of NURSING from 1947 to 1957. She was chosen by the Canadian Nurses' Assoc to evaluate all schools of nursing in Canada from 1957 to 1960. She joined the association and served as its executive director from 1963 to 1981. Mussallem advised many international health agencies, including the World Health Organization, the Red Cross and the Canadian International Development Agency, and was

Helen Mussallem, internationally renowned nursing educator. UBC 1.1/12826

president of the Victorian Order of Nurses for Canada from 1989 to 1992. The author of several important nursing textbooks, she received many awards, including the Order of Canada (1969) and the Florence Nightingale Medal (1981), the highest award of the International Red Cross.

MUSSEL is a marine MOLLUSC belonging to the class Bivalvia. Its soft body is enclosed in a hinged shell with 2 halves (valves). Several species occur in BC waters. The most common species live in dense colonies attached to rocks, pilings or other hard surfaces; others live in the substrate. The shell is anchored by a bundle of fine threads known as the byssus, made from the mucus of a special gland. Most familiar is the Pacific blue (bay) mussel (*Mytilus trossulus*), which has a dark blue to black shell and grows to 11 cm. The blue mussel is common in pro-

A bed of California mussels, the largest mussel species in BC. Rick Harbo photo

tected waters in the intertidal zone, along the beach or clinging to wharfs and piers. Found worldwide, blue mussels once were thought to be one species but are now considered to be several species or subspecies. The thicker-shelled California mussel (*M. californianus*) is the largest mussel species found in BC. It grows to 25 cm and is generally found in extensive beds on surf-exposed rocks, wharfs and seamounts, often in association with the goose BARNACLE.

FIRST NATIONS people ate mussels and used the sharp-edged shells for tools and weapons. Attempts to culture the Pacific blue mussel in BC have been thwarted by heavy predation by the diving DUCK, by market competition from growers on the east coast and in New Zealand, and by a phenomenon known as summer mortality, which claims up to 90% of a crop just as it approaches market size. Biologists speculate that warm summer water temperatures may be the cause of summer mortality. Like other filter feeders, mussels can become toxic to humans through HARMFUL ALGAL BLOOMS. They are used as an indicator species in coastal testing because they accumulate toxins more quickly than other bivalves. *Carol Swann*

MUSSON, Frank W., architect (b 1932, London, England). A graduate of the Architectural Assoc in London, he moved to

Canada in 1955. He first worked for the VANCOUVER firm of Semmons & Simpson, was staff architect for Dominion Construction from 1960 to 1965, then entered private practice in a firm that by 1986 had become the Musson Cattell Mackey Partnership. His better-known buildings in Vancouver include the Bentall Centre (*see* BENTALL CORP), the BC HYDRO Building on Dunsmuir St, Canada Place and the Pan Pacific Hotel. In VICTORIA the firm was responsible for the Hillside Shopping Centre and the Royal Bank and Centra Gas buildings. The Daon Building in downtown Vancouver won a Gov Gen's Medal in 1982.   *Martin Segger*

MYERS, Samuel H., miner, labour activist (b 1838, Ireland; d 3 May 1887, Nanaimo). Myers came to BC in 1858 from his native Ireland to join the Fraser R GOLD RUSH. He made his living at various jobs and MINING claims around the Interior before settling in NANAIMO in the mid-1870s to work in the COAL mines (*see* COAL MINING, VANCOUVER ISLAND). At the end of 1883 he organized the first assembly of the radical KNIGHTS OF LABOR in BC. By mid-1887 the Knights had 6 local assemblies in the province. But Myers, the "father" of the Knights of Labor in BC, had been killed earlier that year in a mine explosion.

MYNCASTER, 40 km west of GRAND FORKS near the US boundary, was a border settlement and station on the GREAT NORTHERN RWY from 1907 to the early 1930s, when the line was abandoned.

It was named for Thomas and William McMynn, early settlers who ran the nearby Harpur Ranch, which dates from 1862.   *AS*

MYRTLE POINT overlooks Malaspina Strait just south of POWELL RIVER, about 115 km northwest of VANCOUVER. Nils Frolander operated a 19th-century store and post office here named Froek. BLOEDEL, STEWART & WELCH had a large RAILWAY LOGGING show here from 1911 until the mid-1920s and went on to become one of BC's largest forest companies (*see also* FOREST INDUSTRY). Today the area is mostly residential; it is also the site of a golf course and regional park.

AS

with the disruption of the war most people left the district.   AS

NAIKOON PROVINCIAL PARK, 726.4 km², is a low-lying coastal wilderness area in the northeast corner of Graham Island, the largest of the QUEEN CHARLOTTE ISLANDS. It is known particularly for its sand dunes and long stretches of windswept beach. The name comes from a HAIDA word meaning "long-nose," a reference to Rose Spit, an ECOLOGICAL RESERVE and one of the park's dominant features. Established in 1973, the park has been occupied by the Haida for at least 8,000 years. *See also* PARKS, PROVINCIAL.

Sandy beaches at Naikoon Provincial Park.
Duane Sept photo

NAKIMU CAVES are located in the Cougar Valley in GLACIER NATIONAL PARK, just west of ROGERS PASS. They are Canada's third largest cave system. The name derives from an aboriginal word describing the sound of water flowing underground. Discovered in 1904 by Charles Deutschmann, a prospector, they became a popular attraction for travellers on the CPR and guests at nearby GLACIER HOUSE. Rerouting of the rail line resulted in a decline in TOURISM and the government closed the caves in 1935. After extensive study they were reopened to the public in 1995. *See also* KARST FORMATIONS.

NADEN HARBOUR, an inlet on the north coast of Graham Island in the QUEEN CHARLOTTE ISLANDS, was the site of a WHALING station 34 km west of MASSET. Built in 1911 by Canadian North Pacific Fisheries, it was acquired by Consolidated Whaling of Toronto in 1918 and operated continuously until 1942, with 3 ships pursuing mostly finback and sperm WHALES. The name is a HAIDA word that refers to the harbour's numerous aboriginal settlements.   AS

NADINA RIVER, 58 km southwest of BURNS LAKE at the west end of FRANÇOIS LK, was a WET'SUWET'EN community. The first white settler, Mike Gallagher, came in about 1910. After the road arrived in 1930, a lively village developed with a store, hotel, school, hall and wharf. Residents trapped, ranched (*see* CATTLE INDUSTRY), prospected and hacked railway ties, but most drifted away in the 1940s. The name is a DAKELH (Carrier) word meaning "log thrown across a creek to serve as a bridge." The Nadina R itself flows into François Lk from Nadina Lk to the west. It is a productive SALMON river and its valley supports a significant population of MOOSE.   AS

NAHATLATCH RIVER flows 20 km west via a chain of lakes into the FRASER R north of BOSTON BAR. It lies in the territory of the NLAKA'PAMUX (Thompson) First Nation, who called it the "salmon river" because of the plentiful runs of SALMON. It is a swiftly flowing river with rapids and a narrow canyon that make it one of the most popular in the province for whitewater river rafting. *See also* RIVERS.

NAHMINT BAY is located on the west side of ALBERNI INLET 25 km south of PORT ALBERNI. It is named for a group of NUU-CHAH-NULTH (Nootka) who lived in the area. Frank Gerrard, a prospector, settled in the bay with his family in 1894, at which time the area's COPPER deposits

were attracting interest. MINING never did develop, but between the world wars an extensive RAILWAY LOGGING operation was centred in the bay. In the 1950s Gus Beurling, developer of the Beurling fishing plug, built one of the first successful sport FISHING lodges on the west coast of VANCOUVER ISLAND, catering to visitors from around the world. Nahmint Lodge operated until 1974; that year it was towed to a new location in BARKLEY SOUND.

NAHUN, on the west side of OKANAGAN LK 22 km north of KELOWNA, was named by Howard B. Kennard, first postmaster (1905) after an OKANAGAN First Nation legend explaining the origin of a large rock near the wharf. The FUR BRIGADES of the HBC knew it as the Golden Gate, because they could easily confine their horses here when they camped. The area was settled prior to WWI but

Nakimu Caves, Glacier National Park, c 1931.
Revelstoke Museum & Archives P970

NAKUSP, village, pop 1,736, overlooks the east side of Upper ARROW LK in the SELKIRK MTS of southeastern BC, midway between REVELSTOKE and CASTLEGAR. The name comes from an aboriginal word indicating that the lakeshore site gave CANOES shelter from the wind. The community was established in 1893 as the western terminus of the Nakusp & Slocan Rwy that built into the Slocan Valley, offering Nakusp the prospect of becoming a major shipping and smelting centre. This did not occur since shipments of Slocan ore were diverted south via KOOTENAY LK and SLOCAN LK to SMELTERS at NELSON and TRAIL. The CPR maintained a SHIPBUILDING operation at Nakusp for its Arrow Lks fleet, which after 1915 continued to offer localized service until 1954. LOGGING and fruit growing have dominated the economy since early in the century; later MINING and TOURISM injected new economic vigour. The village, incorporated in 1964, owns the nearby Nakusp HOT SPRINGS.

NAKWAKTO RAPIDS form the 300-m-wide entrance to SEYMOUR and BELIZE inlets on the mainland coast, opposite the north end of VANCOUVER ISLAND. The tidal rapids through the narrows reach 30 km/h, making it the fastest tidal channel on the coast. It is named for the local KWAKWAKA'WAKW First Nation, who occupied the area before moving to PORT HARDY in 1962.

NAMU is a FISHING community on the Central Coast, near the mouth of Burke Channel. There is evidence the site has been used by aboriginal people for at least 11,000 years, making it the oldest recorded place of human habitation on the coast and the longest continuously occupied site in Canada (*see also* ARCHAEOLOGY). Robert Draney built a cannery in 1893 and it remained in operation, under varied ownership, until 1969. Since 1991 Namu has been a privately owned supply centre for commercial fishing and pleasure boats. Namu is a HEILTSUK word meaning "place of high winds."

Salmon seiners returning to Namu, c 1940.
NAC PA145357

NANAIMO overlooks a fine harbour on the east coast of VANCOUVER ISLAND, 110 km north of VICTORIA. The name derives from SNUNEYMUXW, the name of the Island HALKOMELEM people

who still inhabit the area. The HBC built a fortified post in 1849 after COAL was discovered here. When the company began MINING the coal in 1852, it called the settlement Colvile Town, after the company governor, Andrew Colvile; by 1860, however, it was known as Nanaimo. The Bastion, dating from 1853, is the oldest preserved HBC fort in Canada. The Vancouver Coal Mining and Land Co bought the HBC mine in 1862 and operations were expanded; in 1886 the construction of the ESQUIMALT & NANAIMO RWY gave the industry a further boost (*see* COAL MINING, VANCOUVER ISLAND). Coal sustained the city—production peaked at 1 million tonnes in 1923—until WWII, when the main seams played out (the last mines closed in the 1950s). Blessed with good port facilities and proximity to rich timber resources, the city was able to make the transition to a diversified regional business and manufacturing centre. FOREST PRODUCTS are shipped from Duke Point Industrial Park. Nanaimo became the island's busiest export centre and in 1999 was the third-fastest growing community in BC. Ferries from nearby Departure Bay link the island to the mainland at HORSESHOE BAY and TSAWWASSEN, and the CPR also maintains a ferry dock. The city's industrial downtown waterfront was cleaned up during the 1990s and made accessible to pedestrians. TOURISM has become vital to the Nanaimo economy; each July participants in a famed bathtub race cross GEORGIA STRAIT to Vancouver's ENGLISH BAY. NEWCASTLE ISLAND, a provincial PARK reachable only by boat, lies opposite the city; Petroglyph Park, with its prehistoric sandstone carvings (*see* ROCK ART), is just to the south. The Nanaimo District Museum has exhibits on the region's history and culture.

Hudson's Bay Co Bastion, Nanaimo.
Reimut Lieder/Image Makers

Malaspina University College (*see* COMMUNITY COLLEGES) sprawls across the lower slopes of Mt Benson.
Population: 70,130
Rank in BC: 15th
Population increase since 1981: 49%
Date of incorporation: city 24 Dec 1874
Land area: 125.61 km²
Location: Nanaimo Regional District
Economic base: pulp, lumber, fishing, distribution centre

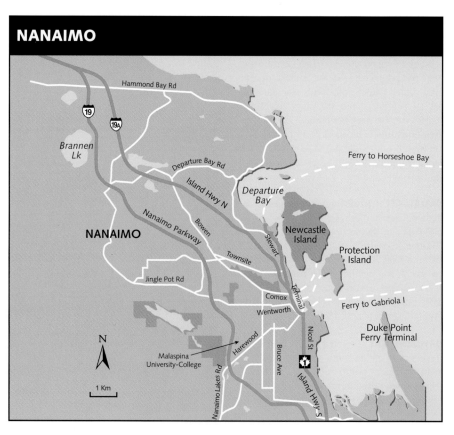

NANAIMO

NANAIMO BARS are the creamy, chocolatey, 3-layer squares that have delighted dessert lovers around the world since at least the 1940s. While the popularity of this unique BC confection is undisputed, its origins are less certain. The most common legend says that an unknown post-WWII homemaker entered her chocolate square recipe in a contest, naming it after her hometown. A more obscure legend credits British families who sent the bars to their COAL miner relatives in NANAIMO, assuming they needed cheering up. The owner of the Scotch Bakery, "Home of the World Famous Nanaimo Bar," knows only that she found the recipe in a church cookbook. And Joyce Hardcastle, winner of the Ultimate Nanaimo Bar Recipe Contest held in 1986 by Mayor Graeme Roberts, knows that the most important thing about Nanaimo bars is not where they came from but how delicious they taste.   *Research by Lynne Bowen*

NANAIMO COMMONWEALTH HOLDING SOCIETY was a non-profit organization at the centre of a political scandal that surfaced in 1992. At that time the *VANCOUVER SUN* began publishing stories alleging that the society, founded in the 1950s to raise money for socialist causes, was taking funds raised for charities and using them to support the provincial NDP. In 1994 the society and 3 related organizations, all with links to the NDP, were convicted of gambling-related offences but "Bingogate," as it came to be called, continued to bedevil the NDP. Mike HARCOURT stepped down as PREMIER in 1996, hoping to lay the matter to rest (he was not implicated personally in the scandal), but the controversy continued to simmer. Finally in May 1998 police investigations led to fraud charges against 4 NDP officials, including long-time party stalwart David STUPICH. In 1999 Stupich pleaded guilty to charges of fraud and illegally operating a lottery scheme; charges against his common-law wife, daughter and another NDP official were all stayed.

NANAIMO First Nation; *see* SNUNEYMUXW.

NANOOSE BAY lies 15 km north of NANAIMO on the east coast of VANCOUVER ISLAND. This well-protected bay is the site of the Canadian Forces Maritime Experimental and Test Ranges (CFMETR), which since 1965 has been used by both Canada and the US Navy as a testing ground for anti-submarine warfare technology. Although controversial and much-protested, Canada's agreement with the US permitting US nuclear-capable submarines to use the base has been renewed every decade since its inception. Actual testing takes place at 4 underwater ranges offshore, known as Whiskey Golf. In 1999, the federal government expropriated the underwater test ranges after negotiations to renew its lease with the provincial government broke down. The province wanted guarantees that no nuclear weapons would be aboard US ships using the test site. The bay, rich in OYSTERS, eelgrass beds and HERRING spawn, is overlooked by Nanoose Hill. The Nanoose First Nation, the Snaw-naw-as,

have a RESERVE opposite the naval docks. White settlement began in the area in the 1880s and several communities formed: Red Gap, site of a major SAWMILL from 1912 to 1942; Brynmarl; and at the head of the harbour, Nanoose Bay itself. The highway passes the Arlington Hotel, originally an inn on the Nanaimo–Alberni wagon road. A large explosives plant also operated on the bay from 1912 to 1925.

NARAMATA, pop 1,998, occupies benchland overlooking the east shore of OKANAGAN LK 16 km north of PENTICTON. It was founded in 1907,

the third of 3 townsites developed by John Moore ROBINSON, the other 2 being PEACHLAND and SUMMERLAND. In addition to the townsite he established orchard properties (*see* TREE FRUITS). The name is said to originate with a seance at which Robinson heard the spirit of an aboriginal chief intone the name of his wife, Nar-ra-mat-tah. The movie *My American Cousin* was filmed here and in Penticton.

NARCOSLI CREEK, 26 km south of QUESNEL in the CHILCOTIN, is on the west side of the FRASER R. An isolated community hall and school (1933) served as the heart of a remote ranching and farming district (*see* CATTLE INDUSTRY; AGRICULTURE). A post office operated from 1937 to 1956.   *AS*

NARDWUAR THE HUMAN SERVIETTE, radio host, musician, journalist (b 5 July 1968, N Vancouver). At UBC in 1986 he joined the campus radio station, and the following year he started his own show, interviewing a wide variety of celebrity subjects, including *Leave it to Beaver*'s Jerry Mathers, former Prime Minister Pierre Trudeau, the punk icon Iggy Pop and former US Vice President Dan Quayle. He became known for either perplexing or annoying his subjects

with uniquely bizarre questions: once he asked Mikhail Gorbachev, "Of all the political leaders you have encountered, who has the largest pants?" It was Nardwuar who asked the question about the RCMP pepper-spraying incident at the 1998 ASIA PACIFIC ECONOMIC COOPERATION (APEC) summit in VANCOUVER that prompted Prime Minister Jean Chretien to make his controversial reply, "For me—pepper—I put it on my plate." Nardwuar also became one of Vancouver's most popular live performers/singers fronting 2 bands, the Evaporators and Thee Goblins, which released albums and merchandise through his label Nardwuar Records.   *SW*

A view of Okanagan Lk across Naramata.
Bernie Pawlik/Image Makers

NARVAEZ, José Maria, Spanish marine pilot (b 1768, Cádiz, Spain; d 1840, Guadalajara, Mexico). He was the first European to explore GEORGIA STRAIT. Commanding the *Santa Saturnina* in 1791, he navigated as far as present-day COMOX and named TEXADA ISLAND. His chart, which includes his surveys of CLAYOQUOT and BARKLEY sounds and is one of the most important early charts of the BC coast, is in the Museo Naval in Madrid. He had earlier (1788) sailed to Alaska with Estéban José MARTINEZ. Exploring ESPERANZA INLET in the captured NORTH WEST AMERICA, he was present in Friendly Cove during the NOOTKA SOUND CONTROVERSY. *See also* SPANISH EXPLORATION.   *Robin Inglis*

NASH, Steve, basketball player (b 7 Feb 1974, Johannesburg, S Africa). The most successful BASKETBALL player to come out of BC, he led ST MICHAEL'S UNIV SCHOOL in VICTORIA to the 1992 BC boys' AAA basketball championship where he won MVP honours. Playing at the Univ of Santa Clara in California he became its all-time leader in assists while leading the team to 3 appearances in the NCAA tournament. In 1996 he was picked by the Phoenix Suns 15th overall in the NBA draft, the highest position for a Canadian before the turn of the century. After 2 seasons with the Suns he was traded to the Dallas Mavericks for the 1999 season. He first played for the Canadian national team in 1993,

Steve Nash, NBA star, signing autographs in Halifax, 1997. Basketball Canada

and in 1999 he led the team to an unexpected berth to the 2000 Olympics. *Patrick Francis*

NASHTON, between KOOTENAY and SLOCAN lakes 5 km west of KASLO, became prominent in the 1890s as a service centre for the nearby Mexico, Montezuma and Cork mines. A station on the KASLO & SLOCAN RWY, it was renamed Zwicky after the manager of the Cork mine when the CPR took over the line and rebuilt it in 1912. The post office continued under the name Nashton; when it closed in 1940 only 34 residents remained. A few dilapidated log buildings still marked the site in 1999. *AS*

NASOOKIN, 1,682 gross tonnes, was the most commodious of the PADDLEWHEEL STEAMBOATS to operate north of the 45th parallel and west of the ROCKY MTS. Built of steel at NELSON by the CPR, it was launched in 1913 and worked on the "Crow run" between Nelson and Kootenay Landing, the western terminus of the CPR route through the CROWSNEST PASS. To expedite shipments of ZINC concentrate from KIMBERLEY to the SMELTER at TRAIL, the CPR built a rail link along the southwest shore of KOOTENAY LK in 1930 and terminated the sternwheeler and railcar barge runs on the former lake link. From 1931 to 1947 the *Nasookin* worked as a car ferry across the lake from GRAY CREEK to Fraser's Landing. It was the only sternwheeler in the world to carry a Greyhound bus balanced across its bow every day. After being replaced by a more modern vessel, the *Nasookin* was tied up at Nelson and used to train naval cadets; in 1953 a sudden drop in the lake level caused its hull to ground and break up.

NASS CAMP, 90 km north of TERRACE near the NASS R, was a LOGGING depot from the 1970s to the mid-1980s, when it became a small service centre offering meals and accommodation to local fishers, hunters and MUSHROOM gatherers. *AS*

NASS HARBOUR was an early cannery on Nass Bay at the mouth of the NASS R, 75 km northeast of PRINCE RUPERT. It was often referred to as McLellan's Cannery after James A. McLellan, who built it in 1887 and employed NISGA'A and CHINESE workers. The plant closed in 1928. The post office here, opened in 1890 and spelled Naas Harbour, was the earliest in the region. *AS*

NASS RIVER, 380 km, rises in the Skeena Mts on the south side of the SPATSIZI PLATEAU and flows through the COAST MTS to salt water at PORTLAND INLET, 80 km north of PRINCE RUPERT. The river drains a 21,100 km² watershed. The name derives from a TLINGIT word meaning "food depot," though the NISGA'A know it as Lisims. The lower watershed is the traditional territory of the Nisga'a, about 1,880 of whom inhabit 4 riverside communities: KINCOLITH (Gingolx), New Aiyansh (GITLAKDAMIKS), CANYON CITY (Gitwinksihlkw) and GREENVILLE

Nass R from the Stewart–Cassiar Highway.
Bernie Pawlik/Image Makers

(Laxqalts'ap). About 150 non-aboriginals inhabit the valley, mainly at NASS CAMP. Capt George VANCOUVER was the first European explorer to reach the mouth of the river in 1793. The HBC established Fort Nass here in 1831, and after the post was relocated farther south as FORT SIMPSON 3 years later, it remained a FUR TRADING centre for the Nisga'a. Each spring, the Nass welcomes a plentiful run of EULACHON that the Nisga'a and other FIRST NATIONS have harvested for centuries. During the eulachon run, the river was transformed into the most important First Nations trading entrepôt on the coast. SALMON CANNERIES operated near the mouth of the river from 1879 to 1942. Commercial FISHING and LOGGING were the principal economic activities in the late 1990s. Ownership of the Nass Valley was contested for more than a century by the Nisga'a, who refused to recognize white authority in the area and asserted their title to the land. The issue was finally resolved in 1999 with the approval of the NISGA'A TREATY, though legal testing of the

treaty's constitutionality continued in 2000. *See also* RIVERS.

NATAL, a COAL mining town in the E KOOTENAY, 40 km north of FERNIE, began in 1907 and thrived until it was abandoned in the 1960s in favour of the new community of SPARWOOD. The site was bulldozed and later occupied by a large open-pit mine operated by TECK CORP. The name, which was conferred following the Boer War, refers to a province of S Africa.

NATION, Arthur William "Bill," fishing guide (b 29 June 1881, Bristol, England; d Oct 1940, Kamloops). He is considered the dean of sport FISHING guides from the early days of angling in the BC Interior (*see also* FLY FISHING). After immigrating to the province as a young man, he settled in the KAMLOOPS area and worked mainly out of Echo Lodge on Paul Lk. He invented a series of classic fly patterns, and his knowledge of the Kamloops TROUT and its habitat was unequalled. In the last week of his life he was still guiding anglers.

NATIONALIST PARTY, BC's first labour political party, was organized early in 1894 to prepare for the forthcoming provincial election. Its platform called for WOMEN'S SUFFRAGE, an end to property qualifications for candidates, a system of RECALL, the 8-hour workday, a single tax on land values and public ownership of transport, utilities and banks. The party's candidate, Robert Macpherson, a carpenter by trade, won election to the legislature in 1894 and again in 1898, though he turned out to be a lukewarm defender of the party platform. Another candidate, George MAXWELL, was elected a federal MP in 1896 with LIBERAL PARTY support. After this the party was eclipsed by other socialist and labour groups.

NATIVE BROTHERHOOD OF BC is an organization of coastal FIRST NATIONS. It was created in Dec 1931 after the HAIDA fisher Alfred ADAMS convened a meeting of North Coast chiefs to discuss forming a successor to the ALLIED INDIAN TRIBES OF BC. Because it was prohibited by law from pursuing land claims (*see* ABORIGINAL RIGHTS), the Brotherhood concerned itself mainly with FISHING issues, eventually becoming an aboriginal fishers' union, though it was active on other issues as well. The major cannery owners signed labour agreements with the Brotherhood in 1943 and it has been the chief bargaining agent for aboriginal commercial fishers and some plant workers ever since. It is the longest-lasting aboriginal organization in Canada. *See also* FISHING, COMMERCIAL; LABOUR MOVEMENT; SALMON CANNERIES..

NATURAL HISTORY OF BC; *see essay, this page.*

NATURE TRUST OF BC is a charitable corporation that buys ecologically significant land to preserve it as a public trust. Established in 1971 with a $4.5 million fund from the federal government, The Trust owns about 200 properties, including riparian areas adjacent to SALMON spawning streams and sensitive GRASSLANDS and WETLANDS. For management purposes it leases much of its land to the appropriate government agency.

NAUKANA, William, fur trader, settler (b 1813, Hawaiian Islands; d Dec 1909, Saltspring Island). One of the HAWAIIANS recruited by the HBC to work in the FUR TRADE in BC, he arrived from the Hawaiian Islands in the 1840s and worked at various trading posts around the province, including FORT LANGLEY and FORT VICTORIA. He was living in the San Juan Islands during the 1860s but decided to move back to British territory in 1872, when the islands were given to the US following the infamous PIG WAR. He settled on PORTLAND ISLAND with several other Hawaiian families and passed the rest of his years living there and on SALTSPRING ISLAND. His descendants continue to live on Saltspring.

NAYLOR, Joseph "Joe," miner, labour activist (b 1872, Wigan, England; d 5 Oct 1946, Cumberland). An organizer for the WESTERN FEDERATION OF MINERS before 1910, he came to prominence in CUMBERLAND during the VANCOUVER ISLAND coal miners' strike of 1912–14 as local president of the United Mine Workers of America. After the strike he was blacklisted by the employer (*see* COAL MINING, VANCOUVER ISLAND). In 1918 he was arrested for aiding draft evaders. Charges were dropped but they prevented him from testifying at the hearing of the police constable alleged to have shot Naylor's friend Ginger GOODWIN. Naylor was president of the BC FEDERATION OF LABOUR from 1917 to 1918, a charter member of the Cumberland local of the Socialist Party of Canada and a founding member and key organizer of the radical One Big Union from 1919. In the 1930s he was among the OBU's last active members. A revolutionary socialist, he was the subject of RCMP surveillance until his death.   *Susan Mayse*

NATURAL HISTORY OF BC

Overview

Richard Cannings

British Columbia is home to more species of living things than any other Canadian province (*see* BIODIVERSITY). Although the reasons for this rich assemblage of species can be attributed largely to topographic and climatic diversity, other factors are in BC's favour as well. The intricate topography of the province juxtaposes MOUNTAINS, plateaus, valleys and coastal plains with their associated LAKES, RIVERS and WETLANDS to form myriad complex and varied ecosystems. Some species of animals and plants are endemic to BC, meaning that they are not known to occur anywhere else in the world. Perhaps the best known of these is the Vancouver Island MARMOT, a large, chocolate-brown relative of the woodchuck found only on the high mountain meadows of central VANCOUVER ISLAND. Fewer than 100 of these animals survive, making it one of the rarest mammals in the world. Also endemic to BC are 168 insect and 6 plant species, most of them restricted to the coast.

Two systems that identify and map BC's ecological diversity are widely used today. Vladimir KRAJINA developed a system of BIOGEOCLIMATIC ZONES, which are areas characterized by climatic factors and defined according to the tree and shrub species that dominate in climax FORESTS within them. Examples of the 14 major

Forest in the Caren range, Sunshine Coast. Dean van't Schip photo

zones are the *Coastal Western Hemlock Zone* along most of the coast, the *Ponderosa Pine Zone* in dry Interior valleys, and the *Spruce-Willow-Birch Zone* that occurs interspersed among the boreal forest and alpine tundra zones in the north. The second system is the ECOREGION CLASSIFICATION SYSTEM developed by Dennis Demarchi, in which BC is divided into 10 ecoprovinces, including the *Southern Interior Mountains* in the KOOTENAY and COLUMBIA MTS regions, the *Boreal Plains* around the

PEACE R, and the *Georgia Depression*, which includes eastern Vancouver Island and the Lower Mainland. Both classification systems have many smaller divisions grouped below the main categories.

BC has a rich marine environment that supports several giant species such as the largest OCTOPUS, SEA STAR and CHITON in the world. Cold, upwelling waters bring nutrients to the highly productive coastal ecosystems, which are also enriched at ESTUARIES from the many RIVERS emptying at the coast. These nutrients feed a soup of tiny plants, the phytoplankton, which in turn are eaten by clouds of zooplankton and other small invertebrates such as copepods and EUPHAUSIIDS, or krill. As coastal waters warm up in summer, the phytoplankton are sometimes dominated by dinoflagellates to create a red tide (*see* HARMFUL ALGAL BLOOMS).

The coastal environment is as diverse as the terrestrial environment. In sheltered, rock-bottomed bays, KELP forests sway in the waves sheltering schools of fish and many species of inver-

Rugged west coast of Vancouver Island. Ken Bowen photo

tebrates on the blades of the kelp and on the ocean floor. Shallow, sandy or muddy shorelines are often characterized by eelgrass meadows, underwater prairies of waving grass that host a unique community of animals and attract thousands of waterfowl every year, including the Brant GOOSE. Offshore islands are breeding grounds for millions of seabirds. AUKLETS, MURRELETS, MURRES, PUFFINS and STORM-PETRELS burrow into the turf or lay

their eggs on rocky cliffs in their annual contact with land. TRIANGLE ISLAND, an ECOLOGICAL RESERVE off the northern tip of Vancouver Island, hosts the largest number, including a million Cassin's auklets.

Two wildlife spectacles of note occur annually in BC coastal waters. In spring, Pacific HERRING spawn in huge numbers in bays and channels up and down the coast. These concentrations bring in SEALS, SEA LIONS, thousands of DUCKS, LOONS, GREBES, GULLS and other water birds, and help feed the gray WHALES on their northward migration. The second spectacle is the annual migration of SALMON to their spawning streams. As the schools of big silver fish leave the open ocean and pass

Eagle feeding on salmon carcass.
Ken Bowen photo

through JOHNSTONE STRAIT and down toward the GULF ISLANDS, KILLER WHALES follow them in, providing unparalleled viewing opportunities. The salmon swim inland, up the rivers and streams where they were born, to spawn and die, sometimes hundreds of kilometres from the sea. Their presence and subsequent death provides a tremendous bounty for terrestrial ecosystems and land animals. BEARS, RACCOONS and other mammals catch migrating salmon live, or feast on the carcasses, while mergansers, goldeneye, DIPPERS and other birds dive for the eggs. Thousands of bald EAGLES gather each winter at sites of chum and coho salmon spawns, most notably at BRACKENDALE on the SQUAMISH and CHEAKAMUS rivers and at Chehalis Flats on the Harrison R.

Salmon runs are one reason why the temperate RAIN FORESTS

Sockeye salmon spawning in the Horsefly R east of Williams Lk.
Roy Luckow photo

along the coast of BC are so productive. The mild winters and abundant rainfall are also important factors. Some of the tallest trees in the world grew along the coast, and a few huge DOUGLAS FIRS, western red CEDAR, western HEMLOCK and Sitka SPRUCE remain (*see* TREES, GIANT). Western hemlock forests produce

Chicken of the woods fungus, near Chilliwack. Roy Luckow photo

about 5 tonnes of plant material per hectare each year, and some very rich sites produce more than 30 tonnes per year. In these forests of giant trees, some of the most important organisms are very small. Fungi are essential elements of these ecosystems; some species connect with the roots of trees to provide them an extra boost in obtaining nutrients in return for sugars produced in the greenery above. Other fungi team up with algae to form lichens, once thought to be benign curiosities, but now known to be important providers of nitrates to a nutrient-poor ecosystem.

Important vertebrates include tiny SALAMANDERS, living at a density of about 200 per hectare, and northern flying SQUIRRELS, which eat lichens and fungi, and then spread their valuable spores through the forest.

Along the southeast coast of Vancouver Island and on the Gulf Islands, winter rainfall is considerably less and the summer drought stronger. Here the natural forest is an open savannah of Garry OAK, ARBUTUS and Douglas firs. This habitat is one of the most endangered ecosystems in Canada. At higher elevations in the COAST MTS the winter rains turn to snow and the RAIN FORESTS become snow forests. Mountain hemlocks, yellow cedars and amabilis FIRS manage to germinate and grow in forests where it is common to have 5 m or more of snow on the ground, often lingering into July. With very little chance of summer FOREST FIRES or other large disturbances, these ancient forests were once filled with ancient trees. One yellow cedar on the Sechelt Peninsula's Caren Range was almost 1,700 years old, and there are still a few trees in CYPRESS PROVINCIAL PARK above W VANCOUVER that range between 1,600 and 1,200 years old.

Forests of the Interior mountains and plateaus are quite different from coastal forests, and are dominated by Engelmann SPRUCE and subalpine fir. These forests are characterized by long, cold winters and short, warm summers and are similar in many ways to the boreal forests of northern BC, which are dominated by white and black spruce, WILLOW and BIRCH. Forests of north and south share many of the same animals and their understories are both characterized by MOSSES, lichens, and plants of the heather family—for example kinnikinnick, blueberries, huckleberries, and RHODODENDRONS. Much of the mountain and boreal forests of BC are now covered by lodgepole PINE, an early colonizing species that needs high temperatures to open its cones and cleared areas to germinate in full sunlight. Both needs are met by forest fires, which have cleared thousands of hectares of the Interior over the last century. Another species that benefits from fire is the trembling aspen. The dominant animal in spruce forests is the snowshoe hare (*see* RABBIT AND HARE), which has a dramatic 10-year population cycle. When the hares are abundant, their predators—LYNX,

great horned OWL, red FOX, COYOTE, northern goshawk and others—increase in population as well. This increase in predators drives down the hare population after 2 years, and numbers remain low until they surge upwards about 8 years later. There is some evidence that the population increase is linked to CLIMATE changes locked into the 10-year cycle of sunspot activity.

Sagebrush on the benchlands beside the Thompson R. Keith Thirkell photo

The low elevation forests of the dry western portion of the southern Interior are dominated by Douglas fir and ponderosa pine, with western LARCH growing in moister areas. These dry southern Interior valleys have short, cool winters and long, hot summers, and the forests have an open understorey containing abundant grasses, fescues, SOOPOLALLIE and kinnikinnick. Indeed, as one moves down in elevation, this becomes a parkland environment in pure ponderosa pine stands. These are forests shaped by fire; both the pines and Douglas firs have thick bark to protect them from ground fires that periodically

The antelope-brush grasslands near Osoyoos. They are among Canada's most endangered ecosystems. Kevin Dunn/Osoyoos Desert Society

clear out shrubs and small trees. The larch, like the lodgepole pine, needs fires to create the bare soil it needs to germinate. Ponderosa pine forests in particular have a number of birds restricted to them. The white-headed WOODPECKER, Canada's rarest woodpecker and an ENDANGERED SPECIES, is found only in the pine forests of the south OKANAGAN VALLEY. Pygmy NUTHATCHES are one of the commonest birds in these forests and are hardly ever seen in any other habitat. The flammulated owl, a small insect eating species, is locally common in mixed ponderosa pine and Douglas fir forests.

At lower elevations in the west Kootenay and north to the BOWRON LAKE region, heavy winter snowfalls and frequent summer rains produce a very diverse forest reminiscent of the coastal rain forest. This is the area commonly called the Interior "Wet Belt" and forests here are dominated by western hemlock and western red cedar. Common understorey plants here include devil's club and skunk cabbage.

In southern Interior valley bottoms from the Fraser and Thompson through the Okanagan and in parts of the southern ROCKY MT TRENCH, the summers are too hot and dry to allow tree germination. Here the natural ecosystem is a semi-arid GRASSLAND dominated by bunchgrasses and shrubs, notably big sagebrush, rabbitbrush and antelope-brush. Brittle prickly-pear cactus is common, and the list of animal species sounds very desert-like: scorpions, black widow SPIDERS, RATTLESNAKES and even pygmy short-horned LIZARDS. The grasslands of BC have been divided into 3 groups, roughly based on elevation. The

Rattlesnake in the southern Interior. R. Wayne Campbell photo

lower grasslands are characterized by bluebunch wheatgrass, often growing with big sagebrush, mostly found in the Thompson–Okanagan area. The middle grasslands, dominated by bluebunch wheatgrass and Sandberg's bluegrass, have few shrubs, usually common rabbitbrush, and are typical of the NICOLA Valley. The upper grasslands are usually dominated by fescues, but on the CARIBOO and CHILCOTIN plateaus wheatgrasses and needlegrasses are important species. Much of BC's native grasslands have been converted to intensive AGRICULTURE, and the antelope-brush grasslands of the southern Okanagan are considered one of Canada's 4 most endangered ecosystems.

The other treeless environment in BC is the alpine tundra on mountaintops throughout the province. The treeline in the coastal mountains is relatively low, usually around 1,700 m, set by the tremendous amount of winter snowfall that in many years does not melt until July, if at all. Alpine meadows on the coast are dominated by sedges and low shrubby plants of the heath family, such as mountain heathers and crowberries. Interior treelines are generally set by temperature, especially the length of the summer growing season, and occur at about 2,100 m elevation in the south. Most southern Interior mountains have extensive subalpine meadows, created by various combinations of fire, climate change and, locally, heavy snowfall. These meadows are famous for their midsummer flowers (*see* WILD-FLOWERS), with huge tracts of red paintbrush, blue lupine, yellow arnica and white valerian. Above treeline the plant life is limited to low-growing cushions of moss campion, alpine forget-me-not and other similar species. Animal life is scarce but

Wildflowers blooming in an alpine meadow above New Denver, Slocan Lk. Keith Thirkell photo

easily visible: typical birds include PTARMIGAN, horned LARKS, American PIPITS and grey-crowned rosy FINCHES. INSECTS from BUTTERFLIES and beetles to flies can be locally abundant on mountaintops as they gather in summer mating rituals.

Most of the highly diverse natural areas in BC coincide with areas that have been heavily populated and modified by humans—the southern valleys and coastal plain. Ecosystems that are particularly vulnerable are wetlands, riparian woodlands (those habitats along streams and lakeshores) and grasslands. Old-growth forests throughout the province are rapidly diminishing in size and number; in many places only small remnants can be found. Species that need these forests for survival are becoming very rare. The most famous of these, the spotted owl, has only about 50 individuals left in BC, but others are affected as well. Environmental issues concerned with the marine environment in BC generally deal with pollution and pure over-exploitation. Sea otters and whales were almost eliminated in the early years of European exploration and settlement, but over-harvests have continued with salmon, herring, ABALONE, HALIBUT and many other species. Meanwhile pollution from PULP mills, municipal sewage and agricultural runoff has been a major factor in the decline of some marine species. *See also* ENVIRONMENTAL MOVEMENT.

NAZKO, pop 259, a DAKELH (Carrier) settlement 75 km west of QUESNEL on the Nazko R, was strategically located near the Great Road or NUX-ALK-Carrier Grease Trail (*see* MACKENZIE HERITAGE TRAIL). Today it is the centre of a remote ranching (*see* CATTLE INDUSTRY) and LOGGING district. Farther south, closer to ALEXIS CREEK, Nazko Lks Provincial PARK is a wilderness canoeing destination. The name means "river flowing from the south." AS

N.E. THING CO (NETCO), founded in 1966 and incorporated as a business in 1969, was an umbrella under which Iain and Ingrid Baxter, 2 VANCOUVER artists, carried out a variety of unconventional activities parodying prevailing notions of art, including environmental gallery installations, a photo lab, a pee-wee HOCKEY team and the Eye Scream Restaurant. One of their first installations was *Bagged Place* at the UBC Fine Arts Gallery in 1966, a replica of a 4-room apartment in which every item was displayed in a plastic bag. From the Baxters' N VANCOUVER home, NETCO produced a series of provocative, humorous conceptual art events until it dissolved along with the couple's marriage in 1978.

NECHAKO RIVER, 516 km, rises on the Nechako Plateau east of the COAST MTS south of BURNS LAKE, flows north through FORT FRASER, then east through VANDERHOOF to join the FRASER R at PRINCE GEORGE. The name comes from the DAKELH (Carrier) term Incha-Khoh, "big river." FUR TRADERS arrived on the river in 1806 and the following year Simon FRASER erected Fort George (which later became Prince George) at the Nechako–Fraser confluence. Homesteaders

The Nechako R on the way to its confluence with the Fraser R at Prince George.
Duncan McDougall/Image Makers

reached the area early in the 20th century; one tiny settlement, Nechacco, took its name from the river. The flow of the river was reduced dramatically in the early 1950s when its headwaters were backed up behind the KENNEY DAM in the Nechako Reservoir, a vast network of flooded lakes, and diverted westward to feed the massive ALCAN power project at KEMANO. At the time, the Kenney was the largest rock-filled dam in the world. In 1987 Alcan won approval for a second stage of its Kemano project, involving a further diminishing of the river's flow. The Nechako is

an important SALMON spawning river and concerns about the survival of the fish led to public hearings in 1994, at which time 3 prominent fisheries scientists admitted that federal and provincial government agencies had long been aware of the damage to fish populations in the Nechako–Fraser system. During the ensuing scandal, the provincial government overrode the federal government and cancelled the project early in 1995. *See also* RIVERS.

NEEDLES, 70 km northwest of CASTLEGAR, was a CPR sternwheeler stop on the west side of Lower ARROW LK; a car ferry later began crossing to FAUQUIER at the same site. There was a small AGRICULTURAL and orchard (*see* TREE FRUITS) settlement here, originally named Fire Valley after the region's frequent FOREST FIRES, but it was abandoned when the KEENLEYSIDE DAM caused water levels to rise. The name comes from the spits of sand that ran into the lake. AS

NEEL, Ellen, Kwakwaka'wakw artist (b 1916; d 1966). She was the granddaughter of Charlie JAMES, who taught her to carve in CEDAR. In VANCOUVER in the 1940s she made a living making miniature TOTEM POLES and in 1946 opened Totem Arts Studios, where she sold her work. She was the first Northwest Coast artist to produce silkscreened images on fabric. In 1949 UBC

Ellen Neel, Kwakwaka'wakw carver, 1950.
Vancouver Sun

hired her to restore poles for the MUSEUM OF ANTHROPOLOGY. The following year she returned to her business and was replaced at UBC by her step-uncle Mungo MARTIN. Although she never received the recognition that more famous, male carvers did, she produced several full-size poles for customers across Canada and internationally. One of her poles is displayed in STANLEY PARK.

NEELY, Cam, hockey player (b 6 June 1965, Comox). He was one of the NHL's premier

Cam Neely, hockey standout, 1996.
Les Bazso/Vancouver Province

power forwards of the late 1980s and early 1990s. He moved from BC to Moose Jaw, SK, developing his HOCKEY skills there before his family returned to live in MAPLE RIDGE where he had a brilliant season with the local midget team. As a junior he played for the Portland Winter Hawks of the WHL, scoring a hat trick in the Memorial Cup final to crown them as the first US team to win the Canadian junior championship. He turned professional with the VANCOUVER CANUCKS at the end of 1983 but didn't reach his potential and in 1986 was sent to the Boston Bruins in exchange for Barry PEDERSON, considered to be one of the worst trades in Canucks history. As a Bruin he became one of the most prolific scorers in the NHL, leading Boston to the Stanley Cup finals in 1988 and 1990. Injuries plagued his remaining seasons but in 1993–94 he scored 50 goals in 44 games, the second-fastest rate in NHL history. A hip injury forced his retirement in 1996 and prevented a comeback 2 years later. His instructional book *Hockey for Everybody* was published in 1998. In 1999, he was inducted into the BC SPORTS HALL OF FAME. SW

NEIL, Al, jazz musician, artist (b 1924, Vancouver). An accomplished JAZZ pianist, he began performing in VANCOUVER in the late 1940s and helped organize the Cellar jazz club, which operated from 1956 to 1964. The LP *Kenneth Patchen Reads with Jazz* (Folkways 9718) displays his bebop piano style. During the 1960s he became involved in free improvisation and mixed media. His trio with bassist Richard Anstey and drummer Gregg Simpson presented video/sound/theatrical events around Vancouver. In the 1970s he performed solo in Paris and Amsterdam, lived briefly in Toronto and launched a series of collaborations with the visual artist Carole Itter, including annual multimedia performances at the WESTERN FRONT. In the 1980s Neil began a successful career as a collagist; his works in paper sold briskly in commercial galleries. He has published an autobiographical novel, *Changes* (1975; rev. 1990) and a story collection, *Slammer* (1980). Besides the Patchen LP, his recordings include *The Al Neil Trio Retrospective 1965–1968* (1976), *Solo* (1981) and *Selections: 3 Decades* (1990). *David Lee*

NELSEN, Nels Johan, ski jumper (b 3 June 1894, Salengen, Norway; d 1943). In 1912 he immigrated to REVELSTOKE, the base from which he became the world's top SKI jumper. Not long after he arrived in Canada he began winning national championships and setting world records. His best jump, 240 ft (73.15 m) in 1924, stood as the international benchmark for 7 years. After losing his hand in a hunting accident in 1932 he focussed on coaching; among his pupils was Bobby Lymburne, a world record holder and a participant in the 1932 Los Angeles Olympics. Instrumental in developing his local ski club and tournaments on Mt Revelstoke, Nelsen was inducted into the BC SPORTS HALL OF FAME and the Ski Hall of Fame in Michigan. *SW*

NELSON, city, pop 9,585, overlooks the west arm of KOOTENAY LK 660 km east of VANCOUVER. The townsite was established in 1887 and first named Stanley for the gov gen. It grew quickly as a service centre for the surrounding mines—the Silver King on Toad Mt being the largest—and was the site of a COPPER–lead SMELTER from 1896 to 1907. Incorporated on 18 Mar 1897, it was the largest city between Vancouver and Winnipeg during the 1890s, when it became the terminus and transfer point for railways and lake steamships. With the decline of MINING, AGRICULTURE became important, though orchards (*see* TREE FRUITS) were ruined by disease between 1920 and 1950. LOGGING and SAWMILLING became the major employers, along with TOURISM. About 350 buildings have been given

Hugh Nelson, lt gov of BC 1887–92, shown here in a portrait painted in 1887.
BC Archives A-01848

heritage status, including the courthouse and city hall designed by Francis RATTENBURY. Since 1981 many have been restored and were displayed to good effect in the movie *Roxanne*, starring Steve Martin. Nelson had the smallest streetcar system in the British Empire between 1899 and 1949: 2 cars, 8 km of track (*see also* STREET RAILWAYS). One of the original cars has been restored and returned to service. The city's NOTRE DAME UNIV (later David Thompson Univ Centre) closed in 1984. The city is known for its thriving arts community; there are said to be more artists and craftspeople per capita than in any other place in Canada. Whitewater SKI area is nearby.
Reading: John Norris, *Historic Nelson: The Early Years*, 1995.

NELSON, Hugh, businessman, politician, lt gov 1887–92 (b 25 May 1830, Larne, Northern

Ireland; d 3 Mar 1893, London, England). He arrived in BC in 1858 hoping to make a fortune in the goldfields (*see* GOLD RUSHES). Instead he got into the transport business at YALE, where his BC & Victoria Express connected the CARIBOO to the coast. After selling out to F.J. BARNARD in 1867, he moved to BURRARD INLET and became a partner in Sewell MOODY's North Shore SAWMILL. After Moody's death he managed the mill until 1882. A strong proponent of CONFEDERATION, he was elected MP for NEW WESTMINSTER in 1871 as a follower of John A. Macdonald. During the scandal over the financing of the CPR he left politics briefly, but in 1879 Macdonald appointed him to the Senate, where he served until he became LT GOV. When his term as lt gov ended he retired to England, where he died soon after.

NELSON & FORT SHEPPARD RAILWAY was built by Daniel Corbin, an American rail promoter, to link Northport on the COLUMBIA R just south of the US border to NELSON. The second half of the name was a misspelling of FORT SHEPHERD, an old HBC trading post. The line, which ran up the valley of the SALMON R and arrived at Five Mile Point east of Nelson at the end of 1893, offered a direct connection to Spokane, WA, for ore from Nelson-area mines. In 1898 it was purchased by James J. Hill's GREAT NORTHERN RWY. Passenger service on the line was discontinued in 1941 but freight traffic continued. Along with several other lines it was merged to form the Burlington Northern Rwy in 1970.

NELSON BROS FISHERIES LTD was created in 1929 by Richard and Norman Nelson, fishers on the west coast of VANCOUVER ISLAND. They purchased a FRASER R cannery in 1933 and the next year took control of CEEPEECEE. They also bought plants at MASSET and PRINCE RUPERT, establishing themselves as one of the most important fish companies on the coast. BC PACKERS secretly bought the company in 1960 and dissolved it as a separate entity in 1969. *See also* SALMON CANNING.

NELSON FORKS, 115 km northwest of FORT NELSON at the confluence of the LIARD and Fort Nelson rivers in BC's remote northeast corner, was the site of a DENE-THAH (Slavey) First Nation village and an HBC trading post. It was abandoned in the early 1950s. A US Army weather station operated here during WWII. *AS*

NELSON ISLAND, 127 km², is located at the mouth of JERVIS INLET opposite TEXADA ISLAND in GEORGIA STRAIT. It was named during an 1860 survey for the British naval hero Horatio Nelson. Granite from quarries in Quarry Bay and on nearby Kelly, Fox and HARDY islands was mined from the 1890s to the 1960s and used in the LEGISLATIVE BUILDINGS and on the harbour seawall in VICTORIA, and in many buildings in VANCOUVER and Seattle. Sparsely populated by homesteaders from the 1890s, the island has undergone extensive LOGGING. AQUACULTURE has also taken place here.
Reading: Karen Southern, *The Nelson Island Story*, 1987.

Horse racing through the streets of Nelson, 1 July 1898. UBC BC225

NEMETZ, Nathaniel, jurist (b 8 Sept 1913, Winnipeg, MB; d 21 Oct 1997, Vancouver). He came to VANCOUVER at age 10 with his parents, studied at UBC and, after apprenticing with a legal firm, was called to the bar in 1937. Early in his career he was associated with labour law. Appointed a judge on the BC Supreme Court in 1963, he became chief justice in 1973. Four years later he became chief justice of the Appeal

Nathaniel Nemetz, chief justice of the appeal court of BC 1977–78. UBC 5.1/2234

Court, the top judicial position in BC. He retired from the bench in 1988. Active in many JEWISH organizations, including B'nai B'rith and the Canadian Jewish Congress, he was the first Jewish chancellor of UBC (1972–75) and the first Jewish member of the exclusive Vancouver Club. He was also a founding member of the local branch of the Canadian Civil Liberties Union and a member of the ORDER OF BC (1990). *See also* JUDICIAL SYSTEM.

NEMIAH VALLEY is in the southern CHILCOTIN about 100 km south of HANCEVILLE on Hwy 20 west of WILLIAMS LAKE. The valley is occupied by ranches (*see* CATTLE INDUSTRY), TOURIST resorts and several RESERVES of the Xeni Gwet'in (Nemiah) people, part of the TSILHQOT'IN First Nation. Konni (Xeni) Lk drains via Nemaia Crk into CHILKO LK. In 1989 the Xeni Gwet'in issued the Nemiah Declaration banning all resource-related development in the valley; in 1991 they won a court injunction to stop LOGGING. Their efforts culminated in 1994 with the creation of Ts'yl-os Provincial PARK (2,300 km²), co-managed by the Nemiah band.

NEPHRITE; *see* JADE.

NETTWERK is a VANCOUVER-based group of companies including a record label (Nettwerk Productions) and artist management company (Nettwerk Management). In the late 1990s the record company's stable of artists included Sarah

MCLACHLAN, Skinny Puppy and Delerium; and managed artists included McLachlan, Barenaked Ladies and Moist. Nettwerk was launched in a West End apartment in 1984 as a label for a local pop band, Moev, then grew quickly by representing non-mainstream musicians. It now has offices in the US and Europe. *See also* SOUND RECORDING INDUSTRY.

NEW AIYANSH; *see* GITLAKDAMIKS.

NEW CALEDONIA was the name early FUR TRADERS gave to the central Interior of BC between the ROCKY MTS and the COAST MTS, essentially the region drained by the upper FRASER R and its tributaries. Alexander MACKENZIE was the first European to penetrate the area on his way to the Pacific Ocean in 1793, but it was Simon FRASER who named it when he arrived in 1805 to establish trading posts for the NORTH WEST CO. The name, meaning New Scotland, was a reference to the Scottish Highlands; Fraser had not seen them but his mother had described them to him. The headquarters of the NWC fur-trading district was FORT ST JAMES on Stuart Lk. The NWC merged with the HBC in 1821. By 1828 New Caledonia as an administrative entity was absorbed into the Columbia Department for purposes of accounting and supply, though the name survived in common usage. It was the original name for the mainland colony created by the British in 1858, but to avoid confusion with French possessions of the same name in the S Pacific it was changed at the last minute to BRITISH COLUMBIA, a choice of Queen Victoria. New Caledonia as the informal name for the central Interior slowly faded from use.

NEW DEMOCRATIC PARTY (NDP) of BC, a provincial wing of the federal political party of the same name, was formed in Oct 1961 at a VANCOUVER convention where the CO-OPERATIVE COMMONWEALTH FEDERATION (CCF) joined forces with organized labour (*see* LABOUR MOVEMENT) and adopted a new name. Robert STRACHAN, who had led the CCF since 1956, remained party leader and leader of the opposition with a fairly constant level of electoral support through the 1960s. The NDP espouses moderate social democratic policies, promoting a mixed ECONOMY and gradual reform through parliamentary democracy. It hopes not to eradicate capitalism but rather to ameliorate its excesses and redistribute wealth to its victims. Nonetheless, the SOCIAL CREDIT PARTY under W.A.C. BENNETT was able to maintain a firm grip on power from 1952 to 1972 by convincing voters that New Democrats were rabid "bolshevikii" who threatened the stability of the province. Strachan resigned in 1969 and was succeeded as NDP leader by Tom BERGER, who fared no better in that year's provincial election and gave way in 1970 to Dave BARRETT. Barrett's folksy approachability appealed to voters tired of 2 decades of Socred rule and in 1972 he led the NDP to its first BC election victory, winning a majority of the seats in the legislature with almost 40% of the popular vote. His government was able to accomplish a great deal in its 3 years in power: 367 pieces of legislation were passed, many in the areas of housing, health (*see* HEALTH POLICY) and welfare policy. The NDP introduced a public auto insurance plan (*see* INSURANCE CORP OF BC), the AGRICULTURAL LAND RESERVE and a LABOUR RELATIONS BOARD. Critics accused the new PREMIER of trying to do too much too quickly with too little attention to cost, and overall the government did appear to be disorganized and accident-prone. More important, it alienated powerful business interests by imposing a tax on the MINING industry, and it lost labour support when it introduced back-to-work legislation. In 1975 the NDP lost an election to the revitalized Social Credit Party. Barrett remained leader through 2 more elections, which the NDP also lost, and he was replaced by Bob SKELLY in 1984. After another defeat the party chose Mike HARCOURT, former mayor of Vancouver, as its leader

Nemiah Valley. Rick Blacklaws photo

in 1987; in 1991 he led the party back to power in a surprising election that saw Social Credit reduced to a rump, replaced in opposition by a resurgent LIBERAL PARTY. Harcourt provided low-key, moderate leadership—too moderate for many in his party—and his government championed fiscal restraint, a settlement of aboriginal issues (*see* ABORIGINAL RIGHTS) and the resolution of divisive land use issues. Despite the reasonable popularity of his government, Harcourt was forced to resign as leader in an attempt to defuse a growing scandal over the misuse of charity bingo revenues (*see also* GAMING; NANAIMO COMMONWEALTH HOLDING SOCIETY). Glen CLARK took over as party leader and PREMIER in 1996 and regained enough support for the NDP to squeak back into power in an election later that year. It was the first time in BC that the NDP had won back-to-back elections. But in 1999 an increasingly unpopular Clark was implicated in a separate scandal, and when it was revealed that he was under police investigation he resigned. Dan MILLER served briefly as interim party leader and premier; then the NDP chose Ujjal DOSANJH, former attorney general, as leader early in 2000. It was the first time that an Indo-Canadian (*see* SOUTH ASIANS) had served as leader of a government in Canada. Dosanjh took over as premier with the NDP well behind the Liberals in the opinion polls. *See also* ELECTION RESULTS.

NEW DENVER, village, pop 579, overlooks the east side of SLOCAN LK in the W KOOTENAY. Originally called Eldorado, it was established during 1891–92 as a service centre for the surrounding MINING area, though the Slocan mining boom collapsed after WWI. The present name refers to Denver, CO. During WWII JAPANESE Canadians from the coast were interned here (*see* JAPANESE, RELOCATION OF), and many remained. The Nikkei Internment Memorial Centre opened in 1994 and recalls this period. Small-scale mining, LOGGING and TOURISM have become mainstays of the local economy.

NEW GOLD HARBOUR is a village site at the eastern end of Maude Island in Skidegate Inlet, between the largest of the QUEEN CHARLOTTE ISLANDS, Moresby and Graham. The HAIDA name for the village, Haina (or Xa'ina), means "sunshine town." It was occupied prehistorically, then reoccupied about 1860 by families from villages on the outer coast, one of which was called Gold Harbour (Chaatl) because it was near where GOLD was discovered in 1850, prompting a rush of outsiders to the islands. Diseases contracted from the newcomers were the main factor that forced Haida residents to relocate to New Gold Harbour. During the 1880s they moved again, this time to SKIDEGATE, and the village was abandoned by 1900.

NEW HAZELTON, district municipality, pop 822, developed on the BULKLEY R 6 km east of HAZELTON during the construction of the GRAND TRUNK PACIFIC RWY in 1912. It was promoted by Robert KELLY, a VANCOUVER merchant who owned the townsite, as an alternative location for the

new train station because it was on the same side of the river as the tracks, which Hazelton was not. After prolonged litigation a station was built. Later the Yellowhead Hwy (Hwy 16; *see* ROADS & HWYS) was built through the community, and the FOREST INDUSTRY has become the main economic activity.

NEW STAR BOOKS, a VANCOUVER book publisher, traces its roots to a group of writers associated with the GEORGIA STRAIGHT, who in 1968 began publishing a series of small books known as the Georgia Straight Writing Series. The series evolved into Vancouver Community Press (VCP) which, in the early 1970s, became increasingly interested in social and political non-fiction and less interested in literary publishing. In 1974 VCP changed its name to New Star Books and for the next 16 years published mostly social-justice oriented non-fiction. In 1990 New Star returned to its literary roots; the press now publishes a balanced list of literary works, broadly political non-fiction and books about BC and its people, places and history. New Star authors include Terry GLAVIN, Stan PERSKY (one of the original founders of the press), Sheila Baxter, Brian FAWCETT, Margaret Randall and Rolf Knight. *See also* BOOK PUBLISHING.

NEW WESTMINSTER is located on the north shore of the FRASER R, 20 km east of VANCOUVER, on the site of a former aboriginal village called Skaiametl. Richard MOODY of the ROYAL  ENGINEERS approved of its easily defensible position on high ground and chose the site to be the capital of the mainland colony of British Columbia. Gov James DOUGLAS had chosen DERBY, farther upriver, but agreed to Moody's choice and on 14 Feb 1859 declared the new capital. By June the first lots were surveyed and sold.

Originally the site was known as Queensborough, but Queen Victoria chose the name New Westminster; the city has been known as "the Royal City" or "the Queen City" ever since. (Queensborough later came to refer to the eastern tip of nearby LULU ISLAND, an area within city boundaries.) On 16 July 1860 New Westminster was incorporated as a city, making it the oldest incorporated municipality west of

Ontario. The capital was transferred to VICTORIA in 1868 following union of the 2 colonies, but New Westminster developed as the principal city on the mainland with a healthy economy based on SAWMILLING and SALMON CANNING. It was eclipsed by the rise of Vancouver, but it continued to play an important role as the commercial centre of the burgeoning FRASER VALLEY agricultural district. The Farmers' Market, built in 1892, attracted buyers and sellers from all over the Lower Mainland. The east end of the city became known as Sapperton after the Royal Engineers, or

New Westminster, the day after the great fire of 1898. BC Archives HP-9367

Columbia Street, New Westminster, 1953. The Pattullo Bridge is in the background. Vancouver Sun

"sappers," many of whom settled there. In Sept 1898 a devastating fire destroyed the business district, many public buildings and residences. But the city rebuilt and flourished in the pre-war period. In 1910 an electric INTERURBAN railway connected the city to CHILLIWACK, and in 1915 the CNR line arrived. Wood products have remained an important part of the local economy, but industry has declined since the 1970s, replaced by a boom in commercial and residential building. During the 1980s the city's waterfront was redeveloped, highlighted by the building of the SKYTRAIN light rapid transit line through the area from Vancouver in 1986 and the opening of the Westminster Quay Public Market complex. SkyBridge, the only cable-stayed bridge in the world used exclusively by rapid transit, was built to carry the Skytrain across the Fraser R to SURREY.

Population: 49,350
Rank in BC: 18th

Population increase since 1981: 28%
Date of incorporation: city 16 July 1860
Land area: 18.47 km²
Location: Greater Vancouver Regional District
Economic base: manufacturing, retail,
government services

NEW WESTMINSTER BRUINS, a junior
HOCKEY powerhouse, belonged to the WHL in
1971–81 and again in 1983–88. Under coach
Ernie "Punch" MCLEAN they played with a bruis-
ing, physical style and won 4 consecutive league
championships (1975–78) and 2 Memorial
Cups (1977–78). In 1981 new owner Peter
Pocklington moved the team to KAMLOOPS. The
Bruins were back in the WHL briefly from 1983
until they moved in 1988 to Kennewick, WA.
Notable Bruins included Barry BECK, Brad
Maxwell, Stan SMYL, Cliff RONNING and Bill
Ranford.

NEW WESTMINSTER SALMONBELLIES is
a legendary team in Canadian LACROSSE history.
It began in 1890 with creation of the BC
Amateur Lacrosse Assoc, playing opponents
from VICTORIA and VANCOUVER. The name was
first applied as an insult, then adopted with
pride as a reflection of the city's FISHING industry.
New Westminster first won the Minto Cup as the
top professional team in Canada in 1908, led by
Alex "Dad" Turnbull, then won it every year but
2 until 1934. In 1928 a Salmonbellies team represented Canada at the Amsterdam Olympics,
where field lacrosse was a demonstration sport,

*New Westminster Salmonbellies in action at
Brockton Point, Vancouver, 1912. CVA Sp.P71*

and finished in a 3-way tie for first. With the
switch to box lacrosse in the 1930s Queens Park
Arena in NEW WESTMINSTER became home to the
Salmonbellies. The club has won the Mann Cup
as the top senior amateur team in the country 2
dozen times (and 3 more times under the name

of a sponsor, O'Keefe's), earning New
Westminster the right to claim it is the lacrosse
capital of Canada. *See also* Jack BIONDA; CANADI-
AN LACROSSE HALL OF FAME; Wayne GOSS.

**NEW WESTMINSTER SOUTHERN RAIL-
WAY** was financed by James Jerome Hill as part
of his GREAT NORTHERN RWY empire. Opened on
14 Feb 1891, it ran from the south side of the
FRASER R opposite NEW WESTMINSTER to the
American border east of Blaine, WA, where it
connected with another Hill line, the Fairhaven
& Southern Rwy. It was the first international rail
line west of Winnipeg. When the province completed a road–rail bridge across the Fraser at New
Westminster in 1904, Hill extended his line—by
then part of the Vancouver, Westminster &
Yukon Rwy—into VANCOUVER. Service on the
line ended in 1909 when the Great Northern
opened an alternative route to Vancouver via
WHITE ROCK.

NEWCASTLE ISLAND, 3.36 km², lies in
NANAIMO Harbour on the east coast of VANCOU-
VER ISLAND. The entire island is a provincial
MARINE PARK. In 1853 the HBC, acting on information supplied by the SNUNEYMUXW
(Nanaimo) inhabitants, opened a COAL mine on
the island. The company called it Newcastle after
the English mining town, and coal was mined
there until 1883. A sandstone quarry operated
from 1870 to 1955 and supplied blocks and pillars for buildings far and near, including the
Nanaimo Post Office and the US Mint in San
Francisco. Another quarry, this one producing
pulpstones for the PULP AND PAPER INDUSTRY,
operated from 1923 to 1932. Both quarries were
later opened for exploration by the public. The
island had a significant population of JAPANESE
people; they operated a HERRING saltery and a
shipyard until 1942, when their property was
confiscated and the residents interned (*see* JAPAN-
ESE, RELOCATION OF). The CPR purchased the

island from Canadian Collieries in 1930 and
transformed it into a resort. Facilities included a
dance pavilion, wading pool, tea house, soccer
pitch and floating hotel. The first of these hotels
was the *Charmer*; it was subsequently replaced by
the *PRINCESS VICTORIA*. Steam cruises brought
passengers for dances and picnics. TOURIST traffic
slowed after the war and the City of Nanaimo
bought the island in 1955, then sold it to the
province in 1961 for $1 on the condition that it
become a marine park. A variety of birds and
other wildlife can be seen on the island and
there are some lovely rocky and sandy beaches to
explore. Today it is a popular place for natural
and cultural history study, trail hiking, camping,
boating and swimming. The CPR pavilion was
restored to operate as a visitor centre. The island
can be reached by a small passenger ferry that
runs from behind the civic arena in Nanaimo in
summer. Like other marine parks, it has a dock
for private boats.

NEWCOMBE, Charles Frederic, psychiatrist,
naturalist, field ethnologist (b 1851, Newcastle-
on-Tyne, Scotland; d 1924, Victoria). Trained as
a medical doctor in Scotland, he emigrated to
Oregon in 1884, then moved his family north to
VICTORIA in 1889 and became BC's first psychiatrist. Most of his time was spent indulging his
interests as an amateur naturalist and collector
of aboriginal artifacts. He travelled widely along
the coast as far north as the QUEEN CHARLOTTE
ISLANDS and was hired by various museums to
procure TOTEM POLES, carvings and other artifacts
from the FIRST NATIONS. He worked exclusively
for Chicago's Field Museum from 1902 to 1906;
later acquisitions form a large part of the collections at the ROYAL BC MUSEUM. He was also an
early collector of the works of Emily CARR, who
was a close friend of his son William, also a naturalist.

NEWGATE, formerly called Gateway, was a
CROWSNEST SOUTHERN RWY station and US border
post in the E KOOTENAY, 70 km southeast of
CRANBROOK. The line was abandoned in 1937;
much of it is now beneath KOOCANUSA LK. The
settlement was rebuilt at the mouth of Linklater
Crk on the west side of the lake. LOGGING and the
CATTLE INDUSTRY are the economic mainstays. AS

NEWITTY was a fortified village at Cape Sutil on
the northern tip of VANCOUVER ISLAND occupied
by the Nahwitti, a division of the KWAK-
W̱AḴA'WAKW (Kwakiutl) nation. It was the scene
in 1850–51 of the first use of gunfire against
coastal FIRST NATIONS by the colonial authorities.
The village was occupied by about 3,100 people
who were thought to be hostile to the nearby
HBC post, FORT RUPERT. In June 1850 men from
Newitty killed 3 HBC deserters, perhaps thinking
that was what the company wanted. In October
a naval gunboat arrived and when the Nahwitti
refused to surrender the murderers the naval
force burned one of their camps. The following
July another naval expedition destroyed the village at Cape Sutil. Following these skirmishes
the Nahwitti turned over 3 corpses, claiming

they were the wanted men, and the incident was closed. Subsequently Humdaspe on HOPE ISLAND became the principal Nahwitti village and Europeans sometimes called this place Newitty as well. *See also* COLONIAL GOVERNMENT.

NEWLANDS, a former AGRICULTURAL and LOGGING settlement 42 km northeast of PRINCE GEORGE, was a station on the GRAND TRUNK PACIFIC RWY. A SAWMILL operated here intermittently from the 1920s to the late 1960s. A few hardy homesteaders remain in the area. AS

NEWMAN, Murray Arthur, fish scientist (b 6 Mar 1924, Chicago). He served with the US Navy during WWII and after studying at the Univ of Chicago and the Univ of California at Berkeley, he came to VANCOUVER in 1953 for doctoral studies at UBC. In 1955 he was hired as the first curator of the VANCOUVER AQUARIUM, which opened in STANLEY PARK the following year. During his tenure the facility grew to become one of the most popular visitor attractions in the city. He retired in 1993. His memoir, *Life in a Fishbowl*, appeared in 1994.

NEWMAN, Peter Charles, writer (b 10 May 1929, Vienna, Austria). One of the legendary figures of Canadian magazine journalism, he was editor of *Maclean's* from 1971 to 1982 and supervised its transition from a monthly to a weekly publication. By this time he had already made a reputation in groundbreaking political journalism as a reporter in Ottawa and author of *Renegade in Power* (1963), a chronicle of the

Peter C. Newman, journalist and author, 1998.
Barry Peterson & Blaise Enright-Peterson

career of former prime minister John Diefenbaker. Newman has also indulged a fascination with the lifestyles of the rich and powerful in a series of "Establishment" books, including *Titans: How the New Canadian Establishment Seized Power* (1998). During the 1980s Newman moved to BC and turned his attention to the past, producing a 3-volume history of the HBC (1985–91). From his west coast vantage, he continued to write prolifically about the country's

business and political elite. He has won several writing awards, including a BC BOOK PRIZE for *Titans*. He has been inducted into the Order of Canada, and in 1999 he received an honorary degree from UBC.

NEWSPAPERS in BC are mainly owned by 3 major chains that together operate 17 dailies and 106 community papers, claiming a daily readership in excess of 3 million. Dominating the market is CanWest Global Communications Corp, publisher of the VANCOUVER SUN, the PROVINCE and the *Victoria Daily* TIMES-COLONIST, which together are read by more than 1 million people each day, and smaller market papers in

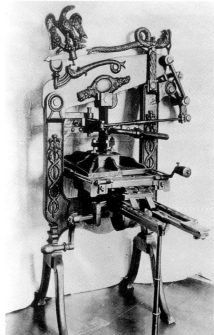

Royal Engineers' printing press, New Westminster. UBC BC1002

NANAIMO and PORT ALBERNI. CanWest's predecessor, Hollinger, still operated dailies in KAMLOOPS, PRINCE GEORGE and 9 smaller markets in 2000. Community newspaper markets are dominated by BLACK PRESS LTD, which publishes dailies in KELOWNA and PENTICTON and 80 smaller papers in western Canada and the US. VANCOUVER'S GEORGIA STRAIGHT is the province's largest alternative newspaper, followed by VICTORIA'S MONDAY MAGAZINE, while 2 national papers, the *Globe and Mail* and the *National Post*, also sell into the market. In addition several non-English-language daily newspapers are published in BC, including 3 CHINESE dailies, *Sing Tao*, *Ming Pao* and *World Journal*.

BC's first newspapers—the *Victoria Gazette* and *Le Courrier de la Nouvelle Calédonie*—were established in 1858 to serve the influx of American miners stampeding to the FRASER R during the GOLD RUSH. Both failed before the year was out but were followed by the *British Colonist*, which has survived as the *Times-Colonist*. Early papers were partisan and often published to further the political ambitions of

their owners or to boost the aspirations of their communities. Amor DE COSMOS used the *Colonist* to campaign against Gov James DOUGLAS and for responsible government. Douglas attempted to suppress the paper with an obscure British statute that permitted him to require the posting of a bond. He set it as $3,000, an astronomical sum for the day, but *Colonist* readers raised the money by public subscription. De Cosmos later used his paper to campaign successfully for BC's entry into CONFEDERATION. In 1872 he became the province's second PREMIER. The first newspaper on the mainland was the *New Westminster Times* in 1860 (*see* NEW WESTMINSTER). It was supplanted by John ROBSON's *British Columbian*, another crusader for the "liberalization" of colonial government. Robson, too, later served as premier. In 1884 the *Victoria Daily Times* was launched. Its LIBERAL PARTY sympathies counterbalanced the CONSERVATIVE PARTY leanings of the *Colonist*. The *Province* followed in 1894; it was first published in Victoria, then relocated to Vancouver to take advantage of the boom generated by the Klondike gold rush, and soon it became BC's leading newspaper. Meanwhile, several pioneering editors established papers in the small towns and MINING camps of the Interior, notably "Colonel" Bob LOWERY, John HOUSTON and, later, Margaret "Ma" MURRAY.

As Vancouver surpassed Victoria to become the economic capital of the province, newspaper competition heated up on the mainland. In

Pacific Press printing plant at Kennedy Heights, Surrey, 1997. Pacific Press

1912 Robert CROMIE obtained a moribund Liberal Party newspaper and resurrected it as the *Vancouver Sun*, one of 5 daily papers in the city. Then markets began to contract. Between 1914 and 1922, 40 daily newspapers folded across Canada. One by one the weaker Vancouver dailies were absorbed by their more vigorous competitors. The *Province* acquired the premises of the *News-Advertiser* and the *Herald*. The *Sun* took over the *World* and the Vancouver market became largely a battlefield for these 2 survivors. The *Province* dominated as the newspaper of record until 1946, when a bitter strike permitted the *Sun* to capture circulation and pass its rival. By the 1950s the *Sun* had the largest circulation of any daily paper in western Canada.

Recent newspaper history in BC has been characterized by volatile ownership and increasing corporate concentration. In Victoria the *Daily Times* and the *Daily Colonist* were acquired by the Thomson Group and merged to form the *Times-Colonist*. In Vancouver Southam and the Cromie family established PACIFIC PRESS in 1957 to print the *Sun* and the *Province*. By 1980 all three papers were owned by Southam, which was swallowed by Hollinger in the 1990s. In 2000 Hollinger sold many Southam properties, including the Victoria and Vancouver dailies, to CanWest.

The rise of electronic media, which provide instant coverage accompanied by dramatic visual images, and the resurgence of community newspapers serving narrow segments of the market, have forced mass-audience papers to rethink their structure and market positions. Some, like the *Province*, have begun to publish shorter articles with lively graphic display that emulates television, along with a heavier emphasis on stories related to crime, scandal, entertainment and sports. Others, like the *Sun*, have tried to provide the depth and context to the news that electronic media can seldom achieve. Most newspapers, from community weeklies to metro dailies, are now exploring news delivery via the Internet. Throughout their turbulent history, BC's newspapers have produced writers and journalists of national calibre. Among the best known are Bruce HUTCHISON, "Torchy" ANDERSON, Benny Nicholas, B.A. MCKELVIE, James K. Nesbitt, Arthur MAYSE, Nancy HODGES, Jim Hume, Pierre BERTON, Mamie Maloney Boggs, Alan FOTHERINGHAM, Pat CARNEY, Marjorie NICHOLS, Barry BROADFOOT and Paul ST PIERRE.   *Stephen Hume*
Reading: David Williams Higgins, *Tales of a Pioneer Journalist*, 1996; Peter Stursberg, *Extra! When the Papers Had the Only News*, 1982; Peter Stursberg, *Those Were the Days*, 1969.

NEWTON, 25 km southeast of VANCOUVER, is an AGRICULTURAL and residential settlement in SURREY that grew up around a BC ELECTRIC RWY CO interurban station (1910) (*see* INTERURBANS) and a strategic crossroads. Named after Elias J. Newton, a saddler and harness-maker who settled in the area in the mid-1880s, it became the site of one of western Canada's first electric-powered SAWMILLS, built in 1910 by King & Farris Lumber Co.   AS

NEWTON, Jack Borden, astronomer (b 13 Aug 1942, Winnipeg). One of the world's best-known amateur astronomers, he was self-taught and supported his lifelong hobby by working as a department store manager. He has written and co-written many books about astronomy and is one of the pioneers of astronomical imaging using computers. He came to BC in 1979 and lived in VICTORIA until his retirement from

business in 1996. He works full-time on astronomy with his wife Alice in OSOYOOS and a winter home in Florida.   *Chris Gainor*

NEWTON, Norman, writer, radio producer, actor, playwright (b 1929, Vancouver). He worked for many years in VANCOUVER as a producer for CBC Radio when it was a centre of literary culture in the province. Along with many radio plays he wrote 3 novels—*The House of Gods* (1961) about the Aztecs; *The One True Man* (1963), also set in Mexico; and *The Big Stuffed Hand of Friendship* (1969), a satire on aboriginal–European relations in small-town BC. He also published a non-fiction book about the HAIDA, *Fire in the Raven's Nest* (1973), and he has written poetry and opera libretti.

NGAN, Wayne, ceramic artist (b 1937, Kwantung, China). He arrived in VANCOUVER from China at age 13 and later attended the Vancouver School of Art (*see* EMILY CARR INSTITUTE OF ART & DESIGN). After graduating in 1963 he established his own pottery studio, taught ceramics at the art school and at UBC, and emerged as one of BC's leading ceramic artists. He subsequently moved to HORNBY ISLAND, where he built a home and studio. His work, for which he won the 1983 Saidye Bronfman Award for Excellence in the Crafts, is heavily influenced by Asian techniques and styles. He is also a sculptor and painter.

NICHOL, Walter Cameron, journalist, lt gov 1920–26 (b 15 Oct 1866, Goderich, ON; d 19 Dec 1928, Victoria). He began a successful career in journalism at the Hamilton *Spectator* newspaper, then moved in 1887 to Toronto, where he launched the original *Saturday Night* magazine. It failed after one issue and he returned to newspaper work in Hamilton and London. In 1897 he and his new wife moved west, to the KOOTENAY briefly, then to VICTORIA, where he became editor of the weekly PROVINCE newspaper. The next year the *Province* moved to VANCOUVER as a daily and Nichol went with it. In 1901 he bought control of the paper. Under his ownership it generally supported the CONSERVATIVE PARTY and was a strong advocate of the war effort. When Lt Gov E.G. PRIOR died suddenly in office, Prime Minister Borden needed to choose a successor quickly. Recalling the loyal support the *Province* had given him, he appointed Nichol on Christmas Day 1920. It is the only time a journalist has been LT GOV. It was a generally prosperous, politically stable period and Nichol's term was uneventful. He retired in Feb 1926 and, having sold the *Province* to the Southam family, lived in Victoria until his death. *See also* NEWSPAPERS.

NICHOLS, Marjorie, journalist (b 1943, Red Deer, AB; d there 29 Dec 1991). Raised on an Alberta farm, she studied journalism at the Univ of Montana and began her career in NEWSPAPERS at the *Ottawa Journal* in 1966. Two years later she became one of the first women in the press gallery covering Parliament Hill, where she began to earn a reputation for her tireless work

Marjorie Nichols, journalist, 1986.

habits and combative, flamboyant personality. In Jan 1972 she joined the VANCOUVER SUN as its bureau chief in VICTORIA. Along with Allan FOTHERINGHAM, Simma HOLT, Jack WASSERMAN and others, she made the *Sun* one of the liveliest, most provocative newspapers in Canada. When an irate Premier Dave BARRETT publicly swore at her during a hallway encounter it made headlines across the country. She returned to Ottawa and worked from 1974 to 1977 as the *Sun*'s parliamentary bureau chief, worked in Washington from 1977 to 1979, then was back in BC with the *Sun* from 1979 to 1987 writing a political column. One of the leading political reporters of her generation, Nichols was working for the *Ottawa Citizen* when she was diagnosed with lung cancer, which eventually took her life.

NICHOLSON, pop 1,057, a residential suburb 7 km south of GOLDEN on the COLUMBIA R, was named after C. Nicholson, the first postmaster. It was the site of the Interior's first RAILWAY LOGGING operation, from the mid-1890s to the 1920s. The Columbia River Lumber Co hauled timber to the river here and floated it downstream to its large SAWMILL at Golden.   AS

NICHOLSON, John Robert, lawyer, politician, lt gov 1968–73 (b 1 Dec 1901, Newcastle, NB; d 8 Oct 1983, Vancouver). After graduating from Dalhousie Univ law school, he moved in 1924 to VANCOUVER, where he became a prominent lawyer and an active Liberal. When WWII began he went to Ottawa as a deputy controller in the department of munitions and supplies. From 1942 to 1951 he was in charge of the Polymer Corp, a CROWN CORPORATION manufacturing artificial rubber, initially for the war effort. In 1952 he moved to Rio de Janeiro as head of the Brazilian Light and Power Co (BRASCAN). He returned to Vancouver in 1956, practised law and served briefly as president of the COUNCIL OF FOREST INDUSTRIES. In 1962 he ran successfully for Parliament as a Liberal in the riding of Vancouver Centre. Under Prime Minister Lester Pearson he held a series of cabinet posts until his retirement from politics prior to the 1968 election. He was sworn in as LT GOV on 2 July 1968 and was in office when the SOCIAL CREDIT PARTY lost its long hold on power in the 1972 provincial election. He retired to his home in Vancouver in 1973.

NICOL, Eric P. humorist (b 28 Dec 1919, Kingston, ON). Raised in VANCOUVER, he served in the RCAF during WWII, after which he studied French at UBC and the Sorbonne. He began his career writing humour for the BBC in London, then returned to Vancouver and began writing a column in the *PROVINCE* newspaper in

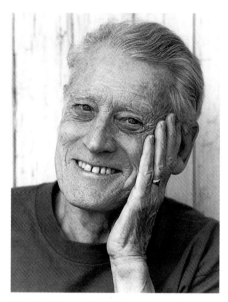

Eric Nicol, humorist, 1998.
Barry Peterson & Blaise Enright-Peterson

1951. This column, along with a steady outpouring of radio and stage plays, television scripts and humorous histories, established him as BC's most popular humorist. *Vancouver*, a history of his hometown, appeared in 1970. Over the years he wrote a series of best-selling books of collected humour, 3 of which were winners of the Leacock Medal for Humour: *The Roving I* (1950), *Shall We Join the Ladies?* (1955) and *Girdle Me a Globe* (1957). *Dickens of the Mounted* (1989) is an inventive edition of the imaginary letters of Frank Dickens, son of Charles and one-time officer in the North West Mounted Police. Nicol's memoirs, *Anything for a Laugh*, were published in 1998.

NICOLA is a historic ranching (*see* CATTLE INDUSTRY) community founded at the south end of Nicola Lk in 1871. By 1882 it was the government and commercial hub of the Nicola Valley, but by 1907 the centre of activity was shifting to MERRITT. The Nicola Ranch, with headquarters at the townsite, was founded in 1919 by Major Charles S. Goldman, a wealthy South African man. Along with cattle, the ranch has the largest fallow-DEER farm in N America.

A view of the Nicola Valley.
Walter Lanz/Image Makers

NICOLA RIVER rises on the Douglas Plateau northeast of PENNASK LK and flows generally westward for 150 km to join the THOMPSON R near SPENCES BRIDGE. The rolling GRASSLANDS through which the upper portion of the river meanders has been cattle country since the first ranchers arrived in the 1870s (*see* CATTLE INDUSTRY). This is the home of the DOUGLAS LAKE CATTLE CO, the largest ranch in Canada, as well as many other smaller spreads. For much longer than that it has been home to the Spaxomin, a branch of the OKANAGAN First Nations. The river is named after Chief Hwistesmetx'quen, called "Nicola" by early FUR TRADERS because it sounded vaguely like "Nicholas" when pronounced phonetically; the mispronunciation has persisted. After it passes through Nicola Lk, the river flows under the COQUIHALLA HWY and merges with the Coldwater R at MERRITT, the largest community along its route. The banks of the lower part of the river, between Merritt and Spences Bridge, become increasingly steep and wooded. Here the original inhabitants are the Sce'exmx, related to the NLAKA'PAMUX (Thompson) First Nations. COAL mining began in the Nicola Valley near Merritt in 1906 and continued until the 1960s. It was followed by COPPER mining at the Craigmont Mine (1961–82) and at the huge open-pit operation in the Highland Valley (since 1971) near LOGAN LAKE. Along with MINING and ranching, LOGGING has been economically important in the watershed. The river is an important SALMON spawning stream and, with its associated lakes, offers some of the best sport FISHING in BC. The area has a number of excellent hiking TRAILS, including historic trails. In the fall, with its many golden aspens, the area is spectacular. *See also* RIVERS.

NICOMEKL RIVER, 25 km, is a slow, shallow stream that meanders through LANGLEY and SURREY south of VANCOUVER to its mouth at MUD BAY north of CRESCENT BEACH. It was used by Coast Salish (*see* SALISHAN FIRST NATIONS) travelling between the BOUNDARY BAY area and the middle

FRASER VALLEY. In 1824 a party of HBC FUR TRADERS also used this route when they came up from the COLUMBIA R to scout the Fraser for a site for the post that became FORT LANGLEY. Prior to flood control measures on the Fraser, the Nicomekl flooded regularly. Now it is a placid stream, popular with anglers for its fall run of coho SALMON. A turn-of-the-century settlement named Nicomekl formed around Maj Robert Hornby's School of Farming, which was aimed at young Englishmen who wished to establish themselves in BC. *See also* RIVERS.

NICOMEN ISLAND, 70 km east of VANCOUVER on the north side of the FRASER R between MISSION and AGASSIZ, was an early FRASER VALLEY farming district (*see* AGRICULTURE). James Codville ran a roadhouse during the GOLD RUSH and opened BC's first rural post office, Codville Landing, in 1865. Several French Canadian settlers farmed here in the 1880s, and Sam McDonald started a cattle ranch. This fertile island, 15 km long, provides important habitat for bald EAGLES, trumpeter SWANS and many other species of waterfowl. The name derives from a HALKOMELEM Salish word meaning "flat part." *AS*

NIEDERMAYER, Scott, hockey player (b 31 Aug 1973, Edmonton). He honed his skills in CRANBROOK and attracted the attention of the KAMLOOPS BLAZERS, for whom he played 3 seasons. He was a West Division all-star, top student-athlete in Canadian junior HOCKEY and a member of the team that won the 1991 world junior championships. He made a memorable pass to set up the game-winning goal that brought the 1992 Blazers their first national junior championship Memorial Cup and brought him honours as the tournament's MVP. Drafted by the New Jersey Devils, he helped the team to win Stanley Cups in 1995 and 2000. He played for Team Canada in the 1996 World Cup and by the late 1990s he had established himself as one of the NHL's premier defencemen. *SW*

NIGEI ISLAND, 62 km², is the largest of a chain of islands off the north end of VANCOUVER ISLAND in Queen Charlotte Strait just west of PORT HARDY. It was visited by the Spanish explorers Dionisio ALCALA-GALIANO and Cayetano VALDES in 1792 and originally named after Alcalá-Galiano. In 1900 the name was changed to avoid confusion with the GULF ISLAND also named for Galiano. Nigei was a local chief of the Nahwitti First Nation, of the KWAKWA̲KA̲ʼWAKW, who gathered food on the island. A small community of fishers and BOATBUILDERS has lived in Cascade Harbour on the outer shore of the island.

NIGHTHAWK and poorwill belong to the nightjar (or goatsucker) family of birds, a group of nocturnal INSECT-eaters with enormous wide mouths, large flat heads, large eyes, tiny bills and intricately patterned brown or grey plumage that conceals them by day when they roost on the ground. The 2 species in BC are the common nighthawk (*Chordeiles minor*), which breeds throughout the province, and the common poorwill (*Phalaenoptilus nuttallii*), which breeds only in the OKANAGAN VALLEY but can be seen farther north in the CHILCOTIN and CARIBOO regions and east to the KOOTENAY. Unlike other nightjars, the common nighthawk feeds both day and night. During courtship the male's wings make a hollow booming sound as it swoops to the ground near its mate. *Kim Goldberg*

NIMPKISH LAKE, 36.5 km², is a long (22 km), narrow lake on northern VANCOUVER ISLAND near PORT MCNEILL. It is fed by the Nimpkish R, rising in the mountains near STRATHCONA PROVINCIAL PARK. The river also drains the lake into Broughton Strait opposite ALERT BAY. An ECOLOGICAL RESERVE in the lower portion of the river protects a stand of some of the tallest DOUGLAS FIRS in Canada. This is the territory of the Nimpkish, or 'Namgis First Nation, a branch of the KWAKWA̲KA̲ʼWAKW. Capt George VANCOUVER visited their village, Xwalkw, in 1792 and called it Cheslakees. Later the 'Namgis moved across the strait to Alert Bay. LOGGING began in the Nimpkish Valley after WWI and developed into one of the largest RAILWAY LOGGING operations on the coast. The FOREST INDUSTRY was still important at the turn of the millennium. The Island Hwy skirts the east side of the lake; Nimpkish Lake Provincial PARK (39.5 km²) is on the west shore. Strong winds make the lake attractive to windsurfers. The Nimpkish system used to be one of the most productive SALMON rivers on the coast but by the 1960s runs had been depleted by over-fishing and logging activities. *See also* LAKES.

NIMPO LAKE, pop 167, on the 9.88 km² lake of the same name about 300 km west of WILLIAMS LAKE on the Chilcotin Hwy (Hwy 20; *see* ROADS AND HWYS), is known as the float plane capital of BC for the constant flow of air traffic servicing the surrounding FISHING sites.

NINE O'CLOCK GUN is a cannon that has boomed across VANCOUVER harbour nightly at 9 pm since 1894, when it was installed at BROCKTON POINT in STANLEY PARK. It was originally

The Nine O'Clock Gun, Brockton Point, Stanley Park, c 1935. The original wooden housing, built in 1894, is now gone. Leonard Frank/VPL 13493

intended as an aid to mariners in synchronizing their chronometers; now it serves as a convenient reminder to Greater Vancouverites to check their clocks. The cannon was moved to its present site, near Hallelujah Point in Stanley Park, in 1954. It fell silent during WWII, and briefly in 1969 when it was stolen by engineering students as a prank; otherwise it is as reliable a sound of the city as the noon-hour rendition of the opening notes of *O Canada* by the horns atop Canada Place.

NINSTINTS, now abandoned, was the main Kunghit HAIDA village on the QUEEN CHARLOTTE ISLANDS. It was located in a sheltered bay on the

Totem poles at Ninstints. Ken Bowen photo

eastern side of Anthony Island. The name comes from the English version of the name of a local chief, Nan stins. During the 1840s the town had 20 houses and a population of 300. A series of epidemics killed many inhabitants until by the 1870s the site was used only as a seasonal camp. Houses and monuments fell into ruins. In 1957 a salvage team from the provincial museum (*see* ROYAL BC MUSEUM) and UBC removed several TOTEM POLES from the site. These are preserved at different museums. In 1958 Anthony Island was made a provincial PARK; in 1981 UNESCO declared Ninstints a WORLD HERITAGE SITE.

NISGA'A are a FIRST NATIONS people occupying the valley of the NASS R in northwest BC. Their language is usually considered to be the northern usage of Nass-Gitksan, but for political reasons is sometimes referred to as a distinct idiom (*see* FIRST NATIONS LANGUAGES; TSIMSHIAN). When the first European explorers arrived at the mouth of the river in 1793 an estimated 8,000 people were living in the Nass Valley. Epidemic diseases reduced that number to less than 900, but since the 1920s the population has recovered. The 1996 population was about 5,300, 1,886 of whom lived in the 4 main villages of Gingolx

Nisga'a pole raising at Gitwinksihlkw (Canyon City) on the Nass R, 1992. Gary Fiegehen photo

(KINCOLITH), Laxqalts'ap (GREENVILLE), Gitwinksihlkw (CANYON CITY) and GITLAKDAMIKS (New Aiyansh). The rest lived outside the territory. The Nisga'a are organized socially into 4 matrilineal totemic clans: KILLER WHALE, WOLF, RAVEN and EAGLE. Clans are further divided into houses, or *wilps*, which hold rights to songs, dances, names and territories. The people occupied villages of CEDAR plank houses (*see* ARCHITECTURE, ABORIGINAL) and engaged in elaborate winter ceremonies, including the POTLATCH. They subsisted on the SALMON and EULACHON fisheries, plus hunting and gathering. Extensive trading networks deep into the Interior linked them with their GITKSAN relatives and other neighbouring groups. Today FISHING and LOGGING are the main employers, though unemployment in the valley

is high. The tradition of wood carving has been revitalized and Nisga'a TOTEM POLES by master carvers such as Norman TAIT and his brother Alver are again being raised in traditional Nisga'a territory and as far away as VANCOUVER, Chicago, England and Australia (*see* ART, NORTHWEST COAST ABORIGINAL). The Nisga'a were the first aboriginal group to initiate a legal land claim against the government (*see* ABORIGINAL RIGHTS), sending a delegation to VICTORIA in 1887. After repeated rebuffs they appealed in a 1913 petition directly to the Privy Council in England, contending that they had never surrendered their territory and asking for recognition of their aboriginal title. In 1955 they formed the Nisga'a Tribal Council to unite the 4 clans in pursuit of their claim. Led by Chief Frank CALDER they initiated another legal case in 1969 (*see* CALDER CASE) that ended at the Supreme Court of Canada. Though the court ruled against the Nisga'a in a split decision, it recognized the principle of aboriginal title and brought about a fundamental shift in government policy. In Aug 1998 the Nisga'a finally initialled a historic treaty settlement with the provincial and federal governments (*see* NISGA'A TREATY).
Reading: Nisga'a Tribal Council, *Nisga'a: People of the Nass River*, 1993.

Canada's youngest lava flow, Nisga'a Memorial Lava Bed Provincial Park. Ian Smith/Vancouver Sun

NISGA'A MEMORIAL LAVA BED PROVINCIAL PARK, 1,768.3 km², is near the town of GITLAKDAMIKS (New Aiyansh) about 105 km north of TERRACE at the NASS R. It features a vast lava plain created by a volcanic eruption in about 1700. The lava flow destroyed two NISGA'A villages and diverted the Nass R. The park, established in 1992, is one of BC's first provincial PARKS to be jointly managed by the province and a FIRST NATION, in this case the Nisga'a, who know it as *Anhluut'ukwsim Laxmihl Angwinga'asanskwhl Nisga'a*.

NISGA'A TREATY is a formal agreement between the NISGA'A people of the NASS R valley and the provincial and federal governments. It was the first treaty made in BC between government and FIRST NATIONS people since TREATY NO 8 was signed 100 years earlier, and it was made possible by a fundamental change in policy on the part of the provincial government, which in 1991 decided to recognize aboriginal title. As such, it is considered a turning point in relations

between aboriginals and non-aboriginals in BC. The agreement resolved a land claim that the Nisga'a first began pursuing in 1887 (*see also* CALDER CASE; ABORIGINAL RIGHTS). Under its terms, the Nisga'a will collectively own 1,992 km² of land in the Nass Valley plus small parcels of land elsewhere (about 8% of what they say was their traditional territory), a $190-million cash settlement (mostly paid by the federal government; *see also* FEDERAL-PROVINCIAL RELATIONS), $11.5 million earmarked for fisheries development, a guaranteed share of fish, animal, timber and mineral resources, and a form of self-government with some jurisdiction over a variety of local services. (The total cost of the agreement is a matter of dispute; estimates have varied from $312 million to $500 million.) In return the Nisga'a agreed to give up their longstanding exemption from taxation under the *Indian Act* and to make no further claims based on aboriginal title. The agreement was initialled on 4 Aug 1998, ratified by the Nisga'a people in a referendum, approved by the provincial legislature on 22 Apr 1999 and ratified by the federal Parliament later in 1999.

During debate over its terms, the Nisga'a Treaty aroused much controversy in the province. Opposition to it centred on 3 arguments. Some people argued that the self-government provisions created a new order of government, thereby amending the Canadian Constitution and, under BC law, requiring approval in a provincewide referendum. Commercial fishers (*see* FISHING, COMMERCIAL) argued that the fishery provisions of the agreement established a fishery based on race (*see also* FISHING, ABORIGINAL). Other commentators argued that the treaty gave the Nisga'a special privileges not enjoyed by all British Columbians. As well, the Gitanyow First Nation of the GITKSAN people argued that the agreement included overlapping land they claim as their own. Treaty proponents, on the other hand, argued that it acknowledged a just claim by the Nisga'a to their traditional lands, that it helped to end the economic uncertainty associated with unresolved land claims, and that a negotiated settlement was a better solution than continued litigation in the courts.

Nitinat Lake, a popular windsurfing spot.
Keith Thirkell photo

NITINAT LAKE, 27.48 km², is a long (24 km), narrow inlet south of BAMFIELD on the west coast

of VANCOUVER ISLAND that is connected to the ocean by a tidal narrows. Boats gained access to the lake by crossing a treacherous bar. Part of the lake is in the Nitinat Triangle portion of the WEST COAST TRAIL section of PACIFIC RIM NATIONAL PARK RESERVE. It was saved from LOGGING in 1972 as the result of a lobbying campaign led by the wilderness activist Ric CARELESS; it was one of the first major successes for the ENVIRONMENTAL MOVEMENT in the province. The area is occupied by the Ditidaht, a NUU-CHAH-NULTH nation, some of whom have lived at a RESERVE at the top end of the lake since the 1960s. Their traditional village of Whyac was located on the ocean at the mouth of the narrows. The lake is a mecca for windsurfers. *See also* LAKES.

NITOBE MEMORIAL GARDEN is a 1.2-ha traditional Japanese garden, considered the most authentic garden of its type outside Japan. Opened in 1960 on the UBC campus near the MUSEUM OF ANTHROPOLOGY, it was designed by the Japanese landscape architect Kannosuke Mori and named for Inazo Nitobe, an educator and diplomat, who died while visiting VICTORIA in 1933. Its layout of rock, gardens, pond and pathways reflects an idealized conception of natural harmony. It also includes a tea house imported from Japan and assembled by Japanese carpenters.

NIVEN, Frederick John, novelist (b 31 Mar 1878, Valparaiso, Chile; d 30 Jan 1944, Vancouver). Born to Scottish parents who were living in Chile, he was raised in Glasgow; many of his novels deal with Scotland and with Scottish immigrants in Canada. Niven himself arrived in BC in 1899, sojourning in the KOOTENAY for treatment of a lung disease. He returned to Scotland the next year and began his writing career by publishing newspaper accounts of his travels. His first novel appeared in 1908; he wrote more than 30 in all. Several are about BC, to which he returned to live permanently in 1920; he settled at Willow Point outside NELSON. He is best known for a trilogy of historical novels: *The Flying Years* (1935) and *Mine Inheritance* (1940) review developments in western Canada from 1811 to WWI; the third novel, *The Transplanted* (1944), deals with MINING and RANCHING in the pre-WWII BC Interior.

NLAKA'PAMUX (Thompson) are an Interior Salish people (*see* SALISHAN FIRST NATIONS) in south-central BC occupying communities along the Fraser Canyon (*see* FRASER R) as far south as YALE, along the lower THOMPSON R and in the NICOLA R valley. They relied on the rich SALMON runs that arrived in the RIVERS every summer, as well as hunting and gathering PLANT foods. They lived communally during the winter in villages of semi-subterranean pit houses (*see* ARCHITECTURE, ABORIGINAL), dispersing in family groups in the spring and summer to gather food. Simon FRASER was the first European to enter their territory; when he passed down the Fraser R in 1808 he reported seeing 1,200 Nlaka'pamux gathered at the village of Kumsheen on the site of LYTTON.

Moccasin made from black tree moss woven with strands of silverberry by Nlaka'pamux weavers. Dorothy Kennedy photo

It was gold traded by the Nlaka'pamux during the 1850s that touched off the GOLD RUSH to the Fraser R in 1858. This brought thousands of miners (*see* MINING) into their territory, followed by road (*see* ROADS AND HWYS) and railway builders, farmers and government agents. Along with the SMALLPOX epidemic of the 1860s, the new arrivals brought important changes for the Nlaka'pamux, who were confined to small RESERVES and forced to adapt to subsistence farming and the wage economy. In 1913 a landslide from rail construction in the Fraser Canyon blocked the annual salmon run and dealt a devastating blow from which the people did not recover for decades (*see* HELLS GATE BLOCKADE). Today the Nlaka'pamux are working with government to maintain salmon stocks in the rivers that they continue to fish as they have done for millennia. There are 11 Nlaka'pamux FIRST NATIONS living in communities throughout the territory, with a total registered population of about 3,500. LOGGING, ranching (*see* CATTLE INDUSTRY) and AGRICULTURE are important employers. Efforts by the Nlaka'pamux to preserve the STEIN R valley from logging led to the creation in 1995 of the Stein Valley Nlaka'pamux Heritage Provincial Park (*see* PARKS, PROVINCIAL).

NON-PARTISAN ASSOCIATION is a civic political organization in VANCOUVER. It formed as an alliance of Liberals and Conservatives in 1937 in reaction to the election of 3 CCF candidates to city council the previous year. Members vowed "to keep politics out of city hall," though in practice this meant keeping socialists and other left-wingers off council. The NPA had no official platform; it merely endorsed candidates it found acceptable. NPA-endorsed candidates largely controlled city council and the parks and school boards from 1938 until the early 1970s when The Electors Action Movement (TEAM) challenged its dominance. During the 1990s the NPA regained its dominant position on city council.

NOOTKA, on the southeast side of Nootka Island in NOOTKA SOUND on the west coast of VANCOUVER ISLAND, was the site of a cannery, pilchard reduction plant (*see* SARDINE, PACIFIC) and boat repair facility from 1917 to 1950. Originally established by the Nootka Packing Co, it was later sold to the CANADIAN FISHING CO.

Many Mowachaht (*see* NUU-CHAH-NULTH) people from nearby YUQUOT worked here. It later became the site of a FISHING resort.   AS

NOOTKA First Nation; *see* NUU-CHAH-NULTH.

NOOTKA SOUND is one of 5 major sounds indenting the west coast of VANCOUVER ISLAND. Capt James COOK named it after what he mistakenly believed the local people called it. Cook, who arrived with 2 ships in 1778, was the first European in the sound. One result of his visit was the beginning of a trade in SEA OTTER pelts; another was a diplomatic squabble between England and Spain over competing claims to the coast (*see* NOOTKA SOUND CONTROVERSY). The sound was home to the Mowachaht and Muchalaht, two NUU-CHAH-NULTH groups, whose village at YUQUOT has been inhabited for thousands of years. Following contact, and the subsequent depopulation due to disease, the Muchalaht merged with the Mowachaht, then relocated to a RESERVE near GOLD RIVER. Later they were called the Mowachaht/Muchalaht First Nation. The sound, with its spectacular mountain scenery, has 3 main arms that penetrate inland: TAHSIS, Tlupana and MUCHALAT inlets. A SALMON CANNERY operated on Nootka Island (526 km²) until the 1950s and a limestone quarry up Tlupana Inlet provided material for the legislative buildings in VICTORIA, but LOGGING was the main economic activity starting in the 1930s. The MV UCHUCK III supplies the various villages and camps.

NOOTKA SOUND CONTROVERSY, 1789–94, was a diplomatic squabble between Spain and Britain for control of the Northwest Coast. During the 1770s Spain actively asserted its claim to the entire west coast of N America by sending expeditions as far north as Alaska from San Blas in Mexico. One of these anchored off NOOTKA SOUND in 1774 (*see* SPANISH EXPLORATION). Britain's counterclaim was based on James COOK's 1778 visit to the BC coast that included a stopover at Nootka. In May 1789 a Spanish expedition under Estéban José MARTINEZ established itself on the site of YUQUOT in Friendly Cove in Nootka Sound, built a fort and later seized British FUR TRADING vessels. This outraged John MEARES, a sponsor of these traders. He

returned to England from China in 1790 and stirred up government and public opinion against Spain with an inflammatory account of events at Friendly Cove. Prime Minister William Pitt took advantage of the inability of France, Spain's traditional European ally, to promise assistance because of the French Revolution; he threatened war over the principle of freedom of the seas and the right of Britons to trade wherever there were no established foreign settlements.

War was averted when Spain agreed to the Nootka Sound Convention on 28 Oct 1790. The Spanish accepted British access to the Northwest Coast and agreed to restore British property with restitution. To attend to the details of the treaty, the 2 countries sent commissioners to Nootka in 1792, but Juan Francisco de la BODEGA Y QUADRA and George VANCOUVER could not reach an agreement; they referred their differing opinions back to Madrid and London. The matter was eventually resolved with the Convention for the Mutual Abandonment of Nootka, 11 Jan 1794, which confirmed the earlier British triumph in gaining access to the coast for the purposes of trade. In Jan 1795, 2 new commissioners, José Manuel de Alava and Thomas Pierce, met in Monterey. They sailed north to Nootka on the *Activa* and arrived on 16 Mar. The fort was dismantled and by 28 Mar the Spanish were ready to abandon their establishment. Alava and Pierce took part in a ceremony in which the British flag was raised, lowered and given to MAQUINNA for safekeeping. The rights of the Mowachaht people were thus restored at Yuquot after imperial manoeuvring in which aboriginal interests had been conspicuously ignored. *See also* FIRST NATIONS; NUU-CHAH-NULTH.   *Robin Inglis*

NORALEE, 55 km southwest of BURNS LAKE at the west end of FRANÇOIS LK, is a LOGGING and summer resort community with a store. The area was first settled in the 1910s though the road did not arrive until 1928. The name comes from Nora and Lee Newgaard, who opened a post office here in 1937.   AS

NORMAN, Percy, swim coach (b 14 Mar 1904, New Westminster; d 26 May 1957, Vancouver). He was Canada's top SWIMMING and DIVING coach for 25 years. As head coach of the VANCOUVER Amateur Swim Club he taught

Captain James Cook's vessels Resolution *and* Discovery *at Nootka Sound, 1778.*

thousands of young people and many of them, including George ATHANS Sr, Joan Langdon, Helen STEWART and Lynda Adams Hunt, dominated their specialties in Canada. His legacy of success continued through coaches he trained including Stewart, Ted Simpson, Bob Gair, Jack POMFRET and Howard Firby. He led the Canadian swim team to the 1932 Los Angeles and 1936 Berlin Olympics and in 1954 he coached the Canadian team at the British Empire Games (*see* BRITISH EMPIRE AND COMMONWEALTH GAMES) in Vancouver, where it collected 6 medals. He was inducted into the BC SPORTS HALL OF FAME in 1967 and the Percy Norman Pool at Vancouver's Little Mountain is named for him.   SW

NORRIS, Leonard Matheson "Len," newspaper cartoonist (b 1 Dec 1913, London, England; d 12 Aug 1997, Langley). He joined the *VANCOUVER SUN* newspaper in 1950 and for 38 years his cartoons were a fixture on the editorial pages. His comic world included an exaggerated version of suburban W VANCOUVER, a.k.a. Amblesnide and Tiddlycove, where he lived for many years. He gave voice to a beleaguered middle class, mocking the pretensions of bureaucrats and the Col Blimps at the "Victoria Conservative Club." His politicians were always fatuous, his children usually brats. His last original cartoon appeared in Dec 1988, though the *Sun* reprinted his work for years. Norris's fame spread far beyond VANCOUVER. He was recognized as the best editorial cartoonist in Canada and annual collections of his work were a staple gift under the Christmas tree for fans around the world. Before coming to Vancouver he worked in advertising and was art director for Maclean Hunter Ltd.

Len Norris at his drafting table, 1963.
Vancouver Sun

NORTH BEND, in the FRASER R canyon 43 km north of YALE, was the CPR's divisional point between VANCOUVER and KAMLOOPS. It was originally known as Yankee Flats. A resort hotel, Fraser Canyon House, was built here in 1886

and replaced in 1935 with a new hotel that lasted until the late 1970s. North Bend was the site of a unique aerial ferry from 1940 to 1986. Two steel cables strung across the river to BOSTON BAR carried a large basket capable of holding a single motor vehicle or 40 passengers. During 46 years of operation the ferry safely transported more than 2 million vehicles and 6 million people on its 3-min crossing. It was replaced by the Cog Harrington Bridge.

NORTH BONAPARTE, a CARIBOO ranching (*see* CATTLE INDUSTRY) centre 115 km southeast of WILLIAMS LAKE, is between Bonaparte and Green lakes on the BONAPARTE PLATEAU. TOURISM has been important to the area, thanks to the dozens of LAKES, good sport FISHING and numerous camping sites in the surrounding region.   AS

NORTH COWICHAN, district municipality, pop 25,305, in the southeast corner of VANCOUVER ISLAND north of DUNCAN, is one of 4 municipalities in the Cowichan Valley Regional District. Home to different Coast Salish nations (*see* SALISHAN FIRST NATIONS), it began attracting farm settlement in the 1860s and was incorporated as a district in 1873, the fourth-oldest municipality in BC. In 1912, 3.45 km² were removed from the southern part of the municipality to become the city of Duncan. The main urban centre has become CHEMAINUS, and the communities of MAPLE BAY, CROFTON and GENOA BAY also are part of the district. DAIRY FARMING was the focus of the AGRICULTURAL economy, while the FOREST INDUSTRY and TOURISM are important economic activities: in 1999 the forest industry employed ³/4 of the municipality's workforce. The first SAWMILL in the region, at Chemainus, began operations in 1862; in 1946 N Cowichan established its own forest reserve. The area's mild CLIMATE and pleasant landscape attract a growing number of retirees.

NORTH PACIFIC CANNERY VILLAGE is a restored SALMON CANNERY in PORT EDWARD south of PRINCE RUPERT. In operation from 1889 to 1972, it is located on Inverness Passage, the northern arm of the SKEENA R. At its peak it employed up

The restored salmon cannery complex at North Pacific Cannery Village, 1996. Allison Eaton photo

to 700 FIRST NATIONS, CHINESE and JAPANESE workers during the summer season. Declared a National Historic Site in 1985, it re-creates a working cannery and the hierarchy of living arrangements for its employees.

NORTH PACIFIC FUR SEAL CONVENTION, 7 July 1911, was an agreement between Canada, Russia, Japan and the US dividing the FUR SEAL harvest of the Pribilof, Commander, Kurile and Robben islands. The agreement ended the pelagic hunt for fur seals that had been carried out since the 1860s by a sealing fleet based in VICTORIA. In return for abandoning the hunt, Canada was compensated with $200,000 and a percentage of the annual value of the land catch still taken by the other signatories. By the late 1990s the convention was still in effect.

NORTH PINE, 20 km north of FORT ST JOHN, is a small AGRICULTURAL settlement in the PEACE R district. It is the site of the annual North Peace Fall Fair, which celebrated its 50th anniversary in 1997.   AS

NORTH VANCOUVER CITY occupies the lower slopes of the North Shore mountains across BURRARD INLET from VANCOUVER, to which it is linked by the SEABUS passenger ferry. It is

surrounded on 3 sides by N VANCOUVER DISTRICT, where 2 bridges afford additional connections to Vancouver. The city developed around 1900 as a commercial district at the bottom of Lonsdale Ave; it incorporated in 1907 with a population of about 2,000. It expanded to its present size in 1915 when it absorbed the SAWMILL community of MOODYVILLE to the east. Sawmilling and SHIPBUILDING were the economic mainstays of the early years. Wallace Shipyards (*see* BURRARD DRY DOCK) was one of the largest in the country; more than 130 vessels were built there. During the Depression, N Vancouver was forced to declare bankruptcy and was managed by a commissioner until 1944. The modern city has lost much of its industrial character and has developed mainly as a residential suburb of Vancouver. The waterfront was revitalized with the addition of Lonsdale Quay (a market, hotel and transportation hub) and Waterfront Park in 1986. Redevelopment of the commercial core continued into the early 21st century.
Population: 41,475
Rank in BC: 20th
Population increase since 1981: 22%
Date of incorporation: city 13 May 1907
Land area: 12.67 km²
Location: Greater Vancouver Regional District
Economic base: retail services, light industry, tourism

NORTH VANCOUVER DISTRICT, pop 80,418, overlooks the north side of BURRARD INLET across

from downtown VANCOUVER. Originally the territory of the MUSQUEAM and SQUAMISH First Nations, it attracted the interest of non-aboriginals in the 1860s when LOGGING began. Pioneer Mills began operation in 1863 and the small settlement that grew up around it became known as MOODYVILLE after Sewell MOODY purchased the SAWMILL. The district incorporated on 10 Aug 1891, encompassing the entire North Shore slope from DEEP COVE to HORSESHOE BAY. Commercial activity focussed on Lonsdale Ave, and in 1907 N VANCOUVER CITY incorporated as a separate jurisdiction. The district also lost W VANCOUVER in 1912 and Moodyville, which joined the city in 1915; as a result it arches across the top of N Vancouver City from the CAPILANO R to Deep Cove and includes such suburbs and former villages as Capilano, Cove Cliff, Lionsview, Lynnmour, Maplewood, Northlands, North Lonsdale, Seymour Heights, Lynn Valley and Upper Lynn. The construction of the original Second Narrows Bridge (1925) (*see* IRONWORKERS MEMORIAL SECOND NARROWS CROSSING) and LIONS GATE BRIDGE (1938) improved access to the North Shore, encouraging its post-war development as a residential suburb of Vancouver. The Depression bankrupted the district in 1932; it was administered by a commissioner until 1951. The district became the terminus of the Pacific Great Eastern Rwy (*see* BC RAIL) in 1956. The busy waterfront is part of the Port of Vancouver, while SEYMOUR and GROUSE mountains, Capilano Canyon and Lynn Headwaters Park attract skiers, hikers and tourists.

NORTH WEST AMERICA was the first European vessel built and launched on the BC coast. It was a 40-ton sloop built in 1788 under the direction of John MEARES at YUQUOT on the west coast of VANCOUVER ISLAND. Launched on 20

Launch of the North West America, *the first European vessel built on the BC coast, in Nootka Sound, 1788, shown here in a painting by John Meares. BC Archives A-02688*

Sept, it was used as a coastal vessel to trade for SEA OTTER pelts. It was one of the ships captured by the Spanish in 1789 (*see* NOOTKA SOUND CONTROVERSY); renamed the *Santa Gertrudis*, it was used for exploration on the west coast of Vancouver Island.

NORTH WEST CO (NWC) was a trading company in Montreal that pioneered the land-based FUR TRADE in BC. The first Nor'wester to arrive west of the ROCKY MTS was Alexander MACKENZIE, who made the first transcontinental crossing to the Pacific in 1793. Afterwards he developed plans to exploit the commercial possibilities of the Northwest Coast. NWC followed up on these plans in 1805 by sending Simon FRASER across the Rockies into the area he christened NEW CALEDONIA, now north-central BC. Fraser and his men built several trading posts: Fort McLeod on MCLEOD LK (1805), FORT ST JAMES on Stuart Lk (1806), FORT FRASER on FRASER LK (1806), and Fort George (site of PRINCE GEORGE) at the confluence of the FRASER and NECHAKO rivers (1807). He descended the river that now bears his name in 1808 but decided it did not provide the passable supply route to the ocean that he was seeking. Farther to the south NWC sought an overland route to the Pacific via the COLUMBIA R. In 1811 David THOMPSON made his way to the mouth of this river, where he found the PACIFIC FUR CO already installed. Two years later the NWC bought out its American competition, taking sole possession of the trade on the Columbia and in New Caledonia. It took over lower Fort George at the mouth of the Columbia, which then became headquarters of the trade beyond the Rockies. The northern district of New Caledonia was supplied by CANOE brigades from the east. In 1813 a party of Nor'westers led by John STUART pioneered the Okanagan brigade route connecting the lower Columbia and the upper Fraser posts via the THOMPSON R and the OKANAGAN VALLEY, but thereafter the NWC chose not to use this route to supply New Caledonia. NWC had no involvement in the maritime FUR TRADE along the coast, nor was it able to achieve Mackenzie's dream of a trading link with China. On 26 Mar 1821 it merged with the HBC, which to that point had no presence west of the mountains. Retaining the HBC name, the new company took over all the NWC posts on the Columbia and in New Caledonia.

NORTHCOTT, Tom, singer (b 29 Aug 1943, Vancouver). A pioneering VANCOUVER folk-rock singer and recording artist, Northcott embodied flower power in the city in the late 1960s, with hit singles such as "Sunny Goodge Street," "1941," "Girl Of The North Country" and "Suzanne." Like many of his contemporaries, Northcott got his first big break on CBC-TV, appearing on the Vancouver-based *Let's Go*. In 1965, he began recording together with Rick Enns (bass) and Kat Hendrikse (drums) as the Tom Northcott Trio; subsequently he signed as a solo act with the major American record label, Warner Brothers. He went on to appear with

groups such as The Who, the Doors and Jefferson Airplane. Following his success as a performer, Northcott established his own recording studio, Studio 3, in Vancouver, and worked with Bruce FAIRBAIRN and David FOSTER, who were novice producers at the time. He also established New Syndrome Records, a label that released records by local acts such as the Collectors (*see* CHILLIWACK). In 1969 Northcott bought a commercial SALMON troller and spent the next decade engaged in commercial FISHING. After completing a law degree at UBC in the 1980s, he returned to the studio and issued two CDs, *So You Thought You Heard It All* (1992) and *Joyful Songs of Leonard Cohen* (1997).   *Mike Harling*

NORTHERN STRAITS First Nations, a division of the Central Coast Salish people (*see* SALISHAN FIRST NATIONS), share a common language (*see* FIRST NATIONS LANGUAGES) and occupy the southern end of VANCOUVER ISLAND, SAN JUAN ISLAND, the southern GULF ISLANDS and the mainland around BOUNDARY BAY. There are 6 groups normally identified as Northern Straits: the T'Sou-ke (Sooke), the LEKWAMMEN (Songhees) in the VICTORIA area, the Saanich (Wsanec) on the SAANICH PENINSULA, the Semiahmoo in Semiahmoo Bay, and the Lummi and the Samish in adjacent Washington state.

NORTHFIELD was a COAL mining community 5 km northwest of downtown NANAIMO on VANCOUVER ISLAND. The VANCOUVER Coal Mining and Land Co, which had purchased the HBC's mining interests in 1861 and was Robert DUNSMUIR's chief competitor in the coal business, developed a colliery here in 1888. It closed in 1895 but was reactivated briefly in the late 1930s. Northfield is now a residential suburb of Nanaimo. *See also* COAL MINING, VANCOUVER ISLAND.   *AS*

NORTHLAND NAVIGATION CO LTD was a marine freight service based in VANCOUVER, founded in 1942 by Capt Harry Terry as the British Columbia Steamship Co operating a single vessel. It changed its name to Northland in 1952 and began to expand its passenger service. In 1958 it took over the CANADIAN PACIFIC NAVIGATION CO steamer service on the west coast of VANCOUVER ISLAND and in 1959 bought the UNION STEAMSHIP CO. But in 1976 Northland withdrew from passenger service to concentrate again on freight operations. It was purchased by Dutch interests, then closed.

NORWEGIANS were among the several groups of Scandinavian immigrants who established isolated colonies on the BC coast toward the end of the 19th century (*see also* FINNS, DANES, SWEDES). John Brae, a Norwegian who came to BC via Minnesota, founded a small settlement in CLAYOQUOT SOUND in 1884 and by 1897 he had been joined there by more than 40 other Norwegian pioneers. Farther north a group of Norwegian immigrants from N Dakota established a short-lived colony called Scandia in QUATSINO SOUND in 1894–95. But the most successful of these coastal ventures was at HAGENSBORG near BELLA COOLA, where a group of colonists led by Rev Christian Saugstad began settling in 1894; descendants of the original pioneers still live in the area. Norwegian farmers also pioneered at MATSQUI and other locations in the FRASER VALLEY. Norwegians were attracted to LOGGING as well as farming, but in the post-WWII era the community became more concentrated in urban areas and began to develop support organizations such as the Sons of Norway, LUTHERAN churches and other ethno-cultural associations. At the 1996 census there were 108,700 people of Norwegian origin living in BC, the largest Norwegian community of any province in Canada. *See also* PEOPLES OF BC.

NOTCH HILL, 20 km northwest of SALMON ARM near SHUSWAP LK, was once a thriving railway community, a base for CPR "pusher" locomotives, with freight and maintenance facilities and a Columbia River Lumber Co SAWMILL. Today it is a quiet farming settlement (*see* AGRICULTURE) with a number of interesting old buildings. It was named by G.M. DAWSON for the gap through the Shuswap Highlands where the railway line now passes.   AS

NOTRE DAME UNIVERSITY OF NELSON opened as Notre Dame College in the city on 6 Sept 1950. Sponsored by the ROMAN CATHOLIC Diocese of Nelson, it offered classes in a former bakery building until moving in 1954 to a new facility erected by faculty and students. In Mar 1963 it obtained the province's second degree-granting charter. NDU was the first Canadian university to offer athletic scholarships and its faculty was the first in English-speaking Canada to unionize. The provincial government announced in June 1974 that it would purchase the university, but closed it in May 1977. The campus reopened as David Thompson Univ Centre and began classes in 1979 as a joint venture between Selkirk College and UNIV OF VICTORIA, making it BC's first university-college. On 1 May 1984 the SOCIAL CREDIT government closed the campus, ostensibly as part of its budgetary restraint program. *See also* EDUCATION, POST-SECONDARY.   *Ron Welwood*

NUCHATLITZ, at the entrance to Nuchatlitz Inlet, on the outer coast of Nootka Island on the west coast of VANCOUVER ISLAND, was a main village of the Nuchatlaht, a NUU-CHAH-NULTH nation. In 1987 most villagers moved to a new site up Espinosa Inlet to be closer to work and conveniences at ZEBALLOS.

NUDIBRANCH, or sea slug, is a MOLLUSC without a shell, and comprises a subclass (Opisthobranchia) of the class Gastropoda, which includes the ABALONE, LIMPET and many other SNAILS. The popular name nudibranchs ("naked gills") refers to the plume-like and tuft-like gill projections of these creatures. There are more than 200 species of nudibranchs in BC waters, exhibiting a spectacular variety of shapes and colours. Nudibranchs prey upon a wide

Dall's dendronotid, a spectacular nudibranch.
Rick Harbo photo

variety of organisms, using specialized tongue-like structures called radulas to "rasp" their food. Species commonly encountered in tidepools and shallow waters include the shaggy mouse nudibranch (*Aeolidia papillosa*), the orange-spotted or clown nudibranch (*Triopha catalinae*), sea lemon (*Archidoris montereyensis*) and the leopard nudibranch (*Diaulula sandiegensis*).

Rick Harbo

NUKKO LAKE, 26 km northwest of PRINCE GEORGE, is a ranching and agricultural district (*see* CATTLE INDUSTRY; AGRICULTURE) with many hobby farms and small acreages. The area around Nukko Lk and Chief Lk, its neighbour to the north, was first settled in about 1910. An early ferry across the NECHAKO R provided access to Prince George.   AS

NURSING became a part of the organized health care system in BC in 1912 with the formation of the Graduate Nurses Assoc of BC (GNABC), the forerunner of the Registered Nurses Assoc of BC. The objective of the association was to prepare legislation, for presentation to government, that would provide for the registration of nurses in the province. On 10 Apr 1918, Bill 68 was passed by the legislature and the *Nurses (Registered) Act* became law. The act enabled the GNABC to examine nurses, approve training schools, keep a current register and set standards by which nursing applicants would be registered. At that time there were approximately 20 nursing training schools scattered throughout BC. Some of these schools were located in small, rural hospitals and provided poor educational programs. Following the passage of Bill 68, the GNABC undertook a survey of nursing schools in the province and subsequently, in 1924, established the first minimum standards for schools of nursing. In 1919 UBC began its nursing programs and by 1923 had graduated the first 3 students with a degree in nursing. In 1935 the GNABC changed its name to the Registered Nurses Assoc of British Columbia (RNABC) and high school graduation became a requirement for admission to a training school. By 1946 there were 3,576 registered nurses in BC.

In 1946 a labour relations committee within

the RNABC was named and certified as the bargaining authority for the first group of nurses at Royal Columbia Hospital. The association launched a labour relations program at the end of 1957 and by 1959 provincial bargaining with the BC Hospital Assoc began, resulting in the establishment of the first uniform salaries for registered nurses. In 1981 collective bargaining procedures changed with the creation of the BC Nurses Union, which is now the bargaining agent for nurses in the province. The RNABC remained responsible for standards and education. By the 1990s nurses were obtaining degrees from UNIV OF VICTORIA as well as UBC and several COMMUNITY COLLEGES offered nursing diplomas. In the year 2000 there were approximately 35,000 registered nurses in BC, 28,000 of whom were practising in a variety of clinical practices, hospitals, health centres and public health programs throughout the province.

Nursing in clinical and acute services focusses on individuals who are sick or in crisis and who have presented themselves for health care. Public health nursing, however, differs in that the main focus is on improving the health of the population through the delivery of programs that focus on self-responsibility for health. These programs are delivered through COMMUNITY DEVELOPMENT projects as well as individual health screening, education and counselling and linking or referral to other specialized service providers within the community. The communicable disease service provision focusses on immunization, risk reduction, outbreak management, and specific disease control and surveillance (*see also* BC CENTRE FOR DISEASE CONTROL). These services are provided in a variety of settings including health units, homes, daycare centres, schools, work sites and community centres. There are approximately 700 public health nurses in BC. Public health nursing services are jointly funded by the ministry of health, the ministry responsible for seniors, and the ministry for children and families. One particularly innovative project, the COMOX Valley Nursing Centre, opened in 1993 with a grant from the ministry of health. This demonstration project, the first of its kind in the province, is run jointly by the ministry and the RNABC and develops programs with input from the local community. All care is provided by nurses with a specific focus on "quality of life" issues such as chronic pain and eating disorders. *See also* HEALTH POLICY.

Claire Sowerbutt

NUTCRACKER, CLARK'S (*Nucifraga columbiana*), is a medium-sized member of the CROW family. It is a white bird with black wing feathers and white wing and tail patches. It is widespread east of the COAST MTS in the southern Interior. Associated specifically with higher-altitude whitebark PINE forests, this bird has a long, pointed black beak with which it extracts the pine cone seeds that form the bulk of its diet. It carries up to 100 seeds at a time in a throat pouch and stores large quantities in caches, sometimes many kilometres from where the seed was collected. The Clark's nutcracker has a

Clark's nutcracker. Duane Sept photo

remarkable ability to remember where the caches are located; the seeds that are not recovered often grow to be new trees.

NUTHATCH is a small, plump bird with a short tail and pointed bill, easily recognized for its habit of walking head first down the trunk of a tree in search of INSECTS and seeds. The name refers to the bird's practice of breaking open hard-shelled seeds with its beak. Often nuthatches are associated with CHICKADEES and other birds in mixed-species foraging, and they are regular visitors to feeding stations in the win-

Red-breasted nuthatch. R. Wayne Campbell photo

ter. Like chickadees, nuthatches nest in cavities in trees. There are 3 species in BC. The least numerous, present mainly in the south-central Interior, is the white-breasted nuthatch (*Sitta carolinensis*). It has a black cap, slate blue back, and white face and breast. Its much more abundant relative, the red-breasted nuthatch (*S. canadensis*), has rust-coloured underparts and a black line through the eye. It is found throughout the province. The pygmy nuthatch (*S. pygmaea*) is associated with the ponderosa PINE forests of the south-central Interior.

NUU-CHAH-NULTH First Nation, formerly called the Nootka, live on the west coast of VAN-COUVER ISLAND. Their traditional territory extends from the BROOKS PENINSULA in the north to the JORDAN R 300 km to the south. Their name means, approximately, "all along the mountainous escarpment" and refers to the location of their territory. It was adopted in 1980 to replace *Nootka*, which was the name mistakenly used by early explorers. When sustained contact with outsiders began in the late 18th century there were about 28,000 Nuu-chah-nulth. Disease and increased warfare depleted their numbers until the population was below 2,000 by the 1930s. By the late 1990s it had grown to about 6,000. The subsistence pattern of the Nuu-chah-nulth was oriented toward the resources of the sea, including shellfish, HALIBUT and, in particular, SALMON. They were the only aboriginal group on the BC coast to hunt whales (*see* WHALING), an activity surrounded by religious ritual. The Nuu-chah-nulth consist of separate tribes, or family groups, speaking dialects of the same language (*see* FIRST NATIONS LANGUAGES) and sharing similar cultural characteristics. Each group originally inhabited particular parts of the territory. At one time there were dozens of groups but since contact with Europeans the number has decreased to 16: the Ka:'yu:'K't'h (Kyuquot) First Nation of KYUQUOT SOUND, the Ehattesaht of ESPERANZA INLET and ZEBALLOS, the Nuchatlaht of Nuchatlitz Inlet and Espinosa Inlet, the Mowachaht (Nootka) near GOLD RIVER, the Hesquiaht at Hesquiat Harbour and HOT SPRINGS COVE, the Ahousaht on FLORES ISLAND, the Tla-o-qui-aht (Clayoquot) in CLAYOQUOT SOUND, the Ucluelet from Ucluelet Inlet, the Toquaht in BARKLEY SOUND, the Uchucklesaht of Uchucklesit Inlet, the Tse-Shaht and Opetchesaht from PORT ALBERNI, and the Huu-ay-aht (Ohiaht) near BAMFIELD. The Diitiidaht (Ditidaht) of NITINAT LK and the Pacheedaht (Pacheenaht) ("people of the sea foam") at Jordan R consider themselves Nuu-chah-nulth (in their cases, formerly known as the Nitinat people) but speak a closely related language. The Makah, who are relatives within the Nootkan subgroup of WAKASHAN, live across JUAN DE FUCA STRAIT on Cape Flattery. Some Nuu-chah-nulth tell stories of contact with non-Natives going back perhaps to Sir Francis DRAKE in the 1570s. Recorded contact began in 1774 with Spanish explorers and in 1778 with the British explorer James COOK. As a result of Cook's visit, a trade in SEA OTTER pelts began and continued until about 1825 (*see* FUR TRADE, MARITIME). From the 1850s permanent trading posts were established on the coast and later the people left home seasonally to hunt SEALS, work in salmon canneries (*see* SALMON CANNING) in the FRASER R and pick hops in Puget Sound. During the 1880s the government allocated RESERVES and missionaries arrived to convert the people. Following WWI canneries and fish plants opened at several locations and commercial FISHING remains an important employer, along with the FOREST INDUSTRY (*see* LOGGING). In several cases traditional villages have moved closer to these jobs and to schools and health facilities

Nuu-chah-nulth female welcome figure carved by Joe David. It is displayed outside the Vancouver Museum. Hilary Stewart photo

so that the people no longer occupy the outer coast as extensively as they did. The Nuu-chah-nulth Tribal Council is located in Port Alberni. *See also* FIRST NATIONS OF BC.
Reading: E.Y. Arima, *The West Coast (Nootka) People*, 1983.

NUXALK, or Bella Coola people (pop about 1,200), are a SALISHAN FIRST NATIONS "outer group" related to but distinct from both the Coast and Interior subgroupings of that language family (*see* FIRST NATIONS LANGUAGES). Traditionally the Nuxalk occupied several permanent villages along the upper DEAN and Burke channels and up the BELLA COOLA R valley. The main tribal groupings were the Bella Coola, the Kimsquit at the head of Dean Channel, the Tallio of S Bentinck Arm and the Kwatna of Kwatna Inlet. Following contact with Europeans and the population decrease that ensued, they

Nuxalk men skimming eulachon oil from a vat, 1977. Dorothy Kennedy photo

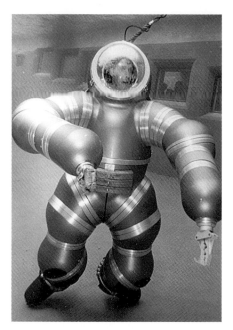

The Newt Suit, developed by Phil Nuytten, a N Vancouver diver and inventor

congregated near the mouth of the Bella Coola R where the main village is now located. Their territory abounded with SALMON, EULACHON, HERRING and sea mammals, allowing them to live sedentarily throughout the year. As well they were oriented to the land, where MOUNTAIN GOAT was the most important resource, providing meat and fat and also wool for blankets. Nuxalk culture was rich in ceremonialism, dominated by 2 secret societies and the POTLATCH. Villages consisted of several households of related families. Everyone belonged to an "ancestral family" or lineage, members of which traced their family back to a single ancestor. Society was less stratified than among other fixed-rank coastal groups. First contact occurred in 1793, when expeditions led by Capt George VANCOUVER and by Alexander MACKENZIE arrived on the coast from different directions. From 1833 to 1844 the HBC operated FORT MCLOUGHLIN at BELLA BELLA; from 1869 to 1882 it had another post at BELLA COOLA. Missionaries arrived in 1883 to begin their transformation of traditional customs. Around 1900, wage-earning in commercial FISHING and LOGGING began to replace the traditional subsistence economy. The 1970s saw a renaissance in traditional singing and dancing and a reawakened sense of aboriginal identity, symbolized by the decision of the Bella Coola to re-adopt publicly their traditional Nuxalk name, which was never abandoned by many of the Elders. *See also* FIRST NATIONS OF BC.

NUYTTEN, Phil, underwater diver, inventor (b 13 Aug 1941, Vancouver). He began scuba diving at age 12 and opened his own diving shop when he was still a teenager. As a commercial diver he worked on heavy construction projects and in the offshore oil industry. His diving company, Can-Dive Services, now Can-Dive Ltd, made him a millionaire. In 1975 he retired from commercial diving to concentrate on inventing. His greatest success was the Newtsuit, a hard-shelled diving suit that allows divers to work at extreme depths while breathing plain air at standard atmospheric pressure. International Hardsuits Inc was established in 1986 to manufacture, sell and lease them; the company was bought by an American manufacturer in 1996. Nuytten heads Nuytco Research Ltd, manufacturers of submersible products, including the "Exosuit," a free-swimming hard suit. A recipient of the ORDER OF BC and a person of myriad interests, he has written on aboriginal ART and he carves masks and TOTEM POLES.

OAK trees occur in N America in many species, but the only one native to BC is the Garry oak (*Quercus garryana*), which is found nowhere else in Canada. It grows on southeast VANCOUVER ISLAND, on the GULF ISLANDS and in 3 isolated

Garry oak.
Kim LaFave drawing

groves in the Lower Mainland. It is far less common than it was a century ago and is considered to be threatened by urban development to the

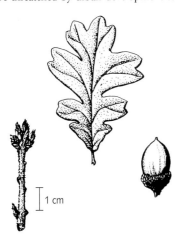

L to r: Winter twig, leaf and fruit of the Garry oak. © T.C. Brayshaw

extent that the Garry oak savannahs of BC are one of Canada's 4 most endangered ecosystems. In eastern Canada the hard, heavy wood of the oak has been used for furniture and flooring, but the BC variety is not abundant enough to have commercial value. It was named by David DOUGLAS after Nicholas Garry, an official of the HBC.

Garry oak, the only oak species native to BC.
Diane Eaton photo

OAK BAY, district municipality, pop 17,865, is a well-to-do residential community occupying the southeast tip of VANCOUVER ISLAND adjacent to VICTORIA, overlooking HARO STRAIT. The first

white settler was John TOD, who arrived in 1850 after a career in the FUR TRADE and developed his Willows Farm on the site. Tod House, built for him in 1851, is the oldest continuously occupied dwelling in western Canada. Oak Bay was a farming and summer cottage area until the 1890s, when the STREET RAILWAY arrived from Victoria and people began building homes. The community has much ARCHITECTURAL interest: a number of houses were designed by Francis RATTENBURY and Samuel MACLURE, among others. Incorporated on 2 July 1906, Oak Bay was named for the many OAK trees on the site. There is no industry and the community is known for its decidedly British flavour. The bay proper welcomes a large number of waterbirds each winter and the offshore Chain Islets contain an ECOLOGICAL RESERVE

that is the second-largest sea bird breeding colony in GEORGIA STRAIT.

OAK BAY MARINE GROUP is N America's largest sport FISHING operator. Founded in VICTORIA in 1962 by Robert Wright, it owns 4 floating hotels, 3 marinas and several lodges including PAINTER'S LODGE in CAMPBELL RIVER, APRIL POINT LODGE on QUADRA ISLAND, King Salmon Resort in RIVERS INLET and Cape Santa Maria Beach Resort in the Bahamas. The company has developed a noticeable presence in Victoria, where it owns several properties, and is a major player in the BC fishing industry.

OAKALLA PRISON FARM, a provincial penal institution, opened on 2 Sept 1912 in BURNABY on a site overlooking Deer Lk. The name, which was changed officially to the Lower Mainland Regional Correctional Centre in 1970, referred to the Royal Oak neighbourhood in which it was located. Between 1919 and 1959, 44 hangings took place. Inmates worked on the farm until the 1970s, and manufactured car licence plates from the early 1930s until 1975. A separate Women's Unit opened in 1940; in 1975 it was renamed the Lakeside Correctional Centre for Women. Oakalla was chronically overcrowded, once holding 1,269 inmates. On 30 June 1991 the entire facility closed; the buildings were razed and the site became a housing development. *See also* PRISONS.

OBERLANDER, Cornelia (Hahn), landscape architect (b 20 June 1924, Muhlheim, Germany). She emigrated with her family to the US near the outbreak of WWII, and after obtaining a BA from Smith College in 1944 she pursued graduate studies at the School of Design at Harvard Univ. In 1953 she moved to VANCOUVER, where she established her own landscape architecture firm and subsequently became one of Canada's leading landscape designers. Early in her career she was associated with low-cost housing projects and children's playgrounds; later she contributed to landmark projects such as Robson Square and the Provincial Courthouse complex in downtown Vancouver, the MUSEUM OF ANTHROPOLOGY at UBC, the National Art Gallery in Ottawa and the Canadian embassy in Washington, DC. She has won many awards and was inducted into the Order of Canada in 1990. She is married to the community planner H. Peter OBERLANDER.

OBERLANDER, H. Peter, community planner (b 1922, Vienna, Austria). He moved to Canada in 1940, graduated in architecture from McGill Univ in 1945, then pursued graduate studies in city planning at Harvard Univ. After working as a federal public servant in Ottawa from 1948 to 1950, he moved to VANCOUVER to join the School of Architecture at UBC, where he taught until 1956, then was founding director of the School of Community and Regional Planning from 1956 to 1970. After another sojourn with the federal public service, he returned to UBC as the founding director of the Centre for Human Settlements and served there from 1973 to 1987. In 1989 he joined the architectural firm of Downs/Archambault as an associate partner. He was inducted into the Order of Canada in 1995. He is married to the landscape architect Cornelia Hahn OBERLANDER.

OBLATES OF MARY IMMACULATE are a congregation of ROMAN CATHOLIC priests founded in 1816 by Eugene de Mazenod in the diocese of Marseilles, France. The Oblates became a missionary congregation with priests and lay brothers going to Oregon in the 1840s. Honoré-Timothée Lempfrit, one of the Oregon missionaries, went for a brief period to assist Modeste DEMERS, the Catholic bishop of VANCOUVER ISLAND, then other Oregon Oblates moved north into Demers's territory in 1858. Louis-Joseph d'HERBOMEZ, the local Oblate superior, was appointed bishop of the BC mainland and focussed his plans on the FIRST NATIONS, the main population of the colony. He designed a system of missions and schools for them, using ST MARY'S MISSION on the FRASER R as a model. There the Oblates ran a RESIDENTIAL SCHOOL and farm, lodged itinerant missionary priests and held annual religious gatherings. In 1868 the SISTERS OF ST ANN began a mission boarding school for girls paralleling the boys' school. The nuns soon taught most classes in both schools. In the 1880s and 1890s the Oblates obtained federal government funding for schools at their St Mary's, KAMLOOPS, CRANBROOK and WILLIAMS LAKE missions. Controversies surrounding residential school management have overshadowed other Oblate contributions to the history of BC. Charles PANDOSY, founder of the OKANAGAN MISSION, began orchards there. Paul DURIEU and Charles Grandidier wrote land claims petitions for the chiefs of the lower Fraser (*see* ABORIGINAL RIGHTS). Other FRANCOPHONE priests like Nicolas COCCOLA and Adrien Gabriel MORICE extended the system of Oblate missions throughout the Interior. As well, a number of Irish Oblates made important contributions, including Brother Patrick Collins, who led the residential school brass bands and did the farm

work that helped support the schools and missions, and James McGuckin, who served 30 years as pastor to First Nations and settlers in the CARIBOO and FRASER VALLEY and later built the Holy Rosary Church, the present-day cathedral, in VANCOUVER.

The modern Oblates minister to urban communities and Interior missions. In the 1990s the Roman Catholic Church in BC was again administered by an Oblate, Adam Exner. He and his fellow Oblates encouraged historic preservation of the cathedral and also of sites administered by First Nations, such as St Paul's Church on the SQUAMISH reserve in N VANCOUVER. *Jacqueline Gresko*

Pulp mill at Ocean Falls, 1920s. UBC BC228

O'BRIAN BAY, a floating LOGGING camp 40 km northeast of PORT HARDY on the north side of Kinnaird Island, was in operation from the mid-1920s to the 1940s with many JAPANESE workers. Myrtle and Bruce Collinson bought the camp in 1945, moved it to nearby SULLIVAN BAY on N Broughton Island and created a thriving float plane base.   *AS*

O'BRIEN, Kathleen, missionary nurse (b 1875, England; d England, date unknown). She arrived on VILLAGE ISLAND in 1920 and at her own expense opened a school and small tuberculosis sanatorium for KWAKWA̱KA̱'WAKW (Kwakiutl) children at MAMALILACULLA, then a principal village site on the island. For many years she was supported by another missionary, Kate Maria Dibben; they officially became part of the COLUMBIA COAST MISSION in 1927, and were legendary on the coast. Dibben became blind and retired to ALERT BAY; O'Brien was named to the Order of the British Empire and she retired to England in 1945.

OBSERVATORY INLET is a long, narrow arm of PORTLAND INLET reaching north from the mouth of the NASS R north of PRINCE RUPERT. It was explored in 1793 by Capt George VANCOUVER, who named it because of astronomical observations he made during his visit. TSIMSHIAN and NISGA'A First Nations have fished at the many

SALMON spawning streams that flow into the inlet (*see* FISHING, ABORIGINAL). The town of ANYOX on Granby Bay near the head of the inlet was the site of a huge COPPER mining operation from 1912 to 1935. MINING also took place in ALICE ARM.

OCEAN FALLS is an almost-abandoned company town at the head of Cousins Inlet, 24 km from the open ocean and 480 km north of VANCOUVER. It is noted for being the rainiest inhabited place in Canada: an average 4,386 mm falls annually. The community sprang to life in 1906, when workers began clearing a site for a mill development. The site was chosen because of the power potential of the WATERFALL that cascades into the inlet from Link Lk. A SAWMILL began operation in 1909 and the Ocean Falls Co opened a PULP AND PAPER mill in 1912. Pacific Mills took over the complex and increased production, and then in 1954 CROWN ZELLERBACH CANADA LTD took control. At its peak the community had a population over 4,000 and gained international renown as the home of a world-class SWIMMING team led by Sandy Gilchrist and Ralph HUTTON. During the 1960s production slowed down and in 1973 the company closed the mill. The NDP government revived the operation as a CROWN CORPORATION but it closed permanently in 1980 and most of the inhabitants moved away. In 1999 there was a permanent population of about 40.

OCEAN FISHERIES LTD is one of the largest seafood processors in BC and Canada's leading producer of SALMON caviar. Incorporated in 1962, it is privately owned by the Safarik family. The company has 3 BC processing plants (in PRINCE RUPERT, VANCOUVER and RICHMOND), which produce fresh, frozen and canned wild salmon. Ocean also processes fresh and frozen HALIBUT and GROUNDFISH fillets. *See also* SALMON CANNING.   *Peter A. Robson*

OCEAN PARK, 20 km south of NEW WESTMINSTER, is a residential suburb of SURREY between CRESCENT BEACH and WHITE ROCK. It was developed in the early 1900s as a waterfront summer resort by a group of Lower Mainland METHODISTS and became the site of a UNITED CHURCH camp. The GREAT NORTHERN RWY had a station here. AS

OCEANIC, at the mouth of the SKEENA R on Smith Island 22 km south of PRINCE RUPERT, was the site of a SALMON CANNERY. It was built in 1903 by the BC Canning Co to replace its ABERDEEN plant, which had burned the previous year. It closed in 1929 and was destroyed by fire in 1935. AS

OCEANOGRAPHY is a discipline that applies the basic principles of biology, chemistry, geology and physics to the study of oceans. The oceanography of the BC coast is complex and only partially understood because studies only began in the early 1950s when pioneer researchers such as J.P. TULLY started their work. The water characteristics on the West Coast, such as temperature, salinity, dissolved oxygen, currents and waves, are influenced by distant events. The mild climate is influenced by the relatively warm waters of the sub-arctic current originating in the western Pacific off Japan. This current flows toward BC through the Gulf of Alaska, transporting millions of cubic metres of water toward the coast every day. Another distant influence is the EL NIÑO phenomenon, which originates near the equator and periodically brings warm water and wet, mild winters from the south. TSUNAMIS are huge waves that may be produced by undersea EARTHQUAKES thousands of kilometres away. The Alaska earthquake in 1964 generated a major tsunami in the N Pacific that reached a height of 2.5 m in ALBERNI INLET, causing extensive damage. Another important determinant of water conditions on the coast, river runoff, is generated closer to home. The discharge from the FRASER R, for example, has a major impact on the oceanography of GEORGIA STRAIT, as water from the river lowers the amount of salt in the surface layer of the ocean. A similar effect is found around the mouths of the SKEENA and other large rivers.

There are several major oceanographic regions in BC, including Georgia Strait, the continental shelf off the west coast of VANCOUVER ISLAND and the QUEEN CHARLOTTE ISLANDS, and the mainland FJORDS. The deep water west of the continental shelf lies within Canada's Exclusive Economic Zone extending 200 km from land. At an average width of 45 km, the continental shelf off BC is narrow relative to others around the world; in comparison, the shelf off Nova Scotia is over 185 km wide. Biological oceanographers recognize it as a very productive region because upwelling (movement of cold deep ocean water to surface layers) brings water rich in nutrients, such as nitrogen and phosphorus, close to the surface where tiny floating marine plants and animals, called phytoplankton and zooplankton, thrive. Phytoplankton are the foundation of the food chain in the ocean and are vital for ocean ecosystems. In the deep water (over 1,000 m) west of the continental shelf, BC oceanographers have discovered undersea volcanoes known as black smokers, where hot water from under the earth's crust is escaping and bringing minerals onto the deep sea floor and overlying water. These black smokers are associated with a unique community of animals, such as giant red worms and CLAMS that are adapted to the darkness, cold temperatures and high pressure of deep-sea conditions.

The shoreline of BC, including all the large and small ISLANDS, fjords and bays, is 27,200 km long, one of the longest in the world governed by a single jurisdiction. Stretched out, it would equal about two-thirds of the earth's circumference at the equator. The fjords were created by glaciers that covered almost all of BC up until about 10,000 years ago (see GLACIATION). As they pushed seaward, the ice masses carved deep gouges in the earth, which then filled with ocean water as the ice melted. Some of the fjords are extremely deep; for example, part of JERVIS INLET is 600 m deep, and HOWE SOUND at BRITANNIA is almost 300 m deep. The fjords bring ocean conditions far inland. BELLA COOLA, for example, is at the head of a long system of fjords more than 100 km from the open sea, and PORT ALBERNI is at the head of a fjord that nearly bisects Vancouver Island. Some of the fjords have unique features of interest to chemical oceanographers, such as SAANICH INLET. Because the deep water in this inlet is only occasionally replaced by new ocean water from off the coast, dissolved oxygen, which marine plants and animals need to live, is almost totally missing. In other fjords, such as Howe Sound, the dissolved oxygen is usually replaced each year. In both cases oceanographers are concerned about disposal of waste material because some waste (wood waste from LOG BOOMING or pulp mills) uses up dissolved oxygen as it decomposes.

Tidal currents along the BC shoreline are among the swiftest in the world, making passages such as SEYMOUR NARROWS near CAMPBELL RIVER tricky to navigate. The tremendous currents at SKOOKUMCHUCK RAPIDS near EGMONT on the SUNSHINE COAST can reach almost 30 km per hour; the earth shakes when these currents are at their maximum strength during spring TIDES.

Biological oceanography is very important to coastal communities because marine ecosystems support all fish populations, including SALMON, HERRING, ROCKFISH, clams, OYSTERS and thousands of other species. Changes in oceanography can result in major differences in marine ecosystems. For example, during El Niño years, when warm water arrives from the south, predatory MACKEREL can move into our region along with it and eat the juvenile salmon. Recreational divers enjoy looking at the diverse species of marine

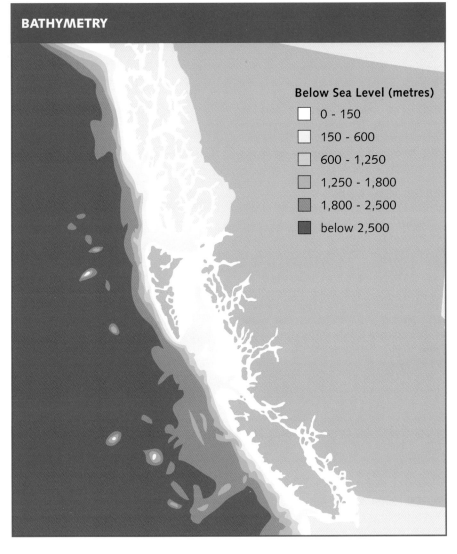

BATHYMETRY

Below Sea Level (metres)

- [ ] 0 - 150
- [ ] 150 - 600
- [ ] 600 - 1,250
- [ ] 1,250 - 1,800
- [ ] 1,800 - 2,500
- [ ] below 2,500

invertebrates that are abundant in tidally swept areas such as Seymour Narrows. Indeed, the clear waters of northern Georgia Strait are sometimes called the "Emerald Sea." In these areas there is an abundance of filter-feeding animals, such as SPONGES, SEA ANEMONES and certain SEA CUCUMBERS that thrive on the food particles brought to them by tidal currents (*see also* BIODIVERSITY; NATURAL HISTORY). The deep inlets on the North Coast (such as at GRENVILLE CHANNEL, near PRINCE RUPERT) are also tidally swept and support diverse animal and plant communities.

Colin Levings

OCHILTREE, a ranching (*see* CATTLE INDUSTRY) district 30 km northeast of WILLIAMS LAKE, was named by William Carson, an early settler and the first postmaster, after his hometown in Scotland. A well-known CARIBOO commune, which still exists under the name CEEDS (Community Enhancement & Economic Development Society), got its start here in the mid-1970s.

AS

OCTOPUS is a carnivorous marine MOLLUSC, related to the CLAM, OYSTER and SNAIL but without the shell. A member of the class Cephalopoda, which also includes SQUID, the

Giant Pacific octopus. Duane Sept photo

octopus has a baglike body and 8 long arms equipped with powerful suckers. Typically octopus are bottom dwellers, living in rock dens on the ocean floor, and they move either by crawling or swimming using water propulsion. They pounce on their prey (fish, CRAB, SCALLOP, SHRIMP), enveloping it in an embrace, then biting with a horny beak and injecting a paralyzing saliva. Like other molluscs they have no teeth but a rough, tongue-like radula, which they use to grind up their food. The octopus has good eyesight and a highly developed brain. Defence mechanisms include ejecting an inky substance into the water to obscure the area while it escapes, and camouflaging itself by altering skin pigmentation to change colour. The male deposits sperm inside the female using a specialized arm, and the female deposits fertilized eggs in her den. The giant Pacific octopus (*Octopus dofleini*) may grow to a 5-m arm span and 80 kg in weight. It has been harvested to provide bait for the HALIBUT fishery and more recently to supply a modest seafood market. A smaller octopus, the red octopus (*O. rubescens*), is often taken incidentally in shrimp and crab traps.

ODDS was a Vancouver pop rock band that began playing local nightclubs in the mid-1980s and rose to brief international success. The quartet—Steven Drake (vocals, guitar, piano), Doug Elliot (bass, vocals), Craig Northey (vocals, guitar), and Paul Brennan (drums), who was replaced by Pat Steward in 1994—began as Dawn Patrol. In 1987 they played their first show as the Odds, featuring original music written by members of the band. In the early 1990s, after relocating to Los Angeles, they came to the attention of the cult rock hero Warren Zevon, who employed them as his backup band for an album and a tour. The Odds released their first album, *Neopolitan*, in 1991. Two years later the group released its second recording, *Bedbugs*, which included its most popular hit, the humorous "Heterosexual Man." Other records followed but the band never made the jump to genuine international stardom, and in 1999 the Odds broke up. Drake focussed on his career as a recording producer while the other band members and DOUG AND THE SLUGS pianist Simon Kendall formed the instrumental group Sharkskin. *See also* SOUND RECORDING INDUSTRY. *Mike Harling*

ODLUM, Edward Faraday, scientist, businessman (b 27 Nov 1850, Tullamore, ON; d 4 May 1935, Vancouver). As a young man he defended Ontario against Fenian invaders. He arrived in VANCOUVER in 1889 from Tokyo, where he had been running a college. A person of wide interests, he travelled extensively, indulging an enthusiasm for ethnography and evolutionary theory and lecturing on the benefits of immigration to Canada. When he was in Vancouver between trips he engaged in real estate and other business affairs that formed the basis of the stock brokerage Odlum Brown. As well he was twice elected alderman, in 1892 and 1904. Among his publications was *A History of British Columbia* (1906).

ODLUM, Victor Wentworth, soldier, journalist (b 21 Oct 1880, Cobourg, ON; d 4 Apr 1971, Vancouver). The son of Edward ODLUM and his first wife Mary Powell, he arrived in VANCOUVER in 1889 with his widowed father. During the Boer War he fought in S Africa with the Royal Canadian Rifles and in WWI he served with distinction on the Western Front. In Nov 1915 he helped organize the first Allied trench raid of the war; it was a tactic that became a regular practice in the British and French armies. He had earlier worked on the *World* newspaper and following the war he owned the sensationalist *Daily Star* (1924–32). He was also a LIBERAL member of the provincial legislature from 1924 to 1928. After again serving in the army in WWII he became a diplomat, serving as Canada's first ambassador to China (1943–46) and ambassador to Turkey (1947–52). In 1964 he came out of retirement to publish the short-lived *Vancouver Times* newspaper. *See also* NEWSPAPERS.

OGDEN, Peter Skene, fur trader (b 1790, Quebec City; d 27 Sept 1854, Oregon City, OR). He grew up in Montreal where his father was a

judge. He joined the NORTH WEST CO in 1810 and served at Ile à la Crosse, SK, where he earned a reputation as a determined, sometimes violent opponent of the HBC. In 1818 the NWC transferred him west of the ROCKY MTS partly to avoid reprisals from the HBC, and he took command at Spokane House (near present-day Spokane, WA). After the merger of the two fur trading companies (*see* FUR TRADE, LAND-BASED) he was allowed to join the HBC and led a series of 6 expeditions during 1824–30: the so-called Snake River expeditions, south as far as southern California and east to Nevada and Idaho, in search of furs. In 1831 he transferred to the North Coast, where he took command at FORT SIMPSON. Ogden was made a chief factor and put in charge of the NEW CALEDONIA district, based at FORT ST JAMES, from 1835 to 1844. In 1846 he returned south to join a triumvirate of HBC officials who took charge of the Columbia District. Ill health forced his retirement in 1854, and he died shortly after.

OGOPOGO is a legendary serpent-like creature believed, but never proved, to inhabit the depths of OKANAGAN LK. The legend derives from First Nations people who called it N'xa'xa'etkw, demon of the lake, and representations occur in ROCK ART. The name *Ogopogo*, a palindrome from a music-hall song, was first used at a business luncheon in VERNON on 23 Aug 1926. Entertainment at the lunch was furnished by a local

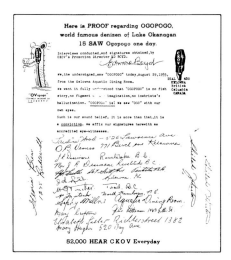

Statement signed by 15 people who claimed to have seen Ogopogo on 29 Aug 1955 at Kelowna. Courtesy Arlene Gaal

troupe who, according to one of its members, sang the light-hearted song including the lines: "I'm looking for the Ogopogo/ The bunny-hugging Ogopogo/ His mother was a mutton, his father was a whale/ I'm going to put a little bit of salt on his tail." The monster is rumoured to nest in underwater caves near Rattlesnake Island opposite PEACHLAND. Even though it has never been proven to exist, "sightings" occur with regularity and the provincial government has declared Ogopogo a protected species.
Reading: Arlene Gaal, *Ogopogo, the Million-Dollar Lake Monster*, 1986.

O'HAGAN, Howard, writer (b 17 Feb 1902, Lethbridge, AB; d Dec 1982, Victoria). He graduated from McGill Univ law school in 1925 but practised only briefly before giving it up to work as a guide and packer in the ROCKY MTS. He then worked as a publicist for the CNR and a railway in Argentina, and he spent time living in various places in Canada, Europe, Australia and the US. In 1974 he returned to live in VICTORIA, where he had worked as a journalist and labourer in the 1950s. He wrote 2 novels and many short stories and articles, mostly adventure tales for maga-

Howard O'Hagan, writer.

zines like *True* and *Argosy*. His book *Tay John* (1939), written when he lived on BOWEN ISLAND, is an imaginative retelling of the *tête jaune* (yellowhead) legend. It has been called the best book to come out of BC pre-WWII and also Canada's first serious work of metafiction.

O'HARA, LAKE, nestles in an amphitheatre of towering peaks in the ROCKY MTS, just west of the Continental Divide in YOHO NATIONAL PARK. Named for Lt Col Robert O'Hara, an early visitor, it is the centre of a network of TRAILS leading to high mountain passes, icefields and alpine meadows. It has been popular with hikers from around the world since the beginning of the century. Lake O'Hara Lodge, built by the CPR in 1926, was still in operation in the late 1990s. *See also* LAKES.

OIL AND GAS INDUSTRY is centred in the PEACE R country in the northeast corner of the province. The earliest commercial quantities of natural gas were produced at POUCE COUPE in 1948 and the first oil was discovered in 1955 at Boundary Lk on the Alberta border, north of the Peace R. These discoveries launched a period of intense development of oil and gas resources, with FORT ST JOHN as the service centre. By 1960 there were 68 oil wells and 200 gas wells in production and by 1980 oil and gas accounted for 27% of the total value of mineral production (*see* MINING). In 1998 the value of oil and gas production was $1.6 billion, about 30% of the

total value of all mineral production. Gas has always been more abundant in BC than oil. The province produces sufficient gas for its own consumption and exports to the US as well, while oil production meets only about 25% of provincial demand and must be supplemented by imports from Alberta. In 1996 the remaining reserves in the northeast were estimated to be 244 billion m³ of gas and 21 million m³ of oil. Extensive reserves may also exist beneath the ocean floor off the north coast of BC. These were estimated in 1998 by the Geological Survey of Canada to be 9.8 billion barrels of oil and 734 million m³ of natural gas, but since 1972 there has been a moratorium on offshore oil and gas exploration because of ENVIRONMENTAL concerns.

A network of PIPELINES carries natural gas from the producing fields in the northeast down through the centre of the province to the Lower Mainland, as well as out to PRINCE RUPERT (*see* WESTCOAST ENERGY INC). Oil is also transported south by pipeline to KAMLOOPS, where it links

BC OIL & GAS REVENUES 1960–98 ($ million)

	Oil	Gas	By-products	Total
1960	-	-	-	9.2
1965	-	-	-	44.1
1970	-	-	-	91.0
1975	-	-	-	320.7
1980	-	-	-	828.3
1986	230.0	486.0	62.0	778.0
1990	318.0	537.0	42.0	897.0
1995	272.0	708.0	57.0	1,037.0
1998	377.6	1,132.9	71.8	1,582.3

BC OIL & GAS INDUSTRY

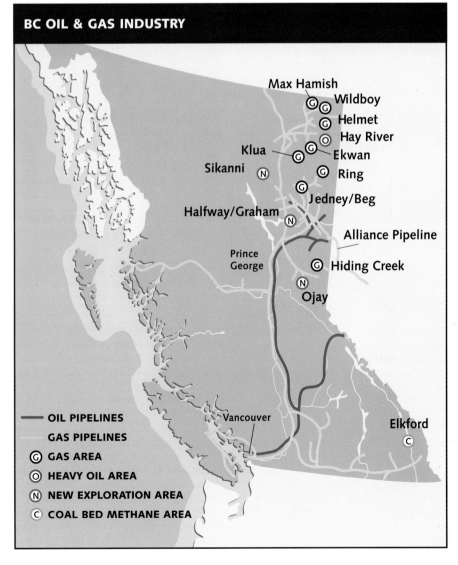

— OIL PIPELINES
— GAS PIPELINES
Ⓖ GAS AREA
◎ HEAVY OIL AREA
Ⓝ NEW EXPLORATION AREA
Ⓒ COAL BED METHANE AREA

Pumping crude oil at a test site in northern BC, 1983. Ralph Bower/Vancouver Sun

with the TRANS MOUNTAIN PIPE LINE COMPANY LTD from Edmonton, which has been supplying oil to VANCOUVER since 1953.

OKANAGAN CENTRE, pop 360, a farming (*see* AGRICULTURE) settlement and former steamship landing, is on the eastern hillsides overlooking OKANAGAN LK 20 km north of KELOWNA. A.B. Knox developed the first orchards here in the early 1900s (*see* TREE FRUITS), and a townsite, laid out in 1908, soon had a hotel, store, post office and school. Grape and wine production (*see* WINE MAKING) have become important in this area.   AS

OKANAGAN FALLS, town, pop 1,874, lies at the twin falls draining SKAHA LK south into the Okanagan R, 20 km south of PENTICTON. Originally called Dogtown, a reference to Skaha, a FIRST NATIONS word for "dog," it was a trading and SALMON fishing site and part of an important CANOE route. In the 1890s it was promoted as a settler's paradise but did not live up to its notices; it is a small TOURISM and orchard (*see* TREE FRUITS) centre. The twin WATERFALLS, which gave the spot its name, have been virtually eliminated by modern flood control.

OKANAGAN First Nation are an Interior Salish people (*see* SALISHAN FIRST NATIONS) who inhabit the OKANAGAN VALLEY south to the confluence of the Okanagan and COLUMBIA rivers in Washington state. Before contact with Europeans their territory extended from SLOCAN LK on the east to the NICOLA valley in the west. The Okanagan language is still spoken by a few hundred people (*see* FIRST NATIONS LANGUAGES). Traditionally the Okanagan inhabited villages that were grouped into loose confederacies, or bands, associated with particular territories. At contact there were 7 such confederacies and an estimated population of 12,000. The people

occupied their villages during the winter when they engaged in ceremonies, feasting and other social and religious activities. Winter lodges called *kekuli* were partly sunk in the ground (*see* ARCHITECTURE, ABORIGINAL). From spring to fall the people dispersed for hunting, gathering and FISHING. Bands had chiefs, or headmen, who enjoyed limited authority. Lesser chiefs might lead war or hunting parties, and religious leaders had some authority as well. Social rank was maintained by wealth, marriage and personal accomplishment, not simply heredity. Warfare between the Okanagan and their neighbours was common, as was trade. Horses were introduced from the south early in the 18th century and the development of an equestrian culture distinguished the Okanagan. The FUR TRADE began in the valley in 1812 from Forts Okanogan and Kamloops. It led to the depletion of food resources and instances of hostility toward traders. The trade was waning by 1858 when the GOLD RUSH on the FRASER R sparked an influx of miners. The rush also attracted settlers who remained to farm and raise cattle (*see* AGRICULTURE; CATTLE INDUSTRY). In the 1860s and 1870s

Okanagan First Nation birch bark basket. Dorothy Kennedy/Canadian Museum of Civilization Artifact iiB17

RESERVES were set aside for the people. By the end of the century the Okanagan were involved increasingly in farming, LOGGING, ranching and wage labour, though discrimination by whites frustrated their attempts to integrate into settler society. Today most people earn their living from wage labour. There are about 4,000 Canadian Okanagan, in 7 bands: the Upper Nicola near MERRITT, the Okanagan near VERNON, the Westbank near KELOWNA, the Penticton, the Upper Similkameen and the Lower Similkameen near KEREMEOS, and the Osoyoos (Inkameep).

OKANAGAN HELICOPTERS LTD; *see* CANADIAN HELICOPTERS LTD.

OKANAGAN LAKE, 360.8 km², extends 128 km from northwest of VERNON to PENTICTON at its south end. Draining south via the Okanagan R toward the US border, it is the largest of a chain of lakes occupying the floor of the OKANAGAN VALLEY in the south-central Interior. The lake is a remnant of a much larger glacial sea—Penticton Lake—left behind by melting ice at the end of the Pleistocene era about 10,000 years ago (*see* GLACIATION). It is surrounded by clay cliffs and grassy benchlands and is the centre of BC's fruit-growing industry (*see* TREE FRUITS), which flourishes thanks to a hot, dry climate and rich alluvial soils deposited by the glaciers. Warm water and sandy beaches attract a growing number of TOURISTS every summer. Part of the traditional

Orchards at Summerland, on the shores of Okanagan Lk. Keith Thirkell photo

territory of the OKANAGAN First Nation, it was visited by Europeans for the first time in 1811, and traders subsequently followed a FUR BRIGADE trail on the west side of the lake. Father Charles PANDOSY founded an OBLATE mission near the present site of KELOWNA in 1860, the first white settlement on the lake. The fruit trees he planted in 1862 were the beginning of the extensive orchards that proliferated after 1900. Steamboat service began on the lake in 1886, when Capt Thomas SHORTS launched the first of his boats (*see* PADDLEWHEEL STEAMBOATS). The SHUSWAP & OKANAGAN RWY connected the lake to the CPR main line at SICAMOUS in 1892 and the CPR launched its own steamer service the following year. Steamers plied the lake until 1937, when the last boat, the SICAMOUS, retired, having been replaced by rail and improved ROAD connections. A floating bridge carries the main highway across the lake at Kelowna. When it opened in 1958, it was the first structure of its kind in Canada. Some people believe Okanagan Lk to be the home of OGOPOGO, a prehistoric underwater creature. *See also* LAKES.

OKANAGAN LANDING, a sheltered landing site on OKANAGAN LK 12 km south of VERNON, was the terminus of the CPR-owned SHUSWAP & OKANAGAN RWY completed from SICAMOUS in 1892, and the northern port for the PADDLEWHEEL STEAMBOATS, which began plying the lake in 1893. The community, which included a lakeside hotel, profited from its strategic location until the 1920s, when CNR built a branch line from KAMLOOPS to KELOWNA. The Landing subsequently became a fashionable residential subdivision, which officially amalgamated with the City of Vernon in 1993.

OKANAGAN MISSION was founded in 1860 by Charles PANDOSY and Pierre Richard, OBLATE missionaries, south of KELOWNA near where Mission Crk enters the east side of OKANAGAN LK. The mission was a base for itinerant priests travelling through the OKANAGAN VALLEY, and Father Pandosy fostered farming and orcharding (*see* TREE FRUITS) there. The small settlement that developed was the first permanent white settlement in the valley. Shortly after Pandosy's death in 1891, the Oblates sold all their property except for the building site, and mission lands became part of AGRICULTURAL developments in the area. The original log buildings survived and were restored as a museum in the 1950s. The modern community of Okanagan Mission, part of Kelowna, is some distance from the Pandosy site.

OKANAGAN VALLEY is a broad U-shaped trough in south-central BC occupied by a chain of lakes that drain south via the Okanagan R to Osoyoos Lk. The lakes, including Swan, OKANAGAN, KALAMALKA, Wood, Duck, SKAHA, VASEUX and Osoyoos, are remnants of a glacial sea—Penticton Lake—that inundated the area some 10,000 years ago (*see* GLACIATION); the largest is Okanagan Lk. Alluvial deposits left behind when the glaciers retreated are the basis of the valley's bountiful agricultural production today. It is bounded on the east by the MONASHEE MTS and on the west by the Thompson–Okanagan Plateau, and it extends about 160 km from VERNON to the US border.

Comprising roughly 3% of the total area of BC, the Okanagan Valley contained about 8% of the provincial population (300,000 people) in 1997, making it the most densely populated region in the Interior. Half a million people were expected to live there by 2021. Most of the population is centred in the 3 largest communities: PENTICTON, KELOWNA and Vernon; each is the economic and administrative focus of its own region. Lying as it does in the rainshadow of the mountains, the valley is sunny and dry, especially south of Penticton. Temperatures are hot in summer and usually mild in winter. The valley is a unique ecosystem that hosts more than 30% of BC's ENDANGERED SPECIES of wildlife as well as 100 rare or endangered PLANTS. Since the 1950s, water-control dams have reduced flooding on the Okanagan R and around Osoyoos Lk.

The valley is the traditional territory of the OKANAGAN First Nation, who occupy several communities. The first outsider known to have visited the area was a fur trader, David Stuart, who in 1811 travelled up the lake on a scouting expedition for the PACIFIC FUR CO. Until 1847, fur traders used the valley to supply Interior posts and carry furs down to the coast (*see* FUR TRADE, LAND-BASED; FUR BRIGADES). A few settlers arrived with the 1858–62 GOLD RUSH, principally to raise cattle and other livestock for the miners. Ranching remained the dominant activity until

the end of the 19th century, when the first irrigation projects were undertaken and orchards were planted (*see* CATTLE INDUSTRY; AGRICULTURE). During the 1920s and 1930s, fruit growing (*see* TREE FRUITS) was established as the valley's main economic activity; at the close of the 20th century the valley was second only to the lower FRASER VALLEY as a source of agricultural products. Since the 1930s, grape growing has expanded dramatically, supplying a WINE MAKING INDUSTRY that in Canada is second in importance only to the Niagara Peninsula.

In 1892 the SHUSWAP & OKANAGAN RWY began operations between OKANAGAN LANDING and SICAMOUS, linking the valley to the outside world via the CPR main line. The CPR then launched PADDLEWHEEL STEAMBOAT service on Okanagan Lk, which lasted until 1937. The south end of the valley got its own rail connection in 1915 with the completion of the KETTLE VALLEY RWY. ROADS AND HWYS eventually replaced rail as the most important transportation link. Since the completion of the COQUIHALLA Connector (Hwy 97C) in 1990, the valley is only about 4 hours from VANCOUVER by car. AIRPORTS are located at Kelowna and Penticton. Along with agriculture, DAIRY FARMING and LOGGING are also economically important, particularly in the north end of the valley. Since the 1960s, TOURISM has become important in both summer and winter. Along with a variety of water-related activities, there are three major ski resorts: Apex Alpine near

O'Keefe Historic Ranch, near Vernon, founded in 1867. Reimut Lieder/Image Makers

Penticton, Big White at Kelowna and Silver Star outside Vernon (*see* SKIING). The valley attracts a growing number of retirees, who appreciate its pleasant climate and scenic beauty; during the 1990s a national magazine picked Penticton and Kelowna as 2 of the top 10 places in Canada to live. However, many people fear that residential and tourist development is threatening farmland and destroying the valley's unique plant and animal life. The Okanagan GRASSLANDS, for example, are considered one of the 4 most endangered ecosystems in Canada.

O'KEEFE, Cornelius, rancher (b 26 July 1838, Fallowfield, ON; d 27 May 1919, Vernon). Raised on a farm in the Ottawa Valley, he came to BC in 1862 to try his luck in the Cariboo goldfields (*see* GOLD RUSH, CARIBOO). He failed to make a strike, so he went to work shipping supplies and building roadhouses, and in 1866 he began importing cattle to supply meat to the miners. In 1867 he and two partners, Thomas Greenhow and Thomas Wood, pre-empted land at the north end of OKANAGAN LK on which to farm and raise cattle for sale (*see* CATTLE INDUSTRY). O'Keefe developed his property into one of the largest ranches in the district, part of which is now the O'KEEFE HISTORIC RANCH. He fathered 17 children and was a prosperous member of the Okanagan social elite until his death.

O'KEEFE HISTORIC RANCH, 12 km north of VERNON in the north OKANAGAN VALLEY, was founded in 1867 by Cornelius O'KEEFE, who was driving cattle north to the goldfields with his partners, Thomas Greenhow and Thomas Wood. The men each pre-empted 66 ha of meadowland to use for ranching (*see* CATTLE INDUSTRY). O'Keefe developed his holdings into one of the largest ranches in the district, diversifying into grain and apple growing and raising pigs and sheep. Much of this land was subsequently sold off for orchards, but the ranch remained in the O'Keefe family and became a historic site in 1967. In 1977 the Devonian Foundation purchased the ranch and gave it to the City of Vernon. A non-profit society now operates the site, which consists of several original buildings depicting ranch life in the early 1900s.

OLAJIDE, Michael Jr "The Silk," boxer (b 8 Dec 1964, Liverpool, England). He grew up in east VANCOUVER and fought as an amateur with the Kingsway BOXING Club for 2 years before he turned professional in 1981. Trained and managed by his father, he won the Canadian middleweight title by defeating Wayne Caplette of Winnipeg on 10 Apr 1985. In 1986 he moved to New York to seek the world crown. Unbeaten in 23 professional matches, he fought for the vacant International Boxing Federation world middleweight title but lost to American Olympic gold medallist Frank Tate in Las Vegas on 10 Oct 1987. The next year he faced another top fighter,

Michael Olajide, 1985 Canadian middleweight champ.

Iran Barkley, but was soundly defeated. Olajide replaced his father with boxing legend Angelo Dundee and arranged to fight the formidable Thomas Hearns at the opening of the Taj Mahal casino on 28 Apr 1990. Olajide lost in 12 rounds in a unanimous decision. When an eye injury permanently forced him out of the sport in 1991, he stayed in New York to become a fitness instructor.

OLALLA, pop 341, in the S OKANAGAN VALLEY, 6 km north of KEREMEOS, was the site of a COPPER mining boom in the 1890s. Briefly it was the bustling centre for several productive mines, but ore deposits did not meet expectations; the town faded and it became a small collection of homes on the highway between Keremeos and PENTICTON. The name comes from a CHINOOK JARGON word for BERRIES, a reference to locally abundant Saskatoon berries.

OLD CURLY was the name given to the first steam locomotive in BC. Built in San Francisco in 1869, it was brought north in 1881 to work on construction of the CPR through the FRASER R Canyon. Following completion of the railway, the locomotive was bought by BC MILLS TIMBER & TRADING CO and used at several RAILWAY LOGGING operations on the coast. The name may be a reference to Satan, although the BROADCASTER Red ROBINSON believes it was named for his grandfather, Curly Surgenor, an early engineer. Today a

Old Curly, a logging locomotive, at the Hastings Mill store, Vancouver, c 1900.
BC Archives A-00312

restored version is on display at BURNABY Heritage Village Museum.

OLIVER, town, pop 4,285, is at the centre of a rich fruit-growing (*see* TREE FRUITS) area in the OKANAGAN VALLEY, 40 km south of PENTICTON. It was created following WWI when the LIBERAL government of John OLIVER decided to irrigate the S Okanagan to provide farmland for returning veterans. Construction of the South Okanagan Lands Project took place during 1920–24, and permanent settlement followed. A 37-km stretch of the nearby Okanagan R was straightened in 1952 to control flooding. Oliver was officially incorporated on 19 Dec 1945. AGRICULTURE has remained the most important activity, followed by MINING, LOGGING and TOURISM, and there are many vineyards and wineries in the vicinity. A museum and archives is housed in a former BC PROVINCIAL POLICE headquarters, built in 1924. Oliver has become increasingly popular as a retirement community. *See also* WINE MAKING INDUSTRY.

OLIVER, John, farmer, politician, premier 6 Mar 1918–17 Aug 1927 (b 31 July 1856, Hartington, England; d 17 Aug 1927, Victoria). The son of a COAL miner, he immigrated to Ontario with his family in 1870 and arrived in BC 7 years later. He worked at labouring jobs before settling on a farm in DELTA. He was drawn into local politics and in 1900 won election as a LIBERAL to the provincial legislature, where he became leader of the opposition. Defeated in 1909, he remained out of politics until his re-election in 1916. During Harlan BREWSTER's government he was minister of agriculture and railways and became PREMIER when Brewster died in office. Oliver was premier during the final months of WWI, the difficult transition period following the war and the economic recession of the early 1920s: he governed in difficult times and did so competently and honestly, never forgetting his humble roots, hence his nickname,

"Honest John." A successful farmer himself, Oliver initiated several irrigation, reclamation and settlement schemes during his tenure, including the draining of Sumas Lk and the irrigation of the southern OKANAGAN VALLEY. His government took over the Pacific Great Eastern Rwy (*see* BC RAIL) and completed it from SQUAMISH to QUESNEL, as well as extending the system of ROADS. He also began BC's first old age pension scheme and finally went ahead with building the new UBC campus at Point Grey in VANCOUVER.

John Oliver, premier of BC, 1918–27, in a 1920 photograph. BC Archives G-06205

He did not accomplish all of this without opposition. In 1924 Oliver lost his seat in an election that his Liberals barely managed to win. He returned to the legislature via a by-election, reasserted his leadership of the party and was enjoying the political advantages of a resurgent economy when he died suddenly of cancer.

OLIVER, William, missionary (b 19 Mar 1848, Bishopston, Scotland; d Feb 1937). He was trained as a ship's carpenter, and as a young man he led a dissolute life at sea. At one point, after a bout of drinking he missed his ship and was stranded in NEW WESTMINSTER; he sought help

from the first church he stumbled into—Mary St Methodist—and was taken in by Rev Ebenezer Robson. From that time on, Oliver's life was devoted to the service of the church (*see* METHODIST CHURCH). In 1884 he volunteered his time to build and operate the *Glad Tidings*, the first powered mission vessel, used by Thomas CROSBY. Oliver was the Methodist marine service's shipwright, skipper and devoted advocate for 50 years, and his work underpinned that of a succession of missionaries, including Crosby and Robert Scott. Oliver's name was a byword in the SALMON CANNERIES, LOGGING camps, LIGHT-HOUSES and aboriginal villages of the coast by the time he retired in 1929.   *HW*
Reading: Robert Scott, *My Captain Oliver*, 1947.

OLSON, Clifford Robert, murderer (b 1940, Richmond). One of the most notorious multiple murderers in Canadian history, he is known to be responsible for the deaths of 11 children in Greater VANCOUVER between Nov 1980 and Aug 1981. He was arrested in Aug and charged with one murder; in a highly controversial move, police and the provincial attorney general agreed to pay $100,000 in trust to his wife and child in return for information about 10 other bodies. Olson initially pleaded not guilty to the murders, but switched his plea and was convicted early in 1982. The families of his victims challenged the payment in court, claiming compensation for the deaths of their children, but their claim was turned down on appeal. His victims and their ages were Sigrun Arnd (18), Teri Lyn Carson (15), Louise Chartrand (17), Ada Court (13), Colleen Daignault (13), Daryn Johnsrude (16), Ray King Jr (15), Judy Kozma (14), Simon Partington (9), Christine Weller (12) and Sandra Wolfsteiner (16).

OMBUDSMAN, Office of, was created in 1979 to conduct investigations into complaints about ministries of the provincial government, CROWN CORPORATIONS, municipalities, universities and the governing bodies of professions. The ombudsman has the power to compel witnesses to appear and to subpoena documents, though findings take the form of recommendations. The ombudsman is appointed by the legislature for a 6-year term.

OMEGA SALMON GROUP LTD is one of the largest producers of farmed salmon in BC. It is owned by the Pan Fish Group of Norway (a public company listed on the Oslo stock exchange) and specializes in raising, processing and marketing farmed Atlantic SALMON and TROUT worldwide. Pan Fish was established in 1992 and BC operations were reorganized and merged as the Omega Salmon Group in 1994. Omega operates 19 salmon farms and 2 salmon hatcheries in BC waters. It has processing facilities in SECHELT and PORT HARDY and produces whole fish, filets and steaks. It employs 140 full-time workers and annually produces 9 million kg of fish with a wholesale value of $60 million, amounting to 20% of the parent company's business. *See also* AQUACULTURE, FIN FISH; FISH HATCHERIES.

OMINECA GOLD RUSH; *see* GOLD RUSH, OMINECA.

ON-TO-OTTAWA TREK, June–July 1935, was a protest by single, unemployed men against conditions in the RELIEF CAMPS established by the federal government during the Depression. Inmates of the camps in BC, organized by the Relief Camp Workers' Union, staged a walkout in Apr 1935 and descended on VANCOUVER, where they subsisted on public charity and demonstrated in support of reforms to the camps. The men finally ran out of patience and decided to carry their protest to Ottawa. On 3 June about 1,000 of them boarded trains and set off for eastern Canada, gathering supporters as they went along. When the trains reached Regina they were halted by authorities; after negotiations with the federal government a delegation of 8 protestors continued on to Ottawa to meet with Prime Minister R.B. Bennett. The meeting did not go well and the delegation returned empty-handed. On 1 July a rally was held in downtown Regina. Police moved in, provoking a riot that led to the death of one officer and the arrest of 120 people. In the end, only 8 men were

100 Mile House, 1870s. UBC BC413

convicted of any crime. The rest left Regina, many returning to Vancouver, where they dispersed back to the relief camps. The following year the government admitted the camps were a failure and closed them.

ONDERDONK, Andrew, railway builder (b 30 Aug 1848, New York City; d 22 June 1905, Oscawana, NY). He supervised construction of 540 km of CPR mainline in BC. As a young engineer he worked for the Central Railroad of New Jersey and on improvements to San Francisco harbour. In 1879 he came to BC under contract to the federal government to supervise construction of the section of the transcontinental railway running from PORT MOODY to Kamloops Lk.

Later he won the contract to continue building east to CRAIGELLACHIE, where the last spike was driven. In order to get the work done he used thousands of low-paid CHINESE labourers, for whom working conditions were frequently dangerous and living conditions often appalling. During most of the construction period he lived at YALE. The work involved complicated logistical challenges and some landmark engineering achievements. After leaving BC he carried out major projects in S America, Chicago and Montreal, and he was working on the New York City subway when he died of heart failure.

100 MILE HOUSE, district municipality, pop 1,850, is in the CARIBOO, 334 km south of PRINCE GEORGE. It was a favourite camping spot for FUR BRIGADES on their way to and from Fort Kamloops, and in 1861 a roadhouse was established to accommodate travellers on the CARIBOO WAGON ROAD. The name refers to its location 100 miles from Mile 0 of that road at LILLOOET. In 1912 the property was bought by the Marquis of Exeter; in 1930 his son, Lord Martin Cecil, became owner and manager of what was by then the Bridge Creek Ranch. Cecil founded a reli-

gious group, the EMISSARIES OF DIVINE LIGHT, whose headquarters remained here. While ranching (*see* CATTLE INDUSTRY) continues to be important, the FOREST INDUSTRY became a mainstay in the 1960s, and there are SAWMILLS and several log-house builders here. All-season TOURISM has also grown in importance, and the area is home to many artists and craftspeople.

150 MILE HOUSE, pop 1,275, on the Cariboo Hwy (*see* ROADS & HWYS) 15 km south of WILLIAMS LAKE, was once an important stopping place on the way to the CARIBOO goldfields (*see* GOLD RUSH, CARIBOO). Originally pre-empted in 1861 by Thomas Davidson, the site flourished after the CARIBOO WAGON ROAD was routed through it 2 years later. The White House was one of the most popular roadhouses in the district. When the Pacific Great Eastern Rwy (*see* BC RAIL) was built through Williams Lake, 150 Mile lost its role as regional distribution centre and later became a bedroom community for its larger neighbour.

O'NEILL, J. Wiggs, riverboat pioneer, writer (b 1882, Barkerville; d 1964). As a youngster he moved with his family to the QUEEN CHARLOTTE ISLANDS and then to Port Simpson (*see* FORT SIMPSON) where his stepfather worked for the HBC. Wiggs began working on a SKEENA R sternwheeler in 1898 and remained on the river until the end of the steamboat era in 1911. He then moved to SMITHERS, where he operated the first power plant and owned an auto agency for 43 years. He was famous as a storyteller and published many articles and books about the Skeena R country. *See also* PADDLEWHEEL STEAMBOATS.

ONLEY, Norman Antony "Toni," artist (b 20 Nov 1928, Douglas, Isle of Man). He learned to paint in his native Isle of Man before coming to Canada in 1948. After working in Ontario he moved to PENTICTON in 1955. During his studies

Toni Onley, artist.

in Mexico in 1957–60 he was influenced by abstract expressionism, then rediscovered his landscape roots in England, where he studied the British watercolourists. He then settled back in VANCOUVER and began painting the watercolour landscapes by which he made his reputation. While teaching fine arts at UBC from 1967 to 1976, he emerged as one of the most commercially successful painters in Canada. He has had many solo exhibitions at galleries across Canada and around the world, and he is an Officer in the Order of Canada. Since 1968 he has flown his own plane to remote locations to paint his landscapes. His books include *Onley's Arctic* (1989), *The Art of Toni Onley* (1999) and, with George WOODCOCK, *The Walls of India* (1985).

OONA RIVER is a small collection of houses sprawling along a river ESTUARY on the eastern side of PORCHER ISLAND, 40 km south of PRINCE RUPERT. It was settled by Scandinavian homesteaders about 1907 in anticipation of the arrival of the railway at Prince Rupert. A SAWMILL was built in the 1920s and LOGGING and commercial FISHING have been the major activities. Ralph EDWARDS retired here from Lonesome Lake in 1966.

OOTSA LAKE, 404 km², lies on the Nechako Plateau south of BURNS LAKE and east of KITIMAT in the traditional territory of the DAKELH (Carrier) and WET'SUWET'EN First Nations. This large lake is now part of central BC's Nechako Reservoir. About 70 km in length and 3–6 km wide, it forms the northern boundary of TWEEDSMUIR PROVINCIAL PARK and was greatly enlarged by the KENNEY DAM. The farming and LOGGING community of Ootsa Lake on the north shore of the lake, 50 km south of Burns Lake, once had a hotel and general store and was a hunting and fishing centre, but when the region was flooded to provide power for the SMELTER at Kitimat, it was reduced to a scattered rural settlement. *Ootsa* is a Dakelh word for "low down." *See also* LAKES. AS

OPEN LEARNING AGENCY is a public educational institution, based in BURNABY, offering distance education via a variety of technologies, including television and the Internet. Since 1988 the OLA has combined the KNOWLEDGE NETWORK with the Open Univ, which offers academic courses, and the Open College, which offers courses leading to professional certification and diplomas. In 1996–97, 13,202 students were enrolled in these courses. It also delivers high school course material and workplace training. It is funded by the provincial government, corporate sponsors and individual fees and donations. *See also* EDUCATION, PUBLIC.

OPOSSUM, North American (*Didelphis virginiana*), is a cat-sized mammal with a white face, long pointed nose, coarse black and white hair, a long prehensile tail and hind feet with an opposable toe adapted for climbing. It is the only opossum species in BC. Native to eastern N America, it was introduced to Washington state in 1925 and had begun to spread north to BC by 1946. It is now found mainly in the lower FRASER VALLEY, where it inhabits deciduous woodlands close to water. Opossums were released on HORNBY ISLAND in 1986 and may be spreading to southern VANCOUVER ISLAND. They den mainly on the ground in burrows dug by other animals, in hollow logs and rock crevices, and feed opportunistically on small animals, insects, fruit and garbage. Young are born in litters of up to 13 after a brief gestation period of 13 days, then suckled in a pouch on the mother's belly until they become independent at about 100 days. They are very short-lived; few survive beyond 2 years. They actually do "play possum": when threatened they fall over and play dead.

OPPENHEIMER, David, businessman, politician (b 1 Jan 1834, Bleiskastel, Germany; d 31 Dec 1897, Vancouver). He moved to the US with his family in 1848; in 1860, after several years in California, he came to BC to work in his brother Charles's supply business, providing goods to the CARIBOO goldfields (*see* GOLD RUSH, CARIBOO). Oppenheimer Bros was headquartered in YALE for many years; it moved to VICTORIA in 1881 and the brothers began to acquire land at the future site of VANCOUVER. By 1887 David and his brothers Charles and Isaac (Ike) were living in

David Oppenheimer, the "Father of Vancouver," c 1896. BC Archives A-02386

Vancouver; together they owned the second-largest chunk of land in the new city. An active city booster, David was involved in all manner of civic improvements and has been called the "Father of Vancouver." After a term as alderman he won election as mayor in 1888 and served 4 terms from 1888 to 1891. The oldest company in Vancouver, Oppenheimer Bros was still in business by the end of the 20th century. Oppenheimer Park in Vancouver is named for him.

ORCA; *see* KILLER WHALE.

ORCA BAY SPORTS AND ENTERTAINMENT, a private company, owned the GRIZZLIES basketball team, GENERAL MOTORS PLACE in downtown VANCOUVER and controlling interest of Northwest Sports Enterprises Ltd, the holding company that owns the VANCOUVER CANUCKS hockey team. Orca Bay was created in 1995 when John McCaw, a Seattle billionaire, purchased the sports empire of the Vancouver entrepreneur Arthur Griffiths. The Grizzlies were sold to Chicago businessman Michael Heisley in 2000.

ORCA BOOK PUBLISHERS is a BOOK PUBLISHING house in VICTORIA, founded in 1984 by Bob Tyrrell. Tyrrell, a former high school English teacher, formed the company to publish his own book, *Island Pubbing*, a guide to VANCOUVER ISLAND pubs. The company focusses on children's books, though it also publishes adult literature and trade non-fiction, including guidebooks. It won Publisher of the Year honours from the Canadian Booksellers Assoc in 1992.

ORCHARDS; *see* TREE FRUITS.

ORDER OF BRITISH COLUMBIA was established on 21 Apr 1989 to honour people "who have served with the greatest distinction and excelled in any field of endeavour benefiting the people of the Province of BC." Nominees suggested by the public are considered by a 7-person

advisory council chaired by the provincial chief justice, and final appointments are made by the LT GOV. The insignia of the order is a medal in the shape of a DOGWOOD with a crowned shield of arms. A ceremony is held once per year to present the order to new members.

OREGON TREATY, 15 June 1846, fixed the southern boundary between BC and the US. Since the Anglo-American Convention of 1818, Britain and the US had agreed to joint occupation of the Oregon Territory, including what is now Washington state, because they could not agree on a border. The Americans wanted a boundary along the 49th parallel of latitude; the British wanted to keep everything south to the COLUMBIA R. Joint occupancy was renewed in 1827 but soon the influx of American settlers into Oregon made it clear that Britain would have to withdraw. Anticipating a withdrawal, the HBC established FORT VICTORIA at the southern tip of VANCOUVER ISLAND in 1843 to replace its trading headquarters, Fort Vancouver, on the Columbia R. During the 1844 American election campaign James Polk, who later won the election, insisted that he would claim territory as far north as 54°40′ N ("Fifty-four Forty or Fight"). The British now wanted to compromise at the 49th parallel, and war with the Americans seemed a possibility. However, Polk toned down his rhetoric and the 2 parties came to an agreement. The 1846 treaty, officially the Treaty of Washington, established the border along the 49th parallel west from the ROCKY MTS to the coast, then south through the GULF ISLANDS and out through the middle of JUAN DE FUCA STRAIT so

MEMBERS of the ORDER OF BC, June 2000

Joan Acosta	1994	John C. Kerr	1997
Bryan ADAMS	1990	Henry Ketcham	1996
Jean Jacques Andre	1999	Kazuko Komatsu	1998
Gerald Andrews	1990	Diana KRALL	2000
Mark Angelo	1998	David C. LAM	1995
F. Gordon Antoine	1993	Dorothy T. Lam	1995
Nava Ashraf	1995	J. Fenwick LANSDOWNE	1995
Unity Bainbridge	1993	Dr Charles Laszlo	1998
Patricia Baird	1992	Robert H. Lee	1990
Michael Conway BAKER	1997	Peter James Lester	1994
Peter John Banks	1996	Victor Ling	2000
Vivien E. Basco	1991	Tong LOUIE	1991
Frank Beinder	1991	Irene MacDonald	1991
Jack T. BELL	1991	Gordon F. MacFarlane	1991
Henry P. BELL-IRVING	1990	William E. McKinney	1997
David A. Boyes	1990	David McLean	1999
Geraldine Braak	1997	Ian MCTAGGART-COWAN	1991
Vernon C. Brink	1990	Kenneth McVay	1995
May Brown	1993	Eleanor Malkin	1996
Bernard O. Brynelsen	1991	Margaret Mitchell	2000
Helen Burnham	2000	Mavor MOORE	1999
Iona CAMPAGNOLO	1998	Basil Morissette	1996
Alex Campbell	1999	Grace Elliott Nelson	2000
R. Wayne CAMPBELL	1992	Nathaniel T. NEMETZ	1990
Brian Canfield	1998	Phil NUYTTEN	1992
Ric CARELESS	1994	Margaret ORMSBY	1990
Eric Charman	1999	Michael O'Shaughnessy	1998
Phyllis Chelsea	1990	Jim PATTISON	1990
Suezone Chow	1992	Elida Peers	1993
Joseph H. Cohen	1990	Barbara PENTLAND	1993
Edna Cooper	1995	Howard E. Petch	1990
Mel Cooper	1992	Leslie Peterson	1990
Robert Cooper	1995	Sophie Mae Pierre	1994
Jean COULTHARD	1994	Derek PORTER	1996
George F. Curtis	1995	Ross Charles Purse	1993
Marilyn Dahl	1993	Barbara Rae	1991
Kathleen & Albert Dalzell	1998	Bill REID	1994
Sushma Datt	1992	Geoffrey Robinson	1999
Robert DAVIDSON	1995	Robert G. ROGERS	1990
Lorne Davies	2000	Jane RULE	1998
Edmund Desjardins	1991	Carole SABISTON	1992
Isabelle Diamond	1995	Martha Salcudean	1998
Jack DIAMOND	1991	William G. Saywell	1994
Beverley Du Gas	1999	Martin T. Schechter	1994
Ronald Eland	1992	Ruth Schiller	1996
Helmut Eppich	1990	Joseph Segal	1992
Frances L. Fleming	1997	Sydney SEGAL	1993
Tom Foord	2000	Jack SHADBOLT	1990
Marguerite Ford	1997	Arthur Skidmore	1995
John A. Fraser	1995	Herbert Skidmore	1995
Timothy Frick	1999	Gordon Appelbe SMITH	2000
Lori FUNG	1990	Michael SMITH	1994
Joan Gentles	1992	Jim SPILSBURY	1993
Ken GEORGETTI	1998	Richard Stace-Smith	1999
Virginia Giles	2000	Dorothy Isabelle Stubbs	1996
Charan Gill	1999	David SUZUKI	1995
Gurdev S. Gill	1990	Alison SYDOR	1999
Murray Goldman	2000	Takao TANABE	1993
Joe GOSNELL	1999	Harvey Thommasen	2000
Hilda Gregory	1998	Roger Tonkin	1998
M. Rendina Hamilton	1994	Nancy TURNER	1999
Rick HANSEN	1990	John J. Verigin	1996
Walter G. Hardwick	1997	Roy Henry VICKERS	1998
Jack K. Harman	1996	Henry Hiroshi Wakabayashi	2000
Tara Singh Hayer	1995	Lawrence J. Wallace	1991
Kathleen HEDDLE	1997	Harry V. WARREN	1991
Jane Heffelfinger	2000	Winnifred Weir	1999
Meg Hickling	1997	Howard WHITE	1997
Richard Hunt	1991	Lorna Williams	1993
Vicky Husband	2000	Peter Wing	1990
Asa Johal	1991	Morris Wosk	1994
Lucille Johnstone	1994	Wolfgang Zimmermann	1992
Douglas JUNG	1997	George B. ZUKERMAN	1996

that Vancouver Island remained in British hands. The line through the Gulf Islands remained in dispute for several more years, leading in 1859 to the PIG WAR. It was finally resolved by international arbitration in 1872.

O'REILLY, Peter, public servant (b 27 Mar 1828, Ince, England; d 3 Sept 1905, Victoria). He was raised in Ireland, where he served in the revenue police before moving to BC in 1858. He was appointed a magistrate on his arrival and also served as high sheriff of the mainland colony until 1866 (*see* COLONIAL GOVERNMENT). He was a gold commissioner in HOPE between 1860 and 1862, then became chief gold commissioner for BC, based in RICHFIELD. In 1863 he married Caroline Trutch, sister of Joseph TRUTCH. After the union of the colonies he served as a county court judge and, from 1864 to 1870, a member of the legislative council. From 1880 to his retirement in 1898 he was Indian reserve commissioner and was responsible for laying out most of the RESERVES in BC (*see* ABORIGINAL RIGHTS; FIRST NATIONS). Meanwhile his investments in land and other business interests made him a wealthy member of VICTORIA's social elite. His home, POINT ELLICE HOUSE, is now a museum.

ORGANIZED CRIME AGENCY OF BC was created in 1999, with an annual budget of $15 million, to counter organized crime throughout the province. It replaced the 25-year-old Coordinated Law Enforcement Unit that was disbanded the previous year after a report cast doubt on its effectiveness. The first head of the new agency was Beverley Ann Busson, a senior RCMP officer and BC's first female police chief. *See also* POLICING.

ORIOLE is a beautiful perching songbird, a summer migrant to BC from southern wintering grounds. Orange or yellow and black in colour, it is found in deciduous woodlands where it builds its hanging sac-shaped nest. The oriole uses its strong, pointed bill to feed on INSECTS and small fruit. Two varieties occur in BC: Bullock's oriole (*Icterus bullockii*) inhabits the western and southern Interior, and its close relative, the Baltimore oriole (*I. galbula*), is found in the PEACE R district. Scientists have debated whether the two are separate species or not; some consider them subspecies of the northern oriole.

ORIOLE, HMCS, a steel-hulled, 101-ft (30.8-m) ketch launched in Massachusetts in 1921, is the oldest commissioned and longest serving vessel in the Canadian navy. Designed by George Owen, a Massachusetts Institute of Technology professor, for a prominent Toronto businessman, *Oriole* was the flagship of the Royal Canadian Yacht Club in Toronto. Acquired by the Royal Canadian Navy in 1949, the vessel was sent to HMCS Cornwallis in Nova Scotia. Since 1954 the *Oriole* has been based at Canadian Forces Base ESQUIMALT where it has been used for officer training. Although its marconi rig and more than 6,600-sq-ft spinnaker have no winches

HMCS Oriole *under full sail.* CF photo

for sail handling, the 81-tonne ketch holds the participation record in the annual SWIFTSURE RACE, with more than 40 races since 1954. It also competes in the biennial VICTORIA–Maui race. During a 7-month, 14,000-km goodwill tour of the S Pacific in 1998, *Oriole* represented Canada at a number of "tall ship" events. *Shirley Hewitt*

ORMSBY, Margaret Anchoretta, historian (b 7 June 1909, Quesnel; d 2 Nov 1996, Coldstream). She was born in QUESNEL and

Margaret Ormsby, BC historian. UBC 5.1/2331

raised in LUMBY. After graduating from UBC and Bryn Mawr College, she joined the history department at McMaster Univ for 3 years, then returned to UBC to teach in 1943. In 1964 she became the first woman head of the history

department. Her book *British Columbia: A History* (1958), commissioned to celebrate the BC centennial, was the standard work for 3 decades. She maintained a lifelong connection with the OKANAGAN VALLEY through her research interests and her support for the Okanagan Historical Society. She was president of the Canadian Historical Assoc in 1965, a member of the Royal Society, and held honorary degrees from 6 universities. After retiring from UBC in 1974, she lived at the family home in COLD-STREAM and continued to write about her native province. She also edited the memoir of Susan Allison, *Pioneer Gentlewoman* (1976). She was named to the ORDER OF BC (1990) and the Order of Canada (1996).

ORPHEUM THEATRE opened in downtown VANCOUVER in 1927 as a venue for vaudeville and live THEATRE. At the time it was the largest theatre in Canada. Later it was converted to a movie theatre, the most palatial along Granville St's theatre row. It was managed by Ivan ACKERY from 1935 to 1969. By the 1970s the building was owned by Famous Players, who planned to convert it to a multiscreen cinema, but the city purchased it

The luxurious interior of the Orpheum Theatre, Vancouver. David Blue/Vancouver Civic Theatres

in 1974 and restored it as a live-performance venue with a seating capacity of 2,780. It became a home for the VANCOUVER SYMPHONY ORCHESTRA.

ORTHODOX CHURCHES are a family of churches commonly known as the Eastern, Greek or Byzantine Churches with a small cluster known as the Oriental Churches. Their historical roots are found in the ancient Near East, eastern Europe, Africa and Asia. The 1991 census indicated that this family of churches was serving 23,540 people in BC, though the churches claim a much larger constituency.

The ancient patriarchal provinces of Rome, Constantinople, Alexandria, Antioch and Jerusalem were established by the 5th century AD. The great schism of 1054 formally separated Rome (the ROMAN CATHOLIC CHURCH) from Constantinople and most of the people of the other 3 jurisdictions (the Orthodox Churches). The Orthodox church in the 20th century includes the ancient patriarchates of Constantinople, Alexandria, Antioch and Jerusalem; the "national" Orthodox Churches of Albania, Bulgaria, Cyprus, Czechoslovakia, Greece, Poland, Romania, Russia, and Serbia; daughter churches of these, formed recently in Europe and N America; and the autonomous churches of Sinai, Finland and Japan. Most Orthodox Christians in BC are affiliated with churches of the Byzantine tradition: Russian, Greek, Ukrainian, Estonian, Serbian and Romanian. The Coptic and Ethiopian communities are part of the Oriental Orthodox Church (non-Calcedonian) with leadership in Cairo and Addis Ababa respectively.

Various jurisdictions of the Orthodox Church are present in BC. Each of these has its own particulars, both as a branch on the tree of Orthodoxy and as a part of the development of ethnic communities in the province. The Ukrainian Orthodox Church of Canada has parishes in CHILLIWACK, NEW WESTMINSTER, KAMLOOPS, KELOWNA, MISSION, PORT ALBERNI, PRINCE GEORGE, VANCOUVER, VERNON and VICTORIA. The Greek Orthodox Church of Canada has parishes in Kamloops, KITIMAT, Vancouver, PENTICTON, Prince George, SURREY and Victoria. The Orthodox Church in America, a denomination with Russian roots, has parishes in LANGLEY, New Westminster and Vancouver. Russian Orthodox Church Abroad has 2 parishes in Vancouver and a mission in Victoria. Various smaller jurisdictions are also present in the province. The Romanian Orthodox Archdiocese in America has parishes in New Westminster and Vancouver. The Ukrainian Orthodox Church, Kievan Patriarchate, has parishes in Langley, Chilliwack (the first English-language parish in BC) and DEWDNEY, along with the CANADIAN ORTHODOX MONASTERY of All Saints of North America. The Serbian Orthodox Church in the US and Canada has 2 parishes in Vancouver. The Estonian Orthodox Church has a parish in Vancouver and the Coptic and Armenian communities also have parishes in Surrey. Antiochian Orthodox Christians and Armenian Orthodox Christians are also present in the Vancouver area. *David J. Goa*

OSLAND, a FISHING and farming settlement on the east side of Smith Island, 20 km southeast of PRINCE RUPERT on the North Coast, was settled about 1913 by a group of Icelanders from Manitoba. The community had a population of 70 in the 1920s, but by 1952 most people had moved to Prince Rupert. *AS*

OSOYOOS, town, pop 4,021, is located at a narrowing of Osoyoos Lk at the south end of the OKANAGAN VALLEY near the US border, 400 km east of VANCOUVER. Sited on an ancient crossing place, it takes its name from an OKANAGAN word meaning "where the lake narrows." The district attracted outside interest with the GOLD RUSHES of the 1860s. In 1861 John Carmichael HAYNES was put in charge of a customs house at the site. He bought up surrounding land, and by the 1880s he was operating a large cattle ranch (*see* CATTLE INDUSTRY). In 1906 Leslie Hill from NELSON established a model orchard, proving that the district was suitable for growing TREE FRUITS, but it was not until the 1920s that the construc-

Osprey. Roy Luckow photo

exclusively on fish, diving from great heights to pluck them from water; they are also known as fish hawks. Normally they build their large stick nests in the open atop high trees or pilings close to water. They are summer visitors, migrating south in the fall.

Aerial view of Osoyoos, 1993. Roy Luckow photo

tion of an irrigation project made possible the expansion of AGRICULTURE. Fruit and vegetable growing have continued to be the mainstays of the economy, along with TOURISM. Incorporated as a village on 14 Jan 1946, the community adopted a Spanish theme in 1974 to attract visitors. ANARCHIST MT provides a stunning view of the surrounding area, and the SKIING at nearby Mt Baldy is excellent. North of town is a famed "pocket desert," Canada's only remaining desert-like habitat. Encompassing about 120 km², it provides a home for several plant and animal species found nowhere else in the country. Part of the "desert" has been protected as an ECOLOGICAL RESERVE; steps are being taken to preserve the endangered burrowing OWL.

OSPREY (*Pandion haliaetus*) is a large white, black and grey bird of prey widely present throughout the southern half of the province, with a particularly significant breeding area around CRESTON and NELSON. Ospreys feed

OTTER was a tiny FRASER VALLEY AGRICULTURAL community in the municipality of LANGLEY. It formed around an intersection on the old Yale Road, had a school and post office, and later became a GREAT NORTHERN RWY station. It was named by an early settler who had served under Colonel William D. Otter during the Red River Rebellion. *AS*

OTTER, SS, the first propeller-driven steamship in the N Pacific, was built in 1852 for the HBC in England by Green, Wigrams and Green. The vessel was 37.2 m long, 6 m wide and 220 tons burden. Superior to the SS BEAVER in size, speed and efficiency, the *Otter* was sent to the coast to assist its famous predecessor but soon developed a reputation of its own. The ship arrived in VICTORIA on 5 Aug 1853 and went into general trading and TOWBOATING service under Capt H.G. Lewis. The *Otter* frequently made freight hauls to San Francisco and on one of these trips, in 1857, is reputed to have touched off the FRASER R GOLD RUSH when it deposited gold at the US Mint. The ship continued to play a pivotal role in the stampede by offering miners regular service between Victoria and the mainland. In 1862 it provided similar service during the Stikine gold rush, and again in 1874 during the CASSIAR rush. In 1862 it carried crews and supplies to the head of BUTE INLET to start the ill-fated wagon road that led to the CHILCOTIN WAR. The *Otter* outlasted less lucky vessels, plying the coast until 1886 when it was burned for its copper on BENTINCK ISLAND. In 1900 a second coastal steamer named *Otter* appeared on the coast. Built in Victoria for the CANADIAN PACIFIC NAVIGATION CO, the 39-m vessel toiled in general freight service until May 1937, when it was destroyed by fire in Malkscope Inlet.

OTTER, RIVER (*Lutra canadensis*), is common in BC and most abundant on the coast in bays and inland waters. It is not considered a marine mammal because it is also found in LAKES, RIVERS and marshes. Unlike the SEA OTTER, it makes its

River otter feeding on salmon.
Ian McAllister photo

home on land, where it builds a nest and nurtures its young. The river otter has a slender body up to 1.5 m long, with a long, tapered tail; it weighs up to 13.6 kg. It has a broad, flat head and a longer neck than a sea otter. The river otter uses a unique shrill whistle to communicate, as well as "chuckles" and grunts to signal other otters. An otter seen in the sea is often a river otter. *Rick Harbo*

OTTER, SEA, *see* SEA OTTER

OUR LADY OF GOOD HOPE was an OBLATE mission established in 1873 near FORT ST JAMES at Stuart Lk as headquarters for missionary activity across northern BC. The church, still standing, is BC's oldest Catholic church and third-oldest church of any denomination. There was a RESIDENTIAL SCHOOL at the mission from 1917 until it was replaced by the school at LEJAC in 1922.

OVERLANDERS were GOLD seekers from Ontario who trekked across the western Interior to the CARIBOO in the summer of 1862. They

A party of Overlanders descending the N Thompson R, 1862, shown in a painting by Robert John Banks. BC Archives PDP-00806

gathered at the Red River Settlement in Manitoba, and the largest group of about 150 people, led by Thomas MCMICKING, set out early in June. Two smaller groups followed. Most of the Overlanders were young men of limited means who hoped to make their fortunes in the GOLD RUSH. The main party's only woman, Catherine SCHUBERT, travelled with her husband and three young children; their fourth child was born after they arrived in BC. The Overlanders journeyed by Red River cart and packhorse. They crossed the plains to Fort Edmonton, then took the YELLOWHEAD PASS across the ROCKY MTS to the headwaters of the FRASER R. It was a perilous trip, full of hardships, but the party safely reached TÊTE JAUNE CACHE on 1 Sept and officially disbanded there. Most of the men travelled the rest of the way down the Fraser by CANOE and raft. Another group went overland south toward KAMLOOPS; 2 were drowned along the way and the rest almost starved. None of the Overlanders struck it rich in the Cariboo, but many remained in BC and went on to have successful careers.

OVERWAITEA FOOD GROUP is a grocery store chain founded by Robert Kidd in NEW WESTMINSTER in 1915. Kidd was an aggressive merchandiser who specialized in discount pricing: the stores' peculiar name derives from Kidd's practice of adding 2 extra ounces (57 grams) to every pound (450 g) of tea he sold ("overweight tea"). In 1968 Jim PATTISON purchased the chain and steadily expanded it until 1982, when Lower Mainland stores were reborn as a new chain, Save-on-Foods & Drugs. The Overwaitea Food Group, part of the Jim Pattison Group, has stores throughout BC and Alberta, as well as a wholesale operation, and is the second-largest grocery store chain in BC (after Safeway) with 27% of the retail market. In 1999 it added Cooper's Foods, a 9-store supermarket chain in the Interior.

OWEEKENO First Nation traditionally occupied the central coast around RIVERS INLET and OWIKENO LK and its drainage. Their language is Oowekyala, a form of the northern WAKASHAN Oowekyala-Heiltsuk language; as a result they are usually grouped with the Heiltsuk (Bella Bella) and HAIHAIS (XaiXais) FIRST NATIONS as the HEILTSUK people (*see* FIRST NATIONS LANGUAGES). Because of their location at the head of the inlet their seasonal subsistence pattern was more oriented to inland resources than that of other coastal groups, though they did visit sites on the outer coast. Their basic social unit was the local group, comprised of related families with their own chief, names, village sites and so on. Society was divided into chiefs, commoners and slaves (*see* SLAVERY), most of whom were war captives. During the mid-1800s epidemics ravaged the population, which declined by 90%. By about 1900 LOGGING and canning activity had centralized settlement at the village of Oweekeno (pop 60; also called Katit) on the Wannock R at the head of Rivers Inlet, accessible only by float plane or boat. Although the canneries have shut down, logging and commercial FISHING remain important.

OWEN, Walter Stewart, lawyer, lt gov 1973–78 (b 26 Jan 1904, Atlin; d 13 Jan 1981, Vancouver). He was born in the ATLIN jail, son of a BC PROVINCIAL POLICE officer who later became warden at OAKALLA PRISON FARM. After studying at UBC law school, he was called to the bar in 1928 and set up in practice in VANCOUVER. When he was named crown prosecutor in 1933 he was the youngest ever appointed in Canada to that time. He returned to private practice in 1942 and became one of the leading Vancouver lawyers of his generation, specializing particularly in industrial relations. He was president of the Canadian Bar Assoc in 1958 and a director of several major corporations. In 1956 he bought radio station CKNW with Frank GRIFFITHS, forming Western Broadcasting, which later grew into the BROADCASTING giant (WIC) WESTERN INTERNATIONAL COMMUNICATIONS. After leaving his post as LT GOV he lived in retirement in Vancouver.

OWEN BAY is on the south side of SONORA ISLAND in the jumble of islands between

VANCOUVER ISLAND and the mainland, about 200 km north of VANCOUVER. It looks across a set of rapids in Okisollo Channel at the north end of QUADRA ISLAND. It was named by a British naval survey after Frederick John Owen Evans of the Admiralty Hydrographic Office. LOGGING began in the 1890s and by the 1920s the bay was being homesteaded, notably by Logan Schibler and his family. A small community developed, including a school, government dock, post office, store and SAWMILL. By the late 1960s, however, the community had dispersed. The bay has a reputation among coastal boaters for being haunted.

OWIKENO LAKE, 101.8 km², is a narrow body of water extending eastward into the COAST MTS from the head of RIVERS INLET on the Mid-Coast about 120 km northeast of PORT HARDY. Draining westward into the inlet via the very short Wannock R, it is situated in the territory of the OWEEKENO First Nation, now centred at the village of Katit. Extensive LOGGING has taken place in the watershed. *See also* LAKES.

OWL is a carnivorous bird of prey, usually active at night and known for its eerie hooting. Its diet consists mainly of rodents, though some species will eat insects, larger mammals and other birds. Owls do not build their own nests; they occupy hollow trees, other birds' nests, cliff ledges or even holes in the ground. There are 15 owl species in BC, more than in any other province, and each is adapted to a different habitat. The short-eared owl (*Asio flammeus*) prefers open country and nests on the ground, as does the white snowy owl (*Nyctea scandiaca*), a winter visitor from its Arctic breeding ground. The burrowing owl (*Athene cunicularia*) nests underground. It once bred in the south-central Interior and the FRASER R delta but because of habitat destruction is no longer found regularly in BC. The barn owl (*Tyto alba*), with its distinctive heart-shaped face, is found in meadow/ pasture/GRASSLAND habitat. Other species are associated with forested habitats. They include the great grey owl (*Strix nebulosa*), the largest

Northern saw-whet owl. Glen Ryder photo

species; the great horned owl (*Bubo virginianus*), a large, ferocious nocturnal hunter; the flammulated owl (*Otus flammeolus*), a small, insect-eating species present in Canada only in southern BC; the tiny northern pygmy owl (*Glaucidium gnoma*); and the northern hawk owl (*Surnia ulula*), the boreal owl (*Aegolius funereus*), the northern saw-whet owl (*Aegolius acadicus*), the western screech owl (*Otus kennicottii*), the barred owl (*Strix varia*) and the long-eared owl (*Asio otus*). The spotted owl (*Strix occidentalis*) is at the centre of debates about the environmental impact of LOGGING. An ENDANGERED SPECIES, it inhabits the province's old-growth FORESTS; it is feared that as these disappear, so will the spotted owl.

OWL CREEK, 30 km northeast of WHISTLER on the BC RAIL line, grew up around a federal government FISH HATCHERY, established in 1905, and a SAWMILL. In 1917 Sam Spetch opened a store and post office. Spetch had settled in 1908 near BIRKEN to the north, on the Summit Ranch, where his post office was called Pemberton Portage after the early TRAIL from PEMBERTON to ANDERSON LK. The hatchery shut down in 1936 and Spetch's son Bill moved the store to MOUNT

CURRIE. Today Owl Creek is the site of a FOREST SERVICE campground.   AS

OYAMA, pop 1,500, lies on a narrow isthmus separating Wood and KALAMALKA lakes east of OKANAGAN LK, 16 km north of KELOWNA. It is part of the LAKE COUNTRY District (pop 9,007), which also includes OKANAGAN CENTRE, WINFIELD and SUNNYWOLD (Carr's Landing). The townsite was established in 1908 to serve the surrounding orchards. It was named for Japanese Prince Iwao Oyama, a hero in the Russo-Japanese war.

OYSTER is a member of the bivalve class of MOLLUSCS. Its soft body is protected by 2 halves (valves) of a hard, rough shell that usually attaches to a rock or other hard surface along the coast. It feeds by filtering algae (*see* SEAWEED) from seawater and thus can be affected by waterborne toxins (*see* HARMFUL ALGAL BLOOMS). At least 4 species of oysters are found in BC. The Olympia oyster (*Ostrea conchaphila*), the only native species, has become uncommon in most areas, probably because of pollution and overharvesting. The edible flat oyster (*O. edulis*) was introduced for experimental culturing and has not established itself in the wild. The American oyster (*Crassostrea virginica*) is the common edible oyster of the east coast of N America. It has been introduced to several west coast sites but only a small population in BOUNDARY BAY has persisted in the wild. The dominant oyster in BC is the large (up to 25 cm), heavily fluted Pacific, or Japanese, oyster (*C. gigas*), which was introduced from Japan in the early 1900s. It continues to have sporadic spawnings that colonize GEORGIA STRAIT and adjacent waters. It was also introduced to a few locations on VANCOUVER ISLAND's west coast. In 1998, production of the Pacific oyster—all of it cultured—was 5,300 tonnes with a wholesale value of $6 million. There is no wild commercial harvest. BAYNES SOUND on the east coast of Vancouver Island is BC's most productive shellfish growing area, accounting for 39% of oyster production. The SUNSHINE COAST, the GULF ISLANDS and the west

Barred owl. R. Wayne Campbell photo

Great grey owl. R. Wayne Campbell photo

Snowy owl. R. Wayne Campbell photo

Olympia oyster, the only oyster species native to BC. Duane Sept photo

coast of Vancouver Island also have successful oyster culture areas. The growing time from seed to market for Pacific oysters varies from 1½–4 years, depending on water temperature, food abundance, culture techniques and desired market size. Two basic methods are employed by oyster farmers. In bottom culture, oyster seed is placed on the beach in the low to mid-intertidal zone and grows in much the same way as naturally seeded oysters. In deep-water or off-bottom culture, the oysters are suspended from floats or rafts using ropes, trays or cages to contain them as they grow. There are many innovative variations in deep-water culture techniques, and some growers use a combination of bottom and deep-water methods in a single production cycle. *See also* AQUACULTURE, SHELLFISH.

OYSTER RIVER flows from VANCOUVER ISLAND's FORBIDDEN PLATEAU into GEORGIA STRAIT 22 km north of COURTENAY, a distance of about 40 km. The river is a favourite with FLY FISHERS; a recreational community formed at its mouth around an early resort and store called the Fisherman's Lodge. Sandy Saratoga Beach is nearby, as are Miracle Beach Provincial PARK and the Oyster R and Oyster Bay Shoreline regional parks. *See also* RIVERS. AS

OYSTERCATCHER, black (*Haematopus bachmani*), is a CROW-sized coastal bird with black plumage set off by pink legs and a long orange-red bill. It is seen in all seasons on islets and rocky shorelines along the coast from Alaska to Baja California. It eats exclusively shellfish, but despite its name principally MUSSELS and LIMPETS, which it opens by inserting its bill between the shells of a bivalve and slicing the hinge muscles. The oystercatcher nests on offshore ISLANDS in shallow depressions lined with shell and bits of debris.

Oystercatcher. Dean van't Schip photo

PACHENA POINT is located in the traditional territory of the Huu-ay-aht (Ohiaht) First Nation on the west coast of VANCOUVER ISLAND, south of BAMFIELD and overlooking the entrance to JUAN DE FUCA STRAIT. This is the stretch of coastline known as the "Graveyard of the Pacific" because of the number of ships that have been wrecked

Lighthouse at Pachena Point. Jim Ryan photo

there. A LIGHTHOUSE was erected in 1907 and in 1999 remained in operation, the only wooden light station left in the province. The northern end of the WEST COAST TRAIL is nearby.

PACIFIC, a small settlement and VIA Rail station 35 km northeast of TERRACE on the west side of

the SKEENA R, was originally called Nicholl. It was renamed because the Pacific Division of the GRAND TRUNK PACIFIC RWY began here. There is little left at the site today.   AS

PACIFIC BIOLOGICAL STATION is a federal marine research facility established in Departure Bay at NANAIMO in 1908. Rev George Taylor, a naturalist and Anglican cleric, was a strong advocate for the creation of the station, and he served as its first director. Over the years PBS staff developed much of our current knowledge of fisheries in BC, and conducted pioneering research on OCEANOGRAPHY and limnology (*see* LAKES) while unravelling the life cycle of the SALMON. Under Dr W.A. Clemens, director from 1924 to 1940, the station underwent significant expansion; this work continued after WWII. About 150 scientific staff are based there, as well as the fisheries research vessel *W.E. Ricker*, named for William "Bill" RICKER who worked at the PBS for many years. Formerly operated under the Fisheries Research Board of Canada, the station is now part of the science branch of Fisheries and Oceans Canada.   *Colin Levings*

PACIFIC COACH LINES was formed in 1979 by a merger of Pacific Stage Lines (PSL) and Vancouver Island Coach Lines. PSL was an intercity bus company created in 1922 by Ivor Neil. It expanded into one of the largest bus lines in Canada, offering scheduled service to Seattle and throughout the FRASER VALLEY. In 1932 it became a wholly owned subsidiary of BC ELECTRIC RWY CO. It was also agent for Gray Line Sightseeing, the largest bus tour company in N America. In the 1960s PSL and Vancouver Island Coach Lines began operating service to and on VANCOUVER ISLAND, and they merged in 1979.

PACIFIC COAST CHILDREN'S MISSION began in 1944 when Alf Bayne and his wife Margaret purchased a work boat, renamed it the *Goforth* and began visiting BC's coast communities as far north as PRINCE RUPERT as an offshoot of the Child for Christ Crusade. Since 1948 the mission has been based at its Homewood property overlooking Gowlland Harbour on QUADRA ISLAND, providing Christian outreach through Sunday schools, Bible classes, summer camps and outdoor education programs.

PACIFIC COAST HOCKEY ASSOCIATION, 1911–26, was founded by the PATRICK family: Joe and HOCKEY-playing sons Lester and Frank. Lester played professionally with the Montreal Wanderers and both sons starred with the Renfrew Millionaires in Ottawa in 1909–10 before retiring temporarily to work in Joe's LOGGING and SAWMILLING business in NELSON. In 1911 Joe sold his company and used the proceeds to back his sons in starting their professional hockey league with teams in VANCOUVER (*see* VANCOUVER MILLIONAIRES, later named the Maroons), VICTORIA (the Senators, later the VICTORIA COUGARS), NEW WESTMINSTER (the Royals, moved to Portland in 1914 to become the Rosebuds) and later Seattle (the Metropolitans 1915–24) and Spokane (the Canaries 1916–17). The Patricks built Canada's first artificial-ice rinks in Victoria and Vancouver. The Vancouver rink at Denman and Georgia seated 10,500; it was the world's largest ice rink and, after Madison Square Garden in New York, the second-biggest sports building in N America. The Patricks stocked the new league with players from the National Hockey Assoc. Cyclone TAYLOR joined the Vancouver team in 1913 and helped the Millionaires win the Stanley Cup in 1915. In 1917 the cup went to a US team for the first time when Seattle won. After the Seattle franchise folded in 1924 the remaining PCHA teams, Vancouver and Victoria, joined the professional prairies league, the Western Canada Hockey League (known as the "Western

Hockey League" in its final season, 1925–26). Victoria brought the Stanley Cup back to the coast for the last time in 1925 by beating the Montreal Canadiens. Player salaries of up to $10,000 a year made it difficult for the WHL to compete and the Patricks arranged to fold the league after the 1925–26 season, selling players' rights to the NHL as it expanded into the US market. A minor professional league known as the Pacific Coast Hockey League, which also featured teams in Vancouver, Victoria, New Westminster, Seattle and Portland, lasted from 1945 until 1952, when it too amalgamated with a prairie league under the Western Hockey League name. Major professional hockey did not return to the coast until 1970 when the VANCOUVER CANUCKS joined the NHL.

PACIFIC COLISEUM opened on the PNE grounds in east VANCOUVER on 8 Jan 1968 with the touring Ice Capades show. The arena was home to the VANCOUVER CANUCKS, then of the WESTERN HOCKEY LEAGUE. On 9 Oct 1970 the Canucks played their first NHL game there. The arena had a seating capacity of 16,500 but the largest crowd exceeded 19,000 for a 1972 concert by the Canadian-born rock singer Neil Young. Others who have appeared at the Coliseum include Queen Elizabeth, Mother Teresa, Frank Sinatra, the Rolling Stones and Michael Jordan. Originally owned by the PNE, the building passed to the city at the end of 1996 after the Canucks moved to their new home, GENERAL MOTORS PLACE.

PACIFIC FLYWAY is one of 4 major generalized north–south migration routes for N American waterfowl. Based on observations made by the 1940s, the Atlantic, Mississippi, Central and Pacific flyways were considered to be the principal routes of migrating birds in N America, and flyway councils were set up in the 1950s. While millions of birds do migrate out of interior lands and from the Arctic to the coast, it has since been learned that this description oversimplifies highly complex migrations, and it applies more to geese (see GOOSE), SWANS and CRANES than to DUCKS and other groups of birds. Nonetheless the concept remained and the flyways became the basis of administrative divisions for international co-operative management of waterfowl populations and of setting migratory waterfowl hunting regulations in both Canada and the US. What is considered the Pacific Flyway encompasses important breeding, staging and winter nesting areas for significant numbers of waterfowl along BC's coastal WETLANDS. Only about 3% of our coastal habitats are suitable for waterfowl and shorebirds; among these are the broad wetlands and deltas of the FRASER, Kitimat and STIKINE rivers, and ESTUARIES and mudflats at SQUAMISH, BOUNDARY BAY, COWICHAN, COMOX, TOFINO and other areas. BC estuaries support the largest populations of waterbirds in Canada. At various times of the year, the Pacific Flyway's skies are alive with millions of birds migrating along BC's coast. *See also* NATURAL HISTORY.

Maggie Paquet

PACIFIC FOREST PRODUCTS LTD began as Pacific Logging Co in 1962 to manage timberland acquired by the CPR when it purchased the ESQUIMALT & NANAIMO RWY on eastern VANCOUVER ISLAND. Although it operated primarily as a forest management and market LOGGING company on 1,258 km² of private land, Pacific Logging acquired interests in several Island SAWMILLING operations. In 1978 it teamed up with Mitsubishi to build the Mayo Forest Products sawmill in NANAIMO. In 1981 Canadian Pacific bought the Tahsis Company, with a pulp mill at GOLD RIVER, 2 sawmills at TAHSIS and extensive timber rights on the west coast of the Island. Tahsis and Pacific Logging were merged into CP Forest, a company formed by Canadian Pacific to oversee its forest operations in BC and Ontario. In 1993 CP Forest changed its name to Avenor Inc and its forest lands, timber harvesting rights and sawmills at LADYSMITH, Tahsis and Nanaimo were placed under the control of a new company, Pacific Forest Products. The company pioneered the selective logging of second-growth coastal forests. Its revenues in 1996 were $383.6 million. In 1997 Avenor sold the company to TimberWest Forest Holdings Ltd. As well, it sold the company's 3 sawmills and Crown timber operations to DOMAN INDUSTRIES. *See also* FOREST INDUSTRY. *Ken Drushka*

PACIFIC FUR CO was formed in 1809 by the wealthy New York merchant John Jacob Astor, who planned to supply the China market with furs from the Pacific Northwest. Astor took on 4 NORTH WEST CO traders as partners and hired several Canadian voyageurs to travel overland to establish a post at the mouth of the COLUMBIA R. At the same time he dispatched a ship, the *Tonquin*, to sail around Cape Horn for the same destination. After a troubled voyage the *Tonquin* arrived at the river mouth in the spring of 1811 and the crew erected a post, called Astoria. The *Tonquin* sailed north to trade. At CLAYOQUOT SOUND the captain offended the local NUU-CHAH-NULTH (Nootka), who retaliated by attacking the vessel. It had been booby-trapped and it exploded, killing about 200 aboriginals. None of the crew survived the incident. Meanwhile the overland party reached Astoria early in 1812 and the company began establishing posts up the Columbia and north into NEW CALEDONIA, where a fort was built at KAMLOOPS in 1812. With the outbreak of the War of 1812, however, the company supply ship failed to arrive and in Oct 1813 the people at Astoria sold out to the Nor'westers, ending the brief history of the Pacific Fur Co.

PACIFIC GREAT EASTERN RAILWAY; *see* BC RAIL.

PACIFIC NATIONAL EXHIBITION (PNE), originally the Vancouver Industrial Exhibition, was an annual agricultural–industrial fair held at Hastings Park, VANCOUVER, from 1910 to 2000. From its beginnings as a small exhibition designed to promote Vancouver's economic development, it grew to include a midway, an

Poster advertising the PNE, 1948.

Playland at the PNE, Vancouver.
Mark Van Manen/Vancouver Sun

amusement park, concerts and major sports facilities. By 1930, when the New Westminster Exhibition closed following a fire, the PNE was the province's main exhibition. It was cancelled during 1942–46 when the military took over the park, using it initially as a transshipment point for residents of Japanese descent who were being interned (see JAPANESE, RELOCATION OF). The fair resumed in 1947 as the Pacific National Exhibition, with a new emphasis on entertainment. At the same time Hastings Park was renamed Exhibition Park. The Shrine Circus was added the following year, along with a Miss PNE beauty pageant. In 1954 Empire Stadium was built for the BRITISH EMPIRE AND COMMONWEALTH GAMES; afterwards it was home to the BC LIONS football team until it moved to BC PLACE STADIUM in 1983. Playland was added in 1958, replacing the smaller Happyland amusement park. Professional HOCKEY was also played on the grounds, first at the Forum, then from 1968 to 1995 at the PACIFIC COLISEUM. In 1973 the provincial government took control of the PNE board. At the beginning of 1997 the city took over the site, by then known as Hastings Park again, with plans to turn it into a large urban park, and the fair began its search for a new home.

PACIFIC PRESS publishes both the *VANCOUVER SUN* and the *PROVINCE*. It was formed in 1957 as a partnership of Sun Publishing, owned by the CROMIE family and publisher of the *Sun*, and Southam Press, publisher of the *Province*, to print the 2 daily NEWSPAPERS. Because the *Sun* was the larger partner, the Cromies received an equalization payment of $3.85 million. The papers continued to be owned separately—the *Province* by Southam and the *Sun* by the Cromies to 1963; then by FP Publications until 1980, when Southam also bought the *Sun*. Hollinger International took over Southam in 1996, but sold most of it, including Pacific Press, to Canwest Global Communications Corp. in 2000.

PACIFIC RIM refers to the countries around the edge of the Pacific Ocean and more specifically to N America, the countries of western S America, Australia, New Zealand and the Pacific Islands and Southeast and East Asia—the so-called Asia–Pacific region. As Canada's Pacific province, BC is most influenced by changing relations with the Pacific Rim. The region has always been an important destination for BC products; for example, furs were exported to China (*see* FUR TRADE) and the first shipments of wood products went to Australia. By the early 19th century the Hawaiian Islands, then known as the Sandwich Islands, were an important stopover for trading ships from the coast bound for China and Europe. But after WWII, and particularly since the 1960s, trans-Pacific trade has exploded and now exceeds trans-Atlantic trade. As a result of this shift VANCOUVER has become the second-largest port on the Pacific Coast of N America in terms of total tonnage handled (after Long Beach, CA). Japan has become the second most valuable trading partner, after the US, for both Canada and BC. In 1996, 25% of BC's exports went to Japan, and a further 11% to other Asian countries, more than any other province and much more than the country as a whole, which ships only 9% of its exports to the Pacific Rim. Wheat, COAL, sulphur and FOREST PRODUCTS are the main exports. At the same time the BC economy attracted Asian investors, particularly the Japanese, who invested heavily in COAL MINING, PULP AND PAPER, FORESTRY and financial services. This 2-way traffic in goods and capital was hit hard by the Asian economic crisis of 1997–98, delivering a serious blow to the BC economy, which had become so dependent on Asian markets.

The last 3 decades of the 20th century saw a huge increase in the movement of people across the Pacific as well as goods; this trend became even stronger in the 1990s. Early in the century public attitudes and public policy opposed immigration from Asian countries (*see* ASIATIC EXCLUSION LEAGUE; HEAD TAX). This situation changed, however, and during the 1960s the final special restrictions on Asian immigration were removed. In 1991 about 33% of all immigrants coming to live in BC were from Asian countries. By 1996, 80% of Vancouver's immigrants were from Asia and the Pacific, while for Canada as a whole the percentage was only 55%.

In hosting tourists from Asia, BC also grew to surpass any other part of the world except the US. Most Asian tourists to BC are Japanese (306,000 in 1996) and Japanese investors are heavily involved in tourist-related services such as hotels and golf courses. Again, this trend slowed in 1998 as economic problems in Asia led to a reduction in the flow of Asian tourists. Still, the Asia–Pacific region is expected to be the major contributor to BC's economic growth and cultural diversity in the 21st century. *See also* APEC; CHINESE; ECONOMY; JAPANESE; PEOPLES OF BC; SOUTH ASIANS; TOURISM.

PACIFIC RIM NATIONAL PARK RESERVE, 513 km², is a narrow strip of beach, foreshore and islands on the west coast of VANCOUVER ISLAND extending 105 km from south of TOFINO in the

Green Point, Pacific Rim National Park.
Duane Sept photo

north to PORT RENFREW in the south. It has 3 distinct units: LONG BEACH (81 km²), the BROKEN GROUP ISLANDS in BARKLEY SOUND and the WEST COAST TRAIL. The borders of the park extend offshore to protect the contiguous ocean environment. Long Beach is the most accessible section, 175 km by Hwy 4 (*see* ROADS AND HWYS) across the island from NANAIMO. The NUU-CHAH-NULTH First Nations have occupied the entire area since before recorded history. They were joined early in the century by a handful of white settlers, then in the 1960s, when camping was allowed on the long stretches of white sand beach, by a small number of squatters and a shifting population of surfers, hippies and TOURISTS. After becoming a park reserve in 1970, the beach was regulated more closely. Cars are not permitted to use the flat sand as a speedway and tenting is confined to authorized campgrounds. Visitors enjoy SURFING in the frigid water, hiking, shell gathering, kayaking or simply observing the many moods of the open Pacific as it crashes onto the shore. GRAY WHALES migrate past the park on their travels between Baja California and the Bering Sea.

PACIFIC SALMON COMMISSION was established in 1985 by the governments of Canada and the US to implement the PACIFIC SALMON TREATY. It represents the interests of commercial and recreational fisheries; federal, state and tribal governments; and environmental agencies.

The commission provides regulatory recommendations to the 2 countries but does not regulate the salmon fisheries. Its fundamental role is to conserve Pacific SALMON in order to achieve optimum production, and to divide harvests so that both countries benefit. It is responsible for all salmon originating in the waters of one country that are subject to interception by the other, or that affect management of the other country's salmon or that affect biologically the stocks of the other country. Canada and the US have one vote each in the commission, and the agreement of both is required for any recommendation or decision. Four regional panels—the Southern, Northern, Transboundary and Fraser River—provide technical and regulatory advice to the commission. The commission receives administrative support from its secretariat, whose headquarters are in VANCOUVER. Secretariat staff members also provide technical information and advice concerning FRASER R sockeye and pink salmon harvests. The Pacific Salmon Commission may recommend that the countries implement harvest limitations, time and area closures, gear restrictions or other measures to control harvests. In addition, the commission may recommend use of enhancement techniques to strengthen weak runs, and mitigate for damage done by LOGGING, MINING, dam-building or other activities. *See also* FISHING, ABORIGINAL; FISHING, COMMERCIAL; FISHING, SPORT.

PACIFIC SALMON TREATY (PST) is an agreement between the US and Canada to co-operate in the sharing, conservation, management, research and enhancement of Pacific SALMON stocks of mutual concern. After many years of negotiation, the PST was ratified in Mar 1985.

Pacific salmon migrate long distances, spending several years at sea. In the course of their migratory cycle, some stocks of fish hatched in US waters enter the fishery zones of Canada, and some Canadian-origin fish enter the fishery zones of the US. These are known as stocks of mutual concern. A fishery in which one country harvests fish spawned in the other is known as an interception fishery. Experience has shown that these fisheries encourage overharvest and discourage investment in conservation and enhancement, especially if the fish produced in one country are caught by fishers of another nation. One nation may harvest too many of the other country's stocks and jeopardize the home country's management plans, unless the 2 countries agree on management policies and conservation concerns. Interception fisheries have been the subject of discussion and controversy between Canada and the US for more than a century. The first agreement to deal with the issue was signed in 1937. Known as the INTERNATIONAL PACIFIC SALMON FISHERIES CONVENTION (IPSFC), this treaty initially allowed the US to harvest approximately 50% of the returns of FRASER R sockeye and pink salmon. Although the convention was slightly modified from the late 1950s onward, significant problems began to emerge. Concerns included the need to deal with

Protestors lobby government to protect Canada's share of the salmon harvest, Vancouver, 1975. Dan Scott/Vancouver Sun

interceptions of other salmon species, Canada's increasing dissatisfaction with the 50/50 sharing agreement, each country's increased fishing (and interception) capacity and the lack of assurance that enhancement programs would provide benefits to the country undertaking such measures.

The Pacific Salmon Treaty replaced the IPSFC in 1985. It covered the area from southeast Alaska south, including the coasts of BC, Washington and Oregon. The new treaty was much broader and included salmon returning to the SKEENA R and NASS R and smaller transboundary rivers. The agreement also addressed interception of chinook, coho, pink and chum salmon. The PST committed the 2 countries to carry out their salmon fisheries and enhancement programs so as to prevent overfishing, provide for optimum production and ensure that both countries receive benefits equal to the production of salmon originating in their waters. As well, both countries agreed to the importance of reducing interceptions, avoiding undue disruption of existing fisheries, and accounting for annual variations in abundance of stocks. Canada's objectives in signing the treaty were threefold.

First, Canada wanted to begin to rebuild its stocks with the assurance that it would receive the benefits of increased production (under the old treaty, increased production would be shared

equally with the USA).

Second, Canada wanted to achieve equity in interceptions. The equity principle in the treaty provides for balancing the value of one country's interceptions against the value of interceptions by the other country. Canada has long held that the US has always benefited substantially more from interceptions of Canadian salmon than Canada has benefited from interceptions of US salmon. The US disagrees. Despite the lack of agreement, which through the late 1980s was aggravated by escalating interceptions in southeast Alaska, both parties to the PST agreed on catch-sharing arrangements through 1992; but by 1999 the disagreement was still preventing the equity principle from being implemented. The issue has been extremely important to Canada, and has been the occasion of 2 significant protests. In 1994 Canada slapped a $1,000 (US) fee on US fishing vessels transiting Canadian waters, and in 1997 angry Canadian fishers blockaded an Alaska State ferry in PRINCE RUPERT harbour for several days. Both measures were effective in bringing the US back to the negotiating table, though in both cases the US sued Canada and recovered some of its losses.

Third, Canada wanted to improve conservation and management of its salmon stocks, particularly chinook stocks. Conservation efforts in Canada were proving to be of limited benefit in helping the stocks rebuild since the Alaskan catch of Canadian chinook and coho stocks was largely unrestricted. The PST included a coastwide chinook conservation plan; after the treaty was signed, chinook stocks began rebuilding, but further management actions were needed to deal with specific stocks of concern.

The main implementing body for the PST is the PACIFIC SALMON COMMISSION, which meets annually to review fisheries plans in both countries and ensure treaty obligations are met. The last comprehensive agreement developed by the commission was for the 1992 fishing season. After 1992, negotiations between the 2 countries deteriorated to the extent that the long-term future of the treaty was at risk. In 1999 both parties signed 10-year catch-sharing agreements for most interception fisheries and a 12-year agreement for Fraser R sockeye and pink salmon. However, the new agreement did not provide any direction on implementation of the equity principle. While having an agreement in place provides certain stability and benefits, many BC fishers, environmental groups and aboriginal groups, as well as the BC government, have publicly and persistently denounced the federal government for signing an agreement too favourable to the US. *See also* ENVIRONMENTAL MOVEMENT; FISHING, ABORIGINAL; FISHING, COMMERCIAL.   *Bud Graham and Peter A. Robson*

PACIFIC SPACE CENTRE; *see* MACMILLAN, H.R., SPACE CENTRE.

PACIFIC STAGE LINES; *see* PACIFIC COACH LINES.

PACIFIC WESTERN AIRLINES (PWA) was

created in 1953 when CENTRAL BC AIRWAYS changed its name and embarked on a period of rapid growth, absorbing other regional airlines and winning the contract to provide services for the construction of the DEW Line in the western Arctic. The airline was based in VANCOUVER and soon had more than 600 employees and a fleet of 75 aircraft. In 1974 the Alberta government purchased PWA and soon after moved the company's headquarters to Calgary. In 1983 PWA Corp was created as a holding company to buy shares of the airline from Alberta. In 1987 PWA Corp acquired CP Air and amalgamated it with PWA, Nordair and Eastern Provincial Airways to form a single airline, Canadian Airlines International, which was purchased by Air Canada in 1999.
Reading: Peter Pigott, *Wing Walkers: A History of Canadian Airlines International*, 1998.

PACIFICA PAPERS INC is a paper manufacturing company created in 1998 when the FOREST INDUSTRY giant MACMILLAN BLOEDEL spun off its paper operations into a separate operation. Pacifica owns the paper mill complexes formerly owned by MacBlo at POWELL RIVER and PORT ALBERNI. *See also* PULP AND PAPER.

PACOFI, on Moresby Island, 47 km south of SKIDEGATE in the QUEEN CHARLOTTE ISLANDS, was the site of a fish plant that opened in 1909 and soon went out of business. The name is an abbreviation for Pacific Coast Fisheries, headed by Alvo von ALVENSLEBEN. Rumour circulated that he was a German spy and that Pacofi was a submarine base in disguise. A SALMON saltery and cannery (*see* SALMON CANNING) operated here from 1927 to 1949.   *AS*

PADDLEWHEEL STEAMBOATS plied the RIVERS, LAKES and coastal waters of BC from 1836, when the HBC sidewheeler *BEAVER* arrived from England, to 1980 when the sternwheel snag boat *Samson V* was retired. The original wooden steamboats were sidewheelers, active on

SS Beaver, c 1874. It was the first steamboat on the BC coast. VPL 799

the coast until the end of the 19th century, when advances in design favoured the use of screw-propelled vessels, but because they needed docks for landing and were difficult to manoeuvre, sidewheelers were little used on Interior lakes and rivers where the shallow-draft sternwheeler was the vessel of choice.

Building a sternwheel steamboat on the Fraser R, 1870s. BC Archives A-00163

The western-style sternwheel steamboat, developed on the Sacramento and Willamette rivers in the 1850s, was well adapted to inland navigation in BC. It was essentially a flat-bottomed barge, 4 to 5 times as long as it was wide. To balance the fixed load on the hull, a locomotive-type boiler with smokestack was installed on the main deck near the bow and was offset at the stern by the engines and the paddlewheel. A well-designed hull would thus remain buoyant

The Inlander *entering Kitselas Canyon on the Skeena R. Narrow beam and shallow draft made sternwheelers the ideal craft for BC's treacherous rivers. BC Archives B-01268*

even when carrying a heavy cargo. Few loaded vessels drew more than a metre of water; some drew less than half that. In the days before highways and heavy-duty internal combustion vehicles, the sternwheeler worked on just about every navigable stretch of fresh water in the province. It could make a landing simply by shoving its prow against the bank while keeping the sternwheel out in deeper water, and an ingenious set of rudders permitted fast manoeuvring in rapid water.

Sternwheelers were first used on the lower FRASER R in 1858 to carry men and supplies from VICTORIA to the GOLD RUSH diggings in the canyon. The first steamer reached HOPE on 6 June 1858; the first sternwheeler on the river, the

Umatilla, reached YALE, the terminus of the lower Fraser run, on 21 July 1858. With the completion of the CPR in 1885, sternwheelers lost their transportation monopoly in the FRASER VALLEY, but they continued to perform a necessary service until the construction of the INTERURBAN line to CHILLIWACK in 1910. Following WWI only one paddlewheeler, the *Skeena,* continued to operate on the lower Fraser until it was retired in 1925. Meanwhile sternwheelers began to work on the upper Fraser in 1863 when the *Enterprise,* working between SODA CREEK and QUESNEL, became a vital link in the CARIBOO WAGON ROAD.

Sternwheelers continued to be used on the upper Fraser as far as TÊTE JAUNE CACHE, as well as to points on the NECHAKO R system, until 1921, by which time a system of ROADS supplementing railways had met transportation demands.

Gold rush activity, followed by the ill-fated COLLINS OVERLAND TELEGRAPH, introduced steamboating to the SKEENA and STIKINE rivers. Capt William MOORE diverted his lower Fraser R sternwheeler *Flying Dutchman* to the Stikine in 1862, and in 1864 Capt Tom Coffin worked the *Union* up the Skeena as far as the site of TERRACE, though neither vessel lasted past the first season. In 1891 the HBC placed the sternwheeler *Caledonia* in regular service on the Skeena, working as far up as HAZELTON, 288 km from the ocean. Two decades of strenuous competition ensued, but the completion of the GRAND TRUNK PACIFIC RWY in 1914 ended steamboat service on the river. On the Stikine, a second discovery of GOLD in the CASSIAR area in 1873 ushered in a

more stable era of steamboating that lasted until 1916. Farther north, as an offshoot of the Klondike gold rush, a fleet of very small sternwheelers was commissioned to work between Lk Bennett, at the north end of the Chilkoot Trail, and the Whitehorse Rapids on the Yukon R. The completion of the WHITE PASS & YUKON ROUTE in 1900 spelled the end of this service, but steamers continued to work on the Tagish Lk branch to cope with trade to ATLIN. The large sternwheeler *Tutshi* worked from Carcross, YT, to the south end of Tagish Lk until 1953. Smaller sternwheelers also worked on Atlin Lk to connect the MINING camps to the Tagish Lk portage from 1899 to 1918, after which the redoubtable screw-propelled motor vessel *Tarahne* was commissioned for this service.

The 1865 GOLD RUSH at Big Bend prompted the HBC to commission the sternwheeler *Marten* to ply the Shuswap system between SAVONA and the head of SEYMOUR ARM on SHUSWAP LK. Shipments destined for the Big Bend camps then

Luxurious lounge on the R.P. Rithet. VMM

had to be transported over a formidable pass in the MONASHEE MTS. When the rush petered out, so did steamer traffic, though sternwheelers remained active on the Shuswap system, shipping produce, lumber and COAL. Business declined with the construction of the CPR, but one boat, the *C.R. Lamb,* owned by Capt William Louie, remained active in the KAMLOOPS area until 1948.

On the PEACE R, CATHOLIC missionaries launched their own sternwheeler in 1903 to carry supplies from the Alberta side as far up the river as HUDSON'S HOPE. Two years later the HBC launched its sternwheeler, the *Peace River,* on the same route, and steamers continued to operate on the Peace until 1930 when the final boat, the *D.A. Thomas,* left the river.

The construction of the CPR through EAGLE and ROGERS passes in 1885 prompted the commissioning of the sternwheeler *Kootenai* to ship supplies north from Fort Colville to the construction camp that became REVELSTOKE via the COLUMBIA R and ARROW LKS system. The completion of the railway also stimulated agrarian settlement in the lush valley of the upper Columbia R. There Frank P. Armstrong, a former survey crew member, initiated more than 30 years of steamboating in 1886 when he worked his

The SS Skuzzy, on the Fraser R above Yale, 1883. It was the first steamer to pass through Hells Gate. VMM

homemade sternwheeler *Duchess* up the Columbia from GOLDEN to Columbia Lk. Subsequent mining and LOGGING in the valley swelled the demand for steamer service until the Kootenay Central Railway was completed from FORT STEELE to Golden in 1915, making boats on the upper Columbia obsolescent. Service ended in 1920 with the last trip of the sternwheeler *Nowitka*.

The discovery of large deposits of SILVER–lead–ZINC ore in the E KOOTENAY prompted steamer service on the upper KOOTENAY R. A tote road from the North Star mine to a landing on the river above Fort Steele was built in 1892–93, and small sternwheelers began running down the treacherous stretch of river to the port of Jennings, MT, to connect with the rail line there. The completion in 1898 of the BC Southern Rwy from CROWSNEST PASS to Kootenay Landing, at the south end of KOOTENAY LK, provided a better way to ship North Star ore, so steamer service dwindled until it ceased altogether in 1901.

When the Northern Pacific Railroad reached the shore of Pend d'Oreille Lk in Idaho in 1882, interest in the galena lodes around Kootenay Lk was reawakened. In 1884 W.A. BAILLIE-GROHMAN launched a small steam launch, the *Midge*, on the lower Kootenay system to assist with his reclamation project at the Kootenay Flats, the lowland area at the south end of the lake. The completion of the Columbia & Kootenay Rwy between ROBSON on the Arrow Lks route and NELSON caused the COLUMBIA & KOOTENAY STEAM NAVIGATION CO to commission the sternwheeler *Nelson* in 1891 to work between Nelson, Bonners Ferry, ID, and various mining camps on Kootenay Lk. Over the next 6 years both the CKSN and rival concerns added boats to service burgeoning mining camps and link up railheads at Nelson, KASLO and Bonners Ferry. On 1 Feb 1897 the CPR acquired the entire fleet of the CKSN; when it decided the following year to make Kootenay Landing the western terminus of its Crowsnest Pass line, and to use sternwheelers, tugs and barges to connect with other rail lines radiating out of Nelson, steamboating became

very active on Kootenay Lk. It remained so until 1930 when the CPR completed a rail link along the southwest shore of the lake to expedite shipments of ore from the SULLIVAN MINE at KIMBERLEY to the COMINCO smelter at TRAIL. The larger sternwheelers went out of CPR service at that time, though the smaller MOYIE and the tug *Granthall* were retained to provide service to remote points at the north end of the lake. The *Moyie* was BC's sole remaining passenger sternwheeler when it was retired in 1957 and is now preserved as a National Historic Site at Kaslo (*see also* NASOOKIN and CITY OF AINSWORTH).

The CPR also worked sternwheelers and tugs on SLOCAN LK and Trout Lk in the W Kootenay in order to link remote camps in the LARDEAU and Slocan mining divisions with rail service to SMELTERS at Trail, Nelson and elsewhere. Construction of branch lines and spurs also enabled the CPR to discard some of the more

Lks run became localized. The larger sternwheelers were gradually retired, leaving the smaller *Minto* to maintain service until 1954.

On OKANAGAN LK the first steamboat, a screw-propelled vessel, was launched by Capt Thomas SHORTS in 1886. Shorts had a monopoly on the business until 1893, when the CPR built the first sternwheeler on the lake, the *Aberdeen*, to connect with the recently completed SHUSWAP & OKANAGAN RWY. Its successors were the *Okanagan* of 1907 and the steel-hulled SICAMOUS, launched

SS Moyie, launched in 1898, now a national historic site on the Kaslo waterfront.
Keith Thirkell photo

by the CPR in 1914 and not retired until 1937. The *Sicamous* was sold to the city of PENTICTON and installed on the waterfront, where it is now one of only 3 sternwheelers preserved in BC. In addition to the *Moyie* and the *Sicamous*, the snag boat *Samson V* is berthed at the NEW WESTMINSTER waterfront.   *Edward L. Affleck*

Reading: Art Downs, *Paddlewheels on the Frontier*, 2 vols, 1967, 1971.

SS Sicamous *on Okanagan Lk, 1930s.*
SS Sicamous Restoration Society

treacherous reaches of the fabled Columbia R–Arrow Lks route. From 1898 to 1915 the CPR's Arrow Lks steamer, run between ARROWHEAD and Robson West (near CASTLEGAR), served as the major link for the railway's service between southeast BC and the Pacific Coast. After the completion of the KETTLE VALLEY RWY, coast-bound traffic followed that route and the Arrow

PAGE, Patricia Kathleen "P.K.," writer, artist (b 23 Nov 1916, Swanage, England). She came to Canada as a child with her parents and lived in Alberta and Manitoba. After art studies she moved to Saint John, NB, then to Montreal, where she helped found *Preview* magazine in 1943 and published her first poetry. After working as a scriptwriter for the National Film Board she married Arthur Irwin, NFB commissioner, in 1950. She lived with him abroad for several years on diplomatic postings before settling in

P.K. Page, poet. Barry Peterson & Blaise Enright-Peterson

VICTORIA in 1964. (Irwin died in 1999.) Her first novel, *The Sun and the Moon*, was published pseudonymously in 1944, after which she published mainly poetry in several collections. *The Metal and the Flower* won a GOV GEN'S LITERARY AWARD in 1954, while her memoir *Brazilian Journal* won a BC BOOK PRIZE and was nominated for a Gov Gen's Literary Award in 1987. In 1998 she published *The Hidden Room: The Collected Poems of P.K. Page*. She was inducted into the Order of Canada in 1977 and has several honorary degrees. She also works as a visual artist under the name P.K. Irwin.

PAINTER'S LODGE is a world-famous fishing resort at CAMPBELL RIVER on VANCOUVER ISLAND. Ned Painter was a boat builder who arrived in Campbell River with his wife June in 1924. He built wooden rowboats and sold and rented them, and in 1926 the couple opened a rustic camp, known as Spit Camp, at the mouth of the river. In 1930 they built a small cottage resort and in 1938 opened Painter's Lodge. Over the years it became associated with the growth of SALMON fishing (*see* FISHING, SPORT) at Campbell River and welcomed many celebrities as guests. The original historic lodge burned in 1985 and was replaced with a modern facility, now owned by the OAK BAY MARINE GROUP.

PALDI was a SAWMILL community 10 km west of DUNCAN on the way to COWICHAN LK. It was founded in 1917 by a syndicate led by Mayo SINGH and Kapoor Singh and was originally called Mayo. In 1936 the name changed to Paldi after Mayo Singh's home village in India. Community life centred on the SIKH temple, one of the first opened in BC in 1919, though there were also numerous JAPANESE Canadian millhands and their families. The original mill closed in 1945 but the community survived, with some residents working at operations owned by the Mayo Lumber Co elsewhere on the Island.

PALLING, a farming (*see* AGRICULTURE) settlement and GRAND TRUNK PACIFIC RWY station on the Endako R, 20 km northwest of BURNS LAKE, was first settled in the 1910s by the Carroll brothers, who also supplied major quantities of ties to the railway. William Lukens opened a store in 1920. There is a WET'SUWET'EN (Carrier) community at nearby Broman Lk. Palling is named after a town in England.   AS

PALLISER, a CPR SAWMILLING settlement 17 km east of GOLDEN, provided much of the timber for building the railway line through the ROCKY MTS. In operation from 1884 to 1908, it was named for Capt John Palliser, who led the Palliser Expedition (1857–1859) that searched for passes through the Rockies.   AS

PALMANTIER, Leonard, cowboy (b Nov 1888; d 24 Oct 1960). He made his first trip to the CARIBOO in 1914 to sell a string of horses, and returned permanently in 1919. He worked at various ranches, then operated his own spread at RISKE CREEK with his wife Josephine Grambush, a TSILHQOT'IN (Chilcotin) woman from Toosey. An avid RODEO participant, Palmantier was acknowledged to be the "best all-round COWBOY in the Cariboo," specializing in bronc riding. Three sons were also rodeo champions, as was his daughter Joan Palmantier Gentles, one of the first women certified as a rodeo judge.

PALMER, E.J., lumberman (b 1856, PA; d 11 Jan 1924, Chemainus). Known throughout his working life as "Old Hickory" because of his tough manner, Palmer began as a brakeman on the Chicago & Northwestern Rwy in 1876. After he had been promoted to conductor he met Frederick Weyerhaeuser on a train, and the lumberman was so impressed with Palmer he hired him to work at one of his Idaho sawmills. When VICTORIA LUMBER & MANUFACTURING CO began in 1889, Palmer was sent to BC to run it. He served as general manager for 34 years, earning a reputation as a tough, cantankerous, but competent and innovative administrator. He introduced many new methods into the LOGGING and SAWMILLING business, including the first use of steam yarders and one of the first steam locomotives. On 17 Nov 1923, the CHEMAINUS mill burned to the ground, and a few weeks later Palmer suffered a fatal heart attack.   *Ken Drushka*

PANDOSY, Charles, Roman Catholic missionary (b 22 Nov 1824, Marseilles, France; d 6 Feb 1891, Penticton). He went to the Oregon Territory in 1847 as an OBLATE missionary and worked among the Yakima Indians until 1858, when he moved to VANCOUVER ISLAND with instructions to open a mission in southern BC. In summer 1859 he and a party travelled to the OKANAGAN VALLEY and established the Immaculate Conception mission near present-day KELOWNA. It was the first permanent non-aboriginal settlement in the valley. He served all over the province before finally settling in the Okanagan in 1887. He did a great deal to stimulate farming and fruit growing in the valley, where he remains a folk hero. *See also* AGRICULTURE; TREE FRUITS.

PANYCH, Morris Stephen, playwright (b 30 June 1952, Calgary). He came to VANCOUVER in 1973 and studied creative writing at UBC. After attending acting school in London, England, he returned to Vancouver and emerged as a playwright in 1982 with *Last Call: A Post-Nuclear Cabaret*, produced at TAMAHNOUS THEATRE. Tamahnous, where he was artistic director from 1984 to 1986, staged several of his musical plays. He has since written 3 dark comedies—*7 Stories* (1989), *The Ends of the Earth* (1993, winner of a GOV GEN'S LITERARY AWARD) and *Vigil* (1995)—and participated in several innovative stage adaptations of classic works. In 1999 his comedy *The History of Things to Come* premiered at the

Painter's Lodge, Campbell River, c 1995.
Oak Bay Marine Group

Morris Panych, playwright (r), with Ken MacDonald, set designer, 1998.
Barry Peterson & Blaise Enright-Peterson

VANCOUVER PLAYHOUSE, and in 2000 *The Overcoat*, a wordless play based on a Nikolai Gogol short story that he co-directed with Wendy Gorling, toured Canada. *See also* THEATRE.

PARKER, Jon Kimura "Jackie," concert pianist (b 25 Dec 1959, Burnaby). He made his concert debut at age 5 with the VANCOUVER Youth Orchestra. After studies with his uncle, Edward Parker, and at the Vancouver Academy of Music and UBC, he attended the Juilliard School of Music in New York as a student of Adele Marcus. In 1984 he won the Leeds International Piano Competition and since then has established himself among the world's leading concert pianists. A recipient of the Gov Gen's Performing Arts Award (1996), he has given command performances for Queen Elizabeth II, toured with the Toronto Symphony and the National Arts Centre Orchestra and made several recordings on the Telarc label. A passionate ambassador of music, he regularly performs in small communities across Canada as a member of Piano Six. On New Year's Eve 1995 he gave a concert in war-torn Sarajevo, Bosnia; the performance was televised live to 59 countries. He was named to the Order of Canada in 1999.

PARKS, NATIONAL are areas of land designated by the federal government to protect representative elements of the natural environment and to encourage public appreciation of the national heritage. As of 1999 there were 38 national parks and park reserves in Canada. (A park reserve is an area that has been designated but is part of an unresolved aboriginal land claim; *see* ABORIGINAL RIGHTS). National parks account for about 2% of the Canadian land mass. Of the 38 parks and park reserves, 6 are located in BC. They are YOHO, GLACIER, MT REVELSTOKE, KOOTENAY, PACIFIC RIM and GWAII HAANAS.

PARKS, PROVINCIAL, are areas of land and water designated by the provincial government for purposes of recreation and conservation. BC has one of the largest, most complex parks systems in the world. As of 1999 there were about 550 provincial parks and 140 ECOLOGICAL RESERVES covering about 10.5% of public lands and a few marine areas in the province. The agency responsible is BC Parks, a department of the Ministry of Environment, Lands and Parks. The goal set by BC Parks was to have at least 12% of each separate terrestrial and marine ecosystem in BC included in the parks system by the year 2000.

The provincial parks system began with establishment of STRATHCONA PROVINCIAL PARK on VANCOUVER ISLAND in 1911. Mt ROBSON was added in 1913, followed by GARIBALDI PROVINCIAL PARK (1920) and KOKANEE GLACIER PROVINCIAL PARK (1922). Initially, the purpose of these parks was to set aside large, scenic mountain wilderness areas, accessible by railway and largely for the use of TOURISTS. By the 1940s, the idea of parks as recreation showpieces for the wealthy had expanded to a new multiple-use goal that included commercial and industrial uses. The FOREST SERVICE had principal responsibility for parks at this time. TWEEDSMUIR PROVINCIAL PARK in the west and HAMBER PROVINCIAL PARK in the east were both well over 10,000 km² when established, but were subsequently carved up for industrial use. Hamber, in the ROCKY MTS, was reduced by almost 10,000 km² to its present size of 245 km² in response to FOREST INDUSTRY pressure and in anticipation of HYDROELECTRIC expansion under the terms of the COLUMBIA RIVER TREATY. Nearly 5,000 km² were removed from Tweedsmuir when the northern portion was flooded to meet hydroelectric needs at KEMANO for the aluminum SMELTER at KITIMAT. Major controversy over these events made it apparent that before parks were established, extensive studies should be done to eliminate or at least reduce conflicts over resource uses.

By the mid-1950s, 2 other factors affected

Lake of the Hanging Glacier Provincial Park.
Walter Lanz/Image Makers

BC's growing park system: cities were growing; and as people became more mobile, more roads were being built. City dwellers' demand for roadside parks and destination campgrounds skyrocketed. As well, public consciousness of conservation ethics and benefits had begun to grow: more and more people believed resource extraction should be prohibited in some areas. A Parks Branch independent of the Forest Service was created and in 1965 a revised *Park Act* was passed to provide more detailed classifications of parks and establish guidelines for conservation and recreation. By the mid-1970s there were 375 parks, including destination campgrounds such as CULTUS LAKE, GOLDSTREAM and Rathtrevor Beach provincial parks, and large wilderness areas for the conservation of wildlife and specific types of natural environments, such as NAIKOON, SPATSIZI PLATEAU, PURCELL WILDERNESS and WELLS GRAY. To confer higher protection status on some PLANTS, animals and natural environments, the province enacted the *Ecological Reserves Act* in 1971. BC was the first jurisdiction in the world to establish an ecological reserves program.

By the 1980s a strong ENVIRONMENTAL MOVEMENT had emerged and was putting new pressure on government to establish parks. The participants included biologists, natural historians and other professionals who were alarmed at the loss of wilderness and plant and animal species. British Columbians shared this concern and the government was spurred into action. Between the mid-1980s and 1999, more than 200 new parks were established, many of them large wilderness areas encompassing entire watersheds. Parks such as CARMANAH–WALBRAN, Pinecone Burke, AKAMINA–Kishinena, TATSHENSHINI–ALSEK and a number in CLAYOQUOT SOUND came into being. The large region of protected areas and special management zones known as the Northern Rockies, announced in 1997, was one of the most innovative models of park establishment to date, and was the largest land-use decision of its kind in N America. It established

MAJOR BC PARKS & PROTECTED AREAS

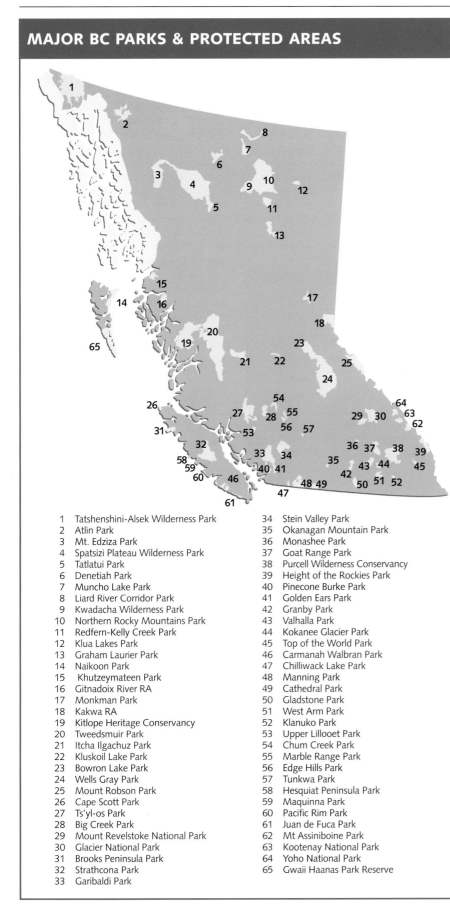

1	Tatshenshini-Alsek Wilderness Park	34	Stein Valley Park
2	Atlin Park	35	Okanagan Mountain Park
3	Mt. Edziza Park	36	Monashee Park
4	Spatsizi Plateau Wilderness Park	37	Goat Range Park
5	Tatlatui Park	38	Purcell Wilderness Conservancy
6	Denetiah Park	39	Height of the Rockies Park
7	Muncho Lake Park	40	Pinecone Burke Park
8	Liard River Corridor Park	41	Golden Ears Park
9	Kwadacha Wilderness Park	42	Granby Park
10	Northern Rocky Mountains Park	43	Valhalla Park
11	Redfern-Kelly Creek Park	44	Kokanee Glacier Park
12	Klua Lakes Park	45	Top of the World Park
13	Graham Laurier Park	46	Carmanah Walbran Park
14	Naikoon Park	47	Chilliwack Lake Park
15	Khutzeymateen Park	48	Manning Park
16	Gitnadoix River RA	49	Cathedral Park
17	Monkman Park	50	Gladstone Park
18	Kakwa RA	51	West Arm Park
19	Kitlope Heritage Conservancy	52	Klanuko Park
20	Tweedsmuir Park	53	Upper Lillooet Park
21	Itcha Ilgachuz Park	54	Chum Creek Park
22	Kluskoil Lake Park	55	Marble Range Park
23	Bowron Lake Park	56	Edge Hills Park
24	Wells Gray Park	57	Tunkwa Park
25	Mount Robson Park	58	Hesquiat Peninsula Park
26	Cape Scott Park	59	Maquinna Park
27	Ts'yl-os Park	60	Pacific Rim Park
28	Big Creek Park	61	Juan de Fuca Park
29	Mount Revelstoke National Park	62	Mt Assiniboine Park
30	Glacier National Park	63	Kootenay National Park
31	Brooks Peninsula Park	64	Yoho National Park
32	Strathcona Park	65	Gwaii Haanas Park Reserve
33	Garibaldi Park		

11,700 km² of parks surrounded by 32,400 km² of special management zones, in which resource development would be managed with conservation objectives in mind. The package included legislating access management and setting up a trust fund and public advisory board for the core region bounded by the MUSKWA and KECHIKA rivers. As well, in recognition of aboriginal land claims (*see* ABORIGINAL RIGHTS), some parks, such as Tseax Lava Beds (NISGA'A), STEIN Valley (NLAKA'-PAMUX), KITLOPE (HAISLA), and Ts'yl-os (TSIL-HQOT'IN), were established through negotiations and co-management agreements with FIRST NATIONS.

The number of people visiting BC's provincial parks grew from about 3 million visits annually in the early 1960s to 26.2 million annual visits in 1998. Almost 90% of BC residents have used a provincial park at some time, and about 60% use one each year. Recreational facilities in BC parks include more than 3,000 km of hiking TRAILS, 11,941 campsites, 119 boat launches and 234 parks with facilities for disabled visitors. Many destination parks have amphitheatres and indoor facilities for natural history and public education programs. Natural and special features protected in BC parks and ecological reserves include DELLA FALLS in Strathcona, the endangered Vancouver Island MARMOT in the Haley Lake Ecological Reserve, the grizzly BEAR sanctuary at KHUTZEYMATEEN, and Tatshenshini-Alsek, part of the world's largest UNESCO WORLD HERITAGE SITE. *Maggie Paquet*

PARKSVILLE, city, pop 9,472, is on the east coast of VANCOUVER ISLAND overlooking GEORGIA STRAIT, 37 km north of NANAIMO. Known originally as Englishman's River after the nearby river, it was named in 1890 for the first postmaster, Nelson Parks. Farm settlement began in the 1870s and it was a regular stop on the wagon road from Nanaimo to PORT ALBERNI after it opened in 1886. Population grew more rapidly with the arrival of the ESQUIMALT & NANAIMO RWY in 1910. The city, incorporated in 1945, has developed as a commercial centre for LOGGING and AGRICULTURE and as a popular summer recreation spot, known for its sport FISHING and its long stretches of sandy beach. The population grew rapidly during the 1990s, a trend that was expected to continue. TOURISM facilities line the highway between Parksville and QUALICUM BEACH. Parksville has also become a bedroom community for commuters to Nanaimo and attracts a large number of retirees. In July it hosts a week-long sandcastle contest. There are numerous recreation areas and provincial PARKS in the vicinity.

PARLIAMENT BUILDINGS, *see* LEGISLATIVE BUILDINGS.

PARSNIP RIVER, 230 km, is an important tributary of the PEACE R in northeast BC. It rises in the ROCKY MT TRENCH near MONKMAN PROVINCIAL PARK and flows northwest through a 20,000 km² drainage area. Much of its northern valley was flooded by the WILLISTON RESERVOIR, created in 1968 after the building of the BENNETT DAM at HUDSON'S HOPE, so that it now flows into the south end of the reservoir. The river is named for the abundant wild parsnips (also called "Indian rhubarb") growing on its banks. *AS*

PARSON, pop 84, a LOGGING and former SAWMILLING community on the COLUMBIA R

35 km southeast of GOLDEN, is on Hwy 95 and the CPR. Prospectors still pan for GOLD at nearby Canyon Crk. It was named after Henry G. Parson, a Golden merchant, NEWSPAPER publisher and MLA in the early 1900s. *AS*

PARTRIDGE, grey (*Perdix perdix*), is a game bird occupying the OKANAGAN VALLEY, to which it spread from Washington state early in the 20th century. Grey-brown in colour with an orange face, it occupies an open habitat of dry rangeland and cultivated fields. Grey partridges are generally found in coveys, which flush together in a flurry of calls and beating wings when disturbed. They were introduced to VANCOUVER ISLAND and the Lower Mainland after 1900, but were extirpated by hunters and urban development.

PASSAGE ISLAND, 13 ha, sits in the entrance to HOWE SOUND between POINT ATKINSON and BOWEN ISLAND, just north of VANCOUVER. It was named by Capt George VANCOUVER during his 1792 survey of the sound. Rugged and windswept, the island was owned for many years by J.C. Keith, former reeve of N VANCOUVER. It was purchased from the Keith family in 1959 and eventually subdivided into lots for about 2 dozen homes.

PASSAGLIA, Lui, football player (b 7 June 1954, Vancouver). A veteran of 23 seasons in the CFL, he holds every record in the league for longevity. After playing college FOOTBALL as a quarterback, receiver and kicker for SFU, he joined the BC LIONS in 1976. Though he scored his first points as a pass receiver, he quickly established himself as the team's durable punter and place kicker. In his first year he broke the team record for most single-season points and he continued breaking records right through the turn of the millennium. By the mid-1980s, Passaglia had established himself as one of the premiere kickers in the CFL or NFL, recording a professional record 50.2-yard punting average over the 1983 season. He also holds the world professional football career scoring record by a margin well over 1,200 points, along with scores of CFL records. His toe has carried the Lions to many key victories, earning Most Valuable Canadian honours in the Lions' defeat of Hamilton for the 1985 Grey Cup and kicking the winning field goal on the last play of the 1994 Grey Cup game against Baltimore. He was a member of 4 CFL All-star teams and led the league in scoring 3 times. Except for a brief tryout for the NFL's Cleveland Browns in 1988, Passaglia remained with the Lions straight through his 40s, breaking CFL records for most seasons, most games played, most field goals, most singles, most converts and most consecutive converts. During the 1998 season he kicked 7 field goals in one game, winning player-of-the-week honours, the oldest player ever to do so. During his off-seasons, he worked as an executive with ICBC. *SW*

PATERSON, 15 km southwest of TRAIL on Little Sheep Crk in the W KOOTENAY, is a border

crossing and former station on GREAT NORTHERN's Red Mountain Rwy. The proposed post office name, was Barney, after a hopeful settler, but it was rejected; Thomas W. PATERSON, railway contractor and BC LT GOV from 1909 to 1914, was honoured instead. *AS*

PATERSON, Thomas Wilson, railway contractor, politician, lt gov 1909–14 (b 6 Dec 1851, Darnel, Scotland; d 28 Aug 1921, Victoria). After immigrating to Canada as a youngster with his parents, he grew up in Ontario, where he got his first job as a labourer on railway construction. Soon he was a partner in a contracting firm and moved to BC seeking new opportunities for his company. In 1883 he won the contract to build the ESQUIMALT & NANAIMO RWY line on VANCOU-

Thomas Wilson Paterson, lt gov of BC 1909–14.
BC Archives A-01687

VER ISLAND; after several other building jobs he became general manager of the VICTORIA & SIDNEY RWY in 1895. He also had investments in shipping, farming and logging. Paterson was elected to the legislature in 1902 for a VICTORIA riding. A LIBERAL, and extremely wealthy, he was considered a friend of big business, an image that eventually hurt him with voters. In 1907 he ran for the mayoralty of Victoria; he lost, then lost his seat in the legislature later the same year. He returned to his business affairs and on 11 Dec 1909 was appointed LT GOV. It was a prosperous period and a politically stable one, and his term of office was uneventful. He retired in 1914 to a home in OAK BAY and a large farm, Inverholm, near LADNER.

PATKAU ARCHITECTS is an architectural firm founded in Edmonton in 1978 by the husband and wife team of John and Patricia Patkau. The couple had met at the Univ of Winnipeg, where John was studying ARCHITECTURE and Patricia interior design. She later received an MA in architecture from Yale Univ. In 1984, after 6 years in Edmonton, the firm moved to VANCOUVER and became one of Canada's leading designers of innovative small and medium-sized

buildings. Among the firm's award-winning designs are the Seabird Island School in AGASSIZ, the Newton Library in SURREY and several private residences.

PATRICK, Curtis Lester, hockey player, coach, general manager (b 31 Dec 1883, Drummondville, QC; d 1 June 1960, Victoria). He was raised in Montreal and excelled in a variety of sports but eventually concentrated on HOCKEY. As a member of the Montreal Wanderers he won his first Stanley Cup in 1906, then joined Ottawa's Renfrew Millionaires of the National Hockey Assoc, forerunner of the NHL. In 1911 he and his brother Frank PATRICK used money provided by the sale of their father's lumber business to organize the PACIFIC COAST HOCKEY ASSOC. Lester played for and ran the VICTORIA COUGARS franchise and in 1925 it won the Stanley Cup, the last time a non-NHL team did so. The brothers made so many refinements to the hockey rulebook—including the addition of the blue line, numbers on jerseys, and the penalty shot—that they may be called the inventors of the modern game. After the Patricks sold the rights of all the players in their league to the new NHL in 1926, the Cougars became an expansion franchise in Detroit (later the Falcons and Red Wings). Lester went to New York as coach of the newly formed Rangers and in only their second season they won the Stanley Cup; in one memorable game of the final series Patrick, aged 44, came off the bench to play goal when the regular netminder was injured. Lester left coaching in 1939 but remained general manager in New York until 1946. After he returned to VICTORIA he organized a new team named the Victoria Cougars to begin play in the minor-professional Pacific Coast Hockey League (later named Western Hockey League) in 1949–50. The father of Lynn and Muzz PATRICK and grandfather of US hockey builder and NHL general manager Craig Patrick, he is a member of the Hockey Hall of Fame and the BC SPORTS HALL OF FAME. The Lester Patrick Trophy, first awarded in 1966, recognizes "contributions to American hockey."
Reading: Eric Whitehead, *The Patricks, Hockey's Royal Family*, 1980.

PATRICK, Frank Alexis, hockey player, general manager (b 23 Dec 1885, Drummondville, QC; d 28 June 1960, Vancouver). He was raised in Montreal and starred as a defenceman for McGill Univ before playing the 1909–10 season with his brother Lester PATRICK and Cyclone TAYLOR on Ottawa's Renfrew Millionaires. In 1910 he scored 6 goals in one game, a mark for defencemen that stood as a major professional record throughout the 20th century. Frank and Lester moved west to NELSON to work in their father Joe's new LOGGING and SAWMILLING operation. When Joe sold the company in 1911 Frank proposed using the proceeds to build Canada's first artificial-ice arenas and start a professional HOCKEY league on the West Coast. Lester thought it too risky to offer hockey in an area where it was almost unknown, but $400,000 later arenas were built in VICTORIA and VANCOUVER. Denman St Arena in Vancouver was the world's largest ice rink and the second-largest sports facility on the continent after Madison Square Garden. The Patricks raided the eastern National Hockey Assoc and brought some of its greatest stars to play for the VANCOUVER MILLIONAIRES, the Victoria Senators (later Aristocrats, VICTORIA COUGARS) and New Westminster Royals (who moved to Portland in 1914) in their PACIFIC COAST HOCKEY ASSOC. Frank was coach and captain of the Millionaires, who played the first pro hockey game in Vancouver on 5 Jan 1912, beating New Westminster 8-3. After Frank signed ex-teammate Cyclone Taylor to Vancouver the 10,500-seat arena was regularly filled and the team won the Stanley Cup in 1915. As well as managing, coaching and playing for Vancouver, Frank served as president of the league. He conceptualized many of the rules of modern hockey including the penalty shot, the blue line, unrestricted passing, and 2 ideas that spread to all sports in N America: assigning numbers to players and organizing a standard playoff series. In 1926 he managed the largest transaction in hockey history by selling virtually all the league's players to the NHL, where he later served as league managing director in 1933, coach of the Boston Bruins in 1933–34 and general manager of the Montreal Canadiens in 1935–36. He was inducted into the Hockey Hall of Fame in 1958 and the BC SPORTS HALL OF FAME in 1966.   *SW*

PATRICK, Frederick Murray "Muzz," hockey player, coach, manager (b 28 June 1915, Victoria; d 1998). The son of Lester PATRICK and younger brother of Lynn PATRICK, he excelled in HOCKEY, BASKETBALL, RUGBY, SOCCER, BOXING and CYCLING while growing up in VICTORIA. He joined his brother on the Canadian basketball champions Victoria Blue Ribbons in 1933 and he won the Canadian amateur heavyweight boxing championship in 1936. He was an exceptional track (*see* TRACK AND FIELD) athlete, running under coach Archie MCKINNON at the YMCA. In 1938 Muzz joined his father and brother on the NY Rangers and played with that team for 4 years, winning the Stanley Cup in 1940. He coached in Tacoma, WA, before becoming head coach of the NY Rangers in 1953 and then general manager (1955–64). Patrick worked in the front office at Madison Square Garden before retiring to Connecticut. He was inducted into the BC SPORTS HALL OF FAME in 1968.   *SW*

PATRICK, Lynn, hockey player, coach, manager (b 3 Feb 1912, Victoria; d 26 Jan 1980, St. Louis, MO). The eldest son of HOCKEY pioneer Lester PATRICK and brother to Muzz PATRICK, he was the highest-scoring British Columbian in the early years of the NHL and a brilliant all-around athlete. In VICTORIA he played BASKETBALL with Muzz on the 1933 Canadian amateur champions Victoria Blue Ribbons. He was a star RUGBY player on the BC Reps team and in 1934 played FOOTBALL for the Winnipeg Blue Bombers. The next year he moved to New York to play under his father with the Rangers for 10 years, placing in the top 5 NHL scorers in 1940–43, leading the

league in goals (32) in 1941–42 and winning the Stanley Cup in 1940. Patrick was an NHL first-team all-star at left wing in 1942 and second-team all-star the next year. After retiring as a player he coached the Boston Bruins during 1950–55, managed them for the next 10 years and became the first general manager of the St Louis Blues in 1967, occasionally taking the coaching reins as well. Later he was Blues vice-president. He was inducted into the BC SPORTS HALL OF FAME in 1968 and the Hockey Hall of Fame in 1980. His son Craig (b 20 May, 1946, Detroit) played in the NHL, became an important builder of the US national team and served as an NHL general manager for the New York Rangers and Pittsburgh Penguins, with whom he won the Stanley Cup in 1991 and 1992.   *SW*

PATTISON, James Allen "Jimmy," entrepreneur (b 1 Oct 1928, Luseland, SK). He moved to VANCOUVER with his family when he was 7 and grew up on the east side. In 1952 he dropped out of university to sell used cars and after 9 years borrowed enough money to open his own dealership. In 1967 he purchased Neon Products, an electrical sign manufacturer and lessor, changed

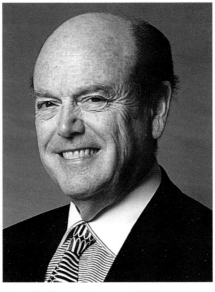

Jimmy Pattison, entrepreneur, 1998.

the name to Neonex International and began buying what became a stable of 50 companies, including airlines, auto dealerships, magazine distributors, supermarkets (OVERWAITEA and Save-On-Foods), a fish processor, Ripley's Believe It Or Not! museums, the largest billboard company in Canada and *BEAUTIFUL BC* magazine. Since 1977 they have been part of the Jim Pattison Group, BC's largest and Canada's third-largest privately owned corporation. Revenues in 1999 totalled $4.6 billion. A deeply religious man, Pattison annually donates a percentage of his income to charity. The Jim Pattison Foundation is the fourth-largest charitable foundation in Canada by value of grants. In 1986 he served as president of EXPO 86. He is a member of the Order of Canada (1987) and the ORDER OF BC (1990).

PATTULLO, Thomas Dufferin "Duff," businessman and premier 15 Nov 1933–9 Dec 1941 (b 19 Jan 1873, Woodstock, ON; d 29 Mar 1956, Victoria). After graduating from school, he tried his hand at banking and newspaper editing before entering politics. He used his father's LIBERAL PARTY connections in 1897 to land a job with an official delegation sent by the federal government to establish a territorial administration in the Yukon. He trekked across the CHILKOOT PASS and arrived in Dawson City in

Duff Pattullo, premier of BC 1933–41.

May 1898. There he eventually went to work in the office of the gold commissioner, married, and settled for 10 years. In 1904 Pattullo served a term on Dawson city council, marking the beginning of his political career. He moved to PRINCE RUPERT in 1908 and became involved in real estate and construction, hoping to take advantage of the arrival of the GRAND TRUNK PACIFIC RWY. His business endeavours did not prosper, but his political career did. In 1910 he was elected to Prince Rupert's first city council and served a term as mayor before being elected a Liberal member of the legislature in 1916. He held his Prince Rupert seat until 1945, when he moved to VICTORIA and joined the cabinet of the new Liberal government as minister of lands.

A dapper dresser with a convivial personality and an appetite for hard work, Pattullo emerged during the 1920s as a leading voice for his party. When the Liberals lost the 1928 election and John MACLEAN quit, Pattullo was chosen house leader, then confirmed as leader of the Liberals and leader of the opposition in May 1930. In the election of Nov 1933 he led his resurgent party to victory against the fragmented CONSERVATIVES and a newly formed CO-OPERATIVE COMMONWEALTH FEDERATION.

Pattullo believed in the necessity of state intervention and tackled the crisis of the Depression with a "little new deal" of reform programs, including a health insurance scheme, a higher minimum wage, a program of public works, increased money to schools and

measures to ease the plight of the poor and unemployed. The Pattullo Bridge across the FRASER R opened on 15 Nov 1937. But his most ambitious plans were foiled by his inability to obtain adequate financial help from the federal government. Indeed, he spent much of his time as PREMIER arguing with Ottawa over financial and constitutional matters, a quarrel that culminated in the federal-provincial conference of Jan 1941; Pattullo, along with the Alberta and Ontario premiers, objected strongly to the centralist recommendations of the Rowell-Sirois Royal Commission. He was widely criticized for his so-called obstructionism, especially in wartime, and the issue followed him into the election of Oct 1941, when the Liberals were reduced to a minority in the legislature. Late in the year the party voted in favour of forming a COALITION with the Conservatives, and Pattullo, who opposed the coalition, resigned as party leader and premier. He held his seat as an independent Liberal until his defeat in the election of Oct 1945. He spent the last years of his life in retirement in Victoria.
Reading: Robin Fisher, *Duff Pattullo,* 1991.

PAULL, Andrew, Squamish leader (b 26 Feb 1892, Squamish; d 28 July 1959, Vancouver). He was raised on the SQUAMISH Nation RESERVE in N VANCOUVER and attended St Paul's RESIDENTIAL SCHOOL on the reserve. He worked in a VANCOUVER law office, then as a longshoreman before joining the MCKENNA–MCBRIDE COMMISSION as an interpreter in 1913. His work for the commission led to a leading role in the ALLIED INDIAN TRIBES OF BC from 1916 to 1927. After the Allied Tribes collapsed, he withdrew from politics, working during the Depression as a sports journalist and promoting aboriginal community activities. He organized the all-Native North Shore Indians LACROSSE team of the 1930s. In 1942 he became an organizer for the NATIVE BROTHERHOOD OF BC and in 1943 president of the North American Indian Brotherhood, a national aboriginal organization. For the rest of his life he played a leading role in the movement for ABORIGINAL RIGHTS in BC. At the same time he was a colourful promoter of BASEBALL and LACROSSE, famous for staging publicity stunts to attract crowds to his games. Typical of his antics was the time he sneaked into the ballpark at night and moved second base closer to first. During the next day's game his Squamish Indians team set a "record" for stolen bases before the opposition noticed. Paull was inducted into the BC SPORTS HALL OF FAME in 1999.

PAULSON, a CPR flag station on McRae Crk 32 km northeast of GRAND FORKS in the W KOOTENAY, was named after the Paulson brothers, who operated a store, post office, hotel and stables here in the early 1900s. The station was originally called Bonanza Siding, as ore from the nearby Inland Empire & Bonanza mine was shipped at this point. *AS*

PAVELIC, Myfanwy (Spencer), artist (b 27 Apr 1916, Victoria). Her grandfather was the founder of Spencer's department store in VICTORIA and she lives on the family's large property, Spencerwood, near SIDNEY on VANCOUVER ISLAND. While she was a teenager her paintings impressed Emily CARR, who organized an exhibition of her work in 1934. Pavelic spent most of the 1940s studying in New York, where she met her husband Nikola, a member of a prominent CROATIAN family. The couple returned to Vancouver Island in 1950 and she has lived there ever since, except for a second sojourn in New York from 1955 to 1960. Primarily a figurative painter, she has an international reputation as a portraitist. Her famous commissions include portraits of the violinist Yehudi Menuhin, which hangs in the National Portrait Gallery in London, and former Canadian prime minister Pierre Trudeau.

PAVILION, 35 km north of LILLOOET, began as a ranch owned by an American prospector, Robert Carson, who came to BC in 1858 seeking GOLD but homesteaded on the high meadows above the FRASER R instead. It is a stop on the BC RAIL line. The local SECWEPEMC (Shuswap) people know it as Ts'kw'aylaxw, "frosty ground."

PAXTON VALLEY, a farming and ranching district (*see* AGRICULTURE; CATTLE INDUSTRY) 45 km east of KAMLOOPS, was named after Samuel Paxton, who settled in the area in 1872 after participating in the GOLD RUSH to the CARIBOO. He was followed by Joseph St Laurent in 1890. The valley runs east of MONTE LK along Paxton and St Laurent creeks. *AS*

PEACE ARCH is a towering (20.4 m) white gate straddling the Canada–US border south of VANCOUVER at WHITE ROCK. It was dedicated on 6 Sept 1921 and commemorates peaceful relations between the 2 countries. Money to pay for the arch was raised by schoolchildren in BC and Washington state; the names of the young donors are embedded in the structure. Within the arch 2 iron gates remain symbolically open.

The Peace Arch at the Canada–US border, south of Vancouver. Les Bazso/Vancouver Sun

The grounds surrounding the arch have been a provincial PARK since 1939.

PEACE RIVER flows from WILLISTON RESERVOIR east through the ROCKY MTS, across the provincial boundary and out onto the rolling lowlands and high prairie of northern Alberta, where it eventually joins the Slave R near Athabasca Lk 1,923 km from its source. With the headwaters of its source rivers in the Omineca Mts east of the ROCKY MT TRENCH, it is the only river on the

Peace R meandering through northeast BC. Roy Luckow photo

continent that flows completely through the entire Rocky Mt range. The BC portion drains a watershed 99,000 km². Major tributaries include the Beatton, HALFWAY and Pine rivers. In BC the river is deeply entrenched in a meandering, steep-sided valley where AGRICULTURE takes place along the floodplain. Originally the Peace was formed from the confluence of the FINLAY and PARSNIP rivers but during the 1960s, as part of the TWO RIVERS POLICY of the W.A.C. BENNETT government, the original watercourse was dammed 22 km west of HUDSON'S HOPE, flooding the river valleys behind and creating the Williston Reservoir. In 1980 the Peace Canyon Dam was added 23 km below the original BENNETT DAM; these power stations now produce a third of the province's output of HYDROELECTRICITY. Fur traders began using the river as a route across the mountains in 1793 when Alexander MACKENZIE travelled up it on his way to the Pacific. The NORTH WEST CO built ROCKY MOUNTAIN FORT near the present site of FORT ST JOHN in 1794 and several other trading posts followed (*see* FUR TRADE, LAND-BASED). Miners heading for the Klondike during the GOLD RUSH ascended to the headwaters of the Peace and steamboats plied the river from 1903 to 1931.

The Peace R District is rich in natural resources. Agriculture predominated until the 1950s, when large-scale development of OIL AND GAS discoveries began and followed at a rapid rate. This was followed in the 1980s by the development of COAL mines southwest of DAWSON CREEK. With the arrival of the BC RAIL line in 1958, the district was linked more directly to the rest of BC. Still, its prairie landscape and location east of the Rockies tends to set the area apart and there are periodic murmurings that it would be better off as part of Alberta. The name *Peace R* refers to an armistice believed to have been made between the Cree and DUNNE-ZA (Beaver) First Nations in about 1765 at a spot on the Alberta portion of the river known as Peace Point. The Peace is a BC HERITAGE RIVER.
Reading: Gordon E. Bowes, ed, *Peace River Chronicles*, 1963.

PEACE RIVER BLOCK was a 14,170 km² block of land straddling the PEACE R in the northeast corner of BC. The province gave it to the federal government in 1883 as part of the land transfers that made possible the construction of the CPR. Ottawa did not select the exact location of the Block until 1907, and it was opened for homesteading in 1912. In 1930 the federal government returned to BC the parts of the Block that it still owned.

PEACHLAND, district municipality, pop 4,524, adjoins the west side of OKANAGAN LK between PENTICTON and KELOWNA. It was founded in 1897 as the first of several OKANAGAN VALLEY settlement schemes proposed by John Moore ROBINSON, a promoter. Robinson actually was seeking GOLD when he tasted the local peaches and realized the agricultural potential of the area. Incorporated on 1 Jan 1909, Peachland has developed as a fruit-growing (*see* TREE FRUITS)

Peachland, on Okanagan Lk.
Jan Drozdzenski/ Image Makers

and WINE-MAKING centre. Just to the north is the 106-km Okanagan Connector highway, which joins the COQUIHALLA HWY at MERRITT and brought the Okanagan within 4 hours of VANCOUVER by road.

PEARDONVILLE, a farming (*see* AGRICULTURE) settlement 42 km southeast of NEW WESTMINSTER and now in the City of ABBOTSFORD, developed in the 1890s near the US border on the old trail leading from Whatcom (Bellingham) to MOUNT LEHMAN. It was named after Richard Peardon, an early settler and the first postmaster. *AS*

PEARKES, George Randolph, soldier, politician, lt gov 1960–68 (b 26 Feb 1888, Watford, England; d 30 May 1984, Victoria). After finishing school he immigrated to Alberta in 1906 with his brother and they homesteaded near Red Deer. Prior to WWI he served with the North-

George Pearkes, lt gov of BC 1960–68.

West Mounted Police in the Yukon. In Mar 1915 he enlisted in VICTORIA with the 2nd Canadian Mounted Rifles. He fought in the trenches for the entire war, was wounded 5 times and was awarded the VICTORIA CROSS at the Battle of Passchendaele. Following the war he became a career officer in the army and was general staff officer at the Royal Military College in Kingston, ON, from 1922 to 1933. He commanded the 2nd Canadian Infantry Brigade at the beginning of WWII and later the 1st Canadian Division. He opposed the ill-fated Dieppe Raid in 1942 and was transferred back to Canada to take over as commanding officer on the West Coast. Disagreeing with the government's conscription policy, he retired from the army in 1945 and ran successfully for Parliament as a Conservative. When the Conservatives came to power in 1957 he became minister of defence, a position he held until he was installed as LT GOV on 13 Oct 1960. He was a popular choice with the public and became one of the few lt govs to agree to an extended term. He finally stepped down in July 1968 and lived his retirement in Victoria. He was grand president of the Royal Canadian Legion from 1966 to 1976.

PEARSE, J.B., surveyor (b 1832, Devonshire, England; d 1902, Victoria). He arrived at FORT VICTORIA in 1851 and soon after was appointed surveyor to the colony of VANCOUVER ISLAND. Among his many tasks was surveying the townsite of VICTORIA, overseeing the erection of government buildings and, with J.D. PEMBERTON, laying out most of the first ROADS on the Island. Pearse was also active in politics, serving on the executive council of Vancouver Island and on Victoria City Council. Following CONFEDERATION he was provincial engineer with the Dominion Works Department. He served for some years on the Victoria sewage commission, when it introduced piped sewers to the city in the early 1890s. In 1860 he built for himself the famous mansion Fernwood, since destroyed; its estate later became the prestigious residential district of the same name. *Martin Segger*

PEARSE, Peter Hector, economist (b 26 Nov 1932, Vernon). After attending UBC and Edinburgh Univ, he returned to UBC as professor of economics and later professor of FORESTRY. An expert in natural resources management, he conducted royal commissions on the BC FOREST INDUSTRY in 1975–76 and Canada's Pacific fisheries in 1981–82 (*see also* FISHERIES POLICY), and also chaired inquiries into water policy and freshwater fisheries. His reports have had a major impact on natural resources policy in Canada. He has also advised foreign governments, World Bank and other international organizations. Professor emeritus at UBC and a private consultant, Pearse is a member of the Order of Canada (1988) and a fellow of the Royal Society of the Arts.

PEARSON, Kathleen Margaret "Kit," writer (b 30 Apr 1947, Edmonton). She worked as a children's librarian for 10 years before becoming

a full-time writer. Her first novel, *The Daring Game* (1986), is based on her experiences as a boarder at CROFTON HOUSE SCHOOL in VANCOUVER in the 1960s. *The Sky is Falling* (1989), the first of a trilogy of historical novels set during WWII, won several awards and launched her career as one of Canada's most successful writers for young people. It was followed by *Looking at the Moon* (1991) and *When the Lights Go On Again* (1993). Her 1996 book, *Awake and Dreaming*, won a GOV GEN'S LITERARY AWARD. She lives in Vancouver.

PECK, Ted "Uncle Stumbly," sport fisher, guide (b 8 May 1929). He grew up in Fisherman's Cove in W VANCOUVER and became one of BC's best-known sport fishers of the 1960s. Peck fished throughout his childhood and began saltwater and freshwater guiding at the age of 15. During the 1940s and 1950s he helped pioneer the art of mooching and became one of the first anglers to use a downrigger by employing a broom handle, pulley, 5-pound sash weight and a clothespin to release the line. After 9 years in the Canadian Armed Forces, Peck started broadcasting fishing reports on VANCOUVER radio stations. His BROADCASTING career led to a stint as host of a television show, *Tides and Trails* (1960–66), which followed him on over 300 fishing and hunting expeditions throughout western Canada and, eventually, the world. After the show went off the air, Peck focussed on his charter business and continued in radio with his reports and a 2-hour open-line show on CKWX radio. In 1987 he left the charter business and turned his energies to working in a PORT COQUITLAM tackle shop and teaching courses on fishing. In 1996 he published a guide, *12 Basic Skills of Fly Fishing. See also* FISHING, SPORT; FLY FISHING.

SW

PEDEN, Douglas, athlete, journalist (b 1916, Victoria). Considered by many the greatest all-around athlete in BC history, he excelled at several sports. As a teenager he was a member of Canada's junior TENNIS team and the Victoria Blue Ribbons BASKETBALL team that won the national championship in 1935. At the 1936 Berlin Olympics he was high scorer for the Canadian basketball team that won a silver medal. After the Olympics he joined his brother Torchy PEDEN on the professional 6-day CYCLING race tours and in 1939 won the Canadian cycling sprint championship. As a RUGBY player he was the only Canadian to score a try against the touring New Zealand All Blacks in 1936. During WWII he played minor-league BASEBALL in the Pittsburgh Pirates' farm system. War service overseas may have spoiled his chance to make the big leagues, though he was a manager in the Pittsburgh system from 1945 to 1951. When he returned to VICTORIA he was a reporter and later sports editor for the *Victoria Times* until his retirement in 1981. He was runner-up to Lionel Conacher for designation in 1950 as Canada's athlete of the half century. Peden was inducted into the Canadian Sports Hall of Fame and the BC SPORTS HALL OF FAME.

PEDEN, William "Torchy," cyclist (b 16 Apr 1906, Victoria; d 25 Jan 1980, Chicago, IL). An all-around athlete, he starred in BASEBALL, HOCKEY, FOOTBALL and SWIMMING before concentrating on bicycle road racing. He represented Canada at the 1928 Olympics in Amsterdam and turned professional 2 years later, competing in the gruelling 6-day CYCLING races that were a fad during the 1930s and 1940s. Nicknamed "Torchy" for his red hair, he was a household name in N America and one of the highest-paid athletes in

"Torchy" Peden, professional cyclist. BCSHF

the world. At a time when most pro sports stars were paid well under $10,000 per season, he was capable of collecting $60,000; he once made $25,000 in a single 6-day race. In 1929 he set a world speed record of 81 mph (130.3 km/h) that stood for 12 years and in 1931 he set a record time for the mile. He retired in 1948 with 38 wins in 149 pro races, a record that stood until 1965. He is a member of the Canadian Sports Hall of Fame and the BC SPORTS HALL OF FAME.

PEDERSON, Barry, hockey player (b 13 Mar 1961, Big River, SK). He grew up in NANAIMO and played his junior HOCKEY for the VICTORIA COUGARS. In his second WHL season (1979–80) he finished 3rd in league scoring and helped Victoria reach the WHL championship final. The next season he again was 3rd in scoring, led the team to a Memorial Cup berth and won recognition as the WHL's outstanding player. Drafted by the Boston Bruins in 1980 he made an easy transition to the NHL, setting a Bruins rookie-points record of 92 and scoring 44 goals. The following season, at 22 he became the youngest player to lead Boston in scoring, with 107 points. In 1984-85, doctors found a non-malignant tumour in his upper right arm and after surgery he never really recovered his scoring touch. In 1986 he was traded to the VANCOUVER CANUCKS for Cam NEELY and a first-round draft pick. In 2 of his seasons Pederson earned over 70 points for Vancouver but Neely turned into a star with

Boston. Pederson was traded to Pittsburgh in 1990 before playing his final NHL season, 1991-92, for Hartford and Boston.

SW

PEETZ, Boris, fishing tackle maker (b 1883, Moscow, Russia; d 12 Jan 1954, Victoria). He arrived in Canada in 1910 and worked briefly as a silversmith for the CPR in Montreal before travelling west to VICTORIA in 1911. He established a jewellery business, but in his leisure time he loved to fish and by the 1920s he was designing and making his own fishing reels. He established the BC Peetz Manufacturing Co, maker of beautiful mahogany and brass reels that were the pride of west coast sport fishers. In 1947 his son Ivan joined the business, which became Peetz and Son. At his death his children ran the business until 1977, then sold it. In 2000 the Peetz Manufacturing (1977) Co continued to make quality fishing tackle in the tradition of its founder. *See also* FISHING, SPORT.

PELICAN, American white (*Pelecanus erythrorhynchos*), is a migrant from southern California and Mexico, arriving each spring to breed at Stum Lk in the CHILCOTIN. It is the only pelican colony in BC. About 150 pairs of birds nest on 5 islands in the lake. They feed on INSECTS and small fish, which they herd into shallows before scooping them into their distinctive long yellow bills. Officially an ENDANGERED SPECIES, pelicans are protected within the confines of White Pelican Provincial Park (27.6 km²), created specifically for them in 1971. White pelicans have a wingspan of 3 m and weigh up to 14 kg. The brown pelican (*P. occidentalis*) is a marine species that occasionally visits the BC coast from the southern US.

PEMBERTON, village, pop 855, lies in the mountains 160 km north of VANCOUVER. It was named for Joseph Despard PEMBERTON, a government surveyor. The community was established in 1858 near the head of Lillooet Lk as a stop along the trail to the goldfields between HARRISON LK and the FRASER R (*see* GOLD RUSH,

Countryside near Pemberton. Keith Thirkell photo

FRASER R). The PEMBERTON TRAIL was completed to SQUAMISH in 1877; it was used briefly to drive cattle to the coast before it fell into disuse. It was via this route that the Pacific Great Eastern Railway (see BC RAIL) arrived from Squamish in 1914. Settlement began in the 1880s and farming (see AGRICULTURE), especially of seed potatoes, was the main economic activity for many years. The post office was first named Pemberton Meadows, which later referred to an agricultural area farther up the LILLOOET R valley, and then Agerton for many years. Large-scale LOGGING became important in the 1950s. Incorporated on 20 July 1956, the village has benefitted from the rapid growth of the resort community of WHISTLER, 35 km to the south.

PEMBERTON, Joseph Despard, engineer, surveyor (b 23 July 1821, Dublin, Ireland; d 11 Nov 1893, Oak Bay). After several years as an engineer on railway construction in Ireland and England, he joined the HBC as surveyor of VANCOUVER ISLAND and arrived in the colony in 1851. As an HBC employee and surveyor general of the colony from 1859 to 1864, he carried out most of the early surveys of southern Vancouver Island, organized the construction of ROADS and bridges, and laid out townsites along the lower FRASER R. He was a member of Vancouver Island's first House of Assembly from 1856 to 1859, was appointed to both the executive and legislative councils in 1864 and, when the colonies united in 1866, was elected to the legislative council. He retired from politics in 1868 to devote all his time to family and business interests. His palatial home, Gonzales, was a gathering place for the local elite. In 1887, with his son Frederick, he established a property and financial company that evolved into the modern investment and real estate firms bearing his name. His daughter Sophia PEMBERTON was a noted painter.

PEMBERTON, Sophia Theresa, artist (b 13 Feb 1869, Victoria; d 31 Oct 1959, Victoria). She was BC's first internationally acclaimed female artist. The daughter of the surveyor J.D. PEMBERTON, she was raised in VICTORIA in circumstances of wealth and privilege and showed artistic talents from a young age. She went to Europe in 1890 and studied painting for 10 years in London and Paris. In 1899 she won the gold medal for students at the prestigious Académie Julian, the first woman to take top prize. After returning to Victoria, she continued to paint, teach and travel in spite of ill health. In 1905 she married an Anglican cleric, Canon Arthur Beanlands, and her work began to take second place to family obligations. A London exhibition of her VANCOUVER ISLAND landscapes in 1909 was her last public showing for almost 50 years. She lived in England until 1947; widowed for a second time, she returned to Victoria, where her work began again to attract notice during the 1950s.

PEMBERTON TRAIL connected LILLOOET with BURRARD INLET via PEMBERTON and SQUAMISH. Completed in 1877 at a cost 4 times the original estimate, the trail was supposed to provide a route for Interior cattle raisers (see CATTLE INDUSTRY) to get their meat to markets around Burrard Inlet. The initial drive proved the trail to be impractical and it fell into disuse. It was resurrected in 1891, when it was made passable for pack horses, and was then used regularly. During WWI the Pacific Great Eastern Rwy (see BC RAIL) was built between Squamish and CLINTON, replacing the trail.

PENDER CANAL was dug in 1911 through an isthmus joining N and S PENDER ISLANDS. In the process 2 archaeological sites were discovered and major excavation took place here from 1984 to 1986. The sites date from between 6,000 and 400 years ago and have provided much of the known information about the middle and late periods in south coastal PREHISTORY. *See also* ARCHAEOLOGY. *Roy Carlson*

PENDER HARBOUR, pop 2,500, is a jumble of islands, bays and lagoons on the SUNSHINE COAST north of SECHELT. It contains the small communities of GARDEN BAY, IRVINES LANDING, Kleindale and MADEIRA PARK. It was charted in 1860 by the British Admiralty and named for Daniel Pender, who surveyed the coast with great zeal from

in 1955. Archaeological excavations at PENDER CANAL have revealed evidence of human occupation going back 6,000 years (see ARCHAEOLOGY; SALISHAN FIRST NATIONS). Most of the 2,000 permanent residents live on N Pender; from the terminal at Otter Bay, ferries travel to both Vancouver Island and TSAWWASSEN (see BC FERRY CORP). Port Washington, Hope Bay and Port Browning are the centres of settlement. Bedwell Harbour, where many S Pender residents live, has a resort and marina and is a Canada Customs port of entry. The islands are named for Daniel Pender, an officer in the Royal Navy engaged in coastal surveys from 1857 to 1870.

PENNASK LAKE, 9.55 km², lies in the high country between MERRITT and KELOWNA, about 80 km southwest of KAMLOOPS near the DOUGLAS LAKE RANCH. Famed for its TROUT FISHING, it is the site of the Pennask Lake Club established in 1929 by James Dole, a pineapple tycoon from Hawaii. In July 1959 the club's lodge hosted Queen Elizabeth II and Prince Philip for 3 days during their royal visit to BC. There is also a provincial PARK at the lake, which can be reached from the COQUIHALLA Connector (Hwy 97C). *See also* LAKES.

Aerial view of Pender Harbour.
Keith Thirkell photo

1857 to 1870 as master of the ships *Plumper*, *Hecate* and BEAVER. Prior to the SMALLPOX epidemic of 1862, the harbour was densely populated each winter by people of the SECHELT nation. Settled after 1900 as a LOGGING and commercial FISHING centre, it now attracts a growing number of retirees and vacationers. It is the home of HARBOUR PUBLISHING, publisher of *The Encyclopedia of British Columbia*.

PENDER ISLANDS, North and South, 34 km², are 2 of the GULF ISLANDS in GEORGIA STRAIT between southern VANCOUVER ISLAND and the mainland. They were once joined by a neck of land called the Indian Portage. Construction of a canal through this land bridge in 1911 separated the islands until a highway bridge rejoined them

PENNY, a LOGGING settlement on VIA Rail and the north side of the FRASER R 100 km east of PRINCE GEORGE, was the site of Roy Spurr's Penny Spruce Mills, which also operated as the Red Mountain Lumber Co. A SAWMILL was established in 1917 and stayed open until the 1960s. A number of people still live in the area despite the fact that Penny has no road access. *AS*

PENSIONS, or retirement income, are largely the responsibility of the federal government and of individuals and their employers. Along with private pension plans, the federal government administers the Canada Pension Plan (CPP), which is a contributory plan, and 2 non-contributory public programs: Old Age Security (OAS) and the Guaranteed Income Supplement (GIS). The OAS and the GIS will be replaced in 2001 with a new low-income public pension called the Seniors Benefit. To supplement these federal programs, the BC government administers 2 non-contributory programs that provide financial aid for seniors who either do not qualify for OAS or GIS or have incomes that fall below a minimum level.

About one-third of BC's labour force participates in an employer-sponsored Registered Pension Plan. As well, there are 9 public sector pension plans for individuals working for the public service, for one of the municipalities, for one of 4 CROWN CORPS or for a college, or working as a schoolteacher or as an MLA. These public sector plans are managed by the BC Investment Management Co, a Crown corporation established at the beginning of 2000. With assets of $54.8 billion, it is the third-largest public sector pension fund in Canada.

PENTECOSTALISM; *see* CONSERVATIVE PROTESTANTISM.

PENTICTON, city, pop 30,987, lies at the southern end of OKANAGAN LK about 390 km east of VANCOUVER. The flat plain between Okanagan and SKAHA lakes was first occupied by OKANAGAN people, and the name derives from a SALISHAN word meaning "a place to stay forever." Fur traders (*see* FUR TRADE, LAND-BASED) began using the valley as a transportation route in 1813. The original settler was Thomas ELLIS, an Irish immigrant who arrived in 1865 and eventually built up a cattle-ranching (*see* CATTLE INDUSTRY) empire encompassing 120 km² of land. In 1892 Ellis sold a small parcel of land to the Penticton Townsite Co but its attempt to develop a settlement failed. More successful was the Southern Okanagan Land Co, which purchased land from Ellis in 1905, expanded the townsite and started commercial TREE FRUIT growing. PADDLEWHEEL STEAMBOATS were active on Okanagan Lk from 1890, and in 1915 the

KETTLE VALLEY RWY arrived. Penticton, which incorporated as a town in 1908 and a city in 1948, developed as the centre of a rich fruit and wine producing area (*see* WINE MAKING). With the completion of the HOPE–PRINCETON HWY in 1949, TOURISM became an important factor. The city gained worldwide fame in Mar 1955 when the PENTICTON VS, a senior amateur team, won the world HOCKEY championship. The hot, dry CLIMATE and sandy beaches attract summer visitors, while skiers (*see* SKIING) flock to nearby Apex Mt in the winter. Along with the rest of the Okanagan, Penticton has grown as a retirement centre. It hosts the annual Ironman Canada Triathlon, the largest event of its kind in Canada.

PENTICTON Vs were among the top amateur men's HOCKEY teams in Canada during the 1950s. Led by playing coach Grant Warwick and his brothers Bill and Dick, the 1954 Vs defeated the Sudbury Wolves for BC's third Allan Cup as Canadian amateur champions. The Vs arrived in Krefeld, Germany, for the 1955 world championship after a gruelling pre-tournament exhibition schedule but won 8 straight games, including a 5-0 victory over powerful Russia in the deciding match. Goaltender Ivan McClelland had 4 shutouts for a 0.75 goals-against average and Bill Warwick scored 14 goals to lead the tournament. The Vs received a raucous welcome when they returned to PENTICTON with the World Cup. Legend has it that when the International Ice Hockey Federation asked for the cup back the Warwicks sent a replica and kept the original on display in their Penticton café. *SW*

PENTLAND, Barbara Lally, composer (b 2 Jan 1912, Winnipeg, MB; d 5 Feb 2000, Vancouver). After studies at the Juilliard School of Music in New York (1936–39) and with Aaron Copland at the Berkshire Music Center in Massachusetts, she joined the Toronto Conservatory of Music and taught there from 1943 to 1949. In 1949 she moved to VANCOUVER and taught in the music department at UBC until

Barbara Pentland, composer. Vancouver Sun

1963. Meanwhile she established her reputation as a leading composer of modern music for piano, voice and larger ensembles. She had honorary degrees from the Univ of Manitoba and SFU, and a Diplôme d'Honneur from the Canadian Conference of the Arts (1977); she was also a Member of the Order of Canada (1989) and the ORDER OF BC (1993).

PENTLATCH were a Northern Coast Salish group occupying the east shore of VANCOUVER ISLAND from PARKSVILLE north to Cape Lazo, as well as the offshore islands including DENMAN and HORNBY. Disease, intertribal warfare and the encroachment of neighbouring groups led to their disappearance in the 19th century. Their language became extinct in 1940. See also FIRST NATIONS LANGUAGES; FIRST NATIONS OF BC; SALISHAN FIRST NATIONS.

PEOPLES OF BC, *see* opposite.

PEP, Tony, boxer (b 14 Sept 1964, New Westminster). Born Anthony Allan Pipke, he learned to box at the Hastings and Kingsway BOXING Centres and fought 12 amateur fights before turning professional at age 17. His controversial attitude made him unpopular with hometown fans and he was booed when he defeated Toronto's Ned Simmons to win the Canadian featherweight championship on 10 Apr 1985. He was booed again when he beat Canadian 1984 Los Angeles Olympics bronze medallist and local hero Dale WALTERS in a heavily promoted bout at the PNE Agrodome in Nov 1986. Pep quit boxing in 1988 after a controversial loss in Copenhagen while seeking the World Boxing Council featherweight crown. Convicted of assault twice in the late 1980s, he moved to Alberta and returned to the ring in 1990 to fight

The Skaha Lk waterfront, Penticton.
Jan Drozdzenski/Image Makers

his way to the Commonwealth super feather-weight crown in Feb 1992. He was ranked 2nd in the world by the WBO before losing a 1995 junior lightweight title bout to Regilio Tuur.

PEREZ, Juan, Spanish naval officer (b circa 1725, Majorca, Spain; d 2 Nov 1775, at sea off California). He was engaged in trade on the Manila galleon route between Mexico and the Philippines and on supply ships to California before being ordered to sail north in the frigate *Santiago* to investigate Russian incursions onto the Northwest Coast. The Spanish claimed sovereignty over the coast and instructed Pérez to take unequivocal possession of it. On 18 July 1774 he arrived off the QUEEN CHARLOTTE ISLANDS, becoming the first European known to have seen the BC coast. He met and traded with the HAIDA, particularly at Langara Island, but did not land. Poor weather frustrated his attempts to proceed farther than the north end of the Charlottes. On its way south, the *Santiago* stopped at the entrance to NOOTKA SOUND, where Perez encountered some NUU-CHAH-NULTH (Nootka) people, but again did not land. The following year he joined a second expedition north but died at sea shortly before his return to San Blas. *See also* SPANISH EXPLORATION.

PERFECT CIRCLE was a secret society of dedicated SOCIAL CREDIT PARTY adherents who kept the Social Credit idea alive in BC during WWII, when the movement attracted almost no popular support. Members identified themselves by a small gold circular pin. The name referred to Socred ideas about the perfect circulation of money.

PEROW, 57 km southeast of SMITHERS on the BULKLEY R and the CNR, developed as a railway and SAWMILLING community, though many residents worked at the GRANISLE COPPER mines in the 1960s and later. It was named after D.A. Perow, general agent of the GRAND TRUNK PACIFIC RWY at VANCOUVER.   *AS*

PERRAULT, Raymond "Ray," politician (b 6 Feb 1926, Vancouver). Raised in VANCOUVER, he graduated from UBC in 1947. He became leader of the provincial LIBERAL PARTY in 1959 and won election to the legislature the following year. He held his seat through 3 elections but did not manage to improve the Liberal's third party status or its 20% of the popular vote. In 1968 he jumped to federal politics, winning the Burnaby–Seymour riding for the Liberals in the "Trudeaumania" election. In 1973 he was appointed to the Senate, where he served as government leader (1974–79 and 1980–82).

PERRY SIDING, on the CPR and the Slocan R, 37 km north of CASTLEGAR, was named after C.E. Perry, a railway engineer. Many DOUKHOBORS settled in the area and named their village Persekovoe, Russian for "land of peaches." Hundreds of Sons of Freedom members were arrested at an encampment here in 1953 and sentenced to jail for public nudity.   *AS*

PEOPLES OF BC

Overview

Daniel Francis

The population of BC in 1996 was 3,724,500, 12.9% of the Canadian total, making it the third most populous province in Canada. The population is distributed unevenly geographically. In 1996 about 86% of residents lived in 3 areas: 56.5% in the province's southwest corner (the LOWER MAINLAND), 18% on VANCOUVER ISLAND and 12.3% in the THOMPSON–OKANAGAN region. Overall population density is 4 people per km², but in the Lower Mainland density jumps to 638 people.

BC is the only province whose population growth rate has consistently exceeded the national growth rate since CONFEDERATION. Some of the growth is natural (excess of births over deaths); the rest is accounted for by migration from the rest of Canada and immigration from other countries. In the period 1986–96 migration and immigration accounted for 80% of population growth. For many years immigration was mainly from Europe and the US, but since the 1960s Asian countries have provided many more immigrants. By 1996, 44% of all immigrants living in BC were from Asian countries; 40% were from Europe. Since WWII, BC's share of total immigration to Canada has been consistently greater than its share of the population. In the mid-1980s, for example, 17% of all immigrants to Canada settled in BC, and the proportion peaked in 1996 at 23%.

The shift in immigration patterns contributed to a shift in the ethnic makeup of the province's people. Until the 1880s, most people in BC were aboriginal. At Confederation in 1871, for instance, aboriginal people made up 71% of the population. Disease and other factors reduced aboriginal numbers dramatically, however (*see* ABORIGINAL DEMOGRAPHY), and waves of immigrants to the province swamped the FIRST NATIONS population. Between 1871 and 1911 the white population increased almost 40-fold. Most newcomers came from Britain, either directly or via other parts of Canada, and by 1900 people of British background accounted for 60% of British Columbians. The proportion of BC residents claiming British heritage peaked at 74% in 1921, then slowly declined. Still, most residents were of British background until 1991; the census that year showed the percentage to have slipped below 50% for the first time in 100 years.

This change resulted partly from relaxation of inter-war restrictions on Asian immigration. Between 1961 and 1981 BC's proportion of people of Asian origin tripled to 7.5% of the total population. By 1996 it had almost tripled again to about 20%, reflecting the province's growing orientation toward the PACIFIC RIM. More generally, visible minorities have become a large proportion of the population. In the 1996 census about a third of all Lower Mainland residents identified themselves as members of visible minorities.

As a frontier society, BC initially attracted many more men than women. This imbalance peaked in 1891, when almost 75% of the population was male; it persisted until about WWI, then declined. By 1921 males accounted for 58.5% of residents; approximate parity was reached in the 1950s.

A large post-WWII baby boom generation influences the age structure of the BC population. The province's overall population has aged with this generation because of low birth rates and continually improving life expectancy. In 1996 the median age in BC was 35.7 years and it was expected to increase. Almost 13% of the population was over 64 years old; by the late 1990s this trend was expected to continue. The mild climate has made BC a favourite destination for retirees, another factor influencing the age structure of the population. Nonetheless, in 1996 BC's concentration of seniors was only the fifth highest of all provinces. Within BC, the Okanagan area had the highest concentration of seniors (23.8% of residents), followed by the VICTORIA area (18.1%).

POPULATION OF BC AND % OF CDN TOTAL

YEAR	POP	%
1871	36,247	1.0
1881	49,459	1.1
1891	98,173	2.0
1901	178,657	3.3
1911	392,480	5.5
1921	524,582	6.0
1931	694,263	6.7
1941	817,861	7.1
1951	1,165,210	8.3
1961	1,629,082	8.9
1971	2,184,625	10.1
1981	2,713,615	11.1
1991	3,282,061	11.7
1996	3,724,505	12.9
1999 (est)	4,023,100	13.2
2006 (proj)	4,428,800	13.7
2016 (proj)	5,098,000	14.8
2026 (proj)	5,715,800	15.8

BC'S GROWING POPULATION

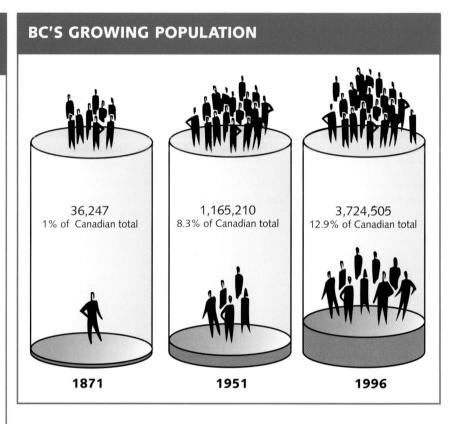

36,247
1% of Canadian total

1,165,210
8.3% of Canadian total

3,724,505
12.9% of Canadian total

1871   **1951**   **1996**

The population of BC is predicted to reach 6 million by 2026, growing by about 70,000 annually (a growth rate of 1–2%). This is a slowdown from the booming growth rate of the early 1990s, when the population grew by more than 100,000 annually, the fastest growth rate of any province in Canada. By 2026, half of the population is expected to be age 42 years or older. *See also* ECONOMY OF BC.

Doukhobor women protesting, 1970.
George Diack/Vancouver Sun

BC POPULATION BY AGE 1996

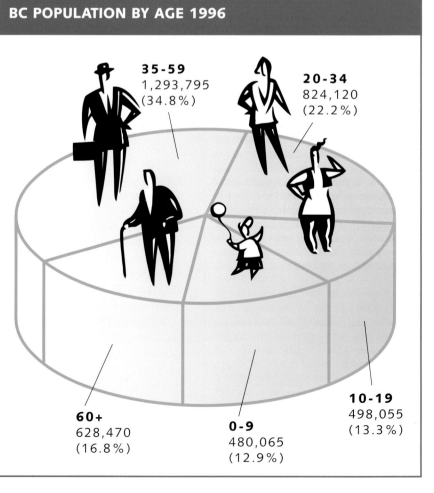

35-59
1,293,795
(34.8%)

20-34
824,120
(22.2%)

60+
628,470
(16.8%)

0-9
480,065
(12.9%)

10-19
498,055
(13.3%)

MEN AND WOMEN

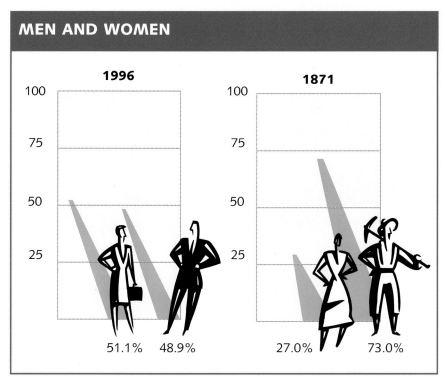

1996	1871
51.1% 48.9%	27.0% 73.0%

BC POPULATION BY GENDER 1871–1996

YEAR	MALE %	FEMALE %
1871	73.0	27.0
1881	74.4	25.6
1891	74.6	25.4
1901	70.9	29.1
1911	70.0	30.0
1921	58.5	41.5
1931	57.3	42.7
1941	54.0	46.0
1951	51.4	48.6
1961	50.7	49.3
1971	50.2	49.8
1981	49.3	50.7
1991	49.1	50.9
1996	48.9	51.1

WHERE WE WERE BORN

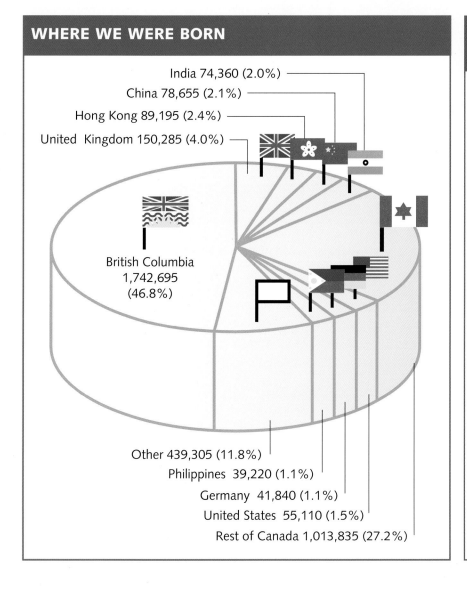

India 74,360 (2.0%)
China 78,655 (2.1%)
Hong Kong 89,195 (2.4%)
United Kingdom 150,285 (4.0%)

British Columbia
1,742,695
(46.8%)

Other 439,305 (11.8%)
Philippines 39,220 (1.1%)
Germany 41,840 (1.1%)
United States 55,110 (1.5%)
Rest of Canada 1,013,835 (27.2%)

BC POPULATION BY PLACE OF BIRTH 1996

British Columbia	**1,742,695**	**46.8%**
Rest of Canada	**1,013,835**	**27.2%**
United Kingdom	150,285	4.0%
Hong Kong	89,195	2.4%
China	78,655	2.1%
India	74,360	2.0%
United States	55,110	1.5%
Germany	41,840	1.1%
Philippines	39,220	1.1%
Taiwan	30,015	0.8%
Netherlands	25,770	0.7%
Italy	20,480	0.5%
Vietnam	20,475	0.5%
Poland	18,275	0.5%
Fiji	14,800	0.4%
South Korea	13,935	0.4%
Iran	10,965	0.3%
Portugal	10,260	0.3%
Hungary	8,425	0.2%
South Africa	8,355	0.2%
Denmark	7,630	0.2%
Yugoslavia	7,550	0.2%
Malaysia	7,130	0.2%
Other immigrants	170,465	4.6%
Total immigrants	**903,195**	**24.3%**
Non-permanent	30,035	0.8%
Unknown, etc	34,740	0.9%

Chinese businessmen in front of their New Westminster shop, 1895.
VPL 8056

Granville Island, Vancouver, a popular meeting place for all peoples.
Jennifer Echols photo

First Nations women and children in Vancouver, 1903. VPL 1869

Japanese fallers on springboard, Englewood.

BC'S MAJOR ETHNIC GROUPS 1871–1991

	British	%	Other European	%	Asian	%	First Nations	%
1871	8,576	23.7	———	—-	1,548	4.3	n/a	n/a
1881	14,660	29.6	2,490	5.0	4,350	8.8	25,661	51.9
1891	n/a	n/a	n/a	n/a	n/a	n/a	27,305	27.8
1901	106,403	60.0	21,784	12.2	19,524	10.9	28,949	16.2
1911	266,295	67.8	69,799	17.8	30,864	7.9	20,174	5.1
1921	387,513	73.9	72,743	13.9	39,739	7.6	22,377	4.3
1931	489,923	70.7	127,246	18.3	50,951	7.3	24,599	3.5
1941	571,336	69.9	175,512	21.5	42,472	5.2	24,882	3.0
1951	766,189	65.8	319,056	27.4	25,644	2.2	28,504	2.4
1961	966,881	59.4	554,712	34.1	40,299	2.5	38,814	2.4
1971	1,265,455	57.9	767,808	35.2	76,695	3.5	52,430	2.4
1981	1,505,467	55.5	874,269	32.2	204,856	7.5	73,670	2.7
1991	1,417,143	43.2	1,287,256	39.2	392,698	12.0	118,731	3.6

n/a (not available)   1871 British total includes Other European figures also

REGIONS OF BC

Scottish family posing for a portrait.
Hannah Maynard/BC Archives F-05032

Sikh cranberry farmer, Fraser Valley, 1992.
Jeff Vinnick/Vancouver Sun

BC POPULATION BY REGION 1881 – 1996

	Vancouver Island	Lower Mainland	Southern Interior	Okanagan/Boundary	Kootenays
1881	17,292	7,939	6,753	817	863
1891	35,744	41,507	8,191	3,360	3,405
1901	50,886	53,641	11,563	12.085	31,962
1911	81,241	183,108	19,031	28,066	50,839
1921	108,792	256,579	24,484	35,522	50,212
1931	120,933	379,858	30,025	40,523	63,021
1941	150,407	449,376	30,710	51,605	69,611
1951	215,003	649,238	41,823	77,686	87,688
1961	290,835	907,531	66,290	94,646	104,951
1971	381,796	1,189,864	102,668	135,472	124,043
1981	491,333	1,432,753	136,059	207,067	144,979
1991	588,256	1,828,912	138,438	251,182	141,466
1996	648,364	2,106,693	142,485	294,987	162,581

	Central Coast	Northwest	Central Interior	Northeast
1881	2,208	2,762	9,825	1,000
1891	2,475	548	2.003	940
1901	3,743	9,270	4,523	984
1911	3,545	16,595	8,411	1,644
1921	10,232	18,986	17,631	2,144
1931	12,658	18,698	21,534	7,013
1941	14,344	18,051	25,276	8,481
1951	18,247	20,854	40,276	14,395
1961	21,325	38,203	74,240	31,061
1971	22,515	56,242	128,205	43,816
1981	26,203	69,433	182,320	54,320
1991	23,398	67,968	181,174	58.267
1996	30,162	69,804	207,091	62,333

BC POPULATION 1921 – 1996

		1921	1941	1951	1961	1971	1981	1991	1996
Vancouver	city	117,217	275,353	344,833	384,522	426,256	414,281	471,844	514,008
Surrey	city	5,814	14,840	33,670	70,838	98,601	147,138	245,173	304,477
Burnaby	city	12,883	30,328	58,376	100,157	125,660	136,494	158,858	179,209
Richmond	city	4,825	10,370	19,186	43,323	62,121	96,154	126,624	148,867
Abbotsford (1)	city	6,062	8,636	15,108	20,781	31,033	54,745	86,928	105,403
Coquitlam	city	2,374	7,949	15,697	29,053	53,073	61,077	84,021	101,820
Saanich	district	10,534	18,173	28,481	48,876	65,040	78,710	95,583	101,388
Delta	district	2,839	4,287	6,701	14,597	45,860	74,692	88,978	95,411
Kelowna	city	2,520	5,118	8,517	13,188	19,412	59,916	75,953	89,442
North Vancouver	district	2,950	5,931	14,469	38,971	57,861	65,367	75,157	80,418
Langley	district	4,881	7,769	12,267	14,585	21,936	44,617	66,040	80,179
Kamloops	city	4,501	5,959	8,099	10,076	26,168	64,048	67,057	76,394
Prince George	city	2,053	2,027	4,703	13,877	33,101	67,559	69,653	75,150
Victoria	city	38,727	44,068	51,331	54,941	61,761	64,379	71,228	73,504
Nanaimo	city	6,304	6,635	7,196	14,135	14,948	47,069	60,129	70,130
Chilliwack	district	3,161	7,787	13,677	18,296	23,739	41,000	49,531	60,186
Maple Ridge	district	3,772	6,476	9,891	16,748	24,476	32,232	48,434	56,173
New Westminster	city	14,495	21,967	28,639	33,654	42,835	38,550	43,585	49,350
Port Coquitlam	city	1,178	1,539	3,232	8,111	19,560	27,535	36,773	46,682
North Vancouver	city	7,652	8,914	15,687	23,656	31,847	33,952	38,436	41,475
West Vancouver	district	2,434	7,669	13,990	25,454	36,440	35,728	38,783	40,882
Vernon	city	3,685	5,209	7,822	10,250	13,283	19,987	27,722	31,326
Penticton	city	3,979	5,777	10,548	13,859	18,146	23,181	27,258	30,987
Mission	district	3,025	4,675	7,135	8,575	10,220	20,056	26,202	30,519
Campbell River	district	——-	——-	1,986	3,737	10,000	15,832	25,259	28,851
North Cowichan	district	2,664	4,590	6,665	9,166	12,170	18,120	21,373	25,305
Langley	city	——-	——-	——-	2,365	4,864	15,124	19,765	22,523
Port Moody	city	1,030	1,512	2,246	4,789	10,778	14,917	17,756	20,847
Port Alberni (2)	city	1,596	6,391	11,168	16,176	20,063	19,892	18,523	18,468
Cranbrook	city	2,725	2,568	3,621	5,549	12,000	15,915	16,447	18,131
Oak Bay	district	4,159	9,240	11,960	16,935	18,426	16,990	17,815	17,865

(1) includes Sumas and Matsqui   *(2) includes Alberni*

PERSKY, Stan, writer, teacher (b 19 Jan 1941, Chicago). After serving in the US navy and working on the San Francisco waterfront, he came to VANCOUVER in 1966. He studied at UBC, where he was an outspoken student radical. At this time he co-founded the GEORGIA STRAIGHT Writing Supplement, which evolved into NEW STAR

Stan Persky, writer, 1998.
Barry Peterson & Blaise Enright-Peterson

BOOKS. Beginning in 1979 with *Son of Socred*, he wrote a series of books chronicling the activities of provincial and civic governments from a leftist perspective and he became well-known as a media commentator during the SOCIAL CREDIT PARTY's years in government. In 1995 he published *Then We Take Berlin*, a collection of essays about eastern Europe, where he spends several weeks each year. His autobiographical novel, *Buddy's: Meditations on Desire* (1989), and a nonfiction collection, *Autobiography of a Tattoo* (1997), both meditate on homosexual desire. Persky's columns have appeared regularly in major daily NEWSPAPERS, and he teaches at Capilano College (*see* COMMUNITY COLLEGES) in N VANCOUVER. *See also* GAY AND LESBIAN RIGHTS.

PETERSON, Roy, cartoonist (b 14 Sept 1936, Winnipeg). He moved to VANCOUVER at age 12

Self-portrait by Roy Peterson, cartoonist.

and, after graduating from high school, worked in department store advertising while attending art school at night. In 1962 he began his long career as editorial cartoonist for the *VANCOUVER SUN*. His work also appears in *Maclean's* magazine and in major newspapers and magazines in the US and Britain. By 1999 the National Newspaper Award for cartooning had been bestowed on him 7 times, making him the most honoured journalist in any category during the awards' 50-year history. His cartoons have won many international awards and he has served as president of both the Assoc of Canadian Editorial Cartoonists and the Assoc of American Editorial Cartoonists. He also illustrates books and has published collections of his cartoons and a children's book.

PETROGLYPHS; *see* ROCK ART.

PEZIM, Murray, stock promoter (b 29 Dec 1921, Toronto; d 22 Apr 1998, Vancouver). A large man with a large personality, "The Pez" went from riches to bankruptcy and back again. He left high school in 1937 to join the family meat business. After serving in the army during WWII, he returned to Toronto and began investing in stocks and working as a broker. In the 1950s he teamed up with Earl Glick and made his first million investing in the famous Denison uranium mine. He moved to VANCOUVER in 1964 and quickly became one of the most flamboyant deal-makers on the VANCOUVER STOCK EXCHANGE. His biggest successes were the financing of GOLD discoveries at Hemlo in northern Ontario and Eskay Crk in northern BC. The latter venture won him Mining

Murray Pezim, stock promoter, 1989. Vancouver Sun

Man of the Year honours in 1989, though trading irregularities concerning the stock also earned him a year's suspension from the VSE. Along with stocks he promoted sporting events and owned the BC LIONS football club from 1989 to 1992. For each big score there were many losses, but most of his friends agreed he was in business more for the excitement than the money. In 1998 he was inducted into the Canadian Mining Hall of Fame.

PHARMACARE is BC's government drug insurance program. Introduced at the beginning of 1974, it assists in paying for eligible drugs and designated medical supplies outside the hospital system. Residents over the age of 65 are fully covered by Pharmacare; others are reimbursed a portion of their expenditure. In 1998–99 Pharmacare spent $504 million.

PHEASANT, RING-NECKED (*Phasianus colchicus*), the only pheasant species resident in BC, is a chicken-sized game bird introduced from England and China between 1880 and 1920.

Ring-necked pheasant. Ken Bowen photo

The male is striking in appearance with mottled plumage, long straight tail, white neck ring and bright red wattles. The female is dull brown. Pheasants nest close to farm fields in the south-central Interior, on eastern VANCOUVER ISLAND, in the FRASER VALLEY and parts of the QUEEN CHARLOTTE ISLANDS. Some populations are threatened by habitat destruction (*see* ENDANGERED SPECIES) and stocking has continued since the initial introduction.

PHILLIPPS, Michael, trader, prospector (b 1842, Hertfordshire, England; d 22 June 1916, Elko). He came to BC in 1863 as an employee of the HBC and was stationed at Fort Kootenai just south of the border in Montana. He relocated to WILD HORSE CRK when the GOLD RUSH began there in 1864, then moved again to Tobacco Plains on the BC–Montana border where he established a private trading post and farm and married a KTUNAXA (Kutenai) woman. In 1873 he became the first white person known to have traversed CROWSNEST PASS, and he was the first person to report on the rich COAL deposits in the area. A prominent local settler, Phillipps served as an Indian agent and a justice of the peace. *See also* COLONIAL GOVERNMENT.

PHILLIPPS-WOLLEY, Edward Clive Oldnall Long, sportsman, writer (b 1854, Dorsetshire, England; d 1918, Duncan). An English military officer and diplomat, he inherited a country estate in 1876, whereupon he resigned his commission and took up a career in the law. Big-game hunting was his passion, however, and in 1890 he was attracted to BC by its sporting potential. With his wife and 4 children he settled in OAK BAY, where he built a large mansion, Woodhall, on 6.5 ha of land. Later the family moved to DUNCAN. Phillipps-Wolley was a widely published writer in both England and BC, and made a great deal of money in real estate and MINING. A committed imperialist, he was knighted in 1915 for his work organizing the Navy League in western Canada.

PHILLIPS, Floyd Eugene "Pan," rancher (b 13 Mar 1910, Pike City, IL; d 28 May 1983, Tsetzi Lk). He grew up on a farm in western Illinois and left home at age 16 to work his way around the West as a harvester and COWBOY. In 1934 he arrived in BC with Richmond HOBSON to begin ranching (see CATTLE INDUSTRY) 150 km north of ANAHIM LK in the BLACKWATER R area. Together they formed the Frontier Cattle Co and established the Home Ranch. Their adventures are chronicled in a popular series of books by Hobson that the CBC used as the basis for a television series in 1998. The partnership dissolved in the 1940s and Phillips ran the Home Ranch with his family. The annual 320-km cattle drive to QUESNEL took 2–3 weeks and was famous as the longest drive in N America at that time; in 1969 the CBC produced a television documentary about it. Phillips sold the Home Ranch in 1970 and moved to nearby Tsetzi Lk, where he operated a FISHING camp with his son until his death.

PHILLIPS ARM, 60 km north of CAMPBELL RIVER beyond E THURLOW ISLAND, was the land of the Kwiakah, a KWAKWAKA'WAKW (Kwakiutl) First Nation whose name means "to club." The Dorth Morden was the largest of a number of mines that flourished between 1890 and 1930. A large FORESTRY camp was located here in the 1970s, and in the early 1990s some innovative LOGGING was done with the assistance of balloons. AS

PHOENIX is an abandoned MINING town in the BOUNDARY DISTRICT outside GREENWOOD. It grew up about 1895 as the centre of the Phoenix COPPER mining camp and was incorporated on 11 Oct 1900 as the highest city in BC (1,400 m).

From 1898 to 1909, ore from the mines was shipped to the Granby SMELTER outside GRAND FORKS via branch lines of 2 competing railways, the CPR and the GREAT NORTHERN RWY. The quality of ore reserves deteriorated after 1909, but demand for copper during WWI kept the operation active until 1919, after which the Granby Mining & Smelting Co focused on its ANYOX operation and the city and mining camp were abandoned. The site was later obliterated by open-pit mining; only the cemetery remained by 2000.

PHOTO RADAR was introduced in BC in 1996 as an attempt to reduce accidents related to traffic speed. Traffic-accident related costs were exceeding $2 billion, with the loss of close to 500 lives and 48,000 injuries annually. BC's photo radar is the only provincial system in Canada, though Calgary and Edmonton have city-run programs and photo radar is used in 75 countries worldwide. The program is staffed by municipal police and RCMP and financed by the Ministry of the Attorney General. Photo radar was greeted sceptically by critics who believed it was simply a "cash cow" for the provincial government. Initial results seemed to indicate that photo radar contributed to decreasing numbers of traffic accidents, though revenues from fines did not reach expected levels. *Toby Rainey*

PHOTOGRAPHY dates back to experiments conducted in the early 1770s in England, but commercially viable photographic processes appeared simultaneously in 1839 in England and France. L.J.M. Daguerre's invention, the daguerreotype, was purchased by the French government and presented to the world (except England, where it was patented). It was a unique image on a silver-plated copper plate. A competing process, the calotype, was developed by W.H. Fox Talbot in England and involved generating a negative and subsequent paper print or positive. Because Fox Talbot also patented his invention, the calotype was not used as widely as the daguerreotype.

By the time photography came to BC in the mid-1850s, the daguerreotype was virtually obsolete and the calotype process had given way to the wet-plate process. Although difficult to master, wet-plate photography produced extraordinarily detailed negatives on glass plates that when printed matched the visual quality and appeal of a daguerreotype. Photographers working outside a fixed location, however, needed to carry a portable darkroom to create each negative. The wet-plate process was replaced in the early 1880s by pre-sensitized dry-plate photography and in the late 1880s by roll film and more durable plastic-like cut sheet negatives. Cameras continued to evolve throughout the 19th century as inventors and manufacturers worked to put photography in the hands of the masses. The most significant technological development relating to photography in the 20th century is the shift from analogue to filmless digital cameras. While still using optical lenses, these cameras store their digital images on memory cards

or electromagnetic storage media. The creation and manipulation of digital images presents society with new opportunities and challenges much as photography did in 1839.

The first photographers in BC were amateurs such as the HBC physician Dr A.R. Benson (d before 1909) and Lt Richard Roche (1831–88) of the Royal Navy. Benson probably took up photography as a hobby in about 1857; Lt Roche apparently had a camera with him when he arrived on HMS *Satellite* in 1858. The first commercial photographers, S.A. Spencer (circa 1829–1911) and George FARDON, arrived in VICTORIA in the wake of the GOLD RUSH on the FRASER R in 1858. Both were primarily portrait photographers. Beginning in the mid-1860s Victoria was also home to several other notable photographers including Frederick DALLY, Charles GENTILE and the wife-and-husband team of Hannah and Richard MAYNARD.

The diverse uses of photography in BC include land survey documentation, portraiture, agricultural, industrial and TOURISM promotion, and photography as an art form. Among the first photographers in BC during 1858–59 were 2 groups of ROYAL ENGINEERS from England. Both documented their activities and FIRST NATIONS

Richard Maynard, photographer, with field camera on tripod, in Hannah Maynard's studio, Victoria, c 1890. BC Archives F-06336

culture. Other important survey photographers included Benjamin F. BALTZLY (Geological Survey of Canada, 1871) and Charles George Horetzky (CPR surveys 1872, 1875, 1879). Edouard Deville, Dominion lands surveyor general of Canada, formulated photographic surveying procedures in the 1880s that were used extensively to map the province's mountainous terrain prior to the beginnings of aerial photographic surveying in the 1920s. Photographers such as Richard Maynard, Charles Macmunn (d Victoria, 1903) and William McFarlane Notman of Montreal (1857–1913) documented construction of the CPR through BC and helped promote the ROCKY and SELKIRK Mts as scenic destinations. Other BC photographers who created significant portfolios of early CPR scenic views were R.H. Trueman (1856–1911) and S.J. Thompson (1864–1929). To further promote BC as a tourist destination the provincial government established its own photographic branch within the Government Travel Bureau in 1939. Two other government ministries, FORESTRY and AGRICULTURE, also operated their own photographic units. Beginning in 1959 some of the photographic output of the Government Travel Bureau was published in *BEAUTIFUL BC* magazine.

Natural resources extraction—MINING, FISHING and LOGGING—and manufacturing and construction activities form the basis of industrial photography. Frederick Dally produced exquisitely detailed photographs of GOLD MINING in the vicinity of BARKERVILLE. First Nations FISHING techniques, recorded by Dally in the 1860s, Maynard from the 1870s to 1880s and Edward S. CURTIS's re-creations in the 1910s, were especially popular with commercial photographers. The amateur photographer F. Dundas Todd (1858–1926), a provincial agriculture inspector, documented fishing and working conditions in SALMON CANNERIES in STEVESTON in 1913. Logging practices were extremely popular with photographers. Outstanding collections were produced by Leonard FRANK on VANCOUVER ISLAND until 1916 and Walter Forest Montgomery in CHASE from the 1910s to the 1930s. Following in the footsteps of Frank, Wilmer Gold documented the logging industry on Vancouver Island during 1940–70.

The practice of systematically documenting BC industrial growth with a camera extends back to at least the 1880s when contractors such as Andrew ONDERDONK hired photographers or offered them the opportunity to record the activity. Of the photographers whose work has survived nearly intact in negative form, industrial and landscape scenery represents the mainstay of C.S. Bailey of Bailey Bros (VANCOUVER, 1888 to the 1890s), Leonard Frank (PORT ALBERNI, 1898–1916; Vancouver, 1917–44), Philip T. Timms (Vancouver, 1900–10), the Wrathall family (HAZELTON/PRINCE RUPERT, 1908–78), Stuart Thomson (Vancouver, 1910–60), Percy Bentley of Dominion Photo Co (Vancouver, 1915–62), the Stocks family (PENTICTON, 1917 to the 1970s) and Otto LANDAUER (Vancouver, 1945–80). Amateur and artistic photographers such as F. Dundas Todd, Mattie GUNTERMAN (Lardeau R district, 1898–1945), James Crookall (Vancouver, 1920s to 1930s), and John VANDERPANT (NEW WESTMINSTER/Vancouver, 1920–46) also left important visual legacies of BC's industrialization. NEWSPAPER staff and freelance photographers compiled extensive collections dating back to the 1910s, many of which were later collected in various archives.

The use of photography as an art form extends back to its beginnings. Amateur photographers, commercial photographers experimenting with the medium, and artist-photographers all contributed to photography's evolution into a means of artistic expression. Among the first photographic salons in BC were those arranged by the commercial photographer John Vanderpant in 1920. His BC contemporaries Harold MORTIMER-LAMB, Johan Helders and James Crookall all created outstanding pictorialist-style images in the 1930s. Although many art galleries began exhibiting photographs and the salons carried on in the 1950s, photography did not fully re-emerge in BC as an art form in its own right until the 1970s. Prominent modern artist-photographers include Marian Penner Bancroft, Roy KIYOOKA, Jeff WALL, Ian WALLACE and Paul WONG.

BC photographers began organizing into clubs and professional associations in the 1890s. The Vancouver Camera Club (1895) appears to have been the first amateur association. The Vancouver Photographic Society of the 1930s, affiliated with the UK Royal Photographic Society, sponsored its first international exhibit in 1940. The POWELL RIVER Camera Club (1939) was an early example of another community club. The Victoria Camera Club, established in

"Milk," a colour transparency in light box by Jeff Wall, 1984.

1944 by a merger of the Victoria Photographic Society (1941) and the Civil Service Camera Club, continues to promote the enjoyment of photography. The Professional Photographers Assoc of BC was organized in 1945 and its members exhibit their works throughout BC. Most BC publications devoted to photography were established by the amateur and professional associations. The principal archival collections of BC photography are the BC Archives in Victoria and the Vancouver Public Library.   *David Mattison*

PHYSICAL GEOGRAPHY OF BC (*see page 549*). (*see page 549*)

PICKETT, Hugh Frank Digby, impresario, Vancouver's "Mr Showbiz" (b 11 Apr 1913, Vancouver). After finishing school he worked as a shipping clerk at Dingwall Cotts & Co and began to indulge his fascination with show

Hugh Pickett, impresario, Vancouver's "Mr Showbiz." BC Entertainment Hall of Fame

business. During WWII he served in the army, then went to work for Hilker Attractions, VANCOUVER's first concert agency, a job that led to ownership of Famous Artists Ltd from 1950 to 1985. During his 40 years as manager, publicist and promoter there was hardly an entertainer in the world whom he did not meet and bring to the city. Stars with whom he had a close association include Marlene Dietrich, Laurence Olivier, Mitzi Gaynor and Katharine Hepburn. He also promoted local talent, not least as longtime publicist for THEATRE UNDER THE STARS. He received the Order of Canada in 1986.

PICTOGRAPHS; *see* ROCK ART.

PIERCE, William Henry, missionary (b 1856, Fort Rupert, Vancouver Island; d 1948, Prince Rupert). The son of a Scottish FUR TRADER and a TSIMSHIAN woman, he was raised at FORT SIMPSON and went to work as a cabin boy on an HBC steamer when he was just 12 years old. After falling under the influence of the missionary Thomas CROSBY, he converted to Methodism (*see* METHODIST CHURCH) and became a missionary himself. He served on the NASS R and at BELLA BELLA and in 1895 opened a mission at KISPIOX on the SKEENA R, where he remained for 15 years. Among other things he helped build a Native-run SAWMILL there. In 1910 he was posted at the cannery village of PORT ESSINGTON, where he organized the Native Fishing Society to protect aboriginal fishing rights. In 1933 he retired to PRINCE RUPERT. His autobiography is *From Potlatch to Pulpit* (1933). Pierce Memorial Church at Kispiox honours his memory. *See also* ABORIGINAL RIGHTS; FISHING, ABORIGINAL.

PIERS ISLAND, 97 ha, in HARO STRAIT near Swartz Bay on VANCOUVER ISLAND, was expropriated by the federal government in 1932 for use as a special prison camp for DOUKHOBOR inmates. The camp, which held as many as 570 inmates, remained open until 1 July 1935, by which time most of the Doukhobor prisoners were released. The island is named for Henry Piers, a Royal Navy surgeon on the coast between 1857 and 1860.

PIG WAR, 1859, was part of a dispute between Great Britain and the US over ownership of the SAN JUAN Islands. The OREGON TREATY of 1846 set the border between American and British territory at the 49th parallel. In the middle of GEORGIA STRAIT the boundary line dipped south to JUAN DE FUCA STRAIT below VANCOUVER ISLAND. The difficulty came in tracing the boundary through the waters between Vancouver Island and the mainland. The British thought that the line ran east of the San Juan Islands, but the US claimed the islands for itself. The matter came to a head in June 1859 when Lyman Cutler, an American settler on San Juan Island, shot a pig belonging to the HBC farm and the HBC demanded compensation. Gov James DOUGLAS dispatched a justice of the peace to the island and at the same time the military commander in Oregon landed a troop of soldiers, ostensibly to defend Americans against attack by aboriginals. Douglas then sent 2 British warships with 800 men as a show of force. An armed clash was averted only by the restraint of British naval officers, who decided the safety of British citizens was not at risk. Negotiators agreed to a joint military occupation of the island, which continued until 1872, when the matter was referred for arbitration to the German emperor. He placed the border through HARO STRAIT and the San Juan Islands became American territory. Meanwhile, Cutler received a small fine for shooting the pig, the incident that almost started a war.

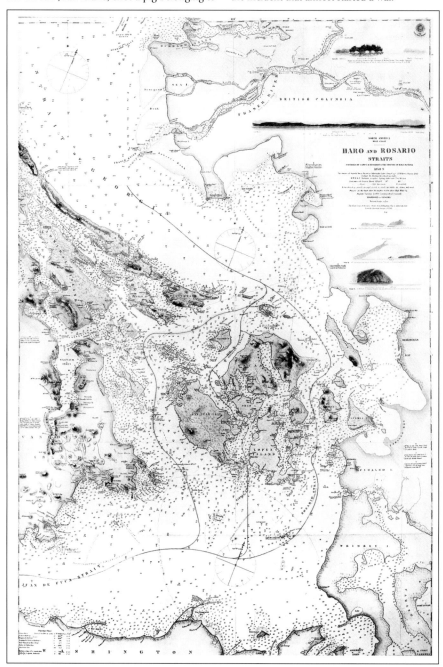

1859 map of the San Juan Islands showing 3 possible US–Canada borders. The map was drawn during a boundary dispute that led to the Pig War. Public Records Office, Surrey, UK/Historical Atlas of BC

PIGEON is a plump, medium-sized bird seen in urban parks and open fields. They strut about in flocks, their heads bobbing as they forage on the ground for seeds, nuts and BERRIES. The female lays only 1 or 2 eggs at a time but may produce as many as 4 broods in a year. Both males and females tend their young, feeding them with a mucus-like mixture known as "pigeon milk" produced in their crops. Of 6 species in Canada, 3 are found in BC. The most common variety is the rock dove (*Columba livia*), introduced from Europe many years ago. It is the blue-grey urban "pigeon" that scrabbles for food at bus stops and park benches, nesting in buildings, on ledges and under bridges. Though often associated with city life, it is actually widely distributed across southern BC. The band-tailed pigeon (*C. fasciata*), the largest species, is primarily a resident of the South Coast. It has blue-grey plumage on its back, with a white mark on the back of the neck, a light buff band across the tip of the tail, and lighter underparts. It prefers to build its flimsy nest in DOUGLAS FIR trees and to forage for food in fields and open woods. The mourning dove (*Zenaida macroura*) is a smaller, more slender bird with a long pointed tail featuring white outer feathers. The rest of the plumage is soft brown to blue-grey. This bird is found primarily in the dry southern Interior, where it keeps to open country and agricultural areas. Most mourning doves migrate south for the winter.

PIGEON GUILLEMOT; *see* GUILLEMOT, PIGEON.

PIKA is a small hamster-like mammal found in mountainous areas in alpine meadows and rocky slopes. Actually pikas are the smallest

Pika. Ken Bowen photo

member of the rabbit order and are sometimes called "rock rabbits." Grey-brown in colour, they blend well with their habitat and are very hard to spot, though they announce their presence with a squeaky call. Females give birth to litters of up to 5, sometimes twice a year. Pikas feed on a variety of plants, which they stack in haypiles during the summer, then store underground for use during the winter. The common, or Rocky Mountain, pika (*Ochotona princeps*) is the most widespread species in BC; there is also a population of collared pikas (*Ochotona collaris*) in the northwest corner of the province.

PIKE, Warburton Mayer, sportsman (b 1861, Dorsetshire, England; d 20 Oct 1915, Bournemouth, England). A well-educated member of a distinguished English family, he arrived in BC in 1884 to indulge his passion for big-game hunting. He bought property on MAYNE and SATURNA islands—including a sheep ranch and profitable sandstone quarry—and in VICTORIA, but his rough clothes and tattered appearance belied his substantial wealth. Trips to the Arctic and Alaska, both involving journeys through northern BC, are described in his classic books *The Barren Grounds of Northern Canada* (1892) and *Through the Sub-Arctic Forest* (1896). Pike returned to England during WWI. There, suffering from poor health and deeply disappointed at being denied active service, he committed suicide.

PILCHARD; *see* SARDINE.

PILOT BAY is on the east side of KOOTENAY LK opposite the West Arm. A settlement grew up when the Davies/Sayward Lumber Co built a SAWMILL at the site in 1890. In 1895 an American syndicate led by Andrew Hendryx and his brother Wilbur (*see* HENDRYX BROS) put in a SMELTER to process low-grade galena from the Bluebell mine at RIONDEL as well as custom ore from other mines in the area. The smelter proved inefficient; after a year it operated mainly as a concentrator until 1906. With the sawmill already closed, the community dwindled away. There is a 3.47 km² provincial MARINE PARK on the site and the remains of the brick smelter stacks could still be seen by the late 1990s. *See also* MINING.

PINANTAN LAKE is a recreational district 28 km east of KAMLOOPS. The Pinantan Valley was an important root-gathering area for people of the SECWEPEMC (Shuswap) First Nations. It was ranched in the 1860s by Donald McPherson. George Wilson was the first settler at the lake in 1887. A former CPR employee, Antoine Pene, built a fishing lodge in the early 1900s. Paul Lake Provincial PARK is nearby. *See also* CATTLE INDUSTRY; FISHING, SPORT; LAKES.   AS

PINCHBECK, William, rancher (b 1831, England; d 31 July 1893, Williams Lake). He was 18 years old when he left England for California. There he ran a roadhouse until news of another GOLD RUSH lured him north to BC. He arrived in WILLIAMS LAKE in 1860 as a constable with Philip Nind, a gold commissioner, and settled there. With William Lyne he established a large ranch (*see* CATTLE INDUSTRY) that occupied most of the Williams Lake valley. He then bought out Lyne and eventually owned a small empire, including a roadhouse and racetrack, a SAWMILL and gristmill, a distillery that made his famous White Wheat Whiskey, and a farm. He also acted as the local police officer, jailer and justice of the peace. Eventually he was overextended by debt, and he was nearly broke when he died. His neatly fenced grave overlooks the Williams Lake Stampede grounds.

PHYSICAL GEOGRAPHY OF BC

Overview

June Ryder

Britanish Columbia is a mosaic of diverse landscapes, ranging from the icefields of the COAST MTS to the pocket deserts of the OKANAGAN VALLEY and the boggy plains of the LIARD R. Although the "SuperNatural" scenery of the province attracts the attention of TOURISTS and residents alike, few people are aware of the manner in which the MOUNTAINS and lowlands, RIVERS, LAKES and COASTLINE have been sculpted by natural forces.

Evolution of the Landscape

The character of a landscape depends upon both the landforms that are present and the earth materials that comprise the landforms. "Landform" refers to the shape of the land surface: valleys, steep slopes and river terraces are examples of landforms. "Earth materials" are the bedrock and younger sediments, or soils, that immediately underlie the land surface; examples are granite, sandstone, beach sand and river gravels. Thus, this account begins with geological history (or origin of the rocks), and continues with a description of how the bedrock was sculpted into its present configuration and how the younger sediments were deposited.

Fraser Plateau (southern part of Central Plateau and Mountains Region): view westward up Churn Creek near the Gang Ranch. The gentle slopes of the upland surface (distance) and thick glacial drift (foreground) have been dissected due to down-cutting by Churn Creek since the last glaciation.

Plate Tectonics and Development of Major Physiographic Regions

About 200 million years ago the part of the globe that is now BC was mostly an empty ocean. To the east, the primeval continent of Pangaea was beginning to disintegrate and the large fragment that would eventually form the ancient crystalline core of N America began to drift slowly westward. Sediments of both marine and terrestrial origin had been accumulating along the western edge of Pangaea for many millions of years. The ocean floor had gradually subsided under the weight of these deposits, resulting in the formation of a deep trough full of fossiliferous muds and oozes interlayered with sand, silt and clay. Sedimentation and subsidence continued along the leading edge of the new continent until the sediments were several thousand metres thick.

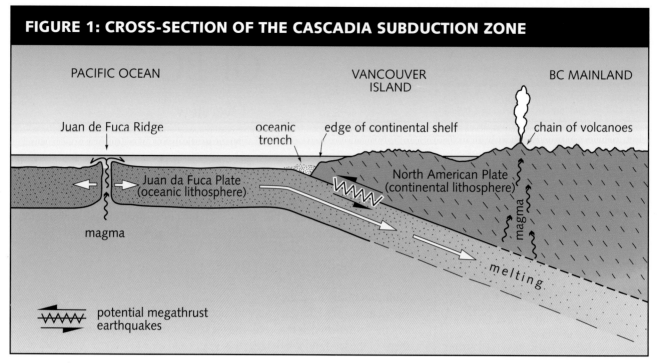

FIGURE 1: CROSS-SECTION OF THE CASCADIA SUBDUCTION ZONE

The ancient Pacific, toward which our continent was drifting, contained several smaller land masses of volcanic origin, similar perhaps to the present-day Hawaiian Islands. These islands and the adjacent shallow seas consisted of coral reefs, lagoons, beaches, deltas and marine sediments, as well as lava rocks and detrital volcanic material such as cinders and ash.

The theory of plate tectonics envisages that the outermost layer of the earth (the crust and upper mantle), the "lithosphere" (solid or rock layer), is subdivided into rigid "plates" that move independently. Where plates are pulling apart, new lithosphere is created by vulcanism. Where plates are converging, one rides up and over the other and pushes the lower plate down (subducts) toward the earth's interior, where it is eventually melted and consumed. A plate boundary of this type, known as a "subduction zone," has formed the western edge of the North American Plate for the past 200 million years (Fig 1). In effect, the continent has been riding westward over the floor

of the Pacific Ocean, inexorably shortening the distance between itself and the volcanic islands of the Pacific.

Several collisions between the oceanic land masses and the continent occurred between about 100 and 50 million years ago. Because the islands consisted of lightweight, relatively buoyant rock, they were not drawn down into the subduction zone and consumed. Instead, they remained at the earth's surface and became attached to the leading edge of the continent. As each new land mass (referred to by geologists as a "terrane") was accreted (collided with and became stuck to the edge of the continental plate), the subduction zone migrated to the new western edge of the continent. During the earliest collisions, the sediments of the previously offshore trough were trapped between the converging land masses, squeezed upward and thrust eastward until they rested on top of the western edge of the original continent. Immense pressure and extremely high temperatures were generated during the accretion of terranes

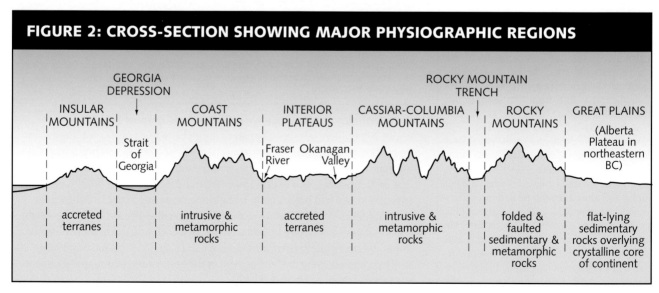

FIGURE 2: CROSS-SECTION SHOWING MAJOR PHYSIOGRAPHIC REGIONS

Nola Johnston illustrations

FIGURE 3: FAULTS, VOLCANIC BELTS AND OTHER TECTONIC FEATURES

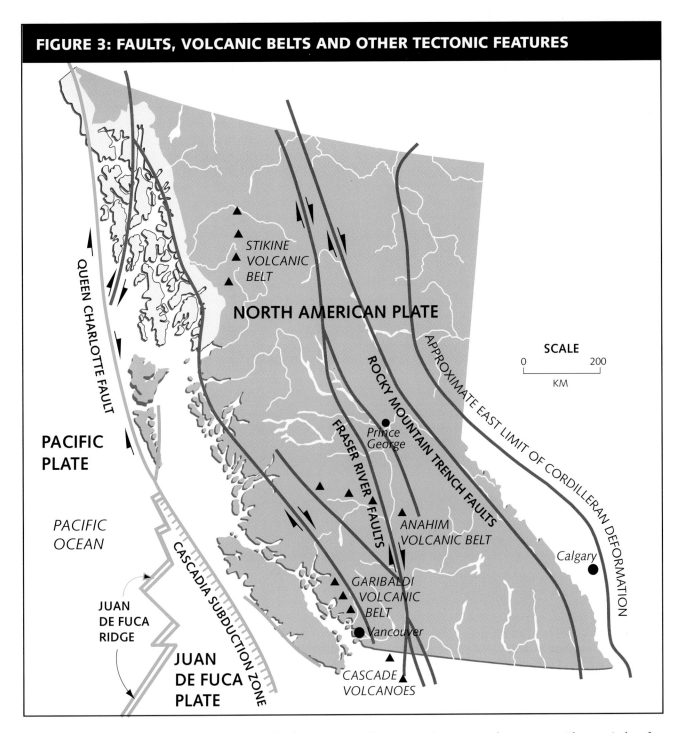

and during the upthrusting of the sedimentary trough. These resulted in the melting of some rocks and the metamorphosis (alteration by extreme heat, extreme pressure, or both) of others. Both intrusion of magma (molten rock) and metamorphism were widespread along the boundaries of major terranes, and the trough sediments were compressed and recrystallized.

Large parts of the western CORDILLERA of N America, as well as BC, were formed as a result of these tectonic processes. The Cordillera flanks the ancient crystalline core of the continent, which is exposed in the Canadian Shield and underlies most of the Great Plains, including the Canadian prairies and Mackenzie R basin. In BC the ancient core underlies the relatively flat lands of the PEACE R–FORT NELSON area; the upthrust

sedimentary rocks comprise the ROCKY MTS. The remainder of the province consists of 2 major groups of terranes, now the Interior Plateaus and the Insular Mountains (VANCOUVER ISLAND and the QUEEN CHARLOTTE ISLANDS), and two mountain belts, now the Coast Mts and the Cassiar-COLUMBIA MTS. Both mountain belts are characterized by the intrusive rocks (formerly magmas) that predominate in the boundary zones between terranes and between the most easterly terrane and the Rocky Mts (Fig 2). This complex history accounts for the great geological diversity of BC.

Faults and Earthquakes
The final phases in the geological development of BC occurred

after the accretion of terranes. Fig 3 shows the familiar north-west–southeast trend of the main physical features of the province. This is partially the result of relatively recent faulting along ruptures that trend parallel to the western edge of the continent. These developed because while the eastern margin of the Pacific Plate was being overridden by the western margin of the N American Plate, it was also moving northwestward; that is, the Pacific Plate was (and still is) rotating in a counter-clock-wise direction. This movement caused slivers of the adjacent continent to be dragged northwestward, generating several major shear zones (transverse faults) where the western side of the fault has moved northwestward relative to the eastern side. The ROCKY MT TRENCH is one such fault zone, and the Fraser Canyon (*see* FRASER R) between HOPE and LILLOOET (the boundary between the Coast and CASCADE MTS) is another (Figs 2 and 3).

No evidence has been found for geologically recent movement along the major transverse faults in eastern and central BC. However, some of the western faults are still active, giving rise to EARTHQUAKES. Tremors are relatively frequent along the Queen Charlotte Fault (Fig 3), which is the present-day boundary between the N American Plate and the Pacific Plate. The St Elias Fault is also active. To the south of the Queen Charlotte Fault, the western boundary of the N American Plate coincides roughly with the edge of the continental shelf off the west coast of Vancouver Island. This boundary is the surface expression of the Cascadia Subduction Zone that plunges down beneath Vancouver Island. Geophysical investigations indicate that this subduction zone is active, although differential movement of the 2 plates that rest against each other here has not been directly recorded. It is thought that a sudden rupture here could cause a great (megathrust) earthquake (Fig 1). Most small and moderate historical earthquakes in southwestern BC have resulted from movements within the North American and Juan de Fuca Plates.

Landform History
The geological history described above formed the framework of BC, as illustrated by the broad relations between tectonic features and the major physiographic regions shown in Fig 2. However, present-day landforms are the products of more recent earth history. In general, the largest landforms, such as plateaus and mountain ranges, have developed since about 50 million years ago (the mid-Tertiary Period); moderately sized landforms, such as coastal FJORDS, date from the GLACIATIONS of the Quaternary Period (2 million to about 12,000 years ago); smaller features, such as river terraces and canyons, have formed since then, during what is called post-glacial time.

The Upland Surface
During the Tertiary Period, there were long intervals of time during which very little upheaval resulted from the movement of the tectonic plates, and the elevations of land and sea remained relatively constant. The most significant of these quiet times, which occurred during mid-Tertiary time, lasted for several million years while erosion and deposition created an erosion surface with a few hundred metres local relief across most of BC (Fig 4a). Then, during the late Tertiary, renewed tectonic action resulted in widespread rising of the land, with uplift

being greatest in the belts that are now our main mountain ranges: the Insular, Coast, Cassiar-Columbia and Rocky mountains (Fig 4b). As uplift progressed, stream gradients were steepened, resulting in increased erosion. Narrow valleys and canyons were cut into the erosion surface, forming landscapes that range from dissected plateaus in areas of moderate uplift to steep-sided mountains where uplift was greatest (Figs 4b and 4c). Today, the products of the more gentle mid-Tertiary erosion are seen in the rolling surface of the Interior plateaus and in the remnants of gently sloping terrain that are found throughout all but the most rugged parts of the mountains. These scattered patches of upland surface are the oldest landforms in BC (Fig 4e).

Vulcanism
Episodes of volcanic activity have occurred sporadically during and since the attachment of the various terranes to the western edge of N America. In BC, a major volcanic interval during early Tertiary time resulted in emplacement of extensive lavas, known as the KAMLOOPS volcanics, in south-central BC.

Another long interval characterized by periodic eruptions of basaltic lava commenced in mid-Tertiary time. This type of magma is very fluid and so it spread widely, forming vast lava lakes. In some regions, most notably the Fraser Plateau, the mid-Tertiary erosion surface became deeply buried by layer upon layer of lava (Fig 4a), and major rivers were impounded and diverted by lava dams. These lava flows, known as the Plateau Basalts, now cap large areas of the Fraser Plateau (Fig 4c), and they commonly form the rimrock along the valleys that dissect the Plateau, such as those of the CHILCOTIN and Fraser rivers. Volcanic activity occurred sporadically for a long time after uplift and dissection of the Plateau. The most recent Plateau Basalts are only about one million years ago.

Tertiary vulcanism also resulted in the formation of some major volcanoes and numerous smaller features, and in many locations eruptions have continued to occur from time to time throughout the ensuing Quaternary Era. Three noteworthy groups of volcanoes have been studied by geologists: Anahim, STIKINE and GARIBALDI volcanic belts (Fig 3). The Anahim belt trends roughly eastward from BELLA COOLA to CLEARWATER, with the age of the volcanoes decreasing eastward. The 3 volcanic centres in the west Chilcotin area—the RAINBOW, ILGACHUZ and Itcha ranges—are the eroded remnants of large, complex volcanoes that were active about 10 million years ago in mid-Tertiary time. In contrast, most of the volcanoes farther east in WELLS GRAY PROVINCIAL PARK formed during the past 3 million years, and the youngest volcanic features here are only about 5,000 years old. The Stikine Volcanic Belt, a chain of volcanoes located along a series of north–south normal faults, is dominated by the massive composite (shield) volcano of MT EDZIZA. This ice-capped mountain is the product of repeated eruptions over the course of many millions of years. Post-glacial eruptions (since about 10,000 years ago) have formed extensive lava flows and small cinder cones on the flanks of the main structure. The well-known Nass (Tseax) lava flow near GITLAKDAMIKS, about 250 years old, is also part of the Stikine belt (*see* NISGA'A MEMORIAL LAVA BED PROVINCIAL PARK). The Garibaldi Volcanic Belt contains many well-known features, such as the BLACK TUSK, the

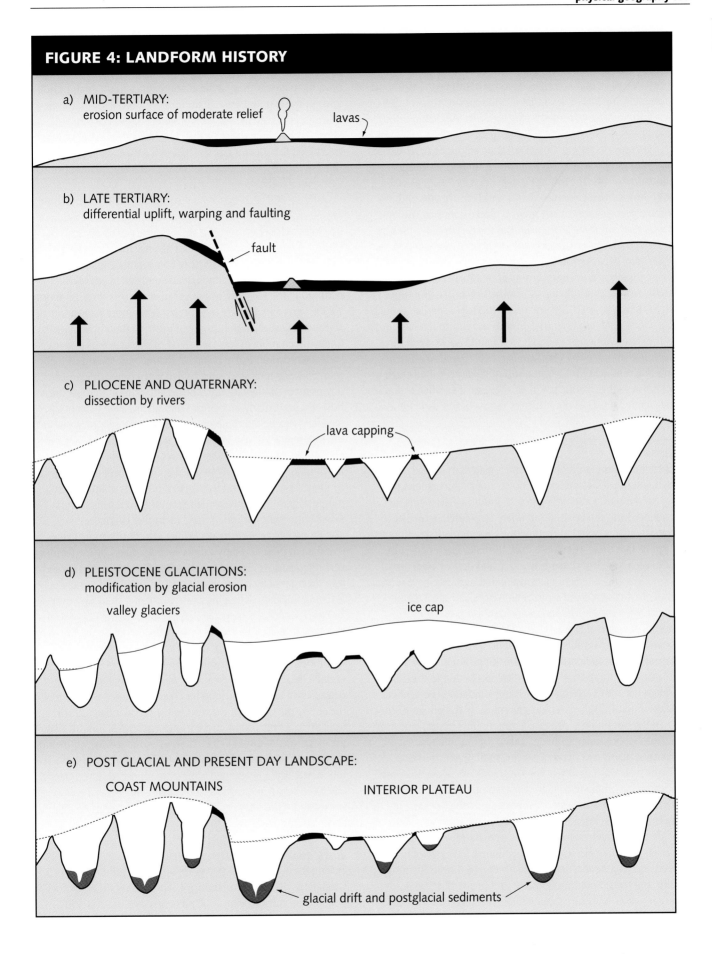

FIGURE 4: LANDFORM HISTORY

a) MID-TERTIARY:
erosion surface of moderate relief — lavas

b) LATE TERTIARY:
differential uplift, warping and faulting — fault

c) PLIOCENE AND QUATERNARY:
dissection by rivers — lava capping

d) PLEISTOCENE GLACIATIONS:
modification by glacial erosion — valley glaciers — ice cap

e) POST GLACIAL AND PRESENT DAY LANDSCAPE:
COAST MOUNTAINS — INTERIOR PLATEAU — glacial drift and postglacial sediments

P

lava flows of the CHEAKAMUS valley near BRANDYWINE FALLS and MEAGER CREEK Hot Springs. It is another north–south trending zone that extends from the upper LILLOOET R to GARIBALDI PROVINCIAL PARK and is continued to the south by the volcanoes of the Cascade Mts in Washington and Oregon. This volcanic belt is thought to be related to the Cascadia Subduction Zone (Fig 1).

On many occasions, violent volcanic eruptions have released vast plumes of volcanic ash that covered thousands of square kilometres of BC. The ash layers deposited by 3 post-glacial eruptions are well preserved in bog and lake deposits and in some places a veneer of ash rests on glacial deposits. The most widespread ash layer originated from the cataclysmic eruption of Mt Mazama (now Crater Lake) in Oregon about 7,000 years ago. Today it can be found throughout much of southern BC, where it ranges in thickness from about 1 to 10 cm; it extends northeastward into Alberta and Saskatchewan. An eruption of Mt St Helens about 3,200 years ago produced a similar, though less widespread, ash layer that extends north through Kamloops to the vicinity of Clearwater. The third and youngest ash layer, deposited about 2,400 years ago, has been traced to a small volcanic vent near Mt Meager north of PEMBERTON (although it is known as the "BRIDGE RIVER" ash because it was first found in the vicinity of that river). A narrow plume of this ash extends eastward to beyond the Rocky Mts.

Glaciation

During the past 2 million years (the Quaternary Period), most high latitude areas have experienced CLIMATE fluctuations that have given rise to alternating glacial and non-glacial episodes. Evidence from the ocean floor, where a complete record of climate change is stored in continuously accumulating sediments, suggests that there were more than 12 major glaciations. On land, each ice advance tends to erode and destroy evidence of its predecessor, so it is not surprising that in BC we have found evidence, in the form of sedimentary layers, of only 3 major glacial episodes. The sediments and landforms of the most recent cool interval (Fraser Glaciation) are well preserved, and wood and other organic material found within the glacial deposits can be radiocarbon-dated. Thus geologists have been able to carry out relatively detailed reconstruction of the timing and events of this interval. Only Fraser Glaciation is described below, but it is likely that older glaciations had a similar history.

At the beginning of Fraser Glaciation, the physical landscape was probably similar to that of today, with mountains, plateaus, plains and rivers occupying their present positions (Fig 4c). About 30,000 years ago, a gradual increase in snowfall, possibly in combination with cooler summers, caused snow-fields and glaciers to begin expanding in the higher parts of the mountains (Fig 5a). For about 10,000 years, as the snowline gradually descended, snow patches were transformed into small glaciers and slow glacier growth continued. Valley glaciers thickened and lengthened, and eventually emerged from the mountains and spread out onto plateaus and plains (Fig 5b). A minor glacier recession about 22,000 years ago was succeeded by renewed and more rapid glacier expansion and thickening. Eventually the ice level rose so high that all but the highest peaks in the mountains were buried and an unbroken ice sheet

extended over plateaus and plains (Fig 5c). This "Cordilleran Ice Sheet" reached its maximum thickness and extent about 15,000 years ago (Figs 5d and 6). In the Interior, the ice spread onto the plateaus from accumulation zones in the high mountains to the east and west, then moved toward gaps in the surrounding mountains, such as the valleys of the Peace, Liard, SKEENA and Stikine rivers. At this time, the Cordilleran Ice Sheet resembled the present-day Greenland ice sheet, with glaciers flowing through mountains to the sea (or to the plains) from a vast central icefield.

After 15,000 years ago, relatively rapid climate amelioration caused rapid shrinking, thinning and disintegration of the Cordilleran Ice Sheet (Figs 5d and 5e). The site of VANCOUVER became ice-free about 13,000 years ago. Ice had disappeared from the southern Interior Plateau and southern valleys by about 11,000 years ago, although a short-lived re-advance occurred in the Lower FRASER VALLEY at about this time. By about 10,000 years ago, glaciers were probably no more extensive than at present. Deglaciation in some of the mountain belts appears to have been more or less the reverse of glacier advance: glacier snouts receded up-valley as the ice shrank back toward its high sources, while meltwater streams deposited outwash gravels downstream on the recently exposed valley floor. In other areas, however, particularly on plateaus and plains, large parts of the ice sheet became disconnected from the accumulation zones in the mountains by high ground that was exposed as the ice melted (Figs 5d and e). These large masses of stagnant (no longer flowing) ice melted slowly in place, gradually becoming covered by melted-out debris and leaving behind tracts of hummocky moraine, gravelly meltwater deposits, and landforms such as eskers (sinuous gravel ridges) and meltwater channels.

During deglaciation, water bodies were much more extensive than at present. Many valleys were dammed by ice, forming very long, narrow glacial lakes (Fig 5e). Fine sediments carried into these lakes by meltwater streams accumulated rapidly, reaching thicknesses ranging from less than 1 m to well over 100 m. Terraces and irregular benchlands underlain by glacial lake silts and clays are prominent features of many Interior valleys, such as the Okanagan, the South THOMPSON Valley near Kamloops, and the Fraser and NECHAKO valleys near PRINCE GEORGE. Along the coast, sea level was relatively high during deglaciation because the land had been depressed relative to the sea by the weight of the ice. On the mainland coast, sea level up to about 200 m above its present level is indicated by the elevations of raised deltas. Glacio-marine sediments, including clay, silt, and stony deposits, accumulated in areas that were inundated. The fine-grained sediments deposited in the glacial lakes and ocean are highly susceptible to erosion and LAND-SLIDES, and today they cause numerous problems for engineers and planners.

Post-glacial Landscape Development

During the 10,000 to 12,000 years since the end of Fraser Glaciation, the glaciated landscape has been modified by rock weathering, gravitational slope processes, and erosion and deposition by streams, waves, and wind (Fig 4e). The results of weathering and slope movements are most apparent in the high mountains and on steep valley sides within the dissected

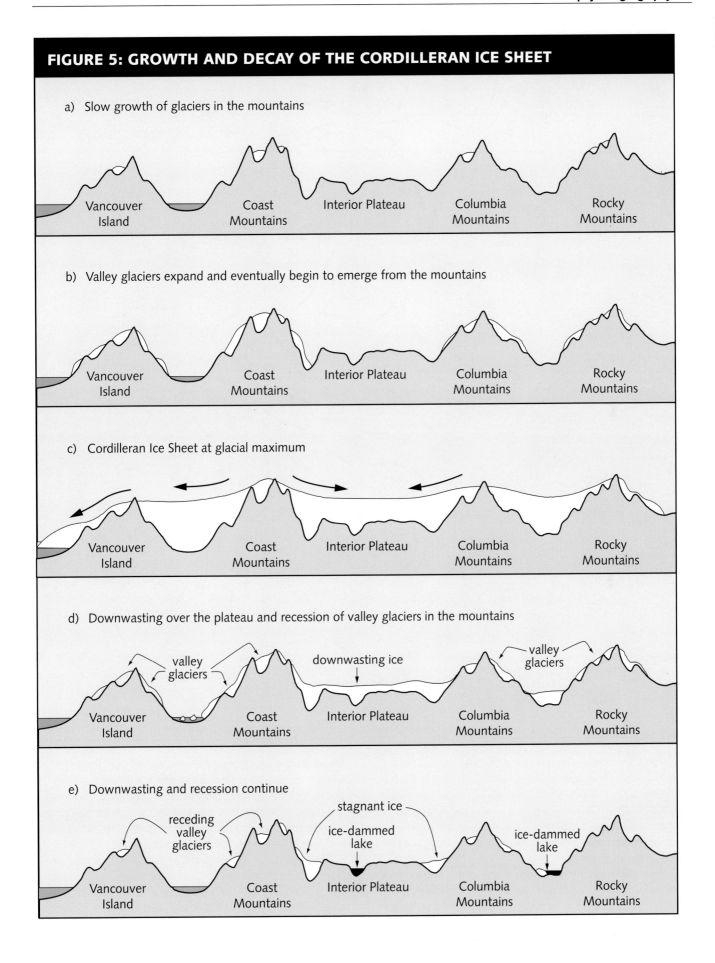

FIGURE 5: GROWTH AND DECAY OF THE CORDILLERAN ICE SHEET

a) Slow growth of glaciers in the mountains

Vancouver Island • Coast Mountains • Interior Plateau • Columbia Mountains • Rocky Mountains

b) Valley glaciers expand and eventually begin to emerge from the mountains

Vancouver Island • Coast Mountains • Interior Plateau • Columbia Mountains • Rocky Mountains

c) Cordilleran Ice Sheet at glacial maximum

Vancouver Island • Coast Mountains • Interior Plateau • Columbia Mountains • Rocky Mountains

d) Downwasting over the plateau and recession of valley glaciers in the mountains

valley glaciers • downwasting ice • valley glaciers

Vancouver Island • Coast Mountains • Interior Plateau • Columbia Mountains • Rocky Mountains

e) Downwasting and recession continue

receding valley glaciers • stagnant ice • ice-dammed lake • ice-dammed lake

Vancouver Island • Coast Mountains • Interior Plateau • Columbia Mountains • Rocky Mountains

FIGURE 6: CORDILLERAN ICE SHEET

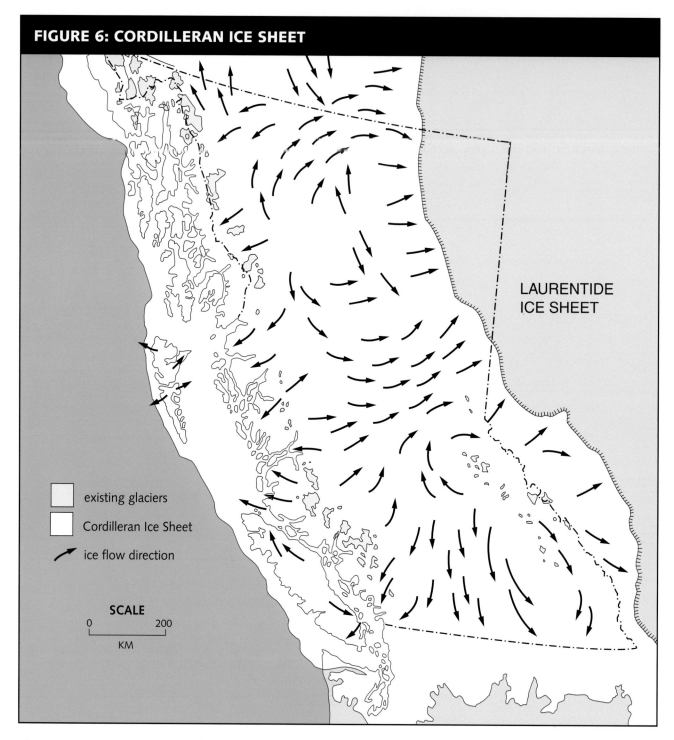

LAURENTIDE
ICE SHEET

existing glaciers

Cordilleran Ice Sheet

ice flow direction

SCALE

0   200

KM

plateaus. Steep slopes have been modified by rockfall, land-slides, debris flows and snow AVALANCHES, resulting in the formation of talus slopes, debris cones and fans, and hummocky landslide debris. Terrace scarps and canyon walls alongside streams that have eroded into glacial materials are commonly unstable, especially where soils are wet and where glacial lake sediments are present.

Post-glacial landforms are also very evident along the floors of major valleys, where rivers have either eroded sideways to form broad floodplains, or cut down into glacial deposits and bedrock, forming river terraces and canyons. Similar but smaller fluvial (related to streams and rivers) landforms can be found along most tributary streams. Alluvial fans, formed where streams emerge from the mountains onto flat terrain, and river deltas are commonly the sites of modern settlement and industry because they may provide the only level or gently sloping, relatively dry land in rugged terrain. Many deltas are also sites of considerable ecological significance.

The importance of post-glacial aeolian (wind) erosion and deposition to present-day land use is far greater than its visible effects would suggest. The wind picks up small sand and silt particles from unvegetated sites, such as floodplains and steep bluffs, and re-deposits them nearby, resulting in the slow accumulation of a layer of loamy, stone-free soil. The effects of this

FIGURE 7: PHYSIOGRAPHIC REGIONS

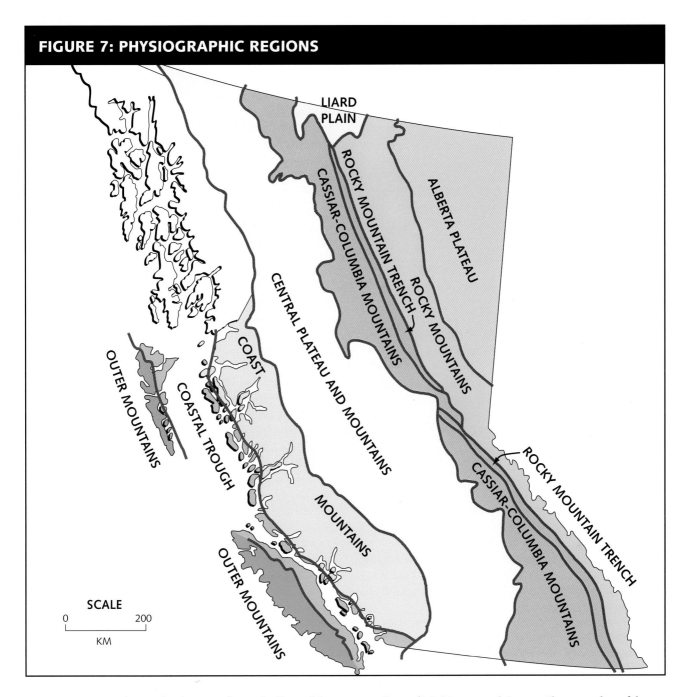

process are most evident in the dry, sparsely treed valleys of the southern Interior, such as the Thompson, Fraser and Okanagan valleys and the Rocky Mt Trench, where the wind-deposited veneer is typically about 1 m thick. This is the basis of the relatively high agricultural capability of these lands. Without the aeolian veneer, soils derived from underlying glacial deposits or river gravels would be exceedingly stony and hard to cultivate. Sand dunes, the more familiar result of wind deposition, are not extensive in BC, but good examples of coastal dunes can be seen at LONG BEACH, and there are cliff-top dunes at FARWELL CANYON near WILLIAMS LAKE and WALHACHIN near CACHE CREEK.

Most of the BC coast is rocky and resistant to wave attack. This, combined with relatively short exposure to wave action (the shoreline has been at its present position for only about 8,000 years), explains the general rarity of landforms such as sea stacks, arches and caves when compared to the unglaciated coastlines of Washington and Oregon. Short stretches of the coast coincide with glacial deposits, which are relatively weak and susceptible to wave erosion. For example, the steep bluffs at Long Beach have been cut into glacial drift, and the sands and gravels recycled to form the beach. Extensive beaches along the east coast of Vancouver Island between NANAIMO and COURTENAY are also backed by glacial materials.

Despite the effects of weathering, slope processes, streams, wind and waves, there are large parts of BC that remain today much the same as they were immediately after they emerged from beneath the ice at the end of Fraser Glaciation. These are areas of low relief and gentle gradients, such as the upland surface of the Interior plateaus, some plains and lowlands, and some broad valley floors. The relict glacial landscape is best seen where it is not hidden by the forest cover, such as in the dry GRASSLANDS of the central and southern Interior. In such places, the casual observer can see signs of post-glacial alteration of till plains, drumlins (streamlined hills of till), eskers and meltwater channels, and even the details of the glacial landscape, such as annual moraines and tiny meltwater channels only 1–2 m high or deep. The volcanic ash layers noted above can also be identified within the soils on the upland surface in south-central BC.

The Physical Landscapes

A diverse array of physical landscapes has resulted from the combined effects of geological framework and landform evolution described above. Areas of similar geology, topography and landform history, known as physiographic regions, are shown in Fig 7.

Mountain Landscapes

The spectacular scenery of the main mountain belts—the Insular, Coast, Cassiar–Columbia and Rocky mountains—is dominated by landforms of glacial erosion: horns and serrated ridges, cirques and glacial troughs with hanging tributary valleys. However, some other aspects of the landscape that derive from the characteristics of the underlying bedrock vary from one mountain region to another. For example, the prominent layering in the sedimentary and meta-sedimentary rocks of the Rocky Mts creates visual details that are quite dissimilar to the more massive, intrusive rocks of the Coast Mts. Some of these sedimentary rocks are also much more susceptible to weathering and disintegration than intrusive rocks, and so slopes covered with rocky debris tend to be relatively extensive in the Rockies.

Present-day snowline rises gradually eastward across the province, and glaciers are part of the mountain landscapes where substantial areas lie above an elevation limit that rises from about 1,700 m on Vancouver Island to about 2,600 m in the Rockies. Glaciers were larger than they are at present during the Little Ice Age of the 17th and 18th centuries, and sparsely vegetated end moraines and outwash plains mark their former extent and recent recession.

Historically the mountain belts have hindered east–west transportation and travel across BC. Even today the influence of the topography is still very evident from a brief glance at the provincial road map, where, for example, the road distance from Vancouver to TRAIL is 628 km as compared to a straight flight path of 400 km. Even where low-elevation passes were utilized, road and rail construction encountered extreme difficulties on steep and unstable slopes, and temporary blockages due to landslides, floods and snow avalanches can still have considerable economic and social impacts. Within the mountains, tens of thousands of kilometres of gravel roads have been constructed to provide access for the LOGGING and MINING industries, and more recently for recreation and tourism. The cost of constructing and maintaining these ROADS is high, as are the costs of identifying and avoiding adverse environmental effects related both to roads and other industrial activities. Attractive mountain scenery of soaring peaks and snowfields is one of the main provincial assets that has allowed development of a significant tourist industry. Backcountry travel attracts both visitors and local residents. As the number of people in the mountains grows, the hazards posed by natural processes, such

as debris flows and floods, are of increasing concern. The greatest danger comes from snow avalanches, which are taking a growing toll of human lives.

Plateau Landscapes

The broad belt of Interior plateaus that extends from the Yukon to the 49th parallel (and beyond) includes level to gently sloping uplands that have undergone various degrees of dissection. For example, broad areas of upland surface in the Chilcotin (western) part of the Fraser Plateau are uninterrupted by deep valleys. By way of contrast, the Thompson Plateau has been segmented by the deep valleys of the Thompson and Okanagan rivers and their tributaries. In physiographic regions that are termed "highlands," such as the Shuswap Highland, dissection is so severe that a large proportion of the area is occupied by steep valley sides. The plateaus also include some areas of greater local relief: hilly areas that were not levelled by Tertiary erosion and the volcanic structures described above.

As mentioned earlier, the variously dissected plateaus existed prior to the onset of Quaternary glaciations. Ice movement across the plateaus resulted in the formation of many landforms that record ice-flow directions (Fig 6), such as drumlins and glacial grooves. Where ice-flow direction coincided with the trend of plateau valleys, the valleys were deepened and widened by glacial erosion. For example, southerly flowing ice in the Okanagan Valley eroded its rocky floor to depths below present sea level. Where ice flowed across the valleys—for example, the east–west section of the Thompson River valley between Cache Creek and MONTE CREEK—the valleys were filled with ice but erosion was much less severe. Ice recession at the end of Fraser Glaciation uncovered extensive till plains and streamlined landforms, and smaller areas of hummocky (stagnant ice) moraine, meltwater deposits and glacial lake sediments. In parts of the northern plateaus, where present and past snowlines are lower than farther south, cirques (and small glaciers at the highest elevations) are common on steep, north-facing slopes, but their headwalls rise up to the level brow of the plateau and glacial horns are absent.

The plateau valleys are typically bounded by steep side-slopes that are separated from the upland surface by a sharp slope break. In the broader valleys, such as the Thompson, Fraser and Stikine, terraces and undulating benchlands underlain by outwash deposits and glacial lake sediments dominate at intermediate elevations, and post-glacial river terraces, alluvial fans and floodplains form the valley floors. Large lakes presently occupy basins formed by glacial erosion and many smaller lakes are impounded by dams of glacial or post-glacial deposits, such as raised deltas and debris flow fans.

Settlement, transportation routes and industry are concentrated in the main valleys of the plateaus. In many places, steep valley sides or deep gullies must be traversed in order to gain access to the benign terrain of the upland surface, so road construction for FORESTRY, mining and the OIL AND GAS INDUSTRY is commonly subject to difficulties similar to those of mountainous terrain. Even within the valleys, geotechnical construction problems arise here and there where terraces are interrupted by deep gullies or erosional scarps alongside the rivers and where glacial deposits and weak volcanic rocks are prone to landslides. Agricultural areas are extensive on level and gently sloping terrain, especially where aeolian soils and glacial lake sediments provide stone-free soils, and where water for irrigation is available in the drier more southern valleys.

The Landscapes of Plains and Lowlands

Relatively small areas of subdued topography, such as the Fraser Basin and the Georgia Depression, are distributed across the province (Fig 7). Most are low-lying because they were least affected by the tectonic uplift that elevated their surroundings. Also, during glaciations, ice tended to converge into these depressions and flow more rapidly there, resulting in increased glacial erosion. In general, these areas are underlain by relatively thick glacial deposits and large rivers flow though them. But all have distinctive individual characteristics.

The Georgia Depression, which lies between Vancouver Island and the mainland and includes the Greater Vancouver area and the Lower Fraser Valley, consists chiefly of narrow coastal plains. Many of these are underlain by remnants of an extensive outwash plain that developed in front of glaciers advancing into the STRAIT OF GEORGIA during the early phase of Fraser Glaciation. The outwash sands can be seen in the sea cliffs at Point Grey, Cowichan Head and near COMOX. At the end of Fraser Glaciation, much of the coastal area was submerged for up to about 3,000 years and covered by marine sediments. During post-glacial time, the Fraser R has formed a broad floodplain and delta. Today, many urban and industrial structures are built on the fine-grained marine deposits and on the deltas of the Fraser and other rivers. Sand and gravel for urban and industrial development is obtained primarily from glacial outwash deposits and from raised deltas along the coast.

The largest area of relatively low relief, northeastern BC, lies east of the Cordillera within the Great Plains physiographic region. It is underlain by flat-lying sedimentary rocks (sandstone, shale) that consist chiefly of detritus that was washed eastward from the young Rocky Mts. These rest upon the crystalline rocks of the old continental core. In general, the higher parts of this region (Alberta Plateau) are underlain by sandstone and the lower lying areas are underlain by shale (Fort Nelson Lowland). The boundary between upland and lowland is a prominent cliff of sandstone. During glaciation, much of this area was covered by the great continental (Laurentide) ice sheet that covered all of central and eastern Canada. Cordilleran ice extended for only a short distance east of the Rockies. At the end of the last glaciation, a large glacial lake occupied the Peace R area because drainage was blocked downstream by Laurentide ice. Many present-day rivers occupy steep-sided valleys cut down through glacial deposits and the underlying sedimentary rocks. Large landslides are common along the valley walls.

Perhaps the most distinctive physical features of the Fraser Basin (e.g., Prince George Lowland) are the numerous drumlins that were formed underneath ice flowing northeastward toward the Peace R gap in the Rocky Mts (Fig 6) and the extensive glacial lake deposits. The lowland around Prince George was occupied by a large glacial lake because southerly drainage (Fraser R) was dammed by ice near QUESNEL. Some drumlins were islands in the glacial lake, while others were inundated

and covered by a layer of clayey lake sediment. The glacial lake sediments can be seen in the city of Prince George in the bluffs alongside the Fraser and Nechako rivers.

The Liard Plain is also underlain by thick glacial sediments, and landforms created by the melting of stagnant ice are common. Numerous low-lying areas are poorly drained, and organic soils with discontinuous permafrost are widespread. In contrast to other lowlands and plains, large parts of the Nass Basin consist of streamlined rocky hills, although glacial deposits are still common. The Rocky Mt Trench, a remarkably continuous,

Boundary Ranges (northern Coast Mts): view westward toward the Alaska Boundary (skyline) and Flood Glacier. The glacier holds back a lake in a tributary valley (behind the forested ridge, left middle-distance), but the lake water periodically spills out from beneath the glacier and drains through the channels visible in the foreground. Glacier outburst floods such as this are a serious, although rare, hazard in parts of the Coast Mts. GSC photo 1998-032

structurally controlled valley (Figs 2 and 3) lying between the Rocky Mts and Cassiar–Columbia Mts, extends the entire length of the province, about 1,350 km. It contains the headwaters of 4 major rivers (Liard, Peace, Fraser and Columbia) and 2 major reservoirs (WILLISTON and KINBASKET). The Trench floor is characterized by thick glacial deposits and broad floodplains.

Summary

BC consists of diverse physiographic regions that share a broadly similar history of tectonics and glaciation but differ considerably in detail. Geological contrasts have resulted from the amalgamation of terranes from various sources, along with sedimentation at continental margins, vulcanism and intrusion of magma. Topographic contrasts have resulted from differential uplift and erosion. Glaciation was sufficiently recent that its effects are still clearly expressed in present-day landscapes: glaciated mountains with sharp crests, horns and ridges, steep-sided cirques, troughs and hanging valleys rising above ice-scoured plains, and plateaus discontinuously veneered by glacial drift. During the short post-glacial interval, steep slopes have been modified to varying extents by gravitational processes ranging from massive landslides to soil creep. Some streams have cut down into their valley floors, resulting in landforms such as canyons and river terraces, while others have created floodplains, alluvial fans and deltas.

Reading: Stuart S. Holland, *Landforms of British Columbia*, 1964; and C.J. Yorath, *Where Terranes Collide*, 1990.

PINCHI LAKE, 135 km northwest of PRINCE GEORGE, is in the traditional territory of the Tl'azt'en, a DAKELH (Carrier) subgroup. There are 4 Tl'azt'en villages (total pop 1,500): Pinchi (Binche) and Tachie (Tache) are on Stuart Lk (Nak'al Bun); Grand Rapids (K'uzche) is on the Tachie R; and MIDDLE RIVER (Dzitl'ainli) is on Trembleur Lk (Dzingha Bun). A cultural festival is held in August. Commercial FISHING, LOGGING and TOURISM support the local economy. *See also* LAKES.

PINE, one of the most commercially significant timber species, occurs in BC in 5 species. Three species are white, softwood pines. Western white pine (*Pinus monticola*), first identified by the pioneer naturalist David DOUGLAS, grows in wet FORESTS on the South Coast and in the southern Interior. Its distinctive, slightly curved cones are the largest of all the pines. It produces lumber used extensively in construction. Whitebark pine (*Pinus albicaulis*) has little commercial importance. It occurs in southern BC on exposed slopes at higher altitudes and can be quite stunted in size. Limber pine (*Pinus flexilis*) is a small, shrub-like tree found only in the southern ROCKY MTS. Two species are yellow, or hardwood, pines. Ponderosa pine (*Pinus ponderosa*) inhabits the southern Interior, where it is well suited to high-temperature, low-moisture locales. Lodgepole pine (*Pinus contorta*) is the most widespread tree in the province. It occurs in 2 varieties: a short, crooked type, also known as shore pine, inhabiting a narrow band along the coast; and a tall, slender type found throughout the Interior. The Interior variant has been used for construction, pulp stock, telegraph poles and railway ties. FIRST NATIONS people used it to make supports for their winter lodges. Forests of lodgepole pine are susceptible to infestations of the mountain pine

Lodgepole pine.
© *T.C. Brayshaw*

beetle (*Dendroctonus ponderosae*). Beetles bore into the trees to lay their eggs and also encourage the spread of fungal infections, destroying vast stretches of forest. Infestation has led to extensive clearcutting throughout the Interior, especially in the CHILCOTIN area.

PINE PASS (el 933 m), the portal to the PEACE R country, is a route through the Hart Ranges of the ROCKY MTS 100 km west of CHETWYND. Located by the railway surveyor Joseph Hunter in 1877, it was at one time considered a possible route through the mountains for the CPR. It is the most northerly, and the lowest, of the highway passes through the Rockies and also carries the BC RAIL main line into the Peace district. The Pine R is a major tributary of the Peace. Bijoux Falls Provincial PARK is located adjacent to the highway at the pass and features a 40-m WATERFALL.

PINK MOUNTAIN, 135 km northwest of FORT ST JOHN, is a roadside settlement at Historic Mile 143 of the ALASKA HWY. There are a number of TOURISM facilities here and some good FISHING and hiking nearby. Several large ranches (*see* CATTLE INDUSTRY) are located to the south. The name comes from the colour of rocks in the vicinity.

AS

PIONEER was a company town associated with the Pioneer GOLD mine on Cadwallader Crk, a tributary of the BRIDGE R, about 160 km north of VANCOUVER in the COAST MTS. The first claim was staked in 1897 and after a number of false starts became a successful operation under David Sloan, a MINING engineer who took charge in 1924. The Pioneer mine, which merged with the adjoining BRALORNE mine in 1959 and closed in 1961, yielded 36.5 tonnes of gold. The townsite was abandoned in the 1970s.

PIONEER LINE of PADDLEWHEEL STEAMBOATS was founded in 1862 by William IRVING and was carried on after his death in 1872 by his son John IRVING. The company's main business was running a regular service between NEW WESTMINSTER and YALE on the FRASER R, though it did

branch out to the STIKINE R with little success in 1874–75. It was especially profitable transporting materials to Yale for construction of the CPR line in the early 1880s. In 1883 it merged with the HBC fleet of steamers running between VICTORIA and New Westminster to form the CANADIAN PACIFIC NAVIGATION CO.

PIPELINES carry oil and natural gas from the fuel-producing northeast corner of BC and from Alberta to populated areas in the central and southern Interior of BC and the Lower Mainland. BC has about 24,570 km of pipeline. Since 1953 TRANS MOUNTAIN PIPE LINE CO LTD has been bringing Alberta oil to southern BC via KAMLOOPS. The first natural gas line was completed in 1957 by Westcoast Transmission (*see* WESTCOAST ENERGY INC) to supply gas from its PEACE R fields to customers in VANCOUVER and the neighbouring US. It has since been extended north to FORT NELSON, west to PRINCE RUPERT and to the SUNSHINE COAST and VANCOUVER ISLAND. *See also* OIL & GAS INDUSTRY.

PIPIT is a SPARROW-sized bird with a slender bill; it feeds on INSECTS and seeds in open fields. The American pipit (*Anthus rubescens*) breeds throughout the province in alpine habitats, with the highest numbers found in the southern Interior MOUNTAINS and the northern boreal mountains. It is not known to nest on VANCOUVER ISLAND or the QUEEN CHARLOTTE ISLANDS. In winter it can be found as low as sea level and it is most numerous on BC's southwest coast, including southeast Vancouver Island. Sprague's pipit breeds on the great plains from Alberta to Manitoba and into the US, but in BC it has been sighted only in a small area in the central Interior, southwest of WILLIAMS LAKE. *Kim Goldberg*

PITKA, John, Estonian pioneer (b 19 Feb 1872, Jalgsemaa, Estonia; d 1944). A hero in the Estonian War of Independence in 1918–19, he was appointed rear admiral of the Estonian navy and knighted by the British for services as an ally against the Russian Bolshevik regime. In 1924 he came to BC with his wife Helene, 4 of their children and 10 other people. They settled on the south shore of Stuart Lk near FORT ST JAMES and attempted to establish a colony. Pitka, his wife and some of their children became Canadian citizens. But he found it impossible to earn a living in such an isolated location and returned to Estonia in 1930. By 1932 all the other settlers had followed and the colony was abandoned. During WWII Pitka and his 3 sons were arrested by the occupying Russian forces and never seen again. Lady Pitka and her daughters came back to BC in 1949 and settled in VANCOUVER.

PITT ISLAND, 1,373 km², is the 5th largest island on the BC coast. Lying just south of the mouth of the SKEENA R on the North Coast, it is divided from the mainland by the narrow GRENVILLE CHANNEL. A steady stream of boats and ships pass the island on their way through the channel, which is part of the INSIDE PASSAGE navigation route. Named by Capt George VANCOUVER

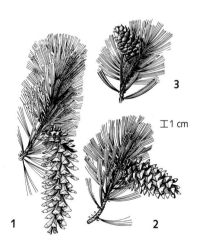

Western white pine (1), limber pine (2), whitebark pine (3). © *T.C. Brayshaw*

Ponderosa pine (1), lodgepole pine (2), shore pine (3). © *T.C. Brayshaw*

for the famous British prime minister, the island is mountainous, wild and uninhabited, though people of the TSIMSHIAN First Nation have long used its shores for food gathering.

PITT LAKE, 53.8 km² and 28 km long, is a widening of the Pitt R, which drains south from GARIBALDI PROVINCIAL PARK through the lake before emptying into the FRASER R near PORT COQUITLAM east of VANCOUVER. The lake, probably named for British Prime Minister William Pitt the Younger, is surrounded by rugged wilderness, which was logged extensively earlier in the century. Accessible by road only at the south

Canoeing on Pitt Lk. Len Mackave photo

end, where there is a managed habitat for waterfowl and other birds, Widgeon Slough, it is bordered on the east by GOLDEN EARS PROVINCIAL PARK and on the west by Pinecone Burke Provincial Park. By the late 1990s LOGGING was still going on in the Upper Pitt Valley.

PITT MEADOWS, district municipality, pop 13,436, occupies the north bank of the FRASER R 30 km east of VANCOUVER. First known as Bonson's Landing, it took its present name from  the Pitt R, its western border, which was probably named for the British Prime Minister William Pitt the Younger. The original inhabitants belonged to the KATZIE Nation of the STO:LO people; their descendants still live on 5 RESERVES in the district and make their living mostly from commercial FISHING. AGRICULTURAL settlement began in the 1870s and CRANBERRIES, blueberries and DAIRY FARMING have continued to be important, along with turf farms, feed lots, nurseries and greenhouses. Many FRENCH CANADIAN and JAPANESE settlers arrived after 1910. Following WWII, DUTCH immigrants reclaimed a large area

of lowlands known as PITT POLDER. Most of the district is rural, with a commercial belt concentrated along the Lougheed Hwy, though many residential subdivisions have appeared since 1990. The FOREST INDUSTRY has also been important and there is a sprinkling of light industry and an AIRPORT. Originally united with MAPLE RIDGE, Pitt Meadows was incorporated separately on 24 Apr 1914.

PITT POLDER, south of PITT LK in the FRASER VALLEY, was the site of an ambitious reclamation project following WWII. Dr Jan Blom purchased 27 km² of marshy lowland on the east bank of the Pitt R used mainly for DUCK hunting and in 1950 formed Pitt Polder Ltd, with capital raised in Holland and locally from the KOERNER family. The company drained and diked the land and sold or leased it to DUTCH immigrant farmers. The area was well suited to dairying and the project was a great success (*see* AGRICULTURE; DAIRY FARMING). There is also an important waterfowl refuge in the area. In Dutch, *polder* means "reclaimed land."

PITTS, Arthur David John, artist (b 1889, London, England; d 1972, Saanich). After leaving school at age 14, he apprenticed as a commercial artist and worked on railway construction in S Africa, then came to Canada in 1914. He was living in VANCOUVER when WWI began, and he enlisted in the Canadian army and spent a year at the front before his arms were shattered by a shell; in 1917 he returned to BC to convalesce. Afterward, while working as a commercial artist in Vancouver, he developed his interest in chronicling FIRST NATIONS culture and made many trips to aboriginal communities. He and his wife lived on her family property in SAANICH from 1933 to 1935 while Pitts worked on a collection of paintings known as his Indian Collection. In 1935 he went to England, where he succeeded as a cartoonist. He returned to BC in 1947 and lived the rest of his life here. The 77 paintings in his Indian

Collection are now divided between the Provincial Archives of BC and the Glenbow Museum in Calgary.

PLANETARIUM; *see* MACMILLAN, H.R., SPACE CENTRE

PLANTS, NATIVE, including trees, shrubs, herbs and grasses, FERNS, MOSSES, liverworts, lichens and fungi, number over 15,000 species in BC. These include an estimated 2,073 vascular plants, about 1,000 bryophytes (mosses and liverworts), 1,600 lichens, 522 species of algae and over 10,000 species of fungi. Some of these plants are huge, such as giant Sitka SPRUCE, western red CEDAR and DOUGLAS FIR (*see also* TREES, GIANT; FORESTS), while others are practically microscopic and are more easily seen when many grow in one location, such as some mosses and lichens. Some of the native plant species in BC are truly ancient—coastal RAIN FORESTS have existed for about 2 million years and contain species that evolved 70 million years ago—and some species have only been here for a few thousand years, having moved northward because of the warmer CLIMATE since the last GLACIATION ended about 10,000 years ago. Remnants of these ancient forests contain trees that are over 1,500 years old. In BC, 595 native vascular plant species, close to 30% of the total, are considered to be at risk (*see* ENDANGERED SPECIES).

Pacific dogwood. Roy Luckow photo

Since the dawn of time, societies have used native plants for sustenance and cultural and economic purposes. In many cases, as in BC, the plants and their uses have in large part helped define a culture. BC's aboriginal inhabitants relied on at least 200 species of native plants for a variety of food, medicinal, ceremonial and technological uses. Depending on the season, they used virtually all parts of various food plants: in spring, the bulbs and shoots; in summer and fall, the flowers, nuts and seeds; and in winter and early spring, the roots. BERRIES were eaten fresh and dried, or mixed with the flesh of fish and other animals to help preserve them, add flavour and increase nutritional content.

Oregon grape. *Dean van't Schip photo*

Wild rhododendron. *Roy Luckow photo*

Skunk cabbage. *Roy Luckow photo*

Western red cedar was one of the principal plants used by coastal people for building and for making clothing, boxes, baskets, CANOES and TOTEM POLES. While LOGGING is the principal use of native trees today, some are gaining a reputation as a source for medicines, such as the cancer drug

Salmonberry. *Rick Blacklaws photo*

taxol, which is derived from YEW. There is a burgeoning industry in picking native MUSHROOMS (fungi), although this practice may turn out to be harmful to the ecosystems in which they grow. SALAL is another native plant that has been harvested commercially by florists for enhancing floral bouquets.

Wildlife populations in BC also depend completely on native plants, since these are the species alongside which they have evolved. When the ecosystems that support native plants are altered or lost, so too are the animal species that depend on them. An example is the dwindling population of mountain CARIBOU in the KOOTENAY region: clearcut logging from valley bottom to mid-elevation into the subalpine there has altered the ecosystems in which arboreal lichens thrive, and arboreal lichens are practically the only food source for mountain caribou throughout 7–8 months of winter conditions. *See also* BIODIVERSITY.   *Maggie Paquet*

PLASKETT, John Stanley, astronomer (b 17 Nov 1865, Hickson, ON; d 17 Oct 1941, Esquimalt). Educated at the Univ of Toronto, he was one of the original staff when the Dominion Observatory was formed in Ottawa in 1903. He became an expert in spectroscopy and pioneered research on the rotation of the Milky Way Galaxy. He successfully pressed the federal government to build a new, larger telescope and supervised construction of the 1.85-m instrument at the DOMINION ASTROPHYSICAL OBSERVATORY north of VICTORIA. He served as director of the observatory from 1917 until his retirement in 1935, and continued his research until his death.   *Chris Gainor*

PLASKETT, Joseph, artist (b 12 July 1918, New Westminster). An internationally acclaimed painter, he lives mainly in Paris and England but continues to sell most of his work in Canada and retains many contacts with his native province. After graduating from UBC in 1938, he was encouraged in his painting by friendships with Lawren HARRIS and J.W.G. MACDONALD. He studied in San Francisco and New York and in 1947–49 was principal of the Winnipeg School of Art. In 1950 he went to Paris and thereafter returned to Canada intermittently, mainly to teach. By 1957 he had settled permanently in Paris but in 1973 began spending summers in Suffolk, England. From the 1950s, when he rejected his early roots in abstract expressionism, his work displayed an individualistic figurative style combining rhythmic brushwork with close attention to detail. Although he painted portraits, he became particularly noted for complex spatial arrangements caught in reflections from windows and mirrors, and "tablescapes" of detritus from elaborate meals. His memoir *A Speaking Likeness* appeared in 1999.   *Martin Segger*

PLEASANT CAMP, 1,200 km northwest of VANCOUVER, is a customs post on the Haines Hwy between Haines, AK, and Haines Junction in the Yukon. The road borders TATSHENSHINI-ALSEK Wilderness PARK and passes through spectacular alpine country with views of the ST ELIAS MTS.   AS

PLOVER is a plump, short-necked, grey-brown and white shorebird, abundant along coastal beaches and Interior lakefronts. Plovers forage for INSECTS and small bivalves on shorelines and mudflats by running in short spurts, then tipping down to eat. Unlike the SANDPIPER, they have 3-toed feet that usually lack the hind digit; this can be seen in the tracks they leave in the sand. Of 10 species in Canada, 5 are found in BC. Black-bellied plovers (*Pluvialis squatarola*) are very common on estuarine mudflats during the winter, when they migrate from their Arctic breeding grounds. The largest number is attracted to BOUNDARY BAY. Black and white in breeding season, they turn a drab grey-brown in fall. American golden plovers (*P. dominicus*) prefer a drier habitat, including fields and pastures, while Pacific golden plovers (*P. fulva*) are rare migrants along the coast in spring and fall. In both species the name refers to the yellow speckles that dot their dark upper parts in spring and summer. Snowy plovers (*Charadrius alexandrinus*) are extremely rare spring and summer visitors to the South Coast. They are small, light-coloured birds that keep to dry sand beaches. Semipalmated plovers (*C. semipalmatus*) occur in flocks in the spring and fall as they migrate to and from their northern nesting grounds. Most abundant on the QUEEN CHARLOTTE ISLANDS, they have grey-brown and white plumage and stubby orange bills with black tips. Killdeer (*C. vociferus*) are common across the southern part of the province in summer in a variety of habitats from seashore to upland LAKES. In the winter they leave the Interior but are common on the South Coast. These noisy birds are distinguished by a double band of black around the neck and breast.

POINT ELLICE BRIDGE COLLAPSE, 26 May 1896, was the worst accident in Canadian transit history, claiming 55 lives. The bridge spanned the Gorge on the streetcar line connecting VICTORIA and ESQUIMALT. It was Victoria Day and a large crowd was heading to Esquimalt to watch a Royal Navy sail-past. At 1:40 pm the middle span of the bridge collapsed as streetcar No 16 was crossing. The vehicle spilled over with 143

Aftermath of the Point Ellice bridge collapse, 1896. BC Archives C-06135

passengers aboard and plunged into the water. Most of the fatalities were passengers; others were people who were on the bridge at the time. In the aftermath of the accident people stopped using the STREET RAILWAY and its owner, Consolidated Railway Co, went bankrupt. The following year, however, a reorganized company emerged, the BC ELECTRIC RWY CO.

POINT ELLICE HOUSE was built on Pleasant St in VICTORIA in 1861 and bought by Peter O'REILLY and his wife Caroline in 1867. The house and its lovely garden remained in the O'Reilly family for more than a century; in 1974 it became a provincial historic site, restored to the pre-WWI period. The house has a reputation for being haunted by the O'Reillys' daughter Kathleen, who lived there until 1945.

POINT ROBERTS forms the western side of BOUNDARY BAY south of TSAWWASSEN. The lower end of the point drops below the US border, a geographical fact that has not stopped British Columbians from flocking there to enjoy the sand beaches, warm water and cold beer at the infamous taverns, The Breakers and The Reef. It is named for Capt Henry Roberts, a British naval officer who served with James COOK. Roberts was supposed to have commanded the ship DISCOVERY when it was sent to survey the northwest coast in 1791. At the last minute he was given other responsibilities and George VANCOUVER sailed in his place.

POLES began coming to BC in the 1890s with the arrival in VANCOUVER of the first known immigrants, the brothers Swiecicki—Adam, Anthony, Joseph and Paul. The Swiecickis and most other Polish immigrants at the time migrated to the West Coast from eastern Canada. The Polish population grew slowly until by the 1920s there were more than 1,000. Most of them lived in the Vancouver area, where they formed the Polish Friendship Society in 1926. Immi-

gration rates remained modest until the end of WWII, when Canada began allowing displaced Europeans into the country. A small group of Poles came to the Lower Mainland at this time to work as farm labourers, settling in the FRASER VALLEY. While immigration from Poland was limited during the early years of the Cold War, Canada admitted large numbers of Poles during the 1980s and 1990s. Every Sept the Polish community in Vancouver comes together for a harvest celebration called *Dozynki*. The 1996 census recorded 102,390 people claiming Polish origin in BC. *Dianne Mackay*

POLESTAR BOOK PUBLISHERS is a literary and trade BOOK PUBLISHER founded in VICTORIA by Julian Ross in 1981. The press was based in WINLAW, near NELSON, and later in VANCOUVER.

The press was purchased by Michelle Benjamin in 1995, and in 1997 its main office returned to Victoria with a marketing branch in Vancouver. Polestar publishes children's fiction and an eclectic mix of fiction, non-fiction and poetry titles. Early in 2000 the press was bought by RAINCOAST BOOKS; under Benjamin's leadership it continued its publishing program as an imprint of Raincoast.

POLICE COMPLAINTS COMMISSIONER oversees the handling of public complaints about municipal police forces (the RCMP has its own complaint process). The office was created by the provincial government in 1998. The first commissioner was a prosecutor from VICTORIA, Don Morrison. Complaints may be filed at a police station or at the commissioner's office. The commissioner, who is independent of the police community and the ministry of the attorney general, has the power to investigate alleged breaches of a new Code of Professional Conduct Regulation applying to all municipal constables. Among other things, the Code governs deceit, neglect of duty, improper disclosures of information, corrupt practices, the use and care of firearms and off-duty conduct. *See also* POLICING. *Russ Francis*

POLICING in BC is carried out by the Royal Canadian Mounted Police under contract with the province or, in the case of 12 municipalities, by local police forces. There are about 4,500 Mounties in BC, which the force designates E Division. These include members of the Federal Force, which is responsible for federal criminal law enforcement; the Provincial Force, which polices rural areas and small communities; and the Municipal Force, which provides policing to 55 municipalities. About 70% of BC's population

BC OFFENCE STATISTICS 1989-98

	1989	1994	1998
Homicide	86	113	90
Attempted murder	104	111	109
Sex offences	5,730	5,865	4,910
Assault (non-sexual)	32,146	42,046	43,019
Robbery	3.342	5,417	5,669
Abduction	124	145	111
Break & enter	56,661	71,809	65,462
Motor vehicle theft	15,691	26,184	29,320
Theft	157,536	187,294	173,414
Fraud	13,318	15,942	13,944
Prostitution	1,076	503	506
Offensive weapons	2,624	3,539	3,697
Drug crimes	13,535	16,387	17,369
Impaired driving	14,338	11,385	9,201
Total violent crimes	41,532	53,697	53,908
Total property crimes	247,386	307,511	287,739
Total "other" crimes*	134,455	154,914	145,157
Grand total	503,505	627,511	595,451

Includes prostitution, gaming & betting, possession of offensive weapons, arson, disturbing the peace, trespassing and vandalism

is served by the RCMP, which took over provincial policing from the BC PROVINCIAL POLICE in 1950. Altogether the force has 143 detachments and (including civilians) 4,987 employees in the province. The 12 communities with their own independent police forces are Central Saanich, DELTA, ESQUIMALT, MATSQUI, NELSON, NEW WESTMINSTER, OAK BAY, PORT MOODY, SAANICH, VANCOUVER, VICTORIA and W VANCOUVER. *See also* ORGANIZED CRIME AGENCY; POLICE COMPLAINTS COMMISSIONER.

POLLEN, Peter, car dealer, politician (b 26 Oct 1927, Regina). A graduate of the Univ of Toronto, he arrived in VICTORIA in 1963 and became a successful car dealer. He joined city council as an alderman in 1969 and won election as mayor for 4 terms (1971–75; 1981–85). He was an outspoken, controversial mayor with strong views about preserving the city as a livable environment. Much of the beautification of Victoria's Inner Harbour took place during his tenure. After leaving municipal politics he served briefly as leader of the provincial CONSERVATIVE PARTY.

POMFRET, Jack, athlete (b 22 Nov 1922, Vancouver). He excelled at BASKETBALL, SWIMMING, FOOTBALL, RUGBY, HOCKEY and BASEBALL and his career spanned every aspect of those sports, from player to coach to administrator. As a basketball player he was captain of his Univ of Washington team before returning to VANCOUVER to lead the Meralomas to one national championship and the Clover Leafs to 3. He was offered a baseball contract with the NY Yankees, while the NY Rangers sought his hockey skills. As a swimmer he set an unofficial world record in the 100-yard freestyle in 1941 and was a member of the Univ of Washington medley relay team that broke the world record the previous year. He coached swimming at the WHITE ROCK Swim Club, Vancouver Amateur Swim Club, Univ of Alberta and UBC. As a basketball coach he guided the UBC Thunderbirds for 15 years and was the assistant with the 1956 Canadian Olympic team in Melbourne. Pomfret became an administrator in swimming and was inducted into the UBC Sports Hall of Fame and the BC SPORTS HALL OF FAME in the all-around category in 1971. *SW*

POPLAR trees occur in BC in 2 native species. Balsam poplar (*Populus balsamifera*) grows in the north and in the PEACE R country. A subspecies, black cottonwood (*balsamifera trichocarpa*), occurs throughout the province and is the largest broad-leaved tree native to BC. These two poplars are distinctive for the fluffy, down-like seeds that fill the air in early summer. The light wood is used for furni-

Trembling aspen.
Kim LaFave drawing

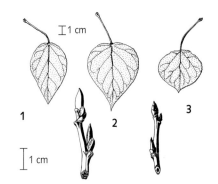

Leaves and twigs of the balsam poplar (1), black cottonwood (2), trembling aspen (3).
© T.C. Brayshaw

Trembling aspen. David Wirzba/Image Makers

ture, plywood, boxes and veneer. A second species, trembling aspen (*Populus tremuloides*), occurs throughout the Interior. It is one of the first trees to colonize areas disturbed by LOGGING or FOREST FIRE, and the gold colour of its leaves is a familiar sign of fall. The name refers to the tendency of the leaves to flutter in a breeze. The wood is used mainly for pulp. Both species are valuable wildlife trees, favoured by WOODPECKERS and other cavity-nesting species.

POPLAR CREEK, a former MINING settlement and ARROWHEAD & KOOTENAY RWY station, is 100 km southeast of REVELSTOKE on the Lardeau R. It was the site of the Lucky Jack GOLD strike in 1903; a townsite with 4 stores, 6 hotels and 7 saloons quickly sprang up, but the gold didn't last and people soon moved away. The village continued as a LOGGING centre until the 1950s but by 1999, little remained. *AS*

POPULATION; *see* PEOPLES OF BC.

PORCHER ISLAND, 531 km², south of PRINCE RUPERT and southwest of the mouth of the SKEENA R, is the territory of the KITKATLA First Nation, a TSIMSHIAN group who live to the south on Dolphin Island. With the development of

Prince Rupert in the early 1900s, many homesteaders arrived. Refuge Bay on the north shore was a steamship port; Hunts Inlet (originally Jap Inlet after the nationality of its first residents) had a school and is still sparsely settled, as are Welcome Harbour and Humpback Bay, site of a short-lived SALMON CANNERY. OONA RIVER is a FISHING village on the east shore. Porcher also had a DOGFISH oil refinery. It was named after Edwin A. Porcher, British naval captain on the coast between 1865 and 1868.

PORCUPINE, North American (*Erethizon dorsatum*), is a large member of the rodent family found in coniferous forests across the province. Weighing up to 18 kg, it has a blunt face and a body covered in long yellow-grey guard hairs. Toward the rear these hairs become stiff, barbed

Porcupine. Ken Bowen photo

quills, up to 8 cm long, which detach and embed painfully in the noses and paws of predators. Porcupines are solitary, nocturnal herbivores. They mate in the autumn and the female gives birth to a single offspring 7 months later.

PORLIER PASS, between VALDES and GALIANO islands, is the middle of 3 main channels leading from outer GEORGIA STRAIT to the calmer inner waters of the GULF ISLANDS (ACTIVE PASS and GABRIOLA PASSAGE are the others). Known also as Cowichan Gap, it has tidal currents up to 9 knots and is considered one of the best FISHING areas in the islands. Dionisio Provincial PARK is on the south side of the pass adjacent to the Race Pt LIGHTHOUSE. The pass was named in 1790 by Spanish explorer José NARVAEZ after a government official in Madrid.

PORPOISE, a toothed WHALE belonging to the family Phocoenidae, is the smallest cetacean in Canadian waters, growing to only about 2 m in length. Porpoises are less gregarious than DOLPHINS and usually travel in groups of 5 or fewer.

Dall's porpoise. Martin Nichols drawing

They use echolocation to manoeuvre underwater and to find their food, mainly fish. Two species are present along the BC coast. Dall's porpoise (*Phocoenoides dalli*), the more common species, is black and white in colour and is sometimes confused with a small KILLER WHALE. It is a fast swimmer and likes to ride the bow waves of moving vessels. It is sometimes distinguished by the "rooster tail" of spray it creates as it surfaces. The harbour porpoise (*Phocoena phocoena*) is chunky in shape and drab grey in colour. Unlike its more acrobatic porpoise and dolphin relatives, it swims quietly in small groups or even alone, shies away from boats and is not particularly active in the water.

PORT ALBERNI, city, pop 18,468, lies at the head of ALBERNI INLET on VANCOUVER ISLAND, 80 km west of NANAIMO. The site was occupied by the Tseshaht nation of the NUU-CHAH-NULTH

(Nootka) before the arrival of the first loggers in 1860. BC's first export SAWMILL, owned by James Thomson & Co, an English shipping firm, went into production in 1861. When the mill closed in 1864 (it burned in 1879), the tiny settlement dwindled but it began to revive with the arrival of farm settlers in the 1880s. MINING was also important in the early days. In 1886 a road (*see* ROADS AND HWYS) opened to Nanaimo and the townsite of Alberni was laid out. Later another site, New Alberni or Stamp Harbour, developed farther south on the east side of the inlet and came to be called Port Alberni. With the arrival of the ESQUIMALT & NANAIMO RWY in 1911, both sites incorporated as cities, Port Alberni on 12 Mar 1912 and Alberni on 1 Jan 1913. In Mar 1964 the communities sustained $10 million damages from a TSUNAMI, caused by an Alaskan EARTHQUAKE, which swept up the inlet and destroyed many buildings. The two communities merged in 1967. Port Alberni is Vancouver Island's main centre for processing FOREST PRODUCTS and manufacturing and servicing FORESTRY equipment. Wood exports have made this the third-largest port in BC with annual shipments of 300,000 tonnes. BC's first paper mill operated here briefly from 1894 to 1895 and several sawmills were established before WWI. In the 1990s the community had to respond to cutbacks in the industry; MACMILLAN BLOEDEL's 2 former lumber operations are now run by WEYERHAEUSER CANADA LTD. PACIFICA PAPER INC operates the paper mill, which received an upgrade dur-

ing the 1990s. Some SHIPBUILDING takes place, as does manufacturing for the AQUACULTURE industry. Port Alberni is also known for its SALMON fishing and as a jumping-off point for PACIFIC RIM NATIONAL PARK. *See also* PULP AND PAPER.

PORT ALBION, or Ittattsoo, pop 479, is a NUU-CHAH-NULTH (Nootka) village on the opposite side of Ucluelet Inlet from UCLUELET on the west coast of VANCOUVER ISLAND. It was the first settlement in the area, and 2 trading posts, one built by Capt Charles Stuart, the other by a man named Sutton, were established there by 1861. During the 1930s and 1940s it was the site of a fish reduction plant and a HERRING cannery but the community dispersed as these facilities shut down. At one time known as Ucluelet East, it was absorbed into the Municipality of Ucluelet.   AS

PORT ALICE, village, pop 1,331, lies at the head of Neroutsos Inlet, an arm of QUATSINO SOUND on the west coast of VANCOUVER ISLAND. The original townsite began with the construction of a pulp mill (*see* PULP AND PAPER) in 1918 by the Whalen Pulp and Paper Co. Alice was the daughter of the founder. The present site, 4 km from the mill, was incorporated in 1965 as BC's first instant municipality.

PORT CLEMENTS, village, pop 558, overlooks Stewart Bay on Masset Inlet about halfway between MASSET and SKIDEGATE on Graham Island, the largest of the QUEEN CHARLOTTE ISLANDS. The area was rich in SALMON and shellfish and there were prehistoric HAIDA villages in the vicinity. The early settlement, dating from 1907, was called Queenstown and was the centre of COAL mining activity. In 1914 the name was changed to Port Clements after H.S. Clements, a politician who brought government projects to the area. LOGGING and SAWMILLING were the basic industries and the population was much larger prior to the Depression, which devastated the local FOREST INDUSTRY. The village was incorporated in 1975 and its economy continued to be based on FORESTS—it became a bedroom community for logging operations at JUSKATLA—but TOURISM has grown in importance as well. A unique attraction is the local museum of Queen Charlotte Islands history.

PORT COQUITLAM is located on the north side of the FRASER R between the Pitt and Coquitlam rivers, 27 km east of VANCOUVER. Burke Mt (el 1,097 m) is a natural boundary to the north.

For thousands of years before white settlement, the area was used by Coast Salish people (*see* SALISHAN FIRST NATIONS), including the Kwikwetl'em people. The name derives from an aboriginal word meaning "little red salmon." The first European settlers were Alexander

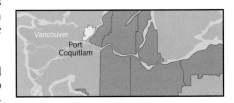

McLean and his family, who began farming beside the Pitt R in 1853. In 1859 the site was almost chosen as the capital of mainland BC instead of NEW WESTMINSTER because of the easily defensible height of land at Mary's Hill. The CPR built a branch line from its main line to New Westminster in 1886, and the community that grew up at the junction was known as Westminster Junction. In 1911 the CPR moved its freight operations from Vancouver to the Junction area and the site incorporated under its present name on 7 Mar 1913. The railway continued to be the main employer, along with LOGGING and AGRICULTURE. Following WWII the city grew rapidly as a residential suburb. In the 1960s the population doubled, and by 1999 it had doubled again since 1970. The economy has diversified with a variety of industrial and commercial developments, including metal fabrication, HIGH-TECHNOLOGY industries and transportation.

Population: 46,682
Rank in BC: 19th
Population increase since 1981: 70%
Date of incorporation: city 7 Mar 1913
Land area: 25.09 km²
Location: Greater Vancouver Regional District

Waterfront at Port Clements, Queen Charlotte Islands, 1938. BC Archives b-03800

Economic base: metal refining and fabricating, poultry processing, light industry, distribution centre

PORT DOUGLAS, an abandoned townsite at the head of HARRISON LK, was established in 1858 next to the ST'AT'IMX (Lillooet) village of Xa'xtsa, when construction began on the DOUGLAS TRAIL. As long as the trail was busy the town flourished as the terminus for steamboats operating on the lake. In its heyday it had 5 hotels and an ANGLICAN CHURCH. On 6 Dec 1859 the first hanging in BC took place here, when an aboriginal man named Wichtakuch was executed for murder. By the mid-1860s the CARIBOO WAGON ROAD had become the main route to the Interior; the trail fell into disuse and people moved away. A SAWMILL operated in the early 1900s but the town disappeared.

PORT EDWARD, district municipality, pop 700, is located just south of PRINCE RUPERT, 560 km up the coast from VANCOUVER. Named after King Edward VII, the townsite was laid out in 1908 in the expectation that it would be the coastal terminus of the GRAND TRUNK PACIFIC RWY. Instead the railway ran to Prince Rupert. Nonetheless, the community developed as a fish canning centre. One of the early canneries, NORTH PACIFIC, built in 1889, has been restored as a museum. By the 1960s the community was the largest fish-processing centre in the north, but the consolidation of canning operations on the coast led to the eventual closure of all the local plants. The district was incorporated on 29 June 1966. *See also* SALMON CANNING.

PORT ESSINGTON is an abandoned townsite near the mouth of the SKEENA R at the junction with the ECSTALL R. It was long a campsite for the TSIMSHIAN, who knew it as Spokeshute, or Spukshut. In 1871 a northern trader, Robert CUNNINGHAM, established a post, which developed into a small village. He gave it the name Capt George VANCOUVER had given the mouth of the river in 1793, after one of his fellow British naval commanders. By 1890 there were 3 SALMON CAN-NERIES and a SAWMILL, and during the next decade the village became a stopover for steamboats operating on the Skeena. Accessible only by water, it had wooden streets and no motorized vehicles. During the period from 1906 to 1910, construction of the GRAND TRUNK PACIFIC RWY on the north side of the river brought much economic activity. At its height the summer population exceeded 2,000. But the choice of PRINCE RUPERT as the railway terminus condemned Port Essington to a slow decline. The last cannery closed in 1936 and by the 1940s only a few residents remained. Fires in 1961 and 1965 destroyed the last buildings and little remains at the site.

Kenneth Campbell

PORT GUICHON is on the south arm of the FRASER R, next door to LADNER in DELTA. Named for Laurent GUICHON, a pioneer farmer who settled here in 1881, it attracted several CROATIAN fishing families and was the first permanent Croatian settlement in Canada. It developed as a small service centre for the surrounding AGRICULTURAL and commercial FISHING communities.

Port Essington on the Skeena R, 1888.
UBC BC124

From 1903 to 1931 a railway ferry ran to SIDNEY, connecting the GREAT NORTHERN RWY main line to VANCOUVER ISLAND.

PORT HAMMOND, on the north shore of the FRASER R 34 km east of VANCOUVER in MAPLE RIDGE, was a CPR depot and SAWMILL town that declined after the Lougheed Hwy was built to the north through HANEY. John Hammond, a farmer, and his brother William, a civil engineer, settled here in 1872 and developed the townsite in hopes that it would become a port for deep-sea SHIPPING.   AS

PORT HARDY, district municipality, pop 5,283, is located at the north end of VANCOUVER ISLAND, 504 km from VICTORIA. It is named for a British naval hero, Sir Thomas Masterman Hardy, the captain of the HMS *Victory*, who comforted Lord Nelson as he died during the Battle of Trafalgar in 1805. The first white settlers, Alec Lyons and his wife Sarah Hunt, arrived in 1904 and opened a store. There was a short-lived land boom in 1912, promoted by a fraudulent land company,

A waterfront park at Port Hardy, 1990.
Peter A. Robson photo

but growth was slow until the opening of the ISLAND COPPER Mine in 1969. It became BC's second-largest COPPER producer before its closure in 1995. Since 1979 Port Hardy has been the terminus of the PRINCE RUPERT ferry and is the regional centre of the North Island. The FOREST INDUSTRY and commercial FISHING are also important. The community is served by North Island College (*see* COMMUNITY COLLEGES).

PORT HUGHES, 26 km northeast of TOFINO at the head of Bedwell Sound, was a short-lived MINING camp on the west coast of VANCOUVER ISLAND. Originally called Bear River, it was established in the 1890s to serve several GOLD and COPPER mines on the Bedwell (then Bear) R. A hotel was built but the boom was soon over. Small-scale mining continued in the area until the 1960s.   AS

PORT KELLS, a neighbourhood in north SURREY, was originally founded on the south shore of the FRASER R opposite BARNSTON ISLAND by

Henry Kells, who laid out a townsite in 1890. The commercial centre he dreamed of never developed, however, and Port Kells became a farming district (*see* AGRICULTURE).

PORT McNEILL, town, pop 2,925, is on the east side of VANCOUVER ISLAND at the top of JOHNSTONE STRAIT, 195 km north of CAMPBELL RIVER. Named for HBC factor William MCNEILL, it was established as a LOGGING community in 1937 and was soon the administrative base for some

Restored steam donkey at Port McNeill.
Keith Thirkell photo

20,000 km² of surrounding forest. It was incorporated on 18 Feb 1966. A ferry connects Port McNeill with SOINTULA and ALERT BAY. Logging has continued to provide employment, along with AQUACULTURE, sport FISHING and eco-tourism.

PORT MANN, on the south side of the FRASER R east of NEW WESTMINSTER, was originally called Bon Accord. It was planned to be the Pacific terminus of the CANADIAN NORTHERN RWY, but a townsite laid out in 1911 and named for Donald Mann, one of the railway's principals, did not attract settlement and the terminus moved to VANCOUVER. The site has been used mainly for

industry. The Port Mann Bridge, completed in 1964, carries the TRANS-CANADA HWY across the river from SURREY to COQUITLAM and is the main access route from the FRASER VALLEY to the Lower Mainland.

PORT MELLON is a pulp mill site at the mouth of the Rainy R, on the west side of HOWE SOUND not far from Langdale. Originally used as a village site by the SQUAMISH nation, it was developed between 1907 to 1909 as a PULP AND PAPER mill by the British-Canadian Wood Pulp and Paper Co and named for one of the company's backers, Henry A. MELLON. Over the years the mill shut down periodically and changed hands several times. The nearby Seaside Hotel, built in 1907, was a popular TOURIST destination until 1958, and continued in business as a pub until the late 1960s. The small townsite of millworkers and their families was accessible only by water until 1953, when the highway opened to GIBSONS. With the opening of road access the townsite gradually disappeared as employees were able to commute by car. In 1951 CANADIAN FOREST PRODUCTS LTD (Canfor) took over the mill and were still operating it in 2000. Port Mellon became notorious for its "black dandruff" of air pollution and the effluent the mill pumped directly into Howe Sound. In 1988 the Oji Paper Co, one of Japan's major paper producers, became joint owner of the Howe Sound Pulp and Paper Co with Canfor. In a major renovation and expansion, a newsprint mill was added and a series of anti-pollution measures were put in place.

PORT MOODY, city, pop 20,847, surrounds the head of BURRARD INLET 15 km east of downtown VANCOUVER. It began when the ROYAL ENGINEERS cut a trail from NEW WESTMINSTER in 1859 to the head of the inlet as a precautionary "back door" in case of an attack from the south.

It was named for Richard MOODY, commander of the engineers. In 1879 the CPR announced Port Moody would be the western terminus of the new transcontinental railway; the first passenger train from Montreal arrived on 4 July 1886. The CPR's decision to shift its end of track down the inlet to Vancouver meant that Port Moody grew less dramatically than anticipated. SAWMILLING and the Imperial Oil development at IOCO (*see also* OIL AND GAS INDUSTRY) were the economic mainstays, along with the port operations. It incorporated as a city on 11 Mar 1913. After WWII it developed mainly as a residential suburb of Vancouver, though its active waterfront handles deep-sea bulk carriers (*see* SHIPPING, DEEP-SEA), and several industries, including a chemical plant, a thermal-electric generating station and a major WINE-MAKING operation are located here. Port Moody also has a campus of Douglas College (*see* COMMUNITY COLLEGES). The West Coast Express commuter train, which uses the existing CPR line, connects Port Moody to downtown Vancouver.

PORT NEVILLE is an inlet on the mainland side of JOHNSTONE STRAIT, opposite and just west of KELSEY BAY. (Port Neville is also the name of the tiny marine community at the inlet's mouth.) It was the site of the first store in the region, established by Hans Hansen in 1891. At that time it was the farthest north of a string of LOGGING "shows" that had sprung up on the coast. There was a SAWMILL at the community until 1925, and extensive RAILWAY LOGGING, as well as limited AGRICULTURE at the head of the inlet near the former site of a KWAKWAKA'WAKW (Kwakiutl) village. This thriving spot was a regular stop for UNION STEAMSHIP CO vessels. Its heyday is past but in 1999 there was still a post office at the inlet and a calm harbour attractive to boaters. It was named by Capt George VANCOUVER in 1792 after John Neville, an officer in the Royal Marines.

PORT RENFREW, pop 400, lies at the mouth of the San Juan R 110 km west of VICTORIA. LOGGING began here in 1906. Wood cut inland was transported to the water by rail, then towed to mills in Victoria. The DAVIS RAFT was pioneered by this operation. Later in the century, TOURISM flourished. Port Renfrew is the jumping-off point for the WEST COAST TRAIL heading north and the JUAN DE FUCA MARINE TRAIL heading south. It was named in 1896 for a British lord who planned to locate settlers nearby.

PORT SIMPSON; *see* FORT SIMPSON.

Port Mann Bridge. Rick Blacklaws photo

Container shipping terminal at the Port of Vancouver, 1988. Roy Luckow photo

PORT OF VANCOUVER is located around the shores of BURRARD INLET. In terms of tonnage handled, it is Canada's largest port and the second-largest port on the west coast of N America, after Long Beach, CA. In 1998 total shipments through the port was close to 72 million tonnes. The port handles 45% of Canada's grain exports and 75% of its COAL exports. International shipping from the port dates back to Nov 1864, when the sailing barque *Ellen Lewis* left for Australia with a cargo of lumber and fence pickets. The port became well established after the arrival of the transcontinental railway in 1886. The federal government created the first central port authority, the Vancouver Harbour Commission, in 1913. It was replaced in 1936 by the National Harbours Board, a CROWN CORPORATION. From 1983 the port was administered by the Vancouver Port Corp, also a Crown agency, which was replaced by the Vancouver Port Authority in 1999. The VPA is an independent agency consisting of representatives from industry and different levels of government. The port handles about 10,000 vessel calls a year from 90 nations. Most coal exports are handled at the associated ROBERTS BANK facility. A huge new container terminal, DeltaPort, opened in 1997 next to Roberts Bank. *See also* CRUISE SHIP INDUSTRY.

PORTAGE MOUNTAIN (el 1,429 m), 85 km west of FORT ST JOHN, forms a natural obstacle to the flow of the PEACE R, which has worn a deep canyon around its southern edge. The powerful rapids that once existed at this site, before the BENNETT and Peace Canyon dams flooded the region and raised the water level, required early river travellers to make a lengthy detour. Portage Mt was also the name of one of the huge construction camps that housed thousands of workers during the building of the Bennett Dam in the 1960s. *AS*

PORTEAU COVE is a provincial MARINE PARK on the east side of HOWE SOUND 24 km north of HORSESHOE BAY. Around 1900 it was the site of a gravel pit, then developed as a resort, Glen Eden, for summer visitors from VANCOUVER. There is a campsite and pier and several vessels have been sunk offshore to form an artificial reef, making it a popular spot for diving.

PORTER, Derek, rower (b 2 Nov 1967, Belfast, Northern Ireland). Raised in VICTORIA, he rowed with the Canadian 8s team that won silver medals at the 1990 and 1991 world championships and gold at the 1992 Barcelona Olympics. In 1993 he switched to single sculls and won gold at the world championships, then silver at the 1996 Olympics in Atlanta. After studying in Ontario to become a chiropractor, he won another gold at the 1999 Pan American Games and returned to BC to pursue his new career while continuing to compete in ROWING. He is a member of the ORDER OF BC (1996) and the BC SPORTS HALL OF FAME (1996). *SW*

PORTLAND INLET is the third-longest of the many FJORDS that indent the BC coast. Surrounded by snow-capped peaks and glaciers, it extends north out of DIXON ENTRANCE 100 km to the town of STEWART at its top end. The lower reaches of the passage are known as Portland Inlet. At the top of Pearse Island it divides: The narrow channel to the west continues as Portland Canal, the channel to the east is OBSERVATORY INLET. The canal forms the southern border between BC and Alaska. The inlet has long been a traditional fishing ground for TSIMSHIAN and NISGA'A First Nations (*see* FISHING, ABORIGINAL). It was named in 1793 by Capt George VANCOUVER for William Bentinck, Duke of Portland, a British politician.

PORTLAND ISLAND, at 1.82 km² one of the smaller GULF ISLANDS, lies just east of Swartz Bay south of SALTSPRING ISLAND. It is named for a 19th-century British warship. Once home to HAWAIIAN settlers, including William NAUKANA, it was owned from the late 1920s to 1937 by Gen Frank "One-Arm" Sutton, a British soldier of fortune who raised racehorses there. The province bought it in 1958 to give to Princess Margaret in commemoration of the BC centennial. Three years later she returned ownership so that it could be turned into Princess Margaret Provincial MARINE PARK. The sunken coastal freighter *G.B. Church* lying offshore was BC's first artificial reef for scuba divers.

PORTLOCK, Nathaniel, maritime fur trader (b circa 1748; d 12 Sept 1812, London, England).

PORT OF VANCOUVER SELECTED STATISTICS

	1991	1998
Total tonnage (000 tonnes)	70,700	71,933
Bulk cargo (000 tonnes)	60,800	60,600
General cargo (000 tonnes)	6,582	4,319
Total foreign containers	383,563	840,098
Cruise passengers	423,928	873,102
IMPORTS & EXPORTS (000 tonnes)	**1995**	**1998**
Japan	22,024	20,653
South Korea	8,181	7,888
China	6,741	5,532
United States	2,577	2,827
Taiwan	2,563	2,628
Brazil	2,683	2,491
Mexico	1,795	1,910
United Kingdom	1,586	1,625
Italy	1,478	1,211
TOP BULK COMMODITIES (000 tonnes)		**1998**
Coal		28,213
Grain		11,070
Fertilizers (potash, phosphates, sulphur, etc)		10,023
Forest products		6,435
Petroleum products		3,843
Chemicals		2,367
Other bulk commodities		9,982
TOP CONTAINERIZED COMMODITIES (000 tonnes)		**1998**
Lumber		508
Animal feeds		408
Meat & fish		383
Wood pulp		360
Grain		359

He entered the Royal Navy in 1772 and was a mate on the *Discovery* during James COOK's visit to the coast in 1778. In 1785 he was chosen by the KING GEORGE'S SOUND CO to lead its first expedition to the coast to trade for SEA OTTER pelts. Portlock commanded the *King George*, with George DIXON in the *Queen Charlotte*. During 1786–87 he made 2 visits to coastal Alaska, where he traded for furs. He returned to England and the navy in 1788. *See also* FUR TRADE, MARITIME.

PORTUGUESE immigration to BC began in 1852 with the arrival of "Portuguese Joe" SILVEY, who ran a store in GASTOWN and later moved to the SUNSHINE COAST with his SECHELT wife. He was followed to the coast by Joe Gonzalves, who arrived in the 1860s from Madeira. Gonzalves, who also married a First Nations woman, helped to found Irvines Landing at PENDER HARBOUR. The nearby village of MADEIRA PARK is named for his homeland. Small but steady immigration continued from the GOLD RUSH period. Significant immigration began in the 1950s as a result of an agreement between the governments of Portugal and Canada. Newcomers, mainly from the Azores Islands, gravitated to AGRICULTURE in the southern OKANAGAN VALLEY and to commercial FISHING. As well, ALCAN ALUMINUM recruited many Portuguese for its smelter at KITIMAT. It has been estimated that by the late 1980s about half the orchard land in the OLIVER–OSOYOOS area was owned by Portuguese, much of it paid for by wages earned at the Alcan smelter. By the end of the century VANCOUVER was the centre of BC's Portuguese community with the third-largest population of Portuguese-Canadians in the country. The Portuguese Club was active and there were several Portuguese-language newspapers and a Portuguese-language radio show. The 1996 census recorded 18,755 Portuguese speakers in BC. *See also* PEOPLES OF BC.   *Dianne Mackay*

POSTAGE STAMPS were used by the colonies of BC and VANCOUVER ISLAND for the prepayment of postage from 1860 to 1871. Under the direction of Gov James DOUGLAS, the 2 colonies jointly issued a stamp in 1860 worth 2 1/2 pence bearing a portrait of Queen Victoria. Issued 20 years after Great Britain produced the world's original postage stamp, this stamp was the first used jointly by 2 separate jurisdictions. In 1865 Vancouver Island issued 2 stamps that were used until it was united with the mainland the following year. BC's next stamp, a 3-pence issued in 1865, bore an unusual design featuring the letter *V* and a crown. This design, in various colours and overprinted with 6 different values, was used until 1871. All stamps for the colonies were printed in England. BC themes have appeared on many Canadian stamps. Canada's 5-cent 1962 Victoria centennial issue reproduces the 1860 BC and Vancouver Island stamp.   *Chris Gainor*

POST-WAR REHABILITATION COUNCIL was created by the provincial COALITION GOVERNMENT in 1942 to help BC adjust to peacetime.

Potlatch at Alert Bay, 1983.
Vickie Jensen photo, courtesy U'Mista Cultural Centre

Chaired by Harry Perry, the minister of education, it included MLAs from all parties, including the opposition leader, Harold WINCH, and a new CONSERVATIVE MLA, W.A.C. BENNETT. The Council toured the province, then prepared 2 reports from 1943 to 1944 recommending that the government get involved in economic development by, among other things, extending the Pacific Great Eastern Rwy (see BC RAIL), investing in a steel industry and creating a publicly owned hydro utility (*see* BC HYDRO). The government ignored the reports but Bennett later adopted many of the recommendations when he became PREMIER.

POTLATCH is an important cultural event celebrated by most of the FIRST NATIONS of the Northwest Coast. The term comes from a NUU-CHAH-NULTH (Nootka) word borrowed into CHINOOK JARGON meaning "to give." The potlatch serves many purposes: to reinforce status in the community, to memorialize the dead, to celebrate a marriage or the construction of a house, to raise a TOTEM POLE, to name children and to pass on the heritable privileges and positions that go with chieftainship. The forms of the potlatch differ among the different coastal First Nations but in general a potlatch validates an individual's role in the community and establishes claims to names, privileges and social rank. This in turn validates the right to resources obtained from specific areas within the tribal territory. Traditionally, potlatch ceremonials were at the heart of First Nations governance and social structure. The event may last several days, during which time guests take part in feasting, speech-making, dancing and gift-giving. The distribution of gifts, which may have become more elaborate following contact with Europeans, affirms the host's wealth and status while at the same time recognizing the status of guests and honouring them for attending. Failing to understand its significance, governments and some

missionaries blamed the potlatch for encouraging idleness and immorality, for squandering wealth and for hindering attempts to convert the First Nations people to Christianity. As a result, in 1884 the federal government banned the potlatch. Aboriginal groups resisted the law and authorities could do little to carry it out. In 1889 the first potlatcher was arrested but Chief Justice Matthew BEGBIE threw the case out of court and ruled that the law as written was unenforceable because it did not define "potlatch." The law was amended in 1895 but it continued to be enforced intermittently. The potlatch was driven underground where it continued in secrecy, especially among the KWAKWA̲KA̲'WAKW (Kwakiutl). For the most part authorities used persuasion rather than coercion in attempting to stamp out the ceremony. For a period following WWI, however, the government pursued the ban with special zeal, making several arrests. In Dec 1921 a Kwakwa̲ka̲'wakw potlatch held by Dan Cranmer at VILLAGE ISLAND resulted in charges being laid against 49 people. In the end, 26 people were jailed. Ceremonial items surrendered as a result of the convictions ended up in the collections of the Canadian Museum of Civilization, the Royal Ontario Museum and the Museum of the American Indian in New York. Many of these items were returned to the coast in 1979–80 and are now on display at the Kwagiulth Museum at We Wai Kai (CAPE MUDGE) and the U'Mista Cultural Centre in ALERT BAY. Traumatic as the suppression of 1921 was, it did not end the potlatch, which remained illegal until the ban was dropped from the revised *Indian Act* in 1951. By the late 1990s, and especially with the revival of aboriginal cultural expression since the 1950s, the potlatch continued to be an important ceremony for coastal people.
Reading: Douglas Cole and Ira Chaikin, *An Iron Hand Upon the People*, 1990; Aldona Jonaitis, *Chiefly Feasts: The Enduring Kwakiutl Potlatch*, 1991.

POTTERS GUILD OF BC, founded in 1955, is an organization of studio ceramic artists. As well as organizing annual exhibitions and sales, sponsoring workshops and sharing information, it owns and operates the Gallery of BC Ceramics, which opened on GRANVILLE ISLAND in VANCOUVER in 1985. The earliest studio potter known to be active in the province was Axel Ebring, a Swedish immigrant labourer who began producing functional pottery at his home near TERRACE in the 1920s. During the 1930s Grace Melvin taught pottery at the Vancouver School of Art (later the EMILY CARR INSTITUTE OF ART & DESIGN), and after WWII Mollie Carter began giving classes through the extension department at UBC. As the number of potters grew, the need for a province-wide organization to coordinate information and activities became evident and the Guild was created. Since that time BC has produced a number of distinguished ceramic artists, working in both the functional and sculptural traditions, whose work has been recognized by galleries, museums and private buyers across N

America. After the Canadian Craft Council established the annual Saidye Bronfman Award for Excellence in the Crafts in 1977 it was won by 3 BC potters: Robin Hopper (1977), Wayne NGAN (1983) and Walter Dexter (1992). Other well-known ceramic artists include Meg Buckley, Jan Grove, Hiro Urakami, Robert Weghsteen, Heinz Laffin, Sally Michener and Tam Irving.

POUCE COUPE, village, pop 894, is in the PEACE R country, 10 km south of DAWSON CREEK. The name belonged to a SEKANI leader known to the early FUR TRADERS. It is located on a fertile prairie where the Dawson Crk flows into the Pouce Coupe R. The pioneer settler was Hector Tremblay, a French Canadian attracted to the country in 1898 by the Klondike GOLD RUSH, who established a trading post. The main influx of homesteaders occurred just prior to WWI from Edmonton over the Edson Trail. The first gas field in BC was discovered nearby in 1921 (*see also* OIL AND GAS INDUSTRY) and the townsite developed during the 1920s. The Northern Alberta Rwy (later the CNR) arrived early in 1931 and the village incorporated the next year. It was the administrative centre of the PEACE RIVER BLOCK and is now a service centre for the surrounding AGRICULTURAL area. Many residents work in Dawson Creek.

POUND, Richard, swimmer, sports administrator (b 22 Mar 1942, St Catharines, ON). Raised in OCEAN FALLS, he emerged from that community's famed swim club to become one of Canada's leading competitors. At the 1960 Rome Olympics he was a 100-m freestyle finalist and a member of the 4th-place medley relay team, and at the 1962 BRITISH EMPIRE GAMES he won gold in the 110-yard freestyle. He moved to Montreal, graduated in law from McGill Univ in 1968 and became a tax lawyer and chartered accountant. After serving as president of the Canadian Olympic Assoc he was appointed to the International Olympic Committee in 1978 and became one of its top administrators. In the late 1990s he was in the news internationally as chair of an ad hoc committee named to investigate allegations of improper conduct by IOC members. He is a member of the Canadian Aquatic and Canadian Sports Halls of Fame. *See also* SWIMMING. *SW*

POWELL, Eric, Anglican missionary (b 9 Nov 1933, Edmonton, AB; d 14 May 1997, Victoria). While studying at the Anglican Theological College in the 1950s he began working summers for the COLUMBIA COAST MISSION in KINGCOME INLET. When he was ordained in 1958 he moved to Kingcome and his experiences with the local KWAKWA̲KA̲'WAKW people formed the basis for Margaret CRAVEN's best-selling novel of the coast, *I Heard the Owl Call My Name* (1967). He moved to POWELL RIVER in 1961 and served as a minister in several other communities. He also worked for BC HYDRO as a liaison with aboriginal communities, served on the BC Council of HUMAN RIGHTS and was a member of the provincial medical ethics committee.

POWELL, Israel Wood, doctor, public servant (b 27 Apr 1836, Port Colborne, ON; d 25 Feb 1915, Victoria). He graduated in medicine from McGill Univ in 1860, then moved to VANCOUVER

Israel Wood Powell, 1874, first superintendent of Indian Affairs, 1872–89. Powell River is named for him. BC Archives F-03704

ISLAND two years later and opened a medical office in VICTORIA. An elected member of the colonial legislature from 1863 to 1866 (*see* COLONIAL GOVERNMENT), he supported union of the colonies and CONFEDERATION with Canada. He was also an active mason, serving as provincial grand master from 1867 to 1875. He declined the offer to become BC's first LT GOV but did serve as the first superintendent of Indian Affairs during 1872–89. He criticized the province's aboriginal policies and supported FIRST NATIONS' attempts to enlarge their RESERVES. In 1890 he was appointed chancellor of UBC, which was then in the planning stages. POWELL RIVER is named for him.

POWELL FOREST CANOE ROUTE is an 80-km circuit through a series of LAKES and connecting portages near POWELL RIVER 145 km north of VANCOUVER. Completed in 1983, the entire trip takes 5–7 days along a route that includes Lois, Horseshoe, Nanton, Dodd, Windsor, Goat and Powell lakes. A shorter "mini" route takes 3 days. Along with the CANOE circuit at BOWRON LAKE PROVINCIAL PARK, it is among the most ambitious paddle circuits in BC.

POWELL RIVER, district municipality, pop 13,131, is located on the mainland coast 130 km north of VANCOUVER. (The population of the surrounding REGIONAL DISTRICT is 19,936.) It  is named for Israel Wood POWELL, who was superintendent of Indian Affairs when he visited the area aboard the Royal Navy vessel HMS

The Pacifica Paper complex at Powell River.

Rocket. Loggers established camps in the area in the 1880s and a PULP AND PAPER mill was constructed between 1910 and 1912 by the Brooks, Scanlon & O'Brien Co. The townsite grew up around the mill, which was owned by the POWELL RIVER CO until 1960, when it merged with MACMILLAN BLOEDEL LTD. At one time it was the world's largest paper mill, with a work force of more than 2,000. The complex has always been the community's major employer, producing newsprint, groundwood printing papers, specialty papers, pulp and lumber, though by 1999, as the mill modernized and downsized under new ownership, PACIFICA PAPER, the number of employees had fallen to 1,031. In 1955 the Powell River Co townsite was sold to the newly formed Corp of the District of Powell River, composed of the villages of Cranberry and Westview and the area of Wildwood. All of the communities continue to have distinct identities. The townsite, which preserves aspects of a classic company town, was declared an official heritage district in 1995 by the federal government. Much of the residential and commercial development since the mid-1960s has been in Westview. There is a campus of Malaspina Univ College (*see* COMMUNITY COLLEGES) and every second summer the KATHAUMIXW International Choral Festival attracts choirs from around the world.

POWELL RIVER CO was started by Dr Dwight Brooks, Michael J. Scanlon and John O'Brien, 3 American lumbermen. The first 2 partners owned the second largest forest company in the US. They came to BC in 1908 and purchased a large stand of timber in the FRASER VALLEY. Later that year they merged their interests with those of O'Brien, who had been logging south of POWELL RIVER since 1900. In 1909 they bought a PULP wood lease at Powell River, including the right

to use the water from Powell Lk for power generation, and formed the Powell River Paper Company Ltd, which opened BC's first newsprint mill in 1912. A model company town was built, another pulp lease obtained, and a LOGGING operation opened at KINGCOME INLET. The subsidiary Kingcome Navigation Co was founded to tow logs to the mill and paper barges to VANCOUVER and Seattle. The mill's capacity was doubled again in 1926, and once more in 1930, making it the largest newsprint mill in the world. In 1932 the company began milling SPRUCE lumber from timber in the QUEEN CHARLOTTE ISLANDS, an operation that was expanded substantially during WWII to supply spruce for aircraft construction. After the war, control and management of the company was turned over to descendants of the founders, plants were upgraded and extensive timber rights acquired. Several mid-sized logging companies were purchased, along with SAWMILLS in Vancouver and NEW WESTMINSTER. Newsprint capacity was expanded further; by the late 1950s, one newspaper out of every 25 in the world was printed on Powell River paper. In Jan 1960 the company merged with Macmillan & Bloedel Ltd to form MacMillan, Bloedel and Powell River Ltd, with Powell River's Harold Foley as vice-chair and his brother Joseph as president. *See also* FOREST INDUSTRY; MACMILLAN BLOEDEL LTD. *Ken Drushka*

PRATT, Charles Edward "Ned," architect (b 15 July 1911, Boston, MA; d 24 Feb 1996, Vancouver). He came to Canada as a youngster, attended BRENTWOOD COLLEGE on VANCOUVER ISLAND and graduated from UBC in 1933. While at UBC he won a bronze medal in rowing at the 1932 Olympics. He studied architecture at the Univ of Toronto, then served in the air force during WWII. When he returned to VANCOUVER, he was a senior partner at the firm of Sharp & Thompson Berwick Pratt from 1945 to 1956 and Thompson Berwick & Pratt from 1956 to 1976. Prominent buildings he designed include UBC's War Memorial Gym, for which he won a Massey silver medal in 1952, the innovative BC HYDRO Building (1957), and the Thea Koerner Graduate Centre at UBC, for which he won a Massey gold medal in 1962. Prominent architects who passed through his firm included Arthur ERICKSON, Ron THOM, Nicholas BAWLF and Barry DOWNS. He died from injuries sustained in a car accident.

PRATT, Walter "Babe," hockey player (b 7 Jan 1916, Stoney Mountain, MB; d 16 Dec 1988, Vancouver). His 12 NHL seasons (1935–47) with the NY Rangers, Toronto Maple Leafs and Boston Bruins earned him 2 Stanley Cups (1940, 1945), a 1944 Hart Trophy as the league's most valuable player and a scoring record for defencemen that stood for 20 years. In 1948 he joined the minor-professional New Westminster Royals as a player and the next season assumed coaching duties as well, leading the team to the PACIFIC COAST HOCKEY LEAGUE championship. After a stint with the Tacoma Rockets he retired

from playing in 1952, returning to the Royals as coach before being fired partway through the season. Following a second career in the FOREST INDUSTRY he returned to HOCKEY as an executive with the VANCOUVER CANUCKS in 1970. A member of the Hockey Hall of Fame, he remained in the team's public relations department until felled by a heart attack during a game. *SW*

PRAWN; *see* SHRIMP.

PREHISTORY refers to the period before there was written history. In BC human prehistory begins with the disappearance of the last glaciers about 13,000 years ago and the subsequent arrival of the earliest inhabitants. Scientists believe that the Americas were populated by migrants from Asia, who crossed an ice-free land

Arnoud Stryd, archaeologist, standing on the spot at Gore Creek where workers found the skeleton of a young male who was killed by a mudslide 9,000 years ago. Roy Carlson photo

Pebble tools from an archaeological site near Yale. Roy Carlson photo

Microblades made of obsidian, dated from 9,000 to 6,000 years ago, excavated at Namu. Roy Carlson photo

bridge between Siberia and Alaska at least 15,000–13,000 years ago, possibly much earlier. These early migrants, known as Paleoindians, may have passed south along the coast, though no evidence has yet been discovered, possibly because rising sea levels have obscured their passage. Paleoindians may also have travelled south in the Interior through an open corridor between retreating ice sheets. It is in this area at CHARLIE LK CAVE north of FORT ST JOHN where stone artifacts and animal bones dating some 11,500 years ago have been found. These remains are the earliest so far discovered in BC.

Archaeologists divide BC prehistory into 3 periods: early, middle and late. During the early period (11,500–6,000 years ago) 5 distinct cultural traditions were present in the province. These traditions are differentiated by the types of stone artifacts associated with each, and by inferences from environmental factors and faunal remains about ways of making a living.

1. The Fluted Point tradition is defined by the presence of large stone spear points that are "fluted," or channelled, at the base to facilitate attachment to the wooden spear shaft. The people who used these points hunted large game such as bison and probably mammoth in parts of the BC Interior and elsewhere in N America. One point was found in the excavations at Charlie Lake Cave.

Excavating a deep shell midden at Namu, 1978.
Roy Carlson photo

2. The Plano tradition, also a hunting tradition of interior N America, replaced the Fluted Point tradition about 11,000 years ago. By this time the mammoth was extinct and bison were the principal game hunted. This tradition centres on the plains and prairies east of the ROCKY MTS. The stone points of this tradition are not fluted, but stemmed at the base, representing a more efficient way of attaching a spear point to its wooden shaft.

3. The Intermontane Stemmed Point tradition, another hunting culture, existed between the Rockies and the COAST MTS from about 11,500–9,000 years ago. Artifacts and remains belonging to this tradition have been found in the KAMLOOPS area, including a young male skeleton dating to about 9,000 years ago, one of the oldest human skeletons recovered in Canada. Stemmed spear points slightly different in style from those of the Plano tradition typify this culture.

4. The Pebble Tool tradition provides the earliest evidence of coastal occupation. The name derives from the fact that many large chopping and scraping tools were made from cobbles and large pebbles. The points belonging to this tradition are neither fluted nor stemmed, but leaf-shaped. Subsistence was based on fishing and sea mammal hunting. Some archaeologists refer to this tradition as the Old Cordilleran culture. Important archaeological sites are at NAMU on the Central Coast and at sites in the QUEEN CHARLOTTE ISLANDS, where artifacts date back 11,000 years, and at younger sites at Bear Cove on northern VANCOUVER ISLAND and GLENROSE and Milliken on the FRASER R. By 7,000 years ago, if not earlier, SALMON fishing was probably established as the most important subsistence activity on the coast.

5. The Microblade tradition is named after the custom of making cutting edges on knives and spear heads by inserting small stone flakes into the edges of antler or wood points and hafts. This method is quite different from that employed in other traditions where a single piece of stone was flaked to make such implements. The tradition appeared about 10,500 years ago in northern BC and gradually spread southward. It is known even earlier in Siberia and Alaska.

The middle period extends from about 6,000–2,000 years ago. On the coast there was considerable cultural elaboration based on the dependable and preservable supply of salmon. The familiar CEDAR plank house and other skills at woodworking, a hierarchical social order with chiefs and SLAVES, and the coastal art tradition all developed during this period. There is also evidence of ritual feasting, an early form of the POTLATCH, and masked dancers. Obsidian artifacts (made from volcanic rock) found far from the places of origin indicate widespread trade, as do artifacts of sea shells found in sites in the Interior. Villages of round pit houses typify the interior cultures of this period, and salmon was also an important mainstay in these upriver regions. In northern regions without access to salmon, people remained nomadic hunters. There is some evidence of raiding and warfare, particularly toward the end of this period. Important middle period sites are Namu, PENDER CANAL, YUQUOT, MARPOLE and KEATLEY CREEK.

The late period extends back 2,000 years before European contact. By the beginning of this period the patterns of culture on both the coast and in the Interior had been set and continued into the historic period. The bow and arrow became common at this time and partially replaced use of the spear thrower. Most of the fortress sites that have been dated belong to this period. These facts suggest an increase in raiding and warfare and its consequences, including population stabilization, increased slavery and increased emphasis on social rank and wealth expressed through the potlatch. Many sites of this period have been excavated throughout the province. *See also* ARCHAEOLOGY.   *Roy Carlson*

PREMIER is the chief minister of the provincial government. He or she is named by the LT GOV but by custom is the elected leader of the political party occupying the most seats in the LEGISLATIVE ASSEMBLY. The premier chooses the CABINET, appoints senior public servants, advises the lt gov and establishes the agenda of the government. He or she may take on one or more cabinet portfolios as well. People who have served as BC premier since CONFEDERATION are listed opposite.

PREMIER, a MINING camp 15 km north of STEWART on the North Coast, was the site of one of the province's richest GOLD–SILVER strikes. Discovered in about 1910, the Premier mine was in serious production from 1919 to 1953 and was still operating intermittently at the end of the 20th century.   *AS*

PRESBYTERIAN CHURCH in Canada is a Reformed and Protestant church in historic continuity with the Church of Scotland, and which follows the spiritual pattern established by John Calvin. The 1991 census indicated that 64,000 people in BC identify themselves as Presbyterians.

PRESBYTERIANS IN BC

Year	Members	% of BC Population
1881	5,753	11.6
1891	15,655	16.0
1901	34,478	19.3
1911	82,735	21.1
1921	123,419	23.5
1931	84,941	12.2
1941	94,554	11.6
1951	97,151	8.3
1961	90,093	5.5
1971	100,940	4.6
1981	89,810	3.3
1991	63,985	2.0

The structure of the Presbyterian Church consists of 4 courts. Members of a congregation, or pastoral charge, are governed by the session, which consists of lay men and women called ruling elders, who are elected by that congregation, and the minister, or teaching elder, who serves as the moderator. Congregations are grouped by geographical area into presbyteries, which are made up of the ministers and one elected elder

PREMIERS of BC

John Foster McCreight		14 Nov 1871–23 Dec 1872
Amor de Cosmos		23 Dec 1872– 11 Feb 1874
George Anthony Walkem		11 Feb 1874–27 Jan 1876
Andrew Charles Elliott		1 Feb 1876 –25 June 1878
George Anthony Walkem		25 June 1878–12 June 1882
Robert Beaven		13 June 1882–29 Jan 1883
William Smithe		29 Jan 1883–29 Mar 1887
A.E.B. Davie		1 Apr 1887–1 Aug 1889
John Robson		2 Aug 1889–29 June 1892
Theodore Davie		2 July 1892–2 Mar 1895
J.H. Turner		4 Mar 1895–8 Aug 1898
Charles A. Semlin		15 Aug 1898–27 Feb 1900
Joseph Martin		28 Feb 1900–14 June 1900
James Dunsmuir		15 June 1900–21 Nov 1902
Edward G. Prior		21 Nov 1902–1 June 1903
Richard McBride	Conservative	1 June 1903–15 Dec 1915
W.J. Bowser	Conservative	15 Dec 1915–23 Nov 1916
Harlan C. Brewster	Liberal	23 Nov 1916–1 Mar 1918
John Oliver	Liberal	6 Mar 1918–17 Aug 1927
J.D. MacLean	Liberal	20 Aug 1927–20 Aug 1928
Simon Fraser Tolmie	Conservative	21 Aug 1928–15 Nov 1933
Duff Pattullo	Liberal	15 Nov 1933–9 Dec 1941
John Hart	Coalition	9 Dec 1941–29 Dec 1947
Byron Johnson	Coalition	29 Dec 1947–1 Aug 1952
W.A.C. Bennett	Social Credit	1 Aug 1952–15 Sept 1972
Dave Barrett	NDP	15 Sept 1972–22 Dec 1975
William Bennett	Social Credit	22 Dec 1975–6 Aug 1986
William Vander Zalm	Social Credit	6 Aug 1986–2 Apr 1991
Rita Johnston	Social Credit	2 Apr 1991–5 Nov 1991
Michael Harcourt	NDP	5 Nov 1991–22 Feb 1996
Glen Clark	NDP	22 Feb 1996–25 Aug 1999
Dan Miller	NDP	25 Aug 1999–24 Feb 2000
Ujjal Dosanjh	NDP	24 Feb 2000–

from each session. Presbyteries oversee congregations and provide support for the ministers. Synods are composed of groups of presbyteries, with similar representation. The national General Assembly is the highest court and principal policy and decision-making body. It is comprised of commissioners elected by presbyteries, and receives reports and recommendations from the agencies and committees of the church. In BC 64 pastoral charges in 5 presbyteries (KOOTENAY, KAMLOOPS, Westminster, VANCOUVER ISLAND and Western Han-Ca, or the Korean Canadian presbytery) form the Synod of BC.

The first Presbyterian minister in BC was John Hall, who arrived in VICTORIA in 1861 as a missionary from the Dublin presbytery of the Irish Presbyterian Church. The following year the first Presbyterian church on Vancouver Island was organized by Hall, and on the mainland at NEW WESTMINSTER by Robert Jamieson, a missionary from the Canadian Presbyterian Church. A Church of Scotland Presbyterian church, St Andrew's, was organized in Victoria in 1866. In 1875, shortly after the various Presbyterian synods and churches united to form the national Presbyterian Church in

Canada, the first presbytery was established in BC, in connection with the Church of Scotland in Edinburgh. Responsibility for the presbytery was transferred in 1887 to the Canadian Church. Missionary work was carried out in the NICOLA VALLEY, the CARIBOO, the OKANAGAN VALLEY and the BOUNDARY region, with ministers travelling long distances to care for members in remote and isolated communities. Congregations were established in Victoria and on the Lower Mainland, primarily but not exclusively attracting Scottish and Irish immigrants. The marine Presbyterian Loggers' Mission was established to serve LOGGING camps on the coast. George C.F. Pringle travelled up and down the coast on the mission boat Sky Pilot to minister to loggers and their families, supported in part by funds raised by provincial and national Presbyterian Women's Missionary Societies. Missions to aboriginal peoples focussed on the west coast of Vancouver Island, and boarding and day schools at AHOUSAT and PORT ALBERNI were established.

In 1925, about 30% of Presbyterians in the province (28 congregations with buildings and 19 groups without buildings) chose not to join the UNITED CHURCH, but instead to remain

distinctly Presbyterian. Presbyterians in BC are active in a variety of social ministries, including outdoor camps and educational programs, and hospital and prison chaplaincies, as well as supporting missions in other countries. Theological education is available through the Vancouver School of Theology, and St Andrew's Hall, the Presbyterian residence and chaplaincy, which opened in 1957 and was expanded in 1995 to provide additional residential units on campus. In 1997, planning for a program of theological education for ruling and teaching elders through the St Andrew's Institute for Elder's Education was begun. *Gail Edwards*

PRESPATOU, 75 km north of FORT ST JOHN at the northern limits of the PEACE R district, is a grain-farming and cattle-ranching district with a store, gas station and 2 churches. It was formed in 1963 by a group of MENNONITES. About 400 people live in the area and at the neighbouring community of ALTONA. *AS*

PRESS GANG PUBLISHERS is a feminist BOOK PUBLISHING collective started in Vancouver in 1975 by a group of women associated with a small independent printing company, Press Gang Printers. The printer, the last worker-controlled feminist print shop in N America, folded in 1993 but the publishing house continued as one of only 2 in Canada specializing in feminist and lesbian fiction and non-fiction. The press's best-known title is the underground classic *Daughters of Copper Woman* by Anne CAMERON. *See also* GAY AND LESBIAN RIGHTS.

PRETTY, Charles N., logger, timber broker (b 7 Mar 1890, Sault Ste Marie, ON; d 6 Apr 1992, Chilliwack). He came to BC a few months after his birth, with his father, Charles Fenn Pretty, a pioneer in the commercial FISHING industry. They settled in NEW WESTMINSTER and Pretty's father sent the first shipment of SALMON on ice east from VANCOUVER by rail. He then homesteaded on the Harrison R, near CHILLIWACK, and in 1908 entered the timber brokerage business with an office in Vancouver. He purchased several billion board ft of timber in the POWELL RIVER area, which was later sold to the Brooks Scanlon Co to launch the Powell River PULP AND PAPER mill. The younger Pretty, after a brief period in the real estate business, joined his father in the brokerage firm. When that business faltered at mid-century, he began LOGGING in the upper FRASER VALLEY and founded Pretty's Timber Co. The company survived; by the late 1990s, managed by Pretty's son Ivan, it was one of the largest independent logging companies in the province. In 1991, when he was 101, Charles Pretty was the first person inducted into the Fraser River Hall of Fame, honouring pioneers of the Fraser Valley. *Ken Drushka*

PREVOST ISLAND lies amidst the southern GULF ISLANDS east of SALTSPRING ISLAND on the BC FERRY route between Swartz Bay and TSAWWASSEN. Its deeply indented shoreline offers several sheltered anchorages for boaters. It is the only Gulf

Island of any size that has no ferry service, but it is populated and boasts one of the largest farms in the islands, owned for many years by the de Burgh family. The island is named for Capt James Prevost of HMS *Satellite*, a British naval vessel posted to the coast between 1857 and 1860. Prevost was British commissioner in the unsuccessful negotiations to settle the boundary dispute with the Americans that led to the PIG WAR.

PRICE, Thomas "Tom," Haida chief (b circa 1860, Ninstints, Queen Charlotte Islands; d 1927). He was Chief Ninstints, the last of a line of HAIDA leaders from the village of NINSTINTS on Anthony Island in the QUEEN CHARLOTTE ISLANDS (Haida Gwaii). He moved to SKIDEGATE in 1875 after SMALLPOX ravaged his own village, and he became an accomplished carver in ARGILLITE and later in SILVER and wood. He served as a Haida authority and teacher to several anthropologists and collectors, notably C.F. NEWCOMBE. When he died, his chiefly line died with him.

PRIEST CAMP, at Garnett Lk in SUMMERLAND, is the probable site of St Joseph's Station, a Jesuit mission founded by Father Giovanni Nobili between 1845 and 1848. St Joseph's was the first non-aboriginal settlement in the OKANAGAN VALLEY. The camp was also used by FUR TRADERS travelling the Okanagan FUR BRIGADE trail, by miners heading for the Cariboo goldfields (*see* GOLD RUSH, CARIBOO) and by ranchers driving cattle north to the rail construction camps. In 1998 Summerland designated the site a 20-ha historic park.   *David Gregory*

PRIESTLEY was a LOGGING community 20 km east of BURNS LAKE on the CNR. The station here was originally named Sheraton after a place in England. The first homesteaders arrived after WWI and a school was established in the 1920s, as was a camp for cutting railway ties. The post office closed in 1952 and by 1999 little remained of the settlement.   *AS*

PRIESTLEY, Jason Bradford, actor (b 28 Aug 1969, Vancouver). He got his start at age 4 acting in a television commercial, and later appeared in

Jason Priestley, actor. Vancouver Sun

locally shot movies and TV shows such as *21 Jump Street*, *Danger Bay* and *MacGyver*. After moving to Los Angeles he became an international celebrity and sex symbol as Brandon Walsh in the teen-oriented TV series *Beverly Hills 90210*, which first aired in 1990. He also acted in movies, including *The Boy Who Could Fly* (1986), *Calendar Girl* (1993), *Coldblooded* (1995), *Love and Death on Long Island* (1997), *The Highwayman* (1999) and *Dill Scallion* (1999). SW

PRINCE, Rose, Dakelh holy woman (b 1915, Fort St James; d 19 Aug 1949, Lejac). Born into the DAKELH (Carrier) nation, she entered the RESIDENTIAL SCHOOL at LEJAC in 1922 and stayed on after graduation to work around the institution. She was disabled by curvature of the spine. Prince was a devout Roman Catholic and a favourite of the nuns at the school. She died of tuberculosis at age 34. In 1951, when her casket was disinterred for removal to a new cemetery, her body was discovered to be perfectly preserved; this was taken by many as a sign of holiness. People began to pray to her, to make pilgrimages to her graveside and to report miraculous cures, and a movement began to have her canonized by the ROMAN CATHOLIC CHURCH as a saint. Meanwhile her grave continues to attract many pilgrims.

PRINCE GEORGE lies at the confluence of the NECHAKO and FRASER rivers near the geographical centre of the province, 780 km north of VANCOUVER. For many years it was BC's third-largest population centre after Vancouver and VICTORIA, but it has been surpassed in size by other centres.

Prince George main street, 1965.

Prince George lies in the traditional territory of the Lheit-Lit'en people, a subgroup of the DAKELH (Carrier), whose main RESERVE is located northeast of the city at SHELLEY. When Simon FRASER extended the FUR TRADE into NEW CALEDONIA for the NORTH WEST CO, he established Fort George on the site in 1807, naming it after King George III of England. For several decades the fort was on the route of the FUR BRIGADES connecting the Interior to the coast. Extensive settlement did not begin until the construction of the GRAND TRUNK PACIFIC RWY (now the CNR) ignited a land boom after 1908. In 1915 Fort George closed and the community was incorporated as Prince George, after the then Duke of Kent. The highway to Vancouver opened in 1926 but it was not until the post-WWII period that Prince George prospered, due largely to the FOREST INDUSTRY. In 1952 the HART HWY was completed between Prince George and DAWSON CREEK and the Pacific Great Eastern Rwy (*see* BC RAIL) was extended to the city from QUESNEL. In the 1960s, as a result of milling efficiencies and an increased utilization of wood wastes, 3 pulp mills opened

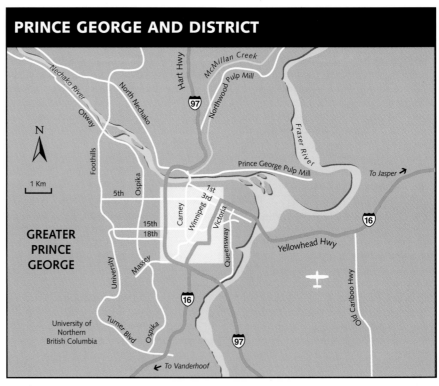

PRINCE GEORGE AND DISTRICT

A view of Prince George, 1990s.
Rick Blacklaws photo

PRINCE RUPERT, city, pop 16,714, is located on Kaien Island (49 km²) near the mouth of the SKEENA R on the North Coast, 730 km west of PRINCE GEORGE on the Yellowhead Hwy (Hwy 16; *see* ROADS AND HWYS). It is officially Canada's cloudiest place with an average of 6,123 overcast hours annually. The site was selected as the Pacific terminus for the GRAND TRUNK PACIFIC RWY, which began clearing a townsite in 1906. The name, which refers to the first governor of the HBC, was chosen in a contest. Alleged shady deals over railway land grants between the province and the GTP sparked a scandal in the legislature in 1906, but the committee formed to study it, the Kaien Island Investigation, found in favour of the government's actions. The city was incorporated on 3 Mar 1910. Founders expected

in Prince George (*see also* PULP AND PAPER). The community's population exploded from less than 14,000 in 1961 to over 33,000 in 1971. By the 1980s there were 15 SAWMILLS, an oil refinery, chemical plants and a brewery, and Prince George had become the major distribution centre for north-central BC. It is the terminus for BC Rail passenger service and an important service depot for the CNR. The city has a full range of cultural institutions, including a symphony orchestra, a regional museum and a major art gallery, and is the site of the UNBC, opened in 1994. Sport FISHING, hunting and cross-country SKIING are important area recreations.

Population: 75,150
Rank in BC: 13th
Population increase since 1981: 11%
Date of incorporation: city 6 Mar 1915
Land area: 322.49 km²
Location: Fraser-Fort George Regional District
Economic base: sawmilling, farming, pulp mills, oil refinery, chemical plants, wood manufacturing

PRINCE LINE of coastal steamships belonged to the Grand Trunk Pacific Steamship Co, incorporated in 1910, a subsidiary of the GRAND TRUNK PACIFIC RWY. The Prince ships inaugurated regular passenger service between PRINCE RUPERT and the South Coast. The *Prince George* and the *Prince Rupert* were large luxury vessels and competed with the CPR's PRINCESS LINE. After WWI the GTP became part of the CNR system and the marine service became Canadian National Steamships Ltd. The line reduced its operations during the 1930s and by the end of WWII was down to 2 vessels running scenic cruises to Prince Rupert and Alaska. In 1975, with the sale of the *Prince George*, CNS ended its Pacific coast operations.
Reading: Norman Hacking, *Prince Ships of Northern British Columbia*, 1995.

Fish boats at Prince Rupert, 1995.
Peter A. Robson photo

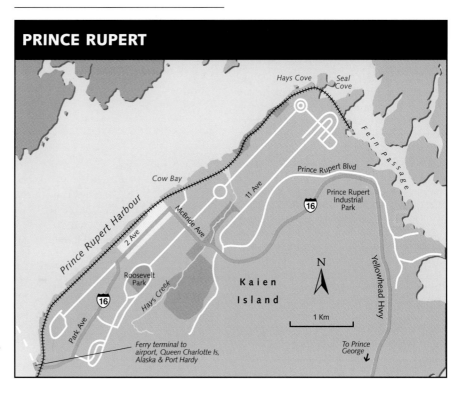

PRINCE RUPERT

Hays Cove · Seal Cove · Fern Passage · Prince Rupert Harbour · Cow Bay · Prince Rupert Blvd · 11 Ave · McBride Ave · 2 Ave · Prince Rupert Industrial Park · Roosevelt Park · Hays Creek · Kaien Island · Yellowhead Hwy · Park Ave · 1 Km · N · Ferry terminal to airport, Queen Charlotte Is, Alaska & Port Hardy · To Prince George

it to become a major seaport, economic rival to VANCOUVER, but it did not. Instead it developed as a commercial FISHING centre. During WWII Prince Rupert became a strategic base for the Canadian services and thousands of American military transshipped here for Alaska and the Far East. Roosevelt Park on the hill overlooking the city commemorates this period. Prince Rupert is the transportation centre of the North Coast with rail service by CNR and VIA Rail, an AIRPORT on Digby Island (34 km²), opened in 1961, and a seaplane base with flights to surrounding coastal communities. In the 1980s grain and COAL terminals were erected on nearby Ridley Island, so in a small way the city has become the international seaport its founders envisioned. In 1998 cargo shipments totalling 9 million tonnes—mainly grain and coal bound for Asia—passed through the port. BC FERRY CORP operates year-round service to PORT HARDY at the north end of VANCOUVER ISLAND and to the QUEEN CHARLOTTE ISLANDS, and the Alaska Marine Hwy has regular ferry service to Alaska. In the late 1990s the city's economy was hit hard by declines in both the fishing and LOGGING industries.

PRINCE RUPERT FISHERMEN'S CO-OPER-ATIVE ASSOCIATION was chartered in 1931 to promote the interests of North Coast fishers. The CO-OP opened fish camps and collecting stations, bought packers and in 1940 established the Prince Rupert Fishermen's CREDIT UNION. During WWII the co-op opened its own fish plant; it expanded over the years into a full processing facility on the PRINCE RUPERT waterfront. An industry downturn forced the company to close in 1996 and its assets were purchased by J.S. McMillan Fisheries Ltd. See also CO-OPERA-TIVES; FISHING, COMMERCIAL.
Reading: A.V. Hill, *Tides of Change: A History of Fishermen's Co-operatives in BC*, 1967.

PRINCE LINE of elegant steamships, owned by the CPR, provided the most important steamship service along the BC coast for nearly 60 years. The fleet began when the CPR purchased the CANADIAN PACIFIC NAVIGATION CO in 1901, forming its BC Coast Steamship Service and revitalizing coastal service with new Princess vessels and new routes. Ships plied the Triangle Route between VICTORIA, VANCOUVER and Seattle, up the coast as far as Alaska and along the west coast of VANCOUVER ISLAND. Following WWI car traffic grew dramatically; the first car ferry, the *Motor Princess*, entered service in 1923. From 1929 to 1950 it ran daily between STEVESTON and SIDNEY. During WWII a pair of Princess vessels was requisitioned by the military for use as troop transports in the Mediterranean. One, *PRINCESS MARGUERITE*, was sunk by torpedoes; the other, *Princess Kathleen*, returned to service on the coast. By the 1950s travellers were demanding fast, efficient transport rather than elegant comfort. At the same time the BLACK BALL LINE moved north from Puget Sound to begin competing on the Vancouver Island run. A labour dispute in 1958 shut down the Princess ships for 2 months and

led to reductions in service and fleet size, including the famous night sailing between Vancouver and Victoria. With the creation of the BC FERRY CORP in 1960 the CPR found it harder to compete and withdrew passenger service in 1981. The CPR continued to operate truck and rail car ferries between the Lower Mainland and Vancouver Island until 1998, when it sold the service (Coastal Marine Operations) to the SOUTHERN RAILWAY OF BC.
Reading: Robert D. Turner, *The Pacific Princesses: An Illustrated History of the Canadian Pacific's Princess Fleet*, 1977.

PRINCESS LOUISA INLET, a narrow, 8-km FJORD near the head of JERVIS INLET, is one of the scenic high points of the coast. It is accessible by

Chatterbox Falls at the head of Princess Louisa Inlet. Ian Douglas photo

boat via Malibu Rapids. Streams of meltwater cascade down the sides of the towering granite walls. At the head of the inlet is a MARINE PARK of the same name (65 ha) and the foaming turbulence of the spectacular Chatterbox Falls (40 m). The site was purchased for $400 by James "Mac" Macdonald, an American man of leisure, in 1927. In 1953 he turned it over to a non-profit society for the perpetual use of boaters. The society transferred it to the provincial government in the 1960s. Macdonald last visited the inlet in 1972; he died 6 years later. Thomas Hamilton, an AVIATION tycoon, built Malibu Lodge overlooking the rapids, but the operation quickly went broke and in 1954 became a Christian youth camp run by Young Life.

PRINCESS LOUISE was a wooden sidewheel steamboat purchased by the HBC in 1878 to carry passengers between VICTORIA and NEW WESTMIN-STER. It inaugurated steamer service between Victoria and BURRARD INLET in 1883 as part of the newly organized CANADIAN PACIFIC NAVIGATION CO. Later it was part of the PRINCESS LINE of coastal vessels owned by the CPR. In 1906 when it was sold and converted to a barge it was the last surviving sidewheeler in the coastal passenger service. The second *Princess Louise* was a 3,630-tonne steel vessel, 97 m long, built at Wallace Shipyards (*see* BURRARD DRY DOCK) in N VANCOUVER in 1921 for the Princess Line. The largest passenger vessel built in BC to that time, it was put on the night run between Victoria and VANCOUVER and in the summer cruised to Skagway, AK. It was retired in 1962, sold and towed to Los Angeles to become a floating restaurant.

PRINCESS MAQUINNA, a 71-m supply vessel owned by the CPR, was a familiar sight on the west coast of VANCOUVER ISLAND from 1913 to 1952. A combination passenger and freight vessel, it was built to handle the heavy seas of the outer coast. Twice a month it travelled between VICTORIA and PORT ALICE, stopping at fish plants, LOGGING camps and villages along the way. When airplanes took over the freight and

Princess Maquinna at Bamfield, 1948.
BC Archives I-26182

passenger business, the famous vessel was converted to an ore carrier, then scrapped in 1962.

PRINCESS MARGUERITE was for 50 years a familiar member of the PRINCESS LINE of coastal steamers owned by the CPR. The original *Marguerite*, named for a daughter of CPR president Thomas SHAUGHNESSY, took over service on

The CP coastal liner Princess Marguerite *leaving Victoria, 1974. Robert D. Turner photo*

the "triangle run" (VICTORIA–VANCOUVER–Seattle) in 1925. A flagship of the fleet during the 1930s, it was 106 m long, weighed 5,288 tonnes and featured 147 first-class staterooms. Requisitioned by the military during WWII, it was torpedoed and sank in the Mediterranean in 1942. A new *Princess Marguerite* went into service in 1949. A close replica of the original, it was one of the last ocean liner-type coastal ferries, and when it was retired in Sept 1974 it was the last survivor from the triangle run.

PRINCESS ROYAL ISLAND, 2,274 km², on the coast north of BELLA BELLA at Caamaño Sound, is the fourth-largest coastal island after VANCOUVER ISLAND and the 2 main QUEEN CHARLOTTE ISLANDS. It is separated from the mainland by Princess Royal Channel, a narrow passage surveyed by George VANCOUVER in 1793 and later used by ferries and CRUISE SHIPS on their routes through the INSIDE PASSAGE. It was named in 1788 by Charles DUNCAN, a British FUR TRADE captain, after his sloop. The TSIMSHIAN First Nation used the island seasonally. There have been 2 communities on the island: BUTEDALE on the east coast, site of a SALMON CANNERY village from 1909 to 1978; and SURF INLET, a MINING town on the west coast from 1917 to 1943. Once covered in a lush temperate RAIN FOREST of HEMLOCK, SPRUCE and CEDAR, the island has undergone considerable LOGGING; the effects of this activity on the sizeable local population of kermode BEARS have raised concerns among biologists and ENVIRONMENTALISTS.

PRINCESS SOPHIA, 74.5 m, was built in 1911 in Scotland and belonged to the PRINCESS LINE of CPR steamers plying the coast from Alaska to Seattle. Early on 24 Oct 1918, as it sailed south from Skagway, it grounded on Vanderbilt Reef in the Lynn Canal during a storm. The vessel remained high and dry for most of 2 days but the

foul weather made it difficult to offload any of the passengers to waiting rescue ships. At about 5:00 pm on 25 Oct the vessel broke up and sank. There were no survivors among the 343 people on board, the most fatalities of any shipwreck in BC history.

PRINCESS VICTORIA was the pride of the PRINCESS LINE of coastal steamers owned by the CPR. A twin-screw steel-hulled vessel, it was 91 m long with a capacity of 1,000 passengers. It entered service in 1903 and could make its regular VICTORIA–VANCOUVER run in 3¹/₂ hours, a record for the time. From 1904 to 1908 it made return trips from Victoria to Vancouver and from Victoria to Seattle every day, then in 1908 inaugurated the famous "triangle run" between the 3 cities that remained a familiar part of coastal passenger service for 40 years. The "Old Vic" was rebuilt in 1930 to accommodate automobiles and placed on the Victoria–Seattle run. After a stint as a floating hotel at NEWCASTLE ISLAND it was used as an excursion boat and backup ferry. It was retired in 1950 with its original machinery still working. The hull was sold as a fuel barge but sank in 1953. The ship's bell is in the BC Provincial Archives and its whistle belongs to the MARITIME MUSEUM OF BC in Victoria.

PRINCETON, town, pop 2,826, lies at the junction of the SIMILKAMEEN and Tulameen rivers, 136 km east of HOPE. It was originally named Red Earth Forks or Vermilion Forks for the red ochre

A view along Bridge Street, Princeton, c 1900. BC Archives C-08181

on the banks of the Tulameen. The pioneer settler was John Fall ALLISON, who established a ranch (*see* CATTLE INDUSTRY) in 1859, one year before Gov James DOUGLAS laid out a townsite and named it in honour of the Prince of Wales's visit to Canada. Princeton grew as the supply centre for an extensive MINING district. At one time GOLD, COAL and COPPER were all mined in the area. During WWI the KETTLE VALLEY RWY linked

Princeton to VANCOUVER and the completion of the HOPE-PRINCETON HWY (*see* ROADS AND HWYS) in 1949 put the town on another major transportation route. LOGGING has supplemented mining as an economic mainstay.

PRIOR, Edward Gawler, engineer, businessman, politician, premier 21 Nov 1902–1 June 1903, lt gov 1919–20 (b 21 May 1853, Dallaghgill, England; d 12 Dec 1920, Victoria). The son of a village parson in Yorkshire, he

E.G. Prior, premier of BC 1902–03, shown here in 1896. BC Archives B-03365

trained as a mining engineer and came to BC in 1873 as assistant manager of a NANAIMO coal mining company (*see* COAL MINING, VANCOUVER ISLAND). In 1878 he became inspector of mines, then held a series of government posts until 1880, when he resigned to go into the hardware business. A CONSERVATIVE, Prior won election to the legislature in 1886, then served as MP for VICTORIA from 1888 to 1896, when he lost his seat because of election irregularities. He was re-elected to the provincial legislature in 1900 and became minister of mines. When James

DUNSMUIR resigned as PREMIER, the lt gov chose Prior to succeed him. Prior's was the last of a series of unstable administrations before party government was established in BC. His term as premier ended in scandal when the lt gov dismissed him because his firm had received government contracts. He ran for election again in 1904 but was defeated. Prior was active in the militia and in his business until 18 Dec 1919, when he was appointed LT GOV. A year later he became the only BC lt gov to die in office.

PRISM was a VANCOUVER rock band that achieved its greatest commercial success in the late 1970s with hits such as "Spaceship Superstar," "Armageddon," "Virginia" and "Young and Restless." The group emerged in 1976 when Jim VALLANCE, using the alias Rodney

The Vancouver rock band Prism (l to r): Rocket Norton, Lindsay Mitchell, Ron Tabak, Allen Harlow, John Hall, 1979. D. Lippingwell photo

Higgs, and Bruce FAIRBAIRN, alumni of a Vancouver rhythm & blues/funk/JAZZ band, Sunshyne, recruited Lindsay Mitchell, Tom Lavin, Ron Tabak, Ab Bryant and Tom Keenlyside to record the band's self-titled debut album. The first single, "Spaceship Superstar," was a national success, but the original members of Prism departed for other projects. As they left, Mitchell replaced them with former members of the Seeds of Time, his late-1960s group notorious for sounding like the Rolling Stones onstage and behaving far worse offstage. In 1978, Tabak (vocals), Mitchell (guitar), John Hall (keyboards), Rocket Norton (drums) and Allen Harlow (guitar/bass) recorded Prism's second album, *See Forever Eyes*. Henry Small replaced Tabak as lead singer in 1981 and the band had some success with the album *Small Change*. Prism released a greatest hits album in 1988, followed by *Immortal*, the Seeds of Time's greatest hits, in 1991. *See also* SOUND RECORDING INDUSTRY. *Mike Harling*

PRISONS are administered by both the federal Department of the Solicitor General and the provincial Ministry of the Attorney General. Federal institutions receive prisoners who are serving sentences of 2 years or more, while provincial institutions are for inmates serving less than 2 years. Jails, also called remand or detention centres and administered by the province, accommodate persons who are awaiting trial or who have received short sentences.

BC Penitentiary, 1964.

The federal government operates 8 correctional facilities in BC: one maximum security prison (Kent Insitution at AGASSIZ), 4 medium security (Mountain Institution at Agassiz, Mission Institution at MISSION, William Head near VICTORIA and Matsqui Institution), 2 minimum security (Elbow Lake near HARRISON LK and Ferndale at Mission) and the Sumas community correctional centre in Abbotsford, mainly for prisoners on day parole. The province operates 19 provincial institutions. Five are secure correctional centres: Vancouver Island Regional in Victoria, the BURNABY Correctional Centre for Women, Fraser Regional in MAPLE RIDGE, KAMLOOPS Regional and PRINCE GEORGE Regional. Two are specialized pre-trial centres (Vancouver and SURREY). Ten are Open Correctional Centres: NANAIMO, New Haven in Burnaby, the Open Living Unit at the Burnaby Correctional Centre for Women, Alouette River and Stave Lake in Maple Ridge, Mt Thurston and Ford Mountain in CHILLIWACK, Rayleigh in Kamloops, Bear Creek in CLEARWATER and Hutda Lake in Prince George. And 2 are community correctional centres: Chilliwack and TERRACE. Mentally disturbed offenders are held in a special section of the Vancouver Pretrial Services Centre or at the Forensic Psychiatric Unit in PORT COQUITLAM. *See also* MENTAL HEALTH POLICY.

PRITCHARD is at the heart of a large ranching district (*see* CATTLE INDUSTRY) on both sides of the S THOMPSON R, 40 km east of KAMLOOPS. The 8,500-year-old remains of a man trapped and drowned in an ancient mud flow were found in this area. Walter Pritchard, an OKANAGAN VALLEY stage driver, built a store and hotel south of the river on the CPR line in 1912, when many new settlers were arriving. A ferry crossed the Thompson R at this point until a bridge was constructed in 1920. *AS*

PRITCHARD, William Arthur, labour leader (b 1889, Salford, England; d 24 Oct 1982, Los Angeles). After arriving in VANCOUVER in 1911 he became head of the Longshoremen's Union and an activist in the Socialist Party of Canada. At the Western Labour Conference in Calgary in 1919 he was a member of the committee set up to organize the One Big Union. He visited Winnipeg during the 1919 general strike and was arrested on his way back to Vancouver. Convicted of seditious conspiracy for his part in the strike, he served a year in prison. His politics later moderated somewhat and he was reeve of BURNABY (1930–32), president of the Union of BC Municipalities and active in the formation of the provincial CCF. *See also* LABOUR MOVEMENT.

PRITCHETT, Harold, union leader (b 1904, Birmingham, England; d 1982, Vancouver). He came to BC when his family immigrated in

Harold Pritchett, labour leader.
UBC BC1532/2098/1

1912. They settled in PORT MOODY and he began working in a shingle mill at age 15. He was a founder of the International Woodworkers of America (IWA Canada; later renamed INDUSTRIAL, WOOD AND ALLIED WORKERS OF CANADA) in 1937, eventually serving as its first non-American president, the first Canadian to lead an international union. He had to resign when his permit to work in the US was revoked because of his membership in the Communist Party, but he continued to be president of the BC district of the IWA until he was expelled during the anti-Communist purge of BC leaders organized by the International leadership in 1948.

PROCTER, 26 km northeast of NELSON on the south shore of the west arm of KOOTENAY LK, is a small resort community. The CPR built a line from Nelson in 1901 and Procter served as an ice-free port for steamships. For many years it was the site of the CPR's handsome Outlet Hotel. The name was originally Proctor, after a local rancher, but changed as a result of confusion with T.G. Procter, a Nelson realtor. *AS*

PROGRESS, an AGRICULTURAL community 33 km west of DAWSON CREEK in the PEACE R district, was first settled in 1916 by the Rosenau and Kerr families. During a meeting to decide on a village name, the secretary of the school board reportedly noticed a watermark in his notepaper that spelled out the word *progress*.　　　　AS

PROGRESSIVE DEMOCRATIC ALLIANCE

(PDA) was a provincial political party created in 1993 by Gordon WILSON, former leader of the BC LIBERAL PARTY. Wilson had led the Liberals to a surprising second-place finish in the 1991 provincial election but proved ineffective at consolidating support. Trouble with his caucus forced him to call a leadership contest in 1993 and when he was ousted he formed the PDA. It found few supporters for its middle-of-the-road policies and in the 1996 provincial election won just 5.7% of the popular vote. Wilson retained his seat in the legislature but the party seemed to lack any future and early in 1999 Wilson joined the NDP government as minister of aboriginal affairs and minister in charge of the BC FERRY CORP. The PDA disbanded in the wake of Wilson's defection.

PROHIBITION

took effect in BC on 1 Oct 1917. A bill banning the sale of liquor except for medicinal, sacramental and industrial purposes had passed the legislature the previous year and was approved by referendum during the 1917 provincial election. The new law met with only qualified success. Enforcement was difficult and expensive. Medical practitioners freely prescribed liquor, bootlegging flourished and alcohol could still be imported for personal use from outside the province. Bars remained open, selling a low-alcohol beer known as "near-beer" legally and other alcohol illegally. In a plebiscite on 20 Oct 1920 voters abandoned prohibition, approving instead a system of government control and sale of alcohol. Following on the results of the plebiscite, in 1921 new legislation created government liquor stores and a 3-person Liquor Control Board (*see* LIQUOR DISTRIBUTION BRANCH) to regulate liquor policy. Prohibition was repealed officially on 15 June 1921, the same day that the first government liquor stores opened. Every province introduced some sort of prohibition before and during WWI; BC was the first province in English Canada to rescind it.

PROPHET RIVER

pop 99, on the ALASKA HWY 90 km south of FORT NELSON, is a FIRST NATIONS community, home to DUNNE-ZA (Beaver), SEKANI and DENE-THAH (Slavey) people. The name refers to the Sekani prophet Zacharie Dakodoa, who encouraged resistance to white encroachment. In 1911 the local band adhered to TREATY NO 8.

PROVINCE

is one of VANCOUVER's two daily NEWSPAPERS. It was founded in VICTORIA in 1894 as a weekly by Hewitt BOSTOCK, who later teamed up with Walter NICHOL. They moved the paper to Vancouver and relaunched it as the *Vancouver Daily Province* on 26 Mar 1898. Nichol took over the entire operation in 1901, then sold it to the Southam chain in 1923. The *Province* had the largest circulation in the city until 1949 when, hurt by a 41-month printers' strike, it was surpassed by the VANCOUVER SUN. When owners of the 2 papers formed PACIFIC PRESS in 1957, the

Province became a morning paper; since 2 Aug 1983 it has been a tabloid. Notable staffers have included Paddy Sherman, who rose to become editor, humorist Eric NICOL, columnist Himie Koshevoy, sports columnist Clancy LORANGER and marine editor Norman HACKING. In 1997 the circulation was 158,500 daily and 192,300 on Sunday. In 2000 ownership of most Southam dailies, including the *Province*, passed from Conrad Black's Hollinger International to Israel Asper's CanWest Global Communications Corp.

PROVINCE EXPLORING EXPEDITION, 1894–

96, accomplished the first crossing of VANCOUVER ISLAND from north to south. Named for the *PROVINCE* newspaper, then a VICTORIA weekly, the expedition was led by Rev William Washington Bolton, headmaster of a Victoria boys' school. It got underway 7 July 1894 from Cape Sutil at the north end of the Island and travelled by foot, raft and CANOE as far as WOSS LK. At Woss Lk the expedition turned toward the West Coast, reaching TAHSIS overland, then canoeing down the coast to PORT ALBERNI, from where members returned to Victoria along a well-travelled route. This left the middle portion of the Island unexplored, but it was not until the summer of 1896 that Bolton was able to remount the expedition. Starting from Woss Lk, he and 4 companions travelled down the Gold R, east across the mountains to BUTTLE LK and south to GREAT CENTRAL LK and Alberni. This trek, which completed the expedition's agenda, took them through much of what later became STRATHCONA PROVINCIAL PARK. A hiking trail built the length of Vancouver Island during the 1990s includes sections of the route pioneered by the expedition.

PROVINCIAL PARTY

was a short-lived political party launched in 1922 by an alliance of disaffected CONSERVATIVES who objected to the leadership of William BOWSER, and members of the UNITED FARMERS OF BC who wished to extend their movement into electoral politics. The driving force in the party was the VANCOUVER millionaire A.D. MCRAE, who financed much of its activity and served as party president. It was agreed that a leader would be chosen later from among members elected to the legislature. The party organ was a muckraking broadsheet, the *Searchlight*, which promoted "clean government" and attempted to expose the corruption of old-line parties. In the election of June 1924 the Provincials elected 3 members with a respectable 24.2% of the vote. Their participation contributed to the personal defeat of Bowser and Premier John OLIVER. But the party began disintegrating soon after as prominent members returned to the Conservatives. By the election of 1928, the Provincial Party no longer existed.

PROVINCIAL POLICE

were established in 1858 to maintain order in the goldfields of the new colony of mainland BC. Known until 1895 as the BC Constabulary, the small force patrolled a vast frontier territory by canoe, horse and wagon, enforcing liquor and games laws, maintaining peace between aboriginals and the first

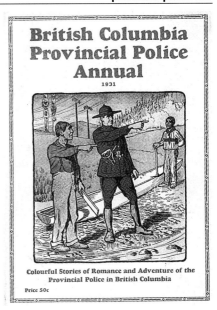

British Columbia Provincial Police Annual 1931

Colourful Stories of Romance and Adventure of the Provincial Police in British Columbia

Price 50c

Cover of the only issue of the force's annual, 1931.

A.W. Stone in uniform of the BC Provincial Police, adopted in 1924.

settlers, policing strikes, controlling smuggling and generally enforcing provincial statutes. The force obtained the first patrol boat for its marine service in 1898. In 1923 it began policing municipalities on contract. The uniform, not adopted until 1924, featured khaki jacket and pants with green trim and a Stetson hat. When the government merged the force with the RCMP in 1950 for reasons of economy, it numbered about 500 men. Chief superintendents were: Chartres BREW (1858–70), John Howe Sullivan (1870–74), Charles Todd (1875–84), Herbert Roycraft (1884–91), Premier Theodore DAVIE (1891–93), Frederick Hussey (1893–1911), Colin S. Campbell (1911–16), William G. McMynn (1917–23), John H. McMullin (1923–39), T.W.S. Parson (1939–47), John Shirras (1947–50) and Roger Peachey (1950). *See also* COLONIAL GOVERNMENT; GOLD RUSHES

PTARMIGAN is a chicken-sized game bird related to GROUSE, from which it is distinguished by its alpine habitat, feathered feet and white winter plumage. In summer the bird's colouring is mottled brown and grey. Ptarmigan nest on the ground. All 3 species occur in BC. Willow

Rock ptarmigan. Ervio Sian photo

ptarmigan (*Lagopus lagopus*), the largest, are found in the north at high elevations and in the WILLOW shrub tundra. Rock ptarmigan (*L. mutus*) are usually found in alpine meadows in the COAST MTS and across the north. The smallest and most widespread species is the white-tailed ptarmigan (*L. leucurus*), which lacks the black tail common to the others.

PUFFIN is a medium-sized seabird, upright in posture, distinguished by its large, bright-coloured, parrot-like bill. Puffins breed in the summer in colonies on islets on the outer coast, where they nest in long burrows. They spend the rest of the time at sea, feeding on fish. Two species occur on the coast. The tufted puffin (*Fratercula cirrhata*) has a black body, white face, orange legs and bill and long yellowish tufts that droop behind the eyes. The smaller, less abundant horned puffin (*F. corniculata*) has a black back, white belly and face and a yellow bill with a red tip. Its name refers to the black fleshy "horns" protruding above each eye.

PUGET SOUND NAVIGATION CO was founded in the late 1890s, based in Seattle. Until 1927 it was owned by Joshua Green. As well as operating steamship service in Puget Sound, it offered passenger service to VICTORIA and

VANCOUVER for many years, in competition with the CPR's PRINCESS LINE. During the so-called "Rate War" of 1908–9 the two companies competed fiercely for business on the Victoria–Seattle route, dropping their one-way fare as low as 25 cents. Peace was eventually restored and PSN continued to operate a Seattle–Victoria service until the 1950s. In 1951 when Washington state took over many PSN routes in Puget Sound, the company created a subsidiary, the BLACK BALL LINE, to operate in Canadian waters.

PUGET'S SOUND AGRICULTURAL CO (PSAC) was established in 1839, separate from but affiliated with the HBC to engage in AGRICULTURE and stock raising (*see* CATTLE INDUSTRY) in the Columbia District of the HBC's fur-trading empire. It was expected that company farms would produce a variety of crops along with wool, hides and tallow for Russian settlements to the north and for export to Hawaii and Great Britain. Initially farms were located at Nisqually and Cowlitz in what is now Washington state. After the Columbia territory was ceded to the US by the 1846 boundary settlement (*see* OREGON TREATY), PSAC moved its operations north to VANCOUVER ISLAND. It established 4 farms around ESQUIMALT harbour and put bailiffs in charge of each: Edward Langford at COLWOOD, Kenneth McKenzie at CRAIGFLOWER, Thomas SKINNER at Constance Cove and Douglas Macauley at Viewfield. Settlers were imported to work the farms and by the mid-1850s most of the immigrant population on Vancouver Island were employed by PSAC. The farms eventually were subdivided and sold, though some of the land remained with the HBC until the 1930s, when it was taken over by the municipality of Esquimalt.

PULICE, Alfred "Foncie," street photographer (b 1914, Vancouver). From the 1930s through the 1970s he stationed himself on the downtown streets of VANCOUVER and snapped candid photographs of passing pedestrians. He broke into the business in 1934, first working for another photographer and then striking out on

Alfred Pulice ("Foncie"), photographer, at work on the streets of Vancouver. Deni Eaglund/Vancouver Sun

his own after WWII. At his busiest he ran 3 operations, taking 8,000 photographs daily. In 1979 he retired and moved to KELOWNA. His camera, with its flash powered by a car battery, is in the collection of the VANCOUVER MUSEUM. *See also* PHOTOGRAPHY.

PULP AND PAPER industry uses several processes to convert wood fibre into cellulose pulp, which is then manufactured into paper, newsprint, cardboard and thousands of other products. The basic pulp process is to reduce wood to fibre by mechanical means or by heating in chemical solutions. To make paper, the fibres are mixed with water and extruded in continuous sheets, which are pressed and dried. Some BC mills produce pulp only, which is shipped to other mills at home or abroad for use in paper or chemical manufacturing. Some mills also produce newsprint, while several mills use BC pulp to manufacture writing, photocopy and other fine papers. In 1998 there were 26 pulp and paper mills operating in the province.

Tufted puffin, Triangle Island. Ian McAllister photo

PULP AND PAPER MAKING AT PORT MELLON

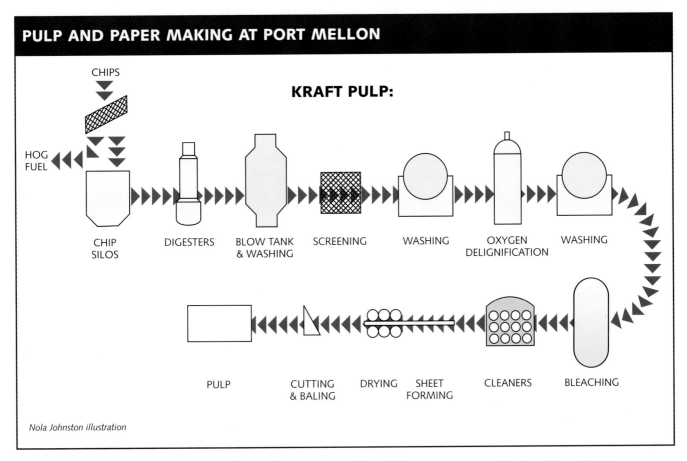

KRAFT PULP:

CHIPS

HOG FUEL

CHIP SILOS · DIGESTERS · BLOW TANK & WASHING · SCREENING · WASHING · OXYGEN DELIGNIFICATION · WASHING

PULP · CUTTING & BALING · DRYING · SHEET FORMING · CLEANERS · BLEACHING

Nola Johnston illustration

All paper making involves taking wood, breaking it down to wood fibre, then arranging the fibres so that they form a consistent, uniform sheet. The process used to accomplish this varies according to what the finished product will be, either kraft pulp or newsprint. Newsprint is what daily newspapers and flyers are printed on; kraft pulp is an intermediate product that other manufacturers use to make a variety of paper products such as fine writing paper, air filters, paper towel, and disposable surgical garments. The first step in any paper production is pulping. Wood fibres are held together by a natural glue called lignin. The basic task of kraft pulping is to break this natural bond while leaving the wood fibres intact—the longer the wood fibres, the stronger the final product. Kraft pulp is known for its strength, therefore the pulping process must produce long fibres. This is accomplished using a chemical called white liquor (sodium sulfide and sodium hydroxide) to "cook" the chips in a large tank called a digester. From there the chips go into a series of tanks where the cooking chemicals are recovered so that they can be recycled and reintroduced into the digester, uncooked chips are screened out, and oxygen is used to remove more of the lignin. At this point the pulp is still brown, so it is washed and sent to the bleach plant, where it is whitened with the application of oxygen, chlorine dioxide, sodium hydroxide and hydrogen peroxide. Next the pulp is sprayed onto a synthetic mesh and the sheet is dried. It is then cut into smaller sheets, bailed and sent to the warehouse for storage.

Howe Sound Pulp and Paper mill at Port Mellon, c 1998. Dean van't Schip photo

BC's first paper mill was opened by the BC Paper Manufacturing Co at PORT ALBERNI in 1894. Because it was designed to use rags as raw material it was unable to utilize local wood for pulp; it failed after 2 years. A few years later the provincial government made pulp leases on Crown timber available to encourage the development of a pulp and paper industry. Several companies were formed and obtained leases, but it was not until 1909 that mills began operating: one a pulp mill at SWANSON BAY on the North Coast, and the second a pulp and paper mill at PORT MELLON on HOWE SOUND. The POWELL RIVER newsprint mill, the first in BC and one of the largest in the world, began production in 1912. The same year the Whalen family opened a pulp and paper mill at WOODFIBRE on Howe Sound and in 1916 they took over the Swanson Bay mill, which operated for another decade. A Whalen-owned pulp mill also began operating

P

PULP AND PAPER MAKING AT PORT MELLON

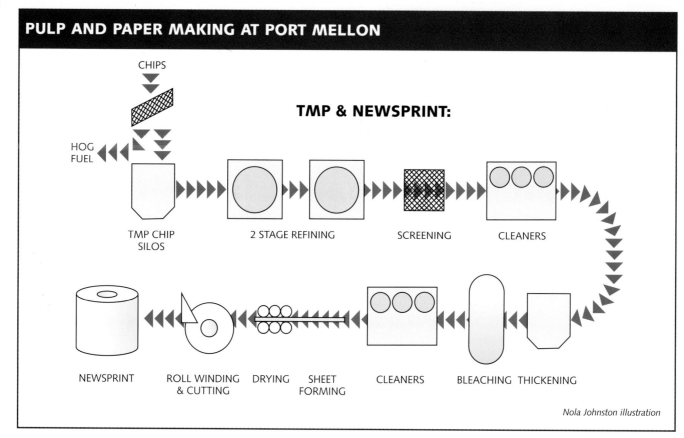

TMP & NEWSPRINT:

CHIPS

HOG FUEL

TMP CHIP SILOS — 2 STAGE REFINING — SCREENING — CLEANERS

NEWSPRINT — ROLL WINDING & CUTTING — DRYING — SHEET FORMING — CLEANERS — BLEACHING THICKENING

Nola Johnston illustration

Making newsprint has some features in common with the Kraft process, but begins differently. Newsprint wood fibres do not have to be as long as those in kraft pulp, so the method of producing the fibres can be more aggressive. In one process, Thermo-Mechanical Pulping, wood chips are steamed in order to make them softer, then sent through primary and secondary refiners, large grinders with combed plates in the middle. A 19,000-hp motor spins the plates as wood chips enter through the centre.

Chips are forced outward past "teeth" that are spaced progressively closer together, and the chips break into smaller and smaller pieces. The pulp is then screened and cleaned, and kraft pulp is added for increased strength. Newsprint pulp is then given a touch of dye to give the paper a slight colour. It is saturated with 99% water, and sent to the high-speed paper machine to be formed into a continuous sheet and dried. The paper is then wound onto 1-tonne rolls and sent to the warehouse.

Text courtesy Howe Sound Pulp and Paper

at PORT ALICE on the northwest coast of VANCOUVER ISLAND in 1918. In 1917 Pacific Mills opened the province's second newsprint mill at OCEAN FALLS; it operated until 1980, then closed for lack of timber. In 1912 the Sidney Roofing & Paper Co built a small paper mill on the SAANICH PENINSULA to manufacture asphalt roofing material and construction paper, and in 1923 Westminster Paper Mills (later SCOTT PAPER LTD), opened a tissue paper mill in NEW WESTMINSTER. This was the last new mill until after WWII.

During the war many chemical-based uses for cellulose were discovered; when the war ended there was an immense demand for pulp. Two new mills were built shortly after armistice, one by BLOEDEL, STEWART & WELCH at Port Alberni, and another by the H.R. MACMILLAN Export Co at Harmac, near NANAIMO. When Forest Management Licence tenures were created in 1948 (*see* FOREST POLICY) they were used to spur development of several pulp mills. The American Celanese Corp opened pulp mills at PRINCE RUPERT (1951) and CASTLEGAR (1960)—the Interior's first pulp mill. CROWN ZELLERBACH's Elk Falls pulp and newsprint mill at CAMPBELL RIVER opened in 1952. BC FOREST PRODUCTS start-

ed production at its CROFTON pulp mill in 1958, and in 1964 a newsprint mill was added. MACMILLAN BLOEDEL opened the Island Paper fine paper mill in VANCOUVER in 1960. The

Tahsis Company opened a pulp mill at GOLD RIVER in 1967, to which a newsprint mill was added in 1990. (By 1999 both operations had shut down.) Eurocan Pulp and Paper Co

Paper being manufactured at Howe Sound Pulp and Paper mill, Port Mellon, c 1998.
Dean van't Schip photo

opened a pulp and paper mill at KITIMAT in 1969. Throughout the late 1960s and 1970s large integrated FOREST PRODUCTS complexes were built in the Interior. These mills obtained most of their raw material in the form of waste from SAWMILLS and plywood plants. The development of a new type of high-speed saw, the Chip-n-Saw, cut small logs into lumber, with the unused portion turned into pulp chips. In 1966, 3 new mills opened in the Interior, one at KAMLOOPS and 2 at PRINCE GEORGE. Two years later Intercontinental Pulp Co opened Prince George's third pulp mill. CRESTBROOK FOREST INDUSTRIES opened a pulp mill at SKOOKUM-CHUCK in the E KOOTENAY in 1969. A small groundwood mill, the first in BC using this process, was opened by Finlay Forest Products at MACKENZIE in 1971. (This mill was later sold to the Montreal company Donahue Inc) In 1972 Cariboo Pulp and Paper opened a mill at QUESNEL and BC Forest Products opened a mill at Mackenzie. WEST FRASER TIMBER opened Quesnel's second mill in 1980. In 1987 a consortium of Interior sawmills opened the Fibreco pulp mill at TAYLOR, and in 1991 Louisiana Pacific began operations at its CHETWYND pulp mill.

As the timber supply tightened during the 1980s and 1990s, large sums were invested in rebuilding many of the established mills to make them more efficient. Others expanded their capacity, and all of them spent large amounts of money installing new equipment to reduce toxins in the effluents dumped into river and ocean waters (*see* ENVIRONMENTAL MOVEMENT). In 1991 Newstech Recycling opened BC's first paper recycling plant in New Westminster, producing de-inked pulp. In 1997 the BC pulp and paper industry employed 10,700 people. It produced 4.1 million metric tonnes of market pulp and 1.5 million tonnes of newsprint. Total value of pulp and newsprint sales was $3.7 billion. But as the decade drew to a close the industry seemed to be in crisis. Pulp from coastal mills had become the highest priced in the world and was losing market share to lower-cost producers. The SKEENA CELLULOSE mill at Prince Rupert had to be rescued with provincial government funds, the Celgar mill at Castlegar closed in bankruptcy, and several other mills were losing money. *See also* FOREST INDUSTRY. *Ken Drushka*

PUNCHAW, 65 km southwest of PRINCE GEORGE on the Chilako R, is the centre of a remote ranching (*see* CATTLE INDUSTRY) and LOGGING district. There is a FOREST SERVICE campsite 10 km east on Punchaw Lk. The name is a DAKELH (Carrier) word meaning "big lake." *AS*

PUNTLEDGE, a COAL mining settlement 5 km southwest of COURTENAY on VANCOUVER ISLAND, was the site of the No 8 Mine, which first operated from 1914 to 1916. A townsite was built here, then abandoned, then reoccupied after WWI when LOGGING activity went on in the area. The mine reopened in 1937 for several years but the community was mostly deserted by the late 1940s. *AS*

PUNTZI LAKE is a small community in the central CHILCOTIN about 65 km west of ALEXIS CREEK. The name derives from a DAKELH (Carrier) word meaning "small lake." William Manning homesteaded here during the GOLD RUSH era and ran a stopping place. He was murdered during the so-called CHILCOTIN WAR and it was in this area that the TSILHQOT'IN (Chilcotin) warriors, who took part in the "war," surrendered to authorities. In 1952 Puntzi became an air base as part of the Pinetree Line, a chain of early-warning radar stations. A civilian community grew around the base, which was demobilized in 1965. The lake is a feeding area for white PELICANS and trumpeter SWANS.

PURCELL MOUNTAINS are one of 4 ranges in south-central BC (the others are the MONASHEE, SELKIRK and CARIBOO Mts) that form the COLUMBIA MTS. Extending south from GOLDEN to the US border, they are considered the dividing line between east and west KOOTENAY. Generally

View of the Purcell Mts. Keith Thirkell photo

lower than the ROCKY MTS, they nonetheless feature several peaks that soar as high as 3,400 m. The highest is Mt Farnham (3,457 m). Nestled in the southern part of the range, KIMBERLEY is the highest city in Canada. In the north the BUGABOOS offer some of the most spectacular backcountry SKIING in the world. The PURCELL WILDERNESS CONSERVANCY protects the vast, isolated central section of the range. MINING and FORESTRY have been the main economic activities. The range is named for Goodwin Purcell, an Irish academic.

PURCELL STRING QUARTET was BC's leading chamber music ensemble for 20 years. Founded in 1969 by 4 VANCOUVER SYMPHONY ORCHESTRA string players—Norman Nelson and Raymond Ovens (violins), Simon Streatfield (viola) and Ian Hampton (cello)—it toured across Canada and internationally, broadcast regularly on radio and made several recordings. In 1972–82 it was quartet-in-residence at SFU. At various times Philippe Etter, Sydney Humphreys,

Bryan King, Marc Destrubé, Frederick Nelson, Robert Growcott, Joseph Peleg and Heather Hay belonged to the ensemble, which ceased performing in 1990.

PURCELL WILDERNESS CONSERVANCY, 1,315.23 km², established in 1974, is a wilderness area in the PURCELL MTS northeast of KOOTENAY LK. It is dominated by several high peaks, in particular Mt Findlay and Hamill Peak. The main access route is the Earl Grey Pass Trail, named for a former gov gen of Canada who crossed the trail from INVERMERE to ARGENTA on horseback and foot in 1908. The trail was used formerly by local aboriginal people and prospectors (*see* GOLD RUSH). Grey built a cabin on TOBY CREEK and touted the region as a future national PARK. No official action took place until 1971, when the town of Argenta re-established the trail as a BC Centennial project. Subsequently the province established the wilderness conservancy, the only such designation in BC, banning the use of combustion engines and all commercial and industrial activity except that devoted to non-mechanized outdoor recreation.

PURDY, Alfred Wellington "Al," writer (b 30 Dec 1918, Wooler, ON; d 21 Apr 2000, Sidney). He is considered one of Canada's greatest poets. Raised in Trenton, ON, he dropped out of high school and rode the rails to VANCOUVER, where he began the life of an itinerant labourer. During WWII he served in the Canadian air force and lived in BC from 1942 to 1944; he also published his first book of poems, *The Enchanted Echo*, which he later pronounced "atrocious." He served a long apprenticeship as a poet, finally breaking through with *The Cariboo Horses* (1965), which won the GOV GEN'S LITERARY AWARD. From that time forward he was able to support himself full-time by writing. He and his wife Eurithe travelled widely while alternating their permanent residence between BC and Ontario. They lived in BC full-time from 1949 to 1956 and in 1985 began spending winters in the VICTORIA area. Purdy published 33 books of poetry, along with a novel, *A Splinter in the Heart*

Al Purdy, poet, 1998.
Barry Peterson & Blaise Enright-Peterson

(1990); an autobiography, *Reaching for the Beaufort Sea* (1993); and 9 collections of essays and correspondence. His *Collected Poems* (1986) won a second Gov Gen's Award. Other collections include *Poems for all the Annettes* (1962), *North of Summer: Poems from Baffin Island*

(1967), *Wild Grape Wine* (1968), *Sex & Death* (1973), *Sundance at Dusk* (1976), *The Stone Bird* (1981), *Piling Blood* (1984), *The Woman on the Shore* (1990), *Naked With Summer in Your Mouth* (1994), *Rooms for Rent in the Outer Planets: Selected Poems* (1996), *To Paris Never Again* (1997) and a second collected poems, *Beyond Remembering: The Collected Poems of Al Purdy* (2000). He was appointed to the Order of Canada in 1983 and the Order of Ontario in 1987. A strong nationalist, he achieved greatness in a way different—and perhaps more fittingly Canadian—than any writer before him. It came not from great learning or heightened sensitivity or stylized rhetoric, but rather by giving voice to the vernacular idiom of ordinary Canadians. Although he cherished the idea of being a writer from age 13, Purdy had little formal education and travelled from coast to coast working at odd jobs until he was in his forties, which gave him a worm's-eye view of Canadian reality that he never lost. Not only did he write naturally and unaffectedly in the language of the mattress-factory lunch room, he also wrote about its subjects: hating the boss, savouring a game of hockey, brewing homemade beer, parting with a beloved old car, rowing with a spouse. This was a highly original choice in a profession where linguistic artifice and intellectual refinement are the norm, but what makes Purdy's best work

great is that it shows the language of ordinary life to have resources of humour, intellect and lyricism fully as rich as those of more formal writing. This was an innovation not only of national but of worldwide significance, and Purdy has been justly honoured for it.   *Howard White*

PUTMAN-WEIR COMMISSION was a review of education appointed by the provincial government in 1924. Commissioners were J.H. Putman, an Ottawa school inspector, and George M. WEIR, professor of education at UBC and later a provincial minister of education. Both were considered progressive reformers. They held over 200 public hearings, visited 150 schools and issued a report, *Survey of the School System* in 1925, containing many recommendations. Among those implemented: an emphasis on child-centred learning and co-operative classroom work, creation of junior high schools for grades 7–9, increased emphasis on manual training and domestic science, the use of IQ testing and measures to improve the standard of teacher education and to encourage students to remain in school longer. The commission is considered a high-water mark of progressive educational thought in Canada during the inter-war period. *See also* EDUCATION, PUBLIC.

southern Interior, principally the OKANAGAN VALLEY, where it feeds on seeds and INSECTS. Two species occur in BC. The California quail (*Callipepla californica*), the most widespread, was first introduced in the 1860s. The male is distinguished by a black and white head with a prominent curved plume. Body plumage is grey-blue-brown with white slash marks. In fall, California quail gather in large coveys. They roost in trees and scatter widely when alarmed. The mountain quail (*Oreortyx pictus*) is confined almost exclusively to southern Vancouver Island, where it is now very rare. It is distinguished by a chestnut throat and a long, straight head plume. It occupies shrubby hills and mountainsides, though it winters at lower elevations.

QUALICUM BEACH, town, pop 6,728, is a retirement/resort community on the east side of VANCOUVER ISLAND, 47 km north of NANAIMO. The name derives from a PENTLATCH word for chum SALMON. The earliest settlers arrived at the

Street scene, Qualicum Beach, 1999.
L. Randal Berry photo

QLT PHOTOTHERAPEUTICS INC is one of BC's leading BIOTECHNOLOGY companies and is a pioneer in photodynamic therapy (PDT), a field of medicine utilizing light-activated drugs in the treatment of cancer and other diseases. The company was founded as Quadra Logic Technologies in 1981 by a group of medical scientists based at UBC, including Dr Julia Levy, who became president of the company in 1995.

QUADRA, Juan Francisco de la Bodega y, *see* BODEGA Y QUADRA, JUAN FRANCISCO DE LA.

QUADRA ISLAND, 276 km², pop 1,960, is one of a group of islands lying between VANCOUVER ISLAND and the mainland at the north end of GEORGIA STRAIT opposite CAMPBELL RIVER.

Originally called Valdes Island, it was renamed in 1903 for the Spanish explorer BODEGA Y QUADRA. Capt George VANCOUVER landed at CAPE MUDGE in 1792 at a large village that is thought to have been Coast Salish (*see* SALISHAN FIRST NATIONS). There are more than 50 petroglyphs on the beach below the old village site (*see* ROCK ART). Early in the 19th century these original inhabitants were replaced by KWAKWAKA'WAKW (Kwakiutl), who now occupy Cape Mudge Village. The Kwagiulth Museum, opened in 1979, displays ceremonial items that were seized by the government during the years when the POTLATCH was banned and subsequently reclaimed by the Kwakwaka'wakw. In the 1880s LOGGING began on the island, which became known for its fine timber. Settlers followed, and by 1901 the island had 4 steamboat landings, 2 hotels, 2 stores and a school. MINING was tried at several sites. The most famous was the Lucky Jim Mine, which opened in 1910 but petered out by 1925. Commercial FISHING was also important, and a cannery operated in QUATHIASKI COVE from 1904 to 1941. CROWN ZELLERBACH received a Forest Management Licence in 1947 that gave them long-term control over much of the north end of the island. By this time Campbell River had taken over as the economic hub of the region. Islanders got their first car ferry service to Campbell River in 1960, and many residents now commute to work there. Rebecca Spit Provincial PARK (1.77 km²), with its gorgeous views of the snow-covered COAST MTS, is a favourite destination for boaters and picnickers. Located on the PACIFIC FLYWAY, a major bird migration route, the island is an important stopover for a variety of waterfowl. The 2 main commercial centres are Quathiaski Cove, where the ferry from Campbell River arrives, and HERIOT BAY, where the ferry to CORTES ISLAND departs.

QUAIL is a small game bird inhabiting brushy habitat on southern VANCOUVER ISLAND and the

May Day on Quadra Island. Ian Douglas photo

mouth of the Little Qualicum R in the 1880s and in 1894 the wagon road arrived from Nanaimo. A village was laid out in 1910, though it was not incorporated until 1942. The community took advantage of its fine CLIMATE, sandy beaches and excellent sport FISHING to develop as a resort. The most notable TOURIST facility was the luxurious Qualicum Beach Hotel, built in 1913, and neighbouring golf course, which attracted celebrity visitors from around the world until it closed in 1969. So many retirees have chosen to live here that in 1999 it had the most senior citizens of any community in BC, with 35% of its population over 65 years of age.

QUAMICHAN, a farming district (*see* AGRICULTURE) on Quamichan Lk, 46 km northwest of

VICTORIA on VANCOUVER ISLAND, is essentially a suburb of DUNCAN. There was a village of the COWICHAN Nation in this area and the name is an Island HALKOMELEM word meaning "humped back," after the shape of a nearby hill.   AS

QUATHIASKI COVE is a small coastal community on the southwest corner of QUADRA ISLAND overlooking DISCOVERY PASSAGE. A fish cannery operated in the cove from 1904 to 1941, forming the nucleus of a thriving settlement, which for a time was the economic hub of the entire region. By the mid-1920s it was eclipsed by CAMPBELL RIVER, but it continues to be one of the 2 commercial centres on Quadra (HERIOT BAY is the other). A car ferry service across Discovery Passage links Quathiaski to Campbell River.

QUATSINO SOUND is a deep, multi-armed FJORD on the northwest corner of VANCOUVER ISLAND. Its name derives from one of the 4 KWAK-WAKA'WAKW (Kwakiutl) First Nations that occupy the area. The sound has 3 major arms: Neroutsos, Holberg and Rupert inlets; and 5 small communities: WINTER HARBOUR, PORT ALICE, COAL HARBOUR, HOLBERG and Quatsino. Among the earliest non-aboriginal settlers was a group of NORWEGIAN immigrants from N Dakota, who established a colony called Scandia in 1894–95 that evolved into the tiny hamlet of Quatsino. A WHALING station operated at Coal Harbour from 1947 to 1967, and recently the huge open-pit ISLAND COPPER MINE in Rupert Inlet closed after 25 years of operation. Otherwise, commercial FISHING and LOGGING have been the main economic activities.

QUEEN CHARLOTTE AIRLINES was founded in 1946 by the coastal pioneer Jim SPILSBURY. The airline began when Spilsbury purchased a float plane for his VANCOUVER-based radio telephone company. Soon QCA (a.k.a. Queer Collection of Aircraft) was flying a regular service to LOGGING camps and other small communities on the coast. By 1949 it was the third-largest airline in

River mouth at Gregory Beach, Rennell Sound, Queen Charlotte Islands.
Brent Matsuda/Image Makers

Canada. Spilsbury sold QCA to Russ BAKER's PACIFIC WESTERN AIRLINES in 1955.
Reading: Jim Spilsbury and Howard White, *The Accidental Airline*, 1988.

QUEEN CHARLOTTE CITY, pop 1,222, is on Bearskin Bay at the south end of Graham Island, 5 km west of the BC FERRY terminal at Skidegate Landing on the QUEEN CHARLOTTE ISLANDS. It is the administrative centre of the islands and the headquarters of the GWAII HAANAS NATIONAL PARK RESERVE. The original townsite grew up around a SAWMILL that went into operation in 1908. Soon there was a hospital, school, hotel and several businesses. The FOREST INDUSTRY has continued to be important to the local economy, along with FISHING and, increasingly, TOURISM.

QUEEN CHARLOTTE ISLANDS are an archipelago of several hundred islands and islets covering 9,596 km² on the North Coast across HECATE STRAIT from PRINCE RUPERT. The 2 largest islands are Graham in the north and Moresby in the south; most of the others are small and uninhabited. The archipelago is roughly 300 km long and 85 km across at its greatest width. It is the homeland of the HAIDA people, who call it Haida Gwaii ("Islands of the People") and have lived here for thousands of years. As their population was decimated by disease in the 19th century, they abandoned many of their villages and today there are 2 principal Haida communities, Old Masset (or Haida) and Skidegate Mission, both on Graham Island. One of the abandoned sites, NINSTINTS on Anthony Island, is a UN WORLD HERITAGE SITE. Parts of the islands may not have been GLACIATED; this and their isolation make them an ecologically unique area, home to animals and plants that occur nowhere else on earth, or only in distant places such as Japan and Ireland. As a result they are often called the "Galapagos of the North." The western side of the archipelago is rugged and steep with spectacular FJORDS. Much of the interior is covered by lush RAIN FORESTS, while the eastern side is low, with many fine beaches.

The first recorded outsiders to arrive were SPANISH EXPLORERS in 1774. Capt George DIXON, a British navigator, named the archipelago in 1787 after his ship, which in turn was named after the wife of King George III. He initiated the trade in SEA OTTER pelts, which peaked about 1820 and continued until the mid-19th century. There was a brief GOLD RUSH in the 1850s but settlers did not begin arriving in any number until early in the 1900s. Between 1910 and WWII, WHALING took place from shore stations at ROSE HARBOUR in the south and NADEN HARBOUR in the north. Loggers were active from the end of the 19th century, and during WWI 26 million board ft of SPRUCE were exported from the islands for use in war plane production. But by the 1970s, as loggers moved south on Moresby Island, some residents grew alarmed at the environmental damage the industry created. A bitter struggle to preserve a large part of Moresby Island from resource development began in 1974 and lasted to 1987, when the governments of BC and Canada signed agreements leading to

One of the Queen Charlotte Airlines fleet of Stranraer flying boats, c 1950.

the creation of the GWAII HAANAS NATIONAL PARK RESERVE, co-managed by the Haida (*see also* ENVIRONMENTAL MOVEMENT). Duu Guusd Tribal Park, encompassing the northwest corner of Graham Island, was created by the Haida in 1981. By the late 1990s the population of the islands was about 6,000, mostly employed in FISHING, LOGGING and TOURISM-related activities. The main communities are QUEEN CHARLOTTE CITY, PORT CLEMENTS, SKIDEGATE, where the main AIRPORT is, and MASSET, the largest community in the Charlottes.
Reading: George F. MacDonald, *Haida Monumental Art*, 1983; Kathleen E. Dalzell, *The Queen Charlotte Islands, Vol. 1: 1774–1966*, 1967, and *The Beloved Island: The Queen Charlotte Islands, Vol. 3*, 1989.

QUEEN CHARLOTTE SOUND is a broad expanse of open water extending 175 km from the north end of VANCOUVER ISLAND to the QUEEN CHARLOTTE ISLANDS. It was named in 1786 by the captain of a trading vessel after the wife of King George III. It is one of only 2 stretches on the coast where the mainland is exposed to the open Pacific without islands to protect it; thus it sometimes presents a hazardous challenge to mariners. Most boat traffic ducks into the INSIDE PASSAGE as soon as possible to avoid the outer waters of the sound. Cape Caution on the mainland near the south end of the sound is considered the dividing line between the north and south coast.

QUEEN ELIZABETH PARK (53 ha) is a landscaped oasis of gardens and trees in south VANCOUVER. The highest point in the city (el 152 m), it is known to locals as Little Mountain (also the name of the surrounding neighbourhood), though it was named officially to commemorate the 1939 visit of King George VI and Queen Elizabeth, the Queen Mother. The park was once the site of 2 quarries, where stone was obtained for building roads. One of them was converted

in 1908 to a city water reservoir, which still perches at the summit of the park. The city purchased the property in 1929 and the park was developed over the next 30 years as the remaining quarry areas were transformed into beautiful sunken gardens. The park also contains tennis courts, a pitch-and-putt golf course and a lawn bowling club. The reservoir and surrounding property were later covered by the Bloedel Conservatory, a 1969 gift to the city from Prentice BLOEDEL and his wife Virginia. Under a Plexiglas geodesic dome 21 m high, the conservatory houses a wide variety of tropical and desert plants, and tropical birds.

QUEEN MARGARET'S SCHOOL, one of BC's most venerable private schools, was founded in DUNCAN in 1921 by Nora Denny, a front-line nurse during WWI who had recently arrived on VANCOUVER ISLAND, and Dorothy Geoghegan, a local teacher. In 1999 the school had 280 students, 80 of whom were boarders. It is co-educational at the junior (kindergarten to grade 7) level with a girls-only high school. The school accommodates 40 horses and offers a horsemastership program and training in riding and stable

management. *See also* EDUCATION, PRIVATE; EQUESTRIAN SPORTS.

QUEENS BAY, a former steamship landing homesteaded in the 1890s by patriotic British immigrants, is today a recreational settlement on the west side of KOOTENAY LK, 30 km northeast of NELSON. The lovely community hall is a former ANGLICAN CHURCH, St Francis-in-the-Woods, constructed in 1915. AS

QUESNEL, city, pop 8,468, the commercial centre of the N CARIBOO, lies at the confluence of the FRASER and Quesnel rivers, 117 km south of PRINCE GEORGE. The name refers to Jules-Maurice QUESNEL, a fur trader who accompanied Simon FRASER on his exploration of the river in 1808. Settlement began in the 1860s with the discovery of GOLD in the Cariboo; the townsite developed as a supply centre for the goldfields. MINING continued to be significant into the 1930s and the city celebrates its links to the GOLD RUSH every July with Billy Barker Days (*see* William "Billy" BARKER). In 1921 the Pacific Great Eastern Rwy (*see* BC RAIL) arrived from SQUAMISH, and until 1952 Quesnel was the end of the line.

Early settlement at Quesnel. UBC BC972

View of Quesnel, 1996. Rick Blacklaws photo

Sunken gardens and Bloedel Conservatory, Queen Elizabeth Park, Vancouver.
Mike Steele photo

During WWII the FOREST INDUSTRY became important, based on the local BIRCH, which was used in the construction of fighter aircraft. The forest industry continued to be the main employer, with pulp mills (*see* PULP AND PAPER), a plywood plant and several SAWMILLS. Quesnel also has a large ranching (*see* CATTLE INDUSTRY) community, and it is the recreational gateway to BARKERVILLE and BOWRON LAKE PROVINCIAL PARK. Incorporated as a village in 1928, it became a city in 1979.

QUESNEL, Jules-Maurice, fur trader (b 25 Oct 1786, Montreal; d 20 May 1842, Montreal). After joining the NORTH WEST CO, he served at different posts in Alberta before coming to NEW CALEDONIA in 1807. He accompanied Simon FRASER on his expedition down the FRASER R to its mouth in 1808. The town of QUESNEL, the river and the lake are named for him. He remained in New Caledonia for 3 years although he disliked the country: "there is nothing to be had but misery and boredom," he wrote. After returning to Montreal in 1811, he left the fur trade (*see* FUR TRADE, LAND-BASED) to pursue various commercial interests in Upper and Lower Canada. He was a leading businessman, active in the public issues of his day, a member of the legislative council of the United Canadas and a Montreal city councillor.

QUESNEL FORKS (originally spelled Quesnelle Forks) is an abandoned townsite in the mountains at the forks of the Quesnel R near the west end of QUESNEL LK. Settled in 1860 and officially surveyed by the ROYAL ENGINEERS in 1861, it was the first of the CARIBOO gold camps. Briefly, it was the largest settlement in the mainland colony,

but as the GOLD RUSH moved on so did most of the miners. After the 1860s it was occupied mainly by CHINESE miners, who worked small claims in the area. Gradually they too moved away and the site became a ghost town; work began in the 1990s to restore it as a historic site.

QUESNEL LAKE, 264 km², northeast of WILLIAMS LAKE, is the largest lake in the CARIBOO. Extending 100 km end to end with a 49-km-long North Arm reaching up into Cariboo Mountains Provincial Park between BOWRON LAKE and WELLS GRAY provincial PARKS, it drains northwest via the Quesnel R to the FRASER R at QUESNEL. It is the deepest lake in BC (530 m) and the second-deepest in Canada after Great Slave Lk. Placer mining for GOLD began in 1859 as part of the Cariboo GOLD RUSH and continued for many years after the rush petered out. Despite the near destruction of SALMON stocks by dams and other MINING-related activity, the lake and its tributaries, especially the Horsefly R, now produce more than half the sockeye salmon in the entire Fraser basin. LOGGING activity has raised concerns that the fish may once again be threatened by habitat degradation. *See also* LAKES.

QUICK, a LOGGING and AGRICULTURAL settlement 26 km southeast of SMITHERS on the BULKLEY R and the CNR, was named for Sam Quick, a GRAND TRUNK PACIFIC RWY section foreman. Waldham Paddon operated a general store here from 1921 to the late 1970s. Many residents relocated from the railway across the river to Hwy 16 in the late 1940s. *AS*

QUILCHENA, overlooking Nicola Lk 23 km east of MERRITT, is the headquarters of the

Quilchena Cattle Co, operated by Guy Rose, great-grandson of Joseph Guichon (*see* GUICHON FAMILY), and his family. In addition to the ranch (*see* CATTLE INDUSTRY), one of the largest in the district, the Roses operate the Quilchena Hotel, built in 1908, and store, established in 1912. A golf course next to the hotel was once a polo field. The name derives from an aboriginal word meaning "place where the willows grow."

QUIMPER, Manuel, Spanish naval officer (dates unknown). He was the first European to undertake a sustained exploration of JUAN DE FUCA STRAIT. Commanding the *Princesa Real* (originally the British FUR TRADING vessel *Princess Royal*, captured by the Spanish in 1789), he left NOOTKA SOUND at the end of May 1790, charted CLAYOQUOT SOUND and made a survey of the northern and southern shores of Juan de Fuca, visiting the harbours of today's PORT RENFREW, SOOKE and ESQUIMALT in BC and Port Discovery and Neah Bay in Washington. His report of HARO STRAIT leading north through the SAN JUAN ISLANDS led to further SPANISH EXPLORATION in 1791–92. Quimper's chart is in the Archivo Historico Nacional in Madrid. *Robin Inglis*

QUINSAM, 14 km west of CAMPBELL RIVER on VANCOUVER ISLAND, was a major RAILWAY LOGGING camp (pop 350) and maintenance centre until truck LOGGING took over in 1953. Today it is a regional base for TimberWest Forest Ltd (Camp 8). The Quinsam R, with its SALMON hatchery (*see* FISH HATCHERIES), links Upper Quinsam R and Quinsam Lks to the Campbell R near DISCOVERY PASSAGE. *AS*

R

RABBIT and **HARE** are small, furry mammals belonging, like the PIKA, to the family Leporidae in the order Lagomorpha. Rabbits and hares are herbivores and both are important links in the food chain, providing meat for larger predators. Hares are slightly larger than rabbits and give birth to young that are fully furred, sighted and ready to hop within minutes, whereas newborn rabbits (called leverets) are hairless, blind and helpless. Two rabbit species occur in BC. Nuttall's cottontail (*Sylvilagus nuttallii*) is found mainly in dry GRASSLAND areas of the Interior; it is Blue-listed by the Conservation Data Centre (*see* ENDANGERED SPECIES). The eastern cottontail (*S. floridanus*), an introduced species, is more common in the Lower Mainland. Of the 4 hare species in Canada, two occur in BC. The most common is the snowshoe hare (*Lepus americanus*), widespread in forested areas. This species is well known for its extreme population fluctuations, its numbers peaking approximately every 10 years followed by a population crash. This fluctuation has been shown to have a direct effect on the numbers of its predators. The white-tailed jackrabbit (*L. townsendii*) is another grassland species; it is an endangered species and is on the provincial Red List. *See also* LYNX; NATURAL HISTORY.

RACCOON (*Procyon lotor*) is an omnivorous feeder, equally at home in the FOREST, where it eats fruits, BERRIES, nuts and small animals, and in urban backyards, where it forages in fish ponds and garbage pails. Distinguished by a humpbacked walk and masked-bandit face, raccoons are not shy of humans and may become aggressive in defence of food or offspring. It weighs up to 25 kg, though half that is more common. The forepaws, equipped with sharp claws, are very sensitive and capable of fine motor activity. Active mainly at night, raccoons den in ravines, hollow logs, even the attics and

Raccoon. R. Wayne Campbell photo

crawl spaces of houses. The female gives birth in the spring to a litter of up to 7 kits, which stick close to their mother for about 6 months. Raccoons are found along the coast and in southern Interior valleys. They have also been introduced to the QUEEN CHARLOTTE ISLANDS, where they prey on seabirds.

RACE ROCKS, the most southerly point in western Canada, is a jumble of tiny islets in JUAN DE FUCA STRAIT off the southern tip of VANCOUVER ISLAND. A danger to mariners, they have been the scene of numerous shipwrecks and claimed many lives over the years. The second LIGHTHOUSE on the coast was built on Great Race Rock in 1860 and was still operating in 2000. The rocks attract a large number of seabirds and SEA LIONS and have been declared an ECOLOGICAL RESERVE. When the lighthouse was automated in 1996 the buildings were turned into a marine research station affiliated with LESTER B. PEARSON COLLEGE OF THE PACIFIC.

RACETTE, Gordon Louis Joseph "Gordy," boxer and "tough guy," (b 28 June 1955, Prince Albert, SK). A NANAIMO bouncer, he dominated the Pacific Northwest "So You Think You're Tough?" circuit before VANCOUVER manager Tony Dowling encouraged him to enter pro BOXING in the early 1980s and declared him "Canada's new heavyweight sensation." Racette began facing world-class opponents including Jimmy Young (1981) and Trevor Berbick (1982), both in Nanaimo. After defeating former title contender Scott LeDoux (1982), he reached the heavyweight ranking of 13th in the world before shifting his focus to kickboxing,

The light station at Race Rocks, as shown in a painting by Buzz Walker.

winning the 1985 World Kickboxing Assoc superheavyweight championship. He continued to box periodically, making a pro comeback in the early 1990s but aborting it in 1992.

RADIUM HOT SPRINGS, village, pop 530, overlooks the COLUMBIA R at the edge of KOOTE-NAY NATIONAL PARK in the ROCKY MTS, 134 km southwest of Banff. It is a resort community famous for its odourless mineral springs. The springs were used by the KTUNAXA (Kutenai) people long before they were officially discovered by HBC Gov George SIMPSON in 1841. Originally called Sinclair Hot Springs after the FUR TRADER James Sinclair, the site took its present name in 1915. The springs were expropriated by the federal government in 1922 to become part of the national PARK. The local economy relies on TOURISM and the FOREST INDUSTRY is also important. The village was incorporated on 10 Dec 1990.

RAE-ARTHUR, Ada Annie (Jordan) "Cougar Annie," coastal pioneer (b 19 June 1888, Sacramento, CA; d 28 Apr 1985, Port Alberni). Of legendary status on the west coast of VAN-COUVER ISLAND, this tiny, formidable pioneer lived for nearly 70 years surrounded by the garden she established at Boat Basin in the remote northern reaches of CLAYOQUOT SOUND. She arrived there in 1915 with her first husband, Willie Rae-Arthur, and 3 small children, and she remained until she was in her mid-90s. She bore 8 more children, 3 of whom died as infants. Having hacked a 2-ha clearing out of the RAIN FOREST, she imported hundreds of varieties of plants and created a mail-order nursery garden business, shipping her plants across Canada. From 1936 she ran the Boat Basin post office, which remained open until the early 1980s, by which time she was the only customer. She was a crack shot who killed so many COUGARS and BEARS in defence of her property that she became known up and down the coast as "Cougar Annie." She outlived 4 husbands and is rumoured to have killed at least one of them. Her remarkable garden still thrives in the wilderness, in the care of the non-profit Boat Basin Foundation. *Margaret Horsfield*
Reading: Margaret Horsfield, *Cougar Annie's Garden*, 1999.

RAFFI; *see* CAVOUKIAN, Raffi.

RAIL is a small marsh bird, usually tawny or grey-brown in colour, inhabiting freshwater and brackish WETLANDS where it nests just above water level and feeds on SNAILS, INSECTS, FROGS and plants. The rail has bare, stalky legs and long toes, which enables it to manoeuvre through its weedy habitat. It is a shy bird, more often heard than seen, and when it takes to the air, which is rarely, it flies with legs dangling. The bird can squeeze through very narrow openings in the marshy undergrowth, hence the expression "thin as a rail." In BC the family Rallidae includes 4 species. Virginia rails (*Rallus limicola*) have long, reddish bills and inhabit the southern half of the

province. Soras (*Porzana carolina*) are chunky birds with short, yellow bills and long, green-yellow legs. They occur commonly along southeast VANCOUVER ISLAND and across the Interior in summer, and migrate to the southern US in winter. American coots (*Fulica americana*) inhabit ponds and marshes across southern BC and north into the PEACE R area. They are about the size of a small duck, slate grey in colour with short white bills and undertails. Their lobed toes aid them in swimming, which they do more than the other rail species, and diving to feed. While swimming, they make a characteristic bobbing motion with their heads. The yellow rail (*Coturnicops noveboracensis*) is a very rare summer visitor to sedge marshes in northeastern BC.

RAILWAY LOGGING flourished in BC FORESTS from the 1890s to the 1930s. The term refers to the use of steam railways to haul logs from the woods to the SAWMILLS or LOG BOOMING grounds. Logging railways operated throughout the province but were most useful in areas of flat terrain, principally along the east coast of VANCOU-VER ISLAND, in the FRASER VALLEY and, pre-WWII, in the E KOOTENAY. Lines required the construction of elaborate log trestles and bridges to cross swamps, ravines and RIVERS. One of these structures, the Bear Crk bridge on the west side of Vancouver Island, built in 1939, was at 74 m the highest wooden structure in Canada. Rail lines were usually short-lived: once the timber supply in an area was exhausted the track was ripped up and relocated. By the mid-1920s, the high point of railway logging on the coast, there were 79 rail operations, some only a few km long but some with as many as 80 km of track. During the Depression many lines closed. At the same time, trucks were being introduced as a replacement for railways in the woods. A rising demand for FOREST PRODUCTS during WWII revitalized railway logging briefly, but conversion to trucks resumed after the war. By the end of the 1950s

Logs on railway flatbeds, all cut from a single Douglas fir, 1930s. UBC BC479

only 3 rail operations remained, all on Vancouver Island. Two of these operations switched to diesel power during the 1960s, leaving MACMILLAN BLOEDEL to run the last steam logging railway in BC until 1969. In 1999 only one logging railway remained in operation, run by CANADIAN FOREST PRODUCTS LTD in the NIMPKISH valley. *See also* LOGGING.
Reading: Robert Turner, *Logging By Rail*, 1990.

RAIN FOREST, temperate, is a term applied to the luxuriant coastal forests of the Pacific Northwest from California north to the Alaska panhandle. Temperate rain forests are found in the middle latitudes as opposed to the tropical rain forests, or jungles, of equatorial latitudes. They receive a huge volume of precipitation, at least 1,000 mm annually, and are characterized by extremely tall trees and a diverse understory of shrubs, MOSSES, FERNS and arboreal (hanging) and terrestrial lichens. It has been estimated that at one time .2% of the earth's surface was covered by temperate rain forest, only 10% of which remains. Of the remaining 10%, about one-quarter is in BC. The dominant tree species in the temperate rain forest include western red CEDAR, Sitka SPRUCE, western HEMLOCK and DOU-GLAS FIR. Many plant and animal species rely on

Rain forest at Clayoquot Sound, 1993.
Gerrit Sommer/WCWC

the rain forest environment for their survival. Extensive LOGGING of BC's rain forests prompted intense opposition from ENVIRONMENTAL groups during the 1980s and 1990s. *See also* BIODIVERSITY; BIOGEOCLIMATIC ZONES; ECOREGION CLASSIFICATION SYSTEM; NATURAL HISTORY.

RAINBOW RANGE is a range of multicoloured volcanic peaks in south TWEEDSMUIR PROVINCIAL PARK west of ANAHIM LAKE. They are the remnants of volcanoes that were active about 10 million years ago. Through the actions of weathering,

Rainbow Range, Tweedsmuir Provincial Park.
Rick Blacklaws photo

erosion and oxidation of the various minerals that make up the mountains, they are stained and streaked with red, yellow and purple hues. This colouring is so dramatic that aboriginal people used to call them the "Bleeding Mountains."

RAINCOAST BOOKS is a VANCOUVER book distribution and publishing company. It was founded in 1979 by Allan MacDougall and Mark Stanton solely as a distribution operation, then expanded into wholesale and began publishing its own titles. By 2000 it represented 40 British and American publishers in Canada and its distribution arm, Book Express, was one of the largest in Canada. In the 1990s Raincoast enjoyed international success with the *Griffin & Sabine* series by Nick BANTOCK; in 1999 the company had a sales and distribution success with the Canadian rights to the hugely popular *Harry Potter* series of books for young readers. In 1999 revenues approached $50 million. *See also* BOOK PUBLISHING.

RAINCOAST CHRONICLES is a journal of BC coast history and folklore started in 1972 by Howard WHITE for the stated aim of "placing BC character on the record." Parallelling such American back-to-the-land publications as *Foxfire* and *Sand County Almanac*, it told the stories of BC coast pioneers. It touched a nerve with Canadians at a time when interest in the country's rural roots was peaking, and it became a cultural landmark on the West Coast, establishing "raincoast" in the lexicon of BC nicknames. The *Chronicles* were first published as a periodical; then they became a series of books that appear about once a year as cultural and historical anthologies, which

include stories, articles, memoirs, poetry, oral history and other West Coast lore.

RANCHING; *see* CATTLE INDUSTRY.

RAND, Paul (born Otto Schellenberger), artist (b 27 Nov 1896, Bonn, Germany; d 27 Jan 1970, Vancouver). He was in Canada on an extended trip when WWI broke out and as an "enemy alien" he was forbidden to return to Germany. During and after the war he worked on a ranch and as a builder in southern Alberta, then moved to VANCOUVER in 1926 to attend art school. He studied at the Vancouver School of Decorative and Applied Arts (*see* EMILY CARR INSTITUTE OF ART & DESIGN) with Fred VARLEY and Jock MACDONALD, and from the mid-1930s to 1965 he worked as a commercial artist. For much of this time he was art director at the VANCOUVER SUN newspaper. He was naturalized in 1930; in 1941, because of anti-German sentiment, he changed his name to Paul Rand. Though he never made a living from his painting, he produced a substantial body of work. He was a realist painter who was drawn to the BC landscape and also created several documentary paintings of industrial and labour scenes.

RANDALL, Samuel W. "Sam," racetrack owner (b 25 Sept 1882, Toronto; d 2 Nov 1961, Vancouver). In 1908 he moved to VANCOUVER and sold home appliances until after WWI, when he became involved in HORSE RACING and took control of the HASTINGS PARK track. For 35 years he was president of the Ascot Jockey Club, which leased Hastings Park. He also built and owned Lansdowne Park on LULU ISLAND (1924–45) and ran the Willows track in VICTORIA to 1947. After WWII he centred his activities on Hastings Park until 1960, when the Ascot Club and entrepreneur Jack DIAMOND formed the BC Jockey Club, codirected by Randall's son Bill. He is a member of the Canadian Sports Hall of Fame and the BC SPORTS HALL OF FAME.

RANDONNEURING is a "challenge" CYCLING sport encompassing competitive and recreational aspects. Cyclists are timed on the total time it takes, including rest, to cover a long distance, usually without outside support. VANCOUVER rider John Hathaway sparked interest in randonneuring in BC by finishing the trans-Canada route in 24 days, 13 hours in 1957 and later by

entering the *Guinness Book of Records* for including every continent during a 81,300-km ride from Nov 1974 to Oct 1976. Wayne Phillips of RICHMOND reduced the trans-Canada record to 20 days in 1977 and to 15 (with motorhome support) in 1982. Since 1979 BC riders have regularly attended the quadrennial world randonneuring event, the Paris–Brest–Paris Randoné in France, with Vancouver's Keith Fraser recording the best time ever by a Canadian, 50 hrs, 9 mins in 1995. The Rocky Mt 1200, a BC–Alberta randonneuring event inaugurated in 1996, passes through KAMLOOPS, CLEARWATER, BLUE RIVER, TETE JAUNE CACHE and REVELSTOKE. To 1999, VICTORIA's Ken Bonner had posted the best times on the popular 1,000-km individual route running from Victoria to PORT HARDY. *SW*

RANKIN, Harry, lawyer, civic politician (b 8 May 1920, Vancouver). For 2 decades he was the most popular and controversial alderman on VANCOUVER city council. He graduated from UBC law school following service in WWII and was called to the bar in 1950. A self-declared socialist from his student days, he gained a reputation as the defender of the underprivileged with a special interest in labour law and civil liberties. He won election to city council for the first time in 1966 and two years later was instrumental in the creation of a left-wing civic party, the Committee of Progressive Electors (COPE), to challenge the dominant NON-PARTISAN ASSOC. At times the lone left-wing voice on council, he consistently topped the polls in civic elections until he decided to test his popularity by running for mayor in 1986. He lost to Gordon CAMPBELL, and retired to his legal practice.

RASCALZ is BC's first successful hip-hop act. After meeting each other at VANCOUVER breakdancing competitions in 1989, the group officially formed as the Ragamuffin Rascalz and released their debut recording, *Really Livin'*, in 1991. (A re-released album under the Rascalz name with all new tracks sold 20,000 units.) The members known as Misfit and Red 1 performed as MCs, while Kemo worked the turntables as DJ/producer and Zebroc and Dedos continued to breakdance. They started their own independent record label, Figure IV, in 1994, then in 1997 became only the second Canadian rap group to sign with a major label. That year's *Cash Crop* earned the group gold sales status (over 60,000 albums sold) and a 1998 Juno award for best rap recording. However, they declined the Juno to protest the exclusion of any live performances of urban/hip-hop music in the televised ceremonies. The next year the Junos featured a televised sequence of Rascalz winning another Juno for best rap recording, as well as a live performance of "Northern Touch," a single that reached No 1 video on the Muchmusic Countdown. Also in 1999, they released their critically acclaimed *Global Warning* album. *SW*

RATTENBURY, Francis Mawson, architect (b 11 Oct 1867, Leeds, England; d 28 Mar 1935, Bournemouth, England). He trained as an

Francis Rattenbury, architect, c 1924.
BC Archives F02163

architect in England with his uncles and was already an award-winning designer when he immigrated to BC in 1892. He opened an office in VANCOUVER; less than a year later he won a competition to design the new LEGISLATIVE BUILDINGS in VICTORIA. He moved to the capital, which remained his home for the next 3 decades. During the Klondike GOLD RUSH he founded a transportation company, but it was not a success and he returned to ARCHITECTURE, designing many landmark buildings in the province, including the EMPRESS HOTEL, the Vancouver Courthouse (now the VANCOUVER ART GALLERY), the Crystal Garden in Victoria, and several banks and hotels. At one time he was chief architect for the CPR and the Bank of Montreal. In 1925 he divorced his first wife and married Alma Clarke Pakenham, a talented musician almost 30 years his junior. The social scandal, coupled with financial reverses related to a land development scheme, caused the Rattenburys to move to England in 1930. They settled in Bournemouth and Alma became a successful writer and performer of popular music. Rattenbury was fatally beaten by his chauffeur, who was carrying on an affair with Alma. The chauffeur was convicted of murder; Alma was acquitted at the sensational trial but committed suicide soon after.

RATTLESNAKE, western (*Crotalus viridis*), is the only seriously poisonous snake in BC. It inhabits rocky outcrops in the arid OKANAGAN,

Western rattlesnake. R. Wayne Campbell photo

THOMPSON and NICOLA valleys. After hibernating communally all winter, rattlers emerge to feed on RODENTS, shrews and sometimes small birds. Coloured brown, tan, olive or grey, with a series of large, dark-brown splotches along the back, this snake grows to about 1.5 m in length. Its bite can cause serious tissue damage to humans but is rarely fatal, and rattlesnakes are not aggressive unless disturbed. The rattle, located at the tail, consists of a series of loosely interlocked horny segments (modified and fused scutes) and is used to warn away intruders. The western rattlesnake has been placed on the provincial Blue list of ENDANGERED SPECIES; it is needlessly persecuted and human encroachment has curtailed its habitat.

RAVEN, common (*Corvus corax*), is a large, black bird very similar in appearance to the CROW, but larger, with a heavier bill and a croaking voice rather than a "caw." The raven has fringed throat feathers (hackles) that give its head a shaggy

Common raven in flight, Queen Charlotte Islands. Duane Sept photo

appearance. It is a soaring, acrobatic flyer and an aggressive scavenger, and it plays a significant role in FIRST NATIONS mythology.

RAWHIDING was an unusual technique for transporting ore from mines located high in the mountains of the Interior. The ore was placed on a large cow hide that was wrapped and tied securely with leather thongs. This "package" was then skidded down the mountainside by horse or donkey. The hide was always placed hair side out to create some drag to assist the animals. It was said that on steep slopes experienced animals knew enough to sit on the load and ride it down. Rawhiding was also used to haul supplies up to the mines. *See also* MINING.

RAYLEIGH, MOUNT, a residential suburb 16 km north of KAMLOOPS on Hwy 97 and the east side of the N THOMPSON R, was once an active farming district (*see* AGRICULTURE). John McIver was the pioneer rancher here in 1869. It was named after the English home of E.T. Webb, another early settler. *AS*

RAZUTIS, Al, filmmaker (b 28 Apr 1946, Bamberg, Germany). He became involved with experimental film in 1967, while studying

sciences at California Western Univ. The next year he moved to VANCOUVER and joined the newly formed INTERMEDIA artists' co-operative. In 1972, combining arts activism with technical innovation, he established the Visual Alchemy Studio, a production facility equipped with an animation stand, holography lab and BC's first optical printer. Razutis is a prolific avant-garde filmmaker and critic who used the movie medium to explore the workings of the unconscious. He also taught at the Vancouver School of Art (*see* EMILY CARR INSTITUTE OF ART & DESIGN) and at SFU. In 1980 his film *A Message From Our Sponsor*, an analysis of the sexual subtext of the beauty industry, was banned in Ontario; the event became an artistic *cause célèbre. See also* FILMMAKING INDUSTRY. *Michael Walsh*

READ, Frank Harold, rowing coach (b 1 Mar 1911, Vancouver; d 22 Jan 1994). Raised in VANCOUVER and on VANCOUVER ISLAND, he played FOOTBALL and rowed as a youth before turning to coaching with the UBC rowing team in 1949. He became Canada's greatest ROWING coach, leading his 8-oared with cox UBC team to a gold medal at the 1954 British Empire Games (*see* BRITISH EMPIRE AND COMMONWEALTH GAMES) in Vancouver and an upset win over the powerful Russian team at the Henley Regatta in England in 1955. At the 1956 Melbourne Olympics his 4-man team won the gold medal while his UBC 8s brought home the silver. He ended his coaching career soon after his 8s won another silver at the 1960 Rome Olympics, but he remained active in the VANCOUVER ROWING CLUB for many years. A self-made millionaire and owner of 3 hotels, he was among the first inductees to the BC SPORTS HALL OF FAME in 1966 and belongs to the UBC Sports Hall of Fame. *SW*

READ ISLAND is one of the Discovery Islands, a tightly massed archipelago at the north end of GEORGIA STRAIT between VANCOUVER ISLAND and the mainland. It is named for a British naval officer, William Viner Read. First occupied by Coast Salish people (*see* SALISHAN FIRST NATIONS), it attracted loggers and the first settlers in the late 1880s. Its remoteness seemed to make the island a haven for flamboyant characters. Foremost among them was a former Dakota Territory police chief, Edgar Wilmot Wylie, who in 1888 opened a hotel and boat dock in Burdwood Bay, and whose name became linked to seamy tales of bootlegging and murder. By the 1920s SURGE NARROWS had become the economic hub for a small population of loggers and ranchers. "The Surge" continues to offer a boat dock, store and an old-fashioned one-room school, one of the last on the coast. There is no ferry service to the island. *Jeanette Taylor*

REBAGLIATI, Ross, snowboarder (b 14 July 1971, N Vancouver). He started SNOWBOARDING seriously while attending high school in VANCOUVER, moved to WHISTLER to train and earned his first major World Cup wins in the super giant slalom at Whistler in 1996 and in the giant slalom at Sestriere, Italy, in 1996 and 1997. He

Ross Rebagliati, snowboarder, returning home to Whistler with his Olympic gold medal, 1998. *Mark van Manen/Vancouver Sun*

was ranked 3rd overall in the 1995–96 and 1996–97 World Cup seasons and won European and US Open championships. He became a household name during the 1998 Winter Olympics in Nagano, Japan, when he won snowboarding's first gold medal in the giant slalom. He drew even greater publicity days later when traces of MARIJUANA were found in his drug test and his medal was revoked by the International Olympic Committee, then returned on the technicality that marijuana was not on the IOC's list of banned drugs. (Rebagliati contended that the marijuana must have been inhaled second-hand at a party.) The decision sparked an international debate on marijuana and drug regulations for athletes. *SW*

RECALL is a method by which voters may reconsider the election of their legislators between general elections, giving constituents more influence over the conduct of their MLAs. In a referendum during the 1991 provincial election, a strong majority of BC voters approved some form of recall legislation. The NDP government introduced a limited system in 1994. Recall may not be initiated until at least 18 months after a general election. Constituents must circulate a petition; at least 40% of registered voters in a constituency must sign it within 60 days. If the chief electoral officer accepts it, the petition forces the resignation of the MLA; a by-election is held to choose a successor. The recall procedure can be used only once in any riding between general elections.

The first recall campaigns under the new legislation were launched in Nov 1997 in the ridings of Prince George North and Skeena; both were unsuccessful. A third campaign was intended to remove LIBERAL MLA Paul Reitsma from his Parksville–Qualicum seat after he admitted to writing letters under a false name to a local newspaper. In June 1998, when the campaign appeared certain to succeed, Reitsma resigned. Otherwise, by mid-2000, recall had not successfully removed an elected MLA from office.

RECCHI, Mark, hockey player (b 1 Feb 1968, Kamloops). He played his junior HOCKEY with the KAMLOOPS BLAZERS in the WHL. Underrated because of his small size, he was drafted only in the fourth round but surprised everyone by proving to be a prolific NHL scorer. In his second full

season with the Pittsburgh Penguins (1990–91) he finished first on the team and 4th in the league in scoring. The Penguins won the 1991 Stanley Cup thanks in large part to his play, but they traded him to Philadelphia midway through the next season. With the Flyers in 1992–93, he scored a career-high 53 goals and 123 points, a points record that stands alongside

Mark Recchi, hockey player, in Montreal Canadiens uniform. *Vancouver Canucks Photo Archives*

his 73 assists (1990-91) as the highest totals in the 20th century by any player born and raised in BC. In 1995 he was traded to Montreal and was a member of Team Canada at the 1998 Winter Olympics in Nagano. The Flyers reacquired him in 1998-99 and he led the team in scoring a season later. *SW*

RED LAKE, 40 km northwest of KAMLOOPS, is a ranching (*see* CATTLE INDUSTRY) and recreational district at the southern edge of the CARIBOO. There are many cottages around the lake itself and small acreages in the general area. A post office operated from 1920 to 1962. *AS*

RED MOUNTAIN SKI AREA, consisting of Red and Granite Mts, is a ski resort at ROSSLAND in the W KOOTENAY. It was the site of the first Canadian downhill championships in 1897, and the first chairlift in western Canada in 1947. The area has produced more members of the national ski team than any other, including Nancy GREENE and Kerrin LEE-GARTNER, both Olympic gold medallists.

RED PASS, 63 km west of Jasper, AB, at the west end of Moose Lk in the ROCKY MTS, is a junction point on the CNR. In the 1920s it developed as a small hunting and FISHING centre with a hotel and school, and a police station that later served as headquarters for Mt ROBSON Provincial Park

(*see* PARKS, PROVINCIAL). A camp of Japanese Canadian internees (*see* JAPANESE, RELOCATION OF) was based here during WWII. Red Pass was later abandoned. *AS*

RED ROCK is a small ranching (*see* CATTLE INDUSTRY), LOGGING and former SAWMILLING settlement on BC RAIL and Hwy 97 (*see* ROADS AND HWYS), 25 km south of PRINCE GEORGE. It is named after a red bluff on the riverbank. *AS*

REDMOND, Fanny Byron (Sister Frances), nurse (b 1854, England; d 15 Apr 1932, Vancouver). She arrived in Canada in 1877 with her naval officer husband and settled first in Winnipeg. After the couple separated she trained as a nurse at Laval Univ in Quebec City, then came west to VANCOUVER in 1887. In the wake of the great fire (*see* DISASTERS) she spearheaded the construction of the city's first hospital, St Luke's, on land purchased from the CPR and next door to St James' ANGLICAN CHURCH. Primarily a maternity hospital, St Luke's also ministered to victims of epidemic diseases such as typhoid and smallpox. Her work there earned her the nickname "Vancouver's Florence Nightingale" and she was the city's first public health nurse.

Peggy Imredy

REDONDA ISLANDS, 280 km², are a pair of high, wooded islands at the mouth of TOBA INLET on the Central Coast north of DESOLATION SOUND. In 1792 the Spanish explorers Dionisio ALCALA-GALIANO and Cayetano VALDES mistook them for a single circular land mass and named them Redonda, Spanish for "round." In fact they are divided by the narrow Waddington Channel. Teakerne Arm indents the west side of W Redonda, while Pendrell Sound, with some of the warmest water on the coast, almost divides E Redonda in half. A SALMON CANNERY operated at Redonda Bay during the 1920s and 1930s, along with a store, post office and major LOGGING operation, making it the centre of activity on the islands. Later, however, REFUGE COVE at the southern tip of W Redonda became the main supply centre and a favourite stopping-in spot for coastal boaters. Logging has been the main economic activity on the islands, along with some AGRICULTURE and MINING, and by the late 1990s there was a growing TOURISM industry with some resorts, ocean kayaking providers and ecotourism opportunities.

REDSTONE, pop 190, 105 km west of WILLIAMS LAKE on the Chilcotin Hwy (Hwy 20; *see* ROADS AND HWYS) at the confluence of the Chilcotin and Chilanko rivers, is named for a nearby reddish cliff. E.P. Lee started a ranch in 1895; a trading post also dates from that time. Today it is a TSILHQOT'IN (Chilcotin) community, Tsi Del Del, whose members first moved here 40 years ago to be closer to schools and services. *AS*

REES, Gareth, rugby player (b 30 June 1967, Duncan). A graduate of ST MICHAEL'S UNIV SCHOOL in VICTORIA, he accepted a year's scholarship to Harrow school in England where he

Gareth Rees, rugby player.

played RUGBY with the first division London Wasps as an 18-year-old. Competing for Canada, he was the youngest player in the first World Cup tournament in 1987. After graduating from the UNIV OF VICTORIA he returned to England to study at Oxford and continued to play for the Wasps through the late 1990s. Acknowledged as one of the top place-kickers in the world, he was the English League's top points scorer in 1996, the same year the team won the league title. He led the Wasps to the championship again in 1998, equalling the British Cup single-game points record in the process. In 1999 he signed with a new club in England, Bedford RFC. A longtime captain of the Canadian national team, he is one of Canada's most-capped players and the only person anywhere to have played in 4 World Cups. In 1999 he stood 8th in all-time scoring at the international level. As a high school teacher, he earned a position at the highly esteemed Eton School, where one of his students was Prince William.   *SW*

REFORM PARTY of British Columbia was formed in 1985 by a group of disgruntled former SOCIAL CREDIT PARTY supporters led by Ron Gamble. (The party was not formally associated with the federal Reform Party of Canada, which was not founded until 1987.) The party did poorly in the 1991 provincial election but shortly afterwards 4 Social Credit MLAs from non-urban ridings defected to Reform, giving it the third-largest contingent in the legislature. In 1995 one of the former Socreds, Jack Weisgerber, was chosen party leader and Reformers were confident about their chances in the 1996 election, especially given the results of the 1993 federal election when 36% of the BC electorate voted Reform. Federal support did not translate into provincial support, however, and BC Reform elected only 2 MLAs in 1996. Weisgerber resigned as leader and in 1997 the party chose

Wilf Hanni, an oil-industry consultant, to be its new leader and to try to consolidate a position on the centre-right of the political spectrum. Shortly after, the 2 MLAs quit the party and BC Reform appeared to be declining into political irrelevance. At a 1998 party convention, Hanni was ousted from the leadership and former Socred Premier Bill VANDER ZALM re-emerged from retirement to take on the leadership of the party. But Vander Zalm's poor showing in a by-election late in 1999—he was soundly beaten by the LIBERAL candidate—suggested that BC Reform remained unpopular with provincial voters.

REFUGE COVE nestles in a quiet harbour at the south end of W REDONDA ISLAND near the entrance to DESOLATION SOUND. HANDLOGGERS were active on the island from about 1900 and the large lagoon behind the cove attracted settlers prior to WWI. In 1914 a school opened to serve the children of these pioneer families, and a store made the cove a provisioning centre for the area. Owned for many years by Jack Tindall and then by Norman and Doris Hope, the store was still operating in 2000, attracting coastal boaters in need of fuel and supplies. Since the early 1970s a group of families and individuals have run Refuge Cove as an unusual CO-OPERATIVE venture, expanding the facilities to include moorage, a fuel dock, boat rental, post office, café and liquor store.

REGENT COLLEGE is a school of theology at UBC, established in 1968 with the backing of the Plymouth Brethren. In 1980 the school entered into a co-operative arrangement with Carey Hall, a seminary overseen by the Baptist Union of Western Canada; Regent College was established as an evangelical alternative to Canada's largest Baptist college, the Baptist McMaster Divinity School in Ontario. Although it was funded by the Plymouth Brethren, the school is officially "transdenominational" and trains graduate students from a wide range of CONSERVATIVE PROTESTANT denominations. It is unique among Protestant seminaries in that it offers graduate-level theological training to lay people from a variety of professions. It is the largest graduate theological college in Canada.   *Dianne Mackay*

REGIONAL DISTRICTS are units of local government created in 1965 to deliver services to people living outside municipal areas and to allow municipalities to provide common services on a shared basis. Districts are governed by boards that are partly elected directly and partly appointed by municipal councils within the district. The province is divided into 28 regional districts, listed alphabetically opposite, with their populations. *See* GOVERNMENT, LOCAL.

REID, Irene (Hoffar), artist (b 2 Sept 1908, Vancouver). The daughter of Henry HOFFAR, a boatbuilder, she attended the Vancouver School of Decorative and Applied Arts (later EMILY CARR INSTITUTE OF ART & DESIGN) from 1925 to 1930, studying with Fred VARLEY and Charles SCOTT.

After further studies in London, England, she taught at the Vancouver School of Art from 1933 to 1937 and had a long and productive career as a painter and mixed-media artist. Twice president of the BC Society of Artists, she was awarded a Centennial Medal for service in the arts in 1967. After living for many years in W VANCOUVER, she moved to SIDNEY on VANCOUVER ISLAND in 1979.

REID, William Ronald "Bill," artist (b 12 Jan 1920, Victoria; d 13 Mar 1998, Vancouver). His mother was a HAIDA schoolteacher, his father an American-born hotelkeeper. Reid was raised in VICTORIA and northern BC. After finishing school he became a radio broadcaster, eventually for the CBC in eastern Canada. He first studied jewellery-making in Toronto in 1948, and when he returned to VANCOUVER in 1950 he began making pieces in his own workshop, developing a style that drew on his Haida heritage. In 1958 he left BROADCASTING to become a full-time artist. His first project was to direct the construction of

Bill Reid, Haida carver, with his monumental sculpture, The Raven and the First Men, *c 1983.*
Bill McLennan/UBC/MOA

Haida-style houses and TOTEM POLES on the UBC campus. Despite the onset of Parkinson's disease in the 1970s, Reid gained an international reputation for his jewellery and increasingly for his monumental sculptures of wood and bronze, including *The Raven and the First Men* (1983) at the MUSEUM OF ANTHROPOLOGY at UBC, *The Chief of the Undersea World* (1984) outside the VANCOUVER AQUARIUM and the *Spirit of Haida Gwaii* (1991), a 6-m canoe spilling over with human and mythological figures at the Canadian embassy in Washington, DC. A second casting of the canoe was installed at the VANCOUVER INTERNATIONAL AIRPORT in 1996. Reid has been widely honoured for his work—he won a Molson Prize for outstanding contributions to Canadian culture in 1977 and is a member of the Order of BC

BC REGIONAL DISTRICT (RD) POPULATION, 1976–99

	1976	1981	1986	1991	1996	1999
Alberni-Clayoquot	32,957	33,397	31,354	32,048	31,652	33,284
Bulkley-Nechako	33,453	39,362	38,794	39,400	41,642	45,169
Capital	236,245	255,879	275,043	307,643	317,989	334,368
Cariboo	52,896	60, 813	62,468	62,855	66,475	72,988
Central Coast	4,287	3,123	3,273	3,639	3,921	4,320
Central Fraser Valley (2, 3)	90,189	118,062	141,763	89,707	-	-
Central Kootenay	50,218	53,449	50,937	52,342	58,099	61,466
Central Okanagan	72,925	87,314	92,776	114,673	136,541	150,755
Columbia-Shuswap	36,407	41,127	41,418	42,721	48,116	52,653
Comox-Strathcona	58,592	70,400	73,558	85,054	97,666	105,321
Cowichan Valley	48,271	54,067	54,411	62,199	70,978	76,386
Dewdney-Alouette (3)	53,743	63,614	71,930	92,394	-	-
East Kootenay	47,599	55,141	54,893	53,746	56,366	61,163
Fraser-Cheam (3)	52,647	58,358	59,988	70,468	-	-
Fraser-Fort George	81,704	91,920	92,511	93,301	98,974	106,526
Fraser Valley (3)	-	-	-	-	222,397	240,601
Greater Vancouver (2,3)	1,118,245	1,208,236	1,324,375	1,585,880	1,831,665	1,990,961
Kitimat-Stikine (4)	39,741	43,603	40,912	43,249	43,618	46,622
Kootenay-Boundary	32,451	34,065	31,351	31,974	32,906	34,136
Mount Waddington	12,840	15,114	15,508	14,293	14,601	15,181
Nanaimo	63,335	78,994	84,888	104,296	121,783	133,404
Northern Rockies (1)	-	-	-	5,192	5,856	6,465
North Okanagan	47,993	55,704	56,906	63,288	71,607	76,640
Okanagan-Similkameen	52,674	58,497	61,010	68,280	75,933	80,370
Peace River (1)	-	-	-	54,844	56,477	60,370
Peace River-Liard (1)	45,974	57,059	59,233	-	-	-
Powell River	20,101	19,834	18,971	19,689	19,936	21,182
Skeena-Queen Charlotte (4)	23,259	24,707	23,901	24,460	24,795	25,467
Squamish-Lillooet	16,232	19,512	20,491	25,067	29,401	35,911
Stikine	1,586	2,005	2,235	2,215	1,391	1,475
Sunshine Coast	12,828	15,906	17,351	21,334	24,914	27,248
Thompson-Nicola	94,401	104,668	101,825	107,148	118,801	128,821

1999 figures are government estimates

(1) The Peace River-Liard RD was split into the Peace River and Fort Nelson-Liard RDs in 1987. The Fort Nelson-Liard RD was renamed the Northern Rockies RD in 1999.

(2) The City and District of Langley were transferred from the Central Fraser Valley RD to the Greater Vancouver RD in 1989.

(3) The Fraser-Cheam, Central Fraser Valley and Dewdney-Alouette RDs were amalgamated in 1995 and apportioned between the Greater Vancouver RD and the new Fraser Valley RD.

(4) Boundary changes were made in 1993/94.

(1994)—and he is credited with reviving a coastal aboriginal artistic tradition that was in danger of dying out. *See also* ART, NORTHWEST COAST ABORIGINAL; FIRST NATIONS.
Reading: Doris Shadbolt, *Bill Reid,* 1998.

REIFEL, GEORGE C., MIGRATORY BIRD SANCTUARY comprises about 3.45 km² of fore-shore at the north end of WESTHAM ISLAND in the mouth of the south arm of the FRASER R. Land for the refuge was leased from a local farmer, George H. Reifel, who donated it to the Crown in 1973. The refuge is named for his father, George C. Reifel, and is operated by the BC WATERFOWL SOCI-ETY. Situated on the PACIFIC FLYWAY, it welcomes over 240 species of migrating birds every year, including tens of thousands of snow geese, which arrive each fall.

REIMER, Eugene "Gene," wheelchair athlete (b 21 Jan 1940, Swift Current, SK). He had polio at age 4 and was left a paraplegic. A longtime resident of ABBOTSFORD, he became one of Canada's first wheelchair athletes in the late 1960s, participating in weightlifting, archery, SWIMMING, BASKETBALL, VOLLEYBALL and all TRACK AND FIELD events. During the 1970s he competed internationally and by his retirement in 1980 he had amassed 9 international and 50 national gold medals. His best year was 1972 when he set world records in the discus and pentathlon at the Paralympics in Heidelberg, Germany, and was named Canada's outstanding male athlete of the year, the first time a disabled athlete had earned such an honour anywhere. In 1974 he received the Order of Canada and in 1993 the W.A.C. BENNETT Award from the BC SPORTS HALL OF FAME. *SW*

REIMER, Kevin Michael, baseball player (b 28 June 1964, Macon, GA). His father Gerry had played his way through the Philadelphia Phillies system before a career-ending injury precluded a chance with the major-league club. Kevin developed his skills under his father's tutelage in ENDERBY and at Orange State College, where he was drafted by the Texas Rangers. Called up from the minor leagues with VANCOUVER pitcher Steve Wilson in 1988, he spent 3 seasons shuttling between Texas and the minors. In his first full season with the Rangers in 1991 he hit for a .269 average with 20 home runs and 69 RBIs. Traded to the Milwaukee Brewers, he had a disappointing 1993 season and spent the next 2 years playing for the Fukuoka Daiei Hawks in Japan where he was a league all-star. Back in N America, he ended his career in the minor leagues. *SW*

RELIEF CAMPS were created across Canada during the Depression to relieve the destitution of single unemployed men. The first camps in BC were organized by the provincial government in 1931. They were absorbed by the federal government in 1932 when the Department of National Defence took over responsibility for a national program of relief camps. In return for clearing brush, planting trees, digging sewers, working on road construction and doing other similar jobs, inmates received accommodation, meals, work clothes, medical attention and a daily cash allowance of 20 cents. In BC there were 237 relief camps, more than in any other province. For the most part the men worked on airstrip construction and ROAD AND HIGHWAY improvements. Projects included construction of the HOPE–PRINCETON HWY, the BIG BEND HWY and the SEA TO SKY HWY between SQUAMISH and Britannia Beach.

By early 1935 discontent in the camps had reached the boiling point. Men objected to the paltry allowance, the quality of the food, and their dehumanizing treatment at the hands of camp officials. Representatives of the Relief Camp Workers' Union, an affiliate of the Communist-backed Workers' Unity League, met in KAMLOOPS in March to plan a protest. Among their demands were decent wages for work, the right to vote (because they had no fixed address, inmates lost their vote), the right to organize freely, a 5-day work week and a system of unemployment insurance. On 4 Apr hundreds of men left the camps and made their way to VANCOUVER,

Harrison Mills relief camp, 1937. VPL 8834

where they were determined to stay until the government met their demands. Sleeping in rented halls and cheap hotels, subsisting on meal tickets paid for by public charity, the men held regular protest meetings and "tin-canned" on street corners to raise money. On 23 Apr one group of protestors invaded the HBC's downtown store and forced a confrontation with police that caused Mayor Gerry MCGEER to read the Riot Act. On 18 May another group invaded the Carnegie Library, which also housed the city museum. But despite McGeer's anti-Communist fulminations, the Vancouver "occupation" was orderly and disciplined. It was also unsuccessful, so on 3 June about 1,000 men boarded freight trains to carry their protest east to Ottawa. This expedition, the ON-TO-OTTAWA TREK, collapsed in Regina. Most men returned to the camps, which remained open for another year; the federal government closed them as of 30 June 1936. In BC they were replaced temporarily by a system of FORESTRY work camps but these too were closed in Apr 1938, largely because they were attracting migrants from across the country. This sparked another Vancouver protest that ended in a violent confrontation known as BLOODY SUNDAY.
Reading: Victor Howard, "We Were the Salt of the Earth!": A Narrative of the On-to-Ottawa Trek and the Regina Riot, 1985.

REMAC, 28 km southeast of TRAIL on the Pend d'Oreille R just north of the US border, was named after the founders of Reeves MacDonald Mines Ltd. Lead–ZINC–SILVER deposits were discovered in 1918 but commercial MINING did not begin until 1949, when a mill and townsite were developed. The ore was exhausted by 1975 and the mine shut down and dismantled. *AS*

REMO, a riverboat stop on the north side of the SKEENA R just west of TERRACE, was originally known as Bateman's Landing after a pioneer family. In the early 1900s, before the arrival of the GRAND TRUNK PACIFIC RWY, it was the main settlement in the area and boasted a hotel and store. By 1912 a ferry ran to Breckenridge Landing, also named after an early settler, on the opposite shore. Kitsumgallum Timber Co operated a mill at Remo in the late 1910s (*see* SAWMILLING). *AS*

RENATA, on the southwest shore of Lower ARROW LK, was one of the small lakeside hamlets flooded out in 1969 by the construction of the KEENLEYSIDE DAM near CASTLEGAR. In 1907 the site was developed for fruit growing by a Winnipeg land company and renamed from Dog Creek to Renata ("reborn"). The community was a mix of many nationalities. Growers formed a CO-OPERATIVE; since there was no road access, they exported their fruit by steamboat. The buildings were all burned prior to flooding and the population dispersed. Nearby was the KETTLE VALLEY RWY boomtown of Brooklyn, which sprang to life in 1898, boasted 10 hotels, a hospital, a NEWSPAPER and 1,000 residents, then was destroyed by fire in 1900 and abandoned.

REPTILES; *see* SALAMANDER; SNAKE.

RESERVES are areas of land allocated for the exclusive use of FIRST NATIONS and held in trust for them by the federal government. Bands (nations) are the primary unit of administration under the federal *Indian Act* and are usually associated with one or more reserves, though some bands have no reserves. There are 197 bands in BC and 1,613 reserves amounting to 3,437.41 km² or .36% of the province's total land area. They range in size from less than 1 ha to more than 180 km². Only about one-quarter are occupied. Somewhere between 25% and 50% of the aboriginal population of BC lives on reserves. A third of the people who live on reserves are not of aboriginal ancestry and are living on land leased from the reserve.

The earliest reserves were on VANCOUVER ISLAND, created under the terms of the DOUGLAS TREATIES between 1850 and 1854, and in the southwest corner of the mainland colony. By CONFEDERATION there were 80 reserves established, a total of 115.08 km², mostly around villages or at food-gathering sites. Little or no consultation with the aboriginal people took place because the provincial government refused to acknowledge aboriginal title (*see* ABORIGINAL RIGHTS). At 5 ha per family, BC reserves were much smaller than in the rest of Canada, and the federal government requested that the province increase reserve size. The province argued that BC aboriginals did not need as much land as aboriginals elsewhere because they were mainly fishers (*see* FISHING, ABORIGINAL). Instead many reserves were reduced in size over the years as white settlement took precedence over aboriginal title. In 1875 the province and the federal government created a 3-person Joint Commission for the Settlement of Indian Reserves. Members were A.C. ANDERSON, Archibald McKinley and G.M. SPROAT. The commission began by dealing with the reserves already established in southern BC and allotted or confirmed 152 reserves (874.50 km²) in its first year. The province was a reluctant participant and in 1878 the 3-person commission was dissolved and Sproat continued as the only commissioner. He was replaced in 1880 by Peter O'REILLY, who was much less sympathetic to aboriginal demands. Most reserves (1,010) were allotted by 1900. A

Royal Commission, the MCKENNA–MCBRIDE COMMISSION, was established in 1913 to make a final determination of BC reserves. It ran for 3 years and reported in 1916. In 1924 the federal government changed the contours of many reserves, adding land in some places, taking it away in others, all without the consent of the First Nations of BC. Then in 1927 the federal *Indian Act* was amended to make it illegal for First Nations organizations to pursue their grievances. With minor exceptions this was how the reserve question stood until the 1980s, when provincial government policy changed. Some of the so-called cut-off lands were returned to aboriginal bands, or compensation was paid, resolving a long-standing grievance. In 1990 the province agreed to enter into a treaty-making process with BC First Nations and the federal government, a process that will inevitably affect the future of reserves (*see* BC TREATY COMMISSION). Under the terms of the *Indian Act*, registered or "status" Indians are not required to pay tax on income earned working on a reserve or sales tax on items purchased there.

RESIDENTIAL SCHOOLS were government-funded, church-operated boarding schools for FIRST NATIONS children. The first ones opened in Ontario in the 1840s and the government extended them across the country during the 1880s. In BC before that time First Nations chil-

Former Alert Bay residential school, 1995.
Les Bazso/Vancouver Province

dren attended either the available public schools with other children or the several schools established by missionaries (*see* EDUCATION). Along with providing a basic education, residential schools, also known as industrial schools, tried to suppress traditional aboriginal language and culture in the absence of parental influence, in order to assimilate First Nations children into mainstream society. No matter how well-meaning administrators may have been in their desire to educate First Nations for economic self-sufficiency, the schools in many cases had devastating effects on children and their families. Many children died at the institutions, which were incubators for fatal diseases. Others were brutally disciplined, and sexually and psychologically abused. The schools were phased out beginning in the 1960s, when the government ended its

partnership arrangement with the churches and either closed or handed schools over to First Nations bands to operate. In 1992 a report by the Royal Commission on Aboriginal Peoples blamed the schools for contributing to the high rates of substance abuse, suicide and family dysfunction among First Nations people. The previous year an OBLATE brother had been convicted of gross indecency involving children at St Joseph's Mission in WILLIAMS LAKE. An investigation by a special BC task force established in 1994 led to ongoing charges and more convictions. In 1998, 10 people who were abused at St Joseph's reached an out-of-court settlement with the federal government and the ROMAN CATHOLIC CHURCH, the first agreement of its kind in Canada. Churches have apologized for their role in the administration of the schools, as did the federal government early in 1998.

There were 17 residential schools in BC; 10 were operated by Catholic missionaries, 5 by the United Church and 2 by Anglicans.
Roman Catholic
    LOWER POST
    LEJAC School, FRASER LAKE
    St Joseph's Mission, Williams Lake
    Christie School, Meares Island, CLAYOQUOT SOUND
    KUPER ISLAND
    St. Augustine's, SECHELT
    St Paul's, N VANCOUVER
    St Mary's, MISSION
    KAMLOOPS
    St Eugene, CRANBROOK
United Church
    Alberni, PORT ALBERNI
    Coqualeetza, CHILLIWACK
    Ahousat, Clayoquot Sound
    Port Simpson (*see* FORT SIMPSON)
    Kitamaat (*see* KITIMAT)
Anglican
    St George's, LYTTON
    St Michael's, ALERT BAY

REVELSTOKE, city, pop 8,047, is located on the COLUMBIA R between the SELKIRK and

MONASHEE MTS at the western entrance to ROGERS PASS, 575 km west of VANCOUVER. Fur traders on the Columbia called the site Big Eddy after a large, treacherous whirlpool that impeded their brigades. Arthur Farwell, a government surveyor, laid out the original townsite in 1884, calling it after himself. When the CPR arrived, it created its own townsite just east of Farwell and in 1886 called it Revelstoke after Lord Revelstoke, head of the London banking firm Baring Bros, which invested heavily in the railway. The city incorporated on 1 Mar 1899, just 2 months after the CPR transferred its divisional point there. The presence of the railway sparked an economic boom that lasted until WWI. The railway remains an important employer, along with MINING and the FOREST INDUSTRY. Two national PARKS, GLACIER and MOUNT REVELSTOKE, attract TOURISM, as do ski facilities at Mt Mackenzie. Snowmobiling and helicopter skiing are also popular. In 1986 Revelstoke undertook a major downtown revitalization project, restoring more than 2 dozen heritage buildings. Revelstoke Dam, 4 km north on the Columbia R, is one of the highest concrete dams (175 m) in Canada. MICA DAM, 130 km farther north, is the highest earth-filled dam (242 m) in N America.

REXMOUNT, a ranching and mining settlement on the north side of what used to be the BRIDGE R at the mouth of Jones Crk 165 km north of VANCOUVER, is now under the waters of CARPENTER LK. It was active in the 1910s and 1920s.   AS

REYNOLDS, Ted, sports commentator (b 22 Jan 1925). Working in television and radio BROADCASTING around BC, he became a familiar face on national TV as he reported on sports from around the world. He went to the CBC in 1956 after working for radio stations in KAMLOOPS and VICTORIA. He covered the Summer Olympics 6 times, the Winter Olympics 4 times, the Commonwealth Games 8 times, the Pan American Games 4 times, the Canada Winter Games 5 times and the Canada Summer Games

Construction of powerhouse at Revelstoke Dam, 1980s. Revelstoke Museum & Archives P1904

for its first 20 years, as well as numerous championships in various sports. He did TV play-by-play for the VANCOUVER Mounties BASEBALL broadcasts, for the BC LIONS and for 5 Grey Cups. He was the first Vancouver host of *Hockey Night in Canada* when the VANCOUVER CANUCKS entered the NHL in 1970. As well as sports, he covered the RIPPLE ROCK explosion in 1958 and 3 royal visits to BC in the 1950s. *SW*

RHODES, Donnelly, actor (b 1932, Winnipeg). He is a veteran stage and television actor with a long list of feature films to his credit. He performed Shakespeare at the Stratford Festival in the 1960s and during the 1970s had a regular role on the daytime TV soap opera *The Young and the Restless*. Since then he has appeared in guest spots on many popular TV programs and he starred in the made-in-BC family adventure series *Danger Bay*. In 1998 he joined the cast of another local series, the award-winning *Da Vinci's Inquest*.

RHODODENDRON, wild, is a shrub of the heather family (Ericaceae) characterized by large, leathery, generally evergreen leaves and clusters of showy flowers. Three species are native to BC. Pacific rhododendron (*Rhododendron macrophyllum*) grows to 8 m in height and has thick evergreen leaves up to 20 cm long; its pink to rose-purple flowers are 5 cm long and grow in terminal clusters. Its BC range is restricted to the southern CASCADE MTS and two locations on southern VANCOUVER ISLAND, where it prefers moist woods in shady habitat. Rhododendron Flats in MANNING PROVINCIAL PARK 33 km east of HOPE is one of the best places to view this flowering giant in June. White rhododendron (*R. albiflorum*) is a smaller species (up to 2.5 m tall), more widely distributed, that grows in moist subalpine habitats. Its leaves are up to 8 cm long and are deciduous, and the flowers are about 2 cm long and grow in lateral clusters. It is one of the largest and showiest flowering alpine shrubs

Rhododendrons in Manning Provincial Park, 1992. Roy Luckow photo

in BC's mountains. In some areas it grows so densely that hikers bushwhacking through the backcountry call it "mountain misery." Its leaves have been reported to be poisonous to livestock. Lapland rosebay (*R. lapponicum*), also native to BC, is a dwarf, ground-hugging shrub with evergreen leaves and few—but showy and aromatic—deep purple flowers. This species grows on rocky alpine slopes and cliffs primarily in the northeast and northern Interior.

RICHARDS, Albert Norton, lawyer, lt gov 1876–81 (b 8 Dec 1822, Brockville, Upper Canada; d 6 Mar 1897, Victoria). A prominent lawyer in his native Brockville, he was also active in politics, winning election as a Liberal to the Canadian Assembly (1863) and to Parliament (1872). In 1874 he emigrated to BC with his family. His Liberal connections in Ottawa stood him in good stead and on 28 July 1876 he was sworn in as the province's second LT GOV. The appointment was protested by many people who associated him with the Liberal government in Ottawa, which was unpopular because of its railway policy. Richards was accused of being a carpetbagger who had not been in BC long enough to deserve the job. He turned out to be a capable if uninspiring lt gov. After his term expired in 1881 he lived in Ontario for 3 years, then returned to BC and practised law in VICTORIA.

RICHARDS, Dallas Murray "Dal," musician (b 5 Jan 1918, Vancouver). A member of the KITSILANO BOYS BAND in his youth, he began his professional career in the late 1930s playing clarinet and saxophones in the VANCOUVER dance bands

Dal Richards, legendary Vancouver band leader, Dec 1999. Glenn Baglo/Vancouver Sun

of Sandy DeSantis and Stan Patton. In 1940 he succeeded Mart KENNEY in directing the orchestra at the Hotel Vancouver's Panorama Roof. He remained there for 25 years, performing, broadcasting on CBC Radio and producing the album *Dance Date with Dal* (1964). After leaving "the Roof" in 1965 he remained a fixture on the local music scene, so much so that 3 Feb 1984 was declared Dal Richards Day in Vancouver. He and his band helped usher in the new millennium at the public First Night celebration in Vancouver, New Year's Eve 1999. *David Lee*

RICHARDS, George Henry, naval surveyor (b Feb 1819, Cornwall, England; d 14 Nov 1896, Bath, England). He entered the Royal Navy as a teenager and served around the world, including the Arctic, where in the 1850s he took part in the search for the missing Franklin expedition. In 1857 he arrived at ESQUIMALT in command of the vessel *Plumper* to survey the waters between VANCOUVER ISLAND and the American mainland as part of the boundary commission (*see* BOUNDARIES). When the GOLD RUSH began, his vessel was used to provide transport and carry out surveys on the FRASER R. In 1860 the paddle sloop *Hecate* replaced the *Plumper*, and in 1860–62 Richards carried out extensive surveys of the lower coast. He left BC at the end of 1862 to take up a new position as hydrographer to the Royal Navy. He retired in 1874, was knighted 3 years later and reached the rank of admiral.

RICHFIELD was a GOLD RUSH town on Williams Crk near BARKERVILLE in the CARIBOO. Established in 1861, it consisted of a series of rough wooden miners' shacks the first summer that GOLD was mined on the creek. When the mines turned out to be the richest in the district, stores, restaurants and, above all, saloons, were added. In 1862 Lt Henry Palmer, deputy commissioner of lands and works, named the town Richfield. It became the site of government buildings for the area, with a jail, courthouse and police barracks. As the gold rush waned, so did the town, until it was virtually abandoned. The original courthouse was replaced with a new one in 1882; in 1999 it was the only building remaining from the prosperous boomtown. *Ken Mather*

RICHMOND occupies most of LULU ISLAND, SEA ISLAND (site of VANCOUVER INTERNATIONAL AIRPORT) and 12 smaller islands (including Mitchell, Twigg and Deadman) at the mouth of the FRASER R, immediately south of VANCOUVER. Farming began in 1862 with the arrival of Hugh McRoberts, who named his property Richmond View after a place in his native Australia. It incorporated as a municipality in 1879. During the 1880s SALMON CANNING began at STEVESTON; at its height that community had 49 canneries. In 1889 Richmond was connected to the mainland by a bridge; the first railway link was in 1902 and the airport opened in

1931. The CPR built a train which was electrified by BC ELECTRIC RWY CO and operated as an INTERURBAN line until 1955. Many JAPANESE people were attracted to the community by the commercial FISHING industry at Steveston; after WWII CHINESE immigrants began to comprise a large portion of the population. When it opened in 1990, the Aberdeen Centre, the first of several shopping malls catering to the Asian community, was the largest enclosed Asian mall in N America. The rich alluvial farmland was protected from inundation by a system of dikes. Since the 1960s most of this land has been taken over by housing and commercial development, and today Richmond is primarily a mixed commercial/residential suburb, though several thousand hectares are preserved in the AGRICULTURAL LAND RESERVE. During the 1980s dozens of HIGH-TECHNOLOGY companies located here. In 1992 the Richmond Library and Cultural Centre opened with its gallery, archives and museum. Richmond reincorporated as a city in 1990.
Population: 148,867
Rank in BC: 4th
Population increase since 1981: 55%
Date of incorporation: district 10 Nov 1879; city 3 Dec 1990
Land area: 168.19 km²
Location: Greater Vancouver Regional District
Economic base: fishing, agriculture, canneries, manufacturing, warehousing

RICHTER, Francis Xavier "Frank," rancher (b 1837, Austria; d Dec 1910). As a young man he moved to the US, then came north to the valley of the SIMILKAMEEN R in 1864, where he worked for the HBC and pre-empted land near CAWSTON. Eventually his "R" Ranch was one of the largest and most prosperous in the southern Interior (see CATTLE INDUSTRY). His youngest son Frank was a SOCIAL CREDIT MLA for the Similkameen and minister of agriculture and of mines in W.A.C. BENNETT's government.

RICKER, William Edwin "Bill," fisheries scientist (b 11 Aug 1908). His accomplishments in fisheries science earned him worldwide recognition. He obtained his BA and PhD from the Univ of Toronto and began working at the PACIFIC BIOLOGICAL STATION (PBS) in NANAIMO in 1931. He subsequently taught at the Univ of Indiana, then returned to the PBS in 1950 and remained there until his retirement in 1973. He is known for developing the "Ricker Curve"—a mathematical formula that describes the fundamental relationship between adult fish and their offspring—and used by fisheries scientists around the world. He also wrote a classic book on fish population dynamics, authored hundreds of scientific papers and collaborated with Russian scientists on a Russian–English dictionary of fisheries and biology terms. The recipient of numerous scientific awards, Ricker was appointed to the Order of Canada in 1986.

RIDLEY, William, Anglican bishop (b 22 July 1836, Brixham, England; d 25 May 1911, England). The son of a Devon stonemason, he worked as a carpenter before training for the mission field. In 1879 he was consecrated first bishop of the new ANGLICAN diocese of Caledonia (northern BC) and came to live at METLAKATLA, his chosen see for the diocese, for nearly 20 years. Ridley's efforts led to confrontation with William DUNCAN, who moved to Alaska with about 800 adherents in 1887. The 3 Caledonia missions operating at Ridley's arrival grew to a dozen as he travelled the diocese by foot and canoe and in his small boat, the *Evangeline*, to areas as distant as MASSET, the STIKINE R and the Bulkley Valley. He translated various publications into FIRST NATIONS dialects and wrote 4 books. He retired to England in 1905.

Peter Botham

RIMMER, David McLellan, filmmaker (b 20 Jan 1942, Vancouver). He dropped out of graduate school at SFU in 1968 to become an artist. While working for CBC television he made his first short film and was one of the central figures at INTERMEDIA, exploring the world of experimental films through his Intermedia Film Co-operative. He taught at UBC and SFU, and in 1984 he joined the faculty of the EMILY CARR INSTITUTE OF ART & DESIGN while continuing to produce a series of experimental films that have won several awards internationally. *See also* FILMMAKING INDUSTRY.

RING-NECKED PHEASANT; *see* PHEASANT, RING-NECKED.

RINGWOOD, Gwen Pharis, dramatist (b 13 Aug 1910, Anatone, WA; d 24 May 1984, Williams Lake). She came to Canada in 1931 to study at the Univ of Alberta and began her career as a prolific playwright in 1935 while working at the Banff School of Fine Arts. After studying drama at the Univ of NC, she returned to Alberta to teach. In 1953 she moved to WILLIAMS LAKE, where she spent the rest of her life. She wrote more than 60 plays for radio and stage, including several musicals and plays for children. Almost all of them were set in western Canada, where Ringwood was a pioneer in community THEATRE. She won a GOV GEN'S AWARD for outstanding service to Canadian drama in 1941 and her book of collected plays (1982) was the first by a Canadian dramatist.

RINKE, Christopher Robert "Chris," wrestler (b 26 Oct 1960, New Westminster). Raised in PORT COQUITLAM, he was a product of SFU's WRESTLING program. He won his first national championship as a junior in 1979 and went on to collect 7 senior titles. His first international medal was a gold in his 82-kg weight class at the 1982 Commonwealth Games and the next year he took a bronze at the Pan American Games. At the 1984 Los Angeles Olympics he won bronze and with SFU teammate Bob Molle's silver brought home Canada's first Olympic wrestling medals since 1936. Rinke won his second Commonwealth gold in Edinburgh in 1986 and his last international competition was the 1988 Seoul Olympics, where he finished 11th.   *SW*

RIONDEL, pop 338, a retirement community on the northeast side of KOOTENAY LK, 88 km north of CRESTON, is the site of the famous Bluebell mine. The low-grade galena deposits of this and adjacent claims were worked from 1885 to 1896 by an American syndicate led by a wealthy brass manufacturer, Andrew Hendryx, and his brother Wilbur (see HENDRYX BROS). The Canadian Metal Co then worked the deposits but it was COMINCO, with its great capacity to smelt low-grade galena, that achieved the greatest success from 1948 to 1971 on the Bluebell claims. Depleted reserves and dewatering problems finally ended MINING activity on the site. The post office that opened in 1907 was named after Count Edouard Riondel, president of the Canadian Metal Co.

RIPPLE ROCK was a dangerous obstacle to navigation lying just below the surface of the water in SEYMOUR NARROWS, DISCOVERY PASSAGE, off the

The blasting of Ripple Rock, 5 Apr 1958.
Bill Dennett/MCR 19984–1, 2, 3, 6

east coast of VANCOUVER ISLAND north of CAMPBELL RIVER. Dozens of vessels were wrecked on the rock and more than 100 people lost their lives. In the 1860s a plan was put forward to link Vancouver Island to the mainland at BUTE INLET, using the twin peaks of Ripple Rock as pilings for a bridge. This plan continued to percolate through the years, promoted by VICTORIA business interests, until finally the decision was taken to destroy the rock to improve safety for mariners. Two attempts were made, one in 1943 and another in 1945—during which 9 men died—but both times the work had to be abandoned. In the late 1950s the government tackled the project again. Tunnels were drilled in the ocean floor out to the rock, then up into its peaks. The rock was honeycombed with passages that were packed with 1,237 tonnes of explosives. At 9:33 a.m. on 5 Apr 1958, the largest non-nuclear peacetime explosion in history destroyed Ripple Rock.

RISK, Sydney, actor, director (b 26 May 1908, Vancouver; d 5 Sept 1985, Vancouver). One of the pioneers of THEATRE in VANCOUVER, he began acting as a student at Kitsilano High School and UBC, where he became director of the Players Club after graduation. During this time he used the stage name Dickson McNaughton. In 1933 he went to England and trained at the Old Vic theatre school under Tyrone Guthrie, while performing with various companies. After returning to Canada in 1938 he taught theatre at UBC, the Banff School of Fine Arts and the Univ of Alberta. In 1946 he founded EVERYMAN THEATRE, Vancouver's first permanent professional theatre company. After its collapse in 1953, Risk rejoined UBC, where he taught until his retirement in 1966.

RISKE CREEK, pop 268, 47 km west of WILLIAMS LAKE on the Chilcotin Hwy (Hwy 20; *see* ROADS AND HWYS), is the CHILCOTIN's oldest pioneer community, named for L.W. Riskie, a farmer who settled in the area in 1868. The name refers to the tiny community and the large geographic area that surrounds it. Becher House, named for Frederick BECHER, was once a famous stopping place on the road. Ranching (*see* CATTLE INDUSTRY) has always been the main activity and Riskie property, known as the Cotton Ranch, was still in business in 2000.

RITCHIE BROS AUCTIONEERS is the world's largest auctioneer of industrial equipment. Now based in RICHMOND, it was founded in KELOWNA in 1963 by Dave Ritchie and his brothers John and Ken, both of whom later retired. By 1999 it had auctioned more than $8.5 billion worth of equipment at more than 1,750 auctions in 16 countries. In 1998 alone it sold more than $1 billion worth of merchandise. Since 1998 it has been listed on the NY Stock Exchange.

RITHET, Robert Paterson, merchant (b 22 Apr 1844, Cleuchhead, Scotland; d 19 Mar 1919, Victoria). He arrived in BC in 1862 in search of gold (*see* GOLD RUSH, CARIBOO). After 2 years in

the CARIBOO he settled in VICTORIA and went to work for a shipping firm. In 1871 he and J. Andrew Welch, a San Francisco merchant, formed a partnership. Their company, which became R.P. Rithet & Co in 1890, engaged in a great variety of enterprises including SALMON CANNING, grocery importing, lumbering, the sugar trade, SHIPPING insurance and sealing (*see* FUR SEAL). One of the wealthiest merchants in BC, Rithet was also active politically, serving as mayor of Victoria in 1885 and MLA from 1894 to 1898.

RIVER OTTER; *see* OTTER.

RIVERS are extremely important in such a mountainous place as BC. They have played, and continue to play, a major role as agents of erosion and shapers of BC's landforms. They cut through mountain ranges, allowing access for people and providing migration routes for spawning SALMON and many other plant and animal species. As well as providing food and settlement areas, they offered a primary means of transportation for FIRST NATIONS people and were the routes followed by railway and highway construction. Rivers were the principal means by which BC was discovered, and exploited, by early explorers and settlers. Rivers facilitated major GOLD RUSHES, and the historic explorations of Alexander MACKENZIE, Simon FRASER and David THOMPSON were conducted down the uncharted rivers that today bear their names. Many of BC's rivers support globally significant salmon populations, as well as opportunities for development of HYDROELECTRICITY. They provide water for AGRICULTURE and industrial and domestic uses, and contribute substantially to the provincial ECONOMY.

BC has 5 major drainage systems: Yukon, PEACE–LIARD (Mackenzie system), COLUMBIA, FRASER, and the coastal system, which is made up of the drainage basins of large and small coastal

THE 10 LARGEST BC WATERSHEDS	
Fraser	231,510 km²
Columbia	102,800 km² *(in BC)*
Peace	99,000 km²
Fort Nelson	55,900 km²
Thompson	55,827 km²
Skeena	54,431 km²
Stikine	49,647 km²
Nechako	47,234 km²
Kootenay	37,685 km² *(in BC)*
Finlay	19,040 km²

AVERAGE WATER FLOW OF BC'S MAJOR RIVERS (m³/sec)	
Columbia (in BC)	2,780
Fraser	2,640
Peace (in BC)	1,330
Liard (in BC)	1,000
Skeena	870
Kootenay (in BC)	860
Nass	810
Pend d'Oreille (in BC)	760
Thompson	750
Stikine	740

rivers such as the SKEENA, STIKINE and NASS; these drainage basins are separated by heights of land. Two-thirds of BC's rivers drain to the Pacific Ocean, while the rest drain north to the Yukon R or northeast to the Mackenzie R. It can also be argued there is a sixth system: the Flathead R system has a headwaters branch in BC's southeast corner. Its watershed is largely in Montana and it drains into the Missouri–Mississippi system and

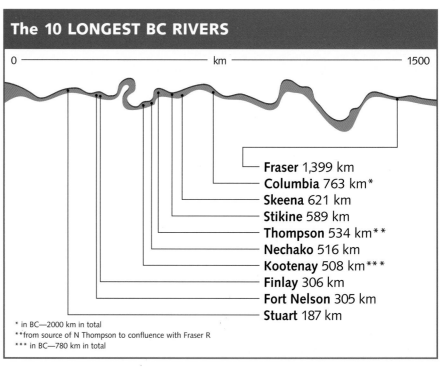

The 10 LONGEST BC RIVERS

0	km	1500

Fraser 1,399 km
Columbia 763 km*
Skeena 621 km
Stikine 589 km
Thompson 534 km**
Nechako 516 km
Kootenay 508 km***
Finlay 306 km
Fort Nelson 305 km
Stuart 187 km

* in BC—2000 km in total
**from source of N Thompson to confluence with Fraser R
*** in BC—780 km in total

The Fraser R at Yale. Rick Blacklaws photo

ultimately to the Atlantic Ocean. This area is called CROWN OF THE CONTINENT in large part because of this major drainage divide.

The northwestern corner of BC lies within the drainage basin of the Yukon R. Large lakes such as Atlin, Tagish and TESLIN are part of this system, which rises in the Jennings Lks in the western end of the Cassiar Mts and is fed by the rivers, LAKES and icefields from Atlin to Teslin lakes. The Liard and Peace rivers and their tributaries are part of the Mackenzie R system and drain about 260,000 km² of northern and northeastern BC. The headwaters of the Peace and the confluence of the FINLAY and PARSNIP rivers were forever altered during the 1960s by construction of the BENNETT DAM and creation of WILLISTON RESERVOIR. Of the major drainage basins, only the Fraser's is completely within BC. From its headwaters at Moose Lk in Mt ROBSON Provincial Park, to its massive ESTUARY at the Pacific Ocean, the Fraser runs 1,399 km. At about 231,500 km², its drainage basin is second in size to the area drained by the Peace–Liard system. As with most of BC's river systems, the Fraser was shaped and successively altered by massive GLACIATION, deposition and subsequent uplift. There is believed to be a close geological linkage between the upper Fraser (as far as MCGREGOR), the Peace and the ROCKY MT TRENCH, but the record of stream piracy is lost in the meltwaters of time. The Columbia R rises in Columbia Lk, flows northward around the top of the SELKIRK MTS, then turns south, draining about 102,845 km² within BC before flowing into the US. The KOOTENAY R, its major tributary, also loops north and south, giving evidence of more stream piracy and a drainage history as complex and equally lost in the geological past as the Fraser's. The fifth drainage system is represented by a number of rivers in the western part of BC that rise on the east side of the COAST MTS and drain most of northwest BC. The 4 largest of these are the Skeena, Nass, Stikine, and TAKU rivers. Geologically they have maintained their courses across the Coast Mts and, with their steep gradients, have expanded their drainage basins at the expense of the other systems that surround them. In time, for instance, the headward expansion of the Taku's tributaries will eventually take over much of what is currently drained by the Yukon R.
Maggie Paquet

Reading: Stuart S. Holland, Landforms of British Columbia, 1976.

RIVERS INLET is a mainland FJORD, 48 km long, off FITZ HUGH SOUND just north of the top of VANCOUVER ISLAND. It was named by Capt George VANCOUVER for George Pitt, First Baron Rivers, a minor British politician. It is known for its productive SALMON fishing. The first SALMON CANNERY opened in 1882, followed over the years by 17 others, including Good Hope, Provincial, Wadhams, Duncanby, Green and Brunswick. Loggers and trappers were also present and the inlet supported a thriving community, also called Rivers Inlet. A hospital operated from 1897 to 1950. The last cannery closed in the 1950s and the inlet was closed to commercial fishing in 1996 because the population of sockeye salmon was dropping precipitously. LOGGING for SPRUCE and HEMLOCK has also been an economic mainstay. The supply centre for the inlet is the small floating community of DAWSON'S LANDING. Oweekeno Village lies at the head of the inlet where the Wannock R drains OWIKENO LK. The OWEEKENO First Nation, who occupy this area, are related to the nearby HEILTSUK (Bella Bella). Penrose Island at the mouth of the inlet is a provincial MARINE PARK. *See also* FISHING, COMMERCIAL.

RIVERSIDE was an early FRASER VALLEY sternwheeler landing on the south shore of the FRASER R, 45 km east of NEW WESTMINSTER. It had a post office from 1881 to 1894. The settlement withered away as a result of the growing importance of MISSION on the opposite side of the river. AS

RIVERVIEW is the site of a hospital, farm and botanical garden in COQUITLAM at the confluence of the Coquitlam and FRASER rivers. As the original Public Hospital for the Insane (later WOODLANDS) became overcrowded, the government purchased land not far away for a new hospital. The land, originally called Colony Farm, was cleared and in 1913 the new psychiatric facility opened. It was originally known as the Hospital for the Mind at Mount Coquitlam; the name was later changed to Essondale, after Provincial Secretary Henry Esson YOUNG. It is now known as Riverview Hospital. It included several buildings, along with the farm, which produced food for patients and was also used as a provincial experimental farm, and a botanical garden established by John DAVIDSON, now the Davidson Arboretum. The only psychiatric hospital in BC, it was slated to be phased out of operation during the 1990s and replaced by several smaller facilities, but in 1999 it still had 800 operating beds.

ROADS AND HIGHWAYS have been an important part of the economic infrastructure in BC since the mid-1850s, when the first wagon road was built, linking FORT VICTORIA to CRAIGFLOWER farm at the head of ESQUIMALT Harbour. In 1862 a TRAIL, later widened for wagons, was driven north across the MALAHAT to the COWICHAN Valley. On the mainland, road building commenced with the discovery of GOLD on the FRASER R. The first route to the Interior was the DOUGLAS TRAIL between HARRISON LK and LILLOOET, built in 1858. Later the CARIBOO WAGON ROAD was completed from YALE to BARKERVILLE in 1862–65.

BC's rugged terrain made road construction difficult; a network of major roads evolved slowly. From 1858 to 1908, bridge and highway construction was the responsibility of the chief commissioner of lands and works. It was an ideal job from which to control development and dispense patronage, and several PREMIERS kept it for themselves. The Cariboo Wagon Road was built with the help of the ROYAL ENGINEERS, but once they withdrew from the colony private contractors took over, entrepreneurs such as Joseph TRUTCH, Thomas SPENCE, Gustavus WRIGHT and Alfred WADDINGTON. Waddington's attempt to push a road across the CHILCOTIN from BUTE INLET touched off the CHILCOTIN WAR in 1864. After BC joined CONFEDERATION in 1871, road construction consumed about 45% of the province's budget. Much of the pick-and-shovel work was carried out by rural settlers labouring for 50 cents to $1 a day.

Close to 9,000 km of roadway criss-crossed the FRASER VALLEY, the KOOTENAY and the central Interior by 1900, and snaked up the east coast of VANCOUVER ISLAND from VICTORIA, but they were little better than dirt tracks. Flooding, LANDSLIDES, snow and other blockages rendered them impassable for long periods of time and little effort was expended maintaining them. For example, the road from Yale to SPENCES BRIDGE was closed from 1891 to 1927, and during this time there was no road connection between the coast and the Interior. Political scandals led Premier Richard MCBRIDE to put highways and bridges under a new department of public works in 1908. The first minister was Thomas "Good Roads" Taylor, who doubled the amount of roadway over the next 6 years. The speed limit at the time was 24 km/h, and while some urban streets were "macadamized," asphalt paving was not introduced until 1910, when Columbia Bitulithic Ltd, the dominant paving company in the province for the rest of the century, was formed.

Construction on a large scale continued in the 1920s, stimulated by the growing popularity of the automobile. The coast was finally connected to the Interior by a new highway up the Fraser Canyon in 1927, though it was not until 1940 that the last link in the trans-provincial highway, known as the BIG BEND HWY, was built between GOLDEN and REVELSTOKE. A significant road-building and general contracting firm that emerged during this period was Dawson Wade Construction Co, founded in 1922 by Fred J. Dawson and Henry Wade. Highway construction slowed during the hard times of the Depression, despite large-scale projects such as the Pattullo Bridge (1937) and LIONS GATE BRIDGE (1938), while during WWII the most important development was the ALASKA HWY, built by the American military.

Some enduring names in BC road construction emerged after WWII as the government tried to make the province accessible to the growing number of people with automobiles. Emil Anderson Contracting Co Ltd began in HOPE in 1946. Its first major contract was the

HOPE–PRINCETON HWY, completed in 1949, and subsequently it was involved in many major highway projects. The companies that later merged as JJM Group also date from the 1940s. By 1950 only 10% of BC highways were paved. In response, new paving and aggregate suppliers entered the market; notably the BA Blacktop Group, with headquarters in N VANCOUVER.

There were 237,000 motor vehicles in BC by 1952, when the election of a SOCIAL CREDIT government ushered in a period of rapid highway construction and improvement. Led by Phil GAGLARDI, minister responsible for highways from 1952 to 1968, the Socreds used road construction as a means of stimulating economic development and a tool of political patronage. By 1966 the province was spending $100 million a year on highways, almost triple what the entire provincial budget had been at the end of the war. Major projects included the George Massey Tunnel, a 4-lane freeway to the US border and another to Hope, 7 Fraser Canyon tunnels, the PORT MANN and Second Narrows (see IRONWORKERS MEMORIAL) bridges, the TSAW-WASSEN ferry (see BC FERRY CORP) causeway and kilometre after kilometre of fresh asphalt. A major new highway project came during the 1980s when the government of Bill BENNETT pushed through the COQUIHALLA HWY against much opposition. In 1988 the Social Credit

government of Bill VANDER ZALM privatized highway and bridge maintenance, making BC the first state or provincial government in N America to get out of the business of looking after its roads. In response, most large contractors set up road maintenance divisions in their companies. Several new firms were created at the same time, 2 of the larger ones being Mainroad Contracting Ltd in SURREY and Emcon Services Ltd in MERRITT. The BC Road Builders and Heavy Construction Assoc, established in 1966 with 12 member companies, grew to 165 members following privatization. In 1993 the NDP government established the BC Transportation Financing Authority to look after transportation infrastructure, including highways. Its wholly owned subsidiary, Highway Constructors Ltd (HCL), employs all construction labour on provincially funded road projects. By 1998 there were 23,710 km of paved highway and 18,730 km of unpaved road in BC available to the 2.2 million motor vehicles in the province.

Major Highways on Vancouver Island

#1, the TRANS-CANADA HWY, begins at Mile 0 at BEACON HILL PARK in Victoria, runs north 113 km to NANAIMO, then crosses by ferry to HORSESHOE BAY on the mainland, goes through VANCOUVER and heads east through the Fraser Valley, following more or less the route of the CPR across BC. Portions of the Vancouver Island section of Hwy #1 were upgraded during the 1990s as part of the Island Highway rebuilding project, the largest construction job in the Island's history.

#17 is the Patricia Bay Hwy, a 32-km stretch connecting Victoria to the ferry terminal at Swartz Bay.

#19 is the northern portion of the Island Hwy from Nanaimo 391 km to PORT HARDY. The section from Nanaimo to CAMPBELL RIVER has been upgraded as part of the Island Hwy rebuilding project. The northern section as far as the top of the Island was only completed in 1979.

#4 runs 140 km across the Island from PARKSVILLE through PORT ALBERNI to PACIFIC RIM NATIONAL PARK and connects UCLUELET and TOFINO on the west coast. The western section was not paved until the early 1970s.

#28 runs 92 km across the middle of the Island from Campbell River to GOLD RIVER.

Major Highways on the Mainland

#3, known also as the Crowsnest Hwy, is the principal route across the southern part of the province just above the US border. It begins at Hope and the 136-km section to PRINCETON through MANNING PROVINCIAL PARK, completed in 1949, is called the Hope–Princeton Hwy. Where #3 crosses Kootenay Pass (el 1,774) between SALMO and CRESTON, it is the highest paved road in Canada.

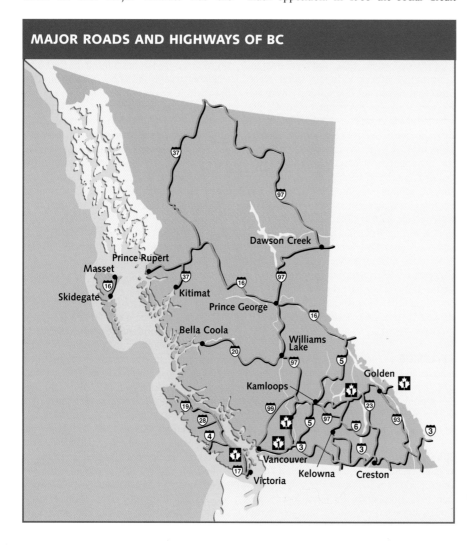

MAJOR ROADS AND HIGHWAYS OF BC

#5 is the Coquihalla Hwy running from Hope 210 km northeast to KAMLOOPS. Completed in 1987, it is BC's only toll highway. North of Kamloops #5 continues 340 km to TÊTE JAUNE CACHE, a section of road known as the Yellowhead South.

#16 is the Yellowhead Hwy stretching from YELLOWHEAD PASS in the ROCKY MTS westward across the province to PRINCE RUPERT via PRINCE GEORGE. It also continues by ferry across HECATE STRAIT to the QUEEN CHARLOTTE ISLANDS where it links MASSET and SKIDEGATE.

#20 is the Chilcotin Road, the third route to the coast, connecting WILLIAMS LAKE 456 km across the Chilcotin Plateau and through the COAST MTS to BELLA COOLA.

#37 is the Stewart-Cassiar Hwy running north 721 km from the GITWANGAK at the SKEENA R east of TERRACE to Watson Lake in the Yukon, where it joins the Alaska Hwy. A section of the Stewart-Cassiar heads west at MEZIADIN LAKE to STEWART. The northern section was not completed until the early 1970s and put an end to scheduled riverboat travel on the lower STIKINE R.

#93 begins at the ROOSVILLE border crossing south of FERNIE and follows the ROCKY MT TRENCH north before crossing the mountains via KOOTENAY NATIONAL PARK and Vermilion Pass (el 1,651 m) to Banff, AB. It connects to highways in the US leading to Seattle, and before 1927 it was the only route from Alberta to the Pacific Ocean.

#97 is the only highway running north–south the length of BC. It begins at the US border near OSOYOOS and travels north through the OKANAGAN VALLEY, then west to Kamloops. At CACHE CREEK it turns north again and is called the Cariboo Hwy; it continues 441 km to Prince George, much of this distance following the old Cariboo Wagon Road. From Prince George north to DAWSON CREEK and the PEACE R country it is called the HART Hwy, after Premier John HART. From Dawson Creek, #97 becomes the Alaska Hwy as it winds its way 2,400 km to Fairbanks.

#99 runs north–south, connecting Vancouver to the US border at Blaine, Wash. To the north it heads up HOWE SOUND, where it is known as the SEA TO SKY HWY, then via WHISTLER and PEMBERTON over the Duffey Lake Road to LILLOOET on the Fraser R. It offers an alternative route to the Interior from the Trans-Canada.

ROBBINS RANGE, an AGRICULTURAL district 28 km east of KAMLOOPS, was named for Cyrus S. Robbins, a New Hampshire prospector who settled here about 1880 and established a substantial horse and CATTLE ranch.   AS

ROBERTS, Morley, writer (b 29 Dec 1857, London, England; d 8 June 1942, London). As a young man he travelled the world, working at a variety of labouring jobs in Australia and the US. He arrived in BC in 1884 and spent the winter of

1884–85 working in a sawmill in NEW WESTMINSTER. After further adventures in BC and California he returned to England and became a prolific writer, publishing more than 2 dozen novels and hundreds of short stories. He also wrote memoirs, biographies and books about cancer and international politics. One of his early novels, *The Mate of the Vancouver* (1892), has been called "the first Vancouver novel." Another, *The Prey of the Strongest* (1906), draws on his experiences working in a SAWMILL.

ROBERTS BANK is a deep-water, COAL-loading "superport" located near TSAWWASSEN south of VANCOUVER. The terminal is a small island built from earth dredged to create a shipping channel. The island is linked to the mainland by a long causeway. The terminal opened in 1970 and was enlarged in 1983. Administered by the PORT OF VANCOUVER, it is operated under a lease arrangement by Westshore Terminals. A huge new container terminal, DeltaPort, opened in 1997.

ROBERTS CREEK, pop 2,477, is an oceanside community on the SUNSHINE COAST, a few minutes north of GIBSONS, named for the pioneering Roberts family—father Thomas, mother Charlotte, and sons Will and Frank—who arrived in 1889. It was a grandson, Harry Roberts, who was most associated with the community, operating a SAWMILL, store and post office until he moved away in the 1920s. AGRICULTURE was the main economic activity, plus catering to summer vacationers. In the 1960s the area attracted a fair number of hippies; they established several communes, most of which faded away, though the community retains a countercultural flavour.

ROBERTSON, Alexander Rocke, lawyer, politician (b 12 May 1841, Chatham, ON; d 1 Dec 1881, Victoria). Trained as a lawyer, he practised in Windsor, ON, until 1864 when he moved to VICTORIA. Colonial regulations did not allow him to practise law on VANCOUVER ISLAND, so after working briefly as a journalist he moved to NEW WESTMINSTER and was admitted to the bar of BC. After union of the colonies in 1866 he moved back to Victoria. A founding member of the Law Society (1869), he swiftly earned a reputation as one of the ablest lawyers in the colony. In 1870 he served a term as mayor of Victoria. He was a vocal proponent of CONFEDERATION and in 1871 won election to the first provincial legislature, joining the CABINET as provincial secretary. After one term he left politics to resume his law practice. In 1880 he was appointed to the provincial Supreme Court. The following summer, when he was only 40 years old, one of his legs was amputated after a swimming accident. He never recovered from the operation and died later that year.

ROBERTSON, Bruce Richard, swimmer (b 27 Apr 1953, Vancouver). He started SWIMMING competitively, for VANCOUVER's Canadian Dolphin Swim Club, at the relatively late age of 16 and won the 100-m butterfly gold medal at the

1971 British championships 2 years later. He was selected for the 1972 Canadian Olympic team and won the silver medal in Munich, placing 2nd to American 7-time gold medal winner Mark Spitz in the 100-m butterfly. During that race Robertson set Canadian and Commonwealth records. He also won a bronze in the freestyle relay. When he won a gold medal in the 100-m butterfly at the 1973 World Aquatic Championships in Belgrade it was Canada's first gold in major international swimming competition since 1912. At the 1974 Commonwealth Games in New Zealand he collected 2 gold, 2 silver, and 2 bronze medals and at the 1975 Pan American Games in Mexico City he won 3 silvers and 2 bronzes. His career honours include the 1973 Norton Crow Trophy as Canadian male athlete of the year, the Order of Canada, and memberships in the Canadian Sports Hall of Fame, the BC SPORTS HALL OF FAME and the Canadian Aquatic Hall of Fame.   SW

ROBERTSON, Edward Alastair "Sandy," athlete (b 23 Feb 1923, Vancouver). He excelled in several sports but particularly in BASKETBALL, BASEBALL and squash. At age 17 he opened his baseball career by pitching a one-hitter with St Regis of the VANCOUVER Senior League. After excelling locally he became the first BC player to sign a major-league baseball contract, in 1946

Sandy Robertson (r) being inducted into the UBC Sports Hall of Fame, with Bob Philip, director of athletics at UBC, 1993.
Fred Hume/UBC Athletic Dept

with the Boston Red Sox. That year he also graduated as a civil engineer and was named Vancouver's sportsman of the year. He continued pitching with the minor-professional Vancouver Capilanos, in one season tying the league record for 12 consecutive victories and being named team MVP. He was the top player on every basketball team he played for—the UBC Thunderbirds, the Clover Leafs and the Meralomas—and helped all win championships. The Meralomas won the Canadian title in 1947 and the Clover Leafs won it in 1948,

1949, 1950 and 1952. In squash he captured 21 regional Pacific Northwest tournaments, the BC championship in 1963 and 1965, and became the first Canadian to win the Pacific Coast Championship in 1964. His son, Bruce ROBERT-SON, was an international SWIMMING champion. Sandy is a member of the UBC Sports Hall of Fame and the BC SPORTS HALL OF FAME (1971). *SW*

ROBIN, American (*Turdus migratorius*), the traditional harbinger of spring, is a plump perching songbird. A member of the thrush family, it is one of the most common birds in N America, and very familiar because it has adapted so well

American robin. R. Wayne Campbell photo

to the presence of humans. It has a black head, tail and wings, striped throat, grey back and brick red breast. In the summer it occurs widely across BC; when the weather turns cold it migrates south or overwinters in the southern part of the province, especially in the Lower Mainland and southern VANCOUVER ISLAND. Robins build their nests of grass, twigs and mud in trees and shrubs and the female lays 3–4 blue-green eggs. They forage on or near the ground for INSECTS, earthworms, fruit and BERRIES.

ROBINSON, Eden, writer (b 1968, Kitamaat). Born and raised on the HAISLA First Nations RESERVE outside KITIMAT, she studied creative WRITING at the UNIV OF VICTORIA. In 1966 her first book, *Traplines*, a collection of short stories, was published; Robinson was hailed as Canada's first Haisla writer. In 2000 she published her first novel, *Monkey Beach*, a portrait of life in a North Coast village.

ROBINSON, Harry, rancher, storyteller (b 8 Oct 1900, Oyama; d 25 Jan 1990, Keremeos). A member of the OKANAGAN First Nation, he grew up in the Similkameen Valley near KEREMEOS, where he heard the stories told by his grandmother and other community elders. As a teenager he worked as a ranch hand around the southern Interior. In 1924 he married Matilda Johnny and the couple acquired a small ranch of their own at Chopaka near Keremeos. Eventually they owned 4 ranches (*see* CATTLE INDUSTRY). By 1973 his wife was dead and Robinson was too old to continue ranching, so he sold out and retired. In his later years he returned to the stories of his youth and became a respected story-

teller and communicator of Okanagan cultural traditions. His stories were collected by Wendy Wickwire in 2 books: *Write It On Your Heart* (1989) and *Nature Power* (1992).

ROBINSON, J. Lewis, geographer (b 9 July 1918, Leamington, ON). After graduating from Syracuse Univ and Clark Univ in Worcester, MA, he became the federal government's first professional geographer when he was hired by the mines department in 1943. In 1946 he came to VANCOUVER to establish a geography program in UBC's department of geology and geography. He served as founding chair of a separate geography department from 1959 until 1968. The leading BC geographer of his generation, he also published many articles and books and was a popular teacher, winning the UBC Master Teacher Award in 1977. He was a pioneer in regional planning and promoted geographical studies in schools and to the public. He retired from UBC in 1983 to become professor emeritus.

ROBINSON, John Moore, teacher, journalist, land developer (b 30 Dec 1855, Williamston County, ON; d 23 Feb 1934, Naramata). He was working as a schoolteacher when he moved west to Portage la Prairie, MB where in 1882 he became editor of a local newspaper and founded a real estate company. Later he founded the Brandon *Times* newspaper and served as a Conservative member in the Manitoba legislature. He was a principal in 2 MINING companies that held claims near CHRISTINA LK and on the west side of OKANAGAN LK. One of the first people to recognize the potential of converting OKANAGAN VALLEY ranch land to irrigated 4-ha fruit farms for settlers, he moved to the Okanagan and formed the Peachland Townsite Co in 1898 to develop PEACHLAND. In 1903 he became the secretary-treasurer and manager of Sir Thomas SHAUGHNESSY's Summerland Development Co, which developed SUMMER-LAND. Robinson gave the community its name, was its first reeve, served as school trustee, helped form the board of trade and created the *Summerland Review* NEWSPAPER. In 1907 he founded the Okanagan Trust Co, which bought land and created the town of NARAMATA, the third of his lakeside communities, where he spent the rest of his life. *David Gregory*

ROBINSON, Robert Gordon "Red," broadcaster (b 30 Mar 1937, Comox). When he was a VANCOUVER high school student in 1953 he began contributing to Al Jordan's afternoon radio show for teenagers on CJOR, *Theme for Teens*, the first scheduled radio program featuring rock 'n' roll in Canada. In 1954, a year before he graduated, he became on-air host and for the next several years was the voice of the teenage generation in the city, playing the new music, hosting live shows and appearing at events around the province. He was so popular that a personal appearance was liable to spark a mob scene. During the 1960s he was a program manager for Vancouver radio stations, and later switched to advertising. In 1988 he opened his

own management company. Inducted into the Canadian Broadcast Hall of Fame in 1997, he is one of only 3 Canadian broadcasters in the Rock and Roll Hall of Fame in the US (1995). *See also* BROADCASTING.

Red Robinson, broadcaster, 1998.

ROBINSON, Spider, writer (b 24 Nov 1948, New York City). He and his wife, the former dancer/choreographer Jeanne Robinson, lived for 10 years in Halifax, then moved to VANCOUVER in 1987. He began writing professionally in 1972 and has published more than 2 dozen books, all speculative fiction. His work has won several awards, including the international Hugo and Nebula Awards for science fiction.

ROBINSON, Svend, politician (b 4 Mar 1952, Minneapolis). A graduate of UBC law school, he won election to the House of Commons as a candidate for the NDP in 1979, when he was 27 years old, and has held his BURNABY riding ever since. He has been one of the most controversial

Svend Robinson, long-time NDP Member of Parliament for Burnaby.

politicians in Canada, taking highly publicized stands on environmental and ABORIGINAL RIGHTS issues, as well as doctor-assisted suicide. He once heckled US President Ronald Reagan, and in 1992 he was expelled from China for protesting human rights abuses there. In 1988 he publicly declared his homosexuality, becoming the country's first openly GAY MP. In the summer of 1994 he served a 14-day prison term for contempt of court following participation in anti-LOGGING protests at CLAYOQUOT SOUND. Robinson is criticized by some for putting self-promotion ahead of party loyalty and for favouring confrontation over compromise, but his admirers say he is one of the few MPs with the courage to speak out on unpopular issues. He ran unsuccessfully for the national leadership of the NDP in 1995 and remained an unrepentant maverick, known as one of the most dedicated constituency politicians in the country.

ROBSON, a residential suburb 4 km northwest of CASTLEGAR, was once a busy CPR terminus, steamship port, ore depot and orchard settlement at the south end of the ARROW LKS. The original landing, located 3 km east in 1891, was named after Gilbert M. SPROAT. In 1902 a railway bridge spanned the COLUMBIA R to W Robson joining the Columbia & Kootenay and COLUMBIA & WESTERN railways. Robson was named after John ROBSON, BC PREMIER from 1889 to 1892. AS

ROBSON, Jim, sports broadcaster (b 17 Jan 1935). He stepped right out of MAPLE RIDGE secondary school and into sports BROADCASTING at CJAV in PORT ALBERNI in 1952. When Bill Stephenson left VANCOUVER's CKWX in 1960, Robson took his place as the voice of the VANCOUVER CANUCKS of HOCKEY and the Vancouver Mounties of BASEBALL. In 1961 he did play-by-play for all 230 games played by the Mounties, Canucks and the BC LIONS, as well as the BC high school boys BASKETBALL championship, the BC Open GOLF tournament and the BC high school track meet (*see* TRACK AND FIELD). In 1970, the Canucks' first year in the NHL, his voice went over the national airwaves on *Hockey Night in Canada* as he joined CBC-TV part-time, a position he kept until 1986. He called Stanley Cup finals in 1975, 1980 and 1982. One of hockey's best play-by-play announcers, he retired from Canucks radio coverage in 1995 but continued to work in TV until 1999. His trademark "special hello to hospital patients and shut-ins, the blind and pensioners and those people who can't get out to the game" is memorized word for word by Vancouver sports fans. He was inducted into the Hockey Hall of Fame in 1992 and into the BC SPORTS HALL OF FAME in 2000.   *SW*

ROBSON, John, journalist, politician, premier 2 Aug 1889–death (b 14 Mar 1824, Perth, ON; d 29 June 1892, London, England). A merchant in western Ontario, he came to BC in 1859 to seek his fortune in the goldfields (*see* GOLD RUSHES). Instead he ended up in NEW WESTMINSTER, where in 1861 he became editor of the *British*

John Robson, premier of BC 1889–92.
BC Archives A-06540

Columbian newspaper. He used the paper to attack the hegemony of Gov James DOUGLAS and the VANCOUVER ISLAND clique and to agitate for more democratic institutions. In 1866, when

Vancouver Island and the mainland joined, he was elected to the legislative council, but when VICTORIA was named capital of the united colony he moved there, becoming editor of the *Daily British Colonist*. An active campaigner for CONFEDERATION, he was a member of the provincial assembly for NANAIMO from 1871 to 1875. By 1882 he had re-established himself in New Westminster with a new *British Columbian* and a

new seat in the legislature. He was a member of the CABINET under William SMITHE and A.E.B. DAVIE until Davie's death, when he became PREMIER. As premier he tried to promote railway building and to control speculation in land and other resources, but his effectiveness was limited by declining health and an inability to control his cabinet. He died of blood poisoning while visiting England. *See also* NEWSPAPERS.

ROBSON, MOUNT (el 3,954 m), the highest peak in the Canadian ROCKY MTS, towers above Berg Lk 72 km west of Jasper. It is the focal point of Mt Robson Provincial Park (2195.34 km²), est 1913, one of the first and largest provincial PARKS. The FRASER R rises in Moose Lk in the park. The mountain is known by the local First Nation as Yuh-hai-has-kun ("Mountain of the Spiral Road") but the origin of the current name is uncertain. The first ascent may have been made by Rev George B. Kinney and Donald "Curly" Phillips on 13 Aug 1909: their climb was later discredited. The mountain was climbed again on 31 July 1913 by W.W. "Billy" FOSTER and Albert H. MacCarthy, led by their guide, Conrad KAIN. It is still a challenging ascent even for the best of MOUNTAINEERS. Mt Robson is also the name of a CNR station and a TOURISM service centre just west of the park.

Mt Robson, the highest peak in the Canadian Rockies. Keith Thirkell photo

ROBSON BIGHT is a small nick in the shoreline on the northeast coast of VANCOUVER ISLAND in JOHNSTONE STRAIT, 20 km south of TELEGRAPH COVE at the mouth of the Tsitika R. It was protected as an ECOLOGICAL RESERVE in 1982 after it was learned that KILLER WHALES frequented the spot to rub their bodies in the rocky shallows. It consists of 12.48 km² of marine reserve and a 5-km² buffer zone on land. In 1991 it was designated the Robson Bight/Michael BIGG ecological reserve in honour of the whale researcher who died a year earlier.

ROBSON VALLEY, part of the ROCKY MT TRENCH, lies between the ROCKY and CARIBOO mts in east-central BC. It takes its name from Mt ROBSON on its eastern edge, the highest peak in the Rockies. VALEMOUNT and MCBRIDE are the main communities. The valley, about 5 km wide and 240 km long, is the traditional territory of the SECWEPEMC (Shuswap) and DAKELH (Carrier) people. The construction of the GRAND TRUNK PACIFIC RWY in 1913 opened the region to development and today both the Yellowhead Hwy (*see* ROADS AND HWYS) and VIA Rail pass through this vital transportation corridor. LOGGING and SAWMILLING are the traditional industries and TOURISM has also become important.   AS

ROCK ART is engravings or paintings done on stone by FIRST NATIONS people and their remote ancestors. Engravings, or *petroglyphs*, were pecked or scratched on the rock surface using a sharp piece of hard stone. Paintings, or *pictographs*, were drawn using pigments made from minerals. Located on boulders and rock faces along the coast, around LAKES and in river valleys, rock art

Petroglyph on a beach boulder at Mackenzie's Rock. Roy Carlson photo

depicts human figures, animals, spirit figures and geometric shapes. The oldest samples in BC date back perhaps 3,000 years. Particularly large collections of pictographs are at Seton Crk on the FRASER R, along the STEIN R, and in the SIMILKAMEEN R Valley between HEDLEY and PRINCETON. A large collection of 111 petroglyphs is located at Thorsen Crk east of BELLA COOLA. Another important coastal site is Chrome Island, off the southern end of DENMAN ISLAND. Rock art usually depicts an important event, an individual's spiritual experience or an attempt to influence the spirit world, and has been interpreted by some researchers as an early form of writing. *Reading:* Annie York, Richard Daly and Chris Arnett, *They Write Their Dreams on the Rocks Forever: Rock Writings in the Stein River Valley*, 1993; Joy Inglis, *Spirit in the Stone*, 1998.

ROCK BAY, on the east side of VANCOUVER ISLAND on JOHNSTONE STRAIT, about 40 km north of CAMPBELL RIVER, was the site of an important

Mid-Coast pictograph depicting ceremonial coppers, a traditional medium of wealth.
Ian McAllister photo

LOGGING camp that operated from about 1900 to the 1940s. The camp, consisting at one point of accommodations for hundreds of loggers, a store, hotel and saloon, originally belonged to BC MILLS TIMBER & TRADING CO, then after 1922 to Merrill Ring & Wilson. The COLUMBIA COAST MISSION operated a hospital in the bay from 1905 to 1945. FOREST INDUSTRY activities relocated in the 1940s and the community was abandoned.

ROCK CLIMBING evolved in BC from its roots in MOUNTAINEERING in the first half of the 20th century to become a popular adventure sport. The most prominent aspect of the sport is freeclimbing, progressing by the use of natural hand- and footholds with ropes and other equipment for safety. Other aspects include aid climbing, which requires the use of direct assistance from devices inserted into the rock on otherwise unclimbable terrain, and bouldering, which is the art of making very short, difficult climbs close to the ground without the use of rope or any equipment. Free and aid climbs in BC typically range from 20 to 600 m in length.

Rock climbing became a practice distinct from mountaineering after completion of the SEA TO SKY HWY to SQUAMISH in 1958 brought the 600-m granite walls of the STAWAMUS CHIEF within easy reach of VANCOUVER. In the 4 decades that followed, over 1,600 individual routes, many of considerable length, were established in the greater Squamish area. Some of the long routes on the Chief, originally climbed with pitons for direct aid, have evolved into freeclimbs that rank among the great rock climbs of the world, including the Baldwin–Cooper Route on the Grand Wall (1961), Freeway (1979), The Northern Lights (1987) and University Wall (1966). Centred on the Stawamus Chief, the entire region from Vancouver to WHISTLER became one of the most important rock climbing destinations in N America and one of the

world's foremost granite climbing areas.

The major centre in the BC Interior is Skaha, just south of PENTICTON, a collection of gneiss crags on about 10 km² of GRASSLAND and scattered woodlands, hosting 600 climbs. With generally short climbs up to 50 m, a warm dry climate and several dozen crags up, Skaha offers a fine complement to Squamish. Climbers were active in the area through the 1980s, but it was

Mark Jones scaling the Stawamus Chief, Squamish. Greg Shea photo

not until the mid-1990s, as more climbs were developed and a guidebook published, that Skaha grew into a popular destination. Two climbers have been responsible for a third of all the climbs: Howie Richardson, author of the guidebook *Skaha Rockclimbs* (1998), and Robin Barley. Hugh Lenney, Dean Hart and other climbers also made significant contributions.

Elsewhere in the Interior, rock climbers have been active since the 1960s, although development amounted to scattered climbs on a variety of crags from the KOOTENAY to PRINCE GEORGE and few records were kept. The primary activist developing climbs in the Interior has been Garry Brace of KAMLOOPS. Marble Canyon, a limestone area between LILLOOET and CACHE CREEK, has been the traditional centre of activity, with approximately 100 climbs up to 400 m high. As rock climbing attracted wider interest in the 1990s, crags were developed at several places, notably REVELSTOKE, NELSON and VANCOUVER ISLAND. HORNE LK, 10 km inland from QUALICUM BEACH on Vancouver Island, is a very steep, 120-m-high limestone crag of 50 or so difficult routes. It is the only developed crag in the province that offers rock climbing that can be compared to the major European limestone crags. Development began in the mid-1990s and it holds a significant place in the evolution of the sport in BC.

The growth of interest in rock climbing has roughly paralleled the steady trend toward outdoor adventure activities since the mid-1980s. Indoor climbing gyms have also accelerated interest. The traditional climbing procedure of using temporary devices inserted in the rock began to be supplemented by the growth of sport climbing in the early 1990s. Sport climbing is a new trend in rock climbing styles that evolved from European practice. Such climbs are generously equipped with permanent expansion bolts for protection in the event of a fall, offering easier progress within each grade of difficulty, despite often being on very steep rock. Almost all climbers today regularly practise both sport and gear climbing.   *Kevin McLane*
Reading: Lyle Knight, *Central BC Rock*, 1996; Kevin McLane, *The Climber's Guide to Squamish*, 1999.

ROCK CREEK, 65 km southeast of PENTICTON on the KETTLE R, was the site of a GOLD RUSH from 1860 to 1861, during which a rowdy boomtown materialized with the usual hotels and saloons (*see* ROCK CREEK WAR). By 1862 most prospectors had left for the CARIBOO, though some MINING continued until the 1930s. A small permanent settlement materialized in the late 1880s around a stop on an early wagon road. By 1913 it had become a centre for apple-raising (*see* TREE FRUITS) and other AGRICULTURAL activities.   AS

ROCK CREEK WAR, 1860, was a dispute between American miners and British authorities over jurisdiction in the goldfields just north of the American border east of OSOYOOS. After the miners had driven GOLD commissioner Peter O'REILLY out of the area by force, Gov James DOUGLAS visited the camps. He promised to improve road access but warned the miners that if they did not obey British law he would return with troops to enforce it. The miners gave in and the "war" ended peacefully. *See also* GOLD RUSHES.

ROCKFISH is a common name for a number of species of scorpionfish (family Scorpaenidae)

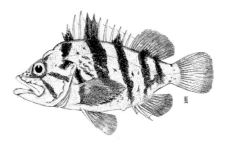

Top: copper rockfish. Rick Harbo photo
Bottom: tiger rockfish.
Courtesy Fisheries & Oceans Canada

exhibiting a variety of shapes, sizes and colours. In BC there are 34 species of rockfish, including quillback, yelloweye (red snapper), tiger and copper—each differing from the others in appearance, habitat and life span. Rockfish grow slowly and do not reproduce until they are relatively old, sometimes 15–20 years old. Some species can live as long as 150 years. Rockfish are harvested commercially (*see* FISHING, COMMERCIAL) by groundfish trawlers and by hook and line vessels. They are also fished recreationally (*see* FISHING, SPORT). Considering their slow growth, they cannot be harvested at the same rate as faster-growing species such as SALMON. Monitoring and research programs in the late 1990s indicated that rockfish stocks in GEORGIA STRAIT were at low levels and, because of their biology, rebuilding was expected to take a long time.

ROCKFORD, 45 km south of KAMLOOPS on the old NICOLA R Valley wagon road to SPENCES BRIDGE, was the site of Robert Scott's Rockford House, an 1880s inn "conducted on temperance principles," according to its post office application. James Aird and William Frisken established ranches (*see* CATTLE INDUSTRY) here in the same era, and Albert Smith built a hotel that burned down in 1901.   AS

ROCKINGHAM, John M., soldier (b 24 Aug 1911, Sydney, Australia; d 24 July 1987, Vancouver). At age 22 he enlisted in the Canadian Scottish Regiment and went overseas as a lieutenant with the regiment in 1941. In 1942 he transferred to the Royal Hamilton Light Infantry (RHLI) as a major. By July 1944 he was promoted to lieutenant colonel to command the RHLI; a month later he was promoted to brigadier to command the 9th Canadian Infantry (Highland) Brigade. By war's end he was considered the best fighting brigadier in the Canadian army, famous for keeping close to his

men in a small armoured scout car. Following the war he held management positions with BC ELECTRIC RWY CO and Pacific Stage Lines (*see* PACIFIC COACH LINES). At the outbreak of war in Korea in 1950 he was appointed to command the 25th Canadian Infantry Brigade, which he led in action in 1950–52. He chose to remain in the regular army and attended the Imperial Defence College in England, then had a distinguished career as a commanding officer in Canada from 1954 to 1966. *See also* MILITARY HISTORY.

ROCKY MOUNTAIN FORT, the first European settlement on the BC mainland, was established in 1794 by NORTH WEST CO (NWC) traders where the Moberly R empties into the PEACE R, south of FORT ST JOHN. It closed in 1804, when it was replaced by another post farther west at the present site of HUDSON'S HOPE. In 1820 the HBC built Fort d'Epinette on the site as part of its competition with the NWC on the Peace. It closed following the merger of the 2 companies the next year.

ROCKY MOUNTAIN PORTAGE HOUSE was a NORTH WEST CO (NWC) trading post established in 1805 on the PEACE R opposite the present site of HUDSON'S HOPE. The jumping-off point for NWC expansion into NEW CALEDONIA, it remained in operation until 1814, when the company decided to supply Interior posts from the coast. The HBC reopened the post for one trading season in 1823–24 and there was another HBC post on the site from the 1860s to 1882, when it moved across the river to the Hudson's Hope side.

ROCKY MOUNTAIN TRENCH is a 1,400-km-long valley, the longest in N America, trending northwest–southeast almost completely through BC from Montana to the Liard Plain just south of the BC–Yukon border. A geological fault zone separating different earth plates, it divides the ROCKY MTS on the east from a series of high mountain ranges and plateaus on the west (from south to north): the COLUMBIA, Omineca and Cassiar Mts. It varies in width from 3 to 16 km. Before the construction of HYDROELECTRIC dams, the floor of the trench was occupied by several major rivers. Today only the FRASER and KECHIKA follow their original routes. The others, including the KOOTENAY, COLUMBIA, PARSNIP, FINLAY and PEACE, have been absorbed or altered by the creation of 2 huge reservoirs, WILLISTON and KINBASKET. The trench has been occupied by human beings for thousands of years, providing an important corridor for movement through the province. Today it is much more populated in the south, where AGRICULTURE, LOGGING, TOURISM and MINING are all economically significant. The communities of CRANBROOK, KIMBERLEY, INVERMERE and GOLDEN all lie in the southern portion of the trench. The northern section is sparsely inhabited.

ROCKY MOUNTAINS, the largest mountain range in N America, runs almost the entire length of BC, about 1,200 km from the US border to just shy of the Yukon border. The Rockies were formed about 120 million years ago when what was then the western edge of N America collided with other land masses, compressing the rock and causing it to fold, fracture and pile up (*see* CORDILLERA). From the US border to the vicinity of Kakwa Pass (well north of Jasper) they form the boundary between BC and Alberta. At Kakwa they continue, trending northwesterly, while the border veers straight north along the 120th degree of longitude. As a result the northeast corner of BC lies on the other side of the mountains. To the west the Rockies are flanked by the ROCKY MT TRENCH; on the east they descend into the rolling foothills of Alberta. The highest peaks are topped by the remnants of the great glaciers that millions of years ago scoured N America, most notably the COLUMBIA ICEFIELD (*see* GLACIATION). The highest peak in the BC Rockies is Mt ROBSON at 3,954 m, followed by Mt Columbia (3,747 m) and MT ASSINIBOINE (3,618 m). As well as a physical barrier, the mountains have thrown up a psychological barrier between BC and the rest of Canada. They are a symbol of BC's uniqueness and separateness.

While FIRST NATIONS people crossed and re-crossed the mountains to trade, hunt and make war, the first Europeans to cross were Alexander MACKENZIE and his party in 1793, using the headwaters of the PEACE R as an avenue into the province. The mountains were subsequently explored by FUR TRADERS seeking practicable routes for transporting furs and supplies, and later by surveyors laying out the routes of the transcontinental railways. The CPR chose KICKING HORSE PASS as the route for its main line, leading to the development of the middle ranges of the mountains as a popular TOURIST destination. Four national parks—Jasper, Banff, YOHO and KOOTENAY—now form a huge reserve that was declared a UNESCO WORLD HERITAGE SITE in 1985 (*see* PARKS, NATIONAL). More recently several million hectares of the Northern Rockies, an area well known for its abundance of wildlife, have been set aside in protected zones. In the

south the CPR completed a line through CROWSNEST PASS in 1898, opening that area to the development of its rich mineral resources. COAL mining continues to be important in the SPARWOOD–ELK R area. The GRAND TRUNK PACIFIC RWY used the YELLOWHEAD PASS west of Jasper as its route to the Pacific, and all 3 railway passes are now used by major highways as well. *See also* ROADS AND HIGHWAYS.

RODDAN, Andrew, United Church minister (b 6 July 1882, Hawick, Scotland; d 25 Apr, 1948, Vancouver). He arrived in VANCOUVER in 1929 from eastern Canada to take up a position as minister at First UNITED CHURCH. An outspoken advocate of social gospel, he organized support for the destitute in the city during the Depression and promoted low-cost housing and welfare services. His Sunday sermons were broadcast over the radio. He was also an amateur painter and a charter member of the VANCOUVER ART GALLERY.

RODE, Ajmer, engineer, writer (b 1 Jan 1940, Punjab, India). He immigrated to Canada in 1966. After completing his MSc at the Univ of Waterloo, he moved to the West Coast and has lived here ever since. He worked as an engineer with BC GAS, and has been writing full-time since 1994. He has published 4 books of poetry—2 in English and 2 in Punjabi—and several plays in Punjabi. In 1998 he published a 1,000-page book of Punjabi poetry, *Leela*, with his brother, also a poet. He is considered a founder of Canadian Punjabi THEATRE and has been a founding member of several Indo-Canadian literary and performing arts associations. In 1994 the Punjab government awarded him the Best Overseas Punjabi Writer prize. *See also* SOUTH ASIANS.

RODENT, a member of the order Rodentia, is one of a large group of mammals characterized by 2 pairs of sharp incisors specialized for gnaw-

ing. These teeth grow continuously and self-sharpen as they are used. Rodents range in size from tiny mice that weigh 10 grams to the largest species, the BEAVER, which grows up to 35 kg. The deer mouse (*Peromyscus maniculatus*) and Townsend's vole (*Microtus townsendi*), 2 of the smallest species, are important prey for a wide range of predators, including WEASELS, HAWKS and OWLS. A group of larger rodents includes

Deer mouse. R. Wayne Campbell photo

rats, 4 species of which occur in BC. The Norway rat (*Rattus norvegicus*), an introduced species, has a short brown coat and a scaly, hairless tail. It lives mainly in burrows and is attracted to urban environments, where it indulges its appetite for garbage and sometimes invades homes and damages woodwork, wires and drains. The roof, or black, rat (*R. rattus*), a similar-sized species and an excellent climber, inhabits only the coastal areas. The bushy-tailed woodrat (*Neotoma cinerea*) has long, soft fur and a distinctive hairy tail. The muskrat (*Ondatra zibethicus*) is a semi-aquatic denizen of riverbanks and other WETLANDS. Its partially webbed hind feet and waterproof fur aid in its aquatic activities. Its name refers to the musk glands beneath its tail with which the animal marks territory. The mountain beaver (*Aplodontia rufa* spp), unrelated to the ordinary beaver, is another rodent genus found in southwestern BC. About the size of a muskrat and without the long, flat beaver tail, it does not venture far from its burrow and so is not often seen. Of the 2 varieties in BC, one is on the province's Red List, the other on the Blue List (*see* ENDANGERED SPECIES). Other rodent groups include MARMOTS, CHIPMUNKS (4 species of which are on the Red List), SQUIRRELS, pocket gophers, jumping mice, PORCUPINES and LEMMINGS.

Some rodents are known to be infected by hantavirus pulmonary syndrome (HPS), a rare respiratory disease caused by a virus. First identified in 1993, the virus has been found in deer mice, rats and other mice. HPS is contracted by inhaling the virus in the droppings, urine or saliva of an infected rodent. The disease is characterized by flu-like symptoms—fever, headaches and difficulty breathing—and may be fatal. Up to 1999 there were 5 cases of HPS in BC, 3 of which resulted in death.

RODEO is a sporting event that features the skills associated with COWBOY life and cattle roundup in a competitive setting. In BC it originated in the

Moraine Lake framed by the Rocky Mountains.
Reimut Lieder/Image Makers

cattle-raising (*see* CATTLE INDUSTRY) districts of the CHILCOTIN–CARIBOO and the NICOLA Valley and evolved over the years from informal gatherings of working cowboys held on ranches or in ranching communities into a regular circuit with professional competition. Many of today's competitors have no ranching experience at all and work in a variety of jobs in the rodeo off-season. There are about a dozen professional rodeos in the province each year, sanctioned by the Canadian Professional Rodeo Assoc, along with 22 semi-professional, 12 high school, 6 "Little Britches" and a variety of other rodeos to a total of about 80 all over the province. The professional circuit culminates in the BC Championship Finals, usually held in KAMLOOPS, an event that invites the top 10 cowboys and cowgirls to compete in 10 events: bareback riding, saddle bronc riding, bull riding, calf roping, barrel racing, steer wrestling, team roping, breakaway roping, junior steer riding and junior

Rodeo at Clinton, 1999. Rick Blacklaws photo

barrel racing. The CLOVERDALE RODEO is the largest in BC—based on number of performances, prize money, attendance and number of competitors—and the second-largest in Canada after the Calgary Stampede. Another major rodeo is the WILLIAMS LAKE Stampede, first held in 1926. There are also many smaller, less commercial events. BC's first professional rodeo star was Kenny MCLEAN of PENTICTON, who emerged as a world champion in the 1960s. Jack Palmantier from RISKE CREEK, the first aboriginal Canadian rodeo star (*see* Leonard PALMANTIER), won the saddle bronc competition at the 1976 International Indian Finals Rodeo in Tulsa, OK. The following year Jim Gladstone became the first competitor from BC (and the first Canadian) to win a world title in the timed event. Other rodeo champions from BC include Daryl Mills of PINK MOUNTAIN, 1994 world bull-riding champion, and Mel Hyland, world saddle bronc champion in 1972.

Rodeo in BC is administered by the BC Rodeo Assoc, created in 1988 from a merger of 3 regional associations.

ROE LAKE, between BRIDGE LK and SHERIDAN LK, 110 km southeast of WILLIAMS LAKE in the CARIBOO, had a post office, school and store in the 1930s and 1940s, when it was a centre for district cattle ranchers (*see* CATTLE INDUSTRY) and DAIRY FARMERS. *AS*

ROGERS, Albert Bowman, civil engineer, located Rogers Pass (b 28 May 1829, Orleans, MA; d 4 May 1889, Waterville, MN). A graduate of Yale Univ (1853), he worked as an engineer on canals and railways in the US before joining the CPR early in 1881. Placed in charge of finding a route through the ROCKY and SELKIRK mountain ranges, he supervised the survey of KICKING HORSE PASS in the southern Rockies, then turned his attention to the Selkirks. It was widely believed that no route existed through this range, but in May 1881 Rogers succeeded in reaching the pass that now bears his name. He was a loud-talking, colourful eccentric whom many of his men found stingy and unlikeable, but his employers praised his work and he was invited to be present at the driving of the Last Spike at CRAIGELLACHIE in 1885. With the CPR finished, he returned to the US. In 1887 a riding accident ended his active career; 2 years later he died of stomach cancer.

ROGERS, Alfred Harold Douglas "Doug," judoka (b 26 Jan 1941, Truro, NS). Raised in St Catharines, Montreal and VANCOUVER, he became Canada's JUDO champion. He trained for 5 years at Japan's Kodokan School of Judo and as a member of the Takushoku Univ judo team, and while in Japan he appeared in several movies including *Godzilla*. In 1964 he won a silver medal at the Tokyo Olympics and the first of 4 consecutive Canadian judo championships. The next year he won bronze at the world championships in Rio de Janiero and gold at the Pan American championships in Guatemala. Also in 1965 he was the first Caucasian to compete in the all-Tokyo and all-Japan university judo team championships, winning gold in both and the top-competitor award. At the 1967 Pan Am Games in Winnipeg he won a gold in the open-

weight category and a silver in the heavyweight. He competed for the last time at the 1972 Munich Olympics where he placed 4th and was Canada's flag-bearer at the opening ceremonies. In retirement he became an airline pilot and had a successful coaching career at UBC. He is a member of the Canadian Sports Hall of the Fame and the BC SPORTS HALL OF FAME. *SW*

ROGERS, Benjamin Tingley, sugar manufacturer (b 21 Oct 1865, Philadelphia, PA; d 17 June 1918, Vancouver). After working at sugar refineries in New Orleans and New York, he came to VANCOUVER at age 24, and with the backing of city council and the CPR he established BC Sugar, now ROGERS SUGAR, in 1890. It was the first refinery in western Canada and the first non-resource-based industry in the city. His West End mansion, Gabriola, designed by the renowned architect Samuel MACLURE, has been preserved as a restaurant. His wife, Mary Isabella Rogers, who outlived her husband by 47 years, was the "grande dame" of Vancouver high society and a generous supporter of the arts.

ROGERS, Charles W., chocolatier (b 1854, Boston, MA; d 1927, Victoria). He began as a grocer in VICTORIA and expanded into the chocolate business in the 1880s. He and his wife Leah, with whom he ran the business and made the chocolates, were notorious eccentrics. They refused to deal with banks, often slept all night in chairs in their store and opened for business only when they felt like it. But their candy was famous the world over and customers lined up around the block to buy it. The couple was wealthy but Leah, who outlived her husband by 25 years, gave away much of the money. Rogers' Chocolates has been located in the same building on Government St in downtown Victoria since 1916.

ROGERS, Frank, union activist (b circa 1878; d 15 Apr 1903, Vancouver). He was BC's first union martyr. A longshoreman and leading socialist in VANCOUVER in the early 1900s (*see* SOCIALIST PARTY OF BC), he led the BC FISHERMEN'S UNION in the FRASER R STRIKE in 1900–01. In 1903 members of the United Brotherhood of Railway Employees went on strike against the CPR, supported by sympathy strikes by various other unions, including the stevedores. While investigating a disturbance near the Vancouver docks during the strike, Rogers was hit by a volley of gunfire from CPR special police. He died 2 days later. His funeral attracted unionists from around the province in a long procession through the city streets. The courts later exonerated a suspect and the company. *See also* LABOUR MOVEMENT.

ROGERS, Jeremiah, logger (b 1818, St Andrews, NB; d 24 Oct 1879, English Bay). An established logger in his native New Brunswick, he moved to Puget Sound in the 1850s and came to BC in 1860 to produce logs for the ANDERSON sawmill at PORT ALBERNI. After the Alberni mill closed in 1864, he moved to PORT NEVILLE, then to ENGLISH BAY in VANCOUVER, where he began LOGGING from a camp at JERICHO BEACH in 1865. (The name Jericho may be a corruption of "Jerry's Cove.") His operation, which cleared much of what is now Kitsilano, provided spars for sailing ships and logs for Edward STAMP's mill on BURRARD INLET. Respected as an innovator, he designed his own axes and used steam-powered tractors to haul his logs to water in what may have been the first application of mechanized power in the BC FOREST INDUSTRY.

ROGERS, Robert Gordon, forestry executive, lt gov 1983–88 (b 19 Aug 1919, Montreal). A graduate of the Royal Military College in Kingston and the Univ of Toronto, he served as a member of a tank regiment in the Canadian Armoured Corps during WWII. Following the war he was a business executive, principally with CROWN ZELLERBACH CANADA where he was chairman and CEO (1975–82). He was also active in the Boy Scouts and the Canadian Council of Christians and Jews. He was serving as chair of the Canada Harbour Place Corp when he was appointed LT GOV. After he left the vice-regal post he was chancellor of UNIV OF VICTORIA (1991–96). Rogers was awarded the ORDER OF BC in 1990.

ROGERS PASS, el 1,323 m, in GLACIER NATIONAL PARK 70 km east of REVELSTOKE through the SELKIRK MTS, is named for A.B. ROGERS, the CPR surveyor who located it in 1881. Construction of the railway over the pass in the summer of 1885 was plagued by FOREST FIRES, mud slides and AVALANCHES of snow, which forced closure of the line during the first winter of operation. In 1886 construction began on 31 snowsheds to protect the track, and in 1916 the CPR built the 8-km CONNAUGHT TUNNEL to reduce the steep grade and to allow trains to avoid this hazardous section. The Mt Macdonald Tunnel, at 14.7 km the longest railway tunnel in N America, was built from 1984 to 1988 to further improve the Rogers Pass section. In 1962 the TRANS-CANADA HWY opened over the pass.

Rogers Pass. Walter Lanz/Image Makers

ROGERS SUGAR is the successor company to BC Sugar, one of the province's oldest manufacturers. Founded in VANCOUVER in 1890 by Benjamin Tingley ROGERS, an American-born entrepreneur, BC Sugar was the city's first major industry not based on LOGGING or commercial FISHING. Starting in the 1930s the company bought into and expanded the beet sugar industry in Alberta and Manitoba; at one time it owned 4 separate factories but only one survived by the year 2000. In the 1980s BC Sugar diversified into paper-based packaging, OIL AND GAS exploration and chemical production, but it divested itself of these non-core businesses early in the 1990s. Starting in 1992 BC Sugar expanded in the sugar business by acquiring Lantic Sugar in eastern Canada, which in turn owned a New York state company, Refined Sugars. These acquisitions made it the largest sugar producer in Canada and the third-largest in N America. In 1997, after a spirited ownership battle, the company was taken over by a consortium consisting of Belcorp and Onex Corp. The sugar companies were split up with the western Canadian operations (Vancouver and Taber, AB) sold on the public market as Rogers Sugar Income Trust. Refined Sugar was sold to US interests and Lantic Sugar remains under the Belcorp-Onex ownership.

ROLLA, 16 km north of DAWSON CREEK, was the commercial centre of the PEACE R district in the 1920s, with banks, hotels and a NEWSPAPER. Grain growing and the CATTLE INDUSTRY were important and a large AGRICULTURAL fair was held annually. The community was first settled by L.H. Miller in 1912 and named after his hometown in Missouri. It lost importance after BC RAIL arrived at Dawson Creek in 1958, with many businesses moving to the larger centre. *AS*

ROLSTON, Tilly Jean, politician (b 23 Feb 1887, Vancouver; d 12 Oct 1953, Vancouver). She was a schoolteacher briefly before she married, then a homemaker before entering politics in mid-life. First elected to the provincial legislature as a CONSERVATIVE for VANCOUVER–Point

Tilly Rolston, first woman cabinet minister with portfolio in Canada. CVA 180-4323

Grey in 1941, she was an early supporter of W.A.C. BENNETT and switched to SOCIAL CREDIT for the 1952 election. Her timely defection gave the new party some much needed credibility. After retaining her seat, she became education minister in Bennett's first CABINET, the first female cabinet minister in Canada with a portfolio. She narrowly lost her seat in the 1953 election and died of cancer soon after.

ROMAN CATHOLIC CHURCH in BC is part of a complex institutional hierarchy that looks to the Pope in Rome for both practical and spiritual leadership. The Pope is aided by his cardinals; patriarchs and primates comprise the next rung of the hierarchy, followed by archbishops, who govern provinces. The Episcopacy is composed of titular and diocesan bishops, as well as apostolic vicars. A diocesan bishop has jurisdiction over a given diocese, over a vicar-general (his chief assistant) and over the diocesan clergy composed of parish priests and canons, who form the cathedral chapter. Lay people compose the body of the church. The Roman Catholic ecclesiastical province of BC is divided into 6 territorial units called dioceses. The archdiocese of VANCOUVER (est 1908), which was originally the diocese of NEW WESTMINSTER created in 1890, is now the episcopal seat of the province. The bishoprics of VICTORIA (1846), KAMLOOPS (1945) and NELSON (1936) are the seats of 3 of the other dioceses. The Vicariate Apostolic of Prince Rupert (1916) was regularized and transferred to PRINCE GEORGE in 1968. The province of BC also includes the diocese of Yukon, based in Whitehorse. New Westminster has been absorbed into the archdiocese of Vancouver but it is also an eparchy (a territorial entity) of the Ukrainian Catholic Church, which practises the Byzantine rites, a branch of Eastern Catholicism. Each diocese has its own cathedral and is composed of smaller geographical units known as parishes.

In 1838 Joseph Signay, the Archbishop of Quebec, sent secular priests François Norbert Blanchet and Modeste DEMERS to the Willamette

ROMAN CATHOLICS IN BC

Year	Members	% of BC Population
1881	14,141	28.6
1891	21,350	21.8
1901	34,020	19.0
1911	58,760	15.0
1921	64,180	12.2
1931	88,106	12.7
1941	109,929	13.4
1951	168,016	14.4
1961	285,184	17.5
1971	408,330	18.7
1981	526,355	19.5
1991	595,315	18.1

Valley, Oregon Territory, in response to requests from French Canadians settled there. The 2 men were to bring Christian order to aboriginals and whites alike, as well as to learn aboriginal languages, regularize marriages and provide education throughout their vast mission field. During their trip west, on 14 Oct 1838, they celebrated the first Mass on the BC mainland at the Big Bend of the COLUMBIA R. In the 1840s Father Demers and Father Nobili (Society of Jesus) made extensive tours through the Interior, the latter going as far north as FORT BABINE, while Father J.B.Z. Bolduc accompanied James DOUGLAS to VANCOUVER ISLAND and preached to aboriginals there. In 1844 the Columbia district was erected as an Apostolic Vicariate composed of 3 dioceses with Norbert Blanchet as Vicar General. Apostolic Vicariates are missionary areas that have not yet been absorbed into the regular church hierarchy. They are governed by the Congregation of the Propaganda of the Faith in Rome under the direct jurisdiction of the Pope. The Apostolic Vicariate of Columbia (which became an archdiocese in 1846) contained the dioceses of Oregon City under the care of Bishop Blanchet, Walla Walla under Bishop A.M. Blanchet (Norbert's brother) and Vancouver Island, NEW CALEDONIA (mainland BC), and the QUEEN CHARLOTTE ISLANDS under Bishop Demers. With no clergy to speak of, the bishops had to call on Europe for help and in 1847 Norbert Blanchet received 5 OBLATES OF MARY IMMACULATE from France. In 1850 Fathers Louis d'HERBOMEZ and Timothée Lempfrit arrived, and in the same year François Jayol, a secular, joined the Oblates. In 1854 Fathers Paul DURIEU and Pierre Richard and 3 lay brothers arrived. During the 19th century, BC acquired most of its personnel from France and Ireland.

The Oblates and Jesuits in the Oregon Territory were soon involved in a bitter dispute with the Bishops Blanchet. This conflict centred on ownership of mission property, and the degree of ecclesiastical authority the bishops would exercise over religious clergy. Religious clergy include monks, members of religious orders (such as the Jesuits) and congregations

(such as the Oblates), as well as nuns and sisters, most of whom are primarily responsible to the Superior General of their order rather than to a secular biship. Secular clergy are directly under the supervision of their diocesan bishop. The squabble was serious enough to be taken to Rome but no solution satisfactory to the Oblates was found, leading them to relocate to ESQUIMALT on Vancouver Island in 1858 and to mainland BC in 1859. A first BC mission (Immaculate Conception) was opened near OKANAGAN LK in that year, a second (St Charles in New Westminster) in 1860, and a third (ST MARY'S) in 1861, up the FRASER R from New Westminster. In 1864 the mainland was erected into the Apostolic Vicariate of BC under the direction of Monsignor Louis d'Herbomez. The Oblates left Vancouver Island in 1866, with the temporary exception of the FORT RUPERT mission (1863–74) and established themselves at New Westminster. The Oblates soon expanded from the South Coast up the Fraser R into the Interior, establishing aboriginal missions at WILLIAMS LAKE (St Joseph's, 1867), Stuart Lk (OUR LADY OF GOOD HOPE, 1873), CRANBROOK (ST EUGENE'S, 1874) and Kamloops (St Louis, 1878). They came to dominate the South Coast and the Interior, leaving much of the rest of the province to their ANGLICAN and METHODIST rivals. In the 1870s and 1880s a new crop of Oblates began to arrive from Europe, most notably Jean-Marie LeJeune and A.G. MORICE, both gifted linguists, and Nicolas COCCOLA, who ministered to railway workers and miners as they moved through the province.

During the last decades of the 19th century and early in the 20th century all denominations active in the province began to focus on the establishment and management of RESIDENTIAL SCHOOLS. The Oblates operated 10 such schools, often with the help of the SISTERS OF ST ANN: St Mary's, Williams Lake, Kamloops, Cranbrook, LEJAC, N Vancouver, SECHELT and LOWER POST on the mainland, and KUPER ISLAND and Christie on Vancouver Island. Education for white children was another priority of the Church and different religious orders established some of the earliest schools in the province. The Sisters of St Ann were particularly active; their original schoolhouse, dating to 1858, is the oldest building in VICTORIA. Until 1977 private Catholic schools were funded by the Church and by parents; since that time the provincial government has provided partial funding (see EDUCATION, PRIVATE). The legacy of the residential schools was one of the most difficult issues facing the church as the 20th century drew to a close: in 1991 the Canadian Catholic Church and the Oblates issued separate apologies to aboriginal people who had been forced to attend the schools.

In 1890 Bishop d'Herbomez died after a long illness and Father Paul Durieu became bishop of the mainland until his own death in 1899. The first decades of the 20th century saw the beginning of numerous changes for Catholics on the mainland. There was a shift in the composition of the Oblates, from French speakers to English speakers, and Irish and Canadians became a majority in the congregation. The administrative

headquarters of the church moved from New Westminster to Vancouver, and in 1908 BC, along the rest of Canada, was removed from the jurisdiction of the Congregation of the Propaganda of the Faith and accepted into the more standard church hierarchy. After the 1908 death of Father Augustine Dontenwill, who had succeeded Durieu as bishop, the Oblates lost their ecclesiastical dominance in BC for more than 70 years, until Father Adam Exner became bishop in the 1990s. The situation on Vancouver Island was somewhat different. While Father Lempfrit worked among the COWICHAN for a few years, the Oblates did not establish any real presence on the Island until their residential schools at Kuper Island (1890) and Christie (1900) opened. As a secular diocese, secular clergy came to dominate, notably Father A.J. BRABANT. Jesuits were active as well, along with Benedictines, who operated schools on the west coast of the Island.

A key figure in the evolution of the church during the first half of the 20th century was William Mark Duke. He came to Vancouver in 1912 to assist Archbishop Timothy Casey, then took over himself as Archbishop of Vancouver in 1933 and served until 1964, the longest tenure of any BC bishop. Bishop Duke established a diocesan seminary and worked for the restoration of the Holy Rosary cathedral. He also extended church involvement in social welfare and charitable work and encouraged the spread of Catholic schools. It was during Bishop Duke's tenure that St Mark's College became affiliated with UBC in 1956. The Church also became involved in Project North, a broad Christian program that aimed to improve the economic and social conditions of aboriginals in the far North. In 1950 BC's second university, Notre Dame College (see NOTRE DAME UNIV OF NELSON), opened in Nelson, sponsored by the Catholic diocese. It continued in operation until it was purchased by the provincial government in the mid-1970s and closed. Along with education, the Catholic Church was active in child welfare until the provincial government took over all children's services in 1973, and established several hospitals and charities. Another prominent bishop was Remi DE ROO, bishop of Vancouver Island from the end of 1962 to 1999.

In Sept 1984 BC Catholics welcomed Pope John Paul II during his tour of Canada, the first time a reigning pope had visited the country and a cause for great celebration among Catholics. In the 1991 census, 595,300 British Columbians identified themselves as Roman Catholic and 7,500 as Catholics of the Ukrainian Church.

Lynn Blake

RONNING, Bernt, pioneer homesteader (b 24 June 1883, Norway; d 1965, Arlington, WA). He came to the HOLBERG area of northern VANCOUVER ISLAND in 1910 and later homesteaded along the historic trail linking Holberg to CAPE SCOTT. Making a living as a trapper, fisher and camp cook, he imported seeds from around the world to indulge his passion for growing trees and shrubs. Over the years his farm's extensive plantation included many giant and exotic specimens.

After his death the farm lay neglected until the early 1980s, when Ron and Julia Moe bought it, restored the gardens and welcomed visitors to view Ronning's legacy.

RONNING, Cliff, hockey player (b 1 Oct 1965, Vancouver). From his record-setting days with the NEW WESTMINSTER BRUINS to his NHL years with the VANCOUVER CANUCKS he was one of the most popular BC HOCKEY players. As a junior with the Bruins in 1983–85 he captured honours as the WHL's rookie of the year, most sportsmanlike player, most valuable player and scoring champion. After a year as star of the Canadian national team he joined the St Louis Blues for 3 seasons before scoring 116 points in only 36 games for a club in Asiago, Italy. After being dealt to the Canucks in 1991, he scored 71 points in 1991–92 and 85 points in 1992–93. The next season, he helped the Canucks reach the 1994 Stanley Cup finals. Fans loved his combination of speed, stickhandling and thirst for hard work and they were dismayed when the Canucks allowed him to sign with the Phoenix Coyotes in 1996. He played with Phoenix for 2 seasons before moving on to the expansion Nashville Predators in 1998. *SW*

ROOSVILLE, pop 40, a customs post and border settlement 80 km southeast of CRANBROOK, was named after Fred Roo, the first postmaster, who settled here about 1899 and built a store and hotel. It is at the southern edge of the KTUNAXA (Kutenai) Tobacco Plains RESERVE. *AS*

ROSE HARBOUR, on the north side of Kunghit Island, looks across Houston Stewart Channel at Moresby Island in the southern QUEEN CHARLOTTE ISLANDS. It was named in 1788 by a fur trader after George Rose, a British public figure. In 1910 the Pacific Whaling Co built a shore WHALING station at the site. The station operated until 1943; at its height it was the most productive whaling station on the coast, employing about 100 men, mainly JAPANESE and CHINESE, from Apr to Oct. In 1999 the site was privately owned, though it is surrounded by GWAII HAANAS NATIONAL PARK RESERVE; almost nothing remains of the station.

ROSE LAKE was a LOGGING and AGRICULTURAL settlement on the GRAND TRUNK PACIFIC RWY and the Endako R, 25 km northwest of BURNS LAKE. An important source of income in the early days for many communities in this region was the production of railway ties. *Rose* is a corruption of the surname of the first homesteader, Charlie Ross, who arrived about 1910. *AS*

ROSE PRAIRIE, pop 50, is an AGRICULTURAL settlement near Roseland Crk 30 km north of FORT ST JOHN in the PEACE R district. It was first settled in about 1940 and is close to the DOIG R First Nation RESERVE. *AS*

ROSEBERY, 4 km northeast of NEW DENVER on SLOCAN LK, was a CPR shipyard and rail barge terminus and a station on the Nakusp & Slocan Rwy. Tref Nault, an early logger in the NAKUSP area, cleared the townsite in 1893, and a SAWMILL and concentrator were built. Ore from the Slocan Valley was unloaded here and barged to SMELTERS at TRAIL and in the US. Rosebery is still a log sorting and booming ground (*see* LOG BOOMING; LOGGING). It was named after the Earl of Rosebery, a CPR director and former prime minister of Great Britain. *AS*

ROSEDALE, 10 km east of CHILLIWACK within Chilliwack municipal boundaries, is an early FRASER VALLEY AGRICULTURAL settlement that developed on the old Yale Road. It had a school, post office and store by the 1890s. The name comes from the wild roses that grew in abundance here. *AS*

ROSENBLATT, Joe, writer, artist (b 26 Dec 1933, Toronto). He left school in grade 10 and spent several years in a series of labouring jobs, notably for the CPR, until he took up writing full-time. He moved west to QUALICUM BEACH in 1980 and has lived there ever since. His writing is known for its wit and eccentricity. His first book of poems, *The Voyage of the Mood*, appeared in 1960, followed by

Joe Rosenblatt, poet and artist, 1998.
Barry Peterson & Blaise Enright-Peterson

more than a dozen others. *Top Soil* won a GOV GEN'S LITERARY AWARD in 1976, and *Poetry Hotel: Selected Poems 1963–85* won a BC BOOK PRIZE. His book *The Voluptuous Gardener* (1996) collected his art and writing from 1973 to 1996. Rosenblatt edited the LITERARY MAGAZINE *Jewish Dialogue* from 1969 to 1983. He has published 2 volumes of memoirs: *Escape from the Glue Factory* (1985) and *The Kissing Goldfish of Siam* (1989).

ROSS, or Ross Spur, 20 km southeast of CRANBROOK, was a station on Daniel Corbin's NELSON & FORT SHEPPARD RWY and named after the first postmaster, S.N. Ross. Post offices were established here and, earlier, at nearby Benton Siding for the use of railway personnel from 1915 to 1951.

ROSS, Flora Amelia, asylum matron (b 1842, San Juan Island, WA; d 2 Nov 1897, New Westminster). She was the daughter of an HBC trader and his mixed-blood wife. After a brief, abusive marriage to Paul Hubbs, an American customs agent, she reverted to her maiden name and in 1870 began working with the mentally ill, an activity she continued for the rest of her life. Her first job was as matron to female "lunatics" in the VICTORIA jail. When the Provincial Lunatic Asylum opened in 1872 she took the same job there and moved to New Westminster when the institution relocated in 1878 (*see* WOODLANDS). Ross was matron of the women's ward until her death, and as long as she was in charge her ward was considered superior to the rest of the institution. She was known for her disdain for mechanical restraints and her humane treatment of patients.

ROSS, Frank Mackenzie, businessman, lt gov 1955–60 (b 14 Apr 1897, Glasgow; d 11 Dec 1971, Vancouver). After emigrating to Canada as a youth he joined the Canadian Bank of Commerce in Montreal. In 1914 he enlisted in the 48th Highlanders and fought in France, where he was severely wounded and decorated for bravery. After the war he joined the St John Drydock and Shipbuilding Co in New Brunswick. He became a wealthy and prominent member of the business community and at the outbreak of WWII joined C.D. Howe's team of "dollar-a-year-men" in Ottawa. During the war he married Phyllis Turner, a senior government administrator. She was a widow with 2 children, one of whom, John Napier TURNER, later became prime minister. The couple settled in VANCOUVER after the war and Ross managed his business interests from there. He was sworn in as LT GOV on 3 Oct 1955. During his term of office, on 15 Apr 1957, fire destroyed Government House (*see* CARY CASTLE) and the Rosses lost most of their personal possessions. A new official residence was reoccupied in 1959. Ross retired from office in 1960. He and his wife returned to Vancouver, to their large home in W Point Grey overlooking Spanish Banks.

ROSS, Paula, dancer, choreographer (b 29 April 1941, Vancouver). She was born Pauline Campbell and later took Paula Ross as a stage name. She studied ballet from a young age and left home at age 15 to join a chorus line at a Montreal casino. She worked the show circuit across Canada and the US for 4 years, then returned to VANCOUVER, where she launched her own modern DANCE company, the Paula Ross Dance Co, in 1965. The company operated for 22 years, presenting distinctive work choreographed by Ross and her dancers. Much of the company's repertoire had a committed political message. Although it could not afford to tour extensively, the Paula Ross Dance gained a national reputation and in 1977 Ross won the Jean A. Chalmers Award for choreography. Finally financial problems became too great a burden; the troupe ceased performing in 1987. Ross moved to VANCOUVER ISLAND, where she continued to dance and create.

ROSS BAY CEMETERY on Fairfield Road in VICTORIA has been in use since 1873 and contains the graves of many prominent BC politicians, including Sir James DOUGLAS and former premiers Amor DE COSMOS, George WALKEM, Alexander DAVIE, John ROBSON and James DUNSMUIR. The prospector Billy BARKER, the artist Emily CARR and the pioneer jurist Matthew BEGBIE are also buried here. The cemetery is notable for its 19th-century design and landscaping and the quality of its monuments. *Guy Robertson*

ROSSLAND, city, pop 3,802, occupies the eroded crater of an extinct volcano in the MONASHEE MTS in southeast BC, 10 km west of TRAIL. The townsite developed in the 1890s as the centre of a GOLD mining district and was named in 1894 for Ross Thompson, a pioneer settler. Pre-WWI Rossland produced 50% of BC's gold. MINING declined in the 1920s, though MOLYBDENUM has been produced since the 1960s. It is mainly a bedroom community for Trail; many residents work at the COMINCO smelter. Some heritage buildings in the downtown area date back to about 1900, and the famous LeRoi gold mine on RED MT is open to visitors. Red Mt is now more famous as a ski centre. The first Canadian downhill ski championships were held there in 1897 and it has produced 2 Olympic medalists: Nancy GREENE Raine and Kerrin LEE-GARTNER (*see* SKIING).

ROTA, Darcy, HOCKEY player (b 16 Feb 1953, Vancouver). Raised in PRINCE GEORGE, he brought his high scoring to the WHL's Edmonton Oil Kings in 1970. In Edmonton he helped the team reach 2 Memorial Cup national championship tournaments, scored a league-leading 73 goals in his final year, and was named a first team all-star. After the Chicago Blackhawks drafted him in 1973 he played 6 seasons with them and part of another with the Atlanta Flames before he joined the VANCOUVER CANUCKS in 1980. He played his best hockey with the Canucks, contributing to their 1982 run to the Stanley Cup finals, scoring 42 goals and 81 points in 1982–83, and representing them in the 1984 NHL all-star game. Rota was forced to end his career in 1984 because of injuries, but he continued working in the front-office side of hockey and later as a coach and general manager in the BC JUNIOR HOCKEY LEAGUE. *SW*

ROUNDS, 55 km southwest of NANAIMO near COWICHAN LK on VANCOUVER ISLAND, was a large RAILWAY LOGGING camp, often called Gordon River, established by the McDonald Murphy Logging Co in 1923. Western Forest Industries, which had a major SAWMILL at nearby HONEYMOON BAY, took over and converted the operation to trucks in 1953. The mill closed in 1981. *AS*

ROWE, Paul, football player (b 25 Jan 1917, Seattle; d 26 Aug 1990, Calgary). An excellent high school RUGBY player, he first played FOOTBALL in 1931, for the VICTORIA Commercial Travellers. After continuing the sport at the Univ of Oregon, he joined the Calgary Bronks (later Stampeders) and played fullback and linebacker for 3 seasons before WWII began. He returned from service overseas to lead the Stampeders to the 1948 Grey Cup. One of the all-time greatest plunging fullbacks in Canadian football, he twice led the Western Conference in scoring (1939, 1948) and was a first-team all-star 5 times before retiring in 1950. He is a member of the Canadian Football Hall of Fame, Canadian Sports Hall of Fame, Alberta Sports Hall of Fame and the BC SPORTS HALL OF FAME. *SW*

ROWING began in BC in 1859 with navy races held in VICTORIA. The first rowing club was formed in Victoria in 1865, followed by the rowing-oriented James Bay Athletic Association in 1882, the Vancouver Boating Club in 1886 and the Burrard Inlet Rowing Club in 1890. Ned Hanlan, the accomplished rowing champion from eastern Canada, visited Victoria in 1884 and put on a well-attended exhibition. The North Pacific Association of Amateur Oarsmen, a body that joined the BC clubs with others in the Pacific Northwest, began in 1891 and held its first regatta in Vancouver the next year. Bob JOHNSTON dominated BC rowing in the 1890s, winning the 1892 Pacific Coast Amateur Sculling Championship, the BC Amateur Championship from 1891 to 1894 and twice defeating the US national champion. In 1898 he was involved in the most significant event in early BC rowing: he challenged and narrowly lost to World Professional Champion Jake Gaudaur Sr in a race in Burrard Inlet. NELSON hosted a rematch, also won by Gaudaur, in 1900. In 1899 the Vancouver Boating Club and Burrard Inlet Club amalgamated to form the VANCOUVER ROWING CLUB. The sport spread throughout the province: in 1906 a regatta took place as PRINCE RUPERT's first sporting event, and clubs in Nelson, KELOWNA and PENTICTON joined the NPAAO the same year. The VRC coxless 4 of Colin Finlayson, Archie Black, George MacKay and William Wood brought home BC's first Olympic rowing medal, a silver from Paris in 1924. Johnston coached Ned PRATT and Noel de Mille to BC's second medal, a bronze in the double sculls at the 1932 Olympics.

Frank READ started volunteering as the coach at UBC in 1949 and he went on to turn rowing into one of the most successful sports in BC and in Canada. His UBC/VRC 8-oared team of Glen Smith, Mike Harris, Tom Toynbee, Doug McDonald, Laurie West, Herman Kovits, Ken Drummond, Bob Wilson and coxswain Ray Sierpina won the gold medal on the Vedder Canal at the 1954 BRITISH EMPIRE AND COMMONWEALTH GAMES in Vancouver. The next year, Read's 8 upset the dominant Russians to finish 2nd at the Henley Royal Regatta. At the 1956 Olympics, his coxless 4 team of Don Arnold, Walter d'Hondt, Lorne Loomer and Archie McKinnon achieved gold and his 8 crew of West, McDonald, William McKerlich, Wayne Pretty, David Helliwell, Bob Wilson, Dick McClure, Philip Kueber and cox Carl Ogawa won the silver. The 1958 British Empire Games yielded another gold in the 8 and 2 silvers in the straight and coxed 4. In the 1960 Olympics, Arnold, d'Hondt, McKerlich, Nelson Kuhn, Glen Mervyn, McKinnon, John Lecky (grandson of H.R. MACMILLAN), cox Tom Biln and future BC Liberal leader and federal cabinet minister David ANDERSON won a second Olympic silver in the 8.

Vancouver Rowing Club, Coal Harbour.
Jon Murray/Vancouver Province

After Read retired, a completely new 8-oared crew coached by West won the 1963 Pan Am Games and George HUNGERFORD combined with future Canadian Olympic Association President Roger Jackson to win the coxless pair gold at the 1964 Tokyo Olympics. UBC/VRC teams won various silvers and bronzes at the Pan Am and British Empire Games of the late 1950s and through the 1960s, but in 1971 national rowing teams replaced club teams in international competition. As members of national teams, VRC rowers and other British Columbians continued to win medals at the Pan Am Games, World Championships and Commonwealth Championships. In Victoria, rowing had lost popularity ever since the James Bay Athletic Association fizzled out in the 1940s, but Lief Gotfredson turned the sport around by reorganizing the Victoria City Rowing Club, later taken over by national team coach Al Morrow. The club's first major triumph was a gold medal by the Bruce Ford-Patrick Walter pair at the 1979 Pan Ams.

At the 1984 Los Angeles Olympics, BC's Dean Crawford, Grant Main, Kevin Neufeld, Pat Turner, Paul Steele and Blair Horne struck gold in the 8, Marilyn Campbell of the women's quad sculls team and pairs rower Tricia SMITH earned silver, and the quad sculls team featuring Ford and Phil Monckton brought home bronze. Ontario medallists Barb Armbrust and Silken LAUMANN were so impressed with the training of the BC Olympians that they moved to Victoria after the Games. Ford, Walter, Main, Neufeld, Smith and Andrea Schreiner were all gold medallists at the 1986 Commonwealth Championships and Kirsten Barnes took gold in the pair at the 1987 Pan Ams. The same year, lightweight doubles rower Janice Mason of Victoria won Canada's first women's rowing world-championship gold in with Ontario partner Heather Hattin.

At the both the 1991 World Championships and 1992 Olympics, Barnes, Jessica Monroe and Brenda Taylor won gold in the 4 and the 8, and Kathleen HEDDLE won gold in the pair and the 8. Victoria's Kelly Mahon also won gold in the 1991 8. Laumann achieved world championship single sculls gold in 1991 and became a national hero the next year for winning Olympic bronze only 2 months after sustaining a career-threatening leg injury. BC's Megan Delehanty and men Derek PORTER, Mike Forgeron, Darren Barber and Michael Rascher also won golds in the 8. Porter also became the single sculls world champion in 1993. In lightweight competition, Gavin Hassett of Victoria won a world championship gold medal with Canada's 8 in 1994.

At the 1996 Atlanta Olympics, Heddle and her pair partner Marnie McBean won again to become the first Canadians ever to win 3 Olympic golds; Laumann (single), Porter (single), Hassett (lightweight straight 4) and Monroe and Theresa Luke (8) took silvers; and Heddle also earned a bronze in the quad. Commonwealth champions include Heddle (pair—1994); Lindsey Turner, Sandi Brouk and Samara Walbohm (lightweight 4—1994); and Luke, Mahon, Julie Jesperson, Jennifer Browett, Anna Van der Camp and Rachel Starr (8—1994).

In Pan Am Games competition, Jesperson won gold (quad) and silver (pair) in 1991 and Luke (coxless pair), Browett (double sculls) and Porter (single sculls) won gold in 1999. Also in 1999, 1956 Olympic silver medallist Dick McClure joined early VRC builders Nelles Stacey, Reggie Woodward and Read in the BC SPORTS HALL OF FAME for his 2 ½ decades of coaching at the world class Burnaby Lake Rowing Club. *SW*

ROXBURGH, Douglas "Doug," amateur golfer (b 28 Dec 1951, Dominican Republic). He was the most successful BC amateur GOLF player of the 20th century. Roxburgh was a 17-year-old VANCOUVER high school student in 1969 when he won the first of his 13 BC amateur championships over 4 different decades, a feat accomplished by no other golfer. He has also won the Canadian junior amateur championship (1970), the Canadian amateur title 4 times (1972, 1974, 1982, 1988) and represented Canada at the world amateur team championship. He is an accountant by profession.

ROY, 60 km north of CAMPBELL RIVER on the mainland coast in Loughborough Inlet, started life as a MINING settlement in the 1890s. A few homesteads sprang up but LOGGING soon became the main employer. Northern Pacific Logging ran one of BC's first truck operations here in 1922, and a shingle mill in the vicinity employed 150. Postmaster D. McGregor named the place after the Scottish outlaw Rob Roy because Roy's real surname, MacGregor, was the same as his own. *AS*

ROY, Reginald H., military historian (b 1922, New Glasgow, NS). He has written 12 books, including regimental histories, biographies and military studies, among them *1944: The Canadians in Normandy*. During WWII he served as an officer with the Cape Breton Highlanders in Italy and Holland. He graduated from UBC in 1951 with an MA and later completed his doctoral studies at the Univ of Washington. He worked on the official history of Canada in WWII under Col C.P. Stacey from 1951 to 1953. He has been on staff at the federal and provincial archives and at ROYAL ROADS, and he was on the faculty at the UNIV OF VICTORIA from 1959 to 1988. He initiated an oral history project to record war veterans' recollections on audiotape.

Ken MacLeod

ROYAL BC MUSEUM opened in VICTORIA in Oct 1886 as the Provincial Museum of Natural History and Anthropology, located in a room in the original LEGISLATIVE BUILDINGS. In 1898 it moved to a wing of the new legislature, where it remained until its present building opened as the BC Provincial Museum in Aug 1968. The first curator was John FANNIN, whose personal collection of stuffed animals formed the core of the museum's natural history collection. Fannin was succeeded as curator/director by Francis Kermode from 1904 to 1940 and Clifford CARL, a marine biologist, from 1940 to 1969. For its

A great mastodon at the Royal BC Museum. RBCM

first 80 years the museum was concerned with the province's NATURAL HISTORY and the cultures of FIRST NATIONS people. In 1967 the mandate expanded to include modern history and the museum inherited a collection of non-aboriginal artifacts from the Provincial Archives. The name of the institution changed from the BC Provincial Museum to the Royal BC Museum on 13 Oct 1987 to commemorate Queen Elizabeth II's visit to Victoria. Other directors have been Bristol Foster (1969–74); Roger Yorke EDWARDS (1974–84); and Bill Barkley (1984–present).

ROYAL ENGINEERS, Columbia Detachment, were sent to BC in 1858, under the command of Col Richard C. MOODY, to initiate a program of public works and to provide a military force to keep peace in the GOLD-mining districts. The first contingent arrived July 12 as part of the British Boundary Commission laying out the border with the US along the 49th parallel between the Pacific and the ROCKY MTS. The main force of the Columbia Detachment arrived in Apr 1859, bringing the number of engineers to 225, plus women and children. The number included a brass band, led by William Haynes, BC's first bandmaster. The men built barracks at Sapperton and began clearing a townsite for the new capital of NEW WESTMINSTER. Over the next 4 years their projects included improving the DOUGLAS TRAIL, building trails from New Westminster to BURRARD INLET, the future site of VANCOUVER, and surveying and constructing parts of the CARIBOO WAGON ROAD. But the force was expensive to maintain; with American territorial ambitions held in check by the Civil War, the Colonial Office recalled the engineers. Most of the men took up the government's offer of 150 acres

(60 ha) of free land and remained in BC as settlers; the rest sailed for England on 11 Nov 1863.

ROYAL HUDSON is the only steam locomotive remaining in regular service in N America. During the summer it hauls a passenger train for sightseers between N VANCOUVER and SQUAMISH. The engine was built for the CPR in 1940. Retired

The historic Royal Hudson steam locomotive.
Courtesy BC Rail

in 1958, it was saved from the scrapyard in 1964 and sent to VANCOUVER to be part of a railway museum. When the museum did not open, the engine was purchased by the BC government and restored. It began its present service with BC RAIL in 1974. Hudson was the name given to a particular class of locomotive, designated Royal after the 1939 visit of King George VI.

ROYAL ROADS UNIVERSITY was founded at ESQUIMALT in 1942 as Royal Roads, a MILITARY college training officers and officer cadets. Initially it was for naval cadets, then in 1948 it became a tri-service college. It occupied HATLEY PARK, the former home of James DUNSMUIR. The government closed the college in 1994 but it reopened 2 years later as Royal Roads Univ and still uses the ornate Dunsmuir home as one of its buildings.

ROYAL VANCOUVER YACHT CLUB was founded as the VANCOUVER Yacht Club in 1903 and received permission to use the prefix "Royal" in 1906. The first elected commodore was real estate dealer Walter E. Graveley, who sailed competitively in the 1876 America's Cup race. Initially located in Coal Harbour, the clubhouse was established at its present site at JERICHO on ENGLISH BAY in 1927. The facility was enlarged in 1978 and again in 1999. At the turn of the century, the club had more than 1,000 active members and owned 7 outstations in the GULF ISLANDS and at the WIGWAM INN in INDIAN ARM, PENDER HARBOUR and farther up the coast.

ROYSTON, pop 1,219, is a seafront community on the east side of VANCOUVER ISLAND, 5 km south of COURTENAY. For many years it was the terminus of a logging railway (*see* RAILWAY LOGGING) owned by the Comox Logging and Railway Co that began LOGGING the central Interior of the Island pre-WWI. The railway hauled the logs to tidewater at Royston, where

they were gathered in booms for towing south to the mills. The logging and LOG BOOMING operations are gone, but offshore the remains of several wrecks have been sunk to provide a breakwater for the booming ground. Royston was also a station on the ESQUIMALT & NANAIMO RWY.

The breakwater at Royston, built using old wrecks. Rick James photo

RUBY CREEK, on the north shore of the FRASER R, 13 km west of HOPE in the FRASER VALLEY, is a former CPR depot. Here crews changed and "helper" locomotives were added to negotiate the mountainous section to the east. Nearby was a STO:LO village named Xwelich, or Wahleach, and the long-deserted AGRICULTURAL settlement of Hunterville, centred on Henry Hunter's pre-

WWI store. Low-quality gemstones are found here and in nearby Garnet Crk.   AS

RUGBY enjoys a special popularity in BC because of the historic connection with Great Britain, home of the sport, and the favourable climate for playing. European football (SOCCER), imported by British settlers and members of the Royal Navy, began to be altered by new "Rugby Union" rules in the 1870s. The first recorded rugby match in the province took place in 1876 at the ESQUIMALT naval base between a Royal Navy side and a group of VICTORIA businessmen. The Vancouver Rugby Union, established in 1888, held games at a muddy Cambie St field filled with stumps and boulders. Rugby became organized provincially under the auspices of the BC Rugby Union, founded in 1889 by players from Victoria, VANCOUVER, NANAIMO and NEW WESTMINSTER, and provincial championships were held the following year.

The first international match involving a BC side occurred in 1893 when a Victoria team visited Oregon. The next year a BC representative side won a tournament over state teams from Oregon and California in San Francisco. Meanwhile attendance at local games climbed and in 1895 the game began to be played at high schools. That year the McKechnie Cup, symbolic of inter-union supremacy in BC, was inaugurated. International play became more common early in the 20th century. The first international match to take place in BC occurred in 1908 when a local team was trounced by a touring Anglo-Welsh side at Brockton Oval. Teams from Australia (1909) and New Zealand (1913) also

defeated local sides, but teams representing BC, Victoria and Vancouver all defeated the New South Wales Waratahs during their 1912 visit. Reggie WOODWARD, considered the father of the game in BC, was instrumental in all these early events.

While Canadian FOOTBALL rose to popularity at the expense of rugby, the Rugby Union of Canada formed in 1929 and soon after interprovincial matches began being played across the country, with the first tour of eastern Canada by a BC rep team happening in 1930. Starting with the Canadian visit to Japan in 1930 featuring British Columbian stars Jack Bain, A.B. Mitchell, Campbell Forbes, G.C. Warnock and Ernest Pinkham, BC has provided more players to the national team than any other province. Notable national stars since WWII have been Douglas "Buzz" MOORE; Ted HUNT; Gerry McGavin of the McGavin's Bread family; George Puil, later a Vancouver alderman and chair of the GREATER VANCOUVER REGIONAL DISTRICT; Denny Veitch, later a VANCOUVER WHITECAPS executive; and Barrie Burnham, Ken Wilke, Ro Hindson, Barry Legh, Gary Johnston, Hans DE GOEDE, Mark WYATT, Glenn Ennis and Gareth REES. The Vancouver Meralomas, UBC, the VANCOUVER ROWING CLUB, Vancouver Ex-Britannia, North Shore All Blacks, the Vancouver Kats and the James Bay Athletic Assoc all have histories as successful local clubs in BC. The first Carling Cup national championship was won by a BC side in 1958 and as of 1998, BC senior men's teams had won

UBC rugby players in action.
Deni Eagland/UBC Athletic Dept

the Canadian championship 29 times in 32 attempts and BC women had won 3 national championships. The BCRU consists of 51 clubs supporting 106 senior men's, 20 senior women's and 34 under-18 and collegiate teams. Individual feats in BC rugby include Moore's Honourary Barbarian title in 1962, Wyatt's world record of 8 penalty goals in a win over Scotland in 1991, Rees's Canadian high for international caps and Burnham's accomplishment as the only player in the world ever to score by all possible means—try, conversion, penalty goal, drop goal and goal from the mark—in one match, at a local Vancouver contest in 1966. Wyatt and de Goede were both captains of the national team and members of All-World teams, selections of the top 15 players in the world. Rugby also boasts 2 BC PREMIERS in its ranks: Byron JOHNSON, a standout fullback for the James Bay Athletic Assoc, and Dave BARRETT, also a fullback

for Ex-Britannia of the Vancouver Rugby Union. At the turn of the 21st century, the future of club rugby was uncertain because of experimentations with semi-pro BC and Canadian leagues, but the McKechnie Cup continued to be awarded as one of Canada's oldest sports trophies. *SW*

RULE, Jane Vance, writer (b 28 Mar 1931, Plainfield, NJ). She came to VANCOUVER from the US in 1956 and taught literature at UBC intermittently until 1976. That year she moved to GALIANO ISLAND, where she has lived ever since. Her first novel, *Desert of the Heart* (1964), a

Jane Rule, writer.
Barry Peterson & Blaise Enright-Peterson

lesbian classic, was the basis for the movie *Desert Hearts*. Several novels and story collections followed, including *The Young in One Another's Arms* (1977), *Memory Board* (1987) and *After the Fire* (1989). A collection of essays, *A Hot-Eyed Moderate*, appeared in 1985. Rule received an honorary doctorate from UBC in 1994. A member of the ORDER OF BC (1998), she is considered one of BC's leading writers of literary fiction.

RUM-RUNNERS were smugglers who carried liquor illegally from BC into the US by boat during American Prohibition from 1920 to 33. The consumption, manufacture, sale or importation of liquor was illegal in the US during this period, creating a huge demand for alcohol from outside the country. Starting from VICTORIA or the GULF ISLANDS, rum-runners crossed under cover of darkness to secluded harbours in Puget Sound, along the coast of the Olympic Peninsula or near the mouth of the COLUMBIA R, where they handed over their illicit cargoes. Sometimes large mother ships acted as seagoing warehouses, waiting outside territorial waters in so-called "Rum Row" off the American west coast while smaller, faster boats ferried the liquor to shore. By the mid-1920s rum-running was earning big profits, attracting big-time criminals and increased attention from the American government. The level of violence increased as smugglers were chased and shot at by hijackers, who wanted to steal the liquor for themselves, and by the US Coast Guard, known as the "dry navy." In one notorious incident in 1924 the fish packer *BERYL G* was intercepted by hijackers at SIDNEY ISLAND, its cargo of liquor was stolen and its 2 crewmen

Rum-runners offloading liquor from the Malahat along the coast of northern California, c 1930.
VMM

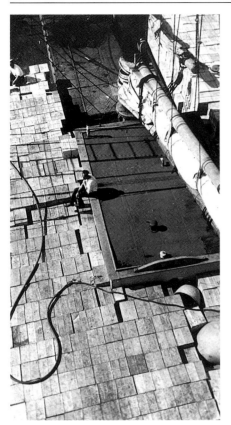

Cases of liquor stacked on the deck of the Malahat, c 1930. VMM

Painting of old sawmill, Ruskin. Rudi Dangelmaier

were murdered and dumped overboard. Nevertheless, rum-running continued to attract small operators such as Johnny SCHNARR, who saw an opportunity to make some money and enjoyed the adventure. More than one prominent BC businessman made a fortune from liquor smuggling before the US repealed the Volsted Act and ended prohibition in 1933.

RUSHTON, Gerald Arnold, office manager, historian (b 20 July 1898, Liverpool, England; d 12 Nov 1993, Tsawwassen). He studied classics before enlisting in the British Army and serving in France during WWI. Following the war he worked for his father's shipping firm and came to BC in 1920 to join its subsidiary, the UNION STEAMSHIP CO. He remained a manager with the company for 38 years, during which time he became an expert on the maritime history of the coast. His book about the company, *Whistle Up the Inlet* (1974), is a BC classic. His wife Margaret Rushton (1907–77) was active in VANCOUVER drama circles and co-founded the Holiday Theatre for children.

RUSKIN was a tiny SAWMILLING community at the mouth of the Stave R, 50 km east of VANCOUVER. It began as a socialist discussion group led by Charles Whetham, an art teacher. The group, inspired by the ideas of the British art critic John Ruskin, formed the Canadian Co-operative Society in 1896 and built the sawmill soon after. The community also featured a communal garden, DAIRY, store and school. The effort collapsed into bankruptcy in 1899 and

the mill was taken over by E.H. Heaps, who ran it until it closed in 1913. The Ruskin HYDRO-ELECTRIC dam upriver was built in 1929. *See also* CO-OPERATIVES.

RUSS, Amos, Haida leader (b circa 1850, Queen Charlotte Islands; d 1934, Queen Charlotte Islands). He was the first HAIDA on the QUEEN CHARLOTTE ISLANDS to convert to Christianity. Born to high status, he was given the name Gedanst and marked as successor to the tribal head, Chief Skidegate. Instead he came under the influence of METHODIST CHURCH missionaries. When the chief ordered him to choose between white and Haida ways he responded by sawing down his family TOTEM POLES and chopping them up for firewood. Ostracized at home, he moved to Port Simpson (*see* FORT SIMPSON) and lived among the TSIMSHIAN; there he married a Haida woman from Alaska. He returned to SKIDEGATE in 1883, bringing with him a teacher from the Port Simpson mission school, George Robinson. Together they made many converts, notably Peter KELLY, later the first ordained aboriginal minister in BC. *HW*

RUSSIAN–AMERICAN CO (RAC), a FUR-TRADING company based at Sitka on Chichagof Island, was formed in 1799 when the Tsar granted it exclusive trading rights in Alaska. These rights were renewed in 1821 and 1844 and made the company the effective government of Russian America. RAC established trading posts at several locations on the Alaskan mainland. In 1834 an attempt by the HBC to establish a trading post on the STIKINE R was met by armed resistance from the Russians, though subsequent negotiations resulted in an 1839 agreement between the 2 trading monopolies, allowing the HBC to trade in the Alaska Panhandle in return for

supplying the Russians with fresh produce and paying an annual rent. When the US purchased Alaska in 1867 the Russian company sold its assets and withdrew.

RUSSIANS were among the earliest explorers and traders on the Northwest Coast. They trapped furs and traded from their base in Alaska (*see* FUR TRADE, MARITIME), although Spain and Britain prevented them from establishing settlements on the BC coast. Russia's presence on the West Coast ended completely with the sale of Alaska to the US in 1867. The first Russian immigrants to BC were left-leaning political emigrés from the Tsarist regime. In 1909 a socialist club, the Russian Progressive Club, was established by these newcomers. The club was dissolved in 1918 after its members were arrested by Canadian authorities in the wake of the Bolshevik Revolution. A large wave of immigrants came to Canada after 1917 to escape the turmoil of the revolution. While most settled in eastern Canada, a small group, mainly army officers and their families, came to BC from the Russian colony of Harbin in Manchuria. Another wave of immigration followed WWII; it included a large group of Russians from Shanghai who came to BC in 1947 to escape the Chinese communist revolution. While immigrants who arrived before the Russian Revolution tended to be poor and illiterate, many of those who came later were well-educated professionals. In 1926 the Russian ORTHODOX Church was established in VANCOUVER, followed by 2 other Orthodox churches, St Nicholas and Holy Trinity. A separate group of Russian immigrants, the DOUKHOBORS, settled in the KOOTENAY and BOUNDARY districts in the early 1900s. Largely because of the Doukhobors, BC has a larger population of Russian origin than any other province: in 1996 76,265 people claimed Russian background. Since the 1970s Russian Jews have been the main immigrants to BC from Russia. The 3 Orthodox churches remain the centre of Russian culture in Vancouver.

Dianne MacKay

RUTLAND, an AGRICULTURAL settlement on the CNR, 8 km east of KELOWNA in the OKANAGAN VALLEY, was named after John Rutland, an Australian settler who grew wheat here in the 1890s. Irrigation helped the community, formerly known as Ellison Flats, become a rich orchard and fruit-packing centre (*see* TREE FRUITS). *AS*

RYAN, on the Moyie R, 44 km southwest of CRANBROOK in the E KOOTENAY, was an early depot on the CPR's NELSON subdivision. It was named after James Ryan, who built the first hotel in Cranbrook. A post office operated from 1903 to 1913. *AS*

RYDER LAKE, 8 km southeast of CHILLIWACK on the slopes of Elk Mt, is a farming (*see* AGRICULTURE) and LOGGING settlement in the FRASER VALLEY. It was named after John Ryder, who homesteaded at Cheam in 1868, then moved here and established an orchard (*see* TREE FRUITS). *AS*

George Ryga, writer. Talonbooks

RYGA, George, writer (b 27 July 1932, Deep Creek, AB; d 18 Nov 1987, Summerland). His parents were immigrants from the Ukraine and he grew up on a rough homestead in northern Alberta. He began writing as a teenager and won a scholarship to study at the Banff School of Fine Arts in 1949. During the 1950s he lived in Edmonton, working at different jobs and struggling to be a writer. In 1962 his first television play was produced, followed by his first novel, *Hungry Hills*, in 1963, the same year that he moved with his wife and children to SUMMERLAND. His first public success was *The Ecstasy of Rita Joe*, a stage play that premiered at the VANCOUVER PLAYHOUSE on 23 Nov 1967. When it opened in Ottawa in 1969 it was the first English-language production at the new National Arts Centre. Other plays followed, including *Grass and Wild Strawberries* (1968), *Captives of the Faceless Drummer* (1971) and *Sunrise on Sarah* (1972), and by the mid-1970s he was recognized as one of Canada's leading playwrights. Ryga was an outspoken social critic, both in his work and in speeches and articles. As well as 15 stage plays, he wrote 5 novels, poetry, short stories and more than 90 scripts for radio and television.

SAANICH INLET is a deep FJORD, 25 km long, at the southeast corner of VANCOUVER ISLAND north of VICTORIA. It separates the SAANICH PENINSULA from the main body of the Island. Originally occupied by Coast Salish (*see* SALISHAN FIRST NATIONS), the inlet now attracts recreational boaters and an increasing number of residents who appreciate its rural setting just a few kilometres from the capital city. Like all fjords, this one has an inlet floor that is shallow at the mouth, then plunges to a maximum depth of 230 m, where water circulates very sluggishly. There are 2 provincial PARKS: GOLDSTREAM at the head of the inlet in FINLAYSON ARM and BAMBERTON. The MALAHAT DRIVE is a scenic stretch of highway above the western side, offering spendid views of the inlet. On the east side the main communities are at Patricia Bay, site of the Institute of Ocean Sciences and Pacific Geo-

Farm on the Saanich Peninsula.
Keith Thirkell photo

science Centre, and at BRENTWOOD BAY, near BUTCHART GARDENS. The smallest ferry in the BC FERRY CORP fleet connects Brentwood Bay to MILL BAY on the west side. Until the mid-1980s, the Inlet had a thriving sport fishery for SALMON, but in the 1990s stocks declined.

SAANICH PENINSULA is an area of rolling farmland along the southeast corner of VANCOUVER ISLAND north of VICTORIA. It is part of the traditional territory of the Wsanec (Saanich) FIRST NATION, who sold it to Gov James DOUGLAS in 1852 (*see* DOUGLAS TREATIES). The Wsanec now occupy 4 communities here. Farmers were attracted by the mild climate, good soil and low relief, and settlement began in the 1860s. The Saanich Agricultural Fair (est 1868) is the oldest continuous fair west of the Great Lks. The highest point is Mt Newton (305 m), known to the Wsanec as Lauwelnew ("place of refuge"). The VICTORIA & SIDNEY RWY ran up the middle of the peninsula during 1894–1919, giving farmers a way to get their produce to market. BC ELECTRIC RWY CO also ran an INTERURBAN train from Victoria to the north end of the peninsula at DEEP BAY from 1913 to 1923. The Victoria International AIRPORT was built in 1938–39 but the peninsula kept its agricultural character until the construction of Hwy 17, the highway linking Victoria to the ferry terminal built at Swartz Bay in 1960 (*see* BC FERRY CORP). This is the main link between the Island and the mainland. Swartz Bay, misnamed after a pioneer settler named L.O. Swart, has been a ferry terminus since 1930 when the Gulf Island Ferry Co began a service to FULFORD HARBOUR on SALTSPRING ISLAND using the small car ferry *Cy Peck*. That service was absorbed by the BC Ferry Authority in 1960. The main urban centre on the peninsula is SIDNEY, with a smaller community at BRENTWOOD BAY near BUTCHART GARDENS. There is a remarkable concentration of government scientific facilities on the peninsula, including an agricultural

research station (est 1912), the Institute of Ocean Sciences, the Pacific Geoscience Centre and the DOMINION RADIO ASTROPHYSICAL OBSERVATORY. Farming continues, though housing developments have encroached on AGRICULTURE since the 1960s and many residents commute to work in Victoria. Today the peninsula is divided into 3 district municipalities: Saanich (pop 101,388), which is part of the Capital Regional District (*see* REGIONAL DISTRICTS), Central Saanich (pop 14,611) and N Saanich (pop 10,411).

SAANICHTON, 20 km north of VICTORIA in Central Saanich district municipality, is a former AGRICULTURAL settlement, now mostly residential, that grew up around a crossroads in the middle of the SAANICH PENINSULA. Henry Simpson farmed here in the late 1850s and built an early hotel. The village was served by both the VICTORIA & SIDNEY RWY and the BC ELECTRIC RWY CO with its INTERURBAN line, but Saanichton declined when bypassed to the east by Hwy 17. The post office here (1892–1922) was named Turgoose after William Turgoose, who arrived in 1865. *AS*

SABISTON, Carole, fibre artist (b 1939, London, England). She came to Canada with her parents in 1948 and studied fine arts at UBC and the UNIV OF VICTORIA. She specializes in large-scale wall hangings, THEATRE sets and costumes, and her work is in private collections and public galleries around the world. Among her many awards are the 1987 Saidye Bronfman Award for Excellence in the Crafts, the ORDER OF BC and an honorary degree from the Univ of Victoria (1995). In 1994 her textile work was featured in the closing ceremonies of the BRITISH EMPIRE AND COMMONWEALTH GAMES in VICTORIA, where she lives.

SABLEFISH (*Anoplopoma fimbria*), commonly known as blackcod, inhabits shelf and slope waters from California around the north Pacific to the Bering Sea and Japan. It is most abundant

Sablefish. Phil Edgell photo; drawing courtesy Fisheries & Oceans Canada

in northern BC and the Gulf of Alaska. The sablefish spawns primarily from Jan to Mar along the continental shelf. It has an elongated black or green-grey body with 2 well-separated, almost equal-sized dorsal fins. The average size of a mature sablefish 4–5 years old is 55 cm; maximum size is about 80 cm. The oldest sablefish on record lived 113 years. Adult sablefish have oily flesh and are considered one of the best smoked fishes, often labelled "smoked Alaska blackcod" in grocery stores. The species has been harvested commercially (*see* FISHING, COMMERCIAL) off BC's coast for more than 40 years. In the mid-1960s, Japan's distant-water fishing fleet targeted Pacific sablefish for more than a decade before foreign fishing was halted with the adoption of Canada's 200-mile Extended Economic Zone in 1977. In the late 1970s, Canadian fishers worked to establish a viable sablefish fishery by pursuing markets in Japan, and experimented with the trap gear as a more effective harvesting method. Both the commercial and the recreational (*see* FISHING, SPORT) sablefish fisheries are open year-round and managed on an annual vessel quota basis. In 1998, the fishery landed 4,500 tonnes with a wholesale value of $32.5 million.

SAILING has a long history in BC, one of the most beautiful cruising and racing areas in the world. However, the first recorded sailing competition, held at ESQUIMALT by the Royal Navy in 1859, failed due to lack of wind. NEW WESTMINSTER's first sailing race was staged at the Queen's Birthday celebrations in 1861. Steamboat racing was also popular around this time. NANAIMO and VICTORIA staged other races and regattas through the turn of the 20th century. The Victoria Yacht Club began in 1892 but experienced difficulty until a revival in 1908. A few different VANCOUVER clubs, including H.O. BELL-IRVING's BURRARD INLET Sailing Club, were active

Yacht under full sail near Heriot Bay, Quadra Island. Ian Douglas photo

during the 1890s but Walter Graveley's ROYAL VANCOUVER YACHT CLUB prevailed after its founding in 1903. The Pacific Northwest's most important sailing event, the Swiftsure Lightship Classic (*see* SWIFTSURE RACE), began in 1930. Competitively, the national women's championships were organized in 1972, following the lead of the West Vancouver Yacht Club's women's regatta. Also that year Canada had its first Olympic success in 40 years as David Millar, Paul Cote and John Ekels from BC won a bronze medal at the Munich Games. Eric Jespersen and Ross MacDonald won BC's second Olympic sailing bronze in the pairs sailing event at the 1992 Barcelona Games. They later earned a second-in-the-world ranking by winning the 1994 Star World Championship, 4 international events in 1995 and the 1996 Olympic trials in Vancouver. *SW*

ST ELIAS MOUNTAINS lie along the BC–Alaska border, tucked into the northwest corner of the province between the Yukon and the Alaska panhandle. The range includes Mt FAIRWEATHER (4,663 m), the highest peak in BC (Mt

Mt St Elias on the BC–Alaska border.
Rick Blacklaws photo

WADDINGTON is the highest peak completely within BC). An area of spectacular alpine scenery rich in wildlife, it is part of TATSHENSHINI–ALSEK Wilderness Provincial PARK (9,580 km², created in 1993) and a vast 8.4 million-ha WORLD HERITAGE SITE created by UNESCO in 1994.

ST EUGENE MISSION, a historic OBLATE mission to the KTUNAXA people, is located on the ST MARY R north of CRANBROOK in the east KOOTENAY. Father Leon Fouquet was the first Oblate to settle here, in 1874. He attracted a band of Ktunaxa led by Chief Joseph, whose descendants are now known as the St Mary's band. In 1897, under the direction of Father Nicolas COCCOLA, a beautiful church was built at the mission using proceeds from the sale of MINING properties at Moyie Lk, which later became the St Eugene SILVER mine. The church was restored in the 1980s;

the RESIDENTIAL SCHOOL that operated between 1912 and 1971 is to become a hotel.

ST GEORGE'S SCHOOL is a private school for boys established in VANCOUVER in 1931 by F.J. Danby-Hunter, an English-born schoolmaster. It began as a private venture but was soon taken over by parents eager to make it an elite school for male offspring of the well-to-do. From 1933 to 1971 the school was led by John Harker, an English-born businessman, and then his younger brother Douglas, a teacher. The school expanded until it outgrew its original location in a private home; a modern senior school was added and then the Convent of the Sacred Heart, a nearby CATHOLIC girls' school, was taken over. *See also* EDUCATION, PRIVATE.

ST JOHNS POST was a NORTH WEST CO (NWC) fur-trading post built in 1806 where the Beatton R flows into the PEACE R east of FORT ST JOHN. The HBC retained the post when it merged with the NWC in 1821, trading with the local SEKANI and DUNNE-ZA (Beaver) people. In the fall of 1823 the HBC made plans to relocate the post farther west. Whether in response to this change or out of animosity toward a trader, local people killed 5 HBC servants at the post. The murderers were never captured and the post never reopened.

ST LEON HOT SPRINGS, 67 km south of REVELSTOKE on the east side of Upper ARROW LK, was a steamship landing and luxurious hotel built in 1902 by Mike Grady, a prospector who struck it rich at SILVERTON. PROHIBITION put the hotel out of business about 1918. It was rebuilt in 1945 but disappeared for good when the Arrow Lks were dammed in 1968. The actual springs were not submerged; they still exist on the hillside above the lake. *AS*

ST MARY RIVER, 117 km, rises in the PURCELL MTS east of KOOTENAY LK and flows southeast through some of the most productive MINING country in BC to its confluence with the KOOTENAY R, opposite historic FORT STEELE. KIMBERLEY and the SULLIVAN MINE lie to the north; the St

Eugene SILVER mine overlooked Moyie Lk to the south. The river flows through the traditional territory of the KTUNAXA (Kutenai) FIRST NATIONS and is named for the Virgin Mary, patron saint of the Oblate missionary order (*see* OBLATES OF MARY IMMACULATE), founders of ST EUGENE MISSION, where one of the Ktunaxa bands, the St Mary's band, now lives. It is a popular stream with anglers, especially for its cutthroat TROUT.

ST MARY'S MISSION, 40 km east of NEW WESTMINSTER on the north bank of the FRASER R, was a mission for aboriginal people founded by the OBLATE missionary Leon Fouquet in 1861. The name refers to St Mary of Egypt, a former prostitute. A RESIDENTIAL SCHOOL for boys opened in 1863; another one, for girls, opened in 1868 and was run by the SISTERS OF ST ANN. From 1864 it hosted an annual retreat that attracted thousands of FIRST NATIONS people from the FRASER VALLEY and VANCOUVER ISLAND. The Oblates also encouraged the settlement of French-speaking farmers from Quebec who congregated at Hatzic Prairie, later DURIEU. A local landmark was the Grotto of Our Lady of Lourdes, a tall, wooden, domed shrine built in 1892 on a hill overlooking the site. The residential schools closed in 1959, replaced 2 years later by a Department of Indian Affairs school, which in turn was phased out in 1984. Mission buildings, including the Grotto, were razed during the 1960s; the site is now Fraser River Heritage Park, within which a full-sized replica of the Grotto has been built.

ST MICHAEL'S UNIVERSITY SCHOOL is a private co-educational school in VICTORIA. It was founded in 1971 when 2 much older private schools were amalgamated. University School was established in Victoria in 1906 to prepare boys from well-to-do families for university entrance. During the 1920s it was briefly a military academy. In the Depression it stumbled into bankruptcy but reopened as a non-profit society. St. Michael's Preparatory School was founded in OAK BAY in 1910 by Kyrle C. Symons, an English-born former cleric. It began in Symons's home, then moved in 1912 to new premises funded by the architect Francis RATTENBURY. When Symons retired in 1946 his sons took over the school. St. Michael's University School has an enrolment of about 850 students, kindergarten to grade 12, one-quarter of whom are boarders. *See also* EDUCATION, PRIVATE.

ST PIERRE, Paul, writer (b 14 Oct 1923, Chicago, IL). He grew up in Nova Scotia, served with the Royal Canadian Air Force during WWII and arrived in VANCOUVER in 1945. He began a career as a NEWSPAPER writer with the NEW WESTMINSTER *Columbian* and the Vancouver *News Herald* before joining the VANCOUVER SUN (1947–68, 1972–79) where he became a popular columnist. In 1958 he began contributing scripts to the CBC television series *CARIBOO COUNTRY*. His first book of stories about CHILCOTIN ranch country, *Breaking Smith's Quarter Horse*, appeared in 1966. He sat as a Liberal Member of

The historic vessel St Roch *on one of its voyages to the eastern Arctic, c 1946. VMM*

Paul St Pierre, writer.

Parliament for the riding of Coast–Chilcotin from 1968 to 1972. His other books include *Chilcotin Holiday* (1970), *Smith and Other Events* (1983) and *Chilcotin and Beyond* (1989), plus books for youngsters and numerous teleplays. In 2000 he received the BC GAS LIFETIME ACHIEVEMENT AWARD.

ST ROCH was an RCMP Arctic patrol vessel. In 1941–42 it made the first west-to-east navigation of the Northwest Passage. The 32-m diesel-powered wooden vessel was launched in N VANCOUVER in 1928 and used to carry supplies and to serve as a floating police detachment. The historic wartime cruise, under Capt Henry Larsen, was intended to assert Canadian sovereignty in the Arctic. In 1944 the ship made the return trip, east-to-west, to became the first vessel to complete the passage in a single season and the first to do so via the more northerly

route down Prince of Wales Strait. It was also the first to make the trip in both directions. The *St Roch* left the Arctic in 1948 and in 1950 became the first ship to circumnavigate N America. It was retired in 1954 when it was purchased by the City of Vancouver; it was then placed in dry dock at the VANCOUVER MARITIME MUSEUM and opened to the public. In 1962 it was declared a national historic site.

SAKIC, Joseph Steve "Joe," hockey player (b 7 July 1969, Burnaby). He first turned heads in the BURNABY Minor HOCKEY Assoc, fuelling rumours that a West Coast Wayne Gretzky was in the making. As a junior he was a standout with the Swift Current Broncos in the WHL and he was selected as Canadian junior player of the year in 1988. The Quebec Nordiques drafted him relatively low, 15th overall, but he proved his doubters wrong and joined the team as soon as he left the junior ranks, soon becoming its captain and best player. He twice scored more

Joe Sakic with the Colorado Avalanche.
Jeff Vinnick/Vancouver Canucks

than 40 goals for Quebec and 3 times earned 100 points before the Nordiques moved to Denver in 1995 to become the Colorado Avalanche. The Avalanche's first season was Sakic's best as he scored 51 goals and 120 points. He won the Conn Smythe Trophy as playoff MVP that year, with 18 goals and 34 points in 22 playoff games to lead the team to its first Stanley Cup. In 1997 the Avalanche re-signed Sakic, agreeing to pay him $17 million US for 1997-98, to that point the highest single-season salary in hockey history. *SW*

SALAL (*Gaultheria shallon*) a member of the heather family (Ericaceae) is one of the most common shrubs in BC's coastal forests, in places forming a dense ground cover. It is characterized

Flowering salal. Peter A. Robson photo

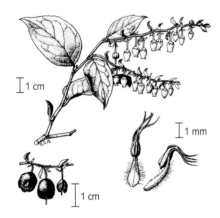

Clockwise from top: flowering branch, stamens, mature and half-grown fruit of the flowering salal. © T.C. Brayshaw

by evergreen leathery leaves and, from May to July, small, pinkish bell- or urn-shaped flowers. The deep blue berries were used extensively by FIRST NATIONS people, either eaten fresh, boiled into a syrup or dried in cakes. Today, many people make jam from them. Branches are harvested commercially for use in floral arrangements. Salal was imported to England by David DOUGLAS for use in gardens.

Ensatina salamander, Sunshine Coast.
Duane Sept photo

SALAMANDER is a small, LIZARD-like, tailed amphibian found in moist wooded areas. Salamanders are both aquatic and terrestrial; the terrestrial species hibernate during the colder months. They feed principally on worms and INSECTS, though larger species also prey on other amphibians, mice and SLUGS. Although they cannot hear, they are sensitive to vibrations. They are egg-laying animals and they engage in complex mating rituals. The male releases sperm, which the female picks up in her cloaca (genital and excretory cavity); the eggs are fertilized as they are laid. Of 19 species native to Canada, 9 occur in BC. The Pacific giant salamander (*Dicamptodon ensatus*), found only in the CHILLIWACK area, is the largest, growing to a length of 33 cm. Other types include the chocolate brown northwestern salamander (*Ambystoma gracile*), found along the West Coast; the long-toed salamander (*A. macrodactylum*), which spends much of its time underground; and the tiger salamander (*A. tigrinum*), common in ponds in the southern OKANAGAN VALLEY. Four lungless species absorb oxygen through their skin; they are active mainly at night and are terrestrial, laying their eggs in moist places on the ground, usually rotten logs. The commonest and most widespread species are the Ensatina salamander (*Ensatina eschscholtzi*) and the western red-backed salamander (*Plethodon vehiculum*), both found only on the South Coast. The clouded salamander (*Aneides ferreus*) is a tree-climbing species occurring on VANCOUVER ISLAND. The Coeur d'Alene salamander, is a rare species found in the spray-zone of creeks in the W KOOTENAY. The rough-skinned newt (*Taricha granulosa*) occurs in coastal forests and in the lower FRASER VALLEY. It has a rough brown body with a bright orange belly and its skin secretes the strongest toxin of any N American amphibian.

SALISHAN FIRST NATIONS are aboriginal peoples speaking languages related within the Salishan family of languages. Although Salishan First Nations originally occupied territories from

Idaho (the Coeur d'Alene) to Oregon (the Tillamook) and were the predominant stock in what is now Washington state, 12 of the 23 Salish tongues were spoken in BC. Some Salishan tongues were spoken in numerous dialectal forms, and a few (OKANAGAN and NORTHERN STRAITS) were spoken by groups that spanned the 49th parallel. The Salishan First Nations divided at an early date into Coast Salish and Interior Salish, and they are contiguous except for outliers on the north (NUXALK) and the south (Tillamook). Although there is no group that calls itself "the Salish," Salishan First Nations are related not only linguistically but historically, since they all descend from a common ancestor group referred to as the proto-Salish. The unproven Mosan Hypothesis, based on similar words for "four" and other common vocabulary, suggested that the Salishan peoples descended from the same original group as the WAKASHAN and Chimakuan peoples (of Washington's Olympic Peninsula). Except for the Nuxalk (Bella Coola), who were influenced culturally by adjacent Wakashan groups, Salishan groups produced art that was more representational than the highly conventionalized Northwest Coast aboriginal ART, and while they did not produce TOTEM POLES they carved elaborate welcoming figures and houseposts for their shed-roofed houses (*see* ARCHITECTURE, ABORIGINAL). The *xwexwe* ritual (with its pectin shell rattles and masks with protruding eyes) developed among the Salish and spread among other groups on the West Coast. Although Salishan ceremonials occasionally included giveaways, the POTLATCH was not a tradition among many groups. Heavy woollen sweaters, scarves and toques, commonly knitted by Salish women, are sometimes referred to as "Salish knitting" and maintain an aboriginal tradition of Salish weaving. *See also* FIRST NATIONS OF BC. *Jay Powell*

SALMO, village, pop 1,202, is 39 km east of CASTLEGAR on the Salmo R. Salmo is Latin for SALMON, a reference to the fish that were plentiful before dam construction destroyed the runs. The village began as a siding on the NELSON & FORT SHEPPARD RWY, constructed in 1893, and

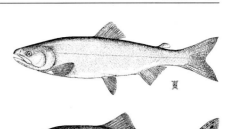

was the centre of the rich SHEEP CREEK MINING area until the 1950s. Today the FOREST INDUSTRY is important and many residents work at the COMINCO operations in TRAIL. Unusual stone murals in the downtown were erected by students from the Kootenay Stone Masonry Training Institution.

SALMON, ATLANTIC (*Salmo salar*) are not native to BC but the species is raised commercially in netpens by the salmon farming industry, mainly in the waters off western and northern VANCOUVER ISLAND (*see* AQUACULTURE, FIN FISH). Surveys conducted in the 1990s discovered small numbers of Atlantic salmon fry in several

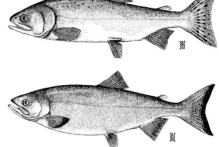

Atlantic salmon. Fisheries & Oceans Canada

Vancouver Island rivers.

In the native habitat the life cycle of the Atlantic salmon is similar to that of the Pacific SALMON. They spawn in the fall in the upper reaches of streams, where the eggs incubate in the gravel. Fry emerge the following spring and young salmon spend 1–2 years in fresh water before migrating to the sea. They return to spawn at 3–5 years of age and then, like STEELHEAD and cutthroat TROUT, they have the ability to return to sea, coming back to spawn a second or third time, though it is estimated that up to 75% of a run dies after spawning once.

The first attempt to introduce Atlantic salmon to BC waters was made in 1905 in the hope of creating an attractive sport FISHING opportunity. The Canada Department of Fisheries (as Fisheries and Oceans Canada was then named) introduced eggs into the COWICHAN LK Hatchery and subsequently released fingerlings into the COWICHAN R and other river systems. This attempt was unsuccessful and was followed by an equally unsuccessful second attempt in 1933–34. In 1985 Ibec Aquaculture Ltd was the first company to receive shipments of Atlantic salmon eggs from Scotland. Government agencies allowed a limited number of egg importations to build a broodstock capacity of domesticated Atlantic salmon for the BC fish farming industry. It was felt that because Atlantic salmon stocks had already been domesticated by several generations of fish farming, they would be easier to raise in captive netpens than undomesticated wild Pacific salmon. Environmentalists warned that escaped Atlantic salmon could survive and spawn, thereby displacing indigenous Pacific salmon runs (*see also* ENVIRONMENTAL MOVEMENT), but based on the dismal results of the earlier attempts at introduction, scientists believed these concerns were unwarranted. In 1998 a handful of Atlantic salmon fry were found in the Tsitika R and small numbers of fry were also found in Amor de Cosmos Crk. Testing revealed that these fry like-

ly were spawned and reared in the system, indicating that Atlantic salmon can spawn and rear fry successfully in a BC river system. Since 1998 other locations on Vancouver Island have been discovered where Atlantic salmon seem to be thriving. *Carol Swann*

SALMON, PACIFIC, genus *Oncorhynchus*, inhabits the coastal waters of northern Pacific Rim countries and is found in N America from San Francisco to Alaska and in coastal areas of Russia, Japan and Korea. Seven species of salmon are recognized: pink (*Oncorhynchus gorbuscha*); chum (*O. keta*); coho (*O. kisutch*); sockeye (*O. nerka*); chinook (*O. tshawytscha*); masu or sakuramasu (*O. masou*); and amago or biwamasu (*O. rhodurus*). The first 5 species listed occur in the eastern Pacific along the central and northern coasts of N America. The other 2 occur in the

Coho salmon. Phil Edgell photo

western Pacific from the southern rivers of the Kamchatka Peninsula south to waters around Taiwan, and are considered to be more trout-like than other members of the genus. An eigth member of this genus that occurs in BC, STEELHEAD (*Oncorhynchus mykiss*), is a sea-run rainbow TROUT. Steelhead are considered by some scientists to resemble the ancestral Pacific salmon type. The fact that there are a number of different species in this genus may be linked with early interglacial periods during the Pleistocene, when the ice melted for a time and sea levels rose to

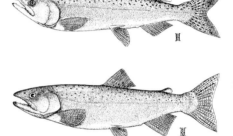

Five species of Pacific salmon, top to bottom: sockeye, pink, chum, chinook, coho. Fisheries & Oceans Canada

incorporate previously landlocked areas in which some evolutionary changes had already begun. This theory would account for the many similarities among the species.

Pacific salmon are considered to be among the most commercially and socially valuable fish

Pink salmon. Phil Edgell photo

in BC. They are large, agile and fast-growing; they perform tremendous migrations; they have complex and interesting behaviour patterns. All Pacific salmon are anadromous, which means the fish spawns in fresh water but spend some, if not all, of its adult life in the salty ocean. The life stages of anadromous salmon are egg, embryo, alevin, fry, smolt and adult (spawner). After emerging from their gravel spawning beds (called redds) in freshwater streams and lakes, the young fry may spend anywhere from a few days to 3 years in fresh water. They then become smolts—physiological changes occur so they can live in salt water and they are on their way to becoming mature adults—and they migrate to the sea. In the ocean they disperse across a wide area of the N Pacific. At the end of their life cycle (1–7 years) mature adults return, generally in summer and fall, to the river systems in which they were born to spawn and die.

The use of salmon for personal consumption and for trading began with FIRST NATIONS hundreds of years ago. Whole cultures, both coastal and inland, were sustained by salmon; for some coastal groups the resource was so rich that particularly intricate cultural, artistic and social lives could flourish; the salmon became a cultural and religious icon among many groups.

The HBC pioneered the commercial fishery when it began salting fish at FORT LANGLEY in the 1830s. Canneries appeared on the lower FRASER R in the 1870s, then spread up the coast as SALMON CANNING developed into a major industry. Canned salmon was almost the only processed product until the 1960s, when improved refrigeration allowed a market for fresh and frozen fish to develop. As well, recreational fishers from around the world are attracted to these magnificent game fish. *See also* FISHERIES POLICY; FISHING, COMMERCIAL; FISHING, SPORT.

Numbers of the various species of salmon fluctuate greatly from year to year depending on many factors, but have been in a generally steady decline since the 1980s. In the late 1990s, the abundance particularly of coho, chinook and sockeye declined sharply due to a combination of factors: primarily overfishing, but also poor ocean survival, loss and deterioration of spawning habitat due mainly to urban and industrial developments in the lower Fraser R and LOGGING in coastal areas, and gear and vessel types that enable large hauls. Governments have responded to this crisis by instituting strict catch limits for both commercial and recreational fisheries, in hopes that stocks will rebuild.

Sockeye (*Oncorhynchus nerka*) primarily spawn in LAKES; a notable exception in BC is the lower STIKINE R system, in which a significant percentage are considered to be "main stem spawners." Young sockeye remain in fresh water generally for a year before migrating to the sea as smolts, where they remain up to 4 years. Average weight at maturity is 1.8–2.3 kg, though some reach up to 7 kg. Their deep red flesh and good flavour appeals to consumers. Sockeye was the mainstay of the early salmon canning industry and by 2000 was still the most important species commercially. The main coastal sockeye spawning areas are the SKEENA, Fraser and NASS rivers, and the Somass–Great Central Lake system on VANCOUVER ISLAND. Between 1986 and 1995 (before the more recent dramatic decline in populations), commercial fishers took an average of 10 million sockeye annually, while sport fishers caught an additional 20,000. KOKANEE are freshwater-resident (commonly called landlocked) sockeye that do not migrate to salt water.

Pink (*O. gorbuscha*) is the most abundant salmon species in BC. After emergence from the gravel, the fry migrate almost immediately to the sea, where they remain for 18 months before returning to their natal rivers. The pink is the smallest species, with an average adult weight of 1–2.5 kg. It has a 2-year lifespan and tends to spawn in ESTUARIES and close to the sea. Pinks are also known as humpbacks, a reference to the hump that develops, particularly in mature males. Between 1986 and 1995 commercial fishers took an average of 14.5 million pink salmon annually, while sport fishers caught an additional 220,000.

Chum, or dog salmon (*O. keta*), are the most widely dispersed salmon, occurring in about 800 BC streams. They generally spawn in the lower portions of RIVERS. At maturity their average weight is 5 kg and many exceed 9 kg. They return to their natal streams 3–7 years after hatching. The chum is the least popular species with consumers, owing to its low oil content. Between 1986 and 1995 commercial fishers took an average of 3.5 million annually.

Chinook (*O. tschawytscha*), also called spring, is the largest Pacific salmon; adults can reach 40 kg and the largest rod-caught specimen on record, taken in the Skeena R in the 1950s, weighed 41.4 kg. Some are stream-type and spend one or more years in fresh water before migrating seaward. Chinook may also return to their natal rivers several months before spawning. Others are ocean-type; they migrate to sea after a few weeks or months and return to their natal streams only to spawn and die. The migration of both types generally peaks in spring, but may take place at any time of year. Chinook are highly sought-after sport fish. An individual exceeding 13.5 kg is known popularly as a TYEE. Between 1986 and 1995 commercial fishers took an annual average of 540,000 chinook, while sport fishers caught an additional 140,000.

Coho (*O. kisutch*) is also a favourite species with anglers. Spawning in about two-thirds of the known salmon-bearing streams in BC, it generally spends a year in fresh water before migrating to the sea. On average coho are 3 years old at maturity and an average mature weight is 3–5 kg.

SALMON LIFE CYCLE

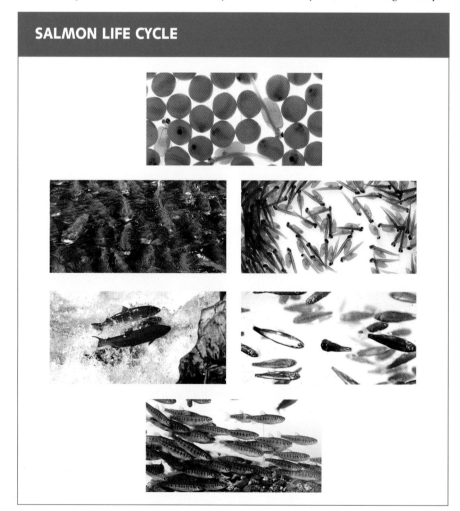

Life cycle of the Pacific salmon, clockwise from top: eggs, alevins, fry, smolts (Rick Blacklaws photos), migrating adult, spawning adult (Roy Luckow photos).

It is rare for an individual to exceed 9 kg. Between 1986 and 1995 commercial fishers took an annual average of 3 million coho. Sport catches during the same period averaged 1.3 million, but had declined drastically to 25,000 by 1998. Much of that decline was due to severe catch restrictions throughout coastal BC, imposed to conserve stocks.

Reading: C. Groot and L. Margolis, eds, *Pacific Salmon Life Histories*, 1991; C. Groot, L. Margolis, W.C. Clarke, *Physiological Ecology of Pacific Salmon*, 1995.

SALMON ARM, district municipality, pop 14,664, lies at the head of the southern arm of SHUSWAP LK on the flood plain of the Salmon R. It is situated on the TRANS-CANADA HWY, halfway between VANCOUVER and Calgary. The name refers

to the once plentiful numbers of SALMON that swarmed up the tributaries draining into the lake. Although GOLD prospectors explored the region briefly in the 1860s, settlement did not begin until the mid-1880s with the arrival of the CPR. The area was incorporated on 15 May 1905 as the District of Salmon Arm and the Municipality of Salmon Arm. The 2 communities combined on 1 Sept 1970. The FOREST INDUSTRY has been the largest employer, with several SAWMILLS and a plywood plant. DAIRY FARMING and soft fruit growing are also important. Salmon Arm is the commercial centre for the Shuswap area, which is increasingly popular with summer vacationers and TOURISTS.

There are more than 20 provincial PARKS and recreation areas on nearby Shuswap Lk. The community boasts a campus of Okanagan Univ College (*see* COMMUNITY COLLEGES), a museum and historical association, and a vibrant performing arts society. The mouth of the Salmon R is a significant nesting area for over 100 bird species.

SALMON CANNING in BC began on the FRASER R near NEW WESTMINSTER in 1867, when James SYME opened the first cannery in an abandoned saltery. His operation failed, but 2 others begun in the same vicinity in 1871 succeeded in launching a permanent industry. By 1881 there were 10 canneries on the Fraser, exporting 142,516 cases of fish. For the most part they concentrated at STEVESTON and LADNER near the mouth of the river. Canneries spread up the coast as well; the first opened on the SKEENA R in

Scow full of salmon being iced down prior to canning, Imperial Cannery dock, Steveston, 1942. *City of Richmond Archives*

1876, the NASS R in 1881 and in RIVERS INLET in 1882. Competition was chaotic and in 1902 BC PACKERS was created to merge and rationalize many of the operations.

Canneries were supplied by a fleet of rowed fishing boats using gillnets in the lower reaches

Cannery processing line. VMM

of the rivers (*see* FISHING, COMMERCIAL). Initially most of the fishers were FIRST NATIONS people from coastal villages, though by 1900 the fleet was mainly JAPANESE and European. Inside the canneries, workers were aboriginal women and CHINESE. They were hired by labour contractors for the canning season, which ran from Mar, when cans were manufactured, to Sept, when the last fish were processed. Workers lived in meagre accommodation provided by the canneries, segregated by race. Fish were butchered, cleaned, cut into pieces and packed in tin cans, all by hand. After tops were soldered on, the cans were cooked in steam retorts, then labelled and shipped. Gradual mechanization (with, for

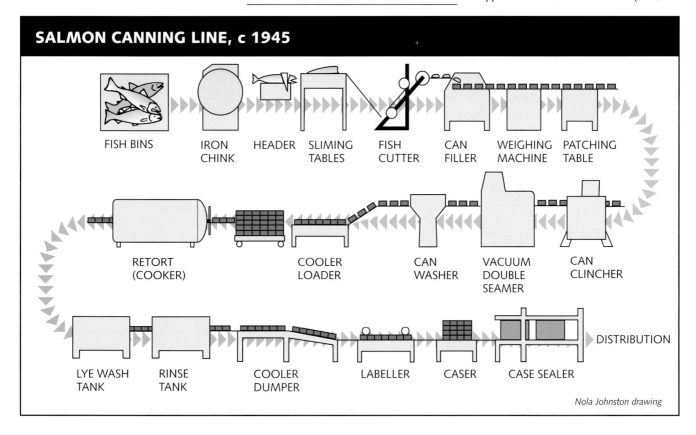

SALMON CANNING LINE, c 1945

FISH BINS — IRON CHINK — HEADER — SLIMING TABLES — FISH CUTTER — CAN FILLER — WEIGHING MACHINE — PATCHING TABLE

RETORT (COOKER) — COOLER LOADER — CAN WASHER — VACUUM DOUBLE SEAMER — CAN CLINCHER

LYE WASH TANK — RINSE TANK — COOLER DUMPER — LABELLER — CASER — CASE SEALER — DISTRIBUTION

Nola Johnston drawing

example, the IRON CHINK) reduced the number of workers and increased the productivity of the canneries. The industry was extremely wasteful: initially it only processed chinook and sockeye;

Filling cans at Brown's Bay Packing, near Campbell River, 1993. Vancouver Province

other species caught in the nets were killed and thrown away. As well, when the supply was so plentiful that the canning lines could not keep up, the excess was discarded. Public complaints caused the government to step in to regulate the industry (*see* FISHERIES POLICY).

From about 1905, new markets opened for pink and chum salmon, encouraging the geographical expansion of the industry. The number of operating canneries peaked at 80 in 1918; in total there were 223 cannery sites on the coast. The Fraser and Skeena rivers always had the highest concentration of canneries, though can-

Display of canned salmon, 1999.
Glenn Baglo/Vancouver Sun

ning took place in many other locations. Production of canned salmon peaked during the 1920s at about 2 million cases annually. With the onset of the Depression the industry began to consolidate and the number of canneries declined steadily. Freezing technology was introduced after WWII, and plants diversified their product lines to stay open year-round. At this time the market for canned fish, much of which had been British, became mainly domestic. Further closures took place in the late 1960s and surviving plants centralized at PRINCE RUPERT and the VANCOUVER area. The CANADIAN FISHING CO cannery at Prince Rupert (owned by BC Packers

until 1999) is the world's largest salmon cannery. There are now fewer canneries than frozen-fish processors. In the late 1990s an average of 1 million 48-lb cases of salmon were canned in BC annually and canned salmon accounted for 40% of the total wholesale value of BC's salmon products, down from 80% in 1955. Specialty markets for frozen, fresh, smoked and salted fish account for the rest. In 1999 there were 8 salmon canneries and 190 fish processing plants operating in BC, concentrated in the Lower Mainland, VANCOUVER ISLAND and Prince Rupert. Along with salmon canning, these processing plants include shellfish processing and fish processing of all types.
Reading: M. Patricia Marchak et al, eds, *Uncommon Property: The Fishing and Fish-Processing Industries in BC,* 1987.

SALMON RIVER rises in the mountains of STRATHCONA PROVINCIAL PARK on VANCOUVER ISLAND and flows northerly for 74 km to empty into JOHNSTONE STRAIT at KELSEY BAY, near SAYWARD north of CAMPBELL RIVER. It is said to have the largest STEELHEAD on the Island. The ESTUARY supports a wide variety of winter waterfowl, including trumpeter SWANS, and has been set aside as a wildlife reserve. Mt Hkusam (el 1,671 m) looms above the east side of the valley near the former site of a KWAKWA̱KA̱'WAKW (Kwakiutl) village of the same name. Farm settlers began arriving in the valley in the 1890s, but LOGGING has been the main economic activity since BC MILLS TIMBER AND TRADING CO began cutting here in 1907. Once the site of one of the largest RAILWAY LOGGING operations on the coast, it later became part of MACMILLAN BLOEDEL's forestry operations. There is another Salmon River in the N OKANAGAN VALLEY that flows by WESTWOLD and FALKLAND and empties into SHUSWAP LK near SALMON ARM.

SALMON VALLEY, 20 km north of PRINCE GEORGE on the SALMON R and near the BC RAIL line, is a small AGRICULTURAL and LOGGING community that was settled in the 1910s and 1920s. A country music festival is held here each year. Most residents commute to Prince George. AS

SALMONID ENHANCEMENT PROGRAM (SEP) was launched in 1977 to rebuild SALMON stocks through the expanded use of enhancement technology. The program encompasses nearly 300 projects and produces coho, chinook, chum, pink and sockeye salmon, as well as small numbers of STEELHEAD and cutthroat TROUT. Projects include FISH HATCHERIES, fishways, spawning and rearing channels, habitat improvements, flow control works, lake fertilization and small classroom incubators, and range in size from spawning channels that release nearly 100 million juveniles annually to schools with classroom incubators that release fewer than 1,000. As many as 10,000 volunteers participate in the program annually.

SALTERY BAY is on the north side of JERVIS INLET near its mouth, 30 km south of POWELL RIVER on the SUNSHINE COAST. It is a terminus for

Canada's first underwater statue, a bronze mermaid sculpted by Simon Morris, Saltery Bay.
Doug Pemberton photo

the ferry that connects the Sunshine Coast Hwy (#101) south across Jervis Inlet to Earls Cove. The name refers to a fish saltery that formerly operated in the bay. The presence of shell MIDDENS indicates that it was used pre-contact by the SECHELT people as a campsite. Saltery Bay Provincial PARK (69 ha) is nearby.

SALTSPRING ISLAND, 193.5 km², pop 9,903 (1998), is the largest and most populous of the GULF ISLANDS between southern VANCOUVER ISLAND and the mainland. The name refers to a group of brine pools at the north end of the island. The FIRST NATIONS people called it Cuan ("each end"), a reference to the mountains located at opposite ends of the island, or Klaathem, a reference to the salt pools. The first group of permanent non-aboriginal settlers arrived in 1859, including several BLACK families from the US. Fruit growing, DAIRY FARMING, mixed farming (*see* AGRICULTURE) and LOGGING were the mainstays of the local economy for many years. One successful enterprise was the Salt Spring Island Creamery, which produced prize-winning butter from 1904 to 1957. Many farms continue to operate on a small scale, though TOURISM has become the island's main economic support. GANGES, the business and service centre, is the largest community in the Gulf Islands, and Mt Bruce (el 709 m) is the highest mountain. Once characterized by a sleepy, rural ambience, the island has experienced dramatic growth since the 1960s as many retirees, artists and other refugees from the urban rat race have discovered its charms. Ferry service began in 1930 when the 20-car *Cy Peck* began a regular run between the island and Swartz Bay. Seventy years later, ferries connect Saltspring to the mainland from Long Harbour and to Vancouver Island from both FULFORD HARBOUR and VESUVIUS BAY.
Reading: Charles Kahn, *Salt Spring: The Story of an Island,* 1998.

SALVATION ARMY is a CONSERVATIVE PROTESTANT religious denomination that originated in Great Britain in 1865 with the work of William Booth, a disaffected METHODIST preacher. It came to BC in 1887 when the first members arrived in VICTORIA. Congregations were established in NEW WESTMINSTER and NANAIMO in 1888 and in KAMLOOPS a year later. By the 1990s the church had corps in every major centre in BC. Initially mocked for its revivalist fervor and street-corner tub-thumping, the "Sally Ann" has become widely admired for its dedication to social work, which it has carried out through a variety of shelters for the homeless, FOOD BANKS, rescue missions, thrift shops, care homes and other services. In VANCOUVER the church opened a 30-bed maternity home in 1907 that evolved into Grace Hospital, the leading maternity centre in the province. When the church handed over control of the hospital to the province in 1994 it was renamed the BC Women's Hospital and Health Centre. In 1991 there were 10,120 members of the Salvation Army in BC.

SAM KEE CO was established in CHINATOWN in VANCOUVER by Chang Toy, an entrepreneur, in about 1888. The company engaged in a variety of commercial activities, including labour contracting, a coastal HERRING saltery and import-export. In 1926, after the city expropriated his land on Pender St, Chang Toy was left with a strip of property 1.8 m wide. Defiantly, he built the world's narrowest commercial building on the site. The Sam Kee Building, which was restored in the 1980s and is the only Canadian building in the *Guinness Book of World Records*, is a tourist attraction in Chinatown.

SAN JOSEF BAY was a pioneer settlement at the mouth of the San Josef R 55 km west of PORT HARDY on the northwest corner of VANCOUVER ISLAND. Many members of the Danish colony at CAPE SCOTT moved here and to nearby Sea Otter Cove in the early 1900s and Henry Ohlsen opened a store (*see* DANES). The

Sea stacks at San Josef Bay. Philip Stone photo

settlers sold farm produce to surrounding LOGGING camps and canneries, but survival was difficult and most people left by WWI. The radar base west of HOLBERG was also known as San Josef.　　　　　　　　　　　　　AS

SAN JUAN ISLAND is an American GULF ISLAND lying at the south end of the GEORGIA STRAIT just south of the US border, across HARO STRAIT from the SAANICH PENINSULA. It is the largest (140 km²) of a group of islands known collectively as the San Juan Islands. It is mainly rural, with the exception of 2 port communities, Friday Harbour and Roche Harbour. San Juan Island was once claimed by the British and was the scene of the infamous PIG WAR between 1859 and 1872, commemorated by a pair of historic sites at opposite ends of the island. It is popular in summer with boaters and other visitors. Ferries reach the island from Anacortes, WA, and from SIDNEY on VANCOUVER ISLAND.

SANCA, a resort community 35 km north of CRESTON, was a former steamship port of call on the east side of KOOTENAY LK. There are TOURISM facilities here for camping, boating and sport FISHING.　　　　　　　　　　　　　　　　AS

SAND DOLLAR is a member of the class Echinoidea in the phylum Echinodermata, a group of spiny-skinned animals that includes the SEA URCHIN. The eccentric sand dollar

Eccentric sand dollar. Rick Harbo photo

(*Dendraster excentricus*) is a disc-shaped marine animal about 10 cm across, inhabiting sand beaches along the Pacific shoreline. They are typically found in large aggregations or "beds." The external surface is covered with short fine spines, which give the animal a velvety texture and dark brown to black-purple coloration. Smooth, light-coloured sand dollar "tests" found on the beach are the skeletons of dead animals. When underwater they burrow into an erect position, exposing most of their surface to the tidal flow or wave action to trap particles of food between their spines. The spines and tube feet direct the food across the body into the mouth, which is located centrally on the lower surface. Like its close relative the sea urchin, each sand dollar is equipped with an Aristotle's lantern, a complex chewing apparatus located inside the mouth. When the TIDE retreats, sand dollars lie flat and

burrow into the sand, where they are often found congregated in large numbers.

SANDERS, Pat, curler. Her Raquet Club of VICTORIA rink, composed of Georgina Hawkes, Louise Herlinveaux and Deb Massullo, achieved international success with BC's second women's world CURLING championship in 1987. To win the right to represent Canada internationally, Sanders defeated former world champion Linda MOORE for the BC championship and Kathy Elwood of Manitoba to capture the national Scott Tournament of Hearts. Held in Chicago, the world championships proved to be a cakewalk for the Sanders rink. The next year, the rink returned to the Scott Tournament of Hearts as Team Canada but finished second.　　　　SW

SANDERSON, Robert, pioneer steamboat captain (b 17 June 1849, Olden, ON; d Sept 1924). He was a mechanical engineer with extensive experience in wharf building and bridge construction when he arrived in BC in 1885, having been employed to build a bridge across the COLUMBIA R at REVELSTOKE. Once that project was finished he got into steamboating on the ARROW LKS. He worked for the COLUMBIA & KOOTENAY STEAM NAVIGATION CO and after the CPR purchased the company in 1897 he became a pilot on the lake boats. At the same time he developed the property at HALCYON HOT SPRINGS during 1890–97. He also owned a lime kiln at Pingston Crk and operated a dredge between Upper and Lower Arrow Lks. He is buried in the Halcyon cemetery.

SANDHILL CRANE; *see* CRANE, SANDHILL.

SANDON is located in the mountains near SLOCAN LK about 10 km east of NEW DENVER. Named for John Sandon, a prospector, it rose to prominence in 1895 with the arrival of 2 rail lines, one

Rock-drilling contest, Sandon, 1904. UBC BC235

leading to KOOTENAY LK and the other to Slocan Lk. Sandon incorporated as a city in 1898 and at its peak boasted a population of 4,000, 2 dozen hotels, an opera house and a popular red light district. A severe fire in May 1900 wiped out most of the business section and the city never regained its initial glory, since reserves of high-grade galena ore were already diminishing (*see* MINING). A demand for ZINC during WWI revived activity in the Sandon camp, but production fell off after the war's end. It was virtually abandoned by 1941, when Japanese Canadians from the coast were interned here (*see* JAPANESE, RELOCATION OF). Most of the remaining buildings were destroyed in a flood in 1955. The province has undertaken to restore some of the buildings as a historic site.

SANDPIPER is the common name for a large, varied family of shorebirds, the Scolopacidae. They have long, slender bills, relatively long legs for wading and a hind toe. They prefer wet shorelines, either fresh or salt water, where they congregate in flocks and forage for food. Along with true sandpipers, the family includes yellowlegs, willets, tattlers, whimbrels, curlews, godwits, turnstones, surfbirds, knots, sanderlings, dunlins, ruffs, dowitchers, snipes and phalaropes. The vast majority are migrants, passing through BC from their northern breeding grounds to their winter ranges in the south. Most remark-

Yellowlegs sandpiper. Ken Bowen photo

able in this regard is the Baird's sandpiper (*Calidris bairdii*), which flies between the high Arctic and Tierra del Fuego in as little as 6 weeks. Only the following species breed in BC: red-necked phalarope (*Phalaropus lobatus*), Wilson's phalarope (*P. tricolor*), common snipe (*Gallinago gallinago*), short-billed dowitcher (*Limnodromus griseus*), least sandpiper (*Calidris minutilla*), long-billed curlew (*Numenius americanum*), spotted sandpiper (*Actitus macularia*), wandering tattler (*Heteroscelus incanus*), solitary sandpiper (*Tringa solitaria*) and the greater and lesser yellowlegs (*Tringa melanoleuca; T. flavipes*).

SANDSPIT, pop 568, is a small community on the northeast tip of Moresby Island at the entrance to Skidegate Inlet in the QUEEN CHAR-

LOTTE ISLANDS. LOGGING began in the area in 1940 and in 1943 the Royal Canadian Air Force built an airstrip that is now the main AIRPORT in the Islands, with scheduled flights to VANCOUVER and PRINCE RUPERT. The ferry to SKIDEGATE on Graham Island goes from nearby ALLIFORD BAY.

SANDWICK, 3 km northeast of COURTENAY on VANCOUVER ISLAND, on the north side of the Tsolum R, was an AGRICULTURAL community first settled in the 1880s. It was named by Eric Duncan, an early farmer and storekeeper, after his home parish in the Shetland Islands. A post office operated here from 1889 to 1948.   AS

SANNIES were the original passenger ferries operated between HORSESHOE BAY and BOWEN ISLAND. The Sannie Transportation Co was founded in 1921 by John H. Brown, who named it for an Australian racehorse. Tommy White took over the business in 1922 and ran regular ferries to Snug Cove and Hood Point on Bowen Island, as well as excursions to other locations around HOWE SOUND. The vessels were long and narrow with 2 rows of bus-like seating inside. The UNION STEAMSHIP CO bought the business in 1944 and maintained the Sannies until the 1950s, when car ferry service made them obsolete.
Reading: Peter D. Ommundsen, *Bowen Island Passenger Ferries: The Sannie Transportation Company 1921–1956*, 1997.

SARDINE, PACIFIC (*Sardinops sagax*), commonly called pilchard, is a long, narrow fish growing to a maximum length of 33 cm. It is dark metallic blue or green on the dorsal surface and silver on the sides and belly, with black spots in a wide variety of sizes and patterns. Its diet consists of small planktonic organisms.

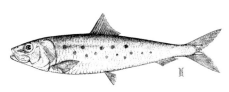

Pacific sardine. Daniel Ware photo/photo and drawing courtesy Fisheries & Oceans Canada

Sardines off the west coast of N America, from California to BC, are considered part of a single widespread stock known as the northern sardine stock. The population experiences large fluctuations in abundance due to changing ocean temperatures every 60 to 80 years. About 10% of the stock's total biomass (its northern edge) enters BC waters in summer to forage. The biomass

then moves south and spawns off central and southern California in spring.

The sardine dominated west coast fisheries from 1925 to 1946. An average of 40,000 tonnes a year were caught by purse seining and reduced to fish meal and oil. A small amount was canned. During this period 15 reduction plants were built along the west coast of VANCOUVER ISLAND and the fishery was the largest single species fishery in BC (*see also* FISHING, COMMERCIAL). The sardine population collapsed in 1947 due to a combination of massive overfishing and unfavourable environmental conditions. The collapse worked its way south until 1974 when the entire stock was estimated to consist of a single 10,000–tonne school of fish, down from an estimated historic high of 7 million tonnes. With the lack of fishing pressure and an improved ocean climate, stocks began rebuilding and sardines once again appeared off the west coast of Vancouver Island in the early 1990s. By 1999 scientists estimated the total biomass of the stock had increased to 1.6 million tonnes. Also in 1999 the first large-scale test fishery was undertaken in BC with an estimated catch of 1,300 tonnes, marketed as either frozen whole fish or canned.

SARDIS, 4 km south of CHILLIWACK in Chilliwack municipality, is an early FRASER VALLEY farming community. Allen C. Wells settled here in 1866 and built a large progressive farm, Eden Bank, site of BC's first creamery and cheese factory (1885) and first DAIRY co-operative. A Methodist RESIDENTIAL SCHOOL for aboriginal children, the Coqualeetza Institute, opened in the 1890s. A training centre for army engineers, now closed, was established in 1949. The name of the community was chosen from the Bible at random by Mrs A. Vedder; Sardis, one of the "seven churches of Asia," is today a ruin in western Turkey.   AS

SARITA, on the east side of BARKLEY SOUND at the mouth of the Sarita R, 45 km south of PORT ALBERNI, was a winter village of the Huu-ay-aht (Ohiaht) people, who are part of the NUU-CHAH-NULTH Nation. It was the site of an early VANCOUVER ISLAND Catholic mission (1877) and a pilchard reduction plant in the 1920s and 1930s (*see* SARDINE, PACIFIC). BLOEDEL, STEWART & WELCH had a large LOGGING camp here from 1947 to 1959.   AS

SASQUATCH is a "wild man" creature rarely sighted but thought to inhabit the woods of the Pacific Northwest. It is a cryptid, a hypothetical animal not recognized by science. Sasquatches have been reported from California—where they are known as Bigfoot—to Alaska. The mountains around HARRISON LK have been particularly productive of sightings. The sasquatch is described as a hairy, broad-shouldered creature, extremely reclusive, standing at least 2 m tall. Evidence for its existence includes references in explorers' journals and FIRST NATIONS legends, muddy photographs, unauthenticated footprints and many personal encounters. The term, an

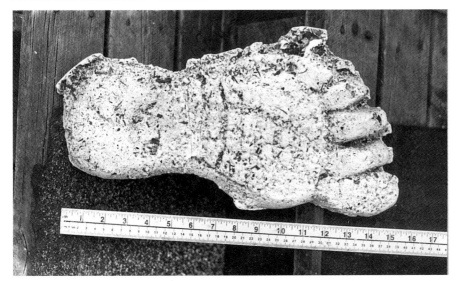

Plaster cast of what is thought to be a 38-cm Sasquatch footprint, Strathcona Provincial Park, 1988. From North America's Great Ape: The Sasquatch *by John A. Bindernagel*

anglicization of a SALISHAN FIRST NATIONS word, came into popular use in the 1920s.

Reading: John Bindernagel, *North America's Great Ape: the Sasquatch*, 1998.

SATURNA ISLAND, 31 km², is one of the GULF ISLANDS between southern VANCOUVER ISLAND and the mainland, south of MAYNE ISLAND and east of the PENDER ISLANDS. It is named for the Spanish explorer José Maria NARVAEZ's ship *Saturnina*. Settlement began in the 1870s and the permanent population now numbers about 300. The Saturna post office was originally named Pikes Landing after Warburton PIKE, an early settler. The island is quite mountainous, so AGRICULTURE has been limited. The only industry was a quarry operation during the 1960s. The island offers little tourist accommodation and is the most isolated of the larger Gulf Islands. The northwest corner of the island, formerly the site of a gravel quarry, was designated Winter Cove Provincial MARINE PARK (92 ha) in 1979. It looks across at the much smaller Samuel Island, once owned by the Toronto industrialist E.P. Taylor and used by him to raise race horses.

SAULTEAUX First Nation are Ojibway-speaking people who migrated west from Manitoba to the PEACE R district after 1870 and settled eventually at the east end of MOBERLY LK north of CHETWYND. Today the population of about 600 is a mix of DUNNE-ZA (Beaver), Cree and Saulteaux people.

SAVARY ISLAND is an arc-shaped island ringed by white sand beaches in GEORGIA STRAIT north of POWELL RIVER. It was first mapped by Capt George VANCOUVER in 1792 and possibly named for a French admiral. The original settler, Jack Green, who arrived in the 1880s, was murdered in 1893. After 1910 the island was developed by a VANCOUVER real estate syndicate that sold lots and built a hotel. The island has under-

Aerial view of Savary Island, looking south.
Photex Studio

gone LOGGING but otherwise there has been no industrial activity. The warm water and mild climate attracted steamboat excursionists, and well-to-do Vancouver families built summer homes. In the late 20th century the island has experienced a rapid increase in population, putting a strain on water and other resources. It is accessible by plane or via a short water-taxi crossing from LUND.

SAVONA, pop 541, is a small community 44 km west of KAMLOOPS, where the THOMPSON R leaves Kamloops Lk. When FUR TRADERS arrived, the site was being used seasonally by aboriginal people. It was originally known as Savona's Ferry after François Saveneux, who settled in 1858 and operated a cable ferry across the river. Ranching developed during the 1870s, an early hotel was built and the community enjoyed a brief boom while the CPR was being constructed from 1882 to 1885. The Monarch SAWMILL opened in 1906. Savona subsequently assumed the role of service centre to the surrounding AGRICULTURAL area and is the site of an AINSWORTH LUMBER CO specialty plywood mill.

SAWMILLING began at various locations on the coast around the middle of the 19th century. Small steam- or water-powered mills at ESQUIMALT, VICTORIA, SOOKE, NANAIMO, YALE, NEW WESTMINSTER and PORT DOUGLAS sold most of their lumber to local markets, though small amounts were exported. The first export mill, ANDERSON MILL, organized by Capt Edward STAMP, began operating at PORT ALBERNI in 1861. It ceased operating in 1865; in 1867 Stamp opened another mill, the HASTINGS MILL, at the site of what later became VANCOUVER. It and another mill at the present site of N VANCOUVER, Pioneer Sawmill, were the first successful large export mills, with most of their production going to various world markets. By 1900 large export mills had also opened in New Westminster, Victoria and CHEMAINUS. The first Interior sawmill began near BARKERVILLE in 1860 and small mills started at KAMLOOPS in the late 1860s. Numerous mills were established during CPR construction in the 1880s, and by the early 1900s several Interior mills were shipping lumber east to prairie markets.

In the early years of the 20th century, BC was invaded by an influx of US lumbermen, who had exhausted timber supplies in the northeastern states and were lured to BC by new leases offered by the provincial government. By the outbreak of WWI, several large new mills had opened in and around Vancouver, on VANCOUVER ISLAND and in the southeastern Interior. US lumber brokers quickly dominated the lumber export business. On the coast, the mills were designed to cut large-diameter logs, primarily CEDAR and FIR, for export abroad. In the Interior, smaller BUSH MILLS, with a few larger mills on some of the major LAKES and RIVERS, cut smaller-diameter species into lumber for railway construction and sale to prairie settlers. The BC lumber industry collapsed at the beginning of WWI because US brokers were reluctant to ship BC products past German naval vessels on the north Pacific. The province's chief forester, H.R. MACMILLAN, was sent on a round-the-world trip to drum up lumber sales. His success in selling orders to British Empire markets revived the

Water-powered sawmill near Barkerville, 1865.
BC Archives G-00804

industry and put control of its sales in local hands. During the 1920s the lumber industry expanded steadily, mostly on the coast, with Interior mills devoted primarily to local markets. Throughout WWII BC was the largest single supplier of lumber to the UK. Most production was transported across Canada by rail and then shipped across the Atlantic. After the war many of the large coastal mills became part of large integrated FOREST INDUSTRY operations, which also included LOGGING divisions, PULP AND PAPER mills and plywood plants. In the Interior a pulp industry was built around the use of sawmill wastes. Several hundred small Interior sawmills were replaced during the 1960s and 1970s by relatively few large mills concentrated in centres such as PRINCE GEORGE, Kamloops, WILLIAMS LAKE, MACKENZIE, REVELSTOKE and GOLDEN. Gradually the major market shifted from the UK to the US, to such an extent that American lumber producers retaliated with attempts to have tariffs imposed on Canadian lumber imports (see SOFT-WOOD LUMBER AGREEMENT). In the late 1990s considerable attention was paid to the production of higher-value FOREST PRODUCTS to replace export

The Chip-N-Saw, which performed several sawmilling operations at once. It was the most revolutionary advance in sawmill technology in the 20th century. USNR Cockums CanCar

shipments of low-value dimensional lumber and raw pulp. Numerous small companies and some new mills built by the large integrated companies have been established to produce higher grades of lumber, manufactured products and fine papers for export. However, the large forest companies had had control of about 85% of the provincial timber supply since the late 1980s,

Cutting specialty lumber, Youbou sawmill, 1994. Ian Lindsay/Vancouver Sun

and it was difficult for the value-added forest producers to obtain raw materials.

In 1997 BC sawmills produced 13.9 billion board ft of lumber, almost double the production of 20 years previously, and close to half of the Canadian total. That year, 7.5 billion board ft were sold in the US, 3.5 billion in Canada and 2 billion in Japan. Lumber sales were worth $7.9 billion. Sawmills in the province employed almost 23,000 people in 1997.   *Ken Drushka*

SAYWARD, village, pop 440, is a LOGGING community near the mouth of the SALMON R on JOHNSTONE STRAIT, 75 km north of CAMPBELL RIVER on VANCOUVER ISLAND. Originally called Salmon River, it took its present name in 1911 from William P. SAYWARD, a pioneer mill owner. Nearby KELSEY BAY was the southern terminus for the BC FERRIES run to PRINCE RUPERT (1966–79) until it was moved to PORT HARDY. The river is

known for its STEELHEAD fishing and the strait is a popular WHALE WATCHING destination.

SAYWARD, William Parsons, lumberman (b 9 Dec 1818, Thomaston, ME; d 1 Feb 1905, San Francisco). A carpenter by trade, he came west to the California goldfields in 1849, then moved north to VICTORIA in 1858 and went into business supplying Puget Sound lumber to local builders. By the 1860s he was the pre-eminent lumber dealer on VANCOUVER ISLAND. He owned SAWMILLS at SHAWNIGAN LK and in Victoria, had extensive timber limits on the island and invested in a variety of other businesses. He sold the Victoria mill in 1892; in 1896 he turned over what remained of his empire to his son and retired to California. The community of SAYWARD is named for him.

SCALLOP, a MOLLUSC of the bivalve class, is familiar for its beautiful fan-shaped shell with pronounced radial ribs. FIRST NATIONS people used these shells for jewellery, rattles and also to make paint. There are 16 or more species in BC waters but only 4 are considered common. Three of these are free-swimming for their entire lives; that is, they can propel themselves through the

Weathervane scallop. Duane Sept photo

water by clapping their shells and expelling water. These are the smooth pink (*Chlamys rubida*), the spiny pink (*C. hastata*) and the weathervane (*Patinopecten caurinus*) scallops. The pink (to 6 cm) and the spiny pink (to 8 cm) are much smaller than the weathervane, which grows to 28 cm and is said to be the largest scallop in the world, though the giant rock scallop (*Crassadoma gigantea*) may grow larger. The rock scallop has a swimming stage when very young, then cements itself to a hard object and stays put for life. It is very slow growing and may live up to 50 years. There are modest commercial DIVE and TRAWL fisheries for pink and spiny scallops, while rock scallops are protected for aboriginal and recreational harvest only (see FISHING, ABORIGINAL). The weathervane scallop, found in local abundance in the GULF ISLANDS, the QUEEN CHARLOTTE ISLANDS and several other regions, is not abundant enough for a significant commercial harvest.

Initial culture experiments with native species were unsuccessful; in the early 1980s Japanese scallops (*Mizuhopecten yessoensis*) were imported to the PACIFIC BIOLOGICAL STATION in NANAIMO. They were cultured and in 1988 their offspring were "outplanted" at several locations along the coast to test their potential for culturing. Island

Scallops Ltd of BOWSER pioneered this initiative. Cultured scallops are spawned and reared in enclosed hatchery tanks, and the young seed is then transferred to rearing facilities for the early part of the animals' lives. Later "seed" scallops are suspended in lantern nets or individually tethered to ropes suspended in the water column at several coastal locations. Small quantities of these cultured scallops are now being marketed in BC. *See also* AQUACULTURE, SHELLFISH.

SCE'EXMX ("people of the creeks") are an Interior Salish nation (*see* SALISHAN FIRST NATIONS) living in the dry uplands of the NICOLA R watershed between SPENCES BRIDGE and MERRITT. Their 4 main communities are Shackan, Nooaitch, Lower Nicola and Coldwater. Closely related to the NLAKA'PAMUX (Thompson), their neighbours to the west, they engage in ranching (*see* CATTLE INDUSTRY), the FOREST INDUSTRY and FISHING for the SALMON that has always been central to their way of life. Their administrative centre is the Nicola Valley Tribal Council in Merritt. The council also includes a fifth group, the Spaxomin First Nation, who live at Douglas Lake. Originally OKANAGAN people from the east, the Spaxomin arrived in the 18th century and have lived here ever since.

SCHNARR, August, coastal pioneer (b 29 Aug 1886, Centralia, WA; d 1981, Heriot Bay). Raised on a Washington homestead, he came to BC in 1909 to work in a LOGGING camp on CRACROFT ISLAND. By 1911 he and brothers Gus and Johnny SCHNARR lived year-round on the coast, logging in summer and trapping furs in winter in BUTE INLET. After serving in the US army during WWI, he returned to the coast, married Zaida Lansell and settled in SHOAL BAY on E THURLOW ISLAND.

August Schnarr and his neighbour, Mrs Williams, with cougar, Bute Inlet, 1940.
MCR 8493

In 1926 they installed a FLOATHOUSE in Bute Inlet. When Zaida died in 1932 he moved with his daughters to OWEN BAY on SONORA ISLAND but remained associated with Bute Inlet where he trapped, fished and logged for 50 years.

SCHNARR, Johnny, logger, fisher, rum-runner (b 16 Nov 1894, near Centralia, Washington; d date unavailable). Raised in poverty on a Washington state homestead, he came to BC when he was 15 years old, with his brothers Gus and August SCHNARR, to work in a LOGGING camp on CRACROFT ISLAND. He remained on the coast trapping and logging until WWI, when he served overseas with the US army. Following the war and the introduction of prohibition in the US, he became a RUM-RUNNER, hauling liquor illegally by boat across the border into Washington. When prohibition ended in 1933 he logged for a while on VANCOUVER ISLAND, then worked in commercial FISHING out of BAMFIELD. He retired in 1969.
Reading: Marion Parker and Robert Tyrrell, *Rumrunner: The Life and Times of Johnny Schnarr*, 1988.

SCHOFIELD, Wilf, botanist (b 19 July 1927, NS). He worked as a schoolteacher in Nova Scotia during the 1940s and 1950s while pursuing academic studies at Acadia Univ. After earning an MA from Stanford Univ in 1956 and a PhD from Duke Univ in 1960, he came to BC to teach in the botany department at UBC. During 34 years there he was recognized as a world authority on plant biology, particularly bryophytes. His many publications include *Some Common Mosses of British Columbia* (1969, now in second printing) and *Introduction to Bryology* (1985). He wrote the entry on bryophytes in the latest edition of the *Encyclopedia Britannica*. In 1990 he received an honorary degree from Acadia Univ. He retired from UBC in 1994 and became professor emeritus. *See also* MOSS; PLANTS, NATIVE. *Dianne Mackay*

SCHROEDER, Andreas Peter, writer (b 26 Nov 1946, Hoheneggelsen, Germany). Raised in an immigrant MENNONITE family, he nurtured an

Andreas Schroeder, writer, 1998.
Barry Peterson & Blaise Enright-Peterson

interest in experimental WRITING while studying at UBC and the Univ of Toronto. He founded and edited *Contemporary Literature in Translation* (1968–83) and has been a full-time writer since 1971. His work includes poetry, drama, translation, a non-fiction account of his stay in PRISON for possession of hashish, *Shaking it Rough* (1976), and the documentary novel *Dust-Ship Glory* (1986). Active in literary politics, he was the first BC chair of The Writers' Union of Canada (1976–77), and all writers in the country owe him a debt of gratitude for leading the campaign that resulted in 1986 in the creation of the Public Lending Right, which pays royalties to writers whose books are in circulation in LIBRARIES.

SCHUBERT, Catherine O'Hare, pioneer settler (b 23 Apr 1835, Rathfryland, Ireland; d 18 July 1918, Armstrong). She moved to America in 1850 with her family and lived in New York until her marriage in 1856 to Augustus Schubert, a German immigrant. The couple moved west to St Paul, MN, then in 1860 north to Fort Garry, where they ran an inn. Two years later they joined a party of OVERLANDERS trekking west to the goldfields (*see* GOLD RUSH, CARIBOO). Catherine, with her 3 young children, was the only woman with the party and she gave birth to a fourth child shortly after her arrival at KAMLOOPS. The couple settled at LILLOOET and began farming. When Augustus was absent prospecting for gold, she ran the farm and a local school. They moved to land near ARMSTRONG in 1883.

SCHWENGERS, Bernhard Peter "Bernie," athlete (b 26 May 1880, Surrey, England; d 6 Dec 1947). Based in VICTORIA for most of his life, he was a brilliant all-around athlete and among Canada's greatest TENNIS players. As well as dominating the provincial tennis scene during the early 20th century, he won the Pacific Northwest singles championship 5 times and was the Canadian Open singles champ twice (1911, 1912). He was the key component of the 1913–14 Davis Cup team that defeated Belgium and S Africa on its way to the European zone finals. In TRACK AND FIELD, he broke the BC record in 1900 by running the 100-yard dash in 10.2 secs. He also played for Victoria sports clubs that won BC championships in RUGBY and SOCCER, and his BASEBALL team was the best on the Pacific coast 1904–5. The St Louis Browns offered him a lucrative contract to play professional baseball but he remained an amateur. A member of the BC SPORTS HALL OF FAME (1966), he was also a standout in CRICKET, GOLF, the hammer throw, discus, polo, FIELD HOCKEY and BASKETBALL. *SW*

SCIENCE WORLD BC is a science and technology centre overlooking FALSE CREEK in downtown VANCOUVER. It offers educational exhibits to the general public. Originally a partnership of the Junior League of Greater Vancouver and the City of Vancouver, it began operations as the Arts, Science & Technology Centre in Jan 1982 in a downtown storefront on Granville St. In 1988

Science World BC, Vancouver.

it moved to its permanent location in the former Expo Centre (*see* EXPO 86) geodesic dome. A refurbished and expanded Science World BC opened on 6 May 1989. It includes 5 main galleries, 2 presentation stages and the ALCAN Omnimax Theatre, featuring one of the largest domed screens in the world. The centre, with 70 staff and more than 130 volunteers, has community extension programs that serve the entire province.

SCOBIE, Stephen, poet, teacher (b 31 Dec 1943, Carnoustie, Scotland). He immigrated to Canada in 1965 and completed a PhD in English at UBC 4 years later. After teaching for 12 years at the Univ of Alberta, he moved to the UNIV OF VICTORIA; he has taught there ever since and has been an active presence in the Canadian literary scene. His first books of poetry appeared in the 1970s. He has published more than a dozen in all and one of them, *McAlmon's Chinese Opera*, won a GOV GEN'S LITERARY AWARD in 1980. He has also written critical works on Canadian literature, on Bob Dylan and on cubism, and was a co-founder of Longspoon Press.

SCOTCH CREEK, pop 1,100, is an AGRICULTURAL and resort village 26 km north of SALMON ARM on the north shore of SHUSWAP LK. It is the commercial centre for north Shuswap communities along the SQUILAX–ANGLEMONT Road with many TOURISM services but still enough old barns for rural appeal. It was named for Scottish prospectors who panned GOLD here in the 1860s.   AS

SCOTT, Blayney, fishing equipment manufacturer (b 4 July 1924, Calgary; d 26 Apr 2000, Victoria). After serving in the merchant marine during WWII, he built a troller and fished the BC coast until 1952, when he founded Scott Plastics Ltd in VICTORIA. The company pioneered the use of plastics in the manufacture of fishing gear and by 1999 was turning out more than 750 products under the "Scotty" trademark. Although fishing, marine and outdoors products comprise the majority of sales, the company also produces custom plastic molded parts for a variety of industries. One of Blayney Scott's major contributions to sport FISHING was the development of the first downrigger trolling rig on the West Coast. The company also produces an egg "incubator" system that allows FISH eggs to develop to

The downrigger, a trolling device developed by Blayney Scott.

the swimming fry stage while protected in a plastic container, a device that is expected to become a valuable tool in ensuring healthy fish populations. *See also* FISHING, COMMERCIAL.

SCOTT, Charles Hepburn, artist (b 1886, Newmilns, Scotland; d 1964, Vancouver). After training at the Glasgow School of Art he immigrated to Canada in 1912 to take up the job of supervisor of art for the Calgary school system. Two years later he moved west to take the same job with the VANCOUVER School Board. During WWI he served with the army overseas, and returned to his job at the school board at war's end. In 1926 he became principal of the Vancouver School of Decorative and Applied Arts, later the Vancouver School of Art (*see* EMILY CARR INSTITUTE OF ART & DESIGN), where he stayed until his retirement in 1956. He was one of the driving forces behind the creation of the VANCOUVER ART GALLERY in 1931 and he also taught for many years at UBC. Though known primarily as a teacher and administrator, he was also a respected painter, chiefly of landscapes reminiscent of the Group of Seven. *See also* ART, VISUAL.

SCOTT, Jack, journalist (b 1916, Vancouver; d 22 Jan 1980, Saltspring Island). He began his NEWSPAPER career as a 15-year-old copy boy in the offices of the VANCOUVER *News-Herald*. He became a reporter and editor and in 1940 began writing his daily "Our Town" column. After a stint in the army during WWII he joined the VANCOUVER SUN and resumed his column. It was a popular feature of the paper for the next 12 years and propelled Scott to the front ranks of Canadian journalists. During the 1960s he was a foreign correspondent for the *Sun* and the Toronto *Star*. He then retired to SALTSPRING ISLAND, where he wrote a column for the VICTORIA *Daily Times* from 1970 to 1976 and contributed occasionally to other papers.

SCOTT PAPER LTD operates BC's only tissue paper mill in NEW WESTMINSTER. It was opened in 1922 by the Herb family as Westminster Paper Mills to produce fruit-wrapping tissue for OKANAGAN VALLEY orchardists. The original mill burned in 1929 and was immediately rebuilt. In 1955 Scott Paper of Philadelphia purchased 50% of the company shares. Beginning in 1957, the company expanded into tissue production in Quebec and purchased 3 mills, including the White Swan division of the E.B. Eddy Co in 1989. In 1984 Scott Paper obtained the first Tree Farm Licence in BC devoted to growing and harvesting cottonwood. In the mid-1990s its American parent was taken over by the Dallas company Kimberly Clark Corp and in 1995 the Canadian head office moved to Ontario. In 1997 Kruger Inc of Montreal purchased Scott Paper Ltd, returning ownership of the company to Canadian hands. *See also* FOREST INDUSTRY.

Ken Drushka

SCOW, Alfred John, jurist (b 10 Apr 1927, Alert Bay). His father, William Scow, was a prominent KWAKWAKA'WAKW chief and his mother, Alice Whonnock, was the daughter of chiefs. He began working in commercial FISHING when he was in his teens, while at the same time attending high school and then university. In 1961 he became the first aboriginal person in BC to graduate from law school (UBC) and the next year he became the first aboriginal called to the BC bar. After practising as a lawyer in VANCOUVER, he served as prosecutor for the City of NEW WESTMINSTER until his appointment as the Canadian member on the Amerindian Lands Commission in Guyana, S America. In 1971 he became the first legally trained aboriginal to be named a BC provincial court judge, a position he held until his retirement in 1994. He has received many honours, including the Aboriginal Achievement Award (1995) and an honorary doctor of laws degree from UBC (1997).

SCULPIN is a member of the Cottidae family of fish, with approximately 40 local species, including the sculpin, Irish lord and cabezon. Adult sculpin are bottom dwellers and live in boreal and temperate waters of the northern hemisphere. A sculpin has a large spiny head with eyes placed high on the skull. In some species, the uppermost preopercular spine has developed into a long horn-like structure. Many

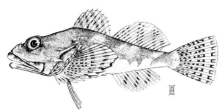

Staghorn sculpin (top); Phil Edgell photo. Great sculpin (bottom); drawing courtesy Fisheries & Oceans Canada

species have no scales at all, while others have a few scales that form thick plates. Pectoral fins on most sculpin are large and fan-like. The males of some species of sculpin are distinguished by an extremely well-developed anal papilla. The colours of the many different species vary markedly. In some species there are even dramatic colour differences between the sexes. Although it is generally a small fish, some sculpin, such as the great sculpin (*Myoxocephalus polyacanthocephalus*), can grow to more than 60 cm in length. Sculpins inhabit a wide range of environments, including tide pools, shallow shoreline waters and deep-ocean realms. A few species inhabit fresh water and are known as bullheads, miller's thumbs and muddlers.

SEA ANEMONE is a marine invertebrate belonging to the phylum Cnidaria (which also includes JELLIES and CORALS). Columnar in shape

Painted anemone. Rick Harbo photo

and flaccid in texture, anemones almost always attach themselves to hard surfaces along the rocky coastal shoreline in the intertidal zone and subtidally to great depths. They are often brightly coloured and when their tentacles drift gracefully in the current they resemble exotic flowers; in fact they are carnivorous predators. Depending on their size they feed on a variety of organisms from tiny plankton to small fish and crustaceans. Food is ingested through the mouth, located at the top of the stalk-like body and surrounded by tentacles. The tentacles direct food into the mouth, which is also the anus. Eggs and sperm are released through the mouth and fertilization occurs externally, though some species reproduce asexually, dividing in 2 or regenerating from parts of the parent. When the TIDE recedes, anemones retract into themselves to conserve moisture, taking on the appearance of rounded lumps of jelly. Of 65 species in Canada, only a few are found with any regularity by beachcombers in BC. Aggregating anemones (*Anthopleura elegantissima*) often occur in groups in tidal pools. These groups are not evidence of sociability; they are the result of budding, or asexual reproduction. Giant green anemones (*A. xanthogrammica*) are the common large species on the outer coast, growing up to 25 cm across. Their deep green colour is caused by algae growing in the cells; when they are removed from the light, the algae die and the anemones become quite pale. Other common species include the proliferating anemone (*Epiactis prolifera*), which is multicoloured and quite small; plumose anemones (*Metridium senile* and *M. giganteum*), which have clouds of thread-like tentacles; and the painted anemone (*Urticina crassicornis*), a thick-tentacled species occuring mainly along the low-tide line and subtidally.

SEA CUCUMBER is a soft-bodied, cylindrical marine creature, a relative of the SEA STAR, SAND DOLLAR and SEA URCHIN, inhabiting the rocky shore along the low TIDE line and to great depths beyond. Superficially resembling a large caterpillar, they attach themselves under rocks and in crevasses using rows of tube feet, or bury themselves in sandy substrate. The mouth is sur-

rounded by tentacles, quite bushy in some types, that collect food; the animal then draws the tentacles into the mouth one at a time to be licked clean. Some species of sea cucumber are known to expel their own internal organs in response to an extreme threat. The predator gets a meal; the cucumber generates a new set of organs. Another deterrent to predators is a poison known as *holothurin*, secreted in the skin. The largest species living in BC coastal waters is the giant California sea cucumber (*Parastichopus californicus*), which grows up to 41 cm in length. Red-brown to yellow and sometimes white in colour, it is covered in warty "spikes" and resembles a squishy pickle. California sea cucumbers have

California sea cucumber. Duane Sept photo

been harvested commercially on the coast since 1980. Destined mainly for the Chinese market, some 500–700 tonnes with a wholesale value of about $2.5 million are landed annually. The red sea cucumber (*Cucumaria miniata*), when it is upright and feeding, looks more like a plant than an animal with its mop-top of 10 bushy tentacles waving in the water. The stiff-footed, or white sea cucumber (*Eupentacta quinquesemita*), the creeping pedal sea cucumber (*Psolus chitonoides*) and the burrowing sea cucumber (*Leptosynapta clarki*) are other local species.

SEA ISLAND, 14.32 km², at the mouth of the north arm of the FRASER R, is one of the Fraser delta islands south of VANCOUVER that comprise RICHMOND. Settlement began in the 1860s when Hugh McRoberts began a farm, called Richmond View, which grew to become the largest in the British Empire (*see* AGRICULTURE). The northeast corner of the island, site of a hotel and cannery, was known as Eburne after Harry Eburne, a pioneer storekeeper. The island was predominantly agricultural until the VANCOUVER INTERNATIONAL AIRPORT opened in 1931. When it expanded in the 1960s, the airport swallowed up most of the remaining farms.

SEA KAYAKING is a very popular marine recreation on the Pacific coast. Since organized tours began in 1978 the number of kayakers has grown to more than 15,000 and the choice of tour companies to 90. Almost the entire COASTLINE is available to kayakers, but favourite tour destinations include the INSIDE PASSAGE between VANCOUVER ISLAND and the mainland (particularly ROBSON BIGHT in JOHNSTONE STRAIT), the larger sounds on the west coast of the Island, the GULF

Sea kayaking off the Saanich Peninsula, 1997.
Les Bazso/Vancouver Province

ISLANDS, DESOLATION SOUND and the QUEEN CHARLOTTE ISLANDS. In some places kayakers had become so numerous that the number of tours allowed is now limited. The Assoc of Canadian Sea Kayak Guides, which includes most of the major tour companies, was formed in the early 1990s to regulate the industry and set safety standards.

SEA LION is a variety of SEAL. Two species occur on the coast. The Steller (northern) sea lion (*Eumetopias jubatus*) breeds at 3 main rookeries: in HECATE STRAIT, at the south end of the QUEEN CHARLOTTE ISLANDS and at Scott Island off northwest VANCOUVER ISLAND. The male is enormous, weighing up to 1,100 kg—more than a bear—and the female is much smaller. Stellers are tawny brown in colour and feed mainly on fish. They were once hunted for blubber and skins, and for many years the killing of sea lions was encouraged because they were thought to be depleting commercial fish stocks. Hunting Stellers has been banned in Canada since 1970; the BC breeding population, about 8,000, appears to be stable but more northerly groups in the Bering Sea and Gulf of Alaska have suf-

fered a marked, unexplained population decline since the 1970s. In 1990 the US added the Steller to its list of threatened species. The VANCOUVER AQUARIUM is one of only 2 facilities in N America to keep Stellers.

California sea lions (*Zalophus californianus*) are smaller. They appear black when wet, and congregate in large groups on rocks and islands. They breed to the south but in the fall and winter migrate as far north as the northern tip of Vancouver Island to feed on HERRING, COD and SQUID. Individuals of this species are familiar as trained seals in zoos and circuses. Populations are growing on the BC coast.

SEA OTTER (*Enhydra lutris*) is the largest member of the weasel family. It inhabits coastal kelp beds from Alaska to California, spending almost all of its time in the water and feeding on SEA URCHINS, shellfish and SEA STARS. Its feeding patterns control the number of sea urchins, which in turn allows KELP to thrive. The sea otter has long moustache-like whiskers and often floats on its back. It is the only mammal, other than primates, that uses tools to feed: it grasps rocks and smashes shells open to gather food. Its thick fur coat is very dense, which helps keep the animal warm and buoyant; it is also black and lustrous, and at the end of the 18th century it became the most valuable fur on world markets, worth about 10 times as much as a BEAVER. The Russians called it "soft gold." As a result the sea otter was hunted almost to extinction (*see* FUR TRADE, MARITIME). By the mid-19th century, only remnant populations survived in Alaska, California and the QUEEN CHARLOTTE ISLANDS. In 1911 an international treaty banned the killing of sea otter, but the last BC population had died out by the 1920s. Elsewhere on the coast, populations recovered slowly until 1965–72, when 89 animals from Alaska were relocated successfully to Bunsby Island on the west coast of VANCOUVER ISLAND. By 1995 the population was estimated to be 1,500 animals and their range had expanded from Bunsby to BC's central coast. Sea otter have

been protected by law since 1970 and still are considered an ENDANGERED SPECIES.

SEA STAR, sometimes called starfish, is a bottom-dwelling marine animal of the phylum Echinodermata. Most species have 5 arms (rays) arranged symmetrically around a central disk, or body. Some have 6 arms or more, but begin life with 5. The sunflower star (*Pycnopodia helianthoides*), BC's largest, measuring up to 1 m across, has anywhere from 15 to 24 rays. The sea star is an echinoderm; that is, it has an internal skeleton, radial symmetry and a vascular system in which water pressure is used to move the tube feet. The feet, contained in a furrow running the

Sunflower star, the largest and fastest sea star in the Pacific Northwest. Duane Sept photo

length of the underside of each arm, are used for locomotion and also to attach to objects. The animal's mouth is located centrally on the underside of its body and the anus is on the top. The main sense organs are light-sensitive eyespots at the tip of each arm. A sea star's body often is covered with tiny spines. There are about 2,000 species worldwide, 68 of which occur in BC coastal waters. Of these, 3 dozen species are found between shore and a depth of 200 m, where they prey on a wide variety of sea life, including the BARNACLE, CLAM, CRAB, MUSSEL, SEA CUCUMBER, SEA URCHIN, SNAIL and much smaller food. The most likely species for beachcombers to encounter is the purple or ochre star (*Pisaster ochraceus*) with its stiff arms and arched central body, usually found firmly attached to rocks at low TIDE. Other common types include the giant pink star (*P. brevispinus*), the largest 5-armed star on the coast; the 6-rayed star (*Leptasterias hexactis*), the only small, 6-armed variety; the red, thin-armed blood star (*Henricia leviuscula*); and the bat star (*Patiria miniata*), most common on the west coast of VANCOUVER ISLAND and in the QUEEN CHARLOTTE ISLANDS. Most species reproduce by shedding eggs and sperm directly into the water, where fertilization takes place. Females of some species, including the 6-rayed star, retain the eggs for brooding. The sea star regenerates an arm to replace one that is lost, and if the lost arm includes a portion of the main body, it will grow into an entirely new animal.

SEA TO SKY HIGHWAY (Hwy 99) runs 37 km along the east side of HOWE SOUND between

Steller sea lions near Pachena Point, Vancouver Island. R. Wayne Campbell photo

Sea to Sky Hwy (Hwy 99) at Porteau Cove.
Keith Thirkell photo

HORSESHOE BAY and SQUAMISH. Originally called the Seaview Hwy, it was first carved out by labourers during the Depression as a rough track from BRITANNIA to Murrin Lk. It was 1955 before BC began constructing a road to link Squamish to the Lower Mainland. The highway, blasted out of the mountainside at a cost of $10 million, opened on 7 Aug 1958. With the development of ski facilities at WHISTLER, the paved highway was extended north in 1964. Rockfalls and flooding plague the spectacularly scenic highway; an alternative inland route between VANCOUVER and Whistler has been a topic of discussion for years. *See also* ROADS AND HWYS.

SEA URCHIN is a spherical marine invertebrate occuring along the rocky coastal shoreline at the tide line and subtidally. Urchins are related to the SEA STAR and SAND DOLLAR, all members of the phylum Echinodermata ("spiny-skinned").

Red sea urchins. Rick Harbo photo

The urchin's lumpish body is covered in spines, which are used for defence and movement. Between the spines are slender tube feet, which pass bits of food collected from the water to the animal's mouth, located in the middle of its underside and surrounded by small teeth. Like other echinoids, urchins are equipped with a complicated chewing apparatus of bone and muscle just inside the mouth, known as Aristotle's lantern after the Greek philosopher who first described it. Of many hundreds of species worldwide, 3 are found commonly along the BC coast. Green sea urchins (*Strongylocentrotus droebachiensis*) occur abundantly in tidal pools and KELP beds from Alaska to Puget Sound. Purple sea urchins (*S. purpuratus*) occur on rocky substrate along exposed shores, where they scrape out depressions in the stone. Giant red sea urchins (*S. franciscanus*), the largest of the local species (up to 17 cm across), actually range from pink to purple in colour and usually congregate in large beds. A commercial fishery (*see* FISHING, COMMERCIAL) for red urchins established in 1978 supplies roe to Japan as a delicacy, and there has been a fishery on the South Coast since 1987 to export live green urchins. Urchins are harvested using hand rakes and mesh bags.

SEABIRD ISLAND, pop 496, is in the FRASER R between AGASSIZ and HOPE. It is named for a PADDLEWHEEL STEAMBOAT that ran aground in 1858. It has been a STO:LO First Nations reserve since 1879 and became the site of the annual Earth Voice Festival, the successor to the Voices for the Wilderness Festival in the STEIN Valley.

SEABOARD LUMBER SALES was established in 1935 to act as an overseas sales agent for the Association of Timber Exporting Companies (Astexo), a consortium of the province's large SAWMILLING companies. From its inception, Seaboard engaged in fierce competition with BC's largest independent exporting company, H.R. MACMILLAN Export, and during its almost 60 years of existence became one of the world's largest lumber exporters. An associated shipping company carried Seaboard lumber around the world and an associated terminal in N VANCOUVER assembled lumber for shipment. In 1993 Seaboard was absorbed by its largest producing member company, INTERNATIONAL FOREST PRODUCTS. *See also* FOREST INDUSTRY. *Ken Drushka*

SEABUS is the high-speed passenger ferry crossing BURRARD INLET from N VANCOUVER to downtown VANCOUVER. It is a reincarnation of the ferry service that used to ply the inlet before the bridges were built. Operated as part of the transit system by the Greater Vancouver Transportation Authority, known since 1999 as TransLink, SeaBus vessels have a capacity of 400 passengers. They have catamaran-style hulls and can move in any direction to avoid traffic. When it opened in June 1977, SeaBus was the first marine transit system of its kind in the world.

SeaBus crossing Burrard Inlet. Coast Mt Bus Co

SEAFOOD PRODUCTS CO LTD, one of the oldest SALMON, HERRING and HALIBUT processing companies in BC, began in 1927 as a single operation in VANCOUVER, then expanded to include a cannery in PRINCE RUPERT and in 1966 another cannery in PORT HARDY. During peak times, the company employs more than 600 people. Port Hardy and Vancouver are the main plants; Prince Rupert acts as the gateway into Canada for fish from Alaska. Most of the products (canned, frozen, fresh and filets) are shipped to Japan. Since 1995 the company has been owned by Maple Leaf Foods Inc. Annual sales range from $35 to $55 million.

SEAGRASSES (phylum Anthophyta), flowering vascular plants, are not true grasses but are related to lilies. Eel-grass (*Zostera marina* and the dwarf *Zostera japonica*) is a pale green ribbon-like plant that grows in abundant meadows, rooted in sand-mud bottoms in protected or sheltered waters. It is a common surface for the deposit of HERRING spawn and provides shelter for a variety of organisms. Surf-grass, the most common species of which is *Phyllospadix scouleri*, is a brighter emerald green in color and is found on rocky shorelines exposed to wave action. Seagrasses provide food for a variety of waterfowl and a sheltered habitat for several marine species (*see also* SEAWEED; KELP). Sea asparagus, or pickleweed (*Salicornia virginica*), is a flowering plant found on the foreshore. It is harvested commercially just before summer flowering, and sold as a fresh salad item.

SEAL is a sleek, torpedo-shaped mammal common to inshore waters along the BC coast. Its limbs are modified into flippers and it moves awkwardly on land, but it is highly adapted to the marine environment. Seals feed on a wide variety of FISH, SQUID and crustaceans. The most

Pacific harbour seals, Trail Islands, Sunshine Coast. Duane Sept photo

common BC seal is the Pacific harbour seal (*Phoca vitulina*), widespread along the coast and often seen basking on rock ledges, mud flats and log booms in groups of varying size, up to several hundred individuals. When this seal is hauled out on land it often assumes an arched position, which gives it a banana-like shape. It is mottled white-black-brown in colour. Adult males weigh up to 140 kg and approach 2 m in length; females are smaller. Harbour seals give birth between June and Sept and pups take to the water within a few hours. These animals were hunted commercially and for bounty in BC during 1913–69, but since being protected in 1970 the population has grown rapidly. Another species found in BC is the northern elephant seal (*Mirounga angustirostris*), recognizable by its bulbous proboscis. It breeds in southern areas but sometimes migrates into BC waters in the spring. *See also* FUR SEAL.

SEALING; *see* FUR SEAL, NORTHERN.

SEAMOUNTS are underwater volcanic peaks rising steeply from the ocean floor. There are many thousands of these formations in the Pacific basin. The 2 largest along the BC coastline are named Bowie and Union. Bowie Seamount lies about 180 km west of the QUEEN CHARLOTTE ISLANDS, where it rises almost 3,000 m to within 37 m of the ocean surface. At one time some of the peak was visible above water. Union Seamount, 108 km west of ESTEVAN POINT on the west coast of VANCOUVER ISLAND, is 5 km across at the base and its summit lies 293 m below the surface.

SEARCH AND RESCUE (SAR) in BC, both land and sea, is carried out by a combination of Coast Guard and federal defence department personnel, along with a variety of volunteer agencies and individuals. The geography of the province—its treacherous COASTLINE, countless inland waterways and almost impenetrable mountain ranges—has made travel a risky business and the history of BC includes a litany of shipwrecks, missing overland travellers and, in more recent decades, air crashes (*see also* DISASTERS). Marine and air SAR in the province is the responsibility of the Department of National Defence through its Victoria Rescue Co-ordina-

tion Centre (RCC). Air force and Canadian Coast Guard (CCG) personnel are co-located at the facility, which is responsible for resolving marine and air cases in the BC and Yukon and along the coast to a distance of 960 km offshore. The Victoria RCC handles approximately 3,000 SAR cases per year. Marine resources at its disposal include the CCG's 9 shore-based lifeboats and rescue vessels, 2 air cushion vehicles (ACVs) based at VANCOUVER INTERNATIONAL AIRPORT and several large ships used for offshore patrol. In addition, on the volunteer side there are 47 units of the Coast Guard Auxiliary (CGA) located along the coast and 2 vessels operated by the Canadian Lifeboat Institution. Naval vessels based at ESQUIMALT, local POLICE and fire depart-

Searchers coordinate rescue of lost snowboarders, North Shore Mts, 1999.
Wayne Leidenfrost/Vancouver Province

ments and RCMP patrol vessels can also be called upon when required. On the air side, 442 Squadron at Canadian Forces Base (CFB) Comox operates four CH113 Labrador helicopters and six CC115 Buffalo fixed-wing aircraft, the CCG operates one S-61 and four MB 105 helicopters, and the Canadian Air Search and Rescue Association (CASARA) assists by providing volunteer aircraft all over the province. No SAR system would be complete without an effective communications network, and in addition to the military communications system the CCG maintains radio stations for SAR traffic at PRINCE RUPERT, TOFINO, COMOX, VANCOUVER and VICTORIA.

Land SAR in BC has traditionally been the responsibility of the police, which historically included the BC PROVINCIAL POLICE and later the RCMP. Coordination of land cases is now conducted by the Emergency Coordination Centre of the Provincial Emergency Program (PEP). This organization includes dedicated volunteer land SAR units, which are called out when

requested, and also helps to train, coordinate and finance the many land SAR societies that operate around the province for wilderness, mountain and AVALANCHE rescue, a well-known example being the North Shore Rescue Unit in Vancouver. Parks Canada also maintains jurisdiction for SAR within the boundaries of its national PARKS and reserves.

The first organized SAR facilities in the province were established on the west coast of VANCOUVER ISLAND in 1907, when the federal department of Marine and Fisheries placed lifeboats at CLO-OOSE, Pachena Bay, Banfield Creek (now BAMFIELD), UCLUELET and Clayoquot (Tofino). These stations were all located on a notorious stretch of coastline known as the "Graveyard of the Pacific" because of the many sailing ships and steamers that had come to grief there. The creation of these facilities, which included the upgrading of an existing telegraph trail into the famed West Coast Lifesaving Trail from PORT RENFREW to Bamfield (*see* WEST COAST TRAIL) and the construction of the LIGHTHOUSE at PACHENA POINT, was a direct result of lobbying efforts by the merchants of Victoria and American shipping interests after the loss of the VALENCIA in Jan 1906. Interestingly, the Bamfield Station received the first purpose-built motorized lifeboat (MLB) in N America with the arrival in 1908 of an 11-m self-righting, self-bailing vessel designed by the US Lifesaving Service. By the outbreak of WWII, services had diminished somewhat and only the Bamfield and Tofino lifeboat stations remained. In 1942 the sudden threat of a Japanese attack in the Aleutian Islands prompted the construction of air bases all over BC, including at Tofino and SHEARWATER, as well

Rescuers attempting to right an overturned lifeboat after an accident in which one person was killed, Vancouver Harbour, 1998.
Ian Smith/Vancouver Sun

as JERICHO BEACH and SEA ISLAND in Vancouver. By war's end the Royal Canadian Air Force's 442 Squadron, which included DC-3 and Canso flying boats, was designated a Rescue Flight and began to operate from the Sea Island facility, thus creating the first designated air SAR services in the province. Also located at these stations were small rescue vessels known as "crash boats" (*see also* FLYING BOAT STATIONS) which were also operated by the RCAF. In 1962 the Canadian Coast Guard was created under the auspices of the federal Ministry of Transport, and both the existing lifeboat stations and several of the crash boats were amalgamated into the CCG fleet. In 1963 a network of Volunteer Rescue Agents was established along the coast. In 1978 this network evolved into the all-volunteer Canadian Marine Rescue Auxiliary (later renamed the Coast Guard Auxiliary), which helped to expand the SAR network to the more remote locations of the coast through the provision of owner-operated vessels and local community-owned rescue craft. The CGA, which originated in BC, went on to become a national organization. Its establishment was followed by the creation of 2 other volunteer marine rescue organizations in BC: the BC Lifeboat Society (now defunct) and the Canadian Lifeboat Society, founded in 1981.   *Clayton Evans*

SEASPAN INTERNATIONAL LTD, Canada's largest marine transportation company, operates a fleet of 40 tugs, 230 barges, 2 self-propelled train ships and 2 self-loading, self-dumping, 18,000-tonne LOG BARGES. Seaspan belongs to the WASHINGTON MARINE GROUP association of companies owned by the Montana-based entrepreneur Dennis Washington and his 2 sons, Kyle and Kevin, who are involved mainly in coastal and deep-sea transportation, ship repair, SHIPBUILDING and component sales and services to the marine industry. The company originated in the mid-1920s with the creation of 2 TOWBOAT companies, VANCOUVER TUGBOAT CO and ISLAND TUG & BARGE, which merged in 1971 to form Seaspan.

SEAWEED (benthic marine algae) is a large photosynthetic organism typically attached to rocks in the intertidal or shallow subtidal zones to depths of 30–40 m. Approximately 700 species are found on the Pacific coast from Alaska to California, in 3 phyla commonly referred to as green, red and brown seaweeds (*see also* SEAGRASSES). Seaweeds are the largest types of algae. They contain chlorophyll and other pigments that utilize sunlight to manufacture nutrients by photosynthesis. They are generally simpler than land plants: they do not have roots or conducting systems because all parts of the plant obtain nutrients and dissolved gases for growth and reproduction directly from the surrounding water. They are anchored, or attached, by a holdfast. The stem-like portion (stipe) supports the leaf-like or blade-like structures, which are the main sites of photosynthesis and reproduction.

Brown seaweeds (phylum Phaeophyta), which include bull KELP and giant kelp, are the largest in BC. Rockweed, or bladderwrack (*Fucus evanescens*), is commonly found intertidally. Yellow-green to brown in colour, it is recognizable by flattened branchlets with swollen, warty ends containing the gametes. These ends pop when stepped on or pressed between fingers. Another common brown seaweed is Japanese weed (*Sargassum muticum*), a long, soft, matted weed whose many branches are lined with small bladder-like floats. This species

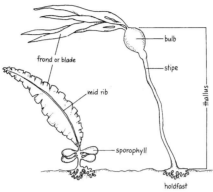

Sea palm(top); Duane Sept photo. Physical features of seaweed(bottom); Jennifer Harbo drawing

was introduced accidentally to the coast from Japan on the shells of OYSTER seed.

Green seaweeds (phylum *Chlorophyta*) form a variety of lettuce-like and ropey or hair-like growths, mats and cushions. Red seaweeds are actually variable in colour from red to brown, purple to black, and also vary in shape from encrusting patches to large, conspicuous single or branched blades. Coral seaweeds belong to this group. The common brick-red to purple Turkish towel (*Chondracanthus exasperatus*) is often washed up on the beach.

SEAWEED, Willie, Kwakwaka'wakw chief, artist (b circa 1873, Nugent Sound; d 1967, Blunden Harbour). A chief of the Nakwaktokw tribe of the KWAKWAKA'WAKW (Kwakiutl), he was a noted carver, singer and orator, one of the key figures who kept POTLATCH traditions alive on the coast during the years the potlatch was illegal. During his life he worked as a fisher and a professional artist, fulfilling commissions for masks, TOTEM POLES and other ceremonial items. He was a masterful innovator who contributed to the development and continuation of the southern Kwakwaka'wakw style of carving and painting. His name is an anglicization of the Kwakwala *Siwid*, meaning "Many Travel by Canoe to be at His Potlatches." *See also* ART, NORTHWEST COAST ABORIGINAL.

SECHART was the site of a WHALING station at the head of BARKLEY SOUND on the west coast of VANCOUVER ISLAND. The Pacific Whaling Co began whaling in 1905, using steam catcher boats to kill the whales offshore and tow them to the station. Soon WHALES began to disappear and whaling ceased in 1917. The buildings served as a PILCHARD packing plant during the 1930s, then were abandoned.

SECHELT, district municipality, pop 7,343, is set on a neck of land separating GEORGIA STRAIT from Sechelt Inlet on the SUNSHINE COAST north of VANCOUVER. It is home to the SECHELT (Shishalh) FIRST NATION, the first aboriginal group in Canada to adopt self-government, whose 725 members occupy the separate Sechelt Indian Government District. The OBLATE missionary Paul DURIEU established a mission here in 1868 and imposed his famous theocratic system on the Sechelt. The district was homesteaded by Thomas John Cook in 1893 but was developed after 1895 by Herbert Whitaker, hotel owner, storekeeper and postmaster. LOGGING and TOURISM fuelled the economy in the early days. Car ferry service linked the Sunshine Coast Hwy to the Lower Mainland in 1951, ending the community's dependence on coastal steamship service (*see also* ROADS AND HWYS). The district incorporated on

Aerial view of Sechelt. Rick Blacklaws photo

30 June 1986, and grew to become the main business centre for the Sunshine Coast. In Aug 1983 it began hosting the Festival of the Written Arts, one of BC's main literary festivals.

SECHELT, or Shishalh Nation, are Northern Coast Salish people (*see* SALISHAN FIRST NATIONS) who occupied the SUNSHINE COAST north of VAN-COUVER, from Gower Point near GIBSONS to SALTERY BAY in JERVIS INLET. At contact with Europeans they occupied some 80 scattered seasonal village sites. The main tribal groupings centred at 4 principal villages: *xenichen* (at the head of Jervis Inlet), *ts'unay* (at Deserted Bay in Jervis Inlet), *tewankw* (in SECHELT INLET) and *kalpalin* (in PENDER HARBOUR). Sechelt traditional territory was bounded on the north by the SLIAMMON and the south by the SQUAMISH Nation. The Sechelt gathered during the Nov–Mar period at one composite winter village on the shores of Pender Harbour, where they formed one of the largest pre-contact FIRST NATIONS communities on the coast. They estimate the original population at more than 20,000; other estimates range between 5,000 and 8,000. By the time of the first official census in 1881 the population had plunged to a mere 167, mostly as a result of introduced diseases, and the survivors had come together at *ch'atlich* near the present site of SECHELT, where there was an Oblate mission and school (*see* OBLATES OF MARY IMMACULATE). By the end of the 20th century the Sechelt Nation numbered about 1,000 members. The modern Sechelt have been involved in the operation of an offshore trawler, a local airline, a SALMON hatchery (*see also* FISH HATCHERIES), an office and cultural complex, a large gravel project, a hotel-marina complex and other business enterprises. In 1986 the Sechelt gained international notice when their long campaign to gain control of their own affairs culminated in the passage of Bill C-93, *The Sechelt Indian Band Self-Government Act*, making them the first First Nation in Canada to achieve self-government. *See also* ABORIGINAL RIGHTS.

SECHELT IMAGE, one of the masterworks of Northwest Coast aboriginal ART, is a prehistoric,

Sechelt Image. Roger Handling photo

50-cm-high granite statuette that children discovered under a tree root near SECHELT in 1921. An ambiguous image, the sculpture may be seen as depicting a mother holding a child or a man clasping a phallus. It was the centrepiece of an exhibition of aboriginal stone sculpture, Images Stone BC, that toured Canada in 1975. A replica is on display at the House of hewhiwus in Sechelt. *See also* PREHISTORY.

SECHELT INLET is a long, narrow FJORD trending south out of JERVIS INLET to form the back side of the Sechelt Peninsula. A short way into the inlet, tidal waters pour through SKOOKUM-CHUCK RAPIDS in Sechelt Narrows. Only a neck of land divides the top of the inlet from GEORGIA STRAIT; the community of SECHELT is situated here. The inlet was widely used by the SECHELT First Nation, who had an important village at Tuwanek. The area was logged extensively early in the century. It is popular with boaters and campers.

SECOND NARROWS BRIDGE; *see* IRONWORK-ERS MEMORIAL SECOND NARROWS CROSSING.

SECRET COVE, a former steamship landing 75 km northwest of VANCOUVER on the SUNSHINE COAST, is today a small but busy recreational community, site of several marinas, hotels and other TOURISM facilities.   AS

SECWEPEMC (Shuswap) are an Interior Salish people (*see* SALISHAN FIRST NATIONS) in central BC whose traditional territories stretch from the FRASER R east to the ROCKY MTS. Today there are about 7,500 Secwepemc occupying 17 communities, 4 of which are allied in the CARIBOO Tribal Council in WILLIAMS LAKE, the rest forming the Shuswap Nation Tribal Council at KAMLOOPS. Traditionally they lived together in small family groups, subsisting by FISHING, hunting and gathering PLANT food. SALMON caught in the rivers running through their territory was particularly important. During the winter they congregated in larger villages of semi-subterranean pit houses (*kekuli; see* ARCHITECTURE, ABORIGINAL). Each village had several chiefs who took leadership roles depending on the activity: hunting, warfare, spiritual observances and so on. FUR TRADERS arrived in Secwepemc territory in 1811, followed by miners and ranchers (*see* MINING; CATTLE INDUSTRY). The SMALLPOX epidemic in 1862 wiped out 13 villages and reduced the population by about 70%. Missionaries began arriving in the 1840s, and in 1867 the OBLATES OF MARY IMMACULATE established St Joseph's mission south of Williams Lake, where a RESIDENTIAL SCHOOL operated from 1891 to 1981. Another Oblate-run school was on the Kamloops RESERVE from 1890 to 1974. The arrival of outsiders resulted in a decline in local food resources and the Secwepemc increasingly entered the wage economy, taking jobs in ranching, LOGGING and rail construction. At the same time they began a political struggle to assert control over their territories, a struggle that continues to the present (*see* ABORIGINAL RIGHTS).

Secwepemc woman preparing animal hide, 1898. Harlan Smith/Secwepemc Museum

Secwepemc communities are at: ADAMS LAKE, Bonaparte (*see* BONAPARTE PLATEAU), CANIM LAKE, Canoe Creek, DOG CREEK, Esketemc (formerly Alkali Lake), High Bar, Kamloops, Little Shuswap, Neskonlith, North Thompson, Skeetchestn (formerly Deadman's Creek), SODA CREEK, SPALLUMCHEEN, Ts'kw'aylaxw (formerly PAVILION), Whispering Pines (formerly CLINTON) and Williams Lake. A group of Secwepemc, the Kinbasket, moved to INVERMERE in the 1850s and came to be grouped politically with the KTUNAXA. *See also* FIRST NATIONS OF BC.

SEGAL, Sydney, doctor (b 28 June 1920, Montreal; d 21 June 1997, Vancouver). After serving with the Canadian army in Europe during WWII, he took a medical degree at Queens Univ, than moved to VANCOUVER to specialize in pediatrics. During a distinguished career as pedi-

Sydney Segal, pediatrician, 1959. UBC 5.1/2771

atrician and professor at UBC, he pioneered several innovative treatment techniques and established himself as an international authority on pediatric medicine. He was associated especially with the care of infants of drug-dependent mothers. Later in his career he became interested in issues of medical ethics. He was a member of the Order of Canada and the ORDER OF BC. *See also* MEDICAL PROFESSION.

SEGHERS, Charles John, Roman Catholic bishop of Vancouver Island in 1873–78 and 1885–86 (b 26 Dec 1839, Ghent, Belgium; d 28 Nov 1886, Alaska). In 1863, after studies in Ghent and Louvain, he was ordained a priest; he then left almost immediately for VANCOUVER ISLAND. He served as parish priest in VICTORIA for 10 years and in 1873 succeeded Modeste DEMERS as bishop of the Island. He particularly strove to extend missionary activity among aboriginal people of the West Coast and Alaska. In 1878 he was transferred to Oregon but in 1885 returned to Vancouver Island. He was murdered by a mentally ill lay assistant during an excursion into central Alaska. *See also* ROMAN CATHOLIC CHURCH.

SEINING; *see* FISHING, COMMERCIAL.

SEKANI are a group of ATHABASCAN-speaking FIRST NATIONS people who inhabit the MOUNTAINS of northeast BC. Their territory is drained by the FINLAY and PARSNIP rivers and they are closely related culturally to their neighbours to the east, the DUNNE-ZA (Beaver) people. Sekani means "people of the rocks, or mountains." Pre-contact with Europeans, the Sekani were hunters and fishers, reliant mainly on big game animals. With the arrival of FUR TRADERS in the 1820s, they spent more time trapping smaller, fur-bearing animals. The Omineca GOLD RUSH attracted many Europeans to the area after 1861. The population of Sekani dropped dramatically and they began gathering at BEAR LK for the winter season. By 1916, when most miners had left, the Sekani population was down to 70. Disruptive change continued in the 1960s with the construction of the BENNETT DAM and the creation of WILLISTON RESERVOIR, which flooded some of their lands and forced a relocation. In 1999 the Sekani numbered 685 and lived mainly in 3 communities: MCLEOD LAKE, FORT WARE (formerly Finlay River) and Tsay Keh Dene (Ingenika).

SELKIRK MOUNTAINS are one of 4 parallel ranges (the others are the PURCELL, MONASHEE and CARIBOO Mts) in south-central BC that form the COLUMBIA MTS system. They are named for the Earl of Selkirk, a 19th-century British colonizer. The Selkirks extend 350 km from the Big Bend of the COLUMBIA R in the north to the US border, creating a natural divide between the ARROW LKS on the west and KOOTENAY LK to the east. Much of the range is protected in GLACIER and MT REVELSTOKE National Parks and in a series of provincial parks: Goat Range, KOKANEE GLACIER, West Arm and Valhalla. Around ROGERS PASS, which carries the CPR and the TRANS-CANADA HWY across the mountains, are several impressive peaks with spectacular relief, including Mt Sir Sandford, at 3,530 m the highest in the range. Named to honour Sir Sandford Fleming, chief engineer of the CPR, this mountain was first climbed on 24 June 1912 by 2 Americans, Howard Palmer and E.W.D. Holway, led by the SWISS GUIDES Rudolph

Selkirk Mts. Keith Thirkell photo

Aemmer and Edward Feuz Jr. The mineral-rich central and southern Selkirks were the scene of successive MINING booms from the late 1880s to the 1920s. Since that time, the FOREST INDUSTRY and more recently TOURISM have been major economic activities. *See also* KOOTENAY.

SELMA PARK was a coastal resort south of SECHELT, developed in 1914 by the ALL RED LINE. It was named for a British luxury yacht that came to BC via Cape Horn in 1911 and was used as a passenger vessel between VANCOUVER and POWELL RIVER. A favourite destination for steamer excursionists, Selma Park was sold to the UNION

Boat Day at Selma Park, c 1920.

STEAMSHIP CO in 1917. Cottages and a large dance hall were added. The Union company sold the property in 1944; it operated as Totem Lodge until it was destroyed by fire in 1952. Since 1990 Selma Park has been part of the Sechelt district.

SEMIAHMOO, 40 km southeast of VANCOUVER on Semiahmoo Bay near the US border, is a sub-

urb of SURREY and site of an early SAWMILL. The Semiahmoo people, who have a RESERVE here at the mouth of the Campbell R, are related to the FIRST NATIONS of southern VANCOUVER ISLAND. The Semiahmoo TRAIL, from the border to the FRASER R opposite NEW WESTMINSTER, was one of the FRASER VALLEY's first primitive roads. AS

SEMLIN, Charles Augustus, teacher, rancher, politician, premier 15 Aug 1898–27 Feb 1900 (b Oct 1836, Barrie, ON; d 3 Nov 1927, Ashcroft). A schoolteacher in his native Ontario, he was attracted to BC in 1862 by the GOLD RUSH but ended up purchasing a ranch in the CARIBOO. First elected to the legislature as a CONSERVATIVE from YALE in 1871, he was defeated in 1875 but re-elected in 1882; he held the seat for the next 18 years. By 1894 he was leader of the opposition, and he became PREMIER following the 1898 election when voters failed to return a strong majority. Lt Gov T.R. MCINNES asked former premier Robert BEAVEN to form a government, but Beaven was unable to do so and the job fell to Semlin. During his brief tenure, Semlin was unable to secure a firm grasp on power, having to mediate the constant bickering between Attorney General Joseph MARTIN and Finance

Minister Francis CARTER-COTTON. Finally Semlin dumped Martin, who then rallied the opposition against him. After limping along for several months, Semlin was defeated in the house. Instead of allowing him to call an election, McInnes called on Martin to form a government, which was immediately defeated. Semlin lost his seat in the ensuing election. He regained it briefly in a 1903 by-election, but rather than face another election later that year, he retired to his CACHE CREEK ranch.

SERL, Don, mountaineer (b 30 Aug 1947, Victoria). He grew up in KAMLOOPS and did not become interested in MOUNTAINEERING until he was in his mid-20s. He took to the sport with a passion and amassed an outstanding record of difficult climbs in the COAST MTS. His ascents include the south face of Mt Tiedemann (1976), the north face of Mt Hickson (1979), the traverse of all the peaks of the Waddington Range (1985), and the west face of Bute Mt (1986). He pioneered many climbs in the Chehalis Range east of VANCOUVER and 2 routes in the St Elias Mts of the Yukon. Educated as a chemist, he worked for many years for MOUNTAIN EQUIPMENT CO-OP. With Bruce Kay, he is the co-author of *West Coast Ice* (1993) and in 2000 he published *The Waddington Guide*, a major guide and history to the most important alpine region in the province. *Chic Scott*

SERVICE, Robert, writer (b 16 Jan 1874, Preston, England; d 11 Sept 1958, Lancieux, France). The "Bard of the Klondike" immigrated to Canada in 1896 and lived near DUNCAN on VANCOUVER ISLAND from 1896 to 1903, working as a farm hand and ranch hand. He began university studies in VICTORIA in 1903 to prepare for

Robert Service, the "Bard of the Klondike," 1958. Cowichan Valley Museum 994.02.9.2

a career in teaching but quit almost immediately and began working for the Canadian Bank of Commerce. The bank sent him to KAMLOOPS in July 1904 and, 4 months later, to its office in Whitehorse, YT. Service published his first collection of poems, *Songs of a Sourdough*, in 1907. He was transferred to Dawson in 1908 but retired from the bank the next year and left the

Klondike for good in 1912. He lived most of the rest of his life in France. His fame was instantaneous and international, and in all he published 13 volumes of poetry, 6 novels, 2 autobiographies and a book on physical fitness. When Germany occupied France during WWII he left, and during the rest of the war he divided his time between VANCOUVER and California.

SETON LAKE, 24.3 km², is in the COAST MTS west of LILLOOET. Lying 244 m above sea level, it is surrounded by mountains soaring to heights over 2,000 m. It was a link in the DOUGLAS TRAIL, the first overland route used by miners to reach the Interior goldfields (*see* GOLD RUSHES). As part of this route, BC's first railway was built in 1861, connecting the west end of the lake at SETON PORTAGE with neighbouring ANDERSON LK. Today the BC RAIL main line runs along its northern shore. A major hydro station is located at the community of SHALALTH; it generates HYDROELEC-TRICITY using water diverted from CARPENTER LK. Seton Lk was named by A.C. ANDERSON, a FUR TRADER, after a childhood friend.

SETON PORTAGE, pop 96, is a tiny community between SETON and ANDERSON lakes, 65 km east of LILLOOET in the COAST MTS. Originally named Seton Lake, it was the site of the first railway in BC, built in 1861 on wooden rails between the lakes as part of the old DOUGLAS TRAIL. The portage was created about 10,000 years ago when a LANDSLIDE divided the original lake into 2. It was formerly known for its apple orchards (*see also* TREE FRUITS) and for many years produced the annual Christmas gift box of McIntosh apples given by Canada to the Queen.

70 MILE HOUSE, pop 923, on Hwy 97 in the south CARIBOO, has declined in importance since the 1920s when it was an important supply centre for the surrounding ranches (*see* CATTLE INDUSTRY). In 1862 Charles Adrian established a historic roadhouse here on the CARIBOO WAGON ROAD; it burned down in 1956. The community was named for its distance from LILLOOET. *AS*

SEWELL INLET, 40 km south of SKIDEGATE on Moresby Island in the QUEEN CHARLOTTE ISLANDS, was home to a number of prospectors in the early 1900s. In 1969, Rayonier established a LOG-GING camp here that is now operated by Western Forest Products. A road from Sewell leads to the west coast of Moresby. *AS*

SEWELL'S MARINA, established in HORSE-SHOE BAY by Dan Sewell in 1931, is the largest boat rental marina of its kind in Canada. Operated by 3 generations of Sewells (Dan, his son Tom and his son Dan), the marina introduced the first motor-powered rowboats in BC, developed the use of HERRING strip as bait in SALMON sport FISHING, and pioneered the broadcasting of weather reports and fishing tips on the radio. In the 1980s Sewell's began bottom-fishing charters with the 19-m *Tarquin II*, a converted crash boat, and followed this initiative in the

1990s with the 54-m *Charlotte Explorer* in the QUEEN CHARLOTTE ISLANDS.

SEWID, James, Kwakwaka'wakw leader, fisher (b 31 Dec 1913, Alert Bay; d 18 May 1988, Campbell River). He grew up on VILLAGE ISLAND and in ALERT BAY. At age 12 he started FISHING on his grandfather's boat. By 1934 he was a skipper and in 1940 he bought his own fish boat. He lived on Village Island until 1945 when he

Chief James Sewid flashing his 1967 Centennial medal. Ross Kenward/Vancouver Province

moved with his family to Alert Bay where in 1950 he became the first elected chief of the 'Namgis (Nimpkish) FIRST NATION. He was heir to numerous high-ranking names and positions and was initiated into the Hamatsa Society. Active also in the ANGLICAN CHURCH, he became a lay reader in 1961. During the 1950s and 1960s he played a key role in encouraging the revival of the POTLATCH and traditional arts (*see* ART, NORTHWEST COAST ABORIGINAL) among the KWAKWAKA'WAKW (Kwakiutl) at Alert Bay. He filled many other leadership positions in his life, including in the NATIVE BROTHERHOOD OF BC, and in his attempts to improve village conditions. His autobiography, *Guests Never Leave Hungry* (ed James P. Spradley) was published in 1969.

SEYMOUR, Frederick, governor of BC 1864–69 (b 6 Sept 1820, Belfast, Ireland; d 10

Frederick Seymour, governor of BC 1864–69.

June 1869, Bella Coola). After serving 16 years as a colonial administrator in the West Indies, he arrived at NEW WESTMINSTER in 1864 to take up his position as governor of the mainland colony (*see* COLONIAL GOVERNMENT). The following year he returned to London to be married; in 1866, when VANCOUVER ISLAND joined the mainland, he returned as the new governor of the united colony. On the issue of whether to join Canada (*see* CONFEDERATION) he remained noncommittal. He died on his way back from talks with the HAIDA and TSIMSHIAN on the North Coast.

SEYMOUR, MOUNT (el 1,453 m) is the most easterly of the North Shore mountains opposite VANCOUVER, overlooking BURRARD INLET on the west side of INDIAN ARM. The first recorded ascent

Mt Seymour. *Jan Drozdzenski/Image Makers*

occurred in 1908. Skiing began in the 1930s and Mt Seymour Provincial Park (35.1 km²) was established in 1936. Road access, completed after WWII, made it one of the most popular destinations in the Lower Mainland for hikers, skiers and naturalists. The Seymour R empties into Burrard Inlet near the IRONWORKERS MEMORIAL SECOND NARROWS CROSSING. The Seymour Dam lies about 20 km from the mouth of the river, creating a reservoir supplying water to Greater Vancouver. The lower valley was opened to hikers and cyclists as the Seymour Demonstration Forest in 1987. All of these features are named for Frederick SEYMOUR, a colonial governor.

SEYMOUR ARM is an isolated hamlet at the head of the north arm of SHUSWAP LK. It flourished briefly as a supply centre during the Big Bend GOLD RUSH in the mid-1860s, then faded. For many years it was the home of artist Charles COLLINGS. The small community, named for Frederick SEYMOUR, governor of BC from 1864 to 1869, is linked to SICAMOUS by ferry.

SEYMOUR INLET is one of the series of long, narrow FJORDS that indent the mainland coast north of VANCOUVER. Located opposite the top end of VANCOUVER ISLAND, it extends 58 km inland from its entrance via NAKWAKTO RAPIDS.

The Seymour R empties into the head of the inlet. It was home to the Nakwaxda'xw band of the KWAKWAKA'WAKW (Kwakiutl) First Nations until they congregated farther south at the village of BLUNDEN HARBOUR in the mid-19th century. The inlet was located during an 1865 survey by the steam vessel *BEAVER*, and it was named for colonial governor Frederick SEYMOUR. The shores of the inlet have undergone extensive LOGGING.

SEYMOUR NARROWS, a narrowing of DISCOVERY PASSAGE, lies between VANCOUVER and QUADRA islands 11 km north of CAMPBELL RIVER, along the major navigation route through the INSIDE PASSAGE. Over the years RIPPLE ROCK was a dangerous obstacle in the channel until it was removed by explosives in 1958, but the Narrows

remains a treacherous stretch of water: currents sometimes exceed 10 knots. It is named for Sir G.F. Seymour, commander of the British navy in the Pacific from 1844 to 1848.

SHADBOLT, Doris Meisel, curator, museum director, writer (b 28 Nov 1919, Preston, ON). Her positions in the museum world have included the Art Gallery of Ontario in Toronto, the National Gallery of Canada in Ottawa, the Metropolitan Museum of Art in New York and 25 years (1950–75) as educator, curator and

Doris Shadbolt, curator and writer, 1998.
Barry Peterson & Blaise Enright-Peterson

associate director of the VANCOUVER ART GALLERY. Her 1967 exhibition *Arts of the Raven* was the first presentation of West Coast FIRST NATIONS art as art rather than ethnological artifact (*see also* ART, NORTHWEST COAST ABORIGINAL). Other major shows she instigated were *Sculpture of the Inuit: Masterworks of the Canadian Arctic* (1969), *New York 13* (1969), *Emily Carr: A Centennial Exhibition* (1971) and *Bill Reid: Retrospective* (1974), the first VAG exhibition to feature a single First Nations artist. She wrote major studies of REID (*Bill Reid*, 1986, winner of 2 BC BOOK PRIZES) and of CARR (*The Art of Emily Carr*, 1979; *Emily Carr*, 1990). She and her husband, the painter Jack SHADBOLT (1909–98), helped build the Shadbolt Centre for the Arts in BURNABY, where they lived together for many years and where Shadbolt still makes her home. In 1988 they co-founded the VANCOUVER INSTITUTE FOR THE VISUAL ARTS, renamed the Jack and Doris Shadbolt Foundation after his death. In 1974 Doris Shadbolt was awarded the Order of Canada and in 2000 she was one of the inaugural winners of the Gov Gen's Award for Voluntarism in the Visual Arts.

SHADBOLT, Jack Leonard, artist (b 4 Feb 1909, Shoeburyness, England; d 22 Nov 1998, Burnaby). He arrived in BC in 1912 with his family. After graduating from teachers' college in VICTORIA, he taught art to children in DUNCAN from 1929 to 1931 and in VANCOUVER from 1932 to 1937. As a young man he met Emily CARR, who strongly influenced his efforts to paint the BC landscape. At the same time he studied in New

Jack Shadbolt with one of his paintings, 1986.
Craig Hodge/Vancouver Sun

York, Paris and London. In 1938 he joined the Vancouver School of Art (*see* EMILY CARR INSTITUTE OF ART & DESIGN), where he taught until 1966. During WWII he served as an official war artist. After working in a social-realist style early in his career, he embraced abstraction following the war, combining modernism with aboriginal traditions and images from the natural world in a unique synthesis through which he sought to create an art expressive of BC's nature and culture. One of Canada's leading painters, he was honoured with many awards, including the Order of Canada (1972), the Molson Prize (1978), the ORDER OF BC (1990), the Gershon Iskowitz Award (1991) and several honorary degrees. He was an influential teacher and mentor for 2 generations of artists in BC and Canada. Dozens of exhibitions of his work have been shown around the world. He also wrote 3 books: *In Search of Form* (1968), *Mind's I* (1973) and *Act of Art* (1981). In 1988 he and his wife, the art critic and curator Doris SHADBOLT, founded the VANCOUVER INSTITUTE FOR THE VISUAL ARTS, which upon his death was renamed the Jack and Doris Shadbolt Foundation. He was also a co-founder of the Artists for Kids Trust, which raises money for art education in schools.

SHALALTH, pop 529, is the site of the BRIDGE R hydro complex, completed in stages from 1931 to 1960, near the west end of SETON LK about 60 km from LILLOOET. Water is diverted from Terzaghi Dam at the foot of CARPENTER LK through Mission Mt to the powerhouses. The name means "the lake" in the ST'AT'IMX (Lillooet) language.

SHANTYMEN'S CHRISTIAN ASSOCIATION (SCA) was a Toronto missionary organization formed in 1914 to evangelize the LOGGING camps in northern Ontario. Backed by the VANCOUVER businessman R.W. Sharpe, it spread to BC in 1919 when a missionary was brought in to minister to a logging camp north of Vancouver. The SCA opened an office in the city in 1920 and began organizing missionaries to work among loggers, fishers and miners in isolated camps and settlements along the coast. A VICTORIA committee was established in 1927 under the leadership of Sammy Whiting. The same year it became a sea-going mission with the purchase of its first boat. The SCA was still active in 1999, operating out of LADYSMITH and using its mission boat, *Coastal Messenger*, to continue serving remote communities.　　　　　　　*Dianne Mackay*

SHARK is a cartilaginous fish, having a skeleton composed of cartilage instead of bone. The most common local species is the spiny DOGFISH,

Six-gill shark. Neil McDaniel photo; drawing courtesy Fisheries & Oceans Canada

taken in commercial and other fisheries. The six-gill shark (*Hexanchus griseus*) grows to a maximum size of 4.7 m and 590 kg. Before WWII it was caught commercially (*see* FISHING, COMMERCIAL) with baited hook for the oil from its huge liver, but synthetic oils put an end to the fishery. In summer these sharks emerge from the depths and are seen by divers in relatively shallow water near HORNBY ISLAND and Tyler Rock off the west coast of VANCOUVER ISLAND. The largest BC shark, the basking shark (*Cetorhinus maximus*), grows to 13 m or more in length and in excess of 4 tonnes. It swims slowly at the surface, using its enormous mouth to strain plankton from the water. Basking sharks' numbers are few and their decline is under investigation. Records of great white sharks washing ashore indicate that they cruise coastal waters, but there have been no recorded shark attacks in BC.

SHAUGHNESSY, Thomas George, railway executive (b 6 Oct 1853, Milwaukee, WI; d 10 Dec 1923, Montreal). He was already an experienced railwayman when he came to Canada in 1882 to join the CPR as general purchasing agent in Montreal. He proved his worth to the company during the construction period of the 1880s, when his careful control of spending was credited with staving off bankruptcy. In 1899 he became president of the company, a position he held until his retirement in 1918. During his tenure the CPR enjoyed unprecedented prosperity and growth, and he was widely considered the most powerful business executive in Canada. In VANCOUVER the company owned a huge block of land granted to it by the provincial government in return for making the city its Pacific terminus. Part of this grant was developed in the years before WWI as an exclusive residential suburb named Shaughnessy Heights, which replaced the West End as the fashionable address for the city's affluent elite.

SHAWNIGAN LAKE, 5.37 km², is on the east side of VANCOUVER ISLAND between VICTORIA and DUNCAN. It is a popular summer recreation spot and home to a growing number of permanent residents, many of whom commute down the Island Hwy to Victoria. A small village at the northeast corner is a service centre for the homes and cottages that completely surround the lake. The ESQUIMALT & NANAIMO RWY passes along the east side; Prime Minister John A. Macdonald hammered the last spike at nearby Cliffside on 13 Aug 1886. LOGGING has taken place here since 1891, when the first SAWMILL was built; it incorporated as the Shawnigan Lake Lumber Co in 1894. Three different mills operated on the site until the last one burned in 1944. SHAWNIGAN LAKE SCHOOL has been offering private education since 1916. There are 2 provincial PARKS and the lake is crowded with watercraft on summer afternoons. The name may be an amalgam of the names of 2 early settlers.

SHAWNIGAN LAKE SCHOOL is a private boarding school at SHAWNIGAN LAKE on VANCOUVER ISLAND. It was established as a school for

boys in 1916 by Christopher W. Lonsdale, a 30-year-old English-born hotel manager, in a building formerly used as a girls' school. It began as an ANGLICAN preparatory school on the English model, designed to produce young gentlemen. The building burned in 1926; it was rebuilt and the school incorporated as a non-profit society and began accepting boys of all grades. Lonsdale remained head until 1952. The school is now limited to the secondary grades and accepts girls. *See also* EDUCATION, PRIVATE.

SHEARER DALE, 35 km north of DAWSON CREEK just south of the PEACE R near the Alberta border, is an AGRICULTURAL settlement named after the Shearer brothers and their families, who arrived in the district in 1927–28.　　AS

SHEARWATER is a medium-sized seabird related to, though smaller than, the ALBATROSS. It is coloured dark above and sometimes white below. Its flight pattern is distinctive, featuring a series of deep wingbeats followed by a long glide on stiffly held wings. Shearwaters are pelagic birds, migrating great distances each year from their breeding colonies in the southern hemisphere off S America and around Australia and New Zealand. For the most part they stay offshore and feed, often in huge numbers, on FISH, SQUID, crustaceans and offal from boats. Several species pay summer visits to the outer BC coast. The most abundant types seen here are the sooty shearwater (*Puffinus griseus*) and the pink-footed shearwater (*P. creatopus*). Other, less common, types are the flesh-footed (*P. carneipes*), Buller's (*P. bulleri*), short-tailed (*P. tenuirostris*) and black-vented (*P. opsithomelas*) shearwaters.

SHEARWATER, on the north side of Denny Island (132 km²), east of BELLA BELLA in the heart of the INSIDE PASSAGE, was the site of an air force base from 1938 to 1947. After WWII it was developed by Andy Widsten as a marine resort. There is a marina, hotel, boatyard and other facilities for mariners.

SHEEP CREEK, a tributary of the Salmo R, 40 km south of NELSON in the W KOOTENAY, was also the name of a MINING camp. About 750,000 oz of GOLD came from the area from 1899 to 1916 and from 1934 to 1942, much of it from the Yellowstone Mine. Lead and ZINC were mined on Iron Mt (1908–26) and at COMINCO's HB site (1953–78), and important tungsten deposits were mined from 1939 to 1958.　　AS

SHELLEY, a DAKELH (Carrier) village and LOGGING settlement 15 km northeast of PRINCE GEORGE on the FRASER R and the CNR, is named after a railway contractor, Sinclair McLean, an innovative logger who moved timber with horse-drawn carriages that ran on pole "rails." He also established a SAWMILL here in 1923; it operated under several different owners until the 1970s.　　AS

SHERE was a LOGGING settlement 50 km southeast of MCBRIDE on the FRASER R and the CNR. The

Etter & McDougall Lumber Co moved its SAWMILL here from CROYDON STATION in 1921 and operated it until the 1940s. AS

SHERIDAN LAKE, also known as Sheridan Corner, is about 35 km southeast of 100 MILE HOUSE in the scenic Interlakes district of the southern CARIBOO. Named after James Sheridan, who first took up land here, it is a commercial centre for surrounding ranchers, resort operators and visitors to the BONAPARTE PLATEAU area. AS

SHIELDS, Ken (b 7 Dec 1945, Beaverlodge, AB) and **Kathy (Williams)** Shields (b 18 Jan 1951, W Vancouver), basketball coaches. Dubbed "Mr and Mrs Basketball," they have won more university BASKETBALL championships than any other coaching couple in the history of the game. In high school Ken starred for the PRINCE RUPERT Rainmakers, leading them to the top of the BC high schools tournament in 1964. After playing university ball in Alberta, he came to UBC in 1969 to coach the UBC women's team to both the 1970 Canadian Intercollegiate Athletic Union title and the senior "A" amateur championships. He later coached the men's team at Laurentian Univ in Sudbury, ON, where Kathy was a member of the women's team that won 2 CIAU championships. The couple married and in 1976 Ken became coach of the men's team at the UNIV OF VICTORIA, where he posted an incredible record of 7 straight CIAU titles. He left UVic in 1989 and coached the Canadian national team from 1990 to 1995, bringing it to within a game of qualifying for the 1992 Olympics. During the late 1990s he coached professional basketball in Japan. He is a member of the Canadian Basketball Hall of Fame and was awarded the Order of Canada in 1999. Kathy Shields, a member of the national women's team in the 1970s, also turned to coaching after her playing days were over and as longtime coach of the UVic women's team won her eighth CIAU championship in 2000. She was also head coach of the national team from 1993 to 1995.

SHINER (*Cymatogaster aggregata*), the silvery saltwater fish caught by children from docks along

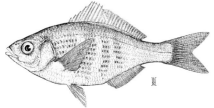

Shiner perch. Phil Edgell photo; drawing courtesy Fisheries & Oceans Canada

the coast, is a species of sea perch. Its flat sides are striped with black, except for the breeding male, which becomes black all over. Young are born alive and fully formed. The fish congregate in bays around pilings and beneath wharves. They grow to about 20 cm, just long enough to give young anglers their first thrill of the catch.

SHINGLE CREEK, an AGRICULTURAL and LOGGING district 14 km west of PENTICTON in the OKANAGAN, was named for the early shingle-cutting operations along its banks. Joe Brent established a large ranch in the area in the early 1900s, which his family maintained for many decades (*see* CATTLE INDUSTRY). AS

SHIPBUILDING on the West Coast began with the construction of the *NORTH WEST AMERICA*, a 40-ton sloop built by CHINESE workers under the direction of John MEARES at YUQUOT in 1788. The

One of the Mabel Brown class of wooden motor sailers, made in N Vancouver during WWI. VMM

ship was something of a novelty, however, and there was no new construction until the discovery of gold on the FRASER R in the 1850s created a demand for ships to transport miners and their supplies (*see* GOLD RUSH, FRASER R). The first ships built at FORT VICTORIA were steam-powered stern-wheelers (*see* PADDLEWHEEL STEAMBOATS), an adaptation of sidewheelers that were impractical for the stormy waters on the coast and in the narrow Fraser Canyon. They were usually about 38 m long, flat bottomed, with a blunt bow and a speed of about 19 km/h. When the hulls wore out, the boilers and engines were used in new vessels. In 1858 the sidewheeler *Caledonia* was launched in VICTORIA harbour, followed by the *Governor Douglas*. Victoria's monopoly on shipbuilding was broken in the 1860s when construction began in NEW WESTMINSTER and BURRARD INLET. The family of John MUIR operated a

SAWMILL at SOOKE in the 1860s and built their own ships to carry lumber to Hawaii and San Francisco. The Muirs' 115-ton schooner *Ann Taylor*, launched in 1861, was the largest ship built in BC to that time. In the 19th century, security in the British Empire depended on sea power. A base for the Royal Navy's Pacific fleet was established at Valparaiso, Chile, in 1837 and in 1862 that base moved north to ESQUIMALT. However, the facilities were used mainly to refit ships, not to build them. An opportunity to construct vessels arose late in the century when the CPR sought to extend its service across the north Pacific to Asia (*see* EMPRESS LINE). The decision to build 3 ships was contingent upon a contract to carry mail for the British post office, and with the mail contract in hand the CPR had the ships built not in Esquimalt but in Barrow-in-Furness, England. BC shipyards continued to rely on ship repair through the depression of the mid-1890s and the subsequent growth of trade and passenger traffic to the Orient. It was not until after 1900 that the first warships—2 minelayers—were constructed at Esquimalt. They were launched in 1903. In addition, the wooden *Princess Beatrice* and *Princess Royal* and the steel *PRINCESS MAQUINNA* were completed by the BC Marine Railways Co between 1904 and 1914 (*see* PRINCESS LINE). The hydrographic survey ship *Lillooet* was built for the Canadian government during the same period. On 1 Jan 1914 it was announced that Sir Alfred Yarrow had purchased the BC Marine Railways Co from Harry F. Bullen. The Scottish company was thus in a position to repair and build ships when WWI broke out.

The war brought significant changes to the pattern of ocean-going trade as resources were directed toward supplying Europe. In BC, export mills were closed for lack of ships to deliver lumber products. Shipbuilding was encouraged by government action. Wallace Shipyards (*see* BURRARD DRY DOCK) on the N VANCOUVER waterfront was perhaps the first to act, contracting to build

The Fort Boise, *one of the 10,000-ton Fort (North Sands) vessels built in BC during WWII.* Allied Shipbuilders

3 auxiliary wooden schooners. Other contracts were let to Wallace and the William Lyall Co, which had purchased Wallace's second yard. When Germany began unrestricted submarine warfare against Allied shipping, a sudden rise in losses resulted in contracts for the construction of 27 more vessels by assorted BC builders. A further 40 were ordered but never built because the war ended. By then, Wallace Shipyards had embarked on the construction of steel ships. Its *War Dog* was the first steel ocean-going freighter launched (1917) and completed in BC. Through 1916 and 1917, John Coughlan & Sons, steel fabricators, built a shipyard on FALSE CREEK and constructed 8 steel ships after American designs. Necessarily built of steel were submarines assembled under contract to the Electric Boat Co of New Jersey by the British Pacific Engineering & Construction Co at BARNET. At least 12 hulls were erected, dismantled and sent in boxes to VANCOUVER for delivery to Vladivostok. With the Bolshevik revolution in Russia, orders ended and the crated submarines were sold for scrap.

The end of WWI brought BC builders more contracts for steel ships, the new standard for ocean-going vessels. As facilities for the construction of wooden ships shut down, contracts for 14 steel ships were given to 4 different yards: Wallace, Coughlan, VICTORIA MACHINERY DEPOT and the dry dock at PRINCE RUPERT, initially owned by the GRAND TRUNK PACIFIC RWY and later incorporated as Prince Rupert Drydock & Shipyard Ltd. Wallace also built a liner for the Alaska TOURIST trade and the *PRINCESS LOUISE*, another of the CPR Princess boats and the largest steel vessel built in BC to that time (1921). With 135 deep-sea vessels (*see also* SHIPPING, DEEP-SEA) built during and immediately after WWI, the future looked bright for BC shipyards, but little construction occurred and again it was repairs that kept the yards busy. A floating dry dock was

built at Burrard Dry Dock in 1924, followed by a new dry dock in Esquimalt; at 358 m long, 38 m wide and 12 m deep this was the largest dry dock in the British Empire and the second-largest in the world after the Commonwealth dock in Boston. Neither dry dock was used as might have been expected, because repair work frequently went to Hong Kong, where prices were lower. When WWII began in 1939, British shipyards were taxed to the limit and orders for new construction came to Canada. The first contracts were for 64 corvettes and 14 minesweepers. North Vancouver Ship Repairs and Burrard Dry Dock received orders for several minesweepers and 2 contracts went to the yard at Prince Rupert, by that time part of the CNR. During 1940, 16 more corvettes and 50 more minesweepers were ordered. A number of passenger ships were also converted for wartime use. But all this activity building or converting armed ships was over-

shadowed by new construction of freighters. Following heavy losses of ships and materiel in early 1940, the British ministry of shipping explored the idea of shipyards in N America, building large numbers of vessels on a standard design known as the North Sands ship. American and Canadian yards responded and construction took place at 6 BC yards: Burrard Dry Dock, N Van Ship Repairs, Prince Rupert Drydock, Victoria Machinery Depot, West Coast Shipbuilders and Yarrows Ltd. In 1942 there were 23,700 men and 360 women at work in BC shipyards, and by the end of the war 253 steel ships had been delivered from BC out of a Canadian total of 402.

Following WWII it became evident that shipbuilding capacity far exceeded peacetime demand, forcing some consolidation of companies. At war's end Burrard Dry Dock and Yarrows merged to form Burrard-Yarrows. In 1951 the floating dry dock at Prince Rupert was sold and later towed to Seattle. Burrard Dry Dock had purchased N Van Ship Repairs during the war, then renamed it Pacific Dry Dock, then closed it after the war. There were also changes in construction methods. Every other shipbuilding nation had earlier adopted welding as the standard method of ship construction and with it the assembly of prefabricated sections. During the war Canada alone used rivetted construction, but this now changed and in 1952 Burrard Dry Dock produced its first all-welded ship, the destroyer escort HMCS *Skeena*. The *Skeena* was one of just 5 such escort vessels built on the West Coast. In 1965 the federal government introduced a new policy of "national competition for new construction" that eliminated the 15–20% differential allowed for West Coast yards. This policy effectively ended new construction for the foreseeable future; part of the fallout was the sale of Burrard Dry Dock to Cornat Industries in 1971. In 1981 a new dry dock was built in Japan and delivered to Versatile Pacific Shipyard, the suc-

Building a high-speed PacifiCat aluminum ferry for BC Ferry Corp. Rob Morris photo

Launch of the offshore supply vessel Lady Alexandra, *built by Allied Shipbuilders for service in the North Sea.*

cessor company to Burrard Dry Dock. This dock allowed repairs to be done to 3/4 of all the ships entering Vancouver harbour. New construction did return with contracts for icebreakers from the Canadian Coast Guard and the *Pierre Radisson* and the *Henry Larsen* were delivered by Versatile Pacific in 1978 and 1987 respectively. But with the loss of the contract to build the *Polar 8* icebreaker, Versatile ceased to be viable, and closed.

Formed in 1959, BC FERRY CORP has been an important customer for the provincial shipbuilding industry. From 1960 to 1999 more than 40 vessels were built for the Crown agency in BC shipyards. During the 1990s these included 2 "Spirit Class" giant ferries designed by Kvaerner Masa Polar Design, a full-service marine consulting company in Vancouver. The provincial government carried this idea forward through Catamaran Ferries International Inc, a wholly owned subsidiary of BC Ferry Corp. The first of 3 high-speed, aluminum catamaran ferries was launched in 1998 and began service on the HORSESHOE BAY–NANAIMO route in 1999. Each vessel was designed to carry 250 vehicles and 1,000 passengers at a service speed of 37 knots, but subsequent revelations about construction cost overruns and operational deficiencies sparked a major political controversy and the government announced that it was going to sell the vessels.
Reading: G.W. Taylor, *Shipyards of British Columbia*, 1986.

SHIPMAN, Nell, actress (b 1892, Victoria; d 1970). Born Helen Foster Barham, she moved to VANCOUVER as a child and joined a vaudeville touring company in her teens. After marrying Ernest Shipman, a theatrical promoter from eastern Canada, in 1911 she moved to California and entered the film industry as a writer, actress and producer. She starred in the silent film *God's Country and the Woman* in 1915 and became an overnight sensation. "The Girl from God's Country" starred in several more action–adventure movies, some of which were filmed in Canada. After separating from her husband in 1920, she turned to producing movies from her home in Idaho, then to writing novels and screenplays. Her popularity faded with the introduction of talkies and she lived the rest of her life in obscurity. Her auto-

biography, *The Silent Screen and My Talking Heart*, appeared after her death.

SHIPPING, DEEP-SEA, based in BC ports, started in 1916 when the provincial government passed the BC Shipping Act to encourage a provincial ship-owning industry free of controls from Ottawa or Britain. As a result of the legislation Canada West Coast Navigation Co was incorporated and 9 diesel auxiliary schooners were constructed, 7 by Wallace Shipyards (*see* Alfred WALLACE) and 2 by Cameron Genoa Mills of VICTORIA. The 5-masted vessels were slow sailers at 76 m long, 13.4 m wide and 2,250 tonnes dwt, often needing help from their Bolinder diesel engines as they delivered BC lumber as far away as Australia and New Zealand. After WWI

City of Victoria, *typical of WWI-era deep-sea ships built in BC.* Courtesy S.C. Heal

they could not compete with faster, larger, more reliable steamships; by 1923 the company had disposed of them all.

Toward the end of the war Wallace Shipyards (later BURRARD DRY DOCK) and the steel-erecting firm J. Coughlan & Sons had received orders to build a series of standard wartime-design steam freighters for the British government (*see* SHIPBUILDING), which led to further orders when the Canadian government set up the CANADIAN GOVERNMENT MERCHANT MARINE LTD to build additional steamships. Coughlan decided to build 3 freighters—*Margaret Coughlan, City of Vancouver* and *City of Victoria*—of 7,920 tonnes dwt, and used them to go into deep-sea tramping, mostly carrying export lumber to N China and Europe. The *Margaret Coughlan* was disposed of in 1925 and when the *City of Victoria* was wrecked on the Japanese coast in 1936, Coughlan decided to sell the third vessel and retire from the shipping business.

During the 1920s the Robert DOLLAR interests of San Francisco, owners of a large SAWMILL at DOLLARTON on BURRARD INLET, transferred some of their vessels to BC under the management of Melville Dollar, son of the founder. The 3 ships were owned by the Canadian-American

Navigation Co, a Canadian corporation, but were registered in Hong Kong. Melville Dollar declared bankrupcty in 1933; a new steamer he had ordered in Scotland was turned over to other owners and the residue of his business was reorganized as Anglo-Canadian Shipping Co. The new owners developed a successful business as brokers and managers and were later partners in Western Canada Steamships Ltd.

Between the wars the CPR registered at VANCOUVER 2 vessels of its trans-Pacific EMPRESS LINE, the *Empress of Russia* and the *Empress of Asia*. As much as anything this was a political strategy, but technically it made the CPR part of the small BC deep-sea shipping fraternity.

At about the same time the Canadian government decided to dispose of its WWI-built, 10,000-ton ships that had been managed by the Crown corporation Park Steamship Co Ltd. Seven new ship owners were registered at Vancouver for the purpose of purchasing, owning and managing a total of 44 ex-Park vessels. The new owners were Canadian Australasian Line (5 ships); Canadian Transport Co, controlled by H.R. MACMILLAN (6); Johnson Walton Steamships, a subsidiary of Danish East Asiatic Co (3); Kerr-Silver Lines (4); Seaboard Shipping Ltd (6); Vancouver Oriental Line, a subsidiary of Counties Ship Management of London, England (2); and Western Canada Steamships Ltd (21). All but 3 of the ships were of the Canadian Victory type; a 4,230-ton vessel owned by Johnson Walton and the 2 Vancouver Oriental ships were North Sands-type COAL burners. A combination of economic, political and union issues brought an end to the Canadian deep-sea merchant marine and by the 1950s all of these vessels had been disposed of and the companies involved had ceased business as ship owners. *S.C. Heal*
Reading: S.C. Heal, *Conceived in War, Born in Peace: Canada's Deep Sea Merchant Marine*, 1992; *A Great Fleet of Ships: The Canadian Forts and Parks*, 1999.

SHIPWORM is not a worm but a bivalve, a marine species of burrowing CLAM, also known as a teredo. It burrows into, eats and eventually destroys unprotected submerged wood. Floating in the water during the larval stage, it settles on the underwater portions of boomed logs, wharves, pilings and boat hulls and with its tiny shells begins to bore inward. As the clam grows, its shells (valves) develop rasping edges which precede the animal like voracious jaws, while the body grows backwards out of the shells like a worm. Wood residue is partially digested to provide food. The clam has 2 pallets at its tail end, which it uses to seal off the burrow. Eggs and sperm are shed into the water, where they produce new larvae. Two species are present in BC: the larger Pacific shipworm (*Bankia setacea*) and the common shipworm (*Teredo navalis*) introduced from the Atlantic. Moving rapidly through their host environments, shipworms can destroy a sizable wooden structure within a year. When removed from the water, however, they die.

SHIRLEY, an AGRICULTURAL and LOGGING settlement 40 km west of VICTORIA on southern VANCOUVER ISLAND, was originally a stop on the Telegraph Trail. It was named by Edwin Clark, the first postmaster, after his home in Hampshire, England. The LIGHTHOUSE at nearby Sheringham Point was automated in 1989. **AS**

SHOAL BAY, on E THURLOW ISLAND, looks onto Cordero Channel 200 km north of VANCOUVER. It began as a LOGGING centre in the 1880s, then was transformed by MINING developments in the 1890s that brought a transient population of several hundred expectant miners and camp followers. The ore petered out and most people moved away but the Thurlow Hotel, owned for many years by Peter and Rose MacDonald, was a coastal landmark until it burned in 1919. The post office here, open from 1896 to 1970, was named Thurlow. With its store, wharf and new hotel, Shoal Bay was still an important local provisioning depot in the late 20th century.

SHOREACRES is a settlement and CPR flag station 16 km northeast of CASTLEGAR, where the Slocan R joins the KOOTENAY R and creates a generous expanse of arable land. A number of DOUKHOBORS settled in the area and named their village Prekrasnoe, Russian for "beautiful." **AS**

SHORTREED, or Shortreed's Corners, 33 km southeast of NEW WESTMINSTER in LANGLEY municipality, was an early farming settlement on the old Yale Road (*see* AGRICULTURE). John and Robert Shortreed arrived here from Ontario in the late 1880s. When the GREAT NORTHERN RWY built its line through nearby ALDERGROVE in 1908, Shortreed faded away. **AS**

SHORTS, Thomas Dolman, steamboat captain (b 1837; d 10 Feb 1921, Hope). He arrived in the OKANAGAN VALLEY in 1883 from the US and was the first settler to pre-empt land on the northwest side of OKANAGAN LK at what is known today as FINTRY. Preferring boating to farming, he began offering passenger and freight service in his rowboat, the *Lucy Shorts*. In 1886 he

Capt Thomas Shorts (r), c 1910, after retiring to Hope. UBC BC837

launched the first steam-driven vessel on the lake, the 9.7-m screw-propelled *Mary Victoria Greenhow*, capable of carrying 5 passengers. Shorts built 3 more vessels and was involved with a syndicate planning to dig a channel linking the SHUSWAP with the Okanagan. That scheme died with the construction in 1892 of the SHUSWAP & OKANAGAN RWY and the following year, when the CPR launched the *Aberdeen*, the first of its Okanagan sternwheelers, Shorts withdrew from the steamboat business. A grateful public recognized his pioneering work by officially dubbing him "Admiral of the Okanagan." He departed the valley for the Klondike GOLD RUSH, then settled at HOPE, where he lived the rest of his life. *See also* PADDLEWHEEL STEAMBOATS.

SHREW (*Plethodon idahoensis*) is a member of the order Insectivore. Among the world's smallest mammals, it is mouselike in appearance, with short legs and hair and a long snout. Most shrews are dull brown, grey or black. Their sight is poor and they function by hearing, smell and touch. They prefer cool, moist environments where they subsist largely on INSECTS, worms, SNAILS and SLUGS. They must feed almost constantly to survive. A benefit to humans is that they eat insect pests that threaten forests. Females give birth to litters of 5–6 young and may produce more than 1 litter annually. Few shrews survive longer than 18 months. Of the 17 species in Canada, 10 occur in BC. The black-backed shrew (*Sorex arcticus*) inhabits WETLANDS in the northeast corner of the province. The Pacific water shrew (*S. bendirii*), the largest BC species at 13 g, is found only in the lower FRASER VALLEY, where it is considered endangered. The common shrew (*S. cinereus*) occurs widely on the mainland. At 4 g the pygmy shrew (*S. hoyi*) is the smallest mammal in N America. It is found in north and central BC but not along the coast. The dusky shrew (*S. monticolus*) is the most

widespread species, found in a variety of habitats. Trowbridge's shrew (*S. trowbridgii*) is restricted to the lower Fraser Valley. The tundra shrew (*S. tundrensis*) occurs only in the extreme northwest corner of the province. The vagrant shrew (*S. vagrans*) inhabits southern BC, including the GULF ISLANDS and VANCOUVER ISLAND. An aquatic species, the water shrew (*S. palustris*) is usually found near streams or around bogs and lakes. Merriam's shrew (*S. merriami*), only discovered in BC early in 1999, is restricted to the dry GRASSLANDS of the south Okanagan.

SHRIKE is a ROBIN-sized perching songbird, grey, black and white in colour with a black mask over the eyes and a hooked bill. In flight the bird shows white patches on black wings.

Northern shrike. R. Wayne Campbell photo

The shrike is a predator, feeding on INSECTS, mice, LIZARDS and other small birds. It sits watchfully on elevated perches, then dives on its prey, catches it, bludgeons it to death, then often hangs the corpse on a thorn bush, barbed wire fence or tree fork for dismembering at leisure. This practice may be part of a courtship display. The 2 species that occur in BC are similar in appearance. The northern shrike (*Lanius excubitor*) migrates into the southern part of the province during winter from its northern breeding grounds. The loggerhead shrike (*L. ludovicianus*) is smaller and much rarer, occasionally visiting the southern edge of the province.

SHRIMP is a marine crustacean with 10 jointed legs and a nearly cylindrical body. There are more than 85 species recorded in BC waters, occurring from the intertidal zone to depths exceeding 5,000 m. Different species prefer different habitats, from rocky bottom to mud and sand. Most species are bottom dwellers but some rise off the bottom at times. Seven shrimp species belonging to the family Pandalidae are important to commercial fisheries: prawn (*Pandalus platyceros*); smooth, or ocean pink (*P. jordani*); northern pink (*P. borealis eous*); flexed pink (*P. goniurus*); sidestripe (*P. dispar*); coonstripe, or dock (*P. danae*); and humpback, or king (*P. hypsinotus*).

Pandalids have a peculiar life history trait in common: in most cases, individuals are male when young and then become female as they grow older. Mature shrimp breed in late autumn or early winter. Developing eggs appear on the female's abdominal swimming legs and are carried there until hatching in spring. After leaving the female, shrimp larvae are thought to swim freely for several months before settling to the bottom as juveniles. Depending on the species, shrimp mature initially as males from 6 to 18 months, then spend 1–2 seasons as sexually active males. Afterwards, adult males turn into females. They usually survive another 1–1.5 years for a total lifespan of 3–4 years.

The prawn is the largest of the harvested shrimp species in BC, growing to 20 cm total

Prawn, the largest species of shrimp in BC.
Rick Harbo photo

length. The minimum commercial size is slightly less than 14 cm. Prawns live in rocky habitats and are typically caught using baited traps at 70–90 m depth. Other species commercially trapped are the coonstripe and humpback shrimp. The commercial prawn trap fishery began prior to 1914, but did not reach prominence until the mid-1970s. Since 1979 it has been monitored to ensure that an adequate number of females spawn. Licence limitation was implemented in 1990 and trap limitation (the maximum number of traps that could be fished by a vessel) in 1995. Between 1993 and 1999 the commercial fishing season was reduced from 276 days to 79 days annually, due to increased in-season monitoring. Although the season was shortened, landings achieved record high levels in 1996–98. The landed value of the fishery peaked in excess of $26 million in 1997, then declined to $18 million due to a downturn in the Japanese market, the major market for more than 90% of the product landed in the trap fishery. There have been several investigative aquaculture projects to assess the feasibility of prawn culture (*see* AQUACULTURE, SHELLFISH).

The shrimp trawl fishery, which is managed separately from prawns, began in the late 1800s with one-man beam trawlers in ENGLISH BAY. It developed in earnest in the 1960s with the development of trawl bottom gear (*see* FISHING, COMMERCIAL). In the mid-1990s a number of events led to a rapid increase in effort and landings in the shrimp trawl fishery. Changes in the management of GROUNDFISH fisheries and poor SALMON returns coincided with a peak abundance of offshore pink shrimp, new fishing areas and markets, and high shrimp prices. In the mid-1990s, both the catch effort and the catch doubled—largely due to salmon fishers redirecting

their efforts to shrimp. In response to the rapid increase in effort and catch, a new management strategy was developed for this fishery. "Total allowable catches" (TAC) are set in most areas and a seasonal opening, generally for the summer months, is set for the offshore pink shrimp fishery off the west coast of VANCOUVER ISLAND. The term TAC refers to a maximum amount of shrimp that is allowed to be taken from an area. Landings in the shrimp trawl fishery peaked at over 7,300 tonnes in 1996 and annual landed

Building the Shuswap & Okanagan Rwy, 1891.
Vernon Museum

values reached $13.7 million in 1995. Landings declined after 1996 to annual levels ranging from 2,000 to 3,000 tonnes worth $5–6 million because of low stock levels in offshore areas and more restrictive management practices.

SHRUM, Gordon Merritt, physicist (b 14 June 1896, Smithville, ON; d 20 June 1985, Vancouver). A veteran of WWI, he graduated with a PhD from the Univ of Toronto in 1923 and came to VANCOUVER to teach at UBC when it opened at its Point Grey campus. He was head of the physics dept from 1938 to 1961 and dean of graduate studies from 1956 to 1961. On his retirement from UBC the SOCIAL CREDIT government named him first chair of the newly created BC HYDRO AND POWER AUTHORITY. As well, in 1963 the government put him in charge of building SFU; he served as its first chancellor from its opening in 1965 until 1968. A true "builder" of Vancouver, Shrum also oversaw the construction of the Robson Square law courts development and the Canada Place convention centre.

SHUSHARTIE BAY opens onto Goletas Channel at the north end of VANCOUVER ISLAND, 30 km west of PORT HARDY. It was a busy little port at the turn of the 20th century, offering a convenient stopover for coastal steamers and fishers. The Skinner family ran a hotel and store from 1906 to WWII and a SALMON cannery operated briefly

during WWI. It was a regular port of call for UNION STEAMSHIP CO vessels into the 1940s. During the 1960s the area was logged extensively and is now largely deserted. The name is a corruption of a Kwakwala (*see* KWAKWA̱KA̱'WAKW) word meaning "place having cockles."

SHUSWAP & OKANAGAN RAILWAY was incorporated in 1886 to build a line from the CPR mainline at SICAMOUS to OKANAGAN LK near VERNON. Major promoters included J.A. MARA,

J.H. TURNER (later premier of BC), Moses Lumby, F.S. BARNARD (later lt gov of BC), Forbes VERNON and R.P. RITHET. The 82-km line, leased by the CPR, was completed in 1892. To link the railway with potential fruit-growing areas to the south, the CPR launched a steamer service connecting OKANAGAN LANDING 105 km down the lake to PENTICTON and other points along the way. The line is still in operation as the Okanagan Valley Rwy.

SHUSWAP First Nation; *see* SECWEPEMC.

SHUSWAP LAKE, 290 km², is a large, multi-armed lake forming the shape of a ragged *H* east of KAMLOOPS and north of the OKANAGAN VALLEY. It is bounded on the east and north by the MONASHEE MTS and Shuswap Highland and on the west by the arid Interior plateau. It drains west via Little Shuswap Lk and the THOMPSON R into the FRASER R. Archaeological evidence indicates the shores of the lake have been inhabited for at least 9,000 years. Early residents were attracted by the plentiful supply of SALMON, which return to the lake each year on their way to spawn. After hatching, the young fish remain for their first year in Shuswap Lk so it is an important nursery site in the life cycle of the BC salmon population.

SECWEPEMC (Shuswap) First Nations communities are clustered near the west end of the lake, having survived in spite of the devastation caused by epidemic diseases in the mid-19th century, when several villages were wiped out.

MINERS and FUR TRADERS passed through the area at that time, and permanent settlement began with the arrival of the CPR main line in the 1880s. The TRANS-CANADA HWY also follows the south shore. A small farming centre named Shuswap developed in the 1880s around a CPR station, hotel and store just west of CHASE, but had disappeared by 1960. AGRICULTURE and LOGGING have become the main economic activities, along with TOURISM, which has flourished since the 1960s. The lake is popular with summer visitors for its sunny climate, warm water and many

View of Shuswap Lk. *Tony Taccone/Image Makers*

sand beaches and provincial PARKS. SICAMOUS is home to a fleet of houseboats that cruise the lake each summer. Sicamous is also home port for the ferry service that connects to the top end of the lake at SEYMOUR ARM; there, in the 1860s, a GOLD RUSH town prospered briefly. SALMON ARM has become the largest urban centre.

SICAMOUS, district municipality, pop 2,827, nestles at the foot of the Eagle Valley on SHUSWAP

SS Sicamous *cruising on Okanagan Lk. Vernon Museum*

and Mara lakes at the junction of the TRANS-CANADA HWY and Hwy 97A. The name is commonly believed to have been taken from the aboriginal *Shick-a-mows*, meaning "in the middle." Permanent settlement began in the 1880s during construction of the CPR in 1885. From its beginning as an outlet for N OKANAGAN farm products, Sicamous attained stature as the northern terminus of the SHUSWAP & OKANAGAN RWY, completed in 1892. The FOREST INDUSTRY and to a lesser degree AGRICULTURE have been important to the local economy, though TOURISM has flourished thanks to the sandy beaches and mild climate of the Shuswap area. Incorporated in 1989, Sicamous bills itself as the "Houseboat Capital of Canada" and boasts the largest fleet of rental houseboats in the country.

SICAMOUS is a 61-m steamboat preserved as a historic site on the PENTICTON beachfront. It was launched in 1914 by the CPR to carry passengers and freight between Penticton and the railhead at OKANAGAN LANDING. The majestic steel-hulled sternwheeler plied the lake for a quarter of a century until improved rail and road communications forced its retirement in 1937. The CPR sold it to the City of Penticton in 1949 and it was moved to the beach location in 1951. Over the years it has been a restaurant, a museum and a community and social centre. During the 1990s it was restored as a heritage vessel. *See also* PADDLEWHEEL STEAMBOATS.

SICKER, MOUNT, (el 701 m), 80 km north of VICTORIA on VANCOUVER ISLAND, was the site of 3 COPPER mines and 2 separate townsites between 1897 and 1907. One mine, the Lenora, was developed by Henry CROFT, who built roads connecting the campsite to DUNCAN and to the ESQUIMALT & NANAIMO RWY. The booming settlement was hailed as the ROSSLAND of Vancouver Island. In 1900 the Lenora, Mt Sicker Rwy was built down the precipitous slopes to the coast at Osborne Bay, where Croft built a smelter in 1902 and the town of CROFTON sprang up. The second

mine, the Tyee, was developed by an English syndicate. It used an aerial tramway to transport its ore off the mountain and built its own smelter near LADYSMITH. A third mine, the Richard III, was short-lived. The high cost of production and declining ore deposits forced closure of the mines and abandonment of the settlements around 1907. *See also* MINING.

SIDEHILL GOUGER is a mythical animal of the arid Interior benchlands beside the FRASER and THOMPSON rivers. Because it grazes on the

The mythical sidehill gouger. Kim LaFave drawing

steep slopes, it is said to have legs shorter on one side of its body than the other, supposedly accounting for the pattern of horizontal tracks circling the hillsides. Of course, this means that the animal cannot turn around without falling down and so it travels in only one direction. Curiously, no specimen has ever been sighted.

SIDMOUTH, 35 km southeast of REVELSTOKE on the COLUMBIA R and the CPR's branch line to ARROWHEAD, was once the site of a small settlement and a large cattle ranch. The area is now underwater after the opening of the KEENLEYSIDE DAM. *AS*

SIDNEY, town, pop 10,701, looks east across HARO STRAIT near the top of the SAANICH PENINSULA, 26 km north of VICTORIA, 8 km south of the Swartz Bay ferry terminal, in the district  municipality of North Saanich. Salish-speaking people first occupied the area (*see* SALISHAN FIRST NATIONS). It is named for nearby SIDNEY ISLAND, which was named in 1859 by a naval survey after Lt Frederick William Sidney, a hydrographer in the British Admiralty. Settlement began in the 1880s and in 1891 the township was incorporated by the Brethour brothers, a family of pioneer settlers. Once the land was logged, the mild climate and fertile soil made farming, particularly

fruit and produce, a thriving activity (*see* AGRI-CULTURE). Sidney became the northern terminus of the VICTORIA & SIDNEY RWY in 1895 and several industries followed, including canning, SAWMILLING and brick-making from local clay deposits. A major fire in the 1920s wiped out much of the early industry. Sidney was incorporated as a village in 1952 and as a town in 1967. Located close to several marinas, it has since become a major BOATBUILDING centre, and the business and TOURIST centre of the Saanich Peninsula.

SIDNEY ISLAND, 8 km², lies 5 km from SIDNEY off the south coast of VANCOUVER ISLAND and at the north end of the SAANICH PENINSULA. Sidney Spit MARINE PARK (est 1961) occupies the north half of the island, which is surrounded by white sand beaches. Originally called Sallas by the Coast Salish (*see* SALISHAN FIRST NATIONS), it was given its present name by an early naval survey, after a British hydrographer. Between 1906 and 1915 it was the site of a factory that produced bricks used in many buildings in VANCOUVER and VICTORIA. The island supports abundant wildlife, including many bird species and about 1,000 fallow deer. A passenger ferry connects the island to Sidney.

SIERRA LEGAL DEFENCE FUND, founded in 1990, is a non-profit environmental organization providing free legal advice on environmental issues or concerns to anyone in Canada who otherwise does not have access to legal counsel. It is independent of the Sierra Club of Canada, local Sierra Club chapters and the Earth Justice Legal Defense Fund (based in the US). Funded by public donations, it has more than 25,000 supporters across Canada and maintains an office in VANCOUVER. *See also* ENVIRONMENTAL MOVEMENT. *Dianne Mackay*

SIHOTA, Munmohan Singh "Moe," politician (b 18 Feb 1955, Duncan). He is the first Indo-Canadian elected to the BC legislature. He was raised in Lake Cowichan, and after studying social work at UBC and working briefly as a social

worker he went to law school at Univ of Victoria and was called to the bar in 1982. While practising law in VICTORIA he launched his political career by winning election to ESQUIMALT municipal council in 1984. In 1986 he was elected for the NDP to the provincial legislature; when the NDP came to power in the 1991 election he

Moe Sihota, politician.

joined Premier Mike HARCOURT's cabinet as minister of labour. Later he served as environment minister (1993–95), minister of education (1996) and minister of the public service (1998). A controversial politician, he was forced to resign from cabinet twice because of inappropriate behaviour, but each time he returned once the controversy had passed. When Ujjal DOSANJH became NDP leader and premier in 2000, Sihota, who had supported a rival candidate for the leadership, was again dumped from the cabinet.

SIKHISM is a religion founded by Guru Nanak in the late 15th century in the northern Indian province of Punjab. Teachings were developed by 10 gurus and are contained in the main scriptures called the Guru Granth Sahib. Sikhism has about 20 million adherents worldwide. It is a monotheistic faith that places emphasis on individual moral responsibility and good conduct, and rejects the caste system. In response to persecution by the Muslim Moguls, Sikhs formed a militant brotherhood called the Khalsa, which adopted the 5 symbols of their faith: unshorn hair worn beneath a covering (Kesh), a small comb (Kanga), a bangle (Kara), a ceremonial dagger (Kirpan) and breeches (Kacha). Male Sikhs took the middle name Singh, meaning lion; females took the middle name Kaur, meaning princess.

The first Sikhs to immigrate to BC arrived between 1904 and 1908, and for many years Sikhs from the Punjab comprised the overwhelming majority of SOUTH ASIAN immigrants to BC. As British subjects they were allowed by law to vote, but the government of BC disen-

franchised them in 1907. That year BC Sikhs established the VANCOUVER Khalsa Diwan Society, the main community organization through which they have fought for equal rights in the province. Securing those rights has required constant vigilance. In 1908 the Canadian government enacted policies to stop immigration from India; in 1914, 376 Sikhs arriving aboard a chartered Japanese ship were refused permission to disembark in Vancouver (see KOMAGATA MARU); Sikhs underwent official and unofficial discrimination in employment, education and access to services; men were drafted for service in WWII although they were denied the right to vote (*see also* ASIATIC EXCLUSION LEAGUE).

In the years following the war, lobbying efforts and a changing political climate had their effect: in 1947 Sikhs were granted the franchise, and by 1967 discriminatory immigration policies had ended. By 1996 about 120,000 Sikhs, some 75% of BC's Indo-Canadian population, lived in BC, most of them in Vancouver and SURREY. Sikhs worship at temples, or gurdwaras, which are also social centres. The first gurdwara opened on W 2nd Avenue in Vancouver in 1908, followed by VICTORIA, NEW WESTMINSTER and ABBOTSFORD in 1912, and temples were established at most other Sikh communities throughout the province. Sikh temples became the subject of much media attention after factional violence exploded in 1996 over control of the Guru Nanak temple in Surrey. The majority faction accused a minority of directing temple funds to India to support the Sikh separatist movement, while the minority accused the temple of failing to acknowledge certain religious practices. After the intervention of police and community leaders the issue was resolved.

In 1986 Moe Sihota became the first Sikh elected to the provincial legislature, and in 2000 Ujjal Dosanjh became premier of BC, the first Sikh elected to the office in Canada.

SILK TRAINS were special freight trains that carried valuable shipments of raw Asian silk from VANCOUVER, where the silk arrived from the Orient by ship, to the east coast. Because the silk was perishable and insurance was paid by the day, speed was critical and the silk trains had priority over all other traffic on the line. From 1900 the CPR dominated the silk run, using its line of ocean steamers and its transcontinental rail connections to deliver silk to New York 13 days after it left Japan. In 1927 CNR also began running silk trains. "Silkers" were a familiar sight until the mid-1930s, when the last of them was replaced by the Panama Canal route and silk declined in importance.

SILLITOE, Acton Windeyer, Anglican bishop (b 1840, Sydney, Australia; d 9 June 1894, New Westminster). He was ordained in England in 1869, then served as chaplain to the British legation at Darmstadt, Germany, and to Princess Alice, daughter of Queen Victoria. In 1879 he married Violet Emily Pelly (b 13 Oct 1855, Essex, England; d 4 July 1934, Vancouver). The following year the couple arrived in NEW WESTMINSTER, where he had been appointed bishop of one of the province's 3 dioceses. The diocese of New Westminster covered southern BC and the bishop and his wife visited most of it by canoe, horse and buggy and steamer. He built schools, launched the *Churchman's Gazette* and raised money for mission churches. He was active in bringing a university to BC and was prominent in the church at the national level (*see also* ANGLICAN CHURCH). Violet's organizational abilities were formidable and she played a key role in support of her husband. After his death she moved to VANCOUVER, where she was active in the St James parish for many years. Several of her brothers and sisters also came to BC.   *Peggy Imredy*

SILVER is a precious metal used in PHOTO-GRAPHIC processes and in a variety of industrial and decorative products. It has been mined in BC since the 1890s, sometimes from galena ores but mainly as a by-product of treating lead–ZINC–COPPER and GOLD ores. In 1998 revenue from BC silver production totalled $119 million, making it the fourth most valuable metallic mineral after copper, gold and zinc.

Silver was first produced in BC at the Eureka Mine on the FRASER R near HOPE in 1871, but large-scale production began as part of the MINING boom in the KOOTENAY, following the discovery of the Silver King Mine near NELSON in 1886. The Bluebell Mine at RIONDEL on the northeast shore of KOOTENAY LK was one of the most famous deposits of silver–lead ore. This lode was worked originally from 1885 to 1896 by an American syndicate but it was COMINCO, with its capacity to smelt low-grade galena, that achieved the greatest success on the Bluebell claims from 1948 to 1971. Other highly productive mines were located on Toad Mt near Nelson, on Red Mt near ROSSLAND and at MOYIE, where the St Eugene Mine was in production from 1893 to 1929. Meanwhile, in the mountains above SLOCAN LK, lead ore high in silver content was easily accessible close to the surface; for a brief period in the mid-1890s Slocan was the most productive mining region in BC. Once this high-grade ore was depleted, production dropped off. Similarly the LARDEAU northeast of Upper ARROW LK enjoyed a boom from the 1890s, but it petered out by WWI. During the war the famous Dolly Varden Mine began production near ALICE ARM in the northeast corner of the province, but it was exhausted quickly and mining ceased in 1921. Silver mining in the mountains east of PENTICTON around BEAVERDELL began in 1901 and continued at different mines to 1991. Much more recently the open-pit Equity Mine near HOUSTON was one of the largest silver producers in the world from 1980 until it closed in 1994. As of 1999 silver was being produced in conjunction with other minerals at Myra Falls on VANCOUVER ISLAND, at Cominco's SULLIVAN MINE and at Eskay Creek north of STEWART. The Eskay Creek mine ranked as the fourth-largest silver producer in the world.

SILVER CREEK is a rich farming district on the

SALMON R, 14 km south of SALMON ARM. A wide variety of AGRICULTURAL goods are produced here: milk, cheese, fruit, hay, turf and Christmas trees. Horses, llamas and beef cattle are raised. There are also a number of TOURISM facilities. *See also* CATTLE INDUSTRY; DAIRY FARMING.   AS

SILVERDALE, 38 km east of NEW WESTMINSTER on the CPR and the north side of the FRASER R in the municipality of MISSION, was an early FRASER VALLEY farming and LOGGING settlement. Bill MINER committed the first train robbery in Canada here in 1904, escaping with about $7,000 in gold and cash.   AS

SILVERTON, village, pop 241, lies on the east side of SLOCAN LK in the heart of the SELKIRK MTS in southeastern BC. It was founded in 1892 by William Hunter and Fred Hume, who opened a store and formed the Slocan Trading and Navigation Co. The original name was Four Mile City because the site was 4 miles (6.4 km) south of NEW DENVER. The permanent name refers to a famous mine of the same name in Colorado. The population peaked at 400 in the late 1920s and the community incorporated on 6 May 1930. LOGGING subsequently became the main economic activity, and later TOURISM as well, thanks to the area's natural beauty.

SILVEY, Joseph "Portuguese Joe," a.k.a. Joe Silvia, storekeeper, fisher (b 1836, Piepika Island, Portugal; d 17 Jan 1902, Reid Island). Born Joseph Silvia Simmons, he arrived in BC in 1852 aboard a WHALING ship. He ran the first

Portuguese Joe Silvey, 1860s. CVA Port.P.656

grocery store in GASTOWN in the 1860s and married a FIRST NATIONS woman from MUSQUEAM, the first marriage between an aboriginal and a non-aboriginal in VANCOUVER. Their daughter Elizabeth was the first child born to a non-aboriginal in Vancouver. After his first wife died, Joe married a SECHELT (Shishalh) woman in 1872; he then moved to the SUNSHINE COAST, where he founded the community of EGMONT and fished for a living. His large family became established

at several different locations around GEORGIA STRAIT. Silva Bay on GABRIOLA ISLAND is named for them. *See also* PORTUGUESE.

SILVICULTURE is the art and science of growing and tending trees. In BC, where the FOREST INDUSTRY has relied heavily on clear-cut systems, silviculture may begin with the preparation of the soil for tree planting by scarification, slash burning or drainage. Seedlings are grown in nurseries from seeds obtained from wild trees or seed orchards. The young trees, usually 1–2 years old, are planted at predetermined densities. Tending of the new forest may include brushing, to prevent other species from inhibiting growth; spacing, to thin out overly dense young FORESTS; fertilizing, to accelerate growth rates; thinning—the selective cutting of young, merchantable

Shannon Lanaway, tree planter, at work on Meadow Mt, 1989. Bill Keay/Vancouver Sun

trees to enhance the growth and value of the remaining stand; and pruning, to remove branches and raise the value of timber obtained from the trees. In more advanced forest countries, silvicultural systems include the seed tree method, where the forest is clear-cut except for seed trees left standing to restock the cleared area naturally; the shelterwood method, in which the original forest is removed in a series of partial cuttings to allow for the regeneration of a new stand under the protection of the older stand; and selection methods, in which uneven-aged stands are maintained by removing individual trees or groups of trees at frequent intervals. Of the 1,896 km² logged in 1995–96 in BC, 1,641.3 km² were clear-cut and 254.8 km² were partially cut. The following silvicultural activity took place that year: site preparation 1,122.18 km²; planting 2,045.98 km²; brushing 658.71 km²; spacing 417.93 km²; fertilizing 65.47 km²; pruning 61.17 km²; 258.9 million trees were planted.

Silviculture has been practised in BC since the 1950s, intensively since about 1985. Practices once focussed on the replenishment of commercial timber stocks, but by the 1980s more attention was being paid to the maintenance of forest ecosystems and BIODIVERSITY. *See also* FORESTRY.   *Ken Drushka*

SIMILKAMEEN RIVER, 251 km, rises in the CASCADE MTS in MANNING PROVINCIAL PARK and flows north and east beside the HOPE-PRINCETON HWY before dipping south across the US border and ultimately flowing into the COLUMBIA R drainage basin. Well-stocked with TROUT, it is

Similkameen R. Robert Pankratz/Image Makers

one of the last major RIVERS in the southern Interior that remains largely pristine. During the 1860s prospectors scoured the river for GOLD (*see* MINING), and important gold and COPPER mines did operate later at HEDLEY and around PRINCETON. The Similkameen flows through the home territories of the Upper and Lower Similkameen bands of the OKANAGAN First Nations. Similkameen was also a station on the GREAT NORTHERN RWY's Vancouver, Victoria and Eastern line from 1907 until the 1940s. The station was located 12 km southeast of KEREMEOS.

SIMON FRASER UNIVERSITY (SFU), atop Burnaby Mt, 30 minutes east of downtown VANCOUVER in BURNABY, opened on 9 Sept 1965 just 2 years after W.A.C. BENNETT's SOCIAL CREDIT government decided to build it. It was created under the leadership of the physicist Gordon SHRUM, who became the first chancellor. The design competition was won by Vancouver architects Arthur ERICKSON and Geoff MASSEY for their daring combination of concrete block and open plazas. The university opened just in time for the student protest movement of the late 1960s, and many of its faculty were American New Leftists, so it was not surprising that the university, dubbed Radical U, was convulsed by occupations and demonstrations from the beginning. For much of the 1970s it operated under censure by the Canadian Assoc of Univ Teachers for alleged interference by the board of governors in acad-

Simon Fraser University, Burnaby. Courtesy SFU

The Academic Quadrangle at Simon Fraser University, Burnaby. James LaBounty/SFU

emic affairs. Political activity on campus was quieter during the 1980s, which were more conservative financially and intellectually. A satellite campus in a converted department store in downtown Vancouver opened on 5 May 1989, mainly to offer mid-career education opportunities. There are now about 22,500 students and 650 faculty. Presidents have been: Patrick MCTAGGART-COWAN (1964–68), Kenneth Strand (1968–74), Pauline JEWETT (the first woman president of a Canadian university, 1974–78), George Pedersen (1978–83), William Saywell (1983–94), John Stubbs (1994–97), Jack Blaney (1998–2000) and Michael Stevenson (appointed in 2000).

SIMONS INTERNATIONAL CORP, BC's largest engineering firm, was founded in Vancouver in 1944 as H.A. Simons by Howard Simons, son of an American engineer. The company expanded its initial involvement in the FOREST INDUSTRY to become active around the world in a wide variety of projects. The company had 1998 revenues of $313 million. In 1999 it was bought by Agra Inc of Oakville, ON.

SIMOOM SOUND, 75 km east of PORT HARDY between KINGCOME INLET and Fife Sound, was the site of a floating LOGGING camp in the early 1900s. The post office, in John Dunseith's general store, was moved to the west side of GILFORD ISLAND in 1936 and then to nearby Echo Bay in 1973 but retained its Simoom Sound name. Echo Bay is a tiny FISHING, LOGGING and TOURISM settlement, site of a school (1929), hotel (1933) and FOREST SERVICE station (1950–68).   *AS*

SIMPSON, Aemilius, hydrographer, fur trader (b 27 July 1792, Scotland; d 2 Sept 1831, Fort Simpson, Nass River). The son of a schoolmaster, he entered the Royal Navy as a young boy and served in the Napoleonic Wars. In 1826 his relative George SIMPSON, governor of the HBC, offered him a post as hydrographer and surveyor with the company. After travelling to Fort Vancouver on the COLUMBIA R he took command of a coastal vessel, the *CADBORO*, trading along the northwest coast. He also produced charts of the lower Columbia and the lower FRASER R. In 1830 Simpson selected the site for a new post near the mouth of the NASS R, and the following summer he helped to establish the post, which was later named after him. He then left on a trading cruise to the north; he fell ill during the journey and died soon after.

SIMPSON, George, HBC governor 1821–60 (b circa 1787, Lochbroom, Scotland; d 7 Sept 1860, Lachine, QC). From the time the HBC absorbed the NORTH WEST CO in 1821, he was the most powerful person in the Canadian FUR TRADE, serving as governor of the Northern and Columbia departments from 1821 to 1826, then overseas governor of the entire HBC domain to

George Simpson, Hudson's Bay Co governor.
Langley Centennial Museum

his death. He made 3 visits to BC. In 1824 he crossed the ROCKY MTS to investigate the management of trade in the Columbia department. He placed Dr John MCLOUGHLIN in charge of the district, based at the new headquarters at Fort Vancouver on the COLUMBIA R, and began a policy of aggressive competition to drive American traders out of the territory south of the river. He also imposed many cost-saving measures and ordered the construction of FORT LANGLEY on the lower FRASER R. In 1828 he returned, making his famous canoe descent of the Fraser and confirming to his disappointment that it was not a navigable waterway for canoe brigades. He also initiated the use of coastal trading vessels and the construction of a string of posts north along the coast. On his last visit, in 1841, he closed many of the coastal posts in favour of visiting steam vessels and made the decision to move HBC headquarters farther north, a decision that led to the establishment of FORT VICTORIA two years later.

SINCLAIR, James "Jimmy," politician (b 26 May 1908, Banff, Scotland; d 7 Feb 1984, W Vancouver). His parents brought him to VANCOUVER as a toddler. After graduating in engineering from UBC he won a Rhodes scholarship to study at Oxford Univ in England. He returned to BC in 1931 and taught school, became an organizer for the provincial LIBERAL PARTY and worked as an assistant to a government minister in VICTORIA. When WWII began he joined the RCAF and saw action in North Africa. Meanwhile he was elected to Parliament for the Liberals in 1940, for the Coast–Capilano riding. He proved to be an independent-minded MP and ran afoul of Prime Minister Mackenzie King,

but once Louis St Laurent became Liberal leader and prime minister in 1948, his career picked up speed. After a stint as assistant to the finance minister, Sinclair joined the cabinet in Oct 1952 as fisheries minister, a position he held until the Liberals were defeated in 1957. In 1955 he became the first Canadian minister to visit the Soviet Union. After losing his seat in the Conservative landslide of 1958 he pursued business interests until his retirement. One of his daughters, Margaret, married Prime Minister Pierre Trudeau in 1971 (*see* Margaret KEMPER).

SINCLAIR, William Brown "Bertrand," writer, fisher (b 9 Jan 1881, Edinburgh, Scotland; d 25 Oct 1972, Pender Harbour). After immigrating to Ontario with his mother in 1889, he ran away to Montana to become a COWBOY at age 14. He began writing western fiction in a new realistic vein in association with Bertha Bower,

Bertrand Sinclair aboard his boat, the Hoo Hoo.

who based the hero of her celebrated novel *Chip of the Flying U* on Sinclair. He married Bower; then he himself became one of the most popular writers of westerns. In 1905 he moved to BC with his second wife. He continued to write, setting most of his subsequent novels in the world of fishers and loggers on the Pacific coast, notably *The Inverted Pyramid* and *Poor Man's Rock*. In 1932 he gave up WRITING as an occupation to become a commercial SALMON troller, thereafter making only occasional contributions to the union newspaper, notably the ballad "Banks Trollers," which became the unofficial anthem of BC's commercial FISHING industry.

SINCLAIR MILLS, 70 km east of PRINCE GEORGE on the FRASER R and VIA Rail, was named after F.N. Sinclair, a railway construction engineer. Don McPhee took over an existing plant in 1925 and developed one of the region's most successful SAWMILLS, noted for the quality of its worker housing. It closed in the late 1960s; in 1999 about 35 people made their home there, relying on LOGGING, mixed farming and TOURISM for their livelihoods.   *AS*

SINGH, Mayo, mill owner (b 1888, Paldi, India; d 23 Feb 1955, Paldi, BC). He arrived in California from his native Punjab in 1906, then worked his way north to join his brother, who was already living in BC. After entering Canada illegally—immigration from India was severely restricted at the time—he found work in a series of SAWMILLS in the BC Interior. By 1912 he was

Mayo Singh, pioneer lumberman.

working at a mill near CHILLIWACK, and when it closed, he and a business partner took it over. In 1917 he went to the Cowichan Valley (*see* COWICHAN R) in search of timber and selected a site for a new mill that became the village of PALDI. From there he expanded his business interests on the island and became a wealthy industrialist and philanthropist.

SINIXT are a small group of Interior Salish people (*see* SALISHAN FIRST NATIONS) from the Slocan Valley, also known as the ARROW LKS band or First Nation. They were almost extinguished by disease in the 19th century and many lived south of the US border, so that when the last registered Canadian band member died the federal government declared them extinct in 1956. However, some Sinixt survived and re-emerged in 1989 to claim their status and their land in Canada. *See also* ABORIGINAL RIGHTS; FIRST NATIONS OF BC.

SIRDAR, pop 50, is a recreational community on Duck Lk 18 km north of CRESTON. It got its start in 1900 as a railway depot and maintenance facility for Kootenay Landing, the CPR's steamship terminal at the south end of nearby KOOTENAY LK. It was named after Lord Kitchener, who became "sirdar" or commander of the Egyptian Army in 1892.   *AS*

SISTERS OF ST ANN is a religious order founded in Montreal in 1850. In 1858, 4 members of the order arrived in VICTORIA to begin teaching and caring for the sick. Eventually the sisters established schools and hospitals across BC and in Alaska. In Victoria they founded several schools, St Joseph's Hospital (1876) and its school of nursing (1900). Their headquarters, St

Ann's Academy, built on Humboldt St in stages from 1871 to 1910, was acquired by the province in the 1970s, received designation as a national historic site, and has been rehabilitated as an office complex. St Ann's Chapel, built in 1858 and moved next to the Academy, is Victoria's oldest surviving religious building. St Ann's Schoolhouse was a 2-room log cabin opened by the Sisters in 1858. The oldest building in the city, it was later moved to a new location and made into a school museum.

SJOLSETH, Minn, artist (b 4 Nov 1919, Oksendahl, Norway; d 7 Nov 1995, Kamloops). After studying art in Oslo she immigrated to Canada in 1953. She continued her studies in Regina and Mexico and in 1956 settled in VAN-COUVER, where she ran 2 art galleries and painted professionally. She is known especially for her oil paintings on aboriginal themes. She moved to the KAMLOOPS area in 1980 with her husband Anthony Carter (1920–92), a photographer and writer, and she continued to paint and hold exhibitions across Canada and in Norway until her death in a motor accident. *See also* ART, VISUAL.

SKAGIT RIVER rises in MANNING PROVINCIAL PARK near Allison Pass and, after following the HOPE-PRINCETON HWY north and west, veers south through Skagit Valley Provincial PARK (279.48 km²) to Ross Lk, a reservoir straddling the US border. It was designated a BC HERITAGE RIVER in 1995. Aboriginal people have used the valley for at least 8,000 years. Their ancient trade route was incorporated in 1858 into the Whatcom TRAIL connecting Washington state to the DEWDNEY TRAIL. H.R. Whitworth pioneered ranching in the valley between 1905 and 1909 (*see* CATTLE INDUSTRY), and there was a brief GOLD RUSH to the STEAMBOAT MT area between 1909 and 1911. HYDROELECTRIC dams on the US side of the border created the Ross Reservoir and threatened to flood parts of the valley in BC, until protestors, led by logger Curley Chittenden, succeeded in halting the project in the 1970s. In 1984 BC HYDRO agreed to provide power to Seattle in return for not raising water levels on the BC side.

SKAHA LAKE, 20 km², is one of a chain of lakes occupying the floor of the OKANAGAN VALLEY; they are the remnants of the vast ancient Penticton glacial sea (*see* GLACIATION). Skaha Lk is a broadening of the Okanagan R, which drains OKANAGAN LK, and extends 20 km from PENTICTON to OKANAGAN FALLS. Originally called Dog Lk, a reference to a historical incident when hungry FUR TRADERS were forced to eat their dogs, it received its present name, the Okanagan word for "dog," in 1930. The surrounding area has become one of Canada's premier ROCK CLIMBING destinations.

SKALBANIA, Nelson, entrepreneur (b 1938, Wilkie, SK). Raised on Vancouver's east side and trained in California as an EARTHQUAKE engineer, he made millions of dollars in the 1970s in real estate deals and became a household name in Canada for his flamboyant lifestyle. He owned a number of professional sports franchises, including the NHL Atlanta Flames (which he moved to Calgary), the CFL Montreal Alouettes and the BASEBALL Vancouver Canadians. He even owned the BC LIONS, briefly, in 1996. It was Skalbania who signed Wayne Gretzky to his first HOCKEY contract. In the recession of the early 1980s his business empire collapsed and Skalbania, called by one business writer "the country's most heroic bankrupt," spent most of the next decade trying to pay back creditors.

SKEENA CELLULOSE INC is a FOREST PRODUCTS company with a large pulp mill (*see* PULP AND PAPER) based in PRINCE RUPERT. Built in 1951 by Columbia Cellulose, it was subsequently owned by Repap Enterprises of Montreal. It had to be rescued by the provincial government in 1997 when it faced bankruptcy. The province became majority owner of the pulp mill, which is Prince Rupert's largest employer, along with 3 SAWMILLS and LOGGING operations. *See also* FOREST INDUSTRY.

SKEENA RIVER, 621 km long, is the second-longest river entirely within BC after the FRASER R and is a major transportation corridor leading from the central Interior to the North Coast. It rises in the Gunanoot Mts just south of the SPATSIZI PLATEAU and flows south and west through the Skeena and COAST MTS to reach the Pacific at PRINCE RUPERT. Its drainage area is 54,431.95 km². Major tributaries include the BABINE, BULKLEY, Kispiox and ECSTALL rivers. The TSIMSHIAN call it K-Shian, "water of the clouds." In the past, rich SALMON and STEELHEAD runs supported a flourishing aboriginal culture for thousands of years. The coastal Tsimshian occupy the lower reaches of the river as high as KITSELAS CANYON, while their close relatives the GITKSAN occupy villages on the upper river. George VANCOUVER reached the mouth of the Skeena in July 1793, but outsiders did not penetrate the river in any number until the 1860s, when preparations were being made for construction of the COLLINS OVERLAND TELEGRAPH. It was at this time that the first PADDLEWHEEL STEAMBOATS appeared on the river. With the Omineca GOLD RUSH of 1870–72, the Skeena became a major supply route to the central Interior. SALMON canneries operated at the mouth of the river beginning in 1876; as many as 18 canneries worked in the area, attracting FIRST NATIONS people for seasonal employment. In 1891 regular steamboat service began to supply trading posts as far up as HAZELTON. The GRAND TRUNK PACIFIC RWY was built through the valley during 1907–1912, followed by the YELLOWHEAD Hwy during WWII, connecting the Skeena with the rest of Canada. Commercial salmon FISHING has continued to be economically important, along with LOGGING, which boomed after the war and is centred at Prince Rupert and TERRACE.

SKELLY, Robert Evans, schoolteacher, politician (b 14 Apr 1943, New Westminster). After graduating from UBC he became a schoolteacher, and won a seat in the provincial legislature for the NDP in 1972. He became leader of the provincial party in 1984 and seemed poised to do well in the 1986 election, when a stumbling kickoff to the campaign was captured on television and his ability as a campaigner proved no match for the charismatic new SOCIAL CREDIT PARTY leader Bill VANDER ZALM. The NDP finished well behind the Socreds and Skelly resigned as leader in 1987. He moved on to federal politics, serving as an MP from 1988 to 1993. After losing his seat he retired to PORT ALBERNI.

SKELTON, Robin, writer, teacher (b 12 Oct 1925, Easington, England; d 22 Aug 1997, Victoria). He taught at Manchester Univ before coming to BC in 1963 to join the English department at the UNIV OF VICTORIA, where he later helped establish the department of creative WRITING. He helped to start UVic's literary magazine, the *Malahat Review*, in 1965 and served as editor from 1971 to 1982. He and his wife Sylvia opened their home for regular literary and artistic salons. He published more than 100 books,

Beach at Skaha Lk. Jan Drozdzenski/Image Makers

Robin Skelton, writer.

including 30 volumes of poetry, short fiction, anthologies, memoirs, criticism, history and books on witchcraft. He was a practising witch and cut a striking figure in his cape, wild beard and assortment of exotic jewellery. In 1982–83 he was chair of the Writers' Union of Canada. He was also an accomplished collagist and a member of the LIMNERS, a VICTORIA visual ARTS group.

SKIDEGATE, pop 695, is on the south side of Graham Island, the largest of the QUEEN CHAR-LOTTE ISLANDS. It is named for the HAIDA chief who met the first FUR TRADERS here in 1787. In 1853 Haida from Skidegate began visiting VICTO-RIA annually to trade and socialize. Diseases they brought back contributed to the drastic decline of the Haida population on the islands. A METHODIST mission was established in 1883 and the village became one of the communities where surviving Haida congregated. LOGGING became the main economic activity. The terminal for the ferry to PRINCE RUPERT and to MORES-BY ISLAND is at nearby Skidegate Landing. The

House fronts at Skidegate, 1890s. BC Archives B-03660

Haida Gwaii Museum has one of the world's largest collections of ARGILLITE carvings. It is also the home of *LOOTAS*, the 15-m dugout CANOE designed and built for EXPO 86 under the supervision of the renowned Haida carver Bill REID.

SKIING is the major outdoor winter recreational activity in BC, involving hundreds of thousands of local enthusiasts along with visitors

Skiing in the Central Interior. Keith Thirkell photo

from around the world (*see* TOURISM). The province's mountainous terrain provides a wide variety of areas with ideal conditions for downhill, cross-country and heli-skiing. BC downhill facilities are considered to offer some of the best skiing in the world. The WHISTLER area, for example, is routinely chosen among the top 5 ski resorts internationally. In 1997 ski tourists spent $616 million in the province.

Recreational skiing developed in conjunction with ski jumping, a sport brought to Canada by

Scandinavian immigrants. In 1891 Scandinavian newcomers at REVELSTOKE created BC's first ski club, principally to encourage jumping. The first national ski jumping championship, held in ROSSLAND in 1898, was won by local jumper Olaus Jeldness. During the 1920s Revelstoke's Nels NELSEN held the world distance record and played a key role in promoting the sport in the province. By this time alpine skiing was becoming more popular. Ski chalets opened on the North Shore mountains opposite VANCOUVER during the 1920s, and in 1946 a lodge opened at DIAMOND HEAD in GARIBALDI PROVINCIAL PARK, attracting the more adventurous backcountry skiers. But it was really in the 1950s that new equipment and new facilities encouraged an explosion of public involvement in the sport. This in turn led to the emergence of BC skiers in international competition, most notably Nancy GREENE of Rossland during the 1960s, Dave MUR-RAY, leader of the "Crazy Canucks" on the Canadian men's ski team in the 1970s, Rob BOYD of Vernon in the 1980s, and Gerry Sorensen (*see* SORENSEN-LENIHAN), Canada's outstanding female athlete in 1982. There are 3 dozen downhill ski facilities in BC, along with several more family-oriented centres offering limited facilities. The main ski resorts are listed opposite.

There are several cross-country ski areas, including Mt Washington near Courtenay, Whistler, Manning Park, 108 Mile Ranch in the CARIBOO, the Kane Valley east of MERRITT, Larch Hills near SALMON ARM, and many others. BC also has become one of the world centres for heli-skiing since wilderness skiing on undeveloped MOUNTAINS began gaining popularity in the early 1960s when the availability of helicopters and snow cats brought previously inaccessible slopes within the reach of the general public. Hans Gmoser, a guide and filmmaker, did much to publicize the sport and in 1962 Michael Wiegele, a ski instructor, produced a feasibility study showing that areas of the CARIBOO, MONASHEE and BUGABOO Mts offered some of the best snow conditions and longest runs to be found anywhere in the world. By 1999 heli-

SKIING AREAS of BC

FRASER VALLEY

Hemlock Valley	14 km north of HARRISON MILLS

LOWER MAINLAND

Cypress Bowl	in CYPRESS PROV PARK above WEST VANCOUVER
GROUSE Mt	in NORTH VANCOUVER
Mt SEYMOUR	in Mt Seymour Prov Park
WHISTLER Mt	north of SQUAMISH
Blackcomb Mt	adjacent to Whistler

VANCOUVER ISLAND

Mt WASHINGTON	31 km west of COURTENAY
FORBIDDEN PLATEAU	23 km west of Courtenay
Mt Arrowsmith Park	east of PORT ALBERNI
Mt Cain Alpine Park	100 north of CAMPBELL RIVER

CENTRAL INTERIOR

Mt Mackenzie	south of REVELSTOKE
Whitetooth Ski area	west of GOLDEN
Gibson Pass	in MANNING PROV PARK
Apex Mt	32 km southwest of PENTICTON
Silver Star Mt	22 km northeast of VERNON
Big White	54 km southeast of KELOWNA
Harper Mt	20 km northeast of KAMLOOPS
Sun Peaks Resort	at Tod Mt, 50 km northeast of Kamloops

KOOTENAYS

Red Mt	near ROSSLAND
Whitewater	20 km southeast of NELSON
Fernie Snow Valley	west of FERNIE
Fairmont Hot Springs	
Panorama Ski Resort	17 km west of INVERMERE in the PURCELL MTS
Phoenix Ski Hill	outside GRAND FORKS
Kimberley Ski Resort	4 km outside the city

NORTHERN INTERIOR

Hudson Bay Mt	22 km west of SMITHERS
Shames Mt Ski Area	20 km west of TERRACE
Murray Ridge Ski Hill	10 km north of FORT ST JAMES
Tabor Mt	20 km east of PRINCE GEORGE
Powder King Ski Village	at PINE PASS, 200 km north of Prince George

skiing operations out of such centres as BLUE RIVER, GOLDEN and Revelstoke were employing 700 people and producing annual revenues of $70 million.

SKINNER, Constance Lindsay, writer (b 7 Dec 1877, Quesnel; d 27 Mar 1939, New York City). Her father Robert Skinner ran the HBC store at QUESNEL, where she spent her childhood. At age 10 she moved with her family to VICTORIA, then to VANCOUVER. She began WRITING at an early age and published stories and NEWSPAPER articles before she was out of her teens. In 1899 she left BC for California and worked as a music and drama critic for the leading papers. She later lived in Chicago, then settled in New York in 1912. Her first novel appeared in 1917 and she went on to have a prolific and influential career, producing 10 novels for young readers, 3 adult novels and several pioneering histories of frontier America, as well as poetry, plays and stories. Though she was far better known in the US than in Canada, much of her output drew its inspiration from her early life on the BC frontier.

SKINNER, Thomas J., pioneer settler (b 1822, West Thurrock, England; d 1889, Cowichan). He was an official with the East India Co in London when he was offered a job as bailiff of one of the PUGET SOUND AGRICULTURAL CO's farms on VANCOUVER ISLAND. He arrived with his family and some other settlers early in 1853; over the next few years he developed at ESQUIMALT a successful farm known as Oaklands. Elected to the first legislative assembly on the Island in 1856, he became a leading member of colonial society. In 1864 he moved his family north to the Cowichan Valley (*see* COWICHAN R), where they started a new farm and where he lived for the rest of his life. One of his granddaughters was the author Constance Lindsay SKINNER.

SKIPPER; *see* BUTTERFLY.

SKOOKUMCHUCK is on the LILLOOET R, 50 km south of MT CURRIE. It was originally a Lil'wat (LILLOOET) village, Ska'tin, located at an important FISHING site. The present name means "strong water" in CHINOOK JARGON. During the 1860s it was a stopping place on the DOUGLAS TRAIL to the Interior. The Church of the Holy Cross, built in 1906, recalls the mission established here by the OBLATES in 1861. The St Agnes Well Hot Springs is nearby.

SKOOKUMCHUCK, 45 km north of CRANBROOK on the KOOTENAY R, is a LOGGING community and site of a CRESTBROOK FOREST INDUSTRIES LTD pulp mill, built in 1969 and purchased by Ontario-based Tembec Inc in 1999 (*see* PULP AND PAPER). The Crows Nest Pass Lumber Co had a RAILWAY LOGGING show here in the 1920s. The name is a CHINOOK JARGON word meaning "strong water." *AS*

SKOOKUMCHUCK RAPIDS is a narrow passage in SECHELT INLET north of SECHELT. The name derives from a CHINOOK JARGON word meaning "strong water." The tide rushing through the narrows creates boiling rapids and whirlpools 4 times a day; the roar can be heard at a distance. Skookumchuck Provincial MARINE PARK provides a popular viewing site on the south side of the narrows.

SKUNK, striped (*Mephitis mephitis*), is a cat-sized member of the weasel family. It is black with white stripes down the length of its back. An omnivore, it feeds on plants, INSECTS, small mammals and birds' eggs. The female gives birth

Striped skunk, Stanley Park, Vancouver. R. Wayne Campbell photo

in May to a litter of 4–7. Skunks are mainly active at night and spend the day sleeping in burrows. They do not hibernate but they may become dormant for a period during the winter. When threatened, they are notorious for spraying an oily, unpleasant-smelling musk, which is secreted by anal glands. This substance not only repels by its smell but causes intense pain if it gets in the eyes. A second species, the spotted skunk (*Spilogale putorius*), occurs in the southwest corner of the province.

SKYTRAIN, the longest fully automated rapid transit system in N America, is a lightweight rail system operating from downtown VANCOUVER through BURNABY to SURREY. Financed jointly by the provincial and federal governments, the system was announced in 1980 and the first phase,

SkyTrain near Metrotown Station, Burnaby, 1999. Ian Lindsay/Vancouver Sun

a 22-km line between Vancouver and NEW WESTMINSTER, opened for revenue service in 1986. Early in 1990 SkyTrain crossed the FRASER R on a 3-km extension into Surrey. SkyTrain is operated by the BC Rapid Transit Co Ltd under contract with the Greater Vancouver Transportation Authority, known since 1999 as TransLink. Powered by electricity, the train is fully automatic. Attendants patrol the system, but the driverless trains are computer controlled. Vehicles travel separate from other traffic on their own guideway, which runs beneath downtown Vancouver through an old railway tunnel and then emerges to continue at grade or elevated 6–8 m above ground. SkyTrain has an average cruising speed of 43.5 km/h and carries about 140,000 riders every weekday.

SLADE, Michael, was originally the pen name for a trio of VANCOUVER lawyers, John Banks, Richard Covell and Jay Clarke, who in 1987 began publishing a series of highly popular thrillers featuring the fictional RCMP Chief Superintendent Robert DeClercq. By the time *Burnt Bones*, the 7th in the series, appeared in 1999, Clarke was writing the books by himself.

SLAVERY was practised by all aboriginal groups on the West Coast prior to contact with Europeans. Slaves were either captured during raids, purchased or traded; they constituted a third order of aboriginal society, below chiefs (nobles) and commoners. They were considered the personal property of their owners, who were free to treat them in any manner whatsoever,

including killing them, usually as an act of wealth destruction. Most slaves were women and children since males were more difficult to restrain. If they were not ransomed by their own people, their status was hereditary; if they wished to be free, their only option was escape. Only rarely did they intermarry with free people. They lived in their owners' houses and their status was closer in function to household servants than to slaves in a plantation economy. The exact proportion of the coastal aboriginal population that were slaves has been placed at anywhere from a quarter to a third. Slavery died out during the 19th century under the influence of the European newcomers. *See also* FIRST NATIONS OF BC.

SLAVEY First Nation; *see* DENE-THAH.

SLESSE, MOUNT (el 2,375 m), in the FRASER VALLEY southeast of CHILLIWACK near the US border, is significant as the site of the worst AVIATION disaster in BC history. On 9 Dec 1956, a Trans Canada Airlines plane heading east out of VANCOUVER carrying 62 passengers and crew smashed into the mountain in bad weather. Everyone on board died, including 5 football players who had participated in the Canadian

Branches covered with herring roe being dried at Sliammon reserve, 1981. Dorothy Kennedy photo

HOMALCO people also reside at the village and are often called Sliammon as well. All 3 groups were formerly known as Mainland COMOX. *See also* FIRST NATIONS OF BC.

Mt Slesse near Chilliwack, site of the worst aviation disaster in BC history. Roy Luckow photo

Football League all-star game at Empire Stadium the day before. The site of the crash was so isolated that it was not discovered by MOUNTAINEERS for 5 months. The coroner landed by helicopter and held a mountaintop funeral ceremony for the victims, whose remains had to be left on the peak.

SLIAMMON people, a First Nation of the Northern Coast Salish people (*see* SALISHAN FIRST NATIONS), occupied the mainland coast of GEORGIA STRAIT from DESOLATION SOUND south to SALTERY BAY in JERVIS INLET. Traditionally their main villages were at Grace Harbour and Sliammon Creek, though the modern population of about 800 is centred at the village of Sliammon, north of POWELL RIVER. KLAHOOSE and

SLOCAN, village, pop 335, at the south end of SLOCAN LK in the W KOOTENAY, began in the 1890s as a service and transportation centre for the area's SILVER-lead mines. Incorporated as a city in 1901, it was at one time the end of line for rail travel into the valley and an important steamboat port. With the passing of the MINING boom it declined. During WWII Japanese Canadians from the Coast were interned at nearby Lemon Creek (*see* JAPANESE, RELOCATION OF). LOGGING and SAWMILLING are the main industries and Slocan, which reincorporated as a village in 1958, is the gateway to Valhalla Provincial PARK, established in 1983.

SLOCAN FOREST PRODUCTS LTD was formed by Ike Barber in 1978 to purchase the timber, LOGGING and SAWMILLING assets of Triangle Pacific Forest Products at SLOCAN. Since then the company has acquired sawmills, timber and PULP AND PAPER facilities throughout the Interior. In June 1997 it completed purchase of the sawmilling operations of TimberWest Forest Co and in 1999 reported revenues of $1.1 billion. *See also* FOREST INDUSTRY.

SLOCAN LAKE, 69.3 km², lies in a deep valley in the SELKIRK MTS of the W KOOTENAY, and drains south via Slocan R for 97 km to the KOOTENAY R just north of CASTLEGAR. Evidence of aboriginal occupation can be seen in pictographs along the shore (*see* ROCK ART). The area was once rich in SALMON, but dam building on the COLUMBIA R

SS William Hunter, *the first propeller-driven vessel on Slocan Lk, at Slocan, c 1895. Silverton Historical Society Archives*

blocked the fish migrations. The area was the scene of frenetic SILVER and lead MINING in the 1890s and most of the communities date from this period. Rail lines from the north and south connected with steamboats on the lake as a vital link in the region's transportation network. A tug and barge service continues to ferry rail cars from SLOCAN to ROSEBERY. Several thousand Japanese Canadians were interned in the Slocan Valley during WWII (*see* JAPANESE, RELOCATION OF). The west side of the lake is part of VALHALLA Provincial Park (est 1983, 498 km²), a mountain wilderness named for the palace where the slain heroes of Norse myth live on.

SLOCAN PARK is a LOGGING and farming settlement 24 km west of NELSON on the SLOCAN R and CPR line. W.C.E. Koch built a SAWMILL nearby in 1904. It was originally called Gutelius after Frederick Passmore Gutelius, general manager of the COLUMBIA & WESTERN RWY, who also contributed his name to Passmore, a neighbouring village and site of a sawmill and lumber company that grew into SLOCAN FOREST PRODUCTS. Many DOUKHOBORS settled in the area.   AS

SLUG is the common name for several species of pulmonate (having a lung rather than gills) gastropod ("belly-foot") MOLLUSCS. "Slug" refers only to body shape: several varieties have apparently evolved separately from different groups of sea snails. Most slugs that occur in BC live near the Mid- and South Coast and on the islands as they prefer moist, temperate conditions. The slug has a long, smooth body with a muscular "foot" along the bottom that moves the slug forward in peristaltic waves. The head has a pair of optic tentacles, a shorter pair for smelling and tasting food and a mouth containing a sawlike radula with which the slug feeds. Enclosed in the mantle, a fleshy hood covering the head and part of the back, is a remnant shell. Slugs are hermaphroditic but mate with themselves only if no other slugs are available. Their hours-long mating ritual includes rearing, lunging, nipping, tail-flapping, mutual penetration and, for the great grey garden slug (*Limax maximus*), a spectacular finish: the slugs dangle, tightly entwined, from a rope of slime. Slugs lay eggs in protected spots, grow to lengths of 1 to 25 cm, can move as fast as 0.04 km/h and live for 1 to 6 years. They eat several times their own body weight every day, mostly soft plant parts and vegetable and animal detritus.

The slug is generally viewed with distaste. It hides during the day and creeps about at night; it destroys gardens and crops and is hard to control; it is covered with slime. Most indigenous slugs do enjoy fresh salad greens, but they also help decompose organic matter, fertilize soil and distribute spores and seeds. Slime, the sticky mucus produced by nearly the whole body surface, protects the slug from dehydration, assists in mating and enables the slug to glide over anything (including broken glass), adhere to any surface at any angle and repel predators.

About 12 species of land slug occur in BC. One of the most common is *Ariolimax columbianus*, the banana slug, so called because many individuals are yellow-green with brown or black spots. At 15–25 cm it is the second-largest slug in the world; it is a peaceful rainforest dweller, not a garden pest. The light brown field slug (*Ariolimax laevis*) lives nearly everywhere in the province and eats a wide variety of vegetation. Most garden and crop destruction can be blamed on the introduced slugs, which have few natural enemies in BC: the nearly omnivorous black slug (*Arion ater*), introduced from Europe in the 1940s; the striped or spotted great grey garden slug (*Limax maximus*), an aggressive, cannibalistic species also from Europe; *Deroceras* species from Europe and Asia; and the greenhouse slug (*Milax gigates*), a Mediterranean import. Several species of sea slugs, which are very different from land slugs, also occur in salt water in BC (*see* NUDIBRANCHS).

Mary Schendlinger

SLUMACH MINE, also known as the Lost Creek Mine, is a legendary GOLD mine in the mountains north of PITT LK in a remote corner of GARIBALDI PROVINCIAL PARK. In 1891 a Coast Salish man named Slumach was hanged for murder. Prior to his death he had been seen around NEW WESTMINSTER with gold nuggets; many people believed that he carried knowledge of a rich gold deposit to his grave. In 1901 an American miner, John Jackson, may have found the mine but he died soon after, leaving a letter hinting at its location. Since then many attempts have been made to find the mine. Some of these have ended in mysterious deaths and disappearances, giving rise to the belief that Slumach placed a curse on the spot. In 1995 an Alberta farmer claimed to have hiked to the site only to find that the deposit had already been mysteriously mined out.

SMALLPOX is an acute infectious disease, potentially fatal, characterized by fever, aches and a pustular rash that may leave scars. The disease runs its course in a month and those who recover have lifelong immunity. It was introduced into BC with the arrival of Europeans and was the disease most responsible for the catastrophic decline in FIRST NATIONS population (*see* ABORIGINAL DEMOGRAPHY). Epidemics occurred periodically from the 1780s to the 1860s. The first occurrence was probably introduced from the south in 1782. It was followed by a virulent epidemic in 1836–38 that is believed to have claimed about a third of the coastal aboriginal population, and another in 1862–63 that accounted for more than 19,000 deaths. This latter outbreak began in VICTORIA, where different First Nations gathered each summer to trade and socialize. A sailor from San Francisco brought the disease ashore and it spread rapidly through the aboriginal camps. Local authorities drove the aboriginal people away; as they travelled up the coast, they carried the disease with them and it spread across the Interior as well.

Smallpox also infected the non-aboriginal population, though less dramatically. After Edward Jenner proved the efficacy of vaccination in the 1790s, it was introduced into America in the early decades of the 19th century. However, there was a strong anti-vaccination movement and resistance to public health efforts was widespread, so isolated outbreaks continued into the 20th century. One of the most celebrated BC incidents occurred in 1892, when smallpox arrived in Victoria from China aboard the ship *Empress of Japan*. The city of VANCOUVER responded by refusing entrance to anyone arriving from Victoria. When a steamer attempted to dock at the harbour, fire hoses were used to keep everyone aboard. An island judge overruled the ban imposed by Vancouver, but the city ignored his decision and continued to put everyone arriving from Victoria into forcible quarantine. Vancouver's mayor, city solicitor and health officer were all arrested for violating the judge's ruling before tempers cooled and the epidemic passed. The last serious outbreak of the disease occurred in Vancouver in 1932: about 100 people became infected and many of them died.

SMEETON, Miles Richard (b 5 Mar 1906, Hovingham, England; d 23 Sept 1988, Calgary) and **Beryl** (b 21 Sept 1905, Tolpuddle, England; d 14 Nov 1979, Cochrane, AB), adventurers. They lived a remarkable life of almost constant adventuring from the time they married in 1938. Miles was a career soldier in the British Army; Beryl had made arduous solo trips by rail, horseback and foot through Siberia, China and S America. In the Himalayas she climbed to the highest altitude of any woman to that time (7,000 m). During WWII they purchased, sight unseen, a property on SALTSPRING ISLAND near Musgrave Landing and farmed there from 1946 to 1950 and 1952 to 1955. From 1955 to 1969 they lived more or less permanently at sea, roaming the world's oceans in their small sailboat. Miles's account of one of these voyages, *Once is Enough* (1959), is considered a classic of sailing literature. It was one of 9 autobiographical books that he published. The couple eventually settled on a farm in Cochrane, AB, in 1969; there they bred animals for release into the wild. One of their accomplishments was to rescue the northern swift fox from extinction. Their daughter Clio carried on their wildlife work.
Reading: Miles Clark, *High Endeavours: The Extraordinary Life and Adventures of Miles and Beryl Smeeton*, 1991.

SMELT, surf (*Hypomesus pretiosus*), is a small silvery fish. During the summer smelts swarm in large numbers along shallow beaches and ESTUARIES, where amateur smelters catch them in nets

Surf smelt. Fisheries & Oceans Canada

or buckets for eating. An important food source for various commercial fishes, the species is common on the Pacific coast from southern California to Alaska and seldom exceeds 30 cm. The smelt family also includes the EULACHON and the capelin. Another species, the pygmy longfin smelt, has freshwater populations in PITT and HARRISON lakes.

SMELTERS are industrial facilities for processing mineral ores to extract metals. Over the years there have been close to 20 operating smelters in BC, though as of 1999 only 2 remained: the COMINCO facility at TRAIL and the ALCAN ALUMINUM CO smelter at KITIMAT. The first smelters in the province were built in the 1880s—south of GOLDEN and in VANCOUVER—to process ores from the booming mining districts, but they ceased operation almost immediately, lacking the necessary supplies of ore, capital and skilled operators. Still, smelters were considered to be symbols of industrial progress and necessary adjuncts to the development of the MINING industry; by processing the ore locally they allowed BC to retain a greater share of the profits from its mineral wealth. The first profitable smelter was the Hall smelter, which went into operation early in 1896 at NELSON. The first enduring smelter was the Trail facility, built later in 1896 by the American mining promoter F.A. HEINZE to process ore from the mines at ROSSLAND. Under CPR–Cominco ownership it put the Hall smelter out of business and developed into one of BC's most important industrial sites. Following construction of the Trail smelter there was a flurry of smelter building lasting to WWI. In the BOUNDARY DISTRICT the Granby Company smelter at GRAND FORKS (1900–19) was for a time the largest copper smelter in the British Empire. Other short-lived smelters were built at GREENWOOD, ANACONDA and BOUNDARY FALLS. On the east side of KOOTENAY LK there was a smelter at PILOT BAY in 1895–96 processing ore from the Bluebell Mine at RIONDEL, and another farther east at MARYSVILLE (1903–08), now part of KIMBERLEY. On VANCOUVER ISLAND, Henry CROFT built a copper smelter to process ore from mines on nearby Mt SICKER (1901–08) and for a short time there was a facility at LADYSMITH. Other smelters were located at VAN ANDA on TEXADA ISLAND (1899–1919) and at ANYOX, north of PRINCE RUPERT (1912–35). With WWI the great era of smelter building drew to a close. The only facilities to go into operation subsequent to 1920 were the Alcan Aluminum smelter at Kitimat in the 1950s and a copper smelter associated with the Afton Mine southwest of KAMLOOPS (1977–97). See chart opposite.

SMITH, Bev, basketball player (b 4 Apr 1960, Armstrong). Raised in SALMON ARM, she won a BASKETBALL scholarship to the Univ of Oregon. She smashed all Oregon scoring records and was named the top defender in college basketball by *Sports Illustrated*. A 2-time all-American, she was runner-up in voting for top player in the US. After graduation she starred in the semiprofessional Italian league, winning the European championship with Vicenza twice. As the centrepiece of the Canadian national team she helped it to 3rd-place finishes at the 1979 and 1989 Pan American Games and the 1979 and 1986 world championships, and to a 4th-place finish at the 1984 Los Angeles Olympics. Frequently cited as one of the top 10 female players in the world, she was named to the world championship all-star team in 1986. In 1988 she was hired as

Bev Smith, basketball player, preparing for the 1996 Olympics. Ralph Bower/Vancouver Sun

coach of the UBC women's basketball team but after a disappointing season she resigned to resume playing in Italy. After winning another 2 European championships, she made her last playing appearance for Canada at the 1996 Atlanta Olympics. She later became head coach of the Canadian women's national team. *SW*

SMITH, Brian R.D., lawyer, business executive, politician (b 7 July 1934, Victoria). A graduate of UBC law school, he entered politics as an alderman, then served as mayor of OAK BAY from 1974 to 1979. He was first elected to the provincial legislature for the SOCIAL CREDIT PARTY in 1979 and joined Premier Bill BENNETT's CABINET as minister of education. Twice re-elected in his Oak Bay–Gordon Head riding, he also served as minister of energy and mines (1982–83) and attorney general (1983–88). During this time he represented the BC government at most of the first ministers' meetings involving constitutional and ABORIGINAL RIGHTS issues. In 1986 he ran for the leadership of the Socreds following Bill Bennett's resignation, but lost to Bill VANDER ZALM. He continued to serve as attorney general in Vander Zalm's cabinet until 1988, when he resigned; subsequently he left politics. He was chairman of CNR from 1989 to 1994 and became chair of BC HYDRO AND POWER AUTHORITY in 1995.

SMITH, Cecil "Cougar," bounty hunter, guide (b 1878, Ashbourne, England; d 1961, Campbell

Cecil Smith (l), famed Vancouver Island cougar hunter. MCR 11538

SMELTER OPERATIONS AT COMINCO

GENERAL FLOWSHEET OF TRAIL OPERATIONS

ZINC OPERATIONS

LEAD OPERATIONS

SULPHUR DIOXIDE (SO₂) OFF-GAS

SO₂ Off Gas

ACID & SO₂ PLANTS

Ammonium Sulphate Solution

Sulphuric Acid

Sulphur Dioxide

Ammonia

Aqueous Ammonia

FERTILIZER PLANTS
Granulator

(NH₄)₂SO₄ Fertilizers

START HERE

Limestone, Silica, Coke etc.

Lead Conc.

FEED PLANT

FEED PREP
Dryer

Blended Feed

SO₂ Off-Gas

Tail Gas to Stack

Liquid SO₂

H₂SO₄

RESIDUE FILTERING
FILTER

Filtered Zinc Residues

KIVCET SMELTER

Steam

GeO₂ Indium

INDIUM / GERMANIUM PLANTS
S X

Steam

Smelter Slag

SLAG FUMING

Steam

Oxygen

Copper Sulphate

Bullion

START HERE

Zinc Conc.

ROASTERS

Steam
Waste Heat Boiler

Zn Calcine

Residues

"Precon"

COAL

COAL PREPARATION
Bowl Mill

Fume

Ferrous Granules (Tail Slag)

Zn Solution

SULPHIDE LEACH

LEACH

PURIFICATION

Zn Slurry

Sulphur Cake

Zinc Conc.

Oxygen

PRESSURE LEACH

Return Acid

OXIDE LEACH
SHRIVER

"Leached Fume"

FUME LEACH
FILTER

Return Acid

Copper Arsenate

Sodium Antimonate

COPPER PRODUCTS

Copper Matte

DROSSING PLANT

Elemental Sulphur

Gypsum

Zinc Electrolyte

Cd Residues

Zinc Dust Slurry

CELL
E & M

Misc. Lead Recycles

LEAD ALLOYS
S.R.F.

As / Sb Dusts

Anode Slimes

LEAD REFINERY
CELL

Lead & Alloys

Return Acid

Zinc Ops Contaminated Water

Lead Ops Contaminated Water

ETP LAGOON
EFFLUENT TREATMENT PLANT

Lime

Sludge to Storage & Recycle

PLANTS

Products

CADMIUM PLANT

Zinc Dust

Zinc & Alloys

1710

Cadmium

Pb Alloys

SILVER REFINERY

Bismuth

Treated Effluent

COLUMBIA RIVER

Silver Gold

Return Acid

LEGEND

Cominco PLANTS Products

▪▪▪▪▪▪▪ Lead Ops. Materials

➤ Zinc Ops. Materials

Text and illustration courtesy Cominco

The Cominco smelter at Trail processes more than 600,000 tonnes of mineral concentrates every year. The smelter's major product is refined zinc. The process (shown above) begins when zinc sulphide concentrate is either burned in the roasters or pressure leached with acid to remove sulphur. Gases from the roasters go to the acid plants via the mercury removal plant. The roasted zinc oxide material is processed in the leaching plants, along with the pressure leach product and the fume from the lead smelter. Several purification stages follow, generating more by-product metals. Residue from the leaching process still contains metals, so it is pumped to the lead smelter for reprocessing. The resulting pure zinc sulphate solution becomes electrolyte in a huge electrolytic process that produces refined zinc. The fertilizer operations convert the sulphur from the zinc and lead operations into useful products. Different grades of ammonium sulphate fertilizer are made from the scrubber solution used to clean the sulphur dioxide from the roasters and lead smelter.

Lead comes to the smelter as lead sulphide concentrate primarily, though increasing quantities of automotive battery scrap are also processed. The lead smelter employs the Russian-developed Kivcet flash smelting process to produce lead bullion from a 2-stage furnace. Dry feed along with fluxing and fuelling agents are injected at the top of the furnace with oxygen. Through chemical reactions and settling, impure lead bullion

and slag are formed and tapped separately from the furnace. Hot sulphur dioxide gas resulting from the process passes through a waste heat boiler to make steam, and then on to an electrostatic precipitator to remove dust particles before being sent to zinc operations for processing into saleable products, including sulphuric acid and liquid sulphur dioxide. Meanwhile, molten slag is transferred to a slag fuming furnace to remove zinc, mainly in the form of zinc oxide fume. The fume is processed to extract more zinc. The remaining black, sand-like barren slag is sold to cement manufacturers. Lead bullion is processed through the drossing plant adjacent to the Kivcet furnace to remove copper and other impurities. The remaining bullion is purified in the electrolytic refinery and cast into the finished product. By-products of the refining process include silver, gold, arsenic, antimony and bismuth. *See also* SMELTERS, opposite.

Lead "pigs" being strapped into bundles at the smelter, for shipment to customers, 1995. Raeff Miles photo

River). He was a son of Amelia and Horace Smith, English immigrants who came to VANCOUVER ISLAND in the 1880s to farm at BLACK CREEK; his brother Eustace SMITH was a famed timber cruiser. Cecil made his living with rod and rifle, becoming a popular hunting and fishing guide and skilled COUGAR tracker in the CAMPBELL RIVER area. At age 14 he killed his first cougar with an old muzzle-loading musket given by a neighbour; reportedly he killed 600 cougars before he stopped counting. He helped the writer Roderick HAIG-BROWN gather information for Haig-Brown's 1934 book *Panther*. Smith was game warden for Campbell River district before he retired. His first wife, Mary Pidcock Smith, was also a crack shot.

SMITH, Eustace, timber cruiser (b 1876, Derbyshire, England; d 1964, Vancouver). At age 11 he came to BC with his family to homestead at BLACK CREEK, near COMOX. After working at various jobs in the coastal FOREST INDUSTRY, he

Eustace Smith, timber cruiser. MCR 10610

established an office in VANCOUVER in 1907, providing timber cruising, brokerage and management services. He established a reputation as the best timber cruiser in BC, having discovered many large stands of valuable timber for his clients, including the NIMPKISH valley. He was well known by most of the major figures in the BC forest industry, and contributed greatly to their success. His trademark was a large S slashed into the corner posts of timber stands he surveyed. His unpublished biography, "The Sign of S," was written by Bruce MCKELVIE. *See also* FORESTRY. *Ken Drushka*

SMITH, Gordon Appelbe, artist (b 18 June 1919, Hove, England). He moved to Winnipeg as a teenager and studied at the Winnipeg School of Art. During WWII he served overseas and was wounded in Sicily. After returning to Canada he moved to VANCOUVER, where he has lived ever since. After completing studies at the Vancouver School of Art (*see* EMILY CARR INSTITUTE OF ART & DESIGN) he served on the faculty there from 1946

until 1956, then at UBC's faculty of education from 1956 to 1982. Meanwhile he developed into one of Canada's leading modernist painters, known for his abstract landscapes that evoke the natural world rather than illustrate it. During the 1950s he belonged to the Art in Living Group, artists who stressed the importance of art in everyday life. The VANCOUVER ART GALLERY staged a major exhibition of his work in 1976 and a 50-year retrospective in 1997. He was inducted into the Order of Canada in 1997 and the ORDER OF BC in 2000.

SMITH, Janet, victim in one of Vancouver's most notorious murders (b 25 June 1902, Perth, Scotland; d 26 July 1924, Vancouver). A nursemaid to the family of wealthy businessman Frederick Baker, she was murdered at her employer's home in Shaughnessy. The police investigation, mishandled from the start, was complicated by political pressure not to embarrass a prominent family. At one point the Baker's CHINESE houseboy, Wong Foon Sing, was abducted, beaten and charged with the murder. He was acquitted and the case, which unfolded against a background of political corruption, Jazz Age excess and widespread racism, was never solved. *Reading:* Edward Starkins, *Who Killed Janet Smith?*, 1984.

SMITH, Mary Ellen (Spear), politician (b 11 Oct 1863, Tavistock, England; d 3 May 1933, Vancouver). She arrived in BC in 1892 and became active in various women's organizations dedicated to the cause of WOMEN'S SUF-

Mary Ellen Smith, politician, in a portrait by Enid Stoddard. BC Archives PDP-03694

FRAGE. In 1917 her husband Ralph SMITH, then finance minister in the LIBERAL provincial government, died. Early in 1918, running as an independent, she won the by-election to succeed him. Subsequently she joined the Liberals and remained an MLA until she lost her seat in the election of 1928. Smith was the first woman in any provincial legislature in Canada and, when she became minister without porfo-

lio in 1921, the first female cabinet minister in the British Empire.

SMITH, Michael, biochemist, Nobel laureate (b 26 Apr 1932, Blackpool, England). After receiving his PhD from the Univ of Manchester he immigrated to Canada in 1956 to work with Har Gobind KHORANA at the BC Research

Michael Smith, Nobel prize-winning UBC biochemist. Gary Fiegehen photo

Council. He moved with Khorana to the Univ of WI in 1960 but returned to UBC the next year to work at the Fisheries Research Board laboratories. In 1966 Smith joined UBC's department of biochemistry where he went on to do groundbreaking research in human genetics. By the 1980s he was receiving recognition for his work on site-directed mutagenesis, a technique allowing genes to be altered in a designated way. He was made a Fellow of the Royal Society in London in 1986 and received the Genetics Society of Canada's Award of Excellence in 1988. Smith also received awards from the Gairdner Foundation (1986) and from the Royal Society of Canada (1992). A year after receiving the Gairdner Foundation award, he became the director of UBC's Biotechnology Lab, a post he held until 1996. Meanwhile, he catapulted to international fame in 1993 as the co-winner of the Nobel Prize in Chemistry for his research on site-directed mutagenesis. Since winning the prize, Smith has received further honours. He became a Peter Wall Distinguished Professor in 1994, received the ORDER OF BC in 1994, the Order of Canada in 1995, and in 1997 he was named Director of the GENOME SEQUENCE CENTRE, Canada's first research centre devoted to decoding human genes. *Dianne Mackay*

SMITH, Ralph, miner, politician (b 8 Aug 1858, Newcastle-on-Tyne, Scotland; d 12 Feb 1917, Victoria). A COAL miner from the age of 11, he immigrated to Canada in 1891 and settled in NANAIMO, where he soon became an official of the Miners & Mine Labourers Protective Assoc. Selected by the local Reform Club to run as a candidate, he failed to get elected in the 1894 provincial election but won a seat in the legislature in 1898. He sat as a labour member until he resigned to run federally in 1900. He won the seat and sat in Parliament as a Liberal and supporter of Wilfrid Laurier until losing in the 1911 election. Smith also was the first BC resident to serve as president of the Trades and Labour Congress of Canada in 1898–1902, though he lost the support of Nanaimo miners for being too moderate. In 1916 he re-entered the provincial assembly, winning election as a LIBERAL from Vancouver and joining Premier BREWSTER's cabinet as minister of finance. He died in office, and his wife Mary Ellen SMITH contested and won his seat. *See also* COAL MINING, VANCOUVER ISLAND; LABOUR MOVEMENT.

SMITH, Shannon, swimmer (b 28 Sept 1961, Vancouver). She began breaking Canadian SWIMMING records at age 10 and continued breaking them until her early retirement from competition in 1978. In 1976, having already amassed 34 Canadian records, she broke the 200-m freestyle Commonwealth mark. She attended the 1976 US nationals and won gold in the 800-m freestyle and bronze in the 400 m. She won her second 400-m bronze that year at the Montreal Olympics. Her time, 4:14:60, was another Commonwealth record and it was later revealed that gold winner Petra Thumer had regularly used steroids, meaning Smith probably deserved the silver. In 1976 she received a Gov Gen's Award, was named Canadian junior female athlete of the year and BC junior athlete of the year. She received this last honour again in 1977 and she was inducted into the BC SPORTS HALL OF FAME in 1983. *SW*

SMITH, Sidney Garfield, logger (b 7 Feb 1882, Saginaw, MI; d 7 Feb 1969, Vancouver). He dropped out of high school in his senior year, moved west and worked at a variety of jobs before joining the Larson Lumber Co at Bellingham, WA, in 1905. In 1911 he came to BC to work for BLOEDEL, STEWART & WELCH at Myrtle Point as an axeman. Two years later he was superintendent of the company's camp near POWELL RIVER. After spending WWI in the US Army, he went to work for Pacific Mills at OCEAN FALLS. He became managing director of BS&W in 1921; under his guidance it became the pre-eminent LOGGING company on the coast. He pioneered the use of modern, mechanized logging equipment and became vice-president of the company in 1942. After the merger of BS&W with H.R. MacMillan Export Co, Smith became a member of the board of directors. His reputation as an innovative and respected logging manager was legendary in the coastal FOREST INDUSTRY.

Ken Drushka

SMITH, Tricia, rower (b Apr 1957, Vancouver). She was a championship-calibre swimmer before beginning competitive ROWING at the VANCOUVER ROWING CLUB and the Burnaby Lake Rowing Club in 1974. Rowing in coxed 4s, 8s and pairs over her career, she collected 5 golds and a silver in national championships competition. She was a regular champion at Canadian meets in all 3 events and as a pairs rower with partner Betty Craig she was never beaten in N America. Smith won many medals in international competition, including 6 bronzes and a silver at world championships and a silver in pairs at the 1984 Los Angeles Olympics. At the 1986 Commonwealth Games, she earned a gold medal as part of Canada's 4s team. Smith, who earned a law degree from UBC in 1985, is a member of the UBC Sports Hall of Fame and the BC SPORTS HALL OF FAME. *SW*

SMITH INLET is one of the smaller FJORDS that indent the mainland coast. Located just north of Cape Caution opposite the north end of VANCOUVER ISLAND, it is guarded by the LIGHTHOUSES on Egg Island at its mouth, which is called Smith Sound. Named in 1786 by James Hanna, a FUR TRADE captain, it was home to the Gwa'sala, the most northerly tribe of the KWAKWA̲KA̲'WAKW (Kwakiutl) First Nation; this group gathered farther south at BLUNDEN HARBOUR in the mid-19th century. Steller's SEA LIONS breed at rookeries on islands at the mouth of the inlet. The several SALMON spawning streams flowing into the inlet made it an important commercial FISHING area from as early as the 1880s. All the canneries in the inlet closed by 1935 and the catch was taken elsewhere for processing.

SMITHE, William, farmer, premier 29 Jan 1883–29 Mar 1887 (b 30 June 1842, Matfen, England; d 28 Mar 1887, Victoria). He came to BC in 1862 and settled on a farm near COWICHAN LK. Establishing himself as a commu-

William Smithe, premier of BC 1883–87, pictured here c 1885. BC Archives H-00791

nity leader, he was named road commissioner for Cowichan in 1865, then ran successfully for the first legislative assembly following CONFEDERATION in 1871. Five years later he joined the cabinet of Premier A.C. ELLIOTT as minister of finance and agriculture. Following the 1878 election he took over leadership of the opposition, though there were no organized parties at the time, and he became PREMIER when Robert BEAVEN failed to command a majority in the legislature. Smithe succeeded in settling a series of long-standing disputes between VANCOUVER ISLAND and the mainland, and between BC and Ottawa. His time as premier was marked by economic expansion fuelled by generous grants of Crown land to private interests for railways and other projects, a policy known as the "Great Potlatch." His government also passed anti-Asian legislation and limited the size of aboriginal RESERVES in favour of non-aboriginal settlers. These policies were endorsed by his victory in the 1886 election, but he died soon after.

SMITHERAM, Henry Arthur "Butch," aboriginal activist (b 8 Jan 1918, Penticton; d 14 Mar 1982, Keremeos). He was deprived of official Indian status when his mother, a member of the OKANAGAN First Nation, married an Englishman. After dropping out of high school he worked at a variety of jobs until he joined the federal Department of Indian Affairs. At KAMLOOPS he became the first aboriginal person in western Canada to be an assistant Indian agent. After returning to school and attending UBC, he began working with the federal Department of Manpower and Immigration in the area of aboriginal employment. In 1968 he began organizing non-status Indians, efforts that led to the creation of the BC Association of Non-Status Indians in 1969. This organization worked to improve conditions for non-status and METIS people. He was also active in the formation of the Native Council of Canada and was made a member of the Order of Canada in 1982.

SMITHERS, town, pop 5,624, lies in the BULKLEY Valley halfway between PRINCE GEORGE and PRINCE RUPERT. It is named for Sir Alfred Waldron Smithers (1850–1924), a London financier and chairman of the GRAND TRUNK PACIFIC RWY when the site was made a major divisional point for the railway in 1913. Nearby EVELYN is named for one of his daughters. Before 1913 the area was barely settled and members of the WET'SUWET'EN

Farmland near Smithers.
Walter Lanz/Image Makers

First Nation were the main inhabitants. Smithers was the first incorporated village in BC (1921) and became a town in 1967. The FOREST INDUSTRY has been the most important employer: there are 2 large sawmills in the area. DAIRY FARMING, the CATTLE INDUSTRY and MINING exploration are also significant. Visitors are attracted by the sport FISHING, game hunting, hiking, rafting, horseback riding and SKIING at Hudson Bay Mt (el 2,621 m), which looms dramatically over the town.

SMYL, Stanley Phillip "Stan" ("Steamer"), hockey player (b 28 Jan 1958, Glendon, AB). One of the most popular players in BC HOCKEY history, he came west in 1974 to play for the WHL's NEW WESTMINSTER BRUINS. In his 3 junior seasons with the Bruins (1975–78) they won the league championship each year and twice won

Stan "Steamer" Smyl, as captain of the Vancouver Canucks.
Vancouver Canucks Photo Archives

the national junior championship Memorial Cup. Smyl joined the VANCOUVER CANUCKS in 1978 and was one of the hardest-working players in the NHL, earning his nickname for his straight-ahead style of play. He was captain of the Canucks for 8 years and in 1982 led them to the Stanley Cup finals. When he retired as a player in 1991 to become a Canucks assistant coach he was the team's career leader in games played (896), goals (262), assists (411) and points (673). His #12 is the only number retired by the Canucks. In 1999 he became head coach with the Canucks' minor-league affiliate in Syracuse, NY. *SW*

SNAIL, a MOLLUSC belonging to the class Gastropoda, has a soft body enclosed in a hard shell. Gastropod means "stomach-foot," a reference to the fleshy, muscular foot running along the underside of the animal, on which it moves about. The snail can retract its body into the shell for protection. It uses its radula, or rasp-like tongue, to feed on plants and/or animals. Carnivorous sea snails use the radula to drill

through the shells of CLAMS, MUSSELS and BARNACLES and to rasp out the soft flesh. A snail may also possess 2 eyes capable of detecting changes in light intensity, and 2 tentacles that act as feelers.

There are hundreds of snail species in BC, both marine and land varieties. Marine snails comprise the greatest number of species. They are found from the high intertidal zone all the way to deep subtidal waters and include periwinkles, moonsnails, hornsnails, whelks and dogwinkles. The black turban snail (*Tegula funebralis*), found on rocks on the open coast, is a common species known to live as long as 100 years. A closely related species, the red turban snail (*Astraea gibberosa*), is commonly found on the rocky shores of the QUEEN CHARLOTTE ISLANDS. Its shell was used for decoration by HAIDA carvers. Lewis's moonsnail (*Polinices lewisii*) is a large species (14 cm high) that lays its eggs in a distinctive sand mold that looks like a collar. Empty clam shells found along the beaches with holes drilled in them are the work of this carnivorous snail, which drills through shells to feed on the flesh. Two of the smallest common snails are the Sitka periwinkle (*Littorina sitkana*) and the checkered periwinkle (*L. scutulata*). They inhabit the high intertidal zone and feed on green algae; they die if they are submerged too long in sea water.

BC has freshwater snails as well, including the Liard hot spring snail (*Physella wrighti*), a rare indigenous species found only at the Liard Hot Springs adjacent to the ALASKA HWY near the Yukon border. The largest terrestrial (land) snail in BC is the common land snail (*Monadenia fidelis*), also known as the striped snail, found in warmer coastal areas. Its nut-brown shell, streaked with light bands, can exceed 3.6 cm in diameter. The European land snail (*Cepaea nemoralis*) is an introduced species, now common in the Lower Mainland. Its striking shell occurs in several colours from yellow to pink and brown. Various species of introduced land snails are familiar visitors to urban gardens.

SNAKE is a long, slender, limbless reptile with a highly flexible body and scaly skin which it sheds periodically. It is a carnivore and kills its prey—small mammals, birds, INSECTS, amphibians—by constriction or poison. Huge jungle snakes such as the python and the anaconda reach lengths of 10 m but BC snakes are much smaller and in most cases harmless to humans. Only the western RATTLESNAKE is seriously poiso-

Northwestern garter snake. *Duane Sept photo*

nous. Like other reptiles, some snake species give birth to live young while others lay eggs. They hibernate during the winter, sometimes in large groups. Aside from the rattler, 6 species are found in BC. Common garter snakes (*Thamnophis sirtalis*) occur in damp habitat and are widespread across the province. Their near relation, the northwestern garter snake (*T. ordinoides*), is the most common species in urban gardens in southwest BC. Despite its name, the western terrestrial garter snake (*T. elegans*) is a semi-aquatic species found across the southern half of the province. The rubber boa (*Charina bottae*) looks like an elongated piece of plasticine. It is a constrictor and a nocturnal animal that occurs in the southern third of the province. The racer (*Coluber constrictor*), a speedy predator with a long, whip-like tail, and the equally aggressive gopher snake (*Pituophis melanoleucus*), grey-yellow with large dark patches, are both denizens of the southern Interior dry belt. Two other species are seen very rarely: the night snake (*Hypsiglena torquata*) of the south Okanagan and the sharptail snake (*Contia tenuis*) of the GULF ISLANDS and southern VANCOUVER ISLAND.

SNAUQ, or Sun'ahk, was a SQUAMISH Nation village on the east side of Kitsilano Point, looking over what is now FALSE CRK in downtown VANCOUVER. It was one of the last aboriginal villages within city limits. The Squamish received a RESERVE at the site in 1876 but as Vancouver grew, the provincial government pressured the inhabitants to move. After 1900 the villagers dispersed to other Squamish communities and by 1913, when the province actually purchased the land, the site was abandoned. In 1977 the Squamish began legal proceedings to win compensation for the land, which is now occupied by Vanier Park, the VANCOUVER MUSEUM and the MACMILLAN SPACE CENTRE. *See also* ABORIGINAL RIGHTS.

SNOWBOARDING spread into BC from Calgary and Mt BAKER in the early 1980s, and the province soon became one of the sport's hotbeds. Snowboards were invented by American skateboarding fanatics in the late 1970s but pioneering BC snowboarders, such as Vancouver's Dave "Raiden" Ewens, concocted homemade boards with planks of plywood and water-ski bindings and took to the local mountains in the winter of 1983–84. The next season, Ewens, Steve Edmundson, Steve Suttie, Cory Campbell and Reggie O'Connor formed the International Snowboarding Association to organize the sport in BC. However, snowboarders were limited to hiking up mountains or sneaking onto chairlifts because snowboards were banned on most local ski hills. In 1985, Cypress Bowl (*see* CYPRESS PROVINCIAL PARK) and Hemlock Valley lifted their ban, followed by VERNON's Big White in 1987, WHISTLER in 1988 and Blackcomb in 1989. To assure administrators of the sport's safety, the ISA focussed on instruction and certification, becoming the Instructors' Snowboard Association of Canada in 1986 (later the Canadian Association of Snowboarding Instructors). Between 1985 and 1990, about 5 organized snowboarding events

David Boyce, snowboarder, at Cypress Bowl, 1998. Rick Loughran/Vancouver Province

were held annually in the province, starting with racing but gradually developing halfpipe, moguls, "big air" and bank slalom categories. The BC Snowboard Association was established in 1991 to administer competition under the Canadian Snowboard Federation. Shirley Hills, president of the BCSNA 1992–98, and Whistler and Blackcomb Snowboard Coordinator Stu Osborne were instrumental in developing the sport in BC during its rise to popularity in the 1990s. British Columbian Bill Smith made a groundbreaking international contribution to the sport by devising the official world snowboard ranking list over the Internet. The Westbeach Classic, BC's most celebrated annual snowboarding event, was first held in 1993, and Whistler later hosted major international meets such as the 1999 Kokanee Summer Surfout and the Sims Invitational World Cup in 2000. Whistler's Ross REBAGLIATI became the biggest name in snowboarding internationally after winning the sport's first Olympic medal in 1998. In the spirit of skateboarding, snowboarding began as a subculture with its own vocabulary and clothing styles, but by 1999 it had become a mainstream sport with more than 146,000 participants in BC.   SW

SNOWSHOE, 40 km northwest of MCBRIDE on the FRASER R and the CNR, was named for nearby Snowshoe Crk. Bob Allan and Fred Thrasher built a SAWMILL here in 1920 on the site of a former GRAND TRUNK PACIFIC RWY construction and engineering camp. It burned down in 1929.   AS

SNUNEYMUXW (Nanaimo) First Nation are a Central Coast Salish (*see* SALISHAN FIRST NATIONS) group of Island HALKOMELEM-speakers who were living around NANAIMO harbour and in the watershed of the Nanaimo R when the first

Europeans arrived. Nanaimo is an anglicized variant of their name. Archaeological evidence shows that ancestors of the Snuneymuxw had been living in the area for thousands of years (*see* ARCHAEOLOGY; PREHISTORY). At contact with Europeans their main winter village was located in Departure Bay near the current BC FERRY CORP terminal, though there were other villages in the harbour and on GABRIOLA ISLAND, and summer FISHING villages were located on the lower FRASER R near the site of FORT LANGLEY. The first meeting with outsiders occurred in June 1792 when the Spanish mariners Dionisio ALCALA-GALIANO and Cayetano VALDES arrived on their exploration of GEORGIA STRAIT. Sustained contact did not begin until the 1850s, after the Snuneymuxw told the HBC about COAL deposits in the harbour and the company established a trading post and began MINING. Initially the Snuneymuxw supplied much of the labour force for the mines. In 1854 Gov James DOUGLAS made the last of his DOUGLAS TREATIES with the local people, buying the coal-rich land for a quantity of trade goods. The Snuneymuxw First Nation, with a population of about 1,200, now has 6 reserves near Nanaimo and on Gabriola Island. *See also* FIRST NATIONS OF BC.

SOCCER was introduced to BC by British settlers on VANCOUVER ISLAND and the ROYAL ENGINEERS headquartered in NEW WESTMINSTER. The first documented games took place in 1862 at the Queen's Birthday celebrations in New Westminster and in 1865 at the annual picnic of the Caledonian Benevolent Society in VICTORIA. The earliest clubs were formed in Victoria and NANAIMO, and in 1890 the first provincial championship medals were presented by the St Andrew's and Caledonian Society. At the start of

the 20th century Victoria had a thriving soccer scene based in BEACON HILL PARK; it included the Victoria West Club, the oldest active club in the province. Other areas where the sport flourished included COQUITLAM, CUMBERLAND, Lake Cowichan, LADYSMITH and ESQUIMALT. Many of the players from central Vancouver Island were British COAL miners. The first tournament resembling a national championship was initiated as the People's Shield in 1906 and the trophy was won in 1913 by Nanaimo's Northfield Violets, but they faced very little competition and as WWI began the trophy was forgotten.

Meanwhile, in 1907 Con JONES and Will Ellis started the Pacific Coast League, with clubs in VANCOUVER, Nanaimo, Victoria, Ladysmith and Seattle. By the end of WWI soccer was so popular that a variety of rival leagues sprang up at the national and provincial levels. In 1921 Ladysmith became the first BC team to compete for a true national title, which originated in 1913 as the Connaught Cup but was later known as the FA Trophy, Dominion Cup, Carling Cup and Challenge Cup. In 1923 the Nanaimo Wanderers became the first of many BC teams to win it, but the real success story of the interwar period was Fred HUME's New Westminster Royals. Featuring Dave TURNER, Austin Delany and future Canadian Soccer Assoc president Aubrey Sanford, the Royals were picked by the Canadian Press news agency as the soccer team of the first half century. Playing in the PCL they won national titles in 1928, 1930, 1931 and 1936, the year Turner retired. The league held many of its games at Vancouver's Con Jones Park, renamed Callister Park in 1942. Players who suceeded Turner and his Royals as BC's finest included goaltender Stan Stronge, North Shore United's

Bruce Wilson, soccer player, in action for Canada against Guatemala, 1985.
Courtesy Univ of Victoria

Jimmy Spencer and Trevor Harvey, and New Westminster Royals goaltender Dan Kulai. Harvey, Spencer and Stronge were all invited to play in England but the first BC player to take up a first (premier)-division offer was Jack COWAN, who starred with Scotland's Dundee United in the early 1950s. During the same period, Gordon "Gogie" Stewart, Errol Crossan, Fre Whittaker and Glen Johnson also played on top British teams with varying degrees of success.

The 3 Lenarduzzi brothers (l to r): Bob, Sam and Dan, at a Vancouver Whitecaps reunion game, 1989.

Through 1950, 7 more national titles went to BC teams, including Vancouver St Andrew's, considered one of Canada's all-time best, Harvey's North Shore United and a Vancouver City team featuring future national team coach Bill McAllister in net and top players Gogie Stewart, Roy "Buster" Cairns and Pat Philley. Led by goaltender Ken Pears, and later with Stewart and Cairns, the Royals returned in the 1950s with another dynasty, winning the championship in 1953, 1955, 1958 and 1960. Pears, Cairns, Stewart and brothers Pat and Brian Philley powered a BC all-star side over visiting Tottenham Hotspur, from Britain, in 1957, then joined 6 other BC players on the World Cup qualifying team later that year. The BC-dominated club beat the US twice before they were eliminated by 2 losses to Mexico. Other noted international soccer events in BC in the 1950s were national-team visits from England (1950) and Ireland (1953); Team BC's first win over international competition, Northern Ireland, in 1953; Vancouver's first major professional game, a 1956 exhibition between UK clubs Aberdeen and Everton in front of 18,000 at Empire Stadium; and a 1956 BC all-star match with Moscow Lokomotiv, the first Soviet sports club to visit North America.

Professional soccer came to Vancouver in 1968 when the United Soccer Association arranged for a team from Sunderland, England, to compete as the Vancouver Royals. The team dropped the direct connection to Sunderland the next year when it picked up other players and joined the new N American Soccer League. With disappointing attendance and unstable ownership, the club folded in 1969. The semi-pro Western Canada Soccer League (1969–1970) included 3 BC teams: the Vancouver Spartans, Vancouver Cougars and Victoria Royals. The Spartans won the league championship in 1969

and the Royals took it the next year. Businessman Herb Capozzi brought a more viable NASL franchise to Vancouver in 1974, and by 1978, when the VANCOUVER WHITECAPS went on a league-record 13-game winning streak, soccer had become the most popular sport in the province. The next year, the Whitecaps garnered the largest reception in BC history when an estimated 100,000 people welcomed them home from their NASL championship triumph. Key players Bob LENARDUZZI and Buzz Parsons were among 4 BC natives playing regularly for the team. Among the many BC players starring in the NASL elsewhere were Victoria's Ian Bridge and one of Canada's greatest-ever defenders, Bruce WILSON. Tony Chursky, a DELTA goaltender out of SFU, was named the NASL's top goaltender in 1976, his rookie year with the Seattle Sounders. He went on to play with various NASL teams to 1982 and to collect 19 international caps playing for Team Canada. In the senior amateur game, Victoria, the birthplace of BC soccer, won national titles in 1975 and again in 1976 and 1979, bookending back-to-back wins by Vancouver Columbus. This heyday of BC soccer in the late 1970s saw women's involvement increase from 3 girls' teams in 1973 to 317 (19 and under) in 1980.

Since the first attempt by a Canadian team to qualify for the 1968 Olympics, BC players have dominated the national team's roster. Two years after reaching the quarter finals at the Los Angeles Olympics, Canada achieved its brightest moment in international soccer by qualifying for the 1986 World Cup. Led by Lenarduzzi, Wilson, Bridge, Vancouver goaltender Paul Dolan and RICHMOND native Randy Samuel, Canada competed well but failed to advance past the first round. Other BC players on the team were Dale Mitchell, George Pakos, David Norman, Mike Sweeney, Randy Ragan and British ex-pats Carl VALENTINE and coach Tony Waiters. Another World Cup player with BC connections was John Van't Schip, a native of FORT ST JOHN who moved to Holland at the age of 9 and became one of that country's top players. After the World Cup, Randy Samuel signed with Dutch powerhouse PSV Eindhoven and Coquitlam's Craig Forrest became Canada's most successful overseas goaltender by playing over 300 games for Ipswich Town in England. Forrest collected over 50 international caps for the Canadian national team and in 2000 he led the team to the Gold Cup, the championship tournament for North, Central and S America and Canada's first international title. The MVP of the event, he was joined on the team by 8 other British Columbians.

After the NASL folded in 1984, the semi-pro Pacific Rim Soccer League formed with 6 teams from the Lower Mainland, Victoria and Nanaimo. It lasted until 1987 and the formation of the pro Canadian Soccer League and the VANCOUVER 86ERS. Tony Waiters and former Canadian Soccer Assoc president Dave Fryatt were both involved in the founding of the team. The 86ers dominated Canadian soccer by capturing 4 straight CSL championships between

1988 and 1991. BC standouts on the team included player-coaches Lenarduzzi and Valentine and players Mitchell, Dolan, and the scoring tandem of Domenic Mobilio and John Catliff, respectively the top 2 CSL goal scorers of all time. Victoria had a semi-professional team called the Riptide in the Western Alliance Challenge Series (with Seattle, Portland and San Jose) in 1985 and placed second. The city later had a CSL team, the Vistas, which lasted from 1989 to 1990. The team featured general manager Bob Bolitho, coach Bruce Wilson and star defender Bridge, all former national stars, in addition to forward Geoff Aunger and likely the world's first heart transplant recipient to play pro sports, midfielder Simon Keith. Amateur soccer continued to thrive in BC as Dick Mosher took over Joe Johnson's successful UBC program and led the men's team to 6 CIAU titles in the 1980s and 1990s. John Buchanan coached SFU to an NAIA title in 1976 and his replacement Keith Watts added two more in 1982 and 1983. At the senior level, teams from Victoria and Vancouver won Challenge Cups in the 1980s and 1990s, giving BC teams a total of 38 national titles at the turn of the century. BC also made strong contributions to a growing women's game, sending goaltender Wendy Hawthorne, defender Andrea Neil, midfielder Geraldine Donnelly and high-scoring forward Silvana Burtini to represent Canada at the first women's World Cup in 1991. Soccer has continued to be the most popular participation sport in BC with a youth registration of nearly 100,000 through 1999.   *SW*

SOCIAL CREDIT LEAGUE OF BC originated in VANCOUVER in 1932 as the Douglas Social Credit Study Group, an informal discussion group organized by journalist Henry Torey to investigate and promote the ideas of Social Credit. Following a visit to Vancouver by Maj C.H. DOUGLAS in 1934, and the electoral success of the SOCIAL CREDIT PARTY in the Alberta election of Aug 1935, the study group incorporated itself as the League and began to organize politically. In the 1937 provincial election it received less than 1% of the vote and largely faded from sight. In 1944 the Social Credit Assoc of Canada organized a BC branch led by Maj A.H. Jukes, but it too failed to attract voter support. A splinter group headed by Lyle Wicks, a Vancouver streetcar driver, formed a new BC Social Credit League in 1949 and received support from the Alberta party. The movement began to attract increased interest when W.A.C. BENNETT joined at the end of 1951. In the election of June 1952, League candidates won 19 seats, one more than the CCF, and formed a new government, led by Bennett. With electoral success, the League transformed itself into the Social Credit Party.

SOCIAL CREDIT PARTY ("Socreds") formed in the wake of the June 1952 provincial election. Its forerunner, the SOCIAL CREDIT LEAGUE OF BC, surprised everyone by winning 19 seats, one more than its nearest opponent, the CCF, and enough to form a minority government. During the election Rev Ernest Hansell led the League, but he had been chosen only for the duration of the campaign. After the vote the elected Socreds met and chose W.A.C. BENNETT to be leader and ultimately PREMIER.

Social Credit adhered nominally to the financial theories of Maj C.H. DOUGLAS, a British engineer who argued that the shortcomings of the capitalist economy resulted from its failure to provide consumers with enough purchasing power. He advocated regular payment of cash dividends, or "social credit," to people to stimulate economic activity. These ideas were embraced by William Aberhart, who led a Social Credit Party to victory in Alberta in 1935. Douglas's theories met with little acceptance in BC. By the time Social Credit won its 1952 election, it had largely discarded the original economic theory and positioned itself as a middle-of-the-road alternative to CCF socialism.

Social Credit retained power in BC for 4 decades, except from 1972 to 1975, by combining anti-socialist scare-mongering and an ambitious program of public works and resource development. Bennett won re-election 6 times and was premier for 20 years. The NDP managed to oust the Socreds in 1972, forcing Bennett's retirement, but under his son Bill BENNETT (leader from Nov 1973) the party came back to win elections in 1975, 1979 and 1983. Bill Bennett's public spending restraint in the mid-1980s met with widespread protests (*see* SOLIDARITY), and he resigned the premiership. His successor William VANDER ZALM carried the party to a solid victory in the 1986 election, but his government struggled with a series of scandals, one of which forced his resignation in 1991. Rita JOHNSTON replaced Vander Zalm as premier; in an election later that year, an NDP win crushed the Socreds. Only a rump of 7 Socreds won seats, setting off a mass exodus from the party. In the 1996 election Social Credit, under its new leader, Larry Gillanders (who resigned partway through the campaign), failed to elect any candidates and the party seemed defunct as an organized political force.
Reading: David Mitchell, *W.A.C. Bennett and the Rise of British Columbia*, 1983; Osborne, J.S. and J.T. Osborne, *Social Credit for Beginners*, 1986.

SOCIAL SERVICES; *see* HUMAN CARE SERVICES.

SOCIALIST PARTY OF BC (SPBC) was formed in VANCOUVER in the summer of 1901. It joined moderate socialist reformers and radical "impossiblists" who believed that reform simply delayed the overthrow of capitalism. In the provincial election of 1903 the party ran 10 candidates, 2 of whom were elected, and it emerged as the leading force for socialism in Canada. In 1904 the SPBC merged with other groups into the Socialist Party of Canada. Its newspaper, the *Western Clarion*, edited by the prominent "impossiblist" E.T. Kingsley, became the official organ of the new party.

SOCIETY FOR THE PREVENTION OF CRUELTY TO ANIMALS (SPCA) is a non-profit animal welfare organization founded originally in England and established in BC in 1895. The society has a central parent body and 32 branches throughout the province, ranging in size from the largest in VANCOUVER to the smallest in the QUEEN CHARLOTTE ISLANDS. As well it engages more than 50 agents in smaller communities. The society operates an animal hospital in Vancouver, a spay and neuter clinic in VICTORIA and more than 2 dozen animal shelters. It responds to complaints of mistreatment, lobbies government for more effective laws and promotes humane education. The society has a paid staff and more than 40,000 volunteers and donors.

SOCIETY FOR PROMOTING ENVIRONMENTAL CONSERVATION (SPEC) is a VANCOUVER-based ENVIRONMENTAL group. Founded in Dec 1968 by Gwen and Derrick MALLARD and a small group of activists, SPEC has campaigned against uranium mining, auto emissions, oil spills and watershed LOGGING. The society is particularly concerned with issues affecting the quality of life in urban areas: traffic congestion, water and air quality, sewage treatment and public transit.

SODA CREEK is located at the head of the upper Fraser Canyon (*see* FRASER R), 33 km north of WILLIAMS LAKE. It lies at the south end of a 650-km stretch of navigable waterway; during the GOLD RUSH in the 1860s it served as a terminus

Soda Creek on the Fraser R. Rick Blacklaws photo

for PADDLEWHEEL STEAMBOATS carrying prospectors and supplies north to QUESNEL and back. The CARIBOO WAGON ROAD arrived in 1863 when the ROYAL ENGINEERS surveyed a townsite. The arrival of the Pacific Great Eastern Rwy (*see* BC RAIL) in 1920 brought about the demise of the sternwheelers, and when the modern highway bypassed the community in 1954 most of the remaining population drifted away. A SEC-WEPEMC (Shuswap) village, Xats'ull, occupied a nearby site on the river for at least 2,000 years;

the Soda Creek FIRST NATION has built a replica of the traditional village that is open to visitors.

SOFTWOOD LUMBER AGREEMENT is a 5-year agreement, effective 1 Apr 1996, between the US and Canada regulating the export of Canadian softwood lumber to the US, which in 1996 accounted for 19% ($4.7 billion) of BC's international exports. This dispute began in 1866, with the end of the first Canada–US free trade agreement, and has reappeared at various times since. This dispute is of great concern to the BC FOREST INDUSTRY, which sells about 60% of its lumber exports in the US. The dispute has been continuous since 1982, when US lumber interests sought to restrict Canadian access to US lumber markets because of perceptions that provincial forest policies had the effect of subsidizing Canadian producers. After Canada endured a series of duties and export taxes, extensive negotiations led to signing of the 1996 agreement limiting lumber exports from BC, Alberta, Ontario and Quebec to 14.7 billion board ft annually. The agreement specified that shipments above that level would incur an escalating export fee, which would be adjusted annually for inflation. *See also* FOREST POLICY.

SOINTULA, pop 637, is on MALCOLM ISLAND, off the east coast of VANCOUVER ISLAND opposite PORT MCNEILL. It was established in 1901 by a party of Finnish socialist utopians led by the journalist and idealist Matti KURIKKA. The FINNS formed the Kalevan Kansa Colonization Co Ltd, which received the island as a grant from the provincial government in return for promises to make improvements. The bulk of the settlers arrived in 1902. *Sointula* is Finnish for "harmony." The utopian commune attracted about 2,000 people during the 4 years of its existence; they published the first printed Finnish-language newspaper in Canada and distributed it worldwide. The commune collapsed in 1905 but many of the settlers remained, making their living in trapping, AGRICULTURE, LOGGING and

Wharves at Sointula, c 1910.
BC Archives D-08473

commercial FISHING. In 1931 Laurie JARVIS, a Sointula Finn, invented the gillnet drum, revolutionizing the commercial fishery. Over the years descendants of the original Finnish colonists have been joined by residents of different backgrounds, particularly during the 1970s, when the back-to-the-land movement brought a wave of latter-day idealists. The community is linked by ferry to Port McNeill.
Reading: Paula Wild, *Sointula: Island Utopia,* 1995.

SOLE is a marine FLATFISH found in waters up to 300 m deep. Like other bottom-dwelling flatfish,

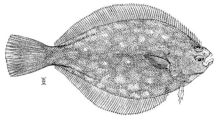

Butter sole. Fisheries & Oceans Canada

Curlfin sole. Phil Edgell photo

sole is asymmetrical as an adult, with its eyes and colour (brown shades) on the right side of its body. A number of sole species dwell in BC, and 10 or more species are landed in the commercial groundfish TRAWL fishery. The most important species are Dover, rock, English and petrale sole. *See also* FLOUNDER; GROUNDFISH.

SOLIDARITY was a coalition of labour unions and community and advocacy groups formed in July 1983 to fight the austerity program (a policy of "restraint") introduced by the SOCIAL CREDIT PARTY government of Bill BENNETT. The coalition was led initially by Art Kube, head of the BC FEDERATION OF LABOUR (BCFL), Renate Shearer, a HUMAN RIGHTS worker, and Father Jim Roberts, a CATHOLIC theologian. Funded by the union movement, it organized one of the largest political demonstrations in BC history as tens of thousands of people took to the streets in rallies and marches to oppose government policies they believed undermined workers' rights and gutted social services. The government responded by holding all-night legislative sessions to force through its program. By Nov, teachers and public employees were on strike and Solidarity was planning a general strike. But a split developed between the labour wing of the coalition officially called Operation Solidarity, which sought to negotiate with the government, and the more radical community groups known as the Solidarity Coalition. Once the public employees won a new contract, labour's enthusiasm for the protest waned. At a meeting in KELOWNA on 13 Nov between Bennett and Jack MUNRO, vice-president of the BCFL, the premier agreed to make small changes to his restraint program and Munro agreed to call off the general strike. The so-called Kelowna Accord outraged many Solidarity members, who felt it was a betrayal of the larger aims of the movement, and the coalition subsequently faded away. *See also* LABOUR MOVEMENT.

SOLSQUA is a tiny farming and LOGGING settlement on the CPR and the north shore of the Eagle R, 30 km northeast of SALMON ARM. The name comes from a SECWEPEMC (Shuswap) word for "water." *AS*

SOMASS RIVER begins at the confluence of the Stamp and Sproat rivers and is the main stem of this river system, which is part of the large Great Central and SPROAT lakes drainage system in central VANCOUVER ISLAND. The word *Somass* means "creek flowing over (or down) an embankment." It flows about 10 km to PORT ALBERNI, where it empties into ALBERNI INLET. Because this area is in a transition ecosystem between the east and west coasts of Vancouver Island, the ESTUARY here is notable for an unusual assemblage of plant species. The region around the river has been occupied for thousands of years. It has been valued for its abundance of FISH and other resources by the Opetchesaht and Tseshaht First Nations, 2 NUU-CHAH-NULTH (Nootka) groups, since before European settlement. The watershed has undergone extensive LOGGING. By the late 1990s the river still supported a sizable SALMON run.

SOMENOS, 50 km north of VICTORIA on the Island Hwy and the ESQUIMALT & NANAIMO RWY, is a VANCOUVER ISLAND farming district (*see* AGRICULTURE) near Somenos Lk. Somenos Marsh is an important nesting and wintering refuge for waterfowl. The name is a COWICHAN word and refers to the "resting places" where paddlers on the COWICHAN R could take a break. *AS*

SOMERSET, Dorothy, theatre pioneer (b 9 June 1900, Perth, Australia; d 11 Aug 1991, Vancouver). A graduate of Radcliffe College, she performed with the Harvard Dramatic Society and studied theatre in England. She was a leading lady in VANCOUVER's Little Theatre in the 1920s and directed annual productions for the University Players Club. She became a permanent member of the UBC Extension Department in 1937. During her tenure there, Somerset established a play-lending library, developed short drama courses, created a radio series called "University Drama School" and founded UBC's Summer School of Theatre. In 1958 she lobbied for the creation of a theatre department at UBC and was subsequently named the

Dorothy Somerset, first head of the UBC theatre department, 1965. UBC 5.1/2868

department's first head. On her retirement in 1965, she received an honorary doctorate.

Dianne Mackay

SOMMERS AFFAIR was a 1955 scandal involving the SOCIAL CREDIT government and its minister of lands and forests, Robert Sommers. Sommers, who had been a school principal in CASTLEGAR before entering politics, was accused by the opposition LIBERALS of improprieties in the granting of a Forest Management Licence to BC FOREST PRODUCTS LTD (BCFP). Judge Arthur Lord investigated the charges and found no basis for them. But the Liberals, especially MLA Gordon GIBSON, refused to lay the matter to rest, claiming that Sommers received money from forest companies in return for favoured treatment. At the end of 1955 the minister responded by suing the VANCOUVER lawyer David Sturdy for libel, a case that dragged on for months and allowed the government of W.A.C. BENNETT to stonewall, even after an RCMP investigation confirmed evidence of wrongdoing. In Feb 1956 Sommers was dropped from the CABINET, but in a general election later that year he was returned to the legislature in an easy victory. He did not fare as well in the courts, however. His libel suit was rejected and in Nov 1957 he was arrested and charged with bribery. A year later he was convicted, along with Wick Gray, a LOGGING operator, and sentenced to 5 years in prison. BCFP was acquitted. Sommers served 28 months before being paroled in mid-1961, after which he operated a piano business on VANCOUVER ISLAND. *See also* FOREST INDUSTRY; FOREST POLICY.

SONGHEES; *see* LEKWAMMEN.

SONO NIS PRESS, a VICTORIA book publisher, was founded in 1968 by J. Michael YATES, a writing professor at UBC. The company originally published literary fiction; in 1976 it was bought by Dick Morriss of Morriss Printing, and it expanded into non-fiction with an emphasis on history and transportation. Morriss died in the

late 1990s and control of the company passed to his daughter Diane. Sono Nis was the name of a character in the first book published by the press, Yates's *The Man in the Glass Octopus*. In Italian *sono* means "I am"; in Anglo-Saxon *nis* means "is not."

SONORA ISLAND, 145 km², lies north of QUADRA ISLAND at the mouth of BUTE INLET in the jumble of islands between VANCOUVER ISLAND and the mainland. It is a high, rugged island surrounded on 3 sides by some of the most treacherous tidal channels on the coast, including the YUCULTAS to the east and the well-known Hole-in-the-Wall on the south. LOGGING began in the 1880s, and from 1914 to 1941 THURSTON BAY on the northwest side of the island was the bustling headquarters of the marine operations of the BC FOREST SERVICE. Since 1970 Thurston Bay has been the site of a provincial MARINE PARK. The only other island settlement is at OWEN BAY. AQUACULTURE began during the 1980s along the island's northwest shore.

SOOKE, pop 11,500, is a LOGGING and FISH-ING community overlooking Sooke Harbour on the southwest coast of VANCOUVER ISLAND, 25 km west of VICTORIA. It was originally inhabited by the

T'sou-ke, a group of NORTHERN STRAITS (Central Coast SALISHAN FIRST NATIONS) people. In 1849 Walter GRANT established a small colony of settlers along the Sooke Basin, the first white set-

East Sooke Regional Park.
Don MacKinnon/ Vancouver Sun

tlers on the Island independent of the HBC. These pioneers were followed by John MUIR, who established his farm, Woodside, in the early 1850s. Sooke was the site of the first steam SAWMILL in BC. In 1864 there was a short-lived GOLD RUSH to nearby Leech R. Whiffen Spit, a wildlife viewing area, protects the harbour from the outside surf. Many residents work in Victoria.

The adjacent settlement of Milnes Landing to the east, named after early resident Ed Milne, has become a suburb of Sooke, while Otter Point to the west and East Sooke across the harbour, site of a regional park, have retained a rural atmosphere. Sooke elected its first mayor and council on 20 Nov 1999 after voting to incorporate as a municipality earlier that year. The district hosts 2 well-known events: the All Sooke Day loggers' celebration in July and a Fine Arts Festival in Aug.

SOOKE LAKE, 16 km north of SOOKE on VAN-COUVER ISLAND, is an important source of water for VICTORIA and was linked to the city by a pipeline built between 1913 and 1915. It was the site of a LOGGING camp in the 1920s and 1930s after the CNR line was built along its eastern shore. *AS*

SOOPOLLALIE (*Shepherdia canadensis*), also called soapberry, is an erect shrub with oval leaves and red, translucent BERRIES that are bitter-tasting and somewhat soapy to the touch. FIRST NATIONS people harvest the berries midsummer and make "Indian ice cream" by whipping them into a foam with water and a sweetener. *See also* PLANTS, NATIVE.

SORBY, Thomas C., architect (b 1836, Wakefield, England; d 1924, Victoria). He was already an accomplished architect in England before he immigrated to Canada in 1883. In Montreal he designed several railway stations and hotels for the CPR, then moved west in 1886 to take part in the post-fire building boom in VANCOUVER. He designed the first Hotel Vancouver, St James Church, the first CPR terminal and a residence for the CPR executive Henry ABBOTT. In VICTORIA he designed several significant residences, including Robert Ward's in Rockland and the parsonage for Christ Church Cathedral. He became fascinated with a scheme to redevelop the Inner Harbour and make Victoria the "super-port" for the West Coast. Though it never developed, Sorby put years of work into promoting the plan. The filling-in of JAMES BAY, the building of large graving docks for marine repairs, development of waterfront recreation parks, dredging of the Inner Harbour—all part of Sorby's 1896 plans, compiled at his own expense—have since become part of Victoria's development history, though the city never officially acknowledged its debt to him. *Martin Segger*

SORENSEN-LENIHAN, Geraldine Ann "Gerry," skier (b 15 Oct 1958, Kimberley). She began SKIING at age 10 and joined the national team in 1979. In 1981 she was the first Canadian woman in more than a decade to win a World Cup race. In Jan 1982 she won the World Cup downhill race in Grindelwald, Switzerland, and the highlight of her career came a month later in Austria when she captured the world alpine downhill championship, the first Canadian to do so since 1958. The Canadian Press news agency named her Canada's outstanding female athlete in 1982. She skied to her fourth World Cup

Gerry Sorensen-Lenihan. Canadian downhill champion, 1983. Ian Lindsay/Vancouver Sun

victory in Puy St Vincent, France, in 1984. She is a member of the Canadian Sports Hall of Fame and the BC SPORTS HALL OF FAME (1986). *SW*

SORRENTO, pop 662, overlooks the west arm of SHUSWAP LK from the TRANS-CANADA HWY 78 km east of KAMLOOPS. It was established as a fruit-growing area in 1910 by J.R. Kinghorn, a promoter, but it became a summer vacation service centre for the western Shuswap area. Kinghorn named the site for the Italian town where he spent his honeymoon.

SOUND RECORDING INDUSTRY in BC is concentrated in VANCOUVER. The city has evolved into an important venue for the recording of popular music owing to the presence of world-class recording studios and skilled technicians and musicians. Sound recording gained popularity with the advent of BROADCAST radio, and many early pop recordings were done in such radio studios as CKWX, CJOR, CFUN and CBC. Private recording studios have operated in Vancouver since the late 1940s, when Al Reusch established the Aragon Recording Studios on Hastings St. Originally Reusch set up Aragon to record highland dance music, but country and western and then early rock 'n' roll predominated. The growing popularity of rock 'n' roll in the 1960s created a demand for studios and several—Studio 3, Psi Chord Studios, Vancouver Sound Recording Studios, R & D Studio—emerged to meet the burgeoning demand. (Record manufacturing also began in the late 1960s; before the advent of the digital format led to its closure in 1988, Marpole's Imperial Records had pressed more than 5,000 titles.) In 1970 the Canadian Radio-Television and Tele-communications Commission introduced Canadian content regulations mandating the proportion of domestic music played on the air-

waves. One of the stipulations of "Cancon" was that the recording studio be located in Canada; this gave the Canadian recording industry a giant boost. Several recording studios opened in Vancouver during the 1970s, including Mushroom, Pinewood, Little Mountain and Blue Wave. These studios attracted local acts such as Bryan ADAMS, LOVERBOY, Heart and the Powder Blues Band, and international acts like Aerosmith, Van Halen and Olivia Newton-John. Several smaller studios such as Profile, Bullfrog and Ocean, were important in the development of Vancouver's alternative music scene. Cancon regulations also spurred the development of local talent, creating a demand for more sophisticated recording technology and personnel. Vancouver became home to some of the world's best recording personnel, including Bruce FAIRBAIRN, Bob Rock, Mike Fraser, Jim VALLANCE, Ron Obvious and David FOSTER. This expertise attracted international acts to the city—including Yes, the Cranberries and Kiss—that used local studios such as Bryan Adams's Warehouse Studio in GASTOWN and Fairbairn's Armoury Studios in Kitsilano. The sound recording industry has also accommodated the demands of the local FILMMAKING INDUSTRY. *Mike Harling*

SOUNDSCAPE PROJECT; *see* WORLD SOUNDSCAPE PROJECT.

SOUTH ASIANS began immigrating to BC from India, Pakistan, Bangladesh and Sri Lanka in 1903, when small numbers of single men arrived to find work in SAWMILLS, road and rail construction, farm labouring and land clearing. By 1908 there were 5,179 S Asians in Canada, almost all in BC. Ironically the exclusionary HEAD TAX placed on CHINESE immigrants created employment opportunities for these newcomers. Almost all the S Asians came from the Punjab area of northern India and almost all of these were Sikhs (*see* SIKHISM). As their number grew, the white community became alarmed and demanded that restrictions already imposed on Chinese and JAPANESE immigrants apply also to S Asians. In 1907 they were deprived of the vote in provincial and municipal jurisdictions, which led to their exclusion from the federal vote, from citizenship and from many jobs and elected offices. At the same time informal restrictions barred access to economic and professional opportunities. Early in 1908 the federal government imposed a regulation requiring immigrants to Canada to arrive on a continuous voyage from their home port. As the government knew, there was no direct shipping connection between India and Canada, so the new requirement had the effect of banning S Asian immigration. The new policy was challenged, most notably during the *KOMAGATA MARU* incident in 1914, but remained in place until 1947. Until 1919 the ban extended to wives and children of men already in BC; as a result the size of the community shrank to about 2,300 by 1911 and 951 in 1921. (Of the small number of women who managed to get into Canada, one was Uday Ram, who in 1911 gave birth to the first S Asian

born in Canada.) Despite economic, political and social discrimination, S Asians managed to make a place for themselves in BC. The FOREST INDUSTRY in particular became an economic mainstay. Pressure to restore the vote increased during the 1930s but the provincial government stalled until 1947 when it granted the franchise. This meant that the federal franchise was automatically restored, and later that year the municipalities followed suit. Immigration policy also changed. The federal government established a quota system in 1951, set initially at 300 S Asian immigrants annually. Further loosening of restrictions followed until S Asians received the same treatment as any other group. One result was that the BC community diversified to include not just Sikhs from the Punjab but many Hindus and Muslims (*see* ISLAM), as well as people from a variety of destinations: Ismailis from Uganda, Goans from E Africa, Indians from Fiji and the Caribbean, Malayalees from Kerala and Sinhalese, Tamils from Sri Lanka, and others. The term "S Asian" now resembles the term "European" in its inclusion of many diverse cultural backgrounds and geographic locations.

Another change in immigration patterns was a shift in destination away from BC, so that by 1971 only 28% of S Asians in Canada lived here. In 1998 about 200,000 people of S Asian background lived in BC, the majority in VANCOUVER, where the Punjabi Market on Main St is one of the largest in N America, and in SURREY. While discrimination has not ended, S Asians are prominent in all walks of life and play leading roles in the economic, social and political life of the province. Their influence became strikingly evident in Feb 2000 when Ujjal DOSANJH, a Vancouver lawyer and MLA, became PREMIER. *Reading:* Norman Buchignani, Doreen M. Indra with Ram Srivastiva, *Continuous Journey: A Social History of South Asians in Canada*, 1985.

SOUTH SLOCAN, pop 142, is a small settlement 18 km west of NELSON on the north shore of the KOOTENAY R, 1 km from the first of the BONNINGTON FALLS dams. Originally known as Slocan Junction, it was the spot where the CPR's Slocan branch, built in 1897, joined the southern CPR mainline. *AS*

SOUTHBANK, 24 km south of BURNS LAKE, is a small LOGGING and AGRICULTURAL settlement on the south shore of FRANÇOIS LK. It has been a ferry terminus since 1916, and a hotel and outpost hospital operated here in the 1920s. The ferry *Omineca Princess* was still running in 2000; its predecessor, the *Jacob Henkel*, honoured a pioneer who came to the area in 1904. Many MENNONITES settled here. *AS*

SOUTHERN RAILWAY OF BC, based in NEW WESTMINSTER and owned since 1994 by the WASHINGTON MARINE GROUP, operates in the lower FRASER VALLEY between New Westminster and CHILLIWACK. It links industrial facilities and ports, hauling freight for local shippers and other railways. A major part of its business involves shipping automobiles to and from ANNACIS ISLAND.

The railway maintains a fleet of 19 locomotives and owns 200 km of track.

SOWARD, Frederick Hubert, historian (b 10 Apr 1899, Minden, Ont; d 1 Jan 1985, Vancouver). A veteran of WWI, he remained in Britain after the war to study at Oxford and Edinburgh. He joined the history department at UBC in 1922 and taught there to his retirement in

F.H. Soward, historian, c 1960. UBC 1.1/15845

1966. He was department head from 1953 to 1963 and dean of graduate studies from 1961 to 1965. An advisor to the Department of External Affairs during WWII, he pioneered the academic study of international relations in Canada.

SPALLUMCHEEN, the largest district municipality in BC by area, pop 5,322, lies north of OKANAGAN LK in the Spallumcheen Valley. The name comes from a Salish word said to mean "beautiful place," or "beautiful valley" (*see* SALISHAN FIRST NATIONS). The earliest settlers arrived in the 1860s. The first community was called Lansdowne, after the gov gen, but it was abandoned when construction of the SHUSWAP & OKANAGAN RWY passed it by and a new settlement sprang up at ARMSTRONG in 1892. The municipality of Spallumcheen received its charter in July 1892. In 1913 Armstrong incorporated as a separate city, creating the unique situation of one municipality surrounded by another. AGRICULTURE has always been the primary industry. TOURIST attractions include the CARAVAN FARM THEATRE and the O'KEEFE HISTORIC RANCH.

SPANISH EXPLORATION of the BC coast in the late 18th century was motivated by concern about a Russian approach to New Spain (Mexico) and later by a search for the Northwest Passage. Spain claimed the entire Pacific coast of America following a late 16th-century papal division of the world between Spain and Portugal. In 1774 Juan PEREZ left San Blas, Mexico, commanding the *Santiago*. On 18 July he sighted the northern end of the QUEEN CHARLOTTE ISLANDS and encountered HAIDA people,

who launched canoes from Langara Island and traded with his crew. He did not land. Later he anchored off NOOTKA SOUND and again traded with local people but neither landed nor officially claimed the area for Spain. These were the first confirmed contacts between Europeans and aboriginal people on the Northwest Coast.

In 1775 Juan Francisco de la BODEGA Y QUADRA in the *Sonora* reached 58°30′ and explored Bucareli Bay off Prince of Wales Island in Alaska. In 1779, learning of James COOK's plan to search for the Northwest Passage, Spain launched a third expedition. Although a year late to intercept the British mariner, it explored as far as Cook Inlet and Kodiak Island.

LAPEROUSE's French expedition to the Northwest Coast in 1786 led to renewed Spanish activity. Estéban José MARTINEZ explored the Alaskan coast north and west to Unalaska Island in 1788, returning to Mexico with information suggesting a Russian plan to occupy Nootka. The Spanish decided to move first. In 1789 Martínez led an expedition to Nootka, where the Spanish established themselves at the present-day village of YUQUOT in Friendly Cove. Here Martínez seized British fur-trading vessels, touching off the NOOTKA SOUND CONTROVERSY. The Spanish withdrew that fall, but in 1790 Francisco ELIZA brought soldiers under the command of Pedro ALBERNI to occupy the site more permanently. While a fort and settlement were under construction, Manuel QUIMPER explored into JUAN DE FUCA STRAIT. The Spanish wintered at Nootka, and in 1791 Eliza continued this exploration with José María NARVAEZ in the tiny schooner *Santa Saturnina*, becoming the first Europeans to enter GEORGIA STRAIT. Scientists attached to a major expedition commanded by Alejandro MALASPINA visited in the summer of that year, exploring and describing Nootka

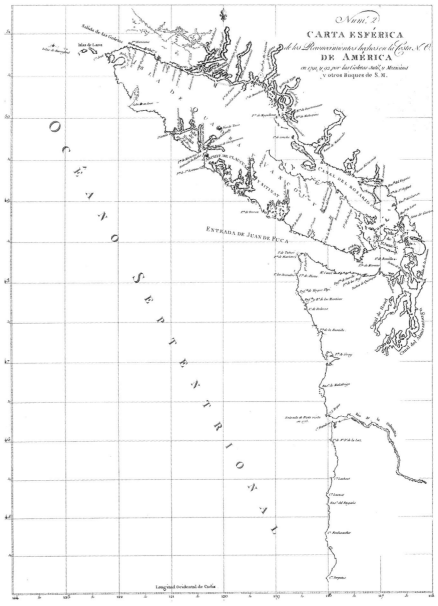

Map from Dionisio Alcalá-Galiano's 1792 expedition. From Relacíon/Historical Atlas of BC

Sound. When Spain and Britain reached a diplomatic agreement over Nootka Sound, Bodega y Quadra was sent there to negotiate the details with George VANCOUVER. Also during his expedition of summer of 1792, Jacinto CAAMANO searched for the Strait of FONTE. Malaspina returned to Mexico in 1791, having learned the details of explorations beyond Juan de Fuca Strait, and persuaded the Viceroy to dispatch 2 officers, Dionisio ALCALA-GALIANO and Cayetano VALDES in the *Sutil* and *Mexicana* to continue searching for a passage to the Atlantic. After visiting Nootka, they entered the strait and encountered Capt Vancouver off Point Grey in late June 1792. For 2 weeks the Spanish and British explored together, sharing information as they sailed among the islands separating VANCOUVER ISLAND from the mainland. After parting from the British, Galiano and Valdes took a more easterly route into Queen Charlotte Strait. They entered the Pacific via Goletas Channel and proceeded to Nootka, completing the first circumnavigation of Vancouver Island by Europeans. That fall Bodega y Quadra and Vancouver failed to settle the competing Spanish and British claims; the Nootka affair was ultimately resolved in Europe. In 1795 Spain ended its occupation of Yuquot and, after one final expedition in 1796, ceased maritime activity north of California.

SPARROW is a small perching bird. Its short, conical bill is adapted to feeding on seeds, but it also eats caterpillars and other INSECTS in summer. Sparrows are primarily birds of brushlands, fields and hedges, nesting and feeding on or near the ground. The house sparrow (*Passer domesticus*) is a member of the family Passeridea; it is a

White-crowned sparrow.
Tim Zurowski photo

very common backyard bird in southern BC but is not native to N America: it was introduced to the eastern US in 1850 and spread rapidly across the continent. Native sparrows are members of the family Emberizidae and are not close relatives of the house sparrow. Males and females generally look alike, most species coloured in patterns of brown and grey. Of the 29 species found in Canada, 21 breed in BC. Common, widespread species include the chipping (*Spizella*

passerina), savannah (*Passerculus sandwichensis*), fox (*Passerella iliaca*), song (*Melospiza melodia*), Lincoln's (*M. lincolnii*) and white-crowned (*Zonotrichia melodia*) sparrows. The American tree sparrow (*Spizella arborea*) breeds only in the northern reaches of the province, and the white-throated (*Zonotrichia albicollis*), LeConte's (*Ammodramus leconteii*), swamp (*Melospiza georgiana*) and Nelson's sharp-tailed (*Ammodramus nelsoni*) sparrows are restricted to the northeast corner of BC. The clay-colored sparrow (*Spizella pallida*) is uncommon in brushy grasslands in the Interior, while the vesper (*Pooecetes gramineus*), lark (*Chondestes grammacus*) and grasshopper (*Ammodramus savannarum*) sparrows are restricted to southern GRASSLANDS. The Brewer's sparrow (*Spizella breweri*) is found in southern sagebrush habitats as well as northern subalpine shrubs. TOWHEES, JUNCOS, snow BUNTINGS and LONGSPURS are also in the family Emberizidae.

SPARROW, Edward Sr, X'muzk'i'um leader (b 24 Dec 1898, Musqueam; d 2 Aug 1998, Musqueam). As a youngster he began working at a SALMON cannery in STEVESTON (*see* SALMON CANNING). After attending RESIDENTIAL SCHOOL at CHILLIWACK he went to work in a SAWMILL and over the years made his living at a variety of occupations up and down the coast. He was a founding member of the NATIVE BROTHERHOOD OF BC, a 3-time chief of the X'muzk'i'um (MUSQUEAM) and a lifelong proponent of their claims to ABORIGINAL RIGHTS. Ronald Sparrow, who launched a landmark lawsuit over aboriginal FISHING rights, is a grandson (*see* SPARROW DECISION). *See also* FIRST NATIONS OF BC.

SPARROW DECISION was a legal case with profound implications for ABORIGINAL RIGHTS in BC. Ronald Sparrow, an elder of the X'muzk'i'um (MUSQUEAM) First Nation in VANCOUVER, was charged in May 1984 with FISHING with an illegal net. He was convicted, but 2 years later the BC Court of Appeal overturned the decision. In 1990 the Supreme Court of Canada upheld the appeal court, ruling that the aboriginal right to catch fish for food is protected by Section 35(1) of the *Constitution Act 1982* and takes priority over other users of the resource. Section 35(1) affirms the aboriginal and treaty rights of aboriginal people; *Sparrow* was the first case involving it to reach the Supreme Court. *See also* FIRST NATIONS OF BC.

SPARWOOD, district municipality, pop 3,982, is a COAL-mining centre in the ELK R Valley in the E KOOTENAY, 28 km north of FERNIE and 21 km from the Alberta border. Railway builders considered the local trees good for ships' spars, hence the name. Constructed to replace the historic MINING towns of MICHEL and NATAL, which were settled in the 1890s, Sparwood was incorporated on 12 May 1966. Kaiser Resources Ltd developed an open-pit mine, now owned by TECK CORP's Elkview Coal, in 1968. The Line Creek Mine, operated by Luscar Ltd, and Byron Creek Collieries opened nearby in the 1970s. FORDING

INC has been the third major player in the coal industry here. Alberta Natural Gas and CRESTBROOK FOREST INDUSTRIES LTD have also been prominent employers. Sparwood is home to the Titan, the world's largest dual-axle dumptruck; more than 500 visitors a day are drawn to view this behemoth in the summer months.

SPATSIZI PLATEAU WILDERNESS PROVINCIAL PARK, 6,567.85 km², lies 325 km north of HAZELTON between the Stikine Plateau and Skeena Mts on the west, the Cassiar Mts on the north and Omineca Mts on the east. One of the largest parks in the province, it is known for its populations of grizzly BEARS, WOLVES, MOOSE, Stone's sheep (*see* MOUNTAIN SHEEP), MOUNTAIN GOATS and BC's largest herd of woodland CARIBOU. More than 140 species of birds are also found here. Gladys Lake ECOLOGICAL RESERVE (485.6 km²), in the west central portion of the park, was established to help protect sheep and goat populations. In the western portion of the park the Eaglenest Range reaches elevations of 2,500 m. The plateau itself is high, rolling upland broken by wide GLACIATED valleys. Excellent hiking, canoeing, rafting, horse-packing, nature study and sport FISHING are afforded by the park, which was created in 1975 largely through the efforts of Tommy and Marian WALKER. The word *Spatsizi* means "red goat" in the TAHLTAN language, a reference to the reddish colour taken on by mountain goats when they roll in the red dust near Cold Fish Lk. The park was established to provide habitat for its wildlife and frequently has been called the "Serengeti of the North."

SPATSIZI RIVER originates on the eastern slopes of the Skeena Mts just outside of the southern boundary of SPATSIZI PLATEAU WILDERNESS PARK. It courses northward for about 70 km through the middle of the park, then easterly before adding its silty flow to the waters of the STIKINE R; it is one of the largest tributaries of the Stikine. Along the way it passes close to Cold Fish Lk and the Gladys Lake ECOLOGICAL RESERVE. Hyland Post was built in 1926 on the upper reaches of the river, just before its confluence with the Stikine, by the Hyland brothers as a base for guide-outfitters and trappers. It was resurrected by Tommy and Marian WALKER when they moved to the area in 1948. The Spatsizi R is a favourite destination for experienced wilderness canoeists.

SPENCE, Thomas, miner, contractor (b circa 1826, Dundee, Scotland; d 7 June 1881, Victoria). He went to San Francisco in 1849 during the California gold rush and came to BC in 1858 when news of another gold find reached the outside world (*see* GOLD RUSH, FRASER R). After a short time prospecting on the FRASER R, he turned his attention to road building and became one of the main contractors for the CARIBOO WAGON ROAD, supervising the construction of 2 long sections. Early in 1865 his men built SPENCES BRIDGE, the first bridge across the THOMPSON R, replacing a ferry operated by Mortimer Cook. After the

Cariboo Wagon Road was completed to BARK-ERVILLE in 1865, the government hired him as superintendent of public works to maintain the road and supervise further construction. Spence was also responsible for improving navigation on the Fraser and other waterways. He retained the position until his accidental death in VICTORIA. *See also* ROADS AND HWYS.

SPENCER, Brian "Spinner," hockey player (b 3 Sept 1949, Fort St James; d 2 June 1988, Riviera Beach, FL). His story is one of the most troubling in NHL history. As a young player in the WHL he shuffled from team to team, failing to put up impressive statistics but building a reputation for great strength. In 1969 he was drafted by the Toronto Maple Leafs. One day in 1970 his father Roy, enraged that CBC-TV was broadcasting a VANCOUVER CANUCKS game instead of allowing him to see his son play, drove to the CBC outlet in PRINCE GEORGE and held employees at gunpoint while demanding that the coverage be switched. He was shot and killed when he opened fire on 2 police officers. Brian spent the rest of his 9-year NHL career with the New York Islanders and Buffalo Sabres before ending it with the Pittsburgh Penguins. He made a poor adjustment to life after hockey, becoming dependent on alcohol and involved in prostitution and drugs. In 1987 he was acquitted of kidnapping and first-degree murder and after the trial tried to straighten out his life, but he was shot and killed as the victim in a roadside robbery attempt. A book about his life, *Gross Misconduct*, was published in 1988, followed by a TV movie of the same name written by Paul Gross and directed by Atom EGOYAN.   *SW*

SPENCER, David, retailer (b 9 Aug 1837, St Athan, Wales; d 2 Mar 1920, Victoria). After apprenticing with a dry goods company in his native Wales, he immigrated to VICTORIA in 1863. He began in business as a bookseller, then entered the dry goods business. In 1873 he bought a Government St store and developed it into the department store David Spencer Ltd. He expanded to NANAIMO in 1890 and to Hastings St in VANCOUVER in 1906, as well as to smaller centres. The stores were known particularly for their British imports. Spencer was a Methodist lay preacher, active in the temperance movement. His eldest child Chris Spencer (1869–1953) took over the chain at his father's death and continued to manage the stores until he sold to Eaton's in 1948. Another son, Victor, vice-president of the chain, built the Tudor-style mansion known as Aberthau, now the West Point Grey Community Centre.

SPENCES BRIDGE, pop 138, is located 37 km north of LYTTON in the arid southern Interior, where the NICOLA R joins the THOMPSON R. It was originally Cook's Ferry, named for the man who ran a ferry across the Thompson; the name changed in 1865 when Thomas SPENCE built the first bridge. It is in the traditional territory of the NLAKA'PAMUX (Thompson) people. Both the TRANS-CANADA HWY and the CPR mainline pass

The bridge for which Spences Bridge is named, 1890s. UBC BC252

through the community. Produce farming (*see* AGRICULTURE) is an active industry and roadside stalls featuring locally-grown produce attract many visitors every summer and fall.

SPERLING STATION was a LOGGING and AGRICULTURAL settlement that developed around a stop on the BC ELECTRIC RWY CO'S INTERURBAN line 26 km southeast of NEW WESTMINSTER, in the municipality of LANGLEY. It was named after R.H. Sperling, general manager of the railway from 1905 to 1914.   *AS*

SPIDER is an arthropod (an animal with jointed limbs) belonging to the class Arachnida, which also includes scorpions and TICKS. A spider's body is divided into 2 parts, the cephalothorax and the much larger abdomen. Along with 8 walking legs, a spider has fangs and poison glands, though most do not produce enough venom to be dangerous to humans. The spider has specialized organs called spinnerets that produce the fine silk used for making webs. It has up to 8 eyes, though it can only distinguish light and dark. There are about 1,300 species of spiders in Canada, several hundred of which occur in BC. The most common include orb weavers, whose familiar webs are constructed to catch flying insects; jumping spiders, which often move by leaping (these spiders have more highly developed eyesight than sedentary web-building spiders); and crab spiders, which grab their prey with crab-like front legs. Spiders feed mainly on INSECTS and play a significant role in helping to control insect pests.

SPILLIMACHEEN, pop 77, is a rural settlement on the COLUMBIA R, 60 km southeast of GOLDEN. The name comes from an OKANAGAN First Nation word for "flat area along edge." Nearby lead, ZINC and SILVER deposits were worked from the 1880s until the late 1950s; the MINING camp was named Galena, another term for lead sulphide ore.   *AS*

SPILSBURY, Ashton James "Jim," businessman, coastal mariner (b 8 Oct 1905, Derbyshire,

England). Raised on SAVARY ISLAND, he became interested in radio communication as a young man. In the 1920s he set up a business selling and servicing radio equipment to the many far-flung small settlements along the coast. During WWII the business moved to VANCOUVER and began manufacturing radio-telephones. In 1944 Spilsbury began using a seaplane to keep in

Jim Spilsbury, coastal pioneer, with his Order of BC medal, 1993.

touch with his customers; this single aircraft eventually grew into QUEEN CHARLOTTE AIRLINES. By the time he sold it in 1955, the airline was the third largest commercial carrier in Canada in terms of air miles flown. Spilsbury then returned to the radio company full-time and built Spilsbury Communications Ltd into one of the country's largest exporters of radio-telephone equipment. Following his retirement in 1981, he wrote 3 bestselling books about his life on the coast, the best known being *Spilsbury's Coast* (with Howard WHITE). He is a member of the ORDER OF BC (1993).

SPIRIT OF THE WEST is a Celtic-influenced pop music group formed in VANCOUVER in 1983 by Geoffrey Kelly, John Mann and J. Knutson. The group originally performed traditional folk music as the Evesdroppers. After its second album, Hugh McMillan replaced Knutson. Other members have included Vince Ditrich and Linda McRae, who subsequently left to pursue a solo career. The band is popular in Canada, in the US and throughout Europe and has recorded 9 albums including their major label debut, *Save This House* (1989), and their first platinum-seller, *Faithlift* (1993). In 1996 the band released a live album with the VANCOUVER SYMPHONY ORCHESTRA, *Open Heart Symphony. See also* SOUND RECORDING INDUSTRY.   *Patrick Francis*

SPOFFORD, Cecilia McNaughton, suffrage campaigner (b 4 Dec 1859, Sydney, NS; d 18 Feb 1938, Victoria). A schoolteacher by profession, she was active in the Woman's Christian Temperance Union; as its president in 1909 she launched a province-wide campaign for WOMEN'S SUFFRAGE. She played an important role in delegations to government and PROHIBITION parades and rallies. An authority on laws affecting women and children, she was the only woman appointed to a provincial commission on public health and NURSING in 1919. At the same time she was elected a VICTORIA school trustee. A plaque in the legislature honours her contribution.

SPONGE is a primitive multi-cellular aquatic animal of the phylum Porifera that filters food from the water as it drifts by. Sponges occur in many colours, including white and black, and in many forms, including thin encrusting mats, attached spheres and erect tube-like, vase-like or branching growths reaching heights of 2 m or more. When broken, some smell like exploded gunpowder. Sponges are common in most marine habitats from the intertidal zone to depths greater than 700 m. More than 260 species live in BC waters, some of which encrust on SCALLOPS. Large sponges provide shelter for fishes and a variety of invertebrates.

Sponge reef mounds (bioherms) occur on glacial till or bedrock in glacially formed troughs in HECATE STRAIT and QUEEN CHARLOTTE SOUND, in water 150–250 m deep. Possibly globally unique, these siliceous Hexactinellid ("glass") sponges form a network around which sediments are deposited. Comprised of broad ridges and mounds to 18 m in height, they form reef complexes up to 300 km². Sponge reefs have occupied some sites continuously since the last GLACIATION and are the focus of scientific research. The live sponges on the surface of these reefs may be 100–150 years old; radiocarbon dating suggests that the oldest mound was formed about 9,000 years ago.   *Rick Harbo*

SPORT BC, formed in 1966, is a nonprofit umbrella organization representing more than 80 BC amateur sports groups. It provides leadership and co-ordination in overall sport issues such as government funding, promotes sport in the province, administers BC athlete-of-the-year awards and the Kidsport Fund and, at its base in VANCOUVER, administers 45 offices for individual sports.

SPORT MEDICINE COUNCIL OF BC (SMCBC) is a non-profit organization that develops, promotes and administers a variety of educational programs, resources and services for the provincial sport, recreation and fitness communities. Founded in 1982 and located in BURNABY at the 8-Rinks Ice Sport Centre, the SMCBC is widely recognized as an authority on fitness, health and exercise. It promotes the ongoing development and coordination of medical, nutritional, psychological and physiological programs and services for provincial team and other elite athletes. It also administers the BC SportsAid Program for individuals interested in upgrading/developing their knowledge and skills in the prevention and first aid care of sport-related injuries. The SMCBC works in co-operation with the Canadian Centre for Ethics in Sport to implement testing, prevention and education programs designed to eliminate doping and promote drug-free sport in Canada. Through a network of physicians, therapists and SportsAid trained volunteers, the council coordinates on-site medical and paramedical assistance at a variety of sporting events, including the VANCOUVER SUN Run. It publishes a quarterly newsletter, the *SportsAider*, along with books and manuals.

Claire Sowerbutt

SPRINGHOUSE, a ranching settlement 24 km south of WILLIAMS LAKE in the CARIBOO, was originally an inn on the earliest trail leading to the goldfields (*see* GOLD RUSHES). It dates from 1862. Augustine Boitano bought the property in 1886 and developed the ranch with his sons Antoine and Clifford. The name acknowledges nearby St Peter's Spring. *See also* CATTLE INDUSTRY.   *AS*

SPROAT, Gilbert Malcolm, entrepreneur, author, Indian commissioner (b 19 Apr 1834, Borgue, Scotland; d 4 June 1913, Victoria). He came to VANCOUVER ISLAND in 1860 as a representative of a London firm helping to finance a sawmill at PORT ALBERNI. In 1863 he succeeded Edward STAMP as manager of ANDERSON MILL, the first export SAWMILL in BC. Meanwhile he became a justice of the peace and pursued business interests in VICTORIA. After the sawmill closed, Sproat returned to England and in 1868 published his classic account of the NUU-CHAH-NULTH people, *Scenes and Studies of Savage Life*. He was appointed BC's first agent general in 1871 and served until 1875. After returning to BC in 1876, he was named one of 3 Indian reserve commissioners appointed to resolve land issues with various FIRST NATIONS bands (*see also* ABORIGINAL RIGHTS; RESERVES). In 1878 the 3-person commission was dissolved and Sproat carried on as the only commissioner. His sympathy for the aboriginal point of view made him unpopular with the provincial government and white settlers, who thought he was being too generous with his land settlements, and in 1880

he was forced to resign. He held other government posts, particularly in the KOOTENAY, where he had a hand in founding REVELSTOKE and NEW DENVER. After retiring from public service in 1889 he promoted real estate in the Interior. Back in Victoria after 1898 he passed his retirement preparing a history of BC that was not completed. SPROAT LK near Port Alberni is named for him.

SPROAT LAKE, 37.8 km², 25 km long with 3 ragged arms at its eastern end, lies just west of PORT ALBERNI on VANCOUVER ISLAND. It drains via the Sproat and SOMASS rivers, major SALMON spawning streams, into the head of ALBERNI INLET. Part of the traditional territory of the Opetchesaht FIRST NATION of the NUU-CHAH-NULTH (Nootka) people, it is the site of well-known petroglyphs showing mythical marine creatures visible along the lakeshore (*see* ROCK ART). The lake was named for Gilbert Malcolm SPROAT in 1856. The surrounding area underwent extensive LOGGING beginning in the 1860s. By the 1990s it had become a well-populated lake abuzz with recreation boats in the summer. Sproat Lake Provincial PARK (39 ha) is situated on the north side.

SPROULE, Robert Evan, miner (b circa 1837, Weeks Mills, ME; d 29 Oct 1886, Victoria). He was the key figure in one of BC's most notorious murder trials. An itinerant prospector, he moved to KOOTENAY LK from the US in 1882 and staked a claim on the ore body that became the Bluebell mine at RIONDEL (*see also* MINING). Later that season another miner, Thomas Hammill, crossed the lake from AINSWORTH and jumped Sproule's claim. In 1883 a judge ruled in favour of Sproule, but the decision was appealed to the BC Supreme Court, where Justice Matthew BEGBIE also ruled in favour of Sproule. On 1 June 1885 Sproule and Hammill were at the lake; Hammill was fatally shot. Sproule, who had left the camp, was pursued and arrested and brought to trial. Despite conflicting testimony and the lack of direct evidence, he was convicted of murder and sentenced to hang. A public outcry, and appeals that went all the way to the Supreme Court of Canada, delayed his execution but in the end the sentence was carried out.

SPRUCE is a coniferous tree occurring in BC in 4 types. White spruce (*Picea glauca*) inhabits most of the Interior in mixed stands with other tree species. Sitka spruce (*P. sitchensis*) grows in a narrow band along the coast, where it is very tolerant of fog and salt spray. It is the tallest variety; the famous Carmanah Giant on VANCOUVER ISLAND soars 96.6 m and is the tallest known tree in Canada (*see also* TREES, GIANT). During both world wars the light, strong wood from Sitka spruce was used

Sitka spruce.
© *T.C. Brayshaw*

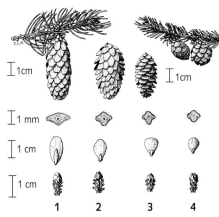

Top to bottom: Branch, cone, cone scale and bract, twig and bud of the Sitka (1), Engelmann (2), white (3) and black (4) spruce.
© T.C. Brayshaw

for airplane construction. Engelmann spruce (*P. engelmannii*) occurs in the Interior, where it usually grows at higher altitudes. Black spruce (*P. mariana*) inhabits the northern Interior, growing mostly in bogs and swamps. All species of spruce have long, straight trunks and scaly bark. It is one of the most commercially important tree species, used for construction, wood containers and pulp stock. *See also* FOREST INDUSTRY; FOREST PRODUCTS.

SPUZZUM, pop 33, is a tiny hamlet in the Fraser Canyon 18 km north of YALE (*see* FRASER R). It was the most southerly village of the NLAKA'PAMUX (Thompson) First Nations and was considered the boundary between their territory and that of the STO:LO of the FRASER VALLEY. Simon FRASER passed a night at the village on his way down the river in 1808. The CPR opened a station in 1885 and during the 1930s the BC PROVINCIAL POLICE had an outpost.

SQUAMISH, district municipality, pop 13,994, lies at the head of HOWE SOUND, 66 km north of VANCOUVER at the mouth of the SQUAMISH R. Originally occupied by the SQUAMISH First

Nation, the site was settled by Europeans in the 1880s and was known briefly as Newport. *Squamish* is a Native word meaning "mother of the wind." Hop farming was important until

Downtown Squamish. *Keith Thirkell photo*

WWI; the FOREST INDUSTRY and BC RAIL, which opened a maintenance depot here, have been the main employers. About a third of the workforce commutes to jobs in Vancouver and WHISTLER. Squamish incorporated as a village in 1948 and a district municipality in 1964, absorbing Paradise Valley, WOODFIBRE, BRACKENDALE and Garibaldi Highlands. It is the gateway to a spectacular outdoor recreation area that includes nearby GARIBALDI PROVINCIAL PARK, the STAWAMUS CHIEF (a sheer granite escarpment popular with ROCK CLIMBERS), Shannon Falls and some of the best windsurfing in N America. In the winter the area attracts large numbers of bald EAGLES. There is a campus of Capilano College (*see* COMMUNITY COLLEGES) and, since 1972, a deep-water port facility.

SQUAMISH First Nation, a division of the Central Coast Salish people (*see* SALISHAN FIRST NATIONS), occupied several traditional village sites in HOWE SOUND and up the drainage of the SQUAMISH and CHEAKAMUS rivers. By about 1850 they also had replaced the MUSQUEAM (now X'muzk'i'um) people in BURRARD INLET. At one point Squamish territory encompassed what is currently part of STANLEY PARK, N VANCOUVER, W VANCOUVER, HORSESHOE BAY and the route of the SEA TO SKY HWY (Hwy 99) all the way to WHISTLER. At contact with Europeans they numbered about 1,700; the 1999 population was 2,910, most of whom live in 9 main RESERVE communities. At the Mission Reserve west of the foot of Lonsdale Ave in N Vancouver the Squamish welcomed OBLATES OF MARY IMMACULATE missionaries and in 1866 erected a chapel, the first ROMAN CATHOLIC church in Greater VANCOUVER. It was replaced by St Paul's Church

Joe Mathias, longtime chief of the Squamish Nation, 1990. *Ian Smith/Vancouver Sun*

in 1886. *See also* FIRST NATIONS OF BC; SALISHAN FIRST NATIONS.

SQUAMISH is a strong winter wind of up to 40 knots blowing out of HOWE SOUND. It takes its name from the community at the head of the inlet. Though the term is often applied to strong outflow winds in other coastal inlets farther north, these usually have their own local names, such as the JERVIS INLET Express. As the wind dissipates over GEORGIA STRAIT it sometimes carries snow showers to the east coast of VANCOUVER ISLAND.

SQUAMISH RIVER flows south from its headwaters in the COAST MTS to empty into the head of HOWE SOUND at the city of SQUAMISH. Its main tributaries are the CHEAKAMUS and Elaho rivers. It drains a watershed of about 3,200 km², a heavily logged area that was the traditional territory of the SQUAMISH First Nation. It is an important river for Pacific SALMON and in Jan and Feb hosts the world's highest concentration of bald EAGLES, which feed on the spawned-out fish. The ESTUARY of the Squamish is also a vital sanctuary for birds. AS

SQUID is a MOLLUSC of the class Cephalopoda, which includes the OCTOPUS, cuttlefish and nautilus (the latter 2 do not occur in BC waters). Unlike the octopus, which has 8 tentacles, the squid typically has 10 tentacles, 2 of which are specialized for breeding. The animal can jet backwards at great speeds and squirt a black inky substance into the water, forming a cloud to obscure it in order to avoid predators. The squid has a horny beak and feeds on small FISH, SHRIMP and other crustaceans. Squid often form schools and are eaten by fish, marine mammals and seabirds. Of the 17 or more species recorded in BC waters, the 2 most commonly encountered are the opal squid (*Loligo opalescens*) and the small stubby squid (*Rossia pacifica*). Occasionally the North Pacific giant squid (*Moroteuthis robusta*)

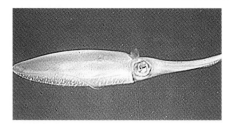

Opal squid. Rick Harbo photo

is taken in trawls off the west coast of VANCOUVER ISLAND or washed ashore. Its body grows to 1.2 m, with another 3.3 m of tentacles.

Opal squid are sometimes seen at night under the lights of docks and are harvested recreationally using squid jigs. Their white sausage-shaped egg cases are found on crab traps or rocks, or even washed ashore. Commercial FISHING vessels in BC use small seine nets to harvest small quantities (generally less than 100 tonnes annually) for bait and food. An experimental fishery using automated jigging machines for offshore flying squid (*Ommastrephes bartrami*) was initiated in 1996. Driftnet fishing for flying squid and other species was banned in 1992 due to the unacceptable capture of non-target species. Schoolmaster gonate squid (*Berryteuthis magister*) have been caught in trawls and experimentally by hook and line in GEORGIA STRAIT. *Rick Harbo*

SQUILAX, pop 256, is a SECWEPEMC community 8 km east of CHASE on Little Shuswap Lk. The name means black BEAR in the Secwepemc language. It has gained fame as the site of the largest colony of Yuma BATS in BC. Quaaout Lodge is a Native-run resort and a large powwow takes place every July.

SQUIRREL is a forest-dwelling member of the order Rodentia. There are 2 types: tree and ground-dwelling. Ground squirrels hibernate,

Northern flying squirrel. R. Wayne Campbell photo

but bushy-tailed tree species are active year-round. They are energetic little animals that often seem agitated; much of their noisy activity has to do with defending their feeding territories from interlopers. They have a varied summer diet of seeds, roots and insects; in winter they feed mainly on seeds from spruce cones. Food is hoarded assiduously by tree squirrels against winter scarcity. There are 5 tree squirrel species in BC. The red squirrel (*Tamiasciurus hudsonicus*) is about 15 cm long with a tail about the same length again. It closely resembles Douglas's squirrel (*T. douglasii*) of the south mainland coast, which is slightly smaller and has an orange belly. The grey squirrel (*Sciurus carolinensis*) is much larger and occurs in grey or black forms. Native to eastern N America, it has been introduced to the Lower Mainland and VICTORIA, where it is now common in parks and gardens. The fox squirrel (*S. niger*) is a close relative of the grey. It was introduced to Washington state from the eastern US and is now found in the south OKANAGAN VALLEY. The northern flying squirrel (*Glaucomys sabrinus*) is common but rarely seen since it is completely nocturnal. Grey-buff in colour, it swoops between tree branches, touching down on the ground occasionally but scampering quickly up a tree again. It is found throughout BC except on VANCOUVER ISLAND and the QUEEN CHARLOTTE ISLANDS. Ground squirrels excavate burrows in the ground or occupy dens in jumbles of debris. They hibernate for about 7 months out of the year. Of the 7 species present in Canada, 4 occur in BC. Columbian ground squirrels (*Spermophilus columbianus*) inhabit the central and southern Interior from the Okanagan east to the ROCKY MTS. Golden-mantled ground squirrels (*S. lateralis*), with colouring similar to the CHIPMUNK, occupy approximately the same range but prefer rocky places from valley-bottom forest to above the treeline. The Cascade mantled ground squirrel (*S. saturatus*) is a similar species confined to the CASCADE MTS, particularly Cathedral (*see* CATHEDRAL LAKES) and MANNING PROVINCIAL PARKS. Arctic ground squirrels (*S. parryii*) live mainly on the tundra of northern Canada but their range dips south to include the far northwest corner of BC.

STAMP, Edward, sawmill manager (b Nov 1814, Alnwick, England; d 17 Jan 1872, London, England). He went to sea as a young man and by 1857 was captain of a vessel that visited Puget Sound to load lumber. The following year he opened a general store in VICTORIA, then returned to England to arrange financing for a SAWMILL at ALBERNI INLET. The mill, known as ANDERSON MILL after its principal backer, was the first export sawmill in BC and operated from 1861 to 1864. Stamp managed the mill until early in 1863. After briefly running a mill at PORT NEVILLE, he built a new one at the foot of Dunlevy St on the south shore of BURRARD INLET. This mill, which went into production in June 1867, became known as the HASTINGS MILL and was the focus of the settlement of GRANVILLE (later VANCOUVER). Also active in politics, Stamp was elected to the united colony's first Legislative Council in 1866

Edward Stamp, early lumberman. CVA Port.P.264

(*see also* COLONIAL GOVERNMENT). Early in 1869 he retired from the sawmill; he then went into the SALMON CANNING business at Sapperton. His attempt to become one of the pioneers of this new industry was cut short when he died suddenly of a heart attack on a visit to England.

STANLEY is an abandoned MINING townsite 65 km east of QUESNEL on the road to BARKERVILLE. It sprang to life when GOLD was discovered at Lightning Crk in 1861. Named for Lord Stanley, British politician and gov gen from 1888 to 1893, it remained a productive mining site for 4 decades, then petered out; by the 1950s it was virtually deserted. During its heyday it had a significant CHINESE population. For most of its life, the post office here was called Van Winkle, after a tributary of Lightning Crk that had its own minor GOLD RUSH.

STANLEY CUP RIOT, 14 June 1994, was one of the worst sports riots in Canadian history and

Disappointed hockey fans venting their anger during the Stanley Cup Riot, Vancouver, 1994. Ric Ernst/Vancouver Province

the largest instance of public unruliness seen in VANCOUVER. The VANCOUVER CANUCKS HOCKEY team had made an incredible run in the Stanley Cup playoffs and that night in New York had lost the seventh game of the final series to the Rangers 3-2. About 80,000 frustrated fans spilled into the downtown area, centred on Robson St. Windows were smashed and stores looted before riot police moved in to disperse the crowd. The damage was estimated at millions of dollars and more than 100 people were arrested and charged with various offences.

STANLEY PARK, 4.05 km², in downtown VAN-COUVER, is the second-largest urban park in Canada (after Nose Hill Park in Calgary). Originally inhabited by FIRST NATIONS people, the park underwent LOGGING during the early

Third Beach, Stanley Park, Vancouver.
Mike Steele photo

days of white settlement. After BC became a colony, the land was set aside as a government reserve for military purposes. It was conveyed to the city for use as a park in 1887 and officially opened on 27 Sept 1888. It is named for Lord Stanley, gov gen from 1888 to 1893. A mixture of developed parkland and natural forest, the park has been called "half savage, half domestic" and is the most popular recreational space in the city. It is surrounded by water on 3 sides and encircled by the seawall, an 8.5-km walkway that took 60 years to complete. Other park features include BROCKTON POINT, where a LIGHTHOUSE has operated since 1890; the NINE O'CLOCK GUN, installed in 1894; Totem Pole Park, a collection of TOTEM POLES from coastal villages; Brockton Oval, once the major sports facility in the Lower Mainland; LUMBERMAN'S ARCH, the site of a First Nations village when the first settlers arrived in Vancouver; Prospect Point, with its panoramic view of LIONS GATE BRIDGE and the North Shore Mts; Siwash Rock; the Stanley Park ZOO; LOST LAGOON; and the VANCOUVER AQUARIUM.

STANTON, Jim, guide (b 1885, Snohomish, WA; d 1978, Knight Inlet). After selling a garage business in Seattle in 1919, he and his wife Laurette bought a boat and cruised up the coast as far as KNIGHT INLET, where they lived for many years trapping furs and guiding hunters and fishers. Laurette died in 1961 but Jim remained at their homestead at the mouth of the Klinaklini R until his death. Their life is described in *Grizzlies In Their Backyard* (1956) by Beth Day.

STANTON, John Herbert Frederic, lawyer (b 13 May 1914, Port Hope, ON). He moved to BC age 10 with his family when his father took a job as a teacher in a private school on VANCOUVER ISLAND. After graduating from SHAWNIGAN LAKE SCHOOL and then UBC, he articled as a lawyer in VANCOUVER and was called to the bar in 1936.

Radicalized by the events of the Depression, he joined the Communist Party but grew increasingly disillusioned and left the party in 1968. He was one of the leading labour lawyers and civil libertarians in BC for 4 decades. Following the death of his wife in 1986 he returned to live in Ontario. His 2 volumes of memoirs are *Never Say Die* (1987) and *My Past is Now* (1994).

STARFISH; *see* SEA STAR.

STARLING, European (*Sturnus vulgaris*), is a gregarious, ROBIN-sized bird. The entire N American population derives from a few dozen released in New York City in 1890. The species thrived and subsequently spread across the entire continent; it was first reported in BC in 1945. The starling is glossy black in colour with a yellow bill for part of the year and beige wing tips that give a speckled appearance. It is an omnivorous feeder that flocks in large numbers. Starlings nest in cavities, both natural and human-made, usually near populated places, and they are sometimes considered an urban nuisance because of their huge winter roosts and their tendency to take over the nests of other species. They are also a major pest on fruit, grape and BERRY crops in the OKANAGAN

European starling. R. Wayne Campbell

and FRASER valleys. Though they are migratory, many remain in BC for the winter, especially in the south.

The crested myna (*Acridotheres cristatellus*) is a close relative. Black with prominent white wing patches and a bushy topknot, it was introduced from Asia at the end of the 19th century. The numbers peaked in the 1930s, then declined; by the late 1990s there were only a handful in the VANCOUVER area, nesting in buildings, power poles and other structures.

STARRET, Martin Stevens, fur trapper, forester (b 17 July 1888, Hope; d 7 Jan 1973, Hope). At age 17 he joined a railway survey crew, then worked as a ranch hand in the Skagit Valley (*see* SKAGIT R). In 1909 he joined his mother at HAZELTON, where she opened a store, and he began crossing to BABINE LK to trap and trade furs. For the next 34 years he lived in the Babine district, ranching, trapping and working for the FOREST SERVICE. At the end of his life he was back running a trap line in the Skagit Valley. His memories of the northern Interior are collected in *Martin: The Story of a Young Fur Trader* (1981). The largest island in Babine Lk is named for him.

ST'AT'IMX (Lillooet) are a FIRST NATIONS people in the south-central Interior, numbering about 5,200 and speaking an Interior Salish language (*see* FIRST NATIONS LANGUAGES; SALISHAN FIRST NATIONS). They divide geographically into 2 groups: those inhabiting the dry Interior benchlands along the FRASER R near LILLOOET as well as ANDERSON and SETON lakes, and those inhabiting the COAST MTS around HARRISON and Lillooet lakes and along the LILLOOET R. The latter group are sometimes called the Lil'wat. Excavations at KEATLEY CREEK north of Lillooet have found evidence of human occupation dating back at least 2,500 years (*see* ARCHAEOLOGY). The St'at'imx were hunters and gatherers but relied for their subsistence mainly on the plentiful runs of SALMON that ascended the major RIVERS. They supplied fish to the early FUR TRADERS but intensive contact with outsiders did not occur until the arrival of miners during the GOLD RUSH of 1858. The diseases that followed depleted the population by an estimated 50%. By 1900 salmon stocks were seriously damaged and the people were experiencing periodic famines. The situation worsened with the Fraser R slides in 1913 and 1914 (*see* HELLS GATE BLOCKADE) and later dam construction. Nonetheless, FISHING and hunting are still important activities, along with wage employment. During the 1980s the Lil'wat people joined their NLAKA'PAMUX (Thompson) neighbours to oppose LOGGING in the STEIN R Valley. Some St'at'imx communities are represented by the Lillooet Tribal Council in Lillooet, others by the In-shuck-ch Councils Administration in MISSION.

STAVE LAKE, 58.6 km², is a widening in the Stave R tucked in the mountains north of MIS-SION. The 27-km long lake, inaccessible by road, was created by construction of a HYDROELECTRIC dam at Stave Falls during 1908–21. It drains south via the river to the FRASER R at RUSKIN. Mt Judge Howay Provincial PARK (61.8 km²) is at its north end. LOGGING, some of which was done by rail, was important in the area, and communities formed on Dewdney Trunk Road at Stave Falls and nearby Steelhead in the 1910s. The name refers to the barrel staves manufactured by the HBC from wood cut in the area.

STAWAMUS CHIEF is a granite dome towering above SQUAMISH, 65 km north of VANCOUVER. It rises abruptly from the edge of Hwy 99 (*see* SEA TO SKY HWY) for 600 m and its smooth walls have made it one of the foremost sites in the world for granite ROCK CLIMBING. The Chief, as it is commonly called, is also the most-used hiking sum-

Stawamus Chief near Squamish, 1993.
Ian Douglas photo

mit in BC via the steep Backside Trail, and was designated a provincial PARK in 1995. The first recorded climb, Peasant's Route, was in 1958 by Les McDonald and Jim Baldwin. With Ed Cooper, an American, Baldwin went on to make the first ascent of the Grand Wall, up the entire height of the Chief, in 1961. It was a 6-week epic that put the community of Squamish in the

national media spotlight. The Chief began its evolution about 94 million years ago, as part of a mass of molten rock 25 km below the earth's surface. Over the next million years or so, magma rose through the crust until it solidified about 10 km below the surface. Over the years the earth above eroded, and then during the last ice age 9,000 to 10,000 years ago, the Chief came to the surface in its present shape.

STEAMBOAT MOUNTAIN, now Shawatum Mt (el 2,158 m), is a prominent landmark over-looking the SKAGIT Valley southeast of HOPE. In 1908 it was the site of a GOLD discovery by 2 American miners. During the ensuing rush, 3 townsites appeared. In 1911 the discovery turned out to be a fraud and the boom turned to bust.

Steelhead. Phil Edgell photo; drawing courtesy Fisheries & Oceans Canada

STEELE, Samuel Benfield, mounted police officer (b 5 Jan 1849, Purbrook, ON; d 30 Jan 1919, London, England). As a teenager in Ontario he joined the militia to repulse the Fenian incursions from the US; in 1870 he went west to Manitoba with the militia to quell the first Red River Rebellion. He joined the North West Mounted Police (NWMP) on its formation in 1873 and participated in its legendary Great March to the foothills of the ROCKY MTS. In a 30-year career with the force he served with distinction during the construction of the CPR, the North-West Rebellion and the Klondike gold rush. His association with BC was brief but significant. In 1884–85 he commanded a troop of NWMP patrolling railway construction camps near GOLDEN. And in July 1887 he led a troop to the KOOTENAY R to pacify a group of KTUNAXA (Kutenai) warriors who objected to whites' encroachments on their land. His men built a log post at the confluence of WILD HORSE CRK and the Kootenay R; it was named FORT STEELE after their commander. It is now a provincial historic site. Steele and his men left BC in Aug 1888. He fought in the Boer War and also commanded the

second contingent of Canadian soldiers to go overseas during WWI. *See also* POLICING.

STEELHEAD (*Oncorhynchus mykiss*) is a member of the SALMON family but is considered to be a sea-going (anadromous) rainbow TROUT. Juveniles remain in fresh water for up to 4 years before migrating to the sea, where they may grow to a weight of 18 kg before returning to their natal streams several years later. Steelhead are powerful swimmers with lots of fight; they

are highly prized by sport fishers, who catch them primarily in rivers. Retention of steelhead by sport and commercial fishers has been restricted in recent years due to declining runs. Unlike salmon, adult steelhead do not always die after spawning but may reproduce more than once. The Steelhead Society of BC, founded in 1970, is a group of anglers engaged in public education and the protection of fish habitat. *See also* FISHING, COMMERCIAL; FISHING, SPORT.

STEEN, David Lee "Dave," decathlete (b 14 Nov 1959, New Westminster). The son of a track coach and former decathlete, he was involved in TRACK AND FIELD from an early age and was SPORT BC's high school athlete of the year in 1977. He trained at the Univ of California at Berkeley and later in Toronto and he was Canada's top decathlete for 10 years, setting the Canadian points record 11 times. He won the silver medal at the Commonwealth Games in 1982, when he became the first Canadian to break the 8,000-point barrier, and again in 1986. In 1983 he won golds at the world university and the Pan American Games and set the first of his 3 world records in the pentathlon. In 1988 he achieved his career-best point total, 8,415, and in Seoul won Canada's first Olympic medal in the

Dave Steen, decathlete, at the 1986 Commonwealth Games, Scotland.
Allsport photo/Courtesy Bill McNulty

decathlon, a bronze. The East German gold and silver medalists were later named on a list of athletes known to have been taking banned steroids. Steen retired shortly after the Olympics. He became a member of the Order of Canada and was inducted into the BC SPORTS HALL OF FAME in 1991. *SW*

STEEVES, Dorothy Gretchen (Biersteker), politician (b 26 May 1891, Amsterdam, Netherlands; d 9 May 1978, Vancouver). She studied law at the Univ of Leyden and practised in Amsterdam and the Hague before joining the Dutch civil service during WWI. Despite a privileged family background, she was a member of

Dorothy Steeves, CCF politician.
BC Archives G-03062

the Socialist Party of Holland, a suffragist and a pacifist. At the end of the war she married Rufus Steeves, a Canadian POW, and immigrated to VANCOUVER in 1919. When the Depression began she once again became active in socialist politics,

joining the local wing of the League for Social Reconstruction and playing an active role in the formation of the provincial section of the CCF. After attending the CCF's first national convention in Regina in 1933, she won election to the provincial legislature in a N VANCOUVER by-election the following year. She served for a decade in the legislature and earned a reputation as a strong feminist and a skilled debater. On the left wing of the party when WWII began, she had to moderate her outspoken pacifism rather than break with her colleagues. After her defeat in the 1945 election she remained active in the CCF, consistently prodding the party to be more radical.

STEIN RIVER, 160 km northwest of VANCOUVER, rises in the COAST MTS and flows 80 km eastward from dense RAIN FOREST through arid drylands to empty into the FRASER R just above LYTTON. The valley and surrounding watershed of the Stein have been used by the NLAKA'PAMUX (Thompson) First Nations and their ancestors for thousands of years. During the 1980s its 1,060 km² watershed was the scene of a protracted environmental dispute. The controversy began in 1976 when BC FOREST PRODUCTS LTD announced plans to begin LOGGING in the valley and on the adjacent slopes. A coalition of environmentalists, recreation organizations and local First Nations people opposed the logging, saying it would destroy a beautiful wilderness area and threaten the cultural heritage of the Nlaka'pamux. In 1985 opponents staged a Labour Day music festival, Voices for the Wilderness, in support of the anti-logging coalition. The festival became an annual event. The dispute dragged on as both sides prepared studies supporting their positions. In Sept 1988 FLETCHER CHALLENGE took over BCFP and announced a moratorium on logging in the Stein. In 1995 the province created Stein Valley Nlaka'pamux Heritage PARK, a 1,070 km² park encompassing the watershed, jointly managed by the Lytton First Nation and BC Parks. *See also* ENVIRONMENTAL MOVEMENT.
Reading: Michael M'Gonigle and Wendy Wickwire, *Stein: The Way of the River*, 1988.

STELLER'S JAY; *see* JAY.

STEPHEN, Alexander Maitland, writer, social activist (b 1882, Hanover, ON; d 1 July 1942, Vancouver). He moved to VICTORIA with his family in 1898 and articled in his uncle's law firm, but he abandoned law in favour of a series of labouring jobs around BC. He then returned to school and studied ARCHITECTURE at the Univ of Chicago, then went to England where he enlisted for military service when WWI began. In 1918 he was invalided back to VANCOUVER, where he launched an engineering company and later took up teaching. As a social activist he founded the Child Welfare Assoc and lobbied for a minimum-wage law, changes to the divorce laws, women's rights, EDUCATION reform and improved social services for poor and disabled children. His politics were left-wing; he ran provincially for the CCF and began his WRITING career as an editor with the *Western Tribune*, a leftist weekly. He published several volumes of poetry, 2 novels and many political pamphlets promoting causes dear to his heart. He enjoyed a national reputation as a writer and critic and corresponded with the leading literary figures of his generation. His poem in praise of his adopted city, "Vancouver" (1934), has been much anthologized.

STEVENS, Henry Herbert, politician (b 8 Dec 1878, Bristol, England; d 14 June 1973 Vancouver). He came to Canada with his widowed father in 1887, settling first in Ontario. The family came west to VERNON in 1894; after working at various jobs and serving briefly with the US Army in the Far East, Stevens settled permanently in VANCOUVER in 1902. He entered politics as an ardent moral reformer (he was an active METHODIST) and in 1909 won election as an alderman. In 1911 he won election in the first of 5 terms as a Conservative MP for the city. During this time he vocally opposed immigration from Asia, but he was also instrumental in the improvement of Vancouver Harbour, especially the construction of a grain elevator in anticipation of the completion of the Panama Canal in 1914. Known as "Steven's Folly" because it attracted little business at first, the facility turned out to be central to Vancouver's emergence as a major grain port.

When Arthur Meighen was prime minister, Stevens served as minister of trade and commerce in 1921 and of customs and excise in 1926. Four years later he won re-election for Kootenay East and joined R.B. Bennett's cabinet as minister of trade and commerce. The Depression sharpened his disenchantment with big business and in 1934 he chaired a parliamentary committee on price spreads, exposing many questionable labour and pricing practices by large corporations. The results embarrassed his leader but catapulted Stevens to public prominence; in 1935 he broke with Bennett and established his own Reconstruction Party. In the Oct election the party won only one seat, Stevens's, and only 9% of the vote. But it did spoil whatever chance Bennett had at re-election. Stevens rejoined the Conservatives in 1939, but after 3 subsequent election defeats and an unsuccessful run at the party leadership in 1942, he left politics to tend to private business in Vancouver.

STEVENS, Homer, union leader (b 1923, Port Guichon). He began fishing when he was 13, gillnetting with a boat owned by his father. In 1946 he became a full-time organizer for the UNITED FISHERMEN AND ALLIED WORKERS' UNION. As leader of the union from 1948 to 1977 he was one of the most prominent and controversial labour leaders in BC. He was a high-profile Communist, and he ran unsuccessfully several times for the Labour Progressive Party in provincial and federal elections. In 1967 he was jailed for a year for contempt of court, having defied an injunction against strike picketing. He led an unsuccessful attempt to organize Atlantic coast fishers into the UFAWU during 1970–71. He retired from the union in 1977 and returned to fishing. *See also* FISHING, COMMERCIAL; LABOUR MOVEMENT.
Reading: Rolf Knight, *Homer Stevens: A Life in Fishing*, 1992.

STEVENSON, Anne (Mackenzie), teacher, community activist (b 7 Sept 1903, Johannesburg, S Africa; d 6 Aug 1995, Cloverdale). She was the daughter of Roderick Mackenzie, a pioneer CARIBOO merchant who established the first permanent store in WILLIAMS LAKE when the community emerged in 1919. A teacher by profession, she was also a 10-year school trustee in Williams Lake and a founder of Cariboo College (now Univ College of the Cariboo). One of her special projects was including aboriginal culture in the school curriculum. Keenly interested in BC history, a member of the first BC Historic Sites advisory board, she was active in the Williams Lake Museum and the BC Historical Assoc (*see* BC HISTORICAL FEDERATION). In 1982 she received an honorary degree from SFU. Her husband, Doug Stevenson, a MINING engineer who later managed the MACKENZIE retail operation, shared her enthusiasm for history and community service.

STEVES, Manoah, pioneer settler (b 18 Dec 1828, Coverdale, NB; d 7 Dec 1897, Steveston). He came west and took up land on LULU ISLAND in 1877. Two years later he was among the petitioners requesting the incorporation of RICHMOND, and he was elected to the first local council in 1881. The DAIRY farm he and his wife established was still in the family in the late 1990s. Steves's eldest son, William Herbert Steves (1860–99), purchased and subdivided the STEVESTON townsite, started a NEWSPAPER and promoted the economic potential of the community. He died of heart disease. Harold Steves (b 1937), a long-time Richmond councillor and former NDP MLA, is the fourth generation of the family to play a prominent role in the community.

STEVESTON village is a historic SALMON CANNING centre in the southwest corner of RICHMOND, at the mouth of the south arm of the FRASER R. The flat, fertile island began attracting settlers in the 1860s. The village is named for

Moncton St, Steveston, 1899.
Courtesy Harold Steves

Manoah STEVES, who arrived with his family in 1878 and began a DAIRY FARM. His son Herbert actually developed the townsite, which became Steveston in 1889. Salmon canning began on the river in 1871; by the 1890s there were 45 canneries, about half at Steveston. Each summer large numbers of JAPANESE, CHINESE, FIRST NATIONS and Euro-Canadian fishers and cannery workers descended on the village. The fishery also supported a significant BOATBUILDING and SHIPBUILDING industry. Sailing ships from around the world visited the harbour to take on cargoes of canned SALMON. The peak of civic aspirations was pre-WWI, when Steveston was promoted as Salmonopolis, a supposed rival of VANCOUVER, but canning activity slowly declined and finally ceased in the 1990s. The GULF OF GEORGIA CANNERY, built in 1894 and at one time the largest plant in BC, was reopened as a national historic site in 1994. Japanese Canadians formed a large part of Steveston's population; their internment during WWII was a serious blow to the community, though some of the internees returned when they were allowed (*see* JAPANESE, RELOCATION OF). Post-war Steveston developed along with Richmond into a residential suburb for Vancouver as farmland was gobbled up for housing. Since the 1970s the community, which remains an active FISHING port, has developed its heritage character and its waterfront to attract business and TOURISM.
Reading: Duncan and Susan Stacey, *Salmonopolis: The Steveston Story*, 1994.

STEWART, district municipality, pop 858, lies at the head of Portland Canal on the Alaska border (*see* PORTLAND INLET). It is named for 2 brothers, John and Robert Stewart, prospectors who settled at the site in 1902. For a while it was a MINING boomtown with a population that reached 10,000. As the mines gave out, residents

Bear Glacier, near Stewart.
Bernie Pawlik/Image Makers

drifted away, and the community continued to depend on the vagaries of the mining industry. Hyder is just across the US border. In the 1990s Hollywood discovered Stewart, and the spectacular mountain scenery has provided a backdrop for several movies. *See also* FILMMAKING INDUSTRY.

STEWART, Helen (Hunt) and **Mary (Mc-Ilwaine)**, swimmers. Helen (b 28 Dec 1938) was taught to swim at the VANCOUVER Amateur Swim Club by Percy NORMAN and Howard Firby. In 1954 she won the silver medal in the 4 x 110-yard freestyle relay at the British Empire Games (*see* BRITISH EMPIRE AND COMMONWEALTH GAMES) and in 1955 she won gold in the 100-m freestyle as well as 2 relay silvers at the Pan American Games in Mexico City. She was named 1955 BC athlete of the year by both the VANCOUVER SUN and the PROVINCE NEWSPAPERS. Married to BC athlete Ted HUNT, she took up volleyball in 1964 and played for Canada's national team 1966–73. Helen's sister Mary (b 8 Dec 1945, Vancouver), who drew attention at an early age as the lion-suited mascot of the BC LIONS, also trained under Firby and won a silver medal with the Canadian freestyle relay team at the 1959 Pan Am Games. After reaching the freestyle finals at the 1960 Rome Olympics, she set her first world record in the 100-m butterfly the next year. In 1962 she set world record times in the 100-m, 100-yard and 110-yard butterfly. At the 1962 British Empire Games she won a gold, a silver and 2 bronze medals and added 4 silvers at the Pan Am Games in 1963. She was the Canadian Press news agency's female athlete of the year in 1961 and 1962. Her final international appearance was at the 1964 Tokyo Olympics where she reached the finals of the 100-m butterfly and 2 relay events. Both sisters are members of Canada's Aquatic Hall of Fame and the BC SPORTS HALL OF FAME (Mary in 1966, Helen in 1968).   *SW*

STEWART, Hilary M., writer, artist (b 3 Nov 1924, St Lucia, West Indies). After graduating from art school in London, England, in 1951 she came to Canada and worked as a designer and

Hilary Stewart, writer, at Heriot Bay on Quadra Island, 1999. Julie Campbell photo

art director. In 1972 she left her job as art director for BCTV in VANCOUVER and turned full time to WRITING and illustrating books about Northwest Coast aboriginal culture. Her book *Cedar: Tree of Life to the Northwest Coast Indians* (1984) won a BC BOOK PRIZE, as did her illustrated edition of *The Adventures and Sufferings of John R. Jewitt* (1987). She is known for her meticulous studies of aboriginal art and material culture (*see also* ART, NORTHWEST COAST ABORIGINAL). From her home on QUADRA ISLAND she has curated museum exhibitions and lectured widely on FIRST NATIONS themes. A 1998 book, *On Island Time*, recounts her life on Quadra.

STEWART, John William, railway contractor (b 1862, Nedd, Scotland; d 24 Sept 1938, Vancouver). Born into a poor crofter's family, he immigrated to Canada in 1882 and began working with the CPR as a member of a survey crew. This work brought him to BC in 1885, and he became part of the crew surveying the line between PORT MOODY and VANCOUVER. While sojourning in the US for several years he continued to gain experience in railway construction. He managed the building of the KASLO & SLOCAN RWY in 1895 and the western portion of the GRAND TRUNK PACIFIC RWY. In 1908 he joined 2 partners to form FOLEY, WELCH & STEWART, the preeminent railway builders in Canada in the prewar period. He was also a principal partner in the LOGGING company BLOEDEL, STEWART & WELCH. In 1916 he organized a battalion of railway construction workers and took them overseas. By the end of WWI he was a major general and director of military railways on the British front. When he returned to BC in 1919 all of his business partners were either dead or ill so he organized his own company, J.W. Stewart & Co, which was involved in major construction projects in Vancouver. He and his wife entertained royalty at their Shaughnessy mansion and were leading members of Vancouver's socioeconomic elite.

STEWART, William, union leader (b 1912, Scotland; d 1974, Vancouver). He immigrated to BC as a young man, and he first became prominent in the LABOUR MOVEMENT as an organizer of the Hotel and Restaurant Workers at a time when the union's mostly female membership was fighting for recognition and better working conditions. During WWII he was an organizer on the waterfront. In 1942 he was elected president of the Boilermakers' Union, along with Malcolm McLeod as secretary. The president of the Canadian Congress of Labour, Aaron Mosher, alarmed at Stewart's radicalism, declared the election void, suspended the union charter and appointed new leaders. When the courts invalidated Mosher's actions, Stewart was re-elected by a huge majority. He remained leader of his union and was one of the most powerful orators in the labour movement until his death.   *Emil Bjarnason*

STIEDA, Alex, cyclist (b 13 Apr 1961 Belleville, ON). Raised in COQUITLAM, he was the first N American cyclist to lead the Tour de France. He

Alex Stieda, cyclist, at the 1986 Tour de France.
John Pierce/Photosport International

won every national junior track-CYCLING event 1979–80 and was 5th in the 3,000-m pursuit at the world junior championships. By age 20 he was one of N America's top cyclists, winning the 1981 Canadian senior track championship while performing well in road races. He won a bronze medal at the 1982 Commonwealth Games and was 4th in overall points at the 1983 world championships. As a member of the 1985 Canadian national team he continued to post excellent finishes including a win, the first by a N American, in the 1985 Paris–Rouen Classic road race. After joining the select 7-Eleven professional racing team in 1986 he raced in Europe and surprised the cycling world by leading the first stage of that year's Tour de France, wearing the leader's yellow jersey for half a day. He didn't reach the Tour de France field again, but raced professionally until 1992.   *SW*

STIKINE RIVER, 640 km (589 km within BC), rises as trickles from a glacier over 1,830 m above headwater lakes in the southeast corner of SPATSIZI PLATEAU WILDERNESS PARK and flows east, north, then west around the edges of the plateau, cuts a deep (330 m), long (nearly 100 km) canyon through the lava beds north and east of MT EDZIZA, runs through a wide but steep valley with numerous glaciers visible from many viewpoints, then slices through the COAST MTS and the Alaska panhandle to empty opposite Wrangell. Along the way, the Stikine courses through 8 of BC's 14 BIOGEOCLIMATIC ZONES. It is BC's fifth-largest river by flow volume and its 49,647.51 km² watershed is the sixth-largest river basin. Its

The Grand Canyon of the Stikine R.
Bernie Pawlik/Image Makers

ESTUARY, a small portion of which lies in BC, forms a huge WETLANDS complex important to hundreds of thousands of migratory birds and waterfowl using the PACIFIC FLYWAY. The lower river wetland habitats are also extremely important for MOOSE, bald EAGLES, grizzly BEARS and endangered pine martens, black swifts and marbled MURRELETS. There is a large, ancient stand of massive cottonwoods here. The Grand Canyon of the Stikine, Canada's longest canyon, is prime habitat for about 300 MOUNTAIN GOATS, which scramble among the steep rock walls.

The river is recognized as having exceptional environmental and cultural heritage significance. It was used by both the TAHLTAN and TLINGIT First Nations for transportation and for SALMON fishing. Stikine means "the Great River" in the Tlingit language. The lower river and its tributary streams and lakes are important salmon spawning habitat for 5 species of Pacific salmon, and commercial and aboriginal FISHING are important here.

While Russian traders became established in Wrangell, the Tlingit maintained their trading activities with the upriver Tahltans. Travelling overland from the Dease R and down the Tanzilla R valley, Robert CAMPBELL of the HBC was the first European to arrive on the banks of the Stikine in 1838 and HBC trading posts were eventually established down the Stikine. From the 1850s through the early 20th century, a series of GOLD RUSHES in the Stikine, CASSIAR, ATLIN, Liard and Klondike areas brought numerous gold seekers up the Stikine and led to the establishment of a tent city at GLENORA and a town at TELEGRAPH CREEK, which today is the only town on the river. The trip up the Stikine, then overland from Telegraph Creek to DEASE LK and up the Dease R to the LIARD R became known as the "all-Canadian" route to the Klondike. PADDLE-WHEEL STEAMBOAT service began in the late 1800s between Wrangell and Telegraph Creek and continued for nearly 100 years into the 1970s. For many years this was the main supply route into the northwest Interior and was the principal means of bringing in people and equipment for construction of the ALASKA HWY during WWII. Today it is considered one of the most exciting paddling rivers of N America, but the canyon is unnavigable. Along its length are spectacular volcanic landscapes, glaciers and icefields. The provincial government designated it a BC HERITAGE RIVER in 1995 and its nomination as the province's second contribution to the Canadian Heritage Rivers System was in the works in the late 1990s.   *Maggie Paquet*

Reading: Jennifer Voss, *Stikine River*, 1998.

STIKINE TERRITORY was a short-lived jurisdiction in northern BC. When mainland BC became a colony in 1858, its northern boundary was set rather vaguely at the STIKINE and FINLAY rivers. Rumours of GOLD discoveries on the Stikine prompted Britain on 19 July 1862 to create a separate territory north of the river to the 62nd parallel and east to the 125th meridian. Gov James DOUGLAS was given jurisdiction over this Stikine Territory. In July 1863 it merged with the mainland colony, the borders of which were then set at their present limits. *See also* BOUNDARIES; COLONIAL GOVERNMENT.

STIKINE TRAIL was part of a proposed "all-Canadian" route through northern BC to the Yukon during the Klondike GOLD RUSH. Early in 1898, prospectors hurried north by steamship to Wrangell, Alaska, where they made their way inland up the STIKINE R to the head of navigation at TELEGRAPH CREEK. The federal government had announced that Donald Mann and William Mackenzie, 2 railway tycoons, would be building a rail line from the river north to TESLIN LK straddling the BC–Yukon border. From Teslin, travellers would complete the trip to Dawson City by water. The railway did not materialize, but thousands of miners struggled on foot over the winding, boggy trail during the next 2 years. *See also* TRAILS.

STILLWATER, on the coast 20 km south of POWELL RIVER, was the site of a major LOGGING operation run by the Brooks, Scanlon & O'Brien Co. The company started the Eagle River and Northern Rwy in 1909 to carry logs down to the water and by WWI was cutting 5 million board feet of DOUGLAS FIR a month and hauling it down 25 km of track. The railway ran for 46 years until truck transport replaced it. *See also* RAILWAY LOGGING.

STO:LO Nation is an alliance of 21 HALKOMELEM communities along the lower FRASER R between NEW WESTMINSTER and HOPE. They have strong cultural ties with other FIRST NATIONS in the FRASER VALLEY and on southern VANCOUVER ISLAND. Their administrative centre is in the former Coqualeetza RESIDENTIAL SCHOOL south of CHILLIWACK. The alliance includes members from Aitchelitz, Chawathil (formerly Hope), Chi:yo:m (Cheam), Qw'ontl'en (Kwantlen), Kwak-wakw-A-pilt, Leq'a:mel (Nicomen), Matsqui, Shxw'ow'hamel (Ohamil), Popkum, Sq'ewlets (Scowlitz), Seabird Island, Ska-wah-look, Skowdale, Skw'atets (Peters), Skway (Chilliwack), Soowhalie, Squiala (Chilliwack), Kw'ekw'i:qw (Sumas), Ch'iyaqtel, Union Bar and Yakweakwioose First Nations. ARCHAEOLOGICAL evidence suggests that ancestors of the Sto:lo have lived in the Fraser Valley for at least 7,000 years. Before contact with Europeans they relied for subsistence mainly on SALMON, which were plentiful in the Fraser and its tributaries. They inhabited villages of several large longhouses, each shared by members of an extended family (*see* ARCHITECTURE, ABORIGINAL). Estimates of the pre-contact population vary considerably, but whatever it was, it declined dramatically when SMALLPOX was introduced in 1782. Later epidemics of smallpox and other diseases were less devastating, though still significant, and the population reached a low point of about 1,300 in 1928. Since then the number has grown; in 1999 the Sto:lo numbered about 6,000.

Sto:lo fishers on the Fraser R, 1993.
Peter A. Robson photo

They became involved in the FUR TRADE with the establishment of FORT LANGLEY by the HBC in 1827. They were especially important to the trade as suppliers of salmon, which the HBC consumed locally and exported. The Fraser R GOLD RUSH brought the first significant number of outsiders into their territory and by the latter half of the 19th century the Sto:lo were being integrated into the wage economy as road and railway builders, cannery workers and farm hands. They received RESERVES in 1864 but subsequently these were reduced in size and the Sto:lo have been petitioning the government for satisfaction of their land claims ever since (*see* ABORIGINAL RIGHTS). The Sto:lo entered into negotiations with the BC TREATY COMMISSION in 1995.

Reading: Keith Thor Carlson, ed., *You Are Asked to Witness: The Sto:lo in Canada's Pacific Coast History*, 1997.

STOLT SEA FARM INC, one of BC's 3 largest producers of farmed Atlantic SALMON, has been in operation in the province since 1985. The company is a subsidiary of Stolt-Nielson, a private company owned by Jacob Stolt-Nielson with its head offices in Norway. Stolt-Nielson is one of the world's largest bulk liquid transporters. The parent company also farms TURBOT in Spain, STURGEON and caviar in California and HALIBUT in both Norway and BC. Stolt Sea Farm employs 130 people who operate 19 salmon farms and 3 hatcheries (*see* FISH HATCHERIES) located off the northeast coast of VANCOUVER ISLAND. As well they are partners in Englewood Packing Co, which processes the salmon at its plant in PORT MCNEILL. Stolt produces in excess of 10,000 tonnes of farmed salmon per year. *See also* AQUACULTURE, FIN FISH. *Peter A. Robson*

STOLTMANN, Randy, environmental activist (b 28 Sept 1962; d 22 May 1994). On a hike into the CARMANAH VALLEY in 1988 he first came across the huge Sitka SPRUCE forest there and began to campaign for its preservation from LOGGING. In 1990 part of the area was protected as a provincial PARK, and has since been expanded to include the neighbouring WALBRAN VALLEY watershed. A grove of Sitka spruce in the park has been

Randy Stoltmann, environmentalist.

named after him, as well as a 2,600 km² wilderness area in the Elaho Valley north of PEMBERTON that environmentalists wish to protect from logging (*see* STOLTMANN WILDERNESS). He died in an AVALANCHE while MOUNTAINEERING west of the KITLOPE VALLEY. *See also* ENVIRONMENTAL MOVEMENT. *Reading:* Randy Stoltmann, *Hiking Guide to the Big Trees of Southwestern BC*, 1991; and *Hiking the Ancient Forests of British Columbia and Washington*, 1996.

STOLTMANN WILDERNESS is 2,600 km² of coastal FOREST at the headwaters of the Elaho R, north of SQUAMISH. Two portions were protected as provincial PARKS in 1996, but INTERNATIONAL FOREST PRODUCTS (Interfor) received permission

to log in the rest and as of 1999 conservationists were fighting to preserve what remained unlogged in the entire area (*see also* ENVIRONMENTAL MOVEMENT). A grove of 1,300-year-old DOUGLAS FIRS beside the Elaho R has become symbolic of the area. The Stoltmann Wilderness is named for Randy STOLTMANN, a poet and a long-time researcher and explorer of the area who fought for its preservation. Stoltmann died in a ski-MOUNTAINEERING accident in 1994.

STONE MOUNTAIN PROVINCIAL PARK, 256.91 km², straddles the ALASKA HWY in the MUSKWA Ranges of the northern ROCKY MTS, 130 km southwest of FORT NELSON. Created in 1957, the PARK is known for its steep, bare mountainous terrain. TRAILS in Stone Mountain provide access to the Wokkpash Gorge Hiking Circuit, a 70-km backpacking trip past Canada's most extensive hoodoo formations, in adjacent Wokkpash Provincial Park.

STONER, 30 km south of PRINCE GEORGE on BC Rail and Hwy 97, is a small ranching and LOGGING settlement and service centre for the surrounding district. The townsite was relocated after being washed away in a 1955 flood. It is named after either a Pacific Great Eastern Rwy (*see* BC RAIL) divisional engineer or a pioneer settler, Walter Stoner. *AS*

STONEY CREEK, pop 564, is a DAKELH (Carrier) community 11 km south of VANDERHOOF. Known in the local language as Sai-kuz, the site became a village during the 1890s as people began moving to it from the surrounding area, attracted by the productive fishery. Trapping, hunting and commercial FISHING have supported the local economy, along with wage employment in LOGGING, MINING and construction. The story of the community is told in the best-selling book by Bridget MORAN, *Stoney Creek Woman* (1988).

STOPS OF INTEREST are roadside markers commemorating significant sites, people, places and events in BC history. The large green-and-yellow signs became familiar to travellers on provincial hwys (*see* ROADS AND HWYS) following the 1958 centennial celebrations. By the mid-1970s more than 100 of these distinctive plaques had been erected, inviting motorists to learn more about the countryside through which they were travelling. Subsequently the government ignored the program, except for a burst of renewed interest in the early 1990s when close to 40 new, redesigned markers went up along the southern Crowsnest Hwy (Hwy 3). Over the years a number of government departments have been responsible for this program and various local community groups have helped to sponsor plaques in their area. *John Atkin*

STORM-PETREL is a small, pelagic seabird (14–25 cm long), usually black or grey in colour with a white rear. Known as the "sea swallow," it feeds on small fish and crustaceans and is distinctive for its habit of fluttering above the ocean

surface, appearing to be walking on water like St Peter. Two species breed along the BC coast at about 40 different island colonies, where they lay their eggs in burrows on the ground. They are the fork-tailed storm-petrel (*Oceanodroma furcata*) and Leach's storm-petrel (*O. leucorhoa*).

STORRS, Monica Melanie, Anglican missionary (b 12 Feb 1888, London, England; d 14 Dec 1967, Liss, England). Her father was a distinguished ANGLICAN cleric and she became active in the church as a young woman. She came to the PEACE R country in 1929 as a lay missionary and remained for 21 years. Based at FORT ST JOHN, she toured the area by wagon and horseback, holding Sunday schools, organizing youth groups and promoting church work of all kinds. By the time she retired to England in 1950 she was widely known as "the Angel of the North Peace." A selection of her diaries was published in 1979 as *God's Galloping Girl: The Peace River Diaries of Monica Storrs, 1929–1931*.

STRACHAN, Robert Martin "Bob," carpenter, politician (b 1 Dec 1913, Glasgow, Scotland; d 21 July 1981, Victoria). He came to Canada in 1931, moved across the West looking for work and ended up in BC in 1935. A carpenter by profession, he made his home in NANAIMO and was at one time provincial leader of the Brotherhood of Carpenters and Joiners. In 1952 he was elected to the provincial legislature for the CCF in Cowichan–Malahat and held the seat for the next 23 years. Prior to the 1956 election he was chosen party leader and became leader of the opposition in the legislature. Under his leadership the CCF (later the NDP) retained its position as official opposition but failed to unseat the ruling SOCIAL CREDIT PARTY. Strachan resigned as party leader prior to the 1969 election, but continued to hold his legislative seat; during Dave BARRETT's NDP government he served in the cabinet as minister of highways (1972–73) and minister of transport and communications (1973–75). He resigned his seat to become BC agent general in London (1975–77).

STRAIGHT, Leland Robert "Lee," journalist, outdoors enthusiast (b 15 Sept 1915,

Lee Straight, outdoors writer.

Vancouver). He was educated at UBC, and for 33 years he was FISHING and outdoors editor for the *VANCOUVER SUN*. An avid sports fisher and hunter with many trophy catches, he left the *Sun* to become recreational fisheries adviser and anglers' ombudsman for the federal government from 1979 to 1985. He was president of the Totem Flyfishers, BC's first FLY FISHING club, and of the STEELHEAD Society of BC (1986–88). A participant in competitive shooting, he qualified for the Canadian international rifle team in the 1950s and managed the national shooting team at the 1962 Pan American Games. He wrote 4 books, and he and his wife Joan published the *BC Freshwater Fishing Guide* and *Sea Angling Guide* annuals before selling them to *BC Outdoors* in 1982. *SW*

STRAITON, a farming settlement on the side of Sumas Mt 7 km northeast of ABBOTSFORD in the FRASER VALLEY (*see* AGRICULTURE), is named after Thomas B. Straiton, an early settler who opened a general store here with his brother. A PIPELINE runs nearby and Straiton is the site of several enormous oil storage tanks. *AS*

STRAITS TOWING & SALVAGE LTD was the largest BC TOWBOATING company in the post-WWII period. It was established at the end of the 19th century when George McKeen started in business as a tugboat operator in NEW WESTMINSTER, and it continued under his son Stanley as Standard Towing. In 1943 Standard merged with Fred Brown's Union Towing to form Straits Towing Ltd. Following the war the company expanded its fleet of tugs and experimented with large, tank-landing ships that were converted into some of the first of the post-war generation of LOG BARGES. Straits built the *Straits Logger*, the first self-loading, self-dumping log barge owned by a private tug company. Straits also was a major carrier of ore from coastal mines destined for SMELTERS at Tacoma and TRAIL. The company merged with River Towing in 1970 to form RivTow Straits, a diversified company owned by the Cosulich family. *S.C. Heal*

STRATHCONA PARK LODGE was built on Upper CAMPBELL LK in 1930 as a summer home for the Swedish-American millionaire Henning Berg. It was later sold and operated as a resort until the BC POWER COMMISSION purchased it in 1956 prior to raising the level of the lake as part of a hydro project. Baikie Brothers, a local LOGGING company, rescued the lodge and moved it to its present site on the east side of the lake, where it reopened under the ownership of Jim BOULDING and his wife Myrna, daughter of Harper Baikie. The original lodge burned in 1973 but was rebuilt and has flourished as a combined resort and wilderness education centre.

STRATHCONA PROVINCIAL PARK, 2,537.73 km², established in 1911, was BC's first provincial park. Located west of CAMPBELL RIVER in the centre of VANCOUVER ISLAND, it is named for Donald Smith, Lord Strathcona, one-time governor of the HBC, president of the Bank of Montreal and

View of the Golden Hinde, Strathcona Park.
Philip Stone photo

backer of the CPR. The mountainous park features the Comox Glacier (Vancouver Island's last remaining icefield; *see* GLACIATION), alpine meadows, several beautiful lakes, the FORBIDDEN PLATEAU and Mt WASHINGTON ski areas, and DELLA FALLS, the highest waterfall in Canada. At 2,200 m, the GOLDEN HINDE is the highest peak on the Island. STRATHCONA PARK LODGE is a popular centre for wilderness education and TOURISM activities. Hwy 28 runs through the park, connecting Campbell River to GOLD RIVER near the head of MUCHALAT INLET on the west side of the Island. Additions to the western and southern portions of Strathcona now link it with contiguous wilderness areas in CLAYOQUOT SOUND. *See also* ENVIRONMENTAL MOVEMENT; PARKS, PROVINCIAL.

STRATHNAVER, pop 21, 35 km north of QUESNEL on BC RAIL, is the site of the Dunkley Lumber Ltd SAWMILL, built in 1950 and sold in the late 1980s to the Novak family. It employs 150 people, many of whom live in neighbouring HIXON, and is one of the most technologically sophisticated mills in N America. The area was settled in 1912 by Scottish immigrants, part of a colonization scheme by the Duke of Sutherland, who bought 16.2 km² of land and came up with the name. In 1913 the duke died and the project was abandoned. *AS*

STRAWBERRY HILL, an AGRICULTURAL settlement 7 km southeast of NEW WESTMINSTER in the City of SURREY, was settled by Japanese BERRY farmers in the early 1900s. Most were interned during WWII and did not return to their farms (*see* JAPANESE, RELOCATION OF). By the late 20th century the area had become mostly residential. *AS*

STREATHAM, a farming (*see* AGRICULTURE) and ranching (*see* CATTLE INDUSTRY) district on the north shore of OOTSA LK, 56 km southwest of BURNS LAKE, was named by the Hinton family, local pioneers who arrived about 1914 and named the place for their home in London, England. Much of this area was submerged when the NECHAKO Reservoir was created in the early 1950s. *AS*

STREET RAILWAYS powered by electricity were the dominant form of urban public transit in the first half of the 20th century. BC's first street railway opened in VICTORIA on 22 Feb 1890, the first such system west of Ontario. Owned by the National Electric Tramway & Lighting Co, it featured 4 cherrywood rail cars running along 15 km of steel rail and receiving electricity from an overhead wire. VANCOUVER inaugurated a similar system on 26 June 1890, followed by NEW WESTMINSTER in Oct 1891. The New Westminster system combined a street railway with N America's first electric INTERURBAN rail line running through BURNABY to downtown Vancouver. The 3 Lower Mainland street railways all went bankrupt in the ensuing depression but

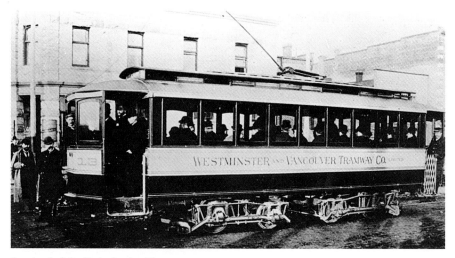

Tramload of dignitaries leaving Vancouver on the inaugural trip of the new interurban line to New Westminster, Oct 1891.
BC Archives 24949

One of the fleet of President's Conference Committee cars, which went into service in Vancouver in 1939.

in 1896 they were reorganized as one company, the Consolidated Railway Co. This new company folded as well, following the POINT ELLICE BRIDGE COLLAPSE, the worst streetcar disaster in Canadian history. Finally, on 15 Apr 1897, BC's street railways achieved financial stability with the creation of the BC ELECTRIC RWY CO (BCER). The new company, based for many years in London, England, ran the transit systems for the next 64 years. The only other electric transit company in BC was the Nelson Electric Tramway Co. Dubbed "the smallest streetcar system in the British Empire," it began operating 2 streetcars on 8 km of track in Nelson at the end of 1899. The city purchased the line in 1914 and ran it to 1949. One of the Nelson streetcars has since been restored to operation.

Before WWI the street railways expanded dramatically along with the cities they served. New track snaked through downtown areas and lines reached out into suburbs. The BCER began manufacturing its own cars at a plant in New Westminster, and by 1914 the fleet numbered 647 pieces of rolling stock. Motor buses began appearing in city streets in the 1920s. The street railway company responded to the competition by purchasing a lighter, faster, smoother-riding car, the President's Conference Committee car, or PCC. The first of 36 PCC cars went into service in Vancouver in 1939. During WWII the transit system handled more passengers than ever before, but after the war the BCER made the decision to replace its aging street railways with motor and trolley buses. The conversion had already been made in New Westminster in 1938. N VANCOUVER followed in 1947 and Victoria in 1948. Vancouver began phasing out its system in 1947, though it was not until 24 Apr 1955 that the last cars in BC were retired in a ceremony at the PNE grounds.

STREPPEL, Greg, swimmer (b 3 June 1968, Galt, ON). During the mid-1990s he was among the top marathon swimmers in the world. Coached by Ron Jacks of Island SWIMMING, he won the 25-km swim at the 1994 World Aquatic

Championships in Italy. That year he also won back-to-back 25-km races in Argentina, then returned in 1995 to duplicate his wins, a feat never matched by another distance swimmer. In all he won 4 major international races in 1995. While the marathon was his specialty, he also competed internationally in various pool events.

STRINGER, Alfred, aviation pioneer (b 26 July 1921, Lancer, SK; d 9 Mar 1997, Victoria). The son of Prairie homesteaders, he joined the Royal Canadian Air Force during WWII and served as engineering officer in the same Commonwealth Air Training Plan squadron as Carl AGAR. After the war he joined Agar and Barney Bent to found Okanagan Helicopters (see CANADIAN HELICOPTERS LTD) in PENTICTON. In 1960 he married Lynn Henson, the widow of the founder of VANCOUVER ISLAND HELICOPTERS, and later took over from his wife as president of the Island company. He retired in 1990 but continued as a consultant. He received numerous honours, including the Lifetime Achievement Award from the BC AVIATION Council and the Air Transport Assoc of Canada. Stringer's death ended 50 years of distinguished service in the helicopter industry.   *Peter Corley-Smith*

STRONG, George Frederick, physician (b 27 Feb 1897, St Paul, MN; d 26 Feb 1957, Montreal). He was educated in St Paul and in 1921 he moved to VANCOUVER, where he became a prominent internist and cardiologist. He was closely associated with Vancouver Hospital (then called Vancouver General Hospital) and helped found the G.F. Strong Rehabilitation Centre (1949). Strong played an important role in establishing several other medical facilities including the BC Medical Research Institute, the UBC Faculty of Medicine and the BC Cancer Foundation. He served as president of the American College of Physicians, the Canadian Heart Foundation and the Vancouver, BC and Canadian medical associations. *See also* MEDICAL PROFESSION.   *AS*

STUART, John, fur trader (b 12 Sept 1780, Leanchoil, Scotland; d 14 Jan 1847 near Forres, Scotland). A trader with the NORTH WEST CO, he joined Simon FRASER in 1805 to carry the fur

trade across the ROCKY MTS into BC, then called NEW CALEDONIA. In 1806 he built a post on FRASER LK. He was second-in-command to Fraser on the arduous 1808 canoe trip down the FRASER R to its mouth. Although the expedition was a disappointment—the river did not turn out to be a usable transport route to the Pacific—Stuart distinguished himself and the next year took command for the NWC in New Caledonia. In 1813 he descended the COLUMBIA R and took part in the purchase of Fort Astoria from American traders. He remained in charge of trade until 1817, when he was transferred to Alberta. When the HBC absorbed the NWC in 1821 Stuart remained with the new concern as chief factor, once again in charge in New Caledonia. In 1824 he left BC and finished his career east of the mountains. *See also* FUR TRADE, LAND-BASED.

STUART ISLAND, 40 km north of CAMPBELL RIVER at the mouth of BUTE INLET, is in the territory of the HOMALCO First Nation. It was first settled in the early 1900s; LOGGING and commercial FISHING are the main employment. There are 2 settlements: BIG BAY on the west side of the island, and Stuart Island at the southern tip, which has a resort, marina, store and post office. Between the two are the fearsome YUCULTAS. Capt George VANCOUVER named the island after John Stuart, the Earl of Bute.   *AS*

STUART RIVER originates at the south end of STUART LK near FORT ST JAMES and flows southeastward for 187 km to join the NECHAKO R 55 km west of PRINCE GEORGE. It is in the territory of the DAKELH (Carrier) First Nation, and the confluence of the Stuart and Nechako rivers was the site of the ancient village of CHUNLAC. Starting in 1806, FUR TRADERS used the river to carry their furs from Fort St James out of the country, and the Stuart is named for John STUART, one of the traders. As part of the FRASER R watershed, it is an important SALMON spawning river; it has been designated a BC HERITAGE RIVER.

STUKUS, Annis, sports personality (b 25 Oct 1914, Toronto). A veteran FOOTBALL player with

Annis Stukus, first coach of the BC Lions, 1999.

the Toronto Argonauts in the 1930s and 1940s, he came west in 1949 to organize and coach the Edmonton Eskimos franchise in the CFL. The team he put together won 3 consecutive Grey Cups in 1954–56, but by that time he had moved to VANCOUVER as coach and manager of the new BC LIONS, which took to the field in 1954; he remained coach until 1956 and returned to Vancouver in 1967 as general manager of the VANCOUVER CANUCKS. Stukus combined careers in sports and journalism, writing for Toronto NEWSPAPERS and doing colour commentary for television football broadcasts. Late in his career he returned to Vancouver again as an announcer with radio station CFUN. Stukus was inducted into the Canadian Sports, Football and Broadcast Halls of Fame. The CFL trophy for coach of the year is named in his honour.

STUMP LAKE is a ranching district (*see* CATTLE INDUSTRY) 32 km south of KAMLOOPS on Hwy 5. In 1873 Peter Fraser had a sheep farm at the north end while William Palmer had a ranch at the south. The lake is a recent formation; early settlers recalled seeing dead stumps there, hence the name. It is a popular windsurfing, sailing and sport FISHING site and it lies along the migration path of 20 species of waterfowl. AS

STUPICH, David, accountant, politician (b 1922). He graduated from UBC in 1949 and began running in elections for the provincial CCF, forerunner of the NDP. In 1963 he was finally elected for the NDP, and he held his NANAIMO riding for the next 3 decades. In Dave BARRETT's NDP government, 1972–75, he served as minister of agriculture and finance minister. After the government's 1975 defeat he continued as opposition finance critic in the legislature and in 1984 made an unsuccessful bid for the party leadership, losing badly to Bob SKELLY. He then moved to federal politics, serving as MP for Nanaimo from 1988 to 1993. Stupich was the leading figure in the NANAIMO COMMONWEALTH HOLDING SOCIETY scandal, and in 1999 he was the only person convicted of related offences. He pleaded guilty to charges of fraud and unlawfully operating a lottery.

STURDY, Martha, designer (b 1942, Vancouver). She dropped out of art school to raise a family and work, and it was not until the mid-1970s that she was able to return to the EMILY CARR INSTITUTE OF ART & DESIGN and complete her degree. Originally known for her bold jewellery made from SHIPBUILDING resin, she subsequently branched out into housewares and furniture and developed her creations into a multi-million-dollar design business with customers around the world.

STURGEON, white (*Acipenser transmontanus*) is the most common sturgeon species in BC. It is a primitive, elongated, cartilaginous fish living mainly in the muddy depths of the province's larger RIVERS and a few LAKES. It is the largest anadromous fish in N America, reaching 6 m in length; a specimen weighing 629 kg was caught

White sturgeon. *Phil Edgell photo; drawing courtesy Fisheries & Oceans Canada*

at NEW WESTMINSTER in 1897. It is extremely slow-growing and may live for well over 100 years. Like all sturgeon species, the white sturgeon has 5 rows of horny plates along its back and sides. Food includes dead and live SALMON, bottom-dwelling invertebrates and other smaller fish. The sturgeon figures prominently in FIRST NATIONS mythology and was an important part of the traditional food fishery. It was also a source of isinglass, a gelatin substance found in the swim bladder, which the HBC sold for various uses. In the 1890s an intense commercial fishery for meat and caviar began on the FRASER R (*see* FISHING, COMMERCIAL). It peaked in 1897, when about 500,000 kg came out of the river, then declined sharply as fish stocks were reduced. In 1994, following the unexplained deaths of many sturgeon in the river, a ban was placed on killing them. They are considered at risk largely because of historic over-exploitation and because diking and HYDROELECTRIC dam construction have altered their habitat. Another, smaller species, the green sturgeon (*Acipenser medirostris*), is found along the coast of VANCOUVER ISLAND and very rarely in the Fraser and SKEENA rivers.
Reading: Terry Glavin, *A Ghost in the Water*, 1994.

STURSBERG, Peter, journalist (b 31 Aug 1913, Chefoo, China). He began his NEWSPAPER career as a reporter with the Victoria Times from 1934 to 1938. As a war correspondent for CBC radio, he covered the landing of Canadian troops in Sicily in 1943, followed the Italian campaign, then reported on the liberation of Holland. He was the only Canadian correspondent to enter both Axis capitals, Rome and Berlin, with the Allies. After the war, from 1950 to 1979, he worked in television for both the CBC and CTV networks, and he wrote several books, including an account of early journalism in Victoria, *Those Were the Days: The Days of Benny Nicholas and the Lotus Eaters* (1969); the autobiography of

Peter Stursberg, journalist, reporting from the Italian front during WWII.

Gordon SHRUM, *Gordon Shrum* (1986); and his memoir *The Sound of War* (1993). He is a member of the Order of Canada and a life member of the Ottawa press gallery.

SUBMARINES were purchased by the provincial government on 4 Aug 1914 just hours before the declaration of WWI. Knowing that war was about to break out and fearing attack by German warships rumoured to be offshore, Premier Richard MCBRIDE authorized spending $1,150,000 for the 2 vessels, which had been built in Seattle for the Chilean navy. He acted quickly before American neutrality laws would make the sale illegal. Renamed the *CC1* and *CC2*, the subs constituted a provincial navy for 3 days (the only one in Canadian history) before ownership was transferred to the national fleet. For 3 years they patrolled the West Coast from their base in ESQUIMALT; in 1917 they were transferred to the Atlantic coast.

SUBSEA TECHNOLOGY is an industry in which BC is a world leader. While the extreme depths of local waters limits scuba diving, the deep coastal FJORDS provide excellent places to develop and test new equipment. Areas of development include both manned and robotic submersibles. Robotic submersibles are of 2 types: Remotely Operated Vehicles (ROVs), where the submersible is connected to the surface operator by a tether or umbilical cable, and Autonomously Operated Underwater Vehicles (AUVs), where the submersible operates without a tether, roaming the sea as long as its power supply lasts. Manned submersibles are primarily

The inventors of the Pisces *submersible (l to r): Don Sorte, Mack Thompson, Al Trice, 1965.*

small, 1- to 3-person submarines called Driver Operated Vehicles (DOVs). Another type of manned subsea equipment is Phil NUYTTEN's Newtsuit, an example of an atmospheric diving suit (ADS). Other notable subsea technology developed in BC includes underwater sonar, survey, navigation and communication systems, Arctic diving systems, sea-floor oil production systems and tourist submarines.

The requirements of the off-shore oil industry in the mid-1970s inspired many BC companies to develop innovative and multi-use vehicles, hardware and software, as well as techniques for subsea work (*see also* OIL AND GAS INDUSTRY). International Hydrodynamics Co Ltd (HYCO), founded by Al TRICE, Don Sorte and Mack Thompson, scored the first major success with the 3-person Pisces class non-military submarine launched in 1966. Many key figures in BC's subsea industry got their start at HYCO. Others working for John Horton of Horton Maritime went on to pursue acoustic research, including positioning and communications systems. By 1999 the largest subsea company in the province was International Submarine Engineering Ltd (ISE) in PORT MOODY. Founded in 1974 by James MCFARLANE, ISE is a world leader in the design and integration of ROVs, AUVs and terrestrial robotics. In total, more than 100 BC companies are involved in some facet of subsea technology.

The federal government began its own subsea research when it set up the Institute of Ocean Sciences (IOS) at Patricia Bay on VANCOUVER ISLAND. Oceanographic studies, as well as subsea technology facilities, are available at 3 of BC's universities (*see also* OCEANOGRAPHY). BC RESEARCH INC at UBC has the province's only large test tank for hydrographic testing. The underwater research lab at SFU has developed a number of mini-ROV and AUV submersibles. And the UNIV OF VICTORIA maintains connections with the IOS at Patricia Bay in SAANICH INLET.

Vickie Jensen

SUDBURY was a 60-m salvage tug famous for its mid-ocean rescues. It began life as a naval corvette, built in Ontario in 1941. After WWII ended, it was converted to a TOWBOAT and Harold Elworthy, owner of ISLAND TUG & BARGE, bought it in 1954. The *Sudbury* and its crew spe-

cialized in deep-sea salvage and completed many dramatic operations, but made their reputation Nov–Dec 1955 when they pulled off the daring N Pacific rescue of the Greek freighter *Makedonia*. The *Sudbury* towed the disabled vessel for 40 days through some of the roughest weather imaginable before arriving safely in VANCOUVER to a hero's welcome. The incident made headlines around the world and for the next decade the *Sudbury* and its 65-m sister vessel *Sudbury II*, purchased by Island Tug in 1958, were the most famous tugs on the Pacific coast. The original *Sudbury* was damaged during repairs and was dismantled for scrap in 1966. Following the mergers that created SEASPAN INTERNATIONAL, the *Sudbury II* remained in service until 1979 when it was sold and converted into a fishing vessel by its new owner. In 1982 it sank in HECATE STRAIT.
Reading: Pat Wastell Norris, *High Seas, High Risk: The Story of the* Sudburys, 1999.

SULLIVAN, 13 km southeast of NEW WESTMINSTER in the City of SURREY, was originally known as Johnston's Settlement after James Johnston, who arrived in 1866. Thomas and Henry Sullivan came in the early 1900s. They farmed and logged, opened a store and post office and built shingle and lumber mills that employed 125 people. Sullivan was a station along BC ELECTRIC RWY CO's INTERURBAN line. *AS*

SULLIVAN BAY is on the north side of N Broughton Island off the top of VANCOUVER ISLAND, about 450 km north of VANCOUVER. In 1945 Myrtle and Bruce Collinson arrived with an old float camp and established a seaplane harbour, fish camp, store and post office. Until the mid-1950s it was the busiest float plane base on the coast. The Collinsons sold out in 1957; in 1971 new ownership converted the facilities to a TOURIST resort.

SULLIVAN MINE, in the mountains at KIMBERLEY, is one of the largest lead–ZINC ore bodies in

The original Sudbury *(r) and the* Sudbury II *at work. Gordon Whittaker/Seaspan International*

the world. The claim was staked in 1892 by 4 American prospectors: Ed Smith, Walter Burchett, John Cleaver and Pat Sullivan. Sullivan died that winter and the claim was named in his honour. In 1896 the 3 surviving partners sold their claim to the LeRoi syndicate. The new owners built a SMELTER at MARYSVILLE, now part of Kimberley, and worked the mine until 1908, when it closed. The Consolidated Mining and Smelting Co, now COMINCO, took over the property in 1910 and developed a profitable means of concentrating and refining the vast deposit of complex ore. By 1937 the mine produced 10% of the world output of lead–zinc, shipping the ore to the Cominco smelter at TRAIL. The mine was expected to run out of ore in the year 2001. *See also* MINING.

SUMAS PRAIRIE is an area of fertile lowlands below Sumas Mt, south of the FRASER R east of ABBOTSFORD. Until the 1920s it was covered by Sumas Lk, which drained into the Fraser via Sumas R. Each spring the lake inundated the surrounding valley. The provincial government began draining Sumas Lk in 1919 and built an extensive network of dikes and canals to divert runoff. As part of this project in 1922 the Chilliwack R was diverted into the Fraser and partly renamed the VEDDER R. The Sumas Reclamation Scheme recovered about 133.65 km² of alluvial soil that began producing crops in 1924. In time, the Prairie became one of the most productive DAIRY FARMING and BERRY and hop-growing areas in the province.

SUMMERLAND, district municipality, pop 10,584, is on the west side of OKANAGAN LK, 16 km north of PENTICTON in the shadow of Giants Head Mt (el 832 m). A community was founded in  1903 by John Moore ROBINSON, a settlement promoter; it was incorporated on 21 Dec 1906 and developed as a major fruit-growing and packing centre. Originally situated right on the lake, the town centre was moved slightly west after 1905. In 1914 the federal government established an AGRICULTURAL research station to serve the TREE FRUIT growers. From 1915 to 1964 Summerland was a stop on the now-defunct KETTLE VALLEY RWY. TOURISM has been another economic mainstay and the area is popular with retirees. Some wood and fibreglass manufacturing takes place, along with several greenhouse operations. Sumac Ridge and other wineries are nearby. *See also* WINE MAKING.

SUMMIT LAKE is a popular place name in mountainous BC, with over 20 listings in the provincial gazetteer. Three communities stand out. The first, 20 km north of PRINCE GEORGE on the Arctic Divide, was originally a trading post. Today it is a LOGGING settlement with TOURISM facilities and a provincial PARK nearby. The

second Summit Lake, on the CPR's Nakusp & Slocan Rwy 100 km southeast of REVELSTOKE, was the site of J.R. Boynton's prosperous pole and tie business and SAWMILL from 1908 until 1920, when it was destroyed by fire. The third is a roadside hamlet on the ALASKA HWY, 115 km west of FORT NELSON in STONE MOUNTAIN PROVINCIAL PARK. *AS*

SUN YAT-SEN CLASSICAL CHINESE GARDEN in Vancouver's CHINATOWN was the first full-scale classical scholar's garden built outside China. It opened on 24 Apr 1986. Modelled after classical gardens developed in Suzhou during the Ming Dynasty (1368–1644), it was constructed, at a cost of $5.3 million, by a team of artisans from Suzhou, who spent months constructing the garden, using no nails, screws or power tools. Most of the building materials were shipped from China, including hand-fired roof tiles for the buildings and convoluted limestone rocks for the grounds. The garden is open to the public year-round.

SUNBURY, 8 km southwest of NEW WESTMINSTER in DELTA municipality, was a unique settlement of

houses on floats and stilts on the south shore of the FRASER R. Apparently named after a steamship, it was home to fishers and cannery workers at nearby ANNIEVILLE and elsewhere in Delta. *See also* FISHING, COMMERCIAL; FLOATHOUSES. *AS*

SUNNYWOLD is an orchard settlement and former steamship landing on the east side of OKANAGAN LK 20 km southwest of VERNON. It is often referred to as Carr's Landing, after Andrew Carr, an early settler who planted the area's first apple, pear and peach trees. *See also* TREE FRUITS. *AS*

SUNRISE VALLEY, 30 km northwest of DAWSON CREEK in the PEACE R district, is an AGRICUL-

TURAL settlement that first took form in the late 1920s. It acquired a school and post office in the early 1930s and a community hall the following decade. Today it is an area of family-owned farms. *AS*

SUN-RYPE PRODUCTS LTD is a fruit products manufacturer based in KELOWNA. The largest pure apple juice packer in Canada, it also produces a wide range of other juices, fruit bars, etc. It was created by fruit growers in 1946 as BC Fruit Processors Ltd, marketing fruit products under the Sun-Rype brand name, and changed its name to Sun-Rype Products Ltd in 1959 to incorporate the brand name. A publicly traded company since 1996, it ceased to be owned by the growers in 1999. Sales in 1998 totalled $83.8 million.

SUNSHINE COAST refers to the coastal strip north of VANCOUVER, from west HOWE SOUND to DESOLATION SOUND. The UNION STEAMSHIP CO borrowed the term in 1925 from Harry Roberts, a ROBERTS CREEK pioneer, and in one of its brochures promised "Sunshine and Sea-charm along Holiday Shores on the Gulf Coast." The

Smuggler Cove on the Sunshine Coast.
Keith Thirkell photo

area actually receives more sunshine than Vancouver but less than VICTORIA. The largest communities are POWELL RIVER, PENDER HARBOUR, SECHELT and GIBSONS, the latter familiar to television viewers as the backdrop for the popular *BEACHCOMBERS* series. The FOREST INDUSTRY has been a mainstay since LOGGING began in the 1890s. The Howe Sound Pulp and Paper Complex at PORT MELLON, jointly owned by CANADIAN FOREST PRODUCTS LTD and Oji Paper of Japan, is the largest employer. In 1990 the Hillside Industrial Park, a 1.9 km² forestry-theme site, opened on Howe Sound close to the mill. Commercial FISHING has also been important. During the 1980s fin fish AQUACULTURE boomed with the opening of numerous salmon farms, but the industry has since collapsed. The Sunshine Coast has been popular with TOURISTS since steamboats began running excursions to summer resorts in the late 1800s. The mild climate, along with reasonable land prices, attract a growing number of people who appreciate a rural ambience within easy reach of Vancouver. The Coast has a population of 25,000, of which about 20% are retirees.

Reading: Howard White, *The Sunshine Coast*, 1997.

SUQUASH, 20 km southeast of PORT HARDY, was the first place that COAL was discovered on VANCOUVER ISLAND, in 1835. Some mining was done there until higher quality seams were found at FORT RUPERT and NANAIMO. Further operations took place in the 1910s. The name is a Kwakwala word meaning "where seals are butchered." *See also* COAL MINING, VANCOUVER ISLAND. AS

SURF INLET, on the west side of PRINCESS ROYAL ISLAND, 175 km southeast of PRINCE RUPERT, was a GOLD and COPPER MINING camp that was in full operation from 1917 to 1926 and again from 1934 to 1942. Ore from several different mine sites was shipped via a chain of lakes to the head of the inlet and then to a Tacoma, WA, SMELTER. The camp had HYDROELECTRIC power, a store, hospital and recreation hall, and a population of 200 at its peak. AS

SURFING takes place year-round at 2 locations on the west coast of VANCOUVER ISLAND. Water temperatures vary from a frigid 4°C to a high of 13°C; wetsuits are suggested even at the height of summer. One community of surfers, whose

Shyna Ellis, surfer, at Long Beach, 1998.
Jon Murray/Vancouver Province

members prefer to see it as a lifestyle rather than a sport, congregates at JORDAN R west of VICTORIA. The other surfs the beaches near TOFINO in PACIFIC RIM NATIONAL PARK. Heli-surfing is possible in more remote locations on the outer coast.

SURGE NARROWS is one of the passages through the jumble of islands between VANCOUVER ISLAND and the mainland at the north end of GEORGIA STRAIT. It lies between QUADRA and MAURELLE islands and is well travelled by boaters using the "middle passage" through the islands. The current in the Narrows reaches 12 knots.

Surge Narrows is also the name of a small community east of the pass on READ ISLAND. Following WWI it was home to Robert and Margaret Tipton, who operated a store, farm and post office and attracted a small group of other settlers. There is still a boat dock, store and one of the last one-room schools on the coast.

SURREY is a sprawling suburban community, the largest in BC in terms of land area, stretching from the banks of the FRASER R south to BOUNDARY BAY and the US border. It is bounded by DELTA on the west and LANGLEY on the east and is the easternmost municipality in the GREATER VANCOUVER REGIONAL DISTRICT. Two rivers, the Serpentine and the NICOMEKL, pass through. In

2000 Surrey was the largest city in BC after VANCOUVER, though it only achieved this ranking during the 1990s. Human occupation dates back several millennia. The Kwantlen and other SALISHAN groups had villages beside the Fraser and on the shores of Boundary and Semiahmoo bays. The Kwantlen village of Kikait later became the townsite of BROWNSVILLE, where Surrey's first hotel was located (1861); a ferry crossed to NEW WESTMINSTER on the north side of the Fraser R from 1884 until 1904, when a bridge was finally built. The initial land pre-emption was taken up in 1861 by James Kennedy. Surrey was incorporated in 1879; its population at the time was less than 1,000. The pioneer settlers, mostly British immigrants, chose the name because they were reminded that Surrey, England, was also located across a river from a place called Westminster. The first city hall (1881) is preserved at the Surrey Museum; the first railway, the NEW WESTMINSTER SOUTHERN, began operating in 1891. Much of the municipality was logged and cleared for farming (*see* AGRICULTURE) before the century ended. Communities such as CLOVERDALE and WHALLEY grew up as commercial centres for an essentially rural economy, but the construction of the Pattullo Bridge across the Fraser in 1937 spurred massive development. After WWII Surrey became the fastest-growing large municipality in Canada. Its population, which is predicted to surpass Vancouver's by 2021, has more than doubled since 1981 and has increased ninefold since 1951, when there were only 33,676 residents. Urban growth has centred around Whalley, Guildford, NEWTON, South

Surrey and Cloverdale, where the Surrey Fall Fair and CLOVERDALE RODEO are held. Ocean-facing CRESCENT BEACH and WHITE ROCK are popular resort communities, though White Rock seceded from Surrey in 1957 and was incorporated as a separate city. In 1990 the SKYTRAIN transit system crossed the Fraser R to Whalley, bringing commuters within half an hour of downtown Vancouver. In 1991 Surrey MLA Rita JOHNSTON briefly became BC's (and Canada's) first female premier. The city boasts a fine arts centre, 16 golf courses, live harness racing at Fraser Downs and more green space per capita than any other Lower Mainland municipality.

Population: 304,477
Rank in BC: 2nd
Increase since 1981: 107%
Date of incorporation: district 10 Nov 1879; city 11 Sept 1993
Land area: 371.4 km²
Location: Greater Vancouver Regional District
Economic base: manufacturing, warehousing, wholesale and retail services, agriculture

SUZUKI, David Takayoshi, scientist, environmentalist (b 24 Mar 1936, Vancouver). He was interned with his family during WWII (*see* JAPANESE, RELOCATION OF), then grew up in Ontario. After studying in the US at Amherst College and the Univ of Chicago, he returned to Canada to teach at the Univ of Alberta in 1962. The next year he joined the department of zoology at UBC and he has been associated with the university

David Suzuki, environmental activist.

ever since, most recently with the Sustainable Development Research Institute. His early research into fruit fly genetics won international recognition. He was made a Fellow of the Royal Society of Canada in 1978 and served on the Science Council of Canada from 1978 to 1984. Increasingly he became involved in public issues related to HUMAN RIGHTS and ENVIRONMENTAL degradation. An effective communicator with the rare ability to convey complicated scientific ideas to a lay public, he has been host and moderator of several radio and television programs, beginning with *Suzuki on Science* (1971–72) and including the award-winning CBC-TV show *The Nature of Things*. His commitment to the environment has been recognized by organizations around the world and continues in the work of the Suzuki Foundation in VANCOUVER. He has written or co-written several books, including *Wisdom of the Elders*, *Genethics*, and the autobiographical *Metamorphosis: Stages in a Life* (1987). The recipient of many honorary degrees, Suzuki was made an officer in the Order of Canada in 1977 and a member of the ORDER OF BC in 1995.

SWALLOW is a small perching bird with long pointed wings and a forked tail. It is an adept flyer and spends most of its time in the air, chasing the INSECTS that form the bulk of its diet. Swallows often nest in colonies and mass in flocks on branches and roadside wires, especially just prior to their southward migration in the

Barn swallow. R. Wayne Campbell photo

fall. Harbingers of spring, the earliest swallows begin arriving on the south coast in Feb. Of dozens of species worldwide, 7 occur in BC. The purple martin (*Progne subis*), the largest species, occurs very rarely along the South Coast; numbers declined at mid-century but later began to recover, thanks in part to a successful nest-box program. Plumage varies from purple-black to dark blue to grey. Martin are known to breed at only a handful of locations around GEORGIA STRAIT and are seen most frequently darting above harbours and river ESTUARIES. More common are the tree swallow (*Tachycineta bicolor*), with its iridescent blue back plumage and white front, and the violet-green swallow (*T. thalassina*), which in Canada is found mainly in BC. Like many species, they nest in cavities or in human-made boxes close to WETLANDS, where their insect prey is plentiful. The bank swallow (*Riparia riparia*) nests colonially in cliffs, riverbanks and construction cuts. For the most part it stays east of the COAST MTS. The northern rough-winged swallow (*Stelgidopteryx serripennis*) nests singly in similar situations. The cliff swallow (*Hirundo pyrrhonota*) is a denizen of open valleys and rangeland. It builds its gourd-shaped nest under bridges and in other high structures wherever there is an overhang. The barn swallow

(*Hirundo rustica*) prefers to nest under the eaves inside buildings. It is easily identified by its deeply forked tail and rust-coloured underparts.

SWAN is a large, white, graceful waterfowl with a long, curved neck and a black or orange bill. It prefers wet, usually freshwater, habitat: ESTUARIES, flooded fields, marshland, LAKES and ponds. Three species occur in BC. The most numerous is the tundra swan (*Cygnus columbianus*), also known as the whistling swan, which migrates through the province to and from its Alaskan

Tundra swan. R. Wayne Campbell

breeding grounds. This species is plentiful along the South Coast and south-central Interior in spring and fall, and many winter in the THOMPSON and OKANAGAN valleys. The PEACE R is also a staging area for migrating birds. The tundra swan may be recognized by a yellow patch ahead of each eye. Trumpeter swans (*Cygnus buccinator*), the largest waterfowl species in N America, are common winter visitors along the South Coast and, to a lesser degree, the south-central Interior. They also breed in the northern portion of the province, principally the Peace lowlands. The estuary of the Courtenay R is the most important wintering site in the world for trumpeters, and VANCOUVER ISLAND as a whole supports 25% of the world population in winter. Valued for their skins, trumpeters were almost eradicated by the 1930s but conservation measures—including the work of Ralph EDWARDS and his family at Lonesome Lk in TWEEDSMUIR PROVINCIAL PARK— have brought the birds back from the brink of extinction. The mute swan (*Cygnus olor*), with its orangey bill, is an introduced species, comparatively sedentary, which is confined mainly to southeast Vancouver Island and the GULF ISLANDS.

SWANGARD, Erwin Michael, journalist, sports supporter (b 11 May 1908, Munich, Germany; d 5 May 1993, Vancouver). He came to Canada as a young man in 1930 and began freelance sports reporting in Saskatoon, where from 1936 to 1944 he was on the permanent staff of the *Star-Phoenix* newspaper. He came to VANCOUVER in 1944 to work for the *PROVINCE*, then the *VANCOUVER SUN* (1951–68), before becoming the news director at radio station CJOR from 1972 to 1977. A football player in his younger days, he was an avid supporter of local athletics and involved in several campaigns to stage major sporting events in Vancouver, including the 1954 BRITISH EMPIRE AND COM-

MONWEALTH GAMES and the 1955 Grey Cup. He was instrumental in acquiring a CFL franchise for the city (*see also* FOOTBALL), as well as a Pacific Coast League BASEBALL team. His role in raising funds for a stadium in BURNABY's Central Park led to it being named Swangard Stadium when it opened in 1969. He also served as president of the PNE. Swangard is a member of the Canadian Football Hall of Fame and was appointed to the Order of Canada in 1989.

SWANSON, Robert Eugene, engineer, poet (b 26 Oct 1905, Reading, England; d 4 Oct 1994, Vancouver). His family immigrated to VANCOUVER ISLAND before WWI, and as a teenager he trained as a steam engineer, finding his first jobs in LOGGING camps on the Island. Eventually he earned his degree as a professional engineer, and

Robert Swanson, logger poet and inventor. Mandelbrot photo

in 1936 he went to work for the provincial government as a steam inspector. During the following years he wrote the folksy poems about logging life that won him the nickname Bard of the Woods. These poems, published in 4 chapbook editions, sold upward of 80,000 copies. They were republished in 1992 as *Rhymes of a Western Logger*. After inventing an air horn for trains, which was used around the world, he went into business as a manufacturer of tuned whistle systems. It is his horn that blasts out the first notes of *O Canada* from the roof of Canada Place on the VANCOUVER waterfront each noon.

SWANSON BAY was a North Coast company town on the mainland shore of Graham Reach, midway up the INSIDE PASSAGE. It was the site of BC's first pulp mill, established in 1909 (*see* PULP AND PAPER). The community, which also was a LOGGING centre with several SAWMILLS, reached a population of 500. The town was named for John Swanson, a steamer captain with the HBC. E.H. Crawford, a local logger, is credited with inventing A-frame LOGGING in the bay. By the mid-1920s the pulp mill had closed but there was a fisheries station and a base for a fleet of 5

Swanson Bay, site of first BC pulp mill in 1909.
BC Archives 24636

Boeing flying boats belonging to Pacific Airways. During WWII the post office closed and the site was virtually abandoned.

SWEDES began arriving in BC toward the end of the 19th century, most of them taking jobs on the construction of the CPR or in the extractive industries: LOGGING, commercial FISHING and MINING. Typical of these early newcomers were the pioneer logger P.B. ANDERSON and the THULIN brothers, Charles and Frederick, founders of LUND and CAMPBELL RIVER. Swedes were also closely associated with the early history of REVELSTOKE. Post-WWII, the Swedish population tended to concentrate in the Lower Mainland, and VANCOUVER came to be called "the largest Swedish city in Canada." The community established self-help societies and cultural associations. Until 1980 the centre of community activities was Swedish Park, a large outdoor facility founded in the 1920s in N VANCOUVER. The Swedish Cultural Society (est 1951) organizes the mid-December Festival of Lights, while the *Swedish Press*, the only surviving Swedish publication in Canada, is a bilingual Swedish-English magazine published since 1929. At the 1996 census, 90,490 people claiming Swedish origin lived in BC.

SWEENEY COOPERAGE LTD, at one time the largest barrel maker in the British Empire, was established in VICTORIA in 1889 by Michael Sweeney, a cooper from Newfoundland. The elder Sweeney ran the company until 1920; that year his son Leo (1886–1977) took over and expanded the business, then called Canadian Western Cooperage, to VANCOUVER. It became Sweeney Cooperage in 1940, and sold barrels to customers in more than 40 countries from its 4-ha site on FALSE CREEK. Business dwindled in the

Barrels piled high at Sweeney Cooperage, Vancouver, 1950s. VPL 3533

1970s with the use of cardboard and plastic containers, and the company closed in 1980.

SWEETWATER, 20 km northwest of DAWSON CREEK in the PEACE R district, developed in the early 1920s around Jimmy Mathews' stopping place on the trail to FORT ST JOHN. By the mid-1930s this farming settlement had a school, store, post office and blacksmith, but FARMINGTON eclipsed it in the following decade. AS

SWIFT is a SWALLOW-like bird, related to the HUMMINGBIRD. It has dull-coloured plumage, a very small bill and feet, and long, slender pointed wings. The swift is known for its great speed and acrobatics in flight. It feeds on the wing, chasing a variety of flying INSECTS. In the S Pacific, swifts' nests, which the birds glue together with saliva, are collected and used to make bird's-nest soup. Three species occur across southern BC. The black swift (*Cypseloides niger*), most abundant in the Lower Mainland and along the east coast of VANCOUVER ISLAND, nests on cliff faces, as does the white-throated swift (*Aeronautes saxatalis*), found mainly in the

OKANAGAN VALLEY. Vaux's swift (*Chaetura vauxi*), the smallest species, prefers to nest in hollow trees, though it is sometimes found in buildings and chimneys.

SWIFTSURE INTERNATIONAL YACHT RACE is an annual yacht race first held in 1930. It runs from VICTORIA out past the mouth of JUAN DE FUCA STRAIT and back, a distance of 140.4 nautical miles. It takes place in late May and has been hosted by the Royal Victoria Yacht Club since 1951. The Juan de Fuca Race, a separate 78.3 nm race for smaller sailboats, was inaugurated in 1962 and the mid-distance (103.4 nm) Cape Flattery Race started in the 1980s. All 3 races now make up the Swiftsure event and attract an average of 200 boats from Alaska to California to Australia. *Shirley Hewitt*

SWIMMING began competitively in VICTORIA during the 1860s but did not become a regular event until it was introduced as part of the Queen's birthday regatta in 1888. The Royal Navy organized many aquatic events for VANCOUVER ISLAND but swimming was unpopular due to the cold waters of the Pacific Northwest and social inhibitions against scantily clad young people bathing in the harbour. In VANCOUVER, lifeguard Joe FORTES helped to popularize the sport recreationally as he taught children to swim at the beach in ENGLISH BAY. However, competitive swimming gradually caught on as the Vancouver Amateur Swimming Club was established in 1903, the YMCA Victoria Swimming Club held its first meeting in 1908 and BC joined the newly formed Canadian Amateur Swimming Association in 1910. By 1915, annual BC swimming championships were being held, alternating between Vancouver and Victoria. Another popular event held at this time was Victoria's 3-Mile swim, first won by Audrey (Griffin) Kieran, a member of the BC SPORTS HALL OF FAME. Racing against men, Kieran won the 3-Mile swim 7 of 10 times, and racing against women she never lost the provincial championship. She was one of the greatest female athletes in BC history, but there was no funding available in the 1920s for her to compete internationally. In 1925, the Crystal Gardens pool opened and became the capital's main location for swimming races. Less populated areas were also getting more serious about competitive swimming, as the CRESCENT BEACH and WHITE ROCK swim clubs bought and christened the Semiahmoo Cup for competition among men's relay teams. An interest in conquering BC's natural waters also developed as Anne (Mundigel) MERAW became the first person to swim to BOWEN ISLAND (1938) and set long-standing distance and endurance records for women by swimming the length of OKANAGAN LK in 1958. She also attempted JUAN DE FUCA STRAIT but her body could not hold up. Bert Thomas, a colourful logger from Tacoma who had rum and coke funnelled to him through a garden hose during his swim, and lit up a Cuban cigar as he backstroked to shore, was the first man to cross the strait in 1955.

The Canada West swimming championships at UBC Aquatic Centre, Vancouver, 1990. The men's swim team was coached by Tom Johnson.
Courtesy Fred Hume/UBC Athletic Dept

In the early 1930s the 2 most important pioneers of Canadian swimming emerged from BC as Percy NORMAN became president of the Vancouver Amateur Swimming Club and Archie MCKINNON debuted as the coach of Canada's national team. Among Norman's first stars were Shirley Muir, Irene Strong, Gerry and Kay McNamee, Ted Simpson, Bill Slater and 2 unofficial world-record holders in short-distance, Jack POMFRET (100-yd freestyle, 1941) and Joan Langdon (50-yd breaststroke, 1940). Langdon, who at age 13 was one of Canada's youngest ever Olympians in 1936, broke more than 20 Canadian records and was named Canada's most outstanding swimmer in 1943. McKinnon taught Peter Salmon, a 2-time Olympic swimmer and 1950 BRITISH EMPIRE GAMES gold medallist, as well as virtually everyone else in Victoria. Though Norman and McKinnon built their own swimming legacies in BC's 2 largest cities, the most impressive BC swimming centre was the small pulp mill community of OCEAN FALLS, which formed its Ocean Falls Amateur Athletic Association in 1921 and built an indoor swimming pool in 1928. Important pioneers were James Wood, Jack Jacquest and Tom Jones, who later became coach for the British Empire Games, but the most influential person at the Ocean Falls Swim Club was George Gate, who became coach in 1950. Ocean Falls had already led Canada to international success earlier that year at Auckland's British Empire Games, with Jim Portelance capturing the silver medal in the 1,650-yd freestyle, and freestyle specialist Allen Gilchrist, the winner of the 1948 Sir Edward Beatty Trophy as Canada's top swimmer, participating in the silver medal-winning freestyle relay team. The club's top female was Lenora Fisher, unbeaten in Canada in the 100-yd, 100-m and 110-yd backstrokes from 1952 to 1956. After winning gold in the 100-m backstroke at the 1953 Pan Am Games, Fisher was declared Canada's top female swimmer that year. Also at the 1953 Games, Percy Norman's prodigy Helen STEWART won the 100-m freestyle. Norman, assisted by Gate, coached the Canadian team at the 1954 British Empire Games in Vancouver, which made use of the new Empire Pool at UBC. Stewart's other coach, Howard Firby, was Canada's 1964 Olympic coach and shaped the careers of Helen's sister Mary STEWART as well as Elaine TANNER, Jane HUGHES and Margaret Iwasaki. At the 1964 games, Hughes finished 5th in the 400-m and set a world record in the 880-yd freestyle later that year. At the 1971 Pan Am Games, Sylvia Dockerill won gold in the 100-m breaststroke. Mary Stewart was a world-record breaker as well, while Tanner, with 4 world records and a double-silver performance at the 1968 Olympics, is considered Canada's best-ever female swimmer.

Soon after Tanner slipped from the spotlight, Vancouver's Leslie CLIFF emerged to win a silver medal at the 1972 Munich Olympics, and Donna-Marie GURR brought home the bronze for the 200-m backstroke. BC men also made marks at Munich as Bill Mahony, a breaststroke specialist who won 4 Commonwealth gold medals over his career, earned a bronze for his participation on the Canadian medley relay team. The 1972 Olympics also marked the last competitive appearance of Ocean Falls "iron man" Ralph HUTTON, who had established himself as BC's most successful swimmer by collecting 24 major international medals. The end of his career also marked the end of the Ocean Falls dynasty: Gate had already left and the CROWN ZELLERBACH paper mill, on which the town's economy was based, closed. Other notable Ocean Falls swimmers included Sandy Gilchrist, the winner of 16 major international medals, Jack Kelso (6 medals), Ian McKenzie (4 medals) and Dick POUND, who won 3 medals and was an Olympic finalist in 1960. Vancouver butterfly specialist Bruce ROBERTSON followed in Hutton's

wake by taking a silver in Munich (along with a bronze in the freestyle relay), then winning Canada's first swimming gold since 1912 at the 1973 World Championships. Wendy COOK followed Cliff as Canada's top woman swimmer by setting a world record in 100-m backstroke and winning 3 gold medals at the 1974 Commonwealth Games. At the 1976 Montreal Olympics, Vancouver's Shannon SMITH emerged to win the bronze in the 400-m freestyle, Gary McDonald and Stephen Pickell won silver in the 4x100 medley relay, and Gail Amundrud, the winner of 12 major international medals, was part of the bronze-winning 400-m freestyle relay team. Smith was coached by Ron Jacks, winner of 11 international medals including the gold in the 110-yd butterfly at the 1966 British Empire Games (and brother of singer Terry JACKS). Lisa Borsholt of Vancouver's Canadian Dolphin Swim Club won the gold in the 200-m breaststroke at the 1978 Commonwealth Games. Other notable BC swimmers between 1970 and 2000 were Wade Flemons, Graham Welbourn, Turlough O'Hare, Kevin Draxinger, Gregg Hamm, Nikki Dryden, Sarah Evanetz, Courtney Chuy and Lauren Van Oosten. In the 1990s Jacks also coached distance swimmers Greg STREPPEL, who won a 1994 World Championship 25-km open water gold, and Kim Dyke, who was ranked fourth in the world in 1993–94. The Canadian Dolphin Swim Club, first brought to the forefront of Canadian swimming by Howard Firby in the 1960s, continued its success as the Pacific Dolphin Swimming Association/UBC Swim Team, with Derek Snelling coaching through the 1970s and Tom Johnson taking the helm in 1979. As well as producing many world-class swimmers, it dominated national team competition from 1961 to 1999 with 50 team titles, more than twice the number of the second and third most successful clubs combined. The Dolphins attracted top talent from across the country; in 1998 they became the first club to capture all 8 national club and CIAU championships, and they repeated the feat in 1999. Also in 1999, homegrown Dolphin Jessica Deglau became the first Canadian swimmer to win 4 golds (200-m freestyle and butterfly, 4x100-m and 4x200-m freestyle relays) at a single Pan Am Games. The Dolphin International Swim Meet, inaugurated in 1963 and later called the Mel Zajac Jr Meet, continued to attract top-level international talent as the longest-running swim meet in N America. *SW*

SWISS GUIDES were brought to Canada by the CPR in 1899 to promote TOURISM at its resort hotels in the ROCKY and COLUMBIA Mts. The first Swiss-trained guides, Christian Haesler Sr and Edward Feuz Sr, were stationed at GLACIER HOUSE near the summit of ROGERS PASS. Over the next few years more of these professional MOUNTAINEERING guides came to Canada to lead well-heeled clients to the previously unclimbed summits. In 1912 three guides—Edward Feuz Jr, Rudolph Aemmer and Christian Haesler Jr—moved with their wives permanently to BC, settling near GOLDEN where the railway built Swiss-

Swiss guides at work in the BC mountains, c 1900, in a photograph used for advertising by the CPR. *UBC BC1291/38*

style homes for them in a small village called Edelweiss. The Swiss guides were largely responsible for bringing mountain culture and traditions to Canada. *Chic Scott*

SYDNEY INLET, a steep-sided FJORD off CLAYOQUOT SOUND 50 km northwest of TOFINO on VANCOUVER ISLAND, is the site of Sydney Inlet Provincial PARK (27.74 km²). A commercial FISHING settlement was located here from the 1920s to the 1940s but was later abandoned. The post office name was spelled "Sidney Inlet." The inlet's western arm, Stewardson Inlet, was the site of a large LOGGING camp that reached a peak of activity in the 1970s. *AS*

SYDOR, Alison Jane, mountain biker (b 9 Sept 1967, Edmonton). Raised in N VANCOUVER, she began bicycle road racing at age 20 and in 1988 joined the Canadian national CYCLING team. In 1991 she won Canada's first medal in women's world championship road racing, a bronze. She competed at the 1992 Barcelona Olympics in the road race and returned to the Olympics in 1996 in Atlanta to compete in the inaugural cross-country mountain biking event. She won a silver medal and was named that year's Canadian female athlete of the year. She is a 3-time mountain bike world champion (1994–96) and 3-time winner of the World Cup series (1996, 1998, 1999). She was named to the ORDER OF BC in 1999.

SYME, James, architect, pioneer salmon canner (b 1832, Edinburgh, Scotland; d 18 Apr 1881, Victoria). He came to BC in 1862 to join the Cariboo GOLD RUSH and worked a claim near BARKERVILLE. He then settled in NEW WESTMINSTER in 1865, making his living as an ornamental plasterer and artist. None of his oil paintings are known to have survived. In 1867, in a saltery at ANNIEVILLE on the FRASER R opposite New Westminster, he began the first commercial SALMON CANNERY in BC, selling locally and exporting to Australia. In 1869 the business failed in the general economic downturn and Syme moved to San Francisco. He returned to BC in 1874 and made his home in VICTORIA, where he worked as an architect, designing and building houses and several major public buildings (*see also* ARCHITECTURE). He died of liver disease at the age of 49.

SYNCHRONIZED SWIMMING in BC started with coach Freddie McDermott's swim team and the Royal Life Saving Society girls' team, which practised pattern and precision swimming in the late 1930s and 1940s, and the first BC Ornamental Swimming Championships held in 1949 at the Crystal Pool in VANCOUVER. Mrs Noel Morrow was instrumental in starting the BC Amateur Synchronized Swimming Assoc in 1952, with 5 associated clubs based in Vancouver, CRESCENT BEACH and VICTORIA. The modern development of the sport largely centred around Order of Canada recipient Donalda Smith, who coached athletes for more than 30 years, wrote the Canadian Synchronized Swimming handbook of rules and served as judge at many international events including the 1984 Olympics. Her daughter, Margaret MacLennan, extended the family legacy by becoming a notable builder herself; after serving as president of Synchro BC and Synchro Canada, she was the first woman named to the Federation Internationale de Natation Amateur, the international governing body of aquatic sports. The province's first international competitive success came in 1970, when the Hollyburn

Alison Sydor at the gold medal presentation, 1996 Mountain Bike World Championships, Cairns, Australia. It was her third consecutive world championship. *Courtesy Univ of Victoria*

Members of the BC Aquasonics Senior A team from Surrey, performing at the Provincial Synchronized Swim Championships, 2000. *Peter Battistoni/Vancouver Sun*

Country Club won the team event at the Copenhagen Invitational, with Cinde Stevens and Karen Rasmussen adding another gold in duets and Stevens capturing a silver for her solo performance. Later that year, Stevens won 2 more medals at international meets and the Hollyburn Club was named "team of the year" by members of the BC sports media. Duet Christine Larsen and Kathy Glen captured BC's first Commonwealth gold in 1990. Larsen later teamed with Janice Bremner to become BC's first Olympic medallists as members of Canada's silver medal team at the 1996 Atlanta Olympics.

SW

SYRINGA CREEK was an AGRICULTURAL settlement and steamship landing 15 km west of CASTLEGAR at the south end of Lower ARROW LK. The community was submerged by the KEENLEY-SIDE DAM but Syringa Provincial PARK offers lake access and protects a rare low-elevation Interior DOUGLAS FIR forest.

AS

SZCZAWINSKI, Adam F., botanist (b 21 Oct 1913, Lwow, Poland). A graduate of the Univ of Lwow, he worked there as a botany instructor until WWII began, then enlisted in the Polish army. For a time he served as director of education for the Polish air force, and from 1944 to 1946 he was a flight lieutenant in the Royal Air Force. When the war ended he immigrated to Canada. After receiving a PhD in botany from UBC in 1953, he became a lecturer in the botany department; in 1955 he joined the BC Provincial Museum (*see* ROYAL BC MUSEUM) as curator and head of the botany division. He worked with Vladimir KRAJINA to develop the ECOLOGICAL RESERVES program and authored and co-authored several books in the museum's handbook series, including *The Orchids of British Columbia* (1959), *The Heather Family of British Columbia* (1962) and *Mushrooms of British Columbia* (1976, with R.J. Bandoni). He was a founding member of the Canadian Botanical Assoc and founded *Syesis*, a research journal published by the RBCM. He retired from the museum in 1975. *See also* MUSHROOMS; PLANTS, NATIVE.

Dianne Mackay

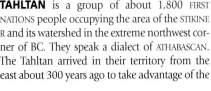

TA TA CREEK, 30 km north of CRANBROOK near the KOOTENAY R, is a small LOGGING and ranching settlement. MINING was important in the early days and a hotel was built here in 1918. The name comes from the last words heard from a horse thief who escaped his capturers at this spot.   AS

TAFT, a CPR siding 32 km west of REVELSTOKE, was named after the manager of the Hood Lumber Co, which was engaged in RAILWAY LOGGING on nearby Crazy Crk. The site was the turning point for "helper" locomotives used on the steep section of rail line due east; the water tank and old station building remained intact until the 1960s.   AS

TAGHUM, pop 142, on the CPR and the north side of the KOOTENAY R in the W KOOTENAY, was originally called Williams Siding. It was the site of A.G. Lambert & Co's lumberyard and planer plant from 1905 to 1933. The LOGGING and milling was done along Sproule Crk to the north and the rough lumber flumed to the planer. Many DOUKHOBORS moved here. The name is a CHINOOK JARGON word for "six"; Taghum was 6 miles (10 km) west of NELSON.   AS

TAGISH are a small group of FIRST NATIONS people who lived in the mountainous region around Tagish Lk in northeast BC and the southern Yukon on the headwaters of the Yukon R. They were hunters and fishers who lived in small family groups following a migratory seasonal cycle. They had extensive trading relations with their southern neighbours, the TLINGIT, and adopted the Tlingit language and aspects of their social organization. It was 2 Tagish men who made the discovery that sparked the Klondike GOLD RUSH in 1898, after which most Tagish congregated at Carcross, YT. There are now no Tagish communities in BC.

TAHLTAN is a group of about 1,800 FIRST NATIONS people occupying the area of the STIKINE R and its watershed in the extreme northwest corner of BC. They speak a dialect of ATHABASCAN. The Tahltan arrived in their territory from the east about 300 years ago to take advantage of the

Tahltan dancers, c 1914. UBC BC672

rich SALMON resource in the river; along with FISHING, they hunted wild game and gathered food PLANTS. Extensive contact with coastal First Nations led to the adoption of the POTLATCH, a system of clans and other aspects of coast culture. Their first exposure to outsiders came with the construction of the COLLINS OVERLAND TELEGRAPH in 1866, followed by GOLD RUSHES to the CASSIAR area (1874) and the Klondike (1898). As disease depleted the population, survivors congregated at 2 main communities, TELEGRAPH CREEK and DEASE LAKE. Wage employment gradually replaced subsistence activities, though the

people still engage in hunting and salmon fishing.

TAHSIS, village, pop 940, is a SAWMILL community at the head of Tahsis Inlet, a long arm of NOOTKA SOUND on the remote west coast of VANCOUVER ISLAND. The site was a winter village of the Mowachaht, a NUU-CHAH-NULTH nation, when George VANCOUVER and Juan BODEGA Y QUADRA visited it in Oct 1792. Its name comes from an aboriginal word meaning "passage" or "crossing," referring to an important trade route up the Tahsis R to WOSS LK. The present community was founded in 1945 when the Gibson brothers built their first sawmill there (*see* J. Gordon GIBSON). The Gibsons sold out to their partners, the East Asiatic Co, in 1952. In 1970 the village was incorporated and taken over from the company by residents. The completion of road access to GOLD RIVER followed 2 years later. A CEDAR mill opened in 1971 but poor markets led to its closure in 1986. The remaining mill complex, now owned by Doman-Western Lumber Ltd, a subsidiary of DOMAN INDUSTRIES, exports most of its product directly to world markets from the village's deep-sea docks.

TAHTSA LAKE, 118 km², is a long (30 km), narrow lake 35 km inland on the east side of the COAST MTS from KEMANO. Fed by glacial streams flowing out of the mountains, it used to empty eastward via the Tahtsa R into OOTSA LK. In 1952 construction of the KENNEY DAM on the NECHAKO R increased water levels in the lake; it began emptying westward through a tunnel excavated through Mt DuBose to Kemano, where water from the lake is used to produce HYDROELECTRICITY for ALCAN's aluminum SMELTER at KITIMAT.

TAIT, Norman, artist (b 1941, Kincolith). A descendant of the master carver Oyai, he was educated by elders in NISGA'A oral tradition and ceremony. He attended RESIDENTIAL SCHOOL in Edmonton, then high school in PRINCE RUPERT before becoming a millwright in a pulp mill. After moving to VANCOUVER in 1971, he began carving seriously. His reputation was established

Norman Tait, Nisga'a carver, at a pole-raising ceremony, 1986. Vickie Jensen photo

in 1973 with his first TOTEM POLE, carved with his father Josiah and erected to commemorate the incorporation of PORT EDWARD. It was the first NISGA'A pole raised in more than 50 years. Other original works are located in Osaka, Phoenix, Chicago, London, N VANCOUVER and at the MUSEUM OF ANTHROPOLOGY at UBC. Tait took part in the carving of a frontal pole for the Native Education Centre in Vancouver, an event documented in Vickie Jensen's book, *Where the People Gather* (1992). *See also* ART, NORTHWEST COAST ABORIGINAL.

TAKAKKAW FALLS, 254 m, the second-highest WATERFALL in BC and in Canada and the highest in the ROCKY MTS, is in YOHO NATIONAL PARK, about 20 km north of FIELD. Water originates from the Daly Glacier and the Waputik Icefield (*see* GLACIATION) straddling the Great Divide. The name derives from a Stoney First Nations word meaning "it is magnificent." (The Stoney, or Nakoda, live in the eastern foothills of the Rockies.) The falls became accessible to visitors following completion of the CPR in 1885, and the railway built Yoho Valley Lodge nearby.

TAKLA LAKE lies northeast of BABINE LK in north-central BC. It empties to the southeast via the MIDDLE R into Trembleur Lk and eventually into the FRASER R (*see also* BC HERITAGE RIVERS). It is part of the traditional territory of the DAKELH First Nation, who have a settlement, pop 250, at Takla Post (Takla Landing) on its northeast shore. BC RAIL has a branch line that runs the entire 100-km length of the lake. While trapping has always been important in the region, and TOURISM has expanded, LOGGING is the primary source of employment. *AS*

TAKU RIVER, flowing through the COAST MTS in the rugged northwest corner of the province,

is formed from the confluence of the Nakina and Inklin rivers. It crosses the border into Alaska to empty via Taku Inlet into Stephens Passage, just south of Juneau. Rich in SALMON, it is the traditional territory of the Taku River TLINGIT, most of whom now live 130 km to the north near the community of ATLIN. The river valley was one of the early overland routes linking the coast to Atlin and TESLIN lakes. In the late 1990s it became the focus of a dispute between a development company and a coalition of FIRST NATIONS people and ENVIRONMENTALISTS: the company planned to build a 140-km road to service an old GOLD MINE (Tulsequah Chief) it wanted to reopen on the Tulsequah R, one of the lower Taku's tributaries. Much of the proposed road route is unroaded wilderness with a high population of grizzly BEARS, so the controversy escalated to include provincial and national environmental groups. Alaskan and other American groups also became involved because the Taku is an important source of salmon for the Alaska commercial fishery.

TAKYSIE LAKE, 40 km south of BURNS LAKE between FRANÇOIS and OOTSA lakes, was first settled in the early 1910s. LOGGING and ranching (*see* CATTLE INDUSTRY) were the economic mainstays. A road was built in 1940 and a number of MENNONITES arrived in 1945. Today the lake has a pleasant resort and a reputation for good sport FISHING. The name is a DAKELH (Carrier) word meaning "three heads." *AS*

TALLMAN, Warren, teacher, literary critic (b 17 Nov 1921, Seattle; d 1 July 1994, Vancouver). He grew up in Olympia, WA, and came to VANCOUVER in 1956 with his wife Ellen to teach in the English department at UBC. During the 1960s their home was a literary drop-in centre where major American poets such as Allen Ginsberg, Robert Creeley and Charles Olson stayed and a new generation of local writers came to meet

Warren Tallman, literary critic.

them. Controversial because of his aggressive advocacy of contemporary US styles in poetry, especially that of the Black Mountain school, he inspired the *TISH* group and influenced a generation of Canadian poets, including George BOWERING, Daphne MARLATT, Fred WAH and bp Nichol. In 1992 he published a collection of his writings, *In the Midst.*

TALON BOOKS LTD (Talonbooks) is a VANCOUVER book publisher founded in 1967 by David Robinson, Jim Brown and others, emerging from the literary MAGAZINE *Talon*. Under the direction of Robinson and Karl Siegler, who joined the company in the early 1970s, Talonbooks became the leading publisher of Canadian plays, in addition to fiction, poetry, ethnography and other genres. The highly successful publication of cookbooks by Umberto MENGHI and Susan Mendelson led to a debate about focus; Siegler and his wife Christy took control of the press in 1985, rededicating it to literary titles. The company claims to be "the largest independent, exclusively literary press in Canada," and maintains more than 240 titles in print. Siegler is active in BC and Canadian publishers' associations in influencing public policy on the arts. *See also* BOOK PUBLISHING.

Bill Schermbrucker

TAMAHNOUS THEATRE originated in VANCOUVER in 1971 as the Vancouver Theatre Workshop, an experimental collective. During its early years members included John GRAY, Larry Lillo, Morris PANYCH, Eric Peterson and John Moffat. In the early 1970s the company mounted a number of daring productions and developed a reputation as BC's leading alternative theatre. Tamahnous was the VANCOUVER EAST CULTURAL CENTRE's resident company during 1976–86, offering such hits as *18 Wheels* and *Last Call: A Post Nuclear Cabaret.* In the late 1980s it lost momentum and mounted fewer and fewer productions; by the late 1990s it had effectively disappeared from the THEATRE scene. Tamahnous is a CHINOOK JARGON word meaning "magic" or "spirits." *AS*

TANABE, Takao, artist (b 16 Sept 1926, Prince Rupert). His family was displaced from the coast during WWII when he was a teenager (*see* JAPANESE, RELOCATION OF). He first studied art at the Winnipeg School of Art, where Joe PLASKETT was one of his teachers, and he continued his studies in New York, London and Tokyo. His first solo exhibition was in 1953 and he has been exhibiting in Canada and occasionally internationally ever since. His continuing interest in small-book design and typography led him to found Periwinkle Press in VANCOUVER in 1956; he published poetry and broadsheets. He taught at the Vancouver School of Art (*see* EMILY CARR INSTITUTE OF ART & DESIGN) from 1962 to 1965 and from 1967 to 1968. He left BC for the US, then taught at the Banff Centre School of Fine Arts from 1973 to 1980. He then returned to the coast where he divides his time between Vancouver and ERRINGTON on VANCOUVER

Takao Tanabe, artist. Eliza Massey

ISLAND. His BC seascapes, as well as Arctic and prairie landscapes, are distinctive in their interpretation of light and space, often in strong horizontal compositions. He holds an honorary diploma from the Emily Carr Institute (1990) and is a member of the ORDER OF BC (1993) and the Order of Canada (1999). *See also* ART, VISUAL; BOOK PUBLISHING.

TANAGER, WESTERN (*Piranga ludoviciana*) is a brilliantly coloured bird found in summer in BC's coniferous and mixed forests, where it eats INSECTS and small fruit. The male's bright red head, yellow body and black wings make this species unmistakable. It winters in Mexico and farther south to Costa Rica.   *Kim Goldberg*

TANNER, Elaine, "Mighty Mouse," swimmer (b 22 Feb 1951, Vancouver). Widely considered Canada's all-time best female swimmer, she specialized in the backstroke, butterfly and individual medley but also competed on medley and freestyle relay teams. She grew up in W VANCOUVER, started SWIMMING when she was 9, began breaking national records in 1965 and

Elaine Tanner, swimmer. She set a new world record for the butterfly stroke.
Bill Cunningham/ Vancouver Province

astonished the swimming world at the 1966 Commonwealth Games in Jamaica by winning 4 gold medals and 3 silvers, an individual record for females. In 1966 she also set a world record in the 220-yard butterfly and at 15 was the youngest person ever to receive the Lou Marsh Trophy as Canada's top athlete. She won it again in 1967, that year capturing 2 golds and 2 silvers while setting 3 world records at the Pan American Games in Winnipeg. Disappointed

Wartime internment camp for Japanese Canadians, Tashme, c 1944.

with 2 silvers and a bronze at the 1968 Olympics in Mexico City, she lost interest in competitive athletics and left the sport at age 19. Canada's only female athlete in any sport with 4 world records to her credit, she is a Member of the Order of Canada and has been inducted into the International Swimming, Canadian Sports and Aquatic Halls of Fame and the BC SPORTS HALL OF FAME (1969).   *SW*

TANTALUS RANGE is a dramatic series of serrate snow-capped peaks at the head of HOWE SOUND along the west side of the SQUAMISH R. Peaks include Ossa (2,260 m), Serratus (2,326 m), Dione (2,590 m) and the highest, Mt Tantalus itself (2,603). Basil Darling, Allan Morkill and Stanley Davies made the first ascent of Tantalus in 1911, and the other summits were climbed by the end of WWI (*see also* MOUNTAINEERING). Lake Lovelywater Recreation Area nestles beneath the range, which is a favourite with hikers and rock climbers.

TAPPEN, 10 km north of SALMON ARM near SHUSWAP LK, is a farming and recreational community at the east end of the Tappen Valley. The name is a mispelling of Tappan, the name of a CPR sub-contractor who worked on the line here in 1884; "helper" locomotives were based at this point for many years. The settlement was originally known as Brightwater.   *AS*

TARRYS, a farming and LOGGING settlement on the CPR and the north shore of the KOOTENAY R 11

km northeast of CASTLEGAR, was named after a pioneer local rancher. Many DOUKHOBORS settled in this area.   *AS*

TASHME, 22 km east of HOPE off the HOPE–PRINCETON HWY, was a community of tarpaper shacks hastily thrown together in 1942 to house Japanese Canadians relocated from the coast (*see* JAPANESE, RELOCATION OF). The population peaked at about 2,600. Most of the men

worked at a SAWMILL or on construction of the highway. At the end of the war, residents were allowed to leave and the community was dismantled in 1946. The name was a combination of the names of the 3 members of the BC Security Commission: Austin TAylor, John SHirras and Frederick MEad.

TASU, on the west coast of Moresby Island 55 km south of SKIDEGATE in the QUEEN CHARLOTTE ISLANDS, was the site of several small COPPER mines from 1914 to 1917. Westfrob Mines, a subsidiary of Falconbridge Nickel, had a large open-pit iron ore operation here (1962–83). The modern townsite had an indoor swimming pool and gymnasium and was home to 400 people. The name is a HAIDA word meaning "lake of plenty," and refers to Tasu Sound.   *AS*

TATALROSE, 35 km southwest of BURNS LAKE and south of FRANÇOIS LK, is a farming and LOGGING district first settled about 1907. MENNONITE families took up land here in the 1940s and a number of GERMANS bought recreational and retirement property in the late 1980s. The post office in the area was originally named Bickle, after a pioneer family.   *AS*

TATLA LAKE, pop 123, lies halfway between WILLIAMS LAKE and BELLA COOLA on the Chilcotin Hwy (#20) in the west CHILCOTIN. Ranching began here about 1890. Bob Graham, a pioneer, purchased the ranch in 1902 and over the years a post office, school, community hall and nursing station were added to the community. The Graham ranch house, built in 1930, is now the Graham Inn, and caters to highway travellers.

TATLATUI PROVINCIAL PARK, 1,058.26 km², is located in the northern Interior immediately southeast of the SPATSIZI Plateau and lies beneath the towering peaks of the Tatlatui Range of the Skeena Mts. Established in 1973, it was the first park to represent the northern Interior of BC west of the ROCKY MTS. This park contains extensive glacial features (*see* GLACIATION) and several high-altitude lakes, including Trygve, Tatlatui and Kitchener lakes. The Firesteel R rises in the park and flows east to join the FINLAY R and thence into the drainage basin of the PEACE R. The park is a favourite with rainbow TROUT fishers (*see also* FISHING, SPORT) and contains an amazing variety of wildlife, including woodland CARIBOU, MOUNTAIN GOATS, MOOSE, grizzly BEARS and black bears. Access is primarily by float plane and on horseback.

TATLAYOKO LAKE, 40 km², is a long, narrow lake in the COAST MTS south of the CHILCOTIN. The HOMATHKO R drains the lake southward and runs between the Homathko Icefield and the base of Mt WADDINGTON into the top of BUTE INLET. The area is remarkable for its mountain scenery, abundant wildlife and excellent sport FISHING. The first rancher arrived around 1910 and ranches are strung out along the road leading north to TATLA LAKE (*see* CATTLE INDUSTRY). TOURISM is an important economic activity in this area and there are several resorts and lodges: fishing, horse-packing and cross-country SKIING are all popular. LIGNUM LTD had a small SAWMILL here in the 1950s. *Tatlayoko* is a TSILHQOT'IN word for "deep rough water."

TATLOW, Robert Garnet, financier, politician (b 6 Sept 1855, Scarva, Ireland; d 11 Apr 1910, Victoria). He made a fortune in VANCOUVER in SHIPPING and real estate and as H.O. BELL-IRVING's partner in the SALMON export business. In 1900 he was elected a CONSERVATIVE member of the legislature, where he became finance minister in Richard MCBRIDE's government in 1903. Breaking with the

Robert Tatlow, Conservative politician, 1909.
BC Archives D-05673

premier over railway policy in 1909, he resigned from the CABINET and did not run for re-election that year. He was killed a few months later when he fell from a runaway carriage. He was an original member of the city's parks board and Tatlow Park in Kitsilano is named in his honour.

TATSHENSHINI RIVER, 193 km, rises in the ST ELIAS MTS in the northwest corner of BC and flows north into the Yukon before looping south to merge with the ALSEK R and empty into the Gulf of Alaska. The area is part of the traditional territory of the Champagne and Aishihik First Nations. Known for its spectacular wilderness scenery, turbulent water and varied wildlife, it has become since 1976 one of the top whitewater rafting rivers in the world. In 1993 the provincial government refused to allow development of a COPPER mine on nearby Windy Craggy Mt that environmentalists argued would damage

Rafting on the Tatshenshini R.
Rick Blacklaws photo

the river. After a protracted campaign by environmental and wilderness recreation groups throughout N America, the BC government created Tatshenshini–Alsek Wilderness Provincial PARK (9,580 km²). It includes the BC side of Mt FAIRWEATHER (el 4,663 m), BC's highest MOUNTAIN, and has a sizable population of grizzly BEARS as well as Canada's only glacier bears, which are a colour phase of black bears known for their unusual blue-grey coat. Other wildlife includes numerous birds, most of the estimated 300 Dall's sheep (*see* MOUNTAIN SHEEP) in BC and several hundred MOUNTAIN GOATS. In Dec 1994 the UN designated the park part of an 84,000 km² UNESCO WORLD HERITAGE SITE that includes Kluane National Park in the Yukon and adjoining national parks in Alaska. *See also* ENVIRONMENTAL MOVEMENT.

TAYLOR, district municipality, pop 1,031, lies at the confluence of the PEACE and Pine rivers on the ALASKA HWY, 18 km south of FORT ST JOHN in the northeast corner of the province. Alexander MACKENZIE passed by in May 1793 on his historic overland expedition to the Pacific Ocean. It is

Peace R at Taylor, 1989. Roy Luckow photo

named for Herbie Taylor, a fur trader, farmer and ferry operator who settled here with his family in 1912. As part of the construction of the Alaska Hwy, the Peace River Suspension Bridge opened in 1943. The largest bridge on the highway, it collapsed on 16 Oct 1957 and was replaced with a new structure in 1960. Incorporated as a village in 1958, Taylor became a district municipality in 1989. Major industries include a pulp mill (*see* PULP AND PAPER), a SAWMILL and a natural gas processing plant.

TAYLOR, Alfred James Towle, engineer, businessman (b 4 Aug 1887, Victoria; d 20 July 1945, NY). He apprenticed as a machinist before moving to VANCOUVER, where he paid for his engineering studies by running a boarding house. In 1912 he founded what became Taylor & Young Engineering, which built various large projects around the province. He moved to England in 1926 and arranged British financial backing, mainly from the Guinness brewing family, for development of an exclusive residential suburb in W VANCOUVER. His British Pacific Properties Ltd developed the BRITISH PROPERTIES during the 1930s and built the LIONS GATE BRIDGE. After returning to Vancouver in 1937, he lived at his estate at Kew Beach, west of Caulfeild in W

Vancouver. He returned to London during WWII to work for the British Ministry of Aircraft Production. Taylor Way, a major stretch of road in W Vancouver, is named after him.

TAYLOR, Austin Cottrell, financier (b 17 Jan 1889, Toronto; d 1 Nov 1965, Vancouver). During WWI the Imperial Munitions Board made him responsible for procuring SPRUCE from the QUEEN CHARLOTTE ISLANDS for airplane construction. He made his fortune in the 1930s as one of the owners of the BRALORNE mine in the BRIDGE R country. A highly profitable GOLD mine, it made Taylor one of the richest and most socially prominent businessmen in VANCOUVER. He raised race horses near LANGLEY (in 1936 his horse Indian Broom ran third in the Kentucky Derby), and in 1936 he purchased the 4-ha Shannon Estate on S Granville St in Vancouver, once the home of B.T. ROGERS. During WWII Taylor was one of C.D. Howe's "dollar-a-year" men, and in 1942 he chaired the BC Security Commission, responsible for removing the Japanese from the coast (see JAPANESE, RELOCATION OF). A staunch Conservative politically, he contributed to various charitable causes. After his death, Shannon Estate was redeveloped into luxury townhouses.

TAYLOR, Frederick "Cyclone," hockey player (b 23 June 1883, Tara, ON; d 9 June 1979, Vancouver). One of the greatest HOCKEY players in history, he began his professional career in 1906 in Michigan and won his first Stanley Cup with the Ottawa Senators in 1909. He came west in 1913 to play for Frank PATRICK's VANCOUVER MILLIONAIRES in the PACIFIC COAST HOCKEY ASSOC and his presence helped make the young league a success with the public. In 1915 he led VANCOUVER to a Stanley Cup championship and he reached the Stanley Cup finals with Vancouver 3 more times (1918, 1921, 1922) before retiring in 1923. He remained active in hockey while working for the federal department of immigration for 30 years. He entered the Hockey Hall of Fame in 1947. *SW*
Reading: Eric Whitehead, *Cyclone Taylor: A Hockey Legend,* 1977.

TAYLOR, Jim, journalist (b 16 Mar 1937, Nipawin, SK). He began his NEWSPAPER career in VICTORIA as a sports reporter with the *Daily Colonist,* but it was as a daily columnist in VANCOUVER with the *VANCOUVER SUN* and the *PROVINCE* from 1971 to 1995 that he won recognition as one of the finest sports writers in the country. Along the way, he published 8 books about athletes as diverse as Wayne Gretzky, Rick HANSEN, Debbie BRILL and Jim YOUNG. His columns were compiled in 2 collections: *Forgive Me My Press Passes* (1993) and *You Mean I Get Paid to Do This?* (1997).

TAYLOR, Louis Denison, longest-serving mayor of Vancouver (b 22 July 1857, Ann Arbor, MI; d 4 June 1946, Vancouver). Despite his electoral success Taylor remains a neglected figure in VANCOUVER's political history, remembered if at all for his habit of wearing a red tie. He arrived in the city in 1896 on his way to go prospecting in Alaska but never reached his destination. Instead he spent the next 2 years in the Interior of BC, mainly working for the CPR. He then settled permanently in Vancouver and became circulation manager for the *PROVINCE* newspaper. From 1905 to 1915 he ran his own daily paper, the *World,* but his principal occupation was politics. Between 1902 and 1938 he ran in 26 elections

Louis D. Taylor, the longest-serving mayor of Vancouver, 1932. CVA Port.P.149

and won 10 times, once as licence commissioner (1902) and 9 times as mayor (1910, 1911, twice in 1915, 1925, 1926, 1927–28, 1931–32, 1933–34). Early in his career Taylor was considered a progressive but his later terms were marred by ill health and the odour of scandal. Investigations into police corruption failed to implicate him but his opponents routinely hinted that he was dishonest. In his later years Taylor was a sad figure, running unsuccessfully in elections, then living as a penniless recluse dependent on the charity of friends.

TCG INTERNATIONAL INC is a retail and wholesale distributor of automobile glass and auto parts with outlets across Canada, in the US and Europe. It was founded in 1946 by 2 brothers, Arthur and Herbert Skidmore, as a single auto glass store. Its 1998 revenues were $226 million, and in 1999 it owned Apple Auto Glass, Speedy Auto Glass, NOVUS windshield repair and a majority interest in Glentel Inc, a mobile communications business. It incorporated under its present name in 1970 and returned to private ownership in 1996. The Skidmores received the ORDER OF BC in 1995.

TCHESINKUT LAKE, 14 km south of BURNS LAKE, was first settled by Tom Kelly, a prospector, in about 1910. More homesteaders arrived after WWI; they built a school and post office and began LOGGING and a SAWMILL operated during the 1930s. TOURISM has become important and the lake, with its resort, is a popular sport FISHING destination. The name is a DAKELH (Carrier) name for "clear waters." *AS*

TEAGUE, John, architect (b 3 June 1835, Cornwall, England; d Oct 1902, Victoria). Lured to N America by the promise of finding GOLD, he erected mine buildings during the California gold rush and in 1859 ventured north (see GOLD RUSH, CARIBOO). Disillusioned with the life of a prospector, he settled in VICTORIA and began constructing buildings for the Royal Navy at ESQUIMALT. He established an ARCHITECTURAL practice and in 1874 obtained the commission for the Church of Our Lord, a congregation of the Reformed Episcopal Church, which counted among its members many of Victoria's civic leaders. Important institutional commissions followed and Teague's distinctive Mansardic roofline and entrance towers contributed greatly to the city's late-19th century cityscape. The final phase of his career was blighted by the depression of the mid-1890s, and his last major commission was the Driard Hotel (1892). *Martin Segger*

TECHNICAL UNIVERSITY OF BC (TechBC) is a post-secondary educational institution established in 1997 to provide university courses in applied and technological fields. The school began offering programs in the fall of 1999, operating from a campus in SURREY and offering courses via on-line technologies. In keeping with its applied focus it maintains close ties with industry. *See also* EDUCATION, POST-SECONDARY.

TECK CORP is a VANCOUVER mining company with roots going back to Teck-Hughes Gold Mines Ltd, operators of a mine at Kirkland Lake, ON, from 1917 to 1968. Through mergers and acquisitions it has become a diversified MINING enterprise whose BC interests include all or part of COMINCO, Highland Valley Copper, the Bullmoose and Quintette COAL mines in northeastern BC (Quintette closed in 2000) and the Elkview coal mine at SPARWOOD. Under its president, Norm Keevil, the company also has interests in GOLD mines in Ontario and Australia, COPPER in Chile and copper–ZINC in Quebec, Mexico and Peru. In 1998 it had revenues of $715 million.

TEIT, James Alexander, ethnographer (b 1864, Shetland Islands, Scotland; d 30 Oct 1922, Spences Bridge). He arrived in BC in 1884 to help at his uncle's general store in SPENCES BRIDGE and the work brought him into contact with the local NLAKA'PAMUX (Thompson) people. He married a Nlaka'pamux woman, Lucy Antko (she died in 1899) and became active in the struggle for ABORIGINAL RIGHTS, helping to form the Interior Tribes of BC and the BC Indian Rights Assoc. In 1894 he met the anthropologist Franz BOAS, who was on a field trip to the Interior, and became his informant and guide. This was the beginning of Teit's ethnological endeavours. He worked with the ethnology division of the Geological Survey of Canada 1911–18, taking many photographs of Interior Salish people (see SALISHAN FIRST NATIONS). After 1918 he worked as a rancher and prospector. He served on the executive of the ALLIED INDIAN TRIBES OF BC from its formation in 1916 to his death.

Aerial view of Telegraph Cove, c 1955.
Courtesy Pat Norris

Church at Telkwa. Walter Lanz/Image Makers

TELEGRAPH COVE is a small village on the northeast coast of VANCOUVER ISLAND, just south of PORT MCNEILL at the western entrance to JOHNSTONE STRAIT. A boardwalk rims the edge of the cove and many of the buildings sit on pilings over the water. The village began in 1912 as a telegraph station on the line between CAMPBELL RIVER and the north end of the Island. In 1929 Fred WASTELL from ALERT BAY, along with his partner Alex Macdonald, opened a SAWMILL to make boxes for shipping SALMON to Japan. Telegraph Cove Mills was the focus of the community until it closed in 1978. Today the cove is home port for summer WHALE WATCHING cruises in Johnstone Strait.
Reading: Pat Wastell Norris, *Time & Tide: A History of Telegraph Cove* (*Raincoast Chronicles* 16), 1995.

TELEGRAPH CREEK, pop 475, is the only town on the STIKINE R, about 260 km upriver from its mouth at the base of the river's Grand Canyon. It is in the territory of the TAHLTAN people and Tahltan village (pop 138) occupies the top of a nearby hill. Settlement began with the discovery of GOLD in 1861, followed by the arrival of the COLLINS OVERLAND TELEGRAPH later in the decade. The community was the gateway to GOLD RUSHES in the CASSIAR (1874–76) and the Klondike (1898–99). In 1928 the road east to DEASE LAKE was improved. During WWII supplies for construction of the ALASKA HWY came through here. More gold discoveries in the 1990s raised expectations of another MINING boom.

TELFORD, James Lyle, doctor, politician (b 21 June 1889, Valens, ON; d 27 Sept 1960, Vancouver). A medical doctor by profession, he was one of the best-known inter-war socialist politicians in BC. He edited his own newspaper, the *Challenge*, and read extremely popular political commentaries on VANCOUVER radio. An early advocate of family planning, Telford opened Canada's second birth control clinic in Vancouver in 1932 at a time when dispensing such information was illegal. He was an energetic promoter of the provincial CCF in its early days; in 1937 he ran successfully for election to the legislature for an East Vancouver seat he shared with Harold WINCH. For a time it looked like he might become leader of the party, but that job went to Winch. Telford ran for mayor of Vancouver instead and won election in Jan 1939. Because the CCF did not allow members to hold 2 elected positions, he left the party and sat in the legislature as an independent while serving his 2-year term as mayor. In the 1941 provincial election he ran again as an independent–labour candidate and lost, which ended his political career.

TELKWA, village, pop 1,194, is situated on the YELLOWHEAD Hwy, 370 km west of PRINCE GEORGE where the Telkwa and BULKLEY rivers meet. Telkwa was on the route of the COLLINS OVERLAND TELEGRAPH, constructed in the 1860s. It became the commercial centre of the Bulkley Valley until pre-WWI construction of the GRAND TRUNK PACIFIC RWY shifted development to SMITHERS.

TELUS COMMUNICATIONS INC was created in 1998 from a merger of BC Telecom, owner of BC Tel, then Canada's second-largest telephone company, and Telus Corp, an Alberta telephone company. The new company, based in BURNABY, had combined assets of $8 billion and annual revenues of $6 billion. It is one of the largest private-sector employers in BC, supporting 14,000 jobs. The objective of the merger was to create a firm large enough to compete with Bell Canada, the country's largest phone company.

BC Tel traced its origins to the Vernon and Nelson Telephone Co, incorporated in 1891 to create a province-wide telephone system. At that

Operators at work in the Seymour Exchange of BC Tel, forerunner of Telus Communications Inc, 1940. Dominion/VPL 25277

time there were more than 3 dozen small phone companies in the province, including the New Westminster & Burrard Inlet Telephone Co in VANCOUVER. Bought by British interests, the latter company changed its name in 1898 to British Columbia Telephones Ltd. It merged with the V&NTC and soon owned subsidiaries on VANCOUVER ISLAND and in the Interior. Ownership returned to BC in 1902 and the company became British Columbia Telephone Co Ltd 2 years later. Local owners of BC Tel sold the company to General Telephone and Electronics Corp of Chicago in 1927 and it was controlled by American owners thereafter. GTE Corp continues to have a 26% share in Telus.

TEMLAXHAM (also known as Tam Lax Aamid, or Dimlahamid, or Prairie Town) was an ancient village of the TSIMISHIAN people located on the SKEENA R near the present site of HAZELTON. According to Tsimshian accounts, it was destroyed in a great flood and the inhabitants dispersed to other communities.

TENNIS was first played in Cowichan and VICTORIA on grass courts around 1885. The Victoria Lawn Tennis Club was formed in 1886 and the COWICHAN BAY Lawn Tennis Club came into being in 1888, holding its first S Cowichan Open in 1912, a summer tournament that continued through the 20th century as the VANCOUVER ISLAND championships. The Cowichan club, the longest-lasting club in BC, still has Canada's only lawn courts. VANCOUVER's first tennis court, circa 1888, belonged to the SALMON CANNING tycoon H.O. BELL-IRVING. The Vancouver Lawn Tennis Club was inaugurated in 1897 with Richard MARPOLE, CPR superintendent and land developer, as its first president.

J.F. Foulkes of Victoria was BC's first real tennis star, clearly establishing himself as the top player in western Canada during the 1890s. Several leading American players—Hazel Hotchkiss Wightman, Dwight Davis, Holcombe Ward and Mal Whitman among them—played in BC in the early 1900s, helping to increase the sport's popularity in the province. Victoria's Marian Pitts defeated Wimbledon superstar Elizabeth Ryan for the Mainland Championship in 1905 to provide BC with its first win over world-calibre opposition. Edward Cardinall was an early BC star; he was BC singles champ 1909–13 and later became an important administrator, the only non-American to win the Marlborough Award for outstanding contribution to tennis. One of the most successful Davis Cup (international team championship) teams in Canadian history was made up entirely of BC players. In 1913 Victoria players Foulkes, Bobby Powell, Bernie SCHWENGERS and H.C. Mayes defeated Belgium and S Africa to reach the European zone finals, which they lost to the USA. Powell, one of BC's earliest participants at Wimbledon, had started the Pacific Northwest Tennis Association in 1904 to link BC, Washington and Oregon. PNW championships remained important competitions for BC players throughout the century.

Competitive tennis had a hiatus during WWI but spread to KELOWNA, VERNON and NELSON in the 1920s and Cardinall was involved in the founding of the BC Lawn Tennis Association in 1921. In Vancouver, Jack WRIGHT emerged as BC's best player in the inter-war period by winning 6 national titles in singles and doubles play. He later was named by the Canadian Press as Canada's tennis player of the first half-century. Marjorie Leeming dominated BC women's tennis during the 1920s when she was a frequent provincial champ. In 1925 she won every title possible in Canada: BC and Canadian singles, doubles and mixed doubles. She also won the Canadian singles title in 1926, the doubles again in 1930 and 1932 and the mixed doubles in 1930. Leeming was named BC's Outstanding Tennis Player 6 times. The STANLEY PARK Tennis Tournament began in 1931, and it became the developing ground of many top competitive players. The BC player of the 1950s was certainly Lorne MAIN, who won the national singles title at age 19 and later made it to the second and third rounds of Wimbledon and captained Canada's Davis Cup team. Bob Puddicombe, another national champion, also qualified for Wimbledon (1966) and was selected to the Davis Cup team in 1965–69.

The first family of BC tennis was undoubtedly the Bardsleys: parents Jim and Jean and sons Tony and Bob. Tony was the most successful of the clan, earning several national titles and 3 Davis Cup selections and being ranked first in Canada in the mid-1970s. During the 1990s the Bardsley brothers continued to win national titles at the Masters level. Other BC Davis Cup stars over the years included Paul Willey, Fred Bolton, Jim Macken, Jim Skelton and Walter Stohlberg. The international women's Federation Cup team featured Victoria's Susan Butt and Wendy (Barlow) Pattenden and Vancouver's Marjorie Blackwood. Pattenden, the Canadian singles champ in 1980, played at Wimbledon and led Canada to the 1980 Championship of the Americas title and fourth place at the Pan Am Games. Blackwood, ranked 48th in the world in 1983, won 3 national championships, represented Canada in the Federation Cup 1972–80 and reached the doubles quarter-finals at Wimbledon twice. In 1987 Vancouver's Hollyburn Country Club hosted the Federation Cup, featuring the world's best women's tennis players from 45 different nations. BC tennis produced 2 of the most successful Canadians in the history of the sport in the 1980s. Helen KELESI rose to 13th in the world in 1989, the highest ranking ever by a player from BC. Grant CONNELL was one of the best doubles players in the world, reaching the Wimbledon finals 3 times and winning the 1995 World Championship with his American partner, Pat Galbraith. *SW*

TENTA, John, wrestler (b 22 June 1963, Surrey). When he visited Japan with his SURREY high school WRESTLING team, he impressed coaches there and was invited to train in the Japanese sumo stable. As an amateur he was Canadian junior champion and won the 1983

John "the Earthquake" Tenta, wrestler, 1992.
Fotogenic Studios

world junior title, Canada's first international gold medal in wrestling. After attending Louisiana State Univ on a wrestling scholarship, he took the Japanese up on their offer and became only the second foreigner—and first Caucasian—to break into sumo. At 200 kg he immediately gained respect from trainers and opponents and he was successful in the ring, but he had trouble adapting to the strict sumo regimen. He left sumo after 21 consecutive wins in 9 months, causing a public uproar in Japan. He then embarked on a professional wrestling career, first as "Big John Tenta" in Japan and later for 6-figure contracts as "the Earthquake" and "the Shark" in the World Wrestling Federation. *SW*

TERN is a mid-sized bird similar in appearance to a small GULL, though its wings are more pointed, its tail is forked and it is generally more

Arctic tern. Ken Bowen photo

streamlined in shape. Grey and white in colour, with a black cap and a pointed red bill, the tern feeds on INSECTS and dives into the water for FISH. Terns nest on the ground in open, flat areas near water. Of 12 species in Canada, 5 occur in BC. The largest N American species is the Caspian tern (*Sterna caspia*), a summer visitor to

GEORGIA STRAIT and the OKANAGAN VALLEY; in the late 20th century it became more prevalent in BC. The common tern (*Sterna hirundo*) passes through southern BC on its migrations to S America and is seen mainly in Georgia Strait. The Arctic tern (*Sterna paradisaea*) breeds in the Arctic and in the northwest corner of BC and migrates off the outer coast, making the longest migration of any bird species to its wintering grounds near the Antarctic Circle. Forster's tern (*Sterna forsteri*) is present mainly in the CRESTON Valley, its only nesting area in the province. The black tern (*Chlidonias niger*), a small, dark bird, breeds in the south-central Interior, then migrates south for the winter.

TERRACE, city, pop 12,779, in the SKEENA Valley 140 km east of PRINCE RUPERT, was created in 1910 with the arrival of the GRAND TRUNK PACIFIC RWY. The townsite was laid out at the  confluence of the Skeena and Kitsumkalum rivers, former site of a TSIMSHIAN village, on land donated by George Little, a pioneer settler. He named the community after the terraced land along the Skeena, which had been formed by GLACIATION during the last ice age. Terrace was incorporated on 31 Dec 1927, and first developed as a SAWMILLING town. During the 1950s it prospered as a supply centre for the construction of KITIMAT, 60 km south. Its strategic location in the heart of northwestern BC has allowed it to become an important transportation hub and one of the fastest-growing centres in the north. TOURISM and the FOREST INDUSTRY are the mainstays of the local economy. The white Kermode BEAR inhabits the area and the city has adopted the animal as its municipal symbol. The heritage of both city and river is remembered each Aug with Riverboat Days.

TERRACE MUTINY, a disturbance among soldiers at the TERRACE army base on 24–29 Nov 1944, was the most serious breach of discipline in the Canadian military during WWII. Soldiers at Terrace belonged to the 15th Brigade and were mainly conscripts; they had been promised that they would not have to serve overseas. When rumours reached the base that the government of Prime Minister Mackenzie King was about to rescind his promise, some of the men refused to obey officers, stole weapons from stores and announced their intention to resist postings overseas. The mutiny petered out when commanding officers regained control of their troops.

TERRY FOX LABORATORY was established in VANCOUVER in 1981 as a joint undertaking between the BC Cancer Agency, the BC Cancer Foundation, UBC and the National Cancer Institute of Canada. It was prompted by a donation of $1 million from the provincial government to the Terry FOX Marathon of Hope in 1980. In the 1990s the TFL's work focussed on developing new technologies to examine cell growth and differentiation, cell aging and gene regulation, with a particular focus on hematology and immunology. Staff are recognized internationally for their work on how cells grow and mature and how this process goes wrong when cancer strikes. A key discovery has been the use of "culture purging," a process whereby leukemic

Shelter Point, Texada Island, known for its "flower rocks," whose natural patterns resemble flowers. Len Mackave photo

cells can be removed from bone marrow taken from a patient. When a patient does not have a suitable marrow donor, his or her own purged bone marrow can then be used for a bone marrow transplant procedure. The TFL is one of only a handful of organizations permitted to use Terry Fox's name in their own. *Claire Sowerbutt*

TESLIN LAKE, 317.2 km² (but only 104.1 km² in BC), is located in remote northern BC and the Yukon and flows via the Teslin R to the Yukon R, which empties into the Bering Sea. The area was first occupied by the TLINGIT people and the name of the lake comes from the Tlingit word for "long narrow water." White explorers and prospectors arrived in the 1870s and 1880s. The area surrounding the lake in BC was virtually uninhabited by the late 1990s. Teslin Lk was part of the "all-Canadian" or Stikine route via TELEGRAPH CREEK during the 1897–98 Klondike GOLD RUSH. AS

TETE JAUNE CACHE, pop 143, is on the Yellowhead Hwy 266 km west of PRINCE GEORGE, where the FRASER R flows out of the mountains into the ROCKY MT TRENCH. During the heyday of the FUR TRADE it was a transshipment point for supplies of leather skins brought across the YELLOWHEAD PASS for distribution to the trading posts in NEW CALEDONIA. The modern community was established in 1911 during the construction of the GRAND TRUNK PACIFIC RWY and grew as PADDLEWHEEL STEAMBOATS arrived up the Fraser R from Prince George. The population spread between Tête Jaune and its short-lived neighbour, Henningville, numbered several thousand. Most people left when the railway was finished. Tête

Jaune ("yellow head") was a blond METIS trapper who guided HBC traders through the Yellowhead Pass in 1820 and who was rumoured to have hidden a fortune in furs nearby.

TEXADA ISLAND, 287 km², pop 1,089, lies adjacent to the SUNSHINE COAST in GEORGIA STRAIT, 80 km north of VANCOUVER. It was named for Felix de Tejeda, an officer with the NARVAEZ expedition in 1791. An extensive industrial history includes MINING, LOGGING and quarrying. Iron ore mining began in 1886 and, with the opening of COPPER and GOLD mines a few years later, the community of VAN ANDA became a small boomtown, billing itself "the mining centre of western North America." Gold mining continued intermittently to 1952, while iron mining continued to 1976. Limestone quarries have been providing material since 1887 and the island is BC's principal supplier of lime rock. BLUBBER BAY at the north end is a well-known anchorage for boaters. The 50-km-long island is connected by car ferry to POWELL RIVER. The 2 main communities are Van Anda (named for the friend of an early mine promoter) and GILLIES BAY.

THEATRE in BC encompasses a variety of live plays, musicals, multimedia and performance events, one-person shows, story theatre, busking, improvisation and powwows, staged by about 35 professional and 70 community theatre companies, as well as many other student, summer and festival groups. Increasingly, categorization is difficult as many companies and individuals draw from 2 or 3 types of performance in their work. Good theatre may be found on the mainstage at the VANCOUVER PLAYHOUSE, at a zone festival in NANAIMO, among students at a coffeehouse in KAMLOOPS, or on a school tour by an aboriginal theatre company in VERNON. British Columbians are finding their dramatic voices after 200 years of colonial and neo-colonial domination in which foreign theatre practices, usually British or American, were promoted while indigenous performances were silenced.

In the late 19th century, performances by Northwest Coast FIRST NATIONS people greatly impressed anthropologists such as Franz BOAS, particularly the hamatsa ceremonies of the KWAKWА̲KА̲'WAKW (Kwakiutl) people, featuring spectacular dancing, singing, masks and stage-craft. European settlers interrupted this ceremonial tradition, with laws banning the POTLATCH and other cultural practices, for example, but late in the 20th century there was a revival of traditional forms with First Nations performance groups such as Atlakim in VANCOUVER and Senklip in Vernon, and with the growing popularity of the powwow.

Non-aboriginal theatre, in its early decades, usually was presented by the military. BC's first play was called *Nootka Sound; or, Britain Prepared* and was staged at the Theatre Royal, Covent Garden, London. This jingoistic piece depicted events during the NOOTKA SOUND CONTROVERSY (1789–94) when Britain and Spain almost went to war over control of VANCOUVER ISLAND. During the 19th century, colonial theatre in BC took place on British warships, where naval officers presented comedies to invited guests. The ROYAL ENGINEERS, a group of surveyors and artisans, performed a season of plays on board their ship the *Thames City* as they sailed to BC; these same "sappers," the province's first dramatic society, also built the first theatre, the Theatre Royal, in NEW WESTMINSTER, where they put on plays. (The Royal Engineers also imported the first recorded LIBRARY in BC.) The Colonial and Royal theatres were built in VICTORIA at about the same time but were operated largely by American touring troupes following the GOLD RUSH. The CARIBOO also enjoyed a flurry of theatrical activity during the 1860s, catering to the tastes of prospectors and other adventurers.

With the arrival of the transcontinental railway in 1887, Vancouver began to supersede Victoria in commerce and in theatre. Pre-WWI, the city boasted major performance spaces at the 1,200-seat VANCOUVER OPERA HOUSE, opened in 1891, and the Pantages Theatre in 1908, part of an American vaudeville circuit. In these theatres, local—or even Canadian—references were rare, though Harry Lindley, perhaps Vancouver's first resident professional, sometimes performed plays with titles such as *In the Cariboo* and *A Scene on Hastings Street* in his stock company. At the same time CHINESE theatre flourished: in Victoria as many as 5 theatres presented Cantonese Opera. During the 1930s a potent form of local theatre emerged as unemployed workers joined the Progressive Arts Club in Vancouver and performed agitprop plays such as *Waiting for Lefty*, a controversial, pro-worker play that the police tried to shut down. Beginning in 1940 popular summer shows, mainly operettas, were presented at Malkin Bowl in STANLEY PARK by THEATRE UNDER THE STARS. Within a decade, the company was fully professional.

With post-WWII prosperity, professional theatre flourished, mainly in Vancouver. In 1946 Sydney RISK founded his EVERYMAN THEATRE, which became the city's first important theatre company and led to others such as Totem (founded in 1951) and Holiday Children's Theatre (1953). A theatrical boom occurred in the early 1960s at about the time the 767-seat

Vancouver Playhouse opened, one of the Canadian regional theatres earmarked for major funding from the Canada Council for the Arts. Under early directors it encouraged local drama and staged such hit plays as George RYGA's *The Ecstasy of Rita Joe* (1967). The ARTS CLUB THEATRE, begun in 1964, was more successful at commercial theatre. Under Bill Millerd, who took over as artistic director in 1972, the company has enjoyed substantial success, moving to a new site on GRANVILLE ISLAND in 1979 and later establishing a third stage at the renovated Stanley Theatre. Arts Club hits such as the musical revue *Jacques Brel is Alive and Well and Living in Paris* and Sherman Snukal's play *Talking Dirty*, which ran for over 1,000 performances, are part of Vancouver's theatrical history. At the same time, John Juliani's Savage God Company was notable for its avant-garde performances, especially during the early 1970s when it staged Samuel Beckett's *Happy Days* in a tree trunk in Stanley Park. TAMAHNOUS THEATRE was an experimental collective practising equality and group creation; its members included John GRAY, Larry Lillo and Morris PANYCH.

In Victoria, the Belfry Theatre, especially under directors James Roy and Glynis Leyshon, has been notable for emphasizing Canadian scripts. Professional companies also exist in Nanaimo, KELOWNA, Kamloops, ARMSTRONG, FORT STEELE, GABRIOLA ISLAND and PRINCE GEORGE. These companies typically present a season of about 6 plays selected from a mix of classical, contemporary and new works appealing to a range of tastes. At their best—as with *The Overcoat*, a wordless musical fable based on a story by Gogol and adapted by Morris Panych and Wendy Gorling, or the 1998 revival of John Gray's Canadian classic *Billy Bishop Goes to War*—exciting works by local playwrights are given memorable productions. Meanwhile, new play development is the focus of the Playwrights Theatre Centre. Founded in 1970 as the New Play Centre, this Vancouver institution receives about 250 scripts a year. Each is scrutinized by a theatre professional; some are developed further with the help of actors; 8 are staged. Amateur community theatre groups, members of the umbrella organization Theatre BC, produce seasons increasingly similar to their professional counterparts. Community theatres normally stage 3–4 productions a year and take a spring production to the zone festivals from which some go on to compete at the annual Mainstage Festival.

Many playwrights are working in BC; in 1999 more than 60 were listed as members of the Playwrights Union of Canada. Four BC writers have won GOV GEN'S LITERARY AWARDS for drama: John Gray for *Billy Bishop Goes to War* (1982), Joan MacLeod for *Amigo's Blue Guitar* (1991), Guillermo Verdecchia for *Fronteras Americanas* (1993) and Morris Panych for *The Ends of the Earth* (1994). Until the late 1950s most serious theatre artists—actors and writers—left the province to train, despite early attempts to establish theatre schools in BC in the 1920s. In NARA-MATA, Carroll Aikins, an orchardist, built a theatre

on his farm under the name Home Theatre. He accepted students from across Canada; they picked apples in the morning, rehearsed in the afternoon and performed in the evening. During the same decade, L. Bullock-Webster operated his BC Dramatic School in Victoria. But these pioneers alone could not provide adequate training opportunities in the province; the need began to be met with the founding of theatre programs at UBC (1958), Vancouver City College (1965) (*see* COMMUNITY COLLEGES) and the UNIV OF VICTORIA (1966). By the year 2000 BC had a growing number of trained actors, directors and designers; the excitement of new, young companies was paired with the experience of several well-established ones; and Fringe Festivals—festivals of small-scale community theatre productions, which encourage local writing and production—had gathered momentum. Theatre professionals, audiences and students were looking forward to a bright future.   *James Hoffman*

A performance of The Sound of Music *at Theatre Under the Stars, Stanley Park, Vancouver, 1974. Jay Morrison photo*

THEATRE UNDER THE STARS (TUTS) was a professional theatre company founded by Gordon Hilker in 1940; shows were performed at Malkin Bowl in STANLEY PARK in VANCOUVER, and the early shows were choreographed by Aida Broadbent. TUTS folded in 1963 but was revived as a semi-professional company in 1969 to present popular musicals in an outdoor setting each summer. The company launched the careers of many performers who went on to national and international stardom, including Brent CARVER, Robert Goulet, Jeff HYSLOP and Ruth Nichol.

THERMOPYLAE was one of the speedy clipper ships that carried tea between China and England in the late 19th century during the heyday of the great Age of Sail. Built for the White Star Line in 1868 in Aberdeen, Scotland, it held

Thermopylae, *the fastest ship on the sea during the golden age of sail, Esquimalt, 1895. MMBC*

all the speed records for transoceanic travel. White Star sold the legendary vessel in 1890 and it was based in VICTORIA from 1891 to 1896, carrying rice from China to N America and lumber and COAL back. The sleek sailing ship returned to England and ended its days as a coal hulk. In 1907, after a respectful ceremony, it was sunk.

THESEN, Sharon, poet, teacher (b 1 Oct 1946, Tisdale, SK). She graduated from SFU in 1974 with an MA in English and 2 years later became an instructor in the department of English at Capilano College (*see* COMMUNITY COLLEGES) in N VANCOUVER. Her first book of poems, *Artemis Hates Romance*, appeared in 1980 and was followed by 7 more collections. Two of her books have been shortlisted for GOV GEN'S LITERARY AWARDS. Formerly the poetry editor at the *Capilano Review*, a literary MAGAZINE, she has contributed essays and reviews to a variety of periodicals.

THETIS ISLAND, 26 km², pop 250, opposite CHEMAINUS, is one of the least developed of the GULF ISLANDS between southern VANCOUVER ISLAND and the mainland. Despite a ferry link to Chemainus, it has no parks and few TOURIST facilities, which suits its small population. It is named for HMS *Thetis*, a 36-gun British naval frigate in the area from 1851 to 1853. It was joined to KUPER ISLAND until 1905, when a canal was dredged between them.

THEYTUS BOOKS, the first BOOK PUBLISHING company in Canada owned and operated by aboriginal people, was founded in 1981 in NANAIMO by Randy Fred. The following year it moved to PENTICTON under new ownership and then became associated with the EN'OWKIN CENTRE there. The name *Theytus* means "to preserve for the purpose of handing down." The press specializes in books by and about aboriginal N Americans.

THOM, Bing Wing, architect (b 8 Dec 1940, Hong Kong). He moved to VANCOUVER as a child and studied ARCHITECTURE at UBC and the Univ of California at Berkeley. In 1963 he joined Arthur

Bing Thom, architect.

ERICKSON's Vancouver office and managed prominent Erickson projects such as Robson Square Courthouse and Roy Thomson Hall at the Univ of Toronto. He established his own firm in 1980. His design for the False Creek Yacht Club (1990) won him a Gov Gen's Award. Other projects included the Canada pavilion at Expo 92 in Seville, Spain, and UBC's Chan Centre for the Performing Arts (1997). During the 1990s he designed an entire city in China, the port of New Dalian. In 1996 he was inducted into the Order of Canada.

THOM, Ronald James, architect (b 15 May 1923, Penticton; d 29 Oct 1986, Toronto). Raised in VANCOUVER, he attended the Vancouver School of Art in 1941–42 and 1945–47 (*see* EMILY CARR INSTITUTE OF ART & DESIGN) and served in the air force during WWII. He articled with Sharp & Thompson, Berwick, Pratt (later Thompson, Berwick & Pratt) in 1949 and became a partner in 1958. He designed many private homes in Vancouver; in the mid-1950s he was a prominent member of the team that designed the BC HYDRO AND POWER AUTHORITY building. In 1960 he won a competition to design Massey College at the Univ of Toronto; by 1963 he had relocated to Toronto and established an office of TBP to direct design of Trent Univ in Peterborough. The office became the independent Thom Partnership in 1970. During the 1970s he was principal designer of several major projects, including LESTER B. PEARSON COLLEGE OF THE PACIFIC, Shaw Festival Theatre in Niagara-on-the-Lake, Metro Toronto Zoo and several homes. Ill health complicated his later years. He was made an officer in the Order of Canada in 1981.

THOMAS, Audrey Callahan, writer (b 17 Nov 1935, Binghamton, NY). She came to BC in 1959 and did graduate studies at UBC. After 2 years in Ghana with her husband, a teacher, she launched her WRITING career with the story collection *Ten Green Bottles* (1967), followed by her first novel, *Mrs. Blood* (1970). Her work, for which she has won 3 BC BOOK PRIZES among many other literary awards, includes *Songs My Mother Taught Me* (1973), *Blown Figures* (1975), *Latakia* (1979), *Intertidal Life* (1984), *The Wild Blue Yonder* (1990), *Coming Down from Wa* (1995) and *Isobel Gunn* (1999). She has also written more than 20 dramas for CBC Radio. A naturalized Canadian, she has lived on GALIANO ISLAND for many years.

THOMAS, François Marie, missionary (b 1868, Brittany, France; d 1957, Williams Lake). A member of the OBLATES OF MARY IMMACULATE, he came to Canada in 1894 and 3 years later was appointed missionary to the aboriginal inhabitants of the CARIBOO-CHILCOTIN region. Based at St Joseph's Mission at 150 MILE HOUSE, he spent 60 years travelling the vast area in all kinds of weather and circumstances, ministering not only to his FIRST NATIONS flock but to all ROMAN CATHOLICS in the region. He made his rounds at least once a year and people travelled great distances to gather at the villages for "priest time."

Diana French

THOMAS, John "Navvy Jack," pioneer settler (b circa 1832, Wales; d circa 1900, Barkerville). He moved to N America as a young man and arrived in BC during the Cariboo GOLD RUSH. After working in the freight business in the Interior he moved to BURRARD INLET in 1866 and ran a short-lived ferry service before establishing a gravel operation at the mouth of the CAPILANO R. For years he supplied gravel to construction sites around the inlet (a mix of sand and gravel is still known as "Navvyjack" to local builders). In 1873 he built a home in W VANCOUVER, making him and wife Rowia, a Squamish woman (*see* SQUAMISH NATION), the first permanent residents of the community. His property included what is now Ambleside. Though much altered, and moved from its original location, the house still stands and is the oldest continuously occupied residence in the Lower Mainland.

THOMPSON, David, fur trader, mapmaker (b 30 Apr 1770, London, England; d 10 Feb 1857, Longueuil, QC). He joined the HBC as an apprentice in 1784 and came out to York Factory on Hudson Bay. While serving inland he studied surveying and mapmaking, and he defected from the HBC to join the NORTH WEST CO in 1797 because his new employer gave him freer rein to indulge his interest in exploring. By 1806 he had completed his surveys of the fur country east of the ROCKY MTS, and with the help of aboriginal guides he began to probe the mountain passes, looking for a way across them. In 1807 he made his way over the Rockies via HOWSE PASS and reached the banks of the COLUMBIA R near present-day GOLDEN. He then travelled south

DAVID THOMPSON'S ROUTE TO THE PACIFIC

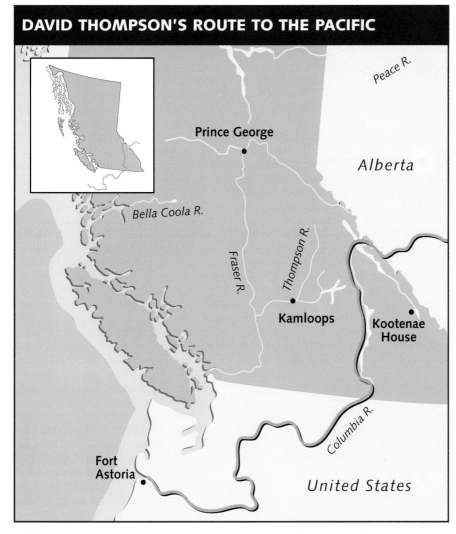

London. Thompson and Sharon McGowan, a filmmaker and producer of *The Lotus Eaters* and *Better Than Chocolate*, were joint winners of the 2000 Woman of the Year Award presented by Women in Film and Video. *See also* FILMMAKING INDUSTRY.

THOMPSON First Nation; *see* NLAKA'PAMUX.

THOMPSON RIVER, the longest tributary of the FRASER R, drains a 55,827.84 km² watershed in central BC. It consists of 2 branches. The N Thompson (365 km) rises in the CARIBOO MTS east of WELLS GRAY PROVINCIAL PARK and flows southerly through wooded country to KAMLOOPS. For most of this distance the CNR and Hwy 5 run parallel to it. At Kamloops the north branch merges with the S Thompson (161 km) flowing in from SHUSWAP LK on the east and the combined river flows west from Kamloops Lk through arid GRASSLANDS for 169 km to the Fraser R. The community of LYTTON overlooks the confluence of the rivers; the ancient aboriginal village of Kumsheen once occupied the site (*see* PREHISTORY). At this end the Thompson flows through the territory of the NLAKA'PAMUX (Thompson) First Nations; from around Kamloops and farther east it is in the territory of the SECWEPEMC (Shuswap). For both groups the river provides the SALMON that have been an important part of their culture and way of life for centuries. FUR TRADERS arrived in the area in 1811 and built a trading post near the present site of Kamloops. They were followed by prospectors during the GOLD RUSH period, then ranchers, who recognized that the rolling grasslands were ideal for grazing cattle (*see* CATTLE INDUSTRY). Construction of the CPR occurred in the valley of the S Thompson during the 1880s, while the CNR follows the northern branch. Ranching is still important in the southern part of the watershed, while LOGGING predominates in the north. TOURISM is a growing economic factor in the watershed. The river was named by Simon FRASER for his fellow explorer David THOMPSON—mistakenly, as it turned out: Thompson never actually saw it.

and built KOOTENAE HOUSE near the present site of INVERMERE; for 2 years he used this site as a base from which to explore and trade in southeast BC, Idaho and Montana. Thompson was on his way back east to Fort William in 1810 when he received orders to re-cross the Rockies immediately and to follow the Columbia to its mouth, where a set of rival American traders was heading. After hiding from a party of hostile Piegans he managed to struggle across the mountains, and in the spring of 1811 he embarked in a CEDAR board canoe for the Pacific Ocean. On 14 July he arrived to find the Americans already installed in Fort Astoria. He then returned east and followed the Columbia to its headwaters, becoming the first person to travel the length of the river and therefore the pioneer of the main FUR TRADE transport route connecting the Interior with the Pacific. Thompson retired from the fur trade in 1812 and lived in Upper Canada, where he completed his maps and worked for many years as a surveyor. Late in his life he wrote his great *Narrative*, one of the classic accounts of fur trade exploration. *See also* FUR TRADE, LAND-BASED.
Reading: Richard Glover, ed, *David Thompson's Narrative 1784–1812*, 1962.

THOMPSON, Peggy, screenwriter, film producer and script editor (b Vancouver). She writes for film, television, radio, stage and print, and is best known for writing 2 films set in BC. *The Lotus Eaters* (1993) drew excellent reviews and won a 1993 Genie Award for best screenplay. *Better Than Chocolate* (1999) premiered at the Berlin Film Festival and was a critical and commercial success in Canada, the USA, and Europe. It won numerous awards, including audience awards for best feature film at GAY AND LESBIAN film festivals in Toronto, Philadelphia and

S Thompson River. Bernie Pawlik/Image Makers

THOMPSON SOUND branches off Tribune Channel west of KNIGHT INLET, 100 km northwest of CAMPBELL RIVER. A large LOGGING camp was located where the Kakweiken R enters the head of the sound. A post office operated here from 1973 to 1978. *AS*

THORBURN, Clifford Charles Devlin, snooker player (b 16 Jan 1948, Victoria). He dropped out of school at age 16 to pursue a career playing pool and became one of the best players in the world. In 1971 he won the N American snooker championship and in 1980 the world championship. Consistently ranked among the top 3 globally, he has won almost every major title in the sport and in 1986 became the first person to win the world master's championship for a third time. His Canadian record of 26 perfect games includes the first in world-championship play, in 1983. He was inducted into the BC SPORTS HALL OF FAME in 1995.

THORMANBY ISLANDS lie at the south end of Malaspina Strait between TEXADA ISLAND and the mainland, just north of SECHELT on the SUNSHINE COAST. The larger southern island was owned by Calvert Simson, who operated a farm on it for half a century (*see* AGRICULTURE). His son gave it to the province in 1975 and most of it is now Simson Provincial MARINE PARK (4.61 km²). Buccaneer Bay in the passage between the 2 islands is another popular marine park. The islands are named for a British racehorse.

THORNTON, Mildred Valley, artist (b 1890, Dresden, ON; d 1967, Vancouver). She studied at the Ontario College of Art and the Art Institute of Chicago and began to paint professionally in the 1920s. Like her better-known contemporary, Emily CARR, she became known for her interest in FIRST NATIONS culture; she completed more than 300 portraits of aboriginal people during her career. In 1934 she moved to VANCOUVER and worked as art critic for the *VANCOUVER SUN* from 1944 to 1959. She wrote about her experiences

Mildred Valley Thornton, artist, wearing a Kwakwa̱ka'wakw robe, 1949. Vancouver Sun

among BC First Nations in the book *Indian Lives and Legends* (1966). Her works are held by the National Gallery in Ottawa, the Glenbow Museum in Calgary, the McMichael Gallery in Kleinburg, ON, and the VANCOUVER ART GALLERY. *See also* ART, VISUAL.

THRASHER; *see* MIMIC THRUSH.

THREE-DAY NOVEL WRITING CONTEST is an annual event occurring on the Labour Day holiday weekend in Sept. Entrants must compose an entire novel during a 72-hour period and the winning entry is published. The contest was launched in 1978 by Pulp Press (now ARSENAL PULP PRESS), a VANCOUVER literary publisher, after the idea was hatched in a hotel beer parlour by Stephen Osborne, founder of the press; William Hoffer, an antiquarian bookseller; and 3 other writers, Mary Beth Knechtel, Laura Lippert and D.M. FRASER. The Toronto writer Tom Walmsley was the winner of the first competition, and his book *Doctor Tin* remains the best-selling contest winner. Nearly 400 entries are received each year; participation peaked in 1986 when 1,200 manuscripts came in (about 90% of entrants actually finish their novels). The three-day novel has been called the only literary genre to originate in Canada. Since 1992 the contest has been run by ANVIL PRESS.

THREE FORKS, an early SILVER mining camp in the W KOOTENAY on the wagon road from KASLO to NEW DENVER, became the terminus of the CPR's Nakusp & Slocan Rwy in 1894. (The line was extended to SANDON in 1895.) The town boomed and reached a peak population of 2,000 in the mid-1890s, but declined in importance as Sandon grew. By 1904, fewer than 100 people lived there. By the 1990s little remained of Three Forks, which was named for the nearby confluence of Kane, Carpenter and Seaton creeks. A hiking trail leads to Sandon. *AS*

THREE GREENHORNS were the first white settlers in, what became VANCOUVER's West End. John MORTON, his brother-in-law Samuel BRIGHOUSE and their friend William Hailstone arrived in BC in 1862. Later that year they bought a 2.2 km² parcel of land between ENGLISH BAY and BURRARD INLET and began making bricks. The men made no money; one by one they sold out. The West End was developed as a residential area by the CPR in the 1880s.

THREE VALLEY GAP, in the Eagle Valley 23 km east of REVELSTOKE on the TRANS-CANADA HWY, was a railway construction camp in the 1880s. It became a reconstructed ghost town of buildings collected from around the province.

THRUMS, pop 312, on the north shore of the KOOTENAY R 7 km northeast of CASTLEGAR, is a DOUKHOBOR settlement. It was named for James Barrie's play, *A Window in Thrums*. Nearly 1,000 Sons of Freedom protest marchers were arrested here in 1932; about 600 of them served 3-year sentences at PIERS ISLAND for public nudity. *AS*

THRUSH is the common name for a number of birds belonging to the same family as BLUEBIRDS and KINGLETS. It includes the familiar American ROBIN (*Turdus migratorius*), which breeds throughout BC. The varied thrush (*Ixoreus naevius*), found in coniferous forests throughout BC, looks like an ornate robin with its black breast-band across a bright orange breast and its orange eye stripe and wing bars. Other thrushes found in BC include Swainson's thrush (*Catharus ustulatus*) and hermit thrush (*C. guttatus*). Both have spotted breasts and occur throughout the province including offshore islands. *Kim Goldberg*

THULIN, Charles Auguste, entrepreneur (b 1863, Sweden; d Apr 1932, Campbell River). He immigrated to the US at age 24, worked his way across the continent and arrived at PORT MOODY in 1888. While LOGGING on the SUNSHINE COAST he pre-empted land on Malaspina Peninsula north of present-day POWELL RIVER; there he and his younger brother **Fred** developed the community of LUND. In 1904 the brothers bought the site of present-day CAMPBELL RIVER and built a store and the Willows Hotel. Charles moved to the new settlement with his wife Mary and their children in 1908. For a quarter-century the Thulins were a driving force behind almost every development in the growing community.

THUNDERBIRD PARK, next door to the ROYAL BC MUSEUM in VICTORIA, was created by the museum in 1941 to display the work of FIRST NATIONS carvers. By 1952 the TOTEM POLES there were deteriorating in the weather and had to be moved inside. The museum hired 3 carvers—Mungo MARTIN, his son David, and Henry HUNT—to make duplicate poles in a new carving shed. Carvers have worked at the park ever since. In 1953 Mungo Martin constructed a traditional KWAKWA̱KA'WAKW big house on-site (*see* ARCHITECTURE, ABORIGINAL) and dedicated it with a POTLATCH.

THURLOW ISLANDS, East (111 km²) and West (85 km²), lie along the north side of JOHNSTONE STRAIT between BUTE and KNIGHT inlets, east of SAYWARD on the north end of VANCOUVER ISLAND. They were named by Capt George VANCOUVER after Baron Thurlow, an 18th-century lord chancellor of England. The islands are in KWAKWA̱KA'WAKW (Kwakiutl) territory. LOGGING began in the 1880s using oxen teams, and mining for GOLD, COPPER and iron took place in the late 1890s; commercial FISHING and TOURISM have become the main economic activities. Settlements are located at BLIND CHANNEL on W Thurlow, which once had a cannery and SAWMILL and is now the site of a resort, and at SHOAL BAY on E Thurlow, which also has a resort. Bickley Bay, 2 km west of Shoal Bay, was settled in the 1890s and had a post office named Channeton. *AS*

THURSTON BAY is on the west side of SONORA ISLAND, 35 km north of CAMPBELL RIVER in the jumble of islands between VANCOUVER ISLAND and the mainland. From 1914 to 1941 it was the regional centre of marine operations for the BC FOREST SERVICE and had maintenance facilities for the fleet of forest patrol vessels. There were several homesteads here as well. In 1970 it became a provincial MARINE PARK for boaters. The post office, located in the bay on Block Island, was named Nodales after the channel between Sonora and E THURLOW ISLAND. R.J. Thurston was an early coastal logger.

THURSTON HARBOUR, on the north shore of Talunkwan Island 50 km southeast of SKIDEGATE in the QUEEN CHARLOTTE ISLANDS, was a WWI LOGGING depot run by the Imperial Munitions Board to mill Sitka SPRUCE for airplane construction. The remote landing was equipped with a hospital, offices, YMCA building and store. The end of the war interrupted the construction of 3 large SAWMILLS and everything was abandoned or sold. The harbour, named after a HALIBUT boat, remained a logging base until the 1970s.   AS

TICK is a small, bloodsucking parasite belonging to the class Arachnida and closely related to the SPIDER. A tick has 4 pairs of legs and highly specialized mouth parts for piercing and attaching to mammals and birds. Ticks often cling to vegetation and wait to lodge on to a passing host. Of the 40 species known in Canada, 2 are

Rocky mountain wood tick (l) and Pacific wood tick. Kim LaFave drawing

found in BC: the Rocky Mountain wood tick (*Dermacentor andersoni*) and the Pacific wood tick (*Ixodes pacificus*). Several diseases are caused by tick bites, most notably Lyme disease, whose symptoms include fever, headache, fatigue and skin rash; if untreated, Lyme disease can damage the heart and nervous system. Between 1991 and 1998, 38 cases were identified in BC. Other diseases harboured and spread by ticks include Rocky Mountain spotted fever, Q fever, Ehrlichiosis, relapsing fever and tularemia.

TIDES are the alternate rising and falling of sea levels along the coast. They are caused by the gravitational pull of the moon and, to a lesser degree, the sun. Much activity along the coast, both human and animal, responds to the rhythm of the tides. There are 3 tidal cycles: daily, monthly and annual. During the daily cycle—actually 24 hrs, 50 mins—the tide fluctuates twice between high and low. One of the fluctuations is usually smaller than the other. Every day tidal peaks occur about an hour later than the previous day. The monthly cycle is affected by the waxing and waning of the moon. At times of the new and full moons, when the gravitational effect of sun and moon are combined, tides are at their highest, the so-called spring tides. The smallest fluctuations—neap tides—occur at the

SOME OF BC'S STRONGEST TIDAL RAPIDS

	Flood		Ebb	
	(km/h)	(knots)	(km/h)	(knots)
Sechelt Rapids	26.8	14.5	29.6	16.0
SEYMOUR NARROWS	29.6	16.0	25.9	14.0
NAKWAKTO RAPIDS	25.9	14.0	29.6	16.0
Gillard Passage	24.1	13.0	18.5	10.0
SURGE NARROWS	22.2	12.0	18.5	10.0
Hole in the Wall	22.2	12.0	18.5	10.0
YUCULTA RAPIDS	14.8	8.0	18.5	10.0
Okisollo Channel	16.7	9.0	16.7	9.0
Arran Rapids	16.7	9.0	16.7	9.0
Malibu Rapids	16.7	9.0	16.7	9.0
Dent Rapids	16.7	9.0	16.7	9.0
GABRIOLA PASSAGE	15.7	8.5	16.7	9.0
Dodd Narrows	16.7	9.0	14.8	8.0
Quatsino Narrows	16.7	9.0	14.8	8.0
PORLIER PASS	16.7	9.0	14.8	8.0
Deception Pass	14.8	8.0	16.7	9.0
ACTIVE PASS	14.8	8.0	14.8	8.0

first and last quarter of the moon when it and the sun are pulling different ways. During the year, tides have their greatest fluctuations near the summer and winter solstices (June and Dec). Tides create brisk currents in the many channels along the coast as water piles up at the ends of narrow passes, waiting to surge through. Some of the best known of these constrictions are ACTIVE PASS and PORLIER PASS in the GULF ISLANDS, SEYMOUR NARROWS at QUADRA ISLAND and the YUCULTAS between STUART and SONORA islands. The currents at NAKWAKTO RAPIDS and the SKOOKUMCHUCK RAPIDS reach 16 knots and are the swiftest tidal currents in the world.

TIEDEMANN, Hermann Otto, architect (b 1821, Berlin, Germany; d 12 Sept 1891, Victoria). Educated in Germany, he arrived on

H.O. Tiedemann, BC's first architect, 1858. BC Archives G-02350

VANCOUVER ISLAND in 1858 and became the colony's first professional architect (*see* ARCHITECTURE). He designed the first LEGISLATIVE BUILDINGS, the so-called Birdcages, which were in use from 1864 to 1898, as well as many other prominent buildings in VICTORIA. He was also a surveyor and from 1862 to 1864 was engaged in building the ill-fated road from BUTE INLET to FORT ALEXANDRIA promoted by Alfred WADDINGTON (*see* CHILCOTIN WAR). Mount Tiedemann and the Tiedemann Glacier are both named for him.

TILIKUM is a 9-m CEDAR dugout CANOE that undertook an epic ocean voyage from VICTORIA to London, England, in May 1901. Crewed by 2 men—John Voss, an experienced sea captain, and Norman Luxton, a young journalist—the canoe crossed the Pacific to Fiji and Australia, continued across the Indian Ocean to the Cape of Good Hope, then cruised north up the coast of Africa to England, arriving at the Thames R in

The Tilikum, *the canoe that travelled the world between 1901 and 1904. MMBC*

Sept 1904. After its 16,000-km journey the *Tilikum* was left to rot in a shipyard on the Thames for 25 years. It was rescued, returned to Victoria, restored and put on public display, first at THUNDERBIRD PARK and, since 1965, in the MARITIME MUSEUM OF BC.

TIMES-COLONIST, VICTORIA, western Canada's oldest NEWSPAPER, was created in 1980 from the merger of the Victoria *Times* (founded 1884) and the Victoria *Colonist* (established in 1858 as the *British Colonist*). The *Colonist's* founder and first editor was Amor DE COSMOS, who sold the paper in 1863, went into politics and eventually became BC's second PREMIER. The paper absorbed other publications and altered its name over the years; it had a number of distinguished editors, including David W. HIGGINS and John ROBSON, another BC premier. It was an outspoken proponent of CONFEDERATION. The *Times-Colonist* was acquired from Thomson Newspapers along with the Nanaimo *Daily News* by Southam Inc in 1998. Its circulation in 2000 was about 80,000. *AS*

TINTAGEL was a railway and LOGGING settlement 12 km east of BURNS LAKE on the CNR. The first homesteaders arrived about 1915. It was named after the castle in Cornwall where King Arthur was supposedly born; in 1967 Britain's Ministry of Works sent a 45-kg stone from the castle as a Canadian centennial gift to BC. It was installed here in a roadside cairn. *AS*

TISH was a VANCOUVER literary periodical launched in Sept 1961 by a group of young UBC writers influenced by the American Black Mountain poets. The first editorial collective consisted of Frank Davey, George BOWERING, Fred WAH, David Dawson and Jamie Reid. Warren TALLMAN, an English literature professor at UBC, provided encouragement. The original editors dispersed in 1963 but publication continued under a series of editors, including Dan McLeod (*see* GEORGIA STRAIGHT), Gladys Hindmarch and Stan PERSKY, until 1969. The name is an anagram.

TLELL, on the east coast of Graham Island, 35 km north of SKIDEGATE in the QUEEN CHARLOTTE ISLANDS, is a residential and AGRICULTURAL district first settled by William Thomas Hodges, or "Mexican Tom." In about 1904 he established a ranch on the banks of the Tlell R that is now the Richardson Ranch (*see also* CATTLE INDUSTRY). An early hotel was built nearby. The name is a HAIDA word of uncertain meaning. *AS*

TLINGIT (Inland, or Taku River), are a small FIRST NATION whose traditional territory in northwest BC and southern Yukon encompasses the TAKU R, and Atlin and TESLIN lakes. They are closely related to the more numerous and widespread coastal Tlingit of the Alaska Panhandle. Originally they lived in nomadic family groups along the Taku R, taking advantage of the plentiful runs of SALMON as well as hunting wild game. During the 19th century they were drawn farther north by the FUR TRADE and the opportunities opened up by the GOLD RUSHES in the Klondike (1898) and around ATLIN, where most now live.

TOAD; *see* FROG.

TOAD RIVER, pop 60, is a roadside settlement with TOURISM facilities on the ALASKA HWY, 150 km west of FORT NELSON. It is located between STONE MT and MUNCHO LK provincial PARKS in an area known for its excellent wildlife viewing. The Toad River Lodge has a collection of over 4,000 hats. *AS*

TOBA INLET, one of the narrow FJORDS indenting the middle coast, doglegs into the COAST MTS just north of DESOLATION SOUND. It extends 32 km from the REDONDA ISLANDS at its mouth to the ESTUARY of the Toba R at the top end. Once the territory of the KLAHOOSE First Nation, whose village sites were around the head of the inlet, it is named for Antonio Toba Arredondo, a Spanish naval officer who sailed with MALASPINA. The steep-sided walls of the inlet show evidence of the extensive LOGGING that has gone on there.

TOBIN, Henry Seymour, soldier, industrialist (b 12 Jan 1877, Ottawa, ON; d Jan 1956, Vancouver). After graduating from the Royal Military College in Kingston, ON, he joined the North West Mounted Police and took part in the survey of the Edmonton-to-Whitehorse route to the Klondike GOLD RUSH in 1898–99. He continued to Dawson City, where he became the first articled law student in the Yukon Territory. He was called to the bar there in 1902, in Alberta in 1905 and in BC in 1910. He founded and commanded the 29th (Vancouver) Battalion, which as part of the Canadian Expeditionary Force during WWI became known as "Tobin's Tigers" for its fierce fighting spirit. After the war he rejoined his VANCOUVER law practice but it gradually took a back seat to his varied business interests. In 1946–47 he was president of the Canadian Manufacturers' Assoc and he served for many years as honorary aide-de-camp to 3 govs gen: Lord Willingdon, Lord Tweedsmuir and the Earl of Athlone.

TOBY CREEK, 115 km south of GOLDEN, was a MINING camp named after Dr Levi Toby from Colville, WA, who prospected here in 1864. The site is on the edge of the PURCELL WILDERNESS CONSERVANCY, 20 km southwest of the ski resort at Panorama Ridge. A lead–ZINC–SILVER–barite deposit was worked from 1953 to 1967 by Sheep Creek Mines Ltd, after which the camp was closed down. *AS*

TOD, John, fur trader (b Oct 1794, Dumbartonshire, Scotland; d 31 Aug 1882, Victoria). He came to Canada in 1811 as a clerk with the HBC attached to Lord Selkirk's group of colonists bound for the Red River. Instead he was sent to a trading post in northern Manitoba, where he remained for several years. Following the HBC's union with the NORTH WEST CO in 1821 he was posted to York Factory, but he got on the wrong side of HBC governor George SIMPSON, who transferred him to NEW CALEDONIA, "the Siberia of the FUR TRADE." In 1823 Tod arrived at Fort George, then spent 1824–32 at Fort McLeod on the PARSNIP R. Discouraged by the isolation and lack of promotion, Tod decided to quit the HBC, but he was talked out of it and spent the rest of the 1830s on leave in England, then back in

John Tod, fur trader. UBC BC1048

Manitoba, where he was finally promoted to chief trader. He returned west in 1839 and took charge of a farm belonging to the PUGET'S SOUND AGRICULTURAL CO at Cowlitz. In 1840 he took command of FORT ALEXANDRIA on the upper FRASER R, and he served as senior officer at Fort Thompson (KAMLOOPS) from 1842 to 1849. In failing health, he retired from the HBC in 1850 after almost 40 years in its service, and settled near FORT VICTORIA on a 40-ha farm overlooking OAK BAY. In 1851 he was appointed to the Legislative Council advising the governor of VANCOUVER ISLAND, a position he held until 1858 when he resigned to devote all his energies to his farm and his sizable family. The Tod home is now a heritage house. Tod Mt near Kamloops is named for him, as is TOD INLET on southern Vancouver Island.

TOD INLET, a narrow arm of SAANICH INLET 16 km northwest of VICTORIA on VANCOUVER ISLAND, was known as Snictel, or "place of the blue grouse," to the Wsanec (Saanich) First Nations people. It was named after John TOD, an HBC officer. The area has become a rural residential community on the SAANICH PENINSULA that borders Gowlland Tod Provincial PARK (12.21 km²) and the BUTCHART GARDENS. *AS*

TODD, Jacob Hunter, merchant, pioneer salmon canner (b 17 Mar 1827, Brampton, ON; d 10 Aug 1899, Victoria). Raised on a farm in Ontario, he moved to VICTORIA in 1862 and established himself as a merchant. From 1863 to 1873 he ran a successful general store in BARKERVILLE. When the gold ran out (*see* GOLD RUSH, CARIBOO) he shifted his business to Victoria and established a wholesale grocery firm, J.H. Todd & Son, which supplied goods to the Interior. He then branched out into SALMON CANNING, which was just beginning on the coast, and eventually he owned 5 canneries known for his Horseshoe brand salmon. At his death he was one of the wealthiest men in the province. His eldest son Charles Fox Todd (1856–1941) took over the canning business, and when Charles died his sons William and Ernest succeeded him. The

Todd canning empire remained in business until the 1960s, when the canneries were sold.

TOFINO, district municipality, pop 1,170, is the jumping-off point for CLAYOQUOT SOUND, just outside the north end of PACIFIC RIM NATIONAL PARK RESERVE on the west coast of VANCOUVER ISLAND, 135 km west of PORT ALBERNI. Situated in the territory of the Tla-o-qui-aht nation (NUU-

Waterfront at Tofino. Keith Thirkell photo

CHAH-NULTH), it was named by Spanish explorers for the hydrographer Vincente Tofino de San Miguel. Since the creation of the park reserve in 1970 and the paving of the road, it has become a major TOURIST centre. Gray WHALE WATCHING is popular, along with other forms of ecotourism in the Sound. LOGGING and commercial FISHING are also important to the local economy.

TOLMIE, Simon Fraser, farmer, politician, premier 21 Aug 1928–15 Nov 1933 (b 25 Jan 1867, Victoria; d 13 Oct 1936, Victoria). His father was William Fraser TOLMIE, a prominent FUR TRADER and politician on VANCOUVER ISLAND, and his grandfather was John WORK, another prominent fur trader. After training as a veterinary surgeon in Ontario, Tolmie managed his father's farm near VICTORIA and was a government cattle inspector. He entered politics in 1917 as a federal candidate for Prime Minister Robert Borden's Union coalition. He won his Victoria riding and 2 years later became federal minister of agriculture. By 1921 the coalition had broken up and Tolmie ran as a Conservative. He won re-election, though the party was relegated to the opposition. In 1926 the provincial CONSERVATIVES met to choose a new leader. With the convention deadlocked, delegates offered the post to Tolmie; he overcame his initial reservations and accepted. Two years later he resigned his federal seat and led the provincial Conservatives to a landslide ELECTION victory, but the Depression set in before

he could build on his success. Tolmie's unimaginative response was to cut government spending and raise taxes. As the financial crisis deepened, the party fractured and he faced challenges from several of his own VANCOUVER MLAs. In 1932 he offered to form a coalition government, but he had no new policies to offer and his undistinguished leadership was increasingly in question. The Conservatives suffered a dismal defeat in the

Simon Fraser Tolmie, premier of BC 1928–33. BC Archives PDP-02226

1933 election; just 3 MLAs were elected. Tolmie retired to his farm. He re-entered federal politics in 1936 by winning a Victoria by-election, but he died 6 months later. He was the last leader of the BC Conservative Party to be PREMIER during the 20th century.

TOLMIE, William Fraser, fur trader, politician (b 3 Feb 1812, Inverness, Scotland; d 8 Dec 1886, Victoria). Trained in medicine, he joined the HBC in 1832 as a clerk and surgeon. He arrived at Fort Vancouver in May 1833 and was posted to the north at FORT MCLOUGHLIN. In 1836 he returned to Fort Vancouver and served there as surgeon and trader; following a furlough home, he took charge of trade and farming operations at Fort Nisqually on Puget Sound. He remained at Nisqually during the years of transition to American rule. In 1859 he moved to VICTORIA and served on the HBC board of management from 1861 to 1870. Meanwhile his political career began in 1860 with his election to the House of Assembly (*see* COLONIAL GOVERNMENT) on VANCOUVER ISLAND. He served until 1866, when the Island merged with BC. A proponent of CONFEDERATION, he was elected to the legislature in 1874 and 1875 but retired following his defeat in 1878. In retirement he lived on a large estate in SAANICH, Cloverdale Farm, and indulged his interest in botany and FIRST NATIONS LANGUAGES. He co-authored *Comparative Vocabularies of the Indian Tribes of British Columbia* in 1884. His son, Simon Fraser TOLMIE, was a PREMIER of BC.

TOMLINSON, Olga, artist (b 1929, Welland, ON). Her UKRAINIAN descent is often celebrated in the subject matter and decorative approach to high realism that is the hallmark of her work. A graduate of the Ontario College of Art (1951), she works in several media, including oil painting, pastel and stone lithography. With her husband, fellow artist Roy Tomlinson, she co-founded Cariboo Stone Press at LONE BUTTE near 100 MILE HOUSE, one of the few independent printmaking ateliers in Canada. She has shown and demonstrated stone lithography in Canada and the US and taken field trips to Japan, the QUEEN CHARLOTTE ISLANDS, and other locations. In 1980 both the Tomlinsons' work was featured in a 30-year retrospective exhibition. *See also* ART, VISUAL. *Martin Segger*

TOMLINSON, Robert, Anglican missionary (b 1842, Ireland; d 1913, Cedarvale). He joined the Church Missionary Society in Ireland (*see* ANGLICAN CHURCH) after medical training at Trinity College and arrived at METLAKATLA in 1867. He served on the NASS R for 11 years; there, with Robert Doolan, he established the mission at KINCOLITH. He moved to Ankitlast on the upper SKEENA R near KISPIOX. In 1883 he moved again, this time to Metlakatla, where William DUNCAN had established his model village. When Duncan was forced to leave in 1887, Tomlinson resigned from the missionary society and returned to the Skeena. He established a non-sectarian mission, Meanskinisht, at CEDARVALE. He rejoined Duncan at New Metlakatla during 1908–12. Tomlinson's son Robert Jr was also a missionary on the North Coast.

TOMSLAKE is a small AGRICULTURAL community 25 km south of DAWSON CREEK near the Alberta border in the PEACE R district. It was founded in 1939 by a group of 518 Sudeten German refugees who had fled their homes in Czechoslovakia to avoid Nazi persecution. They occupied 9,560 ha of rolling bushland belonging to the railway colonization companies. Originally known as Tate Creek, the community took its present name from a nearby lake when a post office opened in 1948.

TOP OF THE WORLD PROVINCIAL PARK, 87.91 km², lies high in the Kootenay ranges of the ROCKY MTS east of KIMBERLEY. Mt Morro (el 2,912 m), the highest point in the park, is one of several spectacular peaks. FIRST NATIONS people traditionally visited to find chert, a rock they used to manufacture tools and weapons. Today the park (est 1973) is known particularly for sport FISHING.

TOPLEY, pop 178, 47 km northwest of BURNS LAKE on the BULKLEY R and the CNR, was first settled during the construction of the GRAND TRUNK PACIFIC RWY. The townsite, named after pioneer William J. Topley, was not surveyed until 1927. LOGGING and MINING have been important in the area.   AS

TOTEM POLES are the most visible example of the rich woodcarving tradition among coastal FIRST NATIONS in BC. Traditionally totem poles served as "documents" in an oral culture, proclaiming cultural identity and displaying a family's history and status. Northwest Coast peoples produced several types of totem poles, including welcome figures, traditionally carved by NUU-

Nuu-chah-nulth welcome figure at UBC Museum of Anthropology, carved by Joe David. Vickie Jensen photo

Totem poles at the Haida village of Ninstints, Anthony Island, Queen Charlotte Islands, 1898. BC Archives G-03254

CHAH-NULTH (Nootka); interior houseposts, by Nuu-chah-nulth and KWAKWAKA'WAKW (Kwakiutl); doorway poles, mostly by HAIDA but also Kwakwaka'wakw, GITKSAN and NUXALK (Bella Coola); mortuary poles, by Haida, TLINGIT and, rarely, TSIMSHIAN; and memorial poles, by Haida, Tlingit, Tsimshian, Kwakwaka'wakw, Nuu-chah-nulth and Nuxalk. Shame poles, erected to ridicule a rival, were uncommon. A new type that has emerged since the 1960s is the commercial pole, commissioned by sources outside the culture for use in non-traditional settings such as museums, corporate parks or offices, schools and shopping malls. Traditionally, Coast Salish (*see* SALISHAN FIRST NATIONS) artists did not carve free-standing totem poles, although they did produce high-relief figures on the walls of

ceremonial dance houses, beam support posts and grave figures.

Each of the coastal groups has a distinct carving style. Poles are carved from western red CEDAR, with carvers looking for gigantic, straight-grained trees with a minimum of knots, rot or twisting. Before contact with Europeans, carving tools included knives, adzes, chisels, gouges and awls made of stone, shell and BEAVER teeth; contemporary carvers use similar metal-bladed tools and chain saws. Most poles range between 3 and 18 m in height. The tallest known 19th-century pole, from the lower NASS R (and now in the Royal Ontario Museum), stands more than 24 m. The tallest contemporary pole, located in ALERT BAY, measures 53 m. The life span of a totem pole in the damp coast CLIMATE averages 60 to 80 years, with some lasting 100 years.

Most totem poles have figures that represent the characters in mythic family or clan narratives. WOLF, EAGLE, RAVEN, FROG, BEAR, beaver,

KILLER WHALE, DOGFISH, thunderbird, sisiutl (double-headed serpent), huxwhukw (cannibal bird), MOUNTAIN GOAT and human figures are common, but PLANTS, celestial bodies and landscape features also appear. It is not possible to "read" a pole by simply identifying the figures carved on it. The figures serve more as an outline of the complex story that the pole represents.

When the first European seafaring explorers ventured to the Pacific coast in the late 1700s they recorded in journals and drawings evidence of interior houseposts among the Nuu-chah-nulth, free-standing exterior carvings among the Tlingit and doorway poles among the Haida. However, the scant mention of these massive wooden carvings suggests that totem poles were not abundant. Trade in SEA OTTER pelts led to a flourishing of totem pole carving as wealthy chiefs commissioned more poles and the introduction of iron tools speeded production. This "golden age of totem poles" peaked in the mid-1860s. Then totem pole carving nearly died out as continuing contact with outsiders brought devastating epidemics, Christian indoctrination and the POTLATCH prohibition of 1884. From 1870 to 1920 the great museums of N America and Europe rushed to collect specimens of the vanishing art.

Beginning in 1925 the few remaining totem poles were recognized as being of interest to TOURISTS, so the Canadian government and the CNR undertook a restoration project on a group of SKEENA R poles. (The US government began a similar project for Alaskan poles in the late 1930s.) In the 1950s Kwakwaka'wakw carver Mungo MARTIN was hired by UBC, and later the ROYAL BC MUSEUM, to train apprentices to repair and replicate totem poles. Slowly a new generation of carvers emerged, including Bill REID and

Raising a Nisga'a doorway pole, carved by Norman Tait and crew, at the Native Education Centre, Vancouver, 1985. Vickie Jensen photo

Robert DAVIDSON (Haida), Doug CRANMER and Tony and Henry HUNT (Kwakwa̲ka̲'wakw), Norman TAIT (NISGA'A), Joe DAVID and Art Thompson (Nuu-chah-nulth), Nathan Jackson (Tlingit), Walter Harris (Gitksan) and many others. In the 1960s First Nations art began a revitalization that has resulted in many new totem poles and a worldwide awareness of the rich Northwest Coast carving tradition. *See also* ART, NORTHWEST COAST ABORIGINAL. *Vickie Jensen*
Reading: Vickie Jensen, *Totem Pole Carving*, 1999; Hilary Stewart, *Totem Poles*, 1990.

TOURISM became one of the major revenue producers in the BC economy during the 1980s and 1990s as a growing number of visitors were attracted by the province's congenial climate and natural beauty. In 1997, 21.3 million overnight visits were recorded. Of these visitors, 10.7 million, or about 50%, were from BC. US visitors accounted for 4.3 million overnight trips, or 20% of the total, and other Canadians paid 4.7 million visits. Overseas visitors made up 7.7% of the tourism market. In 1997 tourists spent an estimated $8.5 billion in BC. Skiers accounted for $616 million, sport fishers $601 million, golfers $118 million, outdoor enthusiasts $865 million, business and convention visitors $1.28 billion, urban tourists $1.9 billion, and touring/sightseeing visitors $1.27 billion. By 1998, all of this activity supported about 16,572 tourism-related businesses and 113,000 direct tourism-related jobs. Tourism British Columbia, a CROWN CORPORATION established in 1997, is mandated to promote tourism in the province.

As the number of visitors to the province increases, so does concern about the impact of tourism on the ENVIRONMENT. Ecotourism—travel that promotes environmental protection and does no harm to the environment—is the fastest growing part of the tourism sector. In 1998 it accounted for just 7% of tourist activity but it is growing 3 times faster than the sector overall. In 1987 several adventure tourism operators created the Wilderness Tourism Council to promote ecotourism and to resist industrial and other developments that threaten natural areas.

TOW HILL, on the north coast of Graham Island, 24 km east of MASSET in the QUEEN CHARLOTTE ISLANDS, was settled in the 1910s and abandoned after WWI. A razor CLAM cannery operated

Tow Hill, Naikoon Provincial Park, Queen Charlotte Islands. Duane Sept photo

here from 1923 to 1930. The hill itself, a 150-m formation of columnar basalt, is the source of many HAIDA legends. The name is a Haida word meaning either "place of food" or "any grease." *AS*

TOWBOATING began its development as a marine transportation industry in BC when the first steam vessel, the BEAVER, arrived to serve the needs of the HBC. While principally a supply vessel, the *Beaver* also worked as a towboat during its long service on the coast. Two distinct needs gave the towboat industry its initial start. One was the need to assist deep-sea sailing ships plying the lumber trade as they made their way to and from coastal ports. ANDERSON MILL, established at PORT ALBERNI in 1860, was the first export SAWMILL, followed by HASTINGS MILL and the MOODYVILLE sawmill, both in BURRARD INLET. Sailing traffic and the need for accompanying tugs grew as more mills joined the exporters. The second need was for towboats to move logs by water from the LOGGING camps to the sawmills. With the development of PULP AND PAPER mills along the coast after 1909, the FOREST INDUSTRY became even more dependent on tugs to transport raw material to the mills and to tow finished product to market. This constant flow of raw logs, wood chip barges and pulp and paper barges remains a common sight on the coast.

Towboating diversified along with the coastal economy and the growth of settlement. Tugs and barges supplied fuel oil and construction materials, moved railcars, performed salvage work and generally were the workhorses of the coast. They evolved from the small, wooden, steam-powered boats that towed the first LOG BOOMS down the INSIDE PASSAGE to modern steel, high-powered vessels such as the SUDBURYs, famous for their mid-ocean rescues, or the smaller tractor tugs that manoeuvre giant freighters around the local harbours.

Hundreds of towboat companies have operated on the coast, and many forest and commercial FISHING outfits maintained their own fleets. A few of the most significant companies were: STRAITS TOWING, founded by Harold Elworthy in VANCOUVER in 1943 and one of the 2 companies that merged in 1969 to form Rivtow Marine Ltd; Kingcome Navigation, the towboating arm of the POWELL RIVER CO and subsequently MACMILLAN BLOEDEL LTD; GULF OF GEORGIA TOWING, founded in Vancouver by George Walkem during WWI and a major coastal barging operation when it sold to SEASPAN INTERNATIONAL in 1977; Vancouver Tug Boat Co., started by Harold Jones and his sister Ruth in 1925 and still flourishing when it merged with ISLAND TUG & BARGE to create Seaspan in 1971; and Pacific Coyle Navigation, another major industry player between 1926 and 1956. (*See also* CATES TOWING.) By the 1990s, however, the industry had consolidated and most of the work was handled by the 2 largest remaining operators, Seaspan International Ltd, part of the WASHINGTON MARINE GROUP, and Rivtow Marine Ltd, founded as River Towing in 1941 by Cecil Cosulich and sold to Smit International in 2000. Other significant companies include the Shields group, Pacific Towing Services and North Arm Transportation. *See also* LOG BARGES.

Notable towboats of the coast include:

Isabel. The first boat built in BC expressly for

SELECTED BC TOURISM STATISTICS 1992–98

	1992	1996	1998
Total tourism revenues ($ million)	n/a	8,314.0	8,760.0
Tourism room revenues ($ million)	747.6	1,093.5	1,201.8
Direct tourism employment	93,870	105,530	112,940
Vancouver International Airport			
arrivals & departures (thousands)	9,935	14,038	15,510
BC Ferries passengers (thousands)	20,667	22,193	21,418
Hotel occupancy (annual average %)	62.4	68.2	62.8
Hotel room rate (annual average $)	81.20	99.90	112.05
Total visitor volume (thousands)	n/a	21,142	21,772
Total visitors to BC parks (thousands)	n/a	23,473	26,290

Breakdown of 1998 visitor volume and tourism revenues:

	Number (thousands)		**Revenue** ($ million)	
Visitors from BC	10,654	48.9%	2,380	27.2%
Visitors from rest of Canada	4,745	21.7%	2,659	30.4%
Visitors from United States	4,782	22.0%	2,167	24.7%
Visitors from Mexico	52	0.2%	36	0.4%
Visitors from Asia & Oceania	774	3.6%	821	9.4%
Visitors from Europe	623	2.9%	625	7.1%
All other overseas visitors	142	0.7%	72	0.8%

TUGBOATS OF THE BC COAST

The steam tug Lorne, built in 1889 in Victoria for the coal baron Robert Dunsmuir to tow coal-carrying sailing ships to the open sea. VMM

The Sudbury, converted from a WWII Royal Canadian Navy corvette by Island Tug and Barge. MMBC

The Rosario Straits, a surplus US Navy tug that Straits Towing purchased when the logging industry boomed in BC after WWII.

The Harmac Cedar, built in the 1960s was an early steel "hot rod" towboat with a steerable nozzle and great log-towing power. Doug Lucas photo

R.N. Hodder, designed by A.G. McIlwain Ltd, a modern multi-purpose tug used for towing barges, log booms and for docking ships. Pat Sayer photo

Rivtow Capt Bob, BC's most powerful tug (6,100 hp) and Rivtow Hercules, a self-dumping log barge. Cim MacDonald photo

Seaspan Commodore (5,700 hp), Seaspan International's flagship, capable of salvage work and worldwide ocean barge-towing. Don Brown photo

Charles H. Cates III, a modern twin Z-drive, reverse tractor tug designed by Robert Allan Ltd for C.H. Cates & Sons.

towing, in 1866, it was a COAL-burning, steam-powered vessel owned by Edward STAMP, owner of the Hastings Mill, and was used to tow lumber ships through JUAN DE FUCA STRAIT to Burrard Inlet. Later owned by Robert DUNSMUIR and used to tow coal ships, it retired in 1898.

Etta White. Owned by the Moodyville sawmill, it went into operation towing ships in and out of Burrard Inlet in 1876. This 28-m steam tug was active on the coast until it burned in 1920.

Maggie. A 22-m steam sidewheeler built in 1873 for the logger Jeremiah ROGERS to tow booms from ENGLISH BAY around to the Hastings Mill, it was the first steamboat built in what would become Vancouver.

Master. The last surviving steam tug on the coast, it was built in FALSE CREEK in 1922 and ties up at the Heritage Harbour at the VANCOUVER MARITIME MUSEUM.

Lorne. It was a 46-m steam-powered tug built by Robert Laing in Victoria in 1889 for Robert Dunsmuir to tow coal ships.

Active. Launched the same year as the *Lorne*, it was used primarily to tow log booms to Burrard Inlet sawmills and remained in service until 1956.

Sea Lion. Built in 1905 for Capt George French, it was considered one of the finest log towers on the coast. It was converted to diesel in the 1950s and continued in service as a marine research vessel.

Ivanhoe. Built in 1907, it belonged for many years to the Kingcome Navigation Co. It was retired in 1971 and went on display at the Vancouver Maritime Museum.

Seaspan Commodore. Built in 1974, it was the flagship of the Seaspan International fleet of tugs in 1999, towing large barges anywhere from Mexico to Alaska.

Rivtow Captain Bob. Named for the Cosulich brothers' late father, it was the most powerful tug on the coast in the late 1990s, at over 6,000 hp.

Reading: Ken Drushka, *Against Wind and Weather: The History of Towboating in BC*, 1981.

TOWHEE is a large SPARROW found in brushy thickets and backyard gardens in southern BC. The spotted towhee (*Pipilo maculatus*), the only species that breeds in the province, has a black hood and red-brown sides. With a characteristic double kicking motion, towhees search for seeds and other food items under fallen leaves.

TOWNSEND, Billy "Blond Tiger," boxer (b 6 May 1909 Durham, England; d 12 May 1985, Vancouver). He moved to NANAIMO with his family at age 2, began BOXING when he was 14 and turned professional 5 years later. After winning the Canadian lightweight and welterweight championships he toured N America, particularly making a name for himself in New York. At Madison Square Garden he starred in 11 main events with classic matches against Eddie Ryan,

Tony Canzoneri, Bat Battalino, Joe Glick, Benny Leonard and Billy Petrolle. Townsend retired in 1934 but returned to the ring 2 years later to win 12 straight matches before being knocked out for the last time. In more than 300 fights he lost only 23, and 4 of those were for world titles. The man who at age 13 had worked in the Nanaimo COAL mines to support his family made an estimated $135,000 through boxing. He was elected to the BC SPORTS HALL OF FAME in 1966.   *SW*

TRACK AND FIELD events were first held in NEW WESTMINSTER, then known as Queensborough, in 1859. Shot put, foot and hurdle races, the caber toss, high and long jumps and the hammer throw were all part of the Queen's birthday celebrations. At the international level, Duncan GILLIS earned BC's first Olympic medal, a silver in the hammer throw, at the 1912 Stockholm Olympics. The next year, VANCOUVER's Bill CHANDLER established himself as one of the world's top distance runners by topping a select field in San Francisco. UBC sent a team led by sprinter Harry WARREN to Saskatoon to compete in western Canada's first intercollegiate track meet in 1923 and joined the Western Canadian Intercollegiate Union a year later.

Hazel Hanson-Monnie finishing first in a 200-m heat during the 1996 BC high school track and field championships. Steve Bosch/Vancouver Sun

Percy WILLIAMS of Vancouver became an international sensation when he tied world records in the 100-m and 100-yd dashes and won gold medals in the 100 m and 200 m at the 1928 Amsterdam Olympics, the first double gold Olympian in 20 years. The 1932 Olympic Games in Los Angeles featured Lillian Palmer and the future Vancouver coach Mary Frizzell helping Canada's 4x100 relay team obtain a silver medal, Duncan MCNAUGHTON winning the high jump and Vancouver's Lee Orr tying an Olympic record in the semi-finals of the 200 m before finishing 5th in the finals. At the 1934

British Empire Games, Bob Dixon won a gold in javelin, and Palmer and Allen Poole took golds in relays. Vancouver's Howie McPhee was BC's next sprinting star as he tied a world record in the 100 m and set several more Canadian and BC records, but he fell short of qualifying for the 100-m finals at the 1936 Berlin Olympics. After starring at UBC in track and rugby, he died tragically of a brain aneurism. VICTORIA also developed a thriving program under coach Archie MCKINNON and many more young athletes strove to follow in the tracks of Williams as track and field became a major summer sport in BC.

In the first half-century of the BRITISH EMPIRE GAMES, BC's outstanding performers included middle distance runners Bill Dale, Jack Hutchins, Doug CLEMENT and Terry Tobacco, sprinters Pat Haley, Harry Nelson and Bruce Springbett, long jumper Jim Panton, javelin thrower Douglas Robinson, hammer thrower Jack Cameron, shot putter John Pavelich, high jumpers Joe Haley and Alice Whitty, pole vaulter Robert Reid and discus thrower Marie Dupree. In the 1950 Games, an all-BC women's 660-yd team of Patricia Jones, Gerry Bemister, Eleanor McKenzie and Elaine Silburn won bronze and N VANCOUVER's Bill Parnell captured a bronze in the 880-yd and a gold in the celebrated mile where he set an Empire record that was broken at Vancouver's famous MIRACLE MILE 4 years later. At the 1948 London Olympics, BC runners Jones and Diane Foster helped secure a bronze medal for Canada in the 400-m relay. On the local scene, the first Vancouver Relays were held in conjunction with the formation of the Vancouver Olympic Club in 1949 and a number of other Lower Mainland track clubs developed, including the Arctic Track Club, Pacific Athletic Club, Quadra Club and New Westminster Olympic Club. The Provincial High School Championships (1947–53) and the Vancouver and District Championships attracted an unprecedented amount of interest during the 1950s.

The Pan American Games were inaugurated in 1959 and immediately became as important as the British Commonwealth Games. At the first Pan Am Games, UBC's Doug Kyle won a silver in the 10,000 m and a bronze in the 5,000 m, and Sally McCallum earned a bronze in the 200 m and combined with Heather Campbell and Valerie Jerome for a 400-m relay bronze. Valerie's brother, Harry JEROME, emerged to stardom that year by tying the world record in the 100 m. He later won a bronze at the 1964 Tokyo Olympics, picked up golds at the 1966 Commonwealths and 1967 Pan Ams and tied the 100-yd dash world record as well. Another BC family act featured shot putter Dave Steen, who won a 1962 Commonwealth bronze medal and golds at the 1966 and 1970 Commonwealths, while his nephew, also Dave STEEN, achieved a bronze in the decathlon at the 1988 Olympics. At the 1963 Pan Am Games, Don Bertoia earned a gold in the 800 m and a bronze in the 1500. Other international performers during the 1960s and '70s period included middle distance runners Sieg Ohlemann, Ken Elmer, Norm Trerise and Bill Smart, high jumpers Diane Gerace, Wilf

Wedmann, John Beers and John Hawkins, decathlete Gerry Moro, javelin thrower Jay Dahlgren, pole vaulters Bob Yard, Kirk Bryde and Alan Kane, sprinters Marjorie Bailey, indoor 880-yd record setter Irene Piotrowski and indoor 60-m world-record setter Patti Loverock, long jumper Mike Mason, hammer thrower Murray Keating, long-distance runners Thelma Wright and Tom Howard, hurdler Bob McLaren and pentathlete Penny May.

In BC, the first coaches' clinic was held in Apr 1963 and interest in track and field spread rapidly through clubs in RICHMOND, BURNABY, the SUNSHINE COAST, TRAIL, SURREY and KIMBERLEY. With his wife Diane, Doug Clement founded the Richmond Kajaks club in 1962. In addition to becoming Canada's leading sports medicine doctor, he coached at least 10 runners to the Olympic level. At the 1971 Pan Am Games, 3 BC female track stars emerged as Brenda Eisler won gold in long jump, Stephanie Berto won gold in the 200 m, setting a Pan Am record, and silver in the 100 m, and Debbie BRILL won gold in high jump. Brill had already achieved gold at the 1970 Commonwealths and went on to win the 1979 World Championships and set an indoor world record. Another high jumper, Greg JOY, emerged from Burnaby in the mid-1970s to win the silver at the 1976 Olympics and set an indoor world record. At the 1975 Pan Ams in Mexico City, Joyce Yakubowich won golds in the 400 m and 4x400-m relay, in addition to a bronze in the 4x100 m relay, and at the 1978 Commonwealth Games Phil Olsen won gold in javelin. Scott Neilson closed the 1970s with a gold in the hammer at the 1979 Pan Am Games. Javelin thrower Laslo Babits and decathlete Steen won golds at the 1983 Pan Ams, Lynn WILLIAMS won a 3,000 gold and 1,500 bronze and Graeme Fell won a gold in the 3,000-m steeplechase at the 1986 Commonwealths. Other international medals in the 1980s and 1990s went to Babits, steeplechaser Greg Duhaime, 800-m specialists Simon Hoogewerf and Charmaine Crooks, 100-m sprinter Philomena Mensah and distance runners Dave Campbell, Debbie Bowker, Robyn Meagher, Jeff Schiebler, Leah Pells and Lynn's husband Paul Williams. Angela CHALMERS won 3,000-m golds in the 1990 and 1994 Commonwealth Games. Olympic successes included Lynn Williams' 1984 bronze in the 1,500 and Chalmers' 1992 bronze in the 3,000. Important builders and coaches over the years have included Willi Krause, Lloyd Swindells, Frederick Rowell, Bob Osborne, Harold Wright, Jack Harrison, Bruce Humber, Lionel Pugh, the Clements and Merv Ferguson. *SW*

TRAIL, city, pop 7,696, straddles the COLUMBIA R 18 km north of the US border in the southeast corner of the province. The original townsite was a steamboat landing, founded in 1890 by Col Eugene Topping and Frank Hanna as a shipping point for the nearby MINING camp of ROSSLAND, where rich mineral deposits were being found. The site was originally called Trail Creek Landing, a reference to the DEWDNEY TRAIL. In 1896 an American entrepreneur, F.A. HEINZE,

Aerial view of Trail, 1999. Larry Doell photo

opened a SMELTER above the townsite to treat ore from the Rossland mines. Two years later the CPR bought the smelter, later combining it with mining properties and a power company to form the Consolidated Mining and Smelting Co, now COMINCO. The smelter grew to become the largest non-ferrous smelting operation in the world. In the year 2000 it was still the world's largest refiner of ZINC and lead. As the smelter expanded, so did Trail, which incorporated on 14 June 1901 and, nearly a century later, was still largely dependent economically on the Cominco operations. Trail is known for its large ITALIAN community and for its sporting heritage: the TRAIL SMOKE EATERS hockey team won the world championship in 1939 and 1961. By the 1970s a serious public health problem had emerged as contaminants from smelting were found to have polluted the air, water and soil. In response Cominco introduced clean-up measures that reduced toxic emissions and residues dramatically.

TRAIL SMOKE EATERS remains the most famous and successful team in BC amateur HOCKEY history. It won 16 provincial senior championships, 3 western championships, 2 Allan Cup Canadian championships and 2 world championships between 1933 and 1987. The name came during the 1928–29 season when a fan in VANCOUVER threw a pipe onto the ice to protest a referee's call in favour of the visiting Trail Senior Hockey Club. Trail playing coach Craig Kendall picked it up and smoked it on his way to the bench, and next morning the

Trail Smoke Eaters, 1961 world champion amateur hockey team. Trail City Archives

PROVINCE newspaper christened the team. The first Smoke Eaters squad to win the national championship, under coach Elmer Piper, defeated the Cornwall Flyers for the Allan Cup in 1938 and then embarked on a gruelling exhibition schedule across Canada and Europe, losing only once in 63 games. The tour ended in Switzerland for the 1939 world championships where Trail outscored the opposition 42-1 over 8 games, returning home with the international crown. Bobby KROMM took over as coach for the 1959–60 season and the team reached the Allan Cup finals but lost to the Chatham Maroons. The Maroons, however, declined to represent Canada at the 1961 world championships and Trail was given the privilege; it beat Russia 5-1 in the final game to win Canada's last international title for 35 years. The Smoke Eaters won another Allan Cup in 1962 but finished 4th at the world championships. The team folded in 1987, one year before its Western International Hockey League suffered the same fate. *SW*

TRAILS were the earliest land transportation routes in BC. Aboriginals used footpaths to travel within their traditional territories to hunting and FISHING sites and to communicate with other groups for purposes of trade and warfare.

Hikers on the West Coast Trail. Vancouver Sun

For example, coastal FIRST NATIONS used a network of "grease trails" between the coast and the Interior, so-called because the people used these corridors to trade EULACHON oil with their inland neighbours. One of these trails is now part of the ALEXANDER MACKENZIE HERITAGE TRAIL, a 420-km hiking trail that follows the route taken by the FUR TRADE explorer Alexander MACKENZIE on his way to the Pacific Ocean in 1793.

When Europeans arrived in the mid-19th century they began constructing trails to link the outlying parts of the colony. On VANCOUVER ISLAND the Goldstream Trail was opened over the Malahat (see MALAHAT DRIVE) in 1862 to connect the VICTORIA area with agricultural settlements farther north. On the mainland the earliest trail was the fur-trade brigade route connecting the

COLUMBIA R to the trading posts of the central Interior via the OKANAGAN VALLEY. It was surveyed in 1811, then used extensively during 1826–47 (see FUR BRIGADES).

The GOLD RUSH that began in 1858 created an immediate need for access routes to the FRASER R canyon. In response, the DOUGLAS TRAIL was built in 1858 linking HARRISON LK to the LILLOOET area. It was improved for wagon use and was the main route to the Interior until it was eclipsed by the CARIBOO WAGON ROAD in the 1860s. The first trail constructed by Europeans in the Lower Mainland was the False Creek Trail, built by ROYAL ENGINEERS in 1860 to connect NEW WEST-MINSTER to the ENGLISH BAY area. The modern Kingsway Ave follows much of its route. The search for gold motivated most of the early trail building in the Interior; chief among these gold rush routes was the DEWDNEY TRAIL, laid across the southern Interior from 1860 to 1865 to access the diggings at WILD HORSE CRK. Two major trails were used by the burgeoning CATTLE INDUSTRY: the PEMBERTON TRAIL, opened in 1877, was an attempt to link Lillooet with BURRARD INLET via SQUAMISH; and the COQUIHALLA TRAIL was used to drive cattle from the NICOLA R valley to HOPE. The Klondike gold rush sparked the construction of an "all-Canadian" route to the

northern goldfields, including a trail from TELE-GRAPH CRK on the STIKINE R. This route is now the basis of the 375-km Telegraph Trail to ATLIN.

On the west coast of Vancouver Island, a life-saving trail was constructed during 1907–10 after the steamship VALENCIA was wrecked near PACHENA POINT. This trail was reopened in 1969 as the WEST COAST TRAIL, now one of the most popular hiking destinations on the continent. In 1995 the West Coast Trail was joined by the shorter JUAN DE FUCA MARINE TRAIL to the south. Of all the hiking trails, the most ambitious is the TRANS-CANADA TRAIL. When completed it will span the continent; the BC section alone is 1,750 km long.

With the construction of railways and ROADS, trails lost their significance as the primary transportation routes and began to be used mainly for recreational purposes. Since the

1960s and the boom in outdoor recreation, the number of trails in the province has grown dramatically. There are thousands of hiking trails, ranging from short urban footpaths to wilderness treks requiring many days to complete. Some trails use part or all of the pioneer routes and many are popular with mountain bikers as well as hikers.

Readings: Bruce Fairley, *A Guide to Climbing and Hiking in Southwestern British Columbia,* 1993; Jack Christie, *Inside Out British Columbia,* 1998.

Some major hiking trails in BC:

Alexander Mackenzie Heritage Trail, from the Fraser R to BELLA COOLA.

Yukon Telegraph Trail, from Telegraph Creek to Atlin.

Sunshine Coast Trail, from SALTERY BAY to DESOLA-TION SOUND.

West Coast Trai, from PORT RENFREW to BAMFIELD.

Baldy Mountain Trail, north of VANDERHOOF to MANSON CREEK.

Stein Heritage Trail, in the STEIN R Valley.

Baden-Powell Trail, from HORSESHOE BAY to DEEP COVE.

Juan de Fuca Trail, from JORDAN RIVER to Port Renfrew.

Sea to Sky Trail, from PEMBERTON to D'ARCY.

Suncoaster Trail, from HALFMOON BAY to Earl's Cove on the SUNSHINE COAST.

TRANQUILLE lies at the mouth of the river of the same name on the north side of Kamloops Lk, 10 km west of KAMLOOPS. It was the site of the first SAWMILL and grist mill in the central Interior, built in 1868 by William FORTUNE and James MCINTOSH. Fortune developed the property as a ranch and farm until he sold it for use as a tuberculosis sanitorium, the first one west of Ontario, in 1907. A new King Edward Sanitorium opened in 1910. From 1959 the buildings were used as a home for the mentally and physically handicapped. The institution closed in 1984. The site, named for a local SECWEPEMC (Shuswap) leader, is an important staging area for migratory waterfowl and bighorn sheep are common.

TRANS-CANADA HIGHWAY (Hwy 1) was completed through BC on 30 July 1962 with the official opening of the 147-km ROGERS PASS section between REVELSTOKE and GOLDEN. The highway was built under the terms of a federal-provincial agreement signed in 1949 and construction began in earnest the next year. Sections through the mountains and the FRASER R canyon were particularly difficult and costly: a 2-km stretch at China Bar north of YALE was the most expensive piece of 2-lane highway constructed in Canada to that time. A continuous highway across BC had been in place since 1940 when the BIG BEND HWY was finished, but this route was superseded by the Rogers Pass route. Today the highway begins at Mile 0 in VICTORIA and travels 113 km north up VANCOUVER ISLAND to NANAIMO,

Mile 0, Trans-Canada Hwy, at Beacon Hill Park in Victoria. Walter Lanz/Image Makers

TRANS-CANADA HIGHWAY

then crosses by ferry to HORSESHOE BAY and the mainland. It continues out the FRASER VALLEY to HOPE, turns north along the Fraser Canyon, then swings east again to cross the Interior via KAMLOOPS, SALMON ARM, Revelstoke and Golden before crossing the KICKING HORSE PASS into Alberta. The Trans-Canada Hwy in BC is 961 km long. *See also* ROADS AND HWYS.

TRANS-CANADA TRAIL runs 16,000 km from VICTORIA to St John's, NF, with a second leg reaching north through Alberta and the Yukon to Tuktoyaktuk near the mouth of the Mackenzie R. The BC section, about 1,750 km long, was substantially completed by the year 2000. It crosses the southern part of the province, follow-

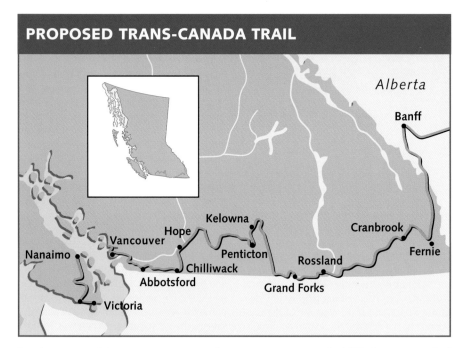

PROPOSED TRANS-CANADA TRAIL

ing the routes of the KETTLE VALLEY RWY, the COLUMBIA & WESTERN RWY and other abandoned railway lines for much of the way. *See also* TRAILS.

TRANS MOUNTAIN PIPE LINE CO LTD supplies 90% of the Lower Mainland's requirements for petroleum products. The company owns and operates a 1,260-km PIPELINE system, built in 1952–53, which transports crude oil

and refined products from Edmonton through KAMLOOPS to its tank farm and marine terminal in BURNABY. Crude oil from northeastern BC is also received at the Kamloops facility for delivery via the pipeline to VANCOUVER. A wholly owned subsidiary owns and operates the portion of the pipeline system that transports crude oil from the border to refineries in Washington. A separate pipeline system transports aviation turbine fuel from Burnaby to VANCOUVER INTERNATIONAL AIRPORT. In 1998 the company had revenues of $133.5 million. *See also* OIL AND GAS INDUSTRY.

TRANSFER PAYMENTS from the federal government to the provinces are of 2 types: equalization payments to the "have not" provinces (BC is not one of these) to counter regional economic disparities, and the Canadian Health and Social Transfer to support health care, post-secondary EDUCATION and social assistance programs. Federal allocations to BC declined sharply during the 1990s as Ottawa struggled to lower its overall deficit by reducing expenditures. Transfers now make up about one-third of BC's spending on HEALTH, education and social assistance, down from one-half in the 1980s. The issue of transfer payments is very much in flux as the provinces and the federal government negotiate new fiscal arrangements in an era of reduced government spending.

TRANSITION HOUSES in BC provide emergency shelter, care and support to abused women and their children. Statistics Canada reported in 1993 that of BC women over the age of 16, 59%—the highest percentage in the country—had experienced male violence at least once. A 1994 survey by the BC Institute Against Family Violence found that the rate of wife assault was highest among women 25–34 years old, women with low incomes and women with disabilities. About 26% of assaults were reported to police. Most communities in BC have counselling and/or support services for abused women, and about 40 counselling programs for wife batterers operate in the province. But the crucial service is provided by transition houses, and designated "safe houses" in smaller centres. Most facilities are maintained at secret locations, as those seeking refuge are often hiding from their abusers. The BC/Yukon Society of Transition Houses, a non-profit association, was founded in 1978; in 1998 its members included 58 transition houses (almost all transition houses in BC), 14 safe home networks, 8 second stage transition houses, 54 Children Who Witness Abuse counselling programs and other groups. The organization seeks to end violence against women and its effects on children, through direct relief services, political advocacy and public education. *See also* HUMAN CARE SERVICES; WOMEN'S MOVEMENT.

TRANSPORTATION ALTERNATIVES have been explored most actively in BC's major centres, where poor air quality and traffic congestion are issues of concern. In the Lower Mainland and FRASER VALLEY, for example, population has mushroomed, and in spite of late 20th-century additions such as SKYTRAIN, SEABUS, West Coast Express commuter trains, articulated buses, new bridges, and highway lanes devoted to buses and high-occupancy vehicles (HOVs), private passenger cars have multiplied. In the mid-1990s some 30,600 vehicles were registered each year in Greater VANCOUVER; it cost taxpayers $600 million per year to build and maintain roads; 30% of the area of Vancouver was used for ROADS and parking areas.

Governments and community groups have been active in promoting alternatives to automobiles in BC, and they have also worked together, most notably on the Go Green program, founded in 1990 and funded by Environment Canada, BC TRANSIT, INSURANCE CORP OF BC and several provincial ministries. Go Green offers British Columbians practical choices for trip reduction. Activities have included extensive public education and a program for workplaces in which managed parking, staggered work hours and other methods are employed to reduce workers' use of cars.

Besides public transit, transportation alternatives include:

Bicycling. Bicycling advocacy groups encourage bicycle commuting and raise public awareness on sharing the road with cyclists. They also give courses on bicycle commuting, provide information on safety and legal issues, and work with local and provincial governments on making policy and planning for bicycle routes. The BC Cycling Coalition, founded in 1998, represents groups in Vancouver, VICTORIA, NANAIMO and the GULF ISLANDS. One member, BEST (Better Environmentally Sound Transportation), a non-profit group founded in 1991, has been effective in the joint project between the BC government, the GREATER VANCOUVER REGIONAL DISTRICT (GVRD) and citizens' groups to establish a unique network of "bikeways" in Vancouver. Bike path systems have also been put in place in RICHMOND, SURREY, N VANCOUVER, MAPLE RIDGE and PITT MEADOWS. To some extent bicycling has been integrated with other transit systems: riders can board the Seabus and the West Coast Express with their bikes; some buses have bicycle racks; BC Transit has installed lockers at park-and-ride stations along the SkyTrain route.

Car pools. A GVRD study showed that the 100 vanpools operating in 1995 were responsible for reducing ground-level exhaust emissions by 135 tonnes, which saved British Columbians $1.3 million, as well as saving commuters money and time (through the use of HOV lanes).

Car Sharing. The Co-operative Auto Network in Vancouver and the Victoria Car Share Co-op, both modelled on long-running programs in Europe and launched in 1997, are non-profit groups whose members own vehicles co-operatively and use them on a per-trip basis for a fraction of the cost of buying, insuring, storing and maintaining their own vehicles (*see also* CO-OPERATIVES).

Still other transportation choices include *walking; in-line skating; telecommuting; alternative fuel vehicles*, which use propane, natural gas, methanol and other substances (see also BC RESEARCH INC; BALLARD POWER SYSTEMS INC); and *shared-ride taxis*, which are still in the planning and research stages.

TRAPP, Ethlyn, doctor (b 18 July 1891, New Westminster; d 31 July 1972, Vancouver). During WWI she worked in military hospitals overseas, then returned to Canada and graduated from medical school at McGill Univ. In VANCOUVER she was an early exponent of the use of radiotherapy for treating cancer. Director of the BC Cancer Institute from 1939 to 1944, she was the first woman president of the BC Medical Assoc

Ethlyn Trapp, medical pioneer, 1954.
UBC 5.1/4216

(1946) and of the National Cancer Institute of Canada (1952). A member of the Order of Canada (1968), she was also an art collector and close friend of Emily CARR. Her N VANCOUVER home, Klee Wyck, is now an arts centre. *See also* MEDICAL PROFESSION.

TRAPP LAKE, a farming settlement 25 km south of KAMLOOPS, was named after Thomas J. Trapp, who first ranched here in 1874 with his partner William R. McDonald. Trapp later ran pack trains for CPR surveyors and became a successful hardware merchant in NEW WESTMINSTER.   AS

TRAWLING; *see* FISHING, COMMERCIAL.

TREATY NO 8 was an agreement between the federal government and the FIRST NATIONS people of northeastern BC and the adjoining parts of Alberta and the NWT. Originally negotiated in 1899, it took several years to collect signatures from all the DUNNE-ZA (Beaver), SEKANI, DENE-THAH (Slavey), Chipewyan and Cree who eventually signed the treaty. Until the initialling of the NISGA'A TREATY in 1998, Treaty No 8 was the only treaty between aboriginal people and the federal government that included any part of BC. The treaty was precipitated by the Klondike GOLD RUSH and the sudden appearance of European prospectors in the north. The local people complained that these intruders stole their horses and drove away fur-bearing animals, and they asked the government for a treaty to protect their rights. For its part the government wished to extinguish any aboriginal claim to the territory in preparation for the peaceful exploitation of northern resources. Under the terms of the treaty the First Nations surrendered their claim to 841,500 km² of land. In BC that includes 270,400 km² east of the ROCKY MTS. In return they received RESERVES, cash, farming equipment and ammunition, teachers, hunting and FISHING rights, and annual payments of $25 for each chief, $15 for each headman and $5 each for everyone else. A parallel Half-breed Commission offered 240 acres (97 ha) of land or $240 cash to MÉTIS within the treaty area. In retrospect it has become clear that the government and the First Nations had different expectations of the treaty. The government believed it was clearing away any aboriginal claim to the territory. The First Nations thought they were getting a guarantee that their traditional way of life and use of the land would not be harmed by the expected influx of outsiders.

TREE FRUITS are produced commercially in BC by 2,000 growers located primarily in the OKANAGAN VALLEY as well as the valley of the SIMILKAMEEN R and around CRESTON. Apples are by far the most important crop, accounting for 80% of the value of tree fruit production. The total annual harvest is 168 million kg of fruit, most of which is sold fresh but some of which is processed into juice and other products. Packing houses store, pack and ship the fresh fruit. The industry employs 7,500 people and has annual sales of about $140 million.

The first tree fruits were grown at HBC posts for consumption by FUR TRADERS, particularly at a nursery planted at FORT LANGLEY in the 1840s. By the 1860s there were small orchards on southern VANCOUVER ISLAND, and with the spread of the GOLD RUSH to the CARIBOO, trees began to be planted in the Interior. The first fruit trees in the Okanagan Valley were planted in 1857 beside Osoyoos Lk, just south of what became the US border, by a former HBC packer named Hiram "Okanogan" Smith. OBLATE missionaries made the first planting in the BC portion of the valley in 1862, near present-day KELOWNA, followed by pioneer settlers such as Thomas ELLIS at PENTICTON (1869) and Alfred Postill at Kelowna (1876). In the Similkameen, Frank RICHTER began planting apple trees on his "R" Ranch in about 1880. In 1889 the BC FRUIT GROWERS' ASSOCIATION (BFGA) was founded in VANCOUVER to serve as an information exchange and voice for the growers. The first formal producers' organization in BC, the BCFGA was still operating in 1999, with 900 members. Before WWI the Okanagan Valley was established as the principal fruit-growing area in the province. Much of this

Workers in a fruit packing plant, Penticton, 1930s.

growing took place on the pioneer ranches or on land purchased from the ranchers, subdivided and sold to orchardists. The initial boom collapsed in 1912, but by that time the industry was entrenched. During the 1920s, thanks largely to government-funded irrigation projects, fruit growing spread south to the OSOYOOS–OLIVER area. In 1939 the BCFGA formed BC Tree Fruits Ltd, a co-operative marketing agency that was still doing business in 1999. Then in 1946 the association formed BC Fruit Processors Ltd to market processed fruit products. The company name was changed to SUN-RYPE PRODUCTS LTD in 1959. Over the years the Pacific Agri-Food Research Centre, established by the federal government in SUMMERLAND in 1914, played a key role in developing new varieties of fruit, controlling INSECT pests and otherwise supporting the industry.

Major commercial fruits are:

Apples. BC produces 30% of the apples grown in Canada, an annual harvest of 150 million kg. Seven varieties predominate: red delicious, golden delicious, McIntosh, Spartan, Gala, Fuji and Jonagold. About 75% of all orchard land is planted in apples, the most valuable edible cash crop in BC.

Peaches. BC's 800 growers produce 5 million kg annually, 20% of total Canadian production.

Apricots. BC is the only province in Canada where apricots are grown commercially. The annual harvest is 300,000 kg, produced by 100 growers.

Pears. BC growers produce 7 million kg, including 50% of the total Canadian production of Bartlett pears and all the commercial production of Anjou, the 2 main varieties.

Cherries. BC growers produce 60% of the annual Canadian crop, about 3 million kg.

Plums. BC growers produce 300,000 kg annually.

TREES, GIANT, are a hallmark of BC, where some of the tallest specimens in the world have been known to grow. The leading "tall tree" species is DOUGLAS FIR, a species that is marvellously contrived for the mild, rainy coastal climate. To obtain the light necessary to its growth, the Douglas fir throws up a tremendous shaft equipped with special cells with spiral thickening to withstand strain. (The Australian eucalypt, the only other tree with these cells, is a broadleaf flowering tree.) The Douglas fir is the tallest

conifer the world has ever seen. The tallest specimen measured by a forester in BC stood near CLOVERDALE in SURREY. It was discovered in 1881 by William Shannon, who was cutting out the Hall's Prairie Road. After it was felled he measured the trunk to be 109.1 m (358 ft) and 3.5 m (11.5 ft) across the stump. Shannon counted the circles and calculated that the tree had been growing for 1,100 years. Stands of giant Douglas fir were soon ravaged by loggers. Forests where Greater VANCOUVER now sprawls contained some of the most majestic trees on earth. Those in Lynn Valley in N VANCOUVER were particularly grand, probably because they were protected from the wind. One, known as "the tallest tree in Lynn Valley," was felled in 1902 and measured by a local landowner at 126.5 m (415 ft), including the stump. The bark was 343 mm (13.5 in) thick. This tree stood on what is now Argyle Rd, off Mountain Highway. In 1907 another very tall Douglas fir was felled in Lynn Valley, measured by loggers at 107.3 m (352 ft). Nearer to the city, an outsized tree was felled in 1896 in the Kerrisdale district. According to Julius Martin Fromme, superintendent at the HASTINGS MILL, it was the biggest fir the mill ever handled, just short of 122 m (400 ft) long, 4.16 m (13 ft 8 in) across the butt with bark as thick as 406 mm (16 in).

In Washington state, several exceptionally tall Douglas firs were recorded. The best known is the Mineral Tree, which stood near the town of Mineral in the foothills of the Cascade Mts and was measured at 119.86 m (393 ft). Not far away, in the drainage of the Nisqually R, a party of surveyors in 1900 measured a downed fir at 116 m (380 ft), and it had a small piece of its top missing. The tallest Douglas fir still standing is in Oregon, the Brummet Fir, at 100.3 m (329 ft).

Some of the notable Douglas firs also had substantial girth. An ancient giant on the east coast of VANCOUVER ISLAND, known as the Westholme Tree, was toppled by a storm in 1919. It had a trunk 5.18 m (17 ft) thick at 1.2 m (4 ft) above the ground. The bole of the Mineral Tree in Washington was 4.9 m (16 ft) at chest height. Perhaps the granddaddy of all Douglas firs was the Conway Snag in the Puget Sound area, with a trunk 5.5 m (18 ft) thick at 1.5 m (5 ft) above the ground. These huge trees were ancient. The annual rings of a time-worn giant in Lynn Valley were counted at 1,280 years; the Westholme Tree was about 1,500 years old (an accurate count was impossible due to butt rot). Another tree in Washington state, the Finney Creek Tree, had 1,400 rings when it was felled.

Of all conifers, including the famed redwoods, the Douglas fir was taller as a tree though not as a forest. The coast redwood (*Sequoia sempervirens*) has produced grander forests but Douglas fir, with its youthful drive and large gene base, has produced the occasional supertall individual tree. Among the flowering plants, the eucalypt (*Eucalyptus regnans*), known as mountain ash in Australia, holds the record. A measurement made in 1879 records a specimen

TREE FRUIT STATISTICS 1971–96 (area in hectares)

	1971	1981	1991	1996
Apples	8,750	7,914	8,030	7,467
Pears	1,437	875	580	524
Prunes & Plums	573	424	277	217
Sweet Cherries	1,131	919	669	689
Sour Cherries	155	151	172	152
Peaches	943	963	727	633
Apricots	311	267	280	245

Douglas fir and gigantic cedar towering over a road near New Westminster, in an 1884 engraving of a drawing by the Marquis of Lorne.

Giant cedar tree, Meares Island Clayoquot Sound. Bernie Pawlik/Image Makers

that reached the incredible height of 132.3 m (434 ft)—without its top, which had broken off.

BC's other 2 tree species that grow to colossal size are Sitka SPRUCE and western red CEDAR. Both are known to have boles greater at the base than those of the Douglas fir. Undoubtedly there were larger trees in the past than remain today. The tallest measured tree in BC in 1999 was a Sitka spruce known as the Carmanah Giant (*see* CARMANAH VALLEY) growing on the southwest coast of Vancouver Island. It is 95.8 m (314 ft) high and is the tallest tree of the species known. However, Sitka spruce is most noticeable for its vast trunk base. Specimens have been known to have trunks more than 6 m (20 ft) through at chest height, though none that size remain standing. Sitka spruce grows rapidly and can live to an age of about 1,350 years. Ancient trees of western red cedar also develop expansive bases. The largest living tree is at Cheewhat Lk on the southwest coast of Vancouver Island. Its bole is 6

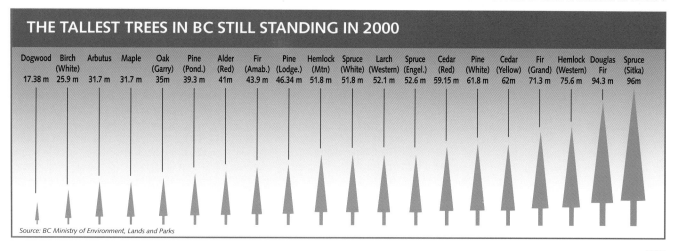

THE TALLEST TREES IN BC STILL STANDING IN 2000

Dogwood	Birch (White)	Arbutus	Maple	Oak (Garry)	Pine (Pond.)	Alder (Red)	Fir (Amab.)	Pine (Lodge.)	Hemlock (Mtn)	Spruce (White)	Larch (Western)	Spruce (Engel.)	Cedar (Red)	Pine (White)	Cedar (Yellow)	Fir (Grand)	Hemlock (Western)	Douglas Fir	Spruce (Sitka)
17.38 m	25.9 m	31.7 m	31.7 m	35m	39.3 m	41m	43.9 m	46.34 m	51.8 m	51.8 m	52.1 m	52.6 m	59.15 m	61.8 m	62m	71.3 m	75.6 m	94.3 m	96m

Source: BC Ministry of Environment, Lands and Parks

One of the huge Sitka spruce trees in the Carmanah Valley. Peter A. Robson photo

m (19.4 ft) in diameter at chest height. The trunk taper of cedar trees is quite pronounced so it is not as tall as Douglas fir or Sitka spruce. The tallest measured, 84.5 m (277 ft), was discovered in the Skwawka Valley on the mainland coast. Red cedar can grow to a notable age. The Cheewhat Lk Tree is estimated to be close to 2,000 years old.

BC is a place of tall trees, especially near the coast, but it does not boast the thickest specimens. The thickest living tree in the province is the Cheewhat Lk Cedar and there is no evidence that there was ever one bigger. In the early days of logging in Washington and Oregon, trees of both species were recorded that were slightly larger: 6.7 m (22 ft) in diameter at chest height for Sitka spruce and 6.8 m (22.3 ft) for red cedar. In California the trunks of some of the giant sequoias are over 7.6 m (25 ft) thick. The same can be said for coast redwoods felled by early loggers. In Mexico there is a Montezuma bald cypress that has a trunk diameter of 11.6 m (38 ft). Baobab trees in Africa attain this size and more. Going back into history there were several notable colossi. The huge sweet chestnut tree on the slope of Mt Etna in Sicily is now a relic, but 200 years ago it had a trunk 18.3 m (60 ft) in diameter at the base. And a plane tree that at one time stood on the banks of the Bosporus near Istanbul had a basal diameter of 13.7 m (45 ft). *See also* STOLTMANN, Randy.   *A.C. Carder*
Reading: A.C. Carder, *Forest Giants of the World*, 1995.

TREGILLUS, Frederick James, pioneer miner (b 31 Oct 1862, Plymouth, England; d 29 Aug 1962, Barkerville). While working on railway construction he was present at the driving of the "Last Spike" at CRAIGELLACHIE in 1885. Later he took up prospecting and made his living in various MINING partnerships. In the 1930s his involvement in quartz mining with Fred Wells led to a GOLD boom and the creation of the town of WELLS. In 1998 his daughter Mildred gave the province the old Tregillus home in BARKERVILLE,

as well as a large collection of period photographs documenting life in the historic town.

TREKKA was the first small Canadian yacht to circle the world. Laurent Giles designed the 6.25-m wooden yawl and John Guzzwell, a British immigrant, built it behind a fish and chip shop in VICTORIA, outfitting it with a 4-hp motor and cotton sails. The name came from the South African word "trek," to make a journey. Guzzwell got off across the Pacific Ocean in Sept 1955 and returned to a hero's welcome 4 years and 52,800 km later. He wrote a book about his voyage, *Trekka Round The World*. After the vessel was sold in 1961, it put many more kilometres under its keel—including a second circumnavigation with new owners—before being donated to the MARITIME MUSEUM OF BC. Guzzwell continued to build and sail boats in Seattle, specializing in the lightweight construction techniques that made *Trekka* such a success.   *Bet Oliver*

TREPANIER, 20 km southwest of KELOWNA on the west side of OKANAGAN LK, was promoted as a fruit-growing settlement by the Peachland Townsite Co in the early 1900s. It had a school and a factory for making concrete pipe in the 1910s. Today it is a recreational area with orchards and vineyards. Trépanier Crk probably got its name from a crude trepanning operation performed on the skull of a SECWEPEMC (Shuswap) chief by Alexander Ross of the NORTH WEST CO in 1817. *See also* TREE FRUITS; WINE MAKING.   *AS*

TRETHEWEY, James, mill owner (b 1833 England; d 24 May 1906, Vancouver). The patriarch of a large family, he arrived in Ontario in the 1850s and prospered as a mill owner and homesteader. In 1875 he came to BC and settled at MISSION, where his wife Mary Ann ran a maternity home, a hotel and a general store. He moved to CHILLIWACK in 1891 to build a mill complex at ELK CREEK and with his sons began the first large-scale LOGGING on HARRISON LK. Five sons engaged in a variety of businesses. William (d 1926) struck it rich in the silver mines of northern Ontario. Arthur (d 1919) bought a SAWMILL on Mill Lk at ABBOTSFORD, renamed it the Abbotsford Timber and Trading Co and built it into the largest employer in the area. At his death his brother and partner Joseph (d 1927) took control of the company. Joe also owned the Chilco Ranch near HANCEVILLE, one of the largest spreads in the CHILCOTIN. Joe's residence, Trethewey House, is a heritage home/museum in Abbotsford. Two other brothers, Sam (d 1929) and Jim (d 1945), also were involved in logging and milling. Joe's son Edgar took over Abbotsford Lumber when his father died, and during the Depression he created Trethewey Logging as a separate company. His wife Margaret was a pioneer EQUESTRIAN in the FRASER VALLEY. Their son Alan built Trethewey Logging into BC's largest independent logging company, and sold it to BC FOREST PRODUCTS in 1971. The Trethewey family has been associated with the Fraser Valley for 5 generations.

TRIANGLE ISLAND, 85 ha, is the outermost of the Scott Islands group about 45 km northwest of the north end of VANCOUVER ISLAND. Tiny, treeless and uninhabited, it is an ECOLOGICAL RESERVE protecting the nesting place for one-fifth of BC's breeding seabirds, more than any other island on the coast. It has the largest colony of Cassin's AUKLETS in the world (360,000 pairs, 40% of the world population) and the largest colony of tufted PUFFINS on the coast south of Alaska (25,000 pairs). As well, there are large numbers of GULLS, MURRES, GUILLEMOTS, CORMORANTS, OYSTERCATCHERS, EAGLES and FALCONS. It is also one of 4 breeding rookeries in BC for Steller's SEA LIONS. The highest LIGHTHOUSE on the coast operated here from 1910 to 1920.

TRIANO, Howard "Jay," basketball player and coach (b 21 Sept 1958, Tilsonburg, ON). His father Howie was a member of the 1964 Canadian Olympic BASKETBALL team. When Jay finished high school in 1977 in his hometown Niagara Falls, ON, he turned down offers from several American universities to play basketball at SFU instead. He immediately became the team's top player and eventually established himself as the best player in SFU history. When he left the university he held 11 basketball records, including most career points (2,616). His #12 was the first number to be retired by SFU Athletics. He captained the Canadian national team 1981–88 and the 1984 and 1988 Olympic teams. He also led the Canadian team that beat the US and Yugoslavia to win gold at the 1983 World University Games. Drafted by the Los Angeles Lakers in 1981, he failed to stick in the NBA and in 1988 retired as a player to become coach at SFU. In 1995 he joined VANCOUVER's new GRIZZLIES NBA organization as director of community relations and radio and television colour commentator. In 1999 he was named head coach of the Canadian men's national basketball team.   *SW*

TRICE, Allan "Al," diver, inventor (b 18 Sept 1929, Vancouver). As a commercial diver using both scuba and hard-hat equipment in the 1950s and 1960s he logged more than 12,000 hours underwater. The allure of deeper diving led to experiments with constant-volume dive suits and the decision that some type of one-atmosphere capsule was a necessity. Frustrated by attempts to buy a 2-person submersible, Trice, Don Sorte and Mack Thompson formed International Hydrodynamics Co (HYCO) in the mid-1960s and built their own. Their prototype working submarine *Pisces* was launched in 1966. Over a 14-year period HYCO built 14 submersibles, including the deepest diving *Pisces VI*, with a depth capability of 2,500 m, and the heaviest submersible *Taurus*, weighing in at 24,516 kg. Many people who went on to invent and market other SUBSEA TECHNOLOGY in BC got their start at HYCO. Trice became project manager for ISE Research, sister company to International Submarine Engineering in PORT MOODY, where he led research and development of underwater vehicles.   *Vickie Jensen*

TRIMEN, Leonard Buttress, architect (b 1846, London, England; d 11 Oct 1891, Victoria). He arrived in BC from England in the early 1880s, and during a brief architectural career in VICTORIA he designed many of the capital city's most prestigious residences. The most significant feature of his practice was the introduction and popularization of the Gothic Vernacular Revival style, later picked up and developed by Samuel MACLURE, Francis RATTENBURY and Percy JAMES, who made it the dominant feature of the Victoria cityscape. *See also* ARCHITECTURE.

TRINITY WESTERN UNIVERSITY was established in 1962 on the site of a former dairy farm in LANGLEY as Trinity Western Junior College by the Evangelical Free Church, a CONSERVATIVE PROTESTANT denomination. The name changed to Trinity Western College in 1971. It began granting a 4-year bachelor's degree in 1979 and became a chartered university in 1985, the first private university in the province. In keeping with religious traditions, students are required to abstain from drinking, smoking and extramarital sex.

TROLLING; *see* FISHING, COMMERCIAL.

TROOPER is a Juno Award-winning rock band that had a string of hits in the 1970s, including "Raise a Little Hell," "The Boys in the Bright White Sports Car," "Two for the Show" and "Oh Pretty Lady." Boyhood friends Ra McGuire (vocals) and Brian Smith (guitar) started out on the VANCOUVER club scene as members of Winter's Green and later as Applejack. When the band was booked to play a MORMON youth dance, they caught the ear of a church member, Randy Bachman of BACHMAN-TURNER OVERDRIVE, who signed the group to his Legend Records label. The band released its first album under the name Trooper in 1975 and won the 1980 Juno Award for group of the year. Heeding its own advice, offered in the song "We're Here for a Good Time (Not a Long Time)," the band has toured the country steadily, billed as Canada's number one party band. *See also* SOUND RECORDING INDUSTRY. *Mike Harling*

TROUP, James, steamboat captain (b Feb 1855, Vancouver, WA; d 1931, Victoria). As a young man he piloted steamboats on the Columbia R on the American side of the border. He came to BC in 1883 and joined the CANADIAN PACIFIC NAVIGATION CO, which had just been organized by his friend John IRVING. Later he took charge of the COLUMBIA & KOOTENAY STEAM NAVIGATION CO on KOOTENAY LK, which the CPR purchased in 1897. After returning to the coast in 1901, Troup took over as manager of the CPR's PRINCESS LINE of coastal steamers, a position he held until his retirement in 1928. Under his direction the fleet of *Princess* ships grew to 19 vessels carrying close to 800,000 passengers and earning $1.3 million annually.

TROUT belongs to the *Salmonidae* family of fish and occurs in the wild in both freshwater and

Cutthroat trout. Phil Edgell photo; drawing courtesy Fisheries & Oceans Canada

sea-run varieties. It is distinguished by dark spots on the lighter background of the back and sides (whereas the closely related CHAR has smaller, brighter scales and light spots on a dark background). All varieties spawn in streams, usually in the spring. Some travel to the sea while others remain in lakes and streams. Beautiful and spirited, they are a favourite with sport fishers. As well they are raised in licensed freshwater "farms," rainbow trout being the most popular. Three species occur in BC. Cutthroat trout (*Oncorhyncus clarki*) are recognizable by the red or orange slash marks on each side of the lower jaw. Young sea-run cutthroats remain in fresh water up to 3 years before migrating to salt water, where they can grow larger than their freshwater relatives. Rainbow trout (*O. mykiss*) include the sea-going STEELHEAD and several resident freshwater strains. The Kamloops trout, found in the lakes of the southern and central Interior, is one of these. The Gerrard trout occurs in the KOOTENAY, where the LARDEAU R, KOOTENAY LK and Jewel Lk contain some of the world's largest rainbow with recorded specimens reaching 23 kg. Brown trout (*Salmo trutta*) were introduced to the COWICHAN and Little Qualicum rivers on VANCOUVER ISLAND during the 1930s, to the KETTLE R in 1957 and to Somenos Lk near DUNCAN. They are distinctive for spawning in the winter. Brown trout average about 1 kg in weight, though larger fish can be found where there is an abundant food supply. *See also* FISHING, SPORT; FLY FISHING.

TROUT LAKE CITY, pop 56, 60 km southeast of REVELSTOKE at the north end of Trout Lk, was created in the early 1890s when GOLD and SILVER were discovered in the LARDEAU country (*see also* MINING). It soon had 5 hotels, a bank, a 6-bed hospital, skating rink, newspaper and 300 inhabitants. The ARROWHEAD & KOOTENAY RWY arrived at the south end of the lake in 1902 and steamboat service was available from 1902 to 1921, but metal prices dropped in the early 1900s and the mines closed. Alice JOWETT's remarkable Windsor Hotel survived into the 1980s along with a handful of hardy modern homesteaders. *AS*

TROWER, Peter, logger, writer (b 25 Aug 1930, St Leonards-on-Sea, England). He came to Canada with his widowed mother and a brother in 1940 and settled in the pulp mill community of PORT MELLON. He left school before graduation and for the next 22 years worked at a variety

Peter Trower, writer, 1998. Barry Peterson & Blaise Enright-Peterson

of jobs, mainly in coastal LOGGING camps. When he turned to writing full-time in 1971 he drew on his logging experiences for a series of poetry collections, including *Moving Through the Mystery*, *Between the Sky and the Splinters*, *Ragged Horizons* and *Where Roads Lead*. His work concerns itself with many subjects other than logging, but he is a legend in coastal WRITING circles as the "logger-poet." In his trilogy of novels—*Grogan's Café* (1993), *Dead Man's Ticket* (1996) and *The Judas Hills* (2000)—he continued to mine this theme.

TRUAX, Barry, composer (b 1947, Chatham, ON). He is one of Canada's leading electro-acoustic composers. He came to VANCOUVER in 1969 to attend UBC. In 1973 he began teaching at SFU in the School of Communication and Contemporary Arts, where, among other things, he has been involved in recording ambient sound for the World Soundscape Project. He is also a member of Vancouver's Urban Noise Task Force, which deals with noise pollution in the city. Truax runs his own CD label, Cambridge Street Records, from his home in BURNABY; there he records his own music using sounds produced electronically. Recordings of his work include *Digital Soundscapes* (1987), a collection of earlier works, *Pacific Rim* (1991), *Song of Songs* (1994) and *Inside* (1996). His multimedia opera, *Powers of Two*, premiered in Montreal in 2000.

TRUCK LOGGERS' ASSOCIATION (TLA) was founded in NANAIMO in 1941 by a group of small, independent coastal loggers. Using the new technology of motor trucks and inexpensive gas-powered LOGGING equipment, truck loggers had become a major force in the coastal logging industry during the 1930s. Over the next 50 years the TLA fought vigorously on behalf of the small-business sector of the provincial FOREST INDUSTRY in the face of continuing growth and expansion by the major integrated companies. It also represents most logging supply companies, which hold associate memberships. Over the years most TLA members sold or lost their timber harvesting rights and became contractors to large corporations. Today only a few members continue as independent market loggers. Based in VANCOUVER, the TLA had 393 industrial and 225 associate members in 1999. *Ken Drushka*

TRUDEAU, Margaret (Sinclair); *see* KEMPER, MARGARET (SINCLAIR) TRUDEAU.

TRUTCH, a small roadside settlement with TOURISM services 210 km northwest of FORT ST JOHN on the ALASKA HWY, was bypassed in 1987 with a new 43-km section of road. The road circumvented a steep winding climb over Trutch Mt, named after Joseph TRUTCH, BC's first LT GOV (1871–76). The US Army had a construction camp here during WWII. *AS*

TRUTCH, Joseph William, surveyor/engineer, lt gov 1871–76 (b 18 Jan 1826, Somerset, England; d 4 March 1904, Somerset). Trained as an engineer, he immigrated to the US in 1849 and 10 years later moved to VICTORIA, where he

Joseph William Trutch, lt gov of BC 1871–76, pictured here in 1875. BC Archives F-07196

found work as a surveyor and road builder. He undertook several projects on the BC mainland, including the construction of the ALEXANDRA BRIDGE at SPUZZUM and construction of parts of the CARIBOO WAGON ROAD. He was elected to the legislative council in 1861. As commissioner of lands and works from 1864 to 1871, he was responsible for creating some of the first RESERVES for FIRST NATIONS. He shared the racist assumptions of his day and ignored aboriginal claims to owning the land (*see* ABORIGINAL RIGHTS). An advocate of CONFEDERATION with Canada, he was

one of the representatives sent to Ottawa in 1870 to negotiate terms. On 14 Aug 1871 he became the new province's first LT GOV, at age 45 the youngest person ever to hold the position. He was a leading critic of responsible government—the principle that CABINET is accountable to an elected legislature—and resisted attempts to democratize government. At his own request he retired after one term of office. In 1877 he received a knighthood but continued to be active, serving as the federal government's agent in BC during the 1880s. Following his wife's death in 1895 he returned to live in England.

TRYGGVASON, Bjarni, engineer, astronaut (b 1946, Iceland). He was the sixth Canadian, and first British Columbian, in space. Raised in KITI-

Madline Seta, a Tsilhqot'in woman, with set net catch, Chilko Lk, 1985. Rick Blacklaws photo

MAT and RICHMOND, he graduated in engineering from UBC in 1972. He joined the Canadian space program in 1984 and was a member of the crew of the US shuttle *Columbia* on an 11-day flight in Aug 1997.

TSAWWASSEN is a suburban community occupying a peninsula in the southwest corner of DELTA, south of VANCOUVER. To the east it overlooks BOUNDARY BAY; to the west it looks across GEORGIA STRAIT to the GULF ISLANDS, and the peninsula receives a less abundant rainfall than the rest of the Lower Mainland. Tsawwassen is chiefly a residential suburb attracting an increasing number of retirees. The original residents were the Tsawwassen people, a branch of the HALKOMELEM, whose RESERVE (est 1878) now occupies the west side of the peninsula. A causeway and BC FERRY CORP terminal were built in 1959 to accommodate ferries travelling to Swartz Bay on VANCOUVER ISLAND. The ROBERTS BANK Superport is just north of the terminal.

TSETSAUT were a group of ATHABASCAN-speaking people who once lived in the mountainous

north-central Interior around MEZIADIN LK. In the 19th century they moved west toward the coast into the headwaters of the Portland Canal (*see* PORTLAND INLET) where eventually they merged with their NISGA'A, GITKSAN and TLINGIT neighbours. A population that numbered about 500 in 1830 declined due to disease, starvation and assimilation; today there are no known descendants.

TSILHQOT'IN (Chilcotin) people inhabit the CHILCOTIN stretching from the FRASER R to the COAST MTS in west-central BC. The Chilcotin Highway (Hwy 20) (*see* ROADS AND HWYS) snakes through the middle of their territory, which is drained by the Chilcotin, HOMATHKO, DEAN and Klinaklini rivers. Traditionally the people lived in small groups, moving seasonally to favourite hunting and FISHING spots. In 1808 Simon FRASER introduced the FUR TRADE to the area and the HBC operated FORT CHILCOTIN from 1829 to 1844, though the Tsilhqot'in did not participate in the trade to the same degree that many other FIRST NATIONS did. With the GOLD RUSH, a pack TRAIL opened across Tsilhqot'in territory and contact with outsiders increased. In 1864, unfriendly relations between aboriginals and Europeans flared into the so-called CHILCOTIN WAR. Following this episode some of the Tsilhqot'in were moved to RESERVES; other reserves were allotted between 1887 and 1904. With the growth of ranching (*see* CATTLE INDUSTRY) after 1880, many Tsilhqot'in became COWBOYS and ranch hands and engaged in haymaking, and some raised small herds of cattle themselves, all of which they combined with traditional subsistence activities. More recently the Tsilhqot'in have faced a dwindling resource base with which to maintain their traditional way of life. In the late 1980s they were particularly concerned by the activities of LOGGING companies in their territory; their response contributed to the creation in 1995 of Ts'yl-os Provincial PARK around CHILKO and Taseko Lks. There are about 2,500 Tsilhqot'in distributed in 6 nations:

Alexandria, Anaham, Stone, ALEXIS CREEK and NEMIAH VALLEY, represented by the Tsilhqot'in National Government; and Toosey, represented by the Carrier-Chilcotin Tribal Council. Both are located in WILLIAMS LAKE.

TSIMSHIAN (meaning "inside the Skeena River") is a grouping of FIRST NATIONS peoples living in northwest BC. It is based on the Tsimshian language family, which relates to the Penutian languages of Oregon and California and includes speakers of 3 languages: Coast Tsimshian, Southern Tsimshian, and Nass-Gitksan, the language of the NISGA'A and the GITKSAN (*see*

Tsimshian woman processing eulachon on the Nass R, 1880s. BC Archives C-07433

FIRST NATIONS LANGUAGES). Aside from that linguistic connotation, Tsimshian usually refers to the first 2 of the groups: the Coast Tsimshian along the lower reaches of the SKEENA R below KITSELAS CANYON, and the Southern Tsimshian along the coast to the south. The ARCHAEOLOGICAL record shows that many of their village sites have been populated for thousands of years. The Tsimshian traditionally inhabited several winter villages that were more or less autonomous units. Each village had its own territory and resource sites and each was represented by hereditary chiefs.

The basic social units were the matrilineal clan and the house. Each clan and each house had its own chief, who controlled resource exploitation and ceremonial privileges. Village chiefs were usually the heads of the highest-ranking houses. Society was divided hierarchically into 4 distinct classes. Summer was devoted to catching and preserving SALMON, the most important food source. Other resources included shellfish, game animals and waterfowl. For the most part winters were spent socializing, feasting and holding POTLATCHES and other ceremonials in the permanent villages, which consisted of large houses constructed of CEDAR planks and timbers (*see* ARCHITECTURE, ABORIGINAL). Housefronts were decorated with crest designs, as were the TOTEM POLES so strongly associated with the Tsimshian (*see* ART, NORTH-

WEST COAST ABORIGINAL).

The Tsimshian became involved in the trade for SEA OTTER pelts beginning with the arrival of the first trading vessel in 1787. The first permanent trading post, FORT SIMPSON, was established on the NASS R in 1831 and resulted in traditional village sites being abandoned as the people relocated near the traders. Trade brought large amounts of wealth into Tsimshian society, encouraging a florescence of artistic production and a destabilization of social structure and rank. Epidemic diseases seriously depleted the population from about 8,500 in 1835 to a low of 3,550 in 1895. (By the late 1990s the population of the Coast and Southern Tsimshian had rebounded to about 10,000.) The activities of missionaries, most notably William DUNCAN, intensified the pace of change, as did the SALMON CANNING industry that flourished at the mouth of the Skeena R after 1876. Many Tsimshian worked seasonally at the canneries.

RESERVES were established in the late 19th century at traditional sites, and villages became bands under the *Indian Act*. The offices of those bands (First Nations) have mainly centralized in PRINCE RUPERT, and FISHING and LOGGING are economic mainstays of the Tsimshian.

TSLEIL WAUTUTH First Nation, pop 350, also called the Burrard band, are Central Coast Salish people (*see* SALISHAN FIRST NATIONS) occupying a 1.1 km² RESERVE on the north shore of BURRARD INLET near the entrance to INDIAN ARM. They are closely related to the neighbouring SQUAMISH Nation. The Tsleil Waututh reserve was the home of Dan GEORGE, actor and writer. Under Chief Leonard George, the people are actively developing the economic potential of their land.

TSUNAMI is a giant wave created by seismic activity below the ocean floor. Travelling in a series, tsunamis spread outward at speeds of several hundred km/h, separated by gaps of 100 to 400 km. At sea they are not high and hardly

Damage caused by tsunami in Port Alberni, 1964. The wave was generated by an earthquake in Alaska. Deni Eagland/Vancouver Sun

betray their presence to ships as they pass. When they arrive on shore they sometimes bring nothing more than a gentle, if substantial, rise and fall in water levels. However, they can arrive in a cresting wall of water as high as a multistorey building and can cause extensive damage and loss of life. The largest recorded tsunami on the BC coast, created by an EARTHQUAKE off southern Alaska, swept up ALBERNI INLET on the night of 27–28 Mar 1964 and crashed into PORT ALBERNI, causing $10 million worth of property damage. Other waves from the same earthquake killed 122 people in Alaska, California and Oregon. A Pacific Tsunami Warning System now enables 24 nations, including Canada, to monitor wave activity.

TULAMEEN is an old townsite on the flats at the junction of Otter Creek and the Tulameen R, 25 km northwest of PRINCETON. Used as a campsite by local FIRST NATIONS people and then by FUR BRIGADES in the 1850s, it was crowded with miners in 1861 during a short-lived GOLD RUSH into the valley. Interest in local mineral deposits was rekindled in the 1880s; in 1901 the provincial government laid out a townsite. Despite initial optimism, the town did not grow to match the ambitions held for it. Tulameen is a Native word meaning "red earth."

TULLY, John Patrick "Jack," oceanographer (b 29 Nov 1906, Brandon, MB; d 19 May 1987, Nanaimo). After graduating from the Univ of Manitoba in 1931 he began his career at the PACIFIC BIOLOGICAL STATION in NANAIMO. He was a founding member of the Pacific Oceanographic Group, which gathered basic information about BC's coast and the north Pacific generally. During WWII he worked on underwater acoustics and sonar. He received a PhD from the Univ of Washington in 1947 and continued to work at the Nanaimo station until his retirement. He was a pioneer in applied OCEANOGRAPHY, especially in ESTUARIES, and studied marine pollution from municipal sewage and pulp mills before pollution research was fashionable. He was also active in international marine science, developing joint studies in the north Pacific with Japan, the US and the former USSR. In 1964 he was elected a fellow of the Royal Society of Canada; in 1985 the government launched the *John P. Tully*, a major oceanographic vessel. *Colin Levings*

TULSEQUAH was a MINING camp 525 km northwest of PRINCE RUPERT, at the confluence of the Tulsequah and TAKU rivers near the Alaska border. GOLD, ZINC, SILVER, COPPER and lead were extracted at a number of sites here from 1925 to the mid-1950s. Controversy erupted in the late 1990s over an attempt to reopen the Tulsequah Chief Mine and build a 160-km road link from ATLIN. *AS*

TUMBLER RIDGE, district municipality, pop 3,775, 115 km southwest of DAWSON CREEK in the foothills of the ROCKY MTS, is a well-planned company town, incorporated on 9 Apr 1981. The name refers to rock slides on a geological formation north of town. It was developed by the BC government to house employees of the huge Quintette and Bullmoose COAL developments nearby, operated by TECK CORP. The 2 open-pit mines produced about 5 million tonnes of coal in 1998. With coal contracts expiring early in the 21st century the community's future is in doubt, especially after WESTCOAST ENERGY INC scrapped plans for a natural gas processing plant and Teck announced the closure of the Quintette mine in 2000. The community is well situated for outdoor recreation, including sport FISHING, hunting, cross country SKIING and snowmobiling. MONKMAN PROVINCIAL PARK, site of the dramatic Kinuseo Falls, is nearby.

TUNA belongs to the family Scombridae (as does MACKEREL) and is found throughout the world's oceans. The tuna that occurs in the largest numbers off the BC coast, albacore tuna

Albacore tuna. *Phil Edgell photo*

(*Thunnus alalunga*), is found offshore erratically during the summer and appears to be part of a single population, known as north Pacific albacore, that migrates seasonally throughout the temperate North Pacific. The albacore resembles the mackerel, though it is much larger and has long, sabre-like pectoral fins and unusually large eyes. The albacore is steely blue on the top and sides, and silvery below. Compared with other tuna, albacore is a small species, growing to 125 cm in length and up to 22 kg in weight. It matures at about 5 years and is thought to live for about 12 years.

The commercial albacore fishery (*see also* FISHING, COMMERCIAL) dates back to the late 1930s. The coastal fishery occurs from July through Oct within 320 km of the coast. Due to the migratory nature of albacore, a Canada–US Albacore Treaty was signed on 26 May 1981. This authorized US fishing vessels to enter certain BC ports and vice versa. Because albacore appear sporadically, the fishery has most often served as a supplemental fishery for SALMON trollers (*see* TROLLING). Up to 370 boats have fished for alba-

core in a given year and recent BC catches are estimated at 3,000 to 4,000 tonnes. Along with the coastal fishery, a handful of Canadian vessels take part in tuna fisheries far out in the Pacific. One of these high-seas fisheries takes place in the North Pacific and follows the migration route of albacore beyond the International Date Line. Another operates in the South Pacific east of Australia from Nov to Apr. Crew members of these 2 fisheries are often at sea for up to 3 months at a time on vessels as small as 10 m in length.

Unlike some other tuna species, albacore do not usually swim with DOLPHINS, and dolphins are not attracted to jigs used by trollers. As a result, commercially harvested and processed albacore meets dolphin-safe labelling requirements. Albacore is the only tuna species that can be canned as "white meat"; all others, such as skipjack and yellowfin, are canned as "light meat."

TUPPER, pop 33, also known as Tupper Creek, is a grain and DAIRY FARMING settlement on Swan Lk near the Alberta border, 30 km south of DAWSON CREEK in the PEACE R district. Ellis Borden opened a store and hotel here about 1920 and the Northern Alberta Rwy arrived in 1931. Many Sudetan German WWII refugees settled nearby at TOMSLAKE in 1939. The creek, and Tupper R north of Swan Lk, were named after Frank Tupper, who surveyed the area.   *AS*

TUPPER, Charles Hibbert, lawyer, politician (b 3 Aug 1855, Amherst, NS; d 30 Mar 1927, Oak Bay). Son of the Conservative prime minister Charles Tupper, he entered politics himself in 1882 as a Conservative MP from Pictou and served in John A. Macdonald's cabinet from 1888 to 1893 as minister of marine and fisheries. He was also minister of justice from 1894 to 1896, and during his father's brief administration in 1896 he was solicitor general. He then left federal politics and moved to VICTORIA to practise law, but he remained prominent in the provincial CONSERVATIVE PARTY. At first he was a supporter of Richard MCBRIDE, but he broke publicly with the premier over railway policy and campaigned actively for the LIBERALS in 1916, in an attempt to defeat McBride's successor, William BOWSER. In the 1920s he joined the PROVINCIAL PARTY movement of disaffected Tories wanting to unseat Bowser, but after its poor showing in the 1924 election, Tupper retired from politics for good.

TURBOT is an alternate name for the arrowtooth FLOUNDER (*Atheresthes stomias*). It is one of

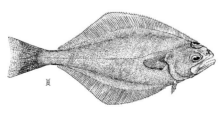

Turbot. *Fisheries & Oceans Canada*

the most abundant FLATFISH landed in commercial trawl GROUNDFISH fisheries (*see* TRAWLING).

TURKEY, wild (*Meleagris gallopavo*), is a large, bare-headed game bird with iridescent plumage and a fan-shaped tail, which the male spreads during courtship. It inhabits wooded areas and feeds on nuts and seeds. Over the years it has been introduced at several locations with mixed success. There are now resident populations on SIDNEY ISLAND and around CRESTON.

TURKEY VULTURE; *see* VULTURE, TURKEY.

TURNER, David, soccer player (b 11 Oct 1903, Edinburgh, Scotland; d 6 Apr 1989, Vancouver). He immigrated with his family to Edmonton in 1914 and moved to VANCOUVER to play SOCCER in 1923. After he and a friend were rejected at a tryout for St Andrew's because they lost the team's new ball in FALSE CRK, he joined the CUMBERLAND United club on VANCOUVER ISLAND and helped it to win the provincial championship in 1925. After a more successful stint with St Andrew's he turned professional, playing first in the US and then for Toronto's Ulster United. When he returned to Vancouver in 1927 from a tour of New Zealand with the Canadian national team he was met by businessman Fred HUME, who arranged for him to be educated at UBC while playing for Hume's NEW WESTMINSTER Royals. Turner led the Royals to an unprecedented 4 Canadian championships before retiring in 1936 to join the BC civil service, in which he was best known for serving as the deputy minister of sport and recreation. He was selected as Canada's outstanding soccer player of the first half-century by the Canadian Press news agency, inducted into the Canadian Sports Hall of Fame in 1951 and named to the BC SPORTS HALL OF FAME in 1966.   *SW*

TURNER, John Herbert, businessman, politician, premier 4 Mar 1895–8 Aug 1898 (b 7 May 1834, Claydon, England; d 9 Dec 1923, Richmond, England). He immigrated to Atlantic Canada in 1856 and settled in Charlottetown, PEI, where he became a successful merchant. He moved to VICTORIA in 1862, where he opened a wholesale business, eventually expanding into SALMON CANNING and insurance and making a substantial fortune. Turner's political career began in 1876 when he won election as a city alderman. After serving as mayor from 1879 to 1881 he retired briefly from politics, but was elected to the provincial legislature in 1886 and remained a member for 16 years. He was finance minister in the governments of 3 premiers during 1887–95 before taking over as PREMIER himself from Theodore DAVIE. A man of affable charm and free-spending policies, Turner had presided as finance minister over a rapid expansion of the provincial debt and this did not change when he became premier. His government was marked by cronyism and generous subsidies to industrialists. Following the 1898 election Lt Gov T.R. MCINNES decided Turner did not have enough support in the legislature to

J.H. Turner, premier of BC 1895–98, pictured here in 1895. BC Archives B-02260

form a government and dismissed him. Turner became leader of the opposition and then minister of finance again in 1900–01, when James DUNSMUIR became premier. In Sept 1901 Turner became BC's first agent general in London, a position he held until his retirement in 1915.

TURNER, John Napier, lawyer, prime minister of Canada 30 June–17 Sept 1984 (b 7 June 1929, Richmond, England). He grew up in Ottawa and at the end of WWII moved west to VANCOUVER with his mother and stepfather, Frank ROSS, a future LT GOV. He attended UBC, where he won a Rhodes scholarship. After studies in Europe he began practising law in Montreal. His political career began with his election as a Liberal to the House of Commons in 1962, and he served in a variety of cabinet posts in the governments of Lester Pearson and Pierre Trudeau. Most prominently he was minister of justice during the terrorist crisis in Quebec in 1970. In 1984 he ran successfully for the leadership of the Liberal Party after Pierre Trudeau's retirement, becoming prime minister on 30 June. He held the job for less than 3 months, as the Liberals were defeated in a Sept election. In that election Turner returned to BC to run for the Vancouver–Quadra seat, which he won. He held the seat as leader of the opposition until 1990 and, subsequently, as a backbencher until his retirement in 1993. Turner was one of 3 Canadian prime ministers to represent a BC constituency (even though in his case he was not prime minister while he held the Vancouver seat)—the other 2 being John A. Macdonald and Kim CAMPBELL—but in fact he spent most of his legal and political career in eastern Canada.

TURNER, Michael, writer (b 1962, N Vancouver). As a teenager he spent his summers working in a fish cannery on the SKEENA R (*see* SALMON CANNING) and his first book, *Company Town* (1992), was a collection of poetic narratives that drew on this experience. After graduating from the UNIV OF VICTORIA he played for 7

years with a hillbilly-punk band, the Hard Rock Miners, which provided material for his second book, *Hard Core Logo* (1993). He won a Genie Award for co-writing 6 original songs for the movie version of *Hard Core Logo*. He has published another poetry collection, *Kingsway* (1995), and 2 novels, *American Whiskey Bar* (1997) and *The Pornographer's Poem* (1999) which won the BC BOOK PRIZE for fiction. He lives in VANCOUVER.

TURNER, Nancy J. (Chapman), ethnobotanist (b 7 Nov 1947, Berkeley, CA). When she moved to VICTORIA with her family at age 5, she was already interested in the outdoors; she joined the Victoria Junior Natural History Society at age 9. She received a BSc degree in biology from the UNIV OF VICTORIA in 1969 and a PhD in botany from UBC in 1974. Her work has focussed on ethnobotanical and environmental knowledge of indigenous peoples of BC, with whom she works closely. She served on the CLAYOQUOT SOUND Scientific Panel on Sustainable Forestry from 1993–95. In 1997 she was awarded the Richard Evans Schultes Award in Ethnobotany from the Healing Forest Conservancy in Washington, DC. She received the first Research Excellence Award of the Faculty of Social Sciences of the Univ of Victoria in 1999. That year she also became a member of the ORDER OF BC and was elected as a Fellow of the Royal Society of Canada. She is past president of the Society of Ethnobiology, and a member of the American Botanical Council and the Advisory Committee of the Centre for the Nutrition and Environment of Indigenous Peoples at McGill Univ. Turner is a prolific writer who has published numerous scientific and popular books, including a series of ROYAL BC MUSEUM publications on ethnobotanies of BC FIRST NATIONS and on edible plants. She is married to the historian Robert D. TURNER. She is a professor in the School of Environmental Studies at the Univ of Victoria.

Maggie Paquet

TURNER, Robert, curator, historian, writer (b 1947). Best known for his authoritative books on historic forms of transportation in BC, he became curator emeritus at the ROYAL BC MUSEUM in VICTORIA after having been their chief of historical collections for many years. He was project historian for the SS MOYIE National Historic Site at KASLO and consulted for many other museums, including the Canadian Museum of Civilization, the Prince George Railway and Forestry Museum, the Dawson City Museum and the Canadian Museum of Rail Travel. His books include *Logging by Rail: The BC Story* (1990), *West of the Great Divide: An Illustrated History of the Canadian Pacific Railway in BC* (1987), *Sternwheelers & Steam Tugs: An Illustrated History of the CPR's BC Lake and River Service* (1984), *The Pacific Empresses: An Illustrated History of the CPR's Trans-Pacific Ocean Liners* (1981) and *The Pacific Princesses: An Illustrated History of the Canadian Pacific's Fleet on the Northwest Coast* (1984).

TURNER LAKES, sometimes known as Hunlen Lakes, are a chain of small lakes surrounded by mountains in southern TWEEDSMUIR PROVINCIAL PARK. Linked by Hunlen Creek, the chain includes Turner, Junker, Widgeon, Kidney, Cutthroat and Vista lakes. They drain via the creek over Hunlen Falls (253 m), the third-highest WATERFALL in BC, into the ATNARKO R, a BC HERITAGE RIVER. They are known for wilderness canoeing and sport FISHING, much of it based at Tweedsmuir Wilderness Camp on Turner Lk.

TURTLE is a small reptile with a soft body encased in a hard, protective shell into which it retracts when threatened. Instead of teeth it possesses a pointed beak to tear at its food. The female lays eggs in a small depression dug in the

Western painted turtle. Ken Bowen photo

ground. During the winter turtles hibernate; the freshwater species native to BC are seen most often in warm weather basking in the sun. By far the most common species in BC is the painted turtle (*Chrysemys picta*), found in lakes, ponds and streams across the southern part of the province, especially in the OKANAGAN VALLEY and KOOTENAY region. Western pond turtles (*Clemmys marmorata*), formerly rare residents of the Lower Mainland, are now completely gone from the area. A sea-going species, the leatherback (*Dermochelys coriacea*), visits the coast but does not breed in the province.

TUSKSHELL, also known as toothshell or dentalum, is an elusive marine MOLLUSC belonging to the class Scaphopoda. The name refers to the curved, tapered shell that resembles a miniature elephant tusk. Open at both ends, it burrows into the ocean floor and lives almost its entire life in the sand, where it uses small tentacles to direct food to its mouth. It is white in colour and grows to 2–5 cm in length. There are 500 species worldwide but only 2 commonly occur in BC, the wampum tuskshell (*Antalis pretiosum*), which was harvested by FIRST NATIONS, particularly the NUU-CHAH-NULTH (Nootka) on the west coast of VANCOUVER ISLAND, and used for ornamentation and as a trade item; and the larger western straight tuskshell (*Rhabdus rectius*).

Tweedsmuir Provincial Park. Keith Thirkell photo

TWEEDSMUIR PROVINCIAL PARK, 9,742.46 km², in west-central BC between BELLA COOLA and ANAHIM Lake, is the largest park in the province. Established in 1938, it is named for Gov Gen John Buchan, Baron Tweedsmuir, who visited the area in 1937. Diverse landscapes feature the towering COAST MTS on its western side, the RAINBOW RANGE on its southeastern side, excellent sport FISHING lakes, rolling forested plateaus and steep-walled valleys. The park also features Hunlen Falls, the third-highest WATERFALL in BC with its vertical drop of 253 m. Wildlife of particular interest includes black BEARS, grizzly bears, woodland CARIBOU, MOUNTAIN GOATS and trumpeter SWANS, which overwinter on LONESOME LAKE. The southern part of the park is accessible from Hwy 20 out of WILLIAMS LAKE; the more isolated northern section is reached via OOTSA and Whitesail lakes. Alexander MACKENZIE passed through the park on his overland excursion to the Pacific in 1793; his route is commemorated in the ALEXANDER MACKENZIE HERITAGE TRAIL, which runs across the southern half of the park. Whether to fish STEELHEAD on the DEAN R, photograph the profusion of WILDFLOWERS, hike the heritage TRAILS or ride horseback through the mountain meadows, visitors make this park one of the most popular wilderness recreation areas in the province.

TWIGG, Alan, critic, publisher (b 1952, Vancouver). As BC's most devoted literary journalist he has written numerous books, including *For Openers: Conversations with 24 Canadian Writers* (1981), *Hubert Evans* (1985), *Vancouver and Its Writers* (1986), and *Twigg's Directory of 1001 BC Writers* (1992). In 1986 he also published the first biography of Premier Bill VANDER ZALM. Twigg is the founding publisher of *BC BookWorld*, Canada's most widely read literary periodical, and he co-founded the BC BOOK PRIZES. In 2000 he became the inaugural winner

Alan Twigg, publisher of BC BookWorld.
Barry Peterson & Blaise Enright-Peterson

of the Gray Campbell Distinguished Service Award, given annually by the BC BOOK PUBLISHING community.

TWIN ISLANDS are 2 small islets, about 80 ha in area when they are joined at low tide, located north of POWELL RIVER near the entrance to DESOLATION SOUND. They were owned from 1961 by Max Markgraf von Baden, a German aristocrat and nephew of Prince Philip. The Prince and Queen Elizabeth stayed at the island's palatial log lodge on 2 occasions. The heavily timbered islands were sold in 1997 and the new owner began LOGGING them. A subsequent sale halted the process.

TWO RIVERS POLICY was PREMIER W.A.C. BENNETT's program of massive HYDROELECTRIC development on the COLUMBIA and PEACE rivers in the 1960s. Bennett wanted new sources of electricity to power industrial development in the province, so he nationalized the BC ELECTRIC RWY CO, created a new CROWN CORPORATION, BC HYDRO, and concluded the COLUMBIA RIVER TREATY, all elements of his "two river" strategy. Dam construction on the rivers—including the BENNETT DAM (1968) on the Peace R and the KEENLEYSIDE (1968), DUNCAN (1967) and MICA (1976) dams on the Columbia R—resulted in a five-fold increase in BC's electrical capacity. More than 80% of BC Hydro's total annual output of electricity is now generated at stations on these 2 rivers. Critics of the policy point to its long-term costs in terms of wildlife habitat degradation and destruction of fish stocks in the Columbia R (*see* ENVIRONMENTAL MOVEMENT).

TYEE, a CHINOOK JARGON word meaning "chief," is the name applied to chinook SALMON weighing more than 13.5 kg. This tradition was inaugurated by the Tyee Club of BC, formed by a group of CAMPBELL RIVER sport fishers in 1924. To be eligible for membership in the club, a fisher has to catch one of the giant salmon using light tackle and a rowboat. The club record, a 32-kg monster, was registered in 1968. *See also* FISHING, SPORT.

TYNEHEAD, originally Tinehead, was an AGRICULTURAL community 13 km southeast of NEW WESTMINSTER in SURREY. It was first known as Bothwell Settlement after the 3 Bothwell brothers, who arrived in the 1880s, but was renamed after Tyne, their Scottish home. LOGGING was important until about 1910. The area is the site of a SALMON hatchery and Surrey's largest regional park.   AS

TYNEMOUTH, SS, was one of 3 "bride ships" carrying unmarried girls and young women from England to settle in BC during 1862–63. The immigration was sponsored by Anglican and women's groups in England in an attempt to elevate the moral tone of the colony by providing European women for marriage. It was also seen as an opportunity for some women to better themselves. The *Tynemouth*, carrying 60 such women among other immigrants, arrived at ESQUIMALT on 17 Sept 1862. Most of the women became domestic servants and governesses, and most did eventually marry.

TZUHALEM, a former VANCOUVER ISLAND farming settlement, now mostly residential, is on the eastern outskirts of DUNCAN and the COWICHAN First Nation reserve. Nearby Mt Tzuhalem was named after a famous Cowichan war chief.   AS

U

UBC PRESS is the BOOK PUBLISHING imprint of the UNIV OF BC. Established in 1971 to publish scholarly books, it grew to become the third-largest university press in Canada, publishing about 30 new non-fiction titles annually. Acknowledged as a leading publisher of books on aboriginal studies, FORESTRY and the FOREST INDUSTRY, the press also publishes in the areas of history, political science, PACIFIC RIM affairs and ENVIRONMENTAL studies. Along with specialist studies, the press publishes textbooks and some general interest books for a broader audience.

UCHUCK ("healing waters") is the name of a series of supply boats that have operated on the west coast of VANCOUVER ISLAND since about 1930. The original *Uchuck* was built in 1928 and used as a cannery tender, then as a freight vessel in BARKLEY SOUND. Capt Richard Porritt built the *Uchuck No 1* in 1941, using it to provide regular passenger and freight service between PORT

ALBERNI and Barkley Sound. Esson Young and George McCandless took over the service in 1946, when they purchased the vessel and formed the Barkley Sound Transportation Co. In 1948 they bought a retired W VANCOUVER ferry, rebuilt it, renamed it *Uchuck II* and put it to work. *Uchuck III*, a converted minesweeper, was added in 1955. As business in Barkley Sound declined with the opening of direct road access to the West Coast, the company shifted operations north to NOOTKA SOUND and changed its name to Nootka Sound Service in 1960. *Uchuck II* was sold in 1966 (*Uchuck No 1* had already been sold in 1956), but in 1999 *Uchuck III* was still operating out of GOLD RIVER, taking freight and passengers to various coastal destinations.

UCLUELET, village, pop 1,658, is a commercial fishing and tourist community located in a deep harbour on the west coast of VANCOUVER ISLAND, at the entrance to BARKLEY SOUND in PACIFIC RIM

NATIONAL PARK RESERVE. The Ucluelet nation (the word means "people with a safe landing place") are a NUU-CHAH-NULTH group. The first white settler, Capt Charles Stuart, established a store near here in 1860. In 1912–13, a LIGHTHOUSE was built at Amphitrite Pt, site of the tragic 1905 wreck of the *Pass of Melfort*, in which 35 people drowned. LOGGING, commercial FISHING and AQUACULTURE are important to the local economy, and TOURISM has boomed since the creation of the park reserve in 1970. In the spring, thousands of visitors are attracted by the annual offshore migration of gray WHALES. On 6 Oct 1967 Ucluelet set a single-day precipitation record for Canada—489.2 mm of rain fell. The village incorporated on 26 Feb 1952.

UKRAINIANS began arriving in BC at the end of the 19th century, part of the huge migration from eastern Europe into western Canada. Most Ukrainians preferred to settle on the prairies, where the Canadian government was successfully enticing immigrants from the Austro-Hungarian Empire with offers of "free land," but some moved on to BC to find work in the MINING, LOGGING and railway construction camps. In BC Ukrainians tended toward heavy labour in industrial and urban areas such as the CROWSNEST PASS, NANAIMO, POWELL RIVER, BRITANNIA MINES and VANCOUVER. Economic conditions led many Ukrainian newcomers to support the socialist labour movement and the Society of Ukrainian Workers and Farmers, later the Association of United Ukrainian Canadians, was created in response to the harsh labour climate. During WWI many Ukrainian-Canadians were interned as enemy aliens; 8 of these internment camps were located in BC at EDGEWOOD, FERNIE, FIELD, Mara Lake, Monashee, Nanaimo, REVELSTOKE and VERNON.

Following the Russian Revolution, Ukraine became a Soviet Republic in 1920 under Russian control. This development split the Ukrainian diaspora into pro-Soviet and anti-Soviet groups. Those supporting a Ukraine free of foreign control eventually formed the Ukrainian Canadian Committee (UCC), which included the Ukrainian National Federation and other associations affiliated with the Ukrainian Orthodox and Ukrainian Catholic Churches. During the 1930s many rural Ukrainians moved to BC from the drought-parched prairies; then, following WWII, a large influx of Ukrainian immigrants from German labour camps (called "DPs," or displaced persons, by many Canadians) strengthened the UCC and gave renewed vigour to its organizations. Regardless of political differences within the community, it has been important for all Ukrainian Canadians to show that their culture survived the oppression of foreign domination. A traditional Ukrainian event each March is the celebration of the birth of Taras Shevchenko, Ukraine's national poet. The first Taras Shevchenko Concert in BC was held in the mining town of HOSMER in 1909. Singing, dancing, drama and craft presentations have become traditional events across the province. A "Ukrainian" float was a regular feature of the

Ucluelet Harbour. Len Mackave photo

PACIFIC NATIONAL EXHIBITION parades from the 1930s to the 1960s, and a successful urban Ukrainian Festival—the only one of its kind in Canada—was held in Vancouver from 1979 to 1985. To celebrate 100 years of the Ukrainian presence in Canada, the Ukrainian Canadian Congress, BC Provincial Council, organized a Ukrainian Canadian Pavilion at the PNE in 1992 that was toured by over 50,000 people.

After the independence of Ukraine in 1991 another wave of immigrants came to BC. In contrast to earlier immigrants, these people arrived from urban centres with professional skills. The Vancouver branch of Ukrainian Canadian Social Services provides assistance to these newcomers. The 1996 census indicated that 168,765 people of Ukrainian origin live in BC. There are cultural centres throughout the province, associations affiliated with the Ukrainian Catholic and Ukrainian Orthodox Churches, branches of the Ukrainian Canadian Congress, the Association of United Ukrainian Canadians and several other organizations that continue to provide valuable services to their members and proudly exhibit their heritage to other British Columbians.

ULRICH, Sharon "Shari," singer/songwriter (b 17 Oct 1951, San Rafael, CA). A Juno Award-winner who is recognized for her catchy melodies and thoughtful lyrics, she achieved professional success after she immigrated to BC in 1972. Two years later, Ulrich joined Rick Scott and Joe Mock in The Pied Pumkin String Ensemble and sang Mock's "Flying," the song for which she became best known. In 1976 she joined the Hometown Band, which performed and recorded with VALDY, and won the 1978 Juno Award for best new band. Her first solo album, *Long Nights*, appeared in 1980 and her second album, *One Step Ahead*, earned her the 1982 Juno for most promising female artist. From 1989 she performed regularly and recorded as a member of UHF, an acoustic trio with Bill Henderson, a former CHILLIWACK member, and Roy FORBES. In the 1990s Ulrich ventured into television as a host, composer and producer. In 1998 she participated in a Pied Pumkin reunion and released her sixth solo album, *The View From Here*. See also SOUND RECORDING INDUSTRY. *Mike Harling*

UNION BAY, pop 615, on BAYNES SOUND south of COURTENAY on VANCOUVER ISLAND, was the site of a large deep-sea loading dock constructed in 1889 by the DUNSMUIR's Union Colliery Co. It was the terminus for an 18-km rail line from the company's coal mines at CUMBERLAND, and had coke ovens, a brickyard and the largest wharf in BC. The mines went into decline after WWII and the wharf complex was demolished in 1966. Several buildings from the original settlement have been restored.

UNION CLUB, founded in 1879 in VICTORIA, was the first gentlemen's club west of Winnipeg. Its name refers to its original purpose, which was to support federation with Canada at a time when the government was threatening secession

Shari Ulrich, singer/songwriter. Victor Dezso photo

if the transcontinental railway was not built. The first president was Judge Matthew Baillie BEGBIE and club members continue to be influential in political affairs. The present club building on Gordon St was built in 1912. It began accepting women as full members in 1994.

UNION OF BC INDIAN CHIEFS, a leading aboriginal political organization, was formed in 1969 by delegates from about 140 aboriginal FIRST NATIONS (then called bands) meeting in KAMLOOPS. The organization united status Indians in the wake of the federal government's 1969 White Paper, which aboriginal people from coast to coast opposed as a denial of ABORIGINAL RIGHTS. The UBCIC's main objective was to pursue a land claims settlement in BC. The organization was run by committee until it chose its first president, George MANUEL, in 1979. He was followed by his son Robert Manuel

(1981–83), Saul Terry (1983–98) and Stewart Phillip. The UBCIC has a resource centre, a research department and a bookstore at its VANCOUVER offices.

UNION OF ELECTORS was a short-lived faction of SOCIAL CREDIT adherents led by Maj A.H. Jukes, head of the BC branch of the Social Credit Assoc. The Union ran 12 candidates in the 1949 provincial election, not one of whom won. It subsequently gave way to the SOCIAL CREDIT LEAGUE as the dominant voice of Social Credit in BC.

UNION STEAMSHIP CO was a shipping line established in 1889 to provide freight and passenger service to the remote LOGGING camps, SALMON CANNERIES and small settlements springing up along the coast. Its first vessel, the 55-m steam yacht *Cutch*, originally owned by an Indian maharajah, began sailing to NANAIMO the next year. By the spring of 1892 the company had assembled 3 steel vessels in VANCOUVER's Coal Harbour—*Coquitlam*, *Comox* and *Capilano*—and had inaugurated its coastal "logging camp run." Among the most familiar ships to follow were the *CASSIAR*, which made the logging run twice weekly from 1901 to 1923, the *CAMOSUN*, which serviced coastal canneries all the way to PRINCE RUPERT from 1906 to 1935, the *CHELOHSIN* and the *CARDENA*. Day excursions became an important part of the company's business as well, especially after 1920, when it purchased a resort complex on BOWEN ISLAND. From 1924 to 1953 the company's vessel *LADY ALEXANDRA* carried thousands of passengers each summer on day excursions and dance cruises. At its peak the company's ships, with their familiar red and black funnels, served more than 200 ports of call, providing for many the only link with the outside world. By the 1950s, however, coastal shipping faced stiff competition from other modes of transportation—chiefly, the automobile

Union Steamship Co dock in Vancouver, 1935. Every ship in the fleet was in port because of a strike. Leonard Frank CVA Wat.P83

and the airplane—and in 1959 Union Steamship was sold to a rival company, NORTHLAND NAVIGATION. One of its former vessels, LADY ROSE, remains in service on the west coast of VANCOUVER ISLAND.

UNITARIAN CHURCH was formed by liberal-thinking Christians who drifted away from mainstream Protestant churches during the 18th and 19th centuries. The main message of Unitarianism is one of faith in the unity of God and the unity of all human beings. Unitarians believe that there is truth in all religions and that all beliefs can be united in spirit if not in doctrine. They held their first public services in BC in VICTORIA in 1871 under the guidance of visiting American minister John Kimball; however, plans to establish a church faltered and the movement was not revived in BC until 1909 when a VANCOUVER schoolteacher, Albert Pino, decided to quit his job and devote himself to promoting Unitarianism. He began services in Vancouver and Victoria, and by 1913 churches had been built in both cities. During the 1920s the church faltered again, though the Vancouver congregation managed to survive under the leadership of Ada Tonkin, Canada's first female Unitarian minister, who raised its profile by organizing free public forums on social and political issues. Since WWII, Unitarianism has grown in popularity and fellowships have been established throughout the province. In 1991 there were 5,115 Unitarians in BC. *Dianne Mackay*

UNITED CHURCH of Canada was formed in 1925 when the METHODIST CHURCH of Canada, the Congregational Union of Canada and two-thirds of the PRESBYTERIAN CHURCH in Canada, together with the Union Churches of Western Canada, joined to form the largest Protestant Christian church in the country. In the 1991 census, 420,800 people living in BC identified the United Church as their religious preference.

The governance of the United Church is structured through an ascending hierarchy of levels, or courts. Members are organized into largely self-governing worshipping communities under the supervision of a minister normally chosen by the congregation. Congregations with church buildings are referred to as preaching places. Particularly in rural areas, up to 5 congregations may be served by a single minister in a pastoral charge. Preaching places and pastoral charges are grouped by geographic region into presbyteries, which elect lay members and members of the order of ministry to be responsible for overseeing the care and well-being of congregations. In turn, presbyteries are grouped into conferences, whose membership is made up of all members of presbyteries. Conferences are responsible for regional administration. They appoint ministers for the conference, and are responsible for overseeing the well-being of presbyteries. Conferences elect representatives, or commissioners, to the national General Council, which is charged with making policy decisions for the church as a whole. In BC in 1999, 211 pastoral charges and 266 preaching places were

served by 177 United Church ministers and organized into 10 presbyteries that form the BC conference. The presbyteries include Cariboo (PRINCE GEORGE to SMITHERS, MACKENZIE and 100 MILE HOUSE), Comox–Nanaimo (VANCOUVER ISLAND north of NANAIMO and POWELL RIVER), Fraser (DELTA to HOPE and AGASSIZ to WHITE ROCK), Kamloops–Okanagan (LILLOOET to KAMLOOPS, GOLDEN to OSOYOOS to PRINCETON), Kootenay (ROCK CREEK to the Alberta border, TRAIL, NELSON, CRANBROOK), Prince Rupert (north coast); Vancouver–Burrard (north of 16th Avenue in VANCOUVER, N and W VANCOUVER, to SQUAMISH and WHISTLER), Vancouver–South (south of 16th Avenue to TSAWWASSEN); Victoria (southern VANCOUVER ISLAND to DUNCAN, and the GULF ISLANDS); and Westminster (BURNABY, NEW WESTMINSTER, COQUITLAM and MAPLE RIDGE).

The particular geographic and demographic challenges posed by BC in the 19th century encouraged many Presbyterian, Methodist and Congregational missionaries and ministers to work co-operatively by sharing churches and preaching places. This co-operative approach to ministry, and a developing shared theology of social reform known as the Social Gospel, was formalized when the national churches articulated a draft Basis of Union in 1908. The strains of WWI further encouraged congregations to share resources through the formation of local union churches. In 1925, 121 Presbyterian pastoral charges, 166 Methodist preaching points, 4 Congregational churches, and 10 local union churches joined in organic union as the BC conference of the United Church. Theological education for the new denomination was provided by Union College, which opened in 1927 on the UBC campus. The immediate challenges faced by the conference included negotiating the amalgamation of churches and the redeployment of ministers. The Depression of the 1930s brought a stronger focus on social outreach and social justice issues. Many United Church ministers and lay men and women were active in providing relief for the unemployed and seeking legislated change as CCF candidates for public office. At union the church inherited extensive mission-

ary work that served remote FISHING and MINING settlements. An active marine mission provided religious services to isolated LOGGING camps and coastal communities. Medical missions had long served northern BC, and lay and ordained missionaries worked with aboriginal people on RESERVES, in urban settings and at the Alberni RESIDENTIAL SCHOOL on Vancouver Island. Active missions to CHINESE and JAPANESE workers drew on the language skills of lay and ordained Chinese and Japanese missionaries and women church workers. During WWII United Church ministers, lay leaders and workers spoke out against the internment of Japanese Canadians. Workers from the Women's Missionary Society accompanied Japanese families into the internment camps and assumed responsibility for education at NEW DENVER, Lemon Creek and TASHME (*see* JAPANESE, RELOCATION OF). The post-war period saw a rapid expansion of new communities throughout the province and the church struggled to serve the rapidly growing population and the demand for new churches. New Christian education programs were instituted and a Christian Leadership Training School opened at NARAMATA in 1947 to provide leadership education for young men and women. An air mission that paralleled the work of the marine missions was established in 1960 to serve missionaries travelling to coastal communities. At the start of the 21st century the United Church faces a declining membership in an increasingly secular society. However, it continues to speak out on major social issues. Theologically liberal, the church has supported a variety of controversial positions, bringing peace and social justice issues to the attention of the wider public and supporting international development work in partnership with indigenous and local churches. *Gail Edwards*

UNITED FARMERS OF BC (UFBC) was an organization formed in Feb 1917 to work for agricultural improvements. Members consistently opposed direct political involvement, and the UFBC never forged the alliance with labour that enabled United Farmers parties to form governments elsewhere in Canada. In 1923 the organization was drawn into politics in support of the short-lived PROVINCIAL PARTY. After its disastrous showing in the 1924 election, the UFBC lost credibility; 4 years later it disbanded. *See also* AGRICULTURE.

UNITED FISHERMEN AND ALLIED WORKERS' UNION (UFAWU) originated in an organizing drive in the early 1940s that unified a number of smaller fishery unions, leaving 2 remaining unions: the United Fishermen's Federal Union (UFFU) and the Fish Cannery, Reduction Plant and Allied Workers' Union. In 1945 these two organizations voted to join forces, creating the UFAWU. UFFU president George Miller became the first president; the cannery workers' union president, Alex Gordon, was elected secretary-treasurer. The new union's early work focussed on establishing a per pound price for SALMON and a uniform coast-wide price

UNITED CHURCH MEMBERS IN BC		
Year	Members	% of BC Population
1881	5,042	10.2
1891	15,440	15.7
1901	26,541	14.9
1911	55,308	14.1
1921	67,590	12.9
1931	166,233	23.9
1941	201,357	24.6
1951	341,914	29.3
1961	504,317	31.0
1971	537,565	24.6
1981	548,360	20.2
1991	420,755	12.8

for sockeye. In the fish packing plants the union fought for equal pay rates for women and an 8-hour day with overtime provisions. Concerned about threats to habitat conservation, in 1957 the UFAWU joined a successful campaign against the proposed Moran Dam on the main stem of the FRASER R. During the 1950s and 1960s the union worked to organize sections of the fishing industry where no contract conditions existed, winning contracts for HALIBUT, HERRING and trawl fishers. Many hard-fought strikes won advances for fish industry workers and the union took part in repeated battles with the federal government over changes to fishing vessel licensing and fleet reduction programs. The UFAWU, led by president Jack Nichol, also played a key role in the fight for a fair PACIFIC SALMON TREATY between Canada and the US. In the late 1990s the union had more than 4,000 members: it was the largest single organization of fishers and fish plant workers on the BC Coast and the only fishing organization that bargained for fish prices with the major fish processing companies. In 1996 the UFAWU membership voted to merge with the Canadian Auto Workers, Canada's largest private sector union, and unionized fishing industry workers from the Atlantic, the Great Lakes and the Pacific joined under one union umbrella. *See also* FISHING, COMMERCIAL; LABOUR MOVEMENT. *David Lane*

UNIVERSITY ENDOWMENT LANDS, pop 6,833, occupy the end of the Point Grey peninsula along the western edge of VANCOUVER. They contain the campus of UBC, an upscale residential suburb known as University Hill, and Pacific Spirit Regional Park. The area underwent extensive LOGGING from the 1860s until it was chosen as the site for a provincial university in 1910. The government set aside 11.74 km² of land at the proposed site to be subdivided and used to underwrite the costs of the university, which opened in 1925. However, these ambitious plans did not work out and during the 1930s the university returned control of the lands to the province. Part of the area was developed for housing, part accommodated the university and the rest remained undeveloped forest. In 1988 the province transferred 7.65 km² of this land to the GREATER VANCOUVER REGIONAL DISTRICT as Pacific Spirit Park. The area's 2 public schools are administered by the Vancouver School Board; otherwise the area is administered directly by the province without any municipal government. In a 1995 referendum, residents voted against becoming a separate municipality.

UNIVERSITY OF BRITISH COLUMBIA (UBC) originated in 1908 with the passage of provincial legislation authorizing creation of a provincial university. The first land was set aside at the proposed site in Point Grey, in VANCOUVER, in 1910 (*see* UNIVERSITY ENDOWMENT LANDS); construction began in 1914, but all progress ceased with the outbreak of WWI that summer. Meanwhile the Vancouver School Board and McGill Univ in Montreal had collaborated to offer undergraduate courses at Vancouver High School since

Students crowding on girders of the unfinished science building at the Pt Grey site of UBC, 1922. They organized the "Great Trek" to encourage the provincial government to proceed with construction of the university. UBC 1.1/1315

Clock tower and main library building at UBC.

1898. This arrangement was formalized as McGill Univ College, which moved into 2 buildings next door to the Vancouver General Hospital in 1912. In 1915 this institution was renamed UBC. Relocation from the so-called "Fairview Shacks" to the Point Grey site was delayed by the war, then by government stalling. On 28 Oct 1922 students and their supporters held a huge downtown rally, then marched to the Point Grey site to pressure the government to act. This "Great Trek" persuaded the province to move ahead with construction and in 1925 classes began at the present site. Expansion has been constant ever since, with the additions of faculties of law (1945), graduate studies (1948), medicine (1950), forestry (1951), education (1956) and commerce (1957). Altogether there are 12 faculties, 9 schools and 11 institutes and research centres. The MUSEUM OF ANTHROPOLOGY, opened in 1976, is a showcase of Northwest Coast aboriginal culture (*see* ART, NORTHWEST COAST ABORIGINAL; FIRST NATIONS), and the campus is home to a variety of scientific research

facilities. In 1999 there were 55,286 students enrolled and 1,800 full-time faculty. Presidents have been: Frank WESBROOK (1913–18), Leonard Klinck (1919–44), Norman MACKENZIE (1944–62), John B. MacDonald (1962–67), Walter Gage (1967–May 1968; Feb 1969–75); Kenneth Hare (June 1968–Jan 1969), Douglas Kenny (1975–83), K. George Pederson (1983–Mar 1985), Robert H.T. Smith (Mar–Nov 1985), David Strangway (Nov 1985–97), and Martha C. Piper (1997–present).

UNIVERSITY OF BC BOTANICAL GARDEN is a 32-ha collection of trees, shrubs and flowers on the grounds of the UBC campus in VANCOUVER. There are more than 10,000 different plants, including Canada's largest collection of RHODODENDRONS. Open to the public, the grounds are divided into 8 separate gardens, each featuring different kinds of plants or plants from different parts of the world. The BC Native Garden, for example, contains PLANTS native to the province and the Alpine Garden is the largest of its type in N America. The Garden carries out extensive botanical research and development programs.

The Univ of BC women's basketball team, en route to the 1930 world championship.
Courtesy Fred Hume/UBC Athletic Dept

UNIVERSITY OF BC WOMEN'S BASKETBALL TEAM

won the world championship in 1930. After taking the 1929–30 VANCOUVER and District Women's Basketball Championship, the team—captain Claire Menton, Rettie Tingley, Jean Whyte, Rene Harris, Mary Campbell, Lois Tourtelotte, Thelma Mahon, Marian Shelly, Florence Carlisle and coach Jack Barberie—narrowly lost to Percy Page's famed Edmonton Grads at the western Canadian championships. However, Edmonton declined to represent N America at the 1930 Women's Olympiad World Championships in Prague and UBC was chosen as the continent's next-best team. After a fundraising campaign brought in $5,500, the team left for Czechoslovakia where it faced European champion France in a single-game final on 8 Sept 1930. In front of 10,000 fans UBC overcame an unfamiliar rules system, a biased referee who spoke no English and an unusual oversized cinder court to win the championship 18-14. The women returned to Vancouver to a huge welcoming crowd at the train station and a reception at the Hotel Vancouver. The trophy is still on display at UBC and the team has been inducted into the UBC Sports Hall of Fame and the BC SPORTS HALL OF FAME.   *SW*

Campus of the Univ of Northern BC.
Courtesy UNBC

began in 1992 and in Aug 1994 Queen Elizabeth presided at the ceremonial opening. Full classes for 1,400 students began in Sept 1994 and by 2000 the university had an enrolment of 3,200. The main campus sits on Cranbrook Hill overlooking the city; there are satellite campuses in PRINCE RUPERT, QUESNEL, FORT ST JOHN and New Aiyansh (*see* GITLAKDAMIKS).

UNIVERSITY OF VICTORIA

(UVic) originated as Victoria College in 1903 offering first-year university courses in affiliation with Montreal's McGill Univ. When UBC began offering courses in VANCOUVER in 1915, the Victoria school closed temporarily; in 1920 it reopened as an affiliate of UBC. It was located in the CRAIGDARROCH mansion from 1921 to 1946, then in the Victoria Normal School. Originally a 2-year college, it expanded to a full 4-year institution in 1961. It

Aerial view of the Univ of Victoria.
UVic Photo Services

UNIVERSITY OF NORTHERN BC

originated in 1990 with the passage of provincial legislation authorizing a university at PRINCE GEORGE. The first president was Geoffrey Weller (1991–95); he was succeeded by George Pedersen (June 1995–Oct 1995) and then Charles Jago (since Oct 1995). Construction of the main campus

was officially proclaimed a university in 1963 and moved to its present location on the site of the old GORDON HEAD Army Camp. Dr Malcolm Taylor was the university's first president. In 2000 UVic had an enrolment of about 17,000 students.

UPHILL, Thomas Aubert, politician (b 26 June 1874, Radstock, England; d 22 Feb 1962, Fernie). At his death he was best known for having fought and won more provincial elections than anyone in Canadian history. He served as the Independent–Labour MLA for FERNIE from 1920 to 1960, watching the turnover of 7 provincial PREMIERS and 8 LT GOVS. After working in the Welsh coal mines as a child, then serving in the Boer War, Uphill came to Canada in 1906. He became secretary of the Fernie local of the miners' union and served as the town's mayor from 1915 to 1917, 1919 and 1946, and from 1949 to 1955. As an MLA he was notorious for his salty language and practical jokes in the legislature, and he was admired for fighting for the rights of workers and the poor. He retired undefeated at 86, the longest-serving MLA in BC history.   *Shannon Emmerson*

UPPER FRASER, a LOGGING community 55 km northeast of PRINCE GEORGE on VIA Rail and the FRASER R, is the site of a SAWMILL established in the 1930s by Don McPhee, Roy Spurr and Edwin Safford and subsequently owned by CANADIAN FOREST PRODUCTS LTD.   AS

UPPER SUMAS, 74 km southeast of VANCOUVER in the City of ABBOTSFORD, is an important DAIRY FARMING district on the southern edge of SUMAS PRAIRIE. It was a stopping place on the Yale Road and later BC ELECTRIC RWY installed an INTERURBAN station here. In the 1920s the community was known as Evanthomas.   AS

UREN, Jane, hotelkeeper (b circa 1831, Cornwall, England; d 1884, Kamloops). She operated the finest hotels in the Interior, first at CLINTON, later at SAVONA. After she was abandoned by her first husband, Peter Toy, she formed a relationship with James Uren. With James away packing so much of the time, she ran the Clinton hotel on her own, as well as bearing several children. The couple moved to Savona in the late 1860s and operated the ferry and another hotel. She was renowned for her good housekeeping and excellent cooking. She and James registered BC's first cattle brand, T, in May 1873. *See also* CATTLE INDUSTRY.

USK is a tiny LOGGING community on the SKEENA R, 20 km northeast of TERRACE. It began in 1912 as a station on the GRAND TRUNK PACIFIC RWY. The Yellowhead Hwy passes on the opposite side of the river and the train does not stop here any more, but the community has maintained its link with the outside world via a cable reaction ferry (*see also* BIG BAR CREEK) across the river.

SS Valencia, *outbound from San Francisco on its final voyage, 1906. BC Archives D-6923*

VALDES Y DE FLORES, Cayetano, Spanish naval officer (b 28 Sept 1767, Seville, Spain; d 6 Feb 1835, Cádiz, Spain). He explored the INSIDE PASSAGE commanding the *Mexicana* and circumnavigated VANCOUVER ISLAND in summer 1792, accompanying Dionisio ALCALA-GALIANO in the *Sutil*. He returned to Spain in 1793 and commanded various warships; he was seriously wounded in the Battle of Trafalgar in 1805. He later played a leading role in political affairs in Spain and was imprisoned and exiled for his liberal views. He was a member of the *Junta de Cédiz* that ruled the country briefly in 1823. *See also* SPANISH EXPLORATION. *Robin Inglis*

VALDES ISLAND, east of NANAIMO, is one of the northern GULF ISLANDS. It is separated from GABRIOLA ISLAND on the north by GABRIOLA PASSAGE and at its south end it looks across PORLIER PASS to GALIANO ISLAND. Both passes carry boaters from outer GEORGIA STRAIT to the inner Gulf Islands. Named for the Spanish explorer Cayetano VALDES, who visited the area in 1792, it is the traditional home of the Lyackson First Nation, a group of Coast Salish (*see* SALISHAN FIRST NATIONS) who have 3 reserves on the island. The notorious Brother XII (*see* Edward Arthur WILSON) had part of his colony on the island before he left the area in 1932.

VALDY, born Paul Valdemar Horsdal, singer, songwriter (b 1 Sept 1945, Ottawa). A SALT-SPRING ISLAND resident, he is a folk singer known for his warm personal manner, his observations on the human condition and the social commentary in his lyrics. His best-known and first hit was "Rock 'n' Roll Song," recorded in 1972. He won Juno Awards for folk singer of the year in 1973 and 1974 based on the success of his albums *Country Man* and *Landscapes*. Other hits include "Simple Life" and "A Good Song." He remains popular

Valdy, singer/songwriter.

thanks to a prodigious touring schedule, his work as a children's performer and his active support of literacy. *Mike Harling*

VALEMOUNT, village, pop 1,303, is located near the north end of KINBASKET LK, 278 km east of PRINCE GEORGE. Named to describe its location in the mountains, it began as a CNR station in 1927 and was originally known as Swift Creek. It was incorporated in 1962. LOGGING and TOURISM have supported the local economy.

VALENCIA, a 77-m iron steamship that worked out of San Francisco, ran aground east of PACHENA PT on the west coast of VANCOUVER ISLAND in Jan 1906. Rescue attempts failed and the ship was dashed to pieces on the rocks. It was the worst marine disaster on the West Coast: 126 of 164 passengers and crew died. This led to construction of the West Coast

Lifesaving Trail, the forerunner of today's WEST COAST TRAIL. *See also* DISASTERS.

VALENTINE, Carl, soccer player, coach (b 4 July 1958, Manchester, England). After starting his professional SOCCER career in England, he signed with the VANCOUVER WHITECAPS in 1978 and became one of VANCOUVER's most popular and recognizable athletes. He made his mark immediately by helping the Whitecaps win the 1979 N American Soccer League championship. By the time the NASL folded in 1984 he was the team's all-time leading scorer. After returning to England for one season, he obtained his Canadian citizenship in 1985 in time to play a key role in Canada's qualification for the 1986 World Cup. He joined the new VANCOUVER 86ERS in 1987 and scored the team's first goal. A Canadian Soccer League all-star in 1989 and 1991, he helped the 86ers win 4 league championships. After the team transferred to the American Professional Soccer League in 1992 he did some interim coaching for Bob LENARDUZZI in 1993 and while continuing to play, became full-time coach in 1994. In 1999 Valentine was fired as coach. He retired from playing with more career N American professional games than any other player. *SW*

VALGARDSON, William Dempsey, writer, teacher (b 7 May 1939, Winnipeg). Raised in the Icelandic community of Gimli, MB, he attended the Univ of Manitoba and taught in high schools in the province during the 1960s. After receiving an MFA from the Univ of Iowa, he worked at a college in Missouri for 4 years. He then moved to BC, where he has taught creative writing at the UNIV OF VICTORIA since 1974. A versatile writer of fiction, he has published 4 story collections, 2 novels, poetry, plays and 3 children's books. His first novel, *Gentle Sinners* (1980), won a *Books in Canada* First Novel Award and was made into a television movie; his second, *The Girl with the Botticelli Face* (1992), won a BC BOOK PRIZE. Through his work at the university he has influenced scores of young writers.

VALHALLA MOUNTAINS are a range in the SELKIRK MTS and loom above the west side of SLOCAN LK, northwest of NELSON. They were named by G.M. DAWSON, a noted geologist, for the Norse legend about a heavenly palace where warriors went after death. Many of the tallest peaks are encompassed in Valhalla Provincial PARK (496 km²) on

The Valhalla Mts, near Nelson.
Len Mackave photo

the west side of Slocan Lk, a dramatic wilderness preserve extending roughly from Gladsheim Peak (el 2,827 m) in the south to Mt Denver (2,758 m) and the New Denver Glacier in the north. This isolated park, created in 1983 after a prolonged campaign by local environmentalists, is a favourite with serious hikers and rock climbers. *See also* ENVIRONMENTAL MOVEMENT.

VALLANCE, Jim, songwriter, record producer (b 1952, Chilliwack). After studying at the UBC School of Music in the early 1970s, he and Bruce FAIRBAIRN formed a rhythm & blues/funk/JAZZ ensemble, Sunshyne. By 1976 Sunshyne had evolved into PRISM, which released a self-titled album in 1977 that featured the songwriting and drumming of Rodney Higgs, a pseudonym adopted by Vallance to conceal his rock 'n' roll involvement from his music school colleagues. After leaving the band in 1978, Vallance met Bryan ADAMS in a Kitsilano music store and the pair began writing and recording demos together. They collaborated on the songwriting and production of Adams's first solo album in 1980, and the partnership continued during Adams's rise to international stardom. The collaboration ended in 1989. Vallance also wrote hit songs for Anne Murray, the American rock group Aerosmith and the Canadian pop rockers Glass Tiger. In the early 1990s he established the Armoury Studios near FALSE CREEK, then sold them to Fairbairn in 1994. *Mike Harling*

VALLEY OF THE THOUSAND FALLS lies east of TETE JAUNE CACHE in Mt ROBSON Provincial Park. Its name refers to the multitude of lacy

waterfalls that tumble from the high cliffs. The Berg Lake Trail, one of the most popular hiking trails in the ROCKY MTS, follows the steep-sided valley. The valley ends at Berg Lk, the outlet of Berg Glacier on the north side of Mt Robson.

VALLICAN is a small AGRICULTURAL and LOGGING settlement on the west side of the Slocan R, 30 km north of CASTLEGAR. Many DOUKHOBOURS moved to this area. In mid-Aug the W KOOTENAY Women's Festival is held here. The name is an abbreviation for Valley of Slocan. *AS*

VAN ANDA, often spelled Vananda, is a village on the northeast side of TEXADA ISLAND in GEORGIA STRAIT, 10 km south of POWELL RIVER. By the early 1900s it was a GOLD and COPPER mining boomtown with hotels, a hospital, opera house, SAWMILL, newspaper and jail. A SMELTER operated intermittently from 1898 to 1919, and MINING continued until the 1950s. Today TOURISM is important and there are many retired residents. It was named after Carl Van Anda, a New York journalist, by his friend Edward Blewitt, a US promoter of the Texada mines. *AS*

VAN DUSEN, Whitford Julian, lumberman, philanthropist (b 18 July 1899, Tara, ON; d 15

W.J. Van Dusen, Vancouver philanthropist.
CVA 134-222

Dec 1978, Vancouver). He was educated at the Univ of Toronto, from which he graduated in 1912 with a degree in forestry. After a brief stint working for the federal Forest Branch, he joined the BC FOREST SERVICE and was appointed Vancouver district forester in 1915. During the late years of WWI he oversaw SPRUCE production for the Imperial Munitions Board in the QUEEN CHARLOTTE ISLANDS, and in 1919 he joined the H.R. MACMILLAN Export Company as manager. He was a principal member of that company and served on its board until 1969. In 1943 Van Dusen set up the VANCOUVER FOUNDATION, and in 1970 he organized the affiliated W.J. Van Dusen Foundation. He was a quiet, frugal and intensely private man who gave most of his large fortune to charity. *Ken Drushka*

VAN DUSEN BOTANICAL GARDEN, 22 ha, was established in 1975 in south VANCOUVER on part of the former Shaughnessy Golf Course, purchased from the CPR with money provided by the forest industry executive W.J. VAN DUSEN. Designed by Bill Livingstone, chief landscaper with the Vancouver Parks Board, and run for its first 20 years by Roy Forster, it is a floral oasis of plants and shrubs in the middle of the city. A library, restaurant and gift shop are located on the site, and guides offer tours of the grounds. Each spring the Garden hosts a giant flower and garden show.

VAN NORMAN, Charles Burwell Kerrens, architect (b 1906, Meaford, ON; d 1975, Vancouver). He arrived in VANCOUVER in 1928 after studies at Univ of Manitoba and joined the firm of Townley and Matheson, then established his own firm in 1930. He was an early exponent of Modern Expressionist ARCHITECTURE in the city. Major commissions included the Burrard Building (1956), the Customs Building on Pender St (1950–54), the Beach Towers apartment complex (the city's first highrise cluster, 1964–68) and Park Royal shopping mall (1950). He also designed the city hall in REVELSTOKE (1938) and many residences. His own Vancouver home on W 61st Ave, torn down in 1994, was a modern classic.

VANARSDOL, a GRAND TRUNK PACIFIC RWY station on the SKEENA R, 8 km northeast of TERRACE, was named after C.C. van Arsdol, a GTP divisional engineer. Many residents of Kitselas moved to this site after the railway had been constructed through KITSELAS CANYON, and the TSIMSHIAN community here became known as New Kitselas. *AS*

VANCITY; *see* VANCOUVER CITY SAVINGS CREDIT UNION.

VANCITY BOOK PRIZE is a $4,000 prize awarded annually to the best book on women's issues by a BC writer. Established in 1992, the prize is co-sponsored by the VANCOUVER CITY SAVINGS CREDIT UNION, the Vancouver Public Library, the BC ministry of women's equality and *BC BookWorld* magazine. Winners have been:

1999 *Inward to the Bones*, Kate BRAID

1998 *Slow Dance: A Story of Stroke, Love and Discovery*, Bonnie Sherr Klein

1997 *The Cure for Death by Lightning*, Gail ANDERSON-DARGATZ

1996 *In Her Nature*, Karen X. Tulchinsky

1995 *The Concubine's Children: Portrait of a Family Divided*, Denise Chong

1994 *Unruly Women: The Politics of Confinement and Resistance*, Karlene Faith

1993 *Portraits: Canadian Women in Focus*, Barbara Woodley

1992 *Under the Viaduct: Homeless in Beautiful BC*, Sheila Baxter

VANCOUVER, city, pop 514,008, is the largest city in BC; Greater Vancouver, which includes the surrounding communities (pop 1,831,665), is the third largest urban area in Canada (*see* GREATER VANCOUVER REGIONAL DISTRICT). Located on a peninsula in the southwest corner of the province, Vancouver occupies 113 km² of land bounded by BURRARD INLET to the north, GEORGIA STRAIT to the west and the FRASER R to the south. The snow-capped COAST MTS north of the city contribute to a dramatically beautiful setting.

Long before English and SPANISH EXPLORERS arrived in 1792, FIRST NATIONS people had settled in the area. The village of MUSQUEAM on the north arm of the Fraser R in what is now southwest Vancouver was a large centre from which the Musqueam people moved to surrounding waters to fish. In Burrard Inlet and FALSE CREEK they encountered other Coast Salish peoples similarly engaged (*see* SALISHAN FIRST NATIONS). Europeans fundamentally disrupted this way of life when drawn to the area by the GOLD RUSH of the late 1850s and 1860s. Lumber mills established on either side of Burrard Inlet in the 1860s marked the onset of industrialism (*see* GRANVILLE), and the pace of change was accelerated further by the decision of the CPR to make the inlet the western terminus of its transcontinental railway. The provincial government encouraged this decision by transferring to the

CPR more than 25 km² of land at the site. On 6 Apr 1886 the legislature incorporated the City of Vancouver, a name chosen by William van Horne, a CPR executive, to give the city a recognizable identity by honouring the British naval explorer George VANCOUVER. Two months later, on 13 June, the fledgling community was dealt a terrible blow when a clearing fire burned out of control and in less than an hour destroyed most of the city (*see* DISASTERS). However, rebuilding began immediately.

Vancouver experienced a recurring cycle of boom followed by recession in the pre-WWI period, including rapid growth spurts from 1897 to 1906 and 1908 to 1912. Renewed growth in the 1920s culminated with the incorporation into Vancouver of South Vancouver and Point Grey in 1929. It was at this time that the city passed Winnipeg as the largest city in western Canada. However, this growth spurt was followed by more hard times in the 1930s. Only since the onset of WWII and the prosperity that followed has the city experienced a long period of relatively sustained economic expansion. The early pattern of boom and bust reflected Vancouver's ties to the provincial economy of MINING, commercial FISHING and the FOREST INDUSTRY, over which it had emerged by the early 1900s as the regional centre. Located on an excellent harbour, it was also an important transportation centre featuring coastal shipping, trans-Pacific steamers and, by

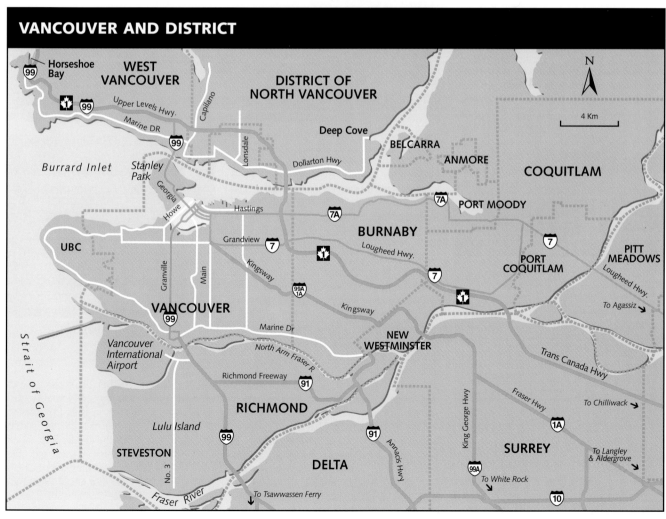

VANCOUVER AND DISTRICT

1915, 2 transcontinental railways. But the city enjoyed much less success as a manufacturing centre, and as recently as the 1960s large SAWMILLS along its Fraser R and False Crk shorelines testified to the city's continuing links to the surrounding resource economy.

In the 1960s Vancouver began to shed its image as "a village at the edge of the rain forest" and to develop the attributes of a big city. As high-rise apartment buildings replaced aging family homes, the West End, once home to the city's elite, evolved into Canada's most densely populated urban neighbourhood. Dozens of new office towers transformed the downtown, while the sawmills and machine shops of False Creek began closing, replaced in the 1970s by condominiums. In a city where as late as 1971 one half of the metropolitan-area population still lived in the urban core, 3 new bridges over waterways around Vancouver and a tunnel under the south arm of the Fraser R accelerated subur-

Opening of the second Granville St Bridge, Vancouver, 1909. BC Archives NA-42000

Damage from the 1886 Vancouver fire, photographed on the next day. UBC BC288/1

banization, creating a band of single-family communities around an increasingly dense centre where singles and families with children chose to reside. These people are able to continue to live in the inner city because in 1967 community activists and urban reformers successfully prevented it from being destroyed by freeways.

From the 1960s to the 1990s Vancouver also emerged as an international city tied less to the

Aerial view of Vancouver, 1939. VPL 6189

VANCOUVER'S POPULATION GROWTH		
Year	Van City	Greater Van
1891	13,709	
1901	27,010	35,395
1911	100,401	142,212
1921	117,217	220,503
1931	246,593	334,389
1941	275,353	388,687
1951	344,833	554,188
1961	384,522	769,006
1971	426,256	985,689
1981	414,281	1,268,183
1991	471,844	1,671,843
1996	514,008	1,831,665

local resource economy and more to other PACIFIC RIM countries through trade, TOURISM and finance. The extraordinary success of EXPO 86 accelerated this transformation and increased the flow of Asian capital into Greater Vancouver. The city's Asian population grew dramatically in the late 1980s and early 1990s, creating in the suburb of RICHMOND a new Chinese commercial centre that rivalled the city's historic CHINATOWN as a community hub. By the 1990s immigrants from Hong Kong and India constituted the 2 largest Asian groups among a great mix of peoples who have given the city its distinctive cosmopolitan character. The new Vancouver contrasts sharply with the overwhelmingly British and Anglo-Canadian city of the past: as recently as 1971 more than 60% of the residents of Greater Vancouver still identified with family ancestry in Britain. The city has also begun to put behind it a long history of racial antipathy by its European majority toward aboriginal and nonwhite minorities, particularly people of Asian heritage. This hostility was highlighted by the 1907 riots in Chinatown and Japantown (*see*

Shopping in Chinatown, 1997.
Jennifer Echols photo

ASIATIC EXCLUSION LEAGUE), the *KOMAGATA MARU* incident in 1914, and the expulsion of JAPANESE residents from the coast in 1942 (*see* JAPANESE, RELOCATION OF). Newcomers from other parts of Asia, as well as Africa, the Middle East, Eastern Europe, South and Central America and other parts of Canada have also contributed their languages, their foods and their arts to Vancouver's distinctive cultural mix.

Vancouver skyline, seen from the south side of False Creek, 1991. Roy Luckow photo

SOME OF VANCOUVER'S LARGEST ETHNO-CULTURAL GROUPS, 1996	
Chinese	288,800
East Indian	107,175
Ukrainian	73,340
Italian	64,280
Polish	50,035
Filipino	42,475
Russian	30,415
Japanese	24,295
Spanish	20,780
Hungarian	19,500

Despite its fast growth during the latter third of the 20th century, Vancouver is generally regarded as a slow-paced, "laid-back" city whose residents take time to enjoy recreation and entertainment. TOURISM has always been an economic mainstay, thanks to the mild climate and magnificent setting, with excellent hiking, ROCK CLIMBING, SKIING, SNOWBOARDING, boating, horseback riding, swimming, beachcombing and birdwatching available nearby. Public gardens and huge parks adjoin areas of dense urban population (see QUEEN ELIZABETH PARK; STANLEY PARK), and Vancouverites support many outdoor events such as the VANCOUVER FOLK MUSIC FESTIVAL, DRAGON BOAT races, Molson Indy Vancouver, Bard on the Beach Shakespeare Festival, Vancouver Children's Festival, Symphony of Fire, celebrations of the Chinese New Year, and an annual lantern festival organized by the Public Dreams Society. The city's cultural life also includes live music, DANCE, literary, THEATRE and sports events; a new public library complex, completed in 1995; the CBC building; the VANCOUVER AQUARIUM; 2 universities—UBC and SFU—as well as the EMILY CARR INSTITUTE OF ART & DESIGN and a number of COMMUNITY COLLEGE campuses; a vital city archives founded by Major J.S. MATTHEWS, located in a large waterfront park which also contains the H.R. MACMILLAN SPACE CENTRE and the VANCOUVER MARITIME MUSEUM.

Not everyone shares in the affluent "latte lifestyle" promoted by the city's boosters. The Downtown Eastside neighbourhood, adjacent to the historic districts of GASTOWN and Chinatown, has gained a reputation as the poorest postal code in Canada. Drug use, crime, prostitution, homelessness and other problems of the modern city are most intense in this small area of 16,000 residents, but they are a fact of life in almost every district of Vancouver. The city also faces serious problems associated with rapid growth, among them increasing traffic congestion and deteriorating air and water quality. These challenges give immediacy to a debate of some years' standing about the future. The noted Vancouver architect Arthur ERICKSON urges

Vancouverites to prepare for dramatic growth, predicting that by the year 2040, Vancouver will be a megacity of 10–25 million people. Others want to curtail expansion and recover the small-city character of the past, marked by low-density housing, peaceful neighbourhoods, quiet streets and courteous drivers. Given the pro-development bias of local government throughout most of Vancouver's history, encouraged by the provincial government's development activities during the years leading up to Expo 86, and given the increasingly integrated nature of economies in Asia and N America, Vancouver's transformation from "urban village" to "world city" is likely to continue.   Robert A.J. McDonald

Reading: Patricia Roy, *Vancouver: An Illustrated History*, 1980; Graeme Wynn and Timothy Oke, eds., *Vancouver and Its Regions*, 1992; Bruce Macdonald, *Vancouver: A Visual History*, 1992; Robert A.J. McDonald, *Making Vancouver: Class, Status and Social Boundaries*, 1996; Chuck Davis, ed, *The Greater Vancouver Book*, 1997.

VANCOUVER, George, British naval officer, explorer (b 22 June 1757, King's Lynn, England; d 12 May 1798, Petersham, England). As a young naval recruit he was appointed midshipman on James COOK's voyages to the S Pacific and the Antarctic (1772–75) and to the coast of BC and Alaska (1776–80). In 1791 Vancouver took command of his own expedition to the northwest coast of America with orders to survey the shoreline from California to Alaska and to resolve a disagreement with Spain over the ownership of the area. He arrived on the coast of California in Apr 1792 in his 297-tonne ship DISCOVERY, and spent the first season exploring north as far as the northern tip of VANCOUVER ISLAND. In June he met 2 Spanish vessels off Point Grey, the present site of VANCOUVER. Relations were cordial and the 2 parties continued together for several days.

After completing his first season of exploration, Vancouver sailed to NOOTKA SOUND to open negotiations with the Spanish commander Juan BODEGA Y QUADRA. The 2 men got on well but did not resolve the diplomatic squabble, which was referred back to Europe (see NOOTKA SOUND CONTROVERSY). After wintering in Hawaii,

Vancouver returned to the coast in May 1793 and continued his survey northward for another 500 km. In DEAN CHANNEL he barely missed meeting Alexander MACKENZIE, who completed his pioneering overland trek to the Pacific 6 weeks after Vancouver passed by. Following another winter in Hawaii, Vancouver returned to the coast in 1794 to complete the survey of the southern shore of Alaska. During his 3 summers on the coast, his crews mapped the entire shoreline of BC and many of its offshore islands. All of this work was done laboriously and meticulously, the men exploring every cove and inlet in small rowboats.

Portrait of George Vancouver.
BC Archives PDP-02252

Vancouver's expedition effectively shattered the dream of a Northwest Passage through N America to the Atlantic and gave Europeans the missing pieces they needed to complete a realistic map of the Pacific basin. *Discovery* arrived back in England in Oct 1795. Vancouver had been in declining health for some time and he spent his last years preparing an account of his voyage with his brother John. It was published shortly after George's death as *A Voyage of Discovery to the North Pacific Ocean and Round the World*.

VANCOUVER AQUARIUM MARINE SCIENCE CENTRE

VANCOUVER AQUARIUM MARINE SCIENCE CENTRE opened in STANLEY PARK in June 1956 as the Vancouver Aquarium, the first public aquarium in Canada. Operated by a non-profit society, it displays more than 8,000 specimens of aquatic life, runs public education programs and does marine research. Since 1964, when it became the first aquarium to have a KILLER WHALE in captivity, it has been home to several of them and in 1990 opened a new habitat for its resident beluga WHALES. Although it features marine life from the Pacific Northwest and the Arctic, the aquarium also houses displays on the

Fountain at the Vancouver Art Gallery.
Diane Eaton photo

Leaping killer whale at the Vancouver Aquarium. Skip Young/Vancouver Aquarium

Amazon and the S Pacific. Bill REID's dramatic sculpture *Killer Whale* was unveiled on the entrance plaza in 1984. The facility has had two directors: Murray NEWMAN (1956–93) and John Nightingale (1993–present). In 1998, when it drew 820,000 visitors, it changed its name to the Vancouver Aquarium Marine Science Centre and in 1999 opened the Pacific Canada Pavilion, profiling marine life in GEORGIA STRAIT. The question of whether whales and other large marine mammals should be kept in captivity has provoked controversy since the 1970s. In Jan 1999, after much debate and a referendum to Vancouver voters, the city and the aquarium agreed that no cetacean would be removed from its wild habitat and brought into Stanley Park, except those animals born in captivity, already living in captivity, or brought in under special circumstances. In 2000 the last killer whale, Bjossa, was removed to another facility.

VANCOUVER ART GALLERY

VANCOUVER ART GALLERY (VAG) opened at its original site on Georgia St in downtown VANCOUVER on 5 Oct 1931. Years of work had been done by an organizing committee led by Henry A. Stone, a Vancouver businessman, who with Charles H. SCOTT chose the 113 works that formed the first permanent collection. In the mid-1940s a large number of works from the estate of Emily CARR were donated to the gallery

and remain in its collection. In 1983 the gallery moved to its present site in the former provincial courthouse, a building designed by Francis RATTENBURY and opened in 1912, and converted for VAG use by Arthur ERICKSON. The gallery's permanent collection now includes more than 5,000 works.

VANCOUVER BACH CHOIR

VANCOUVER BACH CHOIR was founded in 1930 by Herbert Drost, its first conductor, and Harvey Wyness, the first president of the board. The large mixed-voice choir was heard regularly on radio in the 1930s and made the first cross-Canada broadcast of Handel's *Messiah* (1934). Operations were suspended in 1941 due to WWII but the choir was revived in 1950. It made its first recording in 1960 and under conductor Simon Streatfield in the 1970s it toured eastern Canada and Europe. Bruce Pullan was named conductor in 1982.

VANCOUVER BIBLE TRAINING SCHOOL

VANCOUVER BIBLE TRAINING SCHOOL was founded in 1918 to train lay Protestant evangelists for work as missionaries, teachers and pastoral assistants. It was only the second school of its type in Canada. R.W. Sharpe, a Baptist businessman, put up much of the money to run the school, and its longtime principal (1918–44) was Rev Walter Ellis, Vancouver's leading conservative evangelical minister. The name changed in 1950 to Vancouver Bible Institute, and then to Vancouver Bible College after it was taken over by the Baptist Church in 1956. When it closed in 1977, the library and several employees went to TRINITY WESTERN UNIV.

VANCOUVER BLAZERS

VANCOUVER BLAZERS was a professional HOCKEY team in the World Hockey Assoc, a league formed in 1971 to rival the NHL. The Philadelphia Blazers was one of the original WHA teams but had a dismal first season 1972–73 and moved to VANCOUVER when it was bought by entrepreneur Jim PATTISON. Sharing ice time at the PACIFIC COLISEUM with the NHL VANCOUVER CANUCKS, the Blazers missed the playoffs under coaches Andy Bathgate (1973–

74) and Joe Crozier (1974–75) before moving to Calgary in 1975. *Dan Hawthorne*

VANCOUVER CANUCKS

VANCOUVER CANUCKS HOCKEY team is VANCOUVER's entry in the NHL. The name, derived from Canada's WWII mascot Johnny Canuck, was first used by Vancouver's Pacific Coast League minor-professional hockey franchise from 1945 until the NHL's arrival in 1970. A Vancouver group applied for an NHL franchise in 1966 but was passed over in favour of 6 US cities. In 1969, for the price of $6 million each, Vancouver and Buffalo were awarded teams to begin play in the 1970–71 season. Vancouver ownership consisted of majority shareholder Medicor—a company from Minneapolis—and some local minority shareholders including BC Tel chairman Cyrus MacLean. Coley HALL, former owner of the minor-league franchise, was involved as a director.

Headed by general manager Bud Poile, executive assistant Babe PRATT and head coach Hal Laycoe, the team selected castoffs from other NHL squads in the 1970 expansion draft, then lost a "wheel of fortune" spin for the right to draft junior superstar Gilbert Perreault first overall. The Canucks' first game, on 9 Oct at home in the new PACIFIC COLISEUM, was a 3-1 loss to the LA Kings, with Barry Wilkins scoring the team's first goal. Vancouver chalked up its first win 2 days later 5-3 over the Toronto Maple Leafs. Orland Kurtenbach, a former minor-league Canuck, was the team's first captain. Other early stars included playmaker Andre Boudrias, iron man Don Lever, goaltender Gary Smith and play-by-play announcer Jim ROBSON, who had started as the voice of the minor-league team Canucks in 1960 and continued on through the NHL years to the late 1990s.

Frank GRIFFITHS bought Medicor's interest in the team in 1974 and the following year the Canucks reached the playoffs for the first time but lost in the first round. In 1982, led by the spectacular goaltending of Richard Brodeur, they made their initial appearance in the Stanley Cup finals but lost in 4 straight games to the NY Islanders. Other key players in the miracle run were forwards Thomas Gradin, Stan SMYL and Darcy ROTA, fan favourite Harold Snepsts and coach Roger Neilson, who introduced "towel power" to the NHL playoffs by hoisting a white towel of surrender to protest the refereeing in a game against Chicago. The club floundered through the rest of the 1980s but saw Tony Tanti, Patrik Sundstrom and KAMLOOPS defenceman Doug Lidster rewrite many of the team's individual offense records. The latter years of the decade featured the arrival of new coach and GM Pat Quinn in 1987, 1988–89 star rookie Trevor Linden and 1989 signees from the Soviet national team Igor Larionov and Vladimir Krutov. But the Russian with the most impact on the team would be 1991–92 NHL rookie of the year Pavel BURE. Quinn, Linden, Bure and goaltender Kirk MacLean led the Canucks to their second Stanley Cup finals appearance in 1994. In one of the most exciting finals in the modern NHL era, they fought back from a 3-1 deficit against the NY Rangers to tie the series and force a showdown in New York, which they lost 3-2. The effort was marred by a post-game riot in downtown Vancouver involving an estimated 80,000 people (*see* STANLEY CUP RIOT). The team moved to the new 20,000-seat GENERAL MOTORS PLACE for the 1995–96 season. The Canucks were owned by the Griffiths family until 1996 when Arthur Griffiths sold the franchise to Seattle billionaire John McCaw and his ORCA BAY SPORTS AND ENTERTAINMENT. *See also* VANCOUVER MILLIONAIRES; Tiger WILLIAMS; Cam NEELY; Barry PEDERSON; Barry BECK; Mel BRIDGMAN; Cliff RONNING; COURTNALL brothers. *SW*

VANCOUVER CITY SAVINGS CREDIT UNION (VanCity), the largest CREDIT UNION in Canada, was chartered in 1946 as an "open bond" credit union, meaning any VANCOUVER resident could join. It grew rapidly and over the years pioneered a series of innovative financial services, including loans to women in their own name (from its inception); mortgages in low-income areas; Canada's first open mortgage (1959); the daily interest savings account (1967); telephone banking (1985); and Canada's first "ethical" mutual fund, the Ethical Growth Fund (1986). As far as anyone knows VanCity also pioneered the first-in-line teller service now in use at all banks and credit unions. Its most dramatic innovation, however, was the introduction in 1975 of real-time on-line computerization, which eventually led to interbranch service. Beginning in the mid-1980s VanCity continued its tradition of groundbreaking with a series of community initiatives, among them the VanCity Community Foundation; a "community investment" term deposit; micro-lending for small business; and a housing development subsidiary (VanCity Enterprises). By its fiftieth anniversary in 1996 it had 220,000 members and 33 branches. Assets in 1998 totalled $5.9 billion.

VANCOUVER CO-OPERATIVE RADIO is a non-profit, community-owned radio station that broadcasts in the FM band at 102.7 MHz in Greater Vancouver under the call letters CFRO. The station was licensed by the Canadian Radio-Television and Telecommunications Commission (CRTC) in May 1974, after 2 years of organizing by 2 community media research groups, Neighbourhood Radio and Muckrackers. Since going on the air in Apr 1975, CFRO has been broadcasting community events, local music, drama, news and special community interest programs that for commercial and political reasons are not broadcast on commercial or public stations. CFRO is co-operatively owned by approximately 2,000 members, governed by an elected Board of Directors and run by a staff of 3 people, who oversee the programming produced by 100 to 200 volunteers. *See also* BROADCASTING; CO-OPERATIVES. *Norbert Ruebsaat*

VANCOUVER EAST CULTURAL CENTRE is a 350-seat theatre located in a converted church on the east side of VANCOUVER. Opened in 1973 under founding director Chris Wootten, the "Cultch" presents an eclectic mix of DANCE, music, THEATRE and shows for children, by both local performers and touring acts. One of its most enduring shows was *Billy Bishop Goes to War*, by the Vancouver playwright John MacLachlan GRAY, first mounted in 1978. The show went on to become a Canadian classic and returned to Vancouver in 1998 for a twentieth anniversary remount.

VANCOUVER 86ERS became VANCOUVER's professional Canadian SOCCER League franchise in 1987, 3 years after the demise of the North American Soccer League and its popular VANCOUVER WHITECAPS team. Tony Waiters, former coach of the Whitecaps, came up with the name "86ers" to commemorate the founding of the team in 1986 and the founding of Vancouver in 1886. Playing under head coach-player Bob LENARDUZZI and general manager Buzz Parsons out of BURNABY's SWANGARD Stadium, the 86ers recorded their first win on 7 June 1987, but had an unspectacular season and were eliminated from the playoffs. However, the team compiled a 46-game winning streak over the next 2 seasons and then dominated the CSL with 4 consecutive playoff championships (1988–91) and 5 straight regular-season first-place finishes (1988–92). Businessman Milan Ilich bought the team from the nonprofit West Coast Soccer Society in 1989 and in 1992 transferred the club from the floundering CSL to the American Professional Soccer League. After leading the team to the APSL semifinals, Lenarduzzi, who had added the general manager's title to his coaching duties in 1989, resigned to focus on coaching the Canadian national team. Carl VALENTINE became coach and steered the 86ers through 3 losing seasons before posting a 16-12 win-loss record and reaching the newly named A league's Western Conference finals in 1997. Plagued by poor attendance, the club was taken over by BC LIONS owner David Braley that year. Valentine was fired at the end of the 1999 season and replaced by Dale Mitchell. Lenarduzzi returned as general manager and the 86ers introduced a reserve club in ABBOTSFORD and a promising youth development program. *SW*

VANCOUVER FOLK MUSIC FESTIVAL is an annual outdoor music event held in JERICHO BEACH Park during a weekend in July each year. Inspired by the Winnipeg Folk Festival and the Newport Folk Festival, it was initiated by Mitch Podolak and developed by Podolak and Ernie Fladell for its first production in 1978. The organizers wanted to bring in live music that British Columbians had never before heard or seen.

Dancing at the Vancouver Folk Music Festival, 1998. Peter Battistoni/Vancouver Sun

Over the years the "folk music" venue has expanded to include JAZZ, rock, blues, country, gospel, spoken-word and other performances and has presented a number of well-known entertainers. Yet the festival has remained true to its purpose, each year presenting a unique variety of music, rhythm and dance from all over the world, and introducing such BC artists as Stephen Fearing, Veda HILLE, Oh Susannah and Kinnie Starr to its growing audience. The event is still run by a few paid staff and a corps of volunteers—more than 1,000 of them in 1999, compared to 200 when the festival began. In the late 1990s, under the management of Frances Wasserlein and the artistic direction of Dugg Simpson, the event was rated the best festival in VANCOUVER by the *GEORGIA STRAIGHT* Readers' Poll for 3 years running.

VANCOUVER FOUNDATION is Canada's largest community charitable foundation and the fifth largest in N America. Created in 1943 by the lumber executive W.J. VAN DUSEN, it has grown to include 560 separate endowment funds with assets totalling more than $500 million. Each year it distributes about $22 million in grants to community organizations in the province.

VANCOUVER GRIZZLIES basketball team is VANCOUVER's entry in the National Basketball Assoc. The franchise was established in 1994 by Arthur Griffiths (son of Frank GRIFFITHS), then owner of the VANCOUVER CANUCKS hockey team, and shares GENERAL MOTORS PLACE with the Canucks. In Mar 1995 the franchise, the Canucks

Shareef Abdur-Rahim, Vancouver Grizzlies star, 1998. Andy Hayt/NBA

New terminal and runway at the Vancouver International Airport, 1996.
Arlen Redekop/Vancouver Province

and GM Place were purchased by John McCaw, a Seattle billionaire, through his company ORCA BAY SPORTS AND ENTERTAINMENT. The Grizzlies began play in Nov 1995 and won 15 games in their first season under coach Brian Winters. Following a string of defeats, Winters was replaced during the second season by Stu Jackson, the team's general manager. A new head coach, Brian Hill, took over at the start of the third season. The team failed to qualify for the playoffs during the 1990s but banked its hopes on the future with four young stars: Shareef Abdur-Rahim, Bryant "Big Country" Reeves, Michael Dickerson and Mike Bibby. Early in the 1999–2000 season Lionel Hollins took over from Hill as head coach. After the sale of the team to Bill Laurie, a St Louis billionaire, fell through because the new owner would not promise to keep the franchise in Vancouver, McCaw sold the Grizzlies to Michael Heisley, a Chicago entrepreneur, early in 2000.

VANCOUVER INSTITUTE FOR THE VISUAL ARTS (VIVA) was a charitable foundation created in 1988 by Doris and Jack SHADBOLT. Using money donated mainly by the Shadbolts, VIVA presents two $10,000 awards annually to BC artists to support their work, plus a $50,000 "award of honour" every 5 years. The foundation is managed by a volunteer board and award recipients are chosen by an independent selection panel. The first honour award went to the curator and critic Alvin BALKIND in 1992; the second award was shared by the critic Joan Lowndes and the artist Ian WALLACE in 1997. Winners of the annual awards have included Carel Moiseiwitsch, Stan DOUGLAS, Carole Itter, Chick Rice, Terry Ewasiuk and Judy Radul. Following the death of Jack Shadbolt in 1998 the institute was renamed the Jack and Doris Shadbolt Foundation.

VANCOUVER INTERNATIONAL AIRPORT on SEA ISLAND in RICHMOND, south of VANCOUVER, is BC's largest AIRPORT. In 1998 it handled 15.5 million travellers, including 68,000 people on 29 Aug 1998, its busiest day ever in terms of number of passengers. The airport opened on 22 July 1931 and replaced Lansdowne Field on LULU ISLAND, leased by the city since 1928. Flights connected to VICTORIA and Seattle, and in 1938 Trans Canada Airlines began passenger service to Winnipeg and Montreal. During WWII the federal defence department initiated major improvements to the facility. The city retained ownership until 1962, when the federal department of transport purchased the airport for $2.75 million. A new terminal opened in 1968 and was used for domestic flights. As part of the federal government's privatization policy, management of the airport was handed over to the newly created Vancouver International Airport Authority in 1992. This agency embarked on a major expansion, including a $260-million terminal for international flights, which opened on 1 May 1996. There is also a south terminal for local carriers and float planes, and for cargo traffic.

VANCOUVER INTERNATIONAL FESTIVAL was a summer festival of music, THEATRE and film launched in 1958 as part of the provincial centennial celebrations. The Queen Elizabeth Theatre opened in 1959 partly to house the festival, which brought a wide range of international talent to VANCOUVER. "Nothing of the kind on this continent surpasses it in scope and objectives, and it has drawn world attention," wrote Alan Morley, a journalist, in 1969—the same year that the festival was discontinued for lack of money. *See also* MUSIC FESTIVALS.

VANCOUVER INTERNATIONAL FILM FESTIVAL (VIFF), the third largest festival of its kind in N America, takes place each Sept–Oct in selected theatres around VANCOUVER. Started in 1982 by Leonard Schein, it has been directed since 1988 by Alan Franey. In 1999 the 17-day festival exhibited 300 films from 50 countries. The VIFF has distinguished itself among N American festivals by giving special attention to films from the Asia-Pacific region.

A predecessor Vancouver International Film Festival was held for the first time in 1958 as part of the VANCOUVER INTERNATIONAL FESTIVAL. By 1960 this annual event was the largest film festival in N America, but after 1963 funding became increasingly difficult to obtain. The end came in 1969 when acrimony over the alleged censorship of a locally made feature film, *The Plastic Mile*, precipitated the collapse of the already financially troubled organization.

VANCOUVER ISLAND, 31,284 km², is Canada's tenth-largest island and the largest on the Pacific Coast of N America. The exposed top of a submerged mountain system, it lies parallel to the continent on a northeast–southeast axis, extending 460 km from JUAN DE FUCA STRAIT to Queen Charlotte Strait. JOHNSTONE STRAIT in the north and GEORGIA STRAIT in the south separate it from the BC mainland. A rugged spine of mountains rises to altitudes in excess of 2,000 m, including GOLDEN HINDE (el 2,200 m), the Island's highest peak. These mountains separate a rocky, deeply indented west coast from the coastal lowlands and milder climate of the east coast. Deep FJORDS, the longest of which are ALBERNI INLET, MUCHALAT INLET and the various arms of QUATSINO SOUND, almost bisect the Island, which has an average width of 50 km. Its mountains also shelter VANCOUVER and the ESTUARY of the FRASER R from the hurricane-force storms that regularly lash its exposed outer coast. Popularly known as "the Graveyard of the Pacific," the Island's treacherous southwest coast has been the scene of more than 200 shipwrecks. A lifesaving trail built for castaways in the 19th

VANCOUVER ISLAND VITAL STATISTICS

Land area	31,284 km²
Length	460 km
Coastline	3,440 km
Population	671,844

5 largest communities:	
Victoria	73,504
Nanaimo	70,130
Campbell River	28,851
North Cowichan	25,305
Port Alberni	18,468

Three highest mountains:	
Golden Hinde	2,200 m
Elkhorn Mt	2,194 m
Mt Colonel Foster	2,133 m

Highest waterfall	
Della Falls	440 m
(the highest falls in Canada)	

century is now the WEST COAST TRAIL, a unit of PACIFIC RIM NATIONAL PARK RESERVE and one of Canada's most popular wilderness hikes.

HENDERSON LK, near PORT ALBERNI, is the wettest spot in N America, with an average annual precipitation of 6,655 mm; it set a N American rainfall record in 1997 with 8,997.1 mm of precipitation. Vegetation on the west coast is characterized by shorepine bogs and dense temperate RAIN FORESTS of HEMLOCK, CEDAR and SPRUCE; these forests contain some of the largest and oldest trees in the world (*see also* TREES, GIANT). On the east coast, by contrast, the climate is classified as Mediterranean and rated the least severe in Canada. More than 90% of the Island's 671,844 inhabitants (18% of the provincial total) live in this drier, milder climatic zone, which is dominated by DOUGLAS FIR and, in the southern half, ARBUTUS and Garry OAK. Some of

Long Beach, a spectacular stretch along the west coast of Vancouver Island. Roy Luckow photo

these landscapes are protected in a series of major PARKS, the most important being Pacific Rim National Park Reserve and STRATHCONA, BROOKS PENINSULA and CAPE SCOTT provincial PARKS. Most watersheds on the Island are drained by a series of short, steep river systems, providing habitat for once abundant SALMON, STEELHEAD and both anadromous and resident TROUT. Among the best-known rivers are the COWICHAN (a BC HERITAGE RIVER), Nanaimo, Englishman, Qualicum, Oyster, PUNTLEDGE, CAMPBELL, Nitinat, San Juan, Gold, and NIMPKISH rivers.

The Island's first human settlements occurred in the estuaries of these rich salmon streams. Although the ARCHAEOLOGICAL record is still being interpreted, it seems clear that aboriginal peoples from 2 major linguistic groups settled the Island many thousands of years ago (*see* PRE-HISTORY). These speakers of SALISHAN and WAKASHAN FIRST NATIONS LANGUAGES developed a complex village-based tribal culture that was rich in art and material wealth; rank, status and ceremony played significant roles. The aboriginal population at time of contact is unknown but during the 19th century repeated epidemics reduced it by two-thirds or more. Since WWII the aboriginal population has rebounded and

exceeded 7,000 at the end of the 20th century.

Russian, Spanish, British, French and American ships began visiting the region in the 18th century, but it was the visit of Capt James COOK to NOOTKA SOUND in 1778 that led to the beginning of the trade in SEA OTTER skins that attracted many commercial vessels to the coast (*see* FUR TRADE, MARITIME). In 1789 the Spanish established a base at Nootka and the ensuing NOOTKA SOUND CONTROVERSY almost led to a European war. Permanent European settlement of the Island did not begin until 1843, when James DOUGLAS began construction of FORT VICTORIA for the HBC. The European population grew slowly, though the discovery of rich coal fields at NANAIMO sparked the development of a mining industry (*see* COAL MINING, VANCOUVER ISLAND). The Island became a Crown colony in 1849 (*see* VANCOUVER ISLAND, COLONY OF) and entered union with the mainland in 1866, but the provincial capital at VICTORIA was soon eclipsed as an economic power by Vancouver, which took advantage of its location as the Pacific terminus of 3 transcontinental railways. On the Island, settlement concentrated around Victoria, at the coal-mining centres of LADYSMITH, Nanaimo and CUMBERLAND, and in the rich farming regions of the SAANICH PENINSULA and COWICHAN and COMOX valleys (*see* AGRICULTURE). RAILWAY and truck LOGGING exploited the FOREST resource and with the opening of BC's first paper mill on the Alberni Inlet in 1891, the PULP AND PAPER industry soon followed, making the FOREST INDUSTRY the Island's largest employer. The harbour at ESQUIMALT was headquarters for Britain's naval fleet in the Pacific from 1865 and for Canada's Pacific fleet since 1910. Greater Victoria, with over half the Island population, has communicated with its hinterland via the ESQUIMALT & NANAIMO RWY, completed to COURTENAY in 1914. Construction on a new $1.2 billion highway down the rapidly urbanizing east coast began in 1993. Since 1980 the Island's growth has been largely as a TOURISM and retirement destination, a trend that solidified in the late 1990s with the decline in both the COMMERCIAL FISHING and coastal logging industries.

Stephen Hume

Readings: Kim Goldberg, *Where to See Wildlife on*

Vancouver Island, 1997; Lindsay Elms, *Beyond Nootka: A Historical Perspective of Vancouver Island Mountains,* 1997; Charles Lillard, *Seven Shillings a Year: The History of Vancouver Island,* 1986; George Nicholson, *Vancouver Island's West Coast, 1762-1962,* 1965; Ian Smith, *The Unknown Island,* 1973; Rolf Ludvigsen and Graham Beard, *West Coast Fossils: A Guide to the Ancient Life of Vancouver Island,* 1997.

VANCOUVER ISLAND, COLONY OF, existed between 1849 and 1866. It was created by Great Britain as a means of asserting its presence in the area. In return for a payment of 7 shillings, proprietorial rights were awarded to the HBC for 10 years by Charter of Grant dated 13 Jan 1849. Britain retained the right to appoint a governor while the HBC agreed to use revenue from land sales to establish colonists. The arrangement relieved Britain of direct responsibility for the colony and recognized that the HBC, already based at FORT VICTORIA since 1843, was the agency best able to encourage settlement. The first gov was Richard BLANSHARD, whose brief tenure ended in 1851 when he was replaced by HBC chief factor James DOUGLAS. (Douglas resigned from the HBC in 1858 to become governor of the new mainland colony of British Columbia as well.) On 30 May 1859 the HBC lease of Vancouver Island expired and Britain assumed direct responsibility for the island colony. Douglas was assisted by an appointed Council until 1856 when, at the insistence of Britain, an elected 7-member assembly was created. Only 43 colonists owned enough land (8.2 ha, or 20 acres) to qualify as voters. The Assembly opened on 12 Aug 1856. The appointed Council gradually evolved into a legislative body; in 1863 it was dissolved and replaced by an Executive Council and a separate Legislative Council, both appointed. The former consisted of senior officials acting as an advisory body to the governor, while the latter formed an upper house of the legislature. Douglas retired from governorship of the Island in 1863 and was succeeded by Arthur Edward KENNEDY, who feuded incessantly with the assembly.

The colony's economy was dominated by the HBC. Along with the FUR TRADE post, the company operated COAL mines at FORT RUPERT, then NANAIMO, 7 large farms (4 through its subsidiary PUGET'S SOUND AGRICULTURAL CO) and LOGGING and SAWMILLING operations. HBC-sponsored land settlement was not a success. Land was purchased from local aboriginals in a series of 14 agreements negotiated by Gov Douglas from 1850-54 (*see* DOUGLAS TREATIES), but by 1854 there were only 744 white residents, mostly from the British Isles, compared to a FIRST NATIONS population of several thousand. Prospects improved in 1858 when the Fraser R GOLD RUSH created economic opportunities on the Island, inspiring a sudden influx of newcomers. Still the colony continued to have financial problems until Britain merged it with the mainland to form a single colony, British Columbia. On 19 Nov 1866 the colony of Vancouver Island ceased to exist. *See also* COLONIAL GOVERNMENT.

VANCOUVER ISLAND EXPLORING EXPE-DITION (1864), led by the botanist Robert BROWN, was organized by a group of VICTORIA business leaders to explore the interior of the island and look for rumoured GOLD deposits. Members included the artist Frederick WHYMPER; John Meade and Peter John LEECH, former members of the ROYAL ENGINEERS; Henry Thomas Lewis; Alexander Barnston; the botanist John Buttle; John Foley, an experienced prospector; and the colourful adventurer Ranald MACDON-ALD, along with 2 aboriginal guides, Kakalatza and Tomo Antoine. Partly funded by the COLO-NIAL GOVERNMENT, the expedition left Victoria early in June by steamboat, then ascended the COWICHAN R to COWICHAN LK. Members then divided into 2 parties, taking different routes across the island to PORT RENFREW on the west coast. Brown returned briefly to Victoria to remonstrate with his backers about their tight-fistedness and preoccupation with gold seeking. When he rejoined the others at Cowichan Lk they had made a promising gold strike. Dissension broke out and Foley was dismissed. Once again the group divided and followed different routes across the Interior to Port Alberni; there the expedition petered out in Oct and returned to Victoria. Aside from minor COAL and gold discoveries, the expedition's main accomplishment was to describe several parts of Vancouver Island previously unknown to colonists.

VANCOUVER ISLAND HELICOPTERS LTD, the second-oldest operating helicopter company in BC, was founded in 1955 by Ted Henson, a VICTORIA mechanic and pilot. Following in the footsteps of Okanagan Helicopters (*see* CANADI-AN HELICOPTERS LTD), the company performed aerial surveying, MINING exploration, firefighting and power line construction. After Henson disappeared on a flight in 1957, his wife Lynn took over the company and became the first female president of a helicopter company in Canada. When she married Alf STRINGER, one of the founders of Okanagan Helicopters, he became president of VIH in 1965 and held that position until 1985. The company expanded into the air ambulance service and since 1988 has been involved in HELI-LOGGING.

VANCOUVER MARITIME MUSEUM, located in Vanier Park in the Kitsilano neighbourhood of VANCOUVER, opened in 1958 as a provincial centennial project. Among the permanent exhibits is a replica of the forecastle of George VAN-COUVER's ship *DISCOVERY*, a collection of ship models, maritime paintings and other material related to the history of coastal BC. Tied up at the waterfront in the Heritage Harbour is a collection of historic vessels, including the vintage tugs *Ivanhoe* and *Master*, and the *MAPLE LEAF*, the oldest sailing vessel in the province. The RCMP vessel *ST ROCH*, a National Historic Site, is on permanent display next door.

VANCOUVER MILLIONAIRES were original members of BC's first professional HOCKEY league, the PACIFIC COAST HOCKEY ASSOC. Managed and coached by Frank PATRICK, they played their first game on 5 Jan 1912 in the new Denman Arena, the world's largest skating arena and N America's second largest sports facility. Patrick regularly filled the 10,500 seats after he signed scoring sensation Fred "Cyclone" TAYLOR. In 1915 the Millionaires won the league championship and western Canada's first Stanley Cup. Led by playing coach Patrick, Taylor, Mickey MACKAY, Frank Nighbor and goaltender Hugh Lehman, Vancouver dominated the Ottawa Senators 26-6 in a 3-game final series sweep. The win marked not only the first time a team from BC won the Stanley Cup, but the only time in the 20th century Vancouver captured the trophy. The Millionaires made it to the finals again in 1918, 1921 and 1922 but could not regain the championship. In 1922 the club changed its name to the Maroons. It folded when the Patrick family sold the league to the NHL in 1926. *See also* VICTORIA COUGARS. *SW*

VANCOUVER MUSEUM is located near Vanier Park in the Kitsilano neighbourhood of VANCOUVER. It began in 1894 when a group of local history enthusiasts calling themselves the Art, Historical and Scientific Assoc of Vancouver began collecting artifacts. The collection began

Vancouver Museum, with downtown and North Shore Mts in the background. Tourism Vancouver

receiving civic financial support in 1904 and the next year moved into the Carnegie LIBRARY building, where it remained for 6 decades. In 1967, to mark the Canadian centennial, the museum moved to new quarters at its present location, where it houses the largest collection of any civic museum in Canada. Along with material relating to the history of Vancouver and FIRST NATIONS culture, the museum contains a wide variety of other artifacts, including collections of toy soldiers, dolls, costumes, seashells and neon signs.

VANCOUVER OPERA was established in 1960 as the Vancouver Opera Assoc under Irving GUTTMAN, the founding artistic director. International stars who have appeared with the company include Joan Sutherland, Marilyn Horne and Placido Domingo. Guttman was succeeded by Richard Bonynge (1974–78), Hamilton McClymont (1978–82), Brian McMaster (1983–89) and Robert Hallam (1989–99). In 1999 James Wright took over the company, which also stages recitals and runs a successful Opera in the School program.

VANCOUVER OPERA HOUSE was the city's most elegant showcase for the performing arts from 1891 to 1913. It was built by the CPR on Granville St at Robson next door to the first Vancouver Hotel and featured international stars from the worlds of vaudeville, opera, drama and musical theatre. The CPR sold the building in 1911 and it was gutted by fire 2 years later. After reopening as the New Orpheum it remained in operation as a vaudeville house and then a movie theatre until the 1960s, when it was demolished to make way for the Pacific Centre shopping mall and office tower development.

VANCOUVER PLAYHOUSE is a 668-seat theatre built by the city in 1963, when hardly any performance facilities existed for local arts groups. The Vancouver Playhouse Theatre Co staged its first production that year, Brendan Behan's *The Hostage*. In 1967 the company put on the inaugural production of George RYGA's classic, *The Ecstasy of Rita Joe*, and it has shown a commitment to Canadian work from the beginning. Along with the Playhouse's annual series of plays, the building is home to the Friends of Chamber Music, the Festival Concert Society and the Vancouver Recital Society. *See also* THEATRE.

VANCOUVER ROWING CLUB, the city's oldest athletics club, was inaugurated as the VAN-COUVER Boating Club in 1886. It merged with the BURRARD INLET Rowing Club as the VRC in 1899. The club was involved exclusively in rowing until 1908 when it fielded a RUGBY team and a variety of other sports has since been part of the club's agenda. Notable builders in the early days included Bob JOHNSTON, Reggie WOODWARD, Harry Senkler, Nelles Stacey and Col Victor Spencer, but the greatest impact on the club's competitive success came from Frank READ, who became coach of the VRC's UBC student rowers in 1949. He established a winning legacy that included a gold and 2 silver Olympic medals and a gold at the 1954 British Empire Games (*see* BRITISH EMPIRE AND COMMONWEALTH GAMES). In all, the club won 17 international medals in Olympic, Commonwealth and Pan American Games competition before Canada stopped sending club teams in the 1970s. The VRC building, a heritage site in STANLEY PARK, has housed the club since 1911. *SW*

VANCOUVER SCHOOL OF ART; *see* EMILY CARR INSTITUTE OF ART & DESIGN

VANCOUVER STOCK EXCHANGE was founded in 1907 by a group of local business people to raise financing for MINING ventures. Over the years it developed a reputation for shady promotions and lax regulation, at the same time launching many innovative and successful companies. During the 1980s in particular the VSE was plagued by a series of fraudulent manipulations, resulting in a 1993 provincial government investigation into the securities market and the subsequent implementation of new regulations (*see also* BC SECURITIES COMMISSION). By 1999 the exchange had 1,373 listed companies, two-thirds of which were in the resource sector, and was the fourth busiest exchange in N America. That year, as part of a massive reorganization of Canadian stock exchanges, the VSE merged with the Calgary Stock Exchange to form a national junior capital market, surrendering senior stocks to the Toronto Stock Exchange. The new Canadian Venture Exchange (CDNX), with operations centred in VANCOUVER and corporate headquarters in Calgary, had about 2,500 listed companies when it began trading on 29 Nov 1999.

VANCOUVER SUN NEWSPAPER appeared for the first time on 12 Feb 1912. Associated with the LIBERAL PARTY, it was founded as a morning paper by John P. McConnell and R.S. Ford and for several years was one of 4 dailies in VANCOUVER. Robert CROMIE took over in 1917; as he expanded he bought out 2 rivals, the *World* and the *News-Advertiser*, and began publishing in the afternoon. During the 1930s and 1940s the *Sun* competed vigorously with the daily PROVINCE and by the 1950s, under Robert's son Donald CROMIE, it emerged as the largest daily in western Canada, featuring such talented writers as Jack WEBSTER, Jack SCOTT, Simma HOLT, Pierre BERTON and Jack WASSERMAN. The *Province* was owned by the Southam chain and when Donald Cromie sold the *Sun* to FP Publications of Winnipeg in 1963, it marked the end of local newspaper ownership in Vancouver. In 1957 the 2 papers formed PACIFIC PRESS to print both. Since 1937 the *Sun* had been located in the Sun Tower on Beatty St; in 1964 it moved into new headquar-

ters on Granville St. By 1969 it had the second largest daily circulation of any paper in Canada. Bought by Southam in 1980, the *Sun* switched to morning publication 16 Sept 1991. Hollinger International bought Southam in 1996, then sold most of it, including the *Sun*, to CanWest Global Communications in 2000. Daily circulation in 1999 was 202,400.

VANCOUVER SYMPHONY ORCHESTRA (VSO) was established in 1919 by Henry Green, a mysterious, publicity-shy musician from New Zealand, and Mary Isabella Rogers, widow of the

Maestro Bramwell Tovey conducts the Vancouver Symphony, 2000. David Cooper/VSO

sugar baron B.T. ROGERS. Green organized the concerts while Rogers organized financial support, and over the next 2 1/2 years the new orchestra gave 27 performances. Then in 1921, after his salary demands were refused, Green abruptly disappeared and the orchestra collapsed. Thanks to the efforts of Rogers, it revived in 1929, led by the Dutch violist and conductor Allard de Ridder (who later joined the Hart House String Quartet and founded the Ottawa Philharmonic in 1944, before retiring in VANCOUVER in 1952). Over the years the VSO welcomed renowned conductors such as Sir John Barbirolli, Sir Ernest Macmillan, Leonard Bernstein and Otto Klemperer. Under the direction of Kazuyoshi Akiyama in the 1970s, the orchestra enjoyed its greatest success: at one point it had 40,000 subscribers, more than any other N American symphony. During the 1980s, however, the orchestra declined, and early in 1988, teetering on the brink of collapse, it suspended operations. A government bailout saved the orchestra. Under Sergiu Comissiona, the music director, and his successor Bramwell Tovey, who took over in 2000, the VSO continued to play a valued role in the cultural life of the city.

VANCOUVER TUGBOAT CO LTD traces its roots back to 1898, when Harry Jones chartered the small steam tug *On Time*. Jones retired in 1919 and for a while the company was inactive.

It was re-established in 1924 by 2 of Harry's children, Harold and Ruth. During the 1930s the company built up its scow and barge operations, especially the barging of sawmill waste to pulp mills (*see also* PULP AND PAPER; SAWMILLING). When Harold Jones died in 1957 he was succeeded by Arthur Lindsay, who in turn was succeeded by Capt J.C.F. Stewart. More than any of its competitors, VanTug concentrated on providing the largest fleet of chip barges on the coast. In 1970 it merged with ISLAND TUG & BARGE and the following year the new company became SEASPAN INTERNATIONAL.

VANCOUVER WHITECAPS was a professional SOCCER team that played in the North American Soccer League 1974–84. Businessman Herb Capozzi, a former CFL player and BC LIONS manager, put together an ownership group that included C.N. "Chunky" WOODWARD and Denny Veitch. With 13 of its 17 players from BC, the Whitecaps played competitively in their first 2 seasons but missed the playoffs and did not draw the expected crowds. A major turning point came after the 1976 season when Capozzi hired general manager John Best, who replaced 40% of the roster and hired coach Tony Waiters. As Waiters developed a more aggressive, exciting style, fans started to turn out. In 1978 the Whitecaps looked determined to contend, securing star goaltender Phil Parkes and British superstars Kevin Hector and Alan Hinton. Toward the end of the season they won all 13 remaining games, smashing the consecutive-wins record by 4 and drawing crowds of more than 32,000, validating soccer as VANCOUVER's most popular sport. The Whitecaps won their opening playoffs game, but the excitement ended when they lost the second to the Portland Timbers. Waiters won NASL coach-of-the-year honours, Parkes was the league's top goaltender, Hector and John Craven were second-team all-stars and Vancouver native Bob LENARDUZZI was named N American soccer player of the year. For 1979 Best signed Trevor Whymark and 20-year-old star Carl VALENTINE, and the Whitecaps won their division. They raced through the playoffs, finally defeating

Champagne time in the Vancouver Whitecaps dressing room, Sept 1979. L to r: Carl Valentine, Derek Possee, Ray Lewington, Peter Daniel, Bob Bolitho. Kurt Kallberg/Vancouver Province

Tampa Bay to win the NASL championship. Midfielder Alan Ball was named MVP of the play-offs and the team returned to a welcome from some 100,000 roaring fans. Players Lenarduzzi, Buzz Parsons, Steve Nasin and Carl Shearer and assistant coach Leslie Wilson were from BC, and the entire 1979 team was inducted into the BC SPORTS HALL OF FAME in 1988. The franchise continued for another 5 years before folding.   SW

VANDER ZALM, Wilhelmus Nicholaas Theodore Maria Jr (William) "Bill," horticulturalist, politician, premier 6 Aug 1986–2 Apr 1991 (b 29 May 1934, Noordwykerhout, Holland). He grew up in Nazi-occupied Holland and in 1947 moved to the FRASER VALLEY near BRADNER, where his father, who had been in Canada during the war, had started a bulb-producing business. Vander Zalm left high school in 1952 to join the family business after his father

Bill Vander Zalm, premier of BC 1986–91.

suffered a heart attack, and eventually he owned several plant nurseries. He began his political career in SURREY, where he was alderman from 1965 to 1969 and mayor from 1969 to 1975. During this time he also ran unsuccessfully as a federal Liberal, and lost a bid for the leadership of the provincial LIBERAL PARTY in 1972. As mayor of Surrey, Vander Zalm earned a reputation as a crusader against widespread social welfare "fraud." He continued to champion this cause after he was elected a SOCIAL CREDIT MLA in the 1975 provincial election, joining Premier Bill BENNETT's cabinet as minister of human resources. He also served as minister of municipal affairs (1978–81) and of education (1981–83). During his time in cabinet his outspokenness frequently caused controversy, whether he was insulting teachers, French Canadians, unemployed people or his fellow cabinet ministers.

In Apr 1983 Vander Zalm abruptly quit politics shortly before an election, alienating many of his fellow Socreds, who believed he was deserting an unpopular government for his own political advantage. He purchased Fantasy Garden World, a RICHMOND theme park, in 1984; that year he also returned to politics, running unsuccessfully for mayor of VANCOUVER against Mike HARCOURT. In July 1986, following Bennett's mid-term retirement, he won the Socred leadership and the premier's job and 3 months later confirmed the convention's choice by leading the party to victory in a provincial election. Vander Zalm's charm was effective on the campaign trail, but once in power his conservative, even fundamentalist, views on social issues alienated many voters. His term as PREMIER was turbulent until in 1991 his alleged involvement in questionable business dealings forced his resignation and a return to private life. In 1998 he emerged from retirement to take a leading role in the BC REFORM PARTY.

VANDERHOOF, district municipality, pop 4,401, lies in the NECHAKO R Valley at the geographical centre of BC, 97 km west of PRINCE GEORGE. It is within the territory of the DAKELH (Carrier) people; the protohistoric village of CHUNLAC was located nearby. The townsite was laid out by the GRAND TRUNK PACIFIC RWY when it was laying track through to PRINCE RUPERT prior to WWI. It is named for a Chicago promoter, Herbert Vanderhoof, hired by the railway to attract settlers to the area. It was incorporated as a village in 1926. During the 1950s the construction of the KENNEY DAM on the Nechako R provided a boost to the local economy. The other mainstays have been the FOREST INDUSTRY and AGRICULTURE, the valley is the second largest forage producing region in BC. The College of New Caledonia (*see* COMMUNITY COLLEGES) has a satellite campus here. The Vanderhoof International Airshow is the largest camp-in airshow in N America, attracting 25,000 spectators annually.

VANDERPANT, John (Jan van der Pant), photographer (b 11 Jan 1884, Alkmaar, Netherlands; d 24 July 1939, Vancouver). He was internationally renowned during the 1920s and 1930s for his black-and-white silver bromide prints. A Dutch photojournalist, Vanderpant immigrated to southern Alberta in 1911 with his wife Catharina. In Alberta he operated 3 commercial photo studios. The couple and their 2 daughters moved to NEW WESTMINSTER in 1924 and Vanderpant opened a successful portrait studio. In 1926 he and Harold MORTIMER-LAMB opened the VANDERPANT GALLERIES in VANCOUVER. Vanderpant was a member of the Royal Photographic Society and had solo exhibitions in the US, Britain and Europe. He is best known for his distinctive use of light and form in studies of BC's terminal grain elevators and close-ups of fruits and vegetables. *See also* PHOTOGRAPHY.

Sheryl Salloum

Reading: Sheryl Salloum, *Underlying Vibrations: The Photography and Life of John Vanderpant,* 1995.

VANDERPANT GALLERIES, on Robson St in VANCOUVER, was a PHOTOGRAPHY/art gallery opened on 15 Mar 1926 by John VANDERPANT and Harold MORTIMER-LAMB. The partnership dissolved after a year and Vanderpant ran the gallery alone. Through his endeavours the building became a focal point for innovation in music, painting and photography. After his death in 1939, his daughters Anna and Catharina operated a portrait studio at the Galleries until 1941 and 1946 respectively. In 1990 the building that had housed the Galleries, and later the well-known Côte d'Azur restaurant, was demolished.   *Sheryl Salloum*

VANTREIGHT, Geoffrey Arthur, bulb grower, cancer fundraiser (b 1 Jan 1924, Victoria; d 13 May 2000, Saanich). He was raised in VICTORIA. In 1940 he began working at G.A. Vantreight & Sons, his family's large bulb operation, and he became a business and community leader in the SAANICH area. The firm had been established by his grandfather, John Vantreight, an Irish immigrant who homesteaded at GORDON HEAD in 1884, and it was developed in the 1920s and 1930s by his father, who was also named Geoffrey Arthur Vantreight and was known as

BC's "Strawberry King." Vantreight was an avid sports enthusiast and a member of the Victoria Sports Hall of Fame. He was one of the founders of "Daffodil Day," a fundraising campaign for the Canadian Cancer Society, now emulated in many other countries. Vantreight's son, Ian S. Vantreight, the company's general manager, has also been the president of several BC agricultural associations. *AS*

VARGAS ISLAND, 28 km², in CLAYOQUOT SOUND 6 km northwest of TOFINO on the west coast of VANCOUVER ISLAND, was an important

Early motorists at Vaseux Lk. Vernon Museum

summer village site of the Ahousaht First Nation of the NUU-CHAH-NULTH (Nootka). Named by SPANISH EXPLORERS for a government official, it was settled by British immigrant farmers in the 1910s but abandoned by them after WWI. The island's wildness and spectacular beaches, now protected as part of Vargas Island Provincial PARK, have made it a favourite destination for kayakers. *AS*

VARLEY, Frederick Horsman, artist (b 2 Jan 1881, Sheffield, England; d 8 Sept 1969, Toronto). Trained as a painter in Europe, he immigrated to Canada in 1912 and found work as a commercial illustrator in Toronto. He received critical acclaim for his work as an official war artist during WWI and in 1920 he became a founding member of the Group of Seven. During the 1920s he worked chiefly as a portraitist; finding it difficult to make ends meet, he moved west in 1926 to teach at the Vancouver School of Decorative and Applied Arts (*see* EMILY CARR INSTITUTE OF ART & DESIGN). He found VANCOUVER a fertile place to indulge his interest in eastern mysticism and Chinese art. During the decade he lived in BC he played a central role in the local art scene and painted hundreds of landscapes. For 2 years, from 1933 to 1935, he and J.W.G. MACDONALD ran their own art school, the BC College of Arts, on W Georgia St. With the help of the designer Harry Täuber, the college was briefly the centre of the avant-garde in the

city but financial difficulties forced it to close. For much of this time Varley lived in a house in Lynn Canyon in N VANCOUVER. In Apr 1936 he returned east to resume portrait painting and teaching in Ottawa. He spent the rest of his life in eastern Canada, although he made several painting trips to BC. *See also* ART, VISUAL.

VASEUX LAKE, 2.75 km², 14.5 km north of OLIVER in the S OKANAGAN VALLEY, is one of Canada's finest birdwatching areas. A federal wildlife and migratory bird sanctuary, it is an oasis of greenery in the surrounding desert-like terrain. Several rare bird species visit the lake, which also has a population of California bighorn MOUNTAIN SHEEP. Vaseux Lake Provincial PARK (12 ha) was established in 1956 adjacent to the federal wildlife sanctuary. The name is a French word for "muddy," a reference to the shallow, silty water.

VAVENBY, pop 396, is on the N THOMPSON R, 150 km north of KAMLOOPS. It was founded about 1910; the name is a misapplication of Navenby, the English birthplace of an early settler named Daubney Pridgeon. The local economy has relied on 2 SAWMILLS, along with one of the largest sheep ranches in BC.

VEDDER/CHILLIWACK RIVER flows 100 km from CHILLIWACK LK through the Skagit Range of the CASCADE MTS to join the Sumas R shortly before it merges with the FRASER R west of CHILLIWACK. The upper portion (60 km) is known as the Chilliwack R; the lower portion (40 km) was named the Vedder (after an early Dutch settler) when it was rerouted as part of the Sumas Reclamation Scheme in 1922. The river is popular with SALMON fishers during summer and fall and for its winter STEELHEAD fishing. *See also* FISHING, SPORT.

VEDDER CROSSING, 7 km south of CHILLIWACK is a farming community (*see* AGRICULTURE) that got its start in the early 1900s. The Vedder R is named after Volkert Vedder, who arrived in the FRASER VALLEY in 1859 and later acquired land in

this area. His son Adam became a successful farmer and politician. A bridge crosses the Vedder here; upstream of the bridge the river is known as the Chilliwack. *AS*

VERIGIN, Peter Vasilevich "Peter the Lordly," Doukhobor leader (b 29 June 1859, Slavyanka, Russia; d 29 Oct 1924, near Grand Forks). He became leader of the DOUKHOBORS in Russia in 1887 and was immediately arrested by the Tsarist police. Exiled in Siberia for 15 years, he passed the time developing his religious and political ideas. Meanwhile the Doukhobors organized a mass migration to Canada in 1898–99. When Verigin was released from detention in 1902 he followed, and arrived at the Saskatchewan colony at Christmas. When the Canadian government began to renege on promises it had made to the Doukhobors, Verigin came to BC and in 1908 re-established about 5,000 of his followers in the KOOTENAY.

Peter Verigin, Doukhobor leader.
Kootenay Doukhobor Historical Society

Under his leadership they attempted to develop a self-supporting communal society more or less isolated from the outside world. Verigin was killed in a railway explosion, whether intentionally or accidentally has never been determined. His son Peter Petrovich Verigin (1880–1939) had remained in Russia with his mother, the elder Verigin's first wife. After his father died he came to BC in 1927 and assumed leadership of the sect.

VERNON is located in the N OKANAGAN VALLEY on the northeast arm of OKANAGAN LK, nestled between Okanagan, KALAMALKA and Swan lakes, 440 km from VANCOUVER via the COQUIHALLA  HWY. Fur traders began using the west side of Okanagan Lk as a transport route from the lower COLUMBIA R after 1811 (*see* FUR BRIGADES),

Silver Star Mt near Vernon. Keith Thirkell photo

but it was the CATTLE INDUSTRY that brought the first permanent settlement. Between 1862, when the brothers Forbes and Charles VERNON established the COLDSTREAM Ranch, and 1900, thousands of hectares of land were pre-empted and used for cattle raising. Luc Girouard was the first settler in what is now Vernon. In 1861 he built a cabin (which still exists) beside a spot on BX Creek that the aboriginal people called Nintle-moos-chin, or "jumping-over-place." Girouard was joined by an OBLATE missionary and the area became known as Priest's Valley until 1885, when a townsite was laid out and called Centreville. It was incorporated on 31 Dec 1892 and renamed after Forbes Vernon, by then a member of the legislature and major shareholder in the SHUSWAP & OKANAGAN RWY. With the arrival of the railway, the building of an irrigation system and the beginning of steamboat operations on Okanagan Lk, Vernon became part of BC's largest fruit-growing area (*see* TREE FRUITS). During WWI Vernon was the site of the largest army training camp in BC. The camp was enlarged and used again in WWII; in the late 1990s it was still the site of summer cadet training. AGRICULTURE and the FOREST INDUSTRY were the mainstays of the economy for many years, and TOURISM and manufacturing have become important as well. A campus of Okanagan University College (*see* COMMUNITY COLLEGES) is located here, and nearby Silver Star Mt is a popular year-round SKIING and recreation area.

Population: 31,817
Rank in BC: 22nd
Population increase since 1981: 57%
Date of incorporation: city 30 Dec 1892
Land area: 77.1 km²
Location: North Okanagan Regional District
Economic base: agriculture, manufacturing, logging, dairying, wholesale services, tourism

VERNON, Charles Albert, rancher, business promoter (b 1840, Ireland; d 8 Oct 1906,

Victoria). Educated at military college in England, he was an officer in the Lancaster Fusiliers when he resigned his commission to come to Canada with his brother Forbes VERNON to take up land in BC in 1863. After SILVER MINING for 2 years, the brothers settled on property near the north end of OKANAGAN LK and developed a ranch at COLDSTREAM. In 1883 Charles sold his share and moved his family to VICTORIA, where he became a real estate and railway promoter.

VERNON, Forbes George, rancher, politician (b 1843, Ireland; d Jan 1911, London, England). Educated in England, he was an officer in the British army when he resigned his commission and embarked for Canada in 1863 with his brother Charles to take up land in BC. After SILVER MINING for 2 seasons, the brothers settled near the north end of OKANAGAN LK at COLDSTREAM, where they developed a ranch. By 1883 Forbes was the sole owner of the property, which he sold to Gov Gen Lord Aberdeen in 1891. Forbes also belonged to a syndicate that built the SHUSWAP & OKANAGAN RWY linking Okanagan Lk to SICAMOUS in 1892. Meanwhile he served in the legislature from 1875 to 1882 and again from 1886 to 1894 and was chief commissioner of lands and works for almost all of that time. The city of VERNON was named for him. Following his electoral defeat he was BC agent general in London until 1898. He remained in London until his death.

VERNON PREPARATORY SCHOOL was a private school for boys founded in 1914 by Austin C. Mackie, an English-born ANGLICAN cleric, at COLDSTREAM outside VERNON. It was a boarding school, intended to prepare boys for British public school and to mould them into model English gentlemen. Mackie remained head until 1946. The school thrived under his main successor, Charles Twite, from 1948 to 1965, but closed in 1972. *See also* EDUCATION, PRIVATE.

VESAK, Norbert, choreographer (b 22 Oct 1936, Port Moody; d 1990, Charlotte, NC). Trained as a dancer in the US and England, he

returned to VANCOUVER in the early 1960s. He was choreographer at the VANCOUVER PLAYHOUSE, then in 1969 he launched his own DANCE company, Western Dance Theatre. The company folded in 1971 during its second season. The Royal Winnipeg Ballet commissioned him to create a multimedia dance piece based on George RYGA's play *The Ecstasy of Rita Joe*. It was also with the RWB that he created his internationally acclaimed duet "Belong," part of a longer work titled *What to Do 'til the Messiah Comes*. Later he moved to California, where he had a successful international career.

VESUVIUS BAY, on SALTSPRING ISLAND, 52 km north of VICTORIA in the GULF ISLANDS, is a small resort community from which BC FERRY CORP runs a ferry to CROFTON on VANCOUVER ISLAND. A group of BLACK families from the US settled in the area in 1859. Estalon Bittancourt opened a store in 1873. The bay was named after a Royal Navy vessel that had no connection whatsoever with the BC coast. *AS*

VICKERS, Roy Henry, artist (b 4 June 1946, Greenville/Laxgalts'ap). Of mixed British and TSIMSHIAN background, he was raised in the north coastal village of KITKATLA and in HAZELTON and VICTORIA, where he graduated from high

Roy Vickers, artist. Frances Litman photo

school. In the 1970s he studied at the Kitanmaax School of Northwest Coast Indian Art in 'KSAN. After temporarily abandoning his art to work in commercial FISHING, he settled in TOFINO where he opened his own gallery in 1986. Since then his career has flourished, and a second gallery has been opened in Victoria. Vickers' unique style merges traditional aboriginal themes with contemporary design. He was awarded the ORDER OF BC in 1998. *See also* ART, NORTHWEST COAST ABORIGINAL.

VICTORIA is situated at the southern tip of VANCOUVER ISLAND, overlooking JUAN DE FUCA STRAIT. The largest city on the island, it has been the capital of BC since 1868, when capital status shifted from NEW WESTMINSTER. Despite opposition from mainlanders, this decision was reaffirmed in 1898 with the opening of the new LEGISLATIVE BUILDINGS. The city was named for Queen Victoria, who came to the British throne in 1837. Along with several neighbouring communities, it forms the Capital Regional District, the second-largest metropolitan area in BC with a 1996 population of 304,287. The

The Birdcages in Victoria, BC's first legislative buildings, c 1867. Frederick Dally/BC Archives A-02574

The scenic Gorge waterway, Victoria. Diane Eaton photo

area was occupied by Coast Salish (*see* SALISHAN FIRST NATIONS) peoples when the first Europeans arrived. White settlement began with the construction of FORT VICTORIA by the HBC in 1843, supervised by Chief Factor James DOUGLAS, who selected the site and became closely associated with the evolving community. Overlooking an excellent harbour with arable land nearby, the fort became HBC's headquarters for the FUR TRADE on the Pacific coast. A village grew up next to the post at a townsite laid out during 1851–52, also called Victoria. It boomed in 1858 with the arrival of a flood of prospectors during the GOLD RUSH up the FRASER R. The fort, demolished during the 1860s, was superseded by a bustling commercial entrepot; Victoria incorporated as a city in 1862. For many years it was the busiest seaport north of San Francisco; the inner harbour has continued to receive vessels from many ports. SHIPBUILDING, SAWMILLING, commercial FISHING and sealing (*see* FUR SEAL) all were important to the local economy, and the military had a major economic and social presence once ESQUIMALT was made a British naval base in 1865.

The CPR chose BURRARD INLET as its western terminus in 1886, and by the end of the century Victoria's economic fortunes were eclipsed. Sealing ended and maritime shipping became less important, SALMON CANNING centralized on the Fraser R and the city deindustrialized. Victoria was replaced by VANCOUVER as the economic centre of the province, though it continued as the capital and maintained its political role. By the late 1990s most of the labour force was engaged in the service sector, both government and private. TOURISM has become increasingly important, with about 3 million visitors annually, and contributes to the civic attempts to retain an "olde Englande" atmosphere, at least in

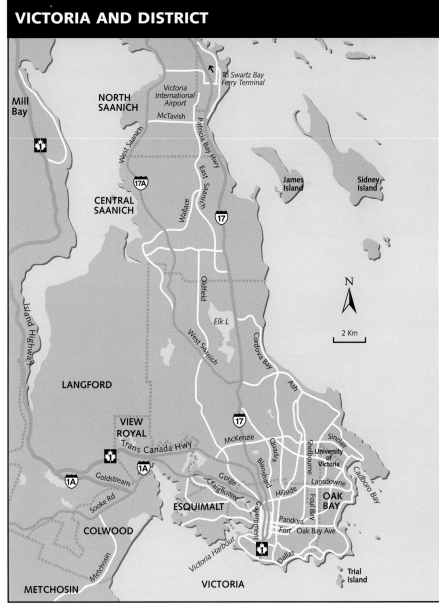

VICTORIA AND DISTRICT

Mill Bay

NORTH SAANICH

To Swartz Bay Ferry Terminal

Victoria International Airport

McTavish

West Saanich

East Saanich

Patricia Bay Hwy

James Island

Sidney Island

CENTRAL SAANICH

Wallace

17

17A

Oldfield

Elk L

West Saanich

Cordova Bay

N

2 Km

LANGFORD

Island Highway

Ash

17

VIEW ROYAL

McKenzie

Quadra

Shelbourne

Sinclair

University of Victoria

Cadboro Bay

Trans Canada Hwy

1A

Goldstream

Blanshard

Lansdowne

Gorge

Hillside

OAK BAY

Craigflower

Foul Bay

Sooke Rd

ESQUIMALT

Government

Pandora

Oak Bay Ave

COLWOOD

Fort

Metchosin

Victoria Harbour

Dallas

Trial Island

METCHOSIN

VICTORIA

The Empress Hotel, Inner Harbour, Victoria, 1990. Roy Luckow photo

Butchart Gardens, a leading attraction of the Victoria area.

Craigdarroch Castle, a Victoria landmark built in 1887.

and the Marine Scenic Drive. The city is connected to the mainland by ferries to Washington state and from nearby Swartz Bay to TSAWWASSEN. The ESQUIMALT & NANAIMO RWY, completed to Victoria in 1888, continues to run north to COURTENAY.

Population: 73,504 (Capital Regional District 304,287)
Rank in BC: 14th
Population increase since 1981: 14%
Date of incorporation: city 2 Aug 1862
Land area: 18.78 km²
Location: Capital Regional District
Economic base: government and retail services, lumber, fishing, shipbuilding, light industry, tourism

VICTORIA & SIDNEY RAILWAY ran up the SAANICH PENINSULA north from VICTORIA 27 km to SIDNEY on southern VANCOUVER ISLAND. Opened in 1894, it was dubbed the "Cordwood Limited" because its early locomotives burned wood for fuel. It was purchased in 1901 by the GREAT NORTHERN RWY, which had ambitions to connect it by ferry to the mainland. Accordingly, in 1903 the converted car ferry SS *Victorian* went into service between Sidney and PORT GUICHON on the FRASER R near LADNER. It was withdrawn for lack of passengers 2 years later. In Apr 1919 the railway closed, forced out of business by bus service and competing rail lines.

VICTORIA COUGARS was originally a professional team playing in the PACIFIC COAST HOCKEY ASSOC under owner, manager and coach Lester PATRICK. Starting as the Aristocrats, the VICTORIA franchise on 3 Jan 1912 hosted the first professional game played west of Ontario and Michigan. The team returned to the league for the 1918–19 season after a 2-year absence and became the Cougars in 1922. In 1925 it won BC's second Stanley Cup after defeating Saskatoon, Calgary and the Montreal Maroons in the playoffs. Led by scoring star Frank FREDRICKSON, the Cougars took advantage of new forward-passing and substitution rules to beat Montreal 3-1. The next year they again met the Maroons in the final but were soundly defeated. In the off-season, Lester's brother Frank PATRICK arranged for the sale of all the PCHA's players to the new NHL. The Cougars became the NHL's Detroit Cougars, which eventually changed its name to Red Wings and became the most successful American franchise in the history of the game. Major professional hockey never returned to Victoria but in 1949 Lester Patrick established a Victoria Cougars club in the minor-professional Pacific Coast Hockey League (later Western Hockey League) featuring Eddie Dorohoy, Roger Lehay and Andy Hebenton and it lasted until 1961. After a stint as a farm team for the Toronto Maple Leafs 1964–67, the Cougars name resurfaced in 1968 as a community owned franchise in the BC JUNIOR HOCKEY LEAGUE. They won the league championship in 1969 and after a group of Calgary businessmen bought the team it was upgraded to the major junior WHL in 1971. WHL coaching legend Pat

the city core, where many picturesque 19th-century buildings have survived. At the same time, the metropolitan area has grown rapidly; in 1994 the city hosted the 15th COMMONWEALTH GAMES, an event that spurred the construction and expansion of various recreational facilities. The actual city is quite small, extending from Foul Bay Rd in the east to Tolmie Ave in the north, and including the old residential suburb of JAMES BAY, which protrudes into Victoria Harbour in the city's southwest corner. Victoria West, located across the harbour next to Esquimalt, is also part of the city proper and is connected to downtown by the Johnson St Bridge. The moderate CLIMATE and relatively affordable real estate make the Victoria area popular with retirees. Post-secondary education is provided by the UNIV OF VICTORIA, Camosun College (*see also* COMMUNITY COLLEGES) and ROYAL ROADS UNIV. Cultural amenities include a civic art gallery, a symphony orchestra, an opera company, the ROYAL BC MUSEUM and the MARITIME MUSEUM OF BC. Other landmarks are the EMPRESS HOTEL, BEACON HILL PARK, THUNDERBIRD PARK, CRAIGDARROCH, the Crystal Garden, CHINATOWN

Ginnell purchased the franchise in 1973 and coached it to a first-place finish in 1974-75. In 1980-81 coach Jack Shupe and players Grant Fuhr, Geoff COURTNALL and Barry PEDERSON led Victoria to its only WHL championship and Memorial Cup appearance. From the mid-1980s to 1995 the Cougars were famously futile, in 1989-90 posting the worst record in WHL history with 5 wins and 65 losses. Their losing streak of 32 games is a record in Canadian junior hockey. After it became apparent that fans had abandoned the team, it moved to PRINCE GEORGE. *SW*

VICTORIA CROSS (VC) was the highest award for military valour in the armed forces of the British Empire and Commonwealth. Instituted by Queen Victoria in 1856 during the Crimean War, it was presented to 93 Canadians before being supplanted in 1972 by Canada's own bravery awards. The VC was awarded to 20 soldiers, sailors and aviators with a connection to BC or to a BC battalion (*see also* MILITARY HISTORY). During WWII, of the 13 VCs awarded to Canadians, 5 went to British Columbians.

BC's VC recipients from all wars are:

Lt Edward Donald Bellew (1882-1961). Born in India, educated in England, he immigrated to BC in 1901 and worked as a construction engineer in NEW WESTMINSTER. He served overseas with the 7th (1st BC Regiment) Battalion. As a machine-gun officer at the 2nd Battle of Ypres, 24 Apr 1915, he prevented the enemy from fully exploiting a gap in the line until his position was overrun and he was taken prisoner. He spent the rest of his life as a dredging inspector on the FRASER R and ranching at MONTE CREEK.

Pte John Chipman Kerr (1887-1963). He left his NS home in 1906, travelling west to work as a logger in the KOOTENAY. He served overseas with the 49th (Edmonton) Battalion. At the Battle of Courcelette on 16 Sept 1916 he single-handedly inflicted heavy losses on the enemy, captured a 240-m section of trench and took 62 prisoners. During WWII he served as a guard for the Royal Canadian Air Force on SEA ISLAND. He retired to PORT MOODY where he took up fishing.

Piper James Richardson (1895-1916). As a child he immigrated with his family from Scotland to CHILLIWACK. He enlisted in Vancouver with the 72nd Seaforth Highlanders of Canada and served overseas with the 16th Canadian Scottish Battalion. During an assault at Regina Trench (Battle of the Somme) on 9 Oct 1916 he played his pipes in full view of the enemy, rallying his comrades for a successful attack. He was killed returning to the firing line to retrieve his pipes.

Pte William Johnstone Milne (1892-1917). He was posted to the 16th (Canadian Scottish) Battalion in June 1916. On 9 Apr 1917 at Vimy Ridge he single-handedly captured 2 machine guns, holding up the advance. He died after capturing the second gun and was awarded the VC.

Sgt Maj Robert Hanna (1887-1967). He immigrated to BC from his native Ireland in 1905 and was working as a logger when WWI began. He

MEN of VALOR
They fight for you

"**When last seen he was collecting Bren and Tommy Guns and preparing a defensive position which successfully covered the withdrawal from the beach.**"— *Excerpt from citation awarding Victoria Cross to Lt-Col. Merritt, South Saskatchewan Regt, Dieppe, Aug. 19, 1942*

Lt Colonel Cecil Merritt, Victoria Cross winner, featured in a WWII poster. NAC C-087124

enlisted in Vancouver with the 29th Battalion. At Hill 70, Lens, France, on 21 Aug 1917 he led a party of men to capture an enemy strongpoint, silencing a machine gun and allowing the attack to succeed. After the war he returned to BC where he ran a logging camp at ALDERGROVE, then farmed at MT LEHMAN.

A/Cpl Filip Konowal (1887-1959). He was awarded the VC while serving with the 47th (New Westminster) Battalion at Hill 70, Lens. Among other brave deeds, he single-handedly wiped out 2 machine-gun emplacements and killed 16 of the enemy.

Pte Michael "Mickey" O'Rourke (1878-1957). He served overseas with the 7th (1st BC Regiment) Battalion as a stretcher bearer. During the fighting at Hill 70 he repeatedly ventured into no man's land under heavy fire to rescue wounded comrades. A pre-war immigrant to BC from Ireland, he worked as a Vancouver longshoreman and was widely known as the feisty "King of the Waterfront."

Maj George PEARKES (1888-1984). A career soldier, he was LT GOV of BC from 1960-68. He won his VC with the 5th Canadian Mounted Rifles at Passchendaele on 30-31 Oct 1917 when, despite a serious leg wound, he led his men forward to capture Source Farm, then held off repeated counterattacks.

Lt Gordon Flowerdew (1885-1918). He enlisted with the 31st BC Horse at WALHACHIN and was serving with Lord Strathcona's Horse on 30 Mar 1918 when he won his VC. He died leading a cavalry charge against enemy infantry positions at Bois de Moreuil that helped to stop the German advance to Amiens.

Lt Rowland Bourke (1885-1958. He was the only Canadian seaman to win a VC during WWI. Rejected by the Canadian services because of

poor eyesight, he went to England and enlisted in the Royal Naval Volunteer Reserve. His medal was won on 10 May 1918 during an assault on a German naval base at Ostend. After the war he returned to his fruit farm near NELSON, then moved to VICTORIA where he worked at the ESQUIMALT naval base. During WWII he helped to organize the GUMBOOT NAVY.

Cpl William Henry Metcalfe (1885-1968). He transferred to the 16th Canadian Scottish in May 1915 and was awarded his VC on 2 Sept 1918 at the Drocourt-Quéant Line for leading a tank under heavy fire against a section of German trench that was holding up the advance.

Lt Col Cyrus Peck (1871-1956). He was the oldest Canadian (47) to win a VC in WWI. While he was at the front he was also MP for the PRINCE RUPERT area where he had lived prior to the war. During 4 years in the trenches he was wounded twice. He won his VC on 2 Sept 1918 at the Drocourt-Quéant Line when, as commanding officer of the 16th Canadian Scottish, he led an assault under intense enemy shelling. Following the war he served as an MLA for the SAANICH and the Islands riding from 1924-33 and was later an aide-de-camp to 2 gov gens.

Cpl Walter Rayfield (1881-1949). He served overseas with the 7th (1st BC Regiment) Battalion and won the VC at the Drocourt-Quéant Line between 2-4 Sept 1918 for several brave actions, including twice rushing a section of trench and capturing 42 prisoners.

Capt John MacGregor (1888-1952). He immigrated from his native Scotland to Canada in 1909 and was a contractor in Prince Rupert when WWI began. He was one of the most decorated Canadians of the war. He won his VC serving with the 2nd Canadian Mounted Rifles between 29 Sept and 3 Oct at Cambrai. While wounded, he stormed an enemy machine-gun nest, killing 4 and taking 8 prisoners. He served as a training officer during WWII, then retired to POWELL RIVER.

Lt Graham Thomson Lyall (1892-1941). He arrived in France with the 4th Canadian Mounted Rifles and served as an officer with the 102nd (Northern BC) Battalion. He was awarded his VC at Bourlon Wood, 27 Sept-1 Oct 1918, for leading his platoon in the capture of 3 enemy strongholds and 195 prisoners. He was killed in action in WWII serving with the British Army.

Lt Col Charles Cecil MERRITT (1908-2000). A native of VANCOUVER, he won his VC for bravery at the Dieppe Raid in 1942. He commanded the South Saskatchewan Regiment (SSR) and his was the only Canadian unit to capture its objectives during the ill-fated raid. He led his men with distinction, wiping out a German pillbox and organizing a rearguard action that allowed more SSR than any other Canadian regiment to get off the beach back to England. He spent the rest of the war as a prisoner of the Germans. After the war he served as a Conservative MP for Vancouver-Burrard from 1945-49 and practised law.

Smokey Smith, the only Canadian private to win the Victoria Cross during WWII.
NAC PA-140011

Major John Mahoney, who won his Victoria Cross during the Italian campaign.
NAC PA-167002

Maj Charles Ferguson Hoey (1914–44). A native of DUNCAN, he went to England in 1933 to enlist in the army. He attended the Royal Military College at Sandhurst and was posted in India before the war. He won his VC during the Burma campaign on 16 Feb 1944 when he died leading an assault on a Japanese machine-gun nest.

Maj John Keefer Mahoney (1911–1990). He was a newspaper reporter with the Vancouver PROVINCE when WWII broke out. He served with the Westminster Regiment and won his VC in Italy on 24 May 1944 for his leadership in establishing a bridgehead across the Melfa R. He remained in the army until 1962, then retired to London, ON.

Pte Ernest "Smokey" Smith (b 1914). Born in New Westminster, he served overseas with the Seaforth Highlanders in Italy. He was the only Canadian private in WWII awarded a VC, which he won on 21–22 Oct 1944 for single-handedly repulsing a German counterattack. Following the war he returned to New Westminster, but joined up again for the Korean War and remained in the army until 1964 when he joined his wife Esther in the travel business in Vancouver. The couple became great ambassadors for Canada, travelling on many veterans' trips from the 1970s to the 1990s.

Lt Robert Hampton Gray (1917–45). Born in TRAIL, he grew up in Nelson, then graduated from UBC in 1940. That year he joined the navy and trained in the British Commonwealth Air Training Plan as a pilot. He won his VC on 9 Aug 1945 when he died attacking a Japanese warship in the Pacific. He was the last Canadian to win the medal, and the only Canadian fighter pilot to win one in WWII. Gray's Peak in KOKANEE GLACIER PARK is named for him and his brother, Jack, who also died in action during the war.

Reading: William Arthur Bishop, *Our Bravest and Our Best: the Story of Canada's Victoria Cross Winners,* 1995; Dr John Blatherwick, *1000 Brave*

Canadians: The Canadian Gallantry Awards, 1854–1989, 1991.

VICTORIA LUMBER & MANUFACTURING CO was established on VANCOUVER ISLAND in 1889 by J.A. Humbird, a US lumberman and protegé of Frederick Weyerhaeuser. Humbird purchased the first tract of timber sold by the ESQUIMALT & NANAIMO RWY, 100,000 acres (400 km²) of the most valuable forest land in BC, for $5 an acre. He abandoned plans to build a SAWMILL in VICTORIA and instead purchased a small mill at CHEMAINUS; it had been built to run on water power in 1862 by A.G. Elliott. Humbird built a new mill on the site, one of the largest and most modern on the Pacific coast, and hired E.J. ("Old Hickory") PALMER, a Weyerhaeuser manager, to run it. VL&M pioneered the use of steam-powered LOGGING equipment, importing the first steam donkey and one of the first steam locomotives. H.R. MACMILLAN gained his first business experience at

VL&M: he worked as assistant manager for less than a year, and resigned after a dispute with Palmer. When MacMillan left he vowed that the next time he walked through the office door, he would own the company. Under Humbird's son Tom and his grandson John, the company remained one of BC's largest and most profitable sawmills. The mill burned to the ground in 1923 and Palmer died soon after. The mill was rebuilt and operated successfully until the early 1940s, when the Humbird family decided to sell, on condition it not be sold to MacMillan. The Toronto industrialist E.P. Taylor bought the mill in 1944; it was later revealed he had purchased it on MacMillan's behalf. The company was folded into the MacMillan company and the Chemainus mill was rebuilt in the 1980s. *See also* FOREST INDUSTRY.   *Ken Drushka*

VICTORIA MACHINERY DEPOT (VMD) was one of the most important and long-lived manufacturing enterprises in VICTORIA. Established in 1882 by Joseph Spratt, also the founder of ALBION IRON WORKS, it was located on Bay St near the POINT ELLICE BRIDGE. VMD initially concentrated on industrial engineering, machinery and foundry work; then it expanded into SHIPBUILDING and ship repair. The company was managed by the Spratt family until 1947. During that time it was an important player in the shipbuilding industry, culminating in the construction during WWII of a succession of corvettes, destroyer escorts and Victory ships. With a second depot at Ogden Point to accommodate its wartime production, VMD employed as many as 3,000 workers at its peak. Post-war production shifted back to commercial vessels, including 12 in the BC FERRY CORP fleet. In 1967 the company sold its shipbuilding and repair operations to BURRARD DRY DOCK, which closed the Ogden Point facility the next year. (The site was later redeveloped by the Coast Guard.) The Bay St location remained in operation until the 1990s.   *Ted Mills*

VICTORIA PIONEER RIFLES was a corps of soldiers organized in 1860 by 45 BLACK residents,

Victoria Pioneer Rifles, formed in 1860.
BC Archives C-06124

The only white person allowed to join was the bandmaster. Largely self-financed, it continued until 1864; that year, not allowed to merge with an all-white corps and snubbed by the governor, the corps disbanded. Known popularly as the African Rifles, it was the first army unit in BC.

VIEW ROYAL, town, pop 6,441, is a residential suburb of VICTORIA about 6 km west of the capital overlooking ESQUIMALT Harbour. First settled by Dr John HELMCKEN in the 1850s, it was incorporated in 1988.

VILLAGE ISLAND is one of the jumble of islands lying between northern VANCOUVER ISLAND and the mainland coast near the entrance to KNIGHT INLET. It is part of the traditional territory of the Malaleleqala, of the KWAKWAKA'WAKW (Kwakiutl) First Nations. Their main village site, MAMALILACULLA, located on the west side of the island, is now largely abandoned, though people return for visits. The missionary Kathleen O'BRIEN ran a school and sanatorium here from 1920 to 1945 and the village was the site of the famous illegal "Christmas POTLATCH" held by Dan Cranmer in 1921.

VINSULLA, 28 km north of KAMLOOPS on the CNR line, is a small AGRICULTURAL settlement situated where Knouff Crk joins the N THOMPSON R. Vinsulla is an anagram for the surname of Michael "Ten Percent" Sullivan, who settled at nearby Sullivan Lk in the 1860s after joining the GOLD RUSH to the CARIBOO. He became a prosperous district landowner with quite a reputation as an entrepreneur. Another tiny farming settlement just to the northeast was named Canough Crk, believed to be a corruption of Knouff Crk. *See also* KNOUFF LK.   AS

VIREO is a small perching songbird, drab olive green in colour with a white or yellowish-white

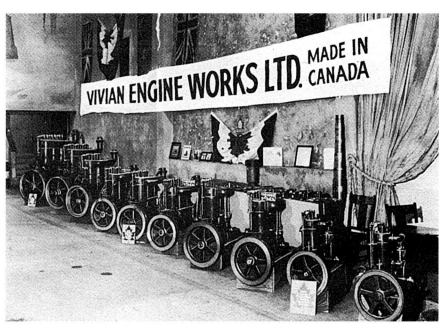

Warbling vireo, a BC songbird. Tim Zurowski photo

chest. It feeds on INSECTS and BERRIES and builds a distinctive cup-shaped nest that hangs suspended from a tree branch. Of 8 species in Canada, 6 occur in BC. The warbling vireo (*Vireo gilvus*) is the most commonly seen in urban

areas. Like Cassin's vireo (*V. cassinii*) and the red-eyed vireo (*V. olivaceus*), it is widely distributed across the province. Hutton's vireo (*V. huttoni*) is resident only on the South Coast, while the Philadelphia vireo (*V. philadelphicus*) and blue-headed vireo (*V. solitarius*) occur mainly in the PEACE R area.

VIVIAN ENGINE WORKS was a marine engine manufacturer, founded in VANCOUVER in 1909 by Will Vivian (1890–1965). It built many of the small gasoline units used to motorize the gillnet FISHING fleet in the years before WWI. In the 1920s Vivian was the first Canadian company to build a marine diesel engine; this unit became its speciality and the key to its expansion. In addition to boat engines, Vivian manufactured engines for a wide variety of uses and for customers around the world. During WWII,

A display of Vivian's small marine engines.

Vivian engines powered many naval vessels and the Vancouver engine works employed more than 800 people. Will Vivian retired in 1950 and sold the company, which was eventually taken over by A.V. Roe.

VOGHT VALLEY, a LOGGING and ranching (*see* CATTLE INDUSTRY) district 90 km southwest of KAMLOOPS, was settled in the 1880s and named after Bill Voght, a local pioneer. His father, William H. Voght, had participated in the FRASER R GOLD RUSH and was an early promoter of COAL MINING and railway construction in the MERRITT area.   AS

VOLUNTEERISM refers to the organized activities of volunteers working with community organizations and governments. Volunteering has been a part of the BC economy since the

Vivian pioneered the development of heavy duty diesel engines.

arrival of European settlers in the 19th century. After firefighting and security concerns were met, concerned citizens organized churches, schools, civic government and systems for the delivery of health care and social services. Recreation, sport and cultural organizations soon followed. Activist volunteers initiated trade unions and organizations to advance the rights of women and minorities. As organizations grew, they hired paid staff and left volunteers to focus on establishing new programs, fundraising and adding a human touch to institutional services.

BC's first volunteer centre was established in VANCOUVER in 1943 as a means of organizing women in support of the war effort. The involvement of more than 30,000 volunteers in sandbagging, rescuing survivors and relieving suffering during the 1948 flooding of the FRASER R (*see also* DISASTERS) demonstrated the value of organized volunteers in the post-war years. The growth of volunteering has advanced to the point where in the late 1990s more than half of all BC adults say they have volunteered. Volunteer BC is an organization that represents 35 volunteer centres in BC; these centres recruit volunteers for community organizations, help those organizations establish and manage volunteer programs, and encourage community involvement in improving the quality of life for everyone. *Roy Crowe*

VULTURE, TURKEY (*Cathartes aura*), a large, bald-headed bird of prey, is Canada's only species of vulture. It breeds across southern BC and is found in greatest abundance around GEORGIA STRAIT and in the OKANAGAN VALLEY. It feeds on carrion and is seen mainly in flight, soaring on its long wings above cliffs and open country. With black plumage and a small, red head, it is distinguishable from the EAGLE in flight by its V-shaped wing position and tendency to tip from side to side as it soars and circles. Eggs are usually laid in a cave or on the ground among rocks. Vultures migrate to S

Turkey vulture. Len Mackave photo

America in winter; hundreds can be seen soaring over southern VANCOUVER ISLAND in September, waiting for winds to carry them across JUAN DE FUCA STRAIT.

WADDINGTON, Alfred Pendrell, entrepreneur (b 6 Oct 1801, London, England; d 27 Feb 1872, Ottawa). Educated in Germany and France, he was involved in a series of failed business ventures before emigrating in 1850 to California. There he prospered as a grocery merchant during the GOLD RUSH. He came north to VICTORIA in 1858 to establish a branch of the business. His book *The Fraser Mines Vindicated* (1858) was the first book published in BC. An advocate of democratic reform, he was elected to the assembly in 1860 but resigned the following year to pursue his road-building schemes. He settled on BUTE INLET as a promising starting point for a road connecting the coast to the Interior, and construction began in 1862. The intrusion of construction workers into the territory of the TSILHQOT'IN people led to the so-called CHILCOTIN WAR. After his road project faltered he became superintendent of schools on VANCOUVER ISLAND and served from 1865 to 1867, then began promoting his scheme for a transcontinental transportation system linking Britain to the Orient via Canada. He was in Ottawa trying to raise support when he caught smallpox and died.

WADDINGTON, MOUNT (el 4,019 m), the highest peak wholly within BC, is located about 300 km north of VANCOUVER in the heart of the COAST MTS. The Coast Salish (*see* SALISHAN FIRST NATIONS) believe it is the keeper of the notorious BUTE INLET wind. The slopes of the MOUNTAIN were an important hunting area for the HOMALCO First Nation. Some of them may have reached its peak, but the area was first explored in the 1920s by Don and Phyllis MUNDAY. The tales of their explorations are among the great epics of Canadian MOUNTAINEERING. Despite repeated attempts between 1926 and 1934, the Mundays were unable to reach the summit. They did manage to climb the lower North West Summit in 1928. The highest point was finally reached

on 21 July 1936 by 2 Americans, Fritz Wiessner and William House. Originally named Mystery Mt by the Mundays, Waddington was renamed to honour Alfred WADDINGTON, a promoter whose attempt to build a road from the coast to the CARIBOO in the 1860s precipitated the CHILCOTIN WAR.

WADE, Frank, actor (b 1897, Liverpool, England; d 1982, Vancouver). After performing in vaudeville in the US and with a Chautauqua company on the prairies, he came to BC in 1926 and made a name for himself in "So This is Canada," a farce about OKANAGAN VALLEY fruit growing. During his long career as one of BC's few full-time professional actors, he took a whistle stop tour across the province, performing in every notable venue, including THEATRE UNDER THE STARS and the ORPHEUM THEATRE, and on

radio and CBC television. He appeared in the Robert Altman film *That Cold Day in the Park* (1969) and closed out his 63 years as a performer with regular appearances on the BEACHCOMBERS television series. Wade retired in 1979.

WAGG, Donald, architect (b 29 Aug 1914, Lancashire, England). After training at the School of Art and Technical College in Manchester, he eventually became city architect for Peterborough. During WWII he served with the ROYAL ENGINEERS, then immigrated to BC, settling in NELSON. There he completed the design for Mt St Francis Hospital. In 1950 he moved to VICTORIA and set up a partnership with retired provincial architect, W.H. Whittaker. The firm specialized in hospital design, carrying out extensive additions to Jubilee and St Joseph's hospitals in Victoria and designing many rural hospitals across BC. Wagg later worked in partnership with Patrick BIRLEY and finally David Hambelton, during which time his firms led the transition in institutional and commercial design from the streamlined Moderne style to a post-war Expressionism based in contemporary European influences. *Martin Segger*

WAH, Fred, writer, teacher (b 1939, Swift Current, SK). He grew up in the W KOOTENAY and while studying at UBC in the early 1960s was part of a group of writers who formed the influential TISH movement. After further studies in the US he returned to the Kootenay and taught at Selkirk College, then helped to create a writing program at David Thompson University Centre (*see* NOTRE DAME UNIV OF NELSON). In 1989 he began teaching at the Univ of Calgary. He has published more than a dozen books of poetry, one of which, *Waiting for Saskatchewan* (1985), won a GOV GEN'S LITERARY AWARD. His first book of prose, *Diamond Grill*, appeared in 1996. He has contributed to many small magazines including *Open Letter* and *Swift Current*, Canada's first electronic literary magazine.

Mt Waddington in the Coast Mts, the highest peak wholly within BC. Tim Briggs/Image Makers

WAIATT BAY, 30 km north of CAMPBELL RIVER at the north end of QUADRA ISLAND, is a former FISHING and LOGGING settlement and steamship port of call. It had a post office, spelled Wyatt Bay, from 1913 to 1946. Octopus Islands MARINE PARK is located here. The name is a Kwakwala (*see* KWAKWAKA'WAKW) word meaning "where there is herring spawn." *AS*

WAKASHAN FIRST NATIONS are people speaking languages related within the Wakashan language family. There are 6 Wakashan tongues: a Northern (or Kwakiutlan) group that includes HAISLA, HEILTSUK and Kwak'wala, the language of the KWAKWAKA'WAKW (Kwakiutl); and a Southern group that includes NUU-CHAH-NULTH (Nootka), Ditidaht and Makah, spoken at Cape Flattery on the Olympic Peninsula in Washington state. Because Kwak'wala is the most southerly of the Northern (Kwakiutlan) subgroup of Wakashan, the Kwakwaka'wakw are occasionally referred to as the "Southern Kwakiutl." All of these groups descend from a single presumed original group known as the proto-Wakashans. These groups attracted the interest of early ethnographers and as a result the Wakashans are among the best described cultural groups in the world. *See also* FIRST NATIONS OF BC; FIRST NATIONS LANGUAGES. *Jay Powell*

WALBRAN, John Thomas, mariner (b 23 Mar 1848, Ripon, England; d 31 Mar 1913, Victoria). He left school at age 14 to train for the British merchant marine and he was chief officer on the steamship *Islander* when it arrived in VICTORIA at the end of 1888. Walbran remained on the West Coast, commanding ships for the CANADIAN PACIFIC NAVIGATION CO and the Canadian government. After retiring in 1904, he turned full-time to his hobby of recording maritime place names, and in 1909 he published the work for which he is best known, *British Columbia Coast Names, 1592–1906*. A classic of BC literature, the book contains a wealth of history and anecdote.

Capt John Walbran, mariner and author, c 1890. BC Archives A-02521

WALBRAN VALLEY is a watershed on the west side of VANCOUVER ISLAND adjacent to the WEST COAST TRAIL south of NITINAT LK. It is an area of luxurious old-growth FOREST mainly of Sitka SPRUCE and western HEMLOCK. In 1990 the first recorded marbled MURRELET nest in BC was found here. The lower portion was included along with the neighbouring CARMANAH VALLEY as part of the 164.5 km² Carmanah Walbran Provincial PARK in 1995.

WALCOTT, 36 km southeast of SMITHERS on the CNR, was the site of a former GRAND TRUNK PACIFIC RWY depot. A footbridge crossed the BULKLEY R here and a one-room school and post office (1925–66) served a small settlement of railway workers and homesteaders. *AS*

WALDO, on the east side of KOOCANUSA LK, 55 km southeast of CRANBROOK, was a busy SAWMILLING community on the CPR and the CROWSNEST SOUTHERN RWY. Baker Lumber and Ross-Saskatoon Lumber both had large mills here in the 1910s and 1920s. The settlement, little of which has survived, was named after William Waldo, a local rancher. *AS*

WALHACHIN was an agricultural settlement along the benchlands of the THOMPSON R, 15 km east of CACHE CREEK. It was established in 1908 by the BC Development Assoc, a London-based development company, as a colony of genteel English farmers. These gentlefolk planted orchards (*see* TREE FRUITS) and rode to hounds, but the area was not suited to AGRICULTURE and when the men returned to England to fight in WWI the colony collapsed. By the late 20th century there was still a tiny village here of retirement and recreational homes; the wooden flumes built to irrigate the fruit trees have mostly rotted away. The name derives from a SECWEPEMC (Shuswap) word meaning "land of round rocks."

WALKEM, George Anthony, lawyer, politician, premier 11 Feb 1874–27 Jan 1876, 25 June 1878–12 June 1882 (b 15 Nov 1834, Newry, Ireland; d 13 Jan 1908, Victoria). He came to Canada with his parents in 1847, and after studying law in Montreal he was called to the bar in Quebec (1858) and Ontario (1861). He moved west to join the Cariboo GOLD RUSH in 1862 and was called to the BC bar the next year. He entered politics in 1864, when he was elected to the legislative council, a position he held until 1870. An advocate of colonial union, then of CONFEDERATION, he was elected to the province's first legislative assembly in 1871 and joined Premier John MCCREIGHT's cabinet as chief commissioner of lands and works. When Amor DE COSMOS took over as PREMIER at the end of 1872, Walkem became his attorney general. By the time he succeeded de Cosmos he had a reputation as a shrewd and pragmatic politician. His first term as premier was marked by discontent over the slow pace of railway construction and a lack of sympathy for aboriginal land claims (*see* ABORIGINAL RIGHTS). He resigned fol-

George Anthony Walkem, premier of BC 1874–76, 1878–82, pictured here in 1897. BC Archives F-08418

lowing a non-confidence motion related to provincial finances. After 2 years in opposition he became premier again. As well as encouraging restrictions on CHINESE immigration, he continued to quarrel with Ottawa over rail policy, going so far as to introduce a resolution in the legislature calling for BC's secession if construction of the line did not begin quickly. He left the premiership to join the BC Supreme Court, where he sat until his retirement in 1903.

WALKER, Alexander, soldier (b 12 May 1764, Collessie, Scotland; d 5 Mar 1831, Edinburgh, Scotland). He joined the East India Co when he was a teenager and went to India as part of the company's private armed force in 1781. In 1785 he took leave to join a trading excursion to the northwest coast of America led by J.C.S. Strange. Walker commanded a small group of soldiers intended to establish a garrison. The expedition arrived on the coast in June 1786 and spent the summer trading, but Strange decided not to establish a post and returned to India. Walker recorded his impressions of the voyage in *An account of a voyage to the north west coast of America in 1785 and 1786*, the first detailed account of coastal FIRST NATIONS people. He remained with the East India Co in India until he retired to Scotland in 1810.

WALKER, Larry, baseball player (b 1 Dec 1966, Maple Ridge). The best player BC has produced, he joined the Montreal Expos organization in 1984. The National League club called him up from the minors in 1989 and he played in Montreal until signing with the Colorado Rockies in 1995. After missing most of the 1996 season due to injury he turned in an all-star year in 1997, leading the NL in home runs (49), finishing 2nd in batting average (.366), runs scored and total hits, and 3rd in runs batted in and doubles. An outfielder, he was the first National Leaguer in 40 years to claim 400 total bases in a season and the third player in BASEBALL history to

Larry Walker in 1994, during his playing days with the Montreal Expos. Vancouver Sun

have 200 hits, 40 home runs and 30 stolen bases in one year. His storybook season won him NL most-valuable-player honours, the first Canadian to be an MVP in the major leagues. In 1998 he led the NL in batting average (.363), becoming the first Canadian to win a major-league batting crown in the modern era, and won the Lou Marsh Trophy for Canadian athlete of the year. He also won his fourth Gold Glove award for defensive play. When he repeated as NL batting champion in 1999 with a .379 average, he became the first major-league player in 68 years to hit .360 or better in 3 consecutive seasons.

WALKER, Michael, economist (b 11 Sept 1945, Corner Brook, NF). After graduating from Univ of Western Ontario in 1969, he worked as an economist with Bank of Canada and the federal finance department in Ottawa until 1974. That year he moved to VANCOUVER and founded a right-wing think tank, the FRASER INSTITUTE. As director of the institute, he wrote for various NEWSPAPERS and made regular radio and television appearances. He and his institute became leading advocates of conservative, market-oriented social and economic policies.

WALKER, Thomas "Tommy," guide, outfitter (b 1904, Gravesend, England; d 26 Dec 1989, Smithers). After studying brewing he worked in the grain importing business in England, then immigrated to BC in 1929. He settled at Stuie in the COAST MTS, on the ATNARKO R 65 km east of BELLA COOLA. He cleared a farm, became a guide and trapper and operated a sport FISHING resort, Stuie (now Tweedsmuir) Lodge. He played a part in the effort to create TWEEDSMUIR PROVINCIAL PARK in 1937. He and his wife Marion travelled by pack train north to the headwaters of the STIKINE R in 1948. They settled at Cold Fish Lk, where they established an outfitting operation and lobbied for the protection of this vast wilderness area, an effort that culminated in the creation of SPATSIZI PLATEAU WILDERNESS PROVINCIAL PARK. In 1974 the Walkers retired to SMITHERS.

Jeff Wall, artist

WALL, Jeffrey David "Jeff," artist, photographer (b 29 Sept 1946, Vancouver). After completing graduate studies in art at UBC (1970) and the Courtauld Institute in England (1970–73), he taught at the Nova Scotia College of Art and Design for a year. He then returned to the West Coast to teach at SFU (1976–87) and UBC (1987–99). In 1977 he produced the first of the works for which he is principally known: large, backlit cibachrome photographs of carefully constructed dramatic scenes. These monumental productions often portray disturbing urban tensions while alluding to art history and modernist theories of representation. Both as a teacher and an artist he has acquired an international reputation. He was hailed by the *Globe and Mail* in 1999 as "Canada's most famous living artist." *See also* ART, VISUAL; PHOTOGRAPHY.

WALLACE, Alfred "Andy," shipbuilder (b 1865, Moricetown, England; d 1 Jan 1929, N Vancouver). He began Wallace Shipyards as a small operation building fishing boats in FALSE CRK in 1894. In 1906 he moved the company to the foot of Lonsdale Ave in N VANCOUVER, where it became BURRARD DRY DOCK. He expanded the business dramatically during WWI, after which his son Clarence WALLACE continued the expansion until the company was one of the biggest

shipbuilders on the coast, employing thousands of workers. The *ST ROCH* was a Wallace-built vessel, as was the *PRINCESS LOUISE* of the CPR's coastal fleet. The company remained in family hands until 1971 (*see also* SHIPBUILDING).

WALLACE, Clarence, shipbuilder, lt gov 1950–55 (b 22 June 1893, Vancouver; d 12 Nov 1982, Palm Desert, CA). The son of the shipbuilder Alfred "Andy" WALLACE, he joined

Clarence Wallace, lt gov of BC 1950–55. BC Archives D-03363

BURRARD DRY DOCK after finishing school. During WWI he served overseas and was wounded at Ypres. By 1929 he was president of the family company, which during WWII built dozens of ships in support of the war effort, earning him a CBE in 1946. He was LT GOV during the final years of the COALITION GOVERNMENT and had to make the constitutionally difficult decision to ask W.A.C. BENNETT to form a government following the indecisive 1952 election. In 1953, when Bennett was defeated in a vote in the legislature, Wallace decided to allow an election rather than ask the CCF to form the government. The family business acquired several competing shipyards in the decades following WWII until the family sold it to Cornat Industries in 1971. *See also* SHIPBUILDING.

WALLACE, Ian, artist (b 25 Aug 1943, Shoreham, England). He was born to Canadian parents who brought him to Canada as a baby. He has lived in VANCOUVER since 1952. A graduate of UBC with an MA (1968), he is known for his conceptual art, large-scale photographic murals and paintings. Also an influential art critic and lecturer, he taught at UBC from 1967 to 1970, then joined the faculty at the EMILY CARR INSTITUTE OF ART & DESIGN in 1972. He is one of a group of contemporary conceptual artists from Vancouver (others include Rodney GRAHAM, Stan DOUGLAS and Jeff WALL) who achieved international reputations. Wallace's work has shown in major exhibitions around the world since the mid-1970s and is in the collections of many prestigious galleries. In 1997 he won an honour award from the VANCOUVER INSTITUTE OF THE VISUAL ARTS.

WALLACE ISLAND, 80 ha, one of the smaller of the GULF ISLANDS, lies off the northeast tip of SALTSPRING ISLAND. It was purchased by David Conover, a California businessman and photographer, and his wife Jeanne, who settled there and developed Wallace Island Resort. Their adventures are recounted in 2 memoirs, *Once Upon an Island* and *One Man's Island*. Conover claimed to have "discovered" Marilyn Monroe when he photographed her on a factory assembly line in 1945. After the Conovers sold their property, the provincial government purchased most of the island in the 1980s; in 1990 it established the Wallace Island Provincial MARINE PARK.

WALLACE SHIPYARDS; *see* BURRARD DRY DOCK.

WALLEYE (*Stizostedion vitreum*) is a popular game fish with widespread distribution in lakes and rivers in Canada and the US. In BC it is found primarily in the COLUMBIA R and in fresh water in the KOOTENAY and northeastern BC. The name refers to the unusually large white or opaque eyes. The fish is cylindrical in shape with a long head, large mouth with many sharp teeth and a prominent white tip on the lower lobe of the tail. Coloration varies from olive to dark green or brown on the back, with yellow sides and a white belly. Flecks of gold, yellow or brown are visible on the upper part of the body and head, and vertical bars can be seen on the back and sides. Walleye spawn in either spring or summer, depending on location. Walleye average 1.4 kg at maturity, but specimens to 9 kg have been recorded.

WALNUT GROVE is a rural district in the municipality of LANGLEY, 35 km east of VANCOUVER, that has grown into a suburb. WindSong, Canada's second co-housing project, is located here (the first is in VICTORIA). Co-housing is a strata-titled residential complex with a significant co-operative element and usually includes a communal kitchen and dining room.   AS

WALTER, Ryan William, hockey player (b 23 Apr 1958, New Westminster). He played minor HOCKEY in BURNABY before moving up to the LANGLEY Lords of the BC JUNIOR HOCKEY LEAGUE and the KAMLOOPS Chiefs and Seattle Breakers of the WHL. He captained Canada at the 1978 world junior championships in Montreal. Drafted 2nd overall by the Washington Capitals, he scored 28 goals during his first NHL season and finished 2nd in rookie-of-the-year voting. At age 21, Walter was one of the youngest captains in NHL history. He had several successful seasons in Washington before being traded to Montreal in 1982. After 9 seasons with the Canadiens, which included winning a Stanley Cup in 1986, he returned to BC in 1991 to play for the VANCOUVER CANUCKS. In 1992 he was named NHL man of the year for his sportsmanship and community work. On retiring he became a television hockey commentator.   SW

WALTERS, Dale, boxer (b 27 Sept 1963, Port Alice) His father Len, a member of the BC SPORTS HALL OF FAME, was named outstanding Canadian amateur athlete in 1951 but a broken hand

Dale Walters, boxer, at a competition in Sweden, 1984.

blocked him from a medal at the 1952 Helsinki Olympics. Dale had better luck, winning a bronze at the 1984 Los Angeles Olympics. Raised in BURNABY, Dale was first known in Canada as an actor in the television series *Ritter's Cove* 1979–80, but by the time he arrived in LA he was the 4th-ranked bantamweight in the world and Canadian champion. He filled in as a CBC-TV colour commentator between bouts en route to the bronze, eventually losing a decision to Mexico's Hector Lopez. Turning professional the next year, he built a 6-0 record before losing on a 10th-round technical knockout to Tony PEP for the Canadian featherweight title. After a series of injuries Dale announced his retirement from BOXING in 1988 and opened Ringside Fitness, a boxing-for-fitness club in downtown VANCOUVER.

WALTERS, Lisa, golfer (b Jan 1960, Prince Rupert). After winning the BC amateur GOLF championship 3 times, she turned professional and qualified for the LPGA tour in 1983. Her first victories were at the 54-hole Hawaiian Open in 1992 and 1993. In 1998 she overcame career-threatening injuries to tie the all-time LPGA scoring record with a 23-under-par 265 over 72 holes to win the Oldsmobile Classic in East Lansing, MI. She finished the year with 6 top-10 finishes and earnings of $309,000, placing her 25th on the LPGA money list. She retired from the LPGA in 2000.

WALTER'S COVE is a remote FISHING settlement on Walters Island, near the entrance to KYUQUOT SOUND on the west coast of VANCOUVER ISLAND. Early residents were Scandinavians from the WHALING station at CACHALOT, which closed in 1924. Long a centre of the commercial SALMON fishery, it has a population of about 30 people served by a store, a school and an outpost hospital established by the Red Cross in 1937. The NUU-CHAH-NULTH (Nootka) village of Houpsitas is opposite and the combined community is usually referred to as Kyuquot.

WALTON, Brian, cyclist (b 18 Dec 1965, Ottawa, ON). Raised in DELTA, he joined the Canadian national CYCLING team and has represented Canada at major international competitions since the 1988 Seoul Olympics. He earned a bronze medal at the 1994 Commonwealth Games (*see* BRITISH EMPIRE AND COMMONWEALTH GAMES), 2 golds and a bronze at the Pan American Games in 1995, and a silver medal in the points race at the 1996 Atlanta Olympics. In 1999 he added his third Pan Am gold medal, winning the road race. Professionally, he has raced for 7-Eleven, Motorola and Saturn teams.

WANETA, situated on the north bank of the Pend d'Oreille R at its confluence with the COLUMBIA R, was designated an outpost of Canada Customs in 1896, replacing the FORT SHEPHERD customs post on the south bank. It was here in 1893 that the NELSON & FORT SHEPPARD RWY, via a bridge across the Pend d'Oreille, connected with the Spokane Falls & Northern

Rwy, providing through rail service from NELSON to Spokane. The settlement was also a distribution centre for prospectors and a small number of settlers homesteading in the Pend d'Oreille valley. In 1953 COMINCO built a power dam nearby. The community has become a suburb of TRAIL.

WAPITI LAKE, 3.76 km², in the ROCKY MTS 60 km south of TUMBLER RIDGE, is the centre of one of the most important FOSSIL finds in N America. The mountains surrounding the lake contain fossilized remains of animals that lived in an ancient sea 210–250 million years ago. The site was discovered in 1947 and has produced evidence of many prehistoric species, mainly fish, that existed before the DINOSAURS.

WARBLER, a small, active songbird in the family Parulidae, breeds in BC in summer, then returns to a tropical home for the winter, usually in Mexico or Central America. In most species, males are brightly coloured, often with patches of yellow, while females have more subtle colouring. While in BC, warblers feed mainly on INSECTS. There are 24 warbler species found regularly in BC. The orange-crowned warbler

Common Yellowthroat. Tim Zurowski photo

(*Vermivora celata*) breeds throughout the province, while its relatives the Nashville (*V. ruficapilla*) and Tennessee (*V. peregrina*) warblers breed only in the southern and northern Interior respectively. The yellow (*Dendroica petechia*), yellow-rumped (*D. coronata*) and Townsend's (*D. townsendi*) warblers are also common, widespread species. The black-throated gray warbler (*D. nigrescens*) is restricted to the South Coast, while the black-throated green warbler (*D. virens*) is found only in the PEACE R area. Other species restricted to the northeast corner of BC include the ovenbird (*Seiurus aurocapillus*), and the magnolia (*Dendroica magnolia*), Cape May (*D. tigrina*), palm (*D. palmarum*), bay-breasted (*D. castanea*), blackpoll (*D. striata*), black-and-white (*Mniotilta varia*), Connecticut (*Oporornis agilis*), mourning (*O. philadelphia*) and Canada (*Wilsonia canadensis*) warblers. The Wilson's (*W. pusilla*) and MacGillivray's (*Oporornis tolmiei*) warblers

are common in moist forests throughout most of the province. The common yellowthroat (*Geothlypis trichas*) is found in marshes and other moist thickets. The northern waterthrush (*Seiurus noveboracensis*) and American redstart (*Setophaga ruticilla*) are found throughout the Interior in moist thickets and deciduous woodlands respectively. The large yellow-breasted chat (*Icteria virens*) is a very rare resident of deciduous thickets in the southern Interior, particularly the southern OKANAGAN VALLEY.

WARDNER, pop 195, is a LOGGING settlement on the CPR's Crowsnest branch and the west side of the KOOTENAY R, 26 km southeast of CRANBROOK. Crows Nest Pass Lumber operated a large SAWMILL here in the 1910s and 1920s. It was named after James F. Wardner, a MINING and railway promoter who developed the townsite in 1896. *AS*

WARFIELD, village, pop 1,788, lies between ROSSLAND and TRAIL in the W KOOTENAY, not far from the US border. Site of an early SAWMILL established by George Merry, it later housed the employees of COMINCO's fertilizer plant, which was located here, and absorbed the neighbouring settlement of Annable, which also had a sawmill. It is named for Carlos Warfield, an associate of F.A. HEINZE, who built the SMELTER at Trail in 1895, and it is essentially a suburb of Trail.

WARNER, David, architect (b 14 Feb 1931, Northampton, England). A graduate of the London Northern Polytechnic in 1954, he practised in London before immigrating to Canada. He worked briefly for Birley and Simpson in VICTORIA, then joined Polson & Siddall Architects in 1958. He had a private practice in Calgary from 1960 to 1968 before returning to Victoria to join Siddall Dennis as an associate. In 1970 the firm became Siddall Dennis Warner Architects. The link with Robert Siddall, who had assumed the practice of P.L. JAMES, can be traced to Francis RATTENBURY. On the retirement of the other principals in 1986 Warner assumed leadership of the firm. Representative work includes the Richard BLANSHARD Building, the City Centre Plaza, Dunsmuir Lodge near SIDNEY, the Workers' Compensation Centre and numerous buildings at the UNIV OF VICTORIA. In 1995 the firm evolved to Warner, James, Johnson Architects and Planners. *See also* ARCHITECTURE. *Martin Segger*

WARREN, Harry Verney, athlete (b 8 Aug 1904, Anacortes, WA). An all-around athlete who participated in CRICKET, RUGBY and FIELD HOCKEY, he won the 100-, 220- and 400-yard sprints at the 1926 BC championships and the 200-yard sprint at the 1927 British Games in London. In 1928 he was named to the Canadian Olympic team as an alternate sprinter and he set an Irish record in winning the 100 m at the 1928 Tailteann Games in Dublin. He is best known, however, as the father of Canadian field hockey. In 1923 he organized the UBC field hockey club and later the Canadian Field Hockey Assoc and the Canadian Women's Field Hockey Assoc. He

was president of the CFHA 1961–64 and the CWFHA in 1963, and was instrumental in sending Canada's first Olympic field hockey entry to Tokyo in 1964. In 1972 he was named an Officer of the Order of Canada and in 1990 he was inducted into the BC SPORTS HALL OF FAME. *SW*

WARREN, James Douglas, master mariner (b 1837, PEI; d 9 Sept 1917, Victoria). He arrived in VICTORIA in 1858 and in the 1860s began trading with aboriginal groups along the coast. In partnership with another Victoria fur dealer, Joseph Boscowitz, he entered the pelagic FUR SEAL hunt and also operated several coastal trading posts. He was a pioneer in the TOWBOATING industry and during the 1870s was captain of the historic steam vessel *BEAVER*. Warren was the first to employ steam vessels in the seal hunt and by the 1880s he and Boscowitz owned the largest fleet of sealing schooners in the industry. He was hit hard financially by vessel seizures associated with the BERING SEA DISPUTE and by legal wrangles with Boscowitz, but managed to recoup his fortune operating vessels in the coastal passenger and freight business during the Klondike GOLD RUSH. He was a principal in the Boscowitz Steamship Co that ran steamers along the coast from 1899 to 1911 until it sold out to the UNION STEAMSHIP CO.

WASA, pop 384, is a MINING and AGRICULTURAL settlement on the CPR and Wasa Lk, near the KOOTENAY R 30 km north of CRANBROOK. It was named after Vasa, a coastal town in Finland, by Nils Hanson, an early settler who became the first postmaster. Wasa Lake Provincial PARK is popular for swimming and boating, and nearby Wasa Slough is a wildlife sanctuary. *AS*

WASHINGTON, MOUNT (el 1,590 m), located 30 km west of COURTENAY on central VANCOUVER ISLAND at the eastern edge of STRATHCONA PROVINCIAL PARK, is one of BC's premier SKIING areas. It is the second busiest winter recreation area in the province after WHISTLER, with its 5 lifts, dozens of downhill runs and 35 km of cross-country ski trails. In 1995 it received more snow than any other ski resort in the world. It is named for Rear Admiral John Washington, a British naval hydrographer.

WASHINGTON, TREATY OF; *see* OREGON TREATY.

WASHINGTON MARINE GROUP, owned by the Montana-based Washington family, is a group of several Canadian transportation companies, some with roots in BC going back more than 100 years. Member companies include CATES TOWING, Kingcome Navigation, SEASPAN INTERNATIONAL LTD, Norsk Pacific Steamship Canada, Seaforth Towing, SOUTHERN RWY OF BC, Vancouver Drydock Co, Vancouver Shipyards Co Ltd and Victoria Shipyards Co Ltd.

WASSERMAN, Jack, journalist (b 17 Feb 1927, Winnipeg, MB; d 6 Apr 1977, Vancouver). He came to VANCOUVER as a youngster and

Jack Wasserman (centre) in the Vancouver Sun newsroom with Len Norris (l) and Roy Peterson, 1966. *Ralph Bower/Vancouver Sun*

attended UBC, where he began reporting for the student newspaper, the *Ubyssey*. He joined the VANCOUVER SUN in 1949 and spent his entire career there, most notably as a columnist reporting on the city's night life and celebrity goings-on. He also hosted radio and television shows. Probably his biggest exclusive was the sudden death of Hollywood film star Errol FLYNN in a West End apartment in 1959. He was so firmly associated with the nightclub scene that a stretch of Hornby St in downtown Vancouver was named "Wasserman's Beat" after his death. *See also* NEWSPAPERS.

WASTELL, Fred, sawmill owner (b 1900, New Westminster; d 1985). He moved to ALERT BAY at 9 years of age when his father A.M. "Duke" Wastell was hired by a FISH processing company to manage a box factory. When the factory closed in 1928, Fred and his wife Emma moved across Broughton Strait to TELEGRAPH COVE, where they established a SAWMILL with a partner, Alex Macdonald. The mill remained in operation to 1978, managed by the Wastells the entire time.

WATER EXPORTS became a contentious political and environmental issue in BC during the 1990s. Though bulk export of fresh water had not yet occurred by 2000, it seemed inevitable that fresh water would one day be traded, like oil and timber, given world population growth rates and the inadequate distribution of fresh water globally. Canada is fortunate to have roughly 9% of the world's fresh-water resources, and BC enjoys the largest share of any province. For many decades the arid regions of America's western states have coveted BC's water, and beginning in the 1960s a massive water transfer project known as the North American Water and Power Alliance was contemplated. However, due to the exorbitant cost and potential ecological implications, the project was terminated before it began. Other medium-scale fresh-water export projects have been considered, though none has come to

fruition. Smaller-scale bulk exports subsequently became a popular approach to transferring BC's fresh water. Proposals have suggested collecting some of the more than 400 million acre-feet of fresh water that flow from BC's coastal streams and RIVERS and drain directly into the Pacific Ocean annually. The water would then be transported to markets in enormous floating "bladders" behind ocean-going freighters, or by tanker trucks. Some BC LAKES could conceivably be used for bulk fresh-water export; Link Lk, behind OCEAN FALLS, for example, receives an annual rainfall of approximately 6.658 billion m³, and all of it drains directly into the ocean over a waterfall. It is estimated that in 20 years the population increase in California will result in a shortfall of roughly 4.932 billion m³ of water annually. In other words, the fresh water from just one of the many BC lakes that flow directly into the Pacific could be harnessed and exported to satisfy the California fresh-water shortfall.

Many Canadians fear that once the country exports even a drop of its fresh water, Canada will lose all control over one of its most precious resources, because both the Canada–US Free Trade Agreement and the North American Free Trade Agreement (NAFTA) failed to deal adequately with the matter of fresh-water exports. Essentially, once fresh water is exported in bulk quantities it becomes a tradable "good"; under the terms of these treaties Canada would have to afford US and Mexican companies "national treatment" with regard to its fresh-water resources—in other words, to provide Americans and/or Mexicans the same access to its fresh water resources as it does its own citizens.

Some Canadian provinces have issued bulk fresh-water export licences, but by the end of the 20th century no water had been exported. The BC government granted a handful of fresh-water export licences, but in Mar 1991 a provincial moratorium on bulk fresh-water exports was issued. Subsequently BC enacted the Water Protection Act, which prohibits bulk fresh-water exports. (The exportation of some bottled water is permitted.) One US company had an export licence to supply the Goleta Water District in California, but the licence was nullified by the provincial moratorium and subsequent legislation. The company sued the government of BC for billions of dollars in damages under the provisions of NAFTA. *Jamie Boyd*

WATERFALLS are a spectacular feature of BC's mountainous terrain. The 3 tallest falls in the country are in BC, and 3 others are also among the 10 tallest in Canada. The designated height of waterfalls depends on whether only the height of the free fall is measured, or the rapids before and after the drop are included. The highest waterfalls in BC, each of them taller than Niagara Falls, are shown opposite. The list is compiled from a variety of sources and measures vertical drop.

WATMOUGH, David Arthur, writer (b 17 Aug 1926, Leyton, England). After active service in the Royal Navy in 1944–45, he studied theology

David Watmough, writer (r) with Floyd St Clair, 1998. *Barry Peterson & Blaise Enright-Peterson*

at the Univ of London. After graduating in 1949 he moved to France, where he wrote his first book, a study of the Catholic worker-priest movement. During the 1950s and early 1960s he lived in California, New York and London before settling in VANCOUVER in 1962. He became a Canadian citizen in 1969. A long-time activist in the literary community, he worked for several years in BROADCASTING and arts journalism, at the same time writing and performing his own plays and monodramas. A prolific writer of fiction, he is best known for a series of novels featuring his gay protagonist, Davey Bryant.

WATSON, Joe (b 6 July 1943) and **Jimmy** (b 19 Aug 1952), hockey players. They starred with the famed Philadelphia Flyers "Broadstreet Bullies" team of the 1970s. Joe played junior HOCKEY in Estevan, SK, and was playing in the professional minor leagues in 1966 when the NHL Boston Bruins brought him up to play defence alongside Bobby Orr. The next season he moved over to Philadelphia where his gritty and

Hunlen Falls, Tweedsmuir Provincial Park. *Ian Douglas photo*

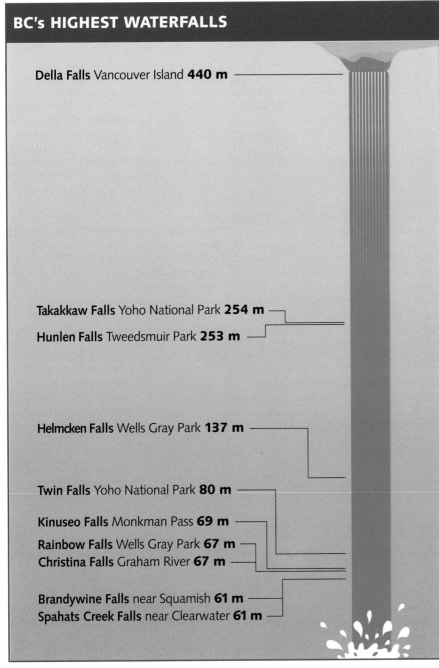

BC's HIGHEST WATERFALLS

Della Falls Vancouver Island **440 m**

Takakkaw Falls Yoho National Park **254 m**

Hunlen Falls Tweedsmuir Park **253 m**

Helmcken Falls Wells Gray Park **137 m**

Twin Falls Yoho National Park **80 m**

Kinuseo Falls Monkman Pass **69 m**

Rainbow Falls Wells Gray Park **67 m**

Christina Falls Graham River **67 m**

Brandywine Falls near Squamish **61 m**

Spahats Creek Falls near Clearwater **61 m**

---

grew restive at Greenpeace's commitment to non-violent protest; in 1977 he left after a dispute over campaign tactics. He immediately founded the Sea Shepherd Conservation Society, bought a boat and launched his own crusade to stop the slaughter of marine wildlife. Watson is willing to use violence to thwart the activities of his targets, who include seal hunters, whalers and drift net fishers. Dubbed a hero by his supporters and a reckless eco-pirate by his detractors, he is one of the most controversial figures active in the ENVIRONMENTAL MOVEMENT. The Sea Shepherd Conservation Society, founded in Vancouver, now has headquarters in California where Watson also teaches.

WATSON, Sheila (Doherty), writer (b 24 Oct 1909, New Westminster; d 1 Feb 1998, Nanaimo). She grew up in the Provincial Asylum for the Insane (*see* WOODLANDS), where her father, Dr Charles DOHERTY, was the superintendent. After graduating from UBC in 1933 she taught school in several small BC towns, one of

Sheila Watson, writer. Barbara Mitchell photo

which, DOG CREEK in the CARIBOO, she used as a setting for her novel *The Double Hook* (1959). She later completed graduate work with Marshall McLuhan and taught at the Univ of Alberta from 1961 to 1975. After her retirement she and her husband, the poet Wilfred WATSON, moved to NANAIMO in 1976. The couple edited the literary journal *White Pelican* from 1971 to 1978 and she published 2 collections of stories and another novel, *Deep Hollow Creek* (1992). *The Double Hook* remains her finest work and one of the classics of Canadian literature.

WATSON, Wilfred, writer, teacher (b 1 May 1911, Rochester, England). He moved to DUNCAN with his parents at age 15 and went to work in a SAWMILL. During WWII he attended UBC, then joined the navy. After graduate work at the Univ of Toronto he taught at the Univ of Alberta until his retirement in 1976; that year he and his wife, the writer Sheila WATSON, moved to NANAIMO. The couple co-founded the literary magazine *White Pelican* (1971–78). His first book of poetry, *Friday's Child* (1955), won a GOV GEN'S LITERARY

---

determined style fitted in perfectly. In 1973 he was joined on the Flyers by Jimmy, who had been a key defenceman with the Calgary Centennials in the WHL. The brothers anchored a blue line that contributed to 2 Stanley Cup championships for Philadelphia (1974, 1975) and both represented the team in NHL all-star games. After a knee injury ended Joe's career in 1978, he took a job in the team's sales department. Jimmy was also plagued by injury and retired in 1982 to become a Flyers talent scout and later a building contractor in Pennsylvania.   *SW*

WATSON, Paul, environmental activist (b 1950, Toronto). Raised in New Brunswick, he joined the Norwegian merchant marine as a teenager, then settled in VANCOUVER. There he became involved in the formation of GREENPEACE and took part in its early campaigns against nuclear testing, WHALING and the SEAL hunt. He

Paul Watson (l) with Bob Hunter, during his days as a member of Greenpeace.
George Diack/Vancouver Sun

AWARD. It was followed by several other poetry collections in which he developed his experiments with typography and an idiosyncratic grid system of "stacking" verse. During the 1960s he was also a prolific playwright, who occasionally collaborated with Marshall McLuhan.

WATTS, George, Nuu-chah-nulth leader (b 1945, Port Alberni). An advocate for ABORIGINAL RIGHTS and autonomy, he has been a prominent leader of the Tseshaht First Nation (NUU-CHAH-NULTH) near PORT ALBERNI for several decades. He served as president of the Nuu-chah-nulth Tribal

George Watts, Nuu-chah-nulth leader, 1990.
Brian Kent/Vancouver Sun

Council from 1970 to 1993 and has represented the Tseshaht as chief negotiator in the treaty process. Active on a variety of committees and boards, including FOREST RENEWAL BC, the Premier's Forest Sector Advisory Committee and the Loan Board of the Nuu-chah-nulth Economic Development Corp, he was a member of the board of BC HYDRO from 1993 to 1997. He is the owner and principal of the Imhahup Consulting Group, which specializes in putting together joint ventures between FIRST NATIONS and non-aboriginal businesses. *Heidi Brown*

WATUN RIVER, on Graham Island, 13 km south of MASSET in the QUEEN CHARLOTTE ISLANDS, was originally known as Woden River. J.B. McDonald, a CATHOLIC priest, built a church and school in 1912 and a group of Seventh Day Adventists also settled here. A BOATBUILDING business and hotel were established, and a cannery opened in the 1920s. When it closed in 1930 the settlement was abandoned. *AS*

WAXWING is a small, multicoloured perching bird. Its plumage shades from grey to brown, highlighted by a backsweeping crest, a black line through the eyes, a yellow-tipped tail and red, waxy tips on some of the wing feathers. The waxwing is gregarious, with a soft, high-pitched call. It feeds on fruit and flying INSECTS. Of 3 species worldwide, 2 occur in BC: the Bohemian

Bohemian waxwing. Tim Zurowski photo

waxwing (*Bombycilla garrulus*) and the cedar waxwing (*B. cedrorum*). The Bohemian, the more northerly species, is found mainly in the Interior and at higher elevations. In the winter it moves south to occupy the Interior range of its relative. The cedar is smaller and is more common along the coast.

WAYMAN, Thomas Ethan, poet, anthologist, teacher (b 13 Aug 1945, Hawkesbury, ON). He is known as a poet of the workplace and a champion of work-related WRITING. He was raised in PRINCE RUPERT and VANCOUVER, and after graduating from UBC and the Univ of California he worked at a vari-

Tom Wayman, writer. Jeremy Addington photo

ety of jobs that provided material for his poetry. His first book, *Waiting for Wayman* (1973), was followed by several other collections of verse, 2 books of essays and 5 poetry anthologies. He was co-founder of the Vancouver Industrial Writers' Union (1979–1995) and the KOOTENAY SCHOOL OF WRITING and he has taught for many years in the BC COMMUNITY COLLEGE system.

WEASEL (*Mustela* spp) is a sleek carnivore with a long, slim body and short legs, belonging to the Mustelidae family of mammals (Mustelids). It feeds on birds, INSECTS, RODENTS and other small mammals. Its brown summer coat, dense and lustrous, changes to white in winter wherever snowfall is significant. All 3 Canadian species are found in BC. The long-tailed weasel (*Mustela frenata*), occupies the southern and central mainland and is the largest weasel in the province, growing up to 45 cm. It is found in almost all habitats from sea level to the alpine. The *altifrontalis* subspecies of the long-tailed weasel is on the provincial Red List (*see* ENDANGERED SPECIES). The short-tailed weasel (*M. erminea*), also known as the ermine, grows to 30 cm in length and is found throughout BC, including VANCOUVER ISLAND, the QUEEN CHARLOTTE ISLANDS, and various other islands along the coast. The Vancouver Island subspecies of ermine is on the provincial Blue List, and another subspecies on the mainland is on the Red List. The least weasel (*M. nivalis*), the smallest of the 3 species, occurs sparsely in the central and northern parts of the mainland.

WEATHERBIE, Vera, painter (b 1909, Vancouver; d 1977, Vancouver). She was a member of the first class at the Vancouver School of Decorative and Applied Arts (*see* EMILY CARR INSTITUTE OF ART & DESIGN) from 1925 to 1930. After further studies at the Royal Academy in London, England, she taught from 1933 to 1935 at the BC College of Art founded by Fred VARLEY and J.W.G. MACDONALD. During the 1930s and 1940s she regularly participated in exhibitions at the VANCOUVER ART GALLERY. In 1942 she married Harold MORTIMER-LAMB; she continued to paint but became less involved in the local art scene. *See also* ART, VISUAL.

WEBB, Phyllis, writer (b 8 Apr 1927, Victoria). After attending UBC in the late 1940s, she left the province and lived for 2 decades in eastern Canada, the US and Europe. During a stint as a

Phyllis Webb, writer, 1998.
Barry Peterson & Blaise Enright-Peterson

radio broadcaster for the CBC in Toronto, she originated the long-running program *Ideas*. She returned to BC in 1969 and has lived on SALT-SPRING ISLAND ever since. Her earliest poetry appeared in the 1950s and she has published steadily. Her 1982 collection, *The Vision Tree: Selected Poems*, won a GOV GEN'S LITERARY AWARD. She also writes cogently about poetry; her prose is collected in *Talking* (1982) and *Nothing But Brush Strokes* (1995). She was inducted into the Order of Canada in 1992.

WEBBER, John, artist (b 6 Oct 1751, London, England; d 29 Apr 1793, London, England). He was an established artist and decorator in London when hired to accompany James COOK's 1776 expedition to the Pacific Coast of N America in search of a Northwest Passage. He made about 200 sketches during the voyage, 29 of which depict the people and places of NOOT-KA SOUND, where the expedition spent a month in 1778. Some of the sketches illustrated the published version of Cook's journal in 1784. They are the earliest representations of coastal FIRST NATIONS.

WEBSTER, Arnold Alexander, teacher, politician (b 1899, Vancouver; d 27 July 1979, Vancouver). Raised in AGASSIZ, he graduated from UBC and was a teacher and school board administrator in VANCOUVER for 40 years. In 1940 he won election to the city parks board and served for 22 years. He was also a member of the UBC Senate for 15 years. He joined the provincial CCF at its creation and was a long-time member of the party executive. After Harold WINCH moved to federal politics in 1953 Webster was chosen party leader and won Winch's East Vancouver seat in the legislature. A low-key, mild-mannered politician, he represented the moderate wing of the party. He managed to maintain the CCF's position as official opposition, but he was replaced prior to the 1956 election and retired from the legislature. He re-entered politics briefly, winning the federal seat of Vancouver–Kingsway for the NDP in 1962 and 1963, before retiring again in 1965. His wife Daisy served as NDP MLA for Vancouver South (1971–75).

WEBSTER, Gloria (Cranmer), 'Namgis (Nimpkish) curator, author (b 4 July 1931, Alert Bay). Her great-grandfather was George HUNT and her father was Dan Cranmer, both of whom worked with the anthropologist Franz BOAS. She studied anthropology at UBC, and after graduating in 1956 she worked as a counsellor at OAKALLA PRISON FARM and with the John Howard Society. In 1971 she joined the MUSEUM OF ANTHROPOLOGY at UBC and began to take part in a series of research projects related to aboriginal people. She was the prime mover in establishing the U'mista Cultural Centre at ALERT BAY and she served as its curator from 1980 to 1991, producing films and books about the KWAKWAKA'WAKW (Kwakiutl) people. As well, she has curated several major museum exhibitions, including *Chiefly Feasts* at

the American Museum of Natural History in New York in 1991.

WEBSTER, John Edgar "Jack," journalist (b 15 Apr 1918, Glasgow, Scotland; d 2 Mar 1999, Vancouver). Raised in a working-class home, he left school at age 14 to work at a newspaper in his native Glasgow. After serving in the British Army during WWII, he moved with his wife Margaret to London to work as a reporter on Fleet St, then immigrated to BC in 1947. He joined the VANCOUVER SUN newspaper, then in 1953 switched to radio as a public affairs commentator and later talk-show host on stations CJOR and CKNW. He was one of the pioneers of the talk format, a pugnacious interviewer who thrived on controversy and confrontation, championing the cause of the underdog against the powerful and the privileged. He loved to intercede in the news, as in a 1963 hostage incident at the BC PENITENTIARY when he was called in to mediate, but he ended up being taken hostage himself. During the 1960s he appeared regularly on the public affairs television show *This Hour*

Jack Webster, broadcaster, 1990. Ian Lindsay/ Vancouver Sun

Has Seven Days, as well as other CBC programs, and in 1978 he left radio to host his own interview show on BCTV. There he cultivated his image as an irascible curmudgeon. He retired in 1987, the same year he was inducted into the Canadian News Hall of Fame. His autobiography, *Webster!* (1990), revealed the extent to which his private life was saddened by the long-term illness of his wife. He was appointed to the Order of Canada in 1988. The Jack Webster Foundation supports annual awards for excellence in reporting. *See also* BROADCASTING.

WEBSTERS CORNERS, 30 km east of NEW WESTMINSTER in MAPLE RIDGE district municipality, is a farming settlement (*see* AGRICULTURE) on the Dewdney Trunk Road. LOGGING was important in the early 1900s, and in 1905 a group of FINNS

arrived from the failed utopian colony at SOINTU-LA. Websters Corners was named for James Webster, who first homesteaded here in 1882. *AS*

WEIR, George Moir, educator, politician (b 10 May 1885, Miami, MB; d 4 Dec 1949, Vancouver). He was teaching at UBC's new department of education in 1924 when he and J.H. Putman, an Ottawa school inspector, were appointed co-chairs of a royal commission into public EDUCATION in the province (*see* PUT-MAN–WEIR COMMISSION). In 1933 he interrupted his duties as head of the UBC education department to win election to the legislature as a LIBER-AL and joined Premier Duff PATTULLO's cabinet as provincial secretary and minister of education. He proposed a public health insurance scheme that later became the basis for the province's first hospital insurance plan (*see* HEALTH POLICY). Defeated in the 1941 election, he returned to the legislature in 1945 and once again served as minister of education until ill health forced his resignation in 1947.

WELDWOOD OF CANADA LTD began operations in 1945, when a predecessor company, Western Plywood, opened a VANCOUVER plywood plant. A second plant was opened at QUESNEL in 1951, and in 1964 the company combined with 2 Ontario plywood firms, Hay and Co and Weldwood Plywood, to form Weldwood of Canada. That year it acquired the assets of Canadian Colliers Resources, including SAWMILLS at SQUAMISH, PORT MOODY and SURREY, and extensive timberlands on VANCOUVER ISLAND and DENMAN ISLAND. Its principal owner was Champion International Corp of New York. In 1969 Weldwood and Daishowa-Marubeni International Ltd formed the Cariboo Pulp and Paper Co at Quesnel, and in the early 1970s started 2 sawmill companies—Babine Forest Products at BURNS LAKE and Houston Forest Products at HOUSTON. In 1988 Weldwood purchased a pulp and sawmill complex at Hinton, AB, and the following year it started a joint distribution company with CANADIAN FOREST PRODUCTS LTD (Canfor), Canfor-Weldwood Distribution. In 1994 Weldwood's private timberlands on the BC coast were sold to the John Hancock Mutual Life Insurance Co, and the following year its coastal sawmills and timber licences were sold to INTERNATIONAL FOREST PRODUCTS LTD. In 1999 Weldwood had sales of close to $1.1 billion. *See also* FOREST INDUSTRY.   *Ken Drushka*

WELLINGTON, 8 km northwest of NANAIMO on VANCOUVER ISLAND, was the site of a major colliery established in the early 1870s by Robert DUNSMUIR. The townsite had 5,000 inhabitants and an opera house in the 1890s. Operations were phased out by 1900 and many buildings were moved to LADYSMITH. Other collieries at S and E Wellington lasted until the 1950s. The mines, connected via tramway to a wharf on Departure Bay, suffered numerous deadly explosions and fires and several bitter strikes. Today the area is a suburb of Nanaimo. *See also* COAL MINING, VANCOUVER ISLAND.   *AS*

WELLS, pop 246, 80 km east of QUESNEL in the CARIBOO, sprang into being in 1933 after Fred Wells, a prospector, finally struck GOLD. His Cariboo Gold Quartz Mine gave birth to a company town that had a population of 4,000 by the end of the decade. The mine continued to operate until 1967: unlike nearby BARKERVILLE the town has remained a functioning community, if much diminished from its heyday, with a thriving arts and crafts community.

Wells, 1991. Roy Luckow photo

WELLS GRAY PROVINCIAL PARK, 5,297.48 km² (est 1939), lies north of CLEARWATER in the COLUMBIA and CARIBOO Mts of the central Interior and encompasses most of the watershed of the Clearwater and other rivers. It is noted for its variety of volcanic formations and spectacular WATERFALLS, in particular HELMCKEN FALLS (137 m), named for J.S. HELMCKEN, a former Speaker of the legislature. Over half of the park is at high elevations and extensive icefields occur in the northern half. It contains 5 major lakes: Murtle (76.3 km²),

Murtle Lake, Wells Gray Provincial Park.
Rick Blacklaws photo

Mahood (32.47 km²), Hobson (39 km²), Clearwater (34.5 km²) and Azure (32 km²), and is a favourite with campers, hikers, canoeists, and cross-country and telemark skiers. The park is also known for its abundant wildlife populations, notably WOLVES, MOOSE and woodland CARIBOU. Parts of it are in the Interior wet belt, which has similar trees and plants as the RAIN FORESTS on the west coast. The park is named for A. Wells Gray, Minister of Lands from 1933 to 1941.

WENNER-GREN, Axel, was a wealthy Swedish entrepreneur who made a fortune manufacturing vacuum cleaners and refrigerators and owned a variety of enterprises worldwide. He was also highly controversial because of his alleged Nazi sympathies during WWII. In 1956 he became interested in the resource potential of the ROCKY MT TRENCH in northern BC. His new subsidiary Wenner-Gren BC Development Co signed an agreement with W.A.C. BENNETT's government promising to build a pulp mill and a railway to the Yukon. Initial surveys revealed the HYDROELECTRICITY potential of the PEACE R and in 1957 he made a new deal with the province to build a huge power project. A railway was begun but never finished and Wenner-Gren's other plans also failed to materialize, though the province itself went ahead with the power project.

WESBROOK, Frank Fairchild, medical scientist (b 12 July 1868, Brant Country, ON; d 20 Oct 1918, Vancouver). After studies at the Univ of Manitoba and in London, Dublin and Cambridge, he became, at age 27, the head of pathology at the Univ of Minnesota. He was dean of medicine there when he was hired away in 1913 to become first president of UBC. Wesbrook was president for the official opening of UBC in 1915, when it took over the McGill Univ College site next to Vancouver General Hospital, but did not survive to see the university move to its Point Grey campus.

WEST COAST TRAIL is an arduous 77-km hiking TRAIL between PORT RENFREW and BAM-

Tsusiat Falls, on the West Coast Trail.
Philip Stone photo

FIELD on the west coast of VANCOUVER ISLAND. Originally the West Coast Lifesaving Trail, it was built during 1907–10, after a telegraph line was strung between VICTORIA and Cape Beale in 1899–1900. The trail allowed boats and lifesaving equipment to be carried to the scene of accidents along the coast. River mouths were crossed by aerial trolleys. Cabins where shipwrecked mariners could find shelter and emergency supplies were located along the trail. By the 1950s the trail was no longer maintained. It was reopened in 1969 as a hiking trail and in 1970 it became part of PACIFIC RIM NATIONAL PARK. The trail is so popular with hikers that reservations are required during open season (May–Sept).

WEST DEMARS, also known as Reid's Landing after John Reid, an early homesteader, was a steamship stop and orchard settlement (*see* TREE FRUITS) 100 km south of REVELSTOKE, at the south end of Upper ARROW LK. LOGGING was important here in the early 1900s. It was named for Nels Demars, a pioneer resident of nearby NAKUSP. The site was flooded during the construction of the KEENLEYSIDE DAM.   AS

WEST FRASER TIMBER CO LTD began in 1955 when the Ketcham family acquired a small planing mill at QUESNEL. Over the next 25 years the company steadily acquired SAWMILLS and related timber-cutting rights in the Interior and developed a chain of retail building-supply stores. In 1979, West Fraser and Daishowa Paper Manufacturing Co of Japan established the Quesnel River Pulp Co with a mill at Quesnel. Two years later West Fraser acquired a portion of Eurocan Pulp and Paper with a pulp mill at KITI-MAT (*see* PULP AND PAPER) and 2 sawmills at other locations. In 1988 the building-supply component of the company was expanded with the purchase of Revelstoke Building Supplies, which also operated a wholesale lumber trading division. The following year a 50% interest in Alberta Newsprint Co's mill at Whitecourt was acquired. In 1993 West Fraser acquired complete control of Eurocan, including its Kitimat pulp mill and sawmills at TERRACE, FRASER LAKE and PRINCE RUPERT. That same year a one-half interest in Houston Forest Products and a portion of Babine Forest Products were acquired. In 1994 the company stunned the FOREST INDUSTRY and the ENVIRONMENTAL community by surrendering LOGGING rights in the KITLOPE VALLEY, a gesture that allowed the 3,170 km² watershed to be preserved. With its acquisition of Ranger Forest Products in northern Alberta in 1995, West Fraser became Canada's biggest lumber producer, with 5,000 employees. Early in 1997 it purchased the Lumberland chain of retail outlets. In 1999 it posted sales of $880 million. *Ken Drushka*

WEST KOOTENAY POWER & LIGHT CO

(WKP) was incorporated in 1897 to provide hydroelectric power (*see* HYDROELECTRICITY) to the ROSSLAND mining camp. It was founded by a consortium of entrepreneurs led by Sir Charles Ross, a Scottish landowner and MINING investor (and later manufacturer of the infamous Ross rifle). CPR bought the company in 1905 and its subsidiary COMINCO took control in 1916. The company's first hydro dam was built at lower BON-NINGTON FALLS on the KOOTENAY R, 13 km west of NELSON. The 51-km transmission line to the mines at Rossland was the longest in the world when it went into operation in 1898. This plant was the first major hydro installation in BC. A second plant opened at upper Bonnington Falls in 1905, mainly to supply power to the smelter at TRAIL, but also to serve an expanding domestic and industrial market. Other W KOOTENAY plants on the river opened at south SLOCAN (1928), Corra Linn (1932) and BRILLIANT (1944) as the company extended service as far west as the OKANAGAN–SIMILKAMEEN district. In 1987 Cominco sold its subsidiary to an American company, Utilicorp in Missouri. In 1998 WKP had revenues of $127 million and celebrated 100 years of providing electricity to the W Kootenay.

WEST MOBERLY LAKE, pop 120, is a DUNNE-ZA (Beaver) community at the west end of MOBER-LY LK, 20 km north of CHETWYND in the PEACE R district. The local FIRST NATION dates back to 1977 when it was one of 2 bands created out of the former Hudson Hope band. At midsummer the community celebrates Treaty Days to commemorate the 1899 signing of TREATY NO 8.

WEST VANCOUVER

spreads across the lower slopes of the North Shore mountains opposite VAN-COUVER from the CAPI-LANO R west to HORSE-SHOE BAY. Originally part of the territory of the SQUAMISH First Nation, it developed from the 1880s as a small community of summer cottagers who, from 1909, were able to commute to Vancouver by ferry. The district incorporated in 1912, when its population was only 700, absorbing a string of tiny waterfront settlements, including Caulfeild, Cypress Park,

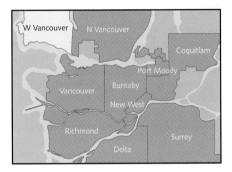

Dundarave, Eagle Harbour, Fisherman's Cove, Horseshoe Bay, Sherman and Wadsley, with Hollyburn as the municipal centre. The decision was taken in 1926 to preserve the residential character of the community by banning any new industry, though a fish cannery operated until 1967. The opening of the LIONS GATE BRIDGE in 1938 improved automobile access; it was a project of the Guinness family, of Irish brewing fame, who undertook to develop the BRITISH PROPERTIES as an elite housing estate. Post-war developments included the Park Royal Shopping Centre, the first covered shopping mall in Canada when it opened in 1950. West Van is now one of the wealthiest communities in the country (it had the highest per capita

income in Canada in 1994) and attracts many visitors to its beaches, retail villages and outdoor facilities at CYPRESS Bowl.
Population: 40,882
Rank in BC: 21st
Population increase since 1981: 14%
Date of incorporation: district 15 Mar 1912
Land area: 98.94 km²
Location: Greater Vancouver Regional District
Economic base: retail services

WESTBANK is a community overlooking the west side of OKANAGAN LK 12 km south and west of KELOWNA. It was on the FUR BRIGADE route used by traders from 1826 to 1847. Settlement began in the 1870s and the community was known as Westside or Hall's Landing until the present name was chosen. A townsite was laid out in 1905 by Ulysses G. Grant, an American land promoter. Surrounded by orchards (*see* TREE FRUITS), Westbank is essentially a residential and commercial suburb of Kelowna. Much of the land between Westbank and Kelowna is part of the Tsinstikeptum RESERVE belonging to the Westbank First Nation, a branch of the OKANA-GAN people.

WESTBRIDGE, pop 80, is a farming community 57 km southeast of PENTICTON where the east and west forks of the KETTLE R merge and a bridge crosses the west fork. A hotel was built in the old days when MINING was important and the KETTLE VALLEY RWY passed through. The Kettle River Provincial Recreation Area is nearby. *AS*

Lighthouse Park, West Vancouver.
Larry Scherban/Image Makers

WESTCOAST ENERGY INC, based in VANCOU-VER, has interests across N America as well as international projects in Mexico and Asia. It was founded as Westcoast Transmission in 1949 by Frank MCMAHON to build a PIPELINE from his gas-producing properties in the PEACE R area to southern BC and the US. Completed in 1957, it was the first major natural gas pipeline in Canada. In 1968 the company completed a branch pipeline to carry natural gas to PRINCE RUPERT. Westcoast Energy subsidiaries include natural gas distribution companies in BC (Centra Gas British Columbia) and Ontario (Union Gas Ltd), as well as power generation

interests in Ontario and a natural gas cogeneration project on VANCOUVER ISLAND. The company also owns energy services businesses across Canada and operates 2,900 km of natural gas gathering pipelines, 16,045 km of gas transmission pipelines and 30,868 km of gas distribution pipelines across Canada. New pipeline projects include a share of the Alliance Pipeline carrying natural gas from northeast BC and Alberta to the American Midwest, and a share of the Maritimes and Northeast Pipeline from Sable Island to markets in Atlantic Canada and New England. Westcoast is the largest corporation in BC. It had revenues of $6.2 billion in 1999.
Reading: Earle Gray, *Wildcatters*, 1982.

WESTERBERG, Andrew Rupert "Ole the Bear," pioneer mail carrier (b 8 May 1879, Vasterbottens, Sweden; d 2 May, 1963, Kamloops). He changed his last name from Westerlund when he arrived in Alberta as a young man to take up ranching and trapping. While on a train to VANCOUVER in 1900 he was recruited by a Big Bend MINING crew (*see* GOLD RUSH, BIG BEND) and got off the train in REVELSTOKE to settle into a life of prospecting, trapping and hunting. In 1914 he began carrying 110 to 220-kg loads of His Majesty's mail by horse up the Big Bend to FRENCH CREEK, a 160-km round trip that could take up to 10 days in the summer and much longer throughout the rest of the year. "Ole the Bear" earned his nickname for his hobby of hunting bears and for narrowly surviving a bear attack while on a mail run. He also gained notoriety for saving a starving horse by building snowshoes for it and leading it home to Revelstoke over a heavily snowed-in trail. When he was home from the mail route and his traplines, he helped his wife Annie, a Norwegian woman, raise their 7 children.

WESTERN CANADA WILDERNESS COMMITTEE is a non-profit conservation society based in VANCOUVER. Since it was founded by Paul George in 1980 it has taken part in many

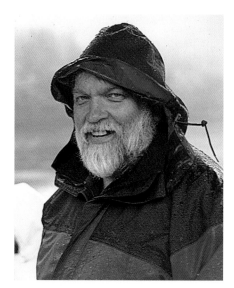

Paul George, founder of the Western Canada Wilderness Committee, 1998. A. Carr/WCWC

high-profile campaigns to preserve forested areas of the province from development, including the STEIN and CARMANAH valleys. It has also engaged in trail building, mapping of wilderness areas, scientific research and a variety of public education projects. In 1991 Environment Canada judged it the most effective ENVIRONMENTAL group in Canada. In the late 1990s it spearheaded a campaign to preserve the STOLTMANN WILDERNESS area north of Vancouver.

WESTERN FEDERATION OF MINERS (WFM) was at the forefront of militant unionism in BC at the end of the 19th century. Created in Montana in 1893 to represent hardrock miners, it crossed the border in 1895 when the first Canadian local was organized at ROSSLAND. By 1900 there were locals in MINING districts across the province, organized as District 6 of the parent union. The union was instrumental in obtaining the 8-hour day for underground mine workers. In 1901 the WFM led a bitter strike at the Rossland mines, where owners were attempting to destroy the union. After failed actions on VANCOUVER ISLAND in 1903, coal miners switched affiliation to the United Mine Workers of America and the WFM concentrated on the metal mining industry in the KOOTENAY. In 1916 it changed its name to the INTERNATIONAL UNION OF MINE, MILL & SMELTER WORKERS, known familiarly as Mine Mill. *See also* LABOUR MOVEMENT.

WESTERN FRONT, one of the first artist-run centres in Canada, was formed in VANCOUVER in 1973 as a collaborative project centred around the critique of media culture through performance art, video and installation. Since then its various members and guests have engaged in an impressive variety of multidisciplinary artistic activities. Founding participants were Martin Bartlett, Mo Van Nostrand, Kate Craig, Henry Greenhow, Glenn LEWIS, Eric Metcalfe, Michael MORRIS and Vincent Trasov, though most used unusual aliases (eg Dr and Lady Brute, Flakey Rose Hip, Mr Peanut). In 1974 the group even ran a candidate—Trasov, campaigning as Mr Peanut—for mayor. The Front provides living and working spaces for artists, and stages readings, screenings, performances and other events. *See also* ART, VISUAL.

WESTERN HOCKEY LEAGUE (WHL) is a major junior league, based in Calgary, consisting of 18 teams from the 4 western provinces and Oregon and Washington states. Created in 1966 as the Canadian Major Junior HOCKEY League with 7 teams from Saskatchewan and Alberta, it expanded into Manitoba the next season and became the Western Canada Hockey League. The first teams from BC joined in 1971. In 1976 the first US franchise, the Portland Winter Hawks, entered and in 1978 the WCHL was renamed the WHL. It is one of 3 major junior leagues that compete annually for the Memorial Cup. Most top junior-aged (17–20) players from BC further their careers through the WHL while others prefer to play a tier lower in the junior A BC JUNIOR HOCKEY LEAGUE to be eligible for US college

recruitment. BC teams in the WHL are the KAMLOOPS BLAZERS, the PRINCE GEORGE Cougars (formerly VICTORIA COUGARS), the KELOWNA Rockets and the KOOTENAY Ice based in CRANBROOK. The WHL also had earlier franchises in NEW WESTMINSTER (1971–81, 1983–88), VANCOUVER (1971–73), Victoria (1971–94), Kelowna (1982–85), and NANAIMO (1982–83). The Blazers and the NEW WESTMINSTER BRUINS are the only BC teams to have won the Memorial Cup. *SW*

WESTERN STAR TRUCKS HOLDINGS LTD, located in KELOWNA and employing about 1,400 people by the late 1990s, is the only major truck manufacturer in BC. Founded by the White Motor Corp in 1967 to make heavy-duty trucks for the resource industries of the Pacific Northwest, the company was sold in 1981 when

Logging truck manufactured by Western Star Trucks Holdings Ltd.

White went bankrupt. In 1991, on the verge of bankruptcy itself, the company was bought by a group of Australian trucking experts who turned its fortunes around by building high-quality specialty trucks for a variety of markets, including the military and resource industries overseas. In 1995 Western Star purchased Orion Bus Industries Inc, once the country's largest builder of transit buses. Sales in 1999 totalled $1.3 billion. In 1999 the provincial government purchased a small share of the company to allow for expansion of its manufacturing plant.

WESTHAM ISLAND lies in the mouth of the south arm of the FRASER R, south of VANCOUVER in DELTA. First settled by farmers in the 1870s, it has retained its AGRICULTURAL character. Many of today's farmers are partners in the effort to provide feeding areas for the hundreds of thousands of migrating waterfowl travelling the PACIFIC FLYWAY. The Canadian Wildlife Service research installation Alaksen and the REIFEL MIGRATORY BIRD SANCTUARY are at the north end.

WESTHOLME, a small farming settlement on VANCOUVER ISLAND in the district municipality of NORTH COWICHAN, 38 km southeast of NANAIMO, was originally known as Hall's Crossing. The postmaster, Capt C.E. Barkley, named the post office after his house, his "home in the west." A picturesque local ANGLICAN church dates from 1880.   AS

WESTLEY, on the CPR and the COLUMBIA R 7 km west of CASTLEGAR, was a railway supply centre and SAWMILLING settlement in the early 1900s. The Yale-Columbia Lumber Co operated a mill from 1902 to 1909, when it burned down. It was rebuilt by the Westley Lumber Co in 1927 but burned again in 1931.   AS

WESTMIN RESOURCES; *see* BOLIDEN (WEST-MIN) CANADA LTD.

WESTON, William Percy, artist (b 30 Nov 1879, London, England; d 20 Dec 1967, New Westminster). He studied at the Putney School of Art in London before moving to Canada in 1909. He settled in VANCOUVER, where he taught high school, then taught at the Provincial Normal School until his retirement in 1946. His

W.P. Weston, artist, 1938, in a portrait by Nan Cheney. BC Archives PDP-04902

influence on the teaching of art in BC schools was immense. Trained as an artist in England, he was affected by the BC landscape and his paintings portray heroic views of wild nature, empty of most signs of human civilization. His work is often compared to that of the Group of Seven; with that group and with his friend Emily CARR he shared an interest in painting the native terrain. He was a charter member of the Canadian Group of Painters, a national association of artists founded in 1933, and he exhibited annually with the BC Society of Fine Arts. *See also* ART, VISUAL.

WESTWOLD, pop 369, is located 60 km northwest of VERNON where the Salmon R valley widens. The first settlers in the 1860s called this area Grande Prairie and the name was in use for many years. A post office near the west end of the prairie was called Adelphi in 1900 but changed in 1926 to Westwold ("wold" being an old English word for a high plain) after the CNR com-

pleted its line from KAMLOOPS to the OKANAGAN VALLEY. AGRICULTURE and LOGGING are the main economic activities. An original settler was Henry Ingram, one of the men responsible for bringing CAMELS to the CARIBOO WAGON ROAD.

WETLANDS are areas of waterlogged soil, meaning the water table is at, near or above the soil surface. They may be constantly flooded or they may be inundated periodically, such as in the case of tidal marshes. Freshwater wetlands include ponds, marshes, bogs, sloughs, swamps

Fresh-water wetlands at Wolf Creek, E Kootenay, 1993. Roy Luckow photo

and fens; saltwater wetlands include tidal flats, salt marshes, ESTUARIES and deltas. About 14% of Canada is covered in wetlands. In BC, where there is much rocky, mountainous terrain (which is not as conducive to their formation as flat land), wetlands account for only about 3% of the total land area, or 31,200 km². This is just a fraction of the wetlands that existed before the arrival of European settlers. It is estimated that 75% of the original wetlands around VICTORIA and the Lower Mainland have been converted to AGRICULTURAL and residential use, while in the OKANAGAN VALLEY as much as 85% of the wetlands are gone. This is significant because wetlands provide important feeding habitat for waterfowl and other animals. The wetlands of BOUNDARY BAY and the FRASER R delta, for example, welcome hundreds of thousands of migrating birds annually. Wetlands also reduce flooding by absorbing excess water and act as filters for purifying water.

WET'SUWET'EN are a FIRST NATIONS people occupying the drainage of the BULKLEY R from about BURNS LAKE west to the SKEENA R. They are an ATHABASCAN-speaking people, closely related to their DAKELH (Carrier) neighbours to the east and north and to the GITKSAN of the Skeena Valley. They have been called Carrier due to a traditional custom: a widow carried a bag containing the ashes of her dead husband for a year following his cremation. The Wet'suwet'en divide themselves

into 5 matrilineal clans and several houses, each house with its own chief. Members of a house are closely related; years ago they occupied the same dwelling at the main village. Wet'suwet'en oral history tells of a large prehistoric village called DIZKLE on the banks of the Bulkley R that the people shared with the Gitksan and other groups and that was abandoned when portents predicted a disaster. Later the Wet'suwet'en established the village of Kyah Wiget near MORICETOWN. They gathered each summer at the Bulkley R to fish for SALMON, the mainstay of their subsistence economy. When the salmon runs petered out in the fall, they dispersed into the hinterlands to fish (*see* FISHING, ABORIGINAL) and hunt game animals. They traded with coastal groups for EULACHON grease, food and ornaments. Relations with the Gitksan have been very close and similar cultural institutions, such as cremating the dead, suggest that the Gitksan may originally have been TSIM-SHIAN-ized Wet'suwet'en. Over time the Wet'suwet'en intermarried and adopted the clan, crest and feasting systems (the POTLATCH) of their Gitksan neighbours.

The Wet'suwet'en were drawn into the FUR TRADE indirectly, chiefly as suppliers of furs to coastal First Nations, who acted as intermediaries. In this way trade goods were obtained, but the people were largely insulated from contact with Europeans until the middle of the 19th century. The SMALLPOX epidemic of the 1860s seriously depleted the population; it is estimated that the Wet'suwet'en numbered only 200 by 1879. Construction of the COLLINS OVERLAND TELEGRAPH brought direct contact. Then came ROMAN CATHOLIC missionaries, who converted many of the people to Christianity. The old village of Kyah Wiget was renamed Moricetown after the Oblate missionary Gabriel MORICE (*see* OBLATES OF MARY IMMACULATE). The first RESERVES were laid out in 1891 by Peter O'REILLY, a reserve commissioner. The arrival of the GRAND TRUNK PACIFIC RWY was followed by expanded settlement. The Wet'suwet'en got jobs packing and guiding and worked on rail construction, and on farms to supplement traditional hunting, fishing and trapping activities. The population began to recover and by the late 1990s there were 4 communities—Moricetown, Broman Lake, HAG-WILGET and Nee-Tahi-Buhn—with a combined registered population of about 2,200. In 1987 the Wet'suwet'en, along with the Gitksan, launched an important court case, known as DELGAMUUKW, claiming jurisdiction over their traditional territories. The results of that case have had a profound impact on ABORIGINAL RIGHTS in BC.
Reading: Terry Glavin, *A Death Feast in Dimlahamid*, 1998.

WEYERHAEUSER CANADA LTD is the Canadian subsidiary of the huge Washington state forest products company, Weyerhaeuser Co. The parent company was established in the Tacoma area in 1900 and by the end of the century was the largest producer of softwood lumber and market pulp in the world (*see* PULP AND PAPER); overall it was the third largest forest company in the US. BC operations began in 1964, when the company formed a partnership to build a pulp mill in KAMLOOPS. In 1971 it took sole ownership of Kamloops Pulp and Paper and renamed it Weyerhaeuser Canada; eventually the company grew to include SAWMILLS and other wood products operations across the West and in Ontario. In 1999 Weyerhaeuser doubled its Canadian holdings by purchasing BC's forest industry giant MACMILLAN BLOEDEL. Shortly after, it moved its Canadian head office from Kamloops to VANCOUVER. *See also* FOREST INDUSTRY.

WHALE is the common name for a number of species of marine mammals of the order Cetacea. There are 2 suborders: Mysticeti, the toothless or baleen whales (filter feeders), and Odontoceti, the toothed whales, which include DOLPHINS and PORPOISES. Many species of whales once visited the BC coast, but a commercial hunt

Killer whale on the move. Phil Edgell photo

that began in the Pacific in the mid-19th century drastically depleted their numbers (*see* WHALING). Today 4 species are present in significant numbers: the gray, humpback and minke whales, which are all baleen whales, and the

KILLER WHALE, a member of the dolphin family.

Gray whales (*Eschrichtius robustus*) breed in warm-water lagoons in Baja California and each spring migrate north along the coast to their summer feeding grounds off Alaska. The round

Gray whale basking near the surface.
Keith Thirkell photo

trip, about 16,000 km, is one of the longest annual migrations of any mammal. The whales pass by the west coast of VANCOUVER ISLAND between March and May, supporting an active WHALE WATCHING industry based in TOFINO and UCLUELET. Grays subsist mainly on amphipods (tiny crustaceans). They grow to 36 tonnes and to 15 m in length, and they live an average of 30 to 40 years. They were valued by hunters for their oil and for the strips of baleen with which they strain food from sea water. Prior to the invention of plastic, baleen was used in manufacturing a wide range of products. A commercial hunt began in Baja in 1845 and the herd of about 20,000 animals was depleted to about 2,000 by 1880. Occasional hunting continued to 1937, when the gray became a protected species. Much to everyone's surprise the population recovered from the devastation of the hunt and apparently

had regained its pre-hunt size by the late 1990s. A number of gray whales spend the summer in the nearshore waters of the BC coast, including the vicinity of PACIFIC RIM NATIONAL PARK, and occasionally a gray strays into GEORGIA STRAIT and the INSIDE PASSAGE.

Humpback whales (*Megaptera novaeangliae*) grow to 18 m in length and weigh up to 41 tonnes. They have long flippers that have been compared to wings. Humpbacks feed mainly on EUPHAUSIIDS but also on HERRING and sand lance (an eel-like fish). They often feed by deploying a "bubble net" as they rapidly circle their prey while exhaling, then swoop up from below with their mouths open. The North Pacific population of humpbacks is estimated at 10,000; over 5,400 individuals have been identified in BC. Each whale has a unique pattern of coloration on the underside of its fluke that can be used for identification. Humpback populations are coming back strongly after being devastated by whaling. The North Pacific population breeds near Hawaii and to a lesser extent Japan between Jan and Apr, then spends the rest of the year off the west coast of N America. On the breeding grounds, males sing long, distinctive songs.

Minke whales (*Balaenoptera acutorostrata*) are the smallest of the baleen whales in BC waters, reaching a length of about 10 m and a weight of about 7 tonnes. With a dark back and a small curved dorsal fin, the minke is inconspicuous and is often missed as it travels through JUAN DE FUCA STRAIT and adjacent waters. When feeding actively on fish, it may show a pointed snout and white bars on the fins. Little is known about minke movement patterns but the whales are seen on the coast throughout the year, usually travelling alone and often feeding in tide rips.
Reading: David A.E. Spalding, *Whales of the West Coast*, 1999.

WHALE WATCHING has become an important sector of the TOURISM industry since 1980, when Bill and Donna Mackay and Jim Borrowman started taking out groups of watchers by boat from TELEGRAPH COVE at the north end of JOHNSTONE STRAIT not far from ROBSON BIGHT. Since then many more operators have entered the industry, offering boat tours out of TOFINO and UCLUELET to view migrating gray WHALES and out of NANAIMO, ALERT BAY and

Humpback whale breaching.
Mark Newman/Image Makers

Whale watching in Johnstone Strait.
Duane Sept photo

VICTORIA to view KILLER WHALES in the INSIDE PASSAGE. In 1999 an estimated 180,000 people went on whale watching tours in Johnstone Strait and in the southern GULF ISLANDS and San Juan Islands. Whale watching is not limited to organized tours. The mammals are visible from land around GEORGIA STRAIT and in PACIFIC RIM NATIONAL PARK and from the decks of passenger ferries on several coastal routes. Whale researchers have raised concerns that whale watching is disturbing the animals in their natural habitat and regulations have been put into place to control the industry.

WHALING was first practised by the NUU-CHAH-NULTH people on the west coast of VANCOUVER ISLAND, long before the arrival of Europeans. The Nuu-chah-nulth pursued the WHALES as they migrated along the coast. Hunters went to sea in log CANOES, armed with harpoons tipped with

A family of visitors posing with the carcass of a giant right whale at the whaling station in Kyuquot, c 1916. BC Archives A-09222

blades of MUSSEL shell. A long line of CEDAR bark and sinew trailed behind the harpoon, dragging several sealskin floats to tire the fleeing animal. Once the kill was made, the carcass was towed back to the village and butchered. Cloaked in elaborate ritual and festivity, whaling played an important role in Nuu-chah-nulth culture. In 1998 the Nuu-chah-nulth served notice that like their Makah relatives in Washington state, they were contemplating a resumption of the hunt, targeting the gray whales that migrate past the coast each year.

Commercial whaling began in the 1830s when American and European ships began

Sei whale, caught at Alert Bay, 1905, by Archie Seymour and others. VMM

Sperm whale being butchered at Kyuquot, c 1916. BC Archives A-09221

Whaler at the harpoon gun, 1908.
BC Archives B-03820

Shore whaling station at Cachalot, Kyuquot Inlet. BC Archives 52843

killing whales on the "Northwest Ground" off the Pacific Coast. A shore-based industry was attempted at stations in GEORGIA STRAIT and on Vancouver Island from 1866 to 1872, but failed. It was not until 1905 that modern shore whaling came to the coast. Using exploding harpoons and speedy catcher boats, whalers hunted the animals offshore, then towed them to the shore stations. Pacific Whaling Co (PWC) operated stations on the west coast of Vancouver Island (SECHART and KYUQUOT SOUND) and on the QUEEN CHARLOTTE ISLANDS (NADEN HARBOUR and ROSE HARBOUR) until 1943. In 1948 PWC was replaced by the Western Whaling Co in COAL HARBOUR, QUATSINO SOUND. It produced whale meat principally for export to Japan and stayed in business until 1967, when commercial whaling on the coast ended. The federal government officially halted the hunt in 1972, by which time the only stations in operation in Canada were on the Atlantic coast.

WHALLEY is the densely urbanized northwest corner of SURREY. Originally it was named Whalley's Corner, after Arthur Whalley, a pioneer settler; the present name was adopted in 1948. The SKYTRAIN arrived in 1994, linking this suburban commercial centre with downtown VANCOUVER.

WHEELER, Anne, filmmaker (b 23 Sept 1946, Edmonton). After completing a science degree, she began her career in film in 1971, forming Filmwest Associates, an Edmonton filmmaking collective. Five years later she chose to freelance, working mainly for the National Film Board making documentaries. In 1981 she began concentrating on dramatic films and feature docudramas. She moved to BC in 1990 and established Wheeler–Hendren Productions Ltd. Her films, which have received numerous Canadian and international awards, include a wide range of documentaries; docu-dramas such as *A War Story* (1981), based on her father's experience as a prisoner of war; and features such as *Loyalties*

Anne Wheeler, filmmaker, 1999.
Rick Loughran/Vancouver Province

(1986), *Bye Bye Blues* (1991), *The Diviners* (1991), *The War Between Us* (1995) and *Better Than Chocolate* (1999). Based in VANCOUVER since the mid-1990s, she has received 6 honorary university degrees and the Order of Canada (1995). *See also* FILMMAKING INDUSTRY.

WHEELER, Arthur Oliver, surveyor, mountaineer (b 1 May 1860, Lyrath, Ireland; d 20 Mar 1945, Banff, AB). He was a land surveyor, trained in the use of PHOTOGRAPHY in map-making who was closely associated with the ROCKY MTS for most of his career. In his work as a surveyor he became a skilled mountain climber. He played a leading role in founding the Alpine Club of Canada and was its first president from 1906 to 1910, as well as editor of the *Canadian Alpine Journal* for 22 years. He also was instrumental in the creation of MT ASSINIBOINE PROVINCIAL PARK in 1922. He directed the BC–Alberta Interprovincial Boundary Survey from 1913 to 1925 and was responsible for naming many features along the Continental Divide. *See also* MOUNTAINEERING.

WHISTLER, district municipality, pop 7,172, BC's only resort municipality, nestles in the COAST MTS 120 km north of VANCOUVER.

Wintertime at Whistler Village.

Originally known as ALTA LAKE, it attracted loggers, miners and a few summer visitors until the 1960s, when winter recreation began. In 1964 a paved road improved access and Whistler Mt opened to the SKIING public. The municipality was incorporated on 6 Sept 1975, when the provincial government began planned development. The resort opened at the end of 1980 and has been growing rapidly ever since. By the year 2000, skiers could choose from more than 200 runs and 32 lifts. Facilities on Whistler (el 2,190 m) and Blackcomb (el 2,440 m) mountains and in Whistler Village, a European-style centre of

contemporary design, have made the area one of the top 5 ski resorts in the world and increasingly an all-season TOURIST destination. In 1999 it attracted 2.3 million visitors. The number of year-round residents is also growing rapidly. The community is named for the hoary MARMOT, an alpine rodent commonly called a "whistler" for the sound it makes.

WHITE, Charlie, sport fisher (b 1925). He moved to VANCOUVER ISLAND from the US after receiving an engineering degree from Cornell Univ and deciding that BC provided the most promising sport FISHING grounds. White helped to create VICTORIA's first television station and also invented one of the first downriggers for trolling, which he developed with Scott Plastics to become the Scotty Downrigger. His next innovation was to attach a camera to the downrigger and to master the filming of fishing from an underwater perspective. The result of his work was *Why Fish Strike*, a film originally named *Salmon Spectacular*, which grossed over $1 million from screenings up and down the West Coast. *In Search of the Ultimate Lure* followed, and White staged seminars around the continent showing his films and providing angling tips. He is the author of several books about fishing. *SW*

WHITE, Howard, writer, book publisher (b 18 Apr 1945, Abbotsford). After studying literature at UBC he founded the periodical RAINCOAST CHRONICLES in 1972 to give voice to the history and culture of the BC coast. This venture expanded in 1974 into a full-fledged BOOK PUBLISHING business, HARBOUR PUBLISHING, which he has operated with his wife Mary White in MADEIRA PARK ever since. Meanwhile he has written and co-written several books of poetry, history and memoir, including *The Men There Were Then* (1983), *A Hard Man to Beat* (1983), *Spilsbury's Coast* (1987), *The Accidental Airline* (1988), *Ghost in the Gears* (1993) and *The Sunshine Coast* (1996). His book of stories and poems, *Writing in the Rain* (1990), won a Leacock Medal for Humour and he has also won a BC BOOK PRIZE (for a collection of *Raincoast Chronicles*) and a career award for regional history from the Canadian Historical Assoc.

WHITE, John Clayton, artist, architect (b 25 Nov 1835, England; d 7 June 1907, Berkeley, CA). He was an artist and draughtsman with the ROYAL ENGINEERS and came to BC with the contingent that arrived in 1858. After the engineers were disbanded he became a surveyor and artist with COLLINS OVERLAND TELEGRAPH, while also working as a draughtsman for the Lands and Works Dept of the COLONIAL GOVERNMENT and later the provincial government. He was well known for his watercolours, oils and scene paintings for local theatres. He left BC in 1867, moving to San Francisco where he continued to work as an artist and draughtsman. *Martin Segger*

WHITE, William Lloyd "Bill," labour leader (b 7 Nov 1905, near Gravenhurst, ON). He was raised on a farm near Yellowgrass, SK. He joined the RCMP in 1930 and sailed into the western Arctic on the ST ROCH, under Henry Larsen. After leaving the RCMP, White became a burner in VANCOUVER's wartime shipyards, and he rose to the presidency of the Marine Workers and Boilermakers Union of Canada, Local 1, a position he held from 1944 to 1955. A militant and uncompromising unionist, he played a key role in achieving many workplace reforms and was instrumental in forcing the establishment of a Royal Commission on the WORKERS' COMPENSATION BOARD under Chief Justice Gordon Sloan in 1950. White is best remembered for his role in defending the closed shop, the key labour practice of requiring all employees at a given workplace to be union members. In 1944 he was named defendant in a well-funded legal challenge to the closed shop; he and his union fought for 7 years, losing at every level in the Canadian court system. Known as *Kuzych vs. White et al*, the case was finally resolved in favour of White and his union on appeal to the Privy Council in London, England, in 1951, establishing an important legal precedent for Canadian unionism. In retirement White collaborated on a book about his labour experiences, *A Hard Man to Beat* (1983). *See also* LABOUR MOVEMENT. *HW*

WHITE PASS & YUKON ROUTE runs 177 km from Skagway, AK, to Whitehorse, YT, across the mountainous northwest corner of BC. The White Pass (el 870 m) straddles the Alaska–BC border and was one of 2 main overland routes followed by prospectors heading for the Klondike during the GOLD RUSH of 1897–98. Construction of a narrow-gauge railway, financed by a British syndicate, began at Skagway in May 1898 and reached Bennett Lk in July 1899. The following summer the line reached Whitehorse and monopolized traffic into the Klondike. After the gold rush ended, the railway survived for 80 years, relying on TOURISM and freight for the local MINING industry. In the 1950s the White Pass pioneered containerization of freight and operated an integrated intermodal system using trucks, rail and ships between the Yukon and VANCOUVER. The mines began to decline and the line closed in 1982. It was reborn in 1988 as a summer excursion railway.

WHITE ROCK, city, pop 17,210, is a beachfront community overlooking Semiahmoo Bay at the US border, 40 km south of VANCOUVER. It was incorporated on 15 Apr 1957, when it  seceded from the municipality of SURREY, which surrounds it on 3 sides. It takes its name from a 437-tonne boulder on the waterfront, painted white to serve as a landmark. Legend has it that a sea god cast the boulder across the ocean to show his strength. Blessed with a long stretch of protected, sandy beach, it began as a community of summer cottages and a TOURIST destination

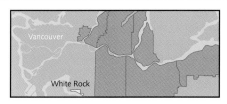

for people from Vancouver. The GREAT NORTHERN RWY provided rail access in 1909, and the long pier extending out into the bay was built in 1914 as a landing dock for coastal steamers. The active waterfront strip still gives the city a beach resort flavour during the summer, though traffic in the other direction is equally heavy as many residents commute into Vancouver to work. Since the 1970s the city, with its mild, dry climate, has experienced rapid growth as a retirement haven; in the late 1990s about half of the population was over 55 years old.

WHITE SPOT restaurant chain was launched on 28 June 1928 when Nat BAILEY opened the first drive-in restaurant in Canada, in the Marpole neighbourhood of VANCOUVER, on Granville St at 67th Ave. In those days the site was considered semi-wilderness. Undaunted, Bailey erected a tiny imitation log cabin, painted a white spot on its roof and borrowed the name from a hamburger operation in Los Angeles. The place became famous for its carhops, its "barbecued sandwiches" and outdoor murals painted by Jim Osborne. White Spot weathered the Depression, expanding in 1937 and adding a fashionable White Spot Dining Room in 1938. When Bailey sold it to General Foods in 1968 for $6.5 million, the business included 11 restaurants, 2 dining rooms, 6 Ernie's Fine Foods outlets, ICL catering services and Newton Farms, the largest private chicken farm in BC (*see also* AGRICULTURE). In 1982 White Spot returned to local ownership under Peter C. Toigo, and by 1997 had grown to 47 outlets, including a new mini-

chain of express outlets called Triple O. It now serves more than 13 million customers yearly and in 1998 posted revenues of $99 million.
Constance Brissenden

WHITECAPS; *see* VANCOUVER WHITECAPS.

WHITEFISH are silvery TROUT-like freshwater fish that occur in many areas of BC. With the exception of one species, the inconnu, they are bottom feeders with small mouths and no teeth. Seven species of whitefish occur in BC. The lake (common) whitefish (*Coregonus clupeaformis*) has been the most important commercial freshwater fish in large LAKES across Canada, though stocks have been depleted (*see* FISHING, COMMERCIAL). In BC it is found mainly in the northern half of the province; attempts have been made to introduce it to southern lakes with only limited success. On average it weighs 1–2 kg, though it may grow much bigger. The mountain whitefish (*Prosopium williamsoni*), more trout-like in appearance, is found in RIVERS and streams throughout the province and is a popular sport fish (*see* FISHING, SPORT). The round whitefish (*P. cylindraceum*) and the broad whitefish (*Coregonus nasus*) are both confined to water systems in the north; the broad whitefish is found only in TESLIN LK. The pygmy whitefish (*Prosopium coulteri*) is small (10–12 cm) and quite rare. The least cisco (*Coregonus sardinella*), also known as the lake herring, occurs in northern lakes that drain into the Yukon R. The largest whitefish species, the inconnu (*Stenodus leucichthys nelma*), occurs in the extreme north of the province. It resembles the pike in appearance and weighs up to 27 kg, and is the only species of whitefish that preys on other fish.

WHITEWATER, an early SILVER MINING camp and SAWMILL in the W KOOTENAY, on the road between KASLO and NEW DENVER, was first known

The waterfront at White Rock, 1924.
Philip Timms/UBC BC1541/3

as Bell's Camp after the Bell brothers, who staked the Whitewater Mine in 1891. It became a station on the KASLO & SLOCAN RWY, which carried ore from the mine. A townsite with hotels, stores, school, an ice plant and 300 inhabitants blossomed briefly; in 1928 it was renamed Retallack after John L. Retallack, owner of the mine. Some abandoned buildings from the 1940s still stand. *AS*

WHONNOCK, also spelled Whonock, 47 km east of VANCOUVER in MAPLE RIDGE municipality, was a STO:LO village site for centuries. Sam Robertson, a HBC boatman at FORT LANGLEY, settled here in 1860 and many others arrived in the mid-1880s along with the CPR. Riverboats stopped here; AGRICULTURE, commercial FISHING and SAWMILLING have been important to the local economy. The name is a HALKOMELEM word meaning "where there are always humpback salmon." *AS*

WHYMPER, Frederick, artist (b 1838, London, England; d 26 Nov 1901, London, England). As a young man he trained with his father, a well-known London engraver and artist. Frederick was in BC from 1862 to 1867 and vis-

Frederick Whymper, artist, during his years in BC. BC Archives A-02535

ited the CARIBOO goldfields (*see also* GOLD RUSH, CARIBOO), accompanied Alfred WADDINGTON's road-building crew to BUTE INLET, was the official artist with the VANCOUVER ISLAND EXPLORING EXPEDITION and took part in the construction of the COLLINS OVERLAND TELEGRAPH. After he returned to England he published *Travel and Adventure in the Territory of Alaska* (1868), which included material on BC. He was one of the most accomplished early painters to work in BC.

WHYTECLIFFE is a small seaside community in HOWE SOUND, just west of HORSESHOE BAY. In 1870 Howe Sound COPPER Mines Ltd began MINING at the site, known as White Cliff Point, and the mine produced for several years. WhyteCliff Park Resort, named for one of the owners, Col

Albert Whyte, began operations in Horseshoe Bay in 1909, and when the Pacific Great Eastern Rwy (*see* BC RAIL) arrived in 1914 the station was named Whytecliff. The UNION STEAMSHIP CO purchased the property in 1939 and began running ferries to BOWEN ISLAND; ferries now leave from the Horseshoe Bay terminal around the corner.

Pounding surf at Wickaninnish Beach. Ucluelet Chamber of Commerce

During WWII the site was a boys' school. W VANCOUVER purchased 16 ha at the point in 1953 to create a park, and the rest is now an expensive residential area. Whytecliff MARINE PARK is Canada's first Marine Protected Area, in which it is illegal to collect any marine life from the underwater sanctuary.

(WIC) WESTERN INTERNATIONAL COMMUNICATIONS was a BROADCASTING company begun in 1956 when Frank GRIFFITHS, then an accountant, and two partners bought NEW WESTMINSTER radio station CKNW. Originally called Western Broadcasting, it grew to include several radio and television stations in the Lower Mainland and the OKANAGAN VALLEY by 1977. In 1985 it took the WIC name and went public with the sale of 6.25 million shares worth $50 million. With the 1991 acquisition of Allarcom, an Alberta broadcaster, it became the largest private broadcaster in Canada. At its peak it owned 11 television stations (including BCTV in VANCOUVER, CHEK in VICTORIA and CHBC in KELOWNA), 12 radio stations, pay TV networks, production facilities, satellite services and wireless communications systems. With the 1997 purchase of Montreal's major English-language television station CFCF, WIC had access to 72% of the English television market in Canada. The 1994 death of Frank Griffiths touched off a challenge to his family's control of the company. Early in 1998 his widow Emily sold controlling interest to Shaw Communications and Cathton Holdings of Edmonton for an estimated $91 million. The sale was challenged by CanWest Global Communications Corp of Winnipeg and WIC became mired in complex legal proceed-

ings related to the division of its assets, which were finally split between Shaw and CanWest Global and WIC was disbanded early in 2000.

WICKANINNISH was a NUU-CHAH-NULTH (Nootka) chief in CLAYOQUOT SOUND on the west coast of VANCOUVER ISLAND at the end of the 18th century. He played a leading role as an intermediary in the SEA OTTER trade. The name means "having no one in front of him in the canoe." Wickaninnish Beach is one of the long stretches of sand forming part of PACIFIC RIM NATIONAL PARK. Migrating gray WHALES are visible offshore during Mar–Apr, as are SEA LIONS clustered on Sea Lion Rocks.

WIGWAM INN is a 40-room lodge built at the head of INDIAN ARM. B.F. Dickens purchased the land in 1906, planning a luxury lodge and cottage resort. Alvo von ALVENSLEBEN joined him as a partner in 1910, the year the first guests arrived.

Royal Vancouver Yacht Club outstation at Wigwam Inn, 1999. Ian Lindsay/Vancouver Sun

The grounds were terraced and emulated a German beer garden. Over the years the inn changed hands several times. In 1962 the RCMP raided it, charging criminal operations, including gambling. The ROYAL VANCOUVER YACHT CLUB purchased the Inn in 1986 for use as an outstation by members. *Doreen Armitage*

WILD, Rowland, journalist (b 30 July 1904, Manchester, England; d 29 Dec 1989, Vancouver). He shot to fame in 1928 as the only reporter able to get inside Afghanistan to write about the political turmoil occurring there. This launched his career as a peripatetic journalist who covered some of the biggest news stories of the century, including Gandhi in India, the Spanish Civil War and post-war reconstruction in Germany. In 1947 he immigrated to VANCOUVER with his wife Barrie, a photographer, and he made his home there for the rest of his life. While contributing regularly to local NEWSPAPERS he wrote several books about Canada, including a biography of Amor DE COSMOS (1958) and a history of Vancouver, and filed stories on BC for the *Daily Telegraph* in London.

WILD HORSE CREEK is a tributary of the KOOTENAY R, near historic FORT STEELE. GOLD was discovered in 1863 and thousands of prospectors rushed to the site. Jack Fisher, a prospector, named the site after the wild horses in the area. The original camp, called Fisherville, was torn down when miners discovered the buildings sat atop a rich gold deposit. The relocated settlement was called Wild Horse, though the post office name was Kootenay until 1895. In 1865 the DEWDNEY TRAIL was extended from HOPE to allow access to the area, but by the next year the height of the rush was over. Several CHINESE miners remained to work the creek; by the end of the 19th century it was virtually abandoned.

WILDFLOWERS occur in BC in spectacular diversity, largely because of the province's widely varied geography (see also PLANTS, NATIVE). Flowers of BC's vast FORESTS may adapt to low wind levels by producing hooked seeds distributed by passing animals, while on nearby mountains alpine plants exploit strong winds with airborne seeds. Plants in the arid regions of the southern Interior may have intricate roots that can extract the most minute amounts of moisture from seemingly dry soil, while wetland plants may float in water with no roots at all. Some 2,073 vascular plants are native to BC, representing all the major families and displaying virtually every floral variation. *See also* pp.770-772.

WILLER, James Sidney Harold "Jim," artist (b 25 Feb 1921, London, England). Educated in England, Amsterdam and Winnipeg, he first exhibited at the VANCOUVER ART GALLERY in 1953 and has had many exhibitions since that time in Canada and the US. His work is in the National Gallery of Canada and other public galleries, and he has long been represented by the Bau-Xi Gallery in VANCOUVER. Willer is a sculptor and muralist as well as a painter. His work, which often juxtaposes realistic and fantastical imagery and makes use of visual illusions and ambiguities, is still representational in style and deeply rooted in nature. Willer also wrote a sci-fi thriller, *Paramind*, published in 1967.   AS

WILLIAM HEAD is a promontory along the south coast of VANCOUVER ISLAND, west of VICTORIA. From 1894 to 1958 it was the site of a quar-

antine station where immigrants were screened for infectious diseases. Since 1959 the premises have been occupied by a minimum security PRISON. William Head is named for the British Arctic explorer William Parry.

WILLIAMS, Bob, politician, town planner, businessman (b 20 Jan 1933, Vancouver). After graduating in planning from UBC, he became the first director of planning for DELTA, then set up his own consulting firm. Raised in VANCOUVER's east end, he ran for city council in 1964 and 2 years later was elected to the provincial legislature as a NDP MLA for Vancouver East. Williams established himself as an aggressive opposition voice and an expert on resource use. As resources minister in the subsequent NDP government from 1972 to 1975, he challenged the large forest companies (*see* FOREST INDUSTRY), reformed land and resource management (*see* AGRICULTURAL LAND RESERVE) and doubled the province's protected lands (*see* PARKS, PROVINCIAL). He was also responsible for the creation of Robson Square in downtown Vancouver and WHISTLER Town Centre. Williams became a lightning rod for anti-socialist attacks, in part for creating a Crown forest sector, while at the same time attracting a loyal following across the province for his concept of the public interest. In 1976, with the NDP again in opposition, he vacated his safe seat to allow for the election of the party leader, Dave BARRETT. He returned to the legislature in a by-election in 1984 and continued as an MLA until 1991, when he retired from politics. As a businessman, Williams was elected to the board of the VANCOUVER CITY SAVINGS CREDIT UNION in 1983 and subsequently led a slate of candidates to take control of the credit union and give it a renewed community orientation. Under the NDP government of Mike HARCOURT, he served as head of the CROWN CORPORATIONS secretariat. In 1998 he was appointed chair of the INSURANCE CORPORATION OF BC. *Herschel Hardin*

WILLIAMS, David James "Tiger," hockey player (b 3 Feb 1954, Weyburn, SK). The NHL leader in career penalty minutes, he earned his

Tiger Williams, hockey player, celebrating a goal. Vancouver Canucks Photo Archives

nickname in minor HOCKEY when he knocked over a referee—his own brother—for calling a penalty on him. After 3 years in the WHL with the Swift Current Broncos he graduated to the NHL with the Toronto Maple Leafs and then joined the VANCOUVER CANUCKS, playing a key role in the team's run to the 1982 Stanley Cup finals. He played for a variety of teams 1984–88 but when he retired from hockey he settled in VANCOUVER where he is a popular sports celebrity, a roller-hockey promoter and a tireless worker for several charities.   SW

WILLIAMS, David Ricardo, lawyer, writer (b 28 Feb 1923, Kamloops; d 29 Jan 1999, Duncan). After graduating from UBC law school following WWII, he practised for many years in DUNCAN and was made a Queen's Counsel in 1969. He also taught law at the UNIV OF VICTORIA. At the same time he indulged an interest in history, writing a series of biographies about important legal and political figures, including Matthew BEGBIE, the VANCOUVER mayor Gerry MCGEER and the outlaw Simon GUNANOOT. His biography of Chief Justice Lyman Poore Duff, *Duff: A Life in the Law*, won a 1985 BC BOOK PRIZE. He also published a novel, *Ace of Pentacles* (1990), and his non-fiction study *With Malice Aforethought* (1993) won a Crime Writers of Canada award. His last book was a history of the Pinkerton's Detective Agency, *Call in Pinkerton's* (1998).

WILLIAMS, Lynn (Kanuka), runner (b 11 July 1960, Regina, SK). She moved to BURNABY in 1982 with her husband Paul, also a runner, to train under coach Doug CLEMENT. Versatile, she

Lynn Williams, distance runner, 1994.
Vancouver Province

was one of Canada's best female road runners between distances of 5 and 15 km and the best in the country over 5,000, 3,000, 1,500 and

(continued on page 773)

Bitter root (Lewisia rediviva) is abundant on arid flatlands unsuited for irrigation, throughout the dry southern Interior. Each 3-cm solitary flower, carried about 5 cm above the ground, has 12 to 18 pale pink petals.

Brittle prickly pear (Opuntia fragilis) is a savagely armed plant. It spreads its mats of fleshy-jointed green stems, bearing brilliant, deep yellow flowers, over the parched hillsides of the dry Interior.

Columbia lily, or tiger lily (Lilium columbianum) is one of 2 BC Lilium species. It may have up to 30 bright orange flowers on a single 80-cm stem, and is found in open woods and logging slashes on both sides of the Cascade Mts and Vancouver Island.

Northern riceroot (Fritillaria camschatcensis) is similar to the chocolate lily but with slightly recurved petals and no speckles. Found near the coast, it ranges from the far north of the province through the Queen Charlotte Islands and northern Vancouver Island.

Ocean spray (Holodiscus discolor) forms thickets of strong stems up to 3 m tall. Its cream-coloured drooping clumps contain hundreds of cream-white flowers, which appear in June or July.

Orange honeysuckle (Lonicera ciliosa) is a showy vine that climbs trees and shrubs in open forests from the coast to the Cascade Mts. Another common species of the genus, Lonicera hispidula, *purple honeysuckle, has a similar range.*

Text by John Trelawny; Hans Roemer photos

Balsam-root (Balsamorhiza sagittata) *forms tufts on dry open slopes in the Interior. The triangular leaves, 8-12 cm wide by 30 cm long, grow on long petioles. Each tuft has large yellow flowers with long stems.*

Harebell, or bluebell (Campanula rotundifolia), *ranges throughout many of the temperate regions of the northern hemisphere and is variable in form. In BC it occurs abundantly in mats in the Rocky Mts; it is more sparse along the coast.*

Easter lily (Erythronium oregonum), *with nodding white flowers on a slender stem, occurs on southern Vancouver Island and the extreme southern coastal mainland of BC in open woodland and grassland in the spring.*

Lady's slipper (Calypso bulbosa) *is a delicate pale purple orchid growing deep in the forests of Vancouver Island and through southern BC.*

Death camas (Zygadenus venenosus) *is one of 3 species of Zygadenus found in BC, all of which are highly toxic. First Nations people were careful to mark this plant while its white flowers were conspicuous so that its bulbs would not be confused with those of the edible* CAMAS. *This species is found in meadows and open places, most commonly in southern BC.*

Few-flowered shooting star (Dodecatheon pulchellum) *belongs to a genus that has strongly reflexed (backward-bending) petals; in this species the flowers are a striking rose-pink. The stamen-tube is ringed with deep yellow at the base, and the single stalk rises from low-lying leaves. The species is found from coastal flats to mountain meadows throughout the province.*

Menzies larkspur (Delphinium menziesii) produces deep blue flowers on single stems. It may be found on coastal bluffs and rocky slopes in May and in mountain meadows in June and July, and it occurs eastward to the Cascade Mts.

Yellow water lily (Nuphar polysepalum) has heart-shaped floating leaves that contrast large cup-shaped golden flowers, making this plant quite unmistakable in ponds and shallow lakes throughout BC.

Yellow avalanche lily (Erythronium grandiflorum) is a sub-alpine species appearing after the receding snow on mountains east of the Cascades and on southern Vancouver Island.

Western anemone, also wind flower (Anemone occidentalis), occurs in alpine meadows. The stems grow up to 20 cm and the terminal flowers are replaced by plumes of seeds. The species ranges from northern BC east to the Rocky Mts and south through the Cascade Mts.

Satin-flower (Sisyrinchium douglasii) has purple flowers, each with 3 yellow anthers, borne on single stalks up to about 20 cm. The flowers bloom as early as mid-February on Vancouver Island, on rocky slopes under Garry oaks. In the Interior the species is found on either side of the Cascade Mts south of Kamloops.

Pink rhododendron (Rhododendron macrophyllum) is a compact, rounded bush about 2 m tall, covered with pink to rose-coloured flowers. It grows in semi-shaded forest edges and can be found along the highway in Manning Park and in the Skagit Valley. Two isolated pockets of this species survive on Vancouver Island.

(continued from page 769)

1,000 m. She won several important road events including a victory over Grete Waitz, one of the world's best. Lynn won a bronze medal in the 1984 Los Angeles Olympics 3,000 m race in which favourites Mary Decker and Zola Budd collided to fall out of contention. At the 1986 Commonwealth Games she earned gold in the 3,000 m and bronze in the 1,500 m. She finished 5th in the 1,500 m and 8th in the 3,000 m at the 1988 Seoul Olympics. Paul, raised in Toronto, was not as successful in Olympic competition but won gold in the 5,000 m at the 1990 Goodwill Games and bronze in the 10,000 m at the 1990 Commonwealth Games. In 1985 Lynn was BC athlete of the year and she was recognized as Canada's top track athlete in 1988 and 1989. Both runners retired in the early 1990s, Lynn with Canadian records in the 1,500, 3,000 and 5,000 m and Paul with Canadian records in the 3,000, 5,000 and 10,000 m. Lynn entered the BC SPORTS HALL OF FAME in 1999. *See also* TRACK AND FIELD. SW

WILLIAMS, Parker, miner, politician (b 1873, Glamorganshire, Wales; d 1958, Nanaimo). He immigrated to Ontario at age 19 and in 1898 moved with his young family to NANAIMO, where he worked in the coal mines (*see* COAL MINING, VANCOUVER ISLAND). In 1903 he was elected to the provincial legislature as a candidate for the SOCIALIST PARTY OF BC (SPBC) and he held his seat through 4 more provincial elections. He belonged to the moderate wing of the SPBC and its successor, the Socialist Party of Canada, and generally supported the CONSERVATIVE government of Richard MCBRIDE in return for small reforms. In 1917 he resigned his seat to become a commissioner on the newly formed Workmen's Compensation Board (now the WORKERS' COMPENSATION BOARD), a position he held until his retirement in 1943.

WILLIAMS, Percy Alfred, sprinter (b 19 May 1908, Vancouver; d 29 Nov 1982, Vancouver). A graduate of King Edward High School in VANCOUVER, he was discovered and trained by coach Bob Granger. Even with his slight build—he weighed only 59 kg—and a heart weakened by

Percy Williams, Olympic double gold medallist in 1928. VPL 22711

childhood disease, he became Canada's leading track athlete. At the 1928 Olympic Games in Amsterdam he won gold medals in both the 100 m and 200 m sprints, the first time a Canadian had won 2 golds in TRACK AND FIELD. (Donovan Bailey repeated the feat in 1996.) Following the Olympics he won a series of indoor races in the US and in 1930 he set a world record for the 100 m (10.3 secs) that lasted for 6 years. Later that year at the British Empire Games in Hamilton he tore a thigh muscle during the 100-yard race but still won gold. The injury never healed properly and he ran for the last time at the 1932 Olympics in Los Angeles. After retiring from track he lived quietly in Vancouver, running an insurance business. He died of a self-inflicted shotgun wound.

Bob Erickson and a horse named Rebel, posing for a photograph to promote the Williams Lake Stampede, 1972. Fred Waterhouse photo

WILLIAMS LAKE, city, pop 10,472, the "Hub of the Cariboo," is located in the rolling rangeland of the central CARIBOO halfway between KAMLOOPS and PRINCE GEORGE. The name, taken from the nearby lake, refers to Chief William, a local SECWEPEMC (Shuswap) leader who is credited with keeping peace between FIRST NATIONS and miners during the GOLD RUSH. White settlement began in 1859 but when the CARIBOO WAGON ROAD bypassed the site in 1863 and built through 150 MILE HOUSE, the community dwindled. The area was long occupied by the large farm and ranch owned by William PINCHBECK and William Lyne. The OBLATES OF MARY IMMACULATE established a mission here in 1867. The arrival of the Pacific Great Eastern Rwy (*see* BC RAIL) in 1919 created an instant village. The community was incorporated as a village on 15 Mar 1929, as a town in 1965 and as a city in 1981. For many years it was the largest cattle shipping point in BC, and it has remained a major ranching centre (*see* CATTLE INDUSTRY) with a new stockyards

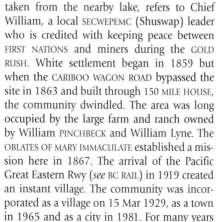

facility opening in 1998. Since the 1970s LOGGING, MINING and TOURISM have also become important. The first Williams Lake Stampede was held in 1926 and has been a major professional RODEO attraction ever since.

WILLISTON, Ray Gillis, teacher, politician (b 1914, Victoria). He began teaching in 1934 at a one-room school south of SALMON ARM; by 1950 he was a school inspector in northern BC. Attracted to politics by a desire to reform the school system, he won election as a SOCIAL CREDIT candidate in PRINCE GEORGE in 1953. The following year he joined Premier W.A.C. BENNETT's CABINET as minister of education. As minister of land and forests in 1956–72, he was central to implementing the Socred TWO RIVERS POLICY and expanding the PROVINCIAL PARKS system. After losing his seat in the 1972 election he became a FOREST INDUSTRY consultant; among other jobs he managed the government-owned PULP AND PAPER mill at OCEAN FALLS until it closed in 1980. BC's largest reservoir, WILLISTON RESERVOIR, is named for him.

WILLISTON RESERVOIR, 1,773 km², lies in the ROCKY MT TRENCH at the headwaters of the PEACE R in north-central BC. The largest body of

Williston Reservoir. BC Hydro

fresh water in the province and the ninth-largest HYDROELECTRIC reservoir in the world, it was created in 1968 with the construction of the W.A.C. BENNETT DAM near HUDSON'S HOPE. Water behind the dam flooded the valleys of the PARSNIP and FINLAY rivers. The town of MACKENZIE was located at the south end of the reservoir as a SAWMILLING centre for the LOGGING that occurs around its shores. It is named for Ray WILLISTON, minister of lands and forests in Bennett's government.

WILLISTON TRANSPORTER is a massive ice-breaking log ferry designed by Polar Design Associates of VANCOUVER and built in 1995 on the shore of WILLISTON RESERVOIR, where it plies the length of the reservoir daily in all seasons. The vessel, 110 m long and 30 m wide, is owned by Findlay Navigation Ltd, an innovator in log transportation on inland LAKES since 1968. The firm has built and operates heavy-duty articulated ferries to carry fully loaded LOGGING trucks, and it has developed underwater bubbling systems to keep ferry routes open after freeze-up.

Robert Allington

WILLOW is a tree occurring widely across BC, usually in moist areas along the banks of streams and lakes. Forty-four species are native to the province, 5 of which are tree-sized; the rest are shrubs. The Pacific Willow (*Salix lucida*, ssp *lasiandra*) is the largest, growing to 15 m in height. Its long, narrow, pointed leaves are typical of many willow species. Scouler's willow (*S. scouleriana*) is named for the Scottish collector John Scouler (1804–71) who visited BC with David DOUGLAS in 1825. It is the more widespread species, mainly on the coast. The inner bark of the willow contains salicylic acid (an ingredient of aspirin) and was chewed by FIRST NATIONS people as a painkiller. The golden weeping willow (*S. chrysocoma*) is an imported but well-known species; examples of it surround LOST LAGOON in STANLEY PARK in VANCOUVER. The peachleaf willow (*S. amygdaloides*) is common in parts of the Interior, especially the OKANAGAN VALLEY.

WILLOW RIVER, a LOGGING and ranching (*see* CATTLE INDUSTRY) community on the Willow R, 27 km northeast of PRINCE GEORGE, is also a VIA Rail station. One of the first SAWMILLS on the new GRAND TRUNK PACIFIC RWY was built here in 1915; several others, long since dismantled, operated over the years. Many residents enjoy the rural setting but commute to Prince George for work. AS

WILMER, a small community on the west side of the COLUMBIA R, 105 km southeast of GOLDEN just north of Windermere Lk , was named for Wilmer Wells, a government official who owned a SAWMILL in the region. It was originally a MINING settlement called Peterborough. Wilmer Marsh is an important refuge for migratory birds and other wildlife. The site of historic KOOTENAE HOUSE is near here. AS

WILSON, Alan "Al" ("Dirt"), football player (b 6 Apr 1960, Duncan). He played high school FOOTBALL with the Cowichan Timbermen and college ball with Montana State Univ, then became a CFL legend with the BC LIONS. He joined the Lions in 1972 and captained the team from 1975 to his retirement in 1986. He was selected as a Western Conference and Canadian all-star for 7 consecutive seasons, won the CFL award for most outstanding offensive lineman (1977) and led the team to 2 Grey Cup finals, winning the trophy in 1985. His number, 52, is retired by the Lions and 28 June 1987 was proclaimed "Al Wilson Day" in VANCOUVER. He was also honoured by DUNCAN, with a street and a public park named for him. He was inducted into the CFL Football Hall of Fame and BC SPORTS HALL OF FAME in 1997. SW

WILSON, Bill, aboriginal activist (b 6 Apr 1944, Comox). As a law student at UBC in the early 1970s he was president of the Native Student Union and the Law Students' Assoc. While still in law school he was hired as executive director of the UNION OF BC INDIAN CHIEFS and he went on to become a leading strategist in

Bill Wilson, aboriginal activist, 1991. Ian Lindsay/ Vancouver Sun

aboriginal politics in the province for more than a decade. He was active in the BC Assoc of Non-Status Indians and founding president of its successor organization, the United Native Nations; he served with UNN from 1976 to 1981. He was also one of the founders of the Native Courtworker and Counselling Association of BC. At the national level he served as vice-president of the Native Council of Canada (1982–83), representing the Council at the 1983 First Ministers Conference. He subsequently retired to VANCOUVER ISLAND, where he became coordinator of the Musgamagw Tribal Council, a KWAKWAKA'WAKW group. *See also* ABORIGINAL RIGHTS; FIRST NATIONS.

WILSON, Bruce, soccer player (b 20 June 1951, Vancouver). He started playing SOCCER in BURNABY, helping his teams win 7 provincial championships before he joined the N American Soccer League's VANCOUVER WHITECAPS in 1974. Renowned for his leadership skills, he played for the Chicago Sting 1978–80, the New York Cosmos 1980–81 (and with them won the 1980 NASL championship), the Toronto Blizzard 1981–84 and the Canadian national team for 13 years. He was the NASL's 1978 defender of the year, a first-team all-star twice and the league's

Bruce Wilson, soccer star, 1985. Courtesy Univ of Victoria

top "iron man," playing in 161 consecutive games. Internationally, he led Canada to the quarter finals at the 1984 Los Angeles Olympics and the 1986 World Cup, where he was named the team's top player. He was once offered a contract to play English first division soccer but remained in Canada. In retirement he became a soccer coach at the UNIV OF VICTORIA. SW

WILSON, Edward Arthur, a.k.a. Brother XII, occult leader (b 25 July 1878, Birmingham, England; d 7 Nov 1934, Neuchatel, Switzerland). As a teenager he went to sea and travelled around the world. From 1907 to 1912 he and his family lived in BC, where he worked on coastal steamers. After abandoning his wife he became an itinerant sea captain again. In the mid-1920s he experienced the mystical visions that changed his life. Wilson believed that astral intelligences had conveyed to him the blueprint for a new spiritual movement. Taking the name Brother XII, he predicted an imminent apocalypse, followed by a new age of enlightenment. In 1927 he returned to BC to establish a colony, the headquarters of the Aquarian Foundation, at Cedar-by-the-Sea on the coast just south of NANAIMO. For a time it flourished, attracting generous donations from followers and expanding to nearby VALDES and De Courcy islands. But Wilson's increasingly erratic behaviour, his sexual involvement with initiates and his tyrannical leadership resulted in divisions within the movement. In 1932 some of his followers took him to court. Wilson ransacked the colony; he absconded with his mistress Madame Zee and a fortune in gold. His death in Switzerland, where apparently he went to seek medical help, was confirmed officially but some people believe Wilson faked his own death; others are convinced the gold remains hidden.

Reading: John Oliphant, *Brother Twelve: The Incredible Story of Canada's False Prophet*, 1991.

WILSON, Eric, writer (b 24 Nov 1940, Ottawa). After graduating from UBC in 1963, he taught in high schools in several BC communities. He published the first of his mysteries for children, *Murder on the Canadian*, in 1976 and has continued to publish at the rate of about a book a year. His work combines elements of suspense with historical settings and a concern for social issues.

WILSON, Ethel (Bryant), writer (b 20 Jan 1888, Port Elizabeth, South Africa; d 22 Dec 1980, Vancouver). The daughter of a Methodist minister, she came to VANCOUVER in 1898 to live with relatives after the death of her parents. Her teenage years were spent at boarding school in England. Returning to Vancouver she taught school until her marriage to Wallace Wilson, a prominent physician, in 1921. She then settled into a comfortable and happy domestic life and did not begin writing until the 1930s. Her first story appeared in *The New Statesman* in 1937 but her major work appeared after WWII. She wrote 5 novels: *Hetty Dorval* (1947), *The Innocent Traveller* (1949), *The Equations of Love* (1952), *Swamp Angel* (1954), considered by many to be her best book, and *Love and Salt Water* (1956). Her short stories were collected in *Mrs Golightly and Other Stories* (1961). Her husband died in 1966 and her own health deteriorated following a stroke. She spent her final years in a nursing home. Since her death, her work has received much praise for its quiet attention to character and its splendid descriptions of Vancouver and the BC landscape. In 1970 she received the Order of Canada Medal of Service. BC's top fiction prize (*see* BC BOOK PRIZES) is named for her.

WILSON, Gordon, teacher, politician (b 1948, Vancouver). He was raised in Kenya, where both of his parents worked. After graduating from UBC with a Master's degree in economic geography, he taught at a COMMUNITY COLLEGE for 17 years. In 1987 he became leader of the provincial LIBERAL PARTY. He made a remarkable impression in the 1991 election and the party staged a surprising comeback, winning 33% of the popular vote, 17 seats (including Wilson's on the SUNSHINE COAST) and official opposition status in the legislature. He was unable to consolidate this success, however. Weakened by party infighting and personal scandal (it was revealed that he was having an extramarital relationship with Judy Tyabji, a fellow Liberal MLA), he was forced to call a leadership contest in 1993. He lost to Gordon CAMPBELL, former mayor of VANCOUVER. Wilson went on to form a new, middle-of-the-road party, the PROGRESSIVE DEMOCRATIC ALLIANCE, with Tyabji, whom he married. The party found few supporters and in the 1996

Gordon Wilson addressing the NDP leadership convention, Feb 2000.
Rick Ernst/Vancouver Province

provincial election won just 5.7% of the popular vote, though Wilson retained his seat in the legislature and continued to be one of the most popular politicians in the province. Early in 1999 he accepted an offer to join the NDP government as minister of aboriginal affairs and minister in charge of the BC FERRY CORP. He later became minister of finance, and when Glen CLARK stepped down as party leader and premier, Wilson joined the contest to succeed him. The leadership was won by Ujjal DOSANJH and Wilson remained in CABINET as minister of employment and investment.

WILSON, Ruth (Plant), athlete (b 27 Apr 1919, Calgary). A top BC all-around athlete, she excelled in BASKETBALL, softball, GOLF and TENNIS. She arrived in VANCOUVER at an early age and as a junior was a champion tennis player at the Vancouver Lawn Tennis Club. Active in sports while attending UBC, she continued her athletics with the Vancouver Hedlunds basketball and BASEBALL teams. She coached and played on 4 straight national basketball championship teams (1943–46) with the Hedlunds and later coached the Vancouver Eilers to 2 Canadian titles (1949, 1950) and the Vancouver Buzz Bombs to another in 1973. Internationally, she managed the Canadian women's basketball entry at the 1959 Pan American Games and won the bronze medal as a coach at the 1967 Pan Am Games. She was the first woman to referee basketball in BC. In softball, she played for Canada at the world championships in 1943 and 1945 and later coached a BC team to the world championships in Portland. As a golfer she played for 8 BC provincial teams and for Team Canada in the international Curtis Cup tournament. She was elected to the BC SPORTS HALL OF FAME (1966) and the UBC Sports Hall of Fame.   *SW*

WILSON, Sandy, writer, director, film producer (b Penticton, 15 Oct 1947). She is a third-generation British Columbian. Her paternal great-grandfather, Falkland Edgeworth Warren (for whom the community of FALKLAND is named),

immigrated from England in 1892, and her mother's father came from England in 1911 and lived at KAMLOOPS and OKANAGAN MISSION. Wilson graduated from SFU in 1969; that year she produced her first film. In 1975 she edited a book about poetry in BC, *Western Windows*, which was short-listed for an Eaton's Book Award. Wilson is best known for her 3 award-winning feature films, *My American Cousin*

Sandy Wilson, filmmaker, 1992. Colin Price/Vancouver Province

(1985), *American Boyfriends* (1989) and *Harmony Cats* (1993), all set in BC. She also wrote and directed the TV movie *Momma's Gonna Buy You a Mockingbird* (1987), and she has directed several episodes of TV series; served as writer, editor and/or director on 8 documentary films, and written and produced 3 short films. *See also* FILMMAKING INDUSTRY.

WILSON, Tracy, figure skater (b 25 Sept 1961, Lachine, QC). She learned to skate at the COQUITLAM Skating Club and trained at the Inlet Skating Club of PORT MOODY. She began her pairs ice dance career with Mark Stokes but when Stokes retired in 1981 she teamed with Nova Scotian Robert McCall and they began training at the North Shore Winter Club. They were Canadian champions 1982–88 and won 3 world championship bronze medals 1986–88. In 1983 they were the first Canadians to win the international "Skate Canada" event and repeated that in 1987. At the 1984 Sarajevo Olympics they finished 8th overall but at the 1988 Calgary Olympics they won bronze, the first medal for Canada in pairs skating. In 1988 Wilson received the Order of Canada and awards as BC senior and overall athlete of the year. After she and McCall toured professionally 1988–90, Wilson became a commentator for CTV Sports. She was inducted into the BC SPORTS HALL OF FAME in 1991. *See also* FIGURE SKATING.   *SW*

WILSON CREEK, a residential district on the SUNSHINE COAST, 50 km northwest of VANCOUVER, developed around Tsawcome, a RESERVE of the SECHELT Nation. The area was first homesteaded in the 1880s and became a steamship landing and LOGGING settlement. It was named after James Wilson, a blacksmith for Burns and Jackson Logging, who had a camp here in the 1930s and 1940s.   *AS*

WILSON LANDING is an AGRICULTURAL and recreational settlement on the west edge of OKANAGAN LK 12 km north of KELOWNA. A former steamship port of call, it was named after Harold F. Wilson, who settled here in 1900. Many other homesteaders arrived before WWI but drifted away after the war. *AS*

WINCH, Ernest Edward, bricklayer, politician (b 22 Mar 1879, Harlow, England; d 11 Jan 1957, Vancouver). He visited Canada and VANCOUVER for the first time when he was 19, but work was scarce and he ended up returning to England. After training as a bricklayer, he came back to BC in 1910 with his wife and children, this time for good. His construction work led him to the LABOUR MOVEMENT and socialist politics. In 1918 he was president of the Vancouver Trades and Labour Council and an organizer for both the longshoremen's and loggers' unions. In the early 1930s he worked as an organizer for the SOCIALIST PARTY OF BC, one of the groups that came together during 1932–33 to form the CCF. In the 1933 provincial election Winch was one of 7 CCFers elected to the legislature. He held his BURNABY seat for the rest of his life. Associated with the left wing of the party, he lost his bid for the leadership to Robert CONNELL and thereafter was content to champion the career of his son Harold WINCH, who became leader of the party in 1939. The Winches, who served together in the legislature until Harold moved to federal politics in 1953, were the longest-serving father-and-son team in Canadian political history. As an MLA, the elder Winch was a persistent and effective critic of conditions in the province's penal and health facilities, and he was widely respected as a tireless worker for the underprivileged and less fortunate.

WINCH, Harold Edward, electrician, politician, leader of the CCF 1939–53 (b 18 June 1907, Loughton, England; d 1 Feb 1993, Vancouver).

Harold Winch, leader of the provincial CCF 1938–53, shown here in 1973. UBC 1.1/13032

The son of the labour leader Ernest WINCH, he was raised in a socialist household (at one point J.S. Woodsworth, the founder of the CCF, was a lodger), and he became politically active during the Depression when he edited the SOCIALIST PARTY OF BC paper, the *Clarion*. Along with his father he won election as a CCF candidate to the legislature for Vancouver East in 1933. Six years later he became party leader, and from 1941 to 1953 he headed the official opposition. His rivalry with SOCIAL CREDIT PARTY leader W.A.C. BENNETT was bitter and personal, and Winch is credited with inventing the nickname "Wacky" to describe his nemesis. He came close to being elected PREMIER twice, but in the 1952 election a new system of transferable ballot gave the Socreds a chance to form a government, despite the CCF winning the highest percentage of the popular vote. Then in Mar 1953 the minority government was defeated in a legislative vote and instead of calling on Winch, the LT GOV allowed Premier Bennett to call an election, which he won. Winch left provincial politics soon after and won election to the House of Commons, where he represented Vancouver East for the CCF (later the NDP) until he retired in 1972.

WINCH, Richard Vance, salmon canner (b 1862, Cobourg, ON; d 31 July 1952, Vancouver). He came west from Ontario as a teenager and worked on CPR construction before settling in VANCOUVER in 1886. He started a food retail business with his brother-in-law George Bower, then branched into SALMON CANNING, establishing Canadian Packers Canning Co on the FRASER R. He was well known in Vancouver as a high roller, with a West End mansion and a pair of Rolls Royces, the first in the city. His Winch Building at Howe and Hastings streets, erected in 1909, still stands as part of the Sinclair Centre heritage development. Winch was hit hard by the post-WWI depression, but he recovered to form Queen Charlotte Fisheries in 1924 and remained active in the canning industry until his death.

WINDERMERE, pop 1,273, overlooks the east side of Windermere Lk, a popular vacation area, 117 km north of CRANBROOK in the E KOOTENAY. The lake was named in 1883 by the surveyor Gilbert SPROAT after the English Lake District. It was developed pre-WWI by Robert Randolph BRUCE as a farming colony for well-to-do British immigrants, but the colony did not live up to its promise and most of the settlers left during the war. It is the site of the famous "stolen church," St Peter's Anglican Church, built in 1887 in Donald on the CPR mainline. When the divisional point moved to REVELSTOKE 10 years later, so did many of the buildings, but 2 settlers who were moving to Windermere decided to take the church with them. Despite protests from Revelstoke, the church stayed where it was, and is.

WINE MAKING INDUSTRY in BC has grown enormously in size and sophistication since the first wineries began producing loganberry wine in the 1920s. The industry is associated with the

OKANAGAN VALLEY but there are also wineries on VANCOUVER ISLAND. The major companies in the early years were GROWERS' WINES (est 1923), CALONA WINES LTD (est 1932), and later MISSION HILL VINEYARDS INC (est 1965). Until the 1970s most BC wines were overly sweet, a result of having to counteract the pungency of the N American grapes being used to make them. More

Joe Busnardo, wine maker, outside his Oliver winery, 1995. Mark van Manen/Vancouver Sun

than anything else it was their sweetness that gave local wines a bad reputation with sophisticated consumers. BC wines "dried out" in the 1970s, when makers switched to superior varieties of imported grapes. Increasingly BC growers replanted their vineyards with higher quality vinifera vines and the modern industry emerged during the 1980s. That decade also saw the appearance of several estate and farm wineries; estate wineries produce wine with BC grapes, 50% of which must come from their own vineyards, while farm wineries are required to produce 75% of their own grapes. Notable examples include Blue Mountain, CedarCreek, Gehringer Bros, Gray Monk, LeComte, Quails' Gate, Sumac Ridge and Summerhill.

The free trade agreement with the US in 1988 was a turning point for the BC industry. The preferential pricing long provided by the provincial government was removed and incentives were given for growers to replace inferior grapes with higher quality vines. In 1988 growers pulled out 13.35 km² of vines; some replanted, some went out of business. The result was an industry capable of producing for the quality end of the market. This new direction was confirmed in 1994 when one of Mission Hill's wines won a prestigious international competition in London, something no one would have predicted for BC wines a quarter of a century earlier. In 1997 there were 27 estate and farm gate wineries in BC and by 2000 there were just over 16 km² of grapes under cultivation. In the year ending 31 Mar 1999 sales of BC wine totalled $177 million.

WINFIELD, an orchard settlement 30 km south of VERNON near Hwy 97 in the OKANAGAN VALLEY, was named after Winfield Lodge, the home of Thomas Wood, justice of the peace, stockraiser and homesteader here in 1871. The village developed as an important fruit-packing centre in the 1920s. *See also* TREE FRUITS. AS

WINGDAM, 35 km east of QUESNEL on Lightning Crk on the road to BARKERVILLE, was a MINING camp. GOLD was discovered in the area in 1861 and the Wingdam mine operated from 1898 to 1938. Some old ruins could still be seen in the late 1990s. Wingdams, built of logs and rocks, are used to divert streams so that miners can work on the exposed riverbed. AS

WINLAW, pop 180, 33 km north of CASTLEGAR, is a farming settlement in the Slocan R valley. John Winlaw built a sawmill here in 1900 and many DOUKHOBORS settled in the area, naming their communal villages Kirpichnoe (Russian for "bricks") and Vesoloe ("merryland"). Valhalla Provincial PARK is nearby.

WINTER HARBOUR, pop 51, is a small fishing village in Forward Inlet, an arm of QUATSINO SOUND on the northwest coast of VANCOUVER ISLAND, 60 km by road from PORT HARDY. Originally called Queenstown, it was the site of a clam cannery built in 1904, and it attracted DANISH, NORWEGIAN and GERMAN settlers from around the North Island. Albert Moore built a floating logging camp at the site in 1936 and LOGGING, commercial FISHING and AQUACULTURE form the basis of the local economy.

WISMER, Gordon Sylvester, lawyer, politician (b 23 Mar 1888, Sutton, ON; d 28 Dec 1968, Vancouver). After arriving in VANCOUVER in 1907 he went into law practice with Gerry MCGEER in 1913. By the 1920s he was one of the most prominent criminal lawyers in the province. A backroom power in the LIBERAL PARTY, he was elected to the legislature for Vancouver Centre in 1933 and served as attorney general from 1937 until his defeat in the 1941 election. He was re-elected in 1945; he rejoined the CABINET as attorney general the next year and served until his defeat in the 1952 election. In 1947 he narrowly lost out to Byron JOHNSON in a bid for the Liberal leadership and the premiership. Known as an old-style political boss, Wismer had no compunction about wielding the powers of patronage.

WISTARIA, a scattered rural settlement on the north side of OOTSA LK 58 km southwest of BURNS LAKE, was first settled about 1907. Trapping, cattle and sheep ranching (*see* CATTLE INDUSTRY), fur farming and LOGGING have all been important to the local economy. Cyril Shelford, a former resident and cabinet minister during W.A.C. BENNETT's SOCIAL CREDIT regime, claims that Wistaria was chosen as a name after Banana, the first choice, was rejected by postal authorities. AS

WOLF (*Canis lupus*), also known as the grey or timber wolf, is a carnivorous mammal, the largest wild member of the dog family. An adult male may weigh up to 45 kg. Wolves prefer remote, timbered habitat and are active

Grey wolf. Mark Newman/Image Makers

mainly at night when their distinctive howl may be heard. They range in colour from white to black though grey-brown is most common. They live in packs of 5–8 related animals, dominated by a lead couple. Each pack roams over its own territory in search of food, consisting of large ungulates (DEER, ELK, CARIBOU, MOOSE, sheep) as well as some smaller animals. The hunt is a highly coordinated attack, depending for success on the amazing stamina of the wolf, which pursues its prey to exhaustion. In each pack only the dominant couple mate. The female produces litters of 4–7 pups, after which she is protected and fed by the pack. Unlike several other provinces where wolves have been exterminated, the BC population is stable at about 8,000 animals. The largest concentrations are on north VANCOUVER ISLAND and in the northeast corner of the province. Despite their reputation for ferocity, healthy wolves do not attack humans.

WOLVERINE (*Gulo gulo*), a carnivorous mammal, is the largest land member of the WEASEL family, about the size of a large dog. Its fur is dark brown, with paler stripes extending along either flank, and is valued as trim for garments because it sheds moisture. Wolverines are known as "skunk bears" because they mark their territory and food with a foul-smelling fluid secreted by anal musk glands. They are strong and aggressive when interfered with. Wolverines are nomadic scavengers; they are active mainly at night and travel long distances in search of food, chiefly carrion, small mammals and birds. They live 8–10 years in the wild. Females become sexually mature at 2 years and may give birth to litters of up to 5 kits annually. There are only a few thousand wolverines in BC, where they are still trapped in small numbers.

WOMEN'S INTERNATIONAL LEAGUE FOR PEACE AND FREEDOM (WILPF) is an organization of peace activists founded in Europe in 1915. A Canadian section was established in Toronto in 1919 and a group of VANCOUVER women, including Laura JAMIESON and Dorothy STEEVES, formed a BC branch in 1921. Over the years the WILPF lobbied against militarism and for disarmament and social justice. During the Cold War, public opinion was not sympathetic to "peaceniks" and the WILPF was accused of communist leanings. In the 1950s the Vancouver branch splintered, losing some of its direction, but it revived and by the early 21st century was still active, one of the oldest women's organizations in the province.

WOMEN'S MOVEMENT, as an organized political movement in BC, had its roots in the women's social reform groups of the 1880s and 1890s. Women of all ethnocultural groups in colonial BC—mostly aboriginal and English-speaking immigrant women, with smaller numbers of Asian and other European women—had informal networks centred on shared domestic work, but as BC's population mushroomed in the frontier society, the colony's white, middle-class women organized more formal groups to rescue sick and destitute people and to improve the moral climate of BC. In 1882 a chapter of the Women's Christian Temperance Union (WCTU) was founded in VICTORIA with 47 members. They opened a "refuge home" for prostitutes, unwed mothers and women who were sick, poor and/or elderly. In 1894 Lady Aberdeen, the wife of Canada's gov gen, set up Local Councils of Women in Victoria and VANCOUVER, as branches of the National Council of Women of Canada, established in 1893 for all Canadian women interested in organized work in any field. In 1898 she also set up a BC branch of the Victorian Order of Nurses, which provided visiting nurses to areas that had no other medical services (*see also* NURSING). The Young Women's Christian Association (YWCA), established in BC before 1900, operated a hostel and employment agency for young single women. Evlyn FARRIS and others created the University Women's Club in 1907, with the long-range goal of improving conditions in education and employment for BC women, and the immediate goal of founding UBC. And in 1909 the BC Department of Agriculture, following a successful model in Ontario, established the BC Women's Institutes, whose stated aims were to promote "household science" and to bring female friendship to women, mostly rural women.

These organizations were instrumental in assisting British Columbians in need and in bringing about social and political change, especially as it affected women and children. The WCTU is remembered mainly for its puritanical views on drinking alcohol, but its members were also tireless promoters of a BC woman's right to run for election as a school trustee, to be paid a higher minimum wage, to receive a "Mother's Pension" from the government if she was a widow with children, and other rights. Members of all women's organizations fought long and hard for WOMEN'S SUFFRAGE, as individuals and through the Political Equality League. When Evlyn Farris was elected to the Senate of the newly formed UBC in 1912, she persuaded the administration to allow women to take science courses. The UWC also campaigned for a shorter work week for women store clerks and organized Vancouver women to do their Christmas shopping early so as to relieve pressure on the clerks; established the first parent-teacher associations in BC; pressed for change in inheritance laws in favour of widows; and lobbied for women's right to practise law in BC.

The women of BC threw themselves into the war effort during WWI, including performing "men's work" in the war industries. In 1915 the Trades and Labour Congress, Canada's central labour organization, dropped its demand to exclude women from factories, workshops and mines, and added a clause about equal pay for equal work. BC women finally got the vote in 1917, and redoubled their efforts on other social reforms. In family law, they lobbied for approved foster homes and CHILD CARE centres and campaigned to keep juvenile offenders out of adult PRISONS. In 1917, the same year Helen Gregory MACGILL became BC's first female judge, the Infants Act was amended so that mothers as well as fathers were considered legal guardians of their own children. After a long campaign, Helena GUTTERIDGE and other BC women succeeded in raising the minimum wage for women in 1918. The Mother's Pension Act, passed in 1920 to provide a monthly subsidy to single mothers, became BC's first social assistance legislation. Through the 1920s the Women's Institutes were instrumental in establishing hospitals and in helping the BC government set up a public health system. Women's groups also lobbied in the areas of child labour and maternity leave. During this same period, Dorothy STEEVES and Laura JAMIESON opened a BC chapter of the WOMEN'S INTERNATIONAL LEAGUE FOR PEACE AND FREEDOM, and the Women's Independent Political Assoc took action on the high cost of living. All of this activity took place before 1929, the year Canadian women were declared to be persons under the law.

During the Depression, women's groups in Vancouver pressured city council to assist the many single women who had lost their jobs and who were ineligible for government relief; meanwhile they organized emergency shelter and food for the women. They took food to men in the RELIEF CAMPS, fought for better conditions in the camps, and fed and supported the men who participated in the protest that culminated in BLOODY SUNDAY. They organized public lectures on divorce law, child care and birth control, which was illegal at the time. And women were more active in supporting the LABOUR MOVEMENT and bringing reforms to trade unions during the 1930s than at any other time in BC history.

When Canada joined WWII in 1939, so did BC women, as nurses and other military personnel and, once again, in the war industries and support efforts at home. This time many women stayed at work after war's end: BC women worked outside the home in greater numbers than ever before. With the more buoyant economy came better public funding in health, education, HUMAN CARE SERVICES and other areas, and better education and employment opportunities for women.

Helena Gutteridge, Vancouver politician and crusader for women's rights, speaking in support of the protests against unemployment, Vancouver, 1938. BC Archives C-07954

The 1960s brought a new awareness of discrimination against women in western society, and for the first time large numbers of women had access to legal, effective birth control. The stage was set for the next wave of the women's movement. In BC as elsewhere, women's subcommittees formed within schools, trade unions, professional associations and non-profit groups. In 1969 a feminist newspaper, the *Pedestal*, began publishing in Vancouver. That year 200 women from Canada and the US attended a Western Regional Conference on Women's Liberation at UBC. In 1970 the federal Royal Commission on the Status of Women published its report, which documented massive discrimination against Canadian women in many areas of life and made 167 recommendations for improvement. The abortion issue was among the most volatile; in the spring of 1970, an "abortion caravan" of a few vehicles set out from Vancouver and BURNS LAKE and proceeded to Ottawa, stopping all along the way to stage demonstrations, garner media attention and pick up supporters. The caravan drew the support of several politicians, including Grace MACINNIS. In May the women arrived in Ottawa and chained themselves to the galleries in the House of Commons in protest. It was the start of an 18-year fight to decriminalize abortion in Canada, and BC women were instrumental in the campaign.

Through the 1970s the women's movement in BC moved in 2 streams: consciousness-raising and political activism. Women's support groups, therapy groups and self-defence workshops sprang up. Women also organized the BC Child Care Federation to lobby for better funding and public policy on child care. They worked within trade unions and political parties; they also established the Service Office and Retail Workers' Union of Canada (SORWUC), predominantly a women's union, which represented workers at day care centres, social service agencies, theatres, pubs and restaurants. Women formed health collectives, explored alternative health care, lobbied for safe, effective birth control and played a more active part in their own pregnancy and childbirth. The first credit courses in women's studies in Canada were offered at UBC in 1971. BC women operated Press Gang Printers, the first all-women's printing company in Canada, which later gave birth to PRESS GANG PUBLISHERS; they opened the Vancouver Women's Bookstore, women's centres, TRANSITION HOUSES and rape crisis centres.

In the 1980s the movement branched out into more focussed interest groups. Domestic workers, most of them non-white immigrant women, continued their campaign to be covered under the BC Labour Standards Act (and finally succeeded in 1995). In 1981 aboriginal women occupied the BC regional office of the Department of Indian Affairs to protest against actions of the DIA and to demand action on deplorable living conditions in their communities (*see* ABORIGINAL RIGHTS; FIRST NATIONS). MediaWatch was established in Vancouver to improve the image of women and girls in the media. Women In Focus, a gallery owned collectively by women artists, was set up in Vancouver (*see also* VISUAL ARTS). A BC chapter of the DisAbled Women's Network (DAWN) was founded in 1985. That year Canada's first Lesbian Centre opened in Vancouver (*see also* GAY AND LESBIAN RIGHTS); BC families successfully challenged the law prohibiting a child from being given the mother's surname without the father's permission; and aboriginal women effected changes to the federal *Indian Act*, which had divested women of their legal Native status if they married white men. Early in 1988 the Supreme Court of Canada struck down the law criminalizing abortion. In Nov of that year, Everywoman's Health Clinic opened its doors in Vancouver and began performing therapeutic abortions, as 300 anti-choice protestors demonstrated outside.

During the late 1980s and 1990s other women's issues surfaced, some of them not even mentioned in the 1970 Royal Commission report. All 4 universities in BC established offices devoted to sexual harassment policy. The extent of violence against women, particularly rape, "domestic abuse" and sexual abuse of children, came more fully to light. By 1990 poverty was still very much a BC women's issue, with women earning an average of 65% of men's wages.

Women have also raised public awareness about lesbian mothers, employment benefits for same-sex couples, censorship and pornography, trans-gendered and cross-gendered people, prostitutes and other sex trade workers; and also the effects on women of the Canada–US Free Trade Agreement, world monetary practices and the federal and BC budgets during less prosperous times. Women have also sounded the alarm about health issues such as the sharp increase in Caesarean sections and hysterectomies, prevention and treatment of breast cancer, and new reproductive technologies. By the beginning of the 21st century, in spite of years' worth of headlines announcing the end of the women's movement, work was continuing on women's issues in all areas of BC life.

WOMEN'S SUFFRAGE was achieved after a long campaign that began in the 1870s. Women in BC cities were first allowed to vote for school trustees in 1884, if certain property qualifications were met, and in 1889 they were allowed to stand for election themselves. They lost these rights in 1891, but new legislation the following year allowed women of means and property to

"The Woman's Cause is Man's"

THE CHAMPION

THE WOMAN'S CAUSE IS MAN'S

The Champion, *publication of the Political Equality League, a women's suffrage group, 1912.*

vote. In 1895 women in cities could be elected school trustees if they owned property; the first woman so elected was Maria GRANT in VICTORIA. Meanwhile MLAs unsuccessfully attempted to pass legislation giving women the provincial vote. In 1906 a loophole in an amendment to the *Municipal Elections Act* permitted women to vote in municipal elections. Victoria women exercised that right for the first time in the civic election of 1907, but the loophole was removed in 1908, and so was the vote.

In 1910 the Political Equality League formed

to lobby for suffrage. It published its own newspaper, *Champion*, and organized chapters across the province. The opposition LIBERAL PARTY endorsed women's suffrage in 1912 but the CONSERVATIVE government of Richard MCBRIDE held out against it. Finally the new premier, William BOWSER, put the issue to referendum during the provincial election of 1916. It passed, and the newly elected Liberal government enacted a bill giving women the provincial vote and the right to run for office as of 5 Apr 1917. They could also vote in municipal elections. BC was the fourth province, after Manitoba, Saskatchewan and Alberta, to grant women the vote.

The federal franchise was granted in 1917 to women in the armed forces and to female relatives of military men. It was extended to all women aged 21 years and older on 24 May 1918. In July 1919 women gained the right to run for federal office, though they were not eligible for appointment to the Senate until 1929.

WONG, Milton, financier (b 1939, Vancouver). A graduate of UBC, he is the founder and chief executive officer of the international investment firm M.K. Wong & Associates and chair of HSBC Asset Management Canada Ltd. He began his career working for National Trustco Ltd in Toronto, then moved back to VANCOUVER in the 1970s and formed his own company in 1980. In 1996 his firm became part of the HONGKONG BANK OF CANADA. Wong is a co-founder of Vancouver's annual International DRAGON BOAT Festival and the founder of the Laurier Institution, a non-profit organization that promotes the benefits of cultural diversity. He was also active in creating SCIENCE WORLD BC. For his commmunity involvement he became a member of the Order of Canada (1997) and in 1999 he became chancellor of SFU.

WONG, Paul, multimedia artist (b 1955, Prince Rupert). He moved to VANCOUVER in 1962 and grew up on the east side. During the 1970s he emerged as a pioneer in the making of video art, as well as the organization of artist-run centres through his association with the WESTERN FRONT. His major video installations include *Murder Research* (1977), a multimedia reconstruction of a murder, and *Confused/Sexual Views* (1984), a controversial piece that the VANCOUVER ART GALLERY cancelled at the last minute, prompting him to sue on the grounds of censorship (the lawsuit was unsuccessful). In 1988 he made a documentary film, *Ordinary Shadows, Chinese Shade*, about a trip to China. Another video installation, *Chinaman's Peak, Walking the Mountain* (1992), deals with his family history and the history of the CHINESE in Canada. He had a major solo retrospective at the National Gallery in Ottawa in 1995 and has exhibited widely internationally.

WONOWON, pop 84, is located on the ALASKA HWY at Historic Mile 101, hence the name. Originally called Blueberry after nearby BLUEBERRY R, it offers services for travellers and is the gateway to a vast recreational wilderness. LOGGING,

the CATTLE INDUSTRY and oil (*see* OIL AND GAS INDUSTRY) are also important to the area. It was the site of a military control gate in WWII.   AS

WOOD, Frederic Gordon Campbell, academic, theatre pioneer (b 26 Jan 1887, Victoria; d 3 June 1976, Vancouver). He graduated from McGill Univ in 1910, and after completing a Master's degree at Harvard Univ he joined the UBC faculty in 1915, the first BC-born faculty member of the newly named institution. He remained a member of the English department until his retirement in 1950. Indulging an interest in THEATRE, he formed the UBC Players Club in 1915 and served as its leader until 1931, conducting an annual tour of student actors across the Interior of the province. It was almost the only theatre troupe in VANCOUVER until 1920, when Wood co-founded the Vancouver Little Theatre as well. The Frederic Wood Theatre on the UBC campus is named after him.

WOODCOCK, George, writer (b 18 May 1912, Winnipeg; d 28 Jan 1995, Vancouver). His parents took him to their native England when he was a youngster and he was raised there. During the 1930s he worked as a railway clerk and began writing poetry. He published his first book in 1940. As editor of the journal *Now* (1940–47), he came to know a wide circle of the British intelligentsia, many of whom later

George Woodcock, writer.

became literary celebrities, including George Orwell, Stephen Spender, V.S. Pritchett and Malcolm Muggeridge. A pacifist and philosophic anarchist, Woodcock spent WWII doing compensatory service as a labourer. Following the war he made a bare living as an editor and reviewer until he and his wife Ingeborg immigrated to Canada in 1949, homesteading on VANCOUVER ISLAND near SOOKE. After this attempt at farming he took a job teaching at UBC, where he was founding editor (1959–1977) of the influential journal *CANADIAN LITERATURE*.

Woodcock was the most prolific serious writer in Canada. He wrote and edited more than 140 books of literary criticism, travel, biography, history and political commentary. As well, he was an accomplished poet and in 1994 published the third volume of an autobiography. His biography of George Orwell, *The Crystal Spirit* (1966), won a GOV GEN'S LITERARY AWARD; his books on anarchism and the DOUKHOBORS remain definitive. Woodcock and his wife led a variety of public causes, including the Canada-India Village Aid Society and the Woodcock Endowment Fund for writers in distress. A year before his death he became the first writer to receive Freedom of the City of VANCOUVER.

WOODFIBRE is the site of a pulp mill on the west side of HOWE SOUND opposite BRITANNIA Beach. The mill opened at the mouth of Mill Creek in 1912, followed by a small townsite of white frame houses for the workers. The complex, which at times included a shingle mill and SAWMILL, obtained water from behind a dam on Henriette Lk in the mountains above. During the 1960s most employees moved off site and began commuting to work by ferry, and the townsite was demolished. Today the mill, owned by Western Forest Products, produces quality kraft paper.

WOODLANDS was a residential and treatment facility for the mentally disabled and ill located in NEW WESTMINSTER. It opened in May 1878 on a 12-ha site overlooking the FRASER R as the Public Asylum for the Insane and grew over the years to accommodate more than 1,000 residents in a series of buildings. In 1897 the name changed to Public Hospital for the Insane. By 1913 another facility, Essondale (now RIVERVIEW), had opened in nearby COQUITLAM and the hospital began to care for the mentally disabled rather than the mentally ill. The name changed in 1950 to the Woodlands School, later simply Woodlands, to reflect this change. Over the years the emphasis shifted from custodial care to training for independence as people with disabilities were integrated into the community. Woodlands downsized in preparation for closure; by the end of 1998 it was almost empty and plans were being made to redevelop the site.

WOODPECKER is a climbing bird with a sharp bill, which it uses to drill holes in tree trunks in search of INSECTS. Its short legs, pointed toes and stiff tail feathers are all adapted to tree climbing. The woodpecker announces itself by the low tapping sound it makes pecking for food. It is also equipped with a long, sticky tongue for catching prey. Woodpeckers nest in holes in trees, mainly aspen. Several species occur in BC. The largest is the pileated woodpecker (*Dryocopus pileatus*), a CROW-sized bird with a conspicous red crest and black and white body, found across southern BC. Lewis' woodpecker (*Melanerpes lewis*) is found mainly in the ponderosa PINE and cottonwood forests of the southern Interior. Black with a pink belly, this species mainly catches insects on the wing rather than drilling for them. The downy woodpecker (*Picoides pubescens*) is a small black and white bird with a white stripe down its back, found throughout the province. The white-

Red-naped sapsucker, a species of woodpecker.
Roy Luckow photo

headed woodpecker (*P. albolarvatus*) occurs only in the south OKANAGAN VALLEY in pine forests. It is distinctive for eating the seeds of ponderosa pines. Other species include the hairy (*P. villosus*), three-toed (*P. tridactylus*) and black-backed (*P. arcticus*) woodpeckers. Another member of the woodpecker family is the sapsucker, notable for drilling holes in tree bark to drink the running sap. Four species occur in BC. Williamson's sapsucker (*Sphyrapicus thyroideus*) is one of the rarest woodpeckers in Canada, found most frequently in the LARCH forests of the south-central Interior. Males are black with red throats and yellow bellies. Other species are the yellow-bellied (*S. varius*), red-naped (*S. nuchalis*) and red-breasted (*S. ruber*) sapsuckers. Another member of the woodpecker family is the northern flicker (*Colaptes auratus*), a ground-feeding species especially fond of ants. It comes in 2 types: the yellow-shafted flicker, which inhabits northern BC, has yellow underwings and tail, black whiskers and a red crescent on the back of the head; the red-shafted flicker, occurring in southern BC, has red underwings and tail and red whiskers at the neck.

WOODPECKER is a tiny ranching settlement and former steamship landing on the BC RAIL line, 45 km south of PRINCE GEORGE on the east side of the FRASER R. Woodpecker Island in the river near here was named for the sound of wood being chopped for fuel for passing riverboats. *AS*

WOODWARD, or Woodward's Landing, was an early AGRICULTURAL settlement on LULU ISLAND, 18 km south of VANCOUVER in the City of RICHMOND. It was named for Nathaniel Woodward, who settled here in 1874, and later became the site of a maintenance and repair depot for BC FERRY CORP. *AS*

WOODWARD, Charles A., merchant (b 19 July 1852, Mono, ON; d 2 June 1937, Vancouver). Raised on a backwoods farm in Ontario, he left to take up storekeeping. In 1875 he moved to Manitoulin Island and established the first WOODWARD'S STORE. He came west to VANCOUVER in 1891 and the next year opened a general store downtown. Woodward prospered during the economic boom associated with the Klondike GOLD RUSH and in 1903 he opened Woodward's Department Store at its long-time location on Hastings St. Two of his sons, Percival and William WOODWARD, became senior managers at the store; Charles "retired" several times but he kept involved in the business until his death. At age 71 he was elected to the provincial legislature as a LIBERAL opposed to the "liquor interest." However, he became alienated from his party and did not run for re-election. He is a member of the Canadian Business Hall of Fame.

WOODWARD, Charles Nanby Wynn "Chunky," retailer, rancher (b 23 Mar 1924, Vancouver; d 27 Apr 1990, Vancouver). Grandson of Charles WOODWARD, who founded WOODWARD'S STORES, and son of William WOODWARD, president of the department store chain, he joined the family business in 1946. He managed the development of Park Royal Shopping Centre,

"Chunky" Woodward, retailer and rancher, 1971. Brian Kent/Vancouver Sun

which opened in W VANCOUVER in 1950, and became president of the company at his father's death in 1957. He remained in charge until 1988, supervising the company's rapid expansion in BC and Alberta. If his business was retail, his great love was ranching (*see* CATTLE INDUSTRY). He owned the DOUGLAS LAKE CATTLE CO from 1959 until his death and was active in promoting RODEO.

WOODWARD, Reginald Percival "Reggie," rugby player (b 8 Feb 1869, Constantinople, Turkey; d 6 July 1957, Vancouver). He arrived in VANCOUVER from England in 1887, helped to found the BC Rugby Union in 1889 and was active in BC RUGBY for 70 years as a player, coach and administrator. He excelled in local, national and international rugby until 1909, by which time he was known as "Mr Rugby." He coached the Vancouver Rugby Union on and off for many years and pioneered the first BC rugby tours to California. He was also active in the VANCOUVER ROWING CLUB, serving in a variety of capacities for 67 years. He was inducted into the BC SPORTS HALL OF FAME in 1967.   *SW*

WOODWARD, William Culham "Willy," retailer, lt gov 1941–46 (b 24 Apr 1885, Gore Bay, ON; d 24 Feb 1957, Hawaii). The son of Charles WOODWARD, founder of WOODWARD'S STORES, he joined the family business as a bookkeeper in 1907, at age 22, after a short stint with the Royal Bank. He and his brother Percival ("Puggy") rose through the ranks to take senior positions at the store. During WWI, Willy served overseas with the First Canadian Heavy Artillery. In 1921 he married Ruth Wynn-Johnson, whose family owned the famed ALKALI LAKE RANCH in the CHILCOTIN. With the death of his father in 1937 he became president of the company. He was also a director of the Bank of Canada and the Royal Bank. During WWII he served as a "dollar-a-year-man" in Ottawa as an advisor to C.D. Howe, then returned to BC to serve as LT GOV. At that time the Woodward's purchased Woodwynn, their farm in SAANICH. Willy remained president of Woodward's until his death, when the company was taken over by his son Charles "Chunky" WOODWARD.

WOODWARD'S STORES LTD was a retail chain founded in VANCOUVER in 1902, when Charles WOODWARD, a local merchant, reorganized the business he had started 10 years earlier. In Nov 1903 what became the flagship of a large regional chain of department stores opened on Hastings St and became a city landmark, known especially for the large neon W atop its roof. Members of the Woodward family remained in charge of the company for almost its entire history: Charles 1902–37, William 1937–57, and "Chunky" 1957–88. Woodward's opened a store in Edmonton in 1926 and PORT ALBERNI in 1948, and in the 1950s the chain began expanding aggressively. It developed the Park Royal Shopping Centre in W VANCOUVER in 1950 and Oakridge Shopping Centre in Vancouver in 1959 and opened stores in VICTORIA (1951), NEW WESTMINSTER (1954) and a variety of smaller communities in BC and Alberta. By the time the business foundered in the early 1990s, it comprised 26 department stores, 33 Woodwynn discount stores, a chain of travel agencies, 4 Abercrombie & Fitch outlets and 3 Commercial Interiors stores. The chain sought protection from creditors in 1992 and was purchased by the HBC in 1993. The building on the original site has been the subject of several redevelopment plans.

WORK, John, fur trader (b 1791, Derry, Ireland; d Dec 1861, Victoria). Born John Wark, he altered his name slightly when he joined the HBC in 1814. He arrived in BC in 1822 and was a

The Haida village of Ninstints, one of 5 BC World Heritage Sites. *Duane Sept photo*

member of the party that explored the lower FRASER R in 1824, locating a site for the future FORT LANGLEY. He was in charge of building Fort Colville on the COLUMBIA R, then took command of the famous Snake River expeditions toward California. He managed the HBC coasting trade from 1834 to 1852 and was in charge at FORT SIMPSON during 1835–46, after which he was one of 3 senior officials put in charge of the company's Columbia department following the resignation of John MCLOUGHLIN in 1846. When Work retired, he settled on a farm called Hillside just north of what is now downtown VICTORIA. He served on the Legislative Council of VANCOUVER ISLAND from 1853 until his death (*see also* COLONIAL GOVERNMENT).

WORKERS' COMPENSATION BOARD was established in 1917 as the Workmen's Compensation Board to provide compensation, medical care, rehabilitation and retraining to workers injured on the job. Prior to that time workers had to sue their employers to receive any payment for job-related injuries. Compensation is paid from a fund financed by employer contributions (there are more than 160,000 participating employers), which are calculated according to the frequency of workplace injuries in particular industries. In the case of fatal injuries, benefits are provided to dependent survivors. In 1998 the WCB handled 179,582 claims and paid out $1.1 billion in benefits. The Board is administered by a 4-person panel of administrators appointed by the provincial minister of labour. As the 20th century ended, the provincial government was considering the recommendations of a 1999 royal commission report reviewing the workers' compensation system.

WORLD HERITAGE SITES are areas of unique cultural and natural importance designated for protection by the United Nations Educational, Scientific and Cultural Organization (UNESCO).

Since the program was launched in 1972, the World Heritage Convention has protected 552 sites around the world. Countries signing the convention agree to protect their own sites and to contribute to the World Heritage Fund to preserve sites internationally. BC has 5 World Heritage Sites: TATSHENSHINI– Alsek Wilderness Provincial Park in the far northwest corner of the province, along with adjacent parks in the Yukon and Alaska (1994); the BURGESS SHALE in YOHO NATIONAL PARK (1980); the abandoned HAIDA village site of NINSTINTS on Anthony Island at the south end of the QUEEN CHARLOTTE ISLANDS (1981); AKAMINA–Kishenina Provincial Park in the extreme southeast corner of the province, as part of the CROWN OF THE CONTINENT site with adjacent parks in Alberta and Montana (1995); and Yoho and KOOTENAY NATIONAL PARKS, which, along with Banff and Jasper National Parks in Alberta, comprise a single ROCKY MTS heritage site called the Four Mountain Parks (1985).

WORLD SOUNDSCAPE PROJECT, a research group founded in the late 1960s with headquarters at SFU, has secured Canada a place in the forefront of the study of soundscape ecology. The project seeks to understand the relationship between human beings and our sonic environment, and ultimately to bring balance and harmony to this relationship. It was initiated by the musician R. Murray Schafer, with Howard Broomfield, Bruce Davis, Peter Huse, Barry TRUAX, Hildegard Westerkamp and Adam Woog. Truax and Westerkamp have maintained and expanded the project since the 1980s, managing the archives, producing a newsletter, distributing recordings and teaching courses on acoustic communication. Schafer and Westerkamp have taken lecture and workshop tours to many parts of the world, igniting wide interest in the project and forming international soundscape networks of people working in science, aesthetics, philosophy, ARCHITECTURE, sociology and other disciplines. An important aspect of the group's work is to raise awareness of the sonic environment, or soundscape, defined as the sum total of all sounds within any defined area: literally to teach people how to listen. Research topics include electroacoustic sounds such as Muzak, radio and the "personal stereo"; lost and disappearing sounds; soundscapes of particular events; the sonic environment of schools; and the effects of urban noise on the delicate balance between listening and soundmaking. Through these and other studies, sound ecologists hope to find ways to reduce sound pollution and design healthier sonic environments.

WOSK, Benjamin, retailer (b 19 Mar 1913, Vradiavka, Russia; d 24 Jan 1995, Honolulu, HI). He moved to VANCOUVER as a teenager with his family and in 1932 began a long career in retail merchandising by selling old stoves. He founded Wosk's Ltd, which specialized in selling furniture and appliances, but he also owned hotels and other real estate. His construction company erected more than 20 Vancouver business and apartment buildings. An active philanthropist and community worker, he was named BC's Good Citizen of the Year in 1975 and joined the Order of Canada in 1978. His brother Morris J. Wosk, also a supporter of non-profit organizations, is a member of the Order of Canada and the ORDER OF BC, and a freeman of the City of Vancouver. The Wosk family is particularly associated with SFU, to which it has donated millions of dollars.

WOSS LAKE lies in the mountainous north-central interior of VANCOUVER ISLAND just north of STRATHCONA PROVINCIAL PARK. Long (25 km) and narrow, it drains north into the NIMPKISH R. It was part of an aboriginal trading route across the island and was used for fishing by the 'Namgis (Nimpkish) group of the KWAK-WAKA'WAKW (Kwakiutl) First Nations, now centred at ALERT BAY. The first white person to visit the lake was John Buttle, a botanist, on the same expedition in 1865 that visited BUTTLE LK. The area surrounding the lake has been extensively logged by one of the largest RAILWAY LOGGING operations in BC. In 1999 residents of the LOGGING camp purchased the site from CANADIAN FOREST PRODUCTS LTD and created the unincorporated community of Woss. The name may be a corruption of an aboriginal word for "fear," a reference to a battle that took place at the lake. Woss Lake Provincial PARK (66.34 km²) lies at the south end.

WRECK BEACH has been VANCOUVER's clothing-optional swimming beach since early in the 1970s. It lies at the foot of the coastal bluffs on the edge of the UBC campus at the western tip of Point Grey, and affords visitors an expansive view of GEORGIA STRAIT. Its name refers to a shipwreck and several wrecked barges located nearby.

WREN is a stubby little grey-brown songbird, noisy and energetic as it goes about its search for INSECTS to eat. The wren is recognizable by its cocked tail held upright when it perches. Wrens build enclosed nests in tree cavities, cliffs, roots or marshes, depending on the species. Of 8

Canadian species, 6 occur in southern BC. Both the rock wren (*Salpinctes obsoletus*) and the canyon wren (*Catherpes mexicanus*) are quite rare. South-central BC is the northern limit of their range; the rock wren nests there in loose rock, the canyon wren in cliff faces and canyon walls. Bewick's wren (*Thryomanes bewickii*) occurs only in the southwest corner of the province, while the house wren (*Troglodytes aedon*) is widespread across the south except in the Lower Mainland. The tiny winter wren (*T. troglodytes*) occurs in forested areas in the province. The marsh wren (*Cistothorus palustris*) frequents cattail marshes, where it constructs sturdy spherical nests out of the vegetation. In fact, the male builds other "dummy" nests that are not occupied.

WRESTLING became a popular competitive sport in BC in the 1880s when organizations such as the St Andrew's and Caledonian Society held "Scotch Backhold," "Collar and Elbow," and "Graeco-Roman" events. By 1888, the Opera houses of VANCOUVER, NEW WESTMINSTER and VICTORIA staged popular professional wrestling bills and the sport was already gaining a reputation for putting on rigged matches for the sake of entertainment. This spectator-oriented brand of the sport peaked in popularity in Vancouver in the 1930s and 1940s. Weekly wrestling showcases promoted by Emil Klank and Percy Hicks attracted world champions such as Jim Londos and Strangler Lewis. Prominent local wrestlers included fireman Jack Forsgren and Victoria's Chief Thunderbird of the LEKWAMMEN First Nation.

Daniel Igali, SFU wrestler (l), 1999 Canadian male athlete of the year. Gerry Kahrmann/ Vancouver Province

Amateur wrestling began as an organized sport in BC in the 1950s and early 1960s, largely due to the work of Paul Nemeth at UBC, the founder and first president of the BC Amateur Wrestling Assoc, and Art Miller of the Vancouver YMCA. BC Wrestling began sending athletes to international competitions in the 1970s and Victoria's Taras Hryb was the first to succeed by capturing a bronze medal at the 1971 Pan Am Games and a gold at the 1974 Commonwealth Games. (Also a 1972 Olympian, Hryb later

became a police officer and won the 90-kg wrestling event at the 1987 World Police and Firefighters' Games.) With strong showings from national intercollegiate champion George Richey, Art Miller's son Jim and YMCA graduate Steve Martin, Canada made its best-ever showing, 10th overall, at the 1974 World Championships. SFU began competitive wrestling in 1972 and hired Mike Jones as coach in 1976. Jim Miller graduated from the YMCA program, participated in the 1976 Olympics, won a Pan Am bronze medal in 1975 and helped to start the Burnaby Mountain Wrestling Club in 1978. Jones and Miller worked co-operatively and in 1984 the club became a National Training Centre. In team competition, the club never lost to another Canadian team and won 15 straight senior national titles to the turn of the century.

Individually, Steve Martin won a silver medal at the 1974 Commonwealths, and PORT COQUITLAM's Chris RINKE won a Commonwealth gold in 1982. John TENTA, a Canadian junior champion from SURREY who trained at Burnaby Mountain, won the 1983 World Junior title, Canada's first international gold medal in wrestling. Tenta went on to become the first Caucasian to break into Japanese sumo and to wrestle professionally in the World Wrestling Federation. SFU also produced BC's first Olympic medallists, in 1984 in Los Angeles, when Bob Molle earned a silver in the 130-kg class and Rinke took the bronze at the 82-kg level. A third BC wrestler, Clark Davis of Victoria and UBC, had won 2 world-championship silvers in the 100-kg class and was favoured for gold at Los Angeles but injured himself in his first match and placed 4th. SFU's Dave McKay and Rinke each captured gold medals at the 1986 Edinburgh Commonwealth Games. McKay, a Winnipeg native, later earned a 5th-place finish in his 68-kg category at the 1988 Olympics. The 1992 Barcelona Olympics yielded BC's next medal, a silver to Jeff Thue in the 130-kg class. Both Molle and Thue were Regina natives attending SFU. Jones and Miller both coached Canada's national team in the 1980s and 1990s and McKay, who had become the coach at Douglas COLLEGE, replaced Miller in 1997.

At the World Championship level, 62-kg SFU wrestler Gary Bohay of Burnaby picked up a silver and Port Coquitlam's Steve Marshall finished 4th in the 100 kg in 1989. Thue won a bronze in 1991 and N VANCOUVER's Janna Penny captured BC's first international women's wrestling medal, a bronze in 1993. One of Canada's greatest wrestlers was North Vancouver's Chris Wilson, a 68-kg SFU competitor who won a 1991 silver and a 1993 bronze at the World Championships, two World Cups (1993 and 1994) and a gold medal at the 1994 Commonwealth Games in Victoria. A remarkable 4 other SFU wrestlers won golds at those games: Scott Bianco from KAMLOOPS (90 kg), Selwyn Tam from Vancouver (52 kg), Greg Edgelow from VERNON (100 kg) and Saskatchewan's Justin Abdou (85 kg). In 1999 another SFU wrestler, Daniel Igali, became the first Canadian man to win a gold medal at the world freestyle championships; Igali was named that year's Canadian male athlete of the year. At the turn of the century, BC Amateur Wrestling had approximately 2,500 members, most of them high school students. *SW*

WRIGHT, Gustavus Blinn, merchant, road builder (b 22 June 1830, Burlington, VT; d 8 Apr 1898, Ainsworth). He arrived in BC from California in 1858 during the gold rush (*see* GOLD RUSH, FRASER R), but instead of prospecting he got involved in the transport business and was soon the most important packer on the DOUGLAS TRAIL. In the 1860s he won contracts to build several sections of the CARIBOO WAGON ROAD and he ran steamboats on both the upper and lower FRASER R (*see* PADDLEWHEEL STEAMBOATS). By the 1880s his ventures included railway surveying, operating general stores and MINING speculation, mostly in the KOOTENAY. Called "the prince of hustlers," he never walked away from an interesting proposition.

WRIGHT, John, architect (b 15 May 1830, Killearn, Scotland; d 23 Aug 1915, Victoria). He immigrated to Ontario in 1845 and began his career as a contractor in Guelph. In 1859 he moved west to VICTORIA, where in less than a decade he designed and built many of the most well-known homes and public buildings still surviving from the early days of the colony. His designs include FISGARD LIGHTHOUSE (1860), the first lighthouse on the coast, which he built with fellow architect H.O. TIEDEMANN; the Wesleyan Methodist Church (1859); Cloverdale, the home of William Fraser TOLMIE; the Richard Carr house, family home of Emily CARR, and POINT ELLICE HOUSE, home of the government official Peter O'REILLY, both restored as heritage sites; and CONGREGATION EMANUEL TEMPLE (1863), the oldest surviving synagogue in Canada. He also designed Victoria's Civic Seal, which in 1999 was still in use. In 1867 he and his partner and brother-in-law, George Sanders, moved to San Francisco, where the architectural firm of Wright and Sanders grew into one of the largest in California.

WRIGHT, John "Jack," tennis player (b 11 Nov 1901, Nelson; d Sept 1949). In 1950 the Canadian Press news agency named him Canada's outstanding TENNIS player of the half century. He won the Canadian singles championship in 1927, 1929 and 1931 and was ranked #1 in Canada for 7 consecutive years. With partner Willard Crocker he also captured the 1923, 1925 and 1929 national doubles titles. Wright played on every Canadian Davis Cup team 1923–33. He was named to the BC SPORTS HALL OF FAME in 1966 and to the Canadian Sports Hall of Fame in 1972. *SW*

WRIGHT, Laurali Ruth "Bunny," writer (b 5 June 1939, Saskatoon, SK). After an itinerant childhood she began a career in journalism, first in MISSION, then at the *Calgary Herald* newspaper from 1968 to 1977. A writing course with

L.R. Wright, writer.

W.O. Mitchell encouraged her to try her hand at fiction. Her first novel, *Neighbours* (1979), won the Alberta First Novel Award but her career really took off in 1985 with the publication of *The Suspect*, a low-key mystery novel set on the SUNSHINE COAST. It was the first Canadian novel to win the Edgar Award for best mystery of the year, given by the Mystery Writers of America,

The town of Wycliffe, site of Staples Mill, 1900–1927. Ft Steele Heritage Town Archives F.S.5.153

and led to a continuing series of novels featuring the fictitious SECHELT RCMP officer Karl Alberg. Two books in the series, *A Chill Rain in January* and *Mother Love*, won the 1990 and 1995 Arthur Ellis Award for best Canadian crime novel. Another book in the series, *Acts of Murder*, was nominated for the 1997 Dashiell Hammett Prize for the year's best crime novel in N America.

WRITING; *see* LITERATURE.

WYATT, Mark, rugby player (b 12 Apr 1961, St George's, Bermuda). Raised in VICTORIA, he started playing RUGBY in high school and eventually developed into one of the top goal kickers in the world. After leading OAK BAY to a 1980 BC high school championship, he enrolled at the UNIV OF VICTORIA and began playing first division rugby for Victoria Velox and internationally for Canada. In 1988 he became the first Canadian to play professionally in Europe when he joined a club in southern France. For the Canadian national team, Wyatt earned 29 international caps, including appearances at the 1987 and 1991 World Cups. He captained the team at the 1991 Cup and the year before in a game against Scotland, he recorded a longstanding international record by kicking 8 penalty goals. Wyatt competed with the world's best when he was selected for All-World teams in 1988 and 1989 and for the Barbarians in 1991. After retiring from rugby, he concentrated on his teaching and coaching career at SHAWNIGAN LAKE SCHOOL. *SW*

WYCLIFFE is an AGRICULTURAL settlement on the CPR and the ST MARY R, 12 km northwest of CRANBROOK. It was the site of a large SAWMILL, operated from the early 1900s to 1927 by the Otis Staples Lumber Co, which had an extensive RAILWAY LOGGING show in the region. Originally known as Bayard, the community was renamed after John Wycliffe, a 14th-century English church reformer. *AS*

WYMAN, Anna, dancer, choreographer (b 1928, Graz, Austria). After working as a dancer in Austria she moved to England in 1952 and opened her own DANCE school. She and her then-husband Max WYMAN immigrated to VANCOUVER in 1967 where the next year she established the Anna Wyman School of Dance Arts, followed by her own dance company, the Anna Wyman Dancers (1971), later the Anna Wyman Dance Theatre (1973–89). The troupe, which mainly performed works choreographed by Wyman, became one of the leading modern dance companies in Canada. In 1975 it was the first modern dance troupe to tour the country and it also travelled extensively abroad: in 1980

Anna Wyman, dancer and choreographer.
Vancouver Province

it made the first tour of China by a Western modern dance company. After the Dance Theatre folded, Wyman continued to operate a school and a student dance company based in W VANCOUVER.

WYMAN, Max, critic, writer (b 14 May 1939, Wellingborough, England). He arrived in VANCOUVER in 1967 from London and got a job as a journalist with the *VANCOUVER SUN* newspaper. Along with writing arts criticism for the *Sun* he became a leading authority on Canadian ballet, about which he has written 3 books: *The Royal Winnipeg Ballet: The First Forty Years; Dance Canada: An Illustrated History;* and *Evelyn Hart: An Intimate Portrait.* Other publications include *Toni Cavelti: A Jeweller's Life* and *Vancouver Forum I*, a collection of essays on BC culture that he edited. He was appointed to the Canada Council in 1995 and to the executive committee of the Canadian Commission for UNESCO in 1998.

WYNNDEL, a railway junction and farming (*see* AGRICULTURE) and LOGGING settlement near the south end of KOOTENAY LK, was first settled around 1900. It was the site of the early Duck Creek Hotel. Much arable land was created in 1940 as a result of the CRESTON flats reclamation. A grain elevator, several food-processing

Max Wyman, 1998.
Barry Peterson & Blaise Enright-Peterson

plants and a specialty SAWMILL, which has been in the Monrad family since 1913, are located here. Wynndel was named for a local fruit grower. *AS*

became his colleagues after the merger. He transferred to FORT ST JAMES and accompanied HBC Governor George SIMPSON on his wild CANOE trip down the FRASER R to the coast in 1828. Yale was posted to FORT LANGLEY and spent the rest of his career there, taking charge of the post in 1834 and becoming a chief trader in 1844. A short, peppery man known as "Little Yale," he turned the fort into an important supplier of cured SALMON and agricultural foodstuffs as well as furs, and was in charge at the post when the first gold miners surged up the river in 1858 (*see* GOLD RUSH, FRASER R; *see also* FUR TRADE, LAND-BASED). In 1860 Yale retired to a farm near VICTORIA, where he lived until his death. The town of YALE, which began as an HBC fort, is named for him.

James Murray Yale, fur trader.
Langley Centennial Museum

X-FILES was the most popular television show ever produced in Canada. A spooky sci-fi thriller, it began filming in the VANCOUVER area on 22 Mar 1993 and aired for the first time that fall, going on to become a cult favourite, especially with young adult viewers. The show was based at Lions Gate Studios in N VANCOUVER and starred David Duchovny as FBI agent Fox Mulder and Gillian Anderson as agent Dana Scully. In 1998, after 5 years in Vancouver, the American producers moved the show to Los Angeles.

YAHK, pop 423, on the Moyie R in the E KOOTENAY, 64 km south of CRANBROOK, was a thriving SAWMILL centre in the early 1900s. By the 1930s the loggers had left and the community, much depleted in size, settled into its role as a local service centre. The name derives from a KTUNAXA word.

YAKOUN RIVER, the largest river on the QUEEN CHARLOTTE ISLANDS, flows north out of Yakoun Lk through the heart of Graham Island to Masset Inlet, where it empties through a large ESTUARY south of PORT CLEMENTS. A popular river with STEELHEAD fishers (*see* FISHING, SPORT), it is also an important SALMON spawning stream. A hatchery (*see* FISH HATCHERIES) at Marie Lk raises salmon for the river. The watershed has been logged extensively, beginning with the massive operation during WWI to harvest Sitka SPRUCE for airplane construction. One unusual tree was the famed Golden Spruce that grew for 300 years on the banks of the river until it was cut down by a vandal in 1997. When exposed to direct sunlight, the chlorophyll in the needles of the tree turned from green to gold.

YALE, pop 169, is on the FRASER R 32 km north of HOPE. Rapids in the river to the north mark the approximate northern extension of Coast SALISHAN territory. Coast Salish people visited this part of the FRASER R Canyon to fish and archaeo-logical evidence of human settlement dates back about 10,000 years. The community began in 1848 as an HBC trading post named for James Murray YALE, chief trader at FORT LANGLEY. During the 1858 GOLD RUSH, Yale was as far as the steamboats could advance up the river and it was the start of the CARIBOO WAGON ROAD to the Interior. It flourished again in the 1880s during CPR construction but then became a virtual ghost town. Today it is a FOREST INDUSTRY and service centre. Yale's St John the Divine Church, built in 1859, is the oldest church in BC on its original foundations. *See also* FISHING, ABORIGINAL; PADDLEWHEEL STEAMBOATS.

YALE, James Murray, fur trader (b circa 1799; d 7 May 1871, Victoria). He joined the HBC in 1815 and was among the first group of HBC workers to settle in NEW CALEDONIA after the merger with the NORTH WEST CO. He was in charge of Fort George 1821–24, during which time a dispute over his aboriginal mistress resulted in the murder of 2 of his men. This incident may have slowed his rise in the company; so did his lack of formal education and his history of enmity toward several NWC partners who

YALE CONVENTION, 14 Sept 1868, was a meeting of 26 delegates from around BC who favoured CONFEDERATION with Canada. Anti-confederationists called it the Yale Conspiracy. The objective of the meeting was to show that union enjoyed widespread support. Delegates passed resolutions in favour of immediate confederation, responsible government, a reduction in the cost of the civil service and reciprocity with the US.

Yale, the head of navigation for steamboats on the Fraser River during the gold rush.
BC Archives F-08515

YARROW is located south of the FRASER R on the eastern edge of SUMAS PRAIRIE, at the base of Vedder Mt. Originally known as Majuba Hill after a battle in the Boer War, the area was settled in the 1890s. In 1910 it became a station on the BC ELECTRIC RWY line from VANCOUVER to CHILLI-WACK. The station was called Yarrow after a local bitter WILDFLOWER, a reference to a feud between the railway and a local landowner. MENNONITE settlers began arriving from the prairies and from Mexico in 1928. While getting established on the land they picked hops and tobacco and worked as loggers. By the 1940s the area was known for its raspberry and strawberry growing (*see* BERRIES). When the berry industry collapsed in 1948–49, Yarrow lost its economic mainstay and became mainly a residential community, part of the Chilliwack district municipality.

YARROWS LTD, *see* BURRARD DRY DOCK.

YATES, J. Michael, writer (b 10 Apr 1938, Fulton, MO). He moved to VANCOUVER in 1967 to teach creative writing at UBC, where he founded SONO NIS PRESS and encouraged the development of a writing style that came to be called West Coast Surrealism. He left teaching in 1971. His own innovative, challenging poetry began appearing in 1967. Collections include *Canticle for Electronic Music* (1967), *The Great Bear Lake Meditations* (1970), *Breath of the Snow Leopard* (1974) and *Schedule of Silence: The Collected Longer Poems, 1960–86* (1986). After he was injured in a car accident in 1978, Yates abandoned writing temporarily; for 12 years he worked as a PRISON guard, an experience he then wrote about in a memoir, *Line Screw* (1993). *See also* LITERATURE.

YELLOWHEAD PASS (el 1,131 m), on the BC–Alberta border 25 km west of Jasper, is a principal transportation corridor across the ROCKY MTS. It is named for a blond METIS trapper who guided HBC traders through the pass in 1820 (*see* FUR TRADE, LAND-BASED), though it was originally called the Leather Pass because the company used it to transport hides to its posts in NEW CALE-DONIA. The nearby town of TETE JAUNE CACHE also reflects the "yellow head" of this blond trapper. A party of OVERLANDERS used it to reach the FRASER R and the Cariboo gold fields in 1862 (*see* GOLD RUSH, CARIBOO). Sir Sandford Fleming recommended it for the main line of the CPR, but when the railway chose a more southerly route the pass fell into obscurity, until 1909–12 when both the GRAND TRUNK PACIFIC and CANADIAN NORTHERN railways chose to cross the mountains via the Yellowhead. In 1922 these 2 lines were reorganized as the single, publicly owned CNR. The first automobile through the pass was driven by Charles Neimeyer and Frank Silverthorne in 1922, using abandoned railway grade most of the way, but the Yellowhead Highway (Hwy 16) was not completed until after WWII. Since 1953 a PIPELINE has carried oil from Alberta through the pass to the Lower Mainland (*see also* OIL AND GAS INDUSTRY). The pass was declared a National Historic Site in 1985.

YENNADON, a farming and LOGGING settlement 38 km east of VANCOUVER in the FRASER VAL-LEY, was first settled by Samuel Edge in 1875. Many JAPANESE families moved here in the 1930s and grew strawberries (*see* BERRIES). An EQUESTRI-AN centre is located here and a university research FOREST is nearby. It was named in 1911 for a place in Devon, England.   AS

YEW is a tree occurring frequently as an ornamental; BC's only native species, the western yew (*Taxus brevifolia*), is also the only yew in BC that reaches tree size. It grows scattered under the canopy of other species along the coast and in the south-

Pacific yew.
© *T.C. Brayshaw*

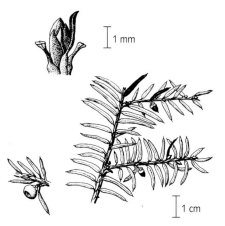

Clockwise from top: Bud, branch and fruit of the western yew. © *T.C. Brayshaw*

eastern Interior. The wood is strong and resilient, favoured by aboriginal people for paddles and bows, though it has had no widespread commercial significance. The leaves are poisonous to livestock. Taxol, a compound found in the bark, has been approved as a cancer treatment.

YIP SANG, VANCOUVER Chinatown pioneer, entrepreneur (b 6 Sept 1845, Canton, China; d 21 July 1927, Vancouver). He left China in 1864 and went to California, where he worked at a variety of jobs. In 1881 he came north to work as a paymaster for CHINESE labourers on the CPR. When the railway was finished he settled in Vancouver and established Wing Sang Co, an import-export business. The Wing Sang Building (1889) is the oldest surviving structure in CHINATOWN in Vancouver and the first brick building constructed there. It was the headquarters for a small empire of businesses. Yip had 4 wives and 23 children and his descendants remain prominent in Vancouver's Asian community. One son, Dock Yip, studied law in Toronto and in 1945 became the first Asian Canadian called to the bar.

YMIR (pronounced *why-mer*) is a former GOLD mining camp on the Salmo R, 28 km south of NELSON. The nearby Ymir Mts were earlier named after the Norse father of the giants. Originally Quartz Creek, Ymir was laid out as a townsite in 1897 by the NELSON & FORT SHEPPARD RWY. After booming briefly as a MINING centre—during the 1890s the Ymir Mine was the largest gold producer in Canada—it was partially destroyed by fire in 1904 and never recovered its former glory.

YOHO NATIONAL PARK, 1,313 km², is in the Main Ranges of the ROCKY MTS west of the Continental Divide. Along with Banff, Jasper and KOOTENAY national PARKS, it encompasses some of the most spectacular mountain scenery in the world; in 1985 these parks were designated a UNESCO WORLD HERITAGE SITE called the Four Mountain Parks. At least half of Yoho Park is above treeline. The name comes from a Cree exclamation of wonder at such natural beauty. The first white explorer in the area was James Hector, surgeon with the PALLISER Expedition,

Mountains in Yoho National Park.
Bernie Pawlik/Image Makers

who visited in 1858 looking for a route through the mountains. Hector almost died when he was kicked in the chest by a horse, and the river he was following was subsequently named the Kicking Horse R. It is the main corridor through the park, followed by the CPR and the TRANS-CANADA HWY. East of FIELD, the CPR climbed a steep grade to reach the summit at KICKING HORSE PASS. Known as the Big Hill, it was the steepest railway grade in N America when the line opened in 1885. It was later replaced by the Spiral Tunnels. The park was created in 1886 as a 26 km² reserve around Mt Stephen in anticipation of TOURIST expansion following completion of the railway. The CPR built a chalet, Mt Stephen House, in Field and promoted the area as "the Canadian Alps." In 1901 the park grew to 2,145.6 km²; it has been reduced over the years to its present size. The glacier-carved valleys and towering peaks make Yoho a favourite destination for hikers. Attractions include EMERALD and O'HARA lakes; the Natural Bridge; the BURGESS SHALE, another World Heritage Site; the trilobite FOSSIL beds on Mt Stephen; TAKAKKAW FALLS, at 254 m the second-highest WATERFALL in Canada; and several icefields (*see* GLACIATION) and remote mountain passes.

YORK, Annie, Nlaka'pamux elder (b 21 Sept 1904, Spuzzum; d 19 Aug 1991, Spuzzum). Her grandfather was the French packer Cataline CAUX. As a young woman York worked as a domestic, trained as a practical nurse and lived at various places in the FRASER VALLEY and the Interior, but in 1932 she returned to SPUZZUM and lived there for the rest of her life. She was an important informant about the customs, language (*see* FIRST NATIONS LANGUAGES) and history of the Nlaka'pamux (Thompson) and contributed to several studies of her people, notably *They Write Their Dreams on the Rock Forever: Rock Writings in the Stein Valley of British Columbia* (1993, with Richard Daly and Chris Arnett) and *Spuzzum: Fraser Canyon Histories 1908–1939* (1998, with Andrea Laforet). *See also* FIRST NATIONS; ROCK ART.

YORK HOUSE SCHOOL in the Shaughnessy district of VANCOUVER is a private school for girls. It was founded in 1932 and named for the English hometown of the first headmistress, Lena (Cotsworth) Clarke. The school, with 600 students from kindergarten to grade 12, has been administered since 1958 by a non-profit society. *See also* EDUCATION, PRIVATE.

YOUBOU is a SAWMILL community on the north shore of COWICHAN LK, 45 km west of DUNCAN on VANCOUVER ISLAND. It was the site of the first sawmill on the lake in 1913. When the CNR reached the community in 1925 it was called Cottonwood; the next year it took the name Youbou after 2 pioneer loggers, Yount and Bouten. The FOREST INDUSTRY has remained the economic mainstay.

YOUNG, Henry Esson, doctor, politician (b 24 Feb 1867, English River, QC; d 20 Oct 1939,

Victoria). As a young man he worked on the construction of the CPR before studying medicine at McGill Univ in Montreal, in England and in the US. He came west to prospect for GOLD at ATLIN, then remained to practise medicine. He was elected to the legislature as a CONSERVATIVE in 1903. He joined Premier Richard MCBRIDE's CABINET in 1907 as provincial secretary and minister of education, and carried out several educational reforms during his tenure. He established UBC and was instrumental in building a new tuberculosis sanatorium at TRANQUILLE and a new mental health facility outside NEW WESTMINSTER, originally called Essondale (*see* RIVERVIEW). He resigned his seat before the 1916 election, following a scandal involving payments from a MINING company. For the rest of his life Young served as provincial medical health officer and is sometimes called BC's "father of public health." *See also* HEALTH POLICY; MEDICAL PROFESSION.

YOUNG, James "Jim" ("Dirty Thirty"), football player (b 6 June, 1943, Hamilton, ON). An all-star on both offence and defence at Queen's Univ, he was a running back for 2 years with the Minnesota Vikings in the NFL before the BC LIONS acquired him from Toronto in 1967. He played in a variety of positions over his FOOTBALL career but primarily was a wide receiver from 1971 until his retirement 8 years later. In 1972 he led the CFL in receiving yards (1,362) and he was named to the all-Canadian team. Nicknamed "Dirty Thirty" because of his aggressive play, he retired as the team leader in pass receptions, receiving touchdowns and total yardage. He was twice chosen the league's outstanding Canadian. In 1989 he joined the Lions coaching staff and later took on additional responsibilities in community relations and business operations. A member of the Canadian Football Hall of Fame and the BC SPORTS HALL OF FAME (1994), he continues to pursue business interests in the Lower Mainland. *SW*

YOUNG, Patricia, poet (b 7 Aug 1954, Victoria). She is the author of 8 books of poetry,

Patricia Young, poet, 1998.
Barry Peterson & Blaise Enright-Peterson

most recently *Ruin and Beauty: New and Selected Poems* (2000). Her collection *All I Ever Needed Was a Beautiful Room* won a BC BOOK PRIZE for poetry in 1988, and her next book, *The Mad and Beautiful Mothers*, won the 1990 Pat LOWTHER Award from the League of Canadian Poets. Her 1993 collection *More Watery Still* was nominated for a GOV GEN'S LITERARY AWARD, and she won her second BC Book Prize in 1998 for *What I Remember From My Time On Earth*. She has taught at the UNIV OF VICTORIA and was the first Ralph Gustafson poet-in-residence at Malaspina University College.

YOUNG, William Alexander George, naval officer, administrator (b circa 1827; d 25 Apr 1885, Accra, Gold Coast). After a distinguished early career in the Royal Navy he came to VANCOUVER ISLAND in 1857 as secretary of the British boundary commission (*see* BOUNDARIES), surveying the 49th parallel. He established a friendship with Gov James DOUGLAS that stood him in good stead for the rest of his stay in the colony. At the end of 1858 Douglas named him colonial secretary for BC and the next year he became acting colonial secretary for Vancouver Island as well, making him the senior civil servant in both colonies. When forced to choose between the 2 positions in 1863 he decided to remain on the Island, where he won election to the LEGISLATIVE ASSEMBLY. When Vancouver Island merged with the mainland in 1866 Young was out of a job, but in 1867 he became acting colonial secretary for the united colony. He was mistrusted for his close ties to political circles in VICTORIA and was replaced in 1868. He left BC the following year and later served as an administrator in Jamaica and governor of the Gold Coast (Ghana), where he died. *See also* COLONIAL GOVERNMENT.

YUCULTAS are a set of rapids between SONORA and STUART islands near the mouth of BUTE INLET in the jumble of islands between VANCOUVER ISLAND and the mainland, about 35 km north of CAMPBELL RIVER. With tidal currents running up to 10 knots, they are a well-known navigational hazard for mariners. The name, often pronounced "Uke-la-taws," refers to a group of KWAKWAKA'WAKW (Kwakiutl) who occupied the area. The Yucultas are part of a series of tidal rapids in Cordero Channel known collectively as the Dents, including the Arran Rapids, Gillard Passage and the Dent Rapids.

YUKON FIELD FORCE was a force of 203 soldiers sent to the Klondike goldfields in 1898 by way of BC to assert Canadian sovereignty and support the North West Mounted Police already stationed there (*see* GOLD RUSHES). Commanded by Lt Col T.D.B. Evans, the force consisted of militia volunteers, mainly from the Royal Canadian Regiment. In May they travelled by boat from VANCOUVER to Wrangell, AK, then steamed up the STIKINE R to TELEGRAPH CREEK, where they set off overland on foot along the rugged Teslin TRAIL. The trail led through northern BC 250 km to the south end of TESLIN LK, where the force established Camp Victoria. They were accompanied on this arduous trek by 4 members of the newly organized Victoria Order of Nurses and by Faith Fenton, a writer for the Toronto *Globe* newspaper. At Camp Victoria the soldiers constructed boats; early in June they continued by water down the lake toward their destination, Fort Selkirk on the Yukon R, where the last of them arrived in mid-Sept. The force remained in the Yukon until mid-1900.

YUQUOT, meaning "windy place," also known as Friendly Cove, is a traditional summer village of the Mowachaht, a FIRST NATION of the NUU-CHAH-NULTH (Nootka) people. It is located at the south end of Nootka Island at the mouth of NOOTKA SOUND on the west coast of VANCOUVER ISLAND. Archaeologists have discovered signs of habitation going back at least 4,200 years and it is one of the longest continuously occupied sites on the coast (*see* ARCHAEOLOGY). Capt James COOK's 2 ships arrived in Resolution Cove at nearby Bligh Island in Mar 1778 and established contact with the local people, whom the visitors described as "friendly." The result was the beginning of a brisk trade in SEA OTTER pelts. In 1788 the British trader John MEARES established a trading and SHIPBUILDING post in the cove. The following year Spanish authorities built a fort, sparking an international crisis (*see* NOOTKA SOUND CONTROVERSY). The Spanish withdrew in 1795 and with the waning of the FUR TRADE the site returned to the Mowachaht. Nearby Jewett's Lk was the site of the famous Whalers' Shrine, where aboriginal whalers purified themselves before the hunt (*see* WHALING). The shrine was subsequently sold and removed to the American Museum of Natural History in New York. From 1917 to the 1950s many Mowachaht found work at a cannery in nearby Boca del Inferno Bay. In 1911 the government built a LIGHTHOUSE on the point adjacent to the village. Until the 1960s there was a ROMAN CATHOLIC church and day school. In 1968 all but one family moved to a RESERVE at the mouth of the GOLD R to be closer to jobs, schools and health care. The Mowachaht–Muchalaht people still use the site regularly for festivals and special events. They welcome visitors in the summer with guided tours of the site and at the end of the 20th century there were plans to build a cultural centre.

YUXWELUPTUN, Lawrence Paul, artist (b 1957, Kamloops). Of Coast Salish (*see* SALISHAN FIRST NATIONS) and OKANAGAN descent, he grew up in KAMLOOPS and RICHMOND. Both his parents were active in aboriginal politics and this family background is reflected in the subject matter of his art. He studied at the EMILY CARR INSTITUTE OF ART & DESIGN from 1978 to 1983. His paintings combine surrealism and other modernist influences with aboriginal imagery and mythology to subvert the romantic tradition of landscape art. They are also outspoken in their portrayal of racism and environmental destruction. *See also* ART, NORTHWEST COAST ABORIGINAL; ART, VISUAL; ENVIRONMENTAL MOVEMENT.

ZEBALLOS, village, pop 232, occupies the delta at the head of Zeballos Inlet, an arm of NOOTKA SOUND on the west coast of VANCOUVER ISLAND. It appeared suddenly in 1935–36 as a result of a GOLD RUSH and the opening of several mines. The site was officially subdivided into lots at the end of 1937. During a hectic decade of MINING, $13 million worth of gold was produced, half of it by the famous Privateer Mine. The last gold mine closed in 1948 and the site was all but abandoned except for a few loggers. From 1962 to 1969 an iron mine operated. In 1969 the Tahsis Co moved its camp here and LOGGING became the main activity. Zeballos is named for Ciriaco Cevallos, one of the Spanish naval officers who explored the inlet in 1791.

ZIMMERMAN, Jeff, baseball pitcher (b 9 Aug 1972, Kelowna). At age 5 he moved with his family to Alberta, where his father Bill raised him and his brother Jordan in baseball. Bill then

Jeff Zimmerman, baseball player, during his 1999 all-star season.

took his sons to Texas to further their baseball prospects, but Jeff graduated from Texas Christian Univ in 1994 without attracting any big-league interest. After pitching in France and for Team Canada, he returned to BC to earn a Master's degree in business administration at SFU. Back in baseball, he joined the Winnipeg Goldeyes and led the independent Northern League in earned-run-average (ERA), garnering him 1997 Rookie-of-the-Year honours. Signing with the Texas Rangers, the only team that offered him a tryout, he finally made the big club in 1999 and took the major leagues by storm, becoming the first Texas pitcher to begin his major league career with 8 straight wins and earning a place on the all-star team. He finished the year 9-3 with a 2.36 ERA. Zimmerman continued to keep an off-season home in VANCOUVER, where he volunteered as pitching coach with the UBC team. In 1999 his brother Jordan was a pitcher in the Seattle Mariners organization.

ZINC, a bluish-white metal used to galvanize steel and in a variety of industrial products, was produced for the first time in Canada in 1916 at the COMINCO facilities at TRAIL using ore from the SULLIVAN MINE. It was one of the first 2 electrolytic zinc refineries in the world. In 1920 Cominco engineers developed an improved method for separating zinc concentrates, allowing the company to become the largest single producer of zinc in the world. As well as the Sullivan Mine, Cominco obtained ore from other sources, including the Bluebell Mine at RIONDEL (1948–71) and the HB Mine near SALMO (1953–78). Zinc ore is also mined at Myra Falls on VANCOUVER ISLAND by BOLIDEN (WESTMIN) CANADA LTD, but this ore is processed offshore. Canada is the world's largest producer of zinc, and BC produces 12.5% of the Canadian total. In 1998 the province produced $231 million worth, making zinc the third most valuable metallic mineral in the province after COPPER and GOLD.

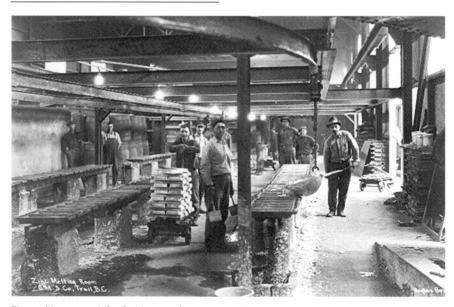

Zinc melting room at the Cominco smelter, Trail, 1930s. Trail City Archives

ZINCTON, between KOOTENAY and SLOCAN lakes on the KASLO & SLOCAN RWY, owed its existence to the Lucky Jim Mine and boasted a population of 200 at its peak in the 1920s. The Zincton post office operated from 1915 to 1932 at the Bear Lake Hotel, an all-purpose establishment run by Scotty Mitchell. Another early MINING townsite in this area, Watson, was destroyed by fire in 1894 and never rebuilt.   *AS*

ZOKOL, Richard "Dick," golfer (b 28 Aug 1958, Kitimat). While attending Brigham Young Univ in Utah he was captain of the GOLF team. In 1981, after graduating from BYU and winning the Canadian amateur golf championship, he turned professional and joined the PGA tour; he won the 1992 Greater Milwaukee Open and the Deposit Guaranty Classic in the same year. In 1992–93 he was voted the Canadian playing professional of the year and was a member of the Canadian Dunhill Cup team. Subsequently he became director of golf at a club in RICHMOND.

Patrick Francis

ZUKERMAN, George, musician (b 22 Feb 1927, England). He is Canada's leading bassoonist, credited with elevating the bassoon from the back rows of the orchestra to centre stage as a solo instrument. He came to BC in

George Zukerman, BC bassoonist, meeting an African trumpeter.

1953 from Israel, where he had played with the Israel Philharmonic Orchestra. After a dozen years with the VANCOUVER SYMPHONY ORCHESTRA and the CBC VANCOUVER CHAMBER ORCHESTRA, he launched a solo career in 1965. Since then he has toured the world playing with leading orchestras, conducting classes, hunting out "lost" repertoire for his instrument and recording all of the major bassoon concertos. He has divided his touring time between major musical centres and countless smaller communities in many of Canada's, and the world's, remotest regions. He is a member of the Order of Canada (1993) and the ORDER OF BC (1996).

Further Reading

Akrigg, G.P.V. and Helen B. *British Columbia Chronicle, 1778–1846 and 1847–1871*, 2 vols. Vancouver: Discovery Press, 1977.

_____. *1001 British Columbia Place Names*. Vancouver: Discovery Press, 1969.

Bancroft, Hubert Howe. *History of British Columbia, 1792–1887*. San Francisco: History Co, 1887.

Barman, Jean. *The West Beyond the West: A History of British Columbia*. Toronto: Univ of Toronto Press, 1991.

Begg, Alexander. *History of British Columbia*. Toronto: William Briggs, 1894.

Bish, Robert L. *Local Government in British Columbia*. Victoria: Union of BC Municipalities, 1987.

Blake, Donald E. *Two Political Worlds: Parties and Voting in British Columbia*. Vancouver: UBC Press, 1985.

Blanchet, M. Wylie. *The Curve of Time*. Sidney: Gray's Publishing, 1968.

Bowen, Lynn. *Boss Whistle: The Coal Miners of Vancouver Island Remember*. Lantzville: Oolichan Books, 1982.

_____. *Three Dollar Dreams*. Lantzville: Oolichan Books, 1987.

Bowering, George. *Bowering's BC: A Swashbuckling History*. Toronto: Penguin, 1996.

Bowes, Gordon E., ed. *Peace River Chronicles*. Vancouver: Prescott Publishing, 1963.

Bringhurst, Robert. *Story as Sharp as a Knife: The Classical Haida Mythtellers and Their World*. Vancouver: Douglas & McIntyre, 1999.

Brody, Hugh. *Maps and Dreams: Indians and the British Columbia Frontier*. Vancouver: Douglas & McIntyre, 1981.

Cail, Robert. *Land, Man and the Law: The Disposal of Crown Lands in British Columbia*. Vancouver: UBC Press, 1974.

Campbell, R. Wayne, et al. *The Birds of British Columbia*, 3 vols. Victoria: Royal BC Museum, 2000.

Cannings, Richard and Sydney Cannings. *British Columbia: A Natural History*. Vancouver: Douglas & McIntyre, 1996.

Carlson, R.L. and L. Dalla Bona, eds. *Early Human Occupation in British Columbia*. Vancouver: UBC Press, 1995.

Carty, R.K., ed. *Politics, Policy and Government in British Columbia*. Vancouver: UBC Press, 1996.

Cole, Douglas. *Captured Heritage: The Scramble for Northwest Coast Artifacts*. Vancouver: Douglas & McIntyre, 1985.

_____ and Ira Chaikin. *An Iron Hand Upon the People: the Law Against the Potlatch on the Northwest Coast*. Vancouver: Douglas & McIntyre, 1990.

Cook, Warren L. *Flood Tide of Empire: Spain and the Pacific Northwest, 1543–1819*. New Haven: Yale University Press, 1973.

Coull, Cheryl. *A Traveller's Guide to Aboriginal BC*. Vancouver: Whitecap Books, 1996.

Davis, Chuck, ed. *The Greater Vancouver Book*. Vancouver: Linkman Press, 1997.

Diamond, Sara. *Women's Labour History in British Columbia: A Bibliography, 1930–1948*. Vancouver: Press Gang Publishers, 1980.

Drucker, Philip. *Cultures of the North Pacific Coast*. San Francisco: Chandler Publishing, 1965.

Drushka, Ken. *HR: A Biography of H.R. MacMillan*. Madeira Park: Harbour Publishing, 1996.

_____. *Tie Hackers to Timber Harvesters: The History of Logging in BC's Interior*. Madeira Park: Harbour Publishing, 1998.

_____. *Working in the Woods: A History of Logging on the West Coast*. Madeira Park: Harbour Publishing, 1992.

Duff, Wilson. *The Indian History of British Columbia*, Vol 1. Victoria: Provincial Museum, 1965.

Farley, A.L. *Atlas of British Columbia*. Vancouver: UBC Press, 1979.

Fisher, Robin. *Contact and Conflict: Indian-European Relations in British Columbia, 1774–1890*. Vancouver: UBC Press, 1977.

_____. *Duff Pattullo of British Columbia*. Toronto: Univ of Toronto Press, 1991.

Fladmark, Knut. *British Columbia Prehistory*. Ottawa: National Museum of Man, 1986.

Freisen, Jean and H.K. Ralston, eds. *Historical Readings on British Columbia*. Toronto: McClelland & Stewart, 1976.

Glavin, Terry. *Dead Reckoning: Confronting the Crisis in Pacific Fisheries*. Vancouver: Douglas & McIntyre, 1996.

_____. *A Death Feast in Dimlahamid*. Vancouver: New Star, 1990.

_____. *This Ragged Place: Travels Across the Landscape*. Vancouver: New Star, 1996.

_____ and Charles Lillard. *A Voice Great Within Us*. Vancouver: New Star, 1998.

Gough, Barry. *Distant Dominion: Britain and the Northwest Coast of North America, 1579–1909*. Vancouver: UBC Press, 1980.

_____. *Gunboat Frontier: British Maritime Authority and Northwest Coast Indians, 1846–1990*. Vancouver: UBC Press, 1984.

_____. *The Northwest Coast: British Navigation, Trade and Discoveries to 1812*. Vancouver: UBC Press, 1992.

Graham, Donald. *Keepers of the Light: A History of British Columbia's Lighthouses and their Keepers*. Madeira Park: Harbour Publishing, 1985.

_____. *Lights of the Inside Passage*. Madeira Park: Harbour Publishing, 1986.

Grainger, M. Allerdale. *Woodsmen of the West*. Toronto: McClelland and Stewart, 1964.

Haig-Brown, Roderick. *The Living Land: An Account of the Natural Resources of British Columbia*. Toronto: Macmillan, 1961.

_____. *A River Never Sleeps*. New York: Lyons & Burford, 1946.

Hale, Linda L. and Jean Barman. *British Columbia Local Histories: A Bibliography*. Victoria: BC Heritage Trust, 1991.

Harris, Cole. *The Resettlement of British Columbia: Essays on Colonialism and Geographical Change*. Vancouver: UBC Press, 1997.

Hendrickson, James E., ed. *Journals of the Colonial Legislatures of the Colonies of Vancouver Island and British Columbia*. Victoria: Provincial Archives of BC, 1980.

Holm, Bill. *Northwest Coast Indian Art: An Analysis of Form*. Seattle: Univ of Washington Press, 1965.

Howay, F.W. *British Columbia from the Earliest Times to the Present*. Vancouver: S.J. Clarke, 1914.

Hutchison, Bruce. *The Fraser*. Toronto: Clarke, Irwin & Co., 1950.

Johnston, Hugh J.M., ed. *The Pacific Province: A History of British Columbia*. Vancouver: Douglas & McIntyre, 1996.

Knight, Rolf. *Indians at Work: An Informal History of Native Indian Labour in British Columbia 1858–1930*, rev ed. Vancouver: New Star, 1996.

Knox, Paul and Philip Resnick, eds. *Essays in BC Political Economy*. Vancouver: New Star, 1974.

Lamb, W. Kaye, ed. *George Vancouver: A Voyage of Discovery to the North Pacific Ocean and Round the World 1791–95*, 4 vols. London: Hakluyt Society, 1970.

_____, ed. *The Journal and Letters of Sir Alexander Mackenzie*. Cambridge: Hakluyt Society, 1970.

_____, ed. *The Letters and Journals of Simon Fraser, 1806–08*. Toronto: Macmillan, 1960.

Lillard, Charles. *Seven Shillings a Year: The History of Vancouver Island*. Ganges: Horsdal & Schubart, 1986.

Lowther, Barbara. *A Bibliography of British Columbia, Vol I: Laying the Foundations, 1849–1899*. Victoria: Univ of Victoria, 1968.

MacDonald, Bruce. *Vancouver: An Illustrated History*. Vancouver: Talon Books, 1992.

MacDonald, George F. *Haida Monumental Art*. Vancouver: UBC Press, 1983.

Mackie, Richard Sommerset. *Trading Beyond the Mountains: The British Fur Trade on the Pacific 1793–1843*. Vancouver: UBC Press, 1996.

Marchak, Patricia. *Green Gold: The Forest Industry in British Columbia*. Vancouver: UBC Press, 1983.

Meggs, Geoff. *Salmon: The Decline of the British Columbia Fishery*. Vancouver: Douglas & McIntyre, 1991.

Mitchell, David J. *W.A.C. Bennett and the Rise of British Columbia*. Vancouver: Douglas & McIntyre, 1983.

Morice, A.G. *The History of the Northern Interior of British Columbia, Formerly New Caledonia*. Toronto: William Briggs, 1904.

Muckle, Robert J. *The First Nations of British Columbia*. Vancouver: UBC Press, 1998.

Newell, Dianne. *Tangled Webs of History: Indians and the Law in Canada's Pacific Coast Fisheries*. Toronto: Univ of Toronto Press, 1993.

Nicholson, George. *Vancouver Island's West Coast, 1762–1962*. Victoria: Morriss Publishing, 1965.

Norris, John. *Strangers Entertained: A History of Ethnic Groups of British Columbia*.Vancouver: Evergreen Press, 1971.

Ormsby, Margaret. *British Columbia: A History*. Toronto: Macmillan, 1958.

Phillips, Paul. *No Power Greater: A Century of Labour in British Columbia*. Vancouver: Boag Foundation, 1967.

Ralston, Keith, and Gerald Friesen, eds. *Historical Essays on British Columbia*. Toronto: McClelland and Stewart, 1976.

Ramsey, Bruce. *Ghost Towns of British Columbia*. Vancouver: Mitchell Press, 1963.

Robin, Martin. *Pillars of Profit: The Company Province 1934–72*. Toronto: McClelland and Stewart, 1973.

_____. *The Rush for Spoils: The Company Province 1871–1933*. Toronto: McClelland and Stewart, 1972.

Robinson, J. Lewis and Walter G. Hardwick. *British Columbia: One Hundred Years of Geographical Change*. Vancouver: Talon Books, 1973.

Roy, Patricia, ed. *A History of British Columbia: Selected Readings*. Toronto: Copp Clark Pittman, 1989.

Sunahara, Ann. *The Politics of Racism: The Uprooting of Japanese Canadians during the Second World War*. Toronto: James Lorimer, 1981.

Suttles, Wayne, ed. *Handbook of North American Indians: Northwest Coast*, Vol 7. Washington: Smithsonian Institution, 1990.

Taylor, G.W. *Builders of British Columbia: An Industrial History*. Victoria: Morriss Publishing, 1982.

_____. *Mining: The History of Mining in British Columbia*. Saanichton: Hancock House, 1978.

_____. *Shipyards of British Columbia*. Victoria: Morriss Publishing, 1986.

_____. *Timber: History of the Forest Industry in BC*. Vancouver: J.J. Douglas, 1975.

Tennant, Paul. *Aboriginal Peoples and Politics: The Indian Land Question in British Columbia, 1849–1989*. Vancouver: UBC Press, 1990.

Turner, Robert D. *The Pacific Empresses: An Illustrated History of Canadian Pacific Railway's Empress Liners on the Pacific Ocean*. Victoria: Sono Nis, 1981.

_____. *The Pacific Princesses*. Victoria: Sono Nis, 1977.

_____. *West of the Great Divide: an Illustrated History of the Canadian Pacific Railway in British Columbia, 1880–1986*. Victoria: Sono Nis, 1987.

Twigg, Alan. *Twigg's Directory of 1001 BC Writers*. Victoria: Crown Publications, 1992.

_____. *Vancouver and its Writers*. Madeira Park: Harbour Publishing, 1986.

Walbran, John T. *British Columbia Coast Names: Their Origin and History*. Ottawa: Government Printing Bureau, 1909.

Ward, W. Peter and Robert A.J. McDonald, eds. *British Columbia: Historical Readings*. Vancouver: Douglas & McIntyre, 1981.

Woodcock, George. *British Columbia: A History of the Province*. Vancouver: Douglas & McIntyre, 1990.

Wynn, Graeme and Timothy Oke, eds. *Vancouver and its Region*. Vancouver: UBC Press, 1992.

Yee, Paul. *Saltwater City: An Illustrated History of the Chinese in Vancouver*. Vancouver: Douglas & McIntyre, 1988.

Young, Cameron. *The Forests of British Columbia*. North Vancouver: Whitecap Books, 1985.

Index

To find the subject you are looking for, please look first in the text of the encyclopedia, in which articles are arranged alphabetically. This index contains only subjects that do not have their own articles in the encyclopedia. Each subject is listed in regular type, followed by the article name (in **boldface** type) in which the subject appears. When there is more than one article, titles of articles are separated by semicolons.